The Carlat Psychiati

Medication Fact Book

For Psychiatric Practice

Third Edition

Talia Puzantian, PharmD, BCPP
Associate Professor, Keck Graduate Institute School of Pharmacy, Claremont, CA

Daniel Carlat, MD
Publisher and Editor-in-Chief, *The Carlat Psychiatry Report*
Associate Clinical Professor, Tufts University School of Medicine, Boston, MA

Published by Carlat Publishing, LLC
PO Box 626, Newburyport, MA 01950

Medication Fact Book

For Psychiatric Practice

Third Edition

Published by Carlat Publishing, LLC
PO Box 626, Newburyport, MA 01950

Publisher and Editor-in-Chief: Daniel Carlat, MD

Deputy Editor: Talia Puzantian, PharmD, BCPP

Executive Editor: Janice Jutras

This CME/CE activity is intended for psychiatrists, psychiatric nurses, psychologists, and other health care professionals with an interest in mental health. The Carlat CME Institute is accredited by the Accreditation Council for Continuing Medical Education to provide continuing medical education for physicians. Carlat CME Institute is approved by the American Psychological Association to sponsor continuing education for psychologists. Carlat CME Institute maintains responsibility for this program and its content. Carlat CME Institute designates this enduring material educational activity for a maximum of eight (8) AMA PRA Category 1 Credits™ or 8 CE for psychologists. Physicians or psychologists should claim credit commensurate only with the extent of their participation in the activity. The American Board of Psychiatry and Neurology has reviewed *The Carlat Psychiatry Report Medication Fact Book* and has approved this program as part of a comprehensive Self-Assessment and CME Program, which is mandated by ABMS as a necessary component of maintenance of certification. CME quizzes must be taken online at www.thecarlatreport.com or http://thecarlatcmeinstitute.com/self-assessment (for ABPN SA course subscribers).

To order, visit www.thecarlatreport.com or call (866) 348-9279

ISBN #: 978-0-692-58378-4

PRINTED IN THE UNITED STATES OF AMERICA

Table of Contents

Introduction 5

ADHD Medications 7

Atomoxetine (Strattera) 11

Dexmethylphenidate (Focalin) 12

Dextroamphetamine (Dexedrine) 13

Guanfacine (Intuniv) 14

Lisdexamfetamine (Vyvanse) 15

Methamphetamine (Desoxyn) 16

Methylphenidate IR (Ritalin) 17

Methylphenidate ER (Concerta, Ritalin-SR and LA) 18

Methylphenidate Transdermal (Daytrana) 19

Mixed Amphetamine Salts (Adderall) 20

Antidepressants 21

Bupropion (Wellbutrin) 26

Desvenlafaxine (Pristiq) 27

Duloxetine (Cymbalta) 28

Levomilnacipran (Fetzima) 29

Mirtazapine (Remeron) 30

Monoamine Oxidase Inhibitors (MAOIs) 31

Selective Serotonin Reuptake Inhibitors (SSRIs) 32

Selegiline Transdermal (EMSAM) 34

Trazodone (Oleptro) 35

Tricyclic Antidepressants (TCAs) 36

Venlafaxine (Effexor XR) 37

Vilazodone (Viibryd) 38

Vortioxetine (Brintellix) 39

Antipsychotics 40

Aripiprazole (Abilify) 46

Asenapine (Saphris) 47

Brexpiprazole (Rexulti) 48

Cariprazine (Vraylar) 49

Chlorpromazine (Thorazine) 50

Clozapine (Clozaril) 51

Fluphenazine (Prolixin) 52

Haloperidol (Haldol) 53

Iloperidone (Fanapt) 54

Loxapine (Loxitane) 55

Lurasidone (Latuda) 56

Olanzapine (Zyprexa) 57

Paliperidone (Invega) 58

Perphenazine (Trilafon) 59

Quetiapine (Seroquel) 60

Risperidone (Risperdal) 61

Thioridazine (Mellaril)..62

Thiothixene (Navane) 63

Trifluoperazine (Stelazine)...64

Ziprasidone (Geodon) 65

Long-Acting Injectable (LAI) Antipsychotics 66

Anxiolytic Medications 70

Alprazolam (Xanax) 72

Buspirone (BuSpar) 73

Clonazepam (Klonopin) 74

Diazepam (Valium) 75

Lorazepam (Ativan) 76

Prazosin (Minipress) 77

Propranolol (Inderal) 78

Dementia Medications 79

Donepezil (Aricept) 81

Galantamine (Razadyne) 82

Memantine (Namenda) 83

Memantine ER/Donepezil (Namzaric) 84

Rivastigmine (Exelon, Exelon Patch) 85

Hypnotics...**86**

Antihistamines (diphenhydramine, doxylamine) 90

Doxepin (Silenor) 91

Eszopiclone (Lunesta).. 92

Ramelteon (Rozerem) 93

Suvorexant (Belsomra)... 94

Temazepam (Restoril) 95

Triazolam (Halcion) 96

Zaleplon (Sonata) 97

Zolpidem (Ambien)... 98

Mood Stabilizers **99**

Carbamazepine (Tegretol) 101

Lamotrigine (Lamictal).. 102

Lithium (Lithobid)... 103

Oxcarbazepine (Trileptal) 104

Valproic Acid (Depakote) 105

Natural Treatments..**106**

L-Methylfolate (Deplin) 108

Melatonin 109

Omega-3 Fatty Acids (Fish Oil)... 110

S-Adenosyl-L-Methionine (SAMe) 111

St. John's Wort 112

Novel Anticonvulsants 113

Gabapentin (Neurontin) 115

Pregabalin (Lyrica) 116

Tiagabine (Gabitril) 117

Topiramate (Topamax) 118

Sexual Dysfunction Medications 119

Avanafil (Stendra) 121

Cyproheptadine 122

Flibanserin (Addyi) 123

Sildenafil (Viagra) 124

Tadalafil (Cialis) 125

Testosterone (various) 126

Vardenafil (Levitra) 127

Sleep Disorder Medications 128

Armodafinil (Nuvigil) 129

Modafinil (Provigil) 130

Sodium Oxybate (Xyrem) 131

Substance Abuse/Dependence Medications 132

Smoking Cessation 133

Acamprosate (Campral) 136

Buprenorphine (Buprenex) 137

Buprenorphine/Naloxone (Suboxone) 138

Bupropion SR (Zyban) 139

Disulfiram (Antabuse) 140

Methadone (Methadose) 141

Naloxone (Evzio, Narcan Nasal Spray) 142

Naltrexone (ReVia, Vivitrol) 143

Nicotine Gum/Lozenge (Nicorette) 144

Nicotine Inhaled (Nicotrol Inhaler) 145

Nicotine Nasal Spray (Nicotrol NS) 146

Nicotine Patch (Nicoderm CQ) 147

Varenicline (Chantix) 148

Appendices 149

Appendix A: Drug Interactions in Psychiatry 150

Appendix B: Psychiatric Medications in Pregnancy and Lactation 158

Appendix C: Schedules of Controlled Substances 162

Appendix D: Lab Monitoring for Psychiatric Medications 163

Index 164

List of Tables

Table 1: ADHD Medications...8

Table 2: Antidepressants... 23

Table 3: Selective Serotonin Reuptake Inhibitors (SSRIs).. 33

Table 3.1: Pharmacokinetics and Drug Interactions of SSRIs 33

Table 4: APA/ADA Monitoring Protocol for Patients on SGAs 42

Table 5: Typical Antipsychotics 43

Table 6: Atypical Antipsychotics 44

Table 7: Long-Acting Injectable Antipsychotics 68

Table 8: Anxiolytic Medications 71

Table 9: Dementia Medications 80

Table 10: Hypnotics 88

Table 11: Mood Stabilizers 100

Table 12: Natural Treatments.. 107

Table 13: Novel Anticonvulsants 114

Table 14: Sexual Dysfunction Medications 120

Table 15: Substance Abuse and Dependence Medications 134

Appendix A Table: CYP450 Drug Interactions for Some Commonly Prescribed Medications......154

Appendix B Table: Psychiatric Medications in Pregnancy and Lactation....................................159

Appendix C Table: Schedules of Controlled Substances...162

Appendix D Table: Lab Monitoring for Psychiatric Medications 163

Introduction

How to Use This Book

Medication information is presented in two ways in this book.

Medication Fact Sheets: In-depth prescribing information for select medications. There are 101 fact sheets in this book. These don't cover all psychiatric medications, but we have included most of the commonly prescribed and newer medications.

Quick-Scan Medication Tables: These are located at the beginning of each therapeutic category and list the very basics: generic and brand names, strengths available, starting doses, and target doses. These tables contain most of the commonly prescribed psychiatric medications.

Changes and Additions to the 3rd Edition

Medication fact sheets have been updated to reflect availability of newer strengths and formulations, as well as generics. New clinical data have been incorporated into the previous edition's fact sheets. Many categories of medications have been expanded to include a larger number of medications: 24 new fact sheets and 4 additional tables are included in this edition.

Categories of Medications

We did our best to categorize medications rationally. However, in some cases a medication can fall into more than one category. In such cases, we went with the types of disorders for which the medication is most often used. If you're having trouble finding a medication in a particular section, look in the index to find its page number.

More on the Medication Fact Sheets

The goal of these fact sheets is to provide need-to-know information that can be easily and quickly absorbed during a busy day of seeing patients. Our main criterion is that all the information should fit on a single page. Please refer to the *PDR (Physicians' Desk Reference)* when you need more in-depth information.

For the most part, each fact sheet contains the following information:

- Both the brand and generic names.
- **A (G) denotes generic availability.**
- FDA-approved indications.
- Off-label uses. We list the more common off-label uses, based on both the medical literature and our own clinical experience. Just because we list a potential use does not imply that we endorse a medication as being particularly effective for that use. We are simply alerting you to the fact that there is some evidence for efficacy.
- Dosage forms, along with available strengths.
- Dosage guidance. We provide recommendations on how to dose medications; these are derived from a variety of sources, including package inserts, clinical trials, and common clinical practice. In other words, don't be surprised when our dosing instructions are at odds with what you find in the *PDR*.
- Cost information. Pricing information for a 1-month supply of a common dosing regimen was obtained from the website GoodRx (www.goodrx.com), accessed in October 2015. These are the prices a patient would have to pay if he or she had no insurance. Because of wide variations in price depending on the pharmacy, in this edition of the *Medication Fact Book* we list price categories rather than the price in dollars. The categories are:
- $: Inexpensive: <$50/month
- $$: Moderate: $50-$100/month
- $$$: Expensive: $100-$200/month
- $$$$: Very expensive: $200-$500/month
- $$$$$: Extremely expensive: >$500/month

This begs the question, what should you do with knowledge of retail pricing? After all, most patients have some type of insurance and are therefore not going to pay retail price, but rather a co-pay. Since there's no clear source for accurately predicting a co-pay, you can use the retail price as a clue. Meds that are very inexpensive will likely require no co-pay, while the most expensive drugs will either require a very expensive co-pay, or, more likely, will not be covered at all without an onerous pre-authorization process.

- Side effects information. We break down side effects into "most common" vs "rare but serious" side effects. We generally define "most common" side effects as those occurring in at least 5% of patients in clinical trials, and which were at least double the rate of the placebo group. Such information is usually found in tables in the drugs' package inserts. We also used post-marketing clinical experience as a guide in determining which side effects were common enough to make the list.
- Mechanism of action. While the mechanism of action is not well-established for most psychiatric drugs, we thought it was important to report the mechanisms most commonly cited.
- Pharmacokinetics, with a focus on drug metabolism and/or half-life.
- Drug interactions.
- Clinical pearls, which typically comment on advantages or disadvantages of a medication in comparison to others in its therapeutic category, tips for dosing or avoiding side effects, types of patients who seem to benefit the most, and so forth.
- Fun facts.
- Lastly, our bottom-line summary or assessment for that particular medication.

Financial Disclosures

Dr. Puzantian and Dr. Carlat have disclosed that they have no relevant relationships or financial interests in any commercial company pertaining to the information provided in this book.

Disclaimer

The medication information in this book was formulated with a reasonable standard of care, and in conformity with professional standards in the field of psychiatry. Medication prescribing decisions are complex, and you should use these fact sheets as only one of many possible sources of medication information. This information is not a substitute for informed medical care. This book is intended for use by licensed professionals only.

If you have any comments or corrections, please let us know by writing to us at info@thecarlatreport.com or *The Carlat Psychiatry Report*, P.O. Box 626, Newburyport, MA 01950.

Note:
Throughout this book,
a [G] or (G) denotes
generic availability.

ADHD Medications

Generally, when you have a patient with ADHD symptoms, your first choice is going to be one of the psychostimulants, because these are usually more effective than the alternatives—atomoxetine, bupropion, and guanfacine. Which psychostimulant will you choose? Here are some of the factors that will influence your decision:

1. Long-acting vs short-acting. Choosing between long- and short-acting stimulants is more art than science. Trial and error, combined with patient preference, will dictate the final regimen. Adults will often start with a long-acting agent so they can take 1 dose in the morning and have it carry through their workday. Kids may do better with short-acting stimulants so that they will have an appetite when the medication wears off at lunch.

2. Amphetamine vs. methylphenidate. Generally, this is a Coke vs. Pepsi decision—some people like one better than the other, and you can't predict this ahead of time. We recommend a methylphenidate over an amphetamine in most cases, because amphetamines tend to have more side effects and are more likely to be abused or diverted.

3. Stimulants vs. non-stimulants. Stimulants are more effective than non-stimulants, so they are your first-line choice for most patients. If you have a substance abuser, start with atomoxetine. Some special clinical circumstances seem to naturally call for other options. For example, bupropion is helpful for ADHD symptoms, as well as for depression, tobacco use, and being overweight, so it might be a great choice for patients with a combination of these problems. Alpha agonists, such as guanfacine and clonidine, are helpful for both ADHD and insomnia, another potential two-fer.

4. Cost. Most ADHD meds are available generically, but some reasonable choices are still branded and therefore more expensive. The most popular of these is Vyvanse, which is a long-acting amphetamine. Vyvanse appears to have a genuine advantage over many other stimulants, mainly in terms of tolerability and less potential for abuse. However, you'll have a hard time convincing insurance companies to cover the cost of Vyvanse unless you can clearly document intolerance to several other trials of stimulants.

Side Effects and Class Warnings

The following apply to all stimulants:

- Potential to cause psychosis or aggression: This is a rare and dose-related effect; it may be more likely in patients with a predisposition for psychosis.

- Worsening or new-onset Tourette's or tic disorders: Stimulants may unmask tics. Of stimulants, methylphenidate is favored. The non-stimulant guanfacine is another alternative.

- Seizures: Stimulants may lower the seizure threshold, although data are contradictory; monitor patients with seizure disorders closely.

- Growth inhibition or weight loss: With long-term use, some growth inhibition may occur occasionally in children, but this is generally not a major problem. Monitoring growth and considering "drug holidays" may limit growth suppression.

- Cardiovascular safety: The FDA issued a serious class warning in 2006 with regard to cardiovascular safety. However, newer data, both in children and adults, have been reassuring. Cardiac events occurred at virtually the same or lower rates among people who took stimulants compared to those who did not. From a practical perspective, we recommend asking about cardiac problems and consulting the child's pediatrician or cardiologist if a problem exists. Amphetamines should be avoided in patients with known or suspected cardiovascular disease.

- All stimulants are controlled substances, schedule 2, which means they can't be refilled or called in. Patients must be given a new prescription every month. In most states, you are allowed to give patients post-dated prescriptions for convenience.

Table 1: ADHD Medications

Brand Name (Generic Name, if different than heading) Year FDA Approved [G] denotes generic availability	Available Strengths (mg except where noted)	Usual Dosage Range (starting–max) (mg)	Duration of Action (hours)	Can It Be Split?	Ages Approved for ADHD	Delivery System/Notes (IR = immediate, CR = controlled, DR = delayed release)
Methylphenidates						
Short-acting						
Focalin [G] (Dexmethylphenidate) 2001	2.5, 5, 10	2.5–10 BID	3–4	Yes (not scored)	6–17	Tablet; D-enantiomer of Ritalin; 2x more potent than methylphenidate
Methylin CT [G] 2003	2.5, 5, 10	2.5 BID–20 TID	3–4	Yes	6–17, adults	Chewable, grape-flavored tablet
Methylin oral solution [G] 2002	5 mg/5 mL, 10 mg/5 mL	2.5 BID–20 TID	3–4	NA	6–17, adults	Clear, grape-flavored liquid
Ritalin [G] 1955	5, 10, 20	2.5 BID–20 TID	3–4	Yes	6–17, adults	IR tablet
Intermediate-acting						
Metadate ER [G] 1999 Branded generic of Ritalin SR	20	10 QAM–30 BID (max 60/day)	6–8	No	6–17, adults	CR tablet (less predictable because of wax matrix)
Methylin ER [G] 2000 Branded generic of Ritalin SR	10, 20	20–60 QAM	4–8	No	6–17, adults	Hydrophilic polymer tablet; possibly more continuous than others in category
Ritalin SR [G] 1982	10, 20	10–60 QAM	4–8	No	6–17, adults	CR tablet (less predictable because of wax matrix)
Long-acting						
Aptensio XR 2015	10, 15, 20, 30, 40, 50, 60	10–60 QAM	8–12	Can be sprinkled; do not crush or chew	6+	Capsule of 40% IR beads & 60% DR beads
Concerta [G] 2000	18, 27, 36, 54	18 QAM–72 QAM	10–16	No	6–12, adults	CR tablet with 22% IR & 78% DR
Daytrana patch (Methylphenidate transdermal system) 2006	10, 15, 20, 30	10–30 QAM Remove after 9 hours	8–12	No	Children >6 years, adults	CR patch; duration can be shortened by decreasing wear time
Focalin XR [G] (Dexmethylphenidate XR) 2005	5, 10, 15, 20, 25, 30, 35, 40	6–17 yrs: 5–30 QAM Adults: 10–40 QAM	8–12	Can be sprinkled; do not crush or chew	6–17, adults	Capsule of 50% IR beads & 50% DR beads; mimics BID dosing; 2x more potent than methylphenidate
Metadate CD [G] 2001	10, 20, 30, 40, 50, 60	20–60 QAM	8–12	Can be sprinkled; do not crush or chew	6+	Capsule of 30% IR beads & 70% DR beads; mimics BID dosing
Quillichew ER 2015	20, 30, 40	20–60 QAM	8–12	Yes	6+	Chewable ER for those who will not swallow pills or take liquid; 30% IR & 70% ER
Quillivant XR 2012	25/5 mL	20–60 QAM	8–12	No	6+	20% IR & 80% ER in oral solution; shake prior to use
Ritalin LA [G] 2002	10, 20, 30, 40, 50, 60	20–60 QAM	8–12	Can be sprinkled; do not crush or chew	6+	Capsule of 50% IR beads & 50% DR beads

Amphetamines

Short-acting	Strengths (mg)	Dosing	Duration (hrs)	Crush/Chew	Age	Notes
Desoxyn [G] (Methamphetamine) 1943	5	5 QAM–10 BID	3–5	Yes	6–17	Slow release tablet
Evekeo (Amphetamine) 2012	5, 10	3–5 yrs: 2.5 QAM–20 BID; 6–17 yrs: 5 QAM–20	3–5	Yes	6–17	Scored tablet
Dexedrine [G] (Dextroamphetamine) 1976	5, 10	3–5 yrs: 2.5 QAM–20 BID; 6–16 yrs: 5 QAM–20 BID	3–5	Yes	3–16	Scored tablet
ProCentra [G] (Dextroamphetamine oral solution) 2008	5 mg/5 mL	5–20 BID	3–5	NA	3–16	Bubblegum-flavored liquid
Zenzedi (Dextroamphetamine) 2013	2.5, 5, 7.5, 10, 15, 20, 30	3–5 yrs: 2.5–20 BID; 6–16 yrs: 5 QAM–20 BID (same as Dexedrine dosing)	3–5	Yes	3–16	Unscored tablet

Intermediate-acting						
Adderall [G] (Mixed amphetamine salts) 1960	5, 7.5, 10, 12.5, 15, 20, 30	3–5 yrs: 2.5 QAM–20 BID; 6–17 yrs: 5 QAM–20 BID; Adults: 5 QAM–20 BID	6–8	Can be crushed	3+	Tablet; mixed salt of l- and d-amphetamine

Long-acting						
Dyanavel XR (Amphetamine) 2015	2.5 mg/mL	6–17 yrs: 2.5 QAM–20 QAM	10–14	Oral suspension	6+	Extended release oral suspension allowing once daily dosing
Adderall XR [G] (Mixed amphetamine salts) 2001	5, 10, 15, 20, 25, 30	6–12 yrs: 5 QAM–30 QAM; 13–17 yrs: 10 QAM–40 QAM; Adults: 20 QAM–60 QAM	8–12	Can be sprinkled; do not crush or chew	6+	Capsule of 50% IR beads & 50% DR beads; mixed salt of l- and d-amphetamine; mimics BID dosing
Dexedrine Spansules [G] (Dextroamphetamine) 1976	5, 10, 15	5 QAM–20 BID	10–14	Can be sprinkled; do not crush or chew	6+	Capsule of 50% IR & 50% sustained release beads

Brand Name (Generic Name, if different than heading) Year FDA Approved [G] denotes generic availability	Available Strengths (mg except where noted)	Usual Dosage Range (starting–max) (mg)	Duration of Action (in hours)	Can It Be Split?	Ages Approved for ADHD	Delivery System/Notes (IR = immediate, CR = controlled, DR = delayed release)
Vyvanse (Lisdexamfetamine) 2007	10, 20, 30, 40, 50, 60, 70	30 QAM–70 QAM	8–12	Can be dissolved in water	6–17, adults	Capsule; lisdexamfetamine is prodrug of dextroamphetamine
Non-stimulants						
Intuniv [G] (Guanfacine ER) [G] 2009	1, 2, 3, 4	1–4 QD (do not increase faster than 1 mg/wk) (adolescents 7 mg/day max)	24	No	6–17	Extended release tablet; do not stop abruptly (orthostatic hypotension); not a 1:1 conversion from IR; do not give with high-fat meals
Kapvay (Clonidine XR) [G] 2009	0.1, 0.2	0.1 QHS; increase by 0.1 mg/day weekly and give divided BID; max 0.4 QD	12–16	No	6–17	Extended release tablet; titrate gradually (orthostatic hypotension); avoid abrupt discontinuation; somnolence
Provigil [G] (Modafinil) 1998	100, 200	100 QAM–400 QAM	18–24	Yes (200 mg tabs are scored)	Not FDA-approved for ADHD	Tablet; studies have shown modafinil to be helpful for ADHD, but low incidence of serious rash; minimal data in children
Strattera (Atomoxetine) 2002	10, 18, 25, 40, 60, 80, 100	Dosage varies. See footnote 1 below.	24	No	6–17: max daily dose of 70 mg; 18+: max dose of 100 mg	Capsule; norepinephrine reuptake inhibitor
Tenex [G] (Guanfacine IR) 1986	1, 2	1–4 QD (do not increase faster than 1 mg/wk)	17	Can be crushed	Not FDA-approved for kids or ADHD. Approved only for adults 18+ for hypertension	Tablet
Wellbutrin [G] (Bupropion) 1985	75, 100	1.4–6 mg/kg/day	6–9	Yes	Not FDA-approved for ADHD	Tablet; bupropion SR & XL versions exist

1Strattera dosing: Weight <70kg, start 0.5 mg/kg, target 1.2 mg/kg, max 1.4 mg/kg; weight >70 kg, 40–100 mg

ATOMOXETINE (Strattera) Fact Sheet

FDA Indications:
ADHD (adults and children >6 years).

Off-Label Uses:
Treatment-resistant depression.

Dosage Forms:
Capsules: 10 mg, 18 mg, 25 mg, 40 mg, 60 mg, 80 mg, 100 mg.

Dosage Guidance:
- Start 40 mg QAM for 3 days, ↑ to 80 mg QAM, may ↑ to 100 mg/day after 2–4 weeks if needed (max 100 mg/day); may divide doses >40 mg/day (morning and late afternoon/early evening).
- Special dosing for children <70 kg:
  Start 0.5 mg/kg QAM for 3 days, ↑ to 1.2 mg/kg QAM, may ↑ to max 1.4 mg/kg/day or 100 mg/day (whichever is less) after 2–4 weeks, if needed; may divide doses >0.5 mg/kg/day.

Cost: $$$$

Side Effects:
- Most common: *Children*: headache, abdominal pain, decreased appetite, fatigue, nausea, vomiting. *Adults*: nausea, dry mouth, decreased appetite, insomnia, constipation, fatigue, erectile dysfunction, abdominal pain, dizziness, urinary hesitation.
- Serious but rare: Class warning for suicidal ideation in children and teens. Severe hepatic injury including increased hepatic enzymes (up to 40 times normal) and jaundice (bilirubin up to 12 times upper limit of normal). Increased blood pressure (↑ 15–20 mmHg) and heart rate (↑ 20 bpm).

Mechanism, Pharmacokinetics, and Drug Interactions:
- Selective norepinephrine reuptake inhibitor (SNRI).
- Metabolized primarily via CYP2D6; t ½: 5 hours.
- Avoid use with MAOIs. Exercise caution with 2D6 inhibitors such as fluoxetine, paroxetine, and quinidine (increased atomoxetine serum levels); use slower titration and do not exceed 80 mg/day.

Clinical Pearls:
- QAM dosing is as effective as BID, but BID dosing has better GI tolerability. Can also be dosed at bedtime if it causes fatigue.
- Appears to be more effective in improving attention than in controlling hyperactivity.
- Labs: Order baseline liver function tests.

Fun Fact:
Atomoxetine was originally known as "tomoxetine"; however, the FDA requested that the name be changed because the similarity to "tamoxifen" could lead to dispensing errors.

Bottom Line:
Advantages: Unlike stimulants, there is no abuse potential, it causes less insomnia and anxiety, and it is unlikely to worsen tics.
Disadvantages: Generally less effective than stimulants, and takes longer to work (2–4 weeks).

DEXMETHYLPHENIDATE (Focalin) Fact Sheet [G]

FDA Indications:
ADHD in adults (XR only) and in children >6 years (IR and XR).

Off-Label Uses:
Narcolepsy, obesity, treatment–resistant depression.

Dosage Forms:
- **Tablets (G):** 2.5 mg, 5 mg, 10 mg.
- **ER capsules (G):** 5 mg, 10 mg, 15 mg, 20 mg, 25 mg, 30 mg, 35 mg, 40 mg.

Dosage Guidance:
- IR: Start 2.5 mg BID, ↑ by 5 mg-10 mg/day every 7 days. Max 20 mg/day; divide IR doses by at least 4 hours.
- ER: Start 10 mg QAM, ↑ by 10 mg/day every 7 days. Max 40 mg/day. For children, start 5 mg QAM, ↑ by 5 mg/day every 7 days. Max (children) 30 mg/day.

Cost: IR: $; ER: $$$

Side Effects:
- Most common: decreased appetite, insomnia, anxiety, GI distress, irritability, tics, headache, tachycardia, hypertension, dry mouth
- Serious but rare: See cardiovascular class warning in chapter introduction.

Mechanism, Pharmacokinetics, and Drug Interactions:
- Stimulant that inhibits reuptake of dopamine and norephinephrine.
- Metabolized primarily via de–esterification, not CYP450; t ½: 2-4.5 hours (2-3 hours in children); ER delivers 50% of dose immediately and 50% about 5 hours later.
- Avoid use with MAOIs.

Clinical Pearls:
- Focalin is the d-isomer of methylphenidate. Dexmethylphenidate is 2x more potent than methylphenidate, which is why it is prescribed at about half the dose.
- Use the same total daily dose of Focalin IR as Focalin XR.
- Focalin XR capsules contain two kinds of beads: Half are immediate release beads and half are enteric coated delayed release beads. A single, once–daily dose of XR capsule provides the same amount of dexmethylphenidate as 2 IR tablets given 4 hours apart.
- The ER capsules cannot be split in half. However, they can be opened and the beads sprinkled over food. The patient should then eat all that food—eating half won't work to split the dose accurately because it won't be possible to determine if the eaten portion contains more immediate release or delayed release beads.
- Give with food if GI side effects occur.

Fun Fact:
With 2 stereoactive centers, methylphenidate has 4 possible stereoisomers. Of the 4, dexmethylphenidate is the most active biologically.

Bottom Line:
Focalin is just Ritalin but more potent. It's available as a generic and may mean fewer tablets for patients. Focalin XR only recently went generic, so it will likely remain quite expensive for a while.

* Throughout this book, a [G] or (G) denotes generic availability.

DEXTROAMPHETAMINE (Dexedrine) Fact Sheet [G]

FDA Indications:
ADHD (adults and children >3 years); **narcolepsy** (adults and children >6 years).

Off-Label Uses:
Obesity, treatment-resistant depression.

Dosage Forms:
- **Tablets (Dexedrine) (G):** 5 mg, 10 mg (scored).
- **Tablets (Zenzedi):** 2.5 mg, 5 mg, 7.5 mg, 10 mg, 15 mg, 20 mg, 30 mg (scored).
- **ER capsules (Dexedrine Spansules) (G):** 5 mg, 10 mg, 15 mg.
- **Liquid (ProCentra) (G):** 5 mg/5 mL.

Dosage Guidance:
- ADHD:
  - Adults and children >6 years: Start 5 mg QAM, ↑ by 5 mg/day at weekly intervals to max 40 mg/day. Divide IR dose QD-TID.
  - Children 3–5 years: Start 2.5 mg QAM, ↑ by 2.5 mg/day weekly to max 40 mg/day; divide IR dose QD-TID.
- Narcolepsy:
  - Start 10 mg QAM, ↑ by 10 mg/day weekly to max 60 mg/day.

Cost: IR: $$; ER: $$$

Side Effects:
- Most common: abdominal pain, anorexia, nausea, tics, insomnia, tachycardia, and headache.
- Serious but rare: See class warnings in chapter introduction.

Mechanism, Pharmacokinetics, and Drug Interactions:
- Stimulant that inhibits reuptake of dopamine and norephinephrine.
- Metabolized primarily through CYP450 2D6 (minor) and glucuronidation; t ½: 10-13 hours.
- Avoid use with MAOIs, antacids.

Clinical Pearls:
- Dextroamphetamine is the more potent d-isomer of amphetamine; potentially less peripheral effects (eg, motor tics) than racemic mix (eg, mixed amphetamine salts like Adderall or methamphetamine).
- IR tablets and oral solution: Doses can be given at intervals of 4-6 hours.
- Dextroamphetamine is the only stimulant, other than Adderall IR, approved for children <6 years (approved for children >3 years).
- New Zenzedi brand offers more dosing flexibility options and may have equivalent pricing to generic IR tablets.
- Also available as D,L racemic mixture of amphetamine as Evekeo brand tablets and as Dyanavel XR oral suspension.

Fun Fact:
Dexys Midnight Runners, the British band famous for its song "Come On Eileen" (1982), derived their name from Dexedrine—"Dexys" after the drug's name and "Midnight Runners" in reference to the energy it provides.

Bottom Line:
Good drug, with very long history of experience, available in short- and long-acting formulations as generics.

GUANFACINE (Intuniv) Fact Sheet [G]

FDA Indications:

ADHD (children ages 6–17), as monotherapy or adjunctive therapy to stimulants (not approved for ADHD in adults).

Off-Label Uses:

Conduct disorder; Tourette's and motor tics; pervasive developmental disorders; migraine prophylaxis; heroin withdrawal.

Dosage Forms:
- **Tablets (G):** 1 mg, 2 mg.
- **ER tablets (G):** 1 mg, 2 mg, 3 mg, 4 mg.

Dosage Guidance:
- IR dosing depends on weight.
  - 27 kg–40.5 kg (55 to 90 lbs): Start 0.5 mg QHS, ↑ by 0.5 mg/day at weekly intervals up to 1.5 mg/day, may ↑ to 2 mg/day after 2 weeks; max 2 mg/day in 2 to 4 divided doses.
  - 40.5 kg–45 kg (90 to 99 lbs): Start 0.5 mg QHS, ↑ by 0.5 mg/day at weekly intervals; max 1 mg per dose, 3 mg/day.
  - >45 kg (99 lbs): Start 1 mg QHS, ↑ by 1 mg/day at weekly intervals up to 3 mg/day, may ↑ to 4 mg/day after 2 weeks; max 1 mg per dose, 4 mg/day.
- ER: Start 1 mg QHS, ↑ by 1 mg/day at weekly intervals; max 4 mg/day. Alternative: 0.05 mg/kg–0.12 mg/kg QD or QHS; max 4 mg/day. Doses up to 7 mg/day ER studied as monotherapy in adolescents.

Cost: IR: $; ER: $

Side Effects:
- Most common: dry mouth, somnolence, dizziness, constipation, fatigue, headache.
- Serious but rare: hypotension, syncope, orthostasis.

Mechanism, Pharmacokinetics, and Drug Interactions:
- Centrally acting, selective alpha–2 adrenergic agonist.
- Metabolized primarily through CYP3A4; t ½: 13–14 hours in children (16–18 in adults).
- Avoid use with MAOIs. Caution with 3A4 inhibitors (eg, clarithromycin, fluvoxamine) and inducers (eg, St. John's wort, carbamazepine).

Clinical Pearls:
- Not a controlled substance.
- Guanfacine IR and ER are not interchangeable on a mg:mg basis. When switching from one formulation to the other, taper and retitrate.
- If patient misses 2 or more consecutive doses, consider repeating titration.
- ER tablets should not be taken with a high-fat meal due to increased medication exposure.
- Minimize side effects, especially somnolence, by administering at bedtime.
- Monitor BP, especially during initial dosing titration.
- Risk of nervousness, anxiety, and possibly rebound hypertension 2–4 days after abrupt discontinuation. Taper dose in 1 mg/day decrements, every 3–7 days.

Fun Fact:

Some prescribers have taken advantage of guanfacine's sympatholytic properties for the treatment of nightmares and dissociative symptoms in PTSD.

Bottom Line:

Advantages over stimulants include no worsening of tic disorders, lack of abuse potential, and no insomnia. However, its delayed onset of effect (2–4 weeks) and lower efficacy rates make it a second-line choice for ADHD generally. ER is now available in generic and easier to use than IR.

LISDEXAMFETAMINE (Vyvanse) Fact Sheet

FDA Indications:

ADHD (adults and children >6 years); **binge eating disorder** (BED).

Off-Label Uses:

Narcolepsy; obesity; treatment-resistant depression.

Dosage Forms:

Capsules: 10 mg, 20 mg, 30 mg, 40 mg, 50 mg, 60 mg, 70 mg.

Dosage Guidance:

- ADHD (adults and children >6 years): Start 30 mg QAM, ↑ by 10 mg–20 mg/day at weekly intervals. Target lowest effective dose; max 70 mg/day.
- Binge eating disorder: Start 30 mg QAM, ↑ by 20 mg/day at weekly intervals to target 50 mg/day; max 70 mg/day.

Cost: $$$$

Side Effects:

- Most common: headache, insomnia, anorexia, abdominal pain, irritability, agitation, tics, decreased appetite, increased heart rate, jitteriness, anxiety.
- Serious but rare: See class warnings in chapter introduction.

Mechanism, Pharmacokinetics, and Drug Interactions:

- Stimulant that inhibits reuptake of dopamine and norephinephrine.
- Metabolized primarily through non-CYP-mediated hepatic and/or intestinal metabolism; t ½: lisdexamfetamine (inactive prodrug) <1 hour; dextroamphetamine (active metabolite) 10–13 hours.
- Avoid use with MAOIs and antacids. Caution with antihypertensives (decreased efficacy of antihypertensive).

Clinical Pearls:

- Lisdexamfetamine is dextroamphetamine with the chemical lysine bound to it, which renders it inactive. It remains inactive until GI enzymes cleave off lysine and convert it to active dextroamphetamine. This means that drug abusers can't get high by snorting it or injecting it.
- Anecdotally, Vyvanse has a more gradual onset and offset than other stimulants, and may cause fewer side effects than other amphetamines.
- Lisdexamfetamine 70 mg is equivalent to 30 mg of mixed amphetamine salts (Adderall).
- While indicated for BED, it is not approved for use as a weight loss or anti-obesity agent.

Fun Fact:

The manufacturer of Vyvanse pursued an indication as an add-on medication for depression, but disappointing results in clinical trials in early 2014 stopped this measure.

Bottom Line:

Vyvanse may have a gentler, "smoother" side effect profile than other amphetamines, and probably has a lower risk of diversion or abuse. However, its high cost means insurance companies don't like to pay for it without prior authorizations.

METHAMPHETAMINE (Desoxyn) Fact Sheet [G]

FDA Indications:

ADHD (children >6 years); **obesity** (adults and adolescents >12 years).

Dosage Forms:

- Tablets (G): 5 mg.

Dosage Guidance:

ADHD (adults and children >6 years): Start 5 mg QAM–BID, ↑ by 5 mg/day at weekly intervals to max 20 mg/day, divided BID.

Cost: $$$

Side Effects:

- Most common: anorexia, tachycardia, dizziness, insomnia, tremor, tics, restlessness, headache, constipation (decreased GI motility). Dental complications, such as poor dental hygiene, diffuse cavities, bruxism, and tooth wear, may develop with abuse.
- Serious but rare: See class warnings in chapter introduction.

Mechanism, Pharmacokinetics, and Drug Interactions:

- Stimulant that inhibits reuptake of dopamine and norephinephrine.
- Metabolized primarily through CYP2D6 to active metabolite (amphetamine); t ½: 4–5 hours.
- Avoid use with MAOIs and antacids.

Clinical Pearls:

- High risk of abuse.
- Not widely used (DEA reports that there were only 16,000 prescriptions written in 2012). When prescribed for obesity, the recommendation is for short-term (ie, a few weeks) use only and as an adjunct to caloric restriction due to its high addiction and diversion potential.
- CNS stimulating effect is approximately equal to or greater than that of amphetamine but less than that of dextroamphetamine; less increase in BP than with amphetamine.

Fun Facts:

Desoxyn is the same as the abused street drug methamphetamine, just pharmaceutical grade. Although methamphetamine and amphetamine were long thought to be available only via laboratories, methamphetamine has been reported to occur naturally in certain acacia trees that grow in West Texas.

Bottom Line:

Highly addictive substance; its use is generally not recommended. Watch the television show "Breaking Bad" if you're not convinced!

METHYLPHENIDATE IR (Ritalin) Fact Sheet [G]

FDA Indications:
ADHD (adults and children >6 years); **narcolepsy.**

Off-Label Uses:
Obesity; treatment-resistant depression.

Dosage Forms:
- **Tablets (G):** 5 mg, 10 mg, 20 mg.
- **Chewable tablets (G):** 2.5 mg, 5 mg, 10 mg.
- **Oral solution (G):** 5 mg/5 mL, 10 mg/5 mL.

Dosage Guidance:
- ADHD
  - Adults: Start 5 mg-10 mg BID, ↑ by 10 mg/day at weekly intervals to max 60 mg/day.
  - Children >6 years: Start 0.3 mg/kg BID or 2.5 mg-5 mg BID before breakfast and lunch, increase by 0.1 mg/kg/dose or 5 mg-10 mg/day at weekly intervals to a max of 2 mg/kg/day or 60 mg/day.
- Narcolepsy: same dosing as ADHD.

Cost: $$

Side Effects:
- Most common: insomnia, headache, nervousness, abdominal pain, nausea, vomiting, anorexia, weight loss, affect lability, tics.
- Serious but rare: See class warnings in chapter introduction.

Mechanism, Pharmacokinetics, and Drug Interactions:
- Stimulant that inhibits reuptake of dopamine and norephinephrine.
- Hepatic metabolism via carboxylesterase CES1A1, not CYP450 isoenzymes; t ½: 2-4 hours.
- Avoid use with MAOIs, antacids.

Clinical Pearls:
- Methylphenidate generally causes fewer side effects than amphetamine preparations—patients are less likely to report feeling "wired."
- While all stimulants may cause tics, a Cochrane review of 8 randomized trials showed that methylphenidate did not worsen tics in children with ADHD and a tic disorder; in some cases it even improved tics.
- Methylin chewable tablet: Administer with at least 8 ounces of water or other fluid.

Fun Fact:
Methylphenidate was synthesized by Ciba (now Novartis) chemist Leandro Panizzon. His wife, Marguerite, had low blood pressure and would take the stimulant before playing tennis. He named the substance "Ritaline," (yes, with the "e" on the end) after his wife's nickname, Rita.

Bottom Line:
Better side effect profile and somewhat lower abuse potential than amphetamines. However, patients often prefer the "kick" they get from Adderall.

METHYLPHENIDATE ER (Concerta, Ritalin-SR and LA) Fact Sheet [G]

FDA Indications:
ADHD (adults and children >6 years); **narcolepsy**.

Off-Label Uses:
Obesity; treatment–resistant depression.

Dosage Forms (more commonly used):
- **SR tablets (Ritalin SR) (G):** 10 mg, 20 mg.
- **ER capsules (Ritalin LA) (G):** 10 mg, 20 mg, 30 mg, 40 mg, 50 mg, 60 mg (50% IR/50% ER).
- **ER capsules (Metadate CD) (G):** 10 mg, 20 mg, 30 mg, 40 mg, 50 mg, 60 mg (30% IR/70% ER).
- **ER capsules (Aptensio XR):** 10 mg, 15 mg, 20 mg, 30 mg, 40 mg, 50 mg, 60 mg (40% IR/60% ER).
- **ER tablets (Concerta) (G):** 18 mg, 27 mg, 36 mg, 54 mg (22% IR/78% ER).
- **ER oral suspension (Quillivant XR):** 25 mg/5 mL (20% IR/80% ER).
- **ER chewable tablets (Quillichew ER):** 20 mg, 30 mg, 40 mg (30% IR/70% ER).

Dosage Guidance:
- Intermediate–acting (Ritalin SR, Metadate ER, Methylin ER):
  - Titrate to effective daily dose with IR, then switch to equivalent 8–hour SR or ER dose QAM-BID (eg, 20 mg ER QAM or BID); max 60 mg/day.
- Long–acting (Aptensio XR, Metadate CD, Ritalin LA, Quillivant XR):
  - Start 20 mg QAM; ↑ by 10 mg–20 mg/day at weekly intervals; max 60 mg/day.
- Long–acting (Concerta):
  - Start 18 mg-36 mg QAM, ↑ by 18 mg/day at weekly intervals; max 72 mg/day.
  - Children >6 years: start 18 mg QAM, ↑ by 18 mg/day in weekly intervals to max 54 mg/day (ages 6-12) or 72 mg/day (age 13+).
- If switching from different form of methylphenidate:
  - 10 mg-15 mg/day: Use 18 mg QAM.
  - 20 mg-30 mg/day: Use 36 mg QAM.
  - 30 mg-45 mg/day: Use 54 mg QAM.
  - 40 mg-60 mg/day: Use 72 mg QAM.
  - 27 mg dose is available for situations in which a dose between 18 mg-36 mg is desired.
- Narcolepsy: Start 10 mg-20 mg ER QAM, ↑ by 10 mg/day at weekly intervals; max 60 mg/day.

Cost: SR: $; LA: $$; ER: $$$

Side Effects and Mechanism, Pharmacokinetics, and Drug Interactions:
See Methylphenidate IR fact sheet.

Clinical Pearls:
- **ER capsules** contain mixture of 30% IR and 70% ER beads. **Aptensio XR,** a new branded formulation of ER capsules, contains a mixture of 40% IR and 60% ER beads. **Ritalin LA** and its generic ER capsules are a combination of 50% IR and 50% DR beads. These products mimic BID dosing of IR.
- **Concerta** is based on the OROS osmotic delivery system (also used for Invega). 22% of dose is immediate (in 1-2 hours) and 78% is delayed.
- To avoid insomnia, dosing of these formulations should be completed by noon.
- **ER capsules** may be opened and contents sprinkled onto small amount (1 tablespoon) of cold applesauce (swallow without chewing).

Bottom Line:
There are many longer-acting methylphenidate preparations. Two good options are Concerta and Ritalin LA, both of which are now available generically.

METHYLPHENIDATE TRANSDERMAL (Daytrana) Fact Sheet

FDA Indications:
ADHD (adults and children >6 years).

Dosage Forms:
Transdermal patch: 10 mg, 15 mg, 20 mg, 30 mg/9 hour.

Dosage Guidance:
Start 10 mg/9 hour patch QAM (for initial therapy or for patients switching from other methylphenidate preparations, regardless of dose). Apply to hip 2 hours before an effect is needed and remove 9 hours after application (drug effects may persist for 5 hours after removal). Increase dose at weekly intervals by using next larger dose system. May be removed in <9 hours if shorter duration is desired or if late-day side effects occur. Rotate application sites. Max 30 mg QD.

Cost: $$$$

Side Effects:
- Most common: headache, insomnia, irritability, decreased appetite, anorexia, nausea, tic, application site reaction (10%-40% incidence in children).
- Serious but rare: allergic contact dermatitis/sensitization, characterized by intense local reactions (eg, edema, papules) that may spread beyond patch site; sensitization may subsequently manifest systemically with other routes of methylphenidate administration.

Mechanism, Pharmacokinetics, and Drug Interactions:
- Stimulant that inhibits reuptake of dopamine and norephinephrine.
- Hepatic metabolism via carboxylesterase CES1A1, not CYP450 isoenzymes; t ½: 3-4 hours.
- Avoid use with MAOIs, antacids.

Clinical Pearls:
- Apply patch to clean, dry area of the hip; don't apply to waistline or to areas under tight clothes, as it may rub off. Alternate sites daily (opposite hip). Absorption not affected by perspiration. Remove after 9 hours. If dislodged, replace with a new patch but remove within the 9-hour total wear time.
- Clinical effect usually seen in 2 hours and lasts approximately 12 hours.
- Exposure of application site to a heat source (eg, hair dryer, heating pad, electric blanket) may increase the amount of drug absorbed.
- In June 2015, the FDA added a warning that Daytrana could cause chemical leukoderma, a permanent loss of skin color. These reactions are irreversible and not harmful but can be disfiguring to patients. Instruct patients to contact their physician if they notice skin color changes or lightening of skin areas; in such cases an alternative medication should be considered.

Fun Fact:
Since 2006, Shire Pharmaceuticals has issued at least 10 recalls of Daytrana patches because users have had difficulty removing the protective cover from the patch. Recall costs have reached into the millions.

Bottom Line:
Daytrana is helpful for kids who, for whatever reason, cannot use any of the wide variety of oral stimulant preparations. Otherwise, we don't recommend it due to high cost, lag time for onset of effect, and the side effect of rash, which is pretty common and unpleasant. .

MIXED AMPHETAMINE SALTS (Adderall) Fact Sheet [G]

FDA Indications:
ADHD (adults and children >3 years for IR, >6 years for XR); **narcolepsy** (adults and children >6 years).

Off-Label Uses:
Obesity; treatment-resistant depression.

Dosage Forms:
- **Tablets (G):** 5 mg, 7.5 mg, 10 mg, 12.5 mg, 15 mg, 20 mg, 30 mg.
- **ER capsules (G):** 5 mg, 10 mg, 15 mg, 20 mg, 25 mg, 30 mg.

Dosage Guidance:
- ADHD
  - Rule of thumb for both preparations: Initial dose should be 0.5 mg/kg, but shoot for a target dose of 1.0 mg/kg-1.2 mg/kg.
  - Adults:
    - IR: Start 5 QAM-BID, max 40 mg/day divided BID.
    - XR: Start 20 mg QAM, increase to max 60 mg/day QAM.
  - Children and adolescents:
    - IR: Start 2.5 mg-5 mg BID, max 40 mg/day divided BID.
    - ER: Start 5 mg-10 mg QAM, increase gradually to max 30 mg/day, or 40 mg/day QAM in adolescents.
- Narcolepsy: Start 10 mg QAM, increase by 10 mg/day at weekly increments; max 60 mg/day.

Cost: IR: $; ER: $$$

Side Effects:
- Most common: insomnia, headache, decreased appetite, abdominal pain, weight loss, agitation.
- Serious but rare: See class warnings in chapter introduction.

Mechanism, Pharmacokinetics, and Drug Interactions:
- Stimulant that inhibits reuptake of dopamine and norephinephrine.
- Metabolized primarily through CYP2D6; t ½: 9-14 hours. Duration of action: 6-8 hours (IR). 8-12 hours (XR).
- Avoid use with MAOIs, antacids.

Clinical Pearls:
- Each dose contains a mixture of amphetamine salts, resulting in a 75:25 ratio of dextro and levo isomers of amphetamine.
- When converting from IR to ER, use the same total daily dose, given QAM.
- Adderall may provide more of a "kick" than methylphenidate preparations. Roughly twice as potent (per mg) as methylphenidate.
- Dextroamphetamine and mixed amphetamine salts are the only stimulants approved for children <6 years (approved for children >3 years).

Fun Fact:
Was briefly pulled from the market in Canada in 2005 because of cardiac concerns.

Bottom Line:
Adderall is effective but is probably the most abused and diverted of all stimulants, which is why we recommend starting most patients on methylphenidate instead.

Antidepressants

What to Prescribe

It's particularly hard to suggest a first-line antidepressant prescription because antidepressants are effective for so many other conditions. Nonetheless, it is helpful to review the most common clinical scenarios:

Medication-naïve patients with "just" depression

For these patients (admittedly unusual in a psychiatric practice), you want something effective and with minimal side effects. This means either an SSRI or bupropion. While most of us start with an SSRI, we recommend considering bupropion as your go-to first-line agent. With bupropion, you get an effective antidepressant with essentially no sexual side effects, no weight gain, no sedation, and a boost in attention. While it has not been approved for any anxiety disorders, bupropion is just as effective as SSRIs for the nonspecific anxiety that usually accompanies depression. On the downside, you have potential insomnia, and a small risk of seizure—but only at doses above 300 mg/day.

If you start with an SSRI, go with escitalopram or sertraline. Both have minimal side effects and minimal drug-drug interactions.

Patients who have comorbid conditions

Patients with depression plus another psychiatric disorder can be tried on "twofer" meds—that is, antidepressants that have clear efficacy for two conditions. Here are some of the common secondary conditions and meds that are effective for them: anxiety disorders (TCAs, SSRIs), bulimia (fluoxetine), smoking cessation (bupropion), ADHD (bupropion), fibromyalgia (duloxetine), diabetic neuropathic pain (duloxetine), and premenstrual dysphoric disorder (SSRIs). Finally, mirtazapine—an antidepressant sometimes shunned because it causes weight gain—is an excellent choice for patients with depression who are underweight and have insomnia.

Patients who have been on other antidepressants

"Treatment-resistant depression" is usually defined as the failure of at least two prior trials of antidepressants at adequate doses and for adequate lengths of time. Such patients fall into two classes: those who have failed the antidepressants on someone else's watch, and those who have failed them on your watch. When a new patient gives you a list of antidepressants that have already been tried, you have a judgment call to make. Some patients may seem more reliable than others, but on the other hand, you may want to obtain records from prior treatment that are credible.

If the patient fails some antidepressants that you prescribed, you can be more confident of a diagnosis of treatment-resistant depression. There's unfortunately no convincing data on what your next step should be. The Star-D trial tried to tease out strategies such as switching vs. augmenting, but it could not find statistical differences between the techniques. That means we're left with a combination of the few clinical trials that have been published, leavened with a great deal of personal preference. Here's a reasonable approach:

- First, try switching to an antidepressant in a different class. Assuming the treatment failures were on SSRIs, the usual sequence of subsequent trials would be: 1) bupropion; 2) an SNRI (venlafaxine, duloxetine, levomilnacipram); 3) an MAOI or a tricyclic.
- Second, try a combination. A suggested combination and order to try are: 1) SSRI/SNRI + bupropion; 2) SSRI/SNRI + atypical antipsychotic; 3) SSRI/SNRI + lithium or thyroid supplementation. There are many more combination possibilities, but these are probably the highest yield with which to begin.
- Third, hit the neurostimulation devices, such as ECT, TMS, and others.

Class Warnings

There are some side effects or warnings that apply to **all** antidepressants. They are listed here in order to minimize repetition in the fact sheets that follow.

Suicide risk

A black box warning regarding an increased risk of suicidal ideation in children and adolescents was added to the labeling on all antidepressants by the FDA in 2004. The warning was based on retrospective reports that showed a very slight increase in suicidal ideation in patients on 9 different antidepressants. The warning was revised in 2007 to also include adolescents and young adults, up to age 24. Since then, more prospective data have emerged that do not support an association, and this warning has been called further into question.

In fact, the data suggest that severity of depression itself is associated with increased risk of suicide. For now, however, the warning remains and is applied to the labeling of all medications approved for the treatment of depression. Thus, you should monitor all patients closely—especially early in therapy or after medication discontinuation—for clinical worsening, changes in behavior, or suicidality.

Mania switch

Activation of mania or hypomania may occur with the use of any antidepressant in individuals who are at risk. Antidepressants should be used with caution in patients with a history of mania or hypomania, or in those with a family history of bipolar disorder.

Serotonin syndrome

A rare but potentially life-threatening condition called serotonin syndrome (agitation, hallucinations, other mental status changes, hyperthermia, tachycardia, labile BP, myoclonus, hyperreflexia, incoordination, nausea, vomiting, diarrhea) has been reported when serotonergic antidepressants have been used with other serotonergic agents (including SSRIs, SNRIs, buspirone, lithium, MAOIs).

Discontinuation syndrome

Abrupt discontinuation of antidepressants, particularly SSRIs and SNRIs, may result in a discontinuation syndrome. While not medically dangerous and generally self-limiting, the discontinuation syndrome may be uncomfortable for patients. Symptoms include dizziness, nausea, headache, irritability, insomnia, diarrhea, agitation, sensory disturbances (eg, electric shock sensations), lethargy, and abnormal dreams. In general, symptoms are more severe with higher-dose and longer-term antidepressant use. Agents that are particularly short-acting may have a higher likelihood of causing a discontinuation syndrome (eg, paroxetine, venlafaxine IR) compared to longer-acting agents (eg, fluoxetine). In cases of planned discontinuation, antidepressant dose should be gradually reduced.

Bleeding risk

Increased bleeding episodes (eg, GI bleed, bruising, nosebleed) have been reported with serotonergic antidepressants, particularly when they are used concomitantly with aspirin, NSAIDs, anticoagulants, or antiplatelet agents.

Table 2: Antidepressants

Generic Name (Brand Name) Year FDA Approved [G] denotes generic availability	Relevant FDA Indication(s)	Available Strengths (mg)	Usual Adult Dosage Range (starting–max) (mg)
Selective serotonin reuptake inhibitor (SSRI)			
Citalopram [G] (Celexa) 1998	MDD	10, 20, 40, 10/5 mL	20–40
Escitalopram [G] (Lexapro) 2002	MDD (12+ yrs), GAD	5, 10, 20, 5/5 mL	10–20
Fluoxetine [G] (Prozac) 1987	MDD (8+ yrs), OCD (7+ yrs), panic disorder, bulimia, PMDD (as Sarafem)	10, 20, 40, 60, 20/5 mL 10, 15, 20 (Sarafem)	20–80
Fluoxetine DR [G] (Prozac Weekly) 2001	MDD, OCD, panic disorder, bulimia	90 DR	90 Qweek
Fluvoxamine [G] Luvox brand discontinued; generic only 1994	OCD	25, 50, 100	50–300
Fluvoxamine ER [G] (Luvox CR) 2008	OCD	100, 150 ER	100–300
Paroxetine [G] (Paxil) 1992 (Pexeva) 2003 (Brisdelle) 2013	MDD, OCD, panic disorder, social anxiety, GAD, PTSD, PMDD, menopausal hot flashes	7.5 (Brisdelle), 10, 20, 30, 40, 10/5 mL	20–60
Paroxetine CR [G] (Paxil CR) 1999	MDD, panic disorder, social anxiety, PMDD	12.5, 25, 37.5 ER	25–62.5
Sertraline [G] (Zoloft) 1991	MDD, OCD (6+ yrs), panic disorder, PTSD, PMDD, social anxiety	25, 50, 100, 150, 200, 20/mL	50–200
Serotonin norepinephrine reuptake inhibitor (SNRI)			
Desvenlafaxine [G] (Khedezla, Pristiq) 2008	MDD	25, 50, 100 ER	50–100
Duloxetine [G] (Cymbalta) 2004	MDD, GAD (7+ yrs) (also diabetic peripheral neuropathy, fibromyalgia, chronic musculoskeletal pain)	20, 30, 40, 60 DR	40–120
Levomilnacipran (Fetzima) 2013	MDD	20, 40, 80, 120 ER	20–120
Venlafaxine [G] 1993 Effexor brand discontinued; generic only	MDD	25, 37.5, 50, 75, 100	75–375
Venlafaxine ER [G] (Effexor XR) 1997	MDD, GAD, social anxiety disorder, panic disorder	37.5, 75, 150, 225 ER	75–225

Generic Name (Brand Name) Year FDA Approved [G] denotes generic availability	Relevant FDA Indication(s)	Available Strengths (mg)	Usual Adult Dosage Range (starting–max) (mg)
Tricyclic antidepressant (TCA)			
Amitriptyline [G] Elavil brand discontinued; generic only 1961	MDD	10, 25, 50, 75, 100, 150	50–300
Clomipramine [G] (Anafranil) 1989	OCD (10+ yrs)	25, 50, 75	25–250
Desipramine [G] (Norpramin) 1964	MDD	10, 25, 50, 75, 100, 150	50–300
Imipramine [G] Tofranil brand discontinued; generic only 1984	MDD	10, 25, 50, 75, 100, 125, 150	25-300
Nortriptyline [G] (Pamelor) 1977	MDD	10, 25, 50, 75, 10/5 mL	25–150
Monoamine oxidase inhibitor (MAOI)			
Isocarboxazid (Marplan) 1959	MDD	10	20–60
Phenelzine [G] (Nardil) 1961	MDD	15	45–90
Selegiline transdermal (EMSAM) 2006	MDD	6, 9, 12/24h patch	6/24h–12/24h
Tranylcypromine [G] (Parnate) 1961	MDD	10	30–60
Dopamine norepinephrine reuptake inhibitor			
Bupropion [G] (Wellbutrin) 1985	MDD	75, 100	200–450
Bupropion SR [G] (Wellbutrin SR, Budeprion SR) 1996	MDD, smoking cessation	100, 150, 200	150–400
Bupropion XL [G] (Wellbutrin XL, Budeprion XL, Forfivo XL) 2003	MDD, seasonal affective disorder	150, 300 (Wellbutrin XL), 450 (Forfivo XL)	150–450
Noradrenergic and specific serotonergic antidepressant (NaSSA)			
Mirtazapine [G] (Remeron) 1996	MDD	7.5, 15, 30, 45	15–45
Mirtazapine ODT [G] (Remeron SolTab) 2001	MDD	15, 30, 45	15–45
Serotonin reuptake inhibitor and 5-HT2A and 5-HT2C antagonist			
Trazodone [G] Desyrel brand discontinued; generic only 1981	MDD	50, 100, 150, 300	50–600
Trazodone ER (Oleptro) 2010	MDD	150, 300	150–375

2016 Medication Fact Book *The Carlat Psychiatry Report*

Generic Name (Brand Name) Year FDA Approved [G] denotes generic availability	Relevant FDA Indication(s)	Available Strengths (mg)	Usual Adult Dosage Range (starting–max) (mg)
Serotonin reuptake inhibitor and 5-HT1A agonist			
Vilazodone (Viibryd) 2011	MDD	10, 20, 40	10–40
Serotonin reuptake inhibitor and 5-HT1A agonist, 5-HT1B partial agonist, and 5-HT3 & 5-HT7 antagonist			
Vortioxetine (Brintellix) 2013	MDD	5, 10, 15, 20	10–20

BUPROPION (Wellbutrin) Fact Sheet [G]

FDA Indications:
Major depression; seasonal affective disorder; smoking cessation.

Off Label Uses:
ADHD; sexual dysfunction; bipolar depression.

Dosage Forms:
- **Tablets (G):** 75 mg, 100 mg.
- **SR tablets (G):** 100 mg, 150 mg, 200 mg.
- **ER tablets** (G): 150 mg, 300 mg, **Forfivo XL:** 450 mg.
- **ER tablets, hydrobromide salt formulation (Aplenzin):** 174 mg, 348 mg, 522 mg (equivalent to 150 mg, 300 mg, 450 mg, respectively).

Dosage Guidance:
- Depression (target dose 300 mg/day):
  - IR: Start 100 mg BID, ↑ to 100 mg TID after >3 days; max dose 450 mg/day, 150 mg/dose, separate doses by at least 6 hours.
  - SR: Start 150 mg QAM, ↑ to 150 mg BID as early as fourth day; max dose 400 mg/day, 200 mg/dose, separate doses by at least 8 hours.
  - ER: Start 150 mg QAM, ↑ to 300 mg QAM as early as fourth day; max dose 450 mg QAM.

Cost: IR/SR/ER: $-$$; Forfivo: $$$$

Side Effects:
- Most common: agitation, insomnia, headache, nausea, vomiting, tremor, tachycardia, dry mouth, weight loss.
- Serious but rare: seizures; risk higher with rapid and large dose increases and in patients at risk for seizures. Risk of seizure depends on dose and formulation: IR: 300 mg/day-450 mg/day (0.4%) vs 450 mg/day-600 mg/day (4%). SR/ER: 100 mg/day-300 mg/day (0.1%) vs 400 mg/day (0.4%). Do not chew, divide, or crush SR or ER tablets as risk of seizures may be increased.

Mechanism, Pharmacokinetics, and Drug Interactions:
- Dopamine and norepinephrine receptor uptake inhibitor.
- Metabolized primarily through CYP2B6; also inhibits CYP2D6; t ½: 21 hours.
- Avoid use with MAOIs.

Clinical Pearls:
- Forfivo XL offers ease of use (1 pill a day) for patients taking 450 mg/day, but it is more expensive and not yet available as generic.
- Aplenzin brand could also be a 1-pill-a-day solution (the 522 mg is equivalent to 450 mg Wellbutrin) but otherwise doesn't offer any real clinical advantage as a different salt (hydrobromide) formulation.
- Give ER dose as early in the morning as possible to minimize insomnia.

Not-So-Fun Fact:
There have been case reports of teenagers and prisoners snorting crushed tablets (believing it to be a stimulant), with subsequent seizures.

Bottom Line:
May be particularly useful for individuals whose depression is associated with fatigue and poor concentration. Absence of sexual side effects and weight gain make this an appealing option for many depressed patients. Although not effective for anxiety disorders, it is effective for the anxiety that often accompanies depression. The seizure risk is not a concern for most patients when dosed appropriately.

DESVENLAFAXINE (Pristiq) Fact Sheet [G]

FDA Indications:

Major depression.

Off-Label Uses:

Fibromyalgia; vasomotor symptoms of menopause; GAD; social anxiety disorder; panic disorder; PTSD; PMDD.

Dosage Forms:

ER tablets (G): 25 mg, 50 mg, 100 mg.

Dosage Guidance:

Start 50 mg QD. Doses up to 400 mg/day have been studied, but there is likely no added benefit of doses >50 mg/day, only an increase in side effects.

Cost: $$$

Side Effects:

- Most common: nausea, dizziness, insomnia, excessive sweating, constipation, dry mouth, somnolence, decreased appetite, anxiety, and sexual side effects.
- Serious but rare: dose–related increases in systolic and diastolic blood pressure (as likely with Pristiq as Effexor). Monitor BP regularly, and if increases are sustained, consider reducing dose or discontinuing.

Mechanism, Pharmacokinetics, and Drug Interactions:

- Serotonin and norepinephrine reuptake inhibitor.
- Active metabolite of venlafaxine, metabolized primarily through conjugation and oxidation via CYP3A4 (minor). Minimally inhibits CYP2D6; t ½: 11 hours.
- Avoid use with MAOIs, other serotonergic medications. Not likely to cause other clinically significant interactions.

Clinical Pearls:

- Desvenlafaxine has not been shown to be any more effective than venlafaxine. Unlike venlafaxine, increasing the dose of desvenlafaxine beyond the recommended 50 mg/day likely does not improve response, but does increase side effects.
- Claims of fewer drug interactions with desvenlafaxine are likely unimportant for the majority of patients as the risk of clinically significant interactions with venlafaxine is already quite low.
- Desvenlafaxine is available in 3 forms: a succinate salt (Pristiq), a base (Khedezla), and a fumarate extended release tablet. Aside from small differences in half-life, there is no difference between these products—all efficacy studies were based on the original Pristiq studies.

Fun Fact:

Desvenlafaxine has not been approved for any indication in the European Union, where regulatory bodies have said that desvenlafaxine is likely less effective than venlafaxine with no advantages in terms of safety and tolerability.

Bottom Line:

For the majority of patients, there are no clear advantages to using desvenlafaxine over other agents, particularly venlafaxine XR.

DULOXETINE (Cymbalta) Fact Sheet [G]

FDA Indications:

Major depression; **generalized anxiety disorder** (kids ages 7+ and adults); **diabetic peripheral neuropathic pain**; **fibromyalgia**; **chronic musculoskeletal pain** (including osteoarthritis and chronic low back pain).

Off-Label Uses:

Other neuropathic or chronic pain disorders; other anxiety disorders; stress urinary incontinence.

Dosage Forms:

Capsules (delayed release) (G): 20 mg, 30 mg, 40 mg, 60 mg.

Dosage Guidance:

All indications: Start 40 mg–60 mg/day; may be divided (20 mg or 30 mg BID) or given as a single daily dose; target dose 60 mg QD; for doses >60 mg/day, titrate in increments of 30 mg/day over 1 week to max 120 mg/day, although doses >60 mg/day not shown to be more effective.

Cost: $

Side Effects:

- Most common: nausea, dry mouth, constipation, diarrhea, decreased appetite, vomiting, fatigue, insomnia, dizziness, agitation, sweating, headache, and sexual side effects.
- Serious but rare: Rare cases of hepatic failure (including fatalities) have been reported (too rare to require routine LFTs in all patients). Hepatitis with abdominal pain, hepatomegaly, elevated transaminases >20 times normal, with and without jaundice observed. May cause orthostatic hypotension or syncope, especially in first week of therapy and after dose increases. Urinary retention reported; hospitalization and/or catheterization were necessary in some cases.

Mechanism, Pharmacokinetics, and Drug Interactions:

- Serotonin and norepinephrine reuptake inhibitor.
- Metabolized primarily through CYP1A2 and 2D6. Inhibitor of CYP2D6; t ½: 12 hours.
- Avoid use with MAOIs, other serotonergic medications. Caution with drugs metabolized by CYP2D6 (eg, paroxetine, fluoxetine, aripiprazole, iloperidone, atomoxetine, beta blockers) as their levels may be increased. Potent inhibitors of CYP2D6 (eg, paroxetine, fluoxetine, quinidine) and CYP1A2 (eg, fluvoxamine, ciprofloxacin) may increase duloxetine levels.

Clinical Pearls:

- Since capsules are delayed release, they should be swallowed whole; do not chew or crush. Although the manufacturer does not recommend opening the capsules, their contents may be sprinkled on applesauce or in apple juice and swallowed immediately.
- Avoid in patients with a history of heavy alcohol use or chronic hepatic disease because of the possibility that duloxetine and alcohol may interact, causing hepatic injury, or the possibility that duloxetine may aggravate preexisting hepatic disease.

Fun Fact:

Duloxetine is approved in Europe for stress urinary incontinence, but the FDA refused this indication in the US because of concerns regarding liver toxicity and potential suicidal ideation.

Bottom Line:

Duloxetine has a niche for depressed patients with various comorbid pain syndromes. However, you should balance this advantage against its potentially serious hepatic side effects.

LEVOMILNACIPRAN (Fetzima) Fact Sheet

FDA Indications:

Major depression.

Off-Label Uses:

Fibromyalgia; anxiety disorders; vasomotor symptoms of menopause; diabetic peripheral neuropathy; chronic musculoskeletal pain.

Dosage Forms:

ER capsules: 20 mg, 40 mg, 80 mg, 120 mg.

Dosage Guidance:

Start 20 mg QD; increase to 40 mg QD after 2 days, then by increments of 40 mg/d every 2 or more days to max 120 mg QD.

Cost: $$$

Side Effects:

- Most common: nausea, vomiting, constipation, sweating, increased heart rate (7–9 beats/minute), erectile dysfunction, and urinary hesitation.
- Serious but rare: urinary retention; increased blood pressure and tachycardia possible.

Mechanism, Pharmacokinetics, and Drug Interactions:

- Serotonin and norepinephrine reuptake inhibitor.
- Metabolized primarily through CYP3A4; t ½: 12 hours.
- Avoid use with MAOIs, other serotonergic medications. Use lower doses (no more than 80 mg/d) in presence of potent 3A4 inhibitors.

Clinical Pearls:

- Three 8–week studies showed greater efficacy than placebo at doses of 40 mg/day and greater. No head–to–head studies versus other antidepressants are available to date.
- According to the manufacturer, levomilnacipran has greater potency for norepinephrine reuptake inhibition than for serotonin reuptake inhibition.
- Noradrenergic effects may contribute to urinary hesitation or retention in about 4%-6% of patients and is dose-related.
- Do not cut, crush, chew, or dissolve; swallow extended release tablets whole with fluid.

Fun Fact:

Levomilnacipran is an enantiomer of milnacipran (Savella, also a Forest drug), an SNRI approved for fibromyalgia. Milnacipran has not shown robust antidepressant efficacy and does not have that indication in the US, although it is used for depression in other countries.

Bottom Line:

More experience will give us a better understanding of the ideal dose and this drug's place in therapy. Until then, consider it as a second-line SNRI.

MIRTAZAPINE (Remeron) Fact Sheet [G]

FDA Indications:

Major depression.

Off-Label Uses:

Panic disorder; PTSD; generalized anxiety disorder; insomnia; nausea; appetite stimulant.

Dosage Forms:

- **Tablets (G):** 7.5 mg, 15 mg, 30 mg, 45 mg.
- **Orally disintegrating tablets (G):** 15 mg, 30 mg, 45 mg.

Dosage Guidance:

- Start 15 mg QHS, ↑ to 15 mg-45 mg/day, ↑ dose every 1-2 weeks. Max 45 mg/day.

Cost: $; ODT: $

Side Effects:

- Most common: somnolence, increased appetite, weight gain.
- Serious but rare: agranulocytosis or severe neutropenia (with or without infection) reported very rarely.

Mechanism, Pharmacokinetics, and Drug Interactions:

- Noradrenergic (via central presynaptic alpha-2 adrenergic receptor antagonist activity) and specific serotonergic (via postsynaptic 5HT2 and 5HT3 antagonist effects) antidepressant.
- Metabolized primarily through CYP1A2, 2D6, and 3A4; t ½: 20-40 hours.
- Avoid use with MAOIs, other serotonergic agents. Caution with inducers of 1A2 or 3A4 (eg, carbamazepine), which could reduce efficacy of mirtazapine.

Clinical Pearls:

- One large meta-analysis reported that mirtazapine has a faster onset of actions than other antidepressants.
- If patients experience too much sedation at initial lower dose, increase dose; mirtazapine has increased noradrenergic effect relative to antihistaminergic effect at higher doses.

Fun Fact:

Esmirtazapine, the (S)-enantiomer, was under development for the treatment of insomnia and hot flashes associated with menopause, but the company pulled the plug in 2010.

Bottom Line:

Mirtazapine is probably under-prescribed, likely due to concerns about weight gain and sedation. It is particularly useful in depressed patients with anxiety or insomnia, those who have had sexual side effects with other antidepressants, and those who may benefit from appetite stimulation (eg, elderly, cancer patients).

MONOAMINE OXIDASE INHIBITORS (MAOIs) Fact Sheet [G]

FDA Indications:

Major depression.

Off-Label Uses:

Treatment-resistant depression; panic disorder; social anxiety disorder.

Dosage Forms:
- Isocarboxazid, **tablets (Marplan):** 10 mg (scored).
- Phenelzine, **tablets (Nardil, G):** 15 mg.
- Tranylcypromine, **tablets (Parnate, G):** 10 mg.

Dosage Guidance:
- Isocarboxazid: Start 10 mg BID, ↑ by 10 mg/day every 2–4 days, to 40 mg/day by end of the first week (divided BID-QID). After first week, may ↑ by up to 20 mg to max 60 mg/day. Use caution in patients on >40 mg/day.
- Phenelzine: Start 15 mg BID, ↑ by 15 mg/day every 2–4 days, up to 60 mg–90 mg/day divided BID.
- Tranylcypromine: Start 10 mg BID, ↑ by 10 mg/day every 2–3 weeks to maximum of 60 mg/day divided BID.

Cost: $$$$ Marplan; $$ phenelzine; $$$$ tranylcypromine

Side Effects:
- Most common: dizziness, headache, orthostatic hypotension, dry mouth, constipation, drowsiness, tremor, sweating, peripheral edema, sexual side effects.
- Serious but rare: hypertensive crisis (see drug interactions).

Mechanism, Pharmacokinetics, and Drug Interactions:
- Non-selective monoamine oxidase inhibitor.
- Metabolized primarily through liver, limited data though likely through oxidative CYP450; t ½ irrelevant as it is an irreversible inhibitor; effects continue for 2 weeks after discontinued.
- Avoid with other antidepressants, serotonergic agents, stimulants, sympathomimetics, dextromethorphan, disulfiram, meperidine. Do not use within 5 weeks of fluoxetine discontinuation or 2 weeks of other antidepressant discontinuation. Discontinue at least 10 days prior to elective surgery. Antihypertensives may exaggerate hypotensive effects.
- Avoid use with foods or supplements high in tyramine, tryptophan, phenylalanine, or tyrosine. Examples include aged cheese, air-dried or cured meats (eg, salami), fava or broad bean pods, tap/draft beers, Marmite concentrate, sauerkraut, soy sauce, or spoiled foods.

Clinical Pearls:
- Studies in the 1970s and 1980s showed that MAOIs were more effective than TCAs for atypical depression, characterized by overeating, oversleeping, rejection sensitivity, and mood reactivity.
- Rough dose equivalents: 20 mg of tranylcypromine = 40 mg of isocarboxazid = 45 mg phenelzine.
- When switching from an MAOI to another antidepressant, wait 2 weeks after MAOI discontinuation. This is because monoamine enzymes are irreversibly inhibited by these MAOIs, and regeneration of enzymes takes 2–3 weeks after discontinuation.

Fun Fact:

MAOIs were the first antidepressants developed, after tuberculosis patients given the antibacterial agent isoniazid (INH) were found to have an elevated mood. Isoniazid was found to be an MAOI and was developed as the first antidepressant in the late 1950s.

Bottom Line:

Not commonly used due to side effects, dietary restrictions, and drug interactions; however, MAOIs should be considered for appropriate patients who do not tolerate or respond to other antidepressants.

SELECTIVE SEROTONIN REUPTAKE INHIBITORS (SSRIs) Fact Sheet [G]

See Tables 3 and 3.1 for **medication names, FDA indication(s), off-label use, supplied as, costs, dosing, pharmacokinetics, and drug interaction information.** (Year of FDA approval can be found in Table 2.)

Side Effects:

- Most common (SSRI with highest incidence in parentheses): nausea (sertraline), insomnia and anxiety (fluoxetine), constipation, sedation, sexual side effects, weight gain (all four paroxetine), apathy, headache.
- Serious but rare: hyponatremia, mainly in the elderly; gastrointestinal bleeding, especially when combined with NSAIDs such as ibuprofen.
- Avoid use with MAOIs (5-week washout period with fluoxetine, 2-week washout period with all others); avoid other serotonergic agents (serotonin syndrome).
- Fluoxetine, fluvoxamine, and paroxetine are most likely to cause clinically significant P450 interaction.

Clinical Pearls:

- All SSRIs are generally equivalent in terms of efficacy. Medication selection is usually made on the basis of side effect profile, potential for drug-drug interactions, insurance coverage, and patient preference.
- Citalopram's maximum daily dose was reduced to 40 mg/day by FDA in August 2011 due to data suggesting increased QTc interval prolongation at doses >40 mg/day. Mean QTc interval prolongation at 60 mg/d was 18.5 msec (vs ziprasidone which has been shown to increase this interval by 20.6 msec). As of this writing, no comparable warning has been issued for escitalopram.
- Escitalopram (which is purified from the racemic mixture, citalopram) is considered the "purest" SSRI and has few, if any, drug-drug interactions.
- Fluoxetine is favored in patients who could use some activation; most likely to cause insomnia, anxiety, decreased appetite.
- Fluvoxamine is used less often due to twice-daily dosing, risk for drug interactions, and fewer data for uses other than OCD even though it's likely just as effective as other SSRIs.
- Paroxetine is least favored due to side effect profile (greatest sexual side effects, weight gain, sedation, constipation) and drug interaction profile.
- Generally, higher doses of SSRIs are required for treating OCD.
- Use lower initial dose for patients with anxiety disorders, particularly panic disorder.
- SSRIs are sometimes prescribed off-label for menopausal symptoms (hot flashes), somatoform disorders, pain syndromes, migraines, and premature ejaculation.

Fun Fact:

SSRIs were the first class of psychotropic drugs discovered using rational drug design, a process that starts with a specific biological target and then creates a molecule designed to affect it.

Bottom Line:

SSRIs have become a mainstay for the treatment of patients with depression and anxiety disorders. Consider them as first-line treatment for many patients and be familiar with at least a couple of agents within the class.

Table 3: Selective Serotonin Reuptake Inhibitors (SSRIs)

Generic Name (Brand Name) [G] denotes generic availability	Relevant FDA Indication(s)	Available Strengths (mg except where noted)	Usual Dosage Range (starting–max) (mg)	Off-Label Use(s)	Cost (Cost for generic, unless otherwise specified)
Citalopram [G] (Celexa)	MDD	10, 20, 40 tabs, 10/5 mL	20 QD–40 QD Increase by 20 mg/d in 7d	OCD, PTSD, social anxiety, GAD, panic disorder, PMDD	$
Escitalopram [G] (Lexapro)	MDD (12+ yrs), GAD	5, 10, 20 tabs, 5/5 mL	10 QD–20 QD Increase by 10 mg/d in 7d	OCD, PTSD, social anxiety, panic disorder, PMDD	$
Fluoxetine [G] (Prozac, Prozac Weekly, Sarafem)	MDD (8+ yrs), OCD (7+ yrs), panic disorder, bulimia, PMDD (as Sarafem)	10, 20, 40, 60 caps/tabs; 90 DR (Prozac weekly); 20/5 mL; 10, 15, 20 tabs (Sarafem)	20 QAM–80 QAM (Starting dose DR: 90 Qweek) Increase 10 mg/d after several weeks	PTSD, social anxiety	$ Sarafem: $$$$
Fluvoxamine [G] (Luvox, Luvox CR)	OCD (8+ yrs)	25, 50, 100 IR tabs; 100, 150 ER caps	50 QHS–300 QHS (Starting dose CR: 100 QHS) Increase by 50 mg/d Qweek	MDD, panic disorder, GAD, PTSD	$
Paroxetine [G] (Brisdelle, Paxil, Paxil CR, Pexeva)	MDD, OCD, panic disorder, social anxiety, GAD, PTSD, PMDD, menopausal hot flashes (Brisdelle)	10, 20, 30, 40 tabs; 10/5 mL; 12.5, 25, 37.5 ER; 7.5 (Brisdelle)	20 mg QHS–60 QHS CR: 25 QD–62.5 QD Increase by 10 mg/d Qweek; CR: 12.5 mg/d Qweek	Premature ejaculation	$ Brisdelle: $$$
Sertraline [G] (Zoloft)	MDD, OCD (6+ yrs), panic disorder, PTSD, PMDD, social anxiety	25, 50, 100, 150, 200 tabs; 20/mL	50 QD–200 QD Increase by 50 mg/d Qweek	GAD	$

Table 3.1: Pharmacokinetics and Drug Interactions of SSRIs

SSRI	Metabolized by (major pathways in bold)	Inhibits (potent inhibition in bold)	Elimination half-life
Citalopram	**2C19, 3A4**, 2D6	2D6 (weak)	35 h
Escitalopram	**2C19, 3A4**, 2D6	2D6 (weak)	27–32 h
Fluoxetine	**2D6**	**2C9/19, 2D6**, 3A4	4–6 days fluoxetine; 9 days norfluoxetine (metabolite)
Fluvoxamine	**1A2, 2D6**	**1A2, 2C9/19, 3A4**	15 h
Paroxetine	**2D6**	**2D6**	21 h
Sertraline	**2C19**, 2D6, 3A4	2D6 (weak), 3A4 (weak)	26 h

SELEGILINE TRANSDERMAL (EMSAM) Fact Sheet

FDA Indications:
Major depression.

Off-Label Uses:
Treatment-resistant depression; panic disorder; treatment-resistant anxiety disorders.

Dosage Forms:
Transdermal patch: 6 mg, 9 mg, 12 mg/24 hour patch.

Dosage Guidance:
- Start 6 mg/24 hours QD; may ↑ in increments of 3 mg/24 h every 2 weeks up to max 12 mg/24 hours.
- Apply to clean, dry, intact skin to upper torso (below neck and above waist), upper thigh, or outer surface of upper arm; apply at the same time each day and rotate application sites; wash hands with soap and water after handling; avoid touching sticky side of patch.

Cost: $$$$$

Side Effects:
- Most common: headache, insomnia, application site reaction, hypotension, diarrhea, dry mouth, weight loss.
- Serious but rare: orthostatic hypotension; caution in patients at risk (elderly, cerebrovascular disease, cardiovascular disease, hypovolemia).

Mechanism, Pharmacokinetics, and Drug Interactions:
- Non-selective monoamine oxidase inhibitor.
- Metabolized primarily through CYP2B6 (also 2C9, 3A4/5) to active (N-desmethylselegiline, amphetamine, methamphetamine) and inactive metabolites; t ½: 18–25 hours.
- Avoid with other antidepressants, serotonergic agents, stimulants, sympathomimetics, dextromethorphan, disulfiram, meperidine. Do not use within 5 weeks of fluoxetine discontinuation or 2 weeks of other antidepressant discontinuation. Discontinue at least 10 days prior to elective surgery. Antihypertensives may exaggerate hypotensive effects. For doses higher than 6 mg, avoid use with foods or supplements high in tyramine, tryptophan, phenylalanine, or tyrosine.
- Wait 2 weeks after discontinuing transdermal selegiline before initiating therapy with serotonergic or any other contraindicated drug.

Clinical Pearls:
- Oral selegiline (Eldepryl) used in Parkinson's disease (≤10 mg/day) is a selective inhibitor of MAO-B, which metabolizes dopamine. When used transdermally as EMSAM, selegiline achieves higher blood levels and non-selectively inhibits both MAO-A and MAO-B. Its antidepressant effect is thought to be due to its MAO-A inhibition, which blocks the breakdown of other centrally active neurotransmitters (norepinephrine, serotonin).
- When using 6 mg/day patch, no special diet required. When using higher doses, tyramine-restricted diet should be followed.
- Patch may contain conducting metal (eg, aluminum); avoid exposure of application site to external heat source, which may increase the amount of drug absorbed.

Fun Fact:
Named "EMSAM" after Emily and Samuel, the children of the CEO of Somerset Pharmaceuticals (original manufacturer).

Bottom Line:
While EMSAM is rarely used, there are some potential advantages, including compliance with patients who do not like swallowing pills; less suicide risk (harder to overdose on a patch than with pills); less likelihood of dietary interactions at 6 mg, and possibly at higher doses too; probably fewer side effects than other MAOIs, such as weight gain and sexual side effects. When MAOIs are indicated, this may be the least risky option to try.

TRAZODONE (Oleptro) Fact Sheet [G]

FDA Indications:

Major depression.

Off-Label Uses:

Insomnia; anxiety.

Dosage Forms:

- **Tablets (G):** 50 mg, 100 mg, 150 mg, 300 mg (scored).
- **ER tablets (Oleptro):** 150 mg, 300 mg (scored).

Dosage Guidance:

- Depression:
  - IR: Start 50 mg TID; ↑ by 50 mg/day every 3-4 days to response (usually 300 mg-400 mg/day); max 600 mg/day.
  - ER: Start 150 mg QHS, ↑ by 75 mg/day every 3 days; max 375 mg/day.
- Insomnia (off-label): Start 25 mg-50 mg QHS; may ↑ by 50 mg increments up to 200 mg QHS.

Cost: IR: $; ER: $$$

Side Effects:

- Most common: drowsiness, dry mouth, dizziness or lightheadedness, orthostatic hypotension, headache, blurred vision, nausea, or vomiting.
- Serious but rare: reports of priapism (painful erection >6 hours in duration); may require surgical or pharmacologic (eg, epinephrine) intervention and may result in impotence or permanent impairment of erectile function. Orthostatic hypotension and syncope reported (less at hypnotic doses).

Mechanism, Pharmacokinetics, and Drug Interactions:

- Serotonin reuptake inhibitor, alpha-1 adrenergic receptor antagonist and serotonin 5HT2A and 5HT2C receptor antagonist.
- Metabolized primarily through CYP3A4 to active metabolite (mCPP); Induces P-glycoprotein; t ½: 7-10 hours.
- Avoid use with MAOIs.

Clinical Pearls:

- If daytime drowsiness occurs, administer the majority of dosage at bedtime or ↓ dose.
- Trazodone's hypnotic effects are not due to anticholinergic nor antihistaminergic effects.
- IR formulation rarely used as antidepressant due to risk for over-sedation and orthostasis at therapeutic doses; majority of IR use currently is for insomnia.

Fun Fact:

As a consequence of the production of mCPP as a metabolite, patients taking trazodone may test positive on urine tests for the presence of MDMA (ecstasy).

Bottom Line:

Fewer sexual side effects and less weight gain compared to other serotonergic antidepressants make this drug appealing for depression. But significant daytime somnolence and dizziness (even with ER formulation), as well as questionable efficacy for depression at doses ≤375 mg/day, limit the utility of trazodone in depression. Trazodone continues to be a go-to drug for many patients with insomnia.

TRICYCLIC ANTIDEPRESSANTS (TCAs) Fact Sheet [G]

FDA Indications:

Major depression, obsessive compulsive disorder (OCD).

Off-Label Uses:

Headache; neuropathic pain; fibromyalgia; anxiety disorders; insomnia.

Dosage Forms:
- **Amitriptyline tablets (G):** 10 mg, 25 mg, 50 mg, 75 mg, 100 mg, 150 mg.
- **Clomipramine capsules (Anafranil, G):** 25 mg, 50 mg, 75 mg.
- **Desipramine tablets (Norpramin, G):** 10 mg, 25 mg, 50 mg, 75 mg, 100 mg, 150 mg.
- **Imipramine tablets and capsules (G):** 10 mg, 25 mg, 50 mg, 75 mg, 100 mg, 125 mg, 150 mg.
- **Nortriptyline capsules (Pamelor, G):** 10 mg, 25 mg, 50 mg, 75 mg, and 10 mg/5 mL oral solution.

Dosage Guidance:
- Amitriptyline or imipramine: Start 25 mg–50 mg QHS and ↑ by 25 mg–50 mg/day intervals every 2–3 days to target dose 150 mg–200 mg/day; max 300 mg/day.
- Clomipramine: Start 25 mg QHS and ↑ by 25 mg/day every 4–7 days to target dose 150 mg–250 mg/day; max 250 mg/day.
- Desipramine: Start 25 mg–50 mg QHS and ↑ by 25 mg–50 mg/day intervals every 2–3 days to target dose 150 mg–200 mg/day; max 300 mg/day.
- Nortriptyline: Start 25 mg–50 mg QHS and ↑ by 25 mg–50 mg/day intervals every 2–3 days to target dose 50 mg–150 mg/day; max 150 mg/day.

Cost: amitriptyline: $; clomipramine: $$$; desipramine: $$; imipramine: $; nortriptyline: $

Side Effects:
- Most common: sedation, dry mouth, constipation, weight gain, sexual side effects, urinary hesitation, blurred vision.
- Serious but rare: seizure; cardiac effects including orthostasis, arrhythmias, QT prolongation, AV block.

Mechanism, Pharmacokinetics, and Drug Interactions:
- Serotonin and norepinephrine reuptake inhibitor.
- Metabolized primarily through liver, limited data though likely through oxidative CYP2D6 primarily; t ½ ranges from 18–44 hrs.
- Avoid use with other serotonergic antidepressants or agents with hypotensive or anticholinergic effects.

Clinical Pearls:
- Using divided doses (BID to TID) may help with tolerability during initiation and titration; but can convert to QHS dosing to minimize daytime sedation.
- Tertiary amines amitriptyline and imipramine are metabolized to secondary amines nortriptyline and imipramine, respectively. Secondary amines generally better tolerated.
- Serum level monitoring established for some TCAs (amitriptyline + nortriptyline: 120–250 ng/mL; desipramine: >115–250 ng/mL; nortriptyline: 50–150 ng/mL).
- Overdose toxicity with potentially serious cardiac effects or fatality with as little as 10-day supply.

Fun Fact:

Imipramine was the first antidepressant approved in the US, developed by tweaking the molecular structure of the antipsychotic Thorazine. It didn't work for psychosis, but was the first wonder drug for depression and anxiety.

Bottom Line:

Not commonly used due to side effects and overdose toxicity risk; however, TCAs should be considered for appropriate patients who do not respond to other antidepressants.

VENLAFAXINE (Effexor XR) Fact Sheet [G]

FDA Indications:
Major depression, social anxiety disorder, GAD, panic disorder.

Off-Label Uses:
PTSD; PMDD; vasomotor symptoms of menopause; diabetic peripheral neuropathy.

Dosage Forms:
- **Tablets (G):** 25 mg, 37.5 mg, 50 mg, 75 mg, 100 mg (scored).
- **ER tablets (G):** 37.5 mg, 75 mg, 150 mg, 225 mg.

Dosage Guidance:
- Depression:
  Start 75 mg/day in 2-3 divided doses or as XR once daily; ↑ dose by 75 mg/day at intervals of 4 or more days; max 375 mg/day (divided TID) or 225 mg/day XR given once daily. IR may be switched to nearest equivalent daily dose of XR QD.
- Anxiety:
  XR: Start 75 mg QD, ↑ by 75 mg/day at weekly intervals; max 225 mg/day; for panic disorder, to minimize exacerbation of panic, start 37.5 mg QD, ↑ to 75 mg QD after 1 week then by 75 mg/day at weekly intervals; max 225 mg/day.

Cost: IR: $; ER: $$

Side Effects:
- Most common: anorexia, constipation, dizziness, dry mouth, nausea, nervousness, somnolence, sweating, sexual side effects, headache, insomnia.
- Serious but rare: sustained, dose-related hypertension reported. May cause hyponatremia or SIADH; use with caution in patients who are volume-depleted, elderly, or taking diuretics.

Mechanism, Pharmacokinetics, and Drug Interactions:
- Serotonin and norepinephrine reuptake inhibitor.
- Metabolized primarily through CYP2D6 to O-desmethylvenlafaxine (ODV), major active metabolite (an SNRI, marketed as Pristiq) and also by CYP3A4; t ½: 5 hrs (11 hrs for ODV).
- Avoid use with MAOIs, other serotonergic agents. Caution with CYP2D6 or 3A4 inhibitors, which may increase venlafaxine levels. Inhibits CYP2D6.

Clinical Pearls
- For patients with nausea, start at lower dose, titrate more slowly, and give with food.
- May cause false-positive PCP in urine drug screen.
- Increase in blood pressure much more likely in doses >225 mg/day.
- Significant discontinuation syndrome, even with XR formulation.
- Theoretically functions as an SSRI in low doses (75 mg/day) and as an SNRI in moderate doses (150 mg–225 mg/day), and affects all monoamines in high doses (>225 mg/day).
- No additional benefit seen with doses >225 mg/day in moderately depressed outpatients, but patients with more severe depression may respond to higher doses (350 mg/day).

Fun Fact:
Venlafaxine is structurally related to the atypical opioid analgesic tramadol (Ultram) (itself a serotonergic agent), but not to any other antidepressant drugs.

Bottom Line:
Venlafaxine is probably somewhat more effective than SSRIs for depression, with a number needed to treat (NNT) of around 15, but its side effect disadvantages relegate it to second-line use.

VILAZODONE (Viibryd) Fact Sheet

FDA Indications:
Major depression.

Off-Label Uses:
OCD; other anxiety disorders.

Dosage Forms:
Tablets: 10 mg, 20 mg, 40 mg.

Dosage Guidance:
- Start 10 mg QD for 7 days; ↑ to 20 mg QD for 7 days, then to recommended dose of 20 mg–40 mg QD (with food). Purpose of dose titration is to minimize GI effects.
- Must take with food, otherwise serum levels are reduced by up to 50%.

Cost: $$$$

Side Effects:
- Most common: diarrhea, nausea, vomiting, dry mouth, insomnia, dizziness.
- Serious but rare: possible hyponatremia or SIADH; use with caution in patients who are volume–depleted, elderly, or taking diuretics.

Mechanism, Pharmacokinetics, and Drug Interactions:
- SSRI plus 5–HT1A partial agonist (buspirone is also 5–HT1A partial agonist).
- Metabolized primarily through CYP3A4; t ½: 25 hours.
- Avoid use with MAOIs, other serotonergic agents. More P450 drug interactions possible with vilazodone than some other SSRIs: Use with 3A4 inhibitors or inducers may require dose adjustment.

Clinical Pearls:
Sometimes marketed as having no or few sexual side effects, but FDA officials wrote an article for *Journal of Clinical Psychiatry* clarifying that studies do not support this claim.

Fun Guess:
The brand name "Viibryd" likely has two origins. First, it rhymes with "hybrid," and the mechanism of action is a hybrid of SSRI and 5–HT1A partial agonism. Second, the word calls to mind "virile," which could be a subliminal suggestion that it does not worsen sexual functioning.

Bottom Line:
Vilazodone appears to be another SSRI (with a little buspirone thrown in). We do not yet know if it has any side effect advantages over other SSRIs. Disadvantages include the slow titration schedule, the need to take it with food in order to achieve a therapeutic blood level, and the many drug interactions. Until further notice, vilazodone should remain a second-line antidepressant.

VORTIOXETINE (Brintellix) Fact Sheet

FDA Indications:
Major depression.

Off-Label Uses:
Generalized anxiety disorder; other anxiety disorders.

Dosage Forms:
Tablets: 5 mg, 10 mg, 15 mg, 20 mg.

Dosage Guidance:
Start 10 mg QD; ↑ to 20 mg QD as tolerated. Consider 5 mg/day for those unable to tolerate higher doses.

Cost: $$$$

Side Effects:
- Most common: nausea, constipation, vomiting, sexual side effects, dry mouth, headache.
- Serious but rare: Serotonergic antidepressants have been rarely associated with bruising or bleeding.

Mechanism, Pharmacokinetics, and Drug Interactions:
- Multi-modal antidepressant.
- Metabolized primarily through CYP 2D6 and, to a lesser extent, via 3A4/5, 2C9/19, 2A6, 2C8, and 2B6; t ½: 66 hours.
- Avoid use with MAOIs, other serotonergic medications. Use lower doses in presence of potent 2D6 inhibitors.

Clinical Pearls:
- The recently approved vortioxetine is a "multimodal" antidepressant or a "serotonin modulator and stimulator." This means it has effects on several receptor sites. Like SSRIs, it is a serotonin reuptake inhibitor, but it also is an agonist at 5-HT1A receptors, a partial agonist at 5-HT1B receptors, and an antagonist at 5-HT3A, 5-HT1D, and 5-HT7 receptors.
- Some data imply a pro-cognitive effect, but at this point it isn't clear if this is a nonspecific byproduct of its antidepressant effects, or a specific advantage of vortioxetine. The studies needed to sort this out have not yet been done.
- Negative findings in some studies were attributed to dose being too low (5–10 mg/d). Higher-dose studies showed vortioxetine to be as effective as both duloxetine and agomelatine, an antidepressant approved in Europe.

Fun Fact:
The brand name Brintellix was apparently crafted to subliminally suggest that the drug helps cognition ("**bring intelli**gence").

Bottom Line:
More experience will give us a better understanding of this drug's place in therapy and if it really is different than other serotonergic antidepressants. Until then, consider it a second-line agent due to its high cost and limited track record.

Antipsychotics

What to Prescribe

Which antipsychotic should you choose? That's probably the most difficult question to answer in psychiatry. There are dozens of options and approved indications. Here are some of the factors you should weigh as you decide which antipsychotic to prescribe for a given patient:

- Efficacy
- Side effects
- Cost

Efficacy

While there's some debate about this, most experts consider clozapine to be the only antipsychotic that is clearly more effective than the others. That's wonderful, except that clozapine also happens to be the drug with one of the worst side effect profiles in psychiatry. Weight gain is the most prominent: You can expect half of all patients who take clozapine to have a 20% or more weight gain over time (Umbricht DS, Pollack S, Kane JM. Clozapine and weight gain. *J Clin Psychiatry.* 1994;55 (suppl B):157-160). When you consider its other major side effects, like sedation, drooling, and life-threatening neutropenia, not to mention the necessity of monthly blood draws, it's no wonder that clozapine is used pretty rarely. Nonetheless, it's incredibly helpful for certain treatment-resistant patients.

Next on the list of drugs that might be more effective than others is olanzapine, another side effect overachiever. It doesn't cause as much weight gain as clozapine, but it's close. In the CATIE trial, 30% of patients gained at least 7% of their initial weight.

Beyond this, there's no consensus that any of the other SGAs differ in efficacy, at least for core symptoms of psychosis. Some people believe that SGAs are more effective than FGAs for negative symptoms. This is probably an artifact of the fact that FGAs are more likely to cause side effects, like EPS, which can mimic negative symptoms. As more SGAs go generic, it is becoming more reasonable to choose them over FGAs for most patients.

Side Effects

SGAs have generally fewer side effects than FGAs, which are more likely to cause extrapyramidal side effects and tardive dyskinesia. Nonetheless, SGAs have plenty of side effects (see Table 6 for a side-by-side comparison), and here are some of the highlights:

- *Weight gain/hyperlipidemia/diabetes.* Clozapine is the worst, followed by Zyprexa, Seroquel, and Risperdal/Invega, in roughly descending order. All of the other SGAs are close to weight-neutral in adults, but we're less confident about this in kids, who tend to balloon up with many supposedly weight-neutral antipsychotics, including Abilify.

- *Sedation.* Clozapine, Zyprexa, and Seroquel tend to be the most sedating, though it's important to note that sedation isn't always bad. Patients who are revved up in a manic psychosis might do particularly well on a sedating antipsychotic—but you might want to switch to an alternative for long-term treatment.

- *Cardiac issues.* Here we are talking about EKG changes, rather than the more indirect cardiac effect of hyperlipidemia. Geodon is the most infamous example, and it does increase the QT interval, which in turn can theoretically cause serious arrhythmias. In practice, however, the actual risk is slight, with a 0.06% rate of clinically relevant QT prolongation. Several other antipsychotics can cause QT prolongation, including thioridizine (Mellaril), iloperidone (Fanapt), and to a lesser extent quetiapine (Seroquel).

- *EPS.* Among the FGAs, Haldol and Prolixin cause the most EPS, while risperidone is the SGA with the highest EPS risk.

- *Akathisia.* Aripiprazole (Abilify) and brexpiprazole (Rexulti) are the SGAs most likely to cause akathisia.

Cost

As of this writing, the following atypicals are available as generics, rendering them relatively inexpensive: aripiprazole, clozapine, olanzapine, paliperidone, quetiapine, risperidone, and ziprasidone.

On the other hand, the following antipsychotics are brand-name only and are often ridiculously expensive (up to $1,000 per month): asenapine (Saphris), brexpiprazole (Rexulti), cariprazine (Vraylar), iloperidone (Fanapt), and lurasidone (Latuda).

Class Warnings

All of the atypical antipsychotics carry the same FDA class warnings. Rather than repeating all of these concerns on each fact sheet, we will mention the warnings here:

- In 2003, the FDA required all manufacturers of atypical antipsychotics to revise their package labeling to reflect the potential risks for weight gain, hyperglycemia, new-onset or worsening diabetes, and hyperlipidemias. While this has become a class warning, it's clear that there are a handful of really bad actors here: Clozapine and olanzapine are the worst, quetiapine and risperidone less so. Patient-specific factors may also play a role. In general, the incidence and severity of weight gain and metabolic effects appear to be greater in the pediatric population.

- A 2004 consensus statement from the American Psychiatric Association and American Diabetes Association recommends the following monitoring protocol for patients on atypical agents. These are the minimal recommendations for monitoring; obviously, more frequent monitoring—for example, in individuals with elevated triglycerides or blood sugar—may be more appropriate for your patients.

Table 4: APA/ADA Monitoring Protocol for Patients on SGAs

	Baseline	4 Weeks	8 Weeks	12 Weeks	Quarterly	Annually	Every 5 Years
Personal/Family History	x					x	
Weight (BMI)	x	x	x	x	x		
Waist Circumference	x					x	
Blood Pressure	x			x		x	
Fasting Plasma Glucose	x			x		x	
Fasting Lipid Profile	x			x			x

Republished with permission of The American Diabetes Association, from *Diabetes Care*, 27(2):2004.
Permission conveyed through Copyright Clearance Center, Inc.

- A black box warning for all agents in this class suggests a substantially **higher mortality rate in geriatric patients with dementia-related psychosis** receiving atypical antipsychotics (4.5%) compared with those receiving placebo (2.6%). Although most fatalities resulted from cardiac-related events (eg, heart failure, sudden death) or infections (mostly pneumonia) as opposed to a clearly direct effect of medication, atypical antipsychotics are *not* approved for the treatment of dementia-related psychosis, and such use should be avoided or minimized when possible.

- **Adverse cerebrovascular events** (eg, stroke, TIA), sometimes fatal, have been reported in geriatric patients (73–97 years of age) with dementia-related psychosis. The FDA has issued a black box warning on atypical antipsychotics to reflect this risk; several studies have shown that cerebrovascular event risk is elevated with typical antipsychotics, as well.

Other warnings that should be considered for all antipsychotic agents (atypicals as well as typical agents) include the following:

- **Neuroleptic malignant syndrome (NMS),** a potentially fatal syndrome characterized by fever, severe muscle rigidity, and autonomic instability, has been reported in patients receiving antipsychotic agents. Treatment requires immediate discontinuation of the drug and intensive symptomatic treatment in a hospital setting.

- **Tardive dyskinesia (TD),** a syndrome of potentially irreversible, involuntary dyskinetic movements, has been reported. TD is more common with first-generation antipsychotics than with atypical agents.

- **Extrapyramidal and withdrawal symptoms** in newborns have been reported with maternal use of typical antipsychotics during the third trimester of pregnancy. Symptoms in the newborn may include agitation, feeding disorder, hypertonia or hypotonia, respiratory distress, and somnolence. These effects vary in severity and may be self-limiting (subsiding within hours or days) or require hospitalization.

Intentionally Left Blank

Table 5: Typical Antipsychotics

Generic Name (Brand Name) Year FDA Approved [G] denotes generic availability	Relevant FDA Indication(s)	Available Strengths (mg)	Dosage Equivalents	Usual Dosage Range (starting–max) (mg)	EPS and Akathisia	Anticholinergic	Relative Sedation and Orthostasis	Notes
Chlorpromazine [G] (Thorazine[1]) 1957	Psychosis, mania, nausea/vomiting	10, 25, 50, 100, 200	100	50–600	Low	Moderate	High	Injectable available; photosensitivity
Fluphenazine [G] (Prolixin[1], Prolixin Decanoate[1]) 1960	Psychosis	1, 2.5, 5, 10	2	2–20	Very high	Low	Low	Oral solution; injectables (short and LAI) available
Haloperidol [G] (Haldol, Haldol Decanoate) 1967	Psychosis, Tourette's disorder	0.5, 1, 2, 5, 10, 20	2	2–20	Very high	Low	Low	Oral solution; injectables (short and LAI) available
Loxapine [G] (Adasuve, Loxitane[1]) 1975	Schizophrenia	5, 10, 25, 50	10	20–100	High	Low	Moderate	10 mg oral inhalation powder available as Adasuve since 2012; available only in enrolled health care facilities
Perphenazine [G] (Trilafon[1]) 1957	Schizophrenia, severe nausea/vomiting	2, 4, 8, 16	8	8–64	High	Low	Low	Mid-potency agent studied and compared to atypicals in CATIE (see fact sheet)
Thioridazine [G] (Mellaril[1]) 1962	Schizophrenia	10, 25, 50, 100	100	50–600	Low	High	High	QT prolongation; irreversible retinal pigmentation at >800mg/d
Thiothixene [G] (Navane) 1967	Schizophrenia	1, 2, 5, 10	4	6–40	High	Low	Low	High-potency agent
Trifluoperazine [G] (Stelazine[1]) 1959	Schizophrenia, non-psychotic anxiety	1, 2, 5, 10	5	4–40	High	Low	Low	High-potency agent

[1]Brand discontinued; no longer available as brand

Table 6: Atypical Antipsychotics

Generic Name (Brand Name) Year FDA Approved [G] denotes generic availability	Relevant FDA Indication(s) (pediatric ages specified where relevant)	Available Strengths (mg)	Usual Dosage Range (starting–max) (mg)*	Weight Gain and Metabolic Effects	EPS and Akathisia	QT Prolongation	Notes
Aripiprazole [G] (Abilify, Abilify Discmelt) 2002 Generic not available for injectable formulations	Schizophrenia (13+) Bipolar mania, monotherapy and adjunctive (10+) Bipolar maintenance, monotherapy and adjunctive Depression adjunct Irritability in autism (6–17) Tourette's disorder (6–18) Agitation in schizophrenia or bipolar (IM only) Acute schizophrenia relapse (LAI Maintena only)	Tablet: 2, 5, 10, 15, 20, 30 ODT: 10, 15 Liquid: 1 mg/mL IM: 9.75 mg/1.3 mL LAI: Maintena (see fact sheet)	10–30 QD	Low	High (mainly akathisia)	Low	Probably most "activating"
Asenapine (Saphris) 2009	Schizophrenia Bipolar mania, monotherapy and adjunctive (10+)	Tablet: 2.5, 5, 10 (sublingual only)	5–10 BID	Moderate	Moderate	Low	Avoid food or drink for 10 minutes after taking; sedating
Brexpiprazole (Rexulti) 2015	Schizophrenia Depression adjunct	Tablet: 0.25, 0.5, 1, 2, 3, 4	1–4 QD	Moderate	High (mainly akathisia)	Low	Newer agent with limited data; weight gain and akathisia most common adverse effects
Cariprazine (Vraylar) 2015	Schizophrenia Bipolar mania and mixed episodes	Capsule: 1.5, 3, 4.5, 6	1.5 – 6 QD	Moderate	Moderate	Low	Newest agent with limited data; possible negative symptom efficacy
Clozapine [G] (Clozaril, FazaClo, Versacloz) 1989 Generic not available for oral suspension	Treatment-resistant schizophrenia Recurrent suicidal behavior in schizophrenia or schizoaffective disorders	Tablet: 12.5, 25, 50, 100, 200 ODT: 12.5, 25, 100, 150, 200 Oral suspension: 50 mg/mL	12.5–450 BID	High	Low	Low	Probably most effective AP

Generic Name (Brand Name) Year FDA Approved [G] denotes generic availability	Relevant FDA Indication(s) (pediatric ages specified where relevant)	Available Strengths (mg)	Usual Dosage Range (starting–max) (mg)*	Weight Gain and Metabolic Effects	EPS and Akathisia	QT Prolongation	Notes
Iloperidone (Fanapt) 2009	Schizophrenia	Tablet: 1, 2, 4, 6, 8, 10, 12	2–12 BID	Moderate	Low	Moderate/high	Orthostatic dizziness; must be titrated
Lurasidone (Latuda) 2010	Schizophrenia, bipolar depression	Tablet: 20, 40, 60, 80, 120	40–160 QD	Low/moderate	Moderate	Low	Sedating; must take with food
Olanzapine [G] (Zyprexa, Zyprexa Zydis) 1996 Generic not available for LAI	Schizophrenia (13+) Bipolar mania, monotherapy and adjunctive (13+) Bipolar maintenance, monotherapy Agitation in schizophrenia or bipolar (IM only)	Tablet: 2.5, 5, 7.5, 10, 15, 20 ODT: 5, 10, 15, 20 IM injection: 10 mg/vial LAI: Relprevv (see fact sheet)	10–20 QD	High	Low/moderate	Low	Greatest weight gain
Paliperidone [G] (Invega) 2006 Generic not available for LAI	Schizophrenia (12+) Schizoaffective disorder	ER tablet: 1.5, 3, 6, 9 LAI: Sustenna and Trinza (see fact sheet)	6–12 QD	Moderate	High	Moderate	Good for those with hepatic impairment; increases prolactin
Quetiapine [G] (Seroquel) 1997 (Seroquel XR) 2007 Generic not available in ER formulation	Schizophrenia (13+) Bipolar mania, monotherapy and adjunctive (10+) Bipolar disorder maintenance Bipolar depression Depression adjunct (approved in ER form)	Tablet: 25, 50, 100, 150, 200, 300, 400 ER tablet: 50, 150, 200, 300, 400	50–800 QD; divided BID to TID 300–800 QHS for XR	Moderate	Low	Moderate	Sedating
Risperidone [G] (Risperdal, Risperdal M-Tab) 1993 Generic not available for LAI	Schizophrenia (13+) Bipolar mania, monotherapy and adjunctive (10+) Irritability in autism (ages 5–16)	Liquid: 1 mg/mL Tablet: 0.25, 0.5, 1, 2, 3, 4 ODT: 0.25, 0.5, 1, 2, 3, 4 LAI: Consta (see fact sheet)	2–6 divided QD to BID	Moderate	High	Low	Increases prolactin
Ziprasidone [G] (Geodon) 2001 Generic not available for IM or oral suspension formulations	Schizophrenia Bipolar mania, monotherapy Bipolar maintenance adjunctive Agitation in schizophrenia (IM injection)	Capsule: 20, 40, 60, 80 Liquid: 10 mg/mL IM injection: 20 mg/mL	20–80 BID	Low	Low	High	Take with food

ODT = orally disintegrating tablet, LAI = long-acting injectable ER, XR = extended release

1For schizophrenia indication

ARIPIPRAZOLE (Abilify) Fact Sheet [G]

FDA Indications:

Schizophrenia (adults, adolescents 13-17 years); **bipolar disorder**, acute treatment of manic and mixed episodes (adults, children 10-17 years); bipolar disorder, maintenance treatment (adults); **major depression**, as adjunct (adults); **irritability in autism** (children 6-17 years); **Tourette's disorder** (children 6-18 years); **acute agitation** in schizophrenia or bipolar disorder (IM); **acute schizophrenia relapse** (Maintena long-acting injectable).

Off-Label Uses:

Bipolar depression; behavioral disturbances; impulse control disorders.

Dosage Forms:

- **Tablets (G):** 2 mg, 5 mg, 10 mg, 15 mg, 20 mg, 30 mg.
- **Orally disintegrating tablets (G):** 10 mg, 15 mg.
- **Oral liquid (G):** 1 mg/mL.
- **IM injectable:** 9.75 mg/1.3 mL.
- **IM depot:** Abilify Maintena: 300 mg and 400 mg; Aristada: 441 mg, 662 mg, 882 mg (see LAI table).

Dosage Guidance:

- Schizophrenia and bipolar disorder: Adults: Start and target dose 10 mg-15 mg/day; max 30 mg/day. Kids: Start 2 mg/day, increase on 3rd day to 5 mg/day; may increase further by 5 mg/day increments weekly to max 30 mg/day.
- Irritability in autism (peds): Start 2 mg/day, increase up to 5 mg/day in weekly increments to max 15 mg/day.
- Depression: Start 2 mg-5 mg/day, ↑ to usual dose 10 mg-15 mg/day, if necessary, as adjunct. Titrate gradually to prevent agitation/akathisia (max 15 mg/day).
- Agitation: 9.75 mg/1.3 mL IM; max 30 mg/day.
- Depot: After oral dose tolerated, start Abilify Maintena 400 mg/4 weeks (continue oral Abilify for first 14 days), target dose 300 mg-400 mg/4 weeks. For Aristada: Start 441 mg, 662 mg, or 882 mg monthly—corresponds to 300 mg, 450 mg, and 600 mg of aripiprazole, respectively. Or, start 882 mg dose every 6 weeks.
- Liquid dosing: Oral solution equivalent to tablet dose up to 25 mg; for 30 mg tablets, give 25 mg oral solution.
- Orally disintegrating tablet: Same as regular tablet dosing.

Cost: $$$$

Side Effects:

- Most common: akathisia, anxiety, insomnia, sedation, tremors.
- Serious but rare: See class warnings in chapter introduction.

Mechanism, Pharmacokinetics, and Drug Interactions:

- Dopamine D2 and serotonin 5HT1A receptor partial agonist and serotonin 5HT2A receptor antagonist.
- Metabolized by CYP450 2D6 and 3A4; t ½: 3 to 6 days.
- Few drug interactions.

Clinical Pearl:

Some prescribers use low-dose aripiprazole to counteract antipsychotic-induced prolactinemia, given its partial agonist properties, but there is little evidence for this strategy.

Fun Fact:

After aripiprazole's generic launch, Otsuka is following up with brexpiprazole (see fact sheet), another dopamine partial agonist, approved for schizophrenia and depression (as adjunct) and in clinical trials for ADHD.

Bottom Line:

Good choice for minimizing risk of weight gain and metabolic side effects, but beware of akathisia. The large number of FDA-approved indications and anecdotal reports of success at a variety of doses make it difficult to predict how each patient will respond at a given dose and for a given indication.

ASENAPINE (Saphris) Fact Sheet

FDA Indications:

Schizophrenia; **bipolar disorder**, acute treatment of manic or mixed episodes (adults, children 10–17 years).

Off-Label Uses:

Bipolar maintenance; bipolar depression; behavioral disturbances; impulse control disorders.

Dosage Forms:

SL tablets: 2.5 mg, 5 mg, 10 mg. (Must be taken sublingually because if swallowed, too much medication is metabolized by the liver during first-pass metabolism.)

Dosage Guidance:

- Schizophrenia: Start 5 mg BID, and increase as needed up to 10 mg BID.
- Bipolar (adults): Same dosing as schizophrenia.
- Bipolar (peds): Start 2.5 mg BID, increase as needed up to 10 mg BID.
- Avoid food or drink for 10 minutes after taking (they significantly reduce absorption and bioavailability).

Cost: $$$$$

Side Effects:

- Most common: akathisia (seems to be dose-related), oral hypoesthesia (numbing of the tongue or decreased oral sensitivity), somnolence, dizziness, extrapyramidal symptoms, weight gain.
- Serious but rare: hypersensitivity reactions including anaphylaxis, angioedema, low blood pressure, rapid heart rate, swollen tongue, difficulty breathing, wheezing, or rash; orthostatic hypotension and syncope, particularly early in treatment (FDA warning, 9/2011).

Mechanism, Pharmacokinetics, and Drug Interactions:

- Dopamine D2 and serotonin 5HT2A receptor antagonist.
- Metabolized by glucuronidation and CYP1A2; inhibitor of 2D6. Smoking may induce metabolism and may lower levels of asenapine via 1A2 induction; adjust dosing. CYP1A2 inhibitors (eg, fluvoxamine) may increase levels of asenapine; adjust dose. May double paroxetine levels. t ½: 24 hours.
- Caution with antihypertensive agents and other drugs that can cause additive hypotension or bradycardia.

Clinical Pearls:

- Has a receptor-binding profile similar to clozapine, although asenapine has very little anticholinergic activity.
- Weight gain does seem to be a problem in many patients.
- Most useful for patients who don't like swallowing pills.

Fun Fact:

Black cherry flavor developed after patients complained about original tablets.

Bottom Line:

Since there are no clear advantages over other atypical antipsychotics, the only reason to prescribe Saphris is if your patient can't or doesn't want to swallow a pill. Mouth numbness, sedation, dizziness, akathisia, weight gain, and potential for allergic reaction are significant liabilities. Not recommended for first-line use.

BREXPIPRAZOLE (Rexulti) Fact Sheet

FDA Indications:
Schizophrenia; depression adjunct.

Off-Label Uses:
Too new to tell.

Dosage Forms:
Tablets: 0.25 mg, 0.5 mg, 1 mg, 2 mg, 3 mg, 4 mg.

Dosage Guidance:
- Schizophrenia: Start 1 mg/day on days 1–4; ↑ to 2 mg/day on days 5–7; then up to max 4 mg/day based on patient response. Usual dose 2 mg–4 mg/day.
- Depression adjunct: Start 0.5 mg–1 mg/day, ↑ at weekly intervals up to max 3 mg/day.

Cost: $$$$$

Side Effects:
- Most common: weight gain, akathisia, somnolence.
- Serious but rare: See class warnings in chapter introduction.

Mechanism, Pharmacokinetics, and Drug Interactions:
- Dopamine D2 and serotonin 5HT1A receptor partial agonist and serotonin 5HT2A receptor antagonist.
- Metabolized by CYP2D6 and 3A4. Poor metabolizers of CYP2D6 metabolize the drug more slowly; may have increased effects; decrease dose by 50%; t ½: 91 hours.
- Caution with potent inhibitors of 2D6 and 3A4 or inducers of 3A4; adjust dose by 50%.

Clinical Pearls:
- As the name suggests, brexpiprazole is chemically and structurally related to its manufacturer's previous blockbuster aripiprazole (Abilify).
- Although the FDA-approved target dose for schizophrenia is 2–4 mg/day, 2 mg/day was no better than placebo in 1 of 2 preclinical registration studies.
- Once-a-day dosing with no regard to meals makes this an easy-to-use option.

Fun Fact:
Plan on seeing more trial results with Rexulti in the future, including those in patients with attention-deficit/hyperactivity disorder, posttraumatic stress disorder, and agitation associated with Alzheimer's dementia.

Bottom Line:
Rexulti may just be a newer spin on Abilify, which is now available as generic. More trial data will indicate whether this is a different chemical entity that warrants a higher price tag. Until then, stick to the cheaper, generic aripiprazole.

CARIPRAZINE (Vraylar) Fact Sheet

FDA Indications:
Schizophrenia; bipolar disorder (manic or mixed episodes).

Off-Label Uses:
Negative symptoms of schizophrenia; major depression; bipolar depression.

Dosage Forms:
Capsules: 1.5 mg, 3 mg, 4.5 mg, 6 mg.

Dosage Guidance:
Schizophrenia and bipolar disorder: Start 1.5 mg/day, increase to 3 mg/day as early as 2nd day. Adjust by 1.5 mg–3 mg/day increments to usual dose 1.5 mg–6 mg/day in schizophrenia and 3 mg–6 mg/day in bipolar disorder.

Cost: Not yet known.

Side Effects:
- Most common: EPS, akathisia, weight gain, sedation.
- Serious but rare: See class warnings in chapter introduction.

Mechanism, Pharmacokinetics, and Drug Interactions:
- Dopamine D2 and D3 and serotonin 5HT1A receptor partial agonist; serotonin 5HT2A receptor antagonist.
- Metabolized primarily by CYP3A4; t ½: 2–4 days for cariprazine (1–3 weeks for active metabolites).
- Caution with CYP3A4 inhibitors and inducers; dose adjustment may be necessary.

Clinical Pearls:
Most recently approved atypical antipsychotic. Most closely similar to aripiprazole with partial D2 agonism. Manufacturer and very early data suggest D3 activity may result in negative symptom improvement.

Fun Fact:
Cariprazine was developed by a Hungarian pharmaceutical company, Gedeon Richter, which was founded in 1901 by a pharmacist. It initially processed extracts from plants to produce herbal drugs.

Bottom Line:
Cariprazine's potential claim to fame will be efficacy for negative symptoms, but the data are too preliminary to make a definitive conclusion. Beyond that, it appears to be another in a series of me-too antipsychotics, with a side effect profile heavy on EPS and akathisia as well as significant potential for weight gain.

CHLORPROMAZINE (Thorazine) Fact Sheet [G]

FDA Indications:
Psychosis; mania; nausea and vomiting; intractable hiccups.

Off-Label Uses:
Bipolar disorder; behavioral disturbances; impulse control disorders.

Dosage Forms:
Tablets (G): 10 mg, 25 mg, 50 mg, 100 mg, 200 mg.

Dosage Guidance:
Schizophrenia: Start 10 mg–25 mg TID; ↑ by 20 mg–50 mg/day increments every 3–4 days to lowest effective dose. Dose range 200 mg–600 mg/day in divided doses; max FDA–approved dose 1000 mg/day.

Cost: $$$

Side Effects:
- Most common: sedation, orthostasis, tachycardia, drowsiness, dry mouth, constipation, blurred vision, prolactin elevation (sexual side effects, amenorrhea, galactorrhea).
- Serious but rare: skin pigmentation and ocular changes (both dose related); jaundice.

Mechanism, Pharmacokinetics, and Drug Interactions:
- Dopamine D2 receptor antagonist.
- Metabolized primarily by CYP2D6, also 1A2 and 3A4. Patients that are poor metabolizers of CYP2D6 metabolize the drug more slowly; may have increased effects; t ½: 23 to 37 hours.
- CYP2D6 inhibitors (eg, fluoxetine, paroxetine, quinidine) may increase chlorpromazine levels.

Clinical Pearls:
- Chlorpromazine is a low–potency conventional (typical) antipsychotic; this leads to less EPS compared to high–potency agents (eg, haloperidol, fluphenazine) and to more anticholinergic side effects compared to mid– and high–potency agents (eg, perphenazine and haloperidol, respectively).
- Extremely sedating agent and often used for this effect. Dosing limited by orthostasis and sedation.

Fun Fact:
Thorazine was developed by a French surgeon in 1948 to induce relaxation and indifference in surgical patients.

Bottom Line:
Not commonly used for core symptoms of schizophrenia; some clinicians use it at low doses (25 mg) as a non–addictive hypnotic/anxiolytic.

CLOZAPINE (Clozaril) Fact Sheet [G]

FDA Indications:

Treatment-resistant schizophrenia; reduction in risk of suicide in schizophrenia and schizoaffective disorder.

Off-Label Uses:

Treatment–resistant bipolar disorder; treatment–resistant aggression and violence in psychotic and other brain disorders.

Dosage Forms:
- **Tablets (Clozaril):** 25 mg, 100 mg (scored).
- **Tablets (G):** 12.5 mg, 25 mg, 50 mg, 100 mg, 200 mg (scored).
- **Orally disintegrating tablets (FazaClo, G):** 12.5 mg, 25 mg, 100 mg, 150 mg, 200 mg.
- **Oral suspension (Versacloz):** 50 mg/mL.

Dosage Guidance:
- Start 12.5 mg once or twice daily; ↑ gradually, in increments of 25 mg–50 mg/day to target dose 300 mg–450 mg/day by end of 2 weeks; may ↑ further in increments ≤100 mg and no more frequently than once or twice weekly. May require doses as high as 600 mg–900 mg/day; max 900 mg/day (usually in 2–3 divided doses). May take 4–6 weeks, or as long as 3–6 months, for response.
- If dosing is interrupted for ≥48 hours, must be retitrated from 12.5 mg–25 mg/day; may be increased more rapidly than initial titration, as tolerated.

Cost: $$$

Side Effects:
- Most common: sedation, orthostatic hypotension, hypersalivation (place towel on pillow), weight gain (15–30 pound average weight gain after 1 year), constipation (risk of toxic megacolon if untreated), tachycardia (can treat with propranolol).
- Serious but rare: potentially life–threatening agranulocytosis (1%–2%); periodic WBC testing (see prescribing information for monitoring details) must occur.

Mechanism, Pharmacokinetics, and Drug Interactions:
- Dopamine D2 and serotonin 5HT2A receptor antagonist.
- Metabolized by several CYP450: 1A2, 2D6, and 3A4; t ½: 12 hours.
- Avoid use with drugs that may cause bone marrow suppression (eg, carbamazepine) and lower seizure threshold. Collapse, respiratory arrest, and cardiac arrest reported during initial clozapine treatment in patients taking benzodiazepines. Inhibitors of 1A2 (eg, fluvoxamine), 2D6 (eg, paroxetine, fluoxetine, quinidine), and 3A4 (eg, erythromycin) may increase clozapine levels. Inducers of 1A2 (eg, smoking) and 3A4 (eg, St. John's wort) may decrease clozapine levels.

Clinical Pearls:
- Risk of agranulocytosis greatest within first 6 months, then incidence declines but can still occur.
- Divided doses may minimize some adverse effects (eg, hypotension, seizures).
- New FDA–required risk evaluation and mitigation strategy (REMS) program requires prescribers to be certified to prescribe clozapine (see www.clozapinerems.com for details).

Fun Facts:

The Quiet Room is a compelling memoir written by a patient, Lori Schiller, who was one of the early users of clozapine.

Bottom Line:

The only drug with convincing evidence based on years of clinical experience to help treatment-resistant schizophrenia. Consider using it after 2 failed trials of other antipsychotics.

FLUPHENAZINE (Prolixin) Fact Sheet [G]

FDA Indications:
Psychosis.

Off-Label Uses:
Bipolar disorder; behavioral disturbances; impulse control disorders.

Dosage Forms:
- **Tablets (G):** 1 mg, 2.5 mg, 5 mg, 10 mg.
- **Oral liquid (G):** 2.5 mg/5 mL, 5 mg/mL.
- **Injection (G):** 2.5 mg/mL.
- **Depot injection (G):** 25 mg/mL (see LAI fact sheet and table).

Dosage Guidance:
Start 1 mg–2.5 mg BID; adjust to lowest effective dose. Dose range 2.5 mg–20 mg/day divided BID; max FDA-approved dose is 40 mg/day, but doses >20 mg/day rarely more effective and difficult to tolerate.

Cost: $

Side Effects:
- Most common: EPS, headache, drowsiness, dry mouth, prolactin elevation (sexual side effects, amenorrhea, galactorrhea).
- Serious but rare: See class warnings in chapter introduction.

Mechanism, Pharmacokinetics, and Drug Interactions:
- Dopamine D2 receptor antagonist.
- Metabolized primarily by CYP2D6. Poor metabolizers of CYP2D6 metabolize the drug more slowly; may have increased effects; t ½: 15 hours.
- CYP2D6 inhibitors (eg, fluoxetine, paroxetine, quinidine) may increase fluphenazine levels.

Clinical Pearls:
- Fluphenazine is a high-potency conventional (typical) antipsychotic; this leads to more EPS compared to mid– or low-potency agents (eg, perphenazine or chlorpromazine, respectively) and to less sedation, less orthostasis, and fewer anticholinergic side effects compared to low-potency agents (eg, chlorpromazine).
- Relatively lower seizure side effect risk compared to lower-potency agents.
- Long-acting decanoate formulation allows option for patients who don't take oral formation reliably.
- Availability of short-acting injectable and oral formulations also allows for more flexibility in administration.

Fun Fact:
Prolixin is the most well-known brand of fluphenazine, but there was also a branded fluphenazine on the market under the name Permitil.

Bottom Line:
Fluphenazine is an effective, inexpensive typical antipsychotic with a long history of experience and use, but clinical utility is limited in some patients due to EPS.

HALOPERIDOL (Haldol) Fact Sheet [G]

FDA Indications:
Psychosis; Tourette's disorder.

Off-Label Uses:
Bipolar disorder; behavioral disturbances; impulse control disorders; delirium.

Dosage Forms:
- **Tablets (G):** 0.5 mg, 1 mg, 2 mg, 5 mg, 10 mg, 20 mg (scored).
- **Oral concentrate (G):** 2 mg/mL.
- **Injectable (G):** 5 mg/mL.
- **Depot injection (G):** 50 mg/mL and 100 mg/mL (see LAI fact sheet and table).

Dosage Guidance:
Schizophrenia: Start 1 mg–2 mg BID (5 mg BID for hospitalized patients); adjust to lowest effective dose. Usual dose range is 5 mg–20 mg/day. Max FDA–approved dose is 100 mg/day, but doses >20 mg/day are rarely used.

Cost: $

Side Effects:
- Most common: EPS, headache, drowsiness, dry mouth, prolactin elevation (sexual side effects, amenorrhea, galactorrhea).
- Serious but rare: See class warnings in chapter introduction.

Mechanism, Pharmacokinetics, and Drug Interactions:
- Dopamine D2 receptor antagonist.
- Metabolized primarily by CYP2D6, also 3A4; may inhibit CYP2D6. Patients that are poor metabolizers of CYP2D6 metabolize the drug more slowly; may have increased effects; t ½: 21 to 24 hours.
- CYP2D6 inhibitors (eg, fluoxetine, paroxetine, quinidine) may increase haloperidol levels. Caution with substrates of 2D6 as haloperidol may increase their levels and effects.

Clinical Pearls:
- Haloperidol is a high–potency conventional (typical) antipsychotic; this leads to more EPS compared to mid– or low–potency agents (eg, perphenazine or chlorpromazine, respectively) and to less sedation, less orthostasis, and fewer anticholinergic side effects compared to low–potency agents (eg, chlorpromazine).
- Relatively lower seizure side effect risk compared to lower–potency agents.
- Availability of short-acting injectable and oral formulations also allows for more flexibility in administration.
- Long–acting decanoate formulation allows option for patients who don't take oral formation reliably.

Fun Fact:
Haldol was discovered in 1958 by Paul Janssen, the founder of Belgian pharmaceutical company Janssen Pharmaceutica.

Bottom Line:
Haloperidol is an effective, inexpensive typical antipsychotic with a long history of experience and use, but clinical utility is limited in some patients due to EPS.

ILOPERIDONE (Fanapt) Fact Sheet

FDA Indications:
Schizophrenia.

Off-Label Uses:
Bipolar disorder; major depression; behavioral disturbances; impulse control disorders.

Dosage Forms:
Tablets: 1 mg, 2 mg, 4 mg, 6 mg, 8 mg, 10 mg, 12 mg.

Dosage Guidance:
Start 1 mg BID; ↑ to 2 mg BID on day 2 and then daily by 4 mg/day to a target dose of 6 mg-12 mg BID daily; max 12 mg BID.

Cost: $$$$$

Side Effects:
• Most common: dizziness (dose-related), dry mouth, fatigue, nasal congestion, orthostatic hypotension (can minimize by gradual dose titration), somnolence, tachycardia (dose-related), moderate weight gain.
• Serious but rare: relatively moderate to high risk of QTc prolongation (risk is increased in patients taking potent CYP2D6 or 3A4 inhibitors, or at higher doses); avoid use in patients with bradycardia, history of MI, hypokalemia, hypomagnesemia, or concomitant use of other drugs that prolong QTc. Priapism reported rarely.

Mechanism, Pharmacokinetics, and Drug Interactions:
• Dopamine D2 and serotonin 5HT2A receptor antagonist.
• Metabolized primarily through CYP 2D6 and also 3A4; t ½: 18 hours (33 hours in poor metabolizers).
• Avoid concomitant use of other drugs known to prolong the QTc interval.
• Potent inhibitors of CYP 2D6 (eg, paroxetine, fluoxetine, quinidine) or 3A4 (eg, ketoconazole, clarithromycin) may increase iloperidone levels; in such cases, decrease iloperidone dose by 50%.

Clinical Pearls:
• Must follow initial titration schedule if treatment has been interrupted for >3 days.
• Minimal data regarding long-term use in schizophrenia and uses other than schizophrenia.

Fun Fact:
Iloperidone was initially on track for FDA approval in 2002, but its approval was delayed to 2009 due to multiple company mergers and out-licensing deals as well as the FDA's request for more data.

Bottom Line:
Not recommended as first-choice agent due to twice-daily dosing, need for titration, QT prolongation (comparable to ziprasidone), dizziness, moderate weight gain, and increases in blood sugar; and because it appears less efficacious than other antipsychotics.

LOXAPINE (Loxitane) Fact Sheet [G]

FDA Indications:
Schizophrenia; acute agitation associated with schizophrenia or acute bipolar mania.

Off-Label Uses:
Bipolar disorder; behavioral disturbances; impulse control disorders.

Dosage Forms:
- **Capsules (G):** 5 mg, 10 mg, 25 mg, 50 mg.
- **Single-use disposable inhaler (Adasuve),** for acute agitation: 10 mg as inhalation powder.

Dosage Guidance:
- Schizophrenia: Start 10 mg BID; adjust to lowest effective dose. Dose range 60 mg–100 mg divided BID–TID; max FDA-approved dose is 250 mg/day, but doses >100 mg/day rarely used.
- Acute agitation (oral inhalation): Give 1 puff every 24 hours as needed (must be given by health care professional).

Cost: capsule: $$; inhalation: $$$

Side Effects:
- Most common: EPS, headache, drowsiness, dry mouth, prolactin elevation (sexual side effects, amenorrhea, galactorrhea), throat irritation (Adasuve).
- Serious but rare: See class warnings in chapter introduction.

Mechanism, Pharmacokinetics, and Drug Interactions:
- Dopamine D2 and serotonin 5HT2A receptor antagonist.
- Metabolized primarily by CYP2D6 and 3A4; t ½: 4–8 hours.
- Caution with inhibitors of CYP2D6 and 3A4 and inducers of 3A4; adjust dose.

Clinical Pearls:
- Loxapine is an intermediate-potency conventional (typical) antipsychotic; this leads to less EPS compared to high-potency agents (eg, haloperidol, fluphenazine) and to less sedation, less orthostasis, and fewer anticholinergic side effects compared to low-potency agents (eg, chlorpromazine).
- Loxapine belongs to the dibenzoxazepine class of antipsychotics and is structurally related to clozapine (which belongs to the chemically akin class of dibenzodiazepines). Some have argued that loxapine may behave as an atypical antipsychotic.
- The new Adasuve oral inhalation version has the advantage of treating agitation quickly without the need for swallowing or a shot. But the risks of bronchospasm and respiratory arrest, along with the contraindication in patients with asthma, COPD, or other lung disease, make this formulation rather unappealing overall.

Fun Fact:
Loxapine is metabolized to the tetracyclic antidepressant amoxapine.

Bottom Line:
Loxapine is an effective, well-tolerated (compared to high-potency and low-potency typical antipsychotics), and inexpensive alternative to atypical antipsychotics.

LURASIDONE (Latuda) Fact Sheet

FDA Indications:

Schizophrenia; bipolar depression (as monotherapy and adjunct).

Off-Label Uses:

Bipolar disorder; treatment-resistant depression; behavioral disturbances; impulse control disorders.

Dosage Forms:

Tablets: 20 mg, 40 mg, 60 mg, 80 mg, 120 mg.

Dosage Guidance:

- Schizophrenia: Start 40 mg QD, with food (at least 350 calories); no titration required. Usual dose 40 mg–160 mg/day. Max dose 160 mg QD.
- Bipolar depression: Start 20 mg QD, with food (at least 350 calories); no titration required. Usual dose 20 mg–120 mg/day. Max dose 120 mg QD, although doses >80 mg/day rarely more effective.

Cost: $$$$$

Side Effects:

- Most common: sedation (dose-related), akathisia (dose-related), nausea, parkinsonism, agitation.
- Serious but rare: orthostatic hypotension and syncope reported (rarely).

Mechanism, Pharmacokinetics, and Drug Interactions:

- Dopamine D2 and serotonin 5HT2A and 5HT7 antagonist; serotonin 5HT1A partial agonist.
- Metabolized primarily through CYP450 3A4; t ½: 18 hours.
- Avoid use with medications that cause orthostasis, potent 3A4 inhibitors (eg, ketoconazole), or inducers (eg, rifampin). Exercise caution/monitor when using in combination with moderate 3A4 inhibitors (eg, diltiazem); use maximum dose of 40 mg/day in patients taking moderate 3A4 inhibitors.

Clinical Pearls:

- Administration with food (at least 350 calories) increases bioavailability roughly threefold; fat content of meal is not important.
- Appears to be relatively weight-neutral and cardiometabolic parameters little affected in company-sponsored trials, although post-marketing observations have been limited.

Fun Fact:

One unique feature of Latuda is its high affinity for the 5-HT7 receptor, which has been linked to depression, learning/memory, cognition, anxiety, and pain. Unfortunately, to date, Latuda has shown no clear benefit over other atypical antipsychotics on these measures.

Bottom Line:

This drug offers some advantages, including no need for titration, once-daily dosing, relatively low-moderate metabolic profile, and relatively low QTc prolongation risk. However, its use is limited by the need to administer with ≥350 calories of food, potential for drug interactions, and side effects including sedation, akathisia, and EPS. In clinical practice, you might lump lurasidone with the other atypicals that cause little weight gain, such as aripiprazole and ziprasidone.

OLANZAPINE (Zyprexa) Fact Sheet [G]

FDA Indications:

Schizophrenia (adults and children >13 years); acute or mixed **bipolar** I manic episodes, as monotherapy or adjunct (adults and children >13 years); maintenance treatment of bipolar disorder; **bipolar depression** (with fluoxetine, sold as Symbyax, adults and children >10 years); **treatment-resistant unipolar depression** (with fluoxetine); **acute agitation** in schizophrenia and bipolar mania (injectable form).

Off-Label Uses:

Behavioral disturbances; impulse control disorders.

Dosage Forms:

- **Tablets (G):** 2.5 mg, 5 mg, 7.5 mg, 10 mg, 15 mg, 20 mg.
- **Orally disintegrating tablets (G):** 5 mg, 10 mg, 15 mg, 20 mg.
- **IM injection (G):** 10 mg.
- **Depot injection:** 210 mg, 300 mg, 405 mg (see LAI fact sheet and table).
- **Fixed combination capsules with fluoxetine (G):** 3/25 mg, 6/25 mg, 6/50 mg, 12/25 mg, 12/50 mg olanzapine/fluoxetine.

Dosage Guidance:

- Schizophrenia, bipolar disorder, depression (adults): Start most patients at 5 mg–10 mg QD, may ↑ by 5 mg QD, in weekly increments, to target dose 10 mg–20 mg QD.
- Acute mania (adults): Start 10 mg–15 mg QD, may ↑ by 5 mg daily, in 24-hour increments, to target dose 10 mg–20 mg QD.
- Max approved dose: 20 mg/day although doses up to 30 mg–50 mg/day have been used.
- Bipolar depression (Symbyax, fixed combination with fluoxetine) (adults): Start 6/25 mg QPM, ↑ as indicated to target dose 6 mg–12 mg/25 mg–50 mg olanzapine/fluoxetine.

Cost: $

Side Effects:

- Most common: somnolence (dose-related), dry mouth (dose-related), constipation, weight gain (up to 40% incidence; may be substantial; 10 to 30 pounds weight gain is common), increased appetite, EPS (dose-related).
- Serious but rare: See class warnings in chapter introduction.

Mechanism, Pharmacokinetics, and Drug Interactions:

- Dopamine D2 and serotonin 5HT2A receptor antagonist.
- Metabolized by CYP 450 1A2, 2D6 (minor), and direct glucuronidation; t ½: 1 to 2 days.
- CYP1A2 inducers (eg, carbamazepine, ritonavir, smoking) may reduce levels significantly.

Clinical Pearls:

Use in children and adolescents may result in increased weight gain and sedation, as well as greater increases in LDL cholesterol, total cholesterol, triglycerides, prolactin, and liver transaminase levels when compared to adults.

Fun Fact:

Olanzapine has been studied for chemotherapy-induced nausea and vomiting (helpful).

Bottom Line:

Good efficacy, particularly in acute schizophrenia and bipolar mania, once-daily dosing, and low risk of QTc interval prolongation make this an appealing drug. However, its high risk for weight gain and metabolic complications make it a second-line choice for many.

PALIPERIDONE (Invega) Fact Sheet [G]

FDA Indications:

Schizophrenia in adults and children ≥12 years; **schizoaffective disorder.**

Off-Label Uses:

Bipolar disorder; behavioral disturbances; impulse control disorders.

Dosage Forms:

- **Controlled release tablets (G):** 1.5 mg, 3 mg, 6 mg, 9 mg (not breakable).
- **Monthly depot injection (Invega Sustenna):** 39 mg, 78 mg, 117 mg, 156 mg, and 234 mg (see LAI fact sheet and table).
- **Every 3-month depot injection (Invega Trinza):** 273 mg, 410 mg, 546 mg, 819 mg (see LAI fact sheet and table).

Dosage Guidance:

Schizophrenia/schizoaffective disorder (adults): Start 6 mg QAM, which may be the effective dose; if required, may ↑ by 3 mg/day at intervals of >5 days to max 12 mg/day.

Cost: $$$$

Side Effects:

- Most common: akathisia, EPS (dose-related), tremor, tachycardia, insomnia, somnolence (especially adolescents), weight gain, orthostatic hypotension, headache, prolactin elevation.
- Serious but rare: modest increase in QTc interval. Orthostatic hypotension and syncope reported. Rarely, controlled release tablet may get caught in GI tract and cause obstructive symptoms in patients with known strictures; avoid use in patients with severe, preexisting GI narrowing (either pathologic or iatrogenic). Esophageal dysmotility and aspiration possible; use caution in patients at risk for aspiration pneumonia (eg, those with advanced Alzheimer's dementia).

Mechanism, Pharmacokinetics, and Drug Interactions:

- Dopamine D2 and serotonin 5HT2A receptor antagonist.
- Not metabolized by liver; t ½: 23 hours.
- Avoid use with drugs known to prolong the QT interval. Paliperidone is the principal active metabolite of risperidone; therefore, avoid use with risperidone. Minimal drug interactions.

Clinical Pearls:

- Warn your patients that they may find what looks like intact capsules in their stool. These are actually empty "ghost pills." They are caused by the fact that Invega (and Concerta, see fact sheet) is an extended release tablet based on the OROS osmotic delivery system: Water from the GI tract enters through a semipermeable membrane coating the tablet, causing the drug to be expelled through laser-drilled holes in the coating. The shell is nonabsorbable and will be expelled in the stool.
- Swallow whole, with fluids; do not chew, divide, or crush.
- Studies suggest paliperidone is not highly effective in acute mania either as monotherapy or in combination with lithium or valproate.
- Along with risperidone, causes the most EPS and hyperprolactinemia of all the atypicals.

Fun Fact:

First drug with FDA approval for schizoaffective disorder, allowing Janssen to carve out a new marketing niche and separate this drug from its competitors (at least from a commercial and marketing perspective).

Bottom Line:

Invega looks like risperidone without drug-drug interactions, but with more QT interval prolongation, more tachycardia, possibly more EPS, and the same amount of hyperprolactinemia. These significant disadvantages make this a second-line option.

PERPHENAZINE (Trilafon) Fact Sheet [G]

FDA Indications:
Schizophrenia; severe nausea and vomiting.

Off-Label Uses:
Bipolar disorder; behavioral disturbances; impulse control disorders.

Dosage Forms:
Tablets (G): 2 mg, 4 mg, 8 mg, 16 mg.

Dosage Guidance:
Schizophrenia: Start 4 mg–8 mg TID (8 mg–16 mg BID-QID for hospitalized patients); adjust to lowest effective dose. Dose range 8 mg–16 mg BID-QID; max FDA-approved dose for non-hospitalized patients is 24 mg/day, but hospitalized psychotic patients can be dosed up to 64 mg/day.

Cost: $

Side Effects:
- Most common: EPS, headache, drowsiness, dry mouth, prolactin elevation (sexual side effects, amenorrhea, galactorrhea).
- Serious but rare: tachycardia (especially with sudden marked increase in dose).

Mechanism, Pharmacokinetics, and Drug Interactions:
- Dopamine D2 receptor antagonist.
- Metabolized primarily by CYP2D6; may inhibit CYP2D6. Poor metabolizers of CYP2D6 metabolize the drug more slowly; may have increased effects; t ½: 9 to 12 hours.
- CYP2D6 inhibitors (eg, fluoxetine, paroxetine, quinidine) may increase perphenazine levels. Caution with substrates of 2D6 as perphenazine may increase their levels and effects.

Clinical Pearls:
- Perphenazine is an intermediate-potency conventional (typical) antipsychotic; this leads to less EPS compared to high-potency agents (eg, haloperidol, fluphenazine) and to less sedation, less orthostasis, and fewer anticholinergic side effects compared to low-potency agents (eg, chlorpromazine).
- Fewer metabolic effects (weight gain, glucose, lipids) than some antipsychotics.
- Based on 18-month, randomized trial of 1,493 patients with schizophrenia (CATIE trial), perphenazine appears similar in efficacy and EPS compared to atypical antipsychotics (olanzapine, quetiapine, risperidone, ziprasidone).

Fun Fact:
Perphenazine has long been available in a formulation with amitriptyline (a tricyclic antidepressant) called Triavil. This combination antipsychotic/antidepressant was first available in 1965, foreshadowing the next such combination drug (Symbyax) by 38 years.

Bottom Line:
Effective, well-tolerated, and inexpensive alternative to atypical antipsychotics.

QUETIAPINE (Seroquel) Fact Sheet [G]

FDA Indications:

Schizophrenia (adults and children ≥13 years); **bipolar**, manic/mixed (adults and children >10 years); **bipolar depression**; maintenance treatment for bipolar; **major depression**, as adjunct.

Off-Label Uses:

Insomnia; anxiety disorders; behavioral disturbances; impulse control disorders.

Dosage Forms:

- **Tablets (G):** 25 mg, 50 mg, 100 mg, 200 mg, 300 mg, 400 mg.
- **ER tablets (Seroquel XR):** 50 mg, 150 mg, 200 mg, 300 mg, 400 mg.

Dosage Guidance:

- Schizophrenia (adults): Start 25 mg BID or 300 mg XR QD.
- Mania (adults): Start 50 mg BID or 300 mg XR QD.
- Depression: Start 50 mg QHS.
- For all indications: may ↑ dose by 50 mg-100 mg/day increments, given in divided doses, every 1-4 days (or up to 300 mg/day XR increments in intervals of >1 day), to target dose.
- Recommended target dose ranges: schizophrenia: 400 mg-800 mg/day; bipolar mania: 400 mg-800 mg/day; bipolar depression: 300 mg/day; bipolar maintenance: 400 mg-800 mg/day; major depression (adjunct): 150 mg-300 mg/day (XR). Max daily dose in adults: 800 mg/day.
- Consider dosing slower and lower in pediatric, elderly, or debilitated patients.

Cost: IR: $; ER: $$$$$

Side Effects:

- Most common: somnolence, hypotension, dry mouth, dizziness, constipation, weight gain.
- Serious but rare: orthostatic hypotension, particularly at high dose or with rapid titration.

Mechanism, Pharmacokinetics, and Drug Interactions:

- Dopamine D2 and serotonin 5HT2A receptor antagonist.
- Metabolized by CYP3A4; t ½: 6 hours (XR: 7 hours).
- Avoid use with agents that may cause additional orthostasis. CYP3A4 inducers (eg, carbamazepine) may lower quetiapine levels; CYP3A4 inhibitors (eg, erythromycin, ketoconazole) may increase quetiapine levels.

Clinical Pearls:

- Swallow XR tablet whole; do not break, crush, or chew; switch between IR and XR at the same total daily dose; dose adjustments may be necessary based on response and tolerability.
- If patient discontinues drug >1 week, retitrate dose as with initial therapy.
- Quetiapine abuse has been reported, particularly in incarcerated populations.

Fun Fact:

Cataracts developed in initial studies with beagle dogs; human studies have not shown an association. However, the label still recommends a slit-lamp exam every 6 months.

Bottom Line:

Low risk for EPS and a broad spectrum of efficacy make this an appealing first-choice agent. However, sedation, weight gain, and orthostasis may limit use. Dosing at bedtime, or switching to XR, may help reduce daytime sedation.

RISPERIDONE (Risperdal) Fact Sheet [G]

FDA Indications:

Schizophrenia (adults and children >13 years); **bipolar disorder, manic/mixed** (adults and children >10 years); **irritability symptoms of autism** (children >5 years).

Off-Label Uses:

Bipolar depression; behavioral disturbances; impulse control disorders.

Dosage Forms:

- **Tablets (G):** 0.25 mg, 0.5 mg, 1 mg, 2 mg, 3 mg, 4 mg.
- **Oral solution (G):** 1 mg/mL.
- **Orally disintegrating tablets (Risperdal M-Tab, G):** 0.25 mg, 0.5 mg, 1 mg, 2 mg, 3 mg, 4 mg.
- **Depot injection (Risperdal Consta):** 12.5 mg, 25 mg, 37.5 mg, 50 mg (see LAI fact sheet and table).

Dosage Guidance:

- Schizophrenia, bipolar (adults): Start 1 mg BID; may ↑ by 1 mg–2 mg/day at intervals ≥24 hours to a recommended dosage range 4 mg–6 mg/day; may be given as a single daily dose once maintenance dose achieved. Max approved dose is 16 mg/day, but daily dosages >6 mg provide no additional benefit, only higher risk for EPS, which is dose-dependent.
- Children, elderly, first-episode psychosis: lower initial dosages (eg, 0.5 mg–1 mg daily) and slower titration to initial target dose of 2 mg daily.
- Autism (children ≥5 years): If <15 kg (33 lbs), use with caution. For 15 kg–20 kg (33 lbs–44 lbs), start 0.25 mg/day, ↑ to 0.5 mg/day after ≥4 days. If response insufficient, may ↑ by 0.25 mg/day in ≥2 week intervals; give QD or BID. For ≥20 kg (44 lbs), start 0.5 mg/day; may ↑ to 1 mg/day after ≥4 days. If response insufficient, may ↑ dose by 0.5 mg/day in ≥2-week intervals; give QD or BID.
- Bipolar mania or schizophrenia (children): Start 0.5 mg QD; ↑ in increments of 0.5 mg–1 mg/day at intervals ≥24 hours to target dose of 2 mg–3 mg/day; doses >3 mg/day do not confer additional benefit and are associated with increased side effects.

Cost: $

Side Effects:

- Most common: EPS, somnolence (particularly in children), anxiety, constipation, nausea, dyspepsia, dizziness, rhinitis, prolactin elevation, weight gain.
- Serious but rare: Orthostatic hypotension may occur, particularly at higher doses or with rapid titration. Hyperprolactinemia with clinical symptoms (galactorrhea, amenorrhea).

Mechanism, Pharmacokinetics, and Drug Interactions:

- Dopamine D2 and serotonin 5HT2A receptor antagonist.
- Metabolized by CYP2D6; t ½: 20 hours.
- CYP2D6 inhibitors (eg, fluoxetine, paroxetine, quinidine) may increase effects of risperidone. Carbamazepine reduces levels and effects of risperidone.

Clinical Pearls:

- Along with paliperidone, causes the most EPS and hyperprolactinemia of all the atypicals.
- When reinitiating after discontinuation, initial titration schedule should be followed.

Fun Fact:

Risperdal M-tabs are marketed in other countries as Risperdal Quicklets.

Bottom Line:

Risperidone has been widely used and is often used first-line. At higher doses (>4 mg/day), risperidone may not provide some of the putative advantages of other atypical antipsychotics, particularly with regard to side effects.

THIORIDAZINE (Mellaril) Fact Sheet [G]

FDA Indications:
Schizophrenia (not for first-line use).

Off-Label Uses:
Anxiety, insomnia.

Dosage Forms:
Tablets (G): Supplied as 10 mg, 25 mg, 50 mg, 100 mg.

Dosage Guidance:
Start 50 mg–100 mg TID; adjust to lowest effective dose. Dose range 200 mg–800 mg/day divided BID-QID; max FDA-approved dose is 800 mg/day due to ocular pigmentation at high doses.

Cost: $$

Side Effects:
- Most common: EPS, headache, sedation, drowsiness, dry mouth, constipation, blurred vision, dizziness, prolactin elevation (sexual side effects, amenorrhea, galactorrhea).
- Serious but rare: QT prolongation and torsade de pointes (highest risk of all antipsychotics); ocular pigmentation and degenerative retinopathies.

Mechanism, Pharmacokinetics, and Drug Interactions:
- Dopamine D2 receptor antagonist.
- Metabolized primarily by CYP2D6; may inhibit CYP2D6. Poor metabolizers of CYP2D6 metabolize the drug more slowly; may have increased effects; t ½: 24 hours.
- CYP2D6 inhibitors (eg, fluoxetine, paroxetine, quinidine) may increase thioridazine levels. Caution with substrates of 2D6 as thioridazine may increase their levels and effects.

Clinical Pearls:
- Thioridazine is a low-potency conventional (typical) antipsychotic; this leads to less EPS and to more sedation, orthostasis, and anticholinergic side effects compared to high-potency agents (eg, haloperidol, fluphenazine).
- Efficacy has not been studied in refractory schizophrenia, but thioridazine is indicated only for and should be reserved for use only in patients who have failed to respond to other medications. This is due to the significant risks associated with thioridazine, particularly QT prolongation.

Fun Fact:
Thioridazine can kill antibiotic-resistant bacteria such as *Staphylococcus aureus* (including MRSA) and extensively drug-resistant (XDR) *Mycobacterium tuberculosis*. Researchers are studying how thioridazine does this (latest studies show a weakening of bacterial cell walls) in order to develop drugs that can target resistant bacteria.

Bottom Line:
Too risky to use for the majority of patients.

THIOTHIXENE (Navane) Fact Sheet [G]

FDA Indications:
Schizophrenia.

Off-Label Uses:
Bipolar disorder; behavioral disturbances; impulse control disorders.

Dosage Forms:
Capsules (G): Supplied as 1 mg, 2 mg, 5 mg, 10 mg.

Dosage Guidance:
Start 2 mg TID–5 mg BID; adjust to lowest effective dose. Usual dose range 20 mg–30 mg/day divided BID–TID; max FDA–approved dose is 60 mg/day but doses >40 mg/day rarely used.

Cost: $$$

Side Effects:
- Most common: EPS, headache, drowsiness, dry mouth, prolactin elevation (sexual side effects, amenorrhea, galactorrhea).
- Serious but rare: See class warnings in chapter introduction.

Mechanism, Pharmacokinetics, and Drug Interactions:
- Dopamine D2 receptor antagonist.
- Metabolized primarily by CYP1A2; t ½: 34 hours.
- Smoking status may affect thiothixene metabolism as smoking is a potent 1A2 inducer; smokers may need higher doses.

Clinical Pearls:
Thiothixene is a high–potency conventional (typical) antipsychotic; this leads to more EPS compared to mid– and low–potency agents (eg, perphenazine or chlorpromazine) and to less sedation, less orthostasis and fewer anticholinergic side effects compared to low–potency agents (eg, chlorpromazine).

Fun Fact:
Pfizer developed thiothixene in the 1960s, and the drug was found to be an effective antidepressant, as well as an antipsychotic. For commercial reasons, the company chose to market it for schizophrenia rather than depression.

Bottom Line:
When using a high–potency typical antipsychotic, most will choose haloperidol or fluphenazine because of greater familiarity with those agents and a range of formulation options (eg, liquid, injectable, long–acting).

TRIFLUOPERAZINE (Stelazine) Fact Sheet [G]

FDA Indications:
Schizophrenia; non-psychotic anxiety.

Off-Label Uses:
Bipolar disorder; behavioral disturbances; impulse control disorders.

Dosage Forms:
Tablets (G): 1 mg, 2 mg, 5 mg, 10 mg.

Dosage Guidance:
Schizophrenia: Start 1 mg–2 mg BID; adjust to lowest effective dose. Usual dose range 5 mg BID–10 mg BID; max FDA-approved dose 40 mg/day.

Cost: $$

Side Effects:
- Most common: EPS, headache, drowsiness, dry mouth, prolactin elevation (sexual side effects, amenorrhea, galactorrhea).
- Serious but rare: See class warnings in chapter introduction.

Mechanism, Pharmacokinetics, and Drug Interactions:
- Dopamine D2 receptor antagonist.
- Metabolized primarily by CYP1A2; t ½: 18 hours.
- Smoking status may affect trifluoperazine metabolism as smoking is a potent 1A2 inducer; smokers may need higher doses.

Clinical Pearls:
- Trifluoperazine is a high-potency conventional (typical) antipsychotic; this leads to more EPS compared to mid- and low-potency agents (eg, perphenazine or chlorpromazine) and to less sedation, less orthostasis, and fewer anticholinergic side effects compared to low-potency agents (eg, chlorpromazine).
- Trifluoperazine was FDA-approved for non-psychotic anxiety at doses of no more than 6 mg/day used for no more than 12 weeks, but is no longer used for this indication.

Fun Fact:
Stelazine was marketed with the tagline slogan "Calm, but still alert."

Bottom Line:
When using a high-potency typical antipsychotic, most will choose haloperidol or fluphenazine because of greater familiarity with those agents and a range of formulation options (eg, liquid, injectable, long-acting).

ZIPRASIDONE (Geodon) Fact Sheet [G]

FDA Indications:

Schizophrenia; bipolar disorder, acute treatment of manic/mixed episode; maintenance treatment of **bipolar disorder** as adjunct; **acute agitation** in patients with schizophrenia (IM only).

Off-Label Uses:

Bipolar disorder; behavioral disturbances; impulse control disorders.

Dosage Forms:
- **Capsules (G):** 20 mg, 40 mg, 60 mg, 80 mg.
- **Oral suspension:** 10 mg/mL.
- **Injection:** 20 mg/mL.

Dosage Guidance:
- Schizophrenia, bipolar disorder: Start 20 mg BID (40 mg BID for acute mania) with meals for 2 to 3 days; ↑ by 40 mg/day increments; can usually ↑ rather quickly to target dose 60 mg BID–80 mg BID. Max approved dose is 160 mg/day, though can go higher in some patients; there are some safety data for doses up to 320 mg/day.
- Schizophrenia, acute agitation: (IM injection) 10 mg Q2 hours or 20 mg Q4 hours; max 40 mg/day. Replace with oral therapy as soon as possible.

Cost: $$$

Side Effects:
- Most common: somnolence, dizziness, akathisia, rash (5%).
- Serious but rare: may result in minor QTc prolongation (dose-related; 10 msec at 160 mg/day). Clinically relevant prolongation (>500 msec) rare (0.06%) and less than placebo (0.23%). Significant QTc prolongation has been associated with the development of malignant ventricular arrhythmias (torsade de pointes) and sudden death. Avoid in patients with hypokalemia, hypomagnesemia, bradycardia, persistent QTc intervals >500 msec, or those receiving other drugs that prolong QTc interval. Patients with symptoms of dizziness, palpitations, or syncope should receive further cardiac evaluation. Drug reaction with eosinophilia and systemic symptoms (DRESS) has been reported with ziprasidone exposure. DRESS begins as a rash that can spread all over the body, may also include swollen lymph nodes, fever, and damage to organs such as the heart, liver, pancreas, or kidneys, and is sometimes fatal; discontinue ziprasidone if DRESS is suspected.

Mechanism, Pharmacokinetics, and Drug Interactions:
- Dopamine D2 and serotonin 5HT2A receptor antagonist.
- Metabolized in liver principally by aldehyde oxidase; less than one-third of clearance mediated by CYP450: CYP3A4 (major), and CYP1A2 (minor); t ½: 7 hours.
- Avoid use with other drugs that prolong QTc interval.

Clinical Pearls:
- Administer twice daily, ideally with meals; ingestion of several hundred calories is necessary to increase absorption up to twofold.
- Causes less weight gain than clozapine, olanzapine, quetiapine, or risperidone. Significant disadvantages, including higher cost, make use of this drug difficult to justify.
- Average increase in QTc greater than any other atypical, although not much more than for quetiapine. Post-marketing surveillance has shown one or two instances of torsade possibly related to ziprasidone use.

Fun Fact:

The brand name Geodon has been suggested to bring to mind the phrase "down (don) to earth (geo)," referring to the goals of the medication.

Bottom Line:

Appealing weight and metabolic profile but dosage titration, twice-daily dosing, and wide range for target dose make this agent more cumbersome to use. QTc interval prolongation risk not clinically important for the majority of patients, but use caution if risk factors exist (bradycardia, low potassium or magnesium).

LONG-ACTING INJECTABLE (LAI) Antipsychotics

Introduction: Do LAIs Work?

These formulations used to be known as "depot" antipsychotics, but the powers that be have renamed them "long-acting injectables" (LAIs), presumably to help remove some of the stigma associated with their use. But no matter what you call them, suddenly every drug company is racing to introduce its own LAI neuroleptic.

Theoretically, LAIs are great solutions for patients who are at high risk of relapse when they stop taking their medications. Indeed, these are the patients in whom we usually entertain the possibility of prescribing an injectable. For example, I have a patient who does quite well when he takes his Clozaril, but when he stops, he ends up isolating himself in his subsidized apartment, the shades drawn, frozen in a series of paranoid delusions. Eventually, someone calls the police and he is involuntarily committed to the hospital, where he is put back on meds and does well—until the cycle repeats itself. Why isn't he on LAIs? Because he refuses to take them. He hates injections. He doesn't want to feel controlled by a medication that stays in his system. This is an example of why it's hard to demonstrate in controlled trials that LAIs prevent relapse any better than orals.

The most recent and largest meta-analysis analyzed 21 randomized controlled trials in which patients with schizophrenia were randomly assigned to either LAIs or orals. There was no difference between the formulations in relapse rates. The exception was that older studies done prior to 1992 showed a benefit of first-generation LAIs (mainly Prolixin Decanoate) over first-generation orals. (Kishimoto T et al, *Schiz Bull* 2014;40(1):192-213).

But as usual with research, there are complications interpreting these studies. While randomized controlled trials are typically the gold standard, in this case, they may not be generalizable to the kinds of patients for whom we would recommend LAIs. Such trials invite all patients, whether or not they are at high risk of non-adherence to pills. In the real world, we would rarely offer LAIs to our patients who are taking their oral medication as directed, but rather to patients who have a history of frequent relapse due to non-adherence.

In fact, naturalistic studies (also known as observational studies) tend to be much more positive about LAIs. These studies make no effort to recruit or to randomize patients to different treatment arms. Instead, they identify patients with schizophrenia in real-world settings who were switched from orals to LAIs by their doctors. The reasons for the switches were typically what you'd expect—poor adherence and poor results on orals. A meta-analysis of 25 of these studies, involving 5,940 patients, found that switching these patients to LAIs strongly decreased the number of hospitalizations (Kishimoto T et al, *J Clin Psychiatry* 2013;74(10):957-65).

The bottom line is that common sense wins the day. Patients who do poorly on pills because of non-adherence are likely to do better on LAIs—if you can get them to agree to get the needle.

With this long-winded introduction out of the way, we can finally get to what you've been waiting for—a comparison of the specific advantages and disadvantages of the many LAIs currently marketed.

Deciding Among the LAIs

General notes on LAIs

- It's best to choose an LAI version of an oral medication that your patient has already taken, so that you can be more confident that the agent is effective and tolerable.

- Be patient. The full therapeutic effect of LAIs can take longer than orals—ie, several months. Don't adjust the LAI dose prematurely.

- Consider oral overlap. Agents differ on how quickly you can titrate up the dose. This is important because for those requiring gradual titration, your patient will need oral pills to make sure he or she has a decent serum level right away. This process is called the "oral overlap" and it has two disadvantages. First, it makes the process of dosing a bit more complex (not a huge deal); second, if the patient is refusing to take oral meds (but accepting an injection, either under court order or voluntarily), you'll have to choose a different LAI or risk a decompensation while waiting for levels to become therapeutic.

- *Never* initiate an LAI on a patient who has a history of neuroleptic malignant syndrome (NMS) on any antipsychotic. That's just asking for trouble.

LAI options

There's a pretty comprehensive table on the following pages that reports, for each LAI, the **FDA indication(s), medication names, costs, available as, dosing information, pharmacokinetics, clinical pearls,** and **notes**. But first, we'll give you a shorthand version of the most clinically relevant points below:

- **Fluphenazine (Prolixin Decanoate)**—Dosed every 2 weeks. Injections are painful. Cheap, but relatively high risk of EPS and TD. Oral overlap required.

- **Haloperidol (Haldol Decanoate)**—Dosed monthly. As cheap as Prolixin, and since it's dosed less often and the pharmacokinetics are more predictable, it's generally the better choice among FGAs. Oral overlap required.

- **Aripiprazole (Abilify Maintena or Aristada)**—Dosed monthly or every 6 weeks (Aristada). Minimal oral overlap required, which makes it easier to dose. Good side effect profile.

- **Olanzapine (Zyprexa Relprevv)**—Dosed either every 2 weeks or monthly, depending on the dose needed. May be the worst choice among all LAIs for multiple reasons. High potential for weight gain. There's a small risk of a post-injection delirium/sedation syndrome, occurring in less than 1% of patients, caused by accidental intravascular injection. For this reason, you have to give the injection at a registered health care facility where patients can be continuously monitored for at least 3 hours after the injection. Restricted use requires physician and facility registration, and additional paperwork with Eli Lilly's program. High cost, restriction of use, monitoring requirement, and risk of adverse outcome all limit use severely. No oral overlap.

- **Paliperidone monthly (Invega Sustenna)**—Monthly dosing. No oral overlap required. Less painful injection than Risperdal Consta or Zyprexa Relprevv. Difficult to initiate because of the need for 2 separate loading injections. Expensive. No oral overlap.

- **Paliperidone every 3 months (Invega Trinza)**—Every-3-month dosing, but your patient must have done well on monthly injections of Sustenna for 4 months before switching to Trinza. Expensive, but given that only 4 doses are needed per year, it may be less expensive than other brand name options. No oral overlap.

- **Risperidone (Risperdal Consta)**—Every-2-week dosing. A 3-week oral overlap and the need for a refrigerated solution make this LAI more cumbersome to use than some of its competitors.

Table 7: Long-Acting Injectable Antipsychotics

Generic Name (Brand Name) Year FDA Approved [G] denotes generic availability	Relevant FDA Indication(s)	Available Strengths	Oral Overlap	Dosing Interval	Initial Dosing	Maintenance Dose	Cost for Monthly Supply at Average Dose (Oct 2015)
Typical Antipsychotics							
Fluphenazine decanoate [G] (Prolixin Decanoate[1]) 1972	Schizophrenia	25 mg/mL	Continue total oral dose for 2–3 days, then ↓ by 50% increments every 2–3 days until discontinued (by next injection)	2 weeks	1.25 X total daily oral dose Q2–3 weeks	Increase in increments of 12.5 mg; do not exceed 100 mg per dose	$$ [G]
Haloperidol decanoate [G] (Haldol Decanoate) 1986	Schizophrenia	50 mg/mL and 100 mg/mL	For 7 days, give usual oral dose, then ↓ by 50% weekly for 2 weeks, then discontinue	4 weeks	10–20 X total oral daily dose Q4 weeks. First dose should be ≤100 mg; if higher dose needed, give remainder in 1–2 weeks.	Lower to 10–15 X total oral daily dose Q4 weeks	$$$ [G] $$$$ Haldol Dec
Atypical Antipsychotics							
Aripiprazole (Abilify Maintena) 2013	Schizophrenia	300 mg and 400 mg vials	For 14 days	4 weeks	400 mg Q4 weeks	400 mg Q4 weeks; decrease to 300 mg Q4 weeks if side effects	$$$$$
Aripiprazole lauroxil (Aristada) 2015	Schizophrenia	441 mg, 662 mg, 882 mg	For 21 days	Monthly or every 6 weeks	441 mg. 662 mg or 882 mg monthly (equiv to 10, 15, and 20 mg/day)	441 mg, 662 mg or 882 mg monthly or 882 mg every 6 weeks	$$$$$
Olanzapine (Zyprexa Relprevv) 2009	Schizophrenia	210, 300, and 405 mg vials	No overlap	2–4 weeks	10 mg/day oral: 210 mg Q2 weeks x 4 doses or 405 mg Q4 weeks x 2 doses; 15 mg/day oral: 300 mg Q2 weeks x 4 doses; 20 mg/day oral: 300 mg Q2 weeks	10 mg/day oral: 150 mg Q2 weeks or 300 mg Q4 weeks; 15 mg/day oral: 210 mg Q2 weeks or 405 mg Q4 weeks; 20 mg/day oral: 300 mg Q2 weeks; Maximum dose: 300 mg Q2 weeks or 405 mg Q4 weeks	$$$$$

Generic Name (Brand Name) Year FDA Approved [G] denotes generic availability	Relevant FDA Indication(s)	Available Strengths	Oral Overlap	Dosing Interval	Initial Dosing	Maintenance Dose	Cost for Monthly Supply at Average Dose (Oct 2015)
Paliperidone palmitate (Invega Sustenna) 2009	Schizophrenia Schizoaffective disorder (monotherapy or adjunct)	39, 78, 117, 156, and 234 mg in prefilled syringes	No overlap	4 weeks	234 mg IM in deltoid, then 156 mg 1 week later	117 mg 3 weeks after 2nd dose then Q month; may adjust monthly dose (maintenance given deltoid or gluteal) Approx. equivalence: 3 mg oral: 39 mg–78 mg 6 mg oral: 117 mg 12 mg oral: 234 mg	$$$$
Paliperidone palmitate (Invega Trinza) 2015	Schizophrenia (only after at least 4 months of adequate treatment on Invega Sustenna)	273, 410, 546, 819 mg in prefilled syringes	No overlap	3 months	Based on previous Invega Sustenna dose: -for 78 mg, give 273 mg Trinza -for 117, give 410 mg Trinza -for 156 mg, give 546 mg Trinza -for 234 mg, give 819 mg Trinza	Give same conversion dose of Trinza every 3 months; adjust if necessary per patient response	$$$$$
Risperidone (Risperdal Consta) 2003	Schizophrenia Bipolar, manic/mixed (monotherapy or adjunct)	12.5, 25, 37.5, and 50 mg vials	With usual oral dose for 3 weeks	2 weeks	Start at 25 mg Q2 weeks. Adjust dose no more frequently than Q 4 weeks as needed for response.	Approx. equivalence: <4 mg/day oral: 25 mg 4 mg–6 mg/day oral: 37.5 mg >6 mg/day oral: 50 mg Maximum dose: 50 mg Q2 weeks	$$$$$

[1] brand discontinued; available as generic only

Anxiolytic Medications

Although antidepressants are arguably the most effective medications for anxiety, in this chapter we focus on benzodiazepines and other drugs used specifically for anxiety disorders.

Psychiatry has long had a love/hate relationship with benzos. They work quickly and predictably, but they often lead to dependence and sometimes to outright addiction.

Assuming you've done a good enough diagnostic evaluation to identify malingerers and drug abusers, here's a reasonable approach to deciding on which anxiolytic medication to prescribe.

1. Start with a long-acting medication such as clonazepam. It's less likely to lead to addiction, because its onset and offset are more gradual.

2. Reserve short-acting benzos, like alprazolam or lorazepam, for patients who have occasional anxiety, and prescribe these on an as-needed basis.

3. When treating anxiety disorders that are responsive to antidepressants (and which aren't?), do the following: Start patients on an SSRI/SNRI plus a benzo. Tell them that in 2 weeks they will be able to stop taking the benzo because the antidepressant will have kicked in.

4. Give buspirone a chance, especially for generalized anxiety disorder. It may not work as reliably as benzos, but it is non-addictive.

5. Don't forget propranolol, which can be really effective for patients who have strong somatic symptoms of anxiety, such as pounding heart and shortness of breath.

6. Finally, prazosin, another blood pressure medication, is effective for PTSD, especially for insomnia and nightmares.

Table 8: Anxiolytic Medications

Generic Name (Brand Name) Year FDA Approved [G] denotes generic availability	Relevant FDA Indication(s)	Available Strengths (mg)	Onset of Action (oral)	Half-Life (hours)	Duration of Action (hours)	Equivalent Dose to Lorazepam 1 mg	Usual Dosage Range (starting–max) (mg)
Alprazolam (Xanax, Xanax XR) [G] 1981	GAD Panic disorder	Tablets: 0.25, 0.5, 1, 2 ER tablets: 0.5, 1, 2, 3 Liquid: 1 mg/mL	30 min (IR) 1–2 hrs (XR)	11–16	3–4 (IR) 10 (XR)	0.5	0.25 mg TID–2 mg TID 0.5 mg–3 mg QD (XR)
Buspirone (BuSpar[1]) [G] 1986	GAD	Tablets: 5, 7.5, 10, 15, 30	1–2 weeks+	2–3	N/A	N/A	5 mg TID–20 mg TID
Clonazepam (Klonopin, Klonopin Wafers[1]) [G] 1975	Panic disorder	Tablets: 0.5, 1, 2 ODT: 0.125, 0.25, 0.5, 1, 2	1 hr	20–80	4–8	0.25–0.5	0.5 mg BID–2 mg TID
Diazepam (Valium) [G] 1963	GAD Alcohol withdrawal	Tablets: 2, 5, 10 Liquid: 5 mg/5 mL, 5 mg/mL Injection: 5 mg/mL	30 min	>100	4–6	5	2 mg BID–10 mg QID
Lorazepam (Ativan) [G] 1977	GAD	Tablets: 0.5, 1, 2 Liquid: 2 mg/mL Injection: 2 mg/mL, 4 mg/mL	30–60 min	10–20	4–6	1	1 mg BID–5 mg BID
Prazosin (Minipress) [G] 1976	PTSD (off-label)	Capsules: 1, 2, 5	1–2 hrs	2–3	4–6	N/A	1 mg/day–10 mg/day QHS or divided BID
Propranolol (Inderal) [G] 1973	Performance anxiety (off-label)	Tablets: 10, 20, 40, 60, 80	60 min	3–6	4–6	N/A	10–40 mg PRN

[1]Brand discontinued; available as generic only

ALPRAZOLAM (Xanax) Fact Sheet [G]

FDA Indications:
Generalized anxiety disorder (GAD); panic disorder.

Off-Label Uses:
Other anxiety disorders; insomnia; acute mania or psychosis; catatonia.

Dosage Forms:
- **Tablets (G):** 0.25, 0.5 mg, 1 mg, 2 mg.
- **ER tablets (Xanax XR, G):** 0.5 mg, 1 mg, 2 mg, 3 mg.
- **Oral concentrate (G):** 1 mg/mL.

Dosage Guidance:
- GAD: Start 0.25 mg–0.5 mg TID; increase by 0.25 mg–0.5 mg/day increments every 3–4 days as needed and tolerated to max dose 4 mg/day divided TID–QID.
- Panic disorder: Start 0.5 mg TID; increase by increments of no more than 1 mg/day every 3–4 days as needed to a target dose 4 mg–6 mg/day divided TID–QID. Max dose 10 mg/day.
- For panic disorder using XR: Start 0.5 mg–1 mg QD; increase by increments of no more than 1 mg/day at intervals of 3–4 days to target dose 3 mg–6 mg QD.

Cost: IR: $; ER: $

Side Effects:
- Most common: sedation, somnolence, memory impairment, slurred speech, incoordination, dependence.
- Serious but rare: anterograde amnesia, increased fall risk, paradoxical reaction (irritability, agitation); respiratory depression (avoid in patients with sleep apnea).

Mechanism, Pharmacokinetics, and Drug Interactions:
- Binds to benzodiazepine receptors to enhance GABA effects.
- Metabolized primarily through CYP3A4; t ½: 11–16 hours.
- Avoid use with other CNS depressants, including alcohol. Adjust dose when given with 3A4 inhibitors or inducers.

Clinical Pearls:
- C–IV controlled substance.
- Benzodiazepines are very effective immediately for GAD and panic disorder, particularly in the early weeks of SSRI therapy while awaiting onset of therapeutic effect.
- Paradoxical reaction of aggression, agitation, and combativeness more likely to occur in elderly or those with brain injury.
- While benzodiazepines are highly abusable, patients with panic disorder rarely self-increase dose when treated adequately, indicating that tolerance to anxiolytic effects does not occur.

Fun Fact:
There are many slang terms for alprazolam; some of the more common ones are Bars, Z–bars, Zannies, Footballs, Blues, or Blue Footballs.

Bottom Line:
Fast-acting and effective for GAD and panic disorder, but short duration of action may contribute to breakthrough symptoms between doses and make withdrawal more difficult.

BUSPIRONE (BuSpar) Fact Sheet [G]

FDA Indications:
Generalized anxiety disorder (GAD).

Off-Label Uses:
Treatment–resistant depression; anxiety symptoms in depression.

Dosage Forms:
Tablets (G): 5 mg, 7.5 mg, 10 mg, 15 mg, 30 mg (scored).

Dosage Guidance:
Start 7.5 mg BID or 5 mg TID; increase by increments of 5 mg/day every 2-3 days to target dose 20 mg-30 mg/day divided BID-TID; max 20 mg TID.

Cost: $

Side Effects:
Most common: dizziness, nervousness, nausea, headache, jitteriness.

Mechanism, Pharmacokinetics, and Drug Interactions:
- Serotonin 5HT1A receptor partial agonist.
- Metabolized primarily through CYP3A4; t ½: 2-3 hours.
- Avoid use with MAOIs; caution with serotonergic agents due to additive effects and risk for serotonin syndrome. Caution with 3A4 inhibitors or inducers as they may affect buspirone serum levels; adjust dose.

Clinical Pearls:
- Similar to antidepressants, buspirone requires 1-2 weeks for onset of therapeutic effects, with full effects occurring over several weeks, and offers no "as-needed" benefits.
- Non-sedating, non-habit-forming alternative to benzodiazepines for anxiety. May be less effective or ineffective in patients who have previously responded to benzos.
- Has only shown efficacy in GAD, not in other anxiety disorders (PTSD, OCD, panic disorder).
- May potentiate antidepressant effects when used in combination with SSRIs in refractory depression.

Fun Fact:
Other psychotropic agents with 5HT1A partial agonist effects include aripiprazole, ziprasidone, and vilazodone.

Bottom Line:
An alternative to benzodiazepine in patients for whom benzos are not appropriate. Don't expect as robust a response though.

CLONAZEPAM (Klonopin) Fact Sheet (G)

FDA Indications:

Seizure disorders; panic disorder.

Off-Label Uses:

Other anxiety disorders; insomnia; acute mania or psychosis; catatonia.

Dosage Forms:

- **Tablets (G):** 0.5 mg, 1 mg, 2 mg.
- **Orally disintegrating tablets (Klonopin Wafers, G):** 0.125 mg, 0.25 mg, 0.5 mg, 1 mg, 2 mg.

Dosage Guidance:

- Dose varies based on patient characteristics (eg, age) and tolerance to benzodiazepines.
- Anxiety: Start 0.5 mg BID; increase by 0.5 mg–1 mg/day increments every 2–4 days to max 6 mg/day divided BID–TID.
- Insomnia (off-label use): Start 0.25 mg–0.5 mg QHS as needed for insomnia. Max 2 mg at bedtime.
- Use lower doses for elderly.

Cost: $

Side Effects:

- Most common: somnolence, daytime grogginess, confusion, ataxia.
- Serious but rare: anterograde amnesia, increased fall risk, paradoxical reaction (irritability, agitation); respiratory depression (avoid in patients with sleep apnea).

Mechanism, Pharmacokinetics, and Drug Interactions:

- Binds to benzodiazepine receptors to enhance GABA effects.
- Metabolized primarily through CYP3A4; t ½: 20–80 hours.
- Avoid concomitant use with other CNS depressants, including alcohol (additive effects). Potent CYP3A4 inhibitors (eg, fluvoxamine, erythromycin) may increase clonazepam levels; CYP3A4 inducers (eg, carbamazepine) may decrease clonazepam levels.

Clinical Pearls:

- C–IV controlled substance.
- High potency, long-acting benzodiazepine with active metabolites that may accumulate.
- Withdrawal effects may not be seen until 3–5 days after abrupt discontinuation and may last 10–14 days due to long half-life and active metabolites of clonazepam.
- Full effects of a particular dose may not be evident for a few days since active metabolites will accumulate with continual use (versus PRN use). Wait several days before increasing dose if patient is taking clonazepam regularly.

Fun Fact:

Klonopin tablets (or "K-pins") have a street value of $2-$5 per tablet, depending on dose and geographic region.

Bottom Line:

Fewer breakthrough symptoms compared to alprazolam when used for anxiety due to longer half-life. May work as a good hypnotic for the short term, although dependence and long half-life limit this use.

DIAZEPAM (Valium) Fact Sheet (G)

FDA Indications:

Generalized anxiety disorder (GAD); alcohol withdrawal; seizures; muscle spasms.

Off-Label Uses:

Other anxiety disorders; insomnia; acute mania or psychosis; catatonia.

Dosage Forms:

- **Tablets (G):** 2 mg, 5 mg, 10 mg (scored).
- **Oral liquid (G):** 5 mg/5 mL, 5 mg/1 mL.
- **Injection (G):** 5 mg/1 mL.

Dosage Guidance:

Anxiety: Start 2 mg BID–5 mg BID; increase by 2 mg–5 mg/day increments every 2–4 days to max 40 mg/day divided BID–QID.

Cost: $

Side Effects:

- Most common: somnolence, daytime grogginess, confusion; ataxia.
- Serious but rare: anterograde amnesia, increased fall risk, paradoxical reaction (irritability, agitation); respiratory depression (avoid in patients with sleep apnea).

Mechanism, Pharmacokinetics, and Drug Interactions:

- Binds to benzodiazepine receptors to enhance GABA effects.
- Metabolized primarily through CYP3A4 and 2C19; t ½: >100 hours.
- Avoid concomitant use with other CNS depressants, including alcohol (additive effects).

Clinical Pearls:

- C–IV controlled substance.
- Long-acting benzodiazepine with active metabolites that may accumulate.
- Tolerance to sedative effect may develop more rapidly (within 2–4 weeks of use) than tolerance to anti-anxiety effect. Benzodiazepines affect the normal sleep architecture; thus, long-term use is discouraged.
- Withdrawal effects may not be seen until 3–5 days after abrupt discontinuation and may last 10–14 days due to long half-life and active metabolites of diazepam.
- Diazepam has the highest lipid solubility of all benzos, which means very rapid distribution into and out of the CNS, resulting in the greatest "rush" felt by patients using in a single-dose manner. This feature makes this the most abusable benzo.

Fun Fact:

Valium has been glorified in music more than once. The Rolling Stones' "little yellow pill" in "Mother's Little Helper" and Lou Reed's "Walk on the Wild Side" ("Jackie is just speeding away/Thought she was James Dean for a day/Then I guess she had to crash/Valium would have helped that bash") are two good examples.

Bottom Line:

Diazepam has a long history of use with good efficacy for anxiety. Its long half-life makes it a particularly effective hypnotic for some patients.

LORAZEPAM (Ativan) Fact Sheet (G)

FDA Indications:
Generalized anxiety disorder (GAD); status epilepticus (IV route).

Off-Label Uses:
Other anxiety disorders; insomnia; acute mania or psychosis; catatonia.

Dosage Forms:
- **Tablets (G):** 0.5 mg, 1 mg, 2 mg.
- **Oral concentrate (G):** 2 mg/mL.
- **Injection (G):** 2 mg/mL, 4 mg/mL.

Dosage Guidance:
- Anxiety: Start 1 mg BID; increase by 0.5 mg–1 mg/day increments every 2–4 days up to 6 mg/day divided BID–TID. Max 10 mg/day divided BID–TID.
- Insomnia (off-label use): Start 0.5 mg–1 mg QHS, 20–30 minutes before bedtime; max 4 mg nightly.
- Use lower doses in elderly.

Cost: $

Side Effects:
- Most common: somnolence, dizziness, weakness, ataxia.
- Serious but rare: anterograde amnesia, increased fall risk, paradoxical reaction (irritability, agitation); respiratory depression (avoid in patients with sleep apnea).

Mechanism, Pharmacokinetics, and Drug Interactions:
- Binds to benzodiazepine receptors to enhance GABA effects.
- Metabolism primarily hepatic (non–CYP450) to inactive compounds; t ½: 10–20 hours.
- Avoid concomitant use with other CNS depressants, including alcohol (additive effects). No risk for CYP450 drug interactions.

Clinical Pearls:
- C–IV controlled substance.
- Lorazepam does not have a long half-life or active metabolites that could accumulate, and poses no CYP450 drug interaction risk.
- Withdrawal symptoms usually seen on the first day after abrupt discontinuation and last 5–7 days in patients receiving short–intermediate half-life benzodiazepines such as lorazepam. A gradual taper is highly recommended, particularly if prolonged treatment on a high dose.
- Tolerance to sedative effect may develop within 2–4 weeks of use, and benzodiazepines affect the normal sleep architecture; thus, long-term use is discouraged.

Fun Fact:
Early Ativan marketing efforts included clever direct-to-consumer advertising campaigns. These included: "Now it can be yours—The Ativan experience" in 1977 and "In a world where certainties are few … no wonder Ativan is prescribed by so many caring clinicians" in 1987.

Bottom Line:
When a benzodiazepine is appropriate for use (short-term; minimal risk of abuse), we consider this to be a first-line agent.

PRAZOSIN (Minipress) Fact Sheet (G)

FDA Indications:
Hypertension.

Off-Label Uses:
PTSD.

Dosage Forms:
Capsules (G): 1 mg, 2 mg, 5 mg.

Dosage Guidance:
- PTSD (off-label): Titrate dose slowly to minimize possibility of "first-dose" orthostatic hypotension. Start 1 mg QHS x 3 days. Then, 2 mg QHS x 4 days. If tolerating but still symptomatic, increase to 3 mg QHS x 7 days. Dose can be increased further, based on response, to 4 mg QHS x 7 days. Target 1 mg–5 mg/day.
- May dose divide BID to target daytime PTSD-associated arousal symptoms.

Cost: $

Side Effects:
- Most common: somnolence, dizziness, headache, weakness.
- Serious but rare: orthostasis and syncope; prolonged erections and priapism have been reported.

Mechanism, Pharmacokinetics, and Drug Interactions:
- Alpha-1 adrenergic receptor antagonist.
- Metabolism primarily hepatic (non-CYP450); t ½: 2–3 hours.
- Caution with other antihypertensive agents, diuretics, and PDE5 inhibitors (eg, Viagra) that may have additive hypotensive effects.

Clinical Pearls:
Initial studies showed improvement in trauma-related nightmares and sleep quality when dosed at bedtime. Subsequent randomized controlled trials have shown positive effects on daytime PTSD symptoms also when dosed BID.

Fun Fact:
Prazosin is an older drug, which is now rarely used for its original indication (hypertension). It's now used as a second-line agent for urinary hesitancy in benign prostatic hyperplasia. It is also being investigated for alcohol dependence.

Bottom Line:
Use prazosin for PTSD, especially for PTSD-associated nightmares.

PROPRANOLOL (Inderal) Fact Sheet (G)

FDA Indications:

Hypertension; angina; post-MI cardioprotection; atrial fibrillation; migraine prophylaxis; essential tremor.

Off-Label Uses:

Performance anxiety.

Dosage Forms:

Tablets (G): 10 mg, 20 mg, 40 mg, 60 mg, 80 mg (scored).

Dosage Guidance:

Performance anxiety (off-label use): Give 10 mg about 60 minutes prior to performance; usual effective dose for most is 10 mg–40 mg.

Cost: $

Side Effects:

Most common: dizziness, fatigue, bradycardia, and hypotension.

Mechanism, Pharmacokinetics, and Drug Interactions:

- Non-selective beta-1 and beta-2 adrenergic receptor antagonist.
- Metabolized primarily through CYP2D6, also 1A2 and 2C19; t ½: 3–6 hours.
- Caution with other hypertensives, CYP2D6 inhibitors, and inhibitors or inducers of 1A2 and 2C19.

Clinical Pearls:

With beta blockade, propranolol reduces some of the somatic symptoms of anxiety (tremor, sweating, flushing, tachycardia).

Fun Fact:

The list of notable people who suffer or have suffered from performance anxiety or stage fright is long. It includes Barbra Streisand, Carly Simon, Van Morrison, Chopin, Renee Fleming, Jay Mohr, Hugh Grant, Laurence Olivier, Mahatma Gandhi, and Thomas Jefferson, among others.

Bottom Line:

Effective and safe for use in performance anxiety, particularly when the sedating or cognitive side effects of benzos could interfere with patient's performance.

Dementia Medications

While it's good that we have a handful of FDA-approved drugs for dementia, the fact is that they do not work very well. In clinical settings, it is usually impossible to know whether they are working at all. This is because they work by slowing the inexorable cognitive decline seen in dementia. It is important to explain this point to family members, who might otherwise expect to see actual improvement in cognition, which is unusual.

For mild to moderate dementia, start with one of the 3 approved cholinesterase inhibitors (CI). These include donepezil, galantamine, and rivastigmine. Start with donepezil (we have the most data and experience with this agent, though the others are equally effective). Titrate donepezil to an effective dose, which is 15 mg–20 mg a day (Doody RS et al, *Drugs Aging* 2008;25(2):163-174).

For moderate to severe Alzheimer's dementia, for an FDA-approved approach, you can start with either memantine IR or high-dose donepezil (either by combining two 10 mgs or using the 23 mg version). Reserve the more expensive memantine XR for those rare situations in which IR is poorly tolerated.

An alternative approach is to follow the same protocol for all your patients with dementia, whether or not it is "severe" or "moderate." Start with a combination of donepezil and memantine, and for patients who have trouble taking two pills, consider Namzaric, which is the combination donepezil/memantine.

All 3 CIs commonly cause nausea, vomiting, and dizziness, and this is why the recommended dosing schedule is excruciatingly slow, generally no faster than 1 increment every 4 weeks. How long should patients be treated with these agents? If they are tolerated, a case can be made that you should never stop them. We say this because very long-term studies have shown that discontinuing donepezil after 6 months causes patients' cognitive scores to plummet to the level of placebo-treated patients. And even when these patients were "rescued" with donepezil, cognitive decline continued. So if a patient has tolerated a CI for several months, keep the prescription going indefinitely.

Table 9: Dementia Medications

Generic Name (Brand Name) Year FDA Approved [G] denotes generic availability	Relevant FDA Indication(s)	Available Strengths (mg except where noted)	Usual Dosage Range (starting–max) (mg)
Donepezil (Aricept, Aricept ODT) [G] 1996	Mild to moderate Alzheimer's dementia (5, 10 mg) Moderate to severe Alzheimer's dementia (10, 23 mg)	Tablets: 5, 10, 23 ODT: 5, 10	5 QAM–23 QAM
Galantamine (Razadyne) [G] 2001	Mild to moderate Alzheimer's dementia	Tablets: 4, 8, 12 Liquid: 4 mg/mL	4 BID–12 BID
Galantamine ER (Razadyne ER) [G] 2004	Mild to moderate Alzheimer's dementia	ER capsules: 8, 16, 24	8 ER QAM–24 ER QAM
Memantine (Namenda) [G] 2003	Moderate to severe Alzheimer's dementia	Tablets: 5, 10 Liquid: 2 mg/mL	5 QAM–10 BID
Memantine ER (Namenda XR) 2010	Moderate to severe Alzheimer's dementia	ER capsules: 7, 14, 21, 28	7–28 QD
Memantine ER/donepezil (Namzaric) 2014	Moderate to severe Alzheimer's dementia (in patients already stabilized on both medications)	ER capsules: 14/10, 28/10	Patients on memantine (10 mg BID or 28 mg XR QD) and donepezil 10 mg QD can be switched to Namzaric 28 mg/10 mg QPM
Rivastigmine (Exelon) [G] 2000	Mild to moderate Alzheimer's dementia Mild to moderate dementia associated with Parkinson's disease	Capsules: 1.5, 3, 4.5, 6	1.5 BID–6 BID
Rivastigmine (Exelon Patch) 2007	Mild to moderate and severe Alzheimer's dementia Mild to moderate dementia associated with Parkinson's disease	ER patches: 4.6, 9.5, 13.3/24 hr	4.6 mg/24 hr QD–13.3 mg/24 hr QD

DONEPEZIL (Aricept) Fact Sheet (G)

FDA Indications:
Mild to moderate Alzheimer's dementia (5 mg, 10 mg); **moderate to severe Alzheimer's dementia** (10 mg, 23 mg).

Off-Label Uses:
Other memory disorders; mild cognitive impairment.

Dosage Forms:
- **Tablets (G):** 5 mg, 10 mg, 23 mg.
- **Orally disintegrating tablets (Aricept ODT, G):** 5 mg, 10 mg.

Dosage Guidance:
- Mild to moderate dementia: Start 5 mg QD and ↑ to 10 mg QD after 4-6 weeks.
- Moderate to severe dementia: May ↑ further to 23 mg QD after ≥3 months (range 10 mg-23 mg/day).

Cost: 5 mg, 10 mg: $; 23 mg: $$$

Side Effects:
- Most common: dose-related diarrhea, nausea, vomiting, weight loss (especially 23 mg/day dose), anorexia, insomnia, abnormal dreams.
- Serious but rare: Cholinesterase inhibitors may have vagotonic effects that may cause bradycardia and/or heart block with or without a history of cardiac disease; syncope reported.

Mechanism, Pharmacokinetics, and Drug Interactions:
- Acetylcholinesterase (AChE) inhibitor.
- Metabolized primarily through CYP 2D6 and 3A4; t ½: 70 hours.
- Avoid use with anticholinergic agents as they will diminish therapeutic effects; avoid beta blockers due to risk of bradycardia. P450 interactions not usually clinically important.

Clinical Pearls:
- The first drug to be approved for dementia, it is also the most prescribed of the 3 CIs. Received additional FDA approval for use in severe dementia (in addition to its initial mild to moderate dementia approval).
- The manufacturer recommends bedtime dosing, but giving it in the morning may prevent the insomnia and vivid dreams some patients report with donepezil.
- Once-a-day dosing and easy titration makes this agent simplest to use.
- GI side effects usually resolve in 1-2 weeks.
- Based on a Cochrane review, donepezil causes fewer side effects than rivastigmine.
- Be mindful of other medications that may have intrinsic anticholinergic activity; these will counteract donepezil's therapeutic effects.
- Donepezil may also be effective in the treatment and prevention of delirium, which has been hypothesized to be due to an overall deficiency of cholinergic tone in the brain.

Fun Fact:
Donepezil has been studied in children for autism, pervasive developmental disorders, ADHD, and tic disorders, however the minimal data do not support such use.

Bottom Line:
First-line agent, but don't expect big improvements.

GALANTAMINE (Razadyne) Fact Sheet (G)

FDA Indications:
Mild to moderate Alzheimer's dementia.

Off-Label Uses:
Other memory disorders; mild cognitive impairment.

Dosage Forms:
- **Tablets (G):** 4 mg, 8 mg, 12 mg.
- **ER capsules (Razadyne ER, G):** 8 mg, 16 mg, 24 mg.
- **Oral solution (G):** 4 mg/mL.

Dosage Guidance:
- IR: Start 4 mg BID (breakfast and dinner), ↑ by 4 mg BID increments every 4 weeks.
- ER: Start 8 mg QAM (breakfast), ↑ by 8 mg/day every 4 weeks.
- For both, max 24 mg/day (target dose: 16 mg–24 mg/day).
- If using oral solution, mix dose with 3–4 ounces of any nonalcoholic beverage; mix well and drink immediately.
- If therapy is interrupted for ≥3 days, restart at the lowest dose and increase to current dose.

Cost: IR: $$; ER: $$

Side Effects:
- Most common: diarrhea, nausea, vomiting, weight loss, anorexia, insomnia, abnormal dreams.
- Serious but rare: Cholinesterase inhibitors may have vagotonic effects that may cause bradycardia and/or heart block with or without a history of cardiac disease; syncope reported.

Mechanism, Pharmacokinetics, and Drug Interactions:
- Acetylcholinesterase (AChE) inhibitor and cholinergic nicotinic receptor modulator.
- Metabolized primarily through CYP2D6 and 3A4; t ½: 7 hours.
- Avoid use with anticholinergic agents as they will diminish therapeutic effects; avoid beta blockers due to risk of bradycardia. P450 interactions not usually clinically important.

Clinical Pearls:
- Galantamine's claim to fame is that it has a "dual" mechanism of action, modulating cholinergic nicotinic receptors in addition to inhibiting acetylcholinesterase. The manufacturer may use this factoid to argue that galantamine is more effective than the other CIs. However, accumulating evidence seems to show no difference in efficacy (Loy C et al, Galantamine in Alzheimer's Disease, *Cochrane Database of Systematic Reviews* 2002. Updated 2006).
- ER formulation seems to be used more often due to ease of once–daily dosing.

Fun Fact:
Razadyne was approved in 2001 with its original name, Reminyl. Pharmacists were sometimes confusing written scripts for Reminyl with Amaryl, a diabetes medication. In April 2005, the trade name was changed to Razadyne to avoid future dispensing errors.

Bottom Line:
No appreciable benefit over donepezil, which has spent a longer time on market and has a greater range of experience given additional indication for severe dementia; consider this a second–line agent.

MEMANTINE (Namenda) Fact Sheet (G)

FDA Indications:
Moderate to severe Alzheimer's dementia.

Off-Label Uses:
Mild to moderate Alzheimer's dementia; other memory disorders; mild cognitive impairment; chronic pain.

Dosage Forms:
- **Tablets (G):** 5 mg, 10 mg.
- **Oral solution (G):** 2 mg/mL.
- **ER capsules (Namenda XR):** 7 mg, 14 mg, 21 mg, 28 mg.

Dosage Guidance:
- IR: 5 mg QD week 1; 5 mg BID week 2; 10 mg QAM and 5 mg QHS week 3; 10 mg BID week 4 and beyond.
- XR: Start 7 mg QD, ↑ by 7 mg/day in increments ≥1 week to max dose 28 mg/day (10 mg BID equivalent to 28 mg XR QD). Can be opened and sprinkled on food.

Cost: IR: $; ER: $$$$

Side Effects:
Most common: dizziness (XR), transient confusion (IR), headache (XR), diarrhea (XR), constipation, sedation.

Mechanism, Pharmacokinetics, and Drug Interactions:
- N–methyl–D–aspartate (NMDA) receptor antagonist.
- Metabolism primarily hepatic, but not P450; t ½: 60–80 hours.
- Pharmacokinetic interactions unlikely.

Clinical Pearls:
- FDA-approved for moderate to severe Alzheimer's dementia only; may also be effective as augmentation added to donepezil in patients with moderate to severe Alzheimer's dementia (see also memantine ER and donepezil fact sheets).
- Data comparing 10 mg BID and 20 mg QD of IR formulation, as well as pharmacokinetic profile, support use of once–daily IR dosing; IR is used QD in Europe.

Fun Fact:
Forest had announced it was discontinuing sales of the IR formulation as of August 15, 2014, in order to "focus on" the XR formulation—just ahead of the IR patent expiration. However, the New York attorney general filed an antitrust lawsuit, claiming this was an anticompetitive move, and Forest was forced to continue offering both Namenda IR and Namenda XR.

Bottom Line:
Memantine's indication (moderate to severe dementia only) may limit its use, but it does boast a unique mechanism of action and has some data to support its usefulness as an augmenter of donepezil. Many prescribers put the majority of their dementia patients on a combination of one of the CIs and memantine; we recommend adding memantine when dementia has progressed to the moderate or severe level, possibly earlier. There's no clinical benefit of using the more expensive XR version.

MEMANTINE ER/DONEPEZIL (Namzaric) Fact Sheet

FDA Indications:
Moderate to severe Alzheimer's dementia.

Off-Label Uses:
Mild to moderate Alzheimer's dementia; other memory disorders; mild cognitive impairment.

Dosage Forms:
Capsules: 14 mg/10 mg, 28 mg/10 mg memantine ER and donepezil.

Dosage Guidance:
- Patients should first be stabilized on the individual medications; patients on memantine (10 mg BID or 28 mg XR QD) and donepezil 10 mg QD can be switched to Namzaric 28 mg/10 mg QPM.
- Patients with severe renal impairment on memantine 5 mg BID or 14 mg XR QD and donepezil 10 mg QD can be switched to Namzaric 14 mg/10 mg QPM.

Cost: $$$$

Side Effects:
- Most common: headache, diarrhea, dizziness, vomiting, weight loss, anorexia, insomnia, abnormal dreams.
- Serious but rare: Cholinesterase inhibitors may have vagotonic effects that may cause bradycardia and/or heart block with or without a history of cardiac disease; syncope reported.

Mechanism, Pharmacokinetics, and Drug Interactions:
- N-methyl-D-aspartate (NMDA) receptor antagonist and acetylcholinesterase (AChE) inhibitor.
- Metabolism: memantine hepatic but not P450 and donepezil primarily through CYP 2D6 and 3A4; t ½: 60–80 hours (memantine) and 70 hours (donepezil).
- Avoid use with anticholinergic agents as they will diminish therapeutic effects; avoid beta blockers due to risk of bradycardia. P450 interactions not usually clinically important.

Clinical Pearls:
- Many experts now stabilize patients on an acetylcholinesterase inhibitor like donepezil and then add memantine.
- The manufacturer recommends bedtime dosing, but taking it in the morning may prevent the insomnia and vivid dreams some patients report with donepezil.
- Once-a-day dosing makes this agent easiest to use.
- Be mindful of other medications that may have intrinsic anticholinergic activity; these will counteract donepezil's therapeutic effects.

Fun Fact:
In 2014, Actavis Pharmaceuticals acquired Forest Pharmaceuticals, manufacturer of Namzaric. That same year, Actavis also acquired Allergan, manufacturer of Botox, another medication targeting the aging process but in a different way.

Bottom Line:
For patients who are already on this regimen but have trouble taking two pills, consider Namzaric.

RIVASTIGMINE (Exelon, Exelon Patch) Fact Sheet (G)

FDA Indications:

Mild to moderate Alzheimer's dementia (capsules); **mild to moderate and severe Alzheimer's dementia** (patch); **dementia associated with Parkinson's disease** (capsules and patch).

Off-Label Uses:

Other memory disorders; mild cognitive impairment.

Dosage Forms:
- **Capsules (G):** 1.5 mg, 3 mg, 4.5 mg, 6 mg.
- **Transdermal patches:** 4.6 mg/24 hour, 9.5 mg/24 hour, 13.3 mg/24 hour, containing rivastigmine 9 mg, 18 mg, and 27 mg, respectively.

Dosage Guidance:
- Start 1.5 mg BID with meals for 4 weeks, ↑ by 1.5 mg BID increments every 4 weeks, up to max 6 mg BID with meals.
- Patch: For mild to moderate dementia, start 4.6 mg/24 hours; if tolerated, ↑ after ≥4 weeks to 9.5 mg/24 hours (target and max dose). For severe dementia, titrate to 13.3 mg/24 hour (effective and max dose).
- Converting oral to patch: <6 mg/day: Use 4.6 mg/24 hour patch; 6 mg–12 mg/day: use 9.5 mg/24 hour patch; apply patch on next day following last oral dose.

Cost: oral: $$$; patch: $$$$

Side Effects:
- Most common: dizziness, headache, diarrhea, anorexia, nausea, vomiting, skin reactions (patch).
- Serious but rare: Cholinesterase inhibitors may have vagotonic effects that may cause bradycardia and/or heart block with or without a history of cardiac disease; syncope reported.

Mechanism, Pharmacokinetics, and Drug Interactions:
- Acetylcholinesterase (AChE) and butyrylcholinesterase (BuChE) inhibitor.
- Metabolized extensively although CYP enzymes minimally involved; t ½: 1.5 hours (oral); 3 hours (after patch removal).
- Avoid use with anticholinergic agents as they will diminish therapeutic effects; avoid beta blockers due to risk of bradycardia. P450 interactions not likely.

Clinical Pearls:
- Only CI with additional indication for Parkinson's-related dementia.
- Rivastigmine inhibits both acetylcholinesterase and the nonspecific butyrylcholinesterase (also known as pseudocholinesterase or BuChE), which is mostly found in the liver and GI tract; this may explain why rivastigmine causes significant GI side effects.
- Rivastigmine transdermal patches may cause less nausea and vomiting.

Fun Fact:

Exelon is also the name of a corporation that provides energy services (electric and natural gas) and is the largest nuclear operator in the United States.

Bottom Line:

Since all CIs are equally effective, we recommend starting with donepezil, which offers once-daily dosing, generic availability, and a good tolerability profile. Rivastigmine remains second-line due to BID dosing, cost, and unacceptably high rates of nausea and vomiting.

Hypnotics

The major challenge in prescribing hypnotics is finding something that works but that does not cause long-term dependence. The best way to achieve this goal is to avoid prescribing benzodiazepines as sleeping pills.

The preferred way to treat insomnia is to treat the underlying cause, which in our case is usually either a psychiatric disorder or a side effect of a medication for that disorder. A common scenario is the patient who presents with major depression with insomnia as one of the depressive symptoms. In this case, either prescribe an antidepressant alone, or an antidepressant plus a 2-week prescription for a hypnotic. In most cases, the antidepressant will have kicked in around the 2-week point, and your patient will no longer need the hypnotic.

If treating the underlying condition doesn't work, you should discuss sleep hygiene techniques, though in our experience these don't do the trick for most psychiatric patients. Although cognitive behavior therapy for chronic insomnia can be effective, it is challenging to find a local therapist who is skilled in the techniques involved.

Once you and your patient have resigned yourselves to a hypnotic, there's a pretty long menu of reasonable offerings. The choices below are not listed in any particular order, because we don't really have any specific recommendations one way or another. We tend to pick and choose among them, which often requires trials of more than one before hitting on the sleep ambrosia for a particular patient.

- **"Z drugs"** (eszopiclone, zaleplon, zolpidem) bind selectively to specific subunits of the GABA receptors that induce sleep, but they don't have the same relaxation effects of benzos, and are probably somewhat less addictive. Zolpidem 5 mg-10 mg has become an old standard. For patients who wake up in the middle of the night, use zaleplon instead, because of its very short duration of action.

- **Antihistamines** (diphenhydramine and doxylamine) are over-the-counter agents that induce sedation by blocking histamine H1 receptors. Start with diphenhydramine 25 mg QHS and increase to 50 mg if needed. The older the patient, the less appropriate this option, as antihistamines can cause confusion when used chronically. While this can occur with anyone, it's more common in the elderly.

- **Benzodiazepines.** While we are aware of the dangers of tolerance, some patients take 0.5 mg of one of the benzos every night and seem to suffer no ill effects, and there is often no dosage creep over many years or even decades.

- **Ramelteon** is a melatonin agonist.

- **Suvorexant** is in a new class of agents called **dual orexin (OX1 and OX2) receptor antagonists,** or DORAs for short.

- **Doxepin** (Silenor) was approved by the FDA for use as a hypnotic. It is an old drug in new clothing—a tricyclic antidepressant being used for its antihistamine properties. Because it is expensive, we suggest using a low dose of generic doxepin to achieve the same effects as Silenor. This may entail prescribing the liquid version in order to get to doses in the 3 mg range.

- **Trazodone,** another antidepressant, is commonly used for insomnia at a dose of 25 mg-50 mg QHS.

Potential Side Effects of Most Hypnotics

Although taken by millions, hypnotics are a high-risk class of medications, especially for the elderly, who are at greater risk for confusion, memory problems, and gait disturbances (sometimes leading to falls). Therefore, try to avoid hypnotics in the elderly, and when you do use them, use the lowest effective dose for the shortest duration of time possible.

Certain precautions apply to most hypnotics, and we'll list them below to minimize repetition in the fact sheets:

- **Daytime grogginess or hangover effect:** most likely to occur with antihistamines or with longer-acting benzodiazepines or extended release zolpidem.

- **Anterograde amnesia:** most likely to occur with benzodiazepines and Z-drugs. Among benzos, triazolam (Halcion) has a particularly bad rep. Just avoid triazolam—there's no need to prescribe it given the wealth of alternatives.

- **CNS depression:** Hypnotics may impair physical or mental abilities and alertness; advise patients to use caution when performing tasks that require alertness (eg, driving).

- **Respiratory depression:** Benzodiazepines in particular may depress respiration; avoid in patients at risk, including those with COPD or apnea, or those taking other depressants such as opiates.
- **Paradoxical reactions,** including hyperactive or aggressive behavior, have been reported, and are particularly seen with benzodiazepines; younger patients, elderly, and those with head injury or organic brain syndromes are at greatest risk.
- **Tolerance** to sedating effects of benzodiazepines generally occurs after several weeks of continuous use (one-third of patients will experience tolerance after 4 weeks of use). Tolerance to anxiolytic effects occurs more slowly, and to anti-seizure effects very little or not at all. Psychological and physical dependence occurs with prolonged use.
- **Discontinuation syndrome:** Withdrawal effects occur with most hypnotics and include rebound insomnia, agitation, anxiety, and malaise. Discontinuation syndromes from benzodiazepines are most severe with longer-term use, higher doses, and shorter-acting agents; in severe cases, discontinuation may include seizures. Use of hypnotics should not be abruptly discontinued; doses should be tapered gradually.
- **Recreational use and abuse** may occur with many hypnotics, particularly the benzodiazepines. Avoid or minimize use in patients who have addiction risk or when abuse is suspected.

Table 10: Hypnotics

Generic Name (Brand Name) Year FDA Approved [G] denotes generic availability	Relevant FDA Indication(s)	Available Strengths (mg except where noted)	Usual Dosage Range for Insomnia (starting–max) (mg at HS)	Equivalent Dose to 1 mg Lorazepam (for benzodiazepines)	Onset of Action[1]	Half-Life (hours)	Duration of Action (hours)[1]
Clonazepam [G] (Klonopin, Klonopin Wafers[1]) 1975	Panic disorder Insomnia (off-label use)	Tablet: 0.5, 1, 2 ODT: 0.125, 0.25, 0.5, 1, 2	0.25 to 0.5–2	0.25–0.5	1 h	20–80	4–8
Diphenhydramine [G] (Benadryl, others) 1946 Available OTC and Rx	Insomnia (adults and children 12+ years)	Capsule: 25, 50 Liquid: 12.5 mg/mL	25–50	NA	1 h	3.5–9	4–6
Doxepin [G] (Silenor) 2010/1969 Generic not available in 3 mg, 6 mg	Insomnia (sleep maintenance)	Tablet: 3, 6 Capsules: 10, 25, 50, 75, 100, 150 Liquid: 10 mg/mL	6	NA	1 h	15	4–6
Doxylamine [G] (Unisom, others) 1978 Available OTC and Rx	Nighttime sleep aid	Tablet: 25	25–50	NA	1 h	10	4–6
Eszopiclone [G] (Lunesta) 2004	Insomnia (sleep onset and sleep maintenance)	Tablet: 1, 2, 3	1–3	NA	30 min	6	6–8
Lorazepam [G] (Ativan) 1977	GAD Insomnia (off-label use)	Tablet: 0.5, 1, 2 Liquid: 2 mg/mL	1–4	1	30–60 min	10–20	4–6
Ramelteon (Rozerem) 2005	Insomnia (sleep onset)	Tablet: 8	8	NA	30 min	1–2.6	Unknown
Suvorexant (Belsomra) 2014	Insomnia (sleep onset and sleep maintenance)	Tablet: 5, 10, 15, 20	10–20	NA	30–60 min	12	6–8
Temazepam [G] (Restoril) 1981	Insomnia (short-term)	Capsule: 7.5, 15, 22.5, 30	15–30	15	30–60 min	9–18	4–6

Generic Name (Brand Name) Year FDA Approved [G] denotes generic availability	Relevant FDA Indication(s)	Available Strengths (mg except where noted)	Usual Dosage Range for Insomnia (starting–max) (mg at HS)	Equivalent Dose to 1 mg Lorazepam (for benzodiazepines)	Onset of Action[1]	Half-Life (hours)	Duration of Action (hours)[1]
Trazodone [G] (Desyrel[2], Oleptro) 1981/2010	Depression Insomnia (off-label use)	Tablet: 50, 100, 150, 300 ER tablet: 150, 300	25 to 50–200	NA	1 h	7–10	Unknown
Triazolam [G] (Halcion) 1982	Insomnia (short-term)	Tablet: 0.125, 0.25	0.25–0.5	0.25	15–30 min	1.5–5.5	Unknown
Zaleplon [G] (Sonata) 1999	Insomnia (short-term, sleep onset)	Capsule: 5, 10	10–20	NA	30 min	1	4
Zolpidem [G] (Ambien, Ambien CR, Edluar, Zolpimist) 1992 Generic not available for Zolpimist	Insomnia (IR: short-term, sleep onset; CR: sleep onset and maintenance)	Tablet: 5, 10 ER tablet: 6.25, 12.5 SL tablet: 5, 10 Oral spray: 5 mg/spray	10, 12.5 CR (5, 6.25 in women)	NA	30 min	2.5–3	6–8
Zolpidem low dose (Intermezzo) 2011	Difficulty falling asleep after middle-of-the-night awakening	SL tablet: 1.75, 3.5	1.75 women; 3.5 men	NA	30 min	2.5	4

[1]Onset and duration vary from person to person, dose to dose, and preparation to preparation
[2]Brand discontinued; available as generic only

ANTIHISTAMINES (diphenhydramine, doxylamine) Fact Sheet [G]

FDA Indications:

Insomnia (adults, children 12–17 years); **allergies; motion sickness; antiparkinsonism.**

Off-Label Uses:

EPS; nausea and vomiting (morning sickness).

Dosage Forms:

- **Tablets, chewable tablets, caplets, capsules, and oral solutions, varies by brand:** 25 mg, 50 mg.
- **Common brand names:**
  - **Diphenhydramine:** Benadryl, Compoz, Nytol, Simply Sleep, Sleep-Eze D, Sominex, Unisom SleepGels, Unisom SleepMelts, and generic.
  - **Doxylamine:** NyQuil, Unisom SleepTabs, and generic.

Dosage Guidance:

Insomnia: Start 25 mg, 30 minutes before bedtime. The dose required to induce sleep can be as low as 6.25 mg, but usual dose is 25 mg. Some patients may require 50 mg at bedtime.

Cost: $

Side Effects:

- Most common: dry mouth, ataxia, urinary retention, constipation, drowsiness, memory problems.
- Serious but rare: blurred vision, tachycardia.

Mechanism, Pharmacokinetics, and Drug Interactions:

- Histamine H1 antagonist.
- Metabolized by liver, primarily CYP2D6; t ½: for diphenhydramine, 3.5–9 hours; for doxylamine, 10 hours (12–15 in elderly).
- Avoid use with other antihistamines or anticholinergics (additive effects).

Clinical Pearls:

- These antihistamines non-selectively antagonize central and peripheral histamine H1 receptors. They also have secondary anticholinergic effects, which can cause side effects including dry mouth and urinary retention, as well as cognitive impairment in susceptible populations.
- Be aware that anticholinergic drugs are often used to treat or prevent extrapyramidal symptoms in patients taking antipsychotics; diphenhydramine is often chosen and dosed at night to take advantage of its sedative effect.

Fun Facts:

The name NyQuil is a portmanteau of "night" and "tranquil."

Bottom Line:

Antihistamines can be very effective sleepers for many patients, although some patients may experience too much grogginess ("hangover") in the morning. Good first-line agents due to low risk of drug tolerance, dependence, or abuse, but exercise caution in the elderly, who may not tolerate peripheral effects.

DOXEPIN (Silenor) Fact Sheet [G]

FDA Indications:

Insomnia (sleep maintenance). Generic doxepin (at higher doses) approved for **depression, anxiety disorders.**

Off-Label Uses:

Headache; neuropathic pain; fibromyalgia; anxiety disorders.

Dosage Forms:
- **Tablets (Silenor):** 3 mg, 6 mg.
- **Capsules (G):** 10 mg, 25 mg, 50 mg, 75 mg, 100 mg, 150 mg.
- **Oral concentrate (G):** 10 mg/mL.

Dosage Guidance:
- **Insomnia:**
- Silenor: Start 6 mg QHS (this is the starting, target, and max dose), taken within 30 minutes of bedtime. Use 3 mg/day in elderly. Avoid meals within 3 hours of taking Silenor.
- Doxepin: Start 10 mg capsule, or achieve a lower dose by using the oral concentrate or by opening the 10 mg capsule, dissolving it in a cup of juice, and drinking a portion of the juice.

Cost: $ generic; $$$$ Silenor

Side Effects:
- Most common: somnolence, nausea, dry mouth, constipation.
- Serious but rare: orthostasis (more likely at higher doses).

Mechanism, Pharmacokinetics, and Drug Interactions:
- Tricyclic antidepressant with norepinephrine and serotonin reuptake inhibition and histamine H1 antagonism.
- Metabolized primarily through CYP2C19 and 2D6 (also 1A2 and 2C9 to lesser extent); t ½: 15 hours.
- Clinically significant drug interactions not likely at the low doses used for hypnotic effects.

Clinical Pearls:
- Silenor is a branded version of generic doxepin, available in lower doses.
- Taking within 3 hours of eating delays therapeutic effect by up to 3 hours. For faster onset and to minimize next-day effects, don't take within 3 hours of a meal.

Fun Fact:

Somaxon Pharmaceuticals, the original but fledgling manufacturer of Silenor, was acquired by Pernix, which hopes to eventually pursue over-the-counter approval.

Bottom Line:

Clinically and pharmacologically, Silenor at 3 mg–6 mg/nightly differs very little from 10 mg/nightly of the generic doxepin, available at a fraction of the price. However, its approval and availability serves as a good reminder that low-dose TCAs may be used as sedatives for their antihistaminic and anticholinergic activity. Silenor/doxepin may be a good agent to put in your arsenal, particularly for those patients in whom you want to avoid benzodiazepines or Z drugs. There appears to be no good reason to use the much more expensive branded product; stick to the low-dose generic.

ESZOPICLONE (Lunesta) Fact Sheet (G)

FDA Indications:

Insomnia (sleep onset and sleep maintenance).

Off-Label Uses:

None.

Dosage Forms:

Tablets (G): 1 mg, 2 mg, 3 mg.

Dosage Guidance:

Start 1 mg QHS; may ↑ to max 3 mg QHS. Use lower doses in elderly (max 2 mg QHS). Take immediately before falling asleep and with at least 7-8 hours before planned awakening time. Avoid administering with high-fat meal (delays onset of effect).

Cost: $$

Side Effects:

- Most common: somnolence, headache, unpleasant taste, dizziness, dry mouth.
- Serious but rare: anaphylaxis; complex sleep-related behavior (sleep-driving, cooking, eating, making phone calls).

Mechanism, Pharmacokinetics, and Drug Interactions:

- Selective GABA-A alpha-1 subunit agonist.
- Metabolized primarily through CYP3A4 and 2E1; t ½: 6 hours (9 hours in elderly).
- Avoid concomitant use with other CNS depressants, including alcohol (additive effects). Potent CYP3A4 inhibitors (eg, fluvoxamine, erythromycin) may increase effects of eszopiclone significantly, whereas CYP3A4 inducers (eg, carbamazepine) may decrease eszopiclone levels; eszopiclone dose adjustments may be necessary.

Clinical Pearls:

- C–IV controlled substance.
- Non-benzodiazepine in structure, but binds to the GABA-benzodiazepine receptor complex like benzodiazepines do; selective for the alpha receptor subtype (causing hypnotic effects but none of the other pharmacologic effects of benzodiazepines); one of the Z drugs. Eszopiclone is the S–enantiomer of zopiclone (a hypnotic agent available in other countries).
- Unlike benzodiazepines, eszopiclone does not disrupt normal sleep architecture (stages).
- Taking after a large, high-fat meal will delay its onset of action (by about an hour). Because of its rapid onset of action, eszopiclone should be taken immediately before bedtime or once difficulty falling asleep has occurred.
- Higher doses increase next-day impairment of driving and alertness.

Fun Fact:

Sepracor, the manufacturer, tried to get Lunesta approved in Europe under the brand name Lunivia. But the European agency determined that eszopiclone was too similar to the already marketed zopiclone to qualify as a patentable product. Sepracor, realizing that it might encounter future generic competition, withdrew its application.

Bottom Line:

Like other Z drugs, eszopiclone is an effective sedative with less potential for dependence than the benzodiazepines. Dosing is simple and, apart from the bitter aftertaste, its rapid onset and long duration of action make it well accepted among patients. As with all sedatives/hypnotics, nightly use should be discouraged.

RAMELTEON (Rozerem) Fact Sheet

FDA Indications:
Insomnia (sleep onset).

Off-Label Uses:
Jet lag; shift-work sleep disorder.

Dosage Forms:
Tablets: 8 mg.

Dosage Guidance:
Start, target, and maximum dose 8 mg QHS, 30 minutes before bedtime. Avoid administering with high-fat meal (delays therapeutic effect by 45 minutes).

Cost: $$$$

Side Effects:
- Most common: headache, somnolence, fatigue, dizziness, nausea.
- Serious but rare: anaphylaxis, angioedema, complex sleep-related behavior (sleep-driving, cooking or eating food, making phone calls), increased prolactin, abnormal cortisol or testosterone levels.

Mechanism, Pharmacokinetics, and Drug Interactions:
- Melatonin-1 and melatonin-2 receptor agonist.
- Metabolized primarily through CYP1A2 (major), and to a lesser extent CYP2C9 and 3A4; t ½: 1–2.6 hours.
- Avoid concomitant use with CNS depressants (additive effects). Exercise caution in patients taking potent CYP1A2 inhibitors (eg, fluvoxamine), which could increase ramelteon effects.

Clinical Pearls:
- Because ramelteon's mechanism of action relates to melatonin receptors and regulation of circadian rhythms, it does not cause patients to "feel" sedated. Often patients say that it doesn't start working for several days—though clinical trials showed efficacy from the first night of use. It's good to warn patients about this ahead of time, or they may conclude it's ineffective after 1 night and stop using it.
- No evidence of abuse potential or physical dependence.
- Hormonal alterations occur very rarely and usually with high-dose (16 mg in one study) and longer-term use (6–12 months). If unexplained amenorrhea, galactorrhea, decreased libido, or fertility problems occur, consider evaluating patient's prolactin or testosterone levels.

Fun Fact:
Another melatonin agonist, agomelatine, has been studied as an antidepressant, partly because circadian rhythms are disrupted in depression (it is approved overseas, but the manufacturer scrapped its development in the US).

Bottom Line:
A good alternative to benzodiazepines and Z drugs for patients at risk for drug abuse or dependence. Compared to other hypnotics, lower risk for respiratory depression and hangover effect (morning grogginess). A good agent to have in your bag of tricks, but consider the possibility of rare hormonal effects. Also consider that over-the-counter melatonin (which ramelteon mimics) may do the same job at a lower price.

SUVOREXANT (Belsomra) Fact Sheet

FDA Indications:
Insomnia (sleep onset and sleep maintenance).

Off-Label Uses:
None.

Dosage Forms:
Tablets: 5 mg, 10 mg, 15 mg, 20 mg.

Dosage Guidance:
Start 10 mg QHS, 30 minutes before bedtime and with at least 7 hours remaining before planned awakening time. If tolerated but not effective, may increase to max 20 mg QHS. For more rapid onset, patients should wait at least an hour after a meal before taking it. Avoid administering within an hour of a high-fat meal (delays therapeutic effect by about 1.5 hours).

Cost: $$$$

Side Effects:
- Most common: somnolence, headache, abnormal dreams, dry mouth.
- Serious but rare: impaired alertness and motor coordination, including impaired driving; sleep paralysis (inability to speak or move for up to a few minutes during the sleep–wake transition), hypnagogic/hypnopompic hallucinations (including vivid and disturbing perceptions), and cataplexy–like symptoms (leg weakness for seconds up to a few minutes both in the nighttime and daytime) reported, especially at higher doses.

Mechanism, Pharmacokinetics, and Drug Interactions:
- "DORA" or dual orexin (OX1 and OX2) receptor antagonist.
- Metabolized primarily through CYP3A4, with minor contribution from 2C19; t ½: 12 hours.
- Caution with CYP3A4 inhibitors and inducers; suvorexant dose adjustment recommended. Caution with alcohol and other CNS depressants.

Clinical Pearls:
- C–IV controlled substance. One study found that drug abusers "liked" suvorexant as much as Ambien.
- Suvorexant has a unique mechanism of action. Unlike other hypnotics, it does not act by stimulating GABA or melatonin receptors or by blocking histamine. Instead, suvorexant blocks orexin receptors (orexins are neurotransmitters that promote wakefulness).
- Risk of next–day impairment increases with dose; caution patients taking 20 mg against next–day driving and other activities requiring mental alertness.

Fun Fact:
Merck expected to gain FDA approval in summer 2013. However, the FDA expressed concerns about safety with the 30 mg–40 mg dosing range Merck was proposing and denied approval. It was finally approved in August 2014.

Bottom Line:
Other than a new mechanism of action, there's not much about suvorexant to recommend. There's no reason to expect it to work any better than the other hypnotics already on the market, and it has the same abuse liability. We're concerned that next–day impairment is a potential side effect at the highest approved dose of 20 mg, particularly since sleepless patients may decide on their own to take even higher doses. It's not a first–line medication hypnotic.

TEMAZEPAM (Restoril) Fact Sheet (G)

FDA Indications:
Insomnia (short term).

Off-Label Uses:
Anxiety disorders; acute mania or psychosis; catatonia.

Dosage Forms:
Capsules (G): 7.5 mg, 15 mg, 22.5 mg, 30 mg.

Dosage Guidance:
Start 15 mg QHS. Max 30 mg nightly. Use lower doses in elderly.

Cost: $

Side Effects:
- Most common: somnolence, dizziness, weakness, ataxia.
- Serious but rare: anterograde amnesia, increased fall risk, paradoxical reaction (irritability, agitation); respiratory depression (avoid in patients with sleep apnea).

Mechanism, Pharmacokinetics, and Drug Interactions:
- Binds to benzodiazepine receptors to enhance GABA effects.
- Metabolized primarily through liver but no CYP450 involvement; t ½: 9–18 hours.
- Avoid concomitant use with other CNS depressants, including alcohol (additive effects). No risk for CYP450 drug interactions.

Clinical Pearls:
- C–IV controlled substance.
- Temazepam has long been a favored hypnotic for the elderly because of the lack of active metabolites, its short half–life, and absence of drug interactions.
- If abruptly discontinued, withdrawal symptoms are usually seen on the first day and last for 5–7 days in patients taking this type of short–intermediate half–life benzodiazepine.
- Tolerance to sedative effect may develop within 2–4 weeks of use, and benzodiazepines affect the normal sleep architecture; thus, long–term use is discouraged.

Fun Facts:
The US Air Force uses temazepam as one of the hypnotics approved as "no-go pills" to help aviators and special duty personnel sleep in support of mission readiness; "ground tests" are required prior to authorization being issued to use the medication in an operational situation.

Bottom Line:
We consider temazepam (and lorazepam) to be first–line agents for insomnia if a benzodiazepine is appropriate for use (short term; minimal risk of abuse).

TRIAZOLAM (Halcion) Fact Sheet (G)

FDA Indications:

Insomnia (short term).

Off-Label Uses:

Anxiety disorders; acute mania or psychosis; catatonia.

Dosage Forms:

Tablets (G): 0.125 mg, 0.25 mg.

Dosage Guidance:

Start 0.25 mg QHS; max 0.5 mg QHS. Take immediately before bedtime. Use lower doses in elderly.

Cost: $

Side Effects:

- Most common: drowsiness, headache, dizziness, ataxia.
- Serious but rare: anterograde amnesia, increased fall risk, paradoxical reaction (irritability, agitation); respiratory depression (avoid in patients with sleep apnea).

Mechanism, Pharmacokinetics, and Drug Interactions:

- Binds to benzodiazepine receptors to enhance GABA effects.
- Metabolized primarily through CYP3A4; t ½: 1.5–5.5 hours.
- Avoid concomitant use with other CNS depressants, including alcohol (additive effects). Avoid use with potent 3A4 inhibitors (eg, erythromycin, ketoconazole, fluvoxamine) as they may increase triazolam levels significantly.

Clinical Pearls:

- C–IV controlled substance.
- Rapid onset of effect; best to take when already in bed.
- Due to its short half–life, triazolam is not effective for patients who suffer from frequent awakenings or early wakening; mostly useful for sleep onset.
- Rebound insomnia and other withdrawal symptoms are more likely and more severe with a short-acting benzodiazepine such as triazolam.
- Tolerance to sedative effect may develop within 2–4 weeks of use, and benzodiazepines affect the normal sleep architecture; thus, long–term use is discouraged.
- May induce more anterograde amnesia than other benzodiazepines; concomitant use of alcohol or use of higher dose (0.5 mg) increases risk.
- Due to studies that suggest the frequency of severe psychiatric disturbances is higher with triazolam compared to other benzodiazepines, the United Kingdom and Brazil have banned it.

Not-So-Fun Fact:

Serial killer Jeffrey Dahmer used triazolam to sedate his victims.

Bottom Line:

There are far better benzodiazepines (lorazepam, temazepam) to use for insomnia in appropriate patients. We cannot recommend using triazolam; some experts have even suggested that it be banned from the US market given the higher likelihood for adverse effects (anterograde amnesia, psychiatric disturbances).

ZALEPLON (Sonata) Fact Sheet (G)

FDA Indications:
Insomnia (short term, sleep onset).

Off-Label Uses:
None.

Dosage Forms:
Capsules (G): 5 mg, 10 mg.

Dosage Guidance:
Start 10 mg QHS, which is the usual dose for most adults. Max 20 mg QHS in those who tolerate but don't benefit from the usual 10 mg dose. Avoid administering with high-fat meal (delays onset of effect by 2 hours). Use lower doses in elderly.

Cost: $

Side Effects:
- Most common: somnolence, dizziness, headache.
- Serious but rare: anaphylaxis, complex sleep-related behavior (sleep-driving, cooking, eating, making phone calls).

Mechanism, Pharmacokinetics, and Drug Interactions:
- Selective GABA-A alpha-1 subunit agonist.
- Metabolized primarily through aldehyde oxidase and also CYP3A4; t ½: 1 hour.
- Avoid concomitant use with other CNS depressants, including alcohol (additive effects). Potent CYP3A4 inhibitors (eg, fluvoxamine, erythromycin) may increase effects of zaleplon significantly, whereas CYP3A4 inducers (eg, carbamazepine) may decrease zaleplon levels; adjust zaleplon dosing.

Clinical Pearls:
- C-IV controlled substance.
- Patients should take it immediately before going to bed or once they are in bed to minimize amnesic episodes.
- Because of zaleplon's very short half-life, it rarely causes next-day impairment.
- Unlike benzodiazepines, zaleplon does not disrupt normal sleep stages.
- Most useful for sleep initiation disorders; does not substantially increase total sleep time or decrease number of awakenings.
- Classified as a Schedule IV drug but, at therapeutic doses, abuse potential is somewhat less than benzodiazepines. However, abuse potential at high doses (2.5-7.5 times recommended dose) is similar to that of benzodiazepines.
- Fewer withdrawal effects than with benzodiazepines, but abrupt discontinuation, particularly from higher doses, can cause withdrawal symptoms (mostly rebound insomnia).

Fun Fact:
The name "Sonata" calls to mind the classical music composition, often for 1 or 2 instruments, with 3 or 4 movements, much like the phases of sleep.

Bottom Line:
Great for inducing sleep, not great for sleep maintenance throughout the night. The only sleeping pill that can be taken at 3 am or 4 am without causing functional impairment when the patient gets out of bed at 7 am or 8 am, although patients should always use caution the next day.

ZOLPIDEM (Ambien) Fact Sheet (G)

FDA Indications:

Insomnia (IR: short term, sleep onset; CR: sleep onset and maintenance; Intermezzo: difficulty falling asleep after middle-of-the-night awakening).

Off-Label Uses:
None.

Dosing:
- **Tablets (G):** 5 mg, 10 mg.
- **ER tablets (G):** 6.25 mg, 12.5 mg.
- **SL tablets (Edluar, G):** 5 mg, 10 mg.
- **SL tablets (Intermezzo):** 1.75 mg, 3.5 mg.
- **Oral spray (Zolpimist):** 5 mg/spray.

Dosage Guidance:
- Start 10 mg QHS (5 mg in women). ER: Start 12.5 mg QHS (6.25 mg in women). Take immediately before bed, with at least 7–8 hours remaining before planned awakening time. Dose may be increased to max 10 mg (or 12.5 mg ER) QHS if no daytime grogginess. Higher doses may lead to greater abuse potential. Use lower doses in elderly.
- Lower doses of 1.75 mg (women), 3.5 mg (men) SL QHS, can be used with ≥4 hours remaining before wake time.

Cost: IR: $; ER: $$; Intermezzo: $$$$; Zolpimist: $$$

Side Effects:
- Most common: headache, somnolence, dizziness, diarrhea.
- Serious but rare: complex sleep-related behavior (sleep-driving, eating, making phone calls).

Mechanism, Pharmacokinetics, and Drug Interactions:
- Selective GABA-A alpha-1 subunit agonist.
- Metabolized primarily through CYP3A4; t ½: 2.5-3 hours.
- Avoid concomitant use with other CNS depressants, including alcohol (additive effects). Potent CYP3A4 inhibitors may increase effects of zolpidem, whereas CYP3A4 inducers (eg, carbamazepine) may decrease zolpidem levels.

Clinical Pearls:
- C-IV controlled substance.
- Unlike benzodiazepines, zolpidem does not disrupt normal sleep stages.
- At therapeutic doses, abuse potential is somewhat less than with benzodiazepines.
- Less withdrawal effects than with benzodiazepines but abrupt discontinuation, particularly from higher doses, can cause withdrawal symptoms (mostly rebound insomnia).
- CR formulation: The dual layer allows some medication to be released immediately, with the rest released gradually, resulting in higher levels through the night.

Fun Fact:
Bioavail Labs received FDA approval for an orally disintegrating tablet form of zolpidem called Tovalt in 2007. It has since been discontinued due to poor sales.

Bottom Line:
Good hypnotic that can also help with sleep maintenance, particularly in the ER formulation. "New" lower-dose version is simply a patent extender, and we find it difficult to justify the higher cost (use generic zaleplon instead for middle-of-the-night awakening).

Mood Stabilizers

There are many medications that we use to treat bipolar disorder. In this chapter, we focus on meds traditionally known as "mood stabilizers"—agents effective not only for acute episodes of mania or depression, but also for preventing cycling (also known as maintenance treatment of bipolar disorder).

In managing bipolar disorder, manic episodes are usually the most straightforward to treat. In fact, many medications qualify as anti-manic agents: Lithium, valproic acid (VPA), carbamazepine, oxcarbazepine, most atypical antipsychotics, typical antipsychotics (in 1974, chlorpromazine was the second drug approved for acute mania after lithium), and benzodiazepines are all effective, owing to their sedative effect.

Bipolar depression, on the other hand, is more challenging as we have fewer proven strategies. Using antidepressants alone may increase cycling by inducing a "switch" into mania, even though, for better or for worse, it is a strategy often employed. One rigorous study (Systematic Treatment Enhancement Program for Bipolar Disorder, or STEP-BD) found that adding bupropion or paroxetine to a mood stabilizer provided no additional benefit. The medications that have received FDA indications for the treatment of bipolar depression include the combination of fluoxetine and olanzapine (Symbyax), quetiapine (Seroquel), and more recently lurasidone (Latuda). In addition, there are data supporting the use of aripiprazole (Abilify) as well as lithium in bipolar depression.

Maintenance treatment of bipolar disorder should include a mood stabilizer with a proven record of reducing cycling and increasing the time period between acute episodes. Only a few medications have such a record. These include lithium (more effective at preventing mania than depression), lamotrigine (more effective at preventing depression than mania), and some atypical antipsychotics (olanzapine, aripiprazole, quetiapine, and ziprasidone, all more effective at preventing mania than depression). The anticonvulsants valproic acid and carbamazepine are commonly used as maintenance treatment. Although they are not indicated by the FDA for this purpose, APA treatment guidelines permit valproic acid and carbamazepine as first-line agents for maintenance treatment of bipolar disorder.

Class Warnings

Several mood stabilizers are also classified as anticonvulsants, and you should note that the FDA issued a black box warning regarding suicide for anticonvulsants as a class. The warning is based on pooled analysis of 199 trials involving various antiepileptics (regardless of indication) that showed an increased risk of suicidal thoughts/behavior (incidence rate: 0.43% of treated patients compared to 0.24% of patients receiving placebo). The risk was observed as early as 1 week after initiation and continued through duration of trials (most trials ≤24 weeks). The risk was higher for patients with seizure disorders compared to those receiving anticonvulsants for other indications.

Another class warning for the anticonvulsants regards a potentially serious, sometimes fatal multi-organ hypersensitivity reaction syndrome (drug rash with eosinophilia and systemic symptoms, or DRESS), which has been reported with some antiepileptic drugs (rare). Symptoms may include fever, rash, and/or lymphadenopathy; monitor for signs and symptoms of possible disparate manifestations associated with lymphatic, hepatic, renal, and/or hematologic organ systems. Early symptoms of hypersensitivity reaction (eg, lymphadenopathy, fever) may occur without rash. If this occurs, discontinuation and conversion to alternate therapy may be required.

Table 11: Mood Stabilizers

Generic Name (Brand Name) Year FDA Approved for Bipolar Disorder or Mania [G] denotes generic availability	Relevant FDA Indication(s)	Available Strengths (mg)	Usual Dosage Range (starting–max) (mg)
Carbamazepine (Carbatrol, Epitol, Equetro, Tegretol, Tegretol XR, Teril) [G] 2004	Bipolar disorder (Equetro: acute mania)	CH: 100, 200 IR: 100, 200, 300, 400 ER: 100, 200, 300, 400 Oral solution: 100 mg/5 mL	200 BID–800 BID
Lamotrigine (Lamictal, Lamictal CD, Lamictal ODT, Lamictal XR) [G] 2003	Bipolar disorder (maintenance)	IR: 5, 25, 50, 100, 150, 200, 250 CH: 2, 5, 25 ODT: 25, 50, 100, 200 ER: 25, 50, 100, 200, 250, 300	25 QD–200 QD 25 QD–100 QD if on VPA
Lithium (Lithobid) [G] 1970	Acute mania Bipolar maintenance	IR: 150, 300, 600 ER: 300, 450 Oral solution: 300 mg/5 mL	300–600 QHS–2400 QD
Oxcarbazepine (Oxtellar XR, Trileptal) [G] 2000	Not approved for any bipolar indication	IR: 150, 300, 600 ER: 150, 300, 600 Oral suspension: 300 mg/5 mL	300 BID–2400 QD
Valproic acid (Depakene, Depakote, Depakote ER, Depakote Sprinkles) [G] 1995	Bipolar disorder (acute mania)	IR: 250 Liquid: 250 mg/5 mL DR: 125, 250, 500 ER: 250, 500	250–500 QHS–4000 QD

CH = chewable, IR = immediate release, ER = extended release, ODT = orally disintegrating tablet, DR = delayed release

CARBAMAZEPINE (Tegretol) Fact Sheet [G]

FDA Indications:

Seizures; trigeminal neuralgia; bipolar disorder (Equetro: acute mania).

Off-Label Uses:

Bipolar maintenance; impulse control disorders; violence and aggression.

Dosage Forms:
- **Chewable tablets (G):** 100 mg, 200 mg (scored).
- **Tablets (Tegretol, Epitol, G):** 100 mg, 200 mg, 300 mg, 400 mg (scored).
- **ER tablets (Tegretol XR, G):** 100 mg, 200 mg, 400 mg.
- **ER capsules (Equetro, Carbatrol, G):** 100 mg, 200 mg, 300 mg.
- **Oral solution (Tegretol, Teril, G):** 100 mg/5 mL.

Dosage Guidance:

Bipolar disorder: Start at 200 mg BID and gradually ↑ by 200 mg/day every 3-4 days, to target 400 mg-600 mg BID (guided by clinical response). Max 800 mg BID. Dosing is the same for IR and ER versions of carbamazepine.

Cost: IR: $; ER: $$

Side Effects:
- Most common: dizziness, somnolence, nausea, headache. (ER versions may cause fewer side effects in some patients, but the evidence is not clear.)
- Serious but rare: hematologic abnormalities including agranulocytosis, aplastic anemia, neutropenia, leukopenia, thrombocytopenia, and pancytopenia reported; hepatic complications including slight increases in hepatic enzymes, cholestatic and heptocellular jaundice, hepatitis and, rarely, hepatic failure, hyponatremia, SIADH; rash (5%-10%), including exfoliation, reported. Severe reactions including toxic epidermal necrolysis and Stevens-Johnson syndrome are rare, but can be fatal.

Mechanism, Pharmacokinetics, and Drug Interactions:
- Sodium channel blocker.
- Metabolized primarily through CYP3A4; t ½: 15 hours (initially 25-65 hours, but induces its own metabolism within 2-4 weeks and then stabilizes).
- High potential for significant interactions: potent inducer of CYP1A2, CYP2B6, CYP2C19, CYP2C8, CYP2C9, CYP3A4, P-glycoprotein; use caution with medications significantly metabolized through these pathways as their levels may become subtherapeutic; caution in patients taking strong CYP3A4 inducers or inhibitors that can affect carbamazepine levels.
- Avoid concomitant use with oral contraceptives (can lower serum levels of these contraceptives and cause unplanned pregnancies) and with clozapine (additive risk of agranulocytosis).

Clinical Pearls:
- Therapeutic levels: 4 mcg/mL-12 mcg/mL in seizure disorders. Studies in bipolar haven't shown correlation between levels and clinical response, so it's best dosed clinically.
- Lab monitoring: Baseline and periodic (at 6 weeks and every 3 months) CBC and LFTs.
- Patients of Asian descent should be screened for the variant HLA-B*1502 allele prior to starting carbamazepine; associated with significantly increased risk of developing Stevens-Johnson syndrome and/ or toxic epidermal necrolysis. Avoid use in such patients.

Fun Fact:

Carbamazepine may cause false-positive serum TCA screen—indeed, its chemical structure contains the familiar tricyclic nucleus common to all TCAs.

Bottom Line:

Equetro is the only FDA-approved formulation for bipolar disorder, but use of other formulations would result in the same effects at a much lower price. However, we do not recommend carbamazepine as a first-line treatment for bipolar disorder due to its side effect profile and high likelihood of significant interactions.

LAMOTRIGINE (Lamictal) Fact Sheet (G)

FDA Indications:
Bipolar disorder (maintenance) in adults; seizures in adults and children.

Off-Label Uses:
Bipolar depression; neuropathic pain; major depression.

Dosage Forms:
- **Tablets (G):** 5 mg, 25 mg, 50 mg, 100 mg, 150 mg, 200 mg, 250 mg (scored).
- **Chewable tablets (Lamictal CD, G):** 2 mg, 5 mg, 25 mg.
- **Orally disintegrating tablets (Lamictal ODT, G):** 25 mg, 50 mg, 100 mg, 200 mg.
- **ER tablets (Lamictal XR, G):** 25 mg, 50 mg, 100 mg, 200 mg, 250 mg, 300 mg.

Dosage Guidance:
- Bipolar disorder: Start 25 mg QD for 2 weeks, ↑ to 50 mg QD for 2 weeks, then 100 mg QD; max 200 mg/day.
- Patients on valproate: Start 25 mg QOD (every other day) for 2 weeks, ↑ to 25 mg QD for 2 weeks, then 50 mg QD; max 100 mg/day (VPA doubles lamotrigine levels).
- Dosing is the same with all versions of lamotrigine.

Cost: IR: $; ER: $$$$

Side Effects:
- Most common: dizziness, headache, nausea, sedation, benign rash (7%).
- Serious but rare: skin reactions (black box warning): severe, potentially life-threatening skin rashes requiring hospitalization reported; incidence is higher in pediatric patients; risk increased by co-administration with valproic acid, higher than recommended starting doses, and exceeding recommended dose titration. The majority of cases occur in the first 8 weeks, but isolated cases may occur beyond 8 weeks or even in patients without risk factors. Discontinue at first sign of rash and do not reinitiate unless rash is clearly not drug-related; rare cases of Stevens-Johnson syndrome, toxic epidermal necrolysis, and angioedema reported.

Mechanism, Pharmacokinetics, and Drug Interactions:
- Sodium channel blocker.
- Metabolism primarily hepatic (non-P450); t ½: 25-33 hours (with VPA 48-70 hours; with carbamazepine 13-14 hours).
- Caution with enzyme-inducing medications (eg, carbamazepine), which may decrease lamotrigine levels. Caution with hormonal contraceptives, which may decrease lamotrigine levels; lamotrigine maintenance dose may need to be increased (twofold). Gradual increases of lamotrigine levels may occur during the inactive "pill-free" week. Lamotrigine may decrease levels of hormonal contraceptives; alternative birth control methods should be considered.

Clinical Pearls:
- Lamotrigine is useful for the maintenance treatment of bipolar disorder, with best efficacy in the prophylaxis of depressive episodes. Not useful in acute episodes.
- If lamotrigine has been stopped/missed >5 half-lives (see above), consider restarting according to initial dosing recommendations to minimize rash risk.

Fun Fact:
The first FDA-approved drug for bipolar disorder (not just acute mania) since lithium, a drug approved more than 30 years earlier (2003 for lamotrigine; 1970 for lithium).

Bottom Line:
Use lamotrigine for maintenance treatment of bipolar disorder, especially to prevent depressive episodes.

LITHIUM (Lithobid) Fact Sheet (G)

FDA Indications:

Acute mania; bipolar disorder (maintenance) in children and adults.

Off-Label Uses:

Bipolar depression; treatment–resistant depression; neutropenia; vascular headache.

Dosage Forms:
- **Tablets (lithium carbonate, G):** 150 mg, 300 mg, 600 mg capsules.
- **ER tablets (Lithobid, G):** 300 mg.
- **ER tablets (Eskalith CR, G):** 450 mg (scored).
- **Oral solution (lithium citrate, G):** 300 mg/5 mL.

Dosage Guidance:

Bipolar: Start 300 mg–600 mg QHS, gradually ↑ to target serum lithium level of 0.8 mEq/L (usually 900 mg–1200 mg/day). Can be dosed BID–TID or all QHS. Max 2,400 mg/day.

Cost: IR: $; ER: $

Side Effects:
- Most common: nausea/diarrhea (take with meals, split dosing, switch to ER), fine tremor (lower dose or use propranolol), polyuria/excessive thirst (dose all at bedtime), memory problems, weight gain, hypothyroidism (7%–8%; 9 times more common in women), acne or worsening psoriasis, benign increase in WBC.
- Serious but rare: Chronic use may result in diminished renal concentrating ability (nephrogenic diabetes insipidus); usually reverses when discontinued or treat with hydrochlorothiazide 25 mg–50 mg/day or amiloride 5 mg–10 mg twice daily. Cardiac: bradycardia, cardiac arrhythmia, flattened or inverted T waves, sinus node dysfunction may occur rarely.

Mechanism, Pharmacokinetics, and Drug Interactions:
- Alters neuronal sodium transport.
- Eliminated by kidneys; t ½: 18–24 hours.
- Drugs that ↑ lithium levels: "**No ACE in the H**ole" (NSAIDs, **ACE** inhibitors, and **H**CTZ); excess sweating can ↑ levels; low-sodium diet may ↑ lithium levels. Caffeine may ↓ levels.

Clinical Pearls:
- Check lithium level, TSH/T4, BUN/Cr, electrolytes after 1 week of treatment, at 1–2 months, then every 6 to 12 months. Target levels for acute mania: 0.8–1.2 mEq/L; maintenance: 0.6–1.0 mEq/L; toxicity >1.5 mEq/L but may see signs at lower levels.
- An increase or decrease of 300 mg/day will change serum level by roughly 0.25±0.1 mEq/L.
- Dehydration: Use with caution in patients with significant fluid loss (protracted sweating, diarrhea, or prolonged fever); temporary reduction or discontinuation may be necessary.

Fun Facts:

The soft drink 7–Up was originally called "Bib-Label Lithiated Lemon–Lime Soda" and contained lithium until 1950.

Bottom Line:

Lithium remains the gold standard for bipolar disorder and is likely underutilized today. It is more useful for euphoric mania than for mixed and rapid–cycling types of bipolar disorder, but it is effective for depressive episodes and maintenance treatment of bipolar disorder. It is also known for its anti–suicide effects in bipolar and unipolar mood disorders. Although it is not free from side effects, most common effects can be managed quite well.

OXCARBAZEPINE (Trileptal) Fact Sheet (G)

FDA Indications:

Seizure disorders in adults and children.

Off-Label Uses:

Bipolar disorder.

Dosage Forms:

- **Tablets (G):** 150 mg, 300 mg, 600 mg (scored).
- **Oral suspension (G):** 300 mg/5 mL.
- **ER tablets (Oxtellar XR):** 150 mg, 300 mg, 600 mg.

Dosage Guidance:

- Bipolar disorder (off-label): Start 300 mg BID, ↑ by 300 mg/day every 3 days or 600 mg/day weekly to target dose 600–1,200 mg BID. Max 2,400 mg/day. No data on use of XR for bipolar disorder; caution as higher doses of XR likely needed when converting from IR to XR.

Cost: IR: $; ER: $$$$

Side Effects:

- Most common: dizziness; somnolence, headache, ataxia, nausea, vomiting.
- Serious but rare: potentially serious, sometimes fatal, dermatologic reactions (eg, Stevens–Johnson, toxic epidermal necrolysis) reported; monitor for skin reactions. Rare cases of anaphylaxis and angioedema reported, even after initial dosing; permanently discontinue should symptoms occur.
- Use caution in patients with previous hypersensitivity to carbamazepine (cross-sensitivity occurs in 25%–30%). Clinically significant hyponatremia (serum sodium <125 mmol/L) may develop (1%–3%; higher rate than with carbamazepine); monitor serum sodium, particularly during first 3 months of therapy, especially in patients at risk for hyponatremia.

Mechanism, Pharmacokinetics, and Drug Interactions:

- Sodium channel blocker and neuronal membrane stabilizer.
- Metabolized primarily through CYP450; potent inducer of CYP3A4 and inhibitor of CYP2C19; t ½: 2 hours (9 hours for active metabolite).
- No auto-induction of metabolism and fewer interactions than with carbamazepine. However, there is still potential for interactions. Avoid concomitant use with medications metabolized by CYP3A4 since oxcarbazepine may reduce their levels. Oxcarbazepine may reduce efficacy of oral contraceptives; nonhormonal measures recommended.

Clinical Pearls:

- Oxcarbazepine is the 10-keto analog of carbamazepine (its "chemical cousin"); it is thought of as a kinder, gentler carbamazepine due to its more favorable side effect and drug interaction profile.
- Not bioequivalent to carbamazepine. Increase total daily dose by 20%–30% if switching from carbamazepine to oxcarbazepine.
- Patients of Asian descent should be screened for the variant HLA-B*1502 allele prior to starting oxcarbazepine; may increase risk of developing Stevens–Johnson syndrome and/ or toxic epidermal necrolysis. Avoid use in such patients.

Fun Fact:

While first synthesized in 1965, oxcarbazepine first appeared on the US market in 2000. In 2010, Novartis pled guilty to marketing oxcarbazepine for neuropathic pain and bipolar disorder in 2000 and 2001.

Bottom Line:

Compared to carbamazepine, oxcarbazepine poses less concern for drug interactions, hepatic or hematologic toxicities, and does not require serum level monitoring. However, due to the paucity of efficacy data in bipolar disorder, it is reserved for second-line use after lithium and valproic acid.

VALPROIC ACID (Depakote) Fact Sheet (G)

FDA Indications:
Seizures; bipolar disorder (acute mania); migraine prophylaxis.

Off-Label Uses:
Bipolar maintenance; impulse control disorders; violence and aggression.

Dosage Forms:
- **Capsules (valproic acid, G):** 250 mg.
- **Oral liquid (Depakene, G):** 250 mg/5 mL.
- **Tablets (delayed release) (Depakote, G):** 125 mg, 250 mg, 500 mg.
- **Capsules (delayed release) (Depakote Sprinkles, G):** 125 mg.
- **ER tablets (Depakote ER, G):** 250 mg, 500 mg.

Dosage Guidance:
- Acute mania: Start 250 mg–500 mg QHS, ↑ rapidly to effective dose (serum level 50 mcg/mL–125 mcg/mL, target 1000 mg–1500 mg/day); max 4000 mg/day, or 60 mg/kg.
- When converting from regular Depakote to Depakote ER, be aware that patients will get about 20% less valproic acid with the ER formulation.

Cost: DR: $; ER: $$

Side Effects:
- Most common: somnolence, nausea, fatigue, dizziness, hair loss, tremor, thrombocytopenia (up to 24% of patients; dose–related).
- Serious but rare: hepatotoxicity—rare idiosyncratic reaction, not dose–related; most cases occur within 3 months; risk factors: age <2 years, multiple anticonvulsants, and presence of neurologic disease in addition to epilepsy. Asymptomatic elevations of liver enzymes may occur, not necessarily associated with hepatic dysfunction. Pancreatitis (rare but potentially fatal). Polycystic ovary syndrome (PCOS) in about 10% of women. Hyperammonemia, encephalopathy (sometimes fatal) reported and may present with normal liver enzymes.

Mechanism, Pharmacokinetics, and Drug Interactions:
- Sodium channel blocker.
- Metabolized primarily by liver but by non–CYP450 enzymes; t ½: 9–16 hours.
- VPA causes ↑ levels of lamotrigine and risk for rash. Taking with topiramate can lead to encephalopathy.

Clinical Pearls:
- ER tablets have 10%–20% less fluctuation in serum concentration than delayed release tablets. Divalproex sodium ER and DR tablets are *not* bioequivalent; increase total daily dose by 10%–20% if switching from DR to ER.
- Monitoring: LFTs and CBC with platelets at baseline and Q6 month intervals, PT/PTT (especially prior to surgery), ammonia (with symptoms of lethargy, mental status change).
- Once steady state levels reached (within 2–4 days of initiation or dose adjustment), trough serum levels should be drawn just before the next dose (ER/DR preparations) or before the morning dose (for immediate release preparations).

Fun Fact:
Valproic acid was first synthesized in 1882 by B.S. Burton as an analogue of valeric acid, found naturally in valerian.

Bottom Line:
Go-to antimanic agent for acute manic episodes with faster onset of response and better adverse effect profile compared to lithium, fewer drug interactions than carbamazepine, and efficacy for rapid cycling and relapse prevention.

Natural Treatments

If you're interested in natural treatments (also known as complementary and alternative medicine, or CAM), you will likely recommend various strategies other than the 5 medications we cover in this section. These would include exercise (helpful for depression and for preventing cognitive impairment), light therapy (for seasonal affective disorder), massage, meditation, and other modalities.

We have included fact sheets on those natural products that have been shown to be effective via standard randomized controlled trials. Some natural products not included here might be effective but have not been adequately tested vs. placebo.

Because most of these products are not regulated by the FDA, there are quality control issues. The amount of active constituents can vary not only from brand to brand, but also from batch to batch, and some products may be adulterated with other herbs, chemicals, drugs, or toxins. We recommend that patients stick to well-known brands sold by trusted retailers.

Table 12: Natural Treatments

Name (Brand Name, if applicable)	Commonly Available Strengths (mg)	Reported Uses in Psychiatry	Usual Dosage Range (starting–max) (mg)
L-methylfolate (Deplin and others)	0.4, 0.8, 1, 3, 5, 7.5, 15	Depression (adjunct)	15
Melatonin	0.5, 1, 2.5, 3, 5, 10	Insomnia	1–20
Omega-3 Fatty Acids (Fish Oil)	500, 1000, 1200	Depression (unipolar, bipolar)	500–2000
S-Adenosyl-L-Methionine (SAMe)	100, 200, 400	Depression	800 BID
St. John's Wort	100, 300, 450	Depression	300 TID

L-METHYLFOLATE (Deplin) Fact Sheet

FDA Indications:

None.

Off-Label Uses:

Adjunctive treatment for depression (considered a "medical food product" by the FDA, not an FDA-approved drug product, although available as prescription only).

Dosage Forms:

- **Capsules (Deplin):** 7.5 mg, 15 mg.
- **Tablets and capsules (various other L-methylfolate products):** 0.4 mg, 0.8 mg, 1 mg, 3 mg, 5 mg.

Dosage Guidance:

Depression (Deplin only): Start 7.5 mg QD; target and max dose 15 mg/day.

Cost: G: $$; Deplin: $$$

Side Effects:

- Most common: not well known; likely well tolerated.
- Serious but rare: Folic acid supplementation may mask symptoms of vitamin B12 deficiency (administration of folic acid may reverse the hematological signs of B12 deficiency, including megaloblastic anemia, while not addressing neurological manifestations). L-methylfolate may be less likely than folic acid to mask B12 deficiency, though the possibility should be considered. May not be a concern with Metanx.

Mechanism, Pharmacokinetics, and Drug Interactions:

- May enhance synthesis of monoamine neurotransmitters.
- No typical drug metabolism pathway as it is naturally stored and used by body; t ½: 3 hours.
- Drug interactions generally unlikely, although L-methylfolate may decrease anticonvulsant levels (including carbamazepine, valproic acid). Drugs that lower folate, such as anticonvulsants (including carbamazepine, valproic acid, lamotrigine), may necessitate higher doses of L-methylfolate.

Clinical Pearls:

- L-methylfolate (Deplin), also known as methyltetrahydrofolate (MTHF), is the active form of folate in the body. L-methylfolate is necessary for the synthesis of monoamines (serotonin, norepinephrine, dopamine). In about 50% of the population, genetic variations impair the function of this enzyme (MTHFR) to a greater or lesser degree. A recent review of the data on one of these genetic polymorphisms (called C677T) found that overall, it did not put people at any higher risk of depression (in fact, schizophrenia was more common).
- A few small studies over the years have shown that both folate (over the counter) and L-methylfolate may be somewhat helpful as adjunctive agents in the treatment of depression, particularly in those with low baseline folate levels.

Fun Fact:

"Medical foods" are foods that are specially formulated and intended for the dietary management of a disease that has distinctive nutritional needs that cannot be met by normal diet alone. These include total parenteral nutrition as well as nasogastric tube feeds and oral rehydration products. Depression has no accepted distinctive nutritional needs.

Bottom Line:

Though the data are not robust, folate supplementation *might* be effective for some patients with depression, but we recommend that patients try the cheap stuff (folic acid) before springing for Deplin (L-methylfolate).

MELATONIN Fact Sheet

FDA Indications:

None.

Off-Label Uses:

Insomnia; jet lag; work-shift sleep disorder.

Dosage Forms:

Supplied over the counter (OTC) in various forms including liquid, tablets, capsules, sublingual, and time-release formulations; usually in 0.5 mg, 1 mg, 2.5 mg, 3 mg, 5 mg, and 10 mg.

Dosage Guidance:

- Insomnia (adults): 0.5 mg-20 mg in early evening. Emerging data suggest lower doses are effective; start low (0.5 mg-1 mg) and gradually increase to desired effect ("normal" melatonin levels vary widely among individuals, and same dose can induce different levels depending on age or health).
- For jet lag, 1 mg-3 mg on day of departure at a time that corresponds to the anticipated bedtime at arrival destination, followed by 1 mg-3 mg at bedtime for next 3-5 days.

Cost: $

Side Effects:

- Most common: Generally well tolerated in the short term. Drowsiness, headaches, and dizziness most common but at similar rates to placebo; next-day grogginess or irritability (higher doses); vivid dreams or nightmares (higher doses).
- Serious but rare: No serious side effects reported; however, long-term human studies have not been conducted. Theoretically, melatonin may alter other hormones (inhibiting ovulation in women and gonadal development in children and adolescents); avoid use in women who are pregnant or are attempting to become pregnant, and use caution in children.

Mechanism, Pharmacokinetics, and Drug Interactions:

- Melatonin receptor agonist.
- Metabolized primarily through CYP1A2, may inhibit CYP1A2; t ½: 35-50 minutes.
- Some suggest melatonin may reduce glucose tolerance and insulin sensitivity and may ↑ efficacy of calcium channel blockers for blood pressure.

Clinical Pearls:

- Melatonin is secreted from the pineal gland in a 24-hour circadian rhythm. It rises at sunset and peaks in middle of night, regulating the normal sleep/wake cycle.
- Melatonin should only be taken in its synthetic form; the "natural" form comes from ground-up cow pineal glands and may spread disease (eg, mad cow disease).
- Melatonin taken at bedtime doesn't seem to affect nocturnal sleep. Taken in the early evening, it appears to be similar to temazepam in hypnotic effect.
- Although melatonin products have been available over the counter in the US since the mid-1990s, many countries require a prescription, and some do not permit its sale.

Fun Fact:

Foods containing melatonin include cherries, bananas, grapes, rice, cereals, herbs, olive oil, wine, and beer.

Bottom Line:

Short-term melatonin treatment appears to only modestly reduce the time it takes to fall asleep (about 12 minutes, might not be considered clinically relevant) and does not appear to significantly improve overall sleep time. However, some patients report minor improvement in subjective feelings of sleep quality. It may be something to consider using in the short term, particularly in older patients (whose endogenous melatonin levels are lower). It is cheaper than ramelteon (Rozerem); however, like ramelteon, we are lacking good long-term safety data, especially with regard to effects on hormones.

OMEGA-3 FATTY ACIDS (Fish Oil) Fact Sheet

FDA Indications:

High triglycerides (as Lovaza); no FDA indications in psychiatry.

Off-Label Uses:

Unipolar and bipolar depression.

Dosage Forms:

- Supplied over the counter in various dosages and formulations; 500 mg, 1000 mg, and 1200 mg softgel capsules most common.
- By prescription only: Lovaza: 1000 mg softgel capsules (GSK). Dosage on label usually reflects fish oil dosage, which is not the same as omega-3 fatty acid dosage (eg, 1000 mg fish oil in some brands may provide 300 mg of omega-3 fatty acids, including EPA and DHA). Dosing recommendations are based on mg of fish oil.

Dosage Guidance:

Effective dose unclear, but studies have used 300 mg to 6 g QD. For depression, start 500 mg/day, increase as tolerated (target dose 1 g-2 g/day); doses >3 g/day should be used cautiously. Dividing dose BID-TID helps with side effect tolerability.

Cost: $

Side Effects:

- Most common: Well tolerated up to 4 g/day. Nausea, loose stools, fishy aftertaste.
- Serious but rare: Caution in those who are allergic to seafood. Increased risk of bleeding, particularly at higher doses.

Mechanism, Pharmacokinetics, and Drug Interactions:

- Exact mechanism unknown, but may improve cell membrane fluidity and membrane function, change neurotransmitter binding, and promote anti-inflammatory effects.
- Metabolism is hepatic, primarily through CYP450; t ½: unknown.
- For most patients, drug interactions not likely an issue; however, may prolong bleeding time. Fish oils may lower blood pressure and have additive effects when used with antihypertensives.

Clinical Pearls:

- Fish oils contain eicosapentaenoic acid (EPA) and docosahexaenoic acid (DHA); both are omega-3 fatty acids (which form the lipid bilayers of cell membranes). Although the body can synthesize these fats from alpha-linolenic acid (ALA), this is believed to be inefficient in many people.
- EPA and DHA are derived from fish; ALA is derived from flax seed and other vegetable matter. Mercury accumulates in fish meat more than in fish oil, which might explain the lack of detectable mercury in most fish oil supplements. Also, the manufacturing process that is used to deodorize fish oil supplements seems to lower the levels of PCBs and other contaminants.

Fun Fact:

Inuit people have been reported to ingest up to 16 g/day (via fish) with no dangerous side effects.

Bottom Line:

The evidence on efficacy in depression is conflicting, and the ideal dose has not been established. However, since omega-3 fatty acids are fairly benign and may offer other health benefits, you may consider using it from time to time. Based on the limited data available, the best use of omega-3 fatty acids (particularly 1 g-2 g with at least 60% EPA), in our opinion, is as an adjunct in the treatment of unipolar and bipolar depression in less severely ill patients; however, there is not enough evidence to recommend omega-3 fatty acids in other disorders at this time.

S-ADENOSYL-L-METHIONINE (SAMe) Fact Sheet

FDA Indications:

None.

Off-Label Uses:

Depression; osteoarthritis.

Dosage Forms:

Supplied over the counter most often as 100 mg, 200 mg, 400 mg tablets, usually enteric coated.

Dosage Guidance:

Effective dose is variable, but most antidepressant studies have used doses of about 400 mg–1600 mg/day (1600 mg most common), usually divided BID.

Cost: $

Side Effects:

- Most common: Well tolerated. Higher doses may result in flatulence, nausea, vomiting, diarrhea, constipation, dry mouth, headache, mild insomnia, anorexia, sweating, dizziness, and nervousness. Anxiety and tiredness have occurred in people with depression, and hypomania in people with bipolar disorder.
- Serious but rare: Theoretical concern of elevated homocysteine since SAMe is converted to this during normal metabolism. No reports to date, but some recommend taking folate and vitamin B supplements anyway.

Mechanism, Pharmacokinetics, and Drug Interactions:

- Methyl group donor that may increase synthesis of neurotransmitters, increase responsiveness of neurotransmitter receptors, and increase fluidity of cell membranes through the production of phospholipids.
- Metabolism similar to endogenous SAMe (transmethylation, transsulphuration, and amino-propylation); t ½: 100 minutes.
- No drug interactions reported. Theoretically, serotonin syndrome possible, but no reports.

Clinical Pearls:

- SAMe is produced by our bodies as a derivative of the amino acid methionine. It functions as a methyl donor and is necessary for the production of serotonin and norepinephrine (and in more than 100 other biochemical reactions) throughout virtually all body tissues and fluids. Concentrations are highest in childhood and decrease with age.
- SAMe is difficult to formulate as a stable oral salt, and the FDA halted trials of an investigational prescription product in 1993 due to concerns about tablet dissolution; concerns have been raised that some supplements may also have these problems.

Fun Facts:

SAMe has been available as a dietary supplement in the US since 1999, but it has been used as a prescription drug in Italy since 1979, in Spain since 1985, and Germany since 1989. Patients in trials of SAMe for depression noted improvement in their arthritis symptoms, suggesting another possible use.

Bottom Line:

Several clinical studies (lasting up to 42 days) have shown that taking SAMe is more effective than placebo and appears to be as effective as TCAs. However, some of these studies are limited by small numbers of patients, inconsistent diagnostic criteria, and short treatment periods. SAMe may have a role as an adjunctive agent in patients who do not respond to antidepressants. Consider using it for those patients with mild to moderate depression who are interested in using alternative therapies, or as an augmentation strategy in partial responders.

ST. JOHN'S WORT Fact Sheet

FDA Indications:

None.

Off-Label Uses:

Depression.

Dosage Forms:

Supplied over the counter most commonly as 100 mg, 300 mg, 450 mg tablets and capsules.

Dosage Guidance:

For mild to moderate depression, most clinical trials have used St. John's wort extract containing 0.3% hypericin and/or 3% hyperforin; most common dose is 300 mg TID. Doses of 1200 mg QD have also been used. Some studies have also used a 0.2% hypericin extract dosed at 250 mg BID. A St. John's wort extract standardized to 5% hyperforin and dosed at 300 mg TID has also been used.

Cost: $

Side Effects:

- Most common: Well tolerated at recommended doses. Insomnia (decrease dose or take in morning), vivid dreams, restlessness, anxiety, agitation, irritability, gastrointestinal discomfort, diarrhea, fatigue, dry mouth, dizziness, and headache reported. Sexual dysfunction may occur, but less often than with SSRIs.
- Serious but rare: risk of severe phototoxic skin reactions and photosensitivity at high doses (2–4 grams/day).

Mechanism, Pharmacokinetics, and Drug Interactions:

- Thought to exert antidepressant effects by modulating effects of monoamines, and may inhibit reuptake of these neurotransmitters.
- Metabolized primarily through the liver; t ½: 24–48 hours.
- Avoid concomitant use with serotonergic agents: rare cases of serotonin syndrome reported. Potent inducer of many CYP450 enzymes (3A4, 2C9, 1A2) and p–glycoprotein transporter, which results in increased metabolism and reduced plasma concentrations of a large number of drugs. St. John's wort can decrease oral contraceptive levels by 13%-15%, resulting in bleeding or unplanned pregnancy; women should use an additional or nonhormonal form of birth control.

Clinical Pearls:

- Also known as *Hypericum perforatum*; active constituents (predominantly hypericin and hyperforin) are derived from the flowering buds.
- St. John's wort is more effective than placebo, likely as effective as low–dose TCAs, and likely as effective as SSRIs in milder forms of depression; however, a study in *JAMA* found it no more effective than placebo or sertraline for moderate to severe depression.
- Avoid abrupt discontinuation due to the risk of withdrawal effects.

Fun Facts:

Although not indigenous to Australia and long considered a weed, St. John's wort is now grown as a cash crop, and Australia produces 20% of the world's supply. The use of St. John's wort dates back to the ancient Greeks; Hippocrates documented the medical use of St. John's wort flowers. St. John's wort is so named because it blooms near June 24th, which is the birthday of John the Baptist. "Wort" is an old English word for plant.

Bottom Line:

St. John's wort can be considered an option along with conventional antidepressants for short–term treatment of mild depression; however, be wary of its many drug interactions.

Novel Anticonvulsants

What to Prescribe

There's a great tradition in psychiatry of adopting antiepileptic drugs for use in psychiatric syndromes. In some cases, such as Depakote, Tegretol, and Lamictal, this strategy has yielded effective treatments. But for the four drugs covered in this chapter (gabapentin, pregabalin, tiagabine, and topiramate), the payoff has been fairly scant. All four were initially touted as having efficacy in bipolar disorder, based on uncontrolled trials. However, subsequent data from randomized controlled trials did not support this indication.

Nonetheless, these drugs have found their places in other spheres, especially disorders related to anxiety. For example, pregabalin is approved for generalized anxiety disorder in parts of Europe. It also has pretty convincing data for effectiveness in helping patients discontinue benzodiazepines. Topiramate seems to have a niche for patients with alcohol dependence and for any patient who wants to lose weight. Gabapentin is a non-addictive alternative to benzodiazepines for anxiety and alcohol dependence. Tiagabine seems to have no place in psychiatric treatment, but we added it because many clinicians sometimes use it anyway.

Oxcarbazepine is covered in our chapter on mood stabilizers because it has pretty good evidence for the treatment of bipolar disorder.

Side Effects

The newer anticonvulsants are appealing because they are generally less toxic than the older agents, do not require serum level monitoring, and in most cases have a lower risk of drug interactions.

However, the antiepileptics have a class warning for increased risk of suicidal thoughts and behavior; this warning stems from pooled analysis of trials (for seizure disorders as well as other indications) that showed a nearly doubled incidence of suicidal thought and behavior (0.43% for anticonvulsants vs 0.24% for placebo).

Table 13: Novel Anticonvulsants

Generic Name (Brand Name) Year FDA Approved [G] denotes generic availability	Off-Label Psychiatric Uses	Available Strengths (mg)	Usual Dosage Range (starting–max) (mg)
Gabapentin (Neurontin) [G] 1993	Anxiety disorders Withdrawal from alcohol or benzodiazepines Alcohol dependence	Capsule: 100, 300, 400 Tablet: 600, 800 Oral solution: 50 mg/mL ER tablet: 300, 600	100 QHS–300 TID
Pregabalin (Lyrica) 2004	Generalized anxiety disorder Withdrawal from alcohol or benzodiazepines Alcohol dependence	Capsule: 25, 50, 75, 100, 150, 200, 225, 300	75 BID–300 BID
Tiagabine [G] (Gabitril) 1997	Anxiety disorders Neuropathic pain	Tablet: 2, 4, 12, 16	2 BID–8 BID
Topiramate (Topamax) [G] 1996	Alcohol dependence Bipolar disorder PTSD Binge-eating disorder Obesity	Tablet: 25, 50, 100, 200 Capsule: 15, 25 ER capsule: 25, 50, 100, 200	25 BID–150 BID

GABAPENTIN (Neurontin) Fact Sheet (G)

FDA Indications:

Partial seizures (Neurontin); **post-herpetic neuralgia** (Gralise, Neurontin); **restless leg syndrome** (Horizant).

Off-Label Uses:

Anxiety disorders; withdrawal from alcohol or benzodiazepines; alcohol dependence.

Dosage Forms:
- **Capsules (G):** 100 mg, 300 mg, 400 mg.
- **Tablets (G):** 600 mg, 800 mg.
- **Oral solution (G):** 50 mg/mL.
- **Tablets, ER (Gralise):** 300 mg, 600 mg.
- **Tablets, ER (Horizant):** 300 mg, 600 mg (gabapentin enacarbil, a prodrug with better bioavailability).

Dosage Guidance:

For anxiety (off-label use), start 100 mg QHS and increase as tolerated to 300 mg TID. Max 3600 mg/day (highest doses often used for pain indications). Use lower doses in patients with renal impairment.

Cost: IR: $; ER: $$$$

Side Effects:
- Most common: dizziness, somnolence, ataxia, weight gain.
- Serious but rare: potentially serious, sometimes fatal multiorgan hypersensitivity (also known as drug reaction with eosinophilia and systemic symptoms, or DRESS).

Mechanism, Pharmacokinetics, and Drug Interactions:
- Blocks voltage-dependent calcium channels and modulates excitatory neurotransmitter release.
- Not metabolized; excreted unchanged by kidneys; t ½: 5-7 hours.
- Few significant drug interactions, although you may see additive sedative effects with other sedating drugs. Analgesic control may be affected when gabapentin is added to opiates, including decreased levels of hydrocodone (Vicodin) or increased levels of morphine.

Clinical Pearls:
- Gabapentin is structurally related to GABA. However, it does not bind to GABA-A or GABA-B receptors, and it does not appear to influence synthesis or uptake of GABA.
- Controlled trials have shown no effect as monotherapy or adjunctive therapy for bipolar disorder.
- There have been reports of recreational use of gabapentin in correctional facilities, some of which have restricted its use.

Fun Facts:

Up to 90% of prescriptions for Neurontin have been for off-label uses. While off-label prescribing is not illegal, the promotion of off-label uses by a drug manufacturer is. A whistleblower lawsuit led to a $430 million settlement by Pfizer for the off-label marketing of Neurontin.

Bottom Line:

Clinicians tend to use gabapentin when they want a non-addictive medication for anxiety and for alcohol dependence. The data for these uses is lukewarm, but not negative. It almost certainly does not work for bipolar disorder *per se*, though it might help with associated symptoms like anxiety and insomnia. If you have a patient with anxiety plus one of the approved uses (such as neuropathic pain and restless leg syndrome), then it's a particularly good choice.

PREGABALIN (Lyrica) Fact Sheet

FDA Indications:

Diabetic peripheral neuropathy; spinal cord injury–associated neuropathic pain; post-herpetic neuralgia; partial seizures; fibromyalgia.

Off-Label Uses:

Generalized anxiety disorder; withdrawal from alcohol or benzodiazepines; alcohol dependence.

Dosage Forms:

Capsules: 25 mg, 50 mg, 75 mg, 100 mg, 150 mg, 200 mg, 225 mg, 300 mg.

Dosage Guidance:

Start 75 mg BID and ↑ as tolerated to max 300 mg BID (based on trials for generalized anxiety disorder, an off-label use). Use lower doses in renal impairment.

Cost: $$$$

Side Effects:

- Most common: peripheral edema, dizziness, somnolence, ataxia, weight gain.
- Serious but rare: hypersensitivity reactions, including skin redness, blistering, hives, rash, dyspnea, and wheezing. Angioedema, possibly life threatening, reported; use with caution in patients with a history of angioedema or patients on ACE inhibitors. Increases in CPK and rare cases of rhabdomyolysis reported.

Mechanism, Pharmacokinetics, and Drug Interactions:

- Binds alpha-2 delta subunit of calcium channels and reduces neurotransmitter release.
- Negligible metabolism; mostly excreted unchanged by kidneys; t ½: 6 hours.
- No significant drug interactions, although you may see additive sedative effects with other sedating drugs.

Clinical Pearls:

- Schedule V controlled substance (same category as cough suppressants containing codeine). Following abrupt withdrawal, insomnia, nausea, headache, or diarrhea may occur; this may be suggestive of physical dependence.
- Pregabalin is related in structure to gabapentin but is more potent, with faster absorption and greater bioavailability.
- For generalized anxiety disorder, pregabalin appears more effective than placebo, but data comparing it to benzodiazepines are inconsistent.

Fun Facts:

Other drugs related to gabapentin and pregabalin are being studied; Pfizer was developing atagabalin for use in insomnia, but it discontinued development due to disappointing trial results.

Bottom Line:

Try pregabalin in a patient with generalized anxiety disorder who has failed or not tolerated SSRI trials. It can also be helpful for patients struggling to discontinue benzodiazepines.

TIAGABINE (Gabitril) Fact Sheet (G)

FDA Indications:

Partial seizures (as adjunctive treatment) in adults and children >12 years.

Off-Label Uses:

Anxiety disorders; neuropathic pain.

Dosage Forms:

Tablets (G): 2 mg, 4 mg, 12 mg, 16 mg.

Dosage Guidance:

- Dosing recommendations in *PDR* are applicable to epileptic patients already on other anticonvulsants that induce tiagabine's metabolism; not applicable to psychiatric dosing.
- Anecdotal reports suggest dosing by starting 2 mg BID and ↑ by 2 mg BID increments as needed; maximum dose used in psychiatry trials is 16 mg/day.

Cost: $$$

Side Effects:

- Most common: decreased concentration, dizziness, nervousness, somnolence, nausea, tremor, weakness, difficulty speaking clearly, tingling in hands and fingers.
- Serious but rare: New-onset seizures and status epilepticus have been associated with tiagabine use for unlabeled indications; often these occurred shortly after initiation or shortly after dose increase. Seizures have also occurred with very low doses or after several months of therapy. In most cases, patients were using concomitant medications (eg, antidepressants, antipsychotics, stimulants, narcotics).

Mechanism, Pharmacokinetics, and Drug Interactions:

- Selective GABA reuptake inhibitor.
- Metabolized primarily through CYP3A4; t ½: 7-9 hours (2-5 hours with enzyme inducers).
- Caution when administering with CYP3A4 inducers or inhibitors; may have additive sedative effects when given with CNS depressants.

Clinical Pearls:

- Based on 3 trials of over 1800 patients with generalized anxiety disorder, tiagabine did not show decrease in anxiety measures.
- No randomized trial evidence evaluating tiagabine for bipolar disorder. No randomized trials of tiagabine for acute mood episodes or for maintenance treatment of bipolar disorder.
- Used sometimes for substance abusers as a non-addictive alternative to benzodiazepines, but evidence for this is lacking.

Fun Facts:

Gabitril is manufactured by Cephalon; the company's name comes from the adjective "cephalic" meaning "related to the head or brain," and it was established primarily to pursue treatments for neurodegenerative diseases. Cephalon also manufactures Provigil.

Bottom Line:

Off-label use is strongly discouraged as tiagabine has, ironically, been associated with new-onset seizures, including status epilepticus. Lack of efficacy data in psychiatric setting make this risk difficult to justify.

TOPIRAMATE (Topamax) Fact Sheet (G)

FDA Indications:

Seizure disorders for patients >2 years; **migraine prophylaxis.**

Off-Label Uses:

Alcohol dependence; bipolar disorder; PTSD; binge-eating disorder; obesity.

Dosage Forms:

- **Tablets (G):** 25 mg, 50 mg, 100 mg, 200 mg.
- **Capsules (G):** 15 mg, 25 mg.
- **Capsules, ER (Trokendi XR, Qudexy XR):** 25 mg, 50 mg, 100 mg, 200 mg.

Dosage Guidance:

Seizures/migraine: Start 25 mg–50 mg QHS and ↑ by 50 mg/day in weekly increments. Doses used in psychiatry have typically been 50 mg–300 mg/day, divided BID.

Cost: IR: $; ER: $$$$$

Side Effects:

- Most common: somnolence, dizziness, nervousness, ataxia, speech problems, memory difficulties, confusion, anorexia.
- Serious but rare: decreases in serum bicarbonate (metabolic acidosis) relatively common but usually mild to moderate; more severe cases, including marked reductions to <17 mEq/L, may occur more rarely. Watch for kidney stones, osteomalacia.

Mechanism, Pharmacokinetics, and Drug Interactions:

- Sodium channel blocker.
- Not metabolized, excreted primarily unchanged; t ½: 21 hours (56 hours for XR); mild CYP3A4 inducer.
- Avoid concomitant use with hydrochlorothiazide: increased risk for hypokalemia; monitor potassium. Additive effects with sedatives or alcohol. Concurrent use with valproic acid may increase risk of hyperammonemia and associated encephalopathy. Higher doses (>200 mg/day) may decrease levels of some drugs, including contraceptives (P450 induction).

Clinical Pearls:

- Many published articles have shown some efficacy in a wide range of disorders, including bipolar disorder, PTSD, alcohol dependence, binge-eating disorder, and obesity.
- Most compelling data is for preventing relapse in alcoholism.
- Some patients may lose weight, but this is not common; greatest decrease in weight seems to occur in heaviest patients (>100 kg). When weight loss occurs, it is often not a large effect (mean of 6 kg) nor is it a sustained effect (patients return to pretreatment weight after 12–18 months).
- A combination of extended release topiramate and phentermine was FDA approved in 2012 for the long-term treatment of obesity as **Qsymia** (Vivus Pharmaceuticals).

Fun Facts:

Dose-related cognitive effects of topiramate have led some to refer to Topamax as "Dopamax."

Bottom Line:

Topiramate is a reasonable off-label choice for alcohol use disorder. Otherwise, relegate it to the "try when out of other ideas" category.

Sexual Dysfunction Medications

Many psychiatric medications cause sexual dysfunction. Most antidepressants (the main exceptions being bupropion and mirtazapine) cause sexual problems, which can include low libido, anorgasmia, and erectile dysfunction. Antipsychotics often lower libido, whether due to increased prolactin or other unknown factors.

Before jumping to treat the side effect of one medication with another medication, try other potential solutions. You can try decreasing the dose of the offending medication, switching to another medication, or prescribing 2- to 3-day drug holidays.

Assuming none of these strategies have worked, you might want to prescribe one of the medications in this section. Here's one approach.

For males who have erectile dysfunction, prescribe one of the PDE-5 inhibitors, of which there are four available options. Sildenafil (Viagra) has the benefit of being well known to patients, a factor which might enhance the placebo effect. Tadalafil (Cialis) has the advantage of a long (up to 36 hours) duration of action. Avanafil (Stendra) works a little more quickly than Viagra—15 minutes as opposed to 30 minutes. Vardenafil (Levitra) is available as a peppermint-flavored orally disintegrating pill—though it has no therapeutic advantages beyond whatever aphrodisiac power peppermint might provide.

For females with low sexual desire, there is one approved medication—flibanserin (Addyi). It doesn't work very well, and it can't be mixed with alcohol, so it's unlikely to become popular. Many believe that its approval was driven more by politics than science.

For both men and women who suffer sexual dysfunction from serotonergic antidepressants, you can try off-label cyproheptadine. It works pretty well sometimes, other times not at all. Adjunctive bupropion sometimes helps as well.

For men with low testosterone, prescribe...testosterone. It will add zip to patients who suffer low libido as a result of low T. However, don't get roped into prescribing this for anyone who asks for it, since there's no evidence it helps men with normal T levels.

Class Warnings for PDE-5 Inhibitors

Avoid concomitant use with nitrates in any form eg, nitroglycerin, isosorbide dinitrate, amyl nitrate or "poppers").

Table 14: Sexual Dysfunction Medications

Generic Name (Brand Name) Year FDA Approved [G] denotes generic availability	Relevant FDA Indication(s)	Available Strengths (mg)	Starting Dose (mg)	Usual Dosage Range (starting–max) (mg)	Special Features
Avanafil (Stendra) 2012	Erectile dysfunction	50, 100, 200	100	50–200	More rapid onset (15 minutes), food doesn't affect absorption
Cyproheptadine [G] 1961 Brand name Periactin discontinued; generic only	None	4; 2/5 mL	4	4–12	Sedating; most effective for anorgasmia
Flibanserin (Addyi) 2015	Hypoactive sexual desire disorder in premenopausal women	100	100	100	Can't be combined with alcohol
Sildenafil (Viagra) 1998 Generic only available as 20 mg tablet	Erectile dysfunction	25, 50, 100	25	25–100	Takes 30 minutes, fatty meals decrease absorption
Tadalafil (Cialis) 2003	Erectile dysfunction	2.5, 5, 10, 20	5	5–20	Takes 1 hour, lasts 36 hours, no meal effect
Testosterone	Hypogonadism	Various formulations and dosages; see fact sheet for details			No evidence for a beneficial effect in the absence of low T
Vardenafil (Levitra) 2003	Erectile dysfunction	2.5, 5, 10, 20	10	10–20	Works in 30 minutes, fatty meals decrease absorption
Vardenafil ODT (Staxyn) 2010	Erectile dysfunction	10 ODT	10	10	Peppermint flavored

AVANAFIL (Stendra) Fact Sheet

FDA Indications:
Erectile dysfunction.

Dosage Forms:
Tablets: 50 mg, 100 mg, 200 mg.

Dosage Guidance:
- Start 100 mg x1 taken 15 minutes before sexual activity. Max dose 200 mg/dose, up to 1 dose/24 hours.
- May be taken with or without food.

Cost: $$$$

Side Effects:
- Most common: headache, nasal congestion, flushing.
- Serious but rare: May cause dose-related impairment of color discrimination. Sudden decrease or loss of hearing has been reported rarely; hearing changes may be accompanied by tinnitus and dizziness. Decreases in blood pressure may occur due to vasodilator effects; concurrent use with alpha-adrenergic antagonists or substantial alcohol consumption may cause symptomatic hypotension. Avoid use with nitrates (see below). Painful erection >6 hours in duration (priapism) may occur rarely.

Mechanism, Pharmacokinetics, and Drug Interactions:
- Phosphodiesterase type 5 (PDE-5) inhibitor.
- Metabolized primarily through CYP3A4, also 2C9/19 to a lesser degree; t ½: 5 hours.
- Avoid concomitant use with nitrates in any form (eg, nitroglycerin, isosorbide dinitrate, amyl nitrate or "poppers"). Use with caution in patients taking alpha-adrenergic blockers; may cause symptomatic hypotension. Use with caution in patients taking strong CYP3A4 inhibitors, which may increase or extend effects of avanafil (maximum of 50 mg in 24 hours).

Clinical Pearls:
Onset of effect is usually 15–30 minutes after a dose (and not affected by meals). About two-thirds of men will have therapeutic effect within 15 minutes. Usual duration is approximately 2 hours.

Fun Fact:
Avanafil was initially approved with the recommendation to take 30 minutes before sexual activity. The company decided it was tough to compete with blockbusters like Viagra and Cialis without some sort of competitive edge, so it presented some data to the FDA and had the dosing changed to "as early as approximately 15 minutes before sexual activity." Spontaneity became the hallmark of the drug's marketing campaign, with taglines like "This time, he was ready before dessert."

Bottom Line:
Avanafil is the newest PDE5 inhibitor to come to market. Its potential advantage is a somewhat faster onset than any of the other ED drugs.

CYPROHEPTADINE Fact Sheet [G]

FDA Indications:

Allergic rhinitis; urticaria.

Off-Label Uses:

Antidepressant-induced sexual dysfunction; anorexia and bulimia nervosa; acute management of serotonin syndrome.

Dosage Forms:

- **Tablets (G):** 4 mg (scored).
- **Syrup (G):** 2 mg/5 mL syrup.

Dosage Guidance:

Take 4 mg–12 mg 1–2 hours before sexual activity.

Cost: $

Side Effects:

Most common: sedation, confusion, weight gain, anticholinergic effects, potential reversal of antidepressant therapeutic effect.

Mechanism, Pharmacokinetics, and Drug Interactions:

- Histamine H1 receptor antagonist with mild antiserotonergic effects.
- Metabolized primarily through hepatic glucuronidation via UGT1A; t ½: 16 hours.
- Avoid concomitant use with MAOIs. Additive effects with other sedating agents.

Clinical Pearls:

Appears to work best for anorgasmia. Average effective dose in one study was 8.6 mg.

Fun Facts:

Cyproheptadine's antagonistic effects at serotonin receptors has been shown to be useful as part of the management of serotonin syndrome. It's been used to counteract the more rarely occurring serotonergic side effects of serotonergic antidepressants, such as sweating and vivid dreams. It is also the most commonly used appetite stimulant for cats.

Bottom Line:

Cyproheptadine is sometimes effective in reversing SSRI-induced anorgasmia, but with continued use it could interfere with antidepressant efficacy. As-needed occasional use is the best strategy.

FLIBANSERIN (Addyi) Fact Sheet

FDA Indications:
Hypoactive sexual desire disorder in premenopausal women.

Dosage Forms:
Tablets: 100 mg.

Dosage Guidance:
Start and continue 100 mg QHS; taking during the daytime may increase risk of hypotension, syncope, and CNS depression. Discontinue after 8 weeks if no improvement.

Cost: $$$$$

Side Effects:
- Most common: dizziness, somnolence, nausea, fatigue, insomnia, dry mouth.
- Serious but rare: May have potential to cause severe hypotension or syncope.

Mechanism, Pharmacokinetics, and Drug Interactions:
- Mixed agonist–antagonist on postsynaptic serotonergic receptors with 5-HT1A agonist and 5-HT2A antagonist effects.
- Metabolized primarily through CYP3A4 and to a lesser extent, 2C19; t ½: 11 hours.
- Avoid concomitant use with alcohol, with CYP3A4 inhibitors, or in patients with hepatic impairment as there may be an increased risk for hypotention and syncope.

Clinical Pearls:
- While studies of Viagra show around 80% of men improving (50%-60% more than placebo), only 8%-13% more women on flibanserin had benefits over placebo.
- Addyi is available only through a restricted program called the Addyi REMS Program because of the increased risk of severe hypotension and syncope due to an interaction between Addyi and alcohol (prescribers must be enrolled, trained, and certified).

Fun Fact:
Based on mediocre efficacy data, Dr. Carlat has made the analogy that "if Viagra is a Starbucks triple espresso, flibanserin is a Dixie cup of cafeteria coffee."

Bottom Line:
This "pink Viagra" is a mildly effective medication with potentially significant side effects. Until we have more data and experience, consider cautiously prescribing it to women who might benefit from it.

SILDENAFIL (Viagra) Fact Sheet

FDA Indications:

Erectile dysfunction; pulmonary arterial hypertension (Revatio brand name).

Dosage Forms:

Tablets: 25 mg, 50 mg, 100 mg.

Dosage Guidance:

Start 50 mg x1 (25 mg if >65 years old or with CYP3A4 inhibitors) 30 minutes–4 hours before sexual activity. Max 100 mg/dose and 1 dose/day. Avoid taking with high-fat meal.

Cost: $$$$

Side Effects:

- Most common: headache, dyspepsia/heartburn, flushing.
- Serious but rare: May cause dose-related impairment of color discrimination. Sudden decrease or loss of hearing has been reported rarely; hearing changes may be accompanied by tinnitus and dizziness. Decreases in blood pressure may occur due to vasodilator effects; concurrent use with alpha-adrenergic antagonists or substantial alcohol consumption may cause symptomatic hypotension. Avoid use with nitrates (see below). Painful erection >6 hours in duration (priapism) may occur rarely.

Mechanism, Pharmacokinetics, and Drug Interactions:

- Phosphodiesterase type 5 (PDE-5) inhibitor.
- Metabolized primarily through CYP3A4 and to a lesser extent, 2C9; t ½: 4 hours.
- Avoid concomitant use with nitrates in any form (eg, nitroglycerin, isosorbide dinitrate, amyl nitrate or "poppers"). Use with caution in patients taking alpha-adrenergic blockers; may cause symptomatic hypotension. Use with caution in patients taking strong CYP3A4 inhibitors, which may increase or extend effects of sildenafil (maximum of 25 mg in 48 hours).

Clinical Pearls:

Onset of effect is usually 15–20 minutes after a dose (but may be delayed 60 minutes by high-fat meal), and usual duration is approximately 2 hours.

Fun Fact:

Sildenafil has been used recreationally. Some users mix it with MDMA (ecstasy) to counteract the erectile dysfunction this recreational drug can cause; this combination is known as "sextasy."

Bottom Line:

Of the agents in this class, sildenafil has the best evidence and longest track record.

TADALAFIL (Cialis) Fact Sheet

FDA Indications:
Erectile dysfunction; benign prostatic hyperplasia; pulmonary arterial hypertension (Adcirca brand name).

Dosage Forms:
Tablets: 2.5 mg, 5 mg, 10 mg, 20 mg.

Dosage Guidance:
- PRN dosing: Start 10 mg x1, 30–60 minutes prior to sexual activity; adjust dose to 5 mg–20 mg based on response. Max 20 mg/dose and 1 dose/24 hours.
- Daily dosing: Start 2.5 mg QD; may increase to max of 5 mg QD based on response.

Cost: $$$$

Side Effects:
- Most common: headache, dyspepsia/nausea, flushing, back pain, muscle aches.
- Serious but rare: May cause dose-related impairment of color discrimination. Sudden decrease or loss of hearing has been reported rarely; hearing changes may be accompanied by tinnitus and dizziness. Decreases in blood pressure may occur due to vasodilator effects; concurrent use with alpha-adrenergic antagonists or substantial alcohol consumption may cause symptomatic hypotension. Avoid use with nitrates (see below). Painful erection >6 hours in duration (priapism) may occur rarely.

Mechanism, Pharmacokinetics, and Drug Interactions:
- Phosphodiesterase type 5 (PDE-5) inhibitor.
- Metabolized primarily through CYP3A4; t ½: 15–17.5 hours.
- Avoid concomitant use with nitrates in any form (eg, nitroglycerin, isosorbide dinitrate, amyl nitrate or "poppers"). Use with caution in patients taking alpha-adrenergic blockers; may cause symptomatic hypotension. Use with caution in patients taking strong CYP3A4 inhibitors, which may increase or extend effects of tadalafil (maximum of 10 mg/dose and 1 dose/72 hours with PRN dosing or 2.5 mg/day with daily dosing).

Clinical Pearls:
- Onset of effect of tadalafil is usually within 1 hour of a dose, and its effects may last 36 hours.
- Daily tadalafil has the advantage of allowing users to always be "ready," but on the downside it can cause daily side effects.

Fun Fact:
Cialis' 36-hour effectiveness earned it the nickname "the weekend pill."

Bottom Line:
Fewer data with tadalafil in psychiatric setting; however, compared to other agents in the class, tadalafil's long duration of action may improve spontaneity, and the lack of interaction with meals may offer advantages.

TESTOSTERONE (various) Fact Sheet [G]

FDA Indications:
Hypogonadism.

Dosage Forms:
- **Capsules (Android):** 10 mg.
- **Buccal ER tablet (Striant):** 30 mg.
- **Topical gel (AndroGel, Androderm):** 1%. 1/62%.
- **Long-acting depot injection (Depo-Testosterone, [G]):** 100 mg/mL, 200 mg/mL.

Dosage Guidance:
- Dosing varies from daily dosing of oral, buccal, and topical agents to Q2–4 week or Q3–6 month dosing of injectable formulations.
- Schedule III controlled substance.

Cost: capsule: $$$$$; buccal: $$$$$; gel: $$$$; depot injectable: $

Side Effects:
- Most common: nausea, headache, insomnia, anxiety, acne, water and electrolyte retention, local effects (eg, gum irritation with buccal formulation, application site irritation with gel, injection site pain with injectables).
- Serious but rare: thromboembolic events (DVT, PE), myocardial infarction, stroke, worsening BPH, risk of prostate cancer.

Mechanism, Pharmacokinetics, and Drug Interactions:
- Anabolic and andronergic testosterone receptor agonist.
- Metabolized primarily through liver (non-CYP450); t ½: varies.

Clinical Pearls:
- Hypogonadism may play a significant role in erectile dysfunction (ED), and a threshold level of testosterone may be necessary for normal erectile function. However, testosterone levels needed for normal sexual function vary widely; some men may have normal function even with age-adjusted lower normal range levels. Testosterone replacement may be appropriate when both clinical symptoms and biochemical evidence of hypogonadism exist.
- Available data indicate that all testosterone products may be equally effective and associated with similar side effect profiles.

Fun Fact:

Stephen Braun, a medical writer, described how he was funded by Abbott Pharmaceuticals to help write a "consensus panel" statement for a physician's organization. Two of his paragraphs casting doubt on the dangers of low testosterone were deleted from the final document (Braun S, *JAMA Internal Medicine* 2013;173(15):1458-60).

Bottom Line:

Successful marketing has convinced the public that "low T" is a public health scourge, leading to over-prescribing of testosterone for patients who don't need it. Prescribe it only for men with demonstrably low testosterone levels and accompanying symptoms.

VARDENAFIL (Levitra) Fact Sheet

FDA Indications:
Erectile dysfunction.

Dosage Forms:
- **Tablets:** 2.5 mg, 5 mg, 10 mg, 20 mg.
- **Orally disintegrating tablets (Staxyn):** 10 mg.

Dosage Guidance:
- Start 10 mg x1, 1 hour prior to sexual activity (5 mg if >65 years old). Max 20 mg/dose and 1 dose/day.
- ODT (Staxyn): Start 10 mg x1, 1 hour prior to sexual activity. Max 10 mg/day.
- Taking with a high-fat meal may decrease serum vardenafil levels by as much as 50%.

Cost: $$$$

Side Effects:
- Most common: flushing, headache, nasal congestion, heartburn.
- Serious but rare: May cause dose-related impairment of color discrimination. Sudden decrease or loss of hearing has been reported rarely; hearing changes may be accompanied by tinnitus and dizziness. Decreases in blood pressure may occur due to vasodilator effects; concurrent use with alpha-adrenergic antagonists or substantial alcohol consumption may cause symptomatic hypotension. Avoid use with nitrates (see below). Painful erection >6 hours in duration (priapism) may occur rarely.

Mechanism, Pharmacokinetics, and Drug Interactions:
- Phosphodiesterase type 5 (PDE-5) inhibitor.
- Metabolized primarily through CYP3A4 and to a lesser extent, 2C9; t ½: 4-5 hours.
- Avoid concomitant use with nitrates in any form (eg, nitroglycerin, isosorbide dinitrate, amyl nitrate or "poppers"). Use with caution in patients taking alpha-blockers; may cause symptomatic hypotension. Use with caution in patients taking strong CYP3A4 inhibitors, which may increase or extend effects of vardenafil (maximum of 5 mg/day).

Clinical Pearls:
Usual onset of effect of vardenafil is within 1 hour of a dose; effects usually last 2 hours.

Fun Fact:
Staxyn, the orally disintegrating tablet form of vardenafil, is peppermint flavored.

Bottom Line:
Vardenafil doesn't offer any benefits compared to sildenafil, which has more data in the psychiatric setting and more clinical experience.

Sleep Disorder Medications

There are only 3 medications in this section (which is why we didn't create a table here)—modafinil (Provigil), armodafinil (Nuvigil), and sodium oxybate (Xyrem). In reality, very few of you will ever prescribe Xyrem, a medication for narcolepsy with cataplexy, both because it's a pretty dangerous drug, and because narcolepsy is a very rare illness (see *TCPR* September 2015 for plenty of info on Xyrem and narcolepsy).

The two "vigil" drugs, on the other hand, are pretty heavily prescribed by psychiatrists for all manner of situations, some legitimate (shift-work disorder, jet lag, antidepressant-induced sleepiness), and others, unbeknownst to the prescribers, pretty marginal (staying up all night to study—or to party). These meds, along with the stimulants, are often used as "cognitive enhancers" by over-achievers. Whether that's a good or a bad thing is a subject of ongoing debate.

There's no clear guidance on which of the vigils to prescribe. Nuvigil lasts a few hours longer than Provigil, which can be a blessing for those who want to stay awake longer or a curse for those who find that it causes them insomnia. Trial and error is the way to go with these agents.

ARMODAFINIL (Nuvigil) Fact Sheet

FDA Indications:
Excessive sleepiness associated with obstructive sleep apnea, narcolepsy, or shift-work disorder.

Off-Label Uses:
ADHD; fatigue; treatment-resistant depression.

Dosage Forms:
Tablets: 50 mg, 150 mg, 200 mg, 250 mg.

Dosage Guidance:
- Obstructive sleep apnea or narcolepsy: 150 mg–250 mg QAM.
- Shift-work sleep disorder: 150 mg QD, 1 hour before start of work shift.

Cost: $$$$$

Side Effects:
- Most common: headache, nausea, dizziness, insomnia, anxiety, irritability.
- Serious but rare: serious rash, including Stevens–Johnson syndrome, multi-organ hypersensitivity reaction, angioedema, and anaphylaxis reported rarely. Rare cases of mania, psychosis, and agitation reported.

Mechanism, Pharmacokinetics, and Drug Interactions:
- Dopamine reuptake inhibitor.
- Metabolized primarily by non-CYP450 liver pathways, but also to some degree by CYP3A4; t ½: 15 hours.
- Duration of action about 8 hours.
- Avoid concomitant use with steroidal contraceptives (hormone levels may be decreased due to 3A4 induction) and with CYP2C19 substrates (eg, omeprazole, phenytoin, diazepam—levels may be increased).

Clinical Pearls:
- Armodafinil is, as the name implies, the R-modafinil enantiomer (modafinil is a 1:1 mixture of both R- and S-enantiomers). Both drugs work by increasing dopamine, likely by inhibiting dopamine reuptake. C-IV controlled substance due to abuse potential, mostly for euphoric and stimulant-like effects.
- Increased heart rate and blood pressure may occur, particularly in patients who don't suffer from excessive sedation or fatigue and at higher doses.

Fun Fact:
In 2010, the FDA declined to approve use of Nuvigil to treat jet lag.

Bottom Line:
Effective wake-promoting agent with some potential for abuse and for drug interactions. Lasts a bit longer than modafinil, but it is more expensive.

MODAFINIL (Provigil) Fact Sheet [G]

FDA Indications:

Excessive sleepiness associated with obstructive sleep apnea, narcolepsy, or shift-work disorder.

Off-Label Uses:

ADHD; fatigue; treatment-resistant depression.

Dosage Forms:

Tablets (G): 100 mg, 200 mg.

Dosage Guidance:

- Obstructive sleep apnea or narcolepsy: 100 mg–400 mg QAM.
- Shift-work sleep disorder: 100 mg–400 mg QD, 1 hour before start of work shift.
- ADHD (off-label): 100 mg–400 mg QAM.
- Treatment-resistant depression, bipolar or unipolar (off-label): 100 mg–400 mg QAM added to antidepressant.

Cost: $$$$

Side Effects:

- Most common: increased heart rate and blood pressure, headache, nausea, jitteriness, rhinitis, diarrhea, back pain, and insomnia.
- Serious but rare: serious rash, including Stevens–Johnson syndrome, multi-organ hypersensitivity reaction, angioedema, and anaphylaxis reported rarely. Rare cases of mania, psychosis, and agitation reported.

Mechanism, Pharmacokinetics, and Drug Interactions:

- Dopamine reuptake inhibitor.
- Metabolized primarily by non-CYP450 liver pathways, but also to some degree by CYP3A4; t ½: 15 hours.
- Duration of action about 6 hours.
- Avoid concomitant use with steroidal contraceptives (hormone levels may be decreased due to 3A4 induction) and with CYP2C9/19 substrates (eg, omeprazole, phenytoin, diazepam—levels may be increased).

Clinical Pearls:

- Works by increasing dopamine, likely by inhibiting dopamine reuptake.
- C–IV controlled substance.
- Increased heart rate and blood pressure may occur, particularly in patients who don't suffer from excessive sedation or fatigue and at higher doses.

Fun Fact:

An ADHD indication was rejected by the FDA because of modafinil's possible association with Stevens–Johnson syndrome.

Bottom Line:

While modafinil can be helpful for many causes of excessive sleepiness, realize that many people may end up using it off-label for lifestyle enhancement, such as working, studying, and partying longer.

SODIUM OXYBATE (Xyrem) Fact Sheet

FDA Indications:
Cataplexy and excessive daytime sedation in narcolepsy.

Off-Label Uses:
Fibromyalgia; chronic pain; neuropathic pain.

Dosage Forms:
Oral solution: 0.5 g/mL.

Dosage Guidance:
Start 4.5 g nightly, given in 2 equal, divided doses (because of extremely short half-life): 2.25 g at bedtime and 2.25 g taken 2.5–4 hours later. Titrate to effect in increments of 1.5 g/night at weekly intervals (0.75 g at bedtime and 0.75 g taken 2.5–4 hours later). Usual dose 6 g–9 g per night. Max 9 g/night.

Cost: $$$$$

Side Effects:
- Most common: nausea, dizziness, vomiting, somnolence, enuresis, tremor, parasomnias (sleepwalking).
- Serious but rare: respiratory depression, depression and suicidality, impaired motor and cognitive function.

Mechanism, Pharmacokinetics, and Drug Interactions:
- CNS depressant.
- Metabolized primarily by conversion to carbon dioxide and then eliminated by expiration; t ½: 0.5–1 hour.
- Avoid concomitant use with alcohol, sedative hypnotics, and other CNS depressants. Valproic acid increases sodium oxybate levels by 25%; adjust valproic acid dose by at least 20%.

Clinical Pearls:
- Sodium oxybate is the sodium salt of gamma hydroxybutyrate (GHB), a Schedule I controlled substance ("date rape" drug).
- Sodium oxybate is a C–III controlled substance and is available only through a restricted distribution program called the Xyrem REMS Program using a centralized pharmacy. Prescribers and patients must enroll in the program (www.XYREMREMS.com or 1–866–XYREM88).
- Xyrem alone was just as effective as modafinil alone for excessive daytime sedation, but the combination was significantly better than either medication used alone in one narcolepsy study.

Fun Fact:
Xyrem is expensive, between $90,000 and $130,000 per year depending on the nightly dose, because it is considered an orphan drug. Jazz Pharmaceuticals is looking to expand its use by pursuing an indication for excessive sedation due to obstructive sleep apnea.

Bottom Line:
Xyrem is often used by sleep specialists as a first-line agent for narcolepsy with cataplexy. It's unlikely that many psychiatrists will ever prescribe it, given its dangers.

Substance Abuse/Dependence Medications

Although medications are helpful in substance abuse, you should combine them with other approaches, such as therapy and 12-step programs. Most patients with substance abuse issues have co-occurring psychiatric disorders. Some clinicians prefer to get the substance abuse under control before treating other disorders, under the theory that substances can both obscure and aggravate the underlying psychiatric symptoms. In practice, however, it takes patients a very long time to get sober, and treatment of other conditions usually can't wait.

Opioid Dependence

- Methadone was first approved by the FDA for use in opioid dependence in 1947. It is a substitute therapy, and while it rarely gets patients off of opiates, it does help decrease the use of illicit forms of opiates. The problem is that patients must show up at methadone clinics to receive their dose for the first few years of treatment, making it hard to carve out a normal work or family life.

- Buprenorphine/naloxone combination (Suboxone) was approved in 2002 and has many advantages over methadone. You can give patients a 30-day supply, allowing them to avoid the methadone lifestyle. Suboxone is probably a little easier to taper off of than methadone for patients who want to attain total opiate sobriety.

Alcohol Dependence

- Disulfiram (Antabuse) is an aversive treatment, causing patients to become ill if they drink while taking the medication. For a long time it was the only approved medication for treating alcohol dependence, and it still has a place in treatment for patients who are very highly motivated to not drink at all (for example, those who are on probation after a DUI, or those who are about to lose jobs or partners if they go on just one more bender).

- Naltrexone (ReVia, Vivitrol) blocks a specific type of opiate receptor in the brain, and is thought to act by reducing cravings and the rewarding effects of alcohol. Most substance abuse specialists consider it the treatment of choice for alcoholism.

- Acamprosate (Campral) is effective in maintaining abstinence after detox. It is thought to "normalize" the brain glutamate system, which becomes unstable after many years of heavy alcohol use. It may work best in patients who are not abusing other substances, who are alcohol-free before starting it, and who have a strong commitment to abstinence.

- Combining medications is another strategy. For example, the combination of acamprosate and disulfiram seems to be more effective than acamprosate alone; however, the combination of naltrexone and acamprosate has not been shown to be more effective than naltrexone alone.

Smoking Cessation

(The following is adapted from a Carlat One-Pager that was originally created for the June 2015 issue of the *Carlat Addiction Treatment Report*. See that issue for the full article.)

Assessment

DSM-5: "Problematic pattern" of tobacco use leading to "significant distress" that lasts at least 12 months.

1. *Determine daily nicotine use.* How many packs per day (20 mg nicotine per pack)? E-cigarettes (nicotine varies)? Chewing tobacco (1 pouch = ¼ pack)? Hookah?
2. *Determine the usage pattern.* When does the patient have his or her first cigarette of the day? Does the patient smoke when sick?
3. *Determine past quitting techniques.* Have any worked—or *not* worked?

Pharmacological Treatment: Which to Choose?

- **Nicotine replacement therapy (NRT).** Start most patients on NRT. Prescribe patch based on nicotine load: 1 ppd = 21 mg. Place it at the same time each day, usually in the morning. Start above the heart and rotate left around the body to prevent skin irritation. Use 0.5% cortisone cream for irritation/rash. Initial dose for 4–8 weeks, then taper monthly or every 2 months. Advise no smoking—patients may note nausea if they do.

- **Combination NRT.** If there are cravings throughout the day even with a patch, add a short-acting agent (gum, lozenge, spray, inhaler). Discuss chewing technique for gum: Chew a few times to activate the release (the sign is bad peppery taste), then park between cheek and gum, and switch sides every few minutes. Each piece is 2–4 mg and lasts about 30 minutes. Spray and inhaler are available by prescription only.

- **Varenicline (Chantix).** Start 0.5 mg per day X 3 days, increase to twice daily for 7–10 days, then quit smoking, then increase gradually to 1 mg twice daily for 3 months. Discuss possible insomnia and vivid dreams (common). Psychiatric side effects, such as depression, suicidal ideation, and aggression, are unusual and likely caused by nicotine withdrawal rather than Chantix.

- **Bupropion (Wellbutrin SR, Zyban).** 150 mg/day is just as effective as the manufacturer's recommended dose of 150 mg BID and carries fewer side effects. Possible side effects of insomnia, nervousness, weight loss (potentially good, especially since many people gain weight after quitting).

- Combination NRT is as effective as Chantix. Bupropion is effective, but less so.

Tips to Improve Success of Treatment

- Normalize failure. Most people need multiple quit attempts before success; if patients know this in advance, they might be more willing to come back and try again.
- The first week after quitting is the hardest in terms of craving. Craving spells last 10–20 minutes; distraction techniques can work to deal with them. Patients can try drinking a large glass of cold water, playing a video game, etc.
- Warn patients that they might cough temporarily after they quit—this is a normal lung response to healing.
- Give phone number 1-800-QUIT-NOW for free support.

Table 15: Substance Abuse and Dependence Medications

Generic Name (Brand Name) Year FDA Approved (Rx status) [G] denotes generic availability	Relevant FDA Indication(s)	Available Strengths (mg)	Usual Dosage Range (mg)
Acamprosate [G] (Campral) 2004 (Rx)	Alcohol	333	666 TID
Buprenorphine [G] (Buprenex, Butrans) 2002 (C-III) Generic not available for patch	Opiate	2, 8 SL 0.3 mg/mL inj 5, 7.5, 10, 15, 20 mcg/h patch	8 QD–16 QD
Buprenorphine and Naloxone [G] (Bunavail, Suboxone, Zubsolv) 2002 (C-III) Generic available for 2/0.5, 8/2 mg SL tablets only	Opiate	2.1/0.3, 4.2/0.7, 6.3/1 buccal film (Bunavail) 2/0.5, 4/1, 8/2, 12/3 SL strips (Suboxone) 2/0.5, 8/2 SL tabs (generic only) 1.4/0.36, 2.9/0.71, 5.7/1.4, 8.6/2.1, 11.4/2.9 SL tabs (Zubsolv)	4–24 QD
Bupropion SR [G] (Zyban) 1997 (Rx)	Smoking	150	150 QAM–150 BID
Disulfiram [G] (Antabuse) 1951 (Rx)	Alcohol	250, 500	125 QPM–500 QPM
Methadone [G] (Dolophine, Methadose) 1947 (C-II)	Opiate	5, 10, 40 10 mg/mL, 10 mg/5 mL, 5 mg/5 mL, oral liquid	20 QD–120 QD
Naloxone (Evzio, Narcan Nasal Spray) 2014 (auto-injector) 2015 (intranasal)	Emergency opioid overdose rescue	0.4 mg/0.4 mL autoinjector 0.4 mg/0.1 mL intranasal	0.4 x1; may repeat every 2–3 minutes
Naltrexone [G] (ReVia) 1984 (Rx)	Alcohol, opiate	50	25 QD–50 QD
Naltrexone ER (Vivitrol) 2006 (Rx)	Alcohol, opiate	380	380 Q4wk

Generic Name (Brand Name) Year FDA Approved (Rx status) [G] denotes generic availability	Relevant FDA Indication(s)	Available Strengths (mg)	Usual Dosage Range (mg)
Nicotine inhaled (Nicotrol Inhaler) 1997 (Rx)	Smoking	4 mg/cartridge	6–16 cartridges per day
Nicotine nasal spray (Nicotrol NS) 1996 (Rx)	Smoking	0.5 mg/spray	1–2 sprays/hour PRN
Nicotine polacrilex [G] (Nicorette Gum, others) 1992 (OTC)	Smoking	2, 4	1 piece PRN up to 24/day
Nicotine polacrilex [G] (Nicorette Lozenge, others) 2009 (OTC)	Smoking	2, 4	1 piece PRN up to 20/day
Nicotine transdermal [G] (Habitrol, Nicoderm CQ) 1991 (OTC)	Smoking	7, 14, 21/24 hours	14–21 QD
Varenicline (Chantix) 2006 (Rx)	Smoking	0.5, 1	0.5 QD–1 BID

ACAMPROSATE (Campral) Fact Sheet [G]

FDA Indications:
Alcohol dependence.

Dosage Forms:
Delayed release tablets (G): 333 mg.

Dosage Guidance:
Start 666 mg TID. Give 333 mg TID in patients with renal impairment.

Cost: $$$

Side Effects:
- Most common: diarrhea (dose related, transient), weakness, peripheral edema, insomnia, anxiety.
- Serious but rare: Acute renal failure reported in a few cases; suicidal ideation, attempts, and completions rare but greater than with placebo in studies.

Mechanism, Pharmacokinetics, and Drug Interactions:
- Mechanism of action is not fully defined; it appears to work by promoting a balance between the excitatory and inhibitory neurotransmitters, glutamate and GABA, respectively (GABA and glutamate activities appear to be disrupted in alcohol dependence).
- Not metabolized, cleared as unchanged drug by kidneys; t ½: 20–33 hours.
- There are no significant drug interactions.

Clinical Pearls:
- Approved by the FDA in 2004, but it has been used in France and other countries since 1989.
- Does not eliminate or treat symptoms of alcohol withdrawal. Usually prescribed for maintenance of abstinence; may continue even if patient relapses with alcohol.
- Clinically, acamprosate has demonstrated efficacy in more than 25 placebo-controlled trials, and has generally been found to be more effective than placebo in reducing risk of returning to any drinking and increasing the cumulative duration of abstinence. However, in reducing heavy drinking, acamprosate appears to be no better than placebo.
- Acamprosate can be used with naltrexone or disulfiram (different mechanism of action), although the combination with naltrexone may not increase efficacy per available studies.
- Taking with food is not necessary, but it may help compliance to do so.
- Compared to naltrexone and disulfiram, acamprosate is unique in that it is not metabolized by the liver and is not impacted by alcohol use, so it can be administered to patients with hepatitis or liver disease and to patients who continue drinking alcohol.

Fun Fact:
Each 333 mg tablet contains 33 mg of elemental calcium (because it is available as acamprosate calcium salt).

Bottom Line:
Acamprosate and naltrexone show similar reduced rates of relapse, but acamprosate is associated with more diarrhea, while naltrexone is associated with more nausea, fatigue, and somnolence; acamprosate is preferred in patients with hepatic impairment.

BUPRENORPHINE (Buprenex) Fact Sheet [G]

FDA Indications:

Opioid dependence, induction; moderate-severe pain (Buprenex, Butrans).

Dosage Forms:
- **SL tablets (G):** 2 mg, 8 mg (scored).
- **Injection (G):** 0.3 mg/mL.
- **Transdermal patch (Butrans):** 5 mcg/h, 7.5 mcg/h, 10 mcg/h, 15 mcg/h, 20 mcg/h.

Dosage Guidance:
- Schedule III controlled substance. Prescribing of SL tablets for opioid dependence is limited to physicians who have met qualification criteria and have received a DEA number specific to buprenorphine (see www.buprenorphine.samhsa.gov).
- Start 2 mg–8 mg SL day 1; then 8 mg–16 mg SL QD (usual induction dose range is 12 mg–16 mg/day and accomplished over 3–4 days). Begin at least 4 hours after last use of heroin or other short-acting opioids and when first signs of withdrawal appear. In essence, if an opioid-dependent patient is not in sufficient withdrawal, introduction of buprenorphine may precipitate withdrawal due to its partial agonist effect. Not for maintenance treatment; patients should be switched to the buprenorphine/naloxone combination product for maintenance and unsupervised therapy.

Cost: SL: $$$

Side Effects:
- Most common: headache, pain, insomnia, nausea, anxiety.
- Serious but rare: Hepatitis reported rarely, ranging from transient, asymptomatic transaminase elevations to hepatic failure; in many cases, patients had preexisting hepatic dysfunction. QT prolongation with higher doses of transdermal patch.

Mechanism, Pharmacokinetics, and Drug Interactions:
- Opioid agonist (delta and mu receptors) and antagonist (kappa receptors).
- Metabolized primarily through CYP3A4; t ½: 31–35 hours.
- Avoid concomitant use with opiate analgesics: diminished pain control. Additive effects with CNS depressants. CYP3A4 inhibitors and inducers may affect levels of buprenorphine.

Clinical Pearls:
- Binds to various opioid receptors, producing agonism at delta receptors, partial agonism at mu receptors, and antagonism at kappa receptors (opioid agonist-antagonist).
- Initially, each approved doctor could treat only 10 patients, but the law was modified to alleviate bottleneck treatment access; now each physician can treat up to 100 patients.

Fun Fact:

A subdermal implantable formulation of buprenorphine, Probuphine, using a polymer matrix sustained release technology, is being developed to minimize risks of noncompliance and diversion. This formulation for maintenance therapy is capable of delivering continuous blood levels of buprenorphine for 6 months.

Bottom Line:

Buprenorphine alone was previously preferred for the initial (induction) phase of treatment, with buprenorphine/naloxone combination (Suboxone) preferred for maintenance treatment (unsupervised administration). Currently, the favored practice is use of the combination for both induction and maintenance as this decreases any abuse or diversion potential.

BUPRENORPHINE/NALOXONE (Suboxone) Fact Sheet [G]

FDA Indications:

Opioid dependence (induction and maintenance).

Dosage Forms:
- **SL tablets (G):** 2/0.5 mg, 8/2 mg (scored).
- **SL film strips (G):** 2/0.5 mg, 4/1 mg, 8/2 mg, 12/3 mg.
- **SL tablets (Zubsolv):** 1.4/0.36 mg, 5.7/1.4 mg.
- **Buccal film (Bunavail):** 2.1/0.3 mg, 4.2/0.7 mg, 6.3/1 mg.

Dosage Guidance:
- Schedule III controlled substance. Prescribing is limited to physicians who have met qualification criteria and have received a DEA number specific to buprenorphine (see www.buprenorphine.samhsa.gov).
- For induction, use strategy described in buprenorphine fact sheet. For maintenance, give combination product (Suboxone or [G]) daily in the equivalent buprenorphine dose on last day of induction; adjust dose in increments of 2 mg or 4 mg to a level that maintains treatment and suppresses opioid withdrawal symptoms (usually 4 mg–24 mg/day); max 32 mg/day.
- Zubsolv 5.7/1.4 mg SL tablet provides equivalent buprenorphine to a Suboxone 8/2 mg SL tablet.
- Bunavail 4.2/0.7 mg buccal film provides equivalent buprenorphine to a Suboxone 8/2 mg SL tablet.

Cost: SL tablet: $$$; film: $$$

Side Effects:
- Most common: headache, pain, vomiting, sweating.
- Serious but rare: Hepatitis reported rarely, ranging from transient, asymptomatic transaminase elevations to hepatic failure; in many cases, patients had preexisting hepatic dysfunction.

Mechanism, Pharmacokinetics, and Drug Interactions:
- Buprenorphine: opioid agonist (delta and mu receptors) and antagonist (kappa receptors); naloxone: opioid antagonist.
- Metabolized primarily through CYP3A4; t ½: 31–35 hours (naloxone: 2–12 hours).
- Avoid concomitant use with opiate analgesics: diminished pain control. Additive effects with CNS depressants. CYP3A4 inhibitors and inducers may affect levels of buprenorphine.

Clinical Pearls:
- Naloxone is an opioid antagonist that is active only when injected; it is added to buprenorphine in order to reduce misuse via intravenous injection of a dissolved tablet.
- The sublingual film formulation is newer; its manufacturer claims it dissolves faster and tastes better than SL tablets. Actually, it is more likely a way for the manufacturer to switch users to a "new" product (with patent protection until 2025) rather than lose patients to forthcoming generics.
- Prescribers should be aware of the high risk for diversion and sale of buprenorphine films and tablets. Some regular opioid abusers periodically buy buprenorphine "off the street" and use it to combat cravings and withdrawal symptoms if their drug of choice is not readily available.

Fun Fact:

The manufacturer of Suboxone, Reckitt Benckiser, generates most of its revenue from selling home and personal care products like Lysol cleaners and Durex condoms.

Bottom Line:

The combination product is preferred over buprenorphine alone for maintenance because the addition of naloxone affords it a lower potential for injection abuse. Although the SL film formulation is currently priced the same as the SL tablets, the SL film strips provide very little (if any) meaningful benefits, and generic SL tablets should be used as a cost-saving measure.

BUPROPION SR (Zyban) Fact Sheet [G]

FDA Indications:
Smoking cessation.

Dosage Forms:
SR tablets (G): 150 mg ER.

Dosage Guidance:
Start 150 mg QAM for 3 days, then 150 mg BID; separate doses by at least 8 hours and administer last dose no later than 6 pm to minimize insomnia. Target smoking quit dates are generally in the second week of treatment.

Cost: $ [G], $$$$ Zyban

Side Effects:
- Most common: agitation, insomnia, headache, nausea, vomiting, tremor, tachycardia, dry mouth, weight loss.
- Serious but rare: seizures; risk higher with rapid and large dose increases and in patients at risk for seizures. Anaphylactoid reactions (eg, pruritus, urticaria, angioedema, dyspnea) reported rarely; reports include Stevens-Johnson syndrome and anaphylactic shock. Class warning regarding suicide risk (see Antidepressants section).

Mechanism, Pharmacokinetics, and Drug Interactions:
- Norepinephrine and dopamine reuptake inhibitor.
- Metabolized primarily through CYP2B6; may inhibit CYP2D6; t ½: 21 hours.
- Avoid use with MAOIs. Levels of drugs metabolized by CYP2D6 (eg, paroxetine, fluoxetine, aripiprazole, iloperidone, atomoxetine, beta blockers) may be increased. Successful cessation of smoking may alter pharmacokinetic properties of other medications (eg, clozapine, olanzapine, theophylline, warfarin, insulin).

Clinical Pearls:
- If patient successfully quits smoking after 7–12 weeks, may consider maintenance therapy based on individual patient risk-benefit. Efficacy of maintenance therapy (150 mg BID) has been shown for up to 6 months. However, if patient has not made significant progress by the seventh week of therapy, success is unlikely and discontinuation should be considered.
- Bupropion slows the weight gain that often occurs in the initial weeks after smoking cessation, but with time, this effect becomes negligible.
- Bupropion and nicotine replacement therapy show similar quit rates: about 25%, or double that seen with placebo, are abstinent at 6 months.
- Equally effective in smokers with or without history of depression.

Fun Fact:
Much of the initial direct-to-consumer advertising that was done for Zyban was via print ads in smoke-free places such as airports.

Bottom Line:
Given the high rate of comorbidity between smoking and depression, this is an attractive intervention for many patients. It is also a particularly good choice for patients who are not able to set a quit date prior to initiating treatment.

DISULFIRAM (Antabuse) Fact Sheet [G]

FDA Indications:
Alcohol dependence.

Dosage Forms:
Tablets (G): 250 mg, 500 mg.

Dosage Guidance:
Start 125 mg QPM (must be abstinent from alcohol >12 hours), increase to 250 mg QPM after several days. Maintenance is usually 250 mg–500 mg QPM, but some patients can drink alcohol without a reaction at the 250 mg/day dose.

Cost: $$

Side Effects:

- Most common: skin eruptions (eg, acne, allergic dermatitis), drowsiness, fatigue, impotence, headache, metallic taste.

- Serious but rare: Severe (very rarely fatal) hepatitis or hepatic failure reported and may occur in patients with or without prior history of abnormal hepatic function. Rare psychotic episodes have been reported. Rarely may cause peripheral neuropathy or optic neuritis.

Mechanism, Pharmacokinetics, and Drug Interactions:

- Aldehyde dehydrogenase inhibitor.

- Metabolized primarily through CYP450; t ½: not defined, but elimination from body is slow, and effects may persist for 1 or 2 weeks after last dose.

- While taking disulfiram, and for 1–2 weeks after stopping, avoid concomitant use of any medications containing alcohol (including topicals), metronidazole, or "disguised" forms of ethanol (cough syrup, some mouthwashes, oral solutions or liquid concentrates containing alcohol such as sertraline). Avoid vinegars, cider, extracts, and foods containing ethanol.

Clinical Pearls:

- Disulfiram inhibits the enzyme aldehyde dehydrogenase; when taken with alcohol, acetaldehyde levels are increased by 5- to 10-fold, causing unpleasant symptoms that include flushing, nausea, vomiting, palpitations, chest pain, vertigo, hypotension, and (in rare instances) cardiovascular collapse and death. This is the basis for its use as aversion therapy. Common advice to patients: "You'll wish you were dead, but it won't kill you."

- Reaction may last from 30–60 minutes to several hours or as long as alcohol remains in the bloodstream.

- Advise patients to carry an identification card or a medical alert bracelet that states they are taking the medication and lists the symptoms of the reaction and clinician contact information.

- Duration of therapy is until the patient is fully recovered and a basis for permanent self-control has been established; maintenance therapy may be required for months or even years.

Fun Fact:
Disulfiram's anti-protozoal activity may be effective in *Giardia* and *Trichomonas* infections.

Bottom Line:
Since craving is not reduced by disulfiram and any alcohol ingestion could result in a reaction, noncompliance can be common. Its use should be reserved for selective, highly motivated patients in conjunction with supportive and psychotherapeutic treatment.

METHADONE (Methadose) Fact Sheet [G]

FDA Indications:
Opioid dependence; severe pain.

Dosage Forms:
- **Tablets (G):** 5 mg, 10 mg, 40 mg (scored),
- **Oral solution (G):** 10 mg/5 mL, 5 mg/5 mL.
- **Oral concentrate (G):** 10 mg/mL.

Dosage Guidance:
- Schedule II controlled substance; distribution of 40 mg dispersible tablets restricted to authorized opioid addiction treatment facilities.
- Start 15–30 mg single dose; then 5–10 mg every 2–4 hours. Adjust dose to prevent withdrawal symptoms; max 40 mg on day 1. 80–120 mg per day is a common maintenance dose for opioid dependence.

Cost: $

Side Effects:
- Most common: constipation, dizziness, sedation, nausea, sweating.
- Serious but rare: May prolong the QTc interval and increase risk for torsade de pointes; caution in patients at risk for QTc prolongation; usually with doses >100 mg/day. Severe respiratory depression may occur; use extreme caution during initiation, titration, and conversion from other opiates to methadone. Respiratory depressant effects occur later and persist longer than analgesic effects, possibly contributing to cases of overdose.

Mechanism, Pharmacokinetics, and Drug Interactions:
- Opioid agonist.
- Metabolized primarily through CYP2B6, 2C19, and 3A4 (major); t ½: 8–59 hours; inhibits CYP2D6.
- High potential for interactions. Avoid concomitant use with other potent sedatives or respiratory depressants. Use with caution in patients on medications metabolized by CYP2D6 that inhibit CYP3A4, prolong the QTc interval, or promote electrolyte depletion.

Clinical Pearls:
- May only be dispensed according to the Substance Abuse and Mental Health Services Administration's (SAMHSA) Center for Substance Abuse Treatment (CSAT) guidelines. Regulations vary by area; consult regulatory agencies and/or methadone treatment facility.
- Methadone accumulates with repeated doses; dose may need reduction after 3–5 days to prevent CNS depressant effects.

Fun Fact:
A persistent but untrue urban legend claims the name "Dolophine" was coined in tribute to Adolf Hitler by its German creators. The name was in fact created after the war by the American branch of Eli Lilly, and the pejorative term "adolphine" (never an actual name of the drug) didn't appear in the US until the early 1970s.

Bottom Line:
Opiate replacement therapy via methadone reduces or eliminates illicit use of opiates and criminality associated with opiate use, allowing patients to improve health and social functioning. It is a successful harm reduction model because it reduces the transmission of infectious diseases associated with opiate injection, such as hepatitis and HIV. Disadvantages include potential for accumulation with repeated doses (which may result in toxicity), interindividual variability in pharmacokinetic parameters, potential for drug interactions, challenges associated with dose titration, stigma associated with opiate replacement therapy, and limited availability of treatment programs (eg, nonexistent in some geographic areas, wait lists in other areas).

NALOXONE (Evzio, Narcan Nasal Spray) Fact Sheet

FDA Indications:
Emergency treatment of known or suspected opioid overdose.

Dosage Forms:
- **Pre-filled auto-injector:** 0.4 mg/0.4 mL.
- **Intranasal (Narcan Nasal Spray [G]):** 4 mg/0.1 mL prefilled syringe with mucosal atomization device.

Dosage Guidance:
- Injectable: Bystander to administer 0.4 mg IM or SC into thigh, through clothing if necessary; may repeat additional doses every 2–3 minutes until emergency response arrives.
- Intranasal: Bystander to spray in each nostril.

Cost: auto-injector: $$$$$; intranasal: $$

Side Effects:
Most common: symptoms of opioid withdrawal, including body aches, fever, sweating, runny nose, sneezing, piloerection, yawning, weakness, shivering or trembling, nervousness, restlessness or irritability, diarrhea, nausea or vomiting, abdominal cramps, increased blood pressure, and tachycardia.

Mechanism, Pharmacokinetics, and Drug Interactions:
- Opioid antagonist.
- Metabolized primarily by conjugation (non-P450) in the liver; t ½: 1.36 hours.

Clinical Pearls:
- Because treatment of overdose with this opioid antagonist must be performed by someone other than the patient, instruct the prescription recipient to inform those around them that they have naloxone rescue and ensure that they have been instructed in recognizing overdose symptoms and how to administer it.
- Evzio comes with printed instructions on the device label as well as electronic voice instructions (there is a speaker that provides instructions to guide the user through each step of the injection).
- Most opioids have a longer duration of action than Evzio, so it's likely that overdose symptoms (CNS depression and respiratory depression) will return after initial improvement. Therefore, patients should continue to be monitored and should receive medical attention after emergency dose(s) provided.
- A new intranasal (IN) form of naloxone rescue administration is available; if broadly distributed, it could make overdose rescue a more acceptable and widespread practice.
- Check out the Prescribe to Prevent website (prescribetoprevent.org) for prescriber resources such as webinars, toolkits, patient education material, and medical-legal resources. This website also provides guidance to physicians on writing a prescription for IN naloxone.

Fun Fact:
Naloxone was first approved for opioid overdose treatment in 1971 and is available as a very inexpensive injectable generic. These newer formulations will come at a much higher price because of the way they are formulated, making them easier to use by non-emergency provider bystanders.

Bottom Line:
Naloxone rescue saves lives. Prescribe it.

NALTREXONE (ReVia, Vivitrol) Fact Sheet [G]

FDA Indications:

Alcohol dependence; opioid addiction (relapse prevention following detox).

Off-Label Uses:

Self–injurious behavior.

Dosage Forms:
- **Tablets (Revia, G):** 50 mg (scored).
- **Long-acting injection (Vivitrol):** 380 mg.

Dosage Guidance:
- Opioid dependence: Start 25 mg for 1 day; if no withdrawal signs, increase to and maintain 50 mg/day (with food); doses >50 mg may increase risk of hepatoxicity.
- Alcohol dependence: Start and maintain 50 mg QD.
- Injection: 380 mg IM (gluteal) Q4 weeks (for opioid or alcohol dependence). Do not initiate therapy until patient is opioid–free for at least 7–10 days (by urinalysis).

Cost: tablet: $; injection: $$$$$

Side Effects:
- Most common: headache, nausea, somnolence, vomiting.
- Serious but rare: Black box warning regarding dose–related hepatocellular injury; the difference between apparent safe and hepatotoxic doses appears to be ≤5–fold (narrow therapeutic window). Discontinue if signs/symptoms of acute hepatitis develop.

Mechanism, Pharmacokinetics, and Drug Interactions:
- Opioid antagonist.
- Metabolized primarily through non–CYP450 pathway; t ½: 4 hours (5–10 days for IM).
- No significant interactions other than avoiding use with opiates (see below).

Clinical Pearls:
- May precipitate acute withdrawal (pain, hypertension, sweating, agitation, and irritability) in opiate–using patients; ensure patient is opioid–free for at least 7–10 days prior to initiating.
- In naltrexone–treated patients requiring emergency pain management, consider alternatives to opiates (eg, regional analgesia, non–opioid analgesics, general anesthesia). If opioid therapy is required, patients should be under the direct care of a trained anesthesia provider.
- Efficacy of oral naltrexone in alcohol dependence (craving and relapse) is more convincing than in opiate dependence. In opiate dependence, craving is not decreased but euphoric effects are blocked. Monthly IM naltrexone may be more effective than oral at maintaining abstinence in opiate dependence, without concern for daily medication adherence.

Fun Fact:

Methylnaltrexone, a closely related drug, is marketed as Relistor for the treatment of opioid–induced constipation.

Bottom Line:

Naltrexone is more frequently used for alcohol dependence than for opiate dependence. It is often used to minimize severity of drinking, while acamprosate is used to prevent relapse. Avoid naltrexone in patients with hepatic impairment or those taking opiate–based pain medications. For opioid dependence, methadone and Suboxone are more effective for most, although naltrexone may be appropriate for highly motivated opiate–dependent patients, with injectable preferred over oral.

NICOTINE GUM/LOZENGE (Nicorette) Fact Sheet [G]

FDA Indications:
Smoking cessation.

Dosage Forms:
- **Gum (G):** 2 mg, 4 mg (over the counter).
- **Lozenge (G):** 2 mg, 4 mg (over the counter).

Dosage Guidance:
- Chew 1 piece of gum PRN urge to smoke, up to 24 pieces/day. Patients who smoke <25 cigarettes/day should start with 2 mg strength; patients smoking ≥25 cigarettes/day should start with the 4 mg strength. Use the following 12-week dosing schedule: weeks 1-6: chew 1 piece of gum every 1-2 hours; to increase chances of quitting, chew at least 9 pieces/day during the first 6 weeks; weeks 7-9: chew 1 piece of gum every 2-4 hours; weeks 10-12: chew 1 piece of gum every 4-8 hours.
- For lozenges: Patients who smoke their first cigarette within 30 minutes of waking should use 4 mg strength; otherwise 2 mg strength is recommended. Use the following 12-week dosing schedule: weeks 1-6: 1 lozenge every 1-2 hours; weeks 7-9: 1 lozenge every 2-4 hours; weeks 10-12: 1 lozenge every 4-8 hours. Use at least 9 lozenges/day during first 6 weeks to improve chances of quitting; do not use more than 1 lozenge at a time; maximum is 5 lozenges every 6 hours or 20 lozenges/day.
- Patients should be advised to completely stop smoking upon initiation of therapy.

Cost: $

Side Effects:
Most common: headache; indigestion; nausea; hiccups; tongue, mouth, and throat irritation or tingling; jaw ache (gum).

Mechanism, Pharmacokinetics, and Drug Interactions:
- Nicotinic-cholinergic receptor agonist.
- Metabolized primarily through liver as well as kidneys and lungs; t ½: 1-2 hours.
- Minimal risk for drug interactions. Successful cessation of smoking may increase serum levels of medications metabolized by CYP1A2 (eg, clozapine, olanzapine, theophylline), which is induced by hydrocarbons in smoke; nicotine itself has no effect.

Clinical Pearls:
- Chew gum slowly until it tingles (about 15 chews), then park gum between cheek and gum until tingle is gone (about 1 minute); repeat until most of tingle is gone (~30 minutes).
- Lozenges should not be chewed or swallowed; allow to dissolve slowly (~20-30 minutes).
- Heavy smokers should use higher-dose gum or lozenge and at least 9 pieces/day to maximize chances of success. Do not use more than 1 piece at a time.
- Each 4 mg lozenge or gum results in 2 mg of absorbed nicotine, equivalent to 2 cigarettes.

Fun Fact:
Nicotine gum is available in a variety of flavors: fruit, mint, cinnamon, orange, cherry, and "original."

Bottom Line:
First-line intervention for those patients who can stop smoking at initiation of therapy; nicotine in the form of gum or lozenge may act as a substitute oral activity, which may aid in behavior modification.

NICOTINE INHALED (Nicotrol Inhaler) Fact Sheet

FDA Indications:
Smoking cessation.

Dosage Forms:
Cartridge: 4 mg delivered per cartridge (prescription required).

Dosage Guidance:
- Use frequent continuous puffing for 20 minutes with each cartridge; 80 deep inhalations over 20 minutes releases 4 mg nicotine, of which 2 mg is absorbed. Use 6–16 cartridges per day. Taper after 6–12 weeks of use by gradual dose reduction over 6–12 additional weeks.
- Patients should be advised to completely stop smoking upon initiation of therapy.

Cost: $$$$

Side Effects:
Most common: headache, mouth/throat irritation, dyspepsia, cough, unpleasant taste, rhinitis, tearing, sneezing.

Mechanism, Pharmacokinetics, and Drug Interactions:
- Nicotinic-cholinergic receptor agonist.
- Metabolized primarily through liver as well as kidneys and lungs; t ½: 1–2 hours.
- Minimal risk for drug interactions. Successful cessation of smoking may increase serum levels of medications metabolized by CYP1A2 (eg, clozapine, olanzapine, theophylline), which is induced by hydrocarbons in smoke; nicotine itself has no effect.

Clinical Pearls:
- Insert cartridge into inhaler and push hard until it pops into place. Replace mouthpiece and twist the top and bottom so that markings do not line up. Inhale deeply into the back of the throat or puff in short breaths. Nicotine in cartridge is used up after about 20 minutes of active puffing.
- Do not eat or drink 15 minutes before or during use. Puff lightly rather than inhale into lungs to minimize coughing.
- Local irritation in the mouth and throat may occur in as many as 40% of patients; coughing (32%) and rhinitis (23%) are also common. These effects are generally mild and occur less frequently with continued use. Use with caution in patients with bronchospastic disease due to potential airway irritation (other forms of nicotine replacement may be preferred).
- Higher ambient temperatures deliver more nicotine; lower temperatures deliver less.
- 1 cartridge delivers 80 puffs or about 2 mg of absorbed nicotine. Roughly 10 cartridges per day is equivalent to the nicotine of smoking 1 pack per day.

Fun Fact:
A nicotine inhaler is not really a true inhaler; puffing deposits the nicotine into the mouth, and it is then absorbed in the same manner as the nicotine gum or lozenge preparations.

Bottom Line:
Very high expense and unpleasant side effects make this form of nicotine replacement therapy difficult to recommend as a first-line option since no single therapy has been shown to be more effective than another.

NICOTINE NASAL SPRAY (Nicotrol NS) Fact Sheet

FDA Indications:
Smoking cessation.

Dosage Forms:
10 mL bottle: 10 mg/mL delivering 0.5 mg/spray in 200 sprays (prescription required).

Dosage Guidance:
- Use 1–2 sprays/hour as needed; do not exceed more than 5 doses (10 sprays) per hour. Max dose is 40 doses/day (80 sprays). Each dose (2 sprays) contains 1 mg of nicotine.
- After initial 8 weeks of treatment, taper dose gradually over 4–6 weeks.
- Patients should be advised to completely stop smoking upon initiation of therapy.

Cost: $$

Side Effects:
- Most common: headache, dyspepsia, rhinitis, nasal irritation, sneezing, coughing.

Mechanism, Pharmacokinetics, and Drug Interactions:
- Nicotinic–cholinergic receptor agonist.
- Metabolized primarily through liver as well as kidneys and lungs; t ½: 1–2 hours.
- Minimal risk for drug interactions. Successful cessation of smoking may increase serum levels of medications metabolized by CYP1A2 (eg, clozapine, olanzapine, theophylline), which is induced by hydrocarbons in smoke; nicotine itself has no effect.

Clinical Pearls:
- Prime pump prior to first use. Blow nose gently prior to use. Tilt head back slightly, breathe through mouth, and spray once in each nostril. Do not sniff, swallow, or inhale through nose.
- Moderate to severe nasal irritation in 94% of patients in the first 2 days of use; severity decreases over time. Nasal congestion and transient changes in sense of smell and taste also reported. Avoid in patients with chronic nasal disorders (eg, allergy, rhinitis, nasal polyps, and sinusitis). Exacerbations of bronchospasm reported in patients with asthma.
- Heavy smokers may well use the maximum amount of 80 sprays/day, meaning they would need a new bottle every 2–3 days. This can be tremendously and prohibitively expensive.
- Potential for abuse and dependence appears to be greater than with other NRT.

Fun Fact:
In a published case report (*Am J Psychiatry* 2001), a 54-year-old man who could no longer afford his Nicotrol NS prescription found a commercial source for nicotine on the Internet (sold as an insecticide). He purchased 25g in a 1 g/mL solution for $30, diluted the nicotine solution with distilled water to 10 mg/mL, and then placed the solution into empty spray bottles.

Bottom Line:
The idea of nasal administration of nicotine is appealing in that it more closely approximates the time course of plasma nicotine levels observed after cigarette smoking than other dosage forms; however, the high cost coupled with unpleasant side effects make this difficult to recommend as a first-line treatment, especially since no one form of nicotine replacement therapy has been shown to be more effective than another.

NICOTINE PATCH (Nicoderm CQ) Fact Sheet [G]

FDA Indications:
Smoking cessation.

Dosage Forms:
Transdermal patch (G): 7 mg, 14 mg, 21 mg/24 hour (over the counter).

Dosage Guidance:
- Apply new patch every 24 hours (same time each day, usually after awakening) to non-hairy, clean, dry skin on the upper body or upper outer arm; each patch should be applied to a different site. Adjustment may be required during initial treatment (move to higher dose if experiencing withdrawal symptoms; lower dose if side effects are experienced). Patients smoking >10 cigarettes/day: Start with 21 mg/day for 6 weeks, then 14 mg/day for 2 weeks, then 7 mg/day for 2 weeks. Patients smoking ≤10 cigarettes/day: Start with 14 mg/day for 6 weeks, then 7 mg/day for 2 weeks.
- Patients should be advised to completely stop smoking upon initiation of therapy.

Cost: $

Side Effects:
- Most common: application site reactions (itching, burning, or redness), diarrhea, dyspepsia, abdominal pain.

Mechanism, Pharmacokinetics, and Drug Interactions:
- Nicotinic-cholinergic receptor agonist.
- Metabolized primarily through liver as well as kidneys and lungs; t ½: 3–6 hours.
- Minimal risk for drug interactions. Successful cessation of smoking may increase serum levels of medications metabolized by CYP1A2 (eg, clozapine, olanzapine, theophylline), which is induced by hydrocarbons in smoke; nicotine itself has no effect.

Clinical Pearls:
- Patch may be worn for 16 or 24 hours. If craving upon awakening, wear patch for 24 hours; if vivid dreams or sleep disruptions occur, wear patch for 16 hours, remove at bedtime.
- Do not cut patch; causes rapid evaporation, making the patch useless.
- Up to 50% of patients will experience a local skin reaction, which is usually mild and self-limiting but may worsen with continued treatment. Local treatment with hydrocortisone cream 1% or triamcinolone cream 0.5% and rotating patch sites may help. In fewer than 5% of patients, such reactions require discontinuation.

Fun Facts:
Studies have found that smoking seems to provide short-term relief from symptoms of ulcerative colitis; recent data have suggested the use of nicotine patches in some patients with flare-ups of ulcerative colitis (not maintenance treatment).

Bottom Line:
Nicotine patches are a first-line intervention in patients who are able to quit smoking at initiation of treatment and who are regular and constant smokers.

VARENICLINE (Chantix) Fact Sheet

FDA Indications:
Smoking cessation.

Dosage Forms:
Tablets: 0.5 mg, 1 mg.

Dosage Guidance:
Start 0.5 mg QD x 3 days, ↑ to 0.5 mg BID x 4 days then ↑ to 1 mg BID for 11 weeks. Titrate slowly and take with food and a full glass of water to decrease GI upset. Start 1 week before target quit date; may consider setting a quit date up to 35 days after starting varenicline (may improve likelihood of abstinence).

Cost: $$$$

Side Effects:
- Most common: nausea, insomnia, headache, abnormal dreams, constipation, flatulence.
- Serious but rare: Black box warning for serious neuropsychiatric events (including depression, suicidal thoughts, suicide, psychosis, hostility) reported, even in those without preexisting psychiatric disease.

Mechanism, Pharmacokinetics, and Drug Interactions:
- Nicotine receptor partial agonist.
- Excreted mostly unchanged with minimal hepatic (non–CYP450) metabolism; t ½: 24 hours.
- Potential lowered tolerance to alcohol, with psychiatric reactions. H2 blockers, quinolones, and trimethoprim may increase varenicline levels. Successful cessation of smoking may alter pharmacokinetic properties of other medications (eg, clozapine, olanzapine, theophylline, warfarin, insulin).

Clinical Pearls:
- Dual mechanism of action: partial agonist at nicotinic receptors, mimicking nicotine effects on the brain and reducing withdrawal symptoms; blocks nicotine from binding to these receptors, thereby decreasing the reinforcing effect of smoking.
- If patient successfully quits smoking after 12 weeks, may continue for another 12 weeks. If not successful in first 12 weeks, then discontinue and reassess factors contributing to failure.
- Similar quit rates as bupropion at 6 months (25%), but higher quit rates compared to bupropion at 1 year if a second 12-week course of varenicline is used.
- Can be combined with bupropion; use with nicotine replacement therapies likely to lead to increased side effects, particularly nausea, headache, vomiting, and dizziness.

Fun Fact:
The show *Saturday Night Live* aired a parody of a Chantix commercial suggesting that side effects of *quitting* smoking could be dangerous (it's on YouTube).

Bottom Line:
Varenicline is the most effective tobacco cessation medication. Psychiatric side effects are usually limited to insomnia or abnormal dreams, but more dramatic reactions are possible, though rare.

Appendices

Appendix A: Drug Interactions in Psychiatry

Drug interactions can be one of the most challenging aspects of psychopharmacology. Today's psychiatrists often use complex medication regimens, while patients frequently take drugs for multiple medical comorbidities. It's impossible to keep track of all of these, but it is important (1) to understand basic concepts of drug-drug interactions, (2) to know where to find information regarding such interactions, and (3) to know which interactions may be clinically relevant.

The majority of interactions in psychiatry will not result in a serious outcome. Many interactions, however, may result in decreased efficacy or increased adverse effects, and these can be easily avoided.

First, let's review some basic concepts. A drug interaction occurs when the pharmacologic action of one drug is altered by the coadministration of another drug. There are two major types of drug interactions: **pharmacodynamic** (what the drug does to the body) and **pharmacokinetic** (what the body does to the drug). Pharmacodynamic interactions impact the effects of the drug at the target site. Pharmacokinetic interactions, on the other hand, impact the amount of time the drug stays in the body and its distribution to active sites.

Pharmacodynamic interactions take place at the level of neurotransmitters and receptors. For example, clonazepam (Klonopin) makes people sleepy by stimulating GABA receptors. Quetiapine (Seroquel) also makes people sleepy, probably by blocking histamine receptors. Combine the two, and patients become *really* sleepy. Pharmacodynamic interactions may also cause two drugs to *oppose* one another. Many of the dementia medications, for example, increase acetylcholine levels, while many psychiatric medications have primary (eg, benztropine) or secondary (eg, clozapine) anticholinergic effects. Giving both together may negate the beneficial effects of the dementia medication.

Some notable—and potentially dangerous—pharmacodynamic interactions in psychiatry include serotonin syndrome (too many serotonergic agents used together); the MAOI-type hypertensive crisis (MAOIs taken with foods high in tyramine); and arrhythmia-causing combinations (medications that increase QT interval, when taken together, may cause life-threatening arrhythmias, such as torsade de pointes). We often try to avoid these problems by doing things like lowering doses or choosing alternative medications. In such cases, we're trying to avoid pharmacodynamic interactions.

Pharmacokinetic interactions are harder to predict, since they are non-intuitive and are unrelated to the pharmacologic action of drugs. Pharmacokinetic interactions depend on where and when two or more drugs come in contact during drug processing. Drugs can interact with one another at four different junctures:

- Absorption (getting the drug into the bloodstream)
- Distribution (ferrying drugs to different tissues once they've been absorbed)
- Metabolism (dismantling drugs into simpler components)
- Excretion (sending drugs into the sewage system)

We'll discuss each one in turn, focusing on some common examples in psychopharmacology.

Absorption. Drug-food, rather than drug-drug, interactions are most relevant during absorption. For example, ziprasidone (Geodon) and lurasidone (Latuda) absorption is decreased by 50%-60% when taken without food, which is why we instruct our patients to take these drugs after a full meal (at least, we *should* be doing this!). Food also speeds absorption of both sertraline (Zoloft) and quetiapine, but only by 25% or so, usually not enough to be clinically relevant. Meanwhile, food famously *slows* absorption of erectile dysfunction drugs such as sildenafil (Viagra) and vardenafil (Levitra)—but not tadalafil (Cialis).

Distribution. Valproic acid (Depakote) is highly protein bound, and only the unbound portion (the "free fraction") of the drug has a therapeutic effect. Aspirin is also highly protein bound, so if your patient combines the two drugs, the aspirin will kick some of the valproic acid off its protein—mainly albumin—which would cause the free fraction of the drug to increase. Standard valproic acid levels in the lab usually do not distinguish between free and bound fractions, so a serum level might be normal, even though the actual functioning valproic acid can be very high—and this could potentially cause side effects. One way to check for this interaction is to order a free valproate level; the normal therapeutic range is about 5 mcg/mL-10 mcg/mL, much less than the total valproic acid therapeutic range of about 40 mcg/mL-100 mcg/mL.

Excretion. Lithium, unlike almost all other drugs in psychiatry, is not metabolized. Instead, it is excreted unchanged in the urine. Because of this, liver disease does not affect lithium levels, but changes in kidney function will affect such levels. Caffeine, for example, speeds up kidney function and can reduce lithium levels. On the other hand, ibuprofen (along with other NSAIDs) and ACE inhibitors decrease lithium excretion, increase lithium levels, and could potentially cause toxic effects.

Liver metabolism. Most drug–drug interactions take place in the liver, where drugs are processed in order to render them water soluble, so that the body can excrete them via the urine or feces. There are two phases of liver metabolism. Phase I involves the famous cytochrome P-450 enzymes, or CYP450. These enzymes attack drugs in a variety of ways, such as hydroxylation (adding a hydroxyl group), dealkylation (taking away an alkyl group), and several others. Unfortunately for those of us trying to remember drug interactions, there are many subfamilies of CYP450 enzymes: CYP 1A2, 2C19, 2D6, 3A4, and several others. Phase II metabolism continues the process of biotransformation, relying mainly on glucuronidation—which is rarely a factor in drug interactions in psychiatric practice.

Practical Implications of Drug-Drug Interactions

To understand drug–drug interactions, you'll need to refamiliarize yourself with some basic terms. Drugs are **substrates** of specific enzymes (the medication relies on that/those enzymatic pathway(s) for metabolism). An **inhibitor** is a drug that binds more tightly to an enzyme than the usual substrate and prevents the enzyme from doing its job; as a result, the substrate for that enzyme gets stuck in a game of musical chairs as it scurries around looking for a free enzyme system to break it down. Since this drug is not getting metabolized as quickly as it otherwise would (the inhibitor is preventing it from doing so), its serum levels become higher than expected. On the other hand, **inducers** stimulate the production of extra enzymes. With more enzymes around, the substrate for that enzyme is broken down more rapidly, leading to lower levels.

Now that you know the basics, how can you most efficiently apply them to your practice? Here are some suggestions.

* Identify the 10 drugs that you most commonly prescribe, and memorize the major drug interactions for each one.
* Antidepressants, antipsychotics, antibiotics, antiretrovirals, and older anticonvulsants have a high likelihood of significant drug interactions—so be particularly vigilant if your patient is taking any of these.
* Recognize the drugs with a narrow therapeutic window, ie, when the toxic dose is not much higher than the therapeutic dose. Commonly used narrow therapeutic window drugs include lithium, carbamazepine (Tegretol), warfarin (Coumadin), digoxin, phenytoin (Dilantin), and phenobarbital.
* Recognize drugs that cause serious side effects and outcomes if blood levels are significantly decreased or increased (eg, oral contraceptives, lamotrigine, clozapine, TCAs, warfarin).
* Drugs with long half-lives, such as diazepam (Valium) or aripiprazole (Abilify), can be particularly troublesome when involved in drug interactions, because metabolic inhibitors—or hepatic dysfunction—can make them ultra long lasting. Be cautious with any new or rarely prescribed drugs: Neither you nor anybody else has had much experience with them, and unreported drug interactions can appear.
* The risk of drug interactions can increase exponentially as the number of drugs increases. Setting a threshold to check for interactions is helpful (eg, any patient on 3 or more drugs).

Another important concern with drug interactions is timing. *Inhibition* happens quickly. It can occur with the first dose of a medication and it can subside quickly. How long it takes to subside depends on the inhibitor's half-life. Generally, the inhibition will stop after 5 half-lives. On the other hand, for *induction* to occur, the body has to synthesize more CYP450 enzymes, and this can take up to 4 weeks. This accounts for the delayed "auto-induction" of carbamazepine. Likewise, for induction to subside, these extra enzymes need to be broken down, a process that could also take several weeks. As a general rule of thumb, any drug prescribed with its inhibitor should be started at half the usual dose and titrated more slowly. Conversely, a drug prescribed with its inducer may need to be dosed higher after the few weeks it takes for induction to occur.

Useful References for Drug Interactions

It's ideal to have a useful resource to use to look up interaction information. The task of keeping track of interactions has become less daunting with the advent of free software from companies like Epocrates (www.epocrates.com) and Medscape (www.medscape.com), which allow you to check for potential interactions among all possible combinations of drugs.

But there are various problems with the computerized databases you'll find at these sites or, if you have one, in your electronic prescribing system. For one, they tend to be overly inclusive, often listing every conceivable interaction, no matter how unlikely. For example, citalopram (Celexa), an SSRI considered by most of us to be a pretty safe choice in combination with just about any drug, looks pretty dangerous in the Epocrates database. Moreover, these databases are often populated with drug-class information rather than medication-specific information, making important nuances unavailable to the user. That's where your clinical judgment and experience come in!

Free

- Medscape (www.medscape.com/druginfo/druginterchecker)
- www.epocrates.com (you'll need to register first)
- www.drugs.com/drug_interactions.html
- medicine.iupui.edu/clinpharm/ddis

Not free

- Lexi-Interact (http://bit.ly/fugKmk), $75 1-year subscription

We also provide a table, CYP450 Drug Interactions for Some Commonly Prescribed Medications, on the following pages for your reference (Adapted from Goren J & Carlat D, *The Carlat Psychiatry Report* 2011;9(2):1-5).

Intentionally Left Blank

Appendix A Table: CYP450 Drug Interactions for Some Commonly Prescribed Medications

CYP450 Family	Inducers	Inhibitors	Substrates ("Victim" Drugs)	Symptoms When Induced	Symptoms When Inhibited
1A2	Carbamazepine Cigarette smoke Modafinil Omeprazole Rifampin Ritonavir St. John's wort	Ciprofloxacin Fluvoxamine (melatonin) Norfloxacin	Asenapine	Loss of efficacy (psychosis)	Insomnia/EPS
			Caffeine	Withdrawal headaches	Jitteriness
			Clozapine	Loss of efficacy (psychosis)	Seizures / sedation / anticholinergic effects
			Duloxetine	Loss of efficacy (depression)	Increased blood pressure
			Fluvoxamine	Loss of efficacy (depression/OCD)	GI/sedation
			Melatonin	Loss of efficacy (insomnia)	Sedation
			Mirtazapine	Loss of efficacy (depression)	Sedation
			Olanzapine	Loss of efficacy (psychosis)	Sedation
			Ramelteon	Loss of efficacy (insomnia)	Sedation
			Thiothixene	Loss of efficacy (psychosis)	EPS
			Trifluoperazine	Loss of efficacy (psychosis)	EPS
2B6	Carbamazepine Phenobarbital Phenytoin Rifampin	Clopidogrel Ketoconazole Ticlopidine	Bupropion	Loss of efficacy (depression)	Seizures/jitteriness/insomnia
			Methadone	Opiate withdrawal	CNS and respiratory depression
			Selegiline	Loss of efficacy (depression)	Insomnia/diarrhea
2C9	Barbiturates Carbamazepine Rifampin St. John's wort	Fluconazole Fluoxetine Fluvoxamine Isoniazid Metronidazole	NSAIDs	Loss of pain control	GI effects
			Methadone	Opiate withdrawal	CNS and respiratory depression
			Oral hypoglycemics	Loss of glycemic control	Hypoglycemia
			Tricyclics	Loss of efficacy (depression/anxiety)	Seizures/arrhythmia/anticholinergic
			Warfarin	Loss of anticoagulant efficacy	Increased bleeding
2C19	Barbiturates Carbamazepine Rifampin	Fluconazole Fluoxetine Fluvoxamine Modafinil Oxcarbazepine	Barbiturates	Loss of efficacy (insomnia / anxiety / seizures)	Sedation/barb intoxication
			Citalopram	Loss of efficacy (depression/anxiety)	GI effects
			Diazepam	Loss of efficacy (insomnia / anxiety / seizures)	Sedation/BZD intoxication
			Doxepin	Loss of efficacy (depression/anxiety/insomnia)	Seizures/arrhythmia/anticholinergic
			Escitalopram	Loss of efficacy (depression/anxiety)	GI effects
			Methadone	Opiate withdrawal	CNS and respiratory depression
			Sertraline	Loss of efficacy (depression/anxiety)	GI effects
			Tricyclics	Loss of efficacy (depression/anxiety)	Seizures/arrhythmia/anticholinergic

CYP450 Family	Inducers	Inhibitors	Substrates ("Victim" Drugs)	Symptoms When Induced	Symptoms When Inhibited
2D6	Not inducible	Asenapine Bupropion Duloxetine Fluoxetine (Haloperidol) Methadone Paroxetine (Perphenazine) (Thioridazine) (Venlafaxine)	Aripiprazole	NA	Akathisia/sedation
			Atomoxetine	NA	GI/constipation
			Brexpiprazole	NA	Akathisia/sedation
			Chlorpromazine	NA	Seizures/sedation/anticholinergic effects
			Clozapine	NA	Seizures/sedation/anticholinergic effects
			Codeine/hydrocodone	NA	Less/no analgesia (not converted to morphine)
			Diphenhydramine	NA	Sedation/anticholinergic
			Doxepin	NA	Sedation/anticholinergic
			Doxylamine	NA	Sedation/anticholinergic
			Duloxetine	NA	Increased BP
			Fluoxetine	NA	GI effects
			Fluphenazine	NA	EPS
			Fluvoxamine	NA	GI effects/sedation
			Galantamine	NA	GI effects
			Haloperidol	NA	EPS
			Iloperidone	NA	Tachycardia/hypotension/stiffness
			Loxapine	NA	EPS/sedation
			Methamphetamine	NA	Insomnia/decreased appetite
			Mirtazapine	NA	Somnolence
			Mixed amphetamine salts	NA	Insomnia/decreased appetite
			Paroxetine	NA	GI effects/anticholinergic/sedation
			Perphenazine	NA	EPS/sedation
			Risperidone	NA	EPS/orthostasis
			Thioridazine	NA	Seizures/sedation/anticholinergic effects/QT prolongation
			Trazodone	NA	Sedation
			Tricyclics	NA	Seizures/arrhythmia/anticholinergic
			Venlafaxine	NA	GI effects
			Vortioxetine	NA	GI effects

CYP450 Family	Inducers	Inhibitors	Substrates ("Victim" Drugs)	Symptoms When Induced	Symptoms When Inhibited
3A4	Barbiturates Carbamazepine Modafinil Oxcarbazepine Phenytoin Rifampin St. John's wort (Topiramate)	Clarithromycin Fluconazole Fluvoxamine Grapefruit juice Ketoconazole Protease inhibitors	Alprazolam	Loss of efficacy (insomnia / anxiety / seizures)	Sedation/BZD intoxication
			Aripiprazole	Loss of efficacy (psychosis)	Akathisia/sedation
			Brexpiprazole	Loss of efficacy (psychosis)	Akathisia/sedation
			Buprenorphine	Opiate withdrawal	CNS and respiratory depression
			Buspirone	Loss of efficacy (anxiety)	GI effects/jitteriness
			Calcium channel blockers	Loss of efficacy (hypertension)	Hypotension
			Carbamazepine	Loss of efficacy/seizures	Sedation/arrhythmia
			Citalopram	Loss of efficacy (depression/anxiety)	GI effects
			Clonazepam	Loss of efficacy (insomnia / anxiety / seizures)	Sedation/BZD intoxication
			Clozapine	Loss of efficacy (psychosis)	Seizures/sedation/anticholinergic effects
			Diazepam	Loss of efficacy (insomnia / anxiety / seizures)	Sedation/BZD intoxication
			Donepezil	Loss of efficacy (dementia)	GI effects
			Escitalopram	Loss of efficacy (depression/anxiety)	GI effects
			Flibanserin	Loss of efficacy (sexual desire)	Nausea/dizziness/sedation
			Galantamine	Loss of efficacy (dementia)	GI effects
			Guanfacine	Loss of efficacy (ADHD)	Sedation/dry mouth/dizziness
			Iloperidone	Loss of efficacy (psychosis)	Sedation/dizziness
			Levomilnacipran	Loss of efficacy (depression)	GI effects
			Loxapine	Loss of efficacy (psychosis)	EPS/sedation
			Lurasidone	Loss of efficacy (psychosis)	Sedation/akathisia
			Methadone	Opiate withdrawal	CNS and respiratory depression
			Mirtazapine	Loss of efficacy (depression/insomnia)	Somnolence
			Oral contraceptives	Loss of efficacy (pregnancy)	GI effects
			Quetiapine	Loss of efficacy (psychosis)	Sedation/orthostasis
			Statins (not pravastatin)	Loss of efficacy (hyperlipidemia)	Rhabdomyolysis
			Sildenafil/tadalafil/vardenafil/avanafil	Loss of efficacy (sexual dysfunction)	Headache/flushing/prolonged erection
			Suvorexant	Loss of efficacy (insomnia)	Sedation/confusion
			Tiagabine	Loss of efficacy (seizures)	Dizziness/somnolence/difficulty concentrating
			Trazodone	Loss of efficacy (insomnia)	Sedation/orthostasis
			Triazolam	Loss of efficacy (insomnia / anxiety / seizures)	Sedation/BZD intoxication
			Tricyclics	Loss of efficacy (depression/anxiety)	Seizures/arrhythmia/anticholinergic

CYP450 Family	Inducers	Inhibitors	Substrates ("Victim")	Symptoms When Induced	Symptoms When Inhibited
			Vilazodone	Loss of efficacy (depression/anxiety)	GI effects
			"Z drugs" (zaleplon, zolpidem, eszopiclone)	Loss of efficacy (insomnia)	Sedation/confusion
			Ziprasidone	Loss of efficacy (psychosis)	Sedation/akathisia

( ) indicates less potent inhibitory effect, therefore generally less of a risk except at higher doses

Appendix B: Psychiatric Medications in Pregnancy and Lactation

Pregnancy presents a unique problem to the psychiatrist. Contrary to what many may think or assume, pregnancy does not protect a woman from an acute episode, a recurrence, or an exacerbation of psychiatric illness. Withholding medications during pregnancy can *sometimes* be an appropriate option, but this is generally not recommended. And since all psychotropic medications cross the placenta to at least *some* degree, their potential effects on the fetus, on labor and delivery, and on the neonate must be considered and balanced with the risk of *not* treating the mother with medication. A similar risk-benefit assessment must be considered in the case of a mother who wishes to breastfeed her child, as psychotropic medications are excreted into breast milk to varying degrees.

One of us (TP) is a pharmacist specializing in psychopharmacology, and I am commonly consulted by psychiatrists to provide updated information on the safety of medications in pregnancy and breastfeeding. It is a difficult task, because the quantity and quality of data vary greatly. I developed the accompanying table by pulling together a variety of sources, including isolated case reports, case series, birth registries, retrospective surveys, prospective comparative cohort studies, case control studies, and meta-analyses. Making judgments about which medication to use—or not use—in a pregnant or lactating woman is a delicate balancing act, involving an assessment of the severity of the underlying illness versus the uncertainties inherent in prescribing medications when the available data are limited.

In reading the following table, keep the following in mind: In the general US population, the baseline rate of major malformations is between 1% and 4%, depending on the population studied and the definitions of "malformations" used. If treatment is necessary, monotherapy with the lowest effective dose and for the shortest duration is prudent. Safety data are generally more robust with older agents, and for that reason older agents—with a few key exceptions—are more preferable than newer drugs with less established safety profiles.

Almost all drugs enter breast milk. The exposure to the infant is described as a percentage of the maternal dose—that is, how much of the weight-adjusted maternal dose is actually excreted into the breast milk. When less than 10% of a mother's dose of medication is excreted into the breast milk, it is generally considered compatible with breastfeeding (with some exceptions) since these low serum levels are unlikely to lead to adverse effects in the infant.

While the table provided here summarizes the current knowledge about psychotropic medication in pregnancy and lactation, it is important to note that information in this area is constantly evolving. If you regularly treat women of childbearing age, we suggest that you keep up with new data, consult with experts in this area, and utilize available resources such as the Organization of Teratology Information Specialists at www.mothertobaby.org or 866-626-6847, Motherisk at www.motherisk.org (see "Drugs in Pregnancy" and "Breastfeeding and Drugs" links), or the LactMed database of the National Library of Medicine at http://1.usa.gov/15eWNH. Another good resource is the MGH Center for Women's Mental Health at womensmentalhealth.org. These resources, along with our table, provide information based upon the available evidence (or lack thereof), but the ultimate clinical decision comes down to careful and individualized consideration between the physician and the patient and her family.

Additional References:

- Cohen LS et al, *Psychiatr Clin N Am* 2010;33(2):273-293
- Einarson A, *Can J Clin Pharmacol* 2009;16(1):e58-e65
- Gentile S, *Schizophrenia Bulletin* 2010;36(3):518-544
- Menson SJ, *Arch Gynecol Obstet* 2008;277:1-13
- Myla ME, *Can J Clin Pharmacol* 2009;16(1):e49-e57
- Oyebode F et al, *Pharmacology & Therapeutics* 2012;135:71-77
- Rowe H et al, *Child Adolesc Psychiatric Clin N Am* 2015;24:1-20
- Sachs HC et al, *Pediatrics* 2013;132(3):e796-e809
- Yonkers KA et al, *General Hospital Psychiatry* 2009;31(5):403-413

Appendix B Table: Psychiatric Medications in Pregnancy and Lactation

Medication	Pregnancy	Breastfeeding	Recommendations
Anxiolytics/hypnotics			
Benzodiazepines (various agents)	Possible increased incidence of cleft lip or palate; floppy infant syndrome; neonatal withdrawal syndrome	Excretion varies with different benzodiazepines, but it is always less than 10%. Excessive sedation in infant, lethargy with consequent feeding difficulty and weight loss reported.	Try to avoid use in first trimester. Lorazepam (Ativan) may be best in class to use due to lack of active metabolites and relatively shorter half-life.
Buspirone (BuSpar)	Fewer data; difficult to determine risks	Low to undetectable infant levels reported	Due to lack of data, other agents with larger safety database should be considered first
Diphenhydramine (Benadryl)	Fairly consistent data show lack of associated malformations	Larger doses or more prolonged use may cause adverse effects in the infant	Considered to be the safest hypnotic in pregnancy and breastfeeding
Suvorexant (Belsomra)	No data	No data	Best to use other agents with data and longer record of experience
Trazodone (Desyrel, Oleptro)	Fewer data show no increased risk of malformations	<1% excretion; not expected to cause adverse effects in breastfed infants	Probably safe
Non-benzodiazepines: Eszopiclone (Lunesta) Zaleplon (Sonata) Zolpidem (Ambien)	Fewer data show no increased risk of malformations	Relatively low levels in breast milk. Most data are with zolpidem. Zolpidem is relatively hydrophilic and excreted rapidly; therefore, may be favored.	Reserve for second-line use due to paucity of data. If unavoidable, use zolpidem, at lowest dose possible.
Mood stabilizers			
Valproate (Depakote)	Most teratogenic of all mood stabilizers, with a 6.2%–20.3% rate of congenital malformations, with neural tube defects most prominent. Teratogenic effects are dose-related with greatest risk at doses >1000 mg per day.	Relatively low excretion (0.68%); considered compatible with breastfeeding	Best to avoid in pregnancy unless absolutely required
Lithium (Eskalith, Lithobid)	Rate of major malformations reported to be 4%–12%. Increased risk of cardiovascular malformation, Ebstein's anomaly; risk is lower than previously thought (0.05%–0.1%). Increased maternal risk of diabetes, polyhydramnios, thyroid dysfunction during pregnancy.	30%–50% excretion; not recommended due to high risk of toxicity	Avoid, particularly in first trimester. Check serum levels and thyroid function frequently during pregnancy. Changes in metabolism and total body water necessitate frequent dose adjustment, particularly in third trimester.
Carbamazepine (Tegretol)	Rate of major malformation reported to be 2.2%–7.9%. Neural tube defects (0.5%–1%), craniofacial defects, cardiovascular malformations, and hypospadias reported.	Relatively high levels in breast milk but with few adverse effects reported. Sedation, poor sucking, withdrawal reactions, and 3 cases of hepatic dysfunction have been reported.	Avoid if possible
Lamotrigine (Lamictal)	Rate of major malformations reported to be 1%–5.6%. Increased risk of oral clefts (0.4%).	Based on limited data, thought to be safe; however, infant exposure can be high and can vary widely (reports of 18%–60% of maternal concentrations); monitor infant. Relatively high infant exposure (22.7%); avoid or exercise caution.	Considered to be the safest of the anticonvulsants, though good safety data is sparse
Oxcarbazepine (Trileptal)	Unlike carbamazepine, there is no epoxide metabolite formed, so oxcarbazepine may be less teratogenic; a Danish study showed no increased risk of major malformation. However, data with oxcarbazepine are limited.	Limited information suggests oxcarbazepine would not be expected to cause adverse effects in breastfed infants, especially if the infant is older than 2 months. Monitor infant for drowsiness, adequate weight gain, and developmental milestones, especially in younger, exclusively breastfed infants and when using combinations of anticonvulsants.	Use caution until more data available

Medication	Pregnancy	Breastfeeding	Recommendations
Antipsychotics			
Conventionals	No increased risk of malformations seen with high-potency agents. Small increased risk with low-potency agents such as chlorpromazine (Thorazine). Transient extrapyramidal side effects; sedation; withdrawal symptoms in neonates.	Relatively low excretion reported although little data available. Sedation and parkinsonism effects possible in breastfed infants.	Haloperidol (Haldol), fluphenazine (Prolixin) favored during pregnancy because of long history of safe use
Atypicals	Fewer data available, most showing no increased risk of malformations. Maternal hyperglycemia, impaired glucose tolerance, and weight gain may lead to maternal complications. Large-for-gestational-age infants reported.	Excretion low, usually <3%, with exception of clozapine (Clozaril), which is seen in relatively high concentrations in breast milk	Second-line after conventional due to paucity of data
Antidepressants			
Tricyclics	Relatively large database; recent meta-analysis of 300,000 live births revealed no increased risk of malformations. Neonatal anticholinergic effects. Transient neonatal withdrawal symptoms reported.	<1%–5% excretion; appear relatively safe during breastfeeding, with possible exception of doxepin	Well characterized and considered reasonable options. Desipramine (Norpramin), nortriptyline (Pamelor) preferred due to lower anticholinergic and orthostatic hypotension risks.
SSRIs	Controversial data regarding cardiovascular malformation with first trimester paroxetine (Paxil) exposure. Larger and more recent studies show no overall increased risk for malformations with SSRIs. Conflicting reports with some showing decreased gestational age, low birth weight, poor neonatal adaptation, low APGAR scores. Conflicting reports regarding SSRI use in later pregnancy and persistent pulmonary hypertension (PPHN). Neonatal toxicity reported as transient jitteriness, tremulousness and tachypnea. No problems detected in behavioral or cognitive development—greatest data with fluoxetine (Prozac).	Relatively low excretion, varies by agent: • Fluoxetine (Zoloft): 3%–9% • Paroxetine: <4% • Sertraline (Zoloft): <2% • Citalopram (Celexa): 5%–10% • Fluvoxamine (Luvox): <2%	Sertraline results in lowest fetal drug exposure and lowest (undetectable) levels in breastfed infants; may be considered favored SSRI. Paroxetine use most controversial. Fluoxetine less favored for breastfeeding due to long half-life and active metabolite; disturbed sleep, colic, irritability, poor feeding reported.
Duloxetine (Cymbalta)	Little data	No published data, though exposure is low	Other agents with more data favored
Levomilnacipran (Fetzima)	No data	No published data	Other agents with more data favored
Mirtazapine (Remeron)	Sparse data, but one small study suggests no increased rate of major malformation	Low excretion; compatible with breastfeeding	May be useful also for pregnancy-associated emesis, insomnia
Venlafaxine/desvenlafaxine (Pristiq)	Earlier data regarding major malformations reassuring, but one more recent study suggested a possible association with birth defects; additional studies needed. Increased maternal blood pressure may be a concern during pregnancy, particularly at higher doses.	2%–9.2% excretion; no adverse outcomes reported	Other agents with more data favored
Vilazodone (Viibryd)	No data	No published data	Other agents with more data favored
Vortioxetine (Brintellix)	No data	No published data	Other agents with more data favored
Bupropion (Wellbutrin)	No increased risk of malformation shown thus far	<1% excretion with no adverse outcomes reported	Well characterized and considered reasonable option. May also help with smoking cessation during pregnancy.

Medication	Pregnancy	Breastfeeding	Recommendations
Stimulants			
Amphetamines and methylphenidate	No apparent congenital malformations; may constrict blood flow to placenta, which reduces oxygen flow to developing fetus. May cause premature delivery, small-for-gestational-age and low-birth-weight babies; however, data inconclusive. Neonatal withdrawal possible.	0.2% excreted into breast milk; adverse effects usually not observed	Caution in pregnancy due to possibility of vasoconstriction and ability to disrupt blood flow to the fetus

Appendix C Table: Schedules of Controlled Substances

In 1970, under the Controlled Substance Act, the FDA created classification schedules that organize drugs into groups based on their risk of abuse or harm. There are 5 classifications of these controlled substances (Schedule I, II, III, IV, and V), and drugs with the highest risk to benefit ratio are considered Schedule I drugs. Most drugs used in psychiatry are not scheduled at all (antidepressants, antipsychotics, etc.). Some of us get confused about whether the most restricted drugs are Schedule I or V. Here's a mnemonic: The number 1 looks like a needle, and a needle is used to inject heroin—which is the prototypical Schedule I drug.

Schedule	Description	Prescribing Implications	Some Examples
I	No accepted medical use, high potential for abuse, illegal to possess or use	Can't be prescribed at all (with the exception of medical marijuana in some states)	• Heroin, LSD, ecstasy, and others • Marijuana (though legalized in some states, it is still illegal at the federal level)
II	High potential for abuse but legal for medical use	Can be prescribed only 1 month at a time, cannot be refilled, cannot be called in, and patient must give pharmacy a paper script (unless you use an e-prescribing program that is certified by DEA to allow prescribing of controlled substances)	• All psychostimulants, such as amphetamine and methylphenidate • Opiates that are especially potent, such as oxycodone, Fentanyl, and others
III	Lower potential for abuse than Schedule I or II, but still pretty abusable	Can be refilled up to 5 times (no more than 6 months), can be called in	• Suboxone (buprenorphine/naloxone) • Ketamine • Xyrem (sodium oxybate) • Some opiates when they are combined with other agents (eg, Vicodin, which is hydrocodone combined with Tylenol) • Tramadol (Ultram) • Carisoprodol (Soma)
IV	Lower potential for abuse than Schedule III	Can be refilled up to 5 times (no more than 6 months), can be called in	• All benzodiazepines (eg, clonazepam, lorazepam, etc.) • Various hypnotics, such as zolpidem, zaleplon, and suvorexant (Belsomra) • Wake-promoting agents, like modafinil and armodafinil
V	Lowest potential for abuse	Can be refilled as many times as prescriber chooses (eg, for 1 year or more), can be called in	• Cough preparations with small amounts of codeine, such as Robitussin AC • Pregabalin (Lyrica)

An updated and more complete list of the schedules is published annually in Title 21 Code of Federal Regulations and can be found here: www.deadiversion.usdoj.gov/21cfr/cfr/2108cfrt.htm

Appendix D Table: Lab Monitoring for Psychiatric Medications

Medications	Recommended Laboratory Tests
Antipsychotics—second generation, primarily clozapine, olanzapine, quetiapine, paliperidone, risperidone[1]	Fasting glucose and lipids
Atomoxetine	LFTs
Carbamazepine	CBZ level, CBC, sodium, LFTs, pregnancy test, HLA-B*1502[2] in Asians
Citalopram	ECG if cardiac disease
Clozapine	Fasting glucose and lipids, complete blood count (CBC)
Desvenlafaxine	Periodic BP
Duloxetine	LFTs if suspect liver disease[3]
Levomilnacipran	Periodic BP/pulse rate
Lithium	Li level, TSH, BUN/creatinine[4], pregnancy test, ECG if cardiac disease
Mirtazapine	Lipids
Naltrexone	LFTs if suspect liver disease
Oxcarbazepine	Sodium, HLA-B*1502[5] in Asians
Paliperidone	Prolactin, fasting glucose and lipids
Phenelzine	LFTs
Risperidone	Prolactin, fasting glucose and lipids
SSRIs	Sodium in elderly if fatigue, dizziness, confusion
Stimulants	ECG if cardiac disease
Topiramate	Bicarbonate
Tricyclic antidepressants	ECG if cardiac disease
Valproic acid	VPA level, LFTs, CBC for platelets, pregnancy test
Venlafaxine	Periodic BP
Ziprasidone	ECG if cardiac disease

[1] Some guidelines recommend monitoring glucose and lipids with all SGAs.

[2] HLA-B*1502 is a gene that increases the risk of developing toxic epidermal necrolysis (TEN) and Stevens-Johnson syndrome (SJS) in response to taking carbamazepine. Asians, especially the Han Chinese, are much more likely to have the gene than other populations.

[3] Duloxetine should not be prescribed in patients with significant alcohol use or evidence of chronic liver disease as it can lead to hepatic failure in rare cases (Cymbalta prescribing information). While the manufacturer does not recommend baseline LFTs for all patients, some clinicians do so anyway to be extra cautious.

[4] The serum creatinine is used to compute the estimated glomerular filtration rate (eGFR), a more precise measure of kidney functioning. Increasingly, laboratory test results include the estimated GFR. You can calculate it yourself using an online calculator at www.niddk.nih.gov/health-information/health-communication-programs/nkdep/lab-evaluation/gfr-calculators/Pages/gfr-calculators.aspx.

[5] HLA-B*1502 is a gene that increases the risk of developing toxic epidermal necrolysis (TEN) and Stevens-Johnson syndrome (SJS) in response to taking carbamazepine. Asians, especially the Han Chinese, are much more likely to have the gene than other populations.

Index

Note: Trade names are capitalized, bolded page numbers are for fact sheets, and non-bolded page numbers are for quick-scan tables.

A

Abilify 44, **46**
Abilify Maintena **46**, 68
acamprosate 134, **136**
Adasuve 43, **55**
Adderall 9, **20**
Adderall XR 9, **20**
Alprazolam 71, **72**
Ambien 89, **98**
amitriptyline 24, **36**
Anafranil 24, **36**
Antabuse 134, **140**
antihistamines **90**
Aplenzin **26**
Aptensio XR 8, **18**
Aricept 80, **81**
aripiprazole 44, **46**, 68
armodafinil **129**
asenapine 44, **47**
Ativan 71, **76**
atomoxetine 10, **11**
avanafil 120, **121**

B

Belsomra 88, **94**
Benadryl 88, **90**
brexpiprazole 44, **48**
Brintellix 25, **39**
Brisdelle 23, **33**
Budeprion SR, XL 24, **26**
Buprenex 134, **137**
buprenorphine 134, **137**
buprenorphine/naloxone 134, **138**
bupropion 10, 24, **26**
BuSpar 71, **73**
buspirone 71, **73**

C

Campral 134, **136**
carbamazepine 100, **101**
cariprazine 44, **49**
Celexa 23, **32**, 33
Chantix 135, **148**
chlorpromazine 43, **50**
Cialis 120, **125**
citalopram 23, **32**, 33
clomipramine 24, **36**
clonazepam 71, **74**
clonidine XR 10
clozapine 44, **51**

Clozaril 44, **51**
Concerta 8, **18**
Cymbalta 23, **28**
cyproheptadine 120, **122**

D

Daytrana 8, **19**
Depakote 100, **105**
Deplin 107, **108**
desipramine 24, **36**
Desoxyn 9, **16**
desvenlafaxine 23, **27**, 160, 163
Dexedrine 9, **13**
Dexedrine Spansules 9, **13**
dexmethylphenidate 8, **12**
dextroamphetamine 9, **13**
diazepam 71, **75**
diphenhydramine 88, **90**
Disulfiram 134, **140**
Dolophine 134, **141**
donepezil 80, **81**
doxepin 88, **91**
doxylamine 88, **90**
duloxetine 23, **28**
Dyanavel XR 9, **13**

E

Effexor 23
Effexor XR 23, **37**
Elavil 24
EMSAM 24, **34**
escitalopram 23, **32**, 33
eszopiclone 88, **92**
Evekeo 9, **13**
Evzio 134, **142**
Exelon 80, **85**
Exelon Patch 80, **85**

F

Fanapt 45, **54**
FazaClo 44, **51**
Fetzima 23, **29**
fish oil 107, **110**
flibanserin 120, **123**
fluoxetine 23, **32**, 33
fluoxetine weekly 23, **33**
fluphenazine 43, **52**
fluphenazine decanoate 68
fluvoxamine 23, **32**, 33
Focalin 8, **12**
Forfivo XL 24, **26**

G

gabapentin 114, **115**
Gabitril 114, **117**
galantamine 80, **82**
Geodon 45, **65**
guanfacine 10, **14**

H

Halcion 89, **96**
Haldol 43, **53**
Haldol Decanoate 43, 68
haloperidol 43, **53**
haloperidol decanoate 43, 68

I

iloperidone 44, **54**
imipramine 24, **36**
Inderal 71, **78**
Intuniv 10, **14**
Invega 45, **58**
Invega Sustenna **58**, 67, 69
Invega Trinza **58**, 67, 69
isocarboxazid 24, **31**

K

Kapvay 10
Klonopin 71, **74**
Klonopin Wafers 71, **74**

L

LAIs **66**, 68–69
Lamictal 100, **102**
lamotrigine 100, **102**
Latuda 45, **56**
Levitra 120, **127**
levomilnacipran 23, **29**
Lexapro 23, **32**, 33
lisdexamfetamine 10, **15**
lithium 100, **103**
Lithobid 100, **103**
L-methylfolate 107, **108**
long-acting injectable antipsychotics **66**, 68–69
lorazepam 71, **76**
Lovaza **110**
loxapine 43, **55**
Loxitane 43, **55**
Lunesta 88, **92**
lurasidone 45, **56**
Luvox IR, CR 23, **32**, 33
Lyrica 114, **116**

M

MAOIs 24. **31**
Marplan 24. **31**
melatonin 107. **109**
Mellaril 43. **62**
Memantine 80. **83**
Memantine ER 80. **84**
Metadate CD 8. **18**
Metadate ER 8. **18**
methadone 134. **141**
Methadose 134. **141**
methamphetamine 9, **16**
Methylin, Methylin CT 8, **17**
Methylin ER 8, **18**
methylphenidate ER 8, **18**
methylphenidate IR 8, **17**
methylphenidate transdermal 8, **19**
Minipress 71, **77**
mirtazapine 24, **30**
mixed amphetamine and dextroamphetamine salts 9, **20**
Modafinil 10, **130**
Monoamine oxidase inhibitors 24, **31**

N

naloxone 134, **142**
naltrexone 134, **143**
Namenda 80, **83**
Namzaric 80, **84**
Narcan Nasal Spray 134, **142**
Nardil 24, **31**
Navane 43, **63**
Neurontin 114, **115**
Nicoderm CQ 135, **147**
Nicorette 135, **144**
Nicorette Gum 135, **144**
Nicorette Lozenge 135, **144**
nicotine inhaled 135, **145**
nicotine nasal spray 135, **146**
nicotine patch 135, **147**
nicotine polacrilex 135, **146**
Nicotrol Inhaler 135, **145**
Nicotrol NS 135, **146**
Norpramin 24, **36**
nortriptyline 24, **36**
Nuvigil 129

O

olanzapine 45, **57**
Oleptro 24, **35**, 89
omega-3 fatty acids 107, **110**
oxcarbazepine 100, **104**

P

paliperidone 45, **58**
Paliperidone palmitate 45, **58**, 69
Pamelor 24, **36**
Parnate 24, **31**
paroxetine 23, **32**, 33
Paxil IR, CR 23, **32**, 33
perphenazine 43, **59**
Pexeva 23, **32**, 33
phenelzine 24, **31**
prazosin 71, **77**
pregabalin 114, **116**
Pristiq 23, **27**, 160, 163
ProCentra 9, **13**
Prolixin 43, **52**
Prolixin Decanoate 68
Propranolol 71, **78**
Provigil 10, **130**
Prozac 23, **32**, 33
Prozac Weekly 23, 33

Q

quetiapine 45, **60**
Quillichew ER 8, **18**
Quillivant XR 8, **18**

R

ramelteon 88, **93**
Razadyne 80, **82**
Remeron 24, **30**
Restoril 88, **95**
ReVia 134, **143**
Rexulti 44, **48**
Risperdal 45, **61**
Risperdal Consta **61**, 69
risperidone 45, **61**, 69
Ritalin 8, **17**
Ritalin LA 8, **18**
Ritalin SR 8, **18**
rivastigmine 80, **85**
Rozerem 88, **93**

S

s-adenosyl-L-methionine 107, **111**
SAMe 107, **111**
Saphris 44, **47**
Sarafem 23, 33
selective serotonin reuptake inhibitors 23, **32**, 33
selegiline transdermal 24, **34**
Seroquel 45, **60**
sertraline 23, **32**, 33
sildenafil 120, **124**
Silenor 88, **91**
sodium oxybate **131**
Sonata 89, **97**
SSRIs 23, **32**, 33
Stelazine 43, **64**
Stendra 120, 121

St. John's wort 107, **112**
Strattera 10, **11**
Suboxone 134, **138**
suvorexant 88, **94**

T

tadalafil 120, **125**
Tegretol 100, **101**
temazepam 88, **95**
testosterone 120, **126**
thioridazine 43, **62**
thiothixene 43, **63**
Thorazine 43, **50**
tiagabine 114, **117**
Topamax 114, **118**
topiramate 114, **118**
tranylcypromine 24, **31**
trazodone 24, **35**, 89
triazolam 89, **96**
trifluoperazine 43, **64**
Trilafon 43, **59**
Trileptal 100, **104**

V

Valium 71, **75**
valproic acid 100, **105**
vardenafil 120, **127**
varenicline 135, **148**
venlafaxine 23, **37**
Versacloz 44, 51
Viagra 120, **124**
Viibryd 25, **38**
vilazodone 25, **38**
Vivitrol 134, **143**
vortioxetine 25, **39**
Vraylar 44, **49**
Vyvanse 10, **15**

W

Wellbutrin 10, 24, **26**

X

Xanax 71, **72**
Xyrem **131**

Z

zaleplon 89, **97**
Zenzedi 9, **13**
ziprasidone 45, **65**
Zoloft 23, **32**, 33
zolpidem 89, **98**
Zyban 134, **139**
Zyprexa 45, **57**
Zyprexa Relprevv 45, 68
Zyprexa Zydis 45

2016 Medication Fact Book

Contents

Volume I

MS-DRG Listing by Major Diagnostic Category iii

Introduction xi

National Average Payment Table xxi

Definitions of the MS-DRGs 1

Pre MDC 1

MDC 1   Diseases And Disorders Of The Nervous System 6

MDC 2   Diseases And Disorders Of The Eye 56

MDC 3   Diseases And Disorders Of The Ear, Nose, Mouth And Throat 67

MDC 4   Diseases And Disorders Of The Respiratory System 89

MDC 5   Diseases And Disorders Of The Circulatory System 108

MDC 6   Diseases And Disorders Of The Digestive System 174

MDC 7   Diseases And Disorders Of The Hepatobiliary System And Pancreas 198

MDC 8   Diseases And Disorders Of The Musculoskeletal System And Connective Tissue 210

MDC 9   Diseases And Disorders Of The Skin, Subcutaneous Tissue And Breast 410

MDC 10   Endocrine, Nutritional And Metabolic Diseases And Disorders 479

MDC 11   Diseases And Disorders Of The Kidney And Urinary Tract 504

MDC 12   Diseases And Disorders Of The Male Reproductive System 521

MDC 13   Diseases And Disorders Of The Female Reproductive System 531

MDC 14   Pregnancy, Childbirth And The Puerperium 544

MDC 15   Newborns And Other Neonates With Conditions Originating In The Perinatal Period 559

MDC 16   Diseases And Disorders Of The Blood And Blood-Forming Organs And Immunological Disorders 571

MDC 17   Myeloproliferative Diseases And Disorders And Poorly Differentiated Neoplasms 580

MDC 18   Infectious And Parasitic Diseases, Systemic or Unspecified Sites 632

MDC 19   Mental Diseases And Disorders 635

MDC 20   Alcohol/Drug Use And Alcohol/Drug-Induced Organic Mental Disorders 637

MDC 21   Injuries, Poisonings And Toxic Effects Of Drugs 638

MDC 22   Burns 782

MDC 23   Factors Influencing Health Status And Other Contacts With Health Services 795

MDC 24   Multiple Significant Trauma 848

MDC 25   Human Immunodeficiency Virus Infections 1041

DRGs Associated with All MDCs 1043

Alphabetic Index to Diseases 1101

Alphabetic Index to Procedures 1377

Volume II

Numeric Index to Diseases 1

Numeric Index to Procedures 95

Alphabetic & Numeric Lists of CCs 195

Alphabetic & Numeric Lists of MCCs 343

MS-DRG Surgical Hierarchy Table 377

MS-LTC-DRG Crosswalk 379

Glossary 395

Diagnosis Codes by MDC 397

DRG Decision Trees 487

Numeric Index to Diseases

Note: The page numbers in this index refer to page numbers in *DRG Expert—Volume I*.

Code	Page	Code	Page	Code	Page	Code	Page	Code	Page	Code	Page
A00*	193	A22.9	633	A50.31	61	A56.1*	518	A84.9	14	B08.02	476
A01*	633	A23*	633	A50.32	633	A56.2	529, 533, 541	A84*	54	B08.03	476
A02.0	193	A24*	633	A50.39	633	A56.3	195	A85.0	1041	B08.04	632
A02.1	634, 1041	A25*	633	A50.40	54	A56.4	2, 86	A85.1	1041	B08.09	632
A02.2*	1041	A26.0	633	A50.41	54	A56.8	529, 533, 541	A85.2	14	B08.1	476
A02.20	633	A26.7	634	A50.42	54	A57	529, 533, 541	A85.8	1041	B08.2*	560, 632
A02.21	14, 54	A26.8	633	A50.43	54	A58	529, 533, 541	A85*	54	B08.3	632
A02.22	104	A26.9	633	A50.44	633	A59.00	529, 533, 541	A86	54, 1041	B08.4	632
A02.23	296	A27.0	633	A50.45	54	A59.01	533, 541	A87*	47	B08.5	2, 86
A02.24	294	A27.8*	14, 54	A50.49	54	A59.02	529	A88.0	47	B08.6*	632
A02.25	633	A27.9	633	A50.5*	633	A59.03	529, 533, 541	A88.1	51	B08.7*	632
A02.29	633	A28.0	633	A50.6	633	A59.09	529, 533, 541	A88.8	54, 1041	B08.8	632
A02.8	633, 1041	A28.1	579	A50.7	633	A59.8	633	A89	54, 1041	B09	632
A02.9	633, 1041	A28.2	633	A50.9	633	A59.9	633	A90	632	B10.0*	14, 54, 560, 1041
A03*	193	A28.8	633	A51.0	529, 533, 541	A60.00	529, 533, 541, 1041	A91	632	B10.8*	476
A04*	193	A28.9	633	A51.1	195	A60.01	529, 1041	A92.0	632	B15*	209
A05.0	193	A30*	633	A51.2	633	A60.02	529	A92.1	632	B16*	209, 560
A05.1	633	A31.0	104	A51.3*	476	A60.03	533, 541	A92.2	14, 54	B17*	209, 560
A05.2	193	A31.1	476	A51.41	14, 54	A60.04	533, 541, 1041	A92.3*	632	B18*	209, 560
A05.3	193	A31.2	633, 1041	A51.42	633	A60.09	529, 533, 541, 1041	A92.4	632	B19.0	560
A05.4	193	A31.8	633, 1041	A51.43	61			A92.5	632	B19.1*	560
A05.5	193	A31.9	633, 1041	A51.44	633	A60.1	529, 533, 541, 1041	A92.8	632	B19.9	560
A05.8	193	A32.0	633	A51.45	209			A92.9	632	B19*	209
A05.9	194	A32.1*	633	A51.46	294	A60.9	529, 533, 541, 1041	A93*	632	B20	1041, 1042
A06.0	193	A32.7	634	A51.49	633			A94	632	B25.0	104
A06.1	193	A32.8*	633	A51.5	633	A63.0	476	A95*	632	B25.1	209
A06.2	193	A32.9	633	A51.9	633	A63.8	529, 533, 541	A96*	632	B25.2	208, 560
A06.3	633	A33	568	A52.00	172	A64	529, 533, 541	A98.0	632	B25.8	632, 1041
A06.4	209	A34	544	A52.01	172	A65	633	A98.1	632	B25.9	632, 1041
A06.5	104	A35	559, 633	A52.02	172	A66.0	476	A98.2	632	B26.0	529, 560
A06.6	14, 54	A36.0	2, 86	A52.03	167	A66.1	476	A98.3	632	B26.1	14, 47, 560
A06.7	476	A36.1	2, 86	A52.04	172	A66.2	476	A98.4	632	B26.2	14, 54, 560
A06.8*	633	A36.2	2, 86	A52.05	172	A66.3	476	A98.5	518	B26.3	208, 560
A06.9	633	A36.3	476	A52.06	172	A66.4	476	A98.8	632	B26.8*	560
A07.3	1041	A36.81	172	A52.09	172	A66.5	2, 86	A99	632	B26.81	209
A07*	193	A36.82	633	A52.10	43	A66.6	296	B00.0	476, 559, 1041	B26.82	632
A08*	194	A36.83	633	A52.11	43	A66.7	633	B00.1	86, 559, 1041	B26.83	632
A09	194	A36.84	633	A52.12	43	A66.8	633	B00.2	2, 87, 559, 1041	B26.84	46
A15*	104, 1041	A36.85	518	A52.13	14, 54	A66.9	633	B00.3	14, 47, 559, 1041	B26.85	632
A17.0	14, 54	A36.86	61	A52.14	14, 54	A67.0	476	B00.4	14, 54, 560, 1041	B26.89	632
A17.1	14, 54	A36.89	633	A52.15	43	A67.1	476	B00.5*	61, 560, 1041	B26.9	632
A17.8*	14, 54	A36.9	633	A52.16	43	A67.2	633	B00.7	560, 634, 1041	B27*	632
A17.9	633	A37*	106	A52.17	43	A67.3	476	B00.81	195, 560, 1041	B30*	61
A17*	1041	A38*	633	A52.19	43	A67.9	633	B00.82	14, 54	B33.0	105
A18.01	212, 294	A39.0	14, 54	A52.2	54	A68*	633	B00.89	560, 632, 1041	B33.1	1041
A18.02	227, 296	A39.1	559, 634	A52.3	43	A69.0	2, 87	B00.9	476, 1041	B33.20	172
A18.03	294	A39.2	634	A52.71	61	A69.1	2, 86	B01.0	560, 632	B33.21	172
A18.09	296	A39.3	634	A52.72	104	A69.2*	633	B01.1*	54	B33.22	172
A18.10	518	A39.4	634	A52.73	633	A69.8	633	B01.11	560	B33.23	172
A18.11	518	A39.5*	559	A52.74	209	A69.9	633	B01.12	14	B33.24	632
A18.12	518	A39.50	172	A52.75	518	A70	632	B01.2	104, 560	B33.3	632
A18.13	518	A39.51	167	A52.76	633	A71*	61	B01.8*	632	B33.4	632
A18.14	529	A39.52	172	A52.77	294	A74.0	61	B01.81	560	B33.8	632
A18.15	529	A39.53	172	A52.78	302	A74.8*	632	B01.89	560	B34*	632
A18.16	533, 541	A39.81	14, 54	A52.79	633	A74.9	632	B01.9	560, 632	B35*	476
A18.17	533, 541	A39.82	60, 559	A52.8	633	A75*	633	B02.0	46, 560, 1041	B36*	476
A18.18	533, 541	A39.83	296, 559	A52.9	633	A77*	633	B02.1	47, 560, 1041	B37.0	2, 87, 1041
A18.2	579	A39.84	296, 559	A53*	633	A78	633	B02.21	46, 560, 1041	B37.1	104, 560, 1041
A18.3*	193	A39.89	634	A54.00	529, 533, 541	A79*	633	B02.22	46, 560, 1041	B37.2	476, 1041
A18.4	476	A39.9	634	A54.01	518	A80.0	14, 54	B02.23	46, 560, 1041	B37.3	533, 541
A18.5*	61	A40.9	559, 1041	A54.02	533, 541	A80.1	14, 54	B02.24	14, 54	B37.4*	529
A18.6	86	A40*	634	A54.03	533, 541	A80.2	14, 54	B02.29	46, 560, 1041	B37.41	533, 541
A18.7	502	A41*	559, 634, 1041	A54.09	529, 533, 541	A80.3*	14, 54	B02.3*	61, 560, 1041	B37.49	533, 541
A18.81	502	A42.0	104	A54.1	529, 533, 541	A80.4	632	B02.7	560, 632, 1041	B37.5	14, 54, 560, 1041
A18.82	633	A42.1	193	A54.21	529, 533, 541	A80.9	14, 54	B02.8	560, 632, 1041	B37.6	167, 560, 1041
A18.83	193	A42.2	476	A54.22	529	A81.1	559	B02.9	453, 560, 1041	B37.7	634
A18.84	633	A42.7	559, 634	A54.23	529	A81.2	1041	B03	632	B37.8*	1041
A18.85	579	A42.8*	633	A54.24	533, 541	A81.82	1041	B04	632	B37.81	193, 560
A18.89	633	A42.9	633	A54.29	529, 533, 541	A81.83	1041	B05.0	14, 54, 560	B37.82	194, 560
A18*	1041	A42*	1041	A54.3*	61	A81.89	1041	B05.1	560, 632	B37.83	2, 87
A19*	633, 1041	A43.0	104	A54.40	296	A81.9	1041	B05.2	104, 560	B37.84	86, 560
A20.0	633	A43.1	476	A54.41	294	A81*	43	B05.3	86, 560	B37.89	633
A20.1	633	A43.8	633	A54.42	227, 296	A82.0	14	B05.4	560, 632	B37.9	633, 1041
A20.2	104	A43.9	633	A54.43	296	A82.1	14	B05.8*	560	B38.0	104
A20.3	633	A43*	1041	A54.49	296	A82.9	14	B05.81	61	B38.1	104
A20.7	634	A44*	633	A54.5	2, 86	A82*	54	B05.89	632	B38.2	104
A20.8	633	A46	454	A54.6	195	A83.0	14	B05.9	632	B38.3	476
A20.9	633	A48.0	559, 633	A54.81	14, 54	A83.1	14	B06.0*	560	B38.4	14, 54, 560
A21.0	633	A48.1	104, 559, 1041	A54.82	633	A83.2	14	B06.00	46	B38.7	560, 633
A21.1	633	A48.2	633	A54.83	172	A83.3	14	B06.01	54	B38.81	476
A21.2	104	A48.3	633	A54.84	633	A83.4	14	B06.02	54	B38.89	560, 633
A21.3	193	A48.4	633	A54.85	193	A83.5	14	B06.09	54	B38.9	633
A21.7	633	A48.5*	633	A54.86	634	A83.6	14	B06.8*	560	B38*	1041
A21.8	633	A48.51	559	A54.89	633	A83.8	14	B06.81	632	B39.0	104, 560
A21.9	633	A48.8	633	A54.9	633	A83.9	14	B06.82	301	B39.1	104, 560
A22.0	476	A49*	633	A55	529, 533, 541	A83*	14	B06.89	632	B39.2	104, 560
A22.1	104	A50.0*	633	A56.0*	533, 541	A84.0	14	B06.9	632	B39.3	633
A22.2	193	A50.1	633	A56.00	529	A84.1	14	B07*	476	B39.4	633
A22.7	634	A50.2	633	A56.01	529	A84.8	14	B08.010	632	B39.5	633
A22.8	633	A50.30	633	A56.09	529			B08.011	632	B39.9	633

Numeric Index to Diseases

Code	Page	Code	Page	Code	Page	Code	Page	Code	Page	Code	Page
B39*	1041	B67.8	209	C32*	2,85	C44.612	476	C50.321	450,454	C79.2	450,453,454
B40*	560,633	B67.90	634	C33	104	C44.619	476	C50.322	450,454	C79.3*	43
B41*	560,633	B67.99	634	C34*	104	C44.621	476	C50.329	450,454	C79.4*	43
B42*	633	B68*	194	C37	605,630	C44.622	476	C50.411	450,454	C79.5*	212,295
B43*	633	B69*	193	C38.0	172	C44.629	476	C50.412	450,454	C79.6*	531,541
B44.0	104	B70.0	194	C38.1	104	C44.691	476	C50.419	450,454	C79.7*	502
B44.1	560,633	B70.1	193	C38.2	104	C44.692	476	C50.421	450,454	C79.81	450,453,454
B44.2	560,633	B71*	193	C38.3	104	C44.699	476	C50.422	450,454	C79.82	523,528,533,541
B44.7	560,633	B72	634	C38.4	104	C44.701	476	C50.429	450,454	C79.89	605,630
B44.81	105	B73*	634	C38.8	104	C44.702	476	C50.511	450,454	C79.9	605,630
B44.89	560,633	B74*	634	C39.0	2,85	C44.709	476	C50.512	450,454	C7A.00	605,630
B44.9	560,633	B75	634	C39.9	104	C44.711	476	C50.519	450,454	C7A.010	193
B45.0	633,1041	B76*	193	C40*	294	C44.712	476	C50.521	450,454	C7A.011	193
B45.1	14,54	B77*	194	C41.1	2	C44.719	476	C50.522	450,454	C7A.012	193
B45.2	633,1041	B78.0	194,1041	C41.2	212	C44.721	476	C50.529	450,454	C7A.019	193
B45.3	633,1041	B78.1	454	C41*	295	C44.722	476	C50.611	450,454	C7A.020	180,193
B45.7	633,1041	B78.7	194,1041	C43.0	453	C44.729	476	C50.612	450,454	C7A.021	193
B45.8	633,1041	B78.9	194,1041	C43.10	61	C44.791	476	C50.619	450,454	C7A.022	193
B45.9	633,1041	B79	194	C43.111	61	C44.792	476	C50.621	450,454	C7A.023	193
B45*	560	B80	195	C43.112	61	C44.799	476	C50.622	450,454	C7A.024	193
B46*	560,633	B81.0	195	C43.121	61	C44.80	476	C50.629	450,454	C7A.025	193
B47.0	560,633	B81.1	195	C43.122	61	C44.81	476	C50.811	450,454	C7A.026	193
B47.1	633,1041	B81.2	195	C43.2*	453	C44.82	476	C50.812	450,454	C7A.029	193
B47.9	476,1041	B81.3	195	C43.3*	453	C44.89	476	C50.819	450,454	C7A.090	104
B48.2	560	B81.4	634	C43.4	453	C44.90	476	C50.821	450,454	C7A.091	605,630
B48.4	560	B81.8	195	C43.5*	453	C44.91	476	C50.822	450,454	C7A.092	193
B48.8	560,1041	B82*	195	C43.6*	453	C44.92	476	C50.829	450,454	C7A.093	504,518
B48*	633	B83.0	634	C43.7*	453	C44.99	476	C50.911	450,454	C7A.094	193
B49	633	B83.1	634	C43.8	453	C45.0	104	C50.912	450,454	C7A.095	193
B50*	633	B83.2	634	C43.9	453	C45.1	193	C50.919	450,454	C7A.096	193
B51*	633	B83.3	634	C44.0*	2	C45.2	172	C50.921	450,454	C7A.098	605,630
B52*	633	B83.4	476	C44.00	476	C45.7	605,630	C50.922	450,454	C7A.1	605,630
B53*	633	B83.8	634	C44.01	476	C45.9	605,630	C50.929	450,454	C7A.8	605,630
B54	633	B83.9	476	C44.02	476	C46.0	476	C50*	453	C7B.00	605,630
B55.0	633	B85*	476	C44.09	476	C46.1	476	C51*	533,541	C7B.01	580,604,630
B55.1	476	B86	476	C44.101	61	C46.2	2,85	C52	533,541	C7B.02	208
B55.2	476	B87*	476	C44.1021	61	C46.3	580,604,630	C53*	533,541	C7B.03	212,295
B55.9	633	B88*	476	C44.1022	61	C46.4	193	C54*	533,541	C7B.04	193
B56*	633	B89	634	C44.1091	61	C46.5*	104	C55	533,541	C7B.09	605,630
B57.0	172	B90.0	51	C44.1092	61	C46.7	476	C56*	531,541	C7B.1	605,630
B57.1	633	B90.1	518	C44.111	61	C46.9	476	C57.0*	531	C7B.8	605,630
B57.2	172	B90.2	374	C44.1121	61	C46*	1041	C57.1*	531	C80.0	605,630
B57.3*	633	B90.8	634	C44.1122	61	C47*	295	C57.2*	531	C80.1	605,630
B57.4*	633	B90.9	105	C44.1191	61	C48.0	605,630	C57.3	531	C80.2	605,630
B57.5	633	B91	51	C44.1192	61	C48.1	193	C57.4	531	C81.01	2
B58.0*	560	B92	634	C44.121	61	C48.2	193	C57.7	533	C81.11	2
B58.00	633	B94.0	61	C44.1221	61	C48.8	193	C57.8	533	C81.21	2
B58.01	61	B94.1	51	C44.1291	61	C49.0	295	C57.9	533	C81.31	2
B58.09	61	B94.2	634	C44.1292	61	C49.10	295	C57*	541	C81.41	2
B58.1	209,560	B94.8	634	C44.131	61	C49.11	295	C58	533,541	C81.71	2
B58.2	14,54,560	B94.9	634	C44.1321	61	C49.12	295	C60*	523,528	C81.91	2
B58.3	104,560	B95*	634	C44.1322	61	C49.20	295	C61	523,528	C81*	580,604,630
B58.8*	560	B96*	634	C44.1391	61	C49.21	295	C62*	523,528	C82.01	2
B58.81	172	B97.4	560	C44.1392	61	C49.22	295	C63*	523,528	C82.11	2
B58.82	633	B97*	634	C44.191	61	C49.3	295	C64*	504,518	C82.21	2
B58.83	633	B99.8	1041	C44.1921	61	C49.4	295	C65*	504,518	C82.31	2
B58.89	633	B99*	634	C44.1922	61	C49.5	295	C66*	504,518	C82.41	2
B58.9	633			C44.1991	61	C49.6	295	C67*	504,518	C82.5*	1041
B58*	1041			C44.1992	61	C49.8	295	C68*	504,518	C82.51	2
B59	104,560,1041			C44.201	476	C49.9	295	C69*	61	C82.61	2
B60.0	633			C44.202	476	C49.A0	193	C70*	43	C82.81	2
B60.10	633			C44.209	476	C49.A1	193	C71*	43	C82.91	2
B60.11	633			C44.211	476	C49.A2	193	C72*	43	C82*	580,604,630
B60.12	61			C44.212	476	C49.A3	193	C73	2,502	C83.0*	1041
B60.13	61			C44.219	476	C49.A4	193	C74*	502	C83.01	2
B60.19	633			C44.221	476	C49.A5	193	C75.0	502	C83.1*	1041
B60.2	633			C44.222	476	C49.A9	193	C75.1	502	C83.3*	1041
B60.8	633,1041			C44.229	476	C4A.111	453	C75.2	502	C83.31	2
B64	633			C44.291	476	C4A.112	453	C75.3	43	C83.51	2
B65.0	518			C44.292	476	C4A.121	453	C75.4	43	C83.7*	1041
B65.1	209			C44.299	476	C4A.122	453	C75.5	43	C83.71	2
B65.2	633			C44.3*	476	C4A*	453	C75.8	502	C83.8*	1041
B65.3	476			C44.40	476	C4A.3*	476	C75.9	502	C83.81	2
B65.8	633			C44.41	476	C50.011	450,454	C76.0	2,85	C83.9*	1041
B65.9	633			C44.42	476	C50.012	450,454	C76.1	104	C83.91	2
B66.0	209			C44.49	476	C50.019	450,454	C76.2	193	C83*	580,604,630
B66.1	209			C44.500	476	C50.021	450,454	C76.3	523,528,533,541	C84.01	2
B66.2	633			C44.501	476	C50.022	450,454	C76.4*	605,630	C84.11	2
B66.3	209			C44.509	476	C50.029	450,454	C76.5*	605,630	C84.4*	1041
B66.4	104			C44.510	476	C50.111	450,454	C76.8	605,630	C84.6*	1041
B66.5	209			C44.511	476	C50.112	450,454	C77.0	2	C84.7*	1041
B66.8	634			C44.519	476	C50.119	450,454	C77*	580,604,630	C84.9*	1041
B66.9	634			C44.520	476	C50.121	450,454	C78.0*	104	C84.91	2
B67.0	209			C44.521	476	C50.122	450,454	C78.1	104	C84.A*	1041
B67.1	104			C44.529	476	C50.129	450,454	C78.2	104	C84.A1	2
B67.2	634			C44.590	476	C50.211	450,454	C78.3*	104	C84.Z*	1041
B67.31	502			C44.591	476	C50.212	450,454	C78.4	193	C84.Z1	2
B67.32	634			C44.599	476	C50.219	450,454	C78.5	193	C84*	580,604,630
B67.39	634			C44.601	476	C50.221	450,454	C78.6	193	C85.11	2
B67.4	634			C44.602	476	C50.222	450,454	C78.7	208	C85.21	2
B67.5	209			C44.609	476	C50.311	450,454	C78.8*	193	C85.81	2
B67.6*	634			C44.611	476	C50.312	450,454	C79.0*	504,518	C85.91	2
B67.7	634					C50.319	450,454	C79.1*	504,518		

Code	Page
C85*	580, 604, 630, 1041
C86.0	2
C86*	580, 604, 630, 1041
C88.4	1041
C88*	580, 604, 630
C90*	580, 604, 630
C91.0*	630
C91.1*	604, 630
C91.3*	604, 630
C91.4*	604, 630
C91.40	2
C91.5*	604, 630
C91.6*	604, 630
C91.9*	604, 630
C91.A*	604, 630
C91.Z*	604, 630
C91*	580
C92.0*	630
C92.1*	604, 630
C92.2*	604, 630
C92.3*	604, 630
C92.4*	630
C92.5*	630
C92.6*	630
C92.9*	604, 630
C92.A*	630
C92.Z*	604, 630
C92*	580
C93.0*	630
C93.1*	604, 630
C93.3*	604, 630
C93.9*	604, 630
C93.Z*	604, 630
C93*	580
C94.0*	630
C94.2*	604, 630
C94.3*	604, 630
C94.4*	604, 630
C94.6*	604, 630
C94.8*	604, 630
C94*	580
C95.0*	630
C95.1*	604, 630
C95.9*	604, 630
C95*	580
C96.0	2, 605, 630
C96.2*	2, 580, 604, 630
C96.4	580, 604, 630
C96.5	502
C96.6	502
C96.9	2, 580, 604, 630
C96.A	2, 580, 604, 630
C96.Z	580, 604, 630
D00.0*	2, 85
D00.1	193
D00.2	193
D01.0	193
D01.1	193
D01.2	193
D01.3	193
D01.4*	193
D01.5	208
D01.7	193
D01.9	193
D02.0	2, 85
D02.1	104
D02.2*	104
D02.3	104
D02.4	104
D03.0	453
D03.10	61
D03.111	61
D03.112	61
D03.121	61
D03.122	61
D03.2*	453
D03.3*	453
D03.4	453
D03.5*	453
D03.6*	453
D03.7*	453
D03.8	453
D03.9	453
D04.0	476
D04.10	61
D04.111	61
D04.112	61
D04.121	61
D04.122	61
D04.2*	476
D04.3*	476
D04.4	476
D04.5	476
D04.6*	476
D04.7*	476
D04.8	476
D04.9	476
D05.00	450, 454
D05.01	450, 454
D05.02	450, 454
D05.10	450, 454
D05.11	450, 454
D05.12	450, 454
D05.80	450, 454
D05.81	450, 454
D05.82	450, 454
D05.90	450, 454
D05.91	450, 454
D05.92	450, 454
D05*	453
D06*	533, 541
D07.0	533, 541
D07.1	533, 541
D07.2	533, 541
D07.3*	533, 541
D07.4	523, 528
D07.5	523, 528
D07.6*	523, 528
D09.0	504, 518
D09.1*	504, 518
D09.2*	61
D09.3	605, 630
D09.8	605, 630
D09.9	605, 630
D10.0	87
D10.1	87
D10.2	87
D10.3*	87
D10.4	86
D10.5	86
D10.6	86
D10.7	86
D10.9	86
D10*	2
D11*	2, 86
D12*	195
D13.0	195
D13.1	195
D13.2	195
D13.3*	195
D13.4	209
D13.5	209
D13.6	208
D13.7	502
D13.9	195
D14.0	2, 86
D14.1	2, 86
D14.2	104
D14.3*	104
D14.4	104
D15.0	579
D15.1	172
D15.2	104
D15.7	104
D15.9	104
D16.00	374
D16.01	374
D16.02	374
D16.10	374
D16.11	374
D16.12	374
D16.20	374
D16.21	374
D16.22	374
D16.30	374
D16.31	374
D16.32	374
D16.4	2, 374
D16.5	2, 87
D16.6	212, 374
D16.7	104
D16.8	374
D16.9	374
D17.0	476
D17.1	476
D17.2*	476
D17.3*	476
D17.4	104
D17.5	195
D17.6	529
D17.71	504, 518
D17.72	504, 518
D17.79	476
D17.9	476
D18.00	2, 172
D18.01	2, 476
D18.02	51
D18.03	195
D18.09	2, 172
D18.1	579
D19.0	104
D19.1	195
D19.7	605, 630
D19.9	605, 630
D20*	195
D21.0	374
D21.10	374
D21.11	374
D21.12	374
D21.20	374
D21.21	374
D21.22	374
D21.3	374
D21.4	374
D21.5	374
D21.6	374
D21.9	374
D22.0	476
D22.10	61
D22.111	61
D22.112	61
D22.121	61
D22.122	61
D22.2*	477
D22.3*	477
D22.4	477
D22.5	477
D22.6*	477
D22.7*	477
D22.9	477
D23.0	476
D23.10	61
D23.111	61
D23.112	61
D23.121	61
D23.122	61
D23.2*	477
D23.3*	477
D23.4	477
D23.5	477
D23.6*	477
D23.7*	477
D23.9	477
D24*	477
D25*	533, 541
D26*	533, 541
D27*	533, 541
D28*	533, 541
D29*	529
D30*	504, 518
D31*	61
D32*	43
D33*	43
D34	2, 502
D35.0*	502
D35.1	502
D35.2	502
D35.3	502
D35.4	43
D35.5	43
D35.6	43
D35.7	502
D35.9	502
D36.0	579
D36.10	374
D36.11	374
D36.12	374
D36.13	374
D36.14	374
D36.15	374
D36.16	374
D36.17	374
D36.7	605, 630
D36.9	605, 630
D37.0*	2, 85
D37.1	194
D37.2	194
D37.3	194
D37.4	194
D37.5	194
D37.6	208
D37.8	194
D37.9	194
D38.0	2, 85
D38.1	104
D38.2	104
D38.3	104
D38.4	104
D38.5	104
D38.6	104
D39.0	533
D39.1*	531
D39.2	533
D39.8	533
D39.9	533
D39*	541
D3A.00	605, 630
D3A.010	195
D3A.011	195
D3A.012	195
D3A.019	195
D3A.020	195
D3A.021	195
D3A.022	195
D3A.023	195
D3A.024	195
D3A.025	195
D3A.026	195
D3A.029	195
D3A.090	104
D3A.091	579
D3A.092	195
D3A.093	504, 518
D3A.094	195
D3A.095	195
D3A.096	195
D3A.8	605, 631
D40*	523, 528
D41*	504, 518
D42*	43
D43*	43
D44.0	502
D44.1*	502
D44.2	502
D44.3	502
D44.5	43
D44.6	43
D44.7	43
D44.9	502
D45	580, 604, 630
D46*	578
D47.0*	580, 604, 630
D47.1	580, 604, 630
D47.2	579
D47.3	579
D47.4	579
D47.9	580, 604, 630
D47.Z1	766
D47.Z2	580, 604, 630
D47.Z9	580, 604, 630
D48.0	212, 295
D48.1	374
D48.2	374
D48.3	194
D48.4	194
D48.5	477
D48.6*	453
D48.60	450, 454
D48.61	450, 454
D48.62	450, 454
D48.7	605, 631
D48.9	605, 631
D49.0	194
D49.1	104
D49.2	212, 374
D49.3	453, 454
D49.4	504, 518
D49.5*	504, 518
D49.6	43
D49.8*	605, 631
D49.9	605, 631
D50*	578
D51*	578
D52*	578
D53*	578
D55*	578
D56.0	560
D56.1	560
D56.2	560
D56.3	560
D56.4	560
D56.5	560
D56.8	560
D56.9	560
D57*	578
D57.4*	560
D58*	578
D59.0	578
D59.1	578
D59.2	560, 578
D59.3	560, 578
D59.4	560, 578
D59.5	560, 578
D59.6	560, 578
D59.8	560, 578
D59.9	560, 578
D60.0	578
D60.1	578
D60.8	578
D60.9	578
D61.0*	578
D61.1	578
D61.2	578
D61.3	578
D61.81*	578
D61.82	580, 604, 630
D61.89	578
D61.9	578
D62	560, 578
D63*	578
D64*	578
D65	560, 579
D66	579
D67	579
D68.0	579
D68.1	579
D68.2	579
D68.311	579
D68.312	579
D68.318	579
D68.32	579
D68.4	579
D68.5*	579
D68.6*	579
D68.8	579
D68.9	579
D69.5*	560
D69*	579
D70.0	578
D70.1	578
D70.2	578
D70.3	578
D70.4	578
D70.8	578
D70.9	578
D71	578
D72.0	578
D72.1	579
D72.8*	579
D72.9	579
D73.0	579
D73.1	579
D73.2	579
D73.3	579
D73.4	579
D73.5	579
D73.8*	579
D73.9	579
D74*	578
D75.0	579
D75.1	579
D75.81	580, 604, 630
D75.82	560, 579
D75.89	579
D75.9	579
D75.A	579
D76.1	579
D76.2	579
D76.3	579
D77	579
D78.1*	560
D78*	766
D80.0	579
D80.1	579
D80.2	579
D80.3	579
D80.4	579
D80.5	579
D80.6	578
D80.7	579
D80.8	578
D80.9	578
D81.0	578
D81.1	578
D81.2	578
D81.3*	502
D81.4	578
D81.5	502
D81.6	578
D81.7	578
D81.810	502
D81.818	501
D81.819	502
D81.89	578
D81.9	578
D82.0	578
D82.1	578
D82.2	579
D82.3	579
D82.4	579
D82.8	579
D82.9	579
D83.0	579
D83.1	579
D83.2	579
D83.8	579
D83.9	579
D84.0	579
D84.1	502
D84.8	579
D84.9	579
D86*	105
D89.0	579
D89.1	580, 604, 630
D89.2	579
D89.3	579
D89.40	579
D89.41	579
D89.42	579
D89.43	579
D89.49	579
D89.810	578
D89.811	578
D89.812	578
D89.813	578
D89.82	296
D89.89	579
D89.9	579
E00*	502
E01*	502
E02	502
E03.0	502
E03.1	502
E03.2	502
E03.3	502
E03.4	2, 502
E03.5	47, 560
E03.8	502
E03.9	502
E04.1	2
E04*	502
E05*	2, 502
E06*	2, 502
E07.0	502
E07.1	502
E07.81	795
E07.89	2, 502
E07.9	2, 502
E08.0*	501
E08.1*	501
E08.2*	519
E08.3*	61
E08.4*	46
E08.5*	167
E08.610	46
E08.618	501
E08.62*	501
E08.63*	501
E08.64*	501
E08.65	501
E08.69	501
E08.8	501
E08.9	501
E08*	1, 2
E09.0*	501
E09.1*	501
E09.2*	519
E09.3*	61
E09.4*	46
E09.5*	167
E09.610	46
E09.618	501
E09.62*	501
E09.63*	501
E09.64*	501
E09.65	501
E09.69	501
E09.8	501
E09.9	501
E09*	1, 2
E10.1*	501
E10.2*	518, 519
E10.3*	61
E10.4*	46

Code	Page	Code	Page	Code	Page	Code	Page	Code	Page	Code	Page
E10.5*	167	E51*	502	E85*	296	F41*	635	F93.0	635	G37.0	44
E10.610	46	E52	502	E86*	502,560	F42.2	635	F93.8	636	G37.1	44
E10.618	501	E53*	502	E87*	502,560	F42.3	635	F93.9	636	G37.2	44
E10.62*	501	E54	502	E88.01	502	F42.4	635	F94*	636	G37.3	14,55
E10.63*	501	E55.0	301	E88.02	605,631	F42.8	635	F95*	51	G37.4	14,55,1041
E10.64*	501	E55.9	502	E88.09	605,631	F42.9	635	F98.0	636	G37.5	44
E10.65	501	E56*	502	E88.1	502	F43.0	635	F98.1	636	G37.8	44
E10.69	501	E58	502	E88.2	502	F43.1*	635	F98.21	635	G37.9	44,1041
E10.8	501	E59	502	E88.3	518,560	F43.20	635	F98.29	636	G40.0*	15
E10.9	501	E60	502	E88.4*	502	F43.21	635	F98.3	636	G40.101	15
E10*	1,2	E61*	502	E88.8*	502	F43.22	635	F98.4	636	G40.109	15
E11.0*	501	E63*	502	E88.9	502	F43.23	635	F98.5	636	G40.111	15
E11.10	501	E64.0	502,560	E89.0	503	F43.24	635	F98.8	636	G40.119	15
E11.11	501	E64.1	502	E89.1	1,2,502	F43.25	635	F98.9	636	G40.2*	15
E11.2*	519	E64.2	502	E89.2	503,560	F43.29	635	F99	635	G40.3*	15
E11.3*	61	E64.3	301	E89.3	503	F43.8	635	G00.0	14	G40.4*	15
E11.4*	46	E64.8	502	E89.4*	533,541	F43.9	635	G00.1	14	G40.5*	15
E11.5*	167	E64.9	502	E89.5	503	F44.0	635	G00.2	14	G40.8*	15
E11.610	46	E65	502	E89.6	503	F44.1	635	G00.3	14	G40.9*	15
E11.618	501	E66.0*	502	E89.8*	766	F44.2	635	G00.8	14	G40.A*	15
E11.62*	501	E66.1	502	F01*	635	F44.4	635	G00.9	14	G40.B*	15
E11.63*	501	E66.2	106	F02*	635	F44.5	635	G00*	54,560	G40*	55
E11.64*	501	E66.3	502	F03.90	1041	F44.6	635	G01	14,54,560	G43*	55
E11.65	501	E66.8	502	F03*	635	F44.7	635	G02	14,54,560	G44*	55
E11.69	501	E66.9	502	F04	635	F44.81	635	G03.0	54,560	G45.0	44,45
E11.8	501	E67*	502	F05	635	F44.89	636	G03.1	54	G45.1	44,45
E11.9	501	E68	502	F06.8	1041	F44.9	635	G03.2	47	G45.2	44,45
E11*	1,2	E70*	502	F06*	635	F45*	635	G03.8	54,560	G45.3	60
E13.0*	501	E71*	502	F07.0	635	F48.1	635	G03.9	54,560	G45.4	45
E13.1*	501	E72*	502	F07.81	55	F48.2	43	G04.0*	14,54	G45.8	44,45
E13.2*	519	E73*	195	F07.89	43	F48.8	635	G04.1	42	G45.9	44,45
E13.3*	61	E74.0*	502	F07.9	635,1041	F48.9	635	G04.2	14,54,560	G46.0	44,45
E13.4*	46	E74.1	195	F09	635,1041	F50.0*	635	G04.3*	14,54	G46.1	44,45
E13.5*	167	E74.2*	502	F11.23	560	F50.2	636	G04.8*	14,55,1041	G46.2	44,45
E13.610	46	E74.3*	195	F11.93	560	F50.8*	636	G04.9*	14,55,1041	G46.3	45
E13.618	501	E74.4	502	F13.230	560	F50.9	636	G05.3	14	G46.4	45
E13.62*	501	E74.8	502	F13.231	560	F51*	636	G05.4	14	G46.5	45
E13.63*	501	E74.9	502	F13.232	560	F52.0	636	G05*	55	G46.6	45
E13.64*	501	E75.0*	43	F13.239	560	F52.1	636	G06.0	14	G46.7	45
E13.65	501	E75.1*	43	F13.930	560	F52.2*	636	G06.1	14	G46.8	45
E13.69	501	E75.21	502	F13.931	560	F52.3*	636	G06.2	14	G47.0*	636
E13.8	501	E75.22	502	F13.932	560	F52.4	636	G06*	54,560	G47.1*	636
E13.9	501	E75.23	43	F13.939	560	F52.5	533,541	G07	560	G47.2*	2,51
E13*	1,2	E75.24*	502	F14.23	560	F52.6	636	G07	14,54	G47.3*	2
E15	502,560	E75.25	43	F15.23	560	F52.8	636	G08	14,51	G47.30	86
E16.0	502	E75.26	43	F15.93	560	F52.9	636	G09	51	G47.31	51
E16.1	502	E75.29	43	F17.200	844	F53.0	635	G10	43	G47.32	106
E16.2	502	E75.3	502	F17.201	844	F53.1	635	G11*	44	G47.33	86
E16.3	502	E75.4	43	F17.203	560	F54	635	G12*	43	G47.34	86
E16.4	194	E75.5	502	F17.210	844	F59	636	G13.0	46	G47.35	51
E16.8	502	E75.6	502	F17.211	844	F60*	635	G13.1	44	G47.36	86
E16.9	502	E76*	502	F17.213	560	F63.0	635	G13.2	43	G47.37	51
E20.0	502,560	E77*	502	F17.220	844	F63.1	636	G13.8	43	G47.39	86
E20.1	502	E78.0*	502	F17.221	844	F63.2	635	G14	51	G47.4*	51
E20.8	502,560	E78.1	502	F17.223	560	F63.3	636	G20	43	G47.5*	2
E20.9	502,560	E78.2	502	F17.290	844	F63.8*	635	G21.0	51	G47.50	86
E21*	502	E78.3	502	F17.291	844	F63.9	636	G21.1*	43	G47.51	51
E22*	502	E78.4*	502	F17.293	560	F64*	636	G21.2	43	G47.52	86
E23.2	560	E78.5	502	F19.230	560	F65*	636	G21.3	43	G47.53	51
E23*	502	E78.6	502	F19.231	560	F66	636	G21.4	43	G47.54	86
E24*	502	E78.70	502	F19.232	560	F68.10	635	G21.8	43	G47.59	86
E25*	503	E78.71	374	F19.239	560	F68.11	635	G21.9	43	G47.6*	2
E26*	503	E78.72	374	F19.930	560	F68.12	635	G23*	43	G47.61	51
E27*	503	E78.79	502	F19.931	560	F68.13	635	G24.0*	51	G47.62	51
E28*	533,541	E78.8*	502	F19.932	560	F68.8	635	G24.1	44	G47.63	86
E29*	503	E78.9	502	F19.939	560	F68.A	635	G24.2	51	G47.69	86
E30*	503	E79.0	795	F20*	635	F69	635	G24.3	51	G47.8	2,86
E31*	503	E79.1	502	F21	635	F70	635	G24.4	51	G47.9	636
E32.0	579	E79.2	502	F22	635	F71	635	G24.5	61	G50*	46
E32.1	560,579	E79.8	502	F23	635	F72	635	G24.8	51	G51.0	46
E32.8	579	E79.9	502	F24	635	F73	635	G24.9	51	G51.1	46
E32.9	579	E80.0	502	F25*	635	F78	635	G25.0	51	G51.2	46
E34*	503	E80.1	502	F28	635,1041	F79	635	G25.1	51	G51.31	46
E35	2,503	E80.2*	502	F29	635,1041	F80.0	636	G25.2	51	G51.32	46
E36.1*	560	E80.3	502	F30*	635	F80.1	636	G25.3	51	G51.33	46
E36*	766	E80.4	209	F31*	635	F80.2	636	G25.4	43	G51.39	46
E40	502	E80.5	209	F32.0	635	F80.4	636	G25.5	43	G51.4	46
E41	502,560	E80.6	209	F32.1	635	F80.81	51	G25.6*	51	G51.8	46
E42	502	E80.7	209	F32.2	635	F80.82	636	G25.7*	51	G51.9	46
E43	502,560	E83.0*	502	F32.3	635	F80.89	636	G25.81	43	G52*	46
E44*	502,560	E83.1*	502	F32.4	635	F80.9	636	G25.82	51	G53	46
E45	502	E83.2	454	F32.5	635	F81*	636	G25.83	51	G54*	46
E46	502,560	E83.3*	502	F32.81	635	F82	636	G25.89	51	G55	46
E50.0	61	E83.4*	502	F32.89	635	F84.0	635	G25.9	43	G56*	46
E50.1	61	E83.5*	502	F32.9	635	F84.2	43	G26	43	G57*	46
E50.2	61	E83.81	502	F33*	635	F84.3	635	G30*	43	G58*	46
E50.3	61	E83.89	502	F34.0	635	F84.5	635	G31*	43	G59	46
E50.4	61	E83.9	502	F34.1	635	F84.8	635	G32.0	51	G60.0	46
E50.5	61	E84.0	104	F34.81	635	F84.9	636	G32.81	44	G60.1	51
E50.6	61	E84.11	559	F34.89	635	F88	636	G32.89	45	G60.2	46
E50.7	61	E84.19	195	F34.9	635	F89	636	G35	44	G60.3	46
E50.8	502	E84.8	502	F39	635	F90*	636	G36.9	1041	G60.8	46
E50.9	502	E84.9	502	F40*	635	F91*	636	G36*	44	G60.9	46

Code	Page	Code	Page	Code	Page	Code	Page	Code	Page	Code	Page
G61.0	54	G96.9	45, 1041	H02.124	62	H02.7*	62	H04.333	60	H10.403	63
G61.1	46	G97.0	51, 560	H02.125	62	H02.811	62	H04.339	60	H10.409	63
G61.8*	46	G97.1	55, 560	H02.126	62	H02.812	62	H04.4*	62	H10.411	63
G61.9	46	G97.2	51, 560	H02.129	62	H02.813	62	H04.5*	62	H10.412	63
G62*	46	G97.3*	51	H02.131	62	H02.814	62	H04.6*	62	H10.413	63
G63	46	G97.4*	560, 766	H02.132	62	H02.815	62	H04.8*	63	H10.419	63
G64	46	G97.5*	766	H02.133	62	H02.816	62	H04.9	63	H10.421	63
G65*	46	G97.61	766	H02.134	62	H02.819	62	H05.00	63	H10.422	63
G70.0*	43	G97.62	766	H02.135	62	H02.821	62	H05.011	60	H10.423	63
G70.1	46	G97.63	766	H02.136	62	H02.822	62	H05.012	60	H10.429	63
G70.2	46	G97.64	766	H02.139	62	H02.823	62	H05.013	60	H10.431	63
G70.80	43	G97.8*	51, 560	H02.141	62	H02.824	62	H05.019	60	H10.432	63
G70.81	43	G98.8	1041	H02.142	62	H02.825	62	H05.021	60	H10.433	63
G70.89	46	G98*	45	H02.143	62	H02.826	62	H05.022	60	H10.439	63
G70.9	46	G99.0	46	H02.144	62	H02.829	62	H05.023	60	H10.44	63
G71.00	51	G99.2	51	H02.145	62	H02.831	62	H05.029	60	H10.45	63
G71.01	51	G99.8	45	H02.146	62	H02.832	62	H05.031	60	H10.501	63
G71.02	51	H00*	61	H02.149	62	H02.833	62	H05.032	60	H10.502	63
G71.09	51	H01.001	61	H02.151	62	H02.834	62	H05.033	60	H10.503	63
G71.11	51	H01.002	61	H02.152	62	H02.835	62	H05.039	60	H10.509	63
G71.12	51	H01.003	61	H02.153	62	H02.836	62	H05.041	60	H10.511	63
G71.13	51	H01.004	61	H02.154	62	H02.839	62	H05.042	60	H10.512	63
G71.14	51	H01.005	61	H02.155	62	H02.841	62	H05.043	60	H10.513	63
G71.19	51	H01.006	61	H02.156	62	H02.842	62	H05.049	60	H10.519	63
G71.2	51	H01.009	61	H02.159	62	H02.843	62	H05.1*	63	H10.521	63
G71.3	51	H01.00A	61	H02.201	62	H02.844	62	H05.20	63	H10.522	63
G71.8	51	H01.00B	61	H02.202	62	H02.845	62	H05.211	60	H10.523	63
G71.9	51	H01.011	61	H02.203	62	H02.846	62	H05.212	60	H10.529	63
G72.0	51	H01.012	61	H02.204	62	H02.849	62	H05.213	60	H10.531	63
G72.1	51	H01.013	61	H02.205	62	H02.851	62	H05.219	60	H10.532	63
G72.2	51	H01.014	61	H02.206	62	H02.852	62	H05.221	63	H10.533	63
G72.3	51	H01.015	61	H02.209	62	H02.853	62	H05.222	63	H10.539	63
G72.4*	296	H01.016	61	H02.20A	62	H02.854	62	H05.223	63	H10.811	63
G72.8*	51	H01.019	61	H02.20B	62	H02.855	62	H05.229	63	H10.812	63
G72.9	51	H01.01A	61	H02.20C	62	H02.856	62	H05.231	63	H10.813	63
G73.1	43	H01.01B	61	H02.211	62	H02.859	62	H05.232	63	H10.819	63
G73.3	43	H01.021	61	H02.212	62	H02.861	62	H05.233	63	H10.821	63
G73.7	51	H01.022	61	H02.213	62	H02.862	62	H05.239	63	H10.822	63
G80.0	42	H01.023	61	H02.214	62	H02.863	62	H05.241	63	H10.823	63
G80.1	42	H01.024	61	H02.215	62	H02.864	62	H05.242	63	H10.829	63
G80.2	42	H01.025	61	H02.216	62	H02.865	62	H05.243	63	H10.89	63
G80.3	43	H01.026	61	H02.219	62	H02.866	62	H05.249	63	H10.9	63
G80.4	51	H01.029	61	H02.21A	62	H02.869	62	H05.251	60	H11*	63
G80.8	51	H01.02A	61	H02.21B	62	H02.871	62	H05.252	60	H15*	63
G80.9	51	H01.02B	61	H02.21C	62	H02.872	62	H05.253	60	H16.001	60
G81*	43	H01.111	61	H02.221	62	H02.873	62	H05.259	60	H16.002	60
G82*	42	H01.112	61	H02.222	62	H02.874	62	H05.261	60	H16.003	60
G83.0	42	H01.113	61	H02.223	62	H02.875	62	H05.262	60	H16.009	60
G83.1*	51	H01.114	61	H02.224	62	H02.876	62	H05.263	60	H16.011	60
G83.2*	51	H01.115	61	H02.225	62	H02.879	62	H05.269	60	H16.012	60
G83.3*	51	H01.116	61	H02.226	62	H02.881	62	H05.3*	63	H16.013	60
G83.4	46	H01.119	61	H02.229	62	H02.882	62	H05.4*	63	H16.019	60
G83.5	51	H01.121	61	H02.22A	62	H02.883	62	H05.5*	63	H16.021	63
G83.8*	51	H01.122	61	H02.22B	62	H02.884	62	H05.811	63	H16.022	63
G83.9	51	H01.123	61	H02.22C	62	H02.885	62	H05.812	63	H16.023	63
G89.0	51	H01.124	61	H02.231	62	H02.886	62	H05.813	63	H16.029	63
G89.1*	795	H01.125	61	H02.232	62	H02.889	62	H05.819	63	H16.031	60
G89.2*	51	H01.126	61	H02.233	62	H02.88A	62	H05.821	60	H16.033	60
G89.3	795	H01.129	61	H02.234	62	H02.88B	62	H05.822	60	H16.039	60
G89.4	51	H01.131	61	H02.235	62	H02.89	62	H05.823	60	H16.041	60
G90.0*	46	H01.132	61	H02.236	62	H02.9	62	H05.829	60	H16.042	63
G90.1	51, 560	H01.133	61	H02.239	62	H04.001	62	H05.89	63	H16.043	63
G90.2	46	H01.134	61	H02.23A	62	H04.002	62	H05.9	63	H16.049	60
G90.3	43	H01.135	61	H02.23B	62	H04.009	62	H10.011	63	H16.051	63
G90.4	46	H01.136	61	H02.23C	62	H04.011	60	H10.012	63	H16.052	63
G90.5*	46	H01.139	61	H02.30	62	H04.012	60	H10.013	63	H16.053	63
G90.8	46	H01.141	61	H02.31	62	H04.013	60	H10.019	63	H16.059	63
G90.9	46	H01.142	61	H02.32	62	H04.019	60	H10.021	63	H16.061	60
G91*	43	H01.143	61	H02.33	62	H04.021	62	H10.022	63	H16.062	60
G92	14, 51, 560	H01.144	61	H02.34	62	H04.022	62	H10.023	63	H16.063	60
G93.0	51	H01.145	61	H02.35	62	H04.023	62	H10.029	63	H16.069	60
G93.1	51, 560	H01.146	61	H02.36	62	H04.029	62	H10.10	63	H16.071	60
G93.2	55	H01.149	61	H02.401	60	H04.031	62	H10.11	63	H16.072	60
G93.3	795	H01.8	61	H02.402	60	H04.032	62	H10.12	63	H16.073	60
G93.4*	45, 1041	H01.9	61	H02.403	60	H04.033	62	H10.13	63	H16.079	60
G93.5	47	H02.0*	61	H02.409	60	H04.039	62	H10.211	63	H16.1*	63
G93.6	47	H02.101	61	H02.411	62	H04.1*	62	H10.212	63	H16.2*	63
G93.7	51	H02.102	61	H02.412	62	H04.2*	62	H10.213	63	H16.301	63
G93.81	45	H02.103	61	H02.413	62	H04.301	62	H10.219	63	H16.302	63
G93.82	47	H02.104	61	H02.419	62	H04.302	62	H10.221	63	H16.303	63
G93.89	45	H02.105	61	H02.421	60	H04.309	62	H10.222	63	H16.309	63
G93.9	45, 1041	H02.106	61	H02.422	60	H04.311	62	H10.223	63	H16.311	60
G94	43	H02.109	61	H02.423	60	H04.312	62	H10.229	63	H16.312	60
G95.0	43	H02.111	62	H02.429	60	H04.313	62	H10.231	63	H16.313	60
G95.1*	51	H02.112	62	H02.431	60	H04.319	62	H10.232	63	H16.319	60
G95.2*	51, 1041	H02.113	62	H02.432	60	H04.321	60	H10.233	63	H16.321	63
G95.8*	51	H02.114	62	H02.433	60	H04.322	60	H10.239	63	H16.322	63
G95.9	51, 1041	H02.115	62	H02.439	60	H04.323	60	H10.30	63	H16.329	63
G96.0	51, 560	H02.116	62	H02.51*	60	H04.329	60	H10.31	63	H16.331	63
G96.11	560, 766	H02.121	62	H02.52*	62	H04.331	60	H10.32	63	H16.332	63
G96.12	51	H02.122	62	H02.53*	62	H04.332	60	H10.33	63	H16.333	63
G96.19	51	H02.123	62	H02.59	60						
G96.8	45			H02.6*	477						

Numeric Index to Diseases

Code	Page	Code	Page	Code	Page	Code	Page	Code	Page	Code	Page
H16.339	63	H35.061	64	H35.363	64	H40.8*	65	H52.6	65	H57.1*	65
H16.391	63	H35.062	64	H35.369	64	H40.9	65	H52.7	65	H57.811	65
H16.392	63	H35.063	64	H35.371	64	H42	65	H53.001	65	H57.812	65
H16.393	63	H35.069	64	H35.372	64	H43*	65	H53.002	65	H57.813	65
H16.399	63	H35.071	64	H35.373	64	H44.0*	60	H53.003	65	H57.819	65
H16.4*	63	H35.072	64	H35.379	64	H44.11*	60	H53.009	65	H57.89	65
H16.8	63	H35.073	64	H35.381	64	H44.121	60	H53.011	65	H57.9	65
H16.9	63	H35.079	64	H35.382	64	H44.122	60	H53.012	65	H59.01*	766
H17*	63	H35.09	64	H35.383	64	H44.123	60	H53.013	65	H59.02*	65
H18*	63	H35.101	64	H35.389	64	H44.129	60	H53.019	65	H59.03*	766
H20*	63	H35.102	64	H35.40	64	H44.13*	65	H53.021	65	H59.09*	766
H21.0*	63	H35.103	64	H35.411	64	H44.19	60	H53.022	65	H59.1*	766
H21.1*	63	H35.109	64	H35.412	64	H44.2*	65	H53.023	65	H59.2*	560, 766
H21.2*	63	H35.111	64	H35.413	64	H44.3*	65	H53.029	65	H59.3*	766
H21.301	63	H35.112	64	H35.419	64	H44.4*	65	H53.031	65	H59.4*	65
H21.302	63	H35.113	64	H35.421	64	H44.5*	65	H53.032	65	H59.8*	766
H21.303	63	H35.119	64	H35.422	64	H44.6*	65	H53.033	65	H60*	86
H21.309	63	H35.121	64	H35.423	64	H44.7*	65	H53.039	65	H61.001	86
H21.311	63	H35.122	64	H35.429	64	H44.8*	65	H53.041	65	H61.002	86
H21.312	63	H35.123	64	H35.431	64	H44.9	65	H53.042	65	H61.003	86
H21.313	63	H35.129	64	H35.432	64	H46*	60	H53.043	65	H61.009	86
H21.319	63	H35.131	64	H35.433	64	H47.0*	60	H53.049	65	H61.011	374
H21.321	63	H35.132	64	H35.439	64	H47.10	51, 560	H53.10	65	H61.012	374
H21.322	63	H35.133	64	H35.441	64	H47.11	51, 560	H53.11	65	H61.013	374
H21.323	63	H35.139	64	H35.442	64	H47.12	65, 560	H53.121	60	H61.019	374
H21.329	63	H35.141	64	H35.443	64	H47.13	65	H53.122	60	H61.021	374
H21.331	60	H35.142	64	H35.449	64	H47.141	51	H53.123	60	H61.022	374
H21.332	60	H35.143	64	H35.451	64	H47.142	51	H53.129	60	H61.023	374
H21.333	60	H35.149	64	H35.452	64	H47.143	51	H53.131	60	H61.029	374
H21.339	60	H35.151	64	H35.453	64	H47.149	51	H53.132	60	H61.031	374
H21.341	63	H35.152	64	H35.459	64	H47.20	60	H53.133	60	H61.032	374
H21.342	63	H35.153	64	H35.461	64	H47.211	60	H53.139	60	H61.033	374
H21.343	63	H35.159	64	H35.462	64	H47.212	60	H53.141	65	H61.039	374
H21.349	63	H35.161	64	H35.463	64	H47.213	60	H53.142	65	H61.1*	86
H21.351	63	H35.162	64	H35.469	64	H47.219	60	H53.143	65	H61.2*	86
H21.352	63	H35.163	64	H35.50	64	H47.22	60	H53.149	65	H61.3*	86
H21.353	63	H35.169	64	H35.51	64	H47.23*	65	H53.15	65	H61.8*	86
H21.359	63	H35.171	64	H35.52	64	H47.291	65	H53.16	65	H61.9*	86
H21.4*	63	H35.172	64	H35.53	64	H47.292	60	H53.19	65	H62*	86
H21.5*	63	H35.173	64	H35.54	64	H47.293	60	H53.2	60	H65*	86
H21.8*	63	H35.179	64	H35.60	64	H47.299	60	H53.3*	65	H66*	86
H21.9	63	H35.20	64	H35.61	64	H47.31*	65	H53.40	60	H67*	86
H22	63	H35.21	64	H35.62	64	H47.321	60	H53.411	60	H68.0*	86
H25*	63	H35.22	64	H35.63	64	H47.322	60	H53.412	60	H68.1*	86
H26*	63	H35.23	64	H35.70	64	H47.323	60	H53.413	60	H69*	86
H27*	63	H35.30	64	H35.711	65	H47.329	60	H53.419	60	H70.0*	86
H28	63	H35.3110	64	H35.712	65	H47.331	60	H53.42*	65	H70.011	560
H30*	63	H35.3111	64	H35.713	65	H47.332	60	H53.431	60	H70.012	560
H31*	63	H35.3112	64	H35.719	65	H47.333	60	H53.432	60	H70.013	560
H32	63	H35.3113	64	H35.721	65	H47.339	60	H53.433	60	H70.019	560
H33.0*	63	H35.3114	64	H35.722	65	H47.39*	65	H53.439	60	H70.1*	86
H33.101	63	H35.3120	64	H35.723	65	H47.4*	51	H53.451	60	H70.2*	86
H33.102	64	H35.3121	64	H35.729	65	H47.5*	51	H53.452	60	H70.8*	86
H33.103	64	H35.3122	64	H35.731	65	H47.6*	51	H53.453	60	H70.811	560
H33.109	64	H35.3123	64	H35.732	65	H47.9	51	H53.459	60	H70.812	560
H33.111	64	H35.3124	64	H35.733	65	H49.0*	60	H53.461	60	H70.813	560
H33.112	64	H35.3130	64	H35.739	65	H49.1*	60	H53.462	60	H70.819	560
H33.113	64	H35.3131	64	H35.81	65	H49.2*	60	H53.469	61	H70.9*	86
H33.119	64	H35.3132	64	H35.82	65	H49.3*	60	H53.47	61	H71*	86
H33.121	60	H35.3133	64	H35.89	65	H49.4*	60	H53.481	61	H72*	86
H33.122	60	H35.3134	64	H35.9	65	H49.81*	502	H53.482	61	H73.0*	86
H33.123	60	H35.3190	64	H36	65	H49.881	60	H53.483	61	H73.1*	86
H33.129	60	H35.3191	64	H40.0*	65	H49.882	60	H53.489	61	H73.2*	86
H33.191	64	H35.3192	64	H40.10*	65	H49.883	60	H53.50	65	H73.8*	86
H33.192	64	H35.3193	64	H40.1110	65	H49.889	60	H53.51	65	H73.9*	86
H33.193	64	H35.3194	64	H40.1111	65	H49.9	60	H53.52	61	H74*	86
H33.199	64	H35.3210	64	H40.1112	65	H50.0*	65	H53.53	65	H75*	86
H33.2*	64	H35.3211	64	H40.1113	65	H50.1*	65	H53.54	65	H80*	86
H33.3*	64	H35.3212	64	H40.1114	65	H50.2*	65	H53.55	65	H81*	86
H33.4*	64	H35.3213	64	H40.1120	65	H50.3*	65	H53.59	65	H82*	86
H33.8	64	H35.3220	64	H40.1121	65	H50.4*	65	H53.6*	65	H83.0*	86
H34*	60	H35.3221	64	H40.1122	65	H50.5*	65	H53.7*	65	H83.1*	86
H35.00	64	H35.3222	64	H40.1123	65	H50.6*	65	H53.8	65	H83.2*	86
H35.011	64	H35.3223	64	H40.1124	65	H50.811	65	H53.9	65	H83.3*	86
H35.012	64	H35.3230	64	H40.1130	65	H50.812	65	H54*	65	H83.8*	86
H35.013	64	H35.3231	64	H40.1131	65	H50.89	60	H55.00	61	H83.9*	86
H35.019	64	H35.3232	64	H40.1132	65	H50.9	65	H55.01	65	H90*	86
H35.021	64	H35.3233	64	H40.1133	65	H51.0	65	H55.02	61	H91*	86
H35.022	64	H35.3290	64	H40.1134	65	H51.1*	65	H55.03	65	H92*	86
H35.023	64	H35.3291	64	H40.1190	65	H51.2*	51	H55.04	61	H93.0*	86
H35.029	64	H35.3292	64	H40.1191	65	H51.8	60	H55.09	65	H93.1*	86
H35.031	64	H35.3293	64	H40.1192	65	H51.9	65	H55.81	61	H93.211	86
H35.032	64	H35.33	64	H40.1193	65	H52.0*	65	H55.89	65	H93.212	86
H35.033	64	H35.341	64	H40.1194	65	H52.1*	65	H57.00	61	H93.213	86
H35.039	64	H35.342	64	H40.12*	60	H52.2*	65	H57.01	43	H93.219	86
H35.041	64	H35.343	64	H40.13*	65	H52.3*	65	H57.02	61	H93.221	86
H35.042	64	H35.349	64	H40.14*	65	H52.4	65	H57.03	61	H93.222	86
H35.043	64	H35.351	64	H40.15*	65	H52.511	60	H57.04	61	H93.223	86
H35.049	64	H35.352	64	H40.2*	65	H52.512	60	H57.051	61	H93.229	86
H35.051	64	H35.353	64	H40.3*	65	H52.513	60	H57.052	61	H93.231	86
H35.052	64	H35.359	64	H40.4*	65	H52.519	60	H57.053	61	H93.232	86
H35.053	64	H35.361	64	H40.5*	65	H52.52*	65	H57.059	61	H93.233	86
H35.059	64	H35.362	64	H40.6*	65	H52.53*	65	H57.09	61	H93.239	86

Code	Page	Code	Page	Code	Page	Code	Page	Code	Page	Code	Page
H93.241	86	I27.0	172	I63.02	44, 45, 561	I65.02	44	I77.74	168	J04.1*	106
H93.242	86	I27.1	172	I63.031	44, 45, 561	I65.03	44	I77.75	168	J04.2	2, 86
H93.243	86	I27.2*	172	I63.032	44, 45, 561	I65.09	44	I77.76	168	J04.3*	2, 86
H93.249	86	I27.81	172	I63.033	44, 45, 561	I65.1	44	I77.77	168	J05*	2, 86
H93.25	636	I27.82	104, 561	I63.039	44, 45, 561	I65.21	44	I77.79	168	J06*	2, 86
H93.291	86	I27.89	172	I63.09	44, 45, 561	I65.22	44	I77.8*	168	J09.X1	105, 561, 1041
H93.292	86	I27.9	172	I63.1*	14	I65.23	44	I77.9	168	J09.X2	105
H93.293	86	I28*	172	I63.10	44, 45, 561	I65.29	44	I78.0	168	J09.X2	561
H93.299	86	I30*	172	I63.111	44, 45, 561	I65.8	44	I78.1	477	J09.X3	632
H93.3*	86	I31.2	561	I63.112	44, 45, 561	I65.9	44	I78.8	168	J09.X9	632
H93.8*	86	I31*	172	I63.113	44, 45, 561	I65*	45	I78.9	168	J10.00	104, 105
H93.9*	86	I32	172, 561	I63.119	44, 45, 561	I66.01	44	I79*	168	J10.01	104, 105
H93.A1	86	I33.0	167	I63.12	44, 45, 561	I66.02	44	I80.0*	168	J10.08	1041
H93.A2	86	I33.9	167	I63.131	44, 45, 561	I66.03	44	I80.1*	167, 561	J10.08	104, 105
H93.A3	86	I33*	561, 1041	I63.132	44, 45, 561	I66.09	44	I80.2*	167, 561	J10.08	561
H93.A9	86	I34*	172	I63.133	44, 45, 561	I66.11	44	I80.3	167, 561	J10.1	105
H94*	86	I35*	172	I63.139	44, 45, 561	I66.12	44	I80.8	168	J10.1	561
H95.0*	86	I36*	172	I63.19	44, 45, 561	I66.13	44	I80.9	168	J10.2	632
H95.1*	86	I37*	172	I63.2*	14	I66.19	44	I81	209	J10.8*	632
H95.2*	766	I38	172, 561	I63.20	44, 45, 561	I66.21	44	I82.0	209	J11.0*	105
H95.3*	560, 766	I39	172, 561	I63.211	44, 45, 561	I66.22	44	I82.1	168	J11.00	104
H95.4*	766	I40.0	561	I63.212	44, 45, 561	I66.23	44	I82.210	168	J11.08	104
H95.51	766	I40*	173, 1041	I63.213	44, 45, 561	I66.29	44	I82.211	168	J11.1	86
H95.52	766	I41	173, 561	I63.219	44, 45, 561	I66.3	44	I82.220	167, 561	J11.2	632
H95.53	766	I42*	173	I63.22	44, 45, 561	I66.8	44	I82.221	167, 561	J11.8*	632
H95.54	766	I43	173, 561	I63.231	44, 45, 561	I66.9	44	I82.290	168	J12.3	1041
H95.8*	766	I44.2	561	I63.232	44, 45, 561	I66*	45, 561	I82.291	168	J12.8*	1041
I00	296	I44*	172	I63.233	44, 45, 561	I67.0	167	I82.3	519	J12.9	1041
I01.0	172	I45.2	561	I63.239	44, 45, 561	I67.1	51	I82.4*	168	J12*	105
I01.1	172	I45.3	561	I63.29	44, 45, 561	I67.2	45	I82.5*	168	J13	105, 561, 1041
I01.2	172	I45.6	561	I63.3*	14	I67.3	43, 1041	I82.6*	168	J14	105, 561, 1041
I01.8	172	I45.89	561	I63.30	44, 45, 561	I67.4	47	I82.7*	168	J15.0	104, 1041
I01.9	172	I45*	172	I63.311	44, 45, 561	I67.5	51	I82.8*	168	J15.1	104, 1041
I02*	172	I46*	167, 561	I63.312	44, 45, 561	I67.6	51	I82.9*	168	J15.2*	104, 1041
I05*	172	I47.0	561	I63.313	44, 45, 561	I67.7	55	I82.A*	168	J15.3	105, 1041
I06*	172	I47.2	561	I63.319	44, 45, 561	I67.81	44, 45	I82.B*	168	J15.4	105, 1041
I07*	172	I47*	172	I63.321	44, 45, 561	I67.82	44, 45	I82.C*	168	J15.5	104, 1041
I08*	172	I48.0	561	I63.322	44, 45, 561	I67.83	46, 1041	I83.0*	168	J15.6	104, 1041
I09.0	172	I48.19	561	I63.323	44, 45, 561	I67.841	44, 45	I83.1*	168	J15.7	105
I09.1	172	I48.21	561	I63.329	44, 45, 561	I67.848	44, 45	I83.2*	168	J15.8	104, 1041
I09.2	172	I48.3	561	I63.331	44, 45, 561	I67.850	46	I83.8*	168	J15.9	105, 1041
I09.81	110, 167, 560	I48.4	561	I63.332	44, 45, 561	I67.858	46	I83.9*	168	J15*	561
I09.89	172	I48.91	561	I63.333	44, 45, 561	I67.89	44, 45	I85.0*	193	J16*	105, 561
I09.9	172	I48.92	561	I63.339	44, 45, 561	I67.9	46	I85.10	195	J17	104
I10	171	I48*	172	I63.341	44, 45, 561	I68.0	46	I85.11	193	J18.0	105, 561
I11.0	110, 167, 560	I49.01	561	I63.342	44, 45, 561	I68.2	55	I86.0	168	J18.1	105, 561, 1041
I11.9	171	I49.02	561	I63.343	44, 45, 561	I68.8	46	I86.1	529	J18.2	105
I12.0	1	I49*	172	I63.349	44, 45, 561	I69*	43	I86.2	529, 533, 541	J18.8	105, 561, 1042
I12*	518	I50*	110, 167, 561	I63.39	44, 45	I70.0	167	I86.3	533, 541	J18.9	105, 561, 1042
I13.0	110, 167, 560	I51.0	173	I63.39	561	I70.1	519	I86.4	168	J20*	106
I13.10	518	I51.1	172	I63.4*	14	I70.2*	167	I86.8	168	J21*	106
I13.11	1	I51.2	172	I63.40	44, 45, 561	I70.261	561	I87.0*	168	J22	106
I13.11	518	I51.3	171	I63.411	44, 45, 561	I70.262	561	I87.1	168	J30*	86
I13.11	518	I51.4	173	I63.412	44, 45, 561	I70.268	561	I87.2	168	J31.1	2
I13.2	1, 110, 167, 560	I51.5	173	I63.413	44, 45, 561	I70.269	561	I87.3*	168	J31.2	2
I15*	171	I51.7	171	I63.419	44, 45, 561	I70.3*	168	I87.8	171	J31*	86
I16.0	171	I51.81	173	I63.421	44, 45, 561	I70.4*	168	I87.9	171	J32*	86
I16.1	172	I51.89	171	I63.422	44, 45, 561	I70.5*	168	I88.0	195	J33*	86
I16.9	172	I51.9	171	I63.423	44, 45, 561	I70.6*	168	I88.1	579	J34.0	569
I20*	172	I52	171	I63.429	44, 45, 561	I70.7*	168	I88.8	579	J34.1	569
I21*	110, 167	I60.0*	6, 14	I63.431	44, 45, 561	I70.8	168	I89.0	477	J34.2	2
I22*	110, 167	I60.1*	6, 14	I63.432	44, 45, 561	I70.9*	168	I89.1	454, 561	J34.81	569
I23.0	172	I60.2	14	I63.433	44, 45, 561	I71*	168	I89.8	579	J34.89	569
I23.1	172	I60.2	6	I63.439	44, 45, 561	I72.0	168	I89.9	579	J34.9	569
I23.2	172	I60.3*	14	I63.441	44, 45, 561	I72.1	168	I95.0	173	J34*	86
I23.3	172	I60.3*	6	I63.442	44, 45, 561	I72.2	519	I95.1	172	J35.0*	2, 86
I23.4	172	I60.4	6, 14	I63.443	44, 45, 561	I72.3	168	I95.2	172	J35.1	2, 86
I23.5	172	I60.5*	6, 14	I63.449	44, 45, 561	I72.4	168	I95.3	172	J35.2	2, 86
I23.6	172	I60.6	6, 14	I63.49	44, 45, 561	I72.5	168	I95.81	172	J35.3	2, 86
I23.7	172	I60.7	6, 14	I63.5*	14	I72.6	168	I95.89	173	J35.8	2, 86
I23.8	172	I60.8	6, 14	I63.50	44, 45, 561	I72.8	168	I95.9	173	J35.9	2, 86
I24.0	172	I60.9	6, 14	I63.511	44, 45, 561	I72.9	168	I96	168, 561	J36	2, 86
I24.1	172	I60*	45, 561	I63.512	44, 45, 561	I73.0*	296	I97.0	173, 561	J37.0	2
I24.8	172	I61.0	6, 14	I63.513	44, 45, 561	I73.1	168	I97.1*	173, 561	J37.1	2
I24.9	172	I61.1	6, 14	I63.519	44, 45, 561	I73.8*	168	I97.2	453, 454	J37*	2
I25.1*	171	I61.2	6, 14	I63.521	44, 45, 561	I73.9	168	I97.3	766	J38.0*	2, 561
I25.2	171	I61.3	6, 14	I63.522	44, 45, 561	I74*	168, 561	I97.4*	766	J38.1	2
I25.3	172, 560	I61.4	6, 14	I63.523	44, 45, 561	I75.0*	168	I97.5*	561, 766	J38.2	2
I25.4*	172	I61.5	6, 14	I63.529	44, 45, 561	I75.81	519	I97.6*	766	J38.3	2
I25.5	171	I61.6	6, 14	I63.531	44, 45, 561	I75.89	168	I97.7*	173, 561	J38.4	2
I25.6	171	I61.8	6, 14	I63.532	44, 45, 561	I76	168, 561	I97.810	51	J38.5	2, 561
I25.7*	171	I61.9	6, 14	I63.533	44, 45, 561	I77.0	168	I97.811	51	J38.6	2
I25.8*	171	I61*	45, 561	I63.539	44, 45, 561	I77.1	168	I97.820	51	J38.7	2
I25.9	171	I62.0*	6	I63.541	44, 45, 561	I77.2	168	I97.821	51	J38*	86
I26.01	104	I62.1	6	I63.542	44, 45, 561	I77.3	168	I97.88	173, 561	J39.0	2, 86, 561
I26.02	104	I62.9	6, 14	I63.543	44, 45, 561	I77.4	195	I97.89	173, 561	J39.1	2, 86
I26.09	104	I62*	45, 561	I63.549	44, 45, 561	I77.5	168	I99*	171	J39.2	2, 86
I26.90	104	I63.0*	14	I63.59	44, 45, 561	I77.6	296	J00	2, 86	J39.3	2, 86
I26.92	104			I63.6	14, 44, 45, 561	I77.70	168	J01*	86	J39.8	2, 106
I26.93	104			I63.81	14, 44, 45, 561	I77.71	168	J02*	2, 86	J39.9	2, 86
I26.94	104			I63.89	14, 44, 45, 561	I77.72	168	J03*	2, 86	J40	106
I26.99	104			I63.9	15, 44, 45, 561	I77.73	519	J04.0	2, 86	J41.0	106
I26*	560			I65.01	44					J41.1	105

Numeric Index to Diseases

Code	Page	Code	Page	Code	Page	Code	Page	Code	Page	Code	Page
J41.8	105	J99	105	K28.2	194	K55.1	195	K68.11	632	L00	453
J42	105	K00.6	569	K28.3	194	K55.20	195	K68.12	193	L01*	453
J43*	105	K00*	2,87	K28.4	194	K55.21	194	K68.19	193	L02.01	3,410,562
J44*	105	K01.0	569	K28.5	194	K55.3*	195	K68.9	193	L02.11	3,410,562
J45.22	561	K01.1	569	K28.6	194	K55.30	562	K68*	562	L02.21*	410,562
J45.32	561	K01*	3,87	K28.7	194	K55.31	562	K70.0	209	L02.31	410,562
J45.42	561	K02.3	3	K28.9	194	K55.32	562	K70.1*	208	L02.41*	410,562
J45.52	561	K02.5*	3	K29.00	195	K55.33	562	K70.2	208	L02.51*	410,562
J45.902	561	K02.6*	3	K29.01	194	K55.8	195	K70.3*	208	L02.61*	410,562
J45*	106	K02.7	3	K29.20	195	K55.9	195	K70.4*	208	L02.81*	410,562
J47*	105	K02.9	3	K29.21	194	K56.0	562	K70.9	208	L02.91	410,562
J60	105	K02*	87	K29.30	195	K56.1	562	K71*	209,562	L02*	454
J61	105	K03*	3,87	K29.31	194	K56.2	562	K72.0*	562	L03.011	454
J62*	105	K04*	3,87	K29.40	195	K56.41	562	K72.9*	562	L03.012	454
J63*	105	K05*	3,87	K29.41	194	K56.49	562	K72*	209	L03.019	454
J64	105	K06*	3,87	K29.50	195	K56.600	562	K73*	209	L03.021	454
J65	105	K08.0	3	K29.51	194	K56.601	562	K74.0	208	L03.022	454
J66*	105	K08.1*	3	K29.60	195	K56.609	562	K74.1	209	L03.029	454
J67*	105	K08.2*	3	K29.61	194	K56.690	562	K74.2	209	L03.031	454
J68.0	106	K08.3	3	K29.70	195	K56.691	562	K74.3	208	L03.032	454
J68.1	105	K08.4*	3	K29.71	194	K56.699	562	K74.4	208	L03.039	454
J68.2	106	K08.5*	3	K29.80	195	K56.7	562	K74.5	208	L03.041	454
J68.3	106	K08.8*	3	K29.81	194	K56*	194	K74.6*	208	L03.042	454
J68.4	105	K08.9	3	K29.90	195	K57.00	195	K75.0	562	L03.049	454
J68.8	105	K08*	87	K29.91	194	K57.01	194	K75.1	562	L03.1*	562
J68.9	105	K09*	3,87	K30	195	K57.10	195	K75.2	562	L03.111	454
J69.0	561	K11*	3,86	K31.0	195,562	K57.11	194	K75.3	562	L03.112	454
J69.8	561	K12.0	3	K31.1	195	K57.12	195	K75.8*	562	L03.113	454
J69*	104	K12.1	3	K31.2	195	K57.13	194	K75.9	562	L03.114	454
J70.0	106,561	K12.2	3	K31.3	195	K57.20	195	K75*	209	L03.115	454
J70.1	105	K12.3*	3	K31.4	195	K57.21	194	K76.0	209	L03.116	454
J70.2	106	K12*	87	K31.5	194	K57.30	195	K76.1	209	L03.119	454
J70.3	106	K13.0	3	K31.6	195	K57.31	194	K76.2	209,562	L03.121	454
J70.4	106	K13.1	3	K31.7	195	K57.32	195	K76.3	209,562	L03.122	454
J70.5	106,788	K13.2*	3	K31.811	194	K57.33	194	K76.4	209,562	L03.123	454
J70.8	106	K13.3	3	K31.819	195	K57.40	195	K76.5	209	L03.124	454
J70.9	106	K13.4	3	K31.82	194	K57.41	194	K76.6	209	L03.125	454
J80	106	K13.5	3	K31.83	195	K57.50	195	K76.7	209,562	L03.126	454
J81.0	561	K13.6	3	K31.84	195	K57.51	194	K76.81	106	L03.129	454
J81*	105	K13.7*	3	K31.89	195	K57.52	195	K76.89	209	L03.2*	3,562
J82	105	K13*	87	K31.9	195	K57.53	194	K76.9	209	L03.211	454
J84.83	561	K14.0	3	K35.2*	193	K57.80	195	K77	209	L03.212	454
J84.84*	561	K14.1	3	K35.20	193	K57.81	194	K80*	209	L03.213	454
J84*	105	K14.2	3	K35.21	180,193	K57.90	195	K81*	209	L03.221	454
J85*	104,561	K14.3	3	K35.3*	193	K57.91	194	K82.A1	209	L03.222	454
J86*	104,561	K14.4	3	K35.30	193	K57.92	195	K82.A2	209	L03.3*	562
J90	105,561	K14.5	3	K35.31	193	K57.93	194	K82*	209	L03.311	454
J91.0	104	K14.6	3	K35.32	180,193	K58*	195	K83.01	209,562	L03.312	454
J91.8	105,561	K14.8	3	K35.33	180,193	K59.0*	195	K83.09	209,562	L03.313	454
J92*	105	K14.9	3	K35.80	195	K59.1	195	K83*	209	L03.314	454
J93*	106	K14*	87	K35.890	195	K59.2	195	K85*	208,562	L03.315	454
J94.0	105,561	K20*	195	K35.891	193	K59.3*	195	K86.2	562	L03.316	454
J94.1	105	K21*	195	K36	195	K59.4	195	K86.3	562	L03.317	454
J94.2	105,561	K22.0	195	K37	195	K59.8	195	K86*	208	L03.319	454
J94.8	105,562	K22.1*	194	K38*	195	K59.9*	195	K87	209	L03.321	454
J94.9	105	K22.2	195	K40.00	562	K60*	195	K90.0	195	L03.322	454
J95.0*	2,106	K22.3	193,562	K40.10	562	K61.0	195,562	K90.1	195	L03.323	454
J95.1	105,562,788	K22.4	195	K40.30	562	K61.1	195,562	K90.2	195	L03.324	454
J95.2	105,562,788	K22.5	195	K40.40	562	K61.2	195,562	K90.3	195	L03.325	454
J95.3	105,562,788	K22.6	193	K40*	195	K61.31	195,562	K90.4*	195	L03.326	454
J95.4	106,562	K22.7*	194	K41.00	562	K61.39	195,562	K90.81	196	L03.327	454
J95.5	106,562	K22.8	195	K41.10	562	K61.4	195,562	K90.89	195	L03.329	454
J95.6*	766	K22.9	195	K41.30	562	K61.5	195,562	K90.9	195	L03.8*	562
J95.7*	562,766	K23	195	K41.40	562	K62.0	195	K91.0	195	L03.811	454
J95.81*	106	K25.0	194	K41*	195	K62.1	195	K91.1	195	L03.818	454
J95.82*	105,788	K25.1	194	K42.0	562	K62.2	195	K91.2	195,562	L03.891	454
J95.830	766	K25.2	194	K42.1	562	K62.3	195	K91.30	194,562	L03.898	454
J95.831	766	K25.3	194	K42*	195	K62.4	196	K91.31	194,562	L03.9*	562
J95.84	106	K25.4	194	K43.0	562	K62.5	194,562	K91.32	194,562	L03.90	454
J95.850	844	K25.5	194	K43.1	562	K62.6	196	K91.5	209	L03.91	454
J95.851	106,562	K25.6	194	K43.3	562	K62.7	196	K91.6*	766	L03*	410
J95.859	106,562	K25.7	194	K43.4	562	K62.8*	196	K91.7*	562,766	L04.0	579
J95.860	766	K25.9	194	K43.6	562	K62.9	196	K91.81	196,562	L04.1	579
J95.861	766	K26.0	194	K43.7	562	K63.0	193	K91.82	196,562	L04.2	579
J95.862	766	K26.1	194	K43*	195	K63.1	196,562	K91.83	196,562	L04.3	579
J95.863	766	K26.2	194	K44.0	195,562	K63.2	196	K91.840	767	L04.8	579
J95.88	106,562	K26.3	194	K44.1	195,562	K63.3	196	K91.841	767	L04.9	579
J95.89	106,562	K26.4	194	K44.9	195	K63.4	196	K91.850	196,562	L04*	562
J96.0*	788	K26.5	194	K45.0	562	K63.5	196	K91.858	196,562	L05*	454
J96.2*	788	K26.6	194	K45.1	562	K63.8*	196	K91.86	196,562	L08.0	454
J96.9*	788	K26.7	194	K45*	195	K63.9	196	K91.870	767	L08.1	477,1042
J96*	105	K26.9	194	K46.0	562	K64*	196	K91.871	767	L08.8*	454
J98.0*	2,106	K27.0	194	K46.1	562	K65.0	193	K91.872	767	L08.9	455,569
J98.1*	106	K27.1	194	K46*	195	K65.1	193	K91.873	767	L10*	453
J98.11	562	K27.2	194	K50*	194	K65.2	193	K91.89	196,562	L11*	477
J98.19	562	K27.3	194	K51*	194	K65.3	196	K92.0	194,562	L12.0	453
J98.2	106,562	K27.4	194	K52.0	195	K65.4	196	K92.1	194,562	L12.1	453
J98.3	106	K27.5	194	K52.1	195,562	K65.8	193	K92.2	194,562	L12.2	477
J98.4	106	K27.6	194	K52.2*	195	K65.9	193	K92.81	195	L12.3*	453
J98.5*	104,562	K27.7	194	K52.3	195	K65*	562	K92.89	196	L12.8	453
J98.6	106	K27.9	194	K52.8*	195	K66.1	562	K92.9	196	L12.9	453
J98.8	106	K28.0	194	K52.9	195	K66*	196	K94*	196	L13.0	477
J98.9	106	K28.1	194	K55.0*	195,562	K67	193,562	K95*	196	L13.1	477

Code	Page	Code	Page	Code	Page	Code	Page	Code	Page	Code	Page
L13.8	453	L89*	410, 453	M06.2*	296	M21.229	374	M23.0*	348	M25.0*	301
L13.9	453	L90*	477	M06.3*	296	M21.231	374	M23.2*	348	M25.1*	302
L14	453	L91*	477	M06.4	301	M21.232	374	M23.3*	348	M25.2*	375
L20*	477	L92*	477	M06.8*	296	M21.239	374	M23.4*	375	M25.3*	375
L21*	477	L92.1	477	M06.9	296	M21.241	374	M23.5*	375	M25.4*	375
L22	477, 569	L92.2	477	M07*	301	M21.242	374	M23.6*	348	M25.5*	302
L23*	477	L92.3	477	M08*	296	M21.249	374	M23.8*	348	M25.6*	302
L24*	477	L92.8	455	M10.0*	301	M21.251	374	M23.9*	348	M25.70	302
L25*	477	L92.9	477	M10.1*	301	M21.252	374	M24.0*	375	M25.711	302
L26	477	L93*	453	M10.2*	301	M21.259	374	M24.10	375	M25.712	302
L27.0	562	L94.0	477	M10.3*	519	M21.261	374	M24.111	348	M25.719	302
L27.1	562	L94.1	477	M10.4*	301	M21.262	374	M24.112	348	M25.721	302
L27*	477	L94.2	477	M10.9	301	M21.269	374	M24.119	348	M25.722	302
L28*	477	L94.3	477	M11*	301	M21.271	374	M24.121	348	M25.729	302
L29.0	477	L94.4	477	M12*	301	M21.272	374	M24.122	348	M25.731	302
L29.1	529	L94.5	453	M13*	301	M21.279	374	M24.129	348	M25.732	302
L29.2	533, 541	L94.6	634	M14*	301	M21.331	46	M24.131	348	M25.739	302
L29.3	529, 534, 541	L94.8	477	M15*	301	M21.332	46	M24.132	348	M25.741	302
L29.8	477	L94.9	477	M16*	301	M21.339	46	M24.139	348	M25.742	302
L29.9	477	L95*	477	M17*	301	M21.371	374	M24.141	348	M25.749	302
L30*	477	L97*	410, 453	M18*	301	M21.372	374	M24.142	348	M25.751	302
L40.0	453	L98.0	455	M19*	301	M21.379	374	M24.149	348	M25.752	302
L40.1	477	L98.1	477	M1A.0*	301	M21.40	374	M24.151	375	M25.759	302
L40.2	453	L98.2	477	M1A.1*	758	M21.41	374	M24.152	375	M25.761	302
L40.3	453	L98.3	410, 455, 562	M1A.2*	301	M21.42	374	M24.159	375	M25.762	302
L40.4	453	L98.4*	410, 453	M1A.3*	301	M21.511	46	M24.171	348	M25.769	302
L40.5*	296	L98.5	477	M1A.4*	301	M21.512	46	M24.172	348	M25.771	302
L40.8	453	L98.6	477	M1A.9*	301	M21.519	46	M24.173	348	M25.772	302
L40.9	453	L98.7	477	M20.001	374	M21.521	46	M24.174	348	M25.773	302
L41*	453	L98.8	477	M20.002	374	M21.522	46	M24.175	348	M25.774	302
L42	477	L98.9	477	M20.009	374	M21.529	46	M24.176	348	M25.775	302
L43*	477	L99	477	M20.011	374	M21.531	46	M24.2*	302	M25.776	302
L44.0	477	M00.00	296	M20.012	374	M21.532	46	M24.30	348	M25.78	297
L44.1	477	M00.011	296	M20.019	374	M21.539	46	M24.311	348	M25.8*	302
L44.2	477	M00.012	296	M20.021	374	M21.541	374	M24.312	348	M25.9	302
L44.3	477	M00.019	296	M20.022	374	M21.542	374	M24.319	348	M26.0*	3
L44.4	632	M00.021	296	M20.029	374	M21.549	374	M24.321	348	M26.1*	3
L44.8	477	M00.022	296	M20.031	374	M21.611	374	M24.322	348	M26.2*	3
L44.9	477	M00.029	296	M20.032	374	M21.612	374	M24.329	348	M26.3*	3
L45	477	M00.031	296	M20.039	374	M21.619	374	M24.331	348	M26.4	3
L49*	477	M00.032	296	M20.091	374	M21.621	374	M24.332	348	M26.5*	3
L50.0	562	M00.039	296	M20.092	374	M21.622	374	M24.339	348	M26.6*	3
L50*	477	M00.041	296	M20.099	374	M21.629	374	M24.341	348	M26.7*	3
L51*	453	M00.042	296	M20.10	374	M21.6X1	374	M24.342	348	M26.8*	3
L52	453	M00.049	296	M20.11	374	M21.6X2	374	M24.349	348	M26.9	3
L53.0	453, 562	M00.051	296	M20.12	374	M21.6X9	374	M24.351	375	M26*	87
L53.1	453, 562	M00.052	296	M20.20	374	M21.70	374	M24.352	375	M27.0	3
L53.2	453, 562	M00.059	296	M20.21	374	M21.721	374	M24.359	375	M27.1	3
L53.3	453, 562	M00.06*	227	M20.30	374	M21.722	374	M24.361	348	M27.2	3
L53.8	477	M00.061	296	M20.31	374	M21.729	374	M24.362	348	M27.3	3
L53.9	477	M00.062	296	M20.32	374	M21.731	374	M24.369	348	M27.4*	3
L54	477	M00.069	296	M20.40	374	M21.732	374	M24.371	348	M27.5*	3
L55*	477	M00.071	296	M20.41	374	M21.733	375	M24.372	348	M27.6*	3
L56*	477	M00.072	296	M20.42	374	M21.734	375	M24.373	348	M27.8	3
L57.3	569	M00.079	297	M20.5X1	374	M21.739	375	M24.374	348	M27.9	3
L57*	477	M00.08	297	M20.5X2	374	M21.751	375	M24.375	348	M27*	87
L58*	477	M00.09	297	M20.5X9	374	M21.752	375	M24.376	348	M30.0	296
L59*	477	M00.1*	297	M20.60	374	M21.759	375	M24.40	375	M30.1	295
L60*	477	M00.161	227	M20.61	374	M21.761	375	M24.411	348	M30.2	296
L62	477	M00.162	227	M20.62	374	M21.762	375	M24.412	348	M30.3	296
L63*	477	M00.169	227	M21.00	374	M21.763	375	M24.419	348	M30.8	296
L64*	477	M00.2*	297	M21.021	374	M21.764	375	M24.421	348	M31.0	296
L65*	477	M00.261	227	M21.022	374	M21.769	375	M24.422	348	M31.1	296
L66*	477	M00.262	227	M21.029	374	M21.80	375	M24.429	348	M31.2	295
L67*	477	M00.269	227	M21.051	374	M21.821	375	M24.431	348	M31.3*	295
L68*	477	M00.8*	297	M21.052	374	M21.822	375	M24.432	348	M31.4	296
L70*	477	M00.861	227	M21.059	374	M21.829	375	M24.439	348	M31.5	296
L71*	477	M00.862	227	M21.061	374	M21.831	375	M24.441	348	M31.6	296
L72*	477	M00.869	227	M21.062	374	M21.832	375	M24.442	348	M31.7	296
L73*	477	M00.9	227, 297	M21.069	374	M21.839	375	M24.443	348	M31.8	168
L74*	477	M01.X61	227	M21.071	374	M21.851	375	M24.444	348	M31.9	168
L75*	477	M01.X62	227	M21.072	374	M21.852	375	M24.445	348	M32*	296
L76.1*	562	M01.X69	227	M21.079	374	M21.859	375	M24.446	348	M33*	296
L76*	767	M01*	297	M21.10	374	M21.861	375	M24.451	375	M34.0	296
L80	477, 569	M02.0*	301	M21.121	374	M21.862	375	M24.452	375	M34.1	296
L81.0	569	M02.1*	301	M21.122	374	M21.869	375	M24.459	375	M34.2	296
L81.1	569	M02.2*	301	M21.129	374	M21.90	375	M24.461	348	M34.81	105
L81.2	569	M02.3*	296	M21.151	374	M21.921	375	M24.462	348	M34.82	296
L81.3	569	M02.8*	297	M21.152	374	M21.922	375	M24.469	348	M34.83	46
L81.4	569	M02.9	301	M21.159	374	M21.929	375	M24.471	348	M34.89	296
L81.5	569	M04*	296	M21.161	374	M21.931	375	M24.472	348	M34.9	296
L81.6	569	M05.0*	296	M21.162	374	M21.932	375	M24.473	348	M35.0*	296
L81.7	569	M05.1*	105	M21.169	374	M21.939	375	M24.474	348	M35.1	296
L81.8	569	M05.2*	296	M21.171	374	M21.941	375	M24.475	348	M35.2	296
L81.9	569	M05.3*	296	M21.172	374	M21.942	375	M24.476	348	M35.3	296
L81*	477	M05.4*	296	M21.179	374	M21.949	375	M24.477	348	M35.4	302
L82*	477	M05.5*	296	M21.20	374	M21.951	375	M24.478	348	M35.5	296
L83	477	M05.6*	296	M21.211	374	M21.952	375	M24.479	348	M35.6	477
L84	477	M05.7*	296	M21.212	374	M21.959	375	M24.5*	375	M35.7	302
L85*	477	M05.8*	296	M21.219	374	M21.961	375	M24.6*	301	M35.8	296
L86	477	M05.9	296	M21.221	374	M21.962	375	M24.7	375	M35.9	296
L87*	477	M06.0*	296	M21.222	374	M21.969	375	M24.8*	375	M36.0	296
L88	455	M06.1	296			M22*	347	M24.9	375	M36.1	301

Code	Page	Code	Page	Code	Page	Code	Page	Code	Page	Code	Page
M36.2	301	M46.4*	297	M51*	297	M79.0	302	M80.051D	303	M80.822P	375
M36.3	301	M46.5*	297	M53.0	46	M79.10	302	M80.051G	303	M80.822S	303
M36.4	301	M46.8*	297	M53.1	46	M79.11	302	M80.051K	375	M80.829A	295, 562
M36.8	296	M46.9*	297	M53.2X1	375	M79.12	302	M80.051P	375	M80.829D	303
M40.00	212	M47*	297	M53.2X2	375	M79.18	302	M80.051S	303	M80.829G	303
M40.04	212	M48.0*	297	M53.2X3	375	M79.2	46	M80.052A	295, 562	M80.829K	375
M40.05	212	M48.1*	297	M53.2X4	375	M79.3	477	M80.052D	303	M80.829P	375
M40.10	212	M48.2*	297	M53.2X5	375	M79.4	477	M80.052G	303	M80.829S	303
M40.14	212	M48.3*	297	M53.2X6	375	M79.5	375	M80.052K	375	M80.831A	295, 562
M40.15	212	M48.40XA	295	M53.2X7	297	M79.6*	302	M80.052P	375	M80.831D	303
M40.204	212	M48.40XD	302	M53.2X8	375	M79.7	302	M80.052S	303	M80.831G	303
M40.205	212	M48.40XG	302	M53.2X9	375	M79.8*	302	M80.059A	295, 562	M80.831K	375
M40.209	212	M48.40XS	297	M53.3	297	M79.9	302	M80.059D	303	M80.831P	375
M40.294	212	M48.41XA	295	M53.8*	297	M79.A*	302	M80.059K	375	M80.831S	303
M40.295	212	M48.41XD	302	M53.9	297	M80.00XA	295, 562	M80.059P	375	M80.832A	295, 562
M40.299	212	M48.41XG	302	M54.00	477	M80.00XD	302	M80.059S	303	M80.832D	303
M40.3*	212	M48.41XS	297	M54.01	477	M80.00XG	302	M80.061A	295, 562	M80.832G	303
M40.4*	212	M48.42XA	295	M54.02	477	M80.00XK	375	M80.061D	303	M80.832K	375
M40.5*	212	M48.42XD	302	M54.03	297	M80.00XP	375	M80.061G	303	M80.832P	375
M40*	297	M48.42XG	302	M54.04	297	M80.00XS	302	M80.061K	375	M80.832S	303
M41.00	212	M48.42XS	297	M54.06	297	M80.011A	295, 562	M80.061P	375	M80.839A	295, 562
M41.04	212	M48.43XA	295	M54.07	297	M80.011D	302	M80.061S	303	M80.839D	303
M41.05	212	M48.43XD	302	M54.08	297	M80.011G	302	M80.062A	295, 562	M80.839G	303
M41.06	212	M48.43XG	302	M54.09	297	M80.011K	375	M80.062D	303	M80.839K	375
M41.07	212	M48.43XS	297	M54.10	46	M80.011P	297	M80.062G	303	M80.839P	375
M41.08	212	M48.44XA	295	M54.11	46	M80.011S	302	M80.062K	375	M80.839S	303
M41.114	212	M48.44XD	302	M54.12	46	M80.012A	295, 562	M80.062P	375	M80.841A	295, 562
M41.115	212	M48.44XG	302	M54.13	46	M80.012D	302	M80.062S	303	M80.841D	303
M41.116	212	M48.44XS	297	M54.14	297	M80.012G	302	M80.069A	295, 562	M80.841G	303
M41.117	212	M48.45XA	295	M54.15	297	M80.012K	375	M80.069D	303	M80.841K	375
M41.119	212	M48.45XD	302	M54.16	297	M80.012P	375	M80.069K	375	M80.841P	375
M41.124	212	M48.45XG	302	M54.17	297	M80.012S	302	M80.069P	375	M80.841S	303
M41.125	212	M48.45XS	297	M54.18	46	M80.019A	295, 562	M80.069S	303	M80.842A	295, 562
M41.126	212	M48.46XA	295	M54.2	297	M80.019D	302	M80.071A	295, 562	M80.842D	303
M41.127	212	M48.46XD	302	M54.3*	297	M80.019K	375	M80.071D	303	M80.842G	303
M41.129	212	M48.46XG	302	M54.4*	297	M80.019P	375	M80.071G	303	M80.842K	375
M41.20	212	M48.46XS	297	M54.5	297	M80.019S	302	M80.071K	375	M80.842P	375
M41.24	212	M48.47XA	295	M54.6	297	M80.021A	295, 562	M80.071P	375	M80.842S	303
M41.25	212	M48.47XD	302	M54.8*	297	M80.021D	302	M80.071S	303	M80.849A	295, 562
M41.26	212	M48.47XG	302	M54.9	297	M80.021G	302	M80.072A	295, 562	M80.849D	303
M41.27	212	M48.47XS	297	M60.0*	302	M80.021K	375	M80.072D	303	M80.849G	303
M41.3*	212	M48.48XA	295	M60.1*	302	M80.021P	375	M80.072G	303	M80.849K	375
M41.40	212	M48.48XD	302	M60.2*	302	M80.021S	302	M80.072K	375	M80.849P	375
M41.44	212	M48.48XG	302	M60.8*	302	M80.022A	295, 562	M80.072P	375	M80.849S	303
M41.45	212	M48.48XS	297	M60.9	302	M80.022D	302	M80.072S	303	M80.851A	295, 562
M41.46	212	M48.50XA	212, 295, 562	M61*	302	M80.022G	302	M80.079A	295, 562	M80.851D	303
M41.47	212	M48.50XD	302	M62.0*	302	M80.022K	375	M80.079D	303	M80.851G	303
M41.50	212	M48.50XG	302	M62.1*	302	M80.022P	375	M80.079G	303	M80.851K	375
M41.54	212	M48.50XS	297	M62.2*	302	M80.022S	303	M80.079K	375	M80.851P	375
M41.55	212, 213	M48.51XA	295, 562	M62.3	302	M80.029A	295, 562	M80.079P	375	M80.851S	303
M41.56	212, 213	M48.51XD	302	M62.4*	302	M80.029D	303	M80.079S	303	M80.852A	295, 562
M41.57	212, 213	M48.51XG	302	M62.5*	302	M80.029G	303	M80.08XA	212, 295, 562	M80.852D	303
M41.80	212	M48.51XS	297	M62.81	302	M80.029K	375	M80.08XD	303	M80.852G	303
M41.84	212	M48.52XA	295, 562	M62.82	302	M80.029P	375	M80.08XG	303	M80.852K	375
M41.85	212	M48.52XD	302	M62.830	297	M80.029S	303	M80.08XK	375	M80.852P	375
M41.86	212	M48.52XG	302	M62.831	302	M80.031A	295, 562	M80.08XP	375	M80.852S	303
M41.87	212	M48.52XS	297	M62.838	302	M80.031D	303	M80.08XS	297	M80.859A	295, 563
M41.9	212	M48.53XA	295, 562	M62.84	302	M80.031G	303	M80.80XA	295, 562	M80.859D	303
M41*	297	M48.53XD	302	M62.89	302	M80.031K	375	M80.80XD	303	M80.859G	375
M42.00	212	M48.53XG	302	M62.9	302	M80.031P	375	M80.80XG	303	M80.859P	375
M42.04	212	M48.53XS	297	M63*	302	M80.031S	303	M80.80XK	375	M80.859S	303
M42.05	212	M48.54XA	212, 295, 562	M65*	302	M80.032A	295, 562	M80.80XP	375	M80.861A	295, 563
M42.06	212	M48.54XD	302	M66*	302	M80.032D	303	M80.80XS	303	M80.861D	303
M42.07	212	M48.54XG	302	M67*	302	M80.032G	303	M80.811A	295, 562	M80.861G	303
M42.08	212	M48.54XS	297	M70.0*	302	M80.032K	375	M80.811D	303	M80.861K	375
M42.09	212	M48.55XA	212, 295, 562	M70.1*	302	M80.032P	375	M80.811G	303	M80.861P	375
M42*	301	M48.55XD	302	M70.2*	302	M80.032S	303	M80.811K	375	M80.861S	303
M43.0*	297	M48.55XG	302	M70.3*	302	M80.039A	295, 562	M80.811P	375	M80.862A	295, 563
M43.1*	297	M48.55XS	297	M70.4*	302	M80.039D	303	M80.811S	303	M80.862D	303
M43.2*	297	M48.56XA	212, 295, 562	M70.5*	302	M80.039G	303	M80.812A	295, 562	M80.862G	303
M43.3	375	M48.56XD	302	M70.6*	302	M80.039K	375	M80.812D	303	M80.862K	375
M43.4	375	M48.56XG	302	M70.7*	302	M80.039P	375	M80.812G	303	M80.862P	375
M43.5*	375	M48.56XS	297	M70.8*	302	M80.039S	303	M80.812K	375	M80.862S	303
M43.6	297	M48.57XA	212, 295, 562	M70.9*	302	M80.041A	295, 562	M80.812P	375	M80.869A	295, 563
M43.8*	297	M48.57XD	302	M71.061	227	M80.041D	303	M80.812S	303	M80.869D	303
M43.8X4	212	M48.57XG	302	M71.062	227	M80.041G	303	M80.819A	295, 562	M80.869G	303
M43.8X5	212	M48.57XS	297	M71.069	227	M80.041K	375	M80.819D	303	M80.869K	375
M43.8X6	212	M48.58XA	212, 295, 562	M71.161	227	M80.041P	375	M80.819G	303	M80.869P	375
M43.8X7	212	M48.58XD	302	M71.162	227	M80.041S	303	M80.819K	375	M80.869S	303
M43.8X8	212	M48.58XG	302	M71.169	227	M80.042A	295, 562	M80.819P	375	M80.871A	295, 563
M43.8X9	212, 213	M48.58XS	297	M71*	302	M80.042D	303	M80.819S	303	M80.871D	303
M43.9	212, 297	M48.8*	296	M72*	302	M80.042G	303	M80.821A	295, 562	M80.871G	303
M45*	296	M48.9	297	M75*	302	M80.042K	375	M80.821D	303	M80.871K	375
M46.0*	297	M49*	297	M76*	302	M80.042P	375	M80.821G	303	M80.871P	375
M46.1	297	M50.0*	297	M77.0*	302	M80.042S	303	M80.821K	375	M80.871S	303
M46.2*	294	M50.10	297	M77.1*	302	M80.049A	295, 562	M80.821P	375	M80.872A	295, 563
M46.20	212	M50.11	297	M77.2*	302	M80.049D	303	M80.821S	303	M80.872D	303
M46.24	212	M50.12*	297	M77.3*	375	M80.049G	303	M80.822A	295, 562	M80.872G	303
M46.25	212	M50.13	297	M77.4*	302	M80.049K	375	M80.822D	303	M80.872K	375
M46.26	212	M50.2*	297	M77.5*	302	M80.049P	375	M80.822G	303	M80.872P	375
M46.27	212	M50.3*	297	M77.8	302	M80.049S	303	M80.822K	375	M80.872S	303
M46.28	212	M50.8*	297	M77.9	302	M80.051A	295, 562			M80.879A	295, 563
M46.3*	294	M50.9*	297								

Code	Page	Code	Page	Code	Page	Code	Page	Code	Page	Code	Page
M80.879D	303	M84.342G	303	M84.371S	304	M84.429G	304	M84.454S	297	M84.48XG	304
M80.879G	303	M84.342K	376	M84.372A	295	M84.429K	376	M84.459A	295, 563	M84.48XK	376
M80.879K	375	M84.342P	376	M84.372D	304	M84.429P	376	M84.459D	304	M84.48XP	376
M80.879P	375	M84.342S	303	M84.372G	304	M84.429S	304	M84.459G	304	M84.48XS	304
M80.879S	303	M84.343A	295	M84.372K	376	M84.431A	295, 563	M84.459K	376	M84.50XA	295, 563
M80.88XA	212, 295, 563	M84.343D	303	M84.372P	376	M84.431D	304	M84.459P	376	M84.50XD	304
M80.88XD	303	M84.343G	303	M84.372S	304	M84.431G	304	M84.459S	304	M84.50XG	304
M80.88XG	303	M84.343K	376	M84.373A	295	M84.431K	376	M84.461A	295, 563	M84.50XK	376
M80.88XK	375	M84.343P	376	M84.373D	304	M84.431P	376	M84.461D	304	M84.50XP	376
M80.88XP	375	M84.343S	303	M84.373G	304	M84.431S	304	M84.461G	304	M84.50XS	304
M80.88XS	297	M84.344A	295	M84.373K	376	M84.432A	295, 563	M84.461K	376	M84.511A	295, 563
M81*	301	M84.344D	303	M84.373P	376	M84.432D	304	M84.461P	376	M84.511D	305
M83*	301	M84.344G	303	M84.373S	304	M84.432G	304	M84.461S	304	M84.511G	305
M84.30XA	295	M84.344K	376	M84.374A	295	M84.432K	376	M84.462A	295, 563	M84.511K	376
M84.30XD	303	M84.344P	376	M84.374D	304	M84.432P	376	M84.462D	304	M84.511P	376
M84.30XG	303	M84.344S	303	M84.374G	304	M84.432S	304	M84.462G	304	M84.511S	305
M84.30XK	375	M84.345A	295	M84.374K	376	M84.433A	295, 563	M84.462K	376	M84.512A	295, 563
M84.30XP	375	M84.345D	303	M84.374P	376	M84.433D	304	M84.462P	376	M84.512D	305
M84.30XS	303	M84.345G	303	M84.374S	304	M84.433G	304	M84.462S	304	M84.512G	305
M84.311A	295	M84.345K	376	M84.375A	295	M84.433K	376	M84.463A	295, 563	M84.512K	376
M84.311D	303	M84.345P	376	M84.375D	304	M84.433P	376	M84.463D	304	M84.512P	376
M84.311G	303	M84.345S	303	M84.375G	304	M84.433S	304	M84.463G	304	M84.512S	305
M84.311K	375	M84.346A	295	M84.375K	376	M84.434A	295, 563	M84.463K	376	M84.519A	295, 563
M84.311P	375	M84.346D	303	M84.375P	376	M84.434D	304	M84.463P	376	M84.519D	305
M84.311S	303	M84.346G	303	M84.375S	304	M84.434G	304	M84.463S	304	M84.519G	305
M84.312A	295	M84.346K	376	M84.376A	295	M84.434K	376	M84.464A	295, 563	M84.519K	376
M84.312D	303	M84.346P	376	M84.376D	304	M84.434P	376	M84.464D	304	M84.519P	376
M84.312G	303	M84.346S	303	M84.376G	304	M84.434S	304	M84.464G	304	M84.519S	305
M84.312K	375	M84.350A	295	M84.376K	376	M84.439A	295, 563	M84.464K	376	M84.521A	295, 563
M84.312P	375	M84.350D	303	M84.376P	376	M84.439D	304	M84.464P	376	M84.521D	305
M84.312S	303	M84.350G	304	M84.376S	304	M84.439G	304	M84.464S	304	M84.521G	305
M84.319A	295	M84.350K	376	M84.377A	295	M84.439K	376	M84.469A	295, 563	M84.521K	376
M84.319D	303	M84.350P	376	M84.377D	304	M84.439P	376	M84.469D	304	M84.521P	376
M84.319G	303	M84.350S	297	M84.377G	304	M84.439S	304	M84.469G	304	M84.521S	305
M84.319K	375	M84.351A	295	M84.377K	376	M84.441A	295, 563	M84.469K	376	M84.522A	295, 563
M84.319P	375	M84.351D	304	M84.377P	376	M84.441D	304	M84.469P	376	M84.522D	305
M84.319S	303	M84.351G	304	M84.377S	304	M84.441G	304	M84.469S	304	M84.522G	305
M84.321A	295	M84.351K	376	M84.378A	295	M84.441K	376	M84.471A	295, 563	M84.522K	376
M84.321D	303	M84.351P	376	M84.378D	304	M84.441P	376	M84.471D	304	M84.522P	376
M84.321G	303	M84.351S	304	M84.378G	304	M84.441S	304	M84.471G	304	M84.522S	305
M84.321K	376	M84.352A	295	M84.378K	376	M84.442A	295, 563	M84.471K	376	M84.529A	295, 563
M84.321P	376	M84.352D	304	M84.378P	376	M84.442D	304	M84.471P	376	M84.529D	305
M84.321S	303	M84.352G	304	M84.378S	304	M84.442G	304	M84.471S	304	M84.529G	305
M84.322A	295	M84.352K	376	M84.379A	295	M84.442K	376	M84.472A	295, 563	M84.529K	376
M84.322D	303	M84.352P	376	M84.379D	304	M84.442P	376	M84.472D	304	M84.529P	376
M84.322G	303	M84.352S	304	M84.379G	304	M84.442S	304	M84.472G	304	M84.529S	305
M84.322K	376	M84.353A	295	M84.379K	376	M84.443A	295, 563	M84.472K	376	M84.531A	295, 563
M84.322P	376	M84.353D	304	M84.379P	376	M84.443D	304	M84.472P	376	M84.531D	305
M84.322S	303	M84.353G	304	M84.379S	304	M84.443G	304	M84.472S	304	M84.531G	305
M84.329A	295	M84.353K	376	M84.38XA	295	M84.443K	376	M84.473A	295, 563	M84.531K	376
M84.329D	303	M84.353P	376	M84.38XD	304	M84.443P	376	M84.473D	304	M84.531P	376
M84.329G	303	M84.353S	304	M84.38XG	304	M84.443S	304	M84.473G	304	M84.531S	305
M84.329K	295	M84.359A	295	M84.38XK	376	M84.444A	295, 563	M84.473K	376	M84.532A	295, 563
M84.329P	376	M84.359D	304	M84.38XP	376	M84.444D	304	M84.473P	376	M84.532D	305
M84.329S	303	M84.359G	304	M84.38XS	304	M84.444G	304	M84.473S	304	M84.532G	305
M84.331A	295	M84.359K	376	M84.40XA	295, 563	M84.444K	376	M84.474A	295, 563	M84.532K	376
M84.331D	303	M84.359P	376	M84.40XD	304	M84.444P	376	M84.474D	304	M84.532P	376
M84.331G	303	M84.359S	304	M84.40XG	304	M84.444S	304	M84.474G	304	M84.532S	305
M84.331K	376	M84.361A	295	M84.40XK	376	M84.445A	295, 563	M84.474K	376	M84.533A	295, 563
M84.331P	376	M84.361D	304	M84.40XP	376	M84.445D	304	M84.474P	376	M84.533D	305
M84.331S	303	M84.361G	304	M84.40XS	304	M84.445G	304	M84.474S	304	M84.533G	305
M84.332A	295	M84.361K	376	M84.411A	295, 563	M84.445K	376	M84.475A	295, 563	M84.533K	376
M84.332D	303	M84.361P	376	M84.411D	304	M84.445P	376	M84.475D	304	M84.533P	376
M84.332G	303	M84.361S	304	M84.411G	304	M84.445S	304	M84.475G	304	M84.533S	376
M84.332K	376	M84.362A	295	M84.411K	376	M84.446A	295, 563	M84.475K	376	M84.534A	295, 563
M84.332P	376	M84.362D	304	M84.411P	376	M84.446D	304	M84.475P	376	M84.534D	305
M84.332S	303	M84.362G	304	M84.411S	304	M84.446G	304	M84.475S	304	M84.534G	305
M84.333A	295	M84.362K	376	M84.412A	295, 563	M84.446K	376	M84.476A	295, 563	M84.534K	376
M84.333D	303	M84.362P	376	M84.412D	304	M84.446P	376	M84.476D	304	M84.534P	376
M84.333G	303	M84.362S	304	M84.412G	304	M84.446S	304	M84.476G	304	M84.534S	305
M84.333K	376	M84.363A	295	M84.412K	376	M84.451A	295, 563	M84.476K	376	M84.539A	295, 563
M84.333P	376	M84.363D	304	M84.412P	376	M84.451D	304	M84.476P	376	M84.539D	305
M84.333S	303	M84.363G	304	M84.412S	304	M84.451G	304	M84.476S	304	M84.539G	305
M84.334A	295	M84.363K	376	M84.419A	295, 563	M84.451K	376	M84.477A	295, 563	M84.539P	376
M84.334D	303	M84.363P	376	M84.419D	304	M84.451P	376	M84.477D	304	M84.539S	305
M84.334G	303	M84.363S	304	M84.419G	304	M84.451S	304	M84.477G	304	M84.541A	295, 563
M84.334K	376	M84.364A	295	M84.419K	376	M84.452A	295, 563	M84.477K	376	M84.541D	305
M84.334P	376	M84.364D	304	M84.419P	376	M84.452D	304	M84.477P	376	M84.541G	305
M84.334S	303	M84.364G	304	M84.419S	304	M84.452G	304	M84.477S	304	M84.541K	376
M84.339A	295	M84.364K	376	M84.421A	295, 563	M84.452K	376	M84.478A	295, 563	M84.541P	376
M84.339D	303	M84.364P	376	M84.421D	304	M84.452P	376	M84.478D	304	M84.541S	305
M84.339G	303	M84.364S	304	M84.421G	304	M84.452S	304	M84.478G	304	M84.542A	296, 563
M84.339K	376	M84.369A	295	M84.421K	376	M84.453A	295, 563	M84.478K	376	M84.542D	305
M84.339P	376	M84.369D	304	M84.421P	376	M84.453D	304	M84.478P	376	M84.542G	305
M84.339S	303	M84.369G	304	M84.421S	304	M84.453G	304	M84.478S	304	M84.542K	376
M84.341A	295	M84.369K	376	M84.422A	295, 563	M84.453K	376	M84.479A	295, 563	M84.542P	376
M84.341D	303	M84.369P	376	M84.422D	304	M84.453S	304	M84.479D	304	M84.542S	305
M84.341G	303	M84.371A	295	M84.422G	304	M84.454A	295, 563	M84.479G	304	M84.549A	296, 563
M84.341K	376	M84.371D	304	M84.422K	376	M84.454D	304	M84.479K	376	M84.549D	305
M84.341P	376	M84.371K	376	M84.422P	376	M84.454K	376	M84.479P	376	M84.549G	305
M84.341S	303	M84.371P	376	M84.422S	304	M84.454P	376	M84.479S	304	M84.549K	376
M84.342A	295			M84.429A	295, 563	M84.48XA	295, 563	M84.48XD	304	M84.549P	376
M84.342D	303			M84.429D	304						

Numeric Index to Diseases

Code	Page	Code	Page	Code	Page	Code	Page	Code	Page	Code	Page
M84.549S	305	M84.576G	305	M84.642S	305	M84.675G	306	M86.169	227	M97.22XA	306
M84.550A	296, 563	M84.576K	377	M84.649A	296, 563	M84.675K	377	M86.18	212	M97.22XD	306
M84.550D	305	M84.576P	377	M84.649D	305	M84.675P	377	M86.261	227	M97.22XS	767
M84.550G	305	M84.576S	305	M84.649G	305	M84.675S	306	M86.262	227	M97.31XA	306
M84.550K	377	M84.58XA	212, 296, 563	M84.649K	377	M84.676A	296, 563	M86.269	227	M97.31XD	306
M84.550P	377	M84.58XD	305	M84.649P	377	M84.676D	306	M86.28	212	M97.31XS	767
M84.550S	297	M84.58XG	305	M84.650A	296, 563	M84.676G	306	M86.361	227	M97.32XA	306
M84.551A	296, 563	M84.58XK	377	M84.650D	305	M84.676K	377	M86.362	227	M97.32XD	306
M84.551D	305	M84.58XP	377	M84.650G	305	M84.676P	377	M86.369	227	M97.32XS	767
M84.551G	305	M84.58XS	297	M84.650K	296, 563	M84.676S	306	M86.38	212	M97.41XA	306
M84.551K	377	M84.60XA	296, 563	M84.650P	377	M84.68XA	212, 296, 563	M86.461	227	M97.41XD	306
M84.551P	377	M84.60XD	305	M84.650S	297	M84.68XD	306	M86.462	227	M97.41XS	767
M84.551S	305	M84.60XG	305	M84.651A	296, 563	M84.68XG	306	M86.469	227	M97.42XA	306
M84.552A	296, 563	M84.60XK	377	M84.651D	305	M84.68XK	377	M86.48	212	M97.42XD	306
M84.552D	305	M84.60XP	377	M84.651G	305	M84.68XP	377	M86.561	227	M97.42XS	767
M84.552G	305	M84.60XS	305	M84.651K	377	M84.68XS	306	M86.562	227	M97.8XXA	306
M84.552K	377	M84.611A	296, 563	M84.651S	305	M84.750A	296, 563	M86.569	227	M97.8XXD	306
M84.552P	377	M84.611D	305	M84.652A	296, 563	M84.750D	306	M86.58	212	M97.8XXS	767
M84.552S	305	M84.611G	305	M84.652G	305	M84.750G	306	M86.661	227	M97.9XXA	306
M84.553A	296, 563	M84.611K	377	M84.652K	377	M84.750K	377	M86.662	227	M97.9XXD	306
M84.553D	305	M84.611P	377	M84.652P	377	M84.750P	377	M86.669	227	M97.9XXS	767
M84.553G	305	M84.611S	305	M84.652S	305	M84.750S	306	M86.68	212	M99.00	302
M84.553K	377	M84.612A	296, 563	M84.653A	296, 563	M84.751A	296, 563	M86.8X6	227	M99.01	297
M84.553P	377	M84.612D	305	M84.653D	305	M84.751D	306	M86.8X8	212	M99.02	297
M84.553S	305	M84.612G	305	M84.653K	377	M84.751G	306	M86*	294	M99.03	297
M84.559A	296, 563	M84.612K	377	M84.653P	377	M84.751K	377	M87*	301	M99.04	297
M84.559D	305	M84.612P	377	M84.653S	305	M84.751P	377	M88*	301	M99.05	302
M84.559G	305	M84.612S	305	M84.659A	296, 563	M84.751S	306	M89.0*	377	M99.06	302
M84.559K	377	M84.619A	296, 563	M84.659D	305	M84.752A	296, 563	M89.1*	377	M99.07	302
M84.559P	377	M84.619D	305	M84.659G	305	M84.752D	306	M89.2*	377	M99.08	302
M84.559S	305	M84.619G	305	M84.659P	377	M84.752G	306	M89.3*	377	M99.09	302
M84.561A	296, 563	M84.619K	377	M84.659S	305	M84.752K	377	M89.4*	301	M99.10	297, 975, 1028
M84.561D	305	M84.619P	377	M84.661A	296, 563	M84.752P	377	M89.5*	377	M99.11	297, 975, 1028
M84.561G	305	M84.619S	305	M84.661G	305	M84.752S	306	M89.6*	377	M99.12	297, 975
M84.561K	377	M84.621A	296, 563	M84.661K	377	M84.753A	296, 563	M89.7*	301	M99.13	297, 975
M84.561P	377	M84.621D	305	M84.661S	305	M84.753D	306	M89.8*	377	M99.14	297, 975
M84.561S	305	M84.621G	305	M84.662A	296, 563	M84.753G	306	M89.9	377	M99.15	297, 975
M84.562A	296, 563	M84.621K	377	M84.662D	305	M84.753K	377	M90*	301	M99.16	348, 975
M84.562D	305	M84.621P	377	M84.662K	377	M84.753P	377	M91*	301	M99.17	348, 975
M84.562G	305	M84.621S	305	M84.662P	377	M84.753S	306	M92*	301	M99.18	104, 975
M84.562K	377	M84.622A	296, 563	M84.662S	305	M84.754A	296, 563	M93*	301	M99.19	348, 975
M84.562P	377	M84.622D	305	M84.663A	296, 563	M84.754D	306	M94.0	106	M99.2*	297
M84.562S	305	M84.622G	305	M84.663D	305	M84.754G	306	M94.1	377	M99.3*	297
M84.563A	296, 563	M84.622K	377	M84.663G	305	M84.754K	377	M94.2*	301	M99.4*	297
M84.563D	305	M84.622P	377	M84.663K	377	M84.754P	377	M94.3*	377	M99.5*	297
M84.563G	305	M84.622S	305	M84.663P	377	M84.754S	306	M94.8*	377	M99.6*	297
M84.563K	377	M84.629A	296, 563	M84.663S	305	M84.755A	296, 563	M94.9	377	M99.7*	297
M84.563P	377	M84.629D	305	M84.664A	296, 563	M84.755D	306	M95.0	86	M99.80	377
M84.563S	305	M84.629G	305	M84.664D	305	M84.755G	306	M95.1*	86	M99.81	377
M84.564A	296, 563	M84.629K	377	M84.664G	305	M84.755K	377	M95.2	377	M99.82	377
M84.564D	305	M84.629P	377	M84.664K	377	M84.755P	377	M95.3	377	M99.83	297
M84.564G	305	M84.629S	305	M84.664P	377	M84.755S	306	M95.4	377	M99.84	297
M84.564K	377	M84.631A	296, 563	M84.664S	305	M84.756A	296, 563	M95.5	377	M99.85	377
M84.564P	377	M84.631D	305	M84.669A	296, 563	M84.756D	306	M95.8	377	M99.86	377
M84.564S	305	M84.631G	305	M84.669D	305	M84.756G	306	M95.9	377	M99.87	377
M84.569A	296, 563	M84.631K	377	M84.669G	305	M84.756K	377	M96.0	306	M99.88	377
M84.569D	305	M84.631P	377	M84.669K	377	M84.756P	377	M96.1	297	M99.89	377
M84.569G	305	M84.631S	305	M84.669P	377	M84.756S	306	M96.2	212, 297	M99.9	377
M84.569K	377	M84.632A	296, 563	M84.669S	305	M84.757A	296, 563	M96.3	212, 297	N00*	519, 563
M84.569P	377	M84.632D	305	M84.671A	296, 563	M84.757D	306	M96.4	212, 297	N01*	519, 563
M84.569S	305	M84.632G	305	M84.671D	305	M84.757G	306	M96.5	212, 297	N02*	519
M84.571A	296, 563	M84.632K	377	M84.671G	305	M84.757K	377	M96.621	306	N03*	519
M84.571D	305	M84.632P	377	M84.671K	377	M84.757P	377	M96.622	306	N04*	519
M84.571G	305	M84.632S	305	M84.671P	377	M84.757S	306	M96.629	306	N05*	519
M84.571K	377	M84.633A	296, 563	M84.671S	305	M84.758A	296, 563	M96.631	306	N06*	519
M84.571P	377	M84.633D	305	M84.672A	296, 563	M84.758D	306	M96.632	306	N07*	519
M84.571S	305	M84.633G	305	M84.672D	305	M84.758G	306	M96.639	306	N08	519
M84.572A	296, 563	M84.633K	377	M84.672G	305	M84.758K	377	M96.65	306	N10	518, 563
M84.572D	305	M84.633P	377	M84.672K	377	M84.758P	377	M96.661	306	N11.0	518
M84.572G	305	M84.633S	305	M84.672P	377	M84.758S	306	M96.662	306	N11.1	519
M84.572K	377	M84.634A	296, 563	M84.672S	305	M84.759A	296, 563	M96.669	306	N11.8	518
M84.572P	377	M84.634D	305	M84.673A	296, 563	M84.759D	306	M96.671	306	N11.9	518, 563
M84.572S	305	M84.634G	305	M84.673D	305	M84.759G	306	M96.672	306	N12	518, 563
M84.573A	296, 563	M84.634K	377	M84.673G	305	M84.759P	377	M96.679	306	N13.0	519, 563
M84.573D	305	M84.634P	377	M84.673K	377	M84.759S	306	M96.69	306	N13.1	519, 563
M84.573G	305	M84.634S	305	M84.673P	377	M84.8*	377	M96.8*	767	N13.2	519, 563
M84.573K	377	M84.639A	296, 563	M84.673S	305	M84.9	377	M96.820	563	N13.3*	563
M84.573P	377	M84.639D	305	M84.674A	296, 563	M85.0*	301	M96.821	563	N13.30	519
M84.573S	305	M84.639G	305	M84.674D	306	M85.1*	377	M97.01XA	306	N13.39	519
M84.574A	296, 563	M84.639K	377	M84.674K	377	M85.2	377	M97.01XD	306	N13.4	519, 563
M84.574D	305	M84.639P	377	M84.674P	377	M85.3*	301	M97.01XS	767	N13.5	518
M84.574G	305	M84.639S	305	M84.674S	306	M85.4*	301	M97.02XA	306	N13.6	518, 563
M84.574K	377	M84.641A	296, 563	M84.675A	296, 563	M85.5*	301	M97.02XD	306	N13.7*	519
M84.574P	377	M84.641D	305	M84.675D	306	M85.6*	301	M97.02XS	767	N13.8	519
M84.574S	305	M84.641G	305			M85.8*	377	M97.11XA	306	N13.9	519, 563
M84.575A	296, 563	M84.641K	377			M85.9	377	M97.11XD	306	N14*	519
M84.575D	305	M84.641P	377			M86.061	227	M97.11XS	767	N15.0	519
M84.575G	305	M84.641S	305			M86.062	227	M97.12XA	306	N15.1	518, 563
M84.575K	377	M84.642A	296, 563			M86.069	227	M97.12XD	306	N15.8	519
M84.575P	377	M84.642D	305			M86.08	212	M97.12XS	767	N15.9	519
M84.575S	305	M84.642K	377			M86.161	227	M97.21XA	306	N16	519
M84.576A	296, 563	M84.642P	377			M86.162	227	M97.21XD	306	N17*	518, 563
M84.576D	305									M97.21XS	767	N18*	1, 518

Code	Page	Code	Page	Code	Page	Code	Page	Code	Page	Code	Page
N19	518	N43.2	529	N73.3	541	N99.522	563	O10.411	547	O22.23	547
N20.0	519	N43.3	529	N73.4	541	N99.523	563	O10.412	547	O22.30	547
N20.1	519	N43.4*	529	N73.5	541	N99.524	563	O10.413	547	O22.31	547
N20.2	519	N44*	529	N73.6	541	N99.528	563	O10.419	547	O22.32	547
N20.9	519	N45*	529	N73.8	541	N99.530	563	O10.42	557	O22.33	547
N21.0	519	N46*	529	N73.9	541	N99.531	563	O10.43	544	O22.40	547
N21.1	519	N47.0	569	N73*	534	N99.532	563	O10.911	547	O22.41	547
N21.8	519	N47.1	569	N74	534, 541	N99.533	563	O10.912	547	O22.42	547
N21.9	519	N47.2	569	N75.0	541	N99.534	563	O10.913	547	O22.43	547
N22	519	N47.3	569	N75.1	541	N99.538	563	O10.919	547	O22.50	547
N23	519	N47.4	569	N75.8	541	N99.6*	767	O10.92	557	O22.51	547
N25*	519	N47.5	569	N75.9	541	N99.7*	563, 767	O10.93	544	O22.52	547
N26.1	519	N47.7	569	N75*	534	N99.81	520, 563	O11.1	547	O22.53	547
N26.2	172	N47.8	569	N76.0	541	N99.820	767	O11.2	547	O22.8X1	547
N26.9	519	N47*	529	N76.1	541	N99.821	767	O11.3	547	O22.8X2	547
N27*	519	N48.0	529	N76.2	541	N99.83	534, 542	O11.4	557	O22.8X3	547
N28.0	519	N48.1	529	N76.3	541	N99.840	767	O11.5	547	O22.8X9	547
N28.1	519	N48.2*	529	N76.4	541	N99.841	767	O11.9	547	O22.90	547
N28.81	519	N48.3*	529	N76.5	541	N99.842	767	O12.00	547	O22.91	547
N28.82	519	N48.5	529	N76.6	541	N99.843	767	O12.01	547	O22.92	547
N28.83	519	N48.6	529	N76.8*	541	N99.85	542	O12.02	547	O22.93	547
N28.84	518, 563	N48.8*	529	N76*	534	N99.89	520, 563	O12.03	547	O23.00	547
N28.85	518, 563	N48.9	529	N77.0	541	O00.00	547	O12.04	557	O23.01	547
N28.86	518, 563	N49*	529	N77.1	541	O00.01	547	O12.05	544	O23.02	547
N28.89	519	N50*	529	N77*	534	O00.101	547	O12.10	547	O23.03	547
N28.9	519	N51	529	N80.0	534, 541	O00.102	547	O12.11	547	O23.10	547
N29	519	N52*	529	N80.1	534, 541	O00.109	547	O12.12	547	O23.11	547
N30.0*	518, 563	N53*	529	N80.2	534, 541	O00.111	547	O12.13	547	O23.12	547
N30.1*	518	N60.01	453	N80.3	534, 541	O00.112	547	O12.14	557	O23.13	547
N30.2*	518	N60.02	453	N80.4	534, 541	O00.119	547	O12.15	544	O23.20	547
N30.3*	519	N60.09	453	N80.5	195	O00.201	547	O12.20	547	O23.21	547
N30.4*	519	N60.11	453	N80.6	477	O00.202	547	O12.21	547	O23.22	547
N30.8*	519, 563	N60.12	453	N80.8	534, 541	O00.209	547	O12.22	547	O23.23	547
N30.9*	519, 563	N60.19	453	N80.9	534, 541	O00.211	547	O12.23	547	O23.30	547
N31.2	563	N60.21	453	N81*	534, 541	O00.212	547	O12.24	557	O23.31	547
N31*	519	N60.22	453	N82.0	534, 541	O00.219	547	O12.25	544	O23.32	547
N32.0	563	N60.29	453	N82.1	534, 541	O00.80	547	O13.1	547	O23.33	547
N32.1	563	N60.31	453	N82.2	196, 563	O00.81	547	O13.2	547	O23.40	547
N32.2	563	N60.32	453	N82.3	196, 563	O00.90	547	O13.3	547	O23.41	547
N32*	520	N60.39	453	N82.4	196, 563	O00.91	547	O13.4	557	O23.42	547
N33	520	N60.41	453	N82.5	534, 541	O01.0	547	O13.5	544	O23.43	547
N34.0	519, 563	N60.42	453	N82.8	534, 541, 563	O01.1	547	O13.9	547	O23.511	547
N34.1	529, 534, 541	N60.49	453	N82.9	534, 541	O01.9	547	O14.00	547	O23.512	547
N34.2	519	N60.81	453	N83.7	563	O02.0	547	O14.02	547	O23.513	547
N34.3	519	N60.82	453	N83*	534, 541	O02.1	545, 557	O14.03	547	O23.519	547
N35.010	519	N60.89	453	N84*	534, 541	O02.81	547	O14.04	557	O23.521	547
N35.011	519	N60.91	453	N85*	534, 541	O02.89	547	O14.05	544	O23.522	548
N35.012	519	N60.92	453	N86	534, 541	O02.9	547	O14.10	547	O23.523	548
N35.013	519	N60.99	453	N87*	534, 541	O03*	545, 557	O14.12	547	O23.529	548
N35.014	519	N60*	454	N88*	534, 541	O04*	545, 557	O14.13	547	O23.591	548
N35.016	519	N61.0	453	N89.8	569	O07*	545, 557	O14.14	557	O23.592	548
N35.021	519	N61.1	453	N89*	534, 541	O08*	544	O14.15	544	O23.593	548
N35.028	519	N61*	454	N90*	534, 542	O09.0*	557	O14.20	547	O23.599	548
N35.111	519	N62	453, 454	N91*	534, 542	O09.1*	557	O14.22	547	O23.90	548
N35.112	519	N63.0	453	N92*	534, 542	O09.2*	557	O14.23	547	O23.91	548
N35.113	519	N63.10	453	N93*	534, 542	O09.3*	557	O14.24	547	O23.92	548
N35.114	519	N63.11	453	N94.0	542	O09.40	557	O14.25	544	O23.93	548
N35.116	519	N63.12	453	N94.1*	542	O09.41	557	O14.90	547	O24.011	548
N35.119	519	N63.13	453	N94.2	542	O09.42	557	O14.92	547	O24.012	548
N35.12	519	N63.14	453	N94.3	542	O09.43	557	O14.93	547	O24.013	548
N35.811	519	N63.20	453	N94.4	542	O09.5*	557	O14.94	557	O24.019	548
N35.812	519	N63.21	453	N94.5	542	O09.6*	557	O14.95	544	O24.02	557
N35.813	519	N63.22	453	N94.6	542	O09.7*	557	O15.00	547	O24.03	544
N35.814	519	N63.23	453	N94.810	541	O09.8*	557	O15.02	547	O24.111	548
N35.816	519	N63.24	453	N94.818	542	O09.9*	557	O15.03	547	O24.112	548
N35.819	519	N63.31	453	N94.819	542	O09.A0	557	O15.1	547	O24.113	548
N35.82	519	N63.32	453	N94.89	542	O09.A1	557	O15.2	544	O24.119	548
N35.911	519	N63.41	453	N94.9	542	O09.A2	557	O15.9	547	O24.12	557
N35.912	519	N63.42	453	N94*	534	O09.A3	557	O16.1	547	O24.13	544
N35.913	519	N63*	454	N95*	534, 542	O10.011	547	O16.2	547	O24.311	548
N35.914	519	N64.0	453	N96	534, 542	O10.012	547	O16.3	547	O24.312	548
N35.916	519	N64.1	453	N97*	534, 542	O10.013	547	O16.4	557	O24.313	548
N35.919	519	N64.2	453	N98.0	563, 632, 634	O10.019	547	O16.5	544	O24.319	548
N35.92	519	N64.3	453	N98.1	767	O10.02	557	O16.9	547	O24.32	557
N36*	520	N64.4	453	N98.2	767	O10.03	544	O20.0	547	O24.33	544
N37	519	N64.51	453	N98.3	767	O10.111	547	O20.8	547	O24.410	548
N39.0	519, 563	N64.52	453	N98.8	767	O10.112	547	O20.9	547	O24.414	548
N39.3	519, 534, 541	N64.53	453	N98.9	767	O10.113	547	O21.0	547	O24.415	548
N39.4*	519	N64.59	453	N99.0	520, 563	O10.119	547	O21.1	547	O24.419	548
N39.8	520	N64.81	453	N99.110	519	O10.12	557	O21.2	547	O24.420	557
N39.9	520	N64.82	453	N99.111	519	O10.13	544	O21.8	547	O24.424	557
N40*	528	N64.89	453	N99.112	519	O10.211	547	O21.9	547	O24.425	557
N41*	529	N64.9	453	N99.113	519	O10.212	547	O22.00	547	O24.429	557
N42.0	529	N64*	454	N99.114	519	O10.213	547	O22.01	547	O24.430	544
N42.1	529	N65.0	453	N99.115	519	O10.219	547	O22.02	547	O24.434	544
N42.3*	529	N65.1	453	N99.116	519	O10.22	557	O22.03	547	O24.435	544
N42.81	529	N65*	453	N99.12	519	O10.23	544	O22.10	547	O24.439	544
N42.82	529	N70*	534, 541	N99.2	534, 542	O10.311	547	O22.11	547	O24.811	548
N42.83	528	N71*	534, 541	N99.3	534, 542	O10.312	547	O22.12	547	O24.812	548
N42.89	529	N72	534, 541	N99.4	196	O10.313	547	O22.13	547	O24.813	548
N42.9	529	N73.0	541	N99.5*	520	O10.319	547	O22.20	547	O24.819	548
N43.0	529	N73.1	541	N99.520	563	O10.32	557	O22.21	547	O24.82	557
N43.1	529	N73.2	541	N99.521	563	O10.33	544	O22.22	547	O24.83	544

Code	Page	Code	Page	Code	Page	Code	Page	Code	Page	Code	Page
O24.911	548	O29.022	548	O30.193	549	O31.12X5	549	O32.0XX0	550	O33.7XX9	550
O24.912	548	O29.023	548	O30.199	549	O31.12X9	549	O32.0XX1	550	O33.8	550
O24.913	548	O29.029	548	O30.201	549	O31.13X0	549	O32.0XX2	550	O33.9	550
O24.919	548	O29.091	548	O30.202	549	O31.13X1	549	O32.0XX3	550	O34.00	550
O24.92	557	O29.092	548	O30.203	549	O31.13X2	549	O32.0XX4	550	O34.01	550
O24.93	544	O29.093	548	O30.209	549	O31.13X3	549	O32.0XX5	550	O34.02	550
O25.10	548	O29.099	548	O30.211	549	O31.13X4	549	O32.0XX9	550	O34.03	550
O25.11	548	O29.111	548	O30.212	549	O31.13X5	549	O32.1XX0	550	O34.10	550
O25.12	548	O29.112	548	O30.213	549	O31.13X9	549	O32.1XX1	550	O34.11	550
O25.13	548	O29.113	548	O30.219	549	O31.20X0	549	O32.1XX2	550	O34.12	550
O25.2	557	O29.119	548	O30.221	549	O31.20X1	549	O32.1XX4	550	O34.13	550
O25.3	544	O29.121	548	O30.222	549	O31.20X2	549	O32.1XX5	550	O34.211	550
O26.00	548	O29.122	548	O30.223	549	O31.20X3	549	O32.1XX9	550	O34.212	550
O26.01	548	O29.123	548	O30.229	549	O31.20X4	549	O32.2XX0	550	O34.219	550
O26.02	548	O29.129	548	O30.231	549	O31.20X5	549	O32.2XX1	550	O34.29	550
O26.03	548	O29.191	548	O30.232	549	O31.20X9	549	O32.2XX2	550	O34.30	550
O26.10	548	O29.192	548	O30.233	549	O31.21X0	549	O32.2XX4	550	O34.31	550
O26.11	548	O29.193	548	O30.239	549	O31.21X1	549	O32.2XX5	550	O34.32	550
O26.12	548	O29.199	548	O30.291	549	O31.21X2	549	O32.3XX0	550	O34.33	550
O26.13	548	O29.211	548	O30.292	549	O31.21X3	549	O32.3XX1	550	O34.40	550
O26.20	548	O29.212	548	O30.293	549	O31.21X4	549	O32.3XX2	550	O34.41	550
O26.21	548	O29.213	548	O30.299	549	O31.21X5	549	O32.3XX4	550	O34.42	550
O26.22	548	O29.219	548	O30.801	549	O31.21X9	549	O32.3XX5	550	O34.43	550
O26.23	548	O29.291	548	O30.802	549	O31.22X0	549	O32.4XX0	550	O34.511	550
O26.30	548	O29.292	548	O30.803	549	O31.22X1	549	O32.4XX1	550	O34.512	550
O26.31	548	O29.293	548	O30.809	549	O31.22X2	549	O32.4XX2	550	O34.513	550
O26.32	548	O29.299	548	O30.811	549	O31.22X3	549	O32.4XX3	550	O34.519	550
O26.33	548	O29.3X1	548	O30.812	549	O31.22X4	549	O32.4XX4	550	O34.521	550
O26.40	548	O29.3X2	548	O30.813	549	O31.22X5	549	O32.4XX5	550	O34.522	550
O26.41	548	O29.3X3	548	O30.819	549	O31.22X9	549	O32.4XX9	550	O34.523	550
O26.42	548	O29.3X9	548	O30.821	549	O31.23X0	549	O32.6XX0	550	O34.529	550
O26.43	548	O29.40	548	O30.822	549	O31.23X1	549	O32.6XX1	550	O34.531	550
O26.50	548	O29.41	548	O30.823	549	O31.23X2	549	O32.6XX2	550	O34.532	550
O26.51	548	O29.42	548	O30.829	549	O31.23X3	549	O32.6XX4	550	O34.533	550
O26.52	548	O29.43	548	O30.831	549	O31.23X5	549	O32.6XX5	550	O34.539	550
O26.53	548	O29.5X1	548	O30.832	549	O31.23X9	549	O32.6XX9	550	O34.591	551
O26.611	548	O29.5X2	548	O30.833	549	O31.30X0	549	O32.8XX0	550	O34.592	551
O26.612	548	O29.5X3	548	O30.839	549	O31.30X1	549	O32.8XX1	550	O34.593	551
O26.613	548	O29.5X9	548	O30.891	549	O31.30X2	549	O32.8XX2	550	O34.599	551
O26.619	548	O29.60	548	O30.892	549	O31.30X3	549	O32.8XX3	550	O34.60	551
O26.62	557	O29.61	548	O30.893	549	O31.30X4	549	O32.8XX4	550	O34.61	551
O26.63	544	O29.62	548	O30.899	549	O31.30X5	549	O32.8XX5	550	O34.62	551
O26.711	548	O29.63	548	O30.90	549	O31.30X9	549	O32.8XX9	550	O34.63	551
O26.712	548	O29.8X1	548	O30.91	549	O31.31X0	549	O32.9XX0	550	O34.70	551
O26.713	548	O29.8X2	548	O30.92	549	O31.31X1	549	O32.9XX1	550	O34.71	551
O26.719	548	O29.8X3	548	O30.93	549	O31.31X2	550	O32.9XX2	550	O34.72	551
O26.72	557	O29.8X9	548	O31.00X0	549	O31.31X3	550	O32.9XX4	550	O34.73	551
O26.73	544	O29.90	548	O31.00X1	549	O31.31X4	550	O32.9XX5	550	O34.80	551
O26.811	548	O29.91	548	O31.00X3	549	O31.31X5	550	O32.9XX9	550	O34.81	551
O26.812	548	O29.92	548	O31.00X4	549	O31.31X9	550	O33.0	550	O34.82	551
O26.813	548	O29.93	548	O31.00X5	549	O31.32X0	550	O33.1	550	O34.83	551
O26.819	548	O30.001	548	O31.00X9	549	O31.32X1	550	O33.2	550	O34.90	551
O26.821	548	O30.002	548	O31.01X0	549	O31.32X2	550	O33.3XX0	550	O34.91	551
O26.822	548	O30.003	548	O31.01X1	549	O31.32X3	550	O33.3XX1	550	O34.92	551
O26.823	548	O30.009	548	O31.01X2	549	O31.32X4	550	O33.3XX2	550	O34.93	551
O26.829	548	O30.011	548	O31.01X3	549	O31.32X5	550	O33.3XX3	550	O35.0XX0	551
O26.831	548	O30.012	548	O31.01X4	549	O31.32X9	550	O33.3XX4	550	O35.0XX1	551
O26.832	548	O30.013	548	O31.01X5	549	O31.33X0	550	O33.3XX5	550	O35.0XX2	551
O26.833	548	O30.019	548	O31.01X9	549	O31.33X1	550	O33.3XX9	550	O35.0XX3	551
O26.839	548	O30.021	549	O31.02X0	549	O31.33X2	550	O33.4XX0	550	O35.0XX4	551
O26.841	548	O30.022	549	O31.02X1	549	O31.33X3	550	O33.4XX1	550	O35.0XX5	551
O26.842	548	O30.023	549	O31.02X2	549	O31.33X4	550	O33.4XX2	550	O35.0XX9	551
O26.843	548	O30.029	549	O31.02X3	549	O31.33X5	550	O33.4XX3	550	O35.1XX0	551
O26.849	548	O30.031	549	O31.02X4	549	O31.33X9	550	O33.4XX4	550	O35.1XX1	551
O26.851	548	O30.032	549	O31.02X5	549	O31.8X10	550	O33.4XX5	550	O35.1XX2	551
O26.852	548	O30.033	549	O31.02X9	549	O31.8X11	550	O33.4XX9	550	O35.1XX3	551
O26.853	548	O30.039	549	O31.03X0	549	O31.8X12	550	O33.5XX0	550	O35.1XX4	551
O26.859	548	O30.041	549	O31.03X1	549	O31.8X13	550	O33.5XX1	550	O35.1XX5	551
O26.86	548	O30.042	549	O31.03X2	549	O31.8X14	550	O33.5XX2	550	O35.1XX9	551
O26.872	548	O30.043	549	O31.03X3	549	O31.8X15	550	O33.5XX3	550	O35.2XX0	551
O26.873	548	O30.049	549	O31.03X4	549	O31.8X19	550	O33.5XX4	550	O35.2XX1	551
O26.879	548	O30.091	549	O31.03X5	549	O31.8X20	550	O33.5XX5	550	O35.2XX2	551
O26.891	548	O30.092	549	O31.03X9	549	O31.8X21	550	O33.5XX9	550	O35.2XX3	551
O26.892	548	O30.093	549	O31.10X0	549	O31.8X22	550	O33.6XX0	550	O35.2XX4	551
O26.893	548	O30.099	549	O31.10X1	549	O31.8X23	550	O33.6XX1	550	O35.2XX5	551
O26.899	548	O30.101	549	O31.10X2	549	O31.8X24	550	O33.6XX2	550	O35.2XX9	551
O26.90	548	O30.102	549	O31.10X3	549	O31.8X25	550	O33.6XX3	550	O35.3XX0	551
O26.91	548	O30.103	549	O31.10X4	549	O31.8X29	550	O33.6XX4	550	O35.3XX1	551
O26.92	548	O30.109	549	O31.10X5	549	O31.8X30	550	O33.6XX5	550	O35.3XX2	551
O26.93	548	O30.111	549	O31.10X9	549	O31.8X31	550	O33.6XX9	550	O35.3XX3	551
O28.0	548	O30.112	549	O31.11X0	549	O31.8X32	550	O33.7XX0	550	O35.3XX4	551
O28.1	548	O30.113	549	O31.11X1	549	O31.8X33	550	O33.7XX1	550	O35.3XX5	551
O28.2	548	O30.119	549	O31.11X2	549	O31.8X34	550	O33.7XX2	550	O35.3XX9	551
O28.3	548	O30.121	549	O31.11X3	549	O31.8X35	550	O33.7XX3	550	O35.4XX0	551
O28.4	548	O30.122	549	O31.11X4	549	O31.8X39	550	O33.7XX4	550	O35.4XX1	551
O28.5	548	O30.123	549	O31.11X5	549	O31.8X90	550	O33.7XX5	550	O35.4XX2	551
O28.8	548	O30.129	549	O31.11X9	549	O31.8X91	550			O35.4XX3	551
O28.9	548	O30.131	549	O31.12X0	549	O31.8X92	550			O35.4XX4	551
O29.011	548	O30.132	549	O31.12X1	549	O31.8X93	550			O35.4XX5	551
O29.012	548	O30.133	549	O31.12X2	549	O31.8X94	550			O35.4XX9	551
O29.013	548	O30.139	549	O31.12X3	549	O31.8X95	550			O35.5XX0	551
O29.019	548	O30.191	549	O31.12X4	549	O31.8X99	550			O35.5XX1	551
O29.021	548	O30.192	549							O35.5XX2	551

Numeric Index to Diseases

Code	Page	Code	Page	Code	Page	Code	Page	Code	Page	Code	Page
O35.5XX3	551	O36.1115	551	O36.5120	552	O36.72X2	552	O36.8394	553	O41.00X9	554
O35.5XX4	551	O36.1119	551	O36.5121	552	O36.72X3	552	O36.8399	553	O41.01X0	554
O35.5XX5	551	O36.1120	551	O36.5122	552	O36.72X4	552	O36.8910	553	O41.01X1	554
O35.5XX9	551	O36.1121	551	O36.5123	552	O36.72X5	552	O36.8911	553	O41.01X2	554
O35.6XX0	551	O36.1122	551	O36.5124	552	O36.72X9	552	O36.8912	553	O41.01X3	554
O35.6XX1	551	O36.1123	551	O36.5125	552	O36.73X0	552	O36.8913	553	O41.01X4	554
O35.6XX2	551	O36.1124	551	O36.5129	552	O36.73X1	552	O36.8914	553	O41.01X5	554
O35.6XX3	551	O36.1125	551	O36.5130	552	O36.73X2	552	O36.8915	553	O41.01X9	554
O35.6XX4	551	O36.1129	551	O36.5131	552	O36.73X3	552	O36.8919	553	O41.02X0	554
O35.6XX5	551	O36.1130	551	O36.5132	552	O36.73X4	552	O36.8920	553	O41.02X1	554
O35.6XX9	551	O36.1131	551	O36.5133	552	O36.73X5	553	O36.8921	553	O41.02X2	554
O35.7XX0	551	O36.1132	551	O36.5134	552	O36.73X9	553	O36.8922	553	O41.02X3	554
O35.7XX1	551	O36.1133	551	O36.5135	552	O36.80X0	553,557	O36.8923	553	O41.02X4	554
O35.7XX2	551	O36.1134	551	O36.5139	552	O36.80X1	553,557	O36.8924	553	O41.02X5	554
O35.7XX3	551	O36.1135	551	O36.5190	552	O36.80X2	553,557	O36.8925	553	O41.02X9	554
O35.7XX4	551	O36.1139	551	O36.5191	552	O36.80X3	553,557	O36.8929	553	O41.03X0	554
O35.7XX5	551	O36.1190	551	O36.5192	552	O36.80X4	553,557	O36.8930	553	O41.03X1	554
O35.7XX9	551	O36.1191	551	O36.5193	552	O36.80X5	553,557	O36.8931	553	O41.03X2	554
O35.8XX0	551	O36.1192	551	O36.5194	552	O36.80X9	553,557	O36.8932	553	O41.03X3	554
O35.8XX1	551	O36.1193	551	O36.5195	552	O36.8120	553	O36.8933	553	O41.03X4	554
O35.8XX2	551	O36.1194	551	O36.5199	552	O36.8121	553	O36.8934	553	O41.03X5	554
O35.8XX3	551	O36.1195	551	O36.5910	552	O36.8122	553	O36.8935	553	O41.03X9	554
O35.8XX4	551	O36.1199	551	O36.5911	552	O36.8123	553	O36.8939	553	O41.1010	554
O35.8XX5	551	O36.1910	552	O36.5912	552	O36.8124	553	O36.8990	553	O41.1011	554
O35.8XX9	551	O36.1911	552	O36.5913	552	O36.8125	553	O36.8991	553	O41.1012	554
O35.9XX0	551	O36.1912	552	O36.5914	552	O36.8129	553	O36.8992	553	O41.1013	554
O35.9XX1	551	O36.1913	552	O36.5915	552	O36.8130	553	O36.8993	553	O41.1014	554
O35.9XX2	551	O36.1914	552	O36.5919	552	O36.8131	553	O36.8994	553	O41.1015	554
O35.9XX3	551	O36.1915	552	O36.5920	552	O36.8132	553	O36.8995	553	O41.1019	554
O35.9XX4	551	O36.1919	552	O36.5921	552	O36.8133	553	O36.8999	553	O41.1020	554
O35.9XX5	551	O36.1920	552	O36.5922	552	O36.8134	553	O36.90X0	553	O41.1021	554
O35.9XX9	551	O36.1921	552	O36.5923	552	O36.8135	553	O36.90X1	553	O41.1022	554
O36.0110	551	O36.1922	552	O36.5924	552	O36.8139	553	O36.90X2	553	O41.1023	554
O36.0111	551	O36.1923	552	O36.5925	552	O36.8190	553	O36.90X3	553	O41.1024	554
O36.0112	551	O36.1924	552	O36.5929	552	O36.8191	553	O36.90X4	553	O41.1025	554
O36.0113	551	O36.1925	552	O36.5930	552	O36.8192	553	O36.90X5	553	O41.1029	554
O36.0114	551	O36.1929	552	O36.5931	552	O36.8193	553	O36.90X9	553	O41.1030	554
O36.0115	551	O36.1930	552	O36.5932	552	O36.8194	553	O36.91X0	553	O41.1031	554
O36.0119	551	O36.1931	552	O36.5933	552	O36.8195	553	O36.91X1	553	O41.1032	554
O36.0120	551	O36.1933	552	O36.5934	552	O36.8199	553	O36.91X3	553	O41.1033	554
O36.0121	551	O36.1934	552	O36.5935	552	O36.8210	553	O36.91X4	553	O41.1034	554
O36.0122	551	O36.1935	552	O36.5939	552	O36.8211	553	O36.91X5	553	O41.1035	554
O36.0123	551	O36.1939	552	O36.5990	552	O36.8212	553	O36.91X9	553	O41.1039	554
O36.0124	551	O36.1990	552	O36.5991	552	O36.8213	553	O36.92X0	553	O41.1090	554
O36.0125	551	O36.1991	552	O36.5992	552	O36.8214	553	O36.92X1	553	O41.1091	554
O36.0129	551	O36.1992	552	O36.5993	552	O36.8215	553	O36.92X2	553	O41.1092	554
O36.0130	551	O36.1993	552	O36.5994	552	O36.8219	553	O36.92X3	553	O41.1093	554
O36.0131	551	O36.1994	552	O36.5995	552	O36.8220	553	O36.92X4	553	O41.1094	554
O36.0132	551	O36.1995	552	O36.5999	552	O36.8221	553	O36.92X5	553	O41.1095	554
O36.0133	551	O36.1999	552	O36.60X0	552	O36.8222	553	O36.92X9	553	O41.1099	554
O36.0134	551	O36.20X0	552	O36.60X1	552	O36.8223	553	O36.93X0	553	O41.1210	554
O36.0135	551	O36.20X1	552	O36.60X2	552	O36.8224	553	O36.93X1	553	O41.1211	554
O36.0139	551	O36.20X2	552	O36.60X3	552	O36.8225	553	O36.93X3	553	O41.1212	554
O36.0190	551	O36.20X3	552	O36.60X4	552	O36.8229	553	O36.93X4	553	O41.1213	554
O36.0191	551	O36.20X4	552	O36.60X5	552	O36.8230	553	O36.93X5	553	O41.1214	554
O36.0192	551	O36.20X5	552	O36.60X9	552	O36.8231	553	O36.93X9	553	O41.1215	554
O36.0193	551	O36.20X9	552	O36.61X0	552	O36.8232	553	O40.1XX0	553	O41.1219	554
O36.0194	551	O36.21X0	552	O36.61X1	552	O36.8233	553	O40.1XX1	553	O41.1220	554
O36.0195	551	O36.21X1	552	O36.61X2	552	O36.8234	553	O40.1XX2	553	O41.1221	554
O36.0199	551	O36.21X2	552	O36.61X3	552	O36.8235	553	O40.1XX3	553	O41.1222	554
O36.0910	551	O36.21X3	552	O36.61X4	552	O36.8239	553	O40.1XX4	553	O41.1223	554
O36.0911	551	O36.21X4	552	O36.61X5	552	O36.8290	553	O40.1XX5	553	O41.1224	554
O36.0912	551	O36.21X5	552	O36.61X9	552	O36.8291	553	O40.1XX9	553	O41.1225	554
O36.0913	551	O36.21X9	552	O36.62X0	552	O36.8292	553	O40.2XX0	553	O41.1229	554
O36.0914	551	O36.22X0	552	O36.62X1	552	O36.8293	553	O40.2XX1	553	O41.1230	554
O36.0915	551	O36.22X1	552	O36.62X2	552	O36.8294	553	O40.2XX2	553	O41.1231	554
O36.0919	551	O36.22X2	552	O36.62X3	552	O36.8295	553	O40.2XX3	553	O41.1232	554
O36.0920	551	O36.22X3	552	O36.62X4	552	O36.8299	553	O40.2XX4	553	O41.1233	554
O36.0921	551	O36.22X4	552	O36.62X5	552	O36.8310	553	O40.2XX5	553	O41.1234	554
O36.0922	551	O36.22X5	552	O36.62X9	552	O36.8311	553	O40.2XX9	553	O41.1235	554
O36.0923	551	O36.22X9	552	O36.63X0	552	O36.8312	553	O40.3XX0	553	O41.1239	554
O36.0924	551	O36.23X0	552	O36.63X1	552	O36.8313	553	O40.3XX1	553	O41.1290	554
O36.0925	551	O36.23X1	552	O36.63X2	552	O36.8314	553	O40.3XX2	553	O41.1291	554
O36.0929	551	O36.23X2	552	O36.63X3	552	O36.8315	553	O40.3XX3	553	O41.1292	554
O36.0930	551	O36.23X3	552	O36.63X4	552	O36.8319	553	O40.3XX4	553	O41.1293	554
O36.0931	551	O36.23X4	552	O36.63X5	552	O36.8320	553	O40.3XX5	553	O41.1294	554
O36.0932	551	O36.23X5	552	O36.63X9	552	O36.8321	553	O40.3XX9	553	O41.1295	554
O36.0933	551	O36.23X9	552	O36.70X0	552	O36.8322	553	O40.9XX0	553	O41.1299	554
O36.0934	551	O36.4XX0	552	O36.70X1	552	O36.8323	553	O40.9XX1	553	O41.1410	554
O36.0935	551	O36.4XX1	552	O36.70X2	552	O36.8324	553	O40.9XX2	553	O41.1411	554
O36.0939	551	O36.4XX2	552	O36.70X3	552	O36.8325	553	O40.9XX3	553	O41.1412	554
O36.0990	551	O36.4XX3	552	O36.70X4	552	O36.8329	553	O40.9XX4	553	O41.1413	554
O36.0991	551	O36.4XX4	552	O36.70X5	552	O36.8330	553	O40.9XX9	553	O41.1414	554
O36.0992	551	O36.4XX5	552	O36.70X9	552	O36.8331	553	O41.00X0	553	O41.1415	554
O36.0993	551	O36.4XX9	552	O36.71X0	552	O36.8332	553	O41.00X1	553	O41.1419	554
O36.0994	551	O36.5110	552	O36.71X1	552	O36.8333	553	O41.00X2	553	O41.1420	554
O36.0995	551	O36.5111	552	O36.71X2	552	O36.8334	553	O41.00X3	553	O41.1421	554
O36.0999	551	O36.5112	552	O36.71X3	552	O36.8335	553	O41.00X4	554	O41.1422	554
O36.1110	551	O36.5113	552	O36.71X4	552	O36.8339	553	O41.00X5	554	O41.1423	554
O36.1111	551	O36.5114	552	O36.71X5	552	O36.8390	553			O41.1424	554
O36.1112	551	O36.5115	552	O36.71X9	552	O36.8391	553			O41.1425	554
O36.1113	551	O36.5119	552	O36.72X0	552	O36.8392	553			O41.1429	554
O36.1114	551			O36.72X1	552	O36.8393	553			O41.1430	554

Numeric Index to Diseases

Code	Page	Code	Page	Code	Page	Code	Page	Code	Page	Code	Page
O41.1431	554	O43.023	555	O46.009	555	O63.2	558	O69.1XX9	558	O75.81	558
O41.1432	554	O43.029	555	O46.011	555	O63.9	555	O69.2XX0	558	O75.82	558
O41.1433	554	O43.101	555	O46.012	555	O64.0XX0	555	O69.2XX1	558	O75.89	558
O41.1434	554	O43.102	555	O46.013	555	O64.0XX1	555	O69.2XX2	558	O75.9	558
O41.1435	554	O43.103	555	O46.019	555	O64.0XX2	555	O69.2XX3	558	O76	558
O41.1439	554	O43.109	555	O46.021	555	O64.0XX3	555	O69.2XX4	558	O77.0	558
O41.1490	554	O43.111	555	O46.022	555	O64.0XX4	555	O69.2XX5	558	O77.1	558
O41.1491	554	O43.112	555	O46.023	555	O64.0XX5	555	O69.2XX9	558	O77.8	558
O41.1492	554	O43.113	555	O46.029	555	O64.0XX9	555	O69.3XX0	558	O77.9	558
O41.1493	554	O43.119	555	O46.091	555	O64.1XX0	555	O69.3XX1	558	O80	558
O41.1494	554	O43.121	555	O46.092	555	O64.1XX1	555	O69.3XX2	558	O82	558
O41.1495	554	O43.122	555	O46.093	555	O64.1XX2	555	O69.3XX3	558	O85	545
O41.1499	554	O43.123	555	O46.099	555	O64.1XX3	555	O69.3XX5	558	O86.00	545
O41.8X10	554	O43.129	555	O46.8X1	555	O64.1XX4	555	O69.3XX9	558	O86.01	545
O41.8X11	554	O43.191	555	O46.8X2	555	O64.1XX5	555	O69.4XX0	558	O86.02	545
O41.8X12	554	O43.192	555	O46.8X9	555	O64.2XX0	555	O69.4XX1	558	O86.03	545
O41.8X13	554	O43.193	555	O46.90	555	O64.2XX1	555	O69.4XX2	558	O86.04	545
O41.8X14	554	O43.199	555	O46.91	555	O64.2XX2	555	O69.4XX3	558	O86.09	545
O41.8X15	554	O43.211	544	O46.92	555	O64.2XX4	555	O69.4XX4	558	O86.1*	545
O41.8X19	554	O43.212	544	O46.93	555	O64.2XX5	555	O69.4XX5	558	O86.2*	545
O41.8X20	554	O43.213	544	O47.00	555	O64.2XX9	555	O69.4XX9	558	O86.4	545
O41.8X21	554	O43.219	544	O47.02	555	O64.3XX0	555	O69.5XX0	558	O86.8*	545
O41.8X22	554	O43.221	544	O47.03	555	O64.3XX1	555	O69.5XX1	558	O87*	545
O41.8X23	554	O43.222	544	O47.1	555	O64.3XX2	555	O69.5XX2	558	O88.011	556
O41.8X24	554	O43.223	544	O47.9	555	O64.3XX3	555	O69.5XX3	558	O88.012	556
O41.8X25	554	O43.229	544	O48.0	555	O64.3XX4	555	O69.5XX5	558	O88.013	556
O41.8X29	554	O43.231	544	O48.1	555	O64.3XX5	555	O69.5XX9	558	O88.019	556
O41.8X30	554	O43.232	544	O60.00	555	O64.3XX9	555	O69.81X0	558	O88.02	558
O41.8X31	554	O43.233	544	O60.02	555	O64.4XX0	555	O69.81X1	558	O88.03	545
O41.8X32	554	O43.239	544	O60.03	555	O64.4XX1	555	O69.81X2	558	O88.111	556
O41.8X33	554	O43.811	555	O60.10X0	557	O64.4XX2	555	O69.81X3	558	O88.112	556
O41.8X34	554	O43.812	555	O60.10X1	557	O64.4XX4	555	O69.81X4	558	O88.113	556
O41.8X35	554	O43.813	555	O60.10X2	557	O64.4XX5	555	O69.81X5	558	O88.119	556
O41.8X39	554	O43.819	555	O60.10X3	557	O64.4XX9	555	O69.81X9	558	O88.12	558
O41.8X90	554	O43.891	555	O60.10X4	557	O64.5XX0	556	O69.82X0	558	O88.13	545
O41.8X91	554	O43.892	555	O60.10X5	557	O64.5XX1	556	O69.82X1	558	O88.211	556
O41.8X92	554	O43.893	555	O60.10X9	557	O64.5XX2	556	O69.82X2	558	O88.212	556
O41.8X93	554	O43.899	555	O60.12X0	557	O64.5XX4	556	O69.82X3	558	O88.213	556
O41.8X94	554	O43.90	555	O60.12X1	557	O64.5XX5	556	O69.82X4	558	O88.219	556
O41.8X95	554	O43.91	555	O60.12X2	557	O64.8XX0	556	O69.82X5	558	O88.22	558
O41.8X99	554	O43.92	555	O60.12X3	557	O64.8XX1	556	O69.82X9	558	O88.23	545
O41.90X0	554	O43.93	555	O60.12X4	557	O64.8XX2	556	O69.89X0	558	O88.311	556
O41.90X1	554	O44.00	555	O60.12X5	557	O64.8XX3	556	O69.89X1	558	O88.312	556
O41.90X2	554	O44.01	555	O60.12X9	557	O64.8XX4	556	O69.89X2	558	O88.313	556
O41.90X3	554	O44.02	555	O60.13X0	557	O64.8XX5	556	O69.89X3	558	O88.319	556
O41.90X4	554	O44.03	555	O60.13X1	557	O64.8XX9	556	O69.89X4	558	O88.32	558
O41.90X5	554	O44.10	555	O60.13X2	557	O64.9XX0	556	O69.89X5	558	O88.33	545
O41.90X9	554	O44.11	555	O60.13X3	557	O64.9XX1	556	O69.89X9	558	O88.811	556
O41.91X0	554	O44.12	555	O60.13X4	557	O64.9XX2	556	O69.9XX0	558	O88.812	556
O41.91X1	554	O44.13	555	O60.13X5	557	O64.9XX4	556	O69.9XX1	558	O88.813	556
O41.91X2	554	O44.20	555	O60.13X9	557	O64.9XX5	556	O69.9XX2	558	O88.819	556
O41.91X3	554	O44.21	555	O60.14X0	557	O64.9XX9	556	O69.9XX3	558	O88.82	558
O41.91X4	554	O44.22	555	O60.14X1	557	O65.0	556	O69.9XX4	558	O88.83	545
O41.91X5	554	O44.23	555	O60.14X2	557	O65.1	556	O69.9XX5	558	O89*	545
O41.91X9	554	O44.30	555	O60.14X3	557	O65.2	556	O69.9XX9	558	O90.0	545
O41.92X0	554	O44.31	555	O60.14X4	557	O65.3	556	O70*	544	O90.1	545
O41.92X1	554	O44.32	555	O60.14X5	557	O65.4	556	O71.00	556	O90.2	545
O41.92X2	554	O44.33	555	O60.14X9	558	O65.5	556	O71.02	556	O90.3	545
O41.92X3	554	O44.40	555	O60.20X0	558	O65.8	556	O71.03	556	O90.4	545
O41.92X4	554	O44.41	555	O60.20X1	558	O65.9	556	O71.1	556	O90.5	545
O41.92X5	554	O44.42	555	O60.20X2	558	O66.0	556	O71.2	544	O90.6	545
O41.92X9	554	O44.43	555	O60.20X3	558	O66.1	556	O71.3	545	O90.8*	545
O41.93X0	554	O44.50	555	O60.20X4	558	O66.2	556	O71.4	545	O90.9	545
O41.93X1	554	O44.51	555	O60.20X5	558	O66.3	556	O71.5	545	O91.011	556
O41.93X2	554	O44.52	555	O60.20X9	558	O66.40	556	O71.6	545	O91.012	556
O41.93X3	554	O44.53	555	O60.22X0	558	O66.41	556	O71.7	545	O91.013	556
O41.93X4	554	O45.001	555	O60.22X1	558	O66.5	556	O71.81	556	O91.019	556
O41.93X5	554	O45.002	555	O60.22X2	558	O66.6	556	O71.82	545	O91.02	545
O41.93X9	554	O45.003	555	O60.22X3	558	O66.8	556	O71.89	545	O91.03	545
O42.00	554	O45.009	555	O60.22X4	558	O66.9	556	O71.9	545	O91.111	556
O42.011	554	O45.011	555	O60.22X5	558	O67.0	558	O72.0	545	O91.112	556
O42.012	554	O45.012	555	O60.22X9	558	O67.8	558	O72.1	545	O91.113	556
O42.013	554	O45.013	555	O60.23X0	558	O67.9	558	O72.2	545	O91.119	556
O42.019	554	O45.019	555	O60.23X1	558	O68	558	O72.3	545	O91.12	545
O42.02	554	O45.021	555	O60.23X2	558	O69.0XX0	558	O73*	545	O91.13	545
O42.10	554	O45.022	555	O60.23X3	558	O69.0XX1	558	O74.0	558	O91.211	556
O42.111	554	O45.023	555	O60.23X4	558	O69.0XX2	558	O74.1	558	O91.212	556
O42.112	554	O45.029	555	O60.23X5	558	O69.0XX3	558	O74.2	558	O91.213	556
O42.113	554	O45.091	555	O60.23X9	558	O69.0XX4	558	O74.3	558	O91.219	556
O42.119	555	O45.092	555	O61.0	555	O69.0XX5	558	O74.4	558	O91.22	545
O42.12	555	O45.093	555	O61.1	555	O69.0XX9	558	O74.5	558	O91.23	545
O42.90	555	O45.099	555	O61.8	555	O69.1XX0	558	O74.6	558	O92.011	556
O42.911	555	O45.8X1	555	O61.9	555	O69.1XX1	558	O74.7	558	O92.012	556
O42.912	555	O45.8X2	555	O62.0	555	O69.1XX3	558	O74.8	558	O92.013	556
O42.913	555	O45.8X3	555	O62.1	555	O69.1XX4	558	O74.9	558	O92.019	556
O42.919	555	O45.8X9	555	O62.2	555	O69.1XX5	558	O75.0	558	O92.02	545
O42.92	555	O45.90	555	O62.3	555			O75.1	558	O92.03	545
O43.011	555	O45.91	555	O62.4	555			O75.2	556	O92.111	556
O43.012	555	O45.92	555	O62.8	555			O75.3	556	O92.112	556
O43.013	555	O45.93	555	O62.9	555			O75.4	545	O92.113	556
O43.019	555	O46.001	555	O63.0	555			O75.5	558	O92.119	556
O43.021	555	O46.002	555	O63.1	555					O92.12	545
O43.022	555	O46.003	555							O92.13	545

Code	Page	Code	Page	Code	Page	Code	Page	Code	Page	Code	Page
O92.2*	545	O99.312	556	O9A.512	557	P07.26	559	P54.9	569	P92.2	569
O92.3	545	O99.313	556	O9A.513	557	P07.3*	559	P55.0	569	P92.3	569
O92.4	545	O99.314	558	O9A.519	557	P08.0	569	P55.1	569	P92.4	569
O92.5	545	O99.315	545	O9A.52	558	P08.1	569	P55.8	559	P92.5	569
O92.6	545	O99.320	556	O9A.53	545	P08.21	569	P55.9	559	P92.6	502
O92.7*	545	O99.321	556	P00.0	568	P08.22	569	P56*	559	P92.8	569
O94	545	O99.322	556	P00.1	568	P09	795	P57*	559	P92.9	569
O98.011	556	O99.323	556	P00.2	569,844	P10*	559	P58*	569	P93*	559
O98.012	556	O99.324	558	P00.3	569	P11.0	559	P59.0	569	P94.0	559
O98.013	556	O99.325	545	P00.4	568	P11.1	568	P59.1	559	P94.1	569
O98.019	556	O99.330	556	P00.5	568	P11.2	559	P59.2*	559	P94.2	569
O98.02	558	O99.331	556	P00.6	568	P11.3	568	P59.3	559	P94.8	569
O98.03	545	O99.332	556	P00.7	568	P11.4	559	P59.8	559	P94.9	569
O98.111	556	O99.333	556	P00.81	568	P11.5	559	P59.9	559	P95	569
O98.112	556	O99.334	558	P00.89	569,844	P11.9	559	P60	559	P96.0	569
O98.113	556	O99.335	545	P00.9	569	P12.0	569	P61.0	559	P96.1	559
O98.119	556	O99.340	556	P01*	568	P12.1	569	P61.1	559	P96.2	559
O98.12	558	O99.341	556	P02.0	568	P12.2	559	P61.2	559	P96.3	569
O98.13	545	O99.342	556	P02.1	568	P12.3	569	P61.3	559	P96.5	569
O98.211	556	O99.343	556	P02.2*	568	P12.4	569	P61.4	559	P96.81	569
O98.212	556	O99.344	558	P02.3	568	P12.81	569	P61.5	559	P96.82	569
O98.213	556	O99.345	545	P02.4	569	P12.89	569	P61.6	559	P96.83	569
O98.219	556	O99.350	556	P02.5	569	P12.9	569	P61.8	559	P96.89	569
O98.22	558	O99.351	556	P02.60	569	P13*	568	P61.9	559	P96.9	569
O98.23	545	O99.352	556	P02.69	569	P14.0	568	P70.0	559	Q00*	51,563
O98.311	556	O99.353	556	P02.70	568	P14.1	568	P70.1	559	Q01*	51,563
O98.312	556	O99.354	558	P02.78	559	P14.2	559	P70.2	559	Q02	51,563
O98.313	556	O99.355	545	P02.8	568	P14.3	568	P70.3	559	Q03*	51,564
O98.319	556	O99.411	556	P02.9	568	P14.8	559	P70.4	559	Q04*	51,564
O98.32	558	O99.412	556	P03.0	569	P14.9	559	P70.8	559	Q05*	51,564
O98.33	545	O99.413	556	P03.1	569	P15*	568	P70.9	569	Q06*	51,564
O98.411	556	O99.419	556	P03.2	569	P19*	568	P71*	559	Q07*	51,564
O98.412	556	O99.42	558	P03.3	569	P22.0	559	P72.0	569	Q10*	65
O98.413	556	O99.43	545	P03.4	559	P22.1	568	P72.1	559	Q11*	65
O98.419	556	O99.511	556	P03.5	568	P22.8	568	P72.2	569	Q12*	65
O98.42	558	O99.512	556	P03.6	568	P22.9	568	P72.8	559	Q13*	65
O98.43	545	O99.513	556	P03.8*	568	P23*	559	P72.9	569	Q14*	65
O98.511	556	O99.519	556	P03.9	569	P24*	559	P74.0	559	Q15*	65
O98.512	556	O99.52	558	P04.0	568	P25*	559	P74.1	559	Q16*	86
O98.513	556	O99.53	545	P04.11	568	P26*	559	P74.21	559	Q17.0	569
O98.519	556	O99.611	556	P04.12	568	P27*	105	P74.22	559	Q17*	87
O98.52	558	O99.612	556	P04.13	568	P28.0	559	P74.31	559	Q18.0	87
O98.53	545	O99.613	556	P04.14	568	P28.1*	568	P74.32	559	Q18.1	87
O98.611	556	O99.619	556	P04.15	568	P28.2	568	P74.41	559	Q18.2	87
O98.612	556	O99.62	556	P04.16	568	P28.3	568	P74.421	559	Q18.3	477
O98.613	556	O99.63	545	P04.17	568	P28.4	568	P74.422	559	Q18.4	87
O98.619	556	O99.711	557	P04.18	568	P28.5	559	P74.49	559	Q18.5	87
O98.62	558	O99.712	557	P04.19	568	P28.8*	568	P74.5	569	Q18.6	87
O98.63	545	O99.713	557	P04.1A	568	P28.9	568	P74.6	569	Q18.7	87
O98.711	556	O99.719	557	P04.2	568	P29.0	568	P74.8	569	Q18.8	87
O98.712	556	O99.72	558	P04.3	568	P29.1*	568	P74.9	569	Q18.9	477
O98.713	556	O99.73	545	P04.40	568	P29.2	568	P76.0	559	Q20*	172
O98.719	556	O99.810	557	P04.41	568	P29.3*	568	P76.1	569	Q21.0	564
O98.72	558	O99.814	558	P04.42	568	P29.4	568	P76.2	559	Q21*	172
O98.73	545	O99.815	545	P04.49	568	P29.89	559	P76.8	569	Q22*	172
O98.811	556	O99.820	557	P04.5	568	P29.9	568	P76.9	569	Q23*	172
O98.812	556	O99.824	558	P04.6	568	P35.0	559	P77*	559	Q24.0	172
O98.813	556	O99.825	545	P04.81	568	P35.1	559	P78.0	559	Q24.1	172
O98.819	556	O99.830	557	P04.89	568	P35.2	559	P78.1	569	Q24.2	172
O98.82	558	O99.834	558	P04.9	568	P35.3	559	P78.2	569	Q24.3	172
O98.83	545	O99.835	545	P05.00	568	P35.4	559	P78.3	569	Q24.4	172
O98.911	556	O99.840	557	P05.01	568	P35.8	559	P78.8*	569	Q24.5	172
O98.912	556	O99.841	557	P05.02	568	P35.9	559	P78.9	569	Q24.6	172
O98.913	556	O99.842	557	P05.03	568	P36*	559	P80.0	569	Q24.8	172
O98.919	556	O99.843	557	P05.04	568	P37.0	559	P80.8	569	Q24.9	172
O98.92	558	O99.844	558	P05.05	568	P37.1	559	P80.9	569	Q25*	172
O98.93	545	O99.845	545	P05.06	568	P37.2	559	P81*	569	Q26.0	172
O99.011	556	O99.89	557	P05.07	568	P37.3	559	P83.0	569	Q26.1	172
O99.012	556	O9A.111	557	P05.08	569	P37.4	559	P83.1	559	Q26.2	172
O99.013	556	O9A.112	557	P05.09	568	P37.5	568	P83.2	559	Q26.3	172
O99.019	556	O9A.113	557	P05.10	568	P37.8	559	P83.3*	569	Q26.4	172
O99.02	558	O9A.119	557	P05.11	559	P37.9	559	P83.4	569	Q26.5	168
O99.03	545	O9A.12	558	P05.12	559	P38*	559	P83.5	569	Q26.6	168
O99.111	556	O9A.13	545	P05.13	559	P39.0	559	P83.6	569	Q26.8	172
O99.112	556	O9A.211	557	P05.14	559	P39.1	568	P83.8*	569	Q26.9	172
O99.113	556	O9A.212	557	P05.15	559	P39.2	559	P83.9	569	Q27*	172
O99.119	556	O9A.213	557	P05.16	559	P39.3	559	P84	569	Q28.0	168
O99.12	558	O9A.219	557	P05.17	559	P39.4	559	P90	559	Q28.1	168
O99.13	545	O9A.22	558	P05.18	569	P39.8	559	P91.0	559	Q28.2	51
O99.210	556	O9A.23	545	P05.19	568	P39.9	559	P91.1	559	Q28.3	51
O99.211	556	O9A.311	557	P05.2	559	P50*	559	P91.2	51,563	Q28.8	168
O99.212	556	O9A.312	557	P05.9	568	P51*	568	P91.3	559	Q28.9	168
O99.213	558	O9A.313	557	P07.00	559	P52*	559	P91.4	559	Q30*	87
O99.214	558	O9A.319	557	P07.01	559	P53	559	P91.5	559	Q31.0	3
O99.215	545	O9A.32	558	P07.02	559	P54.0	568	P91.60	569	Q31.1	3
O99.280	556	O9A.33	545	P07.03	559	P54.1	559	P91.61	569	Q31.2	3
O99.281	556	O9A.411	557	P07.1*	559	P54.2	559	P91.62	569	Q31.3	3
O99.282	556	O9A.412	557	P07.20	569	P54.3	559	P91.63	569	Q31.5	3
O99.283	556	O9A.413	557	P07.21	559	P54.4	559	P91.8*	559	Q31.8	3
O99.284	558	O9A.419	557	P07.22	559	P54.5	569	P91.9	559	Q31.9	3
O99.285	545	O9A.42	558	P07.23	559	P54.6	568	P92.01	559	Q31*	87
O99.310	556	O9A.43	545	P07.24	559	P54.8	568	P92.09	569	Q32.0	3
O99.311	556	O9A.511	557	P07.25	559			P92.1	569	Q32.1	3

Numeric Index to Diseases

Code	Page	Code	Page	Code	Page	Code	Page	Code	Page	Code	Page
Q32.2	3	Q53.02	569	Q77.6	378	R01.0	172	R29.890	51	R40.2364	844
Q32.3	3	Q53.10	569	Q77.7	378	R01.1	172	R29.891	297	R40.2410	844
Q32.4	3	Q53.11*	569	Q77.8	378	R01.2	173	R29.898	302	R40.2411	844
Q32*	87	Q53.12	569	Q77.9	378	R03*	173	R29.9*	51	R40.2412	844
Q33.0	106	Q53.13	569	Q78.0	212, 378	R04.0	86	R30*	519	R40.2413	844
Q33.1	106	Q53.20	569	Q78.1	378	R04.1	3, 87	R31*	519, 564	R40.2414	844
Q33.2	106	Q53.21*	569	Q78.2	378	R04.2	106	R32	519	R40.2420	844
Q33.3	106	Q53.22	569	Q78.3	378	R04.8*	106	R33*	519, 564	R40.2421	844
Q33.4	105	Q53.23	569	Q78.4	378	R04.9	106	R34	518	R40.2422	844
Q33.5	106	Q53.9	569	Q78.5	378	R05	106	R35*	519	R40.2423	844
Q33.6	106	Q53*	529	Q78.6	378	R06.0*	106	R36.0	519	R40.2424	844
Q33.8	106	Q54*	529	Q78.8	378	R06.1	106	R36.1	529	R40.2430	844
Q33.9	106	Q55.22	569	Q78.9	378	R06.2	106	R36.9	519	R40.2431	844
Q34*	106	Q55*	529	Q79.0	106	R06.3	106	R37	636	R40.2432	844
Q35.1	3	Q56.0	529, 534, 542	Q79.1	106	R06.4	106	R39.14	564	R40.2433	844
Q35.3	3	Q56.1	529	Q79.2	196, 564	R06.5	87	R39*	519	R40.2434	844
Q35.5	3	Q56.2	534, 542	Q79.3	196, 564	R06.6	106	R40.0	47	R40.244*	844
Q35.7	3	Q56.3	529, 534, 542	Q79.4	196	R06.7	87	R40.1	47	R40.3	47, 564
Q35.9	3	Q56.4	529, 534, 542	Q79.5*	196	R06.8*	106	R40.20	47, 564	R40.4	635
Q35*	87	Q60*	520	Q79.6*	378	R06.9	106	R40.2110	47, 564	R41.0	795
Q36.0	3	Q61*	520	Q79.8	378	R07.0	87	R40.2111	47, 564	R41.1	795
Q36.1	3	Q62*	520	Q79.9	378	R07.1	106	R40.2112	47, 564	R41.2	795
Q36.9	3	Q63*	520	Q80*	477	R07.2	172	R40.2113	47, 564	R41.3	795
Q36*	87	Q64.0	520	Q81.0	570	R07.81	106	R40.2114	47, 564	R41.4	51
Q37.0	3	Q64.1*	520	Q81.1	570	R07.82	172	R40.2120	47, 564	R41.81	635
Q37.1	3	Q64.2	520	Q81.2	570	R07.89	172	R40.2121	47, 564	R41.82	795
Q37.2	3	Q64.3*	520	Q81.8	570	R07.9	172	R40.2122	47, 564	R41.83	844
Q37.3	3	Q64.4	520	Q81.9	570	R09.0*	106	R40.2123	47, 564	R41.840	636
Q37.4	3	Q64.5	520	Q81*	477	R09.1	105	R40.2124	47, 564	R41.841	635
Q37.5	3	Q64.6	520	Q82.1	570	R09.2	106, 564	R40.2130	844	R41.842	51
Q37.8	3	Q64.7*	520	Q82.2	570	R09.3	106	R40.2131	844	R41.843	635
Q37.9	3	Q64.8	520	Q82.3	570	R09.81	87, 570	R40.2132	844	R41.844	635
Q37*	87	Q64.9	520	Q82.6	570	R09.82	87	R40.2133	844	R41.89	635
Q38.0	3, 87	Q65*	377	Q82.8	570	R09.89	173	R40.2134	844	R41.9	795
Q38.1	3, 87	Q66.50	569	Q82.9	570	R10*	195	R40.2140	844	R42	86
Q38.2	3, 87	Q66.51	569	Q82*	477	R11.0	195	R40.2141	844	R43*	51
Q38.3	3, 87	Q66.52	570	Q83.0	453	R11.10	195	R40.2142	844	R44.0	635
Q38.4	3, 87	Q66.80	570	Q83.1	453	R11.11	195	R40.2143	844	R44.1	65
Q38.5	196	Q66.81	570	Q83.2	453	R11.12	195	R40.2144	844	R44.2	635
Q38.6	3, 87	Q66.82	570	Q83.3	453	R11.13	196	R40.2210	47, 564	R44.3	635
Q38.7	3, 87	Q66*	377	Q83.8	453	R11.14	195	R40.2211	47, 564	R44.8	844
Q38.8	3, 87	Q67.0	377	Q83.9	453	R11.15	196	R40.2212	47, 564	R44.9	844
Q39*	193	Q67.1	377	Q83*	454	R11.2	195	R40.2213	47, 564	R45.0	635
Q40*	196	Q67.2	377	Q84*	477	R12	195	R40.2214	47, 564	R45.1	635
Q41*	196	Q67.3	377	Q85.0*	51	R13*	195	R40.2220	47, 564	R45.2	635
Q42*	196	Q67.4	377	Q85.1	51	R14*	195	R40.2221	47, 564	R45.3	635
Q43.0	194	Q67.5	212, 377	Q85.8	605, 631	R15*	195	R40.2222	47, 564	R45.4	635
Q43.1	196	Q67.6	377	Q85.9	605, 631	R16.0	209	R40.2223	47, 564	R45.5	635
Q43.2	196	Q67.7	377	Q86*	569	R16.1	579	R40.2224	47, 564	R45.6	635
Q43.3	196	Q67.8	377	Q87.0	378	R16.2	209	R40.2230	844	R45.7	635
Q43.4	196	Q68.0	377	Q87.1*	378	R17	209	R40.2231	844	R45.81	635
Q43.5	196	Q68.1	377	Q87.2	378	R18*	795	R40.2232	844	R45.82	635
Q43.6	196	Q68.2	377	Q87.3	378	R19.0*	195	R40.2233	844	R45.83	795
Q43.7	196	Q68.3	377	Q87.4*	172	R19.1*	195	R40.2234	844	R45.84	795
Q43.8	196	Q68.4	377	Q87.5	378	R19.2	195	R40.2240	844	R45.850	844
Q43.9	196	Q68.5	377	Q87.8*	378	R19.3*	196	R40.2241	844	R45.851	635
Q44.0	209	Q68.6	348	Q89.0*	579	R19.4	195	R40.2242	844	R45.86	635
Q44.1	209	Q68.8	377	Q89.1	503	R19.5	195	R40.2243	844	R45.87	635
Q44.2	209	Q69*	377	Q89.2	503	R19.6	87	R40.2244	844	R45.89	635
Q44.3	209	Q70*	377	Q89.3	196	R19.7	195	R40.2250	844	R46*	844
Q44.4	209	Q71*	377	Q89.4	196, 564	R19.8	195	R40.2251	844	R47*	51
Q44.5	209	Q72*	377	Q89.7	378	R20*	51	R40.2252	844	R48.0	636
Q44.6	209	Q73*	377	Q89.8	378	R21	477	R40.2253	844	R48.1	636
Q44.7	209	Q74*	378	Q89.9	844	R22.0	477	R40.2254	844	R48.2	636
Q45.0	208	Q75*	378	Q90*	635	R22.1	477	R40.2310	47, 564	R48.3	65
Q45.1	208	Q76.0	51	Q91*	635	R22.2	477	R40.2311	47, 564	R48.8	636
Q45.2	208	Q76.1	378	Q92*	844	R22.3*	477	R40.2312	47, 564	R48.9	636
Q45.3	208	Q76.2	297	Q93.0	844	R22.4*	477	R40.2313	47, 564	R49*	87
Q45.8	196	Q76.3	212, 378	Q93.1	844	R22.9	477	R40.2314	47, 564	R50*	632
Q45.9	196	Q76.411	297	Q93.2	844	R23.0	795	R40.2320	47, 564	R51	55
Q50*	534, 542	Q76.412	297	Q93.3	635	R23.1	795	R40.2321	47, 564	R52	795
Q51.0	534, 542	Q76.413	297	Q93.4	635	R23.2	795	R40.2322	47, 564	R53.0	795
Q51.10	534, 542	Q76.414	297	Q93.51	635	R23.3	579	R40.2323	47, 564	R53.1	795
Q51.11	534, 542	Q76.415	297	Q93.59	635	R23.4	477	R40.2324	47, 564	R53.2	795
Q51.20	534, 542	Q76.419	297	Q93.7	635	R23.8	477	R40.2330	844	R53.8*	795
Q51.21	534, 542	Q76.42*	212	Q93.8*	635	R23.9	477	R40.2331	844	R54	635
Q51.22	534, 542	Q76.425	378	Q93.82	635	R25*	51	R40.2332	844	R55	172
Q51.28	534, 542	Q76.426	378	Q93.9	635	R26.0	51	R40.2333	844	R56.00	564
Q51.3	534, 542	Q76.427	378	Q95*	844	R26.1	51	R40.2334	844	R56.9	564
Q51.4	534, 542	Q76.428	378	Q96*	534, 542	R26.2	302	R40.2340	47, 564	R56*	55
Q51.5	534, 542	Q76.429	378	Q97*	534, 542	R26.8*	51	R40.2341	47, 564	R57.0	110, 167
Q51.6	534, 542	Q76.49	297	Q98.5	534, 542	R26.9	51	R40.2342	47, 564	R57.1	634
Q51.7	534, 542	Q76.5	378	Q98*	529	R27*	51	R40.2343	47, 564	R57.8	634
Q51.810	534, 542	Q76.6	378	Q99.0	529, 534, 542	R29.0	502, 564	R40.2344	47, 564	R57.9	110, 167, 564
Q51.811	534, 542	Q76.7	378	Q99.1	529, 534, 542	R29.1	51	R40.2350	844	R58	173, 564
Q51.818	534, 542	Q76.8	378	Q99.2	635	R29.2	51	R40.2351	844	R59.0	579
Q51.820	534, 542	Q76.9	378	Q99.8	529, 534, 542	R29.3	51	R40.2352	844	R59.1	579
Q51.821	534, 542	Q77.0	378	Q99.9	844	R29.4	302	R40.2353	844	R59.9	579
Q51.828	534, 542	Q77.1	378	R00.0	172, 564	R29.5	51	R40.2354	844	R60*	795
Q51.9	534, 542	Q77.2	378	R00.1	172	R29.6	51	R40.2360	844	R61	477
Q52*	534, 542	Q77.3	378	R00.2	172	R29.7*	844	R40.2361	844	R62*	502
Q53.00	569	Q77.4	378	R00.8	173	R29.810	51	R40.2362	844	R63*	502
Q53.01	569	Q77.5	378	R00.9	173	R29.818	51	R40.2363	844	R64	795

Code	Page	Code	Page	Code	Page	Code	Page	Code	Page	Code	Page
R65.10	632	R87.620	534, 542	S00.05XA	455, 975	S00.34XA	455, 975	S00.512A	455, 975	S01.02XA	455, 975
R65.11	632	R87.621	534, 542	S00.05XD	796	S00.34XD	796	S00.512D	796	S01.02XD	796
R65.20	634	R87.622	534, 542	S00.05XS	455	S00.34XS	455	S00.512S	455	S01.02XS	455
R65.21	634	R87.623	534, 542	S00.06XA	477, 975	S00.35XA	455, 975	S00.521A	477, 975	S01.03XA	455, 975
R68.0	795	R87.624	534, 542	S00.06XD	796	S00.35XD	796	S00.521D	796	S01.03XD	796
R68.11	795	R87.625	534, 542	S00.06XS	455	S00.35XS	455	S00.521S	455	S01.03XS	455
R68.12	795	R87.628	534, 542	S00.07XA	455, 975	S00.36XA	477, 975	S00.522A	477, 975	S01.04XA	455, 975
R68.13	844	R87.629	570, 796	S00.07XD	796	S00.36XD	796	S00.522D	796	S01.04XD	796
R68.19	844	R87.69	796	S00.07XS	455	S00.36XS	455	S00.522S	455	S01.04XS	455
R68.2	3, 87	R87.7	796	S00.10XA	65, 975	S00.37XA	455, 975	S00.531A	455, 975	S01.05XA	455, 975
R68.3	106	R87.810	534, 542	S00.10XD	796	S00.37XD	796	S00.531D	796	S01.05XD	796
R68.81	795	R87.811	534, 542	S00.10XS	455	S00.37XS	455	S00.531S	455	S01.05XS	455
R68.82	844	R87.820	534, 542	S00.11XA	65, 975	S00.401A	455, 975	S00.532A	455, 975	S01.101A	66, 975
R68.83	795	R87.821	534, 542	S00.11XD	796	S00.401D	796	S00.532D	796	S01.101D	796
R68.84	3, 87	R87.89	796	S00.11XS	455	S00.401S	455	S00.532S	455	S01.101S	456
R68.89	795	R87.9	796	S00.12XA	65, 975	S00.402A	455, 975	S00.541A	455, 975	S01.102A	66, 975
R69	844	R88*	796	S00.12XD	796	S00.402D	796	S00.541D	796	S01.102D	796
R70*	795	R89.0	796	S00.12XS	455	S00.402S	455	S00.541S	455	S01.102S	456
R71*	578	R89.1	796	S00.201A	65, 975	S00.409A	455, 975	S00.542A	455, 975	S01.109A	66, 975
R73*	502	R89.2	796	S00.201D	796	S00.409D	796	S00.542D	796	S01.109D	796
R74*	795	R89.3	796	S00.201S	455	S00.409S	455	S00.542S	455	S01.109S	456
R75	579	R89.4	796	S00.202A	65, 975	S00.411A	455, 975	S00.551A	455, 975	S01.111A	66, 975
R76.0	579	R89.5	796	S00.202D	796	S00.411D	796	S00.551D	796	S01.111D	796
R76.1*	104	R89.6	796	S00.202S	455	S00.411S	455	S00.551S	455	S01.111S	456
R76.8	579	R89.7	796	S00.209A	65, 975	S00.412A	455, 975	S00.552A	455, 975	S01.112A	66, 975
R76.9	579	R89.7	570	S00.209D	796	S00.412D	796	S00.552D	796	S01.112D	796
R77*	795	R89.8	796	S00.209S	455	S00.412S	455	S00.552S	455	S01.112S	456
R78.1	795	R89.9	634	S00.211A	65, 975	S00.419A	455, 975	S00.561A	477, 975	S01.119A	66, 975
R78.2	795	R90.0	477	S00.211D	796	S00.419D	796	S00.561D	796	S01.119D	796
R78.3	795	R90.81	51	S00.211S	455	S00.419S	455	S00.561S	455	S01.119S	456
R78.4	795	R90.82	51	S00.212A	65, 975	S00.421A	477, 975	S00.562A	477, 975	S01.121A	66, 975
R78.5	795	R90.89	796	S00.212D	796	S00.421D	796	S00.562D	796	S01.121D	796
R78.6	795	R91.1	106	S00.212S	455	S00.421S	455	S00.562S	455	S01.121S	456
R78.7*	795	R91.8	106	S00.219A	65, 975	S00.422A	477, 975	S00.571A	455, 975	S01.122A	66, 975
R78.81	564, 634	R92.0	453	S00.219D	796	S00.422D	796	S00.571D	796	S01.122D	796
R78.89	795	R92.1	453	S00.219S	455	S00.422S	455	S00.571S	455	S01.122S	456
R78.9	795	R92.2	453	S00.221A	65, 975	S00.429A	477, 975	S00.572A	455, 975	S01.129A	66, 975
R79*	795	R92.8	453	S00.221D	796	S00.429D	796	S00.572D	796	S01.129D	796
R80.0	519	R92*	454	S00.221S	455	S00.429S	455	S00.572S	455	S01.129S	456
R80.1	519	R93.0	51	S00.222A	65, 975	S00.431A	455, 975	S00.80XA	455, 975	S01.131A	66, 975
R80.2	520	R93.1	171	S00.222D	796	S00.431D	796	S00.80XD	796	S01.131D	796
R80.3	519	R93.2	209	S00.222S	455	S00.431S	455	S00.80XS	455	S01.131S	456
R80.8	519	R93.3	195	S00.229A	65, 975	S00.432A	455, 975	S00.81XA	455, 975	S01.132A	66, 975
R80.9	519	R93.4*	519	S00.229D	796	S00.432D	796	S00.81XD	796	S01.132D	796
R81	501	R93.5	195	S00.229S	455	S00.432S	455	S00.81XS	455	S01.132S	456
R82.0	519, 564	R93.6	378	S00.241A	65, 975	S00.439A	455, 975	S00.82XA	477, 975	S01.139A	66, 975
R82.1	795	R93.7	378	S00.241D	796	S00.439D	796	S00.82XD	796	S01.139D	796
R82.2	209	R93.811	529	S00.241S	455	S00.439S	455	S00.82XS	455	S01.139S	456
R82.3	519	R93.812	529	S00.242A	65, 975	S00.441A	455, 975	S00.83XA	455, 975	S01.141A	66, 975
R82.4	502	R93.813	529	S00.242D	796	S00.441D	796	S00.83XD	796	S01.141D	796
R82.5	519	R93.819	529	S00.242S	455	S00.441S	455	S00.83XS	455	S01.141S	456
R82.6	519	R93.89	796	S00.249A	65, 975	S00.442A	455, 975	S00.84XA	455, 975	S01.142A	66, 975
R82.7*	519	R93.9	796	S00.249D	796	S00.442D	796	S00.84XD	796	S01.142D	796
R82.8*	519	R94.0*	51	S00.249S	455	S00.442S	455	S00.84XS	455	S01.142S	456
R82.90	519	R94.110	65	S00.251A	65, 975	S00.449A	455, 975	S00.85XA	455, 975	S01.149A	66, 975
R82.91	519	R94.111	65	S00.251D	796	S00.449D	796	S00.85XD	796	S01.149D	796
R82.991	519	R94.112	65	S00.251S	455	S00.449S	455	S00.85XS	455	S01.149S	456
R82.992	519	R94.113	65	S00.252A	65, 975	S00.451A	455, 975	S00.86XA	477, 975	S01.151A	66, 975
R82.993	519	R94.118	51	S00.252D	796	S00.451D	796	S00.86XD	796	S01.151D	796
R82.994	519	R94.120	87, 570	S00.252S	455	S00.451S	455	S00.86XS	455	S01.151S	456
R82.998	519	R94.121	87	S00.259A	65, 975	S00.452A	455, 975	S00.87XA	455, 975	S01.152A	66, 975
R83*	51	R94.128	51	S00.259D	796	S00.452D	796	S00.87XD	796	S01.152D	796
R84*	795	R94.130	51	S00.259S	455	S00.452S	455	S00.87XS	455	S01.152S	456
R85.0	795	R94.131	378	S00.261A	65, 975	S00.459A	455, 975	S00.90XA	455, 975	S01.159A	66, 975
R85.1	795	R94.138	51	S00.261D	796	S00.459D	796	S00.90XD	796	S01.159D	796
R85.2	795	R94.2	106	S00.261S	455	S00.459S	455	S00.90XS	455	S01.159S	456
R85.3	795	R94.3*	173	S00.262A	66, 975	S00.461A	477, 975	S00.91XA	455, 975	S01.20XA	3, 87, 975
R85.4	795	R94.4	519	S00.262D	796	S00.461D	796	S00.91XD	796	S01.20XD	796
R85.5	795	R94.5	209	S00.262S	455	S00.461S	455	S00.91XS	455	S01.20XS	456
R85.61*	196	R94.6	503	S00.269A	66, 975	S00.462A	477, 975	S00.92XA	477, 975	S01.21XA	3, 87, 975
R85.69	795	R94.7	503	S00.269D	796	S00.462D	796	S00.92XD	796	S01.21XD	796
R85.7	795	R94.8	519	S00.269S	455	S00.462S	455	S00.92XS	455	S01.21XS	456
R85.81	196	R97.0	796	S00.271A	66, 975	S00.469A	477, 975	S00.93XA	455, 975	S01.22XA	3, 87, 975
R85.82	196	R97.1	796	S00.271D	796	S00.469D	796	S00.93XD	796	S01.22XD	796
R85.89	795	R97.20	796	S00.271S	455	S00.469S	455	S00.93XS	455	S01.22XS	456
R85.9	795	R97.21	796	S00.272A	66, 975	S00.471A	455, 975	S00.94XA	455, 975	S01.23XA	3, 87, 975
R86*	529	R97.8	796	S00.272D	796	S00.471D	796	S00.94XD	796	S01.23XD	796
R87.0	795	R99	844	S00.272S	455	S00.471S	455	S00.94XS	455	S01.23XS	456
R87.1	796	S00.00XA	455, 975	S00.279A	66, 975	S00.472A	455, 975	S00.95XA	455, 975	S01.24XA	3, 87, 975
R87.2	796	S00.00XD	796	S00.279D	796	S00.472D	796	S00.95XD	796	S01.24XD	796
R87.3	796	S00.00XS	455	S00.279S	455	S00.472S	455	S00.95XS	455	S01.24XS	456
R87.4	796	S00.01XA	455, 975	S00.30XA	455, 975	S00.479A	455, 975	S00.96XA	477, 975	S01.25XA	3, 87, 975
R87.5	796	S00.01XD	796	S00.30XD	796	S00.479D	796	S00.96XD	796	S01.25XD	796
R87.610	534, 542	S00.01XS	455	S00.30XS	455	S00.479S	455	S00.96XS	455	S01.25XS	456
R87.611	534, 542	S00.02XA	477, 975	S00.31XA	455, 975	S00.501A	455, 975	S00.97XA	455, 975	S01.301A	87, 975
R87.612	534, 542	S00.02XD	796	S00.31XD	796	S00.501D	796	S00.97XD	796	S01.301D	796
R87.613	534, 542	S00.02XS	455	S00.31XS	455	S00.501S	455	S00.97XS	455	S01.301S	456
R87.614	534, 542	S00.03XA	455, 975	S00.32XA	477, 975	S00.502A	455, 975	S01.00XA	455, 975	S01.302A	87, 975
R87.615	534, 542	S00.03XD	796	S00.32XD	796	S00.502D	796	S01.00XD	796	S01.302D	796
R87.616	534, 542	S00.03XS	455	S00.32XS	455	S00.502S	455	S01.00XS	455	S01.302S	456
R87.618	570, 796	S00.04XA	455, 975	S00.33XA	455, 975	S00.511A	455, 975	S01.01XA	455, 975	S01.309A	87, 975
R87.619	570	S00.04XD	796	S00.33XD	796	S00.511D	796	S01.01XD	796	S01.309D	796
R87.619	796	S00.04XS	455	S00.33XS	455	S00.511S	455	S01.01XS	455	S01.309S	456

Code	Page	Code	Page	Code	Page	Code	Page	Code	Page	Code	Page
S01.311A	87, 976	S01.452A	3, 456, 976	S02.101S	51	S02.11HD	306	S02.40DS	52	S02.620D	306
S01.311D	796	S01.452D	797	S02.102A	48, 50, 976	S02.11HG	306	S02.40EA	3, 88, 976	S02.620G	306
S01.311S	456	S01.452S	456	S02.102B	48, 50, 976, 1024	S02.11HK	378	S02.40EB	3, 88, 976	S02.620K	378
S01.312A	87, 976	S01.459A	3, 456, 976	S02.102D	306	S02.11HS	52	S02.40ED	306	S02.620S	52
S01.312D	796	S01.459D	797	S02.102G	306	S02.121A	48, 50, 976	S02.40EG	306	S02.621A	4, 88, 976
S01.312S	456	S01.459S	456	S02.102K	378	S02.121B	48, 50, 976	S02.40EK	378	S02.621B	4, 88, 976
S01.319A	87, 976	S01.501A	3, 87, 976	S02.102S	51	S02.121D	797	S02.40ES	52	S02.621D	306
S01.319D	796	S01.501D	797	S02.109A	48, 50, 976	S02.121G	797	S02.40FA	3, 88, 976	S02.621G	306
S01.319S	456	S01.501S	456	S02.109B	48, 50, 976, 1024	S02.121K	797	S02.40FB	3, 88, 976	S02.621K	378
S01.321A	87, 976	S01.502A	3, 87, 976	S02.109D	306	S02.121S	767	S02.40FD	306	S02.621S	52
S01.321D	796	S01.502D	797	S02.109G	306	S02.122A	48, 50, 976	S02.40FG	306	S02.622A	4, 88, 976
S01.321S	456	S01.502S	456	S02.109K	378	S02.122B	48, 50, 976	S02.40FK	378	S02.622B	4, 88, 976
S01.322A	87, 976	S01.511A	3, 87, 976	S02.109S	51	S02.122D	797	S02.40FS	52	S02.622D	306
S01.322D	796	S01.511D	797	S02.110A	48, 50, 976	S02.122G	797	S02.411A	88, 976	S02.622G	307
S01.322S	456	S01.511S	456	S02.110B	48, 50, 976	S02.122K	797	S02.411A	3	S02.622K	378
S01.329A	87, 976	S01.512A	3, 87, 976	S02.110D	306	S02.122S	767	S02.411B	3, 88, 976	S02.622S	52
S01.329D	796	S01.512D	797	S02.110G	306	S02.129A	48, 50, 976	S02.411B	3	S02.630A	4, 88, 976
S01.329S	456	S01.512S	456	S02.110K	378	S02.129B	49, 50, 976	S02.411D	306	S02.630B	4, 88, 976
S01.331A	87, 976	S01.521A	3, 87, 976	S02.110S	51	S02.129D	797	S02.411G	306	S02.630D	307
S01.331D	796	S01.521D	797	S02.111A	48, 50, 976	S02.129G	797	S02.411K	378	S02.630G	306
S01.331S	456	S01.521S	456	S02.111B	48, 50, 976	S02.129K	797	S02.411S	52	S02.630K	378
S01.332A	87, 976	S01.522A	3, 87, 976	S02.111D	306	S02.129S	767	S02.412A	88, 976	S02.630S	52
S01.332D	797	S01.522D	797	S02.111G	306	S02.19XA	49, 50, 976	S02.412A	3	S02.631A	4, 88, 976
S01.332S	456	S01.522S	456	S02.111K	378	S02.19XB	49, 50, 976	S02.412B	88, 976	S02.631B	4, 88, 976
S01.339A	87, 976	S01.531A	3, 87, 976	S02.111S	51	S02.19XD	306	S02.412B	3	S02.631D	307
S01.339D	797	S01.531D	797	S02.112A	48, 50, 976	S02.19XG	306	S02.412D	306	S02.631G	307
S01.339S	456	S01.531S	456	S02.112B	48, 50, 976	S02.19XK	378	S02.412G	306	S02.631K	378
S01.341A	87, 976	S01.532A	3, 87, 976	S02.112D	306	S02.19XS	52	S02.412K	378	S02.631S	52
S01.341D	797	S01.532D	797	S02.112G	306	S02.2XXA	87, 976	S02.412S	52	S02.632A	4, 88, 976
S01.341S	456	S01.532S	456	S02.112K	378	S02.2XXB	87, 976	S02.413A	88, 976	S02.632B	4, 88, 976
S01.342A	87, 976	S01.541A	3, 87, 976	S02.112S	51	S02.2XXD	306	S02.413A	3	S02.632D	307
S01.342D	797	S01.541D	797	S02.113A	48, 50, 976	S02.2XXG	306	S02.413B	88, 976	S02.632G	307
S01.342S	456	S01.541S	456	S02.113B	48, 50, 976	S02.2XXK	378	S02.413B	3	S02.632K	378
S01.349A	87, 976	S01.542A	3, 87, 976	S02.113D	306	S02.2XXS	52	S02.413D	306	S02.632S	52
S01.349D	797	S01.542D	797	S02.113G	306	S02.30XA	3, 66, 976	S02.413G	306	S02.640A	4, 88, 976
S01.349S	456	S01.542S	456	S02.113K	378	S02.30XB	3, 66, 976	S02.413K	378	S02.640B	4, 88, 976
S01.351A	87, 976	S01.551A	3, 88, 976	S02.113S	51	S02.30XD	306	S02.413S	52	S02.640D	307
S01.351D	797	S01.551D	797	S02.118A	48, 50, 976	S02.30XG	306	S02.42XA	3, 378, 976	S02.640G	307
S01.351S	456	S01.551S	456	S02.118B	48, 50, 976	S02.30XK	378	S02.42XB	3, 378, 976	S02.640K	378
S01.352A	87, 976	S01.552A	3, 88, 976	S02.118D	306	S02.30XS	52	S02.42XD	306	S02.640S	52
S01.352D	797	S01.552D	797	S02.118G	306	S02.31XA	3, 66, 976	S02.42XG	306	S02.641A	4, 88, 976
S01.352S	456	S01.552S	456	S02.118K	378	S02.31XB	3, 66, 976	S02.42XK	378	S02.641B	4, 88, 976
S01.359A	87, 976	S01.80XA	456, 976	S02.118S	51	S02.31XD	306	S02.42XS	52	S02.641D	307
S01.359D	797	S01.80XD	797	S02.119A	48, 50, 976	S02.31XG	306	S02.5XXA	88, 976	S02.641G	307
S01.359S	456	S01.80XS	456	S02.119B	48, 50, 976	S02.31XK	378	S02.5XXB	88, 976	S02.641K	378
S01.401A	3, 456, 976	S01.81XA	976	S02.119D	306	S02.31XS	52	S02.5XXD	306	S02.641S	52
S01.401D	797	S01.81XA	456	S02.119G	306	S02.32XA	3, 66, 976	S02.5XXG	306	S02.642A	4, 88, 976
S01.401S	456	S01.81XD	797	S02.119S	51	S02.32XB	3, 66, 976	S02.5XXK	378	S02.642B	4, 88, 976
S01.402A	3, 456, 976	S01.81XS	456	S02.11AA	48, 50, 976	S02.32XD	306	S02.5XXS	52	S02.642D	307
S01.402D	797	S01.82XA	976	S02.11AB	48, 50, 976	S02.32XG	306	S02.600A	3, 88, 976	S02.642G	307
S01.402S	456	S01.82XA	456	S02.11AD	306	S02.32XK	378	S02.600B	3, 88, 976	S02.642K	378
S01.409A	3, 456, 976	S01.82XD	797	S02.11AG	306	S02.32XS	52	S02.600D	306	S02.642S	52
S01.409D	797	S01.82XS	456	S02.11AK	378	S02.400A	3, 88, 976	S02.600G	306	S02.650A	4, 88, 976
S01.409S	456	S01.83XA	976	S02.11AS	52	S02.400B	3, 88, 976	S02.600K	378	S02.650B	4, 88, 976
S01.411A	3, 456, 976	S01.83XA	456	S02.11BA	48, 50, 976	S02.400D	306	S02.600S	52	S02.650D	307
S01.411D	797	S01.83XD	797	S02.11BB	48, 50, 976	S02.400G	306	S02.601A	3, 88, 976	S02.650G	307
S01.411S	456	S01.83XS	456	S02.11BD	306	S02.400K	378	S02.601B	3, 88, 976	S02.650K	378
S01.412A	3, 456, 976	S01.84XA	976	S02.11BG	306	S02.400S	52	S02.601D	306	S02.650S	52
S01.412D	797	S01.84XA	456	S02.11BK	378	S02.401A	3, 88, 976	S02.601G	306	S02.651A	4, 88, 976
S01.412S	456	S01.84XD	797	S02.11BS	52	S02.401B	3, 88, 976	S02.601K	378	S02.651B	4, 88, 976
S01.419A	3, 456, 976	S01.84XS	456	S02.11CA	48, 50, 976	S02.401D	306	S02.601S	52	S02.651D	307
S01.419D	797	S01.85XA	456, 976	S02.11CB	48, 50, 976	S02.401K	378	S02.602A	4, 88, 976	S02.651G	307
S01.419S	456	S01.85XD	797	S02.11CD	306	S02.401S	52	S02.602B	4, 88, 976	S02.651K	378
S01.421A	3, 456, 976	S01.85XS	456	S02.11CG	306	S02.402A	3, 88, 976	S02.602D	306	S02.651S	52
S01.421D	797	S01.90XA	456, 976	S02.11CK	378	S02.402B	3, 88, 976	S02.602G	306	S02.652A	4, 88, 976
S01.421S	456	S01.90XD	797	S02.11CS	52	S02.402D	306	S02.602K	378	S02.652B	4, 88, 977
S01.422A	3, 456, 976	S01.90XS	456	S02.11DA	48, 50, 976	S02.402G	306	S02.602S	52	S02.652D	307
S01.422D	797	S01.91XA	456, 976	S02.11DB	48, 50, 976	S02.402K	378	S02.609A	4, 88, 976	S02.652G	307
S01.422S	456	S01.91XD	797	S02.11DD	306	S02.402S	52	S02.609B	4, 88, 976	S02.652K	378
S01.429A	3, 456, 976	S01.91XS	456	S02.11DG	306	S02.40AA	3, 88, 976	S02.609D	306	S02.652S	52
S01.429D	797	S01.92XA	456, 976	S02.11DK	378	S02.40AB	3, 88, 976	S02.609G	306	S02.66XA	4, 88, 977
S01.429S	456	S01.92XD	797	S02.11DS	52	S02.40AD	306	S02.609K	378	S02.66XB	4, 88, 977
S01.431A	3, 456, 976	S01.92XS	456	S02.11EA	48, 50, 976	S02.40AG	306	S02.609S	52	S02.66XD	307
S01.431D	797	S01.93XA	456, 976	S02.11EB	48, 50, 976	S02.40AK	378	S02.610A	4, 88, 976	S02.66XG	307
S01.431S	456	S01.93XD	797	S02.11ED	306	S02.40AS	52	S02.610B	4, 88, 976	S02.66XK	378
S01.432A	3, 456, 976	S01.93XS	456	S02.11EG	306	S02.40BA	3, 88, 976	S02.610D	306	S02.66XS	52
S01.432D	797	S01.94XA	456, 976	S02.11EK	378	S02.40BB	3, 88, 976	S02.610G	306	S02.670A	4, 88, 977
S01.432S	456	S01.94XD	797	S02.11ES	52	S02.40BD	306	S02.610K	378	S02.670B	4, 88, 977
S01.439A	3, 456, 976	S01.94XS	456	S02.11FA	48, 50, 976	S02.40BG	306	S02.610S	52	S02.670D	307
S01.439D	797	S01.95XA	456, 976	S02.11FB	48, 50, 976	S02.40BK	378	S02.611A	4, 88, 976	S02.670G	307
S01.439S	456	S01.95XD	797	S02.11FD	306	S02.40BS	52	S02.611B	4, 88, 976	S02.670K	378
S01.441A	3, 456, 976	S01.95XS	456	S02.11FG	306	S02.40CA	3, 88, 976	S02.611D	306	S02.670S	52
S01.441D	797	S02.0XXA	48, 50, 976	S02.11FK	378	S02.40CB	3, 88, 976	S02.611G	306	S02.671A	4, 88, 977
S01.441S	456	S02.0XXB	48, 50, 976	S02.11FS	52	S02.40CD	306	S02.611K	378	S02.671B	4, 88, 977
S01.442A	3, 456, 976	S02.0XXD	306	S02.11GA	48, 50, 976	S02.40CG	306	S02.611S	52	S02.671D	307
S01.442D	797	S02.0XXG	306	S02.11GB	48, 50, 976	S02.40CK	378	S02.612A	4, 88, 976	S02.671G	307
S01.442S	456	S02.0XXK	378	S02.11GD	306	S02.40CS	52	S02.612B	4, 88, 976	S02.671K	378
S01.449A	3, 456, 976	S02.0XXS	51	S02.11GG	306	S02.40DA	3, 88, 976	S02.612D	306	S02.671S	52
S01.449D	797	S02.101A	48, 50, 976	S02.11GK	378	S02.40DB	3, 88, 976	S02.612G	306	S02.672A	4, 88, 977
S01.449S	456	S02.101B	48, 50, 976, 1024	S02.11GS	52	S02.40DD	306	S02.612K	378	S02.672B	4, 88, 977
S01.451A	3, 456, 976	S02.101D	306	S02.11HA	48, 50, 976	S02.40DG	306	S02.612S	52	S02.672D	307
S01.451D	797	S02.101G	306	S02.11HB	48, 50, 976	S02.40DK	378	S02.620A	4, 88, 976	S02.672G	307
S01.451S	456	S02.101K	378					S02.620B	4, 88, 976	S02.672K	378

Code	Page	Code	Page	Code	Page	Code	Page	Code	Page	Code	Page
S02.672S	52	S03.02XA	4,88,977	S04.41XS	52	S05.41XS	456	S06.2X3A	48,49,977,1024	S06.323D	798
S02.69XA	977	S03.02XD	797	S04.42XA	46,977	S05.42XA	66,977	S06.2X3D	798	S06.323S	52
S02.69XA	4,88	S03.02XS	348	S04.42XD	797	S05.42XD	797	S06.2X3S	52	S06.324A	15,48,49,977,1025
S02.69XB	977	S03.03XA	4,88,977	S04.42XS	52	S05.42XS	456	S06.2X4A	48,49,977,1024	S06.324D	798
S02.69XB	4,88	S03.03XD	797	S04.50XA	46,977	S05.50XA	66,977	S06.2X4D	798	S06.324S	52
S02.69XD	307	S03.03XS	348	S04.50XD	797	S05.50XD	797	S06.2X4S	52	S06.325A	15,48,49,977,1025
S02.69XG	307	S03.1XXA	348,977	S04.50XS	52	S05.50XS	456	S06.2X5A	48,49,977,1024	S06.325D	798
S02.69XK	378	S03.1XXA	797	S04.51XA	46,977	S05.51XA	66,977	S06.2X5D	798	S06.325S	52
S02.69XS	52	S03.1XXS	348	S04.51XD	797	S05.51XD	797	S06.2X5S	52	S06.326A	15,48,49,977,1025
S02.80XA	977	S03.2XXA	88,977	S04.51XS	52	S05.51XS	456	S06.2X6A	48,49,977,1024	S06.326D	798
S02.80XA	4,378	S03.2XXD	797	S04.52XA	46,977	S05.52XA	66,977	S06.2X6D	798	S06.326S	52
S02.80XB	977	S03.2XXS	456	S04.52XD	797	S05.52XD	797	S06.2X6S	52	S06.327A	15,48,49,977,1025
S02.80XB	4,378	S03.40XA	88,977	S04.52XS	52	S05.52XS	456	S06.2X7A	48,49,977,1024	S06.328A	15,48,49,977,1025
S02.80XD	307	S03.40XD	797	S04.60XA	87,977	S05.60XA	66,977	S06.2X8A	48,49,977,1024	S06.329A	15,48,49,977,1025
S02.80XG	307	S03.40XS	348	S04.60XD	797	S05.60XD	797	S06.2X9A	48,49,977,1024	S06.329D	798
S02.80XK	378	S03.41XA	88,977	S04.60XS	52	S05.60XS	456	S06.2X9D	798	S06.329S	52
S02.80XS	52	S03.41XD	797	S04.61XA	87,977	S05.61XA	66,977	S06.2X9S	52	S06.330A	15,49,50,977,1025
S02.81XA	977	S03.41XS	348	S04.61XD	797	S05.61XD	797	S06.300A	49,50,977,1024	S06.330D	798
S02.81XA	4,378	S03.42XA	88,977	S04.61XS	52	S05.61XS	456	S06.300D	798	S06.330S	52
S02.81XB	977	S03.42XD	797	S04.62XA	87,977	S05.62XA	66,977	S06.300S	52	S06.331A	15,49,50,977,1025
S02.81XB	4,378	S03.42XS	348	S04.62XD	797	S05.62XD	797	S06.301A	49,50,977,1024	S06.331D	798
S02.81XD	307	S03.43XA	88,977	S04.62XS	52	S05.62XS	456	S06.301D	798	S06.331S	52
S02.81XG	307	S03.43XD	797	S04.70XA	46,977	S05.70XA	66,977	S06.301S	52	S06.332A	15,49,50,977,1025
S02.81XK	378	S03.43XS	348	S04.70XD	797	S05.70XD	797	S06.302A	49,50,977,1024	S06.332D	798
S02.81XS	52	S03.8XXA	977	S04.70XS	52	S05.70XS	746	S06.302D	798	S06.332S	52
S02.82XA	977	S03.8XXA	378	S04.71XA	46,977	S05.71XA	66,977	S06.302S	52	S06.333A	15,48,49,977,1025
S02.82XA	4,378	S03.8XXD	797	S04.71XD	797	S05.71XD	797	S06.303A	48,49,977,1024	S06.333D	798
S02.82XB	977	S03.8XXS	348	S04.71XS	52	S05.71XS	746	S06.303D	798	S06.333S	52
S02.82XB	4,378	S03.9XXA	348,977	S04.72XA	46,977	S05.72XA	66,977	S06.303S	52	S06.334A	15,48,49,977,1025
S02.82XD	307	S03.9XXD	797	S04.72XD	797	S05.72XD	797	S06.304A	48,49,977,1024	S06.334D	798
S02.82XG	307	S03.9XXS	348	S04.72XS	52	S05.72XS	746	S06.304D	798	S06.334S	52
S02.82XK	378	S04.011A	66,977	S04.811A	46,977	S05.8X1A	66,977	S06.304S	52	S06.335A	15,48,49,977,1025
S02.82XS	52	S04.011D	797	S04.811D	797	S05.8X1D	797	S06.305A	48,49,977,1025	S06.335D	798
S02.831A	4,49,50,977	S04.011S	52	S04.811S	52	S05.8X1S	746	S06.305D	798	S06.335S	52
S02.831B	4,49,50,977	S04.012A	66,977	S04.812A	46,977	S05.8X2A	66,977	S06.305S	52	S06.336A	15,48,49,978,1025
S02.831D	797	S04.012D	797	S04.812D	797	S05.8X2D	797	S06.306A	48,49,977,1025	S06.336D	798
S02.831G	797	S04.012S	52	S04.812S	52	S05.8X2S	746	S06.306D	798	S06.336S	52
S02.831K	797	S04.019A	66,977	S04.819A	46,977	S05.8X9A	66,977	S06.306S	52	S06.337A	15,48,49,978,1025
S02.831S	767	S04.019D	797	S04.819D	797	S05.8X9D	797	S06.307A	48,49,977,1025	S06.338A	15,48,49,978,1025
S02.832A	4,49,50,977	S04.019S	52	S04.819S	52	S05.8X9S	746	S06.308A	48,49,977,1025	S06.339A	15,48,49,978,1025
S02.832B	4,49,50,977	S04.02XA	52,977	S04.891A	46,977	S05.90XA	66,977	S06.309A	48,49,977,1025	S06.339D	798
S02.832D	797	S04.02XD	797	S04.891D	797	S05.90XD	797	S06.309D	798	S06.339S	52
S02.832G	797	S04.02XS	52	S04.891S	52	S05.90XS	746	S06.309S	52	S06.340A	15,49,50,978,1025
S02.832K	797	S04.031A	52,977	S04.892A	46,977	S05.91XA	66,977	S06.310A	15,49,50,977,1025	S06.340D	798
S02.832S	767	S04.031D	797	S04.892D	797	S05.91XD	797	S06.310D	798	S06.340S	52
S02.839A	4,49,50,977	S04.031S	52	S04.892S	52	S05.91XS	746	S06.310S	52	S06.341A	15,49,50,978,1025
S02.839B	4,49,50,977	S04.032A	52,977	S04.899A	46,977	S05.92XA	66,977	S06.311A	15,49,50,977,1025	S06.341D	798
S02.839D	797	S04.032D	797	S04.899D	797	S05.92XD	797	S06.311D	798	S06.341S	52
S02.839G	797	S04.032S	52	S04.899S	52	S05.92XS	746	S06.311S	52	S06.342A	15,49,50,978,1025
S02.839K	797	S04.039A	52,977	S04.9XXA	46,977	S06.0X0A	51,977	S06.312A	15,49,50,977,1025	S06.342D	798
S02.839S	767	S04.039D	797	S04.9XXD	797	S06.0X0D	797	S06.312D	798	S06.342S	52
S02.841A	4,49,50,977	S04.039S	52	S04.9XXS	52	S06.0X0S	52	S06.312S	52	S06.343A	15,48,49,978,1025
S02.841B	4,49,50,977	S04.041A	52,977	S05.00XA	66,977	S06.0X1A	51,977	S06.313A	15,48,49,977,1025	S06.343D	798
S02.841D	797	S04.041D	797	S05.00XD	797	S06.0X1D	797	S06.313D	798	S06.343S	52
S02.841G	797	S04.041S	52	S05.00XS	456	S06.0X1S	52	S06.313S	52	S06.344A	15,48,49,978,1025
S02.841K	797	S04.042A	52,977	S05.01XA	66,977	S06.0X9A	51,977	S06.314A	15,48,49,977,1025	S06.344D	798
S02.841S	768	S04.042D	797	S05.01XD	797	S06.0X9D	797	S06.314D	798	S06.344S	52
S02.842A	4,49,50,977	S04.042S	52	S05.01XS	456	S06.0X9S	52	S06.314S	52	S06.345A	15,48,49,978,1025
S02.842B	4,49,50,977	S04.049A	52,977	S05.02XA	66,977	S06.1X0A	49,50,977,1024	S06.315A	15,48,49,977,1025	S06.345D	798
S02.842D	797	S04.049D	797	S05.02XD	797	S06.1X0D	797	S06.315D	798	S06.345S	52
S02.842G	797	S04.049S	52	S05.02XS	456	S06.1X0S	52	S06.315S	52	S06.346A	15,48,49,978,1025
S02.842K	797	S04.10XA	46,977	S05.10XA	66,977	S06.1X1A	49,50,977,1024	S06.316A	15,48,49,977,1025	S06.346D	798
S02.842S	768	S04.10XD	797	S05.10XD	797	S06.1X1D	797	S06.316D	798	S06.346S	52
S02.849A	4,49,50,977	S04.10XS	52	S05.10XS	456	S06.1X1S	52	S06.316S	52	S06.347A	15,48,49,978,1025
S02.849B	4,49,50,977	S04.11XA	46,977	S05.11XA	66,977	S06.1X2A	49,50,977,1024	S06.317A	15,48,49,977,1025	S06.348A	15,48,49,978,1025
S02.849D	797	S04.11XD	797	S05.11XD	797	S06.1X2D	797	S06.318A	15,48,49,977,1025	S06.349A	15,48,49,978,1025
S02.849G	797	S04.11XS	52	S05.11XS	456	S06.1X2S	52	S06.319A	15,48,49,977,1025	S06.349D	798
S02.849K	797	S04.12XA	46,977	S05.12XA	66,977	S06.1X3A	48,49,977,1024	S06.319D	798		
S02.849S	768	S04.12XD	797	S05.12XD	797	S06.1X3D	797	S06.319S	52		
S02.85XA	4,49,50,977	S04.12XS	52	S05.12XS	456	S06.1X3S	52	S06.320A	15,49,50,977,1025		
S02.85XB	4,49,50,977	S04.20XA	46,977	S05.20XA	66,977	S06.1X4A	48,49,977,1024	S06.320D	798		
S02.85XD	797	S04.20XD	797	S05.20XD	797	S06.1X4D	797	S06.320S	52		
S02.85XG	797	S04.20XS	52	S05.20XS	456	S06.1X4S	52	S06.321A	15,49,50,977,1025		
S02.85XK	797	S04.21XA	46,977	S05.21XA	66,977	S06.1X5A	48,49,977,1024	S06.321D	798		
S02.85XS	768	S04.21XD	797	S05.21XD	797	S06.1X5D	797	S06.321S	52		
S02.91XA	49,50,977,1024	S04.21XS	456	S05.21XS	456	S06.1X5S	52	S06.322A	15,49,50,977,1025		
S02.91XB	49,50,977,1024	S04.22XA	46,977	S05.22XA	66,977	S06.1X6A	48,49,977,1024	S06.322D	798		
S02.91XD	307	S04.22XD	797	S05.22XD	797	S06.1X6D	797	S06.322S	52		
S02.91XG	307	S04.22XS	52	S05.22XS	456	S06.1X6S	52	S06.323A	15,48,49,977,1025		
S02.91XK	378	S04.30XA	46,977	S05.30XA	66,977	S06.1X7A	48,49,977,1024				
S02.91XS	52	S04.30XD	797	S05.30XD	797	S06.1X8A	48,49,977,1024				
S02.92XA	4,378,977	S04.30XS	52	S05.30XS	456	S06.1X9A	48,49,977,1024				
S02.92XA	4,378,977	S04.31XA	46,977	S05.31XA	66,977	S06.1X9D	797				
S02.92XD	307	S04.31XD	797	S05.31XD	797	S06.1X9S	52				
S02.92XG	307	S04.31XS	52	S05.31XS	456	S06.2X0A	49,50,977,1024				
S02.92XK	378	S04.32XA	46,977	S05.32XA	66,977	S06.2X0D	797				
S02.92XS	52	S04.32XD	797	S05.32XD	797	S06.2X0S	52				
S03.00XA	4,88,977	S04.32XS	52	S05.32XS	456	S06.2X1A	49,50,977,1024				
S03.00XD	797	S04.40XA	46,977	S05.40XA	66,977	S06.2X1D	797				
S03.00XS	348	S04.40XD	797	S05.40XD	797	S06.2X1S	52				
S03.01XA	4,88,977	S04.40XS	52	S05.40XS	456	S06.2X2A	49,50,977,1024				
S03.01XD	797	S04.41XA	46,977	S05.41XA	66,977	S06.2X2D	797				
S03.01XS	348	S04.41XD	797	S05.41XD	797	S06.2X2S	52				

Code	Page
S06.349S	52
S06.350A	15, 49, 50, 978, 1025
S06.350D	798
S06.350S	52
S06.351A	15, 49, 50, 978, 1025
S06.351D	798
S06.351S	52
S06.352A	15, 49, 50, 978, 1025
S06.352D	798
S06.352S	52
S06.353A	15, 48, 49, 978, 1025
S06.353D	798
S06.353S	52
S06.354A	15, 48, 49, 978, 1025
S06.354D	798
S06.354S	52
S06.355A	15, 48, 49, 978, 1025
S06.355D	798
S06.355S	52
S06.356A	15, 48, 49, 978, 1025
S06.356D	798
S06.356S	52
S06.357A	15, 48, 49, 978, 1025
S06.358A	15, 48, 49, 978, 1025
S06.359A	15, 48, 49, 978, 1025
S06.359D	798
S06.359S	52
S06.360A	15, 49, 50, 978, 1025
S06.360D	798
S06.360S	52
S06.361A	15, 49, 50, 978, 1025
S06.361D	798
S06.361S	52
S06.362A	15, 49, 50, 978, 1025
S06.362D	798
S06.362S	52
S06.363A	15, 48, 49, 978, 1025
S06.363D	798
S06.363S	52
S06.364A	15, 48, 49, 978, 1025
S06.364D	798
S06.364S	52
S06.365A	15, 48, 49, 978, 1025
S06.365D	798
S06.365S	52
S06.366A	15, 48, 49, 978, 1025
S06.366D	798
S06.366S	53
S06.367A	15, 48, 49, 978, 1025
S06.368A	15, 48, 49, 978, 1025
S06.369A	15, 48, 49, 978, 1025
S06.369D	798
S06.369S	53
S06.370A	15, 49, 50, 978, 1025
S06.370D	798
S06.370S	53
S06.371A	15, 49, 50, 978, 1025
S06.371D	798
S06.371S	53
S06.372A	15, 49, 50, 978, 1025
S06.372D	798
S06.372S	53
S06.373A	15, 48, 49, 978, 1025
S06.373D	798
S06.373S	53
S06.374A	15, 48, 49, 978, 1025
S06.374D	798
S06.374S	53
S06.375A	15, 48, 49, 978, 1025
S06.375D	798
S06.375S	53
S06.376A	15, 48, 49, 978, 1025
S06.376D	798
S06.376S	53
S06.377A	15
S06.377A	48, 49, 978, 1025
S06.378A	15
S06.378A	48, 49, 978, 1025
S06.379A	15, 48, 49, 50, 978, 1025
S06.379D	798
S06.379S	53
S06.380A	15, 49, 50, 978, 1025
S06.380D	798
S06.380S	53
S06.381A	15, 49, 50, 978, 1025
S06.381D	798
S06.381S	53
S06.382A	15, 49, 50, 978, 1025
S06.382D	798
S06.382S	53
S06.383A	15, 48, 49, 978, 1025
S06.383D	798
S06.383S	53
S06.384A	15, 48, 49, 978, 1025
S06.384D	798
S06.384S	53
S06.385A	15, 48, 49, 978, 1025
S06.385D	798
S06.385S	53
S06.386A	15, 48, 49, 978, 1025
S06.386D	798
S06.386S	53
S06.387A	15, 48, 49, 978, 1025
S06.388A	15, 48, 49, 978, 1025
S06.389A	15, 48, 49, 50, 978, 1025
S06.389D	798
S06.389S	53
S06.4X0A	49, 50, 978, 1025
S06.4X0D	798
S06.4X0S	53
S06.4X1A	49, 50, 978, 1025
S06.4X1D	798
S06.4X1S	53
S06.4X2A	49, 50, 978, 1025
S06.4X2D	798
S06.4X2S	53
S06.4X3A	48, 49, 978, 1025
S06.4X3D	798
S06.4X3S	53
S06.4X4A	48, 49, 978, 1025
S06.4X4D	798
S06.4X4S	53
S06.4X5A	48, 49, 978, 1025
S06.4X5D	798
S06.4X5S	53
S06.4X6A	48, 49, 978, 1025
S06.4X6D	798
S06.4X6S	53
S06.4X7A	48, 49, 978, 1025
S06.4X8A	48, 49, 978, 1025
S06.4X9A	48, 49, 978, 1025
S06.4X9D	798
S06.4X9S	53
S06.5X0A	49, 50, 978, 1025
S06.5X0D	798
S06.5X0S	53
S06.5X1A	49, 50, 978, 1025
S06.5X1D	798
S06.5X1S	53
S06.5X2A	49, 50, 978, 1025
S06.5X2D	798
S06.5X2S	53
S06.5X3A	48, 49, 978, 1025
S06.5X3D	798
S06.5X3S	53
S06.5X4A	48, 49, 978, 1025
S06.5X4S	53
S06.5X5A	48, 49, 978, 1025
S06.5X5D	798
S06.5X5S	53
S06.5X6A	48, 49, 978, 1025
S06.5X6D	798
S06.5X6S	53
S06.5X7A	48, 49, 978, 1025
S06.5X8A	48, 49, 978, 1025
S06.5X9A	48, 49, 978, 1025
S06.5X9D	798
S06.5X9S	53
S06.6X0A	15, 49, 50, 978, 1025
S06.6X0D	798
S06.6X0S	53
S06.6X1A	15, 49, 50, 978, 1025
S06.6X1D	798
S06.6X1S	53
S06.6X2A	15, 49, 50, 978, 1025
S06.6X2D	798
S06.6X2S	53
S06.6X3A	15, 48, 49, 978, 1025
S06.6X3D	798
S06.6X3S	53
S06.6X4A	15, 48, 49, 978, 1025
S06.6X4D	798
S06.6X4S	53
S06.6X5A	15, 48, 49, 978, 1025
S06.6X5D	798
S06.6X5S	53
S06.6X6A	15, 48, 49, 978, 1025
S06.6X6D	798
S06.6X6S	53
S06.6X7A	15, 48, 49, 978, 1025
S06.6X8A	15, 48, 49, 978, 1025
S06.6X9A	15, 48, 49, 978, 1025
S06.6X9D	798
S06.6X9S	53
S06.810A	49, 50, 978, 1025
S06.810D	798
S06.810S	53
S06.811A	49, 50, 978, 1025
S06.811D	798
S06.811S	53
S06.812A	49, 50, 978, 1025
S06.812D	798
S06.812S	53
S06.813A	48, 49, 978, 1025
S06.813D	798
S06.813S	53
S06.814A	48, 49, 978, 1025
S06.814D	798
S06.814S	53
S06.815A	48, 49, 978, 1025
S06.815D	798
S06.815S	53
S06.816A	48, 49, 978, 1025
S06.816D	798
S06.816S	53
S06.817A	48, 49, 978, 1025
S06.818A	48, 49, 978, 1025
S06.819A	48, 49, 978, 1025
S06.819D	798
S06.819S	53
S06.820A	49, 50, 978, 1025
S06.820D	798
S06.820S	53
S06.821A	49, 50, 978, 1025
S06.821D	798
S06.821S	53
S06.822A	49, 50, 978, 1025
S06.822D	798
S06.822S	53
S06.823A	48, 49, 978, 1025
S06.823D	798
S06.823S	53
S06.824A	48, 49, 978, 1025
S06.824D	798
S06.824S	53
S06.825A	48, 50, 978, 1025
S06.825D	798
S06.825S	53
S06.826A	48, 50, 978, 1025
S06.826D	798
S06.826S	53
S06.827A	48, 50, 978, 1025
S06.828A	48, 50, 978, 1025
S06.829A	48, 50, 978, 1025
S06.829D	798
S06.829S	53
S06.890A	50, 978, 1025
S06.890D	798
S06.890S	53
S06.891A	50, 978, 1025
S06.891D	798
S06.891S	53
S06.892A	50, 978, 1025
S06.892D	798
S06.892S	53
S06.893A	48, 50, 978, 1025
S06.893D	798
S06.893S	53
S06.894A	48, 50, 978, 1025
S06.894D	798
S06.894S	53
S06.895A	48, 50, 978, 1025
S06.895D	798
S06.895S	53
S06.896A	48, 50, 978, 1025
S06.896D	798
S06.896S	53
S06.897A	48, 50, 978, 1025
S06.898A	48, 50, 978, 1025
S06.899A	48, 50, 978, 1025
S06.899D	798
S06.899S	53
S06.9X0A	50, 978, 1025
S06.9X0D	798
S06.9X0S	53
S06.9X1A	50, 978, 1025
S06.9X1D	798
S06.9X1S	53
S06.9X2A	50, 978, 1025
S06.9X2D	798
S06.9X2S	53
S06.9X3A	48, 49, 978, 1025
S06.9X3D	798
S06.9X3S	53
S06.9X4A	48, 50, 978, 1025
S06.9X4D	798
S06.9X4S	53
S06.9X5A	48, 50, 978, 1025
S06.9X5D	798
S06.9X5S	53
S06.9X6A	48, 50, 978, 1025
S06.9X6D	798
S06.9X6S	53
S06.9X7A	48, 50, 978, 1025
S06.9X8A	48, 50, 978, 1025
S06.9X9A	48, 50, 978, 1025
S06.9X9D	798
S06.9X9S	53
S07.0XXA	4, 746, 978, 1025
S07.0XXD	798
S07.0XXS	456
S07.1XXA	4, 746, 978, 1025
S07.1XXD	798
S07.1XXS	456
S07.8XXA	4, 746, 978, 1025
S07.8XXD	798
S07.8XXS	456
S07.9XXA	4, 746, 978, 1025
S07.9XXD	798
S07.9XXS	456
S08.0XXA	456, 978
S08.0XXD	798
S08.0XXS	456
S08.111A	87, 978
S08.111D	798
S08.111S	456
S08.112A	87, 978
S08.112D	798
S08.112S	456
S08.119A	87, 978
S08.119D	798
S08.119S	456
S08.121A	87, 978
S08.121D	798
S08.121S	456
S08.122A	87, 978
S08.122D	798
S08.122S	456
S08.129A	87, 978
S08.129D	798
S08.129S	456
S08.811A	4, 87, 978
S08.811D	798
S08.811S	456
S08.812A	4, 87, 978
S08.812D	798
S08.812S	456
S08.89XA	456, 978
S08.89XD	798
S08.89XS	456
S09.0XXA	4, 746, 978
S09.0XXD	798
S09.0XXS	168
S09.10XA	4, 746, 978
S09.10XD	798
S09.10XS	746
S09.11XA	4, 746, 978
S09.11XD	798
S09.11XS	348
S09.12XA	456, 978
S09.12XD	798
S09.12XS	456
S09.19XA	4, 746, 978
S09.19XD	798
S09.19XS	746
S09.20XA	87, 978
S09.20XD	798
S09.20XS	746
S09.21XA	87, 978
S09.21XD	798
S09.21XS	456
S09.22XA	87, 978
S09.22XD	798
S09.22XS	456
S09.301A	87, 978
S09.301D	798
S09.301S	746
S09.302A	87, 978
S09.302D	798
S09.302S	746
S09.309A	87, 978
S09.309D	798
S09.309S	746
S09.311A	87, 978
S09.311D	798
S09.311S	456
S09.312A	87, 978
S09.312D	798
S09.312S	456
S09.313A	87, 978
S09.313D	798
S09.313S	456
S09.319A	87, 978
S09.319D	798
S09.319S	456
S09.391A	87, 978
S09.391D	798
S09.391S	746
S09.392A	87, 978
S09.392D	798
S09.392S	746
S09.399A	87, 978
S09.399D	798
S09.399S	746
S09.8XXA	4, 746, 978
S09.8XXD	798
S09.8XXS	746
S09.90XA	4, 746, 978
S09.90XD	798
S09.90XS	746
S09.91XA	87, 978
S09.91XD	798
S09.91XS	746
S09.92XA	4, 746, 978
S09.92XD	798
S09.92XS	746
S09.93XA	4, 746, 978
S09.93XD	798
S09.93XS	746
S10.0XXA	456, 978
S10.0XXD	798
S10.0XXS	456
S10.10XA	456, 978
S10.10XD	798
S10.10XS	456
S10.11XA	456, 978
S10.11XD	798
S10.11XS	456
S10.12XA	477, 978
S10.12XD	798
S10.12XS	456
S10.14XA	456, 978
S10.14XD	799
S10.14XS	456
S10.15XA	456, 978
S10.15XD	799
S10.15XS	456
S10.16XA	477, 978
S10.16XD	799
S10.16XS	456
S10.17XA	456, 978
S10.17XD	799
S10.17XS	457
S10.80XA	978
S10.80XA	457
S10.80XD	799
S10.80XS	457
S10.81XA	457, 978
S10.81XD	799
S10.81XS	457
S10.82XA	978
S10.82XA	477
S10.82XD	799
S10.82XS	457
S10.83XA	457, 978
S10.83XD	799
S10.83XS	457
S10.84XA	978
S10.84XA	457
S10.84XD	799
S10.84XS	457
S10.85XA	979
S10.85XA	457
S10.85XD	799
S10.85XS	457
S10.86XA	477, 979
S10.86XD	799
S10.86XS	457
S10.87XA	979
S10.87XA	457
S10.87XD	799
S10.87XS	457
S10.90XA	457, 979
S10.90XD	799
S10.90XS	457
S10.91XA	457, 979
S10.91XD	799
S10.91XS	457
S10.92XA	477, 979
S10.92XD	799
S10.92XS	457
S10.93XA	457, 979
S10.93XD	799
S10.93XS	457
S10.94XA	457, 979
S10.94XD	799
S10.94XS	457
S10.95XA	457, 979
S10.95XD	799
S10.95XS	457
S10.96XA	477, 979
S10.96XD	799
S10.96XS	457
S10.97XA	457, 979
S10.97XD	799
S10.97XS	457
S11.011A	4, 87, 979
S11.011D	799
S11.011S	457
S11.012A	4, 87, 979, 1026
S11.012D	799
S11.012S	457
S11.013A	4, 87, 979
S11.013D	799
S11.013S	457
S11.014A	4, 87, 979, 1026
S11.014D	799
S11.014S	457
S11.015A	4, 87, 979
S11.015D	799
S11.015S	457
S11.019A	4, 87, 979
S11.019D	799
S11.019S	457
S11.021A	4, 104, 979
S11.021D	799
S11.021S	457
S11.022A	4, 104, 979, 1026
S11.022D	799
S11.022S	457
S11.023A	4, 104, 979
S11.023D	799
S11.023S	457
S11.024A	4, 104, 979, 1026
S11.024D	799
S11.024S	457
S11.025A	4, 104, 979
S11.025D	799
S11.025S	457

Code	Page	Code	Page	Code	Page	Code	Page	Code	Page	Code	Page
S11.029A	4, 104, 979	S11.93XA	4, 457, 979	S12.112A	298, 979	S12.250G	307	S12.431A	298, 979	S12.600G	307
S11.029D	799	S11.93XD	799	S12.112B	298, 979	S12.250K	378	S12.431B	298, 979	S12.600K	379
S11.029S	457	S11.93XS	457	S12.112D	307	S12.250S	298	S12.431D	307	S12.600S	298
S11.031A	4, 87, 979	S11.94XA	4, 457, 979	S12.112K	378	S12.251A	298, 979	S12.431G	307	S12.601A	298, 980
S11.031D	799	S11.94XD	799	S12.112S	298	S12.251B	298, 979	S12.431K	378	S12.601B	298, 980
S11.031S	457	S11.94XS	457	S12.120A	298, 979	S12.251D	307	S12.431S	298	S12.601D	307
S11.032A	4, 87, 979, 1026	S11.95XA	4, 457, 979	S12.120B	298, 979	S12.251G	307	S12.44XA	298, 979	S12.601G	307
S11.032D	799	S11.95XD	799	S12.120D	307	S12.251K	378	S12.44XB	298, 979	S12.601K	379
S11.032S	457	S11.95XS	457	S12.120G	307	S12.251S	298	S12.44XD	307	S12.601S	298
S11.033A	4, 87, 979	S12.000A	297, 979	S12.120K	378	S12.290A	298, 979	S12.44XG	307	S12.630A	298, 980
S11.033D	799	S12.000B	297, 979	S12.120S	298	S12.290B	298, 979	S12.44XK	378	S12.630B	298, 980
S11.033S	457	S12.000D	307	S12.121A	298, 979	S12.290D	307	S12.44XS	298	S12.630D	307
S11.034A	4, 87, 979, 1026	S12.000K	378	S12.121B	298, 979	S12.290G	307	S12.450A	298, 979	S12.630G	307
S11.034D	799	S12.000S	297	S12.121D	307	S12.290K	378	S12.450B	298, 979	S12.630K	379
S11.034S	457	S12.001A	297, 979	S12.121G	307	S12.290S	298	S12.450D	307	S12.630S	298
S11.035A	4, 87, 979	S12.001B	297, 979	S12.121K	378	S12.291A	298, 979	S12.450G	307	S12.631A	298, 980
S11.035D	799	S12.001D	307	S12.121S	298	S12.291B	298, 979	S12.450K	378	S12.631B	298, 980
S11.035S	457	S12.001G	307	S12.130A	298, 979	S12.291D	307	S12.450S	298	S12.631D	307
S11.039A	4, 87, 979	S12.001K	378	S12.130B	298, 979	S12.291G	307	S12.451A	298, 979	S12.631G	307
S11.039D	799	S12.001S	297	S12.130D	307	S12.291K	378	S12.451B	298, 979	S12.631K	379
S11.039S	457	S12.01XA	297, 979	S12.130G	307	S12.291S	298	S12.451D	307	S12.631S	298
S11.10XA	4, 503, 979	S12.01XB	297, 979	S12.130K	378	S12.300A	298, 979	S12.451G	307	S12.64XA	298, 980
S11.10XD	799	S12.01XD	307	S12.130S	298	S12.300B	298, 979	S12.451K	378	S12.64XB	298, 980
S11.10XS	457	S12.01XG	307	S12.131A	298, 979	S12.300D	307	S12.451S	298	S12.64XD	307
S11.11XA	4, 503, 979	S12.01XK	378	S12.131B	298, 979	S12.300G	307	S12.490A	298, 979	S12.64XG	307
S11.11XD	799	S12.01XS	297	S12.131D	307	S12.300K	378	S12.490B	298, 979	S12.64XK	379
S11.11XS	457	S12.02XA	297, 979	S12.131G	307	S12.300S	298	S12.490D	307	S12.64XS	298
S11.12XA	4, 503, 979	S12.02XB	297, 979	S12.131K	378	S12.301A	298, 979	S12.490G	307	S12.650A	298, 980
S11.12XD	799	S12.02XD	307	S12.131S	298	S12.301B	298, 979	S12.490K	378	S12.650B	298, 980
S11.12XS	457	S12.02XG	307	S12.14XA	298, 979	S12.301D	307	S12.490S	298	S12.650D	307
S11.13XA	4, 503, 979	S12.02XK	378	S12.14XB	298, 979	S12.301G	307	S12.491A	298, 979	S12.650G	307
S11.13XD	799	S12.02XS	297	S12.14XD	307	S12.301K	378	S12.491B	298, 979	S12.650K	379
S11.13XS	457	S12.030A	297, 979	S12.14XG	307	S12.301S	298	S12.491D	307	S12.650S	298
S11.14XA	4, 503, 979	S12.030B	297, 979	S12.14XK	378	S12.330A	298, 979	S12.491G	307	S12.651A	298, 980
S11.14XD	799	S12.030D	307	S12.14XS	298	S12.330B	298, 979	S12.491K	379	S12.651B	298, 980
S11.14XS	457	S12.030G	307	S12.150A	298, 979	S12.330D	307	S12.491S	298	S12.651D	307
S11.15XA	4, 503, 979	S12.030K	378	S12.150B	298, 979	S12.330G	307	S12.500A	298, 979	S12.651G	307
S11.15XD	799	S12.030S	297	S12.150D	307	S12.330K	378	S12.500B	298, 979	S12.651K	379
S11.15XS	457	S12.031A	297, 979	S12.150G	307	S12.330S	298	S12.500D	307	S12.651S	298
S11.20XA	4, 87, 979	S12.031B	297, 979	S12.150K	378	S12.331A	298, 979	S12.500G	307	S12.690A	298, 980
S11.20XD	799	S12.031D	307	S12.150S	298	S12.331B	298, 979	S12.500K	379	S12.690B	298, 980
S11.20XS	457	S12.031G	307	S12.151A	298, 979	S12.331D	307	S12.500S	298	S12.690D	307
S11.21XA	4, 87, 979	S12.031K	378	S12.151B	298, 979	S12.331G	307	S12.501A	298, 979	S12.690G	308
S11.21XD	799	S12.031S	297	S12.151G	307	S12.331K	378	S12.501B	298, 979	S12.690K	379
S11.21XS	457	S12.040A	297, 979	S12.151K	378	S12.331S	298	S12.501D	307	S12.690S	298
S11.22XA	4, 87, 979	S12.040B	297, 979	S12.151S	298	S12.34XA	298, 979	S12.501G	307	S12.691A	298, 980
S11.22XD	799	S12.040D	307	S12.190A	298, 979	S12.34XB	298, 979	S12.501K	379	S12.691B	298, 980
S11.22XS	457	S12.040G	307	S12.190B	298, 979	S12.34XD	307	S12.501S	298	S12.691D	307
S11.23XA	4, 87, 979	S12.040K	378	S12.190D	307	S12.34XG	307	S12.530A	298, 979	S12.691G	308
S11.23XD	799	S12.040S	297	S12.190G	307	S12.34XK	378	S12.530B	298, 979	S12.691K	379
S11.23XS	457	S12.041A	297, 979	S12.190K	378	S12.34XS	298	S12.530D	307	S12.691S	298
S11.24XA	4, 87, 979	S12.041B	297, 979	S12.190S	298	S12.350A	298, 979	S12.530G	307	S12.8XXA	4, 87, 980, 1026
S11.24XD	799	S12.041D	307	S12.191A	298, 979	S12.350B	298, 979	S12.530K	379	S12.8XXD	308
S11.24XS	457	S12.041K	378	S12.191B	298, 979	S12.350D	307	S12.530S	298	S12.8XXS	298
S11.25XA	4, 87, 979	S12.041S	297	S12.191D	307	S12.350G	307	S12.531A	298, 979	S12.9XXA	298, 980
S11.25XD	799	S12.090A	297, 979	S12.191G	307	S12.350K	378	S12.531B	298, 979	S12.9XXD	308
S11.25XS	457	S12.090B	297, 979	S12.191S	298	S12.350S	298	S12.531D	307	S12.9XXS	298
S11.80XA	979	S12.090D	307	S12.200A	298, 979	S12.351A	298, 979	S12.531G	307	S13.0XXA	298, 980, 1028
S11.80XA	4, 457	S12.090G	307	S12.200B	298, 979	S12.351B	298, 979	S12.531K	379	S13.0XXD	799
S11.80XD	799	S12.090K	378	S12.200D	307	S12.351D	307	S12.531S	298	S13.0XXS	348
S11.80XS	457	S12.090S	297	S12.200G	307	S12.351G	307	S12.54XA	298, 979	S13.100A	298, 980, 1028
S11.81XA	979	S12.091A	297, 979	S12.200K	378	S12.351K	378	S12.54XB	298, 979	S13.100D	799
S11.81XA	4, 457	S12.091B	297, 979	S12.200S	298	S12.351S	298	S12.54XD	307	S13.100S	348
S11.81XD	799	S12.091D	307	S12.201A	298, 979	S12.390A	298, 979	S12.54XG	307	S13.101A	298, 980, 1028
S11.81XS	457	S12.091G	307	S12.201B	298, 979	S12.390B	298, 979	S12.54XK	379	S13.101D	799
S11.82XA	979	S12.091K	378	S12.201D	307	S12.390D	307	S12.54XS	298	S13.101S	348
S11.82XA	4, 457	S12.091S	297	S12.201G	307	S12.390G	307	S12.550A	298, 979	S13.110A	299, 980, 1028
S11.82XD	799	S12.100A	297, 979	S12.201K	378	S12.390K	378	S12.550B	298, 979	S13.110D	799
S11.82XS	457	S12.100B	297, 979	S12.201S	298	S12.390S	298	S12.550D	307	S13.110S	348
S11.83XA	979	S12.100D	307	S12.230A	298, 979	S12.391A	298, 979	S12.550G	307	S13.111A	299, 980, 1028
S11.83XA	4, 457	S12.100G	307	S12.230B	298, 979	S12.391B	298, 979	S12.550K	379	S13.111D	799
S11.83XD	799	S12.100K	378	S12.230D	307	S12.391D	307	S12.550S	298	S13.111S	348
S11.83XS	457	S12.100S	297	S12.230G	307	S12.391G	307	S12.551A	298, 979	S13.120A	299, 980, 1028
S11.84XA	979	S12.101A	297, 979	S12.230K	378	S12.391K	378	S12.551B	298, 979	S13.120D	799
S11.84XA	4, 457	S12.101B	297, 979	S12.230S	298	S12.391S	298	S12.551D	307	S13.120S	348
S11.84XD	799	S12.101D	307	S12.231A	298, 979	S12.400A	298, 979	S12.551G	307	S13.121A	299, 980, 1028
S11.84XS	457	S12.101G	307	S12.231B	298, 979	S12.400B	298, 979	S12.551K	379	S13.121D	799
S11.85XA	4, 457, 979	S12.101K	378	S12.231D	307	S12.400D	307	S12.551S	298	S13.121S	348
S11.85XD	799	S12.101S	297	S12.231G	307	S12.400G	307	S12.590A	298, 979	S13.130A	299, 980, 1028
S11.85XS	457	S12.110A	297, 979	S12.231S	298	S12.400K	378	S12.590B	298, 979	S13.130D	799
S11.89XA	979	S12.110B	297, 979	S12.24XA	298, 979	S12.400S	298	S12.590D	307	S13.130S	348
S11.89XA	4, 457	S12.110D	307	S12.24XB	298, 979	S12.401A	298, 979	S12.590G	307	S13.131A	299, 980, 1028
S11.89XD	799	S12.110G	307	S12.24XD	307	S12.401B	298, 979	S12.590K	379	S13.131D	799
S11.89XS	457	S12.110K	378	S12.24XG	307	S12.401D	307	S12.590S	298	S13.131S	348
S11.90XA	4, 457, 979	S12.110S	297	S12.24XK	378	S12.401G	307	S12.591A	298, 979	S13.140A	299, 980, 1028
S11.90XD	799	S12.111A	298, 979	S12.24XS	298	S12.401K	378	S12.591B	298, 979	S13.140D	799
S11.90XS	457	S12.111B	298, 979	S12.250A	298, 979	S12.401S	298	S12.591D	307	S13.140S	348
S11.91XA	4, 457, 979	S12.111G	307	S12.250B	298, 979	S12.430A	298, 979	S12.591G	307	S13.141A	299, 980, 1028
S11.91XD	799	S12.111K	378	S12.250D	307	S12.430B	298, 979	S12.591K	379	S13.141D	799
S11.91XS	457	S12.111S	298			S12.430D	307	S12.591S	298	S13.141S	348
S11.92XA	4, 457, 979					S12.430G	307	S12.600A	298, 980	S13.150A	299, 980, 1028
S11.92XD	799					S12.430K	378	S12.600B	298, 980	S13.150D	799
S11.92XS	457					S12.430S	298	S12.600D	307	S13.150S	348

Code	Page	Code	Page	Code	Page	Code	Page	Code	Page	Code	Page
S13.151A	299,980,1028	S14.118S	42	S14.153S	42	S15.111A	4,746,980	S15.312D	800	S20.101D	800
S13.151D	799	S14.119A	42,980,1029	S14.154A	42,980,1029	S15.111D	799	S15.312S	168	S20.101S	457
S13.151S	348	S14.119D	799	S14.154D	799	S15.111S	168	S15.319A	564,746,980,1026	S20.102A	457,981
S13.160A	299,980,1028	S14.119S	42	S14.154S	42	S15.112A	4,746,980			S20.102D	800
S13.160D	799	S14.121A	42,980,1029	S14.155A	42,980,1029	S15.112D	799	S15.319D	800	S20.102S	457
S13.160S	348	S14.121D	799	S14.155D	799	S15.112S	168	S15.319S	168	S20.109A	457,981
S13.161A	299,980,1028	S14.121S	42	S14.155S	42	S15.119A	4,746,980	S15.321A	564,746,980,1026	S20.109D	800
S13.161D	799	S14.122A	42,980,1029	S14.156A	42,980,1029	S15.119D	799			S20.109S	457
S13.161S	348	S14.122D	799	S14.156D	799	S15.119S	168	S15.321D	800	S20.111A	457,981
S13.170A	299,980,1028	S14.122S	42	S14.156S	42	S15.121A	4,746,980	S15.321S	168	S20.111D	800
S13.170D	799	S14.123A	42,980,1029	S14.157A	42,980,1029	S15.121D	799	S15.322A	564,746,980,1026	S20.111S	457
S13.170S	348	S14.123D	799	S14.157D	799	S15.121S	168			S20.112A	457,981
S13.171A	299,980,1028	S14.123S	42	S14.157S	42	S15.122A	4,746,980	S15.322D	800	S20.112D	800
S13.171D	799	S14.124A	42,980,1029	S14.158A	42,980,1029	S15.122D	799	S15.322S	168	S20.112S	457
S13.171S	348	S14.124D	799	S14.158D	799	S15.122S	168	S15.329A	564,746,980,1026	S20.119A	457,981
S13.180A	299,980,1028	S14.124S	42	S14.158S	42	S15.129A	4,746,980			S20.119D	800
S13.180D	799	S14.125A	42,980,1029	S14.159A	42,980,1029	S15.129D	799	S15.329D	800	S20.119S	457
S13.180S	348	S14.125D	799	S14.159D	799	S15.129S	168	S15.329S	168	S20.121A	477,981
S13.181A	299,980,1028	S14.125S	42	S14.159S	42	S15.191A	4,746,980	S15.391A	564,746,980,1026	S20.121D	800
S13.181D	799	S14.126A	42,980,1029	S14.2XXA	46,980	S15.191D	799			S20.121S	457
S13.181S	348	S14.126D	799	S14.2XXD	799	S15.191S	168	S15.391D	800	S20.122A	477,981
S13.20XA	299,980,1028	S14.126S	42	S14.2XXS	53	S15.192A	4,746,980	S15.391S	168	S20.122D	800
S13.20XD	799	S14.127A	42,980,1029	S14.3XXA	46,564,980,1030	S15.192D	799	S15.392A	564,746,980,1026	S20.122S	457
S13.20XS	348	S14.127D	799	S14.3XXD	799	S15.192S	168			S20.129A	477,981
S13.29XA	299,980,1028	S14.127S	42	S14.3XXS	53	S15.199A	4,746,980	S15.392D	800	S20.129D	800
S13.29XD	799	S14.128A	42,980,1029	S14.4XXA	46,980	S15.199D	799	S15.392S	168	S20.129S	457
S13.29XS	348	S14.128D	799	S14.4XXD	799	S15.199S	168	S15.399A	564,746,980,1026	S20.141A	457,981
S13.4XXA	299,980	S14.128S	42	S14.4XXS	53	S15.201A	564,746,980,1025			S20.141D	800
S13.4XXD	799	S14.129A	42,980,1029	S14.5XXA	46,980			S15.399D	800	S20.141S	457
S13.4XXS	348	S14.129D	799	S14.5XXD	799	S15.201D	799	S15.399S	168	S20.142A	457,981
S13.5XXA	379,980	S14.129S	42	S14.5XXS	53	S15.201S	168	S15.8XXA	980,1026	S20.142D	800
S13.5XXD	799	S14.131A	42,980,1029	S14.8XXA	46,980	S15.202A	564,746,980,1025	S15.8XXA	4,746	S20.142S	457
S13.5XXS	348	S14.131D	799	S14.8XXD	799			S15.8XXD	800	S20.149A	457,981
S13.8XXA	980	S14.131S	42	S14.8XXS	53	S15.202D	800	S15.8XXS	168	S20.149D	800
S13.8XXA	299	S14.132A	42,980,1029	S14.9XXA	46,980	S15.202S	168	S15.9XXA	4,746,980	S20.149S	457
S13.8XXD	799	S14.132D	799	S14.9XXD	799	S15.209A	564,746,980,1025	S15.9XXD	800	S20.151A	457,981
S13.8XXS	348	S14.132S	42	S14.9XXS	53			S15.9XXS	168	S20.151D	800
S13.9XXA	299,980	S14.133A	42,980,1029	S15.001A	564,746,980,1025	S15.209D	800	S16.1XXA	299,980	S20.151S	457
S13.9XXD	799	S14.133D	799			S15.209S	168	S16.1XXD	800	S20.152A	457,981
S13.9XXS	348	S14.133S	42	S15.001D	799	S15.211A	564,746,980,1025	S16.1XXS	348	S20.152D	800
S14.0XXA	42,980,1028	S14.134A	42,980,1029	S15.001S	168			S16.2XXA	4,457,980	S20.152S	457
S14.0XXD	799	S14.134D	799	S15.002A	564,746,980,1025	S15.211D	800	S16.2XXD	800	S20.159A	457,981
S14.0XXS	42	S14.134S	42			S15.211S	168	S16.2XXS	457	S20.159D	800
S14.101A	42,980,1028	S14.135A	42,980,1029	S15.002D	799	S15.212A	564,746,980,1026	S16.8XXA	4,746,980	S20.159S	457
S14.101D	799	S14.135D	799	S15.002S	168			S16.8XXD	800	S20.161A	477,981
S14.101S	42	S14.135S	42	S15.009A	564,746,980	S15.212D	800	S16.8XXS	746	S20.161D	800
S14.102A	42,980,1028	S14.136A	42,980,1029	S15.009D	799	S15.212S	168	S16.9XXA	4,746,980	S20.161S	457
S14.102D	799	S14.136D	799	S15.009S	168	S15.219A	564,746,980,1026	S16.9XXD	800	S20.162A	477,981
S14.102S	42	S14.136S	42	S15.011A	564,746,980,1025			S16.9XXS	746	S20.162D	800
S14.103A	42,980,1028	S14.137A	42,980,1029			S15.219D	800	S17.0XXA	4,746,980,1026	S20.162S	457
S14.103D	799	S14.137D	799	S15.011D	799	S15.219S	168	S17.0XXD	800	S20.169A	477,981
S14.103S	42	S14.137S	42	S15.011S	168	S15.221A	564,746,980,1026	S17.0XXS	457	S20.169D	800
S14.104A	42,980,1028	S14.138A	42,980,1029	S15.012A	564,746,980,1025			S17.8XXA	980,1026	S20.169S	457
S14.104D	799	S14.138D	799			S15.221D	800	S17.8XXA	4,746	S20.171A	457,981
S14.104S	42	S14.138S	42	S15.012D	799	S15.221S	168	S17.8XXD	800	S20.171D	800
S14.105A	42,980,1028	S14.139A	42,980,1029	S15.012S	168	S15.222A	564,746,980,1026	S17.8XXS	457	S20.171S	457
S14.105D	799	S14.139D	799	S15.019A	564,746,980,1025			S17.9XXA	4,746,980,1026	S20.172A	457,981
S14.105S	42	S14.139S	42			S15.222D	800	S17.9XXD	800	S20.172D	800
S14.106A	42,980,1028	S14.141A	42,980,1029	S15.019D	799	S15.222S	168	S17.9XXS	457	S20.172S	457
S14.106D	799	S14.141D	799	S15.019S	168	S15.229A	564,746,980,1026	S19.80XA	4,746,980	S20.179A	457,981
S14.106S	42	S14.141S	42	S15.021A	564,746,980,1025			S19.80XD	800	S20.179D	800
S14.107A	42,980,1028	S14.142A	42,980,1029			S15.229D	800	S19.80XS	746	S20.179S	457
S14.107D	799	S14.142D	799	S15.021D	799	S15.229S	168	S19.81XA	4,746,980	S20.20XA	457,981
S14.107S	42	S14.142S	42	S15.021S	168	S15.291A	564,746,980,1026	S19.81XD	800	S20.20XD	800
S14.108A	42,980,1028	S14.143A	42,980,1029	S15.022A	564,746,980,1025			S19.81XS	746	S20.20XS	457
S14.108D	799	S14.143D	799			S15.291D	800	S19.82XA	4,746,980	S20.211A	457,981
S14.108S	42	S14.143S	42	S15.022D	799	S15.291S	168	S19.82XD	800	S20.211D	800
S14.109A	42,980,1029	S14.144A	42,980,1029	S15.022S	168	S15.292A	564,746,980,1026	S19.82XS	746	S20.211S	457
S14.109D	799	S14.144D	799	S15.029A	564,746,980,1025			S19.83XA	4,746,980	S20.212A	457,981
S14.109S	42	S14.144S	42			S15.292D	800	S19.83XD	800	S20.212D	800
S14.111A	42,980,1029	S14.145A	42,980,1029	S15.029D	799	S15.292S	168	S19.83XS	746	S20.212S	457
S14.111D	799	S14.145D	799	S15.029S	168	S15.299A	564,746,980,1026	S19.84XA	4,746,980	S20.219A	457,981
S14.111S	42	S14.145S	42	S15.091A	564,746,980,1025			S19.84XD	800	S20.219D	800
S14.112A	42,980,1029	S14.146A	42,980,1029			S15.299D	800	S19.84XS	746	S20.219S	457
S14.112D	799	S14.146D	799	S15.091D	799	S15.299S	168	S19.85XA	4,746,980	S20.221A	457,981
S14.112S	42	S14.146S	42	S15.091S	168	S15.301A	564,746,980,1026	S19.85XD	800	S20.221D	800
S14.113A	42,980,1029	S14.147A	42,980,1029	S15.092A	564,746,980,1025			S19.85XS	746	S20.221S	457
S14.113D	799	S14.147D	799			S15.301D	800	S19.89XA	4,746,980	S20.222A	457,981
S14.113S	42	S14.147S	42	S15.092D	799	S15.301S	168	S19.89XD	800	S20.222D	800
S14.114A	42,980,1029	S14.148A	42,980,1029	S15.092S	168	S15.302A	564,746,980,1026	S19.89XS	746	S20.222S	457
S14.114D	799	S14.148D	799	S15.099A	564,746,980,1025			S19.9XXA	4,746,980	S20.229A	457,981
S14.114S	42	S14.148S	42			S15.302D	800	S19.9XXD	800	S20.229D	800
S14.115A	42,980,1029	S14.149A	42,980,1029	S15.099D	799	S15.302S	168	S19.9XXS	746	S20.229S	457
S14.115D	799	S14.149D	799	S15.099S	168	S15.309A	564,746,980,1026	S20.00XA	457,980	S20.301A	457,981
S14.115S	42	S14.149S	42	S15.101A	4,746,980			S20.00XD	800	S20.301D	800
S14.116A	42,980,1029	S14.151A	42,980,1029	S15.101D	799	S15.309D	800	S20.00XS	457	S20.301S	457
S14.116D	799	S14.151D	799	S15.101S	168	S15.309S	168	S20.01XA	457,980	S20.302A	457,981
S14.116S	42	S14.151S	42	S15.102A	4,746,980	S15.311A	564,746,980,1026	S20.01XD	800	S20.302D	800
S14.117A	42,980,1029	S14.152A	42,980,1029	S15.102D	799			S20.01XS	457	S20.302S	457
S14.117D	799	S14.152D	799	S15.102S	168	S15.311D	800	S20.02XA	457,980	S20.309A	457,981
S14.117S	42	S14.152S	42	S15.109A	4,746,980	S15.311S	168	S20.02XD	800	S20.309D	800
S14.118A	42,980,1029	S14.153A	42,980,1029	S15.109D	799	S15.312A	564,746,980,1026	S20.02XS	457	S20.309S	457
S14.118D	799	S14.153D	799	S15.109S	168			S20.101A	457,981	S20.311A	457,981

DRG Expert—Volume II

Numeric Index to Diseases

Code	Page	Code	Page	Code	Page	Code	Page	Code	Page	Code	Page
S20.311D	800	S20.452D	800	S21.052D	800	S21.239D	800	S21.421D	801	S22.011K	379
S20.311S	457	S20.452S	458	S21.052S	458	S21.239S	458	S21.421S	459	S22.011S	299
S20.312A	457,981	S20.459A	458,981	S21.059A	458,981	S21.241A	458,981	S21.422A	747,981,1026	S22.012A	299,982
S20.312D	800	S20.459D	800	S21.059D	800	S21.241D	800	S21.422D	801	S22.012B	299,982
S20.312S	457	S20.459S	458	S21.059S	458	S21.241S	458	S21.422S	459	S22.012D	308
S20.319A	457,981	S20.461A	477,981	S21.101A	458,981	S21.242A	458,981	S21.429A	747,981,1026	S22.012K	379
S20.319D	800	S20.461D	800	S21.101D	800	S21.242D	800	S21.429D	801	S22.012S	299
S20.319S	457	S20.461S	458	S21.101S	458	S21.242S	458	S21.429S	459	S22.018A	299,982
S20.321A	477,981	S20.462A	477,981	S21.102A	458,981	S21.249A	458,981	S21.431A	747,981,1026	S22.018B	299,982
S20.321D	800	S20.462D	800	S21.102D	800	S21.249D	800	S21.431D	801	S22.018D	308
S20.321S	457	S20.462S	458	S21.102S	458	S21.249S	458	S21.431S	459	S22.018G	308
S20.322A	477,981	S20.469A	477,981	S21.109A	458,981	S21.251A	458,981	S21.432A	747,981,1026	S22.018K	379
S20.322D	800	S20.469D	800	S21.109D	800	S21.251D	800	S21.432D	801	S22.018S	299
S20.322S	457	S20.469S	458	S21.109S	458	S21.251S	458	S21.432S	459	S22.019A	299,982
S20.329A	477,981	S20.471A	458,981	S21.111A	458,981	S21.252A	458,981	S21.439A	747,981,1026	S22.019B	299,982
S20.329D	800	S20.471D	800	S21.111D	800	S21.252D	800	S21.439D	801	S22.019D	308
S20.329S	457	S20.471S	458	S21.111S	458	S21.252S	458	S21.439S	459	S22.019G	308
S20.341A	457,981	S20.472A	458,981	S21.112A	458,981	S21.259A	458,981	S21.441A	747,981,1026	S22.019K	379
S20.341D	800	S20.472D	800	S21.112D	800	S21.259D	800	S21.441D	801	S22.019S	299
S20.341S	457	S20.472S	458	S21.112S	458	S21.259S	458	S21.441S	459	S22.020A	299,982
S20.342A	457,981	S20.479A	458,981	S21.119A	458,981	S21.301A	746,981,1026	S21.442A	747,981,1026	S22.020B	299,982
S20.342D	800	S20.479D	800	S21.119D	800	S21.301D	801	S21.442D	801	S22.020D	308
S20.342S	457	S20.479S	458	S21.119S	458	S21.301S	458	S21.442S	459	S22.020G	308
S20.349A	457,981	S20.90XA	458,981	S21.121A	746,981	S21.302A	746,981,1026	S21.449A	747,981,1026	S22.020K	379
S20.349D	800	S20.90XD	800	S21.121D	800	S21.302D	801	S21.449D	801	S22.020S	299
S20.349S	457	S20.90XS	458	S21.121S	458	S21.302S	458	S21.449S	459	S22.021A	299,982
S20.351A	457,981	S20.91XA	458,981	S21.122A	746,981	S21.309A	746,981,1026	S21.451A	747,981,1026	S22.021B	299,982
S20.351D	800	S20.91XD	800	S21.122D	800	S21.309D	801	S21.451D	801	S22.021D	308
S20.351S	457	S20.91XS	458	S21.122S	458	S21.309S	458	S21.451S	459	S22.021G	308
S20.352A	457,981	S20.92XA	477,981	S21.129A	746,981	S21.311A	747,981,1026	S21.452A	747,981,1026	S22.021K	379
S20.352D	800	S20.92XD	800	S21.129D	800	S21.311D	801	S21.452D	801	S22.021S	299
S20.352S	457	S20.92XS	458	S21.129S	458	S21.311S	458	S21.452S	459	S22.022A	299,982
S20.359A	457,981	S20.94XA	458,981	S21.131A	458,981	S21.312A	747,981,1026	S21.459A	747,981,1026	S22.022B	299,982
S20.359D	800	S20.94XD	800	S21.131D	800	S21.312D	801	S21.459D	801	S22.022D	308
S20.359S	457	S20.94XS	458	S21.131S	458	S21.312S	458	S21.459S	459	S22.022G	308
S20.361A	477,981	S20.95XA	458,981	S21.132A	458,981	S21.319A	747,981,1026	S21.90XA	459,981	S22.022K	379
S20.361D	800	S20.95XD	800	S21.132D	800	S21.319D	801	S21.90XD	801	S22.022S	299
S20.361S	457	S20.95XS	458	S21.132S	458	S21.319S	458	S21.90XS	459	S22.028A	299,982
S20.362A	477,981	S20.96XA	477,981	S21.139A	458,981	S21.321A	747,981,1026	S21.91XA	459,981	S22.028B	299,982
S20.362D	800	S20.96XD	800	S21.139D	800	S21.321D	801	S21.91XD	801	S22.028D	308
S20.362S	458	S20.96XS	458	S21.139S	458	S21.321S	458	S21.91XS	459	S22.028G	308
S20.369A	477,981	S20.97XA	458,981	S21.141A	746,981	S21.322A	747,981,1026	S21.92XA	747,981	S22.028K	379
S20.369D	800	S20.97XD	800	S21.141D	800	S21.322D	801	S21.92XD	801	S22.028S	299
S20.369S	458	S20.97XS	458	S21.141S	458	S21.322S	458	S21.92XS	459	S22.029A	299,982
S20.371A	458,981	S21.001A	458,981	S21.142A	746,981	S21.329A	747,981,1026	S21.93XA	459,981	S22.029B	299,982
S20.371D	800	S21.001D	800	S21.142D	800	S21.329D	801	S21.93XD	801	S22.029D	308
S20.371S	458	S21.001S	458	S21.142S	458	S21.329S	458	S21.93XS	459	S22.029G	308
S20.372A	458,981	S21.002A	458,981	S21.149A	746,981	S21.331A	747,981,1026	S21.94XA	477,981	S22.029K	379
S20.372D	800	S21.002D	800	S21.149D	800	S21.331D	801	S21.94XD	801	S22.029S	299
S20.372S	458	S21.002S	458	S21.149S	458	S21.331S	458	S21.94XS	459	S22.030A	299,982
S20.379A	458,981	S21.009A	458,981	S21.151A	458,981	S21.332A	747,981,1026	S21.95XA	459,981	S22.030B	299,982
S20.379D	800	S21.009D	800	S21.151D	800	S21.332D	801	S21.95XD	801	S22.030D	308
S20.379S	458	S21.009S	458	S21.151S	458	S21.332S	458	S21.95XS	459	S22.030G	308
S20.401A	458,981	S21.011A	458,981	S21.152A	458,981	S21.339A	747,981,1026	S22.000A	299,981	S22.030K	379
S20.401D	800	S21.011D	800	S21.152D	800	S21.339D	801	S22.000B	299,982	S22.030S	299
S20.401S	458	S21.011S	458	S21.152S	458	S21.339S	458	S22.000D	308	S22.031A	299,982
S20.402A	458,981	S21.012A	458,981	S21.159A	458,981	S21.341A	747,981,1026	S22.000G	308	S22.031B	299,982
S20.402D	800	S21.012D	800	S21.159D	800	S21.341D	801	S22.000K	379	S22.031D	308
S20.402S	458	S21.012S	458	S21.159S	458	S21.341S	458	S22.000S	299	S22.031G	308
S20.409A	458,981	S21.019A	458,981	S21.201A	458,981	S21.342A	747,981,1026	S22.001A	299,982	S22.031K	379
S20.409D	800	S21.019D	800	S21.201D	800	S21.342D	801	S22.001B	299,982	S22.031S	299
S20.409S	458	S21.019S	458	S21.201S	458	S21.342S	458	S22.001D	308	S22.032A	299,982
S20.411A	458,981	S21.021A	458,981	S21.202A	458,981	S21.349A	747,981,1026	S22.001G	308	S22.032B	299,982
S20.411D	800	S21.021D	800	S21.202D	800	S21.349D	801	S22.001K	379	S22.032D	308
S20.411S	458	S21.021S	458	S21.202S	458	S21.349S	458	S22.001S	299	S22.032G	308
S20.412A	458,981	S21.022A	458,981	S21.209A	458,981	S21.351A	747,981,1026	S22.002A	299,982	S22.032K	379
S20.412D	800	S21.022D	800	S21.209D	800	S21.351D	801	S22.002B	299,982	S22.032S	299
S20.412S	458	S21.022S	458	S21.209S	458	S21.351S	458	S22.002D	308	S22.038A	299,982
S20.419A	458,981	S21.029A	458,981	S21.211A	458,981	S21.352A	747,981,1026	S22.002G	308	S22.038B	299,982
S20.419D	800	S21.029D	800	S21.211D	800	S21.352D	801	S22.002K	379	S22.038D	308
S20.419S	458	S21.029S	458	S21.211S	458	S21.352S	459	S22.002S	299	S22.038G	308
S20.421A	477,981	S21.031A	458,981	S21.212A	458,981	S21.359A	747,981,1026	S22.008A	299,982	S22.038S	299
S20.421D	800	S21.031D	800	S21.212D	800	S21.359D	801	S22.008B	299,982	S22.039A	299,982
S20.421S	458	S21.031S	458	S21.212S	458	S21.359S	459	S22.008D	308	S22.039B	299,982
S20.422A	477,981	S21.032A	458,981	S21.219A	458,981	S21.401A	747,981,1026	S22.008G	308	S22.039D	308
S20.422D	800	S21.032D	800	S21.219D	800	S21.401D	801	S22.008K	379	S22.039G	308
S20.422S	458	S21.032S	458	S21.219S	458	S21.401S	459	S22.008S	299	S22.039K	379
S20.429A	477,981	S21.039A	458,981	S21.221A	458,981	S21.402A	747,981,1026	S22.009A	299,982	S22.039S	299
S20.429D	800	S21.039D	800	S21.221D	800	S21.402D	801	S22.009B	299,982	S22.040A	299,982
S20.429S	458	S21.039S	458	S21.221S	458	S21.402S	459	S22.009D	308	S22.040B	299,982
S20.441A	458,981	S21.041A	458,981	S21.222A	458,981	S21.409A	747,981,1026	S22.009G	308	S22.040D	308
S20.441D	800	S21.041D	800	S21.222D	800	S21.409D	801	S22.009K	379	S22.040G	308
S20.441S	458	S21.041S	458	S21.222S	458	S21.409S	459	S22.009S	299	S22.040K	379
S20.442A	458,981	S21.042A	458,981	S21.229A	458,981	S21.411A	747,981,1026	S22.010A	299,982	S22.040S	299
S20.442D	800	S21.042D	800	S21.229D	800	S21.411D	801	S22.010B	299,982	S22.041A	299,982
S20.442S	458	S21.042S	458	S21.229S	458	S21.411S	459	S22.010D	308	S22.041B	299,982
S20.449A	458,981	S21.049A	458,981	S21.231A	458,981	S21.412A	747,981,1026	S22.010G	308	S22.041D	308
S20.449D	800	S21.049D	800	S21.231D	800	S21.412D	801	S22.010K	379	S22.041G	308
S20.449S	458	S21.049S	458	S21.231S	458	S21.412S	459	S22.010S	299	S22.041K	379
S20.451A	458,981	S21.051A	458,981	S21.232A	458,981	S21.419A	747,981,1026	S22.011A	299,982	S22.041S	299
S20.451D	800	S21.051D	800	S21.232D	800	S21.419D	801	S22.011B	299,982	S22.041K	379
S20.451S	458	S21.051S	458	S21.232S	458	S21.419S	459	S22.011D	308	S22.041S	299
S20.452A	458,981	S21.052A	458,981	S21.239A	458,981	S21.421A	747,981,1026	S22.011G	308	S22.042A	299,982

Numeric Index to Diseases

Code	Page
S22.042B	299, 982
S22.042D	308
S22.042G	308
S22.042K	379
S22.042S	299
S22.048A	299, 982
S22.048B	299, 982
S22.048D	308
S22.048G	308
S22.048K	379
S22.048S	299
S22.049A	299, 982
S22.049B	299, 982
S22.049D	308
S22.049G	308
S22.049K	379
S22.049S	299
S22.050A	299, 982
S22.050B	299, 982
S22.050D	308
S22.050G	308
S22.050K	379
S22.050S	299
S22.051A	299, 982
S22.051B	299, 982
S22.051D	308
S22.051G	308
S22.051K	379
S22.051S	299
S22.052A	299, 982
S22.052B	299, 982
S22.052D	308
S22.052G	308
S22.052K	379
S22.052S	299
S22.058A	299, 982
S22.058B	299, 982
S22.058D	299
S22.058G	308
S22.058K	379
S22.058S	299
S22.059A	299, 982
S22.059B	299, 982
S22.059D	308
S22.059G	308
S22.059K	379
S22.059S	299
S22.060A	299, 982
S22.060B	299, 982
S22.060D	308
S22.060G	308
S22.060K	379
S22.060S	299
S22.061A	299, 982
S22.061B	299, 982
S22.061D	308
S22.061G	308
S22.061K	379
S22.061S	299
S22.062A	299, 982
S22.062B	299, 982
S22.062D	308
S22.062G	308
S22.062K	379
S22.062S	299
S22.068A	299, 982
S22.068B	299, 982
S22.068D	308
S22.068G	308
S22.068K	379
S22.068S	299
S22.069A	299, 982
S22.069B	299, 982
S22.069D	308
S22.069G	308
S22.069K	379
S22.069S	299
S22.070A	299, 982
S22.070B	299, 982
S22.070D	308
S22.070G	308
S22.070K	379
S22.070S	299
S22.071A	299, 982
S22.071B	299, 982
S22.071D	308
S22.071G	300, 982
S22.071K	379
S22.071S	299
S22.072A	299, 982
S22.072B	299, 982
S22.072D	308
S22.072G	308
S22.072K	379
S22.072S	299
S22.078A	299, 982
S22.078B	299, 982
S22.078D	308
S22.078G	308
S22.078K	379
S22.078S	299
S22.079A	299, 982
S22.079B	299, 982
S22.079D	308
S22.079G	308
S22.079K	379
S22.079S	299
S22.080A	299, 982
S22.080B	299, 982
S22.080D	308
S22.080G	308
S22.080K	379
S22.080S	299
S22.081A	299, 982
S22.081B	299, 982
S22.081D	308
S22.081G	308
S22.081K	379
S22.081S	299
S22.082A	299, 982
S22.082B	299, 982
S22.082D	308
S22.082G	308
S22.082K	379
S22.082S	299
S22.088A	299, 982
S22.088B	299, 982
S22.088D	308
S22.088G	308
S22.088K	379
S22.088S	299
S22.089A	299, 982
S22.089B	299, 982
S22.089D	308
S22.089G	308
S22.089K	379
S22.089S	299
S22.20XA	379, 982
S22.20XB	379, 982, 1026
S22.20XD	308
S22.20XG	308
S22.20XK	379
S22.20XS	299
S22.21XA	379, 982
S22.21XB	379, 982, 1026
S22.21XD	308
S22.21XG	308
S22.21XK	379
S22.21XS	299
S22.22XA	379, 982
S22.22XB	379, 982, 1026
S22.22XD	308
S22.22XG	308
S22.22XK	379
S22.22XS	299
S22.23XA	379, 982
S22.23XB	379, 982, 1026
S22.23XD	308
S22.23XG	308
S22.23XK	379
S22.23XS	299
S22.24XA	379, 982
S22.24XB	379, 982, 1026
S22.24XD	308
S22.24XG	308
S22.24XK	379
S22.24XS	299
S22.31XA	106, 982
S22.31XB	104, 982
S22.31XD	308
S22.31XG	308
S22.31XK	379
S22.31XS	299
S22.32XA	106, 982
S22.32XB	104, 982
S22.32XD	308
S22.32XG	308
S22.32XK	379
S22.32XS	299
S22.39XA	106, 982
S22.39XB	104, 982
S22.39XD	308
S22.39XG	308
S22.39XS	299
S22.41XA	104, 982
S22.41XB	104, 982, 1026
S22.41XD	308
S22.41XG	308
S22.41XK	379
S22.41XS	299
S22.42XA	104, 982
S22.42XB	104, 982, 1026
S22.42XD	308
S22.42XG	308
S22.42XK	379
S22.42XS	299
S22.43XA	104, 982
S22.43XB	105, 982, 1026
S22.43XD	308
S22.43XG	308
S22.43XK	379
S22.43XS	299
S22.49XA	105, 982
S22.49XB	105, 982
S22.49XD	308
S22.49XG	308
S22.49XK	379
S22.49XS	299
S22.5XXA	105, 982, 1026
S22.5XXB	105, 982, 1026
S22.5XXD	308
S22.5XXG	308
S22.5XXS	299
S22.9XXA	379, 982
S22.9XXB	379, 982, 1029
S22.9XXD	308
S22.9XXG	308
S22.9XXK	379
S22.9XXS	299
S23.0XXA	299, 982
S23.0XXD	801
S23.0XXS	348
S23.100A	299, 982
S23.100D	801
S23.100S	348
S23.101A	299, 982
S23.101D	801
S23.101S	348
S23.110A	300, 982
S23.110D	801
S23.110S	348
S23.111A	300, 982
S23.111D	801
S23.111S	348
S23.120A	300, 982
S23.120D	801
S23.120S	348
S23.121A	300, 982
S23.121D	801
S23.121S	348
S23.122A	300, 982
S23.122D	801
S23.122S	348
S23.123A	300, 982
S23.123D	801
S23.123S	348
S23.130A	300, 982
S23.130D	801
S23.130S	348
S23.131A	300, 982
S23.131D	801
S23.131S	348
S23.132A	300, 982
S23.132D	801
S23.132S	348
S23.133A	300, 982
S23.133D	801
S23.133S	348
S23.140A	300, 982
S23.140D	801
S23.140S	348
S23.141A	300, 982
S23.141D	801
S23.141S	348
S23.142A	300, 982
S23.142D	801
S23.142S	348
S23.143A	300, 982
S23.143D	801
S23.143S	348
S23.150A	300, 982
S23.150D	801
S23.150S	348
S23.151A	300, 982
S23.151D	801
S23.151S	348
S23.152A	300, 982
S23.152D	801
S23.152S	348
S23.153A	300, 982
S23.153D	801
S23.153S	348
S23.160A	300, 982
S23.160D	801
S23.160S	348
S23.161A	300, 982
S23.161D	801
S23.161S	348
S23.162A	300, 982
S23.162D	801
S23.162S	348
S23.163A	300, 982
S23.163D	801
S23.163S	348
S23.170A	300, 982
S23.170D	801
S23.170S	348
S23.171A	300, 982
S23.171D	801
S23.171S	348
S23.20XA	300, 982
S23.20XD	801
S23.20XS	348
S23.29XA	300, 982
S23.29XD	801
S23.29XS	348
S23.3XXA	300, 982
S23.3XXD	801
S23.3XXS	348
S23.41XA	106, 982
S23.41XD	801
S23.41XS	348
S23.420A	106, 982
S23.420D	801
S23.420S	348
S23.421A	106, 982
S23.421D	801
S23.421S	348
S23.428A	106, 982
S23.428D	801
S23.428S	348
S23.429A	106, 982
S23.429D	801
S23.429S	348
S23.8XXA	300, 982
S23.8XXD	801
S23.8XXS	348
S23.9XXA	300, 982
S23.9XXD	801
S23.9XXS	348
S24.0XXA	42, 982, 1029
S24.0XXD	801
S24.0XXS	42
S24.101A	42, 982, 1029
S24.101D	801
S24.101S	42
S24.102A	42, 982, 1029
S24.102D	801
S24.102S	42
S24.103A	42, 982, 1029
S24.103D	801
S24.103S	42
S24.104A	42, 982, 1029
S24.104D	801
S24.104S	42
S24.109A	42, 982, 1029
S24.109D	801
S24.109S	42
S24.111A	42, 982, 1029
S24.111D	801
S24.111S	42
S24.112A	42, 982, 1029
S24.112D	801
S24.112S	42
S24.113A	42, 982, 1029
S24.113D	801
S24.113S	42
S24.114A	42, 982, 1029
S24.114D	801
S24.114S	42
S24.119A	43, 982, 1029
S24.119D	801
S24.119S	43
S24.131A	43, 982, 1029
S24.131D	801
S24.131S	43
S24.132A	43, 982, 1029
S24.132D	801
S24.132S	43
S24.133A	43, 982, 1029
S24.133D	801
S24.133S	43
S24.134A	43, 982, 1029
S24.134D	801
S24.134S	43
S24.139A	43, 982, 1029
S24.139D	801
S24.139S	43
S24.141A	43, 982, 1029
S24.141D	801
S24.141S	43
S24.142A	43, 982, 1029
S24.142D	801
S24.142S	43
S24.143A	43, 982, 1029
S24.143D	801
S24.143S	43
S24.144A	43, 982, 1029
S24.144D	801
S24.144S	43
S24.149A	43, 983, 1029
S24.149D	801
S24.149S	43
S24.151A	43, 983, 1029
S24.151D	801
S24.151S	43
S24.152A	43, 983, 1029
S24.152D	801
S24.152S	43
S24.153A	43, 983, 1029
S24.153D	801
S24.153S	43
S24.154A	43, 983, 1029
S24.154D	801
S24.154S	43
S24.159A	43, 983, 1029
S24.159D	801
S24.159S	43
S24.2XXA	46, 983
S24.2XXD	801
S24.2XXS	53
S24.3XXA	46, 983, 1029
S24.3XXD	801
S24.3XXS	53
S24.4XXA	46, 983
S24.4XXD	801
S24.4XXS	53
S24.8XXA	46, 983, 1029
S24.8XXD	801
S24.8XXS	53
S24.9XXA	46, 983, 1029
S24.9XXD	801
S24.9XXS	53
S25.00XA	564, 747, 983, 1026
S25.00XD	801
S25.00XS	168
S25.01XA	564, 747, 983, 1026
S25.01XD	801
S25.01XS	168
S25.02XA	564, 747, 983, 1026
S25.02XD	801
S25.02XS	168
S25.09XA	564, 747, 983, 1026
S25.09XD	801
S25.09XS	168
S25.101A	564, 747, 983, 1026
S25.101D	801
S25.101S	168
S25.102A	564, 747, 983, 1026
S25.102D	801
S25.102S	168
S25.109A	564, 747, 983, 1026
S25.109D	801
S25.109S	168
S25.111A	564, 747, 983, 1026
S25.111D	801
S25.111S	168
S25.112A	564, 747, 983, 1026
S25.112D	801
S25.112S	168
S25.119A	564, 747, 983, 1026
S25.119D	801
S25.119S	168
S25.121A	564, 747, 983, 1026
S25.121D	801
S25.121S	168
S25.122A	564, 747, 983, 1026
S25.122D	801
S25.122S	168
S25.129A	564, 747, 983, 1026
S25.129D	801
S25.129S	168
S25.191A	564, 747, 983, 1026
S25.191D	801
S25.191S	168
S25.192A	564, 747, 983, 1026
S25.192D	801
S25.192S	168
S25.199A	564, 747, 983, 1026
S25.199D	801
S25.199S	168
S25.20XA	564, 747, 983, 1026
S25.20XD	801
S25.20XS	168
S25.21XA	564, 747, 983, 1026
S25.21XD	801
S25.21XS	168
S25.22XA	564, 747, 983, 1026
S25.22XD	801
S25.22XS	168
S25.29XA	564, 747, 983, 1026
S25.29XD	801
S25.29XS	168
S25.301A	564, 747, 983, 1026
S25.301D	801
S25.301S	168
S25.302A	564, 747, 983, 1026
S25.302D	801
S25.302S	168
S25.309A	564, 747, 983, 1026
S25.309D	801
S25.309S	168
S25.311A	564, 747, 983, 1026
S25.311D	801
S25.311S	168
S25.312A	564, 747, 983, 1026
S25.312D	801
S25.312S	168
S25.319A	564, 747, 983, 1026
S25.319D	801
S25.319S	168
S25.321A	564, 747, 983, 1026
S25.321D	801
S25.321S	168
S25.322A	564, 747, 983, 1026
S25.322D	801
S25.322S	168
S25.329A	564, 747, 983, 1026
S25.329D	801
S25.329S	168
S25.391A	564, 747, 983, 1026
S25.391D	801
S25.391S	168
S25.392A	564, 747, 983, 1026
S25.392D	801
S25.392S	168
S25.399A	564, 747, 983, 1026
S25.399D	801
S25.399S	168
S25.401A	564, 747, 983, 1026
S25.401D	801
S25.401S	168

Code	Page	Code	Page	Code	Page	Code	Page	Code	Page	Code	Page
S25.402A	564,747,983, 1026	S25.819D	801	S27.319D	802	S27.63XD	802	S29.022A	459,983	S30.840A	459,984
S25.402D	801	S25.819S	169	S27.319S	106	S27.63XS	107	S29.022D	802	S30.840D	802
S25.402S	168	S25.891A	983,1026	S27.321A	106,983,1026	S27.69XA	107,983,1027	S29.022S	459	S30.840S	459
S25.409A	564,747,983, 1026	S25.891A	747	S27.321D	802	S27.69XD	802	S29.029A	459,983	S30.841A	459,984
S25.409D	801	S25.891D	801	S27.321S	106	S27.69XS	107	S29.029D	802	S30.841D	802
S25.409S	168	S25.891S	169	S27.322A	106,983,1026	S27.802A	105,983,1027	S29.029S	459	S30.841S	459
S25.411A	564,747,983, 1026	S25.892A	983,1026	S27.322D	802	S27.802D	802	S29.091A	747,983	S30.842A	459,984
S25.411D	801	S25.892A	747	S27.322S	106	S27.802S	107	S29.091D	802	S30.842D	802
S25.411S	168	S25.892D	801	S27.329A	106,983,1026	S27.803A	105,983,1027	S29.091S	747	S30.842S	459
S25.412A	564,747,983, 1026	S25.892S	169	S27.329D	802	S27.803D	802	S29.092A	747,983	S30.843A	459,984
S25.412D	801	S25.899A	983,1026	S27.329S	106	S27.803S	107	S29.092D	802	S30.843D	802
S25.412S	168	S25.899A	747	S27.331A	105,983,1026	S27.808A	105,983,1027	S29.092S	747	S30.843S	459
S25.419A	564,747,983, 1026	S25.899D	801	S27.331D	802	S27.808D	802	S29.099A	747,983	S30.844A	459,984
S25.419D	801	S25.899S	169	S27.331S	106	S27.808S	107	S29.099D	802	S30.844D	802
S25.419S	168	S25.90XA	747,983,1026	S27.332A	105,983,1026	S27.809A	105,983,1027	S29.099S	747	S30.844S	459
S25.421A	564,747,983, 1026	S25.90XD	801	S27.332D	802	S27.809D	802	S29.8XXA	747,983	S30.845A	459,984
S25.421D	801	S25.90XS	169	S27.332S	106	S27.809S	107	S29.8XXD	802	S30.845D	802
S25.421S	168	S25.91XA	747,983,1026	S27.339A	105,983,1026	S27.812A	193,983,1027	S29.8XXS	747	S30.845S	459
S25.422A	564,747,983, 1026	S25.91XD	801	S27.339D	802	S27.812D	802	S29.9XXA	747,983	S30.846A	459,984
S25.422D	801	S25.91XS	169	S27.339S	106	S27.812S	107	S29.9XXD	802	S30.846D	802
S25.422S	168	S25.99XA	747,983,1026	S27.391A	106,983,1026	S27.813A	193,983,1027	S29.9XXS	747	S30.846S	459
S25.429A	564,747,983, 1026	S25.99XD	802	S27.391D	802	S27.813D	802	S30.0XXA	459,983	S30.850A	459,984
S25.429D	801	S25.99XS	169	S27.391S	106	S27.813S	107	S30.0XXD	802	S30.850D	802
S25.429S	168	S26.00XA	173,983,1026	S27.392A	106,983,1026	S27.818A	193,983,1027	S30.0XXS	459	S30.850S	459
S25.491A	564,747,983, 1026	S26.00XD	802	S27.392D	802	S27.818D	802	S30.1XXA	459,983	S30.851A	459,984
S25.491D	801	S26.00XS	106	S27.392S	106	S27.818S	107	S30.1XXD	802	S30.851D	802
S25.491S	168	S26.01XA	173,983,1026	S27.399A	106,983,1026	S27.819A	193,983,1027	S30.1XXS	459	S30.851S	459
S25.492A	564,747,983, 1026	S26.01XD	802	S27.399D	802	S27.819D	802	S30.201A	529,983	S30.852A	459,984
S25.492D	801	S26.01XS	106	S27.399S	106	S27.819S	107	S30.201D	802	S30.852D	802
S25.492S	169	S26.020A	173,983,1026	S27.401A	105,983,1026	S27.892A	983,1027	S30.201S	459	S30.852S	459
S25.499A	564,747,983, 1026	S26.020D	802	S27.401D	802	S27.892A	107	S30.202A	534,542,983	S30.853A	459,984
S25.499D	801	S26.020S	106	S27.401S	106	S27.892D	802	S30.202D	802	S30.853D	802
S25.499S	169	S26.021A	173,983,1026	S27.402A	105,983,1026	S27.892S	107	S30.202S	459	S30.853S	459
S25.501A	747,983	S26.021D	802	S27.402D	802	S27.893A	983,1027	S30.21XA	529,983	S30.854A	459,984
S25.501D	801	S26.021S	106	S27.402S	106	S27.893A	107	S30.21XD	802	S30.854D	802
S25.501S	169	S26.022A	173,983,1026	S27.409A	105,983,1026	S27.893D	802	S30.21XS	459	S30.854S	459
S25.502A	747,983	S26.022D	802	S27.409D	802	S27.893S	107	S30.22XA	529,983	S30.855A	459,984
S25.502D	801	S26.022S	106	S27.409S	106	S27.898A	983,1027	S30.22XD	802	S30.855D	802
S25.502S	169	S26.09XA	173,983,1026	S27.411A	105,983,1026	S27.898A	107	S30.22XS	459	S30.855S	459
S25.509A	747,983	S26.09XD	802	S27.411D	802	S27.898D	802	S30.23XA	534,542,983	S30.856A	459,984
S25.509D	801	S26.09XS	106	S27.411S	106	S27.898S	107	S30.23XD	802	S30.856D	802
S25.509S	169	S26.10XA	173,983,1026	S27.412A	105,983,1026	S27.899A	983,1027	S30.23XS	459	S30.856S	459
S25.511A	747,983	S26.10XD	802	S27.412D	802	S27.899A	107	S30.3XXA	459,983	S30.857A	459,984
S25.511D	801	S26.10XS	106	S27.412S	106	S27.899D	802	S30.3XXD	802	S30.857D	802
S25.511S	169	S26.11XA	173,983,1026	S27.419A	105,983,1026	S27.899S	107	S30.3XXS	459	S30.857S	459
S25.512A	747,983	S26.11XD	802	S27.419D	802	S27.9XXA	747,983,1027	S30.810A	459,984	S30.860A	478,984
S25.512D	801	S26.11XS	106	S27.419S	106	S27.9XXD	802	S30.810D	802	S30.860D	802
S25.512S	169	S26.12XA	173,983,1026	S27.421A	105,983,1026	S27.9XXS	107	S30.810S	459	S30.860S	459
S25.519A	747,983	S26.12XD	802	S27.421D	802	S28.0XXA	747,983,1029	S30.811A	459,984	S30.861A	478,984
S25.519D	801	S26.12XS	106	S27.421S	106	S28.0XXD	802	S30.811D	802	S30.861D	802
S25.519S	169	S26.19XA	173,983,1026	S27.422A	105,983,1026	S28.0XXS	459	S30.811S	459	S30.861S	459
S25.591A	747,983	S26.19XD	802	S27.422D	802	S28.1XXA	459,983	S30.812A	459,984	S30.862A	478,984
S25.591D	801	S26.19XS	106	S27.422S	107	S28.1XXD	802	S30.812D	802	S30.862D	802
S25.591S	169	S26.90XA	173,983,1026	S27.429A	105,983,1027	S28.1XXS	459	S30.812S	459	S30.862S	459
S25.592A	747,983	S26.90XD	802	S27.429D	802	S28.211A	459,983	S30.813A	459,984	S30.863A	478,984
S25.592D	801	S26.90XS	106	S27.429S	106	S28.211D	802	S30.813D	802	S30.863D	802
S25.592S	169	S26.91XA	173,983,1026	S27.431A	105,983,1027	S28.211S	459	S30.813S	459	S30.863S	459
S25.599A	747,983	S26.91XD	802	S27.431D	802	S28.212A	459,983	S30.814A	459,984	S30.864A	478,984
S25.599D	801	S26.91XS	106	S27.431S	107	S28.212D	802	S30.814D	802	S30.864D	802
S25.599S	169	S26.92XA	173,983,1026	S27.432A	105,983,1027	S28.212S	459	S30.814S	459	S30.864S	459
S25.801A	983,1026	S26.92XD	802	S27.432D	802	S28.219A	459,983	S30.815A	459,984	S30.865A	478,984
S25.801A	747	S26.92XS	106	S27.432S	107	S28.219D	802	S30.815D	802	S30.865D	802
S25.801D	801	S26.99XA	173,983,1026	S27.439A	105,983,1026	S28.219S	459	S30.815S	459	S30.865S	459
S25.801S	169	S26.99XD	802	S27.439D	802	S28.221A	459,983	S30.816A	459,984	S30.866A	478,984
S25.802A	983,1026	S26.99XS	106	S27.439S	107	S28.221D	802	S30.816D	802	S30.866D	802
S25.802A	747	S27.0XXA	106,564,983, 1026	S27.491A	105,983,1027	S28.221S	459	S30.816S	459	S30.866S	459
S25.802D	801	S27.0XXD	802	S27.491S	107	S28.222A	459,983	S30.817A	459,984	S30.867A	478,984
S25.802S	169	S27.0XXS	106	S27.492A	105,983,1027	S28.222D	802	S30.817D	802	S30.867D	802
S25.809A	983,1026	S27.1XXA	106,564,983, 1026	S27.492D	802	S28.222S	459	S30.817S	459	S30.867S	459
S25.809A	747	S27.1XXD	802	S27.492S	107	S28.229A	459,983	S30.820A	477,984	S30.870A	459,984
S25.809D	801	S27.1XXS	106	S27.499A	105,983,1027	S28.229D	802	S30.820D	802	S30.870D	802
S25.809S	169	S27.2XXA	106,564,983, 1026	S27.499D	802	S28.229S	459	S30.820S	459	S30.870S	459
S25.811A	983,1026	S27.2XXD	802	S27.499S	107	S29.001A	747,983	S30.821A	477,984	S30.871A	459,984
S25.811A	747	S27.2XXS	106	S27.50XA	107,983,1027	S29.001D	802	S30.821D	802	S30.871D	802
S25.811D	801	S27.301A	106,983,1026	S27.50XD	802	S29.001S	747	S30.821S	459	S30.871S	459
S25.811S	169	S27.301D	802	S27.50XS	107	S29.002A	747,983	S30.822A	478,984	S30.872A	459,984
S25.812A	983,1026	S27.301S	106	S27.51XA	107,983,1027	S29.002D	802	S30.822D	802	S30.872D	802
S25.812A	747	S27.302A	106,983,1026	S27.51XD	802	S29.002S	747	S30.822S	459	S30.872S	459
S25.812D	801	S27.302D	802	S27.51XS	107	S29.009A	747,983	S30.823A	478,984	S30.873A	459,984
S25.812S	169	S27.302S	106	S27.52XA	107,983,1027	S29.009D	802	S30.823D	802	S30.873D	802
S25.819A	983,1026	S27.309A	106,983,1026	S27.52XD	802	S29.009S	747	S30.823S	459	S30.873S	459
S25.819A	747	S27.309D	802	S27.52XS	107	S29.011A	348,983	S30.824A	478,984	S30.874A	459,984
		S27.309S	106	S27.53XA	107,983,1027	S29.011D	802	S30.824D	802	S30.874D	802
		S27.311A	106,983,1026	S27.53XD	802	S29.011S	348	S30.824S	459	S30.874S	459
		S27.311D	802	S27.53XS	107	S29.012A	348,983	S30.825A	478,984	S30.875A	459,984
		S27.311S	106	S27.59XA	107,983,1027	S29.012D	802	S30.825D	802	S30.875D	802
		S27.312A	106,983,1026	S27.59XD	802	S29.012S	348	S30.825S	459	S30.875S	459
		S27.312S	106	S27.59XS	107	S29.019A	348,983	S30.826A	478,984	S30.876A	459,984
		S27.319A	106,983,1026	S27.60XA	107,983,1027	S29.019D	802	S30.826D	802	S30.876D	802
				S27.60XD	802	S29.019S	348	S30.826S	459	S30.876S	459
				S27.60XS	107	S29.021A	459,983	S30.827A	478,984	S30.877A	459,984
				S27.63XA	107,983,1027	S29.021D	802	S30.827D	802	S30.877D	802
						S29.021S	459	S30.827S	459	S30.877S	459

Code	Page	Code	Page	Code	Page	Code	Page	Code	Page	Code	Page
S30.91XA	459, 984	S31.114A	460, 984	S31.20XA	529, 984	S31.601A	196, 984, 1027	S31.644A	196, 984, 1027	S31.834A	747, 985
S30.91XD	802	S31.114D	803	S31.20XD	803	S31.601D	803	S31.644D	803	S31.834D	803
S30.91XS	459	S31.114S	460	S31.20XS	460	S31.601S	460	S31.644S	460	S31.834S	460
S30.92XA	459, 984	S31.115A	460, 984	S31.21XA	529, 984	S31.602A	196, 984, 1027	S31.645A	196, 984, 1027	S31.835A	460, 985
S30.92XD	802	S31.115D	803	S31.21XD	803	S31.602D	803	S31.645D	803	S31.835D	803
S30.92XS	459	S31.115S	460	S31.21XS	460	S31.602S	460	S31.645S	460	S31.835S	460
S30.93XA	459, 984	S31.119A	460, 984	S31.22XA	529, 984	S31.603A	196, 984, 1027	S31.649A	196, 984, 1027	S31.839A	461, 985
S30.93XD	802	S31.119D	803	S31.22XD	803	S31.603D	803	S31.649D	803	S31.839D	803
S30.93XS	459	S31.119S	460	S31.22XS	460	S31.603S	460	S31.649S	460	S31.839S	461
S30.94XA	459, 984	S31.120A	747, 984	S31.23XA	529, 984	S31.604A	196, 984, 1027	S31.650A	196, 985, 1027	S32.000A	300, 985
S30.94XD	802	S31.120D	803	S31.23XD	803	S31.604D	803	S31.650D	803	S32.000B	300, 985
S30.94XS	459	S31.120S	460	S31.23XS	460	S31.604S	460	S31.650S	460	S32.000D	308
S30.95XA	459, 984	S31.121A	747, 984	S31.24XA	529, 984	S31.605A	196, 984, 1027	S31.651A	196, 985, 1027	S32.000G	308
S30.95XD	802	S31.121D	803	S31.24XD	803	S31.605D	803	S31.651D	803	S32.000K	379
S30.95XS	459	S31.121S	460	S31.24XS	460	S31.605S	460	S31.651S	460	S32.000S	300
S30.96XA	459, 984	S31.122A	747, 984	S31.25XA	529, 984	S31.609A	196, 984, 1027	S31.652A	196, 985, 1027	S32.001A	300, 985
S30.96XD	802	S31.122D	803	S31.25XD	803	S31.609D	803	S31.652D	803	S32.001B	300, 985
S30.96XS	459	S31.122S	460	S31.25XS	460	S31.609S	460	S31.652S	460	S32.001D	308
S30.97XA	459, 984	S31.123A	747, 984	S31.30XA	529, 984	S31.610A	196, 984, 1027	S31.653A	196, 985, 1027	S32.001K	379
S30.97XD	802	S31.123D	803	S31.30XD	803	S31.610D	803	S31.653D	803	S32.001S	300
S30.97XS	459	S31.123S	460	S31.30XS	460	S31.610S	460	S31.653S	460	S32.002A	300, 985
S30.98XA	459, 984	S31.124A	747, 984	S31.31XA	529, 984	S31.611A	196, 984, 1027	S31.654A	196, 985, 1027	S32.002B	300, 985
S30.98XD	802	S31.124D	803	S31.31XD	803	S31.611D	803	S31.654D	803	S32.002D	308
S30.98XS	459	S31.124S	460	S31.31XS	460	S31.611S	460	S31.654S	460	S32.002G	308
S31.000A	459, 984	S31.125A	747, 984	S31.32XA	529, 984	S31.612A	196, 984, 1027	S31.655A	196, 985, 1027	S32.002K	379
S31.000D	802	S31.125D	803	S31.32XD	803	S31.612D	803	S31.655D	803	S32.002S	300
S31.000S	459	S31.125S	460	S31.32XS	460	S31.612S	460	S31.655S	460	S32.008A	300, 985
S31.001A	520, 984, 1027	S31.129A	747, 984	S31.33XA	529, 984	S31.613A	196, 984, 1027	S31.659A	196, 985, 1027	S32.008B	300, 985
S31.001D	802	S31.129D	803	S31.33XD	803	S31.613D	803	S31.659D	803	S32.008D	308
S31.001S	459	S31.129S	460	S31.33XS	460	S31.613S	460	S31.659S	460	S32.008G	308
S31.010A	459, 984	S31.130A	460, 984	S31.34XA	529, 984	S31.614A	196, 984, 1027	S31.801A	460, 985	S32.008K	379
S31.010D	802	S31.130D	803	S31.34XD	803	S31.614D	803	S31.801D	803	S32.008S	300
S31.010S	459	S31.130S	460	S31.34XS	460	S31.614S	460	S31.801S	460	S32.009A	300, 985
S31.011A	520, 984, 1027	S31.131A	460, 984	S31.35XA	529, 984	S31.615A	196, 984, 1027	S31.802A	460, 985	S32.009B	300, 985
S31.011D	802	S31.131D	803	S31.35XD	803	S31.615D	803	S31.802D	803	S32.009D	308
S31.011S	459	S31.131S	460	S31.35XS	460	S31.615S	460	S31.802S	460	S32.009G	308
S31.020A	459, 984	S31.132A	460, 984	S31.40XA	534, 542, 984	S31.619A	196, 984, 1027	S31.803A	460, 985	S32.009K	379
S31.020D	802	S31.132D	803	S31.40XD	803	S31.619D	803	S31.803D	803	S32.009S	300
S31.020S	459	S31.132S	460	S31.40XS	460	S31.619S	460	S31.803S	460	S32.010A	300, 985
S31.021A	520, 984, 1027	S31.133A	460, 984	S31.41XA	534, 542, 984	S31.620A	196, 984, 1027	S31.804A	460, 985	S32.010B	300, 985
S31.021D	802	S31.133D	803	S31.41XD	803	S31.620D	803	S31.804D	803	S32.010D	308
S31.021S	459	S31.133S	460	S31.41XS	460	S31.620S	460	S31.804S	460	S32.010G	308
S31.030A	459, 984	S31.134A	460, 984	S31.42XA	534, 542, 984	S31.621A	196, 984, 1027	S31.805A	460, 985	S32.010K	379
S31.030D	802	S31.134D	803	S31.42XD	803	S31.621D	803	S31.805D	803	S32.010S	300
S31.030S	459	S31.134S	460	S31.42XS	460	S31.621S	460	S31.805S	460	S32.011A	300, 985
S31.031A	520, 984, 1027	S31.135A	460, 984	S31.43XA	534, 542, 984	S31.622A	196, 984, 1027	S31.809A	460, 985	S32.011B	300, 985
S31.031D	802	S31.135D	803	S31.43XD	803	S31.622D	803	S31.809D	803	S32.011D	308
S31.031S	459	S31.135S	460	S31.43XS	460	S31.622S	460	S31.809S	460	S32.011G	308
S31.040A	459, 984	S31.139A	460, 984	S31.44XA	534, 542, 984	S31.623A	196, 984, 1027	S31.811A	460, 985	S32.011K	379
S31.040D	802	S31.139D	803	S31.44XD	803	S31.623D	803	S31.811D	803	S32.011S	300
S31.040S	459	S31.139S	460	S31.44XS	460	S31.623S	460	S31.811S	460	S32.012A	300, 985
S31.041A	520, 984, 1027	S31.140A	747, 984	S31.45XA	534, 542, 984	S31.624A	196, 984, 1027	S31.812A	460, 985	S32.012B	300, 985
S31.041D	802	S31.140D	803	S31.45XD	803	S31.624D	803	S31.812D	803	S32.012D	308
S31.041S	459	S31.140S	460	S31.45XS	460	S31.624S	460	S31.812S	460	S32.012G	308
S31.050A	459, 984	S31.141A	747, 984	S31.501A	529, 984	S31.625A	196, 984, 1027	S31.813A	460, 985	S32.012K	379
S31.050D	802	S31.141D	803	S31.501D	803	S31.625D	803	S31.813D	803	S32.012S	300
S31.050S	459	S31.141S	460	S31.501S	529	S31.625S	460	S31.813S	460	S32.018A	300, 985
S31.051A	520, 984, 1027	S31.142A	747, 984	S31.502A	534, 542, 984	S31.629A	196, 984, 1027	S31.814A	460, 985	S32.018B	300, 985
S31.051D	802	S31.142D	803	S31.502D	803	S31.629D	803	S31.814D	803	S32.018D	308
S31.051S	459	S31.142S	460	S31.502S	534, 542	S31.629S	460	S31.814S	460	S32.018G	308
S31.100A	460, 984	S31.143A	747, 984	S31.511A	529, 984	S31.630A	196, 984, 1027	S31.815A	460, 985	S32.018K	379
S31.100D	802	S31.143D	803	S31.511D	803	S31.630D	803	S31.815D	803	S32.018S	300
S31.100S	460	S31.143S	460	S31.511S	529	S31.630S	460	S31.815S	460	S32.019A	300, 985
S31.101A	460, 984	S31.144A	747, 984	S31.512A	534, 542, 984	S31.631A	196, 984, 1027	S31.819A	460, 985	S32.019B	300, 985
S31.101D	802	S31.144D	803	S31.512D	803	S31.631D	803	S31.819D	803	S32.019D	308
S31.101S	460	S31.144S	460	S31.512S	534, 542	S31.631S	460	S31.819S	460	S32.019G	308
S31.102A	460, 984	S31.145A	747, 984	S31.521A	529, 984	S31.632A	196, 984, 1027	S31.821A	460, 985	S32.019K	379
S31.102D	802	S31.145D	803	S31.521D	803	S31.632D	803	S31.821D	803	S32.019S	300
S31.102S	460	S31.145S	460	S31.521S	529	S31.632S	460	S31.821S	460	S32.020A	300, 985
S31.103A	460, 984	S31.149A	747, 984	S31.522A	534, 542, 984	S31.633A	196, 984, 1027	S31.822A	460, 985	S32.020B	300, 985
S31.103D	802	S31.149D	803	S31.522D	803	S31.633D	803	S31.822D	803	S32.020D	308
S31.103S	460	S31.149S	460	S31.522S	534, 542	S31.633S	460	S31.822S	460	S32.020G	308
S31.104A	460, 984	S31.150A	460, 984	S31.531A	529, 984	S31.634A	196, 984, 1027	S31.823A	460, 985	S32.020S	300
S31.104D	802	S31.150D	803	S31.531D	803	S31.634D	803	S31.823D	803	S32.021A	300, 985
S31.104S	460	S31.150S	460	S31.531S	529	S31.634S	460	S31.823S	460	S32.021B	300, 985
S31.105A	460, 984	S31.151A	460, 984	S31.532A	534, 542, 984	S31.635A	196, 984, 1027	S31.824A	460, 985	S32.021D	308
S31.105D	802	S31.151D	803	S31.532D	803	S31.635D	803	S31.824D	803	S32.021G	308
S31.105S	460	S31.151S	460	S31.532S	534, 542	S31.635S	460	S31.824S	460	S32.021K	379
S31.109A	460, 984	S31.152A	460, 984	S31.541A	529, 984	S31.639A	196, 984, 1027	S31.825A	460, 985	S32.021S	300
S31.109D	802	S31.152D	803	S31.541D	803	S31.639D	803	S31.825D	803	S32.022A	300, 985
S31.109S	460	S31.152S	460	S31.541S	529	S31.639S	460	S31.825S	460	S32.022B	300, 985
S31.110A	460, 984	S31.153A	460, 984	S31.542A	534, 542, 984	S31.640A	196, 984, 1027	S31.829A	460, 985	S32.022D	308
S31.110D	802	S31.153D	803	S31.542D	803	S31.640D	803	S31.829D	803	S32.022G	308
S31.110S	460	S31.153S	460	S31.542S	534, 542	S31.640S	460	S31.829S	460	S32.022K	379
S31.111A	460, 984	S31.154A	460, 984	S31.551A	529, 984	S31.641A	196, 984, 1027	S31.831A	460, 985	S32.022S	300
S31.111D	803	S31.154D	803	S31.551D	803	S31.641D	803	S31.831D	803	S32.028A	300, 985
S31.111S	460	S31.154S	460	S31.551S	529	S31.641S	460	S31.831S	460	S32.028B	300, 985
S31.112A	460, 984	S31.155A	460, 984	S31.552A	534, 542, 984	S31.642A	196, 984, 1027	S31.832A	747, 985	S32.028D	308
S31.112D	803	S31.155D	803	S31.552D	803	S31.642D	803	S31.832D	803	S32.028G	308
S31.112S	460	S31.155S	460	S31.552S	534, 542	S31.642S	460	S31.832S	460	S32.028K	379
S31.113A	460, 984	S31.159A	460, 984	S31.600A	196, 984, 1027	S31.643A	196, 984, 1027	S31.833A	460, 985	S32.028S	300
S31.113D	803	S31.159D	803	S31.600D	803	S31.643D	803	S31.833D	803		
S31.113S	460	S31.159S	460	S31.600S	460	S31.643S	460	S31.833S	460		

Code	Page
S32.Ø29A	300, 985
S32.Ø29B	300, 985
S32.Ø29D	308
S32.Ø29G	308
S32.Ø29K	379
S32.Ø29S	300
S32.Ø3ØA	300, 985
S32.Ø3ØB	300, 985
S32.Ø3ØD	308
S32.Ø3ØG	308
S32.Ø3ØK	379
S32.Ø3ØS	300
S32.Ø31A	300, 985
S32.Ø31B	300, 985
S32.Ø31D	308
S32.Ø31G	308
S32.Ø31K	379
S32.Ø31S	300
S32.Ø32A	300, 985
S32.Ø32B	300, 985
S32.Ø32D	308
S32.Ø32G	308
S32.Ø32K	379
S32.Ø32S	300
S32.Ø38A	300, 985
S32.Ø38B	300, 985
S32.Ø38D	308
S32.Ø38G	308
S32.Ø38K	379
S32.Ø38S	300
S32.Ø39A	300, 985
S32.Ø39B	300, 985
S32.Ø39D	308
S32.Ø39G	308
S32.Ø39K	379
S32.Ø39S	300
S32.Ø4ØA	300, 985
S32.Ø4ØB	300, 985
S32.Ø4ØD	308
S32.Ø4ØG	308
S32.Ø4ØK	379
S32.Ø4ØS	300
S32.Ø41A	300, 985
S32.Ø41B	300, 985
S32.Ø41D	308
S32.Ø41G	308
S32.Ø41K	379
S32.Ø41S	300
S32.Ø42A	300, 985
S32.Ø42B	300, 985
S32.Ø42D	308
S32.Ø42G	308
S32.Ø42K	379
S32.Ø42S	300
S32.Ø48A	300, 985
S32.Ø48B	300, 985
S32.Ø48D	308
S32.Ø48G	308
S32.Ø48K	379
S32.Ø48S	300
S32.Ø49A	300, 985
S32.Ø49B	300, 985
S32.Ø49D	308
S32.Ø49G	308
S32.Ø49K	379
S32.Ø49S	300
S32.Ø5ØA	300, 985
S32.Ø5ØB	300, 985
S32.Ø5ØD	308
S32.Ø5ØG	309
S32.Ø5ØK	379
S32.Ø5ØS	300
S32.Ø51A	300, 985
S32.Ø51B	300, 985
S32.Ø51D	309
S32.Ø51G	309
S32.Ø51K	379
S32.Ø51S	300
S32.Ø52A	300, 985
S32.Ø52B	300, 985
S32.Ø52D	309
S32.Ø52G	309
S32.Ø52K	379
S32.Ø52S	300
S32.Ø58A	300, 985
S32.Ø58B	300, 985
S32.Ø58D	309
S32.Ø58G	309
S32.Ø58K	379
S32.Ø58S	300
S32.Ø59A	300, 985
S32.Ø59B	300, 985
S32.Ø59D	309
S32.Ø59G	309
S32.Ø59K	379
S32.Ø59S	300
S32.1ØXA	300, 985, 1029
S32.1ØXB	300, 985, 1029
S32.1ØXD	309
S32.1ØXG	309
S32.1ØXK	379
S32.1ØXS	300
S32.11ØA	300, 985, 1029
S32.11ØB	300, 985, 1029
S32.11ØD	309
S32.11ØG	309
S32.11ØK	379
S32.11ØS	300
S32.111A	300, 985, 1029
S32.111B	300, 985, 1029
S32.111D	309
S32.111G	309
S32.111K	379
S32.111S	300
S32.112A	300, 985, 1029
S32.112B	300, 985, 1029
S32.112D	309
S32.112G	309
S32.112K	379
S32.112S	300
S32.119A	300, 985, 1029
S32.119B	300, 985, 1029
S32.119D	309
S32.119G	309
S32.119K	379
S32.119S	300
S32.12ØA	300, 985, 1029
S32.12ØB	300, 985, 1029
S32.12ØD	309
S32.12ØG	309
S32.12ØK	379
S32.12ØS	300
S32.121A	300, 985, 1029
S32.121B	300, 985, 1029
S32.121D	309
S32.121G	309
S32.121K	379
S32.121S	300
S32.122A	300, 985, 1029
S32.122B	300, 985, 1029
S32.122D	309
S32.122G	309
S32.122K	379
S32.122S	300
S32.129A	300, 985, 1029
S32.129B	300, 985, 1029
S32.129D	309
S32.129G	309
S32.129K	379
S32.129S	300
S32.13ØA	300, 985, 1029
S32.13ØB	300, 985, 1029
S32.13ØD	309
S32.13ØG	309
S32.13ØK	379
S32.13ØS	300
S32.131A	300, 985, 1029
S32.131B	300, 985, 1029
S32.131D	309
S32.131G	309
S32.131K	379
S32.131S	300
S32.132A	300, 985, 1029
S32.132B	300, 985, 1029
S32.132D	309
S32.132G	309
S32.132K	379
S32.132S	300
S32.139A	300, 985, 1029
S32.139B	300, 985, 1029
S32.139D	309
S32.139G	309
S32.139K	379
S32.139S	300
S32.14XA	300, 985, 1029
S32.14XB	300, 985, 1029
S32.14XD	309
S32.14XG	309
S32.14XK	379
S32.14XS	300
S32.15XA	300, 985, 1029
S32.15XB	300, 985, 1029
S32.15XD	309
S32.15XG	309
S32.15XK	379
S32.15XS	300
S32.16XA	300, 985, 1029
S32.16XB	300, 985, 1029
S32.16XD	309
S32.16XG	309
S32.16XK	379
S32.16XS	300
S32.17XA	300, 985, 1029
S32.17XB	300, 985, 1029
S32.17XD	309
S32.17XG	309
S32.17XK	379
S32.17XS	300
S32.19XA	300, 985, 1029
S32.19XB	300, 985, 1029
S32.19XD	309
S32.19XG	309
S32.19XK	379
S32.19XS	300
S32.2XXA	300, 985, 1029
S32.2XXB	301, 985, 1029
S32.2XXD	309
S32.2XXG	309
S32.2XXK	379
S32.2XXS	301
S32.3Ø1A	292, 985, 1029
S32.3Ø1B	292, 985, 1029
S32.3Ø1D	309
S32.3Ø1G	309
S32.3Ø1K	379
S32.3Ø1S	301
S32.3Ø2A	292, 985, 1029
S32.3Ø2B	292, 985, 1029
S32.3Ø2D	309
S32.3Ø2G	309
S32.3Ø2K	379
S32.3Ø2S	301
S32.3Ø9A	292, 985, 1029
S32.3Ø9B	292, 985, 1029
S32.3Ø9D	309
S32.3Ø9G	309
S32.3Ø9K	379
S32.3Ø9S	301
S32.311A	292, 985, 1029
S32.311B	292, 985, 1029
S32.311D	309
S32.311G	309
S32.311K	379
S32.311S	301
S32.312A	292, 985, 1029
S32.312B	292, 985, 1029
S32.312D	309
S32.312G	309
S32.312K	379
S32.312S	301
S32.313A	292, 985, 1029
S32.313B	292, 985, 1029
S32.313D	309
S32.313G	309
S32.313K	379
S32.313S	301
S32.314A	292, 985, 1029
S32.314B	292, 985, 1029
S32.314D	309
S32.314G	309
S32.314K	379
S32.314S	301
S32.315A	292, 985, 1029
S32.315B	292, 985, 1029
S32.315D	309
S32.315G	309
S32.315K	379
S32.315S	301
S32.316A	292, 985, 1029
S32.316B	292, 985, 1029
S32.316D	309
S32.316G	309
S32.316K	379
S32.316S	301
S32.391A	292, 985, 1029
S32.391B	292, 985, 1029
S32.391D	309
S32.391G	309
S32.391K	379
S32.391S	301
S32.392A	292, 985, 1029
S32.392B	292, 985, 1029
S32.392D	309
S32.392G	309
S32.392K	379
S32.392S	301
S32.399A	292, 985, 1029
S32.399B	292, 985, 1029
S32.399D	309
S32.399G	309
S32.399K	379
S32.399S	301
S32.4Ø1A	292, 985, 1029
S32.4Ø1B	292, 985, 1029
S32.4Ø1D	309
S32.4Ø1G	309
S32.4Ø1K	379
S32.4Ø1S	301
S32.4Ø2A	292, 985, 1029
S32.4Ø2B	292, 985, 1029
S32.4Ø2D	309
S32.4Ø2G	309
S32.4Ø2K	379
S32.4Ø2S	301
S32.4Ø9A	292, 985, 1029
S32.4Ø9B	292, 985, 1029
S32.4Ø9D	309
S32.4Ø9G	309
S32.4Ø9K	379
S32.4Ø9S	301
S32.411A	292, 985, 1029
S32.411B	292, 985, 1029
S32.411D	309
S32.411G	309
S32.411K	379
S32.411S	301
S32.412A	292, 985, 1029
S32.412B	292, 985, 1029
S32.412D	309
S32.412G	309
S32.412K	379
S32.412S	301
S32.413A	292, 985, 1029
S32.413B	292, 985, 1029
S32.413D	309
S32.413G	309
S32.413K	379
S32.413S	301
S32.414A	292, 985, 1029
S32.414B	292, 985, 1029
S32.414D	309
S32.414G	309
S32.414K	379
S32.414S	301
S32.415A	292, 985, 1029
S32.415B	292, 985, 1029
S32.415D	309
S32.415G	309
S32.415K	379
S32.415S	301
S32.416A	292, 985, 1029
S32.416B	292, 985, 1029
S32.416D	309
S32.416G	309
S32.416K	379
S32.416S	301
S32.421A	292, 985, 1029
S32.421B	292, 985, 1029
S32.421D	309
S32.421G	309
S32.421K	379
S32.421S	301
S32.422A	292, 985, 1029
S32.422B	292, 986, 1029
S32.422D	309
S32.422G	309
S32.422K	379
S32.422S	301
S32.423A	292, 986, 1029
S32.423B	292, 986, 1029
S32.423D	309
S32.423G	309
S32.423K	379
S32.423S	301
S32.424A	292, 986, 1029
S32.424B	292, 986, 1029
S32.424D	309
S32.424G	309
S32.424K	379
S32.424S	301
S32.425A	292, 986, 1029
S32.425B	292, 986, 1029
S32.425D	309
S32.425G	309
S32.425K	379
S32.425S	301
S32.426A	292, 986, 1029
S32.426B	292, 986, 1029
S32.426D	309
S32.426G	309
S32.426K	379
S32.426S	301
S32.431A	292, 986, 1029
S32.431B	292, 986, 1029
S32.431D	309
S32.431G	309
S32.431K	379
S32.431S	301
S32.432A	292, 986, 1029
S32.432B	292, 986, 1029
S32.432D	309
S32.432G	309
S32.432K	379
S32.432S	301
S32.433A	292, 986, 1029
S32.433B	292, 986, 1030
S32.433D	309
S32.433G	309
S32.433K	379
S32.433S	301
S32.434A	292, 986, 1030
S32.434B	292, 986, 1030
S32.434D	309
S32.434G	309
S32.434K	379
S32.434S	301
S32.435A	292, 986, 1030
S32.435B	292, 986, 1030
S32.435D	309
S32.435G	309
S32.435K	379
S32.435S	301
S32.436A	292, 986, 1030
S32.436B	292, 986, 1030
S32.436D	309
S32.436G	309
S32.436K	379
S32.436S	301
S32.441A	292, 986, 1030
S32.441B	292, 986, 1030
S32.441D	309
S32.441G	309
S32.441K	379
S32.441S	301
S32.442A	292, 986, 1030
S32.442B	292, 986, 1030
S32.442D	309
S32.442G	309
S32.442K	380
S32.442S	301
S32.443A	292, 986, 1030
S32.443B	292, 986, 1030
S32.443D	309
S32.443G	309
S32.443K	380
S32.443S	301
S32.444A	292, 986, 1030
S32.444B	292, 986, 1030
S32.444D	309
S32.444G	309
S32.444K	380
S32.444S	301
S32.445A	292, 986, 1030
S32.445B	292, 986, 1030
S32.445D	309
S32.445G	309
S32.445K	380
S32.445S	301
S32.446A	292, 986, 1030
S32.446B	292, 986, 1030
S32.446D	309
S32.446G	309
S32.446K	380
S32.446S	301
S32.451A	292, 986, 1030
S32.451B	292, 986, 1030
S32.451D	309
S32.451G	309
S32.451K	380
S32.451S	301
S32.452A	292, 986, 1030
S32.452B	292, 986, 1030
S32.452D	309
S32.452G	309
S32.452K	380
S32.452S	301
S32.453A	292, 986, 1030
S32.453B	292, 986, 1030
S32.453D	309
S32.453G	309
S32.453K	380
S32.453S	301
S32.454A	292, 986, 1030
S32.454B	292, 986, 1030
S32.454D	309
S32.454G	309
S32.454K	380
S32.454S	301
S32.455A	292, 986, 1030
S32.455B	292, 986, 1030
S32.455D	309
S32.455G	309
S32.455K	380
S32.455S	301
S32.456A	292, 986, 1030
S32.456B	292, 986, 1030
S32.456D	309
S32.456G	309
S32.456K	380
S32.456S	301
S32.461A	292, 986, 1030
S32.461B	292, 986, 1030
S32.461D	309
S32.461G	309
S32.461K	380
S32.461S	301
S32.462A	292, 986, 1030
S32.462B	292, 986, 1030
S32.462D	309
S32.462G	309
S32.462K	380
S32.462S	301
S32.463A	292, 986, 1030
S32.463B	292, 986, 1030
S32.463D	309
S32.463G	309
S32.463K	380
S32.463S	301
S32.464A	292, 986, 1030
S32.464B	292, 986, 1030
S32.464D	309
S32.464G	309
S32.464K	380
S32.464S	301
S32.465A	292, 986, 1030
S32.465B	292, 986, 1030
S32.465D	309
S32.465G	309
S32.465K	380
S32.465S	301
S32.466A	292, 986, 1030
S32.466B	292, 986, 1030
S32.466D	309
S32.466G	309
S32.466K	380
S32.466S	301
S32.471A	292, 986, 1030
S32.471B	292, 986, 1030
S32.471D	309
S32.471G	309
S32.471K	380
S32.471S	301
S32.472A	292, 986, 1030
S32.472B	292, 986, 1030
S32.472D	309
S32.472G	309
S32.472K	380
S32.472S	301
S32.473A	292, 986, 1030
S32.473B	292, 986, 1030
S32.473D	309
S32.473G	309
S32.473K	380
S32.473S	301
S32.474A	292, 986, 1030
S32.474B	292, 986, 1030
S32.474D	309
S32.474G	309
S32.474K	380
S32.474S	301
S32.475A	292, 986, 1030
S32.475B	292, 986, 1030
S32.475D	309
S32.475G	309
S32.475K	380
S32.475S	301
S32.476A	292, 986, 1030
S32.476B	292, 986, 1030
S32.476D	309
S32.476G	309
S32.476K	380
S32.476S	301
S32.481A	292, 986, 1030
S32.481B	292, 986, 1030
S32.481D	309
S32.481G	309
S32.481K	380
S32.481S	301

Code	Page	Code	Page	Code	Page	Code	Page	Code	Page	Code	Page
S32.482A	292,986,1030	S32.592G	310	S32.811S	301	S34.103D	803	S35.09XA	564,747,987,1027	S35.339D	804
S32.482B	292,986,1030	S32.592K	380	S32.82XA	293,986,1030	S34.103S	43	S35.09XD	804	S35.339S	169
S32.482D	309	S32.592S	301	S32.82XB	293	S34.104A	43,986,1030	S35.09XS	169	S35.341A	747,987,1027
S32.482G	309	S32.599A	292,986,1030	S32.82XB	986,1030	S34.104D	803	S35.10XA	564,747,987,1027	S35.341D	804
S32.482K	380	S32.599B	292,986,1030	S32.82XD	310	S34.104S	43	S35.10XD	804	S35.341S	169
S32.482S	301	S32.599D	310	S32.82XG	310	S34.105A	43,986,1030	S35.10XS	169	S35.348A	747,987,1027
S32.483A	292,986,1030	S32.599G	310	S32.82XK	380	S34.105D	803	S35.11XA	564,747,987,1027	S35.348D	804
S32.483B	292,986,1030	S32.599K	380	S32.82XS	301	S34.105S	169	S35.11XD	804	S35.348S	169
S32.483D	309	S32.599S	301	S32.89XA	986,1030	S34.109A	43,986,1030	S35.11XS	169	S35.349A	747,987,1027
S32.483G	309	S32.601A	292,986,1030	S32.89XA	293	S34.109D	803	S35.12XA	564,747,987,1027	S35.349D	804
S32.483K	380	S32.601B	292,986,1030	S32.89XB	986,1030	S34.109S	43	S35.12XD	804	S35.349S	169
S32.483S	301	S32.601D	310	S32.89XB	293	S34.111A	43,986,1030	S35.12XS	169	S35.401A	747,987,1027
S32.484A	292,986,1030	S32.601G	310	S32.89XD	310	S34.111D	803	S35.19XA	564,747,987,1027	S35.401D	804
S32.484B	292,986,1030	S32.601K	380	S32.89XG	310	S34.111S	43	S35.19XD	804	S35.401S	169
S32.484D	309	S32.601S	301	S32.89XK	380	S34.112A	43,986,1030	S35.19XS	169	S35.402A	747,987,1027
S32.484G	309	S32.602A	292,986,1030	S32.89XS	301	S34.112D	803	S35.211A	747,987,1027	S35.402D	804
S32.484K	380	S32.602B	292,986,1030	S32.9XXA	293,986,1030	S34.112S	43	S35.211D	804	S35.402S	169
S32.484S	301	S32.602D	310	S32.9XXB	293,986,1030	S34.113A	43,986,1030	S35.211S	169	S35.403A	747,987,1027
S32.485A	292,986,1030	S32.602G	310	S32.9XXD	310	S34.113D	803	S35.212A	747,987,1027	S35.403D	804
S32.485B	292,986,1030	S32.602K	380	S32.9XXG	310	S34.113S	43	S35.212D	804	S35.403S	169
S32.485D	309	S32.602S	301	S32.9XXK	380	S34.114A	43,986,1030	S35.212S	169	S35.404A	747,987,1027
S32.485G	309	S32.609A	292,986,1030	S32.9XXS	301	S34.114D	803	S35.218A	747,987,1027	S35.404D	804
S32.485K	380	S32.609B	292,986,1030	S33.0XXA	301,986	S34.114S	43	S35.218D	804	S35.404S	169
S32.485S	301	S32.609D	310	S33.0XXD	803	S34.115A	43,986,1030	S35.218S	169	S35.405A	748,987,1027
S32.486A	292,986,1030	S32.609G	310	S33.0XXS	348	S34.115D	803	S35.219A	747,987,1027	S35.405D	804
S32.486B	292,986,1030	S32.609K	380	S33.100A	301,986	S34.115S	43	S35.219D	804	S35.405S	169
S32.486D	309	S32.609S	301	S33.100D	803	S34.119A	43,986,1030	S35.219S	169	S35.406A	748,987,1027
S32.486G	309	S32.611A	292,986,1030	S33.100S	348	S34.119D	803	S35.221A	747,987,1027	S35.406D	804
S32.486K	380	S32.611B	292,986,1030	S33.101A	301,986	S34.119S	43	S35.221D	804	S35.406S	169
S32.486S	301	S32.611D	310	S33.101D	803	S34.121A	43,986,1030	S35.221S	169	S35.411A	748,987,1027
S32.491A	292,986,1030	S32.611G	310	S33.101S	348	S34.121D	803	S35.222A	747,987,1027	S35.411D	804
S32.491B	292,986,1030	S32.611K	380	S33.110A	301,986	S34.121S	43	S35.222D	804	S35.411S	169
S32.491D	309	S32.611S	301	S33.110D	803	S34.122A	43,986,1030	S35.222S	169	S35.412A	748,987,1027
S32.491G	310	S32.612A	293,986,1030	S33.110S	348	S34.122D	803	S35.228A	747,987,1027	S35.412D	804
S32.491K	380	S32.612B	293,986,1030	S33.111A	301,986	S34.122S	43	S35.228D	804	S35.412S	169
S32.491S	301	S32.612D	310	S33.111D	803	S34.123A	43,987,1030	S35.228S	169	S35.413A	748,987,1027
S32.492A	292,986,1030	S32.612G	310	S33.111S	348	S34.123D	803	S35.229A	747,987,1027	S35.413D	804
S32.492B	292,986,1030	S32.612K	380	S33.120A	301,986	S34.123S	43	S35.229D	804	S35.413S	169
S32.492D	310	S32.612S	301	S33.120D	803	S34.124A	43,987,1030	S35.229S	169	S35.414A	748,987,1027
S32.492G	310	S32.613A	293,986,1030	S33.120S	348	S34.124D	803	S35.231A	747,987,1027	S35.414D	804
S32.492K	380	S32.613B	293,986,1030	S33.121A	301,986	S34.124S	43	S35.231D	804	S35.414S	169
S32.492S	301	S32.613D	310	S33.121D	803	S34.125A	43,987,1030	S35.231S	169	S35.415A	748,987,1027
S32.499A	292,986,1030	S32.613G	310	S33.121S	348	S34.125D	803	S35.232A	747,987,1027	S35.415D	804
S32.499B	292,986,1030	S32.613K	380	S33.130A	301,986	S34.125S	43	S35.232D	804	S35.415S	169
S32.499D	310	S32.613S	301	S33.130D	803	S34.129A	43,987,1030	S35.232S	169	S35.416A	748,987,1027
S32.499G	310	S32.614A	293,986,1030	S33.130S	348	S34.129D	803	S35.238A	747,987,1027	S35.416D	804
S32.499K	380	S32.614B	293,986,1030	S33.131A	301,986	S34.129S	43	S35.238D	804	S35.416S	169
S32.499S	301	S32.614D	310	S33.131D	803	S34.131A	43,987,1030	S35.238S	169	S35.491A	748,987,1027
S32.501A	292,986,1030	S32.614G	310	S33.131S	348	S34.131D	803	S35.239A	747,987,1027	S35.491D	804
S32.501B	292,986,1030	S32.614K	380	S33.140A	301,986	S34.131S	43	S35.239D	804	S35.491S	169
S32.501D	310	S32.614S	301	S33.140D	803	S34.132A	43,987,1030	S35.239S	169	S35.492A	748,987,1027
S32.501G	310	S32.615A	293,986,1030	S33.140S	348	S34.132D	803	S35.291A	747,987,1027	S35.492D	804
S32.501K	380	S32.615B	293,986,1030	S33.141A	301,986	S34.132S	43	S35.291D	804	S35.492S	169
S32.501S	301	S32.615D	310	S33.141D	803	S34.139A	43,987,1030	S35.291S	169	S35.493A	748,987,1027
S32.502A	292,986,1030	S32.615G	310	S33.141S	348	S34.139D	43	S35.292A	747,987,1027	S35.493D	804
S32.502B	292,986,1030	S32.615K	380	S33.2XXA	301,986	S34.21XA	46,987	S35.292D	804	S35.493S	169
S32.502D	310	S32.615S	301	S33.2XXD	803	S34.21XD	803	S35.292S	169	S35.494A	748,987,1027
S32.502G	310	S32.616A	293,986,1030	S33.2XXS	348	S34.21XS	53	S35.298A	747,987,1027	S35.494D	804
S32.502K	380	S32.616B	293,986,1030	S33.30XA	348,986	S34.22XA	46,987	S35.298D	804	S35.494S	169
S32.502S	301	S32.616D	310	S33.30XD	803	S34.22XD	803	S35.298S	169	S35.495A	748,987,1027
S32.509A	292,986,1030	S32.616G	310	S33.30XS	348	S34.22XS	53	S35.299A	747,987,1027	S35.495D	804
S32.509B	292,986,1030	S32.616K	380	S33.39XA	349,986	S34.3XXA	43,987,1030	S35.299D	804	S35.495S	169
S32.509D	310	S32.616S	301	S33.39XD	803	S34.3XXD	804	S35.299S	169	S35.496A	748,987,1027
S32.509G	310	S32.691A	293,986,1030	S33.39XS	349	S34.3XXS	53	S35.311A	747,987,1027	S35.496D	804
S32.509K	380	S32.691B	293,986,1030	S33.4XXA	294,986	S34.4XXA	46,987,1030	S35.311D	804	S35.496S	169
S32.509S	301	S32.691D	310	S33.4XXD	803	S34.4XXD	804	S35.311S	169	S35.50XA	748,987,1027
S32.511A	292,986,1030	S32.691G	310	S33.4XXS	349	S34.4XXS	53	S35.318A	747,987,1027	S35.50XD	804
S32.511B	292,986,1030	S32.691K	380	S33.5XXA	301,986	S34.5XXA	46,987	S35.318D	804	S35.50XS	169
S32.511D	310	S32.691S	301	S33.5XXD	803	S34.5XXD	804	S35.318S	169	S35.511A	748,987,1027
S32.511G	310	S32.692A	293,986,1030	S33.5XXS	349	S34.5XXS	53	S35.319A	747,987,1027	S35.511D	804
S32.511K	380	S32.692B	293,986,1030	S33.6XXA	301,986	S34.6XXA	46,987,1030	S35.319D	804	S35.511S	169
S32.511S	301	S32.692D	310	S33.6XXD	803	S34.6XXD	804	S35.319S	169	S35.512A	748,987,1027
S32.512A	292,986,1030	S32.692G	310	S33.6XXS	349	S34.6XXS	53	S35.321A	747,987,1027	S35.512D	804
S32.512B	292,986,1030	S32.692K	380	S33.8XXA	986	S34.8XXA	46,987,1030	S35.321D	804	S35.512S	169
S32.512D	310	S32.692S	301	S33.8XXA	301	S34.8XXD	804	S35.321S	169	S35.513A	748,987,1027
S32.512G	310	S32.699A	293,986,1030	S33.8XXD	803	S34.8XXS	53	S35.328A	747,987,1027	S35.513D	804
S32.512K	380	S32.699B	293,986,1030	S33.8XXS	349	S34.9XXA	46,987,1030	S35.328D	804	S35.513S	169
S32.512S	301	S32.699D	310	S33.9XXA	301,986	S34.9XXD	804	S35.328S	169	S35.514A	748,987,1027
S32.519A	292,986,1030	S32.699G	310	S33.9XXD	803	S34.9XXS	53	S35.329A	747,987,1027	S35.514D	804
S32.519B	292,986,1030	S32.699K	380	S33.9XXS	349	S35.00XA	564,747,987,1027	S35.329D	804	S35.514S	169
S32.519D	310	S32.699S	301	S34.01XA	43,986,1030	S35.00XD	804	S35.329S	169	S35.515A	748,987,1027
S32.519G	310	S32.810A	293,986,1030	S34.01XD	803	S35.00XS	169	S35.331A	747,987,1027	S35.515D	804
S32.519K	380	S32.810B	293,986,1030	S34.01XS	43	S35.01XA	564,747,987,1027	S35.331D	804	S35.515S	169
S32.519S	301	S32.810D	310	S34.02XA	43,986,1030	S35.01XD	804	S35.331S	169	S35.516A	748,987,1027
S32.591A	292,986,1030	S32.810G	310	S34.02XD	803	S35.01XS	169	S35.338A	747,987,1027	S35.516D	804
S32.591B	292,986,1030	S32.810K	380	S34.02XS	43	S35.02XA	564,747,987,1027	S35.338D	804	S35.516S	169
S32.591D	310	S32.810S	301	S34.101A	43,986,1030	S35.02XD	804	S35.338S	169	S35.531A	748,987,1027
S32.591G	310	S32.811A	293	S34.101D	803	S35.02XS	169	S35.339A	747,987,1027	S35.531D	804
S32.591K	380	S32.811A	986,1030	S34.101S	43					S35.531S	169
S32.591S	301	S32.811B	293,986,1030	S34.102A	43,986,1030					S35.532A	748,987,1027
S32.592A	292,986,1030	S32.811D	310	S34.102D	803					S35.532D	804
S32.592B	292,986,1030	S32.811G	310	S34.102S	43					S35.532S	169
S32.592D	310	S32.811K	380	S34.103A	43,986,1030					S35.533A	748,987,1027

Code	Page
S35.533D	804
S35.533S	169
S35.534A	748, 987, 1027
S35.534D	804
S35.534S	169
S35.535A	748, 987, 1027
S35.535D	804
S35.535S	169
S35.536A	748, 987, 1027
S35.536D	804
S35.536S	169
S35.59XA	748, 987, 1027
S35.59XD	804
S35.59XS	169
S35.8X1A	748, 987, 1027
S35.8X1D	804
S35.8X1S	169
S35.8X8A	987, 1027
S35.8X8A	748
S35.8X8D	804
S35.8X8S	169
S35.8X9A	748, 987, 1027
S35.8X9D	804
S35.8X9S	169
S35.9ØXA	748, 987, 1027
S35.9ØXD	804
S35.9ØXS	169
S35.91XA	748, 987, 1027
S35.91XD	804
S35.91XS	169
S35.99XA	748, 987, 1027
S35.99XD	804
S35.99XS	169
S36.ØØXA	564, 579, 987, 1027
S36.ØØXD	804
S36.ØØXS	196
S36.Ø2ØA	564, 579, 987, 1027
S36.Ø2ØD	804
S36.Ø2ØS	196
S36.Ø21A	564, 579, 987, 1027
S36.Ø21D	804
S36.Ø21S	196
S36.Ø29A	564, 579, 987, 1027
S36.Ø29D	804
S36.Ø29S	196
S36.Ø3ØA	564, 579, 987, 1027
S36.Ø3ØD	804
S36.Ø3ØS	196
S36.Ø31A	564, 579, 987, 1027
S36.Ø31D	804
S36.Ø31S	196
S36.Ø32A	564, 579, 987, 1027
S36.Ø32D	804
S36.Ø32S	196
S36.Ø39A	564, 579, 987, 1027
S36.Ø39D	804
S36.Ø39S	196
S36.Ø9XA	564, 579, 987, 1027
S36.Ø9XD	804
S36.Ø9XS	196
S36.112A	209, 987, 1027
S36.112D	804
S36.112S	196
S36.113A	209, 987, 1027
S36.113D	804
S36.113S	196
S36.114A	209, 987, 1027
S36.114D	804
S36.114S	196
S36.115A	209, 987, 1027
S36.115D	804
S36.115S	196
S36.116A	209, 987, 1027
S36.116D	804
S36.116S	196
S36.118A	209, 987, 1027
S36.118D	804
S36.118S	196
S36.119A	209, 987, 1027
S36.119D	804
S36.119S	196
S36.122A	209, 987, 1027
S36.122D	804
S36.122S	196
S36.123A	209, 987, 1027
S36.123D	804
S36.123S	196
S36.128A	209, 987, 1027
S36.128D	804
S36.128S	196
S36.129A	209, 987, 1027
S36.129D	804
S36.129S	196
S36.13XA	209, 987, 1027
S36.13XD	804
S36.13XS	196
S36.2ØØA	208, 987, 1028
S36.2ØØD	804
S36.2ØØS	196
S36.2Ø1A	208, 987, 1028
S36.2Ø1D	804
S36.2Ø1S	196
S36.2Ø2A	208, 987, 1028
S36.2Ø2D	804
S36.2Ø2S	196
S36.2Ø9A	208, 987, 1028
S36.2Ø9D	804
S36.2Ø9S	196
S36.22ØA	208, 987, 1028
S36.22ØD	804
S36.22ØS	196
S36.221A	208, 987, 1028
S36.221D	804
S36.221S	196
S36.222A	208, 987, 1028
S36.222D	804
S36.222S	196
S36.229A	208, 987, 1028
S36.229D	804
S36.229S	196
S36.23ØA	208, 987, 1028
S36.23ØD	804
S36.23ØS	196
S36.231A	208, 987, 1028
S36.231D	804
S36.231S	196
S36.232A	208, 987, 1028
S36.232D	804
S36.232S	196
S36.239A	208, 987, 1028
S36.239D	804
S36.239S	196
S36.24ØA	208, 987, 1028
S36.24ØD	804
S36.24ØS	196
S36.241A	208, 987, 1028
S36.241D	804
S36.241S	196
S36.242A	208, 987, 1028
S36.242D	804
S36.242S	196
S36.249A	208, 987, 1028
S36.249D	804
S36.249S	196
S36.25ØA	208, 987, 1028
S36.25ØD	804
S36.25ØS	196
S36.251A	208, 987, 1028
S36.251D	804
S36.251S	196
S36.252A	209, 987, 1028
S36.252D	804
S36.252S	196
S36.259A	209, 987, 1028
S36.259D	804
S36.259S	196
S36.26ØA	209, 987, 1028
S36.26ØD	804
S36.26ØS	196
S36.261A	209, 987, 1028
S36.261D	804
S36.261S	196
S36.262A	209, 987, 1028
S36.262D	804
S36.262S	196
S36.269A	209, 987, 1028
S36.269D	804
S36.269S	196
S36.29ØA	209, 987, 1028
S36.29ØD	804
S36.29ØS	196
S36.291A	209, 987, 1028
S36.291D	804
S36.291S	196
S36.292A	209, 987, 1028
S36.292D	804
S36.292S	196
S36.299A	209, 987, 1028
S36.299D	804
S36.299S	196
S36.3ØXA	196, 987, 1028
S36.3ØXD	804
S36.3ØXS	196
S36.32XA	196, 987, 1028
S36.32XD	804
S36.32XS	196
S36.33XA	196, 987, 1028
S36.33XD	804
S36.33XS	196
S36.39XA	196, 987, 1028
S36.39XD	804
S36.39XS	196
S36.4ØØA	196, 987, 1028
S36.4ØØD	804
S36.4ØØS	196
S36.4Ø8A	196, 987, 1028
S36.4Ø8D	804
S36.4Ø8S	196
S36.4Ø9A	196, 987, 1028
S36.4Ø9D	804
S36.4Ø9S	196
S36.41ØA	196, 987, 1028
S36.41ØD	804
S36.41ØS	196
S36.418A	987, 1028
S36.418A	196
S36.418D	804
S36.418S	196
S36.419A	196, 987, 1028
S36.419D	804
S36.419S	196
S36.42ØA	196, 987, 1028
S36.42ØD	804
S36.42ØS	196
S36.428A	196, 987, 1028
S36.428D	804
S36.428S	196
S36.429A	197, 987, 1028
S36.429D	804
S36.429S	197
S36.43ØA	197, 987, 1028
S36.43ØD	804
S36.43ØS	197
S36.438A	197, 987, 1028
S36.438D	804
S36.438S	197
S36.439A	197, 987, 1028
S36.439D	804
S36.439S	197
S36.49ØA	197, 987, 1028
S36.49ØD	804
S36.49ØS	197
S36.498A	197, 987, 1028
S36.498D	804
S36.498S	197
S36.499A	197, 987, 1028
S36.499D	804
S36.499S	197
S36.5ØØA	197, 987, 1028
S36.5ØØD	804
S36.5ØØS	197
S36.5Ø1A	197, 987, 1028
S36.5Ø1D	804
S36.5Ø1S	197
S36.5Ø2A	197, 987, 1028
S36.5Ø2D	804
S36.5Ø2S	197
S36.5Ø3A	197, 987, 1028
S36.5Ø3D	804
S36.5Ø3S	197
S36.5Ø8A	197, 987, 1028
S36.5Ø8D	804
S36.5Ø8S	197
S36.5Ø9A	197, 987, 1028
S36.5Ø9D	804
S36.5Ø9S	197
S36.51ØA	197, 987, 1028
S36.51ØD	804
S36.51ØS	197
S36.511A	197, 987, 1028
S36.511D	804
S36.511S	197
S36.512A	197, 987, 1028
S36.512D	804
S36.512S	197
S36.513A	197, 987, 1028
S36.513D	804
S36.513S	197
S36.518A	197, 987, 1028
S36.518D	804
S36.518S	197
S36.519A	197, 987, 1028
S36.519D	804
S36.519S	197
S36.52ØA	197, 987, 1028
S36.52ØD	804
S36.52ØS	197
S36.521A	197, 987, 1028
S36.521D	804
S36.521S	197
S36.522A	197, 987, 1028
S36.522D	804
S36.522S	197
S36.523A	197, 987, 1028
S36.523D	804
S36.523S	197
S36.528A	197, 987, 1028
S36.528D	804
S36.528S	197
S36.529A	197, 988, 1028
S36.529D	804
S36.529S	197
S36.53ØA	197, 988, 1028
S36.53ØD	804
S36.53ØS	197
S36.531A	197, 988, 1028
S36.531D	804
S36.531S	197
S36.532A	197, 988, 1028
S36.532D	804
S36.532S	197
S36.533A	197, 988, 1028
S36.533D	804
S36.533S	197
S36.538A	197, 988, 1028
S36.538D	804
S36.538S	197
S36.539A	197, 988, 1028
S36.539D	804
S36.539S	197
S36.59ØA	197, 988, 1028
S36.59ØD	804
S36.59ØS	197
S36.591A	197, 988, 1028
S36.591D	804
S36.591S	197
S36.592A	197, 988, 1028
S36.592D	805
S36.592S	197
S36.593A	197, 988, 1028
S36.593D	805
S36.593S	197
S36.598A	197, 988, 1028
S36.598D	805
S36.598S	197
S36.599A	197, 988, 1028
S36.599D	805
S36.599S	197
S36.6ØXA	197, 988, 1028
S36.6ØXD	805
S36.6ØXS	197
S36.61XA	197, 988, 1028
S36.61XD	805
S36.61XS	197
S36.62XA	197, 988, 1028
S36.62XD	805
S36.62XS	197
S36.63XA	197, 988, 1028
S36.63XD	805
S36.63XS	197
S36.69XA	197, 988, 1028
S36.69XD	805
S36.69XS	197
S36.81XA	197, 988, 1030
S36.81XD	805
S36.81XS	197
S36.892A	748, 988, 1028
S36.892D	805
S36.892S	197
S36.893A	748, 988, 1028
S36.893D	805
S36.893S	197
S36.898A	748, 988, 1028
S36.898D	805
S36.898S	197
S36.899A	748, 988, 1028
S36.899D	805
S36.899S	197
S36.9ØXA	197, 988
S36.9ØXD	805
S36.9ØXS	197
S36.92XA	197, 988
S36.92XD	805
S36.92XS	197
S36.93XA	197, 988
S36.93XD	805
S36.93XS	197
S36.99XA	197, 988
S36.99XD	805
S36.99XS	197
S37.ØØ1A	520, 988, 1028
S37.ØØ1D	805
S37.ØØ1S	197
S37.ØØ2A	520, 988, 1028
S37.ØØ2D	805
S37.ØØ2S	197
S37.ØØ9A	520, 988, 1028
S37.ØØ9D	805
S37.ØØ9S	197
S37.Ø11A	520, 988, 1028
S37.Ø11D	805
S37.Ø11S	197
S37.Ø12A	520, 988, 1028
S37.Ø12D	805
S37.Ø12S	197
S37.Ø19A	520, 988, 1028
S37.Ø19D	805
S37.Ø19S	197
S37.Ø21A	520, 988, 1028
S37.Ø21D	805
S37.Ø21S	197
S37.Ø22A	520, 988, 1028
S37.Ø22D	805
S37.Ø22S	197
S37.Ø29A	520, 988, 1028
S37.Ø29D	805
S37.Ø29S	197
S37.Ø31A	520, 988, 1028
S37.Ø31D	805
S37.Ø31S	197
S37.Ø32A	520, 988, 1028
S37.Ø32D	805
S37.Ø32S	197
S37.Ø39A	520, 988, 1028
S37.Ø39D	805
S37.Ø39S	197
S37.Ø41A	520, 988, 1028
S37.Ø41D	805
S37.Ø41S	197
S37.Ø42A	520, 988, 1028
S37.Ø42D	805
S37.Ø42S	197
S37.Ø49A	520, 988, 1028
S37.Ø49D	805
S37.Ø49S	197
S37.Ø51A	520, 988, 1028
S37.Ø51D	805
S37.Ø51S	197
S37.Ø52A	520, 988, 1028
S37.Ø52D	805
S37.Ø52S	197
S37.Ø59A	520, 988, 1028
S37.Ø59D	805
S37.Ø59S	197
S37.Ø61A	520, 988, 1028
S37.Ø61D	805
S37.Ø61S	197
S37.Ø62A	520, 988, 1028
S37.Ø62D	805
S37.Ø62S	197
S37.Ø69A	520, 988, 1028
S37.Ø69D	805
S37.Ø69S	197
S37.Ø91A	520, 988, 1028
S37.Ø91D	805
S37.Ø91S	197
S37.Ø92A	520, 988, 1028
S37.Ø92D	805
S37.Ø92S	197
S37.Ø99A	520, 988, 1028
S37.Ø99D	805
S37.Ø99S	197
S37.1ØXA	520, 988, 1028
S37.1ØXD	805
S37.1ØXS	529, 534, 542
S37.12XA	520, 988, 1028
S37.12XD	805
S37.12XS	529, 534, 542
S37.13XA	520, 988, 1028
S37.13XD	805
S37.13XS	529, 534, 542
S37.19XA	520, 988, 1028
S37.19XD	805
S37.19XS	529, 534, 542
S37.2ØXA	520, 988, 1028
S37.2ØXD	805
S37.2ØXS	529, 534, 542
S37.22XA	520, 988, 1028
S37.22XD	805
S37.22XS	529, 534, 542
S37.23XA	520, 988, 1028
S37.23XD	805
S37.23XS	529, 534, 542
S37.29XA	520, 988, 1028
S37.29XD	805
S37.29XS	529, 534, 542
S37.3ØXA	520, 988, 1028
S37.3ØXD	805
S37.3ØXS	529, 534, 542
S37.32XA	520, 988, 1028
S37.32XD	805
S37.32XS	529, 534, 542
S37.33XA	520, 988, 1028
S37.33XD	805
S37.33XS	529, 534, 542
S37.39XA	520, 988, 1028
S37.39XD	805
S37.39XS	529, 534, 542
S37.4Ø1A	534, 542
S37.4Ø1D	805
S37.4Ø1S	534, 542
S37.4Ø2A	534, 542
S37.4Ø2D	805
S37.4Ø2S	534, 542
S37.4Ø9A	534, 542
S37.4Ø9D	805
S37.4Ø9S	534, 542
S37.421A	534, 542
S37.421D	805
S37.421S	534, 542
S37.422A	534, 542
S37.422D	805
S37.422S	534, 542
S37.429A	534, 542
S37.429D	805
S37.429S	534, 542
S37.431A	534, 542
S37.431D	805
S37.431S	534, 542
S37.432A	534, 542
S37.432D	805
S37.432S	534, 542
S37.439A	534, 542
S37.439D	805
S37.439S	534, 542
S37.491A	534, 542
S37.491D	805
S37.491S	534, 542
S37.492A	534, 542
S37.492D	805
S37.492S	534, 542
S37.499A	534, 542
S37.499D	805
S37.499S	534, 542
S37.5Ø1A	534, 542
S37.5Ø1D	805
S37.5Ø1S	534, 542
S37.5Ø2A	534, 542
S37.5Ø2D	805
S37.5Ø2S	534, 542
S37.5Ø9A	534, 542
S37.5Ø9D	805
S37.5Ø9S	534, 542
S37.511A	534, 542
S37.511D	805
S37.511S	534, 542
S37.512A	534, 542
S37.512D	805
S37.512S	534, 542
S37.519A	534, 542
S37.519D	805
S37.519S	534, 542
S37.521A	534, 542
S37.521D	805
S37.521S	534, 542
S37.522A	534, 542
S37.522D	805
S37.522S	534, 542
S37.529A	534, 542
S37.529D	805
S37.529S	534, 542
S37.531A	534, 542
S37.531D	805
S37.531S	534, 542
S37.532A	534, 542
S37.532D	805
S37.532S	534, 542
S37.539A	534, 542
S37.539D	805

Code	Page	Code	Page	Code	Page	Code	Page	Code	Page	Code	Page
S37.539S	534, 542	S38.02XS	461	S40.011S	461	S40.842S	461	S41.049S	461	S42.012B	349, 989
S37.591A	534, 542	S38.03XA	535, 543, 988	S40.012A	461, 988	S40.849A	461, 988	S41.051A	461, 989	S42.012D	310
S37.591D	805	S38.03XD	805	S40.012D	805	S40.849D	805	S41.051D	806	S42.012G	310
S37.591S	534, 542	S38.03XS	461	S40.012S	461	S40.849S	461	S41.051S	461	S42.012K	380
S37.592A	534, 542	S38.1XXA	748, 988, 1030	S40.019A	461, 988	S40.851A	461, 988	S41.052A	461, 989	S42.012P	380
S37.592D	805	S38.1XXD	805	S40.019D	805	S40.851D	805	S41.052D	806	S42.012S	310
S37.592S	535, 542	S38.1XXS	461	S40.019S	461	S40.851S	461	S41.052S	461	S42.013A	349, 989
S37.599A	535, 542	S38.211A	535, 543, 988	S40.021A	461, 988	S40.852A	461, 988	S41.059A	461, 989	S42.013B	349, 989
S37.599D	805	S38.211D	805	S40.021D	805	S40.852D	805	S41.059D	806	S42.013D	310
S37.599S	535, 542	S38.211S	461	S40.021S	461	S40.852S	461	S41.059S	461	S42.013G	310
S37.60XA	535, 542, 988, 1028	S38.212A	535, 543, 988	S40.022A	461, 988	S40.859A	461, 988	S41.101A	461, 989	S42.013K	380
S37.60XD	805	S38.212D	805	S40.022D	805	S40.859D	805	S41.101D	806	S42.013P	380
S37.60XS	535, 542	S38.212S	461	S40.022S	461	S40.859S	461	S41.101S	461	S42.013S	310
S37.62XA	535, 542, 988, 1028	S38.221A	530, 988	S40.029A	461, 988	S40.861A	478, 988	S41.102A	461, 989	S42.014A	349, 989
S37.62XD	805	S38.221D	805	S40.029D	805	S40.861D	805	S41.102D	806	S42.014B	349, 989
S37.62XS	535, 542	S38.221S	461	S40.029S	461	S40.861S	461	S41.102S	461	S42.014D	310
S37.63XA	535, 542, 988, 1028	S38.222A	530, 988	S40.211A	461, 988	S40.862A	478, 988	S41.109A	461, 989	S42.014G	310
S37.63XD	805	S38.222D	805	S40.211D	805	S40.862D	805	S41.109D	806	S42.014K	380
S37.63XS	535, 542	S38.222S	461	S40.211S	461	S40.862S	461	S41.109S	461	S42.014P	380
S37.69XA	535, 542, 988, 1028	S38.231A	530, 988	S40.212A	461, 988	S40.869A	478, 988	S41.111A	461, 989	S42.014S	310
S37.69XD	805	S38.231D	805	S40.212D	805	S40.869D	805	S41.111D	806	S42.015A	349, 989
S37.69XS	535, 542	S38.231S	461	S40.212S	461	S40.869S	461	S41.111S	461	S42.015B	349, 989
S37.812A	503, 988, 1028	S38.232A	530, 988	S40.219A	461, 988	S40.871A	461, 988	S41.112A	461, 989	S42.015D	310
S37.812D	805	S38.232D	805	S40.219D	805	S40.871D	806	S41.112D	806	S42.015G	310
S37.812S	529, 535, 542	S38.232S	461	S40.219S	461	S40.871S	461	S41.112S	461	S42.015K	380
S37.813A	503, 988, 1028	S38.3XXA	461, 988	S40.221A	461, 988	S40.872A	461, 988	S41.119A	461, 989	S42.015P	380
S37.813D	805	S38.3XXD	805	S40.221D	805	S40.872D	806	S41.119D	806	S42.015S	310
S37.813S	529, 535, 542	S38.3XXS	461	S40.221S	461	S40.872S	461	S41.119S	461	S42.016A	349, 989
S37.818A	503, 988, 1028	S39.001A	748, 988	S40.222A	461, 988	S40.879A	461, 988	S41.121A	748, 989	S42.016B	349, 989
S37.818D	805	S39.001D	805	S40.222D	805	S40.879D	806	S41.121D	806	S42.016D	310
S37.818S	529, 535, 542	S39.001S	748	S40.222S	461	S40.879S	461	S41.121S	461	S42.016G	310
S37.819A	503, 988, 1028	S39.002A	748, 988	S40.229A	461, 988	S40.911A	461, 988	S41.122A	748, 989	S42.016K	380
S37.819D	805	S39.002D	805	S40.229D	805	S40.911D	806	S41.122D	806	S42.016P	380
S37.819S	529, 535, 542	S39.002S	748	S40.229S	461	S40.911S	461	S41.122S	461	S42.016S	310
S37.822A	529	S39.003A	748, 988	S40.241A	461, 988	S40.912A	461, 988	S41.129A	748, 989	S42.017A	349, 989
S37.822D	805	S39.003D	805	S40.241D	805	S40.912D	806	S41.129D	806	S42.017B	349, 989
S37.822S	529	S39.003S	748	S40.241S	461	S40.912S	461	S41.129S	461	S42.017D	310
S37.823A	529	S39.011A	349, 988	S40.242A	461, 988	S40.919A	461, 988	S41.131A	461, 989	S42.017G	310
S37.823D	805	S39.011D	805	S40.242D	805	S40.919D	806	S41.131D	806	S42.017K	380
S37.823S	529	S39.011S	349	S40.242S	461	S40.919S	461	S41.131S	461	S42.017P	380
S37.828A	529	S39.012A	349, 988	S40.249A	461, 988	S40.921A	461, 988	S41.132A	461, 989	S42.017S	310
S37.828D	805	S39.012D	805	S40.249D	805	S40.921D	806	S41.132D	806	S42.018A	349, 989
S37.828S	529	S39.012S	349	S40.249S	461	S40.921S	461	S41.132S	461	S42.018B	349, 989
S37.829A	529	S39.013A	349, 988	S40.251A	461, 988	S40.922A	461, 988	S41.139A	461, 989	S42.018D	310
S37.829D	805	S39.013D	805	S40.251D	805	S40.922D	806	S41.139D	806	S42.018G	310
S37.829S	529	S39.013S	349	S40.251S	461	S40.922S	461	S41.139S	461	S42.018K	380
S37.892A	529, 535, 542, 988, 1028	S39.021A	461, 988	S40.252A	461, 988	S40.929A	461, 988	S41.141A	748, 989	S42.018P	380
S37.892D	805	S39.021D	805	S40.252D	805	S40.929D	806	S41.141D	806	S42.018S	310
S37.892S	529, 535, 542	S39.021S	461	S40.252S	461	S40.929S	461	S41.141S	461	S42.019A	349, 989
S37.893A	529, 535, 542, 988, 1028	S39.022A	461, 988	S40.259A	461, 988	S41.001A	461, 988	S41.142A	748, 989	S42.019B	349, 989
S37.893D	805	S39.022D	805	S40.259D	805	S41.001D	806	S41.142D	806	S42.019D	310
S37.893S	529, 535, 542	S39.022S	461	S40.259S	461	S41.001S	461	S41.142S	461	S42.019G	310
S37.898A	529, 535, 543, 988, 1028	S39.023A	461, 988	S40.261A	478, 988	S41.002A	461, 988	S41.149A	748, 989	S42.019K	380
S37.898D	805	S39.023D	805	S40.261D	805	S41.002D	806	S41.149D	806	S42.019P	380
S37.898S	529, 535, 543	S39.023S	461	S40.261S	461	S41.002S	461	S41.149S	461	S42.019S	310
S37.899A	529, 535, 543, 988, 1028	S39.091A	748, 988	S40.262A	478, 988	S41.009A	461, 988	S41.151A	461, 989	S42.021A	349, 989
S37.899D	805	S39.091D	805	S40.262D	805	S41.009D	806	S41.151D	806	S42.021B	349, 989
S37.899S	529, 535, 543	S39.091S	748	S40.262S	461	S41.009S	461	S41.151S	461	S42.021D	310
S37.90XA	529, 535, 543, 988, 1028	S39.092A	748, 988	S40.269A	478, 988	S41.011A	461, 988	S41.152A	461, 989	S42.021G	310
S37.90XD	805	S39.092D	805	S40.269D	805	S41.011D	806	S41.152D	806	S42.021K	380
S37.90XS	529, 535, 543	S39.092S	748	S40.269S	461	S41.011S	461	S41.152S	461	S42.021P	380
S37.92XA	529, 535, 543, 988, 1028	S39.093A	748, 988	S40.271A	461, 988	S41.012A	461, 988	S41.159A	461, 989	S42.021S	310
S37.92XD	805	S39.093D	805	S40.271D	805	S41.012D	806	S41.159D	806	S42.022A	349, 989
S37.92XS	529, 535, 543	S39.093S	748	S40.271S	461	S41.012S	461	S41.159S	461	S42.022B	349, 989
S37.93XA	529, 535, 543, 988, 1028	S39.81XA	748, 988	S40.272A	461, 988	S41.019A	461, 988	S42.001A	349, 989	S42.022D	310
S37.93XD	805	S39.81XD	805	S40.272D	805	S41.019D	806	S42.001B	349, 989	S42.022G	310
S37.93XS	529, 535, 543	S39.81XS	748	S40.272S	461	S41.019S	461	S42.001G	310	S42.022K	380
S37.99XA	529, 535, 543, 988, 1028	S39.82XA	748, 988	S40.279A	461, 988	S41.021A	748, 988	S42.001K	380	S42.022P	380
S37.99XD	805	S39.82XD	805	S40.279D	805	S41.021D	806	S42.001P	380	S42.022S	310
S37.99XS	529, 535, 543	S39.82XS	748	S40.279S	461	S41.021S	461	S42.001S	310	S42.023A	349, 989
S38.001A	529, 988	S39.83XA	748, 988	S40.811A	461, 988	S41.022A	748, 988	S42.002A	349, 989	S42.023B	349, 989
S38.001D	805	S39.83XD	805	S40.811D	805	S41.022D	806	S42.002B	349, 989	S42.023D	310
S38.001S	461	S39.83XS	748	S40.811S	461	S41.022S	461	S42.002D	310	S42.023G	310
S38.002A	535, 543, 988	S39.840A	748, 988	S40.812A	461, 988	S41.029A	748, 988	S42.002G	310	S42.023K	380
S38.002D	805	S39.840D	805	S40.812D	805	S41.029D	806	S42.002K	380	S42.023P	380
S38.002S	461	S39.840S	748	S40.812S	461	S41.029S	461	S42.002P	380	S42.023S	310
S38.01XA	529, 988	S39.848A	748, 988	S40.819A	461, 988	S41.031A	461, 988	S42.002S	310	S42.024A	349, 989
S38.01XD	805	S39.848D	805	S40.819D	805	S41.031D	806	S42.009A	349, 989	S42.024B	349, 989
S38.01XS	461	S39.848S	748	S40.819S	461	S41.031S	461	S42.009B	349, 989	S42.024D	310
S38.02XA	529, 988	S39.91XA	748, 988	S40.821A	461, 988	S41.032A	461, 988	S42.009D	310	S42.024G	310
S38.02XD	805	S39.91XD	805	S40.821D	805	S41.032D	806	S42.009G	310	S42.024K	380
		S39.91XS	748	S40.821S	461	S41.032S	461	S42.009K	380	S42.024P	380
		S39.92XA	748, 988	S40.822A	461, 988	S41.039A	461, 988	S42.009P	380	S42.024S	310
		S39.92XD	805	S40.822D	805	S41.039D	806	S42.009S	310	S42.025A	349, 989
		S39.92XS	748	S40.822S	461	S41.039S	461	S42.011A	349, 989	S42.025B	349, 989
		S39.93XA	748, 988	S40.829A	461, 988	S41.041A	748, 988	S42.011B	349, 989	S42.025D	310
		S39.93XD	805	S40.829D	805	S41.041D	806	S42.011D	310	S42.025G	310
		S39.93XS	748	S40.829S	461	S41.041S	461	S42.011G	310	S42.025K	380
		S39.94XA	748, 988	S40.841A	461, 988	S41.042A	748, 989	S42.011K	380	S42.025P	380
		S39.94XD	805	S40.841D	805	S41.042D	806	S42.011P	380	S42.025S	310
		S39.94XS	748	S40.841S	461	S41.042S	461	S42.011S	310	S42.026A	349, 989
		S40.011A	461, 988	S40.842A	461, 988	S41.049A	748, 989	S42.012A	349, 989	S42.026B	349, 989
		S40.011D	805	S40.842D	805	S41.049D	806			S42.026D	310

Code	Page	Code	Page	Code	Page	Code	Page	Code	Page	Code	Page
S42.026G	310	S42.114P	380	S42.136A	349,989	S42.191B	989	S42.221P	381	S42.253A	349,990
S42.026K	380	S42.114S	310	S42.136B	349,989	S42.191B	381	S42.221S	311	S42.253B	349,990,1031
S42.026P	380	S42.115A	380,989	S42.136D	311	S42.191D	311	S42.222A	349,989	S42.253D	311
S42.026S	310	S42.115B	380,989	S42.136G	311	S42.191G	311	S42.222B	349,989,1030	S42.253G	311
S42.031A	349,989	S42.115D	310	S42.136K	380	S42.191K	381	S42.222D	311	S42.253K	381
S42.031B	349,989	S42.115G	310	S42.136P	380	S42.191P	381	S42.222G	311	S42.253P	381
S42.031D	310	S42.115K	380	S42.136S	311	S42.191S	311	S42.222K	381	S42.253S	311
S42.031G	310	S42.115P	380	S42.141A	349,989	S42.192A	989	S42.222P	381	S42.254A	349,990
S42.031K	380	S42.115S	310	S42.141B	349,989	S42.192A	381	S42.222S	311	S42.254B	349,990,1031
S42.031P	380	S42.116A	380,989	S42.141D	311	S42.192B	989	S42.223A	349,989	S42.254D	311
S42.031S	310	S42.116B	380,989	S42.141G	311	S42.192B	381	S42.223B	349,989,1030	S42.254G	311
S42.032A	349,989	S42.116D	310	S42.141K	380	S42.192D	311	S42.223D	311	S42.254K	381
S42.032B	349,989	S42.116G	310	S42.141P	380	S42.192G	311	S42.223G	311	S42.254P	381
S42.032D	310	S42.116K	380	S42.141S	311	S42.192K	381	S42.223K	381	S42.254S	311
S42.032G	310	S42.116P	380	S42.142A	349,989	S42.192P	381	S42.223P	381	S42.255A	349,990
S42.032K	380	S42.116S	310	S42.142B	349,989	S42.192S	311	S42.223S	311	S42.255B	349,990,1031
S42.032P	380	S42.121A	349,989	S42.142D	311	S42.199A	989	S42.224A	349,989	S42.255D	311
S42.032S	310	S42.121B	349,989	S42.142G	311	S42.199A	381	S42.224B	349,989,1030	S42.255G	311
S42.033A	349,989	S42.121D	310	S42.142K	380	S42.199B	989	S42.224D	311	S42.255K	381
S42.033B	349,989	S42.121G	310	S42.142P	380	S42.199B	381	S42.224G	311	S42.255P	381
S42.033D	310	S42.121K	380	S42.142S	311	S42.199D	311	S42.224K	381	S42.255S	311
S42.033G	310	S42.121P	380	S42.143A	349,989	S42.199G	311	S42.224P	381	S42.256A	349,990
S42.033K	380	S42.121S	310	S42.143B	349,989	S42.199K	381	S42.224S	311	S42.256B	349,990,1031
S42.033P	380	S42.122A	349,989	S42.143D	311	S42.199P	381	S42.225A	349,989	S42.256D	311
S42.033S	310	S42.122B	349,989	S42.143G	311	S42.199S	311	S42.225B	349,989,1030	S42.256G	311
S42.034A	349,989	S42.122D	310	S42.143K	380	S42.201A	349,989	S42.225D	311	S42.256K	381
S42.034B	349,989	S42.122G	310	S42.143P	380	S42.201B	349,989,1030	S42.225G	311	S42.256P	381
S42.034D	310	S42.122K	380	S42.143S	311	S42.201D	311	S42.225K	381	S42.256S	311
S42.034G	310	S42.122P	380	S42.144A	349,989	S42.201G	311	S42.225P	381	S42.261A	349,990
S42.034K	380	S42.122S	310	S42.144B	349,989	S42.201K	381	S42.225S	311	S42.261B	349,990,1031
S42.034P	380	S42.123A	349,989	S42.144D	311	S42.201P	381	S42.226A	349,989	S42.261D	311
S42.034S	310	S42.123B	349,989	S42.144G	311	S42.201S	311	S42.226B	349,989,1030	S42.261G	311
S42.035A	349,989	S42.123D	310	S42.144K	380	S42.202A	349,989	S42.226D	311	S42.261K	311
S42.035B	349,989	S42.123G	310	S42.144P	380	S42.202B	349,989,1030	S42.226G	311	S42.261P	381
S42.035D	310	S42.123K	380	S42.144S	311	S42.202D	311	S42.226K	381	S42.261S	311
S42.035G	310	S42.123P	380	S42.145A	349,989	S42.202G	311	S42.226P	381	S42.262A	349,990
S42.035K	380	S42.123S	310	S42.145B	349,989	S42.202K	381	S42.226S	311	S42.262B	349,990,1031
S42.035P	380	S42.124A	349,989	S42.145D	311	S42.202P	381	S42.231A	349,989	S42.262D	311
S42.035S	310	S42.124B	349,989	S42.145G	311	S42.202S	311	S42.231B	349,990,1030	S42.262G	311
S42.036A	349,989	S42.124D	310	S42.145K	380	S42.209A	349,989	S42.231D	311	S42.262K	381
S42.036B	349,989	S42.124G	310	S42.145P	380	S42.209B	349,989,1030	S42.231G	311	S42.262P	381
S42.036D	310	S42.124K	380	S42.145S	311	S42.209D	311	S42.231K	381	S42.262S	311
S42.036G	310	S42.124P	380	S42.146A	349,989	S42.209G	311	S42.231P	381	S42.263A	349,990
S42.036K	380	S42.124S	310	S42.146B	349,989	S42.209K	381	S42.231S	311	S42.263B	350,990,1031
S42.036P	380	S42.125A	349,989	S42.146D	311	S42.209P	381	S42.232A	349,989	S42.263D	311
S42.036S	310	S42.125B	349,989	S42.146G	311	S42.209S	311	S42.232B	349,990,1030	S42.263G	311
S42.101A	349,989	S42.125D	310	S42.146K	380	S42.211A	349,989	S42.232D	311	S42.263K	381
S42.101B	349,989	S42.125G	310	S42.146P	380	S42.211B	349,989,1030	S42.232G	311	S42.263P	381
S42.101D	310	S42.125K	380	S42.146S	311	S42.211D	311	S42.232K	381	S42.263S	311
S42.101G	310	S42.125P	380	S42.151A	349,989	S42.211G	311	S42.232P	381	S42.264A	350,990
S42.101K	380	S42.125S	310	S42.151B	349,989	S42.211K	381	S42.232S	311	S42.264B	350,990,1031
S42.101P	380	S42.126A	349,989	S42.151D	311	S42.211P	381	S42.239A	349,989	S42.264D	311
S42.101S	310	S42.126B	349,989	S42.151G	311	S42.211S	311	S42.239B	349,990,1031	S42.264G	311
S42.102A	349,989	S42.126D	310	S42.151K	380	S42.212A	349,989	S42.239D	311	S42.264K	381
S42.102B	349,989	S42.126G	310	S42.151P	380	S42.212B	349,989,1030	S42.239G	311	S42.264P	381
S42.102D	310	S42.126K	380	S42.151S	311	S42.212D	311	S42.239K	381	S42.264S	311
S42.102G	310	S42.126P	380	S42.152A	349,989	S42.212G	311	S42.239P	381	S42.265A	350,990
S42.102K	380	S42.126S	310	S42.152B	349,989	S42.212K	381	S42.239S	311	S42.265B	350,990,1031
S42.102P	380	S42.131A	349,989	S42.152D	311	S42.212P	381	S42.241A	349,990	S42.265D	311
S42.102S	310	S42.131B	349,989	S42.152G	311	S42.212S	311	S42.241B	349,990,1031	S42.265G	311
S42.109A	349,989	S42.131D	311	S42.152K	381	S42.213A	349,989	S42.241D	311	S42.265K	381
S42.109B	349,989	S42.131G	311	S42.152P	381	S42.213B	349,989,1030	S42.241G	311	S42.265P	381
S42.109D	310	S42.131K	380	S42.152S	311	S42.213D	311	S42.241K	381	S42.265S	311
S42.109G	310	S42.131P	380	S42.153A	349,989	S42.213G	311	S42.241P	381	S42.266A	350,990
S42.109K	380	S42.131S	311	S42.153B	349,989	S42.213K	381	S42.241S	311	S42.266B	350,990,1031
S42.109P	380	S42.132A	349,989	S42.153D	311	S42.213P	381	S42.242A	349,990	S42.266D	311
S42.109S	310	S42.132B	349,989	S42.153G	311	S42.213S	311	S42.242B	349,990,1031	S42.266G	311
S42.111A	380,989	S42.132D	311	S42.153K	381	S42.214A	349,989	S42.242D	311	S42.266K	381
S42.111B	380,989	S42.132G	311	S42.153P	381	S42.214B	349,989,1030	S42.242G	311	S42.266P	381
S42.111D	310	S42.132K	380	S42.153S	311	S42.214D	311	S42.242P	381	S42.266S	311
S42.111G	310	S42.132P	380	S42.154A	349,989	S42.214G	311	S42.242S	311	S42.271A	350,990
S42.111K	380	S42.132S	311	S42.154B	349,989	S42.214K	381	S42.249A	349,990	S42.271D	311
S42.111P	380	S42.133A	349,989	S42.154D	311	S42.214P	381	S42.249B	349,990,1031	S42.271G	311
S42.111S	310	S42.133B	349,989	S42.154G	311	S42.214S	311	S42.249D	311	S42.271K	381
S42.112A	380,989	S42.133D	311	S42.154K	381	S42.215A	349,989	S42.249G	311	S42.271P	381
S42.112B	380,989	S42.133G	311	S42.154P	381	S42.215B	349,989,1030	S42.249K	381	S42.271S	311
S42.112D	310	S42.133K	380	S42.154S	311	S42.215D	311	S42.249P	381	S42.272A	350,990
S42.112G	310	S42.133P	380	S42.155A	349,989	S42.215G	311	S42.249S	311	S42.272D	311
S42.112K	380	S42.133S	311	S42.155B	349,989	S42.215K	381	S42.251A	349,990	S42.272G	311
S42.112P	380	S42.134A	349,989	S42.155D	311	S42.215P	381	S42.251B	349,990,1031	S42.272K	381
S42.112S	310	S42.134B	349,989	S42.155G	311	S42.215S	311	S42.251D	311	S42.272P	381
S42.113A	380,989	S42.134D	311	S42.155K	381	S42.216A	349,989	S42.251G	311	S42.272S	311
S42.113B	380,989	S42.134G	311	S42.155P	381	S42.216B	349,989,1030	S42.251K	381	S42.279A	350,990
S42.113D	310	S42.134K	380	S42.155S	311	S42.216D	311	S42.251P	381	S42.279D	311
S42.113G	310	S42.134P	380	S42.156A	349,989	S42.216G	311	S42.251S	311	S42.279G	311
S42.113K	380	S42.134S	311	S42.156B	349,989	S42.216K	381	S42.252A	349,990	S42.279K	381
S42.113P	380	S42.135A	349,989	S42.156D	311	S42.216P	381	S42.252B	349,990,1031	S42.279P	381
S42.113S	310	S42.135B	349,989	S42.156G	311	S42.216S	311	S42.252D	311	S42.279S	311
S42.114A	380,989	S42.135D	311	S42.156K	381	S42.221A	349,989	S42.252G	311	S42.291A	350,990
S42.114B	380,989	S42.135G	311	S42.156P	381	S42.221B	349,989,1030	S42.252K	381	S42.291B	350,990,1031
S42.114D	310	S42.135K	380	S42.156S	311	S42.221D	311	S42.252P	381	S42.291D	311
S42.114G	310	S42.135P	380	S42.191A	989	S42.221G	311	S42.252S	311	S42.291G	311
S42.114K	380	S42.135S	311	S42.191A	381	S42.221K	381			S42.291K	381

Code	Page	Code	Page	Code	Page	Code	Page	Code	Page	Code	Page
S42.291P	381	S42.323G	312	S42.344P	381	S42.366A	350, 990	S42.421D	312	S42.442K	382
S42.291S	311	S42.323K	381	S42.344S	312	S42.366B	350, 990, 1031	S42.421G	312	S42.442P	382
S42.292A	350, 990	S42.323P	381	S42.345A	350, 990	S42.366D	312	S42.421K	382	S42.442S	313
S42.292B	350, 990, 1031	S42.323S	312	S42.345B	350, 990, 1031	S42.366G	312	S42.421P	382	S42.443A	350, 990
S42.292D	312	S42.324A	350, 990	S42.345D	312	S42.366K	382	S42.421S	312	S42.443B	350, 990, 1031
S42.292G	312	S42.324B	350, 990, 1031	S42.345G	312	S42.366P	382	S42.422A	350, 990	S42.443D	313
S42.292K	381	S42.324D	312	S42.345K	381	S42.366S	312	S42.422B	350, 990, 1031	S42.443G	313
S42.292P	381	S42.324G	312	S42.345P	381	S42.391A	350, 990	S42.422D	312	S42.443K	382
S42.292S	312	S42.324K	381	S42.345S	312	S42.391B	350, 990, 1031	S42.422G	312	S42.443P	382
S42.293A	350, 990	S42.324P	381	S42.346A	350, 990	S42.391D	312	S42.422K	382	S42.443S	313
S42.293B	350, 990, 1031	S42.324S	312	S42.346B	350, 990, 1031	S42.391G	312	S42.422P	382	S42.444A	350, 990
S42.293D	312	S42.325A	350, 990	S42.346D	312	S42.391K	382	S42.422S	312	S42.444B	350, 991, 1031
S42.293G	312	S42.325B	350, 990, 1031	S42.346G	312	S42.391P	382	S42.423A	350, 990	S42.444D	313
S42.293K	381	S42.325D	312	S42.346K	381	S42.391S	312	S42.423B	350, 990, 1031	S42.444G	313
S42.293P	381	S42.325G	312	S42.346P	381	S42.392A	350, 990	S42.423D	312	S42.444K	382
S42.293S	312	S42.325K	381	S42.346S	312	S42.392B	350, 990, 1031	S42.423G	312	S42.444P	382
S42.294A	350, 990	S42.325P	381	S42.351A	350, 990	S42.392D	312	S42.423K	382	S42.444S	313
S42.294B	350, 990, 1031	S42.325S	312	S42.351B	350, 990, 1031	S42.392G	312	S42.423P	382	S42.445A	350, 991
S42.294D	312	S42.326A	350, 990	S42.351D	312	S42.392K	382	S42.423S	312	S42.445B	350, 991, 1031
S42.294G	312	S42.326B	350, 990, 1031	S42.351G	312	S42.392P	382	S42.424A	350, 990	S42.445D	313
S42.294K	381	S42.326D	312	S42.351K	381	S42.392S	312	S42.424B	350, 990, 1031	S42.445G	313
S42.294P	381	S42.326G	312	S42.351P	381	S42.399A	350, 990	S42.424D	312	S42.445K	382
S42.294S	312	S42.326K	381	S42.351S	312	S42.399B	350, 990, 1031	S42.424G	312	S42.445P	382
S42.295A	350, 990	S42.326P	381	S42.352A	350, 990	S42.399D	312	S42.424K	382	S42.445S	313
S42.295B	350, 990, 1031	S42.326S	312	S42.352B	350, 990, 1031	S42.399G	312	S42.424P	382	S42.446A	350, 991
S42.295D	312	S42.331A	350, 990	S42.352D	312	S42.399K	382	S42.424S	312	S42.446B	350, 991, 1031
S42.295G	312	S42.331B	350, 990, 1031	S42.352G	312	S42.399P	382	S42.425A	350, 990	S42.446D	313
S42.295K	381	S42.331D	312	S42.352K	381	S42.399S	312	S42.425B	350, 990, 1031	S42.446G	313
S42.295P	381	S42.331G	312	S42.352P	381	S42.401A	350, 990	S42.425D	312	S42.446K	382
S42.295S	312	S42.331K	381	S42.352S	312	S42.401B	350, 990, 1031	S42.425G	312	S42.446P	382
S42.296A	350, 990	S42.331P	381	S42.353A	350, 990	S42.401D	312	S42.425K	382	S42.446S	313
S42.296B	350, 990, 1031	S42.331S	312	S42.353B	350, 990, 1031	S42.401G	312	S42.425P	382	S42.447A	350, 991
S42.296D	312	S42.332A	350, 990	S42.353D	312	S42.401K	382	S42.425S	312	S42.447B	350, 991, 1031
S42.296G	312	S42.332B	350, 990, 1031	S42.353G	312	S42.401P	382	S42.426A	350, 990	S42.447D	313
S42.296K	381	S42.332D	312	S42.353K	381	S42.401S	312	S42.426B	350, 990, 1031	S42.447G	313
S42.296P	381	S42.332G	312	S42.353P	381	S42.402A	350, 990	S42.426D	313	S42.447K	382
S42.296S	312	S42.332K	381	S42.353S	312	S42.402B	350, 990, 1031	S42.426G	313	S42.447P	382
S42.301A	350, 990	S42.332P	381	S42.354A	350, 990	S42.402D	312	S42.426K	382	S42.447S	313
S42.301B	350, 990, 1031	S42.332S	312	S42.354B	350, 990, 1031	S42.402G	312	S42.426P	382	S42.448A	350, 991
S42.301D	312	S42.333A	350, 990	S42.354D	312	S42.402K	382	S42.426S	313	S42.448B	350, 991, 1031
S42.301G	312	S42.333B	350, 990, 1031	S42.354G	312	S42.402P	382	S42.431A	350, 990	S42.448D	313
S42.301K	381	S42.333D	312	S42.354K	381	S42.402S	312	S42.431B	350, 990, 1031	S42.448G	313
S42.301P	381	S42.333G	312	S42.354P	381	S42.409A	350, 990	S42.431D	313	S42.448K	382
S42.301S	312	S42.333K	381	S42.354S	312	S42.409B	350, 990, 1031	S42.431G	313	S42.448P	382
S42.302A	350, 990	S42.333P	381	S42.355A	350, 990	S42.409D	312	S42.431K	382	S42.448S	313
S42.302B	350, 990, 1031	S42.333S	312	S42.355B	350, 990, 1031	S42.409G	312	S42.431P	382	S42.449A	350, 991
S42.302D	312	S42.334A	350, 990	S42.355D	312	S42.409K	382	S42.431S	313	S42.449B	350, 991, 1031
S42.302G	312	S42.334B	350, 990, 1031	S42.355G	312	S42.409P	382	S42.432A	350, 990	S42.449D	313
S42.302K	381	S42.334D	312	S42.355K	381	S42.409S	312	S42.432B	350, 990, 1031	S42.449G	313
S42.302P	381	S42.334G	312	S42.355P	381	S42.411A	350, 990	S42.432D	313	S42.449K	382
S42.302S	312	S42.334K	381	S42.355S	312	S42.411B	350, 990, 1031	S42.432G	313	S42.449P	382
S42.309A	350, 990	S42.334P	381	S42.356A	350, 990	S42.411D	312	S42.432K	382	S42.449S	313
S42.309B	350, 990, 1031	S42.334S	312	S42.356B	350, 990, 1031	S42.411G	312	S42.432P	382	S42.451A	350, 991
S42.309D	312	S42.335A	350, 990	S42.356D	312	S42.411K	382	S42.432S	313	S42.451B	350, 991, 1031
S42.309G	312	S42.335B	350, 990, 1031	S42.356G	312	S42.411P	382	S42.433A	350, 990	S42.451D	313
S42.309K	381	S42.335D	312	S42.356K	381	S42.411S	312	S42.433B	350, 990, 1031	S42.451G	313
S42.309P	381	S42.335G	312	S42.356P	381	S42.412A	350, 990	S42.433D	313	S42.451K	382
S42.309S	312	S42.335K	381	S42.356S	312	S42.412B	350, 990, 1031	S42.433G	313	S42.451P	382
S42.311A	350, 990	S42.335P	381	S42.361A	350, 990	S42.412D	312	S42.433K	382	S42.451S	313
S42.311D	312	S42.335S	312	S42.361B	350, 990, 1031	S42.412G	312	S42.433P	382	S42.452A	350, 991
S42.311G	312	S42.336A	350, 990	S42.361D	312	S42.412K	382	S42.433S	313	S42.452B	350, 991, 1031
S42.311K	381	S42.336B	350, 990, 1031	S42.361G	312	S42.412P	382	S42.434A	350, 990	S42.452D	313
S42.311P	381	S42.336D	312	S42.361K	381	S42.412S	312	S42.434B	350, 990, 1031	S42.452G	313
S42.311S	312	S42.336G	312	S42.361P	381	S42.413A	350, 990	S42.434D	313	S42.452K	382
S42.312A	350, 990	S42.336K	381	S42.361S	312	S42.413B	350, 990, 1031	S42.434G	313	S42.452P	382
S42.312D	312	S42.336P	381	S42.362A	350, 990	S42.413D	312	S42.434K	382	S42.452S	313
S42.312G	312	S42.336S	312	S42.362B	350, 990, 1031	S42.413G	312	S42.434P	382	S42.453A	350, 991
S42.312K	381	S42.341A	350, 990	S42.362D	312	S42.413K	382	S42.434S	313	S42.453B	350, 991, 1031
S42.312P	381	S42.341B	350, 990, 1031	S42.362G	312	S42.413P	382	S42.435A	350, 990	S42.453D	313
S42.312S	312	S42.341D	312	S42.362K	381	S42.413S	312	S42.435B	350, 990, 1031	S42.453G	313
S42.319A	350, 990	S42.341G	312	S42.362P	381	S42.414A	350, 990	S42.435D	313	S42.453K	382
S42.319D	312	S42.341K	381	S42.362S	312	S42.414B	350, 990, 1031	S42.435G	313	S42.453P	382
S42.319G	312	S42.341P	381	S42.363A	350, 990	S42.414D	312	S42.435K	313	S42.453S	313
S42.319K	381	S42.341S	312	S42.363B	350, 990, 1031	S42.414G	312	S42.435P	382	S42.454A	350, 991
S42.319P	381	S42.342A	350, 990	S42.363D	312	S42.414K	382	S42.435S	313	S42.454B	350, 991, 1031
S42.319S	312	S42.342B	350, 990, 1031	S42.363G	312	S42.414P	382	S42.436A	350, 990	S42.454D	313
S42.321A	350, 990	S42.342D	312	S42.363K	381	S42.414S	312	S42.436B	350, 990, 1031	S42.454G	313
S42.321B	350, 990, 1031	S42.342G	312	S42.363P	381	S42.415A	350, 990	S42.436D	313	S42.454K	382
S42.321D	312	S42.342K	381	S42.363S	312	S42.415B	350, 990, 1031	S42.436G	313	S42.454P	382
S42.321G	312	S42.342P	381	S42.364A	350, 990	S42.415D	312	S42.436K	382	S42.454S	313
S42.321K	381	S42.342S	312	S42.364B	350, 990, 1031	S42.415G	312	S42.436P	382	S42.455A	350, 991
S42.321P	381	S42.343A	350, 990	S42.364D	312	S42.415K	382	S42.436S	313	S42.455B	350, 991, 1031
S42.321S	312	S42.343B	350, 990, 1031	S42.364G	312	S42.415P	382	S42.441A	350, 990	S42.455D	313
S42.322A	350, 990	S42.343D	312	S42.364K	381	S42.415S	312	S42.441B	350, 990, 1031	S42.455G	313
S42.322B	350, 990, 1031	S42.343G	312	S42.364P	381	S42.416A	350, 990	S42.441D	313	S42.455K	382
S42.322D	312	S42.343K	381	S42.364S	312	S42.416B	350, 990, 1031	S42.441G	313	S42.455P	382
S42.322G	312	S42.343P	381	S42.365A	350, 990	S42.416D	312	S42.441K	382	S42.455S	313
S42.322K	381	S42.343S	312	S42.365B	350, 990, 1031	S42.416G	312	S42.441P	382	S42.456A	350, 991
S42.322P	381	S42.344A	350, 990	S42.365D	312	S42.416K	382	S42.441S	313	S42.456B	350, 991, 1031
S42.322S	312	S42.344B	350, 990, 1031	S42.365G	312	S42.416P	382	S42.442A	350, 990	S42.456D	313
S42.323A	350, 990	S42.344D	312	S42.365K	382	S42.416S	312	S42.442B	350, 990, 1031	S42.456G	313
S42.323B	350, 990, 1031	S42.344G	312	S42.365P	382	S42.421A	350, 990	S42.442D	313	S42.456K	382
S42.323D	312	S42.344K	381	S42.365S	312	S42.421B	350, 990, 1031	S42.442G	313	S42.456P	382

Code	Page	Code	Page	Code	Page	Code	Page	Code	Page	Code	Page
S42.456S	313	S42.482G	313	S43.011S	351	S43.122S	351	S43.303S	351	S43.50XS	352
S42.461A	350, 991	S42.482K	382	S43.012A	351, 991	S43.129A	351, 991	S43.304A	351, 991	S43.51XA	352, 991
S42.461B	350, 991, 1031	S42.482P	382	S43.012D	806	S43.129D	806	S43.304D	806	S43.51XD	806
S42.461D	313	S42.482S	313	S43.012S	351	S43.129S	351	S43.304S	351	S43.51XS	352
S42.461G	313	S42.489A	351, 991	S43.013A	351, 991	S43.131A	351, 991	S43.305A	351, 991	S43.52XA	352, 991
S42.461K	382	S42.489D	313	S43.013D	806	S43.131D	806	S43.305D	806	S43.52XD	806
S42.461P	382	S42.489G	313	S43.013S	351	S43.131S	351	S43.305S	351	S43.52XS	352
S42.461S	313	S42.489K	382	S43.014A	351, 991	S43.132A	351, 991	S43.306A	351, 991	S43.60XA	352, 991
S42.462A	350, 991	S42.489P	382	S43.014D	806	S43.132D	806	S43.306D	806	S43.60XD	806
S42.462B	350, 991, 1031	S42.489S	313	S43.014S	351	S43.132S	351	S43.306S	351	S43.60XS	352
S42.462D	313	S42.491A	351, 991	S43.015A	351, 991	S43.139A	351, 991	S43.311A	351, 991	S43.61XA	352, 991
S42.462G	313	S42.491B	351, 991, 1031	S43.015D	806	S43.139D	806	S43.311D	806	S43.61XD	806
S42.462K	382	S42.491D	313	S43.015S	351	S43.139S	351	S43.311S	351	S43.61XS	352
S42.462P	382	S42.491G	313	S43.016A	351, 991	S43.141A	351, 991	S43.312A	351, 991	S43.62XA	352, 991
S42.462S	313	S42.491K	382	S43.016D	806	S43.141D	806	S43.312D	806	S43.62XD	806
S42.463A	350	S42.491P	382	S43.016S	351	S43.141S	351	S43.312S	351	S43.62XS	352
S42.463B	351, 991, 1031	S42.491S	313	S43.021A	351, 991	S43.142A	351, 991	S43.313A	351, 991	S43.80XA	991
S42.463D	313	S42.492A	351, 991	S43.021D	806	S43.142D	806	S43.313D	806	S43.80XA	352
S42.463G	313	S42.492B	351, 991, 1031	S43.021S	351	S43.142S	351	S43.313S	351	S43.80XD	806
S42.463K	382	S42.492D	313	S43.022A	351, 991	S43.149A	351, 991	S43.314A	351, 991	S43.80XS	352
S42.463P	382	S42.492G	313	S43.022D	806	S43.149D	806	S43.314D	806	S43.81XA	992
S42.463S	313	S42.492K	382	S43.022S	351	S43.149S	351	S43.314S	351	S43.81XA	352
S42.464A	351, 991	S42.492P	382	S43.023A	351, 991	S43.151A	351, 991	S43.315A	352, 991	S43.81XD	806
S42.464B	351, 991, 1031	S42.492S	313	S43.023D	806	S43.151D	806	S43.315D	806	S43.81XS	352
S42.464D	313	S42.493A	351, 991	S43.023S	351	S43.151S	351	S43.315S	352	S43.82XA	992
S42.464G	313	S42.493B	351, 991, 1031	S43.024A	351, 991	S43.152A	351, 991	S43.316A	352, 991	S43.82XA	352
S42.464K	382	S42.493D	313	S43.024D	806	S43.152D	806	S43.316D	806	S43.82XD	806
S42.464P	382	S42.493G	313	S43.024S	351	S43.152S	351	S43.316S	352	S43.82XS	352
S42.464S	313	S42.493K	382	S43.025A	351, 991	S43.159A	351, 991	S43.391A	352, 991	S43.90XA	352, 992
S42.465A	351, 991	S42.493P	382	S43.025D	806	S43.159D	806	S43.391D	806	S43.90XD	806
S42.465B	351, 991, 1031	S42.493S	313	S43.025S	351	S43.159S	351	S43.391S	352	S43.90XS	352
S42.465D	313	S42.494A	351, 991	S43.026A	351, 991	S43.201A	105, 991	S43.392A	352, 991	S43.91XA	352, 992
S42.465G	313	S42.494B	351, 991, 1031	S43.026D	806	S43.201D	806	S43.392D	806	S43.91XD	806
S42.465K	382	S42.494D	313	S43.026S	351	S43.201S	351	S43.392S	352	S43.91XS	352
S42.465P	382	S42.494G	313	S43.031A	351, 991	S43.202A	105, 991	S43.393A	352, 991	S43.92XA	352, 992
S42.465S	313	S42.494K	382	S43.031D	806	S43.202D	806	S43.393D	806	S43.92XD	806
S42.466A	351, 991	S42.494P	382	S43.031S	351	S43.202S	351	S43.393S	352	S43.92XS	352
S42.466B	351, 991, 1031	S42.494S	313	S43.032A	351, 991	S43.203A	105, 991	S43.394A	352, 991	S44.00XA	46, 992, 1031
S42.466D	313	S42.495A	351, 991	S43.032D	806	S43.203D	806	S43.394D	806	S44.00XD	806
S42.466G	313	S42.495B	351, 991, 1031	S43.032S	351	S43.203S	351	S43.394S	352	S44.00XS	53
S42.466K	382	S42.495D	313	S43.033A	351, 991	S43.204A	105, 991	S43.395A	352, 991	S44.01XA	46, 992, 1031
S42.466P	382	S42.495G	313	S43.033D	806	S43.204D	806	S43.395D	806	S44.01XD	806
S42.466S	313	S42.495K	382	S43.033S	351	S43.204S	351	S43.395S	352	S44.01XS	53
S42.471A	351, 991	S42.495P	382	S43.034A	351, 991	S43.205A	105, 991	S43.396A	352, 991	S44.02XA	46, 992, 1031
S42.471B	351, 991, 1031	S42.495S	313	S43.034D	806	S43.205D	806	S43.396D	806	S44.02XD	806
S42.471D	313	S42.496A	351, 991	S43.034S	351	S43.205S	351	S43.396S	352	S44.02XS	53
S42.471G	313	S42.496B	351, 991, 1031	S43.035A	351, 991	S43.206A	105, 991	S43.401A	352, 991	S44.10XA	46, 992, 1031
S42.471K	382	S42.496D	313	S43.035D	806	S43.206D	806	S43.401D	806	S44.10XD	806
S42.471P	382	S42.496G	313	S43.035S	351	S43.206S	351	S43.401S	352	S44.10XS	53
S42.471S	313	S42.496K	382	S43.036A	351, 991	S43.211A	105, 991	S43.402A	352, 991	S44.11XA	46, 992, 1031
S42.472A	351, 991	S42.496P	382	S43.036D	806	S43.211D	806	S43.402D	806	S44.11XD	806
S42.472B	351, 991, 1031	S42.496S	313	S43.036S	351	S43.211S	351	S43.402S	352	S44.11XS	53
S42.472D	313	S42.90XA	351, 991	S43.081A	351, 991	S43.212A	105, 991	S43.409A	352, 991	S44.12XA	46, 992, 1031
S42.472G	313	S42.90XB	351, 991, 1031	S43.081D	806	S43.212D	806	S43.409D	806	S44.12XD	806
S42.472K	382	S42.90XD	313	S43.081S	351	S43.212S	351	S43.409S	352	S44.12XS	53
S42.472P	382	S42.90XG	313	S43.082A	351, 991	S43.213A	105, 991	S43.411A	352, 991	S44.20XA	46, 992, 1031
S42.472S	313	S42.90XK	382	S43.082D	806	S43.213D	806	S43.411D	806	S44.20XD	806
S42.473A	351, 991	S42.90XP	382	S43.082S	351	S43.213S	351	S43.411S	352	S44.20XS	53
S42.473B	351, 991, 1031	S42.90XS	313	S43.083A	351, 991	S43.214A	105, 991	S43.412A	352, 991	S44.21XA	46, 992, 1031
S42.473D	313	S42.91XA	351, 991	S43.083D	806	S43.214D	806	S43.412D	806	S44.21XD	806
S42.473G	313	S42.91XB	351, 991, 1031	S43.083S	351	S43.214S	351	S43.412S	352	S44.21XS	53
S42.473K	382	S42.91XD	313	S43.084A	351, 991	S43.215A	105, 991	S43.419A	352, 991	S44.22XA	46, 992, 1031
S42.473P	382	S42.91XG	313	S43.084D	806	S43.215D	806	S43.419D	806	S44.22XD	806
S42.473S	313	S42.91XK	382	S43.084S	351	S43.215S	351	S43.419S	352	S44.22XS	53
S42.474A	351, 991	S42.91XP	382	S43.085A	351, 991	S43.216A	105, 991	S43.421A	352, 991	S44.30XA	46, 992, 1031
S42.474B	351, 991, 1031	S42.91XS	313	S43.085D	806	S43.216D	806	S43.421D	806	S44.30XD	806
S42.474D	313	S42.92XA	351, 991	S43.085S	351	S43.216S	351	S43.421S	352	S44.30XS	53
S42.474G	313	S42.92XB	351, 991, 1031	S43.086A	351, 991	S43.221A	105, 991	S43.422A	352, 991	S44.31XA	46, 992, 1031
S42.474K	382	S42.92XD	313	S43.086D	806	S43.221D	806	S43.422D	806	S44.31XD	806
S42.474P	382	S42.92XG	313	S43.086S	351	S43.221S	351	S43.422S	352	S44.31XS	53
S42.474S	313	S42.92XK	382	S43.101A	351, 991	S43.222A	105, 991	S43.429A	352, 991	S44.32XA	46, 992, 1031
S42.475A	351, 991	S42.92XP	382	S43.101D	806	S43.222D	806	S43.429D	806	S44.32XD	806
S42.475B	351, 991, 1031	S42.92XS	313	S43.101S	351	S43.222S	351	S43.429S	352	S44.32XS	53
S42.475D	313	S43.001A	351, 991	S43.102A	351, 991	S43.223A	105, 991	S43.431A	352, 991	S44.40XA	46, 992
S42.475G	313	S43.001D	806	S43.102D	806	S43.223D	806	S43.431D	806	S44.40XD	806
S42.475K	382	S43.001S	351	S43.102S	351	S43.223S	351	S43.431S	352	S44.40XS	53
S42.475P	382	S43.002A	351, 991	S43.109A	351, 991	S43.224A	105, 991	S43.432A	352, 991	S44.41XA	46, 992
S42.475S	313	S43.002D	806	S43.109D	806	S43.224D	806	S43.432D	806	S44.41XD	806
S42.476A	351, 991	S43.002S	351	S43.109S	351	S43.224S	351	S43.432S	352	S44.41XS	53
S42.476B	351, 991, 1031	S43.003A	351, 991	S43.111A	351, 991	S43.225A	105, 991	S43.439A	352, 991	S44.42XA	46, 992
S42.476D	313	S43.003D	806	S43.111D	806	S43.225D	806	S43.439D	806	S44.42XD	806
S42.476G	313	S43.003S	351	S43.111S	351	S43.225S	351	S43.439S	352	S44.42XS	53
S42.476K	382	S43.004A	351, 991	S43.112A	351, 991	S43.226A	105, 991	S43.491A	352, 991	S44.50XA	46, 992
S42.476P	382	S43.004D	806	S43.112D	806	S43.226D	806	S43.491D	806	S44.50XD	806
S42.476S	313	S43.004S	351	S43.112S	351	S43.226S	351	S43.491S	352	S44.50XS	53
S42.481A	351, 991	S43.005A	351, 991	S43.119A	351, 991	S43.301A	351, 991	S43.492A	352, 991	S44.51XA	46, 992
S42.481D	313	S43.005D	806	S43.119D	806	S43.301D	806	S43.492D	806	S44.51XD	806
S42.481G	313	S43.005S	351	S43.119S	351	S43.301S	351	S43.492S	352	S44.51XS	53
S42.481K	382	S43.006A	351, 991	S43.121A	351, 991	S43.302A	351, 991	S43.499A	352, 991	S44.52XA	46, 992
S42.481P	382	S43.006D	806	S43.121D	806	S43.302D	806	S43.499D	806	S44.52XD	806
S42.481S	313	S43.006S	351	S43.121S	351	S43.302S	351	S43.499S	352	S44.52XS	53
S42.482A	351, 991	S43.011A	351, 991	S43.122A	351, 991	S43.303A	351, 991	S43.50XA	352, 991	S44.8X1A	46, 992, 1031
S42.482D	313	S43.011D	806	S43.122D	806	S43.303D	806	S43.50XD	806	S44.8X1D	807

Code	Page	Code	Page	Code	Page	Code	Page	Code	Page	Code	Page
S44.8X1S	53	S45.292S	169	S46.002S	748	S46.229S	462	S46.911S	352	S49.001S	313
S44.8X2A	46,992,1031	S45.299A	748,992,1031	S46.009A	748,992	S46.291A	748,992	S46.912A	352,992	S49.002A	352,993
S44.8X2D	807	S45.299D	807	S46.009D	807	S46.291D	807	S46.912D	807	S49.002D	313
S44.8X2S	53	S45.299S	169	S46.009S	748	S46.291S	748	S46.912S	352	S49.002G	313
S44.8X9A	46,992	S45.301A	748,992,1031	S46.011A	352,992	S46.292A	748,992	S46.919A	352,992	S49.002K	382
S44.8X9D	807	S45.301D	807	S46.011D	807	S46.292D	807	S46.919D	807	S49.002P	382
S44.8X9S	53	S45.301S	169	S46.011S	352	S46.292S	748	S46.919S	352	S49.002S	313
S44.90XA	46,992	S45.302A	748,992,1031	S46.012A	352,992	S46.299A	748,992	S46.921A	382,992	S49.009A	352,993
S44.90XD	807	S45.302D	807	S46.012D	807	S46.299D	807	S46.921D	807	S49.009D	313
S44.90XS	53	S45.302S	169	S46.012S	352	S46.299S	748	S46.921S	462	S49.009K	382
S44.91XA	46,992	S45.309A	748,992,1031	S46.019A	352,992	S46.301A	748,992	S46.922A	382,992	S49.009P	382
S44.91XD	807	S45.309D	807	S46.019D	807	S46.301D	807	S46.922D	807	S49.009S	313
S44.91XS	53	S45.309S	169	S46.019S	352	S46.301S	748	S46.922S	462	S49.011A	352,993
S44.92XA	46,992	S45.311A	748,992,1031	S46.021A	748,992	S46.302A	748,992	S46.929A	382,992	S49.011D	313
S44.92XD	807	S45.311D	807	S46.021D	807	S46.302D	807	S46.929D	807	S49.011G	313
S44.92XS	53	S45.311S	169	S46.021S	461	S46.302S	749	S46.929S	462	S49.011K	382
S45.001A	748,992,1031	S45.312A	748,992,1031	S46.022A	382,992	S46.309A	749,992	S46.991A	749,992	S49.011P	382
S45.001D	807	S45.312D	807	S46.022D	807	S46.309D	807	S46.991D	807	S49.011S	313
S45.001S	169	S45.312S	169	S46.022S	461	S46.309S	749	S46.991S	749	S49.012A	352,993
S45.002A	748,992,1031	S45.319A	748,992,1031	S46.029A	382,992	S46.311A	352,992	S46.992A	749,992	S49.012D	313
S45.002D	807	S45.319D	807	S46.029D	807	S46.311D	807	S46.992D	807	S49.012G	313
S45.002S	169	S45.319S	169	S46.029S	462	S46.311S	352	S46.992S	749	S49.012K	382
S45.009A	748,992,1031	S45.391A	748,992,1031	S46.091A	748,992	S46.312A	352,992	S46.999A	749,992	S49.012P	382
S45.009D	807	S45.391D	807	S46.091D	807	S46.312D	807	S46.999D	807	S49.012S	313
S45.009S	169	S45.391S	169	S46.091S	748	S46.312S	352	S46.999S	749	S49.019A	352,993
S45.011A	748,992,1031	S45.392A	748,992,1031	S46.092A	748,992	S46.319A	352,992	S47.1XXA	749,992,1032	S49.019D	313
S45.011D	807	S45.392D	807	S46.092D	807	S46.319D	807	S47.1XXD	807	S49.019G	313
S45.011S	169	S45.392S	169	S46.092S	748	S46.319S	352	S47.1XXS	462	S49.019K	382
S45.012A	748,992,1031	S45.399A	748,992,1031	S46.099A	748,992	S46.321A	382,992	S47.2XXA	749,992,1032	S49.019P	382
S45.012D	807	S45.399D	807	S46.099D	807	S46.321D	807	S47.2XXD	807	S49.019S	313
S45.012S	169	S45.399S	169	S46.099S	748	S46.321S	462	S47.2XXS	462	S49.021A	352,993
S45.019A	748,992,1031	S45.801A	748,992,1031	S46.101A	748,992	S46.322A	382,992	S47.9XXA	749,992,1032	S49.021D	314
S45.019D	807	S45.801D	807	S46.101D	807	S46.322D	807	S47.9XXD	807	S49.021G	314
S45.019S	169	S45.801S	169	S46.101S	748	S46.322S	462	S47.9XXS	462	S49.021K	382
S45.091A	748,992,1031	S45.802A	748,992,1031	S46.102A	748,992	S46.329A	382,992	S48.011A	749,992,1032	S49.021P	382
S45.091D	807	S45.802D	807	S46.102D	807	S46.329D	807	S48.011D	807	S49.021S	314
S45.091S	169	S45.802S	169	S46.102S	748	S46.329S	462	S48.011S	313	S49.022A	352,993
S45.092A	748,992,1031	S45.809A	748,992,1031	S46.109A	748,992	S46.391A	749,992	S48.012A	749,992,1032	S49.022D	314
S45.092D	807	S45.809D	807	S46.109D	807	S46.391D	807	S48.012D	807	S49.022G	314
S45.092S	169	S45.809S	169	S46.109S	748	S46.391S	749	S48.012S	313	S49.022K	382
S45.099A	748,992,1031	S45.811A	748,992,1031	S46.111A	352,992	S46.392A	749,992	S48.019A	749,992,1032	S49.022P	382
S45.099D	807	S45.811D	807	S46.111D	807	S46.392D	807	S48.019D	807	S49.022S	314
S45.099S	169	S45.811S	169	S46.111S	352	S46.392S	749	S48.019S	313	S49.029A	352,993
S45.101A	748,992,1031	S45.812A	748,992,1031	S46.112A	352,992	S46.399A	749,992	S48.021A	749,992,1032	S49.029D	314
S45.101D	807	S45.812D	807	S46.112D	807	S46.399D	807	S48.021D	807	S49.029G	314
S45.101S	169	S45.812S	169	S46.112S	352	S46.399S	749	S48.021S	313	S49.029K	382
S45.102A	748,992,1031	S45.819A	748,992,1031	S46.119A	352,992	S46.801A	749,992	S48.022A	749,992,1032	S49.029P	382
S45.102D	807	S45.819D	807	S46.119D	807	S46.801D	807	S48.022D	807	S49.029S	314
S45.102S	169	S45.819S	169	S46.119S	352	S46.801S	749	S48.022S	313	S49.031A	352,993
S45.109A	748,992,1031	S45.891A	992,1031	S46.121A	382,992	S46.802A	749,992	S48.029A	749,992,1032	S49.031D	314
S45.109D	807	S45.891A	748	S46.121D	807	S46.802D	807	S48.029D	807	S49.031G	314
S45.109S	169	S45.891D	807	S46.121S	462	S46.802S	749	S48.029S	313	S49.031K	382
S45.111A	748,992,1031	S45.891S	169	S46.122A	382,992	S46.809A	749,992	S48.111A	749,992,1032	S49.031P	382
S45.111D	807	S45.892A	992,1031	S46.122D	807	S46.809D	807	S48.111D	807	S49.031S	314
S45.111S	169	S45.892A	748	S46.122S	462	S46.809S	749	S48.111S	313	S49.032A	352,993
S45.112A	748,992,1031	S45.892D	807	S46.129A	382,992	S46.811A	352,992	S48.112A	749,992,1032	S49.032D	314
S45.112D	807	S45.892S	169	S46.129D	807	S46.811D	807	S48.112D	807	S49.032G	314
S45.112S	169	S45.899A	992,1031	S46.129S	462	S46.811S	352	S48.112S	313	S49.032K	382
S45.119A	748,992,1031	S45.899A	748	S46.191A	748,992	S46.812A	352,992	S48.119A	749,992,1032	S49.032P	382
S45.119D	807	S45.899D	807	S46.191D	807	S46.812D	807	S48.119D	807	S49.032S	314
S45.119S	169	S45.899S	169	S46.191S	748	S46.812S	352	S48.119S	313	S49.039A	352,993
S45.191A	748,992,1031	S45.901A	748,992,1032	S46.192A	748,992	S46.819A	352,992	S48.121A	749,992,1032	S49.039D	314
S45.191D	807	S45.901D	807	S46.192D	807	S46.819D	807	S48.121D	807	S49.039G	314
S45.191S	169	S45.901S	169	S46.192S	748	S46.819S	352	S48.121S	313	S49.039K	382
S45.192A	748,992,1031	S45.902A	748,992,1032	S46.199A	748,992	S46.821A	382,992	S48.122A	749,992,1032	S49.039P	382
S45.192D	807	S45.902D	807	S46.199D	807	S46.821D	807	S48.122D	807	S49.039S	314
S45.192S	169	S45.902S	169	S46.199S	748	S46.821S	462	S48.122S	313	S49.041A	352,993
S45.199A	748,992,1031	S45.909A	748,992,1032	S46.201A	748,992	S46.822A	382,992	S48.129A	749,992,1032	S49.041D	314
S45.199D	807	S45.909D	807	S46.201D	807	S46.822D	807	S48.129D	807	S49.041G	314
S45.199S	169	S45.909S	169	S46.201S	748	S46.822S	462	S48.129S	313	S49.041K	382
S45.201A	748,992,1031	S45.911A	748,992,1032	S46.202A	748,992	S46.829A	382,992	S48.911A	749,992,1032	S49.041P	382
S45.201D	807	S45.911D	807	S46.202D	807	S46.829D	807	S48.911D	807	S49.041S	314
S45.201S	169	S45.911S	169	S46.202S	748	S46.829S	462	S48.911S	313	S49.042A	352,993
S45.202A	748,992,1031	S45.912A	748,992,1032	S46.209A	748,992	S46.891A	749,992	S48.912A	749,992,1032	S49.042D	314
S45.202D	807	S45.912D	807	S46.209D	807	S46.891D	807	S48.912D	807	S49.042G	314
S45.202S	169	S45.912S	169	S46.209S	748	S46.891S	749	S48.912S	313	S49.042K	383
S45.209A	748,992,1031	S45.919A	748,992,1032	S46.211A	352,992	S46.892A	749,992	S48.919A	749,992,1032	S49.042P	383
S45.209D	807	S45.919D	807	S46.211D	807	S46.892D	807	S48.919D	807	S49.042S	314
S45.209S	169	S45.919S	169	S46.211S	352	S46.892S	749	S48.919S	313	S49.049A	352,993
S45.211A	748,992,1031	S45.991A	748,992,1032	S46.212A	352,992	S46.899A	749,992	S48.921A	749,992,1032	S49.049D	314
S45.211D	807	S45.991D	807	S46.212D	807	S46.899D	807	S48.921D	807	S49.049G	314
S45.211S	169	S45.991S	169	S46.212S	352	S46.899S	749	S48.921S	313	S49.049K	383
S45.212A	748,992,1031	S45.992A	748,992,1032	S46.219A	352,992	S46.901A	749,992	S48.922A	749,993,1032	S49.049P	383
S45.212D	807	S45.992D	807	S46.219D	807	S46.901D	807	S48.922D	807	S49.049S	314
S45.212S	169	S45.992S	169	S46.219S	352	S46.901S	749	S48.922S	313	S49.091A	352,993
S45.219A	748,992,1031	S45.999A	748,992,1032	S46.221A	382,992	S46.902A	749,992	S48.929A	749,993,1032	S49.091D	314
S45.219D	807	S45.999D	807	S46.221D	807	S46.902D	807	S48.929D	807	S49.091G	314
S45.219S	169	S45.999S	169	S46.221S	462	S46.902S	749	S48.929S	313	S49.091K	383
S45.291A	748,992,1031	S46.001A	748,992	S46.222A	382,992	S46.909A	749,992	S49.001A	352,993	S49.091P	383
S45.291D	807	S46.001D	807	S46.222D	807	S46.909D	807	S49.001D	313	S49.091S	314
S45.291S	169	S46.001S	748	S46.222S	462	S46.909S	749	S49.001G	313	S49.092A	352,993
S45.292A	748,992,1031	S46.002A	748,992	S46.229A	382,992	S46.911A	352,992	S49.001K	382	S49.092D	314
S45.292D	807	S46.002D	807	S46.229D	807	S46.911D	807	S49.001P	382		

Code	Page	Code	Page	Code	Page	Code	Page	Code	Page	Code	Page
S49.092G	314	S49.142S	314	S50.352S	462	S50.919S	462	S51.841S	462	S52.021J	314
S49.092K	383	S49.149A	352,993	S50.359A	462,993	S51.001A	462,993	S51.842A	749,993	S52.021K	383
S49.092P	383	S49.149D	314	S50.359D	808	S51.001D	808	S51.842D	808	S52.021M	383
S49.092S	314	S49.149G	314	S50.359S	462	S51.001S	462	S51.842S	462	S52.021N	383
S49.099A	352,993	S49.149K	383	S50.361A	478,993	S51.002A	462,993	S51.849A	749,993	S52.021P	383
S49.099D	314	S49.149P	383	S50.361D	808	S51.002D	808	S51.849D	808	S52.021Q	383
S49.099G	314	S49.149S	314	S50.361S	462	S51.002S	462	S51.849S	462	S52.021R	383
S49.099K	383	S49.191A	352,993	S50.362A	478,993	S51.009A	462,993	S51.851A	462,993	S52.021S	314
S49.099P	383	S49.191D	314	S50.362D	808	S51.009D	808	S51.851D	808	S52.022A	993
S49.099S	314	S49.191G	314	S50.362S	462	S51.009S	462	S51.851S	462	S52.022A	352
S49.101A	352,993	S49.191K	383	S50.369A	478,993	S51.011A	462,993	S51.852A	462,993	S52.022B	993
S49.101D	314	S49.191P	383	S50.369D	808	S51.011D	808	S51.852D	808	S52.022B	352,1032
S49.101G	314	S49.191S	314	S50.369S	462	S51.011S	462	S51.852S	462	S52.022C	993
S49.101K	383	S49.192A	352,993	S50.371A	462,993	S51.012A	462,993	S51.859A	462,993	S52.022C	352,1032
S49.101P	383	S49.192D	314	S50.371D	808	S51.012D	808	S51.859D	808	S52.022D	314
S49.101S	314	S49.192G	314	S50.371S	462	S51.012S	462	S51.859S	462	S52.022E	314
S49.102A	352,993	S49.192K	383	S50.372A	462,993	S51.019A	462,993	S52.001B	352,993	S52.022F	314
S49.102D	314	S49.192P	383	S50.372D	808	S51.019D	808	S52.001B	352,993,1032	S52.022G	314
S49.102G	314	S49.192S	314	S50.372S	462	S51.019S	462	S52.001C	352,993,1032	S52.022H	314
S49.102K	383	S49.199A	352,993	S50.379A	462,993	S51.021A	749,993	S52.001D	314	S52.022J	314
S49.102P	383	S49.199D	314	S50.379D	808	S51.021D	808	S52.001E	314	S52.022K	383
S49.102S	314	S49.199G	314	S50.379S	462	S51.021S	462	S52.001F	314	S52.022M	383
S49.109A	352,993	S49.199K	383	S50.811A	462,993	S51.022A	749,993	S52.001G	314	S52.022N	383
S49.109D	314	S49.199P	383	S50.811D	808	S51.022D	808	S52.001H	314	S52.022P	383
S49.109G	314	S49.199S	314	S50.811S	462	S51.022S	462	S52.001J	314	S52.022Q	383
S49.109K	383	S49.80XA	749,993	S50.812A	462,993	S51.029A	749,993	S52.001K	383	S52.022R	383
S49.109P	383	S49.80XD	807	S50.812D	808	S51.029D	808	S52.001M	383	S52.022S	314
S49.109S	314	S49.80XS	749	S50.812S	462	S51.029S	462	S52.001N	383	S52.023A	993
S49.111A	352,993	S49.81XA	749,993	S50.819A	462,993	S51.031A	462,993	S52.001P	383	S52.023A	352
S49.111D	314	S49.81XD	807	S50.819D	808	S51.031D	808	S52.001Q	383	S52.023B	993
S49.111G	314	S49.81XS	749	S50.819S	462	S51.031S	462	S52.001R	383	S52.023B	352,1032
S49.111K	383	S49.82XA	749,993	S50.821A	478,993	S51.032A	462,993	S52.001S	314	S52.023C	993
S49.111P	383	S49.82XD	807	S50.821D	808	S51.032D	808	S52.002A	352,993	S52.023C	352,1032
S49.111S	314	S49.82XS	749	S50.821S	462	S51.032S	462	S52.002B	352,993,1032	S52.023D	314
S49.112A	352,993	S49.90XA	749,993	S50.822A	478,993	S51.039A	462,993	S52.002C	352,993,1032	S52.023E	314
S49.112D	314	S49.90XD	807	S50.822D	808	S51.039D	808	S52.002D	314	S52.023F	314
S49.112G	314	S49.90XS	749	S50.822S	462	S51.039S	462	S52.002E	314	S52.023G	314
S49.112K	383	S49.91XA	749,993	S50.829A	478,993	S51.041A	749,993	S52.002F	314	S52.023H	314
S49.112P	383	S49.91XD	807	S50.829D	808	S51.041D	808	S52.002G	314	S52.023J	314
S49.112S	314	S49.91XS	749	S50.829S	462	S51.041S	462	S52.002H	314	S52.023K	383
S49.119A	352,993	S49.92XA	749,993	S50.841A	462,993	S51.042A	749,993	S52.002J	314	S52.023M	383
S49.119D	314	S49.92XD	807	S50.841D	808	S51.042D	808	S52.002K	383	S52.023N	383
S49.119G	314	S49.92XS	749	S50.841S	462	S51.042S	462	S52.002M	383	S52.023P	383
S49.119K	383	S50.00XA	462,993	S50.842A	462,993	S51.049A	749,993	S52.002N	383	S52.023Q	383
S49.119P	383	S50.00XD	807	S50.842D	808	S51.049D	808	S52.002P	383	S52.023R	383
S49.119S	314	S50.00XS	462	S50.842S	462	S51.049S	462	S52.002Q	383	S52.023S	314
S49.121A	352,993	S50.01XA	462,993	S50.849A	462,993	S51.051A	462,993	S52.002R	383	S52.024A	993
S49.121D	314	S50.01XD	807	S50.849D	808	S51.051D	808	S52.002S	314	S52.024A	352
S49.121G	314	S50.01XS	462	S50.849S	462	S51.051S	462	S52.009A	352,993	S52.024B	993
S49.121K	383	S50.02XA	462,993	S50.851A	462,993	S51.052A	462,993	S52.009B	352,993,1032	S52.024B	352,1032
S49.121P	383	S50.02XD	807	S50.851D	808	S51.052D	808	S52.009C	352,993,1032	S52.024C	993
S49.121S	314	S50.02XS	462	S50.851S	462	S51.052S	462	S52.009D	314	S52.024C	352,1032
S49.122A	352,993	S50.10XA	462,993	S50.852A	462,993	S51.059A	462,993	S52.009E	314	S52.024D	314
S49.122D	314	S50.10XD	807	S50.852D	808	S51.059D	808	S52.009F	314	S52.024E	314
S49.122G	314	S50.10XS	462	S50.852S	462	S51.059S	462	S52.009G	314	S52.024F	314
S49.122K	383	S50.11XA	462,993	S50.859A	462,993	S51.801A	462,993	S52.009H	314	S52.024G	314
S49.122P	383	S50.11XD	807	S50.859D	808	S51.801D	808	S52.009J	314	S52.024H	314
S49.122S	314	S50.11XS	462	S50.859S	462	S51.801S	462	S52.009K	383	S52.024J	314
S49.129A	352,993	S50.12XA	478,993	S50.861A	478,993	S51.802A	462,993	S52.009M	383	S52.024K	383
S49.129D	314	S50.12XD	807	S50.861D	808	S51.802D	808	S52.009N	383	S52.024M	383
S49.129G	314	S50.12XS	462	S50.861S	462	S51.802S	462	S52.009P	383	S52.024N	383
S49.129K	383	S50.311A	462,993	S50.862A	478,993	S51.809A	462,993	S52.009Q	383	S52.024P	383
S49.129P	383	S50.311D	807	S50.862D	808	S51.809D	808	S52.009R	383	S52.024Q	383
S49.129S	314	S50.311S	462	S50.862S	462	S51.809S	462	S52.009S	314	S52.024R	383
S49.131A	352,993	S50.312A	462,993	S50.869A	478,993	S51.811A	462,993	S52.011A	352,993	S52.024S	314
S49.131D	314	S50.312D	807	S50.869D	808	S51.811D	808	S52.011D	314	S52.025A	993
S49.131G	314	S50.312S	462	S50.869S	462	S51.811S	462	S52.011G	314	S52.025A	352
S49.131K	383	S50.319A	462,993	S50.871A	462,993	S51.812A	462,993	S52.011K	383	S52.025B	993
S49.131P	383	S50.319D	807	S50.871D	808	S51.812D	808	S52.011P	383	S52.025B	352,1032
S49.131S	314	S50.319S	462	S50.871S	462	S51.812S	462	S52.011S	314	S52.025C	993
S49.132A	352,993	S50.321A	478,993	S50.872A	462,993	S51.819A	462,993	S52.012A	352,993	S52.025C	352,1032
S49.132D	314	S50.321D	807	S50.872D	808	S51.819D	808	S52.012D	314	S52.025D	314
S49.132G	314	S50.321S	462	S50.872S	462	S51.819S	462	S52.012G	314	S52.025E	314
S49.132K	383	S50.322A	478,993	S50.879A	462,993	S51.821A	749,993	S52.012K	383	S52.025F	314
S49.132P	383	S50.322D	807	S50.879D	808	S51.821D	808	S52.012P	383	S52.025G	314
S49.132S	314	S50.322S	462	S50.879S	462	S51.821S	462	S52.012S	314	S52.025H	314
S49.139A	352,993	S50.329A	478,993	S50.901A	462,993	S51.822A	749,993	S52.019A	352,993	S52.025J	314
S49.139D	314	S50.329D	807	S50.901D	808	S51.822D	808	S52.019D	314	S52.025K	383
S49.139G	314	S50.329S	462	S50.901S	462	S51.822S	462	S52.019G	314	S52.025M	383
S49.139K	383	S50.341A	462,993	S50.902A	462,993	S51.829A	749,993	S52.019K	383	S52.025N	383
S49.139P	383	S50.341D	807	S50.902D	808	S51.829D	808	S52.019P	383	S52.025P	383
S49.139S	314	S50.341S	462	S50.902S	462	S51.829S	462	S52.019S	314	S52.025Q	383
S49.141A	352,993	S50.342A	462,993	S50.909A	462,993	S51.831A	462,993	S52.021A	993	S52.025R	383
S49.141D	314	S50.342D	807	S50.909D	808	S51.831D	808	S52.021A	352	S52.025S	314
S49.141G	314	S50.342S	462	S50.909S	462	S51.831S	462	S52.021B	993	S52.026A	993
S49.141K	383	S50.349A	462,993	S50.911A	462,993	S51.832A	462,993	S52.021B	352,1032	S52.026A	352
S49.141P	383	S50.349D	807	S50.911D	808	S51.832D	808	S52.021C	352,1032	S52.026B	993
S49.141S	314	S50.349S	462	S50.911S	462	S51.832S	462	S52.021D	314	S52.026B	352,1032
S49.142A	352,993	S50.351A	462,993	S50.912A	462,993	S51.839A	462,993	S52.021E	314	S52.026C	993
S49.142D	314	S50.351D	808	S50.912D	808	S51.839D	808	S52.021F	314	S52.026C	352,1032
S49.142G	314	S50.351S	462	S50.912S	462	S51.839S	462	S52.021G	314	S52.026D	314
S49.142K	383	S50.352A	462,993	S50.919A	462,993	S51.841A	749,993	S52.021H	314	S52.026E	314
S49.142P	383	S50.352D	808	S50.919D	808	S51.841D	808			S52.026F	314

Code	Page	Code	Page	Code	Page	Code	Page	Code	Page	Code	Page
S52.026G	314	S52.035E	315	S52.044R	383	S52.101N	384	S52.123G	315	S52.133D	316
S52.026H	314	S52.035F	315	S52.044S	315	S52.101P	384	S52.123H	315	S52.133E	316
S52.026J	314	S52.035G	315	S52.045A	353, 994	S52.101Q	384	S52.123J	315	S52.133F	316
S52.026K	383	S52.035H	315	S52.045B	353, 994, 1032	S52.101R	384	S52.123K	384	S52.133G	316
S52.026M	383	S52.035J	315	S52.045C	353, 994, 1032	S52.101S	315	S52.123M	384	S52.133H	316
S52.026N	383	S52.035K	383	S52.045D	315	S52.102A	353, 994	S52.123N	384	S52.133J	316
S52.026P	383	S52.035M	383	S52.045E	315	S52.102B	353, 994, 1032	S52.123P	384	S52.133K	384
S52.026Q	383	S52.035N	383	S52.045F	315	S52.102C	353, 994, 1032	S52.123Q	384	S52.133M	384
S52.026R	383	S52.035P	383	S52.045G	315	S52.102D	315	S52.123R	384	S52.133N	384
S52.026S	314	S52.035Q	383	S52.045H	315	S52.102E	315	S52.123S	315	S52.133P	384
S52.031A	993	S52.035R	383	S52.045J	315	S52.102F	315	S52.124A	353, 994	S52.133Q	384
S52.031A	352	S52.035S	315	S52.045K	383	S52.102G	315	S52.124B	353, 994, 1032	S52.133R	384
S52.031B	993	S52.036A	993	S52.045M	383	S52.102H	315	S52.124C	353, 994, 1032	S52.133S	315
S52.031B	352, 1032	S52.036A	353	S52.045N	383	S52.102J	315	S52.124D	315	S52.134A	353, 994
S52.031C	993	S52.036B	994	S52.045P	383	S52.102K	384	S52.124E	315	S52.134B	353, 994, 1032
S52.031C	353, 1032	S52.036B	353, 1032	S52.045Q	383	S52.102M	384	S52.124F	315	S52.134C	353, 994, 1032
S52.031D	314	S52.036C	994	S52.045R	383	S52.102N	384	S52.124G	315	S52.134D	316
S52.031E	314	S52.036C	353, 1032	S52.045S	315	S52.102P	384	S52.124H	315	S52.134E	316
S52.031F	314	S52.036D	315	S52.046A	353, 994	S52.102Q	384	S52.124J	315	S52.134F	316
S52.031G	314	S52.036E	315	S52.046B	353, 994, 1032	S52.102R	384	S52.124K	384	S52.134G	316
S52.031H	314	S52.036F	315	S52.046C	353, 994, 1032	S52.102S	315	S52.124M	384	S52.134H	316
S52.031J	314	S52.036G	315	S52.046D	315	S52.109A	353, 994	S52.124N	384	S52.134J	316
S52.031K	383	S52.036H	315	S52.046E	315	S52.109B	353, 994, 1032	S52.124P	384	S52.134K	384
S52.031M	383	S52.036J	315	S52.046F	315	S52.109C	353, 994, 1032	S52.124Q	384	S52.134M	384
S52.031N	383	S52.036K	383	S52.046G	315	S52.109D	315	S52.124R	384	S52.134N	384
S52.031P	383	S52.036M	383	S52.046H	315	S52.109E	315	S52.124S	384	S52.134P	384
S52.031Q	383	S52.036N	383	S52.046J	315	S52.109F	315	S52.125A	353, 994	S52.134Q	384
S52.031R	383	S52.036P	383	S52.046K	383	S52.109G	315	S52.125B	353, 994, 1032	S52.134R	384
S52.031S	314	S52.036Q	383	S52.046M	383	S52.109H	315	S52.125C	353, 994, 1032	S52.134S	316
S52.032A	993	S52.036R	383	S52.046N	384	S52.109J	315	S52.125D	315	S52.135A	353, 994
S52.032A	353	S52.036S	315	S52.046P	384	S52.109K	315	S52.125E	315	S52.135B	353, 994, 1032
S52.032B	993	S52.041A	353, 994	S52.046Q	384	S52.109M	384	S52.125F	315	S52.135C	353, 994, 1032
S52.032B	353, 1032	S52.041B	353, 994, 1032	S52.046R	384	S52.109N	384	S52.125G	315	S52.135D	316
S52.032C	993	S52.041C	353, 994, 1032	S52.046S	315	S52.109P	384	S52.125H	315	S52.135E	316
S52.032C	353, 1032	S52.041D	315	S52.091A	353, 994	S52.109Q	384	S52.125J	315	S52.135F	316
S52.032D	314	S52.041E	315	S52.091B	353, 994, 1032	S52.109R	384	S52.125K	384	S52.135G	316
S52.032E	314	S52.041F	315	S52.091C	353, 994, 1032	S52.109S	315	S52.125M	384	S52.135H	316
S52.032F	314	S52.041G	315	S52.091D	315	S52.111A	353, 994	S52.125N	384	S52.135J	316
S52.032G	314	S52.041H	315	S52.091E	315	S52.111D	315	S52.125P	384	S52.135K	384
S52.032H	314	S52.041J	315	S52.091F	315	S52.111G	315	S52.125Q	384	S52.135M	384
S52.032J	315	S52.041K	383	S52.091G	315	S52.111K	384	S52.125R	384	S52.135N	384
S52.032K	383	S52.041M	383	S52.091H	315	S52.111P	384	S52.125S	315	S52.135P	384
S52.032M	383	S52.041N	383	S52.091J	315	S52.111S	315	S52.126A	353, 994	S52.135Q	384
S52.032N	383	S52.041P	383	S52.091K	384	S52.112A	353, 994	S52.126B	353, 994, 1032	S52.135R	384
S52.032P	383	S52.041Q	383	S52.091M	384	S52.112D	315	S52.126C	353, 994, 1032	S52.135S	316
S52.032Q	383	S52.041R	383	S52.091N	384	S52.112G	315	S52.126D	315	S52.136A	353, 994
S52.032R	383	S52.041S	315	S52.091P	384	S52.112K	384	S52.126E	315	S52.136B	353, 994, 1032
S52.032S	315	S52.042A	353, 994	S52.091Q	384	S52.112P	384	S52.126F	315	S52.136C	353, 994, 1032
S52.033A	993	S52.042B	353, 994, 1032	S52.091R	384	S52.112S	315	S52.126G	315	S52.136D	316
S52.033A	353	S52.042C	353, 994, 1032	S52.091S	315	S52.119A	353, 994	S52.126H	315	S52.136E	316
S52.033B	993	S52.042D	315	S52.092A	353, 994	S52.119D	315	S52.126J	315	S52.136F	316
S52.033B	353, 1032	S52.042E	315	S52.092B	353, 994, 1032	S52.119G	315	S52.126K	384	S52.136G	316
S52.033C	993	S52.042F	315	S52.092C	353, 994, 1032	S52.119K	384	S52.126M	384	S52.136H	316
S52.033C	353, 1032	S52.042G	315	S52.092D	315	S52.119P	384	S52.126N	384	S52.136J	316
S52.033D	315	S52.042H	315	S52.092E	315	S52.119S	315	S52.126P	384	S52.136K	384
S52.033E	315	S52.042J	315	S52.092F	315	S52.121A	353, 994	S52.126Q	384	S52.136M	384
S52.033F	315	S52.042K	383	S52.092G	315	S52.121B	353, 994, 1032	S52.126R	384	S52.136N	384
S52.033G	315	S52.042M	383	S52.092H	315	S52.121C	353, 994, 1032	S52.126S	315	S52.136P	384
S52.033H	315	S52.042N	383	S52.092J	315	S52.121D	315	S52.131A	353, 994	S52.136Q	384
S52.033J	315	S52.042P	383	S52.092K	384	S52.121E	315	S52.131B	353, 994, 1032	S52.136R	384
S52.033K	383	S52.042Q	383	S52.092M	384	S52.121F	315	S52.131C	353, 994, 1032	S52.136S	384
S52.033M	383	S52.042R	383	S52.092N	384	S52.121G	315	S52.131D	315	S52.181A	353, 994
S52.033N	383	S52.042S	315	S52.092P	384	S52.121H	315	S52.131E	315	S52.181B	353, 994, 1032
S52.033P	383	S52.043A	353, 994	S52.092Q	384	S52.121J	315	S52.131F	315	S52.181C	353, 994, 1032
S52.033Q	383	S52.043B	353, 994, 1032	S52.092R	384	S52.121K	384	S52.131G	315	S52.181D	316
S52.033R	383	S52.043C	353, 994, 1032	S52.092S	315	S52.121M	384	S52.131H	315	S52.181E	316
S52.033S	315	S52.043D	315	S52.099A	353, 994	S52.121N	384	S52.131J	315	S52.181F	316
S52.034A	993	S52.043E	315	S52.099B	353, 994, 1032	S52.121P	384	S52.131K	384	S52.181G	316
S52.034A	353	S52.043F	315	S52.099C	353, 994, 1032	S52.121Q	384	S52.131M	384	S52.181H	316
S52.034B	993	S52.043G	315	S52.099D	315	S52.121R	384	S52.131N	384	S52.181J	316
S52.034B	353, 1032	S52.043H	315	S52.099E	315	S52.121S	315	S52.131P	384	S52.181K	384
S52.034C	993	S52.043J	315	S52.099F	315	S52.122A	353, 994	S52.131Q	384	S52.181M	384
S52.034C	353, 1032	S52.043K	383	S52.099G	315	S52.122B	353, 994, 1032	S52.131R	384	S52.181N	384
S52.034D	315	S52.043M	383	S52.099H	315	S52.122C	353, 994, 1032	S52.131S	315	S52.181P	384
S52.034E	315	S52.043N	383	S52.099J	315	S52.122D	315	S52.132A	353, 994	S52.181Q	384
S52.034F	315	S52.043P	383	S52.099K	384	S52.122E	315	S52.132B	353, 994, 1032	S52.181R	384
S52.034G	315	S52.043Q	383	S52.099M	384	S52.122F	315	S52.132C	353, 994, 1032	S52.181S	316
S52.034H	315	S52.043R	383	S52.099N	384	S52.122G	315	S52.132D	315	S52.182A	353, 994
S52.034J	315	S52.043S	315	S52.099P	384	S52.122H	315	S52.132E	315	S52.182B	353, 994, 1032
S52.034K	383	S52.044A	353, 994	S52.099Q	384	S52.122J	315	S52.132F	316	S52.182C	353, 994, 1032
S52.034M	383	S52.044B	353, 994, 1032	S52.099S	315	S52.122K	384	S52.132G	316	S52.182D	316
S52.034N	383	S52.044C	353, 994, 1032	S52.101A	353, 994	S52.122M	384	S52.132H	316	S52.182E	316
S52.034P	383	S52.044D	315	S52.101B	353, 994, 1032	S52.122N	384	S52.132J	316	S52.182F	316
S52.034Q	383	S52.044E	315	S52.101C	353, 994, 1032	S52.122P	384	S52.132K	384	S52.182G	316
S52.034R	383	S52.044F	315	S52.101D	315	S52.122Q	384	S52.132M	384	S52.182H	316
S52.034S	315	S52.044G	315	S52.101E	315	S52.122R	384	S52.132N	384	S52.182J	316
S52.035A	993	S52.044H	315	S52.101F	315	S52.122S	315	S52.132P	384	S52.182K	384
S52.035A	353	S52.044J	315	S52.101G	315	S52.123A	353, 994	S52.132Q	384	S52.182M	384
S52.035B	993	S52.044K	383	S52.101H	315	S52.123B	353, 994, 1032	S52.132R	384	S52.182N	384
S52.035B	353, 1032	S52.044M	383	S52.101J	315	S52.123C	353, 994, 1032	S52.132S	315	S52.182P	384
S52.035C	993	S52.044N	383	S52.101K	384	S52.123D	315	S52.133A	353, 994	S52.182Q	384
S52.035C	353, 1032	S52.044P	383	S52.101M	384	S52.123E	315	S52.133B	353, 994, 1032	S52.182R	384
S52.035D	315	S52.044Q	383			S52.123F	315	S52.133C	353, 994, 1032	S52.182S	316

Code	Page	Code	Page	Code	Page	Code	Page	Code	Page	Code	Page
S52.189A	353,994	S52.221N	384	S52.231J	316	S52.241F	316	S52.251A	353,994	S52.256S	317
S52.189B	353,994,1032	S52.221P	384	S52.231K	385	S52.241G	316	S52.251B	353,994,1032	S52.261A	354,994
S52.189C	353,994,1032	S52.221Q	384	S52.231M	385	S52.241H	316	S52.251C	353,994,1032	S52.261B	354,994,1032
S52.189D	316	S52.221R	384	S52.231N	385	S52.241J	316	S52.251D	317	S52.261C	354,994,1032
S52.189E	316	S52.221S	316	S52.231P	385	S52.241K	385	S52.251E	317	S52.261D	317
S52.189F	316	S52.222A	353,994	S52.231Q	385	S52.241M	385	S52.251F	317	S52.261E	317
S52.189G	316	S52.222B	353,994,1032	S52.231R	385	S52.241N	385	S52.251G	317	S52.261F	317
S52.189H	316	S52.222C	353,994,1032	S52.231S	316	S52.241P	385	S52.251H	317	S52.261G	317
S52.189J	316	S52.222D	316	S52.232A	353,994	S52.241Q	385	S52.251J	317	S52.261H	317
S52.189K	384	S52.222E	316	S52.232B	353,994,1032	S52.241R	385	S52.251K	385	S52.261J	317
S52.189M	384	S52.222F	316	S52.232C	353,994,1032	S52.241S	317	S52.251M	385	S52.261K	385
S52.189N	384	S52.222G	316	S52.232D	316	S52.242A	353,994	S52.251N	385	S52.261M	385
S52.189P	384	S52.222H	316	S52.232E	316	S52.242B	353,994,1032	S52.251P	385	S52.261N	385
S52.189Q	384	S52.222J	316	S52.232F	316	S52.242C	353,994,1032	S52.251Q	385	S52.261P	385
S52.189R	384	S52.222K	384	S52.232G	316	S52.242D	317	S52.251R	385	S52.261Q	385
S52.189S	316	S52.222M	384	S52.232H	316	S52.242E	317	S52.251S	317	S52.261R	385
S52.201A	353,994	S52.222N	384	S52.232J	316	S52.242F	317	S52.252A	353,994	S52.261S	317
S52.201B	353,994,1032	S52.222P	384	S52.232K	385	S52.242G	317	S52.252B	353,994,1032	S52.262A	354,994
S52.201C	353,994,1032	S52.222Q	384	S52.232M	385	S52.242H	317	S52.252C	353,994,1032	S52.262B	354,995,1032
S52.201D	316	S52.222R	384	S52.232N	385	S52.242J	317	S52.252D	317	S52.262C	354,995,1032
S52.201E	316	S52.222S	316	S52.232P	385	S52.242K	385	S52.252E	317	S52.262D	317
S52.201F	316	S52.223A	353,994	S52.232Q	385	S52.242M	385	S52.252F	317	S52.262E	317
S52.201G	316	S52.223B	353,994,1032	S52.232R	385	S52.242N	385	S52.252G	317	S52.262F	317
S52.201H	316	S52.223C	353,994,1032	S52.232S	316	S52.242P	385	S52.252H	317	S52.262G	317
S52.201J	316	S52.223D	316	S52.233A	353,994	S52.242Q	385	S52.252J	317	S52.262H	317
S52.201K	384	S52.223E	316	S52.233B	353,994,1032	S52.242R	385	S52.252K	385	S52.262J	317
S52.201M	384	S52.223F	316	S52.233C	353,994,1032	S52.242S	317	S52.252M	385	S52.262K	385
S52.201N	384	S52.223G	316	S52.233D	316	S52.243A	353,994	S52.252N	385	S52.262M	385
S52.201P	384	S52.223H	316	S52.233E	316	S52.243B	353,994,1032	S52.252P	385	S52.262N	385
S52.201Q	384	S52.223J	316	S52.233F	316	S52.243C	353,994,1032	S52.252Q	385	S52.262P	385
S52.201R	384	S52.223K	384	S52.233G	316	S52.243D	317	S52.252R	385	S52.262Q	385
S52.201S	316	S52.223M	384	S52.233H	316	S52.243E	317	S52.252S	317	S52.262R	385
S52.202A	353,994	S52.223N	385	S52.233J	316	S52.243F	317	S52.253A	353,994	S52.262S	317
S52.202B	353,994,1032	S52.223P	385	S52.233K	385	S52.243G	317	S52.253B	353,994,1032	S52.263A	354,995
S52.202C	353,994,1032	S52.223Q	385	S52.233M	385	S52.243H	317	S52.253C	354,994,1032	S52.263B	354,995,1032
S52.202D	316	S52.223R	385	S52.233N	385	S52.243J	317	S52.253D	317	S52.263C	354,995,1032
S52.202E	316	S52.223S	316	S52.233P	385	S52.243K	385	S52.253E	317	S52.263D	317
S52.202F	316	S52.224A	353,994	S52.233Q	385	S52.243M	385	S52.253F	317	S52.263E	317
S52.202G	316	S52.224B	353,994,1032	S52.233R	385	S52.243N	385	S52.253G	317	S52.263F	317
S52.202H	316	S52.224C	353,994,1032	S52.233S	316	S52.243P	385	S52.253H	317	S52.263G	317
S52.202J	316	S52.224D	316	S52.234A	353,994	S52.243Q	385	S52.253J	317	S52.263H	317
S52.202K	384	S52.224E	316	S52.234B	353,994,1032	S52.243R	385	S52.253K	385	S52.263J	317
S52.202M	384	S52.224F	316	S52.234C	353,994,1032	S52.243S	317	S52.253M	385	S52.263K	385
S52.202N	384	S52.224G	316	S52.234D	316	S52.244A	353,994	S52.253N	385	S52.263M	385
S52.202P	384	S52.224H	316	S52.234E	316	S52.244B	353,994,1032	S52.253P	385	S52.263N	385
S52.202Q	384	S52.224J	316	S52.234F	316	S52.244C	353,994,1032	S52.253Q	385	S52.263P	385
S52.202R	384	S52.224K	385	S52.234G	316	S52.244D	317	S52.253R	385	S52.263Q	385
S52.202S	316	S52.224M	385	S52.234H	316	S52.244E	317	S52.253S	317	S52.263R	385
S52.209A	353,994	S52.224N	385	S52.234J	316	S52.244F	317	S52.254A	354,994	S52.263S	317
S52.209B	353,994,1032	S52.224P	385	S52.234K	385	S52.244G	317	S52.254B	354,994,1032	S52.264A	354,995
S52.209C	353,994,1032	S52.224Q	385	S52.234M	385	S52.244H	317	S52.254C	354,994,1032	S52.264B	354,995,1033
S52.209D	316	S52.224R	385	S52.234N	385	S52.244J	317	S52.254D	317	S52.264C	354,995,1033
S52.209E	316	S52.224S	316	S52.234P	385	S52.244K	385	S52.254E	317	S52.264D	317
S52.209F	316	S52.225A	353,994	S52.234Q	385	S52.244M	385	S52.254F	317	S52.264E	317
S52.209G	316	S52.225B	353,994,1032	S52.234R	385	S52.244N	385	S52.254G	317	S52.264F	317
S52.209H	316	S52.225C	353,994,1032	S52.234S	316	S52.244P	385	S52.254H	317	S52.264G	317
S52.209J	316	S52.225D	316	S52.235A	353,994	S52.244Q	385	S52.254J	317	S52.264H	317
S52.209K	384	S52.225E	316	S52.235B	353,994,1032	S52.244R	385	S52.254K	385	S52.264J	317
S52.209M	384	S52.225F	316	S52.235C	353,994,1032	S52.244S	317	S52.254M	385	S52.264K	385
S52.209N	384	S52.225G	316	S52.235D	316	S52.245A	353,994	S52.254N	385	S52.264M	385
S52.209P	384	S52.225H	316	S52.235E	316	S52.245B	353,994,1032	S52.254P	385	S52.264N	385
S52.209Q	384	S52.225J	316	S52.235F	316	S52.245C	353,994,1032	S52.254Q	385	S52.264P	385
S52.209R	384	S52.225K	385	S52.235G	316	S52.245D	317	S52.254R	385	S52.264Q	385
S52.209S	316	S52.225M	385	S52.235H	316	S52.245E	317	S52.254S	317	S52.264R	385
S52.211A	353,994	S52.225N	385	S52.235J	316	S52.245F	317	S52.255A	354,994	S52.264S	317
S52.211D	316	S52.225P	384	S52.235K	385	S52.245G	317	S52.255B	354,994,1032	S52.265A	354,995
S52.211G	316	S52.225Q	385	S52.235M	385	S52.245H	317	S52.255C	354,994,1032	S52.265B	354,995,1033
S52.211K	384	S52.225R	385	S52.235N	385	S52.245J	317	S52.255D	317	S52.265C	354,995,1033
S52.211P	384	S52.225S	316	S52.235P	385	S52.245K	385	S52.255E	317	S52.265D	317
S52.211S	316	S52.226A	353,994	S52.235Q	385	S52.245M	385	S52.255F	317	S52.265E	317
S52.212A	353,994	S52.226B	353,994,1032	S52.235S	316	S52.245N	385	S52.255G	317	S52.265F	317
S52.212D	316	S52.226C	353,994,1032	S52.236A	353,994	S52.245P	385	S52.255H	317	S52.265G	317
S52.212G	316	S52.226D	316	S52.236B	353,994,1032	S52.245Q	385	S52.255J	317	S52.265H	317
S52.212K	384	S52.226E	316	S52.236C	353,994,1032	S52.245R	385	S52.255K	385	S52.265J	317
S52.212P	384	S52.226F	316	S52.236D	316	S52.245S	317	S52.255M	385	S52.265K	385
S52.212S	316	S52.226G	316	S52.236E	316	S52.246A	353,994	S52.255N	385	S52.265M	385
S52.219A	353,994	S52.226H	316	S52.236F	316	S52.246B	353,994,1032	S52.255P	385	S52.265N	385
S52.219D	316	S52.226J	316	S52.236G	316	S52.246C	353,994,1032	S52.255R	385	S52.265P	385
S52.219G	316	S52.226K	385	S52.236H	316	S52.246D	317	S52.255S	317	S52.265Q	385
S52.219K	384	S52.226M	385	S52.236J	316	S52.246E	317	S52.256A	354,994	S52.265R	385
S52.219P	384	S52.226N	385	S52.236K	385	S52.246F	317	S52.256B	354,994,1032	S52.265S	317
S52.219S	316	S52.226P	385	S52.236M	385	S52.246G	317	S52.256C	354,994,1032	S52.266A	354,995
S52.221A	353,994	S52.226Q	385	S52.236N	385	S52.246H	317	S52.256D	317	S52.266B	354,995,1033
S52.221B	353,994,1032	S52.226R	385	S52.236P	385	S52.246J	317	S52.256E	317	S52.266C	354,995,1033
S52.221C	353,994,1032	S52.226S	316	S52.236Q	385	S52.246K	385	S52.256F	317	S52.266D	317
S52.221D	316	S52.231A	353,994	S52.236R	385	S52.246M	385	S52.256G	317	S52.266E	317
S52.221E	316	S52.231B	353,994,1032	S52.236S	316	S52.246N	385	S52.256H	317	S52.266F	317
S52.221F	316	S52.231C	353,994,1032	S52.241A	353,994	S52.246P	385	S52.256J	317	S52.266G	317
S52.221G	316	S52.231D	316	S52.241B	353,994,1032	S52.246Q	385	S52.256M	385	S52.266H	317
S52.221H	316	S52.231E	316	S52.241C	353,994,1032	S52.246R	385	S52.256N	385	S52.266J	317
S52.221J	316	S52.231F	316	S52.241D	316	S52.246S	317	S52.256P	385	S52.266K	385
S52.221K	384	S52.231G	316	S52.241E	316	S52.251A	353,994	S52.256Q	385	S52.266M	385
S52.221M	384	S52.231H	316					S52.256R	385	S52.266N	385

Code	Page	Code	Page	Code	Page	Code	Page	Code	Page	Code	Page
S52.266P	385	S52.283K	386	S52.309G	318	S52.325B	354, 995, 1033	S52.334R	386	S52.344N	386
S52.266Q	385	S52.283M	386	S52.309H	318	S52.325C	354, 995, 1033	S52.334S	318	S52.344P	386
S52.266R	385	S52.283N	386	S52.309J	318	S52.325D	318	S52.335A	354, 995	S52.344Q	386
S52.266S	317	S52.283P	386	S52.309K	386	S52.325E	318	S52.335B	354, 995, 1033	S52.344R	386
S52.271A	354, 995	S52.283Q	386	S52.309M	386	S52.325F	318	S52.335C	354, 995, 1033	S52.344S	318
S52.271B	354, 995, 1033	S52.283R	386	S52.309N	386	S52.325G	318	S52.335D	318	S52.345A	354, 995
S52.271C	354, 995, 1033	S52.283S	317	S52.309P	386	S52.325H	318	S52.335E	318	S52.345B	354, 995, 1033
S52.271D	317	S52.291A	354, 995	S52.309Q	386	S52.325J	318	S52.335F	318	S52.345C	354, 995, 1033
S52.271E	317	S52.291B	354, 995, 1033	S52.309R	386	S52.325K	386	S52.335G	318	S52.345D	318
S52.271F	317	S52.291C	354, 995, 1033	S52.309S	318	S52.325M	386	S52.335H	318	S52.345E	318
S52.271G	317	S52.291D	317	S52.311A	354, 995	S52.325N	386	S52.335J	318	S52.345F	318
S52.271H	317	S52.291E	317	S52.311D	318	S52.325P	386	S52.335K	386	S52.345G	318
S52.271J	317	S52.291F	317	S52.311G	318	S52.325Q	386	S52.335M	386	S52.345H	318
S52.271K	385	S52.291G	317	S52.311K	386	S52.325R	386	S52.335N	386	S52.345J	318
S52.271M	385	S52.291H	317	S52.311P	386	S52.325S	318	S52.335P	386	S52.345K	386
S52.271N	385	S52.291J	317	S52.311S	318	S52.326A	354, 995	S52.335Q	386	S52.345M	386
S52.271P	385	S52.291K	386	S52.312A	354, 995	S52.326B	354, 995, 1033	S52.335R	386	S52.345N	386
S52.271Q	385	S52.291M	386	S52.312D	318	S52.326C	354, 995, 1033	S52.335S	318	S52.345P	386
S52.271R	385	S52.291N	386	S52.312G	318	S52.326D	318	S52.336A	354, 995	S52.345Q	386
S52.271S	317	S52.291P	386	S52.312K	386	S52.326E	318	S52.336B	354, 995, 1033	S52.345R	386
S52.272A	354, 995	S52.291Q	386	S52.312P	386	S52.326F	318	S52.336C	354, 995, 1033	S52.345S	318
S52.272B	354, 995, 1033	S52.291R	386	S52.312S	318	S52.326G	318	S52.336D	318	S52.346A	354, 995
S52.272C	354, 995, 1033	S52.291S	317	S52.319A	354, 995	S52.326H	318	S52.336E	318	S52.346B	354, 995, 1033
S52.272D	317	S52.292A	354, 995	S52.319D	318	S52.326J	318	S52.336F	318	S52.346C	354, 995, 1033
S52.272E	317	S52.292B	354, 995, 1033	S52.319G	318	S52.326K	386	S52.336G	318	S52.346D	318
S52.272F	317	S52.292C	354, 995, 1033	S52.319K	386	S52.326M	386	S52.336H	318	S52.346E	318
S52.272G	317	S52.292D	317	S52.319P	386	S52.326N	386	S52.336J	318	S52.346F	318
S52.272H	317	S52.292E	317	S52.319S	318	S52.326P	386	S52.336K	386	S52.346G	318
S52.272J	317	S52.292F	317	S52.321A	354, 995	S52.326Q	386	S52.336M	386	S52.346H	318
S52.272K	385	S52.292G	317	S52.321B	354, 995, 1033	S52.326R	386	S52.336N	386	S52.346J	318
S52.272M	385	S52.292H	317	S52.321C	354, 995, 1033	S52.326S	318	S52.336P	386	S52.346K	386
S52.272N	386	S52.292J	318	S52.321D	318	S52.331A	354, 995	S52.336Q	386	S52.346M	386
S52.272P	386	S52.292K	386	S52.321E	318	S52.331B	354, 995, 1033	S52.336R	386	S52.346N	387
S52.272Q	386	S52.292M	386	S52.321F	318	S52.331C	354, 995, 1033	S52.336S	318	S52.346P	387
S52.272R	386	S52.292N	386	S52.321G	318	S52.331D	318	S52.341A	354, 995	S52.346Q	387
S52.272S	317	S52.292P	386	S52.321H	318	S52.331E	318	S52.341B	354, 995, 1033	S52.346R	387
S52.279A	354, 995	S52.292Q	386	S52.321J	318	S52.331F	318	S52.341C	354, 995, 1033	S52.346S	318
S52.279B	354, 995, 1033	S52.292R	386	S52.321K	386	S52.331G	318	S52.341D	318	S52.351A	354, 995
S52.279C	354, 995, 1033	S52.292S	318	S52.321M	386	S52.331H	318	S52.341E	318	S52.351B	354, 995, 1033
S52.279D	317	S52.299A	354, 995	S52.321N	386	S52.331J	318	S52.341F	318	S52.351C	354, 995, 1033
S52.279E	317	S52.299B	354, 995, 1033	S52.321P	386	S52.331K	386	S52.341G	318	S52.351D	318
S52.279F	317	S52.299C	354, 995, 1033	S52.321Q	386	S52.331M	386	S52.341H	318	S52.351E	318
S52.279G	317	S52.299D	318	S52.321R	386	S52.331N	386	S52.341J	318	S52.351F	318
S52.279H	317	S52.299E	318	S52.321S	318	S52.331P	386	S52.341K	386	S52.351G	318
S52.279J	317	S52.299F	318	S52.322A	354, 995	S52.331Q	386	S52.341M	386	S52.351H	318
S52.279K	386	S52.299G	318	S52.322B	354, 995, 1033	S52.331R	386	S52.341N	386	S52.351J	318
S52.279M	386	S52.299H	318	S52.322C	354, 995, 1033	S52.331S	318	S52.341P	386	S52.351K	387
S52.279N	386	S52.299J	318	S52.322D	318	S52.332A	354, 995	S52.341Q	386	S52.351M	387
S52.279P	386	S52.299K	386	S52.322E	318	S52.332B	354, 995, 1033	S52.341R	386	S52.351N	387
S52.279Q	386	S52.299M	386	S52.322F	318	S52.332C	354, 995, 1033	S52.341S	318	S52.351P	387
S52.279R	386	S52.299N	386	S52.322G	318	S52.332D	318	S52.342A	354, 995	S52.351Q	387
S52.279S	317	S52.299P	386	S52.322H	318	S52.332E	318	S52.342B	354, 995, 1033	S52.351R	387
S52.281A	354, 995	S52.299Q	386	S52.322J	318	S52.332F	318	S52.342C	354, 995, 1033	S52.351S	318
S52.281B	354, 995, 1033	S52.299S	318	S52.322K	386	S52.332G	318	S52.342D	318	S52.352A	354, 995
S52.281C	354, 995, 1033	S52.301A	354, 995	S52.322M	386	S52.332H	318	S52.342E	318	S52.352B	354, 995, 1033
S52.281D	317	S52.301B	354, 995, 1033	S52.322N	386	S52.332J	318	S52.342F	318	S52.352C	354, 995, 1033
S52.281E	317	S52.301C	354, 995, 1033	S52.322P	386	S52.332K	386	S52.342G	318	S52.352D	318
S52.281F	317	S52.301D	318	S52.322Q	386	S52.332M	386	S52.342H	318	S52.352E	318
S52.281G	317	S52.301E	318	S52.322R	386	S52.332N	386	S52.342J	318	S52.352F	318
S52.281H	317	S52.301F	318	S52.322S	318	S52.332P	386	S52.342K	386	S52.352G	319
S52.281J	317	S52.301G	318	S52.323A	354, 995	S52.332Q	386	S52.342M	386	S52.352H	319
S52.281K	386	S52.301H	318	S52.323B	354, 995, 1033	S52.332R	386	S52.342N	386	S52.352J	319
S52.281M	386	S52.301J	318	S52.323C	354, 995, 1033	S52.332S	318	S52.342P	386	S52.352K	387
S52.281N	386	S52.301K	386	S52.323D	318	S52.333A	354, 995	S52.342Q	386	S52.352M	387
S52.281P	386	S52.301M	386	S52.323E	318	S52.333B	354, 995, 1033	S52.342R	386	S52.352N	387
S52.281Q	386	S52.301N	386	S52.323F	318	S52.333C	354, 995, 1033	S52.342S	318	S52.352P	387
S52.281R	386	S52.301P	386	S52.323G	318	S52.333D	318	S52.343A	354, 995	S52.352Q	387
S52.281S	317	S52.301Q	386	S52.323H	318	S52.333E	318	S52.343B	354, 995, 1033	S52.352R	387
S52.282A	354, 995	S52.301R	386	S52.323J	318	S52.333F	318	S52.343C	354, 995, 1033	S52.352S	319
S52.282B	354, 995, 1033	S52.301S	318	S52.323K	386	S52.333G	318	S52.343D	318	S52.353A	354, 995
S52.282C	354, 995, 1033	S52.302A	354, 995	S52.323M	386	S52.333H	318	S52.343E	318	S52.353B	354, 995, 1033
S52.282D	317	S52.302B	354, 995, 1033	S52.323N	386	S52.333J	318	S52.343F	318	S52.353C	354, 995, 1033
S52.282E	317	S52.302C	354, 995, 1033	S52.323P	386	S52.333K	386	S52.343G	318	S52.353D	319
S52.282F	317	S52.302D	318	S52.323Q	386	S52.333M	386	S52.343H	318	S52.353E	319
S52.282G	317	S52.302E	318	S52.323R	386	S52.333N	386	S52.343J	318	S52.353F	319
S52.282H	317	S52.302F	318	S52.323S	318	S52.333P	386	S52.343K	386	S52.353G	319
S52.282J	317	S52.302G	318	S52.324A	354, 995	S52.333Q	386	S52.343M	386	S52.353H	319
S52.282K	386	S52.302H	318	S52.324B	354, 995, 1033	S52.333S	318	S52.343N	386	S52.353J	319
S52.282M	386	S52.302J	318	S52.324C	354, 995, 1033	S52.334A	354, 995	S52.343P	386	S52.353K	387
S52.282N	386	S52.302K	386	S52.324D	318	S52.334B	354, 995, 1033	S52.343Q	386	S52.353M	387
S52.282P	386	S52.302M	386	S52.324E	318	S52.334C	354, 995, 1033	S52.343S	318	S52.353N	387
S52.282Q	386	S52.302N	386	S52.324F	318	S52.334D	318	S52.344A	354, 995	S52.353P	387
S52.282R	386	S52.302P	386	S52.324G	318	S52.334E	318	S52.344B	354, 995, 1033	S52.353Q	387
S52.282S	317	S52.302Q	386	S52.324H	318	S52.334F	318	S52.344C	354, 995, 1033	S52.353R	387
S52.283A	354, 995	S52.302R	386	S52.324J	318	S52.334G	318	S52.344D	318	S52.353S	319
S52.283B	354, 995, 1033	S52.302S	318	S52.324K	386	S52.334H	318	S52.344E	318	S52.354A	354, 995
S52.283C	354, 995, 1033	S52.309A	354, 995	S52.324M	386	S52.334J	318	S52.344F	318	S52.354B	354, 995, 1033
S52.283D	317	S52.309B	354, 995, 1033	S52.324N	386	S52.334K	386	S52.344G	318	S52.354C	354, 995, 1033
S52.283E	317	S52.309C	354, 995, 1033	S52.324P	386	S52.334M	386	S52.344H	318	S52.354D	319
S52.283F	317	S52.309D	318	S52.324Q	386	S52.334N	386	S52.344J	318	S52.354E	319
S52.283G	317	S52.309E	318	S52.324R	386	S52.334P	386	S52.344K	386	S52.354G	319
S52.283H	317	S52.309F	318	S52.324S	318	S52.334Q	386	S52.344M	386	S52.354H	319
S52.283J	317			S52.325A	354, 995						

Code	Page	Code	Page	Code	Page	Code	Page	Code	Page	Code	Page
S52.354J	319	S52.364F	319	S52.381C	354, 995, 1033	S52.399S	319	S52.513P	387	S52.532H	320
S52.354K	387	S52.364G	319	S52.381D	319	S52.501A	355, 995	S52.513Q	387	S52.532J	320
S52.354M	387	S52.364H	319	S52.381E	319	S52.501B	355, 995, 1033	S52.513R	387	S52.532K	388
S52.354N	387	S52.364J	319	S52.381F	319	S52.501C	355, 995, 1033	S52.513S	320	S52.532M	388
S52.354P	387	S52.364K	387	S52.381G	319	S52.501D	319	S52.514A	355, 996	S52.532N	388
S52.354Q	387	S52.364M	387	S52.381H	319	S52.501E	319	S52.514B	355, 996, 1033	S52.532P	388
S52.354R	387	S52.364N	387	S52.381J	319	S52.501F	319	S52.514C	355, 996, 1033	S52.532Q	388
S52.354S	319	S52.364P	387	S52.381K	387	S52.501G	319	S52.514D	320	S52.532R	388
S52.355A	354, 995	S52.364Q	387	S52.381M	387	S52.501H	319	S52.514E	320	S52.532S	320
S52.355B	354, 995, 1033	S52.364R	387	S52.381N	387	S52.501J	319	S52.514F	320	S52.539A	355, 996
S52.355C	354, 995, 1033	S52.364S	319	S52.381P	387	S52.501K	387	S52.514G	320	S52.539B	355, 996, 1033
S52.355D	319	S52.365A	354, 995	S52.381Q	387	S52.501M	387	S52.514H	320	S52.539C	355, 996, 1033
S52.355E	319	S52.365B	354, 995, 1033	S52.381R	387	S52.501P	387	S52.514J	320	S52.539D	320
S52.355F	319	S52.365C	354, 995, 1033	S52.381S	319	S52.501Q	387	S52.514K	387	S52.539E	320
S52.355G	319	S52.365D	319	S52.382A	354, 995	S52.501R	387	S52.514M	387	S52.539F	320
S52.355H	319	S52.365E	319	S52.382B	354, 995, 1033	S52.501S	319	S52.514N	387	S52.539G	320
S52.355J	319	S52.365F	319	S52.382C	354, 995, 1033	S52.502A	355, 995	S52.514Q	387	S52.539H	320
S52.355K	387	S52.365G	319	S52.382D	319	S52.502B	355, 996, 1033	S52.514R	387	S52.539J	320
S52.355M	387	S52.365H	319	S52.382E	319	S52.502C	355, 996, 1033	S52.514S	320	S52.539K	388
S52.355N	387	S52.365J	319	S52.382F	319	S52.502D	319	S52.515A	355, 996	S52.539M	388
S52.355P	387	S52.365K	387	S52.382G	319	S52.502E	319	S52.515B	355, 996, 1033	S52.539N	388
S52.355Q	387	S52.365M	387	S52.382H	319	S52.502F	319	S52.515C	355, 996, 1033	S52.539P	388
S52.355R	387	S52.365N	387	S52.382J	319	S52.502G	319	S52.515D	320	S52.539Q	388
S52.355S	319	S52.365P	387	S52.382K	387	S52.502H	319	S52.515E	320	S52.539R	388
S52.356A	354, 995	S52.365Q	387	S52.382M	387	S52.502J	319	S52.515F	320	S52.539S	320
S52.356B	354, 995, 1033	S52.365R	387	S52.382N	387	S52.502K	387	S52.515G	320	S52.541A	355, 996
S52.356C	354, 995, 1033	S52.365S	319	S52.382P	387	S52.502M	387	S52.515H	320	S52.541B	355, 996, 1033
S52.356D	319	S52.366A	354, 995	S52.382Q	387	S52.502N	387	S52.515J	320	S52.541C	355, 996, 1033
S52.356E	319	S52.366B	354, 995, 1033	S52.382R	387	S52.502P	387	S52.515K	387	S52.541D	320
S52.356F	319	S52.366C	354, 995, 1033	S52.382S	319	S52.502Q	387	S52.515M	387	S52.541E	320
S52.356G	319	S52.366D	319	S52.389A	354, 995	S52.502R	387	S52.515N	388	S52.541F	320
S52.356H	319	S52.366E	319	S52.389B	354, 995, 1033	S52.502S	319	S52.515P	388	S52.541G	320
S52.356J	319	S52.366F	319	S52.389C	355, 995, 1033	S52.509A	355, 996	S52.515Q	388	S52.541H	320
S52.356K	387	S52.366G	319	S52.389D	319	S52.509B	355, 996, 1033	S52.515R	388	S52.541J	320
S52.356M	387	S52.366H	319	S52.389E	319	S52.509C	355, 996, 1033	S52.515S	320	S52.541K	388
S52.356N	387	S52.366J	319	S52.389F	319	S52.509D	319	S52.516A	355, 996	S52.541M	388
S52.356P	387	S52.366K	387	S52.389G	319	S52.509E	319	S52.516B	355, 996, 1033	S52.541N	388
S52.356Q	387	S52.366M	387	S52.389H	319	S52.509F	319	S52.516C	355, 996, 1033	S52.541P	388
S52.356R	387	S52.366N	387	S52.389J	319	S52.509G	319	S52.516D	320	S52.541Q	388
S52.356S	319	S52.366P	387	S52.389K	387	S52.509H	319	S52.516E	320	S52.541R	388
S52.361A	354, 995	S52.366Q	387	S52.389M	387	S52.509J	319	S52.516F	320	S52.541S	320
S52.361B	354, 995, 1033	S52.366R	387	S52.389N	387	S52.509K	387	S52.516G	320	S52.542A	355, 996
S52.361C	354, 995, 1033	S52.366S	319	S52.389P	387	S52.509M	387	S52.516H	320	S52.542B	355, 996, 1033
S52.361D	319	S52.371A	354, 995	S52.389Q	387	S52.509N	387	S52.516J	320	S52.542C	355, 996, 1033
S52.361E	319	S52.371B	354, 995, 1033	S52.389S	319	S52.509P	387	S52.516K	388	S52.542D	320
S52.361F	319	S52.371C	354, 995, 1033	S52.391A	355, 995	S52.509Q	387	S52.516M	388	S52.542E	320
S52.361G	319	S52.371D	319	S52.391B	355, 995, 1033	S52.509R	387	S52.516N	388	S52.542F	320
S52.361H	319	S52.371E	319	S52.391C	355, 995, 1033	S52.509S	319	S52.516P	388	S52.542G	320
S52.361J	319	S52.371F	319	S52.391D	319	S52.511A	355, 996	S52.516Q	388	S52.542H	320
S52.361K	387	S52.371G	319	S52.391E	319	S52.511B	355, 996, 1033	S52.516R	388	S52.542J	320
S52.361M	387	S52.371H	319	S52.391F	319	S52.511C	355, 996, 1033	S52.516S	320	S52.542K	388
S52.361N	387	S52.371J	319	S52.391G	319	S52.511D	319	S52.521A	355, 996	S52.542M	388
S52.361P	387	S52.371K	387	S52.391H	319	S52.511E	319	S52.521D	320	S52.542N	388
S52.361Q	387	S52.371M	387	S52.391J	319	S52.511F	319	S52.521G	320	S52.542P	388
S52.361R	387	S52.371N	387	S52.391K	387	S52.511G	319	S52.521K	388	S52.542Q	388
S52.361S	319	S52.371P	387	S52.391M	387	S52.511H	319	S52.521P	388	S52.542R	388
S52.362A	354, 995	S52.371Q	387	S52.391N	387	S52.511J	319	S52.521S	320	S52.542S	320
S52.362B	354, 995, 1033	S52.371R	387	S52.391P	387	S52.511K	387	S52.522A	355, 996	S52.549A	355, 996
S52.362C	354, 995, 1033	S52.371S	319	S52.391Q	387	S52.511M	387	S52.522D	320	S52.549B	355, 996, 1033
S52.362D	319	S52.372A	354, 995	S52.391R	387	S52.511N	387	S52.522G	320	S52.549C	355, 996, 1033
S52.362E	319	S52.372B	354, 995, 1033	S52.391S	319	S52.511Q	387	S52.522K	388	S52.549D	320
S52.362F	319	S52.372C	354, 995, 1033	S52.392A	355, 995	S52.511R	387	S52.522P	388	S52.549E	320
S52.362G	319	S52.372D	319	S52.392B	355, 995, 1033	S52.511S	319	S52.522S	320	S52.549F	320
S52.362H	319	S52.372E	319	S52.392C	355, 995, 1033	S52.512A	355, 996	S52.529A	355, 996	S52.549G	320
S52.362J	319	S52.372F	319	S52.392D	319	S52.512B	355, 996, 1033	S52.529D	320	S52.549H	320
S52.362K	387	S52.372G	319	S52.392E	319	S52.512C	355, 996, 1033	S52.529G	320	S52.549J	320
S52.362M	387	S52.372H	319	S52.392F	319	S52.512D	319	S52.529K	388	S52.549K	388
S52.362N	387	S52.372J	319	S52.392G	319	S52.512E	319	S52.529P	388	S52.549M	388
S52.362P	387	S52.372K	387	S52.392H	319	S52.512F	319	S52.529S	320	S52.549N	388
S52.362Q	387	S52.372M	387	S52.392J	319	S52.512H	319	S52.531A	355, 996	S52.549P	388
S52.362R	387	S52.372N	387	S52.392K	387	S52.512J	319	S52.531B	355, 996, 1033	S52.549Q	388
S52.362S	387	S52.372P	387	S52.392M	387	S52.512K	387	S52.531C	355, 996, 1033	S52.549R	388
S52.363A	354, 995	S52.372Q	387	S52.392N	387	S52.512M	387	S52.531D	320	S52.549S	320
S52.363B	354, 995, 1033	S52.372R	387	S52.392P	387	S52.512N	387	S52.531E	320	S52.551A	355, 996
S52.363C	354, 995, 1033	S52.372S	319	S52.392Q	387	S52.512P	387	S52.531F	320	S52.551B	355, 996, 1033
S52.363D	319	S52.379A	354, 995	S52.392R	387	S52.512Q	387	S52.531G	320	S52.551C	355, 996, 1033
S52.363E	319	S52.379B	354, 995, 1033	S52.392S	319	S52.512R	387	S52.531H	320	S52.551D	320
S52.363F	319	S52.379C	354, 995, 1033	S52.399A	355, 995	S52.512S	319	S52.531J	320	S52.551E	320
S52.363G	319	S52.379D	319	S52.399B	355, 995, 1033	S52.513A	355, 996	S52.531K	388	S52.551F	320
S52.363H	319	S52.379E	319	S52.399C	355, 995, 1033	S52.513B	355, 996, 1033	S52.531M	388	S52.551G	320
S52.363J	319	S52.379F	319	S52.399D	319	S52.513C	355, 996, 1033	S52.531N	388	S52.551H	320
S52.363K	387	S52.379G	319	S52.399E	319	S52.513D	319	S52.531P	388	S52.551J	320
S52.363M	387	S52.379H	319	S52.399F	319	S52.513E	319	S52.531Q	388	S52.551K	388
S52.363N	387	S52.379J	319	S52.399G	319	S52.513F	320	S52.531R	388	S52.551M	388
S52.363P	387	S52.379K	387	S52.399H	319	S52.513G	320	S52.531S	320	S52.551N	388
S52.363Q	387	S52.379M	387	S52.399J	319	S52.513H	320	S52.532A	355, 996	S52.551P	388
S52.363R	387	S52.379N	387	S52.399K	387	S52.513J	320	S52.532B	355, 996, 1033	S52.551Q	388
S52.363S	319	S52.379P	387	S52.399M	387	S52.513K	387	S52.532C	355, 996, 1033	S52.551R	388
S52.364A	354, 995	S52.379Q	387	S52.399N	387	S52.513M	387	S52.532D	320	S52.551S	320
S52.364B	354, 995, 1033	S52.379R	387	S52.399P	387	S52.513N	387	S52.532E	320	S52.552A	355, 996
S52.364C	354, 995, 1033	S52.379S	319	S52.399Q	387			S52.532F	320	S52.552B	355, 996, 1033
S52.364D	319	S52.381A	354, 995	S52.399R	387			S52.532G	320	S52.552C	355, 996, 1033
S52.364E	319	S52.381B	354, 995, 1033							S52.552D	320

Numeric Index to Diseases

Code	Page	Code	Page	Code	Page	Code	Page	Code	Page	Code	Page
S52.552E	320	S52.572B	355,996,1033	S52.601R	388	S52.614N	388	S52.699G	321	S53.016S	355
S52.552F	320	S52.572C	355,996,1033	S52.601S	320	S52.614P	388	S52.699H	321	S53.021A	355,996
S52.552G	320	S52.572D	320	S52.602A	355,996	S52.614Q	388	S52.699J	321	S53.021D	808
S52.552H	320	S52.572E	320	S52.602B	355,996,1033	S52.614R	388	S52.699K	389	S53.021S	355
S52.552J	320	S52.572F	320	S52.602C	355,996,1033	S52.614S	321	S52.699M	389	S53.022A	355,996
S52.552K	388	S52.572G	320	S52.602D	320	S52.615A	355,996	S52.699N	389	S53.022D	808
S52.552M	388	S52.572H	320	S52.602E	320	S52.615B	355,996,1034	S52.699P	389	S53.022S	355
S52.552N	388	S52.572J	320	S52.602F	320	S52.615C	355,996,1034	S52.699Q	389	S53.023A	355,996
S52.552P	388	S52.572K	388	S52.602G	320	S52.615D	321	S52.699R	389	S53.023D	808
S52.552Q	388	S52.572M	388	S52.602H	320	S52.615E	321	S52.699S	321	S53.023S	355
S52.552R	388	S52.572N	388	S52.602J	321	S52.615F	321	S52.90XA	355,996	S53.024A	355,996
S52.552S	320	S52.572P	388	S52.602K	388	S52.615G	321	S52.90XB	355,996,1034	S53.024D	808
S52.559A	355,996	S52.572Q	388	S52.602M	388	S52.615H	321	S52.90XC	355,996,1034	S53.024S	355
S52.559B	355,996,1033	S52.572R	388	S52.602N	388	S52.615J	321	S52.90XD	321	S53.025A	356,996
S52.559C	355,996,1033	S52.572S	320	S52.602P	388	S52.615K	388	S52.90XE	321	S53.025D	808
S52.559D	320	S52.579A	355,996	S52.602Q	388	S52.615M	388	S52.90XF	321	S53.025S	356
S52.559E	320	S52.579B	355,996,1033	S52.602R	388	S52.615N	388	S52.90XG	321	S53.026A	356,996
S52.559F	320	S52.579C	355,996,1033	S52.602S	321	S52.615P	388	S52.90XH	321	S53.026D	808
S52.559G	320	S52.579D	320	S52.609A	355,996	S52.615Q	388	S52.90XJ	321	S53.026S	356
S52.559H	320	S52.579E	320	S52.609B	355,996,1033	S52.615R	388	S52.90XK	389	S53.031A	356,996
S52.559J	320	S52.579F	320	S52.609C	355,996,1033	S52.615S	321	S52.90XM	389	S53.031D	808
S52.559K	388	S52.579G	320	S52.609D	321	S52.616A	355,996	S52.90XN	389	S53.031S	356
S52.559M	388	S52.579H	320	S52.609E	321	S52.616B	355,996,1034	S52.90XP	389	S53.032A	356,996
S52.559N	388	S52.579J	320	S52.609F	321	S52.616C	355,996,1034	S52.90XQ	389	S53.032D	808
S52.559P	388	S52.579K	388	S52.609G	321	S52.616D	321	S52.90XR	389	S53.032S	356
S52.559Q	388	S52.579M	388	S52.609H	321	S52.616E	321	S52.90XS	321	S53.033A	356,996
S52.559R	388	S52.579N	388	S52.609J	321	S52.616F	321	S52.91XA	355,996	S53.033D	808
S52.559S	320	S52.579P	388	S52.609K	388	S52.616G	321	S52.91XB	355,996,1034	S53.033S	356
S52.561A	355,996	S52.579Q	388	S52.609M	388	S52.616H	321	S52.91XC	355,996,1034	S53.091A	356,996
S52.561B	355,996,1033	S52.579R	388	S52.609N	388	S52.616J	321	S52.91XD	321	S53.091D	808
S52.561C	355,996,1033	S52.579S	320	S52.609P	388	S52.616K	388	S52.91XE	321	S53.091S	356
S52.561D	320	S52.591A	355,996	S52.609Q	388	S52.616M	388	S52.91XF	321	S53.092A	356,996
S52.561E	320	S52.591B	355,996,1033	S52.609R	388	S52.616N	389	S52.91XG	321	S53.092D	808
S52.561F	320	S52.591C	355,996,1033	S52.609S	321	S52.616P	389	S52.91XH	321	S53.092S	356
S52.561G	320	S52.591D	320	S52.611A	355,996	S52.616Q	389	S52.91XJ	321	S53.093A	356,996
S52.561H	320	S52.591E	320	S52.611B	355,996,1033	S52.616R	389	S52.91XK	389	S53.093D	808
S52.561J	320	S52.591F	320	S52.611C	355,996,1033	S52.616S	321	S52.91XM	389	S53.093S	356
S52.561K	388	S52.591G	320	S52.611D	321	S52.621A	355,996	S52.91XN	389	S53.094A	356,996
S52.561M	388	S52.591H	320	S52.611E	321	S52.621D	321	S52.91XP	389	S53.094D	808
S52.561N	388	S52.591J	320	S52.611F	321	S52.621G	321	S52.91XQ	389	S53.094S	356
S52.561P	388	S52.591K	388	S52.611G	321	S52.621K	389	S52.91XR	389	S53.095A	356,996
S52.561Q	388	S52.591M	388	S52.611H	321	S52.621P	389	S52.91XS	321	S53.095D	808
S52.561R	388	S52.591N	388	S52.611J	321	S52.621S	321	S52.92XA	355,996	S53.095S	356
S52.561S	320	S52.591P	388	S52.611K	388	S52.622A	355,996	S52.92XB	355,996,1034	S53.096A	356,996
S52.562A	355,996	S52.591Q	388	S52.611M	388	S52.622D	321	S52.92XC	355,996,1034	S53.096D	808
S52.562B	355,996,1033	S52.591R	388	S52.611N	388	S52.622G	321	S52.92XD	321	S53.096S	356
S52.562C	355,996,1033	S52.591S	320	S52.611P	388	S52.622K	389	S52.92XE	321	S53.101A	356,996
S52.562D	320	S52.592A	355,996	S52.611Q	388	S52.622P	389	S52.92XF	321	S53.101D	808
S52.562E	320	S52.592B	355,996,1033	S52.611R	388	S52.622S	321	S52.92XG	321	S53.101S	356
S52.562F	320	S52.592C	355,996,1033	S52.611S	321	S52.629A	355,996	S52.92XH	321	S53.102A	356,996
S52.562G	320	S52.592D	320	S52.612A	355,996	S52.629D	321	S52.92XJ	321	S53.102D	808
S52.562H	320	S52.592E	320	S52.612B	355,996,1033	S52.629G	321	S52.92XK	389	S53.102S	356
S52.562J	320	S52.592F	320	S52.612C	355,996,1033	S52.629K	389	S52.92XM	389	S53.103A	356,996
S52.562K	388	S52.592G	320	S52.612D	321	S52.629P	389	S52.92XN	389	S53.103D	808
S52.562M	388	S52.592H	320	S52.612E	321	S52.629S	321	S52.92XP	389	S53.103S	356
S52.562N	388	S52.592J	320	S52.612F	321	S52.691A	355,996	S52.92XQ	389	S53.104A	356,996
S52.562P	388	S52.592K	388	S52.612G	321	S52.691B	355,996,1034	S52.92XS	321	S53.104D	808
S52.562Q	388	S52.592M	388	S52.612H	321	S52.691C	355,996,1034	S53.001A	355,996	S53.104S	356
S52.562R	388	S52.592N	388	S52.612J	321	S52.691D	321	S53.001D	808	S53.105A	356,996
S52.562S	320	S52.592P	388	S52.612K	388	S52.691E	321	S53.001S	355	S53.105D	808
S52.569A	355,996	S52.592Q	388	S52.612M	388	S52.691F	321	S53.002A	355,996	S53.105S	356
S52.569B	355,996,1033	S52.592R	388	S52.612N	388	S52.691G	321	S53.002D	808	S53.106A	356,996
S52.569C	355,996,1033	S52.592S	320	S52.612Q	388	S52.691H	321	S53.002S	355	S53.106D	808
S52.569D	320	S52.599A	355,996	S52.612R	388	S52.691J	321	S53.003A	355,996	S53.106S	356
S52.569E	320	S52.599B	355,996,1033	S52.612S	321	S52.691K	389	S53.003D	808	S53.111A	356,996
S52.569F	320	S52.599C	355,996,1033	S52.613A	355,996	S52.691M	389	S53.003S	355	S53.111D	808
S52.569G	320	S52.599D	320	S52.613B	355,996,1033	S52.691N	389	S53.004A	355,996	S53.111S	356
S52.569H	320	S52.599E	320	S52.613C	355,996,1033	S52.691P	389	S53.004D	808	S53.112A	356,996
S52.569J	320	S52.599F	320	S52.613D	321	S52.691Q	389	S53.004S	355	S53.112D	808
S52.569K	388	S52.599G	320	S52.613E	321	S52.691R	389	S53.005A	355,996	S53.112S	356
S52.569M	388	S52.599H	320	S52.613F	321	S52.691S	321	S53.005D	808	S53.113A	356,996
S52.569N	388	S52.599J	320	S52.613G	321	S52.692A	355,996	S53.005S	355	S53.113D	808
S52.569P	388	S52.599K	388	S52.613H	321	S52.692B	355,996,1034	S53.006A	355,996	S53.113S	356
S52.569Q	388	S52.599M	388	S52.613J	321	S52.692C	355,996,1034	S53.006D	808	S53.114A	356,996
S52.569R	388	S52.599N	388	S52.613K	388	S52.692D	321	S53.006S	355	S53.114D	808
S52.569S	320	S52.599P	388	S52.613M	388	S52.692E	321	S53.011A	355,996	S53.114S	356
S52.571A	355,996	S52.599Q	388	S52.613N	388	S52.692F	321	S53.011D	808	S53.115A	356,996
S52.571B	355,996,1033	S52.599R	388	S52.613P	388	S52.692G	321	S53.011S	355	S53.115D	808
S52.571C	355,996,1033	S52.599S	320	S52.613Q	388	S52.692H	321	S53.012A	355,996	S53.115S	356
S52.571D	320	S52.601A	355,996	S52.613R	388	S52.692J	321	S53.012D	808	S53.116A	356,996
S52.571E	320	S52.601B	355,996,1033	S52.613S	321	S52.692K	389	S53.012S	355	S53.116D	808
S52.571F	320	S52.601C	355,996,1033	S52.614A	355,996	S52.692M	389	S53.013A	355,996	S53.116S	356
S52.571G	320	S52.601D	320	S52.614B	355,996,1034	S52.692N	389	S53.013D	808	S53.121A	356,996
S52.571H	320	S52.601E	320	S52.614C	355,996,1034	S52.692P	389	S53.013S	355	S53.121D	808
S52.571J	320	S52.601F	320	S52.614D	321	S52.692Q	389	S53.014A	355,996	S53.121S	356
S52.571K	388	S52.601G	320	S52.614E	321	S52.692R	389	S53.014D	808	S53.122A	356,996
S52.571M	388	S52.601H	320	S52.614F	321	S52.692S	321	S53.014S	355	S53.122D	808
S52.571N	388	S52.601J	320	S52.614G	321	S52.699A	355,996	S53.015A	355,996	S53.122S	356
S52.571P	388	S52.601K	388	S52.614H	321	S52.699B	355,996,1034	S53.015D	808	S53.123A	356,996
S52.571Q	388	S52.601M	388	S52.614J	321	S52.699C	355,996,1034	S53.015S	355	S53.123D	808
S52.571R	388	S52.601N	388	S52.614K	388	S52.699E	321	S53.016A	355,996	S53.123S	356
S52.571S	320	S52.601P	388	S52.614M	388	S52.699F	321	S53.016D	808	S53.124A	356,996
S52.572A	355,996	S52.601Q	388							S53.124D	808

Code	Page	Code	Page	Code	Page	Code	Page	Code	Page	Code	Page
S53.124S	356	S53.412S	356	S54.92XS	53	S55.811S	170	S56.104S	749	S56.198S	749
S53.125A	356,996	S53.419A	356,997	S55.001A	749,997,1034	S55.812A	749,997,1034	S56.105A	749,997	S56.199A	749,997
S53.125D	808	S53.419D	808	S55.001D	809	S55.812D	809	S56.105D	809	S56.199D	809
S53.125S	356	S53.419S	356	S55.001S	169	S55.812S	170	S56.105S	749	S56.199S	749
S53.126A	356,996	S53.421A	356,997	S55.002A	749,997,1034	S55.819A	749,997,1034	S56.106A	749,997	S56.201A	749,997
S53.126D	808	S53.421D	808	S55.002D	809	S55.819D	809	S56.106D	809	S56.201D	809
S53.126S	356	S53.421S	356	S55.002S	169	S55.819S	170	S56.106S	749	S56.201S	749
S53.131A	356,996	S53.422A	356,997	S55.009A	749,997,1034	S55.891A	997,1034	S56.107A	749,997	S56.202A	749,997
S53.131D	808	S53.422D	808	S55.009D	809	S55.891A	749	S56.107D	809	S56.202D	809
S53.131S	356	S53.422S	356	S55.009S	169	S55.891D	809	S56.107S	749	S56.202S	750
S53.132A	356,997	S53.429A	356,997	S55.011A	749,997,1034	S55.891S	170	S56.108A	749,997	S56.209A	750,997
S53.132D	808	S53.429D	808	S55.011D	809	S55.892A	997,1034	S56.108D	809	S56.209D	809
S53.132S	356	S53.429S	356	S55.011S	169	S55.892A	749	S56.108S	749	S56.209S	750
S53.133A	356,997	S53.431A	356,997	S55.012A	749,997,1034	S55.892D	809	S56.109A	749,997	S56.211A	356,997
S53.133D	808	S53.431D	808	S55.012D	809	S55.892S	170	S56.109D	809	S56.211D	809
S53.133S	356	S53.431S	356	S55.012S	169	S55.899A	997,1034	S56.109S	749	S56.211S	356
S53.134A	356,997	S53.432A	356,997	S55.019A	749,997,1034	S55.899A	749	S56.111A	356,997	S56.212A	356,997
S53.134D	808	S53.432D	808	S55.019D	809	S55.899D	809	S56.111D	809	S56.212D	809
S53.134S	356	S53.432S	356	S55.019S	169	S55.899S	170	S56.111S	356	S56.212S	356
S53.135A	356,997	S53.439A	356,997	S55.091A	749,997,1034	S55.901A	749,997,1034	S56.112A	356,997	S56.219A	356,997
S53.135D	808	S53.439D	808	S55.091D	809	S55.901D	809	S56.112D	809	S56.219D	809
S53.135S	356	S53.439S	356	S55.091S	169	S55.901S	170	S56.112S	356	S56.219S	356
S53.136A	356,997	S53.441A	356,997	S55.092A	749,997,1034	S55.902A	749,997,1034	S56.113A	356,997	S56.221A	389,997
S53.136D	808	S53.441D	808	S55.092D	809	S55.902D	809	S56.113D	809	S56.221D	809
S53.136S	356	S53.441S	356	S55.092S	169	S55.902S	170	S56.113S	356	S56.221S	463
S53.141A	356,997	S53.442A	356,997	S55.099A	749,997,1034	S55.909A	749,997,1034	S56.114A	356,997	S56.222A	389,997
S53.141D	808	S53.442D	808	S55.099D	809	S55.909D	809	S56.114D	809	S56.222D	809
S53.141S	356	S53.442S	356	S55.099S	169	S55.909S	170	S56.114S	356	S56.222S	463
S53.142A	356,997	S53.449A	356,997	S55.101A	749,997,1034	S55.911A	749,997,1034	S56.115A	356,997	S56.229A	389,997
S53.142D	808	S53.449D	808	S55.101D	809	S55.911D	809	S56.115D	809	S56.229D	809
S53.142S	356	S53.449S	356	S55.101S	169	S55.911S	170	S56.115S	356	S56.229S	463
S53.143A	356,997	S53.491A	356,997	S55.102A	749,997,1034	S55.912A	749,997,1034	S56.116A	356,997	S56.291A	997
S53.143D	808	S53.491D	808	S55.102D	809	S55.912D	809	S56.116D	809	S56.291A	750
S53.143S	356	S53.491S	356	S55.102S	169	S55.912S	170	S56.116S	356	S56.291D	809
S53.144A	356,997	S53.492A	356,997	S55.109A	749,997,1034	S55.919A	749,997,1034	S56.117A	356,997	S56.291S	750
S53.144D	808	S53.492D	808	S55.109D	809	S55.919D	809	S56.117D	809	S56.292A	997
S53.144S	356	S53.492S	356	S55.109S	169	S55.919S	170	S56.117S	356	S56.292A	750
S53.145A	356,997	S53.499A	356,997	S55.111A	749,997,1034	S55.991A	749,997,1034	S56.118A	356,997	S56.292D	809
S53.145D	808	S53.499D	808	S55.111D	809	S55.991D	809	S56.118D	809	S56.292S	750
S53.145S	356	S53.499S	356	S55.111S	169	S55.991S	170	S56.118S	356	S56.299A	997
S53.146A	356,997	S54.00XA	46,997,1034	S55.112A	749,997,1034	S55.992A	749,997,1034	S56.119A	356,997	S56.299A	750
S53.146D	808	S54.00XD	808	S55.112D	809	S55.992D	809	S56.119D	809	S56.299D	809
S53.146S	356	S54.00XS	53	S55.112S	169	S55.992S	170	S56.119S	356	S56.299S	750
S53.191A	356,997	S54.01XA	46,997,1034	S55.119A	749,997,1034	S55.999A	749,997,1034	S56.121A	389,997	S56.301A	997
S53.191D	808	S54.01XD	808	S55.119D	809	S55.999D	809	S56.121D	809	S56.301A	750
S53.191S	356	S54.01XS	53	S55.119S	169	S55.999S	170	S56.121S	462	S56.301D	809
S53.192A	356,997	S54.02XA	46,997,1034	S55.191A	749,997,1034	S56.001A	749,997	S56.122A	389,997	S56.301S	750
S53.192D	808	S54.02XD	808	S55.191D	809	S56.001D	809	S56.122D	809	S56.302A	750
S53.192S	356	S54.02XS	53	S55.191S	169	S56.001S	749	S56.122S	462	S56.302A	997
S53.193A	356,997	S54.10XA	46,997,1034	S55.192A	749,997,1034	S56.002A	749,997	S56.123A	389,997	S56.302D	809
S53.193D	808	S54.10XD	808	S55.192D	809	S56.002D	809	S56.123D	809	S56.302S	750
S53.193S	356	S54.10XS	53	S55.192S	169	S56.002S	749	S56.123S	462	S56.309A	997
S53.194A	356,997	S54.11XA	46,997,1034	S55.199A	749,997,1034	S56.009A	749,997	S56.124A	389,997	S56.309A	750
S53.194D	808	S54.11XD	808	S55.199D	809	S56.009D	809	S56.124D	809	S56.309D	809
S53.194S	356	S54.11XS	53	S55.199S	169	S56.009S	749	S56.124S	462	S56.309S	750
S53.195A	356,997	S54.12XA	47,997,1034	S55.201A	749,997,1034	S56.011A	356,997	S56.125A	389,997	S56.311A	356
S53.195D	808	S54.12XD	808	S55.201D	809	S56.011D	809	S56.125D	809	S56.311A	997
S53.195S	356	S54.12XS	53	S55.201S	169	S56.011S	356	S56.125S	462	S56.311D	809
S53.196A	356,997	S54.20XA	47,997,1034	S55.202A	749,997,1034	S56.012A	356,997	S56.126A	389,997	S56.311S	356
S53.196D	808	S54.20XD	808	S55.202D	809	S56.012D	809	S56.126D	809	S56.312A	357
S53.196S	356	S54.20XS	53	S55.202S	169	S56.012S	356	S56.126S	462	S56.312A	997
S53.20XA	356,997	S54.21XA	47,997,1034	S55.209A	749,997,1034	S56.019A	356,997	S56.127A	389,997	S56.312D	809
S53.20XD	808	S54.21XD	808	S55.209D	809	S56.019D	809	S56.127D	809	S56.312S	357
S53.20XS	356	S54.21XS	53	S55.209S	169	S56.019S	356	S56.127S	462	S56.319A	357
S53.21XA	356,997	S54.22XA	47,997,1034	S55.211A	749,997,1034	S56.021A	389,997	S56.128A	389,997	S56.319A	997
S53.21XD	808	S54.22XD	808	S55.211D	809	S56.021D	809	S56.128D	809	S56.319D	809
S53.21XS	356	S54.22XS	53	S55.211S	169	S56.021S	462	S56.128S	462	S56.319S	357
S53.22XA	356,997	S54.30XA	47,997	S55.212A	749,997,1034	S56.022A	389,997	S56.129A	389,997	S56.321A	389,997
S53.22XD	808	S54.30XD	808	S55.212D	809	S56.022D	809	S56.129D	809	S56.321D	809
S53.22XS	356	S54.30XS	53	S55.212S	169	S56.022S	462	S56.129S	463	S56.321S	463
S53.30XA	356,997	S54.31XA	47,997	S55.219A	749,997,1034	S56.029A	389,997	S56.191A	749,997	S56.322A	389,997
S53.30XD	808	S54.31XD	808	S55.219D	809	S56.029D	809	S56.191D	809	S56.322D	809
S53.30XS	356	S54.31XS	53	S55.219S	170	S56.029S	462	S56.191S	749	S56.322S	463
S53.31XA	356,997	S54.32XA	47,997	S55.291A	749,997,1034	S56.091A	749,997	S56.192A	749,997	S56.329A	389,997
S53.31XD	808	S54.32XD	808	S55.291D	809	S56.091D	809	S56.192D	809	S56.329D	809
S53.31XS	356	S54.32XS	53	S55.291S	170	S56.091S	749	S56.192S	749	S56.329S	463
S53.32XA	356,997	S54.8X1A	47,997,1034	S55.292A	749,997,1034	S56.092A	749,997	S56.193A	749,997	S56.391A	750,997
S53.32XD	808	S54.8X1D	808	S55.292D	809	S56.092D	809	S56.193D	809	S56.391D	809
S53.32XS	356	S54.8X1S	53	S55.292S	170	S56.092S	749	S56.193S	749	S56.391S	750
S53.401A	356,997	S54.8X2A	47,997,1034	S55.299A	749,997,1034	S56.099A	749,997	S56.194A	749,997	S56.392A	750,998
S53.401D	808	S54.8X2D	808	S55.299D	809	S56.099D	809	S56.194D	809	S56.392D	809
S53.401S	356	S54.8X2S	53	S55.299S	170	S56.099S	749	S56.194S	749	S56.392S	750
S53.402A	356,997	S54.8X9A	47,997,1034	S55.801A	749,997,1034	S56.101A	749,997	S56.195A	749,997	S56.399A	750,998
S53.402D	808	S54.8X9D	808	S55.801D	809	S56.101D	809	S56.195D	809	S56.399D	809
S53.402S	356	S54.8X9S	53	S55.801S	170	S56.101S	749	S56.195S	749	S56.399S	750
S53.409A	356,997	S54.90XA	47,997	S55.802A	749,997,1034	S56.102A	749,997	S56.196A	749,997	S56.401A	998
S53.409D	808	S54.90XD	808	S55.802D	809	S56.102D	809	S56.196D	809	S56.401A	750
S53.409S	356	S54.90XS	53	S55.802S	170	S56.102S	749	S56.196S	749	S56.401D	809
S53.411A	356,997	S54.91XA	47,997	S55.809A	749,997,1034	S56.103A	749,997	S56.197A	749,997	S56.401S	750
S53.411D	808	S54.91XD	808	S55.809D	809	S56.103D	809	S56.197D	809	S56.402A	998
S53.411S	356	S54.91XS	53	S55.809S	170	S56.103S	749	S56.197S	749	S56.402A	750
S53.412A	356,997	S54.92XA	47,997	S55.811A	749,997,1034	S56.104A	749,997	S56.198A	749,997	S56.402D	809
S53.412D	808	S54.92XD	808	S55.811D	809	S56.104D	809	S56.198D	809	S56.402S	750

Numeric Index to Diseases

Code	Page
S56.403A	998
S56.403A	750
S56.403D	809
S56.403S	750
S56.404A	998
S56.404A	750
S56.404D	809
S56.404S	750
S56.405A	998
S56.405A	750
S56.405D	809
S56.405S	750
S56.406A	998
S56.406A	750
S56.406D	809
S56.406S	750
S56.407A	998
S56.407A	750
S56.407D	809
S56.407S	750
S56.408A	998
S56.408A	750
S56.408D	809
S56.408S	750
S56.409A	998
S56.409A	750
S56.409D	809
S56.409S	750
S56.411A	357, 998
S56.411D	809
S56.411S	357
S56.412A	357, 998
S56.412D	809
S56.412S	357
S56.413A	357, 998
S56.413D	809
S56.413S	357
S56.414A	357, 998
S56.414D	809
S56.414S	357
S56.415A	357, 998
S56.415D	809
S56.415S	357
S56.416A	357, 998
S56.416D	809
S56.416S	357
S56.417A	357, 998
S56.417D	809
S56.417S	357
S56.418A	357, 998
S56.418D	809
S56.418S	357
S56.419A	357, 998
S56.419D	809
S56.419S	357
S56.421A	389, 998
S56.421D	809
S56.421S	463
S56.422A	389, 998
S56.422D	809
S56.422S	463
S56.423A	389, 998
S56.423D	809
S56.423S	463
S56.424A	389, 998
S56.424D	809
S56.424S	463
S56.425A	389, 998
S56.425D	809
S56.425S	463
S56.426A	389, 998
S56.426D	809
S56.426S	463
S56.427A	389, 998
S56.427D	809
S56.427S	463
S56.428A	389, 998
S56.428D	809
S56.428S	463
S56.429A	389, 998
S56.429D	809
S56.429S	463
S56.491A	750, 998
S56.491D	809
S56.491S	750
S56.492A	750, 998
S56.492D	809
S56.492S	750
S56.493A	750, 998
S56.493D	809
S56.493S	750
S56.494A	750, 998
S56.494D	809
S56.494S	750
S56.495A	750, 998
S56.495D	809
S56.495S	750
S56.496A	750, 998
S56.496D	809
S56.496S	750
S56.497A	750, 998
S56.497D	809
S56.497S	750
S56.498A	750, 998
S56.498D	809
S56.498S	750
S56.499A	750, 998
S56.499D	809
S56.499S	750
S56.501A	998
S56.501A	750
S56.501D	809
S56.501S	750
S56.502A	998
S56.502A	750
S56.502D	809
S56.502S	750
S56.509A	998
S56.509A	750
S56.509D	809
S56.509S	750
S56.511A	357, 998
S56.511D	809
S56.511S	357
S56.512A	357, 998
S56.512D	809
S56.512S	357
S56.519A	357, 998
S56.519D	809
S56.519S	357
S56.521A	389, 998
S56.521D	809
S56.521S	463
S56.522A	389, 998
S56.522D	809
S56.522S	463
S56.529A	389, 998
S56.529D	809
S56.529S	463
S56.591A	750, 998
S56.591D	809
S56.591S	750
S56.592A	750, 998
S56.592D	809
S56.592S	750
S56.599A	750, 998
S56.599D	809
S56.599S	750
S56.801A	750, 998
S56.801D	809
S56.801S	750
S56.802A	750, 998
S56.802D	809
S56.802S	750
S56.809A	750, 998
S56.809D	809
S56.809S	750
S56.811A	357, 998
S56.811D	809
S56.811S	357
S56.812A	357, 998
S56.812D	809
S56.812S	357
S56.819A	357, 998
S56.819D	809
S56.819S	357
S56.821A	389, 998
S56.821D	809
S56.821S	463
S56.822A	389, 998
S56.822D	809
S56.822S	463
S56.829A	389, 998
S56.829D	809
S56.829S	463
S56.891A	750, 998
S56.891D	810
S56.891S	750
S56.892A	750, 998
S56.892D	810
S56.892S	750
S56.899A	750, 998
S56.899D	810
S56.899S	750
S56.901A	750, 998
S56.901D	810
S56.901S	750
S56.902A	750, 998
S56.902D	810
S56.902S	750
S56.909A	750, 998
S56.909D	810
S56.909S	750
S56.911A	357, 998
S56.911D	810
S56.911S	357
S56.912A	357, 998
S56.912D	810
S56.912S	357
S56.919A	357, 998
S56.919D	810
S56.919S	357
S56.921A	389, 998
S56.921D	810
S56.921S	463
S56.922A	389, 998
S56.922D	810
S56.922S	463
S56.929A	389, 998
S56.929D	810
S56.929S	463
S56.991A	750, 998
S56.991D	810
S56.991S	750
S56.992A	750, 998
S56.992D	810
S56.992S	750
S56.999A	750, 998
S56.999D	810
S56.999S	750
S57.00XA	750, 998, 1034
S57.00XD	810
S57.00XS	463
S57.01XA	750, 998, 1034
S57.01XD	810
S57.01XS	463
S57.02XA	750, 998, 1034
S57.02XD	810
S57.02XS	463
S57.80XA	750, 998, 1034
S57.80XD	810
S57.80XS	463
S57.81XA	750, 998, 1034
S57.81XD	810
S57.81XS	463
S57.82XA	750, 998, 1034
S57.82XD	810
S57.82XS	463
S58.011A	750, 998, 1034
S58.011D	810
S58.011S	321
S58.012A	750, 998, 1034
S58.012D	810
S58.012S	321
S58.019A	750, 998, 1034
S58.019D	810
S58.019S	321
S58.021A	750, 998, 1034
S58.021D	810
S58.021S	321
S58.022A	750, 998, 1034
S58.022D	810
S58.022S	321
S58.029A	750, 998, 1034
S58.029D	810
S58.029S	321
S58.111A	750, 998, 1034
S58.111D	810
S58.111S	321
S58.112A	750, 998, 1034
S58.112D	810
S58.112S	321
S58.119A	750, 998, 1034
S58.119D	810
S58.119S	321
S58.121A	750, 998, 1034
S58.121D	810
S58.121S	321
S58.122A	750, 998, 1034
S58.122D	810
S58.122S	321
S58.129A	750, 998, 1034
S58.129D	810
S58.129S	321
S58.911A	750, 998, 1034
S58.911D	810
S58.912A	750, 998, 1034
S58.912D	810
S58.912S	321
S58.919A	750, 998, 1034
S58.919D	810
S58.919S	321
S58.921A	750, 998, 1034
S58.921D	810
S58.921S	321
S58.922A	750, 998, 1034
S58.922D	810
S58.922S	321
S58.929A	750, 998, 1034
S58.929D	810
S58.929S	321
S59.001A	357, 998
S59.001D	321
S59.001G	321
S59.001K	389
S59.001P	389
S59.001S	321
S59.002A	357, 998
S59.002D	321
S59.002G	321
S59.002K	389
S59.002P	389
S59.002S	321
S59.009A	357, 998
S59.009D	321
S59.009G	321
S59.009K	389
S59.009P	389
S59.009S	321
S59.011A	357, 998
S59.011D	321
S59.011G	321
S59.011K	389
S59.011P	389
S59.011S	321
S59.012A	357, 998
S59.012D	321
S59.012G	321
S59.012K	389
S59.012P	389
S59.012S	321
S59.019A	357, 998
S59.019D	321
S59.019G	321
S59.019K	389
S59.019P	389
S59.019S	321
S59.021A	357, 998
S59.021D	321
S59.021G	321
S59.021K	389
S59.021P	389
S59.021S	321
S59.022A	357, 998
S59.022D	321
S59.022G	321
S59.022K	389
S59.022P	389
S59.022S	321
S59.029A	357, 998
S59.029D	321
S59.029G	321
S59.029K	389
S59.029P	389
S59.029S	321
S59.031A	357, 998
S59.031D	321
S59.031G	321
S59.031K	389
S59.031P	389
S59.031S	321
S59.032A	357, 998
S59.032D	321
S59.032G	321
S59.032K	389
S59.032P	389
S59.032S	321
S59.039A	357, 998
S59.039D	321
S59.039G	321
S59.039K	389
S59.039P	389
S59.039S	321
S59.041A	357, 998
S59.041D	321
S59.041G	321
S59.041K	389
S59.041P	389
S59.041S	321
S59.042A	357, 998
S59.042D	321
S59.042G	321
S59.042K	389
S59.042P	389
S59.042S	321
S59.049A	357, 998
S59.049D	321
S59.049G	321
S59.049K	389
S59.049P	389
S59.049S	321
S59.091A	357, 998
S59.091D	321
S59.091G	321
S59.091K	389
S59.091P	389
S59.091S	321
S59.092A	357, 998
S59.092D	321
S59.092G	321
S59.092K	389
S59.092P	389
S59.092S	321
S59.099A	357, 998
S59.099D	321
S59.099G	321
S59.099K	389
S59.099P	389
S59.099S	321
S59.101A	357, 998
S59.101D	322
S59.101G	322
S59.101K	389
S59.101P	389
S59.101S	322
S59.102A	357, 998
S59.102D	322
S59.102G	322
S59.102K	389
S59.102P	389
S59.102S	322
S59.109A	357, 998
S59.109D	322
S59.109G	322
S59.109K	389
S59.109P	389
S59.109S	322
S59.111A	357, 998
S59.111D	322
S59.111G	322
S59.111K	389
S59.111P	389
S59.111S	322
S59.112A	357, 998
S59.112D	322
S59.112G	322
S59.112K	389
S59.112P	389
S59.112S	322
S59.119A	357, 998
S59.119D	322
S59.119G	322
S59.119K	389
S59.119P	389
S59.119S	322
S59.121A	357, 998
S59.121D	322
S59.121G	322
S59.121K	389
S59.121P	389
S59.121S	322
S59.122A	357, 998
S59.122D	322
S59.122G	322
S59.122K	389
S59.122P	389
S59.122S	322
S59.129A	357, 998
S59.129D	322
S59.129G	322
S59.129K	389
S59.129P	389
S59.129S	322
S59.131A	357, 998
S59.131D	322
S59.131G	322
S59.131K	389
S59.131P	389
S59.131S	322
S59.132A	357, 998
S59.132D	322
S59.132G	322
S59.132K	389
S59.132P	389
S59.132S	322
S59.139A	357, 998
S59.139D	322
S59.139G	322
S59.139K	389
S59.139P	389
S59.139S	322
S59.141A	357, 998
S59.141D	322
S59.141G	322
S59.141K	389
S59.141P	389
S59.141S	322
S59.142A	357, 998
S59.142D	322
S59.142G	322
S59.142K	389
S59.142P	389
S59.142S	322
S59.149A	357, 998
S59.149D	322
S59.149G	322
S59.149K	389
S59.149P	389
S59.149S	322
S59.191A	357, 998
S59.191D	322
S59.191G	322
S59.191K	389
S59.191P	389
S59.191S	322
S59.192A	357, 998
S59.192D	322
S59.192G	322
S59.192K	389
S59.192P	389
S59.192S	322
S59.199A	357, 998
S59.199D	322
S59.199G	322
S59.199K	389
S59.199P	389
S59.199S	322
S59.201A	357, 998
S59.201D	322
S59.201G	322
S59.201K	389
S59.201P	389
S59.201S	322
S59.202A	357, 998
S59.202D	322
S59.202G	322
S59.202K	389
S59.202P	389
S59.202S	322
S59.209A	357, 998
S59.209D	322
S59.209G	322
S59.209K	389
S59.209P	389
S59.209S	322
S59.211A	357, 998
S59.211D	322
S59.211G	322
S59.211K	389
S59.211P	389
S59.211S	322
S59.212A	357, 998
S59.212D	322
S59.212G	322
S59.212K	389
S59.212P	389
S59.212S	322
S59.219A	357, 998
S59.219D	322
S59.219G	322
S59.219K	389
S59.219P	389
S59.219S	322
S59.221A	357, 998
S59.221D	322
S59.221G	322
S59.221K	389
S59.221P	389
S59.221S	322
S59.222A	357, 998
S59.222D	322
S59.222G	322
S59.222K	389
S59.222P	322
S59.222S	322
S59.229A	357, 998
S59.229D	322

Code	Page	Code	Page	Code	Page	Code	Page	Code	Page	Code	Page
S59.229G	322	S59.919S	750	S60.152S	463	S60.412S	463	S60.453S	464	S60.522S	464
S59.229K	389	S60.00XA	463, 998	S60.159A	463, 999	S60.413A	463, 999	S60.454A	464, 999	S60.529A	478, 999
S59.229P	389	S60.00XD	810	S60.159D	810	S60.413D	810	S60.454D	810	S60.529D	811
S59.229S	322	S60.00XS	463	S60.159S	463	S60.413S	463	S60.454S	464	S60.529S	464
S59.231A	357, 998	S60.011A	463, 998	S60.211A	463, 999	S60.414A	463, 999	S60.455A	464, 999	S60.541A	464, 999
S59.231D	322	S60.011D	810	S60.211D	810	S60.414D	810	S60.455D	810	S60.541D	811
S59.231G	322	S60.011S	463	S60.211S	463	S60.414S	463	S60.455S	464	S60.541S	464
S59.231K	389	S60.012A	463, 998	S60.212A	463, 999	S60.415A	463, 999	S60.456A	464, 999	S60.542A	464, 999
S59.231P	389	S60.012D	810	S60.212D	810	S60.415D	810	S60.456D	810	S60.542D	811
S59.231S	322	S60.012S	463	S60.212S	463	S60.415S	463	S60.456S	464	S60.542S	464
S59.232A	357, 998	S60.019A	463, 998	S60.219A	463, 999	S60.416A	463, 999	S60.457A	464, 999	S60.549A	464, 999
S59.232D	322	S60.019D	810	S60.219D	810	S60.416D	810	S60.457D	810	S60.549D	811
S59.232G	322	S60.019S	463	S60.219S	463	S60.416S	463	S60.457S	464	S60.549S	464
S59.232K	390	S60.021A	463, 998	S60.221A	463, 999	S60.417A	463, 999	S60.458A	464, 999	S60.551A	464, 999
S59.232P	390	S60.021D	810	S60.221D	810	S60.417D	810	S60.458D	810	S60.551D	811
S59.232S	322	S60.021S	463	S60.221S	463	S60.417S	463	S60.458S	464	S60.551S	464
S59.239A	357, 998	S60.022A	463, 998	S60.222A	463, 999	S60.418A	463, 999	S60.459A	464, 999	S60.552A	464, 999
S59.239D	322	S60.022D	810	S60.222D	810	S60.418D	810	S60.459D	810	S60.552D	811
S59.239G	322	S60.022S	463	S60.222S	463	S60.418S	463	S60.459S	464	S60.552S	464
S59.239K	390	S60.029A	463, 998	S60.229A	463, 999	S60.419A	463, 999	S60.460A	478, 999	S60.559A	464, 999
S59.239P	390	S60.029D	810	S60.229D	810	S60.419D	810	S60.460D	810	S60.559D	811
S59.239S	322	S60.029S	463	S60.229S	463	S60.419S	463	S60.460S	464	S60.559S	464
S59.241A	357, 998	S60.031A	463, 998	S60.311A	463, 999	S60.420A	478, 999	S60.461A	478, 999	S60.561A	478, 999
S59.241D	322	S60.031D	810	S60.311D	810	S60.420D	810	S60.461D	810	S60.561D	811
S59.241G	322	S60.031S	463	S60.311S	463	S60.420S	463	S60.461S	464	S60.561S	464
S59.241K	390	S60.032A	463, 998	S60.312A	463, 999	S60.421A	478, 999	S60.462A	478, 999	S60.562A	478, 999
S59.241P	390	S60.032D	810	S60.312D	810	S60.421D	810	S60.462D	811	S60.562D	811
S59.241S	322	S60.032S	463	S60.312S	463	S60.421S	463	S60.462S	464	S60.562S	464
S59.242A	357, 998	S60.039A	463, 998	S60.319A	463, 999	S60.422A	478, 999	S60.463A	478, 999	S60.569A	478, 999
S59.242D	322	S60.039D	810	S60.319D	810	S60.422D	810	S60.463D	810	S60.569D	811
S59.242G	322	S60.039S	463	S60.319S	463	S60.422S	463	S60.463S	464	S60.569S	464
S59.242K	390	S60.041A	463, 999	S60.321A	478, 999	S60.423A	478, 999	S60.464A	478, 999	S60.571A	464, 999
S59.242P	390	S60.041D	810	S60.321D	810	S60.423D	810	S60.464D	810	S60.571D	811
S59.242S	322	S60.041S	463	S60.321S	463	S60.423S	463	S60.464S	464	S60.571S	464
S59.249A	357, 998	S60.042A	463, 999	S60.322A	478, 999	S60.424A	478, 999	S60.465A	478, 999	S60.572A	464, 999
S59.249D	322	S60.042D	810	S60.322D	810	S60.424D	810	S60.465D	810	S60.572D	811
S59.249G	322	S60.042S	463	S60.322S	463	S60.424S	463	S60.465S	464	S60.572S	464
S59.249K	390	S60.049A	463, 999	S60.329A	478, 999	S60.425A	478, 999	S60.466A	478, 999	S60.579A	464, 999
S59.249P	390	S60.049D	810	S60.329D	810	S60.425D	810	S60.466D	810	S60.579D	811
S59.249S	322	S60.049S	463	S60.329S	463	S60.425S	463	S60.466S	464	S60.579S	464
S59.291A	357, 998	S60.051A	463, 999	S60.341A	463, 999	S60.426A	478, 999	S60.467A	478, 999	S60.811A	464, 999
S59.291D	322	S60.051D	810	S60.341D	810	S60.426D	810	S60.467D	810	S60.811D	811
S59.291G	322	S60.051S	463	S60.341S	463	S60.426S	463	S60.467S	464	S60.811S	464
S59.291K	390	S60.052A	463, 999	S60.342A	463, 999	S60.427A	478, 999	S60.468A	478, 999	S60.812A	464, 999
S59.291P	390	S60.052D	810	S60.342D	810	S60.427D	810	S60.468D	810	S60.812D	811
S59.291S	322	S60.052S	463	S60.342S	463	S60.427S	463	S60.468S	464	S60.812S	464
S59.292A	357, 998	S60.059A	463, 999	S60.349A	463, 999	S60.428A	478, 999	S60.469A	478, 999	S60.819A	464, 999
S59.292D	322	S60.059D	810	S60.349D	810	S60.428D	810	S60.469D	811	S60.819D	811
S59.292G	322	S60.059S	463	S60.349S	463	S60.428S	463	S60.469S	464	S60.819S	464
S59.292K	390	S60.10XA	463, 999	S60.351A	463, 999	S60.429A	478, 999	S60.470A	464, 999	S60.821A	478, 999
S59.292P	390	S60.10XD	810	S60.351D	810	S60.429D	810	S60.470D	811	S60.821D	811
S59.292S	322	S60.10XS	463	S60.351S	463	S60.429S	463	S60.470S	464	S60.821S	464
S59.299A	357, 998	S60.111A	463, 999	S60.352A	463, 999	S60.440A	463, 999	S60.471A	464, 999	S60.822A	478, 999
S59.299D	322	S60.111D	810	S60.352D	810	S60.440D	810	S60.471D	810	S60.822D	811
S59.299G	322	S60.111S	463	S60.352S	463	S60.440S	464	S60.471S	464	S60.822S	464
S59.299K	390	S60.112A	463, 999	S60.359A	463, 999	S60.441A	464, 999	S60.472A	464, 999	S60.829A	478, 999
S59.299P	390	S60.112D	810	S60.359D	810	S60.441D	810	S60.472D	810	S60.829D	811
S59.299S	322	S60.112S	463	S60.359S	463	S60.441S	464	S60.472S	464	S60.829S	464
S59.801A	750, 998	S60.119A	463, 999	S60.361A	478, 999	S60.442A	464, 999	S60.473A	464, 999	S60.841A	464, 999
S59.801D	810	S60.119D	810	S60.361D	810	S60.442D	810	S60.473D	810	S60.841D	811
S59.801S	750	S60.119S	463	S60.361S	463	S60.442S	464	S60.473S	464	S60.841S	464
S59.802A	750, 998	S60.121A	463, 999	S60.362A	478, 999	S60.443A	464, 999	S60.474A	464, 999	S60.842A	464, 999
S59.802D	810	S60.121D	810	S60.362D	810	S60.443D	810	S60.474D	810	S60.842D	811
S59.802S	750	S60.121S	463	S60.362S	463	S60.443S	464	S60.474S	464	S60.842S	464
S59.809A	750, 998	S60.122A	463, 999	S60.369A	478, 999	S60.444A	464, 999	S60.475A	464, 999	S60.849A	464, 999
S59.809D	810	S60.122D	810	S60.369D	810	S60.444D	810	S60.475D	810	S60.849D	811
S59.809S	750	S60.122S	463	S60.369S	463	S60.444S	464	S60.475S	464	S60.849S	464
S59.811A	750, 998	S60.129A	463, 999	S60.371A	463, 999	S60.445A	464, 999	S60.476A	464, 999	S60.851A	464, 999
S59.811D	810	S60.129D	810	S60.371D	810	S60.445D	810	S60.476D	810	S60.851D	811
S59.811S	750	S60.129S	463	S60.371S	463	S60.445S	464	S60.476S	464	S60.851S	464
S59.812A	750, 998	S60.131A	463, 999	S60.372A	463, 999	S60.446A	464, 999	S60.477A	464, 999	S60.852A	464, 999
S59.812D	810	S60.131D	810	S60.372D	810	S60.446D	810	S60.477D	810	S60.852D	811
S59.812S	750	S60.131S	463	S60.372S	463	S60.446S	464	S60.477S	464	S60.852S	464
S59.819A	750, 998	S60.132A	463, 999	S60.379A	463, 999	S60.447A	464, 999	S60.478A	464, 999	S60.859A	464, 999
S59.819D	810	S60.132D	810	S60.379D	810	S60.447D	810	S60.478D	810	S60.859D	811
S59.819S	750	S60.132S	463	S60.379S	463	S60.447S	464	S60.478S	464	S60.859S	464
S59.901A	750, 998	S60.139A	463, 999	S60.391A	463, 999	S60.448A	464, 999	S60.479A	464, 999	S60.861A	478, 999
S59.901D	810	S60.139D	810	S60.391D	810	S60.448D	810	S60.479D	810	S60.861D	811
S59.901S	750	S60.139S	463	S60.391S	463	S60.448S	464	S60.479S	464	S60.861S	464
S59.902A	750, 998	S60.141A	463, 999	S60.392A	463, 999	S60.449A	464, 999	S60.511A	464, 999	S60.862A	478, 999
S59.902D	810	S60.141D	810	S60.392D	810	S60.449D	810	S60.511D	810	S60.862D	811
S59.902S	750	S60.141S	463	S60.392S	463	S60.449S	464	S60.511S	464	S60.862S	464
S59.909A	750, 998	S60.142A	463, 999	S60.399A	463, 999	S60.450A	464, 999	S60.512A	464, 999	S60.869A	478, 999
S59.909D	810	S60.142D	810	S60.399D	810	S60.450D	810	S60.512D	810	S60.869D	811
S59.909S	750	S60.142S	463	S60.399S	463	S60.450S	464	S60.512S	464	S60.869S	464
S59.911A	750, 998	S60.149A	463, 999	S60.410A	463, 999	S60.451A	464, 999	S60.519A	464, 999	S60.871A	464, 999
S59.911D	810	S60.149D	810	S60.410D	810	S60.451D	810	S60.519D	810	S60.871D	811
S59.911S	750	S60.149S	463	S60.410S	463	S60.451S	464	S60.519S	464	S60.871S	464
S59.912A	750, 998	S60.151A	463, 999	S60.411A	463, 999	S60.452A	464, 999	S60.521A	478, 999	S60.872A	464, 999
S59.912D	810	S60.151D	810	S60.411D	810	S60.452D	810	S60.521D	810	S60.872D	811
S59.912S	750	S60.151S	463	S60.411S	463	S60.452S	464	S60.521S	464	S60.872S	464
S59.919A	750, 998	S60.152A	463, 999	S60.412A	463, 999	S60.453A	464, 999	S60.522A	478, 999	S60.879A	464, 999
S59.919D	810	S60.152D	810	S60.412D	810	S60.453D	810	S60.522D	811	S60.879D	811

Code	Page
S60.879S	464
S60.911A	464, 999
S60.911D	811
S60.911S	464
S60.912A	464, 999
S60.912D	811
S60.912S	464
S60.919A	464, 999
S60.919D	811
S60.919S	464
S60.921A	464, 999
S60.921D	811
S60.921S	464
S60.922A	464, 999
S60.922D	811
S60.922S	464
S60.929A	464, 999
S60.929D	811
S60.929S	464
S60.931A	464, 999
S60.931D	811
S60.931S	464
S60.932A	464, 999
S60.932D	811
S60.932S	464
S60.939A	464, 999
S60.939D	811
S60.939S	464
S60.940A	464, 999
S60.940D	811
S60.940S	464
S60.941A	464, 999
S60.941D	811
S60.941S	464
S60.942A	464, 999
S60.942D	811
S60.942S	464
S60.943A	464, 999
S60.943D	811
S60.943S	464
S60.944A	464, 999
S60.944D	811
S60.944S	464
S60.945A	464, 999
S60.945D	811
S60.945S	464
S60.946A	464, 999
S60.946D	811
S60.946S	464
S60.947A	464, 999
S60.947D	811
S60.947S	464
S60.948A	464, 999
S60.948D	811
S60.948S	464
S60.949A	464, 999
S60.949D	811
S60.949S	464
S61.001A	464, 999
S61.001D	811
S61.001S	464
S61.002A	464, 999
S61.002D	811
S61.002S	464
S61.009A	464, 999
S61.009D	811
S61.009S	464
S61.011A	464, 999
S61.011D	811
S61.011S	465
S61.012A	465, 999
S61.012D	811
S61.012S	465
S61.019A	465, 999
S61.019D	811
S61.019S	465
S61.021A	750, 999
S61.021D	811
S61.021S	465
S61.022A	750, 999
S61.022D	811
S61.022S	465
S61.029A	750, 999
S61.029D	811
S61.029S	465
S61.031A	465, 999
S61.031D	811
S61.031S	465
S61.032A	465, 1000
S61.032D	811
S61.032S	465
S61.039A	465, 1000
S61.039D	811
S61.039S	465
S61.041A	750, 1000
S61.041D	811
S61.041S	465
S61.042A	750, 1000
S61.042D	811
S61.042S	465
S61.049A	750, 1000
S61.049D	811
S61.049S	465
S61.051A	465, 1000
S61.051D	811
S61.051S	465
S61.052A	465, 1000
S61.052D	811
S61.052S	465
S61.059A	465, 1000
S61.059D	811
S61.059S	465
S61.101A	465, 1000
S61.101D	811
S61.101S	465
S61.102A	465, 1000
S61.102D	811
S61.102S	465
S61.109A	465, 1000
S61.109D	811
S61.109S	465
S61.111A	465, 1000
S61.111D	811
S61.111S	465
S61.112A	465, 1000
S61.112D	811
S61.112S	465
S61.119A	465, 1000
S61.119D	811
S61.119S	465
S61.121A	750, 1000
S61.121D	811
S61.121S	465
S61.122A	750, 1000
S61.122D	811
S61.122S	465
S61.129A	750, 1000
S61.129D	811
S61.129S	465
S61.131A	465, 1000
S61.131D	811
S61.131S	465
S61.132A	465, 1000
S61.132D	811
S61.132S	465
S61.139A	465, 1000
S61.139D	811
S61.139S	465
S61.141A	750, 1000
S61.141D	811
S61.141S	465
S61.142A	750, 1000
S61.142D	811
S61.142S	465
S61.149A	750, 1000
S61.149D	811
S61.149S	465
S61.151A	465, 1000
S61.151D	811
S61.151S	465
S61.152A	465, 1000
S61.152D	811
S61.152S	465
S61.159A	465, 1000
S61.159D	811
S61.159S	465
S61.200A	465, 1000
S61.200D	811
S61.200S	465
S61.201A	465, 1000
S61.201D	811
S61.201S	465
S61.202A	465, 1000
S61.202D	811
S61.202S	465
S61.203A	465, 1000
S61.203D	811
S61.203S	465
S61.204A	465, 1000
S61.204D	811
S61.204S	465
S61.205A	465, 1000
S61.205D	811
S61.205S	465
S61.206A	465, 1000
S61.206D	811
S61.206S	465
S61.207A	465, 1000
S61.207D	811
S61.207S	465
S61.208A	1000
S61.208A	465
S61.208D	811
S61.208S	465
S61.209A	465, 1000
S61.209D	811
S61.209S	465
S61.210A	465, 1000
S61.210D	811
S61.210S	465
S61.211A	465, 1000
S61.211D	811
S61.211S	465
S61.212A	465, 1000
S61.212D	811
S61.212S	465
S61.213A	465, 1000
S61.213D	811
S61.213S	465
S61.214A	465, 1000
S61.214D	811
S61.214S	465
S61.215A	465, 1000
S61.215D	811
S61.215S	465
S61.216A	465, 1000
S61.216D	811
S61.216S	465
S61.217A	465, 1000
S61.217D	811
S61.217S	465
S61.218A	465, 1000
S61.218D	811
S61.218S	465
S61.219A	465, 1000
S61.219D	811
S61.219S	465
S61.220A	750, 1000
S61.220D	811
S61.220S	465
S61.221A	750, 1000
S61.221D	811
S61.221S	465
S61.222A	750, 1000
S61.222D	811
S61.222S	465
S61.223A	750, 1000
S61.223D	811
S61.223S	465
S61.224A	750, 1000
S61.224D	811
S61.224S	465
S61.225A	750, 1000
S61.225D	811
S61.225S	465
S61.226A	750, 1000
S61.226D	811
S61.226S	465
S61.227A	750, 1000
S61.227D	811
S61.227S	465
S61.228A	750, 1000
S61.228D	811
S61.228S	465
S61.229A	750, 1000
S61.229D	811
S61.229S	465
S61.230A	465, 1000
S61.230D	811
S61.230S	465
S61.231A	465, 1000
S61.231D	811
S61.231S	465
S61.232A	465, 1000
S61.232D	811
S61.232S	465
S61.233A	465, 1000
S61.233D	811
S61.233S	465
S61.234A	465, 1000
S61.234D	811
S61.234S	465
S61.235A	465, 1000
S61.235D	811
S61.235S	465
S61.236A	465, 1000
S61.236D	811
S61.236S	465
S61.237A	465, 1000
S61.237D	811
S61.237S	465
S61.238A	465, 1000
S61.238D	811
S61.238S	465
S61.239A	465, 1000
S61.239D	811
S61.239S	465
S61.240A	750, 1000
S61.240D	811
S61.240S	465
S61.241A	750, 1000
S61.241D	811
S61.241S	465
S61.242A	750, 1000
S61.242D	811
S61.242S	465
S61.243A	750, 1000
S61.243D	811
S61.243S	465
S61.244A	750, 1000
S61.244D	811
S61.244S	465
S61.245A	750, 1000
S61.245D	811
S61.245S	465
S61.246A	750, 1000
S61.246D	811
S61.246S	465
S61.247A	750, 1000
S61.247D	811
S61.247S	465
S61.248A	750, 1000
S61.248D	811
S61.248S	465
S61.249A	750, 1000
S61.249D	811
S61.249S	465
S61.250A	465, 1000
S61.250D	811
S61.250S	465
S61.251A	465, 1000
S61.251D	811
S61.251S	465
S61.252A	465, 1000
S61.252D	811
S61.252S	465
S61.253A	465, 1000
S61.253D	811
S61.253S	465
S61.254A	465, 1000
S61.254D	811
S61.254S	465
S61.255A	465, 1000
S61.255D	811
S61.255S	465
S61.256A	465, 1000
S61.256D	811
S61.256S	465
S61.257A	465, 1000
S61.257D	811
S61.257S	465
S61.258A	465, 1000
S61.258D	811
S61.258S	465
S61.259A	465, 1000
S61.259D	811
S61.259S	465
S61.300A	465, 1000
S61.300D	811
S61.300S	465
S61.301A	465, 1000
S61.301D	811
S61.301S	465
S61.302A	465, 1000
S61.302D	811
S61.302S	465
S61.303A	465, 1000
S61.303D	811
S61.303S	465
S61.304A	465, 1000
S61.304D	811
S61.304S	465
S61.305A	465, 1000
S61.305D	811
S61.305S	465
S61.306A	465, 1000
S61.306D	811
S61.306S	465
S61.307A	465, 1000
S61.307D	811
S61.307S	465
S61.308A	1000
S61.308A	465
S61.308D	811
S61.308S	465
S61.309A	465, 1000
S61.309D	811
S61.309S	465
S61.310A	465, 1000
S61.310D	811
S61.310S	466
S61.311A	466, 1000
S61.311D	811
S61.311S	466
S61.312A	466, 1000
S61.312D	811
S61.312S	466
S61.313A	466, 1000
S61.313D	811
S61.313S	466
S61.314A	466, 1000
S61.314D	811
S61.314S	466
S61.315A	466, 1000
S61.315D	811
S61.315S	466
S61.316A	466, 1000
S61.316D	811
S61.316S	466
S61.317A	466, 1000
S61.317D	811
S61.317S	466
S61.318A	466, 1000
S61.318D	811
S61.318S	466
S61.319A	466, 1000
S61.319D	811
S61.319S	466
S61.320A	750, 1000
S61.320D	811
S61.320S	466
S61.321A	751, 1000
S61.321D	811
S61.321S	466
S61.322A	751, 1000
S61.322D	811
S61.322S	466
S61.323A	751, 1000
S61.323D	811
S61.323S	466
S61.324A	751, 1000
S61.324D	811
S61.324S	466
S61.325A	751, 1000
S61.325D	811
S61.325S	466
S61.326A	751, 1000
S61.326D	811
S61.326S	466
S61.327A	751, 1000
S61.327D	812
S61.327S	466
S61.328A	751, 1000
S61.328D	812
S61.328S	466
S61.329A	751, 1000
S61.329D	812
S61.329S	466
S61.330A	466, 1000
S61.330D	812
S61.330S	466
S61.331A	466, 1000
S61.331D	812
S61.331S	466
S61.332A	466, 1000
S61.332D	812
S61.332S	466
S61.333A	466, 1000
S61.333D	812
S61.333S	466
S61.334A	466, 1000
S61.334D	812
S61.334S	466
S61.335A	466, 1000
S61.335D	812
S61.335S	466
S61.336A	466, 1000
S61.336D	812
S61.336S	466
S61.337A	466, 1000
S61.337D	812
S61.337S	466
S61.338A	466, 1000
S61.338D	812
S61.338S	466
S61.339A	466, 1000
S61.339D	812
S61.339S	466
S61.340A	751, 1000
S61.340D	812
S61.340S	466
S61.341A	751, 1000
S61.341D	812
S61.341S	466
S61.342A	751, 1000
S61.342D	812
S61.342S	466
S61.343A	751, 1000
S61.343D	812
S61.343S	466
S61.344A	751, 1000
S61.344D	812
S61.344S	466
S61.345A	751, 1000
S61.345D	812
S61.345S	466
S61.346A	751, 1000
S61.346D	812
S61.346S	466
S61.347A	751, 1000
S61.347D	812
S61.347S	466
S61.348A	751, 1000
S61.348D	812
S61.348S	466
S61.349A	751, 1000
S61.349D	812
S61.349S	466
S61.350A	466, 1000
S61.350D	812
S61.350S	466
S61.351A	466, 1000
S61.351D	812
S61.351S	466
S61.352A	466, 1000
S61.352D	812
S61.352S	466
S61.353A	466, 1000
S61.353D	812
S61.353S	466
S61.354A	466, 1000
S61.354D	812
S61.354S	466
S61.355A	466, 1000
S61.355D	812
S61.355S	466
S61.356A	466, 1000
S61.356D	812
S61.356S	466
S61.357A	466, 1000
S61.357D	812
S61.357S	466
S61.358A	466, 1000
S61.358D	812
S61.358S	466
S61.359A	466, 1000
S61.359D	812
S61.359S	466
S61.401A	466, 1000
S61.401D	812
S61.401S	466
S61.402A	466, 1000
S61.402D	812
S61.402S	466
S61.409A	466, 1000
S61.409D	812
S61.409S	466
S61.411A	466, 1000
S61.411D	812
S61.411S	466
S61.412A	466, 1000
S61.412D	812
S61.412S	466
S61.419A	466, 1000
S61.419D	812
S61.419S	466
S61.421A	751, 1000
S61.421D	812
S61.421S	466
S61.422A	751, 1000
S61.422D	812
S61.422S	466
S61.429A	751, 1000
S61.429D	812
S61.429S	466
S61.431A	466, 1000
S61.431D	812
S61.431S	466

Code	Page	Code	Page	Code	Page	Code	Page	Code	Page	Code	Page
S61.432A	466, 1000	S62.009B	357, 1001	S62.031G	322	S62.115P	390	S62.141A	358, 1001	S62.162D	323
S61.432D	812	S62.009D	322	S62.031K	390	S62.115S	323	S62.141B	358, 1001	S62.162G	323
S61.432S	466	S62.009G	322	S62.031P	390	S62.116A	357, 1001	S62.141D	323	S62.162K	390
S61.439A	466, 1000	S62.009K	390	S62.031S	322	S62.116B	357, 1001	S62.141G	323	S62.162P	390
S61.439D	812	S62.009P	390	S62.032A	357, 1001	S62.116D	323	S62.141K	390	S62.162S	323
S61.439S	466	S62.009S	322	S62.032B	357, 1001	S62.116G	323	S62.141P	390	S62.163A	358, 1001
S61.441A	751, 1000	S62.011A	357, 1001	S62.032D	322	S62.116K	390	S62.141S	323	S62.163B	358, 1001
S61.441D	812	S62.011B	357, 1001	S62.032G	322	S62.116P	390	S62.142A	358, 1001	S62.163D	323
S61.441S	466	S62.011D	322	S62.032K	390	S62.116S	323	S62.142B	358, 1001	S62.163G	323
S61.442A	751, 1000	S62.011G	322	S62.032P	390	S62.121A	357, 1001	S62.142D	323	S62.163K	390
S61.442D	812	S62.011K	390	S62.032S	322	S62.121B	357, 1001	S62.142G	323	S62.163P	390
S61.442S	466	S62.011P	390	S62.033A	357, 1001	S62.121D	323	S62.142K	390	S62.163S	323
S61.449A	751, 1000	S62.011S	322	S62.033B	357, 1001	S62.121G	323	S62.142P	390	S62.164A	358, 1001
S61.449D	812	S62.012A	357, 1001	S62.033D	322	S62.121K	390	S62.142S	323	S62.164B	358, 1001
S61.449S	466	S62.012B	357, 1001	S62.033G	322	S62.121P	390	S62.143A	358, 1001	S62.164D	323
S61.451A	466, 1000	S62.012D	322	S62.033K	390	S62.121S	323	S62.143B	358, 1001	S62.164G	323
S61.451D	812	S62.012G	322	S62.033P	390	S62.122A	357, 1001	S62.143D	323	S62.164K	390
S61.451S	466	S62.012K	390	S62.033S	322	S62.122B	357, 1001	S62.143G	323	S62.164P	390
S61.452A	466, 1000	S62.012P	390	S62.034A	357, 1001	S62.122D	323	S62.143K	390	S62.164S	323
S61.452D	812	S62.012S	322	S62.034B	357, 1001	S62.122G	323	S62.143P	390	S62.165A	358, 1001
S61.452S	466	S62.013A	357, 1001	S62.034D	322	S62.122K	390	S62.143S	323	S62.165B	358, 1001
S61.459A	466, 1000	S62.013B	357, 1001	S62.034G	322	S62.122P	390	S62.144A	358, 1001	S62.165D	323
S61.459D	812	S62.013D	322	S62.034K	390	S62.122S	323	S62.144B	358, 1001	S62.165G	323
S61.459S	466	S62.013G	322	S62.034P	390	S62.123A	357, 1001	S62.144D	323	S62.165K	390
S61.501A	466, 1000	S62.013K	390	S62.034S	322	S62.123B	357, 1001	S62.144G	323	S62.165P	390
S61.501D	812	S62.013P	390	S62.035A	357, 1001	S62.123D	323	S62.144K	390	S62.165S	323
S61.501S	466	S62.013S	322	S62.035B	357, 1001	S62.123G	323	S62.144P	390	S62.166A	358, 1001
S61.502A	466, 1000	S62.014A	357, 1001	S62.035D	322	S62.123K	390	S62.144S	323	S62.166B	358, 1001
S61.502D	812	S62.014B	357, 1001	S62.035G	322	S62.123P	390	S62.145A	358, 1001	S62.166D	323
S61.502S	466	S62.014D	322	S62.035K	390	S62.123S	323	S62.145B	358, 1001	S62.166G	323
S61.509A	466, 1000	S62.014G	322	S62.035P	390	S62.124A	357, 1001	S62.145D	323	S62.166K	390
S61.509D	812	S62.014K	390	S62.035S	322	S62.124B	357, 1001	S62.145G	323	S62.166P	390
S61.509S	466	S62.014P	390	S62.036A	357, 1001	S62.124D	323	S62.145K	390	S62.166S	323
S61.511A	466, 1000	S62.014S	322	S62.036B	357, 1001	S62.124G	323	S62.145P	390	S62.171A	358, 1001
S61.511D	812	S62.015A	357, 1001	S62.036D	322	S62.124K	390	S62.145S	323	S62.171B	358, 1001
S61.511S	466	S62.015B	357, 1001	S62.036G	322	S62.124P	390	S62.146A	358, 1001	S62.171D	323
S61.512A	466, 1000	S62.015D	322	S62.036K	390	S62.124S	323	S62.146B	358, 1001	S62.171G	323
S61.512D	812	S62.015G	322	S62.036P	390	S62.125A	357, 1001	S62.146D	323	S62.171K	390
S61.512S	466	S62.015K	390	S62.036S	322	S62.125B	357, 1001	S62.146G	323	S62.171P	390
S61.519A	466, 1000	S62.015P	390	S62.101A	357, 1001	S62.125D	323	S62.146K	390	S62.171S	323
S61.519D	812	S62.015S	322	S62.101B	357, 1001	S62.125G	323	S62.146P	390	S62.172A	358, 1001
S61.519S	466	S62.016A	357, 1001	S62.101D	322	S62.125K	390	S62.146S	323	S62.172B	358, 1001
S61.521A	751, 1000	S62.016B	357, 1001	S62.101G	322	S62.125P	390	S62.151A	358, 1001	S62.172D	323
S61.521D	812	S62.016D	322	S62.101K	390	S62.125S	323	S62.151B	358, 1001	S62.172G	323
S61.521S	466	S62.016G	322	S62.101P	390	S62.126A	357, 1001	S62.151D	323	S62.172K	390
S61.522A	751, 1000	S62.016K	390	S62.101S	322	S62.126B	357, 1001	S62.151G	323	S62.172P	390
S61.522D	812	S62.016P	390	S62.102A	357, 1001	S62.126D	323	S62.151K	390	S62.172S	323
S61.522S	466	S62.016S	322	S62.102B	357, 1001	S62.126G	323	S62.151P	390	S62.173A	358, 1001
S61.529A	751, 1000	S62.021A	357, 1001	S62.102D	323	S62.126K	390	S62.151S	323	S62.173B	358, 1001
S61.529D	812	S62.021B	357, 1001	S62.102G	323	S62.126P	390	S62.152A	358, 1001	S62.173D	323
S61.529S	466	S62.021D	322	S62.102K	390	S62.126S	323	S62.152B	358, 1001	S62.173K	390
S61.531A	466, 1000	S62.021G	322	S62.102P	390	S62.131A	357, 1001	S62.152D	323	S62.173P	390
S61.531D	812	S62.021K	390	S62.102S	323	S62.131B	357, 1001	S62.152G	323	S62.173S	323
S61.531S	466	S62.021P	390	S62.109A	357, 1001	S62.131D	323	S62.152K	390	S62.174A	358, 1001
S61.532A	466, 1001	S62.021S	322	S62.109B	357, 1001	S62.131G	323	S62.152P	390	S62.174B	358, 1001
S61.532D	812	S62.022A	357, 1001	S62.109D	323	S62.131K	390	S62.152S	323	S62.174D	323
S61.532S	466	S62.022B	357, 1001	S62.109G	323	S62.131P	390	S62.153A	358, 1001	S62.174G	323
S61.539A	466, 1001	S62.022D	322	S62.109K	390	S62.131S	323	S62.153B	358, 1001	S62.174K	390
S61.539D	812	S62.022G	322	S62.109P	390	S62.132A	357, 1001	S62.153D	323	S62.174P	390
S61.539S	466	S62.022K	390	S62.109S	323	S62.132B	357, 1001	S62.153G	323	S62.174S	323
S61.541A	751, 1001	S62.022P	390	S62.111A	357, 1001	S62.132D	323	S62.153K	390	S62.175A	358, 1001
S61.541D	812	S62.022S	322	S62.111B	357, 1001	S62.132G	323	S62.153P	390	S62.175B	358, 1001
S61.541S	466	S62.023A	357, 1001	S62.111D	323	S62.132K	390	S62.153S	323	S62.175D	323
S61.542A	751, 1001	S62.023B	357, 1001	S62.111G	323	S62.132P	390	S62.154A	358, 1001	S62.175K	390
S61.542D	812	S62.023D	322	S62.111K	390	S62.132S	323	S62.154B	358, 1001	S62.175P	390
S61.542S	466	S62.023G	322	S62.111P	390	S62.133A	357, 1001	S62.154D	323	S62.175S	323
S61.549A	751, 1001	S62.023K	390	S62.111S	323	S62.133B	357, 1001	S62.154G	323	S62.176A	358, 1001
S61.549D	812	S62.023P	390	S62.112A	357, 1001	S62.133D	323	S62.154K	390	S62.176B	358, 1001
S61.549S	466	S62.023S	322	S62.112B	357, 1001	S62.133G	323	S62.154P	390	S62.176D	323
S61.551A	466, 1001	S62.024A	357, 1001	S62.112D	323	S62.133K	390	S62.154S	323	S62.176G	323
S61.551D	812	S62.024B	357, 1001	S62.112G	323	S62.133P	390	S62.155A	358, 1001	S62.176K	390
S61.551S	466	S62.024D	322	S62.112K	390	S62.133S	323	S62.155B	358, 1001	S62.176P	390
S61.552A	466, 1001	S62.024G	322	S62.112P	390	S62.134A	357, 1001	S62.155D	323	S62.176S	323
S61.552D	812	S62.024K	390	S62.112S	323	S62.134B	357, 1001	S62.155G	323	S62.181A	358, 1001
S61.552S	466	S62.024P	390	S62.113A	357, 1001	S62.134D	323	S62.155K	390	S62.181B	358, 1001
S61.559A	466, 1001	S62.024S	322	S62.113B	357, 1001	S62.134G	323	S62.155S	323	S62.181D	323
S61.559D	812	S62.025A	357, 1001	S62.113D	323	S62.134K	390	S62.156A	358, 1001	S62.181K	390
S61.559S	466	S62.025B	357, 1001	S62.113G	323	S62.134P	390	S62.156B	358, 1001	S62.181P	390
S62.001A	357, 1001	S62.025D	322	S62.113K	323	S62.134S	323	S62.156D	323	S62.181S	323
S62.001B	357, 1001	S62.025G	322	S62.113P	390	S62.135A	358, 1001	S62.156G	323	S62.182A	358, 1001
S62.001D	322	S62.025K	390	S62.113S	323	S62.135B	358, 1001	S62.156K	390	S62.182B	358, 1001
S62.001G	322	S62.025P	390	S62.114A	357, 1001	S62.135D	323	S62.156P	390	S62.182D	323
S62.001K	390	S62.025S	322	S62.114B	357, 1001	S62.135G	323	S62.156S	390	S62.182G	323
S62.001P	390	S62.026A	357, 1001	S62.114D	323	S62.135K	390	S62.161A	358, 1001	S62.182K	390
S62.001S	322	S62.026B	357, 1001	S62.114G	323	S62.135P	390	S62.161B	358, 1001	S62.182P	390
S62.002A	357, 1001	S62.026D	322	S62.114K	390	S62.135S	323	S62.161D	323	S62.182S	323
S62.002B	357, 1001	S62.026G	322	S62.114P	390	S62.136A	358, 1001	S62.161G	323	S62.183A	358, 1001
S62.002D	322	S62.026K	390	S62.114S	323	S62.136B	358, 1001	S62.161K	390	S62.183B	358, 1001
S62.002G	322	S62.026P	390	S62.115A	357, 1001	S62.136D	323	S62.161P	390	S62.183D	323
S62.002K	390	S62.026S	322	S62.115B	357, 1001	S62.136G	323	S62.161S	323	S62.183G	323
S62.002P	390	S62.031A	357, 1001	S62.115D	323	S62.136K	390	S62.162A	358, 1001		
S62.002S	322	S62.031B	357, 1001	S62.115G	323	S62.136P	390	S62.162B	358, 1001		
S62.009A	357, 1001	S62.031D	322	S62.115K	390	S62.136S	323				

Code	Page	Code	Page	Code	Page	Code	Page	Code	Page	Code	Page
S62.183K	390	S62.224S	324	S62.246B	358, 1002	S62.303G	324	S62.316P	391	S62.330A	359, 1002
S62.183P	390	S62.225A	358, 1001	S62.246D	324	S62.303K	391	S62.316S	324	S62.330B	359, 1002
S62.183S	323	S62.225B	358, 1001	S62.246G	324	S62.303P	391	S62.317A	358, 1002	S62.330D	324
S62.184A	358, 1001	S62.225D	324	S62.246K	391	S62.303S	324	S62.317B	358, 1002	S62.330G	324
S62.184B	358, 1001	S62.225G	324	S62.246P	391	S62.304A	358, 1002	S62.317D	324	S62.330K	391
S62.184D	323	S62.225K	391	S62.246S	391	S62.304B	358, 1002	S62.317G	324	S62.330P	391
S62.184G	323	S62.225P	391	S62.251A	358, 1002	S62.304D	324	S62.317K	391	S62.330S	324
S62.184K	390	S62.225S	324	S62.251B	358, 1002	S62.304G	324	S62.317P	391	S62.331A	359, 1002
S62.184P	390	S62.226A	358, 1002	S62.251D	324	S62.304K	391	S62.317S	324	S62.331B	359, 1002
S62.184S	323	S62.226B	358, 1002	S62.251G	324	S62.304P	391	S62.318A	358, 1002	S62.331D	324
S62.185A	358, 1001	S62.226D	324	S62.251K	391	S62.304S	324	S62.318B	358, 1002	S62.331G	324
S62.185B	358, 1001	S62.226G	324	S62.251P	391	S62.305A	358, 1002	S62.318D	324	S62.331K	391
S62.185D	323	S62.226K	391	S62.251S	324	S62.305B	358, 1002	S62.318G	324	S62.331P	391
S62.185G	323	S62.226P	391	S62.252A	358, 1002	S62.305D	324	S62.318K	391	S62.331S	324
S62.185K	390	S62.226S	324	S62.252B	358, 1002	S62.305G	324	S62.318P	391	S62.332A	359, 1002
S62.185P	390	S62.231A	358, 1002	S62.252D	324	S62.305K	391	S62.318S	324	S62.332B	359, 1002
S62.185S	323	S62.231B	358, 1002	S62.252G	324	S62.305P	391	S62.319A	358, 1002	S62.332D	324
S62.186A	358, 1001	S62.231D	324	S62.252K	391	S62.305S	324	S62.319B	358, 1002	S62.332G	324
S62.186B	358, 1001	S62.231G	324	S62.252P	391	S62.306A	358, 1002	S62.319D	324	S62.332K	391
S62.186D	323	S62.231K	391	S62.252S	324	S62.306B	358, 1002	S62.319G	324	S62.332P	391
S62.186G	323	S62.231P	391	S62.253A	358, 1002	S62.306D	324	S62.319K	391	S62.332S	324
S62.186K	390	S62.231S	324	S62.253B	358, 1002	S62.306G	324	S62.319P	391	S62.333A	359, 1002
S62.186P	390	S62.232A	358, 1002	S62.253D	324	S62.306K	391	S62.319S	324	S62.333B	359, 1002
S62.186S	323	S62.232B	358, 1002	S62.253G	324	S62.306P	391	S62.320A	358, 1002	S62.333D	324
S62.201A	358, 1001	S62.232D	324	S62.253K	391	S62.306S	324	S62.320B	358, 1002	S62.333G	325
S62.201B	358, 1001	S62.232G	324	S62.253P	391	S62.307A	358, 1002	S62.320D	324	S62.333K	391
S62.201D	323	S62.232K	391	S62.253S	324	S62.307B	358, 1002	S62.320G	324	S62.333P	391
S62.201G	323	S62.232P	391	S62.254A	358, 1002	S62.307D	324	S62.320K	391	S62.333S	325
S62.201K	390	S62.232S	324	S62.254B	358, 1002	S62.307G	324	S62.320P	391	S62.334A	359, 1002
S62.201P	390	S62.233A	358, 1002	S62.254D	324	S62.307K	391	S62.320S	324	S62.334B	359, 1002
S62.201S	323	S62.233B	358, 1002	S62.254G	324	S62.307P	391	S62.321A	358, 1002	S62.334D	325
S62.202A	358, 1001	S62.233D	324	S62.254K	391	S62.307S	324	S62.321B	358, 1002	S62.334G	325
S62.202B	358, 1001	S62.233G	324	S62.254P	391	S62.308A	358, 1002	S62.321D	324	S62.334K	391
S62.202D	323	S62.233K	391	S62.254S	324	S62.308B	358, 1002	S62.321G	324	S62.334P	391
S62.202G	323	S62.233P	391	S62.255A	358, 1002	S62.308D	324	S62.321K	391	S62.334S	325
S62.202K	390	S62.233S	324	S62.255B	358, 1002	S62.308G	324	S62.321P	391	S62.335A	359, 1002
S62.202P	390	S62.234A	358, 1002	S62.255D	324	S62.308K	391	S62.321S	324	S62.335B	359, 1002
S62.202S	323	S62.234B	358, 1002	S62.255G	324	S62.308P	391	S62.322A	359, 1002	S62.335D	325
S62.209A	358, 1001	S62.234D	324	S62.255K	391	S62.308S	391	S62.322B	359, 1002	S62.335K	391
S62.209B	358, 1001	S62.234G	324	S62.255P	391	S62.309A	358, 1002	S62.322D	324	S62.335P	391
S62.209D	323	S62.234K	391	S62.255S	324	S62.309B	358, 1002	S62.322G	324	S62.335S	325
S62.209G	323	S62.234P	391	S62.256A	358, 1002	S62.309D	324	S62.322K	391	S62.336A	359, 1002
S62.209K	390	S62.234S	324	S62.256B	358, 1002	S62.309G	324	S62.322P	391	S62.336B	359, 1002
S62.209P	390	S62.235A	358, 1002	S62.256D	324	S62.309K	391	S62.322S	324	S62.336D	325
S62.209S	323	S62.235B	358, 1002	S62.256G	324	S62.309P	391	S62.323A	359, 1002	S62.336G	325
S62.211A	358, 1001	S62.235D	324	S62.256K	391	S62.309S	324	S62.323B	359, 1002	S62.336K	391
S62.211B	358, 1001	S62.235G	324	S62.256P	391	S62.310A	358, 1002	S62.323D	324	S62.336P	391
S62.211D	323	S62.235K	391	S62.256S	324	S62.310B	358, 1002	S62.323G	324	S62.336S	325
S62.211G	323	S62.235P	391	S62.291A	358, 1002	S62.310D	324	S62.323K	391	S62.337A	359, 1002
S62.211K	390	S62.235S	324	S62.291B	358, 1002	S62.310G	324	S62.323P	391	S62.337B	359, 1002
S62.211P	390	S62.236A	358, 1002	S62.291D	324	S62.310K	391	S62.323S	324	S62.337D	325
S62.211S	323	S62.236B	358, 1002	S62.291G	324	S62.310P	391	S62.324A	359, 1002	S62.337K	391
S62.212A	358, 1001	S62.236D	324	S62.291K	391	S62.310S	324	S62.324B	359, 1002	S62.337P	391
S62.212B	358, 1001	S62.236G	324	S62.291P	391	S62.311A	358, 1002	S62.324D	324	S62.337S	325
S62.212D	323	S62.236K	391	S62.291S	324	S62.311B	358, 1002	S62.324G	324	S62.338A	359, 1002
S62.212G	323	S62.236P	391	S62.292A	358, 1002	S62.311D	324	S62.324K	391	S62.338B	359, 1002
S62.212K	390	S62.236S	324	S62.292B	358, 1002	S62.311G	324	S62.324P	391	S62.338D	325
S62.212P	390	S62.241A	358, 1002	S62.292D	324	S62.311K	391	S62.324S	324	S62.338G	325
S62.212S	323	S62.241B	358, 1002	S62.292G	324	S62.311P	391	S62.325A	359, 1002	S62.338K	391
S62.213A	358, 1001	S62.241D	324	S62.292K	391	S62.311S	324	S62.325B	359, 1002	S62.338P	391
S62.213B	358, 1001	S62.241G	324	S62.292P	391	S62.312A	358, 1002	S62.325D	324	S62.338S	325
S62.213D	323	S62.241K	391	S62.292S	324	S62.312B	358, 1002	S62.325G	324	S62.339A	359, 1002
S62.213G	323	S62.241P	391	S62.299A	358, 1002	S62.312D	324	S62.325K	391	S62.339B	359, 1002
S62.213K	390	S62.241S	324	S62.299B	358, 1002	S62.312G	324	S62.325P	391	S62.339D	325
S62.213P	390	S62.242A	358, 1002	S62.299D	324	S62.312K	391	S62.325S	324	S62.339K	391
S62.213S	323	S62.242B	358, 1002	S62.299G	324	S62.312P	391	S62.326A	359, 1002	S62.339P	391
S62.221A	358, 1001	S62.242D	324	S62.299K	391	S62.312S	324	S62.326B	359, 1002	S62.339S	325
S62.221B	358, 1001	S62.242G	324	S62.299P	391	S62.313A	358, 1002	S62.326D	324	S62.340A	359, 1002
S62.221D	323	S62.242K	391	S62.299S	324	S62.313B	358, 1002	S62.326G	324	S62.340B	359, 1002
S62.221G	323	S62.242P	391	S62.300A	358, 1002	S62.313D	324	S62.326K	391	S62.340D	325
S62.221K	390	S62.242S	324	S62.300B	358, 1002	S62.313G	324	S62.326P	391	S62.340G	325
S62.221P	390	S62.243A	358, 1002	S62.300D	324	S62.313K	391	S62.326S	324	S62.340K	391
S62.221S	323	S62.243B	358, 1002	S62.300G	324	S62.313P	391	S62.327A	359, 1002	S62.340P	391
S62.222A	358, 1001	S62.243D	324	S62.300K	391	S62.313S	324	S62.327B	359, 1002	S62.340S	325
S62.222B	358, 1001	S62.243G	324	S62.300P	391	S62.314A	358, 1002	S62.327D	324	S62.341A	359, 1002
S62.222D	323	S62.243K	391	S62.300S	391	S62.314B	358, 1002	S62.327G	324	S62.341B	359, 1002
S62.222G	323	S62.243P	391	S62.301A	358, 1002	S62.314D	324	S62.327K	391	S62.341D	325
S62.222K	391	S62.243S	324	S62.301B	358, 1002	S62.314G	324	S62.327P	391	S62.341K	391
S62.222P	391	S62.244A	358, 1002	S62.301D	324	S62.314K	391	S62.327S	324	S62.341P	391
S62.222S	323	S62.244B	358, 1002	S62.301G	324	S62.314P	391	S62.328A	359, 1002	S62.341S	325
S62.223A	358, 1001	S62.244D	324	S62.301K	391	S62.314S	324	S62.328B	359, 1002	S62.342A	359, 1002
S62.223B	358, 1001	S62.244G	324	S62.301P	391	S62.315A	358, 1002	S62.328D	324	S62.342B	359, 1002
S62.223D	324	S62.244K	391	S62.301S	324	S62.315B	358, 1002	S62.328G	324	S62.342D	325
S62.223G	324	S62.244P	391	S62.302A	358, 1002	S62.315D	324	S62.328K	391	S62.342G	325
S62.223K	391	S62.244S	324	S62.302B	358, 1002	S62.315G	324	S62.328P	391	S62.342K	391
S62.223P	391	S62.245A	358, 1002	S62.302D	324	S62.315K	391	S62.328S	324	S62.342P	391
S62.223S	324	S62.245B	358, 1002	S62.302G	324	S62.315P	391	S62.329A	359, 1002	S62.342S	325
S62.224A	358, 1001	S62.245D	324	S62.302K	391	S62.315S	324	S62.329B	359, 1002	S62.343A	359, 1002
S62.224B	358, 1001	S62.245G	324	S62.302P	391	S62.316A	358, 1002	S62.329D	324	S62.343B	359, 1002
S62.224D	324	S62.245K	391	S62.302S	324	S62.316B	358, 1002	S62.329G	324		
S62.224G	324	S62.245P	391	S62.303A	358, 1002	S62.316D	324	S62.329K	391		
S62.224K	391	S62.245S	324	S62.303B	358, 1002	S62.316G	324	S62.329P	391		
S62.224P	391	S62.246A	358, 1002	S62.303D	324	S62.316K	391	S62.329S	324		

Code	Page	Code	Page	Code	Page	Code	Page	Code	Page	Code	Page
S62.343D	325	S62.356K	391	S62.369S	325	S62.511B	359, 1003	S62.601G	326	S62.614B	360, 1003
S62.343G	325	S62.356P	391	S62.390A	359, 1003	S62.511D	325	S62.601K	392	S62.614D	326
S62.343K	391	S62.356S	325	S62.390B	359, 1003	S62.511G	325	S62.601P	392	S62.614G	326
S62.343P	391	S62.357A	359, 1002	S62.390D	325	S62.511K	392	S62.601S	326	S62.614K	392
S62.343S	325	S62.357B	359, 1002	S62.390G	325	S62.511P	392	S62.602A	359, 1003	S62.614P	392
S62.344A	359, 1002	S62.357D	325	S62.390K	392	S62.511S	325	S62.602B	359, 1003	S62.614S	326
S62.344B	359, 1002	S62.357G	325	S62.390P	392	S62.512A	359, 1003	S62.602D	326	S62.615A	360, 1003
S62.344D	325	S62.357K	391	S62.390S	325	S62.512B	359, 1003	S62.602G	326	S62.615B	360, 1003
S62.344G	325	S62.357P	391	S62.391A	359, 1003	S62.512D	325	S62.602K	392	S62.615D	326
S62.344K	391	S62.357S	325	S62.391B	359, 1003	S62.512G	325	S62.602P	392	S62.615G	326
S62.344P	391	S62.358A	359, 1002	S62.391D	325	S62.512K	392	S62.602S	326	S62.615K	392
S62.344S	325	S62.358B	359, 1002	S62.391G	325	S62.512P	392	S62.603A	359, 1003	S62.615P	392
S62.345A	359, 1002	S62.358D	325	S62.391K	392	S62.512S	325	S62.603B	359, 1003	S62.615S	326
S62.345B	359, 1002	S62.358G	325	S62.391P	392	S62.513A	359, 1003	S62.603D	326	S62.616A	360, 1003
S62.345D	325	S62.358K	391	S62.391S	325	S62.513B	359, 1003	S62.603G	326	S62.616B	360, 1003
S62.345G	325	S62.358P	391	S62.392A	359, 1003	S62.513D	325	S62.603K	392	S62.616D	326
S62.345K	391	S62.358S	325	S62.392B	359, 1003	S62.513G	325	S62.603P	392	S62.616G	326
S62.345P	391	S62.359A	359, 1002	S62.392D	325	S62.513K	392	S62.603S	326	S62.616K	392
S62.345S	325	S62.359B	359, 1002	S62.392G	325	S62.513P	392	S62.604A	359, 1003	S62.616P	392
S62.346A	359, 1002	S62.359D	325	S62.392K	392	S62.513S	325	S62.604B	359, 1003	S62.616S	326
S62.346B	359, 1002	S62.359G	325	S62.392P	392	S62.514A	359, 1003	S62.604D	326	S62.617A	360, 1003
S62.346D	325	S62.359K	391	S62.392S	325	S62.514B	359, 1003	S62.604G	326	S62.617B	360, 1003
S62.346G	325	S62.359P	391	S62.393A	359, 1003	S62.514D	325	S62.604K	392	S62.617D	326
S62.346K	391	S62.359S	325	S62.393B	359, 1003	S62.514G	325	S62.604P	392	S62.617G	326
S62.346P	391	S62.360A	359, 1002	S62.393D	325	S62.514K	392	S62.604S	326	S62.617K	392
S62.346S	325	S62.360B	359, 1002	S62.393G	325	S62.514P	392	S62.605A	359, 1003	S62.617P	392
S62.347A	359, 1002	S62.360D	325	S62.393K	392	S62.514S	325	S62.605B	359, 1003	S62.617S	326
S62.347B	359, 1002	S62.360G	325	S62.393P	392	S62.515A	359, 1003	S62.605D	326	S62.618A	360, 1003
S62.347D	325	S62.360K	391	S62.393S	325	S62.515B	359, 1003	S62.605G	326	S62.618B	360, 1003
S62.347G	325	S62.360P	391	S62.394A	359, 1003	S62.515D	325	S62.605K	392	S62.618D	326
S62.347K	391	S62.360S	325	S62.394B	359, 1003	S62.515G	325	S62.605P	392	S62.618K	392
S62.347P	391	S62.361A	359, 1002	S62.394D	325	S62.515K	392	S62.605S	326	S62.618P	392
S62.347S	325	S62.361B	359, 1002	S62.394G	325	S62.515P	392	S62.606A	359, 1003	S62.618S	326
S62.348A	359, 1002	S62.361D	325	S62.394K	392	S62.515S	325	S62.606B	359, 1003	S62.619A	360, 1003
S62.348B	359, 1002	S62.361G	325	S62.394P	392	S62.516A	359, 1003	S62.606D	326	S62.619B	360, 1003
S62.348D	325	S62.361K	392	S62.394S	325	S62.516B	359, 1003	S62.606G	326	S62.619D	326
S62.348G	325	S62.361P	392	S62.395A	359, 1003	S62.516D	325	S62.606K	392	S62.619G	326
S62.348K	391	S62.361S	325	S62.395B	359, 1003	S62.516G	325	S62.606P	392	S62.619K	392
S62.348P	391	S62.362A	359, 1002	S62.395D	325	S62.516K	392	S62.606S	326	S62.619P	392
S62.348S	325	S62.362B	359, 1002	S62.395G	325	S62.516P	392	S62.607A	359, 1003	S62.619S	326
S62.349A	359, 1002	S62.362D	325	S62.395K	392	S62.516S	325	S62.607B	359, 1003	S62.620A	360, 1003
S62.349B	359, 1002	S62.362G	325	S62.395P	392	S62.521A	359, 1003	S62.607D	326	S62.620B	360, 1003
S62.349D	325	S62.362K	392	S62.395S	325	S62.521B	359, 1003	S62.607G	326	S62.620D	326
S62.349G	325	S62.362P	392	S62.396A	359, 1003	S62.521D	325	S62.607K	392	S62.620G	326
S62.349K	391	S62.362S	325	S62.396B	359, 1003	S62.521G	325	S62.607P	392	S62.620K	392
S62.349P	391	S62.363A	359, 1002	S62.396D	325	S62.521K	392	S62.607S	326	S62.620P	392
S62.349S	325	S62.363B	359, 1002	S62.396G	325	S62.521P	392	S62.608A	359, 1003	S62.620S	326
S62.350A	359, 1002	S62.363D	325	S62.396K	392	S62.521S	325	S62.608B	359, 1003	S62.621A	360, 1003
S62.350B	359, 1002	S62.363G	325	S62.396P	392	S62.522A	359, 1003	S62.608D	326	S62.621B	360, 1003
S62.350D	325	S62.363K	392	S62.396S	325	S62.522B	359, 1003	S62.608G	326	S62.621D	326
S62.350G	325	S62.363P	392	S62.397A	359, 1003	S62.522D	325	S62.608K	392	S62.621G	326
S62.350K	391	S62.363S	325	S62.397B	359, 1003	S62.522G	325	S62.608P	392	S62.621K	392
S62.350P	391	S62.364A	359, 1002	S62.397D	325	S62.522K	392	S62.608S	326	S62.621P	392
S62.350S	325	S62.364B	359, 1002	S62.397G	325	S62.522P	392	S62.609A	359, 1003	S62.621S	326
S62.351A	359, 1002	S62.364D	325	S62.397K	392	S62.522S	325	S62.609B	359, 1003	S62.622A	360, 1003
S62.351B	359, 1002	S62.364G	325	S62.397P	392	S62.523A	359, 1003	S62.609D	326	S62.622B	360, 1003
S62.351D	325	S62.364K	392	S62.397S	325	S62.523B	359, 1003	S62.609G	326	S62.622D	326
S62.351G	325	S62.364P	392	S62.398A	359, 1003	S62.523D	326	S62.609K	392	S62.622G	326
S62.351K	391	S62.364S	325	S62.398B	359, 1003	S62.523G	326	S62.609P	392	S62.622K	392
S62.351P	391	S62.365A	359, 1003	S62.398D	325	S62.523K	392	S62.609S	326	S62.622P	392
S62.351S	325	S62.365B	359, 1003	S62.398G	325	S62.523P	392	S62.610A	359	S62.622S	326
S62.352A	359, 1002	S62.365D	325	S62.398K	392	S62.523S	326	S62.610A	1003	S62.623A	360, 1003
S62.352B	359, 1002	S62.365G	325	S62.398P	392	S62.524A	359, 1003	S62.610B	359, 1003	S62.623B	360, 1003
S62.352D	325	S62.365K	392	S62.398S	325	S62.524B	359, 1003	S62.610D	326	S62.623D	326
S62.352G	325	S62.365P	392	S62.399A	359, 1003	S62.524D	326	S62.610G	326	S62.623G	326
S62.352K	391	S62.365S	325	S62.399B	359, 1003	S62.524G	326	S62.610K	392	S62.623K	392
S62.352P	391	S62.366A	359, 1003	S62.399D	325	S62.524K	392	S62.610P	392	S62.623P	392
S62.352S	325	S62.366B	359, 1003	S62.399G	325	S62.524P	392	S62.610S	326	S62.623S	326
S62.353A	359, 1002	S62.366D	325	S62.399K	392	S62.524S	326	S62.611A	359	S62.624A	360, 1003
S62.353B	359, 1002	S62.366G	325	S62.399P	392	S62.525A	359, 1003	S62.611A	1003	S62.624B	360, 1003
S62.353D	325	S62.366K	392	S62.399S	325	S62.525B	359, 1003	S62.611B	359, 1003	S62.624D	326
S62.353G	325	S62.366P	392	S62.501A	359, 1003	S62.525D	326	S62.611D	326	S62.624G	326
S62.353K	391	S62.366S	325	S62.501B	359, 1003	S62.525G	326	S62.611G	326	S62.624K	392
S62.353P	391	S62.367A	359, 1003	S62.501D	325	S62.525K	392	S62.611K	392	S62.624P	392
S62.353S	325	S62.367B	359, 1003	S62.501G	325	S62.525P	392	S62.611P	392	S62.624S	326
S62.354A	359, 1002	S62.367D	325	S62.501K	392	S62.525S	326	S62.611S	326	S62.625A	360, 1003
S62.354B	359, 1002	S62.367G	325	S62.501P	392	S62.526A	359, 1003	S62.612A	359	S62.625B	360, 1003
S62.354D	325	S62.367K	392	S62.501S	325	S62.526B	359, 1003	S62.612A	1003	S62.625D	326
S62.354G	325	S62.367P	392	S62.502A	359, 1003	S62.526D	326	S62.612B	359, 1003	S62.625G	326
S62.354K	391	S62.367S	325	S62.502B	359, 1003	S62.526G	326	S62.612D	326	S62.625K	392
S62.354P	391	S62.368A	359, 1003	S62.502D	325	S62.526K	392	S62.612G	326	S62.625P	392
S62.354S	325	S62.368B	359, 1003	S62.502G	325	S62.526P	392	S62.612K	392	S62.625S	326
S62.355A	359, 1002	S62.368D	325	S62.502K	392	S62.526S	326	S62.612P	392	S62.626A	360, 1003
S62.355B	359, 1002	S62.368G	325	S62.502P	392	S62.600A	359, 1003	S62.612S	326	S62.626B	360, 1003
S62.355D	325	S62.368K	392	S62.502S	325	S62.600B	359, 1003	S62.613A	359	S62.626D	326
S62.355G	325	S62.368P	392	S62.509A	359, 1003	S62.600D	326	S62.613A	1003	S62.626G	326
S62.355K	391	S62.368S	325	S62.509B	359, 1003	S62.600G	326	S62.613B	359, 1003	S62.626K	392
S62.355P	391	S62.369A	359, 1003	S62.509D	325	S62.600K	392	S62.613D	326	S62.626P	392
S62.355S	325	S62.369B	325	S62.509G	325	S62.600P	392	S62.613G	326	S62.626S	326
S62.356A	359, 1002	S62.369D	325	S62.509K	392	S62.600S	326	S62.613K	392	S62.627A	360, 1003
S62.356B	359, 1002	S62.369G	325	S62.509P	392	S62.601A	359, 1003	S62.613P	392	S62.627B	360, 1003
S62.356D	325	S62.369K	392	S62.509S	325	S62.601B	359, 1003	S62.613S	326	S62.627D	326
S62.356G	325	S62.369P	392	S62.511A	359, 1003	S62.601D	326	S62.614A	360, 1003		

Code	Page	Code	Page	Code	Page	Code	Page	Code	Page	Code	Page
S62.627G	326	S62.640P	392	S62.654A	360, 1003	S62.667D	327	S63.026S	360	S63.091S	361
S62.627K	392	S62.640S	326	S62.654B	360, 1003	S62.667G	327	S63.031A	360, 1004	S63.092A	361, 1004
S62.627P	392	S62.641A	360, 1003	S62.654D	327	S62.667K	393	S63.031D	812	S63.092D	812
S62.627S	326	S62.641B	360, 1003	S62.654G	327	S62.667P	393	S63.031S	360	S63.092S	361
S62.628A	360, 1003	S62.641D	326	S62.654K	393	S62.667S	327	S63.032A	360, 1004	S63.093A	361, 1004
S62.628B	360, 1003	S62.641G	326	S62.654P	393	S62.668A	360, 1004	S63.032D	812	S63.093D	812
S62.628D	326	S62.641K	392	S62.654S	327	S62.668B	360, 1004	S63.032S	360	S63.093S	361
S62.628G	326	S62.641P	392	S62.655A	360, 1003	S62.668D	327	S63.033A	360, 1004	S63.094A	361, 1004
S62.628K	392	S62.641S	326	S62.655B	360, 1003	S62.668G	327	S63.033D	812	S63.094D	812
S62.628P	392	S62.642A	360, 1003	S62.655D	327	S62.668K	393	S63.033S	360	S63.094S	361
S62.628S	326	S62.642B	360, 1003	S62.655G	327	S62.668P	393	S63.034A	360, 1004	S63.095A	361, 1004
S62.629A	360, 1003	S62.642D	326	S62.655K	393	S62.668S	327	S63.034D	812	S63.095D	812
S62.629B	360, 1003	S62.642G	326	S62.655P	393	S62.669A	360, 1004	S63.034S	360	S63.095S	361
S62.629D	326	S62.642K	392	S62.655S	327	S62.669B	360, 1004	S63.035A	360, 1004	S63.096A	361, 1004
S62.629G	326	S62.642P	392	S62.656A	360, 1003	S62.669D	327	S63.035D	812	S63.096D	812
S62.629K	392	S62.642S	326	S62.656B	360, 1003	S62.669G	327	S63.035S	360	S63.096S	361
S62.629P	392	S62.643A	360, 1003	S62.656D	327	S62.669K	393	S63.036A	360, 1004	S63.101A	361, 1004
S62.629S	326	S62.643B	360, 1003	S62.656G	327	S62.669P	393	S63.036D	812	S63.101D	812
S62.630A	360, 1003	S62.643D	326	S62.656K	393	S62.669S	327	S63.036S	360	S63.101S	361
S62.630B	360, 1003	S62.643G	326	S62.656P	393	S62.90XA	360, 1004	S63.041A	360, 1004	S63.102A	361, 1004
S62.630D	326	S62.643K	392	S62.656S	327	S62.90XB	360, 1004, 1034	S63.041D	812	S63.102D	812
S62.630G	326	S62.643P	392	S62.657A	360, 1004	S62.90XD	327	S63.041S	360	S63.102S	361
S62.630K	392	S62.643S	326	S62.657B	360, 1004	S62.90XG	327	S63.042A	360, 1004	S63.103A	361, 1004
S62.630P	392	S62.644A	360, 1003	S62.657D	327	S62.90XK	393	S63.042D	812	S63.103D	812
S62.630S	326	S62.644B	360, 1003	S62.657G	327	S62.90XP	393	S63.042S	360	S63.103S	361
S62.631A	360, 1003	S62.644D	326	S62.657K	393	S62.90XS	327	S63.043A	360, 1004	S63.104A	361, 1004
S62.631B	360, 1003	S62.644G	326	S62.657P	393	S62.91XA	360, 1004	S63.043D	812	S63.104D	812
S62.631D	326	S62.644K	392	S62.657S	327	S62.91XB	360, 1004	S63.043S	360	S63.104S	361
S62.631G	326	S62.644P	392	S62.658A	360, 1004	S62.91XD	327	S63.044A	360, 1004	S63.105A	361, 1004
S62.631K	392	S62.644S	326	S62.658B	360, 1004	S62.91XG	327	S63.044D	812	S63.105D	812
S62.631P	392	S62.645A	360, 1003	S62.658D	327	S62.91XK	393	S63.044S	360	S63.105S	361
S62.631S	326	S62.645B	360, 1003	S62.658G	327	S62.91XP	393	S63.045A	361, 1004	S63.106A	361, 1004
S62.632A	360, 1003	S62.645D	326	S62.658K	393	S62.91XS	327	S63.045D	812	S63.106D	812
S62.632B	360, 1003	S62.645G	326	S62.658P	393	S62.92XA	360, 1004	S63.045S	361	S63.106S	361
S62.632D	326	S62.645K	392	S62.658S	327	S62.92XB	360, 1004	S63.046A	361, 1004	S63.111A	361, 1004
S62.632G	326	S62.645P	392	S62.659A	360, 1004	S62.92XD	327	S63.046D	812	S63.111D	812
S62.632K	392	S62.645S	326	S62.659B	360, 1004	S62.92XG	327	S63.046S	361	S63.111S	361
S62.632P	392	S62.646A	360, 1003	S62.659D	327	S62.92XK	393	S63.051A	361, 1004	S63.112A	361, 1004
S62.632S	326	S62.646B	360, 1003	S62.659G	327	S62.92XP	393	S63.051D	812	S63.112D	812
S62.633A	360, 1003	S62.646D	326	S62.659K	393	S62.92XS	327	S63.051S	361	S63.112S	361
S62.633B	360, 1003	S62.646G	326	S62.659P	393	S63.001A	360, 1004	S63.052A	361, 1004	S63.113A	361, 1004
S62.633D	326	S62.646K	392	S62.659S	327	S63.001D	812	S63.052D	812	S63.113D	812
S62.633G	326	S62.646P	392	S62.660A	360, 1004	S63.001S	360	S63.052S	361	S63.113S	361
S62.633K	392	S62.646S	326	S62.660B	360, 1004	S63.002A	360, 1004	S63.053A	361, 1004	S63.114A	361, 1004
S62.633P	392	S62.647A	360, 1003	S62.660D	327	S63.002D	812	S63.053D	812	S63.114D	812
S62.633S	326	S62.647B	360, 1003	S62.660G	327	S63.002S	360	S63.053S	361	S63.114S	361
S62.634A	360, 1003	S62.647D	326	S62.660K	393	S63.003A	360, 1004	S63.054A	361, 1004	S63.115A	361, 1004
S62.634B	360, 1003	S62.647G	326	S62.660P	393	S63.003D	812	S63.054D	812	S63.115D	812
S62.634D	326	S62.647K	392	S62.660S	327	S63.003S	360	S63.054S	361	S63.115S	361
S62.634G	326	S62.647P	392	S62.661A	360, 1004	S63.004A	360, 1004	S63.055A	361, 1004	S63.116A	361, 1004
S62.634K	392	S62.647S	326	S62.661B	360, 1004	S63.004D	812	S63.055D	812	S63.116D	812
S62.634P	392	S62.648A	360, 1003	S62.661D	327	S63.004S	360	S63.055S	361	S63.116S	361
S62.634S	326	S62.648B	360, 1003	S62.661G	327	S63.005A	360, 1004	S63.056A	361, 1004	S63.121A	361, 1004
S62.635A	360, 1003	S62.648D	326	S62.661K	393	S63.005D	812	S63.056D	812	S63.121D	812
S62.635B	360, 1003	S62.648G	326	S62.661P	393	S63.005S	360	S63.056S	361	S63.121S	361
S62.635D	326	S62.648K	392	S62.661S	327	S63.006A	360, 1004	S63.061A	361, 1004	S63.122A	361, 1004
S62.635G	326	S62.648P	392	S62.662A	360, 1004	S63.006D	812	S63.061D	812	S63.122D	812
S62.635K	392	S62.648S	326	S62.662B	360, 1004	S63.006S	360	S63.061S	361	S63.122S	361
S62.635P	392	S62.649A	360, 1003	S62.662D	327	S63.011A	360, 1004	S63.062A	361, 1004	S63.123A	361, 1004
S62.635S	326	S62.649B	360, 1003	S62.662G	327	S63.011D	812	S63.062D	812	S63.123D	812
S62.636A	360, 1003	S62.649D	326	S62.662K	393	S63.011S	360	S63.062S	361	S63.123S	361
S62.636B	360, 1003	S62.649G	326	S62.662P	393	S63.012A	360, 1004	S63.063A	361, 1004	S63.124A	361, 1004
S62.636D	326	S62.649K	392	S62.662S	327	S63.012D	812	S63.063D	812	S63.124D	812
S62.636G	326	S62.649P	392	S62.663A	360, 1004	S63.012S	360	S63.063S	361	S63.124S	361
S62.636K	392	S62.649S	326	S62.663B	360, 1004	S63.013A	360, 1004	S63.064A	361, 1004	S63.125A	361, 1004
S62.636P	392	S62.650A	360, 1003	S62.663D	327	S63.013D	812	S63.064D	812	S63.125D	812
S62.636S	326	S62.650B	360, 1003	S62.663G	327	S63.013S	360	S63.064S	361	S63.125S	361
S62.637A	360, 1003	S62.650D	326	S62.663K	393	S63.014A	360, 1004	S63.065A	361, 1004	S63.126A	361, 1004
S62.637B	360, 1003	S62.650G	326	S62.663P	393	S63.014D	812	S63.065D	812	S63.126D	812
S62.637D	326	S62.650K	392	S62.663S	327	S63.014S	360	S63.065S	361	S63.126S	361
S62.637G	326	S62.650P	392	S62.664A	360, 1004	S63.015A	360, 1004	S63.066A	361, 1004	S63.200A	361, 1004
S62.637K	392	S62.650S	326	S62.664B	360, 1004	S63.015D	812	S63.066D	812	S63.200D	812
S62.637P	392	S62.651A	360, 1003	S62.664D	327	S63.015S	360	S63.066S	361	S63.200S	361
S62.637S	326	S62.651B	360, 1003	S62.664G	327	S63.016A	360, 1004	S63.071A	361, 1004	S63.201A	361, 1004
S62.638A	360, 1003	S62.651D	326	S62.664K	393	S63.016D	812	S63.071D	812	S63.201D	812
S62.638B	360, 1003	S62.651G	326	S62.664P	393	S63.016S	360	S63.071S	361	S63.201S	361
S62.638D	326	S62.651K	392	S62.664S	327	S63.021A	360, 1004	S63.072A	361, 1004	S63.202A	361, 1004
S62.638G	326	S62.651P	392	S62.665A	360, 1004	S63.021D	812	S63.072D	812	S63.202D	812
S62.638K	392	S62.651S	326	S62.665B	360, 1004	S63.021S	360	S63.072S	361	S63.202S	361
S62.638P	392	S62.652A	360, 1003	S62.665D	327	S63.022A	360, 1004	S63.073A	361, 1004	S63.203A	361, 1004
S62.638S	326	S62.652B	360, 1003	S62.665G	327	S63.022D	812	S63.073D	812	S63.203D	812
S62.639A	360, 1003	S62.652D	326	S62.665K	393	S63.022S	360	S63.073S	361	S63.203S	361
S62.639B	360, 1003	S62.652G	326	S62.665P	393	S63.023A	360, 1004	S63.074A	361, 1004	S63.204A	361, 1004
S62.639D	326	S62.652K	392	S62.665S	327	S63.023D	812	S63.074D	812	S63.204D	812
S62.639G	326	S62.652P	392	S62.666A	360, 1004	S63.023S	360	S63.074S	361	S63.204S	361
S62.639K	392	S62.652S	326	S62.666B	360, 1004	S63.024A	360, 1004	S63.075A	361, 1004	S63.205A	361, 1004
S62.639P	392	S62.653A	360, 1003	S62.666D	327	S63.024D	812	S63.075D	812	S63.205D	812
S62.639S	326	S62.653B	360, 1003	S62.666G	327	S63.024S	360	S63.075S	361	S63.205S	361
S62.640A	360, 1003	S62.653D	326	S62.666K	393	S63.025A	360, 1004	S63.076A	361, 1004	S63.206A	361, 1004
S62.640B	360, 1003	S62.653G	326	S62.666P	393	S63.025D	812	S63.076D	812	S63.206D	812
S62.640D	326	S62.653K	393	S62.666S	327	S63.025S	360	S63.076S	361	S63.206S	361
S62.640G	326	S62.653P	393	S62.667A	360, 1004	S63.026A	360, 1004	S63.091A	361, 1004	S63.207A	361, 1004
S62.640K	392	S62.653S	326	S62.667B	360, 1004	S63.026D	812	S63.091D	812	S63.207D	812

Code	Page	Code	Page	Code	Page	Code	Page	Code	Page	Code	Page
S63.207S	361	S63.238S	361	S63.269S	362	S63.301S	362	S63.416S	363	S63.497S	363
S63.208A	361, 1004	S63.239A	361, 1004	S63.270A	362, 1005	S63.302A	362, 1005	S63.417A	363, 1005	S63.498A	363, 1005
S63.208D	812	S63.239D	813	S63.270D	813	S63.302D	813	S63.417D	813	S63.498D	813
S63.208S	361	S63.239S	361	S63.270S	362	S63.302S	362	S63.417S	363	S63.498S	363
S63.209A	361, 1004	S63.240A	361, 1004	S63.271A	362, 1005	S63.309A	362, 1005	S63.418A	363, 1005	S63.499A	363, 1005
S63.209D	812	S63.240D	813	S63.271D	813	S63.309D	813	S63.418D	813	S63.499D	813
S63.209S	361	S63.240S	361	S63.271S	362	S63.309S	362	S63.418S	363	S63.499S	363
S63.210A	361, 1004	S63.241A	361, 1004	S63.272A	362, 1005	S63.311A	362, 1005	S63.419A	363, 1005	S63.501A	363, 1005
S63.210D	812	S63.241D	813	S63.272D	813	S63.311D	813	S63.419D	813	S63.501D	813
S63.210S	361	S63.241S	361	S63.272S	362	S63.311S	362	S63.419S	363	S63.501S	363
S63.211A	361, 1004	S63.242A	361, 1004	S63.273A	362, 1005	S63.312A	362, 1005	S63.420A	363, 1005	S63.502A	363, 1005
S63.211D	812	S63.242D	813	S63.273D	813	S63.312D	813	S63.420D	813	S63.502D	813
S63.211S	361	S63.242S	361	S63.273S	362	S63.312S	362	S63.420S	363	S63.502S	363
S63.212A	361, 1004	S63.243A	362, 1004	S63.274A	362, 1005	S63.319A	362, 1005	S63.421A	363, 1005	S63.509A	363, 1005
S63.212D	812	S63.243D	813	S63.274D	813	S63.319D	813	S63.421D	813	S63.509D	813
S63.212S	361	S63.243S	361	S63.274S	362	S63.319S	362	S63.421S	363	S63.509S	363
S63.213A	361, 1004	S63.244A	362, 1004	S63.275A	362, 1005	S63.321A	362, 1005	S63.422A	363, 1005	S63.511A	363, 1005
S63.213D	812	S63.244D	813	S63.275D	813	S63.321D	813	S63.422D	813	S63.511D	813
S63.213S	361	S63.244S	362	S63.275S	362	S63.321S	362	S63.422S	363	S63.511S	363
S63.214A	361, 1004	S63.245A	362, 1004	S63.276A	362, 1005	S63.322A	362, 1005	S63.423A	363, 1005	S63.512A	363, 1005
S63.214D	812	S63.245D	813	S63.276D	813	S63.322D	813	S63.423D	813	S63.512D	813
S63.214S	361	S63.245S	362	S63.276S	362	S63.322S	362	S63.423S	363	S63.512S	363
S63.215A	361, 1004	S63.246A	362, 1004	S63.277A	362, 1005	S63.329A	362, 1005	S63.424A	363, 1005	S63.519A	363, 1005
S63.215D	812	S63.246D	813	S63.277D	813	S63.329D	813	S63.424D	813	S63.519D	813
S63.215S	361	S63.246S	362	S63.277S	362	S63.329S	362	S63.424S	363	S63.519S	363
S63.216A	361, 1004	S63.247A	362, 1004	S63.278A	362, 1005	S63.331A	362, 1005	S63.425A	363, 1005	S63.521A	363, 1005
S63.216D	812	S63.247D	813	S63.278D	813	S63.331D	813	S63.425D	813	S63.521D	813
S63.216S	361	S63.247S	362	S63.278S	362	S63.331S	362	S63.425S	363	S63.521S	363
S63.217A	361, 1004	S63.248A	362, 1004	S63.279A	362, 1005	S63.332A	362, 1005	S63.426A	363, 1005	S63.522A	363, 1005
S63.217D	812	S63.248D	813	S63.279D	813	S63.332D	813	S63.426D	813	S63.522D	813
S63.217S	361	S63.248S	362	S63.279S	362	S63.332S	362	S63.426S	363	S63.522S	363
S63.218A	361, 1004	S63.249A	362, 1004	S63.280A	362, 1005	S63.339A	362, 1005	S63.427A	363, 1005	S63.529A	363, 1005
S63.218D	812	S63.249D	813	S63.280D	813	S63.339D	813	S63.427D	813	S63.529D	813
S63.218S	361	S63.249S	362	S63.280S	362	S63.339S	362	S63.427S	363	S63.529S	363
S63.219A	361, 1004	S63.250A	362, 1004	S63.281A	362, 1005	S63.391A	362, 1005	S63.428A	363, 1005	S63.591A	363, 1005
S63.219D	812	S63.250D	813	S63.281D	813	S63.391D	813	S63.428D	813	S63.591D	813
S63.219S	361	S63.250S	362	S63.281S	362	S63.391S	362	S63.428S	363	S63.591S	363
S63.220A	361, 1004	S63.251A	362, 1004	S63.282A	362, 1005	S63.392A	362, 1005	S63.429A	363, 1005	S63.592A	363, 1005
S63.220D	812	S63.251D	813	S63.282D	813	S63.392D	813	S63.429D	813	S63.592D	813
S63.220S	361	S63.251S	362	S63.282S	362	S63.392S	362	S63.429S	363	S63.592S	363
S63.221A	361, 1004	S63.252A	362, 1004	S63.283A	362, 1005	S63.399A	362, 1005	S63.430A	363, 1005	S63.599A	363, 1005
S63.221D	812	S63.252D	813	S63.283D	813	S63.399D	813	S63.430D	813	S63.599D	813
S63.221S	361	S63.252S	362	S63.283S	362	S63.399S	362	S63.430S	363	S63.599S	363
S63.222A	361, 1004	S63.253A	362, 1004	S63.284A	362, 1005	S63.400A	362, 1005	S63.431A	363, 1005	S63.601A	363, 1005
S63.222D	812	S63.253D	813	S63.284D	813	S63.400D	813	S63.431D	813	S63.601D	813
S63.222S	361	S63.253S	362	S63.284S	362	S63.400S	362	S63.431S	363	S63.601S	363
S63.223A	361, 1004	S63.254A	362, 1004	S63.285A	362, 1005	S63.401A	362, 1005	S63.432A	363, 1005	S63.602A	363, 1005
S63.223D	812	S63.254D	813	S63.285D	813	S63.401D	813	S63.432D	813	S63.602D	813
S63.223S	361	S63.254S	362	S63.285S	362	S63.401S	362	S63.432S	363	S63.602S	363
S63.224A	361, 1004	S63.255A	362, 1004	S63.286A	362, 1005	S63.402A	362, 1005	S63.433A	363, 1005	S63.609A	363, 1005
S63.224D	812	S63.255D	813	S63.286D	813	S63.402D	813	S63.433D	813	S63.609D	813
S63.224S	361	S63.255S	362	S63.286S	362	S63.402S	362	S63.433S	363	S63.609S	363
S63.225A	361, 1004	S63.256A	362, 1004	S63.287A	362, 1005	S63.403A	362, 1005	S63.434A	363, 1005	S63.610A	363, 1005
S63.225D	812	S63.256D	813	S63.287D	813	S63.403D	813	S63.434D	813	S63.610D	813
S63.225S	361	S63.256S	362	S63.287S	362	S63.403S	362	S63.434S	363	S63.610S	363
S63.226A	361, 1004	S63.257A	362, 1004	S63.288A	362, 1005	S63.404A	362, 1005	S63.435A	363, 1005	S63.611A	363, 1005
S63.226D	812	S63.257D	813	S63.288D	813	S63.404D	813	S63.435D	813	S63.611D	813
S63.226S	361	S63.257S	362	S63.288S	362	S63.404S	362	S63.435S	363	S63.611S	363
S63.227A	361, 1004	S63.258A	362, 1004	S63.289A	362, 1005	S63.405A	362, 1005	S63.436A	363, 1005	S63.612A	363, 1005
S63.227D	812	S63.258D	813	S63.289D	813	S63.405D	813	S63.436D	813	S63.612D	813
S63.227S	361	S63.258S	362	S63.289S	362	S63.405S	362	S63.436S	363	S63.612S	363
S63.228A	361, 1004	S63.259A	362, 1004	S63.290A	362, 1005	S63.406A	362, 1005	S63.437A	363, 1005	S63.613A	363, 1005
S63.228D	812	S63.259D	813	S63.290D	813	S63.406D	813	S63.437D	813	S63.613D	813
S63.228S	361	S63.259S	362	S63.290S	362	S63.406S	362	S63.437S	363	S63.613S	363
S63.229A	361, 1004	S63.260A	362, 1004	S63.291A	362, 1005	S63.407A	362, 1005	S63.438A	363, 1005	S63.614A	363, 1005
S63.229D	812	S63.260D	813	S63.291D	813	S63.407D	813	S63.438D	813	S63.614D	813
S63.229S	361	S63.260S	362	S63.291S	362	S63.407S	362	S63.438S	363	S63.614S	363
S63.230A	361, 1004	S63.261A	362, 1004	S63.292A	362, 1005	S63.408A	362, 1005	S63.439A	363, 1005	S63.615A	363, 1005
S63.230D	812	S63.261D	813	S63.292D	813	S63.408D	813	S63.439D	813	S63.615D	813
S63.230S	361	S63.261S	362	S63.292S	362	S63.408S	362	S63.439S	363	S63.615S	363
S63.231A	361, 1004	S63.262A	362, 1004	S63.293A	362, 1005	S63.409A	362, 1005	S63.490A	363, 1005	S63.616A	363, 1005
S63.231D	812	S63.262D	813	S63.293D	813	S63.409D	813	S63.490D	813	S63.616D	813
S63.231S	361	S63.262S	362	S63.293S	362	S63.409S	362	S63.490S	363	S63.616S	363
S63.232A	361, 1004	S63.263A	362, 1004	S63.294A	362, 1005	S63.410A	362, 1005	S63.491A	363, 1005	S63.617A	363, 1005
S63.232D	812	S63.263D	813	S63.294D	813	S63.410D	813	S63.491D	813	S63.617D	813
S63.232S	361	S63.263S	362	S63.294S	362	S63.410S	362	S63.491S	363	S63.617S	363
S63.233A	361, 1004	S63.264A	362, 1004	S63.295A	362, 1005	S63.411A	362, 1005	S63.492A	363, 1005	S63.618A	363, 1005
S63.233D	813	S63.264D	813	S63.295D	813	S63.411D	813	S63.492D	813	S63.618D	813
S63.233S	361	S63.264S	362	S63.295S	362	S63.411S	362	S63.492S	363	S63.618S	363
S63.234A	361, 1004	S63.265A	362, 1004	S63.296A	362, 1005	S63.412A	362, 1005	S63.493A	363, 1005	S63.619A	363, 1005
S63.234D	813	S63.265D	813	S63.296D	813	S63.412D	813	S63.493D	813	S63.619D	813
S63.234S	361	S63.265S	362	S63.296S	362	S63.412S	362	S63.493S	363	S63.619S	363
S63.235A	361, 1004	S63.266A	362, 1004	S63.297A	362, 1005	S63.413A	362, 1005	S63.494A	363, 1005	S63.621A	363, 1005
S63.235D	813	S63.266D	813	S63.297D	813	S63.413D	813	S63.494D	813	S63.621D	813
S63.235S	361	S63.266S	362	S63.297S	362	S63.413S	362	S63.494S	363	S63.621S	363
S63.236A	361, 1004	S63.267A	362, 1004	S63.298A	362, 1005	S63.414A	362, 1005	S63.495A	363, 1005	S63.622A	363, 1005
S63.236D	813	S63.267D	813	S63.298D	813	S63.414D	813	S63.495D	813	S63.622D	813
S63.236S	361	S63.267S	362	S63.298S	362	S63.414S	362	S63.495S	363	S63.622S	363
S63.237A	361, 1004	S63.268A	362, 1004	S63.299A	362, 1005	S63.415A	363, 1005	S63.496A	363, 1005	S63.629A	363, 1005
S63.237D	813	S63.268D	813	S63.299D	813	S63.415D	813	S63.496D	813	S63.629D	813
S63.237S	361	S63.268S	362	S63.299S	362	S63.415S	363	S63.496S	363	S63.629S	363
S63.238A	361, 1004	S63.269A	362, 1004	S63.301A	362, 1005	S63.416A	363, 1005	S63.497A	363, 1005	S63.630A	363, 1005
S63.238D	813	S63.269D	813	S63.301D	813	S63.416D	813	S63.497D	813	S63.630D	813

Numeric Index to Diseases

Code	Page	Code	Page	Code	Page	Code	Page	Code	Page	Code	Page
S63.630S	363	S63.695S	364	S64.497S	53	S65.219S	170	S65.509S	170	S65.901S	170
S63.631A	363, 1005	S63.696A	364, 1005	S64.498A	47, 1006	S65.291A	751, 1006	S65.510A	751, 1006	S65.902A	751, 1006, 1034
S63.631D	813	S63.696D	814	S64.498D	814	S65.291D	814	S65.510D	814	S65.902D	814
S63.631S	363	S63.696S	364	S64.498S	53	S65.291S	170	S65.510S	170	S65.902S	170
S63.632A	363, 1005	S63.697A	364, 1005	S64.8X1A	47, 1006, 1034	S65.292A	751, 1006	S65.511A	751, 1006	S65.909A	751, 1006, 1034
S63.632D	813	S63.697D	814	S64.8X1D	814	S65.292D	814	S65.511D	814	S65.909D	814
S63.632S	363	S63.697S	364	S64.8X1S	53	S65.292S	170	S65.511S	170	S65.909S	170
S63.633A	363, 1005	S63.698A	364, 1005	S64.8X2A	47, 1006, 1034	S65.299A	751, 1006	S65.512A	751, 1006	S65.911A	751, 1006, 1034
S63.633D	813	S63.698D	814	S64.8X2D	814	S65.299D	814	S65.512D	814	S65.911D	814
S63.633S	363	S63.698S	364	S64.8X2S	53	S65.299S	170	S65.512S	170	S65.911S	170
S63.634A	363, 1005	S63.699A	364, 1005	S64.8X9A	47, 1006, 1034	S65.301A	751, 1006	S65.513A	751, 1006	S65.912A	751, 1006, 1034
S63.634D	813	S63.699D	814	S64.8X9D	814	S65.301D	814	S65.513D	814	S65.912D	814
S63.634S	363	S63.699S	363	S64.8X9S	53	S65.301S	170	S65.513S	170	S65.912S	170
S63.635A	363, 1005	S63.8X1A	364, 1005	S64.90XA	47, 1006	S65.302A	751, 1006	S65.514A	751, 1006	S65.919A	751, 1006, 1034
S63.635D	813	S63.8X1D	814	S64.90XD	814	S65.302D	814	S65.514D	814	S65.919D	814
S63.635S	363	S63.8X1S	363	S64.90XS	53	S65.302S	170	S65.514S	170	S65.919S	170
S63.636A	363, 1005	S63.8X2A	364, 1005	S64.91XA	47, 1006	S65.309A	751, 1006	S65.515A	751, 1006	S65.991A	751, 1006, 1034
S63.636D	813	S63.8X2D	814	S64.91XD	814	S65.309D	814	S65.515D	814	S65.991D	814
S63.636S	363	S63.8X2S	364	S64.91XS	53	S65.309S	170	S65.515S	170	S65.991S	170
S63.637A	363, 1005	S63.8X9A	364, 1005	S64.92XA	47, 1006	S65.311A	751, 1006	S65.516A	751, 1006	S65.992A	751, 1006, 1034
S63.637D	813	S63.8X9D	814	S64.92XD	814	S65.311D	814	S65.516D	814	S65.992D	814
S63.637S	363	S63.8X9S	364	S64.92XS	53	S65.311S	170	S65.516S	170	S65.992S	170
S63.638A	363, 1005	S63.90XA	364, 1005	S65.001A	751, 1006, 1034	S65.312A	751, 1006	S65.517A	751, 1006	S65.999A	751, 1006, 1034
S63.638D	813	S63.90XD	814	S65.001D	814	S65.312D	814	S65.517D	814	S65.999D	814
S63.638S	363	S63.90XS	364	S65.001S	170	S65.312S	170	S65.517S	170	S65.999S	170
S63.639A	363, 1005	S63.91XA	364, 1005	S65.002A	751, 1006, 1034	S65.319A	751, 1006	S65.518A	751, 1006	S66.001A	1006
S63.639D	813	S63.91XD	814	S65.002D	814	S65.319D	814	S65.518D	814	S66.001D	814
S63.639S	363	S63.91XS	364	S65.002S	170	S65.319S	170	S65.518S	170	S66.001S	751
S63.641A	363, 1005	S63.92XA	364, 1005	S65.009A	751, 1006, 1034	S65.391A	751, 1006	S65.519A	751, 1006	S66.002A	1006
S63.641D	813	S63.92XD	814	S65.009D	814	S65.391D	814	S65.519D	814	S66.002D	814
S63.641S	363	S63.92XS	364	S65.009S	170	S65.391S	170	S65.519S	170	S66.002S	751
S63.642A	363, 1005	S64.00XA	47, 1005, 1034	S65.011A	751, 1006, 1034	S65.392A	751, 1006	S65.590A	751, 1006	S66.009A	751, 1006
S63.642D	813	S64.00XD	814	S65.011D	814	S65.392D	814	S65.590D	814	S66.009D	814
S63.642S	363	S64.00XS	53	S65.011S	170	S65.392S	170	S65.590S	170	S66.009S	751
S63.649A	363, 1005	S64.01XA	47, 1005, 1034	S65.012A	751, 1006, 1034	S65.399A	751, 1006	S65.591A	751, 1006	S66.011A	364, 1006
S63.649D	813	S64.01XD	814	S65.012D	814	S65.399D	814	S65.591D	814	S66.011D	814
S63.649S	363	S64.01XS	53	S65.012S	170	S65.399S	170	S65.591S	170	S66.011S	364
S63.650A	363, 1005	S64.02XA	47, 1005, 1034	S65.019A	751, 1006, 1034	S65.401A	751, 1006	S65.592A	751, 1006	S66.012A	364, 1006
S63.650D	813	S64.02XD	814	S65.019D	814	S65.401D	814	S65.592D	814	S66.012D	814
S63.650S	363	S64.02XS	53	S65.019S	170	S65.401S	170	S65.592S	170	S66.012S	364
S63.651A	363, 1005	S64.10XA	47, 1005, 1034	S65.091A	751, 1006, 1034	S65.402A	751, 1006	S65.593A	751, 1006	S66.019A	364, 1006
S63.651D	814	S64.10XD	814	S65.091D	814	S65.402D	814	S65.593D	814	S66.019D	814
S63.651S	363	S64.10XS	53	S65.091S	170	S65.402S	170	S65.593S	170	S66.019S	364
S63.652A	363, 1005	S64.11XA	47, 1005, 1034	S65.092A	751, 1006, 1034	S65.409A	751, 1006	S65.594A	751, 1006	S66.021A	393, 1006
S63.652D	814	S64.11XD	814	S65.092D	814	S65.409D	814	S65.594D	814	S66.021D	814
S63.652S	363	S64.11XS	53	S65.092S	170	S65.409S	170	S65.594S	170	S66.021S	466
S63.653A	363, 1005	S64.12XA	47, 1005, 1034	S65.099A	751, 1006, 1034	S65.411A	751, 1006	S65.595A	751, 1006	S66.022A	393, 1006
S63.653D	814	S64.12XD	814	S65.099D	814	S65.411D	814	S65.595D	814	S66.022D	814
S63.653S	363	S64.12XS	53	S65.099S	170	S65.411S	170	S65.595S	170	S66.022S	466
S63.654A	363, 1005	S64.20XA	47, 1005, 1034	S65.101A	751, 1006, 1034	S65.412A	751, 1006	S65.596A	751, 1006	S66.029A	393, 1006
S63.654D	814	S64.20XD	814	S65.101D	814	S65.412D	814	S65.596D	814	S66.029D	814
S63.654S	363	S64.20XS	53	S65.101S	170	S65.412S	170	S65.596S	170	S66.029S	466
S63.655A	363, 1005	S64.21XA	47, 1005, 1034	S65.102A	751, 1006, 1034	S65.419A	751, 1006	S65.597A	751, 1006	S66.091A	751, 1006
S63.655D	814	S64.21XD	814	S65.102D	814	S65.419D	814	S65.597D	814	S66.091D	814
S63.655S	363	S64.21XS	53	S65.102S	170	S65.419S	170	S65.597S	170	S66.091S	751
S63.656A	363, 1005	S64.22XA	47, 1005, 1034	S65.109A	751, 1006, 1034	S65.491A	751, 1006	S65.598A	751, 1006	S66.092A	751, 1006
S63.656D	814	S64.22XD	814	S65.109D	814	S65.491D	814	S65.598D	814	S66.092D	814
S63.656S	363	S64.22XS	53	S65.109S	170	S65.491S	170	S65.598S	170	S66.092S	751
S63.657A	363, 1005	S64.30XA	47, 1006	S65.111A	751, 1006, 1034	S65.492A	751, 1006	S65.599A	751, 1006	S66.099A	751, 1006
S63.657D	814	S64.30XD	814	S65.111D	814	S65.492D	814	S65.599D	814	S66.099D	814
S63.657S	363	S64.30XS	53	S65.111S	170	S65.492S	170	S65.599S	170	S66.099S	751
S63.658A	363, 1005	S64.31XA	47, 1006	S65.112A	751, 1006, 1034	S65.499A	751, 1006	S65.801A	751, 1006, 1034	S66.100A	751, 1006
S63.658D	814	S64.31XD	814	S65.112D	814	S65.499D	814	S65.801D	814	S66.100D	814
S63.658S	363	S64.31XS	53	S65.112S	170	S65.499S	170	S65.801S	170	S66.100S	751
S63.659A	363, 1005	S64.32XA	47, 1006	S65.119A	751, 1006, 1034	S65.500A	751, 1006	S65.802A	751, 1006, 1034	S66.101A	751, 1006
S63.659D	814	S64.32XD	814	S65.119D	814	S65.500D	814	S65.802D	814	S66.101D	814
S63.659S	363	S64.32XS	53	S65.119S	170	S65.500S	170	S65.802S	170	S66.101S	751
S63.681A	363, 1005	S64.40XA	47, 1006	S65.191A	751, 1006, 1034	S65.501A	751, 1006	S65.809A	751, 1006, 1034	S66.102A	751, 1006
S63.681D	814	S64.40XD	814	S65.191D	814	S65.501D	814	S65.809D	814	S66.102D	814
S63.681S	363	S64.40XS	53	S65.191S	170	S65.501S	170	S65.809S	170	S66.102S	751
S63.682A	364, 1005	S64.490A	47, 1006	S65.192A	751, 1006, 1034	S65.502A	751, 1006	S65.811A	751, 1006, 1034	S66.103A	751, 1006
S63.682D	814	S64.490D	814	S65.192D	814	S65.502D	814	S65.811D	814	S66.103D	814
S63.682S	364	S64.490S	53	S65.192S	170	S65.502S	170	S65.811S	170	S66.103S	751
S63.689A	364, 1005	S64.491A	47, 1006	S65.199A	751, 1006, 1034	S65.503A	751, 1006	S65.812A	751, 1006, 1034	S66.104A	751, 1006
S63.689D	814	S64.491D	814	S65.199D	814	S65.503D	814	S65.812D	814	S66.104D	814
S63.689S	364	S64.491S	53	S65.199S	170	S65.503S	170	S65.812S	170	S66.104S	751
S63.690A	364, 1005	S64.492A	47, 1006	S65.201A	751, 1006	S65.504A	751, 1006	S65.819A	751, 1006, 1034	S66.105A	751, 1006
S63.690D	814	S64.492D	814	S65.201D	814	S65.504D	814	S65.819D	814	S66.105D	814
S63.690S	364	S64.492S	53	S65.201S	170	S65.504S	170	S65.819S	170	S66.105S	751
S63.691A	364, 1005	S64.493A	47, 1006	S65.202A	751, 1006	S65.505A	751, 1006	S65.891A	1006, 1034	S66.106A	751, 1006
S63.691D	814	S64.493D	814	S65.202D	814	S65.505D	814	S65.891A	751	S66.106D	814
S63.691S	364	S64.493S	53	S65.202S	170	S65.505S	170	S65.891D	814	S66.106S	751
S63.692A	364, 1005	S64.494A	47, 1006	S65.209A	751, 1006	S65.506A	751, 1006	S65.891S	170	S66.107A	751, 1006
S63.692D	814	S64.494D	814	S65.209D	814	S65.506D	814	S65.892A	1006, 1034	S66.107D	814
S63.692S	364	S64.494S	53	S65.209S	170	S65.506S	170	S65.892A	751	S66.107S	751
S63.693A	364, 1005	S64.495A	47, 1006	S65.211A	751, 1006	S65.507A	751, 1006	S65.892D	814	S66.108A	751, 1006
S63.693D	814	S64.495D	814	S65.211D	814	S65.507D	814	S65.892S	170	S66.108D	814
S63.693S	364	S64.495S	53	S65.211S	170	S65.507S	170	S65.899A	1006, 1034	S66.108S	751
S63.694A	364, 1005	S64.496A	47, 1006	S65.212A	751, 1006	S65.508A	751, 1006	S65.899A	751	S66.109A	751, 1006
S63.694D	814	S64.496D	814	S65.212D	814	S65.508D	814	S65.899D	814	S66.109D	814
S63.694S	364	S64.496S	53	S65.212S	170	S65.508S	170	S65.899S	170	S66.109S	751
S63.695A	364, 1005	S64.497A	47, 1006	S65.219A	751, 1006	S65.509A	751, 1006	S65.901A	751, 1006, 1034		
S63.695D	814	S64.497D	814	S65.219D	814	S65.509D	814	S65.901D	814		

Code	Page	Code	Page	Code	Page	Code	Page	Code	Page	Code	Page
S66.110A	364, 1006	S66.202A	752, 1006	S66.318S	364	S66.491S	752	S66.528S	467	S66.922S	467
S66.110D	814	S66.202D	815	S66.319A	364, 1007	S66.492A	752, 1007	S66.529A	393, 1007	S66.929A	393, 1007
S66.110S	364	S66.202S	752	S66.319D	364	S66.492D	815	S66.529D	815	S66.929D	815
S66.111A	364, 1006	S66.209A	752, 1006	S66.319S	364	S66.492S	752	S66.529S	467	S66.929S	467
S66.111D	814	S66.209D	815	S66.320A	393, 1007	S66.499A	752, 1007	S66.590A	752, 1007	S66.991A	752, 1007
S66.111S	364	S66.209S	752	S66.320D	815	S66.499D	815	S66.590D	815	S66.991D	815
S66.112A	364, 1006	S66.211A	364, 1006	S66.320S	466	S66.499S	752	S66.590S	752	S66.991S	752
S66.112D	814	S66.211D	815	S66.321A	393, 1007	S66.500A	752, 1007	S66.591A	752, 1007	S66.992A	752, 1007
S66.112S	364	S66.211S	364	S66.321D	815	S66.500D	815	S66.591D	815	S66.992D	815
S66.113A	364, 1006	S66.212A	364, 1006	S66.321S	466	S66.500S	752	S66.591S	752	S66.992S	752
S66.113D	815	S66.212D	815	S66.322A	393, 1007	S66.501A	752, 1007	S66.592A	752, 1007	S66.999A	752, 1007
S66.113S	364	S66.212S	364	S66.322D	815	S66.501D	815	S66.592D	815	S66.999D	815
S66.114A	364, 1006	S66.219A	364, 1006	S66.322S	466	S66.501S	752	S66.592S	752	S66.999S	752
S66.114D	815	S66.219D	815	S66.323A	393, 1007	S66.502A	752, 1007	S66.593A	752, 1007	S67.00XA	752, 1007
S66.114S	364	S66.219S	364	S66.323D	815	S66.502D	815	S66.593D	815	S67.00XD	815
S66.115A	364, 1006	S66.221A	393, 1006	S66.323S	466	S66.502S	752	S66.593S	752	S67.00XS	467
S66.115D	815	S66.221D	815	S66.324A	393, 1007	S66.503A	752, 1007	S66.594A	752, 1007	S67.01XA	752, 1007
S66.115S	364	S66.221S	466	S66.324D	815	S66.503D	815	S66.594D	815	S67.01XD	815
S66.116A	364, 1006	S66.222A	393, 1006	S66.324S	466	S66.503S	752	S66.594S	752	S67.01XS	467
S66.116D	815	S66.222D	815	S66.325A	393, 1007	S66.504A	752, 1007	S66.595A	752, 1007	S67.02XA	752, 1007
S66.116S	364	S66.222S	466	S66.325D	815	S66.504D	815	S66.595D	815	S67.02XD	815
S66.117A	364, 1006	S66.229A	393, 1006	S66.325S	466	S66.504S	752	S66.595S	752	S67.02XS	467
S66.117D	815	S66.229D	815	S66.326A	393, 1007	S66.505A	752, 1007	S66.596A	752, 1007	S67.10XA	752, 1007
S66.117S	364	S66.229S	466	S66.326D	815	S66.505D	815	S66.596D	815	S67.10XD	815
S66.118A	364, 1006	S66.291A	752, 1006	S66.326S	466	S66.505S	752	S66.596S	752	S67.10XS	467
S66.118D	815	S66.291D	815	S66.327A	393, 1007	S66.506A	752, 1007	S66.597A	752, 1007	S67.190A	752, 1007
S66.118S	364	S66.291S	752	S66.327D	815	S66.506D	815	S66.597D	815	S67.190D	815
S66.119A	364, 1006	S66.292A	752, 1007	S66.327S	466	S66.506S	752	S66.597S	752	S67.190S	467
S66.119D	815	S66.292D	815	S66.328A	393, 1007	S66.507A	752, 1007	S66.598A	752, 1007	S67.191A	752, 1007
S66.119S	364	S66.292S	752	S66.328D	815	S66.507D	815	S66.598D	815	S67.191D	815
S66.120A	393, 1006	S66.299A	752, 1007	S66.328S	466	S66.507S	752	S66.598S	752	S67.191S	467
S66.120D	815	S66.299D	815	S66.329A	393, 1007	S66.508A	752, 1007	S66.599A	752, 1007	S67.192A	752, 1007
S66.120S	466	S66.299S	752	S66.329D	815	S66.508D	815	S66.599D	815	S67.192D	815
S66.121A	393, 1006	S66.300A	1007	S66.329S	466	S66.508S	752	S66.599S	752	S67.192S	467
S66.121D	815	S66.300A	752	S66.390A	752, 1007	S66.509A	752, 1007	S66.801A	752, 1007	S67.193A	752, 1007
S66.121S	466	S66.300D	815	S66.390D	815	S66.509D	815	S66.801D	815	S67.193D	815
S66.122A	393, 1006	S66.300S	752	S66.390S	752	S66.509S	752	S66.801S	752	S67.193S	467
S66.122D	815	S66.301A	1007	S66.391A	752, 1007	S66.510A	364, 1007	S66.802A	752, 1007	S67.194A	752, 1007
S66.122S	466	S66.301A	752	S66.391D	815	S66.510D	815	S66.802D	815	S67.194D	815
S66.123A	393, 1006	S66.301D	815	S66.391S	752	S66.510S	364	S66.802S	752	S67.194S	467
S66.123D	815	S66.301S	752	S66.392A	752, 1007	S66.511A	364, 1007	S66.809A	752, 1007	S67.195A	752, 1007
S66.123S	466	S66.302A	1007	S66.392D	815	S66.511D	815	S66.809D	815	S67.195D	815
S66.124A	393, 1006	S66.302A	752	S66.392S	752	S66.511S	364	S66.809S	752	S67.195S	467
S66.124D	815	S66.302D	815	S66.393A	752, 1007	S66.512A	364, 1007	S66.811A	364, 1007	S67.196A	752, 1007
S66.124S	466	S66.302S	752	S66.393D	815	S66.512D	815	S66.811D	815	S67.196D	815
S66.125A	393, 1006	S66.303A	752, 1007	S66.393S	752	S66.512S	364	S66.811S	364	S67.196S	467
S66.125D	815	S66.303D	815	S66.394A	752, 1007	S66.513A	364, 1007	S66.812A	364, 1007	S67.197A	752, 1007
S66.125S	466	S66.303S	752	S66.394D	815	S66.513D	815	S66.812D	815	S67.197D	815
S66.126A	393, 1006	S66.304A	752, 1007	S66.394S	752	S66.513S	364	S66.812S	364	S67.197S	467
S66.126D	815	S66.304D	815	S66.395A	752, 1007	S66.514A	364, 1007	S66.819A	364, 1007	S67.198A	752, 1007
S66.126S	466	S66.304S	752	S66.395D	815	S66.514D	815	S66.819D	815	S67.198D	815
S66.127A	393, 1006	S66.305A	752, 1007	S66.395S	752	S66.514S	364	S66.819S	364	S67.198S	467
S66.127D	815	S66.305D	815	S66.396A	752, 1007	S66.515A	364, 1007	S66.821A	393, 1007	S67.20XA	752, 1007
S66.127S	466	S66.305S	752	S66.396D	815	S66.515D	815	S66.821D	815	S67.20XD	815
S66.128A	393, 1006	S66.306A	752, 1007	S66.396S	752	S66.515S	364	S66.821S	467	S67.20XS	467
S66.128D	815	S66.306D	815	S66.397A	752, 1007	S66.516A	364, 1007	S66.822A	393, 1007	S67.21XA	752, 1007
S66.128S	466	S66.306S	752	S66.397D	815	S66.516D	815	S66.822D	815	S67.21XD	815
S66.129A	393, 1006	S66.307A	752, 1007	S66.397S	752	S66.516S	364	S66.822S	467	S67.21XS	467
S66.129D	815	S66.307D	815	S66.398A	752, 1007	S66.517A	364, 1007	S66.829A	393, 1007	S67.22XA	752, 1007
S66.129S	466	S66.307S	752	S66.398D	815	S66.517D	815	S66.829D	815	S67.22XD	815
S66.190A	751, 1006	S66.308A	752	S66.398S	752	S66.517S	364	S66.829S	467	S67.22XS	467
S66.190D	815	S66.308A	1007	S66.399A	752, 1007	S66.518A	364, 1007	S66.891A	752, 1007	S67.30XA	752, 1007
S66.190S	751	S66.308D	815	S66.399D	815	S66.518D	815	S66.891D	815	S67.30XD	815
S66.191A	751, 1006	S66.308S	752	S66.399S	752	S66.518S	364	S66.891S	752	S67.30XS	467
S66.191D	815	S66.309A	752, 1007	S66.401A	752, 1007	S66.519A	364, 1007	S66.892A	752, 1007	S67.31XA	752, 1007
S66.191S	751	S66.309D	815	S66.401D	815	S66.519D	815	S66.892D	815	S67.31XD	815
S66.192A	751, 1006	S66.309S	752	S66.401S	752	S66.519S	364	S66.892S	752	S67.31XS	467
S66.192D	815	S66.310A	364, 1007	S66.402A	752, 1007	S66.520A	393, 1007	S66.899A	752, 1007	S67.32XA	752, 1007
S66.192S	751	S66.310D	815	S66.402D	815	S66.520D	815	S66.899D	815	S67.32XD	815
S66.193A	751, 1006	S66.310S	364	S66.402S	752	S66.520S	466	S66.899S	752	S67.32XS	467
S66.193D	815	S66.311A	364, 1007	S66.409A	752, 1007	S66.521A	393, 1007	S66.901A	752, 1007	S67.40XA	752, 1007
S66.193S	751	S66.311D	815	S66.409D	815	S66.521D	815	S66.901D	815	S67.40XD	816
S66.194A	751, 1006	S66.311S	364	S66.409S	752	S66.521S	466	S66.901S	752	S67.40XS	467
S66.194D	815	S66.312A	364, 1007	S66.411A	364, 1007	S66.522A	393, 1007	S66.902A	752, 1007	S67.41XA	752, 1007
S66.194S	751	S66.312D	815	S66.411D	815	S66.522D	815	S66.902D	815	S67.41XD	816
S66.195A	751, 1006	S66.312S	364	S66.411S	364	S66.522S	466	S66.902S	752	S67.41XS	467
S66.195D	815	S66.313A	364, 1007	S66.412A	364, 1007	S66.523A	393, 1007	S66.909A	752, 1007	S67.42XA	752, 1007
S66.195S	751	S66.313D	815	S66.412D	815	S66.523D	815	S66.909D	815	S67.42XD	816
S66.196A	751, 1006	S66.313S	364	S66.412S	364	S66.523S	466	S66.909S	752	S67.42XS	467
S66.196D	815	S66.314A	364, 1007	S66.419A	364, 1007	S66.524A	393, 1007	S66.911A	364, 1007	S67.90XA	752, 1007
S66.196S	751	S66.314D	815	S66.419D	815	S66.524D	815	S66.911D	815	S67.90XD	816
S66.197A	751, 1006	S66.314S	364	S66.419S	364	S66.524S	466	S66.911S	364	S67.90XS	467
S66.197D	815	S66.315A	364, 1007	S66.421A	393, 1007	S66.525A	393, 1007	S66.912A	364, 1007	S67.91XA	752, 1007
S66.197S	751	S66.315D	815	S66.421D	815	S66.525D	815	S66.912D	815	S67.91XD	816
S66.198A	751, 1006	S66.315S	364	S66.421S	466	S66.525S	466	S66.912S	364	S67.91XS	467
S66.198D	815	S66.316A	364, 1007	S66.422A	393, 1007	S66.526A	393, 1007	S66.919A	364, 1007	S67.92XA	752, 1007
S66.198S	751	S66.316D	815	S66.422D	815	S66.526D	815	S66.919D	815	S67.92XD	816
S66.199A	752, 1006	S66.316S	364	S66.422S	466	S66.526S	467	S66.919S	364	S67.92XS	467
S66.199D	815	S66.317A	364, 1007	S66.429A	393, 1007	S66.527A	393, 1007	S66.921A	393, 1007	S68.011A	752, 1007
S66.199S	752	S66.317D	815	S66.429D	815	S66.527D	815	S66.921D	815	S68.011D	816
S66.201A	752, 1006	S66.317S	364	S66.429S	466	S66.527S	467	S66.921S	467	S68.011S	327
S66.201D	815	S66.318A	364, 1007	S66.491A	752, 1007	S66.528A	393, 1007	S66.922A	393, 1007	S68.012A	752, 1007
S66.201S	752	S66.318D	815	S66.491D	815	S66.528D	815	S66.922D	815	S68.012D	816

Code	Page	Code	Page	Code	Page	Code	Page	Code	Page	Code	Page
S68.012S	327	S68.511S	327	S68.729S	327	S70.311S	467	S71.022S	467	S72.001F	327
S68.019A	752, 1007	S68.512A	753, 1008	S69.80XA	753, 1008	S70.312A	467, 1008	S71.029A	753, 1008	S72.001G	327
S68.019D	816	S68.512D	816	S69.80XD	816	S70.312D	816	S71.029D	816	S72.001H	327
S68.019S	327	S68.512S	327	S69.80XS	753	S70.312S	467	S71.029S	467	S72.001J	327
S68.021A	752, 1007	S68.519A	753, 1008	S69.81XA	753, 1008	S70.319A	467, 1008	S71.031A	467, 1008	S72.001K	393
S68.021D	816	S68.519D	816	S69.81XD	816	S70.319D	816	S71.031D	816	S72.001M	393
S68.021S	327	S68.519S	327	S69.81XS	753	S70.319S	467	S71.031S	467	S72.001N	393
S68.022A	752, 1007	S68.521A	753, 1008	S69.82XA	753, 1008	S70.321A	478, 1008	S71.032A	467, 1008	S72.001P	393
S68.022D	816	S68.521D	816	S69.82XD	816	S70.321D	816	S71.032D	816	S72.001Q	393
S68.022S	327	S68.521S	327	S69.82XS	753	S70.321S	467	S71.032S	467	S72.001R	393
S68.029A	752, 1007	S68.522A	753, 1008	S69.90XA	753, 1008	S70.322A	478, 1008	S71.039A	467, 1008	S72.001S	327
S68.029D	816	S68.522D	816	S69.90XD	816	S70.322D	816	S71.039D	816	S72.002A	293, 564, 1008, 1034
S68.029S	327	S68.522S	327	S69.90XS	753	S70.322S	467	S71.039S	467	S72.002B	293, 564, 1008, 1034
S68.110A	752, 1007	S68.529A	753, 1008	S69.91XA	753, 1008	S70.329A	478, 1008	S71.041A	753, 1008	S72.002C	293, 564, 1008, 1034
S68.110D	816	S68.529D	816	S69.91XD	816	S70.329D	816	S71.041D	816	S72.002D	327
S68.110S	327	S68.529S	327	S69.91XS	753	S70.329S	467	S71.041S	467	S72.002E	327
S68.111A	752, 1007	S68.610A	753, 1008	S69.92XA	753, 1008	S70.341A	467, 1008	S71.042A	753, 1008	S72.002F	327
S68.111D	816	S68.610D	816	S69.92XD	816	S70.341D	816	S71.042D	816	S72.002G	327
S68.111S	327	S68.610S	327	S69.92XS	753	S70.341S	467	S71.042S	467	S72.002H	327
S68.112A	752, 1007	S68.611A	753, 1008	S70.00XA	467, 1008	S70.342A	467, 1008	S71.049A	753, 1008	S72.002J	327
S68.112D	816	S68.611D	816	S70.00XD	816	S70.342D	816	S71.049D	816	S72.002K	393
S68.112S	327	S68.611S	327	S70.00XS	467	S70.342S	467	S71.049S	467	S72.002M	393
S68.113A	752, 1007	S68.612A	753, 1008	S70.01XA	467, 1008	S70.349A	467, 1008	S71.051A	467, 1008	S72.002N	393
S68.113D	816	S68.612D	816	S70.01XD	816	S70.349D	816	S71.051D	816	S72.002P	393
S68.113S	327	S68.612S	327	S70.01XS	467	S70.349S	467	S71.051S	467	S72.002Q	393
S68.114A	752, 1007	S68.613A	753, 1008	S70.02XA	467, 1008	S70.351A	467, 1008	S71.052A	467, 1008	S72.002R	393
S68.114D	816	S68.613D	816	S70.02XD	816	S70.351D	816	S71.052D	816	S72.002S	327
S68.114S	327	S68.613S	327	S70.02XS	467	S70.351S	467	S71.052S	467	S72.009A	293, 564, 1008, 1034
S68.115A	752, 1007	S68.614A	753, 1008	S70.10XA	467, 1008	S70.352A	467, 1008	S71.059A	467, 1008	S72.009B	293, 564, 1008, 1034
S68.115D	816	S68.614D	816	S70.10XD	816	S70.352D	816	S71.059D	816	S72.009C	293, 564, 1008, 1034
S68.115S	327	S68.614S	327	S70.10XS	467	S70.352S	467	S71.059S	467	S72.009D	327
S68.116A	752, 1007	S68.615A	753, 1008	S70.11XA	467, 1008	S70.359A	467, 1008	S71.101A	467, 1008	S72.009E	327
S68.116D	816	S68.615D	816	S70.11XD	816	S70.359D	816	S71.101D	816	S72.009F	327
S68.116S	327	S68.615S	327	S70.11XS	467	S70.359S	467	S71.101S	467	S72.009G	327
S68.117A	752, 1007	S68.616A	753, 1008	S70.12XA	467, 1008	S70.361A	478, 1008	S71.102A	467, 1008	S72.009H	327
S68.117D	816	S68.616D	816	S70.12XD	816	S70.361D	816	S71.102D	816	S72.009J	327
S68.117S	327	S68.616S	327	S70.12XS	467	S70.361S	467	S71.102S	467	S72.009K	393
S68.118A	752, 1007	S68.617A	753, 1008	S70.211A	467, 1008	S70.362A	478, 1008	S71.109A	467, 1008	S72.009M	393
S68.118D	816	S68.617D	816	S70.211D	816	S70.362D	816	S71.109D	816	S72.009N	393
S68.118S	327	S68.617S	327	S70.211S	467	S70.362S	467	S71.109S	467	S72.009P	393
S68.119A	752, 1007	S68.618A	753, 1008	S70.212A	467, 1008	S70.369A	467, 1008	S71.111A	467, 1008	S72.009Q	393
S68.119D	816	S68.618D	816	S70.212D	816	S70.369D	816	S71.111D	816	S72.009R	393
S68.119S	327	S68.618S	327	S70.212S	467	S70.369S	467	S71.111S	467	S72.009S	327
S68.120A	752, 1007	S68.619A	753, 1008	S70.219A	467, 1008	S70.371A	467, 1008	S71.112A	467, 1008	S72.011A	293, 564, 1008, 1035
S68.120D	816	S68.619D	816	S70.219D	816	S70.371D	816	S71.112D	816	S72.011B	293, 564, 1008, 1035
S68.120S	327	S68.619S	327	S70.219S	467	S70.371S	467	S71.112S	467	S72.011C	293, 564, 1008, 1035
S68.121A	752, 1007	S68.620A	753, 1008	S70.221A	478, 1008	S70.372A	467, 1008	S71.119A	467, 1008	S72.011D	327
S68.121D	816	S68.620D	816	S70.221D	816	S70.372D	816	S71.119D	816	S72.011E	327
S68.121S	327	S68.620S	327	S70.221S	467	S70.372S	467	S71.119S	467	S72.011F	327
S68.122A	752, 1007	S68.621A	753, 1008	S70.222A	478, 1008	S70.379A	467, 1008	S71.121A	753, 1008	S72.011G	327
S68.122D	816	S68.621D	816	S70.222D	816	S70.379D	816	S71.121D	816	S72.011H	327
S68.122S	327	S68.621S	327	S70.222S	467	S70.379S	467	S71.121S	467	S72.011J	327
S68.123A	753, 1007	S68.622A	753, 1008	S70.229A	478, 1008	S70.911A	467, 1008	S71.122A	753, 1008	S72.011K	393
S68.123D	816	S68.622D	816	S70.229D	816	S70.911D	816	S71.122D	816	S72.011M	393
S68.123S	327	S68.622S	327	S70.229S	467	S70.911S	467	S71.122S	467	S72.011N	393
S68.124A	753, 1007	S68.623A	753, 1008	S70.241A	467, 1008	S70.912A	467, 1008	S71.129A	753, 1008	S72.011P	393
S68.124D	816	S68.623D	816	S70.241D	816	S70.912D	816	S71.129D	816	S72.011Q	393
S68.124S	327	S68.623S	327	S70.241S	467	S70.912S	467	S71.129S	467	S72.011R	393
S68.125A	753, 1007	S68.624A	753, 1008	S70.242A	467, 1008	S70.919A	467, 1008	S71.131A	467, 1008	S72.011S	327
S68.125D	816	S68.624D	816	S70.242D	816	S70.919D	816	S71.131D	816	S72.012A	293, 564, 1008, 1035
S68.125S	327	S68.624S	327	S70.242S	467	S70.919S	467	S71.131S	467	S72.012B	293, 564, 1008, 1035
S68.126A	753, 1007	S68.625A	753, 1008	S70.249A	467, 1008	S70.921A	467, 1008	S71.132A	467, 1008	S72.012C	293, 564, 1008, 1035
S68.126D	816	S68.625D	816	S70.249D	816	S70.921D	816	S71.132D	816	S72.012D	327
S68.126S	327	S68.625S	327	S70.249S	467	S70.921S	467	S71.132S	467	S72.012E	327
S68.127A	753, 1007	S68.626A	753, 1008	S70.251A	467, 1008	S70.922A	467, 1008	S71.139A	467, 1008	S72.012F	327
S68.127D	816	S68.626D	816	S70.251D	816	S70.922D	816	S71.139D	816	S72.012G	327
S68.127S	327	S68.626S	327	S70.251S	467	S70.922S	467	S71.139S	467	S72.012H	327
S68.128A	753, 1007	S68.627A	753, 1008	S70.252A	467, 1008	S70.929A	467, 1008	S71.141A	753, 1008	S72.012J	327
S68.128D	816	S68.627D	816	S70.252D	816	S70.929D	816	S71.141D	816	S72.012K	393
S68.128S	327	S68.627S	327	S70.252S	467	S70.929S	467	S71.141S	467	S72.012M	393
S68.129A	753, 1007	S68.628A	753, 1008	S70.259A	467, 1008	S71.001A	467, 1008	S71.142A	753, 1008	S72.012N	393
S68.129D	816	S68.628D	816	S70.259D	816	S71.001D	816	S71.142D	816	S72.012P	393
S68.129S	327	S68.628S	327	S70.259S	467	S71.001S	467	S71.142S	467	S72.012Q	393
S68.411A	753, 1007, 1034	S68.629A	753, 1008	S70.261A	478, 1008	S71.002A	467, 1008	S71.149A	753, 1008	S72.012R	393
S68.411D	816	S68.629D	816	S70.261D	816	S71.002D	816	S71.149D	816	S72.012S	327
S68.411S	327	S68.629S	327	S70.261S	467	S71.002S	467	S71.149S	467	S72.019A	293, 565, 1008, 1035
S68.412A	753, 1007, 1034	S68.711A	753, 1008, 1034	S70.262A	478, 1008	S71.009A	467, 1008	S71.151A	467, 1008	S72.019B	293, 565, 1008, 1035
S68.412D	816	S68.711D	816	S70.262D	816	S71.009D	816	S71.151D	816	S72.019C	293, 565, 1008, 1035
S68.412S	327	S68.711S	327	S70.262S	467	S71.009S	467	S71.151S	468		
S68.419A	753, 1007, 1034	S68.712A	753, 1008, 1034	S70.269A	478, 1008	S71.011A	467, 1008	S71.152A	468, 1008		
S68.419D	816	S68.712D	816	S70.269D	816	S71.011D	816	S71.152D	816		
S68.419S	327	S68.712S	327	S70.269S	467	S71.011S	467	S71.152S	468		
S68.421A	753, 1007, 1034	S68.719A	753, 1008, 1034	S70.271A	467, 1008	S71.012A	467, 1008	S71.159A	468, 1008		
S68.421D	816	S68.719D	816	S70.271D	816	S71.012D	816	S71.159D	816		
S68.421S	327	S68.719S	327	S70.271S	467	S71.012S	467	S71.159S	468		
S68.422A	753, 1007, 1034	S68.721A	753, 1008, 1034	S70.272A	467, 1008	S71.019A	467, 1008	S72.001A	293, 564, 1008, 1034		
S68.422D	816	S68.721D	816	S70.272D	816	S71.019D	816				
S68.422S	327	S68.721S	327	S70.272S	467	S71.019S	467	S72.001B	293, 564, 1008, 1034		
S68.429A	753, 1008, 1034	S68.722A	753, 1008, 1034	S70.279A	467, 1008	S71.021A	753, 1008				
S68.429D	816	S68.722D	816	S70.279D	816	S71.021D	816	S72.001C	293, 564, 1008, 1034		
S68.429S	327	S68.722S	327	S70.279S	467	S71.021S	467				
S68.511A	753, 1008	S68.729A	753, 1008, 1034	S70.311A	467, 1008	S71.022A	753, 1008	S72.001D	327		
S68.511D	816	S68.729D	816	S70.311D	816	S71.022D	816	S72.001E	327		

Code	Page
S72.019D	327
S72.019E	327
S72.019F	327
S72.019G	327
S72.019H	327
S72.019J	327
S72.019K	393
S72.019M	393
S72.019N	393
S72.019P	393
S72.019Q	393
S72.019R	393
S72.019S	327
S72.021A	293, 565, 1008, 1035
S72.021B	293, 565, 1008, 1035
S72.021C	293, 565, 1008, 1035
S72.021D	327
S72.021E	327
S72.021F	327
S72.021G	327
S72.021H	327
S72.021J	327
S72.021K	393
S72.021M	393
S72.021N	393
S72.021P	393
S72.021Q	393
S72.021R	393
S72.021S	327
S72.022A	293, 565, 1008, 1035
S72.022B	293, 565, 1008, 1035
S72.022C	293, 565, 1008, 1035
S72.022D	327
S72.022E	327
S72.022F	327
S72.022G	327
S72.022H	328
S72.022J	328
S72.022K	393
S72.022M	393
S72.022N	393
S72.022P	393
S72.022Q	393
S72.022R	393
S72.022S	328
S72.023A	293, 565, 1008, 1035
S72.023B	293, 565, 1008, 1035
S72.023C	293, 565, 1008, 1035
S72.023D	328
S72.023E	328
S72.023F	328
S72.023G	328
S72.023H	328
S72.023J	328
S72.023K	393
S72.023M	393
S72.023N	393
S72.023P	393
S72.023Q	393
S72.023R	393
S72.023S	328
S72.024A	293, 565, 1008, 1035
S72.024B	293, 565, 1008, 1035
S72.024C	293, 565, 1008, 1035
S72.024D	328
S72.024E	328
S72.024F	328
S72.024G	328
S72.024H	328
S72.024J	328
S72.024K	393
S72.024M	393
S72.024N	393
S72.024P	393
S72.024Q	393
S72.024R	393
S72.024S	328
S72.025A	293, 565, 1008, 1035
S72.025B	293, 565, 1008, 1035
S72.025C	293, 565, 1008, 1035
S72.025D	328
S72.025E	328
S72.025F	328
S72.025G	328
S72.025H	328
S72.025J	328
S72.025K	393
S72.025M	393
S72.025N	393
S72.025P	393
S72.025Q	393
S72.025R	393
S72.025S	328
S72.026A	293, 565, 1008, 1035
S72.026B	293, 565, 1008, 1035
S72.026C	293, 565, 1008, 1035
S72.026D	328
S72.026E	328
S72.026F	328
S72.026G	328
S72.026H	328
S72.026J	328
S72.026K	393
S72.026M	393
S72.026N	393
S72.026P	393
S72.026Q	393
S72.026R	393
S72.026S	328
S72.031A	293, 565, 1008, 1035
S72.031B	293, 565, 1008, 1035
S72.031C	293, 565, 1008, 1035
S72.031D	328
S72.031E	328
S72.031F	328
S72.031G	328
S72.031H	328
S72.031J	328
S72.031K	393
S72.031M	393
S72.031N	393
S72.031P	393
S72.031Q	393
S72.031R	393
S72.031S	328
S72.032A	293, 565, 1008, 1035
S72.032B	293, 565, 1008, 1035
S72.032C	293, 565, 1008, 1035
S72.032D	328
S72.032E	328
S72.032F	328
S72.032G	328
S72.032H	328
S72.032J	328
S72.032K	393
S72.032M	393
S72.032N	393
S72.032P	393
S72.032Q	393
S72.032R	393
S72.032S	328
S72.033A	293, 565, 1008, 1035
S72.033B	293, 565, 1008, 1035
S72.033C	293, 565, 1008, 1035
S72.033D	328
S72.033E	328
S72.033F	328
S72.033G	328
S72.033H	328
S72.033J	328
S72.033K	393
S72.033M	393
S72.033N	393
S72.033P	393
S72.033Q	393
S72.033R	394
S72.033S	328
S72.034A	293, 565, 1008, 1035
S72.034B	293, 565, 1008, 1035
S72.034C	293, 565, 1008, 1035
S72.034D	328
S72.034E	328
S72.034F	328
S72.034G	328
S72.034H	328
S72.034J	328
S72.034K	394
S72.034M	394
S72.034N	394
S72.034P	394
S72.034Q	394
S72.034R	394
S72.034S	394
S72.035A	293, 565, 1008, 1035
S72.035B	293, 565, 1008, 1035
S72.035C	293, 565, 1008, 1035
S72.035D	328
S72.035E	328
S72.035F	328
S72.035G	328
S72.035H	328
S72.035J	328
S72.035K	394
S72.035M	394
S72.035N	394
S72.035P	394
S72.035Q	394
S72.035R	394
S72.035S	328
S72.036A	293, 565, 1009, 1035
S72.036B	293, 565, 1009, 1035
S72.036C	293, 565, 1009, 1035
S72.036D	328
S72.036E	328
S72.036F	328
S72.036G	328
S72.036H	328
S72.036J	328
S72.036K	394
S72.036M	394
S72.036N	394
S72.036P	394
S72.036Q	394
S72.036R	394
S72.036S	328
S72.041A	293, 565, 1009, 1035
S72.041B	293, 565, 1009, 1035
S72.041C	293, 565, 1009, 1035
S72.041D	328
S72.041E	328
S72.041F	328
S72.041G	328
S72.041H	328
S72.041J	328
S72.041K	394
S72.041M	394
S72.041N	394
S72.041P	394
S72.041Q	394
S72.041R	394
S72.041S	328
S72.042A	293, 565, 1009, 1035
S72.042B	293, 565, 1009, 1035
S72.042C	293, 565, 1009, 1035
S72.042D	328
S72.042E	328
S72.042F	328
S72.042G	328
S72.042H	328
S72.042J	328
S72.042K	394
S72.042M	394
S72.042N	394
S72.042P	394
S72.042Q	394
S72.042R	394
S72.042S	328
S72.043A	293, 565, 1009, 1035
S72.043B	293, 565, 1009, 1035
S72.043C	293, 565, 1009, 1035
S72.043D	328
S72.043E	328
S72.043F	328
S72.043G	328
S72.043H	328
S72.043J	328
S72.043K	394
S72.043M	394
S72.043N	394
S72.043P	394
S72.043Q	394
S72.043R	394
S72.043S	328
S72.044A	293, 565, 1009, 1035
S72.044B	293, 565, 1009, 1035
S72.044C	293, 565, 1009, 1035
S72.044D	328
S72.044F	328
S72.044G	328
S72.044H	328
S72.044J	328
S72.044K	394
S72.044M	394
S72.044N	394
S72.044P	394
S72.044Q	394
S72.044R	394
S72.044S	328
S72.045A	293, 565, 1009, 1035
S72.045B	293, 565, 1009, 1035
S72.045C	293, 565, 1009, 1035
S72.045D	328
S72.045E	328
S72.045F	328
S72.045G	328
S72.045H	328
S72.045J	328
S72.045K	394
S72.045M	394
S72.045N	394
S72.045P	394
S72.045Q	394
S72.045R	394
S72.045S	328
S72.046A	293, 565, 1009, 1035
S72.046B	293, 565, 1009, 1035
S72.046C	293, 565, 1009, 1035
S72.046D	328
S72.046E	328
S72.046F	328
S72.046G	328
S72.046H	328
S72.046J	328
S72.046K	394
S72.046M	394
S72.046N	394
S72.046P	394
S72.046Q	394
S72.046R	394
S72.046S	328
S72.051A	293, 565, 1009, 1035
S72.051B	293, 565, 1009, 1035
S72.051C	293, 565, 1009, 1035
S72.051D	328
S72.051E	328
S72.051F	328
S72.051G	328
S72.051H	328
S72.051J	328
S72.051K	394
S72.051M	394
S72.051N	394
S72.051P	394
S72.051Q	394
S72.051R	394
S72.051S	328
S72.052A	293, 565, 1009, 1035
S72.052B	293, 565, 1009, 1035
S72.052C	293, 565, 1009, 1035
S72.052D	328
S72.052E	328
S72.052F	328
S72.052G	328
S72.052H	328
S72.052J	328
S72.052K	394
S72.052M	394
S72.052P	394
S72.052Q	394
S72.052R	394
S72.052S	328
S72.059A	293, 565, 1009, 1035
S72.059B	293, 565, 1009, 1035
S72.059C	293, 565, 1009, 1035
S72.059D	328
S72.059E	328
S72.059F	328
S72.059G	328
S72.059H	328
S72.059J	328
S72.059M	394
S72.059N	394
S72.059P	394
S72.059Q	394
S72.059S	328
S72.061A	293, 565, 1009, 1035
S72.061B	293, 565, 1009, 1035
S72.061C	293, 565, 1009, 1035
S72.061D	328
S72.061E	328
S72.061F	328
S72.061G	328
S72.061H	328
S72.061J	328
S72.061K	394
S72.061M	394
S72.061N	394
S72.061P	394
S72.061Q	394
S72.061R	394
S72.061S	328
S72.062A	293, 565, 1009, 1035
S72.062B	293, 565, 1009, 1035
S72.062C	293, 565, 1009, 1035
S72.062D	328
S72.062E	328
S72.062F	328
S72.062G	328
S72.062H	328
S72.062J	328
S72.062K	394
S72.062M	394
S72.062N	394
S72.062P	394
S72.062Q	394
S72.062R	394
S72.062S	328
S72.063A	293, 565, 1009, 1035
S72.063B	293, 565, 1009, 1035
S72.063C	293, 565, 1009, 1035
S72.063D	328
S72.063E	328
S72.063F	328
S72.063G	328
S72.063H	328
S72.063J	328
S72.063K	394
S72.063M	394
S72.063N	394
S72.063P	394
S72.063Q	394
S72.063R	394
S72.063S	328
S72.064A	293, 565, 1009, 1035
S72.064B	293, 565, 1009, 1035
S72.064C	293, 565, 1009, 1035
S72.064D	328
S72.064E	328
S72.064F	328
S72.064G	328
S72.064H	328
S72.064J	328
S72.064K	394
S72.064M	394
S72.064N	394
S72.064P	394
S72.064Q	394
S72.064R	394
S72.064S	328
S72.065A	293, 565, 1009, 1035
S72.065B	293, 565, 1009, 1035
S72.065C	293, 565, 1009, 1035
S72.065D	328
S72.065E	328
S72.065F	328
S72.065G	328
S72.065H	328
S72.065J	328
S72.065K	394
S72.065M	394
S72.065N	394
S72.065P	394
S72.065Q	394
S72.065R	394
S72.065S	328
S72.066A	293, 565, 1009, 1035
S72.066B	293, 565, 1009, 1035
S72.066C	293, 565, 1009, 1035
S72.066D	328
S72.066E	328
S72.066F	328
S72.066G	329
S72.066H	329
S72.066J	329
S72.066K	394
S72.066M	394
S72.066N	394
S72.066P	394
S72.066Q	394
S72.066R	394
S72.066S	329
S72.091A	293, 565, 1009, 1035
S72.091B	293, 565, 1009, 1035
S72.091C	293, 565, 1009, 1035
S72.091D	329
S72.091E	329
S72.091F	329
S72.091G	329
S72.091H	329
S72.091J	329
S72.091K	394
S72.091M	394
S72.091N	394
S72.091P	394
S72.091Q	394
S72.091R	394
S72.091S	329
S72.092A	293, 565, 1009, 1035
S72.092B	293, 565, 1009, 1035
S72.092C	293, 565, 1009, 1035
S72.092D	329
S72.092E	329
S72.092F	329
S72.092G	329
S72.092H	329
S72.092J	329
S72.092K	394

Code	Page	Code	Page	Code	Page	Code	Page	Code	Page	Code	Page
S72.092M	394	S72.111J	329	S72.116G	329	S72.125E	329	S72.134C	294, 565, 1009, 1035	S72.143B	294, 565, 1009, 1035
S72.092N	394	S72.111K	394	S72.116H	329	S72.125F	329	S72.134D	329	S72.143C	294, 565, 1009, 1035
S72.092P	394	S72.111M	394	S72.116J	329	S72.125G	329	S72.134E	329	S72.143D	330
S72.092Q	394	S72.111N	394	S72.116K	395	S72.125H	329	S72.134F	329	S72.143E	330
S72.092R	394	S72.111P	394	S72.116M	395	S72.125J	329	S72.134G	329	S72.143F	330
S72.092S	329	S72.111Q	394	S72.116N	395	S72.125K	395	S72.134H	329	S72.143G	330
S72.099A	293, 565, 1009, 1035	S72.111R	394	S72.116P	395	S72.125M	395	S72.134J	329	S72.143H	330
S72.099B	293, 565, 1009, 1035	S72.111S	329	S72.116Q	395	S72.125N	395	S72.134K	395	S72.143J	330
S72.099C	293, 565, 1009, 1035	S72.112A	293, 565, 1009, 1035	S72.116R	395	S72.125P	395	S72.134M	395	S72.143K	395
S72.099D	329	S72.112B	293, 565, 1009, 1035	S72.116S	329	S72.125Q	395	S72.134N	395	S72.143M	395
S72.099E	329	S72.112C	293, 565, 1009, 1035	S72.121A	293, 565, 1009, 1035	S72.125R	395	S72.134P	395	S72.143N	395
S72.099F	329	S72.112D	329	S72.121B	293, 565, 1009, 1035	S72.125S	329	S72.134Q	395	S72.143P	395
S72.099G	329	S72.112E	329	S72.121C	293, 565, 1009, 1035	S72.126A	294, 565, 1009, 1035	S72.134R	395	S72.143Q	395
S72.099H	329	S72.112F	329	S72.121D	329	S72.126B	294, 565, 1009, 1035	S72.134S	329	S72.143R	395
S72.099J	329	S72.112G	329	S72.121E	329	S72.126C	294, 565, 1009, 1035	S72.135A	294, 565, 1009, 1035	S72.143S	330
S72.099K	394	S72.112H	329	S72.121F	329	S72.126D	329	S72.135B	294, 565, 1009, 1035	S72.144A	294, 565, 1009, 1035
S72.099M	394	S72.112J	329	S72.121G	329	S72.126E	329	S72.135C	294, 565, 1009, 1035	S72.144B	294, 565, 1009, 1035
S72.099N	394	S72.112K	394	S72.121H	329	S72.126F	329	S72.135D	329	S72.144C	294, 565, 1009, 1035
S72.099P	394	S72.112M	394	S72.121J	329	S72.126G	329	S72.135E	329	S72.144D	330
S72.099Q	394	S72.112N	394	S72.121K	395	S72.126H	329	S72.135F	329	S72.144E	330
S72.099R	394	S72.112P	394	S72.121M	395	S72.126J	329	S72.135G	329	S72.144F	330
S72.099S	329	S72.112Q	394	S72.121N	395	S72.126K	395	S72.135H	329	S72.144G	330
S72.101A	293, 565, 1009, 1035	S72.112R	394	S72.121P	395	S72.126M	395	S72.135J	329	S72.144H	330
S72.101B	293, 565, 1009, 1035	S72.112S	329	S72.121Q	395	S72.126N	395	S72.135K	395	S72.144J	330
S72.101C	293, 565, 1009, 1035	S72.113A	293, 565, 1009, 1035	S72.121R	395	S72.126P	395	S72.135M	395	S72.144K	395
S72.101D	329	S72.113B	293, 565, 1009, 1035	S72.121S	329	S72.126Q	395	S72.135N	395	S72.144M	395
S72.101E	329	S72.113C	293, 565, 1009, 1035	S72.122A	293, 565, 1009, 1035	S72.126R	395	S72.135P	395	S72.144N	395
S72.101F	329	S72.113D	329	S72.122B	293, 565, 1009, 1035	S72.126S	329	S72.135Q	395	S72.144P	395
S72.101G	329	S72.113E	329	S72.122C	293, 565, 1009, 1035	S72.131A	294, 565, 1009, 1035	S72.135R	395	S72.144Q	395
S72.101H	329	S72.113F	329	S72.122D	329	S72.131B	294, 565, 1009, 1035	S72.135S	329	S72.144R	395
S72.101J	329	S72.113G	329	S72.122E	329	S72.131C	294, 565, 1009, 1035	S72.136A	294, 565, 1009, 1035	S72.144S	330
S72.101K	394	S72.113H	329	S72.122F	329	S72.131D	329	S72.136B	294, 565, 1009, 1035	S72.145A	294, 565, 1009, 1036
S72.101M	394	S72.113J	329	S72.122G	329	S72.131E	329	S72.136C	294, 565, 1009, 1035	S72.145B	294, 565, 1009, 1036
S72.101N	394	S72.113K	394	S72.122H	329	S72.131F	329	S72.136D	329	S72.145C	294, 565, 1009, 1036
S72.101P	394	S72.113M	394	S72.122J	329	S72.131G	329	S72.136E	329	S72.145D	330
S72.101Q	394	S72.113N	394	S72.122K	395	S72.131H	329	S72.136F	329	S72.145E	330
S72.101R	394	S72.113P	394	S72.122M	395	S72.131J	329	S72.136G	329	S72.145F	330
S72.101S	329	S72.113Q	394	S72.122N	395	S72.131K	395	S72.136H	329	S72.145G	330
S72.102A	293, 565, 1009, 1035	S72.113R	394	S72.122P	395	S72.131M	395	S72.136J	329	S72.145H	330
S72.102B	293, 565, 1009, 1035	S72.113S	329	S72.122Q	395	S72.131N	395	S72.136K	395	S72.145J	330
S72.102C	293, 565, 1009, 1035	S72.114A	293, 565, 1009, 1035	S72.122R	395	S72.131P	395	S72.136M	395	S72.145K	395
S72.102D	329	S72.114B	293, 565, 1009, 1035	S72.122S	329	S72.131Q	395	S72.136N	395	S72.145M	395
S72.102E	329	S72.114C	293, 565, 1009, 1035	S72.123A	293, 565, 1009, 1035	S72.131R	395	S72.136P	395	S72.145N	395
S72.102F	329	S72.114D	329	S72.123B	293, 565, 1009, 1035	S72.131S	329	S72.136Q	395	S72.145P	395
S72.102G	329	S72.114E	329	S72.123C	293, 565, 1009, 1035	S72.132A	294, 565, 1009, 1035	S72.136R	395	S72.145Q	395
S72.102H	329	S72.114F	329	S72.123D	329	S72.132B	294, 565, 1009, 1035	S72.136S	329	S72.145R	395
S72.102J	329	S72.114G	329	S72.123E	329	S72.132C	294, 565, 1009, 1035	S72.141A	294, 565, 1009, 1035	S72.145S	330
S72.102K	394	S72.114H	329	S72.123F	329	S72.132D	329	S72.141B	294, 565, 1009, 1035	S72.146A	294, 565, 1009, 1036
S72.102M	394	S72.114J	329	S72.123G	329	S72.132E	329	S72.141C	294, 565, 1009, 1035	S72.146B	294, 565, 1009, 1036
S72.102N	394	S72.114K	394	S72.123H	329	S72.132F	329	S72.141D	329	S72.146C	294, 565, 1009, 1036
S72.102P	394	S72.114M	394	S72.123J	329	S72.132G	329	S72.141E	329	S72.146D	330
S72.102Q	394	S72.114N	394	S72.123K	395	S72.132H	329	S72.141F	330	S72.146E	330
S72.102R	394	S72.114P	394	S72.123M	395	S72.132J	329	S72.141G	330	S72.146F	330
S72.102S	329	S72.114Q	394	S72.123N	395	S72.132K	395	S72.141H	330	S72.146G	330
S72.109A	293, 565, 1009, 1035	S72.114R	394	S72.123P	395	S72.132M	395	S72.141J	330	S72.146H	330
S72.109B	293, 565, 1009, 1035	S72.114S	329	S72.123Q	395	S72.132N	395	S72.141K	395	S72.146J	330
S72.109C	293, 565, 1009, 1035	S72.115A	293, 565, 1009, 1035	S72.123R	395	S72.132P	395	S72.141M	395	S72.146K	395
S72.109D	329	S72.115B	293, 565, 1009, 1035	S72.123S	329	S72.132Q	395	S72.141N	395	S72.146M	395
S72.109E	329	S72.115C	293, 565, 1009, 1035	S72.124A	293, 565, 1009, 1035	S72.132R	395	S72.141P	395	S72.146N	395
S72.109F	329	S72.115D	329	S72.124B	293, 565, 1009, 1035	S72.132S	329	S72.141Q	395	S72.146P	395
S72.109G	329	S72.115E	329	S72.124C	293, 565, 1009, 1035	S72.133A	294, 565, 1009, 1035	S72.141R	395	S72.146Q	395
S72.109H	329	S72.115F	329	S72.124D	329	S72.133B	294, 565, 1009, 1035	S72.141S	330	S72.146R	395
S72.109J	329	S72.115G	329	S72.124E	329	S72.133C	294, 565, 1009, 1035	S72.142A	294, 565, 1009, 1035	S72.146S	330
S72.109K	394	S72.115H	329	S72.124F	329	S72.133D	329	S72.142B	294, 565, 1009, 1035	S72.21XA	294, 566, 1009, 1036
S72.109M	394	S72.115J	329	S72.124G	329	S72.133E	329	S72.142C	294, 565, 1009, 1035	S72.21XB	294, 566, 1009, 1036
S72.109N	394	S72.115K	394	S72.124H	329	S72.133F	329	S72.142D	330	S72.21XC	294, 566, 1009, 1036
S72.109P	394	S72.115M	394	S72.124J	329	S72.133G	329	S72.142E	330	S72.21XD	330
S72.109Q	394	S72.115N	395	S72.124K	395	S72.133H	329	S72.142F	330	S72.21XE	330
S72.109R	394	S72.115P	394	S72.124M	395	S72.133J	329	S72.142G	330	S72.21XF	330
S72.109S	329	S72.115Q	394	S72.124N	395	S72.133K	395	S72.142H	330	S72.21XG	330
S72.111A	293, 565, 1009, 1035	S72.115R	395	S72.124P	395	S72.133M	395	S72.142J	330	S72.21XH	330
S72.111B	293, 565, 1009, 1035	S72.115S	329	S72.124Q	395	S72.133N	395	S72.142K	395	S72.21XJ	330
S72.111C	293, 565, 1009, 1035	S72.116A	293, 565, 1009, 1035	S72.124R	395	S72.133P	395	S72.142M	395	S72.21XK	395
S72.111D	329	S72.116B	293, 565, 1009, 1035	S72.124S	329	S72.133Q	395	S72.142N	395	S72.21XM	395
S72.111E	329	S72.116C	293, 565, 1009, 1035	S72.125A	294, 565, 1009, 1035	S72.133R	395	S72.142P	395	S72.21XN	395
S72.111F	329	S72.116D	329	S72.125B	294, 565, 1009, 1035	S72.133S	329	S72.142Q	395	S72.21XP	395
S72.111G	329	S72.116E	329	S72.125C	294, 565, 1009, 1035	S72.134A	294, 565, 1009, 1035	S72.142R	395	S72.21XQ	395
S72.111H	329	S72.116F	329	S72.125D	329	S72.134B	294, 565, 1009, 1035	S72.142S	330	S72.21XR	395
								S72.143A	294, 565, 1009, 1035	S72.21XS	330

Code	Page	Code	Page	Code	Page	Code	Page	Code	Page	Code	Page
S72.22XA	294, 566, 1009, 1036	S72.26XR	395	S72.322P	396	S72.331M	396	S72.336J	331	S72.345G	331
S72.22XB	294, 566, 1009, 1036	S72.26XS	330	S72.322Q	396	S72.331N	396	S72.336K	396	S72.345H	331
S72.22XC	294, 566, 1009, 1036	S72.301A	290, 566, 1009, 1036	S72.322R	396	S72.331P	396	S72.336M	396	S72.345J	331
S72.22XD	330	S72.301B	290, 566, 1009, 1036	S72.322S	330	S72.331Q	396	S72.336N	396	S72.345K	396
S72.22XE	330	S72.301C	290, 566, 1009, 1036	S72.323A	290, 566, 1009, 1036	S72.331R	396	S72.336P	396	S72.345M	396
S72.22XF	330	S72.301D	330	S72.323B	290, 566, 1009, 1036	S72.331S	330	S72.336Q	396	S72.345N	396
S72.22XG	330	S72.301E	330	S72.323C	290, 566, 1009, 1036	S72.332A	290, 566, 1010, 1036	S72.336R	396	S72.345P	396
S72.22XH	330	S72.301F	330	S72.323D	330	S72.332B	290, 566, 1010, 1036	S72.336S	331	S72.345Q	396
S72.22XJ	330	S72.301G	330	S72.323E	330	S72.332C	290, 566, 1010, 1036	S72.341A	290, 566, 1010, 1036	S72.345R	396
S72.22XK	395	S72.301H	330	S72.323F	330	S72.332D	330	S72.341B	290, 566, 1010, 1036	S72.345S	331
S72.22XM	395	S72.301J	330	S72.323G	330	S72.332E	330	S72.341C	290, 566, 1010, 1036	S72.346A	290, 566, 1010, 1036
S72.22XN	395	S72.301K	395	S72.323H	330	S72.332F	330	S72.341D	331	S72.346B	290, 566, 1010, 1036
S72.22XP	395	S72.301M	395	S72.323J	330	S72.332G	330	S72.341E	331	S72.346C	290, 566, 1010, 1036
S72.22XQ	395	S72.301N	396	S72.323K	396	S72.332H	330	S72.341F	331	S72.346D	331
S72.22XR	395	S72.301P	395	S72.323M	396	S72.332J	330	S72.341G	331	S72.346E	331
S72.22XS	330	S72.301Q	395	S72.323N	396	S72.332K	396	S72.341H	331	S72.346F	331
S72.23XA	294, 566, 1009, 1036	S72.301R	395	S72.323P	396	S72.332M	396	S72.341J	331	S72.346G	331
S72.23XB	294, 566, 1009, 1036	S72.301S	330	S72.323Q	396	S72.332N	396	S72.341K	396	S72.346H	331
S72.23XC	294, 566, 1009, 1036	S72.302A	290, 566, 1009, 1036	S72.323R	396	S72.332P	396	S72.341M	396	S72.346J	331
S72.23XD	330	S72.302B	290, 566, 1009, 1036	S72.323S	330	S72.332Q	396	S72.341N	396	S72.346K	396
S72.23XE	330	S72.302C	290, 566, 1009, 1036	S72.324A	290, 566, 1010, 1036	S72.332R	396	S72.341P	396	S72.346M	396
S72.23XF	330	S72.302D	330	S72.324B	290, 566, 1010, 1036	S72.332S	330	S72.341Q	396	S72.346N	396
S72.23XG	330	S72.302E	330	S72.324C	290, 566, 1010, 1036	S72.333A	290, 566, 1010, 1036	S72.341R	396	S72.346P	396
S72.23XH	330	S72.302F	330	S72.324D	330	S72.333B	290, 566, 1010, 1036	S72.341S	331	S72.346Q	396
S72.23XJ	330	S72.302G	330	S72.324E	330	S72.333C	290, 566, 1010, 1036	S72.342A	290, 566, 1010, 1036	S72.346R	396
S72.23XK	395	S72.302H	330	S72.324F	330	S72.333D	330	S72.342B	290, 566, 1010, 1036	S72.346S	331
S72.23XM	395	S72.302J	330	S72.324G	330	S72.333E	330	S72.342C	290, 566, 1010, 1036	S72.351A	290, 566, 1010, 1036
S72.23XN	395	S72.302K	395	S72.324H	330	S72.333F	330	S72.342D	331	S72.351B	290, 566, 1010, 1036
S72.23XP	395	S72.302M	395	S72.324J	330	S72.333G	330	S72.342E	331	S72.351C	290, 566, 1010, 1036
S72.23XQ	395	S72.302N	395	S72.324K	396	S72.333H	330	S72.342F	331	S72.351D	331
S72.23XR	395	S72.302P	395	S72.324M	396	S72.333J	330	S72.342G	331	S72.351E	331
S72.23XS	330	S72.302Q	395	S72.324N	396	S72.333K	396	S72.342H	331	S72.351F	331
S72.24XA	294, 566, 1009, 1036	S72.302R	395	S72.324P	396	S72.333M	396	S72.342J	331	S72.351G	331
S72.24XB	294, 566, 1009, 1036	S72.302S	330	S72.324Q	396	S72.333N	396	S72.342K	396	S72.351H	331
S72.24XC	294, 566, 1009, 1036	S72.309A	290, 566, 1009, 1036	S72.324R	396	S72.333P	396	S72.342M	396	S72.351J	331
S72.24XD	330	S72.309B	290, 566, 1009, 1036	S72.324S	330	S72.333Q	396	S72.342N	396	S72.351K	396
S72.24XE	330	S72.309C	290, 566, 1009, 1036	S72.325A	290, 566, 1010, 1036	S72.333R	396	S72.342P	396	S72.351M	396
S72.24XF	330	S72.309D	330	S72.325B	290, 566, 1010, 1036	S72.333S	330	S72.342Q	396	S72.351N	396
S72.24XG	330	S72.309E	330	S72.325C	290, 566, 1010, 1036	S72.334A	290, 566, 1010, 1036	S72.342R	396	S72.351P	396
S72.24XH	330	S72.309F	330	S72.325D	330	S72.334B	290, 566, 1010, 1036	S72.342S	331	S72.351Q	396
S72.24XJ	330	S72.309G	330	S72.325E	330	S72.334C	290, 566, 1010, 1036	S72.343A	290, 566, 1010, 1036	S72.351R	396
S72.24XK	395	S72.309H	330	S72.325F	330	S72.334D	330	S72.343B	290, 566, 1010, 1036	S72.351S	331
S72.24XM	395	S72.309J	330	S72.325G	330	S72.334E	330	S72.343C	290, 566, 1010, 1036	S72.352A	290, 566, 1010, 1036
S72.24XN	395	S72.309K	395	S72.325H	330	S72.334F	330	S72.343D	331	S72.352B	290, 566, 1010, 1036
S72.24XP	395	S72.309M	395	S72.325J	330	S72.334G	330	S72.343E	331	S72.352C	290, 566, 1010, 1036
S72.24XQ	395	S72.309N	395	S72.325K	396	S72.334H	330	S72.343F	331	S72.352D	331
S72.24XR	395	S72.309P	395	S72.325M	396	S72.334J	330	S72.343G	331	S72.352E	331
S72.24XS	330	S72.309Q	395	S72.325N	396	S72.334K	396	S72.343H	331	S72.352F	331
S72.25XA	294, 566, 1009, 1036	S72.309R	395	S72.325P	396	S72.334M	396	S72.343J	331	S72.352G	331
S72.25XB	294, 566, 1009, 1036	S72.309S	330	S72.325Q	396	S72.334N	396	S72.343K	396	S72.352H	331
S72.25XC	294, 566, 1009, 1036	S72.321A	290, 566, 1009, 1036	S72.325R	396	S72.334P	396	S72.343M	396	S72.352J	331
S72.25XD	330	S72.321B	290, 566, 1009, 1036	S72.325S	330	S72.334Q	396	S72.343N	396	S72.352K	396
S72.25XE	330	S72.321C	290, 566, 1009, 1036	S72.326A	290, 566, 1010, 1036	S72.334R	396	S72.343P	396	S72.352M	396
S72.25XF	330	S72.321D	330	S72.326B	290, 566, 1010, 1036	S72.334S	330	S72.343Q	396	S72.352N	396
S72.25XG	330	S72.321E	330	S72.326C	290, 566, 1010, 1036	S72.335A	290, 566, 1010, 1036	S72.343R	396	S72.352P	396
S72.25XH	330	S72.321F	330	S72.326D	330	S72.335B	290, 566, 1010, 1036	S72.343S	331	S72.352Q	396
S72.25XJ	330	S72.321G	330	S72.326E	330	S72.335C	290, 566, 1010, 1036	S72.344A	290, 566, 1010, 1036	S72.352R	396
S72.25XK	395	S72.321H	330	S72.326F	330	S72.335D	330	S72.344B	290, 566, 1010, 1036	S72.352S	331
S72.25XM	395	S72.321J	330	S72.326G	330	S72.335E	331	S72.344C	290, 566, 1010, 1036	S72.353A	290, 566, 1010, 1036
S72.25XN	395	S72.321K	395	S72.326H	330	S72.335F	331	S72.344D	331	S72.353B	290, 566, 1010, 1036
S72.25XP	395	S72.321M	395	S72.326J	330	S72.335G	331	S72.344E	331	S72.353C	290, 566, 1010, 1036
S72.25XQ	395	S72.321N	395	S72.326K	396	S72.335H	331	S72.344F	331	S72.353D	331
S72.25XR	395	S72.321P	395	S72.326M	396	S72.335J	331	S72.344G	331	S72.353E	331
S72.25XS	330	S72.321Q	395	S72.326N	396	S72.335K	396	S72.344H	331	S72.353F	331
S72.26XA	294, 566, 1009, 1036	S72.321R	396	S72.326P	396	S72.335M	396	S72.344J	331	S72.353G	331
S72.26XB	294, 566, 1009, 1036	S72.321S	330	S72.326Q	396	S72.335N	396	S72.344K	396	S72.353H	331
S72.26XC	294, 566, 1009, 1036	S72.322A	290, 566, 1009, 1036	S72.326R	396	S72.335P	396	S72.344M	396	S72.353J	331
S72.26XD	330	S72.322B	290, 566, 1009, 1036	S72.326S	330	S72.335Q	396	S72.344N	396	S72.353K	396
S72.26XE	330	S72.322C	290, 566, 1009, 1036	S72.331A	290, 566, 1010, 1036	S72.335R	396	S72.344P	396	S72.353M	396
S72.26XF	330	S72.322D	330	S72.331B	290, 566, 1010, 1036	S72.335S	331	S72.344Q	396	S72.353N	396
S72.26XG	330	S72.322E	330	S72.331C	290, 566, 1010, 1036	S72.336A	290, 566, 1010, 1036	S72.344R	396	S72.353P	396
S72.26XH	330	S72.322F	330	S72.331D	330	S72.336B	290, 566, 1010, 1036	S72.344S	331	S72.353Q	396
S72.26XJ	330	S72.322G	330	S72.331E	330	S72.336C	290, 566, 1010, 1036	S72.345A	290, 566, 1010, 1036	S72.353R	396
S72.26XK	395	S72.322H	330	S72.331F	330	S72.336D	331	S72.345B	290, 566, 1010, 1036	S72.353S	331
S72.26XM	395	S72.322J	330	S72.331G	330	S72.336E	331	S72.345C	290, 566, 1010, 1036	S72.354A	290, 566, 1010, 1036
S72.26XN	395	S72.322K	396	S72.331H	330	S72.336F	331	S72.345D	331	S72.354B	290, 566, 1010, 1036
S72.26XP	395	S72.322M	396	S72.331J	330	S72.336G	331	S72.345E	331	S72.354C	290, 566, 1010, 1036
S72.26XQ	395	S72.322N	396	S72.331K	396	S72.336H	331	S72.345F	331	S72.354D	331

Code	Page	Code	Page	Code	Page	Code	Page	Code	Page	Code	Page
S72.354E	331	S72.363C	290, 566, 1010, 1036	S72.392B	291, 566, 1010, 1036	S72.411K	397	S72.421G	332	S72.431D	332
S72.354F	331	S72.363D	331	S72.392C	291, 566, 1010, 1036	S72.411M	397	S72.421H	332	S72.431E	332
S72.354G	331	S72.363E	331	S72.392D	331	S72.411N	397	S72.421J	332	S72.431F	332
S72.354H	331	S72.363F	331	S72.392E	331	S72.411P	397	S72.421K	397	S72.431G	332
S72.354J	331	S72.363G	331	S72.392F	331	S72.411Q	397	S72.421M	397	S72.431H	332
S72.354K	396	S72.363H	331	S72.392G	331	S72.411R	397	S72.421N	397	S72.431J	332
S72.354M	396	S72.363J	331	S72.392H	331	S72.411S	332	S72.421P	397	S72.431K	397
S72.354N	396	S72.363K	396	S72.392J	331	S72.412A	291, 1010, 1036	S72.421Q	397	S72.431M	397
S72.354P	396	S72.363M	396	S72.392K	397	S72.412B	291, 1010, 1036	S72.421R	397	S72.431N	397
S72.354Q	396	S72.363N	396	S72.392M	397	S72.412C	291, 1010, 1036	S72.421S	332	S72.431P	397
S72.354R	396	S72.363P	396	S72.392N	397	S72.412D	332	S72.422A	291, 1010, 1036	S72.431Q	397
S72.354S	331	S72.363Q	396	S72.392P	397	S72.412E	332	S72.422B	291, 1010, 1036	S72.431R	397
S72.355A	290, 566, 1010, 1036	S72.363R	396	S72.392Q	397	S72.412F	332	S72.422C	291, 1010, 1036	S72.431S	332
S72.355B	290, 566, 1010, 1036	S72.363S	331	S72.392R	397	S72.412G	332	S72.422D	332	S72.432A	291, 1010, 1037
S72.355C	290, 566, 1010, 1036	S72.364A	291, 566, 1010, 1036	S72.392S	331	S72.412H	332	S72.422E	332	S72.432B	291, 1010, 1037
S72.355D	331	S72.364B	291, 566, 1010, 1036	S72.399A	291, 566, 1010, 1036	S72.412J	332	S72.422F	332	S72.432C	291, 1010, 1037
S72.355E	331	S72.364C	291, 566, 1010, 1036	S72.399B	291, 566, 1010, 1036	S72.412K	397	S72.422G	332	S72.432D	332
S72.355F	331	S72.364D	331	S72.399C	291, 566, 1010, 1036	S72.412M	397	S72.422H	332	S72.432E	332
S72.355G	331	S72.364E	331	S72.399D	331	S72.412N	397	S72.422J	332	S72.432F	332
S72.355H	331	S72.364F	331	S72.399E	331	S72.412P	397	S72.422K	397	S72.432G	332
S72.355J	331	S72.364G	331	S72.399F	331	S72.412Q	397	S72.422M	397	S72.432H	332
S72.355K	396	S72.364H	331	S72.399G	331	S72.412R	397	S72.422N	397	S72.432J	332
S72.355M	396	S72.364J	331	S72.399H	331	S72.412S	332	S72.422P	397	S72.432K	397
S72.355N	396	S72.364K	396	S72.399J	331	S72.413A	291, 1010, 1036	S72.422Q	397	S72.432M	397
S72.355P	396	S72.364M	396	S72.399K	397	S72.413B	291, 1010, 1036	S72.422R	397	S72.432N	397
S72.355Q	396	S72.364N	396	S72.399M	397	S72.413C	291, 1010, 1036	S72.422S	332	S72.432P	397
S72.355R	396	S72.364P	396	S72.399N	397	S72.413D	332	S72.423A	291, 1010, 1036	S72.432Q	397
S72.355S	331	S72.364Q	396	S72.399P	397	S72.413E	332	S72.423B	291, 1010, 1036	S72.432R	397
S72.356A	290, 566, 1010, 1036	S72.364R	396	S72.399Q	397	S72.413F	332	S72.423C	291, 1010, 1036	S72.432S	332
S72.356B	290, 566, 1010, 1036	S72.364S	331	S72.399R	397	S72.413G	332	S72.423D	332	S72.433A	291, 1010, 1037
S72.356C	290, 566, 1010, 1036	S72.365A	291, 566, 1010, 1036	S72.399S	331	S72.413H	332	S72.423E	332	S72.433B	291, 1010, 1037
S72.356D	331	S72.365B	291, 566, 1010, 1036	S72.401A	291, 1010, 1036	S72.413J	332	S72.423F	332	S72.433C	291, 1010, 1037
S72.356E	331	S72.365C	291, 566, 1010, 1036	S72.401B	291, 1010, 1036	S72.413K	397	S72.423G	332	S72.433D	332
S72.356F	331	S72.365D	331	S72.401C	291, 1010, 1036	S72.413M	397	S72.423H	332	S72.433E	332
S72.356G	331	S72.365E	331	S72.401D	331	S72.413N	397	S72.423J	332	S72.433F	332
S72.356H	331	S72.365F	331	S72.401E	331	S72.413P	397	S72.423K	397	S72.433G	332
S72.356J	331	S72.365G	331	S72.401F	331	S72.413Q	397	S72.423M	397	S72.433H	332
S72.356K	396	S72.365H	331	S72.401G	331	S72.413R	397	S72.423N	397	S72.433J	332
S72.356M	396	S72.365J	331	S72.401H	331	S72.413S	332	S72.423P	397	S72.433K	397
S72.356N	396	S72.365K	396	S72.401J	331	S72.414A	291, 1010, 1036	S72.423Q	397	S72.433M	397
S72.356P	396	S72.365M	396	S72.401K	397	S72.414B	291, 1010, 1036	S72.423R	397	S72.433N	397
S72.356Q	396	S72.365N	396	S72.401M	397	S72.414C	291, 1010, 1036	S72.423S	332	S72.433P	397
S72.356R	396	S72.365P	396	S72.401N	397	S72.414D	332	S72.424A	291, 1010, 1036	S72.433Q	397
S72.356S	331	S72.365Q	396	S72.401P	397	S72.414E	332	S72.424B	291, 1010, 1036	S72.433R	397
S72.361A	290, 566, 1010, 1036	S72.365R	396	S72.401Q	397	S72.414F	332	S72.424C	291, 1010, 1036	S72.433S	332
S72.361B	290, 566, 1010, 1036	S72.365S	331	S72.401R	397	S72.414G	332	S72.424D	332	S72.434A	291, 1010, 1037
S72.361C	290, 566, 1010, 1036	S72.366A	291, 566, 1010, 1036	S72.401S	331	S72.414H	332	S72.424E	332	S72.434B	291, 1010, 1037
S72.361D	331	S72.366B	291, 566, 1010, 1036	S72.402A	291, 1010, 1036	S72.414J	332	S72.424F	332	S72.434C	291, 1010, 1037
S72.361E	331	S72.366C	291, 566, 1010, 1036	S72.402B	291, 1010, 1036	S72.414K	397	S72.424G	332	S72.434D	332
S72.361F	331	S72.366D	331	S72.402C	291, 1010, 1036	S72.414M	397	S72.424H	332	S72.434E	332
S72.361G	331	S72.366E	331	S72.402D	331	S72.414N	397	S72.424J	332	S72.434F	332
S72.361H	331	S72.366F	331	S72.402E	331	S72.414P	397	S72.424K	397	S72.434G	332
S72.361J	331	S72.366G	331	S72.402F	331	S72.414Q	397	S72.424M	397	S72.434H	332
S72.361K	396	S72.366H	331	S72.402G	331	S72.414R	397	S72.424N	397	S72.434J	332
S72.361M	396	S72.366J	331	S72.402H	331	S72.414S	332	S72.424P	397	S72.434K	397
S72.361N	396	S72.366K	396	S72.402J	331	S72.415A	291, 1010, 1036	S72.424Q	397	S72.434M	397
S72.361P	396	S72.366M	396	S72.402K	397	S72.415B	291, 1010, 1036	S72.424R	397	S72.434N	397
S72.361Q	396	S72.366N	396	S72.402M	397	S72.415C	291, 1010, 1036	S72.424S	332	S72.434P	397
S72.361R	396	S72.366P	396	S72.402N	397	S72.415D	332	S72.425A	291, 1010, 1036	S72.434Q	397
S72.361S	331	S72.366Q	396	S72.402P	397	S72.415E	332	S72.425B	291, 1010, 1036	S72.434R	397
S72.362A	290, 566, 1010, 1036	S72.366R	397	S72.402R	397	S72.415F	332	S72.425C	291, 1010, 1036	S72.434S	332
S72.362B	290, 566, 1010, 1036	S72.366S	331	S72.402S	331	S72.415G	332	S72.425D	332	S72.435A	291, 1010, 1037
S72.362C	290, 566, 1010, 1036	S72.391A	291, 566, 1010, 1036	S72.409A	291, 1010, 1036	S72.415H	332	S72.425E	332	S72.435B	291, 1010, 1037
S72.362D	331	S72.391B	291, 566, 1010, 1036	S72.409B	291, 1010, 1036	S72.415J	332	S72.425F	332	S72.435C	291, 1010, 1037
S72.362E	331	S72.391C	291, 566, 1010, 1036	S72.409C	291, 1010, 1036	S72.415K	397	S72.425G	332	S72.435D	332
S72.362F	331	S72.391D	331	S72.409D	332	S72.415M	397	S72.425H	332	S72.435E	332
S72.362G	331	S72.391E	331	S72.409E	332	S72.415N	397	S72.425J	332	S72.435F	332
S72.362H	331	S72.391F	331	S72.409F	332	S72.415P	397	S72.425K	397	S72.435G	332
S72.362J	331	S72.391G	331	S72.409G	332	S72.415Q	397	S72.425M	397	S72.435H	332
S72.362K	396	S72.391H	331	S72.409H	332	S72.415R	397	S72.425N	397	S72.435J	332
S72.362M	396	S72.391J	331	S72.409J	332	S72.415S	397	S72.425P	397	S72.435K	397
S72.362N	396	S72.391K	396	S72.409K	397	S72.416A	291, 1010, 1036	S72.425Q	397	S72.435M	397
S72.362P	396	S72.391M	397	S72.409M	397	S72.416B	291, 1010, 1036	S72.425R	397	S72.435N	397
S72.362Q	396	S72.391N	397	S72.409N	397	S72.416C	291, 1010, 1036	S72.425S	332	S72.435P	397
S72.362R	396	S72.391P	397	S72.409P	397	S72.416D	332	S72.426A	291, 1010, 1037	S72.435Q	397
S72.362S	331	S72.391Q	397	S72.409Q	397	S72.416E	332	S72.426B	291, 1010, 1037	S72.435R	397
S72.363A	290, 566, 1010, 1036	S72.391R	397	S72.409R	397	S72.416F	332	S72.426C	291, 1010, 1037	S72.435S	332
		S72.391S	331	S72.409S	332	S72.416G	332	S72.426D	332	S72.436A	291, 1010, 1037
S72.363B	290, 566, 1010, 1036	S72.392A	291, 566, 1010, 1036	S72.411A	291, 1010, 1036	S72.416H	332	S72.426E	332	S72.436B	291, 1010, 1037
				S72.411B	291, 1010, 1036	S72.416J	332	S72.426F	332	S72.436C	291, 1010, 1037
				S72.411C	291, 1010, 1036	S72.416K	397	S72.426G	332	S72.436D	332
				S72.411D	332	S72.416M	397	S72.426H	332	S72.436E	332
				S72.411E	332	S72.416N	397	S72.426J	332	S72.436F	332
				S72.411F	332	S72.416P	397	S72.426K	397	S72.436G	332
				S72.411G	332	S72.416Q	397	S72.426M	397	S72.436H	332
				S72.411H	332	S72.416R	397	S72.426N	397	S72.436J	332
				S72.411J	332	S72.416S	332	S72.426P	397	S72.436K	397
						S72.421A	291, 1010, 1036	S72.426Q	397	S72.436M	397
						S72.421B	291, 1010, 1036	S72.426R	397	S72.436N	397
						S72.421C	291, 1010, 1036	S72.426S	332	S72.436P	397
						S72.421D	332	S72.431A	291, 1010, 1037	S72.436Q	397
						S72.421E	332	S72.431B	291, 1010, 1037	S72.436R	397
						S72.421F	332	S72.431C	291, 1010, 1037	S72.436S	332

Code	Page	Code	Page	Code	Page	Code	Page	Code	Page	Code	Page
S72.441A	291, 1010, 1037	S72.446Q	398	S72.455N	398	S72.464K	398	S72.492R	398	S72.90XS	333
S72.441B	291, 1010, 1037	S72.446R	398	S72.455P	398	S72.464M	398	S72.492S	333	S72.91XA	291, 566, 1011, 1037
S72.441C	291, 1010, 1037	S72.446S	333	S72.455Q	398	S72.464N	398	S72.499A	291, 1011, 1037	S72.91XB	291, 566, 1011, 1037
S72.441D	332	S72.451A	1010	S72.455R	398	S72.464P	398	S72.499B	291, 1011, 1037	S72.91XC	291, 566, 1011, 1037
S72.441E	332	S72.451A	291, 1037	S72.455S	333	S72.464Q	398	S72.499C	291, 1011, 1037	S72.91XD	333
S72.441F	332	S72.451B	1010	S72.456A	1011	S72.464R	398	S72.499D	333	S72.91XE	333
S72.441G	332	S72.451B	291, 1037	S72.456A	291, 1037	S72.464S	333	S72.499E	333	S72.91XF	333
S72.441H	332	S72.451C	1010	S72.456B	1011	S72.465A	1011	S72.499F	333	S72.91XG	333
S72.441J	332	S72.451C	291, 1037	S72.456B	291, 1037	S72.465A	291, 1037	S72.499G	333	S72.91XH	333
S72.441K	397	S72.451D	333	S72.456C	1011	S72.465B	1011	S72.499H	333	S72.91XJ	333
S72.441M	397	S72.451E	333	S72.456C	291, 1037	S72.465B	291, 1037	S72.499J	333	S72.91XK	398
S72.441N	397	S72.451F	333	S72.456D	333	S72.465C	1011	S72.499K	398	S72.91XM	398
S72.441P	397	S72.451G	333	S72.456E	333	S72.465C	291, 1037	S72.499M	398	S72.91XN	398
S72.441Q	397	S72.451H	333	S72.456F	333	S72.465D	333	S72.499N	398	S72.91XP	398
S72.441R	397	S72.451J	333	S72.456G	333	S72.465E	333	S72.499P	398	S72.91XQ	398
S72.441S	332	S72.451K	398	S72.456H	333	S72.465F	333	S72.499Q	398	S72.91XR	398
S72.442A	291, 1010, 1037	S72.451M	398	S72.456J	333	S72.465G	333	S72.499R	398	S72.91XS	333
S72.442B	291, 1010, 1037	S72.451N	398	S72.456K	398	S72.465H	333	S72.499S	333	S72.92XA	291, 566, 1011, 1037
S72.442C	291, 1010, 1037	S72.451P	398	S72.456M	398	S72.465J	333	S72.8X1A	291, 566, 1011, 1037	S72.92XB	291, 566, 1011, 1037
S72.442D	332	S72.451Q	398	S72.456N	398	S72.465K	398	S72.8X1B	291, 566, 1011, 1037	S72.92XC	291, 566, 1011, 1037
S72.442E	332	S72.451R	398	S72.456P	398	S72.465M	398	S72.8X1C	291, 566, 1011, 1037	S72.92XD	333
S72.442F	332	S72.451S	333	S72.456Q	398	S72.465N	398	S72.8X1D	333	S72.92XE	333
S72.442G	332	S72.452A	1011	S72.456R	398	S72.465P	398	S72.8X1E	333	S72.92XF	333
S72.442H	332	S72.452A	291, 1037	S72.456S	333	S72.465Q	398	S72.8X1F	333	S72.92XG	333
S72.442J	332	S72.452B	1011	S72.461A	1011	S72.465R	398	S72.8X1G	333	S72.92XH	333
S72.442K	397	S72.452B	291, 1037	S72.461A	291, 1037	S72.465S	333	S72.8X1H	333	S72.92XJ	333
S72.442M	397	S72.452C	1011	S72.461B	1011	S72.466A	1011	S72.8X1J	333	S72.92XK	398
S72.442N	397	S72.452C	291, 1037	S72.461C	1011	S72.466A	291, 1037	S72.8X1K	398	S72.92XM	398
S72.442P	397	S72.452D	333	S72.461C	291, 1037	S72.466B	1011	S72.8X1N	398	S72.92XN	398
S72.442Q	397	S72.452E	333	S72.461D	333	S72.466B	291, 1037	S72.8X1P	398	S72.92XP	398
S72.442R	397	S72.452F	333	S72.461E	333	S72.466C	1011	S72.8X1Q	398	S72.92XQ	398
S72.442S	332	S72.452G	333	S72.461F	333	S72.466C	291, 1037	S72.8X1R	398	S72.92XR	398
S72.443A	291, 1010, 1037	S72.452H	333	S72.461G	333	S72.466D	333	S72.8X1S	333	S72.92XS	333
S72.443B	291, 1010, 1037	S72.452J	333	S72.461H	333	S72.466E	333	S72.8X2A	291, 566, 1011, 1037	S73.001A	294, 1011
S72.443C	291, 1010, 1037	S72.452K	398	S72.461J	333	S72.466F	333	S72.8X2B	291, 566, 1011, 1037	S73.001D	816
S72.443D	332	S72.452M	398	S72.461K	398	S72.466G	333	S72.8X2C	291, 566, 1011, 1037	S73.001S	364
S72.443E	332	S72.452N	398	S72.461M	398	S72.466H	333	S72.8X2D	333	S73.002A	294, 1011
S72.443F	332	S72.452P	398	S72.461N	398	S72.466J	333	S72.8X2E	333	S73.002D	816
S72.443G	332	S72.452Q	398	S72.461P	398	S72.466K	398	S72.8X2F	333	S73.002S	364
S72.443H	332	S72.452R	398	S72.461Q	398	S72.466M	398	S72.8X2G	333	S73.003A	294, 1011
S72.443J	332	S72.452S	333	S72.461R	398	S72.466N	398	S72.8X2H	333	S73.003D	816
S72.443K	397	S72.453A	1011	S72.461S	333	S72.466P	398	S72.8X2J	333	S73.003S	364
S72.443M	397	S72.453A	291, 1037	S72.462A	1011	S72.466Q	398	S72.8X2K	398	S73.004A	294, 1011
S72.443N	397	S72.453B	1011	S72.462A	291, 1037	S72.466R	398	S72.8X2M	398	S73.004D	816
S72.443P	397	S72.453B	291, 1037	S72.462B	1011	S72.466S	333	S72.8X2N	398	S73.004S	364
S72.443Q	397	S72.453C	1011	S72.462B	291, 1037	S72.471A	291, 1011, 1037	S72.8X2P	398	S73.005A	294, 1011
S72.443R	397	S72.453C	291, 1037	S72.462C	1011	S72.471D	333	S72.8X2Q	398	S73.005D	816
S72.443S	332	S72.453D	333	S72.462C	291, 1037	S72.471G	333	S72.8X2R	398	S73.005S	364
S72.444A	291, 1010, 1037	S72.453E	333	S72.462D	333	S72.471K	398	S72.8X2S	333	S73.006A	294, 1011
S72.444B	291, 1010, 1037	S72.453F	333	S72.462E	333	S72.471P	398	S72.8X9A	291, 566, 1011, 1037	S73.006D	816
S72.444C	291, 1010, 1037	S72.453G	333	S72.462F	333	S72.471S	333	S72.8X9B	291, 566, 1011, 1037	S73.006S	364
S72.444D	332	S72.453H	333	S72.462G	333	S72.472A	291, 1011, 1037	S72.8X9C	291, 566, 1011, 1037	S73.011A	294, 1011
S72.444E	332	S72.453J	333	S72.462H	333	S72.472D	333	S72.8X9D	333	S73.011D	816
S72.444F	332	S72.453K	398	S72.462J	333	S72.472G	333	S72.8X9E	333	S73.011S	364
S72.444G	332	S72.453M	398	S72.462K	398	S72.472K	398	S72.8X9F	333	S73.012A	294, 1011
S72.444H	332	S72.453N	398	S72.462M	398	S72.472P	398	S72.8X9G	333	S73.012D	816
S72.444J	332	S72.453P	398	S72.462M	398	S72.472S	333	S72.8X9H	333	S73.012S	364
S72.444K	397	S72.453Q	398	S72.462N	398	S72.479A	291, 1011, 1037	S72.8X9J	333	S73.013A	294, 1011
S72.444M	397	S72.453R	398	S72.462P	398	S72.479D	333	S72.8X9K	398	S73.013D	816
S72.444N	397	S72.453S	333	S72.462Q	398	S72.479G	333	S72.8X9M	398	S73.013S	364
S72.444P	397	S72.454A	1011	S72.462R	398	S72.479K	398	S72.8X9N	398	S73.014A	294, 1011
S72.444Q	397	S72.454A	291, 1037	S72.462S	333	S72.479P	398	S72.8X9P	398	S73.014D	816
S72.444R	397	S72.454B	1011	S72.463A	1011	S72.479S	333	S72.8X9Q	398	S73.014S	364
S72.444S	332	S72.454B	291, 1037	S72.463A	291, 1037	S72.491A	291, 1011, 1037	S72.8X9R	398	S73.015A	294, 1011
S72.445A	291, 1010, 1037	S72.454C	1011	S72.463B	1011	S72.491B	291, 1011, 1037	S72.8X9S	333	S73.015D	816
S72.445B	291, 1010, 1037	S72.454C	291, 1037	S72.463B	291, 1037	S72.491C	291, 1011, 1037	S72.90XA	291, 566, 1011, 1037	S73.015S	364
S72.445C	291, 1010, 1037	S72.454D	333	S72.463C	1011	S72.491D	333	S72.90XB	291, 566, 1011, 1037	S73.016A	294, 1011
S72.445D	332	S72.454E	333	S72.463C	291, 1037	S72.491F	333	S72.90XC	291, 566, 1011, 1037	S73.016D	816
S72.445E	332	S72.454F	333	S72.463D	333	S72.491G	333	S72.90XD	333	S73.016S	364
S72.445F	332	S72.454G	333	S72.463E	333	S72.491H	333	S72.90XE	333	S73.021A	294, 1011
S72.445G	332	S72.454H	333	S72.463F	333	S72.491J	333	S72.90XF	333	S73.021D	816
S72.445H	332	S72.454J	333	S72.463G	333	S72.491K	398	S72.90XG	333	S73.021S	364
S72.445J	332	S72.454K	398	S72.463H	333	S72.491M	398	S72.90XH	333	S73.022A	294, 1011
S72.445K	397	S72.454M	398	S72.463J	333	S72.491N	398	S72.90XJ	333	S73.022D	816
S72.445M	397	S72.454N	398	S72.463K	398	S72.491P	398	S72.90XK	398	S73.022S	364
S72.445N	397	S72.454P	398	S72.463M	398	S72.491Q	398	S72.90XM	398	S73.023A	294, 1011
S72.445P	397	S72.454Q	398	S72.463N	398	S72.491R	398	S72.90XN	398	S73.023D	817
S72.445Q	397	S72.454R	398	S72.463P	398	S72.491S	333	S72.90XP	398	S73.023S	364
S72.445R	398	S72.454S	333	S72.463Q	398	S72.492A	291, 1011, 1037	S72.90XQ	398	S73.024A	294, 1011
S72.445S	398	S72.455A	1011	S72.463R	398	S72.492B	291, 1011, 1037	S72.90XR	398	S73.024D	817
S72.446A	291, 1010, 1037	S72.455A	291, 1037	S72.463S	333	S72.492C	291, 1011, 1037			S73.024S	364
S72.446B	291, 1010, 1037	S72.455B	1011	S72.464A	1011	S72.492D	333			S73.025A	294, 1011
S72.446C	291, 1010, 1037	S72.455B	291, 1037	S72.464A	291, 1037	S72.492E	333			S73.025D	817
S72.446D	332	S72.455C	1011	S72.464B	1011	S72.492F	333			S73.025S	364
S72.446E	332	S72.455C	291, 1037	S72.464B	291, 1037	S72.492G	333			S73.026A	294, 1011
S72.446F	332	S72.455D	333	S72.464C	1011	S72.492H	333			S73.026D	817
S72.446G	332	S72.455E	333	S72.464C	291, 1037	S72.492J	333			S73.026S	364
S72.446H	332	S72.455F	333	S72.464D	333	S72.492K	398				
S72.446J	332	S72.455G	333	S72.464E	333	S72.492M	398				
S72.446K	398	S72.455H	333	S72.464F	333	S72.492N	398				
S72.446M	398	S72.455J	333	S72.464G	398	S72.492P	398				
S72.446N	398	S72.455K	398	S72.464H	333	S72.492Q	398				
S72.446P	398	S72.455M	398	S72.464J	333						

Code	Page
S73.Ø31A	294, 1011
S73.Ø31D	817
S73.Ø31S	364
S73.Ø32A	294, 1011
S73.Ø32D	817
S73.Ø32S	364
S73.Ø33A	294, 1011
S73.Ø33D	817
S73.Ø33S	364
S73.Ø34A	294, 1011
S73.Ø34D	817
S73.Ø34S	364
S73.Ø35A	294, 1011
S73.Ø35D	817
S73.Ø35S	364
S73.Ø36A	294, 1011
S73.Ø36D	817
S73.Ø36S	364
S73.Ø41A	294, 1011
S73.Ø41D	817
S73.Ø41S	364
S73.Ø42A	294, 1011
S73.Ø42D	817
S73.Ø42S	364
S73.Ø43A	294, 1011
S73.Ø43D	817
S73.Ø43S	364
S73.Ø44A	294, 1011
S73.Ø44D	817
S73.Ø44S	364
S73.Ø45A	294, 1011
S73.Ø45D	817
S73.Ø45S	364
S73.Ø46A	294, 1011
S73.Ø46D	817
S73.Ø46S	364
S73.1Ø1A	294, 1011
S73.1Ø1D	817
S73.1Ø1S	364
S73.1Ø2A	294, 1011
S73.1Ø2D	817
S73.1Ø2S	364
S73.1Ø9A	294, 1011
S73.1Ø9D	817
S73.1Ø9S	364
S73.111A	294, 1011
S73.111D	817
S73.111S	364
S73.112A	294, 1011
S73.112D	817
S73.112S	364
S73.119A	294, 1011
S73.119D	817
S73.119S	364
S73.121A	294, 1011
S73.121D	817
S73.121S	364
S73.122A	294, 1011
S73.122D	817
S73.122S	364
S73.129A	294, 1011
S73.129D	817
S73.129S	364
S73.191A	294, 1011
S73.191D	817
S73.191S	364
S73.192A	294, 1011
S73.192D	817
S73.192S	364
S73.199A	294, 1011
S73.199D	817
S73.199S	364
S74.ØØXA	47, 1011, 1037
S74.ØØXD	817
S74.ØØXS	53
S74.Ø1XA	47, 1011, 1037
S74.Ø1XD	817
S74.Ø1XS	53
S74.Ø2XA	47, 1011, 1037
S74.Ø2XD	817
S74.Ø2XS	53
S74.1ØXA	47, 1011, 1037
S74.1ØXD	817
S74.1ØXS	53
S74.11XA	47, 1011, 1037
S74.11XD	817
S74.11XS	53
S74.12XA	47, 1011, 1037
S74.12XD	817
S74.12XS	53
S74.2ØXA	47, 1011
S74.2ØXD	817
S74.2ØXS	53
S74.21XA	47, 1011
S74.21XD	817
S74.21XS	53
S74.22XA	47, 1011
S74.22XD	817
S74.22XS	53
S74.8X1A	1011, 1037
S74.8X1A	47
S74.8X1D	817
S74.8X1S	53
S74.8X2A	1011, 1037
S74.8X2A	47
S74.8X2D	817
S74.8X2S	53
S74.8X9A	1011, 1037
S74.8X9A	47
S74.8X9D	817
S74.8X9S	54
S74.9ØXA	47, 1011, 1037
S74.9ØXD	817
S74.9ØXS	54
S74.91XA	47, 1011, 1037
S74.91XD	817
S74.91XS	54
S74.92XA	47, 1011, 1037
S74.92XD	817
S74.92XS	54
S75.ØØ1A	753, 1011, 1037
S75.ØØ1D	817
S75.ØØ1S	170
S75.ØØ2A	753, 1011, 1037
S75.ØØ2D	817
S75.ØØ2S	170
S75.ØØ9A	753, 1011, 1037
S75.ØØ9D	817
S75.ØØ9S	170
S75.Ø11A	753, 1011, 1037
S75.Ø11D	817
S75.Ø11S	170
S75.Ø12A	753, 1011, 1037
S75.Ø12D	817
S75.Ø12S	170
S75.Ø19A	753, 1011, 1037
S75.Ø19D	817
S75.Ø19S	170
S75.Ø21A	753, 1011, 1037
S75.Ø21D	817
S75.Ø21S	170
S75.Ø22A	753, 1011, 1037
S75.Ø22D	817
S75.Ø22S	170
S75.Ø29A	753, 1011, 1037
S75.Ø29D	817
S75.Ø29S	170
S75.Ø91A	753, 1011, 1037
S75.Ø91D	817
S75.Ø91S	170
S75.Ø92A	753, 1011, 1037
S75.Ø92D	817
S75.Ø92S	170
S75.Ø99A	753, 1011, 1037
S75.Ø99D	817
S75.Ø99S	170
S75.1Ø1A	753, 1011, 1037
S75.1Ø1D	817
S75.1Ø1S	170
S75.1Ø2A	753, 1011, 1037
S75.1Ø2D	817
S75.1Ø2S	170
S75.1Ø9A	753, 1011, 1037
S75.1Ø9D	817
S75.1Ø9S	170
S75.111A	753, 1011, 1037
S75.111D	817
S75.111S	170
S75.112A	753, 1011, 1037
S75.112D	817
S75.112S	170
S75.119A	753, 1011, 1037
S75.119D	817
S75.119S	170
S75.121A	753, 1011, 1037
S75.121D	817
S75.121S	170
S75.122A	753, 1011, 1037
S75.122D	817
S75.122S	170
S75.129A	753, 1011, 1037
S75.129D	817
S75.129S	170
S75.191A	753, 1011, 1037
S75.191D	817
S75.191S	170
S75.192A	753, 1011, 1037
S75.192D	817
S75.192S	170
S75.199A	753, 1011, 1037
S75.199D	817
S75.199S	170
S75.2Ø1A	753, 1011
S75.2Ø1D	817
S75.2Ø1S	170
S75.2Ø2A	753, 1011
S75.2Ø2D	817
S75.2Ø2S	170
S75.2Ø9A	753, 1011
S75.2Ø9D	817
S75.2Ø9S	170
S75.211A	753, 1011
S75.211D	817
S75.211S	170
S75.212A	753, 1011
S75.212D	817
S75.212S	170
S75.219A	753, 1011
S75.219D	817
S75.219S	170
S75.221A	753, 1011
S75.221D	817
S75.221S	170
S75.222A	753, 1011
S75.222D	817
S75.222S	170
S75.229A	753, 1011
S75.229D	817
S75.229S	170
S75.291A	753, 1011
S75.291D	817
S75.291S	170
S75.292A	753, 1011
S75.292D	817
S75.292S	170
S75.299A	753, 1011
S75.299D	817
S75.299S	170
S75.8Ø1A	753, 1011, 1037
S75.8Ø1D	817
S75.8Ø1S	170
S75.8Ø2A	753, 1011, 1037
S75.8Ø2D	817
S75.8Ø2S	170
S75.8Ø9A	753, 1011, 1037
S75.8Ø9D	817
S75.8Ø9S	170
S75.811A	753, 1011, 1037
S75.811D	817
S75.811S	170
S75.812A	753, 1011, 1037
S75.812D	817
S75.812S	170
S75.819A	753, 1011, 1037
S75.819D	817
S75.819S	170
S75.891A	1011, 1037
S75.891A	753
S75.891D	817
S75.891S	170
S75.892A	1011, 1037
S75.892A	753
S75.892D	817
S75.892S	170
S75.899A	1011, 1037
S75.899A	753
S75.899D	817
S75.899S	170
S75.9Ø1A	753, 1011
S75.9Ø1D	817
S75.9Ø1S	170
S75.9Ø2A	753, 1011
S75.9Ø2D	817
S75.9Ø2S	170
S75.9Ø9A	753, 1011
S75.9Ø9D	817
S75.9Ø9S	170
S75.911A	753, 1011
S75.911D	817
S75.911S	170
S75.912A	753, 1011
S75.912D	817
S75.912S	170
S75.919A	753, 1011
S75.919D	817
S75.919S	170
S75.991A	753, 1011
S75.991D	817
S75.991S	170
S75.992A	753, 1011
S75.992D	817
S75.992S	170
S75.999A	753, 1011
S75.999D	817
S75.999S	170
S76.ØØ1A	753, 1012
S76.ØØ1D	817
S76.ØØ1S	753
S76.ØØ2A	753, 1012
S76.ØØ2D	817
S76.ØØ2S	753
S76.ØØ9A	753, 1012
S76.ØØ9D	817
S76.ØØ9S	753
S76.Ø11A	294, 1012
S76.Ø11D	817
S76.Ø11S	364
S76.Ø12A	294, 1012
S76.Ø12D	817
S76.Ø12S	364
S76.Ø19A	294, 1012
S76.Ø19D	817
S76.Ø19S	364
S76.Ø21A	398, 1012
S76.Ø21D	817
S76.Ø21S	468
S76.Ø22A	398, 1012
S76.Ø22D	817
S76.Ø22S	468
S76.Ø29A	398, 1012
S76.Ø29D	817
S76.Ø29S	468
S76.Ø91A	753, 1012
S76.Ø91D	817
S76.Ø91S	753
S76.Ø92A	753, 1012
S76.Ø92D	817
S76.Ø92S	753
S76.Ø99A	753, 1012
S76.Ø99D	817
S76.Ø99S	753
S76.1Ø1A	753, 1012
S76.1Ø1D	817
S76.1Ø1S	753
S76.1Ø2A	753, 1012
S76.1Ø2D	817
S76.1Ø2S	753
S76.1Ø9A	753, 1012
S76.1Ø9D	817
S76.1Ø9S	753
S76.111A	294, 1012
S76.111D	817
S76.111S	364
S76.112A	294, 1012
S76.112D	817
S76.112S	364
S76.119A	294, 1012
S76.119D	817
S76.119S	364
S76.121A	398, 1012
S76.121D	817
S76.121S	468
S76.122A	398, 1012
S76.122D	817
S76.122S	468
S76.129A	398, 1012
S76.129D	817
S76.129S	468
S76.191A	753, 1012
S76.191D	817
S76.191S	753
S76.192A	753, 1012
S76.192D	817
S76.192S	753
S76.199A	753, 1012
S76.199D	817
S76.199S	753
S76.2Ø1A	753, 1012
S76.2Ø1D	817
S76.2Ø1S	753
S76.2Ø2A	753, 1012
S76.2Ø2D	817
S76.2Ø2S	753
S76.2Ø9A	753, 1012
S76.2Ø9D	817
S76.2Ø9S	753
S76.211A	294, 1012
S76.211D	817
S76.211S	365
S76.212A	294, 1012
S76.212D	817
S76.212S	365
S76.219A	294, 1012
S76.219D	817
S76.219S	365
S76.221A	398, 1012
S76.221D	817
S76.221S	468
S76.222A	398, 1012
S76.222D	817
S76.222S	468
S76.229A	398, 1012
S76.229D	817
S76.229S	468
S76.291A	753, 1012
S76.291D	817
S76.291S	753
S76.292A	753, 1012
S76.292D	817
S76.292S	753
S76.299A	753, 1012
S76.299D	817
S76.299S	753
S76.3Ø1A	753, 1012
S76.3Ø1D	817
S76.3Ø1S	753
S76.3Ø2A	753, 1012
S76.3Ø2D	817
S76.3Ø2S	753
S76.3Ø9A	753, 1012
S76.3Ø9D	817
S76.3Ø9S	753
S76.311A	294, 1012
S76.311D	817
S76.311S	365
S76.312A	294, 1012
S76.312D	817
S76.312S	365
S76.319A	294, 1012
S76.319D	817
S76.319S	365
S76.321A	398, 1012
S76.321D	817
S76.321S	468
S76.322A	398, 1012
S76.322D	817
S76.322S	468
S76.329A	398, 1012
S76.329D	817
S76.329S	468
S76.391A	753, 1012
S76.391D	817
S76.391S	753
S76.392A	753, 1012
S76.392D	817
S76.392S	753
S76.399A	753, 1012
S76.399D	817
S76.399S	753
S76.8Ø1A	753, 1012
S76.8Ø1D	817
S76.8Ø1S	753
S76.8Ø2A	753, 1012
S76.8Ø2D	817
S76.8Ø2S	754
S76.8Ø9A	754, 1012
S76.8Ø9D	817
S76.8Ø9S	754
S76.811A	294, 1012
S76.811D	817
S76.811S	365
S76.812A	294, 1012
S76.812D	817
S76.812S	365
S76.819A	294, 1012
S76.819D	817
S76.819S	365
S76.821A	398, 1012
S76.821D	817
S76.821S	468
S76.822A	398, 1012
S76.822D	817
S76.822S	468
S76.829A	398, 1012
S76.829D	817
S76.829S	468
S76.891A	754, 1012
S76.891D	817
S76.891S	754
S76.892A	754, 1012
S76.892D	817
S76.892S	754
S76.899A	754, 1012
S76.899D	817
S76.899S	754
S76.9Ø1A	754, 1012
S76.9Ø1D	817
S76.9Ø1S	754
S76.9Ø2A	754, 1012
S76.9Ø2D	817
S76.9Ø2S	754
S76.9Ø9A	754, 1012
S76.9Ø9D	817
S76.9Ø9S	754
S76.911A	294, 1012
S76.911D	817
S76.911S	365
S76.912A	294, 1012
S76.912D	817
S76.912S	365
S76.919A	294, 1012
S76.919D	817
S76.919S	365
S76.921A	398, 1012
S76.921D	817
S76.921S	468
S76.922A	398, 1012
S76.922D	817
S76.922S	468
S76.929A	398, 1012
S76.929D	817
S76.929S	468
S76.991A	754, 1012
S76.991D	817
S76.991S	754
S76.992A	754, 1012
S76.992D	817
S76.992S	754
S76.999A	754, 1012
S76.999D	817
S76.999S	754
S77.ØØXA	754, 1012, 1037
S77.ØØXD	817
S77.ØØXS	468
S77.Ø1XA	754, 1012, 1037
S77.Ø1XD	817
S77.Ø1XS	468
S77.Ø2XA	754, 1012, 1037
S77.Ø2XD	817
S77.Ø2XS	468
S77.1ØXA	754, 1012, 1037
S77.1ØXD	817
S77.1ØXS	468
S77.11XA	754, 1012, 1037
S77.11XD	817
S77.11XS	468
S77.12XA	754, 1012, 1037
S77.12XD	818
S77.12XS	468
S77.2ØXA	754, 1012, 1037
S77.2ØXD	818
S77.2ØXS	468
S77.21XA	754, 1012, 1037
S77.21XD	818
S77.21XS	468
S77.22XA	754, 1012, 1037
S77.22XD	818
S77.22XS	468
S78.Ø11A	754, 1012, 1037
S78.Ø11D	818
S78.Ø11S	333
S78.Ø12A	754, 1012, 1037
S78.Ø12D	818
S78.Ø12S	333
S78.Ø19A	754, 1012, 1037
S78.Ø19D	818
S78.Ø19S	333
S78.Ø21A	754, 1012, 1037
S78.Ø21D	818
S78.Ø21S	333
S78.Ø22A	754, 1012, 1037
S78.Ø22D	818
S78.Ø22S	333
S78.Ø29A	754, 1012, 1037
S78.Ø29D	818
S78.Ø29S	333
S78.111A	754, 1012, 1037
S78.111D	818
S78.111S	333
S78.112A	754, 1012, 1037
S78.112D	818
S78.112S	333
S78.119A	754, 1012, 1037
S78.119D	818
S78.119S	333
S78.121A	754, 1012, 1037
S78.121D	818
S78.121S	333

Code	Page	Code	Page	Code	Page	Code	Page	Code	Page	Code	Page
S78.122A	754, 1012, 1037	S79.102A	291, 1012, 1038	S79.192K	399	S80.252A	468, 1012	S80.929A	468, 1013	S81.841A	754, 1013
S78.122D	818	S79.102D	334	S79.192P	399	S80.252D	818	S80.929D	818	S81.841D	818
S78.122S	333	S79.102G	334	S79.192S	334	S80.252S	468	S80.929S	468	S81.841S	468
S78.129A	754, 1012, 1037	S79.102K	399	S79.199A	292, 1012, 1038	S80.259A	468, 1012	S81.001A	468, 1013	S81.842A	754, 1013
S78.129D	818	S79.102P	399	S79.199D	334	S80.259D	818	S81.001D	818	S81.842D	818
S78.129S	333	S79.102S	334	S79.199G	334	S80.259S	468	S81.001S	468	S81.842S	468
S78.911A	754, 1012, 1037	S79.109A	291, 1012, 1038	S79.199K	399	S80.261A	478, 1012	S81.002A	468, 1013	S81.849A	754, 1013
S78.911D	818	S79.109D	399	S79.199P	399	S80.261D	818	S81.002D	818	S81.849D	818
S78.911S	333	S79.109G	334	S79.199S	334	S80.261S	468	S81.002S	468	S81.849S	468
S78.912A	754, 1012, 1037	S79.109K	399	S79.811A	754, 1012	S80.262A	478, 1012	S81.009A	468, 1013	S81.851A	468, 1013
S78.912D	818	S79.109P	399	S79.811D	818	S80.262D	818	S81.009D	818	S81.851D	818
S78.912S	333	S79.109S	334	S79.811S	754	S80.262S	468	S81.009S	468	S81.851S	468
S78.919A	754, 1012, 1037	S79.111A	291, 1012, 1038	S79.812A	754, 1012	S80.269A	478, 1012	S81.011A	468, 1013	S81.852A	468, 1013
S78.919D	818	S79.111D	334	S79.812D	818	S80.269D	818	S81.011D	818	S81.852D	818
S78.919S	333	S79.111G	334	S79.812S	754	S80.269S	468	S81.011S	468	S81.852S	468
S78.921A	754, 1012, 1038	S79.111K	399	S79.819A	754, 1012	S80.271A	468, 1012	S81.012A	468, 1013	S81.859A	469, 1013
S78.921D	818	S79.111P	399	S79.819D	818	S80.271D	818	S81.012D	818	S81.859D	818
S78.921S	333	S79.111S	334	S79.819S	754	S80.271S	468	S81.012S	468	S81.859S	469
S78.922A	754, 1012, 1038	S79.112A	291, 1012, 1038	S79.821A	754, 1012	S80.272A	468, 1012	S81.019A	468, 1013	S82.001A	365, 1013
S78.922D	818	S79.112D	334	S79.821D	818	S80.272D	818	S81.019D	818	S82.001B	365, 1013
S78.922S	333	S79.112G	334	S79.821S	754	S80.272S	468	S81.019S	468	S82.001C	365, 1013
S78.929A	754, 1012, 1038	S79.112K	399	S79.822A	754, 1012	S80.279A	468, 1012	S81.021A	754, 1013	S82.001D	334
S78.929D	818	S79.112P	399	S79.822D	818	S80.279D	818	S81.021D	818	S82.001E	334
S78.929S	334	S79.112S	334	S79.822S	754	S80.279S	468	S81.021S	468	S82.001F	334
S79.001A	294, 566, 1012, 1038	S79.119A	291, 1012, 1038	S79.829A	754, 1012	S80.811A	468, 1012	S81.022A	754, 1013	S82.001G	334
S79.001D	334	S79.119D	334	S79.829D	818	S80.811D	818	S81.022D	818	S82.001H	334
S79.001G	334	S79.119G	334	S79.829S	754	S80.811S	468	S81.022S	468	S82.001J	334
S79.001K	398	S79.119K	399	S79.911A	754, 1012	S80.812A	468, 1012	S81.029A	754, 1013	S82.001K	399
S79.001P	398	S79.119P	399	S79.911D	818	S80.812D	818	S81.029D	818	S82.001M	399
S79.001S	334	S79.119S	334	S79.911S	754	S80.812S	468	S81.029S	468	S82.001N	399
S79.002A	294, 566, 1012, 1038	S79.121A	291, 1012, 1038	S79.912A	754, 1012	S80.819A	468, 1012	S81.031A	468, 1013	S82.001P	399
S79.002D	334	S79.121D	334	S79.912D	818	S80.819D	818	S81.031D	818	S82.001Q	399
S79.002G	334	S79.121G	334	S79.912S	754	S80.819S	468	S81.031S	468	S82.001R	399
S79.002K	398	S79.121K	399	S79.919A	754, 1012	S80.821A	478, 1012	S81.032A	468, 1013	S82.001S	334
S79.002P	398	S79.121P	399	S79.919D	818	S80.821D	818	S81.032D	818	S82.002A	365, 1013
S79.002S	334	S79.121S	334	S79.919S	754	S80.821S	468	S81.032S	468	S82.002B	365, 1013
S79.009A	294, 566, 1012, 1038	S79.122A	291, 1012, 1038	S79.921A	754, 1012	S80.822A	478, 1012	S81.039A	468, 1013	S82.002C	365, 1013
S79.009D	334	S79.122D	334	S79.921D	818	S80.822D	818	S81.039D	818	S82.002D	334
S79.009G	334	S79.122G	334	S79.921S	754	S80.822S	468	S81.039S	468	S82.002E	334
S79.009K	398	S79.122K	399	S79.922A	754, 1012	S80.829A	478, 1012	S81.041A	754, 1013	S82.002F	334
S79.009P	398	S79.122P	399	S79.922D	818	S80.829D	818	S81.041D	818	S82.002G	334
S79.009S	334	S79.122S	334	S79.922S	754	S80.829S	468	S81.041S	468	S82.002H	334
S79.011A	294, 566, 1012, 1038	S79.129A	291, 1012, 1038	S79.929A	754, 1012	S80.841A	468, 1012	S81.042A	754, 1013	S82.002J	334
S79.011D	334	S79.129D	334	S79.929D	818	S80.841D	818	S81.042D	818	S82.002K	399
S79.011G	334	S79.129G	334	S79.929S	754	S80.841S	468	S81.042S	468	S82.002M	399
S79.011K	398	S79.129K	399	S80.00XA	468, 1012	S80.842A	468, 1012	S81.049A	754, 1013	S82.002N	399
S79.011P	398	S79.129P	399	S80.00XD	818	S80.842D	818	S81.049D	818	S82.002P	399
S79.011S	334	S79.129S	334	S80.00XS	468	S80.842S	468	S81.049S	468	S82.002Q	399
S79.012A	294, 566, 1012, 1038	S79.131A	292, 1012, 1038	S80.01XA	468, 1012	S80.849A	468, 1012	S81.051A	468, 1013	S82.002R	399
S79.012D	334	S79.131D	334	S80.01XD	818	S80.849D	818	S81.051D	818	S82.002S	334
S79.012G	334	S79.131G	334	S80.01XS	468	S80.849S	468	S81.051S	468	S82.009A	365, 1013
S79.012K	398	S79.131K	399	S80.02XA	468, 1012	S80.851A	468, 1012	S81.052A	468, 1013	S82.009B	365, 1013
S79.012P	398	S79.131P	399	S80.02XD	818	S80.851D	818	S81.052D	818	S82.009C	365, 1013
S79.012S	334	S79.131S	334	S80.02XS	468	S80.851S	468	S81.052S	468	S82.009D	334
S79.019A	294, 566, 1012, 1038	S79.132A	292, 1012, 1038	S80.10XA	468, 1012	S80.852A	468, 1012	S81.059A	468, 1013	S82.009E	334
S79.019D	334	S79.132D	334	S80.10XD	818	S80.852D	818	S81.059D	818	S82.009F	334
S79.019G	334	S79.132G	334	S80.10XS	468	S80.852S	468	S81.059S	468	S82.009G	334
S79.019K	398	S79.132K	399	S80.11XA	468, 1012	S80.859A	468, 1012	S81.801A	468, 1013	S82.009H	334
S79.019P	398	S79.132P	399	S80.11XD	818	S80.859D	818	S81.801D	818	S82.009J	334
S79.019S	334	S79.132S	334	S80.11XS	468	S80.859S	468	S81.801S	468	S82.009K	399
S79.091A	294, 566, 1012, 1038	S79.139A	292, 1012, 1038	S80.12XA	468, 1012	S80.861A	478, 1013	S81.802A	468, 1013	S82.009M	399
S79.091D	334	S79.139D	334	S80.12XD	818	S80.861D	818	S81.802D	818	S82.009N	399
S79.091G	334	S79.139G	334	S80.12XS	468	S80.861S	468	S81.802S	468	S82.009P	399
S79.091K	398	S79.139K	399	S80.211A	468, 1012	S80.862A	478, 1013	S81.809A	468, 1013	S82.009Q	399
S79.091P	398	S79.139P	399	S80.211D	818	S80.862D	818	S81.809D	818	S82.009R	399
S79.091S	334	S79.139S	334	S80.211S	468	S80.862S	468	S81.809S	468	S82.009S	334
S79.092A	294, 566, 1012, 1038	S79.141A	292, 1012, 1038	S80.212A	468, 1012	S80.869A	478, 1013	S81.811A	468, 1013	S82.011A	365, 1013
S79.092D	334	S79.141D	334	S80.212D	818	S80.869D	818	S81.811D	818	S82.011B	365, 1013
S79.092G	334	S79.141G	334	S80.212S	468	S80.869S	468	S81.811S	468	S82.011C	365, 1013
S79.092K	398	S79.141K	399	S80.219A	468, 1012	S80.871A	468, 1013	S81.812A	468, 1013	S82.011D	334
S79.092P	398	S79.141P	399	S80.219D	818	S80.871D	818	S81.812D	818	S82.011E	334
S79.092S	334	S79.141S	334	S80.219S	468	S80.871S	468	S81.812S	468	S82.011F	334
S79.099A	294, 566, 1012, 1038	S79.142A	292, 1012, 1038	S80.221A	478, 1012	S80.872A	468, 1013	S81.819A	468, 1013	S82.011G	334
S79.099D	334	S79.142D	334	S80.221D	818	S80.872D	818	S81.819D	818	S82.011H	334
S79.099G	334	S79.142G	334	S80.221S	468	S80.872S	468	S81.819S	468	S82.011J	334
S79.099K	398	S79.142K	399	S80.222A	478, 1012	S80.879A	468, 1013	S81.821A	754, 1013	S82.011K	399
S79.099P	399	S79.142P	399	S80.222D	818	S80.879D	818	S81.821D	818	S82.011M	399
S79.099S	334	S79.142S	334	S80.222S	468	S80.879S	468	S81.821S	468	S82.011N	399
S79.101A	291, 1012, 1038	S79.149A	292, 1012, 1038	S80.229A	478, 1012	S80.911A	468, 1013	S81.822A	754, 1013	S82.011P	399
S79.101D	334	S79.149D	334	S80.229D	818	S80.911D	818	S81.822D	818	S82.011Q	399
S79.101G	334	S79.149G	334	S80.229S	468	S80.911S	468	S81.822S	468	S82.011R	399
S79.101K	399	S79.149K	399	S80.241A	468, 1012	S80.912A	468, 1013	S81.829A	754, 1013	S82.011S	334
S79.101P	399	S79.149P	399	S80.241D	818	S80.912D	818	S81.829D	818	S82.012A	365, 1013
S79.101S	334	S79.149S	334	S80.241S	468	S80.912S	468	S81.829S	468	S82.012B	365, 1013
		S79.191A	292, 1012, 1038	S80.242A	468, 1012	S80.919A	468, 1013	S81.831A	468, 1013	S82.012C	365, 1013
		S79.191D	334	S80.242D	818	S80.919D	818	S81.831D	818	S82.012D	334
		S79.191G	334	S80.242S	468	S80.919S	468	S81.831S	468	S82.012E	334
		S79.191K	399	S80.249A	468, 1012	S80.921A	468, 1013	S81.832A	468, 1013	S82.012F	334
		S79.191P	399	S80.249D	818	S80.921D	818	S81.832D	818	S82.012G	334
		S79.191S	334	S80.249S	468	S80.921S	468	S81.832S	468	S82.012H	334
		S79.192A	292, 1012, 1038	S80.251A	468, 1012	S80.922A	468, 1013	S81.839A	468, 1013	S82.012J	334
		S79.192D	334	S80.251D	818	S80.922D	818	S81.839D	818	S82.012K	399
		S79.192G	334	S80.251S	468	S80.922S	468	S81.839S	468	S82.012M	399

Code	Page	Code	Page	Code	Page	Code	Page	Code	Page	Code	Page
S82.012N	399	S82.022J	334	S82.032F	335	S82.042C	365, 1013	S82.091S	335	S82.111P	400
S82.012P	399	S82.022K	399	S82.032G	335	S82.042D	335	S82.092A	365, 1013	S82.111Q	400
S82.012Q	399	S82.022M	399	S82.032H	335	S82.042E	335	S82.092B	365, 1013	S82.111R	400
S82.012R	399	S82.022N	399	S82.032J	335	S82.042F	335	S82.092C	365, 1013	S82.111S	335
S82.012S	334	S82.022P	399	S82.032K	399	S82.042G	335	S82.092D	335	S82.112A	365, 1013
S82.013A	365, 1013	S82.022Q	399	S82.032M	399	S82.042H	335	S82.092E	335	S82.112B	365, 1013, 1038
S82.013B	365, 1013	S82.022R	399	S82.032N	399	S82.042J	335	S82.092F	335	S82.112C	365, 1013, 1038
S82.013C	365, 1013	S82.022S	334	S82.032P	399	S82.042K	399	S82.092G	335	S82.112D	335
S82.013D	334	S82.023A	365, 1013	S82.032Q	399	S82.042M	399	S82.092H	335	S82.112E	335
S82.013E	334	S82.023B	365, 1013	S82.032R	399	S82.042N	399	S82.092J	335	S82.112F	335
S82.013F	334	S82.023C	365, 1013	S82.032S	335	S82.042P	399	S82.092K	400	S82.112G	335
S82.013G	334	S82.023D	334	S82.033A	365, 1013	S82.042Q	399	S82.092M	400	S82.112H	335
S82.013H	334	S82.023E	334	S82.033B	365, 1013	S82.042R	400	S82.092N	400	S82.112J	335
S82.013J	334	S82.023F	334	S82.033C	365, 1013	S82.042S	335	S82.092P	400	S82.112K	400
S82.013K	399	S82.023G	334	S82.033D	335	S82.043A	365, 1013	S82.092Q	400	S82.112M	400
S82.013M	399	S82.023H	334	S82.033E	335	S82.043B	365, 1013	S82.092R	400	S82.112N	400
S82.013N	399	S82.023J	334	S82.033F	335	S82.043C	365, 1013	S82.092S	335	S82.112P	400
S82.013P	399	S82.023K	399	S82.033G	335	S82.043D	335	S82.099A	365, 1013	S82.112Q	400
S82.013Q	399	S82.023M	399	S82.033H	335	S82.043E	335	S82.099B	365, 1013	S82.112R	400
S82.013R	399	S82.023N	399	S82.033J	335	S82.043F	335	S82.099C	365, 1013	S82.112S	335
S82.013S	334	S82.023P	399	S82.033K	399	S82.043G	335	S82.099D	335	S82.113A	365, 1013
S82.014A	365, 1013	S82.023Q	399	S82.033M	399	S82.043H	335	S82.099E	335	S82.113B	365, 1013, 1038
S82.014B	365, 1013	S82.023R	399	S82.033N	399	S82.043J	335	S82.099F	335	S82.113C	365, 1013, 1038
S82.014C	365, 1013	S82.023S	334	S82.033P	399	S82.043K	400	S82.099G	335	S82.113D	335
S82.014D	334	S82.024A	365, 1013	S82.033Q	399	S82.043M	400	S82.099H	335	S82.113E	335
S82.014E	334	S82.024B	365, 1013	S82.033R	399	S82.043N	400	S82.099J	335	S82.113F	335
S82.014F	334	S82.024C	365, 1013	S82.033S	335	S82.043P	400	S82.099K	400	S82.113G	335
S82.014G	334	S82.024D	335	S82.034A	365, 1013	S82.043Q	400	S82.099M	400	S82.113H	335
S82.014H	334	S82.024E	334	S82.034B	365, 1013	S82.043R	400	S82.099N	400	S82.113J	335
S82.014J	334	S82.024F	334	S82.034C	365, 1013	S82.043S	335	S82.099P	400	S82.113K	400
S82.014K	399	S82.024G	334	S82.034D	335	S82.044A	365, 1013	S82.099Q	400	S82.113M	400
S82.014M	399	S82.024H	334	S82.034E	335	S82.044B	365, 1013	S82.099R	400	S82.113N	400
S82.014N	399	S82.024J	334	S82.034F	335	S82.044C	365, 1013	S82.099S	335	S82.113P	400
S82.014P	399	S82.024K	399	S82.034G	335	S82.044D	335	S82.101A	365, 1013	S82.113Q	400
S82.014Q	399	S82.024M	399	S82.034H	335	S82.044E	335	S82.101B	365, 1013, 1038	S82.113R	400
S82.014R	399	S82.024N	399	S82.034J	335	S82.044F	335	S82.101C	365, 1013, 1038	S82.113S	335
S82.014S	334	S82.024P	399	S82.034K	399	S82.044G	335	S82.101D	335	S82.114A	365, 1013
S82.015A	365, 1013	S82.024Q	399	S82.034M	399	S82.044H	335	S82.101E	335	S82.114B	365, 1013, 1038
S82.015B	365, 1013	S82.024R	399	S82.034N	399	S82.044J	335	S82.101F	335	S82.114C	365, 1013, 1038
S82.015C	365, 1013	S82.024S	334	S82.034P	399	S82.044K	400	S82.101G	335	S82.114D	335
S82.015D	334	S82.025A	365, 1013	S82.034Q	399	S82.044M	400	S82.101H	335	S82.114E	335
S82.015E	334	S82.025B	365, 1013	S82.034R	399	S82.044N	400	S82.101J	335	S82.114F	335
S82.015F	334	S82.025C	365, 1013	S82.034S	335	S82.044P	400	S82.101K	400	S82.114G	335
S82.015G	334	S82.025D	334	S82.035A	365, 1013	S82.044Q	400	S82.101M	400	S82.114H	335
S82.015H	334	S82.025E	335	S82.035B	365, 1013	S82.044R	400	S82.101N	400	S82.114J	335
S82.015J	334	S82.025F	335	S82.035C	365, 1013	S82.044S	335	S82.101P	400	S82.114K	400
S82.015K	399	S82.025G	335	S82.035D	335	S82.045A	365, 1013	S82.101Q	400	S82.114M	400
S82.015M	399	S82.025H	335	S82.035E	335	S82.045B	365, 1013	S82.101R	400	S82.114N	400
S82.015N	399	S82.025J	335	S82.035F	335	S82.045C	365, 1013	S82.101S	335	S82.114P	400
S82.015P	399	S82.025K	399	S82.035G	335	S82.045D	335	S82.102A	365, 1013	S82.114Q	400
S82.015Q	399	S82.025M	399	S82.035H	335	S82.045E	335	S82.102B	365, 1013, 1038	S82.114R	400
S82.015R	399	S82.025N	399	S82.035J	335	S82.045F	335	S82.102C	365, 1013, 1038	S82.114S	335
S82.015S	334	S82.025P	399	S82.035K	399	S82.045G	335	S82.102D	335	S82.115A	365, 1013
S82.016A	365, 1013	S82.025Q	399	S82.035M	399	S82.045H	335	S82.102E	335	S82.115B	365, 1013, 1038
S82.016B	365, 1013	S82.025R	399	S82.035N	399	S82.045J	335	S82.102F	335	S82.115C	365, 1013, 1038
S82.016C	365, 1013	S82.025S	335	S82.035P	399	S82.045K	400	S82.102G	335	S82.115D	335
S82.016D	334	S82.026A	365, 1013	S82.035Q	399	S82.045M	400	S82.102H	335	S82.115E	335
S82.016E	334	S82.026B	365, 1013	S82.035R	399	S82.045N	400	S82.102J	335	S82.115F	335
S82.016F	334	S82.026C	365, 1013	S82.035S	335	S82.045P	400	S82.102K	400	S82.115G	335
S82.016G	334	S82.026D	335	S82.036A	365, 1013	S82.045Q	400	S82.102M	400	S82.115H	335
S82.016H	334	S82.026E	335	S82.036B	365, 1013	S82.045R	400	S82.102N	400	S82.115J	335
S82.016J	334	S82.026F	335	S82.036C	365, 1013	S82.045S	335	S82.102P	400	S82.115K	400
S82.016K	399	S82.026G	335	S82.036D	335	S82.046A	365, 1013	S82.102Q	400	S82.115M	400
S82.016M	399	S82.026H	335	S82.036E	335	S82.046B	365, 1013	S82.102R	400	S82.115N	400
S82.016N	399	S82.026J	335	S82.036F	335	S82.046C	365, 1013	S82.102S	335	S82.115P	400
S82.016P	399	S82.026K	399	S82.036G	335	S82.046D	335	S82.109A	365, 1013	S82.115Q	400
S82.016Q	399	S82.026M	399	S82.036H	335	S82.046E	335	S82.109B	365, 1013, 1038	S82.115R	400
S82.016R	399	S82.026N	399	S82.036J	335	S82.046F	335	S82.109C	365, 1013, 1038	S82.115S	335
S82.016S	334	S82.026P	399	S82.036K	399	S82.046G	335	S82.109D	335	S82.116A	365, 1013
S82.021A	365, 1013	S82.026Q	399	S82.036M	399	S82.046H	335	S82.109E	335	S82.116B	365, 1013, 1038
S82.021B	365, 1013	S82.026R	399	S82.036N	399	S82.046J	335	S82.109F	335	S82.116C	365, 1013, 1038
S82.021C	365, 1013	S82.026S	335	S82.036P	399	S82.046K	400	S82.109G	335	S82.116D	336
S82.021D	334	S82.031A	365, 1013	S82.036Q	399	S82.046M	400	S82.109H	335	S82.116E	336
S82.021E	334	S82.031B	365, 1013	S82.036R	399	S82.046N	400	S82.109J	335	S82.116F	336
S82.021F	334	S82.031C	365, 1013	S82.036S	335	S82.046P	400	S82.109K	400	S82.116G	336
S82.021G	334	S82.031D	335	S82.041A	365, 1013	S82.046Q	400	S82.109M	400	S82.116H	336
S82.021H	334	S82.031E	335	S82.041B	365, 1013	S82.046R	400	S82.109N	400	S82.116J	336
S82.021J	334	S82.031F	335	S82.041C	365, 1013	S82.046S	335	S82.109P	400	S82.116K	400
S82.021K	399	S82.031G	335	S82.041D	335	S82.091A	365, 1013	S82.109Q	400	S82.116M	400
S82.021M	399	S82.031H	335	S82.041E	335	S82.091B	365, 1013	S82.109R	400	S82.116N	400
S82.021N	399	S82.031J	335	S82.041F	335	S82.091C	365, 1013	S82.109S	335	S82.116P	400
S82.021P	399	S82.031K	399	S82.041G	335	S82.091D	335	S82.111A	365, 1013	S82.116Q	400
S82.021Q	399	S82.031M	399	S82.041H	335	S82.091E	335	S82.111B	365, 1013, 1038	S82.116R	400
S82.021R	399	S82.031N	399	S82.041J	335	S82.091F	335	S82.111C	365, 1013, 1038	S82.116S	336
S82.021S	334	S82.031P	399	S82.041K	399	S82.091G	335	S82.111D	335	S82.121A	365, 1013
S82.022A	365, 1013	S82.031Q	399	S82.041M	399	S82.091H	335	S82.111E	335	S82.121B	365, 1013, 1038
S82.022B	365, 1013	S82.031R	399	S82.041N	399	S82.091J	335	S82.111F	335	S82.121C	365, 1013, 1038
S82.022C	365, 1013	S82.031S	335	S82.041P	399	S82.091K	335	S82.111G	335	S82.121D	336
S82.022D	334	S82.032A	365, 1013	S82.041Q	399	S82.091M	400	S82.111H	335	S82.121E	336
S82.022E	334	S82.032B	365, 1013	S82.041R	399	S82.091N	400	S82.111J	335	S82.121F	336
S82.022F	334	S82.032C	365, 1013	S82.041S	335	S82.091Q	400	S82.111K	400	S82.121G	336
S82.022G	334	S82.032D	335	S82.042A	365, 1013	S82.091P	400	S82.111M	400	S82.121H	336
S82.022H	334	S82.032E	335	S82.042B	365, 1013	S82.091R	400	S82.111N	400	S82.121J	336

Code	Page	Code	Page	Code	Page	Code	Page	Code	Page	Code	Page
S82.121K	400	S82.131G	336	S82.141D	336	S82.151A	366, 1014	S82.156Q	401	S82.202J	337
S82.121M	400	S82.131H	336	S82.141E	336	S82.151B	366, 1014, 1038	S82.156R	401	S82.202K	401
S82.121N	400	S82.131J	336	S82.141F	336	S82.151C	366, 1014, 1038	S82.156S	337	S82.202M	401
S82.121P	400	S82.131K	400	S82.141G	336	S82.151D	336	S82.161A	366, 1014, 1038	S82.202N	401
S82.121Q	400	S82.131M	400	S82.141H	336	S82.151E	336	S82.161D	337	S82.202P	401
S82.121R	400	S82.131N	400	S82.141J	336	S82.151F	336	S82.161G	337	S82.202Q	401
S82.121S	336	S82.131P	400	S82.141K	400	S82.151G	336	S82.161K	401	S82.202R	401
S82.122A	365, 1013	S82.131Q	400	S82.141M	400	S82.151H	336	S82.161P	401	S82.202S	337
S82.122B	365, 1013, 1038	S82.131R	400	S82.141N	400	S82.151J	336	S82.161S	337	S82.209A	366, 1014
S82.122C	365, 1013, 1038	S82.131S	336	S82.141P	400	S82.151K	401	S82.162A	366, 1014, 1038	S82.209B	366, 1014, 1038
S82.122D	336	S82.132A	365, 1014	S82.141Q	400	S82.151M	401	S82.162D	337	S82.209C	366, 1014, 1038
S82.122E	336	S82.132B	365, 1014, 1038	S82.141R	401	S82.151N	401	S82.162G	337	S82.209D	337
S82.122F	336	S82.132C	365, 1014, 1038	S82.141S	336	S82.151P	401	S82.162K	401	S82.209E	337
S82.122G	336	S82.132D	336	S82.142A	365, 1014	S82.151Q	401	S82.162P	401	S82.209F	337
S82.122H	336	S82.132E	336	S82.142B	365, 1014, 1038	S82.151R	401	S82.162S	337	S82.209G	337
S82.122J	336	S82.132F	336	S82.142C	365, 1014, 1038	S82.151S	336	S82.169A	366, 1014, 1038	S82.209H	337
S82.122K	400	S82.132G	336	S82.142D	336	S82.152A	366, 1014	S82.169D	337	S82.209J	337
S82.122M	400	S82.132H	336	S82.142E	336	S82.152B	366, 1014, 1038	S82.169G	337	S82.209M	401
S82.122N	400	S82.132J	336	S82.142F	336	S82.152C	366, 1014, 1038	S82.169K	401	S82.209N	401
S82.122P	400	S82.132K	400	S82.142G	336	S82.152D	336	S82.169P	401	S82.209P	401
S82.122Q	400	S82.132M	400	S82.142H	336	S82.152E	336	S82.169S	337	S82.209Q	401
S82.122R	400	S82.132N	400	S82.142J	336	S82.152F	336	S82.191A	366, 1014	S82.209R	401
S82.122S	336	S82.132P	400	S82.142K	401	S82.152G	336	S82.191B	366, 1014, 1038	S82.209S	337
S82.123A	365, 1013	S82.132Q	400	S82.142M	401	S82.152H	336	S82.191C	366, 1014, 1038	S82.221A	366, 1014
S82.123B	365, 1013, 1038	S82.132R	400	S82.142N	401	S82.152J	336	S82.191D	337	S82.221B	366, 1014, 1038
S82.123C	365, 1013, 1038	S82.132S	336	S82.142P	401	S82.152K	401	S82.191E	337	S82.221C	366, 1014, 1038
S82.123D	336	S82.133A	365, 1014	S82.142Q	401	S82.152M	401	S82.191F	337	S82.221D	337
S82.123E	336	S82.133B	365, 1014, 1038	S82.142R	401	S82.152N	401	S82.191G	337	S82.221E	337
S82.123F	336	S82.133C	365, 1014, 1038	S82.142S	336	S82.152P	401	S82.191H	337	S82.221F	337
S82.123G	336	S82.133D	336	S82.143A	365, 1014	S82.152Q	401	S82.191J	337	S82.221G	337
S82.123H	336	S82.133E	336	S82.143B	365, 1014, 1038	S82.152R	401	S82.191K	401	S82.221H	337
S82.123J	336	S82.133F	336	S82.143C	365, 1014, 1038	S82.152S	336	S82.191M	401	S82.221J	337
S82.123K	400	S82.133G	336	S82.143D	336	S82.153A	366, 1014	S82.191N	401	S82.221K	401
S82.123M	400	S82.133H	336	S82.143E	336	S82.153B	366, 1014, 1038	S82.191P	401	S82.221M	401
S82.123N	400	S82.133J	336	S82.143F	336	S82.153C	366, 1014, 1038	S82.191Q	401	S82.221N	401
S82.123P	400	S82.133K	400	S82.143G	336	S82.153D	336	S82.191R	401	S82.221P	401
S82.123Q	400	S82.133M	400	S82.143H	336	S82.153E	336	S82.191S	337	S82.221Q	401
S82.123R	400	S82.133N	400	S82.143J	336	S82.153F	336	S82.192A	366, 1014	S82.221R	401
S82.123S	336	S82.133P	400	S82.143K	401	S82.153G	336	S82.192B	366, 1014, 1038	S82.221S	337
S82.124A	365, 1014	S82.133Q	400	S82.143M	401	S82.153H	336	S82.192C	366, 1014, 1038	S82.222A	366, 1014
S82.124B	365, 1014, 1038	S82.133R	400	S82.143N	401	S82.153J	336	S82.192D	337	S82.222B	366, 1014, 1038
S82.124C	365, 1014, 1038	S82.133S	336	S82.143P	401	S82.153K	401	S82.192E	337	S82.222C	366, 1014, 1038
S82.124D	336	S82.134A	365, 1014	S82.143Q	401	S82.153M	401	S82.192F	337	S82.222D	337
S82.124E	336	S82.134B	365, 1014, 1038	S82.143R	401	S82.153N	401	S82.192G	337	S82.222E	337
S82.124F	336	S82.134C	365, 1014, 1038	S82.143S	336	S82.153P	401	S82.192H	337	S82.222F	337
S82.124G	336	S82.134D	336	S82.144A	366, 1014	S82.153Q	401	S82.192J	337	S82.222G	337
S82.124H	336	S82.134E	336	S82.144B	366, 1014, 1038	S82.153R	401	S82.192K	401	S82.222H	337
S82.124J	336	S82.134F	336	S82.144C	366, 1014, 1038	S82.153S	336	S82.192M	401	S82.222J	337
S82.124K	400	S82.134G	336	S82.144D	336	S82.154A	366, 1014	S82.192N	401	S82.222K	401
S82.124M	400	S82.134H	336	S82.144E	336	S82.154B	366, 1014, 1038	S82.192P	401	S82.222M	401
S82.124N	400	S82.134J	400	S82.144F	336	S82.154C	366, 1014, 1038	S82.192Q	401	S82.222N	401
S82.124P	400	S82.134K	400	S82.144G	336	S82.154D	336	S82.192R	401	S82.222P	401
S82.124Q	400	S82.134M	400	S82.144H	336	S82.154E	336	S82.192S	337	S82.222Q	401
S82.124R	400	S82.134N	400	S82.144J	336	S82.154F	336	S82.199A	366, 1014	S82.222R	401
S82.124S	336	S82.134P	400	S82.144K	401	S82.154G	336	S82.199B	366, 1014, 1038	S82.222S	337
S82.125A	365, 1014	S82.134Q	400	S82.144M	401	S82.154H	336	S82.199C	366, 1014, 1038	S82.223A	366, 1014
S82.125B	365, 1014, 1038	S82.134R	400	S82.144N	401	S82.154J	336	S82.199D	337	S82.223B	366, 1014, 1038
S82.125C	365, 1014, 1038	S82.134S	336	S82.144P	401	S82.154K	401	S82.199E	337	S82.223C	366, 1014, 1038
S82.125D	336	S82.135A	365, 1014	S82.144Q	401	S82.154M	401	S82.199F	337	S82.223D	337
S82.125E	336	S82.135B	365, 1014, 1038	S82.144R	401	S82.154N	401	S82.199G	337	S82.223E	337
S82.125F	336	S82.135C	365, 1014, 1038	S82.144S	336	S82.154P	401	S82.199H	337	S82.223F	337
S82.125G	336	S82.135D	336	S82.145A	366, 1014	S82.154Q	401	S82.199J	337	S82.223G	337
S82.125H	336	S82.135E	336	S82.145B	366, 1014, 1038	S82.154R	401	S82.199K	401	S82.223H	337
S82.125J	336	S82.135F	336	S82.145C	366, 1014, 1038	S82.154S	336	S82.199M	401	S82.223J	337
S82.125K	400	S82.135G	336	S82.145D	336	S82.155A	366, 1014	S82.199N	401	S82.223K	401
S82.125M	400	S82.135H	336	S82.145E	336	S82.155B	366, 1014, 1038	S82.199P	401	S82.223M	401
S82.125N	400	S82.135J	336	S82.145F	336	S82.155C	366, 1014, 1038	S82.199Q	401	S82.223N	401
S82.125P	400	S82.135K	400	S82.145G	336	S82.155D	336	S82.199R	401	S82.223P	401
S82.125Q	400	S82.135M	400	S82.145H	336	S82.155E	336	S82.199S	337	S82.223Q	401
S82.125R	400	S82.135N	400	S82.145J	336	S82.155F	336	S82.201A	366, 1014	S82.223R	401
S82.125S	336	S82.135P	400	S82.145K	401	S82.155G	336	S82.201B	366, 1014, 1038	S82.223S	337
S82.126A	365, 1014	S82.135Q	400	S82.145M	401	S82.155H	336	S82.201C	366, 1014, 1038	S82.224A	366, 1014
S82.126B	365, 1014, 1038	S82.135R	400	S82.145N	401	S82.155J	336	S82.201D	337	S82.224B	366, 1014, 1038
S82.126C	365, 1014, 1038	S82.135S	336	S82.145P	401	S82.155K	401	S82.201E	337	S82.224C	366, 1014, 1038
S82.126D	336	S82.136A	365, 1014	S82.145Q	401	S82.155M	401	S82.201F	337	S82.224D	337
S82.126E	336	S82.136B	365, 1014, 1038	S82.145R	401	S82.155N	401	S82.201G	337	S82.224E	337
S82.126F	336	S82.136C	365, 1014, 1038	S82.145S	336	S82.155P	401	S82.201H	337	S82.224F	337
S82.126G	336	S82.136D	336	S82.146A	366, 1014	S82.155Q	401	S82.201J	337	S82.224G	337
S82.126H	336	S82.136E	336	S82.146B	366, 1014, 1038	S82.155R	401	S82.201K	401	S82.224H	337
S82.126J	336	S82.136F	336	S82.146C	366, 1014, 1038	S82.155S	336	S82.201M	401	S82.224J	337
S82.126K	400	S82.136G	336	S82.146D	336	S82.156A	366, 1014	S82.201N	401	S82.224K	401
S82.126M	400	S82.136H	336	S82.146E	336	S82.156B	366, 1014, 1038	S82.201P	401	S82.224M	401
S82.126N	400	S82.136J	336	S82.146F	336	S82.156C	366, 1014, 1038	S82.201Q	401	S82.224N	401
S82.126P	400	S82.136K	400	S82.146G	336	S82.156D	336	S82.201R	401	S82.224P	401
S82.126Q	400	S82.136M	400	S82.146H	336	S82.156E	336	S82.201S	337	S82.224Q	401
S82.126R	400	S82.136N	400	S82.146J	336	S82.156F	336	S82.202A	366, 1014	S82.224S	337
S82.126S	336	S82.136P	400	S82.146K	401	S82.156G	336	S82.202B	366, 1014, 1038	S82.225A	366, 1014
S82.131A	365, 1014	S82.136Q	400	S82.146M	401	S82.156H	336	S82.202C	366, 1014, 1038	S82.225B	366, 1014, 1038
S82.131B	365, 1014, 1038	S82.136R	400	S82.146N	401	S82.156J	336	S82.202D	337	S82.225C	366, 1014, 1038
S82.131C	365, 1014, 1038	S82.136S	336	S82.146P	401	S82.156K	401	S82.202E	337	S82.225D	337
S82.131D	336	S82.141A	365, 1014	S82.146Q	401	S82.156M	401	S82.202F	337	S82.225E	337
S82.131E	336	S82.141B	365, 1014, 1038	S82.146R	401	S82.156N	401	S82.202G	337		
S82.131F	336	S82.141C	365, 1014, 1038	S82.146S	336	S82.156P	401	S82.202H	337		

Code	Page	Code	Page	Code	Page	Code	Page	Code	Page	Code	Page
S82.225F	337	S82.235C	366, 1014, 1038	S82.244S	337	S82.254P	402	S82.264K	402	S82.301G	338
S82.225G	337	S82.235D	337	S82.245A	366, 1014	S82.254Q	402	S82.264M	402	S82.301H	338
S82.225H	337	S82.235E	337	S82.245B	366, 1014, 1038	S82.254R	402	S82.264N	402	S82.301J	338
S82.225J	337	S82.235F	337	S82.245C	366, 1014, 1038	S82.254S	338	S82.264P	402	S82.301K	402
S82.225K	401	S82.235G	337	S82.245D	337	S82.255A	366, 1014	S82.264Q	402	S82.301M	402
S82.225M	401	S82.235H	337	S82.245E	337	S82.255B	366, 1014, 1038	S82.264R	402	S82.301N	402
S82.225N	401	S82.235J	337	S82.245F	337	S82.255C	366, 1014, 1038	S82.264S	338	S82.301P	402
S82.225P	401	S82.235K	401	S82.245G	337	S82.255D	338	S82.265A	366, 1014	S82.301Q	402
S82.225Q	401	S82.235M	401	S82.245H	337	S82.255E	338	S82.265B	366, 1014, 1038	S82.301R	402
S82.225R	401	S82.235N	401	S82.245J	337	S82.255F	338	S82.265C	366, 1014, 1038	S82.301S	338
S82.225S	337	S82.235P	401	S82.245K	402	S82.255G	338	S82.265D	338	S82.302A	366, 1015
S82.226A	366, 1014	S82.235Q	401	S82.245M	402	S82.255H	338	S82.265E	338	S82.302B	366, 1015
S82.226B	366, 1014, 1038	S82.235R	402	S82.245N	402	S82.255J	338	S82.265F	338	S82.302C	366, 1015
S82.226C	366, 1014, 1038	S82.235S	337	S82.245P	402	S82.255K	402	S82.265G	338	S82.302D	338
S82.226D	337	S82.236A	366, 1014	S82.245Q	402	S82.255M	402	S82.265H	338	S82.302E	338
S82.226E	337	S82.236B	366, 1014, 1038	S82.245R	402	S82.255N	402	S82.265J	338	S82.302F	338
S82.226F	337	S82.236C	366, 1014, 1038	S82.245S	337	S82.255P	402	S82.265K	402	S82.302G	338
S82.226G	337	S82.236D	337	S82.246A	366, 1014	S82.255Q	402	S82.265M	402	S82.302H	338
S82.226H	337	S82.236E	337	S82.246B	366, 1014, 1038	S82.255R	402	S82.265N	402	S82.302J	338
S82.226J	337	S82.236F	337	S82.246C	366, 1014, 1038	S82.255S	338	S82.265P	402	S82.302K	402
S82.226K	401	S82.236G	337	S82.246D	337	S82.256A	366, 1014	S82.265Q	402	S82.302M	402
S82.226M	401	S82.236H	337	S82.246E	337	S82.256B	366, 1014, 1038	S82.265R	402	S82.302N	402
S82.226N	401	S82.236J	337	S82.246F	337	S82.256C	366, 1014, 1038	S82.265S	338	S82.302P	402
S82.226P	401	S82.236K	402	S82.246G	338	S82.256D	338	S82.266A	366, 1014	S82.302Q	402
S82.226Q	401	S82.236M	402	S82.246H	338	S82.256E	338	S82.266B	366, 1014, 1038	S82.302R	402
S82.226R	401	S82.236N	402	S82.246J	338	S82.256F	338	S82.266C	366, 1014, 1038	S82.302S	338
S82.226S	337	S82.236P	402	S82.246K	402	S82.256G	338	S82.266D	338	S82.309A	366, 1015
S82.231A	366, 1014	S82.236Q	402	S82.246M	402	S82.256H	338	S82.266E	338	S82.309B	366, 1015
S82.231B	366, 1014, 1038	S82.236R	402	S82.246N	402	S82.256J	338	S82.266F	338	S82.309C	366, 1015
S82.231C	366, 1014, 1038	S82.236S	337	S82.246P	402	S82.256K	402	S82.266G	338	S82.309D	338
S82.231D	337	S82.241A	366, 1014	S82.246Q	402	S82.256M	402	S82.266H	338	S82.309E	338
S82.231E	337	S82.241B	366, 1014, 1038	S82.246R	402	S82.256N	402	S82.266J	338	S82.309F	338
S82.231F	337	S82.241C	366, 1014, 1038	S82.246S	338	S82.256P	402	S82.266K	402	S82.309G	338
S82.231G	337	S82.241D	337	S82.251A	366, 1014	S82.256Q	402	S82.266M	402	S82.309H	338
S82.231H	337	S82.241E	337	S82.251B	366, 1014, 1038	S82.256R	402	S82.266N	402	S82.309J	338
S82.231J	337	S82.241F	337	S82.251C	366, 1014, 1038	S82.256S	338	S82.266P	402	S82.309K	402
S82.231K	401	S82.241G	337	S82.251D	338	S82.261A	366, 1014	S82.266Q	402	S82.309M	402
S82.231M	401	S82.241H	337	S82.251E	338	S82.261B	366, 1014, 1038	S82.266R	402	S82.309N	402
S82.231N	401	S82.241J	337	S82.251F	338	S82.261C	366, 1014, 1038	S82.266S	338	S82.309P	402
S82.231P	401	S82.241K	402	S82.251G	338	S82.261D	338	S82.291A	366, 1015	S82.309Q	402
S82.231Q	401	S82.241M	402	S82.251H	338	S82.261E	338	S82.291B	366, 1015, 1038	S82.309R	402
S82.231R	401	S82.241N	402	S82.251J	338	S82.261F	338	S82.291C	366, 1015, 1038	S82.309S	338
S82.231S	337	S82.241P	402	S82.251K	402	S82.261G	338	S82.291D	338	S82.311A	366, 1015, 1039
S82.232A	366, 1014	S82.241Q	402	S82.251M	402	S82.261H	338	S82.291E	338	S82.311D	338
S82.232B	366, 1014, 1038	S82.241R	402	S82.251N	402	S82.261J	338	S82.291F	338	S82.311G	338
S82.232C	366, 1014, 1038	S82.241S	337	S82.251P	402	S82.261K	402	S82.291G	338	S82.311K	338
S82.232D	337	S82.242A	366, 1014	S82.251Q	402	S82.261M	402	S82.291H	338	S82.311P	402
S82.232E	337	S82.242B	366, 1014, 1038	S82.251R	402	S82.261N	402	S82.291J	338	S82.311S	338
S82.232F	337	S82.242C	366, 1014, 1038	S82.251S	338	S82.261P	402	S82.291K	402	S82.312A	366, 1015, 1039
S82.232G	337	S82.242D	337	S82.252A	366, 1014	S82.261Q	402	S82.291M	402	S82.312D	338
S82.232H	337	S82.242E	337	S82.252B	366, 1014, 1038	S82.261R	402	S82.291N	402	S82.312G	338
S82.232J	337	S82.242F	337	S82.252C	366, 1014, 1038	S82.261S	338	S82.291P	402	S82.312K	402
S82.232K	401	S82.242G	337	S82.252D	338	S82.262A	366, 1014	S82.291Q	402	S82.312P	402
S82.232M	401	S82.242H	337	S82.252E	338	S82.262B	366, 1014, 1038	S82.291R	402	S82.312S	338
S82.232N	401	S82.242J	337	S82.252F	338	S82.262C	366, 1014, 1038	S82.291S	338	S82.319A	366, 1015, 1039
S82.232P	401	S82.242K	402	S82.252G	338	S82.262D	338	S82.292A	366, 1015	S82.319D	338
S82.232Q	401	S82.242M	402	S82.252H	338	S82.262E	338	S82.292B	366, 1015, 1038	S82.319G	338
S82.232R	401	S82.242N	402	S82.252J	338	S82.262F	338	S82.292C	366, 1015, 1039	S82.319K	402
S82.232S	337	S82.242P	402	S82.252K	402	S82.262G	338	S82.292D	338	S82.319P	402
S82.233A	366, 1014	S82.242Q	402	S82.252M	402	S82.262H	338	S82.292E	338	S82.319S	338
S82.233B	366, 1014, 1038	S82.242R	402	S82.252N	402	S82.262J	338	S82.292F	338	S82.391A	366, 1015
S82.233C	366, 1014, 1038	S82.242S	337	S82.252P	402	S82.262K	402	S82.292G	338	S82.391B	366, 1015
S82.233D	337	S82.243A	366, 1014	S82.252Q	402	S82.262M	402	S82.292H	338	S82.391C	366, 1015
S82.233E	337	S82.243B	366, 1014, 1038	S82.252R	402	S82.262N	402	S82.292J	338	S82.391D	338
S82.233F	337	S82.243C	366, 1014, 1038	S82.252S	338	S82.262P	402	S82.292K	402	S82.391E	338
S82.233G	337	S82.243D	337	S82.253A	366, 1014	S82.262Q	402	S82.292M	402	S82.391F	338
S82.233H	337	S82.243E	337	S82.253B	366, 1014, 1038	S82.262R	402	S82.292N	402	S82.391G	338
S82.233J	337	S82.243F	337	S82.253C	366, 1014, 1038	S82.262S	338	S82.292P	402	S82.391H	338
S82.233K	401	S82.243G	337	S82.253D	338	S82.263A	366, 1014	S82.292Q	402	S82.391J	338
S82.233M	401	S82.243H	337	S82.253E	338	S82.263B	366, 1014, 1038	S82.292R	402	S82.391K	402
S82.233N	401	S82.243J	337	S82.253F	338	S82.263C	366, 1014, 1038	S82.292S	338	S82.391M	402
S82.233P	401	S82.243K	402	S82.253G	338	S82.263D	338	S82.299A	366, 1015	S82.391N	402
S82.233Q	401	S82.243M	402	S82.253H	338	S82.263E	338	S82.299B	366, 1015, 1039	S82.391P	402
S82.233R	401	S82.243N	402	S82.253J	338	S82.263F	338	S82.299C	366, 1015, 1039	S82.391Q	402
S82.233S	337	S82.243P	402	S82.253K	402	S82.263G	338	S82.299D	338	S82.391R	402
S82.234A	366, 1014	S82.243Q	402	S82.253M	402	S82.263H	338	S82.299E	338	S82.391S	338
S82.234B	366, 1014, 1038	S82.243R	402	S82.253N	402	S82.263J	338	S82.299F	338	S82.392A	366, 1015
S82.234C	366, 1014, 1038	S82.243S	337	S82.253P	402	S82.263K	402	S82.299G	338	S82.392B	366, 1015
S82.234D	337	S82.244A	366, 1014	S82.253Q	402	S82.263M	402	S82.299H	338	S82.392C	366, 1015
S82.234E	337	S82.244B	366, 1014, 1038	S82.253R	402	S82.263N	402	S82.299J	338	S82.392D	338
S82.234F	337	S82.244C	366, 1014, 1038	S82.253S	338	S82.263P	402	S82.299K	402	S82.392E	338
S82.234G	337	S82.244D	337	S82.254A	366, 1014	S82.263Q	402	S82.299M	402	S82.392F	338
S82.234H	337	S82.244E	337	S82.254B	366, 1014, 1038	S82.263R	402	S82.299N	402	S82.392G	338
S82.234J	337	S82.244F	337	S82.254C	366, 1014, 1038	S82.263S	338	S82.299P	402	S82.392H	338
S82.234K	401	S82.244G	337	S82.254D	338	S82.264A	366, 1014	S82.299Q	402	S82.392J	338
S82.234M	401	S82.244H	337	S82.254E	338	S82.264B	366, 1014, 1038	S82.299R	402	S82.392K	402
S82.234N	401	S82.244J	337	S82.254F	338	S82.264C	366, 1014, 1038	S82.299S	338	S82.392M	402
S82.234P	401	S82.244K	402	S82.254G	338	S82.264D	338	S82.301A	366, 1015	S82.392N	402
S82.234Q	401	S82.244M	402	S82.254H	338	S82.264E	338	S82.301B	366, 1015	S82.392P	402
S82.234R	401	S82.244N	402	S82.254J	338	S82.264F	338	S82.301C	366, 1015	S82.392Q	402
S82.234S	337	S82.244P	402	S82.254K	402	S82.264G	338	S82.301D	338	S82.392R	402
S82.235A	366, 1014	S82.244Q	402	S82.254M	402	S82.264H	338	S82.301E	338	S82.392S	338
S82.235B	366, 1014, 1038	S82.244R	402	S82.254N	402	S82.264J	338	S82.301F	338	S82.399A	366, 1015

Code	Page	Code	Page	Code	Page	Code	Page	Code	Page	Code	Page
S82.399B	366, 1015	S82.422R	403	S82.432N	403	S82.442J	339	S82.452F	339	S82.462C	367, 1015, 1039
S82.399C	366, 1015	S82.422S	339	S82.432P	403	S82.442K	403	S82.452G	339	S82.462D	340
S82.399D	338	S82.423A	367, 1015	S82.432Q	403	S82.442M	403	S82.452H	339	S82.462E	340
S82.399E	338	S82.423B	367, 1015, 1039	S82.432R	403	S82.442N	403	S82.452J	339	S82.462F	340
S82.399F	338	S82.423C	367, 1015, 1039	S82.432S	339	S82.442P	403	S82.452K	403	S82.462G	340
S82.399G	338	S82.423D	339	S82.433A	367, 1015	S82.442Q	403	S82.452M	403	S82.462H	340
S82.399H	338	S82.423E	339	S82.433B	367, 1015, 1039	S82.442R	403	S82.452N	403	S82.462J	340
S82.399J	338	S82.423F	339	S82.433C	367, 1015, 1039	S82.442S	339	S82.452P	403	S82.462K	403
S82.399K	402	S82.423G	339	S82.433D	339	S82.443A	367, 1015	S82.452Q	403	S82.462M	403
S82.399M	402	S82.423H	339	S82.433E	339	S82.443B	367, 1015, 1039	S82.452R	403	S82.462N	403
S82.399N	402	S82.423J	339	S82.433F	339	S82.443C	367, 1015, 1039	S82.452S	339	S82.462P	403
S82.399P	402	S82.423K	403	S82.433G	339	S82.443D	339	S82.453A	367, 1015	S82.462Q	403
S82.399Q	402	S82.423M	403	S82.433H	339	S82.443E	339	S82.453B	367, 1015, 1039	S82.462R	404
S82.399R	402	S82.423N	403	S82.433J	339	S82.443F	339	S82.453C	367, 1015, 1039	S82.462S	340
S82.399S	338	S82.423P	403	S82.433K	403	S82.443G	339	S82.453D	339	S82.463A	367, 1015
S82.401A	366, 1015	S82.423Q	403	S82.433M	403	S82.443H	339	S82.453E	339	S82.463B	367, 1015, 1039
S82.401B	366, 1015, 1039	S82.423R	403	S82.433N	403	S82.443J	339	S82.453F	339	S82.463C	367, 1015, 1039
S82.401C	366, 1015, 1039	S82.423S	339	S82.433P	403	S82.443K	403	S82.453G	339	S82.463D	340
S82.401D	338	S82.424A	367, 1015	S82.433Q	403	S82.443M	403	S82.453H	339	S82.463E	340
S82.401E	338	S82.424B	367, 1015, 1039	S82.433R	403	S82.443N	403	S82.453J	339	S82.463F	340
S82.401F	338	S82.424C	367, 1015, 1039	S82.433S	339	S82.443P	403	S82.453K	403	S82.463G	340
S82.401G	338	S82.424D	339	S82.434A	367, 1015	S82.443Q	403	S82.453M	403	S82.463H	340
S82.401H	338	S82.424E	339	S82.434B	367, 1015, 1039	S82.443R	403	S82.453N	403	S82.463J	340
S82.401J	338	S82.424F	339	S82.434C	367, 1015, 1039	S82.443S	339	S82.453P	403	S82.463K	404
S82.401K	403	S82.424G	339	S82.434D	339	S82.444A	367, 1015	S82.453Q	403	S82.463M	404
S82.401M	403	S82.424H	339	S82.434E	339	S82.444B	367, 1015, 1039	S82.453R	403	S82.463N	404
S82.401N	403	S82.424J	339	S82.434F	339	S82.444C	367, 1015, 1039	S82.453S	339	S82.463P	404
S82.401P	403	S82.424K	403	S82.434G	339	S82.444D	339	S82.454A	367, 1015	S82.463Q	404
S82.401Q	403	S82.424M	403	S82.434H	339	S82.444E	339	S82.454B	367, 1015, 1039	S82.463R	404
S82.401R	403	S82.424N	403	S82.434J	339	S82.444F	339	S82.454C	367, 1015, 1039	S82.463S	340
S82.401S	338	S82.424P	403	S82.434K	403	S82.444G	339	S82.454D	339	S82.464A	367, 1015
S82.402A	366, 1015	S82.424Q	403	S82.434M	403	S82.444H	339	S82.454E	339	S82.464B	367, 1015, 1039
S82.402B	366, 1015, 1039	S82.424R	403	S82.434N	403	S82.444J	339	S82.454F	339	S82.464C	367, 1015, 1039
S82.402C	366, 1015, 1039	S82.424S	339	S82.434P	403	S82.444K	403	S82.454G	339	S82.464D	340
S82.402D	338	S82.425A	367, 1015	S82.434Q	403	S82.444M	403	S82.454H	339	S82.464E	340
S82.402E	338	S82.425B	367, 1015, 1039	S82.434R	403	S82.444N	403	S82.454J	339	S82.464F	340
S82.402F	338	S82.425C	367, 1015, 1039	S82.434S	339	S82.444P	403	S82.454K	403	S82.464G	340
S82.402G	338	S82.425D	339	S82.435A	367, 1015	S82.444Q	403	S82.454M	403	S82.464H	340
S82.402H	338	S82.425E	339	S82.435B	367, 1015, 1039	S82.444R	403	S82.454N	403	S82.464J	340
S82.402J	338	S82.425F	339	S82.435C	367, 1015, 1039	S82.444S	339	S82.454P	403	S82.464K	404
S82.402K	403	S82.425G	339	S82.435D	339	S82.445A	367, 1015	S82.454Q	403	S82.464M	404
S82.402N	403	S82.425H	339	S82.435E	339	S82.445B	367, 1015, 1039	S82.454R	403	S82.464N	404
S82.402P	403	S82.425J	339	S82.435F	339	S82.445C	367, 1015, 1039	S82.454S	339	S82.464P	404
S82.402Q	403	S82.425K	403	S82.435G	339	S82.445D	339	S82.455A	367, 1015	S82.464Q	404
S82.402R	403	S82.425M	403	S82.435H	339	S82.445E	339	S82.455B	367, 1015, 1039	S82.464R	404
S82.402S	338	S82.425N	403	S82.435J	339	S82.445F	339	S82.455C	367, 1015, 1039	S82.464S	340
S82.409A	367, 1015	S82.425P	403	S82.435K	403	S82.445G	339	S82.455D	339	S82.465A	367, 1015
S82.409B	367, 1015, 1039	S82.425Q	403	S82.435M	403	S82.445H	339	S82.455E	339	S82.465B	367, 1015, 1039
S82.409C	367, 1015, 1039	S82.425R	403	S82.435N	403	S82.445J	339	S82.455F	339	S82.465C	367, 1015, 1039
S82.409D	339	S82.425S	339	S82.435P	403	S82.445K	403	S82.455G	339	S82.465D	340
S82.409E	339	S82.426A	367, 1015	S82.435Q	403	S82.445M	403	S82.455H	339	S82.465E	340
S82.409F	339	S82.426B	367, 1015, 1039	S82.435R	403	S82.445N	403	S82.455J	339	S82.465F	340
S82.409G	339	S82.426C	367, 1015, 1039	S82.435S	339	S82.445P	403	S82.455K	403	S82.465G	340
S82.409H	339	S82.426D	339	S82.436A	367, 1015	S82.445Q	403	S82.455M	403	S82.465H	340
S82.409J	339	S82.426E	339	S82.436B	367, 1015, 1039	S82.445R	403	S82.455N	403	S82.465J	340
S82.409K	403	S82.426F	339	S82.436C	367, 1015, 1039	S82.445S	339	S82.455P	403	S82.465K	404
S82.409M	403	S82.426G	339	S82.436D	339	S82.446A	367, 1015	S82.455Q	403	S82.465M	404
S82.409N	403	S82.426H	339	S82.436E	339	S82.446B	367, 1015, 1039	S82.455R	403	S82.465N	404
S82.409P	403	S82.426J	339	S82.436F	339	S82.446C	367, 1015, 1039	S82.455S	339	S82.465P	404
S82.409Q	403	S82.426K	403	S82.436G	339	S82.446D	339	S82.456A	367, 1015	S82.465Q	404
S82.409R	403	S82.426M	403	S82.436H	339	S82.446E	339	S82.456B	367, 1015, 1039	S82.465R	404
S82.409S	339	S82.426N	403	S82.436J	339	S82.446F	339	S82.456C	367, 1015, 1039	S82.465S	340
S82.421A	367, 1015	S82.426P	403	S82.436K	403	S82.446G	339	S82.456D	339	S82.466A	367, 1015
S82.421B	367, 1015, 1039	S82.426Q	403	S82.436M	403	S82.446H	339	S82.456E	339	S82.466B	367, 1015, 1039
S82.421C	367, 1015, 1039	S82.426R	403	S82.436N	403	S82.446J	339	S82.456F	339	S82.466C	367, 1015, 1039
S82.421D	339	S82.426S	339	S82.436P	403	S82.446K	403	S82.456G	339	S82.466D	340
S82.421E	339	S82.431A	367, 1015	S82.436Q	403	S82.446M	403	S82.456H	339	S82.466E	340
S82.421F	339	S82.431B	367, 1015, 1039	S82.436R	403	S82.446N	403	S82.456J	339	S82.466F	340
S82.421G	339	S82.431C	367, 1015, 1039	S82.436S	339	S82.446P	403	S82.456K	403	S82.466G	340
S82.421H	339	S82.431D	339	S82.441A	367, 1015	S82.446Q	403	S82.456M	403	S82.466H	340
S82.421J	339	S82.431E	339	S82.441B	367, 1015, 1039	S82.446R	403	S82.456N	403	S82.466J	340
S82.421K	403	S82.431F	339	S82.441C	367, 1015, 1039	S82.446S	339	S82.456P	403	S82.466K	404
S82.421M	403	S82.431G	339	S82.441D	339	S82.451A	367, 1015	S82.456Q	403	S82.466M	404
S82.421N	403	S82.431H	339	S82.441E	339	S82.451B	367, 1015, 1039	S82.456R	403	S82.466N	404
S82.421P	403	S82.431J	339	S82.441F	339	S82.451C	367, 1015, 1039	S82.456S	340	S82.466P	404
S82.421Q	403	S82.431K	403	S82.441G	339	S82.451D	339	S82.461A	367, 1015	S82.466Q	404
S82.421R	403	S82.431M	403	S82.441H	339	S82.451E	339	S82.461B	367, 1015, 1039	S82.466R	404
S82.421S	339	S82.431N	403	S82.441J	339	S82.451F	339	S82.461C	367, 1015, 1039	S82.466S	340
S82.422A	367, 1015	S82.431P	403	S82.441K	403	S82.451G	339	S82.461D	340	S82.491A	367, 1015
S82.422B	367, 1015, 1039	S82.431Q	403	S82.441M	403	S82.451H	339	S82.461E	340	S82.491B	367, 1015, 1039
S82.422C	367, 1015, 1039	S82.431R	403	S82.441N	403	S82.451J	339	S82.461F	340	S82.491C	367, 1015, 1039
S82.422D	339	S82.431S	339	S82.441P	403	S82.451K	403	S82.461G	340	S82.491D	340
S82.422E	339	S82.432A	367, 1015	S82.441Q	403	S82.451M	403	S82.461H	340	S82.491E	340
S82.422F	339	S82.432B	367, 1015, 1039	S82.441S	339	S82.451N	403	S82.461J	340	S82.491F	340
S82.422G	339	S82.432C	367, 1015, 1039	S82.442A	367, 1015	S82.451P	403	S82.461K	403	S82.491G	340
S82.422H	339	S82.432D	339	S82.442B	367, 1015, 1039	S82.451Q	403	S82.461M	403	S82.491H	340
S82.422J	339	S82.432E	339	S82.442C	367, 1015, 1039	S82.451R	403	S82.461N	403	S82.491J	340
S82.422K	403	S82.432F	339	S82.442D	339	S82.451S	339	S82.461P	403	S82.491K	404
S82.422M	403	S82.432G	339	S82.442E	339	S82.452A	367, 1015	S82.461Q	403	S82.491M	404
S82.422N	403	S82.432H	339	S82.442F	339	S82.452B	367, 1015, 1039	S82.461R	403	S82.491N	404
S82.422P	403	S82.432J	339	S82.442G	339	S82.452C	367, 1015, 1039	S82.461S	340	S82.491P	404
S82.422Q	403	S82.432K	403	S82.442H	339	S82.452D	339	S82.462A	367, 1015	S82.491Q	404
		S82.432M	403			S82.452E	339	S82.462B	367, 1015, 1039	S82.491R	404

Numeric Index to Diseases

Code	Page	Code	Page	Code	Page	Code	Page	Code	Page	Code	Page
S82.491S	340	S82.54XP	404	S82.64XK	404	S82.832C	367, 1016, 1039	S82.844S	341	S82.854P	405
S82.492A	367, 1015	S82.54XQ	404	S82.64XM	404	S82.832D	340	S82.845A	367, 1016	S82.854Q	405
S82.492B	367, 1015, 1039	S82.54XR	404	S82.64XN	404	S82.832E	341	S82.845B	367, 1016	S82.854R	405
S82.492C	367, 1015, 1039	S82.54XS	340	S82.64XP	404	S82.832F	341	S82.845C	367, 1016	S82.854S	341
S82.492D	340	S82.55XA	367, 1015	S82.64XQ	404	S82.832G	341	S82.845D	341	S82.855A	368, 1016
S82.492E	340	S82.55XB	367, 1015	S82.64XR	404	S82.832H	341	S82.845E	341	S82.855B	368, 1016
S82.492F	340	S82.55XC	367, 1015	S82.64XS	340	S82.832J	341	S82.845F	341	S82.855C	368, 1016
S82.492G	340	S82.55XD	340	S82.65XA	367, 1015	S82.832K	404	S82.845G	341	S82.855D	341
S82.492H	340	S82.55XE	340	S82.65XB	367, 1015	S82.832M	404	S82.845H	341	S82.855E	341
S82.492J	340	S82.55XF	340	S82.65XC	367, 1015	S82.832N	404	S82.845J	341	S82.855F	341
S82.492K	404	S82.55XG	340	S82.65XD	340	S82.832P	404	S82.845K	404	S82.855G	341
S82.492M	404	S82.55XH	340	S82.65XE	340	S82.832Q	404	S82.845M	404	S82.855H	341
S82.492N	404	S82.55XJ	340	S82.65XF	340	S82.832R	404	S82.845N	404	S82.855J	341
S82.492P	404	S82.55XK	404	S82.65XG	340	S82.832S	341	S82.845P	404	S82.855K	405
S82.492Q	404	S82.55XM	404	S82.65XH	340	S82.839A	367, 1016	S82.845Q	404	S82.855M	405
S82.492R	404	S82.55XN	404	S82.65XJ	340	S82.839B	367, 1016, 1039	S82.845R	405	S82.855N	405
S82.492S	340	S82.55XP	404	S82.65XK	404	S82.839C	367, 1016, 1039	S82.845S	341	S82.855P	405
S82.499A	367, 1015	S82.55XQ	404	S82.65XM	404	S82.839D	341	S82.846A	367, 1016	S82.855Q	405
S82.499B	367, 1015, 1039	S82.55XR	404	S82.65XN	404	S82.839E	341	S82.846B	367, 1016	S82.855R	405
S82.499C	367, 1015, 1039	S82.55XS	340	S82.65XP	404	S82.839F	341	S82.846C	367, 1016	S82.855S	341
S82.499D	340	S82.56XA	367, 1015	S82.65XQ	404	S82.839G	341	S82.846D	341	S82.856A	368, 1016
S82.499E	340	S82.56XB	367, 1015	S82.65XR	404	S82.839H	341	S82.846E	341	S82.856B	368, 1016
S82.499F	340	S82.56XC	367, 1015	S82.65XS	340	S82.839J	341	S82.846F	341	S82.856C	368, 1016
S82.499G	340	S82.56XD	340	S82.66XA	367, 1015	S82.839K	404	S82.846G	341	S82.856D	341
S82.499H	340	S82.56XE	340	S82.66XB	367, 1015	S82.839M	404	S82.846H	341	S82.856E	341
S82.499J	340	S82.56XF	340	S82.66XC	367, 1015	S82.839N	404	S82.846J	341	S82.856F	341
S82.499K	404	S82.56XG	340	S82.66XD	340	S82.839P	404	S82.846K	404	S82.856G	341
S82.499M	404	S82.56XH	340	S82.66XE	340	S82.839Q	404	S82.846M	405	S82.856H	341
S82.499N	404	S82.56XJ	340	S82.66XF	340	S82.839R	404	S82.846N	405	S82.856J	341
S82.499P	404	S82.56XK	404	S82.66XG	340	S82.839S	341	S82.846P	405	S82.856K	405
S82.499Q	404	S82.56XM	404	S82.66XH	340	S82.841A	367, 1016	S82.846Q	405	S82.856M	405
S82.499R	404	S82.56XN	404	S82.66XJ	340	S82.841B	367, 1016	S82.846R	405	S82.856N	405
S82.499S	340	S82.56XP	404	S82.66XK	404	S82.841C	367, 1016	S82.846S	341	S82.856P	405
S82.51XA	367, 1015	S82.56XQ	404	S82.66XM	404	S82.841D	341	S82.851A	367, 1016	S82.856Q	405
S82.51XB	367, 1015	S82.56XR	404	S82.66XN	404	S82.841E	341	S82.851B	367, 1016	S82.856R	405
S82.51XC	367, 1015	S82.56XS	340	S82.66XP	404	S82.841F	341	S82.851C	367, 1016	S82.856S	341
S82.51XD	340	S82.61XA	367, 1015	S82.66XQ	404	S82.841G	341	S82.851D	341	S82.861A	368, 1016
S82.51XE	340	S82.61XB	367, 1015	S82.66XR	404	S82.841H	341	S82.851E	341	S82.861B	368, 1016, 1039
S82.51XF	340	S82.61XC	367, 1015	S82.66XS	340	S82.841J	341	S82.851F	341	S82.861C	368, 1016, 1039
S82.51XG	340	S82.61XD	340	S82.811A	367, 1016, 1039	S82.841K	404	S82.851G	341	S82.861D	341
S82.51XH	340	S82.61XE	340	S82.811D	340	S82.841M	341	S82.851H	341	S82.861E	341
S82.51XJ	340	S82.61XF	340	S82.811G	340	S82.841N	404	S82.851J	341	S82.861F	341
S82.51XK	404	S82.61XG	340	S82.811K	404	S82.841P	404	S82.851K	405	S82.861G	341
S82.51XM	404	S82.61XH	340	S82.811P	404	S82.841Q	404	S82.851M	405	S82.861H	341
S82.51XN	404	S82.61XJ	340	S82.811S	340	S82.841S	341	S82.851N	405	S82.861J	341
S82.51XP	404	S82.61XK	404	S82.812A	367, 1016, 1039	S82.842A	367, 1016	S82.851P	405	S82.861K	405
S82.51XQ	404	S82.61XM	404	S82.812D	340	S82.842B	367, 1016	S82.851Q	405	S82.861M	405
S82.51XR	404	S82.61XN	404	S82.812G	340	S82.842C	367, 1016	S82.851R	405	S82.861N	405
S82.51XS	340	S82.61XP	404	S82.812K	404	S82.842D	341	S82.851S	341	S82.861P	405
S82.52XA	367, 1015	S82.61XQ	404	S82.812P	404	S82.842E	341	S82.852A	368, 1016	S82.861Q	405
S82.52XB	367, 1015	S82.61XR	404	S82.812S	340	S82.842F	341	S82.852B	368, 1016	S82.861R	405
S82.52XC	367, 1015	S82.61XS	340	S82.819A	367, 1016, 1039	S82.842G	341	S82.852C	368, 1016	S82.861S	341
S82.52XD	340	S82.62XA	367, 1015	S82.819D	340	S82.842H	341	S82.852D	341	S82.862A	368, 1016
S82.52XE	340	S82.62XB	367, 1015	S82.819G	340	S82.842J	341	S82.852E	341	S82.862B	368, 1016, 1039
S82.52XF	340	S82.62XC	367, 1015	S82.819K	404	S82.842K	404	S82.852F	341	S82.862C	368, 1016, 1039
S82.52XG	340	S82.62XD	340	S82.819P	404	S82.842M	404	S82.852G	341	S82.862D	341
S82.52XH	340	S82.62XE	340	S82.819S	340	S82.842N	404	S82.852H	341	S82.862E	341
S82.52XJ	340	S82.62XF	340	S82.821A	367, 1016, 1039	S82.842P	404	S82.852J	341	S82.862F	341
S82.52XK	404	S82.62XG	340	S82.821D	340	S82.842Q	404	S82.852K	405	S82.862G	341
S82.52XM	404	S82.62XH	340	S82.821G	340	S82.842R	404	S82.852M	405	S82.862H	341
S82.52XN	404	S82.62XJ	340	S82.821K	404	S82.842S	341	S82.852N	405	S82.862J	341
S82.52XP	404	S82.62XK	404	S82.821P	404	S82.843A	367, 1016	S82.852P	405	S82.862K	405
S82.52XQ	404	S82.62XM	404	S82.821S	340	S82.843B	367, 1016	S82.852Q	405	S82.862M	405
S82.52XR	404	S82.62XN	404	S82.822A	367, 1016, 1039	S82.843C	367, 1016	S82.852R	405	S82.862N	405
S82.52XS	340	S82.62XP	404	S82.822D	340	S82.843D	341	S82.852S	341	S82.862P	405
S82.53XA	367, 1015	S82.62XQ	404	S82.822G	340	S82.843E	341	S82.853A	368, 1016	S82.862Q	405
S82.53XB	367, 1015	S82.62XR	404	S82.822K	404	S82.843F	341	S82.853B	368, 1016	S82.862R	405
S82.53XC	367, 1015	S82.62XS	340	S82.822P	404	S82.843G	341	S82.853C	368, 1016	S82.862S	341
S82.53XD	340	S82.63XA	367, 1015	S82.822S	340	S82.843H	341	S82.853D	341	S82.863A	368, 1016
S82.53XE	340	S82.63XB	367, 1015	S82.829A	367, 1016, 1039	S82.843J	341	S82.853E	341	S82.863B	368, 1016, 1039
S82.53XF	340	S82.63XC	367, 1015	S82.829D	340	S82.843K	404	S82.853F	341	S82.863C	368, 1016, 1039
S82.53XG	340	S82.63XD	340	S82.829G	340	S82.843M	404	S82.853G	341	S82.863D	341
S82.53XH	340	S82.63XE	340	S82.829K	404	S82.843N	404	S82.853H	341	S82.863E	341
S82.53XJ	340	S82.63XF	340	S82.829P	404	S82.843P	404	S82.853J	341	S82.863F	341
S82.53XK	404	S82.63XG	340	S82.829S	340	S82.843Q	404	S82.853K	405	S82.863G	341
S82.53XM	404	S82.63XH	340	S82.831A	367, 1016	S82.843R	404	S82.853M	405	S82.863H	341
S82.53XN	404	S82.63XJ	340	S82.831B	367, 1016, 1039	S82.843S	341	S82.853N	405	S82.863J	341
S82.53XP	404	S82.63XK	404	S82.831C	367, 1016, 1039	S82.844A	367, 1016	S82.853P	405	S82.863K	405
S82.53XQ	404	S82.63XM	404	S82.831D	340	S82.844B	367, 1016	S82.853Q	405	S82.863M	405
S82.53XR	404	S82.63XN	404	S82.831E	340	S82.844C	367, 1016	S82.853R	405	S82.863N	405
S82.53XS	340	S82.63XP	404	S82.831F	340	S82.844D	341	S82.853S	341	S82.863P	405
S82.54XA	367, 1015	S82.63XQ	404	S82.831G	340	S82.844E	341	S82.854A	368, 1016	S82.863Q	405
S82.54XB	367, 1015	S82.63XR	404	S82.831H	340	S82.844F	341	S82.854B	368, 1016	S82.863R	405
S82.54XC	367, 1015	S82.63XS	340	S82.831J	340	S82.844G	341	S82.854C	368, 1016	S82.863S	341
S82.54XD	340	S82.64XA	367, 1015	S82.831K	404	S82.844H	341	S82.854D	341	S82.864A	368, 1016
S82.54XE	340	S82.64XB	367, 1015	S82.831M	404	S82.844J	341	S82.854E	341	S82.864B	368, 1016, 1039
S82.54XF	340	S82.64XC	367, 1015	S82.831N	404	S82.844K	404	S82.854F	341	S82.864C	368, 1016, 1039
S82.54XG	340	S82.64XD	340	S82.831P	404	S82.844M	404	S82.854G	341	S82.864D	341
S82.54XH	340	S82.64XE	340	S82.831Q	404	S82.844N	404	S82.854H	341	S82.864E	341
S82.54XJ	340	S82.64XF	340	S82.831R	404	S82.844P	404	S82.854J	341	S82.864F	341
S82.54XK	404	S82.64XG	340	S82.831S	340	S82.844Q	404	S82.854K	405	S82.864G	341
S82.54XM	404	S82.64XH	340	S82.832A	367, 1016	S82.844R	404	S82.854M	405	S82.864H	341
S82.54XN	404	S82.64XJ	340	S82.832B	367, 1016, 1039			S82.854N	405	S82.864J	341

Code	Page	Code	Page	Code	Page	Code	Page	Code	Page	Code	Page
S82.864K	405	S82.874G	341	S82.90XD	342	S83.095A	368, 1016	S83.146A	368, 1016	S83.261A	369, 1017
S82.864M	405	S82.874H	341	S82.90XE	342	S83.095D	818	S83.146D	818	S83.261D	819
S82.864N	405	S82.874J	341	S82.90XF	342	S83.095S	368	S83.146S	368	S83.261S	369
S82.864P	405	S82.874K	405	S82.90XG	342	S83.096A	368, 1016	S83.191A	368, 1016	S83.262A	369, 1017
S82.864Q	405	S82.874M	405	S82.90XH	342	S83.096D	818	S83.191D	818	S83.262D	819
S82.864R	405	S82.874N	405	S82.90XJ	342	S83.096S	368	S83.191S	368	S83.262S	369
S82.864S	341	S82.874P	405	S82.90XK	405	S83.101A	368, 1016	S83.192A	368, 1016	S83.269A	369, 1017
S82.865A	368, 1016	S82.874Q	405	S82.90XM	405	S83.101D	818	S83.192D	818	S83.269D	819
S82.865B	368, 1016, 1039	S82.874R	405	S82.90XN	405	S83.101S	368	S83.192S	368	S83.269S	369
S82.865C	368, 1016, 1039	S82.874S	341	S82.90XP	405	S83.102A	368, 1016	S83.193A	368, 1016	S83.271A	369, 1017
S82.865D	341	S82.875A	368, 1016	S82.90XQ	405	S83.102D	818	S83.193D	818	S83.271D	819
S82.865E	341	S82.875B	368, 1016	S82.90XR	405	S83.102S	368	S83.193S	368	S83.271S	369
S82.865F	341	S82.875C	368, 1016	S82.90XS	342	S83.103A	368, 1016	S83.194A	368, 1016	S83.272A	369, 1017
S82.865G	341	S82.875D	341	S82.91XA	368, 1016	S83.103D	818	S83.194D	818	S83.272D	819
S82.865H	341	S82.875E	341	S82.91XB	368, 1016	S83.103S	368	S83.194S	368	S83.272S	369
S82.865J	341	S82.875F	341	S82.91XC	368, 1016	S83.104A	368, 1016	S83.195A	368, 1016	S83.279A	369, 1017
S82.865K	405	S82.875G	341	S82.91XD	342	S83.104D	818	S83.195D	818	S83.279D	819
S82.865M	405	S82.875H	341	S82.91XE	342	S83.104S	368	S83.195S	369	S83.279S	369
S82.865N	405	S82.875J	341	S82.91XF	342	S83.105A	368, 1016	S83.196A	369, 1016	S83.281A	369, 1017
S82.865P	405	S82.875K	405	S82.91XG	342	S83.105D	818	S83.196D	818	S83.281D	819
S82.865Q	405	S82.875M	405	S82.91XH	342	S83.105S	368	S83.196S	369	S83.281S	369
S82.865R	405	S82.875N	405	S82.91XJ	342	S83.106A	368, 1016	S83.200A	369, 1016	S83.282A	369, 1017
S82.865S	341	S82.875P	405	S82.91XK	405	S83.106D	818	S83.200D	818	S83.282D	819
S82.866A	368, 1016	S82.875Q	405	S82.91XM	405	S83.106S	368	S83.200S	369	S83.282S	369
S82.866B	368, 1016, 1039	S82.875R	405	S82.91XN	405	S83.111A	368, 1016	S83.201A	369, 1016	S83.289A	369, 1017
S82.866C	368, 1016, 1039	S82.875S	341	S82.91XP	405	S83.111D	818	S83.201D	818	S83.289D	819
S82.866D	341	S82.876A	368, 1016	S82.91XQ	405	S83.111S	368	S83.201S	369	S83.289S	369
S82.866E	341	S82.876B	368, 1016	S82.91XR	405	S83.112A	368, 1016	S83.202A	369, 1016	S83.30XA	369, 1017
S82.866F	341	S82.876C	368, 1016	S82.91XS	342	S83.112D	818	S83.202D	819	S83.30XD	819
S82.866G	341	S82.876D	342	S82.92XA	368, 1016	S83.112S	368	S83.202S	369	S83.30XS	369
S82.866H	341	S82.876E	342	S82.92XB	368, 1016	S83.113A	368, 1016	S83.203A	369, 1016	S83.31XA	369, 1017
S82.866J	341	S82.876F	342	S82.92XC	368, 1016	S83.113D	818	S83.203D	819	S83.31XD	819
S82.866K	405	S82.876G	342	S82.92XD	342	S83.113S	368	S83.203S	369	S83.31XS	369
S82.866M	405	S82.876H	342	S82.92XE	342	S83.114A	368, 1016	S83.204A	369, 1016	S83.32XA	369, 1017
S82.866N	405	S82.876J	342	S82.92XF	342	S83.114D	818	S83.204D	819	S83.32XD	819
S82.866P	405	S82.876K	405	S82.92XG	342	S83.114S	368	S83.204S	369	S83.32XS	369
S82.866Q	405	S82.876M	405	S82.92XH	342	S83.115A	368, 1016	S83.205A	369, 1016	S83.401A	369, 1017
S82.866R	405	S82.876N	405	S82.92XJ	342	S83.115D	818	S83.205D	819	S83.401D	819
S82.866S	341	S82.876P	405	S82.92XK	405	S83.115S	368	S83.205S	369	S83.401S	369
S82.871A	368, 1016	S82.876Q	405	S82.92XM	405	S83.116A	368, 1016	S83.206A	369, 1016	S83.402A	369, 1017
S82.871B	368, 1016	S82.876R	405	S82.92XN	405	S83.116D	818	S83.206D	819	S83.402D	819
S82.871C	368, 1016	S82.876S	342	S82.92XP	405	S83.116S	368	S83.206S	369	S83.402S	369
S82.871D	341	S82.891A	368, 1016	S82.92XQ	405	S83.121A	368, 1016	S83.207A	369, 1016	S83.409A	369, 1017
S82.871E	341	S82.891B	368, 1016	S82.92XR	405	S83.121D	818	S83.207D	819	S83.409D	819
S82.871F	341	S82.891C	368, 1016	S82.92XS	342	S83.121S	368	S83.207S	369	S83.409S	369
S82.871G	341	S82.891D	342	S83.001A	368, 1016	S83.122A	368, 1016	S83.209A	369, 1016	S83.411A	369, 1017
S82.871H	341	S82.891E	342	S83.001D	818	S83.122D	818	S83.209D	819	S83.411D	819
S82.871J	341	S82.891F	342	S83.001S	368	S83.122S	368	S83.209S	369	S83.411S	369
S82.871K	405	S82.891G	342	S83.002A	368, 1016	S83.123A	368, 1016	S83.211A	369, 1016	S83.412A	369, 1017
S82.871M	405	S82.891H	342	S83.002D	818	S83.123D	818	S83.211D	819	S83.412D	819
S82.871N	405	S82.891J	342	S83.002S	368	S83.123S	368	S83.211S	369	S83.412S	369
S82.871P	405	S82.891K	405	S83.003A	368, 1016	S83.124A	368, 1016	S83.212A	369, 1016	S83.419A	369, 1017
S82.871Q	405	S82.891M	405	S83.003D	818	S83.124D	818	S83.212D	819	S83.419D	819
S82.871R	405	S82.891N	405	S83.003S	368	S83.124S	368	S83.212S	369	S83.419S	369
S82.871S	341	S82.891P	405	S83.004A	368, 1016	S83.125A	368, 1016	S83.219A	369, 1016	S83.421A	369, 1017
S82.872A	368, 1016	S82.891Q	405	S83.004D	818	S83.125D	818	S83.219D	819	S83.421D	819
S82.872B	368, 1016	S82.891R	405	S83.004S	368	S83.125S	368	S83.219S	369	S83.421S	369
S82.872C	368, 1016	S82.891S	342	S83.005A	368, 1016	S83.126A	368, 1016	S83.221A	369, 1016	S83.422A	369, 1017
S82.872D	341	S82.892A	368, 1016	S83.005D	818	S83.126D	818	S83.221D	819	S83.422D	819
S82.872E	341	S82.892B	368, 1016	S83.005S	368	S83.126S	368	S83.221S	369	S83.422S	369
S82.872F	341	S82.892C	368, 1016	S83.006A	368, 1016	S83.131A	368, 1016	S83.222A	369, 1016	S83.429A	369, 1017
S82.872G	341	S82.892D	342	S83.006D	818	S83.131D	818	S83.222D	819	S83.429D	819
S82.872H	341	S82.892E	342	S83.006S	368	S83.131S	368	S83.222S	369	S83.429S	369
S82.872J	341	S82.892F	342	S83.011A	368, 1016	S83.132A	368, 1016	S83.229A	369, 1016	S83.501A	369, 1017
S82.872K	405	S82.892G	342	S83.011D	818	S83.132D	818	S83.229D	819	S83.501D	819
S82.872M	405	S82.892H	342	S83.011S	368	S83.132S	368	S83.229S	369	S83.501S	369
S82.872N	405	S82.892J	342	S83.012A	368, 1016	S83.133A	368, 1016	S83.231A	369, 1017	S83.502A	369, 1017
S82.872P	405	S82.892K	405	S83.012D	818	S83.133D	818	S83.231D	819	S83.502D	819
S82.872Q	405	S82.892M	405	S83.012S	368	S83.133S	368	S83.231S	369	S83.502S	369
S82.872R	405	S82.892N	405	S83.013A	368, 1016	S83.134A	368, 1016	S83.232A	369, 1017	S83.509A	369, 1017
S82.872S	341	S82.892P	405	S83.013D	818	S83.134D	818	S83.232D	819	S83.509D	819
S82.873A	368, 1016	S82.892Q	405	S83.013S	368	S83.134S	368	S83.232S	369	S83.509S	369
S82.873B	368, 1016	S82.892S	342	S83.014A	368, 1016	S83.135A	368, 1016	S83.239A	369, 1017	S83.511A	369, 1017
S82.873C	368, 1016	S82.899A	368, 1016	S83.014D	818	S83.135D	818	S83.239D	819	S83.511D	819
S82.873D	341	S82.899B	368, 1016	S83.014S	368	S83.135S	368	S83.239S	369	S83.511S	369
S82.873E	341	S82.899C	368, 1016	S83.015A	368, 1016	S83.136A	368, 1016	S83.241A	369, 1017	S83.512A	369, 1017
S82.873F	341	S82.899D	342	S83.015D	818	S83.136D	818	S83.241D	819	S83.512D	819
S82.873G	341	S82.899E	342	S83.015S	368	S83.136S	368	S83.241S	369	S83.512S	369
S82.873H	341	S82.899F	342	S83.016A	368, 1016	S83.141A	368, 1016	S83.242A	369, 1017	S83.519A	369, 1017
S82.873J	341	S82.899G	342	S83.016D	818	S83.141D	818	S83.242D	819	S83.519D	819
S82.873K	405	S82.899H	342	S83.016S	368	S83.141S	368	S83.242S	369	S83.519S	369
S82.873M	405	S82.899J	342	S83.091A	368, 1016	S83.142A	368, 1016	S83.249A	369, 1017	S83.521A	369, 1017
S82.873N	405	S82.899K	405	S83.091D	818	S83.142D	818	S83.249D	819	S83.521D	819
S82.873P	405	S82.899M	405	S83.091S	368	S83.142S	368	S83.249S	369	S83.521S	369
S82.873Q	405	S82.899N	405	S83.092A	368, 1016	S83.143A	368, 1016	S83.251A	369, 1017	S83.522A	369, 1017
S82.873R	405	S82.899P	405	S83.092D	818	S83.143D	818	S83.251D	819	S83.522D	819
S82.873S	341	S82.899Q	405	S83.092S	368	S83.143S	368	S83.251S	369	S83.522S	369
S82.874A	368, 1016	S82.899R	405	S83.093A	368, 1016	S83.144A	368, 1016	S83.252A	369, 1017	S83.529A	369, 1017
S82.874B	368, 1016	S82.899S	342	S83.093D	818	S83.144D	818	S83.252D	819	S83.529D	819
S82.874C	368, 1016	S82.90XA	368, 1016	S83.093S	368	S83.144S	368	S83.252S	369	S83.529S	369
S82.874D	341	S82.90XB	368, 1016	S83.094A	368, 1016	S83.145A	368, 1016	S83.259A	369, 1017	S83.60XA	369, 1017
S82.874E	341	S82.90XC	368, 1016	S83.094D	818	S83.145D	818	S83.259D	819	S83.60XD	819
S82.874F	341			S83.094S	368	S83.145S	368	S83.259S	369	S83.60XS	369

Code	Page	Code	Page	Code	Page	Code	Page	Code	Page	Code	Page
S83.61XA	369,1017	S85.091S	171	S85.202S	171	S85.519S	171	S86.029S	469	S86.309S	755
S83.61XD	819	S85.092A	754,1017,1039	S85.209A	754,1017,1039	S85.591A	754,1017,1039	S86.091A	755,1017	S86.311A	369,1018
S83.61XS	369	S85.092D	819	S85.209D	819	S85.591D	819	S86.091D	820	S86.311D	820
S83.62XA	369,1017	S85.092S	171	S85.209S	171	S85.591S	171	S86.091S	755	S86.311S	369
S83.62XD	819	S85.099A	754,1017,1039	S85.211A	754,1017,1039	S85.592A	754,1017,1039	S86.092A	755,1017	S86.312A	369,1018
S83.62XS	369	S85.099D	819	S85.211D	819	S85.592D	819	S86.092D	820	S86.312D	820
S83.8X1A	369,1017	S85.099S	171	S85.211S	171	S85.592S	171	S86.092S	755	S86.312S	369
S83.8X1D	819	S85.101A	754,1017,1039	S85.212A	754,1017,1039	S85.599A	754,1017,1039	S86.099A	755,1017	S86.319A	369,1018
S83.8X1S	369	S85.101D	819	S85.212D	819	S85.599D	819	S86.099D	820	S86.319D	820
S83.8X2A	369,1017	S85.101S	171	S85.212S	171	S85.599S	171	S86.099S	755	S86.319S	369
S83.8X2D	819	S85.102A	754,1017,1039	S85.219A	754,1017,1039	S85.801A	754,1017,1039	S86.101A	755,1017	S86.321A	405,1018
S83.8X2S	369	S85.102D	819	S85.219D	819	S85.801D	819	S86.101D	820	S86.321D	820
S83.8X9A	1017	S85.102S	171	S85.219S	171	S85.801S	171	S86.101S	755	S86.321S	469
S83.8X9A	369	S85.109A	754,1017,1039	S85.291A	754,1017,1039	S85.802A	754,1017,1039	S86.102A	755,1017	S86.322A	405,1018
S83.8X9D	819	S85.109D	819	S85.291D	819	S85.802D	819	S86.102D	820	S86.322D	820
S83.8X9S	369	S85.109S	171	S85.291S	171	S85.802S	171	S86.102S	755	S86.322S	469
S83.90XA	369,1017	S85.111A	754,1017,1039	S85.292A	754,1017,1039	S85.809A	754,1017,1039	S86.109A	755,1017	S86.329A	405,1018
S83.90XD	819	S85.111D	819	S85.292D	819	S85.809D	819	S86.109D	820	S86.329D	820
S83.90XS	369	S85.111S	171	S85.292S	171	S85.809S	171	S86.109S	755	S86.329S	469
S83.91XA	369,1017	S85.112A	754,1017,1039	S85.299A	754,1017,1039	S85.811A	754,1017,1039	S86.111A	369,1017	S86.391A	755,1018
S83.91XD	819	S85.112D	819	S85.299D	819	S85.811D	819	S86.111D	820	S86.391D	820
S83.91XS	369	S85.112S	171	S85.299S	171	S85.811S	171	S86.111S	369	S86.391S	755
S83.92XA	369,1017	S85.119A	754,1017,1039	S85.301A	754,1017	S85.812A	754,1017,1039	S86.112A	369,1017	S86.392A	755,1018
S83.92XD	819	S85.119D	819	S85.301D	819	S85.812D	819	S86.112D	820	S86.392D	820
S83.92XS	369	S85.119S	171	S85.301S	171	S85.812S	171	S86.112S	369	S86.392S	755
S84.00XA	47,1017,1039	S85.121A	754,1017,1039	S85.302A	754,1017	S85.819A	754,1017,1039	S86.119A	369,1017	S86.399A	755,1018
S84.00XD	819	S85.121D	819	S85.302D	819	S85.819D	819	S86.119D	820	S86.399D	820
S84.00XS	54	S85.121S	171	S85.302S	171	S85.819S	171	S86.119S	369	S86.399S	755
S84.01XA	47,1017,1039	S85.122A	754,1017,1039	S85.309A	754,1017	S85.891A	1017,1040	S86.121A	405,1017	S86.801A	755,1018
S84.01XD	819	S85.122D	819	S85.309D	819	S85.891A	754	S86.121D	820	S86.801D	820
S84.01XS	54	S85.122S	171	S85.309S	171	S85.891D	819	S86.121S	469	S86.801S	755
S84.02XA	47,1017,1039	S85.129A	754,1017,1039	S85.311A	754,1017	S85.891S	171	S86.122A	405,1017	S86.802A	755,1018
S84.02XD	819	S85.129D	819	S85.311D	819	S85.892A	1017,1040	S86.122D	820	S86.802D	820
S84.02XS	54	S85.129S	171	S85.311S	171	S85.892A	754	S86.122S	469	S86.802S	755
S84.10XA	47,1017,1039	S85.131A	754,1017,1039	S85.312A	754,1017	S85.892D	819	S86.129A	405,1017	S86.809A	755,1018
S84.10XD	819	S85.131D	819	S85.312D	819	S85.892S	171	S86.129D	820	S86.809D	820
S84.10XS	54	S85.131S	171	S85.312S	171	S85.899A	1017,1040	S86.129S	469	S86.809S	755
S84.11XA	47,1017,1039	S85.132A	754,1017,1039	S85.319A	754,1017	S85.899A	754	S86.191A	1018	S86.811A	369,1018
S84.11XD	819	S85.132D	819	S85.319D	819	S85.899D	819	S86.191A	755	S86.811D	820
S84.11XS	54	S85.132S	171	S85.319S	171	S85.899S	171	S86.191D	820	S86.811S	369
S84.12XA	47,1017,1039	S85.139A	754,1017,1039	S85.391A	754,1017	S85.901A	754,1017	S86.191S	755	S86.812A	369,1018
S84.12XD	819	S85.139D	819	S85.391D	819	S85.901D	819	S86.192A	1018	S86.812D	820
S84.12XS	54	S85.139S	171	S85.391S	171	S85.901S	171	S86.192A	755	S86.812S	369
S84.20XA	47,1017	S85.141A	754,1017,1039	S85.392A	754,1017	S85.902A	754,1017	S86.192D	820	S86.819A	369,1018
S84.20XD	819	S85.141D	819	S85.392D	819	S85.902D	819	S86.192S	755	S86.819D	820
S84.20XS	54	S85.141S	171	S85.392S	171	S85.902S	171	S86.199A	1018	S86.819S	369
S84.21XA	47,1017	S85.142A	754,1017,1039	S85.399A	754,1017	S85.909A	754,1017	S86.199A	755	S86.821A	405,1018
S84.21XD	819	S85.142D	819	S85.399D	819	S85.909D	819	S86.199D	820	S86.821D	820
S84.21XS	54	S85.142S	171	S85.399S	171	S85.909S	171	S86.199S	755	S86.821S	469
S84.22XA	47,1017	S85.149A	754,1017,1039	S85.401A	754,1017	S85.911A	754,1017	S86.201A	755,1018	S86.822A	405,1018
S84.22XD	819	S85.149D	819	S85.401D	819	S85.911D	819	S86.201D	820	S86.822D	820
S84.22XS	54	S85.149S	171	S85.401S	171	S85.911S	171	S86.201S	755	S86.822S	469
S84.801A	1017,1039	S85.151A	754,1017,1039	S85.402A	754,1017	S85.912A	754,1017	S86.202A	755,1018	S86.829A	405,1018
S84.801A	47	S85.151D	819	S85.402D	819	S85.912D	819	S86.202D	820	S86.829D	820
S84.801D	819	S85.151S	171	S85.402S	171	S85.912S	171	S86.202S	755	S86.829S	469
S84.801S	54	S85.152A	754,1017,1039	S85.409A	754,1017	S85.919A	754,1017	S86.209A	755,1018	S86.891A	1018
S84.802A	1017,1039	S85.152D	819	S85.409D	819	S85.919D	819	S86.209D	820	S86.891A	755
S84.802A	47	S85.152S	171	S85.409S	171	S85.919S	171	S86.209S	755	S86.891D	820
S84.802D	819	S85.159A	754,1017,1039	S85.411A	754,1017	S85.991A	754,1017	S86.211A	369,1018	S86.891S	755
S84.802S	54	S85.159D	819	S85.411D	819	S85.991D	819	S86.211D	820	S86.892A	1018
S84.809A	1017,1039	S85.159S	171	S85.411S	171	S85.991S	171	S86.211S	369	S86.892A	755
S84.809A	47	S85.161A	754,1017,1039	S85.412A	754,1017	S85.992A	754,1017	S86.212A	369,1018	S86.892D	820
S84.809D	819	S85.161D	819	S85.412D	819	S85.992D	819	S86.212D	820	S86.892S	755
S84.809S	54	S85.161S	171	S85.412S	171	S85.992S	171	S86.212S	369	S86.899A	1018
S84.90XA	47,1017,1039	S85.162A	754,1017,1039	S85.419A	754,1017	S85.999A	754,1017	S86.219A	369,1018	S86.899A	755
S84.90XD	819	S85.162D	819	S85.419D	819	S85.999D	819	S86.219D	820	S86.899D	820
S84.90XS	54	S85.162S	171	S85.419S	171	S85.999S	171	S86.219S	369	S86.899S	755
S84.91XA	47,1017,1039	S85.169A	754,1017,1039	S85.491A	754,1017	S86.001A	755,1017	S86.221A	405,1018	S86.901A	755,1018
S84.91XD	819	S85.169D	819	S85.491D	819	S86.001D	819	S86.221D	820	S86.901D	820
S84.91XS	54	S85.169S	171	S85.491S	171	S86.001S	755	S86.221S	469	S86.901S	755
S84.92XA	47,1017,1039	S85.171A	754,1017,1039	S85.492A	754,1017	S86.002A	755,1017	S86.222A	405,1018	S86.902A	755,1018
S84.92XD	819	S85.171D	819	S85.492D	819	S86.002D	819	S86.222D	820	S86.902D	820
S84.92XS	54	S85.171S	171	S85.492S	171	S86.002S	755	S86.222S	469	S86.902S	755
S85.001A	754,1017,1039	S85.172A	754,1017,1039	S85.499A	754,1017	S86.009A	755,1017	S86.229A	405,1018	S86.909A	755,1018
S85.001D	819	S85.172D	819	S85.499D	819	S86.009D	819	S86.229D	820	S86.909D	820
S85.001S	170	S85.172S	171	S85.499S	171	S86.009S	755	S86.229S	469	S86.909S	755
S85.002A	754,1017,1039	S85.179A	754,1017,1039	S85.501A	754,1017,1039	S86.011A	369,1017	S86.291A	755,1018	S86.911A	369,1018
S85.002D	819	S85.179D	819	S85.501D	819	S86.011D	819	S86.291D	820	S86.911D	820
S85.002S	170	S85.179S	171	S85.501S	171	S86.011S	369	S86.291S	755	S86.911S	369
S85.009A	754,1017,1039	S85.181A	754,1017,1039	S85.502A	754,1017,1039	S86.012A	369,1017	S86.292A	755,1018	S86.912A	369,1018
S85.009D	819	S85.181D	819	S85.502D	819	S86.012D	819	S86.292D	820	S86.912D	820
S85.009S	170	S85.181S	171	S85.502S	171	S86.012S	369	S86.292S	755	S86.912S	369
S85.011A	754,1017,1039	S85.182A	754,1017,1039	S85.509A	754,1017,1039	S86.019A	369,1017	S86.299A	755,1018	S86.919A	369,1018
S85.011D	819	S85.182D	819	S85.509D	819	S86.019D	819	S86.299D	820	S86.919D	820
S85.011S	170	S85.182S	171	S85.509S	171	S86.019S	369	S86.299S	755	S86.919S	369
S85.012A	754,1017,1039	S85.189A	754,1017,1039	S85.511A	754,1017,1039	S86.021A	405,1017	S86.301A	755,1018	S86.921A	405,1018
S85.012D	819	S85.189D	819	S85.511D	819	S86.021D	819	S86.301D	820	S86.921D	820
S85.012S	170	S85.189S	171	S85.511S	171	S86.021S	469	S86.301S	755	S86.921S	469
S85.019A	754,1017,1039	S85.201A	754,1017,1039	S85.512A	754,1017,1039	S86.022A	405,1017	S86.302A	755,1018	S86.922A	405,1018
S85.019D	819	S85.201D	819	S85.512D	819	S86.022D	819	S86.302D	820	S86.922D	820
S85.019S	171	S85.201S	171	S85.512S	171	S86.022S	469	S86.302S	755	S86.922S	469
S85.091A	754,1017,1039	S85.202A	754,1017,1039	S85.519A	754,1017,1039	S86.029A	405,1017	S86.309A	755,1018	S86.929A	405,1018
S85.091D	819	S85.202D	819	S85.519D	819	S86.029D	820	S86.309D	820	S86.929D	820

Code	Page	Code	Page	Code	Page	Code	Page	Code	Page	Code	Page
S86.929S	469	S89.002S	342	S89.099G	342	S89.149S	342	S89.301G	343	S90.01XS	469
S86.991A	755, 1018	S89.009A	369, 1018	S89.099K	406	S89.191A	370, 1018	S89.301K	406	S90.02XA	469, 1018
S86.991D	820	S89.009D	342	S89.099P	406	S89.191D	342	S89.301P	406	S90.02XD	820
S86.991S	755	S89.009G	342	S89.099S	342	S89.191G	342	S89.301S	343	S90.02XS	469
S86.992A	755, 1018	S89.009K	405	S89.101A	370, 1018	S89.191P	406	S89.302A	370, 1018	S90.111A	469, 1018
S86.992D	820	S89.009P	406	S89.101D	342	S89.191S	342	S89.302D	343	S90.111D	820
S86.992S	755	S89.009S	342	S89.101G	342	S89.192A	370, 1018	S89.302G	343	S90.111S	469
S86.999A	755, 1018	S89.011A	369, 1018	S89.101K	406	S89.192D	342	S89.302K	406	S90.112A	469, 1018
S86.999D	820	S89.011D	342	S89.101P	406	S89.192G	342	S89.302P	406	S90.112D	820
S86.999S	755	S89.011G	342	S89.101S	342	S89.192K	406	S89.302S	343	S90.112S	469
S87.00XA	755, 1018, 1040	S89.011K	406	S89.102A	370, 1018	S89.192P	406	S89.309A	370, 1018	S90.119A	469, 1018
S87.00XD	820	S89.011P	406	S89.102D	342	S89.192S	342	S89.309D	343	S90.119D	820
S87.00XS	469	S89.011S	342	S89.102G	342	S89.199A	370, 1018	S89.309G	343	S90.119S	469
S87.01XA	755, 1018, 1040	S89.012A	369, 1018	S89.102K	406	S89.199D	342	S89.309K	406	S90.121A	469, 1018
S87.01XD	820	S89.012D	342	S89.102P	406	S89.199G	342	S89.309P	406	S90.121D	820
S87.01XS	469	S89.012G	342	S89.102S	342	S89.199K	406	S89.309S	343	S90.121S	469
S87.02XA	755, 1018, 1040	S89.012K	406	S89.109A	370, 1018	S89.199P	406	S89.311A	370, 1018	S90.122A	469, 1018
S87.02XD	820	S89.012P	406	S89.109D	342	S89.199S	342	S89.311D	343	S90.122D	820
S87.02XS	469	S89.012S	342	S89.109G	342	S89.201A	370, 1018	S89.311G	343	S90.122S	469
S87.80XA	755, 1018, 1040	S89.019A	369, 1018	S89.109K	406	S89.201D	343	S89.311K	406	S90.129A	469, 1018
S87.80XD	820	S89.019D	342	S89.109P	406	S89.201G	343	S89.311P	406	S90.129D	820
S87.80XS	469	S89.019G	342	S89.109S	342	S89.201K	406	S89.311S	343	S90.129S	469
S87.81XA	755, 1018, 1040	S89.019K	406	S89.111A	370, 1018	S89.201P	406	S89.312A	370, 1018	S90.211A	469, 1018
S87.81XD	820	S89.019P	406	S89.111D	342	S89.201S	343	S89.312D	343	S90.211D	820
S87.81XS	469	S89.019S	342	S89.111G	342	S89.202A	370, 1018	S89.312G	343	S90.211S	469
S87.82XA	755, 1018, 1040	S89.021A	369, 1018	S89.111K	406	S89.202D	343	S89.312K	406	S90.212A	469, 1018
S87.82XD	820	S89.021D	342	S89.111P	406	S89.202G	343	S89.312P	406	S90.212D	820
S87.82XS	469	S89.021G	342	S89.111S	342	S89.202K	406	S89.312S	343	S90.212S	469
S88.011A	755, 1018, 1040	S89.021K	406	S89.112A	370, 1018	S89.202P	406	S89.319A	370, 1018	S90.219A	469, 1018
S88.011D	820	S89.021P	406	S89.112D	342	S89.202S	343	S89.319D	343	S90.219D	820
S88.011S	342	S89.021S	342	S89.112G	342	S89.209A	370, 1018	S89.319G	343	S90.219S	469
S88.012A	755, 1018, 1040	S89.022A	369, 1018	S89.112K	406	S89.209D	343	S89.319K	406	S90.221A	469, 1018
S88.012D	820	S89.022D	342	S89.112P	406	S89.209G	343	S89.319P	406	S90.221D	820
S88.012S	342	S89.022G	342	S89.112S	342	S89.209K	406	S89.319S	343	S90.221S	469
S88.019A	755, 1018, 1040	S89.022K	406	S89.119A	370, 1018	S89.209P	406	S89.321A	370, 1018	S90.222A	469, 1018
S88.019D	820	S89.022P	406	S89.119D	342	S89.209S	343	S89.321D	343	S90.222D	820
S88.019S	342	S89.022S	342	S89.119G	342	S89.211A	370, 1018	S89.321G	343	S90.222S	469
S88.021A	755, 1018, 1040	S89.029A	369, 1018	S89.119K	406	S89.211D	343	S89.321K	406	S90.229A	469, 1018
S88.021D	820	S89.029D	342	S89.119P	406	S89.211G	343	S89.321P	406	S90.229D	820
S88.021S	342	S89.029G	342	S89.119S	342	S89.211K	406	S89.321S	343	S90.229S	469
S88.022A	755, 1018, 1040	S89.029K	406	S89.121A	370, 1018	S89.211P	406	S89.322A	370, 1018	S90.30XA	469, 1018
S88.022D	820	S89.029P	406	S89.121D	342	S89.211S	343	S89.322D	343	S90.30XD	820
S88.022S	342	S89.029S	342	S89.121G	342	S89.212A	370, 1018	S89.322G	343	S90.30XS	469
S88.029A	755, 1018, 1040	S89.031A	370, 1018	S89.121K	406	S89.212D	343	S89.322K	406	S90.31XA	469, 1018
S88.029D	820	S89.031D	342	S89.121P	406	S89.212G	343	S89.322P	406	S90.31XD	820
S88.029S	342	S89.031G	342	S89.121S	342	S89.212K	406	S89.322S	343	S90.31XS	469
S88.111A	755, 1018, 1040	S89.031K	406	S89.122A	370, 1018	S89.212P	406	S89.329A	370, 1018	S90.32XA	469, 1018
S88.111D	820	S89.031P	406	S89.122D	342	S89.212S	343	S89.329D	343	S90.32XD	820
S88.111S	342	S89.031S	342	S89.122G	342	S89.219A	370, 1018	S89.329G	343	S90.32XS	469
S88.112A	755, 1018, 1040	S89.032A	370, 1018	S89.122K	406	S89.219D	343	S89.329K	406	S90.411A	469, 1018
S88.112D	820	S89.032D	342	S89.122P	406	S89.219G	343	S89.329P	406	S90.411D	820
S88.112S	342	S89.032G	342	S89.122S	342	S89.219K	406	S89.329S	343	S90.411S	469
S88.119A	755, 1018, 1040	S89.032K	406	S89.129A	370, 1018	S89.219P	406	S89.391A	370, 1018	S90.412A	469, 1018
S88.119D	820	S89.032P	406	S89.129D	342	S89.219S	343	S89.391D	343	S90.412D	820
S88.119S	342	S89.032S	342	S89.129G	342	S89.221A	370, 1018	S89.391G	343	S90.412S	469
S88.121A	755, 1018, 1040	S89.039A	370, 1018	S89.129K	406	S89.221D	343	S89.391K	406	S90.413A	469, 1018
S88.121D	820	S89.039D	342	S89.129P	406	S89.221G	343	S89.391P	406	S90.413D	820
S88.121S	342	S89.039G	342	S89.129S	342	S89.221K	406	S89.391S	343	S90.413S	469
S88.122A	755, 1018, 1040	S89.039K	406	S89.131A	370, 1018	S89.221P	406	S89.392A	370, 1018	S90.414A	469, 1018
S88.122D	820	S89.039P	406	S89.131D	342	S89.221S	343	S89.392D	343	S90.414D	820
S88.122S	342	S89.039S	342	S89.131G	342	S89.222A	370, 1018	S89.392G	343	S90.414S	469
S88.129A	755, 1018, 1040	S89.041A	370, 1018	S89.131K	406	S89.222D	343	S89.392K	406	S90.415A	469, 1018
S88.129D	820	S89.041D	342	S89.131P	406	S89.222G	343	S89.392P	406	S90.415D	820
S88.129S	342	S89.041G	342	S89.131S	342	S89.222K	406	S89.392S	343	S90.415S	469
S88.911A	755, 1018, 1040	S89.041K	406	S89.132A	370, 1018	S89.222P	406	S89.399A	370, 1018	S90.416A	469, 1018
S88.911D	820	S89.041P	406	S89.132D	342	S89.222S	343	S89.399D	343	S90.416D	820
S88.911S	342	S89.041S	342	S89.132G	342	S89.229A	370, 1018	S89.399G	343	S90.416S	469
S88.912A	755, 1018, 1040	S89.042A	370, 1018	S89.132K	406	S89.229D	343	S89.399K	406	S90.421A	478, 1018
S88.912D	820	S89.042D	342	S89.132P	406	S89.229G	343	S89.399P	406	S90.421D	820
S88.912S	342	S89.042G	342	S89.132S	342	S89.229K	406	S89.399S	343	S90.421S	469
S88.919A	755, 1018, 1040	S89.042K	406	S89.139A	370, 1018	S89.229P	406	S89.80XA	755, 1018	S90.422A	478, 1018
S88.919D	820	S89.042P	406	S89.139D	342	S89.229S	343	S89.80XD	820	S90.422D	820
S88.919S	342	S89.042S	342	S89.139G	342	S89.291A	370, 1018	S89.80XS	755	S90.422S	469
S88.921A	755, 1018, 1040	S89.049A	370, 1018	S89.139K	406	S89.291D	343	S89.81XA	755, 1018	S90.423A	478, 1018
S88.921D	820	S89.049D	342	S89.139P	406	S89.291G	343	S89.81XD	820	S90.423D	820
S88.921S	342	S89.049G	342	S89.139S	342	S89.291K	406	S89.81XS	755	S90.423S	469
S88.922A	755, 1018, 1040	S89.049K	406	S89.141A	370, 1018	S89.291P	406	S89.82XA	755, 1018	S90.424A	478, 1018
S88.922D	820	S89.049P	406	S89.141D	342	S89.291S	343	S89.82XD	820	S90.424D	820
S88.922S	342	S89.049S	342	S89.141G	342	S89.292A	370, 1018	S89.82XS	755	S90.424S	469
S88.929A	755, 1018, 1040	S89.091A	370, 1018	S89.141K	406	S89.292D	343	S89.90XA	755, 1018	S90.425A	478, 1018
S88.929D	820	S89.091D	342	S89.141P	406	S89.292G	343	S89.90XD	820	S90.425D	820
S88.929S	342	S89.091G	342	S89.141S	342	S89.292K	406	S89.90XS	755	S90.425S	469
S89.001A	369, 1018	S89.091K	406	S89.142A	370, 1018	S89.292P	406	S89.91XA	755, 1018	S90.426A	478, 1018
S89.001D	342	S89.091P	406	S89.142D	342	S89.292S	343	S89.91XD	820	S90.426D	820
S89.001G	342	S89.091S	342	S89.142G	342	S89.299A	370, 1018	S89.91XS	755	S90.426S	469
S89.001K	405	S89.092A	370, 1018	S89.142K	406	S89.299D	343	S89.92XA	755, 1018	S90.441A	469, 1018
S89.001P	405	S89.092D	342	S89.142P	406	S89.299G	343	S89.92XD	820	S90.441D	820
S89.001S	342	S89.092G	342	S89.142S	342	S89.299K	406	S89.92XS	755	S90.441S	469
S89.002A	369, 1018	S89.092K	406	S89.149A	370, 1018	S89.299P	406	S90.00XA	469, 1018	S90.442A	469, 1018
S89.002D	342	S89.092P	406	S89.149D	342	S89.299S	343	S90.00XD	820	S90.442D	820
S89.002G	342	S89.092S	342	S89.149G	342	S89.301A	370, 1018	S90.00XS	469	S90.442S	469
S89.002K	405	S89.099A	370, 1018	S89.149K	406	S89.301D	343	S90.01XA	469, 1018	S90.443A	469, 1018
S89.002P	405	S89.099D	342	S89.149P	406			S90.01XD	820	S90.443D	820

Code	Page	Code	Page	Code	Page	Code	Page	Code	Page	Code	Page
S90.443S	469	S90.551S	469	S90.922S	470	S91.106S	470	S91.152S	470	S91.235S	471
S90.444A	469, 1019	S90.552A	469, 1019	S90.929A	470, 1019	S91.109A	470, 1019	S91.153A	470, 1019	S91.236A	471, 1019
S90.444D	820	S90.552D	820	S90.929D	821	S91.109D	821	S91.153D	821	S91.236D	821
S90.444S	469	S90.552S	469	S90.929S	470	S91.109S	470	S91.153S	470	S91.236S	471
S90.445A	469, 1019	S90.559A	469, 1019	S90.931A	470, 1019	S91.111A	470, 1019	S91.154A	470, 1019	S91.239A	471, 1019
S90.445D	820	S90.559D	820	S90.931D	821	S91.111D	821	S91.154D	821	S91.239D	821
S90.445S	469	S90.559S	469	S90.931S	470	S91.111S	470	S91.154S	470	S91.239S	471
S90.446A	469, 1019	S90.561A	478, 1019	S90.932A	470, 1019	S91.112A	470, 1019	S91.155A	470, 1019	S91.241A	755, 1019
S90.446D	820	S90.561D	820	S90.932D	821	S91.112D	821	S91.155D	821	S91.241D	821
S90.446S	469	S90.561S	469	S90.932S	470	S91.112S	470	S91.155S	470	S91.241S	471
S90.451A	469, 1019	S90.562A	478, 1019	S90.933A	470, 1019	S91.113A	470, 1019	S91.156A	470, 1019	S91.242A	755, 1019
S90.451D	820	S90.562D	820	S90.933D	821	S91.113D	821	S91.156D	821	S91.242D	821
S90.451S	469	S90.562S	469	S90.933S	470	S91.113S	470	S91.156S	470	S91.242S	471
S90.452A	469, 1019	S90.569A	478, 1019	S90.934A	470, 1019	S91.114A	470, 1019	S91.159A	470, 1019	S91.243A	755, 1019
S90.452D	820	S90.569D	820	S90.934D	821	S91.114D	821	S91.159D	821	S91.243D	821
S90.452S	469	S90.569S	469	S90.934S	470	S91.114S	470	S91.159S	470	S91.243S	471
S90.453A	469, 1019	S90.571A	469, 1019	S90.935A	470, 1019	S91.115A	470, 1019	S91.201A	470, 1019	S91.244A	755, 1019
S90.453D	820	S90.571D	820	S90.935D	821	S91.115D	821	S91.201D	821	S91.244D	821
S90.453S	469	S90.571S	469	S90.935S	470	S91.115S	470	S91.201S	470	S91.244S	471
S90.454A	469, 1019	S90.572A	469, 1019	S90.936A	470, 1019	S91.116A	470, 1019	S91.202A	470, 1019	S91.245A	755, 1019
S90.454D	820	S90.572D	820	S90.936D	821	S91.116D	821	S91.202D	821	S91.245D	821
S90.454S	469	S90.572S	469	S90.936S	470	S91.116S	470	S91.202S	470	S91.245S	471
S90.455A	469, 1019	S90.579A	469, 1019	S91.001A	470, 1019	S91.119A	470, 1019	S91.203A	470, 1019	S91.246A	755, 1019
S90.455D	820	S90.579D	820	S91.001D	821	S91.119D	821	S91.203D	821	S91.246D	821
S90.455S	469	S90.579S	469	S91.001S	470	S91.119S	470	S91.203S	470	S91.246S	471
S90.456A	469, 1019	S90.811A	469, 1019	S91.002A	470, 1019	S91.121A	755, 1019	S91.204A	470, 1019	S91.249A	755, 1019
S90.456D	820	S90.811D	820	S91.002D	821	S91.121D	821	S91.204D	821	S91.249D	821
S90.456S	469	S90.811S	469	S91.002S	470	S91.121S	470	S91.204S	470	S91.249S	471
S90.461A	478, 1019	S90.812A	469, 1019	S91.009A	470, 1019	S91.122A	755, 1019	S91.205A	470, 1019	S91.251A	471, 1019
S90.461D	820	S90.812D	820	S91.009D	821	S91.122D	821	S91.205D	821	S91.251D	821
S90.461S	469	S90.812S	469	S91.009S	470	S91.122S	470	S91.205S	470	S91.251S	471
S90.462A	478, 1019	S90.819A	469, 1019	S91.011A	470, 1019	S91.123A	755, 1019	S91.206A	470, 1019	S91.252A	471, 1019
S90.462D	820	S90.819D	820	S91.011D	821	S91.123D	821	S91.206D	821	S91.252D	821
S90.462S	469	S90.819S	469	S91.011S	470	S91.123S	470	S91.206S	470	S91.252S	471
S90.463A	478, 1019	S90.821A	478, 1019	S91.012A	470, 1019	S91.124A	755, 1019	S91.209A	470, 1019	S91.253A	471, 1019
S90.463D	820	S90.821D	820	S91.012D	821	S91.124D	821	S91.209D	821	S91.253D	821
S90.463S	469	S90.821S	469	S91.012S	470	S91.124S	470	S91.209S	470	S91.253S	471
S90.464A	478, 1019	S90.822A	478, 1019	S91.019A	470, 1019	S91.125A	755, 1019	S91.211A	470, 1019	S91.254A	471, 1019
S90.464D	820	S90.822D	820	S91.019D	821	S91.125D	821	S91.211D	821	S91.254D	821
S90.464S	469	S90.822S	469	S91.019S	470	S91.125S	470	S91.211S	470	S91.254S	471
S90.465A	478, 1019	S90.829A	478, 1019	S91.021A	755, 1019	S91.126A	755, 1019	S91.212A	470, 1019	S91.255A	471, 1019
S90.465D	820	S90.829D	820	S91.021D	821	S91.126D	821	S91.212D	821	S91.255D	821
S90.465S	469	S90.829S	469	S91.021S	470	S91.126S	470	S91.212S	470	S91.255S	471
S90.466A	478, 1019	S90.841A	469, 1019	S91.022A	755, 1019	S91.129A	755, 1019	S91.213A	470, 1019	S91.256A	471, 1019
S90.466D	820	S90.841D	820	S91.022D	821	S91.129D	821	S91.213D	821	S91.256D	821
S90.466S	469	S90.841S	469	S91.022S	470	S91.129S	470	S91.213S	470	S91.256S	471
S90.471A	469, 1019	S90.842A	469, 1019	S91.029A	755, 1019	S91.131A	470, 1019	S91.214A	470, 1019	S91.259A	471, 1019
S90.471D	820	S90.842D	820	S91.029D	821	S91.131D	821	S91.214D	821	S91.259D	821
S90.471S	469	S90.842S	469	S91.029S	470	S91.131S	470	S91.214S	470	S91.259S	471
S90.472A	469, 1019	S90.849A	469, 1019	S91.031A	470, 1019	S91.132A	470, 1019	S91.215A	470, 1019	S91.301A	471, 1019
S90.472D	820	S90.849D	821	S91.031D	821	S91.132D	821	S91.215D	821	S91.301D	821
S90.472S	469	S90.849S	469	S91.031S	470	S91.132S	470	S91.215S	470	S91.301S	471
S90.473A	469, 1019	S90.851A	469, 1019	S91.032A	470, 1019	S91.133A	470, 1019	S91.216A	470, 1019	S91.302A	471, 1019
S90.473D	820	S90.851D	821	S91.032D	821	S91.133D	821	S91.216D	821	S91.302D	821
S90.473S	469	S90.851S	469	S91.032S	470	S91.133S	470	S91.216S	470	S91.302S	471
S90.474A	469, 1019	S90.852A	469, 1019	S91.039A	470, 1019	S91.134A	470, 1019	S91.219A	470, 1019	S91.309A	471, 1019
S90.474D	820	S90.852D	821	S91.039D	821	S91.134D	821	S91.219D	821	S91.309D	821
S90.474S	469	S90.852S	469	S91.039S	470	S91.134S	470	S91.219S	470	S91.309S	471
S90.475A	469, 1019	S90.859A	469, 1019	S91.041A	755, 1019	S91.135A	470, 1019	S91.221A	755, 1019	S91.311A	471, 1020
S90.475D	820	S90.859D	821	S91.041D	821	S91.135D	821	S91.221D	821	S91.311D	821
S90.475S	469	S90.859S	469	S91.041S	470	S91.135S	470	S91.221S	470	S91.311S	471
S90.476A	469, 1019	S90.861A	478, 1019	S91.042A	755, 1019	S91.136A	755, 1019	S91.222A	755, 1019	S91.312A	471, 1020
S90.476D	820	S90.861D	821	S91.042D	821	S91.136D	821	S91.222D	821	S91.312D	821
S90.476S	469	S90.861S	469	S91.042S	470	S91.136S	470	S91.222S	470	S91.312S	471
S90.511A	469, 1019	S90.862A	478, 1019	S91.049A	755, 1019	S91.139A	470, 1019	S91.223A	755, 1019	S91.319A	471, 1020
S90.511D	820	S90.862D	821	S91.049D	821	S91.139D	821	S91.223D	821	S91.319D	821
S90.511S	469	S90.862S	470	S91.049S	470	S91.139S	470	S91.223S	470	S91.319S	471
S90.512A	469, 1019	S90.869A	478, 1019	S91.051A	470, 1019	S91.141A	755, 1019	S91.224A	755, 1019	S91.321A	755, 1020
S90.512D	820	S90.869D	821	S91.051D	821	S91.141D	821	S91.224D	821	S91.321D	821
S90.512S	469	S90.869S	470	S91.051S	470	S91.141S	470	S91.224S	470	S91.321S	471
S90.519A	469, 1019	S90.871A	470, 1019	S91.052A	470, 1019	S91.142A	755, 1019	S91.225A	755, 1019	S91.322A	755, 1020
S90.519D	820	S90.871D	821	S91.052D	821	S91.142D	821	S91.225D	821	S91.322D	821
S90.519S	469	S90.871S	470	S91.052S	470	S91.142S	470	S91.225S	470	S91.322S	471
S90.521A	478, 1019	S90.872A	470, 1019	S91.059A	470, 1019	S91.143A	755, 1019	S91.226A	755, 1019	S91.329A	755, 1020
S90.521D	820	S90.872D	821	S91.059D	821	S91.143D	821	S91.226D	821	S91.329D	821
S90.521S	469	S90.872S	470	S91.059S	470	S91.143S	470	S91.226S	470	S91.329S	471
S90.522A	478, 1019	S90.879A	470, 1019	S91.101A	470, 1019	S91.144A	755, 1019	S91.229A	755, 1019	S91.331A	471, 1020
S90.522D	820	S90.879D	821	S91.101D	821	S91.144D	821	S91.229D	821	S91.331D	821
S90.522S	469	S90.879S	470	S91.101S	470	S91.144S	470	S91.229S	470	S91.331S	471
S90.529A	478, 1019	S90.911A	470, 1019	S91.102A	470, 1019	S91.145A	755, 1019	S91.231A	470, 1019	S91.332A	471, 1020
S90.529D	820	S90.911D	821	S91.102D	821	S91.145D	821	S91.231D	821	S91.332D	821
S90.529S	469	S90.911S	470	S91.102S	470	S91.145S	470	S91.231S	470	S91.332S	471
S90.541A	469, 1019	S90.912A	470, 1019	S91.103A	470, 1019	S91.146A	470, 1019	S91.232A	470, 1019	S91.339A	471, 1020
S90.541D	820	S90.912D	821	S91.103D	821	S91.146D	821	S91.232D	821	S91.339D	821
S90.541S	469	S90.912S	470	S91.103S	470	S91.146S	470	S91.232S	470	S91.339S	471
S90.542A	469, 1019	S90.919A	470, 1019	S91.104A	470, 1019	S91.149A	755, 1019	S91.233A	470, 1019	S91.341A	755, 1020
S90.542D	820	S90.919D	821	S91.104D	821	S91.149D	821	S91.233D	821	S91.341D	821
S90.542S	469	S90.919S	470	S91.104S	470	S91.149S	470	S91.233S	470	S91.341S	471
S90.549A	469, 1019	S90.921A	470, 1019	S91.105A	470, 1019	S91.151A	470, 1019	S91.234A	470, 1019	S91.342A	755, 1020
S90.549D	820	S90.921D	821	S91.105D	821	S91.151D	821	S91.234D	821	S91.342D	821
S90.549S	469	S90.921S	470	S91.105S	470	S91.151S	470	S91.234S	471	S91.342S	471
S90.551A	469, 1019	S90.922A	470, 1019	S91.106A	470, 1019	S91.152A	470, 1019	S91.235A	471, 1019	S91.349A	755, 1020
S90.551D	820	S90.922D	821	S91.106D	821	S91.152D	821	S91.235D	821	S91.349D	821

Code	Page
S91.349S	471
S91.351A	471, 1020
S91.351D	821
S91.351S	471
S91.352A	471, 1020
S91.352D	821
S91.352S	471
S91.359A	471, 1020
S91.359D	821
S91.359S	471
S92.001A	370, 1020
S92.001B	370, 1020
S92.001D	343
S92.001G	343
S92.001K	406
S92.001P	406
S92.001S	343
S92.002A	370, 1020
S92.002B	370, 1020
S92.002D	343
S92.002G	343
S92.002K	406
S92.002P	406
S92.002S	343
S92.009A	370, 1020
S92.009B	370, 1020
S92.009D	343
S92.009G	343
S92.009K	406
S92.009P	406
S92.009S	343
S92.011A	370, 1020
S92.011B	370, 1020
S92.011D	343
S92.011G	343
S92.011K	406
S92.011P	406
S92.011S	343
S92.012A	370, 1020
S92.012B	370, 1020
S92.012D	343
S92.012G	343
S92.012K	406
S92.012P	406
S92.012S	343
S92.013A	370, 1020
S92.013B	370, 1020
S92.013D	343
S92.013G	343
S92.013K	406
S92.013P	406
S92.013S	343
S92.014A	370, 1020
S92.014B	370, 1020
S92.014D	343
S92.014G	343
S92.014K	406
S92.014P	406
S92.014S	343
S92.015A	370, 1020
S92.015B	370, 1020
S92.015D	343
S92.015G	343
S92.015K	406
S92.015P	406
S92.015S	343
S92.016A	370, 1020
S92.016B	370, 1020
S92.016D	343
S92.016G	343
S92.016K	406
S92.016P	406
S92.016S	343
S92.021A	370, 1020
S92.021B	370, 1020
S92.021D	343
S92.021G	343
S92.021K	406
S92.021P	406
S92.021S	343
S92.022A	370, 1020
S92.022B	370, 1020
S92.022D	343
S92.022G	343
S92.022K	406
S92.022P	406
S92.022S	343
S92.023A	370, 1020
S92.023B	370, 1020
S92.023D	343
S92.023G	343
S92.023K	406
S92.023P	406
S92.023S	343
S92.024A	370, 1020
S92.024B	370, 1020
S92.024D	343
S92.024G	343
S92.024K	406
S92.024P	406
S92.024S	343
S92.025A	370, 1020
S92.025B	370, 1020
S92.025D	343
S92.025G	343
S92.025K	406
S92.025P	406
S92.025S	343
S92.026A	370, 1020
S92.026B	370, 1020
S92.026D	343
S92.026G	343
S92.026K	406
S92.026P	406
S92.026S	343
S92.031A	370, 1020
S92.031B	370, 1020
S92.031D	343
S92.031G	343
S92.031K	406
S92.031P	406
S92.031S	343
S92.032A	370, 1020
S92.032B	370, 1020
S92.032D	343
S92.032G	343
S92.032K	406
S92.032P	406
S92.032S	343
S92.033A	370, 1020
S92.033B	370, 1020
S92.033D	343
S92.033G	343
S92.033K	406
S92.033P	406
S92.033S	343
S92.034A	370, 1020
S92.034B	370, 1020
S92.034D	343
S92.034G	343
S92.034K	406
S92.034P	406
S92.034S	343
S92.035A	370, 1020
S92.035B	370, 1020
S92.035D	343
S92.035G	343
S92.035K	406
S92.035P	406
S92.035S	343
S92.036A	370, 1020
S92.036B	370, 1020
S92.036D	343
S92.036G	343
S92.036K	406
S92.036P	406
S92.036S	343
S92.041A	1020
S92.041A	370
S92.041B	1020
S92.041B	370
S92.041D	343
S92.041G	343
S92.041K	406
S92.041P	406
S92.041S	343
S92.042A	1020
S92.042A	370
S92.042B	1020
S92.042B	370
S92.042D	343
S92.042G	343
S92.042K	406
S92.042P	406
S92.042S	343
S92.043A	1020
S92.043A	370
S92.043B	1020
S92.043B	370
S92.043D	343
S92.043G	343
S92.043P	406
S92.043S	343
S92.044A	1020
S92.044A	370
S92.044B	1020
S92.044B	370
S92.044D	343
S92.044G	343
S92.044K	406
S92.044P	406
S92.044S	343
S92.045A	1020
S92.045A	370
S92.045B	1020
S92.045B	370
S92.045D	343
S92.045G	343
S92.045K	406
S92.045P	406
S92.045S	343
S92.046A	1020
S92.046A	370
S92.046B	1020
S92.046B	370
S92.046D	343
S92.046G	343
S92.046P	406
S92.046S	343
S92.051A	370
S92.051A	1020
S92.051B	1020
S92.051B	370
S92.051G	343
S92.051K	406
S92.051P	406
S92.051S	343
S92.052A	1020
S92.052A	370
S92.052B	1020
S92.052B	370
S92.052D	343
S92.052G	343
S92.052K	406
S92.052P	406
S92.052S	343
S92.053A	1020
S92.053A	370
S92.053B	1020
S92.053D	343
S92.053G	343
S92.053K	406
S92.053P	407
S92.053S	343
S92.054A	1020
S92.054A	370
S92.054B	1020
S92.054B	370
S92.054D	343
S92.054G	343
S92.054K	407
S92.054P	407
S92.054S	343
S92.055A	1020
S92.055A	370
S92.055B	1020
S92.055B	370
S92.055D	343
S92.055G	343
S92.055K	407
S92.055P	407
S92.055S	343
S92.056A	1020
S92.056A	370
S92.056B	1020
S92.056B	370
S92.056G	343
S92.056K	407
S92.056P	407
S92.056S	343
S92.061A	370, 1020
S92.061B	370, 1020
S92.061D	343
S92.061G	343
S92.061K	407
S92.061P	407
S92.061S	344
S92.062A	370, 1020
S92.062B	370, 1020
S92.062D	344
S92.062G	344
S92.062K	407
S92.062P	407
S92.062S	344
S92.063A	370, 1020
S92.063B	370, 1020
S92.063D	344
S92.063G	344
S92.063K	407
S92.063P	407
S92.063S	344
S92.064A	370, 1020
S92.064B	370, 1020
S92.064D	344
S92.064G	344
S92.064K	407
S92.064S	344
S92.065A	370, 1020
S92.065B	370, 1020
S92.065D	344
S92.065G	344
S92.065P	407
S92.065S	344
S92.066A	370, 1020
S92.066B	370, 1020
S92.066D	344
S92.066G	344
S92.066K	407
S92.066P	407
S92.066S	344
S92.101A	370, 1020
S92.101B	370, 1020
S92.101D	344
S92.101G	344
S92.101K	407
S92.101P	407
S92.101S	344
S92.102A	370, 1020
S92.102B	370, 1020
S92.102D	344
S92.102G	344
S92.102K	407
S92.102P	407
S92.102S	344
S92.109A	370, 1020
S92.109B	370, 1020
S92.109D	344
S92.109G	344
S92.109K	407
S92.109P	407
S92.109S	344
S92.111A	370, 1020
S92.111B	370, 1020
S92.111D	344
S92.111G	344
S92.111K	407
S92.111P	407
S92.111S	344
S92.112A	370, 1020
S92.112B	370, 1020
S92.112D	344
S92.112G	344
S92.112K	407
S92.112P	407
S92.112S	344
S92.113A	370, 1020
S92.113B	370, 1020
S92.113D	344
S92.113G	344
S92.113K	407
S92.113P	407
S92.113S	344
S92.114A	370, 1020
S92.114B	370, 1020
S92.114D	344
S92.114G	344
S92.114P	407
S92.114S	344
S92.115A	370, 1020
S92.115B	370, 1020
S92.115D	344
S92.115G	344
S92.115P	407
S92.115S	344
S92.116A	370, 1020
S92.116B	370, 1020
S92.116D	344
S92.116G	344
S92.116P	407
S92.116S	344
S92.121A	370, 1020
S92.121B	370, 1020
S92.121D	344
S92.121G	344
S92.121K	407
S92.121P	407
S92.121S	344
S92.122A	370, 1020
S92.122B	370, 1020
S92.122D	344
S92.122G	344
S92.122K	407
S92.122P	407
S92.122S	344
S92.123A	370, 1020
S92.123B	370, 1020
S92.123D	344
S92.123G	344
S92.123K	407
S92.123P	407
S92.123S	344
S92.124A	370, 1020
S92.124B	370, 1020
S92.124D	344
S92.124G	344
S92.124K	407
S92.124P	407
S92.124S	344
S92.125A	370, 1020
S92.125B	370, 1020
S92.125D	344
S92.125G	344
S92.125K	407
S92.125P	407
S92.125S	344
S92.126A	370, 1020
S92.126B	370, 1020
S92.126D	344
S92.126G	344
S92.126K	407
S92.126P	407
S92.126S	344
S92.131A	370, 1020
S92.131B	370, 1020
S92.131D	344
S92.131G	344
S92.131K	407
S92.131P	407
S92.131S	344
S92.132A	370, 1020
S92.132B	370, 1020
S92.132D	344
S92.132G	344
S92.132K	407
S92.132P	407
S92.132S	344
S92.133A	370, 1020
S92.133B	370, 1020
S92.133D	344
S92.133G	344
S92.133K	407
S92.133P	407
S92.133S	344
S92.134A	370, 1020
S92.134B	370, 1020
S92.134D	344
S92.134G	344
S92.134K	407
S92.134P	407
S92.134S	344
S92.135A	370, 1020
S92.135B	370, 1020
S92.135D	344
S92.135G	344
S92.135K	407
S92.135P	407
S92.135S	344
S92.136A	370, 1020
S92.136B	370, 1020
S92.136D	344
S92.136G	344
S92.136K	407
S92.136P	407
S92.136S	344
S92.141A	370, 1020
S92.141B	370, 1020
S92.141D	344
S92.141K	407
S92.141P	407
S92.141S	344
S92.142A	370, 1020
S92.142B	371, 1020
S92.142D	344
S92.142G	344
S92.142K	407
S92.142P	407
S92.142S	407
S92.143A	371, 1020
S92.143B	371, 1020
S92.143D	344
S92.143G	344
S92.143K	407
S92.143P	407
S92.143S	344
S92.144A	371, 1020
S92.144B	371, 1020
S92.144D	344
S92.144G	344
S92.144K	407
S92.144P	407
S92.144S	344
S92.145A	371, 1020
S92.145B	371, 1020
S92.145D	344
S92.145G	344
S92.145K	407
S92.145P	407
S92.145S	344
S92.146A	371, 1020
S92.146B	371, 1020
S92.146D	344
S92.146G	344
S92.146K	407
S92.146P	407
S92.146S	344
S92.151A	371, 1020
S92.151B	371, 1020
S92.151D	344
S92.151K	407
S92.151P	407
S92.151S	344
S92.152A	371, 1020
S92.152B	371, 1020
S92.152G	344
S92.152K	407
S92.152P	407
S92.152S	344
S92.153A	371, 1020
S92.153B	371, 1020
S92.153D	344
S92.153G	344
S92.153K	407
S92.153P	407
S92.153S	344
S92.154A	371, 1020
S92.154B	371, 1020
S92.154D	344
S92.154G	344
S92.154K	407
S92.154P	407
S92.154S	344
S92.155A	371, 1020
S92.155B	371, 1020
S92.155D	344
S92.155G	344
S92.155K	407
S92.155P	407
S92.155S	344
S92.156A	371, 1020
S92.156B	371, 1020
S92.156D	344
S92.156G	344
S92.156K	407
S92.156P	407
S92.156S	344
S92.191A	371, 1020
S92.191B	371, 1020
S92.191D	344
S92.191G	344
S92.191K	407
S92.191P	407
S92.191S	344
S92.192A	371, 1020
S92.192B	371, 1020
S92.192D	344
S92.192G	344
S92.192K	407
S92.192P	407
S92.192S	344
S92.199A	371, 1020
S92.199B	371, 1020
S92.199D	344
S92.199G	344
S92.199K	407
S92.199P	407

Code	Page
S92.199S	344
S92.201A	371, 1020
S92.201B	371, 1020
S92.201D	344
S92.201G	344
S92.201K	407
S92.201P	407
S92.201S	344
S92.202A	371, 1020
S92.202B	371, 1020
S92.202D	344
S92.202G	344
S92.202K	407
S92.202P	407
S92.202S	344
S92.209A	371, 1020
S92.209B	371, 1020
S92.209D	344
S92.209G	344
S92.209K	407
S92.209P	407
S92.209S	344
S92.211A	371, 1020
S92.211B	371, 1020
S92.211D	344
S92.211G	344
S92.211K	407
S92.211P	407
S92.211S	344
S92.212A	371, 1020
S92.212B	371, 1021
S92.212D	344
S92.212G	344
S92.212K	407
S92.212P	407
S92.212S	344
S92.213A	371, 1021
S92.213B	371, 1021
S92.213D	344
S92.213G	344
S92.213K	407
S92.213P	407
S92.213S	344
S92.214A	371, 1021
S92.214B	371, 1021
S92.214D	344
S92.214G	344
S92.214K	407
S92.214P	407
S92.214S	344
S92.215A	371, 1021
S92.215B	371, 1021
S92.215D	344
S92.215G	344
S92.215K	407
S92.215P	407
S92.215S	344
S92.216A	371, 1021
S92.216B	371, 1021
S92.216D	344
S92.216G	344
S92.216K	407
S92.216P	407
S92.216S	344
S92.221A	371, 1021
S92.221B	371, 1021
S92.221D	344
S92.221G	344
S92.221K	407
S92.221P	407
S92.221S	344
S92.222A	371, 1021
S92.222B	371, 1021
S92.222D	344
S92.222G	344
S92.222K	407
S92.222P	407
S92.222S	344
S92.223A	371, 1021
S92.223B	371, 1021
S92.223D	344
S92.223G	344
S92.223K	407
S92.223P	407
S92.223S	344
S92.224A	371, 1021
S92.224B	371, 1021
S92.224D	344
S92.224G	344
S92.224K	407
S92.224P	407
S92.224S	344
S92.225A	371, 1021
S92.225B	371, 1021
S92.225D	344
S92.225G	344
S92.225K	407
S92.225P	407
S92.225S	344
S92.226A	371, 1021
S92.226B	371, 1021
S92.226D	344
S92.226G	344
S92.226K	407
S92.226P	407
S92.226S	344
S92.231A	371, 1021
S92.231B	371, 1021
S92.231D	344
S92.231G	344
S92.231K	407
S92.231P	407
S92.231S	344
S92.232A	371, 1021
S92.232B	371, 1021
S92.232D	344
S92.232G	344
S92.232K	407
S92.232P	407
S92.232S	345
S92.233A	371, 1021
S92.233B	371, 1021
S92.233D	345
S92.233G	345
S92.233K	407
S92.233P	407
S92.233S	345
S92.234A	371, 1021
S92.234B	371, 1021
S92.234D	345
S92.234G	345
S92.234K	407
S92.234P	407
S92.234S	345
S92.235A	371, 1021
S92.235B	371, 1021
S92.235D	345
S92.235G	345
S92.235K	407
S92.235P	407
S92.235S	345
S92.236A	371, 1021
S92.236B	371, 1021
S92.236D	345
S92.236G	345
S92.236K	407
S92.236P	407
S92.236S	345
S92.241A	371, 1021
S92.241B	371, 1021
S92.241D	345
S92.241G	345
S92.241K	407
S92.241P	407
S92.241S	345
S92.242A	371, 1021
S92.242B	371, 1021
S92.242D	345
S92.242G	345
S92.242K	407
S92.242P	407
S92.242S	345
S92.243A	371, 1021
S92.243B	371, 1021
S92.243D	345
S92.243G	345
S92.243K	407
S92.243P	407
S92.243S	345
S92.244A	371, 1021
S92.244B	371, 1021
S92.244D	345
S92.244G	345
S92.244K	407
S92.244P	407
S92.244S	345
S92.245A	371, 1021
S92.245B	371, 1021
S92.245D	345
S92.245G	345
S92.245K	407
S92.245P	407
S92.245S	345
S92.246A	371, 1021
S92.246B	371, 1021
S92.246D	345
S92.246G	345
S92.246K	407
S92.246P	407
S92.246S	345
S92.251A	371, 1021
S92.251B	371, 1021
S92.251D	345
S92.251G	345
S92.251K	407
S92.251P	407
S92.251S	345
S92.252A	371, 1021
S92.252B	371, 1021
S92.252D	345
S92.252G	345
S92.252K	407
S92.252P	407
S92.252S	345
S92.253A	371, 1021
S92.253B	371, 1021
S92.253D	345
S92.253G	345
S92.253K	407
S92.253P	407
S92.253S	345
S92.254A	371, 1021
S92.254B	371, 1021
S92.254D	345
S92.254G	345
S92.254K	407
S92.254P	407
S92.254S	345
S92.255A	371, 1021
S92.255B	371, 1021
S92.255D	345
S92.255G	345
S92.255K	407
S92.255P	407
S92.255S	345
S92.256A	371, 1021
S92.256B	371, 1021
S92.256D	345
S92.256G	345
S92.256K	407
S92.256P	407
S92.256S	345
S92.301A	371, 1021
S92.301B	371, 1021
S92.301D	345
S92.301G	345
S92.301K	407
S92.301P	407
S92.301S	345
S92.302A	371, 1021
S92.302B	371, 1021
S92.302D	345
S92.302G	345
S92.302K	407
S92.302P	407
S92.302S	345
S92.309A	371, 1021
S92.309B	371, 1021
S92.309D	345
S92.309G	345
S92.309K	407
S92.309P	407
S92.309S	345
S92.311A	371, 1021
S92.311B	371, 1021
S92.311D	345
S92.311G	345
S92.311K	407
S92.311P	407
S92.311S	345
S92.312A	371, 1021
S92.312B	371, 1021
S92.312D	345
S92.312G	345
S92.312K	407
S92.312P	407
S92.312S	345
S92.313A	371, 1021
S92.313B	371, 1021
S92.313D	345
S92.313G	345
S92.313K	407
S92.313P	407
S92.313S	345
S92.314A	371, 1021
S92.314B	371, 1021
S92.314D	345
S92.314G	345
S92.314K	407
S92.314P	407
S92.314S	345
S92.315A	371, 1021
S92.315B	371, 1021
S92.315D	345
S92.315G	345
S92.315K	407
S92.315P	407
S92.315S	345
S92.316A	371, 1021
S92.316B	371, 1021
S92.316D	345
S92.316G	345
S92.316K	407
S92.316P	408
S92.316S	345
S92.321A	371, 1021
S92.321B	371, 1021
S92.321D	345
S92.321G	345
S92.321K	408
S92.321P	408
S92.321S	345
S92.322A	371, 1021
S92.322B	371, 1021
S92.322D	345
S92.322G	345
S92.322K	408
S92.322P	408
S92.322S	345
S92.323A	371, 1021
S92.323B	371, 1021
S92.323D	345
S92.323G	345
S92.323K	408
S92.323P	408
S92.323S	345
S92.324A	371, 1021
S92.324B	371, 1021
S92.324D	345
S92.324G	345
S92.324K	408
S92.324P	408
S92.324S	345
S92.325A	371, 1021
S92.325B	371, 1021
S92.325D	345
S92.325G	345
S92.325K	408
S92.325P	408
S92.325S	345
S92.326A	371, 1021
S92.326B	371, 1021
S92.326D	345
S92.326G	345
S92.326K	408
S92.326P	408
S92.326S	345
S92.331A	371, 1021
S92.331B	371, 1021
S92.331D	345
S92.331G	345
S92.331K	408
S92.331P	408
S92.331S	345
S92.332A	371, 1021
S92.332B	371, 1021
S92.332D	345
S92.332G	345
S92.332K	408
S92.332P	408
S92.332S	345
S92.333A	371, 1021
S92.333B	371, 1021
S92.333D	345
S92.333G	345
S92.333K	408
S92.333P	408
S92.333S	345
S92.334A	371, 1021
S92.334B	371, 1021
S92.334D	345
S92.334G	345
S92.334K	408
S92.334P	408
S92.334S	345
S92.335A	371, 1021
S92.335B	371, 1021
S92.335D	345
S92.335G	345
S92.335K	408
S92.335P	408
S92.335S	345
S92.336A	371, 1021
S92.336B	371, 1021
S92.336D	345
S92.336G	345
S92.336K	408
S92.336P	408
S92.336S	345
S92.341A	371, 1021
S92.341B	371, 1021
S92.341D	345
S92.341G	345
S92.341K	408
S92.341P	408
S92.341S	345
S92.342A	371, 1021
S92.342B	371, 1021
S92.342D	345
S92.342G	345
S92.342K	408
S92.342P	408
S92.342S	345
S92.343A	371, 1021
S92.343B	371, 1021
S92.343G	345
S92.343K	408
S92.343P	408
S92.343S	345
S92.344A	371, 1021
S92.344B	371, 1021
S92.344G	345
S92.344K	408
S92.344P	408
S92.344S	345
S92.345A	371, 1021
S92.345B	371, 1021
S92.345G	345
S92.345K	408
S92.345P	408
S92.345S	345
S92.346A	371, 1021
S92.346B	371, 1021
S92.346D	345
S92.346K	408
S92.346P	408
S92.346S	345
S92.351A	371, 1021
S92.351B	371, 1021
S92.351D	345
S92.351G	345
S92.351K	408
S92.351P	408
S92.351S	345
S92.352A	371, 1021
S92.352B	371, 1021
S92.352D	345
S92.352G	345
S92.352K	408
S92.352P	408
S92.352S	345
S92.353A	371, 1021
S92.353B	371, 1021
S92.353D	345
S92.353G	345
S92.353K	408
S92.353P	408
S92.353S	345
S92.354A	371, 1021
S92.354B	371, 1021
S92.354D	345
S92.354G	345
S92.354K	408
S92.354P	408
S92.354S	345
S92.355A	371, 1021
S92.355B	371, 1021
S92.355D	345
S92.355G	345
S92.355K	408
S92.355P	408
S92.355S	345
S92.356A	371, 1021
S92.356B	371, 1021
S92.356D	345
S92.356G	345
S92.356K	408
S92.356P	408
S92.356S	345
S92.401A	371, 1021
S92.401B	371, 1021
S92.401D	345
S92.401G	345
S92.401K	408
S92.401P	408
S92.401S	345
S92.402A	371, 1021
S92.402B	371, 1021
S92.402D	345
S92.402G	345
S92.402K	408
S92.402P	408
S92.402S	345
S92.403A	371, 1021
S92.403B	371, 1021
S92.403D	345
S92.403G	345
S92.403K	408
S92.403P	408
S92.403S	345
S92.404A	371, 1021
S92.404B	371, 1021
S92.404D	345
S92.404G	345
S92.404K	408
S92.404P	408
S92.404S	345
S92.405A	371, 1021
S92.405B	371, 1021
S92.405D	345
S92.405G	345
S92.405K	408
S92.405P	408
S92.405S	345
S92.406A	371, 1021
S92.406B	371, 1021
S92.406D	345
S92.406G	345
S92.406K	408
S92.406P	408
S92.406S	345
S92.411A	371, 1021
S92.411B	371, 1021
S92.411D	345
S92.411G	345
S92.411K	408
S92.411P	408
S92.411S	345
S92.412A	371, 1021
S92.412B	372, 1021
S92.412D	345
S92.412G	345
S92.412K	408
S92.412P	408
S92.412S	345
S92.413A	372, 1021
S92.413B	372, 1021
S92.413D	345
S92.413G	345
S92.413K	408
S92.413P	408
S92.413S	346
S92.414A	372, 1021
S92.414B	372, 1021
S92.414D	346
S92.414G	346
S92.414K	408
S92.414P	408
S92.414S	346
S92.415A	372, 1021
S92.415B	372, 1021
S92.415D	346
S92.415G	346
S92.415K	408
S92.415P	408
S92.415S	346
S92.416A	372, 1021
S92.416B	372, 1021
S92.416D	346
S92.416G	346
S92.416K	408
S92.416P	408
S92.416S	346
S92.421A	372, 1021
S92.421B	372, 1021
S92.421D	346
S92.421G	346
S92.421K	408
S92.421P	408
S92.421S	346
S92.422A	372, 1021
S92.422B	372, 1021
S92.422D	346
S92.422G	346

Code	Page	Code	Page	Code	Page	Code	Page	Code	Page	Code	Page
S92.422K	408	S92.506S	346	S92.532B	372, 1022	S92.909G	346	S93.124S	372	S93.322S	373
S92.422P	408	S92.511A	372, 1022	S92.532D	346	S92.909K	408	S93.125A	372, 1022	S93.323A	373, 1022
S92.422S	346	S92.511B	372, 1022	S92.532G	346	S92.909P	408	S93.125D	821	S93.323D	822
S92.423A	372, 1021	S92.511D	346	S92.532K	408	S92.909S	346	S93.125S	372	S93.323S	373
S92.423B	372, 1021	S92.511G	346	S92.532P	408	S92.911A	372, 1022	S93.126A	372, 1022	S93.324A	373, 1022
S92.423D	346	S92.511K	408	S92.532S	346	S92.911B	372, 1022	S93.126D	821	S93.324D	822
S92.423G	346	S92.511P	408	S92.533A	372, 1022	S92.911D	346	S93.126S	372	S93.324S	373
S92.423K	408	S92.511S	346	S92.533B	372, 1022	S92.911G	346	S93.129A	372, 1022	S93.325A	373, 1022
S92.423P	408	S92.512A	372, 1022	S92.533D	346	S92.911K	408	S93.129D	821	S93.325D	822
S92.423S	346	S92.512B	372, 1022	S92.533G	346	S92.911P	408	S93.129S	372	S93.325S	373
S92.424A	372, 1021	S92.512D	346	S92.533K	408	S92.911S	346	S93.131A	372, 1022	S93.326A	373, 1022
S92.424B	372, 1021	S92.512G	346	S92.533P	408	S92.912A	372, 1022	S93.131D	821	S93.326D	822
S92.424D	346	S92.512K	408	S92.533S	346	S92.912B	372, 1022	S93.131S	372	S93.326S	373
S92.424G	346	S92.512P	408	S92.534A	372, 1022	S92.912D	346	S93.132A	372, 1022	S93.331A	373, 1022
S92.424K	408	S92.512S	346	S92.534B	372, 1022	S92.912G	346	S93.132D	821	S93.331D	822
S92.424P	408	S92.513A	372, 1022	S92.534D	346	S92.912K	408	S93.132S	372	S93.331S	373
S92.424S	346	S92.513B	372, 1022	S92.534G	346	S92.912P	408	S93.133A	372, 1022	S93.332A	373, 1022
S92.425A	372, 1021	S92.513D	346	S92.534K	408	S92.912S	346	S93.133D	821	S93.332D	822
S92.425B	372, 1021	S92.513G	346	S92.534P	408	S92.919A	372, 1022	S93.133S	372	S93.332S	373
S92.425D	346	S92.513K	408	S92.534S	346	S92.919B	372, 1022	S93.134A	372, 1022	S93.333A	373, 1022
S92.425G	346	S92.513P	408	S92.535A	372, 1022	S92.919D	346	S93.134D	821	S93.333D	822
S92.425K	408	S92.513S	346	S92.535B	372, 1022	S92.919G	346	S93.134S	372	S93.333S	373
S92.425P	408	S92.514A	372, 1022	S92.535D	346	S92.919K	408	S93.135A	372, 1022	S93.334A	373, 1022
S92.425S	346	S92.514B	372, 1022	S92.535G	346	S92.919P	408	S93.135D	821	S93.334D	822
S92.426A	372, 1021	S92.514D	346	S92.535K	408	S92.919S	346	S93.135S	372	S93.334S	373
S92.426B	372, 1021	S92.514G	346	S92.535P	408	S93.01XA	372, 1022	S93.136A	372, 1022	S93.335A	373, 1022
S92.426D	346	S92.514K	408	S92.535S	346	S93.01XD	821	S93.136D	821	S93.335D	822
S92.426G	346	S92.514P	408	S92.536A	372, 1022	S93.01XS	372	S93.136S	372	S93.335S	373
S92.426K	408	S92.514S	346	S92.536B	372, 1022	S93.02XA	372, 1022	S93.139A	372, 1022	S93.336A	373, 1022
S92.426P	408	S92.515A	372, 1022	S92.536D	346	S93.02XD	821	S93.139D	822	S93.336D	822
S92.426S	346	S92.515B	372, 1022	S92.536G	346	S93.02XS	372	S93.139S	372	S93.336S	373
S92.491A	372, 1021	S92.515D	346	S92.536K	408	S93.03XA	372, 1022	S93.141A	372, 1022	S93.401A	373, 1022
S92.491B	372, 1021	S92.515G	346	S92.536P	408	S93.03XD	821	S93.141D	822	S93.401D	822
S92.491D	346	S92.515K	408	S92.536S	346	S93.03XS	372	S93.141S	373	S93.401S	373
S92.491G	346	S92.515P	408	S92.591A	372, 1022	S93.04XA	372, 1022	S93.142A	372, 1022	S93.402A	373, 1022
S92.491K	408	S92.515S	346	S92.591B	372, 1022	S93.04XD	821	S93.142D	822	S93.402D	822
S92.491P	408	S92.516A	372, 1022	S92.591D	346	S93.04XS	372	S93.142S	372	S93.402S	373
S92.491S	346	S92.516B	372, 1022	S92.591G	346	S93.05XA	372, 1022	S93.143A	372, 1022	S93.409A	373, 1022
S92.492A	372, 1021	S92.516D	346	S92.591K	408	S93.05XD	821	S93.143D	822	S93.409D	822
S92.492B	372, 1021	S92.516G	346	S92.591P	408	S93.05XS	372	S93.143S	372	S93.409S	373
S92.492D	346	S92.516K	408	S92.591S	346	S93.06XA	372, 1022	S93.144A	372, 1022	S93.411A	373, 1022
S92.492G	346	S92.516P	408	S92.592A	372, 1022	S93.06XD	821	S93.144D	822	S93.411D	822
S92.492K	408	S92.516S	346	S92.592B	372, 1022	S93.06XS	372	S93.144S	372	S93.411S	373
S92.492P	408	S92.521A	372, 1022	S92.592D	346	S93.101A	372, 1022	S93.145A	372, 1022	S93.412A	373, 1022
S92.492S	346	S92.521B	372, 1022	S92.592G	346	S93.101D	821	S93.145D	822	S93.412D	822
S92.499A	372, 1021	S92.521D	346	S92.592K	408	S93.101S	372	S93.145S	373	S93.412S	373
S92.499B	372, 1021	S92.521G	346	S92.592P	408	S93.102A	372, 1022	S93.146A	373, 1022	S93.419A	373, 1022
S92.499D	346	S92.521K	408	S92.592S	346	S93.102D	821	S93.146D	822	S93.419D	822
S92.499G	346	S92.521P	408	S92.599A	372, 1022	S93.102S	372	S93.146S	373	S93.419S	373
S92.499K	408	S92.521S	346	S92.599B	372, 1022	S93.103A	372, 1022	S93.149A	373, 1022	S93.421A	373, 1022
S92.499P	408	S92.522A	372, 1022	S92.599D	346	S93.103D	821	S93.149D	822	S93.421D	822
S92.499S	346	S92.522B	372, 1022	S92.599G	346	S93.103S	372	S93.149S	373	S93.421S	373
S92.501A	372, 1021	S92.522D	346	S92.599K	408	S93.104A	372, 1022	S93.301A	373, 1022	S93.422A	373, 1022
S92.501B	372, 1021	S92.522G	346	S92.599P	408	S93.104D	821	S93.301D	822	S93.422D	822
S92.501D	346	S92.522K	408	S92.599S	346	S93.104S	372	S93.301S	373	S93.422S	373
S92.501G	346	S92.522P	408	S92.811A	372, 1022	S93.105A	372, 1022	S93.302A	373, 1022	S93.429A	373, 1022
S92.501K	408	S92.522S	346	S92.811B	372, 1022	S93.105D	821	S93.302D	822	S93.429D	822
S92.501P	408	S92.523A	372, 1022	S92.811D	346	S93.105S	372	S93.302S	373	S93.429S	373
S92.501S	346	S92.523B	372, 1022	S92.811G	346	S93.106A	372, 1022	S93.303A	373, 1022	S93.431A	373, 1022
S92.502A	372, 1021	S92.523D	346	S92.811K	408	S93.106D	821	S93.303D	822	S93.431D	822
S92.502B	372, 1021	S92.523G	346	S92.811P	408	S93.106S	372	S93.303S	373	S93.431S	373
S92.502D	346	S92.523K	408	S92.811S	346	S93.111A	372, 1022	S93.304A	373, 1022	S93.432A	373, 1022
S92.502G	346	S92.523P	408	S92.812A	372, 1022	S93.111D	821	S93.304D	822	S93.432D	822
S92.502K	408	S92.523S	346	S92.812B	372, 1022	S93.111S	372	S93.304S	373	S93.432S	373
S92.502P	408	S92.524A	372, 1022	S92.812D	346	S93.112A	372, 1022	S93.305A	373, 1022	S93.439A	373, 1022
S92.502S	346	S92.524B	372, 1022	S92.812G	346	S93.112D	821	S93.305D	822	S93.439D	822
S92.503A	372, 1021	S92.524D	346	S92.812K	408	S93.112S	372	S93.305S	373	S93.439S	373
S92.503B	372, 1021	S92.524G	346	S92.812P	408	S93.113A	372, 1022	S93.306A	373, 1022	S93.491A	373, 1022
S92.503D	346	S92.524K	408	S92.812S	346	S93.113D	821	S93.306D	822	S93.491D	822
S92.503G	346	S92.524P	408	S92.819A	372, 1022	S93.113S	372	S93.306S	373	S93.491S	373
S92.503K	408	S92.524S	346	S92.819B	372, 1022	S93.114A	372, 1022	S93.311A	373, 1022	S93.492A	373, 1022
S92.503P	408	S92.525A	372, 1022	S92.819D	346	S93.114D	821	S93.311D	822	S93.492D	822
S92.503S	346	S92.525B	372, 1022	S92.819G	346	S93.114S	372	S93.311S	373	S93.492S	373
S92.504A	372, 1021	S92.525D	346	S92.819K	408	S93.115A	372, 1022	S93.312A	373, 1022	S93.499A	373, 1022
S92.504B	372, 1021	S92.525G	346	S92.819P	408	S93.115D	821	S93.312D	822	S93.499D	822
S92.504D	346	S92.525K	408	S92.819S	346	S93.115S	372	S93.312S	373	S93.499S	373
S92.504G	346	S92.525P	408	S92.901A	372, 1022	S93.116A	372, 1022	S93.313A	373, 1022	S93.501A	373, 1022
S92.504K	408	S92.525S	346	S92.901B	372, 1022	S93.116D	821	S93.313D	822	S93.501D	822
S92.504P	408	S92.526A	372, 1022	S92.901D	346	S93.116S	372	S93.313S	373	S93.501S	373
S92.504S	346	S92.526B	372, 1022	S92.901G	346	S93.119A	372, 1022	S93.314A	373, 1022	S93.502A	373, 1022
S92.505A	372, 1021	S92.526D	346	S92.901K	408	S93.119D	821	S93.314D	822	S93.502D	822
S92.505B	372, 1022	S92.526G	346	S92.901P	408	S93.119S	372	S93.314S	373	S93.502S	373
S92.505D	346	S92.526K	408	S92.901S	346	S93.121A	372, 1022	S93.315A	373, 1022	S93.503A	373, 1022
S92.505G	346	S92.526P	408	S92.902A	372, 1022	S93.121D	821	S93.315D	822	S93.503D	822
S92.505K	408	S92.526S	346	S92.902B	372, 1022	S93.121S	372	S93.315S	373	S93.503S	373
S92.505P	408	S92.531A	372, 1022	S92.902D	346	S93.122A	372, 1022	S93.316A	373, 1022	S93.504A	373, 1022
S92.505S	346	S92.531B	372, 1022	S92.902G	346	S93.122D	821	S93.316D	822	S93.504D	822
S92.506A	372, 1022	S92.531D	346	S92.902K	408	S93.122S	372	S93.316S	373	S93.504S	373
S92.506B	372, 1022	S92.531G	346	S92.902P	408	S93.123A	372, 1022	S93.321A	373, 1022	S93.505A	373, 1022
S92.506D	346	S92.531K	408	S92.902S	346	S93.123D	821	S93.321D	822	S93.505D	822
S92.506G	346	S92.531P	408	S92.909A	372, 1022	S93.123S	372	S93.321S	373	S93.505S	373
S92.506K	408	S92.531S	346	S92.909B	372, 1022	S93.124A	372, 1022	S93.322A	373, 1022	S93.506A	373, 1022
S92.506P	408	S92.532A	372, 1022	S92.909D	346	S93.124D	821	S93.322D	822	S93.506D	822

Code	Page	Code	Page	Code	Page	Code	Page	Code	Page	Code	Page
S93.506S	373	S94.10XS	54	S95.192A	755, 1023	S96.002A	756, 1023	S96.229A	408, 1023	S97.02XA	756, 1023
S93.509A	373, 1022	S94.11XA	47, 1023	S95.192D	822	S96.002D	822	S96.229D	823	S97.02XD	823
S93.509D	822	S94.11XD	822	S95.192S	171	S96.002S	756	S96.229S	471	S97.02XS	471
S93.509S	373	S94.11XS	54	S95.199A	755, 1023	S96.009A	756, 1023	S96.291A	756, 1023	S97.101A	756, 1023
S93.511A	373, 1022	S94.12XA	47, 1023	S95.199D	822	S96.009D	822	S96.291D	823	S97.101D	823
S93.511D	822	S94.12XD	822	S95.199S	171	S96.009S	756	S96.291S	756	S97.101S	471
S93.511S	373	S94.12XS	54	S95.201A	755, 1023, 1040	S96.011A	373, 1023	S96.292A	756, 1023	S97.102A	756, 1023
S93.512A	373, 1022	S94.20XA	47, 1023, 1040	S95.201D	822	S96.011D	822	S96.292D	823	S97.102D	823
S93.512D	822	S94.20XD	822	S95.201S	171	S96.011S	373	S96.292S	756	S97.102S	471
S93.512S	373	S94.20XS	54	S95.202A	755, 1023, 1040	S96.012A	373, 1023	S96.299A	756, 1023	S97.109A	756, 1023
S93.513A	373, 1022	S94.21XA	47, 1023, 1040	S95.202D	822	S96.012D	822	S96.299D	823	S97.109D	823
S93.513D	822	S94.21XD	822	S95.202S	171	S96.012S	373	S96.299S	756	S97.109S	471
S93.513S	373	S94.21XS	54	S95.209A	755, 1023, 1040	S96.019A	373, 1023	S96.801A	756, 1023	S97.111A	756, 1023
S93.514A	373, 1022	S94.22XA	47, 1023, 1040	S95.209D	822	S96.019D	822	S96.801D	823	S97.111D	823
S93.514D	822	S94.22XD	822	S95.209S	171	S96.019S	373	S96.801S	756	S97.111S	471
S93.514S	373	S94.22XS	54	S95.211A	755, 1023, 1040	S96.021A	408, 1023	S96.802A	756, 1023	S97.112A	756, 1023
S93.515A	373, 1022	S94.30XA	47, 1023	S95.211D	822	S96.021D	822	S96.802D	823	S97.112D	823
S93.515D	822	S94.30XD	822	S95.211S	171	S96.021S	471	S96.802S	756	S97.112S	471
S93.515S	373	S94.30XS	54	S95.212A	755, 1023, 1040	S96.022A	408, 1023	S96.809A	756, 1023	S97.119A	756, 1023
S93.516A	373, 1022	S94.31XA	47, 1023	S95.212D	822	S96.022D	822	S96.809D	823	S97.119D	823
S93.516D	822	S94.31XD	822	S95.212S	171	S96.022S	471	S96.809S	756	S97.119S	471
S93.516S	373	S94.31XS	54	S95.219A	755, 1023, 1040	S96.029A	408, 1023	S96.811A	373, 1023	S97.121A	756, 1023
S93.519A	373, 1022	S94.32XA	47, 1023	S95.219D	822	S96.029D	822	S96.811D	823	S97.121D	823
S93.519D	822	S94.32XD	822	S95.219S	171	S96.029S	471	S96.811S	373	S97.121S	471
S93.519S	373	S94.32XS	54	S95.291A	755, 1023, 1040	S96.091A	756, 1023	S96.812A	373, 1023	S97.122A	756, 1023
S93.521A	373, 1022	S94.8X1A	47, 1023, 1040	S95.291D	822	S96.091D	822	S96.812D	823	S97.122D	823
S93.521D	822	S94.8X1D	822	S95.291S	171	S96.091S	756	S96.812S	373	S97.122S	471
S93.521S	373	S94.8X1S	54	S95.292A	755, 1023, 1040	S96.092A	756, 1023	S96.819A	373, 1023	S97.129A	756, 1023
S93.522A	373, 1022	S94.8X2A	1023, 1040	S95.292D	822	S96.092D	822	S96.819D	823	S97.129D	823
S93.522D	822	S94.8X2A	47	S95.292S	171	S96.092S	756	S96.819S	373	S97.129S	471
S93.522S	373	S94.8X2D	822	S95.299A	756, 1023, 1040	S96.099A	756, 1023	S96.821A	408, 1023	S97.80XA	756, 1023
S93.523A	373, 1022	S94.8X2S	54	S95.299D	822	S96.099D	822	S96.821D	823	S97.80XD	823
S93.523D	822	S94.8X9A	1023, 1040	S95.299S	171	S96.099S	756	S96.821S	471	S97.80XS	471
S93.523S	373	S94.8X9A	47	S95.801A	756, 1023, 1040	S96.101A	756, 1023	S96.822A	408, 1023	S97.81XA	756, 1023
S93.524A	373, 1022	S94.8X9D	822	S95.801D	822	S96.101D	822	S96.822D	823	S97.81XD	823
S93.524D	822	S94.8X9S	54	S95.801S	171	S96.101S	756	S96.822S	471	S97.81XS	471
S93.524S	373	S94.90XA	47, 1023, 1040	S95.802A	756, 1023, 1040	S96.102A	756, 1023	S96.829A	409, 1023	S97.82XA	756, 1023
S93.525A	373, 1022	S94.90XD	822	S95.802D	822	S96.102D	822	S96.829D	823	S97.82XD	823
S93.525D	822	S94.90XS	54	S95.802S	171	S96.102S	756	S96.829S	471	S97.82XS	471
S93.525S	373	S94.91XA	47, 1023, 1040	S95.809A	756, 1023, 1040	S96.109A	756, 1023	S96.891A	1023	S98.011A	756, 1023, 1040
S93.526A	373, 1022	S94.91XD	822	S95.809D	822	S96.109D	822	S96.891A	756	S98.011D	823
S93.526D	822	S94.91XS	54	S95.809S	171	S96.109S	756	S96.891D	823	S98.011S	346
S93.526S	373	S94.92XA	47, 1023, 1040	S95.811A	756, 1023, 1040	S96.111A	373, 1023	S96.891S	756	S98.012A	756, 1023, 1040
S93.529A	373, 1022	S94.92XD	822	S95.811D	822	S96.111D	822	S96.892A	1023	S98.012D	823
S93.529D	822	S94.92XS	54	S95.811S	171	S96.111S	373	S96.892A	756	S98.012S	346
S93.529S	373	S95.001A	755, 1023, 1040	S95.812A	756, 1023, 1040	S96.112A	373, 1023	S96.892D	823	S98.019A	756, 1023, 1040
S93.601A	373, 1022	S95.001D	822	S95.812D	822	S96.112D	822	S96.892S	756	S98.019D	823
S93.601D	822	S95.001S	171	S95.812S	171	S96.112S	373	S96.899A	1023	S98.019S	346
S93.601S	373	S95.002A	755, 1023, 1040	S95.819A	756, 1023, 1040	S96.119A	373, 1023	S96.899A	756	S98.021A	756, 1023, 1040
S93.602A	373, 1022	S95.002D	822	S95.819D	822	S96.119D	822	S96.899D	823	S98.021D	823
S93.602D	822	S95.002S	171	S95.819S	171	S96.119S	373	S96.899S	756	S98.021S	346
S93.602S	373	S95.009A	755, 1023, 1040	S95.891A	1023, 1040	S96.121A	408, 1023	S96.901A	756, 1023	S98.022A	756, 1023, 1040
S93.609A	373, 1022	S95.009D	822	S95.891A	756	S96.121D	822	S96.901D	823	S98.022D	823
S93.609D	822	S95.009S	171	S95.891D	822	S96.121S	471	S96.901S	756	S98.022S	346
S93.609S	373	S95.011A	755, 1023, 1040	S95.891S	171	S96.122A	408, 1023	S96.902A	756, 1023	S98.029A	756, 1023, 1040
S93.611A	373, 1022	S95.011D	822	S95.892A	1023, 1040	S96.122D	822	S96.902D	823	S98.029D	823
S93.611D	822	S95.011S	171	S95.892A	756	S96.122S	471	S96.902S	756	S98.029S	346
S93.611S	373	S95.012A	755, 1023, 1040	S95.892D	822	S96.129A	408, 1023	S96.909A	756, 1023	S98.111A	756, 1023
S93.612A	373, 1022	S95.012D	822	S95.892S	171	S96.129D	822	S96.909D	823	S98.111D	823
S93.612D	822	S95.012S	171	S95.899A	1023, 1040	S96.129S	471	S96.909S	756	S98.111S	346
S93.612S	373	S95.019A	755, 1023, 1040	S95.899A	756	S96.191A	756, 1023	S96.911A	373, 1023	S98.112A	756, 1023
S93.619A	373, 1022	S95.019D	822	S95.899D	822	S96.191D	822	S96.911D	823	S98.112D	823
S93.619D	822	S95.019S	171	S95.899S	171	S96.191S	756	S96.911S	374	S98.112S	346
S93.619S	373	S95.091A	755, 1023, 1040	S95.901A	756, 1023	S96.192A	756, 1023	S96.912A	374, 1023	S98.119A	756, 1023
S93.621A	373, 1022	S95.091D	822	S95.901D	822	S96.192D	822	S96.912D	823	S98.119D	823
S93.621D	822	S95.091S	171	S95.901S	171	S96.192S	756	S96.912S	374	S98.119S	346
S93.621S	373	S95.092A	755, 1023, 1040	S95.902A	756, 1023	S96.199A	756, 1023	S96.919A	374, 1023	S98.121A	756, 1023
S93.622A	373, 1022	S95.092D	822	S95.902D	822	S96.199D	822	S96.919D	823	S98.121D	823
S93.622D	822	S95.092S	171	S95.902S	171	S96.199S	756	S96.919S	374	S98.121S	346
S93.622S	373	S95.099A	755, 1023, 1040	S95.909A	756, 1023	S96.201A	756, 1023	S96.921A	409, 1023	S98.122A	756, 1023
S93.629A	373, 1022	S95.099D	822	S95.909D	822	S96.201D	822	S96.921D	823	S98.122D	823
S93.629D	822	S95.099S	171	S95.909S	171	S96.201S	756	S96.921S	471	S98.122S	346
S93.629S	373	S95.101A	755, 1023	S95.911A	756, 1023	S96.202A	756, 1023	S96.922A	409, 1023	S98.129A	756, 1023
S93.691A	373, 1022	S95.101D	822	S95.911D	822	S96.202D	822	S96.922D	823	S98.129D	823
S93.691D	822	S95.101S	171	S95.911S	171	S96.202S	756	S96.922S	471	S98.129S	346
S93.691S	373	S95.102A	755, 1023	S95.912A	756, 1023	S96.209A	756, 1023	S96.929A	409, 1023	S98.131A	756, 1023
S93.692A	373, 1022	S95.102D	822	S95.912D	822	S96.209D	822	S96.929D	823	S98.131D	823
S93.692D	822	S95.102S	171	S95.912S	171	S96.209S	756	S96.929S	471	S98.131S	346
S93.692S	373	S95.109A	755, 1023	S95.919A	756, 1023	S96.211A	373, 1023	S96.991A	756, 1023	S98.132A	756, 1023
S93.699A	373, 1023	S95.109D	822	S95.919D	822	S96.211D	822	S96.991D	823	S98.132D	823
S93.699D	822	S95.109S	171	S95.919S	171	S96.211S	373	S96.991S	756	S98.132S	346
S93.699S	373	S95.111A	755, 1023	S95.991A	756, 1023	S96.212A	373, 1023	S96.992A	756, 1023	S98.139A	756, 1023
S94.00XA	47, 1023	S95.111D	822	S95.991D	822	S96.212D	822	S96.992D	823	S98.139D	823
S94.00XD	822	S95.111S	171	S95.991S	171	S96.212S	373	S96.992S	756	S98.139S	346
S94.00XS	54	S95.112A	755, 1023	S95.992A	756, 1023	S96.219A	373, 1023	S96.999A	756, 1023	S98.141A	756, 1023
S94.01XA	47, 1023	S95.112D	822	S95.992D	822	S96.219D	822	S96.999D	823	S98.141D	823
S94.01XD	822	S95.112S	171	S95.992S	171	S96.219S	373	S96.999S	756	S98.141S	346
S94.01XS	54	S95.119A	755, 1023	S95.999A	756, 1023	S96.221A	408, 1023	S97.00XA	756, 1023	S98.142A	756, 1023
S94.02XA	47, 1023	S95.119D	822	S95.999D	822	S96.221D	822	S97.00XD	823	S98.142D	823
S94.02XD	822	S95.119S	171	S95.999S	171	S96.221S	471	S97.00XS	471	S98.142S	346
S94.02XS	54	S95.191A	755, 1023	S96.001A	756, 1023	S96.222A	408, 1023	S97.01XA	756, 1023	S98.149A	756, 1023
S94.10XA	47, 1023	S95.191D	822	S96.001D	822	S96.222D	823	S97.01XD	823	S98.149D	823
S94.10XD	822	S95.191S	171	S96.001S	756	S96.222S	471	S97.01XS	471	S98.149S	346

Code	Page	Code	Page	Code	Page	Code	Page	Code	Page	Code	Page
S98.211A	756, 1023	S99.019K	823	S99.101S	757	S99.149B	757, 1024	S99.231G	824	S99.929A	757, 1024
S98.211D	823	S99.019P	823	S99.102A	757, 1024	S99.149D	824	S99.231K	824	S99.929D	824
S98.211S	346	S99.019S	756	S99.102B	757, 1024	S99.149G	824	S99.231P	824	S99.929S	757
S98.212A	756, 1023	S99.021A	756, 1024	S99.102D	823	S99.149K	824	S99.231S	757	T07.XXXA	757, 1024
S98.212D	823	S99.021B	756, 1024	S99.102G	823	S99.149P	824	S99.232A	757, 1024	T07.XXXD	824
S98.212S	346	S99.021D	823	S99.102K	823	S99.149S	757	S99.232B	757, 1024	T07.XXXS	757
S98.219A	756, 1023	S99.021G	823	S99.102P	823	S99.191A	757, 1024	S99.232G	824	T14.8XXA	757, 1024
S98.219D	823	S99.021K	823	S99.102S	757	S99.191B	757, 1024	S99.232K	824	T14.8XXD	824
S98.219S	346	S99.021P	823	S99.109A	757, 1024	S99.191D	824	S99.232P	824	T14.8XXS	757
S98.221A	756, 1023	S99.021S	756	S99.109B	757, 1024	S99.191G	824	S99.232S	757	T14.90XA	757, 1024
S98.221D	823	S99.022A	756, 1024	S99.109D	823	S99.191K	824	S99.239A	757, 1024	T14.90XD	824
S98.221S	346	S99.022B	756, 1024	S99.109G	823	S99.191P	824	S99.239B	757, 1024	T14.90XS	757
S98.222A	756, 1023	S99.022D	823	S99.109K	823	S99.191S	757	S99.239D	824	T14.91XA	757, 1024
S98.222D	823	S99.022G	823	S99.109P	823	S99.192A	757, 1024	S99.239G	824	T14.91XD	824
S98.222S	346	S99.022K	823	S99.109S	757	S99.192B	757, 1024	S99.239K	824	T14.91XS	757
S98.229A	756, 1023	S99.022P	823	S99.111A	757, 1024	S99.192D	824	S99.239P	824	T15.00XA	66
S98.229D	823	S99.022S	756	S99.111B	757, 1024	S99.192G	824	S99.239S	757	T15.00XD	824
S98.229S	346	S99.029A	756, 1024	S99.111D	823	S99.192K	824	S99.241A	757, 1024	T15.00XS	757
S98.311A	756, 1023, 1040	S99.029B	756, 1024	S99.111G	823	S99.192P	824	S99.241B	757, 1024	T15.01XA	66
S98.311D	823	S99.029D	823	S99.111K	823	S99.192S	757	S99.241D	824	T15.01XD	824
S98.311S	346	S99.029G	823	S99.111P	823	S99.199A	757, 1024	S99.241G	824	T15.01XS	757
S98.312A	756, 1023, 1040	S99.029K	823	S99.111S	757	S99.199B	757, 1024	S99.241K	824	T15.02XA	66
S98.312D	823	S99.029P	823	S99.112A	757, 1024	S99.199D	824	S99.241P	824	T15.02XD	824
S98.312S	346	S99.029S	756	S99.112B	757, 1024	S99.199G	824	S99.241S	757	T15.02XS	757
S98.319A	756, 1023, 1040	S99.031A	756, 1024	S99.112D	823	S99.199K	824	S99.242A	757, 1024	T15.10XA	66
S98.319D	823	S99.031B	756, 1024	S99.112G	823	S99.199P	824	S99.242B	757, 1024	T15.10XD	824
S98.319S	346	S99.031D	823	S99.112K	823	S99.199S	757	S99.242D	824	T15.10XS	757
S98.321A	756, 1023, 1040	S99.031G	823	S99.112P	823	S99.201A	757, 1024	S99.242G	824	T15.11XA	66
S98.321D	823	S99.031K	823	S99.112S	757	S99.201B	757, 1024	S99.242K	824	T15.11XD	824
S98.321S	346	S99.031P	823	S99.119A	757, 1024	S99.201D	824	S99.242P	824	T15.11XS	757
S98.322A	756, 1023, 1040	S99.031S	756	S99.119B	757, 1024	S99.201G	824	S99.242S	757	T15.12XA	66
S98.322D	823	S99.032A	756, 1024	S99.119D	823	S99.201K	824	S99.249A	757, 1024	T15.12XD	824
S98.322S	346	S99.032B	756, 1024	S99.119G	823	S99.201P	824	S99.249B	757, 1024	T15.12XS	757
S98.329A	756, 1023, 1040	S99.032D	823	S99.119K	824	S99.201S	757	S99.249D	824	T15.80XA	66
S98.329D	823	S99.032G	823	S99.119P	824	S99.202A	757, 1024	S99.249G	824	T15.80XD	824
S98.329S	347	S99.032K	823	S99.119S	757	S99.202B	757, 1024	S99.249K	824	T15.80XS	757
S98.911A	756, 1023, 1040	S99.032P	823	S99.121A	757, 1024	S99.202D	824	S99.249P	824	T15.81XA	66
S98.911D	823	S99.032S	756	S99.121B	757, 1024	S99.202G	824	S99.249S	757	T15.81XD	824
S98.911S	347	S99.039A	756, 1024	S99.121D	823	S99.202K	824	S99.291A	757, 1024	T15.81XS	757
S98.912A	756, 1023, 1040	S99.039B	756, 1024	S99.121G	824	S99.202P	824	S99.291B	757, 1024	T15.82XA	66
S98.912D	823	S99.039D	823	S99.121K	824	S99.202S	757	S99.291D	824	T15.82XD	824
S98.912S	347	S99.039G	823	S99.121P	824	S99.209A	757, 1024	S99.291G	824	T15.82XS	757
S98.919A	756, 1023, 1040	S99.039K	823	S99.121S	757	S99.209B	757, 1024	S99.291K	824	T15.90XA	66
S98.919D	823	S99.039P	823	S99.122A	757, 1024	S99.209D	824	S99.291P	824	T15.90XD	824
S98.919S	347	S99.039S	756	S99.122B	757, 1024	S99.209G	824	S99.291S	757	T15.90XS	757
S98.921A	756, 1023, 1040	S99.041A	756, 1024	S99.122D	824	S99.209K	824	S99.292A	757, 1024	T15.91XA	66
S98.921D	823	S99.041B	756, 1024	S99.122G	824	S99.209P	824	S99.292B	757, 1024	T15.91XD	824
S98.921S	347	S99.041D	823	S99.122K	824	S99.209S	757	S99.292D	824	T15.91XS	757
S98.922A	756, 1023, 1040	S99.041G	823	S99.122P	824	S99.211A	757, 1024	S99.292G	824	T15.92XA	66
S98.922D	823	S99.041K	823	S99.122S	757	S99.211B	757, 1024	S99.292K	824	T15.92XD	824
S98.922S	347	S99.041P	823	S99.129A	757, 1024	S99.211D	824	S99.292P	824	T15.92XS	757
S98.929A	756, 1024, 1040	S99.041S	756	S99.129B	757, 1024	S99.211G	824	S99.292S	757	T16.1XXA	87
S98.929D	823	S99.042A	756, 1024	S99.129D	824	S99.211K	824	S99.299A	757, 1024	T16.1XXD	824
S98.929S	347	S99.042B	756, 1024	S99.129G	824	S99.211P	824	S99.299B	757, 1024	T16.1XXS	757
S99.001A	756, 1024	S99.042D	823	S99.129K	824	S99.211S	757	S99.299D	824	T16.2XXA	87
S99.001B	756, 1024	S99.042G	823	S99.129P	824	S99.212A	757, 1024	S99.299G	824	T16.2XXD	824
S99.001D	823	S99.042K	823	S99.129S	757	S99.212B	757, 1024	S99.299K	824	T16.2XXS	757
S99.001G	823	S99.042P	823	S99.131A	757, 1024	S99.212D	824	S99.299P	824	T16.9XXA	87
S99.001K	823	S99.042S	756	S99.131B	757, 1024	S99.212G	824	S99.299S	757	T16.9XXD	824
S99.001P	823	S99.049A	756, 1024	S99.131D	824	S99.212K	824	S99.811A	757, 1024	T16.9XXS	757
S99.001S	756	S99.049B	756, 1024	S99.131G	824	S99.212P	824	S99.811D	824	T17.0XXA	87
S99.002A	756, 1024	S99.049D	823	S99.131K	824	S99.212S	757	S99.811S	757	T17.0XXD	824
S99.002B	756, 1024	S99.049G	823	S99.131S	757	S99.219A	757, 1024	S99.812A	757, 1024	T17.0XXS	757
S99.002D	823	S99.049K	823	S99.132A	757, 1024	S99.219B	757, 1024	S99.812D	824	T17.1XXA	87
S99.002G	823	S99.049P	823	S99.132B	757, 1024	S99.219D	824	S99.812S	757	T17.1XXD	824
S99.002K	823	S99.049S	757	S99.132D	824	S99.219G	824	S99.819A	757, 1024	T17.1XXS	757
S99.002P	823	S99.091A	757, 1024	S99.132G	824	S99.219P	824	S99.819D	824	T17.200A	4, 87
S99.002S	756	S99.091B	757, 1024	S99.132K	824	S99.219S	757	S99.819S	757	T17.200D	824
S99.009A	756, 1024	S99.091D	823	S99.132P	824	S99.221A	757, 1024	S99.821A	757, 1024	T17.200S	757
S99.009B	756, 1024	S99.091G	823	S99.132S	757	S99.221B	757, 1024	S99.821D	824	T17.208A	87
S99.009D	823	S99.091K	823	S99.139A	757, 1024	S99.221D	824	S99.821S	757	T17.208A	4
S99.009G	823	S99.091P	823	S99.139B	757, 1024	S99.221G	824	S99.822A	757, 1024	T17.208D	824
S99.009K	823	S99.091S	757	S99.139D	824	S99.221K	824	S99.822D	824	T17.208S	757
S99.009P	823	S99.092A	757, 1024	S99.139G	824	S99.221P	824	S99.822S	757	T17.210A	4, 87
S99.009S	756	S99.092B	757, 1024	S99.139K	824	S99.221S	757	S99.829A	757, 1024	T17.210D	824
S99.011A	756, 1024	S99.092D	823	S99.139P	824	S99.222A	757, 1024	S99.829D	824	T17.210S	757
S99.011B	756, 1024	S99.092G	823	S99.139S	757	S99.222B	757, 1024	S99.829S	757	T17.218A	87
S99.011D	823	S99.092K	823	S99.141A	757, 1024	S99.222D	824	S99.911A	757, 1024	T17.218A	4
S99.011G	823	S99.092P	823	S99.141B	757, 1024	S99.222G	824	S99.911D	824	T17.218D	824
S99.011K	823	S99.092S	757	S99.141D	824	S99.222K	824	S99.911S	757	T17.218S	757
S99.011P	823	S99.099A	757, 1024	S99.141G	824	S99.222P	824	S99.912A	757, 1024	T17.220A	4, 87
S99.011S	756	S99.099B	757, 1024	S99.141K	824	S99.222S	757	S99.912D	824	T17.220D	824
S99.012A	756, 1024	S99.099D	823	S99.141P	824	S99.229A	757, 1024	S99.912S	757	T17.220S	757
S99.012B	756, 1024	S99.099G	823	S99.141S	757	S99.229B	757, 1024	S99.919A	757, 1024	T17.228A	4, 87
S99.012D	823	S99.099K	823	S99.142A	757, 1024	S99.229D	824	S99.919D	824	T17.228D	824
S99.012G	823	S99.099P	823	S99.142B	757, 1024	S99.229G	824	S99.919S	757	T17.228S	757
S99.012K	823	S99.099S	757	S99.142D	824	S99.229K	824	S99.921A	757, 1024	T17.290A	4, 87
S99.012P	823	S99.101A	757, 1024	S99.142G	824	S99.229P	824	S99.921D	824	T17.290D	824
S99.012S	756	S99.101B	757, 1024	S99.142K	824	S99.229S	757	S99.921S	757	T17.290S	757
S99.019A	756, 1024	S99.101D	823	S99.142P	824	S99.231A	757, 1024	S99.922A	757, 1024	T17.298A	4
S99.019B	756, 1024	S99.101G	823	S99.142S	757	S99.231B	757, 1024	S99.922D	824	T17.298A	87
S99.019D	823	S99.101K	823	S99.149A	757, 1024	S99.231D	824	S99.922S	757	T17.298D	824
S99.019G	823	S99.101P	823							T17.298S	758

Code	Page	Code	Page	Code	Page	Code	Page	Code	Page	Code	Page
T17.300A	4, 87	T17.890D	825	T19.9XXD	825	T20.26XD	825	T20.54XD	825	T21.04XD	825
T17.300D	824	T17.890S	758	T19.9XXS	758	T20.26XS	471	T20.54XS	471	T21.04XS	472
T17.300S	758	T17.898A	107	T20.00XA	791	T20.27XA	791	T20.55XA	791	T21.05XA	791
T17.308A	87	T17.898D	825	T20.00XD	825	T20.27XD	825	T20.55XD	825	T21.05XD	825
T17.308A	4	T17.898S	758	T20.00XS	471	T20.27XS	471	T20.55XS	471	T21.05XS	472
T17.308D	824	T17.900A	107	T20.011A	791	T20.29XA	791	T20.56XA	791	T21.06XA	791
T17.308S	758	T17.900D	825	T20.011D	825	T20.29XD	825	T20.56XD	825	T21.06XD	825
T17.310A	4, 87	T17.900S	758	T20.011S	471	T20.29XS	471	T20.56XS	471	T21.06XS	472
T17.310D	824	T17.908A	107	T20.012A	791	T20.30XA	782, 785, 788, 790	T20.57XA	791	T21.07XA	791
T17.310S	758	T17.908D	825	T20.012D	825	T20.30XD	825	T20.57XD	825	T21.07XD	825
T17.318A	4, 87	T17.908S	758	T20.012S	471	T20.30XS	471	T20.57XS	471	T21.07XS	472
T17.318D	824	T17.910A	107	T20.019A	791	T20.311A	782, 785, 788, 790	T20.59XA	791	T21.09XA	791
T17.318S	758	T17.910D	825	T20.019D	825	T20.311D	825	T20.59XD	825	T21.09XD	825
T17.320A	4, 87	T17.910S	758	T20.019S	471	T20.311S	471	T20.59XS	471	T21.09XS	472
T17.320D	824	T17.918A	107	T20.02XA	791	T20.312A	782, 785, 788, 790	T20.60XA	791	T21.10XA	791
T17.320S	758	T17.918D	825	T20.02XD	825	T20.312D	825	T20.60XD	825	T21.10XD	825
T17.328A	4, 87	T17.918S	758	T20.02XS	471	T20.312S	471	T20.60XS	471	T21.10XS	472
T17.328D	824	T17.920A	107	T20.03XA	791	T20.319A	782, 785, 788, 790	T20.611A	791	T21.11XA	791
T17.328S	758	T17.920D	825	T20.03XD	825	T20.319D	825	T20.611D	825	T21.11XD	825
T17.390A	4, 87	T17.920S	758	T20.03XS	471	T20.319S	471	T20.611S	471	T21.11XS	472
T17.390D	824	T17.928A	107	T20.04XA	791	T20.32XA	782, 785, 788, 790	T20.612A	791	T21.12XA	791
T17.390S	758	T17.928D	825	T20.04XD	825	T20.32XD	825	T20.612D	825	T21.12XD	825
T17.398A	87	T17.928S	758	T20.04XS	471	T20.32XS	471	T20.612S	471	T21.12XS	472
T17.398A	4	T17.990A	107	T20.05XA	791	T20.33XA	782, 785, 788, 790	T20.619A	791	T21.13XA	791
T17.398D	824	T17.990D	825	T20.05XD	825	T20.33XD	825	T20.619D	825	T21.13XD	825
T17.398S	758	T17.990S	758	T20.05XS	471	T20.33XS	471	T20.619S	471	T21.13XS	472
T17.400A	107	T17.998A	107	T20.06XA	791	T20.34XA	782, 785, 788, 790	T20.62XA	791	T21.14XA	791
T17.400D	824	T17.998D	825	T20.06XD	825	T20.34XD	825	T20.62XD	825	T21.14XD	825
T17.400S	758	T17.998S	758	T20.06XS	471	T20.34XS	471	T20.62XS	471	T21.14XS	472
T17.408A	107	T18.0XXA	4, 88	T20.07XA	791	T20.35XA	782, 785, 788, 790	T20.63XA	791	T21.15XA	791
T17.408D	824	T18.0XXD	825	T20.07XD	825	T20.35XD	825	T20.63XD	825	T21.15XD	825
T17.408S	758	T18.0XXS	758	T20.07XS	471	T20.35XS	471	T20.63XS	471	T21.15XS	472
T17.410A	107	T18.100A	197	T20.09XA	791	T20.36XA	782, 785, 788, 790	T20.64XA	791	T21.16XA	791
T17.410D	824	T18.100D	825	T20.09XD	825	T20.36XD	825	T20.64XD	825	T21.16XD	825
T17.410S	758	T18.100S	758	T20.09XS	471	T20.36XS	471	T20.64XS	471	T21.16XS	472
T17.418A	107	T18.108A	197	T20.10XA	791	T20.37XA	782, 785, 788, 790	T20.65XA	791	T21.17XA	791
T17.418D	825	T18.108D	825	T20.10XD	825	T20.37XD	825	T20.65XD	825	T21.17XD	825
T17.418S	758	T18.108S	758	T20.10XS	471	T20.37XS	471	T20.65XS	471	T21.17XS	472
T17.420A	107	T18.110A	197	T20.111A	791	T20.39XA	782, 786, 788, 790	T20.66XA	791	T21.19XA	791
T17.420D	825	T18.110D	825	T20.111D	825	T20.39XD	825	T20.66XD	825	T21.19XD	825
T17.420S	758	T18.110S	758	T20.111S	471	T20.39XS	471	T20.66XS	471	T21.19XS	472
T17.428A	107	T18.118A	197	T20.112A	791	T20.40XA	791	T20.67XA	791	T21.20XA	791
T17.428D	825	T18.118D	825	T20.112D	825	T20.40XD	825	T20.67XD	825	T21.20XD	825
T17.428S	758	T18.118S	758	T20.112S	471	T20.40XS	471	T20.67XS	471	T21.20XS	472
T17.490A	107	T18.120A	197	T20.119A	791	T20.411A	791	T20.69XA	791	T21.21XA	791
T17.490D	825	T18.120D	825	T20.119D	825	T20.411D	825	T20.69XD	825	T21.21XD	825
T17.490S	758	T18.120S	758	T20.119S	471	T20.411S	471	T20.69XS	471	T21.21XS	472
T17.498A	107	T18.128A	197	T20.12XA	791	T20.412A	791	T20.70XA	782, 786, 788, 790	T21.22XA	791
T17.498D	825	T18.128D	825	T20.12XD	825	T20.412D	825	T20.70XD	825	T21.22XD	825
T17.498S	758	T18.128S	758	T20.12XS	471	T20.412S	471	T20.70XS	471	T21.22XS	472
T17.500A	107	T18.190A	197	T20.13XA	791	T20.419A	791	T20.711A	782, 786, 788, 790	T21.23XA	791
T17.500D	825	T18.190D	825	T20.13XD	825	T20.419D	825	T20.711D	825	T21.23XD	825
T17.500S	758	T18.190S	758	T20.13XS	471	T20.419S	471	T20.711S	471	T21.23XS	472
T17.508A	107	T18.198A	197	T20.14XA	791	T20.42XA	791	T20.712A	782, 786, 788, 790	T21.24XA	791
T17.508D	825	T18.198D	825	T20.14XD	825	T20.42XD	825	T20.712D	825	T21.24XD	825
T17.508S	758	T18.198S	758	T20.14XS	471	T20.42XS	471	T20.712S	471	T21.24XS	472
T17.510A	107	T18.2XXA	197	T20.15XA	791	T20.43XA	791	T20.719A	782, 786, 788, 790	T21.25XA	791
T17.510D	825	T18.2XXD	825	T20.15XD	825	T20.43XD	825	T20.719D	825	T21.25XD	825
T17.510S	758	T18.2XXS	758	T20.15XS	471	T20.43XS	471	T20.719S	471	T21.25XS	472
T17.518A	107	T18.3XXA	197	T20.16XA	791	T20.44XA	791	T20.72XA	782, 786, 788, 790	T21.26XA	791
T17.518D	825	T18.3XXD	825	T20.16XD	825	T20.44XD	825	T20.72XD	825	T21.26XD	825
T17.518S	758	T18.3XXS	758	T20.16XS	471	T20.44XS	471	T20.72XS	471	T21.26XS	472
T17.520A	107	T18.4XXA	197	T20.17XA	791	T20.45XA	791	T20.73XA	782, 786, 788, 790	T21.27XA	791
T17.520D	825	T18.4XXD	825	T20.17XD	825	T20.45XD	825	T20.73XD	825	T21.27XD	825
T17.520S	758	T18.4XXS	758	T20.17XS	471	T20.45XS	471	T20.73XS	471	T21.27XS	472
T17.528A	107	T18.5XXA	197	T20.19XA	791	T20.46XA	791	T20.74XA	782, 786, 788, 790	T21.29XA	791
T17.528D	825	T18.5XXD	825	T20.19XD	825	T20.46XD	825	T20.74XD	825	T21.29XD	825
T17.528S	758	T18.5XXS	758	T20.19XS	471	T20.46XS	471	T20.74XS	471	T21.29XS	472
T17.590A	107	T18.8XXA	197	T20.20XA	791	T20.47XA	791	T20.75XA	782, 786, 788, 790	T21.30XA	782, 786, 788, 790
T17.590D	825	T18.8XXD	825	T20.20XD	825	T20.47XD	825	T20.75XD	825	T21.30XD	825
T17.590S	758	T18.8XXS	758	T20.20XS	471	T20.47XS	471	T20.75XS	471	T21.30XS	472
T17.598A	107	T18.9XXA	197	T20.211A	791	T20.49XA	791	T20.76XA	782, 786, 788, 790	T21.31XA	782, 786, 788, 790
T17.598D	825	T18.9XXD	825	T20.211D	825	T20.49XD	825	T20.76XD	825	T21.31XD	825
T17.598S	758	T18.9XXS	758	T20.211S	471	T20.49XS	471	T20.76XS	471	T21.31XS	472
T17.800A	107	T19.0XXA	520	T20.212A	791	T20.50XA	791	T20.77XA	782, 786, 788, 790	T21.32XA	782, 786, 788, 790
T17.800D	825	T19.0XXD	825	T20.212D	825	T20.50XD	825	T20.77XD	825	T21.32XD	825
T17.800S	758	T19.0XXS	758	T20.212S	471	T20.50XS	471	T20.77XS	472	T21.32XS	472
T17.808A	107	T19.1XXA	520	T20.219A	791	T20.511A	791	T20.79XA	782, 786, 788, 790	T21.33XA	782, 786, 788, 790
T17.808D	825	T19.1XXD	825	T20.219D	825	T20.511D	825	T20.79XD	825	T21.33XD	825
T17.808S	758	T19.1XXS	758	T20.219S	471	T20.511S	471	T20.79XS	472	T21.33XS	472
T17.810A	107	T19.2XXA	535, 543	T20.22XA	791	T20.512A	791	T21.00XA	791	T21.34XA	782, 786, 788, 790
T17.810D	825	T19.2XXD	825	T20.22XD	825	T20.512D	825	T21.00XD	825	T21.34XD	825
T17.810S	758	T19.2XXS	758	T20.22XS	471	T20.512S	471	T21.00XS	472	T21.34XS	472
T17.818A	107	T19.3XXA	535, 543	T20.23XA	791	T20.519A	791	T21.01XA	791	T21.35XA	782, 786, 788, 790
T17.818D	825	T19.3XXD	825	T20.23XD	825	T20.519D	825	T21.01XD	825	T21.35XD	825
T17.818S	758	T19.3XXS	758	T20.23XS	471	T20.519S	471	T21.01XS	472	T21.35XS	472
T17.820A	107	T19.4XXA	530	T20.24XA	791	T20.52XA	791	T21.02XA	791	T21.36XA	782, 786, 788, 790
T17.820D	825	T19.4XXD	825	T20.24XD	825	T20.52XD	825	T21.02XD	825	T21.36XD	825
T17.820S	758	T19.4XXS	758	T20.24XS	471	T20.52XS	471	T21.02XS	472	T21.36XS	472
T17.828A	107	T19.8XXA	520	T20.25XA	791	T20.53XA	791	T21.03XA	791	T21.37XA	782, 786, 788, 790
T17.828D	825	T19.8XXD	825	T20.25XD	825	T20.53XD	825	T21.03XD	825	T21.37XD	825
T17.828S	758	T19.8XXS	758	T20.25XS	471	T20.53XS	471	T21.03XS	472	T21.37XS	472
T17.890A	107	T19.9XXA	520	T20.26XA	791	T20.54XA	791	T21.04XA	791	T21.39XA	782, 786, 788, 790

Code	Page	Code	Page	Code	Page	Code	Page	Code	Page	Code	Page
T21.39XD	826	T21.73XD	826	T22.119D	826	T22.249D	826	T22.399D	826	T22.532D	826
T21.39XS	472	T21.73XS	472	T22.119S	472	T22.249S	472	T22.399S	472	T22.532S	473
T21.40XA	791	T21.74XA	782,786,788,790	T22.121A	792	T22.251A	792	T22.40XA	792	T22.539A	792
T21.40XD	826	T21.74XD	826	T22.121D	826	T22.251D	826	T22.40XD	826	T22.539D	826
T21.40XS	472	T21.74XS	472	T22.121S	472	T22.251S	472	T22.40XS	472	T22.539S	473
T21.41XA	791	T21.75XA	782,786,788,790	T22.122A	792	T22.252A	792	T22.411A	792	T22.541A	792
T21.41XD	826	T21.75XD	826	T22.122D	826	T22.252D	826	T22.411D	826	T22.541D	826
T21.41XS	472	T21.75XS	472	T22.122S	472	T22.252S	472	T22.411S	472	T22.541S	473
T21.42XA	791	T21.76XA	782,786,788,790	T22.129A	792	T22.259A	792	T22.412A	792	T22.542A	792
T21.42XD	826	T21.76XD	826	T22.129D	826	T22.259D	826	T22.412D	826	T22.542D	826
T21.42XS	472	T21.76XS	472	T22.129S	472	T22.259S	472	T22.419A	792	T22.542S	473
T21.43XA	791	T21.77XA	782,786,788,790	T22.131A	792	T22.261A	792	T22.419D	826	T22.549A	792
T21.43XD	826	T21.77XD	826	T22.131D	826	T22.261D	826	T22.419S	472	T22.549D	826
T21.43XS	472	T21.77XS	472	T22.131S	472	T22.261S	472	T22.421A	792	T22.549S	473
T21.44XA	791	T21.79XA	782,786,788,790	T22.132A	792	T22.262A	792	T22.421D	826	T22.551A	792
T21.44XD	826	T21.79XD	826	T22.132D	826	T22.262D	826	T22.421S	472	T22.551D	826
T21.44XS	472	T21.79XS	472	T22.132S	472	T22.262S	472	T22.422A	792	T22.551S	473
T21.45XA	791	T22.00XA	792	T22.139A	792	T22.269A	792	T22.422D	826	T22.552A	792
T21.45XD	826	T22.00XD	826	T22.139D	826	T22.269D	826	T22.422S	472	T22.552D	826
T21.45XS	472	T22.00XS	472	T22.139S	472	T22.269S	472	T22.429A	792	T22.552S	473
T21.46XA	792	T22.011A	792	T22.141A	792	T22.291A	792	T22.429D	826	T22.559A	792
T21.46XD	826	T22.011D	826	T22.141D	826	T22.291D	826	T22.429S	472	T22.559D	826
T21.46XS	472	T22.011S	472	T22.141S	472	T22.291S	472	T22.431A	792	T22.559S	473
T21.47XA	792	T22.012A	792	T22.142A	792	T22.292A	792	T22.431D	826	T22.561A	792
T21.47XD	826	T22.012D	826	T22.142D	826	T22.292D	826	T22.431S	472	T22.561D	826
T21.47XS	472	T22.012S	472	T22.142S	472	T22.292S	472	T22.432A	792	T22.561S	473
T21.49XA	792	T22.019A	792	T22.149A	792	T22.299A	792	T22.432D	826	T22.562A	792
T21.49XD	826	T22.019D	826	T22.149D	826	T22.299D	826	T22.432S	472	T22.562D	826
T21.49XS	472	T22.019S	472	T22.149S	472	T22.299S	472	T22.439A	792	T22.562S	473
T21.50XA	792	T22.021A	792	T22.151A	792	T22.30XA	782,786,788,790	T22.439D	826	T22.569A	792
T21.50XD	826	T22.021D	826	T22.151D	826	T22.30XD	826	T22.439S	472	T22.569D	826
T21.50XS	472	T22.021S	472	T22.151S	472	T22.30XS	472	T22.441A	792	T22.569S	473
T21.51XA	792	T22.022A	792	T22.152A	792	T22.311A	782,786,788,790	T22.441D	826	T22.591A	792
T21.51XD	826	T22.022D	826	T22.152D	826	T22.311D	826	T22.441S	472	T22.591D	826
T21.51XS	472	T22.022S	472	T22.152S	472	T22.311S	472	T22.442A	792	T22.591S	473
T21.52XA	792	T22.029A	792	T22.159A	792	T22.312A	782,786,788,790	T22.442D	826	T22.592A	792
T21.52XD	826	T22.029D	826	T22.159D	826	T22.312D	826	T22.442S	472	T22.592D	826
T21.52XS	472	T22.029S	472	T22.159S	472	T22.312S	472	T22.449A	792	T22.592S	473
T21.53XA	792	T22.031A	792	T22.161A	792	T22.319A	782,786,788,790	T22.449D	826	T22.599A	792
T21.53XD	826	T22.031D	826	T22.161D	826	T22.319D	826	T22.449S	473	T22.599D	826
T21.53XS	472	T22.031S	472	T22.161S	472	T22.319S	472	T22.451A	792	T22.599S	473
T21.54XA	792	T22.032A	792	T22.162A	792	T22.321A	782,786,788,790	T22.451D	826	T22.60XA	792
T21.54XD	826	T22.032D	826	T22.162D	826	T22.321D	826	T22.451S	473	T22.60XD	826
T21.54XS	472	T22.032S	472	T22.162S	472	T22.321S	472	T22.452A	792	T22.60XS	473
T21.55XA	792	T22.039A	792	T22.169A	792	T22.322A	782,786,788,790	T22.452D	826	T22.611A	792
T21.55XD	826	T22.039D	826	T22.169D	826	T22.322D	826	T22.452S	473	T22.611D	826
T21.55XS	472	T22.039S	472	T22.169S	472	T22.322S	472	T22.459A	792	T22.611S	473
T21.56XA	792	T22.041A	792	T22.191A	792	T22.329A	782,786,788,790	T22.459D	826	T22.612A	792
T21.56XD	826	T22.041D	826	T22.191D	826	T22.329D	826	T22.459S	473	T22.612D	826
T21.56XS	472	T22.041S	472	T22.191S	472	T22.329S	472	T22.461A	792	T22.612S	473
T21.57XA	792	T22.042A	792	T22.192A	792	T22.331A	782,786,788,790	T22.461D	826	T22.619A	792
T21.57XD	826	T22.042D	826	T22.192D	826	T22.331D	826	T22.461S	473	T22.619D	826
T21.57XS	472	T22.042S	472	T22.192S	472	T22.331S	472	T22.462A	792	T22.619S	473
T21.59XA	792	T22.049A	792	T22.199A	792	T22.332A	782,786,788,790	T22.462D	826	T22.621A	792
T21.59XD	826	T22.049D	826	T22.199D	826	T22.332D	826	T22.462S	473	T22.621D	826
T21.59XS	472	T22.049S	472	T22.199S	472	T22.332S	472	T22.469A	792	T22.621S	473
T21.60XA	792	T22.051A	792	T22.20XA	792	T22.339A	782,786,788,790	T22.469D	826	T22.622A	792
T21.60XD	826	T22.051D	826	T22.20XD	826	T22.339D	826	T22.469S	473	T22.622D	827
T21.60XS	472	T22.051S	472	T22.20XS	472	T22.339S	472	T22.491A	792	T22.622S	473
T21.61XA	792	T22.052A	792	T22.211A	792	T22.341A	782,786,788,790	T22.491D	826	T22.629A	792
T21.61XD	826	T22.052D	826	T22.211D	826	T22.341D	826	T22.491S	473	T22.629D	827
T21.61XS	472	T22.052S	472	T22.211S	472	T22.341S	472	T22.492A	792	T22.629S	473
T21.62XA	792	T22.059A	792	T22.212A	792	T22.342A	782,786,788,790	T22.492D	826	T22.631A	792
T21.62XD	826	T22.059D	826	T22.212D	826	T22.342D	826	T22.492S	473	T22.631D	827
T21.62XS	472	T22.059S	472	T22.212S	472	T22.342S	472	T22.499A	792	T22.631S	473
T21.63XA	792	T22.061A	792	T22.219A	792	T22.349A	782,786,788,790	T22.499D	826	T22.632A	792
T21.63XD	826	T22.061D	826	T22.219D	826	T22.349D	826	T22.499S	473	T22.632D	827
T21.63XS	472	T22.061S	472	T22.219S	472	T22.349S	472	T22.50XA	792	T22.632S	473
T21.64XA	792	T22.062A	792	T22.221A	792	T22.351A	782,786,788,790	T22.50XD	826	T22.639A	792
T21.64XD	826	T22.062D	826	T22.221D	826	T22.351D	826	T22.50XS	473	T22.639D	827
T21.64XS	472	T22.062S	472	T22.221S	472	T22.351S	472	T22.511A	792	T22.639S	473
T21.65XA	792	T22.069A	792	T22.222A	792	T22.352A	782,786,788,790	T22.511D	826	T22.641A	792
T21.65XD	826	T22.069D	826	T22.222D	826	T22.352D	826	T22.511S	473	T22.641D	827
T21.65XS	472	T22.069S	472	T22.222S	472	T22.352S	472	T22.512A	792	T22.641S	473
T21.66XA	792	T22.091A	792	T22.229A	792	T22.359A	782,786,788,790	T22.512D	826	T22.642A	792
T21.66XD	826	T22.091D	826	T22.229D	826	T22.359D	826	T22.512S	473	T22.642D	827
T21.66XS	472	T22.091S	472	T22.229S	472	T22.359S	472	T22.519A	792	T22.642S	473
T21.67XA	792	T22.092A	792	T22.231A	792	T22.361A	782,786,788,790	T22.519D	826	T22.649A	792
T21.67XD	826	T22.092D	826	T22.231D	826	T22.361D	826	T22.519S	473	T22.649D	827
T21.67XS	472	T22.092S	472	T22.231S	472	T22.361S	472	T22.521A	792	T22.649S	473
T21.69XA	792	T22.099A	792	T22.232A	792	T22.362A	782,786,788,790	T22.521D	826	T22.651A	792
T21.69XD	826	T22.099D	826	T22.232D	826	T22.362D	826	T22.521S	473	T22.651D	827
T21.69XS	472	T22.099S	472	T22.232S	472	T22.362S	472	T22.522A	792	T22.651S	473
T21.70XA	782,786,788,790	T22.10XA	792	T22.239A	792	T22.369A	782,786,788,790	T22.522D	826	T22.652A	792
T21.70XD	826	T22.10XD	826	T22.239D	826	T22.369D	826	T22.522S	473	T22.652D	827
T21.70XS	472	T22.10XS	472	T22.239S	472	T22.369S	472	T22.529A	792	T22.652S	473
T21.71XA	782,786,788,790	T22.111A	792	T22.241A	792	T22.391A	782,786,788,790	T22.529D	826	T22.659A	792
T21.71XD	826	T22.111D	826	T22.241D	826	T22.391D	826	T22.529S	473	T22.659D	827
T21.71XS	472	T22.111S	472	T22.241S	472	T22.391S	472	T22.531A	792	T22.659S	473
T21.72XA	782,786,788,790	T22.112A	792	T22.242A	792	T22.392A	782,786,788,790	T22.531D	826	T22.661A	792
T21.72XD	826	T22.112D	826	T22.242D	826	T22.392D	826	T22.531S	473	T22.661D	827
T21.72XS	472	T22.112S	472	T22.242S	472	T22.392S	472	T22.532A	792	T22.661S	473
T21.73XA	782,786,788,790	T22.119A	792	T22.249A	792	T22.399A	782,786,788,790			T22.662A	792

Code	Page	Code	Page	Code	Page	Code	Page	Code	Page	Code	Page
T22.662D	827	T23.012A	792	T23.129A	793	T23.241A	793	T23.352A	782, 786, 789, 790	T23.469A	793
T22.662S	473	T23.012D	827	T23.129D	827	T23.241D	827	T23.352D	827	T23.469D	827
T22.669A	792	T23.012S	473	T23.129S	473	T23.241S	473	T23.352S	473	T23.469S	474
T22.669D	827	T23.019A	792	T23.131A	793	T23.242A	793	T23.359A	782, 786, 789, 790	T23.471A	793
T22.669S	473	T23.019D	827	T23.131D	827	T23.242D	827	T23.359D	827	T23.471D	827
T22.691A	792	T23.019S	473	T23.131S	473	T23.242S	473	T23.359S	474	T23.471S	474
T22.691D	827	T23.021A	792	T23.132A	793	T23.249A	793	T23.361A	782, 786, 789, 790	T23.472A	793
T22.691S	473	T23.021D	827	T23.132D	827	T23.249D	827	T23.361D	827	T23.472D	827
T22.692A	792	T23.021S	473	T23.132S	473	T23.249S	473	T23.361S	474	T23.472S	474
T22.692D	827	T23.022A	792	T23.139A	793	T23.251A	793	T23.362A	782, 786, 789, 790	T23.479A	793
T22.692S	473	T23.022D	827	T23.139D	827	T23.251D	827	T23.362D	827	T23.479D	827
T22.699A	792	T23.022S	473	T23.139S	473	T23.251S	473	T23.362S	474	T23.479S	474
T22.699D	827	T23.029A	792	T23.141A	793	T23.252A	793	T23.369A	782, 786, 789, 790	T23.491A	793
T22.699S	473	T23.029D	827	T23.141D	827	T23.252D	827	T23.369D	827	T23.491D	827
T22.70XA	782, 786, 788, 790	T23.029S	473	T23.141S	473	T23.252S	473	T23.369S	474	T23.491S	474
T22.70XD	827	T23.031A	792	T23.142A	793	T23.259A	793	T23.371A	782, 786, 789, 790	T23.492A	793
T22.70XS	473	T23.031D	827	T23.142D	827	T23.259D	827	T23.371D	827	T23.492D	827
T22.711A	782, 786, 788, 790	T23.031S	473	T23.142S	473	T23.259S	473	T23.371S	474	T23.492S	474
T22.711D	827	T23.032A	792	T23.149A	793	T23.261A	793	T23.372A	782, 786, 789, 790	T23.499A	793
T22.711S	473	T23.032D	827	T23.149D	827	T23.261D	827	T23.372D	827	T23.499D	827
T22.712A	782, 786, 788, 790	T23.032S	473	T23.149S	473	T23.261S	473	T23.372S	474	T23.499S	474
T22.712D	827	T23.039A	792	T23.151A	793	T23.262A	793	T23.379A	782, 786, 789, 790	T23.501A	793
T22.712S	473	T23.039D	827	T23.151D	827	T23.262D	827	T23.379D	827	T23.501D	828
T22.719A	782, 786, 788, 790	T23.039S	473	T23.151S	473	T23.262S	473	T23.379S	474	T23.501S	474
T22.719D	827	T23.041A	792	T23.152A	793	T23.269A	793	T23.391A	782, 786, 789, 790	T23.502A	793
T22.719S	473	T23.041D	827	T23.152D	827	T23.269D	827	T23.391D	827	T23.502D	828
T22.721A	782, 786, 789, 790	T23.041S	473	T23.152S	473	T23.269S	473	T23.391S	474	T23.502S	474
T22.721D	827	T23.042A	792	T23.159A	793	T23.271A	793	T23.392A	782, 786, 789, 790	T23.509A	793
T22.721S	473	T23.042D	827	T23.159D	827	T23.271D	827	T23.392D	827	T23.509D	828
T22.722A	782, 786, 789, 790	T23.042S	473	T23.159S	473	T23.271S	473	T23.392S	474	T23.509S	474
T22.722D	827	T23.049A	792	T23.161A	793	T23.272A	793	T23.399A	782, 786, 789, 790	T23.511A	793
T22.722S	473	T23.049D	827	T23.161D	827	T23.272D	827	T23.399D	827	T23.511D	828
T22.729A	782, 786, 789, 790	T23.049S	473	T23.161S	473	T23.272S	473	T23.399S	474	T23.511S	474
T22.729D	827	T23.051A	792	T23.162A	793	T23.279A	793	T23.401A	793	T23.512A	793
T22.729S	473	T23.051D	827	T23.162D	827	T23.279D	827	T23.401D	827	T23.512D	828
T22.731A	782, 786, 789, 790	T23.051S	473	T23.162S	473	T23.279S	473	T23.401S	474	T23.512S	474
T22.731D	827	T23.052A	792	T23.169A	793	T23.291A	793	T23.402A	793	T23.519A	793
T22.731S	473	T23.052D	827	T23.169D	827	T23.291D	827	T23.402D	827	T23.519D	828
T22.732A	782, 786, 789, 790	T23.052S	473	T23.169S	473	T23.291S	473	T23.402S	474	T23.519S	474
T22.732D	827	T23.059A	792	T23.171A	793	T23.292A	793	T23.409A	793	T23.521A	793
T22.732S	473	T23.059D	827	T23.171D	827	T23.292D	827	T23.409D	827	T23.521D	828
T22.739A	782, 786, 789, 790	T23.059S	473	T23.171S	473	T23.292S	473	T23.409S	474	T23.521S	474
T22.739D	827	T23.061A	792	T23.172A	793	T23.299A	793	T23.411A	793	T23.522A	793
T22.739S	473	T23.061D	827	T23.172D	827	T23.299D	827	T23.411D	827	T23.522D	828
T22.741A	782, 786, 789, 790	T23.061S	473	T23.172S	473	T23.299S	473	T23.411S	474	T23.522S	474
T22.741D	827	T23.062A	792	T23.179A	793	T23.301A	782, 786, 789, 790	T23.412A	793	T23.529A	793
T22.741S	473	T23.062D	827	T23.179D	827	T23.301D	827	T23.412D	827	T23.529D	828
T22.742A	782, 786, 789, 790	T23.062S	473	T23.179S	473	T23.301S	473	T23.412S	474	T23.529S	474
T22.742D	827	T23.069A	792	T23.191A	793	T23.302A	782, 786, 789, 790	T23.419A	793	T23.531A	793
T22.742S	473	T23.069D	827	T23.191D	827	T23.302D	827	T23.419D	827	T23.531D	828
T22.749A	782, 786, 789, 790	T23.069S	473	T23.191S	473	T23.302S	473	T23.419S	474	T23.531S	474
T22.749D	827	T23.071A	793	T23.192A	793	T23.309A	782, 786, 789, 790	T23.421A	793	T23.532A	793
T22.749S	473	T23.071D	827	T23.192D	827	T23.309D	827	T23.421D	827	T23.532D	828
T22.751A	782, 786, 789, 790	T23.071S	473	T23.192S	473	T23.309S	473	T23.421S	474	T23.532S	474
T22.751D	827	T23.072A	793	T23.199A	793	T23.311A	782, 786, 789, 790	T23.422A	793	T23.539A	793
T22.751S	473	T23.072D	827	T23.199D	827	T23.311D	827	T23.422D	827	T23.539D	828
T22.752A	782, 786, 789, 790	T23.072S	473	T23.199S	473	T23.311S	473	T23.422S	474	T23.539S	474
T22.752D	827	T23.079A	793	T23.201A	793	T23.312A	782, 786, 789, 790	T23.429A	793	T23.541A	793
T22.752S	473	T23.079D	827	T23.201D	827	T23.312D	827	T23.429D	827	T23.541D	828
T22.759A	782, 786, 789, 790	T23.079S	473	T23.201S	473	T23.312S	473	T23.429S	474	T23.541S	474
T22.759D	827	T23.091A	793	T23.202A	793	T23.319A	782, 786, 789, 790	T23.431A	793	T23.542A	793
T22.759S	473	T23.091D	827	T23.202D	827	T23.319D	827	T23.431D	827	T23.542D	828
T22.761A	782, 786, 789, 790	T23.091S	473	T23.202S	473	T23.319S	473	T23.431S	474	T23.542S	474
T22.761D	827	T23.092A	793	T23.209A	793	T23.321A	782, 786, 789, 790	T23.432A	793	T23.549A	793
T22.761S	473	T23.092D	827	T23.209D	827	T23.321D	827	T23.432D	827	T23.549D	828
T22.762A	782, 786, 789, 790	T23.092S	473	T23.209S	473	T23.321S	473	T23.432S	474	T23.549S	474
T22.762D	827	T23.099A	793	T23.211A	793	T23.322A	782, 786, 789, 790	T23.439A	793	T23.551A	793
T22.762S	473	T23.099D	827	T23.211D	827	T23.322D	827	T23.439D	827	T23.551D	828
T22.769A	782, 786, 789, 790	T23.099S	473	T23.211S	473	T23.322S	473	T23.439S	474	T23.551S	474
T22.769D	827	T23.101A	793	T23.212A	793	T23.329A	782, 786, 789, 790	T23.441A	793	T23.552A	793
T22.769S	473	T23.101D	827	T23.212D	827	T23.329D	827	T23.441D	827	T23.552D	828
T22.791A	782, 786, 789, 790	T23.101S	473	T23.212S	473	T23.329S	473	T23.441S	474	T23.552S	474
T22.791D	827	T23.102A	793	T23.219A	793	T23.331A	782, 786, 789, 790	T23.442A	793	T23.559A	793
T22.791S	473	T23.102D	827	T23.219D	827	T23.331D	827	T23.442D	827	T23.559D	828
T22.792A	789, 790	T23.102S	473	T23.219S	473	T23.331S	473	T23.442S	474	T23.559S	474
T22.792A	782, 786	T23.109A	793	T23.221A	793	T23.332A	782, 786, 789, 790	T23.449A	793	T23.561A	793
T22.792D	827	T23.109D	827	T23.221D	827	T23.332D	827	T23.449D	827	T23.561D	828
T22.792S	473	T23.109S	473	T23.221S	473	T23.332S	473	T23.449S	474	T23.561S	474
T22.799A	782, 786, 789, 790	T23.111A	793	T23.222A	793	T23.339A	782, 786, 789, 790	T23.451A	793	T23.562A	793
T22.799D	827	T23.111D	827	T23.222D	827	T23.339D	827	T23.451D	827	T23.562D	828
T22.799S	473	T23.111S	473	T23.222S	473	T23.339S	473	T23.451S	474	T23.562S	474
T23.001A	792	T23.112A	793	T23.229A	793	T23.341A	782, 786, 789, 790	T23.452A	793	T23.569A	793
T23.001D	827	T23.112D	827	T23.229D	827	T23.341D	827	T23.452D	827	T23.569D	828
T23.001S	473	T23.112S	473	T23.229S	473	T23.341S	473	T23.452S	474	T23.569S	474
T23.002A	792	T23.119A	793	T23.231A	793	T23.342A	782, 786, 789, 790	T23.459A	793	T23.571A	793
T23.002D	827	T23.119D	827	T23.231D	827	T23.342D	827	T23.459D	827	T23.571D	828
T23.002S	473	T23.119S	473	T23.231S	473	T23.342S	473	T23.459S	474	T23.571S	474
T23.009A	792	T23.121A	793	T23.232A	793	T23.349A	782, 786, 789, 790	T23.461A	793	T23.572A	793
T23.009D	827	T23.121D	827	T23.232D	827	T23.349D	827	T23.461D	827	T23.572D	828
T23.009S	473	T23.121S	473	T23.232S	473	T23.349S	473	T23.461S	474	T23.572S	474
T23.011A	792	T23.122A	793	T23.239A	793	T23.351A	782, 786, 789, 790	T23.462A	793	T23.579A	793
T23.011D	827	T23.122D	827	T23.239D	827	T23.351D	827	T23.462D	827	T23.579D	828
T23.011S	473	T23.122S	473	T23.239S	473	T23.351S	473	T23.462S	474	T23.579S	474

Code	Page	Code	Page	Code	Page	Code	Page	Code	Page	Code	Page
T23.591A	793	T23.702A	782, 786, 789, 790	T24.019A	793	T24.221A	794	T24.422A	794	T24.629A	794
T23.591D	828	T23.702D	828	T24.019D	828	T24.221D	828	T24.422D	828	T24.629D	829
T23.591S	474	T23.702S	474	T24.019S	474	T24.221S	474	T24.422S	475	T24.629S	475
T23.592A	793	T23.709A	782, 786, 789, 790	T24.021A	793	T24.222A	794	T24.429A	794	T24.631A	794
T23.592D	828	T23.709D	828	T24.021D	828	T24.222D	828	T24.429D	828	T24.631D	829
T23.592S	474	T23.709S	474	T24.021S	474	T24.222S	474	T24.429S	475	T24.631S	475
T23.599A	793	T23.711A	782, 786, 789, 790	T24.022A	793	T24.229A	794	T24.431A	794	T24.632A	794
T23.599D	828	T23.711D	828	T24.022D	828	T24.229D	828	T24.431D	828	T24.632D	829
T23.599S	474	T23.711S	474	T24.022S	474	T24.229S	474	T24.431S	475	T24.632S	475
T23.601A	793	T23.712A	782, 786, 789, 790	T24.029A	793	T24.231A	794	T24.432A	794	T24.639A	794
T23.601D	828	T23.712D	828	T24.029D	828	T24.231D	828	T24.432D	828	T24.639D	829
T23.601S	474	T23.712S	474	T24.029S	474	T24.231S	474	T24.432S	475	T24.639S	475
T23.602A	793	T23.719A	782, 786, 789, 790	T24.031A	793	T24.232A	794	T24.439A	794	T24.691A	794
T23.602D	828	T23.719D	828	T24.031D	828	T24.232D	828	T24.439D	828	T24.691D	829
T23.602S	474	T23.719S	474	T24.031S	474	T24.232S	474	T24.439S	475	T24.691S	475
T23.609A	793	T23.721A	782, 786, 789, 790	T24.032A	793	T24.239A	794	T24.491A	794	T24.692A	794
T23.609D	828	T23.721D	828	T24.032D	828	T24.239D	828	T24.491D	828	T24.692D	829
T23.609S	474	T23.721S	474	T24.032S	474	T24.239S	474	T24.491S	475	T24.692S	475
T23.611A	793	T23.722A	782, 786, 789, 790	T24.039A	793	T24.291A	794	T24.492A	794	T24.699A	794
T23.611D	828	T23.722D	828	T24.039D	828	T24.291D	828	T24.492D	828	T24.699D	829
T23.611S	474	T23.722S	474	T24.039S	474	T24.291S	474	T24.492S	475	T24.699S	475
T23.612A	793	T23.729A	782, 786, 789, 790	T24.091A	793	T24.292A	794	T24.499A	794	T24.701A	782, 786, 789, 791
T23.612D	828	T23.729D	828	T24.091D	828	T24.292D	828	T24.499D	828	T24.701D	829
T23.612S	474	T23.729S	474	T24.091S	474	T24.292S	474	T24.499S	475	T24.701S	475
T23.619A	793	T23.731A	782, 786, 789, 790	T24.092A	793	T24.299A	794	T24.501A	794	T24.702A	782, 786, 789, 791
T23.619D	828	T23.731D	828	T24.092D	828	T24.299D	828	T24.501D	828	T24.702D	829
T23.619S	474	T23.731S	474	T24.092S	474	T24.299S	474	T24.501S	475	T24.702S	475
T23.621A	793	T23.732A	782, 786, 789, 790	T24.099A	793	T24.301A	782, 786, 789, 791	T24.502A	794	T24.709A	782, 786, 789, 791
T23.621D	828	T23.732D	828	T24.099D	828	T24.301D	828	T24.502D	828	T24.709D	829
T23.621S	474	T23.732S	474	T24.099S	474	T24.301S	474	T24.502S	475	T24.709S	475
T23.622A	793	T23.739A	782, 786, 789, 790	T24.101A	793	T24.302A	782, 786, 789, 791	T24.509A	794	T24.711A	782, 786, 789, 791
T23.622D	828	T23.739D	828	T24.101D	828	T24.302D	828	T24.509D	828	T24.711D	829
T23.622S	474	T23.739S	474	T24.101S	474	T24.302S	474	T24.509S	475	T24.711S	475
T23.629A	793	T23.741A	782, 786, 789, 791	T24.102A	793	T24.309A	782, 786, 789, 791	T24.511A	794	T24.712A	782, 786, 789, 791
T23.629D	828	T23.741D	828	T24.102D	828	T24.309D	828	T24.511D	828	T24.712D	829
T23.629S	474	T23.741S	474	T24.102S	474	T24.309S	474	T24.511S	475	T24.712S	475
T23.631A	793	T23.742A	782, 786, 789, 791	T24.109A	793	T24.311A	782, 786, 789, 791	T24.512A	794	T24.719A	783, 786, 789, 791
T23.631D	828	T23.742D	828	T24.109D	828	T24.311D	828	T24.512D	828	T24.719D	829
T23.631S	474	T23.742S	474	T24.109S	474	T24.311S	474	T24.512S	475	T24.719S	475
T23.632A	793	T23.749A	782, 786, 789, 791	T24.111A	793	T24.312A	782, 786, 789, 791	T24.519A	794	T24.721A	783, 786, 789, 791
T23.632D	828	T23.749D	828	T24.111D	828	T24.312D	828	T24.519D	828	T24.721D	829
T23.632S	474	T23.749S	474	T24.111S	474	T24.312S	474	T24.519S	475	T24.721S	475
T23.639A	793	T23.751A	782, 786, 789, 791	T24.112A	793	T24.319A	782, 786, 789, 791	T24.521A	794	T24.722A	783, 786, 789, 791
T23.639D	828	T23.751D	828	T24.112D	828	T24.319D	828	T24.521D	828	T24.722D	829
T23.639S	474	T23.751S	474	T24.112S	474	T24.319S	474	T24.521S	475	T24.722S	475
T23.641A	793	T23.752A	782, 786, 789, 791	T24.119A	793	T24.321A	782, 786, 789, 791	T24.522A	794	T24.729A	783, 786, 789, 791
T23.641D	828	T23.752D	828	T24.119D	828	T24.321D	828	T24.522D	828	T24.729D	829
T23.641S	474	T23.752S	474	T24.119S	474	T24.321S	474	T24.522S	475	T24.729S	475
T23.642A	793	T23.759A	782, 786, 789, 791	T24.121A	793	T24.322A	782, 786, 789, 791	T24.529A	794	T24.731A	783, 786, 789, 791
T23.642D	828	T23.759D	828	T24.121D	828	T24.322D	828	T24.529D	828	T24.731D	829
T23.642S	474	T23.759S	474	T24.121S	474	T24.322S	474	T24.529S	475	T24.731S	475
T23.649A	793	T23.761A	782, 786, 789, 791	T24.122A	793	T24.329A	782, 786, 789, 791	T24.531A	794	T24.732A	783, 786, 789, 791
T23.649D	828	T23.761D	828	T24.122D	828	T24.329D	828	T24.531D	828	T24.732D	829
T23.649S	474	T23.761S	474	T24.122S	474	T24.329S	474	T24.531S	475	T24.732S	475
T23.651A	793	T23.762A	782, 786, 789, 791	T24.129A	793	T24.331A	782, 786, 789, 791	T24.532A	794	T24.739A	783, 786, 789, 791
T23.651D	828	T23.762D	828	T24.129D	828	T24.331D	828	T24.532D	828	T24.739D	829
T23.651S	474	T23.762S	474	T24.129S	474	T24.331S	474	T24.532S	475	T24.739S	475
T23.652A	793	T23.769A	782, 786, 789, 791	T24.131A	793	T24.332A	782, 786, 789, 791	T24.539A	794	T24.791A	783, 786, 789, 791
T23.652D	828	T23.769D	828	T24.131D	828	T24.332D	828	T24.539D	828	T24.791D	829
T23.652S	474	T23.769S	474	T24.131S	474	T24.332S	474	T24.539S	475	T24.791S	475
T23.659A	793	T23.771A	782, 786, 789, 791	T24.132A	793	T24.339A	782, 786, 789, 791	T24.591A	794	T24.792A	783, 786, 789, 791
T23.659D	828	T23.771D	828	T24.132D	828	T24.339D	828	T24.591D	828	T24.792D	829
T23.659S	474	T23.771S	474	T24.132S	474	T24.339S	475	T24.591S	475	T24.792S	475
T23.661A	793	T23.772A	782, 786, 789, 791	T24.139A	793	T24.391A	782, 786, 789, 791	T24.592A	794	T24.799A	783, 786, 789, 791
T23.661D	828	T23.772D	828	T24.139D	828	T24.391D	828	T24.592D	828	T24.799D	829
T23.661S	474	T23.772S	474	T24.139S	474	T24.391S	475	T24.592S	475	T24.799S	475
T23.662A	793	T23.779A	782, 786, 789, 791	T24.191A	793	T24.392A	782, 786, 789, 791	T24.599A	794	T25.011A	794
T23.662D	828	T23.779D	828	T24.191D	828	T24.392D	828	T24.599D	828	T25.011D	829
T23.662S	474	T23.779S	474	T24.191S	474	T24.392S	475	T24.599S	475	T25.011S	475
T23.669A	793	T23.791A	782, 786, 789, 791	T24.192A	793	T24.399A	782, 786, 789, 791	T24.601A	794	T25.012A	794
T23.669D	828	T23.791D	828	T24.192D	828	T24.399D	828	T24.601D	828	T25.012D	829
T23.669S	474	T23.791S	474	T24.192S	474	T24.399S	475	T24.601S	475	T25.012S	475
T23.671A	793	T23.792A	782, 786, 789, 791	T24.199A	793	T24.401A	794	T24.602A	794	T25.019A	794
T23.671D	828	T23.792D	828	T24.199D	828	T24.401D	828	T24.602D	828	T25.019D	829
T23.671S	474	T23.792S	474	T24.199S	474	T24.401S	475	T24.602S	475	T25.019S	475
T23.672A	793	T23.799A	782, 786, 789, 791	T24.201A	793	T24.402A	794	T24.609A	794	T25.021A	794
T23.672D	828	T23.799D	828	T24.201D	828	T24.402D	828	T24.609D	828	T25.021D	829
T23.672S	474	T23.799S	474	T24.201S	474	T24.402S	475	T24.609S	475	T25.021S	475
T23.679A	793	T24.001A	793	T24.202A	793	T24.409A	794	T24.611A	794	T25.022A	794
T23.679D	828	T24.001D	828	T24.202D	828	T24.409D	828	T24.611D	829	T25.022D	829
T23.679S	474	T24.001S	474	T24.202S	474	T24.409S	475	T24.611S	475	T25.022S	475
T23.691A	793	T24.002A	793	T24.209A	793	T24.411A	794	T24.612A	794	T25.029A	794
T23.691D	828	T24.002D	828	T24.209D	828	T24.411D	828	T24.612D	829	T25.029D	829
T23.691S	474	T24.002S	474	T24.209S	474	T24.411S	475	T24.612S	475	T25.029S	475
T23.692A	793	T24.009A	793	T24.211A	794	T24.412A	794	T24.619A	794	T25.031A	794
T23.692D	828	T24.009D	828	T24.211D	828	T24.412D	828	T24.619D	829	T25.031D	829
T23.692S	474	T24.009S	474	T24.211S	474	T24.412S	475	T24.619S	475	T25.031S	475
T23.699A	793	T24.011A	793	T24.212A	794	T24.419A	794	T24.621A	794	T25.032A	794
T23.699D	828	T24.011D	828	T24.212D	828	T24.419D	828	T24.621D	829	T25.032D	829
T23.699S	474	T24.011S	474	T24.212S	474	T24.419S	475	T24.621S	475	T25.032S	475
T23.701A	782, 786, 789, 790	T24.012A	793	T24.219A	794	T24.421A	794	T24.622A	794	T25.039A	794
T23.701D	828	T24.012D	828	T24.219D	828	T24.421D	828	T24.622D	829	T25.039D	829
T23.701S	474	T24.012S	474	T24.219S	474	T24.421S	475	T24.622S	475	T25.039S	475

Code	Page
T25.091A	794
T25.091D	829
T25.091S	475
T25.092A	794
T25.092D	829
T25.092S	475
T25.099A	794
T25.099D	829
T25.099S	475
T25.111A	794
T25.111D	829
T25.111S	475
T25.112A	794
T25.112D	829
T25.112S	475
T25.119A	794
T25.119D	829
T25.119S	475
T25.121A	794
T25.121D	829
T25.121S	475
T25.122A	794
T25.122D	829
T25.122S	475
T25.129A	794
T25.129D	829
T25.129S	475
T25.131A	794
T25.131D	829
T25.131S	475
T25.132A	794
T25.132D	829
T25.132S	475
T25.139A	794
T25.139D	829
T25.139S	475
T25.191A	794
T25.191D	829
T25.191S	475
T25.192A	794
T25.192D	829
T25.192S	475
T25.199A	794
T25.199D	829
T25.199S	475
T25.211A	794
T25.211D	829
T25.211S	475
T25.212A	794
T25.212D	829
T25.212S	475
T25.219A	794
T25.219D	829
T25.219S	475
T25.221A	794
T25.221D	829
T25.221S	475
T25.222A	794
T25.222D	829
T25.222S	475
T25.229A	794
T25.229D	829
T25.229S	475
T25.231A	794
T25.231D	829
T25.231S	475
T25.232A	794
T25.232D	829
T25.232S	475
T25.239A	794
T25.239D	829
T25.239S	475
T25.291A	794
T25.291D	829
T25.291S	475
T25.292A	794
T25.292D	829
T25.292S	475
T25.299A	794
T25.299D	829
T25.299S	475
T25.311A	783, 786, 789, 791
T25.311D	829
T25.311S	475
T25.312A	783, 786, 789, 791
T25.312D	829
T25.312S	475
T25.319A	783, 786, 789, 791
T25.319D	829
T25.319S	475
T25.321A	783, 786, 789, 791
T25.321D	829
T25.321S	475
T25.322A	783, 786, 789, 791
T25.322D	829
T25.322S	475
T25.329A	783, 786, 789, 791
T25.329D	829
T25.329S	475
T25.331A	783, 786, 789, 791
T25.331D	829
T25.331S	475
T25.332A	783, 786, 789, 791
T25.332D	829
T25.332S	475
T25.339A	783, 786, 789, 791
T25.339D	829
T25.339S	475
T25.391A	783, 786, 789, 791
T25.391D	829
T25.391S	475
T25.392A	783, 786, 789, 791
T25.392D	829
T25.392S	475
T25.399A	783, 786, 789, 791
T25.399D	829
T25.399S	475
T25.411A	794
T25.411D	829
T25.411S	475
T25.412A	794
T25.412D	829
T25.412S	475
T25.419A	794
T25.419D	829
T25.419S	475
T25.421A	794
T25.421D	829
T25.421S	475
T25.422A	794
T25.422D	829
T25.422S	475
T25.429A	794
T25.429D	829
T25.429S	475
T25.431A	794
T25.431D	829
T25.431S	475
T25.432A	794
T25.432D	829
T25.432S	475
T25.439A	794
T25.439D	829
T25.439S	475
T25.491A	794
T25.491D	829
T25.491S	475
T25.492A	794
T25.492D	829
T25.492S	475
T25.499A	794
T25.499D	829
T25.499S	475
T25.511A	794
T25.511D	829
T25.511S	475
T25.512A	794
T25.512D	829
T25.512S	475
T25.519A	794
T25.519D	829
T25.519S	475
T25.521A	794
T25.521D	829
T25.521S	475
T25.522A	794
T25.522D	829
T25.522S	475
T25.529A	794
T25.529D	829
T25.529S	475
T25.531A	794
T25.531D	829
T25.531S	475
T25.532A	794
T25.532D	829
T25.532S	475
T25.539A	794
T25.539D	829
T25.539S	475
T25.591A	794
T25.591D	829
T25.591S	475
T25.592A	794
T25.592D	829
T25.592S	475
T25.599A	794
T25.599D	829
T25.599S	475
T25.611A	794
T25.611D	829
T25.611S	475
T25.612A	794
T25.612D	829
T25.612S	475
T25.619A	794
T25.619D	829
T25.619S	475
T25.621A	794
T25.621D	829
T25.621S	475
T25.622A	794
T25.622D	829
T25.622S	475
T25.629A	794
T25.629D	829
T25.629S	475
T25.631A	794
T25.631D	829
T25.631S	475
T25.632A	794
T25.632D	829
T25.632S	475
T25.639A	794
T25.639D	829
T25.639S	475
T25.691A	794
T25.691D	829
T25.691S	475
T25.692A	794
T25.692D	829
T25.692S	475
T25.699A	794
T25.699D	829
T25.699S	475
T25.711A	783, 786, 789, 791
T25.711D	829
T25.711S	475
T25.712A	783, 786, 789, 791
T25.712D	829
T25.712S	475
T25.719A	783, 786, 789, 791
T25.719D	829
T25.719S	475
T25.721A	783, 786, 789, 791
T25.721D	829
T25.721S	475
T25.722A	783, 787, 789, 791
T25.722D	829
T25.722S	475
T25.729A	783, 787, 789, 791
T25.729D	829
T25.729S	475
T25.731A	783, 787, 789, 791
T25.731D	829
T25.731S	475
T25.732A	783, 787, 789, 791
T25.732D	829
T25.732S	475
T25.739A	783, 787, 789, 791
T25.739D	829
T25.739S	475
T25.791A	783, 787, 789, 791
T25.791D	829
T25.791S	475
T25.792A	783, 787, 789, 791
T25.792D	829
T25.792S	475
T25.799A	783, 787, 789, 791
T25.799D	829
T25.799S	475
T26.00XA	66
T26.00XD	829
T26.00XS	475
T26.01XA	66
T26.01XD	829
T26.01XS	475
T26.02XA	66
T26.02XD	829
T26.02XS	475
T26.10XA	66
T26.10XD	829
T26.10XS	475
T26.11XA	66
T26.11XD	829
T26.11XS	475
T26.12XA	66
T26.12XD	829
T26.12XS	475
T26.20XA	66
T26.20XD	829
T26.20XS	476
T26.21XA	66
T26.21XD	829
T26.21XS	475
T26.22XA	66
T26.22XD	829
T26.22XS	475
T26.30XA	66
T26.30XD	829
T26.30XS	475
T26.31XA	66
T26.31XD	829
T26.31XS	475
T26.32XA	66
T26.32XD	829
T26.32XS	475
T26.40XA	66
T26.40XD	829
T26.40XS	475
T26.41XA	66
T26.41XD	829
T26.41XS	475
T26.42XA	66
T26.42XD	829
T26.42XS	475
T26.50XA	66
T26.50XD	829
T26.50XS	476
T26.51XA	66
T26.51XD	829
T26.51XS	476
T26.52XA	66
T26.52XD	829
T26.52XS	476
T26.60XA	66
T26.60XD	829
T26.60XS	476
T26.61XA	66
T26.61XD	829
T26.61XS	476
T26.62XA	66
T26.62XD	829
T26.62XS	476
T26.70XA	66
T26.70XD	829
T26.70XS	476
T26.71XA	66
T26.71XD	829
T26.71XS	476
T26.72XA	66
T26.72XD	829
T26.72XS	476
T26.80XA	66
T26.80XD	829
T26.80XS	476
T26.81XA	66
T26.81XD	829
T26.81XS	476
T26.82XA	66
T26.82XD	829
T26.82XS	476
T26.90XA	66
T26.90XD	829
T26.90XS	476
T26.91XA	66
T26.91XD	829
T26.91XS	476
T26.92XA	66
T26.92XD	829
T26.92XS	476
T27.0XXA	107, 788
T27.0XXD	829
T27.0XXS	476
T27.1XXA	107, 788
T27.1XXD	829
T27.1XXS	476
T27.2XXA	107, 788
T27.2XXD	829
T27.2XXS	476
T27.3XXA	107, 788
T27.3XXD	829
T27.3XXS	476
T27.4XXA	107, 788
T27.4XXD	829
T27.4XXS	476
T27.5XXA	107, 788
T27.5XXD	829
T27.5XXS	476
T27.6XXA	107, 788
T27.6XXD	829
T27.6XXS	476
T27.7XXA	107, 788
T27.7XXD	829
T27.7XXS	476
T28.0XXA	4, 87
T28.0XXD	829
T28.0XXS	476
T28.1XXA	193
T28.1XXD	829
T28.1XXS	476
T28.2XXA	197
T28.2XXD	829
T28.2XXS	476
T28.3XXA	794
T28.3XXD	829
T28.3XXS	476
T28.40XA	794
T28.40XD	829
T28.40XS	476
T28.411A	794
T28.411D	829
T28.411S	476
T28.412A	794
T28.412D	829
T28.419A	794
T28.419D	829
T28.419S	476
T28.49XA	794
T28.49XD	829
T28.49XS	476
T28.5XXA	5, 87
T28.5XXD	829
T28.5XXS	476
T28.6XXA	193
T28.6XXD	829
T28.6XXS	476
T28.7XXA	197
T28.7XXD	829
T28.7XXS	476
T28.8XXA	794
T28.8XXD	829
T28.8XXS	476
T28.90XA	794
T28.90XD	830
T28.90XS	476
T28.911A	794
T28.911D	830
T28.911S	476
T28.912A	794
T28.912D	830
T28.912S	476
T28.919A	794
T28.919D	830
T28.919S	476
T28.99XA	794
T28.99XD	830
T28.99XS	476
T30.0	794
T30.4	794
T31.0	794
T31.10	794
T31.11	783, 787, 789, 791
T31.20	794
T31.21	785, 789
T31.22	785, 789
T31.30	794
T31.31	785, 789
T31.32	785, 789
T31.33	785, 789
T31.40	794
T31.41	785, 789
T31.42	785, 789
T31.43	785, 789
T31.44	785, 789
T31.50	794
T31.51	785, 789
T31.52	785, 789
T31.53	785, 789
T31.54	785, 789
T31.55	785, 789
T31.60	794
T31.61	785, 789
T31.62	785, 789
T31.63	785, 789
T31.64	785, 789
T31.65	785, 789
T31.66	785, 789
T31.70	794
T31.71	785, 789
T31.72	785, 789
T31.73	785, 789
T31.74	785, 789
T31.75	785, 789
T31.76	785, 789
T31.77	785, 789
T31.80	794
T31.81	785, 789
T31.82	785, 789
T31.83	785, 789
T31.84	785, 789
T31.85	785, 789
T31.86	785, 789
T31.87	785, 789
T31.88	785, 789
T31.90	794
T31.91	785, 789
T31.92	785, 789
T31.93	785, 789
T31.94	785, 789
T31.95	785, 789
T31.96	785, 789
T31.97	785, 790
T31.98	785, 790
T31.99	785, 790
T32.0	794
T32.10	794
T32.11	783, 787, 789, 791
T32.20	794
T32.21	785, 790
T32.22	785, 790
T32.30	794
T32.31	785, 790
T32.32	785, 790
T32.33	785, 790
T32.40	794
T32.41	785, 790
T32.42	785, 790
T32.43	785, 790
T32.44	785, 790
T32.50	794
T32.51	785, 790
T32.52	785, 790
T32.53	785, 790
T32.54	785, 790
T32.55	785, 790
T32.60	794
T32.61	785, 790
T32.62	785, 790
T32.63	785, 790
T32.64	785, 790
T32.65	785, 790
T32.66	785, 790
T32.70	794
T32.71	785, 790
T32.72	785, 790
T32.73	785, 790
T32.74	785, 790
T32.75	785, 790
T32.76	785, 790
T32.77	785, 790
T32.80	794
T32.81	785, 790
T32.82	785, 790
T32.83	785, 790
T32.84	785, 790
T32.85	785, 790
T32.86	785, 790
T32.87	785, 790
T32.88	785, 790
T32.90	794
T32.91	785, 790
T32.92	785, 790
T32.93	785, 790
T32.94	785, 790
T32.95	785, 790
T32.96	785, 790
T32.97	785, 790
T32.98	785, 790
T32.99	785, 790
T33.011A	768
T33.011D	830
T33.011S	768
T33.012A	768
T33.012D	830
T33.012S	768
T33.019A	768
T33.019D	830
T33.019S	768
T33.02XA	768
T33.02XD	830
T33.02XS	768
T33.09XA	768
T33.09XD	830
T33.09XS	768
T33.1XXA	768
T33.1XXD	830

Code	Page	Code	Page	Code	Page	Code	Page	Code	Page	Code	Page
T33.1XXS	768	T33.99XS	768	T34.822S	768	T36.4X1S	768	T36.92XS	769	T37.4X3S	769
T33.2XXA	768	T34.011A	768	T34.829A	768	T36.4X2A	758	T36.93XA	758	T37.4X4A	759
T33.2XXD	830	T34.011D	830	T34.829D	830	T36.4X2D	830	T36.93XD	830	T37.4X4D	831
T33.2XXS	768	T34.011S	768	T34.829S	768	T36.4X2S	768	T36.93XS	769	T37.4X4S	769
T33.3XXA	768	T34.012A	768	T34.831A	768	T36.4X3A	758	T36.94XA	758	T37.4X5A	566, 759
T33.3XXD	830	T34.012D	830	T34.831D	830	T36.4X3D	830	T36.94XD	830	T37.4X5D	831
T33.3XXS	768	T34.012S	768	T34.831S	768	T36.4X3S	769	T36.94XS	769	T37.4X5S	769
T33.40XA	768	T34.019A	768	T34.832A	768	T36.4X4A	758	T36.95XA	566, 758	T37.4X6A	845
T33.40XD	830	T34.019D	830	T34.832D	830	T36.4X4D	830	T36.95XD	830	T37.4X6D	831
T33.40XS	768	T34.019S	768	T34.832S	768	T36.4X4S	769	T36.95XS	769	T37.4X6S	831
T33.41XA	768	T34.02XA	768	T34.839A	768	T36.4X5A	566, 758	T36.96XA	844	T37.5X1A	759
T33.41XD	830	T34.02XD	830	T34.839D	830	T36.4X5D	830	T36.96XD	830	T37.5X1D	831
T33.41XS	768	T34.02XS	768	T34.839S	768	T36.4X5S	769	T36.96XS	830	T37.5X1S	769
T33.42XA	768	T34.09XA	768	T34.90XA	768	T36.4X6A	844	T37.0X1A	758	T37.5X2A	759
T33.42XD	830	T34.09XD	830	T34.90XD	830	T36.4X6D	830	T37.0X1D	830	T37.5X2D	831
T33.42XS	768	T34.09XS	768	T34.90XS	768	T36.4X6S	830	T37.0X1S	769	T37.5X2S	769
T33.511A	768	T34.1XXA	768	T34.99XA	768	T36.5X1A	758	T37.0X2A	758	T37.5X3A	759
T33.511D	830	T34.1XXD	830	T34.99XD	830	T36.5X1D	830	T37.0X2D	830	T37.5X3D	831
T33.511S	768	T34.1XXS	768	T34.99XS	768	T36.5X1S	769	T37.0X2S	769	T37.5X3S	769
T33.512A	768	T34.2XXA	768	T36.0X1A	758	T36.5X2A	758	T37.0X3A	758	T37.5X4A	759
T33.512D	830	T34.2XXD	830	T36.0X1D	830	T36.5X2D	830	T37.0X3D	830	T37.5X4D	831
T33.512S	768	T34.2XXS	768	T36.0X1S	768	T36.5X2S	769	T37.0X3S	769	T37.5X4S	769
T33.519A	768	T34.3XXA	768	T36.0X2A	758	T36.5X3A	758	T37.0X4A	759	T37.5X5A	566, 759
T33.519D	830	T34.3XXD	830	T36.0X2D	830	T36.5X3D	830	T37.0X4D	830	T37.5X5D	831
T33.519S	768	T34.3XXS	768	T36.0X2S	768	T36.5X3S	769	T37.0X4S	769	T37.5X5S	769
T33.521A	768	T34.40XA	768	T36.0X3A	758	T36.5X4A	758	T37.0X5A	566, 759	T37.5X6A	845
T33.521D	830	T34.40XD	830	T36.0X3D	830	T36.5X4D	830	T37.0X5D	830	T37.5X6D	831
T33.521S	768	T34.40XS	768	T36.0X3S	768	T36.5X4S	769	T37.0X5S	769	T37.5X6S	831
T33.522A	768	T34.41XA	768	T36.0X4A	758	T36.5X5A	566, 758	T37.0X6A	845	T37.8X1A	759
T33.522D	830	T34.41XD	830	T36.0X4D	830	T36.5X5D	830	T37.0X6D	830	T37.8X1D	831
T33.522S	768	T34.41XS	768	T36.0X4S	768	T36.5X5S	769	T37.0X6S	830	T37.8X1S	769
T33.529A	768	T34.42XA	768	T36.0X5A	566, 758	T36.5X6A	844	T37.1X1A	758	T37.8X2A	759
T33.529D	830	T34.42XD	830	T36.0X5D	830	T36.5X6D	830	T37.1X1D	830	T37.8X2D	831
T33.529S	768	T34.42XS	768	T36.0X5S	768	T36.5X6S	830	T37.1X1S	769	T37.8X2S	769
T33.531A	768	T34.511A	768	T36.0X6A	844	T36.6X1A	758	T37.1X2A	758	T37.8X3A	759
T33.531D	830	T34.511D	830	T36.0X6D	830	T36.6X1D	830	T37.1X2D	830	T37.8X3D	831
T33.531S	768	T34.511S	768	T36.0X6S	830	T36.6X1S	769	T37.1X2S	769	T37.8X3S	769
T33.532A	768	T34.512A	768	T36.1X1A	758	T36.6X2A	758	T37.1X3A	759	T37.8X4A	759
T33.532D	830	T34.512D	830	T36.1X1D	830	T36.6X2D	830	T37.1X3D	830	T37.8X4D	831
T33.532S	768	T34.512S	768	T36.1X1S	768	T36.6X2S	769	T37.1X3S	769	T37.8X4S	769
T33.539A	768	T34.519A	768	T36.1X2A	758	T36.6X3A	758	T37.1X4A	759	T37.8X5A	566, 759
T33.539D	830	T34.519D	830	T36.1X2D	830	T36.6X3D	830	T37.1X4D	830	T37.8X5D	831
T33.539S	768	T34.519S	768	T36.1X2S	768	T36.6X3S	769	T37.1X4S	769	T37.8X5S	769
T33.60XA	768	T34.521A	768	T36.1X3A	758	T36.6X4A	758	T37.1X5A	566, 759	T37.8X6A	845
T33.60XD	830	T34.521D	830	T36.1X3D	830	T36.6X4D	830	T37.1X5D	830	T37.8X6D	831
T33.60XS	768	T34.521S	768	T36.1X3S	768	T36.6X4S	769	T37.1X5S	769	T37.8X6S	831
T33.61XA	768	T34.522A	768	T36.1X4A	758	T36.6X5A	566, 758	T37.1X6A	845	T37.91XA	759
T33.61XD	830	T34.522D	830	T36.1X4D	830	T36.6X5D	830	T37.1X6D	830	T37.91XD	831
T33.61XS	768	T34.522S	768	T36.1X4S	768	T36.6X5S	769	T37.1X6S	830	T37.91XS	769
T33.62XA	768	T34.529A	768	T36.1X5A	566, 758	T36.6X6A	844	T37.2X1A	758	T37.92XA	759
T33.62XD	830	T34.529D	830	T36.1X5D	830	T36.6X6D	830	T37.2X1D	830	T37.92XD	831
T33.62XS	768	T34.529S	768	T36.1X5S	768	T36.6X6S	830	T37.2X1S	769	T37.92XS	769
T33.70XA	768	T34.531A	768	T36.1X6A	844	T36.7X1A	758	T37.2X2A	759	T37.93XA	759
T33.70XD	830	T34.531D	830	T36.1X6D	830	T36.7X1D	830	T37.2X2D	830	T37.93XD	831
T33.70XS	768	T34.531S	768	T36.1X6S	830	T36.7X1S	769	T37.2X2S	769	T37.93XS	769
T33.71XA	768	T34.532A	768	T36.2X1A	758	T36.7X2A	758	T37.2X3A	759	T37.94XA	759
T33.71XD	830	T34.532D	830	T36.2X1D	830	T36.7X2D	830	T37.2X3D	830	T37.94XD	831
T33.71XS	768	T34.532S	768	T36.2X1S	768	T36.7X2S	769	T37.2X3S	769	T37.94XS	769
T33.72XA	768	T34.539A	768	T36.2X2A	758	T36.7X3A	758	T37.2X4A	759	T37.95XA	566, 759
T33.72XD	830	T34.539D	830	T36.2X2D	830	T36.7X3D	830	T37.2X4D	830	T37.95XD	831
T33.72XS	768	T34.539S	768	T36.2X2S	768	T36.7X3S	769	T37.2X4S	769	T37.95XS	769
T33.811A	768	T34.60XA	768	T36.2X3A	758	T36.7X4A	758	T37.2X5A	566, 759	T37.96XA	845
T33.811D	830	T34.60XD	830	T36.2X3D	830	T36.7X4D	830	T37.2X5D	830	T37.96XD	831
T33.811S	768	T34.60XS	768	T36.2X3S	768	T36.7X4S	769	T37.2X5S	769	T37.96XS	831
T33.812A	768	T34.61XA	768	T36.2X4A	758	T36.7X5A	566, 758	T37.2X6A	845	T38.0X1A	759
T33.812D	830	T34.61XD	830	T36.2X4D	830	T36.7X5D	830	T37.2X6D	830	T38.0X1D	831
T33.812S	768	T34.61XS	768	T36.2X4S	768	T36.7X5S	769	T37.2X6S	830	T38.0X1S	769
T33.819A	768	T34.62XA	768	T36.2X5A	566, 758	T36.7X6A	844	T37.3X1A	759	T38.0X2A	759
T33.819D	830	T34.62XD	830	T36.2X5D	830	T36.7X6D	830	T37.3X1D	830	T38.0X2D	831
T33.819S	768	T34.62XS	768	T36.2X5S	768	T36.7X6S	830	T37.3X1S	769	T38.0X2S	769
T33.821A	768	T34.70XA	768	T36.2X6A	844	T36.8X1A	758	T37.3X2A	759	T38.0X3A	759
T33.821D	830	T34.70XD	830	T36.2X6D	830	T36.8X1D	830	T37.3X2D	830	T38.0X3D	831
T33.821S	768	T34.70XS	768	T36.2X6S	830	T36.8X1S	769	T37.3X2S	769	T38.0X3S	769
T33.822A	768	T34.71XA	768	T36.3X1A	758	T36.8X2A	758	T37.3X3A	759	T38.0X4A	759
T33.822D	830	T34.71XD	830	T36.3X1D	830	T36.8X2D	830	T37.3X3D	830	T38.0X4D	831
T33.822S	768	T34.71XS	768	T36.3X1S	769	T36.8X2S	769	T37.3X3S	769	T38.0X4S	769
T33.829A	768	T34.72XA	768	T36.3X2A	758	T36.8X3A	758	T37.3X4A	759	T38.0X5A	759
T33.829D	830	T34.72XD	830	T36.3X2D	830	T36.8X3D	830	T37.3X4D	830	T38.0X5D	831
T33.829S	768	T34.72XS	768	T36.3X2S	768	T36.8X3S	769	T37.3X4S	769	T38.0X5S	566
T33.831A	768	T34.811A	768	T36.3X3A	758	T36.8X4A	758	T37.3X5A	566, 759	T38.0X5D	831
T33.831D	830	T34.811D	830	T36.3X3D	830	T36.8X4D	830	T37.3X5D	831	T38.0X5S	769
T33.831S	768	T34.811S	768	T36.3X3S	769	T36.8X4S	769	T37.3X5S	769	T38.0X6A	845
T33.832A	768	T34.812A	768	T36.3X4A	758	T36.8X5A	566, 758	T37.3X6A	845	T38.0X6D	831
T33.832D	830	T34.812D	830	T36.3X4D	830	T36.8X5D	830	T37.3X6D	831	T38.0X6S	831
T33.832S	768	T34.812S	768	T36.3X4S	768	T36.8X5S	769	T37.3X6S	831	T38.1X1A	759
T33.839A	768	T34.819A	768	T36.3X5A	566, 758	T36.8X6A	844	T37.4X1A	759	T38.1X1D	831
T33.839D	830	T34.819D	830	T36.3X5D	830	T36.8X6D	830	T37.4X1D	831	T38.1X1S	769
T33.839S	768	T34.819S	768	T36.3X5S	768	T36.8X6S	830	T37.4X1S	769	T38.1X2A	759
T33.90XA	768	T34.821A	768	T36.3X6A	844	T36.91XA	758	T37.4X2A	759	T38.1X2D	831
T33.90XD	830	T34.821D	830	T36.3X6D	830	T36.91XD	830	T37.4X2D	831	T38.1X2S	769
T33.90XS	768	T34.821S	768	T36.3X6S	830	T36.91XS	769	T37.4X2S	769	T38.1X3A	759
T33.99XA	768	T34.822A	768	T36.4X1A	758	T36.92XA	758	T37.4X3A	759	T38.1X3D	831
T33.99XD	830	T34.822D	830	T36.4X1D	830	T36.92XD	830	T37.4X3D	831	T38.1X3S	769
										T38.1X4A	759

Code	Page	Code	Page	Code	Page	Code	Page	Code	Page	Code	Page
T38.1X4D	831	T38.6X5D	831	T38.906D	831	T39.311D	831	T40.0X2D	832	T40.5X5D	832
T38.1X4S	769	T38.6X5S	769	T38.906S	769	T39.311S	769	T40.0X2S	770	T40.5X5S	770
T38.1X5A	566,759	T38.6X6A	845	T38.991A	759	T39.312A	759	T40.0X3A	759	T40.5X6A	845
T38.1X5D	831	T38.6X6D	831	T38.991D	831	T39.312D	831	T40.0X3D	832	T40.5X6D	832
T38.1X5S	769	T38.6X6S	831	T38.991S	769	T39.312S	769	T40.0X3S	770	T40.5X6S	832
T38.1X6A	845	T38.7X1A	759	T38.992A	759	T39.313A	759	T40.0X4A	760	T40.601A	760
T38.1X6D	831	T38.7X1D	831	T38.992D	831	T39.313D	831	T40.0X4D	832	T40.601D	832
T38.1X6S	831	T38.7X1S	769	T38.992S	769	T39.313S	769	T40.0X4S	770	T40.601S	770
T38.2X1A	759	T38.7X2A	759	T38.993A	759	T39.314A	759	T40.0X5A	567,759	T40.602A	760
T38.2X1D	831	T38.7X2D	831	T38.993D	831	T39.314D	831	T40.0X5D	832	T40.602D	832
T38.2X1S	769	T38.7X2S	769	T38.993S	769	T39.314S	769	T40.0X5S	770	T40.602S	770
T38.2X2A	759	T38.7X3A	759	T38.994A	759	T39.315A	567,759	T40.0X6A	845	T40.603A	760
T38.2X2D	831	T38.7X3D	831	T38.994D	831	T39.315D	831	T40.0X6D	832	T40.603D	832
T38.2X2S	769	T38.7X3S	769	T38.994S	769	T39.315S	769	T40.0X6S	832	T40.603S	770
T38.2X3A	759	T38.7X4A	759	T38.995A	567,759	T39.316A	845	T40.1X1A	759	T40.604A	760
T38.2X3D	831	T38.7X4D	831	T38.995D	831	T39.316D	831	T40.1X1D	832	T40.604D	832
T38.2X3S	769	T38.7X4S	769	T38.995S	769	T39.316S	831	T40.1X1S	770	T40.604S	770
T38.2X4A	759	T38.7X5A	567,759	T38.996A	845	T39.391A	759	T40.1X2A	759	T40.605A	567,760
T38.2X4D	831	T38.7X5D	831	T38.996D	831	T39.391D	831	T40.1X2D	832	T40.605D	832
T38.2X4S	769	T38.7X5S	769	T38.996S	831	T39.391S	769	T40.1X2S	770	T40.605S	770
T38.2X5A	566,759	T38.7X6A	845	T39.011A	759	T39.392A	759	T40.1X3A	759	T40.606A	845
T38.2X5D	831	T38.7X6D	831	T39.011D	831	T39.392D	831	T40.1X3D	832	T40.606D	832
T38.2X5S	769	T38.7X6S	831	T39.011S	769	T39.392S	769	T40.1X3S	770	T40.606S	832
T38.2X6A	845	T38.801A	759	T39.012A	759	T39.393A	759	T40.1X4A	759	T40.691A	760
T38.2X6D	831	T38.801D	831	T39.012D	831	T39.393D	831	T40.1X4D	832	T40.691D	832
T38.2X6S	831	T38.801S	769	T39.012S	769	T39.393S	769	T40.1X4S	770	T40.691S	770
T38.3X1A	759	T38.802A	759	T39.013A	759	T39.394A	759	T40.2X1A	759	T40.692A	760
T38.3X1D	831	T38.802D	831	T39.013D	831	T39.394D	831	T40.2X1D	832	T40.692D	832
T38.3X1S	769	T38.802S	769	T39.013S	769	T39.394S	769	T40.2X1S	770	T40.692S	770
T38.3X2A	759	T38.803A	759	T39.014A	759	T39.395A	567,759	T40.2X2A	759	T40.693A	760
T38.3X2D	831	T38.803D	831	T39.014D	831	T39.395D	831	T40.2X2D	832	T40.693D	832
T38.3X2S	769	T38.803S	769	T39.014S	769	T39.395S	769	T40.2X2S	770	T40.693S	770
T38.3X3A	759	T38.804A	759	T39.015A	567,759	T39.396A	845	T40.2X3A	759	T40.694A	760
T38.3X3D	831	T38.804D	831	T39.015D	831	T39.396D	831	T40.2X3D	832	T40.694D	832
T38.3X3S	769	T38.804S	769	T39.015S	831	T39.396S	831	T40.2X3S	770	T40.694S	770
T38.3X4A	759	T38.805A	567,759	T39.016A	845	T39.4X1A	759	T40.2X4A	759	T40.695A	567,760
T38.3X4D	831	T38.805D	831	T39.016D	831	T39.4X1D	831	T40.2X4D	832	T40.695D	832
T38.3X4S	769	T38.805S	769	T39.016S	831	T39.4X1S	769	T40.2X4S	770	T40.695S	770
T38.3X5A	567,759	T38.806A	845	T39.091A	759	T39.4X2A	759	T40.2X5A	567,759	T40.696A	845
T38.3X5D	831	T38.806D	831	T39.091D	831	T39.4X2D	831	T40.2X5D	832	T40.696D	832
T38.3X5S	769	T38.806S	831	T39.091S	769	T39.4X2S	769	T40.2X5S	770	T40.696S	832
T38.3X6A	845	T38.811A	759	T39.092A	759	T39.4X3A	759	T40.2X6A	845	T40.7X1A	760
T38.3X6D	831	T38.811D	831	T39.092D	831	T39.4X3D	831	T40.2X6D	832	T40.7X1D	832
T38.3X6S	831	T38.811S	769	T39.092S	769	T39.4X3S	769	T40.2X6S	832	T40.7X1S	770
T38.4X1A	759	T38.812A	759	T39.093A	759	T39.4X4A	759	T40.3X1A	759	T40.7X2A	760
T38.4X1D	831	T38.812D	831	T39.093D	831	T39.4X4D	831	T40.3X1D	832	T40.7X2D	832
T38.4X1S	769	T38.812S	769	T39.093S	769	T39.4X4S	769	T40.3X1S	770	T40.7X2S	770
T38.4X2A	759	T38.813A	759	T39.094A	759	T39.4X5A	567,759	T40.3X2A	759	T40.7X3A	760
T38.4X2D	831	T38.813D	831	T39.094D	831	T39.4X5D	831	T40.3X2D	832	T40.7X3D	832
T38.4X2S	769	T38.813S	769	T39.094S	769	T39.4X5S	769	T40.3X2S	770	T40.7X3S	770
T38.4X3A	759	T38.814A	759	T39.095A	567,759	T39.4X6A	845	T40.3X3A	759	T40.7X4A	760
T38.4X3D	831	T38.814D	831	T39.095D	831	T39.4X6D	831	T40.3X3D	832	T40.7X4D	832
T38.4X3S	769	T38.814S	769	T39.095S	769	T39.4X6S	831	T40.3X3S	770	T40.7X4S	770
T38.4X4A	759	T38.815A	567,759	T39.096A	845	T39.8X1A	759	T40.3X4A	759	T40.7X5A	567,760
T38.4X4D	831	T38.815D	831	T39.096D	831	T39.8X1D	831	T40.3X4D	832	T40.7X5D	832
T38.4X4S	769	T38.815S	769	T39.096S	831	T39.8X1S	769	T40.3X4S	770	T40.7X5S	770
T38.4X5A	567,759	T38.816A	845	T39.1X1A	759	T39.8X2A	759	T40.3X5A	567,759	T40.7X6A	845
T38.4X5D	831	T38.816D	831	T39.1X1D	831	T39.8X2D	831	T40.3X5D	832	T40.7X6D	832
T38.4X5S	769	T38.816S	831	T39.1X1S	769	T39.8X2S	769	T40.3X5S	770	T40.7X6S	832
T38.4X6A	845	T38.891A	759	T39.1X2A	759	T39.8X3A	759	T40.3X6A	845	T40.8X1A	760
T38.4X6D	831	T38.891D	831	T39.1X2D	831	T39.8X3D	831	T40.3X6D	832	T40.8X1D	832
T38.4X6S	831	T38.891S	769	T39.1X2S	769	T39.8X3S	769	T40.3X6S	832	T40.8X1S	770
T38.5X1A	759	T38.892A	759	T39.1X3A	759	T39.8X4A	759	T40.4X1A	759	T40.8X2A	760
T38.5X1D	831	T38.892D	831	T39.1X3D	831	T39.8X4D	832	T40.4X1D	832	T40.8X2D	832
T38.5X1S	769	T38.892S	769	T39.1X3S	769	T39.8X4S	769	T40.4X1S	770	T40.8X2S	770
T38.5X2A	759	T38.893A	759	T39.1X4A	759	T39.8X5A	567,759	T40.4X2A	759	T40.8X3A	760
T38.5X2D	831	T38.893D	831	T39.1X4D	831	T39.8X5D	832	T40.4X2D	832	T40.8X3D	832
T38.5X2S	769	T38.893S	769	T39.1X4S	769	T39.8X5S	769	T40.4X2S	770	T40.8X3S	770
T38.5X3A	759	T38.894A	759	T39.1X5A	567,759	T39.8X6A	845	T40.4X3A	759	T40.8X4A	760
T38.5X3D	831	T38.894D	831	T39.1X5D	831	T39.8X6D	832	T40.4X3D	832	T40.8X4D	832
T38.5X3S	769	T38.894S	769	T39.1X5S	769	T39.8X6S	832	T40.4X3S	770	T40.8X4S	770
T38.5X4A	759	T38.895A	567,759	T39.1X6A	845	T39.91XA	759	T40.4X4A	759	T40.901A	760
T38.5X4D	831	T38.895D	831	T39.1X6D	831	T39.91XD	832	T40.4X4D	832	T40.901D	832
T38.5X4S	769	T38.895S	769	T39.1X6S	831	T39.91XS	769	T40.4X4S	770	T40.901S	770
T38.5X5A	567,759	T38.896A	845	T39.2X1A	759	T39.92XA	759	T40.4X5A	567,759	T40.902A	760
T38.5X5D	831	T38.896D	831	T39.2X1D	831	T39.92XD	832	T40.4X5D	832	T40.902D	832
T38.5X5S	769	T38.896S	831	T39.2X1S	769	T39.92XS	770	T40.4X5S	770	T40.902S	770
T38.5X6A	845	T38.901A	759	T39.2X2A	759	T39.93XA	759	T40.4X6A	845	T40.903A	760
T38.5X6D	831	T38.901D	831	T39.2X2D	831	T39.93XD	832	T40.4X6D	832	T40.903D	832
T38.5X6S	831	T38.901S	769	T39.2X2S	769	T39.93XS	770	T40.4X6S	832	T40.903S	770
T38.6X1A	759	T38.902A	759	T39.2X3A	759	T39.94XA	759	T40.5X1A	759	T40.904A	760
T38.6X1D	831	T38.902D	831	T39.2X3D	831	T39.94XD	832	T40.5X1D	832	T40.904D	832
T38.6X1S	769	T38.902S	769	T39.2X3S	769	T39.94XS	770	T40.5X1S	770	T40.904S	770
T38.6X2A	759	T38.903A	759	T39.2X4A	759	T39.95XA	567,759	T40.5X2A	759	T40.905A	567,760
T38.6X2D	831	T38.903D	831	T39.2X4D	831	T39.95XD	832	T40.5X2D	832	T40.905D	832
T38.6X2S	769	T38.903S	769	T39.2X4S	769	T39.95XS	770	T40.5X2S	770	T40.905S	770
T38.6X3A	759	T38.904A	759	T39.2X5A	567,759	T39.96XA	845	T40.5X3A	759	T40.906A	845
T38.6X3D	831	T38.904D	831	T39.2X5D	831	T39.96XD	832	T40.5X3D	832	T40.906D	832
T38.6X3S	769	T38.904S	769	T39.2X5S	769	T39.96XS	832	T40.5X3S	770	T40.906S	832
T38.6X4A	759	T38.905A	567,759	T39.2X6A	845	T40.0X1A	759	T40.5X4A	760	T40.991A	760
T38.6X4D	831	T38.905D	831	T39.2X6S	831	T40.0X1D	832	T40.5X4D	832	T40.991D	832
T38.6X4S	769	T38.905S	769	T39.311A	759	T40.0X1S	770	T40.5X4S	770	T40.991S	770
T38.6X5A	567,759	T38.906A	845			T40.0X2A	759	T40.5X5A	567,760	T40.992A	760

Code	Page	Code	Page	Code	Page	Code	Page	Code	Page	Code	Page
T40.992D	770	T41.3X3D	832	T42.2X4D	832	T42.75XD	833	T43.206D	833	T43.501D	833
T40.992S	770	T41.3X3S	770	T42.2X4S	770	T42.75XS	770	T43.206S	833	T43.501S	771
T40.993A	760	T41.3X4A	760	T42.2X5A	567,760	T42.76XA	845	T43.211A	760	T43.502A	760
T40.993D	832	T41.3X4D	832	T42.2X5D	832	T42.76XD	833	T43.211D	833	T43.502D	833
T40.993S	770	T41.3X4S	770	T42.2X5S	770	T42.76XS	833	T43.211S	770	T43.502S	771
T40.994A	760	T41.3X5A	567,760	T42.2X6A	845	T42.8X1A	760	T43.212A	760	T43.503A	760
T40.994D	832	T41.3X5D	832	T42.2X6D	832	T42.8X1D	833	T43.212D	833	T43.503D	833
T40.994S	770	T41.3X5S	770	T42.2X6S	832	T42.8X1S	770	T43.212S	770	T43.503S	771
T40.995A	567,760	T41.3X6A	845	T42.3X1A	760	T42.8X2A	760	T43.213A	760	T43.504A	760
T40.995D	832	T41.3X6D	832	T42.3X1D	832	T42.8X2D	833	T43.213D	833	T43.504D	833
T40.995S	770	T41.3X6S	832	T42.3X1S	770	T42.8X2S	770	T43.213S	770	T43.504S	771
T40.996A	845	T41.41XA	760	T42.3X2A	760	T42.8X3A	760	T43.214A	760	T43.505A	567,760
T40.996D	832	T41.41XD	832	T42.3X2D	832	T42.8X3D	833	T43.214D	833	T43.505D	833
T40.996S	832	T41.41XS	770	T42.3X2S	770	T42.8X3S	770	T43.214S	770	T43.505S	771
T41.0X1A	760	T41.42XA	760	T42.3X3A	760	T42.8X4A	760	T43.215A	567,760	T43.506A	845
T41.0X1D	832	T41.42XD	832	T42.3X3D	832	T42.8X4D	833	T43.215D	833	T43.506D	833
T41.0X1S	770	T41.42XS	770	T42.3X3S	770	T42.8X4S	770	T43.215S	770	T43.506S	833
T41.0X2A	760	T41.43XA	760	T42.3X4A	760	T42.8X5A	567,760	T43.216A	845	T43.591A	760
T41.0X2D	832	T41.43XD	832	T42.3X4D	832	T42.8X5D	833	T43.216D	833	T43.591D	833
T41.0X2S	770	T41.43XS	770	T42.3X4S	770	T42.8X5S	770	T43.216S	833	T43.591S	771
T41.0X3A	760	T41.44XA	760	T42.3X5A	567,760	T42.8X6A	845	T43.221A	760	T43.592A	760
T41.0X3D	832	T41.44XD	832	T42.3X5D	832	T42.8X6D	833	T43.221D	833	T43.592D	833
T41.0X3S	770	T41.44XS	770	T42.3X5S	770	T42.8X6S	833	T43.221S	770	T43.592S	771
T41.0X4A	760	T41.45XA	567,760	T42.3X6A	845	T43.011A	760	T43.222A	760	T43.593A	760
T41.0X4D	832	T41.45XD	832	T42.3X6D	832	T43.011D	833	T43.222D	833	T43.593D	833
T41.0X4S	770	T41.45XS	770	T42.3X6S	832	T43.011S	770	T43.222S	770	T43.593S	771
T41.0X5A	567,760	T41.46XA	845	T42.4X1A	760	T43.012A	760	T43.223A	760	T43.594A	760
T41.0X5D	832	T41.46XD	832	T42.4X1D	832	T43.012D	833	T43.223D	833	T43.594D	833
T41.0X5S	770	T41.46XS	832	T42.4X1S	770	T43.012S	770	T43.223S	770	T43.594S	771
T41.0X6A	845	T41.5X1A	760	T42.4X2A	760	T43.013A	760	T43.224A	760	T43.595A	567,760
T41.0X6D	832	T41.5X1D	832	T42.4X2D	832	T43.013D	833	T43.224D	833	T43.595D	833
T41.0X6S	832	T41.5X1S	770	T42.4X2S	770	T43.013S	770	T43.224S	770	T43.595S	771
T41.1X1A	760	T41.5X2A	760	T42.4X3A	760	T43.014A	760	T43.225A	567,760	T43.596A	845
T41.1X1D	832	T41.5X2D	832	T42.4X3D	832	T43.014D	833	T43.225D	833	T43.596D	833
T41.1X1S	770	T41.5X2S	770	T42.4X3S	770	T43.014S	770	T43.225S	770	T43.596S	833
T41.1X2A	760	T41.5X3A	760	T42.4X4A	760	T43.015A	567,760	T43.226A	845	T43.601A	760
T41.1X2D	832	T41.5X3D	832	T42.4X4D	832	T43.015D	833	T43.226D	833	T43.601D	833
T41.1X2S	770	T41.5X3S	770	T42.4X4S	770	T43.015S	770	T43.226S	833	T43.601S	771
T41.1X3A	760	T41.5X4A	760	T42.4X5A	567,760	T43.016A	845	T43.291A	760	T43.602A	760
T41.1X3D	832	T41.5X4D	832	T42.4X5D	832	T43.016D	833	T43.291D	833	T43.602D	833
T41.1X3S	770	T41.5X4S	770	T42.4X5S	770	T43.016S	833	T43.291S	770	T43.602S	771
T41.1X4A	760	T41.5X5A	567,760	T42.4X6A	845	T43.021A	760	T43.292A	760	T43.603A	760
T41.1X4D	832	T41.5X5D	832	T42.4X6D	832	T43.021D	833	T43.292D	833	T43.603D	833
T41.1X4S	770	T41.5X5S	770	T42.4X6S	832	T43.021S	770	T43.292S	770	T43.603S	771
T41.1X5A	567,760	T41.5X6A	845	T42.5X1A	760	T43.022A	760	T43.293A	760	T43.604A	760
T41.1X5D	832	T41.5X6D	832	T42.5X1D	832	T43.022D	833	T43.293D	833	T43.604D	833
T41.1X5S	770	T41.5X6S	832	T42.5X1S	770	T43.022S	770	T43.293S	771	T43.604S	771
T41.1X6A	845	T42.0X1A	760	T42.5X2A	760	T43.023A	760	T43.294A	760	T43.605A	567,760
T41.1X6D	832	T42.0X1D	832	T42.5X2D	833	T43.023D	833	T43.294D	833	T43.605D	833
T41.1X6S	832	T42.0X1S	770	T42.5X2S	770	T43.023S	770	T43.294S	771	T43.605S	771
T41.201A	760	T42.0X2A	760	T42.5X3A	760	T43.024A	760	T43.295A	567,760	T43.606A	845
T41.201D	832	T42.0X2D	832	T42.5X3D	833	T43.024D	833	T43.295D	833	T43.606D	833
T41.201S	770	T42.0X2S	770	T42.5X3S	770	T43.024S	770	T43.295S	771	T43.606S	833
T41.202A	760	T42.0X3A	760	T42.5X4A	760	T43.025A	567,760	T43.296A	845	T43.611A	760
T41.202D	832	T42.0X3D	832	T42.5X4D	833	T43.025D	833	T43.296D	833	T43.611D	833
T41.202S	770	T42.0X3S	770	T42.5X4S	770	T43.025S	770	T43.296S	833	T43.611S	771
T41.203A	760	T42.0X4A	760	T42.5X5A	567,760	T43.026A	845	T43.3X1A	760	T43.612A	760
T41.203D	832	T42.0X4D	832	T42.5X5D	833	T43.026D	833	T43.3X1D	833	T43.612D	833
T41.203S	770	T42.0X4S	770	T42.5X5S	770	T43.026S	833	T43.3X1S	771	T43.612S	771
T41.204A	760	T42.0X5A	567,760	T42.5X6A	845	T43.1X1A	760	T43.3X2A	760	T43.613A	760
T41.204D	832	T42.0X5D	832	T42.5X6D	833	T43.1X1D	833	T43.3X2D	833	T43.613D	833
T41.204S	770	T42.0X5S	770	T42.5X6S	833	T43.1X1S	770	T43.3X2S	771	T43.613S	771
T41.205A	567,760	T42.0X6A	845	T42.6X1A	760	T43.1X2A	760	T43.3X3A	760	T43.614A	761
T41.205D	832	T42.0X6D	832	T42.6X1D	833	T43.1X2D	833	T43.3X3D	833	T43.614D	833
T41.205S	770	T42.0X6S	832	T42.6X1S	770	T43.1X2S	770	T43.3X3S	771	T43.614S	771
T41.206A	845	T42.1X1A	760	T42.6X2A	760	T43.1X3A	760	T43.3X4A	760	T43.615A	567,761
T41.206D	832	T42.1X1D	832	T42.6X2D	833	T43.1X3D	833	T43.3X4D	833	T43.615D	833
T41.206S	832	T42.1X1S	770	T42.6X2S	833	T43.1X3S	770	T43.3X4S	771	T43.615S	771
T41.291A	760	T42.1X2A	760	T42.6X3A	760	T43.1X4A	760	T43.3X5A	567,760	T43.616A	845
T41.291D	832	T42.1X2D	832	T42.6X3D	833	T43.1X4D	833	T43.3X5D	833	T43.616D	833
T41.291S	770	T42.1X2S	770	T42.6X3S	770	T43.1X4S	770	T43.3X5S	771	T43.616S	833
T41.292A	760	T42.1X3A	760	T42.6X4A	760	T43.1X5A	567,760	T43.3X6A	845	T43.621A	761
T41.292D	832	T42.1X3D	832	T42.6X4D	833	T43.1X5D	833	T43.3X6D	833	T43.621D	833
T41.292S	770	T42.1X3S	770	T42.6X4S	770	T43.1X5S	770	T43.3X6S	833	T43.621S	771
T41.293A	760	T42.1X4A	760	T42.6X5A	567,760	T43.1X6A	845	T43.4X1A	760	T43.622A	761
T41.293D	832	T42.1X4D	832	T42.6X5D	833	T43.1X6D	833	T43.4X1D	833	T43.622D	833
T41.293S	770	T42.1X4S	770	T42.6X5S	770	T43.1X6S	833	T43.4X1S	771	T43.622S	771
T41.294A	760	T42.1X5A	567,760	T42.6X6A	845	T43.201A	760	T43.4X2A	760	T43.623A	761
T41.294D	832	T42.1X5D	832	T42.6X6D	833	T43.201D	833	T43.4X2D	833	T43.623D	833
T41.294S	770	T42.1X5S	770	T42.6X6S	833	T43.201S	770	T43.4X2S	771	T43.623S	771
T41.295A	567,760	T42.1X6A	845	T42.71XA	760	T43.202A	760	T43.4X3A	760	T43.624A	761
T41.295D	832	T42.1X6D	832	T42.71XD	833	T43.202D	833	T43.4X3D	833	T43.624D	833
T41.295S	770	T42.1X6S	832	T42.71XS	770	T43.202S	770	T43.4X3S	771	T43.624S	771
T41.296A	845	T42.2X1A	760	T42.72XA	760	T43.203A	760	T43.4X4A	760	T43.625A	567,761
T41.296D	832	T42.2X1D	832	T42.72XD	833	T43.203D	833	T43.4X4D	833	T43.625D	833
T41.296S	832	T42.2X1S	770	T42.72XS	770	T43.203S	770	T43.4X4S	771	T43.625S	771
T41.3X1A	760	T42.2X2A	760	T42.73XA	760	T43.204A	760	T43.4X5A	567,760	T43.626A	845
T41.3X1D	832	T42.2X2D	832	T42.73XD	833	T43.204D	833	T43.4X5D	833	T43.626D	833
T41.3X1S	770	T42.2X2S	770	T42.73XS	770	T43.204S	770	T43.4X5S	771	T43.626S	833
T41.3X2A	760	T42.2X3A	760	T42.74XA	760	T43.205A	567,760	T43.4X6A	845	T43.631A	761
T41.3X2D	832	T42.2X3D	832	T42.74XD	833	T43.205D	833	T43.4X6D	833	T43.631D	833
T41.3X3A	760	T42.2X3S	770	T42.74XS	770	T43.205S	770	T43.4X6S	833	T43.631S	771
		T42.2X4A	760	T42.75XA	567,760	T43.206A	845	T43.501A	760	T43.632A	761

Code	Page	Code	Page	Code	Page	Code	Page	Code	Page	Code	Page
T43.632D	833	T44.0X5D	833	T44.5X6D	834	T45.0X1A	761	T45.512A	761	T45.693A	761
T43.632S	771	T44.0X5S	771	T44.5X6S	834	T45.0X1D	834	T45.512D	834	T45.693D	834
T43.633A	761	T44.0X6A	845	T44.6X1A	761	T45.0X1S	771	T45.512S	771	T45.693S	771
T43.633D	833	T44.0X6D	833	T44.6X1D	834	T45.0X2A	761	T45.513A	761	T45.694A	761
T43.633S	771	T44.0X6S	833	T44.6X1S	771	T45.0X2D	834	T45.513D	834	T45.694D	834
T43.634A	761	T44.1X1A	761	T44.6X2A	761	T45.0X2S	771	T45.513S	771	T45.694S	771
T43.634D	833	T44.1X1D	833	T44.6X2D	834	T45.0X3A	761	T45.514A	761	T45.695A	567,761
T43.634S	771	T44.1X1S	771	T44.6X2S	771	T45.0X3D	834	T45.514D	834	T45.695D	834
T43.635A	567,761	T44.1X2A	761	T44.6X3A	761	T45.0X3S	771	T45.514S	771	T45.695S	771
T43.635D	833	T44.1X2D	833	T44.6X3D	834	T45.0X4A	761	T45.515A	567,761	T45.696A	845
T43.635S	771	T44.1X2S	771	T44.6X3S	771	T45.0X4D	834	T45.515D	834	T45.696D	834
T43.636A	845	T44.1X3A	761	T44.6X4A	761	T45.0X4S	771	T45.515S	771	T45.696S	834
T43.636D	833	T44.1X3D	833	T44.6X4D	834	T45.0X5A	567,761	T45.516A	845	T45.7X1A	761
T43.636S	833	T44.1X3S	771	T44.6X4S	771	T45.0X5D	834	T45.516D	834	T45.7X1D	834
T43.641A	761	T44.1X4A	761	T44.6X5A	567,761	T45.0X5S	771	T45.516S	834	T45.7X1S	771
T43.641D	833	T44.1X4D	833	T44.6X5D	834	T45.0X6A	845	T45.521A	761	T45.7X2A	761
T43.641S	771	T44.1X4S	771	T44.6X5S	771	T45.0X6D	834	T45.521D	834	T45.7X2D	834
T43.642A	761	T44.1X5A	567,761	T44.6X6A	845	T45.0X6S	834	T45.521S	771	T45.7X2S	771
T43.642D	833	T44.1X5D	833	T44.6X6D	834	T45.1X1A	761	T45.522A	761	T45.7X3A	761
T43.642S	771	T44.1X5S	771	T44.6X6S	834	T45.1X1D	834	T45.522D	834	T45.7X3D	834
T43.643A	761	T44.1X6A	845	T44.7X1A	761	T45.1X1S	771	T45.522S	771	T45.7X3S	772
T43.643D	833	T44.1X6D	833	T44.7X1D	834	T45.1X2A	761	T45.523A	761	T45.7X4A	761
T43.643S	771	T44.1X6S	833	T44.7X1S	771	T45.1X2D	834	T45.523D	834	T45.7X4D	834
T43.644A	761	T44.2X1A	761	T44.7X2A	761	T45.1X2S	771	T45.523S	771	T45.7X4S	772
T43.644D	833	T44.2X1D	833	T44.7X2D	834	T45.1X3A	761	T45.524A	761	T45.7X5A	567,761
T43.644S	771	T44.2X1S	771	T44.7X2S	771	T45.1X3D	834	T45.524D	834	T45.7X5D	834
T43.691A	761	T44.2X2A	761	T44.7X3A	761	T45.1X3S	771	T45.524S	771	T45.7X5S	772
T43.691D	833	T44.2X2D	833	T44.7X3S	771	T45.1X4A	761	T45.525A	567,761	T45.7X6A	845
T43.691S	771	T44.2X2S	771	T44.7X4A	761	T45.1X4D	834	T45.525D	834	T45.7X6D	834
T43.692A	761	T44.2X3A	761	T44.7X4D	834	T45.1X4S	771	T45.525S	771	T45.7X6S	834
T43.692D	833	T44.2X3D	833	T44.7X4S	771	T45.1X5A	567,761	T45.526A	845	T45.8X1A	761
T43.692S	771	T44.2X3S	771	T44.7X5A	567,761	T45.1X5D	834	T45.526D	834	T45.8X1D	834
T43.693A	761	T44.2X4A	761	T44.7X5D	834	T45.1X5S	771	T45.526S	834	T45.8X1S	772
T43.693D	833	T44.2X4D	834	T44.7X5S	771	T45.1X6A	845	T45.601A	761	T45.8X2A	761
T43.693S	771	T44.2X4S	771	T44.7X6A	845	T45.1X6D	834	T45.601D	834	T45.8X2D	834
T43.694A	761	T44.2X5A	567,761	T44.7X6D	834	T45.1X6S	834	T45.601S	771	T45.8X2S	772
T43.694D	833	T44.2X5D	834	T44.7X6S	834	T45.2X1A	761	T45.602A	761	T45.8X3A	761
T43.694S	771	T44.2X5S	771	T44.8X1A	761	T45.2X1D	834	T45.602D	834	T45.8X3D	834
T43.695A	567,761	T44.2X6A	845	T44.8X1D	834	T45.2X1S	771	T45.602S	771	T45.8X3S	772
T43.695D	833	T44.2X6D	834	T44.8X1S	771	T45.2X2A	761	T45.603A	761	T45.8X4A	761
T43.695S	771	T44.2X6S	834	T44.8X2A	761	T45.2X2D	834	T45.603D	834	T45.8X4D	834
T43.696A	845	T44.3X1A	761	T44.8X2D	834	T45.2X2S	771	T45.603S	771	T45.8X4S	772
T43.696D	833	T44.3X1D	834	T44.8X2S	771	T45.2X3A	761	T45.604A	761	T45.8X5A	567,761
T43.696S	833	T44.3X1S	771	T44.8X3A	761	T45.2X3D	834	T45.604D	834	T45.8X5D	834
T43.8X1A	761	T44.3X2A	761	T44.8X3D	834	T45.2X3S	771	T45.604S	771	T45.8X5S	772
T43.8X1D	833	T44.3X2D	834	T44.8X3S	771	T45.2X4A	761	T45.605A	567,761	T45.8X6A	845
T43.8X1S	771	T44.3X2S	771	T44.8X4A	761	T45.2X4D	834	T45.605D	834	T45.8X6D	834
T43.8X2A	761	T44.3X3A	761	T44.8X4D	834	T45.2X4S	771	T45.605S	771	T45.8X6S	834
T43.8X2D	833	T44.3X3D	834	T44.8X4S	771	T45.2X5A	567,761	T45.606A	845	T45.91XA	761
T43.8X2S	771	T44.3X3S	771	T44.8X5A	567,761	T45.2X5D	834	T45.606D	834	T45.91XD	834
T43.8X3A	761	T44.3X4A	761	T44.8X5D	834	T45.2X5S	771	T45.606S	834	T45.91XS	772
T43.8X3D	833	T44.3X4D	834	T44.8X5S	771	T45.2X6A	845	T45.611A	761	T45.92XA	761
T43.8X3S	771	T44.3X4S	771	T44.8X6A	845	T45.2X6D	834	T45.611D	834	T45.92XD	834
T43.8X4A	761	T44.3X5A	567,761	T44.8X6D	834	T45.2X6S	834	T45.611S	771	T45.92XS	772
T43.8X4D	833	T44.3X5D	834	T44.8X6S	834	T45.3X1A	761	T45.612A	761	T45.93XA	761
T43.8X4S	771	T44.3X5S	771	T44.901A	761	T45.3X1D	834	T45.612D	834	T45.93XD	834
T43.8X5A	567,761	T44.3X6A	845	T44.901D	834	T45.3X1S	771	T45.612S	771	T45.93XS	772
T43.8X5D	833	T44.3X6D	834	T44.901S	771	T45.3X2A	761	T45.613A	761	T45.94XA	761
T43.8X5S	771	T44.3X6S	834	T44.902A	761	T45.3X2D	834	T45.613D	834	T45.94XD	834
T43.8X6A	845	T44.4X1A	761	T44.902D	834	T45.3X2S	771	T45.613S	771	T45.94XS	772
T43.8X6D	833	T44.4X1D	834	T44.902S	771	T45.3X3A	761	T45.614A	761	T45.95XA	567,761
T43.8X6S	833	T44.4X1S	771	T44.903A	761	T45.3X3D	834	T45.614D	834	T45.95XD	834
T43.91XA	761	T44.4X2A	761	T44.903D	834	T45.3X3S	771	T45.614S	771	T45.95XS	772
T43.91XD	833	T44.4X2D	834	T44.903S	771	T45.3X4A	761	T45.615A	567,761	T45.96XA	845
T43.91XS	771	T44.4X2S	771	T44.904A	761	T45.3X4D	834	T45.615D	834	T45.96XD	834
T43.92XA	761	T44.4X3A	761	T44.904D	834	T45.3X4S	771	T45.615S	771	T45.96XS	834
T43.92XD	833	T44.4X3D	834	T44.904S	771	T45.3X5A	567,761	T45.616A	845	T46.0X1A	761
T43.92XS	771	T44.4X3S	771	T44.905A	567,761	T45.3X5D	834	T45.616D	834	T46.0X1D	834
T43.93XA	761	T44.4X4A	761	T44.905D	834	T45.3X5S	771	T45.616S	834	T46.0X1S	772
T43.93XD	833	T44.4X4D	834	T44.905S	771	T45.3X6A	845	T45.621A	761	T46.0X2A	761
T43.93XS	771	T44.4X4S	771	T44.906A	845	T45.3X6D	834	T45.621D	834	T46.0X2D	834
T43.94XA	761	T44.4X5A	567,761	T44.906D	834	T45.3X6S	834	T45.621S	771	T46.0X2S	772
T43.94XD	833	T44.4X5D	834	T44.906S	834	T45.4X1A	761	T45.622A	761	T46.0X3A	761
T43.94XS	771	T44.4X5S	771	T44.991A	761	T45.4X1D	834	T45.622D	834	T46.0X3D	834
T43.95XA	567,761	T44.4X6A	845	T44.991D	834	T45.4X1S	771	T45.622S	771	T46.0X3S	772
T43.95XD	833	T44.4X6D	834	T44.991S	771	T45.4X2A	761	T45.623A	761	T46.0X4A	761
T43.95XS	771	T44.4X6S	834	T44.992A	761	T45.4X2D	834	T45.623D	834	T46.0X4D	834
T43.96XA	845	T44.5X1A	761	T44.992D	834	T45.4X2S	771	T45.623S	771	T46.0X4S	772
T43.96XD	833	T44.5X1D	834	T44.992S	771	T45.4X3A	761	T45.624A	761	T46.0X5A	567,761
T43.96XS	833	T44.5X1S	771	T44.993A	761	T45.4X3D	834	T45.624D	834	T46.0X5D	834
T44.0X1A	761	T44.5X2A	761	T44.993D	834	T45.4X3S	771	T45.624S	771	T46.0X5S	772
T44.0X1D	833	T44.5X2D	834	T44.993S	771	T45.4X4A	761	T45.625A	567,761	T46.0X6A	845
T44.0X1S	771	T44.5X2S	771	T44.994A	761	T45.4X4D	834	T45.625D	834	T46.0X6D	834
T44.0X2A	761	T44.5X3A	761	T44.994D	834	T45.4X4S	771	T45.625S	771	T46.0X6S	834
T44.0X2D	833	T44.5X3D	834	T44.994S	771	T45.4X5A	567,761	T45.626A	845	T46.1X1A	761
T44.0X2S	771	T44.5X3S	771	T44.995A	567	T45.4X5D	834	T45.626D	834	T46.1X1D	834
T44.0X3A	761	T44.5X4A	761	T44.995D	834	T45.4X5S	771	T45.626S	834	T46.1X1S	772
T44.0X3D	833	T44.5X4D	834	T44.995S	771	T45.4X6A	845	T45.691A	761	T46.1X2A	761
T44.0X3S	771	T44.5X4S	771	T44.996A	845	T45.4X6D	834	T45.691D	834	T46.1X2D	834
T44.0X4A	761	T44.5X5A	567,761	T44.996D	834	T45.4X6S	834	T45.691S	771	T46.1X2S	772
T44.0X4D	833	T44.5X5D	834	T44.996S	834	T45.511A	761	T45.692A	761	T46.1X3A	761
T44.0X4S	771	T44.5X5S	771			T45.511D	834	T45.692D	834	T46.1X3D	834
T44.0X5A	567,761	T44.5X6A	845			T45.511S	771	T45.692S	771	T46.1X3S	772

Code	Page	Code	Page	Code	Page	Code	Page	Code	Page	Code	Page
T46.1X4A	761	T46.6X5A	567,762	T47.0X5D	835	T47.5X6D	835	T48.1X1A	762	T48.5X2A	762
T46.1X4D	834	T46.6X5D	835	T47.0X5S	772	T47.5X6S	835	T48.1X1D	835	T48.5X2D	836
T46.1X4S	772	T46.6X5S	772	T47.0X6A	845	T47.6X1A	762	T48.1X1S	772	T48.5X2S	772
T46.1X5A	567,761	T46.6X6A	845	T47.0X6D	835	T47.6X1D	835	T48.1X2A	762	T48.5X3A	762
T46.1X5D	834	T46.6X6D	835	T47.0X6S	835	T47.6X1S	772	T48.1X2D	835	T48.5X3D	836
T46.1X5S	772	T46.6X6S	835	T47.1X1A	762	T47.6X2A	762	T48.1X2S	772	T48.5X3S	772
T46.1X6A	845	T46.7X1A	762	T47.1X1D	835	T47.6X2D	835	T48.1X3A	762	T48.5X4A	762
T46.1X6D	834	T46.7X1D	835	T47.1X1S	772	T47.6X2S	772	T48.1X3D	835	T48.5X4D	836
T46.1X6S	834	T46.7X1S	772	T47.1X2A	762	T47.6X3A	762	T48.1X3S	772	T48.5X4S	772
T46.2X1A	761	T46.7X2A	762	T47.1X2D	835	T47.6X3D	835	T48.1X4A	762	T48.5X5A	567,762
T46.2X1D	834	T46.7X2D	835	T47.1X2S	772	T47.6X3S	772	T48.1X4D	835	T48.5X5D	836
T46.2X1S	772	T46.7X2S	772	T47.1X3A	762	T47.6X4A	762	T48.1X4S	772	T48.5X5S	772
T46.2X2A	761	T46.7X3A	762	T47.1X3D	835	T47.6X4D	835	T48.1X5A	567,762	T48.5X6A	845
T46.2X2D	834	T46.7X3D	835	T47.1X3S	772	T47.6X4S	772	T48.1X5D	835	T48.5X6D	836
T46.2X2S	772	T46.7X3S	772	T47.1X4A	762	T47.6X5A	567,762	T48.1X5S	772	T48.5X6S	836
T46.2X3A	761	T46.7X4A	762	T47.1X4D	835	T47.6X5D	835	T48.1X6A	845	T48.6X1A	762
T46.2X3D	835	T46.7X4D	835	T47.1X4S	772	T47.6X5S	772	T48.1X6D	835	T48.6X1D	836
T46.2X3S	772	T46.7X4S	772	T47.1X5A	567,762	T47.6X6A	845	T48.1X6S	835	T48.6X1S	772
T46.2X4A	761	T46.7X5A	567,762	T47.1X5D	835	T47.6X6D	835	T48.201A	762	T48.6X2A	762
T46.2X4D	835	T46.7X5D	835	T47.1X5S	772	T47.6X6S	835	T48.201D	835	T48.6X2D	836
T46.2X4S	772	T46.7X5S	772	T47.1X6A	845	T47.7X1A	762	T48.201S	772	T48.6X2S	772
T46.2X5A	567,761	T46.7X6A	845	T47.1X6D	835	T47.7X1D	835	T48.202A	762	T48.6X3A	762
T46.2X5D	835	T46.7X6D	835	T47.1X6S	835	T47.7X1S	772	T48.202D	835	T48.6X3D	836
T46.2X5S	772	T46.7X6S	835	T47.2X1A	762	T47.7X2A	762	T48.202S	772	T48.6X3S	772
T46.2X6A	845	T46.8X1A	762	T47.2X1D	835	T47.7X2D	835	T48.203A	762	T48.6X4A	762
T46.2X6D	835	T46.8X1D	835	T47.2X1S	772	T47.7X2S	772	T48.203D	835	T48.6X4D	836
T46.2X6S	835	T46.8X1S	772	T47.2X2A	762	T47.7X3A	762	T48.203S	772	T48.6X4S	772
T46.3X1A	761	T46.8X2A	762	T47.2X2D	835	T47.7X3D	835	T48.204A	762	T48.6X5A	567,762
T46.3X1D	835	T46.8X2D	835	T47.2X2S	772	T47.7X3S	772	T48.204D	835	T48.6X5D	836
T46.3X1S	772	T46.8X2S	772	T47.2X3A	762	T47.7X4A	762	T48.204S	772	T48.6X5S	772
T46.3X2A	761	T46.8X3A	762	T47.2X3D	835	T47.7X4D	835	T48.205A	567,762	T48.6X6A	845
T46.3X2D	835	T46.8X3D	835	T47.2X3S	772	T47.7X4S	772	T48.205D	835	T48.6X6D	836
T46.3X2S	772	T46.8X3S	772	T47.2X4A	762	T47.7X5A	567,762	T48.205S	772	T48.6X6S	836
T46.3X3A	761	T46.8X4A	762	T47.2X4D	835	T47.7X5D	835	T48.206A	845	T48.901A	762
T46.3X3D	835	T46.8X4D	835	T47.2X4S	772	T47.7X5S	772	T48.206D	835	T48.901D	836
T46.3X3S	772	T46.8X4S	772	T47.2X5A	567,762	T47.7X6A	845	T48.206S	835	T48.901S	772
T46.3X4A	762	T46.8X5A	567,762	T47.2X5D	835	T47.7X6D	835	T48.291A	762	T48.902A	762
T46.3X4D	835	T46.8X5D	835	T47.2X5S	772	T47.7X6S	835	T48.291D	835	T48.902D	836
T46.3X4S	772	T46.8X5S	772	T47.2X6A	845	T47.8X1A	762	T48.291S	772	T48.902S	772
T46.3X5A	567,762	T46.8X6A	845	T47.2X6D	835	T47.8X1D	835	T48.292A	762	T48.903A	762
T46.3X5D	835	T46.8X6D	835	T47.2X6S	835	T47.8X1S	772	T48.292D	835	T48.903D	836
T46.3X5S	772	T46.8X6S	835	T47.3X1A	762	T47.8X2A	762	T48.292S	772	T48.903S	772
T46.3X6A	845	T46.901A	762	T47.3X1D	835	T47.8X2D	835	T48.293A	762	T48.904A	762
T46.3X6D	835	T46.901D	835	T47.3X1S	772	T47.8X2S	772	T48.293D	835	T48.904D	836
T46.3X6S	835	T46.901S	772	T47.3X2A	762	T47.8X3A	762	T48.293S	772	T48.904S	772
T46.4X1A	762	T46.902A	762	T47.3X2D	835	T47.8X3D	835	T48.294A	762	T48.905A	567,762
T46.4X1D	835	T46.902D	835	T47.3X2S	772	T47.8X3S	772	T48.294D	835	T48.905D	836
T46.4X1S	772	T46.902S	772	T47.3X3A	762	T47.8X4A	762	T48.294S	772	T48.905S	772
T46.4X2A	762	T46.903A	762	T47.3X3D	835	T47.8X4D	835	T48.295A	567,762	T48.906A	845
T46.4X2D	835	T46.903D	835	T47.3X3S	772	T47.8X4S	772	T48.295D	835	T48.906D	836
T46.4X2S	772	T46.903S	772	T47.3X4A	762	T47.8X5A	567,762	T48.295S	772	T48.906S	836
T46.4X3A	762	T46.904A	762	T47.3X4D	835	T47.8X5D	835	T48.296A	845	T48.991A	762
T46.4X3D	835	T46.904D	835	T47.3X4S	772	T47.8X5S	772	T48.296D	835	T48.991D	836
T46.4X3S	772	T46.904S	772	T47.3X5A	567,762	T47.8X6A	845	T48.296S	835	T48.991S	772
T46.4X4A	762	T46.905A	567	T47.3X5D	835	T47.8X6D	835	T48.3X1A	762	T48.992A	762
T46.4X4D	835	T46.905A	762	T47.3X5S	772	T47.8X6S	835	T48.3X1D	835	T48.992D	836
T46.4X4S	772	T46.905D	835	T47.3X6A	845	T47.91XA	762	T48.3X1S	772	T48.992S	772
T46.4X5A	567,762	T46.905S	772	T47.3X6D	835	T47.91XD	835	T48.3X2A	762	T48.993A	762
T46.4X5D	835	T46.906A	845	T47.3X6S	835	T47.91XS	772	T48.3X2D	835	T48.993D	836
T46.4X5S	772	T46.906D	835	T47.4X1A	762	T47.92XA	762	T48.3X2S	772	T48.993S	772
T46.4X6A	845	T46.906S	835	T47.4X1D	835	T47.92XD	835	T48.3X3A	762	T48.994A	762
T46.4X6D	835	T46.991A	762	T47.4X1S	772	T47.92XS	772	T48.3X3D	835	T48.994D	836
T46.4X6S	835	T46.991D	835	T47.4X2A	762	T47.93XA	762	T48.3X3S	772	T48.994S	772
T46.5X1A	762	T46.991S	772	T47.4X2D	835	T47.93XD	835	T48.3X4A	762	T48.995A	567,762
T46.5X1D	835	T46.992A	762	T47.4X2S	772	T47.93XS	772	T48.3X4D	835	T48.995D	836
T46.5X1S	772	T46.992D	835	T47.4X3A	762	T47.94XA	762	T48.3X4S	772	T48.995S	772
T46.5X2A	762	T46.992S	772	T47.4X3D	835	T47.94XD	835	T48.3X5A	567,762	T48.996A	845
T46.5X2D	835	T46.993A	762	T47.4X3S	772	T47.94XS	772	T48.3X5D	835	T48.996D	836
T46.5X2S	772	T46.993D	835	T47.4X4A	762	T47.95XA	567	T48.3X5S	772	T48.996S	836
T46.5X3A	762	T46.993S	772	T47.4X4D	835	T47.95XA	762	T48.3X6A	845	T49.0X1A	762
T46.5X3D	835	T46.994A	762	T47.4X4S	772	T47.95XD	835	T48.3X6D	835	T49.0X1D	836
T46.5X3S	772	T46.994D	835	T47.4X5A	567,762	T47.95XS	772	T48.3X6S	835	T49.0X1S	772
T46.5X4A	762	T46.994S	772	T47.4X5D	835	T47.96XA	845	T48.4X1A	762	T49.0X2A	762
T46.5X4D	835	T46.995A	567	T47.4X5S	772	T47.96XD	835	T48.4X1D	835	T49.0X2D	836
T46.5X4S	772	T46.995A	762	T47.4X6A	845	T47.96XS	835	T48.4X1S	772	T49.0X2S	772
T46.5X5A	567,762	T46.995D	835	T47.4X6D	835	T48.0X1A	762	T48.4X2A	762	T49.0X3A	762
T46.5X5D	835	T46.995S	772	T47.4X6S	835	T48.0X1D	835	T48.4X2D	835	T49.0X3D	836
T46.5X5S	772	T46.996A	845	T47.5X1A	762	T48.0X1S	772	T48.4X2S	772	T49.0X3S	772
T46.5X6A	845	T46.996D	835	T47.5X1D	835	T48.0X2A	762	T48.4X3A	762	T49.0X4A	762
T46.5X6D	835	T46.996S	835	T47.5X1S	772	T48.0X2D	835	T48.4X3D	835	T49.0X4D	836
T46.5X6S	835	T47.0X1A	762	T47.5X2A	762	T48.0X2S	772	T48.4X3S	772	T49.0X4S	772
T46.6X1A	762	T47.0X1D	835	T47.5X2D	835	T48.0X3A	762	T48.4X4A	762	T49.0X5A	567,762
T46.6X1D	835	T47.0X1S	772	T47.5X2S	772	T48.0X3D	835	T48.4X4D	835	T49.0X5D	836
T46.6X1S	772	T47.0X2A	762	T47.5X3A	762	T48.0X3S	772	T48.4X4S	772	T49.0X5S	772
T46.6X2A	762	T47.0X2D	835	T47.5X3D	835	T48.0X4A	762	T48.4X5A	567,762	T49.0X6A	845
T46.6X2D	835	T47.0X2S	772	T47.5X3S	772	T48.0X4D	835	T48.4X5D	835	T49.0X6D	836
T46.6X2S	772	T47.0X3A	762	T47.5X4A	762	T48.0X4S	772	T48.4X5S	772	T49.0X6S	836
T46.6X3A	762	T47.0X3D	835	T47.5X4D	835	T48.0X5A	567,762	T48.4X6A	845	T49.1X1A	762
T46.6X3D	835	T47.0X3S	772	T47.5X4S	772	T48.0X5D	835	T48.4X6D	835	T49.1X1D	836
T46.6X3S	772	T47.0X4A	762	T47.5X5A	567,762	T48.0X5S	772	T48.4X6S	835	T49.1X1S	772
T46.6X4A	762	T47.0X4D	835	T47.5X5D	835	T48.0X6A	845	T48.5X1A	762	T49.1X2A	762
T46.6X4D	835	T47.0X4S	772	T47.5X5S	772	T48.0X6D	835	T48.5X1D	835	T49.1X2D	836
T46.6X4S	772	T47.0X5A	567,762	T47.5X6A	845	T48.0X6S	835	T48.5X1S	772	T49.1X2S	773

Code	Page	Code	Page	Code	Page	Code	Page	Code	Page	Code	Page
T49.1X3A	762	T49.6X4A	762	T50.1X5A	567, 763	T50.6X6A	845	T50.A11A	763	T50.Z12A	763
T49.1X3D	836	T49.6X4D	836	T50.1X5D	836	T50.6X6D	836	T50.A11D	837	T50.Z12D	837
T49.1X3S	773	T49.6X4S	773	T50.1X5S	773	T50.6X6S	836	T50.A11S	773	T50.Z12S	773
T49.1X4A	762	T49.6X5A	567, 762	T50.1X6A	845	T50.7X1A	763	T50.A12A	763	T50.Z13A	763
T49.1X4D	836	T49.6X5D	836	T50.1X6D	836	T50.7X1D	836	T50.A12D	837	T50.Z13D	837
T49.1X4S	773	T49.6X5S	773	T50.1X6S	836	T50.7X1S	773	T50.A12S	773	T50.Z13S	773
T49.1X5A	567, 762	T49.6X6A	845	T50.2X1A	763	T50.7X2A	763	T50.A13A	763	T50.Z14A	763
T49.1X5D	836	T49.6X6D	836	T50.2X1D	836	T50.7X2D	836	T50.A13D	837	T50.Z14D	837
T49.1X5S	773	T49.6X6S	836	T50.2X1S	773	T50.7X2S	773	T50.A13S	773	T50.Z14S	773
T49.1X6A	845	T49.7X1A	762	T50.2X2A	763	T50.7X3A	763	T50.A14A	763	T50.Z15A	567, 763
T49.1X6D	836	T49.7X1D	836	T50.2X2D	836	T50.7X3D	836	T50.A14D	837	T50.Z15D	837
T49.1X6S	836	T49.7X1S	773	T50.2X2S	773	T50.7X3S	773	T50.A14S	773	T50.Z15S	773
T49.2X1A	762	T49.7X2A	762	T50.2X3A	763	T50.7X4A	763	T50.A15A	567, 763	T50.Z16A	845
T49.2X1D	836	T49.7X2D	836	T50.2X3D	836	T50.7X4D	836	T50.A15D	837	T50.Z16D	837
T49.2X1S	773	T49.7X2S	773	T50.2X3S	773	T50.7X4S	773	T50.A15S	773	T50.Z16S	837
T49.2X2A	762	T49.7X3A	763	T50.2X4A	763	T50.7X5A	567, 763	T50.A16A	845	T50.Z91A	763
T49.2X2D	836	T49.7X3D	836	T50.2X4D	836	T50.7X5D	836	T50.A16D	837	T50.Z91D	837
T49.2X2S	773	T49.7X3S	773	T50.2X4S	773	T50.7X5S	773	T50.A16S	837	T50.Z91S	773
T49.2X3A	762	T49.7X4A	763	T50.2X5A	567, 763	T50.7X6A	845	T50.A21A	763	T50.Z92A	763
T49.2X3D	836	T49.7X4D	836	T50.2X5D	836	T50.7X6D	836	T50.A21D	837	T50.Z92D	837
T49.2X3S	773	T49.7X4S	773	T50.2X5S	773	T50.7X6S	836	T50.A21S	773	T50.Z92S	773
T49.2X4A	762	T49.7X5A	567, 763	T50.2X6A	845	T50.8X1A	763	T50.A22A	763	T50.Z93A	763
T49.2X4D	836	T49.7X5D	836	T50.2X6D	836	T50.8X1D	836	T50.A22D	837	T50.Z93D	837
T49.2X4S	773	T49.7X5S	773	T50.2X6S	836	T50.8X1S	773	T50.A22S	773	T50.Z93S	773
T49.2X5A	567, 762	T49.7X6A	845	T50.3X1A	763	T50.8X2A	763	T50.A23A	763	T50.Z94A	763
T49.2X5D	836	T49.7X6D	836	T50.3X1D	836	T50.8X2D	836	T50.A23D	837	T50.Z94D	837
T49.2X5S	773	T49.7X6S	836	T50.3X1S	773	T50.8X2S	773	T50.A23S	773	T50.Z94S	773
T49.2X6A	845	T49.8X1A	763	T50.3X2A	763	T50.8X3A	763	T50.A24A	763	T50.Z95A	567, 763
T49.2X6D	836	T49.8X1D	836	T50.3X2D	836	T50.8X3D	836	T50.A24D	837	T50.Z95D	837
T49.2X6S	836	T49.8X1S	773	T50.3X2S	773	T50.8X3S	773	T50.A24S	773	T50.Z95S	773
T49.3X1A	762	T49.8X2A	763	T50.3X3A	763	T50.8X4A	763	T50.A25A	567, 763	T50.Z96A	845
T49.3X1D	836	T49.8X2D	836	T50.3X3D	836	T50.8X4D	836	T50.A25D	837	T50.Z96D	837
T49.3X1S	773	T49.8X2S	773	T50.3X3S	773	T50.8X4S	773	T50.A25S	773	T50.Z96S	837
T49.3X2A	762	T49.8X3A	763	T50.3X4A	763	T50.8X5A	567, 763	T50.A26A	845	T51.0X1A	763
T49.3X2D	836	T49.8X3D	836	T50.3X4D	836	T50.8X5D	836	T50.A26D	837	T51.0X1D	837
T49.3X2S	773	T49.8X3S	773	T50.3X4S	773	T50.8X5S	773	T50.A26S	837	T51.0X1S	773
T49.3X3A	762	T49.8X4A	763	T50.3X5A	567, 763	T50.8X6A	845	T50.A91A	763	T51.0X2A	763
T49.3X3D	836	T49.8X4D	836	T50.3X5D	836	T50.8X6D	836	T50.A91D	837	T51.0X2S	773
T49.3X3S	773	T49.8X4S	773	T50.3X5S	773	T50.8X6S	836	T50.A91S	773	T51.0X3A	763
T49.3X4A	762	T49.8X5A	567, 763	T50.3X6A	845	T50.901A	763	T50.A92A	763	T51.0X3D	837
T49.3X4D	836	T49.8X5D	836	T50.3X6D	836	T50.901D	836	T50.A92D	837	T51.0X3S	773
T49.3X4S	773	T49.8X5S	773	T50.3X6S	836	T50.901S	773	T50.A92S	773	T51.0X4A	763
T49.3X5A	567, 762	T49.8X6A	845	T50.4X1A	763	T50.902A	763	T50.A93A	763	T51.0X4D	837
T49.3X5D	836	T49.8X6D	836	T50.4X1D	836	T50.902D	836	T50.A93D	837	T51.0X4S	773
T49.3X5S	773	T49.8X6S	836	T50.4X1S	773	T50.902S	773	T50.A93S	773	T51.1X1A	763
T49.3X6A	845	T49.91XA	763	T50.4X2A	763	T50.903A	763	T50.A94A	763	T51.1X1D	837
T49.3X6D	836	T49.91XD	836	T50.4X2D	836	T50.903D	836	T50.A94D	837	T51.1X1S	773
T49.3X6S	836	T49.91XS	773	T50.4X2S	773	T50.903S	773	T50.A94S	773	T51.1X2A	763
T49.4X1A	762	T49.92XA	763	T50.4X3A	763	T50.904A	763	T50.A95A	567, 763	T51.1X2D	837
T49.4X1D	836	T49.92XD	836	T50.4X3D	836	T50.904D	836	T50.A95D	837	T51.1X2S	773
T49.4X1S	773	T49.92XS	773	T50.4X3S	773	T50.904S	773	T50.A95S	773	T51.1X3A	763
T49.4X2A	762	T49.93XA	763	T50.4X4A	763	T50.905A	567, 763	T50.A96A	845	T51.1X3D	837
T49.4X2D	836	T49.93XD	836	T50.4X4D	836	T50.905D	836	T50.A96D	837	T51.1X3S	773
T49.4X2S	773	T49.93XS	773	T50.4X4S	773	T50.905S	773	T50.A96S	837	T51.1X4A	763
T49.4X3A	762	T49.94XA	763	T50.4X5A	567, 763	T50.906A	845	T50.B11A	763	T51.1X4D	837
T49.4X3D	836	T49.94XD	836	T50.4X5D	836	T50.906D	836	T50.B11D	837	T51.1X4S	773
T49.4X3S	773	T49.94XS	773	T50.4X5S	773	T50.906S	836	T50.B11S	773	T51.2X1A	763
T49.4X4A	762	T49.95XA	567, 763	T50.4X6A	845	T50.911A	763	T50.B12A	763	T51.2X1D	837
T49.4X4D	836	T49.95XD	836	T50.4X6D	836	T50.911D	836	T50.B12D	837	T51.2X1S	773
T49.4X4S	773	T49.95XS	773	T50.4X6S	836	T50.911S	773	T50.B12S	773	T51.2X2A	763
T49.4X5A	567, 762	T49.96XA	845	T50.5X1A	763	T50.912A	763	T50.B13A	763	T51.2X2D	837
T49.4X5D	836	T49.96XD	836	T50.5X1D	836	T50.912D	836	T50.B13D	837	T51.2X2S	773
T49.4X5S	773	T49.96XS	773	T50.5X1S	773	T50.912S	773	T50.B13S	773	T51.2X3A	763
T49.4X6A	845	T50.0X1A	763	T50.5X2A	763	T50.913A	763	T50.B14A	763	T51.2X3D	837
T49.4X6D	836	T50.0X1D	836	T50.5X2D	836	T50.913D	836	T50.B14D	837	T51.2X3S	773
T49.4X6S	836	T50.0X1S	773	T50.5X2S	773	T50.913S	773	T50.B14S	773	T51.2X4A	763
T49.5X1A	762	T50.0X2A	763	T50.5X3A	763	T50.914A	763	T50.B15A	567, 763	T51.2X4D	837
T49.5X1D	836	T50.0X2D	836	T50.5X3D	836	T50.914D	836	T50.B15D	837	T51.2X4S	773
T49.5X1S	773	T50.0X2S	773	T50.5X3S	773	T50.914S	773	T50.B15S	773	T51.3X1A	763
T49.5X2A	762	T50.0X3A	763	T50.5X4A	763	T50.915A	567, 763	T50.B16A	845	T51.3X1D	837
T49.5X2D	836	T50.0X3D	836	T50.5X4D	836	T50.915D	836	T50.B16D	837	T51.3X1S	773
T49.5X2S	773	T50.0X3S	773	T50.5X4S	773	T50.915S	773	T50.B16S	837	T51.3X2A	763
T49.5X3A	762	T50.0X4A	763	T50.5X5A	567, 763	T50.916A	845	T50.B91A	763	T51.3X2D	837
T49.5X3D	836	T50.0X4D	836	T50.5X5D	836	T50.916D	836	T50.B91D	837	T51.3X2S	773
T49.5X3S	773	T50.0X4S	773	T50.5X5S	773	T50.916S	773	T50.B91S	773	T51.3X3A	763
T49.5X4A	762	T50.0X5A	567, 763	T50.5X6A	845	T50.991A	763	T50.B92A	763	T51.3X3D	837
T49.5X4D	836	T50.0X5D	836	T50.5X6D	836	T50.991D	836	T50.B92D	837	T51.3X3S	773
T49.5X4S	773	T50.0X5S	773	T50.5X6S	836	T50.991S	773	T50.B92S	773	T51.3X4A	763
T49.5X5A	567, 762	T50.0X6A	845	T50.6X1A	763	T50.992A	763	T50.B93A	763	T51.3X4D	837
T49.5X5D	836	T50.0X6D	836	T50.6X1D	836	T50.992D	837	T50.B93D	837	T51.3X4S	773
T49.5X5S	773	T50.0X6S	836	T50.6X1S	773	T50.992S	773	T50.B93S	773	T51.8X1A	763
T49.5X6A	845	T50.1X1A	763	T50.6X2A	763	T50.993A	763	T50.B94A	763	T51.8X1D	837
T49.5X6D	836	T50.1X1D	836	T50.6X2D	836	T50.993D	837	T50.B94D	837	T51.8X1S	773
T49.5X6S	836	T50.1X1S	773	T50.6X2S	773	T50.993S	773	T50.B94S	773	T51.8X2A	763
T49.6X1A	762	T50.1X2A	763	T50.6X3A	763	T50.994A	763	T50.B95A	567, 763	T51.8X2D	837
T49.6X1D	836	T50.1X2D	836	T50.6X3D	836	T50.994D	837	T50.B95D	837	T51.8X2S	773
T49.6X1S	773	T50.1X2S	773	T50.6X3S	773	T50.994S	773	T50.B95S	773	T51.8X3A	763
T49.6X2A	762	T50.1X3A	763	T50.6X4A	763	T50.995A	567, 763	T50.B96A	845	T51.8X3D	837
T49.6X2D	836	T50.1X3D	836	T50.6X4D	836	T50.995D	837	T50.B96D	837	T51.8X3S	773
T49.6X2S	773	T50.1X3S	773	T50.6X4S	773	T50.995S	773	T50.B96S	837	T51.8X4A	763
T49.6X3A	762	T50.1X4A	763	T50.6X5A	567, 763	T50.996A	845	T50.Z11A	763	T51.8X4D	837
T49.6X3D	836	T50.1X4D	836	T50.6X5D	836	T50.996D	837	T50.Z11D	837	T51.8X4S	773
T49.6X3S	773	T50.1X4S	773	T50.6X5S	773	T50.996S	837	T50.Z11S	773		

Code	Page	Code	Page	Code	Page	Code	Page	Code	Page	Code	Page
T51.91XA	763	T52.94XA	763	T53.7X3A	764	T55.1X2A	764	T56.7X1A	764	T57.3X4A	764
T51.91XD	837	T52.94XD	837	T53.7X3D	837	T55.1X2D	837	T56.7X1D	838	T57.3X4D	838
T51.91XS	773	T52.94XS	774	T53.7X3S	774	T55.1X2S	774	T56.7X1S	774	T57.3X4S	774
T51.92XA	763	T53.0X1A	763	T53.7X4A	764	T55.1X3A	764	T56.7X2A	764	T57.8X1A	764
T51.92XD	837	T53.0X1D	837	T53.7X4D	837	T55.1X3D	837	T56.7X2D	838	T57.8X1D	838
T51.92XS	773	T53.0X1S	774	T53.7X4S	774	T55.1X3S	774	T56.7X2S	774	T57.8X1S	774
T51.93XA	763	T53.0X2A	763	T53.91XA	764	T55.1X4A	764	T56.7X3A	764	T57.8X2A	764
T51.93XD	837	T53.0X2D	837	T53.91XD	837	T55.1X4D	837	T56.7X3D	838	T57.8X2D	838
T51.93XS	773	T53.0X2S	774	T53.91XS	774	T55.1X4S	774	T56.7X3S	774	T57.8X2S	838
T51.94XA	763	T53.0X3A	763	T53.92XA	764	T56.0X1A	764	T56.7X4A	764	T57.8X3A	764
T51.94XD	837	T53.0X3D	837	T53.92XD	837	T56.0X1D	837	T56.7X4D	838	T57.8X3D	838
T51.94XS	773	T53.0X3S	774	T53.92XS	774	T56.0X1S	774	T56.7X4S	774	T57.8X3S	774
T52.0X1A	763	T53.0X4A	763	T53.93XA	764	T56.0X2A	764	T56.811A	764	T57.8X4A	764
T52.0X1D	837	T53.0X4D	837	T53.93XD	837	T56.0X2D	837	T56.811D	838	T57.8X4D	838
T52.0X1S	773	T53.0X4S	774	T53.93XS	774	T56.0X2S	774	T56.811S	774	T57.8X4S	774
T52.0X2A	763	T53.1X1A	763	T53.94XA	764	T56.0X3A	764	T56.812A	764	T57.91XA	764
T52.0X2D	837	T53.1X1D	837	T53.94XD	837	T56.0X3D	837	T56.812D	838	T57.91XD	838
T52.0X2S	773	T53.1X1S	774	T53.94XS	774	T56.0X3S	774	T56.812S	774	T57.91XS	774
T52.0X3A	763	T53.1X2A	763	T54.0X1A	764	T56.0X4A	764	T56.813A	764	T57.92XA	764
T52.0X3D	837	T53.1X2D	837	T54.0X1D	837	T56.0X4D	838	T56.813D	838	T57.92XD	838
T52.0X3S	773	T53.1X2S	774	T54.0X1S	774	T56.0X4S	774	T56.813S	774	T57.92XS	774
T52.0X4A	763	T53.1X3A	763	T54.0X2A	764	T56.1X1A	764	T56.814A	764	T57.93XA	764
T52.0X4D	837	T53.1X3D	837	T54.0X2D	837	T56.1X1D	838	T56.814D	838	T57.93XD	838
T52.0X4S	773	T53.1X3S	774	T54.0X2S	774	T56.1X1S	774	T56.814S	774	T57.93XS	774
T52.1X1A	763	T53.1X4A	763	T54.0X3A	764	T56.1X2A	764	T56.891A	764	T57.94XA	764
T52.1X1D	837	T53.1X4D	837	T54.0X3D	837	T56.1X2D	838	T56.891D	838	T57.94XD	838
T52.1X1S	773	T53.1X4S	774	T54.0X3S	774	T56.1X2S	774	T56.891S	774	T57.94XS	774
T52.1X2A	763	T53.2X1A	763	T54.0X4A	764	T56.1X3A	764	T56.892A	764	T58.01XA	764
T52.1X2D	837	T53.2X1D	837	T54.0X4D	837	T56.1X3D	838	T56.892D	838	T58.01XD	838
T52.1X2S	773	T53.2X1S	774	T54.0X4S	774	T56.1X3S	774	T56.892S	774	T58.01XS	774
T52.1X3A	763	T53.2X2A	763	T54.1X1A	764	T56.1X4A	764	T56.893A	764	T58.02XA	764
T52.1X3D	837	T53.2X2D	837	T54.1X1D	837	T56.1X4D	838	T56.893D	838	T58.02XD	838
T52.1X3S	773	T53.2X2S	774	T54.1X1S	774	T56.1X4S	774	T56.893S	774	T58.02XS	774
T52.1X4A	763	T53.2X3A	763	T54.1X2A	764	T56.2X1A	764	T56.894A	764	T58.03XA	764
T52.1X4D	837	T53.2X3D	837	T54.1X2D	837	T56.2X1D	838	T56.894D	838	T58.03XD	838
T52.1X4S	773	T53.2X3S	774	T54.1X2S	774	T56.2X1S	774	T56.894S	774	T58.03XS	774
T52.2X1A	763	T53.2X4A	763	T54.1X3A	764	T56.2X2A	764	T56.91XA	764	T58.04XA	764
T52.2X1D	837	T53.2X4D	837	T54.1X3D	837	T56.2X2D	838	T56.91XD	838	T58.04XD	838
T52.2X1S	773	T53.2X4S	774	T54.1X3S	774	T56.2X2S	774	T56.91XS	774	T58.04XS	774
T52.2X2A	763	T53.3X1A	763	T54.1X4A	764	T56.2X3A	764	T56.92XA	764	T58.11XA	764
T52.2X2D	837	T53.3X1D	837	T54.1X4D	837	T56.2X3D	838	T56.92XD	838	T58.11XD	838
T52.2X2S	773	T53.3X1S	774	T54.1X4S	774	T56.2X3S	774	T56.92XS	774	T58.11XS	774
T52.2X3A	763	T53.3X2A	763	T54.2X1A	764	T56.2X4A	764	T56.93XA	764	T58.12XA	764
T52.2X3D	837	T53.3X2D	837	T54.2X1D	837	T56.2X4D	838	T56.93XD	838	T58.12XD	838
T52.2X3S	774	T53.3X2S	774	T54.2X1S	774	T56.2X4S	774	T56.93XS	774	T58.12XS	774
T52.2X4A	763	T53.3X3A	764	T54.2X2A	764	T56.3X1A	764	T56.94XA	764	T58.13XA	764
T52.2X4D	837	T53.3X3D	837	T54.2X2D	837	T56.3X1D	838	T56.94XD	838	T58.13XD	838
T52.2X4S	774	T53.3X3S	774	T54.2X2S	774	T56.3X1S	774	T56.94XS	774	T58.13XS	774
T52.3X1A	763	T53.3X4A	764	T54.2X3A	764	T56.3X2A	764	T57.0X1A	764	T58.14XA	764
T52.3X1D	837	T53.3X4D	837	T54.2X3D	837	T56.3X2D	838	T57.0X1D	838	T58.14XD	838
T52.3X1S	774	T53.3X4S	774	T54.2X3S	774	T56.3X2S	774	T57.0X1S	774	T58.14XS	774
T52.3X2A	763	T53.4X1A	764	T54.2X4A	764	T56.3X3A	764	T57.0X2A	764	T58.2X1A	764
T52.3X2D	837	T53.4X1D	837	T54.2X4D	837	T56.3X3D	838	T57.0X2D	838	T58.2X1D	838
T52.3X2S	774	T53.4X1S	774	T54.2X4S	774	T56.3X3S	774	T57.0X2S	774	T58.2X1S	774
T52.3X3A	763	T53.4X2A	764	T54.3X1A	764	T56.3X4A	764	T57.0X3A	764	T58.2X2A	764
T52.3X3D	837	T53.4X2D	837	T54.3X1D	837	T56.3X4D	838	T57.0X3D	838	T58.2X2D	838
T52.3X3S	774	T53.4X2S	774	T54.3X1S	774	T56.3X4S	774	T57.0X3S	774	T58.2X2S	774
T52.3X4A	763	T53.4X3A	764	T54.3X2A	764	T56.4X1A	764	T57.0X4A	764	T58.2X3A	764
T52.3X4D	837	T53.4X3D	837	T54.3X2D	837	T56.4X1D	838	T57.0X4D	838	T58.2X3D	838
T52.3X4S	774	T53.4X3S	774	T54.3X2S	774	T56.4X1S	774	T57.0X4S	774	T58.2X3S	774
T52.4X1A	763	T53.4X4A	764	T54.3X3A	764	T56.4X2A	764	T57.1X1A	764	T58.2X4A	764
T52.4X1D	837	T53.4X4D	837	T54.3X3D	837	T56.4X2D	838	T57.1X1D	838	T58.2X4D	838
T52.4X1S	774	T53.4X4S	774	T54.3X3S	774	T56.4X2S	774	T57.1X1S	774	T58.2X4S	774
T52.4X2A	763	T53.5X1A	764	T54.3X4A	764	T56.4X3A	764	T57.1X2A	764	T58.8X1A	764
T52.4X2D	837	T53.5X1D	837	T54.3X4D	837	T56.4X3D	838	T57.1X2D	838	T58.8X1D	838
T52.4X2S	774	T53.5X1S	774	T54.3X4S	774	T56.4X3S	774	T57.1X2S	774	T58.8X1S	774
T52.4X3A	763	T53.5X2A	764	T54.91XA	764	T56.4X4A	764	T57.1X3A	764	T58.8X2A	764
T52.4X3D	837	T53.5X2D	837	T54.91XD	837	T56.4X4D	838	T57.1X3D	838	T58.8X2D	838
T52.4X3S	774	T53.5X2S	774	T54.91XS	774	T56.4X4S	774	T57.1X3S	774	T58.8X2S	774
T52.4X4A	763	T53.5X3A	764	T54.92XA	764	T56.5X1A	764	T57.1X4A	764	T58.8X3A	764
T52.4X4D	837	T53.5X3D	837	T54.92XD	837	T56.5X1D	838	T57.1X4D	838	T58.8X3D	838
T52.4X4S	774	T53.5X3S	774	T54.92XS	774	T56.5X1S	774	T57.1X4S	774	T58.8X3S	774
T52.8X1A	763	T53.5X4A	764	T54.93XA	764	T56.5X2A	764	T57.2X1A	764	T58.8X4A	764
T52.8X1D	837	T53.5X4D	837	T54.93XD	837	T56.5X2D	838	T57.2X1D	838	T58.8X4D	838
T52.8X1S	774	T53.5X4S	774	T54.93XS	774	T56.5X2S	774	T57.2X1S	774	T58.8X4S	774
T52.8X2A	763	T53.6X1A	764	T54.94XA	764	T56.5X3A	764	T57.2X2A	764	T58.91XA	764
T52.8X2D	837	T53.6X1D	837	T54.94XD	837	T56.5X3D	838	T57.2X2D	838	T58.91XD	838
T52.8X2S	774	T53.6X1S	774	T54.94XS	774	T56.5X3S	774	T57.2X2S	774	T58.91XS	774
T52.8X3A	763	T53.6X2A	764	T55.0X1A	764	T56.5X4A	764	T57.2X3A	764	T58.92XA	764
T52.8X3D	837	T53.6X2D	837	T55.0X1D	837	T56.5X4D	838	T57.2X3D	838	T58.92XD	838
T52.8X3S	774	T53.6X2S	774	T55.0X1S	774	T56.5X4S	774	T57.2X3S	774	T58.92XS	774
T52.8X4A	763	T53.6X3A	764	T55.0X2A	764	T56.6X1A	764	T57.2X4A	764	T58.93XA	764
T52.8X4D	837	T53.6X3D	837	T55.0X2D	837	T56.6X1D	838	T57.2X4D	838	T58.93XD	838
T52.8X4S	774	T53.6X3S	774	T55.0X2S	774	T56.6X1S	774	T57.2X4S	774	T58.93XS	774
T52.91XA	763	T53.6X4A	764	T55.0X3A	764	T56.6X2A	764	T57.3X1A	764	T58.94XA	764
T52.91XD	837	T53.6X4D	837	T55.0X3D	837	T56.6X2D	838	T57.3X1D	838	T58.94XD	838
T52.91XS	774	T53.6X4S	774	T55.0X3S	774	T56.6X2S	774	T57.3X2A	764	T58.94XS	774
T52.92XA	763	T53.7X1A	764	T55.0X4A	764	T56.6X3A	764	T57.3X2D	838	T59.0X1A	764
T52.92XD	837	T53.7X1D	837	T55.0X4D	837	T56.6X3D	838	T57.3X2S	774	T59.0X1D	838
T52.92XS	774	T53.7X1S	774	T55.0X4S	774	T56.6X3S	774	T57.3X3A	764	T59.0X1S	774
T52.93XA	763	T53.7X2A	764	T55.1X1A	764	T56.6X4A	764	T57.3X3D	838	T59.0X2A	764
T52.93XD	837	T53.7X2D	837	T55.1X1D	837	T56.6X4D	838	T57.3X3S	774	T59.0X2D	838
T52.93XS	774	T53.7X2S	774	T55.1X1S	774	T56.6X4S	774			T59.0X2S	774

Numeric Index to Diseases

Code	Page	Code	Page	Code	Page	Code	Page	Code	Page	Code	Page
T59.0X3A	764	T59.812A	764, 788	T60.8X1A	765	T61.94XA	765	T63.023A	765	T63.122A	765
T59.0X3D	838	T59.812D	838	T60.8X1D	838	T61.94XD	839	T63.023D	839	T63.122D	839
T59.0X3S	774	T59.812S	775	T60.8X1S	775	T61.94XS	775	T63.023S	775	T63.122S	775
T59.0X4A	764	T59.813A	764, 788	T60.8X2A	765	T62.0X1A	765	T63.024A	765	T63.123A	765
T59.0X4D	838	T59.813D	838	T60.8X2D	838	T62.0X1D	839	T63.024D	839	T63.123D	839
T59.0X4S	774	T59.813S	775	T60.8X2S	775	T62.0X1S	775	T63.024S	775	T63.123S	775
T59.1X1A	764	T59.814A	764, 788	T60.8X3A	765	T62.0X2A	765	T63.031A	765	T63.124A	765
T59.1X1D	838	T59.814D	838	T60.8X3D	838	T62.0X2D	839	T63.031D	839	T63.124D	839
T59.1X1S	775	T59.814S	775	T60.8X3S	775	T62.0X2S	775	T63.031S	775	T63.124S	775
T59.1X2A	764	T59.891A	765, 788	T60.8X4A	765	T62.0X3A	765	T63.032A	765	T63.191A	765
T59.1X2D	838	T59.891D	838	T60.8X4D	838	T62.0X3D	839	T63.032D	839	T63.191D	839
T59.1X2S	775	T59.891S	775	T60.8X4S	775	T62.0X3S	775	T63.032S	775	T63.191S	775
T59.1X3A	764	T59.892A	765, 788	T60.91XA	765	T62.0X4A	765	T63.033A	765	T63.192A	765
T59.1X3D	838	T59.892D	838	T60.91XD	838	T62.0X4D	839	T63.033D	839	T63.192D	839
T59.1X3S	775	T59.892S	775	T60.91XS	775	T62.0X4S	775	T63.033S	775	T63.192S	775
T59.1X4A	764	T59.893A	765, 788	T60.92XA	765	T62.1X1A	765	T63.034A	765	T63.193A	765
T59.1X4D	838	T59.893D	838	T60.92XD	838	T62.1X1D	839	T63.034D	839	T63.193D	839
T59.1X4S	775	T59.893S	775	T60.92XS	775	T62.1X1S	775	T63.034S	775	T63.193S	775
T59.2X1A	764	T59.894A	765, 788	T60.93XA	765	T62.1X2A	765	T63.041A	765	T63.194A	765
T59.2X1D	838	T59.894D	838	T60.93XD	838	T62.1X2D	839	T63.041D	839	T63.194D	839
T59.2X1S	775	T59.894S	775	T60.93XS	775	T62.1X2S	775	T63.041S	775	T63.194S	775
T59.2X2A	764	T59.91XA	765, 788	T60.94XA	765	T62.1X3A	765	T63.042A	765	T63.2X1A	765
T59.2X2D	838	T59.91XD	838	T60.94XD	838	T62.1X3D	839	T63.042D	839	T63.2X1D	839
T59.2X2S	775	T59.91XS	775	T60.94XS	775	T62.1X3S	775	T63.042S	775	T63.2X1S	775
T59.2X3A	764	T59.92XA	765, 788	T61.01XA	765	T62.1X4A	765	T63.043A	765	T63.2X2A	765
T59.2X3D	838	T59.92XD	838	T61.01XD	838	T62.1X4D	839	T63.043D	839	T63.2X2D	839
T59.2X3S	775	T59.92XS	775	T61.01XS	775	T62.1X4S	775	T63.043S	775	T63.2X2S	775
T59.2X4A	764	T59.93XA	765, 788	T61.02XA	765	T62.2X1A	765	T63.044A	765	T63.2X3A	765
T59.2X4D	838	T59.93XD	838	T61.02XD	838	T62.2X1D	839	T63.044D	839	T63.2X3D	839
T59.2X4S	775	T59.93XS	775	T61.02XS	775	T62.2X1S	775	T63.044S	775	T63.2X3S	775
T59.3X1A	764	T59.94XA	765, 788	T61.03XA	765	T62.2X2A	765	T63.061A	765	T63.2X4A	765
T59.3X1D	838	T59.94XD	838	T61.03XD	838	T62.2X2D	839	T63.061D	839	T63.2X4D	839
T59.3X1S	775	T59.94XS	775	T61.03XS	775	T62.2X2S	775	T63.061S	775	T63.2X4S	775
T59.3X2A	764	T60.0X1A	765	T61.04XA	765	T62.2X3A	765	T63.062A	765	T63.301A	765
T59.3X2D	838	T60.0X1D	838	T61.04XD	838	T62.2X3D	839	T63.062D	839	T63.301D	839
T59.3X2S	775	T60.0X1S	775	T61.04XS	775	T62.2X3S	775	T63.062S	775	T63.301S	775
T59.3X3A	764	T60.0X2A	765	T61.11XA	765	T62.2X4A	765	T63.063A	765	T63.302A	765
T59.3X3D	838	T60.0X2D	838	T61.11XD	838	T62.2X4D	839	T63.063D	839	T63.302D	839
T59.3X3S	775	T60.0X2S	775	T61.11XS	775	T62.2X4S	775	T63.063S	775	T63.302S	775
T59.3X4A	764	T60.0X3A	765	T61.12XA	765	T62.8X1A	765	T63.064A	765	T63.303A	765
T59.3X4D	838	T60.0X3D	838	T61.12XD	838	T62.8X1D	839	T63.064D	839	T63.303D	839
T59.3X4S	775	T60.0X3S	775	T61.12XS	775	T62.8X1S	775	T63.064S	775	T63.303S	775
T59.4X1A	764	T60.0X4A	765	T61.13XA	765	T62.8X2A	765	T63.071A	765	T63.304A	765
T59.4X1D	838	T60.0X4D	838	T61.13XD	838	T62.8X2D	839	T63.071D	839	T63.304D	839
T59.4X1S	775	T60.0X4S	775	T61.13XS	775	T62.8X2S	775	T63.071S	775	T63.304S	775
T59.4X2A	764	T60.1X1A	765	T61.14XA	765	T62.8X3A	765	T63.072A	765	T63.311A	765
T59.4X2D	838	T60.1X1D	838	T61.14XD	838	T62.8X3D	839	T63.072D	839	T63.311D	839
T59.4X2S	775	T60.1X1S	775	T61.14XS	775	T62.8X3S	775	T63.072S	775	T63.311S	775
T59.4X3A	764	T60.1X2A	765	T61.771A	765	T62.8X4A	765	T63.073A	765	T63.312A	765
T59.4X3D	838	T60.1X2D	838	T61.771D	838	T62.8X4D	839	T63.073D	839	T63.312D	839
T59.4X3S	775	T60.1X2S	775	T61.771S	775	T62.8X4S	775	T63.073S	775	T63.312S	775
T59.4X4A	764	T60.1X3A	765	T61.772A	765	T62.91XA	765	T63.074A	765	T63.313A	765
T59.4X4D	838	T60.1X3D	838	T61.772D	838	T62.91XD	839	T63.074D	839	T63.313D	839
T59.4X4S	775	T60.1X3S	775	T61.772S	775	T62.91XS	775	T63.074S	775	T63.313S	775
T59.5X1A	764	T60.1X4A	765	T61.773A	765	T62.92XA	765	T63.081A	765	T63.314A	765
T59.5X1D	838	T60.1X4D	838	T61.773D	838	T62.92XD	839	T63.081D	839	T63.314D	839
T59.5X1S	775	T60.1X4S	775	T61.773S	775	T62.92XS	775	T63.081S	775	T63.314S	775
T59.5X2A	764	T60.2X1A	765	T61.774A	765	T62.93XA	765	T63.082A	765	T63.321A	765
T59.5X2D	838	T60.2X1D	838	T61.774D	838	T62.93XD	839	T63.082D	839	T63.321D	839
T59.5X2S	775	T60.2X1S	775	T61.774S	775	T62.93XS	775	T63.082S	775	T63.321S	775
T59.5X3A	764	T60.2X2A	765	T61.781A	765	T62.94XA	765	T63.083A	765	T63.322A	765
T59.5X3D	838	T60.2X2D	838	T61.781D	838	T62.94XD	839	T63.083D	839	T63.322D	839
T59.5X3S	775	T60.2X2S	775	T61.781S	775	T62.94XS	775	T63.083S	775	T63.322S	775
T59.5X4A	764	T60.2X3A	765	T61.782A	765	T63.001A	765	T63.084A	765	T63.323A	765
T59.5X4D	838	T60.2X3D	838	T61.782D	838	T63.001D	839	T63.084D	839	T63.323D	839
T59.5X4S	775	T60.2X3S	775	T61.782S	775	T63.001S	775	T63.084S	775	T63.323S	776
T59.6X1A	764	T60.2X4A	765	T61.783A	765	T63.002A	765	T63.091A	765	T63.324A	765
T59.6X1D	838	T60.2X4D	838	T61.783D	838	T63.002D	839	T63.091D	839	T63.324D	839
T59.6X1S	775	T60.2X4S	775	T61.783S	775	T63.002S	775	T63.091S	775	T63.324S	776
T59.6X2A	764	T60.3X1A	765	T61.784A	765	T63.003A	765	T63.092A	765	T63.331A	765
T59.6X2D	838	T60.3X1D	838	T61.784D	838	T63.003D	839	T63.092D	839	T63.331D	839
T59.6X2S	775	T60.3X1S	775	T61.784S	775	T63.003S	775	T63.092S	775	T63.331S	776
T59.6X3A	764	T60.3X2A	765	T61.8X1A	765	T63.004A	765	T63.093A	765	T63.332A	765
T59.6X3D	838	T60.3X2D	838	T61.8X1D	838	T63.004D	839	T63.093D	839	T63.332D	839
T59.6X3S	775	T60.3X2S	775	T61.8X1S	775	T63.004S	775	T63.093S	775	T63.332S	776
T59.6X4A	764	T60.3X3A	765	T61.8X2A	765	T63.011A	765	T63.094A	765	T63.333A	765
T59.6X4D	838	T60.3X3D	838	T61.8X2D	839	T63.011D	839	T63.094D	839	T63.333D	839
T59.6X4S	775	T60.3X3S	775	T61.8X2S	775	T63.011S	775	T63.094S	775	T63.333S	776
T59.7X1A	764	T60.3X4A	765	T61.8X3A	765	T63.012A	765	T63.111A	765	T63.334A	765
T59.7X1D	838	T60.3X4D	838	T61.8X3D	839	T63.012D	839	T63.111D	839	T63.334D	839
T59.7X1S	775	T60.3X4S	775	T61.8X3S	775	T63.012S	775	T63.111S	775	T63.334S	776
T59.7X2A	764	T60.4X1A	765	T61.8X4A	765	T63.013A	765	T63.112A	765	T63.391A	765
T59.7X2D	838	T60.4X1D	838	T61.8X4D	839	T63.013D	839	T63.112D	839	T63.391D	839
T59.7X2S	775	T60.4X1S	775	T61.8X4S	775	T63.013S	775	T63.112S	775	T63.391S	776
T59.7X3A	764	T60.4X2A	765	T61.91XA	765	T63.014A	765	T63.113A	765	T63.392A	765
T59.7X3D	838	T60.4X2D	838	T61.91XD	839	T63.014D	839	T63.113D	839	T63.392D	839
T59.7X3S	775	T60.4X2S	775	T61.91XS	775	T63.014S	775	T63.113S	775	T63.392S	776
T59.7X4A	764	T60.4X3A	765	T61.92XA	765	T63.021A	765	T63.114A	765	T63.393A	765
T59.7X4D	838	T60.4X3D	838	T61.92XD	839	T63.021D	839	T63.114D	839	T63.393D	839
T59.7X4S	775	T60.4X3S	775	T61.92XS	775	T63.021S	775	T63.114S	775	T63.393S	776
T59.811A	764, 788	T60.4X4A	765	T61.93XA	765	T63.022A	765	T63.121A	765	T63.394A	765
T59.811D	838	T60.4X4D	838	T61.93XD	839	T63.022D	839	T63.121D	839	T63.394D	839
T59.811S	775	T60.4X4S	775	T61.93XS	775	T63.022S	775	T63.121S	775	T63.394S	776

Code	Page	Code	Page	Code	Page	Code	Page	Code	Page	Code	Page
T63.411A	765	T63.514A	766	T63.813A	766	T65.1X2A	766	T65.811A	766	T67.8XXA	777
T63.411D	839	T63.514D	839	T63.813D	839	T65.1X2D	840	T65.811D	840	T67.8XXD	840
T63.411S	776	T63.514S	776	T63.813S	776	T65.1X2S	776	T65.811S	776	T67.8XXS	777
T63.412A	765	T63.591A	766	T63.814A	766	T65.1X3A	766	T65.812A	766	T67.9XXA	777
T63.412D	839	T63.591D	839	T63.814D	839	T65.1X3D	840	T65.812D	840	T67.9XXD	840
T63.412S	776	T63.591S	776	T63.814S	776	T65.1X3S	776	T65.812S	776	T67.9XXS	777
T63.413A	765	T63.592A	766	T63.821A	766	T65.1X4A	766	T65.813A	766	T68.XXXA	777
T63.413D	839	T63.592D	839	T63.821D	839	T65.1X4D	840	T65.813D	840	T68.XXXD	840
T63.413S	776	T63.592S	776	T63.821S	776	T65.1X4S	776	T65.813S	776	T68.XXXS	777
T63.414A	765	T63.593A	766	T63.822A	766	T65.211A	766	T65.814A	766	T69.011A	777
T63.414D	839	T63.593D	839	T63.822D	839	T65.211D	840	T65.814D	840	T69.011D	840
T63.414S	776	T63.593S	776	T63.822S	776	T65.211S	776	T65.814S	776	T69.011S	777
T63.421A	765	T63.594A	766	T63.823A	766	T65.212A	766	T65.821A	766	T69.012A	777
T63.421D	839	T63.594D	839	T63.823D	839	T65.212D	840	T65.821D	840	T69.012D	840
T63.421S	776	T63.594S	776	T63.823S	776	T65.212S	776	T65.821S	776	T69.012S	777
T63.422A	765	T63.611A	766	T63.824A	766	T65.213A	766	T65.822A	766	T69.019A	777
T63.422D	839	T63.611D	839	T63.824D	839	T65.213D	840	T65.822D	840	T69.019D	840
T63.422S	776	T63.611S	776	T63.824S	776	T65.213S	776	T65.822S	776	T69.019S	777
T63.423A	765	T63.612A	766	T63.831A	766	T65.214A	766	T65.823A	766	T69.021A	777
T63.423D	839	T63.612D	839	T63.831D	839	T65.214D	840	T65.823D	840	T69.021D	840
T63.423S	776	T63.612S	776	T63.831S	776	T65.214S	776	T65.823S	776	T69.021S	777
T63.424A	765	T63.613A	766	T63.832A	766	T65.221A	766	T65.824A	766	T69.022A	777
T63.424D	839	T63.613D	839	T63.832D	839	T65.221D	840	T65.824D	840	T69.022D	840
T63.424S	776	T63.613S	776	T63.832S	776	T65.221S	776	T65.824S	776	T69.022S	777
T63.431A	765	T63.614A	766	T63.833A	766	T65.222A	766	T65.831A	766	T69.029A	777
T63.431D	839	T63.614D	839	T63.833D	839	T65.222D	840	T65.831D	840	T69.029D	840
T63.431S	776	T63.614S	776	T63.833S	776	T65.222S	776	T65.831S	776	T69.029S	777
T63.432A	765	T63.621A	766	T63.834A	766	T65.223A	766	T65.832A	766	T69.1XXA	777
T63.432D	839	T63.621D	839	T63.834D	839	T65.223D	840	T65.832D	840	T69.1XXD	840
T63.432S	776	T63.621S	776	T63.834S	776	T65.223S	776	T65.832S	776	T69.1XXS	777
T63.433A	765	T63.622A	766	T63.891A	766	T65.224A	766	T65.833A	766	T69.8XXA	777
T63.433D	839	T63.622D	839	T63.891D	839	T65.224D	840	T65.833D	840	T69.8XXD	840
T63.433S	776	T63.622S	776	T63.891S	776	T65.224S	776	T65.833S	776	T69.8XXS	777
T63.434A	765	T63.623A	766	T63.892A	766	T65.291A	766	T65.834A	766	T69.9XXA	777
T63.434D	839	T63.623D	839	T63.892D	839	T65.291D	840	T65.834D	840	T69.9XXD	840
T63.434S	776	T63.623S	776	T63.892S	776	T65.291S	776	T65.834S	776	T69.9XXS	777
T63.441A	765	T63.624A	766	T63.893A	766	T65.292A	766	T65.891A	766	T70.0XXA	86
T63.441D	839	T63.624D	839	T63.893D	839	T65.292D	840	T65.891D	840	T70.0XXD	840
T63.441S	776	T63.624S	776	T63.893S	776	T65.292S	776	T65.891S	776	T70.0XXS	777
T63.442A	765	T63.631A	766	T63.894A	766	T65.293A	766	T65.892A	766	T70.1XXA	86
T63.442D	839	T63.631D	839	T63.894D	840	T65.293D	840	T65.892D	840	T70.1XXD	840
T63.442S	776	T63.631S	776	T63.894S	776	T65.293S	776	T65.892S	776	T70.1XXS	777
T63.443A	765	T63.632A	766	T63.91XA	766	T65.294A	766	T65.893A	766	T70.20XA	777
T63.443D	839	T63.632D	839	T63.91XD	840	T65.294D	840	T65.893D	840	T70.20XD	840
T63.443S	776	T63.632S	776	T63.91XS	776	T65.294S	776	T65.893S	776	T70.20XS	777
T63.444A	765	T63.633A	766	T63.92XA	766	T65.3X1A	766	T65.894A	766	T70.29XA	777
T63.444D	839	T63.633D	839	T63.92XD	840	T65.3X1D	840	T65.894D	840	T70.29XD	840
T63.444S	776	T63.633S	776	T63.92XS	776	T65.3X1S	776	T65.894S	776	T70.29XS	777
T63.451A	765	T63.634A	766	T63.93XA	766	T65.3X2A	766	T65.91XA	766	T70.3XXA	777
T63.451D	839	T63.634D	839	T63.93XD	840	T65.3X2D	840	T65.91XD	840	T70.3XXD	840
T63.451S	776	T63.634S	776	T63.93XS	776	T65.3X2S	776	T65.91XS	776	T70.3XXS	777
T63.452A	765	T63.691A	766	T63.94XA	766	T65.3X3A	766	T65.92XA	766	T70.4XXA	777
T63.452D	839	T63.691D	839	T63.94XD	840	T65.3X3D	840	T65.92XD	840	T70.4XXD	840
T63.452S	776	T63.691S	776	T63.94XS	776	T65.3X3S	776	T65.92XS	776	T70.4XXS	777
T63.453A	765	T63.692A	766	T64.01XA	766	T65.3X4A	766	T65.93XA	766	T70.8XXA	777
T63.453D	839	T63.692D	839	T64.01XD	840	T65.3X4D	840	T65.93XD	840	T70.8XXD	840
T63.453S	776	T63.692S	776	T64.01XS	776	T65.3X4S	776	T65.93XS	776	T70.8XXS	777
T63.454A	765	T63.693A	766	T64.02XA	766	T65.4X1A	766	T65.94XA	766	T70.9XXA	777
T63.454D	839	T63.693D	839	T64.02XD	840	T65.4X1D	840	T65.94XD	840	T70.9XXD	840
T63.454S	776	T63.693S	776	T64.02XS	776	T65.4X1S	776	T65.94XS	776	T70.9XXS	777
T63.461A	765	T63.694A	766	T64.03XA	766	T65.4X2A	766	T66.XXXA	776	T71.111A	777
T63.461D	839	T63.694D	839	T64.03XD	840	T65.4X2D	840	T66.XXXD	840	T71.111D	840
T63.461S	776	T63.694S	776	T64.03XS	776	T65.4X2S	776	T66.XXXS	776	T71.111S	777
T63.462A	765	T63.711A	766	T64.04XA	766	T65.4X3A	766	T67.01XA	776	T71.112A	777
T63.462D	839	T63.711D	839	T64.04XD	840	T65.4X3D	840	T67.01XD	840	T71.112D	840
T63.462S	776	T63.711S	776	T64.04XS	776	T65.4X3S	776	T67.01XS	776	T71.112S	777
T63.463A	766	T63.712A	766	T64.81XA	766	T65.4X4A	766	T67.02XA	776	T71.113A	777
T63.463D	839	T63.712D	839	T64.81XD	840	T65.4X4D	840	T67.02XD	840	T71.113D	840
T63.463S	776	T63.712S	776	T64.81XS	776	T65.4X4S	776	T67.02XS	776	T71.113S	777
T63.464A	766	T63.713A	766	T64.82XA	766	T65.5X1A	766	T67.09XA	776	T71.114A	777
T63.464S	776	T63.713D	839	T64.82XD	840	T65.5X1D	840	T67.09XD	840	T71.114D	840
T63.481A	766	T63.713S	776	T64.82XS	776	T65.5X1S	776	T67.09XS	776	T71.114S	777
T63.481D	839	T63.714A	766	T64.83XA	766	T65.5X2A	766	T67.1XXA	776	T71.121A	777
T63.481S	776	T63.714D	839	T64.83XD	840	T65.5X2D	840	T67.1XXD	840	T71.121D	840
T63.482A	766	T63.714S	776	T64.83XS	776	T65.5X2S	776	T67.1XXS	776	T71.121S	777
T63.482D	839	T63.791A	766	T64.84XA	766	T65.5X3A	766	T67.2XXA	776	T71.122A	777
T63.482S	776	T63.791D	839	T64.84XD	840	T65.5X3D	840	T67.2XXD	840	T71.122D	840
T63.483A	766	T63.791S	776	T64.84XS	776	T65.5X3S	776	T67.2XXS	776	T71.122S	777
T63.483D	839	T63.792A	766	T65.0X1A	766	T65.5X4A	766	T67.3XXA	776	T71.123A	777
T63.483S	776	T63.792D	839	T65.0X1D	840	T65.5X4D	840	T67.3XXD	840	T71.123D	840
T63.484A	766	T63.792S	776	T65.0X1S	776	T65.5X4S	776	T67.3XXS	776	T71.123S	777
T63.484D	839	T63.793A	766	T65.0X2A	766	T65.6X1A	766	T67.4XXA	776	T71.124A	777
T63.484S	776	T63.793D	839	T65.0X2D	840	T65.6X1D	840	T67.4XXD	840	T71.124D	840
T63.511A	766	T63.793S	776	T65.0X2S	776	T65.6X1S	776	T67.4XXS	776	T71.124S	777
T63.511D	839	T63.794A	766	T65.0X3A	766	T65.6X2A	766	T67.5XXA	776	T71.131A	777
T63.511S	776	T63.794D	839	T65.0X3D	840	T65.6X2D	840	T67.5XXD	840	T71.131D	840
T63.512A	766	T63.794S	776	T65.0X3S	776	T65.6X2S	776	T67.5XXS	776	T71.131S	777
T63.512D	839	T63.811A	766	T65.0X4A	766	T65.6X3A	766	T67.6XXA	776	T71.132A	777
T63.512S	776	T63.811D	839	T65.0X4D	840	T65.6X3D	840	T67.6XXD	840	T71.132D	840
T63.513A	766	T63.811S	776	T65.0X4S	776	T65.6X3S	776	T67.6XXS	776	T71.132S	777
T63.513D	839	T63.812A	766	T65.1X1A	766	T65.6X4A	766	T67.7XXA	777	T71.133A	777
T63.513S	776	T63.812D	839	T65.1X1D	840	T65.6X4D	840	T67.7XXD	840	T71.133D	840
		T63.812S	776	T65.1X1S	776	T65.6X4S	776	T67.7XXS	777	T71.133S	777

Numeric Index to Diseases

Numeric Index to Diseases

Code	Page	Code	Page	Code	Page	Code	Page	Code	Page	Code	Page
T71.134A	777	T73.3XXA	777	T75.89XA	778	T78.8XXA	778	T80.319D	841	T81.31XD	841
T71.134D	840	T73.3XXD	840	T75.89XD	840	T78.8XXD	841	T80.319S	778	T81.31XS	778
T71.134S	777	T73.3XXS	777	T75.89XS	778	T78.8XXS	778	T80.39XA	567, 578	T81.32XA	767
T71.141A	777	T73.8XXA	777	T76.01XA	778	T79.0XXA	104, 567, 1024, 1027	T80.39XD	841	T81.32XD	841
T71.141D	840	T73.8XXD	840	T76.01XD	841			T80.39XS	778	T81.32XS	778
T71.141S	777	T73.8XXS	777	T76.01XS	778	T79.0XXD	841	T80.40XA	567, 578	T81.33XA	767
T71.143A	777	T73.9XXA	777	T76.02XA	778	T79.0XXS	758	T80.40XD	841	T81.33XD	841
T71.143D	840	T73.9XXD	840	T76.02XD	841	T79.1XXA	104, 567, 1024, 1027	T80.40XS	778	T81.33XS	778
T71.143S	777	T73.9XXS	777	T76.02XS	778			T80.410A	567, 578	T81.40XA	568, 632
T71.144A	777	T74.01XA	777	T76.11XA	778	T79.1XXD	841	T80.410D	841	T81.40XD	841
T71.144D	840	T74.01XD	840	T76.11XD	841	T79.1XXS	758	T80.410S	778	T81.40XS	778
T71.144S	777	T74.01XS	777	T76.11XS	778	T79.2XXA	567, 778, 1024	T80.411A	567, 578	T81.41XA	568, 632
T71.151A	777	T74.02XA	777	T76.12XA	778	T79.2XXD	841	T80.411D	841	T81.41XD	841
T71.151D	840	T74.02XD	840	T76.12XD	841	T79.2XXS	758	T80.411S	778	T81.41XS	778
T71.151S	777	T74.02XS	777	T76.12XS	778	T79.4XXA	567, 778, 1024	T80.419A	567, 578	T81.42XA	568, 632
T71.152A	777	T74.11XA	777	T76.21XA	778	T79.4XXD	841	T80.419D	841	T81.42XD	841
T71.152D	840	T74.11XD	840	T76.21XD	841	T79.4XXS	758	T80.419S	778	T81.42XS	778
T71.152S	777	T74.11XS	777	T76.21XS	778	T79.5XXA	518, 567, 1024	T80.49XA	567, 578	T81.43XA	568, 632
T71.153A	777	T74.12XA	777	T76.22XA	778	T79.5XXD	841	T80.49XD	841	T81.43XD	841
T71.153D	840	T74.12XD	840	T76.22XD	841	T79.5XXS	758	T80.49XS	778	T81.43XS	778
T71.153S	777	T74.12XS	777	T76.22XS	778	T79.6XXA	409, 1024, 1034	T80.51XA	567, 758	T81.44XA	568, 632
T71.154A	777	T74.21XA	777	T76.31XA	778	T79.6XXD	841	T80.51XD	841	T81.44XD	841
T71.154D	840	T74.21XD	840	T76.31XD	841	T79.6XXS	758	T80.51XS	778	T81.44XS	778
T71.154S	777	T74.21XS	777	T76.31XS	778	T79.7XXA	106, 567, 1024	T80.52XA	567, 758	T81.49XA	568, 632
T71.161A	777	T74.22XA	777	T76.32XA	778	T79.7XXD	841	T80.52XD	841	T81.49XD	841
T71.161D	840	T74.22XD	840	T76.32XD	841	T79.7XXS	758	T80.52XS	778	T81.49XS	778
T71.161S	777	T74.22XS	777	T76.32XS	778	T79.8XXA	778, 1024	T80.59XA	567, 758	T81.500A	568, 767
T71.162A	777	T74.31XA	777	T76.51XA	778	T79.8XXD	841	T80.59XD	841	T81.500D	841
T71.162D	840	T74.31XD	840	T76.51XD	841	T79.8XXS	758	T80.59XS	778	T81.500S	778
T71.162S	777	T74.31XS	777	T76.51XS	778	T79.9XXA	778, 1024	T80.61XA	567, 758	T81.501A	568, 767
T71.163A	777	T74.32XA	777	T76.52XA	778	T79.9XXD	841	T80.61XD	841	T81.501D	841
T71.163D	840	T74.32XD	840	T76.52XD	841	T79.9XXS	758	T80.61XS	778	T81.501S	778
T71.163S	777	T74.32XS	777	T76.52XS	778	T79.A0XA	778, 1024	T80.62XA	567, 758	T81.502A	568, 767
T71.164A	777	T74.4XXA	777	T76.61XA	778	T79.A0XD	841	T80.62XD	841	T81.502D	841
T71.164D	840	T74.4XXD	840	T76.61XD	841	T79.A0XS	758	T80.62XS	778	T81.502S	778
T71.164S	777	T74.4XXS	777	T76.61XS	778	T79.A11A	778, 1024, 1034	T80.69XA	568, 758	T81.503A	568, 767
T71.191A	777	T74.51XA	777	T76.62XA	778	T79.A11D	841	T80.69XD	841	T81.503D	841
T71.191D	840	T74.51XD	840	T76.62XD	841	T79.A11S	758	T80.69XS	778	T81.503S	778
T71.191S	777	T74.51XS	777	T76.62XS	778	T79.A12A	778, 1024, 1034	T80.810A	173, 568	T81.504A	568, 767
T71.192A	777	T74.52XA	777	T76.91XA	778	T79.A12D	841	T80.810D	841	T81.504D	841
T71.192D	840	T74.52XD	840	T76.91XD	841	T79.A12S	758	T80.810S	778	T81.504S	778
T71.192S	777	T74.52XS	777	T76.91XS	778	T79.A19A	778, 1024, 1034	T80.818A	173, 568	T81.505A	568, 767
T71.193A	777	T74.61XA	777	T76.92XA	778	T79.A19D	841	T80.818D	841	T81.505D	841
T71.193D	840	T74.61XD	840	T76.92XD	841	T79.A19S	758	T80.818S	778	T81.505S	778
T71.193S	777	T74.61XS	777	T76.92XS	778	T79.A21A	778, 1024, 1040	T80.89XA	568, 578	T81.506A	568, 767
T71.194A	777	T74.62XA	777	T78.00XA	758	T79.A21D	841	T80.89XD	841	T81.506D	841
T71.194D	840	T74.62XD	840	T78.00XD	841	T79.A21S	758	T80.89XS	778	T81.506S	778
T71.194S	777	T74.62XS	777	T78.00XS	778	T79.A22A	778, 1024, 1040	T80.90XA	173, 568	T81.507A	568, 767
T71.20XA	777	T74.91XA	758	T78.01XA	758	T79.A22D	841	T80.90XD	841	T81.507D	841
T71.20XD	840	T74.91XD	840	T78.01XD	841	T79.A22S	758	T80.90XS	778	T81.507S	778
T71.20XS	777	T74.91XS	758	T78.01XS	778	T79.A29A	778, 1024, 1040	T80.910A	568, 578	T81.508A	767
T71.21XA	777	T74.92XA	758	T78.02XA	758	T79.A29D	841	T80.910D	841	T81.508A	568
T71.21XD	840	T74.92XD	840	T78.02XD	841	T79.A29S	758	T80.910S	778	T81.508D	841
T71.21XS	777	T74.92XS	758	T78.02XS	778	T79.A3XA	778, 1024, 1028	T80.911A	568, 578	T81.508S	778
T71.221A	777	T75.00XA	777	T78.03XA	758	T79.A3XD	841	T80.911D	841	T81.509A	568, 767
T71.221D	840	T75.00XD	840	T78.03XD	841	T79.A3XS	758	T80.911S	778	T81.509D	841
T71.221S	777	T75.00XS	777	T78.03XS	778	T79.A9XA	778, 1024	T80.919A	568, 578	T81.509S	778
T71.222A	777	T75.01XA	777	T78.04XA	758	T79.A9XD	841	T80.919D	841	T81.510A	568, 767
T71.222D	840	T75.01XD	840	T78.04XD	841	T79.A9XS	758	T80.919S	778	T81.510D	841
T71.222S	777	T75.01XS	777	T78.04XS	778	T80.0XXA	104, 567	T80.92XA	568, 578	T81.510S	778
T71.223A	777	T75.09XA	777	T78.05XA	758	T80.0XXD	841	T80.92XD	841	T81.511A	568, 767
T71.223D	840	T75.09XD	840	T78.05XD	841	T80.0XXS	778	T80.92XS	778	T81.511D	841
T71.223S	777	T75.09XS	777	T78.05XS	778	T80.1XXA	173, 567	T80.A0XA	568, 578	T81.511S	778
T71.224A	777	T75.1XXA	777	T78.06XA	758	T80.1XXD	841	T80.A0XD	841	T81.512A	568, 767
T71.224D	840	T75.1XXD	840	T78.06XD	841	T80.1XXS	778	T80.A0XS	778	T81.512D	841
T71.224S	777	T75.1XXS	777	T78.06XS	778	T80.211A	173	T80.A10A	568, 578	T81.512S	778
T71.231A	777	T75.20XA	777	T78.07XA	758	T80.211D	841	T80.A10D	841	T81.513A	568, 767
T71.231D	840	T75.20XD	840	T78.07XD	841	T80.211S	778	T80.A10S	778	T81.513D	841
T71.231S	777	T75.20XS	777	T78.07XS	778	T80.212A	173	T80.A11A	568, 578	T81.513S	778
T71.232A	777	T75.21XA	777	T78.08XA	758	T80.212D	841	T80.A11D	841	T81.514A	568, 767
T71.232D	840	T75.21XD	840	T78.08XD	841	T80.212S	778	T80.A11S	778	T81.514D	841
T71.232S	777	T75.21XS	777	T78.08XS	778	T80.218A	173	T80.A19A	568, 579	T81.514S	778
T71.233A	777	T75.22XA	777	T78.09XA	758	T80.218D	841	T80.A19D	841	T81.515A	568, 767
T71.233D	840	T75.22XD	840	T78.09XD	841	T80.218S	778	T80.A19S	778	T81.515D	841
T71.233S	777	T75.22XS	777	T78.09XS	778	T80.219A	173	T80.A9XA	568, 579	T81.515S	778
T71.234A	777	T75.23XA	778	T78.1XXA	778	T80.219D	841	T80.A9XD	841	T81.516A	568, 767
T71.234D	840	T75.23XD	840	T78.1XXD	841	T80.219S	778	T80.A9XS	778	T81.516D	841
T71.234S	777	T75.23XS	778	T78.1XXS	778	T80.22XA	567, 632, 634	T81.10XA	568, 767	T81.516S	778
T71.29XA	777	T75.29XA	778	T78.2XXA	758	T80.22XD	841	T81.10XD	841	T81.517A	568, 767
T71.29XD	840	T75.29XD	840	T78.2XXD	841	T80.22XS	778	T81.10XS	778	T81.517D	841
T71.29XS	777	T75.29XS	778	T78.2XXS	778	T80.29XA	567, 632, 634	T81.11XA	568, 767	T81.517S	778
T71.9XXA	777	T75.3XXA	86	T78.3XXA	758	T80.29XD	841	T81.11XD	841	T81.518A	767
T71.9XXD	840	T75.3XXD	840	T78.3XXD	841	T80.29XS	778	T81.11XS	778	T81.518A	568
T71.9XXS	777	T75.3XXS	778	T78.3XXS	778	T80.30XA	567, 578	T81.12XA	568, 767	T81.518D	841
T73.0XXA	777	T75.4XXA	778	T78.40XA	758	T80.30XD	841	T81.12XD	841	T81.518S	778
T73.0XXD	840	T75.4XXD	840	T78.40XD	841	T80.30XS	778	T81.12XS	778	T81.519A	568, 767
T73.0XXS	777	T75.4XXS	778	T78.40XS	778	T80.310A	567, 578	T81.19XA	568, 767	T81.519D	841
T73.1XXA	777	T75.81XA	777	T78.41XA	567, 766	T80.310D	841	T81.19XD	841	T81.519S	778
T73.1XXD	840	T75.81XD	840	T78.41XD	841	T80.310S	778	T81.19XS	778	T81.520A	568, 767
T73.1XXS	777	T75.81XS	778	T78.41XS	778	T80.311A	567, 578	T81.30XA	767	T81.520D	841
T73.2XXA	777	T75.82XA	778	T78.49XA	758	T80.311D	841	T81.30XD	841	T81.520S	778
T73.2XXD	840	T75.82XD	840	T78.49XD	841	T80.311S	778	T81.30XS	778	T81.521A	568, 767
T73.2XXS	777	T75.82XS	778	T78.49XS	778	T80.319A	567, 578	T81.31XA	767	T81.521D	841

Code	Page	Code	Page	Code	Page	Code	Page	Code	Page	Code	Page
T81.521S	778	T81.61XS	779	T82.218S	779	T82.512S	779	T82.7XXS	779	T83.091S	779
T81.522A	568,767	T81.69XA	568,767	T82.221A	173	T82.513A	173	T82.817A	173	T83.092A	520
T81.522D	841	T81.69XD	841	T82.221D	842	T82.513D	842	T82.817D	842	T83.092D	842
T81.522S	778	T81.69XS	779	T82.221S	779	T82.513S	779	T82.817S	779	T83.092S	779
T81.523A	568,767	T81.710A	197,568	T82.222A	173	T82.514A	173	T82.818A	173	T83.098A	520
T81.523D	841	T81.710D	841	T82.222D	842	T82.514D	842	T82.818D	842	T83.098D	842
T81.523S	778	T81.710S	779	T82.222S	779	T82.514S	779	T82.818S	779	T83.098S	779
T81.524A	568,767	T81.711A	520,568	T82.223A	173	T82.515A	173	T82.827A	173	T83.110A	520
T81.524D	841	T81.711D	841	T82.223D	842	T82.515D	842	T82.827D	842	T83.110D	842
T81.524S	778	T81.711S	779	T82.223S	779	T82.515S	779	T82.827S	779	T83.110S	779
T81.525A	568,767	T81.718A	171,568	T82.228A	173	T82.518A	173	T82.828A	173	T83.111A	520
T81.525D	841	T81.718D	841	T82.228D	842	T82.518D	842	T82.828D	842	T83.111D	842
T81.525S	778	T81.718S	779	T82.228S	779	T82.518S	779	T82.828S	779	T83.111S	779
T81.526A	568,767	T81.719A	171,568	T82.310A	173	T82.519A	173	T82.837A	173	T83.112A	520
T81.526D	841	T81.719D	841	T82.310D	842	T82.519D	842	T82.837D	842	T83.112D	842
T81.526S	778	T81.719S	779	T82.310S	779	T82.519S	779	T82.837S	779	T83.112S	779
T81.527A	568,767	T81.72XA	171,568	T82.311A	173	T82.520A	173	T82.838A	173	T83.113A	520
T81.527D	841	T81.72XD	841	T82.311D	842	T82.520D	842	T82.838D	842	T83.113D	842
T81.527S	778	T81.72XS	779	T82.311S	779	T82.520S	779	T82.838S	779	T83.113S	779
T81.528A	767	T81.81XA	767	T82.312A	173	T82.521A	173	T82.847A	173	T83.118A	520
T81.528A	568	T81.81XD	841	T82.312D	842	T82.521D	842	T82.847D	842	T83.118D	842
T81.528D	841	T81.81XS	779	T82.312S	779	T82.521S	779	T82.847S	779	T83.118S	779
T81.528S	778	T81.82XA	767	T82.318A	173	T82.522A	173	T82.848A	173	T83.120A	520
T81.529A	568,767	T81.82XD	841	T82.318D	842	T82.522D	842	T82.848D	842	T83.120D	842
T81.529D	841	T81.82XS	779	T82.318S	779	T82.522S	779	T82.848S	779	T83.120S	779
T81.529S	778	T81.83XA	568,767	T82.319A	173	T82.523A	173	T82.855A	173	T83.121A	520
T81.530A	568,767	T81.83XD	841	T82.319D	842	T82.523D	842	T82.855D	842	T83.121D	842
T81.530D	841	T81.83XS	779	T82.319S	779	T82.523S	779	T82.855S	779	T83.121S	779
T81.530S	778	T81.89XA	767	T82.320A	173	T82.524A	173	T82.856A	173	T83.122A	520
T81.531A	568,767	T81.89XD	841	T82.320D	842	T82.524D	842	T82.856D	842	T83.122D	842
T81.531D	841	T81.89XS	779	T82.320S	779	T82.524S	779	T82.856S	779	T83.122S	779
T81.531S	778	T81.9XXA	568,767	T82.321A	173	T82.525A	173	T82.857A	173	T83.123A	520
T81.532A	568,767	T81.9XXD	841	T82.321D	842	T82.525D	842	T82.857D	842	T83.123D	842
T81.532D	841	T81.9XXS	779	T82.321S	779	T82.525S	779	T82.857S	779	T83.123S	779
T81.532S	778	T82.01XA	172	T82.322A	173	T82.528A	173	T82.858A	173	T83.128A	520
T81.533A	568,767	T82.01XD	841	T82.322D	842	T82.528D	842	T82.858D	842	T83.128D	842
T81.533D	841	T82.01XS	779	T82.322S	779	T82.528S	779	T82.858S	779	T83.128S	779
T81.533S	778	T82.02XA	172	T82.328A	173	T82.529A	173	T82.867A	173	T83.190A	520
T81.534A	568,767	T82.02XD	841	T82.328D	842	T82.529D	842	T82.867D	842	T83.190D	842
T81.534D	841	T82.02XS	779	T82.328S	779	T82.529S	779	T82.867S	779	T83.190S	779
T81.534S	778	T82.03XA	172	T82.329A	173	T82.530A	173	T82.868A	173	T83.191A	520
T81.535A	568,767	T82.03XD	841	T82.329D	842	T82.530D	842	T82.868D	842	T83.191D	842
T81.535D	841	T82.03XS	779	T82.329S	779	T82.530S	779	T82.868S	779	T83.191S	779
T81.535S	778	T82.09XA	172	T82.330A	173	T82.531A	173	T82.897A	173	T83.192A	520
T81.536A	568,767	T82.09XD	841	T82.330D	842	T82.531D	842	T82.897D	842	T83.192D	842
T81.536D	841	T82.09XS	779	T82.330S	779	T82.531S	779	T82.897S	779	T83.192S	779
T81.536S	778	T82.110A	172	T82.331A	173	T82.532A	173	T82.898A	173	T83.193A	520
T81.537A	568,767	T82.110D	841	T82.331D	842	T82.532D	842	T82.898D	842	T83.193D	842
T81.537D	841	T82.110S	779	T82.331S	779	T82.532S	779	T82.898S	779	T83.193S	779
T81.537S	778	T82.111A	172	T82.332A	173	T82.533A	173	T82.9XXA	173	T83.198A	520
T81.538A	767	T82.111D	841	T82.332D	842	T82.533D	842	T82.9XXD	842	T83.198D	842
T81.538A	568	T82.111S	779	T82.332S	779	T82.533S	779	T82.9XXS	779	T83.198S	779
T81.538D	841	T82.118A	173	T82.338A	173	T82.534A	173	T83.010A	520	T83.21XA	520
T81.538S	778	T82.118D	841	T82.338D	842	T82.534D	842	T83.010D	842	T83.21XD	842
T81.539A	568,767	T82.118S	779	T82.338S	779	T82.534S	779	T83.010S	779	T83.21XS	779
T81.539D	841	T82.119A	173	T82.339A	173	T82.535A	173	T83.011A	520	T83.22XA	520
T81.539S	778	T82.119D	841	T82.339D	842	T82.535D	842	T83.011D	842	T83.22XD	842
T81.590A	568,767	T82.119S	779	T82.339S	779	T82.535S	779	T83.011S	779	T83.22XS	779
T81.590D	841	T82.120A	172	T82.390A	173	T82.538A	173	T83.012A	520	T83.23XA	520
T81.590S	778	T82.120D	841	T82.390D	842	T82.538D	842	T83.012D	842	T83.23XD	842
T81.591A	568,767	T82.120S	779	T82.390S	779	T82.538S	779	T83.012S	779	T83.23XS	779
T81.591D	841	T82.121A	172	T82.391A	173	T82.539A	173	T83.018A	520	T83.24XA	520
T81.591S	778	T82.121D	841	T82.391D	842	T82.539D	842	T83.018D	842	T83.24XD	842
T81.592A	568,767	T82.121S	779	T82.391S	779	T82.539S	779	T83.018S	779	T83.24XS	779
T81.592D	841	T82.128A	173	T82.392A	173	T82.590A	173	T83.020A	520	T83.25XA	520
T81.592S	778	T82.128D	841	T82.392D	842	T82.590D	842	T83.020D	842	T83.25XD	842
T81.593A	568,767	T82.128S	779	T82.392S	779	T82.590S	779	T83.020S	779	T83.25XS	779
T81.593D	841	T82.129A	173	T82.398A	173	T82.591A	173	T83.021A	520	T83.29XA	520
T81.593S	778	T82.129D	842	T82.398D	842	T82.591D	842	T83.021D	842	T83.29XD	842
T81.594A	568,767	T82.129S	779	T82.398S	779	T82.591S	779	T83.021S	779	T83.29XS	779
T81.594D	841	T82.190A	172	T82.399A	173	T82.592A	173	T83.022A	520	T83.31XA	535,543
T81.594S	778	T82.190D	842	T82.399D	842	T82.592D	842	T83.022D	842	T83.31XD	842
T81.595A	568,767	T82.190S	779	T82.399S	779	T82.592S	779	T83.022S	779	T83.31XS	779
T81.595D	841	T82.191A	172	T82.41XA	173	T82.593A	173	T83.028A	520	T83.32XA	535,543
T81.595S	778	T82.191D	842	T82.41XD	842	T82.593D	842	T83.028D	842	T83.32XD	842
T81.596A	568,767	T82.191S	779	T82.41XS	779	T82.593S	779	T83.028S	779	T83.32XS	779
T81.596D	841	T82.198A	173	T82.42XA	173	T82.594A	173	T83.030A	520	T83.39XA	535,543
T81.596S	778	T82.198D	842	T82.42XD	842	T82.594D	842	T83.030D	842	T83.39XD	842
T81.597A	568,767	T82.198S	779	T82.42XS	779	T82.594S	779	T83.030S	779	T83.39XS	779
T81.597D	841	T82.199A	173	T82.43XA	173	T82.595A	173	T83.031A	520	T83.410A	520
T81.597S	778	T82.199D	842	T82.43XD	842	T82.595D	842	T83.031D	842	T83.410D	842
T81.598A	767	T82.199S	779	T82.43XS	779	T82.595S	779	T83.031S	779	T83.410S	779
T81.598A	568	T82.211A	173	T82.49XA	173	T82.598A	173	T83.032A	520	T83.411A	520
T81.598D	841	T82.211D	842	T82.49XD	842	T82.598D	842	T83.032D	842	T83.411D	842
T81.598S	778	T82.211S	779	T82.49XS	779	T82.598S	779	T83.032S	779	T83.411S	779
T81.599A	568,767	T82.212A	173	T82.510A	173	T82.599A	173	T83.038A	520	T83.418A	520
T81.599D	841	T82.212D	842	T82.510D	842	T82.599D	842	T83.038D	842	T83.418D	842
T81.599S	778	T82.212S	779	T82.510S	779	T82.599S	779	T83.038S	779	T83.418S	779
T81.60XA	568,767	T82.213A	173	T82.511A	173	T82.6XXA	173	T83.090A	520	T83.420A	520
T81.60XD	841	T82.213D	842	T82.511D	842	T82.6XXD	842	T83.090D	842	T83.420D	842
T81.60XS	779	T82.213S	779	T82.511S	779	T82.6XXS	779	T83.090S	779	T83.420S	779
T81.61XA	568,767	T82.218A	173	T82.512A	173	T82.7XXA	173	T83.091A	520	T83.421A	520
T81.61XD	841	T82.218D	842	T82.512D	842	T82.7XXD	842	T83.091D	842	T83.421D	842

Numeric Index to Diseases

Code	Page	Code	Page	Code	Page	Code	Page	Code	Page	Code	Page
T83.421S	779	T83.82XS	780	T84.060S	780	T84.191S	780	T84.498S	780	T84.89XS	780
T83.428A	520	T83.83XA	520	T84.061A	347	T84.192A	347	T84.50XA	347	T84.9XXA	347
T83.428D	842	T83.83XD	842	T84.061D	843	T84.192D	843	T84.50XD	843	T84.9XXD	843
T83.428S	779	T83.83XS	780	T84.061S	780	T84.192S	780	T84.50XS	780	T84.9XXS	780
T83.490A	520	T83.84XA	520	T84.062A	347	T84.193A	347	T84.51XA	347	T85.01XA	54
T83.490D	842	T83.84XD	842	T84.062D	843	T84.193D	843	T84.51XD	843	T85.01XD	843
T83.490S	779	T83.84XS	780	T84.062S	780	T84.193S	780	T84.51XS	780	T85.01XS	780
T83.491A	520	T83.85XA	520	T84.063A	347	T84.194A	347	T84.52XA	347	T85.02XA	54
T83.491D	842	T83.85XD	842	T84.063D	843	T84.194D	843	T84.52XD	843	T85.02XD	843
T83.491S	779	T83.85XS	780	T84.063S	780	T84.194S	780	T84.52XS	780	T85.02XS	780
T83.498A	520	T83.86XA	520	T84.068A	347	T84.195A	347	T84.53XA	227, 347	T85.03XA	54
T83.498D	842	T83.86XD	842	T84.068D	843	T84.195D	843	T84.53XD	843	T85.03XD	843
T83.498S	779	T83.86XS	780	T84.068S	780	T84.195S	780	T84.53XS	780	T85.03XS	780
T83.510A	520	T83.89XA	520	T84.069A	347	T84.196A	347	T84.54XA	227, 347	T85.09XA	54
T83.510D	842	T83.89XD	842	T84.069D	843	T84.196D	843	T84.54XD	843	T85.09XD	843
T83.510S	779	T83.89XS	780	T84.069S	780	T84.196S	780	T84.54XS	780	T85.09XS	780
T83.511A	520	T83.9XXA	520	T84.090A	347	T84.197A	347	T84.59XA	347	T85.110A	54
T83.511D	842	T83.9XXD	842	T84.090D	843	T84.197D	843	T84.59XD	843	T85.110D	843
T83.511S	779	T83.9XXS	780	T84.090S	780	T84.197S	780	T84.59XS	780	T85.110S	780
T83.512A	520	T84.010A	347	T84.091A	347	T84.199A	347	T84.60XA	347	T85.111A	54
T83.512D	842	T84.010D	842	T84.091D	843	T84.199D	843	T84.60XD	843	T85.111D	843
T83.512S	779	T84.010S	780	T84.091S	780	T84.199S	780	T84.60XS	780	T85.111S	780
T83.518A	520	T84.011A	347	T84.092A	347	T84.210A	347	T84.610A	347	T85.112A	54
T83.518D	842	T84.011D	842	T84.092D	843	T84.210D	843	T84.610D	843	T85.112D	843
T83.518S	779	T84.011S	780	T84.092S	780	T84.210S	780	T84.610S	780	T85.112S	780
T83.590A	520	T84.012A	347	T84.093A	347	T84.213A	347	T84.611A	347	T85.113A	54
T83.590D	842	T84.012D	842	T84.093D	843	T84.213D	843	T84.611D	843	T85.113D	843
T83.590S	779	T84.012S	780	T84.093S	780	T84.213S	780	T84.611S	780	T85.113S	780
T83.591A	520	T84.013A	347	T84.098A	347	T84.216A	347	T84.612A	347	T85.118A	54
T83.591D	842	T84.013D	842	T84.098D	843	T84.216D	843	T84.612D	843	T85.118D	843
T83.591S	779	T84.013S	780	T84.098S	780	T84.216S	780	T84.612S	780	T85.118S	780
T83.592A	520	T84.018A	347	T84.099A	347	T84.218A	347	T84.613A	347	T85.120A	54
T83.592D	842	T84.018D	843	T84.099D	843	T84.218D	843	T84.613D	843	T85.120D	843
T83.592S	779	T84.018S	780	T84.099S	780	T84.218S	780	T84.613S	780	T85.120S	780
T83.593A	520	T84.019A	347	T84.110A	347	T84.220A	347	T84.614A	347	T85.121A	54
T83.593D	842	T84.019D	843	T84.110D	843	T84.220D	843	T84.614D	843	T85.121D	843
T83.593S	779	T84.019S	780	T84.110S	780	T84.220S	780	T84.614S	780	T85.121S	780
T83.598A	520	T84.020A	347	T84.111A	347	T84.223A	347	T84.615A	347	T85.122A	54
T83.598D	842	T84.020D	843	T84.111D	843	T84.223D	843	T84.615D	843	T85.122D	843
T83.598S	779	T84.020S	780	T84.111S	780	T84.223S	780	T84.615S	780	T85.122S	780
T83.61XA	520	T84.021A	347	T84.112A	347	T84.226A	347	T84.619A	347	T85.123A	54
T83.61XD	842	T84.021D	843	T84.112D	843	T84.226D	843	T84.619D	843	T85.123D	843
T83.61XS	779	T84.021S	780	T84.112S	780	T84.226S	780	T84.619S	780	T85.123S	780
T83.62XA	520	T84.022A	347	T84.113A	347	T84.228A	347	T84.620A	227, 347	T85.128A	54
T83.62XD	842	T84.022D	843	T84.113D	843	T84.228D	843	T84.620D	843	T85.128D	843
T83.62XS	779	T84.022S	780	T84.113S	780	T84.228S	780	T84.620S	780	T85.128S	780
T83.69XA	520	T84.023A	347	T84.114A	347	T84.290A	347	T84.621A	227, 347	T85.190A	54
T83.69XD	842	T84.023D	843	T84.114D	843	T84.290D	843	T84.621D	843	T85.190D	843
T83.69XS	779	T84.023S	780	T84.114S	780	T84.290S	780	T84.621S	780	T85.190S	780
T83.711A	535, 543	T84.028A	347	T84.115A	347	T84.293A	347	T84.622A	227, 347	T85.191A	54
T83.711D	842	T84.028D	843	T84.115D	843	T84.293D	843	T84.622D	843	T85.191D	843
T83.711S	779	T84.028S	780	T84.115S	780	T84.293S	780	T84.622S	780	T85.191S	780
T83.712A	520	T84.029A	347	T84.116A	347	T84.296A	347	T84.623A	227, 347	T85.192A	54
T83.712D	842	T84.029D	843	T84.116D	843	T84.296D	843	T84.623D	843	T85.192D	843
T83.712S	780	T84.029S	780	T84.116S	780	T84.296S	780	T84.623S	780	T85.192S	780
T83.713A	520	T84.030A	347	T84.117A	347	T84.298A	347	T84.624A	227, 347	T85.193A	54
T83.713D	842	T84.030D	843	T84.117D	843	T84.298D	843	T84.624D	843	T85.193D	843
T83.713S	780	T84.030S	780	T84.117S	780	T84.298S	780	T84.624S	780	T85.193S	780
T83.714A	520	T84.031A	347	T84.119A	347	T84.310A	347	T84.625A	227, 347	T85.199A	54
T83.714D	842	T84.031D	843	T84.119D	843	T84.310D	843	T84.625D	843	T85.199D	843
T83.714S	780	T84.031S	780	T84.119S	780	T84.310S	780	T84.625S	780	T85.199S	780
T83.718A	520	T84.032A	347	T84.120A	347	T84.318A	347	T84.629A	227, 347	T85.21XA	66
T83.718D	842	T84.032D	843	T84.120D	843	T84.318D	843	T84.629D	843	T85.21XD	843
T83.718S	780	T84.032S	780	T84.120S	780	T84.318S	780	T84.629S	780	T85.21XS	780
T83.719A	520	T84.033A	347	T84.121A	347	T84.320A	347	T84.63XA	347	T85.22XA	66
T83.719D	842	T84.033D	843	T84.121D	843	T84.320D	843	T84.63XD	843	T85.22XD	843
T83.719S	780	T84.033S	780	T84.121S	780	T84.320S	780	T84.63XS	780	T85.22XS	780
T83.721A	535, 543	T84.038A	347	T84.122A	347	T84.328A	347	T84.69XA	347	T85.29XA	66
T83.721D	842	T84.038D	843	T84.122D	843	T84.328D	843	T84.69XD	843	T85.29XD	843
T83.721S	780	T84.038S	780	T84.122S	780	T84.328S	780	T84.69XS	780	T85.29XS	780
T83.722A	520	T84.039A	347	T84.123A	347	T84.390A	347	T84.7XXA	227, 347	T85.310A	767
T83.722D	842	T84.039D	843	T84.123D	843	T84.390D	843	T84.7XXD	843	T85.310D	843
T83.722S	780	T84.039S	780	T84.123S	780	T84.390S	780	T84.7XXS	780	T85.310S	780
T83.723A	520	T84.050A	347	T84.124A	347	T84.398A	347	T84.81XA	347	T85.311A	767
T83.723D	842	T84.050D	843	T84.124D	843	T84.398D	843	T84.81XD	843	T85.311D	843
T83.723S	780	T84.050S	780	T84.124S	780	T84.398S	780	T84.81XS	780	T85.311S	780
T83.724A	520	T84.051A	347	T84.125A	347	T84.410A	347	T84.82XA	347	T85.318A	66
T83.724D	842	T84.051D	843	T84.125D	843	T84.410D	843	T84.82XD	843	T85.318D	843
T83.724S	780	T84.051S	780	T84.125S	780	T84.410S	780	T84.82XS	780	T85.318S	780
T83.728A	520	T84.052A	347	T84.126A	347	T84.418A	347	T84.83XA	347	T85.320A	767
T83.728D	842	T84.052D	843	T84.126D	843	T84.418D	843	T84.83XD	843	T85.320D	843
T83.728S	780	T84.052S	780	T84.126S	780	T84.418S	780	T84.83XS	780	T85.320S	780
T83.729A	520	T84.053A	347	T84.127A	347	T84.420A	347	T84.84XA	347	T85.321A	767
T83.729D	842	T84.053D	843	T84.127D	843	T84.420D	843	T84.84XD	843	T85.321D	843
T83.729S	780	T84.053S	780	T84.127S	780	T84.420S	780	T84.84XS	780	T85.321S	780
T83.79XA	520	T84.058A	347	T84.129A	347	T84.428A	347	T84.85XA	347	T85.328A	66
T83.79XD	842	T84.058D	843	T84.129D	843	T84.428D	843	T84.85XD	843	T85.328D	843
T83.79XS	780	T84.058S	780	T84.129S	780	T84.428S	780	T84.85XS	780	T85.328S	780
T83.81XA	520	T84.059A	347	T84.190A	347	T84.490A	347	T84.86XA	347	T85.390A	767
T83.81XD	842	T84.059D	843	T84.190D	843	T84.490D	843	T84.86XD	843	T85.390D	843
T83.81XS	780	T84.059S	780	T84.190S	780	T84.490S	780	T84.86XS	780	T85.390S	780
T83.82XA	520	T84.060A	347	T84.191A	347	T84.498A	347	T84.89XA	347	T85.391A	767
T83.82XD	842	T84.060D	843	T84.191D	843	T84.498D	843	T84.89XD	843	T85.391D	843

Numeric Index to Diseases

Code	Page	Code	Page	Code	Page	Code	Page	Code	Page	Code	Page
T85.391S	780	T85.631S	781	T85.860S	781	Z00*	845	Z20.821	846	Z42*	478
T85.398A	66	T85.633A	767	T85.868A	767	Z01.10	570	Z20.828	846	Z43.0	107
T85.398D	843	T85.633D	844	T85.868D	844	Z01.110	570	Z20.89	846	Z43.1	197
T85.398S	780	T85.635A	54	T85.868S	781	Z01.118	570	Z20.89	570	Z43.2	197
T85.41XA	453, 454	T85.635D	844	T85.890A	54	Z01.12	570	Z20.9	846	Z43.3	197
T85.41XD	843	T85.635S	781	T85.890D	844	Z01*	845	Z21	632	Z43.4	197
T85.41XS	780	T85.638A	767	T85.890S	781	Z02.6	570	Z22.0	846	Z43.5	520
T85.42XA	453, 454	T85.638D	844	T85.898A	767	Z02.82	570	Z22.1	846	Z43.6	520
T85.42XD	843	T85.638S	781	T85.898D	844	Z02.89	570	Z22.2	846	Z43.7	535, 543
T85.42XS	780	T85.690A	767	T85.898S	781	Z02*	845	Z22.3*	846	Z43.8	846
T85.43XA	454	T85.690D	844	T85.9XXA	767	Z03*	845	Z22.4	846	Z43.9	846
T85.43XD	843	T85.690S	781	T85.9XXD	844	Z04.1	781	Z22.6	846	Z44.001	347
T85.43XS	780	T85.691A	767	T85.9XXS	781	Z04.2	781	Z22.7	846	Z44.002	347
T85.44XA	454	T85.691D	520	T86.0*	578	Z04.3	781	Z22.8	846	Z44.009	347
T85.44XD	843	T85.691S	781	T86.1*	520	Z04.4*	845	Z22.9	846	Z44.011	347
T85.44XS	780	T85.692A	767	T86.2*	173	Z04.6	845	Z23	570, 846	Z44.012	347
T85.49XA	454	T85.692D	844	T86.3*	173	Z04.7*	845	Z28.01	570, 846	Z44.019	347
T85.49XD	843	T85.692S	781	T86.4*	209	Z04.81	845	Z28.02	570, 846	Z44.021	347
T85.49XS	781	T85.693A	767	T86.5	767	Z04.82	845	Z28.03	570, 846	Z44.022	347
T85.510A	767	T85.693D	844	T86.810	107	Z04.89	845	Z28.04	570, 846	Z44.029	347
T85.510D	843	T85.693S	781	T86.811	107	Z04.9	845	Z28.09	846	Z44.101	347
T85.510S	781	T85.694A	767	T86.812	107	Z05.0	845	Z28.09	570	Z44.102	347
T85.511A	767	T85.694D	844	T86.818	107	Z05.1	845	Z28.1	570, 846	Z44.109	347
T85.511D	843	T85.694S	781	T86.819	107	Z05.2	845	Z28.20	570, 846	Z44.111	347
T85.511S	781	T85.695A	54	T86.82*	767	Z05.3	845	Z28.21	570, 846	Z44.112	347
T85.518A	767	T85.695D	844	T86.83*	767	Z05.41	846	Z28.29	846	Z44.119	347
T85.518D	843	T85.695S	781	T86.840	66	Z05.42	846	Z28.29	570	Z44.121	347
T85.518S	781	T85.698A	767	T86.841	66	Z05.43	846	Z28.3	846	Z44.122	347
T85.520A	767	T85.698D	844	T86.842	767	Z05.5	846	Z28.81	570, 846	Z44.129	347
T85.520D	843	T85.698S	781	T86.848	767	Z05.6	846	Z28.82	570, 846	Z44.2*	846
T85.520S	781	T85.71XA	767	T86.849	767	Z05.71	846	Z28.83	570, 846	Z44.3*	846
T85.521A	767	T85.71XD	844	T86.85*	767	Z05.72	846	Z28.89	570, 846	Z44.8	795
T85.521D	843	T85.71XS	781	T86.890	209	Z05.73	846	Z28.9	570, 846	Z44.9	795
T85.521S	781	T85.72XA	767	T86.891	209	Z05.8	846	Z29.11	846	Z45.0*	173
T85.528A	767	T85.72XD	844	T86.892	209	Z05.9	846	Z29.12	846	Z45.1	795
T85.528D	843	T85.72XS	781	T86.898	209	Z05*	570	Z29.13	846	Z45.1	844
T85.528S	781	T85.730A	54	T86.899	209	Z08	605, 630, 631	Z29.14	846	Z45.2	795
T85.590A	767	T85.730D	844	T86.9*	767	Z09	846	Z29.3	846	Z45.2	844
T85.590D	843	T85.730S	781	T87.0X1	347	Z11*	846	Z29.8	846	Z45.3*	54
T85.590S	781	T85.731A	54	T87.0X2	347	Z12*	846	Z29.9	846	Z45.4*	54
T85.591A	767	T85.731D	844	T87.0X9	347	Z13.0	846	Z30.0*	846	Z45.8*	846
T85.591D	843	T85.731S	781	T87.1X1	347	Z13.1	846	Z30.2	530, 535, 543	Z45.9	846
T85.591S	781	T85.732A	54	T87.1X2	347	Z13.21	846	Z30.4*	846	Z46.0	846
T85.598A	767	T85.732D	844	T87.1X9	347	Z13.220	846	Z30.8	846	Z46.1	846
T85.598D	843	T85.732S	781	T87.2	347	Z13.228	570, 846	Z30.9	846	Z46.2	54
T85.598S	781	T85.733A	54	T87.3*	409	Z13.29	846	Z31.0	530, 535, 543	Z46.3	846
T85.610A	54	T85.733D	844	T87.4*	409	Z13.30	846	Z31.4*	846	Z46.4	846
T85.610D	843	T85.733S	781	T87.5*	409	Z13.31	846	Z31.5	846	Z46.51	197
T85.610S	781	T85.734A	54	T87.8*	409	Z13.32	846	Z31.6*	846	Z46.59	197
T85.611A	767	T85.734D	844	T87.9	409	Z13.39	846	Z31.7	846	Z46.6	520
T85.611D	843	T85.734S	781	T88.0XXA	568, 632, 634	Z13.40	846	Z31.8*	846	Z46.81	795
T85.611S	781	T85.735A	54	T88.0XXD	844	Z13.41	846	Z31.9	846	Z46.82	795, 844
T85.612A	767	T85.735D	844	T88.0XXS	781	Z13.42	846	Z32*	846	Z46.89	846
T85.612D	843	T85.735S	781	T88.1XXA	632	Z13.49	846	Z33.1	846	Z46.9	846
T85.612S	781	T85.738A	54	T88.1XXD	844	Z13.5	846	Z33.2	545, 557	Z47.1	347
T85.613A	767	T85.738D	844	T88.1XXS	781	Z13.6	846	Z33.3	846	Z47.2	347
T85.613D	843	T85.738S	781	T88.2XXA	568, 781	Z13.71	846	Z34*	846	Z47.3*	347
T85.613S	781	T85.79XA	767	T88.2XXD	844	Z13.79	846	Z36*	846	Z47.81	347
T85.614A	767	T85.79XD	844	T88.2XXS	781	Z13.810	846	Z37*	544, 546, 846	Z47.82	347
T85.614D	843	T85.79XS	781	T88.3XXA	781	Z13.811	846	Z38.00	569	Z47.89	347
T85.614S	781	T85.810A	54	T88.3XXD	844	Z13.818	846	Z38.01	569	Z48.00	846
T85.615A	54	T85.810D	844	T88.3XXS	781	Z13.820	846	Z38.1	569	Z48.01	846
T85.615D	843	T85.810S	781	T88.4XXA	767	Z13.828	846	Z38.2	569	Z48.02	846
T85.615S	781	T85.818A	767	T88.4XXD	844	Z13.83	846	Z38.30	569	Z48.03	795, 844
T85.618A	767	T85.818D	844	T88.4XXS	781	Z13.84	846	Z38.31	569	Z48.1	795, 844
T85.618D	843	T85.818S	781	T88.51XA	781	Z13.850	846	Z38.4	569	Z48.2*	844
T85.618S	781	T85.820A	54	T88.51XD	844	Z13.858	846	Z38.5	569	Z48.21	795
T85.620A	54	T85.820D	844	T88.51XS	781	Z13.88	846	Z38.61	569	Z48.22	795
T85.620D	843	T85.820S	781	T88.52XA	766	Z13.89	846	Z38.62	569	Z48.23	795
T85.620S	781	T85.828A	767	T88.52XD	844	Z13.9	846	Z38.63	569	Z48.24	795
T85.621A	767	T85.828D	844	T88.52XS	781	Z14*	846	Z38.64	569	Z48.280	795
T85.621D	843	T85.828S	781	T88.53XA	568, 766	Z15*	846	Z38.65	569	Z48.288	795
T85.621S	781	T85.830A	54	T88.53XD	844	Z16*	634	Z38.66	569	Z48.290	795
T85.622A	767	T85.830D	844	T88.53XS	781	Z17*	846	Z38.68	569	Z48.298	795
T85.622D	843	T85.830S	781	T88.59XA	568, 766	Z18*	846	Z38.69	569	Z48.3	795, 844
T85.622S	781	T85.838A	767	T88.59XD	844	Z19.1	846	Z38.7	569	Z48.8*	844
T85.623A	767	T85.838D	844	T88.59XS	781	Z19.2	846	Z38.8	569	Z48.810	795
T85.623D	843	T85.838S	781	T88.6XXA	758	Z20.01	846	Z39.0	545	Z48.811	795
T85.623S	781	T85.840A	54	T88.6XXD	844	Z20.09	846	Z39.1	846	Z48.812	795
T85.624A	767	T85.840D	844	T88.6XXS	781	Z20.09	570	Z39.2	846	Z48.813	795
T85.624D	843	T85.840S	781	T88.7XXA	767	Z20.1	846	Z3A*	846	Z48.814	795
T85.624S	781	T85.848A	767	T88.7XXD	844	Z20.2	846	Z40.00	846	Z48.815	795
T85.625A	54	T85.848D	844	T88.7XXS	781	Z20.3	846	Z40.01	454	Z48.816	795
T85.625D	843	T85.848S	781	T88.8XXA	767	Z20.4	846	Z40.02	535, 543	Z48.817	795
T85.625S	781	T85.850A	54	T88.8XXD	844	Z20.5	846	Z40.03	535, 543	Z48.89	795
T85.628A	767	T85.850D	844	T88.8XXS	781	Z20.6	846	Z40.09	846	Z49.01	520
T85.628D	843	T85.850S	781	T88.9XXA	767	Z20.7	846	Z40.8	846	Z49.02	520
T85.628S	781	T85.858A	767	T88.9XXD	844	Z20.7	846	Z40.9	846	Z49.31	520
T85.630A	54	T85.858D	844	T88.9XXS	781	Z20.810	570, 846	Z41.1	478	Z49.32	520
T85.630D	844	T85.858S	781	Z00.110	570	Z20.811	846	Z41.2	529, 570	Z51.0	605, 631
T85.630S	781	T85.860A	54	Z00.111	570	Z20.818	846	Z41.3	570, 846	Z51.1*	605, 630, 631
T85.631A	767	T85.860D	844	Z00.121	570	Z20.818	570	Z41.8	846	Z51.5	846
T85.631D	844			Z00.129	570	Z20.820	846	Z41.9	846	Z51.6	846

Code	Page	Code	Page	Code	Page
Z51.8*	844	Z81.8	570	Z91.15	847
Z51.81	795	Z81*	847	Z91.19	847
Z52.0*	846	Z82.0	570	Z91.410	847
Z52.1*	478	Z82.49	570	Z91.411	847
Z52.2*	409	Z82*	570	Z91.412	847
Z52.3	846	Z83.0	847	Z91.419	847
Z52.4	520	Z83.1	570, 847	Z91.42	847
Z52.5	846	Z83.2	847	Z91.49	847
Z52.6	209	Z83.3	570, 847	Z91.5	847
Z52.8*	846	Z83.41	847	Z91.81	847
Z52.9	846	Z83.42	570, 847	Z91.82	847
Z53.01	570	Z83.430	570, 847	Z91.83	847
Z53.09	570	Z83.438	570, 847	Z91.841	847
Z53.1	570	Z83.49	570, 847	Z91.842	847
Z53.20	570	Z83.511	847	Z91.843	847
Z53.21	570	Z83.518	847	Z91.849	847
Z53.29	570	Z83.52	847	Z91.89	847
Z53.8	570	Z83.6	847	Z92.0	847
Z53.9	570	Z83.71	847	Z92.2*	844
Z53*	846	Z83.79	847	Z92.3	847
Z55*	846	Z84*	847	Z92.8*	847
Z56*	846	Z85.0*	631	Z92.82	45
Z57*	846	Z85.1*	631	Z93*	847
Z59*	846	Z85.2*	631	Z94.0	1, 520
Z60*	846	Z85.21	5	Z94.1	173
Z62.0	846	Z85.3	631	Z94.2	107
Z62.1	846	Z85.4*	631	Z94.3	173
Z62.21	846	Z85.5*	631	Z94.4	209
Z62.22	846	Z85.6	631	Z94.5	478
Z62.29	846	Z85.7*	631	Z94.6	409
Z62.3	846	Z85.8*	631	Z94.7	66
Z62.6	846	Z85.810	5	Z94.81	579
Z62.810	846	Z85.818	5	Z94.82	847
Z62.811	846	Z85.819	5	Z94.83	209
Z62.812	846	Z85.9	631	Z94.84	579
Z62.813	846	Z85*	605	Z94.89	847
Z62.819	846	Z86*	847	Z94.9	847
Z62.820	846	Z87.0*	847	Z95.0	847
Z62.821	846	Z87.1*	847	Z95.1	847
Z62.822	846	Z87.2	847	Z95.2	173
Z62.890	846	Z87.3*	847	Z95.3	173
Z62.891	846	Z87.410	605, 631	Z95.4	173
Z62.898	846	Z87.411	847	Z95.5	847
Z62.9	846	Z87.412	847	Z95.810	847
Z63*	846	Z87.42	847	Z95.811	173
Z64.0	545, 557	Z87.430	847	Z95.812	173
Z64.1	535, 543	Z87.438	847	Z95.818	847
Z64.4	846	Z87.440	847	Z95.820	173
Z65*	847	Z87.441	847	Z95.828	173
Z66	847	Z87.442	847	Z95.9	847
Z67*	847	Z87.448	847	Z96.0	520
Z68.1	847	Z87.5*	847	Z96.1	66
Z68.2*	847	Z87.7*	847	Z96.2*	847
Z68.3*	847	Z87.81	847	Z96.3	847
Z68.4*	502	Z87.820	847	Z96.4*	847
Z68.5*	847	Z87.821	847	Z96.49	1
Z69*	847	Z87.828	847	Z96.5	847
Z70*	847	Z87.890	636	Z96.6*	409
Z71*	847	Z87.891	847	Z96.7	409
Z72.0	847	Z87.892	847	Z96.8*	847
Z72.3	847	Z87.898	847	Z96.89	1
Z72.4	847	Z88*	847	Z96.9	1, 847
Z72.5*	847	Z89*	847	Z97.0	66
Z72.6	847	Z90.01	66	Z97.1*	409
Z72.810	635	Z90.02	847	Z97.2	847
Z72.811	635	Z90.09	847	Z97.3	847
Z72.820	847	Z90.1*	847	Z97.4	847
Z72.821	847	Z90.2	107	Z97.5	847
Z72.89	847	Z90.3	847	Z97.8	847
Z72.9	847	Z90.4*	847	Z98*	847
Z73*	847	Z90.5	847	Z99*	847
Z74*	847	Z90.6	520		
Z75*	847	Z90.7*	535, 543		
Z76.2	570	Z90.79	530		
Z76*	847	Z90.8*	847		
Z77*	847	Z91.010	847		
Z78*	847	Z91.011	847		
Z79.0*	844	Z91.012	847		
Z79.1	844	Z91.013	847		
Z79.2	844	Z91.018	847		
Z79.3	844	Z91.02	847		
Z79.4	844	Z91.030	847		
Z79.5*	844	Z91.038	847		
Z79.810	847	Z91.040	847		
Z79.811	847	Z91.041	847		
Z79.818	847	Z91.048	847		
Z79.82	844	Z91.09	847		
Z79.83	844	Z91.11	847		
Z79.84	844	Z91.120	847		
Z79.890	847	Z91.128	847		
Z79.891	844	Z91.130	847		
Z79.899	844	Z91.138	847		
Z80*	847	Z91.14	847		

Numeric Index to Procedures

Note: The page numbers in this index refer to page numbers in *DRG Expert—Volume I.*

Code	Page
0016070	22, 580, 605, 853
0016071	22, 580, 605, 853
0016072	22, 580, 605, 853
0016073	22, 580, 605, 853
0016074	22, 580, 605, 853
0016075	22, 580, 605, 853
0016076	22, 580, 605, 853
0016077	22, 580, 605, 853
0016078	22, 580, 605, 853
0016370	22, 580, 605, 853
0016371	22, 580, 605, 853
0016372	22, 580, 605, 853
0016373	22, 580, 605, 853
0016374	22, 580, 605, 853
0016375	22, 580, 605, 853
0016376	22, 580, 605, 853
0016377	22, 580, 605, 853
0016378	22, 580, 605, 853
0016470	22, 580, 605, 853
0016471	22, 580, 605, 853
0016472	22, 580, 605, 853
0016473	22, 580, 605, 853
0016474	22, 580, 605, 853
0016475	22, 580, 605, 854
0016476	22, 580, 605, 854
0016477	22, 580, 605, 854
0016478	22, 580, 605, 854
0210083	115
0210088	115
0210089	115
0210093	115
0210098	115
0210099	115
0210344	111
0210444	111
0210483	116
0210488	116
0210489	116
0210493	116
0210498	116
0210499	116
0211083	116
0211088	116
0211089	116
0211093	116
0211098	116
0211099	116
0211344	111
0211444	111
0211483	116
0211488	116
0211489	116
0211493	116
0211498	116
0211499	116
0212083	116
0212088	116
0212089	116
0212093	116
0212098	116
0212099	116
0212344	111
0212444	111
0212483	116
0212488	116
0212489	116
0212493	116
0212498	116
0212499	116
0213083	117
0213088	117
0213089	117
0213093	117
0213098	117
0213099	117
0213344	111
0213444	111
0213483	117
0213488	117
0213489	117
0213493	117
0213498	117
0213499	117
0270046	112
0270056	112
0270066	112
0270076	112
0270346	117, 119, 120, 121, 122
0270356	117, 119, 120, 121, 122
0270366	117, 119, 120, 121, 122
0270376	117, 119, 120, 121, 122
0270446	117, 119, 120, 121, 122
0270456	117, 119, 120, 121, 122
0270466	117, 119, 120, 121, 122
0270476	117, 119, 120, 121, 122
0271046	112
0271056	112
0271066	112
0271076	112
0271346	117, 120, 121, 122
0271356	117, 120, 121, 122
0271366	117, 120, 121, 122
0271376	117, 120, 121, 122
0271446	117, 120, 121, 122
0271456	117, 120, 121, 122
0271466	117, 120, 121, 122
0271476	117, 120, 121, 122
0272046	113
0272056	113
0272066	113
0272076	113
0272346	118, 120, 121, 122
0272356	118, 120, 121, 122
0272366	118, 120, 121, 122
0272376	118, 120, 121, 122
0272446	118, 120, 121, 122
0272456	118, 120, 121, 122
0272466	118, 120, 121, 122
0272476	118, 120, 121, 122
0273046	113
0273056	113
0273066	113
0273076	113
0273346	118, 120, 121, 122
0273356	118, 120, 121, 122
0273366	118, 120, 121, 122
0273376	118, 120, 121, 122
0273446	118, 120, 121, 122
0273456	118, 120, 121, 122
0273466	118, 120, 121, 122
0273476	118, 120, 121, 122
0313090	125
0313091	125
0313092	125
0313093	125
0313094	125
0313095	125
0313096	125
0313097	125
0313098	125
0313099	125
0314090	126
0314091	126
0314092	126
0314093	126
0314094	126
0314095	126
0314096	126
0314097	126
0314098	126
0314099	126
0315090	23, 96, 203, 412, 484, 657
0316091	23, 96, 203, 412, 484, 657
0317090	126
0317093	126
0318091	126
0318094	126
0319093	126
0410090	156
0410091	156
0410092	156
0410093	149, 504, 664, 873
0410094	149, 504, 664, 873
0410095	149, 504, 664, 873
0410096	156, 413, 664
0410097	156, 413, 664
0410098	156, 413, 664
0410099	156, 413, 664
0410490	156
0410491	156
0410492	156
0410493	149, 504, 664, 873
0410494	149, 504, 664, 873
0410495	149, 504, 664, 873
0410496	156, 413, 664
0410497	156, 413, 664
0410498	156, 413, 664
0410499	156, 413, 664
0413093	149, 504, 665, 873
0413094	149, 504, 665, 873
0413095	149, 504, 665, 873
0413493	149, 504, 665, 873
0413494	149, 504, 665, 873
0413495	149, 504, 665, 873
0414093	157
0414094	157
0414095	157
0414493	157
0414494	157
0414495	157
0470341	26, 97, 185, 204, 274, 415, 486, 511, 666, 873
0471341	26, 97, 185, 204, 274, 415, 486, 511, 666, 873
0472341	26, 97, 185, 204, 274, 415, 486, 511, 667, 873
0473341	26, 97, 185, 205, 274, 416, 486, 511, 667, 873
0474341	26, 97, 185, 205, 274, 416, 486, 511, 667, 874
0475341	26, 97, 185, 205, 274, 416, 487, 512, 667, 874
0476341	26, 97, 185, 205, 274, 416, 487, 512, 667, 874
0477341	27, 97, 185, 205, 274, 416, 487, 512, 667, 874
0478341	27, 97, 185, 205, 274, 416, 487, 512, 667, 874
0479341	27, 97, 185, 205, 275, 416, 487, 512, 667, 874
0610075	162
0610076	162
0610095	162
0610096	162
0610475	163
0610476	163
0610495	163
0610496	163
0016*	649
001607A	7, 848
001607B	7, 580, 605, 848
00160J0	22, 580, 605, 853
00160J1	22, 580, 605, 853
00160J2	22, 580, 605, 853
00160J3	22, 580, 605, 853
00160J4	22, 580, 605, 853
00160J5	22, 580, 605, 853
00160J6	22, 580, 605, 853
00160J7	22, 580, 605, 853
00160J8	22, 580, 605, 853
00160JA	7, 848
00160JB	7, 580, 605, 848
00160K0	22, 580, 605, 853
00160K1	22, 580, 605, 853
00160K2	22, 580, 605, 853
00160K3	22, 580, 605, 853
00160K4	22, 580, 605, 853
00160K5	22, 580, 605, 853
00160K6	22, 580, 605, 853
00160K7	22, 580, 605, 853
00160K8	22, 580, 605, 853
00160KA	7, 848
00160KB	7, 580, 605, 848
00160ZB	7, 848
001637A	7, 848
001637B	7, 580, 605, 848
00163J0	22, 580, 605, 853
00163J1	22, 580, 605, 853
00163J2	22, 580, 605, 853
00163J3	22, 580, 605, 853
00163J4	22, 580, 605, 853
00163J5	22, 580, 605, 853
00163J6	22, 580, 605, 853
00163J7	22, 580, 605, 853
00163J8	22, 580, 605, 853
00163JA	7, 848
00163JB	7, 580, 605, 848
00163K0	22, 580, 605, 853
00163K1	22, 580, 605, 853
00163K2	22, 580, 605, 853
00163K3	22, 580, 605, 853
00163K4	22, 580, 605, 853
00163K5	22, 580, 605, 853
00163K6	22, 580, 605, 853
00163K7	22, 580, 605, 853
00163K8	22, 580, 605, 853
00163KA	7, 848
00163KB	7, 580, 605, 848
00163ZB	7, 848
001647A	7, 848
001647B	7, 580, 605, 848
00164J0	22, 580, 605, 854
00164J1	22, 580, 605, 854
00164J2	22, 580, 605, 854
00164J3	22, 580, 605, 854
00164J4	22, 580, 605, 854
00164J5	22, 580, 605, 854
00164J6	22, 580, 605, 854
00164J7	22, 580, 605, 854
00164J8	22, 580, 605, 854
00164JA	7, 848
00164JB	7, 580, 605, 848
00164K0	22, 580, 605, 854
00164K1	22, 580, 605, 854
00164K2	22, 580, 605, 854
00164K3	22, 580, 605, 854
00164K4	22, 580, 605, 854
00164K5	22, 580, 606, 854
00164K6	22, 580, 606, 854
00164K7	22, 580, 606, 854
00164K8	22, 580, 606, 854
00164KA	7, 848
00164KB	7, 580, 606, 848
00164ZB	7, 848
001U072	16, 580, 606
001U074	16, 580, 606
001U076	16, 580, 606
001U077	16, 580, 606
001U079	16, 580, 606
001U0J2	16, 580, 606
001U0J4	16, 580, 606
001U0J6	16, 580, 606
001U0J7	16, 580, 606
001U0J9	16, 580, 606
001U0K2	16, 580, 606
001U0K4	16, 580, 606
001U0K6	16, 580, 606
001U0K7	16, 580, 606
001U0K9	16, 580, 606
001U372	16, 580, 606
001U374	16, 580, 606
001U376	16, 580, 606
001U377	16, 580, 606
001U379	16, 580, 606
001U3J2	16, 580, 606
001U3J4	16, 580, 606
001U3J6	16, 580, 606
001U3J7	16, 580, 606
001U3J9	16, 580, 606
001U3K2	16, 580, 606
001U3K4	16, 580, 606
001U3K6	16, 580, 606
001U3K7	16, 580, 606
001U3K9	16, 580, 606
001U472	16, 580, 606
001U474	16, 580, 606
001U476	16, 580, 606
001U477	16, 581, 606
001U479	16, 581, 606
001U4J2	16, 581, 606
001U4J4	16, 581, 606
001U4J6	16, 581, 606
001U4J7	16, 581, 606
001U4J9	16, 581, 606
001U4K2	16, 581, 606
001U4K4	16, 581, 606
001U4K6	16, 581, 606
001U4K7	16, 581, 606
001U4K9	16, 581, 606
0050*	7, 649, 848
00500ZZ	581, 606
00503ZZ	581, 606
00504ZZ	581, 606
0051*	7, 848
00510ZZ	581, 606
00513ZZ	581, 606
00514ZZ	581, 606
0052*	7, 848
00520ZZ	581, 606
00523ZZ	581, 606
00524ZZ	581, 606
0056*	7, 848
0057*	7, 649, 848
00570ZZ	581, 606
00573ZZ	581, 606
00574ZZ	581, 606
0058*	7, 848
00580ZZ	581, 606
00583ZZ	581, 606
00584ZZ	581, 606
0059*	7, 649, 848
00590ZZ	581, 606
00593ZZ	581, 606
00594ZZ	581, 606
005A*	7, 649, 848
005A0ZZ	581, 606
005A3ZZ	581, 606
005A4ZZ	581, 606
005B*	7, 649, 848
005B0ZZ	581, 606
005B3ZZ	581, 606
005B4ZZ	581, 606
005C*	7, 649, 848
005C0ZZ	581, 606
005C3ZZ	581, 606
005C4ZZ	581, 606
005D*	7, 649, 848
005D0ZZ	581, 606
005D3ZZ	581, 606
005D4ZZ	581, 606
005T*	288
005T0ZZ	16, 581, 606
005T3ZZ	16, 581, 606
005T4ZZ	16, 581, 606
005W*	288
005W0ZZ	16, 581, 606
005W3ZZ	16, 581, 606
005W4ZZ	16, 581, 606
005X*	288
005X0ZZ	16, 581, 606
005X3ZZ	16, 581, 606
005X4ZZ	16, 581, 606
005Y*	288
005Y0ZZ	16, 581, 606
005Y3ZZ	16, 581, 606
005Y4ZZ	16, 581, 606
00760ZZ	7, 649, 848
00763ZZ	7, 649, 848
00764ZZ	7, 649, 848
0080*	7, 649, 848
00800ZZ	581, 606
00803ZZ	581, 606
00804ZZ	581, 606
0087*	7, 649, 848
00870ZZ	581, 606
00873ZZ	581, 606
00874ZZ	581, 606
0088*	7, 848
00880ZZ	581, 606
00883ZZ	581, 606
00884ZZ	581, 606
008F*	28, 69, 271, 649
008F0ZZ	854
008F3ZZ	854
008F4ZZ	854
008G*	28, 69, 271, 649
008G0ZZ	854
008G3ZZ	854
008G4ZZ	854
008H*	28, 69, 271, 649
008H0ZZ	854
008H3ZZ	854
008H4ZZ	854
008J*	28, 69, 271, 649
008J0ZZ	854
008J3ZZ	854
008J4ZZ	854
008K*	28, 69, 649
008K0ZZ	854
008K3ZZ	854
008K4ZZ	854
008L*	28, 69, 271, 649
008L0ZZ	854
008L3ZZ	854
008L4ZZ	854
008M*	28, 69, 271, 649
008M0ZZ	854
008M3ZZ	854
008M4ZZ	854
008N*	28, 69, 271, 649
008N0ZZ	854
008N3ZZ	854
008N4ZZ	854
008P*	7, 69
008Q*	28, 69, 95, 174
008R*	28, 69, 271, 649
008R0ZZ	854
008R3ZZ	854
008R4ZZ	854
008S*	28, 69, 271, 649
008S0ZZ	854
008S3ZZ	854
008S4ZZ	854
008W*	203, 649
008W0ZZ	16, 581, 606, 854
008W3ZZ	16, 581, 606, 854
008W4ZZ	16, 581, 606, 854
008X*	203, 649
008X0ZZ	16, 581, 606, 854
008X3ZZ	16, 581, 606, 854
008X4ZZ	16, 581, 606, 854
008Y*	203, 649
008Y0ZZ	16, 581, 606, 854
008Y3ZZ	16, 581, 606, 854
008Y4ZZ	16, 581, 606, 854
009000Z	7, 649, 848
00900ZX	7, 581, 606
00900ZZ	7, 649, 848
009030Z	7, 649, 848
00903ZZ	7, 649, 848
009040Z	7, 649, 848
00904ZZ	7, 649, 848
009100Z	7, 581, 606, 649, 848
00910ZX	7, 581, 606
00910ZZ	7, 581, 606, 649, 848
009130Z	7
00913ZZ	7
009140Z	7
00914ZZ	7
009200Z	7, 581, 606, 649, 848
00920ZX	7, 581, 606
00920ZZ	7, 581, 606, 649, 848
009230Z	7
00923ZZ	7
009240Z	7
00924ZZ	8
009300Z	8, 649, 848
00930ZX	8, 581, 606
00930ZZ	8, 649, 848
009330Z	8, 649, 848
00933ZZ	8, 649, 848
009340Z	8, 649, 848
00934ZZ	8, 649, 848
009400Z	8, 581, 606, 649, 848
00940ZX	8, 581, 606
00940ZZ	8, 581, 606, 649, 848
009430Z	8
00943ZZ	8
009440Z	8
00944ZZ	8
009500Z	8, 581, 606, 649, 848
00950ZX	8, 581, 606
00950ZZ	8, 581, 606, 649, 848
009530Z	8
00953ZZ	8
009540Z	8
00954ZZ	8
009600Z	8, 581, 606, 649, 848
00960ZX	8, 581, 606
00960ZZ	8, 649, 848

Numeric Index to Procedures

Code	Page	Code	Page	Code	Page	Code	Page	Code	Page	Code	Page
009630Z	8, 581, 606, 649, 848	009J0ZX	29, 69, 271, 649, 854	009W4ZX	16, 288, 581, 606	00BB4ZZ	8, 582, 607, 650, 848	00BQ0ZZ	29, 70, 271, 650, 1043	00CA4ZZ	9, 582, 607
00963ZZ	8	009J0ZZ	29	009W4ZZ	16, 288, 581, 606, 650, 848			00BQ3ZZ	29, 70, 271, 650, 1043	00CB*	650, 848
009640Z	8, 581, 606, 649, 848	009J30Z	29	009X00Z	16, 288, 581, 606, 650, 854	00BC0ZX	8, 582, 607			00CB0ZZ	9
		009J3ZZ	29			00BC0ZZ	8, 582, 607, 650, 848	00BQ4ZZ	29, 70, 271, 650, 1043	00CB3ZZ	9
00964ZZ	8	009J40Z	29	009X0ZX	16, 288, 581, 606	00BC3ZX	8, 582, 607			00CB4ZZ	9
009700Z	8, 649, 848	009J4ZZ	29	009X0ZZ	16, 288, 581, 606, 650, 854	00BC3ZZ	8, 582, 607, 650, 848	00BR0ZX	29, 70, 271, 650, 854	00CC*	650, 848
00970ZX	8, 581, 606	009K00Z	29							00CC0ZZ	9
009730Z	8, 649, 848	009K0ZX	29, 69, 271, 649, 854	009X40Z	16, 288, 581, 606, 650, 854	00BC4ZX	8, 582, 607	00BR0ZZ	29, 70, 271, 650, 1043	00CC3ZZ	9
00973ZZ	8, 649, 848	009K0ZZ	29	009X4ZX	16, 288, 581, 606	00BC4ZZ	8, 582, 607, 650, 848			00CC4ZZ	9
009740Z	8, 649, 848	009K30Z	29	009X4ZZ	16, 288, 581, 606, 650, 854			00BR3ZZ	29, 70, 271, 650, 1043	00CD*	650, 848
00974ZZ	8, 649, 848	009K40Z	29			00BD0ZX	8, 582, 607			00CD0ZZ	9
009800Z	8, 581, 606, 848	009K4ZZ	29	009Y00Z	16, 288, 581, 607, 650, 854	00BD0ZZ	8, 582, 607, 650, 848	00BR4ZZ	29, 70, 271, 650, 1043	00CD3ZZ	9
00980ZX	8, 581, 606	009L00Z	29	009Y0ZX	16, 288, 581, 607					00CD4ZZ	9
00980ZZ	8, 581, 606, 848	009L0ZX	29, 69, 271, 650, 854	009Y0ZZ	16, 288, 581, 607, 650, 854	00BD3ZX	8, 582, 607	00BS0ZX	29, 70, 271, 650, 854	00CF*	29
009830Z	8, 581, 606, 848					00BD3ZZ	8, 582, 607, 650, 848			00CG*	29
00983ZZ	8, 581, 606, 848	009L0ZZ	29	009Y40Z	16, 288, 581, 607, 650, 854			00BS0ZZ	29, 70, 271, 650, 1043	00CH*	29
009840Z	8, 581, 606, 848	009L30Z	29			00BD4ZX	8, 582, 607			00CJ*	29
00984ZZ	8, 581, 606, 848	009L3ZZ	29	009Y4ZX	16, 288, 581, 607	00BD4ZZ	8, 582, 607, 650, 848	00BS3ZZ	29, 70, 271, 650, 1043	00CK*	29
009900Z	8, 581, 606, 649, 848	009L40Z	29	009Y4ZZ	16, 288, 581, 607, 650, 854					00CL*	29
		009L4ZZ	29			00BF0ZX	29, 69, 271, 650, 854	00BS4ZZ	29, 70, 271, 650, 1043	00CM*	29
00990ZX	8, 581, 606	009M00Z	29	00B00ZX	8, 581, 607	00BF0ZZ	29, 69, 271, 650, 1043			00CN*	29
00990ZZ	8, 581, 606, 649, 848	009M0ZX	29, 69, 271, 650, 854	00B00ZZ	8, 581, 607, 650, 848			00BT*	288	00CP*	29
						00BF3ZZ	29, 69, 271, 650, 1043	00BT0ZX	16, 582, 607	00CQ*	29
009930Z	8, 581, 606, 649, 848	009M0ZZ	29	00B03ZX	8, 581, 607			00BT0ZZ	16, 582, 607	00CR*	29
		009M30Z	29	00B03ZZ	8, 581, 607, 650, 848	00BF4ZZ	29, 69, 271, 650, 1043	00BT3ZX	16, 582, 607	00CS*	29
00993ZZ	8, 581, 606, 649, 848	009M3ZZ	29					00BT3ZZ	16, 582, 607	00CT*	650
		009M40Z	29	00B04ZX	8, 581, 607	00BG0ZX	29, 69, 271, 650, 854	00BT4ZX	16, 582, 607	00CT0ZZ	16, 854
009940Z	8, 581, 606, 649, 848	009M4ZZ	29	00B04ZZ	8, 581, 607, 650, 848			00BT4ZZ	16, 582, 607	00CT3ZZ	16, 854
		009N00Z	29			00BG0ZZ	29, 69, 271, 650, 1043	00BW*	288	00CT4ZZ	16, 854
00994ZZ	8, 581, 606, 649, 848	009N0ZX	29, 69, 271, 650, 854	00B10ZX	8, 581, 607			00BW0ZX	16, 582, 607	00CU0ZZ	16, 650, 854
				00B10ZZ	8, 581, 607, 848	00BG3ZZ	29, 69, 271, 650, 1043	00BW0ZZ	16, 582, 607	00CU3ZZ	16, 650, 854
009A00Z	8, 581, 606, 649, 848	009N0ZZ	29	00B13ZX	8, 581, 607			00BW3ZX	16, 582, 607	00CU4ZZ	16, 650, 854
		009N30Z	29	00B13ZZ	8, 581, 607, 848	00BG4ZZ	29, 69, 271, 650, 1043	00BW3ZZ	16, 582, 607	00CW*	650
009A0ZX	8, 581, 606	009N3ZZ	29	00B14ZX	8, 581, 607			00BW4ZX	16, 582, 607	00CW0ZZ	16, 854
009A0ZZ	8, 581, 606, 649, 848	009N40Z	29	00B14ZZ	8, 581, 607, 848	00BH0ZX	29, 69, 271, 650, 854	00BW4ZZ	16, 582, 607	00CW3ZZ	16, 854
		009N4ZZ	29	00B20ZX	8, 581, 607			00BX*	288	00CW4ZZ	16, 854
009A30Z	8, 581, 606, 649, 848	009P00Z	29	00B20ZZ	8, 581, 607, 848	00BH0ZZ	29, 69, 271, 650, 1043	00BX0ZX	16, 582, 607	00CX*	650
009A3ZZ	8, 581, 606, 649, 848	009P0ZX	29, 69, 271, 650, 854	00B23ZX	8, 581, 607			00BX0ZZ	16, 582, 607	00CX0ZZ	16, 854
				00B23ZZ	8, 581, 607, 848	00BH3ZZ	29, 69, 271, 650, 1043	00BX3ZX	16, 582, 607	00CX3ZZ	16, 854
009A40Z	8, 581, 606, 649, 848	009P0ZZ	29	00B24ZX	8, 581, 607			00BX3ZZ	16, 582, 607	00CX4ZZ	16, 854
		009P30Z	29	00B24ZZ	8, 581, 607, 848	00BH4ZZ	29, 70, 271, 650, 1043	00BX4ZX	16, 582, 607	00CY*	650
009A4ZZ	8, 581, 606, 649, 848	009P3ZZ	29	00B60ZX	8, 581, 607			00BX4ZZ	16, 582, 607	00CY0ZZ	16, 854
		009P40Z	29	00B60ZZ	8, 581, 607, 650, 848	00BJ0ZX	29, 70, 271, 650, 854	00BY*	288	00CY3ZZ	16, 854
009B00Z	8, 649, 848	009P4ZZ	29					00BY0ZX	16, 582, 607	00CY4ZZ	16, 854
009B0ZX	8, 581, 606	009Q00Z	29	00B63ZX	8, 581, 607	00BJ0ZZ	29, 70, 271, 650, 1043	00BY0ZZ	16, 582, 607	00D1*	848
009B0ZZ	8, 649, 848	009Q0ZX	29, 69, 271, 650, 854	00B63ZZ	8, 581, 607, 650, 848			00BY3ZX	16, 582, 607	00D10ZZ	9, 582, 607
009B30Z	8, 649, 848					00BJ3ZZ	29, 70, 271, 650, 1043	00BY3ZZ	16, 582, 607	00D13ZZ	9, 582, 607
009B3ZZ	8, 649, 848	009Q0ZZ	29	00B64ZX	8, 581, 607			00BY4ZX	16, 582, 607	00D14ZZ	9, 582, 607
009B40Z	8, 649, 848	009Q30Z	29	00B64ZZ	8, 581, 607, 650, 848	00BJ4ZZ	29, 70, 271, 650, 1043	00BY4ZZ	16, 582, 607	00D2*	848
009B4ZZ	8, 649, 848	009Q3ZZ	29					00C0*	650, 848	00D20ZZ	9, 582, 607
009C00Z	8, 649, 848	009Q40Z	29	00B70ZX	8, 581, 607	00BK0ZX	29, 70, 271, 650, 854	00C00ZZ	8	00D23ZZ	9, 582, 607
009C0ZX	8, 581, 606	009Q4ZZ	29	00B70ZZ	8, 581, 607, 650, 848	00BK0ZZ	29, 70, 271, 650, 854, 1043	00C03ZZ	8	00D24ZZ	9, 582, 607
009C0ZZ	8, 649, 848	009R00Z	29					00C04ZZ	8	00DF*	29, 70, 272, 650
009C30Z	8, 649, 848	009R0ZX	29, 69, 271, 650, 854	00B73ZX	8, 581, 607	00BK3ZZ	29, 70, 271, 650, 854, 1043	00C1*	650, 848	00DF0ZZ	1043
009C3ZZ	8, 649, 848			00B73ZZ	8, 581, 607, 650, 848			00C10ZZ	8, 582, 607	00DF3ZZ	1043
009C40Z	8, 649, 848	009R0ZZ	29			00BK4ZZ	29, 70, 271, 650, 854, 1043	00C13ZZ	8, 582, 607	00DF4ZZ	1043
009C4ZZ	8, 649, 848	009R30Z	29	00B74ZX	8, 581, 607			00C14ZZ	8, 582, 607	00DG*	29, 70, 272, 650
009D00Z	8, 649, 848	009R3ZZ	29	00B74ZZ	8, 581, 607, 650, 848	00BL0ZX	29, 70, 271, 650, 854	00C2*	650, 848	00DG0ZZ	1043
009D0ZX	8, 581, 606	009R40Z	29					00C20ZZ	8, 582, 607	00DG3ZZ	1043
009D0ZZ	8, 649, 848	009R4ZZ	29	00B80ZX	8, 581, 607	00BL0ZZ	29, 70, 271, 650, 1043	00C23ZZ	8, 582, 607	00DG4ZZ	1043
009D30Z	8, 649, 848	009S00Z	29	00B80ZZ	8, 581, 607, 848			00C24ZZ	8, 582, 607	00DH*	29, 70, 272, 650
009D3ZZ	8, 649, 848	009S0ZX	29, 69, 271, 650, 854	00B83ZX	8, 582, 607	00BL3ZZ	29, 70, 271, 650, 1043	00C3*	650	00DH0ZZ	1043
009D40Z	8, 649, 848			00B83ZZ	8, 582, 607, 848			00C30ZZ	8, 854	00DH3ZZ	1043
009D4ZZ	8, 649, 848	009S0ZZ	29	00B84ZX	8, 582, 607	00BL4ZZ	29, 70, 271, 650, 1043	00C33ZZ	8, 854	00DH4ZZ	1043
009F00Z	28	009S30Z	29	00B84ZZ	8, 582, 607, 848			00C34ZZ	8, 854	00DJ*	29, 70, 272, 650
009F0ZX	28, 69, 271, 649, 854	009S3ZZ	29	00B90ZX	8, 582, 607	00BM0ZX	29, 70, 271, 650, 854	00C4*	650, 848	00DJ0ZZ	1043
		009S40Z	29	00B90ZZ	8, 582, 607, 650, 848			00C40ZZ	8, 582, 607	00DJ3ZZ	1043
009F0ZZ	28	009S4ZZ	29			00BM0ZZ	29, 70, 271, 650, 1043	00C43ZZ	8, 582, 607	00DJ4ZZ	1043
009F30Z	28	009T00Z	16, 288, 581, 606, 650, 854	00B93ZX	8, 582, 607			00C44ZZ	8, 582, 607	00DK*	29, 70, 272, 650
009F3ZZ	29			00B93ZZ	8, 582, 607, 650, 848	00BM3ZZ	29, 70, 271, 650, 1043	00C5*	650, 848	00DK0ZZ	1043
009F40Z	29	009T0ZX	16, 288, 581, 606					00C50ZZ	8, 582, 607	00DK3ZZ	1043
009F4ZZ	29	009T0ZZ	16, 288, 581, 606, 650, 854	00B94ZX	8, 582, 607	00BM4ZZ	29, 70, 271, 650, 1043	00C53ZZ	8, 582, 607	00DK4ZZ	1043
009G00Z	29			00B94ZZ	8, 582, 607, 650, 848			00C54ZZ	8, 582, 607	00DL*	29, 70, 272, 650
009G0ZX	29, 69, 271, 649, 854	009T40Z	16, 288, 581, 606, 650, 854			00BN0ZX	29, 70, 271, 650, 854	00C6*	650, 848	00DL0ZZ	1043
		009T4ZX	16, 288, 581, 606	00BA0ZX	8, 582, 607			00C60ZZ	8	00DL3ZZ	1043
009G0ZZ	29	009T4ZZ	16, 288, 581, 606, 650, 854	00BA0ZZ	8, 582, 607, 650, 848	00BN0ZZ	8, 70	00C63ZZ	8	00DL4ZZ	1043
009G30Z	29			00BA3ZX	8, 582, 607	00BN3ZZ	29, 70, 271, 650, 1043	00C64ZZ	8	00DM*	29, 70, 272, 650
009G3ZZ	29	009U00Z	16, 288, 581, 607, 650, 854	00BA3ZZ	8, 582, 607, 650, 848			00C7*	650, 848	00DM0ZZ	1043
009G40Z	29	009U0ZX	16, 288, 581, 606			00BN4ZZ	29, 70, 271, 650, 1043	00C70ZZ	8	00DM3ZZ	1043
009G4ZZ	29	009U0ZZ	16, 288, 581, 606, 650, 854	00BA4ZX	8, 582, 607			00C73ZZ	8	00DM4ZZ	1043
009H00Z	29			00BA4ZZ	8, 582, 607, 650, 848	00BP0ZX	29, 70, 271, 650, 854	00C74ZZ	8	00DN*	29, 70, 272, 650
009H0ZX	29, 69, 271, 649, 854	009W00Z	16, 288, 581, 606, 650, 854	00BB0ZX	8, 582, 607	00BP0ZZ	29, 70, 271, 650, 1043	00C8*	848	00DN0ZZ	1043
				00BB0ZZ	8, 582, 607, 650, 848			00C80ZZ	8, 582, 607	00DN3ZZ	1043
009H0ZZ	29	009W0ZX	16, 288, 581, 606			00BP3ZZ	29, 70, 271, 650, 1043	00C83ZZ	8, 582, 607	00DN4ZZ	1043
009H30Z	29	009W0ZZ	16, 288, 581, 606, 650, 854	00BB3ZX	8, 582, 607			00C84ZZ	8, 582, 607	00DP*	29, 70, 272, 650
009H3ZZ	29			00BB3ZZ	8, 582, 607, 650, 848	00BP4ZZ	29, 70, 271, 650, 1043	00C9*	650, 848	00DP0ZZ	1043
009H40Z	29	009W40Z	16, 288, 581, 606, 650, 854	00BB4ZX	8, 582, 607	00BQ0ZX	29, 70, 271, 650, 854	00C90ZZ	8, 582, 607	00DP3ZZ	1043
009H4ZZ	29							00C93ZZ	8, 582, 607	00DP4ZZ	1043
009J00Z	29							00C94ZZ	9, 582, 607	00DQ*	29, 70, 272, 650
								00CA*	650, 848	00DQ0ZZ	1043
								00CA0ZZ	9, 582, 607	00DQ3ZZ	1043
								00CA3ZZ	9, 582, 607	00DQ4ZZ	1043
										00DR*	29, 70, 272, 650

DRG Expert—Volume II

Numeric Index to Procedures

Code	Page
00DR0ZZ	1043
00DR3ZZ	1043
00DR4ZZ	1043
00DS*	29, 70, 272, 650
00DS0ZZ	1043
00DS3ZZ	1043
00DS4ZZ	1043
00DT*	288, 650
00DT0ZZ	16, 582, 607, 854
00DT3ZZ	16, 582, 607, 854
00DT4ZZ	16, 582, 607, 854
00F30ZZ	9, 650, 848
00F33ZZ	9, 650, 848
00F34ZZ	9, 650, 848
00F40ZZ	9, 650, 849
00F43ZZ	9, 650, 849
00F44ZZ	9, 650, 849
00F50ZZ	9, 650, 849
00F53ZZ	9, 650, 849
00F54ZZ	9, 650, 849
00F60ZZ	9, 650, 849
00F63ZZ	9, 650, 849
00F64ZZ	9, 650, 849
00FU*	288, 650
00FU0ZZ	16, 582, 607, 854
00FU3ZZ	16, 582, 607, 854
00FU4ZZ	16, 582, 607, 854
00FUXZZ	16, 582, 607, 854
00H002Z	9, 650, 849
00H003Z	9, 650, 849
00H004Z	14, 15
00H00MZ	9, 15, 582, 607, 650, 854
00H00YZ	9, 650, 849
00H032Z	9, 650, 849
00H033Z	9, 582, 607, 650, 849
00H03MZ	9, 15, 582, 607, 650, 854
00H03YZ	9, 650, 849
00H042Z	9, 650, 849
00H043Z	9, 650, 849
00H04MZ	9, 15, 582, 607, 650, 854
00H04YZ	9, 650, 849
00H602Z	9, 650, 849
00H603Z	9, 650, 849
00H60MZ	15, 582, 607, 650, 854
00H60MZ	9
00H60YZ	9, 650, 849
00H632Z	9, 650, 849
00H633Z	9, 650, 849
00H63MZ	15, 582, 607, 650, 854
00H63MZ	9
00H63YZ	9, 650, 849
00H642Z	9, 650, 849
00H643Z	9, 650, 849
00H64MZ	15, 582, 607, 650, 854
00H64MZ	9
00H64YZ	9, 650, 849
00HE02Z	29
00HE03Z	29
00HE0MZ	29, 42, 70, 124, 272, 509, 523, 537, 650, 854
00HE0YZ	29
00HE33Z	29
00HE3MZ	29, 42, 70, 124, 272, 509, 523, 537, 650, 854
00HE42Z	29
00HE43Z	29
00HE4MZ	29, 42, 70, 124, 272, 509, 523, 537, 650, 854
00HU02Z	16, 288, 582, 607, 650, 854
00HU0MZ	16, 22, 288, 290, 509, 523, 537, 582, 607, 650, 854
00HU0YZ	16, 288, 582, 607, 650, 854
00HU3MZ	16, 22, 288, 290, 509, 523, 537, 582, 607, 650, 854
00HU42Z	16, 288, 582, 607, 650, 854
00HU4MZ	16, 22, 288, 290, 509, 523, 537, 582, 607, 651, 854
00HV02Z	16, 288, 582, 607, 651, 854
00HV0MZ	16, 22, 288, 290, 509, 523, 537, 582, 607, 651, 854
00HV0YZ	16, 288, 582, 607, 651, 854
00HV3MZ	16, 22, 288, 290, 509, 523, 537, 582, 607, 651, 854
00HV3YZ	16, 288, 582, 607, 651, 854
00HV42Z	16, 288, 582, 607, 651, 854
00HV4MZ	16, 22, 288, 290, 509, 523, 537, 582, 607, 651, 854
00HV4YZ	16, 288, 582, 607, 651, 854
00J00ZZ	9, 67, 582, 607, 651, 849
00J04ZZ	9, 582, 607, 651, 854
00JE0ZZ	29
00JE4ZZ	29
00JU0ZZ	16, 288, 582, 607, 651, 854
00JU4ZZ	16, 288, 582, 607
00JV0ZZ	16, 288, 582, 607, 651, 854
00JV4ZZ	16, 288, 582, 607
00K*	651
00K00ZZ	9, 582, 607, 854
00K03ZZ	9, 582, 607, 854
00K04ZZ	9, 582, 607, 854
00K70ZZ	9, 582, 607, 854
00K73ZZ	9, 582, 607, 854
00K74ZZ	9, 582, 607, 854
00K80ZZ	9, 582, 607, 854
00K83ZZ	9, 582, 607, 854
00K84ZZ	9, 582, 607, 854
00K90ZZ	9, 582, 607, 854
00K93ZZ	9, 582, 607, 854
00K94ZZ	9, 582, 607, 854
00KA0ZZ	9, 582, 607, 854
00KA3ZZ	9, 582, 607, 854
00KA4ZZ	9, 582, 607, 854
00KB0ZZ	9, 582, 607, 854
00KB3ZZ	9, 582, 607, 854
00KB4ZZ	9, 582, 608, 855
00KC0ZZ	9, 582, 608, 855
00KC3ZZ	9, 582, 608, 855
00KC4ZZ	9, 582, 608, 855
00KD0ZZ	9, 582, 608, 855
00KD3ZZ	9, 582, 608, 855
00KD4ZZ	9, 582, 608, 855
00N*	651
00N00ZZ	9, 582, 608, 855
00N03ZZ	9, 582, 608, 855
00N04ZZ	9, 582, 608, 855
00N10ZZ	9, 582, 608, 855
00N13ZZ	9, 582, 608, 855
00N14ZZ	9, 582, 608, 855
00N20ZZ	9, 582, 608, 855
00N23ZZ	9, 582, 608, 855
00N24ZZ	9, 582, 608, 855
00N6*	849
00N60ZZ	9
00N63ZZ	9
00N64ZZ	9
00N70ZZ	9, 582, 608, 855
00N73ZZ	9, 582, 608, 855
00N74ZZ	9, 582, 608, 855
00N8*	849
00N80ZZ	9
00N83ZZ	9
00N84ZZ	9
00N9*	849
00N90ZZ	9, 582, 608
00N93ZZ	9, 582, 608
00N94ZZ	9, 582, 608
00NA*	849
00NA0ZZ	9, 582, 608
00NA3ZZ	9, 582, 608
00NA4ZZ	9, 582, 608
00NB*	849
00NB0ZZ	9
00NB3ZZ	9
00NB4ZZ	9
00NC*	849
00NC0ZZ	9
00NC3ZZ	9
00NC4ZZ	9
00ND*	849
00ND0ZZ	9
00ND3ZZ	9
00ND4ZZ	9
00NF*	29, 70
00NF0ZZ	855, 1043
00NF3ZZ	855, 1043
00NF4ZZ	855, 1043
00NG*	29, 70
00NG0ZZ	855, 1043
00NG3ZZ	855, 1043
00NG4ZZ	855, 1043
00NH*	29, 70
00NH0ZZ	855, 1043
00NH3ZZ	855, 1043
00NH4ZZ	855, 1043
00NJ*	29, 70
00NJ0ZZ	855, 1043
00NJ3ZZ	855, 1043
00NJ4ZZ	855, 1043
00NK*	70, 849
00NK0ZZ	9, 1043
00NK3ZZ	9, 1043
00NK4ZZ	9, 1043
00NL*	29, 70
00NL0ZZ	855, 1043
00NL3ZZ	855, 1043
00NL4ZZ	855, 1043
00NM*	29, 70
00NM0ZZ	855, 1043
00NM3ZZ	855, 1043
00NM4ZZ	855, 1043
00NN*	29, 70
00NN0ZZ	855, 1043
00NN3ZZ	855, 1043
00NN4ZZ	855, 1043
00NP*	29, 70
00NP0ZZ	855, 1043
00NP3ZZ	855, 1043
00NP4ZZ	855, 1043
00NQ*	29, 70
00NQ0ZZ	855, 1043
00NQ3ZZ	855, 1043
00NQ4ZZ	855, 1043
00NR*	29, 70
00NR0ZZ	855, 1043
00NR3ZZ	855, 1043
00NR4ZZ	855, 1043
00NS*	29, 70
00NS0ZZ	855, 1043
00NS3ZZ	855, 1043
00NS4ZZ	855, 1043
00NT*	288
00NT0ZZ	16, 582, 608, 855
00NT3ZZ	16, 582, 608, 855
00NT4ZZ	16, 582, 608, 855
00NW*	288
00NW0ZZ	16, 582, 608, 855
00NW3ZZ	16, 582, 608, 855
00NW4ZZ	16, 582, 608, 855
00NX*	288
00NX0ZZ	16, 582, 608, 855
00NX3ZZ	16, 582, 608, 855
00NX4ZZ	16, 582, 608, 855
00NY*	288
00NY0ZZ	16, 582, 608, 855
00NY3ZZ	16, 582, 608, 855
00NY4ZZ	16, 582, 608, 855
00P000Z	9, 651, 849
00P002Z	9, 651, 849
00P003Z	9, 651, 849
00P007Z	9, 651, 849
00P00JZ	9, 651, 849
00P00KZ	9, 651, 849
00P00MZ	9, 582, 608
00P00YZ	9, 651, 849
00P037Z	9, 651, 849
00P03JZ	9, 651, 849
00P03KZ	9, 651, 849
00P03MZ	9, 583, 608
00P040Z	9, 651, 849
00P042Z	9, 651, 849
00P043Z	9, 651, 849
00P047Z	9, 651, 849
00P04JZ	9, 651, 849
00P04KZ	9, 651, 849
00P04MZ	9, 583, 608
00P600Z	9, 651, 849
00P602Z	9, 651, 849
00P603Z	9, 651, 849
00P60JZ	22, 651, 855
00P60MZ	9, 583, 608
00P60YZ	9, 651, 849
00P63JZ	22, 651, 855
00P63MZ	9, 583, 608
00P640Z	9, 651, 849
00P642Z	9, 651, 849
00P643Z	9, 651, 849
00P64JZ	22, 651, 855
00P64MZ	9, 583, 608
00PE00Z	29
00PE02Z	30
00PE03Z	30
00PE07Z	30
00PE0MZ	30, 70, 272, 523, 537, 651, 855
00PE0YZ	30
00PE37Z	30
00PE3MZ	30, 70, 272, 523, 537, 651, 855
00PE40Z	30
00PE42Z	30
00PE43Z	30
00PE47Z	30
00PE4MZ	30, 70, 272, 523, 537, 651, 855
00PU00Z	16, 288, 583, 608, 651, 855
00PU02Z	16, 288, 583, 608, 651, 855
00PU03Z	17, 288, 583, 608, 651, 855
00PU0JZ	17, 288, 651, 855
00PU0MZ	17, 288, 509, 523, 537, 651, 855
00PU0YZ	17, 288, 583, 608, 651, 855
00PU3JZ	17, 288, 651, 855
00PU3MZ	17, 288, 509, 523, 537, 651, 855
00PU40Z	17, 288, 583, 608, 651, 855
00PU42Z	17, 288, 583, 608, 651, 855
00PU43Z	17, 288, 583, 608, 651, 855
00PU4JZ	17, 288, 651, 855
00PU4MZ	17, 288, 509, 523, 537, 651, 855
00PV00Z	17, 203, 583, 608, 651, 855
00PV02Z	17, 203, 583, 608, 651, 855
00PV03Z	17, 203, 583, 608, 651, 855
00PV07Z	17, 203, 583, 608, 651, 855
00PV0JZ	17, 203, 583, 608, 651, 855
00PV0KZ	17, 203, 583, 608, 651, 855
00PV0MZ	17, 288, 509, 524, 537, 651, 855
00PV0YZ	17, 203, 583, 608, 651, 855
00PV37Z	17, 203, 583, 608, 651, 855
00PV3JZ	17, 203, 583, 608, 651, 855
00PV3KZ	17, 203, 583, 608, 651, 855
00PV3MZ	17, 288, 509, 524, 537, 651, 855
00PV40Z	17, 203, 583, 608, 651, 855
00PV42Z	17, 203, 583, 608, 651, 855
00PV43Z	17, 203, 583, 608, 651, 855
00PV47Z	17, 203, 583, 608, 651, 855
00PV4JZ	17, 203, 583, 608, 651, 855
00PV4KZ	17, 203, 583, 608, 651, 855
00PV4MZ	17, 288, 509, 524, 537, 651, 855
00Q*	651
00Q0*	849
00Q00ZZ	9
00Q03ZZ	9
00Q04ZZ	9
00Q1*	849
00Q10ZZ	9
00Q13ZZ	9
00Q14ZZ	9
00Q2*	849
00Q20ZZ	9
00Q23ZZ	9
00Q24ZZ	9
00Q6*	849
00Q60ZZ	9
00Q63ZZ	9
00Q64ZZ	9
00Q7*	849
00Q70ZZ	9
00Q73ZZ	9
00Q74ZZ	9
00Q8*	849
00Q80ZZ	9
00Q83ZZ	9
00Q84ZZ	9
00Q9*	849
00Q90ZZ	9, 583, 608
00Q93ZZ	9, 583, 608
00Q94ZZ	9, 583, 608
00QA*	849
00QA0ZZ	9, 583, 608
00QA3ZZ	9, 583, 608
00QA4ZZ	9, 583, 608
00QB*	849
00QB0ZZ	9
00QB3ZZ	9
00QB4ZZ	9
00QC*	849
00QC0ZZ	9
00QC3ZZ	10
00QC4ZZ	10
00QD*	849
00QD0ZZ	10
00QD3ZZ	10
00QD4ZZ	10
00QF*	30, 70
00QF0ZZ	855
00QF3ZZ	855
00QF4ZZ	855
00QG*	30, 70
00QG0ZZ	855
00QG3ZZ	855
00QG4ZZ	855
00QH*	30, 70
00QH0ZZ	855
00QH3ZZ	855
00QH4ZZ	855
00QJ*	30, 70
00QJ0ZZ	855
00QJ3ZZ	855
00QJ4ZZ	855
00QK*	30, 70
00QK0ZZ	855
00QK3ZZ	855
00QK4ZZ	855
00QL*	30, 70
00QL0ZZ	855
00QL3ZZ	855
00QL4ZZ	855
00QM*	30, 70
00QM0ZZ	855
00QM3ZZ	855
00QM4ZZ	855
00QN*	30, 70
00QN0ZZ	855
00QN3ZZ	855
00QN4ZZ	855
00QP*	30, 70
00QP0ZZ	855
00QP3ZZ	855
00QP4ZZ	855
00QQ*	30, 70
00QQ0ZZ	855
00QQ3ZZ	855
00QQ4ZZ	855
00QR*	30, 70
00QR0ZZ	855
00QR3ZZ	855
00QR4ZZ	855
00QS*	30, 70
00QS0ZZ	855
00QS3ZZ	855
00QS4ZZ	855
00QT*	288
00QT0ZZ	17, 583, 608, 855
00QT3ZZ	17, 583, 608, 855
00QT4ZZ	17, 583, 608, 855
00QW*	288
00QW0ZZ	17, 583, 608, 855
00QW3ZZ	17, 583, 608, 855
00QW4ZZ	17, 583, 608, 855
00QX*	288
00QX0ZZ	17, 583, 608, 855
00QX3ZZ	17, 583, 608, 855
00QX4ZZ	17, 583, 608, 855
00QY*	288
00QY0ZZ	17, 583, 608, 855
00QY3ZZ	17, 583, 608, 855
00QY4ZZ	17, 583, 608, 855
00R107Z	10, 651, 849
00R10JZ	10, 651, 849
00R10KZ	10, 651, 849
00R147Z	10, 651, 849
00R14JZ	10, 651, 849
00R14KZ	10, 651, 849
00R207Z	10, 651, 849
00R20JZ	10, 651, 849
00R20KZ	10, 651, 849
00R247Z	10, 651, 849
00R24JZ	10, 651, 849
00R24KZ	10, 651, 849
00R607Z	10, 651, 849
00R60JZ	10, 651, 849
00R60KZ	10, 651, 849
00R647Z	10, 651, 849
00R64JZ	10, 651, 849
00R64KZ	10, 651, 849
00RF07Z	30, 70, 651, 855
00RF0JZ	30, 70, 651, 855
00RF0KZ	30, 70, 651, 855
00RF47Z	30, 70, 651, 855
00RF4JZ	30, 70, 651, 855
00RF4KZ	30, 70, 651, 855
00RG07Z	30, 70, 651, 855
00RG0JZ	30, 70, 651, 855
00RG0KZ	30, 70, 651, 855
00RG47Z	30, 70, 651, 855
00RG4JZ	30, 70, 651, 855
00RG4KZ	30, 70, 651, 855
00RH07Z	30, 70, 651, 855
00RH0JZ	30, 70, 651, 855
00RH0KZ	30, 70, 651, 855
00RH47Z	30, 70, 651, 855
00RH4JZ	30, 70, 651, 855
00RH4KZ	30, 70, 651, 855
00RJ07Z	30, 70, 651, 855
00RJ0JZ	30, 70, 651, 855
00RJ0KZ	30, 70, 651, 855
00RJ47Z	30, 70, 651, 855
00RJ4JZ	30, 70, 651, 855
00RJ4KZ	30, 70, 651, 855
00RK07Z	30, 70, 651, 856
00RK0JZ	30, 70, 651, 856
00RK0KZ	30, 70, 651, 856
00RK47Z	30, 70, 651, 856
00RK4JZ	30, 70, 651, 856
00RK4KZ	30, 70, 651, 856
00RL07Z	30, 70, 651, 856
00RL0JZ	30, 70, 651, 856
00RL0KZ	30, 70, 651, 856
00RL47Z	30, 70, 651, 856
00RL4JZ	30, 70, 651, 856
00RL4KZ	30, 70, 651, 856
00RM07Z	30, 70, 651, 856
00RM0JZ	30, 70, 651, 856
00RM0KZ	30, 70, 651, 856
00RM47Z	30, 70, 651, 856
00RM4JZ	30, 70, 651, 856
00RM4KZ	30, 70, 651, 856
00RN07Z	30, 70, 651, 856
00RN0JZ	30, 70, 651, 856
00RN0KZ	30, 70, 651, 856
00RN47Z	30, 70, 651, 856
00RN4JZ	30, 70, 651, 856
00RN4KZ	30, 70, 651, 856
00RP07Z	30, 70, 651, 856
00RP0JZ	30, 70, 651, 856
00RP0KZ	30, 70, 651, 856
00RP47Z	30, 70, 651, 856
00RP4JZ	30, 70, 651, 856
00RP4KZ	30, 70, 651, 856
00RQ07Z	30, 70, 651, 856
00RQ0JZ	30, 70, 651, 856
00RQ0KZ	30, 70, 651, 856
00RQ47Z	30, 70, 651, 856
00RQ4JZ	30, 70, 651, 856
00RQ4KZ	30, 70, 651, 856
00RR07Z	30, 70, 651, 856
00RR0JZ	30, 70, 651, 856
00RR0KZ	30, 70, 651, 856
00RR47Z	30, 70, 651, 856
00RR4JZ	30, 70, 651, 856
00RR4KZ	30, 70, 651, 856
00RS07Z	30, 70, 651, 856
00RS0JZ	30, 70, 651, 856

Numeric Index to Procedures

Numeric Index to Procedures

Code	Page
00RS0KZ	30, 70, 651, 856
00RS47Z	30, 70, 651, 856
00RS4JZ	30, 70, 651, 856
00RS4KZ	30, 70, 651, 856
00RT07Z	17, 288, 583, 608, 651, 856
00RT0JZ	17, 288, 583, 608, 651, 856
00RT0KZ	17, 288, 583, 608, 651, 856
00RT47Z	17, 288, 583, 608, 651, 856
00RT4JZ	17, 288, 583, 608, 651, 856
00RT4KZ	17, 288, 583, 608, 651, 856
00SF*	30
00SF0ZZ	856
00SF3ZZ	856
00SF4ZZ	856
00SG*	30
00SG0ZZ	856
00SG3ZZ	856
00SG4ZZ	856
00SH*	30
00SH0ZZ	856
00SH3ZZ	856
00SH4ZZ	856
00SJ*	30
00SJ0ZZ	856
00SJ3ZZ	856
00SJ4ZZ	856
00SK*	30
00SK0ZZ	856
00SK3ZZ	856
00SK4ZZ	856
00SL*	30
00SL0ZZ	856
00SL3ZZ	856
00SL4ZZ	856
00SM*	30
00SM0ZZ	856
00SM3ZZ	856
00SM4ZZ	856
00SN*	30
00SN0ZZ	856
00SN3ZZ	856
00SN4ZZ	856
00SP*	30
00SP0ZZ	856
00SP3ZZ	856
00SP4ZZ	856
00SQ*	30
00SQ0ZZ	856
00SQ3ZZ	856
00SQ4ZZ	856
00SR*	30
00SR0ZZ	856
00SR3ZZ	856
00SR4ZZ	856
00SS*	30
00SS0ZZ	856
00SS3ZZ	856
00SS4ZZ	856
00SW*	288, 651
00SW0ZZ	17, 583, 608, 856
00SW3ZZ	17, 583, 608, 856
00SW4ZZ	17, 583, 608, 856
00SX*	288, 652
00SX0ZZ	17, 583, 608, 856
00SX3ZZ	17, 583, 608, 856
00SX4ZZ	17, 583, 608, 856
00SY*	288, 652
00SY0ZZ	17, 583, 608, 856
00SY3ZZ	17, 583, 608, 856
00SY4ZZ	17, 583, 608, 856
00T*	652, 849
00T70ZZ	10, 583, 608
00T73ZZ	10, 583, 608
00T74ZZ	10, 583, 608
00U*	652
00U1*	849
00U107Z	10
00U10JZ	10
00U10KZ	10
00U137Z	10
00U13JZ	10
00U13KZ	10
00U147Z	10
00U14JZ	10
00U14KZ	10
00U2*	849
00U207Z	10
00U20JZ	10
00U20KZ	10
00U237Z	10
00U23JZ	10
00U23KZ	10
00U247Z	10
00U24JZ	10
00U24KZ	10
00U607Z	10, 849
00U60JZ	10, 849
00U60KZ	10, 849
00U637Z	10, 849
00U63JZ	10, 849
00U63KZ	10, 849
00U647Z	10, 849
00U64JZ	10, 849
00U64KZ	10, 849
00UF*	30
00UF07Z	856
00UF0JZ	70, 856
00UF0KZ	70, 856
00UF37Z	856
00UF3JZ	70, 856
00UF3KZ	70, 856
00UF47Z	856
00UF4JZ	70, 856
00UF4KZ	70, 856
00UG*	30
00UG07Z	856
00UG0JZ	70, 856
00UG0KZ	70, 856
00UG37Z	856
00UG3JZ	70, 856
00UG3KZ	70, 856
00UG47Z	856
00UG4JZ	70, 856
00UG4KZ	70, 856
00UH*	30
00UH07Z	856
00UH0JZ	70, 856
00UH0KZ	70, 856
00UH37Z	856
00UH3JZ	70, 856
00UH3KZ	70, 856
00UH47Z	856
00UH4JZ	70, 856
00UH4KZ	70, 856
00UJ*	30
00UJ07Z	856
00UJ0JZ	70, 856
00UJ0KZ	70, 856
00UJ37Z	856
00UJ3JZ	70, 856
00UJ3KZ	70, 856
00UJ47Z	856
00UJ4JZ	70, 856
00UJ4KZ	70, 856
00UK*	30
00UK07Z	856
00UK0JZ	71, 856
00UK0KZ	71, 856
00UK37Z	856
00UK3JZ	71, 856
00UK3KZ	71, 856
00UK47Z	856
00UK4JZ	71, 856
00UK4KZ	71, 856
00UL*	30
00UL07Z	856
00UL0JZ	71, 856
00UL0KZ	71, 856
00UL37Z	856
00UL3JZ	71, 856
00UL3KZ	71, 856
00UL47Z	856
00UL4JZ	71, 856
00UL4KZ	71, 856
00UM*	30
00UM07Z	856
00UM0JZ	71, 856
00UM0KZ	71, 856
00UM37Z	856
00UM3JZ	71, 856
00UM3KZ	71, 856
00UM47Z	856
00UM4JZ	71, 856
00UM4KZ	71, 856
00UN*	30
00UN07Z	856
00UN0JZ	71, 856
00UN0KZ	71, 856
00UN37Z	856
00UN3JZ	71, 856
00UN3KZ	71, 856
00UN47Z	856
00UN4JZ	71, 856
00UN4KZ	71, 856
00UP*	30
00UP07Z	856
00UP0JZ	71, 856
00UP0KZ	71, 856
00UP37Z	856
00UP3JZ	71, 857
00UP3KZ	71, 857
00UP47Z	857
00UP4JZ	71, 857
00UP4KZ	71, 857
00UQ*	30
00UQ07Z	857
00UQ0JZ	71, 857
00UQ0KZ	71, 857
00UQ37Z	857
00UQ3JZ	71, 857
00UQ3KZ	71, 857
00UQ47Z	857
00UQ4JZ	71, 857
00UQ4KZ	71, 857
00UR*	30
00UR07Z	857
00UR0JZ	71, 857
00UR0KZ	71, 857
00UR37Z	857
00UR3JZ	71, 857
00UR3KZ	71, 857
00UR47Z	857
00UR4JZ	71, 857
00UR4KZ	71, 857
00US*	30
00US07Z	857
00US0JZ	71, 857
00US0KZ	71, 857
00US37Z	857
00US3JZ	71, 857
00US3KZ	71, 857
00US47Z	857
00US4JZ	71, 857
00US4KZ	71, 857
00UT*	288
00UT07Z	17, 583, 608, 857
00UT0JZ	17, 583, 608, 857
00UT0KZ	17, 583, 608, 857
00UT37Z	17, 583, 608, 857
00UT3JZ	17, 583, 608, 857
00UT3KZ	17, 583, 608, 857
00UT47Z	17, 583, 608, 857
00UT4JZ	17, 583, 608, 857
00UT4KZ	17, 583, 608, 857
00W000Z	10, 652, 849
00W002Z	10, 652, 849
00W003Z	10, 652, 849
00W007Z	10, 652, 849
00W00JZ	10
00W00KZ	10
00W00MZ	10, 652, 849
00W00YZ	10, 652, 849
00W030Z	10, 652, 849
00W032Z	10, 652, 849
00W033Z	10, 652, 849
00W037Z	10, 652, 849
00W03JZ	10, 652, 849
00W03KZ	10, 652, 849
00W03MZ	10, 652, 849
00W040Z	10, 652, 849
00W042Z	10, 652, 849
00W043Z	10, 652, 849
00W047Z	10, 652, 849
00W04JZ	10, 652, 849
00W04KZ	10, 652, 849
00W04MZ	10, 652, 849
00W600Z	10, 652, 849
00W602Z	10, 652, 849
00W603Z	10, 652, 849
00W60JZ	22, 583, 608, 652, 857
00W60MZ	10, 652, 849
00W60YZ	10, 652, 849
00W630Z	10, 652, 849
00W632Z	10, 652, 849
00W63JZ	22, 583, 608, 652, 857
00W63MZ	10, 652, 849
00W640Z	10, 652, 849
00W642Z	10, 652, 849
00W643Z	10, 652, 849
00W64JZ	22, 583, 608, 652, 857
00W64MZ	10, 652, 849
00WE00Z	30
00WE02Z	30
00WE03Z	30
00WE07Z	30
00WE0MZ	30
00WE0YZ	30
00WE30Z	30
00WE32Z	30
00WE33Z	30
00WE37Z	30
00WE3MZ	30
00WE40Z	30
00WE42Z	30
00WE43Z	30
00WE47Z	30
00WE4MZ	30
00WU00Z	17, 288, 583, 608, 652, 857
00WU02Z	17, 288, 583, 608, 652, 857
00WU03Z	17, 288, 583, 608, 652, 857
00WU0JZ	17, 288, 583, 608, 652, 857
00WU0MZ	17, 288, 583, 608, 652, 857
00WU0YZ	17, 288, 583, 608, 652, 857
00WU30Z	17, 288, 583, 608, 652, 857
00WU32Z	17, 288, 583, 608, 652, 857
00WU33Z	17, 288, 583, 608, 652, 857
00WU3JZ	17, 288, 583, 608, 652, 857
00WU3MZ	17, 288, 583, 608, 652, 857
00WU40Z	17, 288, 583, 608, 652, 857
00WU42Z	17, 288, 583, 608, 652, 857
00WU43Z	17, 288, 583, 608, 652, 857
00WU4JZ	17, 288, 583, 608, 652, 857
00WU4MZ	17, 288, 583, 608, 652, 857
00WV00Z	17, 203, 583, 608, 652, 857
00WV02Z	17, 203, 583, 608, 652, 857
00WV03Z	17, 203, 583, 608, 652, 857
00WV07Z	17, 203, 583, 608, 652, 857
00WV0JZ	17, 203, 583, 608, 652, 857
00WV0KZ	17, 203, 583, 608, 652, 857
00WV0MZ	17, 203, 583, 608, 652, 857
00WV0YZ	17, 203, 583, 608, 652, 857
00WV30Z	17, 203, 583, 608, 652, 857
00WV32Z	17, 203, 583, 608, 652, 857
00WV33Z	17, 203, 583, 608, 652, 857
00WV37Z	17, 203, 583, 608, 652, 857
00WV3JZ	17, 203, 583, 608, 652, 857
00WV3KZ	17, 203, 583, 608, 652, 857
00WV3MZ	17, 203, 583, 608, 652, 857
00WV40Z	17, 203, 583, 608, 652, 857
00WV42Z	17, 203, 583, 608, 652, 857
00WV43Z	17, 203, 583, 608, 652, 857
00WV47Z	17, 203, 583, 608, 652, 857
00WV4JZ	17, 203, 583, 608, 652, 857
00WV4KZ	17, 203, 583, 608, 652, 857
00WV4MZ	17, 203, 583, 608, 652, 857
00X*	30, 652
00XF0ZF	857
00XF0ZG	857
00XF0ZH	857
00XF0ZJ	857
00XF0ZK	857
00XF0ZL	857
00XF0ZM	857
00XF0ZN	857
00XF0ZP	857
00XF0ZQ	857
00XF0ZR	857
00XF0ZS	857
00XF4ZF	857
00XF4ZG	857
00XF4ZH	857
00XF4ZJ	857
00XF4ZK	857
00XF4ZL	857
00XF4ZM	857
00XF4ZN	857
00XF4ZP	857
00XF4ZQ	857
00XF4ZS	857
00XG0ZF	857
00XG0ZG	857
00XG0ZH	857
00XG0ZJ	857
00XG0ZK	857
00XG0ZL	857
00XG0ZM	857
00XG0ZN	857
00XG0ZP	857
00XG0ZQ	857
00XG0ZS	857
00XG4ZF	857
00XG4ZG	857
00XG4ZH	857
00XG4ZJ	857
00XG4ZK	857
00XG4ZL	857
00XG4ZM	857
00XG4ZN	857
00XG4ZP	857
00XG4ZQ	857
00XG4ZS	857
00XH0ZF	857
00XH0ZG	857
00XH0ZH	857
00XH0ZJ	857
00XH0ZK	857
00XH0ZL	857
00XH0ZM	857
00XH0ZN	857
00XH0ZP	857
00XH0ZQ	857
00XH0ZR	857
00XH0ZS	857
00XH4ZF	857
00XH4ZG	857
00XH4ZH	857
00XH4ZJ	857
00XH4ZK	857
00XH4ZL	857
00XH4ZM	857
00XH4ZN	857
00XH4ZP	857
00XH4ZQ	857
00XH4ZR	857
00XH4ZS	857
00XJ0ZF	857
00XJ0ZG	857
00XJ0ZH	857
00XJ0ZJ	857
00XJ0ZK	857
00XJ0ZL	857
00XJ0ZM	857
00XJ0ZN	857
00XJ0ZP	857
00XJ0ZQ	857
00XJ0ZS	857
00XJ4ZF	857
00XJ4ZG	857
00XJ4ZH	857
00XJ4ZJ	857
00XJ4ZK	857
00XJ4ZL	857
00XJ4ZM	857
00XJ4ZN	858
00XJ4ZP	858
00XJ4ZQ	858
00XJ4ZS	858
00XK0ZF	858
00XK0ZG	858
00XK0ZH	858
00XK0ZJ	858
00XK0ZK	858
00XK0ZL	858
00XK0ZM	858
00XK0ZN	858
00XK0ZP	858
00XK0ZQ	858
00XK0ZR	858
00XK0ZS	858
00XK4ZG	858
00XK4ZH	858
00XK4ZJ	858
00XK4ZK	858
00XK4ZL	858
00XK4ZM	858
00XK4ZN	858
00XK4ZP	858
00XK4ZR	858
00XK4ZS	858
00XL0ZF	858
00XL0ZG	858
00XL0ZH	858
00XL0ZJ	858
00XL0ZK	858
00XL0ZL	858
00XL0ZM	858
00XL0ZN	858
00XL0ZP	858
00XL0ZQ	858
00XL0ZR	858
00XL0ZS	858
00XL4ZF	858
00XL4ZG	858
00XL4ZH	858
00XL4ZJ	858
00XL4ZK	858
00XL4ZL	858
00XL4ZM	858
00XL4ZN	858
00XL4ZP	858
00XL4ZQ	858
00XL4ZR	858
00XL4ZS	858
00XM0ZF	858
00XM0ZG	858
00XM0ZH	858
00XM0ZJ	858
00XM0ZK	858
00XM0ZL	858
00XM0ZM	858
00XM0ZN	858
00XM0ZP	858
00XM0ZQ	858
00XM0ZR	858
00XM0ZS	858
00XM4ZF	858
00XM4ZH	858
00XM4ZJ	858
00XM4ZK	858
00XM4ZL	858
00XM4ZM	858
00XM4ZN	858
00XM4ZQ	858
00XM4ZR	858
00XM4ZS	858
00XN0ZF	858
00XN0ZG	858
00XN0ZH	858
00XN0ZJ	858
00XN0ZK	858
00XN0ZL	858
00XN0ZM	858
00XN0ZN	858
00XN0ZP	858
00XN0ZQ	858
00XN0ZS	858
00XN4ZF	858
00XN4ZG	858
00XN4ZH	858

Code	Page
00XN4ZJ	858
00XN4ZK	858
00XN4ZL	858
00XN4ZM	858
00XN4ZN	858
00XN4ZP	858
00XN4ZQ	858
00XN4ZR	858
00XN4ZS	858
00XP0ZF	858
00XP0ZG	858
00XP0ZH	858
00XP0ZJ	858
00XP0ZK	858
00XP0ZL	858
00XP0ZM	858
00XP0ZN	858
00XP0ZP	858
00XP0ZQ	858
00XP0ZR	858
00XP0ZS	858
00XP4ZF	858
00XP4ZG	858
00XP4ZH	858
00XP4ZJ	858
00XP4ZK	858
00XP4ZL	858
00XP4ZM	858
00XP4ZN	858
00XP4ZP	858
00XP4ZQ	858
00XP4ZR	858
00XP4ZS	858
00XQ0ZF	858
00XQ0ZG	858
00XQ0ZH	858
00XQ0ZJ	858
00XQ0ZK	858
00XQ0ZL	858
00XQ0ZM	858
00XQ0ZN	858
00XQ0ZP	858
00XQ0ZQ	858
00XQ0ZR	858
00XQ0ZS	858
00XQ4ZF	858
00XQ4ZG	858
00XQ4ZH	858
00XQ4ZJ	858
00XQ4ZK	858
00XQ4ZL	858
00XQ4ZM	858
00XQ4ZN	858
00XQ4ZP	858
00XQ4ZQ	858
00XQ4ZR	858
00XQ4ZS	858
00XR0ZF	858
00XR0ZG	858
00XR0ZH	858
00XR0ZJ	858
00XR0ZK	858
00XR0ZL	858
00XR0ZM	71, 858
00XR0ZN	858
00XR0ZP	858
00XR0ZQ	858
00XR0ZR	858
00XR0ZS	71, 858
00XR4ZF	858
00XR4ZG	858
00XR4ZH	858
00XR4ZJ	858
00XR4ZK	858
00XR4ZL	858
00XR4ZM	71, 858
00XR4ZN	858
00XR4ZP	858
00XR4ZQ	858
00XR4ZR	858
00XR4ZS	71, 858
00XS0ZF	858
00XS0ZG	859
00XS0ZH	859
00XS0ZJ	859
00XS0ZK	859
00XS0ZL	859
00XS0ZM	71, 859
00XS0ZN	859
00XS0ZP	859
00XS0ZQ	859
00XS0ZR	859
00XS0ZS	859
00XS4ZF	859
00XS4ZG	859
00XS4ZH	859
00XS4ZJ	859
00XS4ZK	859
00XS4ZL	859
00XS4ZM	71, 859
00XS4ZN	859
00XS4ZP	859
00XS4ZQ	859
00XS4ZR	859
00XS4ZS	859
01510ZZ	17, 288, 583, 608, 652, 859
01514ZZ	17, 288, 583, 608, 652, 859
01580ZZ	17, 288, 583, 608, 652, 859
01584ZZ	17, 288, 583, 608, 652, 859
015B0ZZ	17, 288, 583, 608, 652, 859
015B4ZZ	17, 288, 583, 608, 652, 859
015K*	30, 71, 143
015L*	30, 143
015M*	30, 143
015N*	30, 143
015N0ZZ	1043
015N3ZZ	1043
015N4ZZ	1043
015P*	30, 143, 531
015R0ZZ	17, 288, 583, 608, 652, 859
015R4ZZ	17, 288, 583, 608, 652, 859
0180*	30, 272, 652
01800ZZ	859
01803ZZ	859
01804ZZ	859
0181*	288, 652
01810ZZ	17, 583, 608, 859
01813ZZ	17, 583, 608, 859
01814ZZ	17, 583, 608, 859
0182*	30, 272, 652
01820ZZ	859
01823ZZ	859
01824ZZ	859
0183*	30, 272, 652
01830ZZ	859
01833ZZ	859
01834ZZ	859
0184*	30, 272, 652
01840ZZ	859
01843ZZ	859
01844ZZ	859
0185*	30, 272, 652
01850ZZ	859
01853ZZ	859
01854ZZ	859
0186*	30, 272, 652
01860ZZ	859
01863ZZ	859
01864ZZ	859
0188*	288, 652
01880ZZ	17, 583, 608, 859
01883ZZ	17, 583, 608, 859
01884ZZ	17, 583, 608, 859
0189*	30, 272, 652
01890ZZ	859
01893ZZ	859
01894ZZ	859
018A*	30, 272, 652
018A0ZZ	859
018A3ZZ	859
018A4ZZ	859
018B*	288, 652
018B0ZZ	17, 583, 608, 859
018B3ZZ	17, 583, 608, 859
018B4ZZ	17, 583, 608, 859
018C*	30, 272, 652
018C0ZZ	859
018C3ZZ	859
018C4ZZ	859
018D*	30, 272, 652
018D0ZZ	859
018D3ZZ	859
018D4ZZ	859
018F*	30, 272, 652
018F0ZZ	859
018F3ZZ	859
018F4ZZ	859
018G*	30, 272, 652
018G0ZZ	859
018G3ZZ	859
018G4ZZ	859
018H*	30, 272, 652
018H0ZZ	859
018H3ZZ	859
018H4ZZ	859
018K*	30, 143
018L*	30, 143
018M*	30, 143, 479
018N*	30, 143
018P*	30, 143
018Q*	30, 272, 652
018Q0ZZ	859
018Q3ZZ	859
018Q4ZZ	859
018R*	288, 652
018R0ZZ	17, 583, 608, 859
018R3ZZ	17, 583, 608, 859
018R4ZZ	17, 583, 608, 859
019000Z	30
01900ZX	30, 272, 652, 859
01900ZZ	30
019040Z	30
01904ZZ	30
019100Z	30
01910ZX	30, 272, 652, 859
01910ZZ	30
019140Z	30
01914ZZ	30
019200Z	30
01920ZX	30, 272, 652, 859
01920ZZ	30
019240Z	31
01924ZZ	31
019300Z	31
01930ZX	31, 272, 652, 859
01930ZZ	31
019340Z	31
01934ZZ	31
019400Z	31
01940ZX	31, 272, 652, 859
01940ZZ	31
019440Z	31
01944ZZ	31
019500Z	31
01950ZX	31, 272, 652, 859
01950ZZ	31
019540Z	31
01954ZZ	31
019600Z	31
01960ZX	31, 272, 652, 859
01960ZZ	31
019640Z	31
01964ZZ	31
019800Z	31
01980ZX	31, 272, 652, 859
01980ZZ	31
019840Z	31
01984ZZ	31
019900Z	31
01990ZX	31, 272, 652, 859
01990ZZ	31
019940Z	31
01994ZZ	31
019A00Z	31
019A0ZX	31, 272, 652, 859
019A0ZZ	31
019A40Z	31
019A4ZZ	31
019B00Z	31
019B0ZZ	31, 272, 652, 859
019B40Z	31
019B4ZZ	31
019C00Z	31
019C0ZX	31, 272, 652, 859
019C0ZZ	31
019C40Z	31
019C4ZZ	31
019D00Z	31
019D0ZX	31, 272, 652, 859
019D0ZZ	31
019D40Z	31
019D4ZZ	31
019F00Z	31
019F0ZX	31, 272, 652, 859
019F40Z	31
019F4ZZ	31
019G00Z	31
019G0ZX	31, 272, 652, 859
019G0ZZ	31
019G40Z	31
019G4ZZ	31
019H00Z	31
019H0ZZ	31, 272, 652, 859
019H40Z	31
019H4ZZ	31
019K00Z	31
019K00Z	143
019K0ZX	31
019K0ZZ	31, 143
019K3ZX	31
019K40Z	31
019K40Z	143
019K4ZX	31
019K4ZZ	31, 143
019L00Z	31
019L00Z	143
019L0ZX	31
019L0ZZ	31, 143
019L3ZX	31
019L40Z	31
019L40Z	143
019L4ZX	31
019L4ZZ	31, 143
019M00Z	31
019M00Z	143
019M0ZX	31
019M3ZX	31
019M40Z	31
019M40Z	143
019M4ZX	31
019M4ZZ	31, 143
019N00Z	31
019N00Z	143
019N0ZX	31
019N0ZZ	31, 143
019N3ZX	31
019N40Z	31
019N40Z	143
019N4ZX	31
019N4ZZ	31, 143
019P00Z	31
019P00Z	143
019P0ZX	31
019P0ZZ	31, 143
019P3ZX	31
019P40Z	31
019P40Z	143
019P4ZX	31
019P4ZZ	31, 143
019Q00Z	31
019Q0ZX	31, 272, 652, 859
019Q0ZZ	31
019Q40Z	31
019R00Z	31
019R0ZX	31, 272, 652, 859
019R0ZZ	31
019R40Z	31
019R4ZZ	31
01B00ZX	31, 272, 652, 859
01B00ZZ	31, 272, 652, 1043
01B03ZZ	31, 272, 652, 1043
01B04ZZ	31, 272, 652, 1043
01B10ZX	31, 272, 652, 859
01B10ZZ	31, 272, 652, 1043
01B13ZZ	31, 272, 652, 1043
01B14ZZ	31, 272, 652, 1043
01B20ZX	31, 272, 652, 859
01B20ZZ	31, 272, 652, 1043
01B23ZZ	31, 272, 652, 1043
01B24ZZ	31, 272, 652, 1043
01B30ZX	31, 272, 652, 859
01B30ZZ	31, 272, 652, 1043
01B33ZZ	31, 272, 652, 1043
01B34ZZ	31, 272, 652, 1043
01B40ZX	31, 272, 652, 859
01B40ZZ	31, 272, 652, 1043
01B43ZZ	31, 272, 652, 1044
01B44ZZ	31, 272, 652, 1044
01B50ZX	31, 272, 652, 859
01B50ZZ	31, 272, 652, 1044
01B53ZZ	31, 272, 652, 1044
01B54ZZ	31, 272, 652, 1044
01B60ZX	31, 272, 652, 859
01B63ZZ	31, 272, 652, 1044
01B64ZZ	31, 272, 652, 1044
01B80ZX	31, 272, 652, 859
01B80ZZ	31, 272, 652, 1044
01B83ZZ	31, 272, 652, 1044
01B84ZZ	31, 272, 652, 1044
01B90ZX	31, 272, 652, 859
01B90ZZ	31, 272, 652, 1044
01B93ZZ	31, 272, 652, 1044
01B94ZZ	31, 272, 652, 1044
01BA0ZX	31, 272, 652, 859
01BA0ZZ	31, 272, 652, 1044
01BA3ZZ	31, 272, 652, 1044
01BA4ZZ	31, 272, 652, 1044
01BB0ZX	31, 272, 652, 859
01BB0ZZ	31, 272, 652, 1044
01BB3ZZ	31, 272, 652, 1044
01BB4ZZ	31, 272, 652, 1044
01BC0ZX	31, 272, 652, 859
01BC0ZZ	31, 272, 652, 1044
01BC3ZZ	31, 272, 652, 1044
01BC4ZZ	31, 272, 652, 1044
01BD0ZX	31, 272, 652, 859
01BD0ZZ	31, 272, 652, 1044
01BD3ZZ	31, 272, 652, 1044
01BD4ZZ	31, 272, 652, 1044
01BF0ZX	31, 272, 653, 859
01BF0ZZ	31, 272, 652, 1044
01BF3ZZ	31, 272, 652, 1044
01BF4ZZ	31, 272, 652, 1044
01BG0ZX	31, 272, 653, 859
01BG0ZZ	31, 272, 652, 1044
01BG3ZZ	31, 272, 653, 1044
01BG4ZZ	31, 272, 652, 1044
01BH0ZX	31, 272, 653, 859
01BH0ZZ	31, 272, 653, 1044
01BH3ZZ	32, 272, 653, 1044
01BH4ZZ	32, 272, 653, 1044
01BK*	32
01BK0ZZ	71, 143
01BK3ZZ	71, 143
01BK4ZZ	71, 143
01BL*	32
01BL0ZZ	143
01BL3ZZ	143
01BL4ZZ	143
01BM*	32
01BM0ZZ	143
01BM3ZZ	143
01BM4ZZ	143
01BN*	32
01BN0ZZ	143, 1044
01BN3ZZ	143, 1044
01BN4ZZ	143, 1044
01BP*	32
01BP0ZZ	143, 537
01BP3ZZ	143, 537
01BP4ZZ	143, 537
01BQ0ZX	32, 272, 653, 859
01BQ0ZZ	32, 272, 653, 1044
01BQ3ZZ	32, 272, 653, 1044
01BQ4ZZ	32, 272, 653, 1044
01BR0ZX	32, 272, 653, 859
01BR0ZZ	32, 272, 653, 1044
01BR3ZZ	32, 272, 653, 1044
01BR4ZZ	32, 272, 653, 1044
01C*	32
01CK*	143
01CL*	143
01CM*	143
01CN*	143
01CP*	143
01D*	32
01D0*	272, 653
01D00ZZ	1044
01D04ZZ	1044
01D1*	272, 653
01D10ZZ	1044
01D13ZZ	1044
01D14ZZ	1044
01D2*	272, 653
01D20ZZ	1044
01D23ZZ	1044
01D24ZZ	1044
01D3*	272, 653
01D33ZZ	1044
01D34ZZ	1044
01D4*	272, 653
01D40ZZ	1044
01D43ZZ	1044
01D44ZZ	1044
01D5*	272, 653
01D50ZZ	1044
01D53ZZ	1044
01D54ZZ	1044
01D6*	272, 653
01D60ZZ	1044
01D63ZZ	1044
01D64ZZ	1044
01D8*	272, 653
01D80ZZ	1044
01D83ZZ	1044
01D84ZZ	1044
01D9*	272, 653
01D90ZZ	1044
01D93ZZ	1044
01D94ZZ	1044
01DA*	272, 653
01DA0ZZ	1044
01DA3ZZ	1044
01DA4ZZ	1044
01DB*	272, 653
01DB0ZZ	1044
01DB3ZZ	1044
01DB4ZZ	1044
01DC*	272, 653
01DC0ZZ	1044
01DC3ZZ	1044
01DC4ZZ	1044
01DD*	272, 653
01DD0ZZ	1044
01DD3ZZ	1044
01DD4ZZ	1044
01DF*	272, 653
01DF0ZZ	1044
01DF3ZZ	1044
01DF4ZZ	1044
01DG*	272, 653
01DG0ZZ	1044
01DG3ZZ	1044
01DG4ZZ	1044
01DH*	272, 653
01DH0ZZ	1044
01DH3ZZ	1044
01DH4ZZ	1044
01DK*	71, 143
01DL*	143
01DM*	143
01DN*	143
01DN0ZZ	1044
01DN3ZZ	1044
01DN4ZZ	1044
01DP*	143, 537
01DQ*	272, 653
01DQ0ZZ	1044
01DQ3ZZ	1044
01DQ4ZZ	1044
01DR*	272, 653
01DR0ZZ	1044
01DR3ZZ	1044
01DR4ZZ	1044
01HY0Z2	32
01HY0MZ	32, 42, 71, 124, 272, 509, 524, 537, 653, 859
01HY0YZ	32
01HY32Z	32
01HY3MZ	32, 42, 71, 124, 272, 509, 524, 537, 653, 859
01HY42Z	32
01HY4MZ	32, 42, 71, 124, 272, 509, 524, 537, 653, 859
01JY0ZZ	32
01JY4ZZ	32
01N*	32
01N0*	272, 653
01N00ZZ	859, 1044
01N03ZZ	859, 1044
01N04ZZ	859, 1044
01N1*	272, 653
01N10ZZ	859, 1044
01N13ZZ	859, 1044
01N14ZZ	859, 1044
01N2*	272, 653
01N20ZZ	859, 1044
01N23ZZ	859, 1044
01N24ZZ	859, 1044
01N3*	272, 653
01N30ZZ	859, 1044
01N33ZZ	859, 1044
01N34ZZ	859, 1044
01N4*	272, 653
01N40ZZ	859, 1044
01N43ZZ	859, 1044
01N44ZZ	859, 1044
01N5*	268
01N50ZZ	640, 859, 1044

Numeric Index to Procedures

Code	Page	Code	Page	Code	Page	Code	Page	Code	Page	Code	Page
01N53ZZ	640, 859, 1044	01Q8*	272, 653	01RD0JZ	32, 273, 653, 860	01U14KZ	273, 861	01UH0KZ	273, 861	021109C	116
01N54ZZ	640, 859, 1044	01Q80ZZ	860	01RD0KZ	32, 273, 653, 860	01U207Z	861	01UH37Z	861	021109F	116
01N6*	272, 653	01Q83ZZ	860	01RD47Z	32, 273, 653, 860	01U20JZ	273, 861	01UH3JZ	273, 861	021109W	116
01N60ZZ	859, 1044	01Q84ZZ	860	01RD4JZ	32, 273, 653, 860	01U20KZ	273, 861	01UH3KZ	273, 861	02110A3	116
01N63ZZ	859, 1044	01Q9*	272, 653	01RD4KZ	32, 273, 653, 860	01U237Z	861	01UH47Z	861	02110A8	116
01N64ZZ	859, 1044	01Q90ZZ	860	01RF07Z	32, 273, 653, 860	01U23JZ	273, 861	01UH4JZ	273, 861	02110A9	116
01N8*	272, 653	01Q93ZZ	860	01RF0JZ	32, 273, 653, 860	01U23KZ	273, 861	01UH4KZ	273, 861	02110AC	116
01N80ZZ	859, 1044	01Q94ZZ	860	01RF0KZ	32, 273, 653, 860	01U247Z	861	01UR07Z	861	02110AF	116
01N83ZZ	859, 1044	01QA*	272, 653	01RF47Z	32, 273, 653, 860	01U24JZ	273, 861	01UR0JZ	861	02110AW	116
01N84ZZ	859, 1044	01QA0ZZ	860	01RF4JZ	32, 273, 653, 860	01U24KZ	273, 861	01UR0KZ	861	02110J3	116
01N9*	272, 653	01QA3ZZ	860	01RF4KZ	32, 273, 653, 860	01U407Z	861	01UR37Z	861	02110J8	116
01N90ZZ	859, 1044	01QA4ZZ	860	01RG07Z	32, 273, 653, 860	01U40JZ	273, 861	01UR3JZ	861	02110J9	116
01N93ZZ	859, 1044	01QB*	272, 653	01RG0JZ	32, 273, 653, 860	01U40KZ	273, 861	01UR3KZ	861	02110JC	116
01N94ZZ	859, 1044	01QB0ZZ	860	01RG0KZ	32, 273, 653, 860	01U437Z	861	01UR47Z	861	02110JF	116
01NA*	272, 653	01QB3ZZ	860	01RG47Z	32, 273, 653, 860	01U43JZ	273, 861	01UR4JZ	861	02110JW	116
01NA0ZZ	859, 1044	01QB4ZZ	860	01RG4JZ	32, 273, 653, 860	01U43KZ	273, 861	01UR4KZ	861	02110K3	116
01NA3ZZ	859, 1044	01QC*	272, 653	01RG4KZ	32, 273, 653, 860	01U447Z	861	01WY00Z	32	02110K8	116
01NA4ZZ	859, 1044	01QC0ZZ	860	01RH07Z	32, 273, 653, 860	01U44JZ	273, 861	01WY02Z	32	02110K9	116
01NB*	272, 653	01QC3ZZ	860	01RH0JZ	32, 273, 653, 860	01U44KZ	273, 861	01WY07Z	32	02110KC	116
01NB0ZZ	859, 1044	01QC4ZZ	860	01RH0KZ	32, 273, 653, 860	01U507Z	861	01WY0MZ	32	02110KF	116
01NB3ZZ	859, 1044	01QD*	273, 653	01RH47Z	32, 273, 653, 860	01U50JZ	273, 861	01WY0YZ	32	02110KW	116
01NB4ZZ	859, 1044	01QD0ZZ	860	01RH4JZ	32, 273, 653, 860	01U50KZ	273, 861	01WY30Z	32	02110Z3	116
01NC*	272, 653	01QD3ZZ	860	01RH4KZ	32, 273, 653, 860	01U537Z	861	01WY32Z	32	02110Z8	116
01NC0ZZ	859, 1044	01QD4ZZ	860	01RR07Z	32, 653, 860	01U53JZ	273, 861	01WY37Z	32	02110Z9	116
01NC3ZZ	859, 1044	01QF*	273, 653	01RR0JZ	32, 653, 860	01U53KZ	273, 861	01WY3MZ	32	02110ZC	116
01NC4ZZ	859, 1044	01QF0ZZ	860	01RR0KZ	32, 653, 860	01U547Z	861	01WY40Z	32	02110ZF	116
01ND*	272, 653	01QF3ZZ	860	01RR47Z	32, 653, 860	01U54JZ	273, 861	01WY42Z	32	02113D4	111
01ND0ZZ	859, 1044	01QF4ZZ	860	01RR4JZ	32, 653, 860	01U54KZ	273, 861	01WY47Z	32	021148C	116
01ND3ZZ	859, 1044	01QG*	273, 653	01RR4KZ	32, 653, 860	01U607Z	861	01WY4MZ	32	021148F	116
01ND4ZZ	859, 1044	01QG0ZZ	860	01S*	32	01U60JZ	273, 861	01X*	32	021148W	116
01NF*	272, 653	01QG3ZZ	860	01S00ZZ	860	01U60KZ	273, 861	021008C	115	021149C	116
01NF0ZZ	859, 1044	01QG4ZZ	860	01S03ZZ	860	01U637Z	861	021008F	115	021149F	116
01NF3ZZ	859, 1044	01QH*	273, 653	01S04ZZ	860	01U63JZ	273, 861	021008W	115	021149W	116
01NF4ZZ	859, 1044	01QH0ZZ	860	01S10ZZ	860	01U63KZ	273, 861	021009C	115	02114A3	116
01NG*	257, 653	01QH3ZZ	860	01S13ZZ	860	01U647Z	861	021009F	115	02114A8	116
01NG0ZZ	859, 1044	01QH4ZZ	860	01S14ZZ	860	01U64JZ	273, 861	021009W	115	02114A9	116
01NG3ZZ	859, 1044	01QQ*	273, 653	01S20ZZ	860	01U64KZ	273, 861	02100A3	115	02114AC	116
01NG4ZZ	859, 1044	01QQ0ZZ	860	01S23ZZ	860	01U807Z	861	02100A8	115	02114AF	116
01NH*	272, 653	01QQ3ZZ	860	01S24ZZ	860	01U80JZ	273, 861	02100A9	116	02114AW	116
01NH0ZZ	859, 1044	01QQ4ZZ	860	01S30ZZ	860	01U80KZ	273, 861	02100AC	116	02114D4	111
01NH3ZZ	859, 1044	01QR*	653	01S33ZZ	860	01U837Z	861	02100AF	116	02114J3	116
01NH4ZZ	859, 1044	01QR0ZZ	860	01S34ZZ	860	01U83JZ	273, 861	02100AW	116	02114J8	116
01NQ*	272, 653	01QR3ZZ	860	01S40ZZ	860	01U83KZ	273, 861	02100J3	116	02114J9	116
01NQ0ZZ	859, 1044	01QR4ZZ	860	01S43ZZ	860	01U847Z	861	02100J8	116	02114JC	116
01NQ3ZZ	859, 1044	01R107Z	32, 273, 653, 860	01S44ZZ	860	01U84JZ	273, 861	02100J9	116	02114JF	116
01NQ4ZZ	860, 1044	01R10JZ	32, 273, 653, 860	01S50ZZ	860	01U84KZ	273, 861	02100JC	116	02114JW	116
01NR*	272, 653	01R10KZ	32, 273, 653, 860	01S53ZZ	860	01UB07Z	861	02100JF	116	02114K3	116
01NR0ZZ	860, 1044	01R147Z	32, 273, 653, 860	01S54ZZ	860	01UB0JZ	273, 861	02100JW	116	02114K8	116
01NR3ZZ	860, 1044	01R14JZ	32, 273, 653, 860	01S60ZZ	860	01UB0KZ	273, 861	02100K3	116	02114K9	116
01NR4ZZ	860, 1044	01R14KZ	32, 273, 653, 860	01S63ZZ	860	01UB37Z	861	02100K8	116	02114KC	116
01PY00Z	32	01R207Z	32, 273, 653, 860	01S64ZZ	860	01UB3JZ	273, 861	02100K9	116	02114KF	116
01PY02Z	32	01R20JZ	32, 273, 653, 860	01S80ZZ	860	01UB3KZ	273, 861	02100KC	116	02114KW	116
01PY07Z	32	01R20KZ	32, 273, 653, 860	01S83ZZ	860	01UB47Z	861	02100KF	116	02114Z3	116
01PY0MZ	32, 71, 272, 524, 537, 653, 860	01R247Z	32, 273, 653, 860	01S84ZZ	860	01UB4JZ	273, 861	02100KW	116	02114Z8	116
01PY0YZ	32	01R24JZ	32, 273, 653, 860	01S90ZZ	860	01UB4KZ	273, 861	02100Z3	116	02114Z9	116
01PY37Z	32	01R24KZ	32, 273, 653, 860	01S93YZ	860	01UC07Z	861	02100Z8	116	02114ZC	116
01PY3MZ	32, 71, 272, 524, 537, 653, 860	01R407Z	32, 273, 653, 860	01S94ZZ	860	01UC0JZ	273, 861	02100Z9	116	02114ZF	116
01PY40Z	32	01R40JZ	32, 273, 653, 860	01SA0ZZ	860	01UC0KZ	273, 861	02100ZC	116	021208C	116
01PY42Z	32	01R40KZ	32, 273, 653, 860	01SA3ZZ	860	01UC37Z	861	02100ZF	116	021208F	116
01PY47Z	32	01R447Z	32, 273, 653, 860	01SA4ZZ	860	01UC3JZ	273, 861	02103D4	111	021208W	116
01PY4MZ	32, 71, 272, 524, 537, 653, 860	01R44JZ	32, 273, 653, 860	01SB0ZZ	860	01UC3KZ	273, 861	021048C	116	021209C	116
01Q*	32	01R44KZ	32, 273, 653, 860	01SB3ZZ	860	01UC47Z	861	021048F	116	021209F	116
01Q0*	272, 653	01R507Z	32, 273, 653, 860	01SB4ZZ	860	01UC4JZ	273, 861	021048W	116	021209W	116
01Q00ZZ	860	01R50JZ	32, 273, 653, 860	01SC0ZZ	860	01UC4KZ	273, 861	021049C	116	02120A3	116
01Q03ZZ	860	01R50KZ	32, 273, 653, 860	01SC3ZZ	860	01UD07Z	861	021049F	116	02120A8	116
01Q04ZZ	860	01R547Z	32, 273, 653, 860	01SC4ZZ	861	01UD0JZ	273, 861	021049W	116	02120A9	116
01Q1*	272, 653	01R54JZ	32, 273, 653, 860	01SD0ZZ	861	01UD0KZ	273, 861	02104A3	116	02120AC	116
01Q10ZZ	860	01R54KZ	32, 273, 653, 860	01SD3ZZ	861	01UD37Z	861	02104A8	116	02120AF	116
01Q13ZZ	860	01R607Z	32, 273, 653, 860	01SD4ZZ	861	01UD3JZ	273, 861	02104A9	116	02120AW	116
01Q14ZZ	860	01R60JZ	32, 273, 653, 860	01SF0ZZ	861	01UD3KZ	273, 861	02104AC	116	02120J3	116
01Q2*	272, 653	01R60KZ	32, 273, 653, 860	01SF3ZZ	861	01UD47Z	861	02104AF	116	02120J8	116
01Q20ZZ	860	01R647Z	32, 273, 653, 860	01SF4ZZ	861	01UD4JZ	273, 861	02104AW	116	02120J9	116
01Q23ZZ	860	01R64JZ	32, 273, 653, 860	01SG0ZZ	861	01UD4KZ	273, 861	02104D4	111	02120JC	116
01Q24ZZ	860	01R64KZ	32, 273, 653, 860	01SG3ZZ	861	01UF07Z	861	02104J3	116	02120JW	116
01Q3*	272, 653	01R807Z	32, 273, 653, 860	01SG4ZZ	861	01UF0JZ	273, 861	02104J8	116	02120K3	116
01Q30ZZ	860	01R80JZ	32, 273, 653, 860	01SH0ZZ	861	01UF0KZ	273, 861	02104J9	116	02120K8	116
01Q33ZZ	860	01R80KZ	32, 273, 653, 860	01SH3ZZ	861	01UF37Z	861	02104JC	116	02120K9	116
01Q34ZZ	860	01R847Z	32, 273, 653, 860	01SH4ZZ	861	01UF3JZ	273, 861	02104JF	116	02120KC	116
01Q4*	272, 653	01R84JZ	32, 273, 653, 860	01SQ0ZZ	861	01UF3KZ	273, 861	02104JW	116	02120KF	116
01Q40ZZ	860	01R84KZ	32, 273, 653, 860	01SQ3ZZ	861	01UF47Z	861	02104K3	116	02120KW	116
01Q43ZZ	860	01RB07Z	32, 273, 653, 860	01SQ4ZZ	861	01UF4JZ	273, 861	02104K8	116	02120Z3	116
01Q44ZZ	860	01RB0JZ	32, 273, 653, 860	01SR0ZZ	861	01UF4KZ	273, 861	02104K9	116	02120Z8	116
01Q5*	272, 653	01RB0KZ	32, 273, 653, 860	01SR3ZZ	861	01UG07Z	861	02104KC	116	02120Z9	116
01Q50ZZ	860	01RB47Z	32, 273, 653, 860	01SR4ZZ	861	01UG0JZ	273, 861	02104KF	116	02120ZC	116
01Q53ZZ	860	01RB4JZ	32, 273, 653, 860	01U*	32, 653	01UG0KZ	273, 861	02104KW	116	02120ZF	116
01Q54ZZ	860	01RB4KZ	32, 273, 653, 860	01U107Z	861	01UG37Z	861	02104Z3	116	02123D4	111
01Q6*	272, 653	01RC07Z	32, 273, 653, 860	01U10JZ	273, 861	01UG3JZ	273, 861	02104Z8	116	021248C	116
01Q60ZZ	860	01RC0JZ	32, 273, 653, 860	01U10KZ	273, 861	01UG3KZ	273, 861	02104Z9	116	021248F	116
01Q63ZZ	860	01RC47Z	32, 273, 653, 860	01U137Z	861	01UG47Z	861	02104ZC	116	021248W	116
01Q64ZZ	860	01RC4JZ	32, 273, 653, 860	01U13JZ	273, 861	01UG4JZ	273, 861	02104ZF	116	021249C	116
		01RC4KZ	32, 273, 653, 860	01U13KZ	273, 861	01UG4KZ	273, 861	021108C	116	021249F	116
		01RD07Z	32, 273, 653, 860	01U147Z	861	01UH07Z	861	021108F	116	021249W	116
				01U14JZ	273, 861	01UH0JZ	273, 861	021108W	116		

Code	Page	Code	Page	Code	Page	Code	Page	Code	Page	Code	Page
02124A3	116	02160JP	111	02174KS	111, 654, 861	021L4KP	112	021R0JA	95, 124, 654, 862	021V4KU	112, 654, 862
02124A8	117	02160JQ	111	02174KT	111, 654, 861	021L4KQ	112	021R0JB	95, 124, 654, 862	021V4ZP	150
02124A9	117	02160JR	111	02174KU	111, 654, 861	021L4KR	112	021R0JD	95, 124, 654, 862	021V4ZQ	150
02124AC	117	02160KP	111	02174ZP	111	021L4Z5	112	021R0KA	95, 124, 654, 862	021V4ZR	150
02124AF	117	02160KQ	111	02174ZQ	111	021L4Z8	112	021R0KB	95, 124, 654, 862	021V4ZS	112, 654, 862
02124AW	117	02160KR	111	02174ZR	111	021L4Z9	112	021R0KD	95, 124, 654, 862	021V4ZT	112, 654, 862
02124D4	111	02160Z7	150, 653	02174ZS	111, 654, 861	021L4ZC	112	021R0ZA	95, 124, 654, 862	021V4ZU	112, 654, 862
02124J3	117	02160ZP	111	02174ZT	111, 654, 861	021L4ZF	112	021R0ZB	95, 124, 654, 862	021W08A	23, 150, 654, 862
02124J8	117	02160ZQ	111	02174ZU	111, 654, 861	021L4ZP	112	021R0ZD	95, 124, 654, 862	021W08B	23, 150, 654, 862
02124J9	117	02160ZR	111	021K08P	111	021L4ZQ	112	021R48A	95, 124, 654, 862	021W08D	23, 150, 654, 862
02124JC	117	02163Z7	150, 653	021K08Q	111	021L4ZR	112	021R48B	95, 124, 654, 862	021W08F	150
02124JF	117	021648P	111	021K08R	111	021L4ZW	112	021R48D	95, 124, 654, 862	021W08G	23, 150, 654, 862
02124JW	117	021648Q	111	021K09P	111	021P08A	95, 124, 654, 861	021R49A	95, 124, 654, 862	021W08H	23, 150, 654, 862
02124K3	117	021648R	111	021K09Q	111	021P08B	95, 124, 654, 861	021R49B	95, 124, 654, 862	021W08P	150
02124K8	117	021649P	111	021K09R	111	021P08D	95, 124, 654, 862	021R49D	95, 124, 654, 862	021W08Q	
02124K9	117	021649Q	111	021K0AP	111	021P09A	95, 124, 654, 862	021R4AA	95, 124, 654, 862	021W08R	150
02124KC	117	021649R	111	021K0AQ	111	021P09B	95, 124, 654, 862	021R4AB	95, 124, 654, 862	021W08V	150
02124KF	117	02164AP	111	021K0AR	111	021P09D	95, 124, 654, 862	021R4AD	95, 124, 654, 862	021W09A	23, 150, 654, 862
02124KW	117	02164AQ	111	021K0JP	111	021P0AA	95, 124, 654, 862	021R4JA	95, 124, 654, 862	021W09B	23, 150, 655, 862
02124Z3	117	02164AR	111	021K0JQ	111	021P0AB	95, 124, 654, 862	021R4JB	95, 124, 654, 862	021W09D	23, 150, 654, 862
02124Z8	117	02164JP	111	021K0JR	111	021P0AD	95, 124, 654, 862	021R4JD	95, 124, 654, 862	021W09F	150
02124Z9	117	02164JQ	111	021K0KP	111	021P0JA	95, 124, 654, 862	021R4KA	95, 124, 654, 862	021W09G	23, 150, 655, 862
02124ZC	117	02164JR	111	021K0KQ	111	021P0JB	95, 124, 654, 862	021R4KB	95, 124, 654, 862	021W09H	23, 150, 655, 862
02124ZF	117	02164KP	111	021K0KR	111	021P0JD	95, 124, 654, 862	021R4KD	95, 124, 654, 862	021W09P	150
021308C	117	02164KQ	111	021K0Z5	111	021P0KA	95, 124, 654, 862	021R4ZA	95, 124, 654, 862	021W09Q	150
021308F	117	02164KR	111	021K0Z8	111	021P0KB	95, 124, 654, 862	021R4ZB	95, 124, 654, 862	021W09R	150
021308W	117	02164Z7	150, 653	021K0Z9	112	021P0KD	95, 124, 654, 862	021R4ZD	95, 124, 654, 862	021W09V	150
021309C	117	02164ZP	111	021K0ZC	112	021P0ZA	95, 124, 654, 862	021V08P	150	021W0AA	23, 150, 655, 862
021309F	117	02164ZQ	111	021K0ZF	112	021P0ZB	95, 124, 654, 862	021V08Q	150	021W0AB	23, 150, 655, 862
021309W	117	02164ZR	111	021K0ZP	112	021P0ZD	95, 124, 654, 862	021V08R	150	021W0AD	23, 150, 655, 862
02130A3	117	021708P	111	021K0ZQ	112	021P48A	95, 124, 654, 862	021V08S	112, 654, 862	021W0AF	150
02130A8	117	021708Q	111	021K0ZR	112	021P48B	95, 124, 654, 862	021V08T	112, 654, 862	021W0AG	23, 150, 655, 862
02130A9	117	021708R	111	021K0ZW	112	021P48D	95, 124, 654, 862	021V09P	150	021W0AH	23, 150, 655, 862
02130AC	117	021708S	111, 653, 861	021K48P	112	021P49A	95, 124, 654, 862	021V09Q	150	021W0AP	150
02130AF	117	021708T	111, 653, 861	021K48Q	112	021P49B	95, 124, 654, 862	021V09R	150	021W0AQ	150
02130AW	117	021708U	111, 653, 861	021K48R	112	021P49D	95, 124, 654, 862	021V09S	112, 654, 862	021W0AR	150
02130J3	117	021709P	111	021K49P	112	021P4AA	95, 124, 654, 862	021V09T	112, 654, 862	021W0AV	150
02130J8	117	021709Q	111	021K49Q	112	021P4AB	95, 124, 654, 862	021V09U	112, 654, 862	021W0JA	23, 150, 655, 862
02130J9	117	021709R	111	021K49R	112	021P4AD	95, 124, 654, 862	021V0AP	150	021W0JB	23, 150, 655, 862
02130JC	117	021709S	111, 653, 861	021K4AP	112	021P4JA	95, 124, 654, 862	021V0AQ	150	021W0JD	23, 150, 655, 862
02130JF	117	021709T	111, 653, 861	021K4AQ	112	021P4JB	95, 124, 654, 862	021V0AR	150	021W0JF	150
02130JW	117	021709U	111, 653, 861	021K4AR	112	021P4JD	95, 124, 654, 862	021V0AS	112, 654, 862	021W0JG	23, 150, 655, 862
02130K3	117	02170AP	111	021K4JP	112	021P4KA	95, 124, 654, 862	021V0AT	112, 654, 862	021W0JH	23, 150, 655, 862
02130K8	117	02170AQ	111	021K4JQ	112	021P4KB	95, 124, 654, 862	021V0AU	112, 654, 862	021W0JP	150
02130K9	117	02170AR	111	021K4JR	112	021P4KD	95, 124, 654, 862	021V0JP	150	021W0JQ	150
02130KC	117	02170AS	111, 653, 861	021K4KP	112	021P4ZA	95, 124, 654, 862	021V0JQ	150	021W0JR	150
02130KF	117	02170AT	111, 653, 861	021K4KQ	112	021P4ZB	95, 124, 654, 862	021V0JR	150	021W0JV	150
02130KW	117	02170AU	111, 653, 861	021K4KR	112	021P4ZD	95, 124, 654, 862	021V0JS	112, 654, 862	021W0KA	23, 150, 655, 862
02130Z3	117	02170JP	111	021K4ZW	112	021Q08A	95, 124, 654, 862	021V0JT	112, 654, 862	021W0KB	23, 150, 655, 862
02130Z8	117	02170JQ	111	021K4Z5	112	021Q08B	95, 124, 654, 862	021V0JU	112, 654, 862	021W0KD	23, 150, 655, 862
02130Z9	117	02170JR	111	021K4Z9	112	021Q08D	95, 124, 654, 862	021V0KP	150	021W0KF	150
02130ZC	117	02170JS	111, 653, 861	021K4ZC	112	021Q09A	95, 124, 654, 862	021V0KQ	150	021W0KG	23, 150, 655, 862
02130ZF	117	02170JT	111, 653, 861	021K4ZF	112	021Q09B	95, 124, 654, 862	021V0KR	150	021W0KH	23, 150, 655, 862
02133D4	111	02170JU	111, 653, 861	021K4ZP	112	021Q09D	95, 124, 654, 862	021V0KS	112, 654, 862	021W0KP	150
021348C	117	02170KP	111	021K4ZQ	112	021Q0AA	95, 124, 654, 862	021V0KT	112, 654, 862	021W0KQ	150
021348F	117	02170KQ	111	021K4ZR	112	021Q0AB	95, 124, 654, 862	021V0KU	112, 654, 862	021W0KR	150
021348W	117	02170KR	111	021L08P	112	021Q0AD	95, 124, 654, 862	021V0ZP	150	021W0KV	150
021349C	117	02170KS	111, 654, 861	021L08Q	112	021Q0JA	95, 124, 654, 862	021V0ZQ	150	021W0ZA	23, 150, 655, 862
021349F	117	02170KT	111, 654, 861	021L08R	112	021Q0JB	95, 124, 654, 862	021V0ZR	150	021W0ZB	23, 150, 655, 862
021349W	117	02170KU	111, 654, 861	021L09P	112	021Q0JD	95, 124, 654, 862	021V0ZS	112, 654, 862	021W0ZD	23, 150, 655, 862
02134A3	117	02170ZP	111	021L09Q	112	021Q0KA	95, 124, 654, 862	021V0ZT	112, 654, 862	021W0ZP	150
02134A8	117	02170ZQ	111	021L09R	112	021Q0KB	95, 124, 654, 862	021V0ZU	112, 654, 862	021W0ZQ	150
02134A9	117	02170ZR	111	021L0AP	112	021Q0KD	95, 124, 654, 862	021V48P	150	021W0ZR	150
02134AC	117	02170ZS	111, 654, 861	021L0AQ	112	021Q0ZA	95, 124, 654, 862	021V48Q	150	021W48A	23, 150, 655, 862
02134AF	117	02170ZT	111, 654, 861	021L0AR	112	021Q0ZB	95, 124, 654, 862	021V48R	150	021W48B	23, 150, 655, 862
02134AW	117	02170ZU	111, 654, 861	021L0JP	112	021Q0ZD	95, 124, 654, 862	021V48S	112, 654, 862	021W48D	23, 150, 655, 862
02134D4	111	021748P	111	021L0JQ	112	021Q48A	95, 124, 654, 862	021V48T	112, 654, 862	021W48P	150
02134J3	117	021748Q	111	021L0JR	112	021Q48B	95, 124, 654, 862	021V48U	654, 862	021W48Q	150
02134J8	117	021748R	111	021L0KP	112	021Q48D	95, 124, 654, 862	021V49P	150	021W48R	150
02134J9	117	021748S	111, 654, 861	021L0KQ	112	021Q49A	95, 124, 654, 862	021V49Q	150	021W49A	23, 150, 655, 862
02134JC	117	021748T	111, 654, 861	021L0KR	112	021Q49D	95, 124, 654, 862	021V49R	150	021W49B	23, 150, 655, 863
02134JF	117	021748U	111, 654, 861	021L0Z5	112	021Q4AA	95, 124, 654, 862	021V49S	112, 654, 862	021W49D	23, 150, 655, 863
02134JW	117	021749P	111	021L0Z8	112	021Q4AB	95, 124, 654, 862	021V49T	112, 654, 862	021W49P	150
02134K3	117	021749Q	111	021L0Z9	112	021Q4AD	95, 124, 654, 862	021V49U	112, 654, 862	021W49Q	150
02134K8	117	021749R	111	021L0ZC	112	021Q4JA	95, 124, 654, 862	021V4AP	150	021W49R	150
02134K9	117	021749S	111, 654, 861	021L0ZF	112	021Q4JB	95, 124, 654, 862	021V4AQ	150	021W4AA	23, 150, 655, 863
02134KC	117	021749T	111, 654, 861	021L0ZP	112	021Q4JD	95, 124, 654, 862	021V4AR	150	021W4AB	23, 150, 655, 863
02134KF	117	021749U	111, 654, 861	021L0ZQ	112	021Q4KA	95, 124, 654, 862	021V4AS	112, 654, 862	021W4AD	23, 150, 655, 863
02134KW	117	02174AP	111	021L0ZR	112	021Q4KB	95, 124, 654, 862	021V4AT	112, 654, 862	021W4AP	150
02134Z3	117	02174AQ	111	021L0ZW	112	021Q4KD	95, 124, 654, 862	021V4AU	112, 654, 862	021W4AQ	150
02134Z8	117	02174AR	111	021L48P	112	021Q4ZA	95, 124, 654, 862	021V4JP	150	021W4AR	150
02134Z9	117	02174AS	111, 654, 861	021L48Q	112	021Q4ZB	95, 124, 654, 862	021V4JQ	150	021W4JA	23, 150, 655, 863
02134ZC	117	02174AT	111, 654, 861	021L48R	112	021Q4ZD	95, 124, 654, 862	021V4JR	150	021W4JB	23, 150, 655, 863
02134ZF	117	02174AU	111, 654, 861	021L49P	112	021R08A	95, 124, 654, 862	021V4JS	112, 654, 862	021W4JD	23, 150, 655, 863
021608P	111	02174JP	111	021L49Q	112	021R08B	95, 124, 654, 862	021V4JT	112, 654, 862	021W4JP	150
021608Q	111	02174JQ	111	021L49R	112	021R08D	95, 124, 654, 862	021V4JU	112, 654, 862	021W4JQ	150
021608R	111	02174JR	111	021L4AP	112	021R09A	95, 124, 654, 862	021V4KP	150	021W4JR	150
021609P	111	02174JS	111	021L4AQ	112	021R09B	95, 124, 654, 862	021V4KQ	150	021W4KA	23, 150, 655, 863
021609Q	111	02174JT	111, 654, 861	021L4AR	112	021R09D	95, 124, 654, 862	021V4KR	150	021W4KB	23, 150, 655, 863
021609R	111	02174JU	111, 654, 861	021L4JP	112	021R0AA	95, 124, 654, 862	021V4KS	112, 654, 862	021W4KD	23, 150, 655, 863
02160AP	111	02174KP	111	021L4JQ	112	021R0AB	95, 124, 654, 862	021V4KT	112, 654, 862	021W4KP	150
02160AQ	111	02174KQ	111	021L4JR	112	021R0AD	95, 124, 654, 862			021W4KQ	150
02160AR	111	02174KR	111									021W4KR	151

Numeric Index to Procedures

Code	Page	Code	Page	Code	Page	Code	Page	Code	Page	Code	Page
021W4ZA	23, 151, 655, 863	02573ZZ	166	02703D6	117, 119, 121, 122, 123	02713ZZ	117, 123	027306Z	113	027J3DZ	118, 166
021W4ZB	23, 151, 655, 863	02574ZK	166	02703DZ	117, 119, 121, 122, 123	027144Z	117, 120, 121, 122	027307Z	113	027J3ZZ	118, 166
021W4ZD	23, 151, 655, 863	02574ZZ	112	02703E6	117, 119, 121, 122, 123	027145Z	117, 120, 121, 122	02730D6	113	027J44Z	118, 166
021W4ZP	151	02580ZZ	112			027146Z	117, 120, 121, 122	02730DZ	113	027J4DZ	118, 166
021W4ZQ	151	02583ZZ	166	02703EZ	117, 119, 121, 122, 123	027147Z	117, 120, 121, 122	02730E6	113	027J4ZZ	118, 166
021W4ZR	151	02584ZZ	112	02703F6	117, 119, 121, 122, 123	02714D6	117, 120, 121, 122, 123	02730EZ	113	027K*	655
021X08A	23, 151, 655, 863	02590ZZ	112			02714DZ	117, 120, 121, 122, 123	02730F6	113	027K04Z	151
021X08B	23, 151, 655, 863	02593ZZ	166	02703FZ	117, 119, 121, 122, 123			02730FZ	113	027K0DZ	151
021X08D	23, 151, 655, 863	02594ZZ	112	02703G6	117, 119, 121, 122, 123	02714E6	117, 120, 121, 122, 123	02730G6	113	027K0ZZ	151
021X08P	151	025D0ZZ	112			02714EZ	117, 120, 121, 122, 123	02730GZ	113	027K34Z	151
021X08Q	151	025D3ZZ	112	02703GZ	117, 119, 121, 122, 123	02714F6	117, 120, 121, 122, 123	02730T6	113	027K3DZ	151
021X08R	151	025D4ZZ	112					02730TZ	113	027K3ZZ	151
021X09A	23, 151, 655, 863	025F0ZZ	112	02703T6	117, 119, 121, 122, 123	02714FZ	117, 120, 121, 122, 123	02730Z6	113	027K44Z	151
021X09B	23, 151, 655, 863	025F3ZZ	166			02714G6	117, 120, 121, 122, 123	02730ZZ	113	027K4DZ	151
021X09D	23, 151, 655, 863	025F4ZZ	112	02703TZ	117, 119, 121, 122, 123			027334Z	118, 120, 121, 122	027K4ZZ	151
021X09P	151	025G0ZZ	112			02714GZ	117, 120, 121, 122, 123	027335Z	118, 120, 121, 122	027L04Z	151, 655
021X09Q	151	025G3ZZ	166	02703Z6	117, 123			027336Z	118, 120, 121, 122	027L0DZ	151, 655
021X09R	151	025G4ZZ	112	02703ZZ	117, 123	02714T6	117, 120, 121, 122, 123	027337Z	118, 120, 121, 122	027L0ZZ	151, 655
021X0AA	23, 151, 655, 863	025H0ZZ	112	027044Z	117, 119, 120, 121, 122			02733D6	118, 120, 121, 122, 123	027L34Z	151, 655
021X0AB	23, 151, 655, 863	025H3ZZ	166			02714TZ	117, 120, 121, 122, 123			027L3DZ	151, 655
021X0AD	23, 151, 655, 863	025H4ZZ	112	027045Z	117, 119, 120, 121, 122	02714Z6	117, 123	02733DZ	118, 120, 121, 122, 123	027L3ZZ	151, 655
021X0AP	151	025J0ZZ	112			02714ZZ	117, 123			027L44Z	151, 655
021X0AQ	151	025J3ZZ	166	027046Z	117, 119, 120, 121, 122	027204Z	113	02733E6	118, 120, 121, 122, 123	027L4DZ	151, 655
021X0AR	151	025J4ZZ	112			027205Z	113			027L4ZZ	151, 655
021X0JA	23, 151, 655, 863	025K0ZZ	112	027047Z	117, 119, 120, 121, 122	027206Z	113	02733EZ	118, 120, 121, 122, 123	027P*	124
021X0JB	23, 151, 655, 863	025K3ZZ	166			027207Z	113			027Q*	124
021X0JD	23, 151, 655, 863	025K4ZZ	112	02704D6	117, 119, 121, 122, 123	02720D6	113	02733F6	118, 120, 121, 122, 123	027R04T	151, 655
021X0JP	151	025L0ZZ	112			02720DZ	113			027R04Z	124
021X0JQ	151	025L3ZZ	166	02704DZ	117, 119, 121, 122, 123	02720E6	113	02733FZ	118, 120, 121, 122, 123	027R0DT	151, 655
021X0JR	151	025L4ZZ	112			02720EZ	113			027R0DZ	124
021X0KA	23, 151, 655, 863	025M0ZZ	112	02704E6	117, 119, 121, 122, 123	02720F6	113	02733G6	118, 120, 122, 123	027R0ZT	151, 655
021X0KB	23, 151, 655, 863	025M3ZZ	166			02720FZ	113	02733GZ	118, 120, 122, 123	027R0ZZ	124
021X0KD	23, 151, 655, 863	025M4ZZ	112	02704EZ	117, 119, 121, 122, 123	02720G6	113	02733T6	118, 120, 121, 122, 123	027R34T	151, 655
021X0KP	151	025N*	89, 655			02720GZ	113			027R34Z	124
021X0KQ	151	025N0ZZ	151, 583, 608, 863	02704F6	117, 119, 121, 122, 123	02720T6	113	02733TZ	118, 120, 121, 122, 123	027R3DT	151, 655
021X0KR	151	025N3ZZ	151, 583, 608, 863			02720TZ	113			027R3DZ	124
021X0ZA	23, 151, 655, 863	025N4ZZ	151, 583, 609, 863	02704FZ	117, 119, 121, 122, 123	02720Z6	113	02733Z6	118, 123	027R3ZT	151, 655
021X0ZB	23, 151, 655, 863	025P*	89			02720ZZ	113	02733ZZ	118, 123	027R3ZZ	124
021X0ZD	23, 151, 655, 863	025P0ZZ	151	02704G6	117, 119, 121, 122, 123	027234Z	118, 120, 121, 122	027344Z	118, 120, 121, 122	027R44T	151, 655
021X0ZP	151	025P3ZZ	151			027235Z	118, 120, 121, 122	027345Z	118, 120, 121, 122	027R44Z	124
021X0ZQ	151	025P4ZZ	151	02704GZ	117, 119, 121, 122, 123	027236Z	118, 120, 121, 122	027346Z	118, 120, 121, 122	027R4DT	151, 655
021X0ZR	151	025Q*	89			027237Z	118, 120, 121, 122	027347Z	118, 120, 121, 122	027R4DZ	124
021X48A	23, 151, 655, 863	025Q0ZZ	151	02704T6	117, 119, 121, 122, 123	02723D6	118, 120, 121, 122, 123	02734D6	118, 120, 121, 122, 123	027R4ZT	151, 655
021X48B	23, 151, 655, 863	025Q3ZZ	151							027R4ZZ	124
021X48D	23, 151, 655, 863	025Q4ZZ	151	02704TZ	117, 119, 121, 122, 123	02723DZ	118, 120, 121, 122, 123	02734DZ	118, 120, 121, 122, 123	027S*	124
021X48P	151	025R*	89							027T*	124
021X48Q	151	025R0ZZ	151	02704Z6	117, 123	02723E6	118, 120, 121, 122, 123	02734E6	118, 120, 121, 122, 123	027V*	124
021X48R	151	025R3ZZ	151	02704ZZ	117, 123					027W*	124
021X49A	23, 151, 655, 863	025R4ZZ	151	027104Z	112	02723EZ	118, 120, 121, 122, 123	02734EZ	118, 120, 121, 122, 123	027X04Z	124
021X49B	23, 151, 655, 863	025S*	89	027105Z	112					027X0DZ	124
021X49D	23, 151, 655, 863	025S0ZZ	151	027106Z	112	02723F6	118, 120, 121, 122, 123	02734F6	118, 120, 121, 122, 123	027X34Z	124
021X49P	151	025S3ZZ	151	027107Z	112					027X3DZ	124
021X49Q	151	025S4ZZ	151	02710D6	113	02723FZ	118, 120, 121, 122, 123	02734FZ	118, 120, 121, 122, 123	027X3ZZ	124
021X49R	151	025T*	89	02710DZ	113					027X44Z	124
021X4AA	23, 151, 655, 863	025T0ZZ	151	02710E6	113	02723G6	118, 120, 122, 123	02734G6	118, 120, 122, 123	027X4DZ	124
021X4AB	23, 151, 655, 863	025T3ZZ	151	02710EZ	113	02723GZ	118, 120, 122, 123	02734GZ	118, 120, 122, 123	027X4ZZ	124
021X4AD	23, 151, 655, 863	025T4ZZ	151	02710F6	113	02723T6	118, 120, 121, 122, 123	02734T6	118, 120, 121, 122, 123	02880ZZ	151
021X4AP	151	025V*	89	02710FZ	113					02883ZZ	151
021X4AQ	151	025V0ZZ	151	02710G6	113	02723TZ	118, 120, 121, 122, 123	02734TZ	118, 120, 121, 122, 123	02884ZZ	151
021X4AR	151	025V3ZZ	151	02710GZ	113					02890ZZ	113
021X4JA	23, 151, 655, 863	025V4ZZ	151	02710T6	113	02723Z6	118, 123	02734Z6	118, 123	02893ZZ	113
021X4JB	23, 151, 655, 863	025W*	89	02710TZ	113	02723ZZ	118, 123	02734ZZ	118, 123	02894ZZ	113
021X4JD	23, 151, 655, 863	025W0ZZ	151	02710Z6	113	027244Z	118, 120, 121, 122	027F04Z	108	028D0ZZ	113
021X4JP	151	025W3ZZ	151	02710ZZ	113	027245Z	118, 120, 121, 122	027F0DZ	108	028D3ZZ	113
021X4JQ	151	025W4ZZ	151	027134Z	117, 120, 121, 122	027246Z	118, 120, 121, 122	027F0ZZ	108	028D4ZZ	113
021X4JR	151	025X0ZZ	89, 151	027135Z	117, 120, 121, 122	027247Z	118, 120, 121, 122	027F34Z	118, 166	02B40ZZ	113
021X4KA	23, 151, 655, 863	025X3ZZ	89, 151	027136Z	117, 120, 121, 122	02724D6	118, 120, 121, 122, 123	027F3DZ	118, 166	02B43ZZ	113
021X4KB	23, 151, 655, 863	025X4ZZ	89, 151	027137Z	117, 120, 121, 122			027F3ZZ	118, 166	02B44ZZ	113
021X4KD	23, 151, 655, 863	027004Z	112	02713D6	117, 120, 121, 122, 123	02724DZ	118, 120, 121, 122, 123	027F44Z	118, 166	02B50ZZ	113
021X4KP	151	027005Z	112					027F4DZ	118, 166	02B53ZZ	166
021X4KQ	151	027006Z	112	02713DZ	117, 120, 121, 122, 123	02724E6	118, 120, 121, 122, 123	027F4ZZ	118, 166	02B54ZZ	113
021X4KR	151	027007Z	112			02724EZ	118, 120, 121, 122, 123	027G04Z	108	02B60ZZ	113
021X4ZA	23, 151, 655, 863	02700D6	112	02713E6	117, 120, 121, 122, 123			027G0DZ	108	02B63ZZ	166
021X4ZB	23, 151, 655, 863	02700DZ	112			02724F6	118, 120, 121, 122, 123	027G0ZZ	108	02B64ZZ	113
021X4ZD	23, 151, 655, 863	02700E6	112	02713EZ	117, 120, 121, 122, 123			027G34Z	118, 166	02B70ZK	124
021X4ZP	151	02700EZ	112			02724FZ	118, 120, 121, 122, 123	027G3DZ	118, 166	02B70ZZ	113
021X4ZQ	151	02700F6	112	02713F6	117, 120, 121, 122, 123			027G44Z	118, 166	02B73ZK	166
021X4ZR	151	02700FZ	112			02724G6	118, 120, 122, 123	027G4DZ	118, 166	02B73ZZ	113
024F*	108	02700G6	112	02713FZ	117, 120, 121, 122, 123	02724GZ	118, 120, 122, 123	027G4ZZ	118, 166	02B74ZK	166
024G*	108	02700GZ	112			02724T6	118, 120, 121, 122, 123	027H04Z	108	02B74ZZ	113
024J*	108	02700T6	112	02713G6	117, 120, 121, 122, 123			027H0DZ	108	02B80ZZ	113
02540ZZ	112	02700TZ	112			02724TZ	118, 120, 121, 122, 123	027H0ZZ	108	02B83ZZ	166
02543ZZ	112	02700Z6	112	02713GZ	117, 120, 121, 122, 123			027H34Z	118, 166	02B84ZZ	113
02544ZZ	112	02700ZZ	112			02724Z6	118, 123	027H3DZ	118, 166	02B90ZZ	113
02550ZZ	112	027034Z	117, 119, 120, 121, 122	02713T6	117, 120, 121, 122, 123	02724ZZ	118, 123	027H3ZZ	118, 166	02B93ZZ	166
02553ZZ	166					027304Z	113	027H44Z	118, 166	02B94ZZ	113
02554ZZ	112	027035Z	117, 119, 120, 121, 122	02713TZ	117, 120, 121, 122, 123	027305Z	113	027H4DZ	118, 166	02BD0ZZ	113
02560ZZ	112	027036Z	117, 119, 120, 121, 122					027H4ZZ	118, 166	02BD3ZZ	113
02563ZZ	166			02713Z6	117, 123			027J04Z	108	02BD4ZZ	113
02564ZZ	112	027037Z	117, 119, 120, 121, 122					027J0DZ	108	02BF0ZZ	113
02570ZK	123							027J0ZZ	108	02BF3ZZ	166
02570ZZ	112							027J34Z	118, 166	02BF4ZZ	113
02573ZK	166										

Code	Page	Code	Page	Code	Page	Code	Page	Code	Page	Code	Page
02BG0ZZ	113	02C13ZZ	118, 120, 123	02CX0ZZ	149	02H703Z	113	02HN02Z	89, 152, 583, 609, 655, 863	02HV4DZ	32, 95, 125, 184, 203, 273, 484, 509, 524, 537, 571, 655, 863
02BG3ZZ	166	02C14Z6	120, 123	02CX3ZZ	184, 655, 863	02H70DZ	113				
02BG4ZZ	113	02C14ZZ	120, 123	02CX3ZZ	149	02H70JZ	119, 141	02HN0JZ	110, 119, 142		
02BH0ZZ	113	02C20Z6	113	02CX4ZZ	184, 655, 863	02H70KZ	110, 148	02HN0KZ	110, 148		
02BH3ZZ	166	02C20ZZ	113	02CX4ZZ	149	02H70MZ	119, 141	02HN0MZ	110, 119, 142	02HV4YZ	143
02BH4ZZ	113	02C23Z6	118, 120, 123	02FN0ZZ	152, 655	02H70NZ	113	02HN0YZ	89, 152, 583, 609, 655, 863	02HW0Z2	152
02BJ0ZZ	113	02C23ZZ	118, 120, 123	02FN3ZZ	152, 655	02H70YZ	143			02HW0DZ	152
02BJ3ZZ	166	02C24Z6	120, 123	02FN4ZZ	152, 655	02H730Z	143	02HN30Z	89, 152, 583, 609, 655, 863	02HW0YZ	152
02BJ4ZZ	113	02C24ZZ	120, 123	02H00DZ	113	02H73DZ	113			02HW3DZ	152
02BK0ZZ	113	02C30Z6	113	02H00YZ	113	02H73JZ	41, 119, 141, 746, 863	02HN3JZ	110, 119, 142	02HW3YZ	152
02BK3ZZ	113	02C30ZZ	113	02H03DZ	118, 120, 121, 122, 123			02HN3KZ	110, 149	02HW42Z	152
02BK4ZZ	113	02C33ZZ	118, 120, 123			02H73KZ	110, 148	02HN3MZ	110, 119, 142	02HW4DZ	152
02BL0ZZ	113	02C33ZZ	118, 120, 123	02H03YZ	118, 120, 121, 122, 123	02H73MZ	119, 141	02HN3YZ	89, 152, 583, 609, 655, 863	02HW4YZ	152
02BL3ZZ	113	02C34Z6	120, 123			02H73NZ	113			02HX02Z	152
02BL4ZZ	113	02C34ZZ	120, 123	02H04DZ	113	02H73YZ	143	02HN40Z	89, 152, 583, 609, 655, 863	02HX0DZ	152
02BM0ZZ	113	02C40ZZ	113	02H04YZ	113	02H742Z	114, 655, 863			02HX32Z	152
02BM3ZZ	166	02C43ZZ	113	02H10DZ	113	02H743Z	114	02HN42Z	89, 152, 583, 609, 655, 863	02HX3DZ	152
02BM4ZZ	113	02C44ZZ	113	02H10YZ	113	02H74DZ	114			02HX42Z	152
02BN*	89	02C50ZZ	113	02H13DZ	118, 120, 121, 122, 123	02H74JZ	119, 141	02HN4JZ	110, 119, 142	02HX4DZ	152
02BN0ZX	151, 583, 609	02C53ZZ	113			02H74KZ	110, 148	02HN4KZ	110, 149	02JA0ZZ	89, 143, 509, 583, 609, 655, 863
02BN0ZZ	151, 583, 609, 655, 863	02C54ZZ	113	02H13YZ	118, 120, 121, 122, 123	02H74MZ	119, 141	02HN4MZ	110, 119, 142		
		02C60ZZ	113			02H74NZ	114	02HN4YZ	89, 152, 583, 609, 655, 863	02JA4ZZ	71, 95, 143, 571, 583, 609
02BN3ZX	151, 583, 609	02C63ZZ	113	02H14DZ	113	02H74YZ	143				
02BN3ZZ	151, 583, 609, 655, 863	02C64ZZ	113	02H14YZ	113	02H20DZ	113	02HP0DZ	152	02JY0ZZ	89, 143, 509, 583, 609, 655, 863
		02C70ZZ	113	02H20YZ	113	02HA0QZ	1	02HP0YZ	152		
02BN4ZX	151, 583, 609	02C73ZZ	113	02H23DZ	118, 120, 121, 122, 123	02HA0RJ	108	02HP3DZ	152	02JY4ZZ	71, 95, 143, 571, 583, 609
02BN4ZZ	151, 583, 609, 655, 863	02C74ZZ	113			02HA0RS	1, 108	02HP3YZ	152		
		02C80ZZ	113	02H23YZ	118, 120, 121, 122, 123	02HA0YZ	152	02HP4DZ	152	02K80ZZ	120, 124
02BP0ZX	124, 1044	02C83ZZ	113			02HA3QZ	1	02HP4YZ	152	02K83ZZ	166
02BP0ZZ	89, 151	02C84ZZ	113	02H24DZ	113	02HA3RJ	108	02HQ00Z	143	02K84ZZ	166
02BP3ZX	124, 1044	02C90ZZ	113	02H24YZ	113	02HA3RS	1, 108	02HQ0DZ	152	02L70CK	124
02BP3ZZ	89, 151, 174, 655, 863	02C93ZZ	113	02H30DZ	113	02HA3RZ	108	02HQ0YZ	143	02L70DK	124
		02C94ZZ	113	02H30YZ	113	02HA3YZ	152	02HQ30Z	143	02L70ZK	124
02BP4ZX	124, 1044	02CD0ZZ	113	02H33DZ	118, 120, 121, 122, 123	02HA4QZ	1	02HQ3DZ	152	02L73CK	166
02BP4ZZ	89, 151	02CD3ZZ	113			02HA4RJ	108	02HQ3YZ	143	02L73DK	166
02BQ0ZX	124, 1044	02CD4ZZ	113	02H33YZ	118, 120, 121, 122, 123	02HA4RS	1, 108	02HQ40Z	143	02L73ZK	166
02BQ0ZZ	89, 151	02CF0ZZ	113			02HA4RZ	1, 108	02HQ4DZ	152	02L74CK	166
02BQ3ZX	124, 1044	02CF3ZZ	151	02H34DZ	113	02HA4YZ	152	02HQ4YZ	143	02L74DK	166
02BQ3ZZ	89, 151, 174, 655, 863	02CF4ZZ	151	02H34YZ	113	02HK00Z	141	02HR00Z	143	02L74ZK	166
		02CG0ZZ	113	02H400Z	143	02HK02Z	141	02HR0DZ	143	02LH0CZ	152, 655
02BQ4ZX	124, 1044	02CG3ZZ	151	02H402Z	113	02HK03Z	114	02HR0YZ	143	02LH0DZ	152, 655
02BQ4ZZ	89, 151	02CG4ZZ	151	02H403Z	113	02HK0DZ	114	02HR30Z	143	02LH0ZZ	152, 655
02BR0ZX	124, 1044	02CH0ZZ	113	02H40DZ	113	02HK0JZ	119, 141	02HR3DZ	152	02LH3CZ	152, 655
02BR0ZZ	89, 151	02CH3ZZ	151	02H40JZ	119, 141	02HK0KZ	110, 148	02HR3YZ	143	02LH3DZ	152, 655
02BR3ZX	124, 1044	02CH4ZZ	151	02H40KZ	110, 148	02HK0MZ	119, 141	02HR40Z	143	02LH3ZZ	152, 655
02BR3ZZ	89, 151, 174, 655, 863	02CJ0ZZ	113	02H40MZ	119, 141	02HK0NZ	114	02HR4DZ	152	02LH4CZ	152, 655
		02CJ3ZZ	151	02H40NZ	113	02HK0YZ	141	02HR4YZ	143	02LH4DZ	152, 655
02BR4ZX	124, 1044	02CJ4ZZ	151	02H40YZ	143	02HK32Z	142	02HS00Z	143	02LH4ZZ	152, 655
02BR4ZZ	89, 151	02CK0ZZ	113	02H430Z	143	02HK3DZ	114	02HS02Z	152	02LP0CZ	95, 125, 655, 863
02BS0ZX	124, 1044	02CK3ZZ	113	02H43DZ	113	02HK3JZ	41, 119, 141, 142, 746, 863	02HS0DZ	152	02LP0DZ	95, 125, 655, 863
02BS0ZZ	89, 151	02CK4ZZ	113	02H43JZ	110, 119, 141			02HS0YZ	143	02LP0ZZ	95, 125, 655, 863
02BS3ZX	124, 1044	02CL0ZZ	113	02H43KZ	110, 148	02HK3KZ	110, 148	02HS30Z	143	02LP3CZ	95, 125, 655, 863
02BS3ZZ	89, 151, 174, 655, 863	02CL3ZZ	113	02H43MZ	110, 119, 141	02HK3MZ	119, 142	02HS3DZ	152	02LP3DZ	95, 125, 655, 863
		02CL4ZZ	113	02H43NZ	113	02HK3NZ	114	02HS3YZ	143	02LP3ZZ	95, 125, 655, 863
02BS4ZX	124, 1044	02CM0ZZ	113	02H43YZ	143	02HK3YZ	141	02HS40Z	143	02LP4CZ	95, 125, 655, 863
02BS4ZZ	89, 151	02CM3ZZ	113	02H440Z	143	02HK40Z	141	02HS42Z	152	02LP4DZ	95, 125, 655, 863
02BT0ZX	124, 1044	02CM4ZZ	113	02H442Z	113	02HK42Z	141	02HS4DZ	152	02LP4ZZ	95, 125, 655, 863
02BT0ZZ	89, 151	02CN*	89, 655	02H443Z	113	02HK43Z	114	02HS4YZ	143	02LQ0CZ	95, 125, 655, 863
02BT3ZX	124, 1044	02CN0ZZ	151, 583, 609, 863	02H44DZ	113	02HK4DZ	114	02HT00Z	143	02LQ0DZ	95, 125, 655, 863
02BT3ZZ	89, 151, 174, 655, 863	02CN3ZZ	151, 583, 609, 863	02H44JZ	119, 141	02HK4JZ	119, 142	02HT02Z	152	02LQ0ZZ	95, 125, 655, 863
		02CN4ZZ	151, 583, 609, 863	02H44KZ	110, 148	02HK4KZ	110, 148	02HT0DZ	152	02LQ3CZ	95, 125, 655, 863
02BT4ZX	124, 1044	02CP*	89, 655	02H44MZ	119, 141	02HK4MZ	119, 142	02HT0YZ	143	02LQ3DZ	95, 125, 655, 863
02BT4ZZ	89, 151	02CP0ZZ	151, 863	02H44NZ	113	02HK4NZ	114	02HT30Z	143	02LQ3ZZ	95, 125, 655, 863
02BV0ZX	124, 1044	02CP3ZZ	152, 863	02H44YZ	143	02HK4YZ	141	02HT3DZ	152	02LQ4CZ	95, 125, 655, 863
02BV0ZZ	89, 151	02CP4ZZ	152, 863	02H600Z	143	02HL00Z	143	02HT3YZ	143	02LQ4ZZ	95, 125, 655, 863
02BV3ZX	124, 1044	02CQ*	89, 655	02H602Z	113, 655, 863	02HL02Z	114, 655, 863	02HT40Z	143	02LR0CT	152, 655
02BV3ZZ	89, 151, 174, 655, 863	02CQ0ZZ	152, 863	02H603Z	113	02HL03Z	114	02HT42Z	152	02LR0CZ	95, 125, 656, 863
		02CQ3ZZ	152, 863	02H60DZ	113	02HL0DZ	114	02HT4DZ	152	02LR0DT	152, 656
02BV4ZX	124, 1044	02CQ4ZZ	152, 863	02H60JZ	119, 141	02HL0JZ	119, 142	02HT4YZ	143	02LR0DZ	95, 125, 656, 863
02BV4ZZ	89, 151	02CR*	89, 655	02H60KZ	110, 148	02HL0KZ	110, 148	02HV00Z	143	02LR0ZT	152, 656
02BW0ZX	125, 1044	02CR0ZZ	152, 863	02H60MZ	119, 141	02HL0MZ	110, 119, 142	02HV02Z	32, 95, 125, 184, 203, 273, 484, 509, 524, 537, 571, 655, 863	02LR0ZZ	152, 656
02BW0ZZ	149, 184, 655, 863	02CR3ZZ	152, 863	02H60NZ	113	02HL0NZ	114			02LR3CT	152, 656
02BW3ZX	125, 1045	02CR4ZZ	152, 863	02H60YZ	143	02HL0YZ	143			02LR3CZ	95, 125, 656, 863
02BW3ZZ	89, 151, 174, 655, 863	02CS*	89, 655	02H630Z	143	02HL30Z	143			02LR3DT	152, 656
		02CS0ZZ	152, 863	02H63DZ	113	02HL3DZ	114	02HV0DZ	32, 95, 125, 184, 203, 273, 484, 509, 524, 537, 571, 655, 863	02LR3DZ	95, 125, 656, 863
02BW4ZX	125, 1045	02CS3ZZ	152, 863	02H63JZ	41, 119, 141, 746, 863	02HL3JZ	41, 119, 142, 746, 863			02LR3ZT	152, 656
02BW4ZZ	149, 184, 655, 863	02CS4ZZ	152, 863							02LR3ZZ	95, 125, 656, 863
02BX0ZX	125, 1045	02CT*	89, 655	02H63KZ	110, 148	02HL3KZ	110, 148			02LR4CT	152, 656
02BX0ZZ	149, 184, 655, 863	02CT0ZZ	152, 863	02H63MZ	119, 141	02HL3MZ	110, 119, 142	02HV0YZ	143	02LR4CZ	95, 125, 656, 863
02BX3ZX	125, 1045	02CT3ZZ	152, 863	02H63NZ	113	02HL3NZ	114	02HV30Z	143	02LR4DT	152, 656
02BX3ZZ	89, 151, 174, 655, 863	02CT4ZZ	152, 863	02H63YZ	143	02HL3YZ	143	02HV3DZ	32, 95, 125, 184, 203, 273, 484, 509, 524, 537, 571, 655, 863	02LR4DZ	95, 125, 656, 863
		02CV*	89, 655	02H640Z	143	02HL40Z	143			02LR4ZT	152, 656
02BX4ZX	125, 1045	02CV0ZZ	152, 863	02H642Z	113, 655, 863	02HL42Z	114, 655, 863			02LR4ZZ	95, 125, 656, 863
02BX4ZZ	149, 184, 655, 863	02CV3ZZ	152, 863	02H643Z	113	02HL43Z	114	02HV3YZ	143	02LS0CZ	152, 656
02C00Z6	113	02CV4ZZ	152, 863	02H64DZ	113	02HL4DZ	114	02HV40Z	143	02LS0DZ	152, 656
02C00ZZ	113	02CW*	184, 655	02H64JZ	119, 141	02HL4JZ	119, 142	02HV42Z	32, 95, 125, 184, 203, 273, 484, 509, 524, 537, 571, 655, 863	02LS0ZZ	152, 656
02C03Z6	118, 120, 123	02CW0ZZ	863	02H64KZ	110, 148	02HL4KZ	110, 148			02LS3CZ	152, 656
02C03ZZ	118, 120, 123	02CW0ZZ	149	02H64MZ	119, 141	02HL4MZ	110, 119, 142			02LS3DZ	152, 656
02C04Z6	120, 123	02CW3ZZ	863	02H64NZ	113	02HL4NZ	114			02LS3ZZ	152, 656
02C04ZZ	120, 123	02CW3ZZ	149	02H64YZ	143	02HL4YZ	143			02LS4CZ	152, 656
02C10Z6	113	02CW4ZZ	863	02H700Z	143	02HN00Z	89, 152, 583, 609, 655, 863			02LS4DZ	152, 656
02C10ZZ	113	02CW4ZZ	149	02H702Z	113, 655, 863					02LS4ZZ	152, 656
02C13Z6	118, 120, 123	02CX0ZZ	184, 655, 863								

Code	Page	Code	Page	Code	Page	Code	Page	Code	Page	Code	Page
02LT0CZ	152, 656	02PA03Z	114	02QA0ZZ	89, 152, 583, 609, 863	02R60KZ	153	02RJ4KZ	108	02RW47Z	108, 864
02LT0DZ	152, 656	02PA07Z	114	02QA3ZZ	152	02R647Z	153	02RK07Z	114	02RW48Z	108, 864
02LT0ZZ	152, 656	02PA08Z	114	02QA4ZZ	152	02R648Z	153	02RK08Z	153, 656	02RW4JZ	108, 864
02LT3CZ	152, 656	02PA0CZ	114	02QB0ZZ	114	02R64JZ	153	02RK0JZ	1, 153, 656	02RW4KZ	108, 864
02LT3DZ	152, 656	02PA0DZ	114	02QB3ZZ	114	02R64KZ	153	02RK0KZ	114	02RX*	108
02LT3ZZ	152, 656	02PA0JZ	114	02QB4ZZ	114	02R7*	656	02RK47Z	114	02RX07Z	89, 656, 864
02LT4CZ	152, 656	02PA0KZ	114	02QC0ZZ	114	02R707Z	153	02RK48Z	153, 656	02RX08Z	89, 656, 864
02LT4DZ	152, 656	02PA0MZ	32, 141, 656, 863	02QC3ZZ	114	02R708Z	153	02RK4JZ	153, 656	02RX0JZ	89, 656, 864
02LT4ZZ	152, 656	02PA0QZ	149	02QC4ZZ	114	02R70JZ	153	02RK4KZ	114	02RX0KZ	89, 656, 864
02LV*	32, 95, 125, 184, 203, 273, 484, 509, 524, 537, 571 656	02PA0RS	149	02QD0ZZ	114	02R70KZ	153	02RL07Z	114	02RX47Z	89, 656, 864
02LV0CZ	656, 863	02PA0RZ	1, 149	02QD3ZZ	114	02R747Z	153	02RL08Z	153, 656	02RX48Z	89, 656, 864
02LV0DZ	656, 863	02PA0YZ	114	02QD4ZZ	114	02R748Z	153	02RL0JZ	1, 153, 656	02RX4JZ	89, 656, 864
02LV0ZZ	656, 863	02PA37Z	114	02QF0ZJ	108	02R74JZ	153	02RL0KZ	114	02RX4KZ	89, 656, 864
02LV3CZ	656, 863	02PA38Z	114	02QF0ZZ	108	02R74KZ	153	02RL47Z	114	02S*	125, 656
02LV3DZ	656, 863	02PA3CZ	114	02QF3ZJ	166	02R907Z	114	02RL48Z	153, 656	02S00ZZ	864
02LV3ZZ	656, 863	02PA3JZ	114	02QF3ZZ	166	02R908Z	114	02RL4JZ	153, 656	02S10ZZ	864
02LV4CZ	656, 863	02PA3KZ	114	02QF4ZJ	108	02R90JZ	114	02RL4KZ	114	02SP0ZZ	864
02LV4DZ	656, 863	02PA3MZ	32, 141, 656, 863	02QF4ZZ	108	02R90KZ	114	02RM07Z	114	02SQ0ZZ	864
02LV4ZZ	656, 863	02PA3NZ	114	02QG0ZE	108	02R947Z	114	02RM08Z	153, 656	02SR0ZZ	864
02LW3DJ	152, 656	02PA3QZ	149	02QG0ZZ	108	02R948Z	114	02RM0JZ	114	02SS0ZZ	864
02N00ZZ	114	02PA3RS	149	02QG3ZE	166	02R94JZ	114	02RM0KZ	114	02ST0ZZ	864
02N03ZZ	114	02PA3RZ	1, 149	02QG3ZZ	166	02R94KZ	114	02RM47Z	114	02SV0ZZ	864
02N04ZZ	114	02PA42Z	114	02QG4ZE	108	02RD07Z	114	02RM48Z	153, 656	02SW0ZZ	864
02N10ZZ	114	02PA43Z	114	02QG4ZZ	108	02RD08Z	114	02RM4JZ	114	02SX0ZZ	864
02N13ZZ	114	02PA47Z	114	02QH0ZZ	108	02RD0JZ	114	02RM4KZ	114	02T50ZZ	114
02N14ZZ	114	02PA48Z	114	02QH3ZZ	166	02RD0KZ	114	02RN*	656	02T53ZZ	114
02N20ZZ	114	02PA4CZ	114	02QH4ZZ	108	02RD47Z	114	02RN07Z	153	02T54ZZ	114
02N23ZZ	114	02PA4DZ	114	02QJ0ZG	108	02RD48Z	114	02RN08Z	153	02T80ZZ	114
02N24ZZ	114	02PA4JZ	114	02QJ0ZZ	108	02RD4JZ	114	02RN0JZ	153	02T83ZZ	166
02N30ZZ	114	02PA4KZ	114	02QJ3ZG	166	02RD4KZ	114	02RN0KZ	153	02T84ZZ	114
02N33ZZ	114	02PA4MZ	32, 141, 656, 863	02QJ3ZZ	166	02RF07Z	108	02RN47Z	153	02T90ZZ	114
02N34ZZ	114	02PA4NZ	114	02QJ4ZG	108	02RF08Z	108	02RN48Z	153	02T93ZZ	114
02N4*	656	02PA4QZ	149	02QJ4ZZ	108	02RF0JZ	108	02RN4JZ	153	02T94ZZ	114
02N40ZZ	152	02PA4RS	149	02QK*	656	02RF0KZ	108	02RN4KZ	153	02TD0ZZ	114
02N43ZZ	152	02PA4RZ	1, 149	02QK0ZZ	152	02RF37H	149	02RP*	89, 656	02TD3ZZ	114
02N44ZZ	152	02PY02Z	152	02QK3ZZ	152	02RF37Z	149	02RP07Z	108, 864	02TD4ZZ	114
02N50ZZ	114	02PY03Z	152	02QK4ZZ	152	02RF38H	149	02RP08Z	108, 864	02TH0ZZ	114
02N53ZZ	114	02PY07Z	152	02QL*	656	02RF38Z	149	02RP0JZ	108, 864	02TH3ZZ	166
02N54ZZ	114	02PY08Z	152	02QL0ZZ	152	02RF3JH	149	02RP0KZ	108, 864	02TH4ZZ	114
02N60ZZ	114	02PY0CZ	152	02QL3ZZ	152	02RF3JZ	149	02RP47Z	108, 864	02TM0ZZ	114
02N63ZZ	114	02PY0DZ	152	02QL4ZZ	152	02RF3KH	149	02RP48Z	108, 864	02TM3ZZ	114
02N64ZZ	114	02PY0JZ	152	02QM0ZZ	114	02RF3KZ	149	02RP4JZ	108, 864	02TM4ZZ	114
02N70ZZ	114	02PY0KZ	152	02QM3ZZ	114	02RF47Z	108	02RP4KZ	108, 864	02TN*	89, 656
02N73ZZ	114	02PY0YZ	152	02QM4ZZ	114	02RF48Z	108	02RQ*	89, 656	02TN0ZZ	153, 583, 609, 864
02N74ZZ	114	02PY37Z	152	02QN*	656	02RF4JZ	108	02RQ07Z	108, 864	02TN3ZZ	153, 583, 609, 864
02N8*	656	02PY38Z	152	02QN0ZZ	152	02RF4KZ	108	02RQ08Z	108, 864	02TN4ZZ	153, 583, 609, 864
02N80ZZ	152	02PY3CZ	152	02QN3ZZ	152	02RG07Z	108	02RQ0JZ	108, 864	02U007Z	153, 656
02N83ZZ	152	02PY3JZ	152	02QN4ZZ	152	02RG08Z	108	02RQ0KZ	108, 864	02U008Z	153, 656
02N84ZZ	152	02PY3KZ	152	02QP*	95, 125, 656	02RG0JZ	108	02RQ47Z	108, 864	02U00JZ	149
02N90ZZ	114	02PY42Z	152	02QP0ZZ	863	02RG0KZ	108	02RQ48Z	108, 864	02U00KZ	153, 656
02N93ZZ	114	02PY43Z	152	02QP3ZZ	863	02RG37H	149	02RQ4JZ	108, 864	02U037Z	123
02N94ZZ	114	02PY47Z	152	02QP4ZZ	863	02RG37Z	149	02RQ4KZ	108, 864	02U038Z	123
02ND0ZZ	114	02PY48Z	152	02QQ*	95, 125, 656	02RG38H	149	02RR*	89, 656	02U03JZ	123
02ND3ZZ	114	02PY4CZ	152	02QQ0ZZ	863	02RG38Z	149	02RR07Z	108, 864	02U03KZ	123
02ND4ZZ	114	02PY4DZ	152	02QQ3ZZ	863	02RG3JH	149	02RR08Z	108, 864	02U047Z	153, 656
02NF0ZZ	108	02PY4JZ	152	02QQ4ZZ	863	02RG3JZ	149	02RR0JZ	108, 864	02U048Z	153, 656
02NF3ZZ	152	02PY4KZ	152	02QR*	95, 125, 656	02RG3KH	149	02RR0KZ	108, 864	02U04JZ	149
02NF4ZZ	152	02Q00ZZ	114	02QR0ZZ	863	02RG3KZ	149	02RR47Z	108, 864	02U04KZ	153, 656
02NG0ZZ	108	02Q03ZZ	114	02QR3ZZ	863	02RG47Z	108	02RR48Z	108, 864	02U107Z	153, 656
02NG3ZZ	152	02Q04ZZ	114	02QR4ZZ	863	02RG48Z	108	02RR4JZ	108, 864	02U108Z	153, 656
02NG4ZZ	152	02Q10ZZ	114	02QS*	142, 656	02RG4JZ	108	02RR4KZ	108, 864	02U10JZ	149
02NH0ZZ	108	02Q13ZZ	114	02QS0ZZ	863	02RG4KZ	108	02RS*	89, 656	02U10KZ	153, 656
02NH3ZZ	152	02Q14ZZ	114	02QS3ZZ	863	02RH07Z	108	02RS07Z	108, 864	02U137Z	123
02NH4ZZ	152	02Q20ZZ	114	02QS4ZZ	863	02RH08Z	108	02RS08Z	108, 864	02U138Z	123
02NJ0ZZ	108	02Q23ZZ	114	02QT*	142, 656	02RH0JZ	108	02RS0JZ	108, 864	02U13JZ	123
02NJ3ZZ	152	02Q24ZZ	114	02QT0ZZ	864	02RH0KZ	108	02RS0KZ	108, 864	02U13KZ	123
02NJ4ZZ	152	02Q30ZZ	114	02QT3ZZ	864	02RH37H	149	02RS47Z	108, 864	02U147Z	153, 656
02NK0ZZ	114	02Q33ZZ	114	02QT4ZZ	864	02RH37Z	149	02RS48Z	108, 864	02U148Z	153, 656
02NK3ZZ	114	02Q34ZZ	114	02QV*	142, 656	02RH38H	149	02RS4JZ	108, 864	02U14JZ	149
02NK4ZZ	114	02Q40ZZ	114	02QV0ZZ	864	02RH38Z	149	02RS4KZ	108, 864	02U14KZ	153, 656
02NL0ZZ	114	02Q43ZZ	114	02QV3ZZ	864	02RH3JH	149	02RT*	89, 656	02U207Z	153, 656
02NL3ZZ	114	02Q44ZZ	114	02QV4ZZ	864	02RH3JZ	149	02RT07Z	108, 864	02U208Z	153, 656
02NL4ZZ	114	02Q50ZZ	114	02QW*	95, 656	02RH3KH	149	02RT08Z	108, 864	02U20JZ	149
02NM0ZZ	114	02Q53ZZ	114	02QW0ZZ	149, 864	02RH3KZ	149	02RT0JZ	108, 864	02U20KZ	153, 656
02NM3ZZ	114	02Q54ZZ	114	02QW3ZZ	149, 864	02RH47Z	108	02RT0KZ	108, 864	02U237Z	123
02NM4ZZ	114	02Q6*	656	02QW4ZZ	149, 864	02RH48Z	108	02RT47Z	108, 864	02U238Z	123
02NN*	89, 656	02Q60ZZ	152	02QX0ZZ	95, 149, 656, 864	02RH4JZ	108	02RT48Z	108, 864	02U23JZ	123
02NN0ZZ	152, 583, 609, 863	02Q63ZZ	152	02QX3ZZ	95, 149, 656, 864	02RH4KZ	108	02RT4JZ	108, 864	02U23KZ	123
02NN3ZZ	152, 583, 609, 863	02Q64ZZ	152	02QX4ZZ	95, 149, 656, 864	02RJ07Z	108	02RT4KZ	108, 864	02U247Z	153, 656
02NN4ZZ	152, 583, 609, 863	02Q7*	656	02R5*	656	02RJ08Z	108	02RV*	89, 656	02U248Z	153, 656
02NP*	125	02Q70ZZ	152	02R507Z	152	02RJ0JZ	108	02RV07Z	108, 864	02U24JZ	149
02NQ*	125	02Q73ZZ	152	02R508Z	152	02RJ0KZ	108	02RV08Z	108, 864	02U24KZ	153, 656
02NR*	125	02Q74ZZ	152	02R50JZ	152	02RJ37H	149	02RV0JZ	108, 864	02U307Z	153, 656
02NS*	125	02Q8*	656	02R50KZ	152	02RJ37Z	149	02RV0KZ	108, 864	02U308Z	153, 656
02NT*	125	02Q80ZZ	152	02R547Z	152	02RJ38H	149	02RV47Z	108, 864	02U30JZ	149
02NV*	125	02Q83ZZ	152	02R548Z	152	02RJ38Z	149	02RV48Z	108, 864	02U30KZ	153, 656
02NW*	125	02Q84ZZ	152	02R54JZ	152	02RJ3JH	149	02RV4JZ	108, 864	02U337Z	123
02NX0ZZ	125	02Q90ZZ	114	02R54KZ	152	02RJ3JZ	149	02RV4KZ	108, 864	02U338Z	123
02NX3ZZ	125	02Q93ZZ	114	02R6*	656	02RJ3KH	149	02RW*	89, 656	02U33JZ	123
02NX4ZZ	125	02Q94ZZ	114	02R607Z	152	02RJ3KZ	149	02RW07Z	108, 864	02U33KZ	123
02PA02Z	114	02QA*	656	02R608Z	152	02RJ47Z	108	02RW08Z	108, 864	02U347Z	153, 656
				02R60JZ	153	02RJ48Z	108	02RW0JZ	108, 864	02U348Z	153, 656
						02RJ4JZ	108	02RW0KZ	108, 864	02U34JZ	149

Code	Page	Code	Page	Code	Page	Code	Page	Code	Page	Code	Page
02U34KZ	153, 656	02UF4JJ	108	02UM38Z	115	02UX07Z	125, 656, 864	02VW0ZZ	153, 657	02WH37Z	167
02U507Z	114	02UF4JZ	109	02UM3JZ	115	02UX08Z	125, 656, 864	02VW3CZ	125	02WH38Z	167
02U508Z	114	02UF4KJ	109	02UM3KZ	115	02UX0JZ	125, 656	02VW3DZ	109, 509, 657, 865	02WH3JZ	167
02U50JZ	114	02UF4KZ	109	02UM47Z	115	02UX37Z	125, 656, 864	02VW3EZ	109, 509, 657, 865	02WH3KZ	167
02U50KZ	114	02UG07E	109	02UM48Z	115	02UX38Z	125, 657, 864	02VW3FZ	109, 509, 657, 865	02WH47Z	115
02U537Z	114	02UG07Z	109	02UM4JZ	115	02UX3JZ	109, 509, 657, 864	02VW3ZZ	153, 657	02WH48Z	115
02U538Z	114	02UG08E	109	02UM4KZ	115	02UX3KZ	125, 657, 864	02VW4CZ	125	02WH4JZ	115
02U53JZ	166	02UG08Z	109	02UN*	656	02UX47Z	125, 657, 864	02VW4DZ	109, 509, 657, 865	02WJ07Z	115
02U53KZ	114	02UG0JE	109	02UN07Z	153	02UX48Z	125, 657, 864	02VW4EZ	109, 509, 657, 865	02WJ08Z	115
02U547Z	114	02UG0JZ	109	02UN08Z	153	02UX4JZ	109, 509, 657, 864	02VW4FZ	109, 509, 657, 865	02WJ0JZ	115
02U548Z	114	02UG0KE	109	02UN0JZ	153	02UX4KZ	125, 657, 864	02VW4ZZ	153, 657	02WJ0KZ	115
02U54JZ	166	02UG0KZ	109	02UN0KZ	153	02VA*	657	02VX0CZ	125	02WJ37Z	167
02U54KZ	114	02UG37E	149	02UN37Z	153	02VA0CZ	153	02VX0DZ	109, 509, 657, 865	02WJ38Z	167
02U607Z	114	02UG37Z	149	02UN38Z	153	02VA0ZZ	153	02VX0EZ	109, 509, 657, 865	02WJ3KZ	167
02U608Z	114	02UG38E	149	02UN3JZ	153	02VA3CZ	153	02VX0FZ	109, 509, 657, 865	02WJ47Z	115
02U60JZ	153, 656	02UG38Z	149	02UN3KZ	153	02VA3ZZ	153	02VX0ZZ	153, 657	02WJ4JZ	115
02U60KZ	115	02UG3JE	118, 149	02UN47Z	153	02VA4CZ	153	02VX3CZ	125	02WJ4KZ	115
02U637Z	153, 656	02UG3JZ	149	02UN48Z	153	02VA4ZZ	153	02VX3DZ	109, 509, 657, 865	02WM0JZ	115
02U638Z	153, 656	02UG3KE	149	02UN4JZ	153	02VG0ZZ	109	02VX3EZ	109, 509, 657, 865	02WM4JZ	115
02U63JZ	153, 656	02UG3KZ	149	02UN4KZ	153	02VG4ZZ	109	02VX3FZ	109, 509, 657, 865	02WY02Z	153
02U63KZ	153, 656	02UG47E	109	02UP*	125, 656	02VP0CZ	125	02VX3ZZ	153, 657	02WY03Z	153
02U647Z	153, 656	02UG47Z	109	02UP07Z	864	02VP0DZ	153, 657	02VX4CZ	125	02WY07Z	153
02U648Z	153, 656	02UG48E	109	02UP08Z	864	02VP0ZZ	153, 657	02VX4DZ	109, 509, 657, 865	02WY08Z	153
02U64JZ	153, 656	02UG48Z	109	02UP0KZ	864	02VP3CZ	125	02VX4EZ	109, 509, 657, 865	02WY0CZ	153
02U64KZ	153, 656	02UG4JE	109	02UP37Z	864	02VP3DZ	153, 657	02VX4FZ	109, 509, 657, 865	02WY0DZ	153
02U707Z	115	02UG4JZ	109	02UP38Z	864	02VP3ZZ	153, 657	02VX4ZZ	153, 657	02WY0JZ	153
02U708Z	115	02UG4KE	109	02UP3KZ	864	02VP4CZ	125	02W50JZ	115	02WY0KZ	153
02U70JZ	153, 656	02UG4KZ	109	02UP47Z	864	02VP4DZ	153, 657	02W54JZ	115	02WY0YZ	153
02U70KZ	115	02UH07Z	109	02UP48Z	864	02VP4ZZ	153, 657	02WA02Z	115	02WY37Z	153
02U737Z	115	02UH08Z	109	02UP4KZ	864	02VQ0CZ	153	02WA03Z	115	02WY38Z	153
02U738Z	115	02UH0JZ	109	02UQ*	125, 656	02VQ0DZ	153, 657	02WA07Z	115	02WY3CZ	154
02U73JZ	124	02UH0KZ	109	02UQ07Z	864	02VQ0ZZ	153, 657	02WA08Z	115	02WY3JZ	154
02U73KZ	115	02UH37Z	149	02UQ08Z	864	02VQ3CZ	153	02WA0CZ	115	02WY3KZ	154
02U747Z	115	02UH38Z	149	02UQ0KZ	864	02VQ3DZ	153, 657	02WA0DZ	115	02WY42Z	154
02U748Z	115	02UH3JZ	149	02UQ38Z	864	02VQ3ZZ	153, 657	02WA0JZ	108	02WY43Z	154
02U74JZ	124	02UH3KZ	149	02UQ3JZ	864	02VQ4CZ	153	02WA0KZ	115, 657, 865	02WY47Z	154
02U74KZ	115	02UH47Z	109	02UQ3KZ	864	02VQ4DZ	153, 657	02WA0MZ	32, 141, 657, 865	02WY48Z	154
02U907Z	115	02UH48Z	109	02UQ47Z	864	02VQ4ZZ	153, 657	02WA0NZ	115	02WY4CZ	154
02U908Z	115	02UH4JZ	109	02UQ48Z	864	02VR0CT	125	02WA0QZ	1, 108	02WY4DZ	154
02U90JZ	115	02UH4KZ	109	02UQ4KZ	864	02VR0CZ	125	02WA0RS	108	02WY4JZ	154
02U90KZ	115	02UJ07G	109	02UR*	125, 656	02VR0DT	153, 657	02WA0RZ	1, 108	02WY4KZ	154
02U937Z	115	02UJ07Z	109	02UR07Z	864	02VR0DZ	153, 657	02WA0YZ	115	02YA0Z0	1
02U938Z	115	02UJ08G	109	02UR08Z	864	02VR0ZT	153, 657	02WA37Z	115	02YA0Z1	1
02U93JZ	115	02UJ08Z	109	02UR0KZ	864	02VR0ZZ	153, 657	02WA38Z	115	02YA0Z2	1
02U93KZ	115	02UJ0JG	109	02UR37Z	864	02VR3CT	125	02WA3CZ	115	0312*	125
02U947Z	115	02UJ0JZ	109	02UR38Z	864	02VR3CZ	153	02WA3KZ	115, 657, 865	031209W	657, 865
02U948Z	115	02UJ0KG	109	02UR3KZ	864	02VR3DT	153, 657	02WA3MZ	32, 141, 657, 865	03120AW	657, 865
02U94JZ	115	02UJ0KZ	109	02UR47Z	864	02VR3DZ	153, 657	02WA3NZ	115	03120JW	657, 865
02U94KZ	115	02UJ37Z	149	02UR48Z	864	02VR3ZT	153, 657	02WA3QZ	1, 108	03120KW	657, 865
02UA07Z	153, 656	02UJ38G	149	02UR4KZ	864	02VR3ZZ	153, 657	02WA3RS	108	03120ZW	657, 865
02UA08Z	153, 656	02UJ38Z	149	02US*	125, 656	02VR4CT	125	02WA3RZ	1, 108	031309B	125
02UA0JZ	149	02UJ3JG	149	02US07Z	864	02VR4CZ	153	02WA42Z	115	031309C	125
02UA0KZ	153, 656	02UJ3JZ	149	02US08Z	864	02VR4DT	153, 657	02WA43Z	115	031309D	125
02UA37Z	153, 656	02UJ3KG	149	02US0KZ	864	02VR4DZ	153, 657	02WA47Z	115	031309F	125
02UA38Z	153, 656	02UJ3KZ	149	02US37Z	864	02VR4ZT	153, 657	02WA48Z	115	031309J	125
02UA3JZ	149	02UJ47G	109	02US38Z	864	02VR4ZZ	153, 657	02WA4CZ	115	031309K	125
02UA3KZ	153, 656	02UJ47Z	109	02US3KZ	864	02VS0CZ	125	02WA4DZ	115	031309M	154
02UA47Z	153, 656	02UJ48G	109	02US47Z	864	02VS0DZ	153, 657	02WA4JZ	115, 657, 865	031309N	154
02UA48Z	153, 656	02UJ48Z	109	02US48Z	864	02VS0ZZ	153, 657	02WA4KZ	115, 657, 865	031309W	125, 657, 865
02UA4JZ	149	02UJ4JG	109	02US4KZ	864	02VS3CZ	125	02WA4MZ	32, 141, 657, 865	03130A0	125
02UA4KZ	153, 656	02UJ4JZ	109	02UT*	125, 656	02VS3DZ	153, 657	02WA4NZ	115	03130A1	125
02UD07Z	115	02UJ4KG	109	02UT07Z	864	02VS3ZZ	153, 657	02WA4QZ	1, 108	03130A2	125
02UD08Z	115	02UJ4KZ	109	02UT08Z	864	02VS4CZ	125	02WA4RS	108	03130A3	125
02UD0JZ	115	02UK07Z	153, 656	02UT0KZ	864	02VS4DZ	153, 657	02WA4RZ	1, 108	03130A4	125
02UD0KZ	115	02UK08Z	153, 656	02UT37Z	864	02VS4ZZ	153, 657	02WF07Z	115	03130A5	125
02UD37Z	115	02UK0JZ	153, 656	02UT38Z	864	02VT0CZ	125	02WF08Z	115	03130A6	125
02UD38Z	115	02UK0KZ	115	02UT3KZ	864	02VT0DZ	153, 657	02WF0JZ	115	03130A7	125
02UD3JZ	115	02UK37Z	153, 656	02UT47Z	864	02VT0ZZ	153, 657	02WF0KZ	115	03130A8	125
02UD3KZ	115	02UK38Z	153, 656	02UT48Z	864	02VT3CZ	125	02WF37Z	109	03130A9	125
02UD47Z	115	02UK3JZ	153, 656	02UT4KZ	864	02VT3DZ	153, 657	02WF38Z	167	03130AB	125
02UD48Z	115	02UK3KZ	115	02UV*	125, 656	02VT3ZZ	153, 657	02WF3JZ	167	03130AC	125
02UD4JZ	115	02UK47Z	153, 656	02UV07Z	864	02VT4CZ	125	02WF3KZ	167	03130AD	125
02UD4KZ	115	02UK48Z	153, 656	02UV08Z	864	02VT4DZ	153, 657	02WF47Z	115	03130AF	125
02UF07J	108	02UK4JZ	153, 656	02UV0KZ	864	02VT4ZZ	153, 657	02WF48Z	115	03130AJ	125
02UF07Z	108	02UK4KZ	115	02UV37Z	864	02VV*	32, 96, 125, 184, 203, 273, 484, 509, 524, 537, 571, 657	02WF4JZ	115	03130AK	125
02UF08J	108	02UL07Z	108	02UV38Z	864	02VV0CZ	864	02WF4KZ	115	03130AM	154
02UF08Z	108	02UL08Z	153, 656	02UV3KZ	864	02VV0DZ	864	02WG07Z	115	03130AN	154
02UF0JJ	108	02UL0JZ	153, 656	02UV47Z	864	02VV0ZZ	864	02WG08Z	115	03130AW	125, 657, 865
02UF0JZ	108	02UL0KZ	115	02UV48Z	864	02VV3DZ	864	02WG0JZ	115	03130J0	125
02UF0KJ	108	02UL37Z	153, 656	02UV4KZ	864	02VV3ZZ	864	02WG0KZ	115	03130J1	125
02UF0KZ	108	02UL38Z	153, 656	02UW*	656	02VV4CZ	864	02WG37Z	167	03130J2	125
02UF37J	149	02UL3JZ	153, 656	02UW07Z	125, 864	02VV4DZ	864	02WG38Z	167	03130J3	125
02UF37Z	149	02UL3KZ	115	02UW08Z	125, 864	02VV4ZZ	865	02WG3JZ	167	03130J4	125
02UF38J	149	02UL47Z	153, 656	02UW0KZ	125	02VW0CZ	125	02WG3KZ	167	03130J5	125
02UF38Z	149	02UL48Z	153, 656	02UW37Z	125, 864	02VW0DZ	109, 509, 657, 865	02WG47Z	115	03130J6	125
02UF3JJ	149	02UL4JZ	153, 656	02UW38Z	125, 864	02VW0EZ	109, 509, 657, 865	02WG48Z	115	03130J7	125
02UF3JZ	149	02UL4KZ	115	02UW3KZ	125, 864	02VW0FZ	109, 509, 657, 865	02WG4JZ	115	03130J8	125
02UF3KJ	149	02UM07Z	115	02UW47Z	125, 864			02WG4KZ	115	03130J9	125
02UF3KZ	149	02UM08Z	153, 656	02UW4JZ	109, 509, 864			02WH07Z	115	03130JB	125
02UF47J	108	02UM0JZ	115	02UW4KZ	125, 864			02WH08Z	115	03130JC	125
02UF47Z	108	02UM0KZ	115					02WH0JZ	115		
02UF48J	108	02UM37Z	115					02WH0KZ	115		
02UF48Z	108										

Code	Page
03130JD	125
03130JF	125
03130JJ	125
03130JK	125
03130JM	154
03130JN	154
03130JW	125, 657, 865
03130K0	125
03130K1	125
03130K2	125
03130K3	125
03130K4	125
03130K5	125
03130K6	125
03130K7	125
03130K8	125
03130K9	125
03130KB	125
03130KC	125
03130KD	125
03130KF	125
03130KJ	125
03130KK	125
03130KM	154
03130KN	154
03130KW	125, 657, 865
03130Z0	125
03130Z1	125
03130Z2	125
03130Z3	125
03130Z4	125
03130Z5	125
03130Z6	125
03130Z7	126
03130Z8	126
03130Z9	126
03130ZC	126
03130ZD	126, 184, 484, 509, 657, 865
03130ZF	126
03130ZJ	126
03130ZK	126
03130ZM	154
03130ZN	154
03130ZW	126, 657, 865
031409B	126
031409C	126
031409D	126
031409F	126
031409J	126
031409K	126
031409M	154
031409N	154
031409W	126, 657, 865
03140A0	126
03140A1	126
03140A2	126
03140A3	126
03140A4	126
03140A5	126
03140A6	126
03140A7	126
03140A8	126
03140A9	126
03140AB	126
03140AC	126
03140AD	126
03140AF	126
03140AJ	126
03140AK	126
03140AM	154
03140AN	154
03140AW	126, 657, 865
03140J0	126
03140J1	126
03140J2	126
03140J3	126
03140J4	126
03140J5	126
03140J6	126
03140J7	126
03140J8	126
03140J9	126
03140JB	126
03140JC	126
03140JD	126
03140JF	126
03140JJ	126
03140JK	126
03140JM	154
03140JN	154
03140JW	126, 657, 865
03140K0	126
03140K1	126
03140K2	126
03140K3	126
03140K4	126
03140K5	126
03140K6	126
03140K7	126
03140K8	126
03140K9	126
03140KB	126
03140KC	126
03140KD	126
03140KF	126
03140KJ	126
03140KK	126
03140KM	154
03140KN	154
03140KW	126, 657, 865
03140Z0	126
03140Z1	126
03140Z2	126
03140Z3	126
03140Z4	126
03140Z5	126
03140Z6	126
03140Z7	126
03140Z8	126
03140Z9	126
03140ZB	126
03140ZC	126
03140ZD	126, 184, 484, 509, 657, 865
03140ZF	126
03140ZJ	126
03140ZK	126
03140ZM	154
03140ZN	154
03140ZW	126, 657, 865
0315*	126
031509W	412, 484, 657, 865
03150A0	23, 96, 203, 412, 484, 657
03150AW	412, 484, 657, 865
03150J0	23, 96, 203, 412, 484, 657
03150JW	412, 484, 657, 865
03150K0	23, 96, 203, 412, 484, 657
03150KW	412, 484, 657, 865
03150Z0	23, 96, 203, 412, 484, 657
03150ZD	184, 484, 509, 657, 865
03150ZT	184, 484, 509, 657, 865
03150ZV	184, 484, 509, 657, 865
03150ZW	412, 484, 657, 865
0316*	126
031609W	412, 484, 657, 865
03160A1	23, 96, 203, 412, 484, 657
03160AW	412, 484, 657, 865
03160J1	23, 96, 203, 412, 484, 657
03160JW	412, 484, 657, 865
03160K1	23, 96, 203, 412, 484, 657
03160KW	412, 484, 657, 865
03160Z1	23, 96, 203, 412, 484, 657
03160ZD	184, 484, 509, 657, 865
03160ZT	184, 484, 509, 657, 865
03160ZV	184, 484, 509, 657, 865
03160ZW	412, 484, 657, 865
031709D	143, 484, 510, 657, 865
031709F	143, 484, 510, 657, 865
031709V	143, 484, 510, 657, 865
031709W	126, 412, 484, 657, 865
03170A0	126
03170A3	126
03170AD	143, 484, 510, 657, 865
03170AF	143, 484, 510, 657, 865
03170AV	143, 484, 510, 657, 865
03170AW	126, 412, 484, 657, 865
03170J0	126
03170J3	126
03170JD	143, 484, 510, 657, 865
03170JF	143, 484, 510, 657, 865
03170JV	143, 484, 510, 657, 865
03170JW	126, 412, 484, 657, 865
03170K0	126
03170K3	126
03170KD	143, 484, 510, 657, 865
03170KF	143, 484, 510, 657, 865
03170KV	143, 484, 510, 657, 865
03170KW	126, 412, 484, 657, 865
03170Z0	126
03170Z3	126
03170ZD	143, 184, 484, 510, 657, 865
03170ZF	143, 484, 510, 657, 865
03170ZV	143, 184, 484, 510, 657, 865
03170ZW	126, 412, 484, 657, 865
031809D	144, 484, 510, 657, 865
031809F	144, 184, 484, 510, 657, 865
031809V	144, 484, 510, 657, 865
031809W	126, 412, 484, 657, 865
03180A1	126
03180A4	126
03180AD	144, 484, 510, 657, 865
03180AF	144, 484, 510, 657, 865
03180AV	144, 484, 510, 657, 865
03180AW	126, 412, 484, 657, 865
03180J1	126
03180J4	126
03180JD	144, 484, 510, 657, 865
03180JF	144, 484, 510, 657, 865
03180JV	144, 484, 510, 657, 865
03180JW	126, 412, 484, 657, 865
03180K1	126
03180K4	126
03180KD	144, 484, 510, 657, 865
03180KF	144, 484, 510, 657, 865
03180KV	144, 484, 510, 657, 865
03180KW	126, 412, 484, 657, 865
03180Z1	126
03180Z4	126
03180ZD	144, 184, 484, 510, 657, 865
03180ZF	144, 484, 510, 657, 865
03180ZV	144, 184, 484, 510, 657, 865
03180ZW	126, 412, 484, 657, 865
031909F	144, 484, 510, 657, 865
03190A3	126
03190AF	144, 484, 510, 657, 865
03190J3	126
03190JF	144, 484, 510, 657, 865
03190K3	126
03190KF	144, 484, 510, 657, 865
03190Z3	126
03190ZF	144, 184, 484, 510, 657, 865
03193ZF	144, 184, 484, 510, 657, 865
031A094	126
031A09F	144, 484, 510, 657, 865
031A0A4	126
031A0AF	144, 484, 510, 657, 865
031A0J4	126
031A0JF	144, 484, 510, 657, 865
031A0K4	126
031A0KF	144, 484, 510, 657, 865
031A0Z4	126
031A0ZF	144, 484, 510, 657, 865
031A3ZF	144, 184, 484, 510, 657, 865
031B093	126
031B09F	144, 484, 510, 657, 865
031B0A3	126
031B0AF	144, 484, 510, 657, 865
031B0J3	126
031B0JF	144, 484, 510, 658, 865
031B0K3	126
031B0KF	144, 484, 510, 658, 865
031B0Z3	126
031B0ZF	144, 184, 484, 510, 658, 865
031B3ZF	144, 184, 484, 510, 658, 865
031C094	126
031C09F	144, 484, 510, 658, 865
031C0A4	126
031C0AF	144, 484, 510, 658, 865
031C0J4	126
031C0JF	144, 484, 510, 658, 865
031C0K4	126
031C0KF	144, 484, 510, 658, 865
031C0Z4	126
031C0ZF	144, 184, 484, 510, 658, 865
031C3ZF	144, 184, 484, 510, 658, 865
031G*	126
031H09G	6, 10, 658, 865
031H09J	23, 96, 126, 203, 412, 484, 658, 865
031H09K	23, 126, 658, 865
031H09Y	23, 96, 126, 203, 412, 484, 658, 865
031H0AG	6, 10, 658, 865
031H0AJ	23, 96, 126, 203, 412, 484, 658, 865
031H0AK	23, 126, 658, 865
031H0AY	24, 96, 126, 203, 412, 484, 658, 865
031H0JG	6, 10, 658, 865
031H0JJ	24, 96, 126, 203, 412, 484, 658, 865
031H0JK	24, 126, 658, 865
031H0JY	24, 96, 126, 203, 412, 484, 658, 865
031H0KG	6, 10, 658, 865
031H0KJ	24, 96, 126, 203, 412, 484, 658, 865
031H0KK	24, 126, 658, 865
031H0KY	24, 96, 126, 203, 412, 484, 658, 865
031H0ZG	6, 10, 658, 865
031H0ZJ	24, 96, 126, 203, 412, 484, 658, 865
031H0ZK	24, 126, 658, 865
031H0ZY	24, 96, 126, 203, 412, 484, 658, 865
031J09G	6, 10, 658, 865
031J09J	24, 96, 126, 203, 412, 484, 658, 865
031J09K	24, 96, 126, 203, 412, 484, 658, 865
031J09Y	24, 96, 126, 203, 412, 484, 658, 865
031J0AG	6, 10, 658, 865
031J0AJ	24, 126, 658, 865
031J0AK	24, 96, 126, 203, 412, 484, 658, 865
031J0AY	24, 96, 126, 203, 412, 484, 658, 865
031J0JG	6, 10, 658, 865
031J0JJ	24, 126, 658, 865
031J0JK	24, 96, 126, 203, 412, 484, 658, 865
031J0JY	24, 96, 126, 203, 412, 484, 658, 865
031J0KG	6, 10, 658, 865
031J0KJ	24, 126, 658, 865
031J0KK	24, 96, 126, 203, 412, 484, 658, 865
031J0KY	24, 96, 127, 203, 412, 484, 658, 865
031J0ZG	6, 10, 658, 865
031J0ZJ	24, 127, 658, 865
031J0ZK	24, 96, 127, 203, 412, 484, 658, 865
031J0ZY	24, 96, 127, 203, 412, 484, 658, 865
031K*	658
031K09J	24, 96, 127, 203, 412, 484, 865
031K09K	24, 127, 865
031K0AJ	24, 96, 127, 203, 412, 484, 865
031K0AK	24, 127, 865
031K0JJ	24, 96, 127, 203, 412, 484, 865
031K0JK	24, 127, 865
031K0KJ	24, 96, 127, 203, 412, 484, 865
031K0KK	24, 127, 865
031K0ZJ	24, 96, 127, 203, 412, 484, 865
031K0ZK	24, 127, 865
031L*	658
031L09J	24, 127, 866
031L09K	24, 96, 127, 203, 412, 484, 866
031L0AJ	24, 127, 866
031L0AK	24, 96, 127, 203, 412, 484, 866
031L0JJ	24, 127, 866
031L0JK	24, 96, 127, 203, 412, 484, 866
031L0KJ	24, 127, 866
031L0KK	24, 96, 127, 203, 412, 484, 866
031L0ZJ	24, 127, 866
031L0ZK	24, 96, 127, 203, 412, 484, 866
031M*	658
031M09J	24, 96, 127, 203, 412, 484, 866
031M09K	24, 127, 866
031M0AJ	24, 96, 127, 203, 412, 484, 866
031M0AK	24, 127, 866
031M0JJ	24, 96, 127, 203, 412, 484, 866
031M0JK	24, 127, 866
031M0KJ	24, 96, 127, 203, 412, 484, 866
031M0KK	24, 127, 866
031M0ZJ	24, 96, 127, 203, 412, 484, 866
031M0ZK	24, 127, 866
031N*	658
031N09J	24, 127, 866
031N09K	24, 96, 127, 203, 412, 484, 866
031N0AJ	24, 127, 866
031N0AK	24, 96, 127, 203, 412, 484, 866
031N0JJ	24, 127, 866
031N0JK	24, 96, 127, 203, 412, 484, 866
031N0KJ	24, 127, 866
031N0KK	24, 96, 127, 203, 412, 484, 866
031N0ZJ	24, 127, 866
031N0ZK	24, 96, 127, 203, 412, 484, 866
031S*	658
031S09G	6, 10, 866
031S0AG	6, 10, 866
031S0JG	6, 10, 866
031S0KG	6, 10, 866
031S0ZG	6, 10, 866
031T*	658
031T09G	6, 10, 866
031T0AG	6, 10, 866
031T0JG	6, 10, 866
031T0KG	6, 10, 866
031T0ZG	6, 10, 866
0350*	89
03500ZZ	154
03503ZZ	154
03504ZZ	154
0351*	89
03510ZZ	154
03513ZZ	154
03514ZZ	154
0352*	89
03520ZZ	154
03523ZZ	154
03524ZZ	154
0353*	89
03530ZZ	154
03533ZZ	154
03534ZZ	154
0354*	89
03540ZZ	154
03543ZZ	154
03544ZZ	154
0355*	127, 484, 658
0356*	127, 484, 658
0357*	127, 484, 658
0358*	127, 484, 658
0359*	127, 484, 658
035A*	127, 484, 658
035B*	127, 484, 658
035C*	127, 484, 658
035D*	127, 484, 658
035F*	127, 484, 658
035G*	658
035G0ZZ	6, 10, 866
035G3ZZ	6, 10, 866
035G4ZZ	6, 10, 866
035H*	24, 127, 658
035J*	24, 127, 658
035K*	24, 127, 658
035L*	24, 127, 658
035M*	24, 127, 658
035N*	24, 127, 658
035P*	24, 127, 658
035Q*	24, 127, 658
035R*	24
035R*	127, 658
035S*	24, 127, 658
035T*	24, 127, 658
035U*	24, 127, 658
035V*	24, 127, 658
035Y*	127, 484, 658
037*	127
037334Z	24, 96, 184, 203, 273, 412, 484, 510, 658, 866
037335Z	24, 96, 184, 203, 273, 412, 484, 510, 658, 866
037336Z	24, 96, 184, 203, 273, 412, 484, 510, 658, 866
037337Z	24, 96, 184, 203, 273, 412, 484, 510, 658, 866
03733D1	24, 96, 184, 203, 273, 412, 484, 510, 658, 866
03733DZ	24, 96, 184, 203, 273, 412, 484, 510, 658, 866
03733EZ	24, 96, 184, 203, 273, 412, 484, 510, 658, 866
03733FZ	24, 96, 184, 203, 273, 412, 485, 510, 658, 866
03733GZ	24, 96, 184, 203, 273, 412, 485, 510, 658, 866
03733Z1	24, 96, 184, 203, 273, 412, 485, 510, 658, 866
03733ZZ	24, 96, 184, 204, 273, 412, 485, 510, 658, 866
037434Z	24, 96, 184, 204, 273, 412, 485, 510, 658, 866

Code	Page
037435Z	24, 96, 184, 204, 273, 412, 485, 510, 658, 866
037436Z	24, 96, 184, 204, 273, 412, 485, 510, 658, 866
037437Z	24, 96, 184, 204, 273, 412, 485, 510, 658, 866
03743D1	24, 96, 184, 204, 273, 412, 485, 510, 658, 866
03743DZ	24, 96, 184, 204, 273, 412, 485, 510, 658, 866
03743EZ	24, 96, 184, 204, 273, 412, 485, 510, 658, 866
03743FZ	24, 96, 184, 204, 274, 412, 485, 510, 658, 866
03743GZ	24, 96, 184, 204, 274, 412, 485, 510, 658, 866
03743Z1	24, 96, 184, 204, 274, 412, 485, 510, 658, 866
03743ZZ	24, 96, 184, 204, 274, 412, 485, 510, 658, 866
037734Z	24, 96, 184, 204, 274, 412, 485, 510, 658, 866
037735Z	24, 96, 184, 204, 274, 412, 485, 510, 658, 866
037736Z	24, 96, 184, 204, 274, 412, 485, 510, 658, 866
037737Z	24, 96, 184, 204, 274, 412, 485, 510, 658, 866
03773D1	24, 96, 184, 204, 274, 412, 485, 510, 658, 866
03773DZ	24, 96, 184, 204, 274, 412, 485, 510, 658, 866
03773EZ	24, 96, 184, 204, 274, 412, 485, 510, 658, 866
03773FZ	24, 96, 184, 204, 274, 412, 485, 510, 658, 866
03773GZ	24, 96, 184, 204, 274, 412, 485, 510, 658, 866
03773Z1	24, 96, 184, 204, 274, 412, 485, 510, 658, 866
03773ZZ	24, 96, 184, 204, 274, 412, 485, 510, 658, 866
037834Z	24, 96, 184, 204, 274, 412, 485, 510, 658, 866
037835Z	24, 96, 184, 204, 274, 412, 485, 510, 658, 866
037836Z	24, 96, 184, 204, 274, 412, 485, 510, 658, 866
037837Z	24, 96, 184, 204, 274, 412, 485, 510, 658, 866
03783D1	24, 96, 184, 204, 274, 412, 485, 510, 658, 866
03783DZ	24, 96, 184, 204, 274, 412, 485, 510, 658, 866
03783EZ	24, 96, 184, 204, 274, 412, 485, 510, 658, 866
03783FZ	24, 96, 184, 204, 274, 412, 485, 510, 658, 866
03783GZ	24, 96, 184, 204, 274, 412, 485, 510, 658, 866
03783Z1	24, 96, 184, 204, 274, 412, 485, 510, 658, 866
03783ZZ	24, 96, 184, 204, 274, 412, 485, 510, 658, 866
037934Z	24, 96, 184, 204, 274, 412, 485, 510, 658, 866
037935Z	24, 96, 184, 204, 274, 412, 485, 510, 658, 866
037936Z	24, 96, 184, 204, 274, 412, 485, 510, 658, 866
037937Z	24, 96, 184, 204, 274, 413, 485, 510, 658, 866
03793D1	24, 96, 184, 204, 274, 413, 485, 510, 658, 866
03793DZ	24, 96, 184, 204, 274, 413, 485, 510, 658, 866
03793EZ	24, 96, 184, 204, 274, 413, 485, 510, 658, 866
03793FZ	24, 96, 184, 204, 274, 413, 485, 510, 658, 866
03793GZ	24, 96, 184, 204, 274, 413, 485, 510, 658, 866
03793Z1	24, 96, 184, 204, 274, 413, 485, 510, 658, 866
03793ZZ	24, 96, 184, 204, 274, 413, 485, 510, 658, 866
037A34Z	24, 96, 184, 204, 274, 413, 485, 510, 658, 866
037A35Z	24, 96, 184, 204, 274, 413, 485, 510, 658, 866
037A36Z	24, 96, 184, 204, 274, 413, 485, 510, 658, 866
037A37Z	24, 96, 184, 204, 274, 413, 485, 510, 658, 866
037A3D1	24, 96, 184, 204, 274, 413, 485, 510, 658, 866
037A3DZ	24, 96, 184, 204, 274, 413, 485, 510, 658, 866
037A3EZ	24, 96, 184, 204, 274, 413, 485, 510, 658, 866
037A3FZ	24, 96, 184, 204, 274, 413, 485, 510, 658, 866
037A3GZ	24, 96, 184, 204, 274, 413, 485, 510, 658, 866
037A3Z1	24, 96, 184, 204, 274, 413, 485, 510, 658, 866
037A3ZZ	24, 96, 184, 204, 274, 413, 485, 510, 658, 866
037G34Z	10, 658, 866
037G35Z	10, 658, 866
037G36Z	10, 658, 866
037G37Z	10, 658, 866
037G3DZ	10, 658, 866
037G3EZ	10, 658, 866
037G3FZ	10, 658, 866
037G3GZ	10, 658, 866
037G3ZZ	10, 658, 866
037G44Z	10, 658, 866
037G45Z	10, 658, 866
037G46Z	10, 658, 866
037G47Z	10, 658, 866
037G4DZ	10, 658, 866
037G4EZ	10, 658, 866
037G4FZ	10, 658, 866
037G4GZ	10, 658, 866
037G4ZZ	10, 658, 866
037H04Z	24
037H0DZ	22
037H0ZZ	24
037H34Z	22, 658, 866
037H35Z	22, 658, 866
037H36Z	22, 658, 866
037H37Z	22, 658, 866
037H3DZ	22, 658, 866
037H3EZ	22, 658, 866
037H3FZ	22, 658, 866
037H3GZ	22, 658, 866
037H3ZZ	24, 658, 866
037H44Z	22, 659, 866
037H45Z	22, 659, 866
037H46Z	22, 659, 866
037H47Z	22, 659, 866
037H4DZ	22, 659, 866
037H4EZ	22, 659, 866
037H4FZ	22, 659, 866
037H4GZ	22, 659, 866
037H4ZZ	24, 659, 866
037J04Z	24
037J0DZ	22
037J0ZZ	24
037J34Z	22, 659, 866
037J35Z	22, 659, 866
037J36Z	22, 659, 866
037J37Z	22, 659, 866
037J3DZ	22, 659, 866
037J3EZ	22, 659, 866
037J3FZ	22, 659, 866
037J3GZ	22, 659, 866
037J3ZZ	24, 659, 866
037J44Z	22, 659, 866
037J45Z	22, 659, 866
037J46Z	22, 659, 866
037J47Z	22, 659, 866
037J4DZ	22, 659, 866
037J4EZ	22, 659, 866
037J4FZ	22, 659, 866
037J4GZ	22, 659, 866
037J4ZZ	24, 659, 866
037K04Z	24
037K0DZ	22
037K0ZZ	24
037K34Z	22, 659, 866
037K35Z	22, 659, 866
037K36Z	22, 659, 866
037K37Z	23, 659, 866
037K3DZ	23, 659, 866
037K3EZ	23, 659, 866
037K3FZ	23, 659, 866
037K3GZ	23, 659, 866
037K3ZZ	24, 659, 866
037K44Z	23, 659, 866
037K45Z	23, 659, 866
037K46Z	23, 659, 867
037K47Z	23, 659, 867
037K4DZ	23, 659, 867
037K4EZ	23, 659, 867
037K4FZ	23, 659, 867
037K4GZ	23, 659, 867
037K4ZZ	24, 659, 867
037L04Z	24
037L0DZ	23
037L0ZZ	24
037L34Z	23, 659, 867
037L35Z	23, 659, 867
037L36Z	23, 659, 867
037L37Z	23, 659, 867
037L3DZ	23, 659, 867
037L3EZ	23, 659, 867
037L3FZ	23, 659, 867
037L3GZ	23, 659, 867
037L3ZZ	24, 659, 867
037L44Z	23, 659, 867
037L45Z	23, 659, 867
037L46Z	23, 659, 867
037L47Z	23, 659, 867
037L4DZ	23, 659, 867
037L4EZ	23, 659, 867
037L4FZ	23, 659, 867
037L4GZ	23, 659, 867
037L4ZZ	24, 659, 867
037M04Z	24
037M0DZ	23
037M0ZZ	24
037M34Z	23, 659, 867
037M35Z	23, 659, 867
037M36Z	23, 659, 867
037M37Z	23, 659, 867
037M3DZ	23, 659, 867
037M3EZ	23, 659, 867
037M3FZ	23, 659, 867
037M3GZ	23, 659, 867
037M3ZZ	24, 659, 867
037M44Z	23, 659, 867
037M45Z	23, 659, 867
037M46Z	23, 659, 867
037M47Z	23, 659, 867
037M4DZ	23, 659, 867
037M4EZ	23, 659, 867
037M4FZ	23, 659, 867
037M4GZ	23, 659, 867
037M4ZZ	24, 659, 867
037N04Z	24
037N0DZ	23
037N0ZZ	24
037N34Z	23, 659, 867
037N35Z	23, 659, 867
037N36Z	23, 659, 867
037N37Z	23, 659, 867
037N3DZ	23, 659, 867
037N3EZ	23, 659, 867
037N3FZ	23, 659, 867
037N3GZ	23, 659, 867
037N3ZZ	24, 659, 867
037N44Z	23, 659, 867
037N45Z	23, 659, 867
037N46Z	23, 659, 867
037N47Z	23, 659, 867
037N4DZ	23, 659, 867
037N4EZ	23, 659, 867
037N4FZ	23, 659, 867
037N4GZ	23, 659, 867
037N4ZZ	24, 659, 867
037P04Z	24
037P0DZ	24
037P0ZZ	24
037P34Z	24, 659, 867
037P35Z	24, 659, 867
037P36Z	24, 659, 867
037P37Z	25, 659, 867
037P3DZ	25, 659, 867
037P3EZ	25, 659, 867
037P3FZ	25, 659, 867
037P3GZ	25, 659, 867
037P3ZZ	25, 659, 867
037P44Z	25, 659, 867
037P45Z	25, 659, 867
037P46Z	25, 659, 867
037P47Z	25, 659, 867
037P4DZ	25, 659, 867
037P4EZ	25, 659, 867
037P4FZ	25, 659, 867
037P4GZ	25, 659, 867
037P4ZZ	25, 659, 867
037Q04Z	25
037Q0DZ	25
037Q0ZZ	25
037Q34Z	25, 659, 867
037Q35Z	25, 659, 867
037Q36Z	25, 659, 867
037Q37Z	25, 659, 867
037Q3DZ	25, 659, 867
037Q3EZ	25, 659, 867
037Q3FZ	25, 659, 867
037Q3GZ	25, 659, 867
037Q3ZZ	25, 659, 867
037Q44Z	25, 659, 867
037Q45Z	25, 659, 867
037Q46Z	25, 659, 867
037Q47Z	25, 659, 867
037Q4DZ	25, 659, 867
037Q4EZ	25, 659, 867
037Q4FZ	25, 659, 867
037Q4GZ	25, 659, 867
037Q4ZZ	25, 659, 867
037Y04Z	25
037Y0DZ	25
037Y0ZZ	25
037Y34Z	25, 96, 184, 204, 274, 413, 485, 510, 659, 867
037Y35Z	25, 96, 184, 204, 274, 413, 485, 510, 659, 867
037Y36Z	25, 96, 184, 204, 274, 413, 485, 510, 659, 867
037Y37Z	25, 96, 184, 204, 274, 413, 485, 510, 659, 867
037Y3DZ	25, 96, 184, 204, 274, 413, 485, 510, 659, 867
037Y3EZ	25, 96, 185, 204, 274, 413, 485, 510, 659, 867
037Y3FZ	25, 96, 185, 204, 274, 413, 485, 510, 659, 867
037Y3GZ	25, 96, 185, 204, 274, 413, 485, 510, 659, 867
037Y3ZZ	25, 96, 185, 204, 274, 413, 485, 510, 659, 867
03900ZX	127, 1045
03904ZX	127, 1045
03910ZX	127, 1045
03914ZX	127, 1045
03920ZX	127, 1045
03924ZX	127, 1045
03930ZX	127, 1045
03934ZX	1045
03934ZX	127
03940ZX	127, 1045
03944ZX	127, 1045
03950ZX	127, 1045
03954ZX	127, 1045
03960ZX	127, 1045
03964ZX	127, 1045
03970ZX	127, 1045
03974ZX	127, 1045
03980ZX	127, 1045
03984ZX	127, 1045
03990ZX	127, 1045
03994ZX	127, 1045
039A0ZX	127, 1045
039A4ZX	127, 1045
039B0ZX	127, 1045
039B4ZX	127, 1045
039C0ZX	127, 1045
039C4ZX	127, 1045
039D0ZX	127, 1045
039D4ZX	127, 1045
039F0ZX	127, 1045
039F4ZX	127, 1045
039G0ZX	127, 1045
039G4ZX	127, 1045
039H0ZX	127, 1045
039H4ZX	127, 1045
039J0ZX	127, 1045
039J4ZX	127, 1045
039K0ZX	127, 1045
039K4ZX	127, 1045
039L0ZX	127, 1045
039L4ZX	127, 1045
039M0ZX	127, 1045
039M4ZX	127, 1045
039N0ZX	127, 1045
039N4ZX	127, 1045
039P0ZX	127, 1045
039P4ZX	127, 1045
039Q0ZX	127, 1045
039Q4ZX	127, 1045
039R0ZX	127, 1045
039R4ZX	127, 1045
039S0ZX	32, 57, 71, 96, 127, 274, 485, 510, 1045
039S4ZX	32, 57, 71, 96, 127, 274, 485, 510, 1045
039T0ZX	32, 57, 71, 96, 127, 274, 485, 510, 1045
039T4ZX	32, 57, 71, 96, 127, 274, 485, 510, 1045
039U0ZX	127, 1045
039U4ZX	127, 1045
039V0ZX	127, 1045
039V4ZX	127, 1045
039Y0ZX	127, 1045
039Y4ZX	127, 1045
03B00ZX	127, 1045
03B00ZZ	89, 154
03B03ZX	127, 1045
03B03ZZ	89, 154, 174, 659, 867
03B04ZX	127, 1045
03B04ZZ	89, 154
03B10ZX	127, 1045
03B10ZZ	89, 154
03B13ZX	127, 1045
03B13ZZ	89, 154, 174, 659, 867
03B14ZX	127, 1045
03B14ZZ	89, 154
03B20ZX	127, 1045
03B20ZZ	89, 154
03B23ZX	127, 1045
03B23ZZ	89, 154, 174, 659, 867
03B24ZX	127, 1045
03B24ZZ	89, 154
03B30ZX	127, 1045
03B30ZZ	89, 154
03B33ZX	127, 1045
03B33ZZ	89, 154, 174, 659, 867
03B34ZX	127, 1045
03B34ZZ	89, 154
03B40ZX	127, 1045
03B40ZZ	89, 154
03B43ZX	127, 1045
03B43ZZ	89, 154, 174, 659, 867
03B44ZX	127, 1045
03B44ZZ	89, 154
03B5*	127
03B50ZX	1045
03B50ZZ	485, 659, 867
03B53ZX	1045
03B53ZZ	485, 659, 867
03B54ZX	1045
03B54ZZ	485, 659, 867
03B6*	127
03B60ZX	1045
03B60ZZ	485, 659, 867
03B63ZX	1045
03B63ZZ	485, 659, 867
03B64ZX	1045
03B64ZZ	485, 659, 867
03B7*	127
03B70ZX	1045
03B70ZZ	485, 659, 867
03B73ZX	1045
03B73ZZ	485, 659, 867
03B74ZX	1045
03B74ZZ	485, 659, 867
03B8*	127
03B80ZX	1045
03B80ZZ	485, 659, 867
03B83ZX	1045
03B83ZZ	485, 659, 867
03B84ZX	1045
03B84ZZ	485, 659, 867
03B9*	127
03B90ZX	1045
03B90ZZ	485, 659, 867
03B93ZX	1045
03B93ZZ	485, 659, 867
03B94ZX	1045
03B94ZZ	485, 659, 867
03BA*	127
03BA0ZX	1045
03BA0ZZ	485, 659, 867
03BA3ZX	1045
03BA3ZZ	485, 659, 867
03BA4ZX	1045
03BA4ZZ	485, 659, 867
03BB*	127
03BB0ZX	1045
03BB0ZZ	485, 659, 867
03BB3ZX	1045
03BB3ZZ	485, 659, 867
03BB4ZX	1045
03BB4ZZ	485, 659, 867
03BC*	127
03BC0ZX	1045
03BC0ZZ	485, 659, 867
03BC3ZX	1045
03BC3ZZ	485, 659, 867
03BC4ZX	1045
03BC4ZZ	485, 659, 867
03BD*	127
03BD0ZX	1045
03BD0ZZ	485, 659, 867
03BD3ZX	1045
03BD3ZZ	485, 660, 867
03BD4ZX	1045
03BD4ZZ	485, 660, 867
03BF*	127
03BF0ZX	1045
03BF0ZZ	485, 660, 867
03BF3ZX	1045
03BF3ZZ	485, 660, 867
03BF4ZX	1045
03BF4ZZ	485, 660, 867
03BG0ZX	127, 1045
03BG0ZZ	6, 10, 660, 867
03BG3ZX	127, 1045
03BG3ZZ	6, 10, 660, 867
03BG4ZX	127, 1045

Numeric Index to Procedures

Code	Page	Code	Page	Code	Page	Code	Page	Code	Page	Code	Page
03BG4ZZ	6, 10, 660, 867	03BV0ZZ	25, 71, 660, 868	03CL3Z7	10, 660, 868	03H64DZ	96, 128, 584, 609, 660, 868	03HN0DZ	71, 128, 584, 609, 661, 869	03L33CZ	154
03BH*	127	03BV3ZX	1045	03CL3ZZ	10, 660, 868			03HN3DZ	71, 128, 584, 609, 661, 869	03L33DZ	154
03BH0ZX	1045	03BV3ZZ	25, 71, 660, 868	03CL4ZZ	10, 660, 868	03H70DZ	128, 584, 609, 660, 868			03L33ZZ	154
03BH0ZZ	25, 71, 660, 867	03BV4ZX	1045	03CM0ZZ	25, 71, 128, 485, 660, 868			03HN4DZ	71, 128, 584, 609, 661, 869	03L34CZ	154
03BH3ZX	1045	03BV4ZZ	25, 71, 660, 868	03CM3Z7	10, 660, 868	03H73DZ	128, 584, 609, 660, 868			03L34DZ	154
03BH3ZZ	25, 71, 660, 867	03BY*	127	03CM3ZZ	10, 660, 868			03HP0DZ	71, 128, 584, 609, 661, 869	03L34ZZ	154
03BH4ZX	1045	03BY0ZX	1045	03CM4ZZ	10, 660, 868	03H74DZ	128, 584, 609, 660, 868			03L4*	89, 174, 661
03BH4ZZ	25, 71, 660, 867	03BY0ZZ	485, 660, 868	03CN0ZZ	25, 71, 128, 485, 660, 868			03HP3DZ	71, 128, 584, 609, 661, 869	03L40CZ	154
03BJ*	127	03BY3ZX	1045	03CN3Z7	10, 660, 868	03H80DJ	128, 584, 609, 660, 868			03L40DZ	154
03BJ0ZX	1045	03BY3ZZ	485, 660, 868	03CN3ZZ	10, 660, 868			03HP4DZ	71, 128, 584, 609, 661, 869	03L40ZZ	154
03BJ0ZZ	25, 71, 660, 867	03BY4ZX	1045	03CN4ZZ	10, 660, 868	03H83DZ	128, 584, 609, 661, 868			03L43CZ	154
03BJ3ZX	1045	03BY4ZZ	485, 660, 868	03CP0ZZ	25, 71, 128, 485, 660, 868			03HQ0DZ	71, 128, 584, 609, 661, 869	03L43DZ	154
03BJ3ZZ	25, 71, 660, 867	03C0*	89	03CP3Z7	660, 868	03H84DZ	128, 584, 609, 661, 868			03L43ZZ	154
03BJ4ZX	1045	03C00ZZ	154, 660, 868	03CP3Z7	10			03HQ3DZ	71, 128, 584, 609, 661, 869	03L44CZ	154
03BJ4ZZ	25, 71, 660, 867	03C03ZZ	154, 660, 868	03CP3ZZ	10, 660, 868	03H90DZ	128, 584, 609, 661, 868			03L44DZ	154
03BK*	127	03C04ZZ	154, 660, 868	03CP4ZZ	10, 660, 868			03HQ4DZ	71, 128, 584, 609, 661, 869	03L44ZZ	154
03BK0ZX	1045	03C1*	89	03CQ0ZZ	25, 71, 128, 485, 660, 868	03H93DZ	128, 584, 609, 661, 868			03L5*	661
03BK0ZZ	25, 71, 660, 867	03C10ZZ	154, 660, 868	03CQ3Z7	10, 660, 868			03HR0DZ	71, 128, 584, 609, 661, 869	03L50CZ	128, 485, 869
03BK3ZX	1045	03C13ZZ	154, 660, 868	03CQ3ZZ	10, 660, 868	03H94DZ	128, 584, 609, 661, 868			03L50DZ	128, 869
03BK3ZZ	25, 71, 660, 867	03C14ZZ	154, 660, 868	03CQ4ZZ	10, 660, 868			03HR3DZ	71, 128, 584, 609, 661, 869	03L53CZ	128, 485, 869
03BK4ZX	1045	03C2*	89	03CR0ZZ	25, 71, 128, 485, 660, 868	03HA0DZ	128, 584, 609, 661, 868			03L53DZ	128, 869
03BK4ZZ	25, 71, 660, 867	03C20ZZ	154, 660, 868	03CR3ZZ	10, 660, 868			03HR4DZ	71, 128, 584, 609, 661, 869	03L53ZZ	128, 485, 869
03BL*	127	03C23ZZ	154, 660, 868	03CR4ZZ	10, 660, 868	03HA3DZ	128, 584, 609, 661, 868			03L54CZ	128, 485, 869
03BL0ZX	1045	03C24ZZ	154, 660, 868	03CS0ZZ	25, 71, 128, 485, 660, 868			03HS0DZ	71, 128, 584, 609, 661, 869	03L54DZ	128, 869
03BL0ZZ	25, 71, 660, 867	03C3*	89	03CS3ZZ	10, 660, 868	03HA4DZ	128, 584, 609, 661, 868			03L54ZZ	128, 485, 869
03BL3ZX	1045	03C30ZZ	154, 660, 868	03CS4ZZ	10, 660, 868			03HS3DZ	71, 128, 584, 609, 661, 869	03L6*	661
03BL3ZZ	25, 71, 660, 867	03C33ZZ	154, 660, 868	03CT0ZZ	25, 71, 128, 485, 660, 868	03HB0DZ	128, 584, 609, 661, 868			03L60CZ	128, 485, 869
03BL4ZX	1045	03C34ZZ	154, 660, 868	03CT3ZZ	10, 660, 868			03HS4DZ	71, 128, 584, 609, 661, 869	03L60DZ	128, 869
03BL4ZZ	25, 71, 660, 867	03C4*	89	03CT4ZZ	10, 660, 868	03HB3DZ	128, 584, 609, 661, 868			03L63CZ	128, 485, 869
03BM*	127	03C40ZZ	154, 660, 868	03CU0ZZ	25, 71, 128, 485, 660, 868			03HT0DZ	71, 128, 584, 609, 661, 869	03L63DZ	128, 869
03BM0ZX	1045	03C43ZZ	154, 660, 868	03CU3ZZ	10, 660, 868	03HB4DZ	128, 584, 609, 661, 868			03L63ZZ	128, 485, 869
03BM0ZZ	25, 71, 660, 867	03C44ZZ	154, 660, 868	03CU4ZZ	10, 660, 868			03HT3DZ	71, 128, 584, 609, 661, 869	03L64CZ	128, 485, 869
03BM3ZX	1045	03C5*	127, 485	03CV0ZZ	25, 71, 128, 485, 660, 868	03HC0DZ	128, 584, 609, 661, 868			03L64DZ	128, 869
03BM3ZZ	25, 71, 660, 867	03C50ZZ	660, 868	03CV3ZZ	10, 660, 868			03HT4DZ	71, 128, 584, 609, 661, 869	03L64ZZ	128, 485, 869
03BM4ZX	1045	03C53ZZ	660, 868	03CV4ZZ	10, 660, 868	03HC3DZ	128, 584, 609, 661, 868			03L7*	661
03BM4ZZ	25, 71, 660, 867	03C54ZZ	660, 868	03CY*	25			03HU0DZ	71, 128, 584, 609, 661, 869	03L70CZ	128, 485, 869
03BN*	127	03C6*	127, 485	03CY*	128, 185, 204, 485, 510	03HC4DZ	128, 584, 609, 661, 868			03L70DZ	128, 869
03BN0ZX	1045	03C60ZZ	660, 868					03HU3DZ	71, 128, 584, 609, 661, 869	03L70ZZ	128, 485, 869
03BN0ZZ	25, 71, 660, 867	03C63ZZ	660, 868	03CY0ZZ	660, 868	03HD0DZ	128, 584, 609, 661, 868			03L73CZ	128, 485, 869
03BN3ZX	1045	03C64ZZ	660, 868	03CY3ZZ	660, 868			03HU4DZ	71, 128, 584, 609, 661, 869	03L73DZ	128, 869
03BN3ZZ	25, 71, 660, 867	03C7*	127, 485	03CY4ZZ	660, 868	03HD3DZ	128, 584, 609, 661, 868			03L73ZZ	128, 485, 869
03BN4ZX	1045	03C70ZZ	660, 868	03H00DZ	96, 128, 609, 660, 868			03HV0DZ	71, 128, 584, 609, 661, 869	03L74CZ	128, 485, 869
03BN4ZZ	25, 71, 660, 867	03C73ZZ	660, 868	03H00DZ	583	03HD4DZ	128, 584, 609, 661, 868			03L74DZ	128, 869
03BP*	127	03C74ZZ	660, 868	03H03DZ	96, 128, 609, 660, 868			03HV3DZ	71, 128, 584, 609, 661, 869	03L74ZZ	128, 485, 869
03BP0ZX	1045	03C8*	128, 485	03H03DZ	583	03HF0DZ	128, 584, 609, 661, 868			03L8*	661
03BP0ZZ	25, 71, 660, 867	03C80ZZ	660, 868	03H04DZ	96, 128, 583, 609, 660, 868			03HV4DZ	71, 128, 584, 609, 661, 869	03L80CZ	128, 485, 869
03BP3ZX	1045	03C83ZZ	660, 868	03H10DZ	96, 128, 583, 609, 660, 868	03HF3DZ	128, 584, 609, 661, 868			03L80DZ	128, 869
03BP3ZZ	25, 71, 660, 867	03C84ZZ	660, 868	03H13DZ	96, 128, 583, 609, 660, 868			03HY02Z	128	03L80ZZ	128, 485, 869
03BP4ZX	1045	03C9*	128, 485	03H14DZ	96, 128, 583, 609, 660, 868	03HF4DZ	128, 584, 609, 661, 868	03HY0DZ	71, 128, 584, 609, 661, 869	03L83CZ	128, 485, 869
03BP4ZZ	25, 71, 660, 867	03C90ZZ	660, 868	03H20DZ	71, 128, 583, 609, 660, 868	03HG0DZ	128, 584, 609, 661, 868	03HY0YZ	128	03L83DZ	128, 869
03BQ*	127	03C93ZZ	660, 868	03H23DZ	71, 128, 583, 609, 660, 868			03HY3DZ	71, 128, 584, 609, 661, 869	03L83ZZ	128, 485, 869
03BQ0ZX	1045	03C94ZZ	660, 868	03H24DZ	71, 128, 583, 609, 660, 868	03HG3DZ	128, 584, 609, 661, 868	03HY42Z	128	03L84CZ	128, 485, 869
03BQ0ZZ	25, 71, 660, 867	03CA*	128, 485	03H30DZ	96, 128, 584, 609, 660, 868	03HG4DZ	128, 584, 609, 661, 868	03HY4DZ	71, 128, 584, 609, 661, 869	03L84DZ	128, 869
03BQ3ZX	1045	03CA0ZZ	660, 868	03H33DZ	96, 128, 584, 609, 660, 868			03JY0ZZ	128	03L84ZZ	128, 485, 869
03BQ3ZZ	25, 71, 660, 867	03CA3ZZ	660, 868	03H34DZ	96, 128, 584, 609, 660, 868	03HH0DZ	128, 584, 609, 661, 868	03L0*	661	03L9*	661
03BQ4ZX	1045	03CA4ZZ	660, 868	03H40DZ	96, 128, 584, 609, 660, 868	03HH3DZ	128, 584, 609, 661, 868	03L00CZ	154	03L90CZ	128, 485, 869
03BQ4ZZ	25, 71, 660, 867	03CB*	128, 485	03H43DZ	96, 128, 584, 609, 660, 868	03HH4DZ	128, 584, 609, 661, 868	03L00DZ	154	03L90DZ	128, 869
03BR*	127	03CB0ZZ	660, 868	03H44DZ	96, 128, 584, 609, 660, 868	03HJ0DZ	71, 128, 584, 609, 661, 868	03L00ZZ	154	03L90ZZ	128, 485, 869
03BR0ZX	1045	03CB3ZZ	660, 868	03H50DZ	96, 128, 584, 609, 660, 868	03HJ3DZ	71, 128, 584, 609, 661, 868	03L03CZ	154	03L93CZ	128, 485, 869
03BR0ZZ	25, 71, 660, 867	03CB4ZZ	660, 868	03H53DZ	96, 128, 584, 609, 660, 868	03HJ4DZ	71, 128, 584, 609, 661, 868	03L03DZ	154	03L93DZ	128, 869
03BR3ZX	1045	03CC*	128, 485	03H54DZ	96, 128, 584, 609, 660, 868	03HK0DZ	71, 128, 584, 609, 661, 868	03L03ZZ	154	03L93ZZ	128, 485, 869
03BR3ZZ	25, 71, 660, 867	03CC0ZZ	660, 868	03H60DZ	96, 128, 584, 609, 660, 868	03HK0MZ	128	03L04CZ	154	03L94CZ	128, 485, 869
03BR4ZX	1045	03CC3ZZ	660, 868	03H63DZ	96, 128, 584, 609, 660, 868	03HK3DZ	71, 128, 584, 609, 661, 868	03L04DZ	154	03L94DZ	128, 869
03BR4ZZ	25, 71, 660, 867	03CC4ZZ	660, 868			03HK3MZ	128	03L04ZZ	154	03L94ZZ	128, 485, 869
03BS*	71, 127	03CD*	128, 485			03HK4DZ	71, 128, 584, 609, 661, 868	03L1*	661	03LA*	661
03BS0ZX	32, 57, 96, 274, 485, 510, 1045	03CD0ZZ	660, 868			03HK4MZ	128	03L10CZ	154	03LA0CZ	128, 485, 869
		03CD3ZZ	660, 868			03HL0DZ	128, 584, 609, 661, 868	03L10DZ	154	03LA0DZ	128, 869
03BS0ZZ	25, 660, 867	03CD4ZZ	660, 868			03HL0MZ	128	03L10ZZ	154	03LA0ZZ	128, 485, 869
03BS3ZX	32, 57, 96, 274, 485, 510, 1045	03CF*	128, 485			03HL3DZ	128, 584, 609, 661, 868	03L13CZ	154	03LA3CZ	128, 485, 869
		03CF0ZZ	660, 868			03HL3MZ	128	03L13DZ	154	03LA3DZ	128, 869
03BS3ZZ	25, 660, 867	03CF3ZZ	660, 868			03HL4DZ	128, 584, 609, 661, 868	03L13ZZ	154	03LA3ZZ	128, 485, 869
03BS4ZX	32, 57, 96, 274, 485, 510, 1045	03CF4ZZ	660, 868			03HL4MZ	128	03L14CZ	154	03LA4CZ	129, 485, 869
03BT*	71, 127	03CG0ZZ	6, 10, 660, 868			03HM0DZ	71, 128, 584, 609, 661, 868	03L14DZ	154	03LA4DZ	129, 869
03BT0ZX	32, 57, 96, 274, 485, 510, 1045	03CG3Z7	10, 128, 660, 868			03HM3DZ	71, 128, 584, 609, 661, 868	03L14ZZ	154	03LA4ZZ	129, 485, 869
		03CG4ZZ	6, 10, 660, 868					03L2*	89	03LB*	661
03BT0ZZ	25, 660, 868	03CH0ZZ	25, 71, 128, 485, 660, 868			03HM4DZ	71, 128, 584, 609, 661, 868	03L2*	174, 661	03LB0CZ	129, 485, 869
03BT3ZX	32, 57, 96, 274, 485, 510, 1045	03CH3Z7	10, 660, 868					03L20CZ	154	03LB0DZ	129, 869
		03CH3ZZ	10, 660, 868					03L20DZ	154	03LB0ZZ	129, 485, 869
03BT3ZZ	25, 660, 868	03CH4ZZ	10, 660, 868					03L20ZZ	154	03LB3CZ	129, 485, 869
03BT4ZX	32, 57, 96, 274, 485, 510, 1045	03CJ0ZZ	25, 71, 128, 485, 660, 868					03L23CZ	154	03LB3DZ	129, 869
		03CJ3Z7	10, 660, 868					03L23DZ	154	03LB3ZZ	129, 486, 869
03BT4ZZ	25, 660, 868	03CJ3ZZ	10, 660, 868					03L23ZZ	154	03LB4CZ	129, 486, 869
03BU*	127	03CJ4ZZ	10, 660, 868					03L24CZ	154	03LB4DZ	129, 869
03BU0ZX	1045	03CK0ZZ	25, 71, 128, 485, 660, 868					03L24DZ	154	03LB4ZZ	129, 486, 869
03BU0ZZ	25, 71, 660, 868	03CK3Z7	10, 660, 868					03L24ZZ	154	03LC*	661
03BU3ZX	1045	03CK3ZZ	10, 660, 868					03L3*	89, 174, 661	03LC0CZ	129, 869
03BU3ZZ	25, 71, 660, 868	03CK4ZZ	10, 660, 868					03L30CZ	154	03LC0DZ	129, 869
03BU4ZX	1045	03CL0ZZ	25, 71, 128, 485, 660, 868					03L30DZ	154	03LC0ZZ	129, 486, 869
03BU4ZZ	25, 71, 660, 868									03L30ZZ	154	03LC3CZ	129, 486, 869
03BV*	127											03LC3DZ	129, 869
03BV0ZX	1045											03LC3ZZ	129, 486, 869

Code	Page
03LC4CZ	129, 486, 869
03LC4DZ	129, 869
03LC4ZZ	129, 486, 869
03LD*	661
03LD0CZ	129, 486, 869
03LD0DZ	129, 869
03LD0ZZ	129, 486, 869
03LD3CZ	129, 486, 869
03LD3DZ	129, 869
03LD3ZZ	129, 486, 869
03LD4CZ	129, 486, 869
03LD4DZ	129, 869
03LD4ZZ	129, 486, 869
03LF*	661
03LF0CZ	129, 486, 869
03LF0DZ	129, 869
03LF0ZZ	129, 486, 869
03LF3CZ	129, 486, 869
03LF3DZ	129, 869
03LF3ZZ	129, 486, 869
03LF4CZ	129, 486, 869
03LF4DZ	129, 869
03LF4ZZ	129, 486, 869
03LG*	661
03LG0BZ	6, 10, 154, 510, 869
03LG0CZ	6, 10, 849
03LG0DZ	10, 154, 510, 869
03LG0DZ	6
03LG0ZZ	6, 10, 849
03LG3BZ	6, 11, 154, 510, 869
03LG3CZ	6, 11, 849
03LG3DZ	11, 154, 510, 869
03LG3DZ	6
03LG3ZZ	6, 11, 849
03LG4BZ	6, 11, 154, 510, 869
03LG4CZ	6, 11, 849
03LG4DZ	11, 154, 510, 869
03LG4DZ	6
03LG4ZZ	6, 11, 849
03LH*	661
03LH0BZ	6, 11, 154, 510, 869
03LH0CZ	32, 71, 129, 869
03LH0DZ	11, 154, 510, 869
03LH0DZ	6
03LH0ZZ	32, 71, 129, 869
03LH3BZ	6, 11, 154, 510, 869
03LH3CZ	32, 71, 129, 869
03LH3DZ	11, 154, 510, 869
03LH3DZ	6
03LH3ZZ	32, 71, 129, 869
03LH4BZ	6, 11, 154, 510, 869
03LH4CZ	32, 71, 129, 869
03LH4DZ	11, 154, 510, 869
03LH4DZ	6
03LH4ZZ	32, 71, 129, 869
03LJ*	661
03LJ0BZ	6, 11, 154, 510, 869
03LJ0CZ	32, 71, 129, 869
03LJ0DZ	11, 154, 510, 869
03LJ0DZ	6
03LJ0ZZ	32, 71, 129, 869
03LJ3BZ	6, 11, 154, 510, 869
03LJ3CZ	32, 71, 129, 869
03LJ3DZ	11, 154, 510, 869
03LJ3DZ	6
03LJ3ZZ	32, 71, 129, 869
03LJ4BZ	6, 11, 154, 510, 869
03LJ4CZ	32, 71, 129, 869
03LJ4DZ	11, 154, 510, 869
03LJ4DZ	6
03LJ4ZZ	32, 71, 129, 869
03LK0BZ	6, 11, 154, 510, 661, 869
03LK0CZ	6, 11, 129
03LK0DZ	11, 154, 510, 661, 869
03LK0DZ	6
03LK0ZZ	6, 11, 129
03LK3BZ	6, 11, 154, 510, 661, 869
03LK3CZ	6, 11, 129
03LK3DZ	11, 154, 510, 661, 869
03LK3DZ	6
03LK3ZZ	6, 11, 129
03LK4BZ	6, 11, 154, 510, 661, 869
03LK4CZ	6, 11, 129
03LK4DZ	11, 154, 510, 661, 869
03LK4DZ	6
03LK4ZZ	6, 11, 129
03LL0BZ	6, 11, 154, 510, 661, 869
03LL0CZ	6, 11, 129
03LL0DZ	11, 154, 510, 661, 869
03LL0DZ	6
03LL0ZZ	6, 11, 129
03LL3BZ	6, 11, 154, 510, 661, 869
03LL3CZ	6, 11, 129
03LL3DZ	11, 154, 510, 661, 869
03LL3DZ	6
03LL3ZZ	6, 11, 129
03LL4BZ	6, 11, 154, 510, 661, 869
03LL4CZ	6, 11, 129
03LL4DZ	11, 154, 510, 661, 869
03LL4DZ	6
03LL4ZZ	6, 11, 129
03LM*	661
03LM0BZ	6, 11, 154, 510, 869
03LM0CZ	32, 71, 129, 869
03LM0DZ	11, 154, 510, 869
03LM0DZ	6
03LM0ZZ	32, 71, 129, 869
03LM3BZ	6, 11, 154, 510, 869
03LM3CZ	32, 71, 129, 869
03LM3DZ	11, 154, 510, 869
03LM3DZ	6
03LM3ZZ	32, 72, 129, 869
03LM4BZ	6, 11, 154, 511, 869
03LM4CZ	32, 72, 129, 869
03LM4DZ	11, 154, 511, 869
03LM4DZ	6
03LM4ZZ	32, 72, 129, 869
03LN*	661
03LN0BZ	6, 11, 154, 510, 869
03LN0CZ	33, 72, 129, 869
03LN0DZ	11, 154, 510, 869
03LN0DZ	6
03LN0ZZ	33, 72, 129, 870
03LN3BZ	6, 11, 154, 511, 870
03LN3CZ	33, 72, 129, 870
03LN3DZ	11, 154, 511, 870
03LN3DZ	6
03LN3ZZ	33, 72, 129, 870
03LN4BZ	6, 11, 154, 511, 870
03LN4CZ	33, 72, 129, 870
03LN4DZ	11, 154, 511, 870
03LN4DZ	6
03LN4ZZ	33, 72, 129, 870
03LP*	661
03LP0BZ	6, 11, 154, 511, 870
03LP0CZ	33, 72, 129, 870
03LP0DZ	11, 154, 511, 870
03LP0DZ	6
03LP0ZZ	33, 72, 129, 870
03LP3BZ	6, 11, 154, 511, 870
03LP3CZ	33, 72, 129, 870
03LP3DZ	11, 154, 511, 870
03LP3DZ	6
03LP3ZZ	33, 72, 129, 870
03LP4BZ	6, 11, 154, 511, 870
03LP4CZ	33, 72, 129, 870
03LP4DZ	11, 154, 511, 870
03LP4DZ	6
03LP4ZZ	33, 72, 129, 870
03LQ*	661
03LQ0BZ	6, 11, 154, 511, 870
03LQ0CZ	33, 72, 129, 870
03LQ0DZ	11, 154, 511, 870
03LQ0DZ	6
03LQ0ZZ	33, 72, 129, 870
03LQ3BZ	6, 11, 154, 511, 870
03LQ3CZ	33, 72, 129, 870
03LQ3DZ	11, 154, 511, 870
03LQ3DZ	6
03LQ3ZZ	33, 72, 129, 870
03LQ4BZ	6, 11, 154, 511, 870
03LQ4CZ	33, 72, 129, 870
03LQ4DZ	11, 155, 511, 870
03LQ4DZ	6
03LR*	661
03LR0CZ	33, 72, 129, 870
03LR0DZ	11, 155, 511, 870
03LR0DZ	6
03LR0ZZ	33, 72, 129, 870
03LR3CZ	33, 72, 129, 870
03LR3DZ	11, 155, 511, 870
03LR3DZ	6
03LR3ZZ	33, 72, 129, 870
03LR4CZ	33, 72, 129, 870
03LR4DZ	11, 155, 511, 870
03LR4DZ	6
03LR4ZZ	33, 72, 129, 870
03LS*	661
03LS0CZ	33, 72, 129, 870
03LS0DZ	11, 155, 511, 870
03LS0DZ	6
03LS0ZZ	33, 72, 129, 870
03LS3CZ	33, 72, 129, 870
03LS3DZ	11, 155, 511, 870
03LS3DZ	6
03LS3ZZ	33, 72, 129, 870
03LS4CZ	33, 72, 129, 870
03LS4DZ	11, 155, 511, 870
03LS4DZ	6
03LS4ZZ	33, 72, 129, 870
03LT*	661
03LT0CZ	33, 72, 129, 870
03LT0DZ	11, 155, 511, 870
03LT0DZ	6
03LT0ZZ	33, 72, 129, 870
03LT3CZ	33, 72, 129, 870
03LT3DZ	11, 155, 511, 870
03LT3DZ	6
03LT3ZZ	33, 72, 129, 870
03LT4CZ	33, 72, 129, 870
03LT4DZ	11, 155, 511, 870
03LT4DZ	6
03LT4ZZ	33, 72, 129, 870
03LU*	483, 661
03LU0CZ	870
03LU0DZ	870
03LU0ZZ	870
03LU3CZ	870
03LU3DZ	870
03LU3ZZ	870
03LU4CZ	870
03LU4DZ	870
03LU4ZZ	870
03LV*	483, 661
03LV0CZ	870
03LV0DZ	870
03LV0ZZ	870
03LV3CZ	870
03LV3DZ	870
03LV3ZZ	870
03LV4CZ	870
03LV4DZ	870
03LV4ZZ	870
03LY*	661
03LY0CZ	129, 870
03LY0DZ	129, 870
03LY0ZZ	129, 870
03LY3CZ	129, 870
03LY3DZ	129, 870
03LY3ZZ	129, 870
03LY4CZ	129, 870
03LY4DZ	129, 870
03LY4ZZ	129, 870
03N*	129
03PY00Z	129
03PY02Z	129
03PY03Z	129
03PY07Z	144, 511, 661, 870
03PY0CZ	129
03PY0DZ	129
03PY0JZ	144, 511, 661, 870
03PY0KZ	144, 511, 661, 870
03PY0MZ	129
03PY0YZ	129
03PY37Z	144, 511, 661, 870
03PY3BZ	129
03PY3JZ	144, 511, 661, 870
03PY3KZ	144, 511, 661, 870
03PY3MZ	129
03PY40Z	129
03PY42Z	129
03PY43Z	129
03PY47Z	144, 511, 661, 870
03PY4CZ	129
03PY4DZ	129
03PY4JZ	144, 511, 661, 870
03PY4KZ	144, 511, 661, 870
03PY4MZ	129
03Q*	129, 661
03Q0*	96
03Q00ZZ	870
03Q03ZZ	870
03Q04ZZ	870
03Q1*	96
03Q10ZZ	870
03Q13ZZ	870
03Q14ZZ	870
03Q2*	96
03Q20ZZ	870
03Q23ZZ	870
03Q24ZZ	870
03Q3*	96
03Q30ZZ	870
03Q33ZZ	870
03Q34ZZ	870
03Q4*	96
03Q40ZZ	870
03Q44ZZ	870
03Q5*	486
03Q50ZZ	413, 870
03Q53ZZ	413, 870
03Q54ZZ	413, 870
03Q6*	486
03Q60ZZ	413, 870
03Q63ZZ	413, 870
03Q64ZZ	413, 870
03Q7*	486
03Q70ZZ	413, 870
03Q73ZZ	413, 870
03Q74ZZ	413, 870
03Q8*	486
03Q80ZZ	413, 870
03Q83ZZ	413, 870
03Q84ZZ	413, 870
03Q9*	486
03Q90ZZ	413, 870
03Q93ZZ	413, 870
03Q94ZZ	413, 870
03QA*	486
03QA0ZZ	413, 870
03QA3ZZ	413, 870
03QA4ZZ	413, 870
03QB*	486
03QB0ZZ	413, 870
03QB3ZZ	413, 870
03QB4ZZ	413, 870
03QC*	486
03QC0ZZ	413, 870
03QC3ZZ	413, 870
03QC4ZZ	413, 870
03QD*	486
03QD0ZZ	413, 870
03QD3ZZ	413, 870
03QD4ZZ	413, 870
03QF*	486
03QF0ZZ	413, 870
03QF3ZZ	413, 870
03QF4ZZ	413, 870
03QG0ZZ	870
03QG3ZZ	870
03QG4ZZ	870
03QH*	25
03QH0ZZ	870
03QH3ZZ	870
03QH4ZZ	870
03QJ*	25
03QJ0ZZ	870
03QJ3ZZ	870
03QJ4ZZ	870
03QK*	25
03QK0ZZ	870
03QK3ZZ	870
03QK4ZZ	870
03QL*	25
03QL0ZZ	870
03QL3ZZ	870
03QL4ZZ	870
03QM*	25
03QM0ZZ	870
03QM3ZZ	870
03QM4ZZ	870
03QN*	25
03QN0ZZ	870
03QN3ZZ	870
03QN4ZZ	870
03QP*	25
03QP0ZZ	870
03QP3ZZ	870
03QP4ZZ	870
03QQ*	25
03QQ0ZZ	870
03QQ3ZZ	870
03QQ4ZZ	870
03QR*	25
03QR0ZZ	870
03QR3ZZ	870
03QR4ZZ	870
03QS*	25
03QS0ZZ	870
03QS3ZZ	870
03QS4ZZ	870
03QT*	25
03QT0ZZ	871
03QT3ZZ	871
03QT4ZZ	871
03QU0ZZ	871
03QU3ZZ	871
03QU4ZZ	871
03QV0ZZ	871
03QV3ZZ	871
03QV4ZZ	871
03QY*	185, 204, 486, 511
03QY0ZZ	871
03QY3ZZ	871
03QY4ZZ	871
03R0*	89, 661
03R007ZZ	109, 871
03R00JZ	109, 871
03R00KZ	109, 871
03R047Z	109, 871
03R04JZ	109, 871
03R04KZ	109, 871
03R1*	89, 661
03R107Z	109, 871
03R10JZ	109, 871
03R10KZ	109, 871
03R147Z	109, 871
03R14JZ	109, 871
03R14KZ	109, 871
03R2*	89
03R2*	661
03R207Z	109
03R207Z	871
03R20JZ	109
03R20JZ	871
03R20KZ	109
03R20KZ	871
03R247Z	109
03R247Z	871
03R24JZ	109
03R24JZ	871
03R24KZ	109
03R24KZ	871
03R3*	89, 661
03R307ZZ	109, 871
03R30JZ	109, 871
03R30KZ	109, 871
03R347Z	109, 871
03R34JZ	109, 871
03R34KZ	109, 871
03R4*	89, 661
03R407Z	109, 871
03R40JZ	109, 871
03R40KZ	109, 871
03R447Z	109, 871
03R44JZ	109, 871
03R44KZ	109, 871
03R5*	129, 661
03R6*	129, 661
03R7*	129, 661
03R8*	129, 661
03R9*	129, 661
03RA*	129, 661
03RB*	129, 661
03RC*	129, 661
03RD*	129, 661
03RF*	129, 661
03RG*	661
03RG0ZZ	6, 11, 871
03RG0JZ	6, 11, 871
03RG0KZ	6, 11, 871
03RG47Z	6, 11, 871
03RG4JZ	6, 11, 871
03RG4KZ	6, 11, 871
03RH*	33, 129
03RJ*	33, 129
03RK*	33, 129
03RL*	33, 129
03RM*	33, 129
03RN*	33, 129
03RP*	33, 129
03RQ*	33, 129
03RR*	33
03RR*	129
03RS*	33, 129
03RT*	33, 129
03RU*	33, 129
03RV*	33, 129
03RY*	129, 661
03S*	129, 661
03S00ZZ	871
03S03ZZ	871
03S04ZZ	871
03S10ZZ	871
03S13ZZ	871
03S14ZZ	871
03S20ZZ	871
03S23ZZ	871
03S24ZZ	871
03S30ZZ	871
03S33ZZ	871
03S34ZZ	871
03S43ZZ	871
03S44ZZ	871
03S50ZZ	413, 871
03S53ZZ	413, 871
03S54ZZ	413, 871
03S60ZZ	413, 871
03S63ZZ	413, 871
03S64ZZ	413, 871
03S70ZZ	413, 871
03S73ZZ	413, 871
03S74ZZ	413, 871
03S80ZZ	413, 871
03S83ZZ	413, 871
03S84ZZ	413, 871
03S90ZZ	413, 871
03S93ZZ	413, 871
03S94ZZ	413, 871
03SA0ZZ	413, 871
03SA3ZZ	413, 871
03SA4ZZ	413, 871
03SB0ZZ	413, 871
03SB3ZZ	413, 871
03SB4ZZ	413, 871
03SC0ZZ	413, 871
03SC3ZZ	413, 871
03SC4ZZ	413, 871
03SD0ZZ	413, 871
03SD3ZZ	413, 871
03SD4ZZ	413, 871
03SF0ZZ	413, 871
03SF3ZZ	413, 871
03SF4ZZ	413, 871
03SG0ZZ	871
03SG3ZZ	871
03SG4ZZ	871
03SH*	25
03SH0ZZ	871
03SH3ZZ	871
03SH4ZZ	871
03SJ*	25
03SJ0ZZ	871
03SJ3ZZ	871
03SJ4ZZ	871
03SK*	25
03SK0ZZ	871
03SK3ZZ	871
03SK4ZZ	871
03SL*	25
03SL0ZZ	871
03SL3ZZ	871
03SL4ZZ	871
03SM*	25
03SM0ZZ	871
03SM3ZZ	871
03SM4ZZ	871
03SN*	25
03SN0ZZ	871
03SN3ZZ	871
03SN4ZZ	871
03SP*	25

Numeric Index to Procedures

Code	Page	Code	Page	Code	Page	Code	Page	Code	Page	Code	Page
03SP0ZZ	871	03UA47Z	662, 871	03UT0JZ	662	03V74DZ	155, 663, 872	03VH0BZ	6, 11, 155, 511, 663, 872	03VL4DZ	7
03SP3ZZ	871	03UA4JZ	662	03UT37Z	662, 872	03V74ZZ	155, 663	03VH0CZ	130	03VL4HZ	26, 130, 663, 872
03SP4ZZ	871	03UB07Z	662, 871	03UT3JZ	662	03V80CZ	130	03VH0DZ	11, 155, 511, 663, 872	03VL4ZZ	155, 663
03SQ*	25	03UB0JZ	662	03UT47Z	662, 872	03V80DZ	155, 663, 872	03VH0DZ	6	03VM0BZ	7, 11, 155, 511, 663, 872
03SQ0ZZ	871	03UB37Z	662, 871	03UT4JZ	662	03V80ZZ	155, 663	03VH0HZ	25, 130, 663, 872	03VM0CZ	130
03SQ3ZZ	871	03UB3JZ	662	03UU07Z	662, 872	03V83CZ	130	03VH0ZZ	155, 663	03VM0DZ	11, 155, 511, 663, 872
03SQ4ZZ	871	03UB47Z	662, 871	03UU0JZ	662	03V83DZ	155, 663, 872	03VH3BZ	6, 11, 155, 511, 663, 872	03VM0DZ	7
03SR*	25	03UB4JZ	662	03UU3JZ	662	03V83ZZ	155, 663	03VH3CZ	130	03VM0HZ	26, 130, 663, 872
03SR0ZZ	871	03UC07Z	662, 872	03UU47Z	662, 872	03V84CZ	130	03VH3DZ	11, 155, 511, 663, 872	03VM0ZZ	155, 663
03SR3ZZ	871	03UC0JZ	662	03UU4JZ	662	03V84DZ	155, 663, 872	03VH3DZ	6	03VM3BZ	7, 11, 155, 511, 663, 872
03SR4ZZ	871	03UC37Z	662, 872	03UV0JZ	662	03V84ZZ	155, 663	03VH3HZ	25, 130, 663, 872	03VM3CZ	130
03SS*	25	03UC3JZ	662	03UV07Z	662, 872	03V90CZ	130	03VH3ZZ	155, 663	03VM3DZ	11, 155, 511, 663, 872
03SS0ZZ	871	03UC47Z	662, 872	03UV37Z	662, 872	03V90DZ	155, 663, 872	03VH4BZ	7, 11, 155, 511, 663, 872	03VM3DZ	7
03SS3ZZ	871	03UC4JZ	662	03UV3JZ	662	03V90ZZ	155, 663	03VH4CZ	130	03VM3HZ	26, 130, 663, 872
03SS4ZZ	871	03UD07Z	662, 872	03UV47Z	662, 872	03V93CZ	130	03VH4DZ	11, 155, 511, 663, 872	03VM3ZZ	155, 663
03ST*	25	03UD0JZ	662	03UV4JZ	662	03V93DZ	155, 663, 872	03VH4DZ	7	03VM4BZ	7, 11, 155, 511, 663, 872
03ST0ZZ	871	03UD37Z	662, 872	03UY07Z	662, 872	03V93ZZ	155, 663	03VH4HZ	25, 130, 663, 872	03VM4CZ	130
03ST3ZZ	871	03UD3JZ	662	03UY0JZ	662	03V94CZ	130	03VH4ZZ	155, 663	03VM4DZ	11, 155, 511, 663, 872
03ST4ZZ	871	03UD47Z	662, 872	03UY37Z	662, 872	03V94DZ	155, 663, 872	03VJ0BZ	7, 11, 155, 511, 663, 872	03VM4DZ	7
03SU0ZZ	871	03UD4JZ	662	03UY3JZ	662	03V94ZZ	155, 663	03VJ0CZ	130	03VM4HZ	26, 130, 663, 872
03SU3ZZ	871	03UF07Z	662, 872	03UY4JZ	662	03VA0CZ	130	03VJ0DZ	11, 155, 511, 663, 872	03VM4ZZ	155, 663
03SU4ZZ	871	03UF0JZ	662	03V00CZ	129	03VA0DZ	155, 663, 872	03VJ0DZ	7	03VN0BZ	7, 11, 155, 511, 663, 872
03SV0ZZ	871	03UF37Z	662, 872	03V00DZ	155, 662, 872	03VA0ZZ	155, 663	03VJ0HZ	26, 130, 663, 872	03VN0CZ	130
03SV3ZZ	871	03UF3JZ	662	03V00ZZ	155, 662	03VA3CZ	130	03VJ0ZZ	155, 663	03VN0DZ	11, 155, 511, 663, 872
03SV4ZZ	871	03UF47Z	662, 872	03V03CZ	129	03VA3DZ	155, 663, 872	03VJ3BZ	7, 11, 155, 511, 663, 872	03VN0DZ	7
03SY0ZZ	871	03UF4JZ	662	03V03DZ	155, 662, 872	03VA3ZZ	155, 663	03VJ3CZ	130	03VN0HZ	26, 130, 663, 872
03SY3ZZ	871	03UG07Z	662, 872	03V03ZZ	155, 662	03VA4CZ	130	03VJ3DZ	11, 155, 511, 663, 872	03VN0ZZ	155, 663
03SY4ZZ	871	03UG0JZ	662	03V04CZ	129	03VA4DZ	155, 663, 872	03VJ3DZ	7	03VN3BZ	7, 11, 155, 511, 663, 872
03U*	129	03UG37Z	662, 872	03V04DZ	155, 662, 872	03VB0CZ	130	03VJ3HZ	26, 130, 663, 872	03VN3CZ	130
03U007Z	661, 871	03UG3JZ	662	03V04ZZ	155, 662	03VB0DZ	155, 663, 872	03VJ3ZZ	155, 663	03VN3DZ	11, 155, 511, 663, 872
03U00JZ	661	03UG47Z	662, 872	03V10CZ	129	03VB0ZZ	155, 663	03VJ4BZ	7, 11, 155, 511, 663, 872	03VN3DZ	7
03U037Z	661, 871	03UG4JZ	662	03V10DZ	155, 662, 872	03VB3CZ	130	03VJ4CZ	130	03VN3HZ	26, 130, 663, 872
03U03JZ	661	03UH07Z	25, 662, 872	03V10ZZ	155, 662	03VB3DZ	155, 663, 872	03VJ4DZ	11, 155, 511, 663, 872	03VN4BZ	7, 11, 155, 511, 663, 872
03U047Z	661, 871	03UH0JZ	25, 662	03V13CZ	129	03VB3ZZ	155, 663	03VJ4DZ	7	03VN4CZ	130
03U04JZ	661	03UH37Z	25, 662, 872	03V13DZ	155, 662, 872	03VB4CZ	130	03VJ4HZ	26, 130, 663, 872	03VN4DZ	11, 155, 511, 663, 872
03U107Z	661	03UH3JZ	25, 662	03V13ZZ	155, 662	03VB4DZ	155, 663, 872	03VJ4ZZ	155, 663	03VN4DZ	7
03U10JZ	661	03UH47Z	25, 662, 872	03V14CZ	129	03VB4ZZ	155, 663	03VK0BZ	7, 11, 155, 511, 663, 872	03VN4HZ	26, 130, 663, 872
03U137Z	661, 871	03UH4JZ	25, 662	03V14DZ	155, 662, 872	03VC0CZ	130	03VK0CZ	7, 11, 130	03VN4ZZ	155, 663
03U13JZ	661	03UJ07Z	25, 662, 872	03V14ZZ	155, 662	03VC0DZ	155, 663, 872	03VK0DZ	11, 155, 511, 663, 872	03VP0BZ	7, 11, 155, 511, 663, 872
03U147Z	661	03UJ0JZ	25, 662	03V20CZ	129	03VC0ZZ	155, 663	03VK0DZ	7	03VP0CZ	130
03U14JZ	661	03UJ37Z	25, 662, 872	03V20DZ	155, 662, 872	03VC3CZ	130	03VK0HZ	26, 130, 663, 872	03VP0DZ	7, 11, 155, 511, 663, 872
03U207Z	661, 871	03UJ3JZ	25, 662	03V20ZZ	155, 662	03VC3DZ	155, 663, 872	03VK0ZZ	155, 663	03VP0HZ	26, 130, 663, 872
03U20JZ	661	03UJ47Z	25, 662, 872	03V23CZ	129	03VC3ZZ	155, 663	03VK3BZ	7, 11, 155, 511, 663, 872	03VP0ZZ	155, 663
03U237Z	661, 871	03UJ4JZ	25, 662	03V23DZ	155, 662, 872	03VC4CZ	130	03VK3CZ	7, 11, 130	03VP3BZ	7, 11, 155, 511, 663, 872
03U23JZ	661	03UK07Z	25, 662, 872	03V23ZZ	155, 662	03VC4DZ	155, 663, 872	03VK3DZ	11, 155, 511, 663, 872	03VP3CZ	130
03U247Z	661, 871	03UK0JZ	25, 662	03V24CZ	129	03VC4ZZ	155, 663	03VK3DZ	7	03VP3DZ	7, 11, 155, 511, 663, 872
03U24JZ	661	03UK37Z	25, 662, 872	03V24DZ	155, 662, 872	03VD0CZ	130	03VK3HZ	26, 130, 663, 872	03VP3HZ	26, 130, 663, 872
03U307Z	661, 871	03UK3JZ	25, 662	03V24ZZ	155, 662	03VD0DZ	155, 663, 872	03VK3ZZ	155, 663	03VP3ZZ	155, 663
03U30JZ	661	03UK47Z	25, 662, 872	03V30CZ	129	03VD0ZZ	155, 663	03VK4BZ	7, 11, 155, 511, 663, 872	03VP4BZ	7, 11, 155, 511, 663, 872
03U337Z	661, 871	03UK4JZ	25, 662	03V30DZ	155, 662, 872	03VD3CZ	130	03VK4CZ	7, 11, 130	03VP4CZ	130
03U33JZ	661	03UL07Z	25, 662, 872	03V30ZZ	155, 662	03VD3DZ	155, 663, 872	03VK4DZ	11, 155, 511, 663, 872	03VP4DZ	7, 11, 155, 511, 663, 872
03U347Z	661, 871	03UL0JZ	25, 662	03V33CZ	129	03VD3ZZ	155, 663	03VK4DZ	7	03VP4HZ	26, 130, 663, 872
03U34JZ	661	03UL37Z	25, 662, 872	03V33DZ	155, 662, 872	03VD4CZ	130	03VK4HZ	26, 130, 663, 872	03VP4ZZ	156, 663
03U407Z	661, 871	03UL3JZ	25, 662	03V33ZZ	155, 662	03VD4DZ	155, 663, 872	03VK4ZZ	155, 663	03VQ0BZ	7, 11, 156, 511, 663, 872
03U40JZ	661	03UL47Z	25, 662, 872	03V34CZ	129	03VD4ZZ	155, 663	03VL0BZ	7, 11, 155, 511, 663, 872	03VQ0CZ	130
03U437Z	661, 871	03UL4JZ	25, 662	03V34DZ	155, 662, 872	03VF0CZ	130	03VL0CZ	7, 11, 130	03VQ0DZ	7, 11, 156, 511, 663, 872
03U43JZ	661	03UM07Z	25, 662, 872	03V34ZZ	155, 662	03VF0DZ	155, 663, 872	03VL0DZ	11, 155, 511, 663, 872	03VQ0HZ	26, 130, 663, 872
03U447Z	661, 871	03UM0JZ	25, 662	03V40CZ	129	03VF0ZZ	155, 663	03VL0DZ	7	03VQ0ZZ	156, 663
03U44JZ	661	03UM37Z	25, 662, 872	03V40DZ	155, 662, 872	03VF3CZ	130	03VL0HZ	26, 130, 663, 872	03VQ3BZ	7, 11, 156, 511, 663, 872
03U507Z	661, 871	03UM3JZ	25, 662	03V40ZZ	155, 662	03VF3DZ	155, 663, 872	03VL0ZZ	155, 663	03VQ3CZ	130
03U50JZ	661	03UM47Z	25, 662, 872	03V43CZ	129	03VF3ZZ	155, 663	03VL3BZ	7, 11, 155, 511, 663, 872	03VQ3DZ	7, 11, 156, 511, 663, 873
03U537Z	661, 871	03UM4JZ	25, 662	03V43DZ	155, 662, 872	03VF4CZ	130	03VL3CZ	7, 11, 130	03VQ3HZ	26, 130, 663, 873
03U53JZ	661	03UN07Z	25, 662, 872	03V43ZZ	155, 662	03VF4DZ	155, 663, 872	03VL3DZ	11, 155, 511, 663, 872	03VQ3ZZ	156, 663
03U547Z	661, 871	03UN0JZ	25, 662	03V44CZ	129	03VF4ZZ	155, 663	03VL3DZ	7	03VQ4BZ	7, 11, 156, 511, 663, 873
03U54JZ	661	03UN37Z	25, 662, 872	03V44DZ	155, 662, 872	03VG0BZ	6, 11, 155, 511, 663, 872	03VL3HZ	26, 130, 663, 872	03VQ4CZ	130
03U607Z	661, 871	03UN3JZ	25, 662	03V44ZZ	155, 662	03VG0CZ	6, 11, 130	03VL3ZZ	155, 663	03VQ4DZ	7, 11, 156, 511, 663, 873
03U60JZ	661	03UN47Z	25, 662, 872	03V50CZ	129	03VG0DZ	11, 155, 511, 663, 872	03VL4BZ	7, 11, 155, 511, 663, 872	03VQ4HZ	26, 130, 663, 873
03U637Z	661, 871	03UN4JZ	25, 662	03V50DZ	155, 663, 872	03VG0DZ	6	03VL4CZ	7, 11, 130	03VQ4ZZ	156, 663
03U63JZ	661	03UP07Z	25, 662, 872	03V50ZZ	155, 662	03VG0HZ	6, 11, 155, 511, 663, 872	03VL4DZ	11, 155, 511, 663, 872		
03U647Z	661, 871	03UP0JZ	25, 662	03V53CZ	129	03VG0ZZ	6, 11, 155, 663				
03U64JZ	662	03UP37Z	25, 662, 872	03V53DZ	155, 662, 872	03VG3BZ	6, 11, 155, 511, 663, 872				
03U707Z	662, 871	03UP3JZ	25, 662	03V53ZZ	155, 662	03VG3CZ	6, 11, 130				
03U70JZ	662	03UP47Z	25, 662, 872	03V54CZ	130	03VG3DZ	11, 155, 511, 663, 872				
03U737Z	662, 871	03UP4JZ	25, 662	03V54DZ	155, 662, 872	03VG3DZ	6				
03U73JZ	662	03UQ07Z	25, 662, 872	03V54ZZ	155, 663	03VG3HZ	6, 11, 155, 511, 663, 872				
03U747Z	662, 871	03UQ0JZ	25, 662	03V60CZ	130	03VG3ZZ	6, 11, 155, 663				
03U74JZ	662	03UQ37Z	25, 662, 872	03V60DZ	155, 663, 872	03VG4BZ	6, 11, 155, 511, 663, 872				
03U807Z	662, 871	03UQ3JZ	25, 662	03V60ZZ	155, 663	03VG4CZ	6, 11, 130				
03U80JZ	662	03UQ47Z	25, 662, 872	03V63CZ	130	03VG4DZ	11, 155, 511, 663, 872				
03U837Z	662, 871	03UQ4JZ	25, 662	03V63DZ	155, 663, 872	03VG4DZ	6				
03U83JZ	662	03UR07Z	662, 872	03V63ZZ	155, 663	03VG4HZ	6, 11, 155, 511, 663, 872				
03U847Z	662, 871	03UR0JZ	662	03V64CZ	130	03VG4ZZ	6, 11, 155, 663				
03U84JZ	662	03UR37Z	662, 872	03V64DZ	155, 663, 872						
03U907Z	662, 871	03UR3JZ	662	03V64ZZ	155, 663						
03U90JZ	662	03UR47Z	662, 872	03V70CZ	130						
03U937Z	662, 871	03UR4JZ	662	03V70DZ	155, 663, 872						
03U93JZ	662	03US07Z	662, 872	03V70ZZ	155, 663						
03U947Z	662, 871	03US0JZ	662	03V73CZ	130						
03U94JZ	662	03US3JZ	662	03V73DZ	155, 663, 872						
03UA07Z	662, 871	03US47Z	662, 872	03V73ZZ	155, 663						
03UA0JZ	662	03US4JZ	662	03V74CZ	130						
03UA37Z	662, 871	03UT07Z	662, 872								
03UA3JZ	662										

Code	Page
03VR0CZ	130
03VR0DZ	7, 11, 156, 511, 663, 873
03VR0ZZ	156, 663
03VR3CZ	130
03VR3DZ	7, 11, 156, 511, 663, 873
03VR3ZZ	156, 663
03VR4CZ	130
03VR4DZ	7, 11, 156, 511, 663, 873
03VR4ZZ	156, 663
03VS0CZ	130
03VS0DZ	7, 11, 156, 511, 663, 873
03VS0ZZ	156, 663
03VS3CZ	130
03VS3DZ	7, 11, 156, 511, 663, 873
03VS3ZZ	156, 663
03VS4CZ	130
03VS4DZ	7, 11, 156, 511, 663, 873
03VS4ZZ	156, 664
03VT0CZ	130
03VT0DZ	7, 11, 156, 511, 664, 873
03VT0ZZ	156, 664
03VT3CZ	130
03VT3DZ	7, 11, 156, 511, 664, 873
03VT3ZZ	156, 664
03VT4CZ	130
03VT4DZ	7, 11, 156, 511, 664, 873
03VT4ZZ	156, 664
03VU0CZ	130
03VU0DZ	7, 11, 156, 511, 664, 873
03VU0ZZ	156, 664
03VU3CZ	130
03VU3DZ	7, 11, 156, 511, 664, 873
03VU3ZZ	156, 664
03VU4CZ	130
03VU4DZ	7, 11, 156, 511, 664, 873
03VU4ZZ	156, 664
03VV0CZ	130
03VV0DZ	7, 11, 156, 511, 664, 873
03VV0ZZ	156, 664
03VV3CZ	130
03VV3DZ	7, 11, 156, 511, 664, 873
03VV3ZZ	156, 664
03VV4CZ	130
03VV4DZ	7, 11, 156, 511, 664, 873
03VV4ZZ	156, 664
03VY0CZ	130
03VY0DZ	156, 664, 873
03VY0ZZ	156, 664
03VY3CZ	130
03VY3DZ	156, 664, 873
03VY3ZZ	156, 664
03VY4CZ	130
03VY4DZ	156, 664, 873
03VY4ZZ	156, 664
03WY00Z	130
03WY02Z	130
03WY03Z	130
03WY07Z	130, 1045
03WY0CZ	130
03WY0DZ	130
03WY0JZ	130, 511
03WY0KZ	130, 1045
03WY0MZ	130
03WY0YZ	130
03WY37Z	130, 1045
03WY3CZ	130
03WY3JZ	130, 511
03WY3KZ	130, 1045
03WY3MZ	130
03WY40Z	130
03WY42Z	130
03WY43Z	130
03WY47Z	130, 1045
03WY4CZ	130
03WY4DZ	130
03WY4JZ	130, 511
03WY4KZ	130, 1045
03WY4MZ	130
041009B	156, 413, 664
041009C	156, 413, 664
041009D	156, 413, 664
041009F	156, 413, 664
041009G	156, 413, 664
041009H	156, 413, 664
041009J	156, 413, 664
041009K	156, 413, 664
041009Q	156, 413, 664
041009R	156, 413, 664
04100A0	156
04100A1	156
04100A2	156
04100A3	149, 504, 664, 873
04100A4	149, 504, 664, 873
04100A5	149, 504, 664, 873
04100A6	156, 413, 664
04100A7	156, 413, 664
04100A8	156, 413, 664
04100A9	156, 413, 664
04100AB	156, 413, 664
04100AC	156, 413, 664
04100AD	156, 413, 664
04100AF	156, 413, 664
04100AG	156, 413, 664
04100AH	156, 413, 664
04100AJ	156, 413, 664
04100AK	156, 413, 664
04100AQ	156, 413, 664
04100AR	156, 413, 664
04100J0	156
04100J1	156, 185, 504
04100J2	156, 185, 504
04100J3	149, 504, 664, 873
04100J4	149, 504, 664, 873
04100J5	149, 504, 664, 873
04100J6	156, 413, 664
04100J7	156, 413, 664
04100J8	156, 413, 664
04100J9	156, 413, 664
04100JB	156, 413, 664
04100JC	156, 413, 664
04100JD	156, 413, 664
04100JF	156, 413, 664
04100JG	156, 413, 664
04100JH	156, 413, 664
04100JJ	156, 413, 664
04100JK	156, 413, 664
04100JQ	156, 413, 664
04100JR	156, 413, 664
04100K0	156
04100K1	156
04100K2	156
04100K3	149, 504, 664, 873
04100K4	149, 504, 664, 873
04100K5	149, 504, 664, 873
04100K6	156, 413, 664
04100K7	156, 413, 664
04100K8	156, 413, 664
04100K9	156, 413, 664
04100KB	156, 413, 664
04100KC	156, 413, 664
04100KD	156, 413, 664
04100KF	156, 413, 664
04100KG	156, 413, 664
04100KH	156, 413, 664
04100KJ	156, 413, 664
04100KK	156, 413, 664
04100KQ	156, 413, 664
04100KR	156, 413, 664
04100Z0	156
04100Z1	156, 185, 504
04100Z2	156, 185, 504
04100Z3	149, 504, 664, 873
04100Z4	149, 504, 664, 873
04100Z5	149, 504, 664, 873
04100Z6	156, 413, 664
04100Z7	156, 413, 664
04100Z8	156, 413, 664
04100Z9	156, 413, 664
04100ZB	156, 413, 664
04100ZC	156, 413, 664
04100ZD	156, 413, 664
04100ZF	156, 413, 664
04100ZG	156, 413, 664
04100ZH	156, 413, 664
04100ZJ	156, 413, 664
04100ZK	156, 413, 664
04100ZQ	156, 413, 664
04100ZR	156, 413, 664
041049B	156, 413, 664
041049C	156, 413, 664
041049D	156, 413, 664
041049F	156, 413, 664
041049G	156, 413, 664
041049H	156, 413, 664
041049J	156, 413, 664
041049K	156, 413, 664
041049Q	156, 413, 664
041049R	156, 413, 664
04104A0	156
04104A1	156
04104A2	156
04104A3	149, 504, 664, 873
04104A4	149, 504, 664, 873
04104A5	149, 504, 664, 873
04104A6	156, 413, 664
04104A7	156, 413, 664
04104A8	156, 414, 664
04104A9	156, 414, 664
04104AB	156, 414, 664
04104AC	156, 414, 664
04104AD	156, 414, 664
04104AF	156, 414, 664
04104AG	156, 414, 664
04104AH	156, 414, 664
04104AJ	156, 414, 664
04104AK	156, 414, 664
04104AQ	156, 414, 664
04104AR	156, 414, 664
04104J0	156
04104J1	156
04104J2	156
04104J3	149, 504, 664, 873
04104J4	149, 504, 664, 873
04104J5	149, 504, 664, 873
04104J6	156, 414, 664
04104J7	156, 414, 664
04104J8	156, 414, 664
04104J9	156, 414, 664
04104JB	156, 414, 664
04104JC	156, 414, 664
04104JD	157, 414, 664
04104JF	157, 414, 664
04104JG	157, 414, 664
04104JH	157, 414, 664
04104JJ	157, 414, 664
04104JK	157, 414, 664
04104JQ	157, 414, 664
04104JR	157, 414, 664
04104K0	157
04104K1	157
04104K2	157
04104K3	149, 504, 664, 873
04104K4	149, 504, 664, 873
04104K5	149, 504, 664, 873
04104K6	157, 414, 664
04104K7	157, 414, 664
04104K8	157, 414, 664
04104K9	157, 414, 664
04104KB	157, 414, 664
04104KC	157, 414, 664
04104KD	157, 414, 664
04104KF	157, 414, 664
04104KG	157, 414, 664
04104KH	157, 414, 664
04104KJ	157, 414, 665
04104KK	157, 414, 665
04104KQ	157, 414, 665
04104KR	157, 414, 665
04104Z0	157
04104Z1	157
04104Z2	157
04104Z3	149, 504, 665, 873
04104Z4	149, 504, 665, 873
04104Z5	149, 504, 665, 873
04104Z6	157, 414, 665
04104Z7	157, 414, 665
04104Z8	157, 414, 665
04104Z9	157, 414, 665
04104ZB	157, 414, 665
04104ZC	157, 414, 665
04104ZD	157, 414, 665
04104ZF	157, 414, 665
04104ZG	157, 414, 665
04104ZH	157, 414, 665
04104ZJ	157, 414, 665
04104ZK	157, 414, 665
04104ZQ	157, 414, 665
04104ZR	157, 414, 665
04130A3	149, 504, 665, 873
04130A4	149, 504, 665, 873
04130A5	149, 504, 665, 873
04130J3	149, 504, 665, 873
04130J4	149, 504, 665, 873
04130J5	149, 504, 665, 873
04130K3	149, 504, 665, 873
04130K4	149, 504, 665, 873
04130K5	149, 504, 665, 873
04130Z3	149, 504, 665, 873
04130Z4	149, 504, 665, 873
04130Z5	149, 504, 665, 873
04134A3	149, 504, 665, 873
04134A4	149, 504, 665, 873
04134A5	149, 504, 665, 873
04134J3	149, 504, 665, 873
04134J4	149, 504, 665, 873
04134J5	150, 504, 665, 873
04134K3	150, 504, 665, 873
04134K4	150, 504, 665, 873
04134K5	150, 504, 665, 873
04134Z3	150, 504, 665, 873
04134Z4	150, 504, 665, 873
04134Z5	150, 504, 665, 873
04140A3	157
04140A4	157
04140A5	157
04140J3	157
04140J4	157
04140J5	157
04140K3	157
04140K4	157
04140K5	157
04140Z3	157
04140Z4	157
04140Z5	157
04144A3	157
04144A4	157
04144A5	157
04144J3	157
04144J4	157
04144J5	157
04144K3	157
04144K4	157
04144K5	157
04144Z3	157
04144Z4	157
04144Z5	157
041C*	157
041C09H	414, 665
041C09J	414, 665
041C09K	414, 665
041C0AH	414, 665
041C0AJ	414, 665
041C0AK	414, 665
041C0J3	185, 504
041C0J4	185, 504
041C0J5	185, 504
041C0JH	414, 665
041C0JJ	414, 665
041C0JK	414, 665
041C0KH	414, 665
041C0KJ	414, 665
041C0KK	414, 665
041C0Z3	185, 504
041C0Z4	185, 504
041C0Z5	185, 505
041C0ZH	414, 665
041C0ZJ	414, 665
041C0ZK	414, 665
041C49H	414, 665
041C49J	414, 665
041C49K	414, 665
041C4AH	414, 665
041C4AJ	414, 665
041C4AK	414, 665
041C4J3	185, 505
041C4J4	185, 505
041C4J5	185, 505
041C4JH	414, 665
041C4JJ	414, 665
041C4JK	414, 665
041C4KH	414, 665
041C4KJ	414, 665
041C4KK	414, 665
041C4Z3	185, 505
041C4Z4	185, 505
041C4Z5	185, 505
041C4ZH	414, 665
041C4ZJ	414, 665
041C4ZK	414, 665
041D*	157
041D09H	414, 665
041D09J	414, 665
041D09K	414, 665
041D0AH	414, 665
041D0AJ	414, 665
041D0AK	414, 665
041D0J3	185, 505
041D0J4	185, 505
041D0J5	185, 505
041D0JH	414, 665
041D0JJ	414, 665
041D0JK	414, 665
041D0KH	414, 665
041D0KJ	414, 665
041D0KK	414, 665
041D0Z3	185, 505
041D0Z4	185, 505
041D0Z5	185, 505
041D0ZH	414, 665
041D0ZJ	414, 665
041D0ZK	414, 665
041D49H	414, 665
041D49J	414, 665
041D49K	414, 665
041D4AH	414, 665
041D4AJ	414, 665
041D4AK	414, 665
041D4J3	185, 505
041D4J4	185, 505
041D4J5	185, 505
041D4JH	414, 665
041D4JJ	414, 665
041D4JK	414, 665
041D4KH	414, 665
041D4KJ	414, 665
041D4KK	414, 665
041D4Z3	185, 505
041D4Z4	185, 505
041D4Z5	185, 505
041D4ZH	414, 665
041D4ZJ	414, 665
041D4ZK	414, 665
041E*	157
041E09H	414, 665
041E09J	414, 665
041E09K	414, 665
041E0AH	414, 665
041E0AJ	414, 665
041E0AK	414, 665
041E0JH	414, 665
041E0JJ	414, 665
041E0JK	414, 665
041E0KH	414, 665
041E0KJ	414, 665
041E0KK	414, 665
041E0ZH	414, 665
041E0ZJ	414, 665
041E0ZK	414, 665
041E49H	414, 665
041E49J	414, 665
041E49K	414, 665
041E4AH	414, 665
041E4AJ	414, 665
041E4AK	414, 665
041E4JH	414, 665
041E4JJ	414, 665
041E4JK	414, 665
041E4KH	414, 665
041E4KJ	414, 665
041E4KK	414, 665
041E4ZH	414, 665
041E4ZJ	414, 665
041E4ZK	414, 665
041F*	157
041F09H	414, 665
041F09J	414, 665
041F09K	414, 665
041F0AH	414, 665
041F0AJ	414, 665
041F0AK	414, 665
041F0JH	414, 665
041F0JJ	414, 665
041F0JK	414, 665
041F0KH	414, 665
041F0KJ	414, 665
041F0KK	414, 665
041F0ZH	414, 665
041F0ZJ	414, 665
041F0ZK	414, 665
041F49H	414, 665
041F49J	414, 665
041F49K	414, 665
041F4AH	414, 665
041F4AJ	414, 665
041F4AK	414, 665
041F4JH	414, 665
041F4JJ	414, 665
041F4JK	414, 665
041F4KH	414, 665
041F4KJ	414, 665
041F4KK	414, 665
041F4ZH	414, 665
041F4ZJ	414, 665
041F4ZK	414, 665
041H*	157
041H09H	415, 665
041H09J	415, 665
041H09K	415, 665
041H0AH	415, 666
041H0AJ	415, 666
041H0AK	415, 666
041H0JH	415, 666
041H0JJ	415, 666
041H0JK	415, 666
041H0KH	415, 666
041H0KJ	415, 666
041H0KK	415, 666
041H0ZH	415, 666
041H0ZJ	415, 666
041H0ZK	415, 666
041H49H	415, 666
041H49J	415, 666
041H49K	415, 666
041H4AH	415, 666
041H4AJ	415, 666
041H4AK	415, 666
041H4JH	415, 666
041H4JJ	415, 666
041H4JK	415, 666
041H4KH	415, 666
041H4KJ	415, 666
041H4KK	415, 666
041H4ZH	415, 666
041H4ZJ	415, 666
041H4ZK	415, 666
041J*	157
041J09H	415, 666
041J09J	415, 666
041J09K	415, 666
041J0AH	415, 666
041J0AJ	415, 666
041J0AK	415, 666
041J0JH	415, 666
041J0JJ	415, 666
041J0JK	415, 666
041J0KH	415, 666
041J0KJ	415, 666
041J0KK	415, 666
041J0ZH	415, 666
041J0ZJ	415, 666
041J0ZK	415, 666
041J49H	415, 666
041J49J	415, 666
041J49K	415, 666
041J4AH	415, 666
041J4AJ	415, 666
041J4AK	415, 666
041J4JH	415, 666
041J4JJ	415, 666
041J4JK	415, 666
041J4KH	415, 666
041J4KJ	415, 666
041J4KK	415, 666
041J4ZH	415, 666
041J4ZJ	415, 666
041J4ZK	415, 666
041K*	130
041K09H	26, 96, 204, 415, 486, 666
041K09J	26, 96, 204, 415, 486, 666
041K09K	26, 96, 204, 415, 486, 666
041K09L	26, 96, 204, 415, 486, 666
041K0AH	26, 96, 204, 415, 486, 666
041K0AJ	26, 96, 204, 415, 486, 666
041K0AK	26, 96, 204, 415, 486, 666
041K0AL	26, 96, 204, 415, 486, 666
041K0JH	26, 96, 204, 415, 486, 666
041K0JJ	26, 96, 204, 415, 486, 666
041K0JK	26, 96, 204, 415, 486, 666
041K0JL	26, 96, 204, 415, 486, 666
041K0KH	26, 96, 204, 415, 486, 666

Numeric Index to Procedures

Numeric Index to Procedures

Code	Page	Code	Page	Code	Page	Code	Page	Code	Page	Code	Page
041K0KJ	26, 96, 204, 415, 486, 666	041L0ZL	26, 97, 204, 415, 486, 666	041T4JS	131	041W4AS	131	045R3ZZ	873	047234Z	26, 97, 185, 204, 274, 415, 486, 511, 667, 873
041K0KK	26, 96, 204, 415, 486, 666	041L49H	26, 97, 204, 415, 486, 666	041T4KP	131	041W4JP	131	045R4ZZ	873		
041K0KL	26, 97, 204, 415, 486, 666	041L49J	26, 97, 204, 415, 486, 666	041T4KQ	131	041W4JQ	131	045S*	131, 486, 666	047235Z	26, 97, 185, 204, 274, 415, 486, 511, 667, 873
041K0ZH	26, 97, 204, 415, 486, 666			041T4KS	131	041W4JS	131	045S0ZZ	873		
041K0ZJ	26, 97, 204, 415, 486, 666	041L49K	26, 97, 204, 415, 486, 666	041T4ZP	131	041W4KP	131	045S3ZZ	873	047236Z	26, 97, 185, 205, 274, 415, 486, 511, 667, 873
041K0ZK	26, 97, 204, 415, 486, 666	041L49L	26, 97, 204, 415, 486, 666	041T4ZQ	131	041W4KQ	131	045S4ZZ	873		
041K0ZL	26, 97, 204, 415, 486, 666	041L4AH	26, 97, 204, 415, 486, 666	041T4ZS	131	041W4KS	131	045T*	131, 486, 666	047237Z	26, 97, 185, 205, 274, 415, 486, 511, 667, 873
041K49H	26, 97, 204, 415, 486, 666	041L4AJ	26, 97, 204, 415, 486, 666	041U09P	131	041W4ZP	131	045T0ZZ	873		
041K49J	26, 97, 204, 415, 486, 666	041L4AK	26, 97, 204, 415, 486, 666	041U09Q	131	041W4ZQ	131	045T3ZZ	873	04723D1	26, 97, 185, 205, 274, 415, 486, 511, 667, 873
041K49K	26, 97, 204, 415, 486, 666	041L4AL	26, 97, 204, 415, 486, 666	041U09S	131	041W4ZS	131	045T4ZZ	873		
041K49L	26, 97, 204, 415, 486, 666	041L4JH	26, 97, 204, 415, 486, 666	041U0AP	131	0450*	185, 666	045U*	131, 486, 666	04723DZ	26, 97, 185, 205, 274, 415, 486, 511, 667, 873
041K4AH	26, 97, 204, 415, 486, 666	041L4JJ	26, 97, 204, 415, 486, 666	041U0AQ	131	04500ZZ	150, 873	045U0ZZ	873		
041K4AJ	26, 97, 204, 415, 486, 666	041L4JK	26, 97, 204, 415, 486, 666	041U0AS	131	04503ZZ	150, 873	045U3ZZ	873	04723EZ	26, 97, 185, 205, 274, 415, 486, 511, 667, 873
041K4AK	26, 97, 204, 415, 486, 666	041L4JL	26, 97, 204, 415, 486, 666	041U0JP	131	04504ZZ	150, 873	045U4ZZ	873		
041K4AL	26, 97, 204, 415, 486, 666	041L4KH	26, 97, 204, 415, 486, 666	041U0JQ	131	04510ZZ	157	045V*	131, 486, 666	04723FZ	26, 97, 185, 205, 274, 415, 486, 511, 667, 873
041K4JH	26, 97, 204, 415, 486, 666	041L4KJ	26, 97, 204, 415, 486, 666	041U0JS	131	04513ZZ	157	045V0ZZ	873		
041K4JJ	26, 97, 204, 415, 486, 666	041L4KK	26, 97, 204, 415, 486, 666	041U0KP	131	04514ZZ	157	045V3ZZ	873	04723GZ	26, 97, 185, 205, 274, 415, 486, 511, 667, 873
041K4JK	26, 97, 204, 415, 486, 666	041L4KL	26, 97, 204, 415, 486, 666	041U0KQ	131	04520ZZ	157	045V4ZZ	873		
041K4JL	26, 97, 204, 415, 486, 666	041L4ZH	26, 97, 204, 415, 486, 666	041U0KS	131	04523ZZ	157	045W*	131, 486, 666	04723Z1	26, 97, 185, 205, 274, 416, 486, 511, 667, 873
041K4KH	26, 97, 204, 415, 486, 666	041L4ZJ	26, 97, 204, 415, 486, 666	041U0ZP	131	04524ZZ	157	045W0ZZ	873		
041K4KJ	26, 97, 204, 415, 486, 666	041L4ZK	26, 97, 204, 415, 486, 666	041U0ZQ	131	04530ZZ	157	045W3ZZ	873	04723ZZ	26, 97, 185, 205, 274, 416, 486, 511, 667, 873
041K4KK	26, 97, 204, 415, 486, 666	041L4ZL	26, 97, 204, 415, 486, 666	041U0ZS	131	04533ZZ	157	045W4ZZ	873		
041K4KL	26, 97, 204, 415, 486, 666	041M*	130	041U3JQ	131	04534ZZ	157	045Y*	131, 486, 666	047334Z	26, 97, 185, 205, 274, 416, 486, 511, 667, 873
041K4ZH	26, 97, 204, 415, 486, 666	041N*	130	041U3JS	131	04540ZZ	157	045Y0ZZ	873		
041K4ZJ	26, 97, 204, 415, 486, 666	041P0JQ	130	041U49P	131	04543ZZ	157	045Y3ZZ	873	047335Z	26, 97, 185, 205, 274, 416, 486, 511, 667, 873
041K4ZK	26, 97, 204, 415, 486, 666	041P0JS	130	041U49Q	131	04544ZZ	157	045Y4ZZ	873		
041K4ZL	26, 97, 204, 415, 486, 666	041P3JQ	130	041U49S	131	04550ZZ	157	047*	131	047336Z	26, 97, 185, 205, 274, 416, 486, 511, 667, 873
041L*	130	041P3JS	130	041U4AP	131	04553ZZ	157	047034Z	26, 97, 185, 204, 274, 415, 486, 511, 666, 873		
041L09H	26, 97, 204, 415, 486, 666	041P4JQ	130	041U4AQ	131	04554ZZ	157			047337Z	26, 97, 185, 205, 274, 416, 486, 511, 667, 873
041L09J	26, 97, 204, 415, 486, 666	041P4JS	130	041U4AS	131	04560ZZ	157	047035Z	26, 97, 185, 204, 274, 415, 486, 511, 666, 873		
041L09K	26, 97, 204, 415, 486, 666	041Q0JQ	130	041U4JP	131	04563ZZ	157			04733D1	26, 97, 185, 205, 274, 416, 486, 511, 667, 873
041L09L	26, 97, 204, 415, 486, 666	041Q0JS	130	041U4JQ	131	04564ZZ	157	047036Z	26, 97, 185, 204, 274, 415, 486, 511, 666, 873		
041L0AH	26, 97, 204, 415, 486, 666	041Q3JQ	130	041U4JS	131	04570ZZ	157			04733DZ	26, 97, 185, 205, 274, 416, 486, 511, 667, 873
041L0AJ	26, 97, 204, 415, 486, 666	041Q3JS	130	041U4KP	131	04573ZZ	157	047037Z	26, 97, 185, 204, 274, 415, 486, 511, 666, 873		
041L0AK	26, 97, 204, 415, 486, 666	041Q4JQ	130	041U4KQ	131	04574ZZ	157			04733EZ	26, 97, 185, 205, 274, 416, 486, 511, 667, 873
041L0AL	26, 97, 204, 415, 486, 666	041Q4JS	130	041U4KS	131	04580ZZ	157	04703D1	26, 97, 185, 204, 274, 415, 486, 511, 666, 873		
041L0JH	26, 97, 204, 415, 486, 666	041R0JQ	130	041U4ZP	131	04583ZZ	157			04733FZ	26, 97, 185, 205, 274, 416, 486, 511, 667, 873
041L0JJ	26, 97, 204, 415, 486, 666	041R0JS	130	041U4ZQ	131	04584ZZ	157	04703DZ	26, 97, 185, 204, 274, 415, 486, 511, 666, 873		
041L0JK	26, 97, 204, 415, 486, 666	041R3JQ	130	041U4ZS	131	0459*	511			04733GZ	26, 97, 185, 205, 274, 416, 486, 511, 667, 873
041L0JL	26, 97, 204, 415, 486, 666	041R3JS	130	041V09P	131	04590ZZ	157	04703EZ	26, 97, 185, 204, 274, 415, 486, 511, 666, 873		
041L0KH	26, 97, 204, 415, 486, 666	041R4JQ	130	041V09Q	131	04593ZZ	157			04733Z1	26, 97, 185, 205, 274, 416, 486, 511, 667, 873
041L0KJ	26, 97, 204, 415, 486, 666	041R4JS	130	041V09S	131	04594ZZ	157	04703FZ	26, 97, 185, 204, 274, 415, 486, 511, 666, 873		
041L0KK	26, 97, 204, 415, 486, 666	041S0JQ	130	041V0AP	131	045A*	511			04733ZZ	26, 97, 185, 205, 274, 416, 486, 511, 667, 873
041L0KL	26, 97, 204, 415, 486, 666	041S0JS	130	041V0AQ	131	045A0ZZ	157	04703GZ	26, 97, 185, 204, 274, 415, 486, 511, 666, 873		
041L0ZH	26, 97, 204, 415, 486, 666	041S3JQ	130	041V0AS	131	045A3ZZ	157			047434Z	26, 97, 185, 205, 274, 416, 487, 511, 667, 874
041L0ZJ	26, 97, 204, 415, 486, 666	041S3JS	130	041V0JP	131	045A4ZZ	157	04703Z1	26, 97, 185, 204, 274, 415, 486, 511, 666, 873		
041L0ZK	26, 97, 204, 415, 486, 666	041S4JQ	130	041V0JQ	131	045B0ZZ	157			047435Z	26, 97, 185, 205, 274, 416, 487, 511, 667, 874
		041S4JS	130	041V0JS	131	045B3ZZ	157	04703ZZ	26, 97, 185, 204, 274, 415, 486, 511, 666, 873		
		041T09P	130	041V0KP	131	045B4ZZ	157			047436Z	26, 97, 185, 205, 274, 416, 487, 511, 667, 874
		041T09Q	130	041V0KQ	131	045C0ZZ	157	047134Z	26, 97, 185, 204, 274, 415, 486, 511, 666, 873		
		041T09S	130	041V0KS	131	045C3ZZ	157			047437Z	26, 97, 185, 205, 274, 416, 487, 511, 667, 874
		041T0AP	130	041V0ZP	131	045C4ZZ	157	047135Z	26, 97, 185, 204, 274, 415, 486, 511, 666, 873		
		041T0AQ	130	041V0ZQ	131	045D0ZZ	157			04743D1	26, 97, 185, 205, 274, 416, 487, 511, 667, 874
		041T0AS	130	041V0ZS	131	045D3ZZ	157	047136Z	26, 97, 185, 204, 274, 415, 486, 511, 666, 873		
		041T0JP	130	041V3JQ	131	045D4ZZ	157			04743DZ	26, 97, 185, 205, 274, 416, 487, 511, 667, 874
		041T0JQ	130	041V3JS	131	045E0ZZ	157	047137Z	26, 97, 185, 204, 274, 415, 486, 511, 666, 873		
		041T0JS	130	041V49P	131	045E3ZZ	157			04743EZ	26, 97, 185, 205, 274, 416, 487, 511, 667, 874
		041T0KP	130	041V49Q	131	045E4ZZ	157	04713D1	26, 97, 185, 204, 274, 415, 486, 511, 666, 873		
		041T0KQ	130	041V49S	131	045F0ZZ	157			04743FZ	26, 97, 185, 205, 274, 416, 487, 511, 667, 874
		041T0KS	130	041V4AP	131	045F3ZZ	157	04713DZ	26, 97, 185, 204, 274, 415, 486, 511, 666, 873		
		041T0ZP	130	041V4AQ	131	045F4ZZ	157			04743GZ	26, 97, 185, 205, 274, 416, 487, 511, 667, 874
		041T0ZQ	130	041V4AS	131	045H0ZZ	157	04713EZ	26, 97, 185, 204, 274, 415, 486, 511, 666, 873		
		041T0ZS	130	041V4JP	131	045H3ZZ	157				
		041T3JQ	130	041V4JQ	131	045H4ZZ	157	04713FZ	26, 97, 185, 204, 274, 415, 486, 511, 666, 873		
		041T3JS	130	041V4JS	131	045J0ZZ	157				
		041T49P	130	041V4KP	131	045J3ZZ	157	04713GZ	26, 97, 185, 204, 274, 415, 486, 511, 666, 873		
		041T49Q	130	041V4KQ	131	045J4ZZ	157				
		041T49S	130	041V4KS	131	045K*	131, 486, 666	04713Z1	26, 97, 185, 204, 274, 415, 486, 511, 666, 873		
		041T4AP	130	041V4ZP	131	045K0ZZ	873				
		041T4AQ	130	041V4ZQ	131	045K3ZZ	873				
		041T4AS	130	041V4ZS	131	045K4ZZ	873	04713ZZ	26, 97, 185, 204, 274, 415, 486, 511, 666, 873		
		041T4JP	130	041W09P	131	045L*	131, 486, 666				
		041T4JQ	130	041W09Q	131	045L0ZZ	873				
				041W09S	131	045L3ZZ	873				
				041W0AP	131	045L4ZZ	873				
				041W0AQ	131	045M*	131, 486, 666				
				041W0AS	131	045M0ZZ	873				
				041W0JP	131	045M3ZZ	873				
				041W0JQ	131	045M4ZZ	873				
				041W0JS	131	045N*	131, 486, 666				
				041W0KP	131	045N0ZZ	873				
				041W0KQ	131	045N3ZZ	873				
				041W0KS	131	045N4ZZ	873				
				041W0ZP	131	045P*	131, 486, 666				
				041W0ZQ	131	045P0ZZ	873				
				041W0ZS	131	045P3ZZ	873				
				041W3JQ	131	045P4ZZ	873				
				041W3JS	131	045Q*	131, 486, 666				
				041W49P	131	045Q0ZZ	873				
				041W49Q	131	045Q3ZZ	873				
				041W49S	131	045Q4ZZ	873				
				041W4AP	131	045R*	131, 486, 666				
				041W4AQ	131	045R0ZZ	873				

Code	Page	Code	Page	Code	Page	Code	Page	Code	Page	Code	Page
04743Z1	26, 97, 185, 205, 274, 416, 487, 512, 667, 874	04773FZ	27, 97, 185, 205, 274, 416, 487, 512, 667, 874	047A3D1	27, 98, 185, 205, 275, 416, 487, 512, 667, 874	047D341	27, 98, 186, 205, 275, 416, 487, 512, 667, 874	047F3EZ	27, 98, 186, 205, 275, 416, 487, 512, 667, 874	047K0Z1	27, 98, 186, 206, 275, 417, 487, 512, 668, 874
04743ZZ	26, 97, 185, 205, 274, 416, 487, 512, 667, 874	04773GZ	27, 97, 185, 205, 274, 416, 487, 512, 667, 874	047A3DZ	27, 98, 185, 205, 275, 416, 487, 512, 667, 874	047D34Z	27, 98, 186, 205, 275, 416, 487, 512, 667, 874	047F3FZ	27, 98, 186, 205, 275, 416, 487, 512, 667, 874	047K341	27, 98, 186, 206, 275, 417, 487, 512, 668, 874
047534Z	26, 97, 185, 205, 274, 416, 487, 512, 667, 874	04773Z1	27, 97, 185, 205, 274, 416, 487, 512, 667, 874	047A3EZ	27, 98, 185, 205, 275, 416, 487, 512, 667, 874	047D35Z	27, 98, 186, 205, 275, 416, 487, 512, 667, 874	047F3GZ	27, 98, 186, 205, 275, 416, 487, 512, 667, 874	047K34Z	27, 98, 186, 206, 275, 417, 487, 512, 668, 874
047535Z	26, 97, 185, 205, 274, 416, 487, 512, 667, 874	04773ZZ	27, 97, 185, 205, 274, 416, 487, 512, 667, 874	047A3FZ	27, 98, 185, 205, 275, 416, 487, 512, 667, 874	047D36Z	27, 98, 186, 205, 275, 416, 487, 512, 667, 874	047F3Z1	27, 98, 186, 205, 275, 416, 487, 512, 667, 874	047K35Z	27, 98, 186, 206, 275, 417, 487, 512, 668, 874
047536Z	26, 97, 185, 205, 274, 416, 487, 512, 667, 874	047834Z	27, 97, 185, 205, 274, 416, 487, 512, 667, 874	047A3GZ	27, 98, 185, 205, 275, 416, 487, 512, 667, 874	047D37Z	27, 98, 186, 205, 275, 416, 487, 512, 667, 874	047F3ZZ	27, 98, 186, 205, 275, 416, 487, 512, 667, 874	047K36Z	27, 98, 186, 206, 275, 417, 487, 512, 668, 875
047537Z	26, 97, 185, 205, 274, 416, 487, 512, 667, 874	047835Z	27, 97, 185, 205, 274, 416, 487, 512, 667, 874	047A3Z1	27, 98, 185, 205, 275, 416, 487, 512, 667, 874	047D3D1	27, 98, 186, 205, 275, 416, 487, 512, 667, 874	047H341	27, 98, 186, 205, 275, 416, 487, 512, 667, 874	047K37Z	27, 98, 186, 206, 275, 417, 487, 512, 668, 875
04753D1	26, 97, 185, 205, 274, 416, 487, 512, 667, 874	047836Z	27, 97, 185, 205, 274, 416, 487, 512, 667, 874	047A3ZZ	27, 98, 185, 205, 275, 416, 487, 512, 667, 874	047D3DZ	27, 98, 186, 205, 275, 416, 487, 512, 667, 874	047H34Z	27, 98, 186, 205, 275, 416, 487, 512, 667, 874	047K3D1	27, 98, 186, 206, 275, 417, 488, 512, 668, 875
04753DZ	26, 97, 185, 205, 274, 416, 487, 512, 667, 874	047837Z	27, 97, 185, 205, 274, 416, 487, 512, 667, 874	047B341	27, 98, 185, 205, 275, 416, 487, 512, 667, 874	047D3EZ	27, 98, 186, 205, 275, 416, 487, 512, 667, 874	047H35Z	27, 98, 186, 205, 275, 416, 487, 512, 667, 874	047K3DZ	27, 98, 186, 206, 275, 417, 488, 512, 668, 875
04753EZ	26, 97, 185, 205, 274, 416, 487, 512, 667, 874	04783D1	27, 97, 185, 205, 274, 416, 487, 512, 667, 874	047B34Z	27, 98, 185, 205, 275, 416, 487, 512, 667, 874	047D3FZ	27, 98, 186, 205, 275, 416, 487, 512, 667, 874	047H36Z	27, 98, 186, 205, 275, 416, 487, 512, 667, 874	047K3EZ	27, 98, 186, 206, 275, 417, 488, 512, 668, 875
04753FZ	26, 97, 185, 205, 274, 416, 487, 512, 667, 874	04783DZ	27, 97, 185, 205, 274, 416, 487, 512, 667, 874	047B35Z	27, 98, 185, 205, 275, 416, 487, 512, 667, 874	047D3GZ	27, 98, 186, 205, 275, 416, 487, 512, 667, 874	047H37Z	27, 98, 186, 205, 275, 416, 487, 512, 667, 874	047K3FZ	27, 98, 186, 206, 275, 417, 488, 512, 668, 875
04753GZ	26, 97, 185, 205, 274, 416, 487, 512, 667, 874	04783EZ	27, 97, 185, 205, 274, 416, 487, 512, 667, 874	047B36Z	27, 98, 185, 205, 275, 416, 487, 512, 667, 874	047D3Z1	27, 98, 186, 205, 275, 416, 487, 512, 667, 874	047H3D1	27, 98, 186, 205, 275, 416, 487, 512, 668, 874	047K3GZ	27, 98, 186, 206, 275, 417, 488, 512, 668, 875
04753Z1	26, 97, 185, 205, 274, 416, 487, 512, 667, 874	04783FZ	27, 97, 185, 205, 274, 416, 487, 512, 667, 874	047B37Z	27, 98, 185, 205, 275, 416, 487, 512, 667, 874	047D3ZZ	27, 98, 186, 205, 275, 416, 487, 512, 667, 874	047H3DZ	27, 98, 186, 205, 275, 416, 487, 512, 668, 874	047K3Z1	27, 98, 186, 206, 275, 417, 488, 512, 668, 875
04753ZZ	26, 97, 185, 205, 274, 416, 487, 512, 667, 874	04783GZ	27, 97, 185, 205, 274, 416, 487, 512, 667, 874	047B3D1	27, 98, 185, 205, 275, 416, 487, 512, 667, 874	047E341	27, 98, 186, 205, 275, 416, 487, 512, 667, 874	047H3EZ	27, 98, 186, 205, 275, 416, 487, 512, 668, 874	047K3ZZ	27, 98, 186, 206, 275, 417, 488, 512, 668, 875
047634Z	27, 97, 185, 205, 274, 416, 487, 512, 667, 874	04783Z1	27, 97, 185, 205, 274, 416, 487, 512, 667, 874	047B3DZ	27, 98, 185, 205, 275, 416, 487, 512, 667, 874	047E34Z	27, 98, 186, 205, 275, 416, 487, 512, 667, 874	047H3FZ	27, 98, 186, 205, 275, 416, 487, 512, 668, 874	047K441	27, 98, 186, 206, 275, 417, 488, 512, 668, 875
047635Z	27, 97, 185, 205, 274, 416, 487, 512, 667, 874	04783ZZ	27, 97, 185, 205, 275, 416, 487, 512, 667, 874	047B3EZ	27, 98, 186, 205, 275, 416, 487, 512, 667, 874	047E35Z	27, 98, 186, 205, 275, 416, 487, 512, 667, 874	047H3GZ	27, 98, 186, 205, 275, 416, 487, 512, 668, 874	047K4D1	27, 98, 186, 206, 275, 417, 488, 513, 668, 875
047636Z	27, 97, 185, 205, 274, 416, 487, 512, 667, 874	047934Z	27, 98, 185, 205, 275, 416, 487, 512, 667, 874	047B3FZ	27, 98, 186, 205, 275, 416, 487, 512, 667, 874	047E36Z	27, 98, 186, 205, 275, 416, 487, 512, 667, 874	047H3Z1	27, 98, 186, 205, 275, 416, 487, 512, 668, 874	047K4Z1	27, 98, 186, 206, 275, 417, 488, 513, 668, 875
047637Z	27, 97, 185, 205, 274, 416, 487, 512, 667, 874	047935Z	27, 98, 185, 205, 275, 416, 487, 512, 667, 874	047B3GZ	27, 98, 186, 205, 275, 416, 487, 512, 667, 874	047E37Z	27, 98, 186, 205, 275, 416, 487, 512, 667, 874	047H3ZZ	27, 98, 186, 205, 275, 416, 487, 512, 668, 874	047L041	27, 98, 186, 206, 275, 417, 488, 513, 668, 875
04763D1	27, 97, 185, 205, 274, 416, 487, 512, 667, 874	047936Z	27, 98, 185, 205, 275, 416, 487, 512, 667, 874	047B3Z1	27, 98, 186, 205, 275, 416, 487, 512, 667, 874	047E3D1	27, 98, 186, 205, 275, 416, 487, 512, 668, 874	047J341	27, 98, 186, 206, 275, 416, 487, 512, 668, 874	047L0D1	27, 98, 186, 206, 275, 417, 488, 513, 668, 875
04763DZ	27, 97, 185, 205, 274, 416, 487, 512, 667, 874	047937Z	27, 98, 185, 205, 275, 416, 487, 512, 667, 874	047B3ZZ	27, 98, 186, 205, 275, 416, 487, 512, 667, 874	047E3DZ	27, 98, 186, 205, 275, 416, 487, 512, 667, 874	047J34Z	27, 98, 186, 206, 275, 416, 487, 512, 668, 874	047L0Z1	27, 98, 186, 206, 275, 417, 488, 513, 668, 875
04763EZ	27, 97, 185, 205, 274, 416, 487, 512, 667, 874	04793D1	27, 98, 185, 205, 275, 416, 487, 512, 667, 874	047C341	27, 98, 186, 205, 275, 416, 487, 512, 667, 874	047E3EZ	27, 98, 186, 205, 275, 416, 487, 512, 667, 874	047J35Z	27, 98, 186, 206, 275, 416, 487, 512, 668, 874	047L341	27, 98, 186, 206, 275, 417, 488, 513, 668, 875
04763FZ	27, 97, 185, 205, 274, 416, 487, 512, 667, 874	04793DZ	27, 98, 185, 205, 275, 416, 487, 512, 667, 874	047C34Z	27, 98, 186, 205, 275, 416, 487, 512, 667, 874	047E3FZ	27, 98, 186, 205, 275, 416, 487, 512, 667, 874	047J36Z	27, 98, 186, 206, 275, 416, 487, 512, 668, 874	047L34Z	27, 98, 186, 206, 275, 417, 488, 513, 668, 875
04763GZ	27, 97, 185, 205, 274, 416, 487, 512, 667, 874	04793EZ	27, 98, 185, 205, 275, 416, 487, 512, 667, 874	047C35Z	27, 98, 186, 205, 275, 416, 487, 512, 667, 874	047E3GZ	27, 98, 186, 205, 275, 417, 487, 512, 667, 874	047J37Z	27, 98, 186, 206, 275, 417, 487, 512, 668, 874	047L35Z	27, 98, 186, 206, 275, 417, 488, 513, 668, 875
04763Z1	27, 97, 185, 205, 274, 416, 487, 512, 667, 874	04793FZ	27, 98, 185, 205, 275, 416, 487, 512, 667, 874	047C36Z	27, 98, 186, 205, 275, 416, 487, 512, 667, 874	047E3Z1	27, 98, 186, 205, 275, 416, 487, 512, 667, 874	047J3D1	27, 98, 186, 206, 275, 417, 487, 512, 668, 874	047L36Z	27, 98, 186, 206, 275, 417, 488, 513, 668, 875
04763ZZ	27, 97, 185, 205, 274, 416, 487, 512, 667, 874	04793GZ	27, 98, 185, 205, 275, 416, 487, 512, 667, 874	047C37Z	27, 98, 186, 205, 275, 416, 487, 512, 667, 874	047E3ZZ	27, 98, 186, 205, 275, 416, 487, 512, 667, 874	047J3DZ	27, 98, 186, 206, 275, 417, 487, 512, 668, 874	047L37Z	27, 98, 186, 206, 275, 417, 488, 513, 668, 875
047734Z	27, 97, 185, 205, 274, 416, 487, 512, 667, 874	04793Z1	27, 98, 185, 205, 275, 416, 487, 512, 667, 874	047C3D1	27, 98, 186, 205, 275, 416, 487, 512, 667, 874	047F341	27, 98, 186, 205, 275, 416, 487, 512, 667, 874	047J3EZ	27, 98, 186, 206, 275, 417, 487, 512, 668, 874	047L3D1	27, 98, 186, 206, 275, 417, 488, 513, 668, 875
047735Z	27, 97, 185, 205, 274, 416, 487, 512, 667, 874	04793ZZ	27, 98, 185, 205, 275, 416, 487, 512, 667, 874	047C3DZ	27, 98, 186, 205, 275, 416, 487, 512, 667, 874	047F34Z	27, 98, 186, 205, 275, 416, 487, 512, 667, 874	047J3FZ	27, 98, 186, 206, 275, 417, 487, 512, 668, 874	047L3DZ	27, 98, 186, 206, 275, 417, 488, 513, 668, 875
047736Z	27, 97, 185, 205, 274, 416, 487, 512, 667, 874	047A341	27, 98, 185, 205, 275, 416, 487, 512, 667, 874	047C3EZ	27, 98, 186, 205, 275, 416, 487, 512, 667, 874	047F35Z	27, 98, 186, 205, 275, 417, 487, 512, 667, 874	047J3GZ	27, 98, 186, 206, 275, 417, 487, 512, 668, 874	047L3EZ	27, 98, 186, 206, 275, 417, 488, 513, 668, 875
047737Z	27, 97, 185, 205, 274, 416, 487, 512, 667, 874	047A34Z	27, 98, 185, 205, 275, 416, 487, 512, 667, 874	047C3FZ	27, 98, 186, 205, 275, 416, 487, 512, 667, 874	047F36Z	27, 98, 186, 205, 275, 416, 487, 512, 667, 874	047J3Z1	27, 98, 186, 206, 275, 417, 487, 512, 668, 874	047L3FZ	27, 98, 186, 206, 275, 417, 488, 513, 668, 875
04773D1	27, 97, 185, 205, 274, 416, 487, 512, 667, 874	047A35Z	27, 98, 185, 205, 275, 416, 487, 512, 667, 874	047C3GZ	27, 98, 186, 205, 275, 416, 487, 512, 667, 874	047F37Z	27, 98, 186, 205, 275, 416, 487, 512, 667, 874	047J3GZ	27, 98, 186, 206, 275, 417, 487, 512, 668, 874	047L3GZ	27, 98, 186, 206, 275, 417, 488, 513, 668, 875
04773DZ	27, 97, 185, 205, 274, 416, 487, 512, 667, 874	047A36Z	27, 98, 185, 205, 275, 416, 487, 512, 667, 874	047C3Z1	27, 98, 186, 205, 275, 416, 487, 512, 667, 874	047F3D1	27, 98, 186, 205, 275, 416, 487, 512, 667, 874	047K041	27, 98, 186, 206, 275, 417, 487, 512, 668, 874	047L3Z1	28, 98, 186, 206, 275, 417, 488, 513, 668, 875
04773EZ	27, 97, 185, 205, 274, 416, 487, 512, 667, 874	047A37Z	27, 98, 185, 205, 275, 416, 487, 512, 667, 874	047C3ZZ	27, 98, 186, 205, 275, 416, 487, 512, 667, 874	047F3DZ	27, 98, 186, 205, 275, 416, 487, 512, 667, 874	047K0D1	27, 98, 186, 206, 275, 417, 487, 512, 668, 874	047L3ZZ	28, 98, 186, 206, 275, 417, 488, 513, 668, 875

Numeric Index to Procedures
DRG Expert—Volume II

Code	Page
047L441	28, 98, 186, 206, 275, 417, 488, 513, 668, 875
047L4D1	28, 98, 186, 206, 275, 417, 488, 513, 668, 875
047L4Z1	28, 98, 186, 206, 275, 417, 488, 513, 668, 875
047M041	28, 98, 186, 206, 275, 417, 488, 513, 668, 875
047M0D1	28, 98, 186, 206, 275, 417, 488, 513, 668, 875
047M0Z1	28, 98, 186, 206, 275, 417, 488, 513, 668, 875
047M341	28, 98, 186, 206, 275, 417, 488, 513, 668, 875
047M3D1	28, 98, 186, 206, 275, 417, 488, 513, 668, 875
047M3Z1	28, 98, 186, 206, 275, 417, 488, 513, 668, 875
047M441	28, 98, 186, 206, 275, 417, 488, 513, 668, 875
047M4D1	28, 98, 186, 206, 275, 417, 488, 513, 668, 875
047M4Z1	28, 98, 186, 206, 275, 417, 488, 513, 668, 875
047N041	28, 98, 186, 206, 275, 417, 488, 513, 668, 875
047N0D1	28, 98, 186, 206, 275, 417, 488, 513, 668, 875
047N0Z1	28, 98, 186, 206, 275, 417, 488, 513, 668, 875
047N341	28, 98, 186, 206, 275, 417, 488, 513, 668, 875
047N3D1	28, 98, 186, 206, 275, 417, 488, 513, 668, 875
047N3Z1	28, 98, 186, 206, 275, 417, 488, 513, 668, 875
047N441	28, 98, 186, 206, 275, 417, 488, 513, 668, 875
047N4D1	28, 98, 186, 206, 275, 417, 488, 513, 668, 875
047N4Z1	28, 98, 186, 206, 275, 417, 488, 513, 668, 875
047Y341	28, 98, 186, 206, 275, 417, 488, 513, 668, 875
047Y34Z	28, 98, 186, 206, 275, 417, 488, 513, 668, 875
047Y35Z	28, 98, 186, 206, 275, 417, 488, 513, 668, 875
047Y36Z	28, 98, 186, 206, 275, 417, 488, 513, 668, 875
047Y37Z	28, 98, 186, 206, 275, 417, 488, 513, 668, 875
047Y3D1	28, 98, 186, 206, 275, 417, 488, 513, 668, 875
047Y3DZ	28, 98, 186, 206, 275, 417, 488, 513, 668, 875
047Y3EZ	28, 98, 186, 206, 275, 417, 488, 513, 668, 875
047Y3FZ	28, 98, 186, 206, 275, 417, 488, 513, 668, 875
047Y3GZ	28, 98, 186, 206, 275, 417, 488, 513, 668, 875
047Y3Z1	28, 98, 186, 206, 275, 417, 488, 513, 668, 875
047Y3ZZ	28, 98, 186, 206, 276, 417, 488, 513, 668, 875
04900ZX	131, 1045
04904ZX	131, 1045
04910ZX	131, 1045
04914ZX	131, 1045
04920ZX	131, 1045
04924ZX	131, 1045
04930ZX	131, 1045
04934ZX	131, 1045
04940ZX	131, 1045
04944ZX	131, 1045
04950ZX	131, 1045
04954ZX	131, 1045
04960ZX	131, 1045
04964ZX	131, 1046
04970ZX	131, 1046
04974ZX	131, 1046
04980ZX	131, 1046
04984ZX	131, 1046
04990ZX	131, 1046
04994ZX	131, 1046
049A0ZX	131, 1046
049A4ZX	131, 1046
049B0ZX	131, 1046
049B4ZX	131, 1046
049C0ZX	131, 1046
049C4ZX	131, 1046
049D0ZX	131, 1046
049D4ZX	131, 1046
049E0ZX	131, 1046
049E4ZX	131, 1046
049F0ZX	131, 1046
049F4ZX	131, 1046
049H0ZX	131, 1046
049H4ZX	131, 1046
049J0ZX	131, 1046
049J4ZX	131, 1046
049K0ZX	131, 1046
049K4ZX	131, 1046
049L0ZX	131, 1046
049L4ZX	131, 1046
049M0ZX	131, 1046
049M4ZX	131, 1046
049N0ZX	131, 1046
049N4ZX	131, 1046
049P0ZX	131, 1046
049P4ZX	131, 1046
049Q0ZX	131, 1046
049Q4ZX	131, 1046
049R0ZX	131, 1046
049R4ZX	131, 1046
049S0ZX	131, 1046
049S4ZX	131, 1046
049T0ZX	131, 1046
049T4ZX	131, 1046
049U0ZX	131, 1046
049U4ZX	131, 1046
049V0ZX	131, 1046
049V4ZX	132, 1046
049W0ZX	132, 1046
049W4ZX	132, 1046
049Y0ZX	132, 1046
049Y4ZX	132, 1046
04B00ZX	132, 1046
04B00ZZ	150, 186, 668, 875
04B03ZX	132, 1046
04B03ZZ	150, 186, 668, 875
04B04ZX	132, 1046
04B04ZZ	150, 186, 668, 875
04B10ZX	132, 1046
04B10ZZ	157, 186, 513, 668, 875
04B13ZX	132, 1046
04B13ZZ	157
04B14ZX	132, 1046
04B14ZZ	157, 186, 513, 668, 875
04B20ZX	132, 1046
04B20ZZ	157, 186, 513, 668, 875
04B23ZX	132, 1046
04B23ZZ	157
04B24ZX	132, 1046
04B24ZZ	157, 186, 513, 668, 875
04B30ZX	132, 1046
04B30ZZ	157, 186, 513, 668, 875
04B33ZX	132, 1046
04B33ZZ	157
04B34ZX	132, 1046
04B34ZZ	157, 186, 513, 668, 875
04B40ZX	132, 1046
04B40ZZ	157, 186, 513, 668, 875
04B43ZX	132, 1046
04B43ZZ	157
04B44ZX	132, 1046
04B44ZZ	157, 186, 513, 668, 875
04B50ZX	132, 1046
04B50ZZ	157, 186, 513, 668, 875
04B53ZX	132, 1046
04B53ZZ	157
04B54ZX	132, 1046
04B54ZZ	157, 186, 513, 668, 875
04B60ZX	132, 1046
04B60ZZ	157, 186, 513, 668, 875
04B63ZX	132, 1046
04B63ZZ	157
04B64ZX	132, 1046
04B64ZZ	157, 186, 513, 668, 875
04B70ZX	132, 1046
04B70ZZ	157, 186, 513, 668, 875
04B73ZX	132, 1046
04B73ZZ	157
04B74ZX	132, 1046
04B74ZZ	157, 186, 513, 668, 875
04B80ZX	132, 1046
04B80ZZ	157, 186, 513, 668, 875
04B83ZX	132, 1046
04B83ZZ	157
04B84ZX	132, 1046
04B84ZZ	157, 186, 513, 668, 875
04B90ZX	132, 1046
04B90ZZ	157, 186, 513, 668, 875
04B93ZX	132, 1046
04B93ZZ	157
04B94ZX	132, 1046
04B94ZZ	157, 186, 513, 668, 875
04BA0ZX	132, 1046
04BA0ZZ	157, 186, 513, 668, 875
04BA3ZX	132, 1046
04BA3ZZ	157
04BA4ZX	132, 1046
04BA4ZZ	157, 186, 513, 668, 875
04BB0ZX	132, 1046
04BB0ZZ	157, 186, 513, 668, 875
04BB3ZX	132, 1046
04BB3ZZ	157
04BB4ZX	132, 1046
04BB4ZZ	157, 186, 513, 668, 875
04BC0ZX	132, 1046
04BC0ZZ	157, 186, 513, 668, 875
04BC3ZX	132, 1046
04BC3ZZ	157
04BC4ZX	132, 1046
04BC4ZZ	157, 186, 513, 668, 875
04BD0ZX	132, 1046
04BD0ZZ	157, 186, 513, 668, 875
04BD3ZX	132, 1046
04BD3ZZ	157
04BD4ZX	132, 1046
04BD4ZZ	157, 186, 513, 668, 875
04BE0ZX	132, 1046
04BE0ZZ	157, 186, 513, 668, 875
04BE3ZX	132, 1046
04BE3ZZ	157
04BE4ZX	132, 1046
04BE4ZZ	157, 186, 513, 668, 875
04BF0ZX	132, 1046
04BF0ZZ	157, 187, 513, 668, 875
04BF3ZX	132, 1046
04BF3ZZ	157
04BF4ZX	132, 1046
04BF4ZZ	157, 187, 513, 668, 875
04BH0ZX	132, 1046
04BH0ZZ	158, 187, 513, 668, 875
04BH3ZX	132, 1046
04BH3ZZ	158
04BH4ZX	132, 1046
04BH4ZZ	158, 187, 513, 668, 875
04BJ0ZX	132, 1046
04BJ0ZZ	158, 187, 513, 668, 875
04BJ3ZX	132, 1046
04BJ3ZZ	158
04BJ4ZX	132, 1046
04BJ4ZZ	158, 187, 513, 668, 875
04BK*	132
04BK0ZX	1046
04BK0ZZ	488, 668, 875
04BK3ZX	1046
04BK3ZZ	488, 668, 875
04BK4ZX	1046
04BK4ZZ	488, 668, 875
04BL*	132
04BL0ZX	1046
04BL0ZZ	488, 668, 875
04BL3ZX	1046
04BL3ZZ	488, 668, 875
04BL4ZX	1046
04BL4ZZ	488, 668, 875
04BM*	132
04BM0ZX	1046
04BM0ZZ	488, 668, 875
04BM3ZX	1046
04BM3ZZ	488, 668, 875
04BM4ZX	1046
04BM4ZZ	488, 668, 875
04BN*	132
04BN0ZX	1046
04BN0ZZ	488, 668, 875
04BN3ZX	1046
04BN3ZZ	488, 668, 875
04BN4ZX	1046
04BN4ZZ	488, 668, 875
04BP*	132
04BP0ZX	1046
04BP0ZZ	488, 668, 875
04BP3ZX	1046
04BP3ZZ	488, 668, 875
04BP4ZX	1046
04BP4ZZ	488, 668, 875
04BQ*	132
04BQ0ZX	1046
04BQ0ZZ	488, 668, 875
04BQ3ZX	1046
04BQ3ZZ	488, 668, 875
04BQ4ZX	1046
04BQ4ZZ	488, 668, 875
04BR*	132
04BR0ZX	1046
04BR0ZZ	488, 668, 875
04BR3ZX	1046
04BR3ZZ	488, 668, 875
04BR4ZX	1046
04BR4ZZ	488, 668, 875
04BS*	132
04BS0ZX	1046
04BS0ZZ	488, 668, 875
04BS3ZX	1046
04BS3ZZ	488, 668, 875
04BS4ZX	1046
04BS4ZZ	488, 668, 875
04BT*	132
04BT0ZX	1046
04BT0ZZ	488, 668, 875
04BT3ZX	1046
04BT3ZZ	488, 668, 875
04BT4ZX	1046
04BT4ZZ	488, 668, 875
04BU*	132
04BU0ZX	1046
04BU0ZZ	488, 668, 875
04BU3ZX	1046
04BU3ZZ	488, 668, 875
04BU4ZX	1046
04BU4ZZ	488, 668, 875
04BV*	132
04BV0ZX	1046
04BV0ZZ	488, 668, 875
04BV3ZX	1046
04BV3ZZ	488, 668, 875
04BV4ZX	1046
04BV4ZZ	488, 668, 875
04BW*	132
04BW0ZX	1046
04BW0ZZ	488, 668, 875
04BW3ZX	1046
04BW3ZZ	488, 668, 875
04BW4ZX	1046
04BW4ZZ	488, 668, 875
04BY*	132
04BY0ZX	1046
04BY0ZZ	488, 668, 875
04BY3ZX	1046
04BY3ZZ	488, 668, 875
04BY4ZX	1046
04BY4ZZ	488, 668, 875
04C*	668
04C0*	187
04C00ZZ	150, 875
04C03ZZ	150, 875
04C04ZZ	150, 875
04C1*	187, 513
04C10ZZ	158, 875
04C13ZZ	158, 875
04C14ZZ	158, 875
04C2*	187, 513
04C20ZZ	158, 875
04C23ZZ	158, 875
04C24ZZ	158, 875
04C3*	187, 513
04C30ZZ	158, 875
04C33ZZ	158, 875
04C34ZZ	158, 875
04C4*	187, 513
04C40ZZ	158, 875
04C43ZZ	158, 875
04C44ZZ	158, 875
04C5*	187, 513
04C50ZZ	158
04C50ZZ	875
04C53ZZ	158, 875
04C54ZZ	158, 875
04C6*	187, 513
04C60ZZ	158, 875
04C63ZZ	158, 875
04C64ZZ	158, 875
04C7*	187, 513
04C70ZZ	158, 875
04C73ZZ	158, 875
04C74ZZ	158, 875
04C8*	187, 513
04C80ZZ	158, 875
04C83ZZ	158, 875
04C84ZZ	158, 875
04C9*	187, 513
04C90ZZ	158, 875
04C93ZZ	158, 875
04C94ZZ	158, 875
04CA*	187, 513
04CA0ZZ	158, 875
04CA3ZZ	158, 875
04CA4ZZ	158, 875
04CB*	187, 513
04CB0ZZ	158, 875
04CB3ZZ	158, 875
04CB4ZZ	158, 875
04CC*	187, 513
04CC0ZZ	158, 875
04CC3ZZ	158, 875
04CC4ZZ	158, 876
04CD*	187, 513
04CD0ZZ	158, 876
04CD3ZZ	158, 876
04CD4ZZ	158, 876
04CE*	187, 513
04CE0ZZ	158, 876
04CE3ZZ	158, 876
04CE4ZZ	158, 876
04CF*	187, 513
04CF0ZZ	158, 876
04CF3ZZ	158, 876
04CF4ZZ	158, 876
04CH*	187, 513
04CH0ZZ	158, 876
04CH3ZZ	158, 876
04CH4ZZ	158, 876
04CJ*	187, 513
04CJ0ZZ	158, 876
04CJ3ZZ	158, 876
04CJ4ZZ	158, 876
04CK*	488
04CK0ZZ	132, 609, 876
04CK0ZZ	584
04CK3ZZ	158, 609, 876
04CK3ZZ	584
04CK4ZZ	132, 609, 876
04CK4ZZ	584
04CL*	488
04CL0ZZ	132, 584, 609, 876
04CL3ZZ	158, 584, 609, 876
04CL4ZZ	132, 584, 609, 876
04CM*	488
04CM0ZZ	132, 584, 609, 876
04CM3ZZ	158, 584, 609, 876
04CM4ZZ	132, 584, 609, 876
04CN*	488
04CN0ZZ	132, 584, 609, 876
04CN3ZZ	158, 584, 609, 876
04CN4ZZ	132, 584, 609, 876
04CP*	488
04CP0ZZ	132, 584, 609, 876
04CP3ZZ	158, 584, 609, 876
04CP4ZZ	132, 584, 609, 876
04CQ*	488
04CQ0ZZ	132, 584, 609, 876
04CQ3ZZ	158, 584, 609, 876
04CQ4ZZ	132, 584, 609, 876
04CR*	488
04CR0ZZ	132, 584, 609, 876
04CR3ZZ	584, 609, 876
04CR3ZZ	158
04CR4ZZ	132, 584, 609, 876
04CS*	488
04CS0ZZ	132, 584, 609, 876
04CS3ZZ	584, 609, 876
04CS3ZZ	158
04CS4ZZ	132, 584, 609, 876
04CT*	488
04CT0ZZ	132, 584, 609, 876
04CT3ZZ	158, 584, 609, 876
04CT4ZZ	132, 584, 609, 876
04CU*	488
04CU0ZZ	132, 584, 609, 876
04CU3ZZ	158, 584, 609, 876
04CU4ZZ	132, 584, 609, 876
04CV*	488
04CV0ZZ	132, 584, 609, 876
04CV3ZZ	158, 584, 609, 876
04CV4ZZ	132, 584, 609, 876
04CW*	488
04CW0ZZ	132, 584, 609, 876
04CW3ZZ	158, 584, 609, 876
04CW4ZZ	132, 584, 609, 876
04CY*	28
04CY*	187, 206, 488, 513
04CY0ZZ	132, 584, 609, 876
04CY3ZZ	158, 584, 609, 876
04CY4ZZ	132, 584, 609, 876
04H00DZ	132, 187, 584, 609, 668, 876
04H03DZ	132, 187, 584, 609, 668, 876
04H04DZ	132, 187, 584, 609, 668, 876
04H10DZ	132, 584, 609, 668, 876
04H13DZ	132, 584, 609, 668, 876
04H14DZ	132, 584, 609, 668, 876
04H20DZ	132, 584, 609, 668, 876
04H23DZ	132, 584, 609, 668, 876
04H24DZ	132, 584, 609, 668, 876
04H30DZ	132, 584, 609, 668, 876
04H33DZ	132, 584, 609, 668, 876
04H34DZ	132, 584, 609, 668, 876
04H40DZ	132, 584, 609, 669, 876
04H43DZ	132, 584, 609, 669, 876
04H44DZ	132, 584, 609, 669, 876
04H50DZ	132, 584, 609, 669, 876

Numeric Index to Procedures

Code	Page
04H53DZ	132, 584, 610, 669, 876
04H54DZ	132, 584, 610, 669, 876
04H60DZ	132, 584, 610, 669, 876
04H63DZ	132, 584, 610, 669, 876
04H64DZ	132, 584, 610, 669, 876
04H70DZ	132, 584, 610, 669, 876
04H73DZ	132, 584, 610, 669, 876
04H74DZ	132, 584, 610, 669, 876
04H80DZ	132, 584, 610, 669, 876
04H83DZ	132, 584, 610, 669, 876
04H84DZ	132, 584, 610, 669, 876
04H90DZ	132, 584, 610, 669, 876
04H93DZ	132, 584, 610, 669, 876
04H94DZ	132, 584, 610, 669, 876
04HA0DZ	132, 584, 610, 669, 876
04HA3DZ	132, 584, 610, 669, 876
04HA4DZ	132, 584, 610, 669, 876
04HB0DZ	132, 584, 610, 669, 876
04HB3DZ	132, 584, 610, 669, 876
04HB4DZ	132, 584, 610, 669, 876
04HC0DZ	132, 584, 610, 669, 876
04HC3DZ	132, 584, 610, 669, 876
04HC4DZ	132, 584, 610, 669, 876
04HD0DZ	132, 584, 610, 669, 876
04HD3DZ	132, 584, 610, 669, 876
04HD4DZ	132, 584, 610, 669, 876
04HE0DZ	132, 584, 610, 669, 876
04HE3DZ	132, 584, 610, 669, 876
04HE4DZ	132, 584, 610, 669, 876
04HF0DZ	132, 584, 610, 669, 876
04HF3DZ	132, 584, 610, 669, 876
04HF4DZ	132, 584, 610, 669, 876
04HH0DZ	132, 584, 610, 669, 876
04HH3DZ	132, 584, 610, 669, 876
04HH4DZ	132, 584, 610, 669, 876
04HJ0DZ	132, 584, 610, 669, 876
04HJ3DZ	132, 584, 610, 669, 876
04HJ4DZ	132, 584, 610, 669, 876
04HK0DZ	132, 585, 610, 669, 876
04HK3DZ	132, 585, 610, 669, 876
04HK4DZ	132, 585, 610, 669, 876
04HL0DZ	132, 585, 610, 669, 876
04HL3DZ	132, 585, 610, 669, 876
04HL4DZ	132, 585, 610, 669, 876
04HM0DZ	132, 585, 610, 669, 876
04HM3DZ	132, 585, 610, 669, 876
04HM4DZ	132, 585, 610, 669, 876
04HN0DZ	132, 585, 610, 669, 876
04HN3DZ	132, 585, 610, 669, 876
04HN4DZ	132, 585, 610, 669, 876
04HP0DZ	132, 585, 610, 669, 876
04HP3DZ	132, 585, 610, 669, 876
04HP4DZ	132, 585, 610, 669, 876
04HQ0DZ	132, 585, 610, 669, 876
04HQ3DZ	132, 585, 610, 669, 876
04HQ4DZ	132, 585, 610, 669, 876
04HR0DZ	132, 585, 610, 669, 876
04HR3DZ	132, 585, 610, 669, 876
04HR4DZ	132, 585, 610, 669, 876
04HS0DZ	132, 585, 610, 669, 876
04HS3DZ	133, 585, 610, 669, 876
04HS4DZ	133, 585, 610, 669, 876
04HT0DZ	133, 585, 610, 669, 876
04HT3DZ	133, 585, 610, 669, 876
04HT4DZ	133, 585, 610, 669, 876
04HU0DZ	133, 585, 610, 669, 876
04HU3DZ	133, 585, 610, 669, 876
04HU4DZ	133, 585, 610, 669, 876
04HV0DZ	133, 585, 610, 669, 876
04HV3DZ	133, 585, 610, 669, 876
04HV4DZ	133, 585, 610, 669, 876
04HW0DZ	133, 585, 610, 669, 876
04HW3DZ	133, 585, 610, 669, 876
04HW4DZ	133, 585, 610, 669, 876
04HY02Z	133, 488, 585, 610, 669, 876
04HY0DZ	133, 585, 610, 669, 876
04HY0YZ	133, 488, 585, 610, 669, 876
04HY3DZ	133, 585, 610, 669, 876
04HY42Z	133, 488, 585, 610, 669, 876
04HY4DZ	133, 585, 610, 669, 876
04JY0ZZ	133
04L0*	187, 669
04L00CZ	150, 876
04L00DZ	150, 876
04L00ZZ	150, 876
04L03CZ	150, 876
04L03DJ	150, 876
04L03DZ	150, 876
04L03ZZ	150, 876
04L04CZ	150, 876
04L04DZ	150, 876
04L04ZZ	150, 876
04L1*	187, 669
04L10CZ	158, 876, 1046
04L10DZ	158, 876, 1046
04L10ZZ	158, 876, 1046
04L13CZ	158, 876, 1046
04L13DZ	158, 876, 1046
04L13ZZ	158, 876, 1046
04L14CZ	158, 876, 1046
04L14DZ	158, 876, 1046
04L14ZZ	158, 876, 1046
04L20CZ	158, 187, 669, 876, 1046
04L20DZ	158, 187, 669, 876, 1046
04L20ZZ	158, 187, 669, 876, 1046
04L23CZ	158, 187, 669, 876, 1046
04L23DZ	158, 187, 669, 877, 1046
04L23ZZ	158, 187, 669, 877, 1046
04L24CZ	158, 187, 669, 877, 1046
04L24DZ	158, 187, 669, 877, 1046
04L24ZZ	158, 187, 669, 877, 1046
04L3*	187, 669
04L30CZ	158, 877, 1046
04L30DZ	158, 877, 1046
04L30ZZ	158, 877, 1046
04L33CZ	158, 877, 1046
04L33DZ	158, 877, 1046
04L33ZZ	158, 877, 1046
04L34CZ	158, 877, 1046
04L34DZ	158, 877, 1046
04L34ZZ	158, 877, 1046
04L4*	187, 669
04L40CZ	158, 877, 1046
04L40DZ	158, 877, 1046
04L40ZZ	158, 877, 1046
04L43CZ	158, 877, 1046
04L43DZ	158, 877, 1046
04L43ZZ	158, 877, 1047
04L44CZ	158, 877, 1047
04L44DZ	158, 877, 1047
04L44ZZ	158, 877, 1047
04L5*	187, 669
04L50CZ	158, 877, 1047
04L50DZ	158, 877, 1047
04L50ZZ	158, 877, 1047
04L53CZ	158, 877, 1047
04L53DZ	158, 877, 1047
04L53ZZ	158, 877, 1047
04L54CZ	158, 877, 1047
04L54DZ	158, 877, 1047
04L54ZZ	158, 877, 1047
04L6*	187, 669
04L60CZ	158, 877, 1047
04L60DZ	158, 877, 1047
04L60ZZ	158, 877, 1047
04L63CZ	158, 877, 1047
04L63DZ	158, 877, 1047
04L63ZZ	158, 877, 1047
04L64CZ	158, 877, 1047
04L64DZ	158, 877, 1047
04L64ZZ	158, 877, 1047
04L7*	187, 669
04L70CZ	158, 877, 1047
04L70DZ	158, 877, 1047
04L70ZZ	158, 877, 1047
04L73CZ	158, 877, 1047
04L73DZ	158, 877, 1047
04L73ZZ	158, 877, 1047
04L74CZ	158, 877, 1047
04L74DZ	158, 877, 1047
04L74ZZ	158, 877, 1047
04L8*	187, 669
04L80CZ	158, 877, 1047
04L80DZ	158, 877, 1047
04L80ZZ	158, 877, 1047
04L83CZ	158, 877, 1047
04L83DZ	158, 877, 1047
04L83ZZ	158, 877, 1047
04L84CZ	158, 877, 1047
04L84DZ	158, 877, 1047
04L84ZZ	158, 877, 1047
04L9*	187, 513, 669
04L90CZ	158, 877, 1047
04L90DZ	158, 877, 1047
04L90ZZ	158, 877, 1047
04L93CZ	158, 877, 1047
04L93DZ	158, 877, 1047
04L93ZZ	158, 877, 1047
04L94CZ	158, 877, 1047
04L94DZ	158, 877, 1047
04L94ZZ	158, 877, 1047
04LA*	187, 513, 669
04LA0CZ	158, 877, 1047
04LA0DZ	158, 877, 1047
04LA0ZZ	158, 877, 1047
04LA3CZ	158, 877, 1047
04LA3DZ	158, 877, 1047
04LA3ZZ	158, 877, 1047
04LA4CZ	158, 877, 1047
04LA4DZ	158, 877, 1047
04LA4ZZ	158, 877, 1047
04LB*	187, 669
04LB0CZ	158, 877, 1047
04LB0DZ	158, 877, 1047
04LB3CZ	158, 877, 1047
04LB3DZ	158, 877, 1047
04LB4CZ	158, 877, 1047
04LB4DZ	158, 877, 1047
04LB4ZZ	158, 877, 1047
04LC*	158, 187, 877
04LC0CZ	158, 187, 877
04LC0DZ	158, 187, 877
04LC0ZZ	158, 187, 877, 1047
04LC3CZ	158, 187, 877, 1047
04LC3DZ	158, 187
04LC3ZZ	159, 187, 877, 1047
04LC4CZ	159, 187, 877, 1047
04LC4DZ	159, 877
04LC4ZZ	159, 187, 877, 1047
04LD*	669
04LD0CZ	159, 187, 877, 1047
04LD0DZ	159, 877
04LD0ZZ	159, 187, 877, 1047
04LD3CZ	159, 187, 877, 1047
04LD3DZ	159, 877
04LD3ZZ	159, 187, 877, 1047
04LD4CZ	159, 187, 877, 1047
04LD4DZ	159, 877
04LD4ZZ	159, 187, 877, 1047
04LE0CT	537
04LE0CZ	159, 187, 669, 877, 1047
04LE0DT	537
04LE0DZ	159, 669, 877
04LE0ZT	537
04LE0ZZ	159, 187, 669, 877, 1047
04LE3CT	537
04LE3CZ	159, 187, 669, 877, 1047
04LE3DT	537
04LE3DZ	159, 669, 877
04LE3ZT	537
04LE3ZZ	159, 187, 669, 877, 1047
04LE4CT	537
04LE4CZ	159, 187, 669, 877, 1047
04LE4DT	537
04LE4DZ	159, 669, 877
04LE4ZT	537
04LE4ZZ	159, 187, 669, 877, 1047
04LF0CU	537
04LF0CZ	159, 187, 669, 877, 1047
04LF0DU	537
04LF0DZ	159, 669, 877
04LF0ZU	537
04LF0ZZ	159, 187, 669, 877, 1047
04LF3CU	537
04LF3CZ	159, 187, 669, 877, 1047
04LF3DU	537
04LF3DZ	159, 669, 877
04LF3ZU	537
04LF3ZZ	159, 187, 669, 877, 1047
04LF4CU	537
04LF4CZ	159, 187, 669, 877, 1047
04LF4DU	537
04LF4DZ	159, 669, 877
04LF4ZU	537
04LF4ZZ	159, 187, 669, 877, 1047
04LR*	669
04LH0CZ	159, 187, 877, 1047
04LH0DZ	159, 877
04LH0ZZ	159, 187, 877, 1047
04LH3CZ	159, 187, 877, 1047
04LH3DZ	159, 877
04LH3ZZ	159, 187, 877, 1047
04LH4CZ	159, 187, 877, 1047
04LH4DZ	159, 877
04LH4ZZ	159, 187, 877, 1047
04LJ*	669
04LJ0CZ	159, 187, 877, 1047
04LJ0DZ	159, 877
04LJ0ZZ	159, 187, 877, 1047
04LJ3CZ	159, 187, 877, 1047
04LJ3DZ	159, 877
04LJ3ZZ	159, 187, 877, 1047
04LJ4CZ	159, 187, 877, 1047
04LJ4DZ	159, 877
04LJ4ZZ	159, 187, 877, 1047
04LK*	669
04LK0CZ	133, 877
04LK0DZ	133, 877
04LK0ZZ	133, 877
04LK3CZ	133, 877
04LK3DZ	133, 877
04LK3ZZ	133, 877
04LK4CZ	133, 877
04LK4DZ	133, 877
04LK4ZZ	133, 877
04LL*	669
04LL0CZ	133, 877
04LL0DZ	133, 877
04LL0ZZ	133, 877
04LL3CZ	133, 877
04LL3DZ	133, 877
04LL3ZZ	133, 877
04LL4CZ	133, 877
04LL4DZ	133, 877
04LL4ZZ	133, 877
04LM*	669
04LM0CZ	133, 877
04LM0DZ	133, 877
04LM0ZZ	133, 877
04LM3CZ	133, 877
04LM3DZ	133, 877
04LM3ZZ	133, 877
04LM4CZ	133, 877
04LM4DZ	133, 877
04LM4ZZ	133, 877
04LN*	669
04LN0CZ	133, 877
04LN0DZ	133, 877
04LN0ZZ	133, 877
04LN3CZ	133, 877
04LN3DZ	133, 877
04LN3ZZ	133, 877
04LN4CZ	133, 877
04LN4DZ	133, 878
04LN4ZZ	133, 878
04LP*	669
04LP0CZ	133, 878
04LP0DZ	133, 878
04LP0ZZ	133, 878
04LP3CZ	133, 878
04LP3DZ	133, 878
04LP3ZZ	133, 878
04LP4CZ	133, 878
04LP4DZ	133, 878
04LP4ZZ	133, 878
04LQ*	669
04LQ0CZ	133, 878
04LQ0DZ	133, 878
04LQ0ZZ	133, 878
04LQ3CZ	133, 878
04LQ3DZ	133, 878
04LQ3ZZ	133, 878
04LQ4CZ	133, 878
04LQ4DZ	133, 878
04LQ4ZZ	133, 878
04LR*	669
04LR0CZ	133, 878
04LR0DZ	133, 878
04LR0ZZ	133, 878
04LR3CZ	133, 878
04LR3DZ	133, 878
04LR3ZZ	133, 878
04LR4CZ	133, 878
04LR4DZ	133, 878
04LR4ZZ	133, 878
04LS*	669
04LS0CZ	133, 878
04LS0DZ	133, 878
04LS0ZZ	133, 878
04LS3CZ	133, 878
04LS3DZ	133, 878
04LS3ZZ	133, 878
04LS4CZ	133, 878
04LS4DZ	133, 878
04LS4ZZ	133, 878
04LT*	669
04LT0CZ	133, 878
04LT0DZ	133, 878
04LT0ZZ	133, 878
04LT3CZ	133, 878
04LT3DZ	133, 878
04LT3ZZ	133, 878
04LT4CZ	133, 878
04LT4DZ	133, 878
04LT4ZZ	133, 878
04LU*	669
04LU0CZ	133, 878
04LU0DZ	133, 878
04LU0ZZ	133, 878
04LU3CZ	133, 878
04LU3DZ	133, 878
04LU3ZZ	133, 878
04LU4CZ	133, 878
04LU4DZ	133, 878
04LU4ZZ	133, 878
04LV*	669
04LV0CZ	133, 878
04LV0DZ	133, 878
04LV0ZZ	133, 878
04LV3CZ	133, 878
04LV3DZ	133, 878
04LV3ZZ	133, 878
04LV4CZ	133, 878
04LV4DZ	133, 878
04LV4ZZ	133, 878
04LW*	669
04LW0CZ	133, 878
04LW0DZ	133, 878
04LW0ZZ	133, 878
04LW3CZ	133, 878
04LW3DZ	133, 878
04LW3ZZ	133, 878
04LW4CZ	133, 878
04LW4DZ	133, 878
04LW4ZZ	133, 878
04LY*	669
04LY0CZ	133, 878
04LY0DZ	133, 878
04LY0ZZ	133, 878
04LY3CZ	133, 878
04LY3DZ	133, 878
04LY3ZZ	133, 878
04LY4CZ	133, 878
04LY4DZ	133, 878
04LY4ZZ	133, 878
04N*	133
04N00ZZ	187
04N04ZZ	187
04N10ZZ	187
04N14ZZ	187
04N20ZZ	187
04N24ZZ	187
04N30ZZ	187
04N34ZZ	187
04N40ZZ	187
04N44ZZ	187
04N50ZZ	187
04N54ZZ	187
04N60ZZ	187
04N64ZZ	187
04N70ZZ	187
04N74ZZ	187
04N80ZZ	187
04N84ZZ	187
04N90ZZ	187
04N94ZZ	187
04NA0ZZ	187
04NA4ZZ	187
04NB0ZZ	187

Numeric Index to Procedures

Code	Page	Code	Page	Code	Page	Code	Page	Code	Page	Code	Page
04NB4ZZ	187	04QE3ZZ	417, 878	04R34KZ	159, 879	04RJ07Z	159, 879	04RY0KZ	880	04SQ3ZZ	417, 880
04NC0ZZ	187	04QE4ZZ	417, 878	04R4*	669	04RJ0JZ	159, 879	04RY47Z	880	04SQ4ZZ	417, 880
04NC4ZZ	187	04QF*	488	04R407Z	159, 879	04RJ0KZ	159, 879	04RY4JZ	880	04SR*	670
04ND0ZZ	187	04QF0ZZ	417, 878	04R40JZ	159, 879	04RJ47Z	159, 879	04RY4KZ	880	04SR0ZZ	417, 880
04ND4ZZ	187	04QF3ZZ	417, 878	04R40KZ	159, 879	04RJ4JZ	159, 879	04S*	134	04SR3ZZ	417, 880
04NE0ZZ	187	04QF4ZZ	417, 878	04R447Z	159, 879	04RJ4KZ	159, 879	04S0*	488, 513, 670	04SR4ZZ	417, 880
04NE4ZZ	187	04QH*	488	04R44JZ	159, 879	04RK*	133, 488, 669	04S00ZZ	880	04SS*	670
04NF0ZZ	187	04QH0ZZ	417, 878	04R44KZ	159, 879	04RK07Z	879	04S03ZZ	880	04SS0ZZ	417, 880
04NF4ZZ	187	04QH3ZZ	417, 878	04R5*	669	04RK0JZ	879	04S04ZZ	880	04SS3ZZ	417, 880
04NH0ZZ	187	04QH4ZZ	417, 878	04R507Z	159, 879	04RK0KZ	879	04S1*	488, 513, 670	04SS4ZZ	417, 880
04NH4ZZ	187	04QJ*	488	04R50JZ	159, 879	04RK47Z	879	04S10ZZ	880	04ST*	670
04NJ0ZZ	187	04QJ0ZZ	417, 878	04R50KZ	159, 879	04RK4JZ	879	04S13ZZ	880	04ST0ZZ	417, 880
04NJ4ZZ	187	04QJ3ZZ	417, 878	04R547Z	159, 879	04RK4KZ	879	04S14ZZ	880	04ST3ZZ	417, 880
04PY00Z	133, 488, 585, 610, 669, 878	04QJ4ZZ	417, 878	04R54JZ	159, 879	04RL*	133, 488, 669	04S2*	488, 513, 670	04ST4ZZ	417, 880
04PY02Z	133, 488, 585, 610, 669, 878	04QK*	488	04R54KZ	159, 879	04RL07Z	879	04S20ZZ	880	04SU*	670
04PY03Z	133, 488, 585, 610, 669, 878	04QK0ZZ	417, 878	04R6*	669	04RL0JZ	879	04S23ZZ	880	04SU0ZZ	417, 880
04PY07Z	133, 1047	04QK3ZZ	417, 878	04R607Z	159, 879	04RL0KZ	879	04S24ZZ	880	04SU3ZZ	417, 880
04PY0CZ	133, 488, 585, 610, 669, 878	04QK4ZZ	417, 878	04R60JZ	159, 879	04RL47Z	879	04S3*	488, 513, 670	04SU4ZZ	417, 880
04PY0DZ	133, 488, 585, 610, 669, 878	04QL*	488	04R60KZ	159, 879	04RL4JZ	879	04S30ZZ	880	04SV*	670
04PY0JZ	133, 1047	04QL0ZZ	417, 878	04R647Z	159, 879	04RL4KZ	879	04S33ZZ	880	04SV0ZZ	417, 880
04PY0KZ	133, 1047	04QL3ZZ	417, 878	04R64JZ	159, 879	04RM*	133, 488, 669	04S34ZZ	880	04SV3ZZ	417, 880
04PY0YZ	133, 488, 585, 610, 669, 878	04QL4ZZ	417, 878	04R64KZ	159, 879	04RM07Z	879	04S4*	488, 513, 670	04SV4ZZ	417, 880
04PY37Z	133, 1047	04QM*	488	04R7*	669	04RM0JZ	879	04S40ZZ	880	04SW*	670
04PY3CZ	133, 488, 585, 610, 669, 878	04QM0ZZ	417, 878	04R707Z	159, 879	04RM0KZ	879	04S43ZZ	880	04SW0ZZ	417, 880
04PY3JZ	133, 1047	04QM3ZZ	417, 878	04R70JZ	159, 879	04RM47Z	879	04S44ZZ	880	04SW3ZZ	417, 880
04PY3KZ	133, 1047	04QM4ZZ	417, 878	04R70KZ	159, 879	04RM4JZ	879	04S5*	488, 513, 670	04SW4ZZ	417, 880
04PY40Z	133, 488, 585, 610, 669, 878	04QN*	488	04R747Z	159, 879	04RM4KZ	879	04S50ZZ	880	04SY*	670
04PY42Z	133, 488, 585, 610, 669, 878	04QN0ZZ	417, 878	04R74JZ	159, 879	04RN*	133, 488, 669	04S53ZZ	880	04SY0ZZ	417, 880
04PY43Z	133, 488, 585, 610, 669, 878	04QN3ZZ	417, 878	04R74KZ	159, 879	04RN07Z	879	04S54ZZ	880	04SY3ZZ	417, 880
04PY47Z	133, 1047	04QN4ZZ	417, 878	04R8*	669	04RN0JZ	879	04S6*	488, 513, 670	04SY4ZZ	417, 880
04PY4CZ	133, 488, 585, 610, 669, 878	04QP*	488	04R807Z	159, 879	04RN0KZ	879	04S60ZZ	880	04U007Z	134, 670, 880
04PY4DZ	133, 488, 585, 610, 669, 878	04QP0ZZ	417, 878	04R80JZ	159, 879	04RN47Z	879	04S63ZZ	880	04U00JZ	134, 670
04PY4JZ	133, 1047	04QP3ZZ	417, 878	04R80KZ	159, 879	04RN4JZ	879	04S64ZZ	880	04U00KZ	134
04PY4KZ	133, 1047	04QP4ZZ	417, 878	04R847Z	159, 879	04RN4KZ	879	04S7*	488, 513, 670	04U037Z	134, 670, 880
04Q*	133, 669	04QQ*	488	04R84JZ	159, 879	04RP*	133, 488, 669	04S70ZZ	880	04U03JZ	150, 513, 670, 880
04Q00ZZ	878	04QQ3ZZ	417, 878	04R84KZ	159, 879	04RP07Z	879	04S73ZZ	880	04U03KZ	134
04Q03ZZ	878	04QQ4ZZ	417, 878	04R9*	513	04RP0JZ	879	04S74ZZ	880	04U047Z	134, 670, 880
04Q04ZZ	878	04QR*	488	04R907Z	159	04RP0KZ	879	04S8*	488, 513, 670	04U04JZ	150, 513, 670, 880
04Q10ZZ	878	04QR0ZZ	417, 878	04R90JZ	159	04RP47Z	879	04S80ZZ	880	04U04KZ	134
04Q13ZZ	878	04QR3ZZ	417, 878	04R90KZ	159	04RP4JZ	879	04S83ZZ	880	04U1*	134
04Q14ZZ	878	04QR4ZZ	417, 878	04R947Z	159	04RP4KZ	879	04S84ZZ	880	04U107Z	670, 880
04Q20ZZ	878	04QS*	488	04R94JZ	159	04RQ*	133, 488, 669	04S9*	505	04U10JZ	670
04Q23ZZ	878	04QS0ZZ	417, 878	04R94KZ	159	04RQ07Z	879	04SA*	505	04U137Z	670, 880
04Q24ZZ	878	04QS3ZZ	417, 878	04RA*	513	04RQ0JZ	879	04SB*	488, 513, 670	04U13JZ	670
04Q30ZZ	878	04QS4ZZ	417, 878	04RA07Z	159	04RQ0KZ	879	04SB0ZZ	880	04U147Z	670, 880
04Q33ZZ	878	04QT*	488	04RA0JZ	159	04RQ47Z	879	04SB3ZZ	880	04U14JZ	670
04Q34ZZ	878	04QT0ZZ	417, 878	04RA0KZ	159	04RQ4JZ	879	04SB4ZZ	880	04U2*	134
04Q40ZZ	878	04QT3ZZ	417, 878	04RA47Z	159	04RQ4KZ	879	04SC*	670	04U207Z	670, 880
04Q43ZZ	878	04QT4ZZ	417, 879	04RA4JZ	159	04RR*	133, 488, 670	04SC0ZZ	880	04U20JZ	670
04Q44ZZ	878	04QU*	488	04RA4KZ	159	04RR07Z	879	04SC3ZZ	880	04U237Z	670, 880
04Q50ZZ	878	04QU0ZZ	417, 879	04RB*	669	04RR0JZ	879	04SC4ZZ	880	04U23JZ	670
04Q53ZZ	878	04QU3ZZ	417, 879	04RB07Z	159, 879	04RR0KZ	879	04SD*	670	04U247Z	670, 880
04Q54ZZ	878	04QU4ZZ	417, 879	04RB0JZ	159, 879	04RR47Z	879	04SD0ZZ	880	04U24JZ	670
04Q60ZZ	878	04QV*	488	04RB0KZ	159, 879	04RR4JZ	879	04SD3ZZ	880	04U3*	134
04Q63ZZ	878	04QV0ZZ	417, 879	04RB47Z	159, 879	04RR4KZ	879	04SD4ZZ	880	04U307Z	670, 880
04Q64ZZ	878	04QV3ZZ	417, 879	04RB4JZ	159, 879	04RS*	133, 488, 670	04SE*	670	04U30JZ	670
04Q70ZZ	878	04QV4ZZ	417, 879	04RB4KZ	159, 879	04RS07Z	879	04SE0ZZ	880	04U337Z	670, 880
04Q73ZZ	878	04QW*	488	04RC*	669	04RS0JZ	879	04SE3ZZ	880	04U33JZ	670
04Q74ZZ	878	04QW0ZZ	417, 879	04RC07Z	159, 879	04RS0KZ	879	04SE4ZZ	880	04U347Z	670, 880
04Q80ZZ	878	04QW3ZZ	417, 879	04RC0JZ	159, 879	04RS47Z	879	04SF*	670	04U34JZ	670
04Q83ZZ	878	04QW4ZZ	417, 879	04RC0KZ	159, 879	04RS4JZ	879	04SF0ZZ	880	04U4*	134
04Q84ZZ	878	04QY*	187, 206, 488, 513	04RC47Z	159, 879	04RS4KZ	879	04SF3ZZ	880	04U407Z	670, 880
04Q90ZZ	878	04QY0ZZ	879	04RC4JZ	159, 879	04RT*	133, 488, 670	04SF4ZZ	880	04U40JZ	670
04Q93ZZ	878	04QY3ZZ	879	04RC4KZ	159, 879	04RT07Z	879	04SH*	670	04U437Z	670, 880
04Q94ZZ	878	04QY4ZZ	879	04RD*	669	04RT0JZ	879	04SH0ZZ	880	04U43JZ	670
04QA0ZZ	878	04R0*	669	04RD07Z	159, 879	04RT0KZ	879	04SH3ZZ	880	04U447Z	670, 880
04QA3ZZ	878	04R007Z	150, 879	04RD0JZ	159, 879	04RT47Z	879	04SH4ZZ	880	04U44JZ	670
04QA4ZZ	878	04R00JZ	150, 879	04RD0KZ	159, 879	04RT4JZ	879	04SJ*	670	04U5*	134
04QB0ZZ	878	04R00KZ	150, 879	04RD47Z	159, 879	04RT4KZ	879	04SJ0ZZ	880	04U507Z	670, 880
04QB3ZZ	878	04R047Z	150, 879	04RD4JZ	159, 879	04RU*	133, 488, 670	04SJ3ZZ	880	04U50JZ	670
04QB4ZZ	878	04R04JZ	150, 879	04RD4KZ	159, 879	04RU07Z	879	04SJ4ZZ	880	04U537Z	670, 880
04QC*	488	04R04KZ	150, 879	04RE*	669	04RU0JZ	879	04SK*	670	04U53JZ	670
04QC0ZZ	417, 878	04R1*	669	04RE07Z	159, 879	04RU0KZ	879	04SK0ZZ	417, 880	04U547Z	670, 880
04QC3ZZ	417, 878	04R107Z	159, 879	04RE0JZ	159, 879	04RU47Z	879	04SK3ZZ	417, 880	04U54JZ	670
04QC4ZZ	417, 878	04R10JZ	159, 879	04RE0KZ	159, 879	04RU4JZ	879	04SK4ZZ	417, 880	04U6*	134
04QD*	488	04R10KZ	159, 879	04RE47Z	159, 879	04RU4KZ	879	04SL*	670	04U607Z	670, 880
04QD0ZZ	417, 878	04R147Z	159, 879	04RE4JZ	159, 879	04RV*	133, 488, 670	04SL0ZZ	417, 880	04U60JZ	670
04QD3ZZ	417, 878	04R14JZ	159, 879	04RE4KZ	159, 879	04RV07Z	879	04SL3ZZ	417, 880	04U637Z	670, 880
04QD4ZZ	417, 878	04R14KZ	159, 879	04RF*	669	04RV0JZ	879	04SL4ZZ	417, 880	04U63JZ	670
04QE*	488	04R2*	669	04RF07Z	159, 879	04RV0KZ	879	04SM*	670	04U647Z	670, 880
04QE0ZZ	417, 878	04R207Z	159, 879	04RF0JZ	159, 879	04RV47Z	879	04SM0ZZ	417, 880	04U64JZ	670
		04R20JZ	159, 879	04RF0KZ	159, 879	04RV4JZ	880	04SM3ZZ	417, 880	04U7*	134
		04R20KZ	159, 879	04RF47Z	159, 879	04RV4KZ	880	04SM4ZZ	417, 880	04U707Z	670, 880
		04R247Z	159, 879	04RF4JZ	159, 879	04RW*	133, 488, 670	04SN*	670	04U70JZ	670
		04R24JZ	159, 879	04RF4KZ	159, 879	04RW07Z	880	04SN0ZZ	417, 880	04U737Z	670, 880
		04R24KZ	159, 879	04RH*	669	04RW0JZ	880	04SN3ZZ	417, 880	04U73JZ	670
		04R3*	669	04RH07Z	159, 879	04RW0KZ	880	04SN4ZZ	417, 880	04U747Z	670, 880
		04R307Z	159, 879	04RH0KZ	159, 879	04RW47Z	880	04SP*	670	04U74JZ	670
		04R30JZ	159, 879	04RH47Z	159, 879	04RW4JZ	880	04SP0ZZ	417, 880	04U8*	134
		04R30KZ	159, 879	04RH4JZ	159, 879	04RW4KZ	880	04SP3ZZ	417, 880	04U807Z	670, 880
		04R347Z	159, 879	04RH4KZ	159, 879	04RY*	133, 488, 670	04SP4ZZ	417, 880	04U837Z	670, 880
		04R34JZ	159, 879	04RJ*	669	04RY07Z	880	04SQ*	670	04U83JZ	670
						04RY0JZ	880	04SQ0ZZ	417, 880		

Code	Page
04U847Z	670,880
04U84JZ	670
04U9*	134
04U907Z	513,670,880
04U90JZ	513,670
04U937Z	513,670,880
04U93JZ	513,670
04U947Z	513,670,880
04U94JZ	513,670
04UA*	134
04UA07Z	513,670,880
04UA0JZ	513,670
04UA37Z	513,670,880
04UA3JZ	513,670
04UA47Z	513,670,880
04UA4JZ	513,670
04UB*	134
04UB07Z	670,880
04UB0JZ	670
04UB37Z	670,880
04UB3JZ	670
04UB47Z	670,880
04UB4JZ	670
04UC*	134
04UC07Z	670,880
04UC0JZ	670
04UC37Z	670,880
04UC3JZ	670
04UC47Z	670,880
04UC4JZ	670
04UD*	134
04UD07Z	670,880
04UD0JZ	670
04UD37Z	670,880
04UD3JZ	670
04UD47Z	670,880
04UD4JZ	670
04UE*	134
04UE07Z	670,880
04UE0JZ	670
04UE37Z	670,880
04UE3JZ	670
04UE47Z	670,880
04UE4JZ	670
04UF*	134
04UF07Z	670,880
04UF0JZ	670
04UF37Z	670,880
04UF3JZ	670
04UF47Z	670,880
04UF4JZ	670
04UH*	134
04UH07Z	670,880
04UH0JZ	670
04UH37Z	670,880
04UH3JZ	670
04UH47Z	670,880
04UH4JZ	670
04UJ*	134
04UJ07Z	670,880
04UJ0JZ	670
04UJ37Z	670,880
04UJ3JZ	670
04UJ47Z	670,880
04UJ4JZ	670
04UK*	134
04UK07Z	670,880
04UK0JZ	670
04UK37Z	670,880
04UK3JZ	670
04UK47Z	670,880
04UK4JZ	670
04UL*	134
04UL07Z	670,880
04UL0JZ	670
04UL37Z	670,880
04UL3JZ	670
04UL47Z	670,880
04UL4JZ	670
04UM*	134
04UM07Z	670,880
04UM0JZ	670
04UM37Z	670,880
04UM3JZ	670
04UM47Z	670,880
04UM4JZ	670
04UN*	134
04UN07Z	670,880
04UN0JZ	670
04UN37Z	670,880
04UN3JZ	670
04UN47Z	670,880
04UN4JZ	670
04UP*	134
04UP07Z	670,880
04UP0JZ	670
04UP37Z	670,880
04UP3JZ	670
04UP47Z	670,880
04UP4JZ	670
04UQ*	134
04UQ07Z	671,880
04UQ0JZ	671
04UQ37Z	671,880
04UQ3JZ	671
04UQ47Z	671,881
04UQ4JZ	671
04UR*	134
04UR07Z	671,881
04UR0JZ	671
04UR37Z	671,881
04UR3JZ	671
04UR47Z	671,881
04UR4JZ	671
04US*	134
04US07Z	671,881
04US0JZ	671
04US37Z	671,881
04US3JZ	671
04US47Z	671,881
04US4JZ	671
04UT*	134
04UT07Z	671,881
04UT0JZ	671
04UT37Z	671,881
04UT3JZ	671
04UT47Z	671,881
04UT4JZ	671
04UU*	134
04UU07Z	671,881
04UU0JZ	671
04UU37Z	671,881
04UU3JZ	671
04UU47Z	671,881
04UU4JZ	671
04UV*	134
04UV07Z	671,881
04UV0JZ	671
04UV37Z	671,881
04UV3JZ	671
04UV47Z	671,881
04UV4JZ	671
04UW*	134
04UW07Z	671,881
04UW0JZ	671
04UW37Z	671,881
04UW3JZ	671
04UW47Z	671,881
04UW4JZ	671
04UY*	134
04UY07Z	671,881
04UY0JZ	671
04UY37Z	671,881
04UY3JZ	671
04UY47Z	671,881
04UY4JZ	671
04V00CZ	134
04V00DJ	28,134,671,881
04V00DZ	159,513,671,881
04V00EZ	159,513,671,881
04V00FZ	159,513,671,881
04V00ZZ	159,513,671
04V03CZ	134
04V03DJ	28,134,671,881
04V03DZ	150,513,671,881
04V03EZ	150,513,671,881
04V03FZ	150,513,671,881
04V03ZZ	159,513,671
04V04CZ	134
04V04DJ	28,134,671,881
04V04DZ	150,513,671,881
04V04EZ	150,513,671,881
04V04FZ	150,513,671,881
04V04ZZ	159,513,671
04V10CZ	134
04V10DZ	159,671,881
04V10ZZ	159,513,671
04V13CZ	134
04V13DZ	159,671,881
04V13ZZ	159,513,671
04V14CZ	134
04V14DZ	159,671,881
04V14ZZ	159,513,671
04V20CZ	134
04V20DZ	159,671,881
04V20ZZ	159,513,671
04V23CZ	134
04V23DZ	159,671,881
04V23ZZ	159,513,671
04V24CZ	134
04V24DZ	159,671,881
04V24ZZ	159,513,671
04V30CZ	134
04V30DZ	159,671,881
04V30ZZ	159,513,671
04V33CZ	134
04V33DZ	159,671,881
04V33ZZ	159,513,671
04V34CZ	134
04V34DZ	159,671,881
04V34ZZ	160,513,671
04V40CZ	134
04V40DZ	160,671,881
04V40ZZ	160,513,671
04V43CZ	134
04V43DZ	160,671,881
04V43ZZ	160,513,671
04V44CZ	134
04V44DZ	160,671,881
04V44ZZ	160,513,671
04V50CZ	134
04V50DZ	160,671,881
04V50ZZ	160,513,671
04V53CZ	134
04V53DZ	160,671,881
04V53ZZ	160,513,671
04V54CZ	134
04V54DZ	160,671,881
04V54ZZ	160,513,671
04V60CZ	134
04V60DZ	160,671,881
04V60ZZ	160,513,671
04V63CZ	134
04V63DZ	160,671,881
04V63ZZ	160,513,671
04V64CZ	134
04V64DZ	160,671,881
04V64ZZ	160,513,671
04V70CZ	134
04V70DZ	160,671,881
04V70ZZ	160,513,671
04V73CZ	134
04V73DZ	160,671,881
04V73ZZ	160,513,671
04V74CZ	134
04V74DZ	160,671,881
04V74ZZ	160,513,671
04V80CZ	134
04V80DZ	160,671,881
04V80ZZ	160,513,671
04V83CZ	134
04V83DZ	160,671,881
04V83ZZ	160,513,671
04V84CZ	134
04V84DZ	160,671,881
04V84ZZ	160,513,671
04V90CZ	134
04V90DZ	160,513,671,881
04V90ZZ	160,513,671
04V93CZ	134
04V93DZ	160,513,671,881
04V93ZZ	160,513,671
04V94CZ	134
04V94DZ	160,513,671,881
04V94ZZ	160,513,671
04VA0CZ	134
04VA0DZ	160,513,671,881
04VA3CZ	134
04VA3DZ	160,514,671,881
04VA3ZZ	160,514,671
04VA4CZ	134
04VA4DZ	160,514,671,881
04VA4ZZ	160,514,671
04VB0CZ	134
04VB0DZ	160,514,671
04VB3CZ	134
04VB3DZ	160,671,881
04VB3ZZ	160,514,671
04VB4CZ	134
04VB4DZ	160,671,881
04VB4ZZ	514
04VC0CZ	134
04VC0DZ	160,671,881
04VC0EZ	160,671,881
04VC0ZZ	160,671
04VC3CZ	134
04VC3DZ	160,671,881
04VC3EZ	160,671,881
04VC3ZZ	160,671
04VC4CZ	134
04VC4DZ	160,671,881
04VC4EZ	160,671,881
04VC4ZZ	160,671
04VD0CZ	134
04VD0DZ	160,671,881
04VD0EZ	160,671,881
04VD0ZZ	160,671
04VD3CZ	134
04VD3DZ	160,671,881
04VD3EZ	160,671,881
04VD3ZZ	160,671
04VD4CZ	134
04VD4DZ	160,671,881
04VD4EZ	160,671,881
04VD4ZZ	160,671
04VE0CZ	134
04VE0DZ	160,671,881
04VE0ZZ	160,671
04VE3CZ	134
04VE3DZ	160,671,881
04VE3ZZ	160,671
04VE4CZ	134
04VE4DZ	160,671,881
04VE4ZZ	160,671
04VF0CZ	134
04VF0DZ	160,671,881
04VF0ZZ	160,671
04VF3CZ	134
04VF3DZ	160,671,881
04VF3ZZ	160,671
04VF4CZ	134
04VF4DZ	160,671,881
04VF4ZZ	160,671
04VH0CZ	134
04VH0DZ	160,671,881
04VH0ZZ	160,671
04VH3CZ	134
04VH3DZ	160,671,881
04VH3ZZ	160,671
04VH4CZ	134
04VH4DZ	160,671,881
04VH4ZZ	160,671
04VJ0CZ	134
04VJ0DZ	160,671,881
04VJ0ZZ	160,671
04VJ3CZ	134
04VJ3DZ	160,671,881
04VJ3ZZ	160,671
04VJ4CZ	134
04VJ4DZ	160,671,881
04VJ4ZZ	160,671
04VK0CZ	134
04VK0DZ	160,671,881
04VK0ZZ	160,671
04VK3CZ	134
04VK3DZ	160,671,881
04VK3ZZ	160,672
04VK4CZ	134
04VK4DZ	160,672,881
04VK4ZZ	160,672
04VL0CZ	134
04VL0DZ	160,672,881
04VL0ZZ	160,672
04VL3CZ	134
04VL3DZ	160,672,881
04VL3ZZ	160,672
04VL4CZ	134
04VL4DZ	160,672,881
04VL4ZZ	160,672
04VM0CZ	134
04VM0DZ	160,672,881
04VM0ZZ	160,672
04VM3CZ	134
04VM3DZ	160,672,881
04VM3ZZ	160,672
04VM4CZ	134
04VM4DZ	160,672,881
04VM4ZZ	160,672
04VN0CZ	134
04VN0DZ	160,672,881
04VN0ZZ	160,672
04VN3CZ	134
04VN3DZ	160,672,881
04VN3ZZ	160,672
04VN4CZ	134
04VN4DZ	160,672,881
04VN4ZZ	160,672
04VP0CZ	134
04VP0DZ	160,672,881
04VP0ZZ	160,672
04VP3CZ	134
04VP3DZ	160,672,881
04VP3ZZ	160,672
04VP4CZ	134
04VP4DZ	160,672,881
04VP4ZZ	160,672
04VQ0CZ	134
04VQ0DZ	160,672,881
04VQ0ZZ	160,672
04VQ3CZ	134
04VQ3DZ	160,672,881
04VQ4CZ	134
04VQ4DZ	160,672,881
04VR0CZ	134
04VR0DZ	160,672,881
04VR0ZZ	160,672
04VR3CZ	134
04VR3DZ	160,672,881
04VR3ZZ	160,672
04VR4CZ	134
04VR4DZ	160,672,881
04VR4ZZ	160,672
04VS0CZ	134
04VS0DZ	160,672,881
04VS0ZZ	160,672
04VS3CZ	134
04VS3DZ	160,672,881
04VS4CZ	134
04VS4DZ	160,672,881
04VT0CZ	134
04VT0ZZ	160,672,881
04VT3CZ	134
04VT3DZ	160,672,881
04VT3ZZ	160,672
04VT4CZ	134
04VT4DZ	160,672,881
04VT4ZZ	160,672
04VU0CZ	134
04VU0DZ	160,672,881
04VU3CZ	134
04VU3DZ	160,672,881
04VU3ZZ	160,672
04VU4CZ	134
04VU4DZ	160,672,881
04VU4ZZ	160,672
04VV0CZ	134
04VV0DZ	160,672,881
04VV0ZZ	160,672
04VV3CZ	134
04VV3DZ	160,672,881
04VV4CZ	134
04VV4DZ	160,672,881
04VV4ZZ	160,672
04VW0CZ	134
04VW0DZ	160,672,881
04VW0ZZ	160,672
04VW3CZ	134
04VW3DZ	160,672,881
04VW3ZZ	160,672
04VW4CZ	134
04VW4DZ	160,672,881
04VW4ZZ	160,672
04VY0CZ	134
04VY0DZ	160,672,881
04VY0ZZ	160,672
04VY3CZ	134
04VY3DZ	160,672,881
04VY3ZZ	160,672
04VY4CZ	134
04VY4DZ	160,672,881
04VY4ZZ	160,672
04WY00Z	134,488,585,610,672,881
04WY02Z	134,488,585,610,672,881
04WY03Z	134,488,585,610,672,881
04WY07Z	134,1047
04WY0CZ	134,488,585,610,672,881
04WY0DZ	134,488,585,610,672,881
04WY0JZ	134,1047
04WY0KZ	134,1047
04WY0YZ	134,488,585,610,672,881
04WY37Z	134,1047
04WY3CZ	134,489,585,610,672,881
04WY3JZ	134,1047
04WY3KZ	134,1047
04WY40Z	134,489,585,610,672,881
04WY42Z	134,489,585,610,672,881
04WY43Z	134,489,585,610,672,881
04WY47Z	134,1047
04WY4CZ	134,489,585,610,672,881
04WY4DZ	134,489,585,610,672,881
04WY4JZ	134,1047
04WY4KZ	134,1047
0510*	672
051007Y	160,881
051009Y	160,881
05100AY	160,881
05100JY	160,881
05100KY	160,881
05100ZY	161,881
051047Y	161,881
051049Y	161,881
05104AY	161,881
05104JY	161,881
05104KY	161,881
05104ZY	161,881
0511*	672
051107Y	161,881
051109Y	161,881
05110AY	161,881
05110JY	161,881
05110KY	161,881
05110ZY	161,881
051147Y	161,881
051149Y	161,881
05114AY	161,881
05114JY	161,881
05114KY	161,881
05114ZY	161,881
0513*	672
051307Y	161,881
051309Y	161,881
05130AY	161,881
05130JY	161,881
05130KY	161,881
05130ZY	161,881
051347Y	161,881
051349Y	161,881
05134AY	161,882
05134JY	161,882
05134KY	161,882
05134ZY	161,882
0514*	672
051407Y	161,882
051409Y	161,882
05140AY	161,882
05140JY	161,882
05140KY	161,882
05140ZY	161,882
051447Y	161,882
051449Y	161,882
05144AY	161,882
05144JY	161,882
05144KY	161,882
05144ZY	161,882
0515*	672
051507Y	161,882
051509Y	161,882
05150AY	161,882
05150JY	161,882
05150KY	161,882
05150ZY	161,882
051547Y	161,882
051549Y	161,882
05154AY	161,882
05154JY	161,882
05154KY	161,882
05154ZY	161,882
0516*	672
051607Y	161,882
051609Y	161,882
05160AY	161,882
05160JY	161,882
05160KY	161,882
05160ZY	161,882
051647Y	161,882

Numeric Index to Procedures

Code	Page
05164 9Y	161, 882
05164AY	161, 882
05164JY	161, 882
05164KY	161, 882
05164ZY	161, 882
0517*	134
0518*	134
0519*	134
051A*	134
051B*	134
051C*	134
051D*	134
051F*	134
051G*	134
051H*	134
051L*	134
051M*	134
051N*	134
051P*	134
051Q*	134
051R*	134
051S*	134
051T*	134
051V*	134
0550*	89
05500ZZ	161
05503ZZ	161
05504ZZ	161
0551*	89
05510ZZ	161
05513ZZ	161
05514ZZ	161
0553*	89
05530ZZ	161
05533ZZ	161
05534ZZ	161
0554*	89
05540ZZ	161
05543ZZ	161
05544ZZ	161
0555*	89
05550ZZ	161
05553ZZ	161
05554ZZ	161
0556*	89
05560ZZ	161
05563ZZ	161
05564ZZ	161
0557*	135, 489, 672
0558*	135, 489, 672
0559*	135, 489, 672
055A*	135, 489, 672
055B*	135, 489, 672
055C*	135, 489, 672
055D*	135, 489, 672
055F*	135, 489, 672
055G*	135, 489, 672
055H*	135, 489, 672
055L*	672
055L0ZZ	7, 11, 882
055L3ZZ	7, 11, 882
055L4ZZ	7, 11, 882
055M*	28, 135, 672
055N*	28, 135, 672
055P*	28, 135, 672
055Q*	28, 135, 672
055R*	28, 135, 672
055S*	28, 135, 672
055T*	28, 135, 672
055V*	28, 135, 672
055Y*	135, 489, 672
057*	135
05793D1	28, 98, 187, 206, 276, 417, 489, 514, 672, 882
05793DZ	28, 99, 187, 206, 276, 417, 489, 514, 672, 882
05793Z1	28, 99, 187, 206, 276, 417, 489, 514, 672, 882
05793ZZ	28, 99, 187, 206, 276, 417, 489, 514, 672, 882
057A3D1	28, 99, 187, 206, 276, 417, 489, 514, 672, 882
057A3DZ	28, 99, 187, 206, 276, 417, 489, 514, 672, 882
057A3Z1	28, 99, 187, 206, 276, 417, 489, 514, 672, 882
057A3ZZ	28, 99, 187, 206, 276, 418, 489, 514, 672, 882
057B3D1	28, 99, 187, 206, 276, 418, 489, 514, 672, 882
057B3DZ	28, 99, 187, 206, 276, 418, 489, 514, 672, 882
057B3Z1	28, 99, 187, 206, 276, 418, 489, 514, 672, 882
057B3ZZ	28, 99, 187, 206, 276, 418, 489, 514, 672, 882
057C3D1	28, 99, 187, 206, 276, 418, 489, 514, 672, 882
057C3DZ	28, 99, 187, 206, 276, 418, 489, 514, 672, 882
057C3Z1	28, 99, 187, 206, 276, 418, 489, 514, 672, 882
057C3ZZ	28, 99, 187, 206, 276, 418, 489, 514, 672, 882
057D3D1	28, 99, 187, 206, 276, 418, 489, 514, 672, 882
057D3DZ	28, 99, 187, 206, 276, 418, 489, 514, 672, 882
057D3Z1	28, 99, 187, 206, 276, 418, 489, 514, 672, 882
057D3ZZ	28, 99, 187, 206, 276, 418, 489, 514, 672, 882
057F3D1	28, 99, 187, 206, 276, 418, 489, 514, 672, 882
057F3DZ	28, 99, 187, 206, 276, 418, 489, 514, 672, 882
057F3Z1	28, 99, 187, 206, 276, 418, 489, 514, 672, 882
057F3ZZ	28, 99, 187, 206, 276, 418, 489, 514, 672, 882
057L3DZ	11, 672, 882
057L4DZ	11, 672, 882
057M0DZ	28
057M0ZZ	28
057M3DZ	28, 672, 882
057M4DZ	28, 672, 882
057N0DZ	28
057N0ZZ	28
057N3DZ	28, 672, 882
057N4DZ	28, 672, 882
057P0DZ	28
057P0ZZ	28
057P3DZ	28, 672, 882
057P4DZ	28, 672, 882
057Q0DZ	28
057Q0ZZ	28
057Q3DZ	28, 672, 882
057Q4DZ	28, 672, 882
057R0DZ	28
057R0ZZ	28
057R3DZ	28, 672, 882
057R4DZ	28, 672, 882
057S0DZ	28
057S0ZZ	28
057S3DZ	28, 672, 882
057S4DZ	28, 672, 882
057T0DZ	28
057T0ZZ	28
057T3DZ	28, 672, 882
057T4DZ	28, 672, 882
05900ZX	135, 1047
05904ZX	135, 1047
05910ZX	135, 1047
05914ZX	135, 1047
05930ZX	135, 1047
05934ZX	135, 1047
05940ZX	135, 1047
05944ZX	135, 1047
05950ZX	135, 1047
05954ZX	135, 1047
05960ZX	135, 1047
05964ZX	135, 1047
05970ZX	135, 1047
05974ZX	135, 1047
05980ZX	135, 1047
05984ZX	135, 1047
05990ZX	135, 1047
05994ZX	135, 1047
059A0ZX	135, 1047
059A4ZX	135, 1047
059B0ZX	135, 1047
059C0ZX	135, 1047
059C4ZX	135, 1047
059D0ZX	135, 1047
059D4ZX	135, 1047
059F0ZX	135, 1047
059F4ZX	135, 1047
059G0ZX	135, 1047
059G4ZX	135, 1047
059H0ZX	135, 1047
059H4ZX	135, 1047
059L0ZX	135, 1047
059L4ZX	135, 1047
059M0ZX	135, 1047
059M4ZX	135, 1047
059N0ZX	135, 1047
059N4ZX	135, 1047
059P0ZX	135, 1047
059P4ZX	135, 1047
059Q0ZX	135, 1047
059Q4ZX	135, 1047
059R0ZX	135, 1047
059R4ZX	135, 1047
059S0ZX	135, 1047
059S4ZX	135, 1047
059T0ZX	135, 1047
059T4ZX	135, 1047
059V0ZX	135, 1047
059V4ZX	135, 1047
059Y0ZX	135, 1047
059Y4ZX	135, 1047
05B00ZZ	89, 161
05B03ZX	135, 1048
05B03ZZ	89, 161
05B04ZX	135, 1048
05B04ZZ	89, 161
05B10ZX	135, 1048
05B10ZZ	89, 161
05B13ZZ	89, 161
05B14ZX	135, 1048
05B14ZZ	89, 161
05B30ZX	135, 1048
05B30ZZ	89, 161
05B33ZX	135, 1048
05B33ZZ	89, 161
05B34ZX	135, 1048
05B34ZZ	89, 161
05B40ZX	135, 1048
05B40ZZ	89, 161
05B43ZX	135, 1048
05B43ZZ	89, 161
05B44ZX	135, 1048
05B44ZZ	89, 161
05B50ZX	135, 1048
05B50ZZ	89, 161
05B53ZX	135, 1048
05B53ZZ	89, 161
05B54ZX	135, 1048
05B54ZZ	89, 161
05B60ZX	135, 1048
05B60ZZ	89, 161
05B63ZX	135, 1048
05B63ZZ	89, 161
05B64ZX	135, 1048
05B64ZZ	89, 161
05B7*	135
05B70ZX	1048
05B70ZZ	489, 672, 882
05B73ZX	1048
05B73ZZ	489, 672
05B74ZX	1048
05B74ZZ	489, 672, 882
05B8*	135
05B80ZX	1048
05B80ZZ	489, 672, 882
05B83ZX	1048
05B83ZZ	489, 672
05B84ZX	1048
05B84ZZ	489, 672, 882
05B9*	135
05B90ZX	1048
05B90ZZ	489, 672, 882
05B93ZX	1048
05B93ZZ	489, 672
05B94ZX	1048
05B94ZZ	489, 672, 882
05BA*	135
05BA0ZX	1048
05BA0ZZ	489, 672, 882
05BA3ZX	1048
05BA3ZZ	489, 672
05BA4ZX	1048
05BA4ZZ	489, 672, 882
05BB*	135
05BB0ZX	1048
05BB0ZZ	489, 672, 882
05BB3ZX	1048
05BB3ZZ	489, 672
05BB4ZX	1048
05BB4ZZ	489, 672, 882
05BC*	135
05BC0ZX	1048
05BC0ZZ	489, 672, 882
05BC3ZX	1048
05BC3ZZ	489, 672
05BC4ZX	1048
05BC4ZZ	489, 672, 882
05BD*	135
05BD0ZX	1048
05BD0ZZ	489, 672, 882
05BD3ZX	1048
05BD3ZZ	489, 672
05BD4ZX	1048
05BD4ZZ	489, 672, 882
05BF*	135
05BF0ZX	1048
05BF0ZZ	489, 673, 882
05BF3ZX	1048
05BF3ZZ	489, 673
05BF4ZX	1048
05BF4ZZ	489, 673, 882
05BG*	135
05BG0ZX	1048
05BG0ZZ	489, 673, 882
05BG3ZX	1048
05BG3ZZ	489, 673
05BG4ZX	1048
05BG4ZZ	489, 673, 882
05BH*	135
05BH0ZX	1048
05BH0ZZ	489, 673, 882
05BH3ZX	1048
05BH3ZZ	489, 673
05BH4ZX	1048
05BH4ZZ	489, 673, 882
05BL0ZX	135, 1048
05BL0ZZ	7, 11, 673, 882
05BL3ZX	135, 1048
05BL3ZZ	7, 11, 673, 882
05BL4ZX	135, 1048
05BL4ZZ	7, 12, 673, 882
05BM*	135
05BM0ZX	1048
05BM0ZZ	28, 72, 673, 882
05BM3ZX	1048
05BM3ZZ	28, 673
05BM4ZX	1048
05BM4ZZ	28, 72, 673, 882
05BN*	135
05BN0ZX	1048
05BN0ZZ	28, 72, 673, 882
05BN3ZX	1048
05BN3ZZ	28, 673
05BN4ZX	1048
05BN4ZZ	28, 72, 673, 882
05BP*	135
05BP0ZX	1048
05BP0ZZ	28, 72, 673, 882
05BP3ZX	1048
05BP3ZZ	28, 673
05BP4ZX	1048
05BP4ZZ	28, 72, 673, 882
05BQ*	135
05BQ0ZX	1048
05BQ0ZZ	28, 72, 673, 882
05BQ3ZX	1048
05BQ3ZZ	28, 673
05BQ4ZX	1048
05BQ4ZZ	28, 72, 673, 882
05BR*	135
05BR0ZX	1048
05BR0ZZ	28, 72, 673, 882
05BR3ZX	1048
05BR3ZZ	28, 673
05BR4ZX	1048
05BR4ZZ	28, 72, 673, 882
05BS*	135
05BS0ZX	1048
05BS0ZZ	28, 72, 673, 882
05BS3ZX	1048
05BS3ZZ	28, 673
05BS4ZX	1048
05BS4ZZ	28, 72, 673, 882
05BT*	135
05BT0ZX	1048
05BT0ZZ	28, 72, 673, 882
05BT3ZX	1048
05BT3ZZ	28, 673
05BT4ZX	1048
05BT4ZZ	28, 72, 673, 882
05BV*	135
05BV0ZX	1048
05BV0ZZ	28, 72, 673, 882
05BV3ZX	1048
05BV3ZZ	28, 673
05BV4ZX	1048
05BV4ZZ	28, 72, 673, 882
05BY*	135
05BY0ZX	1048
05BY0ZZ	489, 673, 882
05BY3ZX	1048
05BY3ZZ	489, 673, 882
05BY4ZX	1048
05BY4ZZ	489, 673, 882
05C0*	89
05C00ZZ	161
05C03ZZ	161
05C04ZZ	161
05C1*	89
05C10ZZ	161
05C13ZZ	161
05C14ZZ	161
05C3*	89
05C30ZZ	161
05C33ZZ	161
05C34ZZ	161
05C4*	89
05C40ZZ	161
05C43ZZ	161
05C44ZZ	161
05C5*	89
05C50ZZ	161
05C53ZZ	161
05C54ZZ	161
05C6*	89
05C60ZZ	161
05C63ZZ	161
05C64ZZ	161
05C7*	135, 489, 673
05C8*	135, 489, 673
05C9*	135, 489, 673
05CA*	135, 489, 673
05CB*	135, 489, 673
05CC*	135, 489, 673
05CD*	135, 489, 673
05CF*	135, 489, 673
05CG*	135, 489, 673
05CH*	135, 489, 673
05CL*	673
05CL0ZZ	7, 12, 882
05CL3ZZ	12, 135, 882
05CL4ZZ	7, 12, 882
05CM*	33, 72, 135, 489, 673
05CM0ZZ	882
05CM3ZZ	882
05CM4ZZ	882
05CN*	33, 72, 135, 489, 673
05CN0ZZ	882
05CN3ZZ	882
05CN4ZZ	882
05CP*	33, 72, 135, 489, 673
05CP0ZZ	882
05CP3ZZ	882
05CP4ZZ	882
05CQ*	33, 72, 135, 489, 673
05CQ0ZZ	882
05CQ3ZZ	882
05CQ4ZZ	882
05CR*	33, 72, 135, 489, 673
05CR0ZZ	882
05CR3ZZ	882
05CR4ZZ	882
05CS*	33, 72, 135, 489, 673
05CS0ZZ	882
05CS3ZZ	882
05CS4ZZ	882
05CT*	33, 72, 135, 489, 673
05CT0ZZ	882
05CT3ZZ	882
05CT4ZZ	882
05CV*	33, 72, 135, 489, 673
05CV0ZZ	882
05CV3ZZ	882
05CV4ZZ	882
05CY*	135, 187, 206, 489, 514, 673
05CY0ZZ	882
05CY3ZZ	882
05CY4ZZ	882
05D*	142
05H002Z	33, 135
05H00DZ	99, 135, 585, 610, 673, 882
05H00MZ	33, 42, 72, 135, 276, 514, 524, 537, 673, 882
05H032Z	33, 135
05H03DZ	99, 135, 585, 610, 673, 882
05H03MZ	33, 42, 72, 135, 276, 514, 537, 673, 882
05H042Z	33, 135
05H04DZ	99, 135, 585, 610, 673, 882
05H04MZ	33, 42, 72, 135, 276, 514, 524, 537, 673, 882
05H10DZ	99, 135, 585, 610, 673, 882
05H13DZ	99, 135, 585, 610, 673, 882
05H14DZ	99, 135, 585, 610, 673, 882
05H30DZ	99, 135, 585, 610, 673, 882
05H30MZ	33, 42, 72, 135, 276, 514, 524, 537, 673, 882
05H33DZ	99, 135, 585, 610, 673, 882
05H33MZ	33, 42, 72, 135, 276, 514, 524, 537, 673, 882
05H34DZ	99, 135, 585, 610, 673, 882
05H34MZ	33, 42, 72, 135, 276, 514, 524, 537, 673, 882
05H40DZ	99, 135, 585, 610, 673, 882
05H40MZ	33, 42, 72, 135, 276, 514, 524, 537, 673, 882
05H43DZ	99, 135, 585, 610, 673, 882
05H43MZ	33, 42, 72, 135, 276, 514, 524, 537, 673, 882
05H44DZ	99, 135, 585, 610, 673, 883
05H44MZ	33, 42, 72, 135, 276, 514, 524, 537, 673, 883
05H50DZ	99, 135, 585, 610, 673, 883
05H53DZ	99, 135, 585, 610, 673, 883
05H54DZ	99, 135, 585, 610, 673, 883
05H60DZ	99, 135, 585, 610, 673, 883
05H63DZ	99, 135, 585, 610, 673, 883
05H64DZ	99, 135, 585, 610, 673, 883
05H70DZ	135, 585, 610, 673, 883
05H73DZ	135, 585, 610, 673, 883
05H74DZ	135, 585, 610, 673, 883

Code	Page	Code	Page	Code	Page	Code	Page	Code	Page	Code	Page
05H80DZ	135, 585, 610, 673, 883	05HS3DZ	72, 136, 585, 610, 673, 883	05L73DZ	136, 883	05LL4CZ	7, 12	05P00MZ	33, 72, 276, 524, 537, 673, 884	05QC4ZZ	884
05H83DZ	135, 585, 610, 673, 883	05HS4DZ	72, 136, 585, 610, 673, 883	05L73ZZ	136, 489, 883	05LL4DZ	7, 12			05QD*	142
				05L74CZ	136, 489, 883	05LL4ZZ	7, 12	05P03MZ	33, 72, 276, 524, 537, 673, 884	05QD0ZZ	884
05H84DZ	135, 585, 610, 673, 883	05HT0DZ	72, 136, 585, 610, 673, 883	05L74DZ	136, 883	05LM*	33, 72, 136			05QD3ZZ	884
				05L74ZZ	136, 489, 883	05LM0CZ	883	05P04MZ	33, 72, 276, 524, 537, 673, 884	05QD4ZZ	884
05H90DZ	135, 585, 610, 673, 883	05HT3DZ	72, 136, 585, 611, 673, 883	05L80CZ	136, 489, 883	05LM0DZ	883			05QF*	142
05H93DZ	135, 585, 610, 673, 883	05HT4DZ	72, 136, 585, 611, 673, 883	05L80DZ	136, 883	05LM0ZZ	883	05P0XMZ	33, 72, 276, 524, 537, 673, 884	05QF0ZZ	884
				05L80ZZ	136, 489, 883	05LM3CZ	883			05QF3ZZ	884
05H94DZ	135, 585, 610, 673, 883	05HV0DZ	72, 136, 585, 611, 673, 883	05L83CZ	136, 489, 883	05LM3DZ	883	05P30MZ	33, 72, 276, 524, 537, 673, 884	05QF4ZZ	884
				05L83DZ	136, 883	05LM3ZZ	883			05QG*	142
05HA0DZ	135, 585, 610, 673, 883	05HV3DZ	72, 136, 585, 611, 673, 883	05L83ZZ	136, 489, 883	05LM4CZ	883	05P33MZ	33, 72, 276, 524, 537, 673, 884	05QG0ZZ	884
				05L84CZ	136, 489, 883	05LM4DZ	883			05QG3ZZ	884
05HA3DZ	135, 585, 610, 673, 883	05HV4DZ	72, 136, 585, 611, 673, 883	05L84DZ	136, 883	05LN*	33, 72, 136	05P34MZ	33, 72, 276, 524, 537, 673, 884	05QG4ZZ	884
				05L90CZ	136, 489, 883	05LN0CZ	883			05QH*	142
05HA4DZ	135, 585, 610, 673, 883	05HY02Z	33, 72, 136, 489, 673, 883	05L90DZ	136, 883	05LN0DZ	883	05P3XMZ	33, 72, 276, 524, 537, 673, 884	05QH0ZZ	884
				05L90ZZ	136, 489, 883	05LN0ZZ	883			05QH3ZZ	884
05HB0DZ	136, 585, 610, 673, 883	05HY0DZ	72, 99, 136, 187, 585, 611, 673, 883	05L93CZ	136, 489, 883	05LN3CZ	883	05P40MZ	33, 72, 276, 524, 537, 673, 884	05QH4ZZ	884
				05L93DZ	136, 883	05LN3DZ	884			05QL*	142
05HB3DZ	136, 585, 610, 673, 883	05HY0YZ	33, 72, 136, 489, 673, 883	05L93ZZ	136, 489, 883	05LN3ZZ	884	05P43MZ	33, 72, 276, 524, 537, 673, 884	05QL0ZZ	884
				05L94CZ	136, 489, 883	05LN4CZ	884			05QL3ZZ	884
05HB4DZ	136, 585, 610, 673, 883	05HY3DZ	72, 99, 136, 187, 585, 611, 673, 883	05L94DZ	136, 883	05LN4DZ	884	05P44MZ	33, 72, 276, 524, 537, 673, 884	05QL4ZZ	884
				05L94ZZ	136, 489, 883	05LP*	33, 72, 136			05QM*	142
05HC0DZ	136, 585, 610, 673, 883	05HY42Z	33, 72, 136, 489, 673, 883	05LA0CZ	136, 489, 883	05LP0CZ	884	05P4XMZ	33, 72, 276, 524, 538, 673, 884	05QM0ZZ	884
				05LA0DZ	136, 883	05LP0DZ	884			05QM3ZZ	884
05HC3DZ	136, 585, 610, 673, 883	05HY4DZ	72, 99, 136, 187, 585, 611, 673, 883	05LA3CZ	136, 489, 883	05LP0ZZ	884			05QM4ZZ	884
				05LA3DZ	136, 883	05LP3CZ	884	05PY00Z	136	05QN*	142
05HC4DZ	136, 585, 610, 673, 883	05JY0ZZ	136	05LA3ZZ	136, 489, 883	05LP3DZ	884	05PY02Z	136	05QN0ZZ	884
		05JY4ZZ	136	05LA4CZ	136, 489, 883	05LP3ZZ	884	05PY07Z	136, 1048	05QN3ZZ	884
05HD0DZ	136, 585, 610, 673, 883	05L*	673	05LA4DZ	136, 883	05LP4CZ	884	05PY0CZ	136	05QN4ZZ	884
		05L00CZ	161	05LA4ZZ	136, 489, 883	05LP4DZ	884	05PY0DZ	136	05QP*	142
05HD3DZ	136, 585, 610, 673, 883	05L00DZ	161	05LB0CZ	136, 489, 883	05LP4ZZ	884	05PY0JZ	136, 1048	05QP0ZZ	884
		05L00ZZ	161	05LB0DZ	136, 883	05LQ*	33, 72, 136	05PY0KZ	136, 1048	05QP3ZZ	884
05HD4DZ	136, 585, 610, 673, 883	05L03CZ	161	05LB0ZZ	136, 489, 883	05LQ0CZ	884	05PY0YZ	136	05QP4ZZ	884
		05L03DZ	161	05LB3CZ	136, 489, 883	05LQ0DZ	884	05PY3JZ	136, 1048	05QQ*	142
05HF0DZ	136, 585, 610, 673, 883	05L03ZZ	161	05LB3DZ	136, 883	05LQ0ZZ	884	05PY3CZ	136	05QQ0ZZ	884
		05L04CZ	161	05LB3ZZ	136, 489, 883	05LQ3CZ	884	05PY3JZ	136, 1048	05QQ3ZZ	884
05HF3DZ	136, 585, 610, 673, 883	05L04DZ	161	05LB4CZ	136, 489, 883	05LQ3DZ	884	05PY3KZ	136, 1048	05QQ4ZZ	884
		05L04ZZ	161	05LB4DZ	136, 883	05LQ3ZZ	884	05PY40Z	137	05QR*	28, 142
05HF4DZ	136, 585, 610, 673, 883	05L10CZ	161	05LB4ZZ	136, 489, 883	05LQ4CZ	884	05PY42Z	137	05QR0ZZ	884
		05L10DZ	161	05LC0CZ	136, 489, 883	05LQ4DZ	884	05PY43Z	137	05QR3ZZ	884
05HG0DZ	136, 585, 610, 673, 883	05L10ZZ	161	05LC0DZ	136, 883	05LQ4ZZ	884	05PY4CZ	137, 1048	05QR4ZZ	884
		05L13CZ	161	05LC0ZZ	136, 489, 883	05LR*	33, 72, 136	05PY4DZ	137	05QS*	28, 142
05HG3DZ	136, 585, 610, 673, 883	05L13DZ	161	05LC3CZ	136, 489, 883	05LR0CZ	884	05PY4JZ	137, 1048	05QS0ZZ	884
		05L13ZZ	161	05LC3DZ	136, 883	05LR0DZ	884	05PY4KZ	137, 1048	05QS3ZZ	884
05HG4DZ	136, 585, 610, 673, 883	05L14CZ	161	05LC3ZZ	136, 489, 883	05LR0ZZ	884			05QS4ZZ	884
		05L14DZ	161	05LC4CZ	136, 489, 883	05LR3CZ	884	05Q*	673	05QT*	142
05HH0DZ	136, 585, 610, 673, 883	05L14ZZ	161	05LC4DZ	136, 883	05LR3DZ	884	05Q0*	142	05QT0ZZ	884
		05L3*	89, 174	05LC4ZZ	136, 489, 883	05LR3ZZ	884	05Q00ZZ	884	05QT3ZZ	884
05HH3DZ	136, 585, 610, 673, 883	05L30CZ	161	05LD0CZ	136, 489, 883	05LR4CZ	884	05Q03ZZ	884	05QT4ZZ	884
		05L30DZ	161	05LD0DZ	136, 883	05LR4DZ	884	05Q04ZZ	884	05QV*	142
05HH4DZ	136, 585, 610, 673, 883	05L30ZZ	161	05LD0ZZ	136, 489, 883	05LR4ZZ	884	05Q1*	142	05QV0ZZ	884
		05L33CZ	161	05LD3CZ	136, 489, 883	05LS*	33, 72, 136	05Q10ZZ	884	05QV3ZZ	884
05HL0DZ	136, 585, 610, 673, 883	05L33DZ	161	05LD3DZ	136, 883	05LS0CZ	884	05Q13ZZ	884	05QV4ZZ	884
		05L33ZZ	161	05LD3ZZ	136, 489, 883	05LS0DZ	884	05Q14ZZ	884	05QY*	137, 187, 206, 489, 514
05HL3DZ	136, 585, 610, 673, 883	05L34CZ	161	05LD4CZ	136, 489, 883	05LS0ZZ	884	05Q3*	142		
		05L34DZ	161	05LD4DZ	136, 883	05LS3CZ	884	05Q30ZZ	884	05QY0ZZ	884
05HL4DZ	136, 585, 610, 673, 883	05L34ZZ	161	05LD4ZZ	136, 489, 883	05LS3DZ	884	05Q33ZZ	884	05QY3ZZ	884
		05L4*	89, 174	05LF0CZ	136, 489, 883	05LS3ZZ	884	05Q34ZZ	884	05QY4ZZ	884
05HM0DZ	72, 136, 585, 610, 673, 883	05L40CZ	161	05LF0DZ	136, 883	05LS4CZ	884	05Q4*	142	05R0*	89, 673
		05L40DZ	161	05LF0ZZ	136, 489, 883	05LS4ZZ	884	05Q40ZZ	884	05R007Z	109, 884
05HM3DZ	72, 136, 585, 610, 673, 883	05L40ZZ	161	05LF3CZ	136, 489, 883	05LT*	33, 72, 136	05Q43ZZ	884	05R00JZ	109, 884
		05L43CZ	161	05LF3DZ	136, 883	05LT0CZ	884	05Q44ZZ	884	05R00KZ	109, 884
05HM4DZ	72, 136, 585, 610, 673, 883	05L43DZ	161	05LF3ZZ	136, 489, 883	05LT0DZ	884	05Q5*	142	05R047Z	109, 884
		05L43ZZ	161	05LF4CZ	136, 489, 883	05LT0ZZ	884	05Q50ZZ	884	05R04JZ	109, 884
05HN0DZ	72, 136, 585, 610, 673, 883	05L44CZ	161	05LF4DZ	136, 883	05LT3CZ	884	05Q53ZZ	884	05R04KZ	109, 884
		05L44DZ	161	05LF4ZZ	136, 489, 883	05LT3DZ	884	05Q54ZZ	884	05R1*	89, 673
05HN3DZ	72, 136, 585, 610, 673, 883	05L44ZZ	161	05LG0CZ	136, 489, 883	05LT3ZZ	884	05Q6*	142	05R107Z	109, 884
		05L5*	89, 174	05LG0DZ	136, 883	05LT4CZ	884	05Q60ZZ	884	05R10JZ	109, 884
05HN4DZ	72, 136, 585, 610, 673, 883	05L50CZ	161	05LG0ZZ	136, 489, 883	05LT4DZ	884	05Q63ZZ	884	05R10KZ	109, 884
		05L50DZ	161	05LG3CZ	136, 489, 883	05LT4ZZ	884	05Q64ZZ	884	05R147Z	109, 884
05HP0DZ	72, 136, 585, 610, 673, 883	05L50ZZ	161	05LG3DZ	136, 883	05LV*	33, 72, 136	05Q7*	142	05R14JZ	109, 884
		05L53CZ	161	05LG3ZZ	136, 489, 883	05LV0CZ	884	05Q70ZZ	884	05R14KZ	109, 884
05HP3DZ	72, 136, 585, 610, 673, 883	05L53DZ	161	05LG4CZ	136, 489, 883	05LV0DZ	884	05Q73ZZ	884	05R3*	89, 673
		05L53ZZ	161	05LG4DZ	136, 883	05LV0ZZ	884	05Q74ZZ	884	05R307Z	109
05HP4DZ	72, 136, 585, 610, 673, 883	05L54CZ	161	05LG4ZZ	136, 489, 883	05LV3CZ	884	05Q8*	142	05R307Z	884
		05L54DZ	161	05LH0CZ	136, 489, 883	05LV3DZ	884	05Q83ZZ	884	05R30JZ	109
05HQ0DZ	72, 136, 585, 610, 673, 883	05L54ZZ	161	05LH0DZ	136, 883	05LV3ZZ	884	05Q84ZZ	884	05R30JZ	884
		05L6*	89, 174	05LH0ZZ	136, 489, 883	05LV4CZ	884	05Q9*	142	05R30KZ	109
05HQ3DZ	72, 136, 585, 610, 673, 883	05L60CZ	161	05LH3CZ	136, 489, 883	05LV4DZ	884	05Q90ZZ	884	05R30KZ	884
		05L60DZ	161	05LH3DZ	136, 883	05LV4ZZ	884	05Q93ZZ	884	05R347Z	109
05HQ4DZ	72, 136, 585, 610, 673, 883	05L60ZZ	161	05LH3ZZ	136, 489, 883	05LY0CZ	136, 884	05Q94ZZ	884	05R347Z	884
		05L63CZ	161	05LH4CZ	136, 489, 883	05LY0DZ	136	05QA*	142	05R34JZ	109
05HR0DZ	72, 136, 585, 610, 673, 883	05L63DZ	161	05LH4DZ	136, 883	05LY0ZZ	136, 884	05QA0ZZ	884	05R34JZ	884
		05L63ZZ	161	05LH4ZZ	136, 489, 883	05LY3CZ	136, 884	05QA3ZZ	884	05R34KZ	109
05HR3DZ	72, 136, 585, 610, 673, 883	05L64CZ	161	05LL*	849	05LY3DZ	136, 884	05QA4ZZ	884	05R34KZ	885
		05L64DZ	161	05LL0CZ	7, 12	05LY3ZZ	136, 884	05QB*	142	05R4*	89, 673
05HR4DZ	72, 136, 585, 610, 673, 883	05L64DZ	162	05LL0DZ	7, 12	05LY4CZ	136, 884	05QB0ZZ	884	05R407Z	885
		05L70CZ	136, 489, 883	05LL3CZ	7, 12	05LY4DZ	136, 884	05QB3ZZ	884	05R40JZ	109
05HS0DZ	72, 136, 585, 610, 673, 883	05L70DZ	136, 883	05LL3DZ	7, 12	05LY4ZZ	136, 884	05QB4ZZ	884	05R40JZ	885
		05L70ZZ	136, 489, 883	05LL3ZZ	7, 12	05N*	136	05QC*	142	05R40KZ	109
		05L73CZ	136, 489, 883					05QC0ZZ	884	05R40KZ	885
								05QC3ZZ	884	05R447Z	109

Numeric Index to Procedures

Code	Page	Code	Page	Code	Page	Code	Page	Code	Page	Code	Page
05R447Z	885	05SH4ZZ	418,885	05UA0JZ	674	05UV47Z	674,886	05VA3DZ	162,675,886	05VP3DZ	162,675,886
05R44JZ	109	05SL0ZZ	885	05UA37Z	674,885	05UV4JZ	674	05VA3ZZ	162,675	05VP3ZZ	162,675
05R44JZ	885	05SL3ZZ	885	05UA3JZ	674	05UY07Z	674,886	05VA4CZ	137	05VP4CZ	137
05R44KZ	109	05SL4ZZ	885	05UA47Z	674,885	05UY0JZ	674	05VA4DZ	162,675,886	05VP4DZ	162,675,886
05R44KZ	885	05SM0ZZ	885	05UA4JZ	674	05UY37Z	674,886	05VA4ZZ	162,675	05VP4ZZ	162,675
05R5*	89,673	05SM3ZZ	885	05UB07Z	674,885	05UY3JZ	674	05VB0CZ	137	05VQ0CZ	137
05R507Z	109,885	05SM4ZZ	885	05UB0JZ	674	05UY47Z	674,886	05VB0DZ	162,675,886	05VQ0DZ	162,675,886
05R50JZ	109,885	05SN0ZZ	885	05UB37Z	674,885	05UY4JZ	674	05VB0ZZ	162,675	05VQ0ZZ	162,675
05R50KZ	109,885	05SN3ZZ	885	05UB3JZ	674	05V00CZ	137	05VB3CZ	137	05VQ3CZ	137
05R547Z	109,885	05SN4ZZ	885	05UB47Z	674,885	05V00DZ	162,674,886	05VB3DZ	162,675,886	05VQ3DZ	162,675,886
05R54JZ	109,885	05SP0ZZ	885	05UB4JZ	674	05V00ZZ	162,674	05VB3ZZ	162,675	05VQ3ZZ	162,675
05R54KZ	109,885	05SP3ZZ	885	05UC07Z	674,885	05V03CZ	137	05VB4CZ	137	05VQ4CZ	137
05R6*	89,673	05SP4ZZ	885	05UC0JZ	674	05V03DZ	162,674,886	05VB4DZ	162,675,886	05VQ4DZ	162,675,886
05R607Z	109,885	05SQ0ZZ	885	05UC37Z	674,885	05V03ZZ	162,674	05VB4ZZ	162,675	05VQ4ZZ	162,675
05R60JZ	109,885	05SQ3ZZ	885	05UC3JZ	674	05V04DZ	162,674,886	05VC0CZ	137	05VR0CZ	137
05R60KZ	109,885	05SQ4ZZ	885	05UC47Z	674,885	05V04ZZ	162,674	05VC0DZ	162,675,886	05VR0DZ	162,675,886
05R647Z	109,885	05SR0ZZ	885	05UC4JZ	674	05V10CZ	137	05VC0ZZ	162,675	05VR0ZZ	162,675
05R64JZ	109,885	05SR3ZZ	885	05UD07Z	674,885	05V10DZ	162,674,886	05VC3CZ	137	05VR3CZ	137
05R64KZ	109,885	05SR4ZZ	885	05UD0JZ	674	05V10ZZ	162,674	05VC3DZ	162,675,886	05VR3DZ	162,675,886
05R7*	137,673	05SS0ZZ	885	05UD37Z	674,885	05V13CZ	137	05VC3ZZ	162,675	05VR3ZZ	162,675
05R8*	137,673	05SS3ZZ	885	05UD3JZ	674	05V13DZ	162,674,886	05VC4CZ	137	05VR4CZ	137
05R9*	137,673	05SS4ZZ	885	05UD47Z	674,885	05V13ZZ	162,674	05VC4DZ	162,675,886	05VR4DZ	162,675,886
05RA*	137,673	05ST0ZZ	885	05UD4JZ	674	05V14CZ	137	05VC4ZZ	162,675	05VR4ZZ	162,675
05RB*	137,673	05ST3ZZ	885	05UF07Z	674,885	05V14DZ	162,675,886	05VD0CZ	137	05VS0CZ	137
05RC*	137,674	05ST4ZZ	885	05UF0JZ	674	05V14ZZ	162,675	05VD0DZ	162,675,886	05VS0DZ	162,675,886
05RD*	137,674	05SV0ZZ	885	05UF37Z	674,885	05V30CZ	137	05VD0ZZ	162,675	05VS0ZZ	162,675
05RF*	137,674	05SV3ZZ	885	05UF3JZ	674	05V30DZ	162,675,886	05VD3CZ	137	05VS3CZ	137
05RG*	137,674	05SV4ZZ	885	05UF47Z	674,885	05V30ZZ	162,675	05VD3DZ	162,675,886	05VS3DZ	162,675,886
05RH*	137,674	05SY0ZZ	885	05UF4JZ	674	05V33CZ	137	05VD3ZZ	162,675	05VS3ZZ	162,675
05RL*	674	05SY3ZZ	885	05UG07Z	674,885	05V33DZ	162,675,886	05VD4CZ	137	05VS4CZ	137
05RL07Z	7,12,885	05SY4ZZ	885	05UG0JZ	674	05V33ZZ	162,675	05VD4DZ	162,675,886	05VS4DZ	162,675,886
05RL0JZ	7,12,885	05U*	137	05UG37Z	674,885	05V34CZ	137	05VD4ZZ	162,675	05VS4ZZ	162,675
05RL0KZ	7,12,885	05U007Z	674,885	05UG3JZ	674	05V34DZ	162,675,886	05VF0CZ	137	05VT0CZ	137
05RL47Z	7,12,885	05U00JZ	674	05UG47Z	674,885	05V34ZZ	162,675	05VF0DZ	162,675,886	05VT0DZ	162,675,886
05RL4JZ	7,12,885	05U037Z	674,885	05UG4JZ	674	05V40CZ	137	05VF0ZZ	162,675	05VT0ZZ	162,675
05RL4KZ	7,12,885	05U03JZ	674	05UH07Z	674,885	05V40DZ	162,675,886	05VF3CZ	137	05VT3CZ	137
05RM*	33,137	05U047Z	674,885	05UH0JZ	674	05V40ZZ	162,675	05VF3DZ	162,675,886	05VT3DZ	162,675,886
05RN*	33,137	05U04JZ	674	05UH37Z	674,885	05V43CZ	137	05VF3ZZ	162,675	05VT3ZZ	162,675
05RP*	33,137	05U107Z	674,885	05UH3JZ	674	05V43DZ	162,675,886	05VF4CZ	137	05VT4CZ	137
05RQ*	33,137	05U10JZ	674	05UH47Z	674,885	05V43ZZ	162,675	05VF4DZ	162,675,886	05VT4DZ	162,675,886
05RR*	33,137	05U137Z	674,885	05UH4JZ	674	05V44CZ	137	05VF4ZZ	162,675	05VT4ZZ	162,675
05RS*	33,137	05U13JZ	674	05UL07Z	674,885	05V44DZ	162,675,886	05VG0CZ	137	05VV0CZ	137
05RT*	33,137	05U147Z	674,885	05UL0JZ	674	05V44ZZ	162,675	05VG0DZ	162,675,886	05VV0DZ	162,675,886
05RV*	33,137	05U14JZ	674	05UL37Z	674,885	05V50CZ	137	05VG0ZZ	162,675	05VV0ZZ	162,675
05RY*	137,674	05U307Z	674	05UL3JZ	674	05V50DZ	162,675,886	05VG3CZ	137	05VV3CZ	137
05S*	137,674	05U307Z	885	05UL47Z	674,885	05V50ZZ	162,675	05VG3DZ	162,675,886	05VV3DZ	162,675,886
05S00ZZ	885	05U30JZ	674	05UL4JZ	674	05V53CZ	137	05VG3ZZ	162,675	05VV3ZZ	162,675
05S03ZZ	885	05U337Z	674	05UM07Z	674,885	05V53DZ	162,675,886	05VG4CZ	137	05VV4CZ	137
05S04ZZ	885	05U337Z	885	05UM0JZ	674	05V53ZZ	162,675	05VG4DZ	162,675,886	05VV4DZ	162,675,886
05S10ZZ	885	05U33JZ	674	05UM37Z	674,885	05V54CZ	137	05VG4ZZ	162,675	05VV4ZZ	162,675
05S13ZZ	885	05U347Z	674	05UM3JZ	674	05V54DZ	162,675,886	05VH0CZ	137	05VY0CZ	137
05S14ZZ	885	05U347Z	885	05UM47Z	674,885	05V54ZZ	162,675	05VH0DZ	162,675,886	05VY0DZ	162,675
05S30ZZ	885	05U34JZ	674	05UM4JZ	674	05V60CZ	137	05VH0ZZ	162,675	05VY0ZZ	162,675
05S33ZZ	885	05U407Z	674	05UN07Z	674,885	05V60DZ	162,675,886	05VH3CZ	137	05VY3CZ	137
05S34ZZ	885	05U407Z	885	05UN0JZ	674	05V60ZZ	162,675	05VH3DZ	162,675,886	05VY3DZ	162,675
05S40ZZ	885	05U40JZ	674	05UN37Z	674,885	05V63CZ	137	05VH3ZZ	162,675	05VY3ZZ	162,675
05S43ZZ	885	05U437Z	674	05UN3JZ	674	05V63DZ	162,675,886	05VH4CZ	137	05VY4CZ	137
05S44ZZ	885	05U437Z	885	05UN47Z	674,885	05V63ZZ	162,675	05VH4DZ	162,675,886	05VY4DZ	162,675
05S50ZZ	885	05U43JZ	674	05UN4JZ	674	05V64CZ	137	05VH4ZZ	162,675	05VY4ZZ	162,675
05S53ZZ	885	05U447Z	674	05UP07Z	674,885	05V64DZ	162,675,886	05VL0CZ	7,12,137	05W002Z	137
05S54ZZ	885	05U447Z	885	05UP0JZ	674	05V64ZZ	162,675	05VL0DZ	7,12,162,675,886	05W00MZ	33
05S60ZZ	885	05U44JZ	674	05UP37Z	674,885	05V70CZ	137			05W032Z	137
05S63ZZ	885	05U507Z	674,885	05UP3JZ	674	05V70DZ	162,675,886	05VL0ZZ	7,12,162,675	05W03MZ	33
05S64ZZ	885	05U50JZ	674	05UP47Z	674,885	05V70ZZ	162,675	05VL3CZ	7,12,137	05W042Z	137
05S70ZZ	418,885	05U537Z	674,885	05UP4JZ	674	05V73CZ	137	05VL3DZ	7,12,162,675,886	05W04MZ	33
05S73ZZ	418,885	05U53JZ	674	05UQ07Z	674,885	05V73DZ	162,675,886			05W0X2Z	137
05S74ZZ	418,885	05U547Z	674,885	05UQ0JZ	674	05V73ZZ	162,675	05VL3ZZ	7,12,162,675	05W30MZ	33
05S80ZZ	418,885	05U54JZ	674	05UQ37Z	674,885	05V74CZ	137	05VL4CZ	7,12,137	05W33MZ	33
05S83ZZ	418,885	05U607Z	674,885	05UQ3JZ	674	05V74DZ	162,675,886	05VL4DZ	7,12,162,675,886	05W34MZ	33
05S84ZZ	418,885	05U60JZ	674	05UQ47Z	674,885	05V74ZZ	162,675			05W40MZ	33
05S90ZZ	418,885	05U637Z	674,885	05UQ4JZ	674	05V80CZ	137	05VL4ZZ	7,12,162,675	05W43MZ	33
05S93ZZ	418,885	05U63JZ	674	05UR07Z	28,674,885	05V80DZ	162,675,886	05VM0CZ	137	05W44MZ	33
05S94ZZ	418,885	05U647Z	674,885	05UR0JZ	28,674	05V80ZZ	162,675	05VM0DZ	162,675,886	05WY00Z	137
05SA0ZZ	418,885	05U64JZ	674	05UR37Z	28,674,885	05V83CZ	137	05VM0ZZ	162,675	05WY02Z	137
05SA3ZZ	418,885	05U707Z	674,885	05UR3JZ	28,674	05V83DZ	162,675,886	05VM3CZ	137	05WY03Z	137
05SA4ZZ	418,885	05U70JZ	674	05UR47Z	28,674,885	05V83ZZ	162,675	05VM3DZ	162,675,886	05WY07Z	137,1048
05SB0ZZ	418,514,885	05U737Z	674,885	05UR4JZ	28,674	05V84CZ	137	05VM3ZZ	162,675	05WY0CZ	137
05SB3ZZ	418,514,885	05U73JZ	674	05US07Z	28,674,885	05V84DZ	162,675,886	05VM4CZ	137	05WY0DZ	137
05SB4ZZ	418,885	05U747Z	674,885	05US0JZ	28,674	05V84ZZ	162,675	05VM4DZ	162,675,886	05WY0JZ	137,1048
05SC0ZZ	418,514,885	05U74JZ	674	05US37Z	28,674,885	05V90CZ	137	05VM4ZZ	162,675	05WY0KZ	137,1048
05SC3ZZ	418,514,885	05U807Z	674,885	05US3JZ	28,674	05V90DZ	162,675,886	05VN0CZ	137	05WY0ZZ	137
05SC4ZZ	418,885	05U80JZ	674	05US47Z	28,674,885	05V90ZZ	162,675	05VN0DZ	162,675,886	05WY37Z	137,1048
05SD0ZZ	418,885	05U837Z	674,885	05US4JZ	28,674	05V93CZ	137	05VN0ZZ	162,675	05WY3CZ	137
05SD3ZZ	418,885	05U83JZ	674	05UT07Z	674,885	05V93DZ	162,675,886	05VN3CZ	137	05WY3JZ	137,1048
05SD4ZZ	418,885	05U847Z	674,885	05UT0JZ	674	05V93ZZ	162,675	05VN3DZ	162,675,886	05WY3KZ	137,1048
05SF0ZZ	418,885	05U84JZ	674	05UT37Z	674,885	05V94CZ	137	05VN3ZZ	162,675	05WY40Z	137
05SF3ZZ	418,885	05U907Z	674,885	05UT3JZ	674	05V94DZ	162,675,886	05VN4CZ	137	05WY42Z	137
05SF4ZZ	418,885	05U90JZ	674	05UT47Z	674,886	05V94ZZ	162,675	05VN4DZ	162,675,886	05WY43Z	137
05SG0ZZ	418,885	05U937Z	674	05UT4JZ	674	05VA0CZ	137	05VN4ZZ	162,675	05WY4CZ	137
05SG3ZZ	418,885	05U93JZ	674	05UV07Z	674,886	05VA0DZ	162,675,886	05VP0CZ	137	05WY4DZ	137
05SG4ZZ	418,885	05U947Z	674,885	05UV0JZ	674	05VA0ZZ	162,675	05VP0DZ	162,675,886	05WY4JZ	137,1048
05SH0ZZ	418,885	05UA07Z	674,885	05UV37Z	674,886	05VA3CZ	137	05VP0ZZ	162,675	05WY4KZ	137,1048
05SH3ZZ	418,885			05UV3JZ	674			05VP3CZ	137		

Code	Page
061007P	115
061007Q	115
061007R	115
061007Y	162
061009P	115
061009Q	115
061009R	115
061009Y	162
06100A5	162
06100A6	162
06100AP	115
06100AQ	115
06100AR	115
06100AY	162
06100J5	162, 198
06100J5	174
06100J6	162, 174, 198
06100JP	115
06100JQ	115
06100JR	115
06100JY	162, 174, 198
06100K5	162
06100K6	162
06100KP	115
06100KQ	115
06100KR	115
06100KY	162
06100Z5	162, 174, 198
06100Z6	162, 174, 198
06100ZP	115
06100ZQ	115
06100ZR	115
06100ZY	163, 174, 198
061047P	115
061047Q	115
061047R	115
061047Y	163
061049P	115
061049Q	115
061049R	115
061049Y	163
06104A5	163
06104A6	163
06104AP	115
06104AQ	115
06104AR	115
06104AY	163
06104J5	163, 174, 198
06104J6	163, 174, 198
06104JP	115
06104JQ	115
06104JR	115
06104JY	163, 174, 198
06104K5	163
06104K6	163
06104KP	115
06104KQ	115
06104KR	115
06104KY	163
06104Z5	163, 174, 198
06104Z6	163, 174, 198
06104ZP	115
06104ZQ	115
06104ZR	115
06104ZY	163, 174, 198
0611*	163
06110J9	174, 198
06110JB	174, 198
06110JY	174, 198
06110Z9	174, 198
06110ZB	174, 198
06110ZY	174, 198
06114J9	174, 198
06114JB	174, 198
06114JY	174, 198
06114Z9	174, 198
06114ZB	174, 198
06114ZY	174, 198
0612*	163
0613*	137
0614*	163
0615*	163
0616*	163
0617*	163
0618*	163
06180J9	174, 198
06180JB	174, 198
06180JY	174, 198
06180Z9	174, 198
06180ZB	174, 198
06180ZY	174, 198
06183J4	198
06183JY	198
06184J4	174, 198
06184J9	174, 198
06184JB	174, 198
06184JY	174, 198
06184Z9	174, 198
06184ZB	174, 198
06184ZY	174, 198
0619*	163
061B*	163
061C*	137
061D*	137
061F*	137
061G*	137
061H*	137
061J*	163
061M*	137
061N*	137
061P*	137
061Q*	137
061T*	137
061V*	137
06500ZZ	163
06503ZZ	163
06504ZZ	163
06510ZZ	163
06513ZZ	163
06514ZZ	163
06520ZZ	163
06523ZZ	163
06524ZZ	163
0653*	28, 137, 675
06540ZZ	163
06543ZZ	163
06544ZZ	163
06550ZZ	163
06553ZZ	163
06554ZZ	163
06560ZZ	163
06563ZZ	163
06564ZZ	163
06570ZZ	163
06573ZZ	163
06574ZZ	163
06580ZZ	163
06583ZZ	163
06584ZZ	163
06590ZZ	163
06593ZZ	163
06594ZZ	163
065B0ZZ	163
065B3ZZ	163
065B4ZZ	163
065C0ZZ	163
065C3ZZ	163
065D0ZZ	163
065D3ZZ	163
065D4ZZ	163
065F0ZZ	163
065F3ZZ	163
065F4ZZ	163
065G0ZZ	163
065G3ZZ	163
065G4ZY	163
065H0ZZ	163
065H3ZZ	163
065H4ZZ	163
065J0ZZ	163
065J4ZZ	163
065M*	142, 675
065M0ZZ	886
065M3ZZ	886
065M4ZZ	886
065N*	142, 675
065N0ZZ	886
065N3ZZ	886
065N4ZZ	886
065P*	142, 675
065P0ZZ	886
065P3ZZ	886
065P4ZZ	886
065Q*	142, 675
065Q0ZZ	886
065Q3ZZ	886
065Q4ZZ	886
065T*	142, 675
065T0ZZ	886
065T3ZZ	886
065T4ZZ	886
065V*	142, 675
065V0ZZ	886
065V3ZZ	886
065V4ZZ	886
065Y0ZZ	183, 1048
065Y0ZC	142, 675, 886
065Y3ZC	183, 1048
065Y3ZZ	142, 675, 886
065Y4ZC	183, 1048
065Y4ZZ	142, 675, 886
067*	137
06703DZ	28, 99, 187, 206, 276, 418, 489, 514, 675, 886
06703ZZ	28, 99, 187, 206, 276, 418, 489, 514, 675, 886
06900ZX	137, 1048
06904ZX	137, 1048
06910ZX	137, 1048
06914ZX	137, 1048
06920ZX	137, 1048
06924ZX	137, 1048
069300Z	33, 72, 137, 489, 675, 886
06930ZX	137, 1048
06930ZZ	33, 72, 137, 675, 886
069340Z	33, 72, 137, 489, 675, 886
06934ZX	137, 1048
06934ZZ	33, 72, 137, 489, 675, 886
06940ZX	137, 1048
06944ZX	137, 1048
06950ZX	137, 1048
06954ZX	137, 1048
06960ZX	137, 1048
06964ZX	137, 1048
06970ZX	137, 1048
06974ZX	137, 1048
06980ZX	137, 1048
06984ZX	137, 1048
06990ZX	137, 1048
06994ZX	137, 1048
069B0ZX	137, 1048
069B4ZX	137, 1048
069C0ZX	137, 1048
069C4ZX	138, 1048
069D0ZX	138, 1048
069D4ZX	138, 1048
069F0ZX	138, 1048
069F4ZX	138, 1048
069G0ZX	138, 1048
069G4ZX	138, 1048
069H0ZX	138, 1048
069H4ZX	138, 1048
069J0ZX	138, 1048
069J4ZX	138, 1048
069M0ZX	138, 1048
069M4ZX	138, 1048
069N0ZX	138, 1048
069N4ZX	138, 1048
069P0ZX	138, 1048
069P4ZX	138, 1048
069Q0ZX	138, 1048
069Q4ZX	138, 1048
069T0ZX	138, 1048
069T4ZX	138, 1048
069V0ZX	138, 1048
069V4ZX	138, 1048
069Y0ZX	138, 1048
069Y4ZX	138, 1048
06B00ZX	138, 1048
06B00ZZ	163
06B03ZX	138, 1048
06B03ZZ	163
06B04ZX	138, 1048
06B04ZZ	163
06B10ZX	138, 1048
06B10ZZ	163
06B13ZX	138, 1048
06B13ZZ	163
06B14ZX	138, 1048
06B14ZZ	163
06B20ZX	138, 1048
06B20ZZ	163
06B23ZX	138, 1048
06B23ZZ	163
06B24ZX	138, 1048
06B24ZZ	163
06B3*	138
06B30ZX	1048
06B30ZZ	28, 675
06B33ZX	1048
06B33ZZ	28, 675
06B34ZX	1048
06B34ZZ	28, 675
06B40ZX	138, 1048
06B40ZZ	163
06B43ZX	138, 1048
06B43ZZ	163
06B44ZX	138, 1048
06B44ZZ	163
06B50ZX	138, 1048
06B50ZZ	163
06B53ZX	138, 1048
06B53ZZ	163
06B54ZX	138, 1048
06B54ZZ	163
06B60ZX	138, 1048
06B60ZZ	163
06B63ZX	138, 1048
06B63ZZ	163
06B64ZX	138, 1048
06B64ZZ	163
06B70ZX	138, 1048
06B70ZZ	163
06B73ZX	138, 1048
06B73ZZ	163
06B74ZX	138, 1048
06B74ZZ	163
06B80ZX	138, 1048
06B80ZZ	163
06B83ZX	138, 1048
06B83ZZ	163
06B84ZX	138, 1048
06B84ZZ	163
06B90ZX	138, 1048
06B90ZZ	163
06B93ZX	138, 1049
06B93ZZ	163
06B94ZX	138, 1049
06B94ZZ	163
06BB0ZX	138, 1049
06BB0ZZ	163
06BB3ZX	138, 1049
06BB3ZZ	163
06BB4ZX	138, 1049
06BB4ZZ	163
06BC0ZX	138, 1049
06BC0ZZ	163
06BC3ZX	138, 1049
06BC3ZZ	163
06BC4ZX	138, 1049
06BC4ZZ	163
06BD0ZX	138, 1049
06BD0ZZ	163
06BD3ZX	138, 1049
06BD3ZZ	163
06BD4ZX	138, 1049
06BD4ZZ	163
06BF0ZX	138, 1049
06BF0ZZ	163
06BF3ZX	138, 1049
06BF3ZZ	163
06BF4ZX	138, 1049
06BF4ZZ	163
06BG0ZX	138, 1049
06BG0ZZ	163
06BG3ZX	138, 1049
06BG4ZX	138, 1049
06BG4ZZ	163
06BH0ZX	138, 1049
06BH0ZZ	163
06BH3ZX	138, 1049
06BH3ZZ	163
06BH4ZX	138, 1049
06BH4ZZ	163
06BJ0ZX	138, 1049
06BJ0ZZ	163
06BJ3ZX	138, 1049
06BJ3ZZ	163
06BJ4ZX	138, 1049
06BJ4ZZ	163
06BM0ZX	138, 1049
06BM0ZZ	142, 675, 886
06BM3ZX	138, 1049
06BM3ZZ	142, 675, 886
06BM4ZX	138, 1049
06BM4ZZ	142, 675, 886
06BN0ZX	138, 1049
06BN0ZZ	142, 675, 886
06BN3ZX	138, 1049
06BN3ZZ	142, 675, 886
06BN4ZX	138, 1049
06BN4ZZ	142, 675, 886
06BP0ZX	138, 1049
06BP0ZZ	142, 675, 886
06BP3ZX	138, 1049
06BP3ZZ	142, 675, 886
06BP4ZX	138, 1049
06BP4ZZ	142, 675, 886
06BQ0ZX	138, 1049
06BQ0ZZ	142, 676, 886
06BQ3ZX	138, 1049
06BQ3ZZ	142, 676, 886
06BQ4ZX	138, 1049
06BQ4ZZ	142, 676, 886
06BT0ZX	138, 1049
06BT0ZZ	142, 676, 886
06BT3ZX	138, 1049
06BT3ZZ	142, 676, 886
06BT4ZX	138, 1049
06BT4ZZ	142, 676, 886
06BV0ZX	138, 1049
06BV0ZZ	142, 676, 886
06BV3ZX	138, 1049
06BV3ZZ	142, 676, 886
06BV4ZX	138, 1049
06BV4ZZ	142, 676, 886
06BY0ZX	183, 1049
06BY0ZZ	138, 489, 676, 886
06BY3ZC	183, 1049
06BY3ZX	138, 489, 676, 886
06BY4ZC	183, 1049
06BY4ZX	138, 1049
06BY4ZZ	138, 489, 676, 886
06C00ZZ	163
06C03ZZ	163
06C04ZZ	163
06C10ZZ	163
06C13ZZ	163
06C14ZZ	163
06C20ZZ	163
06C23ZZ	163
06C24ZZ	163
06C3*	33, 72, 138, 489, 676
06C30ZZ	886
06C33ZZ	886
06C34ZZ	886
06C40ZZ	163
06C43ZZ	163
06C44ZZ	163
06C50ZZ	163
06C53ZZ	163
06C54ZZ	163
06C60ZZ	163
06C63ZZ	163
06C64ZZ	163
06C70ZZ	163
06C73ZZ	163
06C74ZZ	163
06C80ZZ	163
06C83ZZ	163
06C84ZZ	163
06C9*	514
06C90ZZ	163
06C93ZZ	163
06C94ZZ	163
06CB*	514
06CB0ZZ	163
06CB3ZZ	163
06CB4ZZ	163
06CC0ZZ	163
06CC3ZZ	163
06CC4ZZ	163
06CD0ZZ	163
06CD3ZZ	163
06CD4ZZ	163
06CF0ZZ	163
06CF3ZZ	163
06CF4ZZ	163
06CG0ZZ	163
06CG3ZZ	163
06CG4ZZ	163
06CH0ZZ	163
06CH3ZZ	163
06CH4ZZ	163
06CJ0ZZ	163
06CJ3ZZ	163
06CM*	676
06CM0ZZ	142, 886, 1049
06CM3ZZ	163, 886, 1049
06CM4ZZ	142, 886, 1049
06CN*	676
06CN0ZZ	142, 886, 1049
06CN3ZX	164, 886, 1049
06CN4ZZ	142, 886, 1049
06CP*	676
06CP0ZZ	142, 886, 1049
06CP3ZZ	164, 886, 1049
06CP4ZZ	142, 886, 1049
06CQ*	676
06CQ0ZZ	142, 886, 1049
06CQ3ZZ	164, 886, 1049
06CQ4ZZ	142, 886, 1049
06CT*	676
06CT0ZZ	142, 886, 1049
06CT3ZZ	164, 886, 1049
06CT4ZZ	142, 886, 1049
06CV*	676
06CV0ZZ	142, 886, 1049
06CV3ZZ	164, 886, 1049
06CV4ZZ	142, 886, 1049
06CY*	187, 206, 489, 514, 676
06CY0ZZ	138, 886
06CY3ZZ	164, 886
06CY4ZZ	138, 886
06D*	142
06DM0ZZ	1049
06DM3ZZ	1049
06DM4ZZ	1049
06DN0ZZ	1049
06DN3ZZ	1049
06DN4ZZ	1049
06DP0ZZ	1049
06DP3ZZ	1049
06DP4ZZ	1049
06DQ0ZZ	1049
06DQ3ZZ	1049
06DQ4ZZ	1049
06DT0ZZ	1049
06DT3ZZ	1049
06DT4ZZ	1049
06DV0ZZ	1049
06DV3ZZ	1049
06DV4ZZ	1049
06DY0ZZ	1049
06DY3ZZ	1049
06DY4ZZ	1049
06H00DZ	33, 99, 138, 187, 206, 276, 489, 514, 524, 538, 571, 676, 886
06H03DZ	33, 99, 138, 187, 206, 276, 489, 514, 524, 538, 571, 676, 886
06H04DZ	33, 99, 138, 187, 206, 276, 489, 514, 524, 538, 571, 676, 886
06H10DZ	138, 187, 585, 611, 676, 886
06H13DZ	138, 187, 585, 611, 676, 886
06H14DZ	138, 187, 585, 611, 676, 886
06H20DZ	138, 187, 585, 611, 676, 886
06H23DZ	138, 187, 585, 611, 676, 886
06H24DZ	138, 187, 585, 611, 676, 886
06H30DZ	72, 138, 187, 585, 611, 676, 886
06H33DZ	72, 138, 187, 585, 611, 676, 886
06H34DZ	72, 138, 187, 585, 611, 676, 886
06H40DZ	138, 187, 585, 611, 676, 886
06H43DZ	138, 187, 585, 611, 676, 886
06H44DZ	138, 187, 585, 611, 676, 886
06H50DZ	138, 187, 585, 611, 676, 886
06H53DZ	138, 187, 585, 611, 676, 886
06H54DZ	138, 187, 585, 611, 676, 886
06H60DZ	138, 187, 585, 611, 676, 886
06H63DZ	138, 187, 585, 611, 676, 886
06H64DZ	138, 187, 585, 611, 676, 887

Numeric Index to Procedures

Code	Page
06H70DZ	138, 188, 585, 611, 676, 887
06H73DZ	138, 188, 585, 611, 676, 887
06H74DZ	138, 188, 585, 611, 676, 887
06H80DZ	138, 188, 585, 611, 676, 887
06H83DZ	138, 188, 585, 611, 676, 887
06H84DZ	138, 188, 585, 611, 676, 887
06H90DZ	138, 585, 611, 676, 887
06H93DZ	138, 585, 611, 676, 887
06H94DZ	138, 585, 611, 676, 887
06HB0DZ	138, 585, 611, 676, 887
06HB3DZ	138, 585, 611, 676, 887
06HB4DZ	138, 585, 611, 676, 887
06HC0DZ	138, 586, 611, 676, 887
06HC3DZ	138, 586, 611, 676, 887
06HC4DZ	138, 586, 611, 676, 887
06HD0DZ	138, 586, 611, 676, 887
06HD3DZ	138, 586, 611, 676, 887
06HD4DZ	138, 586, 611, 676, 887
06HF0DZ	138, 586, 611, 676, 887
06HF3DZ	138, 586, 611, 676, 887
06HF4DZ	138, 586, 611, 676, 887
06HG0DZ	138, 586, 611, 676, 887
06HG3DZ	138, 586, 611, 676, 887
06HG4DZ	138, 586, 611, 676, 887
06HH0DZ	138, 586, 611, 676, 887
06HH3DZ	138, 586, 611, 676, 887
06HH4DZ	138, 586, 611, 676, 887
06HJ0DZ	138, 586, 611, 676, 887
06HJ3DZ	138, 586, 611, 676, 887
06HJ4DZ	138, 586, 611, 676, 887
06HM0DZ	138, 586, 611, 676, 887
06HM3DZ	138, 586, 611, 676, 887
06HM4DZ	138, 586, 611, 676, 887
06HN0DZ	138, 586, 611, 676, 887
06HN3DZ	138, 586, 611, 676, 887
06HN4DZ	138, 586, 611, 676, 887
06HP0DZ	138, 586, 611, 676, 887
06HP3DZ	138, 586, 611, 676, 887
06HP4DZ	138, 586, 611, 676, 887
06HQ0DZ	138, 586, 611, 676, 887
06HQ3DZ	138, 586, 611, 676, 887
06HQ4DZ	138, 586, 611, 676, 887
06HT0DZ	138, 586, 611, 676, 887
06HT3DZ	138, 586, 611, 676, 887
06HT4DZ	138, 586, 611, 676, 887
06HV0DZ	138, 586, 611, 676, 887

Code	Page
06HV3DZ	138, 586, 611, 676, 887
06HV4DZ	138, 586, 611, 676, 887
06HY02Z	142, 676, 887, 1049
06HY0DZ	72, 99, 138, 586, 611, 676, 887
06HY0YZ	142, 676, 887, 1049
06HY3DZ	72, 99, 138, 188, 586, 611, 676, 887
06HY42Z	142, 676, 887, 1049
06HY4DZ	72, 99, 138, 188, 586, 611, 676, 887
06JY0ZZ	138
06JY4ZZ	139
06L0*	33, 99, 139, 188, 206, 276, 489, 514, 524, 538, 571, 676
06L00CZ	887
06L00DZ	887
06L00ZZ	887
06L03CZ	887
06L03DZ	887
06L03ZZ	887
06L04CZ	887
06L04DZ	887
06L04ZZ	887
06L1*	188, 676
06L10CZ	164, 887
06L10DZ	164, 887
06L10ZZ	164, 887
06L13CZ	164, 887
06L13DZ	164, 887
06L13ZZ	164, 887
06L14CZ	164, 887
06L14DZ	164, 887
06L14ZZ	164, 887
06L20CZ	164, 188, 676, 887
06L20DZ	164, 188, 676, 887
06L20ZZ	164, 174, 206, 676, 887
06L23CZ	164, 188, 676, 887
06L23DZ	164, 188, 676, 887
06L23ZZ	164, 174, 206, 676, 887
06L24CZ	164, 188, 676, 887
06L24DZ	164, 188, 676, 887
06L24ZZ	164, 174, 206, 676, 887
06L30CZ	164, 188, 206, 676, 887
06L30DZ	164, 188, 206, 676, 887
06L30ZZ	164, 174, 206, 676, 887
06L4*	188, 676
06L40CZ	164, 887
06L40DZ	164, 887
06L40ZZ	164, 887
06L43CZ	164, 887
06L43DZ	164, 887
06L43ZZ	164, 887
06L44CZ	164, 887
06L44DZ	164, 887
06L44ZZ	164, 887
06L5*	188, 676
06L50CZ	164, 887
06L50DZ	164, 887
06L50ZZ	164, 887
06L53CZ	164, 887
06L53DZ	164, 887
06L53ZZ	164, 887
06L54CZ	164, 887
06L54DZ	164, 887
06L54ZZ	164, 887
06L6*	188, 676
06L60CZ	164, 887
06L60DZ	164, 887
06L60ZZ	164, 887
06L63CZ	164, 887
06L63DZ	164, 887
06L63ZZ	164, 887
06L64CZ	164, 887
06L64DZ	164, 887
06L64ZZ	164, 887
06L7*	188, 676
06L70CZ	164, 887
06L70DZ	164, 887
06L70ZZ	164, 887

Code	Page
06L73CZ	164, 887
06L73DZ	164, 887
06L73ZZ	164, 887
06L74CZ	164, 887
06L74DZ	164, 887
06L74ZZ	164, 887
06L8*	188, 676
06L80CZ	164, 887
06L80DZ	164, 887
06L80ZZ	164, 887
06L83CZ	164, 887
06L83DZ	164, 887
06L83ZZ	164, 887
06L84CZ	164, 887
06L84DZ	164, 887
06L84ZZ	164, 887
06L9*	188, 676
06L90CZ	164, 514, 887
06L90DZ	164, 887
06L90ZZ	164, 479, 514, 887
06L93CZ	164, 514, 887
06L93DZ	164, 887
06L93ZZ	164, 479, 514, 887
06L94CZ	164, 514, 887
06L94DZ	164, 887
06L94ZZ	164, 479, 514, 887
06LB*	188, 676
06LB0CZ	164, 514, 887
06LB0DZ	164, 887
06LB0ZZ	164, 479, 514, 887
06LB3CZ	164, 514, 887
06LB3DZ	164, 524, 538, 887
06LB3ZZ	164, 479, 514, 887
06LB4CZ	164, 514, 887
06LB4DZ	164, 887
06LB4ZZ	164, 479, 514, 887
06LC*	676
06LC0CZ	164, 188, 887
06LC0DZ	164, 887
06LC0ZZ	164, 188, 887
06LC3CZ	164, 188, 887
06LC3DZ	164, 887
06LC3ZZ	164, 188, 887
06LC4CZ	164, 188, 887
06LC4DZ	164, 887
06LC4ZZ	164, 188, 887
06LD*	676
06LD0CZ	164, 188, 887
06LD0DZ	164, 887
06LD0ZZ	164, 188, 887
06LD3CZ	164, 188, 887
06LD3DZ	164, 887
06LD3ZZ	164, 188, 887
06LD4CZ	164, 188, 887
06LD4DZ	164, 887
06LD4ZZ	164, 188, 887
06LF*	676
06LF0CZ	164, 188, 887
06LF0DZ	164, 887
06LF0ZZ	164, 188, 887
06LF3CZ	164, 188, 887
06LF3DZ	164, 887
06LF3ZZ	164, 188, 887
06LF4CZ	164, 188, 887
06LF4DZ	164, 887
06LF4ZZ	164, 188, 888
06LG*	676
06LG0CZ	164, 188, 888
06LG0DZ	164, 888
06LG0ZZ	164, 188, 888
06LG3CZ	164, 188, 888
06LG3DZ	164, 888
06LG3ZZ	164, 188, 888
06LG4CZ	164, 188, 888
06LG4DZ	164, 888
06LG4ZZ	164, 188, 888
06LH*	188, 676
06LH0CZ	164, 888
06LH0DZ	164, 888
06LH0ZZ	164, 888
06LH3CZ	164, 888
06LH3DZ	164, 888
06LH3ZZ	164, 888
06LH4CZ	164, 888
06LH4DZ	164, 888
06LH4ZZ	164, 888
06LJ*	188, 676
06LJ0CZ	164, 888
06LJ0DZ	164, 888
06LJ0ZZ	164, 888
06LJ3CZ	164, 888
06LJ3DZ	164, 888
06LJ3ZZ	164, 888

Code	Page
06LJ4CZ	164, 888
06LJ4DZ	164, 888
06LJ4ZZ	164, 888
06LM*	676
06LM0CZ	142, 888
06LM0DZ	142, 888
06LM0ZZ	142, 888
06LM3CZ	142, 888
06LM3DZ	142, 888
06LM3ZZ	142, 888
06LM4CZ	142, 888
06LM4DZ	142, 888
06LM4ZZ	142, 888
06LN*	676
06LN0CZ	142, 888
06LN0DZ	142, 888
06LN0ZZ	142, 888
06LN3CZ	142, 888
06LN3DZ	142, 888
06LN3ZZ	142, 888
06LN4CZ	142, 888
06LN4DZ	142, 888
06LN4ZZ	142, 888
06LP*	676
06LP0CZ	142, 888
06LP0DZ	142, 888
06LP0ZZ	142, 888
06LP3CZ	142, 888
06LP3DZ	142, 888
06LP3ZZ	142, 888
06LP4CZ	142, 888
06LP4DZ	142, 888
06LP4ZZ	142, 888
06LQ*	676
06LQ0CZ	142, 888
06LQ0DZ	142, 888
06LQ0ZZ	142, 888
06LQ3CZ	142, 888
06LQ3DZ	142, 888
06LQ3ZZ	142, 888
06LQ4CZ	142, 888
06LQ4DZ	142, 888
06LQ4ZZ	142, 888
06LT*	676
06LT0CZ	142, 888
06LT0DZ	142, 888
06LT0ZZ	142, 888
06LT3CZ	142, 888
06LT3DZ	142, 888
06LT3ZZ	142, 888
06LT4CZ	142, 888
06LT4DZ	142, 888
06LT4ZZ	142, 888
06LV*	676
06LV0CZ	142, 888
06LV0DZ	142, 888
06LV0ZZ	142, 888
06LV3CZ	142, 888
06LV3DZ	142, 888
06LV3ZZ	142, 888
06LV4CZ	142, 888
06LV4DZ	142, 888
06LV4ZZ	142, 888
06LY0CC	183, 1049
06LY0CZ	139, 676, 888
06LY0DC	183, 1049
06LY0DZ	142, 676, 888
06LY0ZC	183, 1049
06LY0ZZ	139, 676, 888
06LY3CC	183, 1049
06LY3CZ	139, 676, 888
06LY3DC	183, 1049
06LY3DZ	142, 676, 888
06LY3ZC	183, 1049
06LY3ZZ	139, 676, 888
06LY4CC	183, 1049
06LY4CZ	139, 676, 888
06LY4DC	183, 1049
06LY4DZ	142, 676, 888
06LY4ZC	183, 1049
06N*	139
06N00ZZ	188
06N04ZZ	188
06N10ZZ	188
06N14ZZ	188
06N20ZZ	188
06N24ZZ	188
06N30ZZ	188
06N34ZZ	188
06N40ZZ	188
06N44ZZ	188
06N50ZZ	188

Code	Page
06N54ZZ	188
06N60ZZ	188
06N64ZZ	188
06N70ZZ	188
06N74ZZ	188
06N80ZZ	188
06N84ZZ	188
06N90ZZ	188
06N94ZZ	188
06NB0ZZ	188
06NB4ZZ	188
06NC0ZZ	188
06NC4ZZ	188
06ND0ZZ	188
06ND4ZZ	188
06NF0ZZ	188
06NF4ZZ	188
06NG0ZZ	188
06NG4ZZ	188
06NH0ZZ	188
06NH4ZZ	188
06NJ0ZZ	188
06NJ4ZZ	188
06PY00Z	142, 676, 888, 1049
06PY02Z	142, 676, 888, 1049
06PY03Z	142, 676, 888, 1049
06PY07Z	139, 1049
06PY0CZ	142, 676, 888, 1049
06PY0DZ	142, 676, 888, 1049
06PY0JZ	139, 1049
06PY0KZ	139, 1049
06PY0YZ	142, 676, 888, 1049
06PY37Z	139, 1049
06PY3CZ	142, 676, 888, 1049
06PY3JZ	139, 1049
06PY3KZ	139, 1049
06PY40Z	142, 676, 888, 1049
06PY42Z	142, 676, 888, 1049
06PY43Z	142, 676, 888, 1049
06PY47Z	139, 1049
06PY4CZ	142, 676, 888, 1049
06PY4DZ	142, 676, 888, 1049
06PY4JZ	139, 1049
06PY4KZ	139, 1049
06Q0*	142
06Q00ZZ	888
06Q03ZZ	888
06Q04ZZ	888
06Q1*	142
06Q10ZZ	888
06Q13ZZ	888
06Q14ZZ	888
06Q2*	143
06Q20ZZ	888
06Q23ZZ	888
06Q24ZZ	888
06Q3*	143
06Q30ZZ	888
06Q33ZZ	888
06Q34ZZ	888
06Q4*	143
06Q40ZZ	888
06Q43ZZ	888
06Q44ZZ	888
06Q5*	143
06Q50ZZ	888
06Q53ZZ	888
06Q54ZZ	888
06Q6*	143
06Q60ZZ	888
06Q63ZZ	888
06Q64ZZ	888
06Q7*	143
06Q70ZZ	888
06Q73ZZ	888
06Q74ZZ	888
06Q8*	143
06Q80ZZ	888
06Q83ZZ	888
06Q84ZZ	888

Code	Page
06Q9*	143
06Q90ZZ	888
06Q93ZZ	888
06Q94ZZ	888
06QB*	143
06QB0ZZ	888
06QB3ZZ	888
06QB4ZZ	888
06QC*	143
06QC0ZZ	888
06QC3ZZ	888
06QC4ZZ	888
06QD*	143
06QD0ZZ	888
06QD3ZZ	888
06QD4ZZ	888
06QF*	143
06QF0ZZ	888
06QF3ZZ	888
06QF4ZZ	888
06QG*	143
06QG0ZZ	888
06QG3ZZ	888
06QG4ZZ	888
06QH*	143
06QH0ZZ	888
06QH3ZZ	888
06QH4ZZ	888
06QJ*	143
06QJ0ZZ	888
06QJ3ZZ	888
06QJ4ZZ	888
06QM*	143
06QM0ZZ	888
06QM3ZZ	888
06QM4ZZ	888
06QN*	143
06QN0ZZ	888
06QN3ZZ	888
06QN4ZZ	888
06QP*	143
06QP0ZZ	888
06QP3ZZ	888
06QP4ZZ	888
06QQ*	143
06QQ0ZZ	888
06QQ3ZZ	888
06QQ4ZZ	888
06QT*	143
06QT0ZZ	888
06QT3ZZ	888
06QT4ZZ	888
06QV*	143
06QV0ZZ	888
06QV3ZZ	888
06QV4ZZ	888
06QY*	139, 188, 206, 489, 514
06QY0ZZ	888
06QY3ZZ	888
06QY4ZZ	889
06R007Z	164
06R00JZ	164
06R00KZ	164
06R047Z	164
06R04JZ	164
06R04KZ	164
06R107Z	164
06R10JZ	164
06R10KZ	164
06R147Z	164
06R14JZ	164
06R14KZ	164
06R207Z	164
06R20JZ	164
06R20KZ	164
06R247Z	164
06R24JZ	164
06R24KZ	164
06R3*	33, 139
06R407Z	164
06R40JZ	164
06R40KZ	164
06R447Z	164
06R44JZ	164
06R44KZ	164
06R507Z	164
06R50JZ	164
06R50KZ	164
06R547Z	164
06R54JZ	164
06R54KZ	164
06R607Z	165

Code	Page
06R60JZ	165
06R60KZ	165
06R647Z	165
06R64JZ	165
06R64KZ	165
06R707Z	165
06R70JZ	165
06R70KZ	165
06R747Z	165
06R74JZ	165
06R74KZ	165
06R807Z	165
06R80JZ	165
06R80KZ	165
06R847Z	165
06R84JZ	165
06R84KZ	165
06R907Z	165
06R90JZ	165
06R90KZ	165
06R947Z	165
06R94JZ	165
06R94KZ	165
06RB07Z	165
06RB0JZ	165
06RB0KZ	165
06RB47Z	165
06RB4JZ	165
06RB4KZ	165
06RC07Z	165
06RC0JZ	165
06RC0KZ	165
06RC47Z	165
06RC4JZ	165
06RC4KZ	165
06RD07Z	165
06RD0JZ	165
06RD0KZ	165
06RD47Z	165
06RD4JZ	165
06RD4KZ	165
06RF07Z	165
06RF0JZ	165
06RF0KZ	165
06RF47Z	165
06RF4JZ	165
06RF4KZ	165
06RG07Z	165
06RG0JZ	165
06RG0KZ	165
06RG47Z	165
06RG4JZ	165
06RG4KZ	165
06RH07Z	165
06RH0JZ	165
06RH0KZ	165
06RH47Z	165
06RH4JZ	165
06RH4KZ	165
06RJ07Z	165
06RJ0JZ	165
06RJ0KZ	165
06RJ47Z	165
06RJ4JZ	165
06RJ4KZ	165
06RM*	143, 676
06RM07Z	889
06RM0JZ	889
06RM0KZ	889
06RM47Z	889
06RM4JZ	889
06RM4KZ	889
06RN*	143, 676
06RN07Z	889
06RN0JZ	889
06RN0KZ	889
06RN47Z	889
06RN4JZ	889
06RN4KZ	889
06RP*	143, 676
06RP07Z	889
06RP0JZ	889
06RP0KZ	889
06RP47Z	889
06RP4JZ	889
06RP4KZ	889
06RQ*	143, 676
06RQ07Z	889
06RQ0JZ	889
06RQ0KZ	889
06RQ47Z	889
06RQ4JZ	889
06RQ4KZ	889
06RT*	143, 676
06RT07Z	889
06RT0JZ	889
06RT0KZ	889
06RT47Z	889
06RT4JZ	889
06RT4KZ	889
06RV*	143, 676
06RV07Z	889
06RV0JZ	889
06RV0KZ	889
06RV47Z	889
06RV4JZ	889
06RV4KZ	889
06RY*	143, 676
06RY07Z	889
06RY0JZ	889
06RY0KZ	889
06RY47Z	889
06RY4JZ	889
06RY4KZ	889
06S0*	489, 514, 676
06S00ZZ	889
06S03ZZ	889
06S04ZZ	889
06S1*	490, 514, 676
06S10ZZ	889
06S13ZZ	889
06S14ZZ	889
06S2*	490, 514, 676
06S20ZZ	889
06S23ZZ	889
06S24ZZ	889
06S3*	490, 514, 676
06S30ZZ	889
06S33ZZ	889
06S34ZZ	889
06S4*	490, 514, 676
06S40ZZ	889
06S43ZZ	889
06S44ZZ	889
06S5*	490, 514, 676
06S50ZZ	889
06S53ZZ	889
06S54ZZ	889
06S6*	490, 514, 676
06S60ZZ	889
06S63ZZ	889
06S64ZZ	889
06S7*	490, 514, 676
06S70ZZ	889
06S73ZZ	889
06S74ZZ	889
06S8*	490, 514, 676
06S80ZZ	889
06S83ZZ	889
06S84ZZ	889
06S9*	505
06SB*	505
06SC*	676
06SC0ZZ	889
06SC3ZZ	889
06SC4ZZ	889
06SD*	676
06SD0ZZ	889
06SD3ZZ	889
06SD4ZZ	889
06SF*	676
06SF0ZZ	889
06SF3ZZ	889
06SF4ZZ	889
06SG*	676
06SG0ZZ	889
06SG3ZZ	889
06SG4ZZ	889
06SH*	676
06SH0ZZ	889
06SH3ZZ	889
06SH4ZZ	889
06SJ*	676
06SJ0ZZ	889
06SJ3ZZ	889
06SJ4ZZ	889
06SM*	676
06SM0ZZ	418, 889
06SM3ZZ	418, 889
06SM4ZZ	418, 889
06SN*	676
06SN0ZZ	418, 889
06SN3ZZ	418, 889
06SN4ZZ	418, 889
06SP*	677
06SP0ZZ	418, 889
06SP3ZZ	418, 889
06SP4ZZ	418, 889
06SQ*	677
06SQ0ZZ	418, 889
06SQ3ZZ	418, 889
06SQ4ZZ	418, 889
06ST*	677
06ST0ZZ	418, 889
06ST3ZZ	418, 889
06ST4ZZ	418, 889
06SV*	677
06SV0ZZ	418, 889
06SV3ZZ	418, 889
06SV4ZZ	418, 889
06SY*	677
06SY0ZZ	418, 889
06SY3ZZ	418, 889
06SY4ZZ	418, 889
06U*	139
06U007Z	677, 889
06U037Z	677, 889
06U03JZ	677
06U047Z	677, 889
06U04JZ	677
06U107Z	677, 889
06U10JZ	677
06U137Z	677, 889
06U13JZ	677
06U147Z	677, 889
06U14JZ	677
06U207Z	677, 889
06U20JZ	677
06U237Z	677, 889
06U23JZ	677
06U247Z	677, 889
06U24JZ	677
06U307Z	677, 889
06U30JZ	677
06U337Z	677, 889
06U33JZ	677
06U347Z	677, 889
06U34JZ	677
06U407Z	677, 889
06U40JZ	677
06U437Z	677, 889
06U43JZ	677
06U447Z	677, 889
06U44JZ	677
06U507Z	677, 889
06U50JZ	677
06U537Z	677, 889
06U53JZ	677
06U547Z	677, 889
06U54JZ	677
06U607Z	677, 889
06U60JZ	677
06U637Z	677, 889
06U63JZ	677
06U647Z	677, 889
06U64JZ	677
06U707Z	677, 889
06U70JZ	677
06U737Z	677, 889
06U73JZ	677
06U747Z	677, 889
06U74JZ	677
06U807Z	677, 889
06U80JZ	677
06U837Z	677, 889
06U83JZ	677
06U847Z	677, 889
06U84JZ	677
06U907Z	514, 677, 889
06U90JZ	514, 677
06U937Z	514, 677, 889
06U93JZ	514, 677
06U947Z	514, 677, 889
06U94JZ	514, 677
06UB07Z	514, 677, 889
06UB0JZ	514, 677
06UB37Z	514, 677, 889
06UB3JZ	514, 677
06UB47Z	514, 677, 889
06UB4JZ	514, 677
06UC07Z	677, 889
06UC0JZ	677
06UC37Z	677, 889
06UC3JZ	677
06UC47Z	677, 889
06UC4JZ	677
06UD07Z	677, 889
06UD0JZ	677
06UD37Z	677, 889
06UD3JZ	677
06UD47Z	677, 889
06UD4JZ	677
06UF07Z	677, 889
06UF37Z	677, 889
06UF3JZ	677
06UF47Z	677, 889
06UF4JZ	677
06UG07Z	677, 889
06UG0JZ	677
06UG3JZ	677
06UG47Z	677, 889
06UG4JZ	677
06UH07Z	677, 889
06UH37Z	677, 889
06UH3JZ	677
06UH47Z	677, 889
06UH4JZ	677
06UJ07Z	677, 889
06UJ0JZ	677
06UJ37Z	677, 889
06UJ3JZ	677
06UJ4JZ	677
06UM07Z	677, 889
06UM0JZ	677
06UM37Z	677, 889
06UM3JZ	677
06UM47Z	677, 889
06UN07Z	677, 889
06UN0JZ	677
06UN37Z	677, 889
06UN3JZ	677
06UN47Z	677, 889
06UN4JZ	677
06UP07Z	677, 889
06UP0JZ	677
06UP37Z	677, 889
06UP3JZ	677
06UP47Z	677, 889
06UP4JZ	677
06UQ07Z	677, 889
06UQ0JZ	677
06UQ37Z	677, 889
06UQ3JZ	677
06UQ47Z	677, 889
06UQ4JZ	677
06UT07Z	677, 889
06UT0JZ	677
06UT37Z	677, 889
06UT3JZ	677
06UT47Z	677, 890
06UT4JZ	677
06UV07Z	677, 890
06UV0JZ	677
06UV37Z	677, 890
06UV3JZ	677
06UV47Z	677, 890
06UV4JZ	677
06UY07Z	677, 890
06UY0JZ	677
06UY37Z	677, 890
06UY3JZ	677
06UY47Z	677, 890
06UY4JZ	677
06V0*	33, 99, 139, 188, 206, 276, 490, 514, 524, 538, 571, 677
06V00CZ	890
06V00DZ	890
06V00ZZ	890
06V03CZ	890
06V03DZ	890
06V03ZZ	890
06V04CZ	890
06V04DZ	890
06V04ZZ	890
06V10CZ	139
06V10DZ	165, 677, 890
06V10ZZ	165, 514, 677
06V13CZ	139
06V13DZ	165, 677, 890
06V13ZZ	165, 514, 677
06V14CZ	139
06V14DZ	165, 677, 890
06V14ZZ	165, 514, 677
06V20CZ	139
06V20DZ	165, 677, 890
06V20ZZ	165, 514, 677
06V23CZ	139
06V23DZ	165, 677, 890
06V23ZZ	165, 514, 677
06V24CZ	139
06V24DZ	165, 677, 890
06V24ZZ	165, 514, 677
06V30CZ	139
06V30DZ	165, 677, 890
06V30ZZ	165, 514, 677
06V33CZ	139
06V33DZ	165, 677, 890
06V33ZZ	165, 514, 677
06V34CZ	139
06V34DZ	165, 677, 890
06V34ZZ	165, 514, 677
06V40CZ	139
06V40DZ	165, 677, 890
06V40ZZ	165, 514, 677
06V43CZ	139
06V43DZ	165, 677, 890
06V43ZZ	165, 514, 677
06V44CZ	139
06V44DZ	165, 677, 890
06V44ZZ	165, 514, 677
06V50CZ	139
06V50DZ	165, 678, 890
06V50ZZ	165, 514, 678
06V53CZ	139
06V53DZ	165, 678, 890
06V53ZZ	165, 514, 678
06V54CZ	139
06V54DZ	165, 678, 890
06V54ZZ	165, 514, 678
06V60CZ	139
06V60DZ	165, 678, 890
06V60ZZ	165, 514, 678
06V63CZ	139
06V63DZ	165, 678, 890
06V63ZZ	165, 514, 678
06V64CZ	139
06V64DZ	165, 678, 890
06V64ZZ	165, 514, 678
06V70CZ	139
06V70DZ	165, 678, 890
06V70ZZ	165, 514, 678
06V73CZ	139
06V73DZ	165, 678, 890
06V73ZZ	165, 514, 678
06V74CZ	139
06V74DZ	165, 678, 890
06V74ZZ	165, 514, 678
06V80CZ	139
06V80DZ	165, 678, 890
06V80ZZ	165, 514, 678
06V83CZ	139
06V83DZ	165, 678, 890
06V83ZZ	165, 514, 678
06V84CZ	139
06V84DZ	165, 678, 890
06V84ZZ	165, 514, 678
06V90CZ	139
06V90DZ	165, 514, 678, 890
06V90ZZ	165, 514, 678
06V93CZ	139
06V93DZ	165, 678, 890
06V93ZZ	165, 514, 678
06V94CZ	139
06V94DZ	165, 514, 678, 890
06V94ZZ	165, 514, 678
06VB0CZ	139
06VB0DZ	165, 514, 678, 890
06VB0ZZ	165, 514, 678
06VB3CZ	139
06VB3DZ	165, 678, 890
06VB3ZZ	165, 514, 678
06VB4CZ	139
06VB4DZ	165, 514, 678, 890
06VB4ZZ	165, 514, 678
06VC0CZ	139
06VC0DZ	165, 678, 890
06VC0ZZ	165, 678
06VC3CZ	139
06VC3DZ	165, 678, 890
06VC3ZZ	165, 678
06VC4CZ	139
06VC4DZ	165, 678, 890
06VC4ZZ	165, 678
06VD0CZ	139
06VD0DZ	165, 678, 890
06VD0ZZ	165, 678
06VD3CZ	139
06VD3DZ	165, 678, 890
06VD3ZZ	165, 678
06VD4CZ	139
06VD4DZ	165, 678, 890
06VD4ZZ	165, 678
06VF0CZ	139
06VF0DZ	165, 678, 890
06VF0ZZ	165, 678
06VF3CZ	139
06VF3DZ	165, 678, 890
06VF3ZZ	165, 678
06VF4CZ	139
06VF4DZ	165, 678, 890
06VF4ZZ	165, 678
06VG0CZ	139
06VG0DZ	165, 678, 890
06VG0ZZ	165, 678
06VG3CZ	139
06VG3DZ	165, 678, 890
06VG3ZZ	165, 678
06VG4CZ	139
06VG4DZ	165, 678, 890
06VG4ZZ	165, 678
06VH0CZ	139
06VH0DZ	165, 678, 890
06VH0ZZ	165, 678
06VH3CZ	139
06VH3DZ	165, 678, 890
06VH3ZZ	165, 678
06VH4CZ	139
06VH4DZ	165, 678, 890
06VH4ZZ	165, 678
06VJ0CZ	139
06VJ0DZ	165, 678, 890
06VJ0ZZ	165, 678
06VJ3CZ	139
06VJ3DZ	165, 678, 890
06VJ3ZZ	165, 678
06VJ4CZ	139
06VJ4DZ	165, 678, 890
06VJ4ZZ	165, 678
06VM0CZ	139
06VM0DZ	165, 678, 890
06VM0ZZ	165, 678
06VM3CZ	139
06VM3DZ	165, 678, 890
06VM3ZZ	165, 678
06VM4CZ	139
06VM4DZ	165, 678, 890
06VM4ZZ	165, 678
06VN0CZ	139
06VN0DZ	165, 678, 890
06VN0ZZ	165, 678
06VN3CZ	139
06VN3DZ	165, 678, 890
06VN3ZZ	165, 678
06VN4CZ	139
06VN4DZ	165, 678, 890
06VN4ZZ	165, 678
06VP0CZ	139
06VP0DZ	166, 678, 890
06VP0ZZ	166, 678
06VP3CZ	139
06VP3DZ	166, 678, 890
06VP3ZZ	166, 678
06VP4CZ	139
06VP4DZ	166, 678, 890
06VP4ZZ	166, 678
06VQ0CZ	139
06VQ0DZ	166, 678, 890
06VQ0ZZ	166, 678
06VQ3CZ	139
06VQ3DZ	166, 678, 890
06VQ3ZZ	166, 678
06VQ4CZ	139
06VQ4DZ	166, 678, 890
06VQ4ZZ	166, 678
06VT0CZ	139
06VT0DZ	166, 678, 890
06VT0ZZ	166, 678
06VT3CZ	139
06VT3DZ	166, 678, 890
06VT3ZZ	166, 678
06VT4CZ	139
06VT4DZ	166, 678, 890
06VT4ZZ	166, 678
06VV0CZ	139
06VV0DZ	166, 678, 890
06VV0ZZ	166, 678
06VV3CZ	139
06VV3DZ	166, 678, 890
06VV3ZZ	166, 678

Code	Page
06VV4CZ	139
06VV4DZ	166, 678, 890
06VV4ZZ	166, 678
06VY0CZ	139
06VY0DZ	166, 678
06VY0ZZ	166, 678
06VY3CZ	139
06VY3DZ	166, 678
06VY3ZZ	166, 678
06VY4CZ	139
06VY4DZ	166, 678
06VY4ZZ	166, 678
06WY00Z	143, 678, 890, 1049
06WY02Z	143, 678, 890, 1049
06WY03Z	143, 678, 890, 1049
06WY07Z	139, 1049
06WY0CZ	143, 678, 890, 1049
06WY0DZ	143, 678, 890, 1049
06WY0JZ	139, 1049
06WY0KZ	139, 1049
06WY0YZ	143, 678, 890, 1049
06WY37Z	139, 1049
06WY3CZ	143, 678, 890, 1049
06WY3JZ	139, 1049
06WY3KZ	139, 1049
06WY40Z	143, 678, 890, 1049
06WY42Z	143, 678, 890, 1049
06WY43Z	143, 678, 890, 1049
06WY47Z	139, 1049
06WY4CZ	143, 678, 890, 1049
06WY4DZ	143, 678, 890, 1049
06WY4JZ	139, 1049
06WY4KZ	139, 1049
0750*	571, 678
07500ZZ	586, 611
07503ZZ	586, 611
07504ZZ	586, 611
0751*	571, 678
07510ZZ	586, 611
07513ZZ	586, 611
07514ZZ	586, 611
0752*	571, 678
07520ZZ	586, 611
07523ZZ	586, 611
07524ZZ	586, 611
0753*	571, 678
07530ZZ	586, 611
07533ZZ	586, 611
07534ZZ	586, 611
0754*	571, 678
07540ZZ	586, 611
07543ZZ	586, 611
07544ZZ	586, 611
0755*	571, 678
07550ZZ	586, 611
07553ZZ	586, 611
07554ZZ	586, 611
0756*	571, 678
07560ZZ	586, 611
07563ZZ	586, 611
07564ZZ	586, 611
0757*	571, 678
07570ZZ	586, 611
07573ZZ	586, 611
07574ZZ	586, 611
0758*	571, 678
07580ZZ	586, 611
07583ZZ	586, 611
07584ZZ	586, 611
0759*	571, 678
07590ZZ	586, 611
07593ZZ	586, 611
07594ZZ	586, 611
075B*	571, 678
075B0ZZ	586, 611
075B3ZZ	586, 611
075B4ZZ	586, 611
075C*	571, 678
075C0ZZ	586, 611
075C3ZZ	586, 611
075C4ZZ	586, 611
075D*	571, 678
075D0ZZ	586, 611
075D3ZZ	586, 611
075D4ZZ	586, 611
075F*	571, 678
075F0ZZ	586, 611
075F3ZZ	586, 611
075F4ZZ	586, 611
075G*	571, 678
075G0ZZ	586, 611
075G3ZZ	586, 611
075G4ZZ	586, 611
075H*	571, 678
075H0ZZ	586, 611
075H3ZZ	586, 611
075H4ZZ	586, 611
075J*	571, 678
075J0ZZ	586, 611
075J3ZZ	586, 611
075J4ZZ	586, 611
075K*	89
075L*	89
075M*	33, 89, 490, 571, 678
075M0ZZ	586, 611, 890
075M3ZZ	586, 611, 890
075M4ZZ	586, 611, 890
075P*	571, 678
075P0ZZ	586, 611, 890
075P3ZZ	586, 611, 890
075P4ZZ	586, 611, 890
079000Z	418, 571, 1049
07900ZX	33, 72, 144, 276, 418, 490, 571, 1049
07900ZZ	418, 571, 1049
07903ZX	33, 72, 144, 276, 418, 490, 571, 1049
079040Z	418, 571, 1049
07904ZX	33, 72, 144, 276, 418, 490, 571, 1049
07904ZZ	418, 571, 1049
079100Z	418, 571, 1049
07910ZX	33, 72, 144, 276, 418, 490, 571, 1049
07910ZZ	418, 571, 1049
07913ZX	33, 72, 144, 276, 418, 490, 571, 1049
079140Z	418, 571, 1049
07914ZX	33, 72, 144, 276, 418, 490, 571, 1049
07914ZZ	418, 571, 1049
079200Z	418, 571, 1049
07920ZX	33, 72, 144, 276, 418, 490, 571, 1049
07920ZZ	418, 571, 1049
07923ZX	33, 72, 144, 276, 418, 490, 571, 1049
079240Z	418, 571, 1049
07924ZX	33, 72, 144, 276, 418, 490, 571, 1049
07924ZZ	418, 571, 1049
079300Z	418, 571, 1049
07930ZX	33, 144, 276, 418, 490, 571, 1049
07930ZZ	418, 571, 1049
07933ZX	33, 144, 276, 418, 490, 571, 1049
079340Z	418, 571, 1049
07934ZX	33, 144, 276, 418, 490, 571, 1049
07934ZZ	418, 571, 1049
079400Z	418, 571, 1049
07940ZX	33, 144, 276, 418, 490, 571, 1049
07940ZZ	418, 571, 1049
07943ZX	33, 144, 276, 418, 490, 571, 1049
079440Z	418, 571, 1049
07944ZX	33, 144, 276, 418, 490, 571, 1049
07944ZZ	418, 571, 1050
079500Z	418, 571, 1050
07950ZX	33, 144, 276, 418, 490, 571, 1050
07950ZZ	418, 571, 1050
07953ZX	33, 144, 276, 418, 490, 571, 1050
079540Z	418, 571, 1050
07954ZX	33, 144, 276, 418, 490, 571, 1050
07954ZZ	418, 571, 1050
079600Z	418, 571, 1050
07960ZX	33, 144, 276, 418, 490, 571, 1050
07960ZZ	418, 571, 1050
07963ZX	33, 144, 276, 418, 490, 571, 1050
079640Z	418, 571, 1050
07964ZX	33, 144, 276, 418, 490, 571, 1050
07964ZZ	418, 571, 1050
079700Z	418, 571, 1050
07970ZX	33, 99, 144, 276, 418, 490, 571, 1050
07970ZZ	418, 571, 1050
07973ZX	33, 99, 144, 276, 418, 490, 571, 1050
079740Z	418, 571, 1050
07974ZX	33, 99, 144, 276, 418, 490, 571, 1050
07974ZZ	418, 571, 1050
079800Z	418, 571, 1050
07980ZX	33, 144, 276, 418, 490, 571, 1050
07980ZZ	418, 571, 1050
07983ZX	33, 144, 276, 418, 490, 571, 1050
079840Z	418, 571, 1050
07984ZX	33, 144, 276, 418, 490, 571, 1050
07984ZZ	418, 571, 1050
079900Z	418, 571, 1050
07990ZX	33, 144, 276, 418, 490, 571, 1050
07990ZZ	418, 571, 1050
07993ZX	33, 144, 276, 418, 490, 571, 1050
079940Z	418, 571, 1050
07994ZX	33, 144, 276, 418, 490, 571, 1050
07994ZZ	418, 571, 1050
079B00Z	418, 571, 1050
079B0ZX	33, 144, 188, 206, 276, 418, 490, 571, 1050
079B0ZZ	418, 571, 1050
079B3ZX	33, 144, 188, 206, 276, 418, 490, 571, 1050
079B40Z	418, 571, 1050
079B4ZX	33, 144, 188, 206, 276, 418, 490, 571, 1050
079B4ZZ	418, 571, 1050
079C00Z	418, 571, 1050
079C0ZX	33, 144, 188, 206, 276, 418, 490, 514, 524, 538, 571, 1050
079C0ZZ	418, 571, 1050
079C3ZX	33, 144, 188, 206, 276, 418, 490, 514, 524, 538, 571, 1050
079C40Z	418, 572, 1050
079C4ZX	33, 144, 188, 206, 276, 418, 490, 514, 524, 538, 572, 1050
079C4ZZ	418, 572, 1050
079D00Z	418, 572, 1050
079D0ZX	33, 144, 188, 206, 276, 418, 490, 514, 572, 1050
079D0ZZ	418, 572, 1050
079D3ZX	33, 144, 188, 206, 276, 418, 490, 514, 572, 1050
079D40Z	418, 572, 1050
079D4ZX	33, 144, 188, 206, 276, 418, 490, 514, 572, 1050
079D4ZZ	418, 572, 1050
079F00Z	418, 572, 1050
079F0ZX	33, 144, 276, 418, 490, 572, 1050
079F0ZZ	418, 572, 1050
079F3ZX	33, 144, 276, 418, 490, 572, 1050
079F40Z	418, 572, 1050
079F4ZX	33, 144, 276, 418, 490, 572, 1050
079F4ZZ	418, 572, 1050
079G00Z	418, 572, 1050
079G0ZX	33, 144, 276, 418, 490, 572, 1050
079G0ZZ	418, 572, 1050
079G3ZX	33, 144, 276, 418, 490, 572, 1050
079G40Z	418, 572, 1050
079G4ZX	33, 144, 276, 418, 490, 572, 1050
079G4ZZ	419, 572, 1050
079H00Z	419, 572, 1050
079H0ZX	33, 144, 276, 419, 490, 524, 538, 572, 1050
079H0ZZ	419, 572, 1050
079H3ZX	33, 144, 276, 419, 490, 524, 538, 572, 1050
079H40Z	419, 572, 1050
079H4ZX	33, 144, 276, 419, 490, 524, 538, 572, 1050
079H4ZZ	419, 572, 1050
079J00Z	419, 572, 1050
079J0ZX	33, 144, 276, 419, 490, 524, 538, 572, 1050
079J0ZZ	419, 572, 1050
079J3ZX	33, 144, 276, 419, 490, 524, 538, 572, 1050
079J40Z	419, 572, 1050
079J4ZX	33, 144, 276, 419, 490, 524, 538, 572, 1050
079J4ZZ	419, 572, 1050
079K00Z	89, 678, 890
079K0ZX	33, 99, 144, 276, 419, 490, 572, 1050
079K0ZZ	89, 678, 890
079K3ZX	33, 99, 144, 276, 419, 490, 572, 1050
079K40Z	89, 678, 890
079K4ZX	34, 99, 144, 276, 419, 490, 572, 1050
079K4ZZ	89, 678, 890
079L00Z	89, 678, 890
079L0ZX	34, 144, 188, 206, 276, 419, 490, 514, 572, 1050
079L0ZZ	89, 678, 890
079L3ZX	34, 144, 188, 206, 276, 419, 490, 514, 572, 1050
079L40Z	89, 678, 890
079L4ZX	34, 144, 188, 206, 276, 419, 490, 514, 572, 1050
079L4ZZ	89, 678, 890
079M00Z	89, 490, 572, 586, 611, 678, 890
079M0ZX	89, 490, 572, 586, 611
079M0ZZ	89, 490, 572, 586, 611, 678, 890
079M3ZX	89, 490, 572, 586, 611
079M40Z	89, 490, 572, 586, 611, 678, 890
079M4ZX	89, 490, 572, 586, 611
079M4ZZ	34, 89, 490, 572, 586, 611, 678, 890
079P00Z	571, 586, 611, 678, 890
079P0ZX	571, 586, 611
079P0ZZ	571, 586, 611, 678, 890
07B0*	572
07B00ZX	34, 72, 144, 276, 419, 490, 1050
07B00ZZ	72, 419, 586, 611, 1050
07B03ZX	34, 72, 144, 276, 419, 490, 1050
07B03ZZ	419, 1050
07B04ZX	34, 72, 144, 276, 419, 490, 1050
07B04ZZ	72, 419, 586, 611, 1050
07B1*	72, 144, 276, 490, 572
07B10ZX	34, 419, 1050
07B10ZZ	99, 188, 419, 1050
07B13ZX	34, 419, 1050
07B13ZZ	99, 188, 419, 1050
07B14ZX	34, 419, 1050
07B14ZZ	99, 188, 419, 1050
07B2*	72, 144, 276, 490, 572
07B20ZX	34, 419, 1050
07B20ZZ	99, 188, 419, 1050
07B23ZX	34, 419, 1050
07B23ZZ	99, 188, 419, 1050
07B24ZX	34, 419, 1050
07B24ZZ	99, 188, 419, 1050
07B3*	572
07B30ZX	34, 144, 276, 419, 490, 1050
07B30ZZ	144, 276, 419, 490, 586, 611, 1050
07B33ZX	34, 144, 276, 419, 490, 1050
07B33ZZ	419, 1050
07B34ZX	34, 144, 276, 419, 490, 1050
07B34ZZ	144, 276, 419, 490, 586, 611, 1050
07B4*	572
07B40ZX	34, 144, 276, 419, 490, 1050
07B40ZZ	144, 276, 419, 490, 586, 611, 1050
07B43ZX	34, 144, 276, 419, 490, 1050
07B43ZZ	419, 1050
07B44ZX	34, 144, 276, 419, 490, 1050
07B44ZZ	144, 276, 419, 490, 586, 611, 1050
07B5*	144, 276, 572
07B50ZX	34, 419, 490, 1050
07B50ZZ	72, 99, 188, 419, 1050
07B53ZX	34, 419, 490, 1050
07B53ZZ	72, 99, 188, 419, 1050
07B54ZX	34, 419, 490, 1050
07B54ZZ	72, 99, 188, 419, 1050
07B6*	144, 276, 572
07B60ZX	34, 419, 490, 1050
07B60ZZ	72, 99, 188, 419, 1050
07B63ZX	34, 419, 490, 1050
07B63ZZ	72, 99, 188, 419, 1050
07B64ZX	34, 419, 490, 1050
07B64ZZ	72, 99, 188, 419, 1050
07B7*	572
07B70ZX	34, 99, 144, 276, 419, 490, 1050
07B70ZZ	99, 144, 276, 419, 490, 586, 611, 1050
07B73ZX	34, 99, 144, 276, 419, 490, 1050
07B73ZZ	419, 1050
07B74ZX	34, 99, 144, 276, 419, 490, 1050
07B74ZZ	99, 144, 276, 419, 490, 586, 611, 1050
07B8*	572
07B80ZX	34, 144, 276, 419, 490, 1050
07B80ZZ	89, 419
07B83ZX	34, 144, 276, 419, 490, 1050
07B83ZZ	89, 419
07B84ZX	34, 144, 276, 419, 490, 1050
07B84ZZ	90, 419
07B9*	572
07B90ZX	34, 144, 276, 419, 490, 1050
07B90ZZ	90, 419
07B93ZX	34, 144, 276, 419, 490, 1050
07B93ZZ	90, 419
07B94ZX	34, 144, 276, 419, 490, 1050
07B94ZZ	90, 419
07BB*	188, 572
07BB0ZX	34, 144, 206, 276, 419, 490, 1050
07BB0ZZ	419, 490, 586, 611, 1050
07BB3ZX	34, 144, 206, 276, 419, 490, 1050
07BB3ZZ	419, 1050
07BB4ZX	34, 144, 206, 276, 419, 490, 1050
07BB4ZZ	419, 490, 586, 611, 1050
07BC*	188, 572
07BC0ZX	34, 144, 206, 276, 419, 490, 514, 524, 538, 1050
07BC0ZZ	419, 1050
07BC3ZX	34, 144, 206, 276, 419, 490, 514, 524, 538, 1050
07BC3ZZ	419, 1050
07BC4ZX	34, 144, 206, 276, 419, 490, 514, 524, 538, 1050
07BC4ZZ	419, 1050
07BD*	188, 572
07BD0ZX	34, 144, 206, 276, 419, 490, 514, 1050
07BD0ZZ	419, 1050
07BD3ZX	34, 144, 206, 276, 419, 490, 514, 1050
07BD3ZZ	419, 1050
07BD4ZX	34, 144, 206, 276, 419, 490, 514, 1050
07BD4ZZ	419, 1050
07BF*	572
07BF0ZX	34, 144, 276, 419, 490, 1050
07BF0ZZ	144, 276, 419, 490, 586, 611, 1050
07BF3ZX	34, 144, 276, 419, 490, 1050
07BF3ZZ	419, 1050
07BF4ZX	34, 144, 276, 419, 490, 1050
07BF4ZZ	144, 276, 419, 490, 586, 611, 1050
07BG*	572
07BG0ZX	34, 144, 276, 419, 490, 1050
07BG0ZZ	144, 276, 419, 490, 586, 611, 1050
07BG3ZX	34, 144, 276, 419, 490, 1050
07BG3ZZ	419, 1050
07BG4ZX	34, 144, 276, 419, 490, 1050
07BG4ZZ	144, 276, 419, 490, 586, 611, 1051
07BH*	144, 276, 524, 538, 572
07BH0ZX	34, 419, 490, 1051
07BH0ZZ	99, 188, 419, 514, 531, 1051
07BH3ZX	34, 419, 490, 1051
07BH3ZZ	99, 188, 419, 514, 1051
07BH4ZX	34, 419, 490, 1051
07BH4ZZ	99, 188, 419, 514, 531, 1051
07BJ*	144, 276, 524, 538, 572

Code	Page	Code	Page	Code	Page	Code	Page	Code	Page	Code	Page
07BJ0ZX	34, 419, 490, 1051	07CG3ZZ	419, 572, 1051	07L44ZZ	573, 587, 612	07LH0ZZ	573, 587, 612	07NG0ZZ	573, 587, 612	07PN3JZ	574, 588, 613, 679
07BJ0ZZ	99, 188, 419, 514, 531, 1051	07CG4ZZ	419, 572, 1051	07L50CZ	573, 587, 612	07LH3CZ	573, 587, 612	07NG3ZZ	574, 587, 613	07PN3KZ	574, 588, 613, 679
07BJ3ZX	34, 419, 490, 1051	07CH0ZZ	420, 572, 1051	07L50DZ	573, 587, 612	07LH3DZ	573, 587, 612	07NG4ZZ	574, 587, 613	07PN40Z	420, 574, 1051
07BJ3ZZ	99, 188, 419, 514, 1051	07CH3ZZ	420, 572, 1051	07L50ZZ	573, 587, 612	07LH4CZ	573, 587, 612	07NH*	679	07PN43Z	420, 574, 1051
07BJ4ZX	34, 419, 490, 1051	07CH4ZZ	420, 572, 1051	07L53CZ	573, 587, 612	07LH4DZ	573, 587, 612	07NH0ZZ	574, 587, 613	07PN47Z	574, 588, 613, 679
07BJ4ZZ	99, 188, 419, 514, 531, 1051	07CJ0ZZ	420, 572, 1051	07L53DZ	573, 587, 612	07LH4ZZ	573, 587, 612	07NH3ZZ	574, 587, 613	07PN4CZ	420, 574, 1051
07BK0ZX	34, 99, 144, 276, 419, 490, 572, 1051	07CJ3ZZ	420, 572, 1051	07L53ZZ	573, 587, 612	07LJ0CZ	573, 587, 612	07NH4ZZ	574, 587, 613	07PN4DZ	420, 574, 1051
		07CJ4ZZ	420, 572, 1051	07L54CZ	573, 587, 612	07LJ0DZ	573, 587, 612	07NJ*	679	07PN4JZ	574, 588, 613, 679
07BK0ZZ	90	07CK0ZZ	420, 572, 1051	07L54DZ	573, 587, 612	07LJ0ZZ	573, 587, 612	07NJ0ZZ	574, 587, 613	07PN4KZ	574, 588, 613, 679
07BK3ZX	34, 99, 144, 276, 419, 490, 572, 1051	07CK3ZZ	420, 572, 1051	07L54ZZ	573, 587, 612	07LJ3CZ	573, 587, 612	07NJ3ZZ	574, 587, 613	07PP00Z	571, 588, 613, 679, 890
		07CK4ZZ	420, 572, 1051	07L60CZ	573, 587, 612	07LJ3DZ	573, 587, 612	07NJ4ZZ	574, 587, 613		
07BK3ZZ	90	07CL0ZZ	420, 572, 1051	07L60DZ	573, 587, 612	07LJ3ZZ	573, 587, 612	07NK*	90	07PP03Z	571, 588, 613, 679, 890
07BK4ZX	34, 99, 144, 276, 419, 490, 572, 1051	07CL3ZZ	420, 572, 1051	07L60ZZ	573, 587, 612	07LJ4CZ	573, 587, 612	07NL*	90	07PP0YZ	571, 588, 613, 679, 890
		07CM*	90, 490, 678	07L63CZ	573, 587, 612	07LJ4DZ	573, 587, 612	07NM*	90, 490, 679		
07BK4ZZ	90	07CM0ZZ	572, 586, 611, 890	07L63DZ	573, 587, 612	07LJ4ZZ	573, 587, 612	07NM0ZZ	574, 587, 613, 890	07PP30Z	571, 588, 613, 679, 890
07BL0ZX	34, 144, 188, 206, 276, 419, 490, 514, 572, 1051	07CM3ZZ	572, 586, 611, 890	07L63ZZ	573, 587, 612	07LK*	90	07NM3ZZ	574, 587, 613, 890	07PP33Z	571, 588, 613, 679, 890
		07CM4ZZ	34, 572, 586, 611, 890	07L64CZ	573, 587, 612	07LK0CZ	890	07NM4ZZ	34, 574, 587, 613, 890	07PP40Z	571, 588, 613, 679, 890
07BL0ZZ	90			07L64DZ	573, 587, 612	07LK0DZ	890				
07BL3ZX	34, 144, 188, 206, 276, 419, 490, 514, 572, 1051	07CP0ZZ	571, 586, 611, 678, 890	07L64ZZ	573, 587, 612	07LK0ZZ	890	07NP*	571, 679	07PP43Z	571, 588, 613, 679, 890
		07HK0YZ	90, 678, 890	07L70CZ	573, 587, 612	07LK3CZ	890	07NP0ZZ	587, 613, 890		
		07HK4YZ	90, 678, 890	07L70DZ	573, 587, 612	07LK3DZ	890	07NP3ZZ	588, 613, 890	07Q0*	679
07BL3ZZ	90	07HL0YZ	90, 678, 890	07L70ZZ	573, 587, 612	07LK3ZZ	890	07NP4ZZ	588, 613, 890	07Q00ZZ	574, 588, 613
07BL4ZX	34, 144, 188, 206, 276, 419, 490, 514, 572, 1051	07HL4YZ	90, 678, 890	07L73CZ	573, 587, 612	07LK4CZ	890	07PK00Z	90	07Q03ZZ	574, 588, 613
		07HM0YZ	90, 490, 572, 586, 611, 678, 890	07L73DZ	573, 587, 612	07LK4DZ	890	07PK03Z	90	07Q04ZZ	574, 588, 613
07BL4ZZ	90			07L73ZZ	573, 587, 612	07LK4ZZ	890	07PK07Z	574, 588, 613, 679	07Q08ZZ	574, 588, 613
07BM*	90, 490	07HM4YZ	90, 490, 572, 586, 611, 678, 890	07L74CZ	573, 587, 612	07LL*	90	07PK0CZ	90	07Q1*	679
07BM0ZX	572, 586, 611			07L74DZ	573, 587, 612	07LL0CZ	890	07PK0DZ	90	07Q10ZZ	574, 588, 613
07BM0ZZ	34, 572, 586, 611, 678, 890	07HN0YZ	420, 572, 1051	07L74ZZ	573, 587, 612	07LL0DZ	890	07PK0JZ	574, 588, 613, 679	07Q13ZZ	574, 588, 613
		07HP0YZ	571, 586, 612, 678, 890	07L80CZ	573, 587, 612	07LL0ZZ	890	07PK0KZ	574, 588, 613, 679	07Q14ZZ	574, 588, 613
07BM3ZX	572, 586, 611			07L80DZ	573, 587, 612	07LL3CZ	890	07PK0YZ	90	07Q18ZZ	574, 588, 613
07BM3ZZ	34, 572, 586, 611, 678, 890	07JK0ZZ	420, 572, 1051	07L80ZZ	573, 587, 612	07LL3DZ	890	07PK30Z	90	07Q2*	679
		07JK4ZZ	420, 572, 1051	07L83CZ	573, 587, 612	07LL3ZZ	890	07PK33Z	90	07Q20ZZ	574, 588, 613
07BM4ZX	572, 586, 611	07JL0ZZ	420, 572, 1051	07L83DZ	573, 587, 612	07LL4CZ	890	07PK37Z	574, 588, 613, 679	07Q23ZZ	574, 588, 613
07BM4ZZ	34, 572, 586, 611, 678, 890	07JL4ZZ	420, 572, 1051	07L83ZZ	573, 587, 612	07LL4DZ	890	07PK3CZ	90	07Q24ZZ	574, 588, 613
		07JM0ZZ	90, 490, 572, 586, 612, 679, 890	07L84CZ	573, 587, 612	07LL4ZZ	890	07PK3DZ	90	07Q28ZZ	574, 588, 613
07BP0ZX	571, 586, 611			07L84DZ	573, 587, 612	07N0*	679	07PK3KZ	574, 588, 613, 679	07Q3*	679
07BP0ZZ	276, 571, 586, 611, 678, 890	07JM4ZZ	34, 90, 490, 572, 586, 612, 679, 890	07L84ZZ	573, 587, 612	07N00ZZ	573, 587, 612	07PK40Z	90	07Q30ZZ	574, 588, 613
				07L90CZ	573, 587, 612	07N03ZZ	573, 587, 612	07PK43Z	90	07Q33ZZ	574, 588, 613
07BP3ZZ	276, 571, 586, 611, 678, 890	07JN0ZZ	188, 420, 572, 1051	07L90DZ	573, 587, 612	07N04ZZ	573, 587, 612	07PK47Z	574, 588, 613, 679	07Q34ZZ	574, 588, 613
		07JN4ZZ	188, 420, 572, 1051	07L93CZ	573, 587, 612	07N1*	679	07PK4CZ	90	07Q4*	679
07BP4ZZ	276, 571, 586, 611, 678, 890			07L93DZ	573, 587, 612	07N10ZZ	573, 587, 612	07PK4DZ	90	07Q40ZZ	574, 588, 613
		07JP0ZZ	99, 144, 188, 202, 420, 490, 514, 521, 538, 572, 586, 612, 679, 890	07L93ZZ	573, 587, 612	07N13ZZ	573, 587, 612	07PK4JZ	574, 588, 613, 679	07Q43ZZ	574, 588, 613
07C00ZZ	419, 572, 1051			07L94CZ	573, 587, 612	07N14ZZ	573, 587, 612	07PK4KZ	574, 588, 613, 679	07Q44ZZ	574, 588, 613
07C03ZZ	419, 572, 1051	07L*	679	07L94DZ	573, 587, 612	07N2*	679	07PL00Z	90	07Q48ZZ	574, 588, 613
07C04ZZ	419, 572, 1051	07L00CZ	572, 586, 612	07L94ZZ	573, 587, 612	07N20ZZ	573, 587, 612	07PL03Z	90	07Q5*	679
07C10ZZ	419, 572, 1051	07L00DZ	572, 586, 612	07LB0CZ	573, 587, 612	07N23ZZ	573, 587, 612	07PL07Z	574, 588, 613, 679	07Q50ZZ	574, 588, 613
07C13ZZ	419, 572, 1051	07L00ZZ	572, 586, 612	07LB0DZ	573, 587, 612	07N24ZZ	573, 587, 612	07PL0CZ	90	07Q53ZZ	574, 588, 613
07C14ZZ	419, 572, 1051	07L03CZ	572, 586, 612	07LB0ZZ	573, 587, 612	07N3*	679	07PL0DZ	90	07Q54ZZ	574, 588, 613
07C20ZZ	419, 572, 1051	07L03DZ	572, 586, 612	07LB3CZ	573, 587, 612	07N30ZZ	573, 587, 612	07PL0JZ	574, 588, 613, 679	07Q58ZZ	574, 588, 613
07C23ZZ	419, 572, 1051	07L03ZZ	572, 586, 612	07LB3DZ	573, 587, 612	07N33ZZ	573, 587, 612	07PL0KZ	574, 588, 613, 679	07Q6*	679
07C24ZZ	419, 572, 1051	07L04CZ	572, 586, 612	07LB3ZZ	573, 587, 612	07N34ZZ	573, 587, 612	07PL0YZ	90	07Q60ZZ	574, 588, 613
07C30ZZ	419, 572, 1051	07L04DZ	572, 586, 612	07LB4CZ	573, 587, 612	07N4*	679	07PL30Z	90	07Q63ZZ	574, 588, 613
07C33ZZ	419, 572, 1051	07L04ZZ	572, 586, 612	07LB4DZ	573, 587, 612	07N40ZZ	573, 587, 612	07PL33Z	90	07Q64ZZ	574, 588, 613
07C34ZZ	419, 572, 1051	07L10CZ	572, 586, 612	07LB4ZZ	573, 587, 612	07N43ZZ	573, 587, 612	07PL37Z	574, 588, 613, 679	07Q68ZZ	574, 588, 613
07C40ZZ	419, 572, 1051	07L10DZ	572, 586, 612	07LC0CZ	573, 587, 612	07N44ZZ	573, 587, 612	07PL3CZ	90	07Q7*	679
07C43ZZ	419, 572, 1051	07L10ZZ	572, 586, 612	07LC0DZ	573, 587, 612	07N5*	679	07PL3DZ	90	07Q70ZZ	574, 588, 613
07C44ZZ	419, 572, 1051	07L13CZ	572, 586, 612	07LC0ZZ	573, 587, 612	07N50ZZ	573, 587, 612	07PL3JZ	574, 588, 613, 679	07Q73ZZ	574, 588, 613
07C50ZZ	419, 572, 1051	07L13DZ	572, 586, 612	07LC3CZ	573, 587, 612	07N53ZZ	573, 587, 612	07PL3KZ	574, 588, 613, 679	07Q74ZZ	574, 588, 613
07C53ZZ	419, 572, 1051	07L13ZZ	572, 586, 612	07LC3DZ	573, 587, 612	07N54ZZ	573, 587, 612	07PL40Z	90	07Q78ZZ	574, 588, 613
07C54ZZ	419, 572, 1051	07L14CZ	572, 586, 612	07LC3ZZ	573, 587, 612	07N6*	679	07PL43Z	90	07Q8*	679
07C60ZZ	419, 572, 1051	07L14DZ	572, 586, 612	07LC4CZ	573, 587, 612	07N60ZZ	573, 587, 613	07PL47Z	574, 588, 613, 679	07Q80ZZ	574, 588, 613
07C63ZZ	419, 572, 1051	07L14ZZ	572, 586, 612	07LC4DZ	573, 587, 612	07N63ZZ	573, 587, 613	07PL4CZ	90	07Q83ZZ	574, 588, 613
07C64ZZ	419, 572, 1051	07L20CZ	572, 586, 612	07LC4ZZ	573, 587, 612	07N64ZZ	573, 587, 613	07PL4JZ	574, 588, 613, 679	07Q84ZZ	574, 588, 613
07C70ZZ	419, 572, 1051	07L20DZ	572, 586, 612	07LD0CZ	573, 587, 612	07N7*	679	07PL4KZ	574, 588, 613, 679	07Q88ZZ	574, 588, 613
07C73ZZ	419, 572, 1051	07L20ZZ	572, 586, 612	07LD0DZ	573, 587, 612	07N70ZZ	573, 587, 613	07PM00Z	90, 490, 574, 588, 613, 679, 890	07Q9*	679
07C74ZZ	419, 572, 1051	07L23CZ	572, 586, 612	07LD0ZZ	573, 587, 612	07N73ZZ	573, 587, 613			07Q90ZZ	574, 588, 613
07C80ZZ	419, 572, 1051	07L23DZ	573, 586, 612	07LD3CZ	573, 587, 612	07N74ZZ	573, 587, 613	07PM03Z	90, 490, 574, 588, 613, 679, 890	07Q93ZZ	574, 588, 613
07C83ZZ	419, 572, 1051	07L23ZZ	573, 586, 612	07LD3DZ	573, 587, 612	07N8*	679			07Q94ZZ	574, 588, 613
07C84ZZ	419, 572, 1051	07L24CZ	573, 586, 612	07LD3ZZ	573, 587, 612	07N80ZZ	573, 587, 613	07PM0YZ	90, 490, 574, 588, 613, 679, 890	07Q98ZZ	574, 588, 613
07C90ZZ	419, 572, 1051	07L24DZ	573, 586, 612	07LD4CZ	573, 587, 612	07N83ZZ	573, 587, 613			07QB*	679
07C93ZZ	419, 572, 1051	07L24ZZ	573, 586, 612	07LD4DZ	573, 587, 612	07N84ZZ	573, 587, 613	07PM30Z	90, 490, 574, 588, 613, 679, 890	07QB0ZZ	574, 588, 613
07C94ZZ	419, 572, 1051	07L30CZ	573, 586, 612	07LD4ZZ	573, 587, 612	07N9*	679			07QB3ZZ	574, 588, 613
07CB0ZZ	419, 572, 1051	07L30DZ	573, 586, 612	07LF0CZ	573, 587, 612	07N90ZZ	573, 587, 613	07PM33Z	90, 490, 574, 588, 613, 679, 890	07QB4ZZ	574, 588, 613
07CB3ZZ	419, 572, 1051	07L30ZZ	573, 586, 612	07LF0DZ	573, 587, 612	07N93ZZ	573, 587, 613			07QB8ZZ	574, 588, 613
07CB4ZZ	419, 572, 1051	07L33CZ	573, 586, 612	07LF0ZZ	573, 587, 612	07N94ZZ	573, 587, 613	07PM40Z	90, 490, 574, 588, 613, 679, 890	07Q9*	679
07CC0ZZ	419, 572, 1051	07L33DZ	573, 586, 612	07LF3CZ	573, 587, 612	07NB*	679			07QC0ZZ	574, 588, 613
07CC3ZZ	419, 572, 1051	07L33ZZ	573, 586, 612	07LF3DZ	573, 587, 612	07NB0ZZ	573, 587, 613	07PM43Z	90, 490, 574, 588, 613, 679, 890	07QC3ZZ	574, 588, 613
07CC4ZZ	419, 572, 1051	07L34CZ	573, 586, 612	07LF3ZZ	573, 587, 612	07NB3ZZ	573, 587, 613			07QC4ZZ	574, 588, 613
07CD3ZZ	419, 572, 1051	07L34DZ	573, 587, 612	07LF4CZ	573, 587, 612	07NB4ZZ	573, 587, 613	07PN00Z	420, 574, 1051	07QC8ZZ	574, 588, 613
07CD4ZZ	419, 572, 1051	07L34ZZ	573, 587, 612	07LF4DZ	573, 587, 612	07NC*	679	07PN03Z	420, 574, 1051	07QD*	679
07CF0ZZ	419, 572, 1051	07L40CZ	573, 587, 612	07LF4ZZ	573, 587, 612	07NC0ZZ	573, 587, 613	07PN07Z	574, 588, 613, 679	07QD0ZZ	574, 588, 613
07CF3ZZ	419, 572, 1051	07L40DZ	573, 587, 612	07LG0CZ	573, 587, 612	07NC3ZZ	573, 587, 613	07PN0CZ	420, 574, 1051	07QD3ZZ	574, 588, 613
07CF4ZZ	419, 572, 1051	07L40ZZ	573, 587, 612	07LG0DZ	573, 587, 612	07NC4ZZ	573, 587, 613	07PN0JZ	574, 588, 613, 679	07QD4ZZ	574, 588, 613
07CG0ZZ	419, 572, 1051	07L43CZ	573, 587, 612	07LG0ZZ	573, 587, 612	07ND*	679	07PN0KZ	574, 588, 613, 679	07QD8ZZ	574, 588, 613
		07L43DZ	573, 587, 612	07LG3CZ	573, 587, 612	07ND0ZZ	573, 587, 613	07PN0YZ	420, 574, 1051	07QF*	679
		07L43ZZ	573, 587, 612	07LG3ZZ	573, 587, 612	07ND3ZZ	573, 587, 613	07PN30Z	420, 574, 1051	07QF0ZZ	574, 588, 613
		07L44CZ	573, 587, 612	07LG4CZ	573, 587, 612	07ND4ZZ	573, 587, 613	07PN33Z	420, 574, 1051	07QF3ZZ	574, 588, 613
		07L44DZ	573, 587, 612	07LG4DZ	573, 587, 612	07NF*	679	07PN37Z	574, 588, 613, 679	07QF4ZZ	574, 588, 613
				07LH0CZ	573, 587, 612	07NF0ZZ	573, 587, 613	07PN3CZ	420, 574, 1051	07QF8ZZ	574, 588, 613
				07LH0DZ	573, 587, 612	07NF3ZZ	573, 587, 613	07PN3DZ	420, 574, 1051		
						07NF4ZZ	573, 587, 613				
						07NG*	679				

Code	Page
07QG*	679
07QG0ZZ	574, 588, 613
07QG3ZZ	574, 588, 613
07QG4ZZ	574, 588, 613
07QG8ZZ	574, 588, 613
07QH*	679
07QH0ZZ	574, 588, 613
07QH3ZZ	574, 588, 613
07QH4ZZ	574, 588, 613
07QH8ZZ	574, 588, 613
07QJ*	679
07QJ0ZZ	574, 588, 613
07QJ3ZZ	574, 588, 613
07QJ4ZZ	574, 588, 613
07QJ8ZZ	574, 588, 613
07QK*	90, 679
07QK0ZZ	890
07QK3ZZ	890
07QK4ZZ	891
07QK8ZZ	891
07QL*	90
07QM*	90, 490, 679
07QM0ZZ	574, 588, 613, 891
07QM3ZZ	574, 588, 613, 891
07QM4ZZ	34, 574, 588, 613, 891
07QP*	571, 679
07QP0ZZ	588, 613, 891
07QP3ZZ	588, 613, 891
07QP4ZZ	588, 613, 891
07S*	679
07SM0ZZ	90, 490, 574, 588, 613, 891
07SP0ZZ	571, 588, 613, 891
07T0*	67, 99, 188, 514, 524, 531
07T00ZZ	420, 574, 588, 613
07T04ZZ	420, 574, 588, 613
07T1*	67, 99, 490
07T10ZZ	420, 574, 588, 613
07T14ZZ	420, 574, 588, 613
07T2*	67, 99, 490
07T20ZZ	420, 574, 588, 613
07T24ZZ	420, 574, 588, 613
07T3*	67, 99, 188, 514, 524, 531
07T30ZZ	420, 574, 588, 613
07T34ZZ	420, 574, 588, 613
07T4*	67, 99, 188, 514, 524, 531
07T40ZZ	420, 574, 588, 613
07T44ZZ	420, 574, 588, 613
07T5*	188, 276
07T50ZZ	420, 450, 451, 452, 574, 588, 613
07T54ZZ	420, 574, 588, 613
07T6*	188, 276
07T60ZZ	420, 450, 451, 452, 574, 588, 613
07T64ZZ	420, 574, 588, 613
07T7*	67, 99, 188, 514, 524, 531
07T70ZZ	420, 450, 451, 452, 574, 588, 613
07T74ZZ	420, 574, 588, 613
07T8*	67, 99, 188, 276, 505, 521, 531
07T80ZZ	420, 450, 451, 452, 453, 574, 588, 613
07T84ZZ	420, 574, 588, 614
07T9*	67, 99, 188, 276, 505, 521, 531
07T90ZZ	420, 450, 451, 452, 453, 574, 588, 614
07T94ZZ	420, 574, 588, 614
07TB*	67, 99, 188, 514, 524, 531
07TB0ZZ	420, 574, 588, 614
07TB4ZZ	420, 574, 588, 614
07TC*	188, 276, 490, 505, 521, 531
07TC0ZZ	420, 574, 588, 614
07TC4ZZ	420, 574, 588, 614
07TD*	90, 188, 276, 490, 505, 521, 531
07TD0ZZ	420, 574, 588, 614
07TD4ZZ	420, 574, 588, 614
07TF*	67, 99, 188, 514, 524, 531
07TF0ZZ	420, 574, 588, 614
07TF4ZZ	420, 574, 588, 614
07TG*	67, 99, 188, 514, 524, 531
07TG0ZZ	420, 574, 588, 614
07TG4ZZ	420, 574, 588, 614
07TH*	188, 277, 505, 521, 531
07TH0ZZ	420, 574, 588, 614
07TH4ZZ	420, 574, 588, 614
07TJ*	188, 277, 505, 521, 531
07TJ0ZZ	420, 574, 588, 614
07TJ4ZZ	420, 574, 588, 614
07TK*	90
07TL*	90
07TM*	34, 90, 490, 679
07TM0ZZ	574, 588, 614, 891
07TM4ZZ	574, 588, 614, 891
07TP*	144, 188, 277, 571, 679
07TP0ZZ	588, 614, 891
07TP4ZZ	588, 614, 891
07U0*	679
07U007Z	574, 588, 614
07U00JZ	574, 588, 614
07U00KZ	574, 588, 614
07U047Z	574, 588, 614
07U04JZ	574, 588, 614
07U04KZ	574, 588, 614
07U1*	679
07U107Z	574, 588, 614
07U10JZ	574, 588, 614
07U10KZ	575, 588, 614
07U147Z	575, 588, 614
07U14JZ	575, 588, 614
07U14KZ	575, 588, 614
07U2*	679
07U207Z	575, 588, 614
07U20JZ	575, 588, 614
07U20KZ	575, 588, 614
07U247Z	575, 588, 614
07U24JZ	575, 588, 614
07U24KZ	575, 589, 614
07U3*	679
07U307Z	575, 589, 614
07U30JZ	575, 589, 614
07U30KZ	575, 589, 614
07U347Z	575, 589, 614
07U34JZ	575, 589, 614
07U34KZ	575, 589, 614
07U4*	679
07U407Z	575, 589, 614
07U40JZ	575, 589, 614
07U40KZ	575, 589, 614
07U447Z	575, 589, 614
07U44JZ	575, 589, 614
07U44KZ	575, 589, 614
07U5*	679
07U507Z	575, 589, 614
07U50JZ	575, 589, 614
07U50KZ	575, 589, 614
07U547Z	575, 589, 614
07U54JZ	575, 589, 614
07U54KZ	575, 589, 614
07U6*	679
07U607Z	575, 589, 614
07U60JZ	575, 589, 614
07U60KZ	575, 589, 614
07U647Z	575, 589, 614
07U64JZ	575, 589, 614
07U64KZ	575, 589, 614
07U7*	679
07U707Z	575, 589, 614
07U70JZ	575, 589, 614
07U70KZ	575, 589, 614
07U747Z	575, 589, 614
07U74JZ	575, 589, 614
07U74KZ	575, 589, 614
07U8*	679
07U807Z	575, 589, 614
07U80JZ	575, 589, 614
07U80KZ	575, 589, 614
07U847Z	575, 589, 614
07U84JZ	575, 589, 614
07U84KZ	575, 589, 614
07U9*	679
07U907Z	575, 589, 614
07U90JZ	575, 589, 614
07U90KZ	575, 589, 614
07U947Z	575, 589, 614
07U94JZ	575, 589, 614
07U94KZ	575, 589, 614
07UB*	679
07UB07Z	575, 589, 614
07UB0JZ	575, 589, 614
07UB0KZ	575, 589, 614
07UB47Z	575, 589, 614
07UB4JZ	575, 589, 614
07UB4KZ	575, 589, 614
07UC*	679
07UC07Z	575, 589, 614
07UC0JZ	575, 589, 614
07UC0KZ	575, 589, 614
07UC47Z	575, 589, 614
07UC4JZ	575, 589, 614
07UC4KZ	575, 589, 614
07UD*	679
07UD07Z	575, 589, 614
07UD0JZ	575, 589, 614
07UD0KZ	575, 589, 614
07UD47Z	575, 589, 614
07UD4JZ	575, 589, 614
07UD4KZ	575, 589, 614
07UF*	679
07UF07Z	575, 589, 614
07UF0JZ	575, 589, 614
07UF0KZ	575, 589, 614
07UF47Z	575, 589, 614
07UF4JZ	575, 589, 614
07UF4KZ	575, 589, 614
07UG*	679
07UG07Z	575, 589, 614
07UG0JZ	575, 589, 614
07UG0KZ	575, 589, 614
07UG47Z	575, 589, 614
07UG4JZ	575, 589, 614
07UG4KZ	575, 589, 614
07UH*	679
07UH07Z	575, 589, 614
07UH0JZ	575, 589, 614
07UH0KZ	575, 589, 614
07UH47Z	575, 589, 614
07UH4JZ	575, 589, 614
07UH4KZ	575, 589, 614
07UJ*	679
07UJ07Z	575, 589, 614
07UJ0JZ	575, 589, 614
07UJ0KZ	575, 589, 614
07UJ47Z	575, 589, 614
07UJ4JZ	575, 589, 614
07UJ4KZ	575, 589, 614
07UK*	90
07UL*	90
07V0*	679
07V00CZ	575, 589, 614
07V00DZ	575, 589, 614
07V00ZZ	575, 589, 614
07V03CZ	575, 589, 614
07V03DZ	575, 589, 614
07V03ZZ	575, 589, 614
07V04CZ	575, 589, 614
07V04DZ	575, 589, 614
07V04ZZ	575, 589, 614
07V1*	679
07V10CZ	575, 589, 614
07V10DZ	575, 589, 614
07V10ZZ	575, 589, 614
07V13CZ	575, 589, 614
07V13DZ	575, 589, 614
07V13ZZ	575, 589, 614
07V14CZ	575, 589, 614
07V14DZ	575, 589, 614
07V14ZZ	575, 589, 614
07V2*	679
07V20CZ	575, 589, 614
07V20DZ	575, 589, 614
07V20ZZ	575, 589, 614
07V23CZ	575, 589, 614
07V23DZ	575, 589, 614
07V23ZZ	575, 589, 614
07V24CZ	575, 589, 614
07V24DZ	575, 589, 614
07V24ZZ	575, 589, 614
07V3*	679
07V30CZ	575, 589, 614
07V30DZ	575, 589, 614
07V30ZZ	575, 589, 614
07V33CZ	575, 589, 614
07V33DZ	575, 589, 614
07V33ZZ	575, 589, 614
07V34CZ	575, 589, 614
07V34DZ	575, 589, 614
07V34ZZ	575, 589, 614
07V4*	679
07V40CZ	575, 589, 614
07V40DZ	575, 589, 614
07V40ZZ	575, 589, 614
07V43CZ	575, 589, 614
07V43DZ	575, 589, 614
07V43ZZ	575, 589, 614
07V44CZ	575, 589, 614
07V44DZ	575, 589, 614
07V44ZZ	575, 589, 614
07V5*	679
07V50CZ	575, 589, 614
07V50DZ	575, 589, 614
07V50ZZ	575, 589, 614
07V53CZ	575, 589, 614
07V53DZ	575, 589, 614
07V53ZZ	575, 589, 614
07V54CZ	575, 589, 615
07V54DZ	575, 589, 615
07V54ZZ	575, 589, 615
07V6*	679
07V60CZ	575, 589, 615
07V60DZ	575, 589, 615
07V60ZZ	575, 589, 615
07V63CZ	575, 589, 615
07V63DZ	575, 589, 615
07V63ZZ	575, 589, 615
07V64CZ	575, 589, 615
07V64DZ	575, 589, 615
07V64ZZ	575, 589, 615
07V7*	679
07V70CZ	575, 589, 615
07V70DZ	575, 589, 615
07V70ZZ	575, 589, 615
07V73CZ	575, 589, 615
07V73DZ	575, 589, 615
07V73ZZ	575, 589, 615
07V74CZ	575, 589, 615
07V74DZ	575, 589, 615
07V74ZZ	575, 589, 615
07V8*	679
07V80CZ	575, 589, 615
07V80DZ	575, 589, 615
07V80ZZ	575, 589, 615
07V83CZ	575, 589, 615
07V83DZ	575, 589, 615
07V83ZZ	575, 589, 615
07V84CZ	575, 589, 615
07V84DZ	575, 589, 615
07V84ZZ	576, 589, 615
07V9*	679
07V90CZ	576, 589, 615
07V90DZ	576, 589, 615
07V90ZZ	576, 589, 615
07V93CZ	576, 589, 615
07V93DZ	576, 589, 615
07V93ZZ	576, 589, 615
07V94CZ	576, 589, 615
07V94DZ	576, 589, 615
07V94ZZ	576, 590, 615
07VB*	679
07VB0CZ	576, 590, 615
07VB0DZ	576, 590, 615
07VB0ZZ	576, 590, 615
07VB3CZ	576, 590, 615
07VB3DZ	576, 590, 615
07VB3ZZ	576, 590, 615
07VB4CZ	576, 590, 615
07VB4DZ	576, 590, 615
07VB4ZZ	576, 590, 615
07VC*	679
07VC0CZ	576, 590, 615
07VC0DZ	576, 590, 615
07VC0ZZ	576, 590, 615
07VC3CZ	576, 590, 615
07VC3DZ	576, 590, 615
07VC3ZZ	576, 590, 615
07VC4CZ	576, 590, 615
07VC4DZ	576, 590, 615
07VC4ZZ	576, 590, 615
07VD*	679
07VD0CZ	576, 590, 615
07VD0DZ	576, 590, 615
07VD0ZZ	576, 590, 615
07VD3CZ	576, 590, 615
07VD3DZ	576, 590, 615
07VD3ZZ	576, 590, 615
07VD4CZ	576, 590, 615
07VD4DZ	576, 590, 615
07VD4ZZ	576, 590, 615
07VF*	679
07VF0CZ	576, 590, 615
07VF0DZ	576, 590, 615
07VF0ZZ	576, 590, 615
07VF3CZ	576, 590, 615
07VF3DZ	576, 590, 615
07VF3ZZ	576, 590, 615
07VF4CZ	576, 590, 615
07VF4DZ	576, 590, 615
07VF4ZZ	576, 590, 615
07VG*	679
07VG0CZ	576, 590, 615
07VG0DZ	576, 590, 615
07VG0ZZ	576, 590, 615
07VG3CZ	576, 590, 615
07VG3DZ	576, 590, 615
07VG3ZZ	576, 590, 615
07VG4CZ	576, 590, 615
07VG4DZ	576, 590, 615
07VG4ZZ	576, 590, 615
07VH*	679
07VH0CZ	576, 590, 615
07VH0DZ	576, 590, 615
07VH0ZZ	576, 590, 615
07VH3CZ	576, 590, 615
07VH3DZ	576, 590, 615
07VH3ZZ	576, 590, 615
07VH4CZ	576, 590, 615
07VH4DZ	576, 590, 615
07VH4ZZ	576, 590, 615
07VJ*	679
07VJ0CZ	576, 590, 615
07VJ0DZ	576, 590, 615
07VJ0ZZ	576, 590, 615
07VJ3CZ	576, 590, 615
07VJ3DZ	576, 590, 615
07VJ3ZZ	576, 590, 615
07VJ4CZ	576, 590, 615
07VJ4DZ	576, 590, 615
07VJ4ZZ	576, 590, 615
07VK*	90
07VL*	90
07WK00Z	90
07WK03Z	90
07WK07Z	576, 590, 615, 679
07WK0CZ	90
07WK0DZ	90
07WK0JZ	576, 590, 615, 679
07WK0KZ	576, 590, 615, 679
07WK0YZ	90
07WK30Z	90
07WK33Z	90
07WK37Z	576, 590, 615, 679
07WK3CZ	90
07WK3DZ	90
07WK3JZ	576, 590, 615, 679
07WK3KZ	576, 590, 615, 679
07WK40Z	90
07WK43Z	90
07WK47Z	576, 590, 615, 679
07WK4CZ	90
07WK4DZ	90
07WK4JZ	576, 590, 615, 679
07WK4KZ	576, 590, 615, 679
07WL00Z	90
07WL03Z	90
07WL07Z	576, 590, 615, 679
07WL0CZ	90
07WL0DZ	90
07WL0JZ	576, 590, 615, 679
07WL0KZ	576, 590, 615, 679
07WL0YZ	90
07WL30Z	90
07WL33Z	90
07WL37Z	576, 590, 615, 679
07WL3CZ	90
07WL3DZ	90
07WL3JZ	576, 590, 615, 679
07WL3KZ	576, 590, 615, 679
07WL40Z	90
07WL43Z	90
07WL47Z	576, 590, 615, 679
07WL4CZ	90
07WL4DZ	90
07WL4JZ	576, 590, 615, 679
07WL4KZ	576, 590, 615, 679
07WM00Z	90, 490, 576, 590, 615, 679, 891
07WM03Z	90, 490, 576, 590, 615, 679, 891
07WM0YZ	90, 490, 576, 590, 615, 679, 891
07WM30Z	90, 490, 576, 590, 615, 679, 891
07WM33Z	90, 490, 576, 590, 615, 679, 891
07WM40Z	90, 490, 576, 590, 615, 679, 891
07WM43Z	90, 490, 576, 590, 615, 679, 891
07WN00Z	420, 576, 1051
07WN03Z	420, 576, 1051
07WN07Z	576, 590, 615, 679
07WN0CZ	420, 576, 1051
07WN0DZ	420, 576, 1051
07WN0JZ	576, 590, 615, 679
07WN0KZ	576, 590, 615, 679
07WN0YZ	420, 576, 1051
07WN30Z	420, 576, 1051
07WN33Z	420, 576, 1051
07WN37Z	576, 590, 615, 679
07WN3CZ	420, 576, 1051
07WN3DZ	420, 576, 1051
07WN3JZ	576, 590, 615, 679
07WN3KZ	576, 590, 615, 679
07WN40Z	420, 576, 1051
07WN43Z	420, 576, 1051
07WN47Z	576, 590, 615, 679
07WN4CZ	420, 576, 1051
07WN4DZ	420, 576, 1051
07WN4JZ	576, 590, 615, 679
07WN4KZ	576, 590, 615, 679
07WP00Z	571, 590, 615, 679, 891
07WP03Z	571, 590, 615, 679, 891
07WP0YZ	571, 590, 615, 679, 891
07WP30Z	571, 590, 615, 679, 891
07WP33Z	571, 590, 615, 679, 891
07WP40Z	571, 590, 615, 679, 891
07WP43Z	571, 590, 615, 679, 891
07YM*	90, 490
07YM0Z0	576, 590, 615
07YM0Z1	576, 590, 615
07YM0Z2	576, 590, 615
07YP*	571
07YP0Z0	590, 615
07YP0Z1	590, 615
07YP0Z2	590, 615
081*	679
0812*	59
08123J4	891
08123K4	891, 1051
08123Z4	490, 891, 1051
0813*	59
08133J4	891
08133K4	891, 1051
08133Z4	490, 891, 1051
081X*	57, 72
081X0J3	891, 1051
081X0K3	891, 1051
081X0Z3	891, 1051
081X3J3	891, 1051
081X3K3	891, 1051
081X3Z3	891, 1051
081Y*	57, 72
081Y0J3	891, 1051
081Y0K3	891, 1051
081Y0Z3	891, 1051
081Y3J3	891, 1051
081Y3K3	891, 1051
081Y3Z3	891, 1051
0850XZZ	57, 1051
0851XZZ	57, 1051
08523ZZ	59, 679, 891, 1051
08533ZZ	59, 679, 891, 1051
08543ZZ	59, 679, 891, 1051
08553ZZ	59, 679, 891, 1051
0856XZZ	57, 679, 891, 1051
0857XZZ	57, 679, 891, 1051
0858XZZ	57, 679, 891, 1051
0859XZZ	57, 679, 891, 1051
085A*	59, 679
085A0ZZ	891, 1051
085A3ZZ	891, 1051
085B*	59, 679
085B0ZZ	891, 1051
085B3ZZ	891, 1051
085C3ZZ	59, 490, 679, 891, 1051
085D3ZZ	59, 490, 680, 891, 1051
085G3ZZ	59, 680, 891, 1051
085H3ZZ	59, 680, 891, 1051
085J3ZZ	59, 1051
085K3ZZ	59, 1051
085L*	57, 680
085L0ZZ	891, 1051

Code	Page
085L3ZZ	891, 1051
085M*	57, 680
085M0ZZ	891, 1051
085M3ZZ	891, 1051
085N*	57, 680
085N0ZZ	420, 891, 1051
085N3ZZ	420, 891, 1051
085NXZZ	420, 891, 1051
085P*	57, 680
085P0ZZ	420, 891, 1051
085P3ZZ	420, 891, 1051
085PXZZ	420, 891, 1051
085Q*	57, 680
085Q0ZZ	420, 891, 1051
085Q3ZZ	420, 891, 1051
085QXZZ	420, 891, 1051
085R*	57, 680
085R0ZZ	420, 891, 1051
085R3ZZ	420, 891, 1051
085RXZZ	420, 891, 1051
085SXZZ	57, 680, 891, 1051
085TXZZ	57, 680, 891, 1051
085V*	57, 680
085V0ZZ	891, 1051
085V3ZZ	891, 1051
085W*	57, 680
085W0ZZ	891, 1051
085W3ZZ	891, 1051
085X*	57, 680
085X0ZZ	891, 1051
085X3ZZ	891, 1051
085X7ZZ	891, 1051
085X8ZZ	891, 1051
085Y*	57, 680
085Y0ZZ	891, 1051
085Y3ZZ	891, 1051
085Y7ZZ	891, 1051
085Y8ZZ	891, 1052
087*	57, 72
087X0DZ	680, 891
087X0DZ	1052
087X0ZZ	1052
087X3DZ	680, 891
087X3DZ	1052
087X3ZZ	1052
087X7DZ	680, 891
087X7DZ	1052
087X7ZZ	1052
087X8DZ	680, 891
087X8DZ	1052
087X8ZZ	1052
087Y0DZ	680, 891
087Y0DZ	1052
087Y0ZZ	1052
087Y3DZ	680, 891
087Y3DZ	1052
087Y3ZZ	1052
087Y7DZ	680, 891
087Y7DZ	1052
087Y7ZZ	1052
087Y8DZ	680, 891
087Y8DZ	1052
087Y8ZZ	1052
0890X0Z	57, 1052
0891X0Z	57, 1052
0892*	59, 680
089230Z	891, 1052
08923ZX	891, 1052
08923ZZ	891, 1052
0893*	59, 680
089330Z	891, 1052
08933ZX	891, 1052
08933ZZ	891, 1052
0894*	59
089430Z	490, 680, 891, 1052
08943ZX	1052
08943ZZ	491, 680, 891, 1052
0895*	59
089530Z	491, 680, 891, 1052
08953ZX	1052
08953ZZ	491, 680, 891, 1052
0896X0Z	57, 680, 891, 1052
0897X0Z	57, 680, 891, 1052
0898X0Z	59, 680, 891, 1052
0899X0Z	59, 680, 891, 1052
089A*	59
089A00Z	680, 891, 1052
089A0ZX	1052
089A0ZZ	680, 891, 1052
089A30Z	680, 891, 1052
089A3ZX	1052
089A3ZZ	680, 891, 1052
089B*	59
089B00Z	680, 891, 1052
089B0ZX	1052
089B0ZZ	680, 891, 1052
089B30Z	680, 891, 1052
089B3ZX	1052
089B3ZZ	680, 891, 1052
089C*	59, 680
089C30Z	891, 1052
089C3ZX	891, 1052
089C3ZZ	891, 1052
089D*	59, 680
089D30Z	891, 1052
089D3ZX	891, 1052
089D3ZZ	891, 1052
089E*	59
089E30Z	680, 891, 1052
089E3ZX	1052
089E3ZZ	680, 891, 1052
089F*	59
089F30Z	680, 891, 1052
089F3ZX	1052
089F3ZZ	680, 891, 1052
089G*	59
089G30Z	680, 891, 1052
089G3ZX	1052
089G3ZZ	680, 891, 1052
089H*	59
089H30Z	680, 891, 1052
089H3ZX	1052
089H3ZZ	680, 891, 1052
089J*	59, 680
089J30Z	891, 1052
089J3ZX	891, 1052
089J3ZZ	891, 1052
089K*	59, 680
089K30Z	891, 1052
089K3ZX	891, 1052
089K3ZZ	891, 1052
089L*	57
089L00Z	680, 891, 1052
089L0ZX	1052
089L0ZZ	680, 891, 1052
089L30Z	680, 891, 1052
089L3ZX	1052
089L3ZZ	680, 891, 1052
089M*	57
089M00Z	680, 891, 1052
089M0ZX	1052
089M0ZZ	680, 891, 1052
089M30Z	680, 891, 1052
089M3ZX	1052
089M3ZZ	680, 891, 1052
089N0ZX	57, 680, 891, 1052
089P0ZX	57, 680, 891, 1052
089Q0ZX	57, 680, 891, 1052
089R0ZX	57, 680, 891, 1052
089SX0Z	57, 1052
089TX0Z	57, 1052
089V*	57
089V00Z	1052
089V0ZX	680, 891, 1052
089V0ZZ	1052
089V30Z	1052
089V3ZX	680, 891, 1052
089V3ZZ	1052
089W*	57
089W00Z	1052
089W0ZX	680, 891, 1052
089W0ZZ	1052
089W30Z	1052
089W3ZX	680, 891, 1052
089W3ZZ	1052
089X*	57
089X00Z	1052
089X0ZX	72, 1052
089X0ZZ	1052
089X30Z	1052
089X3ZX	72, 1052
089X3ZZ	1052
089X70Z	680, 891, 1052
089X7ZX	72, 1052
089X7ZZ	680, 891, 1052
089X80Z	680, 891, 1052
089X8ZX	72, 1052
089X8ZZ	680, 891, 1052
089Y*	57
089Y00Z	1052
089Y0ZX	72, 1052
089Y0ZZ	1052
089Y30Z	1052
089Y3ZX	72, 1052
089Y3ZZ	1052
089Y70Z	680, 891, 1052
089Y7ZX	72, 1052
089Y7ZZ	680, 891, 1052
089Y80Z	680, 891, 1052
089Y8ZX	72, 1052
089Y8ZZ	680, 891, 1052
08B00ZX	56, 1052
08B00ZZ	57, 420, 680, 891, 1052
08B03ZX	56, 1052
08B03ZZ	57, 420, 680, 891, 1052
08B0XZX	56, 1052
08B0XZZ	57, 420, 680, 891, 1052
08B10ZX	56, 1052
08B10ZZ	57, 420, 680, 891, 1052
08B13ZX	56, 1052
08B13ZZ	57, 420, 680, 891, 1052
08B1XZX	56, 1052
08B1XZZ	57, 420, 680, 891, 1052
08B4*	59
08B43ZX	1052
08B43ZZ	680, 891, 1052
08B5*	59
08B53ZX	1052
08B53ZZ	680, 891, 1052
08B6*	680
08B6XZX	59, 892, 1052
08B6XZZ	57, 892, 1052
08B7*	680
08B7XZX	59, 892, 1052
08B7XZZ	57, 892, 1052
08B8*	57, 680
08B8XZX	892, 1052
08B8XZZ	892, 1052
08B9*	57, 680
08B9XZX	892, 1052
08B9XZZ	892, 1052
08BA*	59
08BA0ZX	1052
08BA0ZZ	680, 892, 1052
08BA3ZX	1052
08BA3ZZ	680, 892, 1052
08BB*	59
08BB0ZX	1052
08BB0ZZ	680, 892, 1052
08BB3ZX	1052
08BB3ZZ	680, 892, 1052
08BC*	59, 680
08BC3ZX	892, 1052
08BC3ZZ	892, 1052
08BD*	59, 680
08BD3ZX	892, 1052
08BD3ZZ	892, 1052
08BE*	59
08BE3ZX	1052
08BE3ZZ	1052
08BF*	59
08BF3ZX	1052
08BF3ZZ	1052
08BJ*	59
08BJ3ZX	680, 892, 1052
08BJ3ZZ	1052
08BK*	59
08BK3ZX	680, 892, 1052
08BK3ZZ	1052
08BL*	57
08BL0ZX	1052
08BL0ZZ	1052
08BL3ZX	1052
08BL3ZZ	1052
08BM*	57
08BM0ZX	1052
08BM0ZZ	1053
08BM3ZX	1053
08BM3ZZ	1053
08BN*	57, 680
08BN0ZX	892, 1053
08BN0ZZ	420, 491, 892, 1053
08BN3ZX	892, 1053
08BN3ZZ	420, 491, 892, 1053
08BNXZX	892, 1053
08BNXZZ	420, 491, 892, 1053
08BP*	57, 680
08BP0ZX	892, 1053
08BP0ZZ	420, 491, 892, 1053
08BP3ZX	892, 1053
08BP3ZZ	420, 491, 892, 1053
08BPXZX	892, 1053
08BPXZZ	420, 491, 892, 1053
08BQ*	57, 680
08BQ0ZX	892, 1053
08BQ0ZZ	420, 491, 892, 1053
08BQ3ZX	892, 1053
08BQ3ZZ	420, 491, 892, 1053
08BQXZX	892, 1053
08BQXZZ	420, 491, 892, 1053
08BR*	57, 680
08BR0ZX	892, 1053
08BR0ZZ	420, 491, 892, 1053
08BR3ZX	892, 1053
08BR3ZZ	420, 491, 892, 1053
08BRXZX	892, 1053
08BRXZZ	420, 491, 892, 1053
08BS*	57
08BSXZX	1053
08BSXZZ	680, 892, 1053
08BT*	57
08BTXZX	1053
08BTXZZ	680, 892, 1053
08BV*	57, 680
08BV0ZX	892, 1053
08BV0ZZ	892, 1053
08BV3ZX	892, 1053
08BV3ZZ	892, 1053
08BW*	57, 680
08BW0ZX	892, 1053
08BW0ZZ	892, 1053
08BW3ZX	892, 1053
08BW3ZZ	892, 1053
08BX*	57
08BX0ZX	72, 1053
08BX0ZZ	680, 892, 1053
08BX3ZX	72, 1053
08BX3ZZ	680, 892, 1053
08BX7ZX	72, 1053
08BX7ZZ	680, 892, 1053
08BX8ZX	72, 1053
08BX8ZZ	680, 892, 1053
08BY*	57
08BY0ZX	72, 1053
08BY0ZZ	680, 892, 1053
08BY3ZX	72, 1053
08BY3ZZ	680, 892, 1053
08BY7ZX	72, 1053
08BY7ZZ	680, 892, 1053
08BY8ZX	72, 1053
08BY8ZZ	680, 892, 1053
08C23ZZ	59, 680, 892, 1053
08C33ZZ	59, 680, 892, 1053
08C4*	59, 680
08C43ZZ	892, 1053
08C4XZZ	892, 1053
08C5*	59, 680
08C53ZZ	892, 1053
08C5XZZ	892, 1053
08C8XZZ	57, 680, 892, 1053
08C9XZZ	57, 680, 892, 1053
08CA*	59, 680
08CA0ZZ	892, 1053
08CA3ZZ	892, 1053
08CAXZZ	892, 1053
08CB*	59, 680
08CB0ZZ	892, 1053
08CB3ZZ	892, 1053
08CBXZZ	892, 1053
08CC*	59, 680
08CC3ZZ	892, 1053
08CCXZZ	892, 1053
08CD*	59, 680
08CD3ZZ	892, 1053
08CDXZZ	892, 1053
08CE*	59, 680
08CE3ZZ	892, 1053
08CEXZZ	892, 1053
08CF*	59, 680
08CF3ZZ	892, 1053
08CFXZZ	892, 1053
08CG*	59, 680
08CG3ZZ	892, 1053
08CGXZZ	892, 1053
08CH*	59, 680
08CH3ZZ	892, 1053
08CHXZZ	892, 1053
08CJ*	59, 680
08CJ3ZZ	892, 1053
08CJXZZ	892, 1053
08CK*	59, 680
08CK3ZZ	892, 1053
08CKXZZ	892, 1053
08CL*	680
08CL0ZZ	57, 892, 1053
08CL3ZZ	57, 892, 1053
08CLXZZ	59, 892, 1053
08CM*	680
08CM0ZZ	57, 892, 1053
08CM3ZZ	57, 892, 1053
08CMXZZ	59, 892, 1053
08CV0ZZ	57, 1053
08CV3ZZ	57, 680, 892, 1053
08CVXZZ	59, 680, 892, 1053
08CW0ZZ	57, 1053
08CW3ZZ	57, 680, 892, 1053
08CWXZZ	59, 680, 892, 1053
08CX*	57
08CX0ZZ	1053
08CX3ZZ	1053
08CX7ZZ	1053
08CX8ZZ	1053
08CY*	57
08CY0ZZ	1053
08CY3ZZ	1053
08CY7ZZ	1053
08CY8ZZ	1053
08D8*	57
08D8XZX	1053
08D8XZZ	1053
08D9*	57
08D9XZX	1053
08D9XZZ	1053
08DJ3ZZ	59, 491, 1053
08DK3ZZ	59, 491, 1053
08F43ZZ	59, 680, 892, 1053
08F53ZZ	59, 680, 892, 1053
08H005Z	59, 680, 892
08H00YZ	59, 680, 892
08H031Z	34, 59, 680, 1053
08H033Z	57, 1053
08H0X1Z	34, 59, 680, 1053
08H0X3Z	57, 1053
08H105Z	59, 680, 892
08H10YZ	59, 680, 892
08H131Z	34, 59, 680, 1053
08H133Z	57, 1053
08H1X1Z	34, 59, 680, 1053
08H1X3Z	57, 1053
08JL0ZZ	57, 1053
08JM0ZZ	57, 1053
08L*	57, 680
08LX0CZ	892, 1053
08LX0DZ	892
08LX0DZ	1053
08LX0ZZ	892, 1053
08LX3CZ	892, 1053
08LX3DZ	892
08LX3DZ	1053
08LX3ZZ	892, 1053
08LX7DZ	892
08LX7DZ	1053
08LX7ZZ	892, 1053
08LX8DZ	892
08LX8DZ	1053
08LX8ZZ	892, 1053
08LY0CZ	892, 1053
08LY0DZ	892
08LY0DZ	1053
08LY0ZZ	892, 1053
08LY3CZ	892, 1053
08LY3DZ	892
08LY3DZ	1053
08LY3ZZ	892, 1053
08LY7DZ	892
08LY7DZ	1053
08LY7ZZ	892, 1053
08LY8DZ	892
08LY8DZ	1053
08LY8ZZ	892, 1053
08M*	57, 680
08MNXZZ	420, 892, 1053
08MPXZZ	420, 892, 1053
08MQXZZ	420, 892, 1053
08MRXZZ	420, 892, 1053
08N0XZZ	57, 1053
08N1XZZ	57, 1053
08N23ZZ	59, 680, 892, 1053
08N33ZZ	59, 680, 892, 1053
08N43ZZ	59, 680, 892, 1053
08N53ZZ	59, 680, 892, 1053
08N6XZZ	57, 680, 892, 1053
08N7XZZ	57, 680, 892, 1053
08N8XZZ	59, 680, 892, 1053
08N9XZZ	59, 680, 892, 1053
08NA*	59, 680
08NA0ZZ	892, 1053
08NA3ZZ	892, 1053
08NB*	59, 680
08NB0ZZ	892, 1053
08NB3ZZ	892, 1053
08NC3ZZ	59, 680, 892, 1053
08ND3ZZ	59, 680, 892, 1053
08NE3ZZ	59, 680, 892, 1053
08NF3ZZ	59, 680, 892, 1053
08NG3ZZ	59, 680, 892, 1053
08NH3ZZ	59, 680, 892, 1053
08NJ3ZZ	59, 680, 892, 1053
08NK3ZZ	59, 680, 892, 1053
08NL*	57, 680
08NL0ZZ	892, 1053
08NL3ZZ	892, 1053
08NM*	57, 680
08NM0ZZ	892, 1053
08NM3ZZ	892, 1053
08NN*	34, 57, 680
08NN0ZZ	420, 892, 1053
08NN3ZZ	420, 892, 1054
08NNXZZ	420, 892, 1054
08NP*	34, 57, 680
08NP0ZZ	420, 892, 1054
08NP3ZZ	420, 892, 1054
08NPXZZ	420, 892, 1054
08NQ*	34, 57, 680
08NQ0ZZ	420, 892, 1054
08NQ3ZZ	420, 892, 1054
08NQXZZ	420, 892, 1054
08NR*	34, 57, 680
08NR0ZZ	420, 892, 1054
08NR3ZZ	420, 892, 1054
08NRXZZ	420, 892, 1054
08NSXZZ	57, 1054
08NTXZZ	57, 1054
08NV*	57, 680
08NV0ZZ	892, 1054
08NV3ZZ	892, 1054
08NW*	57, 680
08NW0ZZ	892, 1054
08NW3ZZ	892, 1054
08NX*	57, 73, 680
08NX0ZZ	892, 1054
08NX3ZZ	892, 1054
08NX7ZZ	892, 1054
08NX8ZZ	892, 1054
08NY*	57, 73, 681
08NY0ZZ	893, 1054
08NY3ZZ	893, 1054
08NY7ZZ	893, 1054
08NY8ZZ	893, 1054
08P000Z	57, 1054
08P001Z	57, 1054
08P003Z	56, 681, 893, 1054
08P007Z	57, 1054
08P00CZ	57, 1054
08P00DZ	57, 1054
08P00JZ	56, 681, 893, 1054
08P00KZ	57, 1054
08P00YZ	57, 1054
08P030Z	57, 1054
08P031Z	57, 1054
08P033Z	57, 1054
08P037Z	57, 1054
08P03CZ	57, 1054
08P03DZ	57, 1054
08P03JZ	57, 491, 681, 893, 1054
08P03KZ	57, 1054
08P071Z	57, 1054
08P077Z	57, 1054
08P07CZ	57, 1054
08P07JZ	57, 1054
08P07KZ	57, 1054
08P081Z	57, 1054
08P087Z	57, 1054
08P08CZ	57, 1054
08P08JZ	57, 1054

Numeric Index to Procedures

DRG Expert—Volume II

Code	Page
Ø8PØ8KZ	57, 1054
Ø8PØX7Z	57, 1054
Ø8PØXKZ	57, 1054
Ø8P1ØØZ	57, 1054
Ø8P1Ø1Z	57, 1054
Ø8P1Ø3Z	56, 681, 893, 1054
Ø8P1Ø7Z	57, 1054
Ø8P1ØCZ	57, 1054
Ø8P1ØDZ	57, 1054
Ø8P1ØJZ	56, 681, 893, 1054
Ø8P1ØKZ	57, 1054
Ø8P1ØYZ	57, 1054
Ø8P13ØZ	57, 1054
Ø8P131Z	57, 1054
Ø8P133Z	57, 1054
Ø8P137Z	57, 1054
Ø8P13CZ	57, 1054
Ø8P13DZ	57, 1054
Ø8P13JZ	57, 491, 681, 893, 1054
Ø8P13KZ	57, 1054
Ø8P171Z	57, 1054
Ø8P177Z	57, 1054
Ø8P17CZ	57, 1054
Ø8P17JZ	57, 1054
Ø8P17KZ	57, 1054
Ø8P181Z	57, 1054
Ø8P187Z	57, 1054
Ø8P18CZ	57, 1054
Ø8P18JZ	57, 1054
Ø8P18KZ	57, 1054
Ø8P1X7Z	57, 1054
Ø8P1XKZ	57, 1054
Ø8PJ3JZ	59, 681, 893, 1054
Ø8PK3JZ	59, 681, 893, 1054
Ø8PLØØZ	57, 681, 893, 1054
Ø8PLØ7Z	57, 1054
Ø8PLØJZ	57, 1054
Ø8PLØKZ	57, 1054
Ø8PLØYZ	57, 681, 893, 1054
Ø8PL3ØZ	58, 681, 893, 1054
Ø8PL37Z	58, 1054
Ø8PL3JZ	58, 1054
Ø8PL3KZ	58, 1054
Ø8PMØØZ	58, 681, 893, 1054
Ø8PMØ7Z	58, 1054
Ø8PMØJZ	58, 1054
Ø8PMØKZ	58, 1054
Ø8PMØYZ	58, 681, 893, 1054
Ø8PM3ØZ	58, 681, 893, 1054
Ø8PM37Z	58, 1054
Ø8PM3JZ	58, 1054
Ø8PM3KZ	58, 1054
Ø8QØXZZ	56, 67, 681, 893, 1054
Ø8Q1XZZ	56, 67, 681, 893, 1054
Ø8Q23ZZ	59, 681, 893, 1054
Ø8Q33ZZ	59, 681, 893, 1054
Ø8Q43ZZ	59, 681, 893, 1054
Ø8Q53ZZ	59, 681, 893, 1054
Ø8Q6XZZ	59, 681, 893, 1054
Ø8Q7XZZ	59, 681, 893, 1054
Ø8Q8XZZ	59, 681, 893, 1054
Ø8Q9XZZ	59, 681, 893, 1054
Ø8QA*	59, 681
Ø8QAØZZ	893, 1054
Ø8QA3ZZ	893, 1054
Ø8QB*	59, 681
Ø8QBØZZ	893, 1054
Ø8QB3ZZ	893, 1054
Ø8QC3ZZ	59, 491, 681, 893, 1054
Ø8QD3ZZ	59, 491, 681, 893, 1054
Ø8QE3ZZ	59, 491, 681, 893, 1054
Ø8QF3ZZ	59, 491, 681, 893, 1054
Ø8QG3ZZ	59, 681, 893, 1054
Ø8QH3ZZ	59, 681, 893, 1054
Ø8QJ3ZZ	59, 681, 893, 1054
Ø8QK3ZZ	59, 681, 893, 1054
Ø8QL*	58, 681
Ø8QLØZZ	893, 1054
Ø8QL3ZZ	893, 1054
Ø8QM*	58, 681
Ø8QMØZZ	893, 1054
Ø8QM3ZZ	893, 1054
Ø8QSXZZ	58, 681, 893, 1054
Ø8QTXZZ	58, 681, 893, 1054
Ø8QV*	681
Ø8QVØZZ	58, 893, 1054
Ø8QV3ZZ	58, 893, 1054
Ø8QW*	58, 681
Ø8QWØZZ	893, 1054
Ø8QW3ZZ	893, 1054
Ø8QX*	58, 681
Ø8QXØZZ	893, 1054
Ø8QX3ZZ	893, 1054
Ø8QX7ZZ	420, 893, 1054
Ø8QX8ZZ	420, 893, 1054
Ø8QY*	58, 681
Ø8QYØZZ	893, 1054
Ø8QY3ZZ	893, 1054
Ø8QY7ZZ	420, 893, 1054
Ø8QY8ZZ	420, 893, 1054
Ø8R*	681
Ø8RØØ7Z	56, 893, 1054
Ø8RØØJZ	56, 893, 1054
Ø8RØØKZ	58, 491, 893, 1054
Ø8RØ37Z	56, 893, 1054
Ø8RØ3JZ	58, 491, 893, 1054
Ø8RØ3KZ	56, 893, 1054
Ø8R1Ø7Z	56, 893, 1054
Ø8R1ØJZ	56, 893, 1054
Ø8R1ØKZ	58, 491, 893, 1054
Ø8R137Z	56, 893, 1054
Ø8R13JZ	58, 491, 893, 1054
Ø8R13KZ	56, 893, 1054
Ø8R4*	59, 491
Ø8R437Z	893, 1054
Ø8R43JZ	893, 1054
Ø8R43KZ	893, 1054
Ø8R5*	59, 491
Ø8R537Z	893, 1054
Ø8R53JZ	893, 1054
Ø8R53KZ	893, 1054
Ø8R6*	58
Ø8R6X7Z	893, 1054
Ø8R6XJZ	893, 1054
Ø8R6XKZ	893, 1054
Ø8R7*	58
Ø8R7X7Z	893, 1054
Ø8R7XJZ	893, 1054
Ø8R7XKZ	893, 1054
Ø8R837Z	59, 893, 1054
Ø8R83JZ	59, 893, 1054
Ø8R83KZ	59, 893, 1054
Ø8R8X7Z	58, 893, 1054
Ø8R8XJZ	59, 893, 1054
Ø8R8XKZ	59, 893, 1054
Ø8R937Z	59, 893, 1054
Ø8R93JZ	59, 893, 1055
Ø8R93KZ	59, 893, 1055
Ø8R9X7Z	58, 893, 1055
Ø8R9XJZ	59, 893, 1055
Ø8R9XKZ	59, 893, 1055
Ø8RA*	59
Ø8RAØ7Z	893, 1055
Ø8RAØJZ	893, 1055
Ø8RAØKZ	893, 1055
Ø8RA37Z	893, 1055
Ø8RA3JZ	893, 1055
Ø8RA3KZ	893, 1055
Ø8RB*	59
Ø8RBØ7Z	893, 1055
Ø8RBØJZ	893, 1055
Ø8RBØKZ	893, 1055
Ø8RB37Z	893, 1055
Ø8RB3JZ	893, 1055
Ø8RB3KZ	893, 1055
Ø8RC*	59
Ø8RC37Z	893, 1055
Ø8RC3JZ	893, 1055
Ø8RC3KZ	893, 1055
Ø8RD*	59
Ø8RD37Z	893, 1055
Ø8RD3JZ	893, 1055
Ø8RD3KZ	893, 1055
Ø8RG*	59
Ø8RG37Z	893, 1055
Ø8RG3JZ	893, 1055
Ø8RG3KZ	893, 1055
Ø8RH*	59
Ø8RH37Z	893, 1055
Ø8RH3JZ	893, 1055
Ø8RH3KZ	893, 1055
Ø8RJ*	59
Ø8RJ3ØZ	893, 1055
Ø8RJ37Z	893, 1055
Ø8RJ3JZ	893, 1055
Ø8RJ3KZ	893, 1055
Ø8RK*	59
Ø8RK3ØZ	893, 1055
Ø8RK37Z	893, 1055
Ø8RK3JZ	893, 1055
Ø8RK3KZ	893, 1055
Ø8RN*	58
Ø8RNØ7Z	420, 893, 1055
Ø8RNØJZ	420, 491, 893, 1055
Ø8RNØKZ	420, 893, 1055
Ø8RN37Z	420, 893, 1055
Ø8RN3JZ	420, 491, 893, 1055
Ø8RN3KZ	420, 893, 1055
Ø8RNX7Z	420, 893, 1055
Ø8RNXJZ	420, 491, 893, 1055
Ø8RNXKZ	420, 893, 1055
Ø8RP*	58
Ø8RPØ7Z	420, 893, 1055
Ø8RPØJZ	420, 491, 893, 1055
Ø8RPØKZ	420, 893, 1055
Ø8RP37Z	420, 893, 1055
Ø8RP3JZ	420, 491, 893, 1055
Ø8RP3KZ	420, 893, 1055
Ø8RPX7Z	420, 893, 1055
Ø8RPXJZ	420, 491, 893, 1055
Ø8RPXKZ	420, 893, 1055
Ø8RQ*	58
Ø8RQØ7Z	420, 893, 1055
Ø8RQØJZ	420, 491, 893, 1055
Ø8RQØKZ	420, 893, 1055
Ø8RQ37Z	420, 893, 1055
Ø8RQ3JZ	420, 491, 893, 1055
Ø8RQ3KZ	420, 893, 1055
Ø8RQX7Z	420, 893, 1055
Ø8RQXJZ	420, 491, 893, 1055
Ø8RQXKZ	420, 893, 1055
Ø8RR*	58
Ø8RRØ7Z	420, 893, 1055
Ø8RRØJZ	420, 491, 893, 1055
Ø8RRØKZ	420, 893, 1055
Ø8RR37Z	420, 893, 1055
Ø8RR3JZ	420, 491, 893, 1055
Ø8RR3KZ	420, 893, 1055
Ø8RRX7Z	420, 893, 1055
Ø8RRXJZ	420, 491, 893, 1055
Ø8RRXKZ	420, 893, 1055
Ø8RS*	58
Ø8RSX7Z	893, 1055
Ø8RSXJZ	893, 1055
Ø8RSXKZ	893, 1055
Ø8RT*	58
Ø8RTX7Z	893, 1055
Ø8RTXJZ	893, 1055
Ø8RTXKZ	893, 1055
Ø8RX*	58
Ø8RXØ7Z	420, 893, 1055
Ø8RXØJZ	420, 893, 1055
Ø8RXØKZ	420, 893, 1055
Ø8RX37Z	420, 893, 1055
Ø8RX3JZ	420, 893, 1055
Ø8RX3KZ	420, 893, 1055
Ø8RX77Z	420, 894, 1055
Ø8RX7JZ	420, 894, 1055
Ø8RX7KZ	421, 894, 1055
Ø8RX87Z	421, 894, 1055
Ø8RX8JZ	421, 894, 1055
Ø8RX8KZ	421, 894, 1055
Ø8RY*	58
Ø8RYØ7Z	421, 894, 1055
Ø8RYØJZ	421, 894, 1055
Ø8RYØKZ	421, 894, 1055
Ø8RY37Z	421, 894, 1055
Ø8RY3JZ	421, 894, 1055
Ø8RY3KZ	421, 894, 1055
Ø8RY77Z	421, 894, 1055
Ø8RY7JZ	421, 894, 1055
Ø8RY7KZ	421, 894, 1055
Ø8RY87Z	421, 894, 1055
Ø8RY8JZ	421, 894, 1055
Ø8RY8KZ	421, 894, 1055
Ø8SC3ZZ	59, 681, 894, 1055
Ø8SD3ZZ	59, 681, 894, 1055
Ø8SG3ZZ	59, 681, 894, 1055
Ø8SH3ZZ	59, 681, 894, 1055
Ø8SJ3ZZ	59, 681, 894, 1055
Ø8SK3ZZ	59, 681, 894, 1055
Ø8SL*	58
Ø8SLØZZ	1055
Ø8SL3ZZ	1055
Ø8SM*	58
Ø8SMØZZ	1055
Ø8SM3ZZ	1055
Ø8SN*	34, 58, 491, 681
Ø8SNØZZ	421, 894, 1055
Ø8SN3ZZ	421, 894, 1055
Ø8SNXZZ	421, 894, 1055
Ø8SP*	34, 58, 491, 681
Ø8SPØZZ	421, 894, 1055
Ø8SP3ZZ	421, 894, 1055
Ø8SPXZZ	421, 894, 1055
Ø8SQ*	34, 58, 491, 681
Ø8SQØZZ	421, 894, 1055
Ø8SQ3ZZ	421, 894, 1055
Ø8SQXZZ	421, 894, 1055
Ø8SR*	34, 58, 491, 681
Ø8SRØZZ	421, 894, 1055
Ø8SR3ZZ	421, 894, 1055
Ø8SRXZZ	421, 894, 1055
Ø8SV*	58, 681
Ø8SVØZZ	894, 1055
Ø8SV3ZZ	894, 1055
Ø8SW*	58, 681
Ø8SWØZZ	894, 1055
Ø8SW3ZZ	894, 1055
Ø8SX*	58, 73, 681
Ø8SXØZZ	894, 1055
Ø8SX3ZZ	894, 1055
Ø8SX7ZZ	894, 1055
Ø8SX8ZZ	894, 1055
Ø8SY*	58, 73, 681
Ø8SYØZZ	894, 1055
Ø8SY3ZZ	894, 1055
Ø8SY7ZZ	894, 1055
Ø8SY8ZZ	894, 1055
Ø8TØXZZ	56, 67, 277, 681, 894, 1055
Ø8T1XZZ	56, 67, 277, 681, 894, 1055
Ø8T43ZZ	59, 681, 894, 1055
Ø8T53ZZ	59, 681, 894, 1055
Ø8T8XZZ	59, 681, 894, 1055
Ø8T9XZZ	59, 681, 894, 1055
Ø8TC3ZZ	59, 681, 894, 1055
Ø8TD3ZZ	59, 681, 894, 1055
Ø8TJ3ZZ	59, 681, 894, 1055
Ø8TK3ZZ	59, 681, 894, 1055
Ø8TL*	58
Ø8TLØZZ	1055
Ø8TL3ZZ	1055
Ø8TM*	58
Ø8TMØZZ	1055
Ø8TM3ZZ	1055
Ø8TN*	58, 681
Ø8TNØZZ	421, 894, 1055
Ø8TNXZZ	421, 894, 1055
Ø8TP*	58, 681
Ø8TPØZZ	421, 894, 1055
Ø8TPXZZ	421, 894, 1055
Ø8TQ*	58, 681
Ø8TQØZZ	421, 894, 1055
Ø8TQXZZ	421, 894, 1055
Ø8TR*	58, 681
Ø8TRØZZ	421, 894, 1055
Ø8TRXZZ	421, 894, 1055
Ø8TV*	58, 681
Ø8TVØZZ	894, 1055
Ø8TV3ZZ	894, 1055
Ø8TW*	58, 681
Ø8TWØZZ	894, 1055
Ø8TW3ZZ	894, 1055
Ø8TX*	58, 73, 681
Ø8TXØZZ	894, 1055
Ø8TX3ZZ	894, 1055
Ø8TX7ZZ	894, 1055
Ø8TX8ZZ	894, 1055
Ø8TY*	58, 73, 681
Ø8TYØZZ	894, 1055
Ø8TY3ZZ	894, 1055
Ø8TY7ZZ	894, 1055
Ø8TY8ZZ	894, 1055
Ø8UØ*	58, 491, 681
Ø8UØØ7Z	894, 1055
Ø8UØØJZ	894, 1055
Ø8UØØKZ	894, 1055
Ø8UØ37Z	894, 1056
Ø8UØ3JZ	894, 1056
Ø8UØ3KZ	894, 1056
Ø8U1*	58, 491, 681
Ø8U1Ø7Z	894, 1056
Ø8U1ØJZ	894, 1056
Ø8U1ØKZ	894, 1056
Ø8U137Z	894, 1056
Ø8U13JZ	894, 1056
Ø8U13KZ	894, 1056
Ø8U8*	681
Ø8U8Ø7Z	59, 894, 1056
Ø8U8ØJZ	59, 894, 1056
Ø8U8ØKZ	59, 894, 1056
Ø8U837Z	59, 894, 1056
Ø8U83JZ	59, 894, 1056
Ø8U83KZ	59, 894, 1056
Ø8U8X7Z	58, 894, 1056
Ø8U8XJZ	59, 894, 1056
Ø8U8XKZ	59, 894, 1056
Ø8U9*	681
Ø8U9Ø7Z	59, 894, 1056
Ø8U9ØJZ	59, 894, 1056
Ø8U9ØKZ	59, 894, 1056
Ø8U937Z	59, 894, 1056
Ø8U93JZ	59, 894, 1056
Ø8U93KZ	59, 894, 1056
Ø8U9X7Z	58, 894, 1056
Ø8U9XJZ	59, 894, 1056
Ø8U9XKZ	59, 894, 1056
Ø8UC*	59, 681
Ø8UCØ7Z	894, 1056
Ø8UCØJZ	894, 1056
Ø8UCØKZ	894, 1056
Ø8UC37Z	894, 1056
Ø8UC3JZ	894, 1056
Ø8UC3KZ	894, 1056
Ø8UD*	59, 681
Ø8UDØ7Z	894, 1056
Ø8UDØJZ	894, 1056
Ø8UDØKZ	894, 1056
Ø8UD37Z	894, 1056
Ø8UD3JZ	894, 1056
Ø8UD3KZ	894, 1056
Ø8UE*	59
Ø8UEØ7Z	1056
Ø8UEØJZ	681, 894, 1056
Ø8UEØKZ	1056
Ø8UE37Z	1056
Ø8UE3JZ	681, 894, 1056
Ø8UE3KZ	1056
Ø8UF*	59
Ø8UFØ7Z	1056
Ø8UFØJZ	681, 894, 1056
Ø8UFØKZ	1056
Ø8UF37Z	1056
Ø8UF3JZ	681, 894, 1056
Ø8UF3KZ	1056
Ø8UG*	59, 681
Ø8UGØ7Z	894, 1056
Ø8UGØJZ	894, 1056
Ø8UGØKZ	894, 1056
Ø8UG37Z	894, 1056
Ø8UG3JZ	894, 1056
Ø8UG3KZ	894, 1056
Ø8UH*	59, 681
Ø8UHØ7Z	894, 1056
Ø8UHØJZ	894, 1056
Ø8UHØKZ	894, 1056
Ø8UH37Z	894, 1056
Ø8UH3JZ	894, 1056
Ø8UH3KZ	894, 1056
Ø8UL*	58, 681
Ø8ULØ7Z	894, 1056
Ø8ULØJZ	894, 1056
Ø8ULØKZ	894, 1056
Ø8UL37Z	894, 1056
Ø8UL3JZ	894, 1056
Ø8UL3KZ	894, 1056
Ø8UM*	58, 681
Ø8UMØ7Z	894, 1056
Ø8UMØJZ	894, 1056
Ø8UMØKZ	894, 1056
Ø8UM37Z	894, 1056
Ø8UM3JZ	894, 1056
Ø8UM3KZ	894, 1056
Ø8UN*	58, 681
Ø8UNØ7Z	421, 894, 1056
Ø8UNØJZ	421, 491, 894, 1056
Ø8UNØKZ	421, 894, 1056
Ø8UN37Z	421, 894, 1056
Ø8UN3JZ	421, 491, 894, 1056
Ø8UN3KZ	421, 894, 1056
Ø8UNX7Z	421, 894, 1056
Ø8UNXJZ	421, 491, 894, 1056
Ø8UNXKZ	421, 894, 1056
Ø8UP*	58, 681
Ø8UPØ7Z	421, 894, 1056
Ø8UPØJZ	421, 491, 894, 1056
Ø8UPØKZ	421, 894, 1056
Ø8UP37Z	421, 894, 1056
Ø8UP3JZ	421, 491, 894, 1056
Ø8UP3KZ	421, 894, 1056
Ø8UPX7Z	421, 894, 1056
Ø8UPXJZ	421, 491, 894, 1056
Ø8UPXKZ	421, 894, 1056
Ø8UQ*	58, 681
Ø8UQØ7Z	421, 894, 1056
Ø8UQØJZ	421, 491, 894, 1056
Ø8UQØKZ	421, 894, 1056
Ø8UQ37Z	421, 894, 1056
Ø8UQ3JZ	421, 491, 894, 1056
Ø8UQ3KZ	421, 894, 1056
Ø8UQX7Z	421, 894, 1056
Ø8UQXJZ	421, 491, 894, 1056
Ø8UQXKZ	421, 895, 1056
Ø8UR*	58, 681
Ø8URØ7Z	421, 895, 1056
Ø8URØJZ	421, 491, 895, 1056
Ø8URØKZ	421, 895, 1056
Ø8UR37Z	421, 895, 1056
Ø8UR3JZ	421, 491, 895, 1056
Ø8UR3KZ	421, 895, 1056
Ø8URX7Z	421, 895, 1056
Ø8URXJZ	421, 491, 895, 1056
Ø8URXKZ	421, 895, 1056
Ø8UX*	58, 681
Ø8UXØ7Z	421, 895, 1056
Ø8UXØJZ	421, 895, 1056
Ø8UXØKZ	421, 895, 1056
Ø8UX37Z	421, 895, 1056
Ø8UX3JZ	421, 895, 1056
Ø8UX3KZ	421, 895, 1056
Ø8UX77Z	421, 895, 1056
Ø8UX7JZ	421, 895, 1056
Ø8UX7KZ	421, 895, 1056
Ø8UX87Z	421, 895, 1056
Ø8UX8JZ	421, 895, 1056
Ø8UX8KZ	421, 895, 1056
Ø8UY*	58, 681
Ø8UYØ7Z	421, 895, 1056
Ø8UYØJZ	421, 895, 1056
Ø8UYØKZ	421, 895, 1056
Ø8UY37Z	421, 895, 1056
Ø8UY3JZ	421, 895, 1056
Ø8UY3KZ	421, 895, 1056
Ø8UY77Z	421, 895, 1056
Ø8UY7JZ	421, 895, 1056
Ø8UY7KZ	421, 895, 1056
Ø8UY87Z	421, 895, 1056
Ø8UY8JZ	421, 895, 1056
Ø8UY8KZ	421, 895, 1056
Ø8V*	58, 73, 681
Ø8VXØCZ	895, 1056
Ø8VXØDZ	895
Ø8VXØDZ	1056
Ø8VXØZZ	895, 1056
Ø8VX3CZ	895, 1056
Ø8VX3DZ	895
Ø8VX3DZ	1056
Ø8VX3ZZ	895, 1056
Ø8VX7DZ	895
Ø8VX7DZ	1056
Ø8VX7ZZ	895, 1056
Ø8VX8DZ	895
Ø8VX8DZ	1056
Ø8VX8ZZ	895, 1056
Ø8VYØCZ	895, 1056
Ø8VYØDZ	895
Ø8VYØDZ	1056
Ø8VYØZZ	895, 1056
Ø8VY3CZ	895, 1056
Ø8VY3DZ	895
Ø8VY3DZ	1056
Ø8VY3ZZ	895, 1056
Ø8VY7DZ	895
Ø8VY7DZ	1056

Numeric Index to Procedures

Code	Page
08VY7ZZ	895, 1056
08VY8DZ	895
08VY8DZ	1056
08VY8ZZ	895, 1056
08W000Z	58, 1056
08W003Z	58, 1056
08W007Z	58, 1056
08W00CZ	58, 1056
08W00DZ	58, 1056
08W00JZ	56, 681, 895, 1056
08W00KZ	58, 1056
08W00YZ	58, 1056
08W030Z	58, 1056
08W033Z	58, 1056
08W037Z	58, 1056
08W03CZ	58, 1056
08W03DZ	58, 1056
08W03JZ	56, 681, 895, 1056
08W03KZ	58, 1056
08W070Z	58, 1056
08W073Z	58, 1056
08W077Z	58, 1056
08W07CZ	58, 1056
08W07DZ	58, 1057
08W07JZ	58, 1057
08W07KZ	58, 1057
08W080Z	58, 1057
08W083Z	58, 1057
08W087Z	58, 1057
08W08CZ	58, 1057
08W08DZ	58, 1057
08W08JZ	58, 1057
08W08KZ	58, 1057
08W100Z	58, 1057
08W103Z	58, 1057
08W107Z	58, 1057
08W10CZ	58, 1057
08W10DZ	58, 1057
08W10JZ	56, 681, 895, 1057
08W10KZ	58, 1057
08W10YZ	58, 1057
08W130Z	58, 1057
08W133Z	58, 1057
08W137Z	58, 1057
08W13CZ	58, 1057
08W13DZ	58, 1057
08W13JZ	56, 681, 895, 1057
08W13KZ	58, 1057
08W170Z	58, 1057
08W173Z	58, 1057
08W177Z	58, 1057
08W17CZ	58, 1057
08W17DZ	58, 1057
08W17JZ	58, 1057
08W17KZ	58, 1057
08W180Z	58, 1057
08W183Z	58, 1057
08W187Z	58, 1057
08W18CZ	58, 1057
08W18DZ	58, 1057
08W18JZ	58, 1057
08W18KZ	58, 1057
08WJ3JZ	59, 681, 895, 1057
08WK3JZ	59, 681, 895, 1057
08WL00Z	58, 681, 895, 1057
08WL07Z	58, 1057
08WL0JZ	58, 1057
08WL0KZ	58, 1057
08WL0YZ	58, 681, 895, 1057
08WL30Z	58, 681, 895, 1057
08WL37Z	58, 1057
08WL3JZ	58, 1057
08WL3KZ	58, 1057
08WM00Z	58, 681, 895, 1057
08WM07Z	58, 1057
08WM0JZ	58, 1057
08WM0KZ	58, 1057
08WM0YZ	58, 681, 895, 1057
08WM30Z	58, 681, 895, 1057
08WM37Z	58, 1057
08WM3JZ	58, 1057
08WM3KZ	58, 1057
08X*	58
08XL0ZZ	1057
08XL3ZZ	1057
08XM0ZZ	1057
08XM3ZZ	1057
090*	73, 681
090007Z	421, 895, 1057
09000JZ	421, 895, 1057
09000KZ	421, 895, 1057
09000ZZ	421, 895, 1057
090037Z	421, 895, 1057
09003JZ	421, 895, 1057
09003KZ	421, 895, 1057
09003ZZ	421, 895, 1057
090047Z	421, 895, 1057
09004JZ	421, 895, 1057
09004KZ	421, 895, 1057
09004ZZ	421, 895, 1057
0900X7Z	421, 895, 1057
0900XJZ	421, 895, 1057
0900XKZ	421, 895, 1057
0900XZZ	421, 895, 1057
090107Z	421, 895, 1057
09010JZ	421, 895, 1057
09010KZ	421, 895, 1057
09010ZZ	421, 895, 1057
090137Z	421, 895, 1057
09013JZ	421, 895, 1057
09013KZ	421, 895, 1057
09013ZZ	421, 895, 1057
090147Z	421, 895, 1057
09014JZ	421, 895, 1057
09014KZ	421, 895, 1057
09014ZZ	421, 895, 1057
0901X7Z	421, 895, 1057
0901XJZ	421, 895, 1057
0901XKZ	421, 895, 1057
0901XZZ	421, 895, 1057
090207Z	421, 895, 1057
09020JZ	421, 895, 1057
09020KZ	421, 895, 1057
09020ZZ	421, 895, 1057
090237Z	421, 895, 1057
09023JZ	421, 895, 1057
09023KZ	421, 895, 1057
09023ZZ	421, 895, 1057
090247Z	421, 895, 1057
09024JZ	421, 895, 1057
09024KZ	421, 895, 1057
09024ZZ	421, 895, 1057
0902X7Z	421, 895, 1057
0902XJZ	421, 895, 1057
0902XKZ	421, 895, 1057
0902XZZ	421, 895, 1057
090K*	277
090K07Z	421, 895, 1057
090K0JZ	421, 895, 1057
090K0KZ	421, 895, 1057
090K0ZZ	421, 895, 1057
090K37Z	421, 895, 1057
090K3JZ	421, 895, 1057
090K3KZ	421, 895, 1057
090K3ZZ	421, 895, 1057
090K47Z	421, 895, 1057
090K4JZ	421, 895, 1057
090K4KZ	421, 895, 1057
090K4ZZ	421, 895, 1057
090KX7Z	421, 895, 1057
090KXJZ	421, 895, 1057
090KXKZ	421, 895, 1057
090KXZZ	421, 895, 1057
091*	73
09550Z	73
09558ZZ	73
09560Z	73
09568ZZ	73
0957*	73
0958*	73
095090Z	73
09598ZZ	73, 1057
095A0Z	73, 1057
095A8Z	73, 1057
095B*	82
095C*	82
095D0ZZ	73
095D8ZZ	73
095E0Z	73
095E8ZZ	73
095L*	73
095N*	73, 174
095P*	82
095Q*	82
095R*	82
095S*	82
095T*	82
095U*	82
095U0ZZ	1057
095U3ZZ	1057
095U4ZZ	1057
095U8ZZ	1057
095V*	82
095V0ZZ	1057
095V3ZZ	1057
095V4ZZ	1057
095V8ZZ	1057
095W*	82
095X*	82
098*	73
098L*	681
098L0ZZ	895, 1057
098L3ZZ	895, 1057
098L4ZZ	895, 1057
098L7ZZ	895, 1057
098L8ZZ	895, 1057
099500Z	73, 1057
099508Z	73, 1057
099570Z	73, 1057
099600Z	73, 1057
09960ZX	73, 1057
099670Z	73, 1057
099700Z	73, 1057
09970ZX	73, 1057
09970ZZ	73, 1057
099730Z	73, 1057
09973ZX	73, 1057
099740Z	73, 1057
09974ZX	73, 1057
099770Z	73, 1057
099780Z	73, 1057
099800Z	73, 1057
09980ZX	73, 1057
099830Z	73, 1057
09983ZX	73, 1057
099840Z	73, 1057
09984ZX	73, 1057
099870Z	73, 1057
099880Z	73, 1057
099900Z	73
09990ZX	73, 1057
09990ZZ	73
099A00Z	73
099A0ZX	73, 1057
099A0ZZ	73
099B00Z	82, 1057
099B0ZX	73, 1057
099B0ZZ	82, 1057
099B3ZX	73, 1057
099B40Z	82, 1057
099B4ZX	73, 1057
099B4ZZ	82, 1058
099C00Z	82, 1058
099C0ZX	73, 1058
099C0ZZ	82, 1058
099C3ZX	73, 1058
099C40Z	82, 1058
099C4ZX	73, 1058
099C4ZZ	82, 1058
099D00Z	73
099D0ZX	73, 1058
099D0ZZ	73
099E00Z	73
099E0ZX	73, 1058
099E0ZZ	73
099F0ZX	73, 1058
099F3ZX	73, 1058
099F4ZX	73, 1058
099G0ZX	73, 1058
099G3ZX	73, 1058
099G4ZZ	73, 1058
099N00Z	73, 681, 895
099N0ZZ	73, 681, 895
099N40Z	73, 681, 895
099N4ZZ	73, 681, 895
099N70Z	73, 681, 895
099N7ZZ	73, 681, 895
099N80Z	73, 681, 895
099N8ZZ	73, 681, 895
099P00Z	82
099P0ZX	82
099P0ZZ	82
099Q00Z	82
099Q0ZX	82
099Q0ZZ	82
099R00Z	82
099R0ZX	82
099R0ZZ	82
099S00Z	82
099S0ZX	82
099S0ZZ	82
099T00Z	82
099T0ZX	82
099T0ZZ	82
099U00Z	82
099U0ZX	82
099U0ZZ	82
099V00Z	82
099V0ZX	82
099V0ZZ	82
099W00Z	82
099W0ZX	82
099W0ZZ	82
099X00Z	82
099X0ZX	82
099X0ZZ	82
09B5*	73
09B50ZX	1058
09B50ZZ	1058
09B58ZX	1058
09B58ZZ	1058
09B6*	73
09B60ZX	1058
09B60ZZ	1058
09B68ZX	1058
09B68ZZ	1058
09B7*	73
09B70ZX	1058
09B70ZZ	1058
09B73ZX	1058
09B73ZZ	1058
09B74ZX	1058
09B74ZZ	1058
09B77ZX	1058
09B77ZZ	1058
09B78ZX	1058
09B78ZZ	1058
09B8*	73
09B80ZX	1058
09B80ZZ	1058
09B83ZX	1058
09B83ZZ	1058
09B84ZX	1058
09B84ZZ	1058
09B87ZX	1058
09B87ZZ	1058
09B88ZX	1058
09B88ZZ	1058
09B9*	73
09B90ZX	1058
09B90ZZ	1058
09B98ZX	1058
09B98ZZ	1058
09BA*	73
09BA0ZX	1058
09BA0ZZ	1058
09BA8ZX	1058
09BA8ZZ	1058
09BB0ZX	73, 1058
09BB0ZZ	82
09BB3ZX	73, 1058
09BB3ZZ	82
09BB4ZX	73, 1058
09BB4ZZ	82
09BB8ZX	73, 1058
09BB8ZZ	82
09BC0ZX	73, 1058
09BC0ZZ	82
09BC3ZX	73, 1058
09BC3ZZ	82
09BC4ZX	73, 1058
09BC4ZZ	82
09BC8ZX	73, 1058
09BC8ZZ	82
09BD*	73
09BD0ZX	1058
09BD8ZX	1058
09BE*	73
09BE0ZX	1058
09BE8ZX	1058
09BL0ZZ	73, 681, 895, 1058
09BL3ZZ	73, 681, 895, 1058
09BL4ZZ	73, 681, 895, 1058
09BL7ZZ	73, 681, 895, 1058
09BL8ZZ	73, 681, 895, 1058
09BM0ZZ	73, 681, 895, 1058
09BM3ZZ	73, 681, 895, 1058
09BM4ZZ	73, 681, 895, 1058
09BM8ZZ	73, 681, 895, 1058
09BN0ZZ	73, 174
09BN3ZZ	73, 174
09BN4ZZ	73, 174
09BN7ZZ	73, 174
09BN8ZZ	73, 174
09BP0ZX	82
09BP0ZZ	82
09BP3ZZ	82
09BP4ZZ	82
09BP8ZZ	82
09BQ0ZX	82
09BQ0ZZ	82, 277
09BQ3ZZ	82, 277
09BQ4ZZ	82, 277
09BQ8ZZ	82, 277
09BR0ZX	82
09BR0ZZ	82, 277
09BR3ZZ	82, 277
09BR4ZZ	82, 277
09BR8ZZ	82, 277
09BS0ZX	82
09BS0ZZ	82
09BS3ZZ	82
09BS4ZZ	82
09BS8ZZ	82
09BT0ZX	82
09BT0ZZ	82
09BT3ZZ	82
09BT4ZZ	82
09BT8ZZ	82
09BU0ZX	82
09BU0ZZ	82, 1058
09BU3ZZ	82, 1058
09BU8ZZ	82, 1058
09BV0ZX	82
09BV0ZZ	82, 1058
09BV3ZZ	82, 1058
09BV4ZZ	82, 1058
09BV8ZZ	82, 1058
09BW0ZX	82
09BW0ZZ	82
09BW3ZZ	82
09BW8ZZ	82
09BX0ZX	82
09BX0ZZ	82
09BX3ZZ	82
09BX4ZZ	82
09BX8ZZ	82
09C50ZZ	73, 1058
09C58ZZ	73, 1058
09C60ZZ	73, 1058
09C68ZZ	73, 1058
09C90ZZ	73
09C98ZZ	73
09CA0ZZ	73
09CA8ZZ	73
09CB*	82
09CB0ZZ	1058
09CB3ZZ	1058
09CB4ZZ	1058
09CB8ZZ	1058
09CC*	82
09CC0ZZ	1058
09CC3ZZ	1058
09CC4ZZ	1058
09CC8ZZ	1058
09CD0ZZ	73
09CD8ZZ	73
09CE0ZZ	73
09CE8ZZ	73
09CN*	73, 681
09CN0ZZ	895
09CN3ZZ	895
09CN4ZZ	895
09CN7ZZ	895
09CN8ZZ	895
09CP*	82
09CQ*	82
09CR*	82
09CS*	82
09CT*	82
09CU*	82
09CV*	82
09CW*	82
09CX*	82
09D7*	73
09D8*	73
09D90ZZ	73, 1058
09DA0ZZ	73, 1058
09DB*	82
09DC*	82
09DL*	73, 681
09DL0ZZ	895, 1058
09DL3ZZ	895, 1058
09DL4ZZ	895, 1058
09DL7ZZ	895, 1058
09DL8ZZ	895, 1058
09DM*	73, 681
09DM0ZZ	421, 895, 1058
09DM3ZZ	421, 895, 1058
09DM4ZZ	421, 895, 1058
09DP*	82
09DQ*	82
09DR*	82
09DS*	82
09DT*	82
09DU*	82
09DU0ZZ	1058
09DU3ZZ	1058
09DU4ZZ	1058
09DV*	82
09DV0ZZ	1058
09DV3ZZ	1058
09DV4ZZ	1058
09DW*	82
09DX*	82
09HD04Z	73
09HD05Z	67
09HD06Z	67
09HD0SZ	67
09HD34Z	73
09HD35Z	67
09HD3SZ	67
09HD44Z	73
09HD45Z	67
09HD46Z	67
09HD4SZ	67
09HE04Z	73
09HE05Z	67
09HE06Z	67
09HE0SZ	67
09HE34Z	67
09HE35Z	67
09HE36Z	67
09HE3SZ	67
09HE44Z	67
09HE45Z	67
09HE46Z	67
09HE4SZ	67
09HH0YZ	67
09HJ0YZ	67
09HY0YZ	82
09J70ZZ	73, 1058
09J74ZZ	73, 1058
09J80ZZ	73, 1058
09J84ZZ	73, 1058
09JD0ZZ	73, 1058
09JD4ZZ	73, 1058
09JE0ZZ	73, 1058
09JE4ZZ	73, 1058
09M*	73, 681
09M0XZZ	895, 1058
09M1XZZ	895, 1058
09MKXZZ	277, 421, 895, 1058
09N00ZZ	73, 421, 681, 895, 1058
09N03ZZ	73, 421, 681, 895, 1058
09N04ZZ	73, 421, 681, 895, 1058
09N10ZZ	73, 421, 681, 895, 1058
09N13ZZ	73, 421, 681, 895, 1058
09N14ZZ	73, 421, 681, 895, 1058
09N30ZZ	73, 421, 681, 896, 1058
09N33ZZ	73, 421, 681, 896, 1058
09N34ZZ	73, 421, 681, 896, 1058
09N37ZZ	73, 421, 681, 896, 1058
09N38ZZ	73, 422, 681, 896, 1058
09N40ZZ	73, 422, 681, 896, 1058
09N43ZZ	73, 422, 681, 896, 1058
09N44ZZ	73, 422, 681, 896, 1058
09N47ZZ	73, 422, 681, 896, 1058
09N48ZZ	73, 422, 681, 896, 1058
09N50ZZ	73, 1058
09N58ZZ	73, 1058
09N60ZZ	73, 1058
09N68ZZ	73, 1058
09N7*	73
09N8*	73
09N90ZZ	73
09N98ZZ	73
09NA0ZZ	73
09NA8ZZ	73

Numeric Index to Procedures

Code	Page
09NB*	73
09NC*	73
09ND0ZZ	73
09ND8ZZ	73
09NE0ZZ	74
09NE8ZZ	74
09NN*	74
09NP*	82
09NQ*	82
09NR*	82
09NS*	82
09NT*	83
09NU*	83
09NV*	83
09NW*	83
09NX*	83
09PD*	74
09PE*	74
09PH00Z	74
09PH07Z	74
09PH0DZ	74
09PH0JZ	74
09PH0KZ	74
09PH0YZ	74
09PH37Z	74
09PH3DZ	74
09PH47Z	74
09PH4DZ	74
09PH77Z	74
09PH7JZ	74
09PH7KZ	74
09PH87Z	74
09PH8JZ	74
09PH8KZ	74
09PJ00Z	74
09PJ07Z	74
09PJ0DZ	74
09PJ0JZ	74
09PJ0KZ	74
09PJ0YZ	74
09PJ37Z	74
09PJ3DZ	74
09PJ47Z	74
09PJ4DZ	74
09PJ77Z	74
09PJ7JZ	74
09PJ7KZ	74
09PJ87Z	74
09PJ8JZ	74
09PJ8KZ	74
09PY00Z	83
09PY0YZ	83
09PY30Z	83
09PY40Z	83
09Q00ZZ	74, 422, 681, 896, 1058
09Q03ZZ	74, 422, 681, 896, 1058
09Q04ZZ	74, 422, 681, 896, 1058
09Q10ZZ	74, 422, 681, 896, 1058
09Q13ZZ	74, 422, 681, 896, 1058
09Q14ZZ	74, 422, 681, 896, 1058
09Q20ZZ	74, 422, 681, 896, 1058
09Q23ZZ	74, 422, 681, 896, 1058
09Q24ZZ	74, 422, 681, 896, 1058
09Q30ZZ	74, 422, 681, 896, 1058
09Q33ZZ	74, 422, 681, 896, 1058
09Q34ZZ	74, 422, 681, 896, 1058
09Q37ZZ	74, 422, 681, 896, 1058
09Q38ZZ	74, 422, 681, 896, 1058
09Q40ZZ	74, 422, 681, 896, 1058
09Q43ZZ	74, 422, 681, 896, 1058
09Q44ZZ	74, 422, 681, 896, 1058
09Q47ZZ	74, 422, 681, 896, 1058
09Q48ZZ	74, 422, 681, 896, 1058
09Q50ZZ	74, 1058
09Q58ZZ	74, 1058
09Q60ZZ	74, 1058
09Q68ZZ	74, 1058
09Q7*	74
09Q70ZZ	1058
09Q73ZZ	1058
09Q74ZZ	1058
09Q77ZZ	1058
09Q78ZZ	1058
09Q8*	74
09Q80ZZ	1058
09Q83ZZ	1058
09Q84ZZ	1058
09Q87ZZ	1058
09Q88ZZ	1058
09Q90ZZ	74
09Q98ZZ	74
09QA0ZZ	74
09QA8ZZ	74
09QB*	83
09QC*	83
09QD0ZZ	74
09QD8ZZ	74
09QE0ZZ	74
09QE8ZZ	74
09QK0ZZ	74, 277, 422, 681, 896, 1058
09QK3ZZ	74, 277, 422, 681, 896, 1059
09QK4ZZ	74, 277, 422, 681, 896, 1059
09QK8ZZ	74, 277, 422, 681, 896, 1059
09QL*	74, 681
09QL0ZZ	422, 896, 1059
09QL3ZZ	422, 896, 1059
09QL4ZZ	422, 896, 1059
09QL7ZZ	422, 896, 1059
09QL8ZZ	422, 896, 1059
09QM*	74, 277, 681
09QM0ZZ	422, 896, 1059
09QM3ZZ	422, 896, 1059
09QM4ZZ	422, 896, 1059
09QM8ZZ	422, 896, 1059
09QN*	34, 74, 681
09QN0ZZ	896
09QN3ZZ	896
09QN4ZZ	896
09QN7ZZ	896
09QN8ZZ	896
09QP*	83
09QQ*	83
09QR*	83
09QS*	83
09QT*	83
09QU*	83
09QV*	83
09QW*	83
09QX*	83
09R*	74
09R0*	682
09R007Z	422, 896, 1059
09R00JZ	422, 896, 1059
09R00KZ	422, 896, 1059
09R0X7Z	422, 896, 1059
09R0XJZ	422, 896, 1059
09R0XKZ	422, 896, 1059
09R1*	682
09R107Z	422, 896, 1059
09R10JZ	422, 896, 1059
09R10KZ	422, 896, 1059
09R1X7Z	422, 896, 1059
09R1XJZ	422, 896, 1059
09R1XKZ	422, 896, 1059
09R2*	682
09R207Z	422, 896, 1059
09R20JZ	422, 896, 1059
09R20KZ	422, 896, 1059
09R2X7Z	422, 896, 1059
09R2XJZ	422, 896, 1059
09R2XKZ	422, 896, 1059
09R507Z	1059
09R50JZ	1059
09R50KZ	1059
09R607Z	1059
09R60JZ	1059
09R60KZ	1059
09R907Z	1059
09R90JZ	1059
09R90KZ	1059
09RA07Z	1059
09RA0JZ	1059
09RA0KZ	1059
09RK*	277, 682
09RK07Z	144, 422, 896, 1059
09RK0JZ	422, 896, 1059
09RK0KZ	422, 896, 1059
09RKX7Z	422, 896, 1059
09RKXJZ	422, 896, 1059
09RKXKZ	422, 896, 1059
09RL*	682
09RL07Z	422, 896, 1059
09RL0JZ	422, 896, 1059
09RL0KZ	422, 896, 1059
09RL37Z	422, 896, 1059
09RL3JZ	422, 896, 1059
09RL3KZ	422, 896, 1059
09RL47Z	422, 896, 1059
09RL4JZ	422, 896, 1059
09RL4KZ	422, 896, 1059
09RL77Z	422, 896, 1059
09RL7JZ	422, 896, 1059
09RL7KZ	422, 896, 1059
09RL87Z	422, 896, 1059
09RL8JZ	422, 896, 1059
09RL8KZ	422, 896, 1059
09RM*	277, 682
09RM07Z	422, 896, 1059
09RM0JZ	422, 896, 1059
09RM0KZ	422, 896, 1059
09RM37Z	422, 896, 1059
09RM3JZ	422, 896, 1059
09RM3KZ	422, 896, 1059
09RM47Z	422, 896, 1059
09RM4JZ	422, 896, 1059
09RM4KZ	422, 896, 1059
09RN*	34, 682
09RN07Z	896, 1059
09RN0JZ	896, 1059
09RN0KZ	896, 1059
09RN77Z	896, 1059
09RN7JZ	896, 1059
09RN7KZ	896, 1059
09RN87Z	896, 1059
09RN8JZ	896, 1059
09RN8KZ	896, 1059
09S0*	74, 682
09S00ZZ	422, 896, 1059
09S04ZZ	422, 896, 1059
09S0XZZ	422, 896, 1059
09S1*	74, 682
09S10ZZ	422, 896, 1059
09S14ZZ	422, 896, 1059
09S1XZZ	422, 896, 1059
09S2*	74, 682
09S20ZZ	422, 896, 1059
09S24ZZ	422, 896, 1059
09S2XZZ	422, 896, 1059
09S7*	74
09S70ZZ	1059
09S74ZZ	1059
09S77ZZ	1059
09S78ZZ	1059
09S8*	74
09S80ZZ	1059
09S84ZZ	1059
09S87ZZ	1059
09S88ZZ	1059
09S9*	74
09SA*	74
09SK*	74, 277, 682
09SK0ZZ	422, 896, 1059
09SK4ZZ	422, 896, 1059
09SKXZZ	422, 896, 1059
09SL*	74, 682
09SL0ZZ	896, 1059
09SL4ZZ	896, 1059
09SL7ZZ	896, 1059
09SL8ZZ	896, 1059
09SM*	74, 277, 682
09SM0ZZ	422, 896, 1059
09SM4ZZ	422, 896, 1059
09T0*	74, 682
09T00ZZ	422, 896, 1059
09T04ZZ	422, 896, 1059
09T0XZZ	422, 896, 1059
09T1*	74, 682
09T10ZZ	422, 896, 1059
09T14ZZ	422, 896, 1059
09T1XZZ	422, 896, 1059
09T50ZZ	74
09T58ZZ	74
09T60ZZ	74
09T68ZZ	74
09T7*	74
09T8*	74
09T90ZZ	74, 1059
09T98ZZ	74, 1059
09TA0ZZ	74, 1059
09TA8ZZ	74, 1059
09TB*	83
09TC*	83
09TD0ZZ	74
09TD8ZZ	74
09TE0ZZ	74
09TE8ZZ	74
09TK*	67, 682
09TK07Z	422, 896
09TK4ZZ	422, 896
09TK8ZZ	422, 896
09TKXZZ	422, 896
09TL*	74, 682
09TL0ZZ	896, 1059
09TL4ZZ	896, 1059
09TL7ZZ	896, 1059
09TL8ZZ	896, 1059
09TM*	74, 682
09TM0ZZ	896, 1059
09TM4ZZ	896, 1059
09TM8ZZ	896, 1059
09TN*	74, 174
09TP*	83
09TQ*	83, 277
09TR*	83, 277
09TS*	83
09TT*	83
09TU*	83
09TU0ZZ	1059
09TU4ZZ	1059
09TU8ZZ	1059
09TV*	83
09TV0ZZ	1059
09TV4ZZ	1059
09TV8ZZ	1059
09TW*	83
09TX*	83
09U0*	682
09U007Z	74, 422, 896, 1059
09U00JZ	74, 422, 896, 1059
09U00KZ	74, 422, 896, 1059
09U0X7Z	74, 422, 896, 1059
09U0XJZ	74, 422, 896, 1059
09U0XKZ	74, 422, 896, 1059
09U1*	682
09U107Z	74, 422, 896, 1059
09U10JZ	74, 422, 896, 1059
09U10KZ	74, 422, 896, 1059
09U1X7Z	74, 422, 896, 1059
09U1XJZ	74, 422, 896, 1059
09U1XKZ	74, 422, 896, 1059
09U2*	682
09U207Z	74, 422, 896, 1059
09U20JZ	74, 422, 896, 1059
09U20KZ	74, 422, 896, 1059
09U2X7Z	74, 422, 896, 1059
09U2XJZ	74, 422, 896, 1059
09U2XKZ	74, 422, 896, 1059
09U507Z	74, 1059
09U50JZ	74, 1059
09U50KZ	74, 1059
09U587Z	74, 1059
09U58JZ	74, 1059
09U58KZ	74, 1059
09U607Z	74, 1059
09U60JZ	74, 1059
09U60KZ	74, 1059
09U687Z	74, 1059
09U68JZ	74, 1059
09U68KZ	74, 1059
09U707Z	74, 1059
09U70JZ	74, 1059
09U70KZ	74, 1059
09U777Z	74, 75, 1059
09U77JZ	75, 1059
09U77KZ	75, 1059
09U787Z	75, 1059
09U78JZ	75, 1059
09U78KZ	75, 1059
09U807Z	75, 1059
09U80JZ	75, 1059
09U80KZ	75, 1059
09U877Z	75, 1059
09U87JZ	75, 1059
09U87KZ	75, 1060
09U887Z	75, 1060
09U88JZ	75, 1060
09U88KZ	75, 1060
09U907Z	75, 1060
09U90JZ	75, 1060
09U90KZ	75, 1060
09U987Z	75, 1060
09U98JZ	75, 1060
09U98KZ	75, 1060
09UA07Z	75, 1060
09UA0JZ	75, 1060
09UA0KZ	75, 1060
09UA87Z	75, 1060
09UA8JZ	75, 1060
09UA8KZ	75, 1060
09UB07Z	83
09UB0JZ	83
09UB0KZ	83
09UB37Z	83
09UB3JZ	83
09UB3KZ	83
09UB47Z	83
09UB4JZ	83
09UB4KZ	83
09UB77Z	83
09UB7JZ	83
09UB7KZ	83
09UB87Z	83
09UB8JZ	83
09UB8KZ	83
09UC07Z	83
09UC0JZ	83
09UC0KZ	83
09UC37Z	83
09UC3JZ	83
09UC3KZ	83
09UC47Z	83
09UC4JZ	83
09UC4KZ	83
09UC77Z	83
09UC7JZ	83
09UC7KZ	83
09UC87Z	83
09UC8JZ	83
09UC8KZ	83
09UD07Z	75
09UD0JZ	75
09UD0KZ	75
09UD87Z	75
09UD8JZ	75
09UD8KZ	75
09UE07Z	75
09UE0JZ	75
09UE0KZ	75
09UE87Z	75
09UE8JZ	75
09UE8KZ	75
09UK*	277, 682
09UK07Z	75, 422, 896, 1060
09UK0JZ	75, 422, 896, 1060
09UK0KZ	75, 422, 896, 1060
09UK87Z	75, 422, 896, 1060
09UK8JZ	75, 422, 896, 1060
09UK8KZ	75, 422, 896, 1060
09UKX7Z	75, 422, 896, 1060
09UKXJZ	75, 422, 896, 1060
09UKXKZ	75, 422, 896, 1060
09UL*	682
09UL07Z	75, 422, 896, 1060
09UL0JZ	75, 422, 896, 1060
09UL0KZ	75, 422, 896, 1060
09UL37Z	75, 422, 896, 1060
09UL3JZ	75, 422, 896, 1060
09UL3KZ	75, 422, 896, 1060
09UL47Z	75, 422, 896, 1060
09UL4JZ	75, 422, 896, 1060
09UL4KZ	75, 422, 897, 1060
09UL77Z	75, 422, 897, 1060
09UL7JZ	75, 422, 897, 1060
09UL7KZ	75, 422, 897, 1060
09UL87Z	75, 422, 897, 1060
09UL8JZ	75, 422, 897, 1060
09UL8KZ	75, 422, 897, 1060
09UM*	277, 682
09UM07Z	75, 422, 897, 1060
09UM0JZ	75, 422, 897, 1060
09UM0KZ	75, 422, 897, 1060
09UM37Z	75, 422, 897, 1060
09UM3JZ	75, 422, 897, 1060
09UM3KZ	75, 422, 897, 1060
09UM47Z	75, 422, 897, 1060
09UM4JZ	75, 422, 897, 1060
09UM4KZ	75, 422, 897, 1060
09UM8JZ	75, 422, 897, 1060
09UM8KZ	75, 422, 897, 1060
09UN*	34, 682
09UN07Z	75, 897, 1060
09UN0JZ	75, 897, 1060
09UN0KZ	75, 897, 1060
09UN77Z	75, 897, 1060
09UN7JZ	75, 897, 1060
09UN7KZ	75, 897, 1060
09UN87Z	75, 897, 1060
09UN8JZ	75, 897, 1060
09UN8KZ	75, 897, 1060
09UP07Z	83
09UP0JZ	83
09UP0KZ	83
09UP37Z	83
09UP3JZ	83
09UP3KZ	83
09UP47Z	83
09UP4JZ	83
09UP4KZ	83
09UP77Z	83
09UP7JZ	83
09UP7KZ	83
09UP87Z	83
09UP8JZ	83
09UP8KZ	83
09UQ07Z	83
09UQ0JZ	83
09UQ0KZ	83
09UQ37Z	83
09UQ3JZ	83
09UQ3KZ	83
09UQ47Z	83
09UQ4JZ	83
09UQ4KZ	83
09UQ77Z	83
09UQ7JZ	83
09UQ7KZ	83
09UQ87Z	83
09UQ8JZ	83
09UQ8KZ	83
09UR07Z	83
09UR0JZ	83
09UR0KZ	83
09UR37Z	83
09UR3JZ	83
09UR3KZ	83
09UR47Z	83
09UR4JZ	83
09UR4KZ	83
09UR77Z	83
09UR7JZ	83
09UR7KZ	83
09UR87Z	83
09UR8JZ	83
09US07Z	83
09US0JZ	83
09US0KZ	83
09US37Z	83
09US3JZ	83
09US3KZ	83
09US47Z	83
09US4KZ	83
09US77Z	83
09US7JZ	83
09US7KZ	83
09US87Z	83
09US8JZ	83
09US8KZ	83
09UT07Z	83
09UT0JZ	83
09UT0KZ	83
09UT37Z	83
09UT3JZ	83
09UT3KZ	83
09UT47Z	83
09UT4JZ	83
09UT4KZ	83
09UT77Z	83
09UT7JZ	83
09UT7KZ	83
09UT87Z	83
09UT8JZ	83
09UT8KZ	83
09UU07Z	83
09UU0JZ	83
09UU0KZ	83
09UU37Z	83
09UU3JZ	83
09UU47Z	83
09UU4JZ	83
09UU4KZ	83

Code	Page	Code	Page	Code	Page	Code	Page	Code	Page	Code	Page
09UU77Z	83	09WJ80Z	76	0B5P3ZZ	590, 615, 897	0B9B30Z	91	0B9M0ZX	91, 144, 277, 514, 590, 616	0BBG0ZZ	91, 590, 616
09UU7JZ	83	09WJ87Z	76	0B5P4ZZ	590, 615, 897	0B9B3ZZ	91			0BBG3ZZ	91, 590, 616
09UU7KZ	83	09WJ8JZ	76	0B5T0ZZ	90, 277	0B9B40Z	91	0B9M30Z	100	0BBG4ZX	100, 145, 277, 515
09UU8JZ	83	09WJ8KZ	76	0B5T3ZZ	90, 277	0B9B4ZZ	91	0B9M3ZZ	100	0BBG4ZZ	91, 590, 616, 682, 897
09UU8KZ	83	09WY00Z	84	0B5T4ZZ	90, 277	0B9C00Z	91, 682	0B9M40Z	100	0BBG7ZX	100, 145, 1060
09UV07Z	83	09WY0YZ	84	0B71*	76, 99, 682	0B9C0ZX	91, 144, 277, 514, 590, 615	0B9M4ZZ	100	0BBG7ZZ	91, 590, 616
09UV0JZ	83	09WY30Z	84	0B710DZ	897			0B9M70Z	100	0BBG8ZX	100, 145, 1060
09UV0KZ	83	09WY40Z	84	0B710ZZ	897	0B9C0ZZ	91, 682	0B9M7ZZ	100	0BBH0ZX	91, 145, 277, 515, 590, 616
09UV37Z	83	0B110F4	1, 5	0B713DZ	897	0B9C30Z	99	0B9M80Z	100		
09UV3JZ	83	0B110Z4	1, 5	0B713ZZ	897	0B9C3ZZ	99	0B9N40Z	100	0BBH0ZZ	91, 590, 616
09UV3KZ	83	0B113F4	1, 5	0B714DZ	897	0B9C40Z	99	0B9N4ZZ	100	0BBH3ZZ	91, 590, 616
09UV47Z	83	0B113Z4	1, 5	0B714ZZ	897	0B9C4ZZ	99	0B9P40Z	100	0BBH4ZX	100, 145, 277, 515
09UV4JZ	83	0B114F4	1, 5	0B717DZ	897	0B9C70Z	99	0B9P4ZZ	100	0BBH4ZZ	91, 590, 616, 682, 897
09UV4KZ	83	0B114Z4	1, 5	0B717ZZ	897	0B9C7ZZ	99	0B9T00Z	91	0BBH7ZX	100, 145, 1060
09UV77Z	83	0B51*	76, 99	0B718DZ	897	0B9C80Z	99	0B9T0ZX	91	0BBH7ZZ	91, 590, 616
09UV7JZ	83	0B52*	76, 99	0B718ZZ	897	0B9D00Z	91, 682	0B9T0ZZ	91	0BBH8ZX	100, 145, 1060
09UV7KZ	83	0B530ZZ	90	0B72*	76, 99, 682	0B9D0ZX	91, 144, 277, 514, 590, 616	0BB10ZX	76, 100	0BBJ0ZX	91, 145, 277, 515, 590, 616
09UV87Z	83	0B533ZZ	90	0B720DZ	897			0BB10ZZ	76, 100		
09UV8JZ	83	0B537ZZ	90	0B720ZZ	897	0B9D0ZZ	91, 682	0BB13ZZ	76, 100	0BBJ0ZZ	91, 590, 616
09UV8KZ	83	0B538ZZ	90	0B723DZ	897	0B9D30Z	99	0BB14ZZ	76, 100	0BBJ3ZZ	91, 590, 616
09UW07Z	83	0B540ZZ	90	0B723ZZ	897	0B9D3ZZ	99	0BB17ZZ	76, 100	0BBJ4ZX	100, 145, 277, 515
09UW0JZ	83	0B543ZZ	90	0B724DZ	897	0B9D40Z	99	0BB18ZZ	76, 100	0BBJ4ZZ	91, 590, 616, 682, 897
09UW0KZ	83	0B547ZZ	90	0B724ZZ	897	0B9D4ZZ	99	0BB20ZX	76, 100	0BBJ7ZX	100, 145, 1060
09UW37Z	83	0B548ZZ	90	0B727DZ	897	0B9D70Z	99	0BB20ZZ	76, 100	0BBJ7ZZ	91, 590, 616
09UW3JZ	83	0B550ZZ	90	0B727ZZ	897	0B9D7ZZ	99	0BB23ZZ	76, 100	0BBJ8ZX	100, 145, 1060
09UW3KZ	83	0B553ZZ	90	0B728DZ	897	0B9D80Z	99	0BB24ZZ	76, 100	0BBK0ZX	91, 145, 277, 515, 591, 616
09UW47Z	83	0B557ZZ	90	0B728ZZ	897	0B9F00Z	91, 682	0BB27ZZ	76, 100		
09UW4JZ	83	0B558ZZ	90	0B9100Z	99	0B9F0ZX	91, 144, 277, 514, 590, 616	0BB28ZZ	76, 100	0BBK0ZZ	91, 591, 616
09UW4KZ	84	0B560ZZ	90	0B910ZX	76, 99			0BB30ZX	91	0BBK3ZZ	91, 591, 616
09UW77Z	84	0B563ZZ	90	0B910ZZ	99	0B9F0ZZ	91, 682	0BB30ZZ	91	0BBK4ZX	100, 145, 277, 515
09UW7JZ	84	0B567ZZ	90	0B9130Z	99	0B9F30Z	99	0BB33ZZ	91	0BBK4ZZ	91, 591, 616, 682, 897
09UW7KZ	84	0B568ZZ	90	0B913ZZ	99	0B9F3ZZ	99	0BB37ZZ	91	0BBK7ZX	100, 145, 1060
09UW87Z	84	0B570ZZ	90	0B9140Z	99	0B9F40Z	99	0BB40ZX	91	0BBK7ZZ	91, 591, 616
09UW8JZ	84	0B573ZZ	90	0B914ZZ	99	0B9F4ZZ	99	0BB40ZZ	91	0BBK8ZX	100, 145, 1060
09UW8KZ	84	0B577ZZ	90	0B9200Z	99	0B9F70Z	99	0BB43ZZ	91	0BBL0ZX	91, 145, 277, 515, 591, 616
09UX07Z	84	0B578ZZ	90	0B920ZX	76, 99	0B9F7ZZ	99	0BB47ZZ	91		
09UX0JZ	84	0B580ZZ	90	0B920ZZ	99	0B9F80Z	99	0BB50ZX	91	0BBL0ZZ	91, 591, 616
09UX0KZ	84	0B583ZZ	90	0B9230Z	99	0B9G00Z	91, 682	0BB50ZZ	91	0BBL3ZZ	91, 591, 616
09UX37Z	84	0B587ZZ	90	0B923ZZ	99	0B9G0ZX	91, 144, 277, 514, 590, 616	0BB53ZZ	91	0BBL4ZX	100, 145, 277, 515
09UX3JZ	84	0B588ZZ	90	0B9240Z	99			0BB57ZZ	91	0BBL4ZZ	91, 591, 616, 682, 897
09UX3KZ	84	0B590ZZ	90	0B924ZZ	99	0B9G0ZZ	91, 682	0BB60ZX	91	0BBL7ZX	100, 145, 1060
09UX47Z	84	0B593ZZ	90	0B9300Z	90	0B9G30Z	99	0BB60ZZ	91	0BBL7ZZ	91, 591, 616
09UX4JZ	84	0B597ZZ	90	0B930ZX	90	0B9G3ZZ	99	0BB63ZZ	91	0BBL8ZX	100, 145, 1060
09UX4KZ	84	0B598ZZ	90	0B930ZZ	90	0B9G40Z	99	0BB67ZZ	91	0BBM0ZX	91, 145, 277, 515, 591, 616
09UX77Z	84	0B5B0ZZ	90	0B9330Z	90	0B9G4ZZ	99	0BB70ZX	91		
09UX7JZ	84	0B5B3ZZ	90	0B933ZZ	90	0B9G70Z	99	0BB70ZZ	91	0BBM0ZZ	91, 591, 616, 682, 897
09UX7KZ	84	0B5B7ZZ	90	0B9340Z	90	0B9G7ZZ	99	0BB73ZZ	91	0BBM3ZZ	91, 591, 616, 682, 897
09UX87Z	84	0B5B8ZZ	90	0B934ZZ	91	0B9G80Z	99	0BB77ZZ	91	0BBM4ZX	100, 145, 1060
09UX8JZ	84	0B5C0ZZ	90, 590, 615	0B9400Z	91	0B9H00Z	91, 682	0BB80ZX	91	0BBM7ZX	100, 145, 1060
09UX8KZ	84	0B5C3ZZ	99	0B940ZX	91	0B9H0ZX	91, 144, 277, 514, 590, 616	0BB80ZZ	91	0BBM7ZZ	91, 591, 616, 682, 897
09W7*	75	0B5C4ZZ	90, 590, 615	0B940ZZ	91			0BB83ZZ	91	0BBM8ZX	100, 145, 1060
09W8*	75	0B5C7ZZ	90	0B9430Z	91	0B9H0ZZ	91, 682	0BB87ZZ	91	0BBN0ZZ	91, 682, 897
09W9*	75	0B5D0ZZ	90, 590, 615	0B943ZZ	91	0B9H30Z	99	0BB90ZX	91	0BBN3ZZ	91, 682, 897
09WA*	75	0B5D3ZZ	99	0B9440Z	91	0B9H3ZZ	99	0BB90ZZ	91	0BBN4ZZ	100
09WD*	75	0B5D4ZZ	90, 590, 615	0B944ZZ	91	0B9H40Z	99	0BB93ZZ	91	0BBN8ZX	100
09WE*	75	0B5D7ZZ	90	0B9500Z	91	0B9H4ZZ	99	0BB97ZZ	91	0BBN8ZZ	91, 682, 897
09WH00Z	75	0B5F0ZZ	90, 590, 615	0B950ZX	91	0B9H70Z	99	0BBB0ZX	91	0BBP0ZZ	91, 682, 897
09WH07Z	76	0B5F3ZZ	99	0B950ZZ	91	0B9H7ZZ	99	0BBB0ZZ	91	0BBP3ZZ	91, 682, 897
09WH0DZ	76	0B5F4ZZ	90, 590, 615	0B9530Z	91	0B9H80Z	99	0BBB3ZZ	91	0BBP4ZX	100
09WH0JZ	76	0B5F7ZZ	90	0B953ZZ	91	0B9J00Z	91, 682	0BBB7ZZ	91	0BBP4ZZ	91, 682, 897
09WH0KZ	76	0B5G0ZZ	90, 590, 615	0B9540Z	91	0B9J0ZX	91, 144, 277, 514, 590, 616	0BBC0ZX	91, 144, 277, 514, 590, 616	0BBP8ZX	100
09WH0YZ	76	0B5G3ZZ	99	0B954ZZ	91					0BBP8ZZ	91, 682, 897
09WH30Z	76	0B5G4ZZ	90, 590, 615	0B9600Z	91	0B9J0ZZ	91, 682	0BBC0ZZ	91, 590, 616	0BBT0ZX	91
09WH37Z	76	0B5G7ZZ	90	0B960ZX	91	0B9J30Z	99	0BBC3ZZ	91, 590, 616	0BBT0ZZ	91, 277
09WH3DZ	76	0B5H0ZZ	90, 590, 615	0B960ZZ	91	0B9J3ZZ	99	0BBC4ZX	100, 144, 277, 514	0BBT3ZX	91
09WH40Z	76	0B5H3ZZ	99	0B9630Z	91	0B9J40Z	99	0BBC4ZZ	91, 590, 616, 682, 897	0BBT3ZZ	91, 277
09WH47Z	76	0B5H4ZZ	90, 590, 615	0B963ZZ	91	0B9J4ZZ	99			0BBT4ZX	91
09WH4DZ	76	0B5H7ZZ	90	0B9640Z	91	0B9J70Z	99	0BBC7ZX	100, 145, 1060	0BBT4ZZ	91, 277
09WH70Z	76	0B5J0ZZ	90, 590, 615	0B964ZZ	91	0B9J7ZZ	99	0BBC7ZZ	91, 590, 616	0BC10ZZ	100
09WH77Z	76	0B5J3ZZ	99	0B9700Z	91	0B9J80Z	99	0BBC8ZX	100, 145, 1060	0BC13ZZ	100
09WH7JZ	76	0B5J4ZZ	90, 590, 615	0B970ZX	91	0B9K00Z	91, 682	0BBD0ZX	91, 145, 277, 514, 590, 616	0BC14ZZ	100
09WH7KZ	76	0B5J7ZZ	90	0B970ZZ	91	0B9K0ZX	91, 144, 277, 514, 590, 616			0BC20ZZ	100
09WH80Z	76	0B5K0ZZ	90, 590, 615, 682, 897	0B9730Z	91			0BBD0ZZ	91, 590, 616	0BC23ZZ	100
09WH87Z	76			0B973ZZ	91	0B9K0ZZ	91, 682	0BBD3ZZ	91, 590, 616	0BC24ZZ	100
09WH8JZ	76	0B5K3ZZ	99	0B9740Z	91	0B9K30Z	99	0BBD4ZX	100, 145, 277, 514	0BC30ZZ	91
09WH8KZ	76	0B5K4ZZ	90, 590, 615	0B974ZZ	91	0B9K3ZZ	99	0BBD4ZZ	91, 590, 616, 682, 897	0BC33ZZ	91
09WJ00Z	76	0B5K7ZZ	90, 682, 897	0B9800Z	91	0B9K40Z	99			0BC34ZZ	91
09WJ07Z	76	0B5L0ZZ	90, 590, 615, 682, 897	0B980ZX	91	0B9K4ZZ	99	0BBD7ZX	100, 145, 1060	0BC40ZZ	91
09WJ0DZ	76			0B980ZZ	91	0B9K70Z	99	0BBD7ZZ	91, 590, 616	0BC43ZZ	92
09WJ0JZ	76	0B5L3ZZ	99	0B9830Z	91	0B9K7ZZ	99	0BBD8ZX	100, 145, 1060	0BC44ZZ	92
09WJ0KZ	76	0B5L4ZZ	90, 590, 615	0B983ZZ	91	0B9K80Z	99	0BBF0ZX	91, 145, 277, 514, 590, 616	0BC50ZZ	92
09WJ0YZ	76	0B5L7ZZ	90, 682, 897	0B9840Z	91	0B9L00Z	91, 682			0BC53ZZ	92
09WJ30Z	76	0B5M0ZZ	90, 590, 615, 682, 897	0B984ZZ	91	0B9L0ZX	91, 144, 277, 514, 590, 616	0BBF0ZZ	91, 590, 616	0BC54ZZ	92
09WJ37Z	76	0B5M3ZZ	90	0B9900Z	91			0BBF3ZZ	91, 590, 616	0BC60ZZ	92
09WJ3DZ	76	0B5M4ZZ	90, 590, 615	0B990ZX	91	0B9L0ZZ	91, 682	0BBF4ZX	100, 145, 277, 514		
09WJ40Z	76	0B5M7ZZ	90, 682, 897	0B990ZZ	91	0B9L30Z	100	0BBF4ZZ	91, 590, 616, 682, 897		
09WJ47Z	76	0B5N*	90, 682	0B9930Z	91	0B9L3ZZ	100				
09WJ4DZ	76	0B5N0ZZ	590, 615, 897	0B993ZZ	91	0B9L40Z	100	0BBF7ZX	100, 145, 1060		
09WJ70Z	76	0B5N3ZZ	590, 615, 897	0B9940Z	91	0B9L4ZZ	100	0BBF7ZZ	91, 590, 616		
09WJ77Z	76	0B5N4ZZ	590, 615, 897	0B994ZZ	91	0B9L70Z	100	0BBF8ZX	100, 145, 1060		
09WJ7JZ	76	0B5P*	90, 682	0B9B00Z	91	0B9L7ZZ	100	0BBG0ZX	91, 145, 277, 515, 590, 616		
09WJ7KZ	76	0B5P0ZZ	590, 615, 897	0B9B0ZX	91	0B9L80Z	100				
				0B9B0ZZ	91	0B9M00Z	91, 682				

Numeric Index to Procedures

Code	Page	Code	Page	Code	Page	Code	Page	Code	Page	Code	Page
0BC63ZZ	92	0BH002Z	92	0BHT0MZ	92, 682, 897	0BNP4ZZ	897	0BPL32Z	93, 683	0BQ94ZZ	898
0BC64ZZ	92	0BH003Z	92	0BHT0YZ	92	0BNT0ZZ	93	0BPL33Z	93, 683	0BQ97ZZ	898
0BC70ZZ	92	0BH00DZ	92	0BHT32Z	92	0BNT3ZZ	93	0BPL40Z	93, 683	0BQ98ZZ	898
0BC73ZZ	92	0BH00YZ	92	0BHT3MZ	92, 682, 897	0BNT4ZZ	93	0BPL41Z	93, 683	0BQB*	683
0BC74ZZ	92	0BH031Z	100, 682, 1060	0BHT42Z	92	0BP000Z	93	0BPL42Z	93, 683	0BQB0ZZ	898
0BC80ZZ	92	0BH032Z	92	0BHT4MZ	92, 682, 897	0BP001Z	93	0BPL43Z	93, 683	0BQB3ZZ	898
0BC83ZZ	92	0BH033Z	92	0BHT4YZ	92, 682, 897	0BP002Z	93	0BPL4YZ	93, 683	0BQB4ZZ	898
0BC84ZZ	92	0BH03DZ	92	0BJ00ZZ	100	0BP003Z	100	0BPL71Z	93, 683	0BQB7ZZ	898
0BC90ZZ	92	0BH041Z	100, 682, 1060	0BJ04ZZ	100, 145, 682, 897	0BP007Z	100	0BPL81Z	93, 683	0BQB8ZZ	898
0BC93ZZ	92	0BH042Z	92	0BJ10ZZ	100	0BP00CZ	93	0BPL8YZ	93, 683	0BQK*	683
0BC94ZZ	92	0BH043Z	92	0BJK0ZZ	100	0BP00DZ	93	0BPQ0YZ	93, 683, 897	0BQK0ZZ	898
0BCB0ZZ	92	0BH04DZ	92	0BJK4ZZ	100, 145, 682, 897	0BP00JZ	93	0BPQ4YZ	93, 683	0BQK3ZZ	898
0BCB3ZZ	92	0BH04YZ	92	0BJL0ZZ	100	0BP00KZ	93	0BPQ8YZ	93, 683	0BQK4ZZ	898
0BCB4ZZ	92	0BH071Z	100, 682, 1060	0BJL4ZZ	100, 145, 682, 897	0BP00YZ	93	0BPT00Z	93	0BQK7ZZ	898
0BCC0ZZ	92, 682	0BH081Z	100, 682, 1060	0BJQ0ZZ	100	0BP030Z	93	0BPT02Z	93	0BQK8ZZ	898
0BCC3ZZ	92, 682	0BH102Z	100	0BJQ4ZZ	100	0BP031Z	93	0BPT07Z	93	0BQL*	683
0BCC4ZZ	92, 682	0BH10DZ	100	0BJT0ZZ	100	0BP032Z	93	0BPT0JZ	93	0BQL0ZZ	898
0BCC7ZZ	92, 682	0BH10YZ	100	0BJT4ZZ	100	0BP033Z	100	0BPT0KZ	93	0BQL3ZZ	898
0BCC8ZZ	92, 682	0BH13DZ	100	0BL1*	76, 100, 682	0BP037Z	100	0BPT0MZ	93	0BQL4ZZ	898
0BCD*	92, 682	0BH14DZ	100	0BL10CZ	897	0BP03CZ	93	0BPT0YZ	93	0BQL7ZZ	898
0BCF*	92, 682	0BH14YZ	100	0BL10DZ	897	0BP03DZ	93	0BPT30Z	93	0BQL8ZZ	898
0BCG*	92, 682	0BH30GZ	92	0BL10ZZ	897	0BP03JZ	93	0BPT32Z	93	0BQM*	683
0BCH*	92, 682	0BH33GZ	92	0BL13CZ	897	0BP03KZ	93	0BPT37Z	93	0BQM0ZZ	898
0BCJ*	92, 682	0BH34GZ	92	0BL13DZ	897	0BP040Z	93	0BPT3JZ	93	0BQM3ZZ	898
0BCK*	92, 682	0BH37GZ	92	0BL13ZZ	897	0BP041Z	93	0BPT3KZ	93	0BQM4ZZ	898
0BCL*	92, 682	0BH38GZ	95	0BL14CZ	897	0BP042Z	93	0BPT40Z	93	0BQM7ZZ	898
0BCM*	92, 682	0BH40GZ	92	0BL14DZ	897	0BP043Z	100	0BPT42Z	93	0BQM8ZZ	898
0BCN0ZZ	92	0BH43GZ	92	0BL14ZZ	897	0BP047Z	100	0BPT47Z	93	0BQN*	683
0BCN4ZZ	92	0BH44GZ	92	0BL17DZ	897	0BP04CZ	93	0BPT4JZ	93	0BQN0ZZ	898
0BCP0ZZ	92	0BH47GZ	92	0BL17ZZ	897	0BP04DZ	93	0BPT4KZ	93	0BQN3ZZ	898
0BCP4ZZ	92	0BH48GZ	95	0BL18DZ	897	0BP04JZ	93	0BPT4MZ	93	0BQN4ZZ	898
0BCT0ZZ	92	0BH50GZ	92	0BL18ZZ	897	0BP04KZ	93	0BPT4YZ	93	0BQP*	683
0BCT3ZZ	92	0BH53GZ	92	0BL2*	76, 100, 682	0BP071Z	93	0BPT77Z	93	0BQP0ZZ	898
0BCT4ZZ	92	0BH54GZ	92	0BL20CZ	897	0BP077Z	100	0BPT7JZ	93	0BQP3ZZ	898
0BDN0ZX	92, 591, 616, 682, 897	0BH57GZ	92	0BL20DZ	897	0BP07CZ	100	0BPT7KZ	93	0BQP4ZZ	898
0BDN0ZZ	92, 591, 616, 682, 897	0BH58GZ	95	0BL20ZZ	897	0BP07JZ	100	0BPT7MZ	93	0BQT0ZZ	174, 683, 898
		0BH60GZ	92	0BL23CZ	897	0BP07KZ	100	0BPT87Z	93	0BQT3ZZ	174, 683, 898
0BDN3ZX	92, 591, 616, 682, 897	0BH63GZ	92	0BL23DZ	897	0BP081Z	93	0BPT8JZ	93	0BQT4ZZ	174, 683, 898
0BDN3ZZ	92, 591, 616, 682, 897	0BH64GZ	92	0BL23ZZ	897	0BP087Z	100	0BPT8KZ	93	0BR107Z	76, 93, 145, 422, 683, 898
		0BH67GZ	92	0BL24CZ	897	0BP08CZ	100	0BPT8MZ	93	0BR10JZ	76, 93, 145, 422, 683, 898
0BDN4ZX	92, 591, 616, 682, 897	0BH68GZ	95	0BL24DZ	897	0BP08JZ	100	0BQ*	93		
0BDN4ZZ	92, 591, 616, 682, 897	0BH70GZ	92	0BL24ZZ	897	0BP08KZ	100	0BQ1*	76, 145, 683	0BR10KZ	76, 93, 145, 422, 683, 898
		0BH73GZ	92	0BL27DZ	897	0BP100Z	100	0BQ10ZZ	422, 897		
0BDP0ZX	92, 591, 616, 682, 897	0BH74GZ	92	0BL27ZZ	897	0BP102Z	100	0BQ13ZZ	422, 897	0BR147Z	76, 93, 145, 422, 683, 898
0BDP0ZZ	92, 591, 616, 682, 897	0BH77GZ	92	0BL28DZ	897	0BP107Z	100	0BQ14ZZ	422, 897		
		0BH78GZ	95	0BL28ZZ	897	0BP10CZ	100	0BQ17ZZ	422, 897	0BR14JZ	76, 93, 145, 422, 683, 898
0BDP3ZX	92, 591, 616, 682, 897	0BH80GZ	92	0BL3*	92	0BP10DZ	100	0BQ18ZZ	422, 897		
0BDP3ZZ	92, 591, 616, 682, 897	0BH83GZ	92	0BL4*	92	0BP10JZ	100	0BQ2*	76, 683	0BR14KZ	76, 93, 145, 423, 683, 898
		0BH84GZ	92	0BL5*	92	0BP10KZ	100	0BQ20ZZ	897		
0BDP4ZX	92, 591, 616, 682, 897	0BH87GZ	92	0BL6*	92	0BP130Z	100	0BQ23ZZ	897	0BR207Z	76, 93, 683, 898
0BDP4ZZ	92, 591, 616, 682, 897	0BH88GZ	95	0BL7*	92	0BP132Z	100	0BQ24ZZ	897	0BR20JZ	76, 93, 683, 898
		0BH90GZ	92	0BL8*	92	0BP137Z	100	0BQ27ZZ	897	0BR20KZ	76, 93, 683, 898
0BF10ZZ	76, 92, 682, 897	0BH93GZ	92	0BL9*	92	0BP13CZ	100	0BQ28ZZ	897	0BR247Z	76, 93, 683, 898
0BF13ZZ	76, 92, 682, 897	0BH94GZ	92	0BLB*	92	0BP13DZ	100	0BQ3*	683	0BR24JZ	76, 93, 683, 898
0BF14ZZ	76, 92, 682, 897	0BH97GZ	92	0BM*	92	0BP13JZ	100	0BQ30ZZ	897	0BR24KZ	76, 93, 683, 898
0BF17ZZ	76, 92, 682, 897	0BH98GZ	95	0BM10ZZ	76, 682, 897	0BP13KZ	100	0BQ33ZZ	897	0BR307Z	93, 683, 898
0BF18ZZ	76, 92, 682, 897	0BHB0GZ	92	0BM20ZZ	76, 682, 897	0BP140Z	100	0BQ34ZZ	897	0BR30JZ	93, 683, 898
0BF20ZZ	76, 92, 682, 897	0BHB3GZ	92	0BN1*	76, 100, 682	0BP142Z	100	0BQ37ZZ	897	0BR30KZ	93, 683, 898
0BF23ZZ	76, 92, 682, 897	0BHB7GZ	92	0BN10ZZ	897	0BP147Z	100	0BQ38ZZ	897	0BR347Z	93, 683, 898
0BF24ZZ	76, 92, 682, 897	0BHB8GZ	95	0BN13ZZ	897	0BP14CZ	100	0BQ4*	683	0BR34JZ	93, 683, 898
0BF27ZZ	76, 92, 682, 897	0BHK01Z	100, 682, 1060	0BN14ZZ	897	0BP14DZ	100	0BQ40ZZ	897	0BR34KZ	93, 683, 898
0BF28ZZ	76, 92, 682, 897	0BHK02Z	92, 682	0BN17ZZ	897	0BP14JZ	100	0BQ43ZZ	897	0BR407Z	93, 683, 898
0BF30ZZ	92	0BHK03Z	92, 682	0BN18ZZ	897	0BP14KZ	100	0BQ44ZZ	897	0BR40JZ	93, 683, 898
0BF33ZZ	92	0BHK0YZ	92, 682	0BN2*	76, 100, 682	0BP177Z	100	0BQ47ZZ	897	0BR40KZ	93, 683, 898
0BF34ZZ	92	0BHK31Z	100, 682, 1060	0BN20ZZ	897	0BP17CZ	100	0BQ48ZZ	897	0BR447Z	93, 683, 898
0BF40ZZ	92	0BHK32Z	92, 682	0BN23ZZ	897	0BP17JZ	100	0BQ5*	683	0BR44JZ	93, 683, 898
0BF43ZZ	92	0BHK33Z	92, 682	0BN24ZZ	897	0BP17KZ	100	0BQ50ZZ	897	0BR44KZ	93, 683, 898
0BF44ZZ	92	0BHK41Z	100, 682, 1060	0BN27ZZ	897	0BP187Z	100	0BQ53ZZ	898	0BR507Z	93, 683, 898
0BF50ZZ	92	0BHK42Z	92, 682	0BN28ZZ	897	0BP18CZ	100	0BQ54ZZ	898	0BR50JZ	93, 683, 898
0BF53ZZ	92	0BHK43Z	92, 682	0BN3*	92	0BP18DZ	100	0BQ57ZZ	898	0BR50KZ	93, 683, 898
0BF54ZZ	92	0BHK4YZ	92, 682	0BN4*	92	0BP18JZ	100	0BQ58ZZ	898	0BR547Z	93, 683, 898
0BF60ZZ	92	0BHK71Z	100, 682, 1060	0BN5*	92	0BP18KZ	100	0BQ6*	683	0BR54JZ	93, 683, 898
0BF63ZZ	92	0BHK81Z	100, 682, 1060	0BN6*	92	0BPK00Z	93, 682	0BQ60ZZ	898	0BR54KZ	93, 683, 898
0BF64ZZ	92	0BHK8YZ	92, 682	0BN7*	92	0BPK01Z	93, 682	0BQ63ZZ	898	0BR607Z	93, 683, 898
0BF70ZZ	92	0BHL01Z	100, 682, 1060	0BN8*	92	0BPK02Z	93, 682	0BQ64ZZ	898	0BR60JZ	93, 683, 898
0BF73ZZ	92	0BHL02Z	92, 682	0BN9*	92	0BPK03Z	93, 682	0BQ67ZZ	898	0BR60KZ	93, 683, 898
0BF74ZZ	92	0BHL03Z	92, 682	0BNB*	92	0BPK0YZ	93, 682	0BQ68ZZ	898	0BR647Z	93, 683, 898
0BF80ZZ	92	0BHL0YZ	92, 682	0BNC*	93	0BPK30Z	93, 682	0BQ7*	683	0BR64JZ	93, 683, 898
0BF83ZZ	92	0BHL31Z	100, 682, 1060	0BND*	93	0BPK31Z	93, 682	0BQ70ZZ	898	0BR64KZ	93, 683, 898
0BF84ZZ	92	0BHL32Z	92, 682	0BNF*	93	0BPK32Z	93, 682	0BQ73ZZ	898	0BR707Z	93, 683, 898
0BF90ZZ	92	0BHL33Z	92, 682	0BNG*	93	0BPK33Z	93, 682	0BQ74ZZ	898	0BR70JZ	93, 683, 898
0BF93ZZ	92	0BHL41Z	100, 682, 1060	0BNH*	93	0BPK40Z	93, 682	0BQ77ZZ	898	0BR70KZ	93, 683, 898
0BF94ZZ	92	0BHL42Z	92, 682	0BNJ*	93	0BPK41Z	93, 682	0BQ78ZZ	898	0BR747Z	93, 683, 898
0BFB0ZZ	92	0BHL43Z	92, 682	0BNK*	93	0BPK42Z	93, 682	0BQ8*	683	0BR74JZ	93, 683, 898
0BFB3ZZ	92	0BHL4YZ	92, 682	0BNL*	93	0BPK43Z	93, 682	0BQ80ZZ	898	0BR74KZ	93, 683, 898
0BFB4ZZ	92	0BHL71Z	100, 682, 1060	0BNM*	93	0BPK4YZ	93, 682	0BQ83ZZ	898	0BR807Z	93, 683, 898
0BH001Z	100, 682, 1060	0BHL81Z	100, 682, 1060	0BNN*	100, 682	0BPK8YZ	93, 682	0BQ84ZZ	898	0BR80JZ	93, 683, 898
		0BHL8YZ	92, 682	0BNN0ZZ	897	0BPL00Z	93, 682	0BQ87ZZ	898	0BR80KZ	93, 683, 898
		0BHQ0YZ	92, 682	0BNN3ZZ	897	0BPL01Z	93, 683	0BQ88ZZ	898	0BR847Z	93, 683, 898
		0BHQ4YZ	92, 682	0BNN4ZZ	897	0BPL02Z	93, 683	0BQ9*	683	0BR84JZ	93, 683, 898
0BH001Z	100, 682, 1060	0BHQ8YZ	92, 682	0BNP*	100, 682	0BPL0YZ	93, 683	0BQ90ZZ	898	0BR84KZ	93, 683, 898
		0BHT02Z	92	0BNP0ZZ	897	0BPL30Z	93, 683	0BQ93ZZ	898	0BR907Z	93, 683, 898
				0BNP3ZZ	897	0BPL31Z	93, 683				

Numeric Index to Procedures

Code	Page
0BR90JZ	93, 683, 898
0BR90KZ	93, 683, 898
0BR947Z	93, 683, 898
0BR94JZ	93, 683, 898
0BR94KZ	93, 683, 898
0BRB07Z	93, 683, 898
0BRB0JZ	93, 683, 898
0BRB0KZ	93, 683, 898
0BRB47Z	93, 683, 898
0BRB4JZ	93, 683, 898
0BRB4KZ	93, 683, 898
0BRT07Z	93, 174, 683, 898
0BRT0JZ	93, 174, 683, 898
0BRT0KZ	93, 174, 683, 898
0BRT47Z	93, 174, 683, 898
0BRT4JZ	93, 174, 683, 898
0BRT4KZ	93, 174, 683, 898
0BS*	93
0BS10ZZ	76, 683, 898
0BS20ZZ	76, 683, 898
0BT*	683
0BT1*	76, 93
0BT10ZZ	898
0BT14ZZ	898
0BT2*	76, 93
0BT20ZZ	898
0BT24ZZ	898
0BT3*	93
0BT30ZZ	898
0BT34ZZ	898
0BT4*	93
0BT40ZZ	898
0BT44ZZ	898
0BT5*	93
0BT50ZZ	898
0BT54ZZ	898
0BT6*	93
0BT60ZZ	898
0BT64ZZ	898
0BT7*	94
0BT70ZZ	898
0BT74ZZ	898
0BT8*	94
0BT80ZZ	898
0BT84ZZ	898
0BT9*	94
0BT90ZZ	898
0BT94ZZ	898
0BTB*	94
0BTB0ZZ	898
0BTB4ZZ	898
0BTC*	94
0BTC0ZZ	898
0BTC4ZZ	898
0BTD*	94
0BTD0ZZ	898
0BTD4ZZ	898
0BTF*	94
0BTF0ZZ	898
0BTF4ZZ	898
0BTG*	94
0BTG0ZZ	898
0BTG4ZZ	898
0BTH*	94
0BTH0ZZ	591, 616, 898
0BTH4ZZ	591, 616, 898
0BTJ*	94
0BTJ0ZZ	898
0BTJ4ZZ	898
0BTK*	94
0BTK0ZZ	898
0BTK4ZZ	898
0BTL*	94
0BTL0ZZ	898
0BTL4ZZ	898
0BTM*	94
0BTM0ZZ	898
0BTM4ZZ	898
0BTT0ZZ	100, 898
0BTT4ZZ	100, 898
0BU*	
0BU1*	76, 683
0BU107Z	898
0BU10JZ	898
0BU10KZ	898
0BU147Z	898
0BU14JZ	898
0BU14KZ	898
0BU187Z	898
0BU18JZ	898
0BU18KZ	898
0BU2*	76, 683
0BU207Z	898
0BU20JZ	898
0BU20KZ	898
0BU247Z	898
0BU24JZ	899
0BU24KZ	899
0BU287Z	899
0BU28JZ	899
0BU28KZ	899
0BUT07Z	174, 683, 899
0BUT0JZ	174, 683, 899
0BUT0KZ	174, 683, 899
0BUT47Z	174, 683, 899
0BUT4JZ	174, 683, 899
0BUT4KZ	174, 683, 899
0BV*	94
0BV1*	76, 683
0BV10CZ	899
0BV10DZ	899
0BV10ZZ	899
0BV13CZ	899
0BV13DZ	899
0BV13ZZ	899
0BV14CZ	899
0BV14DZ	899
0BV14ZZ	899
0BV17DZ	899
0BV17ZZ	899
0BV18DZ	899
0BV18ZZ	899
0BV2*	76, 683
0BV20CZ	899
0BV20DZ	899
0BV20ZZ	899
0BV23CZ	899
0BV23DZ	899
0BV23ZZ	899
0BV24CZ	899
0BV24DZ	899
0BV24ZZ	899
0BV27DZ	899
0BV27ZZ	899
0BV28DZ	899
0BV28ZZ	899
0BW000Z	94
0BW002Z	94
0BW003Z	100
0BW007Z	100
0BW00CZ	94
0BW00DZ	94
0BW00JZ	94
0BW00KZ	94
0BW00YZ	94
0BW030Z	94
0BW032Z	94
0BW033Z	100
0BW037Z	100
0BW03CZ	94
0BW03DZ	94
0BW03JZ	94
0BW03KZ	94
0BW040Z	94
0BW042Z	94
0BW043Z	100
0BW047Z	94
0BW04CZ	94
0BW04DZ	94
0BW04JZ	94
0BW04KZ	94
0BW070Z	94
0BW077Z	100
0BW07JZ	100
0BW07KZ	100
0BW080Z	94
0BW087Z	100
0BW08CZ	100
0BW08JZ	100
0BW08KZ	100
0BW100Z	100
0BW102Z	100
0BW10CZ	100
0BW10DZ	100
0BW10FZ	76, 100, 145, 423, 683, 899
0BW10JZ	100
0BW10KZ	100
0BW130Z	100
0BW132Z	100
0BW137Z	101
0BW13CZ	101
0BW13DZ	101
0BW13FZ	76, 101, 145, 423, 683, 899
0BW13JZ	101
0BW13KZ	101
0BW140Z	101
0BW142Z	101
0BW147Z	101
0BW14CZ	101
0BW14DZ	101
0BW14FZ	76, 101, 145, 423, 683, 899
0BW14JZ	101
0BW14KZ	101
0BW170Z	101
0BW172Z	101
0BW177Z	101
0BW17CZ	101
0BW17DZ	101
0BW17FZ	101
0BW17JZ	101
0BW17KZ	101
0BW180Z	101
0BW182Z	101
0BW187Z	101
0BW18CZ	101
0BW18DZ	101
0BW18FZ	101
0BW18JZ	101
0BW18KZ	101
0BWK00Z	94, 683
0BWK02Z	94, 683
0BWK03Z	94, 683
0BWK0YZ	94, 683
0BWK30Z	94, 683
0BWK32Z	94, 683
0BWK33Z	94, 683
0BWK40Z	94, 683
0BWK42Z	94, 683
0BWK43Z	94, 683
0BWK4YZ	94, 683
0BWK8YZ	94, 683
0BWL00Z	94, 683
0BWL02Z	94, 683
0BWL03Z	94, 683
0BWL0YZ	94, 683
0BWL30Z	94, 683
0BWL32Z	94, 683
0BWL33Z	94, 683
0BWL40Z	94, 683
0BWL43Z	94, 683
0BWL4YZ	94, 683
0BWL8YZ	94, 683
0BWQ4YZ	94, 683
0BWQ8YZ	94, 683
0BWT00Z	94
0BWT02Z	94
0BWT07Z	94
0BWT0JZ	94
0BWT0KZ	94
0BWT0MZ	94
0BWT0YZ	94
0BWT30Z	94
0BWT32Z	94
0BWT37Z	94
0BWT3JZ	94
0BWT3KZ	94
0BWT3MZ	94
0BWT40Z	94
0BWT42Z	94
0BWT47Z	94
0BWT4JZ	94
0BWT4KZ	94
0BWT4MZ	94
0BWT4YZ	94
0BWT70Z	94
0BWT72Z	94
0BWT77Z	94
0BWT7JZ	94
0BWT7KZ	94
0BWT7MZ	94
0BWT80Z	94
0BWT82Z	94
0BWT87Z	94
0BWT8JZ	94
0BWT8KZ	94
0BWT8MZ	94
0BYC0Z0	1
0BYC0Z2	1
0BYD0Z0	1
0BYD0Z1	1
0BYD0Z2	1
0BYF0Z0	1
0BYF0Z1	1
0BYF0Z2	1
0BYG0Z0	1
0BYG0Z1	1
0BYG0Z2	1
0BYH0Z0	1
0BYH0Z1	1
0BYH0Z2	1
0BYJ0Z0	1
0BYJ0Z1	1
0BYJ0Z2	1
0BYK0Z0	1
0BYK0Z1	1
0BYK0Z2	1
0BYL0Z0	1
0BYL0Z1	1
0BYL0Z2	1
0BYM0Z0	1
0BYM0Z1	1
0BYM0Z2	1
0C0*	84, 683
0C00X7Z	423, 899, 1060
0C00XJZ	423, 899, 1060
0C00XKZ	423, 899, 1060
0C00XZZ	423, 899, 1060
0C01X7Z	423, 899, 1060
0C01XJZ	423, 899, 1060
0C01XKZ	423, 899, 1060
0C01XZZ	423, 899, 1060
0C50*	84
0C500ZZ	423, 1060
0C503ZZ	423, 1060
0C50XZZ	423, 1060
0C51*	84
0C510ZZ	423, 1060
0C513ZZ	423, 1060
0C51XZZ	423, 1060
0C52*	84
0C520ZZ	1060
0C523ZZ	1060
0C52XZZ	1060
0C53*	84, 683
0C530ZZ	899, 1060
0C533ZZ	899, 1060
0C53XZZ	899, 1060
0C54*	84, 683
0C540ZZ	899, 1060
0C543ZZ	899, 1060
0C54XZZ	899, 1060
0C57*	84, 145
0C570ZZ	1060
0C573ZZ	1060
0C57XZZ	1060
0C58*	85
0C580ZZ	1060
0C583ZZ	1060
0C59*	85
0C590ZZ	1060
0C593ZZ	1060
0C5B*	85
0C5B0ZZ	1060
0C5B3ZZ	1060
0C5C*	85
0C5C0ZZ	1060
0C5C3ZZ	1060
0C5D*	85
0C5D0ZZ	1060
0C5D3ZZ	1060
0C5F*	85
0C5F0ZZ	1060
0C5F3ZZ	1060
0C5G*	85
0C5G0ZZ	1060
0C5G3ZZ	1060
0C5H*	85
0C5H0ZZ	1060
0C5H3ZZ	1060
0C5J*	85
0C5J0ZZ	1060
0C5J3ZZ	1060
0C5M*	76, 174
0C5N*	84
0C5N0ZZ	1060
0C5N3ZZ	1060
0C5NXZZ	1060
0C5P*	76
0C5Q*	76
0C5R*	76, 101, 683
0C5R3ZZ	899
0C5R4ZZ	899
0C5R7ZZ	899
0C5R8ZZ	899
0C5S*	76, 101
0C5S0ZZ	1060
0C5S3ZZ	1060
0C5S4ZZ	1060
0C5S7ZZ	1060
0C5S8ZZ	1060
0C5T*	76, 101
0C5T0ZZ	1060
0C5T3ZZ	1060
0C5T4ZZ	1060
0C5T7ZZ	1060
0C5T8ZZ	1060
0C5V*	76, 101
0C5V0ZZ	1060
0C5V3ZZ	1060
0C5V4ZZ	1060
0C5V7ZZ	1060
0C5V8ZZ	1060
0C7S*	76, 101
0C7S0DZ	1060
0C7S0ZZ	1060
0C7S3ZZ	1060
0C7S4DZ	1060
0C7S4ZZ	1060
0C7S7DZ	1060
0C7S7ZZ	1060
0C7S8DZ	1060
0C9000Z	84, 423, 683, 899
0C900ZZ	84, 423, 683, 899
0C90XZZ	84, 423, 683, 899
0C9100Z	84, 423, 683, 899
0C910ZZ	84, 423, 683, 899
0C91X0Z	84, 423, 683, 899
0C91XZZ	84, 423, 683, 899
0C9200Z	84
0C920ZX	84, 1060
0C920ZZ	84
0C923ZX	84, 1060
0C92X0Z	84
0C92XZX	84, 1060
0C92XZZ	84
0C9300Z	84
0C930ZX	84, 1060
0C930ZZ	84
0C933ZX	84, 1060
0C93X0Z	84
0C93XZX	84, 1060
0C93XZZ	84
0C9400Z	84, 423, 683, 899
0C940ZZ	84, 423, 683, 899
0C94X0Z	84, 423, 683, 899
0C94XZZ	84, 423, 683, 899
0C9700Z	84
0C970ZX	84
0C970ZZ	84
0C97X0Z	84
0C97XZZ	84
0C980ZX	85, 1060
0C980ZZ	85, 1061
0C990ZX	85, 1061
0C990ZZ	85, 1061
0C9B0ZX	85, 1061
0C9C0ZX	85, 1061
0C9D0ZX	85, 1061
0C9F0ZX	85, 1061
0C9G0ZX	85, 1061
0C9G0ZZ	85, 1061
0C9H0ZX	85, 1061
0C9H0ZZ	85, 1061
0C9J0ZX	85, 1061
0C9M00Z	76, 683, 899
0C9M0ZZ	76, 683, 899
0C9M40Z	76, 683, 899
0C9M4ZZ	76, 683, 899
0C9M70Z	76, 683, 899
0C9M7ZZ	76, 683, 899
0C9M80Z	76, 683, 899
0C9M8ZZ	76, 683, 899
0C9N00Z	84, 1061
0C9N0ZX	84, 1061
0C9N0ZZ	84, 1061
0C9N3ZX	84, 1061
0C9NX0Z	84, 1061
0C9NXZX	84, 1061
0C9NXZZ	84, 1061
0C9P00Z	76
0C9P0ZX	76, 1061
0C9P0ZZ	76
0C9P3ZX	76, 1061
0C9PX0Z	76
0C9PXZX	76, 1061
0C9PXZZ	76
0C9Q00Z	76
0C9Q0ZX	76, 1061
0C9Q0ZZ	76
0C9Q3ZX	76, 1061
0C9QX0Z	76
0C9QXZX	76, 1061
0C9QXZZ	76
0C9R00Z	76
0C9R0ZX	76, 101
0C9R0ZZ	76
0C9R40Z	76
0C9R4ZZ	76
0C9R70Z	76
0C9R7ZZ	76
0C9R80Z	76
0C9R8ZZ	76
0C9S00Z	76
0C9S0ZX	76, 101
0C9S0ZZ	76
0C9S40Z	76
0C9S4ZZ	76
0C9S70Z	76
0C9S7ZZ	76
0C9S8ZZ	76
0C9T00Z	76
0C9T0ZX	76, 101
0C9T0ZZ	76
0C9T40Z	76
0C9T4ZZ	76
0C9T70Z	76
0C9T7ZZ	76
0C9T80Z	76
0C9T8ZZ	76
0C9V00Z	76
0C9V0ZX	76, 101
0C9V0ZZ	76
0C9V40Z	76
0C9V4ZZ	76
0C9V70Z	76
0C9V7ZZ	76
0C9V80Z	76
0C9V8ZZ	76
0CB00ZZ	84, 423, 1061
0CB03ZZ	84, 423, 1061
0CB0XZZ	84, 423, 1061
0CB10ZZ	84, 423, 1061
0CB13ZZ	84, 423, 1061
0CB1XZZ	84, 423, 1061
0CB2*	84
0CB20ZX	1061
0CB20ZZ	1061
0CB23ZX	1061
0CB23ZZ	1061
0CB2XZX	1061
0CB2XZZ	1061
0CB3*	84
0CB30ZX	1061
0CB30ZZ	683, 899, 1061
0CB33ZX	1061
0CB33ZZ	683, 899, 1061
0CB3XZX	1061
0CB3XZZ	683, 899, 1061
0CB40ZZ	84, 683, 899, 1061
0CB43ZZ	84, 683, 899, 1061
0CB4XZZ	84, 684, 899, 1061
0CB70ZX	84
0CB70ZZ	84, 483
0CB73ZZ	84, 483
0CB7XZZ	84, 483
0CB80ZX	85, 1061
0CB80ZZ	85, 1061
0CB83ZZ	85, 1061
0CB90ZX	85, 1061
0CB90ZZ	85, 1061
0CB93ZZ	85, 1061
0CBB0ZX	85, 1061
0CBB0ZZ	85, 1061
0CBB3ZZ	85, 1061
0CBC0ZX	85, 1061
0CBC0ZZ	85, 1061
0CBC3ZZ	85, 1061
0CBD0ZX	85, 1061
0CBD0ZZ	85, 1061
0CBD3ZZ	85, 1061
0CBF0ZX	85, 1061
0CBF3ZZ	85, 1061
0CBG0ZX	85, 1061
0CBG0ZZ	85, 1061

Code	Page	Code	Page	Code	Page	Code	Page	Code	Page	Code	Page
0CBG3ZZ	85, 1061	0CDT8ZZ	1061	0CPS0DZ	77	0CQH0ZZ	900	0CR6X7Z	900	0CSR*	77, 101, 684
0CBH0ZX	85, 1061	0CDV*	77, 101	0CPS0JZ	77, 101, 1061	0CQH3ZZ	900	0CR6XJZ	900	0CST*	77, 101, 684
0CBH0ZZ	85, 1061	0CDV0ZZ	1061	0CPS0KZ	77	0CQJ*	85, 684	0CR6XKZ	900	0CSV*	77, 101, 684
0CBH3ZZ	85, 1061	0CDV3ZZ	1061	0CPS0YZ	77	0CQJ0ZZ	900	0CR7*	84, 684	0CT0*	84, 684
0CBJ0ZX	85, 1061	0CDV4ZZ	1061	0CPS30Z	77	0CQJ3ZZ	900	0CR707Z	900	0CT00ZZ	900, 1062
0CBJ0ZZ	85, 1061	0CDV7ZZ	1061	0CPS37Z	77	0CQM*	34, 77, 684	0CR70JZ	900	0CT0XZZ	900, 1062
0CBJ3ZZ	85, 1061	0CDV8ZZ	1061	0CPS3DZ	77	0CQM0ZZ	423, 900	0CR70KZ	900	0CT1*	84, 684
0CBM0ZZ	76, 174	0CH7*	77, 684	0CPS3JZ	77, 101, 1061	0CQM3ZZ	423, 900	0CR737Z	900	0CT10ZZ	900, 1062
0CBM3ZZ	76, 174	0CH701Z	1061	0CPS3KZ	77	0CQM4ZZ	423, 900	0CR73JZ	900	0CT1XZZ	900, 1062
0CBM4ZZ	76, 174	0CH731Z	1061	0CPS77Z	77	0CQM7ZZ	423, 900	0CR73KZ	900	0CT2*	67
0CBM7ZZ	76, 174	0CH7X1Z	1061	0CPS7JZ	77, 101, 1061	0CQM8ZZ	423, 900	0CR7X7Z	900	0CT20ZZ	1062
0CBM8ZZ	76, 174	0CHA0YZ	77, 684, 1061	0CPS7KZ	77	0CQN*	84	0CR7XJZ	900	0CT2XZZ	1062
0CBN*	84	0CL*	85	0CPS87Z	77	0CQN0ZZ	1061	0CR7XKZ	900	0CT3*	84, 684
0CBN0ZX	1061	0CM00ZZ	84, 423, 684, 899, 1061	0CPS8JZ	77, 101, 1061	0CQN3ZZ	1061	0CRB*	85, 684	0CT30ZZ	900, 1062
0CBN0ZZ	1061	0CM10ZZ	84, 423, 684, 899, 1061	0CPS8KZ	77	0CQNXZZ	1061	0CRB07Z	900	0CT3XZZ	900, 1062
0CBN3ZX	1061	0CM30ZZ	84, 423, 684, 899, 1061	0CPY00Z	84, 423, 684, 899, 1061	0CQP*	77	0CRB0JZ	900	0CT7*	67
0CBN3ZZ	1061	0CM70ZZ	84, 684, 899	0CPY01Z	84, 423, 684, 899, 1061	0CQQ*	77	0CRB0KZ	900	0CT80ZZ	85, 1062
0CBNXZX	1061	0CMN0ZZ	84, 1061	0CPY07Z	84, 423, 684, 899, 1061	0CQR*	77, 101, 684	0CRB37Z	900	0CT90ZZ	85, 1062
0CBNXZZ	1061	0CN2*	84, 684	0CPY0DZ	84, 423, 684, 899, 1061	0CQS*	77, 101, 684	0CRB3JZ	900	0CTB0ZZ	85, 1062
0CBP*	76	0CN20ZZ	423, 899, 1061	0CPY0JZ	84, 423, 684, 899, 1061	0CQS0ZZ	900	0CRB3KZ	900	0CTC0ZZ	85, 1062
0CBP0ZX	1061	0CN23ZZ	423, 899, 1061	0CPY0KZ	84, 423, 684, 899, 1061	0CQS3ZZ	900	0CRC*	85, 684	0CTD0ZZ	85, 1062
0CBP3ZX	1061	0CN2XZZ	423, 899, 1061	0CPY0YZ	84, 423, 684, 900, 1061	0CQS4ZZ	900	0CRC07Z	900	0CTF0ZZ	85, 1062
0CBPXZX	1061	0CN3*	84, 684	0CPY30Z	84, 423, 684, 900, 1061	0CQS7ZZ	900	0CRC0JZ	900	0CTG0ZZ	85, 1062
0CBQ*	76	0CN30ZZ	423, 899, 1061	0CPY31Z	84, 423, 684, 900, 1061	0CQS8ZZ	900	0CRC0KZ	900	0CTH0ZZ	85, 1062
0CBQ0ZX	1061	0CN33ZZ	423, 899, 1061	0CPY37Z	84, 423, 684, 900, 1061	0CQT*	77, 101, 684	0CRC37Z	900	0CTJ0ZZ	85, 1062
0CBQ3ZX	1061	0CN3XZZ	423, 899, 1061	0CPY3DZ	84, 423, 684, 900, 1061	0CQV*	77, 101, 684	0CRC3JZ	900	0CTM*	77, 174
0CBQXZX	1061	0CN40ZZ	84, 423, 684, 899, 1061	0CPY3JZ	84, 423, 684, 900, 1061	0CR0*	84, 684	0CRC3KZ	900	0CTN*	84
0CBR0ZX	76, 101	0CN43ZZ	84, 423, 684, 899, 1061	0CPY3KZ	84, 423, 684, 900, 1061	0CR007Z	423, 900, 1061	0CRM*	34, 77, 684	0CTN0ZZ	1062
0CBR0ZZ	76, 101, 684, 899	0CN8*	85, 684	0CPY71Z	77, 684, 900	0CR00JZ	423, 900, 1061	0CRM07Z	900, 1062	0CTNXZZ	1062
0CBR3ZZ	76, 101, 684, 899	0CN80ZZ	899	0CPY77Z	77, 684, 900	0CR00KZ	423, 900, 1061	0CRM0JZ	900, 1062	0CTP*	77
0CBR4ZZ	77, 101, 684, 899	0CN83ZZ	899	0CPY7JZ	77, 684, 900	0CR037Z	423, 900, 1061	0CRM0KZ	900, 1062	0CTP0ZZ	1062
0CBR7ZZ	77, 101, 684, 899	0CN9*	85, 684	0CPY7KZ	77, 684, 900	0CR03JZ	423, 900, 1061	0CRM77Z	900, 1062	0CTPXZZ	1062
0CBR8ZZ	77, 101, 684, 899	0CN90ZZ	899	0CPY81Z	77, 684, 900	0CR03KZ	423, 900, 1061	0CRM7JZ	900, 1062	0CTQ*	77
0CBS0ZX	77, 101	0CN93ZZ	899	0CPY87Z	77, 684, 900	0CR0X7Z	423, 900, 1061	0CRM7KZ	900, 1062	0CTR*	77, 101, 684
0CBS0ZZ	67, 101, 684, 899	0CNB*	85, 684	0CPY8JZ	77, 684, 900	0CR0XJZ	423, 900, 1061	0CRM87Z	900, 1062	0CTR0ZZ	900
0CBS3ZZ	67, 101, 684, 899	0CNB0ZZ	899	0CPY8KZ	77, 684, 900	0CR0XKZ	423, 900, 1061	0CRM8JZ	900, 1062	0CTR4ZZ	900
0CBS4ZZ	67, 101, 684, 899	0CNB3ZZ	899	0CQ00ZZ	84, 423, 684, 900, 1061	0CR1*	84, 684	0CRM8KZ	900, 1062	0CTR7ZZ	900
0CBS7ZZ	67, 101, 684, 899	0CNC*	85, 684	0CQ03ZZ	84, 423, 684, 900, 1061	0CR107Z	423, 900, 1061	0CRN*	84	0CTR8ZZ	900
0CBS8ZZ	67, 101, 684, 899	0CNC0ZZ	899	0CQ10ZZ	84, 423, 684, 900, 1061	0CR10JZ	423, 900, 1061	0CRN07Z	1062	0CTS0ZZ	2
0CBT0ZX	77, 101	0CNC3ZZ	899	0CQ13ZZ	84, 423, 684, 900, 1061	0CR10KZ	423, 900, 1061	0CRN0JZ	1062	0CTS4ZZ	2
0CBT0ZZ	77, 101, 684, 899	0CND*	85, 684	0CQ2*	34, 77, 684	0CR137Z	423, 900, 1061	0CRN0KZ	1062	0CTS7ZZ	2
0CBT3ZZ	77, 101, 684, 899	0CND0ZZ	899	0CQ20ZZ	423, 900	0CR13JZ	423, 900, 1061	0CRN37Z	1062	0CTS8ZZ	2
0CBT4ZZ	77, 101, 684, 899	0CND3ZZ	899	0CQ23ZZ	423, 900	0CR13KZ	423, 900, 1061	0CRN3JZ	1062	0CTT*	77, 101, 684
0CBT7ZZ	77, 101, 684, 899	0CNF*	85, 684	0CQ2XZZ	423, 900	0CR1X7Z	423, 900, 1061	0CRN3KZ	1062	0CTT0ZZ	900
0CBT8ZZ	77, 101, 684, 899	0CNF0ZZ	899	0CQ3*	34, 77, 684	0CR1XJZ	423, 900, 1061	0CRNX7Z	1062	0CTT4ZZ	900
0CBV0ZX	77, 101	0CNF3ZZ	899	0CQ30ZZ	423, 900	0CR1XKZ	423, 900, 1061	0CRNXJZ	1062	0CTT7ZZ	900
0CBV0ZZ	77, 101, 684, 899	0CNG*	85, 684	0CQ33ZZ	423, 900	0CR2*	34, 77	0CRNXKZ	1062	0CTT8ZZ	900
0CBV3ZZ	77, 101, 684, 899	0CNG0ZZ	899	0CQ3XZZ	423, 900	0CR207Z	423	0CRR*	77, 101, 684	0CTV*	77, 101, 684
0CBV4ZZ	77, 101, 684, 899	0CNG3ZZ	899	0CQ40ZZ	84, 423, 684, 900, 1061	0CR20JZ	423	0CRS*	77, 101, 684	0CTV0ZZ	900
0CBV7ZZ	77, 101, 684, 899	0CNH*	85, 684	0CQ43ZZ	84, 423, 684, 900, 1061	0CR20KZ	423	0CRT*	77, 101	0CTV4ZZ	900
0CBV8ZZ	77, 101, 684, 899	0CNH0ZZ	899	0CQ70ZZ	84	0CR237Z	423	0CRT07Z	684	0CTV7ZZ	900
0CC00ZZ	84, 423, 684, 899, 1061	0CNH3ZZ	899	0CQ73ZZ	84	0CR23JZ	423	0CRT0JZ	1062	0CTV8ZZ	900
0CC03ZZ	84, 423, 684, 899, 1061	0CNJ*	85, 684	0CQ8*	85, 684	0CR23KZ	423	0CRT0KZ	684	0CU0*	84, 684
0CC10ZZ	84, 423, 684, 899, 1061	0CNJ0ZZ	899	0CQ80ZZ	900	0CR2X7Z	423	0CRT77Z	684	0CU007Z	423, 900, 1062
0CC13ZZ	84, 423, 684, 899, 1061	0CNJ3ZZ	899	0CQ83ZZ	900	0CR2XJZ	423	0CRT7JZ	1062	0CU00JZ	423, 900, 1062
0CC20ZZ	84	0CNM*	77	0CQ9*	85, 684	0CR2XKZ	423	0CRT7KZ	684	0CU00KZ	423, 900, 1062
0CC23ZZ	84	0CNN*	84	0CQ90ZZ	900	0CR3*	34, 77	0CRT87Z	684	0CU037Z	423, 900, 1062
0CC30ZZ	84	0CNN0ZZ	1061	0CQ93ZZ	900	0CR307Z	423	0CRT8JZ	1062	0CU03JZ	423, 900, 1062
0CC33ZZ	84	0CNN3ZZ	1061	0CQB*	85, 684	0CR30JZ	423	0CRT8KZ	684	0CU03KZ	423, 900, 1062
0CC40ZZ	84, 423, 684, 899, 1061	0CNNXZZ	1061	0CQB0ZZ	900	0CR30KZ	423	0CRV*	77, 101	0CU0X7Z	423, 900, 1062
0CC43ZZ	84, 423, 684, 899, 1061	0CNP*	77	0CQB3ZZ	900	0CR337Z	423	0CRV07Z	684	0CU0XJZ	423, 900, 1062
0CC70ZZ	84	0CNQ*	77	0CQC*	85, 684	0CR33JZ	423	0CRV0JZ	1062	0CU0XKZ	423, 900, 1062
0CC73ZZ	84	0CNR*	77, 101, 684	0CQC0ZZ	900	0CR33KZ	423	0CRV0KZ	684	0CU1*	84, 684
0CC80ZZ	85, 1061	0CNR3ZZ	899	0CQC3ZZ	900	0CR3X7Z	423	0CRV77Z	684	0CU107Z	423, 900, 1062
0CC90ZZ	85, 1061	0CNR4ZZ	899	0CQD*	85, 684	0CR3XJZ	423	0CRV7JZ	1062	0CU10JZ	423, 900, 1062
0CCG0ZZ	85, 1061	0CNR7ZZ	899	0CQD0ZZ	900	0CR3XKZ	423	0CRV7KZ	684	0CU10KZ	423, 900, 1062
0CCH0ZZ	85, 1061	0CNR8ZZ	899	0CQD3ZZ	900	0CR4*	84, 684	0CRV87Z	1062	0CU137Z	423, 900, 1062
0CCM0ZZ	77, 684, 899	0CNS*	77, 101, 684	0CQF*	85, 684	0CR407Z	423, 900, 1061	0CRV8JZ	684	0CU13JZ	423, 900, 1062
0CCM3ZZ	77, 684, 899	0CNS0ZZ	899	0CQF0ZZ	900	0CR40JZ	423, 900, 1061	0CRV8KZ	684	0CU13KZ	423, 900, 1062
0CCM4ZZ	77, 684, 899	0CNS3ZZ	899	0CQF3ZZ	900	0CR40KZ	423, 900, 1061	0CS0*	84, 684	0CU1X7Z	423, 900, 1062
0CCN0ZZ	84, 1061	0CNS4ZZ	899	0CQG*	85, 684	0CR437Z	423, 900, 1061	0CS00ZZ	423, 900, 1062	0CU1XJZ	423, 901, 1062
0CCN3ZZ	84, 1061	0CNS7ZZ	899	0CQG0ZZ	900	0CR43JZ	423, 900, 1062	0CS0XZZ	423, 900, 1062	0CU1XKZ	423, 901, 1062
0CCP0ZZ	77, 684, 899	0CNS8ZZ	899	0CQG3ZZ	900	0CR43KZ	423, 900, 1062	0CS1*	84, 684	0CU207Z	34, 77, 423
0CCP3ZZ	77, 684, 899	0CNT*	77, 101, 684	0CQH*	85, 684	0CR4X7Z	423, 900, 1062	0CS10ZZ	423, 900, 1062	0CU20KZ	34, 77, 423
0CCQ0ZZ	77, 684, 899	0CNT3ZZ	899			0CR4XJZ	423, 900, 1062	0CS1XZZ	423, 900, 1062	0CU237Z	34, 77, 423
0CCQ3ZZ	77, 684, 899	0CNT4ZZ	899			0CR4XKZ	423, 900, 1062	0CS2*	34, 77	0CU23KZ	34, 77, 423
0CCR*	77	0CNT7ZZ	899			0CR5*	84, 684	0CS20ZZ	423	0CU2X7Z	34, 77, 423
0CCS0ZZ	77	0CNT8ZZ	899			0CR507Z	900	0CS2XZZ	423	0CU2XJZ	34, 77
0CCS3ZZ	77	0CNV*	77, 101, 684			0CR50JZ	900	0CS3*	34, 77	0CU2XKZ	34, 77, 423
0CCS4ZZ	77	0CNV3ZZ	899			0CR50KZ	900	0CS30ZZ	423	0CU3*	34, 77
0CCT*	77	0CNV4ZZ	899			0CR537Z	900	0CS3XZZ	423	0CU307Z	423
0CCV*	77	0CNV7ZZ	899			0CR53JZ	900	0CS7*	84, 684	0CU30JZ	423
0CDT*	77, 101	0CNV8ZZ	899			0CR53KZ	900	0CS70ZZ	900	0CU30KZ	423
0CDT0ZZ	1061	0CPS00Z	77			0CR5X7Z	900	0CS7XZZ	900	0CU337Z	423
0CDT3ZZ	1061	0CPS07Z	77			0CR5XJZ	900	0CSB*	85, 684	0CU33JZ	423
0CDT4ZZ	1061					0CR5XKZ	900	0CSB0ZZ	900	0CU33KZ	423
0CDT7ZZ	1061					0CR6*	84, 684	0CSB3ZZ	900	0CU3X7Z	423
						0CR607Z	900	0CSC*	85, 684	0CU3XJZ	423
						0CR60JZ	900	0CSC0ZZ	900	0CU3XKZ	423
						0CR60KZ	900	0CSC3ZZ	900	0CU4*	84, 684
						0CR637Z	900	0CSN*	84	0CU407Z	423, 901, 1062
						0CR63JZ	900	0CSN0ZZ	1062	0CU40JZ	423, 901, 1062
						0CR63KZ	900	0CSNXZZ	1062	0CU40KZ	423, 901, 1062

Code	Page
0CU437Z	423, 901, 1062
0CU43JZ	423, 901, 1062
0CU43KZ	424, 901, 1062
0CU4X7Z	424, 901, 1062
0CU4XJZ	424, 901, 1062
0CU4XKZ	424, 901, 1062
0CU5*	84, 684
0CU507Z	901
0CU50JZ	901
0CU50KZ	901
0CU537Z	901
0CU53JZ	901
0CU53KZ	901
0CU5X7Z	901
0CU5XJZ	901
0CU5XKZ	901
0CU6*	84, 684
0CU607Z	901
0CU60JZ	901
0CU60KZ	901
0CU637Z	901
0CU63JZ	901
0CU63KZ	901
0CU6X7Z	901
0CU6XJZ	901
0CU6XKZ	901
0CU7*	84, 684
0CU707Z	901
0CU70JZ	901
0CU70KZ	901
0CU737Z	901
0CU73JZ	901
0CU73KZ	901
0CU7X7Z	901
0CU7XJZ	901
0CU7XKZ	901
0CUM*	34, 77, 684
0CUM07Z	901, 1062
0CUM0JZ	901, 1062
0CUM0KZ	901, 1062
0CUM77Z	901, 1062
0CUM7JZ	901, 1062
0CUM7KZ	901, 1062
0CUM8JZ	901, 1062
0CUM8KZ	901, 1062
0CUN*	84
0CUN07Z	1062
0CUN0JZ	1062
0CUN0KZ	1062
0CUN37Z	1062
0CUN3JZ	1062
0CUN3KZ	1062
0CUNX7Z	1062
0CUNXJZ	1062
0CUNXKZ	1062
0CUR*	77, 101, 684
0CUS*	77, 101, 684
0CUT*	77, 101, 684
0CUV*	77, 101, 684
0CV*	85
0CVB7DZ	684, 901
0CVB7ZZ	684, 901
0CVB8DZ	684, 901
0CVB8ZZ	684, 901
0CVC7DZ	684, 901
0CVC7ZZ	684, 901
0CVC8DZ	684, 901
0CVC8ZZ	684, 901
0CWS00Z	77
0CWS07Z	77
0CWS0DZ	77
0CWS0JZ	77
0CWS0KZ	77
0CWS0YZ	77
0CWS30Z	77
0CWS37Z	77
0CWS3DZ	77
0CWS3JZ	77
0CWS3KZ	77
0CWS70Z	77
0CWS77Z	77
0CWS7DZ	77
0CWS7JZ	77
0CWS7KZ	77
0CWS80Z	77
0CWS87Z	77
0CWS8DZ	77
0CWS8JZ	77
0CWS8KZ	77
0CWY00Z	84, 424, 684, 901, 1062
0CWY01Z	84, 424, 684, 901, 1062
0CWY0DZ	84, 424, 684, 901, 1062
0CWY0JZ	84, 424, 684, 901, 1062
0CWY0KZ	84, 424, 684, 901, 1062
0CWY0YZ	84, 424, 684, 901, 1062
0CWY30Z	84, 424, 684, 901, 1062
0CWY31Z	84, 424, 684, 901, 1062
0CWY37Z	84, 424, 684, 901, 1062
0CWY3DZ	84, 424, 684, 901, 1062
0CWY3JZ	85, 424, 684, 901, 1062
0CWY3KZ	85, 424, 684, 901, 1062
0CWY70Z	77, 684, 901
0CWY71Z	77, 684, 901
0CWY77Z	77, 684, 901
0CWY7DZ	77, 684, 901
0CWY7JZ	77, 684, 901
0CWY7KZ	77, 684, 901
0CWY80Z	77, 685, 901
0CWY81Z	77, 685, 901
0CWY87Z	77, 685, 901
0CWY8DZ	77, 685, 901
0CWY8JZ	77, 685, 901
0CWY8KZ	77, 685, 901
0CX*	85, 685
0CX00ZZ	424, 901, 1062
0CX0XZZ	424, 901, 1062
0CX10ZZ	424, 901, 1062
0CX1XZZ	424, 901, 1062
0CX30ZZ	424, 901, 1062
0CX3XZZ	424, 901, 1062
0CX40ZZ	424, 901, 1062
0CX4XZZ	424, 901, 1062
0CX50ZZ	424, 901, 1062
0CX5XZZ	424, 901, 1062
0CX60ZZ	424, 901, 1062
0CX6XZZ	424, 901, 1062
0CX70ZZ	901
0CX7XZZ	901
0D11*	174
0D11074	77, 591, 616, 685, 901
0D11076	77, 591, 616, 685, 901
0D110J4	77, 591, 616, 685, 901
0D110J6	77, 591, 616, 685, 901
0D110K4	77, 591, 616, 685, 901
0D110K6	77, 591, 616, 685, 901
0D110Z4	77, 591, 616, 685, 901
0D110Z6	77, 591, 616, 685, 901
0D113J4	77, 591, 616, 685, 901
0D11474	77, 591, 616, 685, 901
0D11476	77, 591, 616, 685, 901
0D114J4	77, 591, 616, 685, 901
0D114J6	77, 591, 616, 685, 901
0D114K4	77, 591, 616, 685, 901
0D114K6	77, 591, 616, 685, 901
0D114Z4	77, 591, 616, 685, 901
0D114Z6	77, 591, 616, 685, 901
0D11874	77, 591, 616, 685, 901
0D11876	77, 591, 616, 685, 901
0D118J4	77, 591, 616, 685, 901
0D118J6	77, 591, 616, 685, 901
0D118K4	77, 591, 616, 685, 901
0D118K6	77, 591, 616, 685, 901
0D118Z4	77, 591, 616, 685, 901
0D118Z6	77, 591, 616, 685, 901
0D12*	174
0D12074	77, 591, 616, 685, 901
0D12076	77, 591, 616, 685, 901
0D120J4	77, 591, 616, 685, 901
0D120J6	77, 591, 616, 685, 901
0D120K4	77, 591, 616, 685, 901
0D120K6	77, 591, 616, 685, 901
0D120Z4	77, 591, 616, 685, 901
0D120Z6	77, 591, 616, 685, 901
0D123J4	77, 591, 616, 685, 901
0D12474	77, 591, 616, 685, 901
0D12476	77, 591, 616, 685, 901
0D124J4	78, 591, 616, 685, 901
0D124J6	78, 591, 616, 685, 901
0D124K4	78, 591, 616, 685, 901
0D124K6	78, 591, 616, 685, 901
0D124Z4	78, 591, 616, 685, 901
0D124Z6	78, 591, 616, 685, 901
0D12874	78, 591, 616, 685, 901
0D12876	78, 591, 616, 685, 901
0D128J4	78, 591, 616, 685, 901
0D128J6	78, 591, 616, 685, 901
0D128K4	78, 591, 616, 685, 901
0D128K6	78, 591, 616, 685, 901
0D128Z4	78, 591, 616, 685, 901
0D128Z6	78, 591, 616, 685, 901
0D13*	174
0D13074	78, 591, 616, 685, 901
0D13076	78, 591, 616, 685, 901
0D130J4	78, 591, 616, 685, 901
0D130J6	78, 591, 616, 685, 901
0D130K4	78, 591, 616, 685, 901
0D130K6	78, 591, 616, 685, 901
0D130Z4	78, 591, 616, 685, 901
0D130Z6	78, 591, 616, 685, 901
0D133J4	78, 591, 616, 685, 901
0D13474	78, 591, 616, 685, 901
0D13476	78, 591, 616, 685, 901
0D134J4	78, 591, 616, 685, 901
0D134J6	78, 591, 616, 685, 901
0D134K4	78, 591, 616, 685, 901
0D134K6	78, 591, 616, 685, 901
0D134Z4	78, 591, 616, 685, 901
0D134Z6	78, 591, 616, 685, 901
0D13874	78, 591, 616, 685, 901
0D13876	78, 591, 616, 685, 901
0D138J4	78, 591, 616, 685, 901
0D138J6	78, 591, 616, 685, 901
0D138K4	78, 591, 616, 685, 901
0D138K6	78, 591, 616, 685, 901
0D138Z4	78, 591, 616, 685, 901
0D138Z6	78, 591, 616, 685, 901
0D15*	78, 174, 685
0D15074	591, 616, 901
0D15076	591, 616, 901
0D15079	591, 616, 901
0D1507A	591, 616, 901
0D1507B	591, 616, 901
0D150J4	591, 616, 901
0D150J6	591, 616, 902
0D150J9	591, 616, 902
0D150JB	591, 616, 902
0D150K4	591, 616, 902
0D150K6	591, 616, 902
0D150K9	591, 616, 902
0D150KA	591, 616, 902
0D150KB	591, 616, 902
0D150Z4	591, 616, 902
0D150Z6	591, 616, 902
0D150Z9	591, 616, 902
0D150ZA	591, 616, 902
0D150ZB	591, 616, 902
0D153J4	591, 616, 902
0D15474	591, 616, 902
0D15476	591, 616, 902
0D15479	591, 616, 902
0D1547A	591, 616, 902
0D1547B	591, 616, 902
0D154J4	591, 616, 902
0D154J6	591, 616, 902
0D154J9	591, 616, 902
0D154JA	591, 616, 902
0D154JB	591, 616, 902
0D154K4	591, 616, 902
0D154K6	591, 616, 902
0D154K9	591, 617, 902
0D154KA	591, 617, 902
0D154KB	591, 617, 902
0D154Z4	591, 617, 902
0D154Z6	591, 617, 902
0D154Z9	591, 617, 902
0D154ZA	591, 617, 902
0D154ZB	591, 617, 902
0D15874	591, 617, 902
0D15876	591, 617, 902
0D15879	591, 617, 902
0D1587A	591, 617, 902
0D1587B	591, 617, 902
0D158J4	591, 617, 902
0D158J6	591, 617, 902
0D158J9	591, 617, 902
0D158JA	591, 617, 902
0D158JB	591, 617, 902
0D158K4	591, 617, 902
0D158K6	591, 617, 902
0D158K9	591, 617, 902
0D158KA	591, 617, 902
0D158KB	591, 617, 902
0D158Z4	591, 617, 902
0D158Z6	591, 617, 902
0D158Z9	591, 617, 902
0D158ZA	591, 617, 902
0D158ZB	591, 617, 902
0D16079	145, 174, 206, 479, 591, 617
0D1607A	145, 174, 206, 479, 591, 617
0D1607B	145, 174, 206, 479, 591, 617
0D1607L	145, 174, 206, 479, 591, 617
0D160J9	145, 174, 206, 479, 591, 617
0D160JA	145, 174, 206, 479, 591, 617
0D160JB	145, 174, 206, 479, 591, 617
0D160JL	145, 174, 206, 479, 591, 617
0D160K9	145, 174, 206, 479, 591, 617
0D160KA	145, 174, 206, 479, 591, 617
0D160KB	145, 174, 206, 479, 592, 617
0D160KL	145, 174, 206, 479, 592, 617
0D160Z9	145, 174, 206, 479, 592, 617
0D160ZA	145, 174, 206, 480, 592, 617
0D160ZB	145, 174, 206, 480, 592, 617
0D160ZL	145, 174, 206, 480, 592, 617
0D16479	145, 174, 206, 480, 592, 617
0D1647A	145, 174, 206, 480, 592, 617
0D1647B	145, 174, 206, 480, 592, 617
0D1647L	145, 174, 206, 480, 592, 617
0D164J9	145, 174, 206, 480, 592, 617
0D164JA	145, 174, 206, 480, 592, 617
0D164JB	145, 174, 206, 480, 592, 617
0D164JL	145, 174, 206, 480, 592, 617
0D164K9	145, 174, 206, 480, 592, 617
0D164KA	145, 174, 206, 480, 592, 617
0D164KB	145, 174, 207, 480, 592, 617
0D164KL	145, 174, 207, 480, 592, 617
0D164Z9	145, 174, 207, 480, 592, 617
0D164ZA	145, 174, 207, 480, 592, 617
0D164ZB	145, 174, 207, 480, 592, 617
0D164ZL	145, 174, 207, 480, 592, 617
0D16879	145, 174, 207, 480, 592, 617
0D1687A	145, 174, 207, 480, 592, 617
0D1687B	145, 174, 207, 480, 592, 617
0D1687L	145, 174, 207, 480, 592, 617
0D168J9	145, 174, 207, 480, 592, 617
0D168JA	145, 174, 207, 480, 592, 617
0D168JB	145, 174, 207, 480, 592, 617
0D168JL	145, 174, 207, 480, 592, 617
0D168K9	145, 174, 207, 480, 592, 617
0D168KA	145, 174, 207, 480, 592, 617
0D168KB	145, 174, 207, 480, 592, 617
0D168KL	145, 174, 207, 480, 592, 617
0D168Z9	145, 174, 207, 480, 592, 617
0D168ZA	145, 174, 207, 480, 592, 617
0D168ZB	145, 174, 207, 480, 592, 617
0D168ZL	145, 174, 207, 480, 592, 617
0D18074	177, 592, 617, 685, 902
0D18078	177, 480, 592, 617, 685, 902
0D1807H	177, 491, 592, 617, 685, 902
0D1807K	177, 491, 592, 617, 685, 902
0D1807L	177, 491, 592, 617, 685, 902
0D1807M	177, 491, 592, 617, 685, 902
0D1807N	177, 491, 592, 617, 685, 902
0D1807P	177, 592, 617, 685, 902
0D1807Q	177, 592, 617, 685, 902
0D180J4	177, 592, 617, 685, 902
0D180J8	177, 480, 592, 617, 685, 902
0D180JH	177, 491, 592, 617, 685, 902
0D180JK	177, 491, 592, 617, 685, 902
0D180JL	177, 491, 592, 617, 685, 902
0D180JM	177, 491, 592, 617, 685, 902
0D180JN	177, 491, 592, 617, 685, 902
0D180JP	177, 592, 617, 685, 902
0D180JQ	177, 592, 617, 685, 902
0D180K4	177, 592, 617, 685, 902
0D180K8	177, 480, 592, 617, 685, 902
0D180KH	177, 491, 592, 617, 685, 902
0D180KK	177, 491, 592, 617, 685, 902
0D180KL	177, 491, 592, 617, 685, 902
0D180KM	177, 491, 592, 617, 685, 902
0D180KN	177, 491, 592, 617, 685, 902
0D180KP	177, 592, 617, 685, 902
0D180KQ	177, 592, 617, 685, 902
0D180Z4	177, 592, 617, 685, 902
0D180Z8	177, 480, 592, 617, 685, 902
0D180ZH	177, 491, 592, 617, 685, 902
0D180ZK	177, 491, 592, 617, 685, 902
0D180ZL	177, 491, 592, 617, 685, 902
0D180ZM	177, 491, 592, 617, 685, 902
0D180ZN	177, 491, 592, 617, 685, 902
0D180ZP	177, 592, 617, 685, 902
0D180ZQ	177, 592, 617, 685, 902
0D18474	177, 592, 617, 685, 902
0D18478	177, 480, 592, 617, 685, 902
0D1847H	177, 491, 592, 617, 685, 902
0D1847K	177, 491, 592, 617, 685, 902
0D1847L	177, 491, 592, 617, 685, 902
0D1847M	177, 491, 592, 617, 685, 902
0D1847N	177, 491, 592, 617, 685, 902
0D1847P	177, 592, 617, 685, 902
0D1847Q	177, 592, 617, 685, 902
0D184J4	177, 592, 617, 685, 902
0D184J8	177, 480, 592, 617, 685, 902
0D184JH	177, 491, 592, 617, 685, 902
0D184JK	177, 491, 592, 617, 685, 902
0D184JL	177, 491, 592, 617, 685, 902

Numeric Index to Procedures
DRG Expert—Volume II

Code	Page
ØD184JM	177, 491, 592, 617, 685, 902
ØD184JN	177, 491, 592, 617, 685, 902
ØD184JP	177, 592, 617, 685, 902
ØD184JQ	177, 592, 617, 685, 902
ØD184K4	177, 592, 617, 685, 902
ØD184K8	177, 480, 592, 617, 685, 902
ØD184KH	177, 491, 592, 617, 685, 902
ØD184KK	177, 491, 592, 617, 685, 902
ØD184KL	177, 491, 592, 617, 685, 902
ØD184KM	177, 491, 592, 617, 685, 902
ØD184KN	177, 491, 592, 617, 685, 902
ØD184KP	177, 592, 617, 685, 902
ØD184KQ	177, 592, 617, 685, 902
ØD184Z4	177, 592, 617, 685, 902
ØD184Z8	177, 480, 592, 617, 685, 902
ØD184ZH	177, 491, 592, 617, 685, 902
ØD184ZK	177, 491, 592, 617, 685, 902
ØD184ZL	177, 491, 592, 617, 685, 902
ØD184ZM	177, 491, 592, 617, 685, 902
ØD184ZN	177, 491, 592, 617, 685, 902
ØD184ZP	177, 592, 617, 685, 902
ØD184ZQ	177, 592, 617, 685, 902
ØD18874	177, 592, 617, 685, 902
ØD18878	177, 480, 592, 617, 685, 902
ØD1887H	145, 177, 491, 592, 617, 685, 902
ØD1887K	177, 491, 592, 617, 685, 902
ØD1887L	177, 491, 592, 617, 685, 902
ØD1887M	177, 491, 592, 617, 685, 902
ØD1887N	177, 491, 592, 617, 685, 902
ØD1887P	177, 592, 617, 685, 902
ØD1887Q	177, 592, 617, 685, 902
ØD188J4	177, 592, 617, 685, 902
ØD188J8	177, 480, 592, 617, 685, 902
ØD188JH	145, 177, 491, 592, 617, 685, 902
ØD188JK	177, 491, 592, 617, 685, 902
ØD188JL	177, 491, 592, 617, 685, 902
ØD188JM	177, 491, 592, 617, 685, 902
ØD188JN	177, 491, 592, 617, 685, 902
ØD188JP	177, 592, 617, 685, 902
ØD188JQ	177, 592, 617, 685, 902
ØD188K4	177, 592, 617, 685, 902
ØD188K8	177, 480, 592, 617, 686, 902
ØD188KH	145, 177, 491, 592, 617, 686, 902
ØD188KK	177, 491, 592, 617, 686, 902
ØD188KL	177, 491, 592, 617, 686, 902
ØD188KM	177, 491, 592, 617, 686, 902
ØD188KN	177, 491, 592, 617, 686, 902
ØD188KP	177, 592, 617, 686, 902
ØD188KQ	177, 592, 618, 686, 902
ØD188Z4	177, 592, 618, 686, 902
ØD188Z8	177, 480, 592, 618, 686, 902
ØD188ZH	177, 480, 592, 618, 686, 902
ØD188ZK	177, 491, 592, 618, 686, 902
ØD188ZL	177, 491, 592, 618, 686, 902
ØD188ZM	177, 491, 592, 618, 686, 902
ØD188ZN	177, 491, 592, 618, 686, 902
ØD188ZP	177, 592, 618, 686, 902
ØD188ZQ	177, 592, 618, 686, 902
ØD19*	177, 686
ØD19Ø74	592, 618, 902
ØD19Ø79	480, 592, 618, 902
ØD19Ø7A	480, 592, 618, 902
ØD19Ø7B	480, 592, 618, 902
ØD19Ø7L	491, 592, 618
ØD19ØJ4	592, 618, 902
ØD19ØJ9	480, 592, 618, 902
ØD19ØJA	480, 592, 618, 902
ØD19ØJB	480, 592, 618, 902
ØD19ØJL	491, 592, 618
ØD19ØK4	592, 618, 902
ØD19ØK9	480, 592, 618, 902
ØD19ØKA	480, 592, 618, 902
ØD19ØKB	480, 592, 618, 903
ØD19ØKL	491, 592, 618
ØD19ØZ4	592, 618, 903
ØD19ØZ9	480, 592, 618, 903
ØD19ØZA	480, 592, 618, 903
ØD19ØZB	480, 592, 618, 903
ØD19ØZL	491, 592, 618
ØD193J4	592, 618, 903
ØD19474	592, 618, 903
ØD19479	480, 592, 618, 903
ØD1947A	480, 592, 618, 903
ØD1947B	480, 592, 618, 903
ØD1947L	491, 592, 618
ØD194J4	592, 618, 903
ØD194J9	480, 592, 618, 903
ØD194JA	480, 593, 618, 903
ØD194JB	480, 593, 618, 903
ØD194JL	491, 593, 618
ØD194K4	593, 618, 903
ØD194K9	480, 593, 618, 903
ØD194KA	480, 593, 618, 903
ØD194KB	480, 593, 618, 903
ØD194KL	491, 593, 618
ØD194Z4	593, 618, 903
ØD194Z9	480, 593, 618, 903
ØD194ZA	480, 593, 618, 903
ØD194ZB	480, 593, 618, 903
ØD194ZL	491, 593, 618
ØD19874	593, 618, 903
ØD19879	480, 593, 618, 903
ØD1987A	480, 593, 618, 903
ØD1987B	480, 593, 618, 903
ØD1987L	491, 593, 618
ØD198J4	593, 618, 903
ØD198J9	480, 593, 618, 903
ØD198JA	480, 593, 618, 903
ØD198JB	480, 593, 618, 903
ØD198JL	491, 593, 618
ØD198K4	593, 618, 903
ØD198K9	480, 593, 618, 903
ØD198KA	480, 593, 618, 903
ØD198KB	480, 593, 618, 903
ØD198KL	491, 593, 618
ØD198Z4	593, 618, 903
ØD198Z9	480, 593, 618, 903
ØD198ZA	480, 593, 618, 903
ØD198ZB	480, 593, 618, 903
ØD198ZL	491, 593, 618
ØD1A*	177, 686
ØD1AØ74	593, 618, 903
ØD1AØ7A	480, 593, 618, 903
ØD1AØ7B	480, 593, 618, 903
ØD1AØ7H	491, 593, 618
ØD1AØ7K	491, 593, 618
ØD1AØ7L	491, 593, 618
ØD1AØ7M	491, 593, 618
ØD1AØ7N	491, 593, 618
ØD1AØ7P	593, 618, 903
ØD1AØ7Q	593, 618, 903
ØD1AØJ4	593, 618, 903
ØD1AØJA	480, 593, 618, 903
ØD1AØJB	480, 593, 618, 903
ØD1AØJH	491, 593, 618
ØD1AØJK	491, 593, 618
ØD1AØJL	491, 593, 618
ØD1AØJM	491, 593, 618
ØD1AØJN	491, 593, 618
ØD1AØJP	593, 618, 903
ØD1AØJQ	593, 618, 903
ØD1AØK4	593, 618, 903
ØD1AØKA	480, 593, 618, 903
ØD1AØKB	480, 593, 618, 903
ØD1AØKH	491, 593, 618
ØD1AØKK	491, 593, 618
ØD1AØKL	491, 593, 618
ØD1AØKM	491, 593, 618
ØD1AØKN	491, 593, 618
ØD1AØKP	593, 618, 903
ØD1AØKQ	593, 618, 903
ØD1AØZ4	593, 618, 903
ØD1AØZA	480, 593, 618, 903
ØD1AØZB	480, 593, 618, 903
ØD1AØZH	491, 593, 618
ØD1AØZK	491, 593, 618
ØD1AØZL	491, 593, 618
ØD1AØZM	491, 593, 618
ØD1AØZN	491, 593, 618
ØD1AØZP	593, 618, 903
ØD1AØZQ	593, 618, 903
ØD1A3J4	593, 618, 903
ØD1A474	593, 618, 903
ØD1A47A	480, 593, 618, 903
ØD1A47B	480, 593, 618, 903
ØD1A47H	491, 593, 618
ØD1A47K	491, 593, 618
ØD1A47L	491, 593, 618
ØD1A47M	491, 593, 618
ØD1A47N	491, 593, 618
ØD1A47P	593, 618, 903
ØD1A47Q	593, 618, 903
ØD1A4J4	593, 618, 903
ØD1A4JA	480, 593, 618, 903
ØD1A4JB	480, 593, 618, 903
ØD1A4JH	491, 593, 618
ØD1A4JK	491, 593, 618
ØD1A4JL	491, 593, 618
ØD1A4JM	491, 593, 618
ØD1A4JN	491, 593, 618
ØD1A4JP	593, 618, 903
ØD1A4JQ	593, 618, 903
ØD1A4K4	593, 618, 903
ØD1A4KA	480, 593, 618, 903
ØD1A4KB	480, 593, 618, 903
ØD1A4KH	491, 593, 618
ØD1A4KK	491, 593, 618
ØD1A4KL	491, 593, 618
ØD1A4KM	491, 593, 618
ØD1A4KN	491, 593, 618
ØD1A4KP	593, 618, 903
ØD1A4KQ	593, 618, 903
ØD1A4Z4	593, 618, 903
ØD1A4ZA	480, 593, 618, 903
ØD1A4ZB	480, 593, 618, 903
ØD1A4ZH	491, 593, 618
ØD1A4ZK	491, 593, 618
ØD1A4ZL	491, 593, 618
ØD1A4ZM	491, 593, 618
ØD1A4ZN	491, 593, 618
ØD1A4ZP	593, 618, 903
ØD1A4ZQ	593, 618, 903
ØD1A874	593, 618, 903
ØD1A87A	480, 593, 618, 903
ØD1A87B	480, 593, 618, 903
ØD1A87H	145, 491, 593, 618, 903
ØD1A87K	491, 593, 618
ØD1A87L	491, 593, 618
ØD1A87M	491, 593, 618
ØD1A87N	492, 593, 618
ØD1A87P	593, 618, 903
ØD1A87Q	593, 618, 903
ØD1A8J4	593, 618, 903
ØD1A8JA	480, 593, 618, 903
ØD1A8JB	480, 593, 618, 903
ØD1A8JH	145, 492, 593, 618, 903
ØD1A8JK	492, 593, 618
ØD1A8JL	492, 593, 618
ØD1A8JM	492, 593, 618
ØD1A8JN	492, 593, 618
ØD1A8JP	593, 618, 903
ØD1A8JQ	593, 618, 903
ØD1A8K4	593, 618, 903
ØD1A8KA	480, 593, 618, 903
ØD1A8KB	480, 593, 619, 903
ØD1A8KH	145, 492, 593, 619, 903
ØD1A8KK	492, 593, 619
ØD1A8KL	492, 593, 619
ØD1A8KM	492, 593, 619
ØD1A8KN	492, 593, 619
ØD1A8KP	593, 619, 903
ØD1A8KQ	593, 619, 903
ØD1A8Z4	593, 619, 903
ØD1A8ZA	480, 593, 619, 903
ØD1A8ZB	480, 593, 619, 903
ØD1A8ZH	480, 593, 619, 903
ØD1A8ZK	492, 593, 619
ØD1A8ZL	492, 593, 619
ØD1A8ZM	492, 593, 619
ØD1A8ZN	492, 593, 619
ØD1A8ZP	593, 619, 903
ØD1A8ZQ	593, 619, 903
ØD1B*	177, 686
ØD1BØ74	593, 619, 903
ØD1BØ7B	480, 593, 619, 903
ØD1BØ7H	492, 593, 619
ØD1BØ7K	492, 593, 619
ØD1BØ7L	492, 593, 619
ØD1BØ7M	492, 593, 619
ØD1BØ7N	492, 593, 619
ØD1BØ7P	593, 619, 903
ØD1BØ7Q	593, 619, 903
ØD1BØJ4	593, 619, 903
ØD1BØJB	480, 593, 619, 903
ØD1BØJH	492, 593, 619
ØD1BØJK	492, 593, 619
ØD1BØJL	492, 593, 619
ØD1BØJM	492, 593, 619
ØD1BØJN	492, 593, 619
ØD1BØJP	593, 619, 903
ØD1BØJQ	593, 619, 903
ØD1BØK4	593, 619, 903
ØD1BØKB	480, 593, 619, 903
ØD1BØKH	492, 594, 619
ØD1BØKK	492, 594, 619
ØD1BØKL	492, 594, 619
ØD1BØKM	492, 594, 619
ØD1BØKN	492, 594, 619
ØD1BØKP	594, 619, 903
ØD1BØKQ	594, 619, 903
ØD1BØZ4	594, 619, 903
ØD1BØZB	480, 594, 619, 903
ØD1BØZH	492, 594, 619
ØD1BØZK	492, 594, 619
ØD1BØZL	492, 594, 619
ØD1BØZM	492, 594, 619
ØD1BØZN	492, 594, 619
ØD1BØZP	594, 619, 903
ØD1BØZQ	594, 619, 903
ØD1B3J4	594, 619, 903
ØD1B474	594, 619, 903
ØD1B47B	480, 594, 619, 903
ØD1B47H	492, 594, 619
ØD1B47K	492, 594, 619
ØD1B47L	492, 594, 619
ØD1B47M	492, 594, 619
ØD1B47N	492, 594, 619
ØD1B47P	594, 619, 903
ØD1B47Q	594, 619, 903
ØD1B4J4	594, 619, 903
ØD1B4JB	480, 594, 619, 903
ØD1B4JH	492, 594, 619
ØD1B4JK	492, 594, 619
ØD1B4JL	492, 594, 619
ØD1B4JM	492, 594, 619
ØD1B4JN	492, 594, 619
ØD1B4JP	594, 619, 903
ØD1B4JQ	594, 619, 903
ØD1B4K4	594, 619, 903
ØD1B4KB	480, 594, 619, 903
ØD1B4KH	492, 594, 619
ØD1B4KK	492, 594, 619
ØD1B4KL	492, 594, 619
ØD1B4KM	492, 594, 619
ØD1B4KN	492, 594, 619
ØD1B4KP	594, 619, 903
ØD1B4KQ	594, 619, 903
ØD1B4Z4	594, 619, 903
ØD1B4ZB	480, 594, 619, 903
ØD1B4ZH	492, 594, 619
ØD1B4ZK	492, 594, 619
ØD1B4ZL	492, 594, 619
ØD1B4ZM	492, 594, 619
ØD1B4ZN	492, 594, 619
ØD1B4ZP	594, 619, 903
ØD1B4ZQ	594, 619, 903
ØD1B874	594, 619, 903
ØD1B87B	480, 594, 619, 903
ØD1B87H	145, 492, 594, 619, 903
ØD1B87K	492, 594, 619
ØD1B87L	492, 594, 619
ØD1B87M	492, 594, 619
ØD1B87N	492, 594, 619
ØD1B87P	594, 619, 903
ØD1B87Q	594, 619, 903
ØD1B8J4	594, 619, 903
ØD1B8JB	480, 594, 619, 903
ØD1B8JH	145, 492, 594, 619, 903
ØD1B8JK	492, 594, 619
ØD1B8JL	492, 594, 619
ØD1B8JM	492, 594, 619
ØD1B8JN	492, 594, 619
ØD1B8JP	594, 619, 903
ØD1B8JQ	594, 619, 903
ØD1B8K4	594, 619, 903
ØD1B8KB	480, 594, 619, 903
ØD1B8KH	145, 492, 594, 619, 903
ØD1B8KK	492, 594, 619
ØD1B8KL	492, 594, 619
ØD1B8KM	492, 594, 619
ØD1B8KN	492, 594, 619
ØD1B8KP	594, 619, 903
ØD1B8KQ	594, 619, 903
ØD1B8Z4	594, 619, 903
ØD1B8ZB	480, 594, 619, 903
ØD1B8ZH	480, 594, 619, 903
ØD1B8ZK	492, 594, 619
ØD1B8ZL	492, 594, 619
ØD1B8ZM	492, 594, 619
ØD1B8ZN	492, 594, 619
ØD1B8ZP	594, 619, 903
ØD1B8ZQ	594, 619, 903
ØD1EØ74	177, 594, 619, 686, 903
ØD1EØ7E	177, 492, 686, 903
ØD1EØ7P	177, 492, 686, 903
ØD1EØJ4	177, 594, 619, 686, 903
ØD1EØJE	177, 492, 686, 903
ØD1EØJP	177, 492, 686, 903
ØD1EØK4	178, 594, 619, 686, 903
ØD1EØKE	178, 492, 686, 903
ØD1EØKP	178, 492, 686, 903
ØD1EØZ4	145, 178, 594, 619, 686, 903
ØD1EØZE	178, 492, 686, 903
ØD1EØZP	178, 492, 686, 903
ØD1E474	178, 594, 619, 686, 903
ØD1E47E	178, 492, 686, 903
ØD1E47P	178, 492, 686, 903
ØD1E4J4	178, 594, 619, 686, 903
ØD1E4JE	178, 492, 686, 903
ØD1E4JP	178, 492, 686, 903
ØD1E4K4	178, 594, 619, 686, 904
ØD1E4KE	178, 492, 686, 904
ØD1E4KP	178, 492, 686, 904
ØD1E4Z4	145, 178, 594, 619, 686, 904
ØD1E4ZE	178, 492, 686, 904
ØD1E4ZP	178, 492, 686, 904
ØD1E874	178, 594, 619, 686, 904
ØD1E87E	178, 492, 594, 619, 686, 904
ØD1E87P	178, 492, 594, 619, 686, 904
ØD1E8J4	178, 594, 619, 686, 904
ØD1E8JE	178, 492, 594, 619, 686, 904
ØD1E8JP	178, 492, 594, 619, 686, 904
ØD1E8K4	178, 594, 619, 686, 904
ØD1E8KE	178, 492, 594, 619, 686, 904
ØD1E8KP	178, 492, 594, 619, 686, 904
ØD1E8Z4	145, 178, 594, 619, 686, 904
ØD1E8ZE	178, 492, 594, 619, 686, 904
ØD1E8ZP	178, 492, 594, 619, 686, 904
ØD1H*	178, 686
ØD1HØ74	594, 619, 904
ØD1HØ7H	492
ØD1HØ7K	492
ØD1HØ7L	492
ØD1HØ7M	492
ØD1HØ7N	492
ØD1HØ7P	492
ØD1HØJ4	594, 619, 904
ØD1HØJH	492
ØD1HØJK	492
ØD1HØJL	492
ØD1HØJM	492
ØD1HØJN	492
ØD1HØJP	492
ØD1HØK4	594, 619, 904
ØD1HØKH	492
ØD1HØKK	492
ØD1HØKL	492
ØD1HØKM	492
ØD1HØKN	492
ØD1HØKP	492
ØD1HØZ4	594, 619, 904
ØD1HØZH	492
ØD1HØZK	492
ØD1HØZL	492
ØD1HØZM	492
ØD1HØZN	492
ØD1HØZP	492
ØD1H3J4	594, 619, 904
ØD1H474	594, 619, 904
ØD1H47H	492
ØD1H47K	492
ØD1H47L	492
ØD1H47M	492
ØD1H47N	492
ØD1H47P	492
ØD1H4J4	594, 619, 904
ØD1H4JH	492
ØD1H4JK	492
ØD1H4JL	492
ØD1H4JM	492
ØD1H4JN	492
ØD1H4JP	492
ØD1H4K4	594, 619, 904
ØD1H4KH	492
ØD1H4KK	492
ØD1H4KL	492
ØD1H4KM	492
ØD1H4KN	492
ØD1H4KP	492
ØD1H4Z4	594, 619, 904
ØD1H4ZH	492
ØD1H4ZK	492
ØD1H4ZL	492
ØD1H4ZM	492
ØD1H4ZN	492
ØD1H4ZP	492
ØD1H874	594, 619, 904
ØD1H87H	492
ØD1H87K	492
ØD1H87L	492
ØD1H87M	492
ØD1H87N	492
ØD1H87P	594, 619, 904
ØD1H8J4	594, 619, 904
ØD1H8JH	492
ØD1H8JK	492
ØD1H8JL	492
ØD1H8JM	492
ØD1H8JN	492
ØD1H8JP	594, 619, 904
ØD1H8K4	594, 619, 904
ØD1H8KH	492
ØD1H8KK	492
ØD1H8KL	492
ØD1H8KM	492
ØD1H8KN	492
ØD1H8KP	594, 619, 904
ØD1H8Z4	594, 619, 904
ØD1H8ZH	492
ØD1H8ZK	492
ØD1H8ZL	492
ØD1H8ZM	492
ØD1H8ZN	492

Numeric Index to Procedures

Code	Page
0D1H8ZP	594, 619, 904
0D1K*	178, 686
0D1K074	594, 619, 904
0D1K07K	492
0D1K07L	492
0D1K07M	492
0D1K07N	492
0D1K07P	492
0D1K0J4	594, 619, 904
0D1K0JK	492
0D1K0JL	492
0D1K0JM	492
0D1K0JN	493
0D1K0JP	493
0D1K0K4	594, 619, 904
0D1K0KK	493
0D1K0KL	493
0D1K0KM	493
0D1K0KN	493
0D1K0KP	493
0D1K0Z4	145, 594, 619, 904
0D1K0ZK	493
0D1K0ZL	493
0D1K0ZM	493
0D1K0ZN	493
0D1K0ZP	493
0D1K3J4	594, 619, 904
0D1K474	594, 619, 904
0D1K47K	493
0D1K47L	493
0D1K47M	493
0D1K47N	493
0D1K47P	493
0D1K4J4	594, 619, 904
0D1K4JK	493
0D1K4JL	493
0D1K4JM	493
0D1K4JN	493
0D1K4JP	493
0D1K4K4	594, 619, 904
0D1K4KK	493
0D1K4KL	493
0D1K4KM	493
0D1K4KN	493
0D1K4KP	493
0D1K4Z4	145, 594, 619, 904
0D1K4ZK	493
0D1K4ZL	493
0D1K4ZM	493
0D1K4ZN	493
0D1K4ZP	493
0D1K874	594, 619, 904
0D1K87K	493
0D1K87L	493
0D1K87M	493
0D1K87N	493
0D1K87P	493
0D1K8J4	594, 620, 904
0D1K8J*	493
0D1K8JL	493
0D1K8JM	493
0D1K8JN	493
0D1K8JP	493
0D1K8K4	594, 620, 904
0D1K8KK	493
0D1K8KL	493
0D1K8KM	493
0D1K8KN	493
0D1K8KP	493
0D1K8Z4	145, 594, 620, 904
0D1K8ZK	493
0D1K8ZL	493
0D1K8ZM	493
0D1K8ZN	493
0D1K8ZP	493
0D1L*	178, 686
0D1L074	594, 620, 904
0D1L07L	493
0D1L07M	493
0D1L07N	493
0D1L07P	493
0D1L0J4	594, 620, 904
0D1L0JL	493
0D1L0JM	493
0D1L0JN	493
0D1L0JP	493
0D1L0K4	594, 620, 904
0D1L0KL	493
0D1L0KM	493
0D1L0KN	493
0D1L0KP	493
0D1L0Z4	145, 594, 620, 904
0D1L0ZL	493
0D1L0ZM	493
0D1L0ZN	493
0D1L0ZP	493
0D1L3J4	594, 620, 904
0D1L474	594, 620, 904
0D1L47L	493
0D1L47M	493
0D1L47N	493
0D1L4J4	594, 620, 904
0D1L4JL	493
0D1L4JM	493
0D1L4JN	493
0D1L4JP	493
0D1L4K4	594, 620, 904
0D1L4KL	493
0D1L4KM	493
0D1L4KN	493
0D1L4KP	493
0D1L4Z4	145, 594, 620, 904
0D1L4ZL	493
0D1L4ZM	493
0D1L4ZP	493
0D1L874	594, 620, 904
0D1L87L	493
0D1L87M	493
0D1L87N	493
0D1L87P	493
0D1L8J4	594, 620, 904
0D1L8JL	493
0D1L8JM	493
0D1L8JN	493
0D1L8JP	493
0D1L8K4	594, 620, 904
0D1L8KL	493
0D1L8KM	493
0D1L8KN	493
0D1L8KP	493
0D1L8Z4	145, 594, 620, 904
0D1L8ZL	493
0D1L8ZM	493
0D1L8ZN	493
0D1L8ZP	493
0D1M*	178, 686
0D1M074	594, 620, 904
0D1M07M	493
0D1M07N	493
0D1M07P	493
0D1M0JM	493
0D1M0JN	493
0D1M0JP	493
0D1M0K4	594, 620, 904
0D1M0KM	493
0D1M0KN	493
0D1M0Z4	594, 620, 904
0D1M0ZM	493
0D1M0ZN	493
0D1M0ZP	493
0D1M3J4	594, 620, 904
0D1M474	594, 620, 904
0D1M47N	493
0D1M47P	493
0D1M4J4	594, 620, 904
0D1M4JM	493
0D1M4JN	493
0D1M4JP	493
0D1M4K4	594, 620, 904
0D1M4KM	493
0D1M4KN	493
0D1M4KP	493
0D1M4Z4	493
0D1M4ZM	493
0D1M4ZN	493
0D1M4ZP	493
0D1M874	594, 620, 904
0D1M87M	493
0D1M87N	493
0D1M87P	493
0D1M8J4	594, 620, 904
0D1M8JM	493
0D1M8JN	493
0D1M8JP	493
0D1M8K4	594, 620, 904
0D1M8KM	493
0D1M8KN	493
0D1M8KP	493
0D1M8Z4	594, 620, 904
0D1M8ZM	493
0D1M8ZN	493
0D1M8ZP	493
0D1N*	178
0D1N074	594, 620, 686, 904
0D1N07N	493, 686
0D1N07P	493, 686
0D1N0J4	594, 620, 686, 904
0D1N0JN	493, 686
0D1N0JP	493, 686
0D1N0K4	594, 620, 686, 904
0D1N0KN	493, 686
0D1N0KP	493, 686
0D1N0ZN	493, 686
0D1N0ZP	493, 686
0D1N3J4	594, 620, 686, 904
0D1N474	594, 620, 686, 904
0D1N47N	493, 686
0D1N47P	493, 686
0D1N4J4	594, 620, 686, 904
0D1N4JN	493, 686
0D1N4JP	493, 686
0D1N4K4	594, 620, 686, 904
0D1N4KN	493, 686
0D1N4KP	493, 686
0D1N4Z4	594, 620, 686, 904
0D1N4ZN	493, 686
0D1N874	594, 620, 686, 904
0D1N87N	493, 686
0D1N87P	493, 686
0D1N8J4	595, 620, 686, 904
0D1N8JN	493, 686
0D1N8JP	493, 686
0D1N8K4	595, 620, 686, 904
0D1N8KN	493, 686
0D1N8KP	493, 686
0D1N8Z4	595, 620, 686, 904
0D1N8ZN	493, 686
0D1N8ZP	493, 686
0D510ZZ	78, 174, 595, 620
0D513ZZ	78, 174, 595, 620
0D517ZZ	78, 174, 595, 620
0D520ZZ	78, 174, 595, 620
0D523ZZ	78, 174, 595, 620
0D527ZZ	78, 174, 595, 620
0D530ZZ	78, 174, 595, 620
0D533ZZ	78, 174, 595, 620
0D537ZZ	78, 174, 595, 620
0D540ZZ	78, 174, 595, 620
0D543ZZ	78, 174, 595, 620
0D547ZZ	78, 174, 595, 620
0D550ZZ	78, 174, 595, 620
0D553ZZ	78, 174, 595, 620
0D557ZZ	78, 174, 595, 620
0D560ZZ	174, 1062
0D563ZZ	174, 1062
0D567ZZ	174, 1062
0D570ZZ	175, 1062
0D573ZZ	175, 1062
0D577ZZ	175, 1062
0D580ZZ	180, 595, 620, 1062
0D583ZZ	180, 595, 620, 1062
0D584ZZ	180, 595, 620, 1062
0D587ZZ	180, 595, 620, 1062
0D590ZZ	175, 207, 595, 620, 1062
0D593ZZ	175, 207, 595, 620, 1062
0D597ZZ	175, 207, 595, 620, 1062
0D5A0ZZ	180, 595, 620, 1062
0D5A3ZZ	180, 595, 620, 1062
0D5A4ZZ	180, 595, 620, 1062
0D5A7ZZ	180, 595, 620, 1062
0D5B0ZZ	180, 595, 620, 1062
0D5B3ZZ	180, 595, 620, 1062
0D5B4ZZ	180, 595, 620, 1062
0D5B7ZZ	180, 595, 620, 1062
0D5C0ZZ	180, 595, 620, 1062
0D5C3ZZ	180, 595, 620, 1062
0D5C4ZZ	180, 595, 620, 1062
0D5C7ZZ	180, 595, 620, 1062
0D5E0ZZ	180, 595, 620, 1062
0D5E3ZZ	180, 595, 620, 1062
0D5E7ZZ	180, 595, 620, 1062
0D5F0ZZ	180, 595, 620, 1062
0D5F3ZZ	180, 595, 620, 1062
0D5F7ZZ	180, 595, 620, 1062
0D5G0ZZ	180, 595, 620, 1062
0D5G3ZZ	180, 595, 620, 1062
0D5G7ZZ	180, 595, 620, 1062
0D5H0ZZ	180, 595, 620, 1062
0D5H3ZZ	180, 595, 620, 1062
0D5H7ZZ	180, 595, 620, 1062
0D5J*	180
0D5K0ZZ	180, 595, 620, 1062
0D5K3ZZ	180, 595, 620, 1062
0D5K7ZZ	180, 595, 620, 1062
0D5L0ZZ	181, 595, 620, 1062
0D5L3ZZ	181, 595, 620, 1062
0D5L7ZZ	181, 595, 620, 1062
0D5M0ZZ	181, 595, 620, 1062
0D5M3ZZ	181, 595, 620, 1062
0D5M7ZZ	181, 595, 620, 1062
0D5N0ZZ	181, 595, 620, 1062
0D5N3ZZ	181, 595, 620, 1062
0D5N7ZZ	181, 595, 620, 1062
0D5Q0ZZ	183, 424, 1063
0D5Q3ZZ	183, 424, 1063
0D5Q7ZZ	183, 424, 1063
0D5QXZZ	183, 424, 1063
0D5R0ZZ	183, 424, 1063
0D5R3ZZ	183, 424, 1063
0D5U0ZZ	188, 207, 493, 538, 595, 620, 1063
0D5U3ZZ	188, 207, 493, 538, 595, 620, 1063
0D5U4ZZ	188, 207, 493, 538, 595, 620, 1063
0D5V*	188, 207, 493, 538
0D5V0ZZ	595, 620, 1063
0D5V3ZZ	595, 620, 1063
0D5V4ZZ	595, 620, 1063
0D5W*	188, 207, 493, 538
0D5W0ZZ	595, 620, 1063
0D5W3ZZ	595, 620, 1063
0D5W4ZZ	595, 620, 1063
0D710DZ	175, 595, 620, 686, 904
0D710ZZ	175, 595, 620, 686, 904
0D713DZ	175, 595, 620, 686, 904
0D713ZZ	175, 595, 620, 686, 904
0D714DZ	175, 595, 620, 686, 904
0D714ZZ	175, 595, 620, 686, 904
0D720DZ	175, 595, 620, 686, 904
0D720ZZ	175, 595, 620, 686, 904
0D723DZ	175, 595, 620, 686, 904
0D723ZZ	175, 595, 620, 686, 904
0D724DZ	175, 595, 620, 686, 904
0D724ZZ	175, 595, 620, 686, 904
0D730DZ	175, 595, 620, 686, 904
0D730ZZ	175, 595, 620, 686, 904
0D733DZ	175, 595, 620, 686, 904
0D733ZZ	175, 595, 620, 686, 904
0D734DZ	175, 595, 620, 686, 904
0D734ZZ	175, 595, 620, 686, 904
0D740DZ	175, 595, 620, 686, 904
0D740ZZ	175, 595, 620, 686, 904
0D743DZ	175, 595, 620, 686, 904
0D743ZZ	175, 595, 620, 686, 904
0D744DZ	175, 595, 620, 686, 904
0D744ZZ	175, 595, 620, 686, 904
0D750DZ	175, 595, 620, 686, 904
0D750ZZ	175, 595, 620, 686, 904
0D753DZ	175, 595, 620, 686, 904
0D753ZZ	175, 595, 620, 686, 904
0D754DZ	175, 595, 620, 686, 904
0D754ZZ	175, 595, 620, 686, 904
0D760DZ	175, 480, 686, 904
0D760ZZ	175, 480, 686, 904
0D763DZ	175, 480, 686, 904
0D763ZZ	175, 480, 686, 904
0D764DZ	175, 480, 686, 904
0D764ZZ	175, 480, 686, 904
0D770DZ	175
0D770ZZ	175
0D773DZ	175
0D773ZZ	175
0D774DZ	175
0D774ZZ	175
0D780DZ	178
0D783ZZ	178
0D784ZZ	178
0D790DZ	178
0D793ZZ	178
0D794ZZ	178
0D7A0ZZ	178
0D7A3ZZ	178
0D7A4ZZ	178
0D7B0ZZ	178
0D7B3ZZ	178
0D7B4ZZ	178
0D7C0ZZ	178
0D7C3ZZ	178
0D7C4ZZ	178
0D7E0ZZ	178
0D7E3ZZ	178
0D7E4ZZ	178
0D7F0ZZ	178
0D7F3ZZ	178
0D7F4ZZ	178
0D7G0ZZ	178
0D7G3ZZ	178
0D7G4ZZ	178
0D7H0ZZ	178
0D7H3ZZ	178
0D7H4ZZ	178
0D7K0ZZ	178
0D7K3ZZ	178
0D7K4ZZ	178
0D7L0ZZ	178
0D7L3ZZ	178
0D7L4ZZ	178
0D7M0ZZ	178
0D7M3ZZ	178
0D7M4ZZ	178
0D7N0ZZ	178
0D7N3ZZ	178
0D7N4ZZ	178
0D7P0DZ	178
0D7P0ZZ	178
0D7P3DZ	178
0D7P3ZZ	178
0D7P4DZ	178
0D7P4ZZ	178
0D7Q0DZ	183, 686, 904
0D7Q0ZZ	183, 686, 904
0D7Q3DZ	183, 686, 904
0D7Q3ZZ	183, 686, 904
0D7Q4DZ	183, 686, 904
0D7Q4ZZ	183, 686, 904
0D84*	78, 175, 686
0D840ZZ	595, 620, 904
0D843ZZ	595, 620, 904
0D844ZZ	595, 620, 904
0D847ZZ	595, 620, 904
0D848ZZ	595, 620, 904
0D870ZZ	175
0D873ZZ	175
0D874ZZ	175
0D877ZZ	175
0D878ZZ	175
0D8R*	183
0D8R0ZZ	1063
0D8R3ZZ	1063
0D9100Z	175, 686
0D910ZX	78, 175, 595, 620
0D910ZZ	175, 686
0D9140Z	175, 686
0D914ZZ	175, 686
0D9170Z	175, 686
0D917ZZ	175, 686
0D9180Z	175, 686
0D918ZZ	175, 686
0D9200Z	175, 686
0D920ZX	78, 175, 595, 620
0D920ZZ	175, 686
0D9240Z	175, 686
0D924ZZ	175, 686
0D9270Z	175, 686
0D927ZZ	175, 686
0D9280Z	175, 686
0D928ZZ	175, 686
0D9300Z	175, 686
0D930ZX	78, 175, 595, 620
0D930ZZ	175, 686
0D9340Z	175, 686
0D934ZZ	175, 686
0D9370Z	175, 686
0D937ZZ	175, 686
0D9380Z	175, 686
0D938ZZ	175, 686
0D9400Z	175, 686
0D940ZX	78, 175, 595, 620
0D940ZZ	175, 686
0D9440Z	175, 686
0D944ZZ	175, 686
0D9470Z	175, 686
0D947ZZ	175, 686
0D9480Z	175, 686
0D948ZZ	175, 686
0D9500Z	175, 686
0D950ZX	78, 175, 595, 620
0D950ZZ	175, 686
0D9540Z	175, 686
0D954ZZ	175, 687
0D9570Z	175, 687
0D957ZZ	175, 687
0D9580Z	175, 687
0D958ZZ	175, 687
0D9600Z	175, 207, 687
0D960ZX	175, 1063
0D960Z	175, 207, 687
0D9640Z	175, 207, 687
0D964ZZ	175, 207, 687
0D9670Z	175, 207, 687
0D967ZZ	175, 207, 687
0D9680Z	175, 207, 687
0D968ZZ	175, 207, 687
0D9700Z	175
0D970ZX	175, 1063
0D970Z	175
0D9740Z	175
0D974ZZ	175
0D977ZZ	175
0D978ZZ	175
0D9800Z	181, 595, 620, 687
0D980ZX	181
0D980ZZ	181, 595, 620, 687
0D9840Z	181, 595, 620, 687
0D984ZZ	181, 595, 620, 687
0D987ZZ	181, 595, 620, 687
0D988ZZ	181, 595, 620, 687

Numeric Index to Procedures

DRG Expert—Volume II

Code	Page
ØD99ØØZ	175, 207, 687, 904
ØD99ØZX	181
ØD99ØZZ	175, 207, 687, 904
ØD994ØZ	175, 207, 687, 904
ØD994ZZ	175, 207, 687, 904
ØD997ZZ	175, 207, 687, 904
ØD998ZZ	175, 207, 687, 904
ØD9AØØZ	181, 595, 620, 687
ØD9AØZX	181
ØD9AØZZ	181, 595, 620, 687
ØD9A4ØZ	181, 595, 620, 687
ØD9A4ZZ	181, 595, 620, 687
ØD9A7ZZ	181, 595, 620, 687
ØD9A8ZZ	181, 595, 620, 687
ØD9BØØZ	181, 595, 620, 687
ØD9BØZX	181
ØD9BØZZ	181, 595, 620, 687
ØD9B4ØZ	181, 595, 620, 687
ØD9B4ZZ	181, 595, 620, 687
ØD9B7ZZ	181, 595, 620, 687
ØD9B8ZZ	181, 595, 620, 687
ØD9CØØZ	181, 595, 620, 687
ØD9CØZX	181
ØD9CØZZ	181, 595, 620, 687
ØD9C4ØZ	181, 595, 620, 687
ØD9C4ZZ	181, 595, 620, 687
ØD9C7ØZ	181, 595, 620, 687
ØD9C7ZZ	181, 595, 620, 687
ØD9C8ØZ	181, 595, 620, 687
ØD9C8ZZ	181, 595, 620, 687
ØD9EØØZ	181, 687
ØD9EØZX	181, 1063
ØD9EØZZ	181, 687
ØD9E4ØZ	181, 687
ØD9E4ZZ	181, 687
ØD9E7ZZ	181, 687
ØD9E8ZZ	181, 687
ØD9FØØZ	181, 687
ØD9FØZX	181, 1063
ØD9FØZZ	181, 687
ØD9F4ØZ	181, 687
ØD9F4ZZ	181, 687
ØD9F7ZZ	181, 687
ØD9F8ZZ	181, 687
ØD9GØØZ	181, 687
ØD9GØZX	181, 1063
ØD9GØZZ	181, 687
ØD9G4ØZ	181, 687
ØD9G4ZZ	181, 687
ØD9G7ZZ	181, 687
ØD9G8ZZ	181, 687
ØD9HØØZ	181, 687
ØD9HØZX	181, 1063
ØD9HØZZ	181, 687
ØD9H4ØZ	181, 687
ØD9H4ZZ	181, 687
ØD9H7ZZ	181, 687
ØD9H8ZZ	181, 687
ØD9JØØZ	180
ØD9JØZX	180
ØD9JØZZ	180
ØD9J3ZX	180
ØD9J4ØZ	180
ØD9J4ZX	180
ØD9J4ZZ	180
ØD9J7ØZ	180
ØD9J7ZX	180
ØD9J7ZZ	180
ØD9J8ØZ	180
ØD9J8ZX	180
ØD9J8ZZ	180
ØD9KØØZ	181, 687
ØD9KØZX	181, 1063
ØD9KØZZ	181, 687
ØD9K4ØZ	181, 687
ØD9K4ZZ	181, 687
ØD9K7ZZ	181, 687
ØD9K8ZZ	181, 687
ØD9LØØZ	181, 687
ØD9LØZX	181, 1063
ØD9LØZZ	181, 687
ØD9L4ØZ	181, 687
ØD9L4ZZ	181, 687
ØD9L7ZZ	181, 687
ØD9L8ZZ	181, 687
ØD9MØØZ	181, 687
ØD9MØZX	181, 1063
ØD9MØZZ	181, 687
ØD9M4ØZ	181, 687
ØD9M4ZZ	181, 687
ØD9M7ZZ	181, 687
ØD9M8ZZ	181, 687
ØD9NØØZ	181, 687
ØD9NØZX	181, 1063
ØD9NØZZ	181, 687
ØD9N4ØZ	181, 687
ØD9N4ZZ	181, 687
ØD9N7ZZ	181, 687
ØD9N8ZZ	181, 687
ØD9PØØZ	178, 687, 904
ØD9PØZX	145, 181, 1063
ØD9PØZZ	181, 687, 904
ØD9P4ØZ	178, 687, 904
ØD9P4ZZ	181, 687, 904
ØD9P7ZZ	181, 687, 904
ØD9P8ZZ	181, 687, 904
ØD9QØØZ	183, 424
ØD9QØZZ	183, 424
ØD9Q4ØZ	183, 424
ØD9Q4ZZ	183, 424
ØD9Q7ØZ	183, 424
ØD9Q7ZZ	183, 424
ØD9Q8ØZ	183, 424
ØD9Q8ZZ	183, 424
ØD9QXØZ	183, 424
ØD9QXZZ	183, 424
ØD9RØØZ	183, 1063
ØD9RØZZ	183, 1063
ØD9R4ØZ	183, 1063
ØD9R4ZZ	183, 1063
ØD9UØØZ	188, 687
ØD9UØZX	188, 202, 538, 576
ØD9UØZZ	188, 687
ØD9U4ZX	188, 202, 538, 576
ØD9VØØZ	188, 687
ØD9VØZX	188, 202, 538, 576
ØD9VØZZ	188, 687
ØD9V4ZX	188, 202, 538, 576
ØD9WØØZ	188, 687
ØD9WØZX	188, 202, 538, 576
ØD9WØZZ	188, 687
ØD9W4ZX	188, 202, 538, 576
ØDB1ØZX	78, 175, 595, 621
ØDB1ØZZ	78, 175, 595, 621, 687, 904
ØDB13ZZ	78, 175, 595, 621, 687, 904
ØDB17ZZ	78, 175, 595, 621, 687, 904
ØDB2ØZX	78, 175, 595, 621
ØDB2ØZZ	78, 175, 595, 621, 687, 904
ØDB23ZZ	78, 175, 595, 621, 687, 904
ØDB27ZZ	78, 175, 595, 621, 687, 904
ØDB3ØZX	78, 175, 595, 621
ØDB3ØZZ	78, 175, 595, 621, 687, 904
ØDB33ZZ	78, 175, 595, 621, 687, 904
ØDB37ZZ	78, 175, 595, 621, 687, 904
ØDB4ØZX	78, 175, 595, 621
ØDB4ØZZ	175, 595, 621, 687, 904
ØDB43ZZ	175, 595, 621, 687, 904
ØDB44ZZ	175, 595, 621, 687, 904
ØDB47ZZ	175, 595, 621, 687, 904
ØDB5ØZX	78, 175, 595, 621
ØDB5ØZZ	78, 175, 595, 621, 687, 904
ØDB53ZZ	78, 175, 595, 621, 687, 904
ØDB57ZZ	78, 175, 595, 621, 687, 904
ØDB6ØZ3	145, 175, 480, 595, 621, 687, 904
ØDB6ØZX	175, 1063
ØDB6ØZZ	145, 175, 480, 595, 621, 687, 904
ØDB63Z3	145, 175, 480, 595, 621, 687, 904
ØDB63ZZ	145, 175, 480, 595, 621, 687, 904
ØDB64Z3	145, 175, 480, 595, 621, 687, 904
ØDB67Z3	145, 175, 480, 595, 621, 687, 904
ØDB67ZZ	145, 175, 480, 595, 621, 687, 904
ØDB68Z3	145, 175, 480, 595, 621, 687, 904
ØDB7ØZX	175, 1063
ØDB7ØZZ	175, 207, 493
ØDB73ZZ	175, 207, 493
ØDB77ZZ	175, 207, 493
ØDB8ØZX	181
ØDB8ØZZ	145, 178, 493, 595, 621, 687, 904
ØDB83ZZ	183, 595, 621, 1063
ØDB84ZZ	145, 178, 493, 595, 621, 687, 904
ØDB87ZZ	183, 595, 621, 687, 904, 1063
ØDB88ZZ	183, 595, 621, 1063
ØDB9ØZX	181
ØDB9ØZZ	175, 207, 595, 621, 1063
ØDB93ZZ	175, 207, 595, 621, 1063
ØDB97ZZ	687, 904
ØDBAØZX	181
ØDBAØZZ	178, 1063
ØDBA3ZZ	183, 1063
ØDBA4ZZ	183, 1063
ØDBA7ZZ	183, 595, 621, 687, 904, 1063
ØDBA8ZZ	183, 1063
ØDBBØZX	181
ØDBBØZZ	178, 1063
ØDBB3ZZ	183, 1063
ØDBB4ZZ	183, 1063
ØDBB7ZZ	183, 595, 621, 687, 905, 1063
ØDBB8ZZ	183, 1063
ØDBCØZX	181
ØDBCØZZ	183, 1063
ØDBC3ZZ	183, 1063
ØDBC4ZZ	183, 1063
ØDBC7ZZ	183, 596, 621, 1063
ØDBC8ZZ	183, 1063
ØDBEØZX	181, 1063
ØDBEØZZ	145, 178, 493, 596, 621, 687, 905
ØDBE3ZZ	145, 178, 493, 596, 621, 687, 905
ØDBE4ZZ	145, 178, 596, 621, 687, 905
ØDBE7ZZ	183, 493, 1063
ØDBFØZX	181, 1063
ØDBFØZZ	145, 178, 493, 596, 621, 687, 905
ØDBF3ZZ	145, 178, 494, 596, 621, 687, 905
ØDBF4ZZ	145, 178, 596, 621, 687, 905
ØDBF7ZZ	183, 494, 1063
ØDBGØZX	181, 1063
ØDBGØZZ	145, 178, 494, 596, 621, 687, 905
ØDBG3ZZ	145, 178, 494, 596, 621, 687, 905
ØDBG4ZZ	145, 178, 596, 621, 687, 905
ØDBG7ZZ	183, 494, 1063
ØDBGFZZ	183, 494, 1063
ØDBHØZX	181, 1063
ØDBHØZZ	145, 178, 494, 596, 621, 687, 905
ØDBH3ZZ	145, 178, 494, 596, 621, 687, 905
ØDBH4ZZ	145, 178, 596, 621, 687, 905
ØDBH7ZZ	183, 494, 1063
ØDBJ*	180
ØDBKØZX	181, 1063
ØDBKØZZ	145, 178, 494, 596, 621, 687, 905
ØDBK3ZZ	145, 178, 494, 596, 621, 687, 905
ØDBK4ZZ	145, 178, 596, 621, 687, 905
ØDBK7ZZ	183, 494, 1063
ØDBLØZX	181, 1063
ØDBLØZZ	145, 178, 494, 596, 621, 687, 905
ØDBL3ZZ	145, 178, 494, 596, 621, 687, 905
ØDBL4ZZ	145, 178, 596, 621, 687, 905
ØDBL7ZZ	183, 494, 1063
ØDBLFZZ	183, 494, 1063
ØDBMØZX	181, 1063
ØDBMØZZ	145, 178, 494, 596, 621, 687, 905
ØDBM3ZZ	145, 178, 494, 596, 621, 687, 905
ØDBM4ZZ	145, 178, 596, 621, 687, 905
ØDBM7ZZ	183, 494, 1063
ØDBMFZZ	183, 494, 1063
ØDBNØZX	181, 1063
ØDBNØZZ	145, 178, 494, 596, 621, 687, 905
ØDBN3ZZ	145, 178, 494, 596, 621, 687, 905
ØDBN4ZZ	145, 178, 596, 621, 687, 905
ØDBN7ZZ	183, 494, 1063
ØDBNFZZ	183, 494, 1063
ØDBPØZX	145, 181, 1063
ØDBPØZZ	145, 179, 521, 596, 621, 687, 905
ØDBP3ZZ	145, 183, 424, 687, 905, 1063
ØDBP4ZZ	145, 179, 521, 596, 621, 687, 905
ØDBP7ZZ	145, 183, 424, 687, 905, 1063
ØDBQØZZ	183, 424, 687, 905, 1063
ØDBQ3ZZ	183, 424, 687, 905, 1063
ØDBQ4ZZ	183, 424, 687, 905, 1063
ØDBQ7ZZ	183, 1063
ØDBQXZZ	183, 1063
ØDBRØZZ	183, 1063
ØDBR3ZZ	183, 1063
ØDBR4ZZ	183, 1063
ØDBUØZX	188, 202, 538, 576
ØDBUØZZ	188, 207, 494, 538, 596, 621, 1063
ØDBU3ZZ	188, 207, 494, 538, 596, 621, 1063
ØDBU4ZZ	188, 207, 494, 538, 596, 621, 1063
ØDBVØZX	188, 202, 538, 576
ØDBVØZZ	188, 207, 494, 538, 596, 621, 1063
ØDBV3ZZ	188, 207, 494, 538, 596, 621, 1063
ØDBV4ZZ	188, 207, 494, 538, 596, 621, 1063
ØDBWØZX	188, 202, 538, 576
ØDBWØZZ	188, 207, 494, 538, 596, 621, 1063
ØDBW3ZZ	188, 207, 494, 538, 596, 621, 1063
ØDBW4ZZ	188, 207, 494, 538, 596, 621, 1063
ØDC1ØZZ	175, 687
ØDC13ZZ	175, 687
ØDC14ZZ	175, 687
ØDC2ØZZ	175, 687
ØDC23ZZ	175, 687
ØDC24ZZ	175, 687
ØDC3ØZZ	175, 687
ØDC33ZZ	175, 687
ØDC34ZZ	175, 687
ØDC4ØZZ	175, 687
ØDC43ZZ	175, 688
ØDC44ZZ	175, 688
ØDC5ØZZ	175, 688
ØDC53ZZ	175, 688
ØDC54ZZ	175, 688
ØDC6ØZZ	175, 207, 688
ØDC63ZZ	175, 207, 688
ØDC64ZZ	175, 207, 688
ØDC7ØZZ	175
ØDC73ZZ	176
ØDC74ZZ	176
ØDC8ØZZ	181, 596, 621, 688
ØDC83ZZ	181, 596, 621, 688
ØDC84ZZ	181, 596, 621, 688
ØDC9ØZZ	176, 207, 688, 905
ØDC93ZZ	176, 207, 688, 905
ØDC94ZZ	176, 207, 688, 905
ØDCAØZZ	181, 596, 621, 688
ØDCA3ZZ	181, 596, 621, 688
ØDCA4ZZ	181, 596, 621, 688
ØDCBØZZ	181, 596, 621, 688
ØDCB3ZZ	181, 596, 621, 688
ØDCB4ZZ	181, 596, 621, 688
ØDCCØZZ	181, 596, 621, 688
ØDCC3ZZ	181, 596, 621, 688
ØDCC4ZZ	181, 596, 621, 688
ØDCEØZZ	181, 688
ØDCE3ZZ	181, 688
ØDCE4ZZ	181, 688
ØDCFØZZ	181, 688
ØDCF3ZZ	181, 688
ØDCF4ZZ	181, 688
ØDCGØZZ	181, 688
ØDCG3ZZ	181, 688
ØDCG4ZZ	181, 688
ØDCHØZZ	181, 688
ØDCH3ZZ	181, 688
ØDCH4ZZ	181, 688
ØDCJ*	180
ØDCKØZZ	181, 688
ØDCK3ZZ	181, 688
ØDCK4ZZ	181, 688
ØDCLØZZ	181, 688
ØDCL3ZZ	181, 688
ØDCL4ZZ	181, 688
ØDCMØZZ	181, 688
ØDCM3ZZ	181, 688
ØDCM4ZZ	181, 688
ØDCNØZZ	181, 688
ØDCN3ZZ	181, 688
ØDCN4ZZ	181, 688
ØDCPØZZ	181, 688, 905
ØDCP3ZZ	181, 688, 905
ØDCP4ZZ	181, 688, 905
ØDCQØZZ	183
ØDCQ3ZZ	183
ØDCQ4ZZ	183
ØDCR*	183
ØDCRØZZ	1063
ØDCR3ZZ	1063
ØDCR4ZZ	1063
ØDCUØZZ	188, 515, 688, 905
ØDCU3ZZ	188, 515, 688, 905
ØDCU4ZZ	189, 515, 688, 905
ØDCV*	189, 515, 688
ØDCVØZZ	905
ØDCV3ZZ	905
ØDCV4ZZ	905
ØDCW*	189, 515, 688
ØDCWØZZ	905
ØDCW3ZZ	905
ØDCW4ZZ	905
ØDDJ3ZX	180
ØDDJ4ZX	180
ØDDJ8ZX	180
ØDF5ØZZ	176, 688
ØDF53ZZ	176, 688
ØDF54ZZ	176, 688
ØDF57ZZ	176, 688
ØDF58ZZ	176, 688
ØDF6ØZZ	176, 480, 688, 905
ØDF63ZZ	176, 480, 688, 905
ØDF64ZZ	176, 480, 688, 905
ØDF67ZZ	176, 480, 688, 905
ØDF68ZZ	176, 480, 688, 905
ØDF8ØZZ	178, 688
ØDF83ZZ	178, 688
ØDF84ZZ	178, 688
ØDF87ZZ	178, 688
ØDF88ZZ	178, 688
ØDF9ØZZ	178, 688
ØDF93ZZ	178, 688
ØDF94ZZ	178, 688
ØDF97ZZ	178, 688
ØDF98ZZ	178, 688
ØDFAØZZ	178, 688
ØDFA3ZZ	178, 688
ØDFA4ZZ	178, 688
ØDFA7ZZ	178, 688
ØDFA8ZZ	178, 688
ØDFBØZZ	178, 688
ØDFB3ZZ	178, 688
ØDFB4ZZ	178, 688
ØDFB7ZZ	178, 688
ØDFB8ZZ	178, 688
ØDFEØZZ	178, 688
ØDFE3ZZ	178, 688
ØDFE4ZZ	178, 688
ØDFE7ZZ	178, 688
ØDFE8ZZ	178, 688
ØDFFØZZ	178, 688
ØDFF3ZZ	178, 688
ØDFF4ZZ	178, 688
ØDFF7ZZ	178, 688
ØDFF8ZZ	178, 688
ØDFGØZZ	178, 688
ØDFG3ZZ	178, 688
ØDFG4ZZ	178, 688
ØDFG7ZZ	178, 688
ØDFG8ZZ	178, 688
ØDFHØZZ	178, 688
ØDFH3ZZ	178, 688
ØDFH4ZZ	178, 688
ØDFH7ZZ	178, 688
ØDFH8ZZ	178, 688
ØDFJØZZ	180
ØDFJ3ZZ	180
ØDFJ4ZZ	180
ØDFJ7ZZ	180
ØDFJ8ZZ	180
ØDFKØZZ	178, 688
ØDFK3ZZ	178, 688
ØDFK4ZZ	178, 688
ØDFK7ZZ	178, 688
ØDFK8ZZ	178, 688
ØDFLØZZ	178, 688
ØDFL3ZZ	178, 688
ØDFL4ZZ	178, 688
ØDFL7ZZ	178, 688
ØDFL8ZZ	178, 688
ØDFMØZZ	178, 688
ØDFM3ZZ	178, 688
ØDFM4ZZ	178, 688
ØDFM7ZZ	178, 688
ØDFM8ZZ	178, 688
ØDFNØZZ	178, 688
ØDFN3ZZ	178, 688
ØDFN4ZZ	178, 688
ØDFN7ZZ	178, 688
ØDFN8ZZ	178, 688
ØDFPØZZ	183, 688, 905
ØDFP3ZZ	183, 688, 905
ØDFP4ZZ	183, 688, 905
ØDFP7ZZ	183, 688, 905
ØDFP8ZZ	183, 688, 905
ØDFQØZZ	183, 688, 905
ØDFQ3ZZ	183, 688, 905
ØDFQ4ZZ	183, 688, 905
ØDFQ7ZZ	183, 688, 905
ØDFQ8ZZ	183, 688, 905
ØDH5Ø1Z	189, 688, 1063
ØDH5Ø2Z	176, 688
ØDH5Ø3Z	176, 688
ØDH5ØYZ	176, 688
ØDH531Z	189, 688, 1063
ØDH532Z	176, 688
ØDH533Z	176, 688
ØDH541Z	189, 688, 1063
ØDH542Z	176, 688
ØDH543Z	176, 688
ØDH571Z	189, 688, 1063
ØDH581Z	189, 688, 1063
ØDH6Ø2Z	176, 688
ØDH6Ø3Z	176, 688
ØDH6ØDZ	176, 480, 688, 905
ØDH6ØMZ	34, 42, 78, 139, 277, 515, 524, 538, 688, 905
ØDH6ØUZ	34, 176, 494, 688
ØDH6ØYZ	176, 688
ØDH632Z	176, 688
ØDH633Z	176, 688
ØDH63DZ	176, 480, 688, 905
ØDH63MZ	34, 42, 78, 139, 277, 515, 524, 538, 688, 905
ØDH642Z	176, 688
ØDH643Z	176, 688
ØDH64DZ	176, 480, 688, 905
ØDH64MZ	34, 42, 78, 139, 277, 515, 524, 538, 688, 905
ØDH8Ø2Z	181, 688
ØDH8Ø3Z	181, 688
ØDH832Z	181, 688
ØDH833Z	181, 688
ØDH842Z	181, 688
ØDH843Z	181, 688
ØDH9Ø2Z	176, 207, 688, 905
ØDH9Ø3Z	176, 207, 688, 905
ØDH932Z	176, 207, 688, 905

Numeric Index to Procedures

Code	Page	Code	Page	Code	Page	Code	Page	Code	Page	Code	Page
0DH933Z	176, 207, 688, 905	0DL73CZ	905	0DNB4ZZ	179, 207, 515, 538, 689, 905	0DNW4ZZ	906	0DPD02Z	182, 689	0DQB0ZZ	183, 906
0DH942Z	176, 207, 688, 905	0DL73DZ	905	0DNC*	689	0DP000Z	181, 689	0DPD03Z	182, 690	0DQB3ZZ	906
0DH943Z	176, 207, 688, 905	0DL73ZZ	905	0DNC0ZZ	179, 207, 494, 515, 538, 905	0DP002Z	182, 689	0DPD07Z	182, 690	0DQB4ZZ	906
0DHA02Z	181, 688	0DL74CZ	905			0DP003Z	182, 689	0DPD0CZ	182, 690	0DQB7ZZ	906
0DHA03Z	181, 689	0DL74DZ	905	0DNC3ZZ	179, 207, 494, 515, 538, 905	0DP007Z	182, 689	0DPD0DZ	182, 690	0DQB8ZZ	906
0DHA32Z	181, 689	0DL74ZZ	905	0DNC4ZZ	179, 207, 515, 538, 905	0DP00CZ	182, 689	0DPD0JZ	182, 690	0DQC*	179, 690
0DHA33Z	181, 689	0DL77DZ	905			0DP00DZ	182, 689	0DPD0KZ	182, 690	0DQE*	179, 690
0DHA42Z	181, 689	0DL77ZZ	905	0DNC7ZZ	179	0DP00JZ	182, 689	0DPD0UZ	182, 690	0DQE0ZZ	183, 906
0DHA43Z	181, 689	0DL78DZ	905	0DNC8ZZ	179	0DP00KZ	182, 689	0DPD0YZ	182, 690	0DQE3ZZ	906
0DHB02Z	181, 689	0DL78ZZ	905	0DNE0ZZ	179, 207, 494, 515, 538, 689, 905	0DP00UZ	182, 689	0DPD30Z	182, 690	0DQE4ZZ	906
0DHB03Z	181, 689	0DL8*	178, 207			0DP00YZ	182, 689	0DPD32Z	182, 690	0DQE7ZZ	906
0DHB32Z	181, 689	0DL9*	178, 207	0DNE3ZZ	179, 207, 494, 515, 538, 689, 905	0DP030Z	182, 689	0DPD33Z	182, 690	0DQE8ZZ	906
0DHB33Z	181, 689	0DLA*	178			0DP032Z	182, 689	0DPD37Z	182, 690	0DQF*	179, 183
0DHB42Z	181, 689	0DLB*	178	0DNE4ZZ	179, 207, 515, 538, 689, 905	0DP033Z	182, 689	0DPD3CZ	182, 690	0DQF3ZZ	179, 690
0DHB43Z	181, 689	0DLC*	179	0DNF0ZZ	179, 207, 494, 515, 538, 689, 905	0DP037Z	182, 689	0DPD3DZ	182, 690	0DQF4ZZ	179, 690
0DHP01Z	189, 689, 1063	0DLE*	179			0DP03CZ	182, 689	0DPD3KZ	182, 690	0DQF7ZZ	179, 690
0DHP31Z	189, 689, 1063	0DLF*	179	0DNF3ZZ	179, 207, 494, 515, 538, 689, 905	0DP03DZ	182, 689	0DPD3UZ	182, 690	0DQF8ZZ	179, 690
0DHP41Z	189, 689, 1063	0DLG*	179			0DP03JZ	182, 689	0DPD40Z	182, 690	0DQG0ZZ	179, 183
0DHP71Z	189, 689, 1063	0DLH*	179	0DNF4ZZ	179, 207, 515, 538, 689, 905	0DP03KZ	182, 689	0DPD42Z	182, 690	0DQG3ZZ	179, 690
0DHP81Z	189, 689, 1063	0DLK*	179	0DNG0ZZ	179, 207, 494, 515, 538, 689, 905	0DP03UZ	182, 689	0DPD43Z	182, 690	0DQG4ZZ	179, 690
0DHQ*	689	0DLL*	179			0DP040Z	182, 689	0DPD47Z	182, 690	0DQG7ZZ	179, 690
0DHQ0DZ	183, 905	0DLM*	179	0DNG3ZZ	180, 207, 494, 515, 538, 689, 905	0DP042Z	182, 689	0DPD4CZ	182, 690	0DQG8ZZ	179, 690
0DHQ0LZ	179, 424, 905	0DLN*	179			0DP043Z	182, 689	0DPD4DZ	182, 690	0DQH*	179, 690
0DHQ3DZ	183, 905	0DLP*	183	0DNG4ZZ	180, 207, 515, 538, 689, 905	0DP047Z	182, 689	0DPD4JZ	182, 690	0DQH0ZZ	183, 906
0DHQ3LZ	179, 424, 905	0DLQ*	183, 689			0DP04CZ	182, 689	0DPD4KZ	182, 690	0DQH3ZZ	906
0DHQ4DZ	183, 905	0DLQ0CZ	905	0DNH0ZZ	180, 207, 494, 515, 538, 689, 905	0DP04DZ	182, 689	0DPD4UZ	182, 690	0DQH4ZZ	906
0DHQ4LZ	179, 424, 905	0DLQ0DZ	905	0DNH3ZZ	180, 207, 494, 515, 538, 689, 905	0DP04JZ	182, 689	0DPD77Z	182, 690	0DQH7ZZ	906
0DHQ7DZ	183, 905	0DLQ0ZZ	905			0DP04KZ	182, 689	0DPD7CZ	182, 690	0DQH8ZZ	906
0DHQ8DZ	183, 905	0DLQ3CZ	905	0DNH4ZZ	180, 207, 515, 538, 689, 905	0DP04UZ	182, 689	0DPD7JZ	182, 690	0DQJ*	180, 690
0DHR*	183	0DLQ3DZ	905	0DNJ0ZZ	180, 207, 494, 515, 538, 689, 905	0DP077Z	182, 689	0DPD7KZ	182, 690	0DQJ0ZZ	906
0DJ00ZZ	101, 145, 189, 202, 424, 494, 515, 521, 538, 576, 596, 621, 689, 905	0DLQ3ZZ	905			0DP07CZ	182, 689	0DPD87Z	182, 690	0DQJ3ZZ	906
		0DLQ4CZ	905	0DNJ3ZZ	180, 207, 494, 515, 538, 689, 905	0DP07JZ	182, 689	0DPD8CZ	182, 690	0DQJ4ZZ	906
		0DLQ4DZ	905			0DP07KZ	182, 689	0DPD8JZ	182, 690	0DQJ7ZZ	906
		0DLQ4ZZ	905	0DNJ4ZZ	180, 207, 515, 538, 689, 905	0DP087Z	182, 689	0DPD8KZ	182, 690	0DQJ8ZZ	906
0DJ04ZZ	78, 176, 596, 621, 689, 905	0DLQ7DZ	905	0DNJ7ZZ	180	0DP08CZ	182, 689	0DPP01Z	182, 690, 906	0DQK*	179, 690
		0DLQ7ZZ	905	0DNJ8ZZ	180	0DP08JZ	182, 689	0DPP31Z	182, 690, 906	0DQK0ZZ	183, 906
0DJ60ZZ	101, 145, 189, 202, 424, 494, 515, 521, 538, 576, 596, 621, 689, 905	0DLQ8DZ	905	0DNK0ZZ	180, 207, 494, 515, 538, 689, 905	0DP08KZ	182, 689	0DPP41Z	182, 690, 906	0DQK4ZZ	906
		0DLQ8ZZ	905			0DP501Z	176, 689	0DPQ*	179, 690	0DQK7ZZ	906
		0DLQXCZ	905	0DNK3ZZ	180, 207, 494, 515, 538, 689, 906	0DP502Z	176, 689	0DPQ0LZ	424, 906	0DQK8ZZ	906
		0DLQXDZ	905			0DP503Z	176, 689	0DPQ3LZ	424, 906	0DQL*	179, 183
0DJ64ZZ	176, 202, 596, 621, 689, 905	0DLQXZZ	905	0DNK4ZZ	180, 207, 515, 538, 689, 906	0DP50UZ	176, 689	0DPQ4LZ	424, 906	0DQL3ZZ	179, 690
		0DM*	689	0DNL0ZZ	180, 207, 494, 515, 538, 689, 906	0DP50YZ	176, 689	0DPQ7LZ	424, 906	0DQL4ZZ	179, 690
0DJD0ZZ	101, 145, 189, 202, 424, 494, 515, 521, 538, 576, 596, 621, 689, 905	0DM5*	176			0DP531Z	176, 689	0DPQ8LZ	424, 906	0DQL7ZZ	179, 690
		0DM6*	176, 480	0DNL3ZZ	180, 207, 494, 515, 538, 689, 906	0DP532Z	176, 689	0DPR*	34, 78, 277, 524, 538, 690	0DQL8ZZ	179, 690
		0DM60ZZ	905			0DP533Z	176, 689			0DQM0ZZ	179, 183
		0DM64ZZ	905	0DNL4ZZ	180, 207, 515, 538, 689, 906	0DP53UZ	176, 689	0DPR0MZ	906	0DQM3ZZ	179, 690
0DJD4ZZ	181, 596, 621, 689, 905, 1063	0DM8*	179	0DNM0ZZ	180, 207, 494, 515, 538, 689, 906	0DP541Z	176, 689	0DPR3MZ	906	0DQM7ZZ	179, 690
		0DM9*	179			0DP542Z	176, 689	0DPR4MZ	906	0DQM8ZZ	179, 690
0DJU0ZZ	101, 145, 189, 202, 424, 494, 515, 521, 538, 576, 596, 621, 689, 905	0DMA*	179	0DNM3ZZ	180, 207, 494, 515, 538, 689, 906	0DP543Z	176, 689	0DPU*	189	0DQN*	179, 690
		0DMB*	179			0DP54UZ	176, 689	0DPV*	189	0DQN0ZZ	183, 906
		0DME*	179	0DNM4ZZ	180, 207, 515, 538, 689, 906	0DP600Z	176, 689	0DPW*	189	0DQN3ZZ	906
		0DMF*	179			0DP602Z	176, 689	0DQ1*	176, 690	0DQN4ZZ	906
		0DMG*	179	0DNN0ZZ	180, 207, 494, 515, 538, 689, 906	0DP603Z	176, 689	0DQ2*	176, 690	0DQN7ZZ	906
0DJU4ZZ	189, 202, 424, 515, 535, 576, 689, 905, 1063	0DMH*	179			0DP607Z	176, 689	0DQ3*	176, 690	0DQN8ZZ	906
		0DMK*	179	0DNN3ZZ	180, 207, 494, 515, 538, 689, 906	0DP60CZ	176, 689	0DQ4*	176, 690	0DQP*	179, 690
		0DML*	179			0DP60DZ	176, 689	0DQ40ZZ	906	0DQP0ZZ	424, 906
0DJV0ZZ	101, 145, 189, 202, 424, 494, 515, 521, 538, 576, 596, 621, 689, 905	0DMM*	179	0DNN4ZZ	180, 207, 515, 538, 689, 906	0DP60JZ	176, 689	0DQ44ZZ	906	0DQP3ZZ	424, 906
		0DMN*	179	0DNP*	183, 689	0DP60KZ	176, 689	0DQ47ZZ	906	0DQP4ZZ	424, 906
		0DMP*	179	0DNP0ZZ	424, 906, 1063	0DP60MZ	34, 78, 277, 524, 538, 689, 906	0DQ48ZZ	906	0DQP7ZZ	424, 906
		0DN1*	176, 689	0DNP3ZZ	424, 906, 1063			0DQ5*	78, 94, 176, 690	0DQP8ZZ	424, 906
		0DN2*	176, 689	0DNP4ZZ	424, 906, 1063	0DP60UZ	176, 689	0DQ50ZZ	596, 621, 906	0DQQ*	183, 690
0DJV4ZZ	189, 202, 424, 515, 535, 576, 689, 905, 1063	0DN3*	176, 689	0DNP7ZZ	424, 906, 1063	0DP60YZ	176, 689	0DQ53ZZ	596, 621, 906	0DQQ0ZZ	424, 906
		0DN4*	176, 689	0DNP8ZZ	424, 906, 1063	0DP630Z	176, 689	0DQ54ZZ	596, 621, 906	0DQQ3ZZ	424, 906
		0DN5*	78, 176, 689	0DNQ*	183	0DP632Z	176, 689	0DQ57ZZ	596, 621, 906	0DQQ4ZZ	424, 906
		0DN6*	176, 480, 689	0DNR*	183, 689	0DP637Z	176, 689	0DQ58ZZ	596, 621, 906	0DQQ7ZZ	424, 906
0DJW0ZZ	101, 145, 189, 202, 424, 494, 515, 521, 538, 576, 596, 621, 689, 905	0DN60ZZ	905	0DNR0ZZ	424, 906, 1063	0DP63CZ	176, 689	0DQ6*	176, 480, 690	0DQQXZZ	424, 906
		0DN63ZZ	905	0DNR3ZZ	424, 906, 1063	0DP63DZ	176, 689	0DQ60ZZ	207, 596, 621, 906	0DQR*	183, 690
		0DN64ZZ	905	0DNR4ZZ	424, 906, 1063	0DP63JZ	176, 689	0DQ63ZZ	207, 596, 621, 906	0DQR0ZZ	424, 906, 1063
		0DN67ZZ	905	0DNU0ZZ	180, 207, 494, 515, 538, 689, 906	0DP63KZ	176, 689	0DQ64ZZ	906, 1063	0DQR3ZZ	424, 906, 1063
0DJW4ZZ	189, 202, 424, 515, 535, 576, 689, 905, 1063	0DN68ZZ	905			0DP63MZ	34, 78, 277, 524, 538, 689, 906	0DQ67ZZ	207, 596, 621, 906	0DQR4ZZ	424, 906, 1063
		0DN7*	176	0DNU3ZZ	180, 207, 494, 515, 538, 689, 906			0DQ68ZZ	207, 596, 621, 906	0DQU*	184
		0DN80ZZ	179, 207, 494, 515, 538, 689, 905			0DP63UZ	176, 689	0DQ7*	176	0DQV*	189, 207, 690
0DL6*	176, 480, 689			0DNU4ZZ	180, 207, 515, 538, 689, 906	0DP640Z	176, 689	0DQ8*	179, 690	0DQV0ZZ	596, 621, 906
0DL60CZ	905	0DN83ZZ	179, 207, 494, 515, 538, 689, 905	0DNV*	180, 207, 515, 538, 689	0DP642Z	176, 689	0DQ80ZZ	183, 906	0DQV3ZZ	596, 621, 906
0DL60DZ	905			0DNV0ZZ	494, 906	0DP643Z	480, 1063	0DQ83ZZ	906	0DQV4ZZ	596, 621, 906
0DL60ZZ	905	0DN84ZZ	179, 207, 515, 538, 689, 905	0DNV3ZZ	494, 906	0DP647Z	176, 689	0DQ84ZZ	906	0DQW*	189, 207, 690
0DL63CZ	905	0DN90ZZ	179, 207, 494, 515, 538, 689, 905	0DNV4ZZ	906	0DP64CZ	176, 480, 1063	0DQ87ZZ	906	0DQW0ZZ	596, 621, 906, 1063
0DL63DZ	905			0DNW*	180, 207, 515, 538, 689	0DP64DZ	176, 689	0DQ88ZZ	906		
0DL63ZZ	905	0DN93ZZ	179, 207, 494, 515, 538, 689, 905			0DP64JZ	176, 689	0DQ9*	176, 690	0DQW3ZZ	596, 621, 906, 1063
0DL64CZ	905			0DNW0ZZ	494, 906	0DP64KZ	176, 689	0DQ90ZZ	183, 906		
0DL64DZ	905	0DN94ZZ	179, 207, 515, 538, 689, 905	0DNW3ZZ	494, 906	0DP64MZ	34, 78, 277, 524, 538, 689, 906	0DQ93ZZ	906	0DQW4ZZ	596, 621, 906, 1063
0DL64ZZ	905	0DNA0ZZ	179, 207, 494, 515, 538, 689, 905					0DQ94ZZ	906		
0DL67DZ	905					0DP64UZ	176, 689	0DQ97ZZ	906	0DR*	690
0DL67ZZ	905	0DNA3ZZ	179, 207, 494, 515, 538, 689, 905			0DP677Z	176, 689	0DQ98ZZ	906	0DR5*	78, 176
0DL68DZ	905					0DP67CZ	176, 689	0DQA*	179, 690	0DR507Z	596, 621, 906
0DL68ZZ	905	0DNA4ZZ	179, 207, 515, 538, 689, 905			0DP67JZ	176, 689	0DQA0ZZ	183, 906	0DR50JZ	596, 621, 906
0DL7*	176, 480, 689	0DNB0ZZ	179, 207, 494, 515, 538, 689, 905			0DP67KZ	176, 689	0DQA3ZZ	906	0DR50KZ	596, 621, 906
0DL70CZ	905					0DP687Z	176, 689	0DQA4ZZ	906	0DR547Z	596, 621, 906
0DL70DZ	905	0DNB3ZZ	179, 207, 494, 515, 538, 689, 905			0DP68CZ	176, 689	0DQA7ZZ	906	0DR54JZ	596, 621, 906
0DL70ZZ	905					0DP68JZ	176, 689	0DQA8ZZ	906	0DR54KZ	596, 621, 906
						0DP68KZ	176, 689	0DQB*	179, 690		
						0DPD00Z	182, 689				

Code	Page
ØDR577Z	596, 621, 906
ØDR57JZ	596, 621, 906
ØDR57KZ	596, 621, 906
ØDR587Z	596, 621, 906
ØDR58JZ	596, 621, 906
ØDR58KZ	596, 621, 906
ØDRR*	183
ØDRRØ7Z	424, 906, 1063
ØDRRØJZ	424, 906, 1063
ØDRRØKZ	424, 906, 1063
ØDRR47Z	424, 906, 1063
ØDRR4JZ	424, 906, 1063
ØDRR4KZ	424, 906, 1063
ØDRUØ7Z	189, 207, 596, 621, 906
ØDRUØJZ	189, 207, 596, 621, 906
ØDRUØKZ	189, 207, 596, 621, 906
ØDRU47Z	189, 207, 596, 621, 906
ØDRU4JZ	189, 207, 596, 621, 906
ØDRU4KZ	189, 207, 596, 621, 906
ØDRV*	189, 207
ØDRVØ7Z	596, 621, 906
ØDRVØJZ	596, 621, 906
ØDRVØKZ	596, 621, 906
ØDRV47Z	596, 621, 906
ØDRV4JZ	596, 621, 906
ØDRV4KZ	596, 621, 906
ØDRW*	189, 207
ØDRWØ7Z	596, 621, 906
ØDRWØJZ	596, 621, 906
ØDRWØKZ	596, 621, 906
ØDRW47Z	596, 621, 906
ØDRW4JZ	596, 621, 906
ØDRW4KZ	596, 621, 906
ØDS5ØZZ	176, 690
ØDS54ZZ	176, 690
ØDS57ZZ	176, 690
ØDS58ZZ	176, 690
ØDS6ØZZ	176, 690, 906
ØDS64ZZ	176, 690, 906
ØDS67ZZ	176, 207, 494, 690, 906
ØDS68ZZ	176, 207, 494, 690, 906
ØDS8ØZZ	179, 690, 906
ØDS84ZZ	179, 690, 906
ØDS87ZZ	179, 690, 906
ØDS88ZZ	179, 690, 906
ØDS9ØZZ	182
ØDS94ZZ	182
ØDS97ZZ	182
ØDS98ZZ	182
ØDSAØZZ	182
ØDSA4ZZ	182
ØDSA7ZZ	182
ØDSA8ZZ	182
ØDSBØZZ	179, 207, 596, 621, 690, 906
ØDSB4ZZ	179, 207, 596, 621, 690, 906
ØDSB7ZZ	179, 207, 596, 621, 690, 906
ØDSB8ZZ	179, 207, 596, 621, 690, 906
ØDSEØZZ	179, 690, 906
ØDSE4ZZ	179, 690, 906
ØDSE7ZZ	179, 690, 906
ØDSE8ZZ	179, 690, 906
ØDSHØZZ	179, 207, 596, 621, 690, 907
ØDSH4ZZ	179, 207, 596, 621, 690, 907
ØDSH7ZZ	179, 207, 596, 621, 690, 907
ØDSH8ZZ	179, 207, 596, 621, 690, 907
ØDSKØZZ	182
ØDSK4ZZ	182
ØDSK7ZZ	182
ØDSK8ZZ	182
ØDSLØZZ	182
ØDSL4ZZ	182
ØDSL7ZZ	182
ØDSL8ZZ	182
ØDSMØZZ	182
ØDSM4ZZ	182
ØDSM7ZZ	182
ØDSM8ZZ	182

Code	Page
ØDSNØZZ	182
ØDSN4ZZ	182
ØDSN7ZZ	182
ØDSN8ZZ	182
ØDSPØZZ	179, 690, 907
ØDSP4ZZ	179, 690, 907
ØDSP7ZZ	179, 690, 907
ØDSP8ZZ	179, 690, 907
ØDSQØZZ	183
ØDSQ4ZZ	183
ØDSQ7ZZ	183
ØDSQ8ZZ	183
ØDT1*	78, 176, 690
ØDT1ØZZ	596, 621, 907
ØDT14ZZ	596, 621, 907
ØDT17ZZ	596, 621, 907
ØDT18ZZ	596, 621, 907
ØDT2*	78, 176, 690
ØDT2ØZZ	596, 621, 907
ØDT24ZZ	596, 621, 907
ØDT27ZZ	596, 621, 907
ØDT28ZZ	596, 621, 907
ØDT3*	78, 176, 690
ØDT3ØZZ	596, 621, 907
ØDT34ZZ	596, 621, 907
ØDT37ZZ	596, 621, 907
ØDT38ZZ	596, 621, 907
ØDT4*	176, 690
ØDT4ØZZ	596, 621, 907
ØDT44ZZ	596, 621, 907
ØDT47ZZ	596, 621, 907
ØDT48ZZ	596, 621, 907
ØDT5*	78, 176, 690
ØDT5ØZZ	596, 621, 907
ØDT54ZZ	596, 621, 907
ØDT57ZZ	596, 621, 907
ØDT58ZZ	596, 621, 907
ØDT6*	145, 176, 690
ØDT6ØZZ	596, 621, 907
ØDT64ZZ	596, 621, 907
ØDT67ZZ	596, 621, 907
ØDT68ZZ	596, 621, 907
ØDT7*	145, 176, 690
ØDT7ØZZ	596, 621, 907
ØDT74ZZ	596, 621, 907
ØDT77ZZ	596, 622, 907
ØDT78ZZ	596, 622, 907
ØDT8*	179, 690
ØDT8ØZZ	596, 622, 907
ØDT84ZZ	596, 622, 907
ØDT87ZZ	596, 622, 907
ØDT88ZZ	596, 622, 907
ØDT9*	145, 179, 494, 690
ØDT9ØZZ	177, 596, 622, 907
ØDT94ZZ	596, 622, 907
ØDT97ZZ	596, 622, 907
ØDT98ZZ	596, 622, 907
ØDTA*	145, 179, 494, 690
ØDTAØZZ	596, 622, 907
ØDTA4ZZ	596, 622, 907
ØDTA7ZZ	596, 622, 907
ØDTA8ZZ	596, 622, 907
ØDTB*	145, 179, 494, 690
ØDTBØZZ	596, 622, 907
ØDTB4ZZ	596, 622, 907
ØDTB7ZZ	596, 622, 907
ØDTB8ZZ	596, 622, 907
ØDTC*	145, 179, 494, 690
ØDTCØZZ	596, 622, 907
ØDTC4ZZ	596, 622, 907
ØDTC7ZZ	596, 622, 907
ØDTC8ZZ	596, 622, 907
ØDTE*	145, 179, 690
ØDTEØZZ	596, 622, 907
ØDTE4ZZ	596, 622, 907
ØDTE7ZZ	596, 622, 907
ØDTE8ZZ	596, 622, 907
ØDTF*	145, 179, 690
ØDTFØZZ	596, 622, 907
ØDTF4ZZ	596, 622, 907
ØDTF7ZZ	596, 622, 907
ØDTF8ZZ	596, 622, 907
ØDTG*	145, 179, 494, 690
ØDTGØZZ	596, 622, 907
ØDTG4ZZ	596, 622, 907
ØDTG7ZZ	596, 622, 907
ØDTG8ZZ	596, 622, 907
ØDTGFZZ	596, 622, 907
ØDTH*	145, 179, 690
ØDTHØZZ	907
ØDTH4ZZ	907
ØDTH7ZZ	907
ØDTH8ZZ	907

Code	Page
ØDTJ*	180, 538, 690
ØDTJØZZ	145, 907
ØDTJ4ZZ	907
ØDTJ7ZZ	145, 907
ØDTJ8ZZ	145, 907
ØDTK*	145, 179, 690
ØDTKØZZ	596, 622, 907
ØDTK4ZZ	596, 622, 907
ØDTK7ZZ	596, 622, 907
ØDTK8ZZ	597, 622, 907
ØDTL*	146, 179, 690
ØDTLØZZ	597, 622, 907
ØDTL4ZZ	597, 622, 907
ØDTL7ZZ	597, 622, 907
ØDTL8ZZ	597, 622, 907
ØDTLFZZ	597, 622, 907
ØDTM*	146, 179, 690
ØDTMØZZ	597, 622, 907
ØDTM4ZZ	597, 622, 907
ØDTM7ZZ	597, 622, 907
ØDTM8ZZ	597, 622, 907
ØDTMFZZ	597, 622, 907
ØDTN*	179, 690
ØDTNØZZ	515, 597, 622, 907
ØDTN4ZZ	597, 622, 907
ØDTN7ZZ	597, 622, 907
ØDTN8ZZ	597, 622, 907
ØDTNFZZ	597, 622, 907
ØDTP*	179
ØDTPØZZ	146, 597, 622, 690, 907
ØDTP4ZZ	146, 597, 622, 690, 907
ØDTP7ZZ	597, 622
ØDTP8ZZ	597, 622
ØDTQ*	183
ØDTQØZZ	1063
ØDTQ4ZZ	1063
ØDTQ7ZZ	1063
ØDTQ8ZZ	1063
ØDTR*	183
ØDTRØZZ	1063
ØDTR4ZZ	1063
ØDTUØZZ	189, 207, 494, 538, 597, 622, 1063
ØDTU4ZZ	189, 207, 494, 538, 597, 622, 1063
ØDU1*	78, 176, 690
ØDU1Ø7Z	597, 622, 907
ØDU1ØJZ	597, 622, 907
ØDU1ØKZ	597, 622, 907
ØDU147Z	597, 622, 907
ØDU14JZ	597, 622, 907
ØDU14KZ	597, 622, 907
ØDU177Z	597, 622, 907
ØDU17JZ	597, 622, 907
ØDU17KZ	597, 622, 907
ØDU187Z	597, 622, 907
ØDU18JZ	597, 622, 907
ØDU18KZ	597, 622, 907
ØDU2*	78, 176, 690
ØDU2Ø7Z	597, 622, 907
ØDU2ØJZ	597, 622, 907
ØDU2ØKZ	597, 622, 907
ØDU247Z	597, 622, 907
ØDU24JZ	597, 622, 907
ØDU24KZ	597, 622, 907
ØDU277Z	597, 622, 907
ØDU27JZ	597, 622, 907
ØDU27KZ	597, 622, 907
ØDU287Z	597, 622, 907
ØDU28JZ	597, 622, 907
ØDU28KZ	597, 622, 907
ØDU3*	78, 176, 690
ØDU3Ø7Z	597, 622, 907
ØDU3ØJZ	597, 622, 907
ØDU3ØKZ	597, 622, 907
ØDU347Z	597, 622, 907
ØDU34JZ	597, 622, 907
ØDU34KZ	597, 622, 907
ØDU377Z	597, 622, 907
ØDU37JZ	597, 622, 907
ØDU37KZ	597, 622, 907
ØDU387Z	597, 622, 907
ØDU38JZ	597, 622, 907
ØDU38KZ	597, 622, 907
ØDU4*	176, 690
ØDU4Ø7Z	907
ØDU4ØJZ	907
ØDU4ØKZ	907
ØDU447Z	907

Code	Page
ØDU44JZ	907
ØDU44KZ	907
ØDU477Z	907
ØDU47JZ	907
ØDU47KZ	907
ØDU487Z	907
ØDU48JZ	907
ØDU48KZ	907
ØDU5*	78, 176, 690
ØDU5Ø7Z	597, 622, 907
ØDU5ØJZ	597, 622, 907
ØDU5ØKZ	597, 622, 907
ØDU547Z	597, 622, 907
ØDU54JZ	597, 622, 907
ØDU54KZ	597, 622, 907
ØDU577Z	597, 622, 907
ØDU57JZ	597, 622, 907
ØDU57KZ	597, 622, 907
ØDU587Z	597, 622, 907
ØDU58JZ	597, 622, 907
ØDU58KZ	597, 622, 907
ØDU6*	176, 480, 690
ØDU6Ø7Z	907
ØDU6ØJZ	907
ØDU6ØKZ	907
ØDU647Z	907
ØDU64JZ	907
ØDU64KZ	907
ØDU677Z	907
ØDU67JZ	907
ØDU67KZ	907
ØDU687Z	907
ØDU68JZ	907
ØDU68KZ	907
ØDU7*	176
ØDU8*	179, 690
ØDU9*	179, 690
ØDUA*	179, 690
ØDUB*	179, 690
ØDUC*	179, 690
ØDUE*	179, 690
ØDUF*	179, 690
ØDUG*	179, 690
ØDUH*	179, 690
ØDUK*	179, 690
ØDUL*	179, 690
ØDUM*	179, 690
ØDUN*	179, 690
ØDUP*	183, 690
ØDUPØ7Z	907
ØDUPØJZ	907
ØDUPØKZ	907
ØDUP47Z	907
ØDUP4JZ	908
ØDUP4KZ	908
ØDUP77Z	908
ØDUP7JZ	908
ØDUP7KZ	908
ØDUP87Z	908
ØDUP8JZ	908
ØDUP8KZ	908
ØDUQ*	183, 690
ØDUQØ7Z	908
ØDUQØJZ	908
ØDUQØKZ	908
ØDUQ47Z	908
ØDUQ4JZ	908
ØDUQ4KZ	908
ØDUQ77Z	908
ØDUQ7JZ	908
ØDUQ7KZ	908
ØDUQ87Z	908
ØDUQ8JZ	908
ØDUQ8KZ	908
ØDUQX7Z	908
ØDUQXJZ	908
ØDUQXKZ	908
ØDUR*	183, 690
ØDURØ7Z	424, 908, 1063
ØDURØJZ	424, 908, 1063
ØDURØKZ	424, 908, 1063
ØDUR47Z	424, 908, 1063
ØDUR4JZ	424, 908, 1063
ØDUR4KZ	424, 908, 1063
ØDUUØ7Z	189, 207, 597, 622, 690, 908
ØDUUØJZ	189, 207, 597, 622, 690, 908
ØDUUØKZ	189, 207, 597, 622, 690, 908
ØDUU47Z	189, 207, 597, 622, 690, 908

Code	Page
ØDUU4JZ	189, 207, 597, 622, 690, 908
ØDUU4KZ	189, 207, 597, 622, 690, 908
ØDUV*	189, 207, 690
ØDUVØ7Z	597, 622, 908
ØDUVØJZ	597, 622, 908
ØDUVØKZ	597, 622, 908
ØDUV47Z	597, 622, 908
ØDUV4JZ	597, 622, 908
ØDUV4KZ	597, 622, 908
ØDUW*	189, 207, 690
ØDUWØ7Z	597, 622, 908
ØDUWØJZ	597, 622, 908
ØDUWØKZ	597, 622, 908
ØDUW47Z	597, 622, 908
ØDUW4JZ	597, 622, 908
ØDUW4KZ	597, 622, 908
ØDV1*	176, 690
ØDV2*	176, 690
ØDV3*	176, 690
ØDV4*	176, 690
ØDV4ØCZ	908
ØDV4ØDZ	908
ØDV4ØZZ	908
ØDV43CZ	908
ØDV43DZ	908
ØDV43ZZ	908
ØDV44CZ	908, 1063
ØDV44DZ	908
ØDV44DZ	1063
ØDV44ZZ	908, 1063
ØDV47DZ	908
ØDV47ZZ	908
ØDV48DZ	908
ØDV48ZZ	908
ØDV5*	176, 690
ØDV6ØCZ	176, 480, 690, 908
ØDV6ØDZ	176, 480, 690, 908
ØDV6ØZZ	176, 480, 690, 908
ØDV63CZ	176, 480, 690, 908
ØDV63DZ	176, 480, 690, 908
ØDV63ZZ	176, 480, 690, 908
ØDV64CZ	176, 480, 690, 908, 1063
ØDV64DZ	176, 480, 690, 908
ØDV64ZZ	176, 480, 690, 908
ØDV67ZZ	176, 480, 690, 908
ØDV68ZZ	176, 480, 690, 908
ØDV7*	176
ØDV8*	179, 691
ØDV9*	179, 691
ØDVA*	179, 691
ØDVB*	179, 691
ØDVC*	179, 691
ØDVE*	179, 691
ØDVF*	179, 691
ØDVG*	179, 691
ØDVH*	179, 691
ØDVK*	179, 691
ØDVL*	179, 691
ØDVM*	179, 691
ØDVN*	179, 691
ØDVP*	183, 691
ØDVPØCZ	908
ØDVPØDZ	908
ØDVPØZZ	908
ØDVP3CZ	908
ØDVP3DZ	908
ØDVP3ZZ	908
ØDVP4CZ	908
ØDVP4DZ	908
ØDVP4ZZ	908
ØDVP7DZ	908
ØDVP7ZZ	908
ØDVP8DZ	908
ØDVP8ZZ	908
ØDVQ*	183
ØDVQØCZ	424
ØDVQØDZ	424
ØDVQØZZ	424
ØDVQ3CZ	424
ØDVQ3DZ	424
ØDVQ3ZZ	424
ØDVQ4CZ	424
ØDVQ4DZ	424
ØDVQ4ZZ	424
ØDVQ7DZ	424
ØDVQ7ZZ	424
ØDVQ8DZ	424
ØDVQ8ZZ	424
ØDVQXCZ	424
ØDVQXDZ	424

Code	Page
ØDVQXZZ	424
ØDWØØØZ	182, 691
ØDWØØ2Z	182, 691
ØDWØØ3Z	182, 691
ØDWØØ7Z	182, 691
ØDWØØCZ	182, 691
ØDWØØDZ	182, 691
ØDWØØJZ	182, 691
ØDWØØKZ	182, 691
ØDWØØUZ	182, 691
ØDWØØYZ	182, 691
ØDWØ3ØZ	182, 691
ØDWØ32Z	182, 691
ØDWØ33Z	182, 691
ØDWØ37Z	182, 691
ØDWØ3CZ	182, 691
ØDWØ3DZ	182, 691
ØDWØ3JZ	182, 691
ØDWØ3KZ	182, 691
ØDWØ3UZ	182, 691
ØDWØ4ØZ	182, 691
ØDWØ42Z	182, 691
ØDWØ43Z	182, 691
ØDWØ47Z	182, 691
ØDWØ4CZ	182, 691
ØDWØ4DZ	182, 691
ØDWØ4JZ	182, 691
ØDWØ4KZ	182, 691
ØDWØ4UZ	176, 207, 480, 597, 622
ØDWØ7ØZ	182, 691
ØDWØ72Z	182, 691
ØDWØ73Z	182, 691
ØDWØ77Z	182, 691
ØDWØ7CZ	182, 691
ØDWØ7DZ	182, 691
ØDWØ7JZ	182, 691
ØDWØ7KZ	182, 691
ØDWØ7UZ	182, 691
ØDWØ8ØZ	182, 691
ØDWØ82Z	182, 691
ØDWØ83Z	182, 691
ØDWØ87Z	182, 691
ØDWØ8CZ	182, 691
ØDWØ8DZ	182, 691
ØDWØ8JZ	182, 691
ØDWØ8KZ	182, 691
ØDWØ8UZ	182, 691
ØDW57DZ	176, 691
ØDW58DZ	176, 691
ØDW6ØØZ	176, 691
ØDW6Ø2Z	176, 691
ØDW6Ø3Z	176, 691
ØDW6Ø7Z	176, 691
ØDW6ØCZ	176, 691
ØDW6ØDZ	176, 691
ØDW6ØJZ	176, 691
ØDW6ØKZ	176, 691
ØDW6ØMZ	176, 691
ØDW6ØUZ	176, 691
ØDW6ØYZ	176, 691
ØDW63ØZ	176, 691
ØDW632Z	176, 691
ØDW633Z	176, 691
ØDW637Z	176, 691
ØDW63CZ	176, 691
ØDW63DZ	176, 691
ØDW63JZ	176, 691
ØDW63KZ	176, 691
ØDW63MZ	176, 691
ØDW63UZ	176, 691
ØDW64ØZ	176, 691
ØDW642Z	176, 691
ØDW643Z	480, 1063
ØDW647Z	177, 691
ØDW64CZ	177, 480, 1063
ØDW64DZ	177, 691
ØDW64JZ	177, 691
ØDW64KZ	177, 691
ØDW64MZ	177, 691
ØDW64UZ	177, 691
ØDW67ØZ	177, 691
ØDW672Z	177, 691
ØDW673Z	177, 691
ØDW677Z	177, 691
ØDW67CZ	177, 691
ØDW67DZ	177, 691
ØDW67JZ	177, 691
ØDW67KZ	177, 691
ØDW67UZ	177, 691
ØDW68ØZ	177, 691
ØDW682Z	177, 691
ØDW683Z	177, 691

Code	Page
ØDW687Z	177, 691
ØDW68CZ	177, 691
ØDW68DZ	177, 691
ØDW68JZ	177, 691
ØDW68KZ	177, 691
ØDW68UZ	177, 691
ØDW8*	179, 691
ØDW8Ø7Z	908
ØDW8ØJZ	908
ØDW8ØKZ	908
ØDW847Z	908
ØDW84JZ	908
ØDW84KZ	908
ØDW877Z	908
ØDW87JZ	908
ØDW87KZ	908
ØDW887Z	908
ØDW88JZ	908
ØDW88KZ	908
ØDWDØØZ	182, 691
ØDWDØ2Z	182, 691
ØDWDØ3Z	182, 691
ØDWDØ7Z	182, 691
ØDWDØCZ	182, 691
ØDWDØDZ	182, 691
ØDWDØJZ	182, 691
ØDWDØKZ	182, 691
ØDWDØUZ	182, 691
ØDWDØYZ	182, 691
ØDWD3ØZ	182, 691
ØDWD32Z	182, 691
ØDWD33Z	182, 691
ØDWD37Z	182, 691
ØDWD3CZ	182, 691
ØDWD3DZ	182, 691
ØDWD3JZ	182, 691
ØDWD3KZ	182, 691
ØDWD3UZ	182, 691
ØDWD4ØZ	182, 691
ØDWD42Z	182, 691
ØDWD43Z	182, 691
ØDWD47Z	182, 691
ØDWD4CZ	182, 691
ØDWD4DZ	182, 691
ØDWD4JZ	182, 691
ØDWD4KZ	182, 691
ØDWD4UZ	182, 691
ØDWD7ØZ	182, 691
ØDWD72Z	182, 691
ØDWD73Z	182, 691
ØDWD77Z	183, 691
ØDWD7CZ	183, 691
ØDWD7DZ	183, 691
ØDWD7JZ	183, 691
ØDWD7KZ	183, 691
ØDWD7UZ	183, 691
ØDWD8ØZ	183, 691
ØDWD82Z	183, 691
ØDWD83Z	183, 691
ØDWD87Z	183, 691
ØDWD8CZ	183, 691
ØDWD8DZ	183, 691
ØDWD8JZ	183, 691
ØDWD8KZ	183, 691
ØDWD8UZ	183, 691
ØDWE*	179, 691
ØDWEØ7Z	908
ØDWEØJZ	908
ØDWEØKZ	908
ØDWE47Z	908
ØDWE4JZ	908
ØDWE4KZ	908
ØDWE77Z	908
ØDWE7JZ	908
ØDWE7KZ	908
ØDWE87Z	908
ØDWE8JZ	908
ØDWE8KZ	908
ØDWQ*	179, 691
ØDWQØLZ	424, 908
ØDWQ3LZ	424, 908
ØDWQ4LZ	424, 908
ØDWQ7LZ	424, 908
ØDWQ8LZ	424, 908
ØDWR*	183
ØDWUØ7Z	189
ØDWUØJZ	189
ØDWUØKZ	189
ØDWU37Z	189
ØDWU3JZ	189
ØDWU3KZ	189
ØDWU47Z	189
ØDWU4JZ	189
ØDWU4KZ	189
ØDWVØ7Z	189
ØDWVØJZ	189
ØDWVØKZ	189
ØDWV37Z	189
ØDWV3JZ	189
ØDWV3KZ	189
ØDWV47Z	189
ØDWV4JZ	189
ØDWV4KZ	189
ØDWWØ7Z	189
ØDWWØJZ	34, 146, 189, 207, 515, 691
ØDWWØKZ	189
ØDWW37Z	189
ØDWW3JZ	34, 146, 189, 207, 515, 691
ØDWW3KZ	189
ØDWW47Z	189
ØDWW4JZ	34, 146, 189, 207, 515, 691
ØDWW4KZ	189
ØDX*	691
ØDX6ØZ5	78, 177, 597, 622, 908
ØDX64Z5	78, 177, 597, 622, 908
ØDX8ØZ5	78, 177, 597, 622, 908
ØDX84Z5	78, 177, 597, 622, 908
ØDXEØZ5	78, 177, 597, 622, 908
ØDXEØZ7	537, 908
ØDXE4Z5	78, 177, 597, 622, 908
ØDXE4Z7	537, 908
ØDY6*	177, 480, 691
ØDY6ØZØ	908
ØDY6ØZ1	908
ØDY6ØZ2	908
ØDY8ØZØ	1
ØDY8ØZ1	1
ØDY8ØZ2	1
ØDYEØZØ	1
ØDYEØZ1	1
ØDYEØZ2	1
ØF1*	691
ØF14*	199
ØF14ØD3	189, 597, 622, 908
ØF14ØD4	597, 622, 908
ØF14ØD5	597, 622, 908
ØF14ØD6	597, 622, 908
ØF14ØD7	597, 622, 908
ØF14ØD8	597, 622, 908
ØF14ØD9	597, 622
ØF14ØD9	908
ØF14ØDB	189, 597, 622, 908
ØF14ØZ3	189, 597, 622, 908
ØF14ØZ4	597, 622, 908
ØF14ØZ5	597, 622, 908
ØF14ØZ6	597, 622, 908
ØF14ØZ7	597, 622, 908
ØF14ØZ8	597, 622, 908
ØF14ØZ9	622
ØF14ØZ9	597, 908
ØF14ØZB	189, 597, 622, 908
ØF144D3	189, 597, 622, 908
ØF144D4	597, 622, 908
ØF144D5	597, 622, 908
ØF144D6	597, 622, 908
ØF144D7	597, 622, 908
ØF144D8	597, 622, 908
ØF144D9	597, 622
ØF144D9	908
ØF144DB	189, 597, 622, 908
ØF144Z3	189, 597, 622, 908
ØF144Z4	597, 622, 908
ØF144Z5	597, 622, 908
ØF144Z6	597, 622, 908
ØF144Z7	597, 622, 908
ØF144Z8	597, 622, 908
ØF144Z9	622
ØF144Z9	597, 908
ØF144ZB	189, 597, 622, 908
ØF15*	200
ØF15ØD3	189, 597, 622, 908
ØF15ØD4	189, 597, 622, 908
ØF15ØD5	597, 622, 908
ØF15ØD6	597, 622, 908
ØF15ØD7	597, 622, 908
ØF15ØD8	597, 622, 908
ØF15ØD9	597, 622
ØF15ØD9	908
ØF15ØDB	189, 597, 622, 908
ØF15ØZ3	189, 597, 622, 908
ØF15ØZ4	189, 597, 623, 908
ØF15ØZ5	597, 623, 908
ØF15ØZ6	597, 623, 908
ØF15ØZ7	597, 623, 908
ØF15ØZ8	597, 623, 908
ØF15ØZ9	623
ØF15ØZ9	597, 908
ØF15ØZB	189, 597, 623, 908
ØF154D3	189, 597, 623, 908
ØF154D4	189, 597, 623, 908
ØF154D5	597, 623, 909
ØF154D6	597, 623, 909
ØF154D7	597, 623, 909
ØF154D8	597, 623, 909
ØF154D9	597, 623
ØF154D9	909
ØF154DB	189, 597, 623, 909
ØF154Z3	189, 597, 623, 909
ØF154Z4	189, 597, 623, 909
ØF154Z5	597, 623, 909
ØF154Z6	597, 623, 909
ØF154Z7	597, 623, 909
ØF154Z8	597, 623, 909
ØF154Z9	597, 623
ØF154Z9	909
ØF154ZB	189, 597, 623, 909
ØF16*	200
ØF16ØD3	189, 597, 623, 909
ØF16ØD4	189, 597, 623, 909
ØF16ØD5	597, 623, 909
ØF16ØD6	597, 623, 909
ØF16ØD7	597, 623, 909
ØF16ØD8	597, 623, 909
ØF16ØD9	597, 623
ØF16ØD9	909
ØF16ØDB	189, 597, 623, 909
ØF16ØZ3	189, 597, 623, 909
ØF16ØZ4	189, 597, 623, 909
ØF16ØZ5	597, 623, 909
ØF16ØZ6	597, 623, 909
ØF16ØZ7	597, 623, 909
ØF16ØZ8	597, 623, 909
ØF16ØZ9	623
ØF16ØZ9	597, 909
ØF16ØZB	189, 598, 623, 909
ØF164D3	189, 598, 623, 909
ØF164D4	189, 598, 623, 909
ØF164D5	598, 623, 909
ØF164D6	598, 623, 909
ØF164D7	598, 623, 909
ØF164D8	598, 623, 909
ØF164D9	598, 623
ØF164D9	909
ØF164DB	189, 598, 623, 909
ØF164Z3	189, 598, 623, 909
ØF164Z4	189, 598, 623, 909
ØF164Z5	598, 623, 909
ØF164Z6	598, 623, 909
ØF164Z7	598, 623, 909
ØF164Z8	598, 623, 909
ØF164Z9	598, 623
ØF164Z9	909
ØF164ZB	189, 598, 623, 909
ØF17ØD3	189, 200, 598, 623, 909
ØF17ØD4	189, 200, 598, 623, 909
ØF17ØD5	200, 598, 623, 909
ØF17ØD6	200, 598, 623, 909
ØF17ØD7	200, 598, 623, 909
ØF17ØD8	200, 598, 623, 909
ØF17ØD9	200, 598, 623, 909
ØF17ØDB	189, 200, 598, 623, 909
ØF17ØZ3	189, 200, 598, 623, 909
ØF17ØZ4	189, 200, 598, 623, 909
ØF17ØZ5	200, 598, 623, 909
ØF17ØZ6	200, 598, 623, 909
ØF17ØZ7	200, 598, 623, 909
ØF17ØZ8	200, 598, 623, 909
ØF17ØZ9	200, 598, 623
ØF17ØZ9	909
ØF17ØZB	189, 200, 598, 623, 909
ØF174D3	189, 200, 598, 623, 909
ØF174D4	189, 200, 598, 623, 909
ØF174D5	598, 623, 909
ØF174D5	200
ØF174D6	200
ØF174D6	598, 623, 909
ØF174D7	200
ØF174D7	598, 623, 909
ØF174D8	200
ØF174D8	598, 623, 909
ØF174D9	200
ØF174D9	598, 623, 909
ØF174DB	189, 598, 623, 909
ØF174DB	200
ØF174Z3	189, 200, 598, 623, 909
ØF174Z4	189, 200, 598, 623, 909
ØF174Z5	200, 598, 623, 909
ØF174Z6	200, 598, 623, 909
ØF174Z7	200, 598, 623, 909
ØF174Z8	200, 598, 623, 909
ØF174Z9	200, 598, 623
ØF174Z9	909
ØF174ZB	189, 200, 598, 623, 909
ØF18*	200
ØF18ØD3	189, 598, 623, 909
ØF18ØD4	598, 623, 909
ØF18ØD5	598, 623, 909
ØF18ØD6	598, 623, 909
ØF18ØD7	598, 623, 909
ØF18ØD8	598, 623, 909
ØF18ØD9	598, 623
ØF18ØD9	909
ØF18ØDB	189, 598, 623, 909
ØF18ØZ3	189, 598, 623, 909
ØF18ØZ4	598, 623, 909
ØF18ØZ5	598, 623, 909
ØF18ØZ6	598, 623, 909
ØF18ØZ7	598, 623, 909
ØF18ØZ8	598, 623, 909
ØF18ØZ9	598, 623
ØF18ØZ9	909
ØF18ØZB	189, 598, 623, 909
ØF184D3	189, 598, 623, 909
ØF184D4	598, 623, 909
ØF184D5	598, 623, 909
ØF184D6	598, 623, 909
ØF184D7	598, 623, 909
ØF184D8	598, 623, 909
ØF184D9	598, 623
ØF184D9	909
ØF184DB	189, 598, 623, 909
ØF184Z3	189, 598, 623, 909
ØF184Z4	598, 623, 909
ØF184Z5	598, 623, 909
ØF184Z6	598, 623, 909
ØF184Z7	598, 623, 909
ØF184Z8	598, 623, 909
ØF184Z9	598, 623
ØF184Z9	909
ØF184ZB	189, 598, 623, 909
ØF19*	200
ØF19ØD3	189, 598, 623, 909
ØF19ØD4	598, 623, 909
ØF19ØD5	598, 623, 909
ØF19ØD6	598, 623, 909
ØF19ØD7	598, 623, 909
ØF19ØD8	598, 623, 909
ØF19ØD9	598, 623, 909
ØF19ØDB	189, 598, 623, 909
ØF19ØZ3	189, 598, 623, 909
ØF19ØZ4	598, 623, 909
ØF19ØZ5	598, 623, 909
ØF19ØZ6	598, 623, 909
ØF19ØZ7	598, 623, 909
ØF19ØZ8	598, 623, 909
ØF19ØZ9	598, 623
ØF19ØZ9	909
ØF19ØZB	189, 598, 623, 909
ØF194D3	189, 598, 623, 909
ØF194D4	598, 623, 909
ØF194D5	598, 623, 909
ØF194D6	598, 623, 909
ØF194D7	598, 623, 909
ØF194D8	598, 623, 909
ØF194D9	598, 623, 909
ØF194DB	189, 598, 623, 909
ØF194Z3	189, 598, 623, 909
ØF194Z4	598, 623, 909
ØF194Z5	598, 623, 909
ØF194Z6	598, 623, 909
ØF194Z7	598, 623, 909
ØF194Z8	598, 623, 909
ØF194Z9	598, 623
ØF194Z9	909
ØF194ZB	189, 598, 623, 909
ØF1D*	198
ØF1DØD3	909
ØF1DØDB	909
ØF1DØDC	909
ØF1DØZ3	909
ØF1DØZB	909
ØF1DØZC	909
ØF1D4D3	909
ØF1D4DB	909
ØF1D4DC	909
ØF1D4Z3	909
ØF1D4ZB	909
ØF1D4ZC	909
ØF1F*	198
ØF1FØD3	909
ØF1FØDB	909
ØF1FØDC	909
ØF1FØZ3	909
ØF1FØZB	909
ØF1FØZC	909
ØF1F4D3	909
ØF1F4DB	909
ØF1F4DC	909
ØF1F4Z3	909
ØF1F4ZB	909
ØF1F4ZC	909
ØF1G*	198
ØF1GØD3	909
ØF1GØDB	909
ØF1GØDC	909
ØF1GØZ3	909
ØF1GØZB	909
ØF1GØZC	909
ØF1G4D3	909
ØF1G4DB	909
ØF1G4DC	910
ØF1G4Z3	910
ØF1G4ZB	910
ØF1G4ZC	910
ØF5Ø*	189, 198
ØF5ØØZF	189, 198
ØF5Ø3ZF	189, 198
ØF5Ø4ZF	189, 198
ØF51*	189, 198
ØF51ØZF	189, 198
ØF513ZF	189, 198
ØF514ZF	189, 198
ØF52*	189, 198
ØF52ØZF	189, 198
ØF523ZF	189, 198
ØF524ZF	189, 198
ØF54*	202, 691
ØF54ØZZ	202, 598, 623, 910
ØF543ZZ	202, 598, 623, 910
ØF544ZZ	202, 598, 623, 910
ØF548ZZ	202, 598, 623, 910
ØF55ØZZ	189, 200
ØF553ZZ	189, 200
ØF557ZZ	189, 200
ØF56ØZZ	189, 200
ØF563ZZ	189, 200
ØF567ZZ	189, 200
ØF57ØZZ	189, 200
ØF573ZZ	189, 200
ØF577ZZ	189, 200
ØF58ØZZ	189, 200
ØF583ZZ	189, 200
ØF587ZZ	189, 200
ØF59ØZZ	189, 200
ØF593ZZ	189, 200
ØF597ZZ	189, 200
ØF5CØZZ	189, 200
ØF5C3ZZ	189, 200
ØF5C7ZZ	189, 200
ØF5DØZZ	198, 494
ØF5D3ZZ	198, 494
ØF5D7ZZ	198, 494
ØF5FØZZ	198, 494
ØF5F3ZZ	198, 494
ØF5F7ZZ	198, 494
ØF5GØZF	198, 494
ØF5GØZZ	198, 494
ØF5G3ZF	198, 494
ØF5G3ZZ	198, 494
ØF75ØDZ	200, 691, 910
ØF75ØZZ	200, 691, 910
ØF757ZZ	200, 691, 910
ØF76ØDZ	200, 691, 910
ØF76ØZZ	200, 691, 910
ØF767ZZ	200, 691, 910
ØF77ØDZ	200, 691, 910
ØF77ØZZ	200, 691, 910
ØF777ZZ	200, 691, 910
ØF78ØDZ	200, 691, 910
ØF78ØZZ	200, 692, 910
ØF787ZZ	200, 692, 910
ØF79ØDZ	200, 692, 910
ØF79ØZZ	200, 692, 910
ØF797ZZ	200, 692, 910
ØF7CØDZ	189, 200, 692, 910
ØF7CØZZ	189, 200, 692, 910
ØF7C3DZ	189, 200, 692, 910
ØF7C3ZZ	189, 200, 692, 910
ØF7C4DZ	189, 200, 692, 910
ØF7C4ZZ	189, 200, 692, 910
ØF7C7DZ	189, 200, 692, 910
ØF7C7ZZ	189, 200, 692, 910
ØF7DØDZ	189, 198, 598, 623, 692, 910
ØF7DØZZ	189, 198, 692, 910
ØF7D3DZ	189, 198, 598, 623, 692, 910
ØF7D3ZZ	189, 198, 692, 910
ØF7D7ZZ	198, 692, 910
ØF7FØDZ	190, 198, 598, 623, 692, 910
ØF7FØZZ	190, 198, 692, 910
ØF7F3DZ	190, 198, 598, 623, 692, 910
ØF7F3ZZ	190, 198, 692, 910
ØF7F7DZ	190, 198, 598, 623, 692, 910
ØF7F7ZZ	198, 692, 910
ØF8*	198
ØF8GØZZ	177, 692, 910
ØF8G3ZZ	177, 692, 910
ØF9ØØØZ	198, 692, 910
ØF9ØØZX	78, 101, 146, 190, 202, 277, 424, 494, 515, 524, 538, 576, 598, 623, 692, 910
ØF9ØØZZ	198, 692, 910
ØF91ØØZ	198, 692, 910
ØF91ØZX	78, 101, 146, 190, 202, 277, 424, 494, 515, 524, 538, 576, 598, 623, 692, 910
ØF91ØZZ	198, 692, 910
ØF92ØØZ	198, 692, 910
ØF92ØZX	78, 101, 146, 190, 202, 277, 424, 494, 515, 524, 538, 576, 598, 623, 692, 910
ØF92ØZZ	198, 692, 910
ØF94ØØZ	200
ØF94ØZX	190, 202
ØF94ØZZ	190, 200
ØF95ØØZ	190, 200, 692
ØF95ØZX	190, 202
ØF95ØZZ	190, 200, 692
ØF954ØZ	190, 200, 692
ØF954ZZ	190, 200, 692
ØF957ØZ	190, 200, 692
ØF957ZZ	190, 200, 692
ØF96ØØZ	190, 200, 692
ØF96ØZX	190, 202
ØF96ØZZ	190, 200, 692
ØF964ØZ	190, 200, 692
ØF964ZZ	190, 200, 692
ØF967ØZ	190, 200, 692
ØF967ZZ	190, 200, 692
ØF97ØØZ	190, 200, 692
ØF97ØZX	190, 202
ØF97ØZZ	190, 200, 692
ØF98ØØZ	190, 200, 692
ØF98ØZX	190, 202
ØF98ØZZ	190, 200, 692
ØF984ØZ	190, 200, 692
ØF984ZZ	190, 200, 692
ØF987ØZ	190, 200, 692
ØF987ZZ	190, 200, 692
ØF99ØØZ	202
ØF99ØZX	190, 202
ØF99ØZZ	202
ØF994ØZ	202
ØF997ØZ	198, 598, 623, 692, 910
ØF9CØØZ	200, 692, 910
ØF9CØZX	190, 202
ØF9CØZZ	200, 692, 910

Numeric Index to Procedures

Code	Page
0F9C70Z	200, 692, 910
0F9C7ZZ	200, 692, 910
0F9D00Z	198
0F9D0ZX	190, 202
0F9D0ZZ	198
0F9D40Z	198
0F9D4ZZ	198
0F9D70Z	198
0F9D7ZZ	198
0F9F00Z	198
0F9F0ZX	190, 202, 494, 598, 623, 692, 910
0F9F0ZZ	198
0F9F40Z	198
0F9F4ZZ	198
0F9F70Z	198
0F9F7ZZ	198
0F9G00Z	198
0F9G0ZX	190, 202, 494, 598, 623, 692, 910
0F9G0ZZ	198
0F9G40Z	198
0F9G4ZZ	198
0FB00ZX	78, 101, 146, 190, 202, 277, 424, 494, 515, 524, 538, 576, 598, 623, 692, 910
0FB00ZZ	198, 692, 910
0FB03ZZ	198, 692, 910
0FB04ZX	190, 202, 424, 515, 576, 598, 623, 692, 910
0FB04ZZ	198, 692, 910
0FB10ZX	78, 101, 146, 190, 202, 277, 424, 494, 515, 524, 538, 576, 598, 623, 692, 910
0FB10ZZ	198, 692, 910
0FB13ZZ	198, 692, 910
0FB14ZX	190, 202, 424, 515, 576, 598, 623, 692, 910
0FB14ZZ	198, 692, 910
0FB20ZX	78, 101, 146, 190, 202, 277, 424, 494, 515, 524, 538, 576, 598, 623, 692, 910
0FB20ZZ	198, 692, 910
0FB23ZZ	198, 692, 910
0FB24ZX	190, 202, 424, 515, 576, 598, 623, 692, 910
0FB24ZZ	198, 692, 910
0FB40ZX	190, 202
0FB40ZZ	202, 598, 623, 692, 910
0FB43ZZ	202, 598, 623, 692, 910
0FB44ZZ	202, 598, 624, 692, 910
0FB48ZZ	202, 598, 624, 692, 910
0FB50ZX	190, 202
0FB50ZZ	190, 200
0FB53ZZ	190, 200
0FB57ZZ	190, 200
0FB60ZX	190, 202
0FB60ZZ	190, 200
0FB63ZZ	190, 200
0FB67ZZ	190, 200
0FB70ZX	190, 202
0FB70ZZ	190, 200
0FB73ZZ	190, 200
0FB77ZZ	190, 200
0FB80ZX	190, 202
0FB80ZZ	200, 692, 910
0FB83ZZ	200, 692, 910
0FB87ZZ	200, 692, 910
0FB90ZX	190, 202
0FB90ZZ	190, 200
0FB93ZZ	190, 200
0FB97ZZ	190, 200
0FBC0ZX	190, 202
0FBC0ZZ	190, 200
0FBC3ZZ	190, 200
0FBC7ZZ	190, 200
0FBD0ZX	190, 202, 494, 598, 624, 692, 910
0FBD0ZZ	198, 494
0FBD3ZZ	198, 494
0FBD7ZZ	198, 494
0FBF0ZX	598, 624, 692, 910
0FBF0ZZ	198, 494
0FBF3ZZ	198, 494
0FBF7ZZ	198, 494
0FBG0ZX	190, 202, 494, 598, 624, 692, 910
0FBG0ZZ	198, 494, 692, 910
0FBG3ZZ	198, 494, 692, 910
0FBG4ZZ	198, 494, 692, 910
0FBG8ZZ	198, 494, 692, 910
0FC0*	198, 692
0FC00ZZ	910
0FC03ZZ	910
0FC04ZZ	910
0FC1*	198, 692
0FC10ZZ	910
0FC13ZZ	910
0FC14ZZ	910
0FC2*	198, 692
0FC20ZZ	910
0FC23ZZ	910
0FC24ZZ	910
0FC4*	200
0FC50ZZ	200, 598, 624
0FC60ZZ	200, 598, 624
0FC70ZZ	200, 598, 624
0FC80ZZ	200, 598, 624
0FC90ZZ	202, 598, 624, 692, 910
0FCC0ZZ	177, 198, 692, 910
0FCC3ZZ	200, 598, 624
0FCC7ZZ	200, 692, 910
0FCD0ZZ	198
0FCD7ZZ	198
0FCF0ZZ	198
0FCF7ZZ	198
0FCG*	198
0FD04ZX	190, 202, 424, 515, 576, 598, 624, 692, 910
0FD14ZX	190, 202, 424, 515, 576, 598, 624, 692, 910
0FD24ZX	190, 202, 424, 515, 576, 598, 624, 692, 910
0FF40ZZ	200
0FF43ZZ	200
0FF44ZZ	200
0FF47ZZ	200
0FF50ZZ	200, 598, 624
0FF53ZZ	200, 598, 624
0FF54ZZ	200, 598, 624
0FF57ZZ	200, 598, 624
0FF60ZZ	200, 598, 624
0FF63ZZ	200, 598, 624
0FF64ZZ	200, 598, 624
0FF67ZZ	200, 598, 624
0FF70ZZ	200, 598, 624
0FF73ZZ	200, 598, 624
0FF74ZZ	200, 598, 624
0FF77ZZ	200, 598, 624
0FF80ZZ	200, 598, 624
0FF83ZZ	200, 598, 624
0FF84ZZ	200, 598, 624
0FF87ZZ	200, 598, 624
0FF90ZZ	200, 598, 624
0FF93ZZ	200, 598, 624
0FF94ZZ	200, 598, 624
0FF97ZZ	200, 598, 624
0FFC0ZZ	200, 598, 624
0FFC3ZZ	200, 598, 624
0FFC4ZZ	200, 598, 624
0FFC7ZZ	200, 598, 624
0FFD0ZZ	198
0FFD3ZZ	198
0FFD4ZZ	198
0FFD7ZZ	198
0FFF0ZZ	198
0FFF3ZZ	198
0FFF4ZZ	198
0FFF7ZZ	198
0FH002Z	198, 692, 910
0FH00YZ	198, 692, 910
0FH032Z	198, 692, 910
0FH042Z	198, 692, 910
0FH102Z	198, 692, 910
0FH132Z	198, 692, 910
0FH142Z	198, 692, 910
0FH202Z	198, 692, 910
0FH232Z	198, 692, 910
0FH242Z	198, 692, 910
0FH402Z	200
0FH40YZ	200
0FH432Z	200
0FH442Z	200
0FHB01Z	692, 1063
0FHB02Z	200, 692
0FHB0DZ	190, 200, 598, 624, 692, 910
0FHB0YZ	200, 692
0FHB31Z	692, 1063
0FHB32Z	200, 692
0FHB3DZ	190, 200, 599, 624, 692, 910
0FHB41Z	692, 1063
0FHB42Z	200, 692
0FHB71Z	692, 1063
0FHB7DZ	190, 200, 599, 624, 692, 910
0FHB81Z	692, 1063
0FHD01Z	692, 1063
0FHD02Z	198
0FHD0DZ	190, 198, 599, 624, 692, 910
0FHD0YZ	198
0FHD31Z	692, 1063
0FHD32Z	198
0FHD3DZ	190, 198, 599, 624, 692, 910
0FHD41Z	692, 1063
0FHD42Z	198
0FHD71Z	692, 1063
0FHD7DZ	190, 198, 599, 624, 692, 910
0FHD81Z	692, 1063
0FHG02Z	198
0FHG0YZ	198
0FHG32Z	198
0FHG42Z	198
0FJ00ZZ	101, 146, 190, 202, 424, 494, 515, 521, 538, 576, 599, 624, 692, 910
0FJ04ZZ	190, 202, 424, 515, 535, 576, 692, 910, 1063
0FJ40ZZ	190, 202
0FJ44ZZ	190, 202, 424, 515, 535, 576, 692, 910, 1063
0FJB0ZZ	202
0FJB4ZZ	202
0FJD0ZZ	190, 203, 494, 599, 624, 692, 910
0FJD4ZZ	190, 203, 424, 515, 535, 576, 692, 910, 1063
0FJG0ZZ	190, 203, 494, 599, 624, 692, 910
0FJG4ZZ	190, 203, 424, 515, 535, 576, 692, 910, 1063
0FL50CZ	200, 599, 624, 692, 910, 1063
0FL50DZ	200, 599, 624, 692, 910
0FL50DZ	1063
0FL50ZZ	200, 599, 624, 692, 910, 1063
0FL60CZ	200, 599, 624, 692, 910, 1063
0FL60DZ	200, 599, 624, 692, 910
0FL60DZ	1063
0FL60ZZ	200, 599, 624, 692, 910, 1063
0FL70CZ	200, 599, 624, 692, 910, 1064
0FL70DZ	201, 599, 624, 692, 910, 1064
0FL70DZ	1064
0FL70ZZ	201, 599, 624, 692, 910, 1064
0FL80CZ	201, 599, 624, 692, 910, 1064
0FL80DZ	201, 599, 624, 692, 910
0FL80DZ	1064
0FL80ZZ	201, 599, 624, 692, 910, 1064
0FL90CZ	201, 599, 624, 692, 910, 1064
0FL90DZ	201, 599, 624, 692, 910
0FL90DZ	1064
0FL90ZZ	201, 599, 624, 692, 910, 1064
0FLC*	201, 692
0FLC0CZ	910
0FLC0DZ	910
0FLC0ZZ	910
0FLC3CZ	910
0FLC3DZ	910
0FLC3ZZ	910
0FLC4CZ	910
0FLC4DZ	910
0FLC4ZZ	910
0FLC7DZ	910
0FLC7ZZ	910
0FLC8DZ	910
0FLC8ZZ	910
0FLD*	190, 198, 692
0FLD0CZ	910
0FLD0DZ	910
0FLD0ZZ	910
0FLD3CZ	910
0FLD3DZ	910
0FLD3ZZ	910
0FLD4CZ	910
0FLD4DZ	910
0FLD4ZZ	910
0FLD7DZ	910
0FLD7ZZ	910
0FLD8DZ	910
0FLD8ZZ	910
0FLF*	190, 198, 692
0FLF0CZ	910
0FLF0DZ	910
0FLF0ZZ	910
0FLF3CZ	910
0FLF3DZ	910
0FLF3ZZ	911
0FLF4CZ	911
0FLF4DZ	911
0FLF4ZZ	911
0FLF7DZ	911
0FLF7ZZ	911
0FLF8DZ	911
0FLF8ZZ	911
0FM0*	198, 692
0FM00ZZ	911
0FM04ZZ	911
0FM1*	198, 692
0FM10ZZ	911
0FM14ZZ	911
0FM2*	199, 692
0FM20ZZ	911
0FM24ZZ	911
0FM40ZZ	201, 599, 624, 692, 911, 1064
0FM50ZZ	201, 692, 911
0FM60ZZ	201, 692, 911
0FM70ZZ	201, 692, 911
0FM80ZZ	201, 692, 911
0FM90ZZ	201, 692, 911
0FMC*	201, 692
0FMC0ZZ	911
0FMC4ZZ	911
0FMD*	199, 692
0FMD0ZZ	911
0FMD4ZZ	911
0FMF*	199, 692
0FMF0ZZ	911
0FMF4ZZ	911
0FMG*	199, 692
0FMG0ZZ	911
0FMG4ZZ	911
0FN*	180, 207, 515, 692
0FN0*	538
0FN00ZZ	494, 911
0FN03ZZ	494, 911
0FN04ZZ	911
0FN1*	538
0FN13ZZ	494, 911
0FN14ZZ	911
0FN2*	538
0FN20ZZ	494, 911
0FN23ZZ	494, 911
0FN24ZZ	911
0FN4*	538
0FN40ZZ	494, 911
0FN43ZZ	494, 911
0FN44ZZ	911
0FN48ZZ	911
0FN5*	538
0FN50ZZ	494, 911
0FN53ZZ	494, 911
0FN54ZZ	911
0FN57ZZ	494, 911
0FN58ZZ	494, 911
0FN6*	538
0FN60ZZ	494, 911
0FN63ZZ	494, 911
0FN64ZZ	911
0FN67ZZ	494, 911
0FN68ZZ	494, 911
0FN70ZZ	494, 538, 911
0FN73ZZ	494, 538, 911
0FN74ZZ	538, 911
0FN77ZZ	494, 538, 911
0FN78ZZ	494, 538, 911
0FN8*	538
0FN80ZZ	494, 911
0FN83ZZ	494, 911
0FN84ZZ	911
0FN87ZZ	494, 911
0FN88ZZ	494, 911
0FN9*	538
0FN90ZZ	494, 911
0FN93ZZ	494, 911
0FN94ZZ	911
0FN97ZZ	494, 911
0FN98ZZ	494, 911
0FNC*	538
0FNC0ZZ	494, 911
0FNC3ZZ	494, 911
0FNC4ZZ	911
0FNC7ZZ	494, 911
0FNC8ZZ	494, 911
0FND*	538
0FND0ZZ	494, 911
0FND3ZZ	494, 911
0FND4ZZ	911
0FND7ZZ	494, 911
0FND8ZZ	494, 911
0FNF*	538
0FNF0ZZ	494, 911
0FNF3ZZ	494, 911
0FNF4ZZ	911
0FNF7ZZ	494, 911
0FNF8ZZ	494, 911
0FNG*	538
0FNG0ZZ	494, 911
0FNG3ZZ	494, 911
0FNG4ZZ	911
0FNG8ZZ	911
0FP000Z	199, 692, 911
0FP002Z	199, 692, 911
0FP003Z	199, 692, 911
0FP00YZ	199, 692, 911
0FP030Z	199, 693, 911
0FP032Z	199, 693, 911
0FP033Z	199, 693, 911
0FP040Z	199, 693, 911
0FP042Z	199, 693, 911
0FP043Z	199, 693, 911
0FP400Z	201
0FP402Z	201
0FP403Z	201
0FP40DZ	201, 599, 624, 693, 911
0FP40YZ	201
0FP430Z	201
0FP432Z	201
0FP433Z	201
0FP43DZ	201, 599, 624, 693, 911
0FP440Z	201
0FP442Z	201
0FP443Z	201
0FP44DZ	201, 599, 624, 693, 911
0FPB00Z	201, 693
0FPB01Z	201, 693
0FPB02Z	201, 693
0FPB03Z	201, 693
0FPB07Z	201, 693
0FPB0CZ	201, 693
0FPB0DZ	201, 693
0FPB0JZ	201, 693
0FPB0KZ	201, 693
0FPB0YZ	201, 693
0FPB30Z	201, 693
0FPB31Z	201, 693
0FPB32Z	201, 693
0FPB33Z	201, 693
0FPB37Z	201, 693
0FPB3CZ	201, 693
0FPB3DZ	201, 693
0FPB3JZ	201, 693
0FPB3KZ	201, 693
0FPB40Z	201, 693
0FPB41Z	201, 693
0FPB42Z	201, 693
0FPB43Z	201, 693
0FPB47Z	201, 693
0FPB4CZ	201, 693
0FPB4DZ	201, 693
0FPB4JZ	201, 693
0FPB4KZ	201, 693
0FPB71Z	201, 693
0FPB77Z	201, 693
0FPB7CZ	201, 693
0FPB7JZ	201, 693
0FPB7KZ	201, 693
0FPB81Z	201, 693
0FPB87Z	201, 693
0FPB8CZ	201, 693
0FPB8JZ	201, 693
0FPB8KZ	201, 693
0FPD00Z	199
0FPD01Z	199
0FPD02Z	199
0FPD03Z	199
0FPD07Z	199
0FPD0CZ	199
0FPD0DZ	199
0FPD0JZ	199
0FPD0KZ	199
0FPD0YZ	199
0FPD30Z	199
0FPD31Z	199
0FPD32Z	199
0FPD33Z	199
0FPD37Z	199
0FPD3CZ	199
0FPD3DZ	199
0FPD3JZ	199
0FPD3KZ	199
0FPD40Z	199
0FPD41Z	199
0FPD42Z	199
0FPD43Z	199
0FPD47Z	199
0FPD4DZ	199
0FPD4JZ	199
0FPD4KZ	199
0FPD71Z	199
0FPD77Z	199
0FPD7CZ	199
0FPD7JZ	199
0FPD7KZ	199
0FPD81Z	199
0FPD87Z	199
0FPD8CZ	199
0FPD8JZ	199
0FPD8KZ	199
0FPG00Z	199
0FPG02Z	199
0FPG03Z	199
0FPG0DZ	199
0FPG0YZ	199
0FPG32Z	199
0FPG33Z	199
0FPG3DZ	199
0FPG40Z	199
0FPG42Z	199
0FPG43Z	199
0FPG4DZ	199
0FPGXDZ	199
0FQ*	693
0FQ0*	199
0FQ00ZZ	911
0FQ04ZZ	911
0FQ1*	199
0FQ10ZZ	911
0FQ13ZZ	911
0FQ14ZZ	911
0FQ2*	199
0FQ20ZZ	911
0FQ23ZZ	911
0FQ24ZZ	911
0FQ4*	201
0FQ43ZZ	599, 624, 911
0FQ44ZZ	599, 624, 911
0FQ48ZZ	599, 624, 911
0FQ5*	201

Code	Page
0FQ50ZZ	599, 624, 911
0FQ53ZZ	599, 624, 911
0FQ54ZZ	599, 624, 911
0FQ57ZZ	599, 624, 911
0FQ58ZZ	599, 624, 911
0FQ6*	201
0FQ60ZZ	599, 624, 911
0FQ63ZZ	599, 624, 911
0FQ64ZZ	599, 624, 911
0FQ67ZZ	599, 624, 911
0FQ68ZZ	599, 624, 911
0FQ70ZZ	201, 599, 624, 911
0FQ73ZZ	201, 599, 624, 911
0FQ74ZZ	201, 599, 624, 911
0FQ77ZZ	201, 599, 624, 911
0FQ78ZZ	201, 599, 624, 911
0FQ8*	201
0FQ80ZZ	599, 624, 911
0FQ83ZZ	599, 624, 911
0FQ84ZZ	599, 624, 911
0FQ87ZZ	599, 624, 911
0FQ88ZZ	599, 624, 911
0FQ9*	201
0FQ90ZZ	599, 624, 911
0FQ93ZZ	599, 624, 911
0FQ94ZZ	599, 624, 911
0FQ97ZZ	599, 624, 911
0FQ98ZZ	599, 624, 911
0FQC*	177, 199
0FQC0ZZ	911
0FQC3ZZ	911
0FQC4ZZ	911
0FQC7ZZ	911
0FQC8ZZ	911
0FQD*	199
0FQD0ZZ	911
0FQD3ZZ	911
0FQD4ZZ	911
0FQD7ZZ	911
0FQD8ZZ	911
0FQF*	199
0FQF0ZZ	911
0FQF3ZZ	911
0FQF4ZZ	911
0FQF7ZZ	911
0FQF8ZZ	911
0FQG*	199
0FQG0ZZ	911
0FQG3ZZ	911
0FQG4ZZ	911
0FQG8ZZ	911
0FR*	693
0FR5*	201
0FR507Z	911
0FR50JZ	599, 624, 911, 1064
0FR50KZ	911
0FR547Z	911
0FR54JZ	599, 624, 911, 1064
0FR54KZ	911
0FR587Z	911
0FR58JZ	599, 624, 911, 1064
0FR58KZ	911
0FR6*	201
0FR607Z	911
0FR60JZ	599, 624, 911, 1064
0FR60KZ	911
0FR647Z	911
0FR64JZ	599, 624, 911, 1064
0FR64KZ	911
0FR687Z	911
0FR68JZ	599, 624, 911, 1064
0FR68KZ	911
0FR707Z	201, 911
0FR70JZ	201, 599, 624, 912, 1064
0FR70KZ	201, 912
0FR747Z	201, 912
0FR74JZ	201, 599, 624, 912, 1064
0FR74KZ	201, 912
0FR787Z	201, 912
0FR78JZ	201, 599, 624, 912, 1064
0FR78KZ	201, 912
0FR8*	201
0FR807Z	912
0FR80JZ	599, 624, 912, 1064
0FR80KZ	912
0FR847Z	912
0FR84JZ	599, 624, 912, 1064
0FR84KZ	912
0FR887Z	912
0FR88JZ	599, 624, 912, 1064
0FR88KZ	912
0FR9*	201
0FR907Z	912
0FR90JZ	599, 624, 912, 1064
0FR90KZ	912
0FR947Z	912
0FR94JZ	599, 624, 912, 1064
0FR94KZ	912
0FR987Z	912
0FR98JZ	599, 624, 912, 1064
0FR98KZ	912
0FRC*	201
0FRC07Z	912
0FRC0JZ	912
0FRC0KZ	912
0FRC47Z	912
0FRC4JZ	912
0FRC4KZ	912
0FRC87Z	912
0FRC8JZ	912
0FRC8KZ	912
0FRD*	199
0FRD07Z	912
0FRD0JZ	912
0FRD0KZ	912
0FRD47Z	912
0FRD4JZ	912
0FRD4KZ	912
0FRD87Z	912
0FRD8JZ	912
0FRD8KZ	912
0FRF*	199
0FRF07Z	912
0FRF0JZ	912
0FRF0KZ	912
0FRF47Z	912
0FRF4JZ	912
0FRF4KZ	912
0FRF87Z	912
0FRF8JZ	912
0FRF8KZ	912
0FS0*	199, 693
0FS00ZZ	912
0FS04ZZ	912
0FS4*	201, 693
0FS40ZZ	599, 624, 912, 1064
0FS44ZZ	599, 624, 912, 1064
0FS5*	201, 693
0FS50ZZ	912
0FS54ZZ	912
0FS6*	201, 693
0FS60ZZ	912
0FS64ZZ	912
0FS70ZZ	201, 693, 912
0FS74ZZ	201, 693, 912
0FS8*	201, 693
0FS80ZZ	912
0FS84ZZ	912
0FS9*	201, 693
0FS90ZZ	912
0FS94ZZ	912
0FSC*	201, 693
0FSC0ZZ	912
0FSC4ZZ	912
0FSD*	199, 693
0FSD0ZZ	912
0FSD4ZZ	912
0FSF*	199, 693
0FSF0ZZ	912
0FSF4ZZ	912
0FSG*	199
0FT0*	199, 693
0FT00ZZ	912
0FT1*	199, 693
0FT10ZZ	912
0FT14ZZ	912
0FT2*	199, 693
0FT20ZZ	912
0FT24ZZ	912
0FT4*	190, 202, 693
0FT40ZZ	202, 599, 624, 912
0FT44ZZ	202, 599, 624, 912, 1064
0FT5*	190, 201
0FT6*	190, 201
0FT70ZZ	190, 201
0FT74ZZ	190, 201
0FT77ZZ	190, 201
0FT78ZZ	190, 201
0FT8*	190, 201
0FT9*	190, 201
0FTC*	190, 201
0FTD0ZZ	199, 494
0FTD7ZZ	199, 494
0FTF0ZZ	199, 494
0FTF7ZZ	199, 494
0FTG*	199, 693
0FTG0ZZ	177, 912
0FTG4ZZ	912
0FU*	693
0FU5*	201
0FU507Z	912
0FU50JZ	912
0FU50KZ	912
0FU537Z	912
0FU53JZ	912
0FU53KZ	912
0FU547Z	912
0FU54JZ	912
0FU54KZ	912
0FU587Z	912
0FU58JZ	912
0FU58KZ	912
0FU6*	201
0FU607Z	912
0FU60JZ	912
0FU60KZ	912
0FU637Z	912
0FU63JZ	912
0FU63KZ	912
0FU647Z	912
0FU64JZ	912
0FU64KZ	912
0FU687Z	912
0FU68JZ	912
0FU68KZ	912
0FU707Z	201, 912
0FU70KZ	201, 912
0FU737Z	201, 912
0FU73JZ	201, 912
0FU73KZ	201, 912
0FU747Z	201, 912
0FU74JZ	201, 912
0FU74KZ	201, 912
0FU787Z	201, 912
0FU78JZ	201, 912
0FU78KZ	201, 912
0FU8*	201
0FU807Z	912
0FU80JZ	912
0FU80KZ	912
0FU837Z	912
0FU83JZ	912
0FU83KZ	912
0FU847Z	912
0FU84JZ	912
0FU84KZ	912
0FU887Z	912
0FU88JZ	912
0FU88KZ	912
0FU9*	201
0FU907Z	912
0FU90JZ	912
0FU90KZ	912
0FU937Z	912
0FU93JZ	912
0FU93KZ	912
0FU947Z	912
0FU94JZ	912
0FU94KZ	912
0FU987Z	912
0FU98JZ	912
0FU98KZ	912
0FUC*	201
0FUC07Z	912
0FUC0JZ	912
0FUC0KZ	912
0FUC37Z	912
0FUC3JZ	912
0FUC3KZ	912
0FUC47Z	912
0FUC4JZ	912
0FUC4KZ	912
0FUC87Z	912
0FUC8JZ	912
0FUC8KZ	912
0FUD*	199
0FUD07Z	912
0FUD0JZ	912
0FUD0KZ	912
0FUD3JZ	190, 599, 624, 912
0FUD3KZ	912
0FUD47Z	190, 599, 624, 912
0FUD4JZ	912
0FUD4KZ	912
0FUD87Z	190, 599, 624, 912
0FUD8JZ	912
0FUD8KZ	912
0FUF*	199
0FUF07Z	912
0FUF0JZ	912
0FUF0KZ	912
0FUF37Z	912
0FUF3JZ	912
0FUF3KZ	912
0FUF47Z	912
0FUF4JZ	913
0FUF4KZ	913
0FUF87Z	913
0FUF8JZ	913
0FUF8KZ	913
0FV50CZ	201, 599, 624, 693, 913, 1064
0FV50DZ	201, 599, 624, 693, 913
0FV50DZ	1064
0FV50ZZ	201, 599, 624, 693, 913, 1064
0FV60CZ	201, 599, 624, 693, 913, 1064
0FV60DZ	201, 599, 624, 693, 913
0FV60DZ	1064
0FV60ZZ	201, 599, 624, 693, 913, 1064
0FV70CZ	201, 599, 624, 693, 913, 1064
0FV70DZ	201, 599, 624, 693, 913
0FV70DZ	1064
0FV70ZZ	201, 599, 624, 693, 913, 1064
0FV80CZ	201, 599, 624, 693, 913, 1064
0FV80DZ	201, 599, 624, 693, 913
0FV80DZ	1064
0FV80ZZ	201, 599, 624, 693, 913, 1064
0FV90CZ	201, 599, 624, 693, 913, 1064
0FV90DZ	201, 599, 624, 693, 913
0FV90DZ	1064
0FV90ZZ	201, 599, 624, 693, 913, 1064
0FVC*	201, 693
0FVC0CZ	913
0FVC0DZ	913
0FVC0ZZ	913
0FVC3CZ	913
0FVC3DZ	913
0FVC3ZZ	913
0FVC4CZ	913
0FVC4DZ	913
0FVC4ZZ	913
0FVC7DZ	913
0FVC7ZZ	913
0FVC8DZ	913
0FVC8ZZ	913
0FVD*	199, 693
0FVD0CZ	913
0FVD0DZ	913
0FVD0ZZ	913
0FVD3CZ	913
0FVD3DZ	913
0FVD3ZZ	913
0FVD4CZ	913
0FVD4DZ	913
0FVD4ZZ	913
0FVD7DZ	913
0FVD7ZZ	913
0FVD8DZ	913
0FVD8ZZ	913
0FVF*	199, 693
0FVF0CZ	913
0FVF0DZ	913
0FVF0ZZ	913
0FVF3CZ	913
0FVF3ZZ	913
0FVF4CZ	913
0FVF4DZ	913
0FVF4ZZ	913
0FVF7DZ	913
0FVF7ZZ	913
0FVF8DZ	913
0FVF8ZZ	913
0FW000Z	199, 693, 913
0FW002Z	199, 693, 913
0FW003Z	199, 693, 913
0FW00YZ	199, 693, 913
0FW030Z	199, 693, 913
0FW032Z	199, 693, 913
0FW033Z	199, 693, 913
0FW040Z	199, 693, 913
0FW043Z	199, 693, 913
0FW400Z	201
0FW402Z	201
0FW403Z	201
0FW40DZ	201
0FW40YZ	201
0FW430Z	201
0FW432Z	201
0FW433Z	201
0FW43DZ	201
0FW440Z	201
0FW442Z	201
0FW443Z	201
0FW44DZ	201
0FWB00Z	201, 693
0FWB02Z	201, 693
0FWB03Z	201, 693
0FWB07Z	201, 693
0FWB0CZ	201, 693
0FWB0DZ	201, 693
0FWB0JZ	201, 693
0FWB0KZ	201, 693
0FWB0YZ	201, 693
0FWB30Z	201, 693
0FWB32Z	201, 693
0FWB33Z	201, 693
0FWB37Z	201, 693
0FWB3CZ	201, 693
0FWB3DZ	201, 693
0FWB3JZ	201, 693
0FWB3KZ	201, 693
0FWB40Z	201, 693
0FWB42Z	201, 693
0FWB43Z	201, 693
0FWB47Z	201, 693
0FWB4CZ	202, 693
0FWB4DZ	202, 693
0FWB4JZ	202, 693
0FWB4KZ	202, 693
0FWB70Z	202, 693
0FWB72Z	202, 693
0FWB73Z	202, 693
0FWB77Z	202, 693
0FWB7CZ	202, 693
0FWB7DZ	202, 693
0FWB7JZ	202, 693
0FWB7KZ	202, 693
0FWB83Z	202, 693
0FWB87Z	202, 693
0FWB8CZ	202, 693
0FWB8JZ	202, 693
0FWB8KZ	202, 693
0FWD00Z	199
0FWD02Z	199
0FWD03Z	199
0FWD07Z	199
0FWD0DZ	199
0FWD0JZ	199
0FWD0KZ	199
0FWD0YZ	199
0FWD30Z	199
0FWD33Z	199
0FWD37Z	199
0FWD3CZ	199
0FWD3DZ	199
0FWD3JZ	199
0FWD3KZ	199
0FWD40Z	199
0FWD42Z	199
0FWD43Z	199
0FWD47Z	199
0FWD4CZ	199
0FWD4JZ	199
0FWD4KZ	199
0FWD70Z	199
0FWD72Z	199
0FWD73Z	199
0FWD77Z	199
0FWD7CZ	199
0FWD7DZ	199
0FWD7JZ	199
0FWD7KZ	199
0FWD83Z	199
0FWD87Z	199
0FWD8CZ	199
0FWD8JZ	199
0FWD8KZ	199
0FWG00Z	199
0FWG02Z	199
0FWG03Z	199
0FWG0DZ	199
0FWG0YZ	199
0FWG30Z	199
0FWG32Z	199
0FWG33Z	199
0FWG3DZ	199
0FWG40Z	199
0FWG42Z	199
0FWG43Z	199
0FWG4DZ	199
0FY00Z0	1
0FY00Z1	1
0FY00Z2	1
0FYG*	2, 199, 494
0G50*	479
0G500ZZ	12, 424
0G503ZZ	12, 424
0G504ZZ	12, 424
0G51*	479
0G510ZZ	12
0G513ZZ	12
0G514ZZ	12
0G52*	479
0G53*	479
0G54*	479
0G560ZZ	139
0G563ZZ	139
0G564ZZ	139
0G570ZZ	139
0G573ZZ	139
0G574ZZ	139
0G580ZZ	139
0G583ZZ	139
0G584ZZ	139
0G590ZZ	139
0G593ZZ	139
0G594ZZ	139
0G5B0ZZ	139
0G5B3ZZ	139
0G5B4ZZ	139
0G5C0ZZ	139
0G5C3ZZ	139
0G5C4ZZ	139
0G5D0ZZ	139
0G5D3ZZ	139
0G5D4ZZ	139
0G5F0ZZ	139
0G5F3ZZ	139
0G5F4ZZ	139
0G5G*	483
0G5H*	483
0G5K*	483
0G5L*	483, 515
0G5M*	483, 515
0G5N*	483, 515
0G5P*	483, 515
0G5Q*	483, 515
0G5R*	483, 515
0G80*	479
0G800ZZ	12
0G803ZZ	12
0G804ZZ	12
0G8J*	483
0G900Z	12, 424, 479
0G900ZX	12, 479
0G900ZZ	12, 424, 479
0G903ZX	12, 479

Code	Page
0G9040Z	12, 424, 479
0G904ZX	12, 479
0G904ZZ	12, 424, 479
0G9100Z	12, 479
0G910ZX	12, 479
0G910ZZ	12, 479
0G913ZX	12, 479
0G9140Z	12, 479
0G914ZX	12, 479
0G914ZZ	12, 479
0G9200Z	479
0G920ZX	479
0G920ZZ	479
0G9240Z	479
0G924ZZ	479
0G9300Z	479
0G930ZX	479
0G930ZZ	479
0G9340Z	479
0G934ZZ	479
0G9400Z	479
0G940ZX	479
0G940ZZ	479
0G9440Z	479
0G944ZZ	479
0G9600Z	139
0G960ZX	139
0G960ZZ	139
0G963ZX	139
0G9640Z	139
0G964ZX	139
0G964ZZ	139
0G9700Z	139
0G970ZX	139
0G970ZZ	139
0G973ZX	139
0G9740Z	139
0G974ZX	139
0G974ZZ	139
0G9800Z	139
0G980ZX	139
0G980ZZ	139
0G983ZX	139
0G9840Z	139
0G984ZX	139
0G984ZZ	139
0G9900Z	139
0G990ZX	139
0G990ZZ	139
0G993ZX	139
0G9940Z	139
0G994ZX	139
0G994ZZ	139
0G9B00Z	139
0G9B0ZX	139
0G9B0ZZ	139
0G9B3ZX	139
0G9B40Z	139
0G9B4ZX	139
0G9B4ZZ	139
0G9C00Z	139
0G9C0ZX	139
0G9C0ZZ	139
0G9C3ZX	139
0G9C40Z	139
0G9C4ZX	139
0G9C4ZZ	139
0G9D00Z	139
0G9D0ZX	139
0G9D0ZZ	139
0G9D3ZX	139
0G9D40Z	140
0G9D4ZX	140
0G9D4ZZ	140
0G9F00Z	140
0G9F0ZX	140
0G9F0ZZ	140
0G9F3ZX	140
0G9F40Z	140
0G9F4ZX	140
0G9F4ZZ	140
0G9G00Z	78, 424, 483, 913
0G9G0ZX	483
0G9G0ZZ	78, 424, 483, 693, 913
0G9H00Z	78, 424, 483, 693, 913
0G9H0ZX	483
0G9H0ZZ	78, 424, 483, 693, 913
0G9K00Z	78, 424, 483, 693, 913
0G9K0ZX	483
0G9K0ZZ	78, 424, 483, 693, 913
0G9L00Z	78, 424, 483, 693, 913
0G9L0ZX	277, 483
0G9L0ZZ	78, 424, 483, 693, 913
0G9L3ZX	277, 483
0G9L4ZX	277, 483
0G9M00Z	78, 424, 483, 693, 913
0G9M0ZX	277, 483
0G9M0ZZ	78, 424, 483, 693, 913
0G9M3ZX	277, 483
0G9M4ZX	277, 483
0G9N00Z	78, 424, 483, 693, 913
0G9N0ZX	277, 483
0G9N0ZZ	78, 424, 483, 693, 913
0G9N3ZX	277, 483
0G9N4ZX	277, 483
0G9P00Z	693
0G9P0ZX	277, 483
0G9P0ZZ	78, 424, 483, 693, 913
0G9P3ZX	277, 483
0G9P4ZX	277, 483
0G9Q00Z	78, 424, 483, 693, 913
0G9Q0ZX	277, 483
0G9Q0ZZ	78, 424, 483, 693, 913
0G9Q3ZX	277, 483
0G9Q4ZX	277, 483
0G9R00Z	78, 424, 483, 693, 913
0G9R0ZX	277, 483
0G9R0ZZ	78, 424, 483, 693, 913
0G9R3ZX	277, 483
0G9R4ZX	277, 483
0GB0*	479
0GB00ZX	12
0GB00ZZ	12, 424
0GB03ZX	12
0GB03ZZ	12, 424
0GB04ZX	12
0GB04ZZ	12, 424
0GB1*	479
0GB10ZX	12
0GB10ZZ	12
0GB13ZX	12
0GB13ZZ	12
0GB14ZX	12
0GB14ZZ	12
0GB20ZX	479
0GB20ZZ	479
0GB23ZZ	479
0GB24ZZ	479
0GB30ZX	479
0GB30ZZ	479
0GB33ZZ	479
0GB34ZZ	479
0GB40ZX	479
0GB40ZZ	479
0GB43ZZ	479
0GB44ZZ	479
0GB60ZX	140
0GB60ZZ	140
0GB63ZX	140
0GB63ZZ	140
0GB64ZX	140
0GB64ZZ	140
0GB70ZX	140
0GB70ZZ	140
0GB73ZX	140
0GB73ZZ	140
0GB74ZX	140
0GB74ZZ	140
0GB80ZX	140
0GB80ZZ	140
0GB83ZX	140
0GB83ZZ	140
0GB84ZX	140
0GB90ZX	140
0GB90ZZ	140
0GB93ZX	140
0GB93ZZ	140
0GB94ZX	140
0GB94ZZ	140
0GBB0ZX	140
0GBB0ZZ	140
0GBB3ZX	140
0GBB3ZZ	140
0GBB4ZX	140
0GBB4ZZ	140
0GBC0ZX	140
0GBC0ZZ	140
0GBC3ZX	140
0GBC3ZZ	140
0GBC4ZX	140
0GBC4ZZ	140
0GBD0ZX	140
0GBD0ZZ	140
0GBD3ZX	140
0GBD3ZZ	140
0GBD4ZX	140
0GBD4ZZ	140
0GBF0ZX	140
0GBF0ZZ	140
0GBF3ZX	140
0GBF3ZZ	140
0GBF4ZX	140
0GBF4ZZ	140
0GBG0ZX	483
0GBG0ZZ	483
0GBG3ZZ	483
0GBG4ZZ	483
0GBH0ZX	483
0GBH0ZZ	483
0GBH3ZZ	483
0GBH4ZZ	483
0GBJ0ZX	483
0GBJ0ZZ	483
0GBJ3ZZ	483
0GBJ4ZZ	483
0GBL*	483
0GBL0ZX	277
0GBL0ZZ	515
0GBL3ZX	277
0GBL3ZZ	515
0GBL4ZX	277
0GBL4ZZ	515
0GBM*	483
0GBM0ZX	277
0GBM0ZZ	515
0GBM3ZX	277
0GBM3ZZ	515
0GBM4ZX	277
0GBM4ZZ	515
0GBN*	483
0GBN0ZX	277
0GBN0ZZ	515
0GBN3ZX	277
0GBN3ZZ	515
0GBN4ZX	277
0GBN4ZZ	515
0GBP*	483
0GBP0ZX	277
0GBP0ZZ	515
0GBP3ZX	277
0GBP3ZZ	515
0GBP4ZX	277
0GBP4ZZ	515
0GBQ*	483
0GBQ0ZX	277
0GBQ0ZZ	515
0GBQ3ZX	277
0GBQ3ZZ	515
0GBQ4ZX	277
0GBQ4ZZ	515
0GBR*	483
0GBR0ZX	277
0GBR0ZZ	515
0GBR3ZX	277
0GBR3ZZ	515
0GBR4ZX	277
0GBR4ZZ	515
0GC0*	479
0GC00ZZ	12, 424
0GC03ZZ	12, 424
0GC04ZZ	12, 424
0GC1*	479
0GC10ZZ	12
0GC13ZZ	12
0GC14ZZ	12
0GC2*	479
0GC3*	479
0GC4*	479
0GC60ZZ	140
0GC63ZZ	140
0GC64ZZ	140
0GC70ZZ	140
0GC73ZZ	140
0GC74ZZ	140
0GC80ZZ	140
0GC83ZZ	140
0GC84ZZ	140
0GC90ZZ	140
0GC93ZZ	140
0GC94ZZ	140
0GCB0ZZ	140
0GCB3ZZ	140
0GCB4ZZ	140
0GCC0ZZ	140
0GCC3ZZ	140
0GCC4ZZ	140
0GCD0ZZ	140
0GCD3ZZ	140
0GCD4ZZ	140
0GCF0ZZ	140
0GCF3ZZ	140
0GCF4ZZ	140
0GCG*	78, 483, 693
0GCG0ZZ	424, 913
0GCG3ZZ	424, 913
0GCG4ZZ	424, 913
0GCH*	78, 483, 693
0GCH0ZZ	424, 913
0GCH3ZZ	424, 913
0GCH4ZZ	425, 913
0GCK*	78, 483, 693
0GCK0ZZ	425, 913
0GCK3ZZ	425, 913
0GCK4ZZ	425, 913
0GCL*	78, 483, 693
0GCL0ZZ	425, 913
0GCL3ZZ	425, 913
0GCL4ZZ	425, 913
0GCM*	78, 483, 693
0GCM0ZZ	425, 913
0GCM3ZZ	425, 913
0GCM4ZZ	425, 913
0GCN*	78, 483, 693
0GCN0ZZ	425, 913
0GCN3ZZ	425, 913
0GCN4ZZ	425, 913
0GCP*	78, 483, 693
0GCP0ZZ	425, 913
0GCP3ZZ	425, 913
0GCP4ZZ	425, 913
0GCQ*	78, 483, 693
0GCQ0ZZ	425, 913
0GCQ3ZZ	425, 913
0GCQ4ZZ	425, 913
0GCR*	78, 483, 693
0GCR0ZZ	425, 913
0GCR3ZZ	425, 913
0GCR4ZZ	425, 913
0GHS02Z	78, 425, 483, 693, 913
0GHS03Z	78, 425, 483, 693, 913
0GHS0YZ	78, 425, 483, 693, 913
0GHS32Z	78, 425, 483, 693, 913
0GHS33Z	78, 425, 483, 693, 913
0GHS42Z	78, 425, 483, 693, 913
0GHS43Z	78, 425, 483, 693, 913
0GJ00ZZ	12, 479
0GJ04ZZ	12, 479
0GJ10ZZ	12, 479
0GJ14ZZ	12, 479
0GJ50ZZ	479
0GJ54ZZ	479
0GJK0ZZ	78, 425, 483, 693, 913
0GJK4ZZ	277, 483
0GJR0ZZ	78, 425, 483, 693, 913
0GJR4ZZ	277, 483
0GJS0ZZ	78, 425, 483, 693, 913
0GJS4ZZ	277, 483
0GM2*	479, 693
0GM20ZZ	913
0GM24ZZ	913
0GM3*	479, 693
0GM30ZZ	913
0GM34ZZ	913
0GMG*	483
0GMH*	483
0GML*	483
0GMM*	483
0GMN*	483
0GMP*	483
0GMQ*	483
0GMR*	483
0GN0*	479
0GN00ZZ	12, 425
0GN03ZZ	12, 425
0GN04ZZ	12, 425
0GN1*	479
0GN10ZZ	12
0GN13ZZ	12
0GN14ZZ	12
0GN2*	479, 693
0GN20ZZ	913
0GN23ZZ	913
0GN24ZZ	913
0GN3*	479, 693
0GN30ZZ	913
0GN33ZZ	913
0GN34ZZ	913
0GN4*	479, 693
0GN40ZZ	913
0GN43ZZ	913
0GN44ZZ	913
0GN60ZZ	140
0GN63ZZ	140
0GN64ZZ	140
0GN70ZZ	140
0GN73ZZ	140
0GN74ZZ	140
0GN80ZZ	140
0GN83ZZ	140
0GN84ZZ	140
0GN90ZZ	140
0GN93ZZ	140
0GN94ZZ	140
0GNB0ZZ	140
0GNB3ZZ	140
0GNB4ZZ	140
0GNC0ZZ	140
0GNC3ZZ	140
0GNC4ZZ	140
0GND0ZZ	140
0GND3ZZ	140
0GND4ZZ	140
0GNF0ZZ	140
0GNF3ZZ	140
0GNF4ZZ	140
0GNG*	483
0GNH*	483
0GNK*	483
0GNL*	483
0GNM*	483
0GNN*	483
0GNP*	483
0GNQ*	483
0GNR*	483
0GP000Z	12, 425, 479
0GP030Z	12, 425, 479
0GP040Z	12, 425, 479
0GP100Z	12, 479
0GP130Z	12, 479
0GP140Z	12, 479
0GP500Z	479
0GP530Z	479
0GP540Z	479
0GPK00Z	78, 425, 483, 694, 913
0GPK30Z	78, 425, 483, 694, 913
0GPK40Z	78, 425, 483, 694, 913
0GPR00Z	78, 425, 483, 694, 913
0GPR30Z	78, 425, 483, 694, 913
0GPR40Z	78, 425, 483, 694, 913
0GPS00Z	140
0GPS02Z	140
0GPS03Z	140
0GPS0YZ	140
0GPS30Z	140
0GPS32Z	140
0GPS33Z	140
0GPS40Z	140
0GPS42Z	140
0GPS43Z	140
0GQ0*	479
0GQ00ZZ	12, 425
0GQ03ZZ	12, 425
0GQ04ZZ	12, 425
0GQ1*	479
0GQ10ZZ	12
0GQ13ZZ	12
0GQ14ZZ	12
0GQ2*	479, 694
0GQ20ZZ	913
0GQ23ZZ	913
0GQ24ZZ	913
0GQ3*	479, 694
0GQ30ZZ	913
0GQ33ZZ	913
0GQ34ZZ	913
0GQ4*	479, 694
0GQ40ZZ	913
0GQ43ZZ	913
0GQ44ZZ	913
0GQ60ZZ	140
0GQ63ZZ	140
0GQ64ZZ	140
0GQ70ZZ	140
0GQ73ZZ	140
0GQ74ZZ	140
0GQ80ZZ	140
0GQ83ZZ	140
0GQ84ZZ	140
0GQ90ZZ	140
0GQ93ZZ	140
0GQ94ZZ	140
0GQB0ZZ	140
0GQB3ZZ	140
0GQB4ZZ	140
0GQC0ZZ	140
0GQC3ZZ	140
0GQC4ZZ	140
0GQD0ZZ	140
0GQD3ZZ	140
0GQD4ZZ	140
0GQF0ZZ	140
0GQF3ZZ	140
0GQF4ZZ	140
0GQG*	483, 694
0GQG0ZZ	913
0GQG3ZZ	913
0GQG4ZZ	913
0GQH*	483, 694
0GQH0ZZ	913
0GQH3ZZ	913
0GQH4ZZ	913
0GQJ*	483, 694
0GQJ0ZZ	913
0GQJ3ZZ	913
0GQJ4ZZ	913
0GQK*	483, 694
0GQK0ZZ	913
0GQK3ZZ	913
0GQK4ZZ	913
0GQL*	483
0GQM*	483
0GQN*	483
0GQP*	483
0GQQ*	483
0GQR*	483
0GS2*	479, 694
0GS20ZZ	913
0GS24ZZ	913
0GS3*	479, 694
0GS30ZZ	913
0GS34ZZ	913
0GSG*	483
0GSH*	483
0GSL*	483
0GSM*	483
0GSN*	483
0GSP*	483
0GSQ*	483
0GSR*	483
0GT0*	479
0GT00ZZ	12, 425
0GT04ZZ	12, 425
0GT1*	479
0GT10ZZ	12
0GT14ZZ	12
0GT2*	479
0GT20ZZ	425
0GT24ZZ	425
0GT3*	479
0GT30ZZ	425
0GT34ZZ	425
0GT4*	479
0GT40ZZ	425

Numeric Index to Procedures

Code	Page	Code	Page	Code	Page	Code	Page	Code	Page	Code	Page
0GT44ZZ	425	0H54XZD	445	0HBT0ZZ	450, 451, 480, 694, 914, 1064	0HHV31Z	425, 694, 1064	0HNDXZZ	425, 694, 914, 1065	0HR1X73	481, 638, 783, 914
0GT60ZZ	140	0H54XZZ	445			0HHV3NZ	451, 694, 914, 1064	0HNEXZZ	425, 694, 914, 1065	0HR1X74	481, 638, 783, 914
0GT64ZZ	140	0H55XZD	445	0HBT3ZZ	450, 451, 480, 694, 914, 1064	0HHV71Z	425, 694, 1064			0HR1XJ3	481, 638, 783, 914
0GT70ZZ	140	0H55XZZ	445			0HHV7NZ	451, 694, 914, 1064	0HNFXZZ	425, 694, 914, 1065	0HR1XJ4	481, 638, 783, 915
0GT74ZZ	140	0H56XZD	445	0HBT7ZZ	451, 495, 694, 914, 1064	0HHV81Z	425, 694, 1064			0HR1XJZ	481, 638, 783, 915
0GT80ZZ	140	0H56XZZ	445			0HHV8NZ	451, 694, 914, 1064	0HNGXZZ	425, 694, 914, 1065	0HR1XK3	146, 481, 638, 783, 915
0GT84ZZ	140	0H57XZD	445	0HBT8ZZ	451, 495, 694, 1064	0HHW01Z	425, 694, 1064			0HR1XK4	146, 481, 638, 783, 915
0GT90ZZ	140	0H57XZZ	445	0HBU0ZX	451, 495, 694, 914, 1064	0HHW0NZ	451, 694, 914, 1064	0HNHXZZ	425, 694, 914, 1065	0HR2*	79, 695
0GT94ZZ	140	0H58XZD	445			0HHW31Z	425, 694, 1064	0HNJXZZ	425, 694, 914, 1065	0HR2X72	425, 915, 1065
0GTB0ZZ	140	0H58XZZ	445	0HBU0ZZ	450, 451, 480, 694, 914, 1064	0HHW3NZ	451, 694, 914, 1064			0HR2X73	425, 915, 1065
0GTB4ZZ	140	0H59XZD	445			0HHW71Z	425, 694, 1064	0HNKXZZ	425, 694, 914, 1065	0HR2X74	425, 915, 1065
0GTC0ZZ	140	0H59XZZ	445	0HBU3ZZ	450, 451, 480, 694, 914, 1064	0HHW7NZ	451, 694, 914, 1064			0HR2XJ3	425, 915, 1065
0GTC4ZZ	140	0H5AXZD	445			0HHW81Z	425, 694, 1064	0HNLXZZ	425, 695, 914, 1065	0HR2XJ4	425, 915, 1065
0GTD0ZZ	140	0H5AXZZ	445	0HBU7ZZ	451, 495, 694, 914, 1064	0HHW8NZ	451, 694, 914, 1064			0HR2XJZ	425, 915, 1065
0GTD4ZZ	140	0H5BXZD	445			0HHWX1Z	425, 694, 1064	0HNMXZZ	425, 695, 914, 1065	0HR2XK3	425, 915, 1065
0GTF0ZZ	140	0H5BXZZ	445	0HBU8ZZ	451, 495, 694, 914, 1064	0HHX01Z	425, 694, 1064			0HR2XK4	425, 915, 1065
0GTF4ZZ	140	0H5CXZD	445	0HBV0ZX	451, 495, 694, 1064	0HHX0NZ	451, 694, 914, 1064	0HNNXZZ	425, 694, 914, 1065	0HR3*	79, 695
0GTG*	483	0H5CXZZ	445			0HHX31Z	425, 694, 1064	0HNQXZZ	425, 695, 1065	0HR3X72	425, 915, 1065
0GTH*	483	0H5DXZD	445	0HBV0ZZ	450, 451, 480, 694, 914, 1064	0HHX3NZ	451, 694, 914, 1064	0HNRXZZ	425, 695, 1065	0HR3X73	425, 915, 1065
0GTJ0ZZ	483	0H5DXZZ	445			0HHX71Z	425, 694, 1064	0HNT*	451	0HR3X74	425, 915, 1065
0GTJ4ZZ	483	0H5EXZD	445	0HBV3ZZ	450, 451, 480, 694, 914, 1064	0HHX7NZ	451, 694, 914, 1064	0HNU*	451	0HR3XJ3	425, 915, 1065
0GTK*	483	0H5EXZZ	445			0HHX81Z	425, 694, 1064	0HNV*	451	0HR3XJ4	425, 915, 1065
0GTL*	483, 515	0H5FXZD	445	0HBV7ZZ	451, 495, 694, 914, 1064	0HHX8NZ	451, 694, 914, 1064	0HNW*	451	0HR3XJZ	425, 915, 1065
0GTM*	483, 515	0H5FXZZ	445			0HHXX1Z	425, 694, 1064	0HNX*	451	0HR3XK3	425, 915, 1065
0GTN*	483, 515	0H5GXZD	445	0HBV8ZZ	451, 495, 694, 914, 1064	0HM1XZZ	78, 425, 694, 1064	0HPT0JZ	451, 695, 914, 1065	0HR3XK4	425, 915, 1065
0GTP*	483, 515	0H5GXZZ	445	0HBW0ZX	451, 495, 694, 914, 1064	0HM2XZZ	425, 694, 914, 1064			0HR4*	34, 79, 214, 410, 787
0GTQ*	483, 515	0H5HXZD	445			0HM3XZZ	78, 425, 694, 914, 1064	0HPT0NZ	451, 695, 914, 1065	0HR4X72	481, 638, 783, 915
0GTR*	483, 515	0H5HXZZ	445	0HBW0ZZ	451, 694, 914	0HM4XZZ	78, 425, 694, 1064	0HPT0YZ	451, 695, 914, 1065	0HR4X73	481, 638, 783, 915
0GW000Z	12, 425, 479	0H5JXZD	445	0HBW3ZZ	451, 694, 914	0HM5XZZ	425, 694, 1064			0HR4X74	481, 638, 783, 915
0GW030Z	12, 425, 479	0H5JXZZ	445	0HBW7ZZ	451, 694, 914	0HM6XZZ	425, 694, 1064	0HPT3JZ	451, 695, 914, 1065	0HR4XJ3	481, 638, 783, 915
0GW040Z	12, 425, 479	0H5KXZD	445	0HBW8ZZ	451, 694, 914	0HM7XZZ	425, 480, 694, 1064	0HPT3NZ	451, 695, 914, 1065	0HR4XJ4	481, 638, 783, 915
0GW100Z	12, 479	0H5KXZZ	445	0HBWXZZ	451, 694, 914	0HM8XZZ	425, 694, 1064			0HR4XJZ	481, 638, 783, 915
0GW130Z	12, 479	0H5LXZD	445	0HBX0ZX	451, 495, 694, 914, 1064	0HM9XZZ	78, 425, 480, 694, 914, 1064	0HPU0JZ	451, 695, 914, 1065	0HR4XK3	146, 481, 638, 783, 915
0GW140Z	12, 479	0H5LXZZ	445	0HBX0ZZ	451, 694, 914	0HMAXZZ	425, 694, 1064	0HPU0NZ	451, 695, 914, 1065	0HR4XK4	146, 481, 638, 783, 915
0GW500Z	479	0H5MXZD	445	0HBX3ZZ	451, 694, 914	0HMBXZZ	425, 694, 1064	0HPU0YZ	451, 695, 914, 1065	0HR5*	34, 146, 214, 410, 787
0GW530Z	479	0H5MXZZ	445	0HBX7ZZ	451, 694, 914	0HMCXZZ	425, 694, 1064			0HR5X72	101, 190, 481, 638, 783, 915
0GW540Z	479	0H5NXZD	445	0HBX8ZZ	451, 694, 914	0HMDXZZ	425, 694, 1064	0HPU3JZ	451, 695, 914, 1065	0HR5X73	190, 481, 638, 783, 915
0GWK00Z	78, 425, 483, 694, 913	0H5NXZZ	445	0HBXXZZ	451, 694, 914	0HMEXZZ	425, 694, 1064	0HPU3NZ	451, 695, 914, 1065	0HR5X74	101, 190, 481, 638, 783, 915
		0H5QXZZ	445	0HBY0ZX	451, 495, 694, 914, 1064	0HMFXZZ	425, 694, 1064	0HQ9XZZ	535, 537	0HR5XJ3	190, 481, 638, 783, 915
0GWK30Z	78, 425, 483, 694, 913	0H5RXZZ	445	0HBY0ZZ	451, 694, 914	0HMGXZZ	425, 694, 1064	0HQQXZZ	425, 695, 914	0HR5XJ4	190, 481, 638, 783, 915
		0H5T*	451, 694	0HBY3ZZ	451, 694, 914	0HMHXZZ	425, 694, 1064	0HQRXZZ	425, 695, 914	0HR5XJZ	190, 481, 638, 783, 915
0GWK40Z	78, 425, 483, 694, 913	0H5T0ZZ	914, 1064	0HBY7ZZ	451, 694, 914	0HMJXZZ	425, 694, 1064	0HQT0ZZ	451, 695, 914	0HR5XK3	79, 481, 638, 783, 915
		0H5T3ZZ	914, 1064	0HBY8ZZ	451, 694, 914	0HMKXZZ	425, 694, 1064	0HQT3ZZ	451, 695, 914	0HR5XK4	79, 481, 638, 783, 915
0GWR00Z	78, 425, 483, 694, 913	0H5T7ZZ	914, 1064	0HCT0ZZ	451, 495, 694, 914, 1064	0HMLXZZ	425, 694, 1064	0HQT7ZZ	451, 695, 914	0HR6*	34, 146, 214, 410, 787
		0H5T8ZZ	914, 1064	0HCU0ZZ	451, 495, 694, 914, 1064	0HMMXZZ	425, 694, 1064	0HQT8ZZ	451, 695, 914	0HR6X72	101, 190, 481, 638, 783, 915
0GWR30Z	78, 425, 483, 694, 913	0H5U*	451, 694	0HCV0ZZ	451, 495, 694, 1064	0HMTXZZ	451	0HQU0ZZ	451, 695, 914	0HR6X73	190, 481, 638, 783, 915
		0H5U0ZZ	914, 1064	0HCW0ZZ	451, 495, 694, 914, 1064	0HMUXZZ	451	0HQU3ZZ	451, 695, 914	0HR6X74	101, 190, 481, 638, 783, 915
0GWR40Z	78, 425, 483, 694, 913	0H5U3ZZ	914, 1064	0HCX0ZZ	451, 495, 694, 914, 1064	0HMVXZZ	451	0HQU7ZZ	451, 695, 914	0HR6XJ3	190, 481, 638, 783, 915
		0H5U7ZZ	914, 1064	0HDT0ZZ	243, 425, 694, 914	0HMWXZZ	451, 694, 914	0HQU8ZZ	451, 695, 914	0HR6XJ4	190, 481, 638, 783, 915
0GWS00Z	140	0H5U8ZZ	914, 1064	0HDU0ZZ	243, 425, 694, 914	0HMXXZZ	451, 694, 914	0HQV0ZZ	451	0HR6XJZ	190, 481, 638, 783, 915
0GWS02Z	140	0H5V*	451, 694	0HDV0ZZ	243, 425, 694, 914	0HN0XZZ	78, 425, 694, 914, 1064	0HQV3ZZ	451	0HR6XK3	79, 481, 638, 783, 915
0GWS03Z	140	0H5V3ZZ	914, 1064	0HDY0ZZ	243, 425, 694, 914			0HQV7ZZ	451	0HR6XK4	79, 481, 638, 783, 915
0GWS0YZ	140	0H5V7ZZ	914, 1064	0HHT01Z	425, 694, 1064	0HN1XZZ	78, 425, 694, 914, 1064	0HQV8ZZ	451	0HR7*	34, 146, 214, 410, 787
0GWS30Z	140	0H5V8ZZ	914, 1064	0HHT0NZ	451, 694, 914, 1064	0HN2XZZ	78, 425, 694, 914, 1064	0HQW*	451, 695	0HR7X72	101, 190, 481, 638, 783, 915
0GWS32Z	140	0H5W*	451, 694	0HHT0YZ	451, 694, 914, 1064	0HN3XZZ	78, 425, 694, 914, 1064	0HQW0ZZ	914	0HR7X73	190, 481, 638, 783, 915
0GWS33Z	140	0H5W3ZZ	914	0HHT31Z	425, 694, 1064	0HN4XZZ	78, 425, 694, 914, 1064	0HQW3ZZ	914	0HR7X74	101, 190, 481, 638, 783, 915
0GWS40Z	140	0H5W7ZZ	914	0HHT3NZ	451, 694, 914, 1064	0HN5XZZ	425, 694, 914, 1065	0HQW7ZZ	914	0HR7XJ3	190, 481, 638, 783, 915
0GWS42Z	140	0H5W8ZZ	914	0HHT71Z	425, 694, 1064	0HN6XZZ	425, 694, 914, 1065	0HQW8ZZ	914	0HR7XJ4	190, 481, 638, 783, 915
0GWS43Z	140	0H5WXZZ	914	0HHT7NZ	451, 694, 914, 1064	0HN7XZZ	425, 694, 914, 1065	0HQWXZZ	914	0HR7XJZ	190, 481, 638, 783, 915
0H0T07Z	451, 694, 914, 1064	0H5X*	451, 694	0HHT81Z	425, 694, 1064	0HN8XZZ	425, 694, 914, 1065	0HQX*	451, 695	0HR7XK3	481, 638, 783, 915
0H0T0JZ	451, 1064	0H5X0ZZ	914	0HHT8NZ	451, 694, 914, 1064	0HN9XZZ	425, 694, 914, 1065	0HQX0ZZ	914	0HR7XK3	79
0H0T0KZ	451, 1064	0H5X3ZZ	914	0HHU01Z	425, 694, 1064	0HNAXZZ	425, 694, 914, 1065	0HQX3ZZ	914	0HR7XK4	481, 638, 783, 915
0H0T0ZZ	451	0H5X7ZZ	914	0HHU0NZ	451, 694, 914, 1064	0HNBXZZ	425, 694, 914, 1065	0HQX7ZZ	914	0HR7XK4	79
0H0T37Z	451, 694, 914, 1064	0H5X8ZZ	914	0HHU0YZ	451, 694, 914, 1064	0HNCXZZ	425, 694, 914, 1065	0HQX8ZZ	914		
0H0T3KZ	451, 1064	0H5XXZZ	914	0HHU31Z	425, 694, 1064			0HQXXZZ	914		
0H0T3ZZ	451	0H99X0Z	425, 535, 1064	0HHU3NZ	451, 694, 914, 1064			0HQY0ZZ	451		
0H0U07Z	451, 694, 914, 1064	0H99XZZ	425, 535, 1064	0HHU71Z	425, 694, 1064			0HQY3ZZ	451		
0H0U0JZ	451, 1064	0H9T0ZX	451, 494, 694, 914, 1064	0HHU7NZ	451, 694, 914, 1064			0HQY7ZZ	451		
0H0U0KZ	451, 1064	0H9T0ZZ	451, 494, 694, 914, 1064	0HHU81Z	425, 694, 1064			0HQY8ZZ	451		
0H0U0ZZ	451			0HHU8NZ	451, 694, 914, 1064			0HR0*	34, 79, 214, 410, 787		
0H0U37Z	451, 694, 914, 1064	0H9U0ZX	451, 494, 694, 914, 1064	0HHV01Z	425, 694, 1064			0HR0X72	481, 638, 783, 914		
0H0U3KZ	451, 1064	0H9U0ZZ	451, 494, 694, 914, 1064	0HHV0NZ	451, 694, 914, 1064			0HR0X73	481, 638, 783, 914		
0H0U3ZZ	451	0H9V0ZX	451, 494, 694, 914, 1064					0HR0X74	481, 638, 783, 914		
0H0V07Z	451, 694, 914, 1064	0H9V0ZZ	451, 494, 694, 914, 1064					0HR0XJ3	481, 638, 783, 914		
0H0V0JZ	450, 451, 694, 914, 1064	0H9W0ZX	451, 494, 694, 914, 1064					0HR0XJ4	481, 638, 783, 914		
0H0V0KZ	451, 694, 914, 1064	0H9W0ZZ	451, 494, 694, 914, 1064					0HR0XJZ	481, 638, 783, 914		
0H0V0ZZ	451	0H9X0ZX	451, 494, 694, 914, 1064					0HR0XK3	146, 481, 638, 783, 914		
0H0V37Z	451, 694, 914, 1064	0H9X0ZZ	451, 494, 694, 914, 1064					0HR0XK4	146, 481, 638, 783, 914		
0H0V3KZ	451, 694, 914, 1064	0HB9XZZ	445					0HR1*	34, 146, 214, 410, 787		
0H0V3ZZ	451	0HBT0ZX	451, 495, 694, 914, 1064					0HR1X72	481, 638, 783, 914		
0H50XZD	445										
0H50XZZ	445										
0H51XZD	445										
0H51XZZ	445										

Code	Page
ØHR8*	34, 146, 214, 410, 787
ØHR8X72	481, 638, 783, 915
ØHR8X73	190, 481, 638, 783, 915
ØHR8X74	481, 638, 783, 915
ØHR8XJ3	190, 481, 638, 783, 915
ØHR8XJ4	190, 481, 638, 783, 915
ØHR8XJZ	190, 481, 638, 783, 915
ØHR8XK3	79, 481, 638, 783, 915
ØHR8XK4	79, 481, 638, 783, 915
ØHR9*	535, 695
ØHR9X72	915, 1065
ØHR9X73	915, 1065
ØHR9X74	915, 1065
ØHR9XJ3	915, 1065
ØHR9XJ4	915, 1065
ØHR9XJZ	915, 1065
ØHR9XK3	915, 1065
ØHR9XK4	915, 1065
ØHRA*	34, 146, 214, 410, 787
ØHRAX72	481, 638, 783, 915
ØHRAX73	481, 638, 783, 915
ØHRAX74	481, 638, 783, 915
ØHRAXJ3	481, 638, 783, 915
ØHRAXJ4	481, 638, 783, 915
ØHRAXJZ	481, 638, 783, 915
ØHRAXK3	638, 783, 915
ØHRAXK4	638, 783, 915
ØHRB*	34, 146, 214, 410, 787
ØHRBX72	481, 638, 783, 915
ØHRBX73	481, 638, 783, 915
ØHRBX74	481, 638, 783, 915
ØHRBXJ3	481, 638, 783, 915
ØHRBXJ4	481, 638, 783, 915
ØHRBXJZ	481, 638, 783, 915
ØHRBXK3	638, 783, 915
ØHRBXK4	638, 783, 915
ØHRC*	34, 146, 214, 410, 787
ØHRCX72	481, 638, 783, 915
ØHRCX73	481, 638, 783, 915
ØHRCX74	481, 638, 783, 915
ØHRCXJ3	481, 638, 783, 915
ØHRCXJ4	481, 638, 783, 915
ØHRCXJZ	481, 638, 783, 915
ØHRCXK3	638, 783, 915
ØHRCXK4	638, 783, 915
ØHRD*	34, 146, 214, 410, 787
ØHRDX72	481, 638, 783, 915
ØHRDX73	481, 638, 783, 915
ØHRDX74	481, 638, 783, 915
ØHRDXJ3	481, 638, 783, 915
ØHRDXJ4	481, 638, 783, 915
ØHRDXJZ	481, 638, 783, 915
ØHRDXK3	638, 783, 915
ØHRDXK4	638, 783, 915
ØHRE*	34, 146, 214, 410, 787
ØHREX72	481, 638, 783, 915
ØHREX73	481, 638, 783, 915
ØHREX74	481, 638, 783, 915
ØHREXJ3	481, 638, 783, 915
ØHREXJ4	481, 638, 783, 915
ØHREXJZ	481, 638, 783, 915
ØHREXK3	638, 783, 915
ØHREXK4	638, 783, 915
ØHRF*	34, 146, 268, 410, 787
ØHRFX72	640, 783, 915, 1065
ØHRFX73	640, 783, 915
ØHRFX74	640, 783, 915, 1065
ØHRFXJ3	481, 638, 783, 915
ØHRFXJ4	481, 638, 783, 915
ØHRFXJZ	481, 638, 783, 915
ØHRFXK3	638, 783, 915
ØHRFXK4	638, 783, 915
ØHRG*	34, 146, 268, 410, 787
ØHRGX72	640, 783, 915, 1065
ØHRGX73	640, 783, 915
ØHRGX74	640, 783, 915, 1065
ØHRGXJ3	481, 638, 783, 915
ØHRGXJ4	481, 638, 783, 915
ØHRGXJZ	481, 638, 783, 915
ØHRGXK3	638, 783, 915
ØHRGXK4	638, 783, 915
ØHRH*	34, 146, 214, 410, 787
ØHRHX72	481, 638, 783, 915
ØHRHX73	481, 638, 783, 915
ØHRHX74	481, 638, 783, 915
ØHRHXJ3	481, 638, 783, 915
ØHRHXJ4	481, 638, 783, 915
ØHRHXJZ	481, 638, 783, 915
ØHRHXK3	638, 783, 915
ØHRHXK4	638, 783, 915
ØHRJ*	34, 146, 214, 410, 787
ØHRJX72	481, 638, 783, 915
ØHRJX73	481, 638, 783, 915
ØHRJX74	481, 638, 783, 915
ØHRJXJ3	481, 638, 783, 915
ØHRJXJ4	481, 638, 783, 915
ØHRJXJZ	481, 638, 783, 915
ØHRJXK3	638, 783, 915
ØHRJXK4	638, 783, 915
ØHRK*	34, 146, 214, 410, 787
ØHRKX72	481, 638, 783, 915
ØHRKX73	481, 638, 783, 915
ØHRKX74	481, 638, 783, 915
ØHRKXJ3	481, 638, 783, 915
ØHRKXJ4	481, 638, 783, 915
ØHRKXJZ	481, 639, 784, 915
ØHRKXK3	639, 784, 915
ØHRKXK4	639, 784, 915
ØHRL*	34, 146, 214, 410, 787
ØHRLX72	481, 639, 784, 915
ØHRLX73	481, 639, 784, 915
ØHRLX74	481, 639, 784, 915
ØHRLXJ3	481, 639, 784, 915
ØHRLXJ4	481, 639, 784, 915
ØHRLXJZ	481, 639, 784, 915
ØHRLXK3	639, 784, 915
ØHRLXK4	639, 784, 915
ØHRM*	34, 146, 214, 410, 787
ØHRMX72	481, 639, 784, 915
ØHRMX73	481, 639, 784, 915
ØHRMX74	481, 639, 784, 915
ØHRMXJ3	481, 639, 784, 915
ØHRMXJ4	481, 639, 784, 915
ØHRMXJZ	481, 639, 784, 915
ØHRMXK3	639, 784, 915
ØHRMXK4	639, 784, 915
ØHRN*	34, 146, 214, 410, 787
ØHRNX72	482, 639, 784, 915
ØHRNX73	482, 639, 784, 915
ØHRNX74	482, 639, 784, 915
ØHRNXJ3	482, 639, 784, 915
ØHRNXJ4	482, 639, 784, 915
ØHRNXJZ	482, 639, 784, 915
ØHRNXK3	639, 784, 915
ØHRNXK4	639, 784, 915
ØHRQ*	695
ØHRQX7Z	425, 915
ØHRQXJZ	425, 915
ØHRQXKZ	425, 916
ØHRR*	695
ØHRRX7Z	425, 916
ØHRRXJZ	425, 916
ØHRRXKZ	425, 916
ØHRSXJZ	425, 695, 1065
ØHRSXKZ	425, 695, 1065
ØHRTØ75	450, 451, 695, 916
ØHRTØ76	450, 451, 695, 916
ØHRTØ77	450, 451, 695, 916
ØHRTØ78	450, 451, 695, 916
ØHRTØ79	450, 451, 695, 916
ØHRTØ7Z	450, 451, 695, 916
ØHRTØJZ	450, 451, 695, 916
ØHRTØKZ	450, 451, 695, 916
ØHRT37Z	451, 453
ØHRT3JZ	450, 451, 695, 916
ØHRT3KZ	451
ØHRUØ75	450, 451, 695, 916
ØHRUØ76	450, 451, 695, 916
ØHRUØ77	450, 451, 695, 916
ØHRUØ78	450, 451, 695, 916
ØHRUØ79	450, 451, 695, 916
ØHRUØ7Z	450, 451, 695, 916
ØHRUØJZ	450, 451, 695, 916
ØHRUØKZ	450, 451, 695, 916
ØHRU37Z	451, 453
ØHRU3JZ	450, 452, 695, 916
ØHRU3KZ	452
ØHRVØ75	450, 452, 695, 916
ØHRVØ76	450, 452, 695, 916
ØHRVØ77	450, 452, 695, 916
ØHRVØ78	450, 452, 695, 916
ØHRVØ79	450, 452, 695, 916
ØHRVØ7Z	452
ØHRVØJZ	450, 452, 695, 916
ØHRVØKZ	452
ØHRV37Z	452, 453
ØHRV3JZ	450, 452, 695, 916
ØHRV3KZ	452
ØHRW*	452, 695
ØHRWØ7Z	916
ØHRWØJZ	916
ØHRWØKZ	916
ØHRW37Z	916
ØHRW3JZ	916
ØHRW3KZ	916
ØHRWX7Z	916
ØHRWXJZ	916
ØHRWXKZ	916
ØHRX*	452, 695
ØHRXØ7Z	916
ØHRXØJZ	916
ØHRXØKZ	916
ØHRX37Z	916
ØHRX3JZ	916
ØHRX3KZ	916
ØHRXX7Z	916
ØHRXXJZ	916
ØHRXXKZ	916
ØHSTØZZ	452, 695, 916
ØHSUØZZ	452, 695, 916
ØHSVØZZ	452, 695, 916
ØHSWXZZ	452, 695, 916
ØHSXXZZ	452, 695, 916
ØHTTØZZ	450, 452, 695, 916
ØHTUØZZ	450, 452, 695, 916
ØHTVØZZ	450, 451, 452, 695, 916
ØHTWXZZ	452, 695, 916
ØHTXXZZ	452, 695, 916
ØHTYØZZ	452, 695, 916
ØHUTØ7Z	452
ØHUTØJZ	452
ØHUTØKZ	452
ØHUT37Z	452
ØHUT3JZ	452
ØHUT3KZ	452
ØHUT77Z	452
ØHUT7JZ	452
ØHUT7KZ	452
ØHUT87Z	452
ØHUT8JZ	452
ØHUT8KZ	452
ØHUUØ7Z	452
ØHUUØJZ	452
ØHUUØKZ	452
ØHUU37Z	452
ØHUU3KZ	452
ØHUU77Z	452
ØHUU7JZ	452
ØHUU7KZ	452
ØHUU87Z	452
ØHUU8JZ	452
ØHUU8KZ	452
ØHUVØ7Z	452
ØHUVØJZ	452
ØHUVØKZ	452
ØHUV37Z	452
ØHUV3KZ	452
ØHUV77Z	452
ØHUV7JZ	452
ØHUV7KZ	452
ØHUV87Z	452
ØHUV8JZ	452
ØHUV8KZ	452
ØHUW*	695
ØHUWØ7Z	452, 916
ØHUWØJZ	452, 916
ØHUWØKZ	452, 916
ØHUW37Z	452, 916
ØHUW3JZ	452, 916
ØHUW3KZ	452, 916
ØHUW77Z	452, 916
ØHUW7JZ	452, 916
ØHUW7KZ	452, 916
ØHUW87Z	452, 916
ØHUW8JZ	452, 916
ØHUW8KZ	452, 916
ØHUWX7Z	452, 916
ØHUWXJZ	452, 916
ØHUWXKZ	452, 916
ØHUX*	695
ØHUXØ7Z	452, 916
ØHUXØJZ	452, 916
ØHUXØKZ	452, 916
ØHUX37Z	452, 916
ØHUX3JZ	452, 916
ØHUX3KZ	452, 916
ØHUX77Z	452, 916
ØHUX7JZ	452, 916
ØHUX7KZ	452, 916
ØHUX87Z	452, 916
ØHUX8JZ	452, 916
ØHUX8KZ	452, 916
ØHUXX7Z	452, 916
ØHUXXJZ	452, 916
ØHUXXKZ	452, 916
ØHWTØJZ	452, 695, 916, 1065
ØHWTØYZ	452, 695, 916, 1065
ØHWT3JZ	452, 695, 916, 1065
ØHWUØJZ	452, 695, 916, 1065
ØHWUØYZ	452, 695, 916, 1065
ØHWU3JZ	452, 695, 916, 1065
ØHX*	79
ØHXØXZZ	34, 146, 190, 214, 410, 482, 639, 784, 787, 916
ØHX1XZZ	34, 146, 190, 214, 410, 482, 639, 784, 787, 916
ØHX2XZZ	425, 695, 916, 1065
ØHX3XZZ	425, 695, 916, 1065
ØHX4XZZ	34, 146, 190, 214, 410, 482, 639, 784, 787, 916
ØHX5XZZ	34, 146, 190, 214, 410, 482, 639, 784, 787, 916
ØHX6XZZ	34, 146, 190, 214, 410, 482, 639, 784, 787, 916
ØHX7XZZ	34, 146, 190, 214, 410, 482, 639, 784, 787, 916
ØHX8XZZ	34, 146, 190, 214, 410, 482, 639, 784, 787, 916
ØHX9XZZ	34, 146, 190, 214, 410, 482, 639, 784, 787, 916
ØHXAXZZ	34, 146, 190, 214, 410, 482, 639, 784, 787, 916
ØHXBXZZ	34, 146, 190, 214, 410, 482, 639, 784, 787, 916
ØHXCXZZ	34, 146, 190, 214, 410, 482, 639, 784, 787, 916
ØHXDXZZ	34, 146, 190, 214, 410, 482, 639, 784, 787, 916
ØHXEXZZ	34, 146, 190, 214, 410, 482, 639, 784, 787, 916
ØHXFXZZ	34, 146, 190, 214, 410, 482, 639, 784, 787, 916
ØHXGXZZ	34, 146, 190, 214, 410, 482, 639, 784, 787, 916
ØHXHXZZ	34, 146, 190, 214, 410, 482, 639, 784, 787, 916
ØHXJXZZ	34, 146, 190, 214, 410, 482, 639, 784, 787, 916
ØHXKXZZ	34, 146, 190, 214, 410, 482, 639, 784, 787, 916
ØHXLXZZ	34, 146, 190, 214, 410, 482, 639, 784, 787, 916
ØHXMXZZ	34, 146, 190, 214, 410, 482, 639, 784, 787, 916
ØHXNXZZ	34, 146, 190, 214, 410, 482, 639, 784, 787, 916
ØJØ*	695
ØJØ1*	79
ØJØ1ØZZ	425, 916, 1065
ØJØ13ZZ	425, 916, 1065
ØJØ4*	481
ØJØ4ØZZ	425, 1065
ØJØ43ZZ	425, 1065
ØJØ5*	481
ØJØ5ØZZ	425, 1065
ØJØ53ZZ	425, 1065
ØJØ6*	481
ØJØ6ØZZ	425, 1065
ØJØ63ZZ	426, 1065
ØJØ7*	481
ØJØ7ØZZ	426, 1065
ØJØ73ZZ	426, 1065
ØJØ8*	481
ØJØ8ØZZ	426, 1065
ØJØ83ZZ	426, 1065
ØJØ9*	481
ØJØ9ØZZ	426, 1065
ØJØ93ZZ	426, 1065
ØJØD*	481
ØJØDØZZ	426, 1065
ØJØD3ZZ	426, 1065
ØJØF*	481
ØJØFØZZ	426, 1065
ØJØF3ZZ	426, 1065
ØJØG*	481
ØJØGØZZ	426, 1065
ØJØG3ZZ	426, 1065
ØJØH*	481
ØJØHØZZ	426, 1065
ØJØH3ZZ	426, 1065
ØJØL*	481
ØJØLØZZ	426, 1065
ØJØL3ZZ	426, 1065
ØJØM*	481
ØJØMØZZ	426, 1065
ØJØM3ZZ	426, 1065
ØJØN*	481
ØJØNØZZ	426, 1065
ØJØN3ZZ	426, 1065
ØJØP*	481
ØJØPØZZ	426, 1065
ØJØP3ZZ	426, 1065
ØJ5ØØZZ	445
ØJ5Ø3ZZ	445
ØJ51ØZZ	445
ØJ513ZZ	445
ØJ54ØZZ	445
ØJ543ZZ	445
ØJ55ØZZ	445
ØJ553ZZ	445
ØJ56ØZZ	445
ØJ563ZZ	445
ØJ57ØZZ	445
ØJ573ZZ	445
ØJ58ØZZ	445
ØJ583ZZ	445
ØJ59ØZZ	445
ØJ593ZZ	445
ØJ5BØZZ	445
ØJ5B3ZZ	445
ØJ5CØZZ	445
ØJ5C3ZZ	445
ØJ5DØZZ	445
ØJ5D3ZZ	445
ØJ5FØZZ	445
ØJ5F3ZZ	445
ØJ5GØZZ	445
ØJ5G3ZZ	445
ØJ5HØZZ	446
ØJ5H3ZZ	446
ØJ5JØZZ	446
ØJ5J3ZZ	446
ØJ5KØZZ	446
ØJ5K3ZZ	446
ØJ5LØZZ	446
ØJ5L3ZZ	446
ØJ5MØZZ	446
ØJ5M3ZZ	446
ØJ5NØZZ	446
ØJ5N3ZZ	446
ØJ5PØZZ	446
ØJ5P3ZZ	446
ØJ5QØZZ	446
ØJ5Q3ZZ	446
ØJ5RØZZ	446
ØJ5R3ZZ	446
ØJ8Ø*	34, 243, 695
ØJ8ØØZZ	426, 916
ØJ8Ø3ZZ	426, 916
ØJ81*	56, 67, 695
ØJ81ØZZ	916, 1065
ØJ813ZZ	916, 1065
ØJ84*	34, 243, 695
ØJ84ØZZ	426, 916
ØJ843ZZ	426, 916
ØJ85*	34, 243, 695
ØJ85ØZZ	426, 916
ØJ853ZZ	426, 916
ØJ86*	34, 243, 695
ØJ86ØZZ	426, 916
ØJ863ZZ	426, 916
ØJ87*	34, 243, 695
ØJ87ØZZ	426, 916
ØJ873ZZ	426, 916
ØJ88*	34, 243, 695
ØJ88ØZZ	426, 916
ØJ883ZZ	426, 916
ØJ89*	34, 243, 695
ØJ89ØZZ	426, 916
ØJ893ZZ	426, 916
ØJ8B*	34, 243, 695
ØJ8BØZZ	426, 916
ØJ8B3ZZ	426, 916
ØJ8C*	34, 243, 695
ØJ8CØZZ	426, 916
ØJ8C3ZZ	426, 916
ØJ8D*	34, 243, 695
ØJ8DØZZ	426, 916
ØJ8D3ZZ	426, 916
ØJ8F*	34, 243, 695
ØJ8FØZZ	426, 916
ØJ8F3ZZ	426, 916
ØJ8G*	34, 243, 695
ØJ8GØZZ	426, 916
ØJ8G3ZZ	426, 916
ØJ8H*	34, 243, 695
ØJ8HØZZ	426, 916
ØJ8H3ZZ	426, 916
ØJ8J*	268
ØJ8JØZZ	426, 640, 916, 1065
ØJ8J3ZZ	426, 640, 916, 1065
ØJ8K*	268
ØJ8KØZZ	426, 640, 916, 1065
ØJ8K3ZZ	426, 640, 916, 1065
ØJ8L*	34, 243, 695
ØJ8LØZZ	426, 916
ØJ8L3ZZ	426, 916
ØJ8M*	34, 243, 695
ØJ8MØZZ	426, 916
ØJ8M3ZZ	426, 916
ØJ8N*	34, 243, 695
ØJ8NØZZ	426, 916
ØJ8N3ZZ	426, 916
ØJ8P*	34, 243, 695
ØJ8PØZZ	426, 916
ØJ8P3ZZ	426, 916
ØJ8Q*	34, 243, 695
ØJ8QØZZ	426, 916
ØJ8Q3ZZ	426, 916
ØJ8R*	34, 243, 695
ØJ8RØZZ	426, 916
ØJ8R3ZZ	426, 916
ØJ8S*	34, 243, 695
ØJ8SØZZ	426, 916
ØJ8S3ZZ	426, 916
ØJ8T*	35, 243, 695
ØJ8TØZZ	426, 916
ØJ8T3ZZ	426, 916
ØJ8V*	35, 243, 695
ØJ8VØZZ	426, 916
ØJ8V3ZZ	426, 916
ØJ8W*	35, 243, 695
ØJ8WØZZ	426, 916
ØJ8W3ZZ	426, 916
ØJ9ØØZZ	243, 426, 695, 916, 1065
ØJ91ØZZ	85, 426, 695, 916
ØJ94ØZZ	243, 426, 695, 916, 1065

Numeric Index to Procedures

Code	Page	Code	Page	Code	Page	Code	Page	Code	Page	Code	Page
ØJ95ØZZ	243, 426, 695, 917, 1065	ØJBCØZZ	35, 58, 79, 1Ø1, 146, 19Ø, 2Ø7, 214, 41Ø, 482, 515, 524, 538, 576, 638, 917	ØJD93ZZ	453	ØJH63VZ	35, 1Ø1, 146, 19Ø, 2Ø8, 277, 426, 495, 515, 524, 538, 577, 695, 917	ØJHDØNZ	35, 146, 214, 41Ø, 482, 639, 784, 787, 917	ØJHL3VZ	35, 1Ø1, 146, 191, 2Ø8, 277, 426, 495, 515, 524, 538, 577, 695, 917
ØJ96ØZZ	243, 426, 695, 917, 1065			ØJDBØZZ	35, 243, 426, 695, 917						
ØJ97ØZZ	243, 426, 695, 917, 1065			ØJDCØZZ	35, 243, 426, 695, 917			ØJHDØVZ	35, 1Ø1, 146, 191, 2Ø8, 277, 426, 495, 515, 524, 538, 577, 695, 917	ØJHL3WZ	446, 518
ØJ98ØZZ	243, 426, 695, 917, 1065	ØJBC3ZZ	446	ØJDDØZZ	35, 243, 426, 695, 917	ØJH63VZ	446, 518			ØJHL3XZ	446, 518
ØJ99ØZZ	243, 426, 695, 917, 1065	ØJBDØZZ	35, 58, 79, 1Ø1, 146, 19Ø, 2Ø7, 214, 41Ø, 482, 515, 524, 538, 576, 638, 917	ØJDFØZZ	35, 243, 426, 695, 917	ØJH63XZ	446, 518			ØJHMØNZ	35, 146, 214, 41Ø, 482, 639, 784, 787, 917
ØJ9BØZZ	243, 426, 695, 917, 1065			ØJDGØZZ	35, 243, 426, 695, 917	ØJH7*	35	ØJHDØWZ	426, 515		
						ØJH7ØBZ	22, 41, 29Ø	ØJHDØXZ	446, 518		
ØJ9CØZZ	243, 426, 695, 917, 1065			ØJDHØZZ	35, 243, 426, 695, 917	ØJH7ØCZ	22, 41, 29Ø			ØJHMØVZ	35, 1Ø1, 146, 191, 2Ø8, 277, 426, 495, 515, 524, 538, 577, 695, 917
ØJ9DØZZ	243, 426, 695, 917, 1065	ØJBD3ZZ	446			ØJH7ØDZ	15, 22, 41, 29Ø	ØJHD3NZ	35, 146, 214, 41Ø, 482, 639, 784, 787, 917		
		ØJBFØZZ	35, 58, 79, 1Ø1, 146, 19Ø, 2Ø7, 214, 41Ø, 482, 515, 524, 538, 576, 638, 917	ØJDJØZZ	268, 64Ø, 917	ØJH7ØEZ	15, 22, 41, 29Ø				
ØJ9FØZZ	243, 426, 695, 917, 1065			ØJDKØZZ	268, 64Ø, 917	ØJH7ØMZ	14Ø			ØJHMØWZ	426, 515
				ØJDLØZZ	35, 243, 426, 695, 917	ØJH7ØNZ	146, 19Ø, 214, 41Ø, 482, 639, 784, 787, 917	ØJHD3VZ	35, 1Ø1, 146, 191, 2Ø8, 277, 426, 495, 515, 524, 538, 577, 695, 917	ØJHMØXZ	446, 518
ØJ9GØZZ	243, 426, 695, 917, 1065									ØJHM3NZ	35, 146, 214, 41Ø, 482, 639, 784, 787, 917
ØJ9HØZZ	243, 426, 695, 917, 1065	ØJBF3ZZ	446	ØJDL3ZZ	453	ØJH7ØVZ	1Ø1, 146, 191, 2Ø8, 277, 426, 495, 515, 524, 538, 577, 695, 917				
		ØJBGØZZ	35, 58, 79, 1Ø1, 146, 19Ø, 2Ø7, 214, 41Ø, 482, 515, 524, 538, 576, 638, 917	ØJDMØZZ	35, 243, 426, 695, 917			ØJHD3WZ	446, 518		
ØJ9JØZZ	268, 426, 64Ø, 917, 1065			ØJDM3ZZ	453			ØJHD3XZ	446, 518	ØJHM3VZ	35, 1Ø1, 146, 191, 2Ø8, 277, 426, 495, 515, 524, 538, 577, 695, 917
ØJ9KØZZ	268, 426, 64Ø, 917, 1065			ØJDNØZZ	35, 243, 426, 695, 917	ØJH73BZ	22, 41, 29Ø	ØJHFØNZ	35, 146, 214, 41Ø, 482, 639, 784, 787, 917		
						ØJH73CZ	22, 41, 29Ø				
ØJ9LØZZ	243, 426, 695, 917, 1065			ØJDPØZZ	35, 243, 426, 695, 917	ØJH73DZ	15, 22, 41, 29Ø			ØJHM3WZ	446, 518
		ØJBG3ZZ	446			ØJH73EZ	15, 22, 41, 29Ø	ØJHFØVZ	35, 1Ø1, 146, 191, 2Ø8, 277, 426, 495, 515, 524, 538, 577, 695, 917	ØJHM3XZ	446, 518
ØJ9MØZZ	243, 426, 695, 917, 1065	ØJBHØZZ	35, 58, 79, 1Ø1, 146, 19Ø, 2Ø7, 214, 41Ø, 482, 515, 524, 538, 576, 638, 917	ØJDQØZZ	35, 243, 426, 695, 917	ØJH73MZ	14Ø			ØJHNØNZ	35, 146, 214, 41Ø, 482, 639, 784, 787, 917
ØJ9NØZZ	243, 426, 695, 917, 1065			ØJDRØZZ	35, 243, 426, 695, 917	ØJH73NZ	146, 191, 214, 41Ø, 482, 639, 784, 787, 917	ØJHFØWZ	426, 515		
								ØJHFØXZ	446, 518	ØJHNØVZ	35, 1Ø1, 146, 191, 2Ø8, 277, 426, 495, 515, 524, 538, 577, 695, 917
ØJ9PØZZ	243, 426, 695, 917, 1065	ØJBH3ZZ	446	ØJHØ*	35, 79, 146, 19Ø, 214, 41Ø, 482, 787	ØJH73VZ	1Ø1, 146, 191, 2Ø8, 277, 426, 495, 515, 524, 538, 577, 695, 917	ØJHF3NZ	35, 146, 214, 41Ø, 482, 639, 784, 787, 917		
		ØJBJØZZ	268, 426, 64Ø, 917, 1065	ØJHØØNZ	639, 784, 917						
ØJ9QØZZ	243, 426, 695, 917, 1065			ØJHØ3NZ	639, 784, 917					ØJHNØWZ	426, 515
		ØJBJ3ZZ	268, 426, 64Ø, 917, 1065	ØJH1*	35, 79, 146, 19Ø, 214, 41Ø, 482, 787	ØJH8ØØNZ	141	ØJHF3VZ	35, 1Ø1, 146, 191, 2Ø8, 277, 426, 495, 515, 524, 538, 577, 695, 917	ØJHNØXZ	446, 518
ØJ9RØZZ	243, 426, 695, 917, 1065	ØJBKØZZ	268, 426, 64Ø, 917, 1065	ØJH1ØNZ	639, 784, 917	ØJH8Ø2Z	446			ØJHN3HZ	446
				ØJH13NZ	639, 784, 917	ØJH8Ø4Z	119, 141			ØJHN3NZ	35, 146, 214, 41Ø, 482, 639, 784, 787, 917
ØJBØØZZ	35, 58, 79, 1Ø1, 146, 19Ø, 2Ø7, 214, 41Ø, 482, 515, 524, 538, 576, 638, 917	ØJBK3ZZ	268, 426, 64Ø, 917, 1065	ØJH4*	35, 79, 146, 19Ø, 214, 41Ø, 482, 787	ØJH8Ø5Z	119, 141	ØJHF3WZ	446, 518		
				ØJH4ØNZ	639, 784, 917	ØJH8Ø6Z	119, 141	ØJHF3XZ	446, 518		
				ØJH43NZ	639, 784, 917	ØJH8Ø7Z	119, 141	ØJHGØNZ	35, 146, 214, 41Ø, 482, 639, 784, 787, 917	ØJHN3VZ	35, 1Ø1, 146, 191, 2Ø8, 277, 426, 495, 515, 524, 538, 577, 695, 917
		ØJBLØZZ	35, 58, 79, 1Ø1, 146, 19Ø, 2Ø7, 214, 41Ø, 482, 515, 524, 538, 576, 638, 917	ØJH5*	35, 79, 146, 19Ø, 214, 41Ø, 482, 787	ØJH8Ø8Z	11Ø, 119				
				ØJH5ØNZ	639, 784, 917	ØJH8Ø9Z	11Ø, 119	ØJHGØVZ	35, 1Ø1, 146, 191, 2Ø8, 277, 426, 495, 516, 524, 538, 577, 695, 917	ØJHN3WZ	446, 518
ØJBØ3ZZ	446			ØJH53NZ	639, 784, 917	ØJH8ØAZ	11Ø, 119			ØJHN3XZ	446, 518
ØJB1ØZZ	35, 58, 79, 1Ø1, 146, 19Ø, 2Ø7, 214, 41Ø, 482, 515, 524, 538, 576, 638, 917			ØJH6ØØZ	141	ØJH8ØBZ	22, 35, 41, 29Ø			ØJHPØHZ	446
		ØJBL3ZZ	446	ØJH6Ø2Z	35, 141, 426, 695, 917	ØJH8ØCZ	22, 35, 41, 29Ø	ØJHGØWZ	426, 515	ØJHPØNZ	35, 146, 214, 41Ø, 482, 639, 784, 787, 917
		ØJBMØZZ	35, 58, 79, 1Ø1, 146, 19Ø, 2Ø7, 214, 41Ø, 482, 515, 524, 538, 576, 638, 917	ØJH6Ø4Z	119, 141	ØJH8ØDZ	15, 22, 35, 42, 29Ø	ØJHGØXZ	446, 518		
				ØJH6Ø5Z	119, 141	ØJH8ØEZ	15, 22, 35, 42, 29Ø	ØJHG3NZ	35, 146, 214, 41Ø, 482, 639, 784, 787, 917	ØJHPØVZ	35, 1Ø1, 146, 191, 2Ø8, 277, 426, 495, 516, 524, 538, 577, 695, 917
ØJB13ZZ	79, 1065			ØJH6Ø6Z	119, 141	ØJH8ØHZ	446				
ØJB4ØZZ	35, 58, 79, 1Ø1, 146, 19Ø, 2Ø7, 214, 41Ø, 482, 515, 524, 538, 576, 638, 917			ØJH6Ø7Z	119, 141	ØJH8ØMZ	35, 14Ø				
		ØJBM3ZZ	446	ØJH6Ø8Z	11Ø, 119	ØJH8ØNZ	35, 146, 191, 214, 41Ø, 482, 639, 784, 787, 917				
		ØJBNØZZ	35, 58, 79, 1Ø1, 146, 19Ø, 2Ø7, 214, 41Ø, 482, 515, 524, 538, 577, 638, 917	ØJH6Ø9Z	11Ø, 119			ØJHG3VZ	35, 1Ø1, 146, 191, 2Ø8, 277, 426, 495, 516, 524, 538, 577, 695, 917	ØJHPØWZ	426, 516
				ØJH6ØAZ	11Ø, 119					ØJHPØXZ	446, 518
				ØJH6ØBZ	21, 35, 41, 29Ø	ØJH8ØPZ	119, 141			ØJHP3HZ	446
ØJB43ZZ	446			ØJH6ØCZ	21, 35, 41, 29Ø	ØJH8ØVZ	35, 1Ø1, 146, 191, 2Ø8, 277, 426, 495, 515, 524, 538, 577, 695, 917	ØJHG3WZ	446, 518	ØJHP3NZ	35, 146, 214, 41Ø, 482, 639, 784, 787, 917
ØJB5ØZZ	35, 58, 79, 1Ø1, 146, 19Ø, 2Ø7, 214, 41Ø, 482, 515, 524, 538, 576, 638, 917	ØJBN3ZZ	446	ØJH6ØDZ	15, 21, 35, 41, 29Ø			ØJHG3XZ	446, 518		
		ØJBPØZZ	35, 58, 79, 1Ø1, 146, 19Ø, 2Ø7, 214, 41Ø, 482, 515, 524, 538, 576, 638, 917	ØJH6ØEZ	15, 21, 35, 41, 29Ø			ØJHHØNZ	35, 146, 214, 41Ø, 482, 639, 784, 787, 917		
				ØJH6ØFZ	11Ø, 149					ØJHP3VZ	35, 1Ø1, 146, 191, 2Ø8, 277, 426, 495, 516, 524, 538, 577, 695, 917
				ØJH6ØHZ	446	ØJH83ØZ	141				
ØJB53ZZ	446	ØJBP3ZZ	446	ØJH6ØMZ	35, 14Ø	ØJH832Z	446	ØJHHØVZ	35, 1Ø1, 146, 191, 2Ø8, 277, 426, 495, 515, 524, 538, 577, 695, 917		
ØJB6ØZZ	35, 58, 79, 1Ø1, 146, 19Ø, 2Ø7, 214, 41Ø, 482, 515, 524, 538, 576, 638, 917	ØJBQØZZ	35, 58, 79, 1Ø1, 146, 19Ø, 2Ø8, 214, 41Ø, 482, 515, 524, 538, 577, 638, 917	ØJH6ØNZ	35, 146, 19Ø, 214, 41Ø, 482, 639, 784, 787, 917	ØJH834Z	119, 141			ØJHPØWZ	426, 516
						ØJH835Z	119, 141			ØJHP3WZ	446, 518
						ØJH836Z	119, 141			ØJHP3XZ	446, 518
				ØJH6ØPZ	119, 141	ØJH837Z	119, 141	ØJHHØWZ	426, 515	ØJHQ*	35, 146, 214, 41Ø, 482, 787
				ØJH6ØVZ	35, 1Ø1, 146, 19Ø, 2Ø8, 277, 426, 495, 515, 524, 538, 577, 695, 917	ØJH838Z	11Ø, 119	ØJHHØXZ	446, 518		
ØJB63ZZ	446	ØJBQ3ZZ	446			ØJH839Z	11Ø, 119	ØJHH3NZ	35, 146, 214, 41Ø, 482, 639, 784, 787, 917	ØJHQØNZ	639, 784, 917
ØJB7ØZZ	35, 58, 79, 1Ø1, 146, 19Ø, 2Ø7, 214, 41Ø, 482, 515, 524, 538, 576, 638, 917	ØJBRØZZ	35, 58, 79, 1Ø1, 146, 19Ø, 2Ø8, 214, 41Ø, 482, 515, 524, 538, 577, 638, 917			ØJH83AZ	11Ø, 119			ØJHQ3NZ	639, 784, 917
						ØJH83BZ	22, 35, 42, 29Ø			ØJHR*	35, 146, 214, 41Ø, 482, 787
						ØJH83CZ	22, 35, 42, 29Ø	ØJHH3VZ	35, 1Ø1, 146, 191, 2Ø8, 277, 426, 495, 515, 524, 538, 577, 695, 917		
				ØJH6ØWZ	426, 515	ØJH83DZ	15, 22, 35, 42, 29Ø			ØJHRØNZ	639, 784, 917
				ØJH6ØXZ	446, 518	ØJH83EZ	15, 22, 35, 42, 29Ø			ØJHR3NZ	639, 784, 917
ØJB73ZZ	446	ØJBR3ZZ	446	ØJH63ØZ	141	ØJH83HZ	446	ØJHH3WZ	446, 518	ØJHSØ1Z	426, 695, 1065
ØJB8ØZZ	35, 58, 79, 1Ø1, 146, 19Ø, 2Ø7, 214, 41Ø, 482, 515, 524, 538, 576, 638, 917	ØJDØØZZ	35, 243, 426, 695, 917	ØJH632Z	35, 141, 426, 695, 917	ØJH83MZ	35, 14Ø	ØJHH3XZ	446, 518	ØJHSØYZ	426, 695, 1065
						ØJH83NZ	35, 146, 191, 214, 41Ø, 482, 639, 784, 787, 917			ØJHS31Z	426, 695, 1065
		ØJD1ØZZ	35, 243, 426, 695, 917	ØJH634Z	119, 141			ØJHJ*	35, 268, 41Ø, 482, 787	ØJHTØ1Z	426, 696, 1065
		ØJD4ØZZ	35, 243, 426, 695, 917	ØJH635Z	119, 141					ØJHTØVZ	35, 1Ø1, 146, 191, 2Ø8, 277, 426, 495, 516, 524, 539, 696, 917
				ØJH636Z	119, 141			ØJHJØNZ	639, 784, 917		
ØJB83ZZ	446			ØJH637Z	119, 141	ØJH83PZ	119, 141	ØJHJ3NZ	639, 784, 917		
ØJB9ØZZ	35, 58, 79, 1Ø1, 146, 19Ø, 2Ø7, 214, 41Ø, 482, 515, 524, 538, 576, 638, 917	ØJD5ØZZ	35, 243, 426, 695, 917	ØJH638Z	11Ø, 119	ØJH83VZ	35, 1Ø1, 146, 191, 2Ø8, 277, 426, 495, 515, 524, 538, 577, 695, 917	ØJHK*	35, 268, 41Ø, 482, 787	ØJHTØYZ	35, 1Ø1, 146, 191, 2Ø8, 277, 426, 495, 516, 524, 539, 696, 917
		ØJD6ØZZ	35, 243, 426, 695, 917	ØJH639Z	11Ø, 119			ØJHKØNZ	639, 784, 917		
				ØJH63AZ	11Ø, 119			ØJHK3NZ	639, 784, 917		
		ØJD63ZZ	453	ØJH63BZ	22, 35, 41, 29Ø			ØJHLØNZ	35, 146, 214, 41Ø, 482, 639, 784, 787, 917	ØJHT31Z	426, 696, 1065
ØJB93ZZ	446	ØJD7ØZZ	35, 243, 426, 695, 917	ØJH63CZ	22, 35, 41, 29Ø	ØJH83WZ	446, 518			ØJHT3VZ	35, 1Ø1, 146, 191, 2Ø8, 277, 426, 495, 516, 524, 539, 696, 917
ØJBBØZZ	35, 58, 79, 1Ø1, 146, 19Ø, 2Ø7, 214, 41Ø, 482, 515, 524, 538, 576, 638, 917			ØJH63DZ	15, 22, 35, 41, 29Ø	ØJH83XZ	446, 518	ØJHLØVZ	35, 1Ø1, 146, 191, 2Ø8, 277, 426, 495, 515, 524, 538, 577, 695, 917		
		ØJD73ZZ	453	ØJH63EZ	15, 22, 35, 41, 29Ø	ØJH9*	35, 146, 214, 41Ø, 482, 787				
		ØJD8ØZZ	35, 243, 426, 695, 917	ØJH63FZ	11Ø, 149	ØJH9ØNZ	639, 784, 917				
				ØJH63HZ	446	ØJH93NZ	639, 784, 917			ØJHVØ1Z	426, 696, 1065
		ØJD83ZZ	453	ØJH63MZ	35, 14Ø	ØJHB*	35, 146, 214, 41Ø, 482, 787	ØJHLØWZ	426, 515	ØJHVØYZ	426, 696, 1065
ØJBB3ZZ	446	ØJD9ØZZ	35, 243, 426, 695, 917	ØJH63NZ	35, 146, 19Ø, 214, 41Ø, 482, 639, 784, 787, 917	ØJHBØNZ	639, 784, 917	ØJHLØXZ	446, 518	ØJHV31Z	426, 696, 1065
						ØJHB3NZ	639, 784, 917	ØJHL3NZ	35, 146, 214, 41Ø, 482, 639, 784, 787, 917	ØJHWØ1Z	426, 696, 1065
				ØJH63PZ	119, 141	ØJHC*	35, 146, 214, 41Ø, 482, 787			ØJHWØYZ	426, 696, 1065
						ØJHCØNZ	639, 784, 917				
						ØJHC3NZ	639, 784, 917				

Numeric Index to Procedures

Numeric Index to Procedures

Code	Page
ØJHW31Z	426, 696, 1065
ØJN00ZZ	243
ØJN03ZZ	243
ØJN10ZZ	243
ØJN13ZZ	243
ØJN40ZZ	243
ØJN43ZZ	243
ØJN50ZZ	243
ØJN53ZZ	243
ØJN60ZZ	243
ØJN63ZZ	243
ØJN70ZZ	243
ØJN73ZZ	243
ØJN80ZZ	243
ØJN83ZZ	243
ØJN90ZZ	243
ØJN93ZZ	243
ØJNB0ZZ	243
ØJNB3ZZ	243
ØJNC0ZZ	243
ØJNC3ZZ	243
ØJND0ZZ	243
ØJND3ZZ	243
ØJNF0ZZ	243
ØJNF3ZZ	243
ØJNG0ZZ	243
ØJNG3ZZ	243
ØJNH0ZZ	243
ØJNH3ZZ	243
ØJNJ0ZZ	268, 640, 917
ØJNJ3ZZ	268, 640, 917
ØJNK0ZZ	268, 640, 917
ØJNK3ZZ	268, 640, 917
ØJNL0ZZ	243
ØJNL3ZZ	243
ØJNM0ZZ	243
ØJNM3ZZ	243
ØJNN0ZZ	243
ØJNN3ZZ	243
ØJNP0ZZ	243
ØJNP3ZZ	243
ØJNQ0ZZ	243
ØJNQ3ZZ	243
ØJNR0ZZ	243
ØJNR3ZZ	243
ØJPT0FZ	35, 149, 696, 917, 1065
ØJPT0PZ	35, 141, 696, 917, 1065
ØJPT3FZ	35, 149, 696, 917, 1065
ØJPT3PZ	35, 141, 696, 917, 1065
ØJQ00ZZ	35, 243, 426, 696, 917
ØJQ10ZZ	243, 426, 696, 1065
ØJQ40ZZ	243, 426, 696, 1065
ØJQ50ZZ	243, 426, 696, 1065
ØJQ60ZZ	243, 426, 696, 1065
ØJQ70ZZ	243, 426, 696, 1065
ØJQ80ZZ	243, 426, 696, 1065
ØJQ90ZZ	243, 427, 696, 1065
ØJQB0ZZ	243, 427, 495, 696, 917, 1065
ØJQC0ZZ	179, 243, 427, 507, 537, 696
ØJQD0ZZ	243, 427, 495, 696, 1065
ØJQF0ZZ	243, 427, 495, 696, 1065
ØJQG0ZZ	243, 427, 495, 696, 1065
ØJQH0ZZ	243, 427, 495, 696, 1065
ØJQJ0ZZ	35, 268, 427, 640, 917, 1065
ØJQK0ZZ	35, 268, 427, 640, 917, 1065
ØJQL0ZZ	243, 427, 495, 696, 1065
ØJQM0ZZ	243, 427, 495, 696, 1065
ØJQN0ZZ	243, 427, 495, 696, 1065
ØJQP0ZZ	243, 427, 495, 696, 1065
ØJQQ0ZZ	243, 427, 495, 696, 1065
ØJQR0ZZ	243, 427, 495, 696, 1065
ØJR0*	243, 696
ØJR007Z	427
ØJR00JZ	427
ØJR00KZ	427
ØJR037Z	79, 427, 481, 917
ØJR03JZ	427
ØJR03KZ	427
ØJR1*	244, 696
ØJR107Z	56, 67, 427, 917
ØJR10JZ	427
ØJR10KZ	56, 67, 427, 917
ØJR137Z	56, 79, 427, 481, 917
ØJR13JZ	427
ØJR13KZ	56, 67, 427, 917
ØJR4*	244, 696
ØJR407Z	427
ØJR40JZ	427
ØJR40KZ	427
ØJR437Z	79, 427, 481, 917
ØJR43JZ	427
ØJR43KZ	427
ØJR5*	244, 696
ØJR507Z	427
ØJR50JZ	427
ØJR50KZ	427
ØJR537Z	79, 427, 481, 917
ØJR53JZ	427
ØJR53KZ	427
ØJR6*	244, 696
ØJR607Z	427
ØJR60JZ	427
ØJR60KZ	427
ØJR637Z	79, 427, 481, 917
ØJR63JZ	427
ØJR63KZ	427
ØJR7*	244, 696
ØJR707Z	427
ØJR70JZ	427
ØJR70KZ	427
ØJR737Z	79, 427, 481, 917
ØJR73JZ	427
ØJR73KZ	427
ØJR8*	244, 696
ØJR807Z	427
ØJR80KZ	427
ØJR837Z	79, 427, 481, 917
ØJR83JZ	427
ØJR83KZ	427
ØJR9*	244, 696
ØJR907Z	427
ØJR90JZ	427
ØJR90KZ	427
ØJR937Z	79, 427, 481, 917
ØJR93JZ	427
ØJR93KZ	427
ØJRB*	244, 696
ØJRB07Z	427
ØJRB0JZ	427
ØJRB0KZ	427
ØJRB37Z	79, 427, 481, 917
ØJRB3JZ	427
ØJRB3KZ	427
ØJRC*	244, 696
ØJRC07Z	427
ØJRC0JZ	427
ØJRC0KZ	427
ØJRC37Z	79, 427, 481, 917
ØJRC3JZ	427
ØJRC3KZ	427
ØJRD*	244, 696
ØJRD07Z	427
ØJRD0JZ	427
ØJRD0KZ	427
ØJRD37Z	79, 427, 481, 917
ØJRD3JZ	427
ØJRD3KZ	427
ØJRF*	244, 696
ØJRF07Z	427
ØJRF0JZ	427
ØJRF0KZ	427
ØJRF37Z	79, 427, 481, 917
ØJRF3JZ	427
ØJRF3KZ	427
ØJRG*	244, 696
ØJRG07Z	427
ØJRG0JZ	427
ØJRG0KZ	427
ØJRG3JZ	427
ØJRG3KZ	427
ØJRH*	244, 696
ØJRH07Z	427
ØJRH0JZ	427
ØJRH0KZ	427
ØJRH37Z	79, 427, 481, 917
ØJRH3JZ	427
ØJRH3KZ	427
ØJRJ07Z	35, 268, 427, 640, 917
ØJRJ0JZ	35, 268, 427, 640, 917
ØJRJ0KZ	35, 268, 427, 640, 917
ØJRJ37Z	79, 427, 481, 696, 917
ØJRJ3JZ	35, 268, 427, 640, 917
ØJRJ3KZ	35, 268, 427, 640, 917
ØJRK07Z	35, 268, 427, 640, 917
ØJRK0JZ	35, 268, 427, 640, 917
ØJRK0KZ	35, 268, 427, 640, 917
ØJRK37Z	79, 427, 481, 696, 918
ØJRK3JZ	35, 268, 427, 640, 918
ØJRK3KZ	35, 268, 427, 640, 918
ØJRL*	244, 696
ØJRL07Z	427
ØJRL0JZ	427
ØJRL0KZ	427
ØJRL37Z	79, 427, 481, 918
ØJRL3JZ	427
ØJRL3KZ	427
ØJRM*	244, 696
ØJRM07Z	427
ØJRM0JZ	427
ØJRM0KZ	427
ØJRM37Z	79, 427, 481, 918
ØJRM3JZ	427
ØJRM3KZ	427
ØJRN*	244, 696
ØJRN07Z	427
ØJRN0JZ	427
ØJRN0KZ	427
ØJRN37Z	79, 427, 481, 918
ØJRN3JZ	427
ØJRN3KZ	427
ØJRP*	244, 696
ØJRP07Z	427
ØJRP0JZ	427
ØJRP0KZ	427
ØJRP37Z	79, 427, 481, 918
ØJRP3JZ	427
ØJRP3KZ	427
ØJRQ*	244, 696
ØJRQ07Z	427
ØJRQ0JZ	427
ØJRQ0KZ	427
ØJRQ37Z	79, 427, 481, 918
ØJRQ3JZ	427
ØJRQ3KZ	427
ØJRR*	244, 696
ØJRR07Z	427
ØJRR0JZ	427
ØJRR0KZ	427
ØJRR37Z	79, 427, 481, 918
ØJRR3JZ	427
ØJRR3KZ	427
ØJU0*	244, 696
ØJU00JZ	427
ØJU00KZ	427
ØJU03JZ	427
ØJU03KZ	427
ØJU1*	244, 696
ØJU107Z	427
ØJU10JZ	427
ØJU10KZ	427
ØJU137Z	427
ØJU13JZ	427
ØJU13KZ	427
ØJU4*	244, 696
ØJU40JZ	427
ØJU40KZ	427
ØJU437Z	427
ØJU43JZ	427
ØJU43KZ	427
ØJU5*	244, 696
ØJU507Z	427
ØJU50JZ	427
ØJU50KZ	427
ØJU537Z	427
ØJU53JZ	427
ØJU6*	244, 696
ØJU607Z	427
ØJU60JZ	427
ØJU60KZ	427
ØJU637Z	427
ØJU63JZ	428
ØJU7*	244, 696
ØJU707Z	428
ØJU70JZ	428
ØJU70KZ	428
ØJU737Z	428
ØJU73JZ	428
ØJU73KZ	428
ØJU8*	244, 696
ØJU807Z	428
ØJU80JZ	428
ØJU80KZ	428
ØJU837Z	428
ØJU83JZ	428
ØJU83KZ	428
ØJU9*	244, 696
ØJU907Z	428
ØJU90JZ	428
ØJU90KZ	428
ØJU937Z	428
ØJU93JZ	428
ØJU93KZ	428
ØJUB*	244, 696
ØJUB07Z	428
ØJUB0JZ	428
ØJUB0KZ	428
ØJUB37Z	428
ØJUB3JZ	428
ØJUB3KZ	428
ØJUC*	179, 244, 504, 537, 696
ØJUC07Z	428
ØJUC0JZ	428
ØJUC0KZ	428
ØJUC37Z	428
ØJUC3JZ	428
ØJUC3KZ	428
ØJUD*	244, 696
ØJUD07Z	428
ØJUD0JZ	428
ØJUD0KZ	428
ØJUD37Z	428
ØJUD3JZ	428
ØJUD3KZ	428
ØJUF*	244, 696
ØJUF07Z	428
ØJUF0JZ	428
ØJUF0KZ	428
ØJUF37Z	428
ØJUF3JZ	428
ØJUF3KZ	428
ØJUG*	244, 696
ØJUG07Z	428
ØJUG0JZ	428
ØJUG0KZ	428
ØJUG37Z	428
ØJUG3JZ	428
ØJUG3KZ	428
ØJUH*	244, 696
ØJUH07Z	428
ØJUH0JZ	428
ØJUH0KZ	428
ØJUH37Z	428
ØJUH3JZ	428
ØJUH3KZ	428
ØJUJ*	35, 268
ØJUJ07Z	428, 640, 918
ØJUJ0JZ	428, 640, 918
ØJUJ0KZ	428, 640, 918
ØJUJ37Z	428, 640, 918
ØJUJ3JZ	428, 640, 918
ØJUJ3KZ	428, 640, 918
ØJUK*	35, 268
ØJUK07Z	428, 640, 918
ØJUK0JZ	428, 640, 918
ØJUK0KZ	428, 640, 918
ØJUK37Z	428, 640, 918
ØJUK3JZ	428, 640, 918
ØJUK3KZ	428, 640, 918
ØJUL*	244, 696
ØJUL07Z	428
ØJUL0JZ	428
ØJUL0KZ	428
ØJUL37Z	428
ØJUL3JZ	428
ØJUL3KZ	428
ØJUM*	244, 696
ØJUM07Z	428
ØJUM0JZ	428
ØJUM0KZ	428
ØJUM37Z	428
ØJUM3JZ	428
ØJUM3KZ	428
ØJUN*	244, 696
ØJUN07Z	428
ØJUN0JZ	428
ØJUN0KZ	428
ØJUN37Z	428
ØJUN3JZ	428
ØJUN3KZ	428
ØJUP*	244, 696
ØJUP07Z	428
ØJUP0JZ	428
ØJUP0KZ	428
ØJUP37Z	428
ØJUP3JZ	428
ØJUP3KZ	428
ØJUQ*	244, 696
ØJUQ07Z	428
ØJUQ0JZ	428
ØJUQ0KZ	428
ØJUQ37Z	428
ØJUQ3JZ	428
ØJUQ3KZ	428
ØJUR*	244, 696
ØJUR07Z	428
ØJUR0JZ	428
ØJUR0KZ	428
ØJUR37Z	428
ØJUR3JZ	428
ØJUR3KZ	428
ØJWS00Z	446
ØJWS03Z	446
ØJWS07Z	446
ØJWS0JZ	446
ØJWS0KZ	446
ØJWS0NZ	446
ØJWS0YZ	446
ØJWS30Z	446
ØJWS33Z	446
ØJWS37Z	446
ØJWS3JZ	446
ØJWS3KZ	446
ØJWS3NZ	446
ØJWS3YZ	446
ØJWT00Z	446
ØJWT02Z	35, 141, 428, 696, 918
ØJWT03Z	446
ØJWT07Z	446
ØJWT0FZ	35, 149, 428, 696, 918
ØJWT0HZ	446
ØJWT0JZ	446
ØJWT0KZ	446
ØJWT0MZ	141
ØJWT0NZ	446
ØJWT0PZ	35, 141, 428, 696, 918
ØJWT0VZ	446
ØJWT0WZ	446
ØJWT0XZ	446
ØJWT0YZ	35, 141, 428, 696, 918
ØJWT30Z	446
ØJWT32Z	35, 141, 428, 696, 918
ØJWT33Z	446
ØJWT37Z	446
ØJWT3FZ	35, 149, 428, 696, 918
ØJWT3HZ	446
ØJWT3JZ	446
ØJWT3KZ	446
ØJWT3MZ	141
ØJWT3NZ	446
ØJWT3PZ	35, 141, 428, 696, 918
ØJWT3VZ	446
ØJWT3WZ	446
ØJWT3XZ	446
ØJWTXMZ	141
ØJWV00Z	446
ØJWV03Z	446
ØJWV07Z	446
ØJWV0HZ	446
ØJWV0JZ	446
ØJWV0KZ	446
ØJWV0NZ	446
ØJWV0VZ	446
ØJWV0WZ	446
ØJWV0XZ	446
ØJWV0YZ	446
ØJWV30Z	446
ØJWV33Z	446
ØJWV37Z	446
ØJWV3HZ	446
ØJWV3JZ	446
ØJWV3KZ	446
ØJWV3NZ	446
ØJWV3VZ	446
ØJWV3WZ	446
ØJWV3XZ	446
ØJWW00Z	446
ØJWW03Z	446
ØJWW07Z	446
ØJWW0HZ	446
ØJWW0JZ	446
ØJWW0KZ	446
ØJWW0NZ	446
ØJWW0VZ	446
ØJWW0WZ	446
ØJWW0YZ	446
ØJWW30Z	446
ØJWW33Z	446
ØJWW37Z	446
ØJWW3HZ	446
ØJWW3JZ	446
ØJWW3KZ	446
ØJWW3NZ	446
ØJWW3VZ	446
ØJWW3WZ	446
ØJWW3XZ	446
ØJWW3YZ	446
ØJX00ZB	35, 79, 146, 191, 214, 410, 482, 639, 784, 787, 918
ØJX00ZC	35, 79, 146, 191, 214, 410, 482, 639, 784, 787, 918
ØJX00ZZ	244, 428, 696
ØJX03ZB	35, 79, 146, 191, 214, 410, 482, 639, 784, 787, 918
ØJX03ZC	35, 79, 146, 191, 214, 410, 482, 639, 784, 787, 918
ØJX03ZZ	244, 428, 696
ØJX10ZB	35, 79, 146, 191, 214, 410, 482, 639, 784, 787, 918
ØJX10ZC	35, 79, 146, 191, 214, 410, 482, 639, 784, 787, 918
ØJX10ZZ	244, 428, 696
ØJX13ZB	35, 79, 146, 191, 214, 410, 482, 639, 784, 787, 918
ØJX13ZC	35, 79, 146, 191, 214, 410, 482, 639, 784, 787, 918
ØJX13ZZ	244, 428, 696
ØJX40ZB	35, 79, 146, 191, 214, 410, 482, 639, 784, 787, 918
ØJX40ZC	35, 79, 146, 191, 214, 410, 482, 639, 784, 787, 918
ØJX40ZZ	244, 428, 696
ØJX43ZB	35, 79, 146, 191, 214, 410, 482, 639, 784, 787, 918
ØJX43ZC	35, 79, 146, 191, 214, 410, 482, 639, 784, 787, 918
ØJX43ZZ	244, 428, 696
ØJX50ZB	35, 79, 146, 191, 214, 410, 482, 639, 784, 787, 918

Code	Page
ØJX5ØZC	35, 79, 146, 191, 214, 41Ø, 482, 639, 784, 787, 918
ØJX5ØZZ	244, 428, 696
ØJX53ZB	35, 79, 146, 191, 214, 41Ø, 482, 639, 784, 787, 918
ØJX53ZC	35, 79, 146, 191, 214, 41Ø, 482, 639, 784, 787, 918
ØJX53ZZ	244, 428, 696
ØJX6ØZB	35, 146, 191, 214, 41Ø, 482, 639, 784, 787, 918
ØJX6ØZC	35, 146, 191, 214, 41Ø, 482, 639, 784, 787, 918
ØJX6ØZZ	244, 428, 696
ØJX63ZB	35, 146, 191, 214, 41Ø, 482, 639, 784, 787, 918
ØJX63ZC	35, 146, 191, 214, 41Ø, 482, 639, 784, 787, 918
ØJX63ZZ	244, 428, 696
ØJX7ØZB	35, 146, 191, 214, 41Ø, 482, 639, 784, 787, 918
ØJX7ØZC	35, 146, 191, 214, 41Ø, 482, 639, 784, 787, 918
ØJX7ØZZ	244, 428, 696
ØJX73ZB	35, 146, 191, 214, 41Ø, 482, 639, 784, 787, 918
ØJX73ZC	35, 146, 191, 214, 41Ø, 482, 639, 784, 787, 918
ØJX73ZZ	244, 428, 696
ØJX8ØZB	35, 146, 191, 214, 41Ø, 482, 639, 784, 787, 918
ØJX8ØZC	35, 146, 191, 215, 41Ø, 482, 639, 784, 787, 918
ØJX8ØZZ	244, 428, 696
ØJX83ZB	35, 146, 191, 215, 41Ø, 482, 639, 784, 787, 918
ØJX83ZC	35, 146, 191, 215, 41Ø, 482, 639, 784, 787, 918
ØJX83ZZ	244, 428, 696
ØJX9ØZB	36, 146, 191, 215, 41Ø, 482, 639, 784, 787, 918
ØJX9ØZC	36, 146, 191, 215, 41Ø, 482, 639, 784, 787, 918
ØJX9ØZZ	244, 428, 696
ØJX93ZB	36, 146, 191, 215, 41Ø, 482, 639, 784, 787, 918
ØJX93ZC	36, 146, 191, 215, 41Ø, 482, 639, 784, 787, 918
ØJX93ZZ	244, 428, 696
ØJXBØZB	36, 146, 191, 215, 41Ø, 482, 639, 784, 787, 918
ØJXBØZC	36, 146, 191, 215, 41Ø, 482, 639, 784, 787, 918
ØJXBØZZ	244, 428, 696
ØJXB3ZB	36, 146, 191, 215, 41Ø, 482, 639, 784, 787, 918
ØJXB3ZC	36, 146, 191, 215, 41Ø, 482, 639, 784, 787, 918
ØJXB3ZZ	244, 428, 696
ØJXCØZB	36, 146, 191, 215, 41Ø, 482, 639, 784, 787, 918
ØJXCØZC	36, 146, 191, 215, 411, 482, 639, 784, 787, 918
ØJXCØZZ	244, 428, 696
ØJXC3ZB	36, 146, 191, 215, 411, 482, 639, 784, 787, 918
ØJXC3ZC	36, 146, 191, 215, 411, 482, 639, 784, 787, 918
ØJXC3ZZ	244, 428, 696
ØJXDØZB	36, 147, 191, 215, 411, 482, 639, 784, 787, 918
ØJXDØZC	36, 147, 191, 215, 411, 482, 639, 784, 787, 918
ØJXDØZZ	244, 428, 696
ØJXD3ZB	36, 147, 191, 215, 411, 482, 639, 784, 787, 918
ØJXD3ZC	36, 147, 191, 215, 411, 482, 639, 784, 787, 918
ØJXD3ZZ	244, 428, 696
ØJXFØZB	36, 147, 191, 215, 411, 482, 639, 784, 787, 918
ØJXFØZC	36, 147, 191, 215, 411, 482, 639, 784, 787, 918
ØJXFØZZ	244, 428, 696
ØJXF3ZB	36, 147, 191, 215, 411, 482, 639, 784, 787, 918
ØJXF3ZC	36, 147, 191, 215, 411, 482, 639, 784, 787, 918
ØJXF3ZZ	244, 428, 696
ØJXGØZB	36, 147, 191, 215, 411, 482, 639, 784, 787, 918
ØJXGØZC	36, 147, 191, 215, 411, 482, 639, 784, 787, 918
ØJXGØZZ	244, 428, 696
ØJXG3ZB	36, 147, 191, 215, 411, 482, 639, 784, 787, 918
ØJXG3ZC	36, 147, 191, 215, 411, 482, 639, 784, 787, 918
ØJXG3ZZ	244, 428, 696
ØJXHØZB	36, 147, 191, 215, 411, 482, 639, 784, 787, 918
ØJXHØZC	36, 147, 191, 215, 411, 482, 639, 784, 787, 918
ØJXHØZZ	244, 428, 696
ØJXH3ZB	36, 147, 191, 215, 411, 482, 639, 784, 787, 918
ØJXH3ZC	36, 147, 191, 215, 411, 482, 639, 784, 787, 918
ØJXH3ZZ	244, 428, 696
ØJXJØZB	268, 411, 64Ø, 784, 787, 918
ØJXJØZC	268, 411, 64Ø, 784, 787, 918
ØJXJØZZ	36, 244, 428, 696
ØJXJ3ZB	268, 411, 64Ø, 784, 787, 918
ØJXJ3ZC	268, 411, 64Ø, 784, 787, 918
ØJXJ3ZZ	36, 244, 428, 696
ØJXKØZB	268, 411, 64Ø, 784, 787, 918
ØJXKØZC	268, 411, 64Ø, 784, 787, 918
ØJXKØZZ	244, 696
ØJXK3ZB	268, 411, 64Ø, 784, 787, 918
ØJXK3ZC	268, 411, 64Ø, 784, 787, 918
ØJXK3ZZ	244, 696
ØJXLØZB	36, 147, 191, 215, 411, 482, 639, 784, 787, 918
ØJXLØZC	36, 147, 191, 215, 411, 482, 639, 784, 787, 918
ØJXLØZZ	244, 428, 696
ØJXL3ZB	36, 147, 191, 215, 411, 482, 639, 784, 787, 918
ØJXL3ZC	36, 147, 191, 215, 411, 482, 639, 784, 787, 918
ØJXL3ZZ	244, 428, 696
ØJXMØZB	36, 147, 191, 215, 411, 482, 639, 784, 787, 918
ØJXMØZC	36, 147, 191, 215, 411, 482, 639, 784, 787, 918
ØJXMØZZ	244, 428, 696
ØJXM3ZB	36, 147, 191, 215, 411, 482, 639, 784, 787, 918
ØJXM3ZC	36, 147, 191, 215, 411, 482, 639, 784, 787, 918
ØJXM3ZZ	244, 428, 696
ØJXNØZB	36, 147, 191, 215, 411, 482, 639, 784, 787, 918
ØJXNØZC	36, 147, 191, 215, 411, 482, 639, 784, 787, 918
ØJXNØZZ	244, 428, 696
ØJXN3ZB	36, 147, 191, 215, 411, 482, 639, 784, 787, 918
ØJXN3ZC	36, 147, 191, 215, 411, 482, 639, 784, 787, 918
ØJXN3ZZ	244, 428, 696
ØJXPØZB	36, 147, 191, 215, 411, 482, 639, 784, 787, 918
ØJXPØZC	36, 147, 191, 215, 411, 482, 639, 784, 787, 918
ØJXPØZZ	244, 428, 696
ØJXP3ZB	36, 147, 191, 215, 411, 482, 639, 784, 787, 918
ØJXP3ZC	36, 147, 191, 215, 411, 482, 639, 784, 787, 918
ØJXP3ZZ	244, 428, 696
ØJXQØZB	36, 147, 191, 215, 411, 482, 639, 784, 787, 918
ØJXQØZC	36, 147, 191, 215, 411, 482, 639, 784, 787, 918
ØJXQØZZ	244, 428, 696
ØJXQ3ZB	36, 147, 191, 215, 411, 482, 639, 785, 787, 918
ØJXQ3ZC	36, 147, 191, 215, 411, 482, 639, 785, 787, 918
ØJXQ3ZZ	244, 428, 696
ØJXRØZB	36, 147, 191, 215, 411, 482, 639, 785, 787, 918
ØJXRØZC	36, 147, 191, 215, 411, 482, 639, 785, 787, 918
ØJXRØZZ	244, 428, 696
ØJXR3ZB	36, 147, 191, 215, 411, 482, 639, 785, 787, 918
ØJXR3ZC	36, 147, 191, 215, 411, 482, 639, 785, 787, 918
ØJXR3ZZ	244, 428, 696
ØK5Ø*	244, 696
ØK5ØØZZ	428, 918, 1Ø65
ØK5Ø3ZZ	428, 918, 1Ø65
ØK5Ø4ZZ	428, 918, 1Ø65
ØK51*	244, 696
ØK51ØZZ	428, 918, 1Ø65
ØK513ZZ	428, 918, 1Ø65
ØK514ZZ	428, 918, 1Ø65
ØK52*	244, 696
ØK52ØZZ	428, 918, 1Ø65
ØK523ZZ	428, 918, 1Ø66
ØK524ZZ	428, 918, 1Ø66
ØK53*	244, 696
ØK53ØZZ	428, 918, 1Ø66
ØK533ZZ	428, 918, 1Ø66
ØK534ZZ	428, 918, 1Ø66
ØK54*	244, 696
ØK54ØZZ	428, 918, 1Ø66
ØK543ZZ	428, 918, 1Ø66
ØK544ZZ	428, 918, 1Ø66
ØK55*	244, 696
ØK55ØZZ	428, 918, 1Ø66
ØK553ZZ	428, 918, 1Ø66
ØK554ZZ	428, 918, 1Ø66
ØK56*	244, 696
ØK56ØZZ	428, 918, 1Ø66
ØK563ZZ	428, 918, 1Ø66
ØK564ZZ	429, 918, 1Ø66
ØK57*	244, 696
ØK57ØZZ	429, 918, 1Ø66
ØK573ZZ	429, 918, 1Ø66
ØK574ZZ	429, 918, 1Ø66
ØK58*	244, 696
ØK58ØZZ	429, 918, 1Ø66
ØK583ZZ	429, 918, 1Ø66
ØK584ZZ	429, 918, 1Ø66
ØK59*	244, 696
ØK59ØZZ	429, 918, 1Ø66
ØK593ZZ	429, 918, 1Ø66
ØK594ZZ	429, 918, 1Ø66
ØK5B*	244, 696
ØK5BØZZ	429, 918, 1Ø66
ØK5B3ZZ	429, 918, 1Ø66
ØK5B4ZZ	429, 918, 1Ø66
ØK5C*	268
ØK5CØZZ	64Ø, 918
ØK5C3ZZ	64Ø, 918
ØK5C4ZZ	64Ø, 918
ØK5D*	268
ØK5DØZZ	64Ø, 918
ØK5D3ZZ	64Ø, 918
ØK5D4ZZ	64Ø, 918
ØK5F*	244, 696
ØK5FØZZ	429, 918, 1Ø66
ØK5F3ZZ	429, 918, 1Ø66
ØK5F4ZZ	429, 918, 1Ø66
ØK5G*	244, 696
ØK5GØZZ	429, 918, 1Ø66
ØK5G3ZZ	429, 918, 1Ø66
ØK5G4ZZ	429, 918, 1Ø66
ØK5H*	244, 696
ØK5HØZZ	429, 918, 1Ø66
ØK5H3ZZ	429, 918, 1Ø66
ØK5H4ZZ	429, 918, 1Ø66
ØK5J*	244, 696
ØK5JØZZ	429, 918, 1Ø66
ØK5J3ZZ	429, 918, 1Ø66
ØK5J4ZZ	429, 918, 1Ø66
ØK5K*	244, 696
ØK5KØZZ	429, 918, 1Ø66
ØK5K3ZZ	429, 918, 1Ø66
ØK5K4ZZ	429, 918, 1Ø66
ØK5L*	244, 696
ØK5LØZZ	429, 918, 1Ø66
ØK5L3ZZ	429, 918, 1Ø66
ØK5L4ZZ	429, 918, 1Ø66
ØK5M*	244, 696
ØK5MØZZ	429, 918, 1Ø66
ØK5M3ZZ	429, 919, 1Ø66
ØK5M4ZZ	429, 919, 1Ø66
ØK5N*	244, 696
ØK5NØZZ	429, 919, 1Ø66
ØK5N3ZZ	429, 919, 1Ø66
ØK5N4ZZ	429, 919, 1Ø66
ØK5P*	244, 696
ØK5PØZZ	429, 919, 1Ø66
ØK5P3ZZ	429, 919, 1Ø66
ØK5P4ZZ	429, 919, 1Ø66
ØK5Q*	244, 696
ØK5QØZZ	429, 919, 1Ø66
ØK5Q3ZZ	429, 919, 1Ø66
ØK5Q4ZZ	429, 919, 1Ø66
ØK5R*	244, 696
ØK5RØZZ	429, 919, 1Ø66
ØK5R3ZZ	429, 919, 1Ø66
ØK5R4ZZ	429, 919, 1Ø66
ØK5S*	244, 696
ØK5SØZZ	429, 919, 1Ø66
ØK5S3ZZ	429, 919, 1Ø66
ØK5S4ZZ	429, 919, 1Ø66
ØK5T*	244, 696
ØK5TØZZ	429, 919, 1Ø66
ØK5T3ZZ	429, 919, 1Ø66
ØK5T4ZZ	429, 919, 1Ø66
ØK5V*	244, 696
ØK5VØZZ	429, 919, 1Ø66
ØK5V3ZZ	429, 919, 1Ø66
ØK5V4ZZ	429, 919, 1Ø66
ØK5W*	244, 696
ØK5WØZZ	429, 919, 1Ø66
ØK5W3ZZ	429, 919, 1Ø66
ØK5W4ZZ	429, 919, 1Ø66
ØK8Ø*	36, 244, 696
ØK8ØØZZ	919
ØK8Ø3ZZ	919
ØK8Ø4ZZ	919
ØK81*	36, 244, 696
ØK81ØZZ	919
ØK813ZZ	919
ØK814ZZ	919
ØK82*	36, 244, 696
ØK82ØZZ	919
ØK823ZZ	919
ØK824ZZ	919
ØK83*	36, 244, 696
ØK83ØZZ	919
ØK833ZZ	919
ØK834ZZ	919
ØK84*	79, 177
ØK85*	36, 244, 696
ØK85ØZZ	919
ØK853ZZ	919
ØK854ZZ	919
ØK86*	36, 244, 696
ØK86ØZZ	919
ØK863ZZ	919
ØK864ZZ	919
ØK87*	36, 244, 696
ØK87ØZZ	919
ØK873ZZ	919
ØK874ZZ	919
ØK88*	36, 244, 696
ØK88ØZZ	919
ØK883ZZ	919
ØK884ZZ	919
ØK89*	36, 244, 696
ØK89ØZZ	919
ØK893ZZ	919
ØK894ZZ	919
ØK8B*	36, 244, 696
ØK8BØZZ	919
ØK8B3ZZ	919
ØK8B4ZZ	919
ØK8C*	268
ØK8CØZZ	64Ø, 919
ØK8C3ZZ	64Ø, 919
ØK8C4ZZ	64Ø, 919
ØK8D*	268
ØK8DØZZ	64Ø, 919
ØK8D3ZZ	64Ø, 919
ØK8D4ZZ	64Ø, 919
ØK8F*	36, 244, 696
ØK8FØZZ	919
ØK8F3ZZ	919
ØK8F4ZZ	919
ØK8G*	36, 244, 696
ØK8GØZZ	919
ØK8G3ZZ	919
ØK8G4ZZ	919
ØK8H*	36, 244, 696
ØK8HØZZ	919
ØK8H3ZZ	919
ØK8H4ZZ	919
ØK8J*	36, 244, 696
ØK8JØZZ	919
ØK8J3ZZ	919
ØK8J4ZZ	919
ØK8K*	36, 244, 696
ØK8KØZZ	919
ØK8K3ZZ	919
ØK8K4ZZ	919
ØK8L*	36, 244, 696
ØK8LØZZ	919
ØK8L3ZZ	919
ØK8L4ZZ	919
ØK8M*	36, 244, 696
ØK8MØZZ	919
ØK8M3ZZ	919
ØK8M4ZZ	919
ØK8N*	36, 244, 696
ØK8NØZZ	919
ØK8N3ZZ	919
ØK8N4ZZ	919
ØK8P*	36, 244, 696
ØK8PØZZ	919
ØK8P3ZZ	919
ØK8P4ZZ	919
ØK8Q*	36, 244, 696
ØK8QØZZ	919
ØK8Q3ZZ	919
ØK8Q4ZZ	919
ØK8R*	36, 244, 697
ØK8RØZZ	919
ØK8R3ZZ	919
ØK8R4ZZ	919
ØK8S*	36, 244, 697
ØK8SØZZ	919
ØK8S3ZZ	919
ØK8S4ZZ	919
ØK8T*	36, 244, 697
ØK8TØZZ	919
ØK8T3ZZ	919
ØK8T4ZZ	919
ØK8V*	36, 244, 697
ØK8VØZZ	919
ØK8V3ZZ	919
ØK8V4ZZ	919
ØK8W*	36, 244, 697
ØK8WØZZ	919
ØK8W3ZZ	919
ØK8W4ZZ	919
ØK9ØØØZ	79, 244, 429, 697, 1Ø66
ØK9ØØZX	36, 244, 429, 577, 1Ø66
ØK9ØØZZ	79, 244, 429, 697, 1Ø66
ØK9Ø3ZX	244
ØK9Ø4ØZ	79, 244, 429, 697, 1Ø66
ØK9Ø4ZX	244
ØK9Ø4ZZ	79, 244, 429, 697, 1Ø66
ØK91ØØZ	79, 244, 429, 697, 1Ø66
ØK91ØZX	36, 244, 429, 577, 1Ø66
ØK91ØZZ	79, 244, 429, 697, 1Ø66
ØK913ZX	244
ØK914ØZ	79, 244, 429, 697, 1Ø66
ØK914ZX	244
ØK914ZZ	79, 244, 429, 697, 1Ø66
ØK92ØØZ	79, 244, 429, 697, 1Ø66
ØK92ØZX	36, 244, 429, 577, 1Ø66
ØK92ØZZ	79, 244, 429, 697, 1Ø66
ØK923ZX	244
ØK924ØZ	79, 244, 429, 697, 1Ø66
ØK924ZX	244
ØK924ZZ	79, 244, 429, 697, 1Ø66
ØK93ØØZ	79, 244, 429, 697, 1Ø66
ØK93ØZX	36, 244, 429, 577, 1Ø66
ØK93ØZZ	79, 244, 429, 697, 1Ø66
ØK933ZX	244
ØK934ØZ	79, 244, 429, 697, 1Ø66
ØK934ZX	244
ØK934ZZ	79, 244, 429, 697, 1Ø66
ØK94ØØZ	244, 429, 697, 1Ø66
ØK94ØZX	36, 244, 429, 577, 1Ø66
ØK94ØZZ	244, 429, 697, 1Ø66
ØK943ZX	244
ØK944ØZ	244, 429, 697, 1Ø66
ØK944ZX	244
ØK944ZZ	244, 429, 697, 1Ø66
ØK95ØØZ	244, 429, 697, 1Ø66
ØK95ØZX	36, 244, 429, 577, 1Ø66
ØK95ØZZ	244, 429, 697, 1Ø66
ØK953ZX	244
ØK954ØZ	244, 429, 697, 1Ø66
ØK954ZX	245
ØK954ZZ	245, 429, 697, 1Ø66
ØK96ØØZ	245, 429, 697, 1Ø66
ØK96ØZX	36, 245, 429, 577, 1Ø66
ØK96ØZZ	245, 429, 697, 1Ø66
ØK963ZX	245

Numeric Index to Procedures

DRG Expert—Volume II

Code	Page
ØK964ØZ	245, 429, 697, 1Ø66
ØK964ZX	245
ØK964ZZ	245, 429, 697, 1Ø66
ØK97ØØZ	245, 429, 697, 1Ø66
ØK97ØZX	36, 245, 429, 577, 1Ø66
ØK97ØZZ	245, 429, 697, 1Ø66
ØK973ZX	245
ØK974ØZ	245, 429, 697, 1Ø66
ØK974ZX	245
ØK974ZZ	245, 429, 697, 1Ø66
ØK98ØØZ	245, 429, 697, 1Ø66
ØK98ØZX	36, 245, 429, 577, 1Ø66
ØK98ØZZ	245, 429, 697, 1Ø66
ØK983ZX	245
ØK984ØZ	245, 429, 697, 1Ø66
ØK984ZX	245
ØK984ZZ	245, 429, 697, 1Ø66
ØK99ØØZ	245, 429, 697, 1Ø66
ØK99ØZX	36, 245, 429, 577, 1Ø66
ØK99ØZZ	245, 429, 697, 1Ø66
ØK993ZX	245
ØK994ØZ	245, 429, 697, 1Ø66
ØK994ZX	245
ØK994ZZ	245, 429, 697, 1Ø66
ØK9BØØZ	245, 429, 697, 1Ø66
ØK9BØZX	36, 245, 429, 577, 1Ø66
ØK9BØZZ	245, 429, 697, 1Ø66
ØK9B3ZX	245
ØK9B4ØZ	245, 429, 697, 1Ø66
ØK9B4ZX	245
ØK9B4ZZ	245, 429, 697, 1Ø66
ØK9CØØZ	268, 64Ø, 919
ØK9CØZX	36, 245, 429, 577, 1Ø66
ØK9CØZZ	268, 64Ø, 919
ØK9C3ZX	245
ØK9C4ØZ	268, 64Ø, 919
ØK9C4ZX	245
ØK9DØØZ	268, 64Ø, 919
ØK9DØZX	36, 245, 429, 577, 1Ø66
ØK9DØZZ	268, 64Ø, 919
ØK9D3ZX	245
ØK9D4ØZ	268, 64Ø, 919
ØK9D4ZX	245
ØK9FØØZ	245, 429, 697, 1Ø66
ØK9FØZX	36, 245, 429, 577, 1Ø66
ØK9FØZZ	245, 429, 697, 1Ø66
ØK9F3ZX	245
ØK9F4ØZ	245, 429, 697, 1Ø66
ØK9F4ZX	245
ØK9F4ZZ	245, 429, 697, 1Ø66
ØK9GØØZ	245, 429, 697, 1Ø66
ØK9GØZX	36, 245, 429, 577, 1Ø66
ØK9GØZZ	245, 429, 697, 1Ø66
ØK9G3ZX	245
ØK9G4ØZ	245, 429, 697, 1Ø66
ØK9G4ZX	245
ØK9G4ZZ	245, 429, 697, 1Ø66
ØK9HØØZ	245, 429, 697, 1Ø66
ØK9HØZX	36, 1Ø1, 245, 429, 577, 1Ø66
ØK9HØZZ	245, 429, 697, 1Ø66
ØK9H3ZX	245
ØK9H4ØZ	245, 429, 697, 1Ø66
ØK9H4ZX	245
ØK9H4ZZ	245, 429, 697, 1Ø66
ØK9JØØZ	245, 429, 697, 1Ø66
ØK9JØZX	36, 1Ø1, 245, 429, 577, 1Ø66
ØK9JØZZ	245, 429, 697, 1Ø66
ØK9J3ZX	245
ØK9J4ØZ	245, 429, 697, 1Ø66
ØK9J4ZX	245
ØK9J4ZZ	245, 429, 697, 1Ø66
ØK9KØØZ	245, 429, 697, 1Ø66
ØK9KØZX	36, 245, 429, 577, 1Ø66
ØK9KØZZ	245, 429, 697, 1Ø66
ØK9K3ZX	245
ØK9K4ØZ	245, 429, 697, 1Ø66
ØK9K4ZX	245
ØK9K4ZZ	245, 429, 697, 1Ø66
ØK9LØØZ	245, 429, 697, 1Ø66
ØK9LØZX	36, 245, 429, 577, 1Ø66
ØK9LØZZ	245, 429, 697, 1Ø66
ØK9L3ZX	245
ØK9L4ØZ	245, 429, 697, 1Ø66
ØK9L4ZX	245
ØK9L4ZZ	245, 429, 697, 1Ø66
ØK9MØØZ	245, 429, 697, 1Ø66
ØK9MØZX	36, 245, 429, 577, 1Ø66
ØK9MØZZ	245, 429, 697, 1Ø66
ØK9M3ZX	245
ØK9M4ØZ	245, 429, 697, 1Ø66
ØK9M4ZX	245
ØK9M4ZZ	245, 429, 697, 1Ø66
ØK9NØØZ	245, 429, 697, 1Ø66
ØK9NØZX	36, 245, 429, 577, 1Ø66
ØK9NØZZ	245, 429, 697, 1Ø66
ØK9N3ZX	245
ØK9N4ØZ	245, 429, 697, 1Ø66
ØK9N4ZX	245
ØK9N4ZZ	245, 429, 697, 1Ø66
ØK9PØØZ	245, 429, 697, 1Ø66
ØK9PØZX	36, 245, 429, 577, 1Ø66
ØK9PØZZ	245, 429, 697, 1Ø66
ØK9P3ZX	245
ØK9P4ØZ	245, 429, 697, 1Ø66
ØK9P4ZX	245
ØK9P4ZZ	245, 429, 697, 1Ø66
ØK9QØØZ	245, 429, 697, 1Ø66
ØK9QØZX	36, 245, 429, 577, 1Ø67
ØK9QØZZ	245, 429, 697, 1Ø67
ØK9Q3ZX	245
ØK9Q4ØZ	245, 429, 697, 1Ø67
ØK9Q4ZX	245
ØK9Q4ZZ	245, 429, 697, 1Ø67
ØK9RØØZ	245, 429, 697, 1Ø67
ØK9RØZX	36, 245, 429, 577, 1Ø67
ØK9RØZZ	245, 429, 697, 1Ø67
ØK9R3ZX	245
ØK9R4ØZ	245, 429, 697, 1Ø67
ØK9R4ZX	245
ØK9R4ZZ	245, 429, 697, 1Ø67
ØK9SØØZ	245, 429, 697, 1Ø67
ØK9SØZX	36, 245, 429, 577, 1Ø67
ØK9SØZZ	245, 429, 697, 1Ø67
ØK9S3ZX	245
ØK9S4ØZ	245, 429, 697, 1Ø67
ØK9S4ZX	245
ØK9S4ZZ	245, 43Ø, 697, 1Ø67
ØK9TØØZ	245, 43Ø, 697, 1Ø67
ØK9TØZX	36, 245, 43Ø, 577, 1Ø67
ØK9TØZZ	245, 43Ø, 697, 1Ø67
ØK9T3ZX	245
ØK9T4ØZ	245, 43Ø, 697, 1Ø67
ØK9T4ZX	245
ØK9T4ZZ	245, 43Ø, 697, 1Ø67
ØK9VØØZ	245, 43Ø, 697, 1Ø67
ØK9VØZX	36, 245, 43Ø, 577, 1Ø67
ØK9VØZZ	245, 43Ø, 697, 1Ø67
ØK9V3ZX	245
ØK9V4ØZ	245, 43Ø, 697, 1Ø67
ØK9V4ZX	245
ØK9V4ZZ	245, 43Ø, 697, 1Ø67
ØK9WØØZ	245, 43Ø, 697, 1Ø67
ØK9WØZX	36, 245, 43Ø, 577, 1Ø67
ØK9WØZZ	245, 43Ø, 697, 1Ø67
ØK9W3ZX	245
ØK9W4ØZ	245, 43Ø, 697, 1Ø67
ØK9W4ZX	245
ØK9W4ZZ	245, 43Ø, 697, 1Ø67
ØKBØ*	245
ØKBØØZX	36, 43Ø, 577, 1Ø67
ØKBØØZZ	36, 43Ø, 697, 919
ØKBØ3ZZ	36, 43Ø, 697, 919
ØKBØ4ZZ	36, 43Ø, 697, 919
ØKB1*	245
ØKB1ØZX	36, 43Ø, 577, 1Ø67
ØKB1ØZZ	36, 43Ø, 697, 919
ØKB13ZZ	36, 43Ø, 697, 919
ØKB14ZZ	36, 43Ø, 697, 919
ØKB2*	245
ØKB2ØZX	36, 43Ø, 577, 1Ø67
ØKB2ØZZ	36, 43Ø, 697, 919
ØKB23ZZ	36, 43Ø, 697, 919
ØKB24ZZ	36, 43Ø, 697, 919
ØKB3*	245
ØKB3ØZX	36, 43Ø, 577, 1Ø67
ØKB3ØZZ	36, 43Ø, 697, 919
ØKB33ZZ	36, 43Ø, 697, 919
ØKB34ZZ	36, 43Ø, 697, 919
ØKB4*	245
ØKB4ØZX	36, 43Ø, 577, 1Ø67
ØKB4ØZZ	36, 43Ø, 697, 919
ØKB43ZZ	36, 43Ø, 697, 919
ØKB44ZZ	36, 43Ø, 697, 919
ØKB5*	245
ØKB5ØZX	36, 43Ø, 577, 1Ø67
ØKB5ØZZ	36, 43Ø, 697, 919
ØKB53ZZ	36, 43Ø, 697, 919
ØKB54ZZ	36, 43Ø, 697, 919
ØKB6*	245
ØKB6ØZX	36, 43Ø, 577, 1Ø67
ØKB6ØZZ	36, 43Ø, 697, 919
ØKB63ZZ	36, 43Ø, 697, 919
ØKB64ZZ	36, 43Ø, 697, 919
ØKB7*	245
ØKB7ØZX	36, 43Ø, 577, 1Ø67
ØKB7ØZZ	36, 43Ø, 697, 919
ØKB73ZZ	36, 43Ø, 697, 919
ØKB74ZZ	36, 43Ø, 697, 919
ØKB8*	245
ØKB8ØZX	36, 43Ø, 577, 1Ø67
ØKB8ØZZ	36, 43Ø, 697, 919
ØKB83ZZ	36, 43Ø, 697, 919
ØKB84ZZ	36, 43Ø, 697, 919
ØKB9*	245
ØKB9ØZX	36, 43Ø, 577, 1Ø67
ØKB9ØZZ	36, 43Ø, 697, 919
ØKB93ZZ	36, 43Ø, 697, 919
ØKB94ZZ	36, 43Ø, 697, 919
ØKBB*	245
ØKBBØZX	36, 43Ø, 577, 1Ø67
ØKBBØZZ	36, 43Ø, 697, 919
ØKBB3ZZ	36, 43Ø, 697, 919
ØKBB4ZZ	36, 43Ø, 697, 919
ØKBCØZX	36, 245, 43Ø, 577, 1Ø67
ØKBCØZZ	268, 64Ø, 919
ØKBC3ZX	245
ØKBC3ZZ	268, 64Ø, 919
ØKBC4ZX	245
ØKBC4ZZ	268, 64Ø, 919
ØKBDØZX	36, 245, 43Ø, 577, 1Ø67
ØKBDØZZ	268, 64Ø, 919
ØKBD3ZX	245
ØKBD3ZZ	268, 64Ø, 919
ØKBD4ZX	245
ØKBD4ZZ	268, 64Ø, 919
ØKBF*	245
ØKBFØZX	36, 43Ø, 577, 1Ø67
ØKBFØZZ	36, 43Ø, 697, 919
ØKBF3ZZ	36, 43Ø, 697, 919
ØKBF4ZZ	36, 43Ø, 697, 919
ØKBG*	245
ØKBGØZX	36, 43Ø, 577, 1Ø67
ØKBGØZZ	36, 43Ø, 697, 919
ØKBG3ZZ	36, 43Ø, 697, 919
ØKBG4ZZ	36, 43Ø, 697, 919
ØKBH*	245
ØKBHØZX	36, 1Ø1, 43Ø, 577, 1Ø67
ØKBHØZZ	36, 43Ø, 697, 919
ØKBH3ZZ	36, 43Ø, 697, 919
ØKBH4ZZ	36, 43Ø, 697, 919
ØKBJ*	245
ØKBJØZX	36, 1Ø1, 43Ø, 577, 1Ø67
ØKBJØZZ	36, 43Ø, 697, 919
ØKBJ3ZZ	36, 43Ø, 697, 919
ØKBJ4ZZ	36, 43Ø, 697, 919
ØKBK*	245
ØKBKØZX	36, 43Ø, 577, 1Ø67
ØKBKØZZ	36, 43Ø, 697, 919
ØKBK3ZZ	36, 43Ø, 697, 919
ØKBK4ZZ	36, 43Ø, 697, 919
ØKBL*	245
ØKBLØZX	36, 43Ø, 577, 1Ø67
ØKBLØZZ	37, 43Ø, 697, 919
ØKBL3ZZ	37, 43Ø, 697, 919
ØKBL4ZZ	37, 43Ø, 697, 919
ØKBM*	245
ØKBMØZX	37, 43Ø, 577, 1Ø67
ØKBMØZZ	37, 43Ø, 697, 919
ØKBM3ZZ	37, 43Ø, 697, 919
ØKBM4ZZ	37, 43Ø, 697, 919
ØKBN*	245
ØKBNØZX	37, 43Ø, 577, 1Ø67
ØKBNØZZ	37, 43Ø, 482, 697, 919
ØKBN3ZZ	37, 43Ø, 697, 92Ø
ØKBN4ZZ	37, 43Ø, 697, 92Ø
ØKBP*	245
ØKBPØZX	37, 43Ø, 577, 1Ø67
ØKBPØZZ	37, 43Ø, 482, 697, 92Ø
ØKBP3ZZ	37, 43Ø, 697, 92Ø
ØKBP4ZZ	37, 43Ø, 697, 92Ø
ØKBQ*	246
ØKBQØZX	37, 43Ø, 577, 1Ø67
ØKBQØZZ	37, 43Ø, 697, 92Ø
ØKBQ3ZZ	37, 43Ø, 697, 92Ø
ØKBQ4ZZ	37, 43Ø, 697, 92Ø
ØKBR*	246
ØKBRØZX	37, 43Ø, 577, 1Ø67
ØKBRØZZ	37, 43Ø, 697, 92Ø
ØKBR3ZZ	37, 43Ø, 697, 92Ø
ØKBR4ZZ	37, 43Ø, 698, 92Ø
ØKBS*	246
ØKBSØZX	37, 43Ø, 577, 1Ø67
ØKBSØZZ	37, 43Ø, 482, 698, 92Ø
ØKBS3ZZ	37, 43Ø, 698, 92Ø
ØKBS4ZZ	37, 43Ø, 698, 92Ø
ØKBT*	246
ØKBTØZX	37, 43Ø, 577, 1Ø67
ØKBTØZZ	37, 43Ø, 482, 698, 92Ø
ØKBT3ZZ	37, 43Ø, 698, 92Ø
ØKBT4ZZ	37, 43Ø, 698, 92Ø
ØKBV*	246
ØKBVØZX	37, 43Ø, 577, 1Ø67
ØKBVØZZ	37, 43Ø, 482, 698, 92Ø
ØKBV3ZZ	37, 43Ø, 698, 92Ø
ØKBV4ZZ	37, 43Ø, 698, 92Ø
ØKBW*	246
ØKBWØZX	37, 43Ø, 577, 1Ø67
ØKBWØZZ	37, 43Ø, 482, 698, 92Ø
ØKBW3ZZ	37, 43Ø, 698, 92Ø
ØKBW4ZZ	37, 43Ø, 698, 92Ø
ØKCØ*	79, 246, 698
ØKCØØZZ	43Ø, 1Ø67
ØKCØ3ZZ	43Ø, 1Ø67
ØKCØ4ZZ	43Ø, 1Ø67
ØKC1*	79, 246, 698
ØKC1ØZZ	43Ø, 1Ø67
ØKC13ZZ	43Ø, 1Ø67
ØKC14ZZ	43Ø, 1Ø67
ØKC2*	79, 246, 698
ØKC2ØZZ	43Ø, 1Ø67
ØKC23ZZ	43Ø, 1Ø67
ØKC24ZZ	43Ø, 1Ø67
ØKC3*	79, 246, 698
ØKC3ØZZ	43Ø, 1Ø67
ØKC33ZZ	43Ø, 1Ø67
ØKC34ZZ	43Ø, 1Ø67
ØKC4*	246, 698
ØKC4ØZZ	43Ø, 1Ø67
ØKC43ZZ	43Ø, 1Ø67
ØKC44ZZ	43Ø, 1Ø67
ØKC5*	246, 698
ØKC5ØZZ	43Ø, 1Ø67
ØKC53ZZ	43Ø, 1Ø67
ØKC54ZZ	43Ø, 1Ø67
ØKC6*	246, 698
ØKC6ØZZ	43Ø, 1Ø67
ØKC63ZZ	43Ø, 1Ø67
ØKC64ZZ	43Ø, 1Ø67
ØKC7*	246, 698
ØKC7ØZZ	43Ø, 1Ø67
ØKC73ZZ	43Ø, 1Ø67
ØKC74ZZ	43Ø, 1Ø67
ØKC8*	246, 698
ØKC8ØZZ	43Ø, 1Ø67
ØKC83ZZ	43Ø, 1Ø67
ØKC84ZZ	43Ø, 1Ø67
ØKC9*	246, 698
ØKC9ØZZ	43Ø, 1Ø67
ØKC93ZZ	43Ø, 1Ø67
ØKC94ZZ	43Ø, 1Ø67
ØKCB*	246, 698
ØKCBØZZ	43Ø, 1Ø67
ØKCB3ZZ	43Ø, 1Ø67
ØKCB4ZZ	43Ø, 1Ø67
ØKCC*	268
ØKCCØZZ	64Ø, 92Ø
ØKCC3ZZ	64Ø, 92Ø
ØKCC4ZZ	64Ø, 92Ø
ØKCD*	268
ØKCDØZZ	64Ø, 92Ø
ØKCD3ZZ	64Ø, 92Ø
ØKCD4ZZ	64Ø, 92Ø
ØKCF*	246, 698
ØKCFØZZ	43Ø, 1Ø67
ØKCF3ZZ	43Ø, 1Ø67
ØKCF4ZZ	43Ø, 1Ø67
ØKCG*	246, 698
ØKCGØZZ	43Ø, 1Ø67
ØKCG3ZZ	43Ø, 1Ø67
ØKCG4ZZ	43Ø, 1Ø67
ØKCH*	246, 698
ØKCHØZZ	43Ø, 1Ø67
ØKCH3ZZ	43Ø, 1Ø67
ØKCH4ZZ	43Ø, 1Ø67
ØKCJ*	246, 698
ØKCJØZZ	43Ø, 1Ø67
ØKCJ3ZZ	43Ø, 1Ø67
ØKCJ4ZZ	43Ø, 1Ø67
ØKCK*	246, 698
ØKCKØZZ	43Ø, 1Ø67
ØKCK3ZZ	43Ø, 1Ø67
ØKCK4ZZ	43Ø, 1Ø67
ØKCL*	246, 698
ØKCLØZZ	43Ø, 1Ø67
ØKCL3ZZ	43Ø, 1Ø67
ØKCL4ZZ	43Ø, 1Ø67
ØKCM*	246, 698
ØKCMØZZ	43Ø, 1Ø67
ØKCM3ZZ	431, 1Ø67
ØKCM4ZZ	431, 1Ø67
ØKCN*	246, 698
ØKCNØZZ	431, 1Ø67
ØKCN3ZZ	431, 1Ø67
ØKCN4ZZ	431, 1Ø67
ØKCP*	246, 698
ØKCPØZZ	431, 1Ø67
ØKCP3ZZ	431, 1Ø67
ØKCP4ZZ	431, 1Ø67
ØKCQ*	246, 698
ØKCQØZZ	431, 1Ø67
ØKCQ3ZZ	431, 1Ø67
ØKCQ4ZZ	431, 1Ø67
ØKCR*	246, 698
ØKCRØZZ	431, 1Ø67
ØKCR3ZZ	431, 1Ø67
ØKCR4ZZ	431, 1Ø67
ØKCS*	246, 698
ØKCSØZZ	431, 1Ø67
ØKCS3ZZ	431, 1Ø67
ØKCS4ZZ	431, 1Ø67
ØKCT*	246, 698
ØKCTØZZ	431, 1Ø67
ØKCT3ZZ	431, 1Ø67
ØKCT4ZZ	431, 1Ø67
ØKCV*	246, 698
ØKCVØZZ	431, 1Ø67
ØKCV3ZZ	431, 1Ø67
ØKCV4ZZ	431, 1Ø67
ØKCW*	246, 698
ØKCWØZZ	431, 1Ø67
ØKCW3ZZ	431, 1Ø67
ØKCW4ZZ	431, 1Ø67
ØKDØØZZ	37, 246, 431, 698, 92Ø
ØKD1ØZZ	37, 246, 431, 698, 92Ø
ØKD2ØZZ	37, 246, 431, 698, 92Ø
ØKD3ØZZ	37, 246, 431, 698, 92Ø
ØKD4ØZZ	37, 246, 431, 698, 92Ø
ØKD5ØZZ	37, 246, 431, 698, 92Ø
ØKD6ØZZ	37, 246, 431, 698, 92Ø
ØKD7ØZZ	37, 246, 431, 698, 92Ø
ØKD8ØZZ	37, 246, 431, 698, 92Ø
ØKD9ØZZ	37, 246, 431, 698, 92Ø
ØKDBØZZ	37, 246, 431, 698, 92Ø
ØKDCØZZ	268, 64Ø, 92Ø
ØKDDØZZ	268, 64Ø, 92Ø
ØKDFØZZ	37, 246, 431, 698, 92Ø
ØKDGØZZ	37, 246, 431, 698, 92Ø
ØKDHØZZ	37, 246, 431, 698, 92Ø
ØKDJØZZ	37, 246, 431, 698, 92Ø
ØKDKØZZ	37, 246, 431, 698, 92Ø
ØKDLØZZ	37, 246, 431, 698, 92Ø
ØKDMØZZ	37, 246, 431, 698, 92Ø
ØKDNØZZ	37, 246, 431, 698, 92Ø
ØKDPØZZ	37, 246, 431, 698, 92Ø
ØKDQØZZ	37, 246, 431, 698, 92Ø
ØKDRØZZ	37, 246, 431, 698, 92Ø

Numeric Index to Procedures

Code	Page
0KDS0ZZ	37, 246, 431, 698, 920
0KDT0ZZ	37, 246, 431, 698, 920
0KDV0ZZ	37, 246, 431, 698, 920
0KDW0ZZ	37, 246, 431, 698, 920
0KHX0MZ	37, 246, 698, 920
0KHX0YZ	37, 246, 698, 920
0KHX3MZ	37, 246, 698, 920
0KHX4MZ	37, 246, 698, 920
0KHY0MZ	37, 246, 698, 920
0KHY0YZ	37, 246, 698, 920
0KHY3MZ	37, 246, 698, 920
0KHY4MZ	37, 246, 698, 920
0KJX0ZZ	246
0KJX4ZZ	246
0KJY0ZZ	246
0KJY4ZZ	246
0KM*	37
0KM0*	246, 698
0KM00ZZ	920
0KM04ZZ	920
0KM1*	246, 698
0KM10ZZ	920
0KM14ZZ	920
0KM2*	246, 698
0KM20ZZ	920
0KM24ZZ	920
0KM3*	246, 698
0KM30ZZ	920
0KM34ZZ	920
0KM4*	246, 698
0KM40ZZ	920
0KM44ZZ	920
0KM5*	246, 698
0KM50ZZ	920
0KM54ZZ	920
0KM6*	246, 698
0KM60ZZ	920
0KM64ZZ	920
0KM7*	246, 698
0KM70ZZ	920
0KM74ZZ	920
0KM8*	246, 698
0KM80ZZ	920
0KM84ZZ	920
0KM9*	246, 698
0KM90ZZ	920
0KM94ZZ	920
0KMB*	246, 698
0KMB0ZZ	920
0KMB4ZZ	920
0KMC*	268
0KMC0ZZ	640, 920
0KMC4ZZ	640, 920
0KMD*	268
0KMD0ZZ	640, 920
0KMD4ZZ	640, 920
0KMF*	246, 698
0KMF0ZZ	920
0KMF4ZZ	920
0KMG*	246, 698
0KMG0ZZ	920
0KMG4ZZ	920
0KMH*	246, 698
0KMH0ZZ	920
0KMH4ZZ	920
0KMJ*	246, 698
0KMJ0ZZ	920
0KMJ4ZZ	920
0KMK*	246, 698
0KMK0ZZ	920
0KMK4ZZ	920
0KML*	246, 698
0KML0ZZ	920
0KML4ZZ	920
0KMM*	246, 698
0KMM0ZZ	920
0KMM4ZZ	920
0KMN*	246, 698
0KMN0ZZ	920
0KMN4ZZ	920
0KMP*	246, 698
0KMP0ZZ	920
0KMP4ZZ	920
0KMQ*	246, 698
0KMQ0ZZ	920
0KMQ4ZZ	920
0KMR*	246, 698
0KMR0ZZ	920
0KMR4ZZ	920
0KMS*	246, 698
0KMS0ZZ	920
0KMS4ZZ	920
0KMT*	246, 698
0KMT0ZZ	920
0KMT4ZZ	920
0KMV*	246, 698
0KMV0ZZ	920
0KMV4ZZ	920
0KMW*	246, 698
0KMW0ZZ	920
0KMW4ZZ	920
0KN00ZZ	246
0KN03ZZ	246
0KN04ZZ	246
0KN10ZZ	246
0KN13ZZ	246
0KN14ZZ	246
0KN20ZZ	246
0KN23ZZ	246
0KN24ZZ	246
0KN30ZZ	246
0KN33ZZ	246
0KN34ZZ	246
0KN40ZZ	246
0KN43ZZ	246
0KN44ZZ	246
0KN50ZZ	246
0KN53ZZ	246
0KN54ZZ	246
0KN60ZZ	246
0KN63ZZ	246
0KN64ZZ	246
0KN70ZZ	246
0KN73ZZ	246
0KN74ZZ	246
0KN80ZZ	246
0KN83ZZ	246
0KN84ZZ	246
0KN90ZZ	246
0KN93ZZ	246
0KN94ZZ	246
0KNB0ZZ	246
0KNB3ZZ	246
0KNB4ZZ	246
0KNC0ZZ	268, 431, 640, 920
0KNC3ZZ	268, 431, 640, 920
0KNC4ZZ	268, 431, 640, 920
0KND0ZZ	268, 431, 640, 920
0KND3ZZ	268, 431, 640, 920
0KND4ZZ	268, 431, 640, 920
0KNF0ZZ	246
0KNF3ZZ	246
0KNF4ZZ	246
0KNG0ZZ	246
0KNG3ZZ	246
0KNG4ZZ	246
0KNH0ZZ	246
0KNH3ZZ	246
0KNH4ZZ	246
0KNJ0ZZ	246
0KNJ3ZZ	246
0KNJ4ZZ	246
0KNK0ZZ	246
0KNK3ZZ	246
0KNK4ZZ	246
0KNL0ZZ	246
0KNL3ZZ	246
0KNL4ZZ	246
0KNM0ZZ	246
0KNM3ZZ	246
0KNM4ZZ	246
0KNN0ZZ	246
0KNN3ZZ	246
0KNN4ZZ	246
0KNP0ZZ	246
0KNP3ZZ	246
0KNP4ZZ	246
0KNQ0ZZ	246
0KNQ3ZZ	246
0KNQ4ZZ	246
0KNR0ZZ	246
0KNR3ZZ	246
0KNR4ZZ	246
0KNS0ZZ	246
0KNS3ZZ	246
0KNS4ZZ	246
0KNT0ZZ	246
0KNT3ZZ	246
0KNT4ZZ	246
0KNV0ZZ	246
0KNV3ZZ	246
0KNV4ZZ	246
0KNW0ZZ	246
0KNW3ZZ	246
0KNW4ZZ	246
0KPX00Z	247, 431, 698, 1067
0KPX07Z	247, 431, 698, 1067
0KPX0JZ	247, 431, 698, 1067
0KPX0KZ	247, 431, 698, 1067
0KPX0MZ	37, 247, 698, 920
0KPX0YZ	247, 431, 698, 1067
0KPX30Z	247, 431, 698, 1067
0KPX37Z	247, 431, 698, 1067
0KPX3JZ	247, 431, 698, 1067
0KPX3KZ	247, 431, 698, 1067
0KPX3MZ	37, 247, 698, 920
0KPX40Z	247, 431, 698, 1067
0KPX47Z	247, 431, 698, 1067
0KPX4JZ	247, 431, 698, 1067
0KPX4KZ	247, 431, 698, 1067
0KPX4MZ	37, 247, 698, 920
0KPY00Z	247, 431, 698, 920, 1067
0KPY07Z	247, 431, 698, 1067
0KPY0JZ	247, 431, 698, 920, 1067
0KPY0KZ	247, 431, 698, 1067
0KPY0MZ	37, 247, 698, 920
0KPY0YZ	247, 431, 698, 920, 1067
0KPY30Z	247, 431, 698, 920, 1067
0KPY37Z	247, 431, 698, 1067
0KPY3JZ	247, 431, 698, 920, 1067
0KPY3KZ	247, 431, 698, 1067
0KPY3MZ	37, 247, 698, 920
0KPY40Z	247, 431, 698, 920, 1067
0KPY47Z	247, 431, 698, 1067
0KPY4JZ	247, 431, 698, 920, 1067
0KPY4KZ	247, 431, 698, 1067
0KPY4MZ	37, 247, 698, 920
0KQ0*	37, 247, 698
0KQ00ZZ	431, 920, 1067
0KQ03ZZ	431, 920, 1067
0KQ04ZZ	431, 920, 1067
0KQ1*	37, 247, 698
0KQ10ZZ	431, 920, 1067
0KQ13ZZ	431, 920, 1067
0KQ14ZZ	431, 920, 1067
0KQ2*	37, 247, 698
0KQ20ZZ	431, 920, 1067
0KQ23ZZ	431, 920, 1067
0KQ24ZZ	431, 920, 1067
0KQ3*	37, 247, 698
0KQ30ZZ	431, 920, 1067
0KQ33ZZ	431, 920, 1067
0KQ34ZZ	431, 920, 1067
0KQ4*	37, 247, 698
0KQ40ZZ	431, 920, 1067
0KQ43ZZ	431, 920, 1068
0KQ44ZZ	431, 920, 1068
0KQ5*	37, 247, 495, 698
0KQ50ZZ	431, 920, 1068
0KQ53ZZ	431, 920, 1068
0KQ54ZZ	431, 920, 1068
0KQ6*	37, 247, 495, 698
0KQ60ZZ	431, 920, 1068
0KQ63ZZ	431, 920, 1068
0KQ64ZZ	431, 920, 1068
0KQ7*	37, 247, 495, 698
0KQ70ZZ	431, 920, 1068
0KQ73ZZ	431, 920, 1068
0KQ74ZZ	431, 920, 1068
0KQ8*	37, 247, 495, 698
0KQ80ZZ	431, 920, 1068
0KQ83ZZ	431, 920, 1068
0KQ84ZZ	431, 920, 1068
0KQ9*	37, 247, 495, 698
0KQ90ZZ	431, 920, 1068
0KQ93ZZ	431, 920, 1068
0KQ94ZZ	431, 920, 1068
0KQB*	37, 247, 495, 698
0KQB0ZZ	431, 920, 1068
0KQB3ZZ	431, 920, 1068
0KQB4ZZ	431, 920, 1068
0KQC*	268
0KQC0ZZ	640, 920, 1068
0KQC3ZZ	640, 921, 1068
0KQC4ZZ	640, 921, 1068
0KQD*	269
0KQD0ZZ	640, 921, 1068
0KQD3ZZ	640, 921, 1068
0KQD4ZZ	640, 921, 1068
0KQF*	37, 247, 698
0KQF0ZZ	431, 921, 1068
0KQF3ZZ	431, 921, 1068
0KQF4ZZ	431, 921, 1068
0KQG*	37, 247, 698
0KQG0ZZ	431, 921, 1068
0KQG3ZZ	431, 921, 1068
0KQG4ZZ	431, 921, 1068
0KQH*	37, 247, 698
0KQH0ZZ	431, 921, 1068
0KQH3ZZ	431, 921, 1068
0KQH4ZZ	431, 921, 1068
0KQJ*	37, 247, 698
0KQJ0ZZ	431, 921, 1068
0KQJ3ZZ	431, 921, 1068
0KQJ4ZZ	431, 921, 1068
0KQK*	37, 247, 698
0KQK0ZZ	431, 921, 1068
0KQK3ZZ	431, 921, 1068
0KQK4ZZ	431, 921, 1068
0KQL*	37, 247, 698
0KQL0ZZ	431, 921, 1068
0KQL3ZZ	431, 921, 1068
0KQL4ZZ	431, 921, 1068
0KQM*	37, 247, 698
0KQM0ZZ	431, 544, 921, 1068
0KQM3ZZ	431, 921, 1068
0KQM4ZZ	431, 921, 1068
0KQN*	37, 247, 495, 698
0KQN0ZZ	431, 921, 1068
0KQN3ZZ	431, 921, 1068
0KQN4ZZ	431, 921, 1068
0KQP*	37, 247, 495, 698
0KQP0ZZ	431, 921, 1068
0KQP3ZZ	431, 921, 1068
0KQP4ZZ	431, 921, 1068
0KQQ*	247, 698
0KQQ0ZZ	921
0KQQ3ZZ	921
0KQQ4ZZ	921
0KQR*	247, 698
0KQR0ZZ	921
0KQR3ZZ	921
0KQR4ZZ	921
0KQS*	37, 247, 495, 698
0KQS0ZZ	431, 921, 1068
0KQS3ZZ	431, 921, 1068
0KQS4ZZ	431, 921, 1068
0KQT*	37, 247, 495, 698
0KQT0ZZ	431, 921, 1068
0KQT3ZZ	431, 921, 1068
0KQT4ZZ	431, 921, 1068
0KQV*	37, 247, 495, 698
0KQV0ZZ	431, 921, 1068
0KQV3ZZ	431, 921, 1068
0KQV4ZZ	431, 921, 1068
0KQW*	37, 247, 495, 698
0KQW0ZZ	431, 921, 1068
0KQW3ZZ	431, 921, 1068
0KQW4ZZ	431, 921, 1068
0KR007Z	37, 247, 431, 698, 921, 1068
0KR00JZ	37, 247, 431, 698, 921, 1068
0KR00KZ	37, 247, 431, 698, 921, 1068
0KR047Z	37, 247, 431, 698, 921, 1068
0KR04JZ	37, 247, 431, 698, 921, 1068
0KR04KZ	37, 247, 431, 698, 921, 1068
0KR107Z	37, 247, 431, 698, 921, 1068
0KR10JZ	37, 247, 431, 698, 921, 1068
0KR10KZ	37, 247, 431, 698, 921, 1068
0KR147Z	37, 247, 431, 698, 921, 1068
0KR14JZ	37, 247, 431, 698, 921, 1068
0KR14KZ	37, 247, 431, 698, 921, 1068
0KR207Z	37, 247, 431, 698, 921, 1068
0KR20JZ	37, 247, 431, 698, 921, 1068
0KR20KZ	37, 247, 431, 698, 921, 1068
0KR247Z	37, 247, 431, 698, 921, 1068
0KR24JZ	37, 247, 431, 698, 921, 1068
0KR24KZ	37, 247, 431, 699, 921, 1068
0KR307Z	37, 247, 432, 699, 921, 1068
0KR30JZ	37, 247, 432, 699, 921, 1068
0KR30KZ	37, 247, 432, 699, 921, 1068
0KR347Z	37, 247, 432, 699, 921, 1068
0KR34JZ	37, 247, 432, 699, 921, 1068
0KR34KZ	37, 247, 432, 699, 921, 1068
0KR407Z	37, 247, 432, 699, 921, 1068
0KR40JZ	37, 247, 432, 699, 921, 1068
0KR40KZ	37, 247, 432, 699, 921, 1068
0KR447Z	37, 247, 432, 699, 921, 1068
0KR44JZ	37, 247, 432, 699, 921, 1068
0KR44KZ	37, 247, 432, 699, 921, 1068
0KR507Z	37, 247, 432, 495, 699, 921, 1068
0KR50JZ	37, 247, 432, 495, 699, 921, 1068
0KR50KZ	37, 247, 432, 495, 699, 921, 1068
0KR547Z	37, 247, 432, 495, 699, 921, 1068
0KR54JZ	37, 247, 432, 495, 699, 921, 1068
0KR54KZ	37, 247, 432, 495, 699, 921, 1068
0KR607Z	37, 247, 432, 495, 699, 921, 1068
0KR60JZ	37, 247, 432, 495, 699, 921, 1068
0KR60KZ	37, 247, 432, 495, 699, 921, 1068
0KR647Z	37, 247, 432, 495, 699, 921, 1068
0KR64JZ	37, 247, 432, 495, 699, 921, 1068
0KR64KZ	37, 247, 432, 495, 699, 921, 1068
0KR707Z	37, 247, 432, 495, 699, 921, 1068
0KR70JZ	37, 247, 432, 495, 699, 921, 1068
0KR70KZ	37, 247, 432, 495, 699, 921, 1068
0KR747Z	37, 247, 432, 495, 699, 921, 1068
0KR74JZ	37, 247, 432, 495, 699, 921, 1068
0KR74KZ	37, 247, 432, 495, 699, 921, 1068
0KR807Z	37, 247, 432, 495, 699, 921, 1068
0KR80JZ	37, 247, 432, 495, 699, 921, 1068
0KR80KZ	37, 247, 432, 495, 699, 921, 1068
0KR847Z	37, 247, 432, 495, 699, 921, 1068
0KR84JZ	37, 247, 432, 495, 699, 921, 1068
0KR84KZ	37, 247, 432, 495, 699, 921, 1068
0KR907Z	37, 247, 432, 495, 699, 921, 1068
0KR90JZ	37, 247, 432, 495, 699, 921, 1068
0KR90KZ	37, 247, 432, 495, 699, 921, 1068
0KR947Z	37, 247, 432, 495, 699, 921, 1068
0KR94JZ	37, 247, 432, 495, 699, 921, 1068
0KR94KZ	37, 247, 432, 495, 699, 921, 1068
0KRB07Z	37, 247, 432, 495, 699, 921, 1068
0KRB0JZ	37, 247, 432, 495, 699, 921, 1068
0KRB0KZ	37, 247, 432, 495, 699, 921, 1068
0KRB47Z	37, 247, 432, 495, 699, 921, 1068
0KRB4JZ	37, 247, 432, 495, 699, 921, 1068
0KRB4KZ	37, 247, 432, 495, 699, 921, 1068
0KRC07Z	269, 640, 921, 1068
0KRC0JZ	269, 640, 921, 1068
0KRC0KZ	269, 640, 921, 1068
0KRC47Z	269, 640, 921, 1068
0KRC4JZ	269, 640, 921, 1068
0KRC4KZ	269, 640, 921, 1068
0KRD07Z	269, 640, 921, 1068
0KRD0JZ	269, 640, 921, 1068
0KRD0KZ	269, 640, 921, 1068
0KRD47Z	269, 640, 921, 1068
0KRD4JZ	269, 640, 921, 1068
0KRD4KZ	269, 640, 921, 1068
0KRF07Z	37, 247, 432, 699, 921, 1068
0KRF0JZ	37, 247, 432, 699, 921, 1068
0KRF0KZ	37, 247, 432, 699, 921, 1068
0KRF47Z	37, 247, 432, 699, 921, 1068
0KRF4JZ	38, 247, 432, 699, 921, 1068
0KRF4KZ	38, 247, 432, 699, 921, 1068
0KRG07Z	38, 247, 432, 699, 921, 1068
0KRG0JZ	38, 247, 432, 699, 921, 1068
0KRG0KZ	38, 247, 432, 699, 921, 1068
0KRG47Z	38, 247, 432, 699, 921, 1068
0KRG4JZ	38, 247, 432, 699, 921, 1068
0KRG4KZ	38, 247, 432, 699, 921, 1068
0KRH07Z	38, 247, 432, 699, 921, 1068
0KRH0JZ	38, 247, 432, 699, 921, 1068
0KRH0KZ	38, 247, 432, 699, 921, 1068
0KRH47Z	38, 247, 432, 699, 921, 1068
0KRH4JZ	38, 247, 432, 699, 921, 1068
0KRH4KZ	38, 247, 432, 699, 921, 1068
0KRJ07Z	38, 247, 432, 699, 921, 1068
0KRJ0JZ	38, 247, 432, 699, 921, 1068

Code	Page	Code	Page	Code	Page	Code	Page	Code	Page	Code	Page
ØKRJØKZ	38, 247, 432, 699, 921, 1068	ØKRTØ7Z	38, 248, 432, 495, 699, 922, 1069	ØKSL4ZZ	922	ØKTP*	38, 248, 700	ØKUBØ7Z	433	ØKURØKZ	433
ØKRJ47Z	38, 247, 432, 699, 921, 1068	ØKRTØJZ	38, 248, 432, 495, 699, 922, 1069	ØKSM*	248, 495, 699	ØKTPØZZ	432	ØKUBØJZ	433	ØKUR47Z	433
ØKRJ4JZ	38, 247, 432, 699, 921, 1068	ØKRTØKZ	38, 248, 432, 495, 699, 922, 1069	ØKSMØZZ	922	ØKTP4ZZ	432	ØKUBØKZ	433	ØKUR4JZ	433
ØKRJ4KZ	38, 247, 432, 699, 921, 1068	ØKRT47Z	38, 248, 432, 495, 699, 922, 1069	ØKSM4ZZ	922	ØKTQ*	38, 248, 700	ØKUB47Z	433	ØKUR4KZ	433
ØKRKØ7Z	38, 247, 432, 699, 921, 1068	ØKRT4JZ	38, 248, 432, 495, 699, 922, 1069	ØKSN*	248, 495, 699	ØKTQØZZ	432	ØKUB4JZ	433	ØKUS*	248, 700
ØKRKØJZ	38, 247, 432, 699, 921, 1068	ØKRT4KZ	38, 248, 432, 495, 699, 922, 1069	ØKSNØZZ	922	ØKTQ4ZZ	432	ØKUB4KZ	433	ØKUSØ7Z	433
ØKRKØKZ	38, 247, 432, 699, 921, 1068	ØKRVØ7Z	38, 248, 432, 495, 699, 922, 1069	ØKSN4ZZ	922	ØKTR*	38, 248, 700	ØKUC*	269	ØKUSØJZ	433
ØKRK47Z	38, 247, 432, 699, 921, 1068	ØKRVØJZ	38, 248, 432, 495, 699, 922, 1069	ØKSP*	248, 495, 699	ØKTRØZZ	432	ØKUCØ7Z	433, 640, 922	ØKUSØKZ	433
ØKRK4JZ	38, 247, 432, 699, 921, 1068	ØKRVØKZ	38, 248, 432, 495, 699, 922, 1069	ØKSPØZZ	922	ØKTR4ZZ	432	ØKUCØJZ	433, 640, 922	ØKUS47Z	433
ØKRK4KZ	38, 247, 432, 699, 921, 1068	ØKRV47Z	38, 248, 432, 495, 699, 922, 1069	ØKSP4ZZ	922	ØKTS*	38, 248, 700	ØKUCØKZ	433, 640, 922	ØKUS4JZ	433
ØKRLØ7Z	38, 247, 432, 699, 921, 1068	ØKRV4JZ	38, 248, 432, 495, 699, 922, 1069	ØKSQ*	248, 495, 699	ØKTSØZZ	432	ØKUC47Z	433, 640, 922	ØKUS4KZ	433
ØKRLØJZ	38, 247, 432, 699, 921, 1068	ØKRV4KZ	38, 248, 432, 495, 699, 922, 1069	ØKSQØZZ	922	ØKTS4ZZ	432	ØKUC4JZ	433, 640, 922	ØKUT*	248, 700
ØKRLØKZ	38, 247, 432, 699, 921, 1069	ØKRWØ7Z	38, 248, 432, 495, 699, 922, 1069	ØKSQ4ZZ	922	ØKTT*	38, 248, 700	ØKUC4KZ	433, 640, 922	ØKUTØ7Z	433
ØKRL47Z	38, 247, 432, 699, 921, 1069	ØKRWØJZ	38, 248, 432, 495, 699, 922, 1069	ØKSR*	248, 495, 699	ØKTTØZZ	432	ØKUD*	269	ØKUTØJZ	433
ØKRL4JZ	38, 247, 432, 699, 921, 1069	ØKRWØKZ	38, 248, 432, 495, 699, 922, 1069	ØKSRØZZ	922	ØKTT4ZZ	432	ØKUDØ7Z	433, 640, 922	ØKUTØKZ	433
ØKRL4KZ	38, 247, 432, 699, 921, 1069	ØKRW47Z	38, 248, 432, 495, 699, 922, 1069	ØKSR4ZZ	922	ØKTV*	38, 248, 700	ØKUDØJZ	433, 640, 922	ØKUT47Z	433
ØKRMØ7Z	38, 247, 432, 699, 921, 1069	ØKRW4JZ	38, 248, 432, 495, 699, 922, 1069	ØKSS*	248, 495, 699	ØKTVØZZ	433	ØKUDØKZ	433, 640, 922	ØKUT4JZ	433
ØKRMØJZ	38, 247, 432, 699, 921, 1069	ØKRW4KZ	38, 248, 432, 495, 699, 922, 1069	ØKSSØZZ	922	ØKTV4ZZ	433	ØKUD47Z	433, 640, 922	ØKUT4KZ	433
ØKRMØKZ	38, 247, 432, 699, 921, 1069	ØKS*	38	ØKSS4ZZ	922	ØKTW*	38, 248, 700	ØKUD4JZ	433, 640, 922	ØKUV*	248, 700
ØKRM47Z	38, 247, 432, 699, 921, 1069	ØKSØ*	248, 495, 699	ØKST*	248, 495, 699	ØKTWØZZ	433	ØKUD4KZ	433, 640, 922	ØKUVØ7Z	433
ØKRM4JZ	38, 247, 432, 699, 921, 1069	ØKSØØZZ	922	ØKSTØZZ	922	ØKTW4ZZ	433	ØKUF*	248, 700	ØKUVØJZ	433
ØKRM4KZ	38, 247, 432, 699, 921, 1069	ØKSØ4ZZ	922	ØKST4ZZ	922	ØKU*	38	ØKUFØ7Z	433	ØKUVØKZ	433
ØKRNØ7Z	38, 247, 432, 495, 699, 921, 1069	ØKS1*	58, 248, 495, 699	ØKSV*	248, 495, 699	ØKUØ*	248, 700	ØKUFØJZ	433	ØKUV4JZ	433
ØKRNØJZ	38, 247, 432, 495, 699, 921, 1069	ØKS1ØZZ	922	ØKSVØZZ	922	ØKUØØ7Z	433	ØKUFØKZ	433	ØKUV4KZ	433
ØKRNØKZ	38, 247, 432, 495, 699, 921, 1069	ØKS14ZZ	922	ØKSV4ZZ	922	ØKUØØJZ	433	ØKUF47Z	433	ØKUW*	248, 700
ØKRN47Z	38, 247, 432, 495, 699, 921, 1069	ØKS2*	248, 495, 699	ØKSW*	248, 495, 699	ØKUØØKZ	433	ØKUF4JZ	433	ØKUWØ7Z	433
ØKRN4JZ	38, 247, 432, 495, 699, 922, 1069	ØKS2ØZZ	922	ØKSWØZZ	922	ØKUØ47Z	433	ØKUF4KZ	433	ØKUWØJZ	433
ØKRN4KZ	38, 247, 432, 495, 699, 922, 1069	ØKS24ZZ	922	ØKSW4ZZ	922	ØKUØ4JZ	433	ØKUG*	248, 700	ØKUWØKZ	433
ØKRPØ7Z	38, 247, 432, 495, 699, 922, 1069	ØKS3*	248, 495, 699	ØKTØ*	38, 248, 699	ØKUØ4KZ	433	ØKUGØ7Z	433	ØKUW47Z	433
ØKRPØJZ	38, 247, 432, 495, 699, 922, 1069	ØKS3ØZZ	922	ØKTØØZZ	432	ØKU1*	248, 700	ØKUGØJZ	433	ØKUW4JZ	433
ØKRPØKZ	38, 248, 432, 495, 699, 922, 1069	ØKS34ZZ	922	ØKTØ4ZZ	432	ØKU1Ø7Z	433	ØKUGØKZ	433	ØKUW4KZ	433
ØKRP47Z	38, 248, 432, 495, 699, 922, 1069	ØKS4*	248, 495, 699	ØKT1*	38, 248, 699	ØKU1ØJZ	433	ØKUG47Z	433	ØKWXØØZ	248, 433, 700, 1069
ØKRP4JZ	38, 248, 432, 495, 699, 922, 1069	ØKS4ØZZ	922	ØKT1ØZZ	432	ØKU1ØKZ	433	ØKUG4JZ	433	ØKWXØ7Z	248, 433, 700, 1069
ØKRP4KZ	38, 248, 432, 495, 699, 922, 1069	ØKS44ZZ	922	ØKT14ZZ	432	ØKU147Z	433	ØKUG4KZ	433	ØKWXØJZ	248, 434, 700, 1069
ØKRQØ7Z	248, 699, 922	ØKS5*	248, 495, 699	ØKT2*	38, 248, 699	ØKU14JZ	433	ØKUH*	248, 700	ØKWXØKZ	248, 434, 700, 1069
ØKRQØJZ	248, 699, 922	ØKS5ØZZ	922	ØKT2ØZZ	432	ØKU14KZ	433	ØKUHØ7Z	433	ØKWXØMZ	248, 434, 700, 1069
ØKRQØKZ	248, 699, 922	ØKS54ZZ	922	ØKT24ZZ	432	ØKU2*	248, 700	ØKUHØJZ	433	ØKWXØYZ	248, 434, 700, 1069
ØKRQ47Z	248, 699, 922	ØKS6*	248, 495, 699	ØKT3*	38, 248, 699	ØKU2Ø7Z	433	ØKUHØKZ	433	ØKWX3ØZ	248, 434, 700, 1069
ØKRQ4JZ	248, 699, 922	ØKS6ØZZ	922	ØKT3ØZZ	432	ØKU2ØJZ	433	ØKUH47Z	433	ØKWX37Z	248, 434, 700, 1069
ØKRQ4KZ	248, 699, 922	ØKS64ZZ	922	ØKT34ZZ	432	ØKU2ØKZ	433	ØKUH4JZ	433	ØKWX3JZ	248, 434, 700, 1069
ØKRRØ7Z	248, 699, 922	ØKS7*	248, 495, 699	ØKT4*	38, 248, 699	ØKU247Z	433	ØKUH4KZ	433	ØKWX3KZ	248, 434, 700, 1069
ØKRRØJZ	248, 699, 922	ØKS7ØZZ	922	ØKT4ØZZ	432	ØKU24JZ	433	ØKUJ*	248, 700	ØKWX3MZ	248, 434, 700, 1069
ØKRRØKZ	248, 699, 922	ØKS74ZZ	922	ØKT44ZZ	432	ØKU24KZ	433	ØKUJØ7Z	433	ØKWX4ØZ	248, 434, 700, 1069
ØKRR47Z	248, 699, 922	ØKS8*	248, 495, 699	ØKT5*	38, 248, 699	ØKU3*	248, 700	ØKUJØJZ	433	ØKWX47Z	248, 434, 700, 1069
ØKRR4JZ	248, 699, 922	ØKS8ØZZ	922	ØKT5ØZZ	432	ØKU3Ø7Z	433	ØKUJØKZ	433	ØKWX4JZ	248, 434, 700, 1069
ØKRR4KZ	248, 699, 922	ØKS84ZZ	922	ØKT54ZZ	432	ØKU3ØJZ	433	ØKUJ47Z	433	ØKWX4KZ	248, 434, 700, 1069
ØKRSØ7Z	38, 248, 432, 495, 699, 922, 1069	ØKS9*	248, 495, 699	ØKT6*	38, 248, 699	ØKU3ØKZ	433	ØKUJ4JZ	433	ØKWX4MZ	248, 434, 700, 1069
ØKRSØJZ	38, 248, 432, 495, 699, 922, 1069	ØKS9ØZZ	922	ØKT6ØZZ	432	ØKU347Z	433	ØKUJ4KZ	433	ØKWYØØZ	248, 434, 700, 922, 1069
ØKRSØKZ	38, 248, 432, 495, 699, 922, 1069	ØKS94ZZ	922	ØKT64ZZ	432	ØKU34JZ	433	ØKUK*	248, 700	ØKWYØ7Z	248, 434, 700, 1069
ØKRS47Z	38, 248, 432, 495, 699, 922, 1069	ØKSB*	248, 495, 699	ØKT7*	38, 248, 699	ØKU34KZ	433	ØKUKØ7Z	433	ØKWYØJZ	248, 434, 700, 922, 1069
ØKRS4JZ	38, 248, 432, 495, 699, 922, 1069	ØKSBØZZ	922	ØKT7ØZZ	432	ØKU4*	248, 700	ØKUKØJZ	433	ØKWYØKZ	248, 434, 700, 1069
ØKRS4KZ	38, 248, 432, 495, 699, 922, 1069	ØKSB4ZZ	922	ØKT74ZZ	432	ØKU4Ø7Z	433	ØKUKØKZ	433	ØKWYØMZ	248, 434, 700, 922, 1069
		ØKSC*	269	ØKT8*	38, 248, 699	ØKU4ØJZ	433	ØKUK47Z	433	ØKWYØYZ	248, 434, 700, 922, 1069
		ØKSCØZZ	640, 922	ØKT8ØZZ	432	ØKU4ØKZ	433	ØKUK4JZ	433	ØKWY3ØZ	248, 434, 700, 1069
		ØKSC4ZZ	640, 922	ØKT84ZZ	432	ØKU447Z	433	ØKUK4KZ	433	ØKWY37Z	248, 434, 700, 1069
		ØKSD*	269	ØKT9*	38, 248, 700	ØKU44JZ	433	ØKUL*	248, 700	ØKWY3JZ	248, 434, 700, 922, 1069
		ØKSDØZZ	640, 922	ØKT9ØZZ	432	ØKU44KZ	433	ØKULØ7Z	433	ØKWY3KZ	248, 434, 700, 1069
		ØKSD4ZZ	640, 922	ØKT94ZZ	432	ØKU5*	248, 700	ØKULØJZ	433	ØKWY3MZ	248, 434, 700, 922, 1069
		ØKSF*	248, 495, 699	ØKTB*	38, 248, 700	ØKU5Ø7Z	433	ØKULØKZ	433	ØKWY4ØZ	248, 434, 700, 1069
		ØKSFØZZ	922	ØKTBØZZ	432	ØKU5ØJZ	433	ØKUL47Z	433	ØKWY47Z	248, 434, 700, 1069
		ØKSF4ZZ	922	ØKTB4ZZ	432	ØKU5ØKZ	433	ØKUL4JZ	433	ØKWY4JZ	248, 434, 700, 922, 1069
		ØKSG*	248, 495, 699	ØKTC*	269	ØKU547Z	433	ØKUL4KZ	433		
		ØKSGØZZ	922	ØKTCØZZ	640, 922	ØKU54JZ	433	ØKUM*	248, 700		
		ØKSG4ZZ	922	ØKTC4ZZ	640, 922	ØKU54KZ	433	ØKUMØ7Z	433		
		ØKSH*	248, 495, 699	ØKTD*	269	ØKU6*	248, 700	ØKUMØJZ	433		
		ØKSHØZZ	922	ØKTDØZZ	640, 922	ØKU6Ø7Z	433	ØKUMØKZ	433		
		ØKSH4ZZ	922	ØKTD4ZZ	640, 922	ØKU6ØJZ	433	ØKUM47Z	433		
		ØKSJ*	248, 495, 699	ØKTF*	38, 248, 700	ØKU6ØKZ	433	ØKUM4JZ	433		
		ØKSJØZZ	922	ØKTFØZZ	432	ØKU647Z	433	ØKUM4KZ	433		
		ØKSJ4ZZ	922	ØKTF4ZZ	432	ØKU64JZ	433	ØKUN*	248, 700		
		ØKSK*	248, 495, 699	ØKTG*	38, 248, 700	ØKU64KZ	433	ØKUNØ7Z	433		
		ØKSKØZZ	922	ØKTGØZZ	432	ØKU7*	248, 700	ØKUNØJZ	433		
		ØKSK4ZZ	922	ØKTG4ZZ	432	ØKU7Ø7Z	433	ØKUNØKZ	433		
		ØKSL*	248, 495, 699	ØKTH*	38, 248, 700	ØKU7ØJZ	433	ØKUN47Z	433		
		ØKSLØZZ	922	ØKTHØZZ	432, 450, 451, 452, 453	ØKU7ØKZ	433	ØKUN4JZ	433		
				ØKTH4ZZ	432	ØKU747Z	433	ØKUN4KZ	433		
				ØKTJ*	38, 248, 700	ØKU74JZ	433	ØKUP*	248, 700		
				ØKTJØZZ	432, 450, 451, 452, 453	ØKU74KZ	433	ØKUPØ7Z	433		
				ØKTJ4ZZ	432	ØKU8*	248, 700	ØKUPØJZ	433		
				ØKTK*	38, 248, 700	ØKU8Ø7Z	433	ØKUPØKZ	433		
				ØKTKØZZ	432	ØKU8ØJZ	433	ØKUP47Z	433		
				ØKTK4ZZ	432	ØKU8ØKZ	433	ØKUP4JZ	433		
				ØKTL*	38, 248, 700	ØKU847Z	433	ØKUP4KZ	433		
				ØKTLØZZ	432	ØKU84JZ	433	ØKUQ*	248, 700		
				ØKTL4ZZ	432	ØKU84KZ	433	ØKUQØ7Z	433		
				ØKTM*	38, 248, 700	ØKU9*	248, 700	ØKUQØJZ	433		
				ØKTMØZZ	432	ØKU9Ø7Z	433	ØKUQØKZ	433		
				ØKTM4ZZ	432	ØKU9ØKZ	433	ØKUQ47Z	433		
				ØKTN*	38, 248, 700	ØKU947Z	433	ØKUQ4JZ	433		
				ØKTNØZZ	432	ØKU94JZ	433	ØKUQ4KZ	433		
				ØKTN4ZZ	432	ØKU94KZ	433	ØKUR*	248, 700		
						ØKUB*	248, 700	ØKURØ7Z	433		
								ØKURØJZ	433		

Code	Page	Code	Page	Code	Page	Code	Page	Code	Page	Code	Page
0KWY4KZ	248, 434, 700, 1069	0KXL0Z2	38, 249	0L5J4ZZ	923	0L8D*	39, 249, 496, 700	0L9500Z	249, 700, 1070	0L9K4ZX	250
0KWY4MZ	248, 434, 700, 1069	0KXL0Z6	450, 452, 700, 922	0L5K*	249, 700	0L8D0ZZ	1069	0L950ZX	249, 434, 1070	0L9K4ZZ	250, 701, 1070
		0KXL0ZZ	38, 249	0L5K0ZZ	923	0L8D3ZZ	1069	0L950ZZ	249, 700, 1070	0L9L00Z	250, 701, 1070
0KX0*	38, 248	0KXL4Z0	38, 249	0L5K3ZZ	923	0L8D4ZZ	1069	0L953ZX	249	0L9L0ZX	250, 434, 1070
0KX1*	38, 248	0KXL4Z1	38, 249	0L5K4ZZ	923	0L8F*	39, 249, 496, 700	0L9540Z	249, 700, 1070	0L9L0ZZ	250, 701, 1070
0KX2*	38, 248	0KXL4Z2	38, 249	0L5L*	249, 700	0L8F0ZZ	1069	0L954ZX	249	0L9L3ZX	250
0KX3*	38, 248	0KXL4Z6	450, 452, 700, 922	0L5L0ZZ	923	0L8F3ZZ	1069	0L954ZZ	249, 701, 1070	0L9L40Z	250, 701, 1070
0KX4*	38, 248	0KXL4ZZ	38, 249	0L5L3ZZ	923	0L8F4ZZ	1069	0L9600Z	249, 701, 1070	0L9L4ZX	250
0KX5*	38, 248	0KXM*	38, 249	0L5L4ZZ	923	0L8G*	39, 249, 496, 700	0L960ZX	249, 434, 1070	0L9L4ZZ	250, 701, 1070
0KX6*	38, 248	0KXN*	38, 249	0L5M*	249, 700	0L8G0ZZ	1069	0L960ZZ	249, 701, 1070	0L9M00Z	250, 701, 1070
0KX7*	38, 248	0KXN0ZZ	411	0L5M0ZZ	923	0L8G3ZZ	1069	0L963ZX	249	0L9M0ZX	250, 434, 1070
0KX8*	38, 248	0KXP*	38, 249	0L5M3ZZ	923	0L8G4ZZ	1069	0L9640Z	249, 701, 1070	0L9M0ZZ	250, 701, 1070
0KX9*	38, 248	0KXP0ZZ	411	0L5M4ZZ	923	0L8H*	39, 249, 496, 700	0L964ZX	249	0L9M3ZX	250
0KXB*	38, 248	0KXQ*	38, 249	0L5N*	249, 700	0L8H0ZZ	1069	0L964ZZ	249, 701, 1070	0L9M40Z	250, 701, 1070
0KXC*	38, 269	0KXR*	38, 249	0L5N0ZZ	923	0L8H3ZZ	1069	0L9700Z	269, 640, 923, 1070	0L9M4ZX	250
0KXC0Z0	640, 922	0KXS*	38, 249	0L5N3ZZ	923	0L8H4ZZ	1069			0L9M4ZZ	250, 701, 1070
0KXC0Z1	640, 922	0KXT*	38, 249	0L5N4ZZ	923	0L8J*	224, 700, 851	0L970ZX	249, 434, 1070	0L9N00Z	250, 701, 1070
0KXC0Z2	640, 922	0KXV*	38, 249	0L5P*	249, 700	0L8K*	224, 700, 851	0L970ZZ	269, 641, 923, 1070	0L9N0ZX	250, 434, 1070
0KXC0ZZ	640, 922	0KXW*	38, 249	0L5P0ZZ	923	0L8L*	39, 249, 496, 700			0L9N0ZZ	250, 701, 1070
0KXC4Z0	640, 922	0L5*	495	0L5P3ZZ	923	0L8L0ZZ	1069	0L973ZX	249	0L9N3ZX	250
0KXC4Z1	640, 922	0L50*	249, 700	0L5P4ZZ	923	0L8L3ZZ	1069	0L9740Z	269, 641, 923, 1070	0L9N40Z	250, 701, 1070
0KXC4Z2	640, 922	0L500ZZ	922	0L5Q*	249, 700	0L8L4ZZ	1069			0L9N4ZX	250
0KXC4ZZ	640, 922	0L503ZZ	922	0L5Q0ZZ	923	0L8M*	39, 249, 496, 700	0L974ZX	249	0L9N4ZZ	250, 701, 1070
0KXD*	38, 269	0L504ZZ	922	0L5Q3ZZ	923	0L8M0ZZ	1069	0L9800Z	269, 641, 923, 1070	0L9P00Z	250, 701, 1070
0KXD0Z0	640, 922	0L51*	249, 700	0L5Q4ZZ	923	0L8M3ZZ	1069			0L9P0ZX	250, 434, 1070
0KXD0Z1	640, 922	0L510ZZ	922	0L5R*	249, 700	0L8M4ZZ	1069	0L980ZX	249, 434, 1070	0L9P0ZZ	250, 701, 1070
0KXD0Z2	640, 922	0L513ZZ	922	0L5R0ZZ	923	0L8N*	257, 700	0L980ZZ	269, 641, 923, 1070	0L9P3ZX	250
0KXD0ZZ	640, 922	0L514ZZ	922	0L5R3ZZ	923	0L8N0ZZ	923			0L9P40Z	250, 701, 1070
0KXD4Z0	640, 922	0L52*	249, 700	0L5R4ZZ	923	0L8N3ZZ	923	0L983ZX	249	0L9P4ZX	250
0KXD4Z1	640, 922	0L520ZZ	922	0L5S*	249, 700	0L8N4ZZ	923	0L9840Z	269, 641, 923, 1070	0L9P4ZZ	250, 701, 1070
0KXD4Z2	640, 922	0L523ZZ	922	0L5S0ZZ	923	0L8P*	257, 700			0L9Q00Z	250, 701, 1070
0KXD4ZZ	640, 922	0L524ZZ	922	0L5S3ZZ	923	0L8P0ZZ	923	0L984ZX	249	0L9Q0ZX	250, 434, 1070
0KXF0Z0	38, 248	0L53*	249, 700	0L5S4ZZ	923	0L8P3ZZ	923	0L9900Z	249, 701, 1070	0L9Q0ZZ	250, 701, 1070
0KXF0Z1	38, 248	0L530ZZ	923	0L5T*	249, 700	0L8P4ZZ	923	0L990ZX	249, 434, 1070	0L9Q3ZX	250
0KXF0Z2	38, 248	0L533ZZ	923	0L5T0ZZ	923	0L8Q*	39, 249, 496, 700	0L990ZZ	249, 701, 1070	0L9Q40Z	250, 701, 1070
0KXF0Z5	450, 452, 700, 922	0L534ZZ	923	0L5T3ZZ	923	0L8Q0ZZ	1069	0L993ZX	249	0L9Q4ZX	250
0KXF0Z7	450, 452, 700, 922	0L54*	249, 700	0L5T4ZZ	923	0L8Q3ZZ	1069	0L9940Z	249, 701, 1070	0L9Q4ZZ	250, 701, 1070
0KXF0Z8	450, 452, 700, 922	0L540ZZ	923	0L5V*	249, 700	0L8Q4ZZ	1069	0L994ZX	249	0L9R00Z	250, 701, 1070
0KXF0Z9	450, 452, 700, 922	0L543ZZ	923	0L5V0ZZ	923	0L8R*	39, 249, 496, 700	0L994ZZ	249, 701, 1070	0L9R0ZX	250, 434, 1070
0KXF0ZZ	38, 248	0L544ZZ	923	0L5V3ZZ	923	0L8R0ZZ	1069	0L9B00Z	249, 701, 1070	0L9R0ZZ	250, 701, 1070
0KXF4Z0	38, 248	0L55*	249, 700	0L5V4ZZ	923	0L8R3ZZ	1069	0L9B0ZX	249, 434, 1070	0L9R3ZX	250
0KXF4Z1	38, 248	0L550ZZ	923	0L5W*	249, 700	0L8R4ZZ	1069	0L9B0ZZ	249, 701, 1070	0L9R40Z	250, 701, 1070
0KXF4Z2	38, 248	0L553ZZ	923	0L5W0ZZ	923	0L8S*	39, 249, 496, 700	0L9B3ZX	249	0L9R4ZX	250
0KXF4Z5	450, 452, 700, 922	0L554ZZ	923	0L5W3ZZ	923	0L8S0ZZ	1069	0L9B40Z	249, 701, 1070	0L9R4ZZ	250, 701, 1070
0KXF4Z7	450, 452, 700, 922	0L56*	249, 700	0L5W4ZZ	923	0L8S3ZZ	1069	0L9B4ZX	249	0L9S00Z	250, 701, 1070
0KXF4Z8	450, 452, 700, 922	0L560ZZ	923	0L80*	38, 249, 495, 700	0L8S4ZZ	1069	0L9C00Z	249, 701, 1070	0L9S0ZX	250, 434, 1070
0KXF4Z9	450, 452, 700, 922	0L563ZZ	923	0L800ZZ	1069	0L8T*	39, 249, 496, 700	0L9C0ZX	249, 434, 1070	0L9S0ZZ	250, 701, 1070
0KXF4ZZ	38, 248	0L564ZZ	923	0L803ZZ	1069	0L8T0ZZ	1069	0L9C0ZZ	249, 701, 1070	0L9S3ZX	250
0KXG0Z0	38, 248	0L57*	269	0L804ZZ	1069	0L8T3ZZ	1069	0L9C3ZX	249	0L9S40Z	250, 701, 1070
0KXG0Z1	38, 248	0L570ZZ	434, 640, 923, 1069	0L81*	38, 249, 495, 700	0L8T4ZZ	1069	0L9C40Z	249, 701, 1070	0L9S4ZX	250
0KXG0Z2	38, 248			0L810ZZ	1069	0L8V*	39, 249, 496, 700	0L9C4ZX	249	0L9S4ZZ	250, 701, 1070
0KXG0Z5	450, 452, 700, 922	0L573ZZ	434, 640, 923, 1069	0L813ZZ	1069	0L8V0ZZ	1069	0L9C4ZZ	249, 701, 1070	0L9T00Z	250, 701, 1070
0KXG0Z7	450, 452, 700, 922			0L814ZZ	1069	0L8V3ZZ	1069	0L9D00Z	249, 701, 1070	0L9T0ZX	250, 434, 1070
0KXG0Z8	450, 452, 700, 922	0L574ZZ	434, 640, 923, 1069	0L82*	38, 249, 495, 700	0L8V4ZZ	1069	0L9D0ZX	249, 434, 1070	0L9T0ZZ	250, 701, 1070
0KXG0Z9	450, 452, 700, 922			0L820ZZ	1069	0L8W*	39, 249, 496, 700	0L9D0ZZ	249, 701, 1070	0L9T3ZX	250
0KXG0ZZ	38, 248	0L58*	269	0L823ZZ	1069	0L8W0ZZ	1069	0L9D3ZX	249	0L9T40Z	250, 701, 1070
0KXG4Z0	38, 248	0L580ZZ	434, 640, 923, 1069	0L824ZZ	1069	0L8W3ZZ	1069	0L9D40Z	249, 701, 1070	0L9T4ZX	250
0KXG4Z1	38, 249			0L83*	38, 249, 495, 700	0L8W4ZZ	1069	0L9D4ZX	249	0L9T4ZZ	250, 701, 1070
0KXG4Z2	38, 249	0L583ZZ	434, 640, 923, 1069	0L830ZZ	1069	0L9000Z	249, 700, 1069	0L9D4ZZ	249, 701, 1070	0L9V00Z	250, 701, 1070
0KXG4Z5	450, 452, 700, 922			0L833ZZ	1069	0L900ZX	249, 434, 1070	0L9F00Z	249, 701, 1070	0L9V0ZX	250, 434, 1070
0KXG4Z7	450, 452, 700, 922	0L584ZZ	434, 640, 923, 1069	0L834ZZ	1069	0L900ZZ	249, 700, 1069	0L9F0ZX	249, 434, 1070	0L9V0ZZ	250, 701, 1070
0KXG4Z8	450, 452, 700, 922			0L84*	38, 249, 495, 700	0L903ZX	249	0L9F0ZZ	249, 701, 1070	0L9V3ZX	250
0KXG4Z9	450, 452, 700, 922	0L59*	249, 700	0L840ZZ	1069	0L9040Z	249, 700, 1069	0L9F3ZX	250	0L9V40Z	250, 701, 1070
0KXG4ZZ	38, 249	0L590ZZ	923	0L843ZZ	1069	0L904ZX	249	0L9F40Z	250, 701, 1070	0L9V4ZX	250
0KXH0Z0	38, 249	0L593ZZ	923	0L844ZZ	1069	0L904ZZ	249, 700, 1069	0L9F4ZX	250	0L9V4ZZ	250, 701, 1070
0KXH0Z1	38, 249	0L594ZZ	923	0L85*	38, 249, 495, 700	0L9100Z	249, 700, 1069	0L9G00Z	250, 701, 1070	0L9W00Z	250, 701, 1070
0KXH0Z2	411, 700, 922	0L5B*	249, 700	0L850ZZ	1069	0L910ZX	249, 434, 1070	0L9G0ZX	250, 434, 1070	0L9W0ZX	250, 434, 1070
0KXH0ZZ	38, 249	0L5B0ZZ	923	0L853ZZ	1069	0L910ZZ	249, 700, 1069	0L9G0ZZ	250, 701, 1070	0L9W0ZZ	250, 701, 1070
0KXH4Z0	38, 249	0L5B3ZZ	923	0L854ZZ	1069	0L913ZX	249	0L9G3ZX	250	0L9W3ZX	250
0KXH4Z1	38, 249	0L5B4ZZ	923	0L86*	39, 249, 495, 700	0L9140Z	249, 700, 1069	0L9G40Z	250, 701, 1070	0L9W40Z	250, 701, 1070
0KXH4Z2	38, 249	0L5C*	249, 700	0L860ZZ	1069	0L914ZX	249	0L9G4ZX	250	0L9W4ZX	250
0KXH4ZZ	411, 700, 922	0L5C0ZZ	923	0L863ZZ	1069	0L914ZZ	249, 700, 1069	0L9H00Z	250, 701, 1070	0L9W4ZZ	250, 701, 1070
0KXJ0Z0	38, 249	0L5C3ZZ	923	0L864ZZ	1069	0L9200Z	249, 700, 1069	0L9H0ZX	250, 434, 1070	0L9B0*	250
0KXJ0Z1	38, 249	0L5C4ZZ	923	0L87*	269	0L920ZX	249, 434, 1070	0L9H0ZZ	250, 701, 1070	0LB00ZX	434, 1070
0KXJ0Z2	411, 700, 922	0L5D*	249, 700	0L870ZZ	640, 923, 1069	0L920ZZ	249, 700, 1069	0L9H3ZX	250	0LB00ZZ	39, 701, 923
0KXJ4Z0	38, 249	0L5D0ZZ	923	0L873ZZ	640, 923, 1069	0L923ZX	249	0L9H40Z	250, 701, 1070	0LB03ZZ	39, 701, 923
0KXJ4Z1	38, 249	0L5D3ZZ	923	0L874ZZ	640, 923, 1069	0L9240Z	249, 700, 1069	0L9H4ZX	250	0LB04ZZ	39, 701, 923
0KXJ4Z2	38, 249	0L5D4ZZ	923	0L88*	269	0L924ZX	249	0L9H4ZZ	250, 701, 1070	0LB1*	250
0KXJ4ZZ	411, 700, 922	0L5F*	249, 700	0L880ZZ	640, 923, 1069	0L924ZZ	249, 700, 1069	0L9J00Z	250, 701, 1070	0LB10ZX	434, 1070
0KXK0Z0	38, 249	0L5F0ZZ	923	0L883ZZ	640, 923, 1069	0L9300Z	249, 700, 1069	0L9J0ZX	250, 434, 1070	0LB10ZZ	39, 701, 923
0KXK0Z1	38, 249	0L5F3ZZ	923	0L884ZZ	640, 923, 1069	0L930ZX	249, 434, 1070	0L9J0ZZ	250, 701, 1070	0LB13ZZ	39, 701, 923
0KXK0Z2	38, 249	0L5F4ZZ	923	0L89*	39, 249, 496, 700	0L930ZZ	249, 700, 1070	0L9J3ZX	250	0LB14ZZ	39, 701, 923
0KXK0Z6	450, 452, 700, 922	0L5G*	249, 700	0L890ZZ	1069	0L933ZX	249	0L9J40Z	250, 701, 1070	0LB2*	250
0KXK0ZZ	38, 249	0L5G0ZZ	923	0L893ZZ	1069	0L9340Z	249, 700, 1070	0L9J4ZX	250	0LB20ZX	434, 1070
0KXK4Z0	38, 249	0L5G3ZZ	923	0L894ZZ	1069	0L934ZX	249	0L9K00Z	250, 701, 1070	0LB20ZZ	39, 701, 923
0KXK4Z1	38, 249	0L5G4ZZ	923	0L8B*	39, 249, 495, 700	0L934ZZ	250, 701, 1070	0L9K0ZX	250, 434, 1070	0LB23ZZ	39, 701, 923
0KXK4Z2	38, 249	0L5H*	249, 700	0L8B0ZZ	1069	0L9400Z	249, 700, 1070	0L9K0ZZ	250, 701, 1070	0LB24ZZ	39, 701, 923
0KXK4Z6	450, 452, 700, 922	0L5H0ZZ	923	0L8B3ZZ	1069	0L940ZX	249, 434, 1070	0L9K3ZX	250	0LB3*	250
0KXK4ZZ	38, 249	0L5H3ZZ	923	0L8B4ZZ	1069	0L940ZZ	249, 700, 1070	0L9K40Z	250, 701, 1070	0LB30ZX	434, 1070
0KXL0Z0	38, 249	0L5H4ZZ	923	0L8C*	39, 249, 495, 700	0L943ZX	249			0LB30ZZ	39, 701, 923
0KXL0Z1	38, 249	0L5J*	249, 700	0L8C0ZZ	1069	0L9440Z	249, 700, 1070			0LB33ZZ	39, 701, 923
		0L5J0ZZ	923	0L8C3ZZ	1069	0L944ZX	249			0LB34ZZ	39, 701, 923
		0L5J3ZZ	923	0L8C4ZZ	1069	0L944ZZ	249, 700, 1070			0LB4*	250

Numeric Index to Procedures

Code	Page	Code	Page	Code	Page	Code	Page	Code	Page	Code	Page
0LB40ZX	434,1070	0LBQ0ZZ	39,701,923	0LCJ0ZZ	1071	0LDS0ZZ	39,251,434,702,924	0LMT0ZZ	924	0LPX07Z	251,702,1071
0LB40ZZ	39,701,923	0LBQ3ZZ	39,701,923	0LCJ3ZZ	1071	0LDT0ZZ	39,251,434,702,924	0LMT4ZZ	924	0LPX0JZ	251,702,1071
0LB43ZZ	39,701,923	0LBQ4ZZ	39,701,923	0LCJ4ZZ	1071	0LDV0ZZ	39,251,434,702,924	0LMV*	251,702	0LPX0KZ	251,702,1071
0LB44ZZ	39,701,923	0LBR*	250	0LCK*	250,702	0LDW0ZZ	39,251,434,702,924	0LMV0ZZ	924	0LPX0YZ	251,702,1071
0LB5*	250	0LBR0ZX	434,1070	0LCK0ZZ	1071	0LHX0YZ	39,251,702,924	0LMV4ZZ	924	0LPX37Z	251,702,1071
0LB50ZX	434,1070	0LBR0ZZ	39,701,923	0LCK3ZZ	1071	0LHY0YZ	39,251,702,924	0LMW*	251,702	0LPX3JZ	251,702,1071
0LB50ZZ	39,701,923	0LBR3ZZ	39,701,923	0LCK4ZZ	1071	0LJX0ZZ	269,641,924,1071	0LMW0ZZ	924	0LPX3KZ	251,702,1071
0LB53ZZ	39,701,923	0LBR4ZZ	39,701,923	0LCL*	250,702	0LJX4ZZ	269,641,924,1071	0LMW4ZZ	924	0LPX40Z	251,702,1071
0LB54ZZ	39,701,923	0LBS*	250	0LCL0ZZ	1071	0LJY0ZZ	251	0LN00ZZ	251	0LPX47Z	251,702,1071
0LB6*	250	0LBS0ZX	434,1070	0LCL3ZZ	1071	0LJY4ZZ	251	0LN03ZZ	251	0LPX4JZ	251,702,1071
0LB60ZX	434,1070	0LBS0ZZ	39,434,701,923	0LCL4ZZ	1071	0LM*	39	0LN04ZZ	251	0LPX4KZ	251,702,1071
0LB60ZZ	39,701,923	0LBS3ZZ	39,701,923	0LCM*	250,702	0LM0*	251,702	0LN10ZZ	251	0LPY00Z	251,702,1071
0LB63ZZ	39,701,923	0LBS4ZZ	39,701,923	0LCM0ZZ	1071	0LM00ZZ	924	0LN13ZZ	251	0LPY07Z	251,702,1071
0LB64ZZ	39,701,923	0LBT*	250	0LCM3ZZ	1071	0LM04ZZ	924	0LN14ZZ	251	0LPY0JZ	251,702,1071
0LB70ZX	250,434,1070	0LBT0ZX	434,1070	0LCM4ZZ	1071	0LM1*	251,702	0LN20ZZ	251	0LPY0KZ	251,702,1071
0LB70ZZ	269,496,641,923	0LBT0ZZ	39,434,701,923	0LCN*	250,702	0LM10ZZ	924	0LN23ZZ	251	0LPY0YZ	251,702,1071
0LB73ZX	250	0LBT3ZZ	39,701,923	0LCN0ZZ	1071	0LM14ZZ	924	0LN24ZZ	251	0LPY37Z	251,702,1071
0LB73ZZ	269,496,641,923	0LBT4ZZ	39,701,923	0LCN3ZZ	1071	0LM2*	251,702	0LN30ZZ	251	0LPY3JZ	251,702,1071
0LB74ZX	250	0LBV*	250	0LCN4ZZ	1071	0LM20ZZ	924	0LN33ZZ	251	0LPY3KZ	251,702,1071
0LB74ZZ	269,496,641,923	0LBV0ZX	434,1070	0LCP*	250,702	0LM24ZZ	924	0LN34ZZ	251	0LPY40Z	251,702,1071
0LB80ZX	250,434,1070	0LBV0ZZ	39,482,701,923	0LCP0ZZ	1071	0LM3*	251,702	0LN40ZZ	251	0LPY47Z	251,702,1071
0LB80ZZ	269,496,641,923	0LBV3ZZ	39,701,923	0LCP3ZZ	1071	0LM30ZZ	924	0LN43ZZ	251	0LPY4JZ	251,702,1071
0LB83ZX	250	0LBV4ZZ	39,701,924	0LCP4ZZ	1071	0LM34ZZ	924	0LN44ZZ	251	0LPY4KZ	251,702,1071
0LB83ZZ	269,496,641,923	0LBW*	250	0LCQ*	250,702	0LM4*	251,702	0LN50ZZ	251	0LQ0*	39,251,702
0LB84ZX	250	0LBW0ZX	434,1070	0LCQ0ZZ	1071	0LM40ZZ	924	0LN53ZZ	251	0LQ00ZZ	434,924
0LB84ZZ	269,496,641,923	0LBW0ZZ	39,482,701,924	0LCQ3ZZ	1071	0LM44ZZ	924	0LN54ZZ	251	0LQ03ZZ	434,924
0LB9*	250	0LBW3ZZ	39,701,924	0LCQ4ZZ	1071	0LM5*	251,702	0LN60ZZ	251	0LQ04ZZ	434,924
0LB90ZX	434,1070	0LBW4ZZ	39,701,924	0LCR*	250,702	0LM50ZZ	924	0LN63ZZ	251	0LQ1*	266,702
0LB90ZZ	39,701,923	0LC0*	250,701	0LCR0ZZ	1071	0LM54ZZ	924	0LN64ZZ	251	0LQ10ZZ	924,1071
0LB93ZZ	39,701,923	0LC00ZZ	1070	0LCR3ZZ	1071	0LM6*	251,702	0LN70ZZ	269,434,641,924	0LQ13ZZ	924,1071
0LB94ZZ	39,701,923	0LC03ZZ	1070	0LCR4ZZ	1071	0LM60ZZ	924	0LN73ZZ	269,434,641,924	0LQ14ZZ	924,1071
0LBB*	250	0LC04ZZ	1070	0LCS*	250,702	0LM64ZZ	924	0LN74ZZ	269,434,641,924	0LQ2*	266,702
0LBB0ZX	434,1070	0LC1*	250,701	0LCS0ZZ	1071	0LM7*	269	0LN80ZZ	269,434,641,924	0LQ20ZZ	924,1071
0LBB0ZZ	39,701,923	0LC10ZZ	1070	0LCS3ZZ	1071	0LM70ZZ	641,924	0LN83ZZ	269,434,641,924	0LQ23ZZ	924,1071
0LBB3ZZ	39,701,923	0LC13ZZ	1070	0LCS4ZZ	1071	0LM74ZZ	641,924	0LN84ZZ	269,434,641,924	0LQ24ZZ	924,1071
0LBB4ZZ	39,701,923	0LC14ZZ	1070	0LCT*	250,702	0LM8*	269	0LN90ZZ	251	0LQ3*	39,251,702
0LBC*	250	0LC2*	250,701	0LCT0ZZ	1071	0LM80ZZ	641,924	0LN93ZZ	251	0LQ30ZZ	434,924
0LBC0ZX	434,1070	0LC20ZZ	1070	0LCT3ZZ	1071	0LM84ZZ	641,924	0LN94ZZ	251	0LQ33ZZ	434,924
0LBC0ZZ	39,701,923	0LC23ZZ	1070	0LCT4ZZ	1071	0LM9*	251,702	0LNB0ZZ	251	0LQ34ZZ	434,924
0LBC3ZZ	39,701,923	0LC24ZZ	1070	0LCV*	250,702	0LM90ZZ	924	0LNB3ZZ	251	0LQ4*	39,251,702
0LBC4ZZ	39,701,923	0LC3*	250,701	0LCV0ZZ	1071	0LM94ZZ	924	0LNB4ZZ	251	0LQ40ZZ	434,924
0LBD*	250	0LC30ZZ	1070	0LCV3ZZ	1071	0LMB*	251,702	0LNC0ZZ	251	0LQ43ZZ	434,924
0LBD0ZX	434,1070	0LC33ZZ	1070	0LCV4ZZ	1071	0LMB0ZZ	924	0LNC3ZZ	251	0LQ44ZZ	434,924
0LBD0ZZ	39,701,923	0LC34ZZ	1070	0LCW*	250,702	0LMB4ZZ	924	0LNC4ZZ	251	0LQ5*	39,251,702
0LBD3ZZ	39,701,923	0LC4*	250,701	0LCW0ZZ	1071	0LMC*	251,702	0LND0ZZ	251	0LQ50ZZ	434,924
0LBD4ZZ	39,701,923	0LC40ZZ	1070	0LCW3ZZ	1071	0LMC0ZZ	924	0LND3ZZ	251	0LQ53ZZ	434,924
0LBF*	250	0LC43ZZ	1070	0LCW4ZZ	1071	0LMC4ZZ	924	0LND4ZZ	251	0LQ54ZZ	434,924
0LBF0ZX	434,1070	0LC44ZZ	1070	0LD00ZZ	39,250,434,702,924	0LMD*	251,702	0LNF0ZZ	251	0LQ6*	39,251,702
0LBF0ZZ	39,701,923	0LC5*	250,701	0LD10ZZ	39,250,434,702,924	0LMD0ZZ	924	0LNF3ZZ	251	0LQ60ZZ	434,924
0LBF3ZZ	39,701,923	0LC50ZZ	1070	0LD20ZZ	39,250,434,702,924	0LMD4ZZ	924	0LNF4ZZ	251	0LQ63ZZ	434,924
0LBF4ZZ	39,701,923	0LC53ZZ	1070	0LD30ZZ	39,250,434,702,924	0LMF*	251,702	0LNG0ZZ	251	0LQ64ZZ	434,924
0LBG*	250	0LC54ZZ	1070	0LD40ZZ	39,250,434,702,924	0LMF0ZZ	924	0LNG3ZZ	251	0LQ7*	39,269
0LBG0ZX	434,1070	0LC6*	250,701	0LD50ZZ	39,250,434,702,924	0LMF4ZZ	924	0LNG4ZZ	251	0LQ70ZZ	434,641,924,1071
0LBG0ZZ	39,701,923	0LC60ZZ	1070	0LD60ZZ	39,250,434,702,924	0LMG*	251,702	0LNH0ZZ	251	0LQ73ZZ	434,641,924,1071
0LBG3ZZ	39,701,923	0LC63ZZ	1070	0LD70ZZ	269,641,924	0LMG0ZZ	924	0LNH3ZZ	251	0LQ74ZZ	434,641,924,1071
0LBG4ZZ	39,701,923	0LC64ZZ	1070	0LD80ZZ	269,641,924	0LMG4ZZ	924	0LNH4ZZ	251	0LQ8*	39,269
0LBH*	250	0LC7*	269	0LD90ZZ	39,250,434,702,924	0LMH*	251,702	0LNJ0ZZ	251	0LQ80ZZ	434,641,924,1071
0LBH0ZX	434,1070	0LC70ZZ	641,924,1070	0LDB0ZZ	39,250,434,702,924	0LMH0ZZ	924	0LNJ3ZZ	251	0LQ83ZZ	434,641,924,1071
0LBH0ZZ	39,701,923	0LC73ZZ	641,924,1070	0LDC0ZZ	39,250,434,702,924	0LMH4ZZ	924	0LNJ4ZZ	251	0LQ84ZZ	434,641,924,1071
0LBH3ZZ	39,701,923	0LC74ZZ	641,924,1070	0LDD0ZZ	39,250,434,702,924	0LMJ*	251,702	0LNK0ZZ	251	0LQ9*	39,251,702
0LBH4ZZ	39,701,923	0LC8*	269	0LDF0ZZ	39,250,434,702,924	0LMJ0ZZ	924	0LNK3ZZ	251	0LQ90ZZ	434,924
0LBJ*	250	0LC80ZZ	641,924,1070	0LDG0ZZ	39,250,434,702,924	0LMJ4ZZ	924	0LNK4ZZ	251	0LQ93ZZ	434,924
0LBJ0ZX	434,1070	0LC83ZZ	641,924,1071	0LDH0ZZ	39,250,434,702,924	0LMK*	251,702	0LNL0ZZ	251	0LQ94ZZ	434,924
0LBJ0ZZ	39,701,923	0LC84ZZ	641,924,1071	0LDJ0ZZ	39,251,434,702,924	0LMK0ZZ	924	0LNL3ZZ	251	0LQB*	39,251,702
0LBJ3ZZ	39,701,923	0LC9*	250,701	0LDK0ZZ	39,251,434,702,924	0LMK4ZZ	924	0LNL4ZZ	251	0LQB0ZZ	434,924
0LBJ4ZZ	39,701,923	0LC90ZZ	1071	0LDL0ZZ	39,251,434,702,924	0LML*	251,702	0LNM0ZZ	251	0LQB3ZZ	434,924
0LBK*	250	0LC93ZZ	1071	0LDM0ZZ	39,251,434,702,924	0LML0ZZ	924	0LNM3ZZ	251	0LQB4ZZ	434,924
0LBK0ZX	434,1070	0LC94ZZ	1071	0LDN0ZZ	39,251,434,702,924	0LML4ZZ	924	0LNM4ZZ	251	0LQC*	39,251,702
0LBK0ZZ	39,701,923	0LCB*	250,701	0LDP0ZZ	39,251,434,702,924	0LMM*	251,702	0LNN0ZZ	251	0LQC0ZZ	434,924
0LBK3ZZ	39,701,923	0LCB0ZZ	1071	0LDQ0ZZ	39,251,434,702,924	0LMM0ZZ	924	0LNN3ZZ	251	0LQC3ZZ	434,924
0LBK4ZZ	39,701,923	0LCB3ZZ	1071	0LDR0ZZ	39,251,434,702,924	0LMM4ZZ	924	0LNN4ZZ	251	0LQC4ZZ	434,924
0LBL*	250	0LCB4ZZ	1071			0LMN*	251,702	0LNP0ZZ	251	0LQD*	39,251,702
0LBL0ZX	434,1070	0LCC*	250,701			0LMN0ZZ	924	0LNP3ZZ	251	0LQD0ZZ	434,924
0LBL0ZZ	39,701,923	0LCC0ZZ	1071			0LMN4ZZ	924	0LNP4ZZ	251	0LQD3ZZ	434,924
0LBL3ZZ	39,701,923	0LCC3ZZ	1071			0LMP*	251,702	0LNQ0ZZ	251	0LQD4ZZ	434,924
0LBL4ZZ	39,701,923	0LCC4ZZ	1071			0LMP0ZZ	924	0LNQ3ZZ	251	0LQF*	39,251,702
0LBM*	250	0LCD*	250,701			0LMP4ZZ	924	0LNQ4ZZ	251	0LQF0ZZ	434,924
0LBM0ZX	434,1070	0LCD0ZZ	1071			0LMQ*	251,702	0LNR0ZZ	251	0LQF3ZZ	434,924
0LBM0ZZ	39,701,923	0LCD3ZZ	1071			0LMQ0ZZ	924	0LNR3ZZ	251	0LQF4ZZ	434,924
0LBM3ZZ	39,701,923	0LCD4ZZ	1071			0LMQ4ZZ	924	0LNR4ZZ	251	0LQG*	39,251,702
0LBM4ZZ	39,701,923	0LCF*	250,701			0LMR*	251,702	0LNS0ZZ	251	0LQG0ZZ	434,924
0LBN*	250	0LCF0ZZ	1071			0LMR0ZZ	924	0LNS3ZZ	251	0LQG3ZZ	434,924
0LBN0ZX	434,1070	0LCF3ZZ	1071			0LMR4ZZ	924	0LNS4ZZ	251	0LQG4ZZ	434,924
0LBN0ZZ	39,701,923	0LCF4ZZ	1071			0LMS*	251,702	0LNT0ZZ	251	0LQH*	39,251,702
0LBN3ZZ	39,701,923	0LCG*	250,701			0LMS0ZZ	924	0LNT3ZZ	251	0LQH0ZZ	434,924
0LBN4ZZ	39,701,923	0LCG0ZZ	1071			0LMS4ZZ	924	0LNT4ZZ	251	0LQH3ZZ	434,924
0LBP*	250	0LCG3ZZ	1071			0LMT*	251,702	0LNV0ZZ	251	0LQH4ZZ	434,924
0LBP0ZX	434,1070	0LCG4ZZ	1071					0LNV3ZZ	251		
0LBP0ZZ	39,701,923	0LCH*	250,701					0LNV4ZZ	251		
0LBP3ZZ	39,701,923	0LCH0ZZ	1071					0LNW0ZZ	251		
0LBP4ZZ	39,701,923	0LCH3ZZ	1071					0LNW3ZZ	251		
0LBQ*	250	0LCH4ZZ	1071					0LNW4ZZ	251		
0LBQ0ZX	434,1070	0LCJ*	250,701					0LPX00Z	251,702,1071		

Code	Page	Code	Page	Code	Page	Code	Page	Code	Page	Code	Page
ØLQJ*	39, 251, 702	ØLS1ØZZ	435, 925	ØLT9*	252, 703	ØLX2ØZZ	925	ØM54*	232, 496, 703	ØM800ZZ	926, 1071
ØLQJØZZ	434, 924	ØLS14ZZ	435, 925	ØLTB*	252, 703	ØLX24ZZ	925	ØM540ZZ	925	ØM803ZZ	926, 1071
ØLQJ3ZZ	434, 924	ØLS2*	252, 702	ØLTC*	252, 703	ØLX3*	252, 496, 703	ØM543ZZ	925	ØM804ZZ	926, 1071
ØLQJ4ZZ	434, 924	ØLS2ØZZ	435, 925	ØLTD*	252, 703	ØLX3ØZZ	925	ØM544ZZ	925	ØM81*	252, 703
ØLQK*	39, 251, 702	ØLS24ZZ	435, 925	ØLTF*	252, 703	ØLX34ZZ	925	ØM55*	269	ØM810ZZ	926, 1071
ØLQKØZZ	434, 924	ØLS3*	252, 702	ØLTG*	252, 703	ØLX4*	252, 496, 703	ØM550ZZ	435, 641, 925	ØM813ZZ	926, 1071
ØLQK3ZZ	434, 924	ØLS3ØZZ	435, 925	ØLTH*	252, 703	ØLX4ØZZ	925	ØM553ZZ	435, 641, 925	ØM814ZZ	926, 1071
ØLQK4ZZ	434, 924	ØLS34ZZ	435, 925	ØLTJ*	252, 703	ØLX44ZZ	925	ØM554ZZ	925	ØM82*	252, 703
ØLQL*	39, 251, 702	ØLS4*	252, 702	ØLTK*	252, 703	ØLX5*	252, 496, 703	ØM554ZZ	435, 641	ØM820ZZ	926, 1071
ØLQLØZZ	435, 924	ØLS4ØZZ	435, 925	ØLTL*	252, 703	ØLX5ØZZ	925	ØM56*	269	ØM823ZZ	926, 1071
ØLQL3ZZ	435, 924	ØLS44ZZ	435, 925	ØLTM*	252, 703	ØLX54ZZ	925	ØM560ZZ	435, 641, 925	ØM824ZZ	926, 1071
ØLQL4ZZ	435, 924	ØLS5*	252, 702	ØLTN*	252, 703	ØLX6*	252, 496, 703	ØM563ZZ	435, 641, 925	ØM83*	252, 703
ØLQM*	39, 251, 702	ØLS5ØZZ	435, 925	ØLTP*	252, 703	ØLX6ØZZ	925	ØM564ZZ	926	ØM830ZZ	926, 1071
ØLQMØZZ	435, 924	ØLS54ZZ	435, 925	ØLTQ*	252, 703	ØLX64ZZ	925	ØM564ZZ	435, 641	ØM833ZZ	926, 1071
ØLQM3ZZ	435, 924	ØLS6*	252, 702	ØLTR*	252, 703	ØLX7*	269	ØM57*	269	ØM834ZZ	926, 1071
ØLQM4ZZ	435, 924	ØLS6ØZZ	435, 925	ØLTS*	252, 703	ØLX7ØZZ	641, 925	ØM570ZZ	641, 926	ØM84*	252, 703
ØLQN*	39, 251, 702	ØLS64ZZ	435, 925	ØLTT*	252, 703	ØLX74ZZ	641, 925	ØM573ZZ	641, 926	ØM840ZZ	926, 1071
ØLQNØZZ	435, 924	ØLS7*	269	ØLTV*	252, 703	ØLX8*	269	ØM574ZZ	641, 926	ØM843ZZ	926, 1071
ØLQN3ZZ	435, 924	ØLS7ØZZ	641, 925	ØLTW*	252, 703	ØLX8ØZZ	641, 925	ØM58*	269	ØM844ZZ	926, 1071
ØLQN4ZZ	435, 924	ØLS74ZZ	641, 925	ØLUØ*	252, 703	ØLX84ZZ	641, 925	ØM580ZZ	641, 926	ØM850ZZ	252
ØLQP*	39, 251, 702	ØLS8*	269	ØLU1*	252, 703	ØLX9*	252, 496, 703	ØM583ZZ	641, 926	ØM853ZZ	252
ØLQPØZZ	435, 924	ØLS8ØZZ	641, 925	ØLU2*	252, 703	ØLX9ØZZ	925	ØM584ZZ	641, 926	ØM854ZZ	252
ØLQP3ZZ	435, 924	ØLS84ZZ	641, 925	ØLU3*	252, 703	ØLX94ZZ	925	ØM59*	232, 703	ØM860ZZ	252
ØLQP4ZZ	435, 924	ØLS9*	252, 702	ØLU4*	252, 703	ØLXB*	252, 496, 703	ØM590ZZ	926	ØM863ZZ	252
ØLQQ*	251, 702	ØLS9ØZZ	435, 925	ØLU5*	252, 703	ØLXBØZZ	925	ØM593ZZ	926	ØM864ZZ	252
ØLQQØZZ	924, 1071	ØLS94ZZ	435, 925	ØLU6*	252, 703	ØLXB4ZZ	925	ØM594ZZ	926	ØM87*	269
ØLQQ3ZZ	924, 1071	ØLSB*	252, 702	ØLU7*	39, 269	ØLXC*	252, 496, 703	ØM5B*	232, 703	ØM870ZZ	641, 926
ØLQQ4ZZ	924, 1071	ØLSBØZZ	435, 925	ØLU7Ø7Z	435, 641, 925	ØLXCØZZ	925	ØM5BØZZ	926	ØM873ZZ	641, 926
ØLQR*	251, 702	ØLSB4ZZ	435, 925	ØLU7ØJZ	435, 641, 925	ØLXC4ZZ	925	ØM5B3ZZ	926	ØM874ZZ	641, 926
ØLQRØZZ	924, 1071	ØLSC*	252, 702	ØLU7ØKZ	435, 641, 925	ØLXD*	252, 496, 703	ØM5B4ZZ	926	ØM88*	269
ØLQR3ZZ	925, 1071	ØLSCØZZ	435, 925	ØLU747Z	435, 641, 925	ØLXDØZZ	925	ØM5C*	232, 703	ØM880ZZ	641, 926
ØLQR4ZZ	925, 1071	ØLSC4ZZ	435, 925	ØLU74JZ	435, 641, 925	ØLXD4ZZ	925	ØM5CØZZ	926	ØM883ZZ	641, 926
ØLQS*	251, 702	ØLSD*	252, 702	ØLU74KZ	435, 641, 925	ØLXF*	252, 496, 703	ØM5C3ZZ	926	ØM884ZZ	641, 926
ØLQSØZZ	925, 1071	ØLSDØZZ	435, 925	ØLU8*	39, 269	ØLXFØZZ	925	ØM5C4ZZ	926	ØM89*	252, 703
ØLQS3ZZ	925, 1071	ØLSD4ZZ	435, 925	ØLU8Ø7Z	435, 641, 925	ØLXF4ZZ	925	ØM5D*	232, 703	ØM890ZZ	926, 1071
ØLQS4ZZ	925, 1071	ØLSF*	252, 702	ØLU8ØJZ	435, 641, 925	ØLXG*	252, 496, 703	ØM5DØZZ	926	ØM893ZZ	926, 1071
ØLQT*	251, 702	ØLSFØZZ	435, 925	ØLU8ØKZ	435, 641, 925	ØLXGØZZ	925	ØM5D3ZZ	926	ØM894ZZ	926, 1071
ØLQTØZZ	925, 1071	ØLSF4ZZ	435, 925	ØLU847Z	435, 641, 925	ØLXG4ZZ	925	ØM5D4ZZ	926	ØM8B*	252, 703
ØLQT3ZZ	925, 1071	ØLSG*	252, 702	ØLU84JZ	435, 641, 925	ØLXH*	252, 496, 703	ØM5F*	232, 703	ØM8BØZZ	926, 1071
ØLQT4ZZ	925, 1071	ØLSGØZZ	435, 925	ØLU84KZ	435, 641, 925	ØLXHØZZ	925	ØM5FØZZ	926	ØM8B3ZZ	926, 1071
ØLQV*	39, 251, 702	ØLSG4ZZ	435, 925	ØLU9*	252, 703	ØLXH4ZZ	925	ØM5F3ZZ	926	ØM8B4ZZ	926, 1071
ØLQVØZZ	435, 925	ØLSH*	252, 702	ØLUB*	252, 703	ØLXJ*	252, 496, 703	ØM5F4ZZ	926	ØM8C*	252, 703
ØLQV3ZZ	435, 925	ØLSHØZZ	435, 925	ØLUC*	252, 703	ØLXJØZZ	925	ØM5G*	232, 703	ØM8CØZZ	926, 1071
ØLQV4ZZ	435, 925	ØLSH4ZZ	435, 925	ØLUD*	252, 703	ØLXJ4ZZ	925	ØM5GØZZ	926	ØM8C3ZZ	926, 1071
ØLQW*	39, 251, 702	ØLSJ*	252, 702	ØLUF*	252, 703	ØLXK*	252, 496, 703	ØM5G3ZZ	926	ØM8C4ZZ	926, 1071
ØLQWØZZ	435, 925	ØLSJØZZ	435, 925	ØLUG*	252, 703	ØLXKØZZ	925	ØM5G4ZZ	926	ØM8D*	252, 703
ØLQW3ZZ	435, 925	ØLSJ4ZZ	435, 925	ØLUH*	252, 703	ØLXK4ZZ	925	ØM5H*	232, 703	ØM8DØZZ	926, 1071
ØLQW4ZZ	435, 925	ØLSK*	252, 702	ØLUJ*	252, 703	ØLXL*	252, 496, 703	ØM5HØZZ	926	ØM8D3ZZ	926, 1071
ØLRØ*	251, 702	ØLSKØZZ	435, 925	ØLUK*	252, 703	ØLXLØZZ	925	ØM5H3ZZ	926	ØM8D4ZZ	926, 1071
ØLR1*	251, 702	ØLSK4ZZ	435, 925	ØLUL*	252, 703	ØLXL4ZZ	925	ØM5H4ZZ	926	ØM8F*	252, 703
ØLR2*	251, 702	ØLSL*	252, 702	ØLUM*	252, 703	ØLXM*	252, 496, 703	ØM5J*	232, 703	ØM8FØZZ	926, 1072
ØLR3*	251, 702	ØLSLØZZ	435, 925	ØLUN*	252, 703	ØLXMØZZ	925	ØM5JØZZ	926	ØM8F3ZZ	926, 1072
ØLR4*	251, 702	ØLSL4ZZ	435, 925	ØLUP*	252, 703	ØLXM4ZZ	925	ØM5J3ZZ	926	ØM8F4ZZ	926, 1072
ØLR5*	251, 702	ØLSM*	252, 702	ØLUQ*	252, 703	ØLXN*	252, 496, 703	ØM5J4ZZ	926	ØM8G*	252, 703
ØLR6*	252, 702	ØLSMØZZ	435, 925	ØLUR*	252, 703	ØLXNØZZ	925	ØM5K*	232, 703	ØM8GØZZ	926, 1072
ØLR7*	39, 269	ØLSM4ZZ	435, 925	ØLUS*	252, 703	ØLXN4ZZ	925	ØM5KØZZ	926	ØM8G3ZZ	926, 1072
ØLR7Ø7Z	435, 641, 925	ØLSN*	252, 702	ØLUT*	252, 703	ØLXP*	252, 496, 703	ØM5K3ZZ	926	ØM8G4ZZ	926, 1072
ØLR7ØJZ	435, 641, 925	ØLSNØZZ	435, 925	ØLUV*	252, 703	ØLXPØZZ	925	ØM5K4ZZ	926	ØM8H*	252, 703
ØLR7ØKZ	435, 641, 925	ØLSN4ZZ	435, 925	ØLUW*	252, 703	ØLXP4ZZ	925	ØM5L*	241, 703	ØM8HØZZ	926, 1072
ØLR747Z	435, 641, 925	ØLSP*	252, 702	ØLWX00Z	252, 703, 1071	ØLXQ*	252, 496, 703	ØM5LØZZ	926	ØM8H3ZZ	926, 1072
ØLR74JZ	435, 641, 925	ØLSPØZZ	435, 925	ØLWX07Z	252, 703, 1071	ØLXQØZZ	925	ØM5L3ZZ	926	ØM8H4ZZ	926, 1072
ØLR74KZ	435, 641, 925	ØLSP4ZZ	435, 925	ØLWXØJZ	252, 703, 1071	ØLXQ4ZZ	925	ØM5L4ZZ	926	ØM8J*	252, 703
ØLR8*	39, 269	ØLSQ*	252, 702	ØLWXØKZ	252, 703, 1071	ØLXR*	252, 496, 703	ØM5M*	241, 703	ØM8JØZZ	926, 1072
ØLR8Ø7Z	435, 641, 925	ØLSQØZZ	435, 925	ØLWXØYZ	252, 703, 1071	ØLXRØZZ	925	ØM5MØZZ	926	ØM8J3ZZ	926, 1072
ØLR8ØJZ	435, 641, 925	ØLSQ4ZZ	435, 925	ØLWX3ØZ	252, 703, 1071	ØLXR4ZZ	925	ØM5M3ZZ	926	ØM8J4ZZ	926, 1072
ØLR8ØKZ	435, 641, 925	ØLSR*	252, 702	ØLWX37Z	252, 703, 1071	ØLXS*	252, 496, 703	ØM5M4ZZ	926	ØM8K*	252, 703
ØLR847Z	435, 641, 925	ØLSRØZZ	435, 925	ØLWX3JZ	252, 703, 1071	ØLXSØZZ	925	ØM5N*	232, 703	ØM8KØZZ	926, 1072
ØLR84JZ	435, 641, 925	ØLSR4ZZ	435, 925	ØLWX3KZ	252, 703, 1071	ØLXS4ZZ	925	ØM5NØZZ	926, 1071	ØM8K3ZZ	926, 1072
ØLR84KZ	435, 641, 925	ØLSS*	252, 702	ØLWX4ØZ	252, 703, 1071	ØLXT*	252, 496, 703	ØM5N3ZZ	926, 1071	ØM8K4ZZ	926, 1072
ØLR9*	252, 702	ØLSSØZZ	435, 925	ØLWX47Z	252, 703, 1071	ØLXTØZZ	925	ØM5N4ZZ	926, 1071	ØM8L*	252, 703
ØLRB*	252, 702	ØLSS4ZZ	435, 925	ØLWX4JZ	252, 703, 1071	ØLXT4ZZ	925	ØM5P*	232, 703	ØM8LØZZ	926, 1072
ØLRC*	252, 702	ØLST*	252, 702	ØLWX4KZ	252, 703, 1071	ØLXV*	252, 496, 703	ØM5PØZZ	926, 1071	ØM8L3ZZ	926, 1072
ØLRD*	252, 702	ØLSTØZZ	435, 925	ØLWY00Z	252, 703, 1071	ØLXVØZZ	925	ØM5P3ZZ	926, 1071	ØM8L4ZZ	926, 1072
ØLRF*	252, 702	ØLST4ZZ	435, 925	ØLWY07Z	252, 703, 1071	ØLXV4ZZ	925	ØM5P4ZZ	926, 1071	ØM8M*	252, 703
ØLRG*	252, 702	ØLSV*	252, 702	ØLWYØJZ	252, 703, 1071	ØLXW*	252, 496, 703	ØM5Q*	229, 703	ØM8MØZZ	926, 1072
ØLRH*	252, 702	ØLSVØZZ	435, 925	ØLWYØKZ	252, 703, 1071	ØLXWØZZ	925	ØM5QØZZ	926	ØM8M3ZZ	926, 1072
ØLRJ*	252, 702	ØLSV4ZZ	435, 925	ØLWYØYZ	252, 703, 1071	ØLXW4ZZ	925	ØM5Q3ZZ	926	ØM8M4ZZ	926, 1072
ØLRK*	252, 702	ØLSW*	252, 702	ØLWY3ØZ	252, 703, 1071	ØM50*	232, 703	ØM5Q4ZZ	926	ØM8N*	252, 703
ØLRL*	252, 702	ØLSWØZZ	435, 925	ØLWY37Z	252, 703, 1071	ØM500ZZ	925	ØM5R*	229, 703	ØM8NØZZ	926, 1072
ØLRM*	252, 702	ØLSW4ZZ	435, 925	ØLWY3JZ	252, 703, 1071	ØM503ZZ	925	ØM5RØZZ	926	ØM8N3ZZ	926, 1072
ØLRN*	252, 702	ØLTØ*	252, 702	ØLWY3KZ	252, 703, 1071	ØM504ZZ	925	ØM5R3ZZ	926	ØM8N4ZZ	926, 1072
ØLRP*	252, 702	ØLT1*	252, 702	ØLWY4ØZ	252, 703, 1071	ØM51*	232, 703	ØM5R4ZZ	926	ØM8P*	252, 703
ØLRQ*	252, 702	ØLT3*	252, 702	ØLWY47Z	252, 703, 1071	ØM510ZZ	925	ØM5S*	257, 496, 703	ØM8PØZZ	926, 1072
ØLRR*	252, 702	ØLT4*	252, 702	ØLWY4JZ	252, 703, 1071	ØM513ZZ	925	ØM5SØZZ	926, 1071	ØM8P3ZZ	926, 1072
ØLRS*	252, 702	ØLT5*	252, 702	ØLWY4KZ	252, 703, 1071	ØM514ZZ	925	ØM5S3ZZ	926, 1071	ØM8P4ZZ	926, 1072
ØLRT*	252, 702	ØLT6*	252, 702	ØLX*	39	ØM52*	232, 703	ØM5S4ZZ	926, 1071	ØM8Q*	253, 703
ØLRV*	252, 702	ØLT7*	269, 496	ØLXØ*	252, 496, 703	ØM520ZZ	925	ØM5T*	257, 496, 703	ØM8QØZZ	926, 1072
ØLRW*	252, 702	ØLT7ØZZ	641, 925	ØLX00ZZ	925	ØM523ZZ	925	ØM5TØZZ	926, 1071	ØM8Q3ZZ	926, 1072
ØLS*	39	ØLT74ZZ	641, 925	ØLX04ZZ	925	ØM524ZZ	925	ØM5T3ZZ	926, 1071	ØM8Q4ZZ	926, 1072
ØLSØ*	252, 702	ØLT8*	269, 496	ØLX1*	252, 496, 703	ØM53*	232, 496, 703	ØM5T4ZZ	926, 1071	ØM8R*	253, 703
ØLSØØZZ	435, 925	ØLT8ØZZ	641, 925	ØLX1ØZZ	925	ØM533ZZ	925	ØM5V*	232	ØM8RØZZ	926, 1072
ØLSØ4ZZ	435, 925	ØLT84ZZ	641, 925	ØLX14ZZ	925	ØM534ZZ	925	ØM5W*	232	ØM8R3ZZ	926, 1072
ØLS1*	252, 702			ØLX2*	252, 496, 703			ØM80*	252, 703	ØM8R4ZZ	926, 1072

Code	Page	Code	Page	Code	Page	Code	Page	Code	Page	Code	Page
0M8S*	253, 703	0M9J3ZX	253	0MB83ZZ	269, 641, 927	0MC1*	253, 704	0MCS0ZZ	927, 1073	0MDM3ZZ	1073
0M8S0ZZ	926, 1072	0M9J4ZX	253	0MB84ZZ	269, 641, 927	0MC10ZZ	927, 1073	0MCS3ZZ	927, 1073	0MDM4ZZ	1073
0M8S3ZZ	926, 1072	0M9K00Z	253, 703, 926, 1072	0MB90ZX	253, 435, 1072	0MC13ZZ	927, 1073	0MCS4ZZ	927, 1073	0MDN*	254, 704
0M8S4ZZ	926, 1072	0M9K0ZX	253, 435, 1072	0MB90ZZ	253, 704, 927, 1072	0MC14ZZ	927, 1073	0MCT*	253, 704	0MDN0ZZ	1073
0M8T*	253, 703	0M9K0ZZ	253, 704, 926, 1072	0MB93ZX	253	0MC2*	253, 704	0MCT0ZZ	927, 1073	0MDN3ZZ	1073
0M8T0ZZ	926, 1072	0M9K3ZX	253	0MB93ZZ	253, 704, 927, 1072	0MC20ZZ	927, 1073	0MCT3ZZ	927, 1073	0MDN4ZZ	1073
0M8T3ZZ	926, 1072	0M9K4ZX	253	0MB94ZZ	253, 704, 927, 1072	0MC23ZZ	927, 1073	0MCT4ZZ	927, 1073	0MDP*	254, 704
0M8T4ZZ	926, 1072	0M9L00Z	253, 704, 926, 1072	0MBB0ZZ	253, 704, 927, 1072	0MC24ZZ	927, 1073	0MCV*	253, 704	0MDP0ZZ	1073
0M8V*	253, 703	0M9L0ZZ	253, 704, 926, 1072	0MBB3ZZ	253, 704, 927, 1072	0MC3*	253, 704	0MCV0ZZ	927, 1073	0MDP3ZZ	1073
0M8V0ZZ	926, 1072	0M9L4ZZ	224, 704	0MBB4ZZ	253, 704, 927, 1072	0MC30ZZ	927, 1073	0MCV3ZZ	927, 1073	0MDP4ZZ	1073
0M8V3ZZ	926, 1072	0M9M00Z	253, 704, 926, 1072	0MBC0ZZ	253, 704, 927, 1072	0MC33ZZ	927, 1073	0MCV4ZZ	927, 1073	0MDQ*	254, 704
0M8V4ZZ	926, 1072	0M9M0ZZ	253, 704, 926, 1072	0MBC3ZZ	253, 704, 927, 1072	0MC34ZZ	927, 1073	0MCW*	253, 704	0MDQ0ZZ	1073
0M8W*	253, 703	0M9M4ZZ	224, 704	0MBC4ZZ	253, 704, 927, 1072	0MC4*	253, 704	0MCW0ZZ	927, 1073	0MDQ3ZZ	1073
0M8W0ZZ	926, 1072	0M9N00Z	253, 704, 926, 1072	0MBD0ZZ	253, 704, 927, 1072	0MC40ZZ	927, 1073	0MCW3ZZ	927, 1073	0MDQ4ZZ	1073
0M8W3ZZ	926, 1072	0M9N0ZZ	253, 704, 926, 1072	0MBD3ZZ	253, 704, 927, 1072	0MC43ZZ	927, 1073	0MCW4ZZ	927, 1073	0MDR*	254, 704
0M8W4ZZ	926, 1072	0M9N40Z	227, 496, 704, 1072	0MBD4ZZ	253, 704, 927, 1072	0MC44ZZ	927, 1073	0MD0*	253, 704	0MDR0ZZ	1073
0M9000Z	253, 703, 926, 1072	0M9P00Z	253, 704, 927, 1072	0MBF0ZZ	253, 704, 927, 1072	0MC5*	261	0MD00ZZ	1073	0MDR3ZZ	1073
0M900ZZ	253, 703, 926, 1072	0M9P0ZZ	253, 704, 927, 1072	0MBF3ZZ	253, 704, 927, 1072	0MC50ZZ	641	0MD03ZZ	1073	0MDR4ZZ	1073
0M9040Z	277	0M9P40Z	227, 496, 704, 1072	0MBF4ZZ	253, 704, 927, 1072	0MC53ZZ	641	0MD04ZZ	1073	0MDS*	254, 704
0M9100Z	253, 703, 926, 1072	0M9Q00Z	253, 704, 927, 1072	0MBG0ZZ	253, 704, 927, 1072	0MC54ZZ	641	0MD1*	253, 704	0MDS0ZZ	1073
0M910ZZ	253, 703, 926, 1072	0M9Q0ZZ	253, 704, 927, 1072	0MBG3ZZ	253, 704, 927, 1072	0MC6*	261	0MD10ZZ	1073	0MDS3ZZ	1073
0M914ZZ	264, 703	0M9Q40Z	229, 704	0MBG4ZZ	253, 704, 927, 1072	0MC60ZZ	641	0MD13ZZ	1073	0MDS4ZZ	1073
0M9200Z	253, 703, 926, 1072	0M9R00Z	253, 704, 927, 1072	0MBH*	253	0MC63ZZ	641	0MD14ZZ	1073	0MDT*	254, 704
0M920ZZ	253, 703, 926, 1072	0M9R0ZZ	253, 704, 927, 1072	0MBH0ZX	435, 1072	0MC64ZZ	641	0MD2*	253, 704	0MDT0ZZ	1073
0M924ZZ	264, 703	0M9R40Z	229, 704	0MBH0ZZ	704, 1072	0MC7*	269	0MD20ZZ	1073	0MDT3ZZ	1073
0M9300Z	253, 703, 926, 1072	0M9S00Z	253, 704, 927, 1072	0MBH3ZZ	704, 1072	0MC70ZZ	641, 927	0MD23ZZ	1073	0MDT4ZZ	1073
0M930ZZ	253, 703, 926, 1072	0M9S0ZZ	253, 704, 927, 1072	0MBH4ZZ	704, 1072	0MC73ZZ	641, 927	0MD24ZZ	1073	0MDV*	254, 704
0M934ZZ	264, 496, 703	0M9S40Z	257, 704, 1072	0MBJ*	253	0MC74ZZ	641, 927	0MD3*	253, 704	0MDV0ZZ	1073
0M9400Z	253, 703, 926, 1072	0M9T00Z	253, 704, 927, 1072	0MBJ0ZX	435, 1072	0MC8*	269	0MD30ZZ	1073	0MDV3ZZ	1073
0M940ZZ	253, 703, 926, 1072	0M9T0ZZ	253, 704, 927, 1072	0MBJ0ZZ	704, 1072	0MC80ZZ	641, 927	0MD33ZZ	1073	0MDV4ZZ	1073
0M944ZZ	264, 496, 703	0M9T40Z	257, 704, 1072	0MBJ3ZZ	704, 1072	0MC83ZZ	641, 927	0MD34ZZ	1073	0MDW*	254, 704
0M9500Z	261, 641	0M9V00Z	253, 704, 927, 1072	0MBJ4ZZ	704, 1072	0MC84ZZ	641, 927	0MD4*	253, 704	0MDW0ZZ	1073
0M950ZZ	261, 641	0M9V0ZX	253, 435, 1072	0MBK*	253	0MC9*	253, 704	0MD40ZZ	1073	0MDW3ZZ	1073
0M954ZZ	261, 641	0M9V0ZZ	253, 704, 927, 1072	0MBK0ZX	435, 1072	0MC90ZZ	927, 1073	0MD43ZZ	1073	0MDW4ZZ	1073
0M9600Z	261, 641	0M9V3ZX	253	0MBK0ZZ	704, 1072	0MC93ZZ	927, 1073	0MD44ZZ	1073	0MHX0YZ	39, 254, 704, 927
0M960ZZ	261, 641	0M9V4ZX	253	0MBK3ZZ	704, 1072	0MC94ZZ	927, 1073	0MD5*	254, 704	0MHY0YZ	39, 254, 704, 927
0M964ZZ	261, 641	0M9W00Z	253, 704, 927, 1072	0MBK4ZZ	704, 1072	0MCB*	253, 704	0MD50ZZ	1073	0MJX0ZZ	222
0M9700Z	269, 641, 926	0M9W0ZX	253, 435, 1072	0MBL0ZZ	253, 704, 1072	0MCB0ZZ	927, 1073	0MD53ZZ	1073	0MJX4ZZ	222
0M970ZZ	269, 641, 926	0M9W0ZZ	253, 704, 927, 1072	0MBL3ZZ	253, 704, 1072	0MCB3ZZ	927, 1073	0MD54ZZ	1073	0MJY0ZZ	222
0M9800Z	269, 641, 926	0M9W3ZX	253	0MBL4ZZ	253, 704, 1072	0MCB4ZZ	927, 1073	0MD6*	254, 704	0MJY4ZZ	222
0M980ZZ	269, 641, 926	0M9W4ZX	253	0MBM0ZZ	253, 704, 1072	0MCC*	253, 704	0MD60ZZ	1073	0MM*	277
0M9900Z	253, 703, 926, 1072	0MB00ZZ	253, 704, 927, 1072	0MBM3ZZ	253, 704, 1072	0MCC0ZZ	927, 1073	0MD63ZZ	1073	0MN00ZZ	254
0M990ZX	253, 435, 1072	0MB03ZZ	253, 704, 927, 1072	0MBM4ZZ	253, 704, 1072	0MCC3ZZ	927, 1073	0MD64ZZ	1073	0MN03ZZ	254
0M990ZZ	253, 703, 926, 1072	0MB04ZZ	253, 704, 927, 1072	0MBN0ZZ	253, 704, 1072	0MCC4ZZ	927, 1073	0MD7*	269	0MN04ZZ	254
0M993ZX	253	0MB10ZZ	253, 704, 1072	0MBN3ZZ	253, 704, 1072	0MCD*	253, 704	0MD70ZZ	641, 927	0MN10ZZ	254
0M994ZX	253	0MB13ZZ	253, 704, 1072	0MBN4ZZ	253, 704, 1072	0MCD0ZZ	927, 1073	0MD73ZZ	641, 927	0MN13ZZ	254
0M9B00Z	253, 703, 926, 1072	0MB14ZZ	253, 704, 1072	0MBP0ZZ	253, 704, 1072	0MCD3ZZ	927, 1073	0MD74ZZ	641, 927	0MN14ZZ	254
0M9B0ZX	253, 435, 1072	0MB20ZZ	253, 704, 1072	0MBP3ZZ	253, 704, 1072	0MCD4ZZ	927, 1073	0MD8*	269	0MN20ZZ	254
0M9B0ZZ	253, 703, 926, 1072	0MB23ZZ	253, 704, 1072	0MBP4ZZ	253, 704, 1072	0MCF*	253, 704	0MD80ZZ	641, 927	0MN23ZZ	254
0M9B3ZX	253	0MB24ZZ	253, 704, 1072	0MBQ0ZZ	253, 704, 1072	0MCF0ZZ	927, 1073	0MD83ZZ	641, 927	0MN24ZZ	254
0M9B4ZX	253	0MB30ZZ	253, 704, 1072	0MBQ3ZZ	253, 704, 1072	0MCF3ZZ	927, 1073	0MD84ZZ	641, 927	0MN30ZZ	254
0M9C00Z	253, 703, 926, 1072	0MB33ZZ	253, 704, 1072	0MBQ4ZZ	253, 704, 1072	0MCF4ZZ	927, 1073	0MD9*	254, 704	0MN33ZZ	254
0M9C0ZZ	253, 703, 926, 1072	0MB34ZZ	253, 704, 1072	0MBR0ZZ	253, 704, 1072	0MCG*	253, 704	0MD90ZZ	1073	0MN34ZZ	254
0M9D00Z	253, 703, 926, 1072	0MB40ZZ	253, 704, 1072	0MBR3ZZ	253, 704, 1072	0MCG0ZZ	927, 1073	0MD93ZZ	1073	0MN40ZZ	254
0M9D0ZZ	253, 703, 926, 1072	0MB43ZZ	253, 704, 1072	0MBR4ZZ	253, 704, 1072	0MCG3ZZ	927, 1073	0MD94ZZ	1073	0MN43ZZ	254
0M9F00Z	253, 703, 926, 1072	0MB44ZZ	253, 704, 1072	0MBS0ZZ	253, 704, 1073	0MCG4ZZ	927, 1073	0MDB*	254, 704	0MN44ZZ	254
0M9F0ZZ	253, 703, 926, 1072	0MB50ZZ	253, 704, 1072	0MBS3ZZ	253, 704, 1073	0MCH*	253, 704	0MDB0ZZ	1073	0MN50ZZ	254
0M9G00Z	253, 703, 926, 1072	0MB53ZZ	253, 704, 1072	0MBS4ZZ	253, 704, 1073	0MCH0ZZ	927, 1073	0MDB3ZZ	1073	0MN53ZZ	254
0M9G0ZZ	253, 703, 926, 1072	0MB54ZZ	253, 704, 1072	0MBT0ZZ	253, 704, 1073	0MCH3ZZ	927, 1073	0MDB4ZZ	1073	0MN54ZZ	254
0M9H00Z	253, 703, 926, 1072	0MB60ZZ	253, 704, 1072	0MBT3ZZ	253, 704, 1073	0MCH4ZZ	927, 1073	0MDC*	254, 704	0MN60ZZ	254
0M9H0ZX	253, 435, 1072	0MB63ZZ	253, 704, 1072	0MBT4ZZ	253, 704, 1073	0MCJ*	253, 704	0MDC0ZZ	1073	0MN63ZZ	254
0M9H0ZZ	253, 703, 926, 1072	0MB64ZZ	253, 704, 1072	0MBV*	253	0MCJ0ZZ	927, 1073	0MDC3ZZ	1073	0MN64ZZ	254
0M9H3ZX	253	0MB70ZZ	269, 641, 927	0MBV0ZX	435, 1073	0MCJ3ZZ	927, 1073	0MDC4ZZ	1073	0MN70ZZ	269, 435, 641, 927
0M9H4ZX	253	0MB73ZZ	269, 641, 927	0MBV0ZZ	704, 927, 1073	0MCJ4ZZ	927, 1073	0MDD*	254, 704	0MN73ZZ	269, 435, 641, 927
0M9J00Z	253, 703, 926, 1072	0MB74ZZ	269, 641, 927	0MBV3ZZ	704, 927, 1073	0MCK*	253, 704	0MDD0ZZ	1073	0MN74ZZ	269, 435, 641, 927
0M9J0ZX	253, 435, 1072	0MB80ZZ	269, 641, 927	0MBV4ZZ	704, 927, 1073	0MCK0ZZ	927, 1073	0MDD3ZZ	1073	0MN80ZZ	269, 435, 641, 927
0M9J0ZZ	253, 703, 926, 1072			0MBW*	253	0MCK3ZZ	927, 1073	0MDD4ZZ	1073	0MN83ZZ	269, 435, 641, 927
				0MBW0ZX	435, 1073	0MCK4ZZ	927, 1073	0MDF*	254, 704	0MN84ZZ	269, 435, 641, 927
				0MBW0ZZ	704, 927, 1073	0MCL*	253, 704	0MDF0ZZ	1073	0MN90ZZ	254
				0MBW3ZZ	704, 927, 1073	0MCL0ZZ	927, 1073	0MDF3ZZ	1073	0MN93ZZ	254
				0MBW4ZZ	704, 927, 1073	0MCL3ZZ	927, 1073	0MDF4ZZ	1073	0MN94ZZ	254
				0MC0*	253, 704	0MCL4ZZ	927, 1073	0MDG*	254, 704	0MNB0ZZ	254
				0MC00ZZ	927, 1073	0MCM*	253, 704	0MDG0ZZ	1073	0MNB3ZZ	254
				0MC03ZZ	927, 1073	0MCM0ZZ	927, 1073	0MDG3ZZ	1073	0MNB4ZZ	254
				0MC04ZZ	927, 1073	0MCM3ZZ	927, 1073	0MDG4ZZ	1073	0MNC0ZZ	254
						0MCM4ZZ	927, 1073	0MDH*	254, 704	0MNC3ZZ	254
						0MCN*	253, 704	0MDH0ZZ	1073	0MNC4ZZ	254
						0MCN0ZZ	927, 1073	0MDH3ZZ	1073	0MND0ZZ	254
						0MCN3ZZ	927, 1073	0MDH4ZZ	1073	0MND3ZZ	254
						0MCN4ZZ	927, 1073	0MDJ*	254, 704	0MND4ZZ	254
						0MCP*	253, 704	0MDJ0ZZ	1073	0MNF0ZZ	254
						0MCP0ZZ	927, 1073	0MDJ3ZZ	1073	0MNF3ZZ	254
						0MCP3ZZ	927, 1073	0MDJ4ZZ	1073	0MNF4ZZ	254
						0MCP4ZZ	927, 1073	0MDK*	254, 704	0MNG0ZZ	254
						0MCQ*	253, 704	0MDK0ZZ	1073	0MNG3ZZ	254
						0MCQ0ZZ	927, 1073	0MDK3ZZ	1073	0MNG4ZZ	254
						0MCQ3ZZ	927, 1073	0MDK4ZZ	1073	0MNH0ZZ	254
						0MCQ4ZZ	927, 1073	0MDL*	254, 704	0MNH3ZZ	254
						0MCR*	253, 704	0MDL0ZZ	1073	0MNH4ZZ	254
						0MCR0ZZ	927, 1073	0MDL3ZZ	1073	0MNJ0ZZ	254
						0MCR3ZZ	927, 1073	0MDL4ZZ	1073	0MNJ3ZZ	254
						0MCR4ZZ	927, 1073	0MDM*	254, 704	0MNJ4ZZ	254
						0MCS*	253, 704	0MDM0ZZ	1073	0MNK0ZZ	254

Code	Page	Code	Page	Code	Page	Code	Page	Code	Page	Code	Page
0MNK3ZZ	254	0MQ7*	254, 705	0MR807Z	255, 705, 928	0MRR47Z	255, 705, 928	0MTD4ZZ	928, 1074	0MWX40Z	255, 705, 928, 1074
0MNK4ZZ	254	0MQ70ZZ	927	0MR80JZ	255, 705, 928	0MRR4JZ	255, 705, 928	0MTF*	255, 705	0MWX47Z	255, 705, 928, 1074
0MNL0ZZ	254	0MQ73ZZ	927	0MR80KZ	255, 705, 928	0MRR4KZ	255, 705, 928	0MTF0ZZ	928, 1074	0MWX4JZ	255, 705, 928, 1074
0MNL3ZZ	254	0MQ74ZZ	927	0MR847Z	255, 705, 928	0MRS07Z	257, 705, 928	0MTF4ZZ	928, 1074	0MWX4KZ	255, 705, 928, 1074
0MNL4ZZ	254	0MQ8*	254, 705	0MR84JZ	255, 705, 928	0MRS0JZ	257, 705, 928	0MTG*	255, 705	0MWY00Z	255, 705, 928, 1074
0MNM0ZZ	254	0MQ80ZZ	927	0MR84KZ	255, 705, 928	0MRS0KZ	257, 705, 928	0MTG0ZZ	928, 1074	0MWY07Z	255, 705, 928, 1074
0MNM3ZZ	254	0MQ83ZZ	927	0MR907Z	255	0MRS47Z	257, 705, 928	0MTG4ZZ	928, 1074	0MWY0JZ	255, 705, 928, 1074
0MNM4ZZ	254	0MQ84ZZ	928	0MR90JZ	255	0MRS4JZ	257, 705, 928	0MTH*	255, 705	0MWY0KZ	255, 705, 928, 1074
0MNN0ZZ	254	0MQ9*	254	0MR947Z	255	0MRS4KZ	257, 705, 928	0MTH0ZZ	1074	0MWY0YZ	255, 705, 928, 1074
0MNN3ZZ	254	0MQB*	254	0MR94JZ	255	0MRT07Z	257, 705, 928	0MTH4ZZ	1074	0MWY30Z	255, 705, 928, 1074
0MNN4ZZ	254	0MQC*	254	0MR94KZ	255	0MRT0JZ	257, 705, 928	0MTJ*	255, 705	0MWY37Z	255, 705, 928, 1074
0MNP0ZZ	254	0MQD*	254	0MRB07Z	255	0MRT0KZ	257, 705, 928	0MTJ0ZZ	1074	0MWY3JZ	255, 705, 928, 1074
0MNP3ZZ	254	0MQF*	254	0MRB0JZ	255	0MRT47Z	257, 705, 928	0MTJ4ZZ	1074	0MWY3KZ	255, 705, 928, 1074
0MNP4ZZ	254	0MQG*	254	0MRB0KZ	255	0MRT4JZ	257, 705, 928	0MTK*	255, 705	0MWY40Z	255, 705, 928, 1074
0MNQ0ZZ	254	0MQH*	254	0MRB47Z	255	0MRT4KZ	257, 705, 928	0MTK0ZZ	1074	0MWY47Z	255, 705, 928, 1074
0MNQ3ZZ	254	0MQJ*	254	0MRB4JZ	255	0MRV07Z	255	0MTK4ZZ	1074	0MWY4JZ	255, 705, 928, 1074
0MNQ4ZZ	254	0MQK*	254	0MRB4KZ	255	0MRV0JZ	255	0MTL*	255, 705	0MWY4KZ	255, 705, 928, 1074
0MNR0ZZ	254	0MQL*	254	0MRC07Z	255	0MRV0KZ	255	0MTL0ZZ	1074	0MX*	255
0MNR3ZZ	254	0MQM*	254	0MRC0JZ	255	0MRV47Z	255	0MTL4ZZ	1074	0N5*	67, 705
0MNR4ZZ	254	0MQN*	227, 705	0MRC0KZ	255	0MRV4JZ	255	0MTM*	255, 705	0N50*	278, 849
0MNS0ZZ	254	0MQN0ZZ	928	0MRC47Z	255	0MRV4KZ	255	0MTM0ZZ	1074	0N500ZZ	12, 599, 624
0MNS3ZZ	254	0MQN3ZZ	928	0MRC4JZ	255	0MRW07Z	255	0MTM4ZZ	1074	0N503ZZ	12, 599, 624
0MNS4ZZ	254	0MQN4ZZ	928	0MRC4KZ	255	0MRW0JZ	255	0MTN*	255, 705	0N504ZZ	12, 599, 624
0MNT0ZZ	254	0MQP*	227, 705	0MRD07Z	255	0MRW0KZ	255	0MTN0ZZ	1074	0N51*	278, 849
0MNT3ZZ	254	0MQP0ZZ	928	0MRD0JZ	255	0MRW47Z	255	0MTN4ZZ	1074	0N510ZZ	12, 599, 624
0MNT4ZZ	254	0MQP3ZZ	928	0MRD0KZ	255	0MRW4JZ	255	0MTP*	255, 705	0N513ZZ	12, 599, 624
0MNV0ZZ	254	0MQP4ZZ	928	0MRD47Z	255	0MRW4KZ	255	0MTP0ZZ	1074	0N514ZZ	12, 599, 624
0MNV3ZZ	254	0MQQ*	254, 705	0MRD4JZ	255	0MS0*	277	0MTP4ZZ	1074	0N53*	278, 849
0MNV4ZZ	254	0MQQ0ZZ	928	0MRD4KZ	255	0MS1*	277	0MTQ*	255, 705	0N530ZZ	12, 599, 624
0MNW0ZZ	254	0MQQ3ZZ	928	0MRF07Z	255	0MS2*	277	0MTQ0ZZ	1074	0N533ZZ	12, 599, 624
0MNW3ZZ	254	0MQQ4ZZ	928	0MRF0JZ	255	0MS4*	277	0MTQ4ZZ	1074	0N534ZZ	12, 599, 624
0MNW4ZZ	254	0MQR*	254, 705	0MRF0KZ	255	0MS5*	277	0MTR*	255, 705	0N54*	278, 849
0MPX00Z	277	0MQR0ZZ	928	0MRF47Z	255	0MS6*	277	0MTR0ZZ	1074	0N540ZZ	12, 599, 624
0MPX07Z	254, 704, 927, 1073	0MQR3ZZ	928	0MRF4JZ	255	0MS7*	277	0MTR4ZZ	1074	0N543ZZ	12, 599, 624
0MPX0JZ	277	0MQR4ZZ	928	0MRF4KZ	255	0MS8*	277	0MTS*	255, 705	0N544ZZ	12, 599, 624
0MPX0KZ	254, 704, 927, 1073	0MQS*	257, 705	0MRG07Z	255	0MS9*	255	0MTS0ZZ	1074	0N55*	278, 849
0MPX0YZ	277	0MQS0ZZ	928	0MRG0JZ	255	0MSB*	255	0MTS4ZZ	1074	0N550ZZ	12, 599, 624
0MPX37Z	254, 704, 927, 1073	0MQS3ZZ	928	0MRG0KZ	255	0MSC*	277	0MTT*	255, 705	0N553ZZ	12, 599, 624
0MPX3JZ	277	0MQS4ZZ	928	0MRG47Z	255	0MSD*	277	0MTT0ZZ	1074	0N554ZZ	12, 599, 624
0MPX3KZ	254, 704, 927, 1073	0MQT*	257, 705	0MRG4JZ	255	0MSF*	277	0MTT4ZZ	1074	0N56*	278, 849
0MPX40Z	277	0MQT0ZZ	928	0MRG4KZ	255	0MSG*	277	0MTV*	255, 705	0N560ZZ	12, 599, 624
0MPX47Z	254, 704, 927, 1073	0MQT3ZZ	928	0MRH07Z	255	0MSH*	277	0MTV0ZZ	928, 1074	0N563ZZ	12, 599, 624
0MPX4JZ	277	0MQT4ZZ	928	0MRH0JZ	255	0MSJ*	277	0MTV4ZZ	928, 1074	0N564ZZ	12, 599, 624
0MPX4KZ	254, 704, 927, 1073	0MQV*	254	0MRH0KZ	255	0MSK*	277	0MTW*	255, 705	0N57*	278, 849
0MPY00Z	277	0MQW*	254	0MRH47Z	255	0MSL*	277	0MTW0ZZ	928, 1074	0N570ZZ	12, 599, 624
0MPY07Z	254, 704, 927, 1073	0MR007Z	254	0MRH4JZ	255	0MSM*	277	0MTW4ZZ	928, 1074	0N573ZZ	12, 599, 624
0MPY0JZ	277	0MR00JZ	254	0MRH4KZ	255	0MSN*	277	0MU0*	255	0N574ZZ	12, 599, 624
0MPY0KZ	254, 704, 927, 1073	0MR00KZ	254	0MRJ07Z	255	0MSP*	277	0MU1*	278	0N5B*	232
0MPY0YZ	277	0MR047Z	254	0MRJ0JZ	255	0MSQ*	277	0MU2*	278	0N5B0ZZ	928, 1074
0MPY37Z	254, 704, 927, 1073	0MR04JZ	254	0MRJ0KZ	255	0MSR*	277	0MU3*	278	0N5B3ZZ	928, 1074
0MPY3JZ	277	0MR04KZ	254	0MRJ47Z	255	0MSS*	277	0MU4*	278	0N5B4ZZ	928, 1074
0MPY3KZ	254, 704, 927, 1073	0MR107Z	254, 705, 928	0MRJ4JZ	255	0MST*	278	0MU5*	278	0N5C*	232
0MPY40Z	277	0MR10JZ	254, 705, 928	0MRJ4KZ	255	0MSV*	255	0MU6*	278	0N5C0ZZ	928, 1074
0MPY47Z	254, 704, 927, 1074	0MR10KZ	254, 705, 928	0MRK07Z	255	0MSW*	255	0MU7*	278	0N5C3ZZ	928, 1074
0MPY4JZ	277	0MR147Z	254, 705, 928	0MRK0JZ	255	0MT0*	255, 705	0MU8*	278	0N5C4ZZ	928, 1074
0MPY4KZ	254, 704, 927, 1074	0MR14JZ	254, 705, 928	0MRK0KZ	255	0MT00ZZ	928, 1074	0MU9*	255	0N5F*	232
0MQ0*	254	0MR14KZ	254, 705, 928	0MRK47Z	255	0MT04ZZ	928, 1074	0MUB*	278	0N5F0ZZ	928, 1074
0MQ1*	254, 704	0MR207Z	254, 705, 928	0MRK4JZ	255	0MT1*	255, 705	0MUC*	278	0N5F3ZZ	928, 1074
0MQ10ZZ	927	0MR20JZ	254, 705, 928	0MRK4KZ	255	0MT10ZZ	1074	0MUD*	278	0N5F4ZZ	928, 1074
0MQ13ZZ	927	0MR20KZ	254, 705, 928	0MRL07Z	255	0MT14ZZ	1074	0MUF*	278	0N5G*	232
0MQ14ZZ	927	0MR247Z	254, 705, 928	0MRL0JZ	255	0MT2*	255, 705	0MUG*	278	0N5G0ZZ	928, 1074
0MQ2*	254, 704	0MR24JZ	254, 705, 928	0MRL0KZ	255	0MT20ZZ	1074	0MUH*	278	0N5G3ZZ	928, 1074
0MQ20ZZ	927	0MR24KZ	254, 705, 928	0MRL47Z	255	0MT24ZZ	1074	0MUJ*	278	0N5G4ZZ	928, 1074
0MQ23ZZ	927	0MR307Z	254, 705, 928	0MRL4JZ	255	0MT3*	255, 705	0MUK*	278	0N5H*	232
0MQ24ZZ	927	0MR30JZ	254, 705, 928	0MRL4KZ	255	0MT30ZZ	1074	0MUL*	278	0N5H0ZZ	928, 1074
0MQ3*	254, 704	0MR30KZ	254, 705, 928	0MRM07Z	255	0MT34ZZ	1074	0MUM*	278	0N5H3ZZ	928, 1074
0MQ30ZZ	927	0MR347Z	254, 705, 928	0MRM0JZ	255	0MT4*	255, 705	0MUN*	278	0N5H4ZZ	928, 1074
0MQ33ZZ	927	0MR34JZ	254, 705, 928	0MRM0KZ	255	0MT40ZZ	1074	0MUP*	278	0N5J*	232
0MQ34ZZ	927	0MR34KZ	254, 705, 928	0MRM47Z	255	0MT44ZZ	1074	0MUQ*	278	0N5J0ZZ	928, 1074
0MQ4*	254, 705	0MR407Z	254, 705, 928	0MRM4JZ	255	0MT5*	255, 705	0MUR*	278	0N5J3ZZ	928, 1074
0MQ40ZZ	927	0MR40JZ	254, 705, 928	0MRM4KZ	255	0MT50ZZ	1074	0MUS*	278	0N5J4ZZ	928, 1074
0MQ43ZZ	927	0MR40KZ	254, 705, 928	0MRN07Z	227, 705, 928	0MT54ZZ	1074	0MUT*	278	0N5K*	232
0MQ44ZZ	927	0MR447Z	254, 705, 928	0MRN0JZ	227, 705, 928	0MT6*	255, 705	0MUV*	255	0N5K0ZZ	928, 1074
0MQ5*	254, 705	0MR44JZ	254, 705, 928	0MRN0KZ	227, 705, 928	0MT60ZZ	1074	0MUW*	255	0N5K3ZZ	928, 1074
0MQ50ZZ	927	0MR44KZ	254, 705, 928	0MRN47Z	227, 705, 928	0MT64ZZ	1074	0MWX00Z	255, 705, 928, 1074	0N5K4ZZ	928, 1074
0MQ53ZZ	927	0MR507Z	254, 705, 928	0MRN4JZ	227, 705, 928	0MT7*	269	0MWX07Z	255, 705, 928, 1074	0N5L*	232
0MQ54ZZ	927	0MR50JZ	254, 705, 928	0MRN4KZ	227, 705, 928	0MT70ZZ	641, 928	0MWX0JZ	255, 705, 928, 1074		
0MQ6*	254, 705	0MR50KZ	254, 705, 928	0MRP07Z	227, 705, 928	0MT74ZZ	641, 928	0MWX0KZ	255, 705, 928, 1074		
0MQ60ZZ	927	0MR547Z	254, 705, 928	0MRP0JZ	227, 705, 928	0MT8*	269	0MWX0YZ	255, 705, 928, 1074		
0MQ63ZZ	927	0MR54JZ	254, 705, 928	0MRP0KZ	227, 705, 928	0MT80ZZ	641, 928	0MWX30Z	255, 705, 928, 1074		
0MQ64ZZ	927	0MR54KZ	254, 705, 928	0MRP47Z	227, 705, 928	0MT84ZZ	641, 928	0MWX37Z	255, 705, 928, 1074		
		0MR607Z	254, 705, 928	0MRP4JZ	227, 705, 928	0MT9*	255, 705	0MWX3JZ	255, 705, 928, 1074		
		0MR60JZ	255, 705, 928	0MRP4KZ	227, 705, 928	0MT90ZZ	928, 1074	0MWX3KZ	255, 705, 928, 1074		
		0MR60KZ	255, 705, 928	0MRQ07Z	255, 705, 928	0MT94ZZ	928, 1074				
		0MR647Z	255, 705, 928	0MRQ0JZ	255, 705, 928	0MTB*	255, 705				
		0MR64JZ	255, 705, 928	0MRQ0KZ	255, 705, 928	0MTB0ZZ	928, 1074				
		0MR64KZ	255, 705, 928	0MRQ47Z	255, 705, 928	0MTB4ZZ	928, 1074				
		0MR707Z	255, 705, 928	0MRQ4JZ	255, 705, 928	0MTC*	255, 705				
		0MR70JZ	255, 705, 928	0MRQ4KZ	255, 705, 928	0MTC0ZZ	928, 1074				
		0MR70KZ	255, 705, 928	0MRR07Z	255, 705, 928	0MTC4ZZ	928, 1074				
		0MR747Z	255, 705, 928	0MRR0KZ	255, 705, 928	0MTD*	255, 705				
		0MR74JZ	255, 705, 928					0MTD0ZZ	928, 1074			
		0MR74KZ	255, 705, 928								

Code	Page
ØN5LØZZ	928, 1074
ØN5L3ZZ	928, 1074
ØN5L4ZZ	929, 1074
ØN5M*	232
ØN5MØZZ	929, 1074
ØN5M3ZZ	929, 1074
ØN5M4ZZ	929, 1074
ØN5N*	232
ØN5NØZZ	929, 1074
ØN5N3ZZ	929, 1074
ØN5N4ZZ	929, 1074
ØN5P*	232
ØN5PØZZ	929, 1074
ØN5P3ZZ	929, 1074
ØN5P4ZZ	929, 1074
ØN5Q*	232
ØN5QØZZ	929, 1074
ØN5Q3ZZ	929, 1074
ØN5Q4ZZ	929, 1074
ØN5R*	232
ØN5RØZZ	929, 1074
ØN5R3ZZ	929, 1074
ØN5R4ZZ	929, 1074
ØN5T*	232
ØN5TØZZ	929, 1074
ØN5T3ZZ	929, 1074
ØN5T4ZZ	929, 1074
ØN5V*	232
ØN5VØZZ	929, 1074
ØN5V3ZZ	929, 1074
ØN5V4ZZ	929, 1074
ØN5X*	232
ØN5XØZZ	929, 1074
ØN5X3ZZ	929, 1074
ØN5X4ZZ	929, 1074
ØN8ØØZZ	12
ØN8Ø3ZZ	12
ØN8Ø4ZZ	12
ØN81ØZZ	12
ØN813ZZ	12
ØN814ZZ	12
ØN83ØZZ	12
ØN833ZZ	12
ØN834ZZ	12
ØN84ØZZ	12
ØN843ZZ	12
ØN844ZZ	12
ØN85ØZZ	12
ØN853ZZ	12
ØN854ZZ	12
ØN86ØZZ	12
ØN863ZZ	12
ØN864ZZ	12
ØN87ØZZ	12
ØN873ZZ	12
ØN874ZZ	12
ØN8C*	79
ØN8F*	79
ØN8G*	79
ØN8H*	79
ØN8J*	79
ØN8K*	79
ØN8L*	79
ØN8M*	79
ØN8N*	79
ØN8P*	56, 67, 705
ØN8PØZZ	929, 1074
ØN8P3ZZ	929, 1074
ØN8P4ZZ	929, 1074
ØN8Q*	56, 67, 705
ØN8QØZZ	929, 1074
ØN8Q3ZZ	929, 1074
ØN8Q4ZZ	929, 1074
ØN8R*	79
ØN8T*	79
ØN8V*	79
ØN8X*	79
ØN9ØØØZ	12, 849
ØN9ØØZX	12, 222, 496
ØN9ØØZZ	12, 849
ØN9Ø3ZX	12, 222, 496
ØN9Ø4ØZ	12, 849
ØN9Ø4ZX	12, 222, 496
ØN9Ø4ZZ	12, 849
ØN91ØØZ	12, 849
ØN91ØZX	12, 222, 496
ØN91ØZZ	12, 849
ØN913ZX	12, 222, 496
ØN914ØZ	12, 849
ØN914ZX	12, 222, 496
ØN914ZZ	12, 849
ØN93ØØZ	12, 849
ØN93ØZX	12, 222, 496

Code	Page
ØN93ØZZ	12, 849
ØN933ZX	12, 222, 496
ØN934ØZ	12, 849
ØN934ZX	12, 222, 496
ØN934ZZ	12, 849
ØN94ØØZ	12, 849
ØN94ØZX	12, 222, 496
ØN94ØZZ	12, 849
ØN943ZX	12, 222, 496
ØN944ØZ	12, 849
ØN944ZX	12, 222, 496
ØN944ZZ	12, 849
ØN95ØØZ	12, 849
ØN95ØZX	12, 222, 496
ØN95ØZZ	12, 849
ØN953ZX	13, 222, 496
ØN954ØZ	13, 849
ØN954ZX	13, 222, 496
ØN954ZZ	13, 849
ØN96ØØZ	13, 849
ØN96ØZX	13, 222, 496
ØN96ØZZ	13, 849
ØN963ZX	13, 222, 496
ØN964ØZ	13, 849
ØN964ZX	13, 222, 496
ØN964ZZ	13, 849
ØN97ØØZ	13, 849
ØN97ØZX	13, 222, 496
ØN97ØZZ	13, 849
ØN973ZX	13, 222, 496
ØN974ØZ	13, 849
ØN974ZX	13, 222, 496
ØN974ZZ	13, 850
ØN9CØØZ	79
ØN9CØZX	79, 222, 1074
ØN9CØZZ	79
ØN9C3ZX	79, 222, 1074
ØN9C4ØZ	79
ØN9C4ZX	79, 222, 1074
ØN9C4ZZ	79
ØN9FØØZ	79
ØN9FØZX	79, 222, 1074
ØN9FØZZ	79
ØN9F3ZX	79, 222, 1074
ØN9F4ØZ	79
ØN9F4ZX	79, 222, 1074
ØN9F4ZZ	79
ØN9GØØZ	79
ØN9GØZX	79, 222, 1074
ØN9GØZZ	79
ØN9G3ZX	79, 222, 1074
ØN9G4ØZ	79
ØN9G4ZX	79, 222, 1074
ØN9G4ZZ	79
ØN9HØØZ	79
ØN9HØZX	79, 222, 1074
ØN9HØZZ	79
ØN9H3ZX	79, 222, 1074
ØN9H4ØZ	79
ØN9H4ZX	79, 222, 1074
ØN9H4ZZ	79
ØN9JØØZ	79
ØN9JØZX	79, 222, 1074
ØN9JØZZ	79
ØN9J3ZX	79, 222, 1074
ØN9J4ØZ	79
ØN9J4ZX	79, 222, 1074
ØN9J4ZZ	79
ØN9KØØZ	79
ØN9KØZX	79, 222, 1074
ØN9KØZZ	79
ØN9K3ZX	79, 222, 1074
ØN9K4ØZ	79
ØN9K4ZX	79, 222, 1074
ØN9K4ZZ	79
ØN9LØØZ	79
ØN9LØZX	79, 222, 1074
ØN9LØZZ	79
ØN9L3ZX	79, 222, 1074
ØN9L4ØZ	79
ØN9L4ZX	79, 222, 1074
ØN9L4ZZ	79
ØN9MØØZ	79
ØN9MØZX	79, 222, 1074
ØN9MØZZ	79
ØN9M3ZX	79, 222, 1074
ØN9M4ØZ	79
ØN9M4ZX	79, 222, 1074
ØN9M4ZZ	79
ØN9NØØZ	79
ØN9NØZX	79, 222, 1074
ØN9NØZZ	79
ØN9N3ZX	79, 222, 1074

Code	Page
ØN9N4ØZ	79
ØN9N4ZX	79, 222, 1074
ØN9N4ZZ	80
ØN9PØØZ	56, 67, 705, 929, 1074
ØN9PØZX	56, 1074
ØN9PØZZ	56, 67, 705, 929, 1074
ØN9P3ZX	56, 1074
ØN9P4ØZ	56, 67, 705, 929, 1074
ØN9P4ZX	56, 1074
ØN9P4ZZ	56, 67, 705, 929, 1074
ØN9QØØZ	56, 67, 705, 929, 1074
ØN9QØZX	56, 1074
ØN9QØZZ	56, 67, 705, 929, 1074
ØN9Q3ZX	56, 1074
ØN9Q4ØZ	56, 67, 705, 929, 1074
ØN9Q4ZX	56, 1074
ØN9Q4ZZ	56, 67, 705, 929, 1075
ØN9RØZX	80, 222, 1075
ØN9R3ZX	80, 222, 1075
ØN9R4ZX	80, 222, 1075
ØN9TØZX	80, 222, 1075
ØN9T3ZX	80, 222, 1075
ØN9T4ZX	80, 222, 1075
ØN9VØZX	80, 222, 1075
ØN9V3ZX	80, 222, 1075
ØN9V4ZX	80, 222, 1075
ØN9XØØZ	80
ØN9XØZX	80, 222, 1075
ØN9XØZZ	80
ØN9X3ZX	80, 222, 1075
ØN9X4ØZ	80
ØN9X4ZX	80, 222, 1075
ØN9X4ZZ	80
ØNBØ*	13
ØNBØØZX	222, 496
ØNBØØZZ	67, 278, 599, 624, 705, 850
ØNBØ3ZX	222, 496
ØNBØ3ZZ	67, 278, 599, 624, 705, 850
ØNBØ4ZX	222, 496
ØNBØ4ZZ	67, 278, 599, 624, 705, 850
ØNB1*	13
ØNB1ØZX	222, 496
ØNB1ØZZ	67, 278, 599, 624, 705, 850
ØNB13ZX	222, 496
ØNB13ZZ	67, 278, 599, 624, 705, 850
ØNB14ZX	222, 496
ØNB14ZZ	67, 278, 599, 624, 705, 850
ØNB3*	13
ØNB3ØZX	222, 496
ØNB3ØZZ	67, 278, 599, 624, 705, 850
ØNB33ZX	222, 496
ØNB33ZZ	67, 278, 599, 624, 705, 850
ØNB34ZX	222, 496
ØNB34ZZ	67, 278, 599, 624, 705, 850
ØNB4*	13
ØNB4ØZX	222, 496
ØNB4ØZZ	67, 278, 599, 624, 705, 850
ØNB43ZX	222, 496
ØNB43ZZ	67, 278, 599, 624, 705, 850
ØNB44ZX	222, 496
ØNB44ZZ	67, 278, 599, 624, 705, 850
ØNB5*	13
ØNB5ØZX	222, 496
ØNB5ØZZ	67, 278, 599, 624, 705, 850
ØNB53ZX	222, 496
ØNB53ZZ	67, 278, 599, 624, 705, 850
ØNB54ZX	222, 496
ØNB54ZZ	67, 278, 599, 624, 705, 850
ØNB6*	13
ØNB6ØZX	222, 496

Code	Page
ØNB6ØZZ	67, 278, 599, 624, 705, 850
ØNB63ZX	222, 496
ØNB63ZZ	67, 278, 599, 624, 706, 850
ØNB64ZX	222, 496
ØNB64ZZ	67, 278, 599, 624, 706, 850
ØNB7*	13
ØNB7ØZX	222, 496
ØNB7ØZZ	67, 278, 599, 624, 706, 850
ØNB73ZX	222, 496
ØNB73ZZ	67, 278, 599, 624, 706, 850
ØNB74ZX	222, 496
ØNB74ZZ	67, 278, 599, 624, 706, 850
ØNBBØZZ	67, 278, 706, 929
ØNBB3ZZ	67, 278, 706, 929
ØNBB4ZZ	67, 278, 706, 929
ØNBCØZX	80, 222, 1075
ØNBCØZZ	67, 278, 706, 929
ØNBC3ZX	80, 222, 1075
ØNBC3ZZ	67, 278, 706, 929
ØNBC4ZX	80, 222, 1075
ØNBC4ZZ	67, 278, 706, 929
ØNBFØZX	80, 222, 1075
ØNBFØZZ	67, 278, 706, 929
ØNBF3ZX	80, 222, 1075
ØNBF3ZZ	67, 278, 706, 929
ØNBF4ZX	80, 222, 1075
ØNBF4ZZ	67, 278, 706, 929
ØNBGØZX	80, 222, 1075
ØNBGØZZ	67, 278, 706, 929
ØNBG3ZX	80, 222, 1075
ØNBG3ZZ	67, 278, 706, 929
ØNBG4ZX	80, 222, 1075
ØNBG4ZZ	67, 278, 706, 929
ØNBHØZX	80, 222, 1075
ØNBHØZZ	67, 278, 706, 929
ØNBH3ZX	80, 222, 1075
ØNBH3ZZ	67, 278, 706, 929
ØNBH4ZX	80, 222, 1075
ØNBH4ZZ	67, 278, 706, 929
ØNBJØZX	80, 222, 1075
ØNBJØZZ	67, 278, 706, 929
ØNBJ3ZX	80, 222, 1075
ØNBJ3ZZ	67, 278, 706, 929
ØNBJ4ZX	80, 222, 1075
ØNBJ4ZZ	67, 278, 706, 929
ØNBKØZX	80, 222, 1075
ØNBKØZZ	67, 278, 706, 929
ØNBK3ZX	80, 222, 1075
ØNBK3ZZ	67, 278, 706, 929
ØNBK4ZX	80, 222, 1075
ØNBK4ZZ	67, 278, 706, 929
ØNBLØZX	80, 222, 1075
ØNBLØZZ	67, 278, 706, 929
ØNBL3ZX	80, 222, 1075
ØNBL3ZZ	67, 278, 706, 929
ØNBL4ZX	80, 222, 1075
ØNBL4ZZ	67, 278, 706, 929
ØNBMØZX	80, 222, 1075
ØNBMØZZ	67, 278, 706, 929
ØNBM3ZX	80, 222, 1075
ØNBM3ZZ	67, 278, 706, 929
ØNBM4ZX	80, 222, 1075
ØNBM4ZZ	67, 278, 706, 929
ØNBNØZX	80, 222, 1075
ØNBNØZZ	67, 278, 706, 929
ØNBN3ZX	80, 222, 1075
ØNBN3ZZ	67, 278, 706, 929
ØNBN4ZX	80, 222, 1075
ØNBN4ZZ	67, 278, 706, 929
ØNBP*	56
ØNBPØZX	1075
ØNBPØZZ	67, 706, 929, 1075
ØNBP3ZX	1075
ØNBP3ZZ	67, 706, 929, 1075
ØNBP4ZX	1075
ØNBP4ZZ	67, 706, 929, 1075
ØNBQ*	56
ØNBQØZX	1075
ØNBQØZZ	67, 706, 929, 1075
ØNBQ3ZX	1075
ØNBQ3ZZ	67, 706, 929, 1075
ØNBQ4ZX	1075
ØNBQ4ZZ	67, 706, 929, 1075
ØNBRØZZ	67, 278, 706, 929
ØNBR3ZZ	67, 278, 706, 929
ØNBR4ZZ	68, 278, 706, 929
ØNBTØZZ	67, 278, 706, 929

Code	Page
ØNBT3ZZ	67, 278, 706, 929
ØNBT4ZZ	67, 278, 706, 929
ØNBVØZZ	67, 278, 706, 929
ØNBV3ZZ	67, 278, 706, 929
ØNBV4ZZ	67, 278, 706, 929
ØNBXØZX	80, 222, 1075
ØNBXØZZ	68, 278, 706, 929
ØNBX3ZX	80, 222, 1075
ØNBX3ZZ	68, 278, 706, 929
ØNBX4ZX	80, 222, 1075
ØNBX4ZZ	68, 278, 706, 929
ØNC1*	13, 68, 706, 850
ØNC1ØZZ	599, 624
ØNC13ZZ	599, 625
ØNC14ZZ	599, 625
ØNC3*	13, 68, 706, 850
ØNC3ØZZ	599, 625
ØNC33ZZ	599, 625
ØNC34ZZ	599, 625
ØNC4*	13, 68, 706, 850
ØNC4ØZZ	599, 625
ØNC43ZZ	599, 625
ØNC44ZZ	599, 625
ØNC5*	13, 68, 706, 850
ØNC5ØZZ	599, 625
ØNC53ZZ	599, 625
ØNC54ZZ	599, 625
ØNC6*	13, 68, 706, 850
ØNC6ØZZ	599, 625
ØNC63ZZ	599, 625
ØNC64ZZ	599, 625
ØNC7*	13, 68, 706, 850
ØNC7ØZZ	599, 625
ØNC73ZZ	599, 625
ØNC74ZZ	599, 625
ØNCC*	80
ØNCF*	80
ØNCG*	80
ØNCH*	80
ØNCJ*	80
ØNCK*	80
ØNCL*	80
ØNCM*	80
ØNCN*	80
ØNCP*	80
ØNCQ*	80
ØNCX*	80
ØNDØØZZ	39, 255, 435, 706, 929
ØND1ØZZ	39, 255, 435, 706, 929
ØND3ØZZ	39, 255, 435, 706, 929
ØND4ØZZ	39, 255, 435, 706, 929
ØND5ØZZ	39, 255, 435, 706, 929
ØND6ØZZ	39, 255, 435, 706, 929
ØND7ØZZ	39, 256, 435, 706, 929
ØNDBØZZ	39, 256, 435, 706, 929
ØNDCØZZ	39, 256, 435, 706, 929
ØNDFØZZ	39, 256, 435, 706, 929
ØNDGØZZ	39, 256, 435, 706, 929
ØNDHØZZ	39, 256, 435, 706, 929
ØNDJØZZ	39, 256, 435, 706, 929
ØNDKØZZ	39, 256, 435, 706, 929
ØNDLØZZ	39, 256, 435, 706, 929
ØNDMØZZ	39, 256, 435, 706, 929
ØNDNØZZ	39, 256, 435, 706, 929
ØNDPØZZ	39, 256, 435, 706, 929
ØNDQØZZ	39, 256, 435, 706, 929
ØNDRØZZ	39, 256, 435, 706, 929
ØNDTØZZ	39, 256, 435, 706, 929
ØNDVØZZ	40, 256, 435, 706, 929
ØNDXØZZ	40, 256, 435, 706, 929

Code	Page
ØNHØØ4Z	13, 278, 706, 850
ØNHØØMZ	13
ØNHØØNZ	15, 40
ØNHØ34Z	13, 278, 706, 850
ØNHØ3MZ	13
ØNHØ44Z	13, 278, 706, 850
ØNHØ4MZ	13
ØNH1*	13, 68, 278, 706, 850
ØNH3*	13, 68, 278, 706, 850
ØNH4*	13, 68, 278, 706, 850
ØNH5Ø4Z	13, 68, 278, 706, 850
ØNH5ØSZ	80
ØNH534Z	13, 68, 278, 706, 850
ØNH53SZ	80
ØNH544Z	13, 68, 278, 706, 850
ØNH54SZ	80
ØNH6Ø4Z	13, 68, 278, 706, 850
ØNH6ØSZ	80
ØNH634Z	13, 68, 278, 706, 850
ØNH63SZ	80
ØNH644Z	13, 68, 278, 706, 850
ØNH64SZ	80
ØNH7*	13, 68, 278, 706, 850
ØNHC*	80
ØNHF*	80
ØNHG*	80
ØNHH*	80
ØNHJ*	80
ØNHK*	80
ØNHL*	80
ØNHM*	80
ØNHN*	80
ØNHP*	80
ØNHQ*	80
ØNHR*	80
ØNHT*	80
ØNHV*	80
ØNHW*	80
ØNHX*	80
ØNJØØZZ	13, 222, 706, 929
ØNJØ4ZZ	13, 222, 706, 929
ØNJBØZZ	68, 222, 706, 929
ØNJB4ZZ	68, 222, 706, 929
ØNJWØZZ	68, 222, 706, 929
ØNJW4ZZ	68, 222, 706, 929
ØNN1*	13, 68, 278, 706, 850
ØNN3*	13, 68, 278, 706, 850
ØNN4*	13, 68, 278, 706, 850
ØNN5*	13, 68, 278, 706, 850
ØNN6*	13, 68, 278, 706, 850
ØNN7*	13, 68, 278, 706, 850
ØNNC*	68, 706
ØNNCØZZ	929
ØNNC3ZZ	929
ØNNC4ZZ	929
ØNNF*	68, 706
ØNNFØZZ	929
ØNNF3ZZ	929
ØNNF4ZZ	929
ØNNG*	68, 706
ØNNGØZZ	929
ØNNG3ZZ	929
ØNNG4ZZ	929
ØNNH*	68, 706
ØNNHØZZ	929
ØNNH3ZZ	929
ØNNH4ZZ	929
ØNNJ*	68, 706
ØNNJØZZ	929
ØNNJ3ZZ	929
ØNNJ4ZZ	929
ØNNK*	68, 706
ØNNKØZZ	929
ØNNK3ZZ	929
ØNNK4ZZ	929
ØNNL*	68, 706
ØNNLØZZ	929

Code	Page
ØNNL3ZZ	929
ØNNL4ZZ	929
ØNNM*	68, 706
ØNNMØZZ	929
ØNNM3ZZ	929
ØNNM4ZZ	929
ØNNN*	68, 706
ØNNNØZZ	929
ØNNN3ZZ	929
ØNNN4ZZ	929
ØNNP*	68, 706
ØNNPØZZ	929
ØNNP3ZZ	929
ØNNP4ZZ	929
ØNNQ*	68, 706
ØNNQØZZ	929
ØNNQ3ZZ	929
ØNNQ4ZZ	929
ØNNR*	68, 706
ØNNRØZZ	929
ØNNR3ZZ	929
ØNNR4ZZ	929
ØNNT*	68, 706
ØNNTØZZ	929
ØNNT3ZZ	929
ØNNT4ZZ	929
ØNNV*	68, 706
ØNNVØZZ	929
ØNNV3ZZ	929
ØNNV4ZZ	929
ØNNX*	85, 706
ØNNXØZZ	435, 929, 1075
ØNNX3ZZ	435, 929, 1075
ØNNX4ZZ	435, 929, 1075
ØNPØØØZ	13
ØNPØØ4Z	13
ØNPØØ5Z	13
ØNPØØ7Z	13
ØNPØØJZ	13, 68, 278, 706, 929
ØNPØØKZ	13
ØNPØØMZ	13, 599, 625
ØNPØØNZ	40
ØNPØØSZ	13
ØNPØ3ØZ	13
ØNPØ34Z	13
ØNPØ37Z	13
ØNPØ3JZ	13, 68, 278, 706, 929
ØNPØ3KZ	13
ØNPØ3MZ	13, 599, 625
ØNPØ3SZ	13
ØNPØ4ØZ	13
ØNPØ44Z	13
ØNPØ47Z	13
ØNPØ4JZ	13, 68, 278, 706, 929
ØNPØ4KZ	13
ØNPØ4MZ	13, 599, 625
ØNPØ4SZ	13
ØNPØX4Z	13
ØNPØXMZ	13, 599, 625
ØNPØXSZ	13
ØNPWØØZ	80, 232
ØNPWØ4Z	68, 232, 706, 929
ØNPWØ7Z	80, 232
ØNPWØJZ	56, 706, 929, 1075
ØNPWØKZ	80, 232
ØNPWØMZ	80, 232
ØNPW3ØZ	80, 232
ØNPW34Z	68, 232, 706, 929
ØNPW37Z	80, 232
ØNPW3JZ	56, 706, 929, 1075
ØNPW3KZ	80, 232
ØNPW3MZ	80, 232
ØNPW4ØZ	80, 232
ØNPW44Z	68, 232, 706, 929
ØNPW47Z	80, 232
ØNPW4JZ	56, 706, 929, 1075
ØNPW4KZ	80, 232
ØNPW4MZ	80, 232
ØNPWX4Z	68, 232, 706, 929
ØNQØØZZ	13, 68, 278, 706, 850
ØNQØ3ZZ	13, 68, 278, 706, 850
ØNQØ4ZZ	13, 68, 278, 706, 850
ØNQ1ØZZ	13, 68, 278, 706, 850
ØNQ13ZZ	13, 68, 278, 706, 850
ØNQ14ZZ	13, 68, 278, 706, 850
ØNQ3ØZZ	13, 68, 278, 706, 850
ØNQ33ZZ	13, 68, 278, 706, 850
ØNQ34ZZ	13, 68, 278, 706, 850
ØNQ4ØZZ	13, 68, 278, 706, 850
ØNQ43ZZ	13, 68, 278, 706, 850
ØNQ44ZZ	13, 68, 278, 706, 850
ØNQ5ØZZ	13, 68, 278, 706, 850
ØNQ53ZZ	13, 68, 278, 706, 850
ØNQ54ZZ	13, 68, 278, 706, 850
ØNQ6ØZZ	13, 68, 278, 706, 850
ØNQ63ZZ	13, 68, 278, 706, 850
ØNQ64ZZ	13, 68, 278, 706, 850
ØNQ7ØZZ	13, 68, 278, 706, 850
ØNQ73ZZ	13, 68, 278, 706, 850
ØNQ74ZZ	13, 68, 278, 706, 850
ØNQBØZZ	80, 278, 435, 706, 929, 1075
ØNQB3ZZ	80, 278, 435, 706, 929, 1075
ØNQB4ZZ	80, 278, 435, 706, 929, 1075
ØNQCØZZ	68, 706, 930
ØNQC3ZZ	68, 706, 930
ØNQC4ZZ	68, 706, 930
ØNQFØZZ	68, 706, 930
ØNQF3ZZ	68, 706, 930
ØNQF4ZZ	68, 706, 930
ØNQGØZZ	68, 706, 930
ØNQG3ZZ	68, 706, 930
ØNQG4ZZ	68, 706, 930
ØNQHØZZ	68, 706, 930
ØNQH3ZZ	68, 706, 930
ØNQH4ZZ	68, 706, 930
ØNQJØZZ	68, 706, 930
ØNQJ3ZZ	68, 706, 930
ØNQJ4ZZ	68, 706, 930
ØNQKØZZ	68, 706, 930
ØNQK3ZZ	68, 706, 930
ØNQK4ZZ	68, 706, 930
ØNQLØZZ	68, 707, 930
ØNQL3ZZ	68, 707, 930
ØNQL4ZZ	68, 707, 930
ØNQMØZZ	68, 707, 930
ØNQM3ZZ	68, 707, 930
ØNQM4ZZ	68, 707, 930
ØNQNØZZ	68, 707, 930
ØNQN3ZZ	68, 707, 930
ØNQN4ZZ	68, 707, 930
ØNQPØZZ	56, 68, 707, 930, 1075
ØNQP3ZZ	56, 68, 707, 930, 1075
ØNQP4ZZ	56, 68, 707, 930, 1075
ØNQQØZZ	56, 68, 707, 930, 1075
ØNQQ3ZZ	56, 68, 707, 930, 1075
ØNQQ4ZZ	56, 68, 707, 930, 1075
ØNQRØZZ	68, 278, 707, 930
ØNQR3ZZ	68, 278, 707, 930
ØNQR4ZZ	68, 278, 707, 930
ØNQTØZZ	68, 278, 707, 930
ØNQT3ZZ	68, 278, 707, 930
ØNQT4ZZ	68, 278, 707, 930
ØNQVØZZ	68, 278, 707, 930
ØNQV3ZZ	68, 278, 707, 930
ØNQV4ZZ	68, 278, 707, 930
ØNQXØZZ	68, 707, 930
ØNQX3ZZ	68, 707, 930
ØNQX4ZZ	68, 707, 930
ØNRØ*	13, 68, 278, 707, 850
ØNR1*	13, 68, 278
ØNR1ØJZ	707, 850
ØNR13JZ	707, 850
ØNR14JZ	707, 850
ØNR3*	13, 68, 278
ØNR3ØJZ	707, 850
ØNR33JZ	707, 850
ØNR34JZ	707, 850
ØNR4*	13, 68, 278
ØNR4ØJZ	707, 850
ØNR43JZ	707, 850
ØNR44JZ	707, 850
ØNR5*	13, 68, 278
ØNR5ØJZ	707, 850
ØNR53JZ	707, 850
ØNR54JZ	707, 850
ØNR6*	13, 68, 278
ØNR6ØJZ	707, 850
ØNR63JZ	707, 850
ØNR64JZ	707, 850
ØNR7*	13, 68, 278
ØNR7ØJZ	707, 850
ØNR73JZ	707, 850
ØNR74JZ	707, 850
ØNRB*	80, 278, 707
ØNRBØ7Z	435, 930, 1075
ØNRBØJZ	435, 930, 1075
ØNRBØKZ	435, 930, 1075
ØNRB37Z	435, 930, 1075
ØNRB3JZ	435, 930, 1075
ØNRB3KZ	435, 930, 1075
ØNRB47Z	435, 930, 1075
ØNRB4JZ	435, 930, 1075
ØNRB4KZ	435, 930, 1075
ØNRC*	68
ØNRCØJZ	56, 278, 707, 930
ØNRC3JZ	56, 278, 707, 930
ØNRC4JZ	56, 278, 707, 930
ØNRF*	68
ØNRFØJZ	56, 278, 707, 930
ØNRF3JZ	56, 278, 707, 930
ØNRF4JZ	56, 278, 707, 930
ØNRG*	68
ØNRGØJZ	56, 278, 707, 930
ØNRG3JZ	56, 278, 707, 930
ØNRG4JZ	56, 278, 707, 930
ØNRH*	68
ØNRHØJZ	56, 278, 707, 930
ØNRH3JZ	56, 278, 707, 930
ØNRH4JZ	56, 278, 707, 930
ØNRJ*	68
ØNRJØJZ	56, 278, 707, 930
ØNRJ3JZ	56, 278, 707, 930
ØNRJ4JZ	56, 278, 707, 930
ØNRK*	68
ØNRKØJZ	56, 278, 707, 930
ØNRK3JZ	56, 279, 707, 930
ØNRK4JZ	56, 279, 707, 930
ØNRL*	68
ØNRLØJZ	56, 279, 707, 930
ØNRL3JZ	56, 279, 707, 930
ØNRL4JZ	56, 279, 707, 930
ØNRM*	68
ØNRMØJZ	56, 279, 707, 930
ØNRM3JZ	56, 279, 707, 930
ØNRM4JZ	56, 279, 707, 930
ØNRN*	68
ØNRNØJZ	56, 279, 707, 930
ØNRN3JZ	56, 279, 707, 930
ØNRN4JZ	56, 279, 707, 930
ØNRP*	68
ØNRPØ7Z	56, 707, 930, 1075
ØNRPØJZ	56, 707, 930, 1075
ØNRP37Z	56, 707, 930, 1075
ØNRP3JZ	56, 707, 930, 1075
ØNRP47Z	56, 707, 930, 1075
ØNRP4JZ	56, 707, 930, 1075
ØNRQ*	68
ØNRQØ7Z	56, 707, 930, 1075
ØNRQØJZ	56, 707, 930, 1075
ØNRQ37Z	56, 707, 930, 1075
ØNRQ3JZ	56, 707, 930, 1075
ØNRQ47Z	56, 707, 930, 1075
ØNRQ4JZ	56, 707, 930, 1075
ØNRR*	68, 707
ØNRRØ7Z	930
ØNRRØJZ	930
ØNRRØKZ	930
ØNRR37Z	930
ØNRR3JZ	930
ØNRR3KZ	930
ØNRR47Z	930
ØNRR4JZ	930
ØNRR4KZ	930
ØNRT*	67, 279, 707
ØNRTØ7Z	930
ØNRTØJZ	930
ØNRTØKZ	930
ØNRT37Z	930
ØNRT3JZ	930
ØNRT3KZ	930
ØNRT47Z	930
ØNRT4JZ	930
ØNRT4KZ	930
ØNRV*	67, 279, 707
ØNRVØ7Z	930
ØNRVØJZ	930
ØNRVØKZ	930
ØNRV37Z	930
ØNRV3JZ	930
ØNRV3KZ	930
ØNRV47Z	930
ØNRV4JZ	930
ØNRV4KZ	930
ØNRX*	68
ØNRXØJZ	56, 279, 707, 930
ØNRX3JZ	56, 279, 707, 930
ØNRX4JZ	56, 279, 707, 930
ØNSØØ4Z	13, 68, 279, 707, 850
ØNSØØ5Z	13, 68, 279, 707, 850
ØNSØØZZ	13, 68, 279, 707, 850
ØNSØ34Z	13, 68, 279, 707, 850
ØNSØ35Z	13, 68, 279, 707, 850
ØNSØ3ZZ	13, 68, 279, 707, 850
ØNSØ44Z	13, 68, 279, 707, 850
ØNSØ45Z	13, 68, 279, 707, 850
ØNSØ4ZZ	13, 68, 279, 707, 850
ØNS1Ø4Z	13, 68, 279, 707, 850
ØNS1ØZZ	13, 68, 279, 707, 850
ØNS134Z	13, 68, 279, 707, 850
ØNS13ZZ	13, 68, 279, 707, 850
ØNS144Z	13, 68, 279, 707, 850
ØNS14ZZ	13, 68, 279, 707, 850
ØNS3Ø4Z	13, 68, 279, 707, 850
ØNS3ØZZ	13, 68, 279, 707, 850
ØNS334Z	13, 68, 279, 707, 850
ØNS33ZZ	13, 68, 279, 707, 850
ØNS344Z	13, 68, 279, 707, 850
ØNS34ZZ	13, 68, 279, 707, 850
ØNS4Ø4Z	13, 68, 279, 707, 850
ØNS4ØZZ	13, 68, 279, 707, 850
ØNS434Z	13, 68, 279, 707, 850
ØNS43ZZ	13, 68, 279, 707, 850
ØNS444Z	13, 68, 279, 707, 850
ØNS44ZZ	13, 68, 279, 707, 850
ØNS5Ø4Z	13, 68, 279, 707, 850
ØNS5ØZZ	13, 68, 279, 707, 850
ØNS534Z	13, 68, 279, 707, 850
ØNS53ZZ	13, 68, 279, 707, 850
ØNS544Z	13, 68, 279, 707, 850
ØNS54ZZ	13, 68, 279, 707, 850
ØNS6Ø4Z	13, 68, 279, 707, 850
ØNS6ØZZ	13, 68, 279, 707, 850
ØNS634Z	13, 68, 279, 707, 850
ØNS63ZZ	13, 68, 279, 707, 850
ØNS644Z	13, 69, 279, 707, 850
ØNS64ZZ	13, 69, 279, 707, 850
ØNS7Ø4Z	13, 69, 279, 707, 850
ØNS7ØZZ	13, 69, 279, 707, 850
ØNS734Z	13, 69, 279, 707, 850
ØNS73ZZ	13, 69, 279, 707, 850
ØNS744Z	13, 69, 279, 707, 850
ØNS74ZZ	13, 69, 279, 707, 850
ØNSBØ4Z	69, 279, 435, 707, 930, 1075
ØNSBØZZ	69, 279, 435, 707, 930, 1075
ØNSCØ4Z	56, 69, 279, 707, 930
ØNSCØZZ	56, 69, 279, 707, 930
ØNSFØ4Z	56, 69, 279, 707, 930
ØNSFØZZ	56, 69, 279, 707, 930
ØNSGØ4Z	56, 69, 279, 707, 930
ØNSGØZZ	56, 69, 279, 707, 930
ØNSHØ4Z	56, 69, 279, 707, 930
ØNSHØZZ	56, 69, 279, 707, 930
ØNSJØ4Z	56, 69, 279, 707, 930
ØNSJØZZ	56, 69, 279, 707, 930
ØNSKØ4Z	56, 69, 279, 707, 930
ØNSKØZZ	56, 69, 279, 707, 930
ØNSLØ4Z	56, 69, 279, 707, 930
ØNSLØZZ	56, 69, 279, 707, 930
ØNSMØ4Z	69, 279, 707, 930
ØNSMØZZ	69, 279, 707, 930
ØNSNØ4Z	69, 279, 707, 930
ØNSNØZZ	69, 279, 707, 930
ØNSPØ4Z	56, 69, 279, 707, 930
ØNSPØZZ	56, 69, 279, 707, 930
ØNSQØ4Z	56, 69, 279, 707, 930
ØNSQØZZ	56, 69, 279, 707, 930
ØNSRØ4Z	69, 279, 707, 930
ØNSRØ5Z	69, 279, 707, 930
ØNSRØZZ	69, 279, 707, 930
ØNSTØ4Z	69, 279, 707, 930
ØNSTØ5Z	69, 279, 707, 930
ØNSTØZZ	69, 279, 707, 930
ØNSVØ4Z	69, 279, 707, 930
ØNSVØ5Z	69, 279, 707, 930
ØNSVØZZ	69, 279, 707, 930
ØNSXØ4Z	56, 69, 279, 707, 930
ØNSXØZZ	56, 69, 279, 707, 930
ØNT*	279, 707
ØNT1ØZZ	13, 69, 599, 625, 850
ØNT3ØZZ	13, 69, 599, 625, 850
ØNT4ØZZ	13, 69, 599, 625, 850
ØNT5ØZZ	13, 69, 599, 625, 850
ØNT6ØZZ	13, 69, 599, 625, 850
ØNT7ØZZ	13, 69, 599, 625, 850
ØNTBØZZ	69, 930
ØNTCØZZ	69, 930
ØNTFØZZ	69, 930
ØNTGØZZ	69, 930
ØNTHØZZ	69, 930
ØNTJØZZ	69, 930
ØNTKØZZ	69, 930
ØNTLØZZ	69, 930
ØNTMØZZ	69, 930
ØNTNØZZ	69, 930
ØNTPØZZ	69, 930
ØNTQØZZ	69, 930
ØNTRØZZ	69, 930
ØNTTØZZ	67, 930
ØNTVØZZ	67, 930
ØNTXØZZ	69, 930
ØNUØ*	13, 69, 279
ØNUØØJZ	707, 850
ØNUØ3JZ	708, 850
ØNUØ4JZ	708, 850
ØNU1*	13, 69, 279
ØNU1ØJZ	708, 850
ØNU13JZ	708, 850
ØNU14JZ	708, 850
ØNU3*	69, 279
ØNU3Ø7Z	13
ØNU3ØJZ	13, 708, 850
ØNU3ØKZ	13
ØNU337Z	13
ØNU33JZ	13, 708, 850
ØNU33KZ	13
ØNU347Z	13
ØNU34JZ	13, 708, 850
ØNU34KZ	13
ØNU4*	13, 69, 279
ØNU4ØJZ	708, 850
ØNU43JZ	708, 850
ØNU44JZ	708, 850
ØNU5*	13, 69, 279
ØNU5ØJZ	708, 850
ØNU53JZ	708, 850
ØNU54JZ	708, 850
ØNU6*	13, 69, 279
ØNU6ØJZ	708, 850
ØNU63JZ	708, 850
ØNU64JZ	708, 850
ØNU7*	13, 69, 279
ØNU7ØJZ	708, 850
ØNU73JZ	708, 850
ØNU74JZ	708, 850
ØNUB*	80, 279, 708
ØNUBØ7Z	435, 931, 1075
ØNUBØJZ	435, 931, 1075
ØNUBØKZ	435, 931, 1075
ØNUB37Z	435, 931, 1075
ØNUB3JZ	435, 931, 1075
ØNUB3KZ	435, 931, 1075
ØNUB47Z	435, 931, 1075
ØNUB4JZ	435, 931, 1075
ØNUB4KZ	435, 931, 1075
ØNUC*	69
ØNUCØJZ	56, 279, 708, 931
ØNUC3JZ	56, 279, 708, 931
ØNUC4JZ	56, 279, 708, 931
ØNUF*	69
ØNUFØJZ	56, 279, 708, 931
ØNUF3JZ	56, 279, 708, 931
ØNUF4JZ	56, 279, 708, 931
ØNUG*	69
ØNUGØJZ	56, 279, 708, 931
ØNUG3JZ	56, 279, 708, 931
ØNUG4JZ	56, 279, 708, 931
ØNUH*	69
ØNUHØJZ	56, 279, 708, 931
ØNUH3JZ	56, 279, 708, 931
ØNUH4JZ	56, 279, 708, 931
ØNUJ*	69
ØNUJØJZ	56, 279, 708, 931
ØNUJ3JZ	56, 279, 708, 931
ØNUJ4JZ	56, 279, 708, 931
ØNUK*	69
ØNUKØJZ	56, 279, 708, 931
ØNUK3JZ	56, 279, 708, 931
ØNUK4JZ	56, 279, 708, 931
ØNUL*	69
ØNULØJZ	56, 279, 708, 931
ØNUL3JZ	56, 279, 708, 931
ØNUL4JZ	56, 279, 708, 931
ØNUM*	69
ØNUMØJZ	56, 279, 708, 931
ØNUM3JZ	56, 279, 708, 931
ØNUM4JZ	56, 279, 708, 931
ØNUN*	69
ØNUNØJZ	56, 279, 708, 931
ØNUN3JZ	56, 279, 708, 931
ØNUN4JZ	56, 279, 708, 931

Code	Page	Code	Page	Code	Page	Code	Page	Code	Page	Code	Page
ØNUP*	69	ØP52*	101, 232, 496, 708	ØP5TØZZ	931, 1076	ØP8P3ZZ	641, 932	ØP960ZX	102, 223, 436, 496, 516, 524, 1076	ØP9F4ZZ	233
ØNUPØJZ	56, 708, 931, 1075	ØP520ZZ	931, 1075	ØP5T3ZZ	931, 1076	ØP8P4ZZ	641, 932	ØP960ZZ	232	ØP9G00Z	233
ØNUP3JZ	56, 708, 931, 1075	ØP523ZZ	931, 1075	ØP5T4ZZ	931, 1076	ØP8Q*	269	ØP963ZX	102, 223, 436, 496, 516, 524, 1076	ØP9G0ZX	223, 436, 496, 516, 524, 1076
ØNUP4JZ	56, 708, 931, 1075	ØP524ZZ	931, 1075	ØP5V*	232, 708	ØP8QØZZ	641, 932	ØP9640Z	233	ØP9G0ZZ	233
ØNUQ*	69	ØP53*	80, 708	ØP5VØZZ	931, 1076	ØP8Q3ZZ	641, 932	ØP964ZX	102, 223, 436, 496, 516, 524, 1076	ØP9G3ZX	223, 436, 496, 516, 524, 1076
ØNUQØJZ	56, 708, 931, 1075	ØP530ZZ	931, 1075	ØP5V3ZZ	931, 1076	ØP8Q4ZZ	641, 932	ØP964ZZ	233	ØP9G40Z	233
ØNUQ3JZ	56, 708, 931, 1075	ØP534ZZ	931, 1075	ØP5V4ZZ	931, 1076	ØP8R*	279, 708	ØP9700Z	233	ØP9G4ZX	223, 436, 496, 516, 524, 1076
ØNUQ4JZ	56, 708, 931, 1075	ØP54*	232, 708	ØP80*	101, 279, 708	ØP8RØZZ	932	ØP970ZX	102, 223, 436, 496, 516, 524, 1076	ØP9G4ZZ	233
ØNUR*	69, 708	ØP540ZZ	931, 1075	ØP800ZZ	931	ØP8R3ZZ	932	ØP970ZZ	233	ØP9H00Z	233
ØNURØ7Z	931	ØP543ZZ	931, 1075	ØP803ZZ	931	ØP8R4ZZ	932	ØP973ZX	102, 223, 436, 496, 516, 524, 1076	ØP9H0ZX	223, 436, 496, 516, 524, 1076
ØNURØJZ	931	ØP544ZZ	931, 1075	ØP804ZZ	931	ØP8S*	279, 708	ØP9740Z	233	ØP9H0ZZ	233
ØNURØKZ	931	ØP55*	101, 232, 496, 708	ØP81*	101, 279, 708	ØP8SØZZ	932	ØP974ZX	102, 223, 436, 496, 516, 524, 1076	ØP9H3ZX	223, 436, 496, 516, 524, 1076
ØNUR37Z	931	ØP550ZZ	931, 1075	ØP810ZZ	931	ØP8S3ZZ	932	ØP974ZZ	233	ØP9H40Z	233
ØNUR3JZ	931	ØP553ZZ	931, 1075	ØP813ZZ	931	ØP8S4ZZ	932	ØP980ZX	102, 223, 436, 496, 516, 524, 1076	ØP9H4ZX	223, 436, 496, 516, 524, 1076
ØNUR3KZ	931	ØP554ZZ	931, 1075	ØP814ZZ	931	ØP8T*	279, 708	ØP980ZZ	233	ØP9H4ZZ	233
ØNUR47Z	931	ØP56*	101, 232, 496, 708	ØP82*	101, 279, 708	ØP8TØZZ	932	ØP983ZX	102, 223, 436, 496, 516, 524, 1076	ØP9J00Z	233
ØNUR4JZ	931	ØP560ZZ	931, 1075	ØP820ZZ	931	ØP8T3ZZ	932	ØP9840Z	233	ØP9J0ZX	223, 436, 496, 516, 524, 1076
ØNUR4KZ	931	ØP563ZZ	931, 1075	ØP823ZZ	931	ØP8T4ZZ	932	ØP984ZX	102, 223, 436, 496, 516, 524, 1076	ØP9J0ZZ	233
ØNUT*	69, 279, 708	ØP564ZZ	931, 1075	ØP824ZZ	931	ØP8V*	279, 708	ØP984ZZ	233	ØP9J3ZX	223, 436, 496, 516, 524, 1076
ØNUTØ7Z	435, 931	ØP57*	101, 232, 496, 708	ØP83*	279, 708	ØP8VØZZ	932	ØP9900Z	233	ØP9J40Z	233
ØNUTØJZ	435, 931	ØP570ZZ	931, 1075	ØP830ZZ	931	ØP8V3ZZ	932	ØP990ZX	102, 223, 436, 496, 516, 524, 1076	ØP9J4ZX	223, 436, 496, 516, 524, 1076
ØNUTØKZ	435, 931	ØP573ZZ	931, 1075	ØP833ZZ	931	ØP8V4ZZ	932	ØP990ZZ	233	ØP9J4ZZ	233
ØNUT37Z	435, 931	ØP574ZZ	931, 1075	ØP834ZZ	931	ØP9000Z	232	ØP993ZX	102, 223, 436, 496, 516, 524, 1076	ØP9K00Z	233
ØNUT3JZ	435, 931	ØP58*	101, 232, 496, 708	ØP84*	279, 708	ØP900ZX	102, 222, 436, 496, 516, 524, 1076	ØP9940Z	233	ØP9K0ZX	223, 436, 496, 516, 524, 1076
ØNUT3KZ	435, 931	ØP580ZZ	931, 1075	ØP840ZZ	931			ØP994ZX	102, 223, 436, 496, 516, 524, 1076	ØP9K0ZZ	233
ØNUT47Z	436, 931	ØP583ZZ	931, 1075	ØP843ZZ	931	ØP900ZZ	232	ØP994ZZ	233	ØP9K3ZX	223, 436, 496, 516, 524, 1076
ØNUT4JZ	436, 931	ØP584ZZ	931, 1075	ØP844ZZ	931	ØP903ZX	102, 222, 436, 496, 516, 524, 1076	ØP9B00Z	233	ØP9K40Z	233
ØNUT4KZ	436, 931	ØP59*	101, 232, 496, 708	ØP85*	101, 279, 708			ØP9B0ZX	102, 223, 436, 496, 516, 524, 1076	ØP9K4ZX	223, 436, 496, 516, 524, 1076
ØNUV*	69, 279, 708	ØP590ZZ	931, 1075	ØP850ZZ	931	ØP9040Z	232			ØP9K4ZZ	233
ØNUVØ7Z	436, 931	ØP593ZZ	931, 1075	ØP853ZZ	931	ØP904ZX	102, 222, 436, 496, 516, 524, 1076	ØP9B0ZZ	233	ØP9L00Z	233
ØNUVØJZ	436, 931	ØP594ZZ	931, 1075	ØP854ZZ	931			ØP9B3ZX	102, 223, 436, 496, 516, 524, 1076	ØP9L0ZX	223, 436, 496, 516, 524, 1076
ØNUVØKZ	436, 931	ØP5B*	101, 232, 496, 708	ØP86*	101, 279, 708	ØP904ZZ	232	ØP9B40Z	233	ØP9L0ZZ	233
ØNUV37Z	436, 931	ØP5BØZZ	931, 1075	ØP860ZZ	931	ØP9100Z	232	ØP9B4ZX	102, 223, 436, 496, 516, 524, 1076	ØP9L3ZX	223, 436, 496, 516, 524, 1076
ØNUV3JZ	436, 931	ØP5B3ZZ	931, 1075	ØP863ZZ	931	ØP910ZX	102, 222, 436, 496, 516, 524, 1076	ØP9B4ZZ	233	ØP9L40Z	233
ØNUV3KZ	436, 931	ØP5B4ZZ	931, 1075	ØP864ZZ	931			ØP9C00Z	233	ØP9L4ZX	223, 436, 496, 516, 524, 1076
ØNUV47Z	436, 931	ØP5C*	232, 708	ØP87*	101, 279, 708	ØP910ZZ	232	ØP9C0ZX	223, 436, 496, 516, 524, 1076	ØP9L4ZZ	233
ØNUV4JZ	436, 931	ØP5CØZZ	931, 1075	ØP870ZZ	932	ØP913ZX	102, 222, 436, 496, 516, 524, 1076	ØP9C0ZZ	233	ØP9M00Z	269
ØNUV4KZ	436, 931	ØP5C3ZZ	931, 1075	ØP873ZZ	932			ØP9C3ZX	223, 436, 496, 516, 524, 1076	ØP9M0ZX	269, 436, 496, 516, 524, 641, 932, 1076
ØNUX*	69	ØP5C4ZZ	931, 1075	ØP874ZZ	932	ØP9140Z	232	ØP9C40Z	233		
ØNUXØJZ	56, 279, 708, 931	ØP5D*	232, 708	ØP88*	102, 279, 708	ØP914ZX	102, 222, 436, 496, 516, 524, 1076	ØP9C4ZX	223, 436, 496, 516, 524, 1076	ØP9M0ZZ	269
ØNUX3JZ	56, 279, 708, 931	ØP5DØZZ	931, 1075	ØP880ZZ	932			ØP9C4ZZ	233	ØP9M3ZX	269, 436, 496, 516, 525, 641, 932, 1076
ØNUX4JZ	56, 279, 708, 931	ØP5D3ZZ	931, 1075	ØP883ZZ	932	ØP914ZZ	232	ØP9D00Z	233		
ØNW000Z	14	ØP5D4ZZ	931, 1075	ØP884ZZ	932	ØP9200Z	232	ØP9D0ZX	223, 436, 496, 516, 524, 1076	ØP9M40Z	269
ØNW004Z	14	ØP5F*	232, 708	ØP89*	102, 279, 708	ØP920ZX	102, 222, 436, 496, 516, 524, 1076	ØP9D0ZZ	233	ØP9M4ZX	269, 436, 496, 516, 525, 641, 932, 1076
ØNW005Z	14	ØP5FØZZ	931, 1075	ØP890ZZ	932			ØP9D3ZX	223, 436, 496, 516, 524, 1076		
ØNW007Z	14	ØP5F3ZZ	931, 1075	ØP893ZZ	932	ØP920ZZ	232	ØP9D40Z	233	ØP9M4ZZ	269
ØNW00JZ	14	ØP5F4ZZ	931, 1075	ØP894ZZ	932	ØP923ZX	102, 223, 436, 496, 516, 524, 1076	ØP9D4ZX	223, 436, 496, 516, 524, 1076	ØP9N00Z	269
ØNW00KZ	14	ØP5G*	232, 708	ØP8B*	102, 279, 708			ØP9D4ZZ	233	ØP9N0ZX	269, 436, 496, 516, 525, 641, 932, 1076
ØNW00MZ	14	ØP5GØZZ	931, 1075	ØP8BØZZ	932	ØP9240Z	232	ØP9F00Z	233		
ØNW00NZ	14	ØP5G3ZZ	931, 1075	ØP8B3ZZ	932	ØP924ZX	102, 223, 436, 496, 516, 524, 1076	ØP9F0ZX	223, 436, 496, 516, 524, 1076	ØP9N0ZZ	269
ØNW00SZ	14	ØP5G4ZZ	931, 1075	ØP8B4ZZ	932			ØP9F0ZZ	233	ØP9N3ZX	269, 436, 496, 516, 525, 641, 932, 1076
ØNW030Z	14	ØP5H*	232, 708	ØP8C*	229, 708	ØP924ZZ	232	ØP9F3ZX	223, 436, 496, 516, 524, 1076		
ØNW034Z	14	ØP5HØZZ	931, 1075	ØP8CØZZ	932	ØP9300Z	232	ØP9F40Z	233	ØP9N40Z	269
ØNW035Z	14	ØP5H3ZZ	931, 1075	ØP8C3ZZ	932	ØP930ZX	80, 223, 577, 1076	ØP9F4ZX	223, 436, 496, 516, 524, 1076	ØP9N4ZX	269, 436, 496, 516, 525, 641, 932, 1076
ØNW037Z	14	ØP5H4ZZ	931, 1075	ØP8C4ZZ	932	ØP933ZX	80, 223, 577, 1076				
ØNW03JZ	14	ØP5J*	232, 708	ØP8D*	229, 708	ØP9340Z	232			ØP9N4ZZ	269
ØNW03KZ	14	ØP5JØZZ	931, 1075	ØP8DØZZ	932	ØP934ZX	80, 223, 577, 1076			ØP9P00Z	269
ØNW03MZ	14	ØP5J3ZZ	931, 1075	ØP8D3ZZ	932	ØP934ZZ	232			ØP9P0ZX	269, 436, 496, 516, 525, 641, 932, 1076
ØNW03SZ	14	ØP5J4ZZ	931, 1075	ØP8D4ZZ	932	ØP9400Z	232				
ØNW040Z	14	ØP5K*	232, 708	ØP8F*	229, 708	ØP940ZX	102, 223, 577, 1076			ØP9P0ZZ	269
ØNW044Z	14	ØP5KØZZ	931, 1075	ØP8FØZZ	932					ØP9P3ZX	269, 436, 496, 516, 525, 641, 932, 1076
ØNW045Z	14	ØP5K3ZZ	931, 1075	ØP8F3ZZ	932	ØP940ZZ	232				
ØNW047Z	14	ØP5K4ZZ	931, 1075	ØP8F4ZZ	932	ØP943ZX	102, 223, 577, 1076			ØP9P40Z	269
ØNW04JZ	14	ØP5L*	232, 708	ØP8G*	229, 708	ØP9440Z	232			ØP9P4ZX	269, 436, 496, 516, 525, 641, 932, 1076
ØNW04KZ	14	ØP5LØZZ	931, 1075	ØP8GØZZ	932	ØP944ZX	102, 223, 577, 1076				
ØNW04MZ	14	ØP5L3ZZ	931, 1075	ØP8G3ZZ	932					ØP9P4ZZ	269
ØNW04SZ	14	ØP5L4ZZ	931, 1075	ØP8G4ZZ	932	ØP944ZZ	232			ØP9Q00Z	269
ØNWW00Z	80	ØP5M*	269	ØP8H*	266, 708	ØP9500Z	232				
ØNWW04Z	80	ØP5MØZZ	641, 931, 1075	ØP8HØZZ	932	ØP950ZX	102, 223, 436, 496, 516, 524, 1076				
ØNWW07Z	80	ØP5M3ZZ	641, 931, 1075	ØP8H3ZZ	932						
ØNWW0JZ	80	ØP5M4ZZ	641, 931, 1075	ØP8H4ZZ	932	ØP950ZZ	232				
ØNWW0KZ	80	ØP5N*	269	ØP8J*	266, 708	ØP953ZX	102, 223, 436, 496, 516, 524, 1076				
ØNWW0MZ	80	ØP5NØZZ	641, 931, 1075	ØP8JØZZ	932						
ØNWW30Z	80	ØP5N3ZZ	641, 931, 1075	ØP8J3ZZ	932	ØP9540Z	232				
ØNWW34Z	80	ØP5N4ZZ	641, 931, 1075	ØP8J4ZZ	932	ØP954ZX	102, 223, 436, 496, 516, 524, 1076				
ØNWW37Z	80	ØP5P*	269	ØP8K*	266, 708						
ØNWW3JZ	80	ØP5PØZZ	641, 931, 1075	ØP8KØZZ	932	ØP954ZZ	232				
ØNWW3KZ	80	ØP5P3ZZ	641, 931, 1075	ØP8K3ZZ	932	ØP9600Z	232				
ØNWW3MZ	80	ØP5P4ZZ	641, 931, 1075	ØP8K4ZZ	932						
ØNWW40Z	80	ØP5Q*	269	ØP8L*	266, 708						
ØNWW44Z	80	ØP5QØZZ	641, 931, 1076	ØP8LØZZ	932						
ØNWW47Z	80	ØP5Q3ZZ	641, 931, 1076	ØP8L3ZZ	932						
ØNWW4JZ	80	ØP5Q4ZZ	641, 931, 1076	ØP8L4ZZ	932						
ØNWW4KZ	80	ØP5R*	232, 708	ØP8M*	269						
ØNWW4MZ	80	ØP5RØZZ	931, 1076	ØP8MØZZ	641, 932						
ØP50*	101, 232, 496, 708	ØP5R3ZZ	931, 1076	ØP8M3ZZ	641, 932						
ØP500ZZ	931, 1075	ØP5R4ZZ	931, 1076	ØP8M4ZZ	641, 932						
ØP503ZZ	931, 1075	ØP5S*	232, 708	ØP8N*	269						
ØP504ZZ	931, 1075	ØP5SØZZ	931, 1076	ØP8NØZZ	641, 932						
ØP51*	101, 232, 496, 708	ØP5S3ZZ	931, 1076	ØP8N3ZZ	641, 932						
ØP510ZZ	931, 1075	ØP5S4ZZ	931, 1076	ØP8N4ZZ	641, 932						
ØP513ZZ	931, 1075	ØP5T*	232, 708	ØP8P*	269						
ØP514ZZ	931, 1075			ØP8PØZZ	641, 932						

Code	Page
0P9Q0ZX	269, 436, 496, 516, 525, 641, 932, 1076
0P9Q0ZZ	269
0P9Q3ZX	269, 436, 496, 516, 525, 641, 932, 1076
0P9Q40Z	269
0P9Q4ZX	269, 436, 496, 516, 525, 641, 932, 1076
0P9Q4ZZ	269
0P9R00Z	233
0P9R0ZX	223, 436, 577, 1076
0P9R0ZZ	233
0P9R3ZX	223, 436, 577, 1076
0P9R40Z	233
0P9R4ZX	223, 436, 577, 1076
0P9R4ZZ	233
0P9S00Z	233
0P9S0ZX	223, 436, 577, 1076
0P9S0ZZ	233
0P9S3ZX	223, 436, 577, 1076
0P9S40Z	233
0P9S4ZX	223, 436, 577, 1076
0P9S4ZZ	233
0P9T0ZZ	233
0P9T0ZX	223, 436, 577, 1076
0P9T0ZZ	233
0P9T3ZX	223, 436, 577, 1076
0P9T40Z	233
0P9T4ZX	223, 436, 577, 1076
0P9T4ZZ	233
0P9V00Z	233
0P9V0ZX	223, 436, 577, 1076
0P9V0ZZ	233
0P9V3ZX	223, 436, 577, 1076
0P9V40Z	233
0P9V4ZX	223, 436, 577, 1076
0P9V4ZZ	233
0PB0*	102
0PB00ZX	223, 436, 496, 516, 525, 1076
0PB00ZZ	17, 279, 708, 932
0PB03ZX	223, 436, 496, 516, 525, 1076
0PB03ZZ	17, 279, 708, 932
0PB04ZX	223, 436, 496, 516, 525, 1076
0PB04ZZ	17, 279, 708, 932
0PB1*	102
0PB10ZX	223, 436, 496, 516, 525, 1076
0PB10ZZ	17, 279, 708, 932
0PB13ZX	223, 436, 496, 516, 525, 1076
0PB13ZZ	17, 279, 708, 932
0PB14ZX	223, 436, 496, 516, 525, 1076
0PB14ZZ	17, 279, 708, 932
0PB2*	102
0PB20ZX	223, 436, 497, 516, 525, 708, 932
0PB20ZZ	17, 279, 708, 932
0PB23ZX	223, 436, 497, 516, 525, 1076
0PB23ZZ	17, 279, 708, 932
0PB24ZX	223, 436, 497, 516, 525, 1076
0PB24ZZ	17, 279, 708, 932
0PB3*	80
0PB30ZX	223, 577, 1076
0PB30ZZ	279, 497, 708, 932
0PB33ZX	223, 577, 1076
0PB33ZZ	279, 497, 708, 932
0PB34ZX	223, 577, 1076
0PB34ZZ	279, 497, 708, 932
0PB40ZX	102, 223, 577, 1076
0PB40ZZ	80, 279, 497, 708, 932
0PB43ZX	102, 223, 577, 1076
0PB43ZZ	80, 279, 497, 708, 932
0PB44ZX	102, 223, 577, 1076
0PB44ZZ	80, 279, 497, 708, 932
0PB5*	102
0PB50ZX	223, 436, 497, 516, 525, 1076
0PB50ZZ	17, 279, 708, 932
0PB53ZX	223, 436, 497, 516, 525, 1076
0PB53ZZ	17, 279, 708, 932
0PB54ZX	223, 436, 497, 516, 525, 1076
0PB54ZZ	17, 279, 708, 932
0PB6*	102
0PB60ZX	223, 436, 497, 516, 525, 1076
0PB60ZZ	17, 279, 708, 932
0PB63ZX	223, 436, 497, 516, 525, 1076
0PB63ZZ	17, 279, 708, 932
0PB64ZX	223, 436, 497, 516, 525, 1076
0PB64ZZ	17, 279, 708, 932
0PB7*	102
0PB70ZX	223, 436, 497, 516, 525, 1076
0PB70ZZ	17, 279, 708, 932
0PB73ZX	223, 436, 497, 516, 525, 1076
0PB73ZZ	17, 280, 708, 932
0PB74ZX	223, 436, 497, 516, 525, 1076
0PB74ZZ	17, 280, 708, 932
0PB8*	102
0PB80ZX	223, 436, 497, 516, 525, 1076
0PB80ZZ	17, 280, 708, 932
0PB83ZX	223, 436, 497, 516, 525, 1076
0PB83ZZ	17, 280, 708, 932
0PB84ZX	223, 436, 497, 516, 525, 1076
0PB84ZZ	17, 280, 708, 932
0PB9*	102
0PB90ZX	223, 436, 497, 516, 525, 1076
0PB90ZZ	17, 280, 708, 932
0PB93ZX	223, 436, 497, 516, 525, 1076
0PB93ZZ	17, 280, 708, 932
0PB94ZX	223, 436, 497, 516, 525, 1076
0PB94ZZ	17, 280, 708, 932
0PBB*	102
0PBB0ZX	223, 436, 497, 516, 525, 1076
0PBB0ZZ	17, 280, 708, 932
0PBB3ZX	223, 436, 497, 516, 525, 1076
0PBB3ZZ	17, 280, 708, 932
0PBB4ZX	223, 436, 497, 516, 525, 1076
0PBB4ZZ	17, 280, 708, 932
0PBC0ZX	223, 436, 497, 516, 525, 1076
0PBC0ZZ	229, 708, 932
0PBC3ZX	223, 436, 497, 516, 525, 1076
0PBC3ZZ	229, 708, 932
0PBC4ZX	223, 436, 497, 516, 525, 1076
0PBC4ZZ	229, 708, 932
0PBD0ZX	223, 436, 497, 516, 525, 1076
0PBD0ZZ	229, 708, 932
0PBD3ZX	223, 436, 497, 516, 525, 1076
0PBD3ZZ	229, 708, 932
0PBD4ZX	223, 436, 497, 516, 525, 1076
0PBD4ZZ	229, 708, 932
0PBF0ZX	223, 436, 497, 516, 525, 1076
0PBF0ZZ	229, 708, 932
0PBF3ZX	223, 436, 497, 516, 525, 1076
0PBF3ZZ	229, 708, 932
0PBF4ZX	223, 436, 497, 516, 525, 1076
0PBF4ZZ	229, 708, 932
0PBG0ZX	223, 436, 497, 516, 525, 1076
0PBG0ZZ	229, 708, 932
0PBG3ZX	223, 436, 497, 516, 525, 1076
0PBG3ZZ	229, 708, 932
0PBG4ZX	223, 436, 497, 516, 525, 1076
0PBG4ZZ	229, 708, 932
0PBH0ZX	223, 436, 497, 516, 525, 1076
0PBH0ZZ	266, 708, 932
0PBH3ZX	223, 436, 497, 516, 525, 1076
0PBH3ZZ	266, 708, 932
0PBH4ZX	223, 436, 497, 516, 525, 1076
0PBH4ZZ	266, 708, 932
0PBJ0ZX	223, 436, 497, 516, 525, 1076
0PBJ0ZZ	266, 708, 932
0PBJ3ZX	223, 436, 497, 516, 525, 1076
0PBJ3ZZ	267, 708, 932
0PBJ4ZX	223, 436, 497, 516, 525, 1076
0PBJ4ZZ	267, 708, 932
0PBK0ZX	223, 436, 497, 516, 525, 1076
0PBK0ZZ	267, 708, 932
0PBK3ZX	223, 436, 497, 516, 525, 1076
0PBK3ZZ	267, 708, 932
0PBK4ZX	223, 436, 497, 516, 525, 1076
0PBK4ZZ	267, 708, 932
0PBL0ZX	223, 436, 497, 516, 525, 1076
0PBL0ZZ	267, 708, 932
0PBL3ZX	223, 436, 497, 516, 525, 1076
0PBL3ZZ	267, 708, 932
0PBL4ZX	223, 436, 497, 516, 525, 1076
0PBL4ZZ	267, 708, 932
0PBM*	269
0PBM0ZX	436, 497, 516, 525, 641, 932, 1076
0PBM0ZZ	641, 932
0PBM3ZX	436, 497, 516, 525, 641, 932, 1076
0PBM3ZZ	642, 932
0PBM4ZX	436, 497, 516, 525, 642, 932, 1076
0PBM4ZZ	642, 932
0PBN*	269
0PBN0ZX	436, 497, 516, 525, 642, 932, 1076
0PBN0ZZ	642, 932
0PBN3ZX	436, 497, 516, 525, 642, 932, 1076
0PBN3ZZ	642, 932
0PBN4ZX	436, 497, 516, 525, 642, 932, 1076
0PBN4ZZ	642, 932
0PBP*	269
0PBP0ZX	436, 497, 516, 525, 642, 932, 1076
0PBP0ZZ	642, 932
0PBP3ZX	436, 497, 516, 525, 642, 932, 1076
0PBP3ZZ	642, 932
0PBP4ZX	436, 497, 516, 525, 642, 932, 1076
0PBP4ZZ	642, 932
0PBQ*	269
0PBQ0ZX	436, 497, 516, 525, 642, 932, 1076
0PBQ0ZZ	642, 932
0PBQ3ZX	436, 497, 516, 525, 642, 932, 1076
0PBQ3ZZ	642, 932
0PBQ4ZX	436, 497, 516, 525, 642, 932, 1076
0PBQ4ZZ	642, 932
0PBR0ZX	223, 436, 577, 1076
0PBR0ZZ	80, 280, 436, 497, 708, 932
0PBR3ZX	223, 436, 577, 1076
0PBR3ZZ	80, 280, 436, 497, 708, 932
0PBR4ZX	223, 436, 577, 1076
0PBR4ZZ	80, 280, 436, 497, 708, 932
0PBS0ZX	223, 436, 577, 1076
0PBS0ZZ	80, 280, 436, 497, 708, 932
0PBS3ZX	223, 436, 577, 1076
0PBS3ZZ	80, 280, 436, 497, 708, 932
0PBS4ZX	223, 436, 577, 1076
0PBS4ZZ	80, 280, 436, 497, 708, 932
0PBT0ZX	223, 436, 577, 1076
0PBT0ZZ	80, 280, 436, 497, 708, 932
0PBT3ZX	223, 436, 577, 1076
0PBT3ZZ	80, 280, 436, 497, 708, 932
0PBT4ZX	223, 436, 577, 1076
0PBT4ZZ	80, 280, 436, 497, 708, 932
0PBV0ZX	223, 436, 577, 1077
0PBV0ZZ	80, 280, 436, 497, 708, 932
0PBV3ZX	223, 436, 577, 1077
0PBV3ZZ	80, 280, 436, 497, 708, 932
0PBV4ZX	223, 436, 577, 1077
0PBV4ZZ	80, 280, 436, 497, 709, 932
0PC0*	102, 280, 709
0PC00ZZ	932
0PC03ZZ	932
0PC04ZZ	932
0PC1*	102, 280, 709
0PC10ZZ	932
0PC13ZZ	932
0PC14ZZ	932
0PC2*	102, 280, 709
0PC20ZZ	932
0PC23ZZ	932
0PC24ZZ	932
0PC3*	280, 709
0PC30ZZ	933
0PC33ZZ	933
0PC34ZZ	933
0PC4*	280, 709
0PC40ZZ	933
0PC43ZZ	933
0PC44ZZ	933
0PC5*	102, 280, 709
0PC50ZZ	933
0PC53ZZ	933
0PC54ZZ	933
0PC6*	102, 280, 709
0PC60ZZ	933
0PC63ZZ	933
0PC64ZZ	933
0PC7*	102, 280, 709
0PC70ZZ	933
0PC73ZZ	933
0PC74ZZ	933
0PC8*	102, 280, 709
0PC80ZZ	933
0PC83ZZ	933
0PC84ZZ	933
0PC9*	102, 280, 709
0PC90ZZ	933
0PC93ZZ	933
0PC94ZZ	933
0PCB*	102, 280, 709
0PCB0ZZ	933
0PCB3ZZ	933
0PCB4ZZ	933
0PCC*	229, 709
0PCC0ZZ	933
0PCC3ZZ	933
0PCC4ZZ	933
0PCD*	229, 709
0PCD0ZZ	933
0PCD3ZZ	933
0PCD4ZZ	933
0PCF*	229, 709
0PCF0ZZ	933
0PCF3ZZ	933
0PCF4ZZ	933
0PCG*	229, 709
0PCG0ZZ	933
0PCG3ZZ	933
0PCG4ZZ	933
0PCH*	267, 709
0PCH3ZZ	933
0PCH4ZZ	933
0PCJ*	267, 709
0PCJ0ZZ	933
0PCJ3ZZ	933
0PCJ4ZZ	933
0PCK*	267, 709
0PCK0ZZ	933
0PCK3ZZ	933
0PCK4ZZ	933
0PCL*	267, 709
0PCL0ZZ	933
0PCL3ZZ	933
0PCL4ZZ	933
0PCM*	269
0PCM0ZZ	642, 933
0PCM3ZZ	642, 933
0PCM4ZZ	642, 933
0PCN*	269
0PCN0ZZ	642, 933
0PCN3ZZ	642, 933
0PCN4ZZ	642, 933
0PCP*	269
0PCP0ZZ	642, 933
0PCP3ZZ	642, 933
0PCP4ZZ	642, 933
0PCQ*	269
0PCQ0ZZ	642, 933
0PCQ3ZZ	642, 933
0PCQ4ZZ	642, 933
0PCR*	280, 709
0PCR0ZZ	933
0PCR3ZZ	933
0PCR4ZZ	933
0PCS*	280, 709
0PCS0ZZ	933
0PCS3ZZ	933
0PCS4ZZ	933
0PCT*	280, 709
0PCT0ZZ	933
0PCT3ZZ	933
0PCT4ZZ	933
0PCV*	280, 709
0PCV0ZZ	933
0PCV3ZZ	933
0PCV4ZZ	933
0PD00ZZ	40, 256, 437, 709, 933
0PD10ZZ	40, 256, 437, 709, 933
0PD20ZZ	40, 256, 437, 709, 933
0PD30ZZ	40, 256, 437, 709, 933
0PD40ZZ	40, 256, 437, 709, 933
0PD50ZZ	40, 256, 437, 709, 933
0PD60ZZ	40, 256, 437, 709, 933
0PD70ZZ	40, 256, 437, 709, 933
0PD80ZZ	40, 256, 437, 709, 933
0PD90ZZ	40, 256, 437, 709, 933
0PDB0ZZ	40, 256, 437, 709, 933
0PDC0ZZ	40, 256, 437, 709, 933
0PDD0ZZ	40, 256, 437, 709, 933
0PDF0ZZ	40, 256, 437, 709, 933
0PDG0ZZ	40, 256, 437, 709, 933
0PDH0ZZ	40, 256, 437, 709, 933
0PDJ0ZZ	40, 256, 437, 709, 933
0PDK0ZZ	40, 256, 437, 709, 933
0PDL0ZZ	40, 256, 437, 709, 933
0PDM0ZZ	269, 642, 933
0PDN0ZZ	269, 642, 933
0PDP0ZZ	269, 642, 933
0PDQ0ZZ	269, 642, 933
0PDR0ZZ	269, 642, 933
0PDS0ZZ	269, 642, 933
0PDT0ZZ	269, 642, 933
0PDV0ZZ	269, 642, 933
0PH0*	102, 280, 709
0PH000Z	147, 933
0PH004Z	933
0PH030Z	147, 933
0PH034Z	933
0PH040Z	147, 933
0PH044Z	933
0PH1*	102, 280, 709
0PH104Z	933
0PH134Z	933
0PH144Z	933
0PH2*	102, 280, 709
0PH204Z	933
0PH234Z	933
0PH244Z	933
0PH3*	280, 709
0PH304Z	933
0PH334Z	933
0PH344Z	933
0PH4*	280, 709
0PH404Z	933
0PH434Z	933
0PH444Z	933
0PH5*	102, 280, 709
0PH504Z	933
0PH534Z	933
0PH544Z	933
0PH6*	102, 280, 709
0PH604Z	933
0PH634Z	933
0PH644Z	933
0PH7*	102, 280, 709
0PH704Z	933
0PH734Z	933
0PH744Z	933
0PH8*	102, 280, 709
0PH804Z	933
0PH834Z	933
0PH844Z	933
0PH9*	102, 280, 709
0PH904Z	933
0PH934Z	933
0PH944Z	933
0PHB*	102, 280, 709
0PHB04Z	933
0PHB34Z	933
0PHB44Z	933
0PHC04Z	229, 709, 933
0PHC05Z	229, 709, 933
0PHC06Z	229, 709, 933
0PHC0BZ	229, 709, 933
0PHC0CZ	229, 709, 933
0PHC0DZ	229, 709, 933
0PHC34Z	229, 709, 933
0PHC35Z	229, 709, 933
0PHC36Z	229, 709, 933
0PHC3BZ	229, 709, 933
0PHC3CZ	229, 709, 933
0PHC3DZ	229, 709, 933
0PHC44Z	229, 709, 933
0PHC45Z	229, 709, 933
0PHC46Z	229, 709, 933
0PHC4CZ	229, 709, 933
0PHC4DZ	229, 709, 933
0PHD04Z	229, 709, 933
0PHD05Z	229, 709, 933
0PHD06Z	229, 709, 933
0PHD0BZ	229, 709, 933

Numeric Index to Procedures

Code	Page	Code	Page	Code	Page	Code	Page	Code	Page	Code	Page
0PHD0CZ	229,709,933	0PHK05Z	267,709,934	0PHY3MZ	934	0PP20JZ	233,710,1077	0PP94KZ	234,710,1077	0PPF44Z	234,711,935,1078
0PHD0DZ	229,709,933	0PHK06Z	267,709,934	0PHY4MZ	934	0PP20KZ	233,710,1077	0PPB04Z	234,710,1077	0PPF45Z	234,711,935,1078
0PHD34Z	229,709,933	0PHK0BZ	267,709,934	0PJY0ZZ	102,223	0PP234Z	233,710,1077	0PPB07Z	234,711,1077	0PPF47Z	234,711,935,1078
0PHD35Z	229,709,933	0PHK0CZ	267,709,934	0PJY4ZZ	102,223	0PP237Z	233,710,1077	0PPB0JZ	234,711,1077	0PPF4JZ	234,711,935,1078
0PHD36Z	229,709,933	0PHK0DZ	267,709,934	0PN0*	102,280,710	0PP23JZ	233,710,1077	0PPB0KZ	234,711,1077	0PPF4KZ	234,711,935,1078
0PHD3BZ	229,709,933	0PHK34Z	267,710,934	0PN1*	102,280,710	0PP23KZ	233,710,1077	0PPB34Z	234,711,1077	0PPG04Z	234,711,935,1078
0PHD3CZ	229,709,933	0PHK35Z	267,710,934	0PN2*	102,280,710	0PP244Z	233,710,1077	0PPB37Z	234,711,1077	0PPG05Z	234,711,935,1078
0PHD3DZ	229,709,933	0PHK36Z	267,710,934	0PN3*	280	0PP247Z	233,710,1077	0PPB3JZ	234,711,1077	0PPG07Z	234,711,935,1078
0PHD44Z	229,709,933	0PHK3BZ	267,710,934	0PN4*	280	0PP24JZ	233,710,1077	0PPB3KZ	234,711,1077	0PPG0JZ	234,711,935,1078
0PHD45Z	229,709,933	0PHK3CZ	267,710,934	0PN5*	102,280,710	0PP24KZ	233,710,1077	0PPB44Z	234,711,1077	0PPG0KZ	234,711,935,1078
0PHD46Z	229,709,933	0PHK3DZ	267,710,934	0PN6*	102,280,710	0PP304Z	233,710,1077	0PPB47Z	234,711,1077	0PPG34Z	234,711,935,1078
0PHD4BZ	229,709,933	0PHK44Z	267,710,934	0PN7*	102,280,710	0PP307Z	233,710,1077	0PPB4JZ	234,711,1077	0PPG35Z	234,711,935,1078
0PHD4CZ	229,709,933	0PHK45Z	267,710,934	0PN8*	102,280,710	0PP30JZ	233,710,1077	0PPB4KZ	234,711,1077	0PPG37Z	234,711,935,1078
0PHD4DZ	229,709,933	0PHK46Z	267,710,934	0PN9*	102,280,710	0PP30KZ	233,710,1077	0PPC04Z	234,711,935,1077	0PPG3JZ	234,711,935,1078
0PHF04Z	229,709,933	0PHK4BZ	267,710,934	0PNB*	102,280,710	0PP334Z	233,710,1077	0PPC05Z	234,711,935,1077	0PPG3KZ	234,711,935,1078
0PHF05Z	229,709,933	0PHK4CZ	267,710,934	0PNC*	229,710	0PP337Z	233,710,1077	0PPC07Z	234,711,935,1077	0PPG44Z	234,711,935,1078
0PHF06Z	229,709,933	0PHK4DZ	267,710,934	0PNC0ZZ	934	0PP33JZ	233,710,1077	0PPC0JZ	234,711,935,1077	0PPG45Z	234,711,935,1078
0PHF07Z	229,709,934	0PHL04Z	267,710,934	0PNC3ZZ	934	0PP33KZ	233,710,1077	0PPC0KZ	234,711,935,1077	0PPG47Z	234,711,935,1078
0PHF0BZ	229,709,934	0PHL05Z	267,710,934	0PNC4ZZ	934	0PP344Z	233,710,1077	0PPC34Z	234,711,935,1077	0PPG4JZ	234,711,935,1078
0PHF0CZ	229,709,934	0PHL06Z	267,710,934	0PND*	229,710	0PP347Z	233,710,1077	0PPC35Z	234,711,935,1077	0PPG4KZ	234,711,935,1078
0PHF0DZ	229,709,934	0PHL0BZ	267,710,934	0PND0ZZ	934	0PP34JZ	233,710,1077	0PPC37Z	234,711,935,1077	0PPH04Z	234,711,935,1078
0PHF34Z	229,709,934	0PHL0CZ	267,710,934	0PND3ZZ	934	0PP34KZ	233,710,1077	0PPC3JZ	234,711,935,1077	0PPH05Z	234,711,935,1078
0PHF35Z	229,709,934	0PHL0DZ	267,710,934	0PND4ZZ	934	0PP404Z	233,710,1077	0PPC3KZ	234,711,935,1077	0PPH07Z	234,711,935,1078
0PHF36Z	229,709,934	0PHL34Z	267,710,934	0PNF*	229,710	0PP407Z	233,710,1077	0PPC44Z	234,711,935,1077	0PPH0JZ	234,711,935,1078
0PHF37Z	229,709,934	0PHL35Z	267,710,934	0PNF0ZZ	934	0PP40JZ	233,710,1077	0PPC45Z	234,711,935,1077	0PPH0KZ	234,711,935,1078
0PHF3BZ	229,709,934	0PHL36Z	267,710,934	0PNF3ZZ	934	0PP40KZ	233,710,1077	0PPC47Z	234,711,935,1077	0PPH34Z	234,711,935,1078
0PHF3CZ	229,709,934	0PHL3BZ	267,710,934	0PNF4ZZ	934	0PP434Z	233,710,1077	0PPC4JZ	234,711,935,1077	0PPH35Z	234,711,935,1078
0PHF3DZ	229,709,934	0PHL3CZ	267,710,934	0PNG*	229,710	0PP437Z	233,710,1077	0PPC4KZ	234,711,935,1077	0PPH37Z	234,711,935,1078
0PHF44Z	229,709,934	0PHL3DZ	267,710,934	0PNG0ZZ	934	0PP43JZ	233,710,1077	0PPD04Z	234,711,935,1077	0PPH3JZ	234,711,935,1078
0PHF45Z	229,709,934	0PHL44Z	267,710,934	0PNG3ZZ	934	0PP43KZ	233,710,1077	0PPD05Z	234,711,935,1077	0PPH3KZ	234,711,935,1078
0PHF46Z	229,709,934	0PHL45Z	267,710,934	0PNG4ZZ	934	0PP444Z	233,710,1077	0PPD07Z	234,711,935,1077	0PPH44Z	234,711,935,1078
0PHF47Z	229,709,934	0PHL46Z	267,710,934	0PNH*	267,710	0PP447Z	233,710,1077	0PPD0JZ	234,711,935,1077	0PPH45Z	234,711,935,1078
0PHF4BZ	229,709,934	0PHL4BZ	267,710,934	0PNH0ZZ	935	0PP44JZ	233,710,1077	0PPD0KZ	234,711,935,1077	0PPH47Z	234,711,935,1078
0PHF4CZ	229,709,934	0PHL4CZ	267,710,934	0PNH3ZZ	935	0PP44KZ	233,710,1077	0PPD34Z	234,711,935,1077	0PPH4JZ	234,711,935,1078
0PHF4DZ	229,709,934	0PHL4DZ	267,710,934	0PNH4ZZ	935	0PP504Z	233,710,1077	0PPD35Z	234,711,935,1077	0PPH4KZ	234,711,935,1078
0PHG04Z	229,709,934	0PHM*	269	0PNJ*	267,710	0PP507Z	233,710,1077	0PPD37Z	234,711,935,1077	0PPJ04Z	234,711,935,1078
0PHG05Z	229,709,934	0PHM04Z	642,934	0PNJ0ZZ	935	0PP50JZ	233,710,1077	0PPD3JZ	234,711,935,1077	0PPJ05Z	234,711,935,1078
0PHG06Z	229,709,934	0PHM05Z	642,934	0PNJ3ZZ	935	0PP50KZ	233,710,1077	0PPD3KZ	234,711,935,1077	0PPJ07Z	234,711,935,1078
0PHG07Z	229,709,934	0PHM34Z	642,934	0PNJ4ZZ	935	0PP534Z	233,710,1077	0PPD44Z	234,711,935,1077	0PPJ0JZ	234,711,935,1078
0PHG0BZ	229,709,934	0PHM35Z	642,934	0PNK*	267,710	0PP537Z	233,710,1077	0PPD45Z	234,711,935,1077	0PPJ0KZ	234,711,935,1078
0PHG0CZ	229,709,934	0PHM44Z	642,934	0PNK0ZZ	935	0PP53JZ	233,710,1077	0PPD47Z	234,711,935,1077	0PPJ34Z	234,711,935,1078
0PHG0DZ	229,709,934	0PHM45Z	642,934	0PNK3ZZ	935	0PP53KZ	233,710,1077	0PPD4JZ	234,711,935,1077	0PPJ35Z	234,711,935,1078
0PHG34Z	229,709,934	0PHN*	269	0PNK4ZZ	935	0PP544Z	233,710,1077	0PPD4KZ	234,711,935,1077	0PPJ37Z	234,711,935,1078
0PHG35Z	229,709,934	0PHN04Z	642,934	0PNL*	267,710	0PP547Z	233,710,1077	0PPF04Z	234,711,935,1077	0PPJ3JZ	234,711,935,1078
0PHG36Z	229,709,934	0PHN05Z	642,934	0PNL0ZZ	935	0PP54JZ	233,710,1077	0PPF05Z	234,711,935,1077	0PPJ3KZ	234,711,935,1078
0PHG37Z	229,709,934	0PHN34Z	642,934	0PNL3ZZ	935	0PP54KZ	233,710,1077	0PPF07Z	234,711,935,1077	0PPJ44Z	234,711,935,1078
0PHG3BZ	229,709,934	0PHN35Z	642,934	0PNL4ZZ	935	0PP604Z	233,710,1077	0PPF0JZ	234,711,935,1077		
0PHG3CZ	229,709,934	0PHN44Z	642,934	0PNM*	269	0PP607Z	233,710,1077	0PPF0KZ	234,711,935,1077		
0PHG3DZ	229,709,934	0PHN45Z	642,934	0PNM0ZZ	642,935	0PP60JZ	233,710,1077	0PPF34Z	234,711,935,1077		
0PHG44Z	229,709,934	0PHP*	269	0PNM3ZZ	642,935	0PP60KZ	233,710,1077	0PPF35Z	234,711,935,1077		
0PHG45Z	229,709,934	0PHP04Z	642,934	0PNM4ZZ	642,935	0PP634Z	233,710,1077	0PPF37Z	234,711,935,1077		
0PHG46Z	229,709,934	0PHP05Z	642,934	0PNN*	269	0PP637Z	233,710,1077	0PPF3JZ	234,711,935,1077		
0PHG47Z	229,709,934	0PHP34Z	642,934	0PNN0ZZ	642,935	0PP63JZ	233,710,1077	0PPF3KZ	234,711,935,1078		
0PHG4BZ	229,709,934	0PHP35Z	642,934	0PNN3ZZ	642,935	0PP63KZ	233,710,1077				
0PHG4CZ	229,709,934	0PHP44Z	642,934	0PNN4ZZ	642,935	0PP644Z	233,710,1077				
0PHG4DZ	229,709,934	0PHP45Z	642,934	0PNP*	269	0PP647Z	233,710,1077				
0PHH04Z	267,709,934	0PHQ*	269	0PNP0ZZ	642,935	0PP64JZ	233,710,1077				
0PHH05Z	267,709,934	0PHQ04Z	642,934	0PNP3ZZ	642,935	0PP64KZ	233,710,1077				
0PHH06Z	267,709,934	0PHQ05Z	642,934	0PNP4ZZ	642,935	0PP704Z	233,710,1077				
0PHH0BZ	267,709,934	0PHQ34Z	642,934	0PNQ*	269	0PP707Z	233,710,1077				
0PHH0CZ	267,709,934	0PHQ35Z	642,934	0PNQ0ZZ	642,935	0PP70JZ	233,710,1077				
0PHH0DZ	267,709,934	0PHQ44Z	642,934	0PNQ3ZZ	642,935	0PP70KZ	233,710,1077				
0PHH34Z	267,709,934	0PHQ45Z	642,934	0PNQ4ZZ	642,935	0PP734Z	233,710,1077				
0PHH35Z	267,709,934	0PHR*	280,710	0PNR*	280	0PP737Z	233,710,1077				
0PHH36Z	267,709,934	0PHR04Z	934	0PNS*	280	0PP73JZ	233,710,1077				
0PHH3BZ	267,709,934	0PHR05Z	934	0PNT*	280	0PP73KZ	233,710,1077				
0PHH3CZ	267,709,934	0PHR34Z	934	0PNV*	280	0PP744Z	233,710,1077				
0PHH3DZ	267,709,934	0PHR35Z	934	0PP004Z	233,710,1077	0PP747Z	233,710,1077				
0PHH44Z	267,709,934	0PHR44Z	934	0PP007Z	233,710,1077	0PP74JZ	233,710,1077				
0PHH45Z	267,709,934	0PHR45Z	934	0PP00JZ	233,710,1077	0PP74KZ	233,710,1077				
0PHH46Z	267,709,934	0PHS*	280,710	0PP00KZ	233,710,1077	0PP804Z	233,710,1077				
0PHH4BZ	267,709,934	0PHS04Z	934	0PP034Z	233,710,1077	0PP807Z	233,710,1077				
0PHH4CZ	267,709,934	0PHS05Z	934	0PP037Z	233,710,1077	0PP80JZ	233,710,1077				
0PHH4DZ	267,709,934	0PHS34Z	934	0PP03JZ	233,710,1077	0PP80KZ	233,710,1077				
0PHJ04Z	267,709,934	0PHS35Z	934	0PP03KZ	233,710,1077	0PP834Z	233,710,1077				
0PHJ05Z	267,709,934	0PHS44Z	934	0PP044Z	233,710,1077	0PP837Z	233,710,1077				
0PHJ06Z	267,709,934	0PHS45Z	934	0PP047Z	233,710,1077	0PP83JZ	233,710,1077				
0PHJ0BZ	267,709,934	0PHT*	280,710	0PP04JZ	233,710,1077	0PP83KZ	233,710,1077				
0PHJ0CZ	267,709,934	0PHT04Z	934	0PP04KZ	233,710,1077	0PP844Z	233,710,1077				
0PHJ0DZ	267,709,934	0PHT05Z	934	0PP104Z	233,710,1077	0PP847Z	233,710,1077				
0PHJ34Z	267,709,934	0PHT34Z	934	0PP107Z	233,710,1077	0PP84JZ	233,710,1077				
0PHJ35Z	267,709,934	0PHT35Z	934	0PP10JZ	233,710,1077	0PP84KZ	233,710,1077				
0PHJ36Z	267,709,934	0PHT44Z	934	0PP10KZ	233,710,1077	0PP904Z	234,710,1077				
0PHJ3BZ	267,709,934	0PHT45Z	934	0PP134Z	233,710,1077	0PP907Z	234,710,1077				
0PHJ3CZ	267,709,934	0PHV*	280,710	0PP137Z	233,710,1077	0PP90JZ	234,710,1077				
0PHJ3DZ	267,709,934	0PHV04Z	934	0PP13JZ	233,710,1077	0PP90KZ	234,710,1077				
0PHJ44Z	267,709,934	0PHV05Z	934	0PP13KZ	233,710,1077	0PP934Z	234,710,1077				
0PHJ45Z	267,709,934	0PHV34Z	934	0PP144Z	233,710,1077	0PP937Z	234,710,1077				
0PHJ46Z	267,709,934	0PHV35Z	934	0PP147Z	233,710,1077	0PP93JZ	234,710,1077				
0PHJ4BZ	267,709,934	0PHV44Z	934	0PP14JZ	233,710,1077	0PP93KZ	234,710,1077				
0PHJ4CZ	267,709,934	0PHV45Z	934	0PP14KZ	233,710,1077	0PP944Z	234,710,1077				
0PHJ4DZ	267,709,934	0PHY*	102,280,710	0PP204Z	233,710,1077	0PP947Z	234,710,1077				
0PHK04Z	267,709,934	0PHY0MZ	934	0PP207Z	233,710,1077	0PP94JZ	234,710,1077				

Code	Page	Code	Page	Code	Page	Code	Page	Code	Page	Code	Page
0PPJ45Z	234, 711, 935, 1078	0PPM47Z	234, 642, 935, 1078	0PPQ4JZ	235, 642, 936, 1078	0PQ80ZZ	102, 280, 712	0PR73JZ	102, 712	0PRM07Z	642, 936
0PPJ47Z	234, 711, 935, 1078	0PPM4JZ	234, 642, 935, 1078	0PPQ4KZ	235, 642, 936, 1078	0PQ83ZZ	102, 280, 712	0PR74JZ	102, 712	0PRM0JZ	642, 936
0PPJ4JZ	234, 711, 935, 1078	0PPM4KZ	234, 642, 935, 1078	0PPR04Z	235, 711, 1078	0PQ84ZZ	102, 280, 712	0PR8*	280	0PRM0KZ	642, 936
0PPJ4KZ	234, 711, 935, 1078	0PPN04Z	234, 642, 935, 1078	0PPR05Z	235, 711, 1078	0PQ90ZZ	102, 280, 712	0PR80JZ	102, 712	0PRM37Z	642, 936
0PPK04Z	234, 711, 935, 1078	0PPN05Z	234, 642, 935, 1078	0PPR07Z	235, 711, 1078	0PQ93ZZ	102, 280, 712	0PR83JZ	102, 712	0PRM3JZ	642, 936
0PPK05Z	234, 711, 935, 1078	0PPN07Z	234, 642, 935, 1078	0PPR0JZ	235, 711, 1078	0PQ94ZZ	102, 280, 712	0PR84JZ	102, 712	0PRM3KZ	642, 936
0PPK07Z	234, 711, 935, 1078	0PPN0JZ	234, 642, 935, 1078	0PPR0KZ	235, 711, 1078	0PQB0ZZ	102, 280, 712	0PR9*	280	0PRM47Z	642, 936
0PPK0JZ	234, 711, 935, 1078	0PPN0KZ	234, 642, 935, 1078	0PPR34Z	235, 711, 1078	0PQB3ZZ	102, 280, 712	0PR90JZ	102, 712	0PRM4KZ	642, 936
0PPK0KZ	234, 711, 935, 1078	0PPN34Z	234, 642, 935, 1078	0PPR35Z	235, 711, 1078	0PQB4ZZ	102, 280, 712	0PR93JZ	102, 712	0PRN*	269
0PPK34Z	234, 711, 935, 1078	0PPN35Z	234, 642, 935, 1078	0PPR37Z	235, 711, 1078	0PQC0ZZ	229, 712, 936	0PR94JZ	102, 712	0PRN07Z	642, 936
0PPK35Z	234, 711, 935, 1078	0PPN37Z	234, 642, 935, 1078	0PPR3JZ	235, 711, 1078	0PQC3ZZ	229, 712, 936	0PRB*	280	0PRN0JZ	642, 936
0PPK37Z	234, 711, 935, 1078	0PPN3JZ	234, 642, 935, 1078	0PPR3KZ	235, 711, 1078	0PQC4ZZ	229, 712, 936	0PRB0JZ	102, 712	0PRN0KZ	642, 936
0PPK3JZ	234, 711, 935, 1078	0PPN3KZ	234, 642, 935, 1078	0PPR44Z	235, 711, 1078	0PQD0ZZ	229, 712, 936	0PRB3JZ	102, 712	0PRN3JZ	642, 936
0PPK3KZ	234, 711, 935, 1078	0PPN44Z	234, 642, 935, 1078	0PPR45Z	235, 711, 1078	0PQD3ZZ	229, 712, 936	0PRB4JZ	102, 712	0PRN3KZ	642, 936
0PPK44Z	234, 711, 935, 1078	0PPN45Z	234, 642, 935, 1078	0PPR47Z	235, 711, 1078	0PQD4ZZ	229, 712, 936	0PRC07Z	229, 712, 936	0PRN47Z	642, 936
0PPK45Z	234, 711, 935, 1078	0PPN47Z	234, 642, 935, 1078	0PPR4JZ	235, 711, 1078	0PQF0ZZ	229, 712, 936	0PRC0JZ	229	0PRN4JZ	642, 936
0PPK47Z	234, 711, 935, 1078	0PPN4JZ	234, 642, 935, 1078	0PPR4KZ	235, 711, 1078	0PQF3ZZ	229, 712, 936	0PRC0KZ	229, 712, 936	0PRN4KZ	642, 936
0PPK4JZ	234, 711, 935, 1078	0PPN4KZ	234, 642, 935, 1078	0PPS04Z	235, 711, 1078	0PQF4ZZ	229, 712, 936	0PRC37Z	229, 712, 936	0PRP*	269
0PPK4KZ	234, 711, 935, 1078	0PPP04Z	235, 642, 936, 1078	0PPS05Z	235, 711, 1078	0PQG0ZZ	229, 712, 936	0PRC3JZ	229, 712, 936	0PRP07Z	642, 936
0PPL04Z	234, 711, 935, 1078	0PPP05Z	235, 642, 936, 1078	0PPS07Z	235, 711, 1078	0PQG3ZZ	229, 712, 936	0PRC3KZ	229, 712, 936	0PRP0JZ	642, 936
0PPL05Z	234, 711, 935, 1078	0PPP07Z	235, 642, 936, 1078	0PPS0JZ	235, 711, 1078	0PQG4ZZ	229, 712, 936	0PRC47Z	229, 712, 936	0PRP0KZ	642, 936
0PPL07Z	234, 711, 935, 1078	0PPP0JZ	235, 642, 936, 1078	0PPS0KZ	235, 711, 1078	0PQH0ZZ	267, 712, 936	0PRC4JZ	229, 712, 936	0PRP37Z	642, 936
0PPL0JZ	234, 711, 935, 1078	0PPP0KZ	235, 642, 936, 1078	0PPS34Z	235, 711, 1078	0PQH3ZZ	267, 712, 936	0PRC4KZ	229, 712, 936	0PRP3JZ	642, 936
0PPL0KZ	234, 711, 935, 1078	0PPP34Z	235, 642, 936, 1078	0PPS35Z	235, 711, 1078	0PQH4ZZ	267, 712, 936	0PRD07Z	229, 712, 936	0PRP3KZ	642, 936
0PPL34Z	234, 711, 935, 1078	0PPP35Z	235, 642, 936, 1078	0PPS37Z	235, 711, 1078	0PQJ0ZZ	267, 712, 936	0PRD0JZ	229	0PRP47Z	642, 936
0PPL35Z	234, 711, 935, 1078	0PPP37Z	235, 642, 936, 1078	0PPS3KZ	235, 711, 1078	0PQJ3ZZ	267, 712, 936	0PRD0KZ	229, 712, 936	0PRP4JZ	643, 936
0PPL37Z	234, 711, 935, 1078	0PPP3JZ	235, 642, 936, 1078	0PPS44Z	235, 711, 1078	0PQJ4ZZ	267, 712, 936	0PRD37Z	229, 712, 936	0PRP4KZ	643, 937
0PPL3JZ	234, 711, 935, 1078	0PPP3KZ	235, 642, 936, 1078	0PPS45Z	235, 711, 1078	0PQK0ZZ	267, 712, 936	0PRD3JZ	229, 712, 936	0PRQ*	269
0PPL3KZ	234, 711, 935, 1078	0PPP44Z	235, 642, 936, 1078	0PPS47Z	235, 711, 1078	0PQK3ZZ	267, 712, 936	0PRD3KZ	229, 712, 936	0PRQ07Z	643, 937
0PPL44Z	234, 711, 935, 1078	0PPP45Z	235, 642, 936, 1078	0PPS4JZ	235, 711, 1078	0PQK4ZZ	267, 712, 936	0PRD47Z	229, 712, 936	0PRQ0JZ	643, 937
0PPL45Z	234, 711, 935, 1078	0PPP47Z	235, 642, 936, 1078	0PPS4KZ	235, 711, 1078	0PQL0ZZ	267, 712, 936	0PRD4JZ	229, 712, 936	0PRQ0KZ	643, 937
0PPL47Z	234, 711, 935, 1078	0PPP4JZ	235, 642, 936, 1078	0PPT04Z	235, 711, 1078	0PQL3ZZ	267, 712, 936	0PRD4KZ	229, 712, 936	0PRQ37Z	643, 937
0PPL4JZ	234, 711, 935, 1078	0PPP4KZ	235, 642, 936, 1078	0PPT05Z	235, 711, 1078	0PQL4ZZ	267, 712, 936	0PRF*	229, 712	0PRQ3JZ	643, 937
0PPL4KZ	234, 711, 935, 1078	0PPQ04Z	235, 642, 936, 1078	0PPT07Z	235, 711, 1078	0PQM0ZZ	269, 642, 936	0PRF07Z	936	0PRQ3KZ	643, 937
0PPM04Z	234, 642, 935, 1078	0PPQ05Z	235, 642, 936, 1078	0PPT0JZ	235, 711, 1079	0PQM3ZZ	269, 642, 936	0PRF0JZ	936	0PRQ47Z	643, 937
0PPM05Z	234, 642, 935, 1078	0PPQ07Z	235, 642, 936, 1078	0PPT0KZ	235, 711, 1079	0PQM4ZZ	269, 642, 936	0PRF0KZ	936	0PRQ4JZ	643, 937
0PPM07Z	234, 642, 935, 1078	0PPQ0JZ	235, 642, 936, 1078	0PPT34Z	235, 711, 1079	0PQN0ZZ	269, 642, 936	0PRF37Z	936	0PRQ4KZ	643, 937
0PPM0JZ	234, 642, 935, 1078	0PPQ0KZ	235, 642, 936, 1078	0PPT35Z	235, 711, 1079	0PQN3ZZ	269, 642, 936	0PRF3JZ	936	0PRR*	280
0PPM0KZ	234, 642, 935, 1078	0PPQ34Z	235, 642, 936, 1078	0PPT37Z	235, 711, 1079	0PQN4ZZ	269, 642, 936	0PRF3KZ	936	0PRR07Z	937
0PPM34Z	234, 642, 935, 1078	0PPQ35Z	235, 642, 936, 1078	0PPT3JZ	235, 711, 1079	0PQP0ZZ	269, 642, 936	0PRF47Z	936	0PRR0KZ	937
0PPM35Z	234, 642, 935, 1078	0PPQ37Z	235, 642, 936, 1078	0PPT3KZ	235, 711, 1079	0PQP3ZZ	269, 642, 936	0PRF4JZ	936	0PRR37Z	937
0PPM37Z	234, 642, 935, 1078	0PPQ3JZ	235, 642, 936, 1078	0PPT44Z	235, 711, 1079	0PQP4ZZ	269, 642, 936	0PRF4KZ	936	0PRR3KZ	937
0PPM3JZ	234, 642, 935, 1078	0PPQ3KZ	235, 642, 936, 1078	0PPT45Z	235, 711, 1079	0PQQ0ZZ	269, 642, 936	0PRG*	229, 712	0PRR47Z	937
0PPM3KZ	234, 642, 935, 1078	0PPQ44Z	235, 642, 936, 1078	0PPT47Z	235, 711, 1079	0PQQ3ZZ	269, 642, 936	0PRG07Z	936	0PRR4KZ	937
0PPM44Z	234, 642, 935, 1078	0PPQ45Z	235, 642, 936, 1078	0PPT4JZ	235, 711, 1079	0PQQ4ZZ	269, 642, 936	0PRG0JZ	936	0PRS*	280
0PPM45Z	234, 642, 935, 1078	0PPQ47Z	235, 642, 936, 1078	0PPV04Z	235, 712, 1079	0PQR0ZZ	280	0PRG0KZ	936	0PRS07Z	937
				0PPV05Z	235, 712, 1079	0PQR3ZZ	280	0PRG37Z	936	0PRS0KZ	937
				0PPV07Z	235, 712, 1079	0PQR4ZZ	280	0PRG3JZ	936	0PRS37Z	937
				0PPV0JZ	235, 712, 1079	0PQS0ZZ	280	0PRG3KZ	936	0PRS3KZ	937
				0PPV0KZ	235, 712, 1079	0PQS3ZZ	280	0PRG47Z	936	0PRS47Z	937
				0PPV34Z	235, 712, 1079	0PQS4ZZ	280	0PRG4JZ	936	0PRS4KZ	937
				0PPV35Z	235, 712, 1079	0PQT0ZZ	280	0PRG4KZ	936	0PRT*	280
				0PPV37Z	235, 712, 1079	0PQT3ZZ	280	0PRH*	267, 712	0PRT07Z	937
				0PPV3JZ	235, 712, 1079	0PQT4ZZ	280	0PRH07Z	936, 1079	0PRT0KZ	937
				0PPV3KZ	235, 712, 1079	0PQV0ZZ	280	0PRH0JZ	936	0PRT37Z	937
				0PPV44Z	235, 712, 1079	0PQV3ZZ	280	0PRH0KZ	936, 1079	0PRT3KZ	937
				0PPV45Z	235, 712, 1079	0PQV4ZZ	280	0PRH37Z	936, 1079	0PRT47Z	937
				0PPV47Z	235, 712, 1079	0PR0*	280	0PRH3JZ	936	0PRT4KZ	937
				0PPV4JZ	235, 712, 1079	0PR00JZ	102, 712	0PRH3KZ	936, 1079	0PRV*	280
				0PPV4KZ	235, 712, 1079	0PR03JZ	102, 712	0PRH47Z	936, 1079	0PRV07Z	937
				0PPY00Z	235, 1079	0PR04JZ	102, 712	0PRH4JZ	936	0PRV0KZ	937
				0PPY0MZ	235, 1079	0PR1*	280	0PRH4KZ	936, 1079	0PRV37Z	937
				0PPY3MZ	235, 712, 1079	0PR10JZ	102, 712	0PRJ*	267, 712	0PRV3KZ	937
				0PPY40Z	235, 1079	0PR13JZ	102, 712	0PRJ07Z	936, 1079	0PRV47Z	937
				0PPY4MZ	235, 712, 1079	0PR14JZ	102, 712	0PRJ0JZ	936	0PRV4KZ	937
				0PQ00ZZ	102, 280, 712	0PR2*	280	0PRJ0KZ	936, 1079	0PS000Z	102, 147, 280, 712, 937
				0PQ03ZZ	102, 280, 712	0PR20JZ	102, 712	0PRJ37Z	936, 1079	0PS004Z	80, 280, 712, 937
				0PQ04ZZ	102, 280, 712	0PR23JZ	102, 712	0PRJ3JZ	936	0PS00ZZ	80, 280, 712, 937
				0PQ10ZZ	102, 280, 712	0PR24JZ	102, 712	0PRJ3KZ	936, 1079	0PS030Z	102, 147, 280, 712, 937
				0PQ13ZZ	102, 280, 712	0PR3*	280	0PRJ47Z	936, 1079	0PS034Z	280, 712, 937
				0PQ14ZZ	102, 280, 712	0PR307Z	936	0PRJ4JZ	936	0PS040Z	102, 147, 280, 712, 937
				0PQ20ZZ	102, 280, 712	0PR30KZ	936	0PRJ4KZ	936, 1079	0PS044Z	280, 712, 937
				0PQ23ZZ	102, 280, 712	0PR337Z	936	0PRK*	267, 712	0PS104Z	80, 102, 280, 712, 937
				0PQ24ZZ	102, 280, 712	0PR33KZ	936	0PRK07Z	936, 1079	0PS10ZZ	80, 102, 280, 712, 937
				0PQ30ZZ	280	0PR347Z	936	0PRK0JZ	936	0PS134Z	102, 280, 712, 937
				0PQ33ZZ	280	0PR34KZ	936	0PRK0KZ	936, 1079	0PS144Z	102, 280, 712, 937
				0PQ34ZZ	280	0PR4*	280	0PRK37Z	936, 1079	0PS204Z	80, 102, 280, 712, 937
				0PQ40ZZ	280	0PR407Z	936	0PRK3JZ	936	0PS20ZZ	80, 102, 280, 712, 937
				0PQ43ZZ	280	0PR40KZ	936	0PRK3KZ	936, 1079	0PS234Z	102, 280, 712, 937
				0PQ44ZZ	280	0PR437Z	936	0PRK47Z	936, 1079	0PS244Z	102, 280, 712, 937
				0PQ50ZZ	102, 280, 712	0PR43KZ	936	0PRK4JZ	936	0PS304Z	17, 288, 599, 625, 712, 937
				0PQ53ZZ	102, 280, 712	0PR447Z	936	0PRK4KZ	936, 1079	0PS30ZZ	17, 288, 599, 625, 712, 937
				0PQ54ZZ	102, 280, 712	0PR44KZ	936	0PRL*	267, 712		
				0PQ60ZZ	102, 280, 712	0PR5*	280	0PRL07Z	936, 1079		
				0PQ63ZZ	102, 280, 712	0PR50JZ	102, 712	0PRL0JZ	936		
				0PQ64ZZ	102, 280, 712	0PR53JZ	102, 712	0PRL0KZ	936, 1079		
				0PQ70ZZ	102, 280, 712	0PR54JZ	102, 712	0PRL37Z	936, 1079		
				0PQ73ZZ	102, 280, 712	0PR6*	280	0PRL3JZ	936		
				0PQ74ZZ	102, 280, 712	0PR60JZ	102, 712	0PRL3KZ	936, 1079		
						0PR63JZ	102, 712	0PRL47Z	936, 1079		
						0PR64JZ	102, 712	0PRL4JZ	936		
						0PR7*	280	0PRL4KZ	936, 1079		
						0PR70JZ	102, 712	0PRM*	269		

Code	Page	Code	Page	Code	Page	Code	Page	Code	Page	Code	Page
0PS334Z	17, 288, 599, 625, 712, 937	0PSF3DZ	230, 713, 937	0PSK4CZ	267, 713, 938	0PT80ZZ	17, 102, 281, 713, 938	0PUD0JZ	938	0PUP3JZ	643, 939
0PS33ZZ	280, 288	0PSF44Z	230, 713, 937	0PSK4DZ	267, 713, 938	0PT90ZZ	17, 102, 281, 713, 938	0PUD0KZ	938	0PUP3KZ	643, 939
0PS344Z	17, 288, 599, 625, 712, 937	0PSF45Z	230, 713, 937	0PSL04Z	267, 713, 938	0PTB0ZZ	17, 102, 281, 713, 938	0PUD37Z	938	0PUP47Z	643, 939
0PS34ZZ	17, 288, 599, 625, 712, 937	0PSF46Z	230, 713, 937	0PSL05Z	267, 713, 938			0PUD3JZ	938	0PUP4JZ	643, 939
0PS404Z	17, 288, 599, 625, 712, 937	0PSF4BZ	230, 713, 937	0PSL06Z	267, 713, 938	0PTC0ZZ	230, 713, 938	0PUD3KZ	939	0PUP4KZ	643, 939
0PS40ZZ	17, 288, 599, 625, 712, 937	0PSF4CZ	230, 713, 937	0PSL0BZ	267, 713, 938	0PTD0ZZ	230, 713, 938	0PUD47Z	939	0PUQ*	270
0PS434Z	17, 288, 599, 625, 712, 937	0PSF4DZ	230, 713, 937	0PSL0CZ	267, 713, 938	0PTF0ZZ	230, 713, 938	0PUD4JZ	939	0PUQ07Z	643, 939
0PS43ZZ	280, 288	0PSG04Z	230, 713, 937	0PSL0DZ	267, 713, 938	0PTG0ZZ	230, 713, 938	0PUD4KZ	939	0PUQ0JZ	643, 939
0PS444Z	288	0PSG05Z	230, 713, 937	0PSL0ZZ	267, 713, 938	0PTH0ZZ	268, 713, 938	0PUF*	230, 714	0PUQ0KZ	643, 939
0PS444Z	17, 599, 625, 712, 937	0PSG06Z	230, 713, 937	0PSL34Z	267, 713, 938, 1079	0PTJ0ZZ	268, 713, 938	0PUF07Z	939	0PUQ37Z	643, 939
0PS44ZZ	17, 288, 599, 625, 712, 937	0PSG0BZ	230, 713, 937	0PSL35Z	267, 713, 938	0PTK0ZZ	268, 713, 938	0PUF0JZ	939	0PUQ3JZ	643, 939
0PS504Z	80, 280, 712, 937	0PSG0CZ	230, 713, 937	0PSL36Z	267, 713, 938, 1079	0PTL0ZZ	268, 714, 938	0PUF0KZ	939	0PUQ3KZ	643, 939
0PS50ZZ	80, 280, 712, 937	0PSG0DZ	230, 713, 937	0PSL3BZ	267, 713, 938	0PTM0ZZ	270, 643, 938	0PUF37Z	939	0PUQ47Z	643, 939
0PS534Z	280, 712, 937	0PSG0ZZ	230, 713, 937	0PSL3CZ	267, 713, 938	0PTN0ZZ	270, 643, 938	0PUF3JZ	939	0PUQ4JZ	643, 939
0PS544Z	280, 712, 937	0PSG34Z	230, 713, 937	0PSL3DZ	267, 713, 938	0PTP0ZZ	270, 643, 938	0PUF3KZ	939	0PUQ4KZ	643, 939
0PS604Z	80, 280, 712, 937	0PSG35Z	230, 713, 937	0PSL44Z	268, 713, 938, 1079	0PTQ0ZZ	270, 643, 938	0PUF47Z	939	0PUR*	281
0PS60ZZ	80, 280, 712, 937	0PSG36Z	230, 713, 937	0PSL45Z	268, 713, 938	0PTR0ZZ	80, 281, 437, 714, 938	0PUF4JZ	939	0PUR07Z	939
0PS634Z	280, 712, 937	0PSG3BZ	230, 713, 937	0PSL46Z	268, 713, 938, 1079	0PTS0ZZ	80, 281, 437, 714, 938	0PUF4KZ	939	0PUR0KZ	939
0PS644Z	280, 712, 937	0PSG3CZ	230, 713, 937	0PSL4BZ	268, 713, 938	0PTT0ZZ	80, 281, 437, 714, 938	0PUG*	230, 714	0PUR37Z	939
0PS704Z	80, 280, 712, 937	0PSG3DZ	230, 713, 937	0PSL4CZ	268, 713, 938	0PTV0ZZ	80, 281, 437, 714, 938	0PUG07Z	939	0PUR3KZ	939
0PS70ZZ	80, 280, 712, 937	0PSG44Z	230, 713, 937	0PSL4DZ	268, 713, 938	0PU0*	281	0PUG0JZ	939	0PUR47Z	939
0PS734Z	280, 712, 937	0PSG45Z	230, 713, 937	0PSM04Z	269, 643, 938	0PU00JZ	102, 714	0PUG0KZ	939	0PUR4KZ	939
0PS744Z	280, 712, 937	0PSG46Z	230, 713, 937	0PSM05Z	269, 643, 938	0PU03JZ	102, 714	0PUG37Z	939	0PUS*	281
0PS804Z	80, 280, 712, 937	0PSG4BZ	230, 713, 937	0PSM06Z	269, 643, 938	0PU04JZ	102, 714	0PUG3JZ	939	0PUS07Z	939
0PS80ZZ	80, 280, 712, 937	0PSG4CZ	230, 713, 937	0PSM34Z	269, 643, 938	0PU1*	281	0PUG3KZ	939	0PUS0KZ	939
0PS834Z	280, 712, 937	0PSG4DZ	230, 713, 937	0PSM35Z	269, 643, 938	0PU10JZ	102, 714	0PUG47Z	939	0PUS37Z	939
0PS844Z	280, 712, 937	0PSH04Z	267, 713, 937	0PSM44Z	269, 643, 938	0PU13JZ	102, 714	0PUG4JZ	939	0PUS3KZ	939
0PS904Z	80, 280, 712, 937	0PSH05Z	267, 713, 937	0PSM45Z	269, 643, 938	0PU14JZ	102, 714	0PUG4KZ	939	0PUS47Z	939
0PS90ZZ	80, 280, 712, 937	0PSH06Z	267, 713, 937	0PSN04Z	270, 643, 938	0PU2*	281	0PUH*	268, 714	0PUS4KZ	939
0PS934Z	280, 712, 937	0PSH0BZ	267, 713, 937	0PSN05Z	270, 643, 938	0PU20JZ	102, 714	0PUH07Z	939, 1079	0PUT*	281
0PS944Z	280, 712, 937	0PSH0CZ	267, 713, 937	0PSN34Z	270, 643, 938	0PU23JZ	102, 714	0PUH0JZ	939	0PUT07Z	939
0PSB04Z	80, 280, 712, 937	0PSH0DZ	267, 713, 937	0PSN35Z	270, 643, 938	0PU24JZ	102, 714	0PUH0KZ	939, 1079	0PUT0KZ	939
0PSB0ZZ	80, 280, 712, 937	0PSH0ZZ	267, 713, 937	0PSN44Z	270, 643, 938	0PU307Z	281, 938	0PUH37Z	939, 1079	0PUT37Z	939
0PSB34Z	280, 712, 937	0PSH34Z	267, 713, 937, 1079	0PSN45Z	270, 643, 938	0PU30KZ	281, 938	0PUH3JZ	939	0PUT3KZ	939
0PSB44Z	280, 712, 937	0PSH35Z	267, 713, 937	0PSP04Z	270, 643, 938	0PU337Z	281, 938	0PUH47Z	939, 1079	0PUT47Z	939
0PSC04Z	229, 712, 937	0PSH36Z	267, 713, 937, 1079	0PSP05Z	270, 643, 938	0PU33JZ	281, 288, 714, 938	0PUH4JZ	939	0PUT4KZ	939
0PSC05Z	229, 712, 937	0PSH3BZ	267, 713, 937	0PSP06Z	270, 643, 938	0PU33KZ	281, 938	0PUH4KZ	939, 1079	0PUV*	281
0PSC06Z	230, 712, 937	0PSH3CZ	267, 713, 937	0PSP34Z	270, 643, 938	0PU347Z	281, 938	0PUJ*	268, 714	0PUV07Z	939
0PSC0BZ	230, 712, 937	0PSH3DZ	267, 713, 937	0PSP35Z	270, 643, 938	0PU34JZ	281, 714, 938	0PUJ0JZ	939	0PUV0KZ	939
0PSC0CZ	230, 712, 937	0PSH44Z	267, 713, 937, 1079	0PSP44Z	270, 643, 938	0PU34KZ	281, 938	0PUJ0KZ	939, 1079	0PUV37Z	939
0PSC0DZ	230, 712, 937	0PSH45Z	267, 713, 937	0PSP45Z	270, 643, 938	0PU4*	281	0PUJ37Z	939, 1079	0PUV3KZ	939
0PSC0ZZ	230, 713, 937	0PSH46Z	267, 713, 938, 1079	0PSQ04Z	270, 643, 938	0PU40JZ	714, 938	0PUJ3JZ	939	0PUV47Z	939
0PSC34Z	230, 713, 937	0PSH4BZ	267, 713, 938	0PSQ05Z	270, 643, 938	0PU40KZ	938	0PUJ3KZ	939, 1079	0PUV4KZ	939
0PSC35Z	230, 713, 937	0PSH4CZ	267, 713, 938	0PSQ0ZZ	270, 643, 938	0PU437Z	938	0PUJ47Z	939, 1079	0PW004Z	235
0PSC36Z	230, 713, 937	0PSH4DZ	267, 713, 938	0PSQ34Z	270, 643, 938	0PU43JZ	288, 714, 938	0PUJ4JZ	939	0PW007Z	235
0PSC3BZ	230, 713, 937	0PSJ04Z	267, 713, 938	0PSQ35Z	270, 643, 938	0PU43KZ	938	0PUJ4KZ	939, 1079	0PW00JZ	235
0PSC3CZ	230, 713, 937	0PSJ05Z	267, 713, 938	0PSQ44Z	270, 643, 938	0PU447Z	938	0PUK*	268, 714	0PW00KZ	235
0PSC3DZ	230, 713, 937	0PSJ06Z	267, 713, 938	0PSQ45Z	270, 643, 938	0PU44JZ	714, 938	0PUK07Z	939, 1079	0PW034Z	235
0PSC44Z	230, 713, 937	0PSJ0BZ	267, 713, 938	0PSR04Z	270, 643, 938	0PU44KZ	938	0PUK0JZ	939	0PW037Z	235
0PSC45Z	230, 713, 937	0PSJ0CZ	267, 713, 938	0PSR05Z	280, 713, 938	0PU5*	281	0PUK0KZ	939, 1079	0PW03JZ	235
0PSC46Z	230, 713, 937	0PSJ0DZ	267, 713, 938	0PSR0ZZ	270, 643, 938	0PU50JZ	102, 714	0PUK37Z	939, 1079	0PW03KZ	235
0PSC4BZ	230, 713, 937	0PSJ0ZZ	267, 713, 938	0PSR34Z	270, 643, 938	0PU53JZ	102, 714	0PUK3JZ	939	0PW044Z	235
0PSC4CZ	230, 713, 937	0PSJ34Z	267, 713, 938, 1079	0PSR35Z	280, 713, 938	0PU54JZ	102, 714	0PUK3KZ	939, 1079	0PW047Z	235
0PSC4DZ	230, 713, 937	0PSJ35Z	267, 713, 938	0PSR44Z	270, 643, 938	0PU6*	281	0PUK47Z	939, 1079	0PW04JZ	235
0PSD04Z	230, 713, 937	0PSJ36Z	267, 713, 938	0PSR45Z	280, 713, 938	0PU60JZ	102, 714	0PUK4JZ	939	0PW04KZ	235
0PSD05Z	230, 713, 937	0PSJ3BZ	267, 713, 938	0PSS04Z	270, 643, 938	0PU63JZ	102, 714	0PUK4KZ	939, 1079	0PW104Z	235
0PSD06Z	230, 713, 937	0PSJ3CZ	267, 713, 938	0PSS05Z	280, 713, 938	0PU64JZ	102, 714	0PUL*	268, 714	0PW107Z	235
0PSD0BZ	230, 713, 937	0PSJ3DZ	267, 713, 938	0PSS0ZZ	270, 643, 938	0PU7*	281	0PUL07Z	939, 1079	0PW10JZ	235
0PSD0CZ	230, 713, 937	0PSJ44Z	267, 713, 938, 1079	0PSS34Z	270, 643, 938	0PU70JZ	102, 714	0PUL0JZ	939	0PW10KZ	235
0PSD0DZ	230, 713, 937	0PSJ45Z	267, 713, 938	0PSS35Z	281, 713, 938	0PU73JZ	102, 714	0PUL0KZ	939, 1079	0PW134Z	235
0PSD0ZZ	230, 713, 937	0PSJ46Z	267, 713, 938, 1079	0PSS44Z	270, 643, 938	0PU74JZ	102, 714	0PUL37Z	939, 1079	0PW137Z	235
0PSD34Z	230, 713, 937	0PSJ4BZ	267, 713, 938	0PSS45Z	281, 713, 938	0PU8*	281	0PUL3JZ	939	0PW13JZ	235
0PSD35Z	230, 713, 937	0PSJ4CZ	267, 713, 938	0PST04Z	270, 643, 938	0PU80JZ	102, 714	0PUL3KZ	939, 1079	0PW13KZ	235
0PSD36Z	230, 713, 937	0PSJ4DZ	267, 713, 938	0PST05Z	281, 713, 938	0PU83JZ	102, 714	0PUL47Z	939, 1079	0PW144Z	235
0PSD3BZ	230, 713, 937	0PSK04Z	267, 713, 938	0PST0ZZ	270, 643, 938	0PU84JZ	102, 714	0PUL4JZ	939	0PW147Z	235
0PSD3CZ	230, 713, 937	0PSK05Z	267, 713, 938	0PST34Z	270, 643, 938	0PU9*	281	0PUL4KZ	939, 1079	0PW14JZ	235
0PSD3DZ	230, 713, 937	0PSK06Z	267, 713, 938	0PST35Z	281, 713, 938	0PU90JZ	102, 714	0PUM*	270	0PW14KZ	235
0PSD44Z	230, 713, 937	0PSK0BZ	267, 713, 938	0PST44Z	270, 643, 938	0PU93JZ	102, 714	0PUM07Z	643, 939	0PW204Z	235
0PSD45Z	230, 713, 937	0PSK0CZ	267, 713, 938	0PST45Z	281, 713, 938	0PU94JZ	102, 714	0PUM0JZ	643, 939	0PW207Z	235
0PSD46Z	230, 713, 937	0PSK0DZ	267, 713, 938	0PSV04Z	270, 643, 938	0PUB*	281	0PUM0KZ	643, 939	0PW20JZ	235
0PSD4BZ	230, 713, 937	0PSK0ZZ	267, 713, 938	0PSV05Z	281, 713, 938	0PUB0JZ	102, 714	0PUM37Z	643, 939	0PW20KZ	235
0PSD4CZ	230, 713, 937	0PSK34Z	267, 713, 938, 1079	0PSV0ZZ	270, 643, 938	0PUB3JZ	103, 714	0PUM3JZ	643, 939	0PW234Z	235
0PSD4DZ	230, 713, 937	0PSK35Z	267, 713, 938	0PSV34Z	270, 643, 938	0PUB4JZ	103, 714	0PUM3KZ	643, 939	0PW237Z	235
0PSF04Z	230, 713, 937	0PSK36Z	267, 713, 938, 1079	0PSV35Z	281, 713, 938	0PUC*	230, 714	0PUM47Z	643, 939	0PW23JZ	235
0PSF05Z	230, 713, 937	0PSK3BZ	267, 713, 938	0PSV44Z	270, 643, 938	0PUC07Z	938	0PUM4JZ	643, 939	0PW23KZ	235
0PSF06Z	230, 713, 937	0PSK3CZ	267, 713, 938	0PSV45Z	281, 713, 938	0PUC0JZ	938	0PUM4KZ	643, 939	0PW244Z	235
0PSF0BZ	230, 713, 937	0PSK3DZ	267, 713, 938	0PT00ZZ	17, 102, 281, 713, 938	0PUC0KZ	938	0PUN*	270	0PW247Z	235
0PSF0CZ	230, 713, 937	0PSK44Z	267, 713, 938, 1079	0PT10ZZ	17, 102, 281, 713, 938	0PUC37Z	938	0PUN07Z	643, 939	0PW24JZ	235
0PSF0DZ	230, 713, 937	0PSK45Z	267, 713, 938	0PT20ZZ	17, 102, 281, 713, 938	0PUC3JZ	938	0PUN0JZ	643, 939	0PW24KZ	235
0PSF0ZZ	230, 713, 937	0PSK46Z	267, 713, 938, 1079			0PUC47Z	938	0PUN0KZ	643, 939	0PW304Z	235
0PSF34Z	230, 713, 937	0PSK4BZ	267, 713, 938	0PT50ZZ	17, 102, 281, 713, 938	0PUC4JZ	938	0PUN37Z	643, 939	0PW307Z	235
0PSF35Z	230, 713, 937					0PUC4KZ	938	0PUN3JZ	643, 939	0PW30JZ	235
0PSF36Z	230, 713, 937			0PT60ZZ	17, 102, 281, 713, 938	0PUD*	230, 714	0PUN3KZ	643, 939	0PW30KZ	235
0PSF3BZ	230, 713, 937					0PUD07Z	938	0PUN47Z	643, 939	0PW334Z	235
0PSF3CZ	230, 713, 937			0PT70ZZ	17, 102, 281, 713, 938			0PUN4JZ	643, 939	0PW337Z	235
								0PUN4KZ	643, 939	0PW33JZ	235
								0PUP*	270	0PW33KZ	235
								0PUP07Z	643, 939	0PW344Z	235
								0PUP0JZ	643, 939	0PW347Z	235
								0PUP0KZ	643, 939	0PW34JZ	235
								0PUP37Z	643, 939	0PW34KZ	235
										0PW404Z	235
										0PW407Z	235

Code	Page	Code	Page	Code	Page	Code	Page	Code	Page	Code	Page
ØPW4ØJZ	235	ØPWC45Z	236	ØPWK4KZ	236	ØPWSØ7Z	237	ØQ5B4ZZ	939,1079	ØQ8FØZZ	940
ØPW4ØKZ	235	ØPWC47Z	236	ØPWLØ5Z	236	ØPWSØJZ	237	ØQ5C*	241	ØQ8F3ZZ	940
ØPW434Z	235	ØPWC4JZ	236	ØPWLØ7Z	236	ØPWSØKZ	237	ØQ5CØZZ	939,1079	ØQ8F4ZZ	940
ØPW437Z	235	ØPWC4KZ	236	ØPWLØJZ	236	ØPWS34Z	237	ØQ5C3ZZ	939,1079	ØQ8G*	230,497
ØPW43JZ	235	ØPWDØ5Z	236	ØPWLØKZ	236	ØPWS35Z	237	ØQ5C4ZZ	939,1079	ØQ8GØZZ	940
ØPW43KZ	235	ØPWDØ7Z	236	ØPWL34Z	236	ØPWS37Z	237	ØQ5D*	237	ØQ8G3ZZ	940
ØPW444Z	235	ØPWDØJZ	236	ØPWL35Z	236	ØPWS3JZ	237	ØQ5DØZZ	939,1079	ØQ8G4ZZ	940
ØPW447Z	235	ØPWD34Z	236	ØPWL37Z	236	ØPWS3KZ	237	ØQ5D3ZZ	939,1079	ØQ8H*	230,497
ØPW44JZ	235	ØPWD35Z	236	ØPWL3JZ	236	ØPWS44Z	237	ØQ5D4ZZ	939,1079	ØQ8HØZZ	940
ØPW44KZ	235	ØPWD37Z	236	ØPWL3KZ	236	ØPWS45Z	237	ØQ5F*	237	ØQ8H3ZZ	940
ØPW504Z	235	ØPWD3JZ	236	ØPWL44Z	236	ØPWS47Z	237	ØQ5FØZZ	939,1079	ØQ8H4ZZ	940
ØPW507Z	235	ØPWD3KZ	236	ØPWL47Z	236	ØPWS4JZ	237	ØQ5F3ZZ	939,1079	ØQ8J*	230,497
ØPW50JZ	235	ØPWD37Z	236	ØPWL4JZ	236	ØPWS4KZ	237	ØQ5F4ZZ	939,1079	ØQ8JØZZ	940
ØPW50KZ	235	ØPWD44Z	236	ØPWL4KZ	236	ØPWTØ4Z	237	ØQ5G*	237	ØQ8J3ZZ	940
ØPW534Z	235	ØPWD45Z	236	ØPWMØ4Z	270	ØPWTØ5Z	237	ØQ5GØZZ	939,1079	ØQ8J4ZZ	940
ØPW537Z	235	ØPWD47Z	236	ØPWMØ5Z	270	ØPWTØ7Z	237	ØQ5G3ZZ	939,1079	ØQ8K*	230,497
ØPW53JZ	235	ØPWD4JZ	236	ØPWMØ7Z	270	ØPWTØJZ	237	ØQ5G4ZZ	939,1079	ØQ8KØZZ	940
ØPW53KZ	235	ØPWD4KZ	236	ØPWMØJZ	270	ØPWTØKZ	237	ØQ5H*	237	ØQ8K3ZZ	940
ØPW544Z	235	ØPWFØ4Z	236	ØPWM34Z	270	ØPWT34Z	237	ØQ5HØZZ	939,1079	ØQ8K4ZZ	940
ØPW547Z	235	ØPWFØ5Z	236	ØPWM35Z	270	ØPWT35Z	237	ØQ5H3ZZ	939,1079	ØQ8L*	257,497
ØPW54JZ	235	ØPWFØ7Z	236	ØPWM37Z	270	ØPWT37Z	237	ØQ5H4ZZ	939,1079	ØQ8LØZZ	940,1079
ØPW54KZ	235	ØPWFØJZ	236	ØPWM3JZ	270	ØPWT3JZ	237	ØQ5J*	237	ØQ8L3ZZ	940,1079
ØPW604Z	235	ØPWFØKZ	236	ØPWM3KZ	270	ØPWT3KZ	237	ØQ5JØZZ	939,1079	ØQ8L4ZZ	940,1079
ØPW607Z	235	ØPWF34Z	236	ØPWM44Z	270	ØPWT44Z	237	ØQ5J3ZZ	939,1079	ØQ8M*	257,497
ØPW60JZ	235	ØPWF35Z	236	ØPWM45Z	270	ØPWT45Z	237	ØQ5J4ZZ	939,1079	ØQ8MØZZ	940,1080
ØPW60KZ	235	ØPWF37Z	236	ØPWM47Z	270	ØPWT47Z	237	ØQ5K*	237	ØQ8M3ZZ	940,1080
ØPW634Z	235	ØPWF3JZ	236	ØPWM3JZ	270	ØPWT4JZ	237	ØQ5KØZZ	939,1079	ØQ8M4ZZ	940,1080
ØPW637Z	235	ØPWF3KZ	236	ØPWM4KZ	270	ØPWT4KZ	237	ØQ5K3ZZ	939,1079	ØQ8N*	257,497
ØPW63JZ	235	ØPWF44Z	236	ØPWN04Z	270	ØPWVØ4Z	237	ØQ5K4ZZ	939,1079	ØQ8NØZZ	940,1080
ØPW63KZ	236	ØPWF45Z	236	ØPWNØ5Z	270	ØPWVØ5Z	237	ØQ5L*	257,497	ØQ8N3ZZ	940,1080
ØPW644Z	236	ØPWF47Z	236	ØPWNØ7Z	270	ØPWVØ7Z	237	ØQ5LØZZ	939,1079	ØQ8N4ZZ	940,1080
ØPW647Z	236	ØPWF4JZ	236	ØPWNØJZ	270	ØPWVØJZ	237	ØQ5L3ZZ	939,1079	ØQ8P*	257,497
ØPW64JZ	236	ØPWF4KZ	236	ØPWNØKZ	270	ØPWVØKZ	237	ØQ5L4ZZ	940,1079	ØQ8PØZZ	940,1080
ØPW64KZ	236	ØPWGØ4Z	236	ØPWNØZZ	270	ØPWV34Z	237	ØQ5M*	257,497	ØQ8P3ZZ	940,1080
ØPW704Z	236	ØPWGØ5Z	236	ØPWN34Z	270	ØPWV35Z	237	ØQ5MØZZ	940,1079	ØQ8P4ZZ	940,1080
ØPW707Z	236	ØPWGØ7Z	236	ØPWN35Z	270	ØPWV37Z	237	ØQ5M3ZZ	940,1079	ØQ8Q*	281
ØPW70JZ	236	ØPWGØJZ	236	ØPWN37Z	270	ØPWV3JZ	237	ØQ5M4ZZ	940,1079	ØQ8QØZZ	940
ØPW70KZ	236	ØPWGØKZ	236	ØPWN3JZ	270	ØPWV3KZ	237	ØQ5N*	257,497	ØQ8Q3ZZ	940
ØPW734Z	236	ØPWG34Z	236	ØPWN3KZ	270	ØPWV44Z	237	ØQ5NØZZ	940,1079	ØQ8Q4ZZ	940
ØPW737Z	236	ØPWG35Z	236	ØPWN44Z	270	ØPWV45Z	237	ØQ5N3ZZ	940,1079	ØQ8R*	281
ØPW73JZ	236	ØPWG37Z	236	ØPWN45Z	270	ØPWV47Z	237	ØQ5N4ZZ	940,1079	ØQ8RØZZ	940
ØPW73KZ	236	ØPWG3JZ	236	ØPWN3KZ	270	ØPWV4JZ	237	ØQ5P*	257,497	ØQ8R3ZZ	940
ØPW744Z	236	ØPWG3KZ	236	ØPWN44Z	270	ØPWV4KZ	237	ØQ5PØZZ	940,1079	ØQ8R4ZZ	940
ØPW747Z	236	ØPWG44Z	236	ØPWN47Z	270	ØPWYØØZ	237	ØQ5P3ZZ	940,1079	ØQ8S*	281
ØPW74JZ	236	ØPWG45Z	236	ØPWN4JZ	270	ØPWYØMZ	237	ØQ5P4ZZ	940,1079	ØQ8SØZZ	940
ØPW74KZ	236	ØPWG47Z	236	ØPWN4KZ	270	ØPWY3ØZ	237	ØQ5Q*	237	ØQ8S3ZZ	940
ØPW804Z	236	ØPWG4JZ	236	ØPWPØ4Z	270	ØPWY3MZ	237	ØQ5QØZZ	940,1079	ØQ8S4ZZ	940
ØPW807Z	236	ØPWG4KZ	236	ØPWPØ5Z	270	ØPWY4ØZ	237	ØQ5Q3ZZ	940,1079	ØQ9ØØØZ	237
ØPW80JZ	236	ØPWHØ4Z	236	ØPWPØ7Z	270	ØPWY4MZ	237	ØQ5Q4ZZ	940,1079	ØQ9ØØZX	223,497,516,
ØPW80KZ	236	ØPWHØ5Z	236	ØPWPØJZ	270	ØQ5*	714	ØQ5R*	237		525,577,1080
ØPW834Z	236	ØPWHØ7Z	236	ØPWPØKZ	270	ØQ5Ø*	237	ØQ5RØZZ	940,1079	ØQ9ØØZZ	237
ØPW837Z	236	ØPWHØJZ	236	ØPWP34Z	270	ØQ5ØØZZ	939,1079	ØQ5R3ZZ	940,1079	ØQ9Ø3ZX	223,497,516,
ØPW83JZ	236	ØPWHØKZ	236	ØPWP35Z	270	ØQ5Ø3ZZ	939,1079	ØQ5R4ZZ	940,1079		525,577,1080
ØPW83KZ	236	ØPWH34Z	236	ØPWP37Z	270	ØQ5Ø4ZZ	939,1079	ØQ5S*	237	ØQ9Ø4ØZ	237
ØPW844Z	236	ØPWH35Z	236	ØPWP3JZ	270	ØQ51*	237	ØQ5SØZZ	940,1079	ØQ9Ø4ZX	223,497,516,
ØPW847Z	236	ØPWH37Z	236	ØPWP3KZ	270	ØQ51ØZZ	939,1079	ØQ5S3ZZ	940,1079		525,577,1080
ØPW84JZ	236	ØPWH3JZ	236	ØPWP44Z	270	ØQ513ZZ	939,1079	ØQ5S4ZZ	940,1079	ØQ9Ø4ZZ	237
ØPW84KZ	236	ØPWH3KZ	236	ØPWP45Z	270	ØQ514ZZ	939,1079	ØQ8*	714	ØQ91ØØZ	237
ØPW904Z	236	ØPWH44Z	236	ØPWP47Z	270	ØQ52*	237	ØQ8Ø*	281	ØQ91ØZX	223,497,516,
ØPW907Z	236	ØPWH45Z	236	ØPWP4JZ	270	ØQ52ØZZ	939,1079	ØQ8ØØZZ	940		525,577,1080
ØPW90JZ	236	ØPWH47Z	236	ØPWP4KZ	270	ØQ523ZZ	939,1079	ØQ8Ø3ZZ	940	ØQ91ØZZ	237
ØPW90KZ	236	ØPWH4JZ	236	ØPWQØ4Z	270	ØQ524ZZ	939,1079	ØQ8Ø4ZZ	940	ØQ913ZX	223,497,516,
ØPW934Z	236	ØPWH4KZ	236	ØPWQØ5Z	270	ØQ53*	237	ØQ81*	281		525,577,1080
ØPW937Z	236	ØPWJØ4Z	236	ØPWQØ7Z	270	ØQ53ØZZ	939,1079	ØQ81ØZZ	940	ØQ914ØZ	237
ØPW93JZ	236	ØPWJØ5Z	236	ØPWQØJZ	270	ØQ533ZZ	939,1079	ØQ813ZZ	940	ØQ914ZX	223,497,516,
ØPW93KZ	236	ØPWJØ7Z	236	ØPWQØKZ	270	ØQ534ZZ	939,1079	ØQ814ZZ	940		525,577,1080
ØPW944Z	236	ØPWJØJZ	236	ØPWQ34Z	270	ØQ54*	237	ØQ82*	281	ØQ914ZZ	237
ØPW947Z	236	ØPWJØKZ	236	ØPWQ35Z	270	ØQ54ØZZ	939,1079	ØQ82ØZZ	940	ØQ92ØØZ	237
ØPW94JZ	236	ØPWJ34Z	236	ØPWQ37Z	270	ØQ543ZZ	939,1079	ØQ823ZZ	940	ØQ92ØZX	223,497,516,
ØPW94KZ	236	ØPWJ35Z	236	ØPWQ3JZ	270	ØQ544ZZ	939,1079	ØQ824ZZ	940		525,577,1080
ØPWBØ4Z	236	ØPWJ37Z	236	ØPWQ3KZ	270	ØQ55*	237	ØQ83*	281	ØQ92ØZZ	237
ØPWBØ5Z	236	ØPWJ3JZ	236	ØPWQ44Z	270	ØQ55ØZZ	939,1079	ØQ83ØZZ	940	ØQ923ZX	223,497,516,
ØPWBØJZ	236	ØPWJ3KZ	236	ØPWQ45Z	270	ØQ553ZZ	939,1079	ØQ833ZZ	940		525,577,1080
ØPWBØKZ	236	ØPWJ44Z	236	ØPWQ47Z	270	ØQ554ZZ	939,1079	ØQ834ZZ	940	ØQ924ØZ	237
ØPWB34Z	236	ØPWJ45Z	236	ØPWQ4JZ	270	ØQ56*	241	ØQ84*	281	ØQ924ZX	223,497,516,
ØPWB37Z	236	ØPWJ47Z	236	ØPWQ4KZ	270	ØQ56ØZZ	939,1079	ØQ84ØZZ	940		525,577,1080
ØPWB3JZ	236	ØPWJ4JZ	236	ØPWRØ4Z	236	ØQ563ZZ	939,1079	ØQ843ZZ	940	ØQ924ZZ	237
ØPWB3KZ	236	ØPWJ4KZ	236	ØPWRØ5Z	237	ØQ564ZZ	939,1079	ØQ844ZZ	940	ØQ93ØØZ	237
ØPWB44Z	236	ØPWKØ4Z	236	ØPWRØ7Z	237	ØQ57*	241	ØQ85*	281	ØQ93ØZX	223,497,516,
ØPWB47Z	236	ØPWKØ5Z	236	ØPWRØJZ	237	ØQ57ØZZ	939,1079	ØQ85ØZZ	940		525,577,1080
ØPWB4JZ	236	ØPWKØ7Z	236	ØPWRØKZ	237	ØQ573ZZ	939,1079	ØQ853ZZ	940	ØQ93ØZZ	237
ØPWB4KZ	236	ØPWKØJZ	236	ØPWR34Z	237	ØQ574ZZ	939,1079	ØQ854ZZ	940	ØQ933ZX	223,497,516,
ØPWCØ4Z	236	ØPWKØKZ	236	ØPWR35Z	237	ØQ58*	241	ØQ86*	224,851		525,577,1080
ØPWCØ5Z	236	ØPWK34Z	236	ØPWR37Z	237	ØQ58ØZZ	939,1079	ØQ87*	224,851	ØQ934ØZ	237
ØPWCØ7Z	236	ØPWK35Z	236	ØPWR3JZ	237	ØQ583ZZ	939,1079	ØQ88*	224,851	ØQ934ZX	223,497,516,
ØPWCØJZ	236	ØPWK37Z	236	ØPWR3KZ	237	ØQ584ZZ	939,1079	ØQ89*	224,851		525,577,1080
ØPWCØKZ	236	ØPWK3JZ	236	ØPWR44Z	237	ØQ59*	241	ØQ8B*	224,851	ØQ934ZZ	237
ØPWC34Z	236	ØPWK3KZ	236	ØPWR45Z	237	ØQ59ØZZ	939,1079	ØQ8C*	224,851	ØQ94ØØZ	237
ØPWC35Z	236	ØPWK44Z	236	ØPWR47Z	237	ØQ593ZZ	939,1079	ØQ8D*	227	ØQ94ØZX	223,497,516,
ØPWC37Z	236	ØPWK45Z	236	ØPWR4JZ	237	ØQ594ZZ	939,1079	ØQ8DØZZ	940		525,577,1080
ØPWC3JZ	236	ØPWK47Z	236	ØPWR4KZ	237	ØQ5B*	241	ØQ8D3ZZ	940	ØQ94ØZZ	237
ØPWC3KZ	236	ØPWK4JZ	236	ØPWSØ4Z	237	ØQ5BØZZ	939,1079	ØQ8D4ZZ	940	ØQ943ZX	223,497,516,
ØPWC44Z	236			ØPWSØ5Z	237	ØQ5B3ZZ	939,1079	ØQ8F*	227		525,577,1080

Numeric Index to Procedures

Numeric Index to Procedures

Code	Page
0Q9440Z	237
0Q944ZX	223, 497, 516, 525, 577, 1080
0Q944ZZ	237
0Q9500Z	237
0Q950ZX	223, 497, 516, 525, 577, 1080
0Q950ZZ	237
0Q953ZX	223, 497, 516, 525, 577, 1080
0Q9540Z	237
0Q954ZX	223, 497, 516, 525, 577, 1080
0Q954ZZ	237
0Q9600Z	241
0Q960ZX	223, 437, 497, 516, 525, 1080
0Q960ZZ	241
0Q963ZX	223, 437, 497, 516, 525, 1080
0Q9640Z	241
0Q964ZX	223, 437, 497, 516, 525, 1080
0Q964ZZ	241
0Q9700Z	241
0Q970ZX	223, 437, 497, 516, 525, 1080
0Q970ZZ	241
0Q973ZX	223, 437, 497, 516, 525, 1080
0Q9740Z	241
0Q974ZX	223, 437, 497, 516, 525, 1080
0Q974ZZ	241
0Q9800Z	241
0Q980ZX	223, 437, 497, 516, 525, 1080
0Q980ZZ	241
0Q983ZX	223, 437, 497, 516, 525, 1080
0Q9840Z	241
0Q984ZX	223, 437, 497, 516, 525, 1080
0Q984ZZ	241
0Q9900Z	241
0Q990ZX	223, 437, 497, 516, 525, 1080
0Q990ZZ	242
0Q993ZX	223, 437, 497, 516, 525, 1080
0Q9940Z	242
0Q994ZX	223, 437, 497, 516, 525, 1080
0Q994ZZ	242
0Q9B00Z	242
0Q9B0ZX	223, 437, 497, 516, 525, 1080
0Q9B0ZZ	242
0Q9B3ZX	223, 437, 497, 516, 525, 1080
0Q9B40Z	242
0Q9B4ZX	223, 437, 497, 516, 525, 1080
0Q9B4ZZ	242
0Q9C00Z	242
0Q9C0ZX	223, 437, 497, 516, 525, 1080
0Q9C0ZZ	242
0Q9C3ZX	223, 437, 497, 516, 525, 1080
0Q9C40Z	242
0Q9C4ZX	223, 437, 497, 516, 525, 1080
0Q9C4ZZ	242
0Q9D00Z	237, 714, 940
0Q9D0ZX	223, 437, 497, 516, 525, 1080
0Q9D0ZZ	237, 714, 940
0Q9D3ZX	223, 437, 497, 516, 525, 1080
0Q9D40Z	237, 714, 940
0Q9D4ZX	223, 437, 497, 516, 525, 1080
0Q9D4ZZ	237, 714, 940
0Q9F00Z	237, 714, 940
0Q9F0ZX	223, 437, 497, 516, 525, 1080
0Q9F0ZZ	237, 714, 940
0Q9F3ZX	223, 437, 497, 517, 525, 1080
0Q9F40Z	237, 714, 940
0Q9F4ZX	224, 437, 497, 517, 525, 1080
0Q9F4ZZ	237, 714, 940
0Q9G00Z	237
0Q9G0ZX	224, 437, 497, 517, 525, 1080
0Q9G0ZZ	237
0Q9G3ZX	224, 437, 497, 517, 525, 1080
0Q9G40Z	237
0Q9G4ZX	224, 437, 497, 517, 525, 1080
0Q9G4ZZ	237
0Q9H00Z	237
0Q9H0ZX	224, 437, 497, 517, 525, 1080
0Q9H0ZZ	237
0Q9H3ZX	224, 437, 497, 517, 525, 1080
0Q9H40Z	237
0Q9H4ZX	224, 437, 497, 517, 525, 1080
0Q9H4ZZ	237
0Q9J00Z	237
0Q9J0ZX	224, 437, 497, 517, 525, 1080
0Q9J0ZZ	237
0Q9J3ZX	224, 437, 497, 517, 525, 1080
0Q9J40Z	237
0Q9J4ZX	224, 437, 497, 517, 525, 1080
0Q9J4ZZ	237
0Q9K00Z	237
0Q9K0ZX	224, 437, 497, 517, 525, 1080
0Q9K0ZZ	237
0Q9K3ZX	224, 437, 497, 517, 525, 1080
0Q9K40Z	237
0Q9K4ZX	224, 437, 497, 517, 525, 1080
0Q9K4ZZ	237
0Q9L00Z	257
0Q9L0ZX	224, 437, 497, 517, 525, 1080
0Q9L0ZZ	257
0Q9L3ZX	224, 437, 497, 517, 525, 1080
0Q9L40Z	257
0Q9L4ZX	224, 437, 497, 517, 525, 1080
0Q9L4ZZ	257
0Q9M00Z	257
0Q9M0ZX	224, 437, 497, 517, 525, 1080
0Q9M0ZZ	257
0Q9M3ZX	224, 437, 497, 517, 525, 1080
0Q9M40Z	257
0Q9M4ZX	224, 437, 497, 517, 525, 1080
0Q9M4ZZ	257
0Q9N00Z	257
0Q9N0ZX	224, 437, 497, 517, 525, 1080
0Q9N0ZZ	257
0Q9N3ZX	224, 437, 497, 517, 525, 1080
0Q9N40Z	257
0Q9N4ZX	224, 437, 497, 517, 525, 1080
0Q9N4ZZ	257
0Q9P00Z	257
0Q9P0ZX	224, 437, 497, 517, 525, 1080
0Q9P0ZZ	257
0Q9P3ZX	224, 437, 497, 517, 525, 1080
0Q9P40Z	257
0Q9P4ZX	224, 437, 497, 517, 525, 1080
0Q9P4ZZ	257
0Q9Q00Z	237
0Q9Q0ZX	224, 437, 577, 1080
0Q9Q0ZZ	237
0Q9Q3ZX	224, 437, 577, 1080
0Q9Q40Z	237
0Q9Q4ZX	224, 437, 577, 1080
0Q9Q4ZZ	237
0Q9R00Z	237
0Q9R0ZX	224, 437, 577, 1080
0Q9R0ZZ	237
0Q9R3ZX	224, 437, 577, 1080
0Q9R40Z	237
0Q9R4ZX	224, 437, 577, 1080
0Q9R4ZZ	237
0Q9S00Z	237
0Q9S0ZX	224, 497, 517, 525, 577, 1080
0Q9S0ZZ	237
0Q9S3ZX	224, 497, 517, 525, 577, 1080
0Q9S40Z	237
0Q9S4ZX	224, 497, 517, 525, 577, 1080
0Q9S4ZZ	237
0QB0*	497
0QB00ZX	224, 517, 525, 577, 1080
0QB00ZZ	80, 281, 714, 940
0QB03ZX	224, 517, 525, 577, 1080
0QB03ZZ	80, 281, 714, 940
0QB04ZX	224, 517, 525, 577, 1080
0QB04ZZ	80, 281, 714, 940
0QB1*	497
0QB10ZX	224, 517, 525, 577, 1080
0QB10ZZ	80, 281, 437, 714, 940
0QB13ZX	224, 517, 525, 577, 1080
0QB13ZZ	80, 281, 714, 940
0QB14ZX	224, 517, 525, 577, 1080
0QB14ZZ	80, 281, 714, 940
0QB2*	497
0QB20ZX	224, 517, 525, 577, 1080
0QB20ZZ	80, 281, 437, 714, 940
0QB23ZX	224, 517, 525, 577, 1080
0QB23ZZ	80, 281, 714, 940
0QB24ZX	224, 517, 525, 577, 1080
0QB24ZZ	80, 281, 714, 940
0QB3*	497
0QB30ZX	224, 517, 525, 577, 1080
0QB30ZZ	80, 281, 437, 714, 940
0QB33ZX	224, 517, 525, 577, 1080
0QB33ZZ	80, 281, 714, 940
0QB34ZX	224, 517, 525, 577, 1080
0QB34ZZ	80, 281, 714, 940
0QB4*	497
0QB40ZX	224, 517, 525, 577, 1080
0QB40ZZ	80, 281, 714, 940
0QB43ZX	224, 517, 525, 577, 1080
0QB43ZZ	80, 281, 714, 940
0QB44ZX	224, 517, 525, 577, 1080
0QB44ZZ	80, 281, 714, 940
0QB5*	497
0QB50ZX	224, 517, 525, 577, 1080
0QB50ZZ	80, 281, 714, 940
0QB53ZX	224, 517, 525, 577, 1080
0QB53ZZ	81, 281, 714, 940
0QB54ZX	224, 517, 525, 577, 1080
0QB54ZZ	81, 281, 714, 940
0QB60ZX	224, 437, 497, 517, 525, 1080
0QB60ZZ	242, 714, 940
0QB63ZX	224, 437, 497, 517, 525, 1080
0QB63ZZ	242, 714, 940
0QB64ZX	224, 437, 497, 517, 525, 1080
0QB64ZZ	242, 714, 940
0QB70ZX	224, 437, 497, 517, 525, 1080
0QB70ZZ	242, 714, 940
0QB73ZX	224, 437, 497, 517, 525, 1080
0QB73ZZ	242, 714, 940
0QB74ZX	224, 437, 497, 517, 525, 1080
0QB74ZZ	242, 714, 940
0QB80ZX	224, 437, 497, 517, 525, 1080
0QB80ZZ	242, 714, 940
0QB83ZX	224, 437, 497, 517, 525, 1080
0QB83ZZ	242, 714, 940
0QB84ZX	224, 437, 497, 517, 525, 1080
0QB84ZZ	242, 714, 940
0QB90ZX	224, 437, 497, 517, 525, 1080
0QB90ZZ	242, 714, 940
0QB93ZX	224, 437, 497, 517, 525, 1080
0QB93ZZ	242, 714, 940
0QB94ZX	224, 437, 497, 517, 525, 1080
0QB94ZZ	242, 714, 940
0QBB0ZX	224, 437, 498, 517, 525, 1080
0QBB0ZZ	242, 714, 940
0QBB3ZX	224, 437, 498, 517, 526, 1080
0QBB3ZZ	242, 714, 940
0QBB4ZX	224, 437, 498, 517, 526, 1080
0QBB4ZZ	242, 714, 940
0QBC0ZX	224, 437, 498, 517, 526, 1080
0QBC0ZZ	242, 714, 940
0QBC3ZX	224, 437, 498, 517, 526, 1080
0QBC3ZZ	242, 714, 940
0QBC4ZX	224, 437, 498, 517, 526, 1080
0QBC4ZZ	242, 714, 940
0QBD0ZX	224, 437, 498, 517, 526, 1080
0QBD0ZZ	227, 714, 940
0QBD3ZX	224, 437, 498, 517, 526, 1080
0QBD3ZZ	227, 714, 940
0QBD4ZX	224, 437, 498, 517, 526, 1080
0QBD4ZZ	227, 714, 940
0QBF0ZX	224, 437, 498, 517, 526, 1080
0QBF0ZZ	227, 714, 940
0QBF3ZX	224, 437, 498, 517, 526, 1080
0QBF3ZZ	228, 714, 940
0QBF4ZX	224, 437, 498, 517, 526, 1080
0QBF4ZZ	228, 714, 940
0QBG0ZX	224, 437, 498, 517, 526, 1080
0QBG0ZZ	230, 714, 940
0QBG3ZX	224, 437, 498, 517, 526, 1080
0QBG3ZZ	230, 714, 940
0QBG4ZX	224, 437, 498, 517, 526, 1080
0QBG4ZZ	230, 714, 940
0QBH0ZX	224, 437, 498, 517, 526, 1080
0QBH0ZZ	230, 714, 940
0QBH3ZX	224, 437, 498, 517, 526, 1080
0QBH3ZZ	230, 714, 940
0QBH4ZX	224, 437, 498, 517, 526, 1080
0QBH4ZZ	230, 714, 940
0QBJ0ZX	224, 437, 498, 517, 526, 1080
0QBJ0ZZ	230, 714, 940
0QBJ3ZX	224, 437, 498, 517, 526, 1080
0QBJ3ZZ	230, 714, 940
0QBJ4ZX	224, 437, 498, 517, 526, 1080
0QBJ4ZZ	230, 714, 940
0QBK0ZX	224, 437, 498, 517, 526, 1080
0QBK0ZZ	230, 714, 940
0QBK3ZX	224, 437, 498, 517, 526, 1080
0QBK3ZZ	230, 714, 940
0QBK4ZX	224, 437, 498, 517, 526, 1080
0QBK4ZZ	230, 714, 940
0QBL*	498
0QBL0ZX	224, 437, 517, 526, 1080
0QBL0ZZ	257, 714, 940, 1080
0QBL3ZX	224, 437, 517, 526, 1080
0QBL3ZZ	257, 714, 940, 1080
0QBL4ZX	224, 437, 517, 526, 1080
0QBL4ZZ	257, 714, 940, 1080
0QBM*	498
0QBM0ZX	224, 437, 517, 526, 1080
0QBM0ZZ	257, 714, 940, 1080
0QBM3ZX	224, 437, 517, 526, 1080
0QBM3ZZ	257, 714, 940, 1080
0QBM4ZX	224, 437, 517, 526, 1080
0QBM4ZZ	257, 714, 940, 1080
0QBN*	498
0QBN0ZX	224, 437, 517, 526, 1080
0QBN0ZZ	257, 714, 940, 1080
0QBN3ZX	224, 437, 517, 526, 1080
0QBN3ZZ	257, 714, 940, 1080
0QBN4ZX	224, 437, 517, 526, 1080
0QBN4ZZ	257, 714, 940, 1080
0QBP*	498
0QBP0ZX	224, 437, 517, 526, 1080
0QBP0ZZ	257, 714, 940, 1080
0QBP3ZX	224, 437, 517, 526, 1080
0QBP3ZZ	257, 714, 940, 1080
0QBP4ZX	224, 437, 517, 526, 1080
0QBP4ZZ	257, 714, 940, 1080
0QBQ0ZX	224, 437, 577, 1080
0QBQ0ZZ	81, 281, 498, 714, 940
0QBQ3ZX	224, 437, 577, 1080
0QBQ3ZZ	81, 281, 498, 714, 940
0QBQ4ZX	224, 437, 577, 1080
0QBQ4ZZ	81, 281, 498, 714, 940
0QBR0ZX	224, 437, 577, 1080
0QBR0ZZ	81, 281, 498, 714, 940
0QBR3ZX	224, 437, 577, 1080
0QBR3ZZ	81, 281, 498, 714, 940
0QBR4ZX	224, 437, 577, 1080
0QBR4ZZ	81, 281, 498, 714, 940
0QBS*	498
0QBS0ZX	224, 517, 526, 577, 1080
0QBS0ZZ	81, 281, 437, 714, 940
0QBS3ZX	224, 517, 526, 577, 1080
0QBS3ZZ	81, 281, 714, 940
0QBS4ZX	224, 517, 526, 578, 1080
0QBS4ZZ	81, 281, 714, 940
0QC*	714
0QC0*	281
0QC00ZZ	940
0QC03ZZ	940
0QC04ZZ	940
0QC1*	281
0QC10ZZ	940
0QC13ZZ	940
0QC14ZZ	940
0QC2*	281
0QC20ZZ	940
0QC23ZZ	940
0QC24ZZ	940
0QC3*	281
0QC30ZZ	940
0QC33ZZ	940
0QC34ZZ	940
0QC4*	281
0QC40ZZ	940
0QC43ZZ	940
0QC44ZZ	940
0QC5*	281
0QC50ZZ	941
0QC53ZZ	941
0QC54ZZ	941
0QC6*	224, 851
0QC7*	224, 851
0QC8*	224, 851
0QC9*	224, 851
0QCB*	224, 851
0QCC*	224, 851
0QCD*	228
0QCD0ZZ	941
0QCD3ZZ	941
0QCD4ZZ	941
0QCF*	228
0QCF0ZZ	941
0QCF3ZZ	941
0QCF4ZZ	941
0QCG*	230
0QCG0ZZ	941
0QCG3ZZ	941
0QCG4ZZ	941
0QCH*	230
0QCH0ZZ	941
0QCH3ZZ	941
0QCH4ZZ	941
0QCJ*	230
0QCJ0ZZ	941
0QCJ4ZZ	941
0QCK*	230
0QCK0ZZ	941
0QCK3ZZ	941
0QCK4ZZ	941
0QCL*	257
0QCL3ZZ	941
0QCL4ZZ	941
0QCM*	257
0QCM0ZZ	941
0QCM3ZZ	941
0QCM4ZZ	941
0QCN*	257
0QCN0ZZ	941
0QCN3ZZ	941
0QCN4ZZ	941
0QCP*	257
0QCP0ZZ	941
0QCP3ZZ	941
0QCP4ZZ	941
0QCQ*	281
0QCQ0ZZ	941
0QCQ3ZZ	941
0QCQ4ZZ	941
0QCR*	281
0QCR0ZZ	941
0QCR3ZZ	941
0QCR4ZZ	941
0QCS*	281
0QCS0ZZ	941
0QCS3ZZ	941
0QCS4ZZ	941
0QD00ZZ	40, 256, 437, 714, 941
0QD10ZZ	40, 256, 437, 714, 941
0QD20ZZ	40, 256, 437, 714, 941
0QD30ZZ	40, 256, 437, 714, 941
0QD40ZZ	40, 256, 437, 714, 941
0QD50ZZ	40, 256, 437, 714, 941

Code	Page	Code	Page	Code	Page	Code	Page	Code	Page	Code	Page
0QD60ZZ	40, 256, 437, 714, 941	0QH645Z	224, 715, 851	0QHC3CZ	225, 715, 851	0QHK3DZ	230, 716, 942	0QNJ4ZZ	942	0QP40KZ	238, 716, 1081
0QD70ZZ	40, 256, 437, 714, 941	0QH646Z	225, 715, 851	0QHC3DZ	225, 715, 851	0QHK44Z	231, 716, 942	0QNK*	231, 716	0QP434Z	238, 716, 1081
0QD80ZZ	40, 256, 437, 714, 941	0QH64BZ	225, 715, 851	0QHC44Z	225, 715, 851	0QHK45Z	231, 716, 942	0QNK0ZZ	942	0QP437Z	238, 716, 1081
		0QH64CZ	225, 715, 851	0QHC45Z	225, 715, 851	0QHK46Z	231, 716, 942	0QNK3ZZ	942	0QP43JZ	238, 716, 1081
0QD90ZZ	40, 256, 437, 714, 941	0QH64DZ	225, 715, 851	0QHC46Z	225, 715, 851	0QHK4BZ	231, 716, 942	0QNK4ZZ	942	0QP43KZ	238, 716, 1081
		0QH704Z	225, 715, 851	0QHC4CZ	225, 715, 851	0QHK4CZ	231, 716, 942	0QNL*	257, 716	0QP444Z	238, 716, 1081
0QDB0ZZ	40, 256, 437, 714, 941	0QH705Z	225, 715, 851	0QHC4DZ	225, 715, 851	0QHK4DZ	231, 716, 942	0QNL0ZZ	942	0QP447Z	238, 716, 1081
0QDC0ZZ	40, 256, 437, 714, 941	0QH706Z	225, 715, 851	0QHD*	228, 715	0QHL*	257, 716	0QNL3ZZ	942	0QP44JZ	238, 716, 1081
		0QH70BZ	225, 715, 851	0QHD04Z	941	0QHL04Z	942	0QNL4ZZ	942	0QP44KZ	238, 716, 1081
0QDD0ZZ	40, 256, 437, 714, 941	0QH70CZ	225, 715, 851	0QHD05Z	941	0QHL05Z	942	0QNM*	257, 716	0QP504Z	238, 716, 1081
		0QH70DZ	225, 715, 851	0QHD34Z	941	0QHL34Z	942	0QNM0ZZ	942	0QP507Z	238, 716, 1081
0QDF0ZZ	40, 256, 437, 714, 941	0QH734Z	225, 715, 851	0QHD35Z	941	0QHL35Z	942	0QNM3ZZ	942	0QP50JZ	238, 716, 1081
		0QH735Z	225, 715, 851	0QHD44Z	941	0QHL44Z	942	0QNM4ZZ	942	0QP50KZ	238, 716, 1081
0QDG0ZZ	40, 256, 437, 714, 941	0QH736Z	225, 715, 851	0QHD45Z	941	0QHL45Z	942	0QNN*	257, 716	0QP534Z	238, 716, 1081
		0QH73BZ	225, 715, 851	0QHF*	228, 715	0QHM*	257, 716	0QNN0ZZ	942	0QP537Z	238, 716, 1081
0QDH0ZZ	40, 256, 437, 714, 941	0QH73CZ	225, 715, 851	0QHF04Z	941	0QHM04Z	942	0QNN3ZZ	942	0QP53JZ	238, 716, 1081
		0QH73DZ	225, 715, 851	0QHF05Z	941	0QHM05Z	942	0QNN4ZZ	942	0QP53KZ	238, 716, 1081
0QDJ0ZZ	40, 256, 437, 714, 941	0QH744Z	225, 715, 851	0QHF34Z	941	0QHM34Z	942	0QNP*	257, 716	0QP544Z	238, 716, 1081
		0QH745Z	225, 715, 851	0QHF35Z	941	0QHM35Z	942	0QNP0ZZ	942	0QP547Z	238, 716, 1081
0QDK0ZZ	40, 256, 437, 714, 941	0QH746Z	225, 715, 851	0QHF44Z	941	0QHM44Z	942	0QNP3ZZ	942	0QP54JZ	238, 716, 1081
		0QH74BZ	225, 715, 851	0QHF45Z	941	0QHM45Z	942	0QNP4ZZ	942	0QP54KZ	238, 716, 1081
0QDL0ZZ	40, 256, 437, 714, 941	0QH74CZ	225, 715, 851	0QHG04Z	230, 715, 941	0QHN*	257, 716	0QNQ*	281	0QP604Z	242, 498, 716, 1081
		0QH74DZ	225, 715, 851	0QHG05Z	230, 715, 941	0QHN04Z	942	0QNR*	281	0QP605Z	242, 498, 716, 1081
0QDM0ZZ	40, 256, 437, 714, 941	0QH804Z	225, 715, 851	0QHG06Z	230, 715, 941	0QHN05Z	942	0QNS*	281	0QP607Z	242, 498, 716, 1081
		0QH805Z	225, 715, 851	0QHG07Z	230, 715, 941	0QHN34Z	942	0QP004Z	237		
0QDN0ZZ	40, 256, 437, 714, 941	0QH806Z	225, 715, 851	0QHG0BZ	230, 715, 941	0QHN35Z	942	0QP004Z	716, 1080	0QP60JZ	242, 498, 716, 1081
		0QH807Z	225, 715, 851	0QHG0CZ	230, 715, 941	0QHN44Z	942	0QP007Z	237	0QP60KZ	242, 498, 716, 1081
0QDP0ZZ	40, 256, 437, 714, 941	0QH80BZ	225, 715, 851	0QHG0DZ	230, 715, 941	0QHN45Z	942	0QP007Z	716, 1081		
		0QH80CZ	225, 715, 851	0QHG34Z	230, 715, 941	0QHP*	257, 716	0QP00JZ	237	0QP634Z	242, 498, 716, 1081
0QDQ0ZZ	40, 256, 437, 714, 941	0QH80DZ	225, 715, 851	0QHG35Z	230, 715, 941	0QHP04Z	942	0QP00JZ	716, 1080	0QP635Z	242, 498, 716, 1081
		0QH834Z	225, 715, 851	0QHG36Z	230, 715, 941	0QHP05Z	942	0QP00KZ	237		
0QDR0ZZ	40, 256, 437, 714, 941	0QH835Z	225, 715, 851	0QHG37Z	230, 715, 941	0QHP34Z	942	0QP00KZ	716, 1081	0QP637Z	242, 498, 716, 1081
		0QH836Z	225, 715, 851	0QHG3BZ	230, 715, 941	0QHP35Z	942	0QP034Z	237		
0QDS0ZZ	40, 256, 437, 714, 941	0QH837Z	225, 715, 851	0QHG3CZ	230, 715, 941	0QHP44Z	942	0QP034Z	716, 1081	0QP63JZ	242, 498, 716, 1081
		0QH83BZ	225, 715, 851	0QHG3DZ	230, 715, 941	0QHP45Z	942	0QP037Z	237		
0QH0*	281, 714	0QH83CZ	225, 715, 851	0QHG44Z	230, 715, 941	0QHQ*	281, 716	0QP037Z	716, 1081	0QP63KZ	242, 498, 716, 1081
0QH004Z	941	0QH83DZ	225, 715, 851	0QHG45Z	230, 715, 941	0QHQ04Z	942	0QP03JZ	237		
0QH005Z	941	0QH844Z	225, 715, 851	0QHG46Z	230, 715, 941	0QHQ05Z	942	0QP03JZ	716, 1081	0QP644Z	242, 498, 716, 1081
0QH034Z	941	0QH845Z	225, 715, 851	0QHG47Z	230, 715, 941	0QHQ34Z	942	0QP03KZ	237		
0QH035Z	941	0QH846Z	225, 715, 851	0QHG4BZ	230, 715, 941	0QHQ35Z	942	0QP03KZ	716, 1081	0QP645Z	242, 498, 716, 1081
0QH044Z	941	0QH84BZ	225, 715, 851	0QHG4CZ	230, 715, 941	0QHQ44Z	942	0QP044Z	237		
0QH045Z	941	0QH84CZ	225, 715, 851	0QHG4DZ	230, 715, 941	0QHQ45Z	942	0QP044Z	716, 1081	0QP647Z	242, 498, 716, 1081
0QH1*	281, 714	0QH84DZ	225, 715, 851	0QHH04Z	230, 715, 941	0QHR*	281, 716	0QP047Z	237		
0QH104Z	941	0QH904Z	225, 715, 851	0QHH05Z	230, 715, 941	0QHR04Z	942	0QP047Z	716, 1081	0QP64JZ	242, 498, 716, 1081
0QH105Z	941	0QH905Z	225, 715, 851	0QHH06Z	230, 715, 941	0QHR05Z	942	0QP04JZ	237		
0QH134Z	941	0QH906Z	225, 715, 851	0QHH07Z	230, 715, 941	0QHR34Z	942	0QP04JZ	716, 1081	0QP64KZ	242, 498, 716, 1081
0QH135Z	941	0QH907Z	225, 715, 851	0QHH0BZ	230, 715, 941	0QHR35Z	942	0QP04KZ	237		
0QH144Z	941	0QH90BZ	225, 715, 851	0QHH0DZ	230, 715, 941	0QHR44Z	942	0QP04KZ	716, 1081	0QP704Z	242, 498, 716, 1081
0QH145Z	941	0QH90CZ	225, 715, 851	0QHH34Z	230, 715, 941	0QHR45Z	942	0QP104Z	237, 716, 1081		
0QH2*	281, 714	0QH90DZ	225, 715, 851	0QHH35Z	230, 715, 941	0QHS*	281, 716	0QP107Z	237, 716, 1081	0QP705Z	242, 498, 716, 1081
0QH204Z	941	0QH934Z	225, 715, 851	0QHH36Z	230, 715, 941	0QHS04Z	942	0QP10JZ	237, 716, 1081		
0QH205Z	941	0QH935Z	225, 715, 851	0QHH37Z	230, 715, 941	0QHS05Z	942	0QP10KZ	237, 716, 1081	0QP707Z	242, 498, 716, 1081
0QH234Z	941	0QH936Z	225, 715, 851	0QHH3BZ	230, 715, 941	0QHS34Z	942	0QP134Z	237, 716, 1081		
0QH235Z	941	0QH937Z	225, 715, 851	0QHH3CZ	230, 715, 941	0QHS35Z	942	0QP137Z	237, 716, 1081	0QP70JZ	242, 498, 716, 1081
0QH244Z	941	0QH93BZ	225, 715, 851	0QHH3DZ	230, 715, 941	0QHS44Z	942	0QP13JZ	237, 716, 1081		
0QH245Z	941	0QH93CZ	225, 715, 851	0QHH44Z	230, 715, 941	0QHS45Z	942	0QP13KZ	237, 716, 1081	0QP70KZ	242, 498, 716, 1081
0QH3*	281, 714	0QH93DZ	225, 715, 851	0QHH45Z	230, 715, 941	0QHY*	281, 716	0QP144Z	237, 716, 1081		
0QH304Z	941	0QH944Z	225, 715, 851	0QHH46Z	230, 715, 941	0QHY0MZ	942	0QP147Z	237, 716, 1081	0QP734Z	242, 498, 716, 1081
0QH305Z	941	0QH945Z	225, 715, 851	0QHH47Z	230, 715, 941	0QHY3MZ	942	0QP14JZ	237, 716, 1081		
0QH334Z	941	0QH946Z	225, 715, 851	0QHH4BZ	230, 715, 941	0QHY4MZ	942	0QP14KZ	237, 716, 1081	0QP735Z	242, 498, 716, 1081
0QH335Z	941	0QH947Z	225, 715, 851	0QHH4CZ	230, 715, 941	0QJY0ZZ	224	0QP204Z	237, 716, 1081		
0QH344Z	941	0QH94BZ	225, 715, 851	0QHH4DZ	230, 715, 941	0QJY4ZZ	224	0QP205Z	237, 716, 1081	0QP737Z	242, 498, 716, 1081
0QH345Z	941	0QH94CZ	225, 715, 851	0QHJ04Z	230, 715, 941	0QN0*	281	0QP207Z	237, 716, 1081		
0QH4*	281, 714	0QH94DZ	225, 715, 851	0QHJ05Z	230, 715, 941	0QN1*	281	0QP20JZ	237, 716, 1081	0QP73JZ	242, 498, 716, 1081
0QH404Z	941	0QHB04Z	225, 715, 851	0QHJ06Z	230, 715, 941	0QN2*	281	0QP20KZ	237, 716, 1081		
0QH405Z	941	0QHB05Z	225, 715, 851	0QHJ0BZ	230, 715, 941	0QN3*	281	0QP234Z	237, 716, 1081	0QP73KZ	242, 498, 716, 1081
0QH434Z	941	0QHB06Z	225, 715, 851	0QHJ0CZ	230, 715, 941	0QN4*	281	0QP235Z	237, 716, 1081		
0QH435Z	941	0QHB0BZ	225, 715, 851	0QHJ0DZ	230, 715, 941	0QN5*	281	0QP237Z	237, 716, 1081	0QP744Z	242, 498, 716, 1081
0QH444Z	941	0QHB0CZ	225, 715, 851	0QHJ34Z	230, 715, 941	0QN6*	225, 716, 851	0QP23JZ	237, 716, 1081		
0QH445Z	941	0QHB0DZ	225, 715, 851	0QHJ36Z	230, 715, 941	0QN7*	225, 716, 851	0QP23KZ	237, 716, 1081	0QP745Z	242, 498, 716, 1081
0QH5*	281, 714	0QHB34Z	225, 715, 851	0QHJ3BZ	230, 715, 941	0QN8*	225, 716, 851	0QP244Z	238, 716, 1081		
0QH504Z	941	0QHB35Z	225, 715, 851	0QHJ3CZ	230, 715, 941	0QN9*	225, 716, 851	0QP245Z	238, 716, 1081	0QP747Z	242, 498, 716, 1081
0QH505Z	941	0QHB36Z	225, 715, 851	0QHJ3DZ	230, 715, 941	0QNB*	225, 716, 851	0QP247Z	238, 716, 1081		
0QH534Z	941	0QHB3BZ	225, 715, 851	0QHJ44Z	230, 715, 941	0QNC*	225, 716, 851	0QP24JZ	238, 716, 1081	0QP74JZ	242, 498, 716, 1081
0QH535Z	941	0QHB3CZ	225, 715, 851	0QHJ45Z	230, 715, 941	0QND*	228, 716	0QP24KZ	238, 716, 1081		
0QH544Z	941	0QHB3DZ	225, 715, 851	0QHJ46Z	230, 715, 941	0QND0ZZ	942	0QP304Z	238, 716, 1081	0QP74KZ	242, 498, 716, 1081
0QH545Z	941	0QHB44Z	225, 715, 851	0QHJ4BZ	230, 715, 941	0QND4ZZ	942	0QP305Z	238, 716, 1081		
0QH604Z	224, 714, 851	0QHB45Z	225, 715, 851	0QHJ4CZ	230, 715, 941	0QNF*	228, 716	0QP307Z	238, 716, 1081	0QP804Z	242, 498, 716, 1081
0QH605Z	224, 714, 851	0QHB46Z	225, 715, 851	0QHJ4DZ	230, 715, 942	0QNF0ZZ	942	0QP30JZ	238, 716, 1081		
0QH606Z	224, 714, 851	0QHB4BZ	225, 715, 851	0QHK04Z	230, 715, 942	0QNF3ZZ	942	0QP30KZ	238, 716, 1081	0QP805Z	242, 498, 716, 1081
0QH60BZ	224, 714, 851	0QHB4CZ	225, 715, 851	0QHK05Z	230, 715, 942	0QNF4ZZ	942	0QP334Z	238, 716, 1081		
0QH60CZ	224, 714, 851	0QHB4DZ	225, 715, 851	0QHK06Z	230, 715, 942	0QNG*	231, 716	0QP335Z	238, 716, 1081	0QP807Z	242, 498, 716, 1081
0QH60DZ	224, 714, 851	0QHC04Z	225, 715, 851	0QHK0BZ	230, 715, 942	0QNG0ZZ	942	0QP337Z	238, 716, 1081		
0QH634Z	224, 714, 851	0QHC05Z	225, 715, 851	0QHK0CZ	230, 715, 942	0QNG3ZZ	942	0QP33JZ	238, 716, 1081	0QP80JZ	242, 498, 716, 1081
0QH635Z	224, 714, 851	0QHC0BZ	225, 715, 851	0QHK0DZ	230, 715, 942	0QNG4ZZ	942	0QP33KZ	238, 716, 1081		
0QH636Z	224, 714, 851	0QHC0CZ	225, 715, 851	0QHK34Z	230, 715, 942	0QNH*	231, 716	0QP344Z	238, 716, 1081	0QP80KZ	242, 498, 716, 1081
0QH63BZ	224, 714, 851	0QHC0DZ	225, 715, 851	0QHK35Z	230, 715, 942	0QNH0ZZ	942	0QP345Z	238, 716, 1081		
0QH63CZ	224, 714, 851	0QHC34Z	225, 715, 851	0QHK36Z	230, 715, 942	0QNH3ZZ	942	0QP347Z	238, 716, 1081	0QP834Z	242, 498, 716, 1081
0QH63DZ	224, 715, 851	0QHC35Z	225, 715, 851	0QHK3BZ	230, 716, 942	0QNJ*	231, 716	0QP34JZ	238, 716, 1081		
0QH644Z	224, 715, 851	0QHC36Z	225, 715, 851	0QHK3CZ	230, 716, 942	0QNJ0ZZ	942	0QP34KZ	238, 716, 1081		
		0QHC3BZ	225, 715, 851			0QNJ3ZZ	942	0QP404Z	238, 716, 1081		
								0QP407Z	238, 716, 1081		
								0QP40JZ	238, 716, 1081		

Numeric Index to Procedures

Code	Page	Code	Page	Code	Page	Code	Page	Code	Page	Code	Page
0QP835Z	242, 498, 716, 1081	0QPC37Z	242, 498, 717, 1081	0QPG3JZ	238, 717, 942, 1082	0QPK3KZ	238, 717, 943, 1082	0QPN44Z	239, 717, 943, 1082	0QQ20ZZ	281
0QP837Z	242, 498, 716, 1081	0QPC3JZ	242, 498, 717, 1081	0QPG3KZ	238, 717, 942, 1082	0QPK44Z	238, 717, 943, 1082	0QPN45Z	239, 717, 943, 1082	0QQ23ZZ	281
0QP83JZ	242, 498, 716, 1081	0QPC3KZ	242, 498, 717, 1081	0QPG44Z	238, 717, 942, 1082	0QPK45Z	238, 717, 943, 1082	0QPN47Z	239, 717, 943, 1082	0QQ24ZZ	281
0QP83KZ	242, 498, 716, 1081	0QPC44Z	242, 498, 717, 1081	0QPG45Z	238, 717, 942, 1082	0QPK47Z	238, 717, 943, 1082	0QPN4JZ	239, 717, 943, 1082	0QQ30ZZ	281
0QP844Z	242, 498, 716, 1081	0QPC45Z	242, 498, 717, 1081	0QPG47Z	238, 717, 942, 1082	0QPK4JZ	238, 717, 943, 1082	0QPN4KZ	239, 717, 943, 1082	0QQ33ZZ	281
0QP845Z	242, 498, 716, 1081	0QPC47Z	242, 498, 717, 1081	0QPG4JZ	238, 717, 942, 1082	0QPK4KZ	238, 717, 943, 1082	0QPP04Z	239, 717, 943, 1082	0QQ34ZZ	281
0QP847Z	242, 498, 716, 1081	0QPC4JZ	242, 498, 717, 1081	0QPG4KZ	238, 717, 942, 1082	0QPL04Z	238, 717, 943, 1082	0QPP05Z	239, 717, 943, 1082	0QQ40ZZ	281
0QP84JZ	242, 498, 716, 1081	0QPC4KZ	242, 498, 717, 1081	0QPH04Z	238, 717, 942, 1082	0QPL05Z	238, 717, 943, 1082	0QPP07Z	239, 717, 943, 1082	0QQ43ZZ	281
0QP84KZ	242, 498, 716, 1081	0QPD04Z	238, 717, 942, 1081	0QPH05Z	238, 717, 942, 1082	0QPL07Z	238, 717, 943, 1082	0QPP0JZ	239, 717, 943, 1082	0QQ44ZZ	281
0QP904Z	242, 498, 716, 1081	0QPD05Z	238, 717, 942, 1081	0QPH07Z	238, 717, 942, 1082	0QPL0JZ	238, 717, 943, 1082	0QPP0KZ	239, 717, 943, 1082	0QQ50ZZ	281
0QP905Z	242, 498, 716, 1081	0QPD07Z	238, 717, 942, 1081	0QPH0JZ	238, 717, 942, 1082	0QPL0KZ	238, 717, 943, 1082	0QPP34Z	239, 717, 943, 1082	0QQ53ZZ	281
0QP907Z	242, 498, 716, 1081	0QPD0JZ	238, 717, 942, 1081	0QPH0KZ	238, 717, 942, 1082	0QPL34Z	238, 717, 943, 1082	0QPP35Z	239, 717, 943, 1082	0QQ54ZZ	281
0QP90JZ	242, 498, 716, 1081	0QPD0KZ	238, 717, 942, 1081	0QPH34Z	238, 717, 942, 1082	0QPL35Z	238, 717, 943, 1082	0QPP37Z	239, 717, 943, 1082	0QQ60ZZ	225, 718, 851
0QP90KZ	242, 498, 716, 1081	0QPD34Z	238, 717, 942, 1081	0QPH35Z	238, 717, 942, 1082	0QPL37Z	238, 717, 943, 1082	0QPP3JZ	239, 717, 943, 1082	0QQ63ZZ	225, 718, 851
0QP934Z	242, 498, 716, 1081	0QPD35Z	238, 717, 942, 1081	0QPH37Z	238, 717, 942, 1082	0QPL3JZ	238, 717, 943, 1082	0QPP3KZ	239, 717, 943, 1082	0QQ64ZZ	225, 718, 851
0QP935Z	242, 498, 716, 1081	0QPD37Z	238, 717, 942, 1081	0QPH3JZ	238, 717, 942, 1082	0QPL3KZ	238, 717, 943, 1082	0QPP44Z	239, 717, 943, 1082	0QQ70ZZ	225, 718, 851
0QP937Z	242, 498, 716, 1081	0QPD3JZ	238, 717, 942, 1081	0QPH3KZ	238, 717, 942, 1082	0QPL44Z	238, 717, 943, 1082	0QPP45Z	239, 717, 943, 1082	0QQ73ZZ	225, 718, 851
0QP93JZ	242, 498, 716, 1081	0QPD3KZ	238, 717, 942, 1082	0QPH44Z	238, 717, 942, 1082	0QPL45Z	238, 717, 943, 1082	0QPP47Z	239, 718, 943, 1082	0QQ74ZZ	225, 718, 851
0QP93KZ	242, 498, 716, 1081	0QPD44Z	238, 717, 942, 1082	0QPH45Z	238, 717, 942, 1082	0QPL47Z	238, 717, 943, 1082	0QPP4JZ	239, 718, 943, 1082	0QQ80ZZ	225, 718, 851
0QP944Z	242, 498, 716, 1081	0QPD45Z	238, 717, 942, 1082	0QPH47Z	238, 717, 942, 1082	0QPL4JZ	238, 717, 943, 1082	0QPP4KZ	239, 718, 943, 1082	0QQ83ZZ	225, 718, 851
0QP945Z	242, 498, 716, 1081	0QPD47Z	238, 717, 942, 1082	0QPH4JZ	238, 717, 942, 1082	0QPL4KZ	238, 717, 943, 1082	0QPQ04Z	239, 718, 1082	0QQ84ZZ	225, 718, 851
0QP947Z	242, 498, 716, 1081	0QPD4JZ	238, 717, 942, 1082	0QPH4KZ	238, 717, 942, 1082	0QPM04Z	238, 717, 943, 1082	0QPQ05Z	239, 718, 1082	0QQ90ZZ	225, 718, 851
0QP94JZ	242, 498, 716, 1081	0QPD4KZ	238, 717, 942, 1082	0QPJ04Z	238, 717, 942, 1082	0QPM05Z	238, 717, 943, 1082	0QPQ07Z	239, 718, 1082	0QQ93ZZ	225, 718, 851
0QP94KZ	242, 498, 716, 1081	0QPF04Z	238, 717, 942, 1082	0QPJ05Z	238, 717, 942, 1082	0QPM07Z	238, 717, 943, 1082	0QPQ0JZ	239, 718, 1082	0QQ94ZZ	225, 718, 851
0QPB04Z	242, 498, 716, 1081	0QPF05Z	238, 717, 942, 1082	0QPJ07Z	238, 717, 942, 1082	0QPM0JZ	238, 717, 943, 1082	0QPQ0KZ	239, 718, 1082	0QQB0ZZ	225, 718, 851
0QPB05Z	242, 498, 716, 1081	0QPF07Z	238, 717, 942, 1082	0QPJ0JZ	238, 717, 942, 1082	0QPM0KZ	238, 717, 943, 1082	0QPQ34Z	239, 718, 1082	0QQB3ZZ	225, 718, 851
0QPB07Z	242, 498, 716, 1081	0QPF0JZ	238, 717, 942, 1082	0QPJ0KZ	238, 717, 942, 1082	0QPM34Z	238, 717, 943, 1082	0QPQ35Z	239, 718, 1082	0QQB4ZZ	225, 718, 851
0QPB0JZ	242, 498, 717, 1081	0QPF0KZ	238, 717, 942, 1082	0QPJ34Z	238, 717, 942, 1082	0QPM35Z	238, 717, 943, 1082	0QPQ37Z	239, 718, 1082	0QQC0ZZ	225, 718, 851
0QPB0KZ	242, 498, 717, 1081	0QPF34Z	238, 717, 942, 1082	0QPJ35Z	238, 717, 942, 1082	0QPM37Z	238, 717, 943, 1082	0QPQ3JZ	239, 718, 1082	0QQC3ZZ	225, 718, 851
0QPB34Z	242, 498, 717, 1081	0QPF35Z	238, 717, 942, 1082	0QPJ37Z	238, 717, 942, 1082	0QPM3JZ	238, 717, 943, 1082	0QPQ3KZ	239, 718, 1082	0QQC4ZZ	225, 718, 851
0QPB35Z	242, 498, 717, 1081	0QPF37Z	238, 717, 942, 1082	0QPJ3JZ	238, 717, 942, 1082	0QPM3KZ	238, 717, 943, 1082	0QPQ44Z	239, 718, 1082	0QQD0ZZ	228, 718, 943
0QPB37Z	242, 498, 717, 1081	0QPF3JZ	238, 717, 942, 1082	0QPJ3KZ	238, 717, 942, 1082	0QPM44Z	238, 717, 943, 1082	0QPQ45Z	239, 718, 1082	0QQD3ZZ	281
0QPB3JZ	242, 498, 717, 1081	0QPF3KZ	238, 717, 942, 1082	0QPJ44Z	238, 717, 942, 1082	0QPM45Z	238, 717, 943, 1082	0QPQ47Z	239, 718, 1082	0QQD4ZZ	228, 718, 943
0QPB3KZ	242, 498, 717, 1081	0QPF44Z	238, 717, 942, 1082	0QPJ45Z	238, 717, 942, 1082	0QPM47Z	238, 717, 943, 1082	0QPQ4JZ	239, 718, 1082	0QQF0ZZ	228, 718, 943
0QPB44Z	242, 498, 717, 1081	0QPF45Z	238, 717, 942, 1082	0QPJ47Z	238, 717, 942, 1082	0QPM4JZ	238, 717, 943, 1082	0QPQ4KZ	239, 718, 1082	0QQF3ZZ	281
0QPB45Z	242, 498, 717, 1081	0QPF47Z	238, 717, 942, 1082	0QPJ4JZ	238, 717, 942, 1082	0QPM4KZ	238, 717, 943, 1082	0QPR04Z	239, 718, 1082	0QQF4ZZ	228, 718, 943
0QPB47Z	242, 498, 717, 1081	0QPF4JZ	238, 717, 942, 1082	0QPJ4KZ	238, 717, 942, 1082	0QPN04Z	238, 717, 943, 1082	0QPR05Z	239, 718, 1082	0QQG0ZZ	231, 718, 943
0QPB4JZ	242, 498, 717, 1081	0QPF4KZ	238, 717, 942, 1082	0QPK04Z	238, 717, 942, 1082	0QPN05Z	238, 717, 943, 1082	0QPR07Z	239, 718, 1082	0QQG3ZZ	231, 718, 943
0QPB4KZ	242, 498, 717, 1081	0QPG04Z	238, 717, 942, 1082	0QPK05Z	238, 717, 942, 1082	0QPN07Z	238, 717, 943, 1082	0QPR0JZ	239, 718, 1082	0QQH0ZZ	231, 718, 943
0QPC04Z	242, 498, 717, 1081	0QPG05Z	238, 717, 942, 1082	0QPK07Z	238, 717, 942, 1082	0QPN0JZ	238, 717, 943, 1082	0QPR0KZ	239, 718, 1082	0QQH3ZZ	231, 718, 943
0QPC05Z	242, 498, 717, 1081	0QPG07Z	238, 717, 942, 1082	0QPK0JZ	238, 717, 942, 1082	0QPN0KZ	238, 717, 943, 1082	0QPR34Z	239, 718, 1082	0QQH4ZZ	231, 718, 943
0QPC07Z	242, 498, 717, 1081	0QPG0JZ	238, 717, 942, 1082	0QPK0KZ	238, 717, 942, 1082	0QPN34Z	238, 717, 943, 1082	0QPR35Z	239, 718, 1082	0QQJ0ZZ	231, 718, 943
0QPC0JZ	242, 498, 717, 1081	0QPG0KZ	238, 717, 942, 1082	0QPK34Z	238, 717, 943, 1082	0QPN35Z	238, 717, 943, 1082	0QPR37Z	239, 718, 1082	0QQJ3ZZ	231, 718, 943
0QPC0KZ	242, 498, 717, 1081	0QPG34Z	238, 717, 942, 1082	0QPK35Z	238, 717, 943, 1082	0QPN37Z	238, 717, 943, 1082	0QPR3JZ	239, 718, 1082	0QQJ4ZZ	231, 718, 943
0QPC34Z	242, 498, 717, 1081	0QPG35Z	238, 717, 942, 1082	0QPK37Z	238, 717, 943, 1082	0QPN3JZ	238, 717, 943, 1082	0QPR3KZ	239, 718, 1082	0QQK0ZZ	231, 718, 943
0QPC35Z	242, 498, 717, 1081	0QPG37Z	238, 717, 942, 1082	0QPK3JZ	238, 717, 943, 1082	0QPN3KZ	238, 717, 943, 1082	0QPR44Z	239, 718, 1082	0QQK3ZZ	231, 718, 943
								0QPR45Z	239, 718, 1082	0QQK4ZZ	231, 718, 943
								0QPR47Z	239, 718, 1082	0QQL0ZZ	257, 718, 943
								0QPR4JZ	239, 718, 1082	0QQL3ZZ	257, 718, 943
								0QPR4KZ	239, 718, 1082	0QQL4ZZ	257, 718, 943
								0QPS04Z	239, 718, 1082	0QQM0ZZ	257, 718, 943
								0QPS07Z	239, 718, 1082	0QQM3ZZ	257, 718, 943
								0QPS0JZ	239, 718, 1082	0QQM4ZZ	257, 718, 943
								0QPS0KZ	239, 718, 1083	0QQN0ZZ	257, 718, 943
								0QPS34Z	239, 718, 1083	0QQN3ZZ	257, 718, 943
								0QPS37Z	239, 718, 1083	0QQN4ZZ	257, 718, 943
								0QPS3JZ	239, 718, 1083	0QQP0ZZ	257, 718, 943
								0QPS3KZ	239, 718, 1083	0QQP3ZZ	257, 718, 943
								0QPS44Z	239, 718, 1083	0QQP4ZZ	257, 718, 943
								0QPS47Z	239, 718, 1083	0QQQ0ZZ	281, 718, 943
								0QPS4JZ	239, 718, 1083	0QQQ3ZZ	281, 718, 943
								0QPS4KZ	239, 718, 1083	0QQQ4ZZ	281, 718, 943
								0QPY00Z	239, 1083	0QQR0ZZ	281, 718, 943
								0QPY0MZ	239, 1083	0QQR3ZZ	281, 718, 943
								0QPY3MZ	239, 718, 1083	0QQR4ZZ	281, 718, 943
								0QPY40Z	239, 1083	0QQS0ZZ	281
								0QPY4MZ	239, 718, 1083	0QQS3ZZ	281
								0QQ00ZZ	281	0QQS4ZZ	281
								0QQ03ZZ	281	0QR0*	281
								0QQ04ZZ	281	0QR007Z	943
								0QQ10ZZ	281	0QR00KZ	943
								0QQ13ZZ	281	0QR037Z	943
								0QQ14ZZ	281	0QR03KZ	943
										0QR047Z	943
										0QR04KZ	943
										0QR1*	281
										0QR107Z	943
										0QR10KZ	943
										0QR137Z	943
										0QR13KZ	943
										0QR147Z	943
										0QR14KZ	943
										0QR2*	281
										0QR207Z	943
										0QR20KZ	943
										0QR237Z	943
										0QR23KZ	943
										0QR247Z	943
										0QR24KZ	943
										0QR3*	281
										0QR307Z	943
										0QR30KZ	943

Code	Page
0QR337Z	943
0QR33KZ	943
0QR347Z	943
0QR34KZ	943
0QR4*	281
0QR407Z	943
0QR40JZ	718, 943
0QR40KZ	943
0QR437Z	943
0QR43JZ	718, 943
0QR43KZ	943
0QR447Z	943
0QR44JZ	718, 943
0QR44KZ	943
0QR5*	281
0QR507Z	943
0QR50JZ	718, 943
0QR50KZ	943
0QR537Z	943
0QR53JZ	718, 943
0QR53KZ	943
0QR547Z	943
0QR54JZ	718, 943
0QR54KZ	943
0QR6*	225, 718, 851
0QR7*	225, 718, 851
0QR8*	225, 718, 851
0QR9*	225, 718, 851
0QRB*	225, 718, 851
0QRC*	225, 718, 851
0QRD*	228, 718
0QRD07Z	943
0QRD0JZ	943
0QRD0KZ	943
0QRD37Z	943
0QRD3JZ	943
0QRD3KZ	943
0QRD47Z	943
0QRD4JZ	943
0QRD4KZ	943
0QRF*	228, 718
0QRF07Z	943
0QRF0JZ	943
0QRF0KZ	943
0QRF37Z	943
0QRF3JZ	943
0QRF3KZ	943
0QRF47Z	943
0QRF4JZ	943
0QRF4KZ	943
0QRG*	231, 718
0QRG07Z	943
0QRG0JZ	943
0QRG0KZ	943
0QRG37Z	943
0QRG3JZ	943
0QRG3KZ	943
0QRG47Z	943
0QRG4JZ	943
0QRG4KZ	943
0QRH*	231, 718
0QRH07Z	943
0QRH0JZ	944
0QRH0KZ	944
0QRH37Z	944
0QRH3JZ	944
0QRH3KZ	944
0QRH47Z	944
0QRH4JZ	944
0QRH4KZ	944
0QRJ*	231, 718
0QRJ07Z	944
0QRJ0JZ	944
0QRJ0KZ	944
0QRJ37Z	944
0QRJ3JZ	944
0QRJ3KZ	944
0QRJ47Z	944
0QRJ4JZ	944
0QRJ4KZ	944
0QRK*	231, 718
0QRK07Z	944
0QRK0JZ	944
0QRK0KZ	944
0QRK37Z	944
0QRK3JZ	944
0QRK3KZ	944
0QRK47Z	944
0QRK4JZ	944
0QRK4KZ	944
0QRL*	257, 718
0QRL07Z	944
0QRL0JZ	944
0QRL0KZ	944
0QRL37Z	944
0QRL3JZ	944
0QRL3KZ	944
0QRL47Z	944
0QRL4JZ	944
0QRL4KZ	944
0QRM*	257, 718
0QRM07Z	944
0QRM0JZ	944
0QRM0KZ	944
0QRM37Z	944
0QRM3JZ	944
0QRM3KZ	944
0QRM47Z	944
0QRM4JZ	944
0QRM4KZ	944
0QRN*	257, 718
0QRN07Z	944
0QRN0JZ	944
0QRN0KZ	944
0QRN37Z	944
0QRN3JZ	944
0QRN3KZ	944
0QRN47Z	944
0QRN4JZ	944
0QRN4KZ	944
0QRP*	257, 718
0QRP07Z	944
0QRP0JZ	944
0QRP0KZ	944
0QRP37Z	944
0QRP3JZ	944
0QRP3KZ	944
0QRP47Z	944
0QRP4JZ	944
0QRP4KZ	944
0QRQ*	281
0QRQ07Z	944
0QRQ0KZ	944
0QRQ37Z	944
0QRQ3KZ	944
0QRQ47Z	944
0QRQ4KZ	944
0QRR*	281
0QRR07Z	944
0QRR0KZ	944
0QRR37Z	944
0QRR3KZ	944
0QRR47Z	944
0QRR4KZ	944
0QRS*	281
0QRS07Z	944
0QRS0KZ	944
0QRS37Z	944
0QRS3KZ	944
0QRS47Z	944
0QRS4KZ	944
0QS004Z	17, 288, 599, 625, 718, 944
0QS00ZZ	17, 288, 600, 625, 718, 944
0QS034Z	17, 288, 600, 625, 718, 944
0QS03ZZ	281, 288
0QS044Z	17, 289, 600, 625, 718, 944
0QS04ZZ	18, 289, 600, 625, 718, 944
0QS104Z	18, 289, 600, 625, 718, 944
0QS10ZZ	18, 289, 600, 625, 718, 944
0QS134Z	18, 289, 600, 625, 718, 944
0QS13ZZ	281, 288
0QS144Z	18, 289, 600, 625, 718, 944
0QS14ZZ	18, 289, 600, 625, 718, 944
0QS204Z	81, 281, 718, 944
0QS205Z	281, 718, 944
0QS20ZZ	81, 281, 718, 944
0QS234Z	281, 718, 944
0QS235Z	281, 718, 944
0QS244Z	281, 718, 944
0QS245Z	281, 718, 944
0QS304Z	81, 281, 718, 944
0QS305Z	281, 718, 944
0QS30ZZ	81, 281, 718, 944
0QS334Z	281, 718, 944
0QS335Z	281, 718, 944
0QS344Z	281, 718, 944
0QS345Z	281, 718, 944
0QS404Z	81, 281, 718, 944
0QS40ZZ	81, 281, 718, 944
0QS434Z	281, 718, 944
0QS444Z	281, 718, 944
0QS504Z	81, 281, 718, 944
0QS50ZZ	81, 281, 718, 944
0QS534Z	281, 718, 944
0QS544Z	281, 718, 944
0QS604Z	225, 498, 718, 851
0QS605Z	225, 718, 851
0QS606Z	225, 498, 718, 851
0QS60BZ	225, 718, 852
0QS60CZ	225, 718, 852
0QS60DZ	225, 718, 852
0QS60ZZ	225, 718, 852
0QS634Z	225, 718, 852
0QS635Z	225, 718, 852
0QS636Z	225, 718, 852
0QS63BZ	225, 718, 852
0QS63CZ	225, 718, 852
0QS63DZ	225, 718, 852
0QS644Z	225, 718, 852
0QS645Z	225, 718, 852
0QS646Z	225, 718, 852
0QS64BZ	225, 718, 852
0QS64CZ	225, 718, 852
0QS64DZ	225, 718, 852
0QS704Z	225, 498, 718, 852
0QS705Z	225, 719, 852
0QS706Z	225, 498, 719, 852
0QS70BZ	225, 719, 852
0QS70CZ	225, 719, 852
0QS70DZ	225, 719, 852
0QS70ZZ	225, 719, 852
0QS734Z	225, 719, 852
0QS735Z	225, 719, 852
0QS736Z	225, 719, 852
0QS73BZ	225, 719, 852
0QS73CZ	225, 719, 852
0QS73DZ	225, 719, 852
0QS744Z	225, 719, 852
0QS745Z	225, 719, 852
0QS746Z	225, 719, 852
0QS74BZ	225, 719, 852
0QS74CZ	225, 719, 852
0QS74DZ	225, 719, 852
0QS804Z	225, 498, 719, 852
0QS805Z	225, 719, 852
0QS806Z	225, 498, 719, 852
0QS80BZ	225, 719, 852
0QS80CZ	225, 719, 852
0QS80DZ	225, 719, 852
0QS80ZZ	226, 719, 852
0QS834Z	226, 719, 852
0QS835Z	226, 719, 852
0QS836Z	226, 719, 852
0QS83BZ	226, 719, 852
0QS83CZ	226, 719, 852
0QS83DZ	226, 719, 852
0QS844Z	226, 719, 852
0QS845Z	226, 719, 852
0QS846Z	226, 719, 852
0QS84BZ	226, 719, 852
0QS84CZ	226, 719, 852
0QS84DZ	226, 719, 852
0QS904Z	226, 498, 719, 852
0QS905Z	226, 719, 852
0QS906Z	226, 498, 719, 852
0QS90BZ	226, 719, 852
0QS90CZ	226, 719, 852
0QS90DZ	226, 719, 852
0QS90ZZ	226, 719, 852
0QS934Z	226, 719, 852
0QS935Z	226, 719, 852
0QS936Z	226, 719, 852
0QS93BZ	226, 719, 852
0QS93CZ	226, 719, 852
0QS93DZ	226, 719, 852
0QS944Z	226, 719, 852
0QS945Z	226, 719, 852
0QS946Z	226, 719, 852
0QS94BZ	226, 719, 852
0QS94CZ	226, 719, 852
0QS94DZ	226, 719, 852
0QSB04Z	226, 498, 719, 852
0QSB05Z	226, 719, 852
0QSB06Z	226, 498, 719, 852
0QSB0BZ	226, 719, 852
0QSB0CZ	226, 719, 852
0QSB0DZ	226, 719, 852
0QSB0ZZ	226, 719, 852
0QSB34Z	226, 719, 852
0QSB35Z	226, 719, 852
0QSB36Z	226, 719, 852
0QSB3BZ	226, 719, 852
0QSB3CZ	226, 719, 852
0QSB3DZ	226, 719, 852
0QSB44Z	226, 719, 852
0QSB45Z	226, 719, 852
0QSB46Z	226, 719, 852
0QSB4BZ	226, 719, 852
0QSB4CZ	226, 719, 852
0QSB4DZ	226, 719, 852
0QSC04Z	226, 498, 719, 852
0QSC05Z	226, 719, 852
0QSC06Z	226, 498, 719, 852
0QSC0BZ	226, 719, 852
0QSC0CZ	226, 719, 852
0QSC0DZ	226, 719, 852
0QSC0ZZ	226, 719, 852
0QSC34Z	226, 719, 852
0QSC35Z	226, 719, 852
0QSC36Z	226, 719, 852
0QSC3BZ	226, 719, 852
0QSC3CZ	226, 719, 852
0QSC3DZ	226, 719, 852
0QSC44Z	226, 719, 852
0QSC45Z	226, 719, 852
0QSC46Z	226, 719, 852
0QSC4BZ	226, 719, 852
0QSC4CZ	226, 719, 852
0QSC4DZ	226, 719, 852
0QSD04Z	81, 281, 719, 944
0QSD05Z	228, 719, 944
0QSD0ZZ	81, 281, 719, 944
0QSD34Z	281, 719, 944
0QSD35Z	228, 719, 944
0QSD44Z	281, 719, 944
0QSD45Z	228, 719, 944
0QSF04Z	81, 282, 719, 944
0QSF05Z	228, 719, 944
0QSF0ZZ	81, 282, 719, 944
0QSF34Z	282, 719, 944
0QSF35Z	228, 719, 944
0QSF44Z	282, 719, 944
0QSF45Z	228, 719, 944
0QSG04Z	231, 719, 944
0QSG05Z	231, 719, 944
0QSG06Z	231, 719, 944
0QSG0BZ	231, 719, 944
0QSG0CZ	231, 719, 944
0QSG0DZ	231, 719, 944
0QSG0ZZ	231, 719, 944
0QSG34Z	231, 719, 944
0QSG35Z	231, 719, 944
0QSG36Z	231, 719, 944
0QSG3BZ	231, 719, 944
0QSG3CZ	231, 719, 944
0QSG3DZ	231, 719, 944
0QSG44Z	231, 719, 944
0QSG45Z	231, 719, 944
0QSG46Z	231, 719, 944
0QSG4BZ	231, 719, 944
0QSG4CZ	231, 719, 944
0QSG4DZ	231, 719, 944
0QSH04Z	231, 719, 944
0QSH05Z	231, 719, 944
0QSH06Z	231, 719, 944
0QSH0BZ	231, 719, 944
0QSH0CZ	231, 719, 944
0QSH0DZ	231, 719, 944
0QSH0ZZ	231, 719, 944
0QSH34Z	231, 719, 944
0QSH35Z	231, 719, 944
0QSH36Z	231, 719, 944
0QSH3BZ	231, 719, 944
0QSH3CZ	231, 719, 944
0QSH3DZ	231, 719, 944
0QSH44Z	231, 719, 944
0QSH45Z	231, 719, 944
0QSH46Z	231, 719, 944
0QSH4BZ	231, 719, 944
0QSH4CZ	231, 719, 944
0QSH4DZ	231, 719, 944
0QSJ04Z	231, 719, 944
0QSJ05Z	231, 719, 944
0QSJ06Z	231, 719, 944
0QSJ0BZ	231, 719, 944
0QSJ0CZ	231, 719, 944
0QSJ0DZ	231, 719, 944
0QSJ0ZZ	231, 719, 944
0QSJ34Z	231, 719, 944
0QSJ35Z	231, 719, 944
0QSJ36Z	231, 719, 944
0QSJ3BZ	231, 719, 945
0QSJ3CZ	231, 719, 945
0QSJ3DZ	231, 719, 945
0QSJ44Z	231, 719, 945
0QSJ45Z	231, 719, 945
0QSJ46Z	231, 719, 945
0QSJ4BZ	231, 719, 945
0QSJ4CZ	231, 719, 945
0QSJ4DZ	231, 719, 945
0QSK04Z	231, 719, 945
0QSK05Z	231, 719, 945
0QSK06Z	231, 719, 945
0QSK0BZ	231, 719, 945
0QSK0CZ	231, 719, 945
0QSK0DZ	231, 719, 945
0QSK0ZZ	231, 719, 945
0QSK34Z	231, 719, 945
0QSK35Z	231, 719, 945
0QSK36Z	231, 720, 945
0QSK3BZ	231, 720, 945
0QSK3CZ	231, 720, 945
0QSK3DZ	231, 720, 945
0QSK44Z	231, 720, 945
0QSK45Z	231, 720, 945
0QSK46Z	231, 720, 945
0QSK4BZ	231, 720, 945
0QSK4CZ	231, 720, 945
0QSK4DZ	231, 720, 945
0QSL04Z	257, 720, 945
0QSL05Z	257, 720, 945
0QSL0ZZ	257, 720, 945
0QSL34Z	257, 720, 945
0QSL35Z	257, 720, 945
0QSL44Z	257, 720, 945
0QSL45Z	257, 720, 945
0QSM04Z	257, 720, 945
0QSM05Z	257, 720, 945
0QSM0ZZ	257, 720, 945
0QSM34Z	257, 720, 945
0QSM35Z	257, 720, 945
0QSM44Z	257, 720, 945
0QSM45Z	257, 720, 945
0QSN042	257, 720, 945
0QSN04Z	257, 720, 945
0QSN052	257, 720, 945
0QSN05Z	257, 720, 945
0QSN0Z2	257, 720, 945
0QSN0ZZ	257, 720, 945
0QSN342	257, 720, 945
0QSN34Z	257, 720, 945
0QSN352	257, 720, 945
0QSN35Z	257, 720, 945
0QSN442	257, 720, 945
0QSN44Z	257, 720, 945
0QSN452	257, 720, 945
0QSN45Z	257, 720, 945
0QSP042	257, 720, 945
0QSP04Z	257, 720, 945
0QSP052	257, 720, 945
0QSP05Z	257, 720, 945
0QSP0Z2	257, 720, 945
0QSP0ZZ	257, 720, 945
0QSP342	257, 720, 945
0QSP34Z	257, 720, 945
0QSP352	257, 720, 945
0QSP35Z	257, 720, 945
0QSP442	257, 720, 945
0QSP44Z	257, 720, 945
0QSP452	257, 720, 945
0QSP45Z	257, 720, 945
0QSQ04Z	257, 720, 945
0QSQ05Z	282, 720, 945
0QSQ0ZZ	257, 720, 945
0QSQ34Z	257, 720, 945
0QSQ35Z	282, 720, 945
0QSQ44Z	257, 720, 945
0QSQ45Z	282, 720, 945
0QSR04Z	257, 720, 945
0QSR05Z	282, 720, 945
0QSR0ZZ	257, 720, 945
0QSR34Z	258, 720, 945
0QSR35Z	282, 720, 945
0QSR44Z	258, 720, 945
0QSR45Z	282, 720, 945
0QSS04Z	18, 289, 600, 625, 720, 945
0QSS0ZZ	18, 289, 600, 625, 720, 945
0QSS34Z	18, 289, 600, 625, 720, 945
0QSS3ZZ	18, 288, 289, 600, 625, 720, 945
0QSS44Z	18, 289, 600, 625, 720, 945
0QSS4ZZ	18, 289, 600, 625, 720, 945
0QT*	720
0QT20ZZ	81, 282, 945
0QT30ZZ	81, 282, 945
0QT40ZZ	81, 282, 498, 945
0QT50ZZ	81, 282, 498, 945
0QT60ZZ	226, 852
0QT70ZZ	226, 852
0QT80ZZ	226, 852
0QT90ZZ	226, 852
0QTB0ZZ	226, 852
0QTC0ZZ	226, 852
0QTD0ZZ	228, 945
0QTF0ZZ	228, 945
0QTG0ZZ	231, 945
0QTH0ZZ	231, 945
0QTJ0ZZ	231, 945
0QTK0ZZ	231, 945
0QTL0ZZ	258, 945, 1083
0QTM0ZZ	258, 945, 1083
0QTN0ZZ	258, 945, 1083
0QTP0ZZ	258, 945, 1083
0QTQ0ZZ	81, 282, 945
0QTR0ZZ	81, 282, 945
0QTS0ZZ	81, 282, 945
0QU0*	282
0QU007Z	945
0QU00JZ	720, 945
0QU00KZ	945
0QU037Z	945
0QU03JZ	288, 720, 945
0QU03KZ	945
0QU047Z	945
0QU04JZ	720, 945
0QU04KZ	945
0QU1*	282
0QU107Z	945
0QU10JZ	720, 945
0QU10KZ	945
0QU137Z	945
0QU13JZ	288, 720, 945
0QU13KZ	945
0QU147Z	945
0QU14JZ	720, 945
0QU14KZ	945
0QU2*	282
0QU207Z	945
0QU20KZ	945
0QU237Z	945
0QU23KZ	945
0QU247Z	945
0QU24KZ	945
0QU3*	282
0QU307Z	945
0QU30KZ	945
0QU337Z	945
0QU33KZ	945
0QU347Z	945
0QU34KZ	945
0QU4*	282
0QU407Z	945
0QU40JZ	720, 945
0QU40KZ	945
0QU437Z	945
0QU43JZ	720, 945
0QU43KZ	945
0QU447Z	945
0QU44JZ	720, 945
0QU44KZ	945
0QU5*	282
0QU507Z	945
0QU50JZ	720, 945
0QU50KZ	945
0QU537Z	945
0QU53JZ	720, 945
0QU53KZ	945
0QU547Z	945
0QU54JZ	720, 945
0QU54KZ	945
0QU6*	226, 720, 852
0QU7*	226, 720, 852
0QU8*	226, 720, 852
0QU9*	226, 720, 852
0QUB*	226, 720, 852
0QUC*	226, 720, 852
0QUD*	228, 720
0QUD07Z	945
0QUD0JZ	945
0QUD0KZ	945
0QUD37Z	945
0QUD3JZ	945
0QUD3KZ	945

Numeric Index to Procedures

Code	Page	Code	Page	Code	Page	Code	Page	Code	Page	Code	Page
ØQUD47Z	945	ØQUQ*	282	ØQW537Z	239	ØQWC45Z	243	ØQWK4KZ	240	ØQWS0JZ	240
ØQUD4JZ	945	ØQUQ07Z	946	ØQW53JZ	239	ØQWC47Z	243	ØQWL04Z	258	ØQWS0KZ	240
ØQUD4KZ	945	ØQUQ0KZ	946	ØQW53KZ	239	ØQWC4JZ	243	ØQWL05Z	258	ØQWS34Z	240
ØQUF*	228, 720	ØQUQ37Z	946	ØQW544Z	239	ØQWC4KZ	243	ØQWL07Z	258	ØQWS37Z	240
ØQUF07Z	945	ØQUQ3KZ	946	ØQW547Z	239	ØQWD04Z	239, 720, 946	ØQWL0JZ	258	ØQWS3JZ	240
ØQUF0JZ	945	ØQUQ47Z	946	ØQW54JZ	239	ØQWD05Z	239, 720, 946	ØQWL0KZ	258	ØQWS3KZ	240
ØQUF0KZ	945	ØQUQ4KZ	946	ØQW54KZ	239	ØQWD07Z	239, 720, 946	ØQWL34Z	258	ØQWS44Z	240
ØQUF37Z	945	ØQUR*	282	ØQW604Z	242	ØQWD0JZ	239, 720, 946	ØQWL35Z	258	ØQWS47Z	240
ØQUF3JZ	945	ØQUR07Z	946	ØQW605Z	242	ØQWD0KZ	239, 720, 946	ØQWL37Z	258	ØQWS4JZ	240
ØQUF3KZ	945	ØQUR0KZ	946	ØQW607Z	242	ØQWD34Z	239, 720, 946	ØQWL3JZ	258	ØQWS4KZ	240
ØQUF47Z	945	ØQUR37Z	946	ØQW60JZ	242	ØQWD35Z	239, 720, 946	ØQWL3KZ	258	ØQWY00Z	240
ØQUF4JZ	945	ØQUR47Z	946	ØQW60KZ	242	ØQWD37Z	239, 720, 946	ØQWL44Z	258	ØQWY0MZ	240
ØQUF4KZ	945	ØQUR4KZ	946	ØQW634Z	242	ØQWD3JZ	239, 720, 946	ØQWL45Z	258	ØQWY30Z	240
ØQUG*	231, 720	ØQUS*	282	ØQW635Z	242	ØQWD3KZ	239, 720, 946	ØQWL47Z	258	ØQWY3MZ	240
ØQUG07Z	945	ØQUS07Z	946	ØQW637Z	242	ØQWD44Z	239, 720, 946	ØQWL4JZ	258	ØQWY40Z	240
ØQUG0JZ	946	ØQUS0KZ	946	ØQW63JZ	242	ØQWD45Z	239, 720, 946	ØQWL4KZ	258	ØQWY4MZ	240
ØQUG0KZ	946	ØQUS37Z	946	ØQW63KZ	242	ØQWD47Z	239, 720, 946	ØQWM04Z	258	ØR50*	240, 720
ØQUG37Z	946	ØQUS3JZ	288	ØQW644Z	242	ØQWD4JZ	239, 720, 946	ØQWM05Z	258	ØR500ZZ	946
ØQUG3JZ	946	ØQUS3KZ	946	ØQW645Z	242	ØQWD4KZ	239, 720, 946	ØQWM07Z	258	ØR503ZZ	946
ØQUG3KZ	946	ØQUS47Z	946	ØQW647Z	242	ØQWF04Z	239, 720, 946	ØQWM0JZ	258	ØR504ZZ	946
ØQUG47Z	946	ØQUS4KZ	946	ØQW64JZ	242	ØQWF05Z	239, 720, 946	ØQWM0KZ	258	ØR51*	240, 720
ØQUG4JZ	946	ØQW004Z	239	ØQW64KZ	242	ØQWF07Z	239, 720, 946	ØQWM34Z	258	ØR510ZZ	946
ØQUG4KZ	946	ØQW007Z	239	ØQW704Z	242	ØQWF0JZ	239, 720, 946	ØQWM35Z	258	ØR513ZZ	946
ØQUH*	231, 720	ØQW00JZ	239	ØQW705Z	242	ØQWF0KZ	239, 720, 946	ØQWM37Z	258	ØR514ZZ	946
ØQUH07Z	946	ØQW00KZ	239	ØQW707Z	242	ØQWF34Z	239, 720, 946	ØQWM3JZ	258	ØR530ZZ	18, 289, 720, 946
ØQUH0JZ	946	ØQW034Z	239	ØQW70JZ	242	ØQWF35Z	239, 720, 946	ØQWM3KZ	258	ØR54*	240, 720
ØQUH0KZ	946	ØQW037Z	239	ØQW70KZ	242	ØQWF37Z	239, 720, 946	ØQWM44Z	258	ØR540ZZ	946
ØQUH37Z	946	ØQW03JZ	239	ØQW734Z	242	ØQWF3JZ	239, 720, 946	ØQWM45Z	258	ØR543ZZ	946
ØQUH3JZ	946	ØQW03KZ	239	ØQW735Z	242	ØQWF3KZ	239, 720, 946	ØQWM47Z	258	ØR544ZZ	946
ØQUH3KZ	946	ØQW044Z	239	ØQW737Z	242	ØQWF44Z	239, 720, 946	ØQWM4JZ	258	ØR550ZZ	18, 289, 720, 946
ØQUH47Z	946	ØQW047Z	239	ØQW73JZ	242	ØQWF45Z	239, 720, 946	ØQWM4KZ	258	ØR56*	240, 720
ØQUH4JZ	946	ØQW04JZ	239	ØQW73KZ	242	ØQWF47Z	239, 720, 946	ØQWN04Z	258	ØR560ZZ	946
ØQUH4KZ	946	ØQW04KZ	239	ØQW744Z	242	ØQWF4JZ	239, 720, 946	ØQWN05Z	258	ØR563ZZ	946
ØQUJ*	231, 720	ØQW104Z	239	ØQW745Z	242	ØQWF4KZ	240, 720, 946	ØQWN07Z	258	ØR564ZZ	946
ØQUJ07Z	946	ØQW107Z	239	ØQW747Z	242	ØQWG04Z	240	ØQWN0JZ	258	ØR590ZZ	18, 289, 720, 946
ØQUJ0JZ	946	ØQW10JZ	239	ØQW74JZ	242	ØQWG05Z	240	ØQWN0KZ	258	ØR5A*	240, 720
ØQUJ0KZ	946	ØQW10KZ	239	ØQW74KZ	242	ØQWG07Z	240	ØQWN34Z	258	ØR5A0ZZ	946
ØQUJ37Z	946	ØQW134Z	239	ØQW804Z	242	ØQWG0JZ	240	ØQWN35Z	258	ØR5A3ZZ	946
ØQUJ3JZ	946	ØQW137Z	239	ØQW805Z	242	ØQWG0KZ	240	ØQWN37Z	258	ØR5A4ZZ	946
ØQUJ3KZ	946	ØQW13JZ	239	ØQW807Z	242	ØQWG34Z	240	ØQWN3JZ	258	ØR5B0ZZ	18, 289, 720, 946
ØQUJ47Z	946	ØQW13KZ	239	ØQW80JZ	242	ØQWG35Z	240	ØQWN3KZ	258	ØR5C*	69, 240, 720
ØQUJ4JZ	946	ØQW144Z	239	ØQW80KZ	242	ØQWG37Z	240	ØQWN44Z	258	ØR5C0ZZ	946, 1083
ØQUJ4KZ	946	ØQW147Z	239	ØQW834Z	242	ØQWG3JZ	240	ØQWN45Z	258	ØR5C3ZZ	946, 1083
ØQUK*	231, 720	ØQW14JZ	239	ØQW835Z	242	ØQWG3KZ	240	ØQWN47Z	258	ØR5C4ZZ	946, 1083
ØQUK07Z	946	ØQW14KZ	239	ØQW837Z	242	ØQWG44Z	240	ØQWN4JZ	258	ØR5D*	69, 240, 720
ØQUK0JZ	946	ØQW204Z	239	ØQW83JZ	242	ØQWG45Z	240	ØQWN4KZ	258	ØR5D0ZZ	946, 1083
ØQUK0KZ	946	ØQW205Z	239	ØQW83KZ	242	ØQWG47Z	240	ØQWP04Z	258	ØR5D3ZZ	946, 1083
ØQUK37Z	946	ØQW207Z	239	ØQW844Z	242	ØQWG4JZ	240	ØQWP05Z	258	ØR5D4ZZ	946, 1083
ØQUK3JZ	946	ØQW20JZ	239	ØQW845Z	242	ØQWG4KZ	240	ØQWP07Z	258	ØR5E*	240, 720
ØQUK3KZ	946	ØQW20KZ	239	ØQW847Z	242	ØQWH04Z	240	ØQWP0JZ	258	ØR5E0ZZ	946
ØQUK47Z	946	ØQW234Z	239	ØQW84JZ	242	ØQWH05Z	240	ØQWP0KZ	258	ØR5E3ZZ	946
ØQUK4JZ	946	ØQW235Z	239	ØQW84KZ	242	ØQWH07Z	240	ØQWP34Z	258	ØR5E4ZZ	946
ØQUK4KZ	946	ØQW237Z	239	ØQW904Z	242	ØQWH0JZ	240	ØQWP35Z	258	ØR5F*	240, 720
ØQUL*	258, 720	ØQW23JZ	239	ØQW905Z	242	ØQWH0KZ	240	ØQWP37Z	258	ØR5F0ZZ	946
ØQUL07Z	946	ØQW23KZ	239	ØQW907Z	242	ØQWH34Z	240	ØQWP3JZ	258	ØR5F3ZZ	946
ØQUL0JZ	946	ØQW244Z	239	ØQW90JZ	242	ØQWH35Z	240	ØQWP3KZ	258	ØR5F4ZZ	946
ØQUL0KZ	946	ØQW245Z	239	ØQW90KZ	242	ØQWH37Z	240	ØQWP44Z	258	ØR5G*	240, 720
ØQUL37Z	946	ØQW247Z	239	ØQW934Z	242	ØQWH3JZ	240	ØQWP45Z	258	ØR5G0ZZ	946
ØQUL3JZ	946	ØQW24JZ	239	ØQW935Z	242	ØQWH3KZ	240	ØQWP47Z	258	ØR5G3ZZ	946
ØQUL3KZ	946	ØQW24KZ	239	ØQW937Z	242	ØQWH44Z	240	ØQWP4JZ	258	ØR5G4ZZ	946
ØQUL47Z	946	ØQW304Z	239	ØQW93JZ	242	ØQWH45Z	240	ØQWP4KZ	258	ØR5H*	240, 720
ØQUL4JZ	946	ØQW305Z	239	ØQW93KZ	242	ØQWH47Z	240	ØQWQ04Z	240	ØR5H0ZZ	946
ØQUL4KZ	946	ØQW307Z	239	ØQW944Z	242	ØQWH4JZ	240	ØQWQ05Z	240	ØR5H3ZZ	946
ØQUM*	258, 720	ØQW30JZ	239	ØQW945Z	243	ØQWH4KZ	240	ØQWQ07Z	240	ØR5H4ZZ	946
ØQUM07Z	946	ØQW30KZ	239	ØQW947Z	243	ØQWJ04Z	240	ØQWQ0JZ	240	ØR5J*	240, 720
ØQUM0JZ	946	ØQW334Z	239	ØQW94JZ	243	ØQWJ05Z	240	ØQWQ0KZ	240	ØR5J0ZZ	946
ØQUM0KZ	946	ØQW335Z	239	ØQW94KZ	243	ØQWJ07Z	240	ØQWQ34Z	240	ØR5J3ZZ	946
ØQUM37Z	946	ØQW337Z	239	ØQWB04Z	243	ØQWJ0JZ	240	ØQWQ35Z	240	ØR5J4ZZ	946
ØQUM3JZ	946	ØQW33JZ	239	ØQWB05Z	243	ØQWJ0KZ	240	ØQWQ37Z	240	ØR5K*	240, 720
ØQUM3KZ	946	ØQW33KZ	239	ØQWB07Z	243	ØQWJ34Z	240	ØQWQ3JZ	240	ØR5K0ZZ	946
ØQUM47Z	946	ØQW344Z	239	ØQWB0KZ	243	ØQWJ35Z	240	ØQWQ3KZ	240	ØR5K3ZZ	946
ØQUM4JZ	946	ØQW345Z	239	ØQWB34Z	243	ØQWJ37Z	240	ØQWQ44Z	240	ØR5K4ZZ	946
ØQUM4KZ	946	ØQW347Z	239	ØQWB35Z	243	ØQWJ3JZ	240	ØQWQ45Z	240	ØR5L*	240, 498, 720
ØQUN*	258, 720	ØQW34JZ	239	ØQWB37Z	243	ØQWJ3KZ	240	ØQWQ47Z	240	ØR5L0ZZ	946
ØQUN07Z	946	ØQW34KZ	239	ØQWB3JZ	243	ØQWJ44Z	240	ØQWQ4JZ	240	ØR5L3ZZ	946
ØQUN0JZ	946	ØQW404Z	239	ØQWB3KZ	243	ØQWJ45Z	240	ØQWQ4KZ	240	ØR5L4ZZ	946
ØQUN0KZ	946	ØQW407Z	239	ØQWB44Z	243	ØQWJ47Z	240	ØQWR04Z	240	ØR5M*	240, 498, 720
ØQUN37Z	946	ØQW40JZ	239	ØQWB45Z	243	ØQWJ4JZ	240	ØQWR05Z	240	ØR5M0ZZ	946
ØQUN3JZ	946	ØQW40KZ	239	ØQWB47Z	243	ØQWJ4KZ	240	ØQWR07Z	240	ØR5M3ZZ	946
ØQUN47Z	946	ØQW434Z	239	ØQWB4JZ	243	ØQWK04Z	240	ØQWR0JZ	240	ØR5M4ZZ	946
ØQUN4JZ	946	ØQW437Z	239	ØQWB4KZ	243	ØQWK05Z	240	ØQWR0KZ	240	ØR5N*	270
ØQUN4KZ	946	ØQW43JZ	239	ØQWC04Z	243	ØQWK07Z	240	ØQWR34Z	240	ØR5N0ZZ	437, 643, 946
ØQUP*	258, 720	ØQW43KZ	239	ØQWC05Z	243	ØQWK0JZ	240	ØQWR35Z	240	ØR5N3ZZ	437, 643, 946
ØQUP07Z	946	ØQW444Z	239	ØQWC07Z	243	ØQWK0KZ	240	ØQWR37Z	240	ØR5N4ZZ	437, 643, 946
ØQUP0JZ	946	ØQW447Z	239	ØQWC0JZ	243	ØQWK34Z	240	ØQWR3JZ	240	ØR5P*	270
ØQUP0KZ	946	ØQW44JZ	239	ØQWC0KZ	243	ØQWK35Z	240	ØQWR3KZ	240	ØR5P0ZZ	437, 643, 946
ØQUP37Z	946	ØQW44KZ	239	ØQWC34Z	243	ØQWK37Z	240	ØQWR44Z	240	ØR5P3ZZ	437, 643, 946
ØQUP3JZ	946	ØQW504Z	239	ØQWC35Z	243	ØQWK3JZ	240	ØQWR45Z	240	ØR5P4ZZ	437, 643, 946
ØQUP3KZ	946	ØQW507Z	239	ØQWC37Z	243	ØQWK3KZ	240	ØQWR47Z	240	ØR5Q*	270
ØQUP47Z	946	ØQW50JZ	239	ØQWC3JZ	243	ØQWK44Z	240	ØQWR4JZ	240	ØR5Q0ZZ	643, 947
ØQUP4JZ	946	ØQW50KZ	239	ØQWC3KZ	243	ØQWK45Z	240	ØQWR4KZ	240	ØR5Q3ZZ	643, 947
ØQUP4KZ	946	ØQW534Z	239	ØQWC44Z	243	ØQWK47Z	240	ØQWS04Z	240	ØR5Q4ZZ	643, 947
						ØQWK4JZ	240	ØQWS07Z	240	ØR5R*	270

Code	Page
0R5R0ZZ	643, 947
0R5R3ZZ	643, 947
0R5R4ZZ	643, 947
0R5S*	270
0R5S0ZZ	643, 947
0R5S3ZZ	643, 947
0R5S4ZZ	643, 947
0R5T*	270
0R5T0ZZ	643, 947
0R5T3ZZ	643, 947
0R5T4ZZ	643, 947
0R5U*	270
0R5U0ZZ	643, 947
0R5U3ZZ	643, 947
0R5U4ZZ	643, 947
0R5V*	270
0R5V0ZZ	643, 947
0R5V3ZZ	643, 947
0R5V4ZZ	643, 947
0R5W*	270
0R5W0ZZ	643, 947
0R5W3ZZ	643, 947
0R5W4ZZ	643, 947
0R5X*	270
0R5X0ZZ	643, 947
0R5X3ZZ	643, 947
0R5X4ZZ	643, 947
0R9000Z	282
0R900ZZ	282
0R9100Z	282
0R910ZZ	282
0R9300Z	282
0R930ZZ	282
0R9400Z	282
0R940ZZ	282
0R9500Z	282
0R950ZZ	282
0R9600Z	282
0R960ZZ	282
0R9900Z	282
0R990ZZ	282
0R9A00Z	282
0R9A0ZZ	282
0R9B00Z	282
0R9B0ZZ	282
0R9C00Z	81
0R9C0ZX	81, 224, 1083
0R9C0ZZ	81
0R9C3ZX	81, 224, 1083
0R9C40Z	81
0R9C4ZX	81, 224, 1083
0R9C4ZZ	81
0R9D00Z	81
0R9D0ZX	81, 224, 1083
0R9D0ZZ	81
0R9D3ZX	81, 224, 1083
0R9D40Z	81
0R9D4ZX	81, 224, 1083
0R9D4ZZ	81
0R9E00Z	264
0R9E00Z	720
0R9E0ZZ	264, 720
0R9F00Z	264
0R9F00Z	720
0R9F0ZZ	264, 720
0R9G00Z	264
0R9G00Z	720
0R9G0ZZ	264, 720
0R9H00Z	264
0R9H00Z	720
0R9H0ZZ	264, 720
0R9J00Z	264, 720
0R9J0ZZ	264, 720
0R9K00Z	264, 720
0R9K0ZZ	264, 720
0R9L00Z	264, 498, 720
0R9L0ZZ	264, 498, 720
0R9M00Z	264, 498, 720
0R9M0ZZ	264, 498, 720
0R9N00Z	261, 643
0R9N0ZZ	261, 643
0R9P00Z	261, 643
0R9P0ZZ	261, 643
0R9Q00Z	261, 643
0R9Q0ZZ	261, 643
0R9R00Z	261, 643
0R9R0ZZ	261, 643
0R9S00Z	261, 643
0R9S0ZZ	261, 643
0R9T00Z	261, 643
0R9T0ZZ	261, 643
0R9U00Z	261, 643
0R9U0ZZ	261, 643
0R9V00Z	261, 643
0R9V0ZZ	261, 643
0R9W00Z	261, 643
0R9W0ZZ	261, 643
0R9X00Z	261, 643
0R9X0ZZ	261, 643
0RB00ZZ	18, 289, 600, 625, 720, 947
0RB03ZZ	18, 289, 600, 625, 720, 947
0RB04ZZ	18, 289, 600, 625, 720, 947
0RB10ZZ	18, 289, 600, 625, 720, 947
0RB13ZZ	18, 289, 600, 625, 720, 947
0RB14ZZ	18, 289, 600, 625, 720, 947
0RB30ZZ	18, 289, 720, 947
0RB33ZZ	18, 289, 720, 947
0RB34ZZ	18, 289, 721, 947
0RB40ZZ	18, 289, 600, 625, 721, 947
0RB43ZZ	18, 289, 600, 625, 721, 947
0RB44ZZ	18, 289, 600, 625, 721, 947
0RB50ZZ	18, 289, 721, 947
0RB53ZZ	18, 289, 721, 947
0RB54ZZ	18, 289, 721, 947
0RB60ZZ	18, 289, 600, 625, 721, 947
0RB63ZZ	18, 289, 600, 625, 721, 947
0RB64ZZ	18, 289, 600, 625, 721, 947
0RB90ZZ	18, 289, 721, 947
0RB93ZZ	18, 289, 721, 947
0RB94ZZ	18, 289, 721, 947
0RBA0ZZ	18, 289, 600, 625, 721, 947
0RBA3ZZ	18, 289, 600, 625, 721, 947
0RBA4ZZ	18, 289, 600, 625, 721, 947
0RBB0ZZ	18, 289, 721, 947
0RBB3ZZ	18, 289, 721, 947
0RBB4ZZ	18, 289, 721, 947
0RBC0ZX	81, 224, 1083
0RBC0ZZ	69, 240, 721, 947, 1083
0RBC3ZX	81, 224, 1083
0RBC3ZZ	69, 240, 721, 947, 1083
0RBC4ZX	81, 224, 1083
0RBC4ZZ	69, 240, 721, 947, 1083
0RBD0ZX	81, 224, 1083
0RBD0ZZ	69, 240, 721, 947, 1083
0RBD3ZX	81, 224, 1083
0RBD3ZZ	69, 240, 721, 947, 1083
0RBD4ZX	81, 224, 1083
0RBD4ZZ	69, 240, 721, 947, 1083
0RBE0ZZ	268, 721, 947, 1083
0RBE3ZZ	268, 721, 947, 1083
0RBE4ZZ	268, 721, 947, 1083
0RBF0ZZ	268, 721, 947, 1083
0RBF3ZZ	268, 721, 947, 1083
0RBF4ZZ	268, 721, 947, 1083
0RBG0ZZ	268, 721, 947, 1083
0RBG3ZZ	268, 721, 947, 1083
0RBG4ZZ	268, 721, 947, 1083
0RBH0ZZ	268, 721, 947, 1083
0RBH3ZZ	268, 721, 947, 1083
0RBH4ZZ	268, 721, 947, 1083
0RBJ0ZZ	268, 721, 947, 1083
0RBJ3ZZ	268, 721, 947, 1083
0RBJ4ZZ	268, 721, 947, 1083
0RBK0ZZ	268, 721, 947, 1083
0RBK3ZZ	268, 721, 947, 1083
0RBK4ZZ	268, 721, 947, 1083
0RBL0ZZ	268, 721, 947, 1083
0RBL3ZZ	268, 721, 947, 1083
0RBL4ZZ	268, 721, 947, 1083
0RBM0ZZ	268, 721, 947, 1083
0RBM3ZZ	268, 721, 947, 1083
0RBM4ZZ	268, 721, 947, 1083
0RBN0ZZ	270, 643, 947, 1083
0RBN3ZZ	270, 643, 947, 1083
0RBN4ZZ	270, 643, 947, 1083
0RBP0ZZ	270, 643, 947, 1083
0RBP3ZZ	270, 643, 947, 1083
0RBP4ZZ	270, 643, 947, 1083
0RBQ0ZZ	270, 643, 947, 1083
0RBQ3ZZ	270, 643, 947, 1083
0RBQ4ZZ	270, 643, 947, 1083
0RBR0ZZ	270, 643, 947, 1083
0RBR3ZZ	270, 643, 947, 1083
0RBR4ZZ	270, 643, 947, 1083
0RBS0ZZ	270, 643, 947, 1083
0RBS3ZZ	270, 643, 947, 1083
0RBS4ZZ	270, 643, 947, 1083
0RBT0ZZ	270, 643, 947, 1083
0RBT3ZZ	270, 643, 947, 1083
0RBT4ZZ	270, 643, 947, 1083
0RBU0ZZ	270, 643, 947, 1083
0RBU3ZZ	270, 643, 947, 1083
0RBU4ZZ	270, 643, 947, 1083
0RBV0ZZ	270, 643, 947, 1083
0RBV3ZZ	270, 643, 947, 1083
0RBV4ZZ	270, 643, 947, 1083
0RBW0ZZ	270, 643, 947, 1083
0RBW3ZZ	270, 643, 947, 1083
0RBW4ZZ	270, 643, 947, 1083
0RBX0ZZ	270, 643, 947, 1083
0RBX3ZZ	270, 643, 947, 1083
0RBX4ZZ	270, 644, 947, 1083
0RC0*	282
0RC1*	282
0RC3*	282
0RC4*	282
0RC5*	282
0RC6*	282
0RC9*	282
0RCA*	282
0RCB*	282
0RCC*	69, 282, 721
0RCC0ZZ	947
0RCC3ZZ	947
0RCC4ZZ	947
0RCD*	69, 282, 721
0RCD0ZZ	947
0RCD3ZZ	947
0RCD4ZZ	947
0RCE*	264, 721
0RCF*	264, 721
0RCG*	264, 721
0RCH*	264, 721
0RCJ*	264, 721
0RCK*	264, 721
0RCL*	264, 498, 721
0RCM*	264, 498, 721
0RCN*	261
0RCN0ZZ	644
0RCN3ZZ	644
0RCN4ZZ	644
0RCP*	261
0RCP0ZZ	644
0RCP3ZZ	644
0RCP4ZZ	644
0RCQ*	261
0RCQ0ZZ	644
0RCQ3ZZ	644
0RCQ4ZZ	644
0RCR*	261
0RCR0ZZ	644
0RCR3ZZ	644
0RCR4ZZ	644
0RCS*	261
0RCS0ZZ	644
0RCS3ZZ	644
0RCS4ZZ	644
0RCT*	261
0RCT0ZZ	644
0RCT3ZZ	644
0RCT4ZZ	644
0RCU*	261
0RCU0ZZ	644
0RCU3ZZ	644
0RCU4ZZ	644
0RCV*	261
0RCV0ZZ	644
0RCV3ZZ	644
0RCV4ZZ	644
0RCW*	261
0RCW0ZZ	644
0RCW3ZZ	644
0RCW4ZZ	644
0RCX*	261
0RCX0ZZ	644
0RCX3ZZ	644
0RCX4ZZ	644
0RG0*	221
0RG0070	18, 721, 947
0RG0071	18, 721, 947
0RG007J	18, 721, 947
0RG00A0	18, 721, 947
0RG00AJ	18, 721, 947
0RG00J0	18, 721, 947
0RG00J1	18, 721, 947
0RG00JJ	18, 721, 947
0RG00K0	18, 721, 947
0RG00K1	18, 721, 947
0RG00KJ	18, 721, 947
0RG0370	18, 721, 947
0RG0371	18, 721, 947
0RG037J	18, 721, 947
0RG03A0	18, 721, 947
0RG03AJ	18, 721, 947
0RG03J0	18, 721, 947
0RG03J1	18, 721, 947
0RG03JJ	18, 721, 947
0RG03K0	18, 721, 947
0RG03K1	18, 721, 947
0RG03KJ	18, 721, 947
0RG0470	18, 721, 947
0RG0471	18, 721, 947
0RG047J	18, 721, 947
0RG04A0	18, 721, 947
0RG04AJ	18, 721, 947
0RG04J0	18, 721, 947
0RG04J1	18, 721, 947
0RG04JJ	18, 721, 947
0RG04K0	18, 721, 947
0RG04K1	18, 721, 947
0RG04KJ	18, 721, 947
0RG1*	221
0RG1070	18, 210, 721, 947
0RG1071	18, 211, 721, 947
0RG107J	18, 210, 721, 947
0RG10A0	18, 210, 721, 947
0RG10AJ	18, 210, 721, 947
0RG10J0	18, 210, 721, 947
0RG10J1	18, 211, 721, 947
0RG10JJ	18, 210, 721, 947
0RG10K0	18, 210, 721, 947
0RG10K1	18, 211, 721, 947
0RG10KJ	18, 210, 721, 947
0RG1370	18, 210, 721, 947
0RG1371	18, 211, 721, 947
0RG137J	18, 210, 721, 947
0RG13A0	18, 210, 721, 947
0RG13AJ	18, 210, 721, 947
0RG13J0	18, 210, 721, 947
0RG13J1	18, 211, 721, 947
0RG13JJ	18, 210, 721, 947
0RG13K0	18, 210, 721, 947
0RG13K1	18, 211, 721, 947
0RG13KJ	18, 210, 721, 947
0RG1470	18, 210, 721, 947
0RG1471	18, 211, 721, 947
0RG147J	18, 210, 721, 948
0RG14A0	18, 210, 721, 948
0RG14AJ	18, 210, 721, 948
0RG14J0	18, 210, 721, 948
0RG14J1	18, 211, 721, 948
0RG14JJ	18, 210, 721, 948
0RG14K0	18, 210, 721, 948
0RG14K1	18, 211, 721, 948
0RG14KJ	18, 210, 721, 948
0RG2*	221
0RG2070	18, 210, 721, 948
0RG2071	18, 211, 721, 948
0RG207J	18, 210, 721, 948
0RG20A0	18, 210, 721, 948
0RG20AJ	18, 210, 721, 948
0RG20J0	18, 210, 721, 948
0RG20J1	18, 211, 721, 948
0RG20JJ	18, 210, 721, 948
0RG20K0	18, 210, 721, 948
0RG20K1	18, 211, 721, 948
0RG20KJ	18, 210, 721, 948
0RG2370	18, 210, 721, 948
0RG2371	18, 211, 721, 948
0RG237J	18, 210, 721, 948
0RG23A0	18, 210, 721, 948
0RG23AJ	18, 210, 721, 948
0RG23J0	18, 210, 721, 948
0RG23J1	18, 211, 721, 948
0RG23JJ	18, 210, 721, 948
0RG23K0	18, 210, 721, 948
0RG23K1	18, 211, 721, 948
0RG23KJ	18, 210, 721, 948
0RG2470	18, 210, 721, 948
0RG2471	18, 211, 721, 948
0RG247J	18, 210, 721, 948
0RG24A0	18, 210, 721, 948
0RG24AJ	18, 210, 721, 948
0RG24J0	18, 210, 721, 948
0RG24J1	18, 211, 721, 948
0RG24JJ	18, 210, 721, 948
0RG24K0	18, 210, 721, 948
0RG24K1	18, 211, 721, 948
0RG24KJ	18, 210, 721, 948
0RG4*	221
0RG4070	18, 210, 721, 948
0RG4071	18, 211, 721, 948
0RG407J	18, 210, 721, 948
0RG40A0	18, 210, 721, 948
0RG40AJ	18, 210, 721, 948
0RG40J0	18, 210, 721, 948
0RG40J1	18, 211, 721, 948
0RG40JJ	18, 210, 721, 948
0RG40K0	18, 210, 721, 948
0RG40K1	18, 211, 721, 948
0RG40KJ	18, 210, 721, 948
0RG4370	18, 210, 721, 948
0RG4371	18, 211, 721, 948
0RG437J	18, 210, 721, 948
0RG43A0	18, 210, 721, 948
0RG43AJ	18, 210, 721, 948
0RG43J0	18, 210, 722, 948
0RG43J1	18, 211, 722, 948
0RG43JJ	18, 210, 722, 948
0RG43K0	18, 210, 722, 948
0RG43K1	18, 211, 722, 948
0RG43KJ	18, 210, 722, 948
0RG4470	18, 210, 722, 948
0RG4471	18, 211, 722, 948
0RG447J	18, 210, 722, 948
0RG44A0	18, 210, 722, 948
0RG44AJ	18, 210, 722, 948
0RG44J0	18, 210, 722, 948
0RG44J1	18, 211, 722, 948
0RG44JJ	18, 210, 722, 948
0RG44K0	18, 210, 722, 948
0RG44K1	18, 211, 722, 948
0RG44KJ	19, 210, 722, 948
0RG6*	213
0RG6070	19, 210, 722, 948
0RG6071	19, 211, 722, 948
0RG607J	19, 210, 722, 948
0RG60A0	19, 210, 722, 948
0RG60AJ	19, 210, 722, 948
0RG60J0	19, 210, 722, 948
0RG60J1	19, 211, 722, 948
0RG60JJ	19, 210, 722, 948
0RG60K0	19, 210, 722, 948
0RG60K1	19, 211, 722, 948
0RG60KJ	19, 210, 722, 948
0RG6370	19, 210, 722, 948
0RG6371	19, 211, 722, 948
0RG637J	19, 210, 722, 948
0RG63A0	19, 210, 722, 948
0RG63AJ	19, 210, 722, 948
0RG63J0	19, 210, 722, 948
0RG63J1	19, 211, 722, 948
0RG63JJ	19, 210, 722, 948
0RG63K0	19, 210, 722, 948
0RG63K1	19, 211, 722, 948
0RG63KJ	19, 210, 722, 948
0RG6470	19, 210, 722, 948
0RG6471	19, 211, 722, 948
0RG647J	19, 210, 722, 948
0RG64A0	19, 210, 722, 948
0RG64AJ	19, 210, 722, 948
0RG64J0	19, 210, 722, 948
0RG64J1	19, 211, 722, 948
0RG64JJ	19, 210, 722, 948
0RG64K0	19, 210, 722, 948
0RG64K1	19, 211, 722, 948
0RG64KJ	19, 210, 722, 948
0RG7*	213
0RG7070	19, 210, 213, 722, 948
0RG7071	19, 211, 213, 722, 948
0RG707J	19, 210, 213, 722, 948
0RG70A0	19, 210, 213, 722, 948
0RG70AJ	19, 210, 213, 722, 948
0RG70J0	19, 210, 213, 722, 948
0RG70J1	19, 211, 213, 722, 948
0RG70JJ	19, 210, 213, 722, 948
0RG70K0	19, 210, 213, 722, 948
0RG70K1	19, 211, 213, 722, 948
0RG70KJ	19, 210, 213, 722, 948
0RG7370	19, 210, 213, 722, 948
0RG7371	19, 211, 213, 722, 948
0RG737J	19, 210, 213, 722, 948
0RG73A0	19, 210, 213, 722, 948
0RG73AJ	19, 210, 213, 722, 948
0RG73J0	19, 210, 213, 722, 948
0RG73J1	19, 211, 213, 722, 948
0RG73JJ	19, 210, 213, 722, 948
0RG73K0	19, 210, 213, 722, 948
0RG73K1	19, 211, 213, 722, 948
0RG73KJ	19, 210, 213, 722, 948
0RG7470	19, 210, 213, 722, 948
0RG7471	19, 211, 213, 722, 948
0RG747J	19, 210, 213, 722, 948
0RG74A0	19, 210, 213, 722, 948
0RG74AJ	19, 210, 213, 722, 948

Numeric Index to Procedures

Code	Page
ØRG74JØ	19, 210, 213, 722, 948
ØRG74J1	19, 211, 213, 722, 948
ØRG74JJ	19, 210, 213, 722, 948
ØRG74KØ	19, 210, 213, 722, 948
ØRG74K1	19, 211, 213, 722, 948
ØRG74KJ	19, 210, 213, 722, 948
ØRG8*	213
ØRG8Ø7Ø	19, 210, 722, 948
ØRG8Ø71	19, 211, 722, 948
ØRG8Ø7J	19, 210, 722, 948
ØRG8ØAØ	19, 210, 722, 948
ØRG8ØAJ	19, 210, 722, 948
ØRG8ØJØ	19, 210, 722, 948
ØRG8ØJ1	19, 211, 722, 948
ØRG8ØJJ	19, 210, 722, 948
ØRG8ØKØ	19, 210, 722, 948
ØRG8ØK1	19, 211, 722, 948
ØRG8ØKJ	19, 210, 722, 948
ØRG837Ø	19, 210, 722, 948
ØRG8371	19, 211, 722, 948
ØRG837J	19, 210, 722, 948
ØRG83AØ	19, 210, 722, 948
ØRG83AJ	19, 210, 722, 948
ØRG83JØ	19, 210, 722, 948
ØRG83J1	19, 211, 722, 948
ØRG83JJ	19, 210, 722, 948
ØRG83KØ	19, 210, 722, 948
ØRG83K1	19, 211, 722, 948
ØRG83KJ	19, 210, 722, 948
ØRG847Ø	19, 210, 722, 948
ØRG8471	19, 211, 722, 948
ØRG847J	19, 210, 722, 948
ØRG84AØ	19, 210, 722, 948
ØRG84AJ	19, 210, 722, 948
ØRG84JØ	19, 210, 722, 948
ØRG84J1	19, 211, 722, 948
ØRG84JJ	19, 210, 722, 948
ØRG84KØ	19, 210, 722, 948
ØRG84K1	19, 211, 722, 948
ØRG84KJ	19, 210, 722, 948
ØRGA*	213
ØRGAØ7Ø	19, 210, 722, 949
ØRGAØ71	19, 211, 722, 949
ØRGAØ7J	19, 210, 722, 949
ØRGAØAØ	19, 210, 722, 949
ØRGAØAJ	19, 210, 722, 949
ØRGAØJØ	19, 210, 722, 949
ØRGAØJ1	19, 211, 722, 949
ØRGAØJJ	19, 210, 722, 949
ØRGAØKØ	19, 210, 722, 949
ØRGAØK1	19, 211, 722, 949
ØRGAØKJ	19, 210, 722, 949
ØRGA37Ø	19, 210, 722, 949
ØRGA371	19, 211, 722, 949
ØRGA37J	19, 210, 722, 949
ØRGA3AØ	19, 210, 722, 949
ØRGA3AJ	19, 210, 722, 949
ØRGA3JØ	19, 210, 722, 949
ØRGA3J1	19, 211, 722, 949
ØRGA3JJ	19, 210, 722, 949
ØRGA3KØ	19, 210, 722, 949
ØRGA3K1	19, 211, 722, 949
ØRGA3KJ	19, 210, 722, 949
ØRGA47Ø	19, 211, 722, 949
ØRGA471	19, 211, 722, 949
ØRGA47J	19, 211, 722, 949
ØRGA4AØ	19, 211, 722, 949
ØRGA4AJ	19, 211, 722, 949
ØRGA4JØ	19, 211, 722, 949
ØRGA4J1	19, 211, 722, 949
ØRGA4JJ	19, 211, 722, 949
ØRGA4KØ	19, 211, 722, 949
ØRGA4K1	19, 211, 722, 949
ØRGA4KJ	19, 211, 722, 949
ØRGC*	69, 282
ØRGCØ4Z	722, 949
ØRGCØ7Z	722, 949
ØRGCØJZ	722, 949
ØRGCØKZ	722, 949
ØRGC34Z	722, 949
ØRGC37Z	722, 949
ØRGC3JZ	722, 949
ØRGC3KZ	722, 949
ØRGC44Z	722, 949
ØRGC47Z	722, 949
ØRGC4JZ	722, 949
ØRGC4KZ	722, 949
ØRGD*	69, 282
ØRGDØ4Z	722, 949
ØRGDØ7Z	722, 949
ØRGDØJZ	722, 949
ØRGDØKZ	722, 949
ØRGD34Z	722, 949
ØRGD37Z	722, 949
ØRGD3JZ	722, 949
ØRGD3KZ	722, 949
ØRGD44Z	722, 949
ØRGD47Z	722, 949
ØRGD4JZ	722, 949
ØRGD4KZ	722, 949
ØRGE*	264
ØRGF*	264
ØRGG*	264
ØRGH*	264
ØRGJ*	264
ØRGK*	264
ØRGL*	264
ØRGLØ4Z	722, 949
ØRGLØ5Z	723, 949
ØRGLØ7Z	723, 949
ØRGLØJZ	723, 949
ØRGLØKZ	723, 949
ØRGL34Z	723, 949
ØRGL35Z	723, 949
ØRGL37Z	723, 949
ØRGL3JZ	723, 949
ØRGL3KZ	723, 949
ØRGL44Z	723, 949
ØRGL45Z	723, 949
ØRGL47Z	723, 949
ØRGL4JZ	723, 949
ØRGL4KZ	723, 949
ØRGM*	264
ØRGMØ4Z	723, 949
ØRGMØ5Z	723, 949
ØRGMØ7Z	723, 949
ØRGMØJZ	723, 949
ØRGMØKZ	723, 949
ØRGM34Z	723, 949
ØRGM35Z	723, 949
ØRGM37Z	723, 949
ØRGM3JZ	723, 949
ØRGM3KZ	723, 949
ØRGM44Z	723, 949
ØRGM45Z	723, 949
ØRGM47Z	723, 949
ØRGM4JZ	723, 949
ØRGM4KZ	723, 949
ØRGN*	270
ØRGNØ4Z	644, 949
ØRGNØ5Z	644, 949
ØRGNØ7Z	644, 949
ØRGNØJZ	644, 949
ØRGNØKZ	644, 949
ØRGN34Z	644, 949
ØRGN35Z	644, 949
ØRGN37Z	644, 949
ØRGN3JZ	644, 949
ØRGN3KZ	644, 949
ØRGN44Z	644, 949
ØRGN45Z	644, 949
ØRGN47Z	644, 949
ØRGN4JZ	644, 949
ØRGN4KZ	644, 949
ØRGP*	270
ØRGPØ4Z	644, 949
ØRGPØ5Z	644, 949
ØRGPØ7Z	644, 949
ØRGPØJZ	644, 949
ØRGPØKZ	644, 949
ØRGP34Z	644, 949
ØRGP35Z	644, 949
ØRGP37Z	644, 949
ØRGP3JZ	644, 949
ØRGP3KZ	644, 949
ØRGP44Z	644, 949
ØRGP45Z	644, 949
ØRGP47Z	644, 949
ØRGP4JZ	644, 949
ØRGP4KZ	644, 949
ØRGQ*	270
ØRGQØ4Z	644, 949
ØRGQØ5Z	644, 949
ØRGQØ7Z	644, 949
ØRGQØJZ	644, 949
ØRGQØKZ	644, 949
ØRGQ34Z	644, 949
ØRGQ35Z	644, 949
ØRGQ37Z	644, 949
ØRGQ3JZ	644, 949
ØRGQ3KZ	644, 949
ØRGQ44Z	644, 949
ØRGQ45Z	644, 949
ØRGQ47Z	644, 949
ØRGQ4JZ	644, 949
ØRGQ4KZ	644, 949
ØRGR*	270
ØRGRØ4Z	644, 949
ØRGRØ5Z	644, 949
ØRGRØ7Z	644, 949
ØRGRØJZ	644, 949
ØRGRØKZ	644, 949
ØRGR34Z	644, 949
ØRGR35Z	644, 949
ØRGR37Z	644, 949
ØRGR3JZ	644, 949
ØRGR3KZ	644, 949
ØRGR44Z	644, 949
ØRGR45Z	644, 949
ØRGR47Z	644, 949
ØRGR4JZ	644, 949
ØRGR4KZ	644, 949
ØRGS*	270
ØRGSØ4Z	644, 949
ØRGSØ5Z	644, 949
ØRGSØ7Z	644, 949
ØRGSØJZ	644, 949
ØRGSØKZ	644, 949
ØRGS34Z	644, 949
ØRGS35Z	644, 949
ØRGS37Z	644, 949
ØRGS3JZ	644, 949
ØRGS3KZ	644, 949
ØRGS44Z	644, 949
ØRGS45Z	644, 949
ØRGS47Z	644, 949
ØRGS4JZ	644, 949
ØRGS4KZ	644, 949
ØRGT*	270
ØRGTØ4Z	644, 949
ØRGTØ5Z	644, 949
ØRGTØ7Z	644, 949
ØRGTØJZ	644, 949
ØRGTØKZ	644, 949
ØRGT34Z	644, 949
ØRGT35Z	644, 949
ØRGT37Z	644, 949
ØRGT3JZ	644, 949
ØRGT3KZ	644, 949
ØRGT44Z	644, 949
ØRGT45Z	644, 949
ØRGT47Z	644, 950
ØRGT4JZ	644, 950
ØRGT4KZ	644, 950
ØRGU*	270
ØRGUØ4Z	644, 950
ØRGUØ5Z	644, 950
ØRGUØ7Z	644, 950
ØRGUØJZ	644, 950
ØRGUØKZ	644, 950
ØRGU34Z	644, 950
ØRGU35Z	644, 950
ØRGU37Z	644, 950
ØRGU3JZ	644, 950
ØRGU3KZ	644, 950
ØRGU44Z	644, 950
ØRGU45Z	644, 950
ØRGU47Z	644, 950
ØRGU4JZ	644, 950
ØRGU4KZ	644, 950
ØRGV*	270
ØRGVØ4Z	644, 950
ØRGVØ5Z	644, 950
ØRGVØ7Z	644, 950
ØRGVØJZ	644, 950
ØRGVØKZ	644, 950
ØRGV34Z	644, 950
ØRGV35Z	644, 950
ØRGV37Z	644, 950
ØRGV3JZ	644, 950
ØRGV3KZ	644, 950
ØRGV44Z	644, 950
ØRGV45Z	644, 950
ØRGV47Z	644, 950
ØRGV4JZ	644, 950
ØRGV4KZ	644, 950
ØRGW*	270
ØRGWØ4Z	644, 950
ØRGWØ5Z	644, 950
ØRGWØ7Z	644, 950
ØRGWØJZ	644, 950
ØRGWØKZ	644, 950
ØRGW34Z	644, 950
ØRGW35Z	644, 950
ØRGW37Z	644, 950
ØRGW3JZ	644, 950
ØRGW3KZ	644, 950
ØRGW44Z	644, 950
ØRGW45Z	644, 950
ØRGW47Z	644, 950
ØRGW4JZ	644, 950
ØRGW4KZ	644, 950
ØRGX*	270
ØRGXØ4Z	644, 950
ØRGXØ5Z	644, 950
ØRGXØ7Z	644, 950
ØRGXØJZ	644, 950
ØRGXØKZ	644, 950
ØRGX34Z	644, 950
ØRGX35Z	644, 950
ØRGX37Z	644, 950
ØRGX3JZ	645, 950
ØRGX3KZ	645, 950
ØRGX44Z	645, 950
ØRGX45Z	645, 950
ØRGX47Z	645, 950
ØRGX4JZ	645, 950
ØRGX4KZ	645, 950
ØRHØØ4Z	282
ØRHØØBZ	19, 289, 723, 950
ØRHØØCZ	19, 289, 723, 950
ØRHØØDZ	19, 289, 723, 950
ØRHØ34Z	282
ØRHØ3BZ	19, 289, 723, 950
ØRHØ3CZ	19, 289, 723, 950
ØRHØ3DZ	19, 289, 723, 950
ØRHØ44Z	282
ØRHØ4BZ	19, 289, 723, 950
ØRHØ4CZ	19, 289, 723, 950
ØRHØ4DZ	19, 289, 723, 950
ØRH1Ø4Z	282
ØRH1ØBZ	19, 289, 723, 950
ØRH1ØCZ	19, 289, 723, 950
ØRH1ØDZ	19, 289, 723, 950
ØRH134Z	282
ØRH13BZ	19, 289, 723, 950
ØRH13CZ	19, 289, 723, 950
ØRH13DZ	19, 289, 723, 950
ØRH144Z	282
ØRH14BZ	19, 289, 723, 950
ØRH14CZ	19, 289, 723, 950
ØRH14DZ	19, 289, 723, 950
ØRH4Ø4Z	282
ØRH4ØBZ	19, 289, 723, 950
ØRH4ØCZ	19, 289, 723, 950
ØRH4ØDZ	19, 289, 723, 950
ØRH434Z	282
ØRH43BZ	19, 289, 723, 950
ØRH43CZ	19, 289, 723, 950
ØRH43DZ	19, 289, 723, 950
ØRH444Z	282
ØRH44BZ	19, 289, 723, 950
ØRH44CZ	19, 289, 723, 950
ØRH44DZ	19, 289, 723, 950
ØRH6Ø4Z	282
ØRH6ØBZ	19, 289, 723, 950
ØRH6ØCZ	19, 289, 723, 950
ØRH6ØDZ	19, 289, 723, 950
ØRH634Z	282
ØRH63BZ	19, 289, 723, 950
ØRH63CZ	19, 289, 723, 950
ØRH63DZ	19, 289, 723, 950
ØRH644Z	282
ØRH64BZ	19, 289, 723, 950
ØRH64CZ	19, 289, 723, 950
ØRH64DZ	19, 289, 723, 950
ØRHAØ4Z	282
ØRHAØBZ	19, 289, 723, 950
ØRHAØCZ	19, 289, 723, 950
ØRHAØDZ	19, 289, 723, 950
ØRHA34Z	282
ØRHA3BZ	19, 289, 723, 950
ØRHA3CZ	19, 289, 723, 950
ØRHA3DZ	20, 289, 723, 950
ØRHA44Z	282
ØRHA4BZ	20, 289, 723, 950
ØRHA4CZ	20, 289, 723, 950
ØRHA4DZ	20, 289, 723, 950
ØRHCØ3Z	81
ØRHCØ4Z	81
ØRHC34Z	81
ØRHC43Z	81
ØRHC44Z	81
ØRHDØ3Z	81
ØRHDØ4Z	81
ØRHD34Z	81
ØRHD43Z	81
ØRHD44Z	81
ØRHEØ4Z	264, 723
ØRHE34Z	264, 723
ØRHE44Z	264, 723
ØRHFØ4Z	264, 723
ØRHF34Z	264, 723
ØRHF44Z	264, 723
ØRHGØ4Z	264, 723
ØRHG34Z	264, 723
ØRHG44Z	264, 723
ØRHHØ4Z	264, 723
ØRHH34Z	264, 723
ØRHH44Z	264, 723
ØRHJØ4Z	264, 723
ØRHJ34Z	264, 723
ØRHJ44Z	264, 723
ØRHKØ4Z	264, 723
ØRHK34Z	264, 723
ØRHK44Z	264, 723
ØRHLØ4Z	264, 723
ØRHLØ5Z	264, 723
ØRHL34Z	264, 723
ØRHL35Z	264, 723
ØRHL44Z	264, 723
ØRHL45Z	264, 723
ØRHMØ4Z	264, 723
ØRHMØ5Z	264, 723
ØRHM34Z	264, 723
ØRHM35Z	264, 723
ØRHM44Z	264, 723
ØRHM45Z	264, 723
ØRHNØ4Z	261, 645
ØRHNØ5Z	261, 645
ØRHN34Z	261, 645
ØRHN35Z	261, 645
ØRHN44Z	261, 645
ØRHN45Z	261, 645
ØRHPØ4Z	261, 645
ØRHPØ5Z	261, 645
ØRHP34Z	261, 645
ØRHP35Z	261, 645
ØRHP44Z	261, 645
ØRHP45Z	261, 645
ØRHQØ4Z	261, 645
ØRHQØ5Z	261, 645
ØRHQ34Z	261, 645
ØRHQ35Z	261, 645
ØRHQ44Z	261, 645
ØRHQ45Z	261, 645
ØRHRØ4Z	261, 645
ØRHRØ5Z	261, 645
ØRHR34Z	261, 645
ØRHR35Z	261, 645
ØRHR44Z	261, 645
ØRHR45Z	261, 645
ØRHSØ4Z	261, 645
ØRHSØ5Z	261, 645
ØRHS34Z	261, 645
ØRHS35Z	261, 645
ØRHS44Z	261, 645
ØRHS45Z	261, 645
ØRHTØ4Z	261, 645
ØRHTØ5Z	261, 645
ØRHT34Z	261, 645
ØRHT35Z	261, 645
ØRHT44Z	261, 645
ØRHT45Z	261, 645
ØRHUØ4Z	261, 645
ØRHUØ5Z	261, 645
ØRHU34Z	261, 645
ØRHU35Z	261, 645
ØRHU44Z	261, 645
ØRHU45Z	261, 645
ØRHVØ4Z	261, 645
ØRHVØ5Z	261, 645
ØRHV34Z	261, 645
ØRHV35Z	261, 645
ØRHV44Z	261, 645
ØRHV45Z	261, 645
ØRHWØ4Z	261, 645
ØRHWØ5Z	261, 645
ØRHW34Z	261, 645
ØRHW35Z	261, 645
ØRHW44Z	261, 645
ØRHW45Z	261, 645
ØRHXØ4Z	261, 645
ØRHXØ5Z	261, 645
ØRHX34Z	261, 645
ØRHX35Z	261, 645
ØRHX44Z	261, 645
ØRHX45Z	261, 645
ØRJØØZZ	282
ØRJØ4ZZ	266, 723, 950
ØRJ1ØZZ	282
ØRJ14ZZ	266, 723, 950
ØRJ3ØZZ	282
ØRJ34ZZ	266, 723, 950
ØRJ4ØZZ	282
ØRJ44ZZ	266, 723, 950
ØRJ5ØZZ	282
ØRJ54ZZ	266, 723, 950
ØRJ6ØZZ	282
ØRJ64ZZ	266, 723, 950
ØRJ9ØZZ	282
ØRJ94ZZ	266, 723, 950
ØRJAØZZ	282
ØRJA4ZZ	266, 723, 950
ØRJBØZZ	282
ØRJB4ZZ	266, 723, 950
ØRJCØZZ	69, 224, 723, 950
ØRJC4ZZ	69, 224, 723, 950
ØRJDØZZ	69, 224, 723, 950
ØRJD4ZZ	69, 224, 723, 950
ØRJEØZZ	264, 723
ØRJE4ZZ	266, 723, 950
ØRJFØZZ	264, 723
ØRJF4ZZ	266, 723, 950
ØRJGØZZ	264, 723
ØRJG4ZZ	266, 723, 950
ØRJHØZZ	264, 723
ØRJH4ZZ	266, 723, 950
ØRJJØZZ	264, 723
ØRJJ4ZZ	266, 723, 950
ØRJKØZZ	264, 723
ØRJK4ZZ	266, 723, 950
ØRJLØZZ	264, 723
ØRJL4ZZ	266, 723, 950
ØRJMØZZ	264, 723
ØRJM4ZZ	266, 723, 950
ØRJNØZZ	261, 645
ØRJN4ZZ	266, 723, 950
ØRJPØZZ	261, 645
ØRJP4ZZ	266, 723, 950
ØRJQØZZ	261, 645
ØRJQ4ZZ	266, 723, 950
ØRJRØZZ	261, 645
ØRJR4ZZ	266, 723, 950
ØRJSØZZ	261, 645
ØRJS4ZZ	266, 723, 950
ØRJTØZZ	261, 645
ØRJT4ZZ	266, 723, 950
ØRJUØZZ	261, 645
ØRJU4ZZ	266, 723, 950
ØRJVØZZ	261, 645
ØRJV4ZZ	266, 723, 950
ØRJWØZZ	261, 645
ØRJW4ZZ	266, 723, 950
ØRJXØZZ	261, 645
ØRJX4ZZ	266, 723, 950
ØRNØØZZ	723, 950
ØRNØ3ZZ	723, 950
ØRNØ4ZZ	723, 950
ØRN1ØZZ	723, 950
ØRN13ZZ	723, 950
ØRN14ZZ	723, 950
ØRN3ØZZ	723, 950
ØRN33ZZ	723, 950
ØRN34ZZ	723, 950
ØRN4ØZZ	723, 950
ØRN43ZZ	723, 950
ØRN44ZZ	723, 950
ØRN5ØZZ	723, 950
ØRN53ZZ	723, 950
ØRN54ZZ	723, 950
ØRN6ØZZ	723, 950
ØRN63ZZ	723, 950
ØRN64ZZ	723, 950
ØRN9ØZZ	723, 950
ØRN93ZZ	723, 950
ØRN94ZZ	723, 950
ØRNAØZZ	723, 950
ØRNA3ZZ	723, 950
ØRNA4ZZ	723, 950
ØRNBØZZ	723, 950
ØRNB3ZZ	723, 950
ØRNB4ZZ	723, 950
ØRNCØZZ	69, 723, 950
ØRNC3ZZ	69, 723, 950
ØRNC4ZZ	69, 723, 950
ØRNDØZZ	69, 723, 950
ØRND3ZZ	69, 724, 950
ØRND4ZZ	69, 724, 950
ØRNEØZZ	268, 724, 950
ØRNE3ZZ	268, 724, 950
ØRNE4ZZ	268, 724, 951

Code	Page	Code	Page	Code	Page	Code	Page	Code	Page	Code	Page
ØRNF0ZZ	268, 724, 951	ØRP14JZ	951	ØRP94KZ	283	ØRPF40Z	265, 724	ØRPM07Z	265, 725	ØRPS04Z	262, 646
ØRNF3ZZ	268, 724, 951	ØRP14KZ	282	ØRPA00Z	283	ØRPF43Z	265, 724	ØRPM0JZ	241, 725, 951	ØRPS05Z	262, 646
ØRNF4ZZ	268, 724, 951	ØRP300Z	282	ØRPA03Z	283	ØRPF44Z	265, 724	ØRPM0KZ	265, 725	ØRPS07Z	262, 646
ØRNG0ZZ	268, 724, 951	ØRP303Z	282	ØRPA04Z	283	ØRPF47Z	265, 724	ØRPM34Z	265, 725	ØRPS0JZ	241, 646, 951
ØRNG3ZZ	268, 724, 951	ØRP307Z	282	ØRPA07Z	283	ØRPF4JZ	241, 724, 951	ØRPM35Z	265, 725	ØRPS0KZ	262, 646
ØRNG4ZZ	268, 724, 951	ØRP30JZ	240, 724	ØRPA0AZ	283	ØRPF4KZ	265, 724	ØRPM37Z	265, 725	ØRPS34Z	262, 646
ØRNH0ZZ	268, 724, 951	ØRP30JZ	951	ØRPA0JZ	240, 724, 951	ØRPG00Z	265, 724	ØRPM3JZ	241, 725, 951	ØRPS35Z	262, 646
ØRNH3ZZ	268, 724, 951	ØRP30KZ	282	ØRPA0KZ	283	ØRPG03Z	265, 724	ØRPM3KZ	265, 725	ØRPS37Z	262, 646
ØRNH4ZZ	268, 724, 951	ØRP337Z	282	ØRPA34Z	283	ØRPG04Z	265, 724	ØRPM40Z	265, 725	ØRPS3JZ	241, 646, 951
ØRNJ0ZZ	268, 724, 951	ØRP33JZ	240, 724	ØRPA37Z	283	ØRPG07Z	265, 724	ØRPM43Z	265, 725	ØRPS3KZ	262, 646
ØRNJ3ZZ	268, 724, 951	ØRP33JZ	951	ØRPA3AZ	283	ØRPG0JZ	241, 724, 951	ØRPM44Z	265, 725	ØRPS40Z	262, 646
ØRNJ4ZZ	268, 724, 951	ØRP33KZ	282	ØRPA3JZ	240, 724, 951	ØRPG0KZ	265, 724	ØRPM45Z	265, 725	ØRPS43Z	262, 646
ØRNK0ZZ	268, 724, 951	ØRP340Z	282	ØRPA3KZ	283	ØRPG34Z	265, 724	ØRPM47Z	265, 725	ØRPS44Z	262, 646
ØRNK3ZZ	268, 724, 951	ØRP343Z	282	ØRPA40Z	283	ØRPG37Z	265, 724	ØRPM4JZ	241, 725, 951	ØRPS45Z	262, 646
ØRNK4ZZ	268, 724, 951	ØRP347Z	282	ØRPA43Z	283	ØRPG3JZ	241, 724, 951	ØRPM4KZ	265, 725	ØRPS47Z	262, 646
ØRNL0ZZ	268, 724, 951	ØRP34JZ	240, 724	ØRPA44Z	283	ØRPG3KZ	265, 724	ØRPN00Z	261, 645	ØRPS4JZ	241, 646, 951
ØRNL3ZZ	268, 724, 951	ØRP34JZ	951	ØRPA47Z	283	ØRPG40Z	265, 724	ØRPN03Z	261, 645	ØRPS4KZ	262, 646
ØRNL4ZZ	268, 724, 951	ØRP34KZ	282	ØRPA4AZ	283	ØRPG43Z	265, 724	ØRPN04Z	261, 645	ØRPT00Z	262, 646
ØRNM0ZZ	268, 724, 951	ØRP400Z	282	ØRPA4JZ	240, 724, 951	ØRPG44Z	265, 724	ØRPN07Z	261, 645	ØRPT03Z	262, 646
ØRNM3ZZ	268, 724, 951	ØRP403Z	282	ØRPA4KZ	283	ØRPG47Z	265, 724	ØRPN0JZ	241, 645, 951	ØRPT04Z	262, 646
ØRNM4ZZ	268, 724, 951	ØRP404Z	282	ØRPB00Z	283	ØRPG4JZ	241, 724, 951	ØRPN0KZ	261, 645	ØRPT05Z	262, 646
ØRNN0ZZ	270, 645, 951	ØRP407Z	282	ØRPB03Z	283	ØRPG4KZ	265, 724	ØRPN34Z	262, 645	ØRPT07Z	262, 646
ØRNN3ZZ	270, 645, 951	ØRP40AZ	282	ØRPB07Z	283	ØRPH00Z	265, 724	ØRPN35Z	262, 645	ØRPT0JZ	241, 646, 951
ØRNN4ZZ	270, 645, 951	ØRP40JZ	240, 724	ØRPB0JZ	240, 724, 951	ØRPH03Z	265, 724	ØRPN37Z	262, 645	ØRPT0KZ	262, 646
ØRNP0ZZ	270, 645, 951	ØRP40JZ	951	ØRPB0KZ	283	ØRPH04Z	265, 724	ØRPN3JZ	241, 645, 951	ØRPT34Z	262, 646
ØRNP3ZZ	270, 645, 951	ØRP40KZ	282	ØRPB37Z	283	ØRPH07Z	265, 724	ØRPN3KZ	262, 645	ØRPT35Z	262, 646
ØRNP4ZZ	270, 645, 951	ØRP434Z	282	ØRPB3JZ	240, 724, 951	ØRPH0JZ	241, 724, 951	ØRPN40Z	262, 645	ØRPT37Z	262, 646
ØRNQ0ZZ	270, 645, 951	ØRP437Z	282	ØRPB3KZ	283	ØRPH0KZ	265, 724	ØRPN44Z	262, 645	ØRPT3JZ	241, 646, 951
ØRNQ3ZZ	270, 645, 951	ØRP43AZ	282	ØRPB40Z	283	ØRPH34Z	265, 724	ØRPN45Z	262, 645	ØRPT3KZ	262, 646
ØRNQ4ZZ	270, 645, 951	ØRP43JZ	240, 724	ØRPB43Z	283	ØRPH37Z	265, 724	ØRPN47Z	262, 645	ØRPT40Z	262, 646
ØRNR0ZZ	270, 645, 951	ØRP43JZ	951	ØRPB47Z	283	ØRPH3JZ	241, 724, 951	ØRPN4JZ	241, 645, 951	ØRPT43Z	262, 646
ØRNR3ZZ	270, 645, 951	ØRP43KZ	282	ØRPB4JZ	240, 724, 951	ØRPH3KZ	265, 724	ØRPN4KZ	262, 645	ØRPT44Z	262, 646
ØRNR4ZZ	270, 645, 951	ØRP440Z	282	ØRPB4KZ	283	ØRPH40Z	265, 724	ØRPP00Z	262, 645	ØRPT45Z	262, 646
ØRNS0ZZ	270, 645, 951	ØRP443Z	282	ØRPC00Z	81, 240	ØRPH43Z	265, 724	ØRPP03Z	262, 645	ØRPT47Z	262, 646
ØRNS3ZZ	270, 645, 951	ØRP444Z	282	ØRPC03Z	81, 240	ØRPH44Z	265, 724	ØRPP04Z	262, 645	ØRPT4JZ	241, 646, 951
ØRNS4ZZ	270, 645, 951	ØRP447Z	282	ØRPC04Z	69, 240, 724, 951	ØRPH47Z	265, 724	ØRPP05Z	262, 645	ØRPT4KZ	262, 646
ØRNT0ZZ	270, 645, 951	ØRP44AZ	282	ØRPC0JZ	81, 240	ØRPH4JZ	241, 724, 951	ØRPP07Z	262, 645	ØRPU00Z	262, 646
ØRNT3ZZ	270, 645, 951	ØRP44JZ	240, 724	ØRPC0KZ	81, 240	ØRPH4KZ	265, 724	ØRPP0JZ	241, 645, 951	ØRPU03Z	262, 646
ØRNT4ZZ	270, 645, 951	ØRP44JZ	951	ØRPC34Z	69, 240, 724, 951	ØRPJ00Z	265, 724	ØRPP0KZ	262, 645	ØRPU04Z	262, 646
ØRNU0ZZ	271, 645, 951	ØRP44KZ	282	ØRPC37Z	81, 240	ØRPJ03Z	265, 724	ØRPP34Z	262, 645	ØRPU05Z	262, 646
ØRNU3ZZ	271, 645, 951	ØRP500Z	282	ØRPC3KZ	81, 240	ØRPJ04Z	265, 724	ØRPP35Z	262, 645	ØRPU07Z	262, 646
ØRNU4ZZ	271, 645, 951	ØRP503Z	282	ØRPC3KZ	81, 240	ØRPJ07Z	265, 724	ØRPP37Z	262, 645	ØRPU0JZ	241, 646, 951
ØRNV0ZZ	271, 645, 951	ØRP507Z	282	ØRPC40Z	81, 240	ØRPJ0JZ	241, 724, 951	ØRPP3JZ	241, 645, 951	ØRPU0KZ	262, 646
ØRNV3ZZ	271, 645, 951	ØRP50JZ	240, 724	ØRPC43Z	81, 240	ØRPJ0KZ	265, 724	ØRPP3KZ	262, 645	ØRPU34Z	262, 646
ØRNV4ZZ	271, 645, 951	ØRP50JZ	951	ØRPC44Z	69, 240, 724, 951	ØRPJ34Z	265, 724	ØRPP40Z	262, 645	ØRPU35Z	262, 646
ØRNW0ZZ	271, 645, 951	ØRP50KZ	282	ØRPC47Z	81, 240	ØRPJ37Z	265, 724	ØRPP43Z	262, 645	ØRPU37Z	262, 646
ØRNW3ZZ	271, 645, 951	ØRP537Z	282	ØRPC4JZ	81, 240	ØRPJ3JZ	241, 724, 951	ØRPP44Z	262, 645	ØRPU3JZ	241, 646, 951
ØRNW4ZZ	271, 645, 951	ØRP53JZ	240, 724	ØRPC4KZ	81, 240	ØRPJ3KZ	265, 724	ØRPP45Z	262, 645	ØRPU3KZ	262, 646
ØRNX0ZZ	271, 645, 951	ØRP53JZ	951	ØRPCX4Z	69, 240, 724, 951	ØRPJ40Z	265, 724	ØRPP47Z	262, 645	ØRPU40Z	262, 646
ØRNX3ZZ	271, 645, 951	ØRP53KZ	282	ØRPD00Z	81, 241	ØRPJ43Z	265, 724	ØRPP4JZ	241, 645, 951	ØRPU43Z	262, 646
ØRNX4ZZ	271, 645, 951	ØRP540Z	282	ØRPD03Z	81, 241	ØRPJ44Z	265, 724	ØRPP4KZ	262, 645	ØRPU44Z	262, 646
ØRP000Z	282	ØRP543Z	282	ØRPD04Z	69, 241, 724, 951	ØRPJ47Z	265, 724	ØRPQ03Z	262, 645	ØRPU45Z	262, 646
ØRP003Z	282	ØRP547Z	282	ØRPD07Z	81, 241	ØRPJ4JZ	241, 724, 951	ØRPQ04Z	262, 645	ØRPU47Z	262, 646
ØRP004Z	282	ØRP54JZ	240, 724	ØRPD0JZ	81, 241	ØRPJ4KZ	265, 724	ØRPQ05Z	262, 645	ØRPU4JZ	241, 646, 951
ØRP007Z	282	ØRP54JZ	951	ØRPD0KZ	81, 241	ØRPK00Z	265, 724	ØRPQ07Z	262, 645	ØRPU4KZ	262, 646
ØRP00AZ	282	ØRP54KZ	282	ØRPD34Z	69, 241, 724, 951	ØRPK03Z	265, 724	ØRPQ0JZ	241, 645, 951	ØRPV00Z	262, 646
ØRP00JZ	240, 724	ØRP600Z	282	ØRPD37Z	81, 241	ØRPK04Z	265, 724	ØRPQ0KZ	262, 645	ØRPV03Z	262, 646
ØRP00JZ	951	ØRP603Z	282	ØRPD3JZ	81, 241	ØRPK07Z	265, 724	ØRPQ34Z	262, 645	ØRPV04Z	262, 646
ØRP00KZ	282	ØRP604Z	282	ØRPD3KZ	81, 241	ØRPK0JZ	241, 724, 951	ØRPQ35Z	262, 645	ØRPV05Z	262, 646
ØRP034Z	282	ØRP607Z	282	ØRPD40Z	81, 241	ØRPK0KZ	265, 724	ØRPQ37Z	262, 645	ØRPV07Z	262, 646
ØRP037Z	282	ØRP60AZ	282	ØRPD43Z	81, 241	ØRPK34Z	265, 724	ØRPQ3JZ	241, 645, 951	ØRPV0JZ	241, 646, 951
ØRP03AZ	282	ØRP60JZ	240, 724	ØRPD44Z	69, 241, 724, 951	ØRPK37Z	265, 724	ØRPQ3KZ	262, 645	ØRPV0KZ	262, 646
ØRP03JZ	240, 724	ØRP60JZ	951	ØRPD47Z	81, 241	ØRPK3JZ	241, 724, 951	ØRPQ40Z	262, 645	ØRPV34Z	262, 646
ØRP03JZ	951	ØRP60KZ	282	ØRPD4JZ	81, 241	ØRPK3KZ	265, 724	ØRPQ43Z	262, 645	ØRPV35Z	262, 646
ØRP03KZ	282	ØRP634Z	282	ØRPD4KZ	81, 241	ØRPK40Z	265, 724	ØRPQ44Z	262, 645	ØRPV37Z	262, 646
ØRP040Z	282	ØRP637Z	282	ØRPDX4Z	69, 241, 724, 951	ØRPK43Z	265, 724	ØRPQ45Z	262, 645	ØRPV3JZ	241, 646, 951
ØRP043Z	282	ØRP63AZ	282	ØRPE00Z	264, 724	ØRPK47Z	265, 724	ØRPQ47Z	262, 645	ØRPV3KZ	262, 646
ØRP044Z	282	ØRP63JZ	240, 724	ØRPE03Z	264, 724	ØRPK4JZ	241, 724, 951	ØRPQ4JZ	241, 645, 951	ØRPV40Z	262, 646
ØRP047Z	282	ØRP63JZ	951	ØRPE04Z	264, 724	ØRPK4KZ	265, 724	ØRPQ4KZ	262, 645	ØRPV43Z	262, 646
ØRP04AZ	282	ØRP63KZ	282	ØRPE07Z	264, 724	ØRPL00Z	265, 724	ØRPR00Z	262, 645	ØRPV44Z	262, 646
ØRP04JZ	240, 724	ØRP640Z	282	ØRPE0JZ	241, 724, 951	ØRPL03Z	265, 724	ØRPR03Z	262, 645	ØRPV45Z	262, 646
ØRP04JZ	951	ØRP643Z	282	ØRPE0KZ	264, 724	ØRPL04Z	265, 724	ØRPR04Z	262, 645	ØRPV47Z	262, 646
ØRP04KZ	282	ØRP644Z	282	ØRPE34Z	264, 724	ØRPL05Z	265, 724	ØRPR05Z	262, 645	ØRPV4JZ	241, 646, 951
ØRP100Z	282	ØRP647Z	282	ØRPE37Z	264, 724	ØRPL07Z	265, 724	ØRPR07Z	262, 645	ØRPV4KZ	262, 646
ØRP103Z	282	ØRP64AZ	282	ØRPE3JZ	241, 724, 951	ØRPL0JZ	241, 724, 951	ØRPR0JZ	241, 645, 951	ØRPW00Z	262, 646
ØRP104Z	282	ØRP64JZ	240, 724	ØRPE3KZ	264, 724	ØRPL0KZ	265, 724	ØRPR0KZ	262, 645	ØRPW03Z	262, 646
ØRP107Z	282	ØRP64JZ	951	ØRPE40Z	264, 724	ØRPL34Z	265, 724	ØRPR34Z	262, 645	ØRPW04Z	262, 646
ØRP10AZ	282	ØRP64KZ	282	ØRPE43Z	264, 724	ØRPL35Z	265, 724	ØRPR35Z	262, 645	ØRPW05Z	262, 646
ØRP10JZ	240, 724	ØRP900Z	282	ØRPE44Z	264, 724	ØRPL37Z	265, 724	ØRPR3JZ	241, 646, 951	ØRPW07Z	262, 646
ØRP10JZ	951	ØRP903Z	282	ØRPE47Z	264, 724	ØRPL3JZ	241, 724, 951	ØRPR3KZ	262, 646	ØRPW0JZ	241, 646, 951
ØRP10KZ	282	ØRP907Z	282	ØRPE4JZ	241, 724, 951	ØRPL3KZ	265, 724	ØRPR40Z	262, 646	ØRPW0KZ	262, 646
ØRP134Z	282	ØRP90JZ	240, 724	ØRPE4KZ	264, 724	ØRPL40Z	265, 724	ØRPR43Z	262, 646	ØRPW34Z	262, 646
ØRP137Z	282	ØRP90JZ	951	ØRPF00Z	264, 724	ØRPL43Z	265, 724	ØRPR44Z	262, 646	ØRPW35Z	262, 646
ØRP13AZ	282	ØRP90KZ	282	ØRPF03Z	264, 724	ØRPL44Z	265, 724	ØRPR45Z	262, 646	ØRPW37Z	262, 646
ØRP13JZ	240, 724	ØRP937Z	282	ØRPF04Z	264, 724	ØRPL45Z	265, 724	ØRPR47Z	262, 646	ØRPW3JZ	241, 646, 951
ØRP13JZ	951	ØRP93JZ	240, 724	ØRPF07Z	264, 724	ØRPL47Z	265, 724	ØRPR4JZ	241, 646, 951	ØRPW3KZ	262, 646
ØRP13KZ	282	ØRP93JZ	951	ØRPF0JZ	241, 725, 951	ØRPL4JZ	241, 725, 951	ØRPR4KZ	262, 646	ØRPW40Z	262, 646
ØRP140Z	282	ØRP93KZ	282	ØRPF0KZ	264, 724	ØRPL4KZ	265, 725	ØRPS00Z	262, 646	ØRPW43Z	262, 646
ØRP143Z	282	ØRP940Z	282	ØRPF34Z	264, 724	ØRPM00Z	265, 725	ØRPS03Z	262, 646	ØRPW45Z	262, 646
ØRP144Z	282	ØRP943Z	282	ØRPF37Z	264, 724	ØRPM03Z	265, 725			ØRPW47Z	262, 646
ØRP147Z	282	ØRP947Z	282	ØRPF3JZ	241, 724, 951	ØRPM04Z	265, 725			ØRPW4JZ	241, 646, 951
ØRP14AZ	282	ØRP94AZ	282	ØRPF3KZ	264, 724	ØRPM05Z	265, 725			ØRPW4KZ	262, 646
ØRP14JZ	240, 724	ØRP94JZ	240, 724								
		ØRP94JZ	951								

Code	Page
ØRPXØØZ	262,646
ØRPXØ3Z	262,646
ØRPXØ4Z	262,646
ØRPXØ5Z	262,646
ØRPXØ7Z	262,646
ØRPXØJZ	241,646,951
ØRPXØKZ	262,646
ØRPX34Z	262,646
ØRPX35Z	262,646
ØRPX37Z	262,646
ØRPX3JZ	241,646,951
ØRPX3KZ	262,646
ØRPX4ØZ	262,646
ØRPX43Z	262,646
ØRPX44Z	262,646
ØRPX45Z	262,646
ØRPX47Z	262,646
ØRPX4JZ	241,646,951
ØRPX4KZ	262,646
ØRQØØZZ	283
ØRQØ3ZZ	283
ØRQØ4ZZ	283
ØRQ1ØZZ	283
ØRQ13ZZ	283
ØRQ14ZZ	283
ØRQ3ØZZ	20,289,600,625,725,951
ØRQ33ZZ	283
ØRQ34ZZ	283
ØRQ4ØZZ	283
ØRQ43ZZ	283
ØRQ44ZZ	283
ØRQ5ØZZ	283
ØRQ53ZZ	283
ØRQ54ZZ	283
ØRQ6ØZZ	283
ØRQ63ZZ	283
ØRQ64ZZ	283
ØRQ9ØZZ	20,289,600,625,725,951
ØRQ93ZZ	283
ØRQ94ZZ	283
ØRQAØZZ	283
ØRQA3ZZ	283
ØRQA4ZZ	283
ØRQBØZZ	20,289,600,625,725,951
ØRQB3ZZ	283
ØRQB4ZZ	283
ØRQCØZZ	81,283,725,951
ØRQC3ZZ	81,283,725,951
ØRQC4ZZ	81,283,725,951
ØRQDØZZ	81,283,725,951
ØRQD3ZZ	81,283,725,951
ØRQD4ZZ	81,283,725,951
ØRQEØZZ	265,725,951,1083
ØRQE3ZZ	265,725,951,1083
ØRQE4ZZ	265,725,951,1083
ØRQFØZZ	265,725,951,1083
ØRQF3ZZ	265,725,951,1083
ØRQF4ZZ	265,725,951,1083
ØRQGØZZ	265,725,951,1083
ØRQG3ZZ	265,725,951,1083
ØRQG4ZZ	265,725,951,1083
ØRQHØZZ	265,725,951,1083
ØRQH3ZZ	265,725,951,1083
ØRQH4ZZ	265,725,951,1083
ØRQJØZZ	265,725,951,1083
ØRQJ3ZZ	265,725,951,1083
ØRQJ4ZZ	265,725,951,1083
ØRQKØZZ	265,725,951,1083
ØRQK3ZZ	265,725,951,1083
ØRQK4ZZ	265,725,951,1083
ØRQLØZZ	265,725,951
ØRQL3ZZ	265,725,951
ØRQL4ZZ	265,725,951
ØRQMØZZ	265,725,951
ØRQM3ZZ	265,725,951
ØRQM4ZZ	265,725,951
ØRQNØZZ	40,262,646,952
ØRQN3ZZ	40,262,646,952
ØRQN4ZZ	40,262,646,952
ØRQPØZZ	40,262,646,952
ØRQP3ZZ	40,262,646,952
ØRQP4ZZ	40,262,646,952
ØRQQØZZ	40,262,646,952
ØRQQ3ZZ	40,262,646,952
ØRQQ4ZZ	40,262,646,952
ØRQRØZZ	40,262,646,952
ØRQR3ZZ	40,262,646,952
ØRQR4ZZ	40,262,646,952
ØRQSØZZ	40,262,646,952
ØRQS3ZZ	40,262,646,952
ØRQS4ZZ	40,262,646,952
ØRQTØZZ	40,262,646,952
ØRQT3ZZ	40,262,646,952
ØRQT4ZZ	40,262,646,952
ØRQUØZZ	40,262,646,952
ØRQU3ZZ	40,263,646,952
ØRQU4ZZ	40,263,646,952
ØRQVØZZ	40,263,646,952
ØRQV3ZZ	40,263,646,952
ØRQV4ZZ	40,263,646,952
ØRQWØZZ	40,263,646,952
ØRQW3ZZ	40,263,646,952
ØRQW4ZZ	40,263,646,952
ØRQXØZZ	40,263,646,952
ØRQX3ZZ	40,263,646,952
ØRQX4ZZ	40,263,646,952
ØRRØØ7Z	283
ØRRØØJZ	283
ØRRØØKZ	283
ØRR1Ø7Z	283
ØRR1ØJZ	283
ØRR1ØKZ	283
ØRR3Ø7Z	283
ØRR3ØJZ	289,725,952
ØRR3ØJZ	20
ØRR3ØKZ	283
ØRR4Ø7Z	283
ØRR4ØJZ	283
ØRR4ØKZ	283
ØRR5Ø7Z	283
ØRR5ØJZ	20,289,725,952
ØRR5ØKZ	283
ØRR6Ø7Z	283
ØRR6ØJZ	283
ØRR6ØKZ	283
ØRR9Ø7Z	283
ØRR9ØJZ	20,289,725,952
ØRR9ØKZ	283
ØRRAØ7Z	283
ØRRAØJZ	283
ØRRAØKZ	283
ØRRBØ7Z	283
ØRRBØJZ	20,289,725,952
ØRRBØKZ	283
ØRRC*	81,283,725
ØRRCØ7Z	952
ØRRCØJZ	952
ØRRCØKZ	952
ØRRD*	81,283,725
ØRRDØ7Z	952
ØRRDØJZ	952
ØRRDØKZ	952
ØRRE*	227,725
ØRREØ7Z	952
ØRREØJZ	952
ØRREØKZ	952
ØRRF*	227,725
ØRRFØ7Z	952
ØRRFØJZ	952
ØRRFØKZ	952
ØRRG*	227,725
ØRRGØ7Z	952
ØRRGØJZ	952
ØRRGØKZ	952
ØRRH*	227,725
ØRRHØ7Z	952
ØRRHØJZ	952
ØRRHØKZ	952
ØRRJ*	227,725
ØRRJØØZ	952
ØRRJØ7Z	952
ØRRJØJ6	952
ØRRJØJ7	952
ØRRJØJZ	952
ØRRJØKZ	952
ØRRK*	227,725
ØRRKØØZ	952
ØRRKØ7Z	952
ØRRKØJ6	952
ØRRKØJ7	952
ØRRKØJZ	952
ØRRKØKZ	952
ØRRL*	227,725
ØRRLØ7Z	952
ØRRLØJZ	952
ØRRLØKZ	952
ØRRM*	227,725
ØRRMØ7Z	952
ØRRMØJZ	952
ØRRMØKZ	952
ØRRN*	227,725
ØRRNØ7Z	952
ØRRNØJZ	952
ØRRNØKZ	952
ØRRP*	227,725
ØRRPØ7Z	952
ØRRPØJZ	952
ØRRPØKZ	952
ØRRQ*	40,263
ØRRQØ7Z	646,952
ØRRQØJZ	646,952
ØRRQØKZ	646,952
ØRRR*	40,263
ØRRRØ7Z	646,952
ØRRRØJZ	646,952
ØRRRØKZ	646,952
ØRRS*	40,263
ØRRSØ7Z	646
ØRRSØ7Z	952
ØRRSØJZ	646
ØRRSØJZ	952
ØRRSØKZ	646
ØRRSØKZ	952
ØRRT*	40,263
ØRRTØ7Z	646
ØRRTØ7Z	952
ØRRTØJZ	646
ØRRTØJZ	952
ØRRTØKZ	646
ØRRTØKZ	952
ØRRU*	40,263
ØRRUØ7Z	646,952
ØRRUØJZ	646,952
ØRRUØKZ	646,952
ØRRV*	40,263
ØRRVØ7Z	646,952
ØRRVØJZ	646,952
ØRRVØKZ	646,952
ØRRW*	40,263
ØRRWØ7Z	646,952
ØRRWØJZ	646,952
ØRRWØKZ	646,952
ØRRX*	40,263
ØRRXØ7Z	647,952
ØRRXØJZ	647,952
ØRRXØKZ	647,952
ØRSØØ4Z	283,725,952
ØRSØØZZ	283,725,952
ØRS1Ø4Z	283,725,952
ØRS1ØZZ	283,725,952
ØRS4Ø4Z	283,725,952
ØRS4ØZZ	283,725,952
ØRS6Ø4Z	283,725,952
ØRS6ØZZ	283,725,952
ØRSAØ4Z	283,725,952
ØRSAØZZ	283,725,952
ØRSCØ4Z	69,283,725,952
ØRSCØZZ	69,283,725,952
ØRSDØ4Z	69,283,725,952
ØRSDØZZ	69,283,725,952
ØRSEØ4Z	268,725
ØRSEØ4Z	952
ØRSEØZZ	268,725,952
ØRSFØ4Z	268,725
ØRSFØ4Z	952
ØRSFØZZ	268,725,952
ØRSGØ4Z	268,725
ØRSGØ4Z	952
ØRSGØZZ	268,725,952
ØRSHØ4Z	268,725
ØRSHØ4Z	952
ØRSHØZZ	268,725,952
ØRSJØ4Z	268,725,952
ØRSJØZZ	268,725,952
ØRSKØ4Z	268,725,952
ØRSKØZZ	268,725,952
ØRSLØ4Z	268,725,952
ØRSLØ5Z	268,725,952
ØRSLØZZ	268,725,952
ØRSMØ4Z	268,725,952
ØRSMØ5Z	268,725,952
ØRSMØZZ	268,725,952
ØRSNØ4Z	271,647,952
ØRSNØ5Z	271,647,952
ØRSNØZZ	271,647,952
ØRSPØ4Z	271,647,952
ØRSPØ5Z	271,647,952
ØRSPØZZ	271,647,952
ØRSQØ4Z	271,647,952
ØRSQØ5Z	271,647,952
ØRSQØZZ	271,647,952
ØRSRØ4Z	271,647,952
ØRSRØ5Z	271,647,952
ØRSRØZZ	271,647,952
ØRSSØ4Z	271,647,952
ØRSSØ5Z	271,647,952
ØRSSØZZ	271,647,952
ØRSTØ4Z	271,647,952
ØRSTØ5Z	271,647,952
ØRSTØZZ	271,647,952
ØRSUØ4Z	271,647,952
ØRSUØ5Z	271,647,952
ØRSUØZZ	271,647,952
ØRSVØ4Z	271,647,952
ØRSVØ5Z	271,647,952
ØRSVØZZ	271,647,952
ØRSWØ4Z	271,647,952
ØRSWØ5Z	271,647,952
ØRSWØZZ	271,647,952
ØRSXØ4Z	271,647,952
ØRSXØ5Z	271,647,952
ØRSXØZZ	271,647,952
ØRT3ØZZ	20,289,725,952
ØRT4ØZZ	20,289,725,952
ØRT5ØZZ	20,289,725,952
ØRT9ØZZ	20,289,725,952
ØRTBØZZ	20,289,725,952
ØRTCØZZ	69,283,725,952
ØRTDØZZ	69,283,725,952
ØRTEØZZ	268,725,952
ØRTFØZZ	268,725,952
ØRTGØZZ	268,725,952
ØRTHØZZ	268,725,952
ØRTJØZZ	268,725,952
ØRTKØZZ	268,725,953
ØRTLØZZ	268,725,953
ØRTMØZZ	268,725,953
ØRTNØZZ	271,647,953
ØRTPØZZ	271,647,953
ØRTQØZZ	271,647,953
ØRTRØZZ	271,647,953
ØRTSØZZ	271,647,953
ØRTTØZZ	271,647,953
ØRTUØZZ	271,647,953
ØRTVØZZ	271,647,953
ØRTWØZZ	271,437,647,953
ØRTXØZZ	271,437,647,953
ØRUØØ7Z	283
ØRUØØJZ	20,289,725,953
ØRUØØKZ	283
ØRUØ37Z	283
ØRUØ3JZ	20,289,725,953
ØRUØ3KZ	283
ØRUØ47Z	283
ØRUØ4JZ	20,289,725,953
ØRUØ4KZ	283
ØRU1Ø7Z	283
ØRU1ØJZ	20,289,725,953
ØRU1ØKZ	283
ØRU137Z	283
ØRU13JZ	20,289,725,953
ØRU13KZ	283
ØRU147Z	283
ØRU14JZ	20,289,725,953
ØRU14KZ	283
ØRU3*	289,725
ØRU3Ø7Z	20,600,625,953
ØRU3ØJZ	20,600,625,953
ØRU3ØKZ	20,600,625,953
ØRU337Z	20,600,625,953
ØRU33JZ	20,600,625,953
ØRU33KZ	20,600,625,953
ØRU347Z	20,600,625,953
ØRU34JZ	20,600,625,953
ØRU34KZ	20,600,625,953
ØRU4Ø7Z	283
ØRU4ØJZ	20,289,725,953
ØRU4ØKZ	283
ØRU437Z	283
ØRU43JZ	20,289,725,953
ØRU43KZ	283
ØRU447Z	283
ØRU44JZ	20,289,725,953
ØRU44KZ	283
ØRU5Ø7Z	283
ØRU5ØJZ	20,289,725,953
ØRU5ØKZ	283
ØRU537Z	283
ØRU53JZ	20,289,725,953
ØRU53KZ	283
ØRU547Z	283
ØRU54JZ	20,289,725,953
ØRU54KZ	283
ØRU6Ø7Z	283
ØRU6ØJZ	20,289,725,953
ØRU6ØKZ	283
ØRU637Z	283
ØRU63JZ	20,290,725,953
ØRU63KZ	283
ØRU647Z	283
ØRU64JZ	20,290,725,953
ØRU64KZ	283
ØRU9*	289,725
ØRU9Ø7Z	20,600,625,953
ØRU9ØJZ	20,600,625,953
ØRU9ØKZ	20,600,625,953
ØRU937Z	20,600,625,953
ØRU93JZ	20,600,625,953
ØRU93KZ	20,600,625,953
ØRU947Z	20,600,625,953
ØRU94JZ	20,600,625,953
ØRU94KZ	20,600,625,953
ØRUAØ7Z	283
ØRUAØJZ	20,290,725,953
ØRUAØKZ	283
ØRUA37Z	283
ØRUA3JZ	20,290,725,953
ØRUA3KZ	283
ØRUA47Z	283
ØRUA4JZ	20,290,725,953
ØRUA4KZ	283
ØRUB*	289,725
ØRUBØ7Z	20,600,625,953
ØRUBØJZ	20,600,625,953
ØRUBØKZ	20,600,625,953
ØRUB37Z	20,600,625,953
ØRUB3JZ	20,600,625,953
ØRUB3KZ	20,600,625,953
ØRUB47Z	20,600,625,953
ØRUB4JZ	20,600,625,953
ØRUB4KZ	20,600,625,953
ØRUC*	81,283,725
ØRUCØ7Z	953
ØRUCØJZ	953
ØRUCØKZ	953
ØRUC37Z	953
ØRUC3JZ	953
ØRUC3KZ	953
ØRUC47Z	953
ØRUC4JZ	953
ØRUC4KZ	953
ØRUD*	81,283,725
ØRUDØ7Z	953
ØRUDØJZ	953
ØRUDØKZ	953
ØRUD37Z	953
ØRUD3JZ	953
ØRUD3KZ	953
ØRUD47Z	953
ØRUD4JZ	953
ØRUD4KZ	953
ØRUE*	265,725
ØRUEØ7Z	953,1083
ØRUEØJZ	953,1083
ØRUEØKZ	953,1083
ØRUE37Z	953,1083
ØRUE3JZ	953,1083
ØRUE3KZ	953,1083
ØRUE47Z	953,1083
ØRUE4JZ	953,1083
ØRUE4KZ	953,1083
ØRUF*	265,725
ØRUFØ7Z	953,1083
ØRUFØJZ	953,1083
ØRUFØKZ	953,1083
ØRUF37Z	953,1083
ØRUF3JZ	953,1083
ØRUF3KZ	953,1083
ØRUF47Z	953,1083
ØRUF4JZ	953,1083
ØRUF4KZ	953,1083
ØRUG*	265,725
ØRUGØ7Z	953,1083
ØRUGØJZ	953,1083
ØRUGØKZ	953,1083
ØRUG37Z	953,1083
ØRUG3JZ	953,1083
ØRUG3KZ	953,1083
ØRUG47Z	953,1083
ØRUG4JZ	953,1083
ØRUG4KZ	953,1083
ØRUH*	265,725
ØRUHØ7Z	953,1083
ØRUHØJZ	953,1083
ØRUHØKZ	953,1083
ØRUH37Z	953,1083
ØRUH3JZ	953,1083
ØRUH3KZ	953,1083
ØRUH47Z	953,1083
ØRUH4JZ	953,1083
ØRUH4KZ	953,1083
ØRUJ*	265,725
ØRUJØ7Z	953,1083
ØRUJØJZ	953,1083
ØRUJØKZ	953,1083
ØRUJ37Z	953,1083
ØRUJ3JZ	953,1083
ØRUJ3KZ	953,1083
ØRUJ47Z	953,1083
ØRUJ4JZ	953,1083
ØRUJ4KZ	953,1083
ØRUK*	265,725
ØRUKØ7Z	953,1083
ØRUKØJZ	953,1083
ØRUKØKZ	953,1083
ØRUK37Z	953,1083
ØRUK3JZ	953,1083
ØRUK3KZ	953,1083
ØRUK47Z	953,1083
ØRUK4JZ	953,1083
ØRUK4KZ	953,1083
ØRUL*	265,725
ØRULØ7Z	953
ØRULØJZ	953
ØRULØKZ	953
ØRUL37Z	953
ØRUL3JZ	953
ØRUL3KZ	953
ØRUL47Z	953
ØRUL4JZ	953
ØRUL4KZ	953
ØRUM*	265,725
ØRUMØ7Z	953
ØRUMØJZ	953
ØRUMØKZ	953
ØRUM37Z	953
ØRUM3JZ	953
ØRUM3KZ	953
ØRUM47Z	953
ØRUM4JZ	953
ØRUM4KZ	953
ØRUN*	40,263
ØRUNØ7Z	647,953
ØRUNØJZ	647,953
ØRUNØKZ	647,953
ØRUN37Z	647,953
ØRUN3JZ	647,953
ØRUN3KZ	647,953
ØRUN47Z	647,953
ØRUN4JZ	647,953
ØRUN4KZ	647,953
ØRUP*	40,263
ØRUPØ7Z	647,953
ØRUPØJZ	647,953
ØRUPØKZ	647,953
ØRUP37Z	647,953
ØRUP3JZ	647,953
ØRUP3KZ	647,953
ØRUP47Z	647,953
ØRUP4JZ	647,953
ØRUP4KZ	647,953
ØRUQ*	40,263
ØRUQØ7Z	647,953
ØRUQØJZ	647,953
ØRUQØKZ	647,953
ØRUQ37Z	647,953
ØRUQ3JZ	647,953
ØRUQ3KZ	647,953
ØRUQ47Z	647,953
ØRUQ4JZ	647,953
ØRUQ4KZ	647,954
ØRUR*	40,263
ØRURØ7Z	647,954
ØRURØJZ	647,954
ØRURØKZ	647,954
ØRUR37Z	647,954
ØRUR3JZ	647,954

Numeric Index to Procedures

Code	Page	Code	Page	Code	Page	Code	Page	Code	Page	Code	Page
ØRUR3KZ	647,954	ØRW04KZ	283	ØRW637Z	284	ØRWD04Z	81	ØRWH38Z	266,726	ØRWM43Z	266,727
ØRUR47Z	647,954	ØRW100Z	283	ØRW638Z	284	ØRWD07Z	81	ØRWH3JZ	284,726,954	ØRWM44Z	266,727
ØRUR4JZ	647,954	ØRW103Z	283	ØRW63AZ	284	ØRWD08Z	81	ØRWH3KZ	266,726	ØRWM45Z	266,727
ØRUR4KZ	647,954	ØRW104Z	283,725,954	ØRW63JZ	284,726,954	ØRWD0JZ	81	ØRWH40Z	266,726	ØRWM47Z	266,727
ØRUS*	40,263	ØRW107Z	283	ØRW63KZ	284	ØRWD0KZ	81	ØRWH43Z	266,726	ØRWM48Z	266,727
ØRUS07Z	647,954	ØRW108Z	283	ØRW640Z	284	ØRWD30Z	81	ØRWH44Z	266,726	ØRWM4JZ	284,727,954
ØRUS0JZ	647,954	ØRW10AZ	283	ØRW643Z	284	ØRWD33Z	81	ØRWH47Z	266,726	ØRWM4KZ	266,727
ØRUS0KZ	647,954	ØRW10JZ	283,725,954	ØRW644Z	284,726,954	ØRWD34Z	81	ØRWH48Z	266,726	ØRWN00Z	263,647
ØRUS37Z	647,954	ØRW10KZ	283	ØRW647Z	284	ØRWD37Z	81	ØRWH4JZ	284,726,954	ØRWN04Z	263,647
ØRUS3JZ	647,954	ØRW130Z	283	ØRW648Z	284	ØRWD38Z	81	ØRWH4KZ	266,726	ØRWN05Z	263,647
ØRUS3KZ	647,954	ØRW133Z	283	ØRW64AZ	284	ØRWD3JZ	81	ØRWJ00Z	266,726	ØRWN07Z	263,647
ØRUS47Z	647,954	ØRW134Z	283,725,954	ØRW64JZ	284,726,954	ØRWD3KZ	81	ØRWJ03Z	266,726	ØRWN08Z	263,647
ØRUS4JZ	647,954	ØRW137Z	283	ØRW64KZ	284	ØRWD40Z	81	ØRWJ04Z	266,726	ØRWN0JZ	284,727,954
ØRUS4KZ	647,954	ØRW138Z	283	ØRW900Z	284	ØRWD43Z	81	ØRWJ07Z	266,726	ØRWN0KZ	263,647
ØRUT*	40,263	ØRW13AZ	284	ØRW903Z	284	ØRWD47Z	81	ØRWJ08Z	266,726	ØRWN33Z	263,647
ØRUT07Z	647,954	ØRW13JZ	284,725,954	ØRW907Z	284	ØRWD48Z	81	ØRWJ0JZ	284,726,954	ØRWN34Z	263,647
ØRUT0JZ	647,954	ØRW13KZ	284	ØRW90JZ	289,726,954	ØRWD4JZ	81	ØRWJ0KZ	266,726	ØRWN35Z	263,647
ØRUT0KZ	647,954	ØRW140Z	284	ØRW90JZ	20	ØRWD4KZ	81	ØRWJ30Z	266,726	ØRWN37Z	263,647
ØRUT37Z	647,954	ØRW143Z	284	ØRW90KZ	284	ØRWE00Z	265,726	ØRWJ33Z	266,726	ØRWN38Z	263,647
ØRUT3JZ	647,954	ØRW144Z	284,725,954	ØRW930Z	284	ØRWE03Z	265,726	ØRWJ34Z	266,726	ØRWN3JZ	284,727,954
ØRUT3KZ	647,954	ØRW147Z	284	ØRW933Z	284	ØRWE04Z	265,726	ØRWJ37Z	266,726	ØRWN40Z	263,647
ØRUT47Z	647,954	ØRW148Z	284	ØRW937Z	284	ØRWE07Z	265,726	ØRWJ38Z	266,726	ØRWN43Z	263,647
ØRUT4JZ	647,954	ØRW14AZ	284	ØRW93JZ	289,726,954	ØRWE08Z	265,726	ØRWJ3JZ	284,726,954	ØRWN44Z	263,647
ØRUT4KZ	647,954	ØRW14JZ	284,725,954	ØRW93JZ	20	ØRWE0JZ	265,726	ØRWJ3KZ	266,726	ØRWN45Z	263,647
ØRUU*	40,263	ØRW14KZ	284	ØRW93KZ	284	ØRWE0KZ	265,726	ØRWJ40Z	266,726	ØRWN47Z	263,647
ØRUU07Z	647,954	ØRW300Z	284	ØRW940Z	284	ØRWE33Z	265,726	ØRWJ43Z	266,726	ØRWN48Z	263,647
ØRUU0JZ	647,954	ØRW303Z	284	ØRW943Z	284	ØRWE34Z	265,726	ØRWJ44Z	266,726	ØRWN4KZ	263,647
ØRUU0KZ	647,954	ØRW307Z	284	ØRW947Z	284	ØRWE37Z	265,726	ØRWJ47Z	266,726	ØRWP00Z	263,647
ØRUU37Z	647,954	ØRW30JZ	20,289,725,954	ØRW94JZ	289,726,954	ØRWE38Z	265,726	ØRWJ48Z	266,726	ØRWP03Z	263,647
ØRUU3JZ	647,954	ØRW30KZ	284	ØRW94JZ	20	ØRWE3JZ	265,726	ØRWJ4JZ	284,726,954	ØRWP04Z	263,647
ØRUU3KZ	647,954	ØRW330Z	284	ØRW94KZ	284	ØRWE3KZ	265,726	ØRWJ4KZ	266,726	ØRWP05Z	263,647
ØRUU47Z	647,954	ØRW333Z	284	ØRWA00Z	284	ØRWE40Z	265,726	ØRWK00Z	266,726	ØRWP07Z	263,647
ØRUU4JZ	647,954	ØRW337Z	284	ØRWA03Z	284	ØRWE43Z	265,726	ØRWK04Z	266,726	ØRWP08Z	263,647
ØRUU4KZ	647,954	ØRW33JZ	20,289,725,954	ØRWA04Z	284,726,954	ØRWE44Z	265,726	ØRWK07Z	266,726	ØRWP0JZ	284,727,954
ØRUV*	40,263	ØRW33KZ	284	ØRWA07Z	284	ØRWE47Z	265,726	ØRWK08Z	266,726	ØRWP0KZ	263,647
ØRUV07Z	647,954	ØRW340Z	284	ØRWA08Z	284	ØRWE48Z	265,726	ØRWK0JZ	284,726,954	ØRWP30Z	263,647
ØRUV0JZ	647,954	ØRW343Z	284	ØRWA0AZ	284	ØRWE4JZ	265,726	ØRWK0KZ	266,726	ØRWP33Z	263,647
ØRUV0KZ	647,954	ØRW347Z	284	ØRWA0JZ	284,726,954	ØRWE4KZ	265,726	ØRWK30Z	266,726	ØRWP34Z	263,647
ØRUV37Z	647,954	ØRW34JZ	20,289,725,954	ØRWA0KZ	284	ØRWF00Z	265,726	ØRWK33Z	266,726	ØRWP35Z	263,647
ØRUV3JZ	647,954	ØRW34KZ	284	ØRWA30Z	284	ØRWF03Z	265,726	ØRWK34Z	266,726	ØRWP37Z	263,647
ØRUV3KZ	647,954	ØRW400Z	284	ØRWA33Z	284	ØRWF04Z	265,726	ØRWK37Z	266,726	ØRWP38Z	263,647
ØRUV47Z	647,954	ØRW403Z	284	ØRWA34Z	284,726,954	ØRWF07Z	265,726	ØRWK38Z	266,726	ØRWP3JZ	284,727,954
ØRUV4JZ	647,954	ØRW404Z	284,725,954	ØRWA37Z	284	ØRWF08Z	265,726	ØRWK3JZ	284,726,954	ØRWP3KZ	263,647
ØRUV4KZ	647,954	ØRW407Z	284	ØRWA38Z	284	ØRWF0JZ	265,726	ØRWK3KZ	266,726	ØRWP40Z	263,647
ØRUW*	40,263	ØRW408Z	284	ØRWA3AZ	284	ØRWF0KZ	265,726	ØRWK40Z	266,726	ØRWP43Z	263,647
ØRUW07Z	647,954	ØRW40AZ	284	ØRWA3JZ	284,726,954	ØRWF30Z	265,726	ØRWK43Z	266,726	ØRWP44Z	263,647
ØRUW0JZ	647,954	ØRW40JZ	284,725,954	ØRWA3KZ	284	ØRWF33Z	265,726	ØRWK44Z	266,726	ØRWP45Z	263,647
ØRUW0KZ	647,954	ØRW40KZ	284	ØRWA40Z	284	ØRWF37Z	265,726	ØRWK47Z	266,726	ØRWP47Z	263,647
ØRUW37Z	647,954	ØRW430Z	284	ØRWA43Z	284	ØRWF38Z	265,726	ØRWK48Z	266,726	ØRWP48Z	263,647
ØRUW3JZ	647,954	ØRW433Z	284	ØRWA44Z	284,726,954	ØRWF3JZ	265,726	ØRWK4JZ	284,726,954	ØRWP4JZ	284,727,954
ØRUW3KZ	647,954	ØRW434Z	284,725,954	ØRWA47Z	284	ØRWF3KZ	265,726	ØRWK4KZ	266,726	ØRWP4KZ	263,648
ØRUW47Z	647,954	ØRW437Z	284	ØRWA48Z	284	ØRWF40Z	265,726	ØRWL00Z	266,726	ØRWQ00Z	263,648
ØRUW4JZ	647,954	ØRW438Z	284	ØRWA4AZ	284	ØRWF43Z	265,726	ØRWL03Z	266,726	ØRWQ03Z	263,648
ØRUW4KZ	647,954	ØRW43AZ	284	ØRWA4JZ	284,726,954	ØRWF44Z	265,726	ØRWL04Z	266,726	ØRWQ04Z	263,648
ØRUX*	40,263	ØRW43JZ	284,725,954	ØRWA4KZ	284	ØRWF47Z	265,726	ØRWL05Z	266,726	ØRWQ05Z	263,648
ØRUX07Z	647,954	ØRW43KZ	284	ØRWB00Z	284	ØRWF48Z	265,726	ØRWL07Z	266,726	ØRWQ07Z	263,648
ØRUX0JZ	647,954	ØRW440Z	284	ØRWB03Z	284	ØRWF4JZ	265,726	ØRWL08Z	266,726	ØRWQ08Z	263,648
ØRUX0KZ	647,954	ØRW443Z	284	ØRWB07Z	284	ØRWF4KZ	265,726	ØRWL0JZ	284,726,954	ØRWQ0JZ	284,727,954
ØRUX37Z	647,954	ØRW444Z	284,725,954	ØRWB0JZ	20,289,726,954	ØRWG00Z	265,726	ØRWL0KZ	266,726	ØRWQ0KZ	263,648
ØRUX3JZ	647,954	ØRW447Z	284	ØRWB0KZ	284	ØRWG03Z	265,726	ØRWL30Z	266,726	ØRWQ30Z	263,648
ØRUX3KZ	647,954	ØRW448Z	284	ØRWB30Z	284	ØRWG04Z	265,726	ØRWL33Z	266,726	ØRWQ33Z	263,648
ØRUX47Z	647,954	ØRW44AZ	284	ØRWB33Z	284	ØRWG07Z	265,726	ØRWL34Z	266,726	ØRWQ34Z	263,648
ØRUX4JZ	647,954	ØRW44JZ	284,725,954	ØRWB37Z	284	ØRWG08Z	265,726	ØRWL35Z	266,726	ØRWQ35Z	263,648
ØRUX4KZ	647,954	ØRW44KZ	284	ØRWB3JZ	20,289,726,954	ØRWG0JZ	284,726,954	ØRWL37Z	266,726	ØRWQ37Z	263,648
ØRW000Z	283	ØRW500Z	284	ØRWB3KZ	284	ØRWG30Z	265,726	ØRWL38Z	266,726	ØRWQ38Z	263,648
ØRW003Z	283	ØRW503Z	284	ØRWB40Z	284	ØRWG33Z	265,726	ØRWL3JZ	284,726,954	ØRWQ3JZ	284,727,954
ØRW004Z	283	ØRW507Z	284	ØRWB43Z	284	ØRWG37Z	265,726	ØRWL3KZ	266,726	ØRWQ3KZ	263,648
ØRW004Z	725,954	ØRW50JZ	725,954	ØRWB47Z	284	ØRWG38Z	265,726	ØRWL40Z	266,726	ØRWQ40Z	263,648
ØRW007Z	283	ØRW50JZ	20,289	ØRWB4JZ	20,289,726,954	ØRWG3JZ	284,726,954	ØRWL43Z	266,726	ØRWQ43Z	263,648
ØRW008Z	283	ØRW50KZ	284	ØRWB4KZ	284	ØRWG3KZ	266,726	ØRWL44Z	266,726	ØRWQ44Z	263,648
ØRW00AZ	283	ØRW530Z	284	ØRWC03Z	81	ØRWG40Z	266,726	ØRWL45Z	266,726	ØRWQ45Z	263,648
ØRW00JZ	283	ØRW533Z	284	ØRWC04Z	81	ØRWG43Z	266,726	ØRWL47Z	266,726	ØRWQ47Z	263,648
ØRW00JZ	725,954	ØRW537Z	284	ØRWC07Z	81	ØRWG44Z	266,726	ØRWL48Z	266,726	ØRWQ48Z	263,648
ØRW00KZ	283	ØRW53JZ	725,954	ØRWC08Z	81	ØRWG47Z	266,726	ØRWL4JZ	284,726,954	ØRWQ4JZ	284,727,954
ØRW030Z	283	ØRW53JZ	20,289	ØRWC0JZ	81	ØRWG48Z	266,726	ØRWL4KZ	266,726	ØRWQ4KZ	263,648
ØRW033Z	283	ØRW53KZ	284	ØRWC0KZ	81	ØRWG4JZ	284,726,954	ØRWM00Z	266,726	ØRWR00Z	263,648
ØRW034Z	283	ØRW540Z	284	ØRWC30Z	81	ØRWG4KZ	266,726	ØRWM03Z	266,726	ØRWR03Z	263,648
ØRW034Z	725,954	ØRW543Z	284	ØRWC33Z	81	ØRWH00Z	266,726	ØRWM04Z	266,726	ØRWR04Z	263,648
ØRW037Z	283	ØRW547Z	284	ØRWC34Z	81	ØRWH03Z	266,726	ØRWM05Z	266,726	ØRWR05Z	263,648
ØRW038Z	283	ØRW54JZ	725,954	ØRWC37Z	81	ØRWH04Z	266,726	ØRWM07Z	266,726	ØRWR07Z	263,648
ØRW03AZ	283	ØRW54JZ	20,289	ØRWC38Z	81	ØRWH07Z	266,726	ØRWM08Z	266,726	ØRWR08Z	263,648
ØRW03JZ	283	ØRW54KZ	284	ØRWC3JZ	81	ØRWH08Z	266,726	ØRWM0JZ	284,726,954	ØRWR0JZ	284,727,954
ØRW03JZ	725,954	ØRW600Z	284	ØRWC3KZ	81	ØRWH0JZ	284,726,954	ØRWM0KZ	266,726	ØRWR0KZ	263,648
ØRW03KZ	283	ØRW603Z	284	ØRWC40Z	81	ØRWH0KZ	266,726	ØRWM30Z	266,727	ØRWR30Z	263,648
ØRW040Z	283	ØRW604Z	284,725,954	ØRWC43Z	81	ØRWH30Z	266,726	ØRWM33Z	266,727	ØRWR33Z	263,648
ØRW043Z	283	ØRW607Z	284	ØRWC44Z	81	ØRWH33Z	266,726	ØRWM34Z	266,727	ØRWR34Z	263,648
ØRW044Z	283	ØRW608Z	284	ØRWC47Z	81	ØRWH34Z	266,726	ØRWM35Z	266,727	ØRWR35Z	263,648
ØRW044Z	725,954	ØRW60AZ	284	ØRWC48Z	81	ØRWH37Z	266,726	ØRWM37Z	266,727	ØRWR37Z	263,648
ØRW047Z	283	ØRW60JZ	284,725,954	ØRWC4JZ	81			ØRWM38Z	266,727	ØRWR38Z	263,648
ØRW048Z	283	ØRW60KZ	284	ØRWC4KZ	81			ØRWM3JZ	284,727,954		
ØRW04AZ	283	ØRW630Z	284	ØRWD00Z	81			ØRWM3KZ	266,727		
ØRW04JZ	725,954	ØRW634Z	284,726,954	ØRWD03Z	81			ØRWM40Z	266,727		

Code	Page	Code	Page	Code	Page	Code	Page	Code	Page	Code	Page
ØRWR3JZ	284, 727, 954	ØRWV35Z	264, 648	ØS584ZZ	955	ØS9K00Z	258, 727, 1084	ØSBJ3ZZ	258, 727, 955, 1084	ØSG0070	20, 211, 727, 955
ØRWR3KZ	263, 648	ØRWV37Z	264, 648	ØS59*	243	ØS9K0ZZ	258, 727, 1084			ØSG0071	20, 211, 727, 955
ØRWR40Z	263, 648	ØRWV38Z	264, 648	ØS590ZZ	955	ØS9L00Z	258, 727, 1084	ØSBJ4ZZ	258, 727, 955, 1084	ØSG007J	20, 211, 727, 955
ØRWR43Z	263, 648	ØRWV3JZ	284, 727, 954	ØS593ZZ	955	ØS9L0ZZ	258, 727, 1084			ØSG00A0	20, 211, 727, 955
ØRWR44Z	263, 648	ØRWV3KZ	264, 648	ØS594ZZ	955	ØS9M00Z	258, 727, 1084	ØSBK0ZZ	258, 727, 955, 1084	ØSG00AJ	20, 211, 727, 955
ØRWR45Z	263, 648	ØRWV40Z	264, 648	ØS5B*	243	ØS9M0ZZ	258, 727, 1084			ØSG00J0	20, 211, 727, 955
ØRWR47Z	263, 648	ØRWV43Z	264, 648	ØS5B0ZZ	955	ØS9N00Z	258, 727, 1084	ØSBK3ZZ	258, 727, 955, 1084	ØSG00J1	20, 211, 727, 955
ØRWR48Z	263, 648	ØRWV44Z	264, 648	ØS5B3ZZ	955	ØS9N0ZZ	258, 727, 1084			ØSG00JJ	20, 211, 727, 955
ØRWR4JZ	284, 727, 954	ØRWV45Z	264, 648	ØS5B4ZZ	955	ØS9P00Z	258, 727, 1084	ØSBK4ZZ	258, 727, 955, 1084	ØSG00K0	20, 211, 727, 955
ØRWR4KZ	263, 648	ØRWV47Z	264, 648	ØS5C*	241	ØS9P0ZZ	258, 727, 1084			ØSG00K1	20, 211, 727, 955
ØRWS00Z	263, 648	ØRWV48Z	264, 648	ØS5C0ZZ	955, 1083	ØS9Q00Z	258, 727, 1084	ØSBL0ZZ	258, 727, 955, 1084	ØSG00KJ	20, 211, 727, 955
ØRWS03Z	263, 648	ØRWV4JZ	284, 727, 954	ØS5C3ZZ	955, 1083	ØS9Q0ZZ	258, 727, 1084	ØSBL3ZZ	258, 727, 955, 1084	ØSG0370	20, 211, 727, 955
ØRWS04Z	263, 648	ØRWV4KZ	264, 648	ØS5C4ZZ	955, 1083	ØSB00ZZ	20, 289, 600, 625, 727, 955			ØSG0371	20, 211, 727, 955
ØRWS05Z	263, 648	ØRWW00Z	264, 648	ØS5D*	241			ØSBL4ZZ	258, 727, 955, 1084	ØSG037J	20, 211, 727, 955
ØRWS07Z	263, 648	ØRWW03Z	264, 648	ØS5D0ZZ	955, 1083	ØSB03ZZ	20, 289, 600, 625, 727, 955			ØSG03A0	20, 211, 727, 955
ØRWS08Z	263, 648	ØRWW04Z	264, 648	ØS5D3ZZ	955, 1083			ØSBM0ZZ	258, 727, 955, 1084	ØSG03AJ	20, 211, 727, 955
ØRWS0JZ	284, 727, 954	ØRWW05Z	264, 648	ØS5D4ZZ	955, 1083	ØSB04ZZ	20, 289, 600, 625, 727, 955			ØSG03J0	20, 211, 727, 955
ØRWS0KZ	263, 648	ØRWW07Z	264, 648	ØS5F*	231			ØSBM3ZZ	258, 727, 955, 1084	ØSG03J1	20, 211, 727, 955
ØRWS30Z	263, 648	ØRWW08Z	264, 648	ØS5F0ZZ	955	ØSB20ZZ	20, 289, 727, 955			ØSG03JJ	20, 211, 727, 955
ØRWS33Z	263, 648	ØRWW0JZ	284, 727, 954	ØS5F3ZZ	955	ØSB23ZZ	20, 289, 727, 955	ØSBM4ZZ	258, 727, 955, 1084	ØSG03K0	20, 211, 728, 955
ØRWS34Z	263, 648	ØRWW0KZ	264, 648	ØS5F4ZZ	955	ØSB24ZZ	20, 289, 727, 955			ØSG03K1	20, 211, 728, 955
ØRWS35Z	263, 648	ØRWW30Z	264, 648	ØS5G*	231	ØSB30ZZ	20, 289, 600, 625, 727, 955	ØSBN0ZZ	258, 727, 955, 1084	ØSG03KJ	20, 211, 728, 955
ØRWS37Z	263, 648	ØRWW33Z	264, 648	ØS5G0ZZ	955					ØSG0470	20, 211, 728, 955
ØRWS38Z	263, 648	ØRWW34Z	264, 648	ØS5G3ZZ	955	ØSB33ZZ	20, 289, 600, 625, 727, 955	ØSBN3ZZ	258, 727, 955, 1084	ØSG0471	20, 211, 728, 955
ØRWS3JZ	284, 727, 954	ØRWW35Z	264, 648	ØS5G4ZZ	955					ØSG047J	20, 211, 728, 955
ØRWS3KZ	263, 648	ØRWW37Z	264, 648	ØS5H*	258, 498	ØSB34ZZ	20, 289, 600, 625, 727, 955	ØSBN4ZZ	258, 727, 955, 1084	ØSG04A0	20, 211, 728, 955
ØRWS40Z	263, 648	ØRWW38Z	264, 648	ØS5H0ZZ	955, 1084					ØSG04AJ	20, 211, 728, 955
ØRWS43Z	263, 648	ØRWW3JZ	284, 727, 954	ØS5H3ZZ	955, 1084	ØSB40ZZ	20, 289, 727, 955	ØSBP0ZZ	258, 727, 955, 1084	ØSG04J0	20, 211, 728, 955
ØRWS44Z	263, 648	ØRWW3KZ	264, 648	ØS5H4ZZ	955, 1084	ØSB43ZZ	20, 289, 727, 955			ØSG04J1	20, 211, 728, 955
ØRWS45Z	263, 648	ØRWW40Z	264, 648	ØS5J*	258, 498	ØSB44ZZ	20, 289, 727, 955	ØSBP3ZZ	258, 727, 955, 1084	ØSG04JJ	20, 211, 728, 955
ØRWS47Z	263, 648	ØRWW43Z	264, 648	ØS5J0ZZ	955, 1084	ØSB50ZZ	20, 289, 600, 625, 727, 955			ØSG04K0	20, 211, 728, 955
ØRWS48Z	263, 648	ØRWW44Z	264, 648	ØS5J3ZZ	955, 1084			ØSBP4ZZ	258, 727, 955, 1084	ØSG04K1	20, 211, 728, 955
ØRWS4JZ	284, 727, 954	ØRWW45Z	264, 648	ØS5J4ZZ	955, 1084	ØSB53ZZ	20, 289, 600, 625, 727, 955			ØSG1*	213
ØRWS4KZ	263, 648	ØRWW47Z	264, 648	ØS5K*	258, 498			ØSBQ0ZZ	258, 727, 955, 1084	ØSG1070	20, 211, 213, 728, 955
ØRWT00Z	263, 648	ØRWW48Z	264, 648	ØS5K0ZZ	955, 1084	ØSB54ZZ	20, 289, 600, 625, 727, 955				
ØRWT03Z	263, 648	ØRWW4JZ	285, 727, 954	ØS5K3ZZ	955, 1084			ØSBQ3ZZ	258, 727, 955, 1084	ØSG1071	20, 212, 213, 728, 955
ØRWT04Z	263, 648	ØRWW4KZ	264, 648	ØS5K4ZZ	955, 1084	ØSB60ZZ	20, 289, 600, 625, 727, 955				
ØRWT05Z	263, 648	ØRWX00Z	264, 648	ØS5L*	258, 498			ØSBQ4ZZ	258, 727, 955, 1084	ØSG107J	20, 211, 213, 728, 955
ØRWT07Z	263, 648	ØRWX03Z	264, 648	ØS5L0ZZ	955, 1084	ØSB63ZZ	20, 289, 600, 625, 727, 955				
ØRWT08Z	263, 648	ØRWX04Z	264, 648	ØS5L3ZZ	955, 1084			ØSC0*	285	ØSG10A0	20, 211, 213, 728, 955
ØRWT0JZ	284, 727, 954	ØRWX05Z	264, 648	ØS5L4ZZ	955, 1084	ØSB64ZZ	20, 289, 600, 625, 727, 955	ØSC2*	285	ØSG10AJ	20, 211, 213, 728, 955
ØRWT0KZ	263, 648	ØRWX07Z	264, 648	ØS5M*	258, 498			ØSC3*	285		
ØRWT30Z	263, 648	ØRWX08Z	264, 648	ØS5M0ZZ	955, 1084	ØSB70ZZ	20, 289, 600, 625, 727, 955	ØSC4*	285	ØSG10J0	20, 211, 213, 728, 955
ØRWT33Z	263, 648	ØRWX0JZ	285, 727, 954	ØS5M3ZZ	955, 1084			ØSC5*	285		
ØRWT34Z	263, 648	ØRWX0KZ	264, 648	ØS5M4ZZ	955, 1084	ØSB73ZZ	20, 289, 600, 625, 727, 955	ØSC6*	285	ØSG10J1	20, 212, 213, 728, 955
ØRWT35Z	263, 648	ØRWX30Z	264, 648	ØS5N*	258, 498			ØSC7*	285		
ØRWT37Z	263, 648	ØRWX33Z	264, 648	ØS5N0ZZ	955, 1084	ØSB74ZZ	20, 289, 600, 625, 727, 955	ØSC8*	285	ØSG10JJ	20, 211, 213, 728, 955
ØRWT38Z	263, 648	ØRWX34Z	264, 648	ØS5N3ZZ	955, 1084			ØSC9*	226, 727		
ØRWT3JZ	284, 727, 954	ØRWX35Z	264, 648	ØS5N4ZZ	955, 1084	ØSB80ZZ	20, 289, 600, 625, 727, 955	ØSCB*	226, 727	ØSG10K0	20, 211, 213, 728, 955
ØRWT3KZ	263, 648	ØRWX37Z	264, 648	ØS5P*	258, 498			ØSCC*	228, 498, 727		
ØRWT40Z	263, 648	ØRWX38Z	264, 648	ØS5P0ZZ	955, 1084	ØSB83ZZ	20, 289, 600, 625, 727, 955	ØSCC0ZZ	1084	ØSG10K1	20, 212, 213, 728, 955
ØRWT43Z	263, 648	ØRWX3JZ	285, 727, 954	ØS5P3ZZ	955, 1084			ØSCC3ZZ	1084		
ØRWT44Z	263, 648	ØRWX3KZ	264, 648	ØS5P4ZZ	955, 1084	ØSB84ZZ	20, 289, 600, 625, 727, 955	ØSCC4ZZ	1084	ØSG10KJ	20, 211, 213, 728, 955
ØRWT45Z	263, 648	ØRWX40Z	264, 648	ØS5Q*	258, 498			ØSCD*	228, 498, 727		
ØRWT47Z	263, 648	ØRWX43Z	264, 648	ØS5Q0ZZ	955, 1084	ØSB90ZZ	226, 727, 852	ØSCD0ZZ	1084	ØSG1370	20, 211, 213, 728, 955
ØRWT48Z	263, 648	ØRWX44Z	264, 648	ØS5Q3ZZ	955, 1084	ØSB93ZZ	226, 727, 852	ØSCD3ZZ	1084		
ØRWT4JZ	284, 727, 954	ØRWX45Z	264, 648	ØS5Q4ZZ	955, 1084	ØSB94ZZ	226, 727, 852	ØSCD4ZZ	1084	ØSG1371	20, 212, 213, 728, 955
ØRWT4KZ	263, 648	ØRWX47Z	264, 648	ØS9000Z	285	ØSBB0ZZ	226, 727, 852	ØSCF*	231, 727		
ØRWU00Z	263, 648	ØRWX48Z	264, 648	ØS900ZZ	285	ØSBB3ZZ	226, 727, 852	ØSCG*	231, 727	ØSG137J	20, 211, 213, 728, 955
ØRWU03Z	263, 648	ØRWX4JZ	285, 727, 954	ØS9200Z	285	ØSBB4ZZ	226, 727, 852	ØSCH*	258, 727		
ØRWU04Z	263, 648	ØRWX4KZ	264, 648	ØS920ZZ	285	ØSBC0ZZ	228, 498, 727, 955, 1084	ØSCH0ZZ	1084	ØSG13A0	20, 211, 213, 728, 955
ØRWU05Z	263, 648	ØS5*	727	ØS9300Z	285			ØSCH3ZZ	1084		
ØRWU07Z	263, 648	ØS50*	241	ØS930ZZ	285	ØSBC3ZZ	228, 498, 727, 955, 1084	ØSCH4ZZ	1084	ØSG13AJ	20, 211, 213, 728, 955
ØRWU08Z	263, 648	ØS500ZZ	954	ØS9400Z	285			ØSCJ*	258, 727		
ØRWU0JZ	284, 727, 954	ØS503ZZ	954	ØS940ZZ	285	ØSBC4ZZ	228, 498, 727, 955, 1084	ØSCJ0ZZ	1084	ØSG13J0	20, 211, 213, 728, 955
ØRWU0KZ	263, 648	ØS504ZZ	954	ØS9500Z	285			ØSCJ3ZZ	1084		
ØRWU30Z	263, 648	ØS52*	289	ØS950ZZ	285	ØSBD0ZZ	228, 498, 727, 955, 1084	ØSCJ4ZZ	1084	ØSG13J1	20, 212, 213, 728, 955
ØRWU33Z	263, 648	ØS520ZZ	20, 954	ØS9600Z	285			ØSCK*	258, 727		
ØRWU34Z	263, 648	ØS523ZZ	20, 954	ØS960ZZ	285	ØSBD3ZZ	228, 498, 727, 955, 1084	ØSCK0ZZ	1084	ØSG13JJ	20, 211, 213, 728, 955
ØRWU35Z	263, 648	ØS524ZZ	20, 954	ØS9700Z	285			ØSCK3ZZ	1084		
ØRWU37Z	263, 648	ØS53*	241	ØS970ZZ	285	ØSBD4ZZ	228, 498, 727, 955, 1084	ØSCK4ZZ	1084	ØSG13K0	20, 211, 213, 728, 955
ØRWU38Z	263, 648	ØS530ZZ	954	ØS9800Z	285			ØSCL*	258, 727		
ØRWU3JZ	284, 727, 954	ØS533ZZ	954	ØS980ZZ	285	ØSBF0ZZ	231, 727, 955, 1084	ØSCL0ZZ	1084	ØSG13K1	20, 212, 213, 728, 955
ØRWU3KZ	263, 648	ØS534ZZ	954	ØS9900Z	226, 727			ØSCL3ZZ	1084		
ØRWU40Z	263, 648	ØS54*	289	ØS990ZZ	226, 727	ØSBF3ZZ	231, 727, 955, 1084	ØSCL4ZZ	1084	ØSG13KJ	20, 211, 213, 728, 955
ØRWU43Z	263, 648	ØS540ZZ	20, 954	ØS9B00Z	226, 727			ØSCM*	258, 727		
ØRWU44Z	263, 648	ØS543ZZ	20, 954	ØS9B0ZZ	226, 727	ØSBF4ZZ	231, 727, 955, 1084	ØSCM0ZZ	1084	ØSG1470	20, 211, 213, 728, 955
ØRWU45Z	263, 648	ØS544ZZ	20, 954	ØS9C00Z	228, 498, 727, 1084			ØSCM3ZZ	1084		
ØRWU47Z	264, 648	ØS55*	241			ØSBG0ZZ	231, 727, 955, 1084	ØSCM4ZZ	1084	ØSG1471	20, 212, 213, 728, 955
ØRWU48Z	264, 648	ØS550ZZ	954	ØS9C0ZZ	228, 498, 727, 1084			ØSCN*	258, 727		
ØRWU4JZ	284, 727, 954	ØS553ZZ	954			ØSBG3ZZ	231, 727, 955, 1084	ØSCN0ZZ	1084	ØSG147J	20, 211, 213, 728, 955
ØRWU4KZ	264, 648	ØS554ZZ	954	ØS9D00Z	228, 498, 727, 1084			ØSCN3ZZ	1084		
ØRWV00Z	264, 648	ØS56*	241			ØSBG4ZZ	231, 727, 955, 1084	ØSCN4ZZ	1084	ØSG14A0	20, 211, 213, 728, 955
ØRWV03Z	264, 648	ØS560ZZ	954	ØS9D0ZZ	228, 498, 727, 1084			ØSCP*	258, 727		
ØRWV04Z	264, 648	ØS563ZZ	954			ØSBH0ZZ	258, 727, 955, 1084	ØSCP0ZZ	1084	ØSG14AJ	20, 211, 213, 728, 955
ØRWV05Z	264, 648	ØS564ZZ	954	ØS9F00Z	231, 727			ØSCP3ZZ	1084		
ØRWV07Z	264, 648	ØS57*	241	ØS9F0ZZ	231, 727	ØSBH3ZZ	258, 727, 955, 1084	ØSCP4ZZ	1084	ØSG14J0	20, 211, 213, 728, 955
ØRWV08Z	264, 648	ØS570ZZ	954	ØS9G00Z	231, 727			ØSCQ*	258, 727		
ØRWV0JZ	284, 727, 954	ØS573ZZ	954	ØS9G0ZZ	231, 727	ØSBH4ZZ	258, 727, 955, 1084	ØSCQ0ZZ	1084	ØSG14J1	20, 212, 213, 728, 955
ØRWV0KZ	264, 648	ØS574ZZ	954	ØS9H00Z	258, 727, 1084			ØSCQ3ZZ	1084		
ØRWV30Z	264, 648	ØS58*	241	ØS9H0ZZ	258, 727, 1084	ØSBJ0ZZ	258, 727, 955, 1084	ØSCQ4ZZ	1084		
ØRWV33Z	264, 648	ØS580ZZ	955	ØS9J00Z	258, 727, 1084			ØSG0*	213		
ØRWV34Z	264, 648	ØS583ZZ	955	ØS9J0ZZ	258, 727, 1084						

DRG Expert—Volume II

Numeric Index to Procedures

Code	Page
ØSG14JJ	20,211,213,728,955
ØSG14KØ	20,211,213,728,955
ØSG14K1	20,212,213,728,955
ØSG14KJ	20,211,213,728,955
ØSG3*	213
ØSG3070	20,211,728,955
ØSG3071	20,212,728,955
ØSG307J	20,211,728,956
ØSG30AØ	20,211,728,956
ØSG30AJ	20,211,728,956
ØSG30JØ	21,211,728,956
ØSG30J1	21,212,728,956
ØSG30JJ	21,211,728,956
ØSG30KØ	21,211,728,956
ØSG30K1	21,212,728,956
ØSG30KJ	21,211,728,956
ØSG3370	21,211,728,956
ØSG3371	21,212,728,956
ØSG337J	21,211,728,956
ØSG33AØ	21,211,728,956
ØSG33AJ	21,211,728,956
ØSG33JØ	21,211,728,956
ØSG33J1	21,212,728,956
ØSG33JJ	21,211,728,956
ØSG33KØ	21,211,728,956
ØSG33K1	21,212,728,956
ØSG33KJ	21,211,728,956
ØSG3470	21,211,728,956
ØSG3471	21,212,728,956
ØSG347J	21,211,728,956
ØSG34AØ	21,211,728,956
ØSG34AJ	21,211,728,956
ØSG34JØ	21,211,728,956
ØSG34J1	21,212,728,956
ØSG34JJ	21,211,728,956
ØSG34KØ	21,211,728,956
ØSG34K1	21,212,728,956
ØSG34KJ	21,211,728,956
ØSG5*	213
ØSG504Z	21,728,956
ØSG507Z	21,728,956
ØSG50JZ	21,728,956
ØSG50KZ	21,728,956
ØSG534Z	21,728,956
ØSG537Z	21,728,956
ØSG53JZ	21,728,956
ØSG53KZ	21,728,956
ØSG544Z	21,728,956
ØSG547Z	21,728,956
ØSG54JZ	21,728,956
ØSG54KZ	21,728,956
ØSG6*	213
ØSG604Z	21,728,956
ØSG607Z	21,728,956
ØSG60JZ	21,728,956
ØSG60KZ	21,728,956
ØSG634Z	21,728,956
ØSG637Z	21,728,956
ØSG63JZ	21,728,956
ØSG63KZ	21,728,956
ØSG644Z	21,728,956
ØSG647Z	21,728,956
ØSG64JZ	21,728,956
ØSG64KZ	21,728,956
ØSG7*	213
ØSG704Z	21,212,728,956
ØSG707Z	21,212,728,956
ØSG70JZ	21,212,728,956
ØSG70KZ	21,212,728,956
ØSG734Z	21,212,728,956
ØSG737Z	21,212,728,956
ØSG73JZ	21,212,728,956
ØSG73KZ	21,212,728,956
ØSG744Z	21,212,728,956
ØSG747Z	21,212,728,956
ØSG74JZ	21,212,728,956
ØSG74KZ	21,212,728,956
ØSG8*	213
ØSG804Z	21,212,728,956
ØSG807Z	21,212,728,956
ØSG80JZ	21,212,728,956
ØSG80KZ	21,212,728,956
ØSG834Z	21,212,728,956
ØSG837Z	21,212,728,956
ØSG83JZ	21,212,728,956
ØSG83KZ	21,212,728,956
ØSG844Z	21,212,728,956
ØSG847Z	21,212,728,956
ØSG84JZ	21,212,728,956

Code	Page
ØSG84KZ	21,212,728,956
ØSG9*	226,852
ØSG904Z	728
ØSG905Z	728
ØSG907Z	728
ØSG90JZ	728
ØSG90KZ	728
ØSG934Z	728
ØSG935Z	728
ØSG937Z	728
ØSG93JZ	728
ØSG93KZ	728
ØSG944Z	728
ØSG945Z	728
ØSG947Z	728
ØSG94JZ	728
ØSG94KZ	728
ØSGB*	226,852
ØSGBØ4Z	728
ØSGBØ5Z	728
ØSGBØ7Z	728
ØSGBØJZ	728
ØSGBØKZ	728
ØSGB34Z	728
ØSGB35Z	728
ØSGB37Z	728
ØSGB3JZ	728
ØSGB3KZ	728
ØSGB44Z	728
ØSGB45Z	728
ØSGB47Z	728
ØSGB4JZ	728
ØSGB4KZ	728
ØSGC*	228
ØSGCØ4Z	728,956
ØSGCØ5Z	728,956
ØSGCØ7Z	728,956
ØSGCØJZ	728,956
ØSGCØKZ	728,956
ØSGC34Z	728,956
ØSGC35Z	728,956
ØSGC37Z	728,956
ØSGC3JZ	728,956
ØSGC3KZ	728,956
ØSGC44Z	728,956
ØSGC45Z	728,956
ØSGC47Z	728,956
ØSGC4JZ	728,956
ØSGC4KZ	728,956
ØSGD*	228
ØSGDØ4Z	728,956
ØSGDØ5Z	729,956
ØSGDØ7Z	729,956
ØSGDØJZ	729,956
ØSGDØKZ	729,956
ØSGD34Z	729,956
ØSGD35Z	729,956
ØSGD37Z	729,956
ØSGD3JZ	729,956
ØSGD3KZ	729,956
ØSGD44Z	729,956
ØSGD45Z	729,956
ØSGD47Z	729,956
ØSGD4JZ	729,956
ØSGD4KZ	729,956
ØSGF*	231,498
ØSGFØ4Z	729,956
ØSGFØ5Z	729,956
ØSGFØ7Z	729,956
ØSGFØJZ	729,956
ØSGFØKZ	729,956
ØSGF34Z	729,956
ØSGF35Z	729,956
ØSGF37Z	729,956
ØSGF3JZ	729,956
ØSGF3KZ	729,956
ØSGF44Z	729,956
ØSGF45Z	729,956
ØSGF47Z	729,956
ØSGF4JZ	729,956
ØSGF4KZ	729,956
ØSGG*	231,498
ØSGGØ4Z	729,956
ØSGGØ5Z	729,956
ØSGGØ7Z	729,956
ØSGGØJZ	729,956
ØSGGØKZ	729,956
ØSGG34Z	729,956
ØSGG35Z	729,956
ØSGG37Z	729,956
ØSGG3JZ	729,956
ØSGG3KZ	729,956
ØSGG44Z	729,956

Code	Page
ØSGG45Z	729,956
ØSGG47Z	729,956
ØSGG4JZ	729,956
ØSGG4KZ	729,956
ØSGH*	258
ØSGHØ4Z	729,956
ØSGHØ5Z	729,956
ØSGHØ7Z	729,956
ØSGHØJZ	729,956
ØSGHØKZ	729,956
ØSGH34Z	729,956
ØSGH35Z	729,956
ØSGH37Z	729,956
ØSGH3JZ	729,956
ØSGH3KZ	729,956
ØSGH44Z	729,956
ØSGH45Z	729,956
ØSGH47Z	729,956
ØSGH4JZ	729,956
ØSGH4KZ	729,956
ØSGJ*	258
ØSGJØ4Z	729,956
ØSGJØ5Z	729,956
ØSGJØ7Z	729,956
ØSGJØJZ	729,956
ØSGJØKZ	729,956
ØSGJ34Z	729,956
ØSGJ35Z	729,956
ØSGJ37Z	729,956
ØSGJ3JZ	729,956
ØSGJ3KZ	729,956
ØSGJ44Z	729,956
ØSGJ45Z	729,956
ØSGJ47Z	729,956
ØSGJ4JZ	729,956
ØSGJ4KZ	729,956
ØSGK*	258
ØSGKØ4Z	729,956
ØSGKØ5Z	729,956
ØSGKØ7Z	729,956
ØSGKØJZ	729,956
ØSGKØKZ	729,956
ØSGK34Z	729,957
ØSGK35Z	729,957
ØSGK37Z	729,957
ØSGK3JZ	729,957
ØSGK3KZ	729,957
ØSGK44Z	729,957
ØSGK45Z	729,957
ØSGK47Z	729,957
ØSGK4JZ	729,957
ØSGK4KZ	729,957
ØSGL*	258
ØSGLØ4Z	729,957
ØSGLØ5Z	729,957
ØSGLØ7Z	729,957
ØSGLØJZ	729,957
ØSGLØKZ	729,957
ØSGL34Z	729,957
ØSGL35Z	729,957
ØSGL37Z	729,957
ØSGL3JZ	729,957
ØSGL3KZ	729,957
ØSGL44Z	729,957
ØSGL45Z	729,957
ØSGL47Z	729,957
ØSGL4JZ	729,957
ØSGL4KZ	729,957
ØSGM*	258
ØSGMØ4Z	729,957
ØSGMØ5Z	729,957
ØSGMØ7Z	729,957
ØSGMØJZ	729,957
ØSGMØKZ	729,957
ØSGM34Z	729,957
ØSGM35Z	729,957
ØSGM37Z	729,957
ØSGM3JZ	729,957
ØSGM3KZ	729,957
ØSGM44Z	729,957
ØSGM45Z	729,957
ØSGM47Z	729,957
ØSGM4JZ	729,957
ØSGM4KZ	729,957
ØSGN*	258
ØSGNØ4Z	729,957
ØSGNØ5Z	729,957
ØSGNØ7Z	729,957
ØSGNØJZ	729,957
ØSGNØKZ	729,957
ØSGN34Z	729,957
ØSGN35Z	729,957
ØSGN37Z	729,957

Code	Page
ØSGN3JZ	729,957
ØSGN3KZ	729,957
ØSGN44Z	729,957
ØSGN45Z	729,957
ØSGN47Z	729,957
ØSGN4JZ	729,957
ØSGN4KZ	729,957
ØSGP*	258
ØSGPØ4Z	1084
ØSGPØ5Z	1084
ØSGPØ7Z	1084
ØSGPØJZ	1084
ØSGPØKZ	1084
ØSGP34Z	1084
ØSGP35Z	1084
ØSGP37Z	1084
ØSGP3JZ	1084
ØSGP3KZ	1084
ØSGP44Z	1084
ØSGP45Z	1084
ØSGP47Z	1084
ØSGP4JZ	1084
ØSGP4KZ	1084
ØSGQ*	258
ØSGQØ4Z	1084
ØSGQØ5Z	1084
ØSGQØ7Z	1084
ØSGQØJZ	1084
ØSGQØKZ	1084
ØSGQ34Z	1084
ØSGQ35Z	1084
ØSGQ37Z	1084
ØSGQ3JZ	1084
ØSGQ3KZ	1084
ØSGQ44Z	1084
ØSGQ45Z	1084
ØSGQ47Z	1084
ØSGQ4JZ	1084
ØSGQ4KZ	1084
ØSHØØ4Z	285
ØSHØØBZ	21,290,729,957
ØSHØØCZ	21,290,729,957
ØSHØØDZ	21,290,729,957
ØSHØ34Z	285
ØSHØ3BZ	21,290,729,957
ØSHØ3CZ	21,290,729,957
ØSHØ3DZ	21,290,729,957
ØSHØ44Z	285
ØSHØ4BZ	21,290,729,957
ØSHØ4CZ	21,290,729,957
ØSHØ4DZ	21,290,729,957
ØSH3Ø4Z	285
ØSH3ØBZ	21,290,729,957
ØSH3ØCZ	21,290,729,957
ØSH3ØDZ	21,290,729,957
ØSH334Z	285
ØSH33BZ	21,290,729,957
ØSH33CZ	21,290,729,957
ØSH33DZ	21,290,729,957
ØSH344Z	285
ØSH34BZ	21,290,729,957
ØSH34CZ	21,290,729,957
ØSH34DZ	21,290,729,957
ØSH5Ø4Z	285
ØSH534Z	285
ØSH544Z	285
ØSH6Ø4Z	285
ØSH634Z	285
ØSH644Z	285
ØSH7Ø4Z	285
ØSH734Z	285
ØSH744Z	285
ØSH8Ø4Z	285
ØSH834Z	285
ØSH844Z	285
ØSH9Ø4Z	226,729
ØSH9Ø5Z	226,729
ØSH9Ø8Z	226,1084
ØSH934Z	226,729
ØSH935Z	226,729
ØSH944Z	226,729
ØSH945Z	226,729
ØSHBØ4Z	226,729
ØSHBØ5Z	226,729
ØSHBØ8Z	226,1084
ØSHB34Z	226,729
ØSHB35Z	226,729
ØSHB44Z	226,729
ØSHB45Z	226,729
ØSHCØ4Z	228,729,1084
ØSHCØ5Z	228,729,1084
ØSHCØ8Z	228,1084
ØSHC34Z	228,729,1084

Code	Page
ØSHC35Z	228,729,1084
ØSHC44Z	228,729,1084
ØSHC45Z	228,729,1084
ØSHDØ4Z	228,729,1084
ØSHDØ5Z	228,729,1084
ØSHDØ8Z	228,1084
ØSHD34Z	228,729,1084
ØSHD35Z	228,729,1084
ØSHD44Z	228,730,1084
ØSHD45Z	228,730,1084
ØSHFØ4Z	231,730
ØSHFØ5Z	231,730
ØSHF34Z	231,730
ØSHF35Z	231,730
ØSHF44Z	231,730
ØSHF45Z	231,730
ØSHGØ4Z	231,730
ØSHGØ5Z	231,730
ØSHG34Z	231,730
ØSHG35Z	231,730
ØSHG44Z	231,730
ØSHG45Z	231,730
ØSHHØ4Z	258,730,1084
ØSHHØ5Z	258,730,1084
ØSHH34Z	258,730,1084
ØSHH35Z	258,730,1084
ØSHH44Z	258,730,1084
ØSHH45Z	258,730,1084
ØSHJØ4Z	258,730,1084
ØSHJØ5Z	258,730,1084
ØSHJ34Z	258,730,1084
ØSHJ35Z	258,730,1084
ØSHJ44Z	258,730,1084
ØSHJ45Z	258,730,1084
ØSHKØ4Z	258,730,1084
ØSHKØ5Z	258,730,1084
ØSHK34Z	258,730,1084
ØSHK35Z	258,730,1084
ØSHK44Z	258,730,1084
ØSHK45Z	258,730,1084
ØSHLØ4Z	258,730,1085
ØSHLØ5Z	258,730,1085
ØSHL34Z	258,730,1085
ØSHL35Z	258,730,1085
ØSHL44Z	258,730,1085
ØSHL45Z	258,730,1085
ØSHMØ4Z	258,730,1085
ØSHMØ5Z	258,730,1085
ØSHM34Z	258,730,1085
ØSHM35Z	258,730,1085
ØSHM44Z	258,730,1085
ØSHM45Z	258,730,1085
ØSHNØ4Z	258,730,1085
ØSHNØ5Z	258,730,1085
ØSHN34Z	258,730,1085
ØSHN35Z	258,730,1085
ØSHN44Z	258,730,1085
ØSHN45Z	258,730,1085
ØSHPØ4Z	258,730,1085
ØSHPØ5Z	258,730,1085
ØSHP34Z	258,730,1085
ØSHP35Z	258,730,1085
ØSHP44Z	259,730,1085
ØSHP45Z	259,730,1085
ØSHQØ4Z	259,730,1085
ØSHQØ5Z	259,730,1085
ØSHQ34Z	259,730,1085
ØSHQ35Z	259,730,1085
ØSHQ44Z	259,730,1085
ØSHQ45Z	259,730,1085
ØSJØØZZ	285
ØSJØ4ZZ	266,730,957
ØSJ2ØZZ	285
ØSJ24ZZ	224
ØSJ3ØZZ	285
ØSJ34ZZ	266,730,957
ØSJ4ØZZ	285
ØSJ44ZZ	224
ØSJ5ØZZ	285
ØSJ54ZZ	266,730,957
ØSJ6ØZZ	285
ØSJ64ZZ	266,730,957
ØSJ7ØZZ	285
ØSJ74ZZ	266,730,957
ØSJ8ØZZ	285
ØSJ84ZZ	266,730,957
ØSJ9ØZZ	226,730
ØSJ94ZZ	266,730,957
ØSJBØZZ	226,730
ØSJB4ZZ	266,730,957
ØSJCØZZ	228,730,1085
ØSJC4ZZ	266,498,730,957,1085

Code	Page
ØSJDØZZ	228,730,1085
ØSJD4ZZ	266,498,730,957,1085
ØSJFØZZ	231,730
ØSJF4ZZ	266,730,957
ØSJGØZZ	231,730
ØSJG4ZZ	266,730,957
ØSJHØZZ	259,730,1085
ØSJH4ZZ	266,730,957
ØSJJØZZ	259,730,1085
ØSJJ4ZZ	266,730,957
ØSJKØZZ	259,730,1085
ØSJK4ZZ	266,730,957
ØSJLØZZ	259,730,1085
ØSJL4ZZ	266,730,957
ØSJMØZZ	259,730,1085
ØSJM4ZZ	266,730,957
ØSJNØZZ	259,730,1085
ØSJN4ZZ	266,730,957
ØSJPØZZ	259,730,1085
ØSJP4ZZ	266,730,957
ØSJQØZZ	259,730,1085
ØSJQ4ZZ	266,730,957
ØSNØØZZ	730,957
ØSNØ3ZZ	730,957
ØSNØ4ZZ	730,957
ØSN2ØZZ	730,957
ØSN23ZZ	730,957
ØSN24ZZ	730,957
ØSN3ØZZ	730,957
ØSN33ZZ	730,957
ØSN34ZZ	730,957
ØSN4ØZZ	730,957
ØSN43ZZ	730,957
ØSN44ZZ	730,957
ØSN5ØZZ	730,957
ØSN53ZZ	730,957
ØSN54ZZ	730,957
ØSN6ØZZ	730,957
ØSN63ZZ	730,957
ØSN64ZZ	730,957
ØSN7ØZZ	730,957
ØSN73ZZ	730,957
ØSN74ZZ	730,957
ØSN8ØZZ	730,957
ØSN83ZZ	730,957
ØSN84ZZ	730,957
ØSN9ØZZ	226,730,852
ØSN93ZZ	226,730,852
ØSN94ZZ	226,730,852
ØSNBØZZ	226,730,852
ØSNB3ZZ	226,730,852
ØSNB4ZZ	226,730,852
ØSNCØZZ	228,730,957,1085
ØSNC3ZZ	228,730,957,1085
ØSNC4ZZ	228,730,957,1085
ØSNDØZZ	228,730,957,1085
ØSND3ZZ	228,730,957,1085
ØSND4ZZ	228,730,957,1085
ØSNFØZZ	231,730,957
ØSNF3ZZ	231,730,957
ØSNF4ZZ	231,730,957
ØSNGØZZ	231,730,957
ØSNG3ZZ	231,730,957
ØSNG4ZZ	231,730,957
ØSNHØZZ	259,730,957
ØSNH3ZZ	259,730,957
ØSNH4ZZ	259,730,957
ØSNJØZZ	259,730,957
ØSNJ3ZZ	259,730,957
ØSNJ4ZZ	259,730,957
ØSNKØZZ	259,730,957
ØSNK3ZZ	259,730,957
ØSNK4ZZ	259,730,957
ØSNLØZZ	259,730,957
ØSNL3ZZ	259,730,957
ØSNL4ZZ	259,730,957
ØSNMØZZ	259,730,957
ØSNM3ZZ	259,730,957
ØSNM4ZZ	259,730,957
ØSNNØZZ	259,730,957
ØSNN3ZZ	259,730,957
ØSNN4ZZ	259,730,957
ØSNPØZZ	259,730,957
ØSNP3ZZ	259,730,957
ØSNP4ZZ	259,730,957
ØSNQØZZ	259,730,957

Numeric Index to Procedures

Numeric Index to Procedures

Code	Page
ØSNQ3ZZ	259, 73Ø, 957
ØSNQ4ZZ	259, 73Ø, 957
ØSPØØØZ	285
ØSPØØ3Z	285
ØSPØØ4Z	285
ØSPØØ7Z	285
ØSPØØAZ	285
ØSPØØJZ	241, 73Ø, 957
ØSPØØKZ	285
ØSPØ34Z	285
ØSPØ37Z	285
ØSPØ3AZ	285
ØSPØ3JZ	241, 73Ø, 957
ØSPØ3KZ	285
ØSPØ4ØZ	285
ØSPØ43Z	285
ØSPØ44Z	285
ØSPØ47Z	285
ØSPØ4AZ	285
ØSPØ4JZ	241, 73Ø, 957
ØSPØ4KZ	285
ØSP2ØØZ	285
ØSP2Ø3Z	285
ØSP2Ø7Z	285
ØSP2ØJZ	241, 73Ø, 957
ØSP2ØKZ	285
ØSP237Z	285
ØSP23JZ	241, 73Ø, 957
ØSP23KZ	285
ØSP24ØZ	285
ØSP243Z	285
ØSP247Z	285
ØSP24JZ	241, 73Ø, 957
ØSP24KZ	285
ØSP3ØØZ	285
ØSP3Ø3Z	285
ØSP3Ø4Z	285
ØSP3Ø7Z	285
ØSP3ØAZ	285
ØSP3ØJZ	241, 73Ø, 957
ØSP3ØKZ	285
ØSP334Z	285
ØSP337Z	285
ØSP33AZ	285
ØSP33JZ	241, 73Ø, 957
ØSP33KZ	285
ØSP34ØZ	285
ØSP343Z	285
ØSP344Z	285
ØSP347Z	285
ØSP34AZ	285
ØSP34JZ	241, 73Ø, 957
ØSP34KZ	285
ØSP4ØØZ	285
ØSP4Ø3Z	285
ØSP4Ø7Z	285
ØSP4ØJZ	241, 73Ø, 957
ØSP4ØKZ	285
ØSP437Z	285
ØSP43JZ	241, 73Ø, 957
ØSP43KZ	285
ØSP44ØZ	285
ØSP443Z	285
ØSP447Z	285
ØSP44JZ	241, 73Ø, 957
ØSP44KZ	285
ØSP5ØØZ	285
ØSP5Ø3Z	285
ØSP5Ø4Z	285
ØSP5Ø7Z	285
ØSP5ØJZ	241, 731, 957
ØSP5ØKZ	285
ØSP534Z	285
ØSP537Z	285
ØSP53JZ	241, 731, 957
ØSP53KZ	285
ØSP54ØZ	285
ØSP543Z	285
ØSP544Z	285
ØSP547Z	285
ØSP54JZ	241, 731, 957
ØSP54KZ	285
ØSP6ØØZ	285
ØSP6Ø3Z	285
ØSP6Ø4Z	285
ØSP6Ø7Z	285
ØSP6ØJZ	241, 731, 957
ØSP6ØKZ	285
ØSP634Z	285
ØSP637Z	285
ØSP63JZ	241, 731, 957
ØSP63KZ	285
ØSP64ØZ	285
ØSP643Z	285
ØSP644Z	285
ØSP647Z	285
ØSP64JZ	241, 731, 957
ØSP64KZ	285
ØSP7ØØZ	285
ØSP7Ø3Z	285
ØSP7Ø4Z	285
ØSP7Ø7Z	285
ØSP7ØJZ	241, 731, 957
ØSP7ØKZ	285
ØSP734Z	285
ØSP737Z	285
ØSP73JZ	241, 731, 957
ØSP73KZ	285
ØSP74ØZ	285
ØSP743Z	285
ØSP744Z	285
ØSP747Z	285
ØSP74JZ	241, 731, 957
ØSP74KZ	285
ØSP8ØØZ	285
ØSP8Ø3Z	285
ØSP8Ø4Z	285
ØSP8Ø7Z	285
ØSP8ØJZ	241, 731, 958
ØSP8ØKZ	285
ØSP834Z	285
ØSP837Z	285
ØSP83JZ	241, 731, 958
ØSP83KZ	285
ØSP84ØZ	285
ØSP843Z	285
ØSP844Z	285
ØSP847Z	285
ØSP84JZ	241, 731, 958
ØSP84KZ	285
ØSP9ØØZ	226, 731
ØSP9Ø3Z	226, 731
ØSP9Ø4Z	226, 731
ØSP9Ø5Z	226, 731
ØSP9Ø7Z	226, 731
ØSP9Ø8Z	216, 217, 226, 499, 1Ø85
ØSP9Ø9Z	215, 216, 217, 499, 731, 852
ØSP9ØBZ	216, 217, 226, 499, 731
ØSP9ØEZ	217, 218, 226, 1Ø85
ØSP9ØJZ	215, 216, 217, 731, 852
ØSP9ØKZ	226, 731
ØSP934Z	226, 731
ØSP935Z	226, 731
ØSP937Z	226, 731
ØSP93JZ	215, 731, 852
ØSP93KZ	226, 731
ØSP94ØZ	226, 731
ØSP943Z	226, 731
ØSP944Z	226, 731
ØSP945Z	226, 731
ØSP947Z	226, 731
ØSP948Z	216, 217, 499
ØSP94JZ	215, 216, 217, 499, 731, 852
ØSP94KZ	226, 731
ØSPAØJZ	215, 216, 217, 731, 852
ØSPA3JZ	215, 731, 852
ØSPA4JZ	215, 216, 217, 499, 731, 852
ØSPBØØZ	226, 731
ØSPBØ3Z	226, 731
ØSPBØ4Z	226, 731
ØSPBØ5Z	226, 731
ØSPBØ7Z	226, 731
ØSPBØ8Z	216, 217, 218, 226, 499, 5ØØ, 1Ø85
ØSPBØ9Z	215, 217, 218, 499, 5ØØ, 731, 852
ØSPBØBZ	216, 217, 218, 226, 499, 5ØØ, 731
ØSPBØEZ	218, 226, 1Ø85
ØSPBØJZ	215, 216, 218, 731, 852
ØSPBØKZ	226, 731
ØSPB34Z	226, 731
ØSPB35Z	226, 731
ØSPB37Z	226, 731
ØSPB3JZ	215, 731, 852
ØSPB3KZ	226, 731
ØSPB4ØZ	226, 731
ØSPB43Z	226, 731
ØSPB44Z	226, 731
ØSPB45Z	226, 731
ØSPB47Z	226, 731
ØSPB48Z	216, 217, 218, 499, 5ØØ
ØSPB4JZ	215, 216, 217, 218, 5ØØ, 731, 852
ØSPB4KZ	226, 731
ØSPCØØZ	228, 731, 1Ø85
ØSPCØ3Z	228, 731, 1Ø85
ØSPCØ4Z	228, 731, 1Ø85
ØSPCØ5Z	228, 731, 1Ø85
ØSPCØ7Z	228, 731, 1Ø85
ØSPCØ8Z	217, 218, 219, 228, 1Ø85
ØSPCØ9Z	215, 217, 218, 219, 228, 5ØØ, 731, 958
ØSPCØEZ	218, 219, 228, 1Ø85
ØSPCØJC	215, 216, 217, 218, 5ØØ, 731, 958
ØSPCØJZ	215, 217, 218, 219, 5ØØ, 731, 958
ØSPCØKZ	228, 731, 1Ø85
ØSPCØLZ	215, 218, 219, 5ØØ, 731, 958
ØSPCØMZ	215, 218, 219, 5ØØ, 731, 958
ØSPCØNZ	215, 218, 219, 5ØØ, 731, 958
ØSPC34Z	228, 731, 1Ø85
ØSPC35Z	228, 731, 1Ø85
ØSPC37Z	228, 731, 1Ø85
ØSPC38Z	217, 218, 219
ØSPC3JC	215, 731, 958
ØSPC3JZ	215, 731, 958
ØSPC3KZ	228, 731, 1Ø85
ØSPC3LZ	215, 731, 958
ØSPC3MZ	215, 731, 958
ØSPC3NZ	215, 731, 958
ØSPC4ØZ	228, 731, 1Ø85
ØSPC43Z	228, 731, 1Ø85
ØSPC44Z	228, 731, 1Ø85
ØSPC45Z	228, 731, 1Ø85
ØSPC47Z	228, 731, 1Ø85
ØSPC48Z	217, 218, 219
ØSPC4JC	215, 216, 217, 218, 219, 5ØØ, 731, 958
ØSPC4JZ	215, 217, 218, 219, 5ØØ, 731, 958
ØSPC4KZ	228, 731, 1Ø85
ØSPC4LZ	215, 218, 219, 5ØØ, 731, 958
ØSPC4MZ	215, 218, 219, 5ØØ, 731, 958
ØSPC4NZ	215, 218, 219, 5ØØ, 731, 958
ØSPDØØZ	228, 731, 1Ø85
ØSPDØ3Z	228, 731, 1Ø85
ØSPDØ4Z	228, 731, 1Ø85
ØSPDØ5Z	228, 731, 1Ø85
ØSPDØ7Z	228, 731, 1Ø85
ØSPDØ8Z	217, 22Ø, 228, 1Ø85
ØSPDØ9Z	215, 217, 219, 22Ø, 228, 5ØØ, 5Ø1, 731, 958
ØSPDØEZ	219, 22Ø, 221, 228, 1Ø85
ØSPDØJC	215, 216, 217, 219, 22Ø, 5Ø1, 731, 958
ØSPDØJZ	215, 217, 219, 22Ø, 5Ø1, 731, 958
ØSPDØKZ	228, 731, 1Ø85
ØSPDØLZ	215, 219, 22Ø, 5ØØ, 5Ø1, 731, 958
ØSPDØMZ	215, 219, 22Ø, 5ØØ, 5Ø1, 731, 958
ØSPDØNZ	215, 219, 22Ø, 5ØØ, 5Ø1, 731, 958
ØSPD34Z	228, 731, 1Ø85
ØSPD35Z	228, 731, 1Ø85
ØSPD37Z	228, 731, 1Ø85
ØSPD38Z	217, 22Ø
ØSPD3JC	215, 731, 958
ØSPD3JZ	215, 731, 958
ØSPD3KZ	228, 731, 1Ø85
ØSPD3LZ	215, 731, 958
ØSPD3MZ	215, 731, 958
ØSPD3NZ	215, 731, 958
ØSPD4ØZ	228, 731, 1Ø85
ØSPD43Z	228, 731, 1Ø85
ØSPD44Z	228, 731, 1Ø85
ØSPD45Z	228, 731, 1Ø85
ØSPD47Z	228, 731, 1Ø85
ØSPD48Z	217, 22Ø
ØSPD4JC	215, 216, 217, 22Ø, 5Ø1, 731, 958
ØSPD4JZ	215, 217, 219, 22Ø, 5Ø1, 731, 958
ØSPD4KZ	228, 731, 1Ø85
ØSPD4LZ	215, 22Ø, 221, 5ØØ, 731, 958
ØSPD4MZ	215, 22Ø, 221, 5ØØ, 731, 958
ØSPD4NZ	215, 22Ø, 221, 5ØØ, 5Ø1, 731, 958
ØSPEØJZ	215, 216, 218, 731, 852
ØSPE3JZ	215, 731, 852
ØSPE4JZ	215, 216, 217, 218, 5ØØ, 731, 852
ØSPFØØZ	231, 731
ØSPFØ3Z	231, 731
ØSPFØ4Z	231, 731
ØSPFØ5Z	231, 731
ØSPFØ7Z	231, 731
ØSPFØJZ	241, 731, 958
ØSPFØKZ	231, 731
ØSPF34Z	231, 731
ØSPF35Z	231, 731
ØSPF37Z	231, 731
ØSPF3JZ	241, 731, 958
ØSPF3KZ	231, 731
ØSPF4ØZ	231, 731
ØSPF43Z	231, 731
ØSPF44Z	231, 731
ØSPF45Z	231, 731
ØSPF47Z	231, 731
ØSPF4JZ	241, 731, 958
ØSPF4KZ	231, 731
ØSPGØØZ	231, 731
ØSPGØ3Z	231, 731
ØSPGØ4Z	231, 731
ØSPGØ5Z	231, 731
ØSPGØ7Z	231, 731
ØSPGØJZ	241, 731, 958
ØSPGØKZ	231, 731
ØSPG34Z	231, 731
ØSPG35Z	231, 731
ØSPG37Z	231, 731
ØSPG3JZ	241, 731, 958
ØSPG3KZ	231, 731
ØSPG4ØZ	231, 731
ØSPG43Z	231, 731
ØSPG44Z	232, 731
ØSPG45Z	232, 731
ØSPG47Z	232, 731
ØSPG4JZ	241, 731, 958
ØSPG4KZ	232, 731
ØSPHØØZ	259, 731, 1Ø85
ØSPHØ3Z	259, 731, 1Ø85
ØSPHØ4Z	259, 731, 1Ø85
ØSPHØ5Z	259, 731, 1Ø85
ØSPHØ7Z	259, 731, 1Ø85
ØSPHØJZ	241, 731, 958
ØSPHØKZ	259, 731, 1Ø85
ØSPH34Z	259, 731, 1Ø85
ØSPH35Z	259, 731, 1Ø85
ØSPH37Z	259, 731, 1Ø85
ØSPH3JZ	241, 731, 958
ØSPH3KZ	259, 731, 1Ø85
ØSPH4ØZ	259, 732, 1Ø85
ØSPH43Z	259, 732, 1Ø85
ØSPH44Z	259, 732, 1Ø85
ØSPH45Z	259, 732, 1Ø85
ØSPH47Z	259, 732, 1Ø85
ØSPH4JZ	241, 732, 958
ØSPH4KZ	259, 732, 1Ø85
ØSPJØØZ	259, 732, 1Ø85
ØSPJØ3Z	259, 732, 1Ø85
ØSPJØ4Z	259, 732, 1Ø85
ØSPJØ5Z	259, 732, 1Ø85
ØSPJØ7Z	259, 732, 1Ø85
ØSPJØJZ	241, 732, 958
ØSPJØKZ	259, 732, 1Ø85
ØSPJ34Z	259, 732, 1Ø85
ØSPJ35Z	259, 732, 1Ø85
ØSPJ37Z	259, 732, 1Ø85
ØSPJ3JZ	241, 732, 958
ØSPJ3KZ	259, 732, 1Ø85
ØSPJ4ØZ	259, 732, 1Ø85
ØSPJ43Z	259, 732, 1Ø85
ØSPJ44Z	259, 732, 1Ø85
ØSPJ45Z	259, 732, 1Ø85
ØSPJ47Z	259, 732, 1Ø85
ØSPJ4JZ	241, 732, 958
ØSPJ4KZ	259, 732, 1Ø85
ØSPKØØZ	259, 732, 1Ø85
ØSPKØ3Z	259, 732, 1Ø85
ØSPKØ4Z	259, 732, 1Ø85
ØSPKØ5Z	259, 732, 1Ø85
ØSPKØ7Z	259, 732, 1Ø85
ØSPKØJZ	241, 732, 958
ØSPKØKZ	259, 732, 1Ø85
ØSPK34Z	259, 732, 1Ø85
ØSPK35Z	259, 732, 1Ø85
ØSPK37Z	259, 732, 1Ø85
ØSPK3JZ	241, 732, 958
ØSPK3KZ	259, 732, 1Ø85
ØSPK4ØZ	259, 732, 1Ø85
ØSPK43Z	259, 732, 1Ø85
ØSPK44Z	259, 732, 1Ø85
ØSPK45Z	259, 732, 1Ø85
ØSPK47Z	259, 732, 1Ø85
ØSPK4JZ	241, 732, 958
ØSPK4KZ	259, 732, 1Ø85
ØSPLØØZ	259, 732, 1Ø85
ØSPLØ3Z	259, 732, 1Ø85
ØSPLØ4Z	259, 732, 1Ø85
ØSPLØ5Z	259, 732, 1Ø85
ØSPLØ7Z	259, 732, 1Ø85
ØSPLØJZ	241, 732, 958
ØSPLØKZ	259, 732, 1Ø85
ØSPL34Z	259, 732, 1Ø85
ØSPL35Z	259, 732, 1Ø85
ØSPL37Z	259, 732, 1Ø85
ØSPL3JZ	241, 732, 958
ØSPL3KZ	259, 732, 1Ø85
ØSPL4ØZ	259, 732, 1Ø85
ØSPL43Z	259, 732, 1Ø85
ØSPL44Z	259, 732, 1Ø85
ØSPL45Z	259, 732, 1Ø85
ØSPL47Z	259, 732, 1Ø85
ØSPL4JZ	241, 732, 958
ØSPL4KZ	259, 732, 1Ø85
ØSPMØØZ	259, 732, 1Ø85
ØSPMØ3Z	259, 732, 1Ø85
ØSPMØ4Z	259, 732, 1Ø85
ØSPMØ5Z	259, 732, 1Ø85
ØSPMØ7Z	259, 732, 1Ø85
ØSPMØJZ	241, 732, 958
ØSPMØKZ	259, 732, 1Ø85
ØSPM34Z	259, 732, 1Ø85
ØSPM35Z	259, 732, 1Ø85
ØSPM37Z	259, 732, 1Ø85
ØSPM3JZ	241, 732, 958
ØSPM3KZ	259, 732, 1Ø85
ØSPM4ØZ	259, 732, 1Ø85
ØSPM43Z	259, 732, 1Ø85
ØSPM44Z	259, 732, 1Ø85
ØSPM45Z	259, 732, 1Ø85
ØSPM47Z	259, 732, 1Ø85
ØSPM4JZ	241, 732, 958
ØSPM4KZ	259, 732, 1Ø85
ØSPNØØZ	259, 732, 1Ø85
ØSPNØ3Z	259, 732, 1Ø85
ØSPNØ4Z	259, 732, 1Ø85
ØSPNØ5Z	259, 732, 1Ø85
ØSPNØ7Z	259, 732, 1Ø85
ØSPNØJZ	241, 732, 958
ØSPNØKZ	259, 732, 1Ø85
ØSPN34Z	259, 732, 1Ø86
ØSPN35Z	259, 732, 1Ø86
ØSPN37Z	259, 732, 1Ø86
ØSPN3JZ	241, 732, 958
ØSPN3KZ	259, 732, 1Ø86
ØSPN4ØZ	259, 732, 1Ø86
ØSPN43Z	259, 732, 1Ø86
ØSPN44Z	259, 732, 1Ø86
ØSPN45Z	259, 732, 1Ø86
ØSPN47Z	259, 732, 1Ø86
ØSPN4JZ	241, 732, 958
ØSPN4KZ	259, 732, 1Ø86
ØSPPØØZ	259, 732, 1Ø86
ØSPPØ3Z	259, 732, 1Ø86
ØSPPØ4Z	259, 732, 1Ø86
ØSPPØ5Z	259, 732, 1Ø86
ØSPPØ7Z	259, 732, 1Ø86
ØSPPØJZ	241, 732, 958
ØSPPØKZ	259, 732, 1Ø86
ØSPP34Z	259, 732, 1Ø86
ØSPP35Z	259, 732, 1Ø86
ØSPP37Z	259, 732, 1Ø86
ØSPP3JZ	241, 732, 958
ØSPP3KZ	259, 732, 1Ø86
ØSPP4ØZ	259, 732, 1Ø86
ØSPP43Z	259, 732, 1Ø86
ØSPP44Z	259, 732, 1Ø86
ØSPP45Z	259, 732, 1Ø86
ØSPP47Z	259, 732, 1Ø86
ØSPP4JZ	241, 732, 958
ØSPP4KZ	259, 732, 1Ø86
ØSPQØØZ	259, 732, 1Ø86
ØSPQØ3Z	259, 732, 1Ø86
ØSPQØ4Z	259, 732, 1Ø86
ØSPQØ5Z	259, 732, 1Ø86
ØSPQØ7Z	259, 732, 1Ø86
ØSPQØJZ	241, 732, 958
ØSPQØKZ	259, 732, 1Ø86
ØSPQ34Z	259, 732, 1Ø86
ØSPQ35Z	259, 732, 1Ø86
ØSPQ37Z	259, 732, 1Ø86
ØSPQ3JZ	241, 732, 958
ØSPQ3KZ	259, 732, 1Ø86
ØSPQ4ØZ	259, 732, 1Ø86
ØSPQ43Z	259, 732, 1Ø86
ØSPQ44Z	259, 732, 1Ø86
ØSPQ45Z	259, 732, 1Ø86
ØSPQ47Z	259, 732, 1Ø86
ØSPQ4JZ	241, 732, 958
ØSPQ4KZ	259, 732, 1Ø86
ØSPRØJZ	215, 216, 217, 732, 852
ØSPR3JZ	215, 732, 852
ØSPR4JZ	215, 216, 217, 499, 732, 852
ØSPSØJZ	215, 216, 218, 732, 852
ØSPS3JZ	215, 732, 852
ØSPS4JZ	215, 216, 217, 218, 5ØØ, 732, 852
ØSPTØJZ	215, 216, 217, 218, 219, 5ØØ, 732, 958
ØSPT3JZ	215, 732, 958
ØSPT4JZ	215, 216, 217, 218, 219, 5ØØ, 732, 958
ØSPUØJZ	215, 216, 217, 22Ø, 5Ø1, 732, 958
ØSPU3JZ	215, 732, 958
ØSPU4JZ	215, 216, 217, 22Ø, 5Ø1, 732, 958
ØSPVØJZ	215, 216, 217, 218, 219, 5ØØ, 732, 958
ØSPV3JZ	215, 732, 958
ØSPV4JZ	215, 216, 217, 218, 219, 5ØØ, 732, 958
ØSPWØJZ	215, 216, 217, 22Ø, 5Ø1, 732, 958
ØSPW3JZ	215, 732, 958
ØSPW4JZ	215, 216, 217, 22Ø, 5Ø1, 732, 958
ØSQØØZZ	285
ØSQØ3ZZ	285
ØSQØ4ZZ	285
ØSQ2ØZZ	21, 289, 6ØØ, 625, 732, 958
ØSQ23ZZ	285
ØSQ24ZZ	285
ØSQ3ØZZ	285
ØSQ33ZZ	285
ØSQ34ZZ	285
ØSQ4ØZZ	21, 289, 6ØØ, 625, 732, 958
ØSQ43ZZ	285
ØSQ44ZZ	285
ØSQ5ØZZ	285
ØSQ53ZZ	285
ØSQ54ZZ	285
ØSQ6ØZZ	285
ØSQ63ZZ	285
ØSQ64ZZ	285
ØSQ7ØZZ	286
ØSQ73ZZ	286
ØSQ74ZZ	286
ØSQ8ØZZ	286
ØSQ83ZZ	286
ØSQ84ZZ	286
ØSQ9ØZZ	226, 732, 852
ØSQ93ZZ	226, 732, 852
ØSQ94ZZ	226, 732, 852
ØSQBØZZ	226, 732, 852
ØSQB3ZZ	226, 732, 852

Code	Page
0SQB4ZZ	226, 732, 852
0SQC0ZZ	228, 732, 958
0SQC3ZZ	228, 732, 958
0SQC4ZZ	228, 732, 958
0SQD0ZZ	228, 732, 958
0SQD3ZZ	228, 732, 958
0SQD4ZZ	228, 732, 958
0SQF0ZZ	232, 732, 958
0SQF3ZZ	232, 732, 958
0SQF4ZZ	232, 733, 958
0SQG0ZZ	232, 733, 958
0SQG3ZZ	232, 733, 958
0SQG4ZZ	232, 733, 958
0SQH0ZZ	286
0SQH3ZZ	286
0SQH4ZZ	286
0SQJ0ZZ	286
0SQJ3ZZ	286
0SQJ4ZZ	286
0SQK0ZZ	286
0SQK3ZZ	286
0SQK4ZZ	286
0SQL0ZZ	286
0SQL3ZZ	286
0SQL4ZZ	286
0SQM0ZZ	286
0SQM3ZZ	286
0SQM4ZZ	286
0SQN0ZZ	286
0SQN3ZZ	286
0SQN4ZZ	286
0SQP0ZZ	286
0SQP3ZZ	286
0SQP4ZZ	286
0SQQ0ZZ	286
0SQQ3ZZ	286
0SQQ4ZZ	286
0SR007Z	286
0SR00JZ	286
0SR00KZ	286
0SR207Z	286
0SR20JZ	21, 290, 733, 958
0SR20KZ	286
0SR307Z	286
0SR30JZ	286
0SR30KZ	286
0SR407Z	286
0SR40JZ	21, 290, 733, 958
0SR40KZ	286
0SR5*	286
0SR6*	286
0SR7*	286
0SR8*	286
0SR9*	213
0SR9019	216, 217, 221, 499, 733, 852
0SR901A	216, 217, 221, 499, 733, 852
0SR901Z	216, 217, 221, 499, 733, 852
0SR9029	216, 217, 221, 499, 733, 852
0SR902A	216, 217, 221, 499, 733, 852
0SR902Z	216, 217, 221, 499, 733, 852
0SR9039	216, 217, 221, 499, 733, 852
0SR903A	216, 217, 221, 499, 733, 852
0SR903Z	216, 217, 221, 499, 733, 852
0SR9049	216, 217, 221, 499, 733, 852
0SR904A	216, 217, 221, 499, 733, 852
0SR904Z	216, 217, 221, 499, 733, 853
0SR9069	216, 217, 221, 499, 733, 853
0SR906A	216, 217, 221, 499, 733, 853
0SR906Z	216, 217, 221, 499, 733, 853
0SR907Z	221, 733, 853
0SR90EZ	217, 226, 733, 853
0SR90J9	216, 217, 221, 499, 733, 853
0SR90JA	216, 217, 221, 499, 733, 853
0SR90JZ	216, 217, 221, 499, 733, 853
0SR90KZ	221, 733, 853
0SRA*	213, 221, 498, 733, 853
0SRA009	216, 217, 499
0SRA00A	216, 218, 499
0SRA00Z	216, 217, 499
0SRA019	216, 217, 499
0SRA01A	216, 218, 499
0SRA01Z	216, 217, 499
0SRA039	216, 217, 499
0SRA03A	216, 218, 499
0SRA03Z	216, 217, 499
0SRA0J9	216, 218, 499
0SRA0JA	216, 217, 499
0SRA0JZ	216, 218, 499
0SRB*	213
0SRB019	216, 218, 221, 500, 733, 853
0SRB01A	216, 218, 221, 500, 733, 853
0SRB01Z	216, 218, 221, 500, 733, 853
0SRB029	216, 218, 221, 500, 733, 853
0SRB02A	216, 218, 221, 500, 733, 853
0SRB02Z	216, 218, 221, 500, 733, 853
0SRB039	216, 218, 221, 500, 733, 853
0SRB03A	216, 218, 221, 500, 733, 853
0SRB03Z	216, 218, 221, 500, 733, 853
0SRB049	216, 218, 221, 500, 733, 853
0SRB04A	216, 218, 221, 500, 733, 853
0SRB04Z	216, 218, 221, 500, 733, 853
0SRB069	216, 218, 221, 500, 733, 853
0SRB06A	216, 218, 221, 500, 733, 853
0SRB06Z	216, 218, 221, 500, 733, 853
0SRB07Z	221, 733, 853
0SRB0EZ	218, 226, 733, 853
0SRB0J9	216, 218, 221, 500, 733, 853
0SRB0JA	216, 218, 221, 500, 733, 853
0SRB0JZ	216, 218, 221, 500, 733, 853
0SRB0KZ	221, 733, 853
0SRC069	213, 217, 218, 221, 500, 733, 958
0SRC06A	213, 217, 218, 219, 221, 500, 733, 958
0SRC06Z	214, 217, 219, 221, 500, 733, 958
0SRC07Z	214, 221, 733, 958
0SRC0EZ	218, 219, 228, 733, 958
0SRC0J9	214, 217, 218, 219, 221, 500, 733, 958
0SRC0JA	214, 217, 219, 221, 500, 733, 958
0SRC0JZ	214, 217, 218, 219, 221, 500, 733, 958
0SRC0KZ	214, 221, 733, 958
0SRC0L9	214, 217, 218, 219, 221, 500, 733, 958
0SRC0LA	214, 217, 219, 221, 500, 733, 958
0SRC0LZ	214, 217, 218, 219, 221, 500, 733, 958
0SRC0M9	214, 218, 219, 221, 500, 733, 958
0SRC0MA	214, 219, 221, 500, 733, 958
0SRC0MZ	214, 218, 219, 221, 500, 733, 958
0SRC0N9	214, 218, 219, 221, 500, 733, 958
0SRC0NA	214, 218, 221, 500, 733, 958
0SRC0NZ	214, 218, 219, 221, 500, 733, 958
0SRD069	214, 217, 219, 220, 221, 501, 733, 958
0SRD06A	214, 217, 219, 220, 221, 501, 733, 958
0SRD06Z	214, 217, 219, 220, 221, 501, 733, 958
0SRD07Z	214, 221, 733, 958
0SRD0EZ	220, 228, 733, 958
0SRD0J9	214, 217, 219, 220, 221, 501, 733, 958
0SRD0JA	214, 217, 220, 221, 501, 733, 958
0SRD0JZ	214, 217, 219, 220, 221, 501, 733, 958
0SRD0KZ	214, 221, 733, 958
0SRD0L9	214, 217, 219, 220, 221, 501, 733, 958
0SRD0LA	214, 217, 220, 221, 501, 733, 958
0SRD0LZ	214, 217, 219, 220, 221, 501, 733, 958
0SRD0M9	214, 220, 221, 500, 733, 958
0SRD0MA	214, 219, 221, 501, 733, 958
0SRD0MZ	214, 220, 221, 500, 733, 958
0SRD0N9	214, 219, 220, 221, 500, 733, 958
0SRD0NA	214, 219, 220, 221, 501, 733, 958
0SRD0NZ	214, 219, 220, 221, 500, 733, 958
0SRE*	214, 221, 498, 733, 853
0SRE009	216, 218, 500
0SRE00A	216, 218, 500
0SRE00Z	216, 218, 500
0SRE019	216, 218, 500
0SRE01A	216, 218, 500
0SRE01Z	216, 218, 500
0SRE039	216, 218, 500
0SRE03A	216, 218, 500
0SRE03Z	216, 218, 500
0SRE0J9	216, 218, 500
0SRE0JA	216, 218, 500
0SRE0JZ	216, 218, 500
0SRF*	214, 733
0SRF07Z	221, 958
0SRF0J9	221, 958
0SRF0JA	221, 958
0SRF0JZ	221, 958
0SRF0KZ	221, 958
0SRG*	214, 733
0SRG07Z	221, 958
0SRG0J9	221, 958
0SRG0JA	221, 958
0SRG0JZ	221, 958
0SRG0KZ	221, 958
0SRH*	259, 733
0SRH07Z	958, 1086
0SRH0JZ	958, 1086
0SRH0KZ	958, 1086
0SRJ*	259, 733
0SRJ07Z	958, 1086
0SRJ0JZ	958, 1086
0SRJ0KZ	958, 1086
0SRK*	259, 733
0SRK07Z	958, 1086
0SRK0JZ	958, 1086
0SRK0KZ	958, 1086
0SRL*	259, 733
0SRL07Z	958, 1086
0SRL0JZ	958, 1086
0SRL0KZ	958, 1086
0SRM*	259, 733
0SRM07Z	958, 1086
0SRM0JZ	958, 1086
0SRM0KZ	958, 1086
0SRN*	259, 733
0SRN07Z	958, 1086
0SRN0JZ	958, 1086
0SRN0KZ	958, 1086
0SRP*	260, 733
0SRP07Z	958, 1086
0SRP0JZ	958, 1086
0SRP0KZ	958, 1086
0SRQ*	260, 733
0SRQ07Z	958, 1086
0SRQ0JZ	958, 1086
0SRQ0KZ	958, 1086
0SRR*	214, 221, 498, 733, 853
0SRR019	216, 218, 499
0SRR01A	216, 217, 499
0SRR01Z	216, 218, 499
0SRR039	216, 218, 499
0SRR03A	216, 217, 499
0SRR03Z	216, 218, 499
0SRR0J9	216, 217, 499
0SRR0JA	216, 218, 499
0SRR0JZ	216, 217, 499
0SRS*	214, 221, 499, 733, 853
0SRS019	216, 218, 500
0SRS01A	216, 218, 500
0SRS01Z	216, 218, 500
0SRS039	216, 218, 500
0SRS03A	216, 218, 500
0SRS03Z	216, 218, 500
0SRS0J9	216, 218, 500
0SRS0JA	216, 218, 500
0SRS0JZ	216, 218, 500
0SRT*	214, 221, 733
0SRT07Z	958
0SRT0J9	217, 218, 219, 500, 958
0SRT0JA	217, 218, 219, 500, 958
0SRT0JZ	217, 218, 219, 500, 958
0SRT0KZ	958
0SRU*	214, 221, 733
0SRU07Z	958
0SRU0J9	217, 220, 500, 501, 958
0SRU0JA	217, 219, 220, 500, 501, 958
0SRU0JZ	217, 220, 501, 958
0SRU0KZ	958
0SRV*	214, 221, 733
0SRV07Z	958
0SRV0J9	217, 219, 500, 959
0SRV0JA	217, 218, 219, 500, 959
0SRV0JZ	217, 219, 500, 959
0SRV0KZ	959
0SRW*	214, 221, 733
0SRW07Z	959
0SRW0J9	217, 219, 220, 500, 501, 959
0SRW0JA	217, 219, 220, 221, 500, 501, 959
0SRW0JZ	217, 220, 500, 501, 959
0SRW0KZ	959
0SS004Z	286, 733, 959
0SS00ZZ	286, 733, 959
0SS304Z	286, 733, 959
0SS30ZZ	286, 733, 959
0SS504Z	286, 733, 959
0SS50ZZ	286, 733, 959
0SS604Z	286, 733, 959
0SS60ZZ	286, 733, 959
0SS704Z	286, 733, 959
0SS70ZZ	286, 733, 959
0SS804Z	286, 733, 959
0SS80ZZ	286, 733, 959
0SS904Z	226, 733, 853
0SS905Z	226, 733, 853
0SS90ZZ	226, 733, 853
0SSB04Z	226, 733, 853
0SSB05Z	226, 733, 853
0SSB0ZZ	226, 733, 853
0SSC04Z	228, 733, 959
0SSC05Z	228, 733, 959
0SSC0ZZ	228, 733, 959
0SSD04Z	228, 733, 959
0SSD05Z	228, 733, 959
0SSD0ZZ	228, 733, 959
0SSF04Z	232, 733, 959
0SSF05Z	232, 733, 959
0SSF0ZZ	232, 733, 959
0SSG04Z	232, 733, 959
0SSG05Z	232, 733, 959
0SSG0ZZ	232, 733, 959
0SSH04Z	260, 733, 959
0SSH05Z	260, 733, 959
0SSH0ZZ	260, 733, 959
0SSJ04Z	260, 733, 959
0SSJ05Z	260, 733, 959
0SSJ0ZZ	260, 733, 959
0SSK04Z	260, 733, 959
0SSK05Z	260, 733, 959
0SSK0ZZ	260, 733, 959
0SSL04Z	260, 733, 959
0SSL05Z	260, 733, 959
0SSL0ZZ	260, 733, 959
0SSM04Z	260, 733, 959
0SSM05Z	260, 733, 959
0SSM0ZZ	260, 733, 959
0SSN04Z	260, 733, 959
0SSN05Z	260, 733, 959
0SSN0ZZ	260, 733, 959
0SSP04Z	260, 733, 959
0SSP05Z	260, 733, 959
0SSP0ZZ	260, 733, 959
0SSQ04Z	260, 733, 959
0SSQ05Z	260, 733, 959
0SSQ0ZZ	260, 733, 959
0ST*	733
0ST20ZZ	21, 289, 959
0ST40ZZ	21, 289, 959
0ST50ZZ	286, 959
0ST60ZZ	286, 959
0ST70ZZ	286, 959
0ST80ZZ	286, 959
0ST90ZZ	226, 853
0STB0ZZ	226, 853
0STC0ZZ	228, 959
0STD0ZZ	228, 959
0STF0ZZ	232, 959
0STG0ZZ	232, 959
0STH0ZZ	260, 499, 959, 1086
0STJ0ZZ	260, 499, 959, 1086
0STK0ZZ	260, 499, 959, 1086
0STL0ZZ	260, 499, 959, 1086
0STM0ZZ	260, 499, 959, 1086
0STN0ZZ	260, 499, 959, 1086
0STP0ZZ	260, 499, 959, 1086
0STQ0ZZ	260, 499, 959, 1086
0SU007Z	286
0SU00JZ	21, 290, 733, 959
0SU00KZ	286
0SU037Z	286
0SU03JZ	21, 290, 733, 959
0SU03KZ	286
0SU047Z	286
0SU04JZ	21, 290, 733, 959
0SU04KZ	286
0SU2*	289, 733
0SU207Z	21, 600, 625, 959
0SU20JZ	21, 600, 625, 959
0SU20KZ	21, 600, 625, 959
0SU237Z	21, 600, 625, 959
0SU23JZ	21, 600, 625, 959
0SU23KZ	21, 600, 625, 959
0SU247Z	21, 600, 625, 959
0SU24JZ	21, 600, 625, 959
0SU24KZ	21, 600, 625, 959
0SU307Z	286
0SU30JZ	21, 290, 733, 959
0SU30KZ	286
0SU337Z	286
0SU33JZ	21, 290, 733, 959
0SU33KZ	286
0SU347Z	286
0SU34JZ	21, 290, 733, 959
0SU34KZ	286
0SU4*	289, 733
0SU407Z	21, 600, 625, 959
0SU40JZ	21, 600, 625, 959
0SU40KZ	21, 600, 625, 959
0SU437Z	21, 600, 625, 959
0SU43JZ	21, 600, 625, 959
0SU43KZ	21, 600, 625, 959
0SU447Z	21, 600, 625, 959
0SU44JZ	21, 600, 625, 959
0SU44KZ	21, 600, 625, 959
0SU507Z	286
0SU50JZ	21, 290, 733, 959
0SU50KZ	286
0SU537Z	286
0SU53JZ	21, 290, 733, 959
0SU53KZ	286
0SU547Z	286
0SU54JZ	21, 290, 733, 959
0SU54KZ	286
0SU607Z	286
0SU60JZ	21, 290, 733, 959
0SU60KZ	286
0SU637Z	286
0SU63JZ	21, 290, 733, 959
0SU63KZ	286
0SU647Z	286
0SU64JZ	21, 290, 733, 959
0SU64KZ	286
0SU7*	286
0SU8*	286
0SU907Z	286
0SU909Z	216, 217, 286, 499
0SU90BZ	214, 221, 733, 853
0SU90JZ	286
0SU90KZ	286
0SU937Z	286
0SU93JZ	286
0SU93KZ	286
0SU947Z	286
0SU94JZ	286
0SU94KZ	286
0SUA09Z	216, 217, 286, 499
0SUA0BZ	214, 221, 499, 733, 853
0SUB07Z	286
0SUB09Z	217, 218, 286, 500
0SUB0BZ	214, 221, 733, 853
0SUB0JZ	286
0SUB0KZ	286
0SUB37Z	286
0SUB3JZ	286
0SUB3KZ	286
0SUB47Z	286
0SUB4JZ	286
0SUB4KZ	286
0SUC*	286
0SUD*	286
0SUE09Z	217, 218, 286, 500
0SUE0BZ	214, 221, 499, 734, 853
0SUF*	286
0SUG*	286
0SUH*	286
0SUH0JZ	734, 959
0SUH3JZ	734, 959
0SUH4JZ	734, 959
0SUJ*	286
0SUJ0JZ	734, 959
0SUJ3JZ	734, 959
0SUJ4JZ	734, 959
0SUK*	286
0SUL*	286
0SUM*	286
0SUN*	286
0SUP*	286
0SUQ*	286
0SUR*	734
0SUR09Z	216, 218, 286, 499, 959
0SUR0BZ	214, 221, 499, 853
0SUS*	734
0SUS09Z	217, 218, 286, 500, 959
0SUS0BZ	214, 221, 499, 853
0SUT09Z	286
0SUU09Z	286
0SUV09Z	228, 286, 734, 959
0SUW09Z	228, 286, 734, 959
0SW000Z	286
0SW003Z	286
0SW004Z	286, 734, 959
0SW007Z	286
0SW008Z	286
0SW00AZ	286
0SW00JZ	286, 734, 959
0SW00KZ	286
0SW030Z	286
0SW033Z	286
0SW034Z	286, 734, 959
0SW037Z	286
0SW038Z	286
0SW03AZ	286
0SW03JZ	286, 734, 959
0SW03KZ	286
0SW040Z	286
0SW043Z	286
0SW044Z	286, 734, 959
0SW047Z	286

Code	Page
0SW048Z	286
0SW04AZ	286
0SW04JZ	286, 734, 959
0SW04KZ	286
0SW200Z	286
0SW203Z	286
0SW207Z	286
0SW20JZ	21
0SW20JZ	289, 734, 959
0SW20KZ	286
0SW230Z	286
0SW233Z	286
0SW237Z	286
0SW23JZ	21
0SW23JZ	289, 734, 959
0SW23KZ	286
0SW240Z	286
0SW243Z	286
0SW247Z	286
0SW24JZ	21
0SW24JZ	289, 734, 959
0SW24KZ	286
0SW300Z	286
0SW303Z	286
0SW304Z	286, 734, 959
0SW307Z	286
0SW308Z	286
0SW30AZ	286
0SW30JZ	286, 734, 959
0SW30KZ	286
0SW330Z	286
0SW333Z	286
0SW334Z	286, 734, 959
0SW337Z	286
0SW338Z	287
0SW33AZ	287
0SW33JZ	287, 734, 959
0SW33KZ	287
0SW340Z	287
0SW343Z	287
0SW344Z	287, 734, 959
0SW347Z	287
0SW348Z	287
0SW34AZ	287
0SW34JZ	287, 734, 959
0SW34KZ	287
0SW400Z	287
0SW403Z	287
0SW407Z	287
0SW40JZ	21, 289, 734, 959
0SW40KZ	287
0SW430Z	287
0SW433Z	287
0SW437Z	287
0SW43JZ	21, 289, 734, 959
0SW43KZ	287
0SW440Z	287
0SW443Z	287
0SW447Z	287
0SW44JZ	21, 289, 734, 959
0SW44KZ	287
0SW500Z	287
0SW503Z	287
0SW504Z	287
0SW507Z	287
0SW508Z	287
0SW50JZ	287
0SW50KZ	287
0SW530Z	287
0SW533Z	287
0SW534Z	287
0SW537Z	287
0SW538Z	287
0SW53JZ	287
0SW53KZ	287
0SW540Z	287
0SW543Z	287
0SW544Z	287
0SW547Z	287
0SW548Z	287
0SW54JZ	287
0SW54KZ	287
0SW600Z	287
0SW603Z	287
0SW604Z	287
0SW607Z	287
0SW608Z	287
0SW60JZ	287
0SW60KZ	287
0SW630Z	287
0SW633Z	287
0SW634Z	287
0SW637Z	287

Code	Page
0SW638Z	287
0SW63JZ	287
0SW63KZ	287
0SW640Z	287
0SW643Z	287
0SW644Z	287
0SW647Z	287
0SW648Z	287
0SW64JZ	287
0SW64KZ	287
0SW700Z	287
0SW703Z	287
0SW704Z	287
0SW707Z	287
0SW708Z	287
0SW70JZ	287
0SW70KZ	287
0SW730Z	287
0SW733Z	287
0SW734Z	287
0SW737Z	287
0SW738Z	287
0SW73JZ	287
0SW73KZ	287
0SW740Z	287
0SW743Z	287
0SW744Z	287
0SW747Z	287
0SW748Z	287
0SW74JZ	287
0SW74KZ	287
0SW800Z	287
0SW803Z	287
0SW804Z	287
0SW807Z	287
0SW808Z	287
0SW80JZ	287
0SW80KZ	287
0SW830Z	287
0SW833Z	287
0SW834Z	287
0SW837Z	287
0SW838Z	287
0SW83JZ	287
0SW83KZ	287
0SW840Z	287
0SW843Z	287
0SW844Z	287
0SW847Z	287
0SW848Z	287
0SW84JZ	287
0SW84KZ	287
0SW900Z	226, 734
0SW903Z	226, 734
0SW904Z	227, 734
0SW905Z	227, 734
0SW907Z	227, 734
0SW908Z	227, 734
0SW909Z	227, 734
0SW90BZ	227, 734
0SW90JZ	216, 499, 734, 853
0SW90KZ	227, 734
0SW930Z	227, 734
0SW933Z	227, 734
0SW934Z	227, 734
0SW935Z	227, 734
0SW937Z	227, 734
0SW938Z	227, 734
0SW93JZ	216, 499, 734, 853
0SW93KZ	227, 734
0SW940Z	227, 734
0SW943Z	227, 734
0SW944Z	227, 734
0SW945Z	227, 734
0SW947Z	227, 734
0SW948Z	227, 734
0SW94JZ	216, 499, 734, 853
0SW94KZ	227, 734
0SWA0JZ	216, 499, 734, 853
0SWA3JZ	216, 499, 734, 853
0SWA4JZ	216, 499, 734, 853
0SWB00Z	227, 734
0SWB03Z	227, 734
0SWB04Z	227, 734
0SWB05Z	227, 734
0SWB07Z	227, 734
0SWB08Z	227, 734
0SWB09Z	227, 734
0SWB0BZ	227, 734
0SWB0JZ	216, 499, 734, 853
0SWB0KZ	227, 734
0SWB30Z	227, 734
0SWB33Z	227, 734

Code	Page
0SWB34Z	227, 734
0SWB35Z	227, 734
0SWB37Z	227, 734
0SWB38Z	227, 734
0SWB3JZ	216, 499, 734, 853
0SWB3KZ	227, 734
0SWB40Z	227, 734
0SWB43Z	227, 734
0SWB44Z	227, 734
0SWB45Z	227, 734
0SWB47Z	227, 734
0SWB48Z	227, 734
0SWB4JZ	216, 499, 734, 853
0SWB4KZ	227, 734
0SWC00Z	228, 734, 1086
0SWC03Z	228, 734, 1086
0SWC04Z	228, 734, 1086
0SWC05Z	228, 734, 1086
0SWC07Z	228, 734, 1086
0SWC08Z	228, 734, 1086
0SWC09Z	228, 734, 1086
0SWC0JC	216, 734, 959
0SWC0JZ	216, 734, 959
0SWC0KZ	228, 734, 1086
0SWC30Z	228, 734, 1086
0SWC33Z	228, 734, 1086
0SWC34Z	228, 734, 1086
0SWC35Z	228, 734, 1086
0SWC37Z	228, 734, 1086
0SWC38Z	228, 734, 1086
0SWC3JC	216, 734, 959
0SWC3JZ	216, 734, 959
0SWC3KZ	228, 734, 1086
0SWC40Z	228, 734, 1086
0SWC43Z	228, 734, 1086
0SWC44Z	228, 734, 1086
0SWC45Z	228, 734, 1086
0SWC47Z	228, 734, 1086
0SWC48Z	228, 734, 1086
0SWC4JC	216, 734, 959
0SWC4JZ	216, 734, 959
0SWC4KZ	228, 734, 1086
0SWD00Z	228, 734, 1086
0SWD03Z	228, 734, 1086
0SWD04Z	228, 734, 1086
0SWD05Z	228, 734, 1086
0SWD07Z	228, 734, 1086
0SWD08Z	228, 734, 1086
0SWD09Z	228, 734, 1086
0SWD0JC	216, 734, 959
0SWD0JZ	216, 734, 959
0SWD0KZ	228, 734, 1086
0SWD30Z	228, 734, 1086
0SWD33Z	228, 734, 1086
0SWD34Z	228, 734, 1086
0SWD35Z	228, 734, 1086
0SWD37Z	228, 734, 1086
0SWD38Z	228, 734, 1086
0SWD3JC	216, 734, 959
0SWD3JZ	216, 734, 959
0SWD3KZ	228, 734, 1086
0SWD40Z	228, 734, 1086
0SWD43Z	228, 734, 1086
0SWD44Z	228, 734, 1086
0SWD45Z	228, 734, 1086
0SWD47Z	228, 734, 1086
0SWD48Z	228, 734, 1086
0SWD4JC	216, 734, 959
0SWD4JZ	216, 734, 959
0SWD4KZ	228, 734, 1086
0SWE0JZ	216, 499, 734, 853
0SWE3JZ	216, 499, 734, 853
0SWE4JZ	216, 499, 734, 853
0SWF00Z	232, 734
0SWF03Z	232, 734
0SWF04Z	232, 734
0SWF05Z	232, 734
0SWF07Z	232, 734
0SWF08Z	232, 734
0SWF0JZ	287, 734, 959
0SWF0KZ	232, 734
0SWF30Z	232, 734
0SWF33Z	232, 734
0SWF34Z	232, 734
0SWF35Z	232, 734
0SWF37Z	232, 734
0SWF38Z	232, 734
0SWF3JZ	287, 734, 959
0SWF3KZ	232, 734
0SWF40Z	232, 734
0SWF43Z	232, 734
0SWF44Z	232, 734
0SWF45Z	232, 734

Code	Page
0SWF47Z	232, 734
0SWF48Z	232, 734
0SWF4JZ	287, 734, 959
0SWF4KZ	232, 734
0SWG00Z	232, 734
0SWG03Z	232, 734
0SWG04Z	232, 734
0SWG05Z	232, 734
0SWG07Z	232, 734
0SWG08Z	232, 734
0SWG0JZ	287, 734, 959
0SWG0KZ	232, 735
0SWG30Z	232, 735
0SWG33Z	232, 735
0SWG34Z	232, 735
0SWG35Z	232, 735
0SWG37Z	232, 735
0SWG38Z	232, 735
0SWG3JZ	287, 735, 959
0SWG3KZ	232, 735
0SWG40Z	232, 735
0SWG43Z	232, 735
0SWG44Z	232, 735
0SWG45Z	232, 735
0SWG47Z	232, 735
0SWG48Z	232, 735
0SWG4JZ	287, 735, 959
0SWG4KZ	232, 735
0SWH00Z	260, 735, 1086
0SWH03Z	260, 735, 1086
0SWH04Z	260, 735, 1086
0SWH05Z	260, 735, 1086
0SWH07Z	260, 735, 1086
0SWH08Z	260, 735, 1086
0SWH0JZ	287, 735, 959
0SWH0KZ	260, 735, 1086
0SWH30Z	260, 735, 1086
0SWH33Z	260, 735, 1086
0SWH34Z	260, 735, 1086
0SWH35Z	260, 735, 1086
0SWH37Z	260, 735, 1086
0SWH38Z	260, 735, 1086
0SWH3JZ	287, 735, 959
0SWH3KZ	260, 735, 1086
0SWH40Z	260, 735, 1086
0SWH43Z	260, 735, 1086
0SWH44Z	260, 735, 1086
0SWH45Z	260, 735, 1086
0SWH47Z	260, 735, 1086
0SWH48Z	260, 735, 1086
0SWH4JZ	287, 735, 959
0SWH4KZ	260, 735, 1086
0SWJ00Z	260, 735, 1086
0SWJ03Z	260, 735, 1086
0SWJ04Z	260, 735, 1086
0SWJ05Z	260, 735, 1086
0SWJ07Z	260, 735, 1086
0SWJ08Z	260, 735, 1086
0SWJ0JZ	287, 735, 959
0SWJ0KZ	260, 735, 1086
0SWJ30Z	260, 735, 1086
0SWJ33Z	260, 735, 1086
0SWJ34Z	260, 735, 1086
0SWJ35Z	260, 735, 1086
0SWJ37Z	260, 735, 1086
0SWJ38Z	260, 735, 1086
0SWJ3JZ	287, 735, 959
0SWJ3KZ	260, 735, 1086
0SWJ40Z	260, 735, 1086
0SWJ43Z	260, 735, 1086
0SWJ44Z	260, 735, 1086
0SWJ45Z	260, 735, 1086
0SWJ47Z	260, 735, 1086
0SWJ48Z	260, 735, 1086
0SWJ4JZ	287, 735, 959
0SWJ4KZ	260, 735, 1086
0SWK00Z	260, 735, 1086
0SWK03Z	260, 735, 1086
0SWK04Z	260, 735, 1086
0SWK05Z	260, 735, 1086
0SWK07Z	260, 735, 1086
0SWK08Z	260, 735, 1086
0SWK0JZ	287, 735, 959
0SWK0KZ	260, 735, 1086
0SWK30Z	260, 735, 1086
0SWK33Z	260, 735, 1086
0SWK34Z	260, 735, 1086
0SWK35Z	260, 735, 1086
0SWK37Z	260, 735, 1086
0SWK38Z	260, 735, 1086
0SWK3JZ	287, 735, 959
0SWK3KZ	260, 735, 1086
0SWK40Z	260, 735, 1087

Code	Page
0SWK43Z	260, 735, 1087
0SWK44Z	260, 735, 1087
0SWK45Z	260, 735, 1087
0SWK47Z	260, 735, 1087
0SWK48Z	260, 735, 1087
0SWK4JZ	287, 735, 959
0SWK4KZ	260, 735, 1087
0SWL00Z	260, 735, 1087
0SWL03Z	260, 735, 1087
0SWL04Z	260, 735, 1087
0SWL05Z	260, 735, 1087
0SWL07Z	260, 735, 1087
0SWL08Z	260, 735, 1087
0SWL0JZ	287, 735, 959
0SWL0KZ	260, 735, 1087
0SWL30Z	260, 735, 1087
0SWL33Z	260, 735, 1087
0SWL34Z	260, 735, 1087
0SWL35Z	260, 735, 1087
0SWL37Z	260, 735, 1087
0SWL38Z	260, 735, 1087
0SWL3JZ	287, 735, 959
0SWL3KZ	260, 735, 1087
0SWL40Z	260, 735, 1087
0SWL43Z	260, 735, 1087
0SWL44Z	260, 735, 1087
0SWL45Z	260, 735, 1087
0SWL47Z	260, 735, 1087
0SWL48Z	260, 735, 1087
0SWL4JZ	287, 735, 959
0SWL4KZ	260, 735, 1087
0SWM00Z	260, 735, 1087
0SWM03Z	260, 735, 1087
0SWM04Z	260, 735, 1087
0SWM05Z	260, 735, 1087
0SWM07Z	260, 735, 1087
0SWM08Z	260, 735, 1087
0SWM0JZ	287, 735, 959
0SWM0KZ	260, 735, 1087
0SWM30Z	260, 735, 1087
0SWM33Z	260, 735, 1087
0SWM34Z	260, 735, 1087
0SWM35Z	260, 735, 1087
0SWM37Z	260, 735, 1087
0SWM38Z	260, 735, 1087
0SWM3JZ	287, 735, 959
0SWM3KZ	260, 735, 1087
0SWM40Z	260, 735, 1087
0SWM43Z	260, 735, 1087
0SWM44Z	260, 735, 1087
0SWM45Z	260, 735, 1087
0SWM47Z	260, 735, 1087
0SWM48Z	260, 735, 1087
0SWM4JZ	287, 735, 959
0SWM4KZ	260, 735, 1087
0SWN00Z	260, 735, 1087
0SWN03Z	260, 735, 1087
0SWN04Z	260, 735, 1087
0SWN05Z	260, 735, 1087
0SWN07Z	260, 735, 1087
0SWN08Z	260, 735, 1087
0SWN0JZ	287, 735, 959
0SWN0KZ	260, 735, 1087
0SWN30Z	260, 735, 1087
0SWN33Z	260, 735, 1087
0SWN34Z	260, 735, 1087
0SWN35Z	260, 735, 1087
0SWN37Z	260, 735, 1087
0SWN38Z	260, 735, 1087
0SWN3JZ	287, 735, 959
0SWN3KZ	260, 735, 1087
0SWN40Z	260, 735, 1087
0SWN43Z	260, 735, 1087
0SWN44Z	260, 735, 1087
0SWN45Z	260, 735, 1087
0SWN47Z	260, 735, 1087
0SWN48Z	260, 735, 1087
0SWN4JZ	287, 735, 959
0SWN4KZ	260, 735, 1087
0SWP00Z	260, 735, 1087
0SWP03Z	260, 735, 1087
0SWP04Z	260, 735, 1087
0SWP05Z	260, 735, 1087
0SWP07Z	260, 735, 1087
0SWP08Z	260, 735, 1087
0SWP0JZ	287, 735, 959
0SWP0KZ	260, 735, 1087
0SWP30Z	260, 735, 1087
0SWP33Z	260, 735, 1087
0SWP34Z	260, 735, 1087
0SWP35Z	260, 735, 1087
0SWP37Z	260, 735, 1087
0SWP38Z	260, 736, 1087

Code	Page
0SWP3JZ	287, 736, 959
0SWP3KZ	260, 736, 1087
0SWP40Z	261, 736, 1087
0SWP43Z	261, 736, 1087
0SWP44Z	261, 736, 1087
0SWP45Z	261, 736, 1087
0SWP47Z	261, 736, 1087
0SWP48Z	261, 736, 1087
0SWP4JZ	287, 736, 959
0SWP4KZ	261, 736, 1087
0SWQ00Z	261, 736, 1087
0SWQ03Z	261, 736, 1087
0SWQ04Z	261, 736, 1087
0SWQ05Z	261, 736, 1087
0SWQ07Z	261, 736, 1087
0SWQ08Z	261, 736, 1087
0SWQ0JZ	287, 736, 959
0SWQ0KZ	261, 736, 1087
0SWQ30Z	261, 736, 1087
0SWQ33Z	261, 736, 1087
0SWQ34Z	261, 736, 1087
0SWQ35Z	261, 736, 1087
0SWQ37Z	261, 736, 1087
0SWQ38Z	261, 736, 1087
0SWQ3JZ	287, 736, 959
0SWQ3KZ	261, 736, 1087
0SWQ40Z	261, 736, 1087
0SWQ43Z	261, 736, 1087
0SWQ44Z	261, 736, 1087
0SWQ45Z	261, 736, 1087
0SWQ47Z	261, 736, 1087
0SWQ48Z	261, 736, 1087
0SWQ4JZ	287, 736, 960
0SWQ4KZ	261, 736, 1087
0SWR0JZ	216, 499, 736, 853
0SWR3JZ	216, 499, 736, 853
0SWR4JZ	216, 499, 736, 853
0SWS0JZ	216, 499, 736, 853
0SWS3JZ	216, 499, 736, 853
0SWS4JZ	216, 499, 736, 853
0SWT0JZ	216, 736, 960
0SWT3JZ	216, 736, 960
0SWT4JZ	216, 736, 960
0SWU0JZ	216, 736, 960
0SWU3JZ	216, 736, 960
0SWU4JZ	216, 736, 960
0SWV0JZ	216, 736, 960
0SWV3JZ	216, 736, 960
0SWV4JZ	216, 736, 960
0SWW0JZ	216, 736, 960
0SWW3JZ	216, 736, 960
0SWW4JZ	216, 736, 960
0T13*	505
0T1307B	526, 539, 600, 625, 736, 960
0T130JB	526, 539, 600, 625, 736, 960
0T130KB	526, 539, 600, 625, 736, 960
0T130ZB	526, 539, 600, 625, 736, 960
0T1347B	526, 539, 600, 625, 736, 960
0T134JB	526, 539, 600, 625, 736, 960
0T134KB	526, 539, 600, 625, 736, 960
0T134ZB	526, 539, 600, 625, 736, 960
0T14*	505
0T1407B	526, 539, 600, 625, 736, 960
0T140JB	526, 539, 600, 625, 736, 960
0T140KB	526, 539, 600, 625, 736, 960
0T140ZB	526, 539, 600, 625, 736, 960
0T1447B	526, 539, 600, 625, 736, 960
0T144JB	526, 539, 600, 625, 736, 960
0T144KB	526, 539, 600, 625, 736, 960
0T144ZB	526, 539, 600, 625, 736, 960
0T16*	505, 736
0T16076	526, 539, 600, 625, 960
0T16077	526, 539, 600, 625, 960
0T16078	526, 539, 600, 625, 960

Code	Page	Code	Page	Code	Page
0T16079	526, 539, 600, 625, 960	0T164K9	526, 539, 600, 626, 960	0T17479	526, 539, 601, 626, 960
0T1607A	526, 539, 600, 625, 960	0T164KA	526, 539, 600, 626, 960	0T1747A	526, 539, 601, 626, 960
0T1607B	960	0T164KB	960	0T1747B	960
0T1607C	526, 539, 600, 625, 960	0T164KC	526, 539, 600, 626, 960	0T1747C	526, 539, 601, 626, 960
0T1607D	526, 539, 600, 625, 960	0T164KD	526, 539, 600, 626, 960	0T1747D	526, 539, 601, 626, 960
0T160J6	526, 539, 600, 625, 960	0T164Z6	526, 539, 600, 626, 960	0T174J6	526, 539, 601, 626, 960
0T160J7	526, 539, 600, 625, 960	0T164Z7	526, 539, 600, 626, 960	0T174J7	526, 539, 601, 626, 960
0T160J8	526, 539, 600, 625, 960	0T164Z8	526, 539, 600, 626, 960	0T174J8	526, 539, 601, 626, 960
0T160J9	526, 539, 600, 625, 960	0T164Z9	526, 539, 600, 626, 960	0T174J9	526, 539, 601, 626, 960
0T160JA	526, 539, 600, 625, 960	0T164ZA	526, 539, 600, 626, 960	0T174JA	526, 539, 601, 626, 960
0T160JB	960	0T164ZB	960	0T174JB	960
0T160JC	526, 539, 600, 625, 960	0T164ZC	526, 539, 600, 626, 960	0T174JC	526, 539, 601, 626, 960
0T160JD	526, 539, 600, 625, 960	0T164ZD	526, 539, 600, 626, 960	0T174JD	526, 539, 601, 626, 960
0T160K6	526, 539, 600, 625, 960	0T17*	505, 736	0T174K6	526, 539, 601, 626, 960
0T160K7	526, 539, 600, 625, 960	0T17076	526, 539, 600, 626, 960	0T174K7	526, 539, 601, 626, 960
0T160K8	526, 539, 600, 625, 960	0T17077	526, 539, 600, 626, 960	0T174K8	526, 539, 601, 626, 960
0T160K9	526, 539, 600, 625, 960	0T17078	526, 539, 600, 626, 960	0T174K9	526, 539, 601, 626, 960
0T160KA	526, 539, 600, 625, 960	0T17079	526, 539, 601, 626, 960	0T174KA	526, 539, 601, 626, 960
0T160KB	960	0T1707A	526, 539, 601, 626, 960	0T174KB	960
0T160KC	526, 539, 600, 625, 960	0T1707B	960	0T174KC	526, 539, 601, 626, 960
0T160KD	526, 539, 600, 625, 960	0T1707C	526, 539, 601, 626, 960	0T174KD	526, 539, 601, 626, 960
0T160Z6	526, 539, 600, 625, 960	0T1707D	526, 539, 601, 626, 960	0T174Z6	526, 539, 601, 626, 960
0T160Z7	526, 539, 600, 626, 960	0T170J6	526, 539, 601, 626, 960	0T174Z7	526, 539, 601, 626, 960
0T160Z8	526, 539, 600, 626, 960	0T170J7	526, 539, 601, 626, 960	0T174Z8	526, 539, 601, 626, 960
0T160Z9	526, 539, 600, 626, 960	0T170J8	526, 539, 601, 626, 960	0T174Z9	526, 539, 601, 626, 960
0T160ZA	526, 539, 600, 626, 960	0T170J9	526, 539, 601, 626, 960	0T174ZA	526, 539, 601, 626, 960
0T160ZB	960	0T170JA	526, 539, 601, 626, 960	0T174ZB	960
0T160ZC	526, 539, 600, 626, 960	0T170JB	960	0T174ZC	526, 539, 601, 626, 960
0T160ZD	526, 539, 600, 626, 960	0T170JC	526, 539, 601, 626, 960	0T174ZD	526, 539, 601, 626, 960
0T163JD	526, 539, 600, 626, 960	0T170JD	526, 539, 601, 626, 960	0T18*	505, 736
0T16476	526, 539, 600, 626, 960	0T170K6	526, 539, 601, 626, 960	0T18076	526, 539, 601, 626, 960
0T16477	526, 539, 600, 626, 960	0T170K7	526, 539, 601, 626, 960	0T18077	526, 539, 601, 626, 960
0T16478	526, 539, 600, 626, 960	0T170K8	526, 539, 601, 626, 960	0T18078	526, 539, 601, 626, 960
0T16479	526, 539, 600, 626, 960	0T170K9	526, 539, 601, 626, 960	0T18079	526, 539, 601, 626, 960
0T1647A	526, 539, 600, 626, 960	0T170KA	526, 539, 601, 626, 960	0T1807A	526, 539, 601, 626, 960
0T1647B	960	0T170KB	960	0T1807B	960
0T1647C	526, 539, 600, 626, 960	0T170KC	526, 539, 601, 626, 960	0T1807C	526, 539, 601, 626, 960
0T1647D	526, 539, 600, 626, 960	0T170KD	526, 539, 601, 626, 960	0T1807D	527, 539, 601, 626, 960
0T164J6	526, 539, 600, 626, 960	0T170Z6	526, 539, 601, 626, 960	0T180J6	527, 539, 601, 626, 960
0T164J7	526, 539, 600, 626, 960	0T170Z7	526, 539, 601, 626, 960	0T180J7	527, 539, 601, 626, 960
0T164J8	526, 539, 600, 626, 960	0T170Z8	526, 539, 601, 626, 960	0T180J8	527, 539, 601, 626, 960
0T164J9	526, 539, 600, 626, 960	0T170Z9	526, 539, 601, 626, 960	0T180J9	527, 539, 601, 626, 960
0T164JA	526, 539, 600, 626, 960	0T170ZA	526, 539, 601, 626, 960	0T180JA	527, 539, 601, 626, 960
0T164JB	960	0T170ZB	960	0T180JB	960
0T164JC	526, 539, 600, 626, 960	0T170ZC	526, 539, 601, 626, 960	0T180JC	527, 539, 601, 626, 960
0T164JD	526, 539, 600, 626, 960	0T170ZD	526, 539, 601, 626, 960	0T180JD	527, 539, 601, 626, 961
0T164K6	526, 539, 600, 626, 960	0T173JD	526, 539, 601, 626, 960	0T180K6	527, 539, 601, 626, 961
0T164K7	526, 539, 600, 626, 960	0T17476	526, 539, 601, 626, 960	0T180K7	527, 539, 601, 626, 961
0T164K8	526, 539, 600, 626, 960	0T17477	526, 539, 601, 626, 960	0T180K8	527, 539, 601, 626, 961
		0T17478	526, 539, 601, 626, 960	0T180K9	527, 539, 601, 626, 961

Code	Page	Code	Page	Code	Page
0T180KA	527, 539, 601, 626, 961	0T1B0KD	504, 601, 626	0T7D4ZZ	508, 527, 736, 961, 1087
0T180KB	961	0T1B0ZC	504, 601, 626	0T82*	505
0T180KC	527, 539, 601, 626, 961	0T1B0ZD	507, 535, 601, 626, 736, 961	0T8C*	507
0T180KD	527, 539, 601, 626, 961	0T1B3JD	504, 601, 626	0T8C0ZZ	1087
0T180Z6	527, 539, 601, 626, 961	0T1B479	504, 601, 626	0T8C3ZZ	1087
0T180Z7	527, 539, 601, 626, 961	0T1B47D	504, 601, 626	0T8C4ZZ	1087
0T180Z8	527, 539, 601, 626, 961	0T1B4J9	504, 601, 626	0T9000Z	505, 736, 961
0T180Z9	527, 539, 601, 626, 961	0T1B4JC	504, 601, 626	0T900ZX	287, 505, 578, 601, 627, 736, 961
0T180ZA	527, 539, 601, 626, 961	0T1B4JD	504, 601, 626	0T900ZZ	505, 736
0T180ZB	961	0T1B4K9	504, 601, 626	0T9040Z	505, 736, 961
0T180ZC	527, 539, 601, 626, 961	0T1B4KC	504, 601, 626	0T9070Z	505, 736, 961
0T180ZD	527, 539, 601, 626, 961	0T1B4KD	504, 601, 626	0T907ZZ	505, 736
0T183JD	527, 539, 601, 626, 961	0T1B4Z9	504, 601, 626	0T9080Z	505, 736, 961
0T18476	527, 539, 601, 626, 961	0T1B4ZC	504, 601, 626	0T908ZZ	505, 736
0T18477	527, 539, 601, 626, 961	0T1B4ZD	507, 535, 601, 626, 736, 961	0T9100Z	505, 736, 961
0T18478	527, 539, 601, 626, 961	0T50*	505	0T910ZX	287, 505, 578, 601, 627, 736, 961
0T18479	527, 539, 601, 626, 961	0T51*	505	0T910ZZ	505, 736
0T1847A	527, 539, 601, 626, 961	0T53*	505	0T9140Z	505, 736, 961
0T1847B	961	0T54*	505	0T9170Z	505, 736, 961
0T1847C	527, 539, 601, 626, 961	0T56*	505, 527, 540, 736	0T917ZZ	505, 736
0T1847D	527, 539, 601, 626, 961	0T560ZZ	961	0T9180Z	505, 736, 961
0T184J6	527, 539, 601, 626, 961	0T563ZZ	961	0T918ZZ	505, 736
0T184J7	527, 539, 601, 626, 961	0T564ZZ	961	0T9300Z	505, 527, 540, 601, 627, 736, 961
0T184J8	527, 539, 601, 626, 961	0T567ZZ	961	0T930ZX	287, 505, 578, 601, 627, 736, 961
0T184J9	527, 539, 601, 626, 961	0T568ZZ	961	0T930ZZ	505, 527, 540, 601, 627, 736, 961
0T184JA	527, 539, 601, 626, 961	0T57*	505, 527, 540, 736	0T9340Z	505, 527, 540, 601, 627, 736, 961
0T184JB	961	0T570ZZ	961	0T9370Z	505, 736, 961, 1087
0T184JC	527, 540, 601, 626, 961	0T573ZZ	961	0T937ZZ	505, 736, 961
0T184JD	527, 540, 601, 626, 961	0T574ZZ	961	0T9380Z	505, 736, 961, 1087
0T184K6	527, 540, 601, 626, 961	0T577ZZ	961	0T938ZZ	505, 736, 961
0T184K7	527, 540, 601, 626, 961	0T578ZZ	961	0T9400Z	505, 527, 540, 601, 627, 736, 961
0T184K8	527, 540, 601, 626, 961	0T5B*	527	0T940ZX	287, 505, 578, 601, 627, 736, 961
0T184K9	527, 540, 601, 626, 961	0T5B0ZZ	507, 540, 601, 627, 1087	0T940ZZ	505, 527, 540, 601, 627, 736, 961
0T184KA	527, 540, 601, 626, 961	0T5B3ZZ	507, 540, 601, 627, 1087	0T9440Z	505, 527, 540, 601, 627, 736, 961
0T184KB	961	0T5B4ZZ	507, 540, 601, 627, 1087	0T9470Z	505, 736, 961, 1087
0T184KC	527, 540, 601, 626, 961	0T5B7ZZ	508, 1087	0T947ZZ	505, 736, 961
0T184KD	527, 540, 601, 626, 961	0T5B8ZZ	508, 1087	0T9480Z	505, 736, 961, 1087
0T184Z6	527, 540, 601, 626, 961	0T5C*	527	0T948ZZ	505, 736, 961
0T184Z7	527, 540, 601, 626, 961	0T5C0ZZ	507, 540, 601, 627, 1087	0T960ZX	505
0T184Z8	527, 540, 601, 626, 961	0T5C3ZZ	507, 540, 601, 627, 1087	0T9600Z	505, 1087
0T184Z9	527, 540, 601, 626, 961	0T5C4ZZ	507, 540, 601, 627, 1087	0T964ZZ	505, 1087
0T184ZA	527, 540, 601, 626, 961	0T5C7ZZ	508, 1087	0T9670Z	505, 1087
0T184ZB	961	0T5C8ZZ	508, 1087	0T968ZZ	505, 1087
0T184ZC	527, 540, 601, 626, 961	0T73*	505	0T970ZX	505
0T184ZD	527, 540, 601, 626, 961	0T74*	505	0T970ZZ	505, 1087
0T1B*	527	0T760ZZ	505, 736, 961, 1087	0T974ZZ	505, 1087
0T1B079	504, 601, 626	0T763ZZ	505, 736, 961, 1087	0T977ZZ	505, 1087
0T1B07C	504, 601, 626	0T764ZZ	505, 736, 961, 1087	0T978ZZ	505, 1087
0T1B07D	504, 601, 626	0T768DZ	505, 736, 961, 1087	0T980ZX	505
0T1B0J9	504, 601, 626	0T768ZZ	505, 736, 961, 1087	0T980ZZ	505, 1087
0T1B0JC	504, 601, 626	0T770ZZ	505, 736, 961, 1087	0T984ZZ	505, 1087
0T1B0JD	504, 601, 626	0T773ZZ	505, 736, 961, 1087	0T987ZZ	505, 1087
0T1B0K9	504, 601, 626	0T774ZZ	505, 736, 961, 1087	0T988ZZ	505, 1087
0T1B0KC	504, 601, 626	0T778DZ	505, 736, 961, 1087	0T9B00Z	507, 527, 535, 601, 627, 736, 961
		0T778ZZ	505, 736, 961, 1087	0T9B0ZX	507, 527, 540, 601, 627
		0T780ZZ	505, 736, 961	0T9B0ZZ	507, 736
		0T783ZZ	505, 736, 961	0T9B3ZX	508, 527, 540, 1087
		0T784ZZ	505, 736, 961	0T9B4ZX	508, 527, 540, 1087
		0T788DZ	505, 736, 961, 1087	0T9B7ZX	508, 527, 540, 1087
		0T7B0DZ	504, 540, 736, 961	0T9B8ZX	508, 527, 540, 1087
		0T7B0ZZ	504, 540, 736, 961	0T9C00Z	507, 736
		0T7B3DZ	504, 540, 736, 961	0T9C0ZX	507, 527, 540, 601, 627
		0T7B3ZZ	504, 540, 736, 961	0T9C0ZZ	507, 736
		0T7B4DZ	504, 540, 736, 961	0T9C3ZX	508, 527, 540, 1087
		0T7B4ZZ	504, 540, 736, 961	0T9C4ZX	508, 527, 540, 1087
		0T7B8DZ	504, 540, 736, 961	0T9C7ZX	508, 527, 540, 1087
		0T7B8ZZ	504, 540, 736, 961	0T9C8ZX	508, 527, 540, 1087
		0T7D0ZZ	508, 527, 736, 961, 1087		
		0T7D3ZZ	508, 527, 736, 961, 1087		

Numeric Index to Procedures
DRG Expert—Volume II

Code	Page
ØT9DØØZ	508, 736, 1087
ØT9DØZZ	508
ØT9D4ØZ	508, 736, 1087
ØT9D4ZZ	508
ØT9D7ØZ	508
ØT9D7ZZ	508
ØT9D8ØZ	508
ØT9D8ZZ	508
ØT9DXØZ	508
ØT9DXZZ	508
ØTBØØZX	287, 505, 578, 601, 627, 736, 961
ØTBØØZZ	505, 527, 601, 627, 736, 961
ØTBØ3ZZ	505, 527, 601, 627, 736, 961
ØTBØ4ZZ	505, 527, 601, 627, 736, 961
ØTBØ7ZZ	505, 736, 961
ØTBØ8ZZ	505, 736, 961
ØTB1ØZX	287, 505, 578, 601, 627, 736, 961
ØTB1ØZZ	505, 527, 601, 627, 736, 961
ØTB13ZZ	505, 527, 601, 627, 736, 961
ØTB14ZZ	505, 527, 601, 627, 736, 961
ØTB17ZZ	505, 736, 961
ØTB18ZZ	505, 736, 961
ØTB3ØZX	287, 505, 578, 601, 627, 736, 961
ØTB3ØZZ	505, 527, 601, 627, 736, 961
ØTB33ZZ	505, 527, 601, 627, 736, 961
ØTB34ZZ	505, 527, 601, 627, 736, 961
ØTB37ZZ	505, 736, 961
ØTB38ZZ	505, 736, 961
ØTB4ØZX	287, 505, 578, 601, 627, 736, 961
ØTB4ØZZ	505, 527, 601, 627, 736, 961
ØTB43ZZ	505, 527, 601, 627, 736, 961
ØTB44ZZ	505, 527, 601, 627, 736, 961
ØTB47ZZ	505, 736, 961
ØTB48ZZ	505, 736, 961
ØTB6ØZX	505
ØTB6ØZZ	505, 527, 540, 736, 961
ØTB63ZZ	505, 527, 540, 736, 961
ØTB64ZZ	505, 527, 540, 736, 961
ØTB67ZZ	505, 527, 540, 736, 961
ØTB68ZZ	505, 527, 540, 736, 961
ØTB7ØZX	505
ØTB7ØZZ	505, 527, 540, 736, 961
ØTB73ZZ	505, 527, 540, 736, 961
ØTB74ZZ	505, 527, 540, 736, 961
ØTB77ZZ	505, 527, 540, 736, 961
ØTB78ZZ	505, 527, 540, 736, 961
ØTBBØZX	507, 527, 540, 601, 627
ØTBBØZZ	504, 521, 540, 601, 627, 736, 961
ØTBB3ZX	508, 527, 540, 1087
ØTBB3ZZ	504, 521, 540, 601, 627, 737, 961
ØTBB4ZX	508, 527, 540, 1087
ØTBB4ZZ	504, 521, 540, 602, 627, 737, 961
ØTBB7ZX	508, 527, 540, 1087
ØTBB7ZZ	508, 527, 1087
ØTBB8ZX	508, 527, 540, 1087
ØTBB8ZZ	508, 527, 1087
ØTBCØZX	507, 527, 540, 602, 627
ØTBCØZZ	504, 521, 540, 602, 627, 737, 961
ØTBC3ZX	508, 527, 540, 1087
ØTBC3ZZ	504, 521, 540, 602, 627, 737, 961
ØTBC4ZX	508, 527, 540, 1087
ØTBC4ZZ	504, 521, 540, 602, 627, 737, 961
ØTBC7ZX	508, 527, 540, 1087
ØTBC7ZZ	508, 527, 1088
ØTBC8ZX	508, 527, 540, 1088
ØTBC8ZZ	508, 527, 1088
ØTBDØZZ	508
ØTBD3ZZ	509
ØTBD4ZZ	509
ØTBD7ZZ	509
ØTBD8ZZ	509
ØTBDXZZ	509
ØTCØ*	505, 737
ØTCØ3ZZ	961
ØTCØ4ZZ	961
ØTC1*	505, 737
ØTC13ZZ	961
ØTC14ZZ	961
ØTC3*	737
ØTC3ØZZ	505, 961
ØTC33ZZ	505, 961
ØTC34ZZ	505, 961
ØTC37ZZ	508, 961, 1088
ØTC38ZZ	508, 961, 1088
ØTC4*	737
ØTC4ØZZ	505, 961
ØTC43ZZ	505, 961
ØTC44ZZ	505, 961
ØTC47ZZ	508, 961, 1088
ØTC48ZZ	508, 961, 1088
ØTC6ØZZ	505, 1088
ØTC63ZZ	505, 1088
ØTC64ZZ	505, 1088
ØTC67ZZ	508, 737, 961, 1088
ØTC68ZZ	508, 737, 961, 1088
ØTC7ØZZ	505, 1088
ØTC73ZZ	505, 1088
ØTC74ZZ	505, 1088
ØTC77ZZ	508, 737, 961, 1088
ØTC78ZZ	508, 737, 961, 1088
ØTCBØZZ	507, 737
ØTCB3ZZ	507, 737
ØTCB4ZZ	507, 737
ØTCCØZZ	507, 737
ØTCC3ZZ	507, 737
ØTCC4ZZ	507, 737
ØTCDØZZ	509, 737, 1088
ØTCD3ZZ	509, 737, 1088
ØTCD4ZZ	509, 737, 1088
ØTDØ*	505
ØTD1*	505
ØTF33ZZ	505, 737, 961
ØTF34ZZ	505, 737, 961
ØTF43ZZ	505, 737, 962
ØTF44ZZ	505, 737, 962
ØTH5Ø2Z	505, 737
ØTH5ØYZ	505, 737
ØTH532Z	505, 737
ØTH542Z	505, 737
ØTH58YZ	505, 737
ØTH9Ø2Z	505, 1088
ØTH9ØMZ	505
ØTH9ØYZ	505, 1088
ØTH932Z	505, 1088
ØTH93MZ	505
ØTH942Z	505, 1088
ØTH94MZ	505
ØTH97MZ	505
ØTH98MZ	505
ØTH98YZ	506, 1088
ØTHBØ2Z	507, 737
ØTHBØLZ	507, 737, 962
ØTHBØMZ	507
ØTHBØYZ	507, 737
ØTHB32Z	507, 737
ØTHB3LZ	507, 737, 962
ØTHB3MZ	507
ØTHB42Z	507, 737
ØTHB4LZ	507, 737, 962
ØTHB4MZ	507
ØTHB7LZ	507, 737, 962
ØTHB7MZ	507
ØTHB8LZ	507, 737, 962
ØTHB8MZ	507
ØTHB8YZ	507, 737
ØTHC*	507, 737
ØTHCØLZ	962
ØTHC3LZ	962
ØTHC4LZ	962
ØTHC7LZ	962
ØTHC8LZ	962
ØTHDØ2Z	509, 737, 1088
ØTHDØLZ	507, 737, 962
ØTHDØYZ	509, 737, 1088
ØTHD32Z	509, 737, 1088
ØTHD3LZ	507, 737, 962
ØTHD42Z	509, 737, 1088
ØTHD4LZ	507, 737, 962
ØTHD7LZ	507, 737, 962
ØTHD8LZ	507, 737, 962
ØTHDX2Z	509, 737, 1088
ØTHDXLZ	507, 737, 962
ØTJ5ØZZ	506, 737
ØTJ9ØZZ	506, 1088
ØTJBØZZ	507, 737, 962
ØTJB4ZZ	507, 527, 602, 627, 737, 962, 1088
ØTJDØZZ	509, 540, 737, 962, 1088
ØTL3*	506, 737
ØTL3ØCZ	962
ØTL3ØDZ	962
ØTL3ØZZ	962
ØTL33CZ	962
ØTL33DZ	962
ØTL33ZZ	962
ØTL34CZ	962
ØTL34DZ	962
ØTL34ZZ	962
ØTL37DZ	962
ØTL37ZZ	962
ØTL38DZ	962
ØTL38ZZ	962
ØTL4*	506, 737
ØTL4ØCZ	962
ØTL4ØDZ	962
ØTL4ØZZ	962
ØTL43CZ	962
ØTL43DZ	962
ØTL43ZZ	962
ØTL44CZ	962
ØTL44DZ	962
ØTL44ZZ	962
ØTL47DZ	962
ØTL47ZZ	962
ØTL48DZ	962
ØTL48ZZ	962
ØTL6*	506, 737
ØTL6ØCZ	962
ØTL6ØDZ	962
ØTL6ØZZ	962
ØTL63CZ	962
ØTL63DZ	962
ØTL63ZZ	962
ØTL64CZ	962
ØTL64DZ	962
ØTL64ZZ	962
ØTL67DZ	962
ØTL67ZZ	962
ØTL68DZ	962
ØTL68ZZ	962
ØTL7*	506, 737
ØTL7ØCZ	962
ØTL7ØDZ	962
ØTL7ØZZ	962
ØTL73CZ	962
ØTL73DZ	962
ØTL73ZZ	962
ØTL74CZ	962
ØTL74DZ	962
ØTL74ZZ	962
ØTL77DZ	962
ØTL77ZZ	962
ØTL78DZ	962
ØTL78ZZ	962
ØTLB*	507, 737
ØTLBØCZ	962
ØTLBØDZ	962
ØTLBØZZ	962
ØTLB3CZ	962
ØTLB3DZ	962
ØTLB3ZZ	962
ØTLB4CZ	962
ØTLB4DZ	962
ØTLB4ZZ	962
ØTLB7DZ	962
ØTLB7ZZ	962
ØTLB8DZ	962
ØTLB8ZZ	962
ØTLC*	507, 737
ØTLCØCZ	962
ØTLCØDZ	962
ØTLCØZZ	962
ØTLC3CZ	962
ØTLC3DZ	962
ØTLC3ZZ	962
ØTLC4CZ	962
ØTLC4DZ	962
ØTLC4ZZ	962
ØTLC7DZ	962
ØTLC7ZZ	962
ØTLC8DZ	962
ØTLC8ZZ	962
ØTLD*	509, 527, 540
ØTLDØCZ	1088
ØTLDØDZ	1088
ØTLDØZZ	1088
ØTLD3CZ	1088
ØTLD3DZ	1088
ØTLD3ZZ	1088
ØTLD4CZ	1088
ØTLD4DZ	1088
ØTLD4ZZ	1088
ØTLD7DZ	1088
ØTLD7ZZ	1088
ØTLD8DZ	1088
ØTLD8ZZ	1088
ØTLDXCZ	1088
ØTLDXDZ	1088
ØTLDXZZ	1088
ØTMØ*	506
ØTM1*	506
ØTM2*	506
ØTM3*	506
ØTM4*	506
ØTM6*	506, 737
ØTM6ØZZ	962
ØTM64ZZ	962
ØTM7*	506, 737
ØTM7ØZZ	962
ØTM74ZZ	962
ØTM8*	506, 737
ØTM8ØZZ	962
ØTM84ZZ	962
ØTMB*	504, 540, 737
ØTMBØZZ	962
ØTMB4ZZ	962
ØTMC*	504, 540, 737
ØTMCØZZ	962
ØTMC4ZZ	962
ØTMD*	509, 521, 540, 737
ØTMDØZZ	962
ØTMD4ZZ	962
ØTNØ*	506, 527, 540, 737
ØTNØØZZ	602, 627, 962
ØTNØ3ZZ	602, 627, 962
ØTNØ4ZZ	602, 627, 962
ØTNØ7ZZ	602, 627, 962
ØTNØ8ZZ	602, 627, 962
ØTN1*	506, 527, 540, 737
ØTN1ØZZ	602, 627, 962
ØTN13ZZ	602, 627, 962
ØTN14ZZ	602, 627, 962
ØTN17ZZ	602, 627, 962
ØTN18ZZ	602, 627, 962
ØTN3*	506, 527, 540, 737
ØTN3ØZZ	602, 627, 962
ØTN33ZZ	602, 627, 962
ØTN34ZZ	602, 627, 962
ØTN37ZZ	602, 627, 962
ØTN38ZZ	602, 627, 962
ØTN4*	506, 527, 540, 737
ØTN4ØZZ	602, 627, 962
ØTN43ZZ	602, 627, 962
ØTN44ZZ	602, 627, 962
ØTN47ZZ	602, 627, 962
ØTN48ZZ	602, 627, 962
ØTN6*	506, 737
ØTN6ØZZ	527, 540, 602, 627, 962
ØTN63ZZ	527, 540, 602, 627, 962
ØTN64ZZ	527, 540, 602, 627, 962
ØTN67ZZ	962
ØTN68ZZ	962
ØTN7*	506, 737
ØTN7ØZZ	527, 540, 602, 627, 962
ØTN73ZZ	527, 540, 602, 627, 962
ØTN74ZZ	527, 540, 602, 627, 962
ØTN77ZZ	962
ØTN78ZZ	962
ØTNBØZZ	507, 737, 962
ØTNB3ZZ	507, 527, 540, 602, 627, 737, 962
ØTNB4ZZ	507, 527, 540, 602, 627, 737, 962
ØTNB7ZZ	508
ØTNB8ZZ	508
ØTNCØZZ	507, 737, 962
ØTNC3ZZ	507, 527, 540, 602, 627, 737, 962
ØTNC4ZZ	507, 527, 540, 602, 627, 737, 962
ØTNC7ZZ	508
ØTNC8ZZ	508
ØTND*	509, 521, 540, 737
ØTNDØZZ	962, 1088
ØTND3ZZ	962, 1088
ØTND4ZZ	962, 1088
ØTND7ZZ	962, 1088
ØTND8ZZ	962, 1088
ØTNDXZZ	962, 1088
ØTP5ØØZ	506, 737
ØTP5Ø2Z	506, 737
ØTP5Ø3Z	506, 737
ØTP5Ø7Z	506, 737
ØTP5ØCZ	506, 737
ØTP5ØDZ	506, 737
ØTP5ØJZ	506, 737
ØTP5ØKZ	506, 737
ØTP5ØYZ	506, 737
ØTP53ØZ	506, 737
ØTP532Z	506, 737
ØTP533Z	506, 737
ØTP537Z	506, 737
ØTP53CZ	506, 737
ØTP53DZ	506, 737
ØTP53JZ	506, 737
ØTP53KZ	506, 737
ØTP54ØZ	506, 737
ØTP542Z	506, 737
ØTP543Z	506, 737
ØTP547Z	506, 737
ØTP54CZ	506, 737
ØTP54DZ	506, 737
ØTP54JZ	506, 737
ØTP54KZ	506, 737
ØTP577Z	506, 737
ØTP57CZ	506, 737
ØTP57JZ	506, 737
ØTP57KZ	506, 737
ØTP587Z	506, 737
ØTP58CZ	506, 737
ØTP58JZ	506, 737
ØTP58KZ	506, 737
ØTP58YZ	506, 737
ØTP9ØØZ	506, 1088
ØTP9Ø2Z	506, 1088
ØTP9Ø3Z	506, 1088
ØTP9Ø7Z	506, 1088
ØTP9ØCZ	506, 1088
ØTP9ØDZ	506, 1088
ØTP9ØJZ	506, 1088
ØTP9ØKZ	506, 1088
ØTP9ØMZ	506
ØTP9ØYZ	506, 1088
ØTP93ØZ	506, 1088
ØTP932Z	506, 1088
ØTP933Z	506, 1088
ØTP937Z	506, 1088
ØTP93CZ	506, 1088
ØTP93DZ	506, 1088
ØTP93JZ	506, 1088
ØTP93KZ	506, 1088
ØTP93MZ	506
ØTP94ØZ	506, 1088
ØTP942Z	506, 1088
ØTP943Z	506, 1088
ØTP947Z	506, 1088
ØTP94CZ	506, 1088
ØTP94DZ	506, 1088
ØTP94JZ	506, 1088
ØTP94KZ	506, 1088
ØTP94MZ	506
ØTP977Z	506, 1088
ØTP97CZ	506, 1088
ØTP97JZ	506, 1088
ØTP97KZ	506, 1088
ØTP97MZ	506
ØTP987Z	506, 1088
ØTP98CZ	506, 1088
ØTP98JZ	506, 1088
ØTP98KZ	506, 1088
ØTP98MZ	506
ØTP98YZ	506, 1088
ØTP9XMZ	506
ØTPBØØZ	507, 737
ØTPBØ2Z	507, 737
ØTPBØ3Z	507, 737
ØTPBØ7Z	507, 737
ØTPBØCZ	507, 737
ØTPBØDZ	507, 737
ØTPBØJZ	507, 737
ØTPBØKZ	507, 737
ØTPBØLZ	507, 737
ØTPBØMZ	507, 1088
ØTPBØYZ	507, 737
ØTPB3ØZ	507, 737
ØTPB32Z	507, 737
ØTPB33Z	507, 737
ØTPB37Z	507, 737
ØTPB3CZ	507, 737
ØTPB3DZ	507, 737
ØTPB3JZ	507, 737
ØTPB3KZ	507, 737
ØTPB3LZ	507, 737
ØTPB3MZ	507, 1088
ØTPB4ØZ	507, 737
ØTPB42Z	507, 737
ØTPB43Z	507, 737
ØTPB47Z	507, 737
ØTPB4CZ	507, 737
ØTPB4DZ	507, 737
ØTPB4JZ	507, 737
ØTPB4KZ	507, 737
ØTPB4LZ	507, 737
ØTPB4MZ	507, 1088
ØTPB77Z	507, 737
ØTPB7CZ	507, 737
ØTPB7JZ	507, 737
ØTPB7KZ	507, 737
ØTPB7LZ	507, 737
ØTPB7MZ	507, 1088
ØTPB87Z	507, 737
ØTPB8CZ	507, 737
ØTPB8JZ	507, 737
ØTPB8KZ	507, 737
ØTPB8LZ	507, 737
ØTPB8MZ	507, 1088
ØTPB8YZ	507, 737
ØTPBXMZ	508, 1088
ØTPDØØZ	509, 737, 1088
ØTPDØ2Z	509, 737, 1088
ØTPDØ3Z	509, 737, 1088
ØTPDØ7Z	509, 737, 1088
ØTPDØCZ	509, 737, 1088
ØTPDØDZ	509, 737, 1088
ØTPDØJZ	509, 737, 1088
ØTPDØKZ	509, 737, 1088
ØTPDØLZ	509, 527, 540, 1088
ØTPDØYZ	509, 737, 1088
ØTPD3ØZ	509, 737, 1088
ØTPD32Z	509, 737, 1088
ØTPD33Z	509, 737, 1088
ØTPD37Z	509, 737, 1088
ØTPD3CZ	509, 737, 1088
ØTPD3DZ	509, 737, 1088
ØTPD3JZ	509, 737, 1088
ØTPD3KZ	509, 737, 1088
ØTPD3LZ	509, 527, 540, 1088
ØTPD4ØZ	509, 737, 1088
ØTPD42Z	509, 737, 1088
ØTPD43Z	509, 738, 1088
ØTPD47Z	509, 738, 1088
ØTPD4CZ	509, 738, 1088
ØTPD4DZ	509, 738, 1088
ØTPD4JZ	509, 738, 1088
ØTPD4KZ	509, 738, 1088
ØTPD4LZ	509, 527, 540, 1088
ØTPD77Z	509, 738, 1088
ØTPD7CZ	509, 738, 1088
ØTPD7JZ	509, 738, 1088
ØTPD7KZ	509, 738, 1088

Numeric Index to Procedures

Code	Page
0TPD7LZ	509, 527, 540, 1088
0TPD87Z	509, 738, 1088
0TPD8CZ	509, 738, 1088
0TPD8JZ	509, 738, 1088
0TPD8KZ	509, 738, 1088
0TPD8LZ	509, 527, 540, 1088
0TPDXLZ	509, 527, 540, 1088
0TQ0*	506, 527
0TQ00ZZ	602, 627
0TQ03ZZ	602, 627
0TQ04ZZ	602, 627
0TQ07ZZ	602, 627
0TQ08ZZ	602, 627
0TQ1*	506, 527
0TQ10ZZ	602, 627
0TQ13ZZ	602, 627
0TQ14ZZ	602, 627
0TQ17ZZ	602, 627
0TQ18ZZ	602, 627
0TQ3*	506, 738
0TQ30ZZ	962
0TQ33ZZ	962
0TQ34ZZ	962
0TQ37ZZ	962
0TQ38ZZ	962
0TQ4*	506, 738
0TQ40ZZ	962
0TQ43ZZ	962
0TQ44ZZ	962
0TQ47ZZ	962
0TQ48ZZ	962
0TQ6*	183, 506, 738
0TQ60ZZ	962
0TQ63ZZ	962
0TQ64ZZ	962
0TQ67ZZ	962
0TQ68ZZ	962
0TQ7*	183, 506, 527, 540, 738
0TQ70ZZ	602, 627, 962
0TQ73ZZ	602, 627, 962
0TQ74ZZ	602, 627, 962
0TQ77ZZ	602, 627, 962
0TQ78ZZ	602, 627, 962
0TQB*	183, 504, 527, 540, 738
0TQB0ZZ	508, 602, 627, 962
0TQB3ZZ	508, 602, 627, 963
0TQB4ZZ	508, 602, 627, 963
0TQB7ZZ	602, 627, 963
0TQB8ZZ	602, 627, 963
0TQC0ZZ	504, 540
0TQC3ZZ	504, 540
0TQC4ZZ	504, 540
0TQC7ZZ	504, 540
0TQC8ZZ	504, 540
0TQD*	521, 738
0TQD0ZZ	508, 602, 627, 963
0TQD3ZZ	508, 602, 627, 963
0TQD4ZZ	508, 602, 627, 963
0TQD7ZZ	509, 602, 627, 963
0TQD8ZZ	509, 602, 627, 963
0TQDXZZ	509, 602, 627, 963
0TR3*	506
0TR4*	506
0TR6*	506, 738
0TR607Z	963
0TR60JZ	963
0TR60KZ	963
0TR647Z	963
0TR64JZ	963
0TR64KZ	963
0TR677Z	963
0TR67JZ	963
0TR67KZ	963
0TR687Z	963
0TR68JZ	963
0TR68KZ	963
0TR7*	506, 738
0TR707Z	963
0TR70JZ	963
0TR70KZ	963
0TR747Z	963
0TR74JZ	963
0TR74KZ	963
0TR777Z	963
0TR77JZ	963
0TR77KZ	963
0TR787Z	963
0TR78JZ	963

Code	Page
0TR78KZ	963
0TRB*	504, 738
0TRB07Z	963
0TRB0JZ	963
0TRB0KZ	963
0TRB47Z	963
0TRB4JZ	963
0TRB4KZ	963
0TRB77Z	963
0TRB7JZ	963
0TRB7KZ	963
0TRB87Z	963
0TRB8JZ	963
0TRB8KZ	963
0TRC*	504, 738
0TRC07Z	963
0TRC0JZ	963
0TRC0KZ	963
0TRC47Z	963
0TRC4JZ	963
0TRC4KZ	963
0TRC77Z	963
0TRC7JZ	963
0TRC7KZ	963
0TRC87Z	963
0TRC8JZ	963
0TRC8KZ	963
0TRD*	509, 521, 738
0TRD07Z	963
0TRD0JZ	963
0TRD0KZ	963
0TRD4JZ	963
0TRD4KZ	963
0TRD77Z	963
0TRD7JZ	963
0TRD7KZ	963
0TRD87Z	963
0TRD8JZ	963
0TRD8KZ	963
0TRDX7Z	963
0TRDXJZ	963
0TRDXKZ	963
0TS0*	506, 738
0TS00ZZ	963
0TS04ZZ	963
0TS1*	506, 738
0TS10ZZ	963
0TS14ZZ	963
0TS2*	506, 738
0TS20ZZ	963
0TS24ZZ	963
0TS3*	506
0TS4*	506
0TS6*	506
0TS7*	506
0TS8*	506
0TSB*	504
0TSC*	508, 537
0TSD*	508, 521, 537
0TT0*	506, 738
0TT00ZZ	963
0TT04ZZ	963
0TT1*	506, 738
0TT10ZZ	963
0TT14ZZ	963
0TT2*	506, 738
0TT20ZZ	963
0TT24ZZ	963
0TT3*	506, 738
0TT30ZZ	963
0TT34ZZ	963
0TT37ZZ	963
0TT38ZZ	963
0TT4*	506, 738
0TT40ZZ	963
0TT44ZZ	963
0TT47ZZ	963
0TT48ZZ	963
0TT6*	506, 738
0TT60ZZ	963
0TT64ZZ	963
0TT67ZZ	963
0TT68ZZ	963
0TT7*	506, 738
0TT70ZZ	963
0TT74ZZ	963
0TT77ZZ	963
0TT78ZZ	963
0TTB*	504, 521, 540, 738
0TTB0ZZ	531, 602, 627, 963
0TTB4ZZ	602, 627, 963
0TTB7ZZ	602, 627, 963

Code	Page
0TTB8ZZ	602, 627, 963
0TTC*	504, 521, 540, 738
0TTC0ZZ	602, 627, 963
0TTC4ZZ	602, 627, 963
0TTC7ZZ	602, 627, 963
0TTC8ZZ	602, 627, 963
0TTD0ZZ	531
0TU3*	506
0TU4*	506
0TU6*	506, 738
0TU607Z	963
0TU60JZ	963
0TU60KZ	963
0TU647Z	963
0TU64JZ	963
0TU64KZ	963
0TU677Z	963
0TU67JZ	963
0TU67KZ	963
0TU687Z	963
0TU68JZ	963
0TU68KZ	963
0TU7*	506, 738
0TU707Z	963
0TU70JZ	963
0TU70KZ	963
0TU747Z	963
0TU74JZ	963
0TU74KZ	963
0TU777Z	963
0TU77JZ	963
0TU77KZ	963
0TU787Z	963
0TU78JZ	963
0TU78KZ	963
0TUB*	504, 738
0TUB07Z	963
0TUB0JZ	963
0TUB0KZ	963
0TUB47Z	963
0TUB4JZ	963
0TUB4KZ	963
0TUB77Z	963
0TUB7JZ	963
0TUB7KZ	963
0TUB87Z	963
0TUB8JZ	963
0TUB8KZ	963
0TUC*	508, 537
0TUC0JZ	1088
0TUC4JZ	1088
0TUC7JZ	1088
0TUC8JZ	1088
0TUD*	509, 521, 738
0TUD07Z	963
0TUD0JZ	963
0TUD0KZ	963
0TUD47Z	963
0TUD4JZ	963
0TUD4KZ	963
0TUD77Z	963
0TUD7JZ	963
0TUD7KZ	963
0TUD87Z	963
0TUD8JZ	963
0TUD8KZ	963
0TUDX7Z	963
0TUDXJZ	963
0TUDXKZ	963
0TV3*	506
0TV4*	506
0TV6*	506, 738
0TV60CZ	963
0TV60DZ	963
0TV60ZZ	963
0TV63CZ	963
0TV63DZ	963
0TV63ZZ	963
0TV64CZ	963
0TV64DZ	963
0TV64ZZ	963
0TV67DZ	963
0TV67ZZ	963
0TV68DZ	963
0TV68ZZ	963
0TV7*	506, 738
0TV70*	963
0TV70DZ	964
0TV73CZ	964
0TV73DZ	964
0TV73ZZ	964
0TV74CZ	964

Code	Page
0TV74DZ	964
0TV74ZZ	964
0TV77DZ	964
0TV77ZZ	964
0TV78DZ	964
0TV78ZZ	964
0TVB*	504, 540, 738
0TVB0CZ	964
0TVB0DZ	964
0TVB0ZZ	964
0TVB3CZ	964
0TVB3DZ	964
0TVB3ZZ	964
0TVB4CZ	964
0TVB4DZ	964
0TVB4ZZ	964
0TVB7DZ	964
0TVB7ZZ	964
0TVB8DZ	964
0TVB8ZZ	964
0TVC*	504, 537
0TVD*	509, 521, 540, 738
0TVD0CZ	964
0TVD0DZ	964
0TVD0ZZ	964
0TVD3CZ	964
0TVD3DZ	964
0TVD3ZZ	964
0TVD4CZ	964
0TVD4DZ	964
0TVD4ZZ	964
0TVD7DZ	964
0TVD7ZZ	964
0TVD8DZ	964
0TVD8ZZ	964
0TVDXZZ	964
0TW500Z	506, 738
0TW502Z	506, 738
0TW503Z	506, 738
0TW507Z	506, 738
0TW50CZ	506, 738
0TW50DZ	506, 738
0TW50JZ	506, 738
0TW50KZ	506, 738
0TW50YZ	506, 738
0TW530Z	506, 738
0TW532Z	506, 738
0TW533Z	506, 738
0TW537Z	506, 738
0TW53CZ	506, 738
0TW53DZ	506, 738
0TW53JZ	506, 738
0TW53KZ	506, 738
0TW540Z	506, 738
0TW542Z	506, 738
0TW543Z	506, 738
0TW547Z	506, 738
0TW54CZ	506, 738
0TW54DZ	506, 738
0TW54JZ	506, 738
0TW54KZ	506, 738
0TW570Z	506, 738
0TW572Z	506, 738
0TW573Z	506, 738
0TW577Z	506, 738
0TW57CZ	506, 738
0TW57DZ	506, 738
0TW57JZ	506, 738
0TW57KZ	506, 738
0TW580Z	506, 738
0TW582Z	506, 738
0TW583Z	506, 738
0TW587Z	506, 738
0TW58CZ	506, 738
0TW58DZ	506, 738
0TW58JZ	506, 738
0TW58KZ	506, 738
0TW58YZ	506, 738
0TW900Z	506, 1088
0TW902Z	506, 1088
0TW903Z	506, 1088
0TW907Z	506, 1088
0TW90CZ	507, 1088
0TW90DZ	507, 1088
0TW90JZ	507, 1088
0TW90KZ	507, 1088
0TW90MZ	507, 1088
0TW90YZ	507, 1088
0TW930Z	507, 1088
0TW933Z	507, 1088
0TW937Z	507, 1088
0TW93CZ	507, 1088

Code	Page
0TW93DZ	507, 1088
0TW93JZ	507, 1088
0TW93KZ	507, 1088
0TW93MZ	507, 1088
0TW940Z	507, 1088
0TW942Z	507, 1088
0TW943Z	507, 1088
0TW947Z	507, 1088
0TW94CZ	507, 1088
0TW94DZ	507, 1088
0TW94JZ	507, 1088
0TW94KZ	507, 1088
0TW94MZ	507, 1088
0TW970Z	507, 1088
0TW972Z	507, 1088
0TW973Z	507, 1088
0TW977Z	507, 1088
0TW97CZ	507, 1088
0TW97DZ	507, 1088
0TW97JZ	507, 1088
0TW97KZ	507, 1088
0TW97MZ	507, 1089
0TW980Z	507, 1088
0TW982Z	507, 1088
0TW983Z	507, 1088
0TW987Z	507, 1088
0TW98CZ	507, 1088
0TW98DZ	507, 1088
0TW98JZ	507, 1089
0TW98KZ	507, 1089
0TW98MZ	507, 1089
0TW98YZ	507, 1089
0TWB00Z	508, 738
0TWB02Z	508, 738
0TWB03Z	508, 738
0TWB07Z	508, 738
0TWB0CZ	508, 738
0TWB0DZ	508, 738
0TWB0JZ	508, 738
0TWB0KZ	508, 738
0TWB0LZ	508, 738
0TWB0MZ	508, 738
0TWB0YZ	508, 738
0TWB30Z	508, 738
0TWB32Z	508, 738
0TWB33Z	508, 738
0TWB37Z	508, 738
0TWB3CZ	508, 738
0TWB3DZ	508, 738
0TWB3JZ	508, 738
0TWB3KZ	508, 738
0TWB3LZ	508, 738
0TWB3MZ	508, 738
0TWB40Z	508, 738
0TWB42Z	508, 738
0TWB43Z	508, 738
0TWB47Z	508, 738
0TWB4CZ	508, 738
0TWB4DZ	508, 738
0TWB4JZ	508, 738
0TWB4KZ	508, 738
0TWB4LZ	508, 738
0TWB4MZ	508, 738
0TWB70Z	508, 738
0TWB72Z	508, 738
0TWB73Z	508, 738
0TWB77Z	508, 738
0TWB7CZ	508, 738
0TWB7DZ	508, 738
0TWB7JZ	508, 738
0TWB7KZ	508, 738
0TWB7LZ	508, 738
0TWB7MZ	508, 738
0TWB80Z	508, 738
0TWB82Z	508, 738
0TWB83Z	508, 738
0TWB87Z	508, 738
0TWB8CZ	508, 738
0TWB8DZ	508, 738
0TWB8JZ	508, 738
0TWB8KZ	508, 738
0TWB8LZ	508, 738
0TWB8MZ	508, 738
0TWB8YZ	508, 738
0TWD00Z	509, 738, 1089
0TWD02Z	509, 738, 1089
0TWD03Z	509, 738, 1089
0TWD07Z	509, 738, 1089
0TWD0CZ	509, 738, 1089
0TWD0DZ	509, 738, 1089
0TWD0JZ	509, 738, 1089
0TWD0KZ	509, 738, 1089

Code	Page
0TWD0LZ	509, 527, 540, 1089
0TWD0YZ	509, 738, 1089
0TWD30Z	509, 738, 1089
0TWD32Z	509, 738, 1089
0TWD33Z	509, 738, 1089
0TWD37Z	509, 738, 1089
0TWD3CZ	509, 738, 1089
0TWD3DZ	509, 738, 1089
0TWD3JZ	509, 738, 1089
0TWD3KZ	509, 738, 1089
0TWD3LZ	509, 527, 540, 1089
0TWD40Z	509, 738, 1089
0TWD42Z	509, 738, 1089
0TWD43Z	509, 738, 1089
0TWD47Z	509, 738, 1089
0TWD4CZ	509, 738, 1089
0TWD4DZ	509, 738, 1089
0TWD4JZ	509, 738, 1089
0TWD4KZ	509, 738, 1089
0TWD4LZ	509, 527, 540, 1089
0TWD70Z	509, 738, 1089
0TWD72Z	509, 738, 1089
0TWD73Z	509, 738, 1089
0TWD77Z	509, 738, 1089
0TWD7CZ	509, 738, 1089
0TWD7DZ	509, 738, 1089
0TWD7JZ	509, 738, 1089
0TWD7KZ	509, 738, 1089
0TWD7LZ	509, 527, 540, 1089
0TWD80Z	509, 738, 1089
0TWD82Z	509, 738, 1089
0TWD83Z	509, 739, 1089
0TWD87Z	509, 739, 1089
0TWD8CZ	509, 739, 1089
0TWD8DZ	509, 739, 1089
0TWD8JZ	509, 739, 1089
0TWD8KZ	509, 739, 1089
0TWD8LZ	509, 527, 540, 1089
0TY*	504
0TY00Z0	1
0TY00Z1	2
0TY00Z2	2
0TY10Z0	2
0TY10Z1	2
0TY10Z2	2
0U1*	531
0U50*	531
0U51*	531
0U52*	531
0U54*	531
0U55*	531
0U56*	531
0U57*	535
0U570ZZ	544, 545, 546, 1089
0U573ZZ	544, 545, 546, 1089
0U574ZZ	544, 545, 546, 1089
0U577ZZ	544, 545, 546, 1089
0U578ZZ	544, 545, 546, 1089
0U59*	531
0U590ZZ	1089
0U593ZZ	1089
0U594ZZ	1089
0U597ZZ	1089
0U598ZZ	1089
0U5B*	531
0U5C*	535
0U5C0ZZ	1089
0U5C3ZZ	1089
0U5C4ZZ	1089
0U5C7ZZ	1089
0U5C8ZZ	1089
0U5F*	535
0U5F0ZZ	1089
0U5F3ZZ	1089
0U5F4ZZ	1089
0U5F7ZZ	1089
0U5F8ZZ	1089
0U5G*	535
0U5G0ZZ	437, 1089
0U5G3ZZ	437, 1089
0U5G4ZZ	437, 1089
0U5G7ZZ	437, 1089
0U5G8ZZ	437, 1089

Numeric Index to Procedures
DRG Expert—Volume II

Numeric Index to Procedures

Code	Page
0U5GXZZ	437, 1089
0U5J*	535
0U5J0ZZ	1089
0U5JXZZ	1089
0U5K*	535
0U5K0ZZ	1089
0U5K3ZZ	1089
0U5K4ZZ	1089
0U5K7ZZ	1089
0U5K8ZZ	1089
0U5KXZZ	1089
0U5L*	535
0U5L0ZZ	438, 1089
0U5LXZZ	438, 1089
0U5M*	535
0U5M0ZZ	438, 1089
0U5MXZZ	438, 1089
0U75*	531
0U76*	531
0U77*	531
0U79*	531, 739
0U790DZ	964
0U790ZZ	964
0U793DZ	964
0U793ZZ	964
0U794DZ	964
0U794ZZ	964
0U797DZ	964
0U797ZZ	964
0U798DZ	964
0U798ZZ	964
0U7G0DZ	535, 739, 964
0U7G0ZZ	535, 739, 964
0U7G3DZ	535, 739, 964
0U7G3ZZ	535, 739, 964
0U7G4DZ	535, 739, 964
0U7G4ZZ	535, 739, 964
0U7K*	537, 739
0U7K0DZ	964
0U7K0ZZ	964
0U7K3DZ	964
0U7K3ZZ	964
0U7K4DZ	964
0U7K4ZZ	964
0U7K7DZ	964
0U7K7ZZ	964
0U7K8DZ	964
0U7K8ZZ	964
0U7KXDZ	964
0U7KXZZ	964
0U80*	531
0U81*	531
0U82*	531
0U84*	537
0U9000Z	531
0U900ZX	531
0U900ZZ	531
0U903ZX	531
0U9040Z	531
0U904ZX	531
0U904ZZ	531
0U90XZZ	531
0U9100Z	531
0U910ZX	531
0U910ZZ	531
0U913ZX	531
0U9140Z	531
0U914ZX	531
0U914ZZ	531
0U91XZZ	531
0U9200Z	531
0U920ZX	531
0U920ZZ	531
0U923ZX	531
0U9240Z	531
0U924ZX	531
0U924ZZ	531
0U92XZZ	531
0U9400Z	537
0U940ZX	531
0U940ZZ	537
0U943ZX	535, 1089
0U9440Z	537
0U944ZX	535, 1089
0U944ZZ	537
0U9500Z	531
0U950ZX	531
0U950ZZ	531
0U953ZX	531
0U9540Z	531
0U954ZX	531
0U9570Z	531
0U957ZX	531

Code	Page
0U9580Z	531
0U958ZX	531
0U9600Z	531
0U960ZX	531
0U960ZZ	531
0U963ZX	531
0U9640Z	531
0U964ZX	531
0U9670Z	531
0U967ZX	531
0U9680Z	531
0U968ZX	531
0U9700Z	531
0U970ZX	531
0U970ZZ	531
0U973ZX	531
0U9740Z	531
0U974ZX	531
0U9770Z	531
0U977ZX	531
0U9780Z	531
0U978ZX	531
0U9900Z	531, 739, 964
0U990ZX	531
0U990ZZ	531, 739, 964
0U993ZX	535, 1089
0U9940Z	531, 739, 964
0U994ZX	535, 1089
0U994ZZ	531, 739, 964
0U9970Z	531, 739, 964
0U997ZX	535, 1089
0U997ZZ	531, 739, 964
0U9980Z	531, 739, 964
0U998ZX	535, 1089
0U998ZZ	531, 739, 964
0U9C00Z	535, 1089
0U9C0ZX	438, 535, 1089
0U9C0ZZ	535, 1089
0U9C3ZX	438, 535, 1089
0U9C40Z	535, 1089
0U9C4ZX	438, 535, 1089
0U9C4ZZ	535, 1089
0U9C70Z	535, 1089
0U9C7ZX	438, 535, 1089
0U9C7ZZ	535, 1089
0U9C80Z	535, 1089
0U9C8ZX	438, 535, 1089
0U9C8ZZ	535, 1089
0U9F00Z	540
0U9F0ZX	535, 1089
0U9F0ZZ	540
0U9F3ZX	535, 1089
0U9F4ZX	535, 1089
0U9F70Z	540
0U9F7ZX	535, 1089
0U9F7ZZ	540
0U9F80Z	540
0U9F8ZX	535, 1089
0U9F8ZZ	540
0U9G00Z	535, 1089
0U9G0ZX	438, 536, 1089
0U9G0ZZ	536, 1089
0U9G3ZX	438, 536, 1089
0U9G40Z	536, 1089
0U9G4ZX	438, 536, 1089
0U9G4ZZ	536, 1089
0U9G70Z	536, 1089
0U9G7ZX	438, 536, 1089
0U9G7ZZ	536, 1089
0U9G80Z	536, 1089
0U9G8ZX	438, 536, 1089
0U9G8ZZ	536, 1089
0U9GX0Z	536, 1089
0U9GXZX	438, 536, 1089
0U9GXZZ	536, 1089
0U9J*	536
0U9J00Z	1089
0U9J0ZX	438, 1089
0U9J0ZZ	1089
0U9JX0Z	1089
0U9JXZX	438, 1089
0U9JXZZ	1089
0U9K0ZX	536, 1089
0U9K3ZX	536, 1089
0U9K4ZX	536, 1089
0U9K7ZX	536, 1089
0U9K8ZX	536, 1089
0U9KXZX	536, 1089
0U9L0ZX	536, 1089
0U9LXZX	536, 1089
0U9M*	536
0U9M00Z	438, 1089
0U9M0ZX	438, 1089

Code	Page
0U9M0ZZ	438, 1089
0U9MX0Z	438, 1089
0U9MXZX	438, 1089
0U9MXZZ	438, 1089
0UB0*	531
0UB00ZZ	499
0UB03ZZ	499
0UB04ZZ	499
0UB07ZZ	499
0UB08ZZ	499
0UB1*	531
0UB10ZZ	499
0UB13ZZ	499
0UB14ZZ	499
0UB17ZZ	499
0UB18ZZ	499
0UB2*	531
0UB20ZZ	499
0UB23ZZ	499
0UB24ZZ	499
0UB27ZZ	499
0UB28ZZ	499
0UB40ZX	531
0UB40ZZ	531
0UB43ZX	535, 1089
0UB43ZZ	531
0UB44ZX	535, 1089
0UB44ZZ	531
0UB47ZX	535, 1089
0UB47ZZ	532
0UB48ZX	535, 1089
0UB48ZZ	532
0UB5*	532
0UB50ZZ	544, 545, 546
0UB53ZZ	544, 545, 546
0UB54ZZ	544, 545, 546
0UB57ZZ	544, 545, 546
0UB58ZZ	544, 545, 546
0UB6*	532
0UB60ZZ	544, 545, 546
0UB63ZZ	544, 545, 546
0UB64ZZ	544, 545, 546
0UB67ZZ	544, 545, 546
0UB68ZZ	544, 545, 546
0UB70ZX	532
0UB70ZZ	535, 544, 545, 546
0UB73ZX	532
0UB73ZZ	535, 544, 545, 546
0UB74ZX	532
0UB74ZZ	535, 544, 545, 546
0UB77ZX	532
0UB77ZZ	535, 544, 545, 546
0UB78ZX	532
0UB78ZZ	535, 544, 545, 546
0UB90ZX	532
0UB90ZZ	532, 1089
0UB93ZX	535, 1089
0UB93ZZ	532, 1089
0UB94ZX	535, 1089
0UB94ZZ	532, 1089
0UB97ZX	535, 1089
0UB97ZZ	532, 1089
0UB98ZX	535, 1089
0UB98ZZ	532, 1089
0UBC0ZX	438, 535, 1089
0UBC0ZZ	438, 536, 1089
0UBC3ZX	438, 535, 1089
0UBC3ZZ	438, 536, 1089
0UBC4ZX	438, 535, 1089
0UBC4ZZ	438, 536, 1089
0UBC7ZX	438, 535, 1090
0UBC7ZZ	438, 536, 1090
0UBC8ZX	438, 535, 1090
0UBC8ZZ	438, 536, 1090
0UBF*	536
0UBF0ZX	1090
0UBF0ZZ	1090
0UBF3ZX	1090
0UBF3ZZ	1090
0UBF4ZX	1090
0UBF4ZZ	1090
0UBF7ZX	1090
0UBF7ZZ	1090
0UBF8ZX	1090
0UBF8ZZ	1090
0UBG*	536
0UBG0ZX	438, 1090
0UBG0ZZ	438, 1090
0UBG3ZX	438, 1090
0UBG3ZZ	438, 1090
0UBG4ZX	438, 1090
0UBG4ZZ	438, 1090
0UBG7ZX	438, 1090

Code	Page
0UBG7ZZ	438, 1090
0UBG8ZX	438, 1090
0UBG8ZZ	438, 1090
0UBGXZX	438, 1090
0UBGXZZ	438, 1090
0UBJ*	536
0UBJ0ZX	1090
0UBJ0ZZ	1090
0UBJXZX	1090
0UBJXZZ	1090
0UBK*	536
0UBK0ZX	1090
0UBK0ZZ	1090
0UBK3ZX	1090
0UBK3ZZ	1090
0UBK4ZX	1090
0UBK4ZZ	1090
0UBK7ZX	1090
0UBK7ZZ	1090
0UBK8ZX	1090
0UBK8ZZ	1090
0UBKXZX	1090
0UBKXZZ	1090
0UBL*	536
0UBL0ZX	1090
0UBL0ZZ	438, 1090
0UBLXZX	1090
0UBLXZZ	438, 1090
0UBM0ZX	438, 536, 1090
0UBM0ZZ	536
0UBMXZX	438, 536, 1090
0UBMXZZ	536
0UC0*	532
0UC1*	532
0UC2*	532
0UC4*	537
0UC5*	532
0UC6*	532
0UC7*	532
0UC90ZZ	532, 739, 964
0UC93ZZ	532, 739, 964
0UC94ZZ	532, 739, 964
0UCB*	540
0UCC*	536, 739
0UCC0ZZ	964
0UCC3ZZ	964
0UCC4ZZ	964
0UCC7ZZ	964
0UCC8ZZ	964
0UCF*	540
0UCG0ZZ	536, 1090
0UCG3ZZ	536, 1090
0UCG4ZZ	536, 1090
0UCJ*	536
0UCJ0ZZ	1090
0UCJXZZ	1090
0UCL*	536
0UCL0ZZ	1090
0UCLXZZ	1090
0UCM0ZZ	438, 536, 1090
0UDB*	535
0UDB7ZX	1090
0UDB7ZZ	1090
0UDB8ZX	1090
0UDB8ZZ	1090
0UDN*	532
0UF50ZZ	532, 739, 964
0UF53ZZ	532, 739, 964
0UF54ZZ	532, 739, 964
0UF57ZZ	532, 739, 964
0UF58ZZ	532, 739, 964
0UF60ZZ	532, 739, 964
0UF63ZZ	532, 739, 964
0UF64ZZ	532, 739, 964
0UF67ZZ	532, 739, 964
0UF68ZZ	532, 739, 964
0UF70ZZ	532, 739, 964
0UF73ZZ	532, 739, 964
0UF74ZZ	532, 739, 964
0UF77ZZ	532, 739, 964
0UF78ZZ	532, 739, 964
0UF90ZZ	540
0UF93ZZ	540
0UF94ZZ	540
0UF97ZZ	540
0UF98ZZ	540
0UHC01Z	535, 739, 1090
0UHC31Z	535, 739, 1090
0UHC41Z	535, 739, 1090
0UHC71Z	535, 739, 1090
0UHC81Z	535, 739, 1090
0UHG01Z	535, 739, 1090
0UHG31Z	535, 739, 1090

Code	Page
0UHG41Z	535, 739, 1090
0UHG71Z	535, 739, 1090
0UHG81Z	535, 739, 1090
0UHGX1Z	535, 739, 1090
0UHH03Z	536, 1090
0UHH0YZ	536, 1090
0UHH33Z	536, 1090
0UHH43Z	536, 1090
0UJ30ZZ	532
0UJ34ZZ	532
0UJ80ZZ	532
0UJ84ZZ	532
0UJD0ZZ	532
0UJD4ZZ	532
0UJH0ZZ	536, 1090
0UJH4ZZ	536, 1090
0UJM0ZZ	438, 536, 544, 1090
0UL5*	532
0UL50CZ	544, 545, 546, 1090
0UL50DZ	544, 545, 546
0UL50DZ	1090
0UL50ZZ	544, 546, 1090
0UL53CZ	544, 546, 1090
0UL53DZ	544, 546
0UL53DZ	1090
0UL53ZZ	544, 546, 1090
0UL54CZ	544, 546, 1090
0UL54DZ	544, 546
0UL54DZ	1090
0UL54ZZ	544, 546, 1090
0UL57DZ	544, 546
0UL57DZ	1090
0UL57ZZ	544, 546, 1090
0UL58DZ	544, 546
0UL58DZ	1090
0UL58ZZ	544, 546, 1090
0UL6*	532
0UL60CZ	544, 546, 1090
0UL60DZ	544, 546
0UL60DZ	1090
0UL60ZZ	544, 546, 1090
0UL63CZ	544, 546, 1090
0UL63DZ	544, 546
0UL63DZ	1090
0UL63ZZ	544, 546, 1090
0UL64CZ	544, 546, 1090
0UL64DZ	544, 546
0UL64DZ	1090
0UL64ZZ	544, 546, 1090
0UL67DZ	544, 546
0UL67DZ	1090
0UL67ZZ	544, 546, 1090
0UL68DZ	544, 546
0UL68DZ	1090
0UL68ZZ	544, 546, 1090
0UL7*	535
0UL70CZ	544, 546, 1090
0UL70DZ	544, 546
0UL70DZ	1090
0UL70ZZ	544, 546, 1090
0UL73CZ	544, 546, 1090
0UL73DZ	544, 546
0UL73DZ	1090
0UL73ZZ	544, 546, 1090
0UL74CZ	544, 546, 1090
0UL74DZ	544, 546
0UL74DZ	1090
0UL74ZZ	544, 546, 1090
0UL77DZ	544, 546
0UL77DZ	1090
0UL77ZZ	544, 546, 1090
0UL78DZ	544, 546
0UL78DZ	1090
0UL78ZZ	544, 546, 1090
0ULF*	536
0ULG*	537
0UM0*	532, 739
0UM00ZZ	964
0UM04ZZ	964
0UM1*	532, 739
0UM10ZZ	964
0UM14ZZ	964
0UM2*	532, 739
0UM20ZZ	964
0UM24ZZ	964
0UM4*	537, 739
0UM40ZZ	964
0UM44ZZ	964
0UM5*	532, 739
0UM50ZZ	964
0UM54ZZ	964

Code	Page
0UM6*	532, 739
0UM60ZZ	964
0UM64ZZ	964
0UM7*	532, 739
0UM70ZZ	964
0UM74ZZ	964
0UM9*	540
0UMC*	540
0UMF*	536
0UMG*	536, 739
0UMG0ZZ	964
0UMG4ZZ	964
0UMJXZZ	536, 1090
0UMK*	536
0UMK0ZZ	1090
0UMK4ZZ	1090
0UMKXZZ	1090
0UMMXZZ	536, 739, 964, 1090
0UN0*	532, 739
0UN00ZZ	964
0UN03ZZ	964
0UN04ZZ	964
0UN08ZZ	964
0UN1*	532, 739
0UN10ZZ	964
0UN13ZZ	964
0UN14ZZ	964
0UN18ZZ	964
0UN2*	532, 739
0UN20ZZ	964
0UN23ZZ	964
0UN24ZZ	964
0UN28ZZ	964
0UN4*	537, 739
0UN40ZZ	964
0UN43ZZ	964
0UN44ZZ	964
0UN48ZZ	964
0UN5*	532, 739
0UN50ZZ	964
0UN53ZZ	964
0UN54ZZ	964
0UN57ZZ	964
0UN58ZZ	964
0UN6*	532, 739
0UN60ZZ	964
0UN63ZZ	964
0UN64ZZ	964
0UN67ZZ	964
0UN68ZZ	964
0UN7*	532, 739
0UN70ZZ	964
0UN73ZZ	964
0UN74ZZ	964
0UN77ZZ	964
0UN78ZZ	964
0UN9*	535
0UNC*	540
0UNF*	536
0UNG*	536, 739
0UNG0ZZ	964
0UNG3ZZ	964
0UNG4ZZ	964
0UNG7ZZ	964
0UNG8ZZ	964
0UNGXZZ	964
0UNJ*	536
0UNJ0ZZ	1090
0UNJXZZ	1090
0UNK*	536
0UNK0ZZ	1090
0UNK3ZZ	1090
0UNK4ZZ	1090
0UNK7ZZ	1090
0UNK8ZZ	1090
0UNKXZZ	1090
0UNL*	536
0UNL0ZZ	1090
0UNLXZZ	1090
0UNM*	536, 739
0UNM0ZZ	964
0UNMXZZ	964
0UP300Z	532
0UP303Z	532
0UP30YZ	532
0UP330Z	532
0UP333Z	532
0UP340Z	532
0UP343Z	532
0UP800Z	532
0UP803Z	532
0UP807Z	532

Code	Page
0UP80CZ	532.
0UP80DZ	532
0UP80JZ	532
0UP80KZ	532
0UP80YZ	532
0UP830Z	532
0UP833Z	532
0UP837Z	532
0UP83CZ	532
0UP83DZ	532
0UP83JZ	532
0UP83KZ	532
0UP840Z	532
0UP843Z	532
0UP847Z	532
0UP84CZ	532
0UP84DZ	532
0UP84JZ	532
0UP84KZ	532
0UP877Z	532
0UP87CZ	532
0UP87JZ	532
0UP87KZ	532
0UP887Z	532
0UP88CZ	532
0UP88JZ	532
0UP88KZ	532
0UPD00Z	532, 739, 964
0UPD01Z	532, 739, 964
0UPD03Z	532, 739, 964
0UPD07Z	532, 739, 964
0UPD0CZ	536, 1090
0UPD0DZ	532, 739, 964
0UPD0HZ	532, 739, 964
0UPD0JZ	532, 739, 964
0UPD0KZ	532, 739, 964
0UPD0YZ	532, 739, 964
0UPD30Z	532, 739, 964
0UPD31Z	532, 739, 964
0UPD33Z	532, 739, 964
0UPD37Z	532, 739, 964
0UPD3DZ	532, 739, 964
0UPD3HZ	532, 739, 964
0UPD3JZ	532, 739, 964
0UPD3KZ	532, 739, 964
0UPD40Z	532, 739, 964
0UPD41Z	532, 739, 964
0UPD43Z	532, 739, 964
0UPD47Z	532, 739, 965
0UPD4DZ	532, 739, 965
0UPD4HZ	532, 739, 965
0UPD4JZ	532, 739, 965
0UPD4KZ	532, 739, 965
0UPD71Z	532, 739, 965
0UPD77Z	532, 739, 965
0UPD7JZ	532, 739, 965
0UPD7KZ	532, 739, 965
0UPD81Z	532, 739, 965
0UPD87Z	532, 739, 965
0UPD8JZ	532, 739, 965
0UPD8KZ	532, 739, 965
0UPH00Z	536, 1090
0UPH01Z	536, 1090
0UPH03Z	536, 1090
0UPH07Z	536, 1090
0UPH0DZ	536, 1090
0UPH0JZ	536, 1090
0UPH0KZ	536, 1090
0UPH0YZ	536, 1090
0UPH30Z	536, 1090
0UPH31Z	536, 1090
0UPH33Z	536, 1090
0UPH37Z	536, 1090
0UPH3DZ	536, 1090
0UPH3JZ	536, 1090
0UPH3KZ	536, 1090
0UPH40Z	536, 1090
0UPH41Z	536, 1090
0UPH43Z	536, 1090
0UPH47Z	536, 1090
0UPH4DZ	536, 1090
0UPH4JZ	536, 1090
0UPH4KZ	536, 1090
0UPH71Z	536, 1090
0UPH77Z	536, 1090
0UPH7JZ	536, 1090
0UPH7KZ	536, 1090
0UPH81Z	536, 1090
0UPH87Z	536, 1090
0UPH8JZ	536, 1090
0UPH8KZ	536, 1090
0UPM00Z	438, 536, 1090
0UPM07Z	438, 536, 1090
0UPM0JZ	438, 536, 1090
0UPM0KZ	438, 536, 1090
0UQ0*	532, 739
0UQ00ZZ	965
0UQ03ZZ	965
0UQ04ZZ	965
0UQ08ZZ	965
0UQ1*	532, 739
0UQ10ZZ	965
0UQ13ZZ	965
0UQ14ZZ	965
0UQ18ZZ	965
0UQ2*	532, 739
0UQ20ZZ	965
0UQ23ZZ	965
0UQ24ZZ	965
0UQ28ZZ	965
0UQ4*	537, 739
0UQ40ZZ	965
0UQ43ZZ	965
0UQ44ZZ	965
0UQ48ZZ	965
0UQ5*	532, 739
0UQ50ZZ	965
0UQ53ZZ	965
0UQ54ZZ	965
0UQ57ZZ	965
0UQ58ZZ	965
0UQ6*	532, 739
0UQ60ZZ	965
0UQ63ZZ	965
0UQ64ZZ	965
0UQ67ZZ	965
0UQ68ZZ	965
0UQ7*	532, 739
0UQ70ZZ	965
0UQ73ZZ	965
0UQ74ZZ	965
0UQ77ZZ	965
0UQ78ZZ	965
0UQ9*	183, 532, 739
0UQ90ZZ	965
0UQ93ZZ	965
0UQ94ZZ	965
0UQ97ZZ	965
0UQ98ZZ	965
0UQC*	536, 739
0UQC0ZZ	965
0UQC3ZZ	965
0UQC4ZZ	965
0UQC7ZZ	965
0UQC8ZZ	965
0UQF*	536
0UQG0ZZ	179, 536, 602, 627, 739, 965
0UQG3ZZ	179, 536, 602, 627, 739, 965
0UQG4ZZ	179, 536, 602, 627, 739, 965
0UQG8ZZ	438, 602, 627, 739, 965
0UQJ*	536
0UQJ0ZZ	1090
0UQJXZZ	1090
0UQK0ZZ	536, 1090
0UQK3ZZ	536, 1090
0UQK4ZZ	536, 1090
0UQK7ZZ	536, 1090
0UQK8ZZ	536, 1090
0UQL*	536
0UQL0ZZ	1091
0UQLXZZ	1091
0UQM0ZZ	183, 438, 536, 739, 965
0US0*	532, 739
0US00ZZ	965
0US04ZZ	965
0US08ZZ	965
0US1*	532, 739
0US10ZZ	965
0US14ZZ	965
0US18ZZ	965
0US2*	532, 739
0US20ZZ	965
0US24ZZ	965
0US28ZZ	965
0US4*	537, 739
0US40ZZ	965
0US44ZZ	965
0US48ZZ	965
0US5*	532, 739
0US50ZZ	965
0US54ZZ	965
0US58ZZ	965
0US6*	532, 739
0US60ZZ	965
0US64ZZ	965
0US68ZZ	965
0US7*	532, 739
0US70ZZ	965
0US74ZZ	965
0US78ZZ	965
0US90ZZ	537
0US94ZZ	537
0US97ZZ	537
0US98ZZ	537
0USC*	532, 739
0USC0ZZ	965
0USC4ZZ	965
0USC8ZZ	965
0USF*	536
0USG*	508, 537
0UT0*	532
0UT00ZZ	438
0UT04ZZ	438
0UT07ZZ	438
0UT08ZZ	438
0UT0FZZ	438
0UT1*	532
0UT10ZZ	438
0UT14ZZ	438
0UT17ZZ	438
0UT18ZZ	438
0UT1FZZ	438
0UT2*	532
0UT20ZZ	438, 531
0UT24ZZ	438
0UT27ZZ	438
0UT28ZZ	438
0UT2FZZ	438
0UT4*	537
0UT40ZZ	531
0UT44ZZ	531
0UT47ZZ	531
0UT48ZZ	531
0UT5*	532
0UT50ZZ	544, 546
0UT54ZZ	544, 546
0UT57ZZ	544, 546
0UT58ZZ	544, 546
0UT5FZZ	544, 546
0UT6*	532
0UT60ZZ	544, 546
0UT64ZZ	544, 546
0UT67ZZ	544, 546
0UT68ZZ	544, 546
0UT6FZZ	544, 546
0UT7*	532
0UT70ZZ	531, 544, 546
0UT74ZZ	544, 546
0UT77ZZ	544, 546
0UT78ZZ	544, 546
0UT7FZZ	544, 546
0UT9*	532
0UT90ZL	1091
0UT90ZZ	531
0UT94ZL	1091
0UT94ZZ	531
0UT97ZL	1091
0UT97ZZ	531, 1091
0UT98ZL	1091
0UT98ZZ	531, 1091
0UT9FZL	1091
0UT9FZZ	531, 1091
0UTC*	536
0UTC0ZZ	531
0UTC4ZZ	531
0UTC7ZZ	531
0UTC8ZZ	531
0UTF*	536
0UTG*	537
0UTG0ZZ	531
0UTJ*	536
0UTJ0ZZ	1091
0UTJXZZ	1091
0UTK*	536
0UTK0ZZ	1091
0UTK4ZZ	1091
0UTK7ZZ	1091
0UTK8ZZ	1091
0UTKXZZ	1091
0UTL*	536
0UTL0ZZ	438, 1091
0UTLXZZ	438, 1091
0UTM*	531, 536
0UTM0ZZ	438
0UTMXZZ	438
0UU4*	537, 739
0UU407Z	965
0UU40JZ	965
0UU40KZ	965
0UU447Z	965
0UU44JZ	965
0UU44KZ	965
0UU5*	532
0UU507Z	739, 965
0UU50KZ	739, 965
0UU547Z	739, 965
0UU54KZ	739, 965
0UU577Z	739, 965
0UU57KZ	739, 965
0UU587Z	739, 965
0UU58KZ	739, 965
0UU6*	532
0UU607Z	739, 965
0UU60KZ	739, 965
0UU647Z	739, 965
0UU64KZ	739, 965
0UU677Z	739, 965
0UU67KZ	739, 965
0UU687Z	739, 965
0UU68KZ	739, 965
0UU7*	532
0UU707Z	739, 965
0UU70KZ	739, 965
0UU747Z	739, 965
0UU74KZ	739, 965
0UU777Z	739, 965
0UU77KZ	739, 965
0UU787Z	739, 965
0UU78KZ	739, 965
0UUF*	536
0UUG*	537, 739
0UUG07Z	965
0UUG0JZ	965
0UUG0KZ	965
0UUG47Z	965
0UUG4JZ	965
0UUG4KZ	965
0UUG77Z	965
0UUG7JZ	965
0UUG7KZ	965
0UUG87Z	965
0UUG8JZ	965
0UUG8KZ	965
0UUGX7Z	965
0UUGXJZ	965
0UUGXKZ	965
0UUJ*	536
0UUJ0JZ	1091
0UUJ0KZ	1091
0UUJX7Z	1091
0UUJXJZ	1091
0UUJXKZ	1091
0UUK*	540
0UUM*	536, 739
0UUM07Z	965, 1091
0UUM0JZ	965, 1091
0UUM0KZ	965, 1091
0UUMX7Z	965, 1091
0UUMXJZ	965, 1091
0UUMXKZ	965, 1091
0UV*	536, 739
0UVC0CZ	965
0UVC0DZ	965
0UVC0ZZ	965
0UVC3CZ	965
0UVC3DZ	965
0UVC3ZZ	965
0UVC4CZ	965
0UVC4DZ	965
0UVC4ZZ	965
0UVC7DZ	965
0UVC7ZZ	965
0UVC8DZ	965
0UVC8ZZ	965
0UW300Z	532
0UW303Z	532
0UW30YZ	532
0UW330Z	532
0UW333Z	532
0UW340Z	532
0UW343Z	532
0UW800Z	532
0UW803Z	532
0UW807Z	532
0UW80CZ	532
0UW80DZ	532
0UW80JZ	532
0UW80KZ	532
0UW80YZ	532
0UW830Z	532
0UW833Z	532
0UW837Z	532
0UW83CZ	532
0UW83DZ	532
0UW83KZ	533
0UW840Z	533
0UW843Z	533
0UW847Z	533
0UW84CZ	533
0UW84DZ	533
0UW84JZ	533
0UW84KZ	533
0UW870Z	533
0UW873Z	533
0UW877Z	533
0UW87CZ	533
0UW87DZ	533
0UW87JZ	533
0UW87KZ	533
0UW880Z	533
0UW883Z	533
0UW887Z	533
0UW88CZ	533
0UW88DZ	533
0UW88JZ	533
0UW88KZ	533
0UWD00Z	533, 739, 965
0UWD01Z	533, 739, 965
0UWD03Z	533, 739, 965
0UWD07Z	533, 739, 965
0UWD0CZ	536, 1091
0UWD0DZ	533, 739, 965
0UWD0HZ	533, 739, 965
0UWD0JZ	533, 739, 965
0UWD0KZ	533, 739, 965
0UWD0YZ	533, 739, 965
0UWD30Z	533, 739, 965
0UWD31Z	533, 739, 965
0UWD33Z	533, 739, 965
0UWD37Z	533, 739, 965
0UWD3CZ	536, 1091
0UWD3DZ	533, 739, 965
0UWD3HZ	533, 739, 965
0UWD3JZ	533, 739, 965
0UWD3KZ	533, 739, 965
0UWD40Z	533, 739, 965
0UWD41Z	533, 739, 965
0UWD43Z	533, 739, 965
0UWD47Z	533, 739, 965
0UWD4CZ	536, 1091
0UWD4DZ	533, 740, 965
0UWD4HZ	533, 740, 965
0UWD4JZ	533, 740, 965
0UWD4KZ	533, 740, 965
0UWD70Z	533, 740, 965
0UWD71Z	533, 740, 965
0UWD73Z	533, 740, 965
0UWD77Z	533, 740, 966
0UWD7CZ	536, 1091
0UWD7DZ	533, 740, 966
0UWD7HZ	533, 740, 966
0UWD7JZ	533, 740, 966
0UWD7KZ	533, 740, 966
0UWD80Z	533, 740, 966
0UWD81Z	533, 740, 966
0UWD83Z	533, 740, 966
0UWD87Z	533, 740, 966
0UWD8CZ	536, 1091
0UWD8DZ	533, 740, 966
0UWD8HZ	533, 740, 966
0UWD8JZ	533, 740, 966
0UWD8KZ	533, 740, 966
0UWH00Z	536, 1091
0UWH01Z	536, 1091
0UWH07Z	536, 1091
0UWH0DZ	536, 1091
0UWH0JZ	536, 1091
0UWH0KZ	536, 1091
0UWH0YZ	536, 1091
0UWH30Z	536, 1091
0UWH31Z	536, 1091
0UWH33Z	536, 1091
0UWH37Z	536, 1091
0UWH3DZ	536, 1091
0UWH3JZ	536, 1091
0UWH3KZ	536, 1091
0UWH40Z	536, 1091
0UWH41Z	536, 1091
0UWH43Z	536, 1091
0UWH47Z	536, 1091
0UWH4DZ	536, 1091
0UWH4JZ	536, 1091
0UWH4KZ	536, 1091
0UWH70Z	536, 1091
0UWH71Z	536, 1091
0UWH73Z	536, 1091
0UWH77Z	536, 1091
0UWH7DZ	536, 1091
0UWH7JZ	536, 1091
0UWH7KZ	536, 1091
0UWH80Z	536, 1091
0UWH81Z	536, 1091
0UWH83Z	536, 1091
0UWH87Z	536, 1091
0UWH8DZ	536, 1091
0UWH8JZ	536, 1091
0UWH8KZ	536, 1091
0UWM00Z	438, 536, 1091
0UWM07Z	438, 536, 1091
0UWM0JZ	438, 536, 1091
0UWM0KZ	438, 536, 1091
0UY00Z0	533
0UY00Z1	533
0UY00Z2	533
0UY10Z0	533
0UY10Z1	533
0UY10Z2	533
0UY90Z0	533
0UY90Z1	533
0UY90Z2	533
0V1*	522
0V50*	508
0V500ZZ	521
0V503ZZ	521
0V504ZZ	521
0V507ZZ	523, 1091
0V508ZZ	523, 1091
0V51*	527
0V52*	527
0V53*	527
0V56*	522
0V57*	522
0V59*	522
0V5B*	522
0V5C*	522
0V5F*	522
0V5F0ZZ	1091
0V5F3ZZ	1091
0V5F4ZZ	1091
0V5F8ZZ	1091
0V5G*	522
0V5G0ZZ	1091
0V5G3ZZ	1091
0V5G4ZZ	1091
0V5G8ZZ	1091
0V5H*	522
0V5H0ZZ	1091
0V5H3ZZ	1091
0V5H4ZZ	1091
0V5H8ZZ	1091
0V5J*	522
0V5J0ZZ	1091
0V5J3ZZ	1091
0V5J4ZZ	1091
0V5J8ZZ	1091
0V5K*	522
0V5K0ZZ	1091
0V5K3ZZ	1091
0V5K4ZZ	1091
0V5K8ZZ	1091
0V5L*	522
0V5L0ZZ	1091
0V5L3ZZ	1091
0V5L4ZZ	1091
0V5L8ZZ	1091
0V5S*	521
0V5S0ZZ	438, 1091
0V5S3ZZ	438, 1091
0V5S4ZZ	438, 1091
0V5SXZZ	438, 1091
0V5T*	521
0V5T0ZZ	438, 1091
0V5T3ZZ	438, 1091
0V5T4ZZ	438, 1091
0V5TXZZ	438, 1091
0V7*	522, 740
0V7N0DZ	966
0V7N0ZZ	966
0V7N3DZ	966
0V7N3ZZ	966

Code	Page	Code	Page	Code	Page	Code	Page	Code	Page	Code	Page
0V7N4DZ	966	0VB64ZZ	522	0VCTXZZ	1092	0VNJ3ZZ	966	0VPM3KZ	523	0VQN3ZZ	967
0V7N4ZZ	966	0VB70ZZ	522, 1091	0VH00*	528, 740	0VNJ4ZZ	966	0VPM40Z	523	0VQN4ZZ	967
0V7P0DZ	966	0VB73ZZ	522	0VH001Z	1092	0VNJ8ZZ	966	0VPM43Z	523	0VQN8ZZ	967
0V7P0ZZ	966	0VB74ZZ	522	0VH031Z	1092	0VNK*	522, 740	0VPM47Z	523	0VQP*	523, 740
0V7P3DZ	966	0VB90ZX	522	0VH041Z	1092	0VNK0ZZ	966	0VPM4CZ	523	0VQP0ZZ	967
0V7P3ZZ	966	0VB90ZZ	522	0VH071Z	1092	0VNK3ZZ	966	0VPM4JZ	523	0VQP3ZZ	967
0V7P4DZ	966	0VB93ZZ	522	0VH081Z	1092	0VNK4ZZ	966	0VPM4KZ	523	0VQP4ZZ	967
0V7P4ZZ	966	0VB94ZZ	522	0VJ40ZZ	528, 1092	0VNK8ZZ	966	0VPM77Z	523	0VQP8ZZ	967
0V7Q0DZ	966	0VBB0ZX	522	0VJ44ZZ	528, 1092	0VNL*	522, 740	0VPM7CZ	523	0VQQ*	523, 740
0V7Q0ZZ	966	0VBB0ZZ	522	0VJD0ZZ	522	0VNL0ZZ	966	0VPM7JZ	523	0VQQ0ZZ	967
0V7Q3DZ	966	0VBB3ZZ	522	0VJD4ZZ	522	0VNL3ZZ	966	0VPM7KZ	523	0VQQ3ZZ	967
0V7Q3ZZ	966	0VBB4ZZ	522	0VJM0ZZ	522, 1092	0VNL4ZZ	966	0VPM87Z	523	0VQQ4ZZ	967
0V7Q4DZ	966	0VBC0ZX	522	0VJM4ZZ	522, 1092	0VNL8ZZ	966	0VPM8CZ	523	0VQQ8ZZ	967
0V7Q4ZZ	966	0VBC0ZZ	522	0VJR0ZZ	522, 1092	0VNN*	522, 740	0VPM8JZ	523	0VQS*	521, 740
0V9000Z	527, 1091	0VBC3ZZ	522	0VJR4ZZ	522, 1092	0VNN0ZZ	966	0VPM8KZ	523	0VQS0ZZ	438, 967, 1092
0V900ZX	508, 527, 1091	0VBC4ZZ	522	0VLN0DZ	522, 740, 966	0VNN3ZZ	966	0VPR0DZ	523	0VQS3ZZ	438, 967, 1092
0V9002Z	527, 1091	0VBF0ZZ	522, 1091	0VLN3DZ	522, 740, 966	0VNN4ZZ	966	0VPR3DZ	523	0VQS4ZZ	438, 967, 1092
0V9070Z	527, 1091	0VBF3ZZ	522, 1091	0VLN4DZ	522, 740, 966	0VNN8ZZ	966	0VPR4DZ	523	0VQSXZZ	967
0V9007Z	527, 1091	0VBF4ZZ	522, 1091	0VLN8DZ	522, 740, 966	0VNP*	522, 740	0VPS00Z	521, 1092	0VQT*	521, 740
0V9080Z	527, 1091	0VBF8ZZ	522, 1091	0VLP0DZ	522, 740, 966	0VNP0ZZ	966	0VPS03Z	521, 1092	0VQT0ZZ	438, 967, 1092
0V9008Z	527, 1091	0VBG0ZZ	522, 1091	0VLP3DZ	522, 740, 966	0VNP3ZZ	966	0VPS07Z	521, 1092	0VQT3ZZ	438, 967, 1092
0V9100Z	527	0VBG3ZZ	522, 1091	0VLP4DZ	522, 740, 966	0VNP4ZZ	966	0VPS0JZ	517, 521, 1092	0VQT4ZZ	438, 967, 1092
0V910ZX	527	0VBG4ZZ	522, 1091	0VLP8DZ	522, 740, 966	0VNP8ZZ	966	0VPS0KZ	521, 1092	0VQTXZZ	438, 967, 1092
0V910ZZ	527	0VBG8ZZ	522, 1091	0VLQ0DZ	522, 740, 966	0VNQ*	522, 740	0VPS0YZ	521, 1092	0VR*	499, 523
0V9200Z	527	0VBH0ZZ	522, 1091	0VLQ3DZ	522, 740, 966	0VNQ0ZZ	966	0VPS30Z	521, 1092	0VS*	523
0V920ZX	527	0VBH3ZZ	522, 1091	0VLQ4DZ	522, 740, 966	0VNQ3ZZ	966	0VPS33Z	521, 1092	0VSF*	740
0V920ZZ	527	0VBH4ZZ	522, 1091	0VLQ8DZ	522, 740, 966	0VNQ4ZZ	966	0VPS37Z	521, 1092	0VSF0ZZ	967
0V9300Z	527	0VBH8ZZ	522, 1091	0VM*	740	0VNQ8ZZ	966	0VPS3JZ	517, 521, 1092	0VSF3ZZ	967
0V930ZX	527	0VBJ0ZZ	522, 1091	0VM5XZZ	522, 966	0VNS*	521	0VPS3KZ	521, 1092	0VSF4ZZ	967
0V930ZZ	527	0VBJ3ZZ	522, 1091	0VM6*	522	0VNS0ZZ	1092	0VPS40Z	521, 1092	0VSF8ZZ	967
0V950ZZ	527, 1091	0VBJ4ZZ	522, 1091	0VM60ZZ	966	0VNS3ZZ	1092	0VPS43Z	521, 1092	0VSG*	740
0V9900Z	522, 740, 966	0VBJ8ZZ	522, 1091	0VM64ZZ	966	0VNS4ZZ	1092	0VPS47Z	521, 1092	0VSG0ZZ	967
0V990ZX	522	0VBK0ZZ	522, 1091	0VM7*	522	0VP400Z	528, 1092	0VPS4KZ	517, 521, 1092	0VSG3ZZ	967
0V9902Z	522, 740, 966	0VBK3ZZ	522, 1091	0VM70ZZ	966	0VP401Z	528, 1092	0VPS4KZ	521, 1092	0VSG4ZZ	967
0V9B00Z	522, 740, 966	0VBK4ZZ	522, 1091	0VM74ZZ	966	0VP403Z	528, 1092	0VPS77Z	521, 1092	0VSG8ZZ	967
0V9B0ZX	522	0VBK8ZZ	522, 1091	0VM9*	522	0VP407Z	528, 1092	0VPS7JZ	517, 521, 1092	0VSH*	740
0V9B0ZZ	522, 740, 966	0VBL0ZZ	522, 1091	0VM90ZZ	966	0VP40JZ	528, 1092	0VPS7KZ	521, 1092	0VSH0ZZ	967
0V9C00Z	522, 740, 966	0VBL3ZZ	522, 1091	0VM94ZZ	966	0VP40KZ	528, 1092	0VPS87Z	521, 1092	0VSH3ZZ	967
0V9C0ZX	522	0VBL4ZZ	522, 1091	0VMB*	522	0VP40YZ	528, 1092	0VPS8JZ	517, 521, 1092	0VSH4ZZ	967
0V9C0ZZ	522, 740, 966	0VBL8ZZ	522, 1091	0VMB0ZZ	966	0VP430Z	528, 1092	0VPS8KZ	521, 1092	0VSH8ZZ	967
0V9J00Z	522	0VBS*	521	0VMB4ZZ	966	0VP431Z	528, 1092	0VQ0*	528, 740	0VT0*	508, 521
0V9J0ZZ	522	0VBS0ZX	438, 1091	0VMC*	522	0VP433Z	528, 1092	0VQ00ZZ	966, 1092	0VT00ZZ	521
0V9J40Z	522	0VBS0ZZ	438, 1091	0VMC0ZZ	966	0VP437Z	528, 1092	0VQ03ZZ	966, 1092	0VT04ZZ	521, 1092
0V9J4ZZ	522	0VBS3ZX	438, 1091	0VMC4ZZ	966	0VP43JZ	528, 1092	0VQ04ZZ	966, 1092	0VT07ZZ	523, 1092
0V9K00Z	522	0VBS3ZZ	438, 1092	0VMF*	522	0VP43KZ	528, 1092	0VQ07ZZ	966, 1092	0VT08ZZ	523, 1092
0V9K0ZZ	522	0VBS4ZX	438, 1092	0VMF0ZZ	966	0VP440Z	528, 1092	0VQ08ZZ	966, 1092	0VT1*	528
0V9K40Z	522	0VBS4ZZ	438, 1092	0VMF4ZZ	966	0VP441Z	528, 1092	0VQ1*	528	0VT2*	528
0V9K4ZZ	522	0VBSXZX	438, 1092	0VMG*	522	0VP443Z	528, 1092	0VQ2*	528	0VT3*	508, 521, 528
0V9L00Z	522	0VBSXZZ	438, 1092	0VMG0ZZ	966	0VP447Z	528, 1092	0VQ3*	528	0VT6*	523
0V9L0ZZ	522	0VC0*	528	0VMG4ZZ	966	0VP44JZ	528, 1092	0VQ9*	523, 740	0VT7*	523
0V9L40Z	522	0VC00ZZ	1092	0VMH*	522	0VP44KZ	528, 1092	0VQ90ZZ	966	0VT9*	523, 740
0V9L4ZZ	522	0VC03ZZ	1092	0VMH0ZZ	966	0VP471Z	528, 1092	0VQ93ZZ	966	0VT90ZZ	967
0V9S00Z	521, 1091	0VC04ZZ	1092	0VMH4ZZ	966	0VP477Z	528, 1092	0VQ94ZZ	966	0VT94ZZ	967
0V9S0ZX	438, 521, 1091	0VC07ZZ	1092	0VMSXZZ	521, 966	0VP47JZ	528, 1092	0VQB*	523, 740	0VTB*	523, 740
0V9S0ZZ	521, 1091	0VC08ZZ	1092	0VN0*	528, 740	0VP47KZ	528, 1092	0VQB0ZZ	966	0VTB0ZZ	967
0V9S3ZX	438, 521, 1091	0VC1*	528	0VN00ZZ	966, 1092	0VP481Z	528, 1092	0VQB3ZZ	966	0VTB4ZZ	967
0V9S40Z	521, 1091	0VC2*	528	0VN03ZZ	966, 1092	0VP487Z	528, 1092	0VQB4ZZ	966	0VTC*	287, 523, 740
0V9S4ZX	438, 521, 1091	0VC3*	528	0VN04ZZ	966, 1092	0VP48JZ	528, 1092	0VQC*	523, 740	0VTC0ZZ	967
0V9S4ZZ	521, 1091	0VC50ZZ	528, 1092	0VN07ZZ	966, 1092	0VP48KZ	528, 1092	0VQC0ZZ	966	0VTC4ZZ	967
0V9SX0Z	521, 1091	0VC9*	522, 740	0VN08ZZ	966, 1092	0VPD00Z	522, 740, 966	0VQC3ZZ	966	0VTF*	523
0V9SXZX	438, 521, 1091	0VC90ZZ	966	0VN1*	528	0VPD03Z	522, 740, 966	0VQC4ZZ	966	0VTF0ZZ	1092
0V9SXZZ	521, 1091	0VC93ZZ	966	0VN2*	528	0VPD07Z	522, 740, 966	0VQF*	523, 740	0VTF4ZZ	1092
0V9T00Z	521, 1091	0VC94ZZ	966	0VN3*	528	0VPD0JZ	522, 740, 966	0VQF0ZZ	966	0VTG*	523
0V9T0ZX	438, 521, 1091	0VCB*	522, 740	0VN5*	522, 740	0VPD0KZ	522, 740, 966	0VQF3ZZ	966	0VTG0ZZ	1092
0V9T0ZZ	521, 1091	0VCB0ZZ	966	0VN50ZZ	966	0VPD0YZ	522, 740, 966	0VQF4ZZ	966	0VTG4ZZ	1092
0V9T3ZX	438, 521, 1091	0VCB3ZZ	966	0VN53ZZ	966	0VPD30Z	522, 740, 966	0VQF8ZZ	966	0VTH*	523
0V9T40Z	521, 1091	0VCB4ZZ	966	0VN54ZZ	966	0VPD33Z	522, 740, 966	0VQG*	523, 740	0VTH0ZZ	1092
0V9T4ZX	438, 521, 1091	0VCC*	522, 740	0VN5XZZ	966	0VPD37Z	522, 740, 966	0VQG0ZZ	966	0VTH4ZZ	1092
0V9T4ZZ	521, 1091	0VCC0ZZ	966	0VN6*	522, 740	0VPD3JZ	522, 740, 966	0VQG3ZZ	966	0VTJ*	523
0V9TX0Z	521, 1091	0VCC3ZZ	966	0VN60ZZ	966	0VPD3KZ	522, 740, 966	0VQG4ZZ	966	0VTK*	523
0V9TXZX	438, 521, 1091	0VCC4ZZ	966	0VN63ZZ	966	0VPD40Z	522, 740, 966	0VQG8ZZ	966	0VTL*	523
0V9TXZZ	521, 1091	0VCF*	522	0VN64ZZ	966	0VPD43Z	522, 740, 966	0VQH*	523, 740	0VTS*	521
0VB00ZX	508, 527, 1091	0VCG*	522	0VN7*	522, 740	0VPD47Z	522, 740, 966	0VQH0ZZ	966	0VU1*	528
0VB00ZZ	527, 1091	0VCH*	522	0VN70ZZ	966	0VPD4JZ	522, 740, 966	0VQH3ZZ	966	0VU2*	528
0VB03ZZ	527, 1091	0VCJ*	522	0VN73ZZ	966	0VPD4KZ	522, 740, 966	0VQH4ZZ	967	0VU3*	528
0VB04ZZ	527, 1091	0VCK*	522	0VN74ZZ	966	0VPD77Z	522, 740, 966	0VQH8ZZ	967	0VU5*	523, 740
0VB07ZZ	508, 523, 1091	0VCL*	522	0VNF*	522, 740	0VPD7JZ	522, 740, 966	0VQJ*	523, 740	0VU507Z	967
0VB08ZZ	508, 523, 1091	0VCS0ZZ	521, 1092	0VNF0ZZ	966	0VPD7KZ	522, 740, 966	0VQJ0ZZ	967	0VU50JZ	967
0VB10ZX	527	0VCS3ZZ	521, 1092	0VNF3ZZ	966	0VPD87Z	522, 740, 966	0VQJ3ZZ	967	0VU50KZ	967
0VB10ZZ	527	0VCS4ZZ	521, 1092	0VNF4ZZ	966	0VPD8JZ	522, 740, 966	0VQJ4ZZ	967	0VU547Z	967
0VB13ZZ	527	0VCT*	521	0VNF8ZZ	966	0VPD8KZ	522, 740, 966	0VQJ8ZZ	967	0VU54JZ	967
0VB14ZZ	527	0VCT0ZZ	1092	0VNG*	522, 740	0VPM00Z	522	0VQK*	523, 740	0VU54KZ	967
0VB20ZX	527	0VCT3ZZ	1092	0VNG0ZZ	966	0VPM07Z	522	0VQK0ZZ	967	0VU5X7Z	967
0VB20ZZ	527	0VCT4ZZ	1092	0VNG3ZZ	966	0VPM0CZ	522	0VQK3ZZ	967	0VU5XJZ	967
0VB23ZZ	527			0VNG4ZZ	966	0VPM0JZ	522	0VQK4ZZ	967	0VU5XKZ	967
0VB24ZZ	528			0VNG8ZZ	966	0VPM0KZ	523	0VQK8ZZ	967	0VU6*	523, 740
0VB30ZZ	528			0VNH*	522, 740	0VPM0YZ	523	0VQL*	523, 740	0VU607Z	967
0VB30ZZ	528			0VNH0ZZ	966	0VPM30Z	523	0VQL0ZZ	967	0VU60JZ	967
0VB33ZZ	528			0VNH3ZZ	966	0VPM33Z	523	0VQL3ZZ	967	0VU60KZ	967
0VB34ZZ	528			0VNH4ZZ	966	0VPM37Z	523	0VQL4ZZ	967	0VU647Z	967
0VB50ZZ	528, 1091			0VNH8ZZ	966	0VPM3CZ	523	0VQL8ZZ	967	0VU64JZ	967
0VB60ZZ	522, 1091			0VNJ*	522, 740	0VPM3JZ	523	0VQN*	523, 740	0VU64KZ	967
0VB63ZZ	522	0VCT4ZZ	1092	0VNJ0ZZ	966			0VQN0ZZ	967	0VU687Z	967

Code	Page
0VU68JZ	967
0VU68KZ	967
0VU7*	523, 740
0VU707Z	967
0VU70JZ	967
0VU70KZ	967
0VU747Z	967
0VU74JZ	967
0VU74KZ	967
0VU787Z	967
0VU78JZ	967
0VU78KZ	967
0VU9*	523, 740
0VU907Z	967
0VU90JZ	967
0VU90KZ	967
0VUB*	523, 740
0VUB07Z	967
0VUB0JZ	967
0VUB0KZ	967
0VUC*	523, 740
0VUC07Z	967
0VUC0JZ	967
0VUC0KZ	967
0VUF*	523, 740
0VUF07Z	967
0VUF0JZ	967
0VUF0KZ	967
0VUF47Z	967
0VUF4JZ	967
0VUF4KZ	967
0VUF87Z	967
0VUF8JZ	967
0VUF8KZ	967
0VUG*	523, 740
0VUG07Z	967
0VUG0JZ	967
0VUG0KZ	967
0VUG47Z	967
0VUG4JZ	967
0VUG4KZ	967
0VUG87Z	967
0VUG8JZ	967
0VUG8KZ	967
0VUH*	523, 740
0VUH07Z	967
0VUH0JZ	967
0VUH0KZ	967
0VUH47Z	967
0VUH4JZ	967
0VUH4KZ	967
0VUH87Z	967
0VUH8JZ	967
0VUH8KZ	967
0VUJ*	523, 740
0VUJ07Z	967
0VUJ0JZ	967
0VUJ0KZ	967
0VUJ47Z	967
0VUJ4JZ	967
0VUJ4KZ	967
0VUJ87Z	967
0VUJ8JZ	967
0VUJ8KZ	967
0VUK*	523, 740
0VUK07Z	967
0VUK0JZ	967
0VUK0KZ	967
0VUK47Z	967
0VUK4JZ	967
0VUK4KZ	967
0VUK87Z	967
0VUK8JZ	967
0VUK8KZ	967
0VUL*	523, 740
0VUL07Z	967
0VUL0JZ	967
0VUL0KZ	967
0VUL47Z	967
0VUL4JZ	967
0VUL4KZ	967
0VUL87Z	967
0VUL8JZ	967
0VUL8KZ	967
0VUN*	523, 740
0VUN07Z	967
0VUN0JZ	967
0VUN0KZ	967
0VUN47Z	967
0VUN4JZ	967
0VUN4KZ	967
0VUN87Z	967
0VUN8JZ	967
0VUN8KZ	967
0VUP*	523, 740
0VUP07Z	967
0VUP0JZ	967
0VUP0KZ	967
0VUP47Z	967
0VUP4JZ	967
0VUP4KZ	967
0VUP87Z	967
0VUP8JZ	967
0VUP8KZ	967
0VUQ*	523, 740
0VUQ07Z	967
0VUQ0JZ	967
0VUQ0KZ	967
0VUQ47Z	967
0VUQ4JZ	967
0VUQ4KZ	967
0VUQ87Z	967
0VUQ8JZ	967
0VUQ8KZ	967
0VUS07Z	521, 740, 967
0VUS0JZ	517, 521, 1092
0VUS0KZ	521, 740, 967
0VUS47Z	521, 740, 967
0VUS4JZ	517, 521, 1092
0VUS4KZ	521, 740, 967
0VUT*	740
0VUT07Z	438, 521, 967, 1092
0VUT0JZ	438, 521, 968, 1092
0VUT0KZ	438, 521, 968, 1092
0VUT47Z	438, 521, 968, 1092
0VUT4JZ	438, 521, 968, 1092
0VUT4KZ	438, 521, 968, 1092
0VUTX7Z	438, 521, 968, 1092
0VUTXJZ	438, 521, 968, 1092
0VUTXKZ	438, 521, 968, 1092
0VW400Z	528, 1092
0VW403Z	528, 1092
0VW407Z	528, 1092
0VW40JZ	528, 1092
0VW40KZ	528, 1092
0VW40YZ	528, 1092
0VW430Z	528, 1092
0VW433Z	528, 1092
0VW437Z	528, 1092
0VW43JZ	528, 1092
0VW43KZ	528, 1092
0VW440Z	528, 1092
0VW443Z	528, 1092
0VW447Z	528, 1092
0VW44JZ	528, 1092
0VW44KZ	528, 1092
0VW470Z	528, 1092
0VW473Z	528, 1092
0VW477Z	528, 1092
0VW47JZ	528, 1092
0VW47KZ	528, 1092
0VW480Z	528, 1092
0VW483Z	528, 1092
0VW487Z	528, 1092
0VW48JZ	528, 1092
0VW48KZ	528, 1092
0VWD00Z	523, 740, 968
0VWD03Z	523, 740, 968
0VWD07Z	523, 740, 968
0VWD0JZ	523, 740, 968
0VWD0KZ	523, 740, 968
0VWD0YZ	523, 740, 968
0VWD30Z	523, 740, 968
0VWD33Z	523, 740, 968
0VWD37Z	523, 740, 968
0VWD3JZ	523, 740, 968
0VWD3KZ	523, 740, 968
0VWD40Z	523, 740, 968
0VWD43Z	523, 740, 968
0VWD47Z	523, 740, 968
0VWD4JZ	523, 740, 968
0VWD4KZ	523, 740, 968
0VWD70Z	523, 740, 968
0VWD73Z	523, 740, 968
0VWD77Z	523, 740, 968
0VWD7JZ	523, 740, 968
0VWD7KZ	523, 740, 968
0VWD80Z	523, 740, 968
0VWD83Z	523, 740, 968
0VWD87Z	523, 740, 968
0VWD8JZ	523, 740, 968
0VWD8KZ	523, 740, 968
0VWM00Z	523
0VWM03Z	523
0VWM07Z	523
0VWM0CZ	523
0VWM0JZ	523
0VWM0KZ	523
0VWM0YZ	523
0VWM30Z	523
0VWM33Z	523
0VWM37Z	523
0VWM3CZ	523
0VWM3JZ	523
0VWM3KZ	523
0VWM40Z	523
0VWM43Z	523
0VWM47Z	523
0VWM4CZ	523
0VWM4JZ	523
0VWM4KZ	523
0VWM70Z	523
0VWM73Z	523
0VWM77Z	523
0VWM7CZ	523
0VWM7JZ	523
0VWM7KZ	523
0VWM80Z	523
0VWM83Z	523
0VWM87Z	523
0VWM8CZ	523
0VWM8JZ	523
0VWM8KZ	523
0VWS00Z	521, 1092
0VWS03Z	521, 1092
0VWS07Z	521, 1092
0VWS0JZ	521, 1092
0VWS0KZ	521, 1092
0VWS0YZ	521, 1092
0VWS30Z	521, 1092
0VWS33Z	521, 1092
0VWS37Z	521, 1092
0VWS3JZ	521, 1092
0VWS3KZ	521, 1092
0VWS40Z	521, 1092
0VWS43Z	521, 1092
0VWS47Z	521, 1092
0VWS4JZ	521, 1092
0VWS4KZ	521, 1092
0VWS70Z	521, 1092
0VWS73Z	521, 1092
0VWS77Z	521, 1092
0VWS7JZ	521, 1092
0VWS7KZ	521, 1092
0VWS80Z	521, 1092
0VWS83Z	521, 1093
0VWS87Z	521, 1093
0VWS8JZ	521, 1093
0VWS8KZ	521, 1093
0VXT0ZD	508, 521, 602, 627, 740, 968
0VXT0ZS	438, 521, 740, 968, 1093
0VXTXZD	509, 521, 602, 627, 740, 968
0VXTXZS	521, 740, 968
0W0*	740
0W0007Z	438, 1093
0W000JZ	438, 1093
0W000KZ	438, 1093
0W000ZZ	438, 1093
0W0037Z	438, 1093
0W003JZ	438, 1093
0W003KZ	438, 1093
0W003ZZ	438, 1093
0W0047Z	438, 1093
0W004JZ	438, 1093
0W004KZ	438, 1093
0W004ZZ	438, 1093
0W02*	81
0W0207Z	438, 968, 1093
0W020JZ	438, 968, 1093
0W020KZ	438, 968, 1093
0W020ZZ	438, 968, 1093
0W0237Z	438, 968, 1093
0W023JZ	438, 968, 1093
0W023KZ	438, 968, 1093
0W023ZZ	438, 968, 1093
0W0247Z	438, 968, 1093
0W024JZ	438, 968, 1093
0W024KZ	438, 968, 1093
0W024ZZ	438, 968, 1093
0W04*	69, 287
0W0407Z	968
0W040JZ	968
0W040KZ	968
0W040ZZ	968
0W0437Z	968
0W043JZ	968
0W043KZ	968
0W043ZZ	968
0W0447Z	968
0W044JZ	968
0W044KZ	968
0W044ZZ	968
0W05*	69, 287
0W0507Z	968
0W050JZ	968
0W050KZ	968
0W050ZZ	968
0W0537Z	968
0W053JZ	968
0W053KZ	968
0W053ZZ	968
0W0547Z	968
0W054JZ	968
0W054KZ	968
0W054ZZ	968
0W06*	81
0W0607Z	438, 968, 1093
0W060JZ	438, 968, 1093
0W060KZ	438, 968, 1093
0W060ZZ	438, 968, 1093
0W0637Z	438, 968, 1093
0W063JZ	438, 968, 1093
0W063KZ	438, 968, 1093
0W063ZZ	438, 968, 1093
0W0647Z	438, 968, 1093
0W064JZ	438, 968, 1093
0W064KZ	438, 968, 1093
0W064ZZ	438, 968, 1093
0W0807Z	438, 1093
0W080JZ	438, 1093
0W080KZ	438, 1093
0W080ZZ	438, 1093
0W0837Z	438, 1093
0W083JZ	438, 1093
0W083KZ	438, 1093
0W083ZZ	438, 1093
0W0847Z	438, 1093
0W084JZ	439, 1093
0W084KZ	439, 1093
0W084ZZ	439, 1093
0W0F*	481
0W0F07Z	439, 1093
0W0F0JZ	439, 1093
0W0F0KZ	439, 1093
0W0F0ZZ	439, 1093
0W0F37Z	439, 1093
0W0F3JZ	439, 1093
0W0F3KZ	439, 1093
0W0F3ZZ	439, 1093
0W0F47Z	439, 1093
0W0F4JZ	439, 1093
0W0F4KZ	439, 1093
0W0F4ZZ	439, 1093
0W0K07Z	439, 1093
0W0K0JZ	439, 1093
0W0K0KZ	439, 1093
0W0K0ZZ	439, 1093
0W0K37Z	439, 1093
0W0K3JZ	439, 1093
0W0K3KZ	439, 1093
0W0K3ZZ	439, 1093
0W0K47Z	439, 1093
0W0K4JZ	439, 1093
0W0K4KZ	439, 1093
0W0K4ZZ	439, 1093
0W0L07Z	439, 1093
0W0L0JZ	439, 1093
0W0L0KZ	439, 1093
0W0L0ZZ	439, 1093
0W0L37Z	439, 1093
0W0L3JZ	439, 1093
0W0L3KZ	439, 1093
0W0L3ZZ	439, 1093
0W0L47Z	439, 1093
0W0L4JZ	439, 1093
0W0L4KZ	439, 1093
0W0L4ZZ	439, 1093
0W0M07Z	439, 1093
0W0M0JZ	439, 1093
0W0M0KZ	439, 1093
0W0M0ZZ	439, 1093
0W0M37Z	439, 1093
0W0M3JZ	439, 1093
0W0M3KZ	439, 1093
0W0M3ZZ	439, 1093
0W0M47Z	439, 1093
0W0M4JZ	439, 1093
0W0M4KZ	439, 1093
0W0M4ZZ	439, 1093
0W0N*	536
0W0N07Z	968, 1093
0W0N0JZ	968, 1093
0W0N0KZ	968, 1093
0W0N0ZZ	968, 1093
0W0N37Z	968, 1093
0W0N3JZ	968, 1093
0W0N3KZ	968, 1093
0W0N3ZZ	968, 1093
0W0N47Z	968, 1093
0W0N4JZ	968, 1093
0W0N4KZ	968, 1093
0W0N4ZZ	968, 1093
0W11*	22, 740
0W110J9	602, 627, 968
0W110JB	602, 627, 968
0W110JG	602, 627, 968
0W110JJ	602, 627, 968
0W190J9	103, 740, 968
0W190JB	103, 740, 968
0W190JJ	103, 740, 968
0W193J9	103, 740, 968
0W193JB	103, 740, 968
0W193JJ	103, 740, 968
0W194J9	103, 740, 968
0W194JB	103, 740, 968
0W194JJ	103, 740, 968
0W1B0J9	103, 740, 968
0W1B0JB	103, 740, 968
0W1B0JJ	103, 740, 968
0W1B3J9	103, 740, 968
0W1B3JB	103, 740, 968
0W1B3JJ	103, 740, 968
0W1B4J9	103, 740, 968
0W1B4JB	103, 740, 968
0W1B4JJ	103, 740, 968
0W1G0J4	147, 191, 208, 517, 602, 627, 740, 968
0W1G0JW	191, 199, 602, 627
0W1G0JY	191, 199, 602, 627
0W1G3J4	147, 191, 208, 517, 602, 627, 740, 968
0W1G3JW	191, 199, 602, 627
0W1G3JY	191, 199, 602, 627
0W1G4J4	147, 191, 208, 517, 602, 627, 740, 968
0W1G4JW	191, 199, 602, 627
0W1G4JY	191, 199, 602, 627
0W1J0J9	540
0W1J0JB	540
0W1J0JG	540
0W1J0JJ	540
0W1J3J9	540
0W1J3JB	540
0W1J3JG	540
0W1J3JJ	540
0W1J4J9	540
0W1J4JB	540
0W1J4JG	540
0W1J4JJ	540
0W30*	81, 147, 499, 740
0W300ZZ	602, 627, 968
0W303ZZ	602, 627, 968
0W304ZZ	602, 627, 968
0W31*	81, 147, 499, 741
0W310ZZ	602, 627, 968
0W313ZZ	602, 627, 968
0W314ZZ	602, 627, 968
0W32*	81, 147, 499, 741
0W320ZZ	602, 627, 968
0W323ZZ	602, 627, 968
0W324ZZ	602, 627, 968
0W33*	147, 499, 602, 741
0W330ZZ	81, 627, 968
0W333ZZ	81, 627, 968
0W334ZZ	81, 627, 968
0W337ZZ	94, 627, 968
0W338ZZ	94, 627, 968
0W33XZZ	94, 627, 968
0W34*	81, 147, 499, 741
0W340ZZ	602, 627, 968
0W343ZZ	602, 627, 968
0W344ZZ	602, 627, 968
0W35*	81, 147, 499, 741
0W350ZZ	602, 627, 968
0W353ZZ	602, 627, 968
0W354ZZ	602, 627, 968
0W36*	81, 147, 499, 741
0W360ZZ	602, 627, 968
0W363ZZ	602, 627, 968
0W364ZZ	602, 627, 968
0W38*	94, 147, 287, 741
0W380ZZ	439, 602, 627, 968
0W383ZZ	439, 602, 627, 968
0W384ZZ	439, 602, 627, 968
0W39*	94, 147, 499, 741
0W390ZZ	602, 627, 968
0W393ZZ	602, 627, 968
0W394ZZ	602, 627, 968
0W3B*	94, 147, 499, 741
0W3B0ZZ	602, 627, 968
0W3B3ZZ	602, 627, 968
0W3B4ZZ	602, 627, 968
0W3C*	140, 499, 741
0W3C0ZZ	968
0W3C3ZZ	968
0W3C4ZZ	968
0W3D*	94, 147, 741
0W3D0ZZ	602, 627, 968
0W3D3ZZ	602, 627, 968
0W3D4ZZ	602, 627, 968
0W3F*	147, 191, 208, 287, 517, 741
0W3F0ZZ	439, 602, 627, 968
0W3F3ZZ	439, 602, 627, 968
0W3F4ZZ	439, 602, 627, 968
0W3G3ZZ	147, 191, 208, 517, 602, 627, 741, 968
0W3G4ZZ	147, 191, 208, 517, 602, 627, 741, 968
0W3H*	191, 208, 517, 741
0W3H0ZZ	540, 602, 627, 968
0W3H3ZZ	147, 602, 627, 968
0W3H4ZZ	147, 602, 627, 968
0W3J*	147, 191, 208, 517, 741
0W3J0ZZ	602, 627, 968
0W3J3ZZ	602, 627, 968
0W3J4ZZ	602, 627, 968
0W3K*	147, 287, 499, 741
0W3K0ZZ	439, 602, 628, 968
0W3K3ZZ	439, 602, 628, 969
0W3K4ZZ	439, 602, 628, 969
0W3L*	147, 287, 499, 741
0W3L0ZZ	439, 602, 628, 969
0W3L3ZZ	439, 602, 628, 969
0W3L4ZZ	439, 602, 628, 969
0W3M*	147, 528, 741
0W3M0ZZ	602, 628, 969
0W3M3ZZ	602, 628, 969
0W3M4ZZ	602, 628, 969
0W3N*	147, 540, 741
0W3N0ZZ	602, 628, 969
0W3N3ZZ	602, 628, 969
0W3N4ZZ	602, 628, 969
0W3P0ZZ	191, 208, 517, 540, 602, 628, 741, 969
0W3P3ZZ	147, 191, 208, 517, 602, 628, 741, 969
0W3P4ZZ	147, 191, 208, 517, 602, 628, 741, 969
0W3P7ZZ	183, 741, 969
0W3Q*	94, 147, 741
0W3Q0ZZ	969
0W3Q3ZZ	499, 602, 628, 969
0W3Q4ZZ	499, 602, 628, 969
0W3Q7ZZ	499, 602, 628, 969
0W3Q8ZZ	602, 628, 969
0W3R*	147, 508, 528, 540, 741
0W3R0ZZ	602, 628, 969
0W3R3ZZ	602, 628, 969
0W3R4ZZ	602, 628, 969
0W3R7ZZ	602, 628, 969
0W3R8ZZ	602, 628, 969
0W4M*	521
0W4N*	537
0W9100Z	14, 69, 602, 628, 741, 850

Numeric Index to Procedures

Code	Page
0W910ZX	14, 602, 628
0W910ZZ	14, 69, 602, 628, 741, 850
0W9200Z	85, 439, 741, 969
0W920ZZ	85, 439, 741, 969
0W9240Z	85, 439, 741, 969
0W924ZZ	85, 439, 741, 969
0W9300Z	85, 439, 741, 969
0W930ZZ	85, 439, 741, 969
0W9340Z	85, 439, 741, 969
0W934ZZ	85, 439, 741, 969
0W9400Z	85, 439, 741, 969
0W940ZZ	85, 439, 741, 969
0W9440Z	85, 439, 741, 969
0W944ZZ	85, 439, 741, 969
0W9500Z	85, 439, 741, 969
0W950ZZ	85, 439, 741, 969
0W9540Z	85, 439, 741, 969
0W954ZZ	85, 439, 741, 969
0W9600Z	81, 439, 483, 741, 969
0W960ZZ	81, 439, 483, 741, 969
0W9640Z	81, 439, 483, 741, 969
0W964ZZ	81, 439, 483, 741, 969
0W9940Z	103
0W994ZX	103
0W994ZZ	103
0W9B40Z	103
0W9B4ZX	103
0W9B4ZZ	103
0W9C00Z	103, 147, 741, 969
0W9C0ZX	103, 147, 499, 578, 602, 628
0W9C0ZZ	103, 147, 741, 969
0W9C40Z	103, 147, 741, 969
0W9C4ZZ	103, 147, 741, 969
0W9D00Z	94, 166, 602, 628, 741, 969
0W9D0ZX	94, 166, 602, 628, 741, 969
0W9D0ZZ	94, 166, 602, 628, 741, 969
0W9D40Z	94, 166, 602, 628, 741, 969
0W9D4ZX	94, 166, 602, 628, 741, 969
0W9D4ZZ	94, 166, 602, 628, 741, 969
0W9F00Z	147, 191, 208, 439, 517, 602, 628, 741
0W9F0ZX	191, 439, 602, 628, 741, 969, 1093
0W9F0ZZ	147, 191, 208, 439, 517, 602, 628, 741
0W9F3ZX	191, 439, 602, 628, 741, 969, 1093
0W9F4ZX	191, 439, 602, 628, 741, 969, 1093
0W9G00Z	147, 191, 203, 517, 540, 578, 602, 628, 741, 969
0W9G0ZX	191, 203, 540, 578, 602, 628, 741, 969, 1093
0W9G0ZZ	147, 191, 203, 517, 540, 578, 602, 628, 741, 969
0W9G4ZX	191, 203, 540, 578, 602, 628, 741, 969, 1093
0W9H00Z	147, 191, 208, 439, 517, 603, 628, 741
0W9H0ZX	191, 203, 540, 578, 603, 628, 741, 969, 1093
0W9H0ZZ	147, 191, 208, 439, 517, 603, 628, 741
0W9H3ZX	191, 203, 540, 578, 603, 628, 741, 969, 1093
0W9H40Z	147, 191, 208, 439, 517, 603, 628, 741
0W9H4ZX	191, 203, 540, 578, 603, 628, 741, 969, 1093
0W9H4ZZ	147, 191, 208, 439, 517, 603, 628, 741
0W9J00Z	40, 147, 191, 208, 517, 741
0W9J0ZX	191, 203, 540, 578, 603, 628, 741, 969, 1093
0W9J0ZZ	40, 147, 191, 208, 517, 741
0W9J40Z	40, 147, 191, 208, 517, 741
0W9J4ZX	191, 203, 540, 578, 603, 628, 741, 969, 1093
0W9J4ZZ	40, 147, 191, 208, 517, 741
0W9N00Z	439, 536, 1093
0W9N0ZZ	439, 536, 1093
0W9N40Z	439, 536, 1093
0W9N4ZZ	439, 536, 1093
0WB00ZZ	40, 58, 81, 147, 256, 411, 741, 969, 1093
0WB03ZZ	40, 58, 81, 147, 256, 411, 741, 969, 1093
0WB04ZZ	40, 58, 81, 147, 256, 411, 741, 969, 1093
0WB0XZZ	40, 58, 81, 147, 256, 411, 741, 969, 1093
0WB20ZZ	40, 58, 81, 147, 256, 411, 741, 969, 1093
0WB23ZZ	40, 58, 81, 147, 256, 411, 741, 969, 1093
0WB24ZZ	40, 58, 81, 147, 256, 411, 741, 969, 1093
0WB2XZZ	40, 58, 81, 147, 256, 411, 741, 969, 1093
0WB30ZX	85, 1093
0WB30ZZ	85, 1093
0WB33ZX	85, 1093
0WB33ZZ	85, 1093
0WB34ZZ	85, 1093
0WB3XZX	85, 1093
0WB3XZZ	85, 1093
0WB40ZZ	40, 81, 147, 256, 411, 741, 969, 1093
0WB43ZZ	40, 81, 147, 256, 411, 741, 969, 1093
0WB44ZZ	40, 81, 147, 256, 411, 741, 969, 1093
0WB4XZZ	40, 81, 147, 256, 411, 741, 969, 1093
0WB50ZZ	40, 81, 147, 256, 411, 741, 969, 1093
0WB53ZZ	40, 81, 147, 256, 411, 741, 969, 1093
0WB54ZZ	40, 81, 147, 256, 411, 741, 969, 1093
0WB5XZZ	40, 81, 147, 256, 411, 741, 969, 1093
0WB60ZZ	40, 81, 147, 256, 411, 741, 969, 1093
0WB63ZZ	40, 81, 147, 256, 411, 741, 969, 1093
0WB64ZZ	40, 81, 147, 256, 411, 741, 969, 1093
0WB6XZZ	81, 103, 147, 439, 741, 969
0WB6XZZ	40, 81, 147, 256, 411, 741, 969, 1093
0WB80ZZ	103, 241, 439, 499, 603, 628, 1093
0WB83ZZ	103, 241, 439, 499, 603, 628, 1093
0WB84ZZ	103, 241, 439, 499, 603, 628, 1093
0WB8XZZ	103, 241, 439, 499, 603, 628, 1093
0WBC0ZX	103, 147, 499, 578, 603, 628
0WBC0ZZ	94, 499, 603, 628, 1093
0WBC3ZZ	94, 499, 603, 628, 1093
0WBC4ZZ	94, 499, 603, 628, 1093
0WBF*	191
0WBF0ZX	439, 603, 628, 741, 969, 1093
0WBF0ZZ	256, 439, 499, 603, 628, 1093
0WBF3ZX	439, 603, 628, 741, 969, 1093
0WBF3ZZ	256, 439, 499, 603, 628, 1093
0WBF4ZX	439, 603, 628, 741, 969, 1093
0WBF4ZZ	256, 439, 499, 603, 628, 1093
0WBFXZ2	256, 439, 499, 603, 628, 1093
0WBFXZX	439, 603, 628, 741, 969, 1093
0WBFXZZ	256, 439, 499, 603, 628, 1093
0WBH0ZX	191, 203, 540, 578
0WBH0ZZ	191, 287, 439, 507, 521, 540, 603, 628
0WBH3ZZ	191, 287, 439, 507, 521, 540, 603, 628
0WBH4ZZ	191, 287, 439, 507, 521, 540, 603, 628
0WBK0ZZ	40, 147, 256, 411, 741, 969, 1093
0WBK3ZZ	40, 147, 256, 411, 741, 969, 1093
0WBK4ZZ	40, 147, 256, 411, 741, 969, 1093
0WBKXZZ	40, 147, 256, 411, 741, 969, 1094
0WBL0ZZ	40, 147, 256, 411, 741, 969, 1094
0WBL3ZZ	40, 147, 256, 411, 741, 969, 1094
0WBL4ZZ	40, 147, 256, 411, 741, 969, 1094
0WBLXZZ	40, 147, 256, 411, 741, 969, 1094
0WBM0ZZ	40, 147, 256, 411, 741, 969, 1094
0WBM3ZZ	40, 147, 256, 411, 741, 969, 1094
0WBM4ZZ	40, 147, 256, 411, 741, 969, 1094
0WBMXZZ	40, 147, 256, 411, 741, 969, 1094
0WBN*	537
0WBN0ZX	439, 1094
0WBN0ZZ	439, 1094
0WBN3ZZ	439, 1094
0WBN4ZX	439, 1094
0WBN4ZZ	439, 1094
0WBNXZX	439, 1094
0WBNXZZ	439, 1094
0WC10ZZ	14, 69, 603, 628, 741, 850
0WC13ZZ	14, 69, 603, 628, 741, 850
0WC14ZZ	14, 69, 603, 628, 741, 850
0WC30ZZ	85, 439, 741, 969, 1094
0WC33ZZ	85, 439, 741, 969, 1094
0WC34ZZ	85, 439, 741, 1094
0WCC0ZZ	103, 147, 741, 969
0WCC3ZZ	103, 147, 741, 969
0WCC4ZZ	103, 147, 741, 969
0WCD0ZZ	94, 166, 603, 628, 741, 969
0WCD3ZZ	94, 166, 603, 628, 741, 969
0WCD4ZZ	94, 166, 603, 628, 741, 969
0WCG0ZZ	191, 517, 741, 969
0WCG3ZZ	191, 517, 741, 969
0WCG4ZZ	191, 517, 741, 969
0WCH0ZZ	191, 517, 741, 969
0WCH3ZZ	191, 517, 741, 969
0WCH4ZZ	191, 517, 741, 969
0WCJ0ZZ	147, 191, 203, 517, 603, 628, 741
0WCJ3ZZ	147, 191, 208, 439, 517, 603, 628, 741
0WCJ4ZZ	147, 191, 208, 439, 517, 603, 628, 741
0WCP0ZZ	147, 191, 203, 517, 603, 628, 741
0WCP3ZZ	147, 191, 208, 439, 517, 603, 628, 741
0WCP4ZZ	147, 191, 208, 439, 517, 603, 628, 741
0WCQ7ZZ	103, 741, 969
0WCQ8ZZ	103, 741, 969
0WCR0ZZ	147, 191, 203, 517, 603, 628, 741
0WCR3ZZ	147, 191, 208, 439, 517, 603, 628, 741
0WCR4ZZ	147, 191, 208, 439, 517, 603, 628, 741
0WF10ZZ	14, 741, 850
0WF13ZZ	14, 741, 850
0WF14ZZ	14, 741, 850
0WF30ZZ	85, 439, 741, 969, 1094
0WF33ZZ	85, 439, 741, 969, 1094
0WF34ZZ	85, 439, 741, 969, 1094
0WF90ZZ	103, 741, 969
0WF93ZZ	103, 741, 969
0WF94ZZ	103, 741, 969
0WFB0ZZ	103, 741, 969
0WFB3ZZ	103, 741, 969
0WFB4ZZ	103, 741, 969
0WFC0ZZ	103, 741, 969
0WFC3ZZ	103, 741, 969
0WFC4ZZ	103, 741, 969
0WFD*	741
0WFD0ZZ	166
0WFD3ZZ	166
0WFD4ZZ	166
0WFDXZZ	166
0WFG0ZZ	191, 208, 603, 628, 741, 969
0WFG3ZZ	191, 208, 603, 628, 741, 969
0WFG4ZZ	191, 208, 603, 628, 741, 969
0WFQ0ZZ	103, 741, 969
0WFQ3ZZ	103, 741, 969
0WFQ4ZZ	103, 741, 969
0WFQ7ZZ	103, 741, 969
0WFQ8ZZ	103, 741, 969
0WH001Z	40, 741, 1094
0WH003Z	446
0WH00YZ	446
0WH01Z	40, 741, 1094
0WH033Z	446
0WH03YZ	446
0WH041Z	40, 741, 1094
0WH043Z	446
0WH04YZ	446
0WH101Z	40, 741, 1094
0WH10YZ	14
0WH131Z	40, 742, 1094
0WH13YZ	14
0WH141Z	40, 742, 1094
0WH14YZ	14
0WH201Z	40, 742, 1094
0WH203Z	446
0WH20YZ	446
0WH231Z	40, 742, 1094
0WH233Z	446
0WH23YZ	446
0WH241Z	40, 742, 1094
0WH24Z	446
0WH24YZ	446
0WH3*	742
0WH301Z	82, 1094
0WH303Z	85, 439, 969, 1094
0WH30YZ	85, 439, 969, 1094
0WH331Z	82, 1094
0WH333Z	85, 439, 969, 1094
0WH33YZ	85, 439, 969, 1094
0WH341Z	82, 1094
0WH343Z	85, 439, 969, 1094
0WH34YZ	85, 439, 969, 1094
0WH401Z	82, 742, 1094
0WH403Z	446
0WH40YZ	446
0WH431Z	82, 742, 1094
0WH433Z	446
0WH43YZ	446
0WH441Z	82, 742, 1094
0WH443Z	446
0WH44YZ	446
0WH501Z	82, 742, 1094
0WH503Z	446
0WH50YZ	446
0WH531Z	82, 742, 1094
0WH533Z	447
0WH53YZ	447
0WH541Z	82, 742, 1094
0WH543Z	447
0WH54YZ	447
0WH601Z	82, 499, 742, 1094
0WH603Z	447
0WH60YZ	447
0WH631Z	82, 499, 742, 1094
0WH633Z	447
0WH63YZ	447
0WH641Z	82, 499, 742, 1094
0WH643Z	447
0WH64YZ	447
0WH801Z	103, 742, 1094
0WH831Z	103, 742, 1094
0WH841Z	103, 742, 1094
0WH901Z	103, 742, 1094
0WH931Z	103, 742, 1094
0WH941Z	103, 742, 1094
0WHB01Z	103, 742, 1094
0WHB31Z	103, 742, 1094
0WHB41Z	103, 742, 1094
0WHC*	147, 742
0WHC01Z	1094
0WHC03Z	103, 969
0WHC0YZ	103, 969
0WHC31Z	1094
0WHC33Z	103, 969
0WHC3YZ	103, 969
0WHC41Z	1094
0WHC43Z	103, 969
0WHC4YZ	103, 969
0WHD*	742
0WHD01Z	147, 1094
0WHD03Z	94, 166, 603, 628, 969
0WHD0YZ	94, 166, 603, 628, 969
0WHD31Z	147, 1094
0WHD33Z	94, 166, 603, 628, 969
0WHD3YZ	94, 166, 603, 628, 969
0WHD41Z	147, 1094
0WHD43Z	94, 166, 603, 628, 969
0WHD4YZ	94, 166, 603, 628, 969
0WHF*	191, 742
0WHF01Z	1094
0WHF31Z	1094
0WHF41Z	1094
0WHG01Z	191, 499, 742, 1094
0WHG03Z	191, 517, 742
0WHG31Z	191, 499, 742, 1094
0WHG3YZ	191
0WHG41Z	192, 499, 742, 1094
0WHG43Z	192, 517, 742
0WHG4YZ	192
0WHH01Z	499, 517, 742, 1094
0WHH03Z	192
0WHH0YZ	192
0WHH31Z	499, 517, 742, 1094
0WHH33Z	192
0WHH3YZ	192
0WHH41Z	499, 517, 742, 1094
0WHH43Z	192
0WHH4YZ	192
0WHJ01Z	528, 535, 742, 1094
0WHJ03Z	192
0WHJ0YZ	192
0WHJ31Z	528, 535, 742, 1094
0WHJ33Z	192
0WHJ3YZ	192
0WHJ41Z	528, 535, 742, 1094
0WHJ43Z	192
0WHJ4YZ	192
0WHK01Z	742, 1094
0WHK03Z	447
0WHK0YZ	447
0WHK31Z	742, 1094
0WHK33Z	447
0WHK3YZ	447
0WHK41Z	742, 1094
0WHK43Z	447
0WHK4YZ	447
0WHL01Z	742, 1094
0WHL03Z	447
0WHL0YZ	447
0WHL31Z	742, 1094
0WHL33Z	447
0WHL3YZ	447
0WHL41Z	742, 1094
0WHL43Z	447
0WHL4YZ	447
0WHM01Z	528, 742, 1094
0WHM03Z	447
0WHM0YZ	447
0WHM31Z	528, 742, 1094
0WHM33Z	447
0WHM3YZ	447
0WHM41Z	528, 742, 1094
0WHM43Z	447
0WHM4YZ	447
0WHN01Z	535, 742, 1094
0WHN03Z	439, 537, 1094
0WHN0YZ	439, 537, 1094
0WHN31Z	535, 742, 1094
0WHN33Z	439, 537, 1094
0WHN3YZ	439, 537, 1094
0WHN41Z	535, 742, 1094
0WHN43Z	439, 537, 1094
0WHN4YZ	439, 537, 1094
0WHP01Z	192, 742, 1094
0WHP03Z	192
0WHP31Z	192, 742, 1094
0WHP41Z	192, 742, 1094
0WHP71Z	192, 742, 1094
0WHP81Z	192, 742, 1094
0WHQ01Z	103, 742, 1094
0WHQ33Z	103, 742, 969
0WHQ3YZ	103, 742, 969
0WHQ41Z	103, 742, 1094
0WHQ4YZ	103, 742, 969
0WHQ71Z	103, 742, 1094
0WHQ81Z	103, 742, 1094
0WHR01Z	517, 528, 535, 742, 1094
0WHR31Z	517, 528, 535, 742, 1094
0WHR41Z	517, 528, 535, 742, 1094
0WHR71Z	517, 528, 535, 742, 1094
0WHR81Z	517, 528, 535, 742, 1094
0WJ00ZZ	191
0WJ10ZZ	14, 69, 603, 628, 742, 850

Code	Page
0WJ14ZZ	14, 603, 628, 742, 969
0WJ20ZZ	447
0WJ40ZZ	447
0WJ50ZZ	447
0WJ60ZZ	82, 439, 483, 742, 969
0WJ64ZZ	287, 483, 742, 969
0WJ80ZZ	103
0WJ84ZZ	103
0WJ90ZZ	94, 147, 517, 603, 628, 742, 969
0WJ94ZZ	103, 147, 742, 969
0WJB0ZZ	94, 147, 517, 603, 628, 742, 969
0WJB4ZZ	103, 147, 742, 969
0WJC0ZZ	94, 147, 517, 603, 628, 742, 969
0WJC4ZZ	82, 103, 147, 578, 603, 628
0WJD4ZZ	82, 103, 147, 578, 603, 628
0WJF0ZZ	147, 192, 208, 439, 517, 603, 628, 742
0WJF4ZZ	192, 203, 439, 517, 535, 578, 742, 969, 1094
0WJG0ZZ	103, 147, 192, 203, 439, 499, 517, 521, 540, 578, 603, 628, 742, 969
0WJG4ZZ	192, 203, 439, 517, 535, 578, 742, 969, 1094
0WJH0ZZ	147, 192, 208, 439, 517, 603, 628, 742
0WJH4ZZ	192, 203, 540, 578, 603, 628, 742, 970, 1094
0WJJ0ZZ	103, 147, 192, 203, 439, 499, 517, 521, 540, 578, 603, 628, 742, 970
0WJJ4ZZ	192, 203, 439, 517, 535, 578, 742, 970, 1094
0WJK0ZZ	447
0WJL0ZZ	447
0WJM0ZZ	447
0WJM4ZZ	447
0WJN0ZZ	540
0WJN4ZZ	540
0WJP0ZZ	103, 147, 192, 203, 439, 499, 517, 521, 540, 578, 603, 628, 742, 970
0WJP4ZZ	192, 203, 439, 517, 535, 578, 742, 970, 1094
0WJQ0ZZ	94, 147, 517, 603, 628, 742, 970
0WJQ4ZZ	103, 147, 742, 970
0WJR0ZZ	103, 147, 192, 203, 439, 499, 517, 521, 540, 578, 603, 628, 742, 970
0WJR4ZZ	192, 203, 439, 517, 535, 578, 742, 970, 1094
0WM*	742
0WM20ZZ	82, 439, 1094
0WM40ZZ	82, 439, 1094
0WM50ZZ	82, 439, 1094
0WM60ZZ	82, 439, 1094
0WM80ZZ	103, 287, 439, 970
0WMF0ZZ	184, 208, 439, 603, 628, 970
0WMK0ZZ	439, 1094
0WML0ZZ	439, 1094
0WMM0ZZ	439, 1094
0WMN0ZZ	537, 970, 1094
0WP100Z	14
0WP101Z	14
0WP10JZ	14
0WP10YZ	14
0WP130Z	14
0WP131Z	14
0WP13JZ	14
0WP13YZ	14
0WP140Z	14
0WP141Z	14
0WP14JZ	14
0WP14YZ	14
0WPC00Z	103, 147, 742, 970
0WPC01Z	103, 147, 742, 970
0WPC03Z	103, 147, 742, 970
0WPC07Z	103, 147, 742, 970
0WPC0JZ	103, 147, 742, 970
0WPC0KZ	103, 147, 742, 970
0WPC0YZ	103, 147, 742, 970
0WPC30Z	103, 147, 742, 970
0WPC31Z	103, 147, 742, 970
0WPC33Z	103, 147, 742, 970
0WPC37Z	103, 147, 742, 970
0WPC3KZ	103, 147, 742, 970
0WPC3YZ	103, 147, 742, 970
0WPC40Z	103, 147, 742, 970
0WPC41Z	103, 147, 742, 970
0WPC43Z	103, 147, 742, 970
0WPC47Z	103, 147, 742, 970
0WPC4JZ	103, 147, 742, 970
0WPC4KZ	103, 148, 742, 970
0WPC4YZ	103, 148, 742, 970
0WPD00Z	94, 166, 603, 628, 742, 970
0WPD01Z	94, 166, 603, 628, 742, 970
0WPD03Z	94, 166, 603, 628, 742, 970
0WPD0YZ	94, 166, 603, 628, 742, 970
0WPD30Z	94, 166, 603, 628, 742, 970
0WPD31Z	94, 166, 603, 628, 742, 970
0WPD33Z	94, 166, 603, 628, 742, 970
0WPD3YZ	94, 166, 603, 628, 742, 970
0WPD40Z	94, 166, 603, 628, 742, 970
0WPD41Z	94, 166, 603, 628, 742, 970
0WPD43Z	94, 166, 603, 628, 742, 970
0WPD4YZ	94, 166, 603, 628, 742, 970
0WPF00Z	192, 742
0WPF01Z	192, 742
0WPF03Z	192, 742
0WPF07Z	192, 742
0WPF0JZ	192, 742
0WPF0KZ	192, 742
0WPF0YZ	192, 742
0WPF30Z	192, 742
0WPF31Z	192, 742
0WPF33Z	192, 742
0WPF37Z	192, 742
0WPF3JZ	192, 742
0WPF3KZ	192, 742
0WPF3YZ	192, 742
0WPF40Z	192, 742
0WPF41Z	192, 742
0WPF43Z	192, 742
0WPF47Z	192, 742
0WPF4JZ	192, 742
0WPF4KZ	192, 742
0WPF4YZ	742
0WPG01Z	192
0WPG03Z	192, 742
0WPG0JZ	192
0WPG0YZ	192
0WPG30Z	192
0WPG31Z	192
0WPG33Z	192
0WPG3JZ	192
0WPG3YZ	192
0WPG40Z	192
0WPG41Z	192
0WPG43Z	192, 742
0WPG4JZ	192
0WPG4YZ	192
0WPH00Z	192
0WPH01Z	192
0WPH0YZ	192
0WPH30Z	192
0WPH31Z	192
0WPH33Z	192
0WPH3YZ	192
0WPH40Z	192
0WPH41Z	192
0WPH43Z	192
0WPH4YZ	192
0WPM07Z	521, 1094
0WPM0KZ	521, 1094
0WPM37Z	522, 1094
0WPM3KZ	522, 1094
0WPM47Z	522, 1094
0WPM4KZ	522, 1094
0WPMX7Z	522, 1094
0WPMXJZ	522, 1094
0WPMXKZ	522, 1094
0WPN00Z	439, 537, 1094
0WPN01Z	439, 537, 1094
0WPN03Z	439, 537, 1094
0WPN07Z	439, 537, 1094
0WPN0JZ	439, 537, 1094
0WPN0KZ	439, 537, 1094
0WPN0YZ	439, 537, 1094
0WPN30Z	439, 537, 1094
0WPN31Z	440, 537, 1094
0WPN33Z	440, 537, 1094
0WPN37Z	440, 537, 1094
0WPN3JZ	440, 537, 1094
0WPN3KZ	440, 537, 1094
0WPN3YZ	440, 537, 1094
0WPN40Z	440, 537, 1094
0WPN41Z	440, 537, 1094
0WPN43Z	440, 537, 1094
0WPN47Z	440, 537, 1094
0WPN4JZ	440, 537, 1094
0WPN4KZ	440, 537, 1094
0WPN4YZ	440, 537, 1094
0WPP01Z	192
0WPP02Z	192
0WPP0YZ	192
0WPQ31Z	103, 742, 970
0WPQ33Z	103, 742, 970
0WPQ3YZ	103, 742, 970
0WPQ41Z	103, 742, 970
0WPQ43Z	103, 742, 970
0WPQ4YZ	103, 742, 970
0WPQ71Z	103, 742, 970
0WPQ7YZ	103, 742, 970
0WPQ81Z	103, 742, 970
0WQ0*	742
0WQ00Z	440, 1094
0WQ03Z	440, 1094
0WQ04Z	440, 1094
0WQ0XZZ	440, 1094
0WQ2*	82, 742
0WQ20Z	440, 1094
0WQ23Z	440, 1094
0WQ24Z	440, 1094
0WQ2XZZ	56, 440, 970, 1094
0WQ30ZZ	40, 82, 440, 742, 970
0WQ33ZZ	40, 82, 440, 742, 970
0WQ34ZZ	40, 82, 440, 742, 970
0WQ3XZZ	40, 82, 440, 742, 970
0WQ4*	82, 742
0WQ40ZZ	440, 1094
0WQ43Z	440, 1094
0WQ44Z	440, 1094
0WQ4XZZ	440, 1094
0WQ5*	82, 742
0WQ50Z	440, 1094
0WQ53Z	440, 1094
0WQ54ZZ	440, 1094
0WQ5YZ	440, 1094
0WQ6*	82, 742
0WQ60Z	440, 1094
0WQ63ZZ	440, 1094
0WQ64Z	440, 1094
0WQ6XZ2	103, 148, 177, 440, 603, 628, 970
0WQ6XZZ	440, 1094
0WQ8*	103, 287, 742
0WQ80ZZ	440, 970
0WQ83ZZ	440, 970
0WQ84ZZ	440, 970
0WQ8XZZ	440, 970
0WQC*	103, 742
0WQC0ZZ	970
0WQC3ZZ	970
0WQC4ZZ	970
0WQF*	540, 742
0WQF0ZZ	184, 507, 528, 603, 628, 970, 1095
0WQF3ZZ	184, 208, 440, 507, 528, 603, 628, 970
0WQF4ZZ	184, 208, 440, 507, 528, 603, 628, 970
0WQFXZ2	183, 508, 528, 603, 628, 970, 1095
0WQFXZZ	184, 208, 440, 508, 528, 603, 628, 970
0WQK*	742
0WQK0ZZ	440, 1095
0WQK3ZZ	440, 1095
0WQK4ZZ	440, 1095
0WQKXZZ	440, 1095
0WQL*	742
0WQL0ZZ	440, 1095
0WQL3ZZ	440, 1095
0WQL4ZZ	440, 1095
0WQLXZZ	440, 1095
0WQM*	742
0WQM0ZZ	440, 1095
0WQM3ZZ	440, 1095
0WQM4ZZ	440, 1095
0WQMXZZ	440, 1095
0WQN0ZZ	537, 742, 970, 1095
0WQN3ZZ	537, 743, 970, 1095
0WQN4ZZ	537, 743, 970, 1095
0WU007Z	215, 785, 788, 1095
0WU00JZ	440, 743, 1095
0WU00KZ	440, 743, 1095
0WU047Z	215, 785, 788, 1095
0WU04JZ	440, 743, 1095
0WU04KZ	440, 743, 1095
0WU2*	743
0WU207Z	40, 215, 440, 785, 788, 970
0WU20JZ	82, 440, 1095
0WU20KZ	82, 440, 1095
0WU247Z	40, 215, 440, 785, 788, 970
0WU24JZ	82, 440, 1095
0WU24KZ	82, 440, 1095
0WU4*	69, 287, 743
0WU407Z	40, 440, 970
0WU40JZ	970
0WU40KZ	970
0WU447Z	40, 440, 970
0WU44JZ	970
0WU44KZ	970
0WU5*	69, 287, 743
0WU507Z	40, 440, 970
0WU50JZ	970
0WU50KZ	970
0WU547Z	40, 440, 970
0WU54JZ	970
0WU54KZ	970
0WU607Z	215, 785, 788, 1095
0WU60JZ	82, 440, 743, 1095
0WU60KZ	82, 440, 743, 1095
0WU647Z	215, 785, 788, 1095
0WU64JZ	82, 440, 743, 1095
0WU64KZ	82, 440, 743, 1095
0WU8*	94
0WU80JZ	287
0WU84JZ	287
0WUC*	103, 743
0WUC07Z	970
0WUC0JZ	970
0WUC0KZ	970
0WUC47Z	970
0WUC4JZ	970
0WUC4KZ	970
0WUF*	184, 743
0WUF07Z	970, 1095
0WUF0JZ	970, 1095
0WUF0KZ	970, 1095
0WUF47Z	970
0WUF4JZ	970
0WUF4KZ	970
0WUK07Z	215, 785, 788, 1095
0WUK0JZ	440, 743, 1095
0WUK0KZ	440, 743, 1095
0WUK47Z	215, 785, 788, 1095
0WUK4JZ	440, 743, 1095
0WUK4KZ	440, 743, 1095
0WUL07Z	215, 785, 788, 1095
0WUL0JZ	440, 743, 1095
0WUL0KZ	440, 743, 1095
0WUL47Z	215, 785, 788, 1095
0WUL4JZ	440, 743, 1095
0WUL4KZ	440, 743, 1095
0WUM07Z	522, 1095
0WUM0JZ	440, 743, 1095
0WUM0KZ	440, 743, 1095
0WUM47Z	522, 1095
0WUM4JZ	440, 743, 1095
0WUM4KZ	440, 743, 1095
0WUN*	537, 743
0WUN07Z	970, 1095
0WUN0JZ	970, 1095
0WUN0KZ	970, 1095
0WUN47Z	970, 1095
0WUN4JZ	970, 1095
0WUN4KZ	970, 1095
0WW000Z	447
0WW001Z	447
0WW003Z	447
0WW007Z	447
0WW00JZ	447
0WW00KZ	447
0WW00YZ	447
0WW030Z	447
0WW031Z	447
0WW033Z	447
0WW037Z	447
0WW03JZ	447
0WW03KZ	447
0WW03YZ	447
0WW040Z	447
0WW041Z	447
0WW043Z	447
0WW047Z	447
0WW04JZ	447
0WW04KZ	447
0WW04YZ	447
0WW100Z	14
0WW101Z	14
0WW103Z	14
0WW10JZ	14
0WW10YZ	14
0WW130Z	14
0WW131Z	14
0WW133Z	14
0WW13JZ	14
0WW13YZ	14
0WW140Z	14
0WW141Z	14
0WW143Z	14
0WW14JZ	14
0WW14YZ	14
0WW200Z	447
0WW201Z	447
0WW203Z	447
0WW207Z	447
0WW20JZ	447
0WW20KZ	447
0WW20YZ	447
0WW230Z	447
0WW231Z	447
0WW233Z	447
0WW237Z	447
0WW23JZ	447
0WW23KZ	447
0WW23YZ	447
0WW240Z	447
0WW241Z	447
0WW243Z	447
0WW247Z	447
0WW24JZ	447
0WW24KZ	447
0WW24YZ	447
0WW400Z	447
0WW401Z	447
0WW403Z	447
0WW407Z	447
0WW40JZ	447
0WW40KZ	447
0WW40YZ	447
0WW430Z	447
0WW431Z	447
0WW433Z	447
0WW437Z	447
0WW43JZ	447
0WW43KZ	447
0WW43YZ	447
0WW440Z	447
0WW441Z	447
0WW443Z	447
0WW447Z	447
0WW44JZ	447
0WW44KZ	447
0WW44YZ	447
0WW500Z	447
0WW501Z	447
0WW503Z	447
0WW507Z	447
0WW50JZ	447
0WW50KZ	447
0WW50YZ	447
0WW530Z	447
0WW531Z	447
0WW533Z	447
0WW537Z	447
0WW53JZ	447
0WW53KZ	447
0WW53YZ	447
0WW540Z	447
0WW541Z	447
0WW543Z	447
0WW547Z	447
0WW54JZ	447
0WW54YZ	447
0WW600Z	447
0WW601Z	447
0WW603Z	447
0WW607Z	447
0WW60JZ	447
0WW60KZ	447
0WW60YZ	447
0WW630Z	447
0WW631Z	447
0WW633Z	447
0WW637Z	447
0WW63JZ	447
0WW63KZ	447
0WW63YZ	447
0WW640Z	447
0WW641Z	447
0WW643Z	447
0WW647Z	447
0WW64JZ	447
0WW64KZ	447
0WW64YZ	447
0WWC00Z	103, 148, 743, 970
0WWC01Z	103, 148, 743, 970
0WWC03Z	103, 148, 743, 970
0WWC07Z	103, 148, 743, 970
0WWC0JZ	103, 148, 743, 970
0WWC0KZ	103, 148, 743, 970
0WWC0YZ	103, 148, 743, 970
0WWC30Z	103, 148, 743, 970
0WWC31Z	103, 148, 743, 970
0WWC33Z	103, 148, 743, 970
0WWC37Z	103, 148, 743, 970
0WWC3JZ	103, 148, 743, 970
0WWC3KZ	103, 148, 743, 970
0WWC3YZ	103, 148, 743, 970
0WWC40Z	103, 148, 743, 970
0WWC41Z	103, 148, 743, 970
0WWC43Z	103, 148, 743, 970
0WWC47Z	103, 148, 743, 970
0WWC4JZ	103, 148, 743, 970
0WWC4KZ	103, 148, 743, 970
0WWC4YZ	103, 148, 743, 970
0WWD00Z	94, 166, 603, 628, 743, 970
0WWD01Z	94, 166, 603, 628, 743, 970
0WWD03Z	94, 166, 603, 628, 743, 970
0WWD0YZ	94, 166, 603, 628, 743, 970
0WWD30Z	94, 166, 603, 628, 743, 970
0WWD31Z	94, 166, 603, 628, 743, 970
0WWD33Z	94, 166, 603, 628, 743, 970
0WWD3YZ	94, 166, 603, 628, 743, 970

Numeric Index to Procedures

Code	Page
ØWWD40Z	94, 166, 603, 628, 743, 970
ØWWD41Z	94, 166, 603, 628, 743, 970
ØWWD43Z	94, 166, 603, 628, 743, 970
ØWWD4YZ	94, 166, 603, 628, 743, 970
ØWWF00Z	192, 743
ØWWF01Z	192, 743
ØWWF03Z	192, 743
ØWWF07Z	192, 743
ØWWF0JZ	192, 743
ØWWF0KZ	192, 743
ØWWF0YZ	192, 743
ØWWF30Z	192, 743
ØWWF31Z	192, 743
ØWWF33Z	192, 743
ØWWF37Z	192, 743
ØWWF3JZ	192, 743
ØWWF3KZ	192, 743
ØWWF3YZ	192, 743
ØWWF40Z	192, 743
ØWWF41Z	192, 743
ØWWF43Z	192, 743
ØWWF47Z	192, 743
ØWWF4JZ	192, 743
ØWWF4KZ	192, 743
ØWWF4YZ	192, 743
ØWWG00Z	192
ØWWG01Z	192
ØWWG03Z	192, 743
ØWWG07Z	192, 743
ØWWG0YZ	192
ØWWG30Z	192
ØWWG31Z	192
ØWWG33Z	192
ØWWG3JZ	192
ØWWG3YZ	192
ØWWG40Z	192
ØWWG41Z	192
ØWWG43Z	192, 743
ØWWG4JZ	192, 743
ØWWG4YZ	192
ØWWH00Z	192
ØWWH01Z	192
ØWWH03Z	192
ØWWH0YZ	192
ØWWH30Z	192
ØWWH31Z	192
ØWWH33Z	192
ØWWH3YZ	192
ØWWH40Z	192
ØWWH41Z	192
ØWWH43Z	192
ØWWH4YZ	192
ØWWJ00Z	192
ØWWJ01Z	192
ØWWJ03Z	192
ØWWJ0JZ	192
ØWWJ0YZ	192
ØWWJ30Z	192
ØWWJ31Z	192
ØWWJ33Z	192
ØWWJ3JZ	192
ØWWJ3YZ	192
ØWWJ40Z	192
ØWWJ41Z	192
ØWWJ43Z	192
ØWWJ4JZ	192
ØWWJ4YZ	192
ØWWK00Z	447
ØWWK01Z	447
ØWWK03Z	447
ØWWK07Z	447
ØWWK0JZ	447
ØWWK0KZ	447
ØWWK0YZ	447
ØWWK30Z	447
ØWWK31Z	447
ØWWK33Z	447
ØWWK37Z	447
ØWWK3JZ	447
ØWWK3KZ	447
ØWWK3YZ	447
ØWWK40Z	447
ØWWK41Z	447
ØWWK43Z	447
ØWWK47Z	447
ØWWK4JZ	447
ØWWK4KZ	447
ØWWK4YZ	447
ØWWL00Z	447
ØWWL01Z	447
ØWWL03Z	447
ØWWL07Z	447
ØWWL0JZ	447
ØWWL0YZ	447
ØWWL30Z	447
ØWWL31Z	447
ØWWL33Z	447
ØWWL37Z	447
ØWWL3JZ	447
ØWWL3KZ	448
ØWWL3YZ	448
ØWWL40Z	448
ØWWL41Z	448
ØWWL43Z	448
ØWWL47Z	448
ØWWL4JZ	448
ØWWL4KZ	448
ØWWL4YZ	448
ØWWM00Z	448
ØWWM01Z	448
ØWWM03Z	448
ØWWM07Z	522, 1095
ØWWM0JZ	448
ØWWM0KZ	522, 1095
ØWWM0YZ	448
ØWWM30Z	448
ØWWM31Z	448
ØWWM33Z	448
ØWWM37Z	522, 1095
ØWWM3JZ	448
ØWWM3KZ	522, 1095
ØWWM3YZ	448
ØWWM40Z	448
ØWWM41Z	448
ØWWM43Z	448
ØWWM47Z	522, 1095
ØWWM4JZ	448
ØWWM4KZ	522, 1095
ØWWM4YZ	448
ØWWN00Z	440, 537, 1095
ØWWN01Z	440, 537, 1095
ØWWN03Z	440, 537, 1095
ØWWN07Z	440, 537, 1095
ØWWN0JZ	440, 537, 1095
ØWWN0KZ	440, 537, 1095
ØWWN0YZ	440, 537, 1095
ØWWN30Z	440, 537, 1095
ØWWN31Z	440, 537, 1095
ØWWN33Z	440, 537, 1095
ØWWN37Z	440, 537, 1095
ØWWN3JZ	440, 537, 1095
ØWWN3KZ	440, 537, 1095
ØWWN3YZ	440, 537, 1095
ØWWN40Z	440, 537, 1095
ØWWN41Z	440, 537, 1095
ØWWN43Z	440, 537, 1095
ØWWN47Z	440, 537, 1095
ØWWN4JZ	440, 537, 1095
ØWWN4KZ	440, 537, 1095
ØWWN4YZ	440, 537, 1095
ØWWP01Z	192
ØWWP03Z	192
ØWWP0YZ	192
ØWWQ31Z	103, 743, 970
ØWWQ33Z	103, 743, 970
ØWWQ3YZ	103, 743, 970
ØWWQ41Z	103, 743, 970
ØWWQ43Z	103, 743, 970
ØWWQ4YZ	103, 743, 970
ØWWQ71Z	103, 743, 970
ØWWQ73Z	103, 743, 970
ØWWQ7YZ	103, 743, 970
ØWWQ81Z	103, 743, 970
ØWWQ83Z	103, 743, 970
ØWWQ8YZ	103, 743, 970
ØWY20Z0	82, 440, 743, 1095
ØWY20Z1	82, 440, 743, 1095
ØX0*	743
ØX0207Z	440, 1095
ØX020JZ	440, 1095
ØX020KZ	440, 1095
ØX020ZZ	440, 1095
ØX0237Z	440, 1095
ØX023JZ	440, 1095
ØX023KZ	440, 1095
ØX023ZZ	440, 1095
ØX0247Z	440, 1095
ØX024JZ	440, 1095
ØX024KZ	440, 1095
ØX024ZZ	440, 1095
ØX0307Z	440, 1095
ØX030JZ	440, 1095
ØX030KZ	440, 1095
ØX030ZZ	440, 1095
ØX0337Z	440, 1095
ØX033JZ	440, 1095
ØX033KZ	440, 1095
ØX033ZZ	440, 1095
ØX0347Z	440, 1095
ØX034JZ	440, 1095
ØX034KZ	440, 1095
ØX034ZZ	440, 1095
ØX0407Z	440, 1095
ØX040JZ	440, 1095
ØX040KZ	440, 1095
ØX0437Z	440, 1095
ØX043JZ	440, 1095
ØX043KZ	440, 1095
ØX043ZZ	440, 1095
ØX0447Z	440, 1095
ØX044JZ	440, 1095
ØX044KZ	440, 1095
ØX044ZZ	440, 1095
ØX0507Z	440, 1095
ØX050JZ	440, 1095
ØX050KZ	440, 1095
ØX050ZZ	440, 1095
ØX0537Z	440, 1095
ØX053JZ	440, 1095
ØX053KZ	440, 1095
ØX053ZZ	440, 1095
ØX0547Z	440, 1095
ØX054JZ	440, 1095
ØX054KZ	440, 1095
ØX054ZZ	440, 1095
ØX0607Z	440, 1095
ØX060JZ	440, 1095
ØX060KZ	440, 1095
ØX060ZZ	440, 1095
ØX0637Z	440, 1095
ØX063JZ	440, 1095
ØX063KZ	440, 1095
ØX063ZZ	440, 1095
ØX0647Z	440, 1095
ØX064JZ	440, 1095
ØX064KZ	440, 1095
ØX064ZZ	440, 1095
ØX0707Z	440, 1095
ØX070JZ	440, 1095
ØX070KZ	440, 1095
ØX070ZZ	440, 1095
ØX0737Z	441, 1095
ØX073JZ	441, 1095
ØX073KZ	441, 1095
ØX073ZZ	441, 1095
ØX0747Z	441, 1095
ØX074JZ	441, 1095
ØX074KZ	441, 1095
ØX074ZZ	441, 1095
ØX0807Z	441, 1095
ØX080JZ	441, 1095
ØX080KZ	441, 1095
ØX080ZZ	441, 1095
ØX0837Z	441, 1095
ØX083JZ	441, 1095
ØX083KZ	441, 1095
ØX083ZZ	441, 1095
ØX0847Z	441, 1095
ØX084JZ	441, 1095
ØX084KZ	441, 1095
ØX084ZZ	441, 1095
ØX0907Z	441, 1095
ØX090JZ	441, 1096
ØX090KZ	441, 1096
ØX090ZZ	441, 1096
ØX0937Z	441, 1096
ØX093JZ	441, 1096
ØX093KZ	441, 1096
ØX093ZZ	441, 1096
ØX0947Z	441, 1096
ØX094JZ	441, 1096
ØX094KZ	441, 1096
ØX094ZZ	441, 1096
ØX0B07Z	441, 1096
ØX0B0JZ	441, 1096
ØX0B0KZ	441, 1096
ØX0B0ZZ	441, 1096
ØX0B37Z	441, 1096
ØX0B3JZ	441, 1096
ØX0B3KZ	441, 1096
ØX0B3ZZ	441, 1096
ØX0B47Z	441, 1096
ØX0B4JZ	441, 1096
ØX0B4KZ	441, 1096
ØX0B4ZZ	441, 1096
ØX0C07Z	441, 1096
ØX0C0JZ	441, 1096
ØX0C0KZ	441, 1096
ØX0C0ZZ	441, 1096
ØX0C37Z	441, 1096
ØX0C3JZ	441, 1096
ØX0C3KZ	441, 1096
ØX0C3ZZ	441, 1096
ØX0C47Z	441, 1096
ØX0C4JZ	441, 1096
ØX0C4KZ	441, 1096
ØX0C4ZZ	441, 1096
ØX0D07Z	441, 1096
ØX0D0JZ	441, 1096
ØX0D0KZ	441, 1096
ØX0D0ZZ	441, 1096
ØX0D37Z	441, 1096
ØX0D3JZ	441, 1096
ØX0D3KZ	441, 1096
ØX0D3ZZ	441, 1096
ØX0D47Z	441, 1096
ØX0D4JZ	441, 1096
ØX0D4KZ	441, 1096
ØX0D4ZZ	441, 1096
ØX0F07Z	441, 1096
ØX0F0JZ	441, 1096
ØX0F0KZ	441, 1096
ØX0F0ZZ	441, 1096
ØX0F37Z	441, 1096
ØX0F3JZ	441, 1096
ØX0F3KZ	441, 1096
ØX0F3ZZ	441, 1096
ØX0F47Z	441, 1096
ØX0F4JZ	441, 1096
ØX0F4KZ	441, 1096
ØX0F4ZZ	441, 1096
ØX0G07Z	441, 1096
ØX0G0JZ	441, 1096
ØX0G0KZ	441, 1096
ØX0G0ZZ	441, 1096
ØX0G37Z	441, 1096
ØX0G3JZ	441, 1096
ØX0G3KZ	441, 1096
ØX0G3ZZ	441, 1096
ØX0G47Z	441, 1096
ØX0G4JZ	441, 1096
ØX0G4KZ	441, 1096
ØX0G4ZZ	441, 1096
ØX0H07Z	441, 1096
ØX0H0JZ	441, 1096
ØX0H0KZ	441, 1096
ØX0H0ZZ	441, 1096
ØX0H37Z	441, 1096
ØX0H3JZ	441, 1096
ØX0H3KZ	441, 1096
ØX0H3ZZ	441, 1096
ØX0H47Z	441, 1096
ØX0H4JZ	441, 1096
ØX0H4KZ	441, 1096
ØX0H4ZZ	441, 1096
ØX3*	148, 287, 743
ØX320ZZ	441, 603, 628, 970
ØX323ZZ	441, 603, 628, 970
ØX324ZZ	441, 603, 628, 970
ØX330ZZ	441, 603, 628, 970
ØX333ZZ	441, 603, 628, 970
ØX334ZZ	441, 603, 628, 970
ØX340ZZ	441, 603, 628, 970
ØX343ZZ	441, 603, 628, 970
ØX344ZZ	441, 603, 628, 970
ØX350ZZ	441, 603, 628, 970
ØX353ZZ	441, 603, 628, 970
ØX354ZZ	441, 603, 628, 970
ØX360ZZ	441, 603, 628, 970
ØX363ZZ	441, 603, 628, 970
ØX364ZZ	441, 603, 628, 970
ØX370ZZ	441, 603, 628, 970
ØX373ZZ	441, 603, 628, 970
ØX374ZZ	441, 603, 628, 970
ØX380ZZ	441, 603, 628, 970
ØX383ZZ	441, 603, 628, 970
ØX384ZZ	441, 603, 628, 970
ØX390ZZ	441, 603, 628, 971
ØX393ZZ	441, 603, 628, 971
ØX394ZZ	441, 603, 628, 971
ØX3B0ZZ	441, 603, 628, 971
ØX3B3ZZ	441, 603, 628, 971
ØX3B4ZZ	441, 603, 628, 971
ØX3C0ZZ	441, 603, 628, 971
ØX3C3ZZ	441, 603, 628, 971
ØX3C4ZZ	441, 603, 628, 971
ØX3D0ZZ	441, 603, 628, 971
ØX3D3ZZ	441, 603, 628, 971
ØX3D4ZZ	441, 603, 629, 971
ØX3F0ZZ	441, 603, 629, 971
ØX3F3ZZ	441, 603, 629, 971
ØX3F4ZZ	441, 603, 629, 971
ØX3G0ZZ	441, 603, 629, 971
ØX3G3ZZ	441, 603, 629, 971
ØX3G4ZZ	441, 603, 629, 971
ØX3H0ZZ	441, 603, 629, 971
ØX3H3ZZ	441, 603, 629, 971
ØX3H4ZZ	441, 603, 629, 971
ØX3J0ZZ	441, 603, 629, 971
ØX3J3ZZ	441, 603, 629, 971
ØX3J4ZZ	441, 603, 629, 971
ØX3K0ZZ	441, 603, 629, 971
ØX3K3ZZ	441, 603, 629, 971
ØX3K4ZZ	441, 603, 629, 971
ØX6*	141
ØX600ZZ	222, 441, 743, 971
ØX610ZZ	222, 441, 743, 971
ØX620ZZ	222, 441, 743, 971
ØX630ZZ	222, 441, 743, 971
ØX68*	222, 743
ØX680Z1	441, 971
ØX680Z2	441, 971
ØX680Z3	441, 971
ØX69*	222, 743
ØX690Z1	441, 971
ØX690Z2	441, 971
ØX690Z3	441, 971
ØX6B0ZZ	222, 441, 743, 971
ØX6C0ZZ	222, 441, 743, 971
ØX6D*	222, 743
ØX6D0Z1	441, 971
ØX6D0Z2	441, 971
ØX6D0Z3	441, 971
ØX6F*	222, 743
ØX6F0Z1	441, 971
ØX6F0Z2	441, 971
ØX6F0Z3	441, 971
ØX6J*	222, 743
ØX6J0Z0	441, 971
ØX6J0Z4	441, 971
ØX6J0Z5	441, 971
ØX6J0Z6	441, 971
ØX6J0Z7	442, 971
ØX6J0Z8	442, 971
ØX6J0Z9	442, 971
ØX6J0ZB	442, 971
ØX6J0ZC	442, 971
ØX6J0ZD	442, 971
ØX6J0ZF	442, 971
ØX6K*	222, 743
ØX6K0Z0	442, 971
ØX6K0Z4	442, 971
ØX6K0Z5	442, 971
ØX6K0Z6	442, 971
ØX6K0Z7	442, 971
ØX6K0Z8	442, 971
ØX6K0Z9	442, 971
ØX6K0ZB	442, 971
ØX6K0ZC	442, 971
ØX6K0ZF	442, 971
ØX6L*	271
ØX6L0Z0	442, 648, 971
ØX6L0Z1	442, 648, 971
ØX6L0Z3	442, 648, 971
ØX6M*	271
ØX6M0Z0	442, 648, 971
ØX6M0Z1	442, 649, 971
ØX6M0Z2	442, 649, 971
ØX6M0Z3	442, 649, 971
ØX6N*	271
ØX6N0Z0	442, 649, 971, 1096
ØX6N0Z1	442, 649, 971, 1096
ØX6N0Z2	442, 649, 971, 1096
ØX6N0Z3	442, 649, 971, 1096
ØX6P*	271
ØX6P0Z0	442, 649, 971, 1096
ØX6P0Z1	442, 649, 971, 1096
ØX6P0Z2	442, 649, 971, 1096
ØX6P0Z3	442, 649, 971, 1096
ØX6Q*	271
ØX6Q0Z0	442, 649, 971, 1096
ØX6Q0Z1	442, 649, 971, 1096
ØX6Q0Z2	442, 649, 971, 1096
ØX6Q0Z3	442, 649, 971, 1096
ØX6R*	271
ØX6R0Z0	442, 649, 971, 1096
ØX6R0Z1	442, 649, 971, 1096
ØX6R0Z2	442, 649, 971, 1096
ØX6R0Z3	442, 649, 971, 1096
ØX6S*	271
ØX6S0Z0	442, 649, 971, 1096
ØX6S0Z1	442, 649, 971, 1096
ØX6S0Z2	442, 649, 971, 1096
ØX6S0Z3	442, 649, 971, 1096
ØX6T*	271
ØX6T0Z0	442, 649, 971, 1096
ØX6T0Z1	442, 649, 971, 1096
ØX6T0Z2	442, 649, 971, 1096
ØX6T0Z3	442, 649, 971, 1096
ØX6V*	271
ØX6V0Z0	442, 649, 971, 1096
ØX6V0Z1	442, 649, 971, 1096
ØX6V0Z2	442, 649, 971, 1096
ØX6V0Z3	442, 649, 971, 1096
ØX6W*	271
ØX6W0Z0	442, 649, 971, 1096
ØX6W0Z1	442, 649, 971, 1096
ØX6W0Z2	442, 649, 971, 1096
ØX6W0Z3	442, 649, 971, 1096
ØXB20ZZ	40, 148, 256, 411, 743, 971, 1096
ØXB23ZZ	40, 148, 256, 411, 743, 971, 1096
ØXB24ZZ	40, 148, 256, 411, 743, 971, 1096
ØXB30ZZ	40, 148, 256, 411, 743, 971, 1096
ØXB33ZZ	40, 148, 256, 411, 743, 971, 1096
ØXB34ZZ	40, 148, 256, 411, 743, 971, 1096
ØXB40ZZ	40, 148, 256, 411, 743, 971, 1096
ØXB43ZZ	40, 148, 256, 411, 743, 971, 1096
ØXB44ZZ	40, 148, 256, 411, 743, 971, 1096
ØXB50ZZ	40, 148, 256, 411, 743, 971, 1096
ØXB53ZZ	40, 148, 256, 411, 743, 971, 1096
ØXB54ZZ	40, 148, 256, 411, 743, 971, 1096
ØXB60ZZ	40, 148, 256, 411, 743, 971, 1096
ØXB63ZZ	40, 148, 256, 411, 743, 971, 1096
ØXB64ZZ	40, 148, 256, 411, 743, 971, 1096
ØXB70ZZ	40, 148, 256, 411, 743, 971, 1096
ØXB73ZZ	40, 148, 256, 411, 743, 971, 1096
ØXB74ZZ	40, 148, 256, 411, 743, 971, 1096
ØXB80ZZ	40, 148, 256, 411, 743, 971, 1096

Code	Page
ØXB83ZZ	40, 148, 256, 411, 743, 971, 1096
ØXB84ZZ	40, 148, 256, 411, 743, 971, 1096
ØXB90ZZ	40, 148, 256, 411, 743, 971, 1096
ØXB93ZZ	40, 148, 256, 411, 743, 971, 1096
ØXB94ZZ	41, 148, 256, 411, 743, 971, 1096
ØXBB0ZZ	41, 148, 256, 411, 743, 971, 1096
ØXBB3ZZ	41, 148, 256, 411, 743, 971, 1096
ØXBB4ZZ	41, 148, 256, 411, 743, 971, 1096
ØXBC0ZZ	41, 148, 256, 411, 743, 971, 1096
ØXBC3ZZ	41, 148, 256, 411, 743, 971, 1096
ØXBC4ZZ	41, 148, 256, 411, 743, 971, 1096
ØXBD0ZZ	41, 148, 256, 411, 743, 971, 1096
ØXBD3ZZ	41, 148, 256, 411, 743, 971, 1096
ØXBD4ZZ	41, 148, 256, 411, 743, 971, 1096
ØXBF0ZZ	41, 148, 256, 411, 743, 971, 1096
ØXBF3ZZ	41, 148, 256, 411, 743, 971, 1096
ØXBF4ZZ	41, 148, 256, 411, 743, 971, 1096
ØXBG0ZZ	41, 148, 256, 411, 743, 971, 1096
ØXBG3ZZ	41, 148, 256, 411, 743, 971, 1096
ØXBG4ZZ	41, 148, 256, 411, 743, 971, 1096
ØXBH0ZZ	41, 148, 256, 411, 743, 971, 1096
ØXBH3ZZ	41, 148, 256, 411, 743, 971, 1096
ØXBH4ZZ	41, 148, 256, 411, 743, 971, 1096
ØXBJ0ZZ	41, 148, 256, 411, 743, 971, 1096
ØXBJ3ZZ	41, 148, 256, 411, 743, 971, 1096
ØXBJ4ZZ	41, 148, 256, 411, 743, 971, 1096
ØXBK0ZZ	41, 148, 256, 411, 743, 971, 1096
ØXBK3ZZ	41, 148, 256, 411, 743, 971, 1096
ØXBK4ZZ	41, 148, 256, 411, 743, 971, 1096
ØXH201Z	743, 1096
ØXH203Z	448
ØXH20YZ	448
ØXH231Z	743, 1096
ØXH233Z	448
ØXH23YZ	448
ØXH241Z	743, 1096
ØXH243Z	448
ØXH24YZ	448
ØXH301Z	743, 1096
ØXH303Z	448
ØXH30YZ	448
ØXH331Z	743, 1096
ØXH333Z	448
ØXH33YZ	448
ØXH341Z	743, 1096
ØXH343Z	448
ØXH34YZ	448
ØXH401Z	743, 1096
ØXH403Z	448
ØXH40YZ	448
ØXH431Z	743, 1096
ØXH433Z	448
ØXH43YZ	448
ØXH441Z	743, 1096
ØXH443Z	448
ØXH44YZ	448
ØXH501Z	743, 1096
ØXH503Z	448
ØXH50YZ	448
ØXH531Z	743, 1096
ØXH533Z	448
ØXH53YZ	448
ØXH541Z	743, 1097
ØXH543Z	448

Code	Page
ØXH54YZ	448
ØXH601Z	744, 1097
ØXH603Z	448
ØXH60YZ	448
ØXH631Z	744, 1097
ØXH633Z	448
ØXH63YZ	448
ØXH641Z	744, 1097
ØXH643Z	448
ØXH64YZ	448
ØXH701Z	744, 1097
ØXH703Z	448
ØXH70YZ	448
ØXH731Z	744, 1097
ØXH733Z	448
ØXH73YZ	448
ØXH741Z	744, 1097
ØXH743Z	448
ØXH74YZ	448
ØXH801Z	744, 1097
ØXH803Z	448
ØXH80YZ	448
ØXH831Z	744, 1097
ØXH833Z	448
ØXH83YZ	448
ØXH841Z	744, 1097
ØXH843Z	448
ØXH84YZ	448
ØXH901Z	744, 1097
ØXH903Z	448
ØXH90YZ	448
ØXH931Z	744, 1097
ØXH933Z	448
ØXH93YZ	448
ØXH941Z	744, 1097
ØXH943Z	448
ØXH94YZ	448
ØXHB01Z	744, 1097
ØXHB03Z	448
ØXHB0YZ	448
ØXHB31Z	744, 1097
ØXHB33Z	448
ØXHB3YZ	448
ØXHB41Z	744, 1097
ØXHB43Z	448
ØXHB4YZ	448
ØXHC01Z	744, 1097
ØXHC0YZ	448
ØXHC31Z	744, 1097
ØXHC3YZ	448
ØXHC41Z	744, 1097
ØXHC4YZ	448
ØXHD01Z	744, 1097
ØXHD03Z	448
ØXHD0YZ	448
ØXHD31Z	744, 1097
ØXHD33Z	448
ØXHD3YZ	448
ØXHD41Z	744, 1097
ØXHD43Z	448
ØXHD4YZ	448
ØXHF01Z	744, 1097
ØXHF03Z	448
ØXHF0YZ	448
ØXHF31Z	744, 1097
ØXHF33Z	448
ØXHF3YZ	448
ØXHF41Z	744, 1097
ØXHF43Z	448
ØXHF4YZ	448
ØXHG01Z	744, 1097
ØXHG03Z	448
ØXHG0YZ	448
ØXHG31Z	744, 1097
ØXHG33Z	448
ØXHG3YZ	448
ØXHG41Z	744, 1097
ØXHG43Z	448
ØXHG4YZ	448
ØXHH01Z	744, 1097
ØXHH03Z	448
ØXHH0YZ	448
ØXHH31Z	744, 1097
ØXHH33Z	448
ØXHH3YZ	448
ØXHH41Z	744, 1097
ØXHH43Z	448
ØXHH4YZ	448
ØXHJ01Z	744, 1097
ØXHJ03Z	448

Code	Page
ØXHJ0YZ	448
ØXHJ31Z	744, 1097
ØXHJ33Z	448
ØXHJ3YZ	448
ØXHJ41Z	744, 1097
ØXHJ43Z	448
ØXHJ4YZ	448
ØXHK01Z	744, 1097
ØXHK03Z	448
ØXHK0YZ	448
ØXHK31Z	744, 1097
ØXHK33Z	448
ØXHK3YZ	448
ØXHK41Z	744, 1097
ØXHK43Z	448
ØXHK4YZ	448
ØXJ20ZZ	448
ØXJ30ZZ	448
ØXJ40ZZ	448
ØXJ50ZZ	448
ØXJ60ZZ	448
ØXJ70ZZ	448
ØXJ80ZZ	448
ØXJ90ZZ	448
ØXJB0ZZ	448
ØXJC0ZZ	448
ØXJD0ZZ	448
ØXJF0ZZ	448
ØXJG0ZZ	448
ØXJH0ZZ	448
ØXJJ0ZZ	448
ØXJJ4ZZ	256
ØXJK0ZZ	448
ØXJK4ZZ	256
ØXM00ZZ	227, 744, 853
ØXM10ZZ	227, 744, 853
ØXM20ZZ	227, 744, 853
ØXM30ZZ	227, 744, 853
ØXM40ZZ	227, 744, 853
ØXM50ZZ	227, 744, 853
ØXM60ZZ	227, 744, 853
ØXM70ZZ	227, 744, 853
ØXM80ZZ	227, 744, 853
ØXM90ZZ	227, 744, 853
ØXMB0ZZ	227, 744, 853
ØXMC0ZZ	227, 744, 853
ØXMD0ZZ	227, 744, 853
ØXMF0ZZ	227, 744, 853
ØXMG0ZZ	227, 744, 853
ØXMH0ZZ	227, 744, 853
ØXMJ0ZZ	227, 744, 853
ØXMK0ZZ	227, 744, 853
ØXML0ZZ	271, 649, 971
ØXMM0ZZ	271, 649, 971
ØXMN0ZZ	271, 649, 971
ØXMP0ZZ	271, 649, 971
ØXMQ0ZZ	271, 649, 971
ØXMR0ZZ	271, 649, 971
ØXMS0ZZ	271, 649, 971
ØXMT0ZZ	271, 649, 971
ØXMV0ZZ	271, 649, 971
ØXMW0ZZ	271, 649, 971
ØXQ*	744
ØXQ20ZZ	971
ØXQ23ZZ	971
ØXQ24ZZ	971
ØXQ2XZZ	971
ØXQ30ZZ	971
ØXQ33ZZ	971
ØXQ34ZZ	971
ØXQ3XZZ	971
ØXQ40ZZ	971
ØXQ43ZZ	971
ØXQ44ZZ	972
ØXQ4XZZ	972
ØXQ50ZZ	972
ØXQ53ZZ	972
ØXQ54ZZ	972
ØXQ5XZZ	972
ØXQ60ZZ	972
ØXQ63ZZ	972
ØXQ64ZZ	972
ØXQ6XZZ	972
ØXQ70ZZ	972
ØXQ73ZZ	972
ØXQ74ZZ	972
ØXQ7XZZ	972
ØXQ80ZZ	972
ØXQ83ZZ	972
ØXQ84ZZ	972
ØXQ8XZZ	972
ØXQ90ZZ	972
ØXQ93ZZ	972

Code	Page
ØXQ94ZZ	972
ØXQ9XZZ	972
ØXQB0ZZ	972
ØXQB3ZZ	972
ØXQB4ZZ	972
ØXQBXZZ	972
ØXQC0ZZ	972
ØXQC3ZZ	972
ØXQC4ZZ	972
ØXQCXZZ	972
ØXQD0ZZ	972
ØXQD3ZZ	972
ØXQD4ZZ	972
ØXQDXZZ	972
ØXQF0ZZ	972
ØXQF4ZZ	972
ØXQFXZZ	972
ØXQG0ZZ	972
ØXQG3ZZ	972
ØXQG4ZZ	972
ØXQGXZZ	972
ØXQH0ZZ	972
ØXQH3ZZ	972
ØXQH4ZZ	972
ØXQHXZZ	972
ØXQJ*	41
ØXQJ0ZZ	972
ØXQJ3ZZ	972
ØXQJ4ZZ	972
ØXQJXZZ	972
ØXQK*	41
ØXQK0ZZ	972
ØXQK3ZZ	972
ØXQK4ZZ	972
ØXQKXZZ	972
ØXQL*	41
ØXQL0ZZ	972
ØXQL3ZZ	972
ØXQL4ZZ	972
ØXQLXZZ	972
ØXQM*	41
ØXQM0ZZ	972
ØXQM3ZZ	972
ØXQM4ZZ	972
ØXQMXZZ	972
ØXQN*	41
ØXQN0ZZ	972
ØXQN3ZZ	972
ØXQN4ZZ	972
ØXQNXZZ	972
ØXQP*	41
ØXQP0ZZ	972
ØXQP3ZZ	972
ØXQP4ZZ	972
ØXQPXZZ	972
ØXQQ*	41
ØXQQ0ZZ	972
ØXQQ3ZZ	972
ØXQQ4ZZ	972
ØXQQXZZ	972
ØXQR*	41
ØXQR0ZZ	972
ØXQR3ZZ	972
ØXQR4ZZ	972
ØXQRXZZ	972
ØXQS*	41
ØXQS0ZZ	972
ØXQS3ZZ	972
ØXQS4ZZ	972
ØXQSXZZ	972
ØXQT*	41
ØXQT0ZZ	972
ØXQT3ZZ	972
ØXQT4ZZ	972
ØXQTXZZ	972
ØXQV*	41
ØXQV0ZZ	972
ØXQV3ZZ	972
ØXQV4ZZ	972
ØXQVXZZ	972
ØXQW*	41
ØXQW0ZZ	972
ØXQW3ZZ	972
ØXQW4ZZ	972
ØXQWXZZ	972
ØXR*	41
ØXRL07N	264, 649, 972
ØXRL07P	264, 649, 972
ØXRL47N	264, 649, 972
ØXRL47P	264, 649, 972
ØXRM07N	264, 649, 972
ØXRM07P	264, 649, 972

Code	Page
ØXRM47N	264, 649, 972
ØXRM47P	264, 649, 972
ØXU207Z	215, 785, 788, 1097
ØXU20JZ	442, 744, 1097
ØXU20KZ	442, 744, 1097
ØXU247Z	215, 785, 788, 1097
ØXU24JZ	442, 744, 1097
ØXU24KZ	442, 744, 1097
ØXU307Z	215, 785, 788, 1097
ØXU30JZ	442, 744, 1097
ØXU30KZ	442, 744, 1097
ØXU347Z	215, 785, 788, 1097
ØXU34JZ	442, 744, 1097
ØXU34KZ	442, 744, 1097
ØXU407Z	215, 785, 788, 1097
ØXU40JZ	442, 744, 1097
ØXU40KZ	442, 744, 1097
ØXU447Z	215, 785, 788, 1097
ØXU44JZ	442, 744, 1097
ØXU44KZ	442, 744, 1097
ØXU507Z	215, 785, 788, 1097
ØXU50JZ	442, 744, 1097
ØXU50KZ	442, 744, 1097
ØXU547Z	215, 785, 788, 1097
ØXU54JZ	442, 744, 1097
ØXU54KZ	442, 744, 1097
ØXU607Z	215, 785, 788, 1097
ØXU60JZ	442, 744, 1097
ØXU60KZ	442, 744, 1097
ØXU647Z	215, 785, 788, 1097
ØXU64JZ	442, 744, 1097
ØXU64KZ	442, 744, 1097
ØXU707Z	215, 785, 788, 1097
ØXU70JZ	442, 744, 1097
ØXU70KZ	442, 744, 1097
ØXU747Z	215, 785, 788, 1097
ØXU74JZ	442, 744, 1097
ØXU74KZ	442, 744, 1097
ØXU807Z	215, 785, 788, 1097
ØXU80JZ	442, 744, 1097
ØXU80KZ	442, 744, 1097
ØXU847Z	215, 785, 788, 1097
ØXU84JZ	442, 744, 1097
ØXU84KZ	442, 744, 1097
ØXU907Z	215, 785, 788, 1097
ØXU90JZ	442, 744, 1097
ØXU90KZ	442, 744, 1097
ØXU947Z	215, 785, 788, 1097
ØXU94JZ	442, 744, 1097
ØXU94KZ	442, 744, 1097
ØXUB07Z	215, 785, 788, 1097
ØXUB0JZ	442, 744, 1097
ØXUB0KZ	442, 744, 1097
ØXUB47Z	215, 785, 788, 1097
ØXUB4JZ	442, 744, 1097
ØXUB4KZ	442, 744, 1097
ØXUC07Z	215, 785, 788, 1097
ØXUC0JZ	442, 744, 1097
ØXUC0KZ	442, 744, 1097
ØXUC47Z	215, 785, 788, 1097
ØXUC4JZ	442, 744, 1097
ØXUC4KZ	442, 744, 1097
ØXUD07Z	215, 785, 788, 1097
ØXUD0JZ	442, 744, 1097
ØXUD0KZ	442, 744, 1097
ØXUD47Z	215, 785, 788, 1097
ØXUD4JZ	442, 744, 1097
ØXUD4KZ	442, 744, 1097
ØXUF07Z	215, 785, 788, 1097
ØXUF0JZ	442, 744, 1097

Code	Page
ØXUF0KZ	442, 744, 1097
ØXUF47Z	215, 785, 788, 1097
ØXUF4JZ	442, 744, 1097
ØXUF4KZ	442, 744, 1097
ØXUG07Z	215, 785, 788, 1097
ØXUG0JZ	442, 744, 1097
ØXUG0KZ	442, 744, 1097
ØXUG47Z	215, 785, 788, 1097
ØXUG4JZ	442, 744, 1097
ØXUG4KZ	442, 744, 1097
ØXUH07Z	215, 785, 788, 1097
ØXUH0JZ	442, 744, 1097
ØXUH0KZ	442, 744, 1097
ØXUH47Z	215, 785, 788, 1097
ØXUH4JZ	442, 744, 1097
ØXUH4KZ	442, 744, 1097
ØXUJ07Z	41, 148, 271, 411, 649, 785, 788, 972, 1097
ØXUJ0JZ	442, 744, 1097
ØXUJ0KZ	442, 744, 1097
ØXUJ47Z	41, 148, 271, 411, 649, 785, 788, 972, 1097
ØXUJ4JZ	442, 744, 1097
ØXUJ4KZ	442, 744, 1097
ØXUK07Z	41, 148, 271, 411, 649, 785, 788, 972, 1097
ØXUK0JZ	442, 744, 1097
ØXUK0KZ	442, 744, 1097
ØXUK47Z	41, 148, 271, 411, 649, 785, 788, 972, 1097
ØXUK4JZ	442, 744, 1097
ØXUK4KZ	442, 744, 1097
ØXUL07Z	41, 148, 271, 411, 649, 785, 788, 972, 1097
ØXUL0JZ	442, 744, 1097
ØXUL0KZ	442, 744, 1097
ØXUL47Z	41, 148, 271, 411, 649, 785, 788, 972, 1097
ØXUL4JZ	442, 744, 1097
ØXUL4KZ	442, 744, 1097
ØXUM07Z	41, 148, 271, 411, 649, 785, 788, 972, 1097
ØXUM0JZ	442, 744, 1097
ØXUM0KZ	442, 744, 1097
ØXUM47Z	41, 148, 271, 411, 649, 785, 788, 972, 1097
ØXUM4JZ	442, 744, 1097
ØXUM4KZ	442, 744, 1097
ØXUN07Z	41, 148, 271, 411, 649, 785, 788, 972, 1097
ØXUN0JZ	442, 744, 1097
ØXUN0KZ	442, 744, 1097
ØXUN47Z	41, 148, 271, 411, 649, 785, 788, 972, 1097
ØXUN4JZ	442, 744, 1097
ØXUN4KZ	442, 744, 1097
ØXUP07Z	41, 148, 271, 411, 649, 785, 788, 972, 1097
ØXUP0JZ	442, 744, 1097
ØXUP0KZ	442, 744, 1097
ØXUP47Z	41, 148, 271, 411, 649, 785, 788, 972, 1097
ØXUP4JZ	442, 744, 1097
ØXUP4KZ	442, 744, 1097
ØXUQ07Z	41, 148, 271, 411, 649, 785, 788, 972, 1097
ØXUQ0JZ	442, 744, 1097
ØXUQ0KZ	442, 744, 1097
ØXUQ47Z	41, 148, 271, 411, 649, 785, 788, 972, 1097
ØXUQ4JZ	442, 744, 1097
ØXUQ4KZ	442, 744, 1097

Code	Page	Code	Page	Code	Page	Code	Page	Code	Page	Code	Page
ØXUR07Z	41, 148, 271, 411, 649, 785, 788, 972, 1097	ØY0*	744	ØY0G47Z	443, 1098	ØY3H4ZZ	443, 604, 629, 972	ØY6U0Z1	444, 973	ØYB6*	192
ØXUR0JZ	442, 744, 1097	ØY0007Z	442, 1098	ØY0G4JZ	443, 1098	ØY3J0ZZ	443, 604, 629, 972	ØY6U0Z2	444, 973	ØYB60ZX	203, 541, 578, 604, 629, 745, 973, 1099
ØXUR0KZ	442, 744, 1097	ØY000JZ	442, 1098	ØY0G4KZ	443, 1098	ØY3J3ZZ	443, 604, 629, 972	ØY6U0Z3	444, 973		
ØXUR47Z	41, 148, 271, 411, 649, 785, 788, 972, 1097	ØY000KZ	442, 1098	ØY0G4ZZ	443, 1098	ØY3J4ZZ	443, 604, 629, 972	ØY6V*	41, 141, 261, 479	ØYB60ZZ	256, 444, 499, 604, 629, 1099
ØXUR4JZ	442, 744, 1097	ØY000ZZ	442, 1098	ØY0H07Z	443, 1098	ØY3K0ZZ	444, 604, 629, 973	ØY6V0Z0	444, 973	ØYB63ZX	203, 541, 578, 604, 629, 745, 973, 1099
ØXUR4KZ	442, 744, 1097	ØY0037Z	442, 1098	ØY0H0JZ	443, 1098	ØY3K3ZZ	444, 604, 629, 973	ØY6V0Z1	444, 973		
ØXUS07Z	41, 148, 271, 411, 649, 785, 788, 972, 1097	ØY003JZ	442, 1098	ØY0H0KZ	443, 1098	ØY3K4ZZ	444, 604, 629, 973	ØY6V0Z2	444, 973	ØYB63ZZ	256, 444, 499, 604, 629, 1099
ØXUS0JZ	442, 744, 1097	ØY003KZ	442, 1098	ØY0H0ZZ	443, 1098	ØY3L0ZZ	444, 604, 629, 973	ØY6V0Z3	444, 973	ØYB64ZX	203, 541, 578, 604, 629, 745, 973, 1099
ØXUS0KZ	442, 744, 1097	ØY003ZZ	442, 1098	ØY0H37Z	443, 1098	ØY3L3ZZ	444, 604, 629, 973	ØY6W*	41, 141, 261, 479		
ØXUS47Z	41, 148, 271, 411, 649, 785, 788, 972, 1097	ØY0047Z	442, 1098	ØY0H3JZ	443, 1098	ØY3L4ZZ	444, 604, 629, 973	ØY6W0Z0	444, 973	ØYB64ZZ	256, 444, 499, 604, 629, 1099
ØXUS4JZ	442, 744, 1097	ØY004JZ	442, 1098	ØY0H3KZ	443, 1098	ØY3M0ZZ	444, 604, 629, 973	ØY6W0Z1	444, 973	ØYB7*	192
ØXUS4KZ	442, 744, 1098	ØY004KZ	442, 1098	ØY0H3ZZ	443, 1098	ØY3M3ZZ	444, 604, 629, 973	ØY6W0Z2	444, 973	ØYB70ZX	203, 541, 578, 604, 629, 745, 973, 1099
ØXUT07Z	41, 148, 271, 411, 649, 785, 788, 972, 1098	ØY004ZZ	442, 1098	ØY0H47Z	443, 1098	ØY3M4ZZ	444, 604, 629, 973	ØY6W0Z3	444, 973		
ØXUT0JZ	442, 744, 1098	ØY0107Z	443, 1098	ØY0H4JZ	443, 1098	ØY3N0ZZ	444, 604, 629, 973	ØY6X*	41, 141, 261, 479	ØYB70ZZ	256, 444, 499, 604, 629, 1099
ØXUT0KZ	442, 744, 1098	ØY010JZ	443, 1098	ØY0H4KZ	443, 1098	ØY3N3ZZ	444, 604, 629, 973	ØY6X0Z0	444, 973	ØYB73ZX	203, 541, 578, 604, 629, 745, 973, 1099
ØXUT47Z	41, 148, 271, 411, 649, 785, 788, 972, 1098	ØY010KZ	443, 1098	ØY0H4ZZ	443, 1098	ØY3N4ZZ	444, 604, 629, 973	ØY6X0Z1	444, 973		
ØXUT4JZ	442, 744, 1098	ØY0137Z	443, 1098	ØY0J07Z	443, 1098	ØY6*	744	ØY6X0Z2	444, 973	ØYB73ZZ	256, 444, 499, 604, 629, 1099
ØXUT4KZ	442, 744, 1098	ØY013JZ	443, 1098	ØY0J0JZ	443, 1098	ØY620ZZ	119, 222, 444, 973	ØY6X0Z3	444, 973	ØYB74ZX	203, 541, 578, 604, 629, 745, 973, 1099
ØXUV07Z	41, 148, 271, 411, 649, 785, 788, 972, 1098	ØY013KZ	443, 1098	ØY0J0KZ	443, 1098	ØY630ZZ	119, 222, 444, 973	ØY6Y*	41, 141, 261, 479		
ØXUV0JZ	442, 744, 1098	ØY013ZZ	443, 1098	ØY0J37Z	443, 1098	ØY640ZZ	119, 222, 444, 973	ØY6Y0Z0	444, 973	ØYB74ZZ	256, 444, 499, 604, 629, 1099
ØXUV0KZ	442, 744, 1098	ØY0147Z	443, 1098	ØY0J3JZ	443, 1098	ØY670ZZ	119, 222, 444, 973	ØY6Y0Z1	444, 973	ØYB8*	192
ØXUV47Z	41, 148, 271, 411, 649, 785, 788, 972, 1098	ØY014JZ	443, 1098	ØY0J3KZ	443, 1098	ØY680ZZ	119, 222, 444, 973	ØY6Y0Z2	444, 973	ØYB80ZX	203, 541, 578, 604, 629, 745, 973, 1099
ØXUV4JZ	442, 744, 1098	ØY014KZ	443, 1098	ØY0J47Z	443, 1098	ØY6C*	41, 119, 222, 479	ØY6Y0Z3	444, 973		
ØXUV4KZ	442, 744, 1098	ØY014ZZ	443, 1098	ØY0J4JZ	443, 1098	ØY6C0Z1	444, 973	ØY9500Z	148, 192, 208, 444, 517, 604, 629, 744	ØYB80ZZ	256, 444, 499, 604, 629, 1099
ØXUW07Z	41, 148, 271, 411, 649, 785, 788, 972, 1098	ØY0907Z	443, 1098	ØY0J4KZ	443, 1098	ØY6C0Z2	444, 973			ØYB83ZX	203, 541, 578, 604, 629, 745, 973, 1099
ØXUW0JZ	442, 744, 1098	ØY090JZ	443, 1098	ØY0J4ZZ	443, 1098	ØY6C0Z3	444, 973	ØY950ZX	192, 203, 540, 578, 604, 629, 744, 973, 1098		
ØXUW0KZ	442, 744, 1098	ØY090KZ	443, 1098	ØY0K07Z	443, 1098	ØY6D*	41, 119, 222, 479			ØYB83ZZ	256, 444, 499, 604, 629, 1099
ØXUW47Z	41, 148, 271, 411, 649, 785, 788, 972, 1098	ØY090ZZ	443, 1098	ØY0K0JZ	443, 1098	ØY6D0Z1	444, 973	ØY950ZZ	148, 192, 208, 444, 517, 604, 629, 744	ØYB84ZX	203, 541, 578, 604, 629, 745, 973, 1099
ØXUW4JZ	442, 744, 1098	ØY0937Z	443, 1098	ØY0K0KZ	443, 1098	ØY6D0Z2	444, 973				
ØXUW4KZ	442, 744, 1098	ØY093JZ	443, 1098	ØY0K0ZZ	443, 1098	ØY6D0Z3	444, 973	ØY953ZX	192, 203, 540, 578, 604, 629, 744, 973, 1098	ØYB84ZZ	256, 444, 499, 604, 629, 1099
ØXW600Z	448	ØY093KZ	443, 1098	ØY0K37Z	443, 1098	ØY6F0ZZ	41, 119, 222, 444, 479, 973			ØYB90ZZ	41, 148, 256, 411, 745, 973, 1099
ØXW603Z	448	ØY093ZZ	443, 1098	ØY0K3JZ	443, 1098			ØY9540Z	148, 192, 208, 444, 517, 604, 629, 744	ØYB93ZZ	41, 148, 256, 411, 745, 973, 1099
ØXW607Z	448	ØY0947Z	443, 1098	ØY0K3KZ	443, 1098	ØY6G0ZZ	41, 119, 222, 444, 479, 973			ØYB94ZZ	41, 148, 256, 411, 745, 973, 1099
ØXW60JZ	448	ØY094JZ	443, 1098	ØY0K3ZZ	443, 1098			ØY954ZX	192, 203, 540, 578, 604, 629, 744, 973, 1098	ØYBB0ZZ	41, 148, 256, 411, 745, 973, 1099
ØXW60KZ	448	ØY094KZ	443, 1098	ØY0K47Z	443, 1098	ØY6H*	41, 119, 222, 479				
ØXW60YZ	448	ØY094ZZ	443, 1098	ØY0K4JZ	443, 1098	ØY6H0Z1	444, 973	ØY954ZZ	148, 192, 208, 444, 517, 604, 629, 744	ØYBB3ZZ	41, 148, 256, 411, 745, 973, 1099
ØXW630Z	448	ØY0B07Z	443, 1098	ØY0K4KZ	443, 1098	ØY6H0Z2	444, 973			ØYBB4ZZ	41, 148, 256, 411, 745, 973, 1099
ØXW633Z	448	ØY0B0JZ	443, 1098	ØY0K4ZZ	443, 1098	ØY6H0Z3	444, 973	ØY9600Z	148, 192, 208, 444, 518, 604, 629, 744	ØYBC0ZZ	41, 148, 256, 411, 745, 973, 1099
ØXW637Z	448	ØY0B0KZ	443, 1098	ØY0L07Z	443, 1098	ØY6J*	41, 119, 222, 479			ØYBC3ZZ	41, 148, 256, 412, 745, 973, 1099
ØXW63JZ	448	ØY0B0ZZ	443, 1098	ØY0L0JZ	443, 1098	ØY6J0Z1	444, 973	ØY960ZX	192, 203, 540, 578, 604, 629, 745, 973, 1098	ØYBC4ZZ	41, 148, 257, 412, 745, 973, 1099
ØXW63YZ	448	ØY0B37Z	443, 1098	ØY0L0KZ	443, 1098	ØY6J0Z2	444, 973				
ØXW640Z	448	ØY0B3JZ	443, 1098	ØY0L0ZZ	443, 1098	ØY6J0Z3	444, 973	ØY960ZZ	148, 192, 208, 444, 518, 604, 629, 745	ØYBD0ZZ	41, 148, 257, 412, 745, 973, 1099
ØXW643Z	448	ØY0B3KZ	443, 1098	ØY0L37Z	443, 1098	ØY6M*	41, 119, 222, 479			ØYBD3ZZ	41, 148, 257, 412, 745, 973, 1099
ØXW647Z	448	ØY0B3ZZ	443, 1098	ØY0L3JZ	443, 1098	ØY6M0Z4	444, 973	ØY963ZX	192, 203, 541, 578, 604, 629, 745, 973, 1098	ØYBD4ZZ	41, 148, 257, 412, 745, 973, 1099
ØXW64JZ	448	ØY0B47Z	443, 1098	ØY0L3KZ	443, 1098	ØY6M0Z5	444, 973			ØYBF0ZZ	41, 148, 257, 412, 745, 973, 1099
ØXW64KZ	448	ØY0B4JZ	443, 1098	ØY0L3ZZ	443, 1098	ØY6M0Z6	444, 973	ØY9640Z	148, 192, 208, 444, 518, 604, 629, 745	ØYBF3ZZ	41, 148, 257, 412, 745, 973, 1099
ØXW64YZ	448	ØY0B4KZ	443, 1098	ØY0L47Z	443, 1098	ØY6M0Z7	444, 973			ØYBF4ZZ	41, 148, 257, 412, 745, 973, 1099
ØXW700Z	448	ØY0C07Z	443, 1098	ØY0L4JZ	443, 1098	ØY6M0Z8	444, 973	ØY964ZX	192, 203, 541, 578, 604, 629, 745, 973, 1098	ØYBG0ZZ	41, 148, 257, 412, 745, 973, 1099
ØXW703Z	448	ØY0C0JZ	443, 1098	ØY0L4KZ	443, 1098	ØY6M0Z9	444, 973			ØYBG3ZZ	41, 148, 257, 412, 745, 973, 1099
ØXW707Z	448	ØY0C0KZ	443, 1098	ØY0L4ZZ	443, 1098	ØY6M0ZB	444, 973	ØY964ZZ	148, 192, 208, 444, 518, 604, 629, 745	ØYBG4ZZ	41, 148, 257, 412, 745, 973, 1099
ØXW70JZ	448	ØY0C0ZZ	443, 1098	ØY3*	148, 287, 744	ØY6M0ZC	444, 973				
ØXW70KZ	448	ØY0C37Z	443, 1098	ØY300ZZ	443, 603, 629, 972	ØY6M0ZD	444, 973	ØYB00ZZ	41, 148, 256, 411, 745, 973, 1098	ØYBH0ZZ	41, 148, 257, 412, 745, 973, 1099
ØXW70YZ	448	ØY0C3JZ	443, 1098	ØY303ZZ	443, 603, 629, 972	ØY6M0ZF	444, 973			ØYBH3ZZ	41, 148, 257, 412, 745, 973, 1099
ØXW730Z	448	ØY0C3KZ	443, 1098	ØY304ZZ	443, 603, 629, 972	ØY6N*	41, 119, 222, 479	ØYB03ZZ	41, 148, 256, 411, 745, 973, 1098		
ØXW733Z	448	ØY0C3ZZ	443, 1098	ØY310ZZ	443, 603, 629, 972	ØY6N0Z4	444, 973			ØYBH4ZZ	41, 148, 257, 412, 745, 973, 1099
ØXW737Z	448	ØY0C47Z	443, 1098	ØY313ZZ	443, 603, 629, 972	ØY6N0Z5	444, 973	ØYB04ZZ	41, 148, 256, 411, 745, 973, 1098	ØYBJ0ZZ	41, 148, 257, 412, 745, 973, 1099
ØXW73JZ	448	ØY0C4JZ	443, 1098	ØY314ZZ	443, 603, 629, 972	ØY6N0Z6	444, 973				
ØXW73KZ	448	ØY0C4KZ	443, 1098	ØY35*	192, 208, 517	ØY6N0Z7	444, 973	ØYB10ZZ	41, 148, 256, 411, 745, 973, 1098		
ØXW73YZ	448	ØY0C4ZZ	443, 1098	ØY350ZZ	443, 603, 629, 972	ØY6N0Z8	444, 973				
ØXW740Z	448	ØY0D07Z	443, 1098	ØY353ZZ	443, 603, 629, 972	ØY6N0Z9	444, 973	ØYB13ZZ	41, 148, 256, 411, 745, 973, 1098		
ØXW743Z	448	ØY0D0JZ	443, 1098	ØY354ZZ	443, 603, 629, 972	ØY6N0ZB	444, 973				
ØXW747Z	448	ØY0D0KZ	443, 1098	ØY36*	192, 208, 517	ØY6N0ZC	444, 973	ØYB14ZZ	41, 148, 256, 411, 745, 973, 1099		
ØXW74JZ	448	ØY0D0ZZ	443, 1098	ØY360ZZ	443, 603, 629, 972	ØY6N0ZD	444, 973				
ØXW74KZ	448	ØY0D37Z	443, 1098	ØY363ZZ	443, 603, 629, 972	ØY6N0ZF	444, 973	ØYB5*	192		
ØXW74YZ	448	ØY0D3JZ	443, 1098	ØY364ZZ	443, 603, 629, 972	ØY6P*	41, 141, 261, 479	ØYB50ZX	203, 541, 578, 604, 629, 745, 973, 1099		
ØXX*	41	ØY0D3KZ	443, 1098	ØY370ZZ	443, 603, 629, 972	ØY6P0Z0	444, 973				
ØXXN0ZL	264, 649, 972	ØY0D3ZZ	443, 1098	ØY373ZZ	443, 603, 629, 972	ØY6P0Z1	444, 973	ØYB50ZZ	256, 444, 499, 604, 629, 1099		
ØXXP0ZM	264, 649, 972	ØY0D47Z	443, 1098	ØY374ZZ	443, 603, 629, 972	ØY6P0Z2	444, 973	ØYB53ZX	203, 541, 578, 604, 629, 745, 973, 1099		
ØXYJ0Z0	41, 744, 972	ØY0D4JZ	443, 1098	ØY380ZZ	443, 603, 629, 972	ØY6P0Z3	444, 973				
ØXYJ0Z1	41, 744, 972	ØY0D4KZ	443, 1098	ØY383ZZ	443, 603, 629, 972	ØY6Q*	41, 141, 261, 479	ØYB53ZZ	256, 444, 499, 604, 629, 1099		
ØXYK0Z0	41, 744, 972	ØY0D4ZZ	443, 1098	ØY384ZZ	443, 603, 629, 972	ØY6Q0Z0	444, 973	ØYB54ZX	203, 541, 578, 604, 629, 745, 973, 1099		
ØXYK0Z1	41, 744, 972	ØY0F07Z	443, 1098	ØY390ZZ	443, 603, 629, 972	ØY6Q0Z1	444, 973				
		ØY0F0JZ	443, 1098	ØY393ZZ	443, 603, 629, 972	ØY6Q0Z2	444, 973	ØYB54ZZ	256, 444, 499, 604, 629, 1099		
		ØY0F0KZ	443, 1098	ØY394ZZ	443, 603, 629, 972	ØY6Q0Z3	444, 973				
		ØY0F0ZZ	443, 1098	ØY3B0ZZ	443, 603, 629, 972	ØY6R*	41, 141, 261, 479				
		ØY0F37Z	443, 1098	ØY3B3ZZ	443, 603, 629, 972	ØY6R0Z0	444, 973				
		ØY0F3JZ	443, 1098	ØY3B4ZZ	443, 603, 629, 972	ØY6R0Z1	444, 973				
		ØY0F3KZ	443, 1098	ØY3C0ZZ	443, 603, 629, 972	ØY6R0Z2	444, 973				
		ØY0F3ZZ	443, 1098	ØY3C3ZZ	443, 603, 629, 972	ØY6R0Z3	444, 973				
		ØY0F47Z	443, 1098	ØY3C4ZZ	443, 603, 629, 972	ØY6S*	41, 141, 261, 479				
		ØY0F4JZ	443, 1098	ØY3D0ZZ	443, 604, 629, 972	ØY6S0Z0	444, 973				
		ØY0F4KZ	443, 1098	ØY3D3ZZ	443, 604, 629, 972	ØY6S0Z1	444, 973				
		ØY0F4ZZ	443, 1098	ØY3D4ZZ	443, 604, 629, 972	ØY6S0Z2	444, 973				
		ØY0G07Z	443, 1098	ØY3F0ZZ	443, 604, 629, 972	ØY6S0Z3	444, 973				
		ØY0G0JZ	443, 1098	ØY3F3ZZ	443, 604, 629, 972	ØY6T*	41, 141, 261, 479				
		ØY0G0KZ	443, 1098	ØY3F4ZZ	443, 604, 629, 972	ØY6T0Z0	444, 973				
		ØY0G0ZZ	443, 1098	ØY3G0ZZ	443, 604, 629, 972	ØY6T0Z1	444, 973				
		ØY0G37Z	443, 1098	ØY3G3ZZ	443, 604, 629, 972	ØY6T0Z3	444, 973				
		ØY0G3JZ	443, 1098	ØY3G4ZZ	443, 604, 629, 972	ØY6U*	41, 141, 261, 479				
		ØY0G3KZ	443, 1098	ØY3H0ZZ	443, 604, 629, 972	ØY6U0Z0	444, 973				
		ØY0G3ZZ	443, 1098	ØY3H3ZZ	443, 604, 629, 972						

Code	Page
0YBJ3ZZ	41, 148, 257, 412, 745, 973, 1099
0YBJ4ZZ	41, 148, 257, 412, 745, 973, 1099
0YBK0ZZ	41, 148, 257, 412, 745, 973, 1099
0YBK3ZZ	41, 148, 257, 412, 745, 973, 1099
0YBK4ZZ	41, 148, 257, 412, 745, 973, 1099
0YBL0ZZ	41, 148, 257, 412, 745, 973, 1099
0YBL3ZZ	41, 148, 257, 412, 745, 973, 1099
0YBL4ZZ	41, 148, 257, 412, 745, 973, 1099
0YBM0ZZ	41, 148, 257, 412, 745, 973, 1099
0YBM3ZZ	41, 148, 257, 412, 745, 973, 1099
0YBM4ZZ	41, 148, 257, 412, 745, 973, 1099
0YBN0ZZ	41, 148, 257, 412, 745, 973, 1099
0YBN3ZZ	41, 148, 257, 412, 745, 973, 1099
0YBN4ZZ	41, 148, 257, 412, 745, 973, 1099
0YH001Z	745, 1099
0YH003Z	448
0YH00Z	448
0YH031Z	745, 1099
0YH033Z	449
0YH03YZ	449
0YH041Z	745, 1099
0YH043Z	449
0YH04YZ	449
0YH101Z	745, 1099
0YH103Z	449
0YH10YZ	449
0YH131Z	745, 1099
0YH133Z	449
0YH13YZ	449
0YH141Z	745, 1099
0YH143Z	449
0YH14YZ	449
0YH501Z	745, 1099
0YH503Z	449
0YH50YZ	449
0YH531Z	745, 1099
0YH533Z	449
0YH53YZ	449
0YH541Z	745, 1099
0YH543Z	449
0YH54YZ	449
0YH601Z	745, 1099
0YH603Z	449
0YH60YZ	449
0YH631Z	745, 1099
0YH633Z	449
0YH63YZ	449
0YH641Z	745, 1099
0YH643Z	449
0YH64YZ	449
0YH701Z	745, 1099
0YH703Z	449
0YH70YZ	449
0YH731Z	745, 1099
0YH733Z	449
0YH73YZ	449
0YH741Z	745, 1099
0YH743Z	449
0YH74YZ	449
0YH801Z	745, 1099
0YH803Z	449
0YH80YZ	449
0YH831Z	745, 1099
0YH833Z	449
0YH83YZ	449
0YH841Z	745, 1099
0YH843Z	449
0YH84YZ	449
0YH901Z	745, 1099
0YH903Z	449
0YH90YZ	449
0YH931Z	745, 1099
0YH933Z	449
0YH93YZ	449
0YH941Z	745, 1099
0YH943Z	449
0YH94YZ	449
0YHB01Z	745, 1099
0YHB03Z	449
0YHB0YZ	449
0YHB31Z	745, 1099
0YHB33Z	449
0YHB3YZ	449
0YHB41Z	745, 1099
0YHB43Z	449
0YHB4YZ	449
0YHC01Z	745, 1099
0YHC03Z	449
0YHC0YZ	449
0YHC31Z	745, 1099
0YHC33Z	449
0YHC3YZ	449
0YHC41Z	745, 1099
0YHC43Z	449
0YHC4YZ	449
0YHD01Z	745, 1099
0YHD03Z	449
0YHD0YZ	449
0YHD31Z	745, 1099
0YHD33Z	449
0YHD3YZ	449
0YHD41Z	745, 1099
0YHD43Z	449
0YHD4YZ	449
0YHF01Z	745, 1099
0YHF03Z	449
0YHF0YZ	449
0YHF31Z	745, 1099
0YHF33Z	449
0YHF3YZ	449
0YHF41Z	745, 1099
0YHF43Z	449
0YHF4YZ	449
0YHG01Z	745, 1099
0YHG03Z	449
0YHG0YZ	449
0YHG31Z	745, 1099
0YHG33Z	449
0YHG3YZ	449
0YHG41Z	745, 1099
0YHG43Z	449
0YHG4YZ	449
0YHH01Z	745, 1099
0YHH03Z	449
0YHH0YZ	449
0YHH31Z	745, 1099
0YHH33Z	449
0YHH3YZ	449
0YHH41Z	745, 1099
0YHH43Z	449
0YHH4YZ	449
0YHJ01Z	745, 1099
0YHJ03Z	449
0YHJ0YZ	449
0YHJ31Z	745, 1099
0YHJ33Z	449
0YHJ3YZ	449
0YHJ41Z	745, 1099
0YHJ43Z	449
0YHJ4YZ	449
0YHK01Z	745, 1099
0YHK03Z	449
0YHK0YZ	449
0YHK31Z	745, 1099
0YHK33Z	449
0YHK3YZ	449
0YHK41Z	745, 1099
0YHK43Z	449
0YHK4YZ	449
0YHL01Z	745, 1099
0YHL03Z	449
0YHL0YZ	449
0YHL31Z	745, 1099
0YHL33Z	449
0YHL3YZ	449
0YHL41Z	745, 1099
0YHL43Z	449
0YHL4YZ	449
0YHM01Z	745, 1099
0YHM03Z	449
0YHM0YZ	449
0YHM31Z	745, 1099
0YHM33Z	449
0YHM3YZ	449
0YHM41Z	745, 1099
0YHM43Z	449
0YHM4YZ	449
0YHN01Z	745, 1099
0YHN03Z	449
0YHN0YZ	449
0YHN31Z	745, 1099
0YHN33Z	449
0YHN3YZ	449
0YHN41Z	745, 1099
0YHN43Z	449
0YHN4YZ	449
0YJ00ZZ	449
0YJ10ZZ	449
0YJ50ZZ	148, 192, 208, 444, 518, 604, 629, 745, 973
0YJ54ZZ	192, 203, 541, 578, 604, 629, 745, 973, 1099
0YJ60ZZ	148, 192, 208, 444, 518, 604, 629, 745, 973
0YJ64ZZ	192, 203, 541, 578, 604, 629, 745, 973, 1099
0YJ70ZZ	148, 193, 208, 444, 518, 604, 629, 745, 973
0YJ74ZZ	193, 203, 541, 578, 604, 629, 745, 973, 1099
0YJ80ZZ	449
0YJ84ZZ	193, 203, 541, 578, 604, 629, 745, 973, 1099
0YJ90ZZ	449
0YJA0ZZ	148, 193, 208, 444, 518, 604, 629, 745, 973
0YJA4ZZ	193, 203, 541, 578, 604, 629, 745, 973, 1099
0YJB0ZZ	449
0YJC0ZZ	449
0YJD0ZZ	449
0YJE0ZZ	449
0YJE4ZZ	193, 203, 541, 578, 604, 629, 745, 973, 1099
0YJF0ZZ	449
0YJG0ZZ	449
0YJH0ZZ	449
0YJJ0ZZ	449
0YJK0ZZ	449
0YJL0ZZ	449
0YJM0ZZ	449
0YJN0ZZ	449
0YM*	745
0YM00ZZ	444, 1099
0YM10ZZ	444, 1099
0YM20ZZ	287, 973
0YM30ZZ	287, 973
0YM40ZZ	287, 973
0YM50ZZ	287, 973
0YM60ZZ	287, 973
0YM70ZZ	221, 853
0YM80ZZ	221, 853
0YM90ZZ	287, 973
0YMB0ZZ	287, 973
0YMC0ZZ	221, 853
0YMD0ZZ	221, 853
0YMF0ZZ	221, 853
0YMG0ZZ	221, 853
0YMH0ZZ	221, 853
0YMJ0ZZ	221, 853
0YMK0ZZ	221, 853
0YML0ZZ	221, 853
0YMM0ZZ	221, 853
0YMN0ZZ	221, 853
0YMP0ZZ	261, 973
0YMQ0ZZ	261, 973
0YMR0ZZ	261, 973
0YMS0ZZ	261, 973
0YMT0ZZ	261, 974
0YMU0ZZ	261, 974
0YMV0ZZ	261, 974
0YMW0ZZ	261, 974
0YMX0ZZ	261, 974
0YMY0ZZ	261, 974
0YQ0*	745
0YQ00ZZ	974
0YQ03ZZ	974
0YQ04ZZ	974
0YQ0XZZ	974
0YQ1*	745
0YQ10ZZ	974
0YQ13ZZ	974
0YQ14ZZ	974
0YQ1XZZ	974
0YQ50ZZ	184, 1099
0YQ53ZZ	184, 1099
0YQ54ZZ	184, 1099
0YQ60ZZ	184, 1099
0YQ63ZZ	184, 1099
0YQ64ZZ	184, 1099
0YQ70ZZ	184, 1099
0YQ73ZZ	184, 1099
0YQ74ZZ	184, 1099
0YQ80ZZ	184, 1099
0YQ83ZZ	184, 1099
0YQ84ZZ	184, 1099
0YQ9*	745
0YQ90ZZ	974
0YQ93ZZ	974
0YQ94ZZ	974
0YQ9XZZ	974
0YQA0ZZ	184, 1099
0YQA3ZZ	184, 1099
0YQA4ZZ	184, 1099
0YQB*	745
0YQB0ZZ	974
0YQB3ZZ	974
0YQB4ZZ	974
0YQBXZZ	974
0YQC*	745
0YQC0ZZ	974
0YQC3ZZ	974
0YQC4ZZ	974
0YQCXZZ	974
0YQD*	745
0YQD0ZZ	974
0YQD3ZZ	974
0YQD4ZZ	974
0YQDXZZ	974
0YQE0ZZ	184, 1099
0YQE3ZZ	184, 1099
0YQE4ZZ	184, 1099
0YQF*	745
0YQF0ZZ	974
0YQF4ZZ	974
0YQFXZZ	974
0YQG*	745
0YQG0ZZ	974
0YQG3ZZ	974
0YQG4ZZ	974
0YQGXZZ	974
0YQH*	745
0YQH0ZZ	974
0YQH3ZZ	974
0YQH4ZZ	974
0YQHXZZ	974
0YQJ*	745
0YQJ0ZZ	974
0YQJ3ZZ	974
0YQJ4ZZ	974
0YQJXZZ	974
0YQK*	745
0YQK0ZZ	974
0YQK3ZZ	974
0YQK4ZZ	974
0YQKXZZ	974
0YQL*	745
0YQL0ZZ	974
0YQL3ZZ	974
0YQL4ZZ	974
0YQLXZZ	974
0YQM*	745
0YQM0ZZ	974
0YQM3ZZ	974
0YQM4ZZ	974
0YQMXZZ	974
0YQN*	745
0YQN0ZZ	974
0YQN3ZZ	974
0YQN4ZZ	974
0YQNXZZ	974
0YQP*	745
0YQP0ZZ	974
0YQP3ZZ	974
0YQP4ZZ	974
0YQPXZZ	974
0YQQ*	745
0YQQ0ZZ	974
0YQQ3ZZ	974
0YQQ4ZZ	974
0YQQXZZ	974
0YQR*	745
0YQR0ZZ	974
0YQR3ZZ	974
0YQR4ZZ	974
0YQRXZZ	974
0YQS*	745
0YQS0ZZ	974
0YQS3ZZ	974
0YQS4ZZ	974
0YQSXZZ	974
0YQT*	745
0YQT0ZZ	974
0YQT3ZZ	974
0YQT4ZZ	974
0YQTXZZ	974
0YQU*	745
0YQU0ZZ	974
0YQU3ZZ	974
0YQU4ZZ	974
0YQUXZZ	974
0YQV*	745
0YQV3ZZ	974
0YQV4ZZ	974
0YQVXZZ	974
0YQW*	745
0YQW0ZZ	974
0YQW3ZZ	974
0YQW4ZZ	974
0YQWXZZ	974
0YQX*	745
0YQX0ZZ	974
0YQX3ZZ	974
0YQX4ZZ	974
0YQXXZZ	974
0YQY*	745
0YQY0ZZ	974
0YQY3ZZ	974
0YQY4ZZ	974
0YQYXZZ	974
0YU0*	745
0YU007Z	444, 1099
0YU00JZ	444, 1099
0YU00KZ	444, 1099
0YU047Z	444, 1099
0YU04JZ	444, 1099
0YU04KZ	444, 1099
0YU1*	745
0YU107Z	444, 1099
0YU10JZ	444, 1099
0YU10KZ	444, 1099
0YU147Z	444, 1099
0YU14JZ	444, 1099
0YU14KZ	444, 1099
0YU5*	184
0YU507Z	1099
0YU50JZ	1099
0YU50KZ	1099
0YU6*	184
0YU607Z	1099
0YU60JZ	1099
0YU60KZ	1099
0YU7*	184
0YU707Z	1099
0YU70JZ	1099
0YU70KZ	1099
0YU747Z	1099
0YU74JZ	1099
0YU74KZ	1099
0YU8*	184
0YU807Z	1099
0YU80JZ	1099
0YU80KZ	1099
0YU847Z	1099
0YU84JZ	1099
0YU84KZ	1099
0YU9*	745
0YU907Z	444, 1099
0YU90JZ	444, 1099
0YU90KZ	444, 1099
0YU947Z	444, 1100
0YU94JZ	444, 1100
0YU94KZ	444, 1100
0YUA*	184
0YUA07Z	1100
0YUA0JZ	1100
0YUA0KZ	1100
0YUB*	745
0YUB07Z	444, 1100
0YUB0JZ	444, 1100
0YUB0KZ	444, 1100
0YUB47Z	444, 1100
0YUB4JZ	444, 1100
0YUB4KZ	444, 1100
0YUC*	745
0YUC07Z	444, 1100
0YUC0JZ	444, 1100
0YUC0KZ	444, 1100
0YUC47Z	444, 1100
0YUC4JZ	444, 1100
0YUC4KZ	444, 1100
0YUD*	745
0YUD07Z	444, 1100
0YUD0JZ	444, 1100
0YUD0KZ	444, 1100
0YUD47Z	444, 1100
0YUD4JZ	444, 1100
0YUD4KZ	444, 1100
0YUE*	184
0YUE07Z	1100
0YUE0JZ	1100
0YUE0KZ	1100
0YUE47Z	1100
0YUE4JZ	1100
0YUE4KZ	1100
0YUF*	745
0YUF07Z	444, 1100
0YUF0JZ	444, 1100
0YUF0KZ	444, 1100
0YUF47Z	444, 1100
0YUF4JZ	444, 1100
0YUF4KZ	444, 1100
0YUG*	745
0YUG07Z	444, 1100
0YUG0JZ	444, 1100
0YUG0KZ	444, 1100
0YUG47Z	444, 1100
0YUG4JZ	444, 1100
0YUG4KZ	444, 1100
0YUH*	745
0YUH07Z	444, 1100
0YUH0JZ	444, 1100
0YUH0KZ	444, 1100
0YUH47Z	444, 1100
0YUH4JZ	444, 1100
0YUH4KZ	444, 1100
0YUJ*	745
0YUJ07Z	444, 1100
0YUJ0JZ	444, 1100
0YUJ0KZ	445, 1100
0YUJ47Z	445, 1100
0YUJ4JZ	445, 1100
0YUJ4KZ	445, 1100
0YUK*	745
0YUK07Z	445, 1100
0YUK0JZ	445, 1100
0YUK0KZ	445, 1100
0YUK47Z	445, 1100
0YUK4JZ	445, 1100
0YUK4KZ	445, 1100
0YUL*	745
0YUL07Z	445, 1100
0YUL0JZ	445, 1100
0YUL0KZ	445, 1100
0YUL47Z	445, 1100
0YUL4JZ	445, 1100
0YUL4KZ	445, 1100
0YUM*	745
0YUM07Z	445, 1100
0YUM0JZ	445, 1100
0YUM0KZ	445, 1100
0YUM47Z	445, 1100
0YUM4JZ	445, 1100
0YUM4KZ	445, 1100
0YUN*	745
0YUN07Z	445, 1100
0YUN0JZ	445, 1100
0YUN0KZ	445, 1100
0YUN47Z	445, 1100
0YUN4JZ	445, 1100
0YUN4KZ	445, 1100
0YUP*	745
0YUP07Z	445, 1100
0YUP0JZ	445, 1100
0YUP0KZ	445, 1100
0YUP47Z	445, 1100
0YUP4JZ	445, 1100
0YUP4KZ	445, 1100
0YUQ*	745
0YUQ07Z	445, 1100
0YUQ0JZ	445, 1100
0YUQ0KZ	445, 1100
0YUQ47Z	445, 1100
0YUQ4JZ	445, 1100
0YUQ4KZ	445, 1100
0YUR*	745
0YUR07Z	445, 1100
0YUR0JZ	445, 1100
0YUR47Z	445, 1100
0YUR4JZ	445, 1100
0YUR4KZ	445, 1100

Numeric Index to Procedures

Code	Page
0YUS*	745
0YUS07Z	445, 1100
0YUS0JZ	445, 1100
0YUS0KZ	445, 1100
0YUS47Z	445, 1100
0YUS4JZ	445, 1100
0YUS4KZ	445, 1100
0YUT*	745
0YUT07Z	445, 1100
0YUT0JZ	445, 1100
0YUT0KZ	445, 1100
0YUT47Z	445, 1100
0YUT4JZ	445, 1100
0YUT4KZ	445, 1100
0YUU*	745
0YUU07Z	445, 1100
0YUU0JZ	445, 1100
0YUU0KZ	445, 1100
0YUU47Z	445, 1100
0YUU4JZ	445, 1100
0YUU4KZ	445, 1100
0YUV*	745
0YUV07Z	445, 1100
0YUV0JZ	445, 1100
0YUV0KZ	445, 1100
0YUV47Z	445, 1100
0YUV4JZ	445, 1100
0YUV4KZ	445, 1100
0YUW*	745
0YUW07Z	445, 1100
0YUW0JZ	445, 1100
0YUW0KZ	445, 1100
0YUW47Z	445, 1100
0YUW4JZ	445, 1100
0YUW4KZ	445, 1100
0YUX*	745
0YUX07Z	445, 1100
0YUX0JZ	445, 1100
0YUX0KZ	445, 1100
0YUX47Z	445, 1100
0YUX4JZ	445, 1100
0YUX4KZ	445, 1100
0YUY*	745
0YUY07Z	445, 1100
0YUY0JZ	445, 1100
0YUY0KZ	445, 1100
0YUY47Z	445, 1100
0YUY4JZ	445, 1100
0YUY4KZ	445, 1100
0YW900Z	449
0YW903Z	449
0YW907Z	449
0YW90JZ	449
0YW90KZ	449
0YW90YZ	449
0YW930Z	449
0YW933Z	449
0YW937Z	449
0YW93JZ	449
0YW93KZ	449
0YW93YZ	449
0YW940Z	449
0YW943Z	449
0YW947Z	449
0YW94JZ	449
0YW94KZ	449
0YW94YZ	449
0YWB00Z	449
0YWB03Z	449
0YWB07Z	449
0YWB0JZ	449
0YWB0KZ	449
0YWB0YZ	449
0YWB30Z	449
0YWB33Z	449
0YWB37Z	449
0YWB3JZ	449
0YWB3KZ	449
0YWB3YZ	449
0YWB40Z	449
0YWB43Z	449
0YWB47Z	449
0YWB4JZ	449
0YWB4KZ	449
0YWB4YZ	449
10A00ZZ	545
10A03ZZ	545
10A04ZZ	545
10A07ZZ	545, 1100
10A08ZZ	545, 1100
10D00Z0	545
10D00Z1	545
10D00Z2	545
10D07Z3	546
10D07Z3	544
10D07Z4	546
10D07Z4	544
10D07Z5	546
10D07Z5	544
10D07Z6	544, 546
10D07Z7	546
10D07Z7	544
10D07Z8	544, 546
10D17Z9	544, 546
10D17ZZ	544, 545, 547
10D18Z9	544, 546
10D18ZZ	544, 545, 547
10D2*	533
10E0XZZ	544, 546
10S2*	541
10T*	533
30230AZ	5
30230G0	5
30230G2	5
30230G3	5
30230G4	5
30230U2	5
30230U3	5
30230U4	5
30230X0	5
30230X2	5
30230X3	5
30230X4	5
30230Y0	5
30230Y2	5
30230Y3	5
30230Y4	5
30233AZ	5
30233G0	5
30233G2	5
30233G3	5
30233G4	5
30233U2	5
30233U3	5
30233U4	5
30233X0	5
30233X2	5
30233X3	5
30233X4	5
30233Y2	5
30233Y3	5
30233Y4	5
30240AZ	5
30240G0	5
30240G2	5
30240G3	5
30240G4	5
30240U2	5
30240U3	5
30240U4	5
30240X0	5
30240X2	5
30240X3	5
30240X4	5
30240Y0	5
30240Y2	5
30240Y3	5
30240Y4	5
30243AZ	5
30243G0	5
30243G2	5
30243G3	5
30243G4	5
30243U2	5
30243U3	5
30243U4	5
30243X0	5
30243X2	5
30243X3	5
30243X4	5
30243Y0	5
30243Y2	5
30243Y3	5
30243Y4	5
3E03002	630
3E03017	44
3E030TZ	28, 143
3E030U0	518
3E030U1	518
3E03302	630
3E03317	44
3E033U0	518
3E033U1	518
3E04002	630
3E04017	44
3E040TZ	28, 143
3E04302	630
3E04317	44
3E05002	630
3E05017	44
3E05302	630
3E05317	44
3E06002	630
3E06017	44
3E06302	630
3E06317	44
3E08017	44
3E08317	44
3E0J3U0	518
3E0J3U1	518
3E0J7U0	518
3E0J7U1	518
3E0J8U0	518
3E0J8U1	518
3E0P3Q0	541
3E0P3Q1	541
3E0P7Q0	541
3E0P7Q1	541
3E0Q005	14, 15
3E0Q305	15
3E0Q705	15
3E0R302	630
3E0S302	630
4A020N6	109, 110, 118, 167
4A020N7	109, 110, 118, 167
4A020N8	109, 110, 118, 167
4A023FZ	109, 166
4A023N6	109, 110, 118, 167
4A023N7	109, 110, 118, 167
4A023N8	109, 110, 118, 167
4A027FZ	109, 166
4A027N6	109, 110, 118, 167
4A027N7	109, 110, 118, 167
4A027N8	109, 110, 118, 167
4A028FZ	109, 166
4A028N6	109, 110, 118, 167
4A028N7	109, 110, 118, 167
4A028N8	109, 110, 118, 167
4A0605Z	445, 578, 1100
4A060BZ	445, 578, 1100
4A0C45Z	193, 203
4A0C4BZ	193, 203
4A1605Z	445, 578, 1100
4A160BZ	445, 578, 1100
5A02110	166
5A02116	109
5A0211D	109
5A02210	166
5A02216	109
5A0221D	109
5A1522F	1
5A1522G	1
5A1522H	1
5A1935Z	107
5A1945Z	107
5A1955Z	1, 107, 634, 783, 789
B20*	109, 110, 118, 167
B2100ZZ	109, 110, 118, 167
B2101ZZ	109, 110, 118, 167
B210YZZ	109, 110, 118, 167
B2110ZZ	109, 110, 118, 167
B2111ZZ	109, 110, 118, 167
B211YZZ	109, 110, 118, 167
B2120ZZ	109, 110, 118, 167
B2121ZZ	109, 110, 118, 167
B212YZZ	109, 110, 118, 167
B2130ZZ	109, 110, 118, 167
B2131ZZ	109, 110, 118, 167
B213YZZ	109, 110, 118, 167
B214*	109, 110, 118, 167
B215*	109, 110, 118, 167
B216*	109, 110, 118, 167
B217*	109, 110, 118, 167
B218*	110, 118, 167
B21F*	110, 118, 167
D02*	41, 501, 605
D0Y0KZZ	14
D0Y1KZZ	14
D0Y6KZZ	94, 528, 604, 629
D0Y7KZZ	94, 528, 604, 629
D72*	41, 501, 605
D82*	41, 501, 605
D92*	41, 501, 605
DB2*	41, 501, 605
DBY0KZZ	94, 452, 528, 604, 629
DBY1KZZ	94, 452, 528, 604, 629
DBY2KZZ	94, 452, 528, 604, 629
DBY5KZZ	94, 452, 528, 604, 629
DBY6KZZ	94, 452, 528, 604, 629
DBY7KZZ	94, 452, 528, 604, 629
DBY8KZZ	94, 452, 528, 604, 629
DD2*	41, 501, 605
DDY0KZZ	94, 528, 604, 629
DDY1KZZ	94, 528, 604, 629
DDY2KZZ	94, 528, 604, 629
DDY3KZZ	94, 528, 604, 629
DDY4KZZ	94, 528, 604, 629
DDY5KZZ	94, 528, 604, 629
DDY7KZZ	94, 528, 604, 629
DDY8KZZ	94, 528, 604, 629
DF2*	41, 501, 605
DFY0KZZ	193, 199
DFY1KZZ	94, 528, 604, 629
DFY2KZZ	94, 528, 604, 629
DFY3KZZ	94, 528, 604, 629
DG2*	41, 501, 605
DGY0KZZ	483, 604, 629
DGY1KZZ	483, 604, 629
DGY2KZZ	94, 528, 604, 629
DGY4KZZ	484, 604, 629
DGY5KZZ	484, 604, 629
DM2*	41, 501, 605
DMY0KZZ	94, 452, 528, 604, 629
DMY1KZZ	94, 452, 528, 604, 629
DT2*	41, 501, 605
DU2*	41, 501, 605
DV2*	41, 501, 605
DVY0KZZ	94, 452, 528, 604, 629
DW2*	41, 501, 605
F00*	795
F01*	795
F02*	795
F06*	795
F07*	795
F08*	795
F09*	795
F0B*	795
F0C*	795
F0DZ05Z	795
F0DZ0ZZ	795
F0DZ11Z	795
F0DZ12Z	795
F0DZ15Z	795
F0DZ1LZ	795
F0DZ1ZZ	795
F0DZ21Z	795
F0DZ22Z	795
F0DZ25Z	795
F0DZ2KZ	795
F0DZ2ZZ	795
F0DZ3MZ	795
F0DZ4SZ	795
F0DZ4VZ	795
F0DZ51Z	795
F0DZ52Z	795
F0DZ55Z	795
F0DZ5KZ	795
F0DZ5LZ	795
F0DZ5ZZ	795
F0DZ6EZ	795
F0DZ6FZ	795
F0DZ6UZ	795
F0DZ6ZZ	795
F0DZ7EZ	795
F0DZ7FZ	795
F0DZ7UZ	795
F0DZ7ZZ	795
F0DZ8EZ	795
F0DZ8FZ	795
F0DZ8UZ	795
F0F*	795
HZ30ZZZ	637
HZ32ZZZ	637
HZ33ZZZ	637
HZ34ZZZ	637
HZ35ZZZ	637
HZ36ZZZ	637
HZ37ZZZ	637
HZ38ZZZ	637
HZ39ZZZ	637
HZ3BZZZ	637
HZ40ZZZ	637
HZ41ZZZ	637
HZ42ZZZ	637
HZ43ZZZ	637
HZ44ZZZ	637
HZ45ZZZ	637
HZ46ZZZ	637
HZ47ZZZ	637
HZ48ZZZ	637
HZ49ZZZ	637
HZ4BZZZ	637
HZ50ZZZ	637
HZ51ZZZ	637
HZ52ZZZ	637
HZ53ZZZ	637
HZ54ZZZ	637
HZ55ZZZ	637
HZ56ZZZ	637
HZ57ZZZ	637
HZ58ZZZ	637
HZ59ZZZ	637
HZ5BZZZ	637
HZ5CZZZ	637
HZ5DZZZ	637
X27H385	103, 140, 193, 208, 287, 445, 499, 518, 745, 974
X27H395	103, 141, 193, 208, 287, 445, 499, 518, 746, 974
X27H3B5	103, 141, 193, 208, 287, 445, 499, 518, 746, 974
X27H3C5	103, 141, 193, 208, 288, 445, 499, 518, 746, 974
X27J385	103, 141, 193, 208, 288, 445, 499, 518, 746, 974
X27J395	103, 141, 193, 208, 288, 445, 499, 518, 746, 974
X27J3B5	103, 141, 193, 208, 288, 445, 499, 518, 746, 974
X27J3C5	103, 141, 193, 208, 288, 445, 499, 518, 746, 974
X27K385	141
X27K395	141
X27K3B5	141
X27K3C5	141
X27L385	141
X27L395	141
X27L3B5	141
X27L3C5	141
X27M385	141
X27M395	141
X27M3B5	141
X27M3C5	141
X27N385	141
X27N395	141
X27N3B5	141
X27N3C5	141
X27P385	141
X27P395	141
X27P3B5	141
X27P3C5	141
X27Q385	141
X27Q395	141
X27Q3B5	141
X27Q3C5	141
X27R385	141
X27R395	141
X27R3B5	141
X27R3C5	141
X27S385	141
X27S395	141
X27S3B5	141
X27S3C5	141
X27T385	141
X27T395	141
X27T3B5	141
X27T3C5	141
X27U385	141
X27U395	141
X27U3B5	141
X27U3C5	141
X2C0361	118, 120, 123
X2C1361	118, 120, 123
X2C2361	118, 120, 123
X2C3361	118, 120, 123
X2RF032	109
X2RF332	149
X2RF432	109
XHRPXL2	41, 82, 148, 215, 412, 482, 537, 639, 785, 788, 974
XNS0032	21, 289, 604, 629, 746, 974
XNS0332	21, 289, 604, 629, 746, 974
XNS3032	21, 289, 604, 629, 746, 974
XNS3332	21, 289, 604, 629, 746, 974
XNS4032	974
XNS4032	21, 289, 604, 629, 746
XNS4332	21, 289, 604, 629, 746, 974
XR2G021	228, 1100
XR2H021	228, 1100
XRG0092	21, 221, 746, 974
XRG00F3	21, 211, 221, 746, 974
XRG1092	21, 211, 221, 746, 974
XRG10F3	21, 211, 221, 746, 974
XRG2092	21, 211, 221, 746, 974
XRG20F3	21, 211, 221, 746, 974
XRG4092	21, 211, 221, 746, 974
XRG40F3	21, 211, 221, 746, 974
XRG6092	21, 211, 213, 746, 974
XRG60F3	21, 211, 213, 746, 974
XRG7092	21, 211, 213, 746, 974
XRG70F3	21, 211, 213, 746, 974
XRG8092	21, 211, 213, 746, 974
XRG80F3	21, 211, 213, 746, 974
XRGA092	21, 211, 213, 746, 974
XRGA0F3	21, 211, 213, 746, 974
XRGB092	21, 211, 213, 746, 974
XRGB0F3	21, 211, 213, 746, 974
XRGC092	21, 211, 213, 746, 974
XRGC0F3	21, 211, 213, 746, 974
XRGD092	21, 211, 213, 746, 974
XRGD0F3	21, 211, 213, 746, 974
XV508A4	508, 523, 1100
XW033C3	5
XW043C3	5

Alphabetic CC List

G91.2	(Idiopathic) normal pressure hydrocephalus
O04.89	(Induced) termination of pregnancy with other complications
O04.80	(Induced) termination of pregnancy with unspecified complications
S42.222A	2-part displaced fracture of surgical neck of left humerus, initial encounter for closed fracture
S42.222P	2-part displaced fracture of surgical neck of left humerus, subsequent encounter for fracture with malunion
S42.222K	2-part displaced fracture of surgical neck of left humerus, subsequent encounter for fracture with nonunion
S42.221A	2-part displaced fracture of surgical neck of right humerus, initial encounter for closed fracture
S42.221P	2-part displaced fracture of surgical neck of right humerus, subsequent encounter for fracture with malunion
S42.221K	2-part displaced fracture of surgical neck of right humerus, subsequent encounter for fracture with nonunion
S42.223A	2-part displaced fracture of surgical neck of unspecified humerus, initial encounter for closed fracture
S42.223P	2-part displaced fracture of surgical neck of unspecified humerus, subsequent encounter for fracture with malunion
S42.223K	2-part displaced fracture of surgical neck of unspecified humerus, subsequent encounter for fracture with nonunion
S42.225A	2-part nondisplaced fracture of surgical neck of left humerus, initial encounter for closed fracture
S42.225P	2-part nondisplaced fracture of surgical neck of left humerus, subsequent encounter for fracture with malunion
S42.225K	2-part nondisplaced fracture of surgical neck of left humerus, subsequent encounter for fracture with nonunion
S42.224A	2-part nondisplaced fracture of surgical neck of right humerus, initial encounter for closed fracture
S42.224P	2-part nondisplaced fracture of surgical neck of right humerus, subsequent encounter for fracture with malunion
S42.224K	2-part nondisplaced fracture of surgical neck of right humerus, subsequent encounter for fracture with nonunion
S42.226A	2-part nondisplaced fracture of surgical neck of unspecified humerus, initial encounter for closed fracture
S42.226P	2-part nondisplaced fracture of surgical neck of unspecified humerus, subsequent encounter for fracture with malunion
S42.226K	2-part nondisplaced fracture of surgical neck of unspecified humerus, subsequent encounter for fracture with nonunion
E71.111	3-methylglutaconic aciduria
S42.232A	3-part fracture of surgical neck of left humerus, initial encounter for closed fracture
S42.232P	3-part fracture of surgical neck of left humerus, subsequent encounter for fracture with malunion
S42.232K	3-part fracture of surgical neck of left humerus, subsequent encounter for fracture with nonunion
S42.231A	3-part fracture of surgical neck of right humerus, initial encounter for closed fracture
S42.231P	3-part fracture of surgical neck of right humerus, subsequent encounter for fracture with malunion
S42.231K	3-part fracture of surgical neck of right humerus, subsequent encounter for fracture with nonunion
S42.239A	3-part fracture of surgical neck of unspecified humerus, initial encounter for closed fracture
S42.239P	3-part fracture of surgical neck of unspecified humerus, subsequent encounter for fracture with malunion
S42.239K	3-part fracture of surgical neck of unspecified humerus, subsequent encounter for fracture with nonunion
S42.242A	4-part fracture of surgical neck of left humerus, initial encounter for closed fracture
S42.242P	4-part fracture of surgical neck of left humerus, subsequent encounter for fracture with malunion
S42.242K	4-part fracture of surgical neck of left humerus, subsequent encounter for fracture with nonunion
S42.241A	4-part fracture of surgical neck of right humerus, initial encounter for closed fracture
S42.241P	4-part fracture of surgical neck of right humerus, subsequent encounter for fracture with malunion
S42.241K	4-part fracture of surgical neck of right humerus, subsequent encounter for fracture with nonunion
S42.249A	4-part fracture of surgical neck of unspecified humerus, initial encounter for closed fracture
S42.249P	4-part fracture of surgical neck of unspecified humerus, subsequent encounter for fracture with malunion
S42.249K	4-part fracture of surgical neck of unspecified humerus, subsequent encounter for fracture with nonunion
A42.1	Abdominal actinomycosis
O00.01	Abdominal pregnancy with intrauterine pregnancy
O00.00	Abdominal pregnancy without intrauterine pregnancy
T80.30XA	ABO incompatibility reaction due to transfusion of blood or blood products, unspecified, initial encounter
T80.310A	ABO incompatibility with acute hemolytic transfusion reaction, initial encounter
T80.311A	ABO incompatibility with delayed hemolytic transfusion reaction, initial encounter
T80.319A	ABO incompatibility with hemolytic transfusion reaction, unspecified, initial encounter
N75.1	Abscess of Bartholin's gland
N45.4	Abscess of epididymis or testis
K63.0	Abscess of intestine
N41.2	Abscess of prostate
K11.3	Abscess of salivary gland
E32.1	Abscess of thymus
N76.4	Abscess of vulva
Q25.41	Absence and aplasia of aorta
G40.A11	Absence epileptic syndrome, intractable, with status epilepticus
G40.A19	Absence epileptic syndrome, intractable, without status epilepticus
B60.10	Acanthamebiasis, unspecified
I97.51	Accidental puncture and laceration of a circulatory system organ or structure during a circulatory system procedure
I97.52	Accidental puncture and laceration of a circulatory system organ or structure during other procedure
K91.71	Accidental puncture and laceration of a digestive system organ or structure during a digestive system procedure
K91.72	Accidental puncture and laceration of a digestive system organ or structure during other procedure
N99.71	Accidental puncture and laceration of a genitourinary system organ or structure during a genitourinary system procedure
N99.72	Accidental puncture and laceration of a genitourinary system organ or structure during other procedure
M96.820	Accidental puncture and laceration of a musculoskeletal structure during a musculoskeletal system procedure
M96.821	Accidental puncture and laceration of a musculoskeletal structure during other procedure
J95.71	Accidental puncture and laceration of a respiratory system organ or structure during a respiratory system procedure
J95.72	Accidental puncture and laceration of a respiratory system organ or structure during other procedure
E36.11	Accidental puncture and laceration of an endocrine system organ or structure during an endocrine system procedure
E36.12	Accidental puncture and laceration of an endocrine system organ or structure during other procedure
H59.213	Accidental puncture and laceration of eye and adnexa during an ophthalmic procedure, bilateral
H59.223	Accidental puncture and laceration of eye and adnexa during other procedure, bilateral
H59.212	Accidental puncture and laceration of left eye and adnexa during an ophthalmic procedure
H59.222	Accidental puncture and laceration of left eye and adnexa during other procedure
G97.48	Accidental puncture and laceration of other nervous system organ or structure during a nervous system procedure
G97.49	Accidental puncture and laceration of other nervous system organ or structure during other procedure
H59.211	Accidental puncture and laceration of right eye and adnexa during an ophthalmic procedure
H59.221	Accidental puncture and laceration of right eye and adnexa during other procedure
L76.11	Accidental puncture and laceration of skin and subcutaneous tissue during a dermatologic procedure
L76.12	Accidental puncture and laceration of skin and subcutaneous tissue during other procedure
H95.31	Accidental puncture and laceration of the ear and mastoid process during a procedure on the ear and mastoid process
H95.32	Accidental puncture and laceration of the ear and mastoid process during other procedure
D78.11	Accidental puncture and laceration of the spleen during a procedure on the spleen
D78.12	Accidental puncture and laceration of the spleen during other procedure
H59.219	Accidental puncture and laceration of unspecified eye and adnexa during an ophthalmic procedure
H59.229	Accidental puncture and laceration of unspecified eye and adnexa during other procedure
G97.41	Accidental puncture or laceration of dura during a procedure
E87.2	Acidosis
D68.4	Acquired coagulation factor deficiency
L12.30	Acquired epidermolysis bullosa, unspecified
D59.9	Acquired hemolytic anemia, unspecified
D68.311	Acquired hemophilia
B47.1	Actinomycetoma
A42.9	Actinomycosis, unspecified
A42.82	Actinomycotic encephalitis
A42.81	Actinomycotic meningitis
D68.51	Activated protein C resistance
A06.0	Acute amebic dysentery
A24.1	Acute and fulminating melioidosis
G36.1	Acute and subacute hemorrhagic leukoencephalitis [Hurst]
H40.213	Acute angle-closure glaucoma, bilateral
H40.212	Acute angle-closure glaucoma, left eye
H40.211	Acute angle-closure glaucoma, right eye

Alphabetic & Numeric Lists of CCs

H40.219	Acute angle-closure glaucoma, unspecified eye
K04.4	Acute apical periodontitis of pulpal origin
K35.20	Acute appendicitis with generalized peritonitis, without abscess
K35.31	Acute appendicitis with localized peritonitis and gangrene, without perforation
K35.30	Acute appendicitis with localized peritonitis, without perforation or gangrene
J21.1	Acute bronchiolitis due to human metapneumovirus
J21.8	Acute bronchiolitis due to other specified organisms
J21.0	Acute bronchiolitis due to respiratory syncytial virus
J21.9	Acute bronchiolitis, unspecified
I67.81	Acute cerebrovascular insufficiency
B57.0	Acute Chagas' disease with heart involvement
B57.1	Acute Chagas' disease without heart involvement
K81.0	Acute cholecystitis
K81.2	Acute cholecystitis with chronic cholecystitis
I24.0	Acute coronary thrombosis not resulting in myocardial infarction
N30.01	Acute cystitis with hematuria
N30.00	Acute cystitis without hematuria
B17.0	Acute delta-(super) infection of hepatitis B carrier
K31.0	Acute dilatation of stomach
G36.9	Acute disseminated demyelination, unspecified
K26.3	Acute duodenal ulcer without hemorrhage or perforation
I82.A13	Acute embolism and thrombosis of axillary vein, bilateral
I82.622	Acute embolism and thrombosis of deep veins of left upper extremity
I82.621	Acute embolism and thrombosis of deep veins of right upper extremity
I82.629	Acute embolism and thrombosis of deep veins of unspecified upper extremity
I82.623	Acute embolism and thrombosis of deep veins of upper extremity, bilateral
I82.413	Acute embolism and thrombosis of femoral vein, bilateral
I82.423	Acute embolism and thrombosis of iliac vein, bilateral
I82.C13	Acute embolism and thrombosis of internal jugular vein, bilateral
I82.A12	Acute embolism and thrombosis of left axillary vein
I82.412	Acute embolism and thrombosis of left femoral vein
I82.422	Acute embolism and thrombosis of left iliac vein
I82.C12	Acute embolism and thrombosis of left internal jugular vein
I82.452	Acute embolism and thrombosis of left peroneal vein
I82.432	Acute embolism and thrombosis of left popliteal vein
I82.B12	Acute embolism and thrombosis of left subclavian vein
I82.442	Acute embolism and thrombosis of left tibial vein
I82.492	Acute embolism and thrombosis of other specified deep vein of left lower extremity
I82.493	Acute embolism and thrombosis of other specified deep vein of lower extremity, bilateral
I82.491	Acute embolism and thrombosis of other specified deep vein of right lower extremity
I82.499	Acute embolism and thrombosis of other specified deep vein of unspecified lower extremity
I82.890	Acute embolism and thrombosis of other specified veins
I82.290	Acute embolism and thrombosis of other thoracic veins
I82.453	Acute embolism and thrombosis of peroneal vein, bilateral
I82.433	Acute embolism and thrombosis of popliteal vein, bilateral
I82.A11	Acute embolism and thrombosis of right axillary vein
I82.411	Acute embolism and thrombosis of right femoral vein
I82.421	Acute embolism and thrombosis of right iliac vein
I82.C11	Acute embolism and thrombosis of right internal jugular vein
I82.451	Acute embolism and thrombosis of right peroneal vein
I82.431	Acute embolism and thrombosis of right popliteal vein
I82.B11	Acute embolism and thrombosis of right subclavian vein
I82.441	Acute embolism and thrombosis of right tibial vein
I82.B13	Acute embolism and thrombosis of subclavian vein, bilateral
I82.612	Acute embolism and thrombosis of superficial veins of left upper extremity
I82.611	Acute embolism and thrombosis of superficial veins of right upper extremity
I82.619	Acute embolism and thrombosis of superficial veins of unspecified upper extremity
I82.613	Acute embolism and thrombosis of superficial veins of upper extremity, bilateral
I82.210	Acute embolism and thrombosis of superior vena cava
I82.443	Acute embolism and thrombosis of tibial vein, bilateral
I82.A19	Acute embolism and thrombosis of unspecified axillary vein
I82.4Z3	Acute embolism and thrombosis of unspecified deep veins of distal lower extremity, bilateral
I82.4Z2	Acute embolism and thrombosis of unspecified deep veins of left distal lower extremity
I82.402	Acute embolism and thrombosis of unspecified deep veins of left lower extremity
I82.4Y2	Acute embolism and thrombosis of unspecified deep veins of left proximal lower extremity
I82.403	Acute embolism and thrombosis of unspecified deep veins of lower extremity, bilateral
I82.4Y3	Acute embolism and thrombosis of unspecified deep veins of proximal lower extremity, bilateral
I82.4Z1	Acute embolism and thrombosis of unspecified deep veins of right distal lower extremity
I82.401	Acute embolism and thrombosis of unspecified deep veins of right lower extremity
I82.4Y1	Acute embolism and thrombosis of unspecified deep veins of right proximal lower extremity
I82.4Z9	Acute embolism and thrombosis of unspecified deep veins of unspecified distal lower extremity
I82.409	Acute embolism and thrombosis of unspecified deep veins of unspecified lower extremity
I82.4Y9	Acute embolism and thrombosis of unspecified deep veins of unspecified proximal lower extremity
I82.419	Acute embolism and thrombosis of unspecified femoral vein
I82.429	Acute embolism and thrombosis of unspecified iliac vein
I82.C19	Acute embolism and thrombosis of unspecified internal jugular vein
I82.459	Acute embolism and thrombosis of unspecified peroneal vein
I82.439	Acute embolism and thrombosis of unspecified popliteal vein
I82.B19	Acute embolism and thrombosis of unspecified subclavian vein
I82.449	Acute embolism and thrombosis of unspecified tibial vein
I82.90	Acute embolism and thrombosis of unspecified vein
I82.602	Acute embolism and thrombosis of unspecified veins of left upper extremity
I82.601	Acute embolism and thrombosis of unspecified veins of right upper extremity
I82.609	Acute embolism and thrombosis of unspecified veins of unspecified upper extremity
I82.603	Acute embolism and thrombosis of unspecified veins of upper extremity, bilateral
J05.10	Acute epiglottitis without obstruction
C94.02	Acute erythroid leukemia, in relapse
C94.01	Acute erythroid leukemia, in remission
C94.00	Acute erythroid leukemia, not having achieved remission
K25.3	Acute gastric ulcer without hemorrhage or perforation
A08.11	Acute gastroenteropathy due to Norwalk agent
A08.19	Acute gastroenteropathy due to other small round viruses
K28.3	Acute gastrojejunal ulcer without hemorrhage or perforation
D89.810	Acute graft-versus-host disease
M86.072	Acute hematogenous osteomyelitis, left ankle and foot
M86.052	Acute hematogenous osteomyelitis, left femur
M86.042	Acute hematogenous osteomyelitis, left hand
M86.022	Acute hematogenous osteomyelitis, left humerus
M86.032	Acute hematogenous osteomyelitis, left radius and ulna
M86.012	Acute hematogenous osteomyelitis, left shoulder
M86.062	Acute hematogenous osteomyelitis, left tibia and fibula
M86.09	Acute hematogenous osteomyelitis, multiple sites
M86.08	Acute hematogenous osteomyelitis, other sites
M86.071	Acute hematogenous osteomyelitis, right ankle and foot
M86.051	Acute hematogenous osteomyelitis, right femur
M86.041	Acute hematogenous osteomyelitis, right hand
M86.021	Acute hematogenous osteomyelitis, right humerus
M86.031	Acute hematogenous osteomyelitis, right radius and ulna
M86.011	Acute hematogenous osteomyelitis, right shoulder
M86.061	Acute hematogenous osteomyelitis, right tibia and fibula
M86.079	Acute hematogenous osteomyelitis, unspecified ankle and foot
M86.059	Acute hematogenous osteomyelitis, unspecified femur
M86.049	Acute hematogenous osteomyelitis, unspecified hand
M86.029	Acute hematogenous osteomyelitis, unspecified humerus
M86.039	Acute hematogenous osteomyelitis, unspecified radius and ulna
M86.019	Acute hematogenous osteomyelitis, unspecified shoulder
M86.00	Acute hematogenous osteomyelitis, unspecified site
M86.069	Acute hematogenous osteomyelitis, unspecified tibia and fibula
T80.910A	Acute hemolytic transfusion reaction, unspecified incompatibility, initial encounter
B16.1	Acute hepatitis B with delta-agent without hepatic coma
B16.9	Acute hepatitis B without delta-agent and without hepatic coma
B17.10	Acute hepatitis C without hepatic coma
B17.2	Acute hepatitis E
R04.81	Acute idiopathic pulmonary hemorrhage in infants
T80.22XA	Acute infection following transfusion, infusion, or injection of blood and blood products, initial encounter
N71.0	Acute inflammatory disease of uterus
E80.21	Acute intermittent (hepatic) porphyria
J84.114	Acute interstitial pneumonitis
I24.9	Acute ischemic heart disease, unspecified
N17.9	Acute kidney failure, unspecified
C95.00	Acute leukemia of unspecified cell type not having achieved remission
C95.02	Acute leukemia of unspecified cell type, in relapse
C95.01	Acute leukemia of unspecified cell type, in remission
L03.321	Acute lymphangitis of abdominal wall
L03.322	Acute lymphangitis of back [any part except buttock]
L03.327	Acute lymphangitis of buttock
L03.323	Acute lymphangitis of chest wall
L03.212	Acute lymphangitis of face
L03.324	Acute lymphangitis of groin
L03.891	Acute lymphangitis of head [any part, except face]
L03.122	Acute lymphangitis of left axilla
L03.126	Acute lymphangitis of left lower limb
L03.124	Acute lymphangitis of left upper limb
L03.222	Acute lymphangitis of neck
L03.898	Acute lymphangitis of other sites
L03.325	Acute lymphangitis of perineum
L03.121	Acute lymphangitis of right axilla
L03.125	Acute lymphangitis of right lower limb
L03.123	Acute lymphangitis of right upper limb
L03.329	Acute lymphangitis of trunk, unspecified
L03.326	Acute lymphangitis of umbilicus
L03.129	Acute lymphangitis of unspecified part of limb
L03.91	Acute lymphangitis, unspecified
C91.00	Acute lymphoblastic leukemia not having achieved remission
C91.02	Acute lymphoblastic leukemia, in relapse
C91.01	Acute lymphoblastic leukemia, in remission

H70.093	Acute mastoiditis with other complications, bilateral
H70.092	Acute mastoiditis with other complications, left ear
H70.091	Acute mastoiditis with other complications, right ear
H70.099	Acute mastoiditis with other complications, unspecified ear
H70.003	Acute mastoiditis without complications, bilateral
H70.002	Acute mastoiditis without complications, left ear
H70.001	Acute mastoiditis without complications, right ear
H70.009	Acute mastoiditis without complications, unspecified ear
C94.20	Acute megakaryoblastic leukemia not having achieved remission
C94.22	Acute megakaryoblastic leukemia, in relapse
C94.21	Acute megakaryoblastic leukemia, in remission
C93.02	Acute monoblastic/monocytic leukemia, in relapse
C93.01	Acute monoblastic/monocytic leukemia, in remission
C93.00	Acute monoblastic/monocytic leukemia, not having achieved remission
C92.02	Acute myeloblastic leukemia, in relapse
C92.01	Acute myeloblastic leukemia, in remission
C92.00	Acute myeloblastic leukemia, not having achieved remission
C92.62	Acute myeloid leukemia with 11q23-abnormality in relapse
C92.61	Acute myeloid leukemia with 11q23-abnormality in remission
C92.60	Acute myeloid leukemia with 11q23-abnormality not having achieved remission
C92.A2	Acute myeloid leukemia with multilineage dysplasia, in relapse
C92.A1	Acute myeloid leukemia with multilineage dysplasia, in remission
C92.A0	Acute myeloid leukemia with multilineage dysplasia, not having achieved remission
C92.52	Acute myelomonocytic leukemia, in relapse
C92.51	Acute myelomonocytic leukemia, in remission
C92.50	Acute myelomonocytic leukemia, not having achieved remission
I30.0	Acute nonspecific idiopathic pericarditis
D89.812	Acute on chronic graft-versus-host disease
N70.02	Acute oophoritis
C94.40	Acute panmyelosis with myelofibrosis not having achieved remission
C94.42	Acute panmyelosis with myelofibrosis, in relapse
C94.41	Acute panmyelosis with myelofibrosis, in remission
N73.0	Acute parametritis and pelvic cellulitis
K27.3	Acute peptic ulcer, site unspecified, without hemorrhage or perforation
I30.9	Acute pericarditis, unspecified
H30.143	Acute posterior multifocal placoid pigment epitheliopathy, bilateral
H30.142	Acute posterior multifocal placoid pigment epitheliopathy, left eye
H30.141	Acute posterior multifocal placoid pigment epitheliopathy, right eye
H30.149	Acute posterior multifocal placoid pigment epitheliopathy, unspecified eye
D62	Acute posthemorrhagic anemia
C92.42	Acute promyelocytic leukemia, in relapse
C92.41	Acute promyelocytic leukemia, in remission
C92.40	Acute promyelocytic leukemia, not having achieved remission
N41.0	Acute prostatitis
B40.0	Acute pulmonary blastomycosis
B38.0	Acute pulmonary coccidioidomycosis
J70.0	Acute pulmonary manifestations due to radiation
N10	Acute pyelonephritis
I01.1	Acute rheumatic endocarditis
I01.9	Acute rheumatic heart disease, unspecified
I01.2	Acute rheumatic myocarditis
I01.0	Acute rheumatic pericarditis
N70.01	Acute salpingitis
N70.03	Acute salpingitis and oophoritis
E06.0	Acute thyroiditis
G37.3	Acute transverse myelitis in demyelinating disease of central nervous system
B17.9	Acute viral hepatitis, unspecified
E27.2	Addisonian crisis
D81.32	Adenosine deaminase 2 deficiency
D81.30	Adenosine deaminase deficiency, unspecified
A85.1	Adenoviral encephalitis
A08.2	Adenoviral enteritis
A87.1	Adenoviral meningitis
T81.516A	Adhesions due to foreign body accidentally left in body following aspiration, puncture or other catheterization, initial encounter
T81.514A	Adhesions due to foreign body accidentally left in body following endoscopic examination, initial encounter
T81.515A	Adhesions due to foreign body accidentally left in body following heart catheterization, initial encounter
T81.511A	Adhesions due to foreign body accidentally left in body following infusion or transfusion, initial encounter
T81.513A	Adhesions due to foreign body accidentally left in body following injection or immunization, initial encounter
T81.512A	Adhesions due to foreign body accidentally left in body following kidney dialysis, initial encounter
T81.518A	Adhesions due to foreign body accidentally left in body following other procedure, initial encounter
T81.517A	Adhesions due to foreign body accidentally left in body following removal of catheter or packing, initial encounter
T81.510A	Adhesions due to foreign body accidentally left in body following surgical operation, initial encounter
T81.519A	Adhesions due to foreign body accidentally left in body following unspecified procedure, initial encounter
E71.521	Adolescent X-linked adrenoleukodystrophy
E27.5	Adrenomedullary hyperfunction
E71.522	Adrenomyeloneuropathy
T74.61XA	Adult forced labor exploitation, confirmed, initial encounter
T76.61XA	Adult forced labor exploitation, suspected, initial encounter
T74.51XA	Adult forced sexual exploitation, confirmed, initial encounter
T76.51XA	Adult forced sexual exploitation, suspected, initial encounter
K31.1	Adult hypertrophic pyloric stenosis
T74.01XA	Adult neglect or abandonment, confirmed, initial encounter
T76.01XA	Adult neglect or abandonment, suspected, initial encounter
T74.11XA	Adult physical abuse, confirmed, initial encounter
T76.11XA	Adult physical abuse, suspected, initial encounter
J84.82	Adult pulmonary Langerhans cell histiocytosis
T74.21XA	Adult sexual abuse, confirmed, initial encounter
T76.21XA	Adult sexual abuse, suspected, initial encounter
C91.50	Adult T-cell lymphoma/leukemia (HTLV-1-associated) not having achieved remission
C91.52	Adult T-cell lymphoma/leukemia (HTLV-1-associated), in relapse
C91.51	Adult T-cell lymphoma/leukemia (HTLV-1-associated), in remission
B56.9	African trypanosomiasis, unspecified
M80.072A	Age-related osteoporosis with current pathological fracture, left ankle and foot, initial encounter for fracture
M80.072P	Age-related osteoporosis with current pathological fracture, left ankle and foot, subsequent encounter for fracture with malunion
M80.072K	Age-related osteoporosis with current pathological fracture, left ankle and foot, subsequent encounter for fracture with nonunion
M80.052A	Age-related osteoporosis with current pathological fracture, left femur, initial encounter for fracture
M80.052P	Age-related osteoporosis with current pathological fracture, left femur, subsequent encounter for fracture with malunion
M80.052K	Age-related osteoporosis with current pathological fracture, left femur, subsequent encounter for fracture with nonunion
M80.032A	Age-related osteoporosis with current pathological fracture, left forearm, initial encounter for fracture
M80.032P	Age-related osteoporosis with current pathological fracture, left forearm, subsequent encounter for fracture with malunion
M80.032K	Age-related osteoporosis with current pathological fracture, left forearm, subsequent encounter for fracture with nonunion
M80.042A	Age-related osteoporosis with current pathological fracture, left hand, initial encounter for fracture
M80.042P	Age-related osteoporosis with current pathological fracture, left hand, subsequent encounter for fracture with malunion
M80.042K	Age-related osteoporosis with current pathological fracture, left hand, subsequent encounter for fracture with nonunion
M80.022A	Age-related osteoporosis with current pathological fracture, left humerus, initial encounter for fracture
M80.022P	Age-related osteoporosis with current pathological fracture, left humerus, subsequent encounter for fracture with malunion
M80.022K	Age-related osteoporosis with current pathological fracture, left humerus, subsequent encounter for fracture with nonunion
M80.062A	Age-related osteoporosis with current pathological fracture, left lower leg, initial encounter for fracture
M80.062P	Age-related osteoporosis with current pathological fracture, left lower leg, subsequent encounter for fracture with malunion
M80.062K	Age-related osteoporosis with current pathological fracture, left lower leg, subsequent encounter for fracture with nonunion
M80.012A	Age-related osteoporosis with current pathological fracture, left shoulder, initial encounter for fracture
M80.012P	Age-related osteoporosis with current pathological fracture, left shoulder, subsequent encounter for fracture with malunion
M80.012K	Age-related osteoporosis with current pathological fracture, left shoulder, subsequent encounter for fracture with nonunion
M80.071A	Age-related osteoporosis with current pathological fracture, right ankle and foot, initial encounter for fracture
M80.071P	Age-related osteoporosis with current pathological fracture, right ankle and foot, subsequent encounter for fracture with malunion
M80.071K	Age-related osteoporosis with current pathological fracture, right ankle and foot, subsequent encounter for fracture with nonunion
M80.051A	Age-related osteoporosis with current pathological fracture, right femur, initial encounter for fracture
M80.051P	Age-related osteoporosis with current pathological fracture, right femur, subsequent encounter for fracture with malunion
M80.051K	Age-related osteoporosis with current pathological fracture, right femur, subsequent encounter for fracture with nonunion
M80.031A	Age-related osteoporosis with current pathological fracture, right forearm, initial encounter for fracture
M80.031P	Age-related osteoporosis with current pathological fracture, right forearm, subsequent encounter for fracture with malunion
M80.031K	Age-related osteoporosis with current pathological fracture, right forearm, subsequent encounter for fracture with nonunion
M80.041A	Age-related osteoporosis with current pathological fracture, right hand, initial encounter for fracture
M80.041P	Age-related osteoporosis with current pathological fracture, right hand, subsequent encounter for fracture with malunion
M80.041K	Age-related osteoporosis with current pathological fracture, right hand, subsequent encounter for fracture with nonunion
M80.021A	Age-related osteoporosis with current pathological fracture, right humerus, initial encounter for fracture
M80.021P	Age-related osteoporosis with current pathological fracture, right humerus, subsequent encounter for fracture with malunion
M80.021K	Age-related osteoporosis with current pathological fracture, right humerus, subsequent encounter for fracture with nonunion
M80.061A	Age-related osteoporosis with current pathological fracture, right lower leg, initial encounter for fracture

M80.061P	Age-related osteoporosis with current pathological fracture, right lower leg, subsequent encounter for fracture with malunion
M80.061K	Age-related osteoporosis with current pathological fracture, right lower leg, subsequent encounter for fracture with nonunion
M80.011A	Age-related osteoporosis with current pathological fracture, right shoulder, initial encounter for fracture
M80.011P	Age-related osteoporosis with current pathological fracture, right shoulder, subsequent encounter for fracture with malunion
M80.011K	Age-related osteoporosis with current pathological fracture, right shoulder, subsequent encounter for fracture with nonunion
M80.079A	Age-related osteoporosis with current pathological fracture, unspecified ankle and foot, initial encounter for fracture
M80.079P	Age-related osteoporosis with current pathological fracture, unspecified ankle and foot, subsequent encounter for fracture with malunion
M80.079K	Age-related osteoporosis with current pathological fracture, unspecified ankle and foot, subsequent encounter for fracture with nonunion
M80.059A	Age-related osteoporosis with current pathological fracture, unspecified femur, initial encounter for fracture
M80.059P	Age-related osteoporosis with current pathological fracture, unspecified femur, subsequent encounter for fracture with malunion
M80.059K	Age-related osteoporosis with current pathological fracture, unspecified femur, subsequent encounter for fracture with nonunion
M80.039A	Age-related osteoporosis with current pathological fracture, unspecified forearm, initial encounter for fracture
M80.039P	Age-related osteoporosis with current pathological fracture, unspecified forearm, subsequent encounter for fracture with malunion
M80.039K	Age-related osteoporosis with current pathological fracture, unspecified forearm, subsequent encounter for fracture with nonunion
M80.049A	Age-related osteoporosis with current pathological fracture, unspecified hand, initial encounter for fracture
M80.049P	Age-related osteoporosis with current pathological fracture, unspecified hand, subsequent encounter for fracture with malunion
M80.049K	Age-related osteoporosis with current pathological fracture, unspecified hand, subsequent encounter for fracture with nonunion
M80.029A	Age-related osteoporosis with current pathological fracture, unspecified humerus, initial encounter for fracture
M80.029P	Age-related osteoporosis with current pathological fracture, unspecified humerus, subsequent encounter for fracture with malunion
M80.029K	Age-related osteoporosis with current pathological fracture, unspecified humerus, subsequent encounter for fracture with nonunion
M80.069A	Age-related osteoporosis with current pathological fracture, unspecified lower leg, initial encounter for fracture
M80.069P	Age-related osteoporosis with current pathological fracture, unspecified lower leg, subsequent encounter for fracture with malunion
M80.069K	Age-related osteoporosis with current pathological fracture, unspecified lower leg, subsequent encounter for fracture with nonunion
M80.019A	Age-related osteoporosis with current pathological fracture, unspecified shoulder, initial encounter for fracture
M80.019P	Age-related osteoporosis with current pathological fracture, unspecified shoulder, subsequent encounter for fracture with malunion
M80.019K	Age-related osteoporosis with current pathological fracture, unspecified shoulder, subsequent encounter for fracture with nonunion
M80.00XA	Age-related osteoporosis with current pathological fracture, unspecified site, initial encounter for fracture
M80.00XP	Age-related osteoporosis with current pathological fracture, unspecified site, subsequent encounter for fracture with malunion
M80.00XK	Age-related osteoporosis with current pathological fracture, unspecified site, subsequent encounter for fracture with nonunion
M80.08XA	Age-related osteoporosis with current pathological fracture, vertebra(e), initial encounter for fracture
M80.08XP	Age-related osteoporosis with current pathological fracture, vertebra(e), subsequent encounter for fracture with malunion
M80.08XK	Age-related osteoporosis with current pathological fracture, vertebra(e), subsequent encounter for fracture with nonunion
Q44.0	Agenesis, aplasia and hypoplasia of gallbladder
Q45.0	Agenesis, aplasia and hypoplasia of pancreas
C96.21	Aggressive systemic mastocytosis
J67.7	Air conditioner and humidifier lung
E70.339	Albinism with hematologic abnormality, unspecified
E70.30	Albinism, unspecified
F10.180	Alcohol abuse with alcohol-induced anxiety disorder
F10.14	Alcohol abuse with alcohol-induced mood disorder
F10.151	Alcohol abuse with alcohol-induced psychotic disorder with hallucinations
F10.159	Alcohol abuse with alcohol-induced psychotic disorder, unspecified
F10.181	Alcohol abuse with alcohol-induced sexual dysfunction
F10.121	Alcohol abuse with intoxication delirium
F10.188	Alcohol abuse with other alcohol-induced disorder
F10.19	Alcohol abuse with unspecified alcohol-induced disorder
F10.280	Alcohol dependence with alcohol-induced anxiety disorder
F10.24	Alcohol dependence with alcohol-induced mood disorder
F10.27	Alcohol dependence with alcohol-induced persisting dementia
F10.251	Alcohol dependence with alcohol-induced psychotic disorder with hallucinations
F10.259	Alcohol dependence with alcohol-induced psychotic disorder, unspecified
F10.281	Alcohol dependence with alcohol-induced sexual dysfunction
F10.221	Alcohol dependence with intoxication delirium
F10.288	Alcohol dependence with other alcohol-induced disorder
F10.29	Alcohol dependence with unspecified alcohol-induced disorder
F10.231	Alcohol dependence with withdrawal delirium
F10.232	Alcohol dependence with withdrawal with perceptual disturbance

F10.230	Alcohol dependence with withdrawal, uncomplicated
F10.239	Alcohol dependence with withdrawal, unspecified
F10.980	Alcohol use, unspecified with alcohol-induced anxiety disorder
F10.94	Alcohol use, unspecified with alcohol-induced mood disorder
F10.951	Alcohol use, unspecified with alcohol-induced psychotic disorder with hallucinations
F10.959	Alcohol use, unspecified with alcohol-induced psychotic disorder, unspecified
F10.981	Alcohol use, unspecified with alcohol-induced sexual dysfunction
F10.921	Alcohol use, unspecified with intoxication delirium
F10.988	Alcohol use, unspecified with other alcohol-induced disorder
F10.99	Alcohol use, unspecified with unspecified alcohol-induced disorder
K86.0	Alcohol-induced chronic pancreatitis
E24.4	Alcohol-induced pseudo-Cushing's syndrome
I42.6	Alcoholic cardiomyopathy
G72.1	Alcoholic myopathy
E87.3	Alkalosis
P74.41	Alkalosis of newborn
B44.81	Allergic bronchopulmonary aspergillosis
D69.0	Allergic purpura
B48.2	Allescheriasis
G31.81	Alpers disease
Q87.81	Alport syndrome
J84.01	Alveolar proteinosis
G45.3	Amaurosis fugax
A06.81	Amebic cystitis
A06.2	Amebic nondysenteric colitis
A06.3	Ameboma of intestine
E85.9	Amyloidosis, unspecified
G12.21	Amyotrophic lateral sclerosis
K61.0	Anal abscess
O70.4	Anal sphincter tear complicating delivery, not associated with third degree laceration
T80.51XA	Anaphylactic reaction due to administration of blood and blood products, initial encounter
T88.6XXA	Anaphylactic reaction due to adverse effect of correct drug or medicament properly administered, initial encounter
T78.08XA	Anaphylactic reaction due to eggs, initial encounter
T78.06XA	Anaphylactic reaction due to food additives, initial encounter
T78.04XA	Anaphylactic reaction due to fruits and vegetables, initial encounter
T78.07XA	Anaphylactic reaction due to milk and dairy products, initial encounter
T78.03XA	Anaphylactic reaction due to other fish, initial encounter
T78.09XA	Anaphylactic reaction due to other food products, initial encounter
T80.59XA	Anaphylactic reaction due to other serum, initial encounter
T78.01XA	Anaphylactic reaction due to peanuts, initial encounter
T78.02XA	Anaphylactic reaction due to shellfish (crustaceans), initial encounter
T78.05XA	Anaphylactic reaction due to tree nuts and seeds, initial encounter
T78.00XA	Anaphylactic reaction due to unspecified food, initial encounter
T80.52XA	Anaphylactic reaction due to vaccination, initial encounter
T78.2XXA	Anaphylactic shock, unspecified, initial encounter
C84.79	Anaplastic large cell lymphoma, ALK-negative, extranodal and solid organ sites
C84.73	Anaplastic large cell lymphoma, ALK-negative, intra-abdominal lymph nodes
C84.76	Anaplastic large cell lymphoma, ALK-negative, intrapelvic lymph nodes
C84.72	Anaplastic large cell lymphoma, ALK-negative, intrathoracic lymph nodes
C84.74	Anaplastic large cell lymphoma, ALK-negative, lymph nodes of axilla and upper limb
C84.71	Anaplastic large cell lymphoma, ALK-negative, lymph nodes of head, face, and neck
C84.75	Anaplastic large cell lymphoma, ALK-negative, lymph nodes of inguinal region and lower limb
C84.78	Anaplastic large cell lymphoma, ALK-negative, lymph nodes of multiple sites
C84.77	Anaplastic large cell lymphoma, ALK-negative, spleen
C84.70	Anaplastic large cell lymphoma, ALK-negative, unspecified site
C84.69	Anaplastic large cell lymphoma, ALK-positive, extranodal and solid organ sites
C84.63	Anaplastic large cell lymphoma, ALK-positive, intra-abdominal lymph nodes
C84.66	Anaplastic large cell lymphoma, ALK-positive, intrapelvic lymph nodes
C84.62	Anaplastic large cell lymphoma, ALK-positive, intrathoracic lymph nodes
C84.64	Anaplastic large cell lymphoma, ALK-positive, lymph nodes of axilla and upper limb
C84.61	Anaplastic large cell lymphoma, ALK-positive, lymph nodes of head, face, and neck
C84.65	Anaplastic large cell lymphoma, ALK-positive, lymph nodes of inguinal region and lower limb
C84.68	Anaplastic large cell lymphoma, ALK-positive, lymph nodes of multiple sites
C84.67	Anaplastic large cell lymphoma, ALK-positive, spleen
C84.60	Anaplastic large cell lymphoma, ALK-positive, unspecified site
B76.0	Ancylostomiasis
P61.2	Anemia of prematurity
I25.3	Aneurysm of heart
I28.1	Aneurysm of pulmonary artery
Q93.51	Angelman syndrome
I20.1	Angina pectoris with documented spasm
C86.5	Angioimmunoblastic T-cell lymphoma
C22.3	Angiosarcoma of liver
B81.0	Anisakiasis
Q45.1	Annular pancreas
Q25.48	Anomalous origin of subclavian artery

Q26.4	Anomalous pulmonary venous connection, unspecified
K61.2	Anorectal abscess
F50.02	Anorexia nervosa, binge eating/purging type
F50.01	Anorexia nervosa, restricting type
F50.00	Anorexia nervosa, unspecified
G93.1	Anoxic brain damage, not elsewhere classified
G46.1	Anterior cerebral artery syndrome
S43.215A	Anterior dislocation of left sternoclavicular joint, initial encounter
S43.214A	Anterior dislocation of right sternoclavicular joint, initial encounter
S43.216A	Anterior dislocation of unspecified sternoclavicular joint, initial encounter
S42.012B	Anterior displaced fracture of sternal end of left clavicle, initial encounter for open fracture
S42.012P	Anterior displaced fracture of sternal end of left clavicle, subsequent encounter for fracture with malunion
S42.012K	Anterior displaced fracture of sternal end of left clavicle, subsequent encounter for fracture with nonunion
S42.011B	Anterior displaced fracture of sternal end of right clavicle, initial encounter for open fracture
S42.011P	Anterior displaced fracture of sternal end of right clavicle, subsequent encounter for fracture with malunion
S42.011K	Anterior displaced fracture of sternal end of right clavicle, subsequent encounter for fracture with nonunion
S42.013B	Anterior displaced fracture of sternal end of unspecified clavicle, initial encounter for open fracture
S42.013P	Anterior displaced fracture of sternal end of unspecified clavicle, subsequent encounter for fracture with malunion
S42.013K	Anterior displaced fracture of sternal end of unspecified clavicle, subsequent encounter for fracture with nonunion
S12.110A	Anterior displaced Type II dens fracture, initial encounter for closed fracture
S12.110K	Anterior displaced Type II dens fracture, subsequent encounter for fracture with nonunion
M47.012	Anterior spinal artery compression syndromes, cervical region
M47.013	Anterior spinal artery compression syndromes, cervicothoracic region
M47.016	Anterior spinal artery compression syndromes, lumbar region
M47.011	Anterior spinal artery compression syndromes, occipito-atlanto-axial region
M47.019	Anterior spinal artery compression syndromes, site unspecified
M47.014	Anterior spinal artery compression syndromes, thoracic region
M47.015	Anterior spinal artery compression syndromes, thoracolumbar region
S43.212A	Anterior subluxation of left sternoclavicular joint, initial encounter
S43.211A	Anterior subluxation of right sternoclavicular joint, initial encounter
S43.213A	Anterior subluxation of unspecified sternoclavicular joint, initial encounter
A22.9	Anthrax, unspecified
D80.6	Antibody deficiency with near-normal immunoglobulins or with hyperimmunoglobulinemia
D68.312	Antiphospholipid antibody with hemorrhagic disorder
D68.61	Antiphospholipid syndrome
M31.4	Aortic arch syndrome [Takayasu]
R47.01	Aphasia
D61.9	Aplastic anemia, unspecified
A96.9	Arenaviral hemorrhagic fever, unspecified
E72.21	Argininemia
E72.22	Arginosuccinic aciduria
Q07.02	Arnold-Chiari syndrome with hydrocephalus
Q07.03	Arnold-Chiari syndrome with spina bifida and hydrocephalus
Q87.82	Arterial tortuosity syndrome
I28.0	Arteriovenous fistula of pulmonary vessels
Q28.0	Arteriovenous malformation of precerebral vessels
Q27.30	Arteriovenous malformation, site unspecified
A69.23	Arthritis due to Lyme disease
M00.872	Arthritis due to other bacteria, left ankle and foot
M00.822	Arthritis due to other bacteria, left elbow
M00.842	Arthritis due to other bacteria, left hand
M00.852	Arthritis due to other bacteria, left hip
M00.862	Arthritis due to other bacteria, left knee
M00.812	Arthritis due to other bacteria, left shoulder
M00.832	Arthritis due to other bacteria, left wrist
M00.871	Arthritis due to other bacteria, right ankle and foot
M00.821	Arthritis due to other bacteria, right elbow
M00.841	Arthritis due to other bacteria, right hand
M00.851	Arthritis due to other bacteria, right hip
M00.861	Arthritis due to other bacteria, right knee
M00.811	Arthritis due to other bacteria, right shoulder
M00.831	Arthritis due to other bacteria, right wrist
M00.879	Arthritis due to other bacteria, unspecified ankle and foot
M00.829	Arthritis due to other bacteria, unspecified elbow
M00.849	Arthritis due to other bacteria, unspecified hand
M00.859	Arthritis due to other bacteria, unspecified hip
M00.80	Arthritis due to other bacteria, unspecified joint
M00.869	Arthritis due to other bacteria, unspecified knee
M00.819	Arthritis due to other bacteria, unspecified shoulder
M00.839	Arthritis due to other bacteria, unspecified wrist
M00.88	Arthritis due to other bacteria, vertebrae
Q74.3	Arthrogryposis multiplex congenita
B77.0	Ascariasis with intestinal complications
B77.89	Ascariasis with other complications
B77.9	Ascariasis, unspecified
T81.61XA	Aseptic peritonitis due to foreign substance accidentally left during a procedure, initial encounter
F84.5	Asperger's syndrome

B44.9	Aspergillosis, unspecified
R09.01	Asphyxia
T71.231A	Asphyxiation due to being trapped in a (discarded) refrigerator, accidental, initial encounter
T71.233A	Asphyxiation due to being trapped in a (discarded) refrigerator, assault, initial encounter
T71.232A	Asphyxiation due to being trapped in a (discarded) refrigerator, intentional self-harm, initial encounter
T71.234A	Asphyxiation due to being trapped in a (discarded) refrigerator, undetermined, initial encounter
T71.221A	Asphyxiation due to being trapped in a car trunk, accidental, initial encounter
T71.223A	Asphyxiation due to being trapped in a car trunk, assault, initial encounter
T71.222A	Asphyxiation due to being trapped in a car trunk, intentional self-harm, initial encounter
T71.224A	Asphyxiation due to being trapped in a car trunk, undetermined, initial encounter
T71.131A	Asphyxiation due to being trapped in bed linens, accidental, initial encounter
T71.133A	Asphyxiation due to being trapped in bed linens, assault, initial encounter
T71.132A	Asphyxiation due to being trapped in bed linens, intentional self-harm, initial encounter
T71.134A	Asphyxiation due to being trapped in bed linens, undetermined, initial encounter
T71.29XA	Asphyxiation due to being trapped in other low oxygen environment, initial encounter
T71.21XA	Asphyxiation due to cave-in or falling earth, initial encounter
T71.161A	Asphyxiation due to hanging, accidental, initial encounter
T71.163A	Asphyxiation due to hanging, assault, initial encounter
T71.162A	Asphyxiation due to hanging, intentional self-harm, initial encounter
T71.164A	Asphyxiation due to hanging, undetermined, initial encounter
T71.191A	Asphyxiation due to mechanical threat to breathing due to other causes, accidental, initial encounter
T71.193A	Asphyxiation due to mechanical threat to breathing due to other causes, assault, initial encounter
T71.192A	Asphyxiation due to mechanical threat to breathing due to other causes, intentional self-harm, initial encounter
T71.194A	Asphyxiation due to mechanical threat to breathing due to other causes, undetermined, initial encounter
T71.121A	Asphyxiation due to plastic bag, accidental, initial encounter
T71.123A	Asphyxiation due to plastic bag, assault, initial encounter
T71.122A	Asphyxiation due to plastic bag, intentional self-harm, initial encounter
T71.124A	Asphyxiation due to plastic bag, undetermined, initial encounter
T71.151A	Asphyxiation due to smothering in furniture, accidental, initial encounter
T71.153A	Asphyxiation due to smothering in furniture, assault, initial encounter
T71.152A	Asphyxiation due to smothering in furniture, intentional self-harm, initial encounter
T71.154A	Asphyxiation due to smothering in furniture, undetermined, initial encounter
T71.141A	Asphyxiation due to smothering under another person's body (in bed), accidental, initial encounter
T71.143A	Asphyxiation due to smothering under another person's body (in bed), assault, initial encounter
T71.144A	Asphyxiation due to smothering under another person's body (in bed), undetermined, initial encounter
T71.111A	Asphyxiation due to smothering under pillow, accidental, initial encounter
T71.113A	Asphyxiation due to smothering under pillow, assault, initial encounter
T71.112A	Asphyxiation due to smothering under pillow, intentional self-harm, initial encounter
T71.114A	Asphyxiation due to smothering under pillow, undetermined, initial encounter
T71.20XA	Asphyxiation due to systemic oxygen deficiency due to low oxygen content in ambient air due to unspecified cause, initial encounter
T71.9XXA	Asphyxiation due to unspecified cause, initial encounter
Q89.01	Asplenia (congenital)
A08.32	Astrovirus enteritis
A52.2	Asymptomatic neurosyphilis
J98.11	Atelectasis
I75.023	Atheroembolism of bilateral lower extremities
I75.013	Atheroembolism of bilateral upper extremities
I75.81	Atheroembolism of kidney
I75.022	Atheroembolism of left lower extremity
I75.012	Atheroembolism of left upper extremity
I75.89	Atheroembolism of other site
I75.021	Atheroembolism of right lower extremity
I75.011	Atheroembolism of right upper extremity
I75.029	Atheroembolism of unspecified lower extremity
I75.019	Atheroembolism of unspecified upper extremity
I25.721	Atherosclerosis of autologous artery coronary artery bypass graft(s) with angina pectoris with documented spasm
I25.728	Atherosclerosis of autologous artery coronary artery bypass graft(s) with other forms of angina pectoris
I25.729	Atherosclerosis of autologous artery coronary artery bypass graft(s) with unspecified angina pectoris
I25.720	Atherosclerosis of autologous artery coronary artery bypass graft(s) with unstable angina pectoris
I70.463	Atherosclerosis of autologous vein bypass graft(s) of the extremities with gangrene, bilateral legs
I70.462	Atherosclerosis of autologous vein bypass graft(s) of the extremities with gangrene, left leg
I70.468	Atherosclerosis of autologous vein bypass graft(s) of the extremities with gangrene, other extremity

I70.461	Atherosclerosis of autologous vein bypass graft(s) of the extremities with gangrene, right leg
I70.469	Atherosclerosis of autologous vein bypass graft(s) of the extremities with gangrene, unspecified extremity
I70.443	Atherosclerosis of autologous vein bypass graft(s) of the left leg with ulceration of ankle
I70.442	Atherosclerosis of autologous vein bypass graft(s) of the left leg with ulceration of calf
I70.444	Atherosclerosis of autologous vein bypass graft(s) of the left leg with ulceration of heel and midfoot
I70.448	Atherosclerosis of autologous vein bypass graft(s) of the left leg with ulceration of other part of lower leg
I70.441	Atherosclerosis of autologous vein bypass graft(s) of the left leg with ulceration of thigh
I70.449	Atherosclerosis of autologous vein bypass graft(s) of the left leg with ulceration of unspecified site
I70.433	Atherosclerosis of autologous vein bypass graft(s) of the right leg with ulceration of ankle
I70.432	Atherosclerosis of autologous vein bypass graft(s) of the right leg with ulceration of calf
I70.434	Atherosclerosis of autologous vein bypass graft(s) of the right leg with ulceration of heel and midfoot
I70.438	Atherosclerosis of autologous vein bypass graft(s) of the right leg with ulceration of other part of lower leg
I70.431	Atherosclerosis of autologous vein bypass graft(s) of the right leg with ulceration of thigh
I70.439	Atherosclerosis of autologous vein bypass graft(s) of the right leg with ulceration of unspecified site
I25.711	Atherosclerosis of autologous vein coronary artery bypass graft(s) with angina pectoris with documented spasm
I25.718	Atherosclerosis of autologous vein coronary artery bypass graft(s) with other forms of angina pectoris
I25.719	Atherosclerosis of autologous vein coronary artery bypass graft(s) with unspecified angina pectoris
I25.710	Atherosclerosis of autologous vein coronary artery bypass graft(s) with unstable angina pectoris
I25.761	Atherosclerosis of bypass graft of coronary artery of transplanted heart with angina pectoris with documented spasm
I25.768	Atherosclerosis of bypass graft of coronary artery of transplanted heart with other forms of angina pectoris
I25.769	Atherosclerosis of bypass graft of coronary artery of transplanted heart with unspecified angina pectoris
I25.760	Atherosclerosis of bypass graft of coronary artery of transplanted heart with unstable angina
I25.812	Atherosclerosis of bypass graft of coronary artery of transplanted heart without angina pectoris
I25.810	Atherosclerosis of coronary artery bypass graft(s) without angina pectoris
I25.700	Atherosclerosis of coronary artery bypass graft(s), unspecified, with unstable angina pectoris
I70.263	Atherosclerosis of native arteries of extremities with gangrene, bilateral legs
I70.262	Atherosclerosis of native arteries of extremities with gangrene, left leg
I70.268	Atherosclerosis of native arteries of extremities with gangrene, other extremity
I70.261	Atherosclerosis of native arteries of extremities with gangrene, right leg
I70.269	Atherosclerosis of native arteries of extremities with gangrene, unspecified extremity
I25.751	Atherosclerosis of native coronary artery of transplanted heart with angina pectoris with documented spasm
I25.758	Atherosclerosis of native coronary artery of transplanted heart with other forms of angina pectoris
I25.759	Atherosclerosis of native coronary artery of transplanted heart with unspecified angina pectoris
I25.750	Atherosclerosis of native coronary artery of transplanted heart with unstable angina
I25.811	Atherosclerosis of native coronary artery of transplanted heart without angina pectoris
I70.563	Atherosclerosis of nonautologous biological bypass graft(s) of the extremities with gangrene, bilateral legs
I70.562	Atherosclerosis of nonautologous biological bypass graft(s) of the extremities with gangrene, left leg
I70.568	Atherosclerosis of nonautologous biological bypass graft(s) of the extremities with gangrene, other extremity
I70.561	Atherosclerosis of nonautologous biological bypass graft(s) of the extremities with gangrene, right leg
I70.569	Atherosclerosis of nonautologous biological bypass graft(s) of the extremities with gangrene, unspecified extremity
I70.543	Atherosclerosis of nonautologous biological bypass graft(s) of the left leg with ulceration of ankle
I70.542	Atherosclerosis of nonautologous biological bypass graft(s) of the left leg with ulceration of calf
I70.544	Atherosclerosis of nonautologous biological bypass graft(s) of the left leg with ulceration of heel and midfoot
I70.548	Atherosclerosis of nonautologous biological bypass graft(s) of the left leg with ulceration of other part of lower leg
I70.541	Atherosclerosis of nonautologous biological bypass graft(s) of the left leg with ulceration of thigh
I70.549	Atherosclerosis of nonautologous biological bypass graft(s) of the left leg with ulceration of unspecified site
I70.533	Atherosclerosis of nonautologous biological bypass graft(s) of the right leg with ulceration of ankle
I70.532	Atherosclerosis of nonautologous biological bypass graft(s) of the right leg with ulceration of calf
I70.534	Atherosclerosis of nonautologous biological bypass graft(s) of the right leg with ulceration of heel and midfoot
I70.538	Atherosclerosis of nonautologous biological bypass graft(s) of the right leg with ulceration of other part of lower leg
I70.531	Atherosclerosis of nonautologous biological bypass graft(s) of the right leg with ulceration of thigh
I70.539	Atherosclerosis of nonautologous biological bypass graft(s) of the right leg with ulceration of unspecified site
I25.731	Atherosclerosis of nonautologous biological coronary artery bypass graft(s) with angina pectoris with documented spasm
I25.738	Atherosclerosis of nonautologous biological coronary artery bypass graft(s) with other forms of angina pectoris
I25.739	Atherosclerosis of nonautologous biological coronary artery bypass graft(s) with unspecified angina pectoris
I25.730	Atherosclerosis of nonautologous biological coronary artery bypass graft(s) with unstable angina pectoris
I70.663	Atherosclerosis of nonbiological bypass graft(s) of the extremities with gangrene, bilateral legs
I70.662	Atherosclerosis of nonbiological bypass graft(s) of the extremities with gangrene, left leg
I70.668	Atherosclerosis of nonbiological bypass graft(s) of the extremities with gangrene, other extremity
I70.661	Atherosclerosis of nonbiological bypass graft(s) of the extremities with gangrene, right leg
I70.669	Atherosclerosis of nonbiological bypass graft(s) of the extremities with gangrene, unspecified extremity
I70.643	Atherosclerosis of nonbiological bypass graft(s) of the left leg with ulceration of ankle
I70.642	Atherosclerosis of nonbiological bypass graft(s) of the left leg with ulceration of calf
I70.644	Atherosclerosis of nonbiological bypass graft(s) of the left leg with ulceration of heel and midfoot
I70.648	Atherosclerosis of nonbiological bypass graft(s) of the left leg with ulceration of other part of lower leg
I70.641	Atherosclerosis of nonbiological bypass graft(s) of the left leg with ulceration of thigh
I70.649	Atherosclerosis of nonbiological bypass graft(s) of the left leg with ulceration of unspecified site
I70.633	Atherosclerosis of nonbiological bypass graft(s) of the right leg with ulceration of ankle
I70.632	Atherosclerosis of nonbiological bypass graft(s) of the right leg with ulceration of calf
I70.634	Atherosclerosis of nonbiological bypass graft(s) of the right leg with ulceration of heel and midfoot
I70.638	Atherosclerosis of nonbiological bypass graft(s) of the right leg with ulceration of other part of lower leg
I70.631	Atherosclerosis of nonbiological bypass graft(s) of the right leg with ulceration of thigh
I70.639	Atherosclerosis of nonbiological bypass graft(s) of the right leg with ulceration of unspecified site
I25.791	Atherosclerosis of other coronary artery bypass graft(s) with angina pectoris with documented spasm
I25.798	Atherosclerosis of other coronary artery bypass graft(s) with other forms of angina pectoris
I25.799	Atherosclerosis of other coronary artery bypass graft(s) with unspecified angina pectoris
I25.790	Atherosclerosis of other coronary artery bypass graft(s) with unstable angina pectoris
I70.763	Atherosclerosis of other type of bypass graft(s) of the extremities with gangrene, bilateral legs
I70.762	Atherosclerosis of other type of bypass graft(s) of the extremities with gangrene, left leg
I70.768	Atherosclerosis of other type of bypass graft(s) of the extremities with gangrene, other extremity
I70.761	Atherosclerosis of other type of bypass graft(s) of the extremities with gangrene, right leg
I70.769	Atherosclerosis of other type of bypass graft(s) of the extremities with gangrene, unspecified extremity
I70.743	Atherosclerosis of other type of bypass graft(s) of the left leg with ulceration of ankle
I70.742	Atherosclerosis of other type of bypass graft(s) of the left leg with ulceration of calf
I70.744	Atherosclerosis of other type of bypass graft(s) of the left leg with ulceration of heel and midfoot
I70.748	Atherosclerosis of other type of bypass graft(s) of the left leg with ulceration of other part of lower leg
I70.741	Atherosclerosis of other type of bypass graft(s) of the left leg with ulceration of thigh
I70.749	Atherosclerosis of other type of bypass graft(s) of the left leg with ulceration of unspecified site
I70.733	Atherosclerosis of other type of bypass graft(s) of the right leg with ulceration of ankle
I70.732	Atherosclerosis of other type of bypass graft(s) of the right leg with ulceration of calf
I70.734	Atherosclerosis of other type of bypass graft(s) of the right leg with ulceration of heel and midfoot
I70.738	Atherosclerosis of other type of bypass graft(s) of the right leg with ulceration of other part of lower leg

I70.731	Atherosclerosis of other type of bypass graft(s) of the right leg with ulceration of thigh
I70.739	Atherosclerosis of other type of bypass graft(s) of the right leg with ulceration of unspecified site
I70.363	Atherosclerosis of unspecified type of bypass graft(s) of the extremities with gangrene, bilateral legs
I70.362	Atherosclerosis of unspecified type of bypass graft(s) of the extremities with gangrene, left leg
I70.368	Atherosclerosis of unspecified type of bypass graft(s) of the extremities with gangrene, other extremity
I70.361	Atherosclerosis of unspecified type of bypass graft(s) of the extremities with gangrene, right leg
I70.369	Atherosclerosis of unspecified type of bypass graft(s) of the extremities with gangrene, unspecified extremity
I70.343	Atherosclerosis of unspecified type of bypass graft(s) of the left leg with ulceration of ankle
I70.342	Atherosclerosis of unspecified type of bypass graft(s) of the left leg with ulceration of calf
I70.344	Atherosclerosis of unspecified type of bypass graft(s) of the left leg with ulceration of heel and midfoot
I70.348	Atherosclerosis of unspecified type of bypass graft(s) of the left leg with ulceration of other part of lower leg
I70.341	Atherosclerosis of unspecified type of bypass graft(s) of the left leg with ulceration of thigh
I70.349	Atherosclerosis of unspecified type of bypass graft(s) of the left leg with ulceration of unspecified site
I70.333	Atherosclerosis of unspecified type of bypass graft(s) of the right leg with ulceration of ankle
I70.332	Atherosclerosis of unspecified type of bypass graft(s) of the right leg with ulceration of calf
I70.334	Atherosclerosis of unspecified type of bypass graft(s) of the right leg with ulceration of heel and midfoot
I70.338	Atherosclerosis of unspecified type of bypass graft(s) of the right leg with ulceration of other part of lower leg
I70.331	Atherosclerosis of unspecified type of bypass graft(s) of the right leg with ulceration of thigh
I70.339	Atherosclerosis of unspecified type of bypass graft(s) of the right leg with ulceration of unspecified site
I25.110	Atherosclerotic heart disease of native coronary artery with unstable angina pectoris
G80.3	Athetoid cerebral palsy
Q21.1	Atrial septal defect
I23.1	Atrial septal defect as current complication following acute myocardial infarction
I44.2	Atrioventricular block, complete
Q21.2	Atrioventricular septal defect
I48.4	Atypical atrial flutter
C92.22	Atypical chronic myeloid leukemia, BCR/ABL-negative, in relapse
C92.21	Atypical chronic myeloid leukemia, BCR/ABL-negative, in remission
C92.20	Atypical chronic myeloid leukemia, BCR/ABL-negative, not having achieved remission
M84.750A	Atypical femoral fracture, unspecified, initial encounter for fracture
M84.750P	Atypical femoral fracture, unspecified, subsequent encounter for fracture with malunion
M84.750K	Atypical femoral fracture, unspecified, subsequent encounter for fracture with nonunion
A81.9	Atypical virus infection of central nervous system, unspecified
R44.0	Auditory hallucinations
F84.0	Autistic disorder
G99.0	Autonomic neuropathy in diseases classified elsewhere
E70.311	Autosomal recessive ocular albinism
S05.72XA	Avulsion of left eye, initial encounter
S05.71XA	Avulsion of right eye, initial encounter
S05.70XA	Avulsion of unspecified eye, initial encounter
B60.0	Babesiosis
R78.81	Bacteremia
A04.9	Bacterial intestinal infection, unspecified
E78.71	Barth syndrome
S52.562A	Barton's fracture of left radius, initial encounter for closed fracture
S52.562P	Barton's fracture of left radius, subsequent encounter for closed fracture with malunion
S52.562K	Barton's fracture of left radius, subsequent encounter for closed fracture with nonunion
S52.562Q	Barton's fracture of left radius, subsequent encounter for open fracture type I or II with malunion
S52.562M	Barton's fracture of left radius, subsequent encounter for open fracture type I or II with nonunion
S52.562R	Barton's fracture of left radius, subsequent encounter for open fracture type IIIA, IIIB, or IIIC with malunion
S52.562N	Barton's fracture of left radius, subsequent encounter for open fracture type IIIA, IIIB, or IIIC with nonunion
S52.561A	Barton's fracture of right radius, initial encounter for closed fracture
S52.561P	Barton's fracture of right radius, subsequent encounter for closed fracture with malunion
S52.561K	Barton's fracture of right radius, subsequent encounter for closed fracture with nonunion
S52.561Q	Barton's fracture of right radius, subsequent encounter for open fracture type I or II with malunion
S52.561M	Barton's fracture of right radius, subsequent encounter for open fracture type I or II with nonunion
S52.561R	Barton's fracture of right radius, subsequent encounter for open fracture type IIIA, IIIB, or IIIC with malunion
S52.561N	Barton's fracture of right radius, subsequent encounter for open fracture type IIIA, IIIB, or IIIC with nonunion
S52.569A	Barton's fracture of unspecified radius, initial encounter for closed fracture
S52.569P	Barton's fracture of unspecified radius, subsequent encounter for closed fracture with malunion
S52.569K	Barton's fracture of unspecified radius, subsequent encounter for closed fracture with nonunion
S52.569Q	Barton's fracture of unspecified radius, subsequent encounter for open fracture type I or II with malunion
S52.569M	Barton's fracture of unspecified radius, subsequent encounter for open fracture type I or II with nonunion
S52.569R	Barton's fracture of unspecified radius, subsequent encounter for open fracture type IIIA, IIIB, or IIIC with malunion
S52.569N	Barton's fracture of unspecified radius, subsequent encounter for open fracture type IIIA, IIIB, or IIIC with nonunion
A44.9	Bartonellosis, unspecified
M35.2	Behcet's disease
G03.2	Benign recurrent meningitis [Mollaret]
S62.212B	Bennett's fracture, left hand, initial encounter for open fracture
S62.212P	Bennett's fracture, left hand, subsequent encounter for fracture with malunion
S62.212K	Bennett's fracture, left hand, subsequent encounter for fracture with nonunion
S62.211B	Bennett's fracture, right hand, initial encounter for open fracture
S62.211P	Bennett's fracture, right hand, subsequent encounter for fracture with malunion
S62.211K	Bennett's fracture, right hand, subsequent encounter for fracture with nonunion
S62.213B	Bennett's fracture, unspecified hand, initial encounter for open fracture
S62.213P	Bennett's fracture, unspecified hand, subsequent encounter for fracture with malunion
S62.213K	Bennett's fracture, unspecified hand, subsequent encounter for fracture with nonunion
S52.382A	Bent bone of left radius, initial encounter for closed fracture
S52.382P	Bent bone of left radius, subsequent encounter for closed fracture with malunion
S52.382K	Bent bone of left radius, subsequent encounter for closed fracture with nonunion
S52.382Q	Bent bone of left radius, subsequent encounter for open fracture type I or II with malunion
S52.382M	Bent bone of left radius, subsequent encounter for open fracture type I or II with nonunion
S52.382R	Bent bone of left radius, subsequent encounter for open fracture type IIIA, IIIB, or IIIC with malunion
S52.382N	Bent bone of left radius, subsequent encounter for open fracture type IIIA, IIIB, or IIIC with nonunion
S52.282A	Bent bone of left ulna, initial encounter for closed fracture
S52.282P	Bent bone of left ulna, subsequent encounter for closed fracture with malunion
S52.282K	Bent bone of left ulna, subsequent encounter for closed fracture with nonunion
S52.282Q	Bent bone of left ulna, subsequent encounter for open fracture type I or II with malunion
S52.282M	Bent bone of left ulna, subsequent encounter for open fracture type I or II with nonunion
S52.282R	Bent bone of left ulna, subsequent encounter for open fracture type IIIA, IIIB, or IIIC with malunion
S52.282N	Bent bone of left ulna, subsequent encounter for open fracture type IIIA, IIIB, or IIIC with nonunion
S52.381A	Bent bone of right radius, initial encounter for closed fracture
S52.381P	Bent bone of right radius, subsequent encounter for closed fracture with malunion
S52.381K	Bent bone of right radius, subsequent encounter for closed fracture with nonunion
S52.381Q	Bent bone of right radius, subsequent encounter for open fracture type I or II with malunion
S52.381M	Bent bone of right radius, subsequent encounter for open fracture type I or II with nonunion
S52.381R	Bent bone of right radius, subsequent encounter for open fracture type IIIA, IIIB, or IIIC with malunion
S52.381N	Bent bone of right radius, subsequent encounter for open fracture type IIIA, IIIB, or IIIC with nonunion
S52.281A	Bent bone of right ulna, initial encounter for closed fracture
S52.281P	Bent bone of right ulna, subsequent encounter for closed fracture with malunion
S52.281K	Bent bone of right ulna, subsequent encounter for closed fracture with nonunion
S52.281Q	Bent bone of right ulna, subsequent encounter for open fracture type I or II with malunion
S52.281M	Bent bone of right ulna, subsequent encounter for open fracture type I or II with nonunion
S52.281R	Bent bone of right ulna, subsequent encounter for open fracture type IIIA, IIIB, or IIIC with malunion
S52.281N	Bent bone of right ulna, subsequent encounter for open fracture type IIIA, IIIB, or IIIC with nonunion
S52.389A	Bent bone of unspecified radius, initial encounter for closed fracture
S52.389P	Bent bone of unspecified radius, subsequent encounter for closed fracture with malunion

S52.389K	Bent bone of unspecified radius, subsequent encounter for closed fracture with nonunion
S52.389Q	Bent bone of unspecified radius, subsequent encounter for open fracture type I or II with malunion
S52.389M	Bent bone of unspecified radius, subsequent encounter for open fracture type I or II with nonunion
S52.389R	Bent bone of unspecified radius, subsequent encounter for open fracture type IIIA, IIIB, or IIIC with malunion
S52.389N	Bent bone of unspecified radius, subsequent encounter for open fracture type IIIA, IIIB, or IIIC with nonunion
S52.283A	Bent bone of unspecified ulna, initial encounter for closed fracture
S52.283P	Bent bone of unspecified ulna, subsequent encounter for closed fracture with malunion
S52.283K	Bent bone of unspecified ulna, subsequent encounter for closed fracture with nonunion
S52.283Q	Bent bone of unspecified ulna, subsequent encounter for open fracture type I or II with malunion
S52.283M	Bent bone of unspecified ulna, subsequent encounter for open fracture type I or II with nonunion
S52.283R	Bent bone of unspecified ulna, subsequent encounter for open fracture type IIIA, IIIB, or IIIC with malunion
S52.283N	Bent bone of unspecified ulna, subsequent encounter for open fracture type IIIA, IIIB, or IIIC with nonunion
I45.2	Bifascicular block
K41.00	Bilateral femoral hernia, with obstruction, without gangrene, not specified as recurrent
K41.01	Bilateral femoral hernia, with obstruction, without gangrene, recurrent
K40.00	Bilateral inguinal hernia, with obstruction, without gangrene, not specified as recurrent
K40.01	Bilateral inguinal hernia, with obstruction, without gangrene, recurrent
F31.31	Bipolar disorder, current episode depressed, mild
F31.30	Bipolar disorder, current episode depressed, mild or moderate severity, unspecified
F31.32	Bipolar disorder, current episode depressed, moderate
F31.5	Bipolar disorder, current episode depressed, severe, with psychotic features
F31.4	Bipolar disorder, current episode depressed, severe, without psychotic features
F31.0	Bipolar disorder, current episode hypomanic
F31.2	Bipolar disorder, current episode manic severe with psychotic features
F31.11	Bipolar disorder, current episode manic without psychotic features, mild
F31.12	Bipolar disorder, current episode manic without psychotic features, moderate
F31.13	Bipolar disorder, current episode manic without psychotic features, severe
F31.10	Bipolar disorder, current episode manic without psychotic features, unspecified
F31.61	Bipolar disorder, current episode mixed, mild
F31.62	Bipolar disorder, current episode mixed, moderate
F31.64	Bipolar disorder, current episode mixed, severe, with psychotic features
F31.63	Bipolar disorder, current episode mixed, severe, without psychotic features
F31.60	Bipolar disorder, current episode mixed, unspecified
F31.81	Bipolar II disorder
C86.4	Blastic NK-cell lymphoma
B40.9	Blastomycosis, unspecified
B40.81	Blastomycotic meningoencephalitis
K90.2	Blind loop syndrome, not elsewhere classified
T80.211A	Bloodstream infection due to central venous catheter, initial encounter
Z68.1	Body mass index (BMI) 19.9 or less, adult
Z68.41	Body mass index (BMI) 40.0-44.9, adult
Z68.42	Body mass index (BMI) 45.0-49.9, adult
Z68.43	Body mass index (BMI) 50.0-59.9, adult
Z68.44	Body mass index (BMI) 60.0-69.9, adult
Z68.45	Body mass index (BMI) 70 or greater, adult
T86.831	Bone graft failure
T86.832	Bone graft infection
T86.830	Bone graft rejection
T86.02	Bone marrow transplant failure
T86.03	Bone marrow transplant infection
T86.01	Bone marrow transplant rejection
Z94.81	Bone marrow transplant status
A30.4	Borderline lepromatous leprosy
A30.3	Borderline leprosy
A30.2	Borderline tuberculoid leprosy
A05.1	Botulism food poisoning
L10.3	Brazilian pemphigus [fogo selvagem]
T82.310A	Breakdown (mechanical) of aortic (bifurcation) graft (replacement), initial encounter
T82.512A	Breakdown (mechanical) of artificial heart, initial encounter
T85.613A	Breakdown (mechanical) of artificial skin graft and decellularized allodermis, initial encounter
T82.513A	Breakdown (mechanical) of balloon (counterpulsation) device, initial encounter
T85.510A	Breakdown (mechanical) of bile duct prosthesis, initial encounter
T82.221A	Breakdown (mechanical) of biological heart valve graft, initial encounter
T85.41XA	Breakdown (mechanical) of breast prosthesis and implant, initial encounter
T82.110A	Breakdown (mechanical) of cardiac electrode, initial encounter
T82.111A	Breakdown (mechanical) of cardiac pulse generator (battery), initial encounter
T82.311A	Breakdown (mechanical) of carotid arterial graft (bypass), initial encounter
T82.211A	Breakdown (mechanical) of coronary artery bypass graft, initial encounter
T85.610A	Breakdown (mechanical) of cranial or spinal infusion catheter, initial encounter

T83.010A	Breakdown (mechanical) of cystostomy catheter, initial encounter
T84.310A	Breakdown (mechanical) of electronic bone stimulator, initial encounter
T85.511A	Breakdown (mechanical) of esophageal anti-reflux device, initial encounter
T82.312A	Breakdown (mechanical) of femoral arterial graft (bypass), initial encounter
T83.21XA	Breakdown (mechanical) of graft of urinary organ, initial encounter
T82.01XA	Breakdown (mechanical) of heart valve prosthesis, initial encounter
T85.110A	Breakdown (mechanical) of implanted electronic neurostimulator of brain electrode (lead), initial encounter
T85.111A	Breakdown (mechanical) of implanted electronic neurostimulator of peripheral nerve electrode (lead), initial encounter
T85.112A	Breakdown (mechanical) of implanted electronic neurostimulator of spinal cord electrode (lead), initial encounter
T85.113A	Breakdown (mechanical) of implanted electronic neurostimulator, generator, initial encounter
T83.410A	Breakdown (mechanical) of implanted penile prosthesis, initial encounter
T83.411A	Breakdown (mechanical) of implanted testicular prosthesis, initial encounter
T83.111A	Breakdown (mechanical) of implanted urinary sphincter, initial encounter
T83.112A	Breakdown (mechanical) of indwelling ureteral stent, initial encounter
T82.514A	Breakdown (mechanical) of infusion catheter, initial encounter
T85.614A	Breakdown (mechanical) of insulin pump, initial encounter
T84.113A	Breakdown (mechanical) of internal fixation device of bone of left forearm, initial encounter
T84.117A	Breakdown (mechanical) of internal fixation device of bone of left lower leg, initial encounter
T84.112A	Breakdown (mechanical) of internal fixation device of bone of right forearm, initial encounter
T84.116A	Breakdown (mechanical) of internal fixation device of bone of right lower leg, initial encounter
T84.213A	Breakdown (mechanical) of internal fixation device of bones of foot and toes, initial encounter
T84.210A	Breakdown (mechanical) of internal fixation device of bones of hand and fingers, initial encounter
T84.115A	Breakdown (mechanical) of internal fixation device of left femur, initial encounter
T84.111A	Breakdown (mechanical) of internal fixation device of left humerus, initial encounter
T84.218A	Breakdown (mechanical) of internal fixation device of other bones, initial encounter
T84.114A	Breakdown (mechanical) of internal fixation device of right femur, initial encounter
T84.110A	Breakdown (mechanical) of internal fixation device of right humerus, initial encounter
T84.119A	Breakdown (mechanical) of internal fixation device of unspecified bone of limb, initial encounter
T84.216A	Breakdown (mechanical) of internal fixation device of vertebrae, initial encounter
T85.21XA	Breakdown (mechanical) of intraocular lens, initial encounter
T85.611A	Breakdown (mechanical) of intraperitoneal dialysis catheter, initial encounter
T84.410A	Breakdown (mechanical) of muscle and tendon graft, initial encounter
T84.318A	Breakdown (mechanical) of other bone devices, implants and grafts, initial encounter
T82.518A	Breakdown (mechanical) of other cardiac and vascular devices and implants, initial encounter
T82.118A	Breakdown (mechanical) of other cardiac electronic device, initial encounter
T85.518A	Breakdown (mechanical) of other gastrointestinal prosthetic devices, implants and grafts, initial encounter
T85.118A	Breakdown (mechanical) of other implanted electronic stimulator of nervous system, initial encounter
T84.418A	Breakdown (mechanical) of other internal orthopedic devices, implants and grafts, initial encounter
T85.615A	Breakdown (mechanical) of other nervous system device, implant or graft, initial encounter
T83.418A	Breakdown (mechanical) of other prosthetic devices, implants and grafts of genital tract, initial encounter
T85.618A	Breakdown (mechanical) of other specified internal prosthetic devices, implants and grafts, initial encounter
T83.118A	Breakdown (mechanical) of other urinary devices and implants, initial encounter
T83.113A	Breakdown (mechanical) of other urinary stents, initial encounter
T82.318A	Breakdown (mechanical) of other vascular grafts, initial encounter
T85.612A	Breakdown (mechanical) of permanent sutures, initial encounter
T85.311A	Breakdown (mechanical) of prosthetic orbit of left eye, initial encounter
T85.310A	Breakdown (mechanical) of prosthetic orbit of right eye, initial encounter
T82.510A	Breakdown (mechanical) of surgically created arteriovenous fistula, initial encounter
T82.511A	Breakdown (mechanical) of surgically created arteriovenous shunt, initial encounter
T82.515A	Breakdown (mechanical) of umbrella device, initial encounter
T82.519A	Breakdown (mechanical) of unspecified cardiac and vascular devices and implants, initial encounter
T82.119A	Breakdown (mechanical) of unspecified cardiac electronic device, initial encounter
T82.319A	Breakdown (mechanical) of unspecified vascular grafts, initial encounter
T83.110A	Breakdown (mechanical) of urinary electronic stimulator device, initial encounter
T82.41XA	Breakdown (mechanical) of vascular dialysis catheter, initial encounter
T85.01XA	Breakdown (mechanical) of ventricular intracranial (communicating) shunt, initial encounter
F23	Brief psychotic disorder
T84.018A	Broken internal joint prosthesis, other site, initial encounter

T84.019A	Broken internal joint prosthesis, unspecified site, initial encounter
T84.011A	Broken internal left hip prosthesis, initial encounter
T84.013A	Broken internal left knee prosthesis, initial encounter
T84.010A	Broken internal right hip prosthesis, initial encounter
T84.012A	Broken internal right knee prosthesis, initial encounter
J47.1	Bronchiectasis with (acute) exacerbation
J47.0	Bronchiectasis with acute lower respiratory infection
J68.0	Bronchitis and pneumonitis due to chemicals, gases, fumes and vapors
A23.9	Brucellosis, unspecified
F50.2	Bulimia nervosa
L12.0	Bullous pemphigoid
C83.79	Burkitt lymphoma, extranodal and solid organ sites
C83.73	Burkitt lymphoma, intra-abdominal lymph nodes
C83.76	Burkitt lymphoma, intrapelvic lymph nodes
C83.72	Burkitt lymphoma, intrathoracic lymph nodes
C83.74	Burkitt lymphoma, lymph nodes of axilla and upper limb
C83.71	Burkitt lymphoma, lymph nodes of head, face, and neck
C83.75	Burkitt lymphoma, lymph nodes of inguinal region and lower limb
C83.78	Burkitt lymphoma, lymph nodes of multiple sites
C83.77	Burkitt lymphoma, spleen
C83.70	Burkitt lymphoma, unspecified site
T27.1XXA	Burn involving larynx and trachea with lung, initial encounter
T28.1XXA	Burn of esophagus, initial encounter
T27.0XXA	Burn of larynx and trachea, initial encounter
T28.2XXA	Burn of other parts of alimentary tract, initial encounter
T27.2XXA	Burn of other parts of respiratory tract, initial encounter
T27.3XXA	Burn of respiratory tract, part unspecified, initial encounter
T21.32XA	Burn of third degree of abdominal wall, initial encounter
T23.362A	Burn of third degree of back of left hand, initial encounter
T23.361A	Burn of third degree of back of right hand, initial encounter
T23.369A	Burn of third degree of back of unspecified hand, initial encounter
T21.35XA	Burn of third degree of buttock, initial encounter
T21.31XA	Burn of third degree of chest wall, initial encounter
T20.33XA	Burn of third degree of chin, initial encounter
T21.37XA	Burn of third degree of female genital region, initial encounter
T20.36XA	Burn of third degree of forehead and cheek, initial encounter
T20.30XA	Burn of third degree of head, face, and neck, unspecified site, initial encounter
T25.312A	Burn of third degree of left ankle, initial encounter
T22.342A	Burn of third degree of left axilla, initial encounter
T20.312A	Burn of third degree of left ear [any part, except ear drum], initial encounter
T22.322A	Burn of third degree of left elbow, initial encounter
T25.322A	Burn of third degree of left foot, initial encounter
T22.312A	Burn of third degree of left forearm, initial encounter
T23.302A	Burn of third degree of left hand, unspecified site, initial encounter
T24.322A	Burn of third degree of left knee, initial encounter
T24.332A	Burn of third degree of left lower leg, initial encounter
T23.352A	Burn of third degree of left palm, initial encounter
T22.362A	Burn of third degree of left scapular region, initial encounter
T22.352A	Burn of third degree of left shoulder, initial encounter
T24.312A	Burn of third degree of left thigh, initial encounter
T23.312A	Burn of third degree of left thumb (nail), initial encounter
T25.332A	Burn of third degree of left toe(s) (nail), initial encounter
T22.332A	Burn of third degree of left upper arm, initial encounter
T23.372A	Burn of third degree of left wrist, initial encounter
T20.32XA	Burn of third degree of lip(s), initial encounter
T21.34XA	Burn of third degree of lower back, initial encounter
T21.36XA	Burn of third degree of male genital region, initial encounter
T23.342A	Burn of third degree of multiple left fingers (nail), including thumb, initial encounter
T23.332A	Burn of third degree of multiple left fingers (nail), not including thumb, initial encounter
T23.341A	Burn of third degree of multiple right fingers (nail), including thumb, initial encounter
T23.331A	Burn of third degree of multiple right fingers (nail), not including thumb, initial encounter
T20.39XA	Burn of third degree of multiple sites of head, face, and neck, initial encounter
T25.392A	Burn of third degree of multiple sites of left ankle and foot, initial encounter
T24.392A	Burn of third degree of multiple sites of left lower limb, except ankle and foot, initial encounter
T22.392A	Burn of third degree of multiple sites of left shoulder and upper limb, except wrist and hand, initial encounter
T23.392A	Burn of third degree of multiple sites of left wrist and hand, initial encounter
T25.391A	Burn of third degree of multiple sites of right ankle and foot, initial encounter
T24.391A	Burn of third degree of multiple sites of right lower limb, except ankle and foot, initial encounter
T22.391A	Burn of third degree of multiple sites of right shoulder and upper limb, except wrist and hand, initial encounter
T23.391A	Burn of third degree of multiple sites of right wrist and hand, initial encounter
T25.399A	Burn of third degree of multiple sites of unspecified ankle and foot, initial encounter
T24.399A	Burn of third degree of multiple sites of unspecified lower limb, except ankle and foot, initial encounter
T22.399A	Burn of third degree of multiple sites of unspecified shoulder and upper limb, except wrist and hand, initial encounter
T23.399A	Burn of third degree of multiple sites of unspecified wrist and hand, initial encounter
T20.37XA	Burn of third degree of neck, initial encounter
T20.34XA	Burn of third degree of nose (septum), initial encounter
T21.39XA	Burn of third degree of other site of trunk, initial encounter

T25.311A	Burn of third degree of right ankle, initial encounter
T22.341A	Burn of third degree of right axilla, initial encounter
T20.311A	Burn of third degree of right ear [any part, except ear drum], initial encounter
T22.321A	Burn of third degree of right elbow, initial encounter
T25.321A	Burn of third degree of right foot, initial encounter
T22.311A	Burn of third degree of right forearm, initial encounter
T23.301A	Burn of third degree of right hand, unspecified site, initial encounter
T24.321A	Burn of third degree of right knee, initial encounter
T24.331A	Burn of third degree of right lower leg, initial encounter
T23.351A	Burn of third degree of right palm, initial encounter
T22.361A	Burn of third degree of right scapular region, initial encounter
T22.351A	Burn of third degree of right shoulder, initial encounter
T24.311A	Burn of third degree of right thigh, initial encounter
T23.311A	Burn of third degree of right thumb (nail), initial encounter
T25.331A	Burn of third degree of right toe(s) (nail), initial encounter
T22.331A	Burn of third degree of right upper arm, initial encounter
T23.371A	Burn of third degree of right wrist, initial encounter
T20.35XA	Burn of third degree of scalp [any part], initial encounter
T22.30XA	Burn of third degree of shoulder and upper limb, except wrist and hand, unspecified site, initial encounter
T23.322A	Burn of third degree of single left finger (nail) except thumb, initial encounter
T23.321A	Burn of third degree of single right finger (nail) except thumb, initial encounter
T21.30XA	Burn of third degree of trunk, unspecified site, initial encounter
T25.319A	Burn of third degree of unspecified ankle, initial encounter
T22.349A	Burn of third degree of unspecified axilla, initial encounter
T20.319A	Burn of third degree of unspecified ear [any part, except ear drum], initial encounter
T22.329A	Burn of third degree of unspecified elbow, initial encounter
T25.329A	Burn of third degree of unspecified foot, initial encounter
T22.319A	Burn of third degree of unspecified forearm, initial encounter
T23.309A	Burn of third degree of unspecified hand, unspecified site, initial encounter
T24.329A	Burn of third degree of unspecified knee, initial encounter
T24.339A	Burn of third degree of unspecified lower leg, initial encounter
T23.349A	Burn of third degree of unspecified multiple fingers (nail), including thumb, initial encounter
T23.339A	Burn of third degree of unspecified multiple fingers (nail), not including thumb, initial encounter
T23.359A	Burn of third degree of unspecified palm, initial encounter
T22.369A	Burn of third degree of unspecified scapular region, initial encounter
T22.359A	Burn of third degree of unspecified shoulder, initial encounter
T23.329A	Burn of third degree of unspecified single finger (nail) except thumb, initial encounter
T24.302A	Burn of third degree of unspecified site of left lower limb, except ankle and foot, initial encounter
T24.301A	Burn of third degree of unspecified site of right lower limb, except ankle and foot, initial encounter
T24.309A	Burn of third degree of unspecified site of unspecified lower limb, except ankle and foot, initial encounter
T24.319A	Burn of third degree of unspecified thigh, initial encounter
T23.319A	Burn of third degree of unspecified thumb (nail), initial encounter
T25.339A	Burn of third degree of unspecified toe(s) (nail), initial encounter
T22.339A	Burn of third degree of unspecified upper arm, initial encounter
T23.379A	Burn of third degree of unspecified wrist, initial encounter
T21.33XA	Burn of third degree of upper back, initial encounter
T26.22XA	Burn with resulting rupture and destruction of left eyeball, initial encounter
T26.21XA	Burn with resulting rupture and destruction of right eyeball, initial encounter
T26.20XA	Burn with resulting rupture and destruction of unspecified eyeball, initial encounter
T31.10	Burns involving 10-19% of body surface with 0% to 9% third degree burns
T31.11	Burns involving 10-19% of body surface with 10-19% third degree burns
T31.20	Burns involving 20-29% of body surface with 0% to 9% third degree burns
T31.30	Burns involving 30-39% of body surface with 0% to 9% third degree burns
T31.40	Burns involving 40-49% of body surface with 0% to 9% third degree burns
T31.50	Burns involving 50-59% of body surface with 0% to 9% third degree burns
T31.60	Burns involving 60-69% of body surface with 0% to 9% third degree burns
T31.70	Burns involving 70-79% of body surface with 0% to 9% third degree burns
T31.80	Burns involving 80-89% of body surface with 0% to 9% third degree burns
T31.90	Burns involving 90% or more of body surface with 0% to 9% third degree burns
R64	Cachexia
T70.3XXA	Caisson disease [decompression sickness], initial encounter
K80.37	Calculus of bile duct with acute and chronic cholangitis with obstruction
K80.36	Calculus of bile duct with acute and chronic cholangitis without obstruction
K80.47	Calculus of bile duct with acute and chronic cholecystitis with obstruction
K80.46	Calculus of bile duct with acute and chronic cholecystitis without obstruction
K80.33	Calculus of bile duct with acute cholangitis with obstruction
K80.32	Calculus of bile duct with acute cholangitis without obstruction
K80.43	Calculus of bile duct with acute cholecystitis with obstruction
K80.42	Calculus of bile duct with acute cholecystitis without obstruction
K80.31	Calculus of bile duct with cholangitis, unspecified, with obstruction
K80.30	Calculus of bile duct with cholangitis, unspecified, without obstruction
K80.41	Calculus of bile duct with cholecystitis, unspecified, with obstruction
K80.40	Calculus of bile duct with cholecystitis, unspecified, without obstruction
K80.35	Calculus of bile duct with chronic cholangitis with obstruction
K80.34	Calculus of bile duct with chronic cholangitis without obstruction
K80.45	Calculus of bile duct with chronic cholecystitis with obstruction
K80.44	Calculus of bile duct with chronic cholecystitis without obstruction
K80.51	Calculus of bile duct without cholangitis or cholecystitis with obstruction

K80.66	Calculus of gallbladder and bile duct with acute and chronic cholecystitis without obstruction
K80.63	Calculus of gallbladder and bile duct with acute cholecystitis with obstruction
K80.62	Calculus of gallbladder and bile duct with acute cholecystitis without obstruction
K80.61	Calculus of gallbladder and bile duct with cholecystitis, unspecified, with obstruction
K80.60	Calculus of gallbladder and bile duct with cholecystitis, unspecified, without obstruction
K80.65	Calculus of gallbladder and bile duct with chronic cholecystitis with obstruction
K80.64	Calculus of gallbladder and bile duct with chronic cholecystitis without obstruction
K80.71	Calculus of gallbladder and bile duct without cholecystitis with obstruction
K80.13	Calculus of gallbladder with acute and chronic cholecystitis with obstruction
K80.12	Calculus of gallbladder with acute and chronic cholecystitis without obstruction
K80.01	Calculus of gallbladder with acute cholecystitis with obstruction
K80.00	Calculus of gallbladder with acute cholecystitis without obstruction
K80.11	Calculus of gallbladder with chronic cholecystitis with obstruction
K80.10	Calculus of gallbladder with chronic cholecystitis without obstruction
K80.19	Calculus of gallbladder with other cholecystitis with obstruction
K80.18	Calculus of gallbladder with other cholecystitis without obstruction
K80.21	Calculus of gallbladder without cholecystitis with obstruction
N20.2	Calculus of kidney with calculus of ureter
N20.1	Calculus of ureter
A08.31	Calicivirus enteritis
A04.5	Campylobacter enteritis
B37.83	Candidal cheilitis
B37.41	Candidal cystitis and urethritis
B37.82	Candidal enteritis
B37.81	Candidal esophagitis
B37.84	Candidal otitis externa
B37.0	Candidal stomatitis
F12.121	Cannabis abuse with intoxication delirium
F12.150	Cannabis abuse with psychotic disorder with delusions
F12.151	Cannabis abuse with psychotic disorder with hallucinations
F12.221	Cannabis dependence with intoxication delirium
F12.250	Cannabis dependence with psychotic disorder with delusions
F12.251	Cannabis dependence with psychotic disorder with hallucinations
F12.921	Cannabis use, unspecified with intoxication delirium
F12.950	Cannabis use, unspecified with psychotic disorder with delusions
F12.951	Cannabis use, unspecified with psychotic disorder with hallucinations
T85.44XA	Capsular contracture of breast implant, initial encounter
E34.0	Carcinoid syndrome
T86.290	Cardiac allograft vasculopathy
O04.86	Cardiac arrest following (induced) termination of pregnancy
O08.81	Cardiac arrest following an ectopic and molar pregnancy
O03.86	Cardiac arrest following complete or unspecified spontaneous abortion
O07.36	Cardiac arrest following failed attempted termination of pregnancy
O03.36	Cardiac arrest following incomplete spontaneous abortion
I51.0	Cardiac septal defect, acquired
I31.4	Cardiac tamponade
I42.7	Cardiomyopathy due to drug and external agent
I43	Cardiomyopathy in diseases classified elsewhere
I42.9	Cardiomyopathy, unspecified
A52.00	Cardiovascular syphilis, unspecified
G45.1	Carotid artery syndrome (hemispheric)
D47.Z2	Castleman disease
A28.1	Cat-scratch disease
F20.2	Catatonic schizophrenia
G83.4	Cauda equina syndrome
Q62.32	Cecoureterocele
I77.4	Celiac artery compression syndrome
K12.2	Cellulitis and abscess of mouth
L03.311	Cellulitis of abdominal wall
L03.312	Cellulitis of back [any part except buttock]
H05.013	Cellulitis of bilateral orbits
L03.317	Cellulitis of buttock
L03.313	Cellulitis of chest wall
L03.211	Cellulitis of face
L03.314	Cellulitis of groin
L03.811	Cellulitis of head [any part, except face]
L03.112	Cellulitis of left axilla
L03.116	Cellulitis of left lower limb
H05.012	Cellulitis of left orbit
L03.114	Cellulitis of left upper limb
L03.221	Cellulitis of neck
L03.818	Cellulitis of other sites
L03.315	Cellulitis of perineum
L03.111	Cellulitis of right axilla
L03.115	Cellulitis of right lower limb
H05.011	Cellulitis of right orbit
L03.113	Cellulitis of right upper limb
L03.319	Cellulitis of trunk, unspecified
L03.316	Cellulitis of umbilicus
H05.019	Cellulitis of unspecified orbit
L03.119	Cellulitis of unspecified part of limb
L03.90	Cellulitis, unspecified
G37.1	Central demyelination of corpus callosum
S73.045A	Central dislocation of left hip, initial encounter
S73.044A	Central dislocation of right hip, initial encounter
S73.046A	Central dislocation of unspecified hip, initial encounter
G37.2	Central pontine myelinolysis
H34.13	Central retinal artery occlusion, bilateral
H34.12	Central retinal artery occlusion, left eye
H34.11	Central retinal artery occlusion, right eye
H34.10	Central retinal artery occlusion, unspecified eye
H34.8132	Central retinal vein occlusion, bilateral, stable
H34.8130	Central retinal vein occlusion, bilateral, with macular edema
H34.8131	Central retinal vein occlusion, bilateral, with retinal neovascularization
H34.8122	Central retinal vein occlusion, left eye, stable
H34.8120	Central retinal vein occlusion, left eye, with macular edema
H34.8121	Central retinal vein occlusion, left eye, with retinal neovascularization
H34.8112	Central retinal vein occlusion, right eye, stable
H34.8110	Central retinal vein occlusion, right eye, with macular edema
H34.8111	Central retinal vein occlusion, right eye, with retinal neovascularization
H34.8192	Central retinal vein occlusion, unspecified eye, stable
H34.8190	Central retinal vein occlusion, unspecified eye, with macular edema
H34.8191	Central retinal vein occlusion, unspecified eye, with retinal neovascularization
S73.042A	Central subluxation of left hip, initial encounter
S73.041A	Central subluxation of right hip, initial encounter
S73.043A	Central subluxation of unspecified hip, initial encounter
B65.3	Cercarial dermatitis
G32.81	Cerebellar ataxia in diseases classified elsewhere
G11.3	Cerebellar ataxia with defective DNA repair
I68.2	Cerebral arteritis in other diseases classified elsewhere
I67.7	Cerebral arteritis, not elsewhere classified
I67.850	Cerebral autosomal dominant arteriopathy with subcortical infarcts and leukoencephalopathy
I67.82	Cerebral ischemia
O22.51	Cerebral venous thrombosis in pregnancy, first trimester
O22.52	Cerebral venous thrombosis in pregnancy, second trimester
O22.53	Cerebral venous thrombosis in pregnancy, third trimester
O22.50	Cerebral venous thrombosis in pregnancy, unspecified trimester
O87.3	Cerebral venous thrombosis in the puerperium
G96.0	Cerebrospinal fluid leak
G97.0	Cerebrospinal fluid leak from spinal puncture
M50.021	Cervical disc disorder at C4-C5 level with myelopathy
M50.022	Cervical disc disorder at C5-C6 level with myelopathy
M50.023	Cervical disc disorder at C6-C7 level with myelopathy
M50.03	Cervical disc disorder with myelopathy, cervicothoracic region
M50.01	Cervical disc disorder with myelopathy, high cervical region
M50.020	Cervical disc disorder with myelopathy, mid-cervical region, unspecified level
M50.00	Cervical disc disorder with myelopathy, unspecified cervical region
O26.872	Cervical shortening, second trimester
O26.873	Cervical shortening, third trimester
O26.879	Cervical shortening, unspecified trimester
Q05.0	Cervical spina bifida with hydrocephalus
O86.11	Cervicitis following delivery
A42.2	Cervicofacial actinomycosis
B57.2	Chagas' disease (chronic) with heart involvement
B57.5	Chagas' disease (chronic) with other organ involvement
B57.30	Chagas' disease with digestive system involvement, unspecified
B57.40	Chagas' disease with nervous system involvement, unspecified
A52.16	Charcot's arthropathy (tabetic)
E70.330	Chediak-Higashi syndrome
J95.4	Chemical pneumonitis due to anesthesia
A92.0	Chikungunya virus disease
T74.62XA	Child forced labor exploitation, confirmed, initial encounter
T76.62XA	Child forced labor exploitation, suspected, initial encounter
T74.02XA	Child neglect or abandonment, confirmed, initial encounter
T76.02XA	Child neglect or abandonment, suspected, initial encounter
T74.12XA	Child physical abuse, confirmed, initial encounter
T76.12XA	Child physical abuse, suspected, initial encounter
T74.32XA	Child psychological abuse, confirmed, initial encounter
T76.32XA	Child psychological abuse, suspected, initial encounter
T74.22XA	Child sexual abuse, confirmed, initial encounter
T76.22XA	Child sexual abuse, suspected, initial encounter
T74.52XA	Child sexual exploitation, confirmed, initial encounter
T76.52XA	Child sexual exploitation, suspected, initial encounter
E71.520	Childhood cerebral X-linked adrenoleukodystrophy
A70	Chlamydia psittaci infections
Q44.4	Choledochal cyst
A00.0	Cholera due to Vibrio cholerae 01, biovar cholerae
A00.1	Cholera due to Vibrio cholerae 01, biovar eltor
A00.9	Cholera, unspecified
H59.813	Chorioretinal scars after surgery for detachment, bilateral
H59.812	Chorioretinal scars after surgery for detachment, left eye
H59.811	Chorioretinal scars after surgery for detachment, right eye
H59.819	Chorioretinal scars after surgery for detachment, unspecified eye
H31.323	Choroidal rupture, bilateral
H31.322	Choroidal rupture, left eye
H31.321	Choroidal rupture, right eye
H31.329	Choroidal rupture, unspecified eye
I31.0	Chronic adhesive pericarditis
J70.1	Chronic and other pulmonary manifestations due to radiation

I48.20	Chronic atrial fibrillation, unspecified
I50.42	Chronic combined systolic (congestive) and diastolic (congestive) heart failure
I31.1	Chronic constrictive pericarditis
I50.32	Chronic diastolic (congestive) heart failure
I82.A23	Chronic embolism and thrombosis of axillary vein, bilateral
I82.722	Chronic embolism and thrombosis of deep veins of left upper extremity
I82.721	Chronic embolism and thrombosis of deep veins of right upper extremity
I82.729	Chronic embolism and thrombosis of deep veins of unspecified upper extremity
I82.723	Chronic embolism and thrombosis of deep veins of upper extremity, bilateral
I82.513	Chronic embolism and thrombosis of femoral vein, bilateral
I82.523	Chronic embolism and thrombosis of iliac vein, bilateral
I82.C23	Chronic embolism and thrombosis of internal jugular vein, bilateral
I82.A22	Chronic embolism and thrombosis of left axillary vein
I82.512	Chronic embolism and thrombosis of left femoral vein
I82.522	Chronic embolism and thrombosis of left iliac vein
I82.C22	Chronic embolism and thrombosis of left internal jugular vein
I82.552	Chronic embolism and thrombosis of left peroneal vein
I82.532	Chronic embolism and thrombosis of left popliteal vein
I82.B22	Chronic embolism and thrombosis of left subclavian vein
I82.542	Chronic embolism and thrombosis of left tibial vein
I82.592	Chronic embolism and thrombosis of other specified deep vein of left lower extremity
I82.593	Chronic embolism and thrombosis of other specified deep vein of lower extremity, bilateral
I82.591	Chronic embolism and thrombosis of other specified deep vein of right lower extremity
I82.599	Chronic embolism and thrombosis of other specified deep vein of unspecified lower extremity
I82.891	Chronic embolism and thrombosis of other specified veins
I82.291	Chronic embolism and thrombosis of other thoracic veins
I82.553	Chronic embolism and thrombosis of peroneal vein, bilateral
I82.533	Chronic embolism and thrombosis of popliteal vein, bilateral
I82.A21	Chronic embolism and thrombosis of right axillary vein
I82.511	Chronic embolism and thrombosis of right femoral vein
I82.521	Chronic embolism and thrombosis of right iliac vein
I82.C21	Chronic embolism and thrombosis of right internal jugular vein
I82.551	Chronic embolism and thrombosis of right peroneal vein
I82.531	Chronic embolism and thrombosis of right popliteal vein
I82.B21	Chronic embolism and thrombosis of right subclavian vein
I82.541	Chronic embolism and thrombosis of right tibial vein
I82.B23	Chronic embolism and thrombosis of subclavian vein, bilateral
I82.712	Chronic embolism and thrombosis of superficial veins of left upper extremity
I82.711	Chronic embolism and thrombosis of superficial veins of right upper extremity
I82.719	Chronic embolism and thrombosis of superficial veins of unspecified upper extremity
I82.713	Chronic embolism and thrombosis of superficial veins of upper extremity, bilateral
I82.211	Chronic embolism and thrombosis of superior vena cava
I82.543	Chronic embolism and thrombosis of tibial vein, bilateral
I82.A29	Chronic embolism and thrombosis of unspecified axillary vein
I82.5Z3	Chronic embolism and thrombosis of unspecified deep veins of distal lower extremity, bilateral
I82.5Z2	Chronic embolism and thrombosis of unspecified deep veins of left distal lower extremity
I82.502	Chronic embolism and thrombosis of unspecified deep veins of left lower extremity
I82.5Y2	Chronic embolism and thrombosis of unspecified deep veins of left proximal lower extremity
I82.503	Chronic embolism and thrombosis of unspecified deep veins of lower extremity, bilateral
I82.5Y3	Chronic embolism and thrombosis of unspecified deep veins of proximal lower extremity, bilateral
I82.5Z1	Chronic embolism and thrombosis of unspecified deep veins of right distal lower extremity
I82.501	Chronic embolism and thrombosis of unspecified deep veins of right lower extremity
I82.5Y1	Chronic embolism and thrombosis of unspecified deep veins of right proximal lower extremity
I82.5Z9	Chronic embolism and thrombosis of unspecified deep veins of unspecified distal lower extremity
I82.509	Chronic embolism and thrombosis of unspecified deep veins of unspecified lower extremity
I82.5Y9	Chronic embolism and thrombosis of unspecified deep veins of unspecified proximal lower extremity
I82.519	Chronic embolism and thrombosis of unspecified femoral vein
I82.529	Chronic embolism and thrombosis of unspecified iliac vein
I82.C29	Chronic embolism and thrombosis of unspecified internal jugular vein
I82.559	Chronic embolism and thrombosis of unspecified peroneal vein
I82.539	Chronic embolism and thrombosis of unspecified popliteal vein
I82.B29	Chronic embolism and thrombosis of unspecified subclavian vein
I82.549	Chronic embolism and thrombosis of unspecified tibial vein
I82.91	Chronic embolism and thrombosis of unspecified vein
I82.702	Chronic embolism and thrombosis of unspecified veins of left upper extremity
I82.701	Chronic embolism and thrombosis of unspecified veins of right upper extremity
I82.709	Chronic embolism and thrombosis of unspecified veins of unspecified upper extremity
I82.703	Chronic embolism and thrombosis of unspecified veins of upper extremity, bilateral
D89.811	Chronic graft-versus-host disease
G61.81	Chronic inflammatory demyelinating polyneuritis
A06.1	Chronic intestinal amebiasis
N18.4	Chronic kidney disease, stage 4 (severe)
N18.5	Chronic kidney disease, stage 5
C95.10	Chronic leukemia of unspecified cell type not having achieved remission
C95.12	Chronic leukemia of unspecified cell type, in relapse
C95.11	Chronic leukemia of unspecified cell type, in remission
C91.12	Chronic lymphocytic leukemia of B-cell type in relapse
C91.11	Chronic lymphocytic leukemia of B-cell type in remission
C91.10	Chronic lymphocytic leukemia of B-cell type not having achieved remission
G03.1	Chronic meningitis
M86.372	Chronic multifocal osteomyelitis, left ankle and foot
M86.352	Chronic multifocal osteomyelitis, left femur
M86.342	Chronic multifocal osteomyelitis, left hand
M86.322	Chronic multifocal osteomyelitis, left humerus
M86.332	Chronic multifocal osteomyelitis, left radius and ulna
M86.312	Chronic multifocal osteomyelitis, left shoulder
M86.362	Chronic multifocal osteomyelitis, left tibia and fibula
M86.39	Chronic multifocal osteomyelitis, multiple sites
M86.38	Chronic multifocal osteomyelitis, other site
M86.371	Chronic multifocal osteomyelitis, right ankle and foot
M86.351	Chronic multifocal osteomyelitis, right femur
M86.341	Chronic multifocal osteomyelitis, right hand
M86.321	Chronic multifocal osteomyelitis, right humerus
M86.331	Chronic multifocal osteomyelitis, right radius and ulna
M86.311	Chronic multifocal osteomyelitis, right shoulder
M86.361	Chronic multifocal osteomyelitis, right tibia and fibula
M86.379	Chronic multifocal osteomyelitis, unspecified ankle and foot
M86.359	Chronic multifocal osteomyelitis, unspecified femur
M86.349	Chronic multifocal osteomyelitis, unspecified hand
M86.329	Chronic multifocal osteomyelitis, unspecified humerus
M86.339	Chronic multifocal osteomyelitis, unspecified radius and ulna
M86.319	Chronic multifocal osteomyelitis, unspecified shoulder
M86.30	Chronic multifocal osteomyelitis, unspecified site
M86.369	Chronic multifocal osteomyelitis, unspecified tibia and fibula
C92.12	Chronic myeloid leukemia, BCR/ABL-positive, in relapse
C92.11	Chronic myeloid leukemia, BCR/ABL-positive, in remission
C92.10	Chronic myeloid leukemia, BCR/ABL-positive, not having achieved remission
C93.10	Chronic myelomonocytic leukemia not having achieved remission
C93.12	Chronic myelomonocytic leukemia, in relapse
C93.11	Chronic myelomonocytic leukemia, in remission
D47.1	Chronic myeloproliferative disease
N03.6	Chronic nephritic syndrome with dense deposit disease
N03.7	Chronic nephritic syndrome with diffuse crescentic glomerulonephritis
N03.4	Chronic nephritic syndrome with diffuse endocapillary proliferative glomerulonephritis
N03.2	Chronic nephritic syndrome with diffuse membranous glomerulonephritis
N03.3	Chronic nephritic syndrome with diffuse mesangial proliferative glomerulonephritis
N03.5	Chronic nephritic syndrome with diffuse mesangiocapillary glomerulonephritis
N03.1	Chronic nephritic syndrome with focal and segmental glomerular lesions
N03.0	Chronic nephritic syndrome with minor glomerular abnormality
N03.8	Chronic nephritic syndrome with other morphologic changes
N03.9	Chronic nephritic syndrome with unspecified morphologic changes
J44.1	Chronic obstructive pulmonary disease with (acute) exacerbation
J44.0	Chronic obstructive pulmonary disease with (acute) lower respiratory infection
N11.1	Chronic obstructive pyelonephritis
M86.472	Chronic osteomyelitis with draining sinus, left ankle and foot
M86.452	Chronic osteomyelitis with draining sinus, left femur
M86.442	Chronic osteomyelitis with draining sinus, left hand
M86.422	Chronic osteomyelitis with draining sinus, left humerus
M86.432	Chronic osteomyelitis with draining sinus, left radius and ulna
M86.412	Chronic osteomyelitis with draining sinus, left shoulder
M86.462	Chronic osteomyelitis with draining sinus, left tibia and fibula
M86.49	Chronic osteomyelitis with draining sinus, multiple sites
M86.48	Chronic osteomyelitis with draining sinus, other site
M86.471	Chronic osteomyelitis with draining sinus, right ankle and foot
M86.451	Chronic osteomyelitis with draining sinus, right femur
M86.441	Chronic osteomyelitis with draining sinus, right hand
M86.421	Chronic osteomyelitis with draining sinus, right humerus
M86.431	Chronic osteomyelitis with draining sinus, right radius and ulna
M86.411	Chronic osteomyelitis with draining sinus, right shoulder
M86.461	Chronic osteomyelitis with draining sinus, right tibia and fibula
M86.479	Chronic osteomyelitis with draining sinus, unspecified ankle and foot
M86.459	Chronic osteomyelitis with draining sinus, unspecified femur
M86.449	Chronic osteomyelitis with draining sinus, unspecified hand
M86.429	Chronic osteomyelitis with draining sinus, unspecified humerus
M86.439	Chronic osteomyelitis with draining sinus, unspecified radius and ulna
M86.419	Chronic osteomyelitis with draining sinus, unspecified shoulder
M86.40	Chronic osteomyelitis with draining sinus, unspecified site
M86.469	Chronic osteomyelitis with draining sinus, unspecified tibia and fibula
J93.81	Chronic pneumothorax

B40.1	Chronic pulmonary blastomycosis
B38.1	Chronic pulmonary coccidioidomycosis
J81.1	Chronic pulmonary edema
I27.82	Chronic pulmonary embolism
J96.12	Chronic respiratory failure with hypercapnia
J96.11	Chronic respiratory failure with hypoxia
J96.10	Chronic respiratory failure, unspecified whether with hypoxia or hypercapnia
I09.2	Chronic rheumatic pericarditis
I50.22	Chronic systolic (congestive) heart failure
I70.92	Chronic total occlusion of artery of the extremities
N11.9	Chronic tubulo-interstitial nephritis, unspecified
K55.1	Chronic vascular disorders of intestine
I87.333	Chronic venous hypertension (idiopathic) with ulcer and inflammation of bilateral lower extremity
I87.332	Chronic venous hypertension (idiopathic) with ulcer and inflammation of left lower extremity
I87.331	Chronic venous hypertension (idiopathic) with ulcer and inflammation of right lower extremity
I87.339	Chronic venous hypertension (idiopathic) with ulcer and inflammation of unspecified lower extremity
I87.313	Chronic venous hypertension (idiopathic) with ulcer of bilateral lower extremity
I87.312	Chronic venous hypertension (idiopathic) with ulcer of left lower extremity
I87.311	Chronic venous hypertension (idiopathic) with ulcer of right lower extremity
I87.319	Chronic venous hypertension (idiopathic) with ulcer of unspecified lower extremity
B18.0	Chronic viral hepatitis B with delta-agent
B18.1	Chronic viral hepatitis B without delta-agent
B18.9	Chronic viral hepatitis, unspecified
J94.0	Chylous effusion
R82.0	Chyluria
E72.23	Citrullinemia
Q79.61	Classical Ehlers-Danlos syndrome
E70.0	Classical phenylketonuria
Q64.12	Cloacal exstrophy of urinary bladder
B66.1	Clonorchiasis
A50.51	Clutton's joints
D68.9	Coagulation defect, unspecified
Q25.1	Coarctation of aorta
F14.150	Cocaine abuse with cocaine-induced psychotic disorder with delusions
F14.151	Cocaine abuse with cocaine-induced psychotic disorder with hallucinations
F14.121	Cocaine abuse with intoxication with delirium
F14.280	Cocaine dependence with cocaine-induced anxiety disorder
F14.250	Cocaine dependence with cocaine-induced psychotic disorder with delusions
F14.251	Cocaine dependence with cocaine-induced psychotic disorder with hallucinations
F14.259	Cocaine dependence with cocaine-induced psychotic disorder, unspecified
F14.281	Cocaine dependence with cocaine-induced sexual dysfunction
F14.282	Cocaine dependence with cocaine-induced sleep disorder
F14.221	Cocaine dependence with intoxication delirium
F14.222	Cocaine dependence with intoxication with perceptual disturbance
F14.229	Cocaine dependence with intoxication, unspecified
F14.288	Cocaine dependence with other cocaine-induced disorder
F14.23	Cocaine dependence with withdrawal
F14.20	Cocaine dependence, uncomplicated
F14.950	Cocaine use, unspecified with cocaine-induced psychotic disorder with delusions
F14.951	Cocaine use, unspecified with cocaine-induced psychotic disorder with hallucinations
F14.921	Cocaine use, unspecified with intoxication delirium
B38.9	Coccidioidomycosis, unspecified
M48.52XA	Collapsed vertebra, not elsewhere classified, cervical region, initial encounter for fracture
M48.53XA	Collapsed vertebra, not elsewhere classified, cervicothoracic region, initial encounter for fracture
M48.56XA	Collapsed vertebra, not elsewhere classified, lumbar region, initial encounter for fracture
M48.57XA	Collapsed vertebra, not elsewhere classified, lumbosacral region, initial encounter for fracture
M48.51XA	Collapsed vertebra, not elsewhere classified, occipito-atlanto-axial region, initial encounter for fracture
M48.58XA	Collapsed vertebra, not elsewhere classified, sacral and sacrococcygeal region, initial encounter for fracture
M48.50XA	Collapsed vertebra, not elsewhere classified, site unspecified, initial encounter for fracture
M48.54XA	Collapsed vertebra, not elsewhere classified, thoracic region, initial encounter for fracture
M48.55XA	Collapsed vertebra, not elsewhere classified, thoracolumbar region, initial encounter for fracture
S52.532A	Colles' fracture of left radius, initial encounter for closed fracture
S52.532P	Colles' fracture of left radius, subsequent encounter for closed fracture with malunion
S52.532K	Colles' fracture of left radius, subsequent encounter for closed fracture with nonunion
S52.532Q	Colles' fracture of left radius, subsequent encounter for open fracture type I or II with malunion
S52.532M	Colles' fracture of left radius, subsequent encounter for open fracture type I or II with nonunion
S52.532R	Colles' fracture of left radius, subsequent encounter for open fracture type IIIA, IIIB, or IIIC with malunion
S52.532N	Colles' fracture of left radius, subsequent encounter for open fracture type IIIA, IIIB, or IIIC with nonunion
S52.531A	Colles' fracture of right radius, initial encounter for closed fracture
S52.531P	Colles' fracture of right radius, subsequent encounter for closed fracture with malunion
S52.531K	Colles' fracture of right radius, subsequent encounter for closed fracture with nonunion
S52.531Q	Colles' fracture of right radius, subsequent encounter for open fracture type I or II with malunion
S52.531M	Colles' fracture of right radius, subsequent encounter for open fracture type I or II with nonunion
S52.531R	Colles' fracture of right radius, subsequent encounter for open fracture type IIIA, IIIB, or IIIC with malunion
S52.531N	Colles' fracture of right radius, subsequent encounter for open fracture type IIIA, IIIB, or IIIC with nonunion
S52.539A	Colles' fracture of unspecified radius, initial encounter for closed fracture
S52.539P	Colles' fracture of unspecified radius, subsequent encounter for closed fracture with malunion
S52.539K	Colles' fracture of unspecified radius, subsequent encounter for closed fracture with nonunion
S52.539Q	Colles' fracture of unspecified radius, subsequent encounter for open fracture type I or II with malunion
S52.539M	Colles' fracture of unspecified radius, subsequent encounter for open fracture type I or II with nonunion
S52.539R	Colles' fracture of unspecified radius, subsequent encounter for open fracture type IIIA, IIIB, or IIIC with malunion
S52.539N	Colles' fracture of unspecified radius, subsequent encounter for open fracture type IIIA, IIIB, or IIIC with nonunion
A93.2	Colorado tick fever
K94.01	Colostomy hemorrhage
K94.02	Colostomy infection
K94.03	Colostomy malfunction
D81.9	Combined immunodeficiency, unspecified
D83.2	Common variable immunodeficiency with autoantibodies to B- or T-cells
D83.0	Common variable immunodeficiency with predominant abnormalities of B-cell numbers and function
D83.1	Common variable immunodeficiency with predominant immunoregulatory T-cell disorders
D83.9	Common variable immunodeficiency, unspecified
G91.0	Communicating hydrocephalus
T79.A0XA	Compartment syndrome, unspecified, initial encounter
K56.601	Complete intestinal obstruction, unspecified as to cause
M84.758A	Complete oblique atypical femoral fracture, left leg, initial encounter for fracture
M84.758P	Complete oblique atypical femoral fracture, left leg, subsequent encounter for fracture with malunion
M84.758K	Complete oblique atypical femoral fracture, left leg, subsequent encounter for fracture with nonunion
M84.757A	Complete oblique atypical femoral fracture, right leg, initial encounter for fracture
M84.757P	Complete oblique atypical femoral fracture, right leg, subsequent encounter for fracture with malunion
M84.757K	Complete oblique atypical femoral fracture, right leg, subsequent encounter for fracture with nonunion
M84.759A	Complete oblique atypical femoral fracture, unspecified leg, initial encounter for fracture
M84.759P	Complete oblique atypical femoral fracture, unspecified leg, subsequent encounter for fracture with malunion
M84.759K	Complete oblique atypical femoral fracture, unspecified leg, subsequent encounter for fracture with nonunion
O03.89	Complete or unspecified spontaneous abortion with other complications
O44.01	Complete placenta previa NOS or without hemorrhage, first trimester
O44.02	Complete placenta previa NOS or without hemorrhage, second trimester
O44.03	Complete placenta previa NOS or without hemorrhage, third trimester
M84.755A	Complete transverse atypical femoral fracture, left leg, initial encounter for fracture
M84.755P	Complete transverse atypical femoral fracture, left leg, subsequent encounter for fracture with malunion
M84.755K	Complete transverse atypical femoral fracture, left leg, subsequent encounter for fracture with nonunion
M84.754A	Complete transverse atypical femoral fracture, right leg, initial encounter for fracture
M84.754P	Complete transverse atypical femoral fracture, right leg, subsequent encounter for fracture with malunion
M84.754K	Complete transverse atypical femoral fracture, right leg, subsequent encounter for fracture with nonunion
M84.756A	Complete transverse atypical femoral fracture, unspecified leg, initial encounter for fracture
M84.756P	Complete transverse atypical femoral fracture, unspecified leg, subsequent encounter for fracture with malunion
M84.756K	Complete transverse atypical femoral fracture, unspecified leg, subsequent encounter for fracture with nonunion
S58.012A	Complete traumatic amputation at elbow level, left arm, initial encounter
S58.011A	Complete traumatic amputation at elbow level, right arm, initial encounter
S58.019A	Complete traumatic amputation at elbow level, unspecified arm, initial encounter
S88.012A	Complete traumatic amputation at knee level, left lower leg, initial encounter
S88.011A	Complete traumatic amputation at knee level, right lower leg, initial encounter
S88.019A	Complete traumatic amputation at knee level, unspecified lower leg, initial encounter

S78.012A	Complete traumatic amputation at left hip joint, initial encounter
S48.012A	Complete traumatic amputation at left shoulder joint, initial encounter
S58.112A	Complete traumatic amputation at level between elbow and wrist, left arm, initial encounter
S58.111A	Complete traumatic amputation at level between elbow and wrist, right arm, initial encounter
S58.119A	Complete traumatic amputation at level between elbow and wrist, unspecified arm, initial encounter
S88.112A	Complete traumatic amputation at level between knee and ankle, left lower leg, initial encounter
S88.111A	Complete traumatic amputation at level between knee and ankle, right lower leg, initial encounter
S88.119A	Complete traumatic amputation at level between knee and ankle, unspecified lower leg, initial encounter
S78.112A	Complete traumatic amputation at level between left hip and knee, initial encounter
S48.112A	Complete traumatic amputation at level between left shoulder and elbow, initial encounter
S78.111A	Complete traumatic amputation at level between right hip and knee, initial encounter
S48.111A	Complete traumatic amputation at level between right shoulder and elbow, initial encounter
S78.119A	Complete traumatic amputation at level between unspecified hip and knee, initial encounter
S48.119A	Complete traumatic amputation at level between unspecified shoulder and elbow, initial encounter
S78.011A	Complete traumatic amputation at right hip joint, initial encounter
S48.011A	Complete traumatic amputation at right shoulder joint, initial encounter
S78.019A	Complete traumatic amputation at unspecified hip joint, initial encounter
S48.019A	Complete traumatic amputation at unspecified shoulder joint, initial encounter
S98.012A	Complete traumatic amputation of left foot at ankle level, initial encounter
S98.912A	Complete traumatic amputation of left foot, level unspecified, initial encounter
S58.912A	Complete traumatic amputation of left forearm, level unspecified, initial encounter
S68.412A	Complete traumatic amputation of left hand at wrist level, initial encounter
S78.912A	Complete traumatic amputation of left hip and thigh, level unspecified, initial encounter
S88.912A	Complete traumatic amputation of left lower leg, level unspecified, initial encounter
S98.312A	Complete traumatic amputation of left midfoot, initial encounter
S48.912A	Complete traumatic amputation of left shoulder and upper arm, level unspecified, initial encounter
S98.011A	Complete traumatic amputation of right foot at ankle level, initial encounter
S98.911A	Complete traumatic amputation of right foot, level unspecified, initial encounter
S58.911A	Complete traumatic amputation of right forearm, level unspecified, initial encounter
S68.411A	Complete traumatic amputation of right hand at wrist level, initial encounter
S78.911A	Complete traumatic amputation of right hip and thigh, level unspecified, initial encounter
S88.911A	Complete traumatic amputation of right lower leg, level unspecified, initial encounter
S98.311A	Complete traumatic amputation of right midfoot, initial encounter
S48.911A	Complete traumatic amputation of right shoulder and upper arm, level unspecified, initial encounter
S98.019A	Complete traumatic amputation of unspecified foot at ankle level, initial encounter
S98.919A	Complete traumatic amputation of unspecified foot, level unspecified, initial encounter
S58.919A	Complete traumatic amputation of unspecified forearm, level unspecified, initial encounter
S68.419A	Complete traumatic amputation of unspecified hand at wrist level, initial encounter
S78.919A	Complete traumatic amputation of unspecified hip and thigh, level unspecified, initial encounter
S88.919A	Complete traumatic amputation of unspecified lower leg, level unspecified, initial encounter
S98.319A	Complete traumatic amputation of unspecified midfoot, initial encounter
S48.919A	Complete traumatic amputation of unspecified shoulder and upper arm, level unspecified, initial encounter
S68.712A	Complete traumatic transmetacarpal amputation of left hand, initial encounter
S68.711A	Complete traumatic transmetacarpal amputation of right hand, initial encounter
S68.719A	Complete traumatic transmetacarpal amputation of unspecified hand, initial encounter
R56.01	Complex febrile convulsions
G90.522	Complex regional pain syndrome I of left lower limb
G90.512	Complex regional pain syndrome I of left upper limb
G90.523	Complex regional pain syndrome I of lower limb, bilateral
G90.59	Complex regional pain syndrome I of other specified site
G90.521	Complex regional pain syndrome I of right lower limb
G90.511	Complex regional pain syndrome I of right upper limb
G90.529	Complex regional pain syndrome I of unspecified lower limb
G90.519	Complex regional pain syndrome I of unspecified upper limb
G90.513	Complex regional pain syndrome I of upper limb, bilateral
G90.50	Complex regional pain syndrome I, unspecified
N98.9	Complication associated with artificial fertilization, unspecified

T81.710A	Complication of mesenteric artery following a procedure, not elsewhere classified, initial encounter
T81.718A	Complication of other artery following a procedure, not elsewhere classified, initial encounter
T81.711A	Complication of renal artery following a procedure, not elsewhere classified, initial encounter
T81.719A	Complication of unspecified artery following a procedure, not elsewhere classified, initial encounter
T81.72XA	Complication of vein following a procedure, not elsewhere classified, initial encounter
N98.3	Complications of attempted introduction of embryo in embryo transfer
N98.2	Complications of attempted introduction of fertilized ovum following in vitro fertilization
T87.2	Complications of other reattached body part
T87.1X2	Complications of reattached (part of) left lower extremity
T87.0X2	Complications of reattached (part of) left upper extremity
T87.1X1	Complications of reattached (part of) right lower extremity
T87.0X1	Complications of reattached (part of) right upper extremity
T87.1X9	Complications of reattached (part of) unspecified lower extremity
T87.0X9	Complications of reattached (part of) unspecified upper extremity
T86.5	Complications of stem cell transplant
I87.1	Compression of vein
G37.5	Concentric sclerosis [Balo] of central nervous system
S06.0X1A	Concussion with loss of consciousness of 30 minutes or less, initial encounter
S06.0X9A	Concussion with loss of consciousness of unspecified duration, initial encounter
A51.31	Condyloma latum
Q42.2	Congenital absence, atresia and stenosis of anus with fistula
Q42.3	Congenital absence, atresia and stenosis of anus without fistula
Q41.0	Congenital absence, atresia and stenosis of duodenum
Q41.2	Congenital absence, atresia and stenosis of ileum
Q41.1	Congenital absence, atresia and stenosis of jejunum
Q42.9	Congenital absence, atresia and stenosis of large intestine, part unspecified
Q42.8	Congenital absence, atresia and stenosis of other parts of large intestine
Q41.8	Congenital absence, atresia and stenosis of other specified parts of small intestine
Q42.0	Congenital absence, atresia and stenosis of rectum with fistula
Q42.1	Congenital absence, atresia and stenosis of rectum without fistula
Q41.9	Congenital absence, atresia and stenosis of small intestine, part unspecified
D69.42	Congenital and hereditary thrombocytopenia purpura
P61.3	Congenital anemia from fetal blood loss
Q25.43	Congenital aneurysm of aorta
Q64.31	Congenital bladder neck obstruction
Q33.4	Congenital bronchiectasis
Q32.2	Congenital bronchomalacia
Q04.6	Congenital cerebral cysts
Q33.0	Congenital cystic lung
Q68.1	Congenital deformity of finger(s) and hand
Q67.5	Congenital deformity of spine
Q39.5	Congenital dilatation of esophagus
Q25.44	Congenital dilation of aorta
Q39.6	Congenital diverticulum of esophagus
Q43.6	Congenital fistula of rectum and anus
Q62.0	Congenital hydronephrosis
Q23.1	Congenital insufficiency of aortic valve
Q31.5	Congenital laryngomalacia
Q76.426	Congenital lordosis, lumbar region
Q76.427	Congenital lordosis, lumbosacral region
Q76.428	Congenital lordosis, sacral and sacrococcygeal region
Q76.425	Congenital lordosis, thoracolumbar region
Q76.429	Congenital lordosis, unspecified region
Q25.40	Congenital malformation of aorta unspecified
Q76.9	Congenital malformation of bony thorax, unspecified
Q28.9	Congenital malformation of circulatory system, unspecified
Q39.9	Congenital malformation of esophagus, unspecified
Q25.9	Congenital malformation of great arteries, unspecified
Q26.9	Congenital malformation of great vein, unspecified
Q43.9	Congenital malformation of intestine, unspecified
Q31.9	Congenital malformation of larynx, unspecified
Q76.7	Congenital malformation of sternum
Q87.3	Congenital malformation syndromes involving early overgrowth
Q87.2	Congenital malformation syndromes predominantly involving limbs
Q43.3	Congenital malformations of intestinal fixation
Q89.09	Congenital malformations of spleen
Q62.2	Congenital megaureter
D74.0	Congenital methemoglobinemia
Q23.3	Congenital mitral insufficiency
Q23.2	Congenital mitral stenosis
Q61.02	Congenital multiple renal cysts
G71.2	Congenital myopathies
G11.0	Congenital nonprogressive ataxia
Q62.10	Congenital occlusion of ureter, unspecified
Q62.11	Congenital occlusion of ureteropelvic junction
Q62.12	Congenital occlusion of ureterovesical orifice
Q45.2	Congenital pancreatic cyst
Q27.4	Congenital phlebectasia
Q64.2	Congenital posterior urethral valves
Q22.2	Congenital pulmonary valve insufficiency
Q22.1	Congenital pulmonary valve stenosis

Q61.00	Congenital renal cyst, unspecified
P35.0	Congenital rubella syndrome
Q76.3	Congenital scoliosis due to congenital bony malformation
Q61.01	Congenital single renal cyst
Q23.0	Congenital stenosis of aortic valve
Q32.3	Congenital stenosis of bronchus
Q26.0	Congenital stenosis of vena cava
Q64.32	Congenital stricture of urethra
Q64.33	Congenital stricture of urinary meatus
Q31.1	Congenital subglottic stenosis
Q32.0	Congenital tracheomalacia
Q62.31	Congenital ureterocele, orthotopic
D61.01	Constitutional (pure) red blood cell aplasia
S37.812A	Contusion of adrenal gland, initial encounter
S36.520A	Contusion of ascending [right] colon, initial encounter
S37.22XA	Contusion of bladder, initial encounter
S36.221A	Contusion of body of pancreas, initial encounter
S36.522A	Contusion of descending [left] colon, initial encounter
S27.802A	Contusion of diaphragm, initial encounter
S36.420A	Contusion of duodenum, initial encounter
S36.122A	Contusion of gallbladder, initial encounter
S36.220A	Contusion of head of pancreas, initial encounter
S26.01XA	Contusion of heart with hemopericardium, initial encounter
S26.11XA	Contusion of heart without hemopericardium, initial encounter
S26.91XA	Contusion of heart, unspecified with or without hemopericardium, initial encounter
S36.112A	Contusion of liver, initial encounter
S27.322A	Contusion of lung, bilateral, initial encounter
S27.321A	Contusion of lung, unilateral, initial encounter
S27.329A	Contusion of lung, unspecified, initial encounter
S36.892A	Contusion of other intra-abdominal organs, initial encounter
S36.528A	Contusion of other part of colon, initial encounter
S36.428A	Contusion of other part of small intestine, initial encounter
S27.892A	Contusion of other specified intrathoracic organs, initial encounter
S37.892A	Contusion of other urinary and pelvic organ, initial encounter
S36.62XA	Contusion of rectum, initial encounter
S36.523A	Contusion of sigmoid colon, initial encounter
S36.32XA	Contusion of stomach, initial encounter
S36.222A	Contusion of tail of pancreas, initial encounter
S27.52XA	Contusion of thoracic trachea, initial encounter
S36.521A	Contusion of transverse colon, initial encounter
S36.92XA	Contusion of unspecified intra-abdominal organ, initial encounter
S36.529A	Contusion of unspecified part of colon, initial encounter
S36.229A	Contusion of unspecified part of pancreas, initial encounter
S36.429A	Contusion of unspecified part of small intestine, initial encounter
S37.92XA	Contusion of unspecified urinary and pelvic organ, initial encounter
S37.12XA	Contusion of ureter, initial encounter
S37.32XA	Contusion of urethra, initial encounter
S37.62XA	Contusion of uterus, initial encounter
S06.385A	Contusion, laceration, and hemorrhage of brainstem with loss of consciousness greater than 24 hours with return to pre-existing conscious level, initial encounter
S06.383A	Contusion, laceration, and hemorrhage of brainstem with loss of consciousness of 1 hour to 5 hours 59 minutes, initial encounter
S06.381A	Contusion, laceration, and hemorrhage of brainstem with loss of consciousness of 30 minutes or less, initial encounter
S06.382A	Contusion, laceration, and hemorrhage of brainstem with loss of consciousness of 31 minutes to 59 minutes, initial encounter
S06.384A	Contusion, laceration, and hemorrhage of brainstem with loss of consciousness of 6 hours to 24 hours, initial encounter
S06.389A	Contusion, laceration, and hemorrhage of brainstem with loss of consciousness of unspecified duration, initial encounter
S06.375A	Contusion, laceration, and hemorrhage of cerebellum with loss of consciousness greater than 24 hours with return to pre-existing conscious level, initial encounter
S06.373A	Contusion, laceration, and hemorrhage of cerebellum with loss of consciousness of 1 hour to 5 hours 59 minutes, initial encounter
S06.371A	Contusion, laceration, and hemorrhage of cerebellum with loss of consciousness of 30 minutes or less, initial encounter
S06.372A	Contusion, laceration, and hemorrhage of cerebellum with loss of consciousness of 31 minutes to 59 minutes, initial encounter
S06.374A	Contusion, laceration, and hemorrhage of cerebellum with loss of consciousness of 6 hours to 24 hours, initial encounter
S06.379A	Contusion, laceration, and hemorrhage of cerebellum with loss of consciousness of unspecified duration, initial encounter
G95.81	Conus medullaris syndrome
E74.03	Cori disease
T86.841	Corneal transplant failure
T86.842	Corneal transplant infection
T86.840	Corneal transplant rejection
T27.5XXA	Corrosion involving larynx and trachea with lung, initial encounter
T28.6XXA	Corrosion of esophagus, initial encounter
T27.4XXA	Corrosion of larynx and trachea, initial encounter
T28.7XXA	Corrosion of other parts of alimentary tract, initial encounter
T27.6XXA	Corrosion of other parts of respiratory tract, initial encounter
T27.7XXA	Corrosion of respiratory tract, part unspecified, initial encounter
T23.769A	Corrosion of third degree back of unspecified hand, initial encounter
T21.72XA	Corrosion of third degree of abdominal wall, initial encounter
T23.762A	Corrosion of third degree of back of left hand, initial encounter

T23.761A	Corrosion of third degree of back of right hand, initial encounter
T21.75XA	Corrosion of third degree of buttock, initial encounter
T21.71XA	Corrosion of third degree of chest wall, initial encounter
T20.73XA	Corrosion of third degree of chin, initial encounter
T21.77XA	Corrosion of third degree of female genital region, initial encounter
T20.76XA	Corrosion of third degree of forehead and cheek, initial encounter
T20.70XA	Corrosion of third degree of head, face, and neck, unspecified site, initial encounter
T25.712A	Corrosion of third degree of left ankle, initial encounter
T22.742A	Corrosion of third degree of left axilla, initial encounter
T20.712A	Corrosion of third degree of left ear [any part, except ear drum], initial encounter
T22.722A	Corrosion of third degree of left elbow, initial encounter
T25.722A	Corrosion of third degree of left foot, initial encounter
T22.712A	Corrosion of third degree of left forearm, initial encounter
T23.702A	Corrosion of third degree of left hand, unspecified site, initial encounter
T24.722A	Corrosion of third degree of left knee, initial encounter
T24.732A	Corrosion of third degree of left lower leg, initial encounter
T23.752A	Corrosion of third degree of left palm, initial encounter
T22.762A	Corrosion of third degree of left scapular region, initial encounter
T22.752A	Corrosion of third degree of left shoulder, initial encounter
T24.712A	Corrosion of third degree of left thigh, initial encounter
T23.712A	Corrosion of third degree of left thumb (nail), initial encounter
T25.732A	Corrosion of third degree of left toe(s) (nail), initial encounter
T22.732A	Corrosion of third degree of left upper arm, initial encounter
T23.772A	Corrosion of third degree of left wrist, initial encounter
T20.72XA	Corrosion of third degree of lip(s), initial encounter
T21.74XA	Corrosion of third degree of lower back, initial encounter
T21.76XA	Corrosion of third degree of male genital region, initial encounter
T23.742A	Corrosion of third degree of multiple left fingers (nail), including thumb, initial encounter
T23.732A	Corrosion of third degree of multiple left fingers (nail), not including thumb, initial encounter
T23.741A	Corrosion of third degree of multiple right fingers (nail), including thumb, initial encounter
T23.731A	Corrosion of third degree of multiple right fingers (nail), not including thumb, initial encounter
T20.79XA	Corrosion of third degree of multiple sites of head, face, and neck, initial encounter
T25.792A	Corrosion of third degree of multiple sites of left ankle and foot, initial encounter
T24.792A	Corrosion of third degree of multiple sites of left lower limb, except ankle and foot, initial encounter
T22.792A	Corrosion of third degree of multiple sites of left shoulder and upper limb, except wrist and hand, initial encounter
T23.792A	Corrosion of third degree of multiple sites of left wrist and hand, initial encounter
T25.791A	Corrosion of third degree of multiple sites of right ankle and foot, initial encounter
T24.791A	Corrosion of third degree of multiple sites of right lower limb, except ankle and foot, initial encounter
T22.791A	Corrosion of third degree of multiple sites of right shoulder and upper limb, except wrist and hand, initial encounter
T23.791A	Corrosion of third degree of multiple sites of right wrist and hand, initial encounter
T25.799A	Corrosion of third degree of multiple sites of unspecified ankle and foot, initial encounter
T24.799A	Corrosion of third degree of multiple sites of unspecified lower limb, except ankle and foot, initial encounter
T22.799A	Corrosion of third degree of multiple sites of unspecified shoulder and upper limb, except wrist and hand, initial encounter
T23.799A	Corrosion of third degree of multiple sites of unspecified wrist and hand, initial encounter
T20.77XA	Corrosion of third degree of neck, initial encounter
T20.74XA	Corrosion of third degree of nose (septum), initial encounter
T21.79XA	Corrosion of third degree of other site of trunk, initial encounter
T25.711A	Corrosion of third degree of right ankle, initial encounter
T22.741A	Corrosion of third degree of right axilla, initial encounter
T20.711A	Corrosion of third degree of right ear [any part, except ear drum], initial encounter
T22.721A	Corrosion of third degree of right elbow, initial encounter
T25.721A	Corrosion of third degree of right foot, initial encounter
T22.711A	Corrosion of third degree of right forearm, initial encounter
T23.701A	Corrosion of third degree of right hand, unspecified site, initial encounter
T24.721A	Corrosion of third degree of right knee, initial encounter
T24.731A	Corrosion of third degree of right lower leg, initial encounter
T23.751A	Corrosion of third degree of right palm, initial encounter
T22.761A	Corrosion of third degree of right scapular region, initial encounter
T22.751A	Corrosion of third degree of right shoulder, initial encounter
T24.711A	Corrosion of third degree of right thigh, initial encounter
T23.711A	Corrosion of third degree of right thumb (nail), initial encounter
T25.731A	Corrosion of third degree of right toe(s) (nail), initial encounter
T22.731A	Corrosion of third degree of right upper arm, initial encounter
T23.771A	Corrosion of third degree of right wrist, initial encounter
T20.75XA	Corrosion of third degree of scalp [any part], initial encounter
T22.70XA	Corrosion of third degree of shoulder and upper limb, except wrist and hand, unspecified site, initial encounter
T23.722A	Corrosion of third degree of single left finger (nail) except thumb, initial encounter

T23.721A	Corrosion of third degree of single right finger (nail) except thumb, initial encounter
T21.70XA	Corrosion of third degree of trunk, unspecified site, initial encounter
T25.719A	Corrosion of third degree of unspecified ankle, initial encounter
T22.749A	Corrosion of third degree of unspecified axilla, initial encounter
T20.719A	Corrosion of third degree of unspecified ear [any part, except ear drum], initial encounter
T22.729A	Corrosion of third degree of unspecified elbow, initial encounter
T25.729A	Corrosion of third degree of unspecified foot, initial encounter
T22.719A	Corrosion of third degree of unspecified forearm, initial encounter
T23.709A	Corrosion of third degree of unspecified hand, unspecified site, initial encounter
T24.729A	Corrosion of third degree of unspecified knee, initial encounter
T24.739A	Corrosion of third degree of unspecified lower leg, initial encounter
T23.749A	Corrosion of third degree of unspecified multiple fingers (nail), including thumb, initial encounter
T23.739A	Corrosion of third degree of unspecified multiple fingers (nail), not including thumb, initial encounter
T23.759A	Corrosion of third degree of unspecified palm, initial encounter
T22.769A	Corrosion of third degree of unspecified scapular region, initial encounter
T22.759A	Corrosion of third degree of unspecified shoulder, initial encounter
T23.729A	Corrosion of third degree of unspecified single finger (nail) except thumb, initial encounter
T24.702A	Corrosion of third degree of unspecified site of left lower limb, except ankle and foot, initial encounter
T24.701A	Corrosion of third degree of unspecified site of right lower limb, except ankle and foot, initial encounter
T24.709A	Corrosion of third degree of unspecified site of unspecified lower limb, except ankle and foot, initial encounter
T24.719A	Corrosion of third degree of unspecified thigh, initial encounter
T23.719A	Corrosion of third degree of unspecified thumb (nail), initial encounter
T25.739A	Corrosion of third degree of unspecified toe(s) (nail), initial encounter
T22.739A	Corrosion of third degree of unspecified upper arm, initial encounter
T23.779A	Corrosion of third degree of unspecified wrist, initial encounter
T21.73XA	Corrosion of third degree of upper back, initial encounter
T26.72XA	Corrosion with resulting rupture and destruction of left eyeball, initial encounter
T26.71XA	Corrosion with resulting rupture and destruction of right eyeball, initial encounter
T26.70XA	Corrosion with resulting rupture and destruction of unspecified eyeball, initial encounter
T32.10	Corrosions involving 10-19% of body surface with 0% to 9% third degree corrosion
T32.11	Corrosions involving 10-19% of body surface with 10-19% third degree corrosion
T32.20	Corrosions involving 20-29% of body surface with 0% to 9% third degree corrosion
T32.30	Corrosions involving 30-39% of body surface with 0% to 9% third degree corrosion
T32.40	Corrosions involving 40-49% of body surface with 0% to 9% third degree corrosion
T32.50	Corrosions involving 50-59% of body surface with 0% to 9% third degree corrosion
T32.60	Corrosions involving 60-69% of body surface with 0% to 9% third degree corrosion
T32.70	Corrosions involving 70-79% of body surface with 0% to 9% third degree corrosion
T32.80	Corrosions involving 80-89% of body surface with 0% to 9% third degree corrosion
T32.90	Corrosions involving 90% or more of body surface with 0% to 9% third degree corrosion
P71.0	Cow's milk hypocalcemia in newborn
A81.00	Creutzfeldt-Jakob disease, unspecified
A98.0	Crimean-Congo hemorrhagic fever
G72.81	Critical illness myopathy
G62.81	Critical illness polyneuropathy
K50.814	Crohn's disease of both small and large intestine with abscess
K50.813	Crohn's disease of both small and large intestine with fistula
K50.812	Crohn's disease of both small and large intestine with intestinal obstruction
K50.818	Crohn's disease of both small and large intestine with other complication
K50.811	Crohn's disease of both small and large intestine with rectal bleeding
K50.819	Crohn's disease of both small and large intestine with unspecified complications
K50.80	Crohn's disease of both small and large intestine without complications
K50.114	Crohn's disease of large intestine with abscess
K50.113	Crohn's disease of large intestine with fistula
K50.112	Crohn's disease of large intestine with intestinal obstruction
K50.118	Crohn's disease of large intestine with other complication
K50.111	Crohn's disease of large intestine with rectal bleeding
K50.119	Crohn's disease of large intestine with unspecified complications
K50.10	Crohn's disease of large intestine without complications
K50.014	Crohn's disease of small intestine with abscess
K50.013	Crohn's disease of small intestine with fistula
K50.012	Crohn's disease of small intestine with intestinal obstruction
K50.018	Crohn's disease of small intestine with other complication
K50.011	Crohn's disease of small intestine with rectal bleeding
K50.019	Crohn's disease of small intestine with unspecified complications
K50.00	Crohn's disease of small intestine without complications
K50.914	Crohn's disease, unspecified, with abscess
K50.913	Crohn's disease, unspecified, with fistula
K50.912	Crohn's disease, unspecified, with intestinal obstruction
K50.918	Crohn's disease, unspecified, with other complication
K50.911	Crohn's disease, unspecified, with rectal bleeding
K50.919	Crohn's disease, unspecified, with unspecified complications
K50.90	Crohn's disease, unspecified, without complications
S07.0XXA	Crushing injury of face, initial encounter
S07.9XXA	Crushing injury of head, part unspecified, initial encounter
S17.0XXA	Crushing injury of larynx and trachea, initial encounter
S77.02XA	Crushing injury of left hip, initial encounter
S77.12XA	Crushing injury of left thigh, initial encounter
S17.9XXA	Crushing injury of neck, part unspecified, initial encounter
S07.8XXA	Crushing injury of other parts of head, initial encounter
S17.8XXA	Crushing injury of other specified parts of neck, initial encounter
S77.01XA	Crushing injury of right hip, initial encounter
S77.11XA	Crushing injury of right thigh, initial encounter
S07.1XXA	Crushing injury of skull, initial encounter
S77.00XA	Crushing injury of unspecified hip, initial encounter
S77.10XA	Crushing injury of unspecified thigh, initial encounter
B45.9	Cryptococcosis, unspecified
J84.116	Cryptogenic organizing pneumonia
A07.2	Cryptosporidiosis
E24.9	Cushing's syndrome, unspecified
L02.211	Cutaneous abscess of abdominal wall
L02.212	Cutaneous abscess of back [any part, except buttock]
L02.31	Cutaneous abscess of buttock
L02.213	Cutaneous abscess of chest wall
L02.01	Cutaneous abscess of face
L02.214	Cutaneous abscess of groin
L02.811	Cutaneous abscess of head [any part, except face]
L02.412	Cutaneous abscess of left axilla
L02.612	Cutaneous abscess of left foot
L02.512	Cutaneous abscess of left hand
L02.416	Cutaneous abscess of left lower limb
L02.414	Cutaneous abscess of left upper limb
L02.419	Cutaneous abscess of limb, unspecified
L02.11	Cutaneous abscess of neck
L02.818	Cutaneous abscess of other sites
L02.215	Cutaneous abscess of perineum
L02.411	Cutaneous abscess of right axilla
L02.611	Cutaneous abscess of right foot
L02.511	Cutaneous abscess of right hand
L02.415	Cutaneous abscess of right lower limb
L02.413	Cutaneous abscess of right upper limb
L02.219	Cutaneous abscess of trunk, unspecified
L02.216	Cutaneous abscess of umbilicus
L02.619	Cutaneous abscess of unspecified foot
L02.519	Cutaneous abscess of unspecified hand
L02.91	Cutaneous abscess, unspecified
A44.1	Cutaneous and mucocutaneous bartonellosis
A22.0	Cutaneous anthrax
B40.3	Cutaneous blastomycosis
B38.3	Cutaneous coccidioidomycosis
B45.2	Cutaneous cryptococcosis
A36.3	Cutaneous diphtheria
C82.69	Cutaneous follicle center lymphoma, extranodal and solid organ sites
C82.63	Cutaneous follicle center lymphoma, intra-abdominal lymph nodes
C82.66	Cutaneous follicle center lymphoma, intrapelvic lymph nodes
C82.62	Cutaneous follicle center lymphoma, intrathoracic lymph nodes
C82.64	Cutaneous follicle center lymphoma, lymph nodes of axilla and upper limb
C82.61	Cutaneous follicle center lymphoma, lymph nodes of head, face, and neck
C82.65	Cutaneous follicle center lymphoma, lymph nodes of inguinal region and lower limb
C82.68	Cutaneous follicle center lymphoma, lymph nodes of multiple sites
C82.67	Cutaneous follicle center lymphoma, spleen
C82.60	Cutaneous follicle center lymphoma, unspecified site
B55.1	Cutaneous leishmaniasis
A32.0	Cutaneous listeriosis
D47.01	Cutaneous mastocytosis
A31.1	Cutaneous mycobacterial infection
A43.1	Cutaneous nocardiosis
C84.A1	Cutaneous T-cell lymphoma, unspecified lymph nodes of head, face, and neck
C84.A9	Cutaneous T-cell lymphoma, unspecified, extranodal and solid organ sites
C84.A3	Cutaneous T-cell lymphoma, unspecified, intra-abdominal lymph nodes
C84.A6	Cutaneous T-cell lymphoma, unspecified, intrapelvic lymph nodes
C84.A2	Cutaneous T-cell lymphoma, unspecified, intrathoracic lymph nodes
C84.A4	Cutaneous T-cell lymphoma, unspecified, lymph nodes of axilla and upper limb
C84.A5	Cutaneous T-cell lymphoma, unspecified, lymph nodes of inguinal region and lower limb
C84.A8	Cutaneous T-cell lymphoma, unspecified, lymph nodes of multiple sites
C84.A7	Cutaneous T-cell lymphoma, unspecified, spleen
C84.A0	Cutaneous T-cell lymphoma, unspecified, unspecified site
P28.2	Cyanotic attacks of newborn
A07.4	Cyclosporiasis
K86.2	Cyst of pancreas
Q61.11	Cystic dilatation of collecting ducts
Q44.6	Cystic disease of liver
E84.19	Cystic fibrosis with other intestinal manifestations
E84.8	Cystic fibrosis with other manifestations

E84.9	Cystic fibrosis, unspecified
Q61.9	Cystic kidney disease, unspecified
B69.0	Cysticercosis of central nervous system
B69.1	Cysticercosis of eye
B69.89	Cysticercosis of other sites
B69.9	Cysticercosis, unspecified
E72.04	Cystinosis
E72.01	Cystinuria
H59.033	Cystoid macular edema following cataract surgery, bilateral
H59.032	Cystoid macular edema following cataract surgery, left eye
H59.031	Cystoid macular edema following cataract surgery, right eye
H59.039	Cystoid macular edema following cataract surgery, unspecified eye
N99.510	Cystostomy hemorrhage
N99.511	Cystostomy infection
N99.512	Cystostomy malfunction
B25.9	Cytomegaloviral disease, unspecified
B25.1	Cytomegaloviral hepatitis
O08.6	Damage to pelvic organs and tissues following an ectopic and molar pregnancy
O04.84	Damage to pelvic organs following (induced) termination of pregnancy
O03.84	Damage to pelvic organs following complete or unspecified spontaneous abortion
O07.34	Damage to pelvic organs following failed attempted termination of pregnancy
O03.34	Damage to pelvic organs following incomplete spontaneous abortion
O22.30	Deep phlebothrombosis in pregnancy, unspecified trimester
E80.3	Defects of catalase and peroxidase
G23.9	Degenerative disease of basal ganglia, unspecified
O72.2	Delayed and secondary postpartum hemorrhage
T80.911A	Delayed hemolytic transfusion reaction, unspecified incompatibility, initial encounter
O08.1	Delayed or excessive hemorrhage following ectopic and molar pregnancy
O07.1	Delayed or excessive hemorrhage following failed attempted termination of pregnancy
Q93.9	Deletion from autosomes, unspecified
Q93.3	Deletion of short arm of chromosome 4
Q93.4	Deletion of short arm of chromosome 5
Q93.7	Deletions with other complex rearrangements
F05	Delirium due to known physiological condition
F02.81	Dementia in other diseases classified elsewhere with behavioral disturbance
G37.9	Demyelinating disease of central nervous system, unspecified
A90	Dengue fever [classical dengue]
A91	Dengue hemorrhagic fever
Z99.11	Dependence on respirator [ventilator] status
M36.0	Dermato(poly)myositis in neoplastic disease
M33.92	Dermatopolymyositis, unspecified with myopathy
M33.99	Dermatopolymyositis, unspecified with other organ involvement
M33.91	Dermatopolymyositis, unspecified with respiratory involvement
M33.93	Dermatopolymyositis, unspecified without myopathy
M33.90	Dermatopolymyositis, unspecified, organ involvement unspecified
J84.117	Desquamative interstitial pneumonia
Q24.0	Dextrocardia
D82.1	Di George's syndrome
E23.2	Diabetes insipidus
E08.52	Diabetes mellitus due to underlying condition with diabetic peripheral angiopathy with gangrene
K44.0	Diaphragmatic hernia with obstruction, without gangrene
B66.2	Dicroceliasis
C82.59	Diffuse follicle center lymphoma, extranodal and solid organ sites
C82.53	Diffuse follicle center lymphoma, intra-abdominal lymph nodes
C82.56	Diffuse follicle center lymphoma, intrapelvic lymph nodes
C82.52	Diffuse follicle center lymphoma, intrathoracic lymph nodes
C82.54	Diffuse follicle center lymphoma, lymph nodes of axilla and upper limb
C82.51	Diffuse follicle center lymphoma, lymph nodes of head, face, and neck
C82.55	Diffuse follicle center lymphoma, lymph nodes of inguinal region and lower limb
C82.58	Diffuse follicle center lymphoma, lymph nodes of multiple sites
C82.57	Diffuse follicle center lymphoma, spleen
C82.50	Diffuse follicle center lymphoma, unspecified site
C83.39	Diffuse large B-cell lymphoma, extranodal and solid organ sites
C83.33	Diffuse large B-cell lymphoma, intra-abdominal lymph nodes
C83.36	Diffuse large B-cell lymphoma, intrapelvic lymph nodes
C83.32	Diffuse large B-cell lymphoma, intrathoracic lymph nodes
C83.34	Diffuse large B-cell lymphoma, lymph nodes of axilla and upper limb
C83.31	Diffuse large B-cell lymphoma, lymph nodes of head, face, and neck
C83.35	Diffuse large B-cell lymphoma, lymph nodes of inguinal region and lower limb
C83.38	Diffuse large B-cell lymphoma, lymph nodes of multiple sites
C83.37	Diffuse large B-cell lymphoma, spleen
C83.30	Diffuse large B-cell lymphoma, unspecified site
G37.0	Diffuse sclerosis of central nervous system
S06.2X5A	Diffuse traumatic brain injury with loss of consciousness greater than 24 hours with return to pre-existing conscious levels, initial encounter
S06.2X3A	Diffuse traumatic brain injury with loss of consciousness of 1 hour to 5 hours 59 minutes, initial encounter
S06.2X1A	Diffuse traumatic brain injury with loss of consciousness of 30 minutes or less, initial encounter
S06.2X2A	Diffuse traumatic brain injury with loss of consciousness of 31 minutes to 59 minutes, initial encounter
S06.2X4A	Diffuse traumatic brain injury with loss of consciousness of 6 hours to 24 hours, initial encounter
S06.2X9A	Diffuse traumatic brain injury with loss of consciousness of unspecified duration, initial encounter
I42.0	Dilated cardiomyopathy
A36.9	Diphtheria, unspecified
A36.81	Diphtheritic cardiomyopathy
A36.86	Diphtheritic conjunctivitis
A36.85	Diphtheritic cystitis
A36.83	Diphtheritic polyneuritis
A36.82	Diphtheritic radiculomyelitis
A36.84	Diphtheritic tubulo-interstitial nephropathy
B70.0	Diphyllobothriasis
G83.0	Diplegia of upper limbs
B71.1	Dipylidiasis
M01.X72	Direct infection of left ankle and foot in infectious and parasitic diseases classified elsewhere
M01.X22	Direct infection of left elbow in infectious and parasitic diseases classified elsewhere
M01.X42	Direct infection of left hand in infectious and parasitic diseases classified elsewhere
M01.X52	Direct infection of left hip in infectious and parasitic diseases classified elsewhere
M01.X62	Direct infection of left knee in infectious and parasitic diseases classified elsewhere
M01.X12	Direct infection of left shoulder in infectious and parasitic diseases classified elsewhere
M01.X32	Direct infection of left wrist in infectious and parasitic diseases classified elsewhere
M01.X9	Direct infection of multiple joints in infectious and parasitic diseases classified elsewhere
M01.X71	Direct infection of right ankle and foot in infectious and parasitic diseases classified elsewhere
M01.X21	Direct infection of right elbow in infectious and parasitic diseases classified elsewhere
M01.X41	Direct infection of right hand in infectious and parasitic diseases classified elsewhere
M01.X51	Direct infection of right hip in infectious and parasitic diseases classified elsewhere
M01.X61	Direct infection of right knee in infectious and parasitic diseases classified elsewhere
M01.X11	Direct infection of right shoulder in infectious and parasitic diseases classified elsewhere
M01.X31	Direct infection of right wrist in infectious and parasitic diseases classified elsewhere
M01.X79	Direct infection of unspecified ankle and foot in infectious and parasitic diseases classified elsewhere
M01.X29	Direct infection of unspecified elbow in infectious and parasitic diseases classified elsewhere
M01.X49	Direct infection of unspecified hand in infectious and parasitic diseases classified elsewhere
M01.X59	Direct infection of unspecified hip in infectious and parasitic diseases classified elsewhere
M01.X0	Direct infection of unspecified joint in infectious and parasitic diseases classified elsewhere
M01.X69	Direct infection of unspecified knee in infectious and parasitic diseases classified elsewhere
M01.X19	Direct infection of unspecified shoulder in infectious and parasitic diseases classified elsewhere
M01.X39	Direct infection of unspecified wrist in infectious and parasitic diseases classified elsewhere
M01.X8	Direct infection of vertebrae in infectious and parasitic diseases classified elsewhere
Q20.5	Discordant atrioventricular connection
I31.9	Disease of pericardium, unspecified
G95.9	Disease of spinal cord, unspecified
O99.411	Diseases of the circulatory system complicating pregnancy, first trimester
O99.412	Diseases of the circulatory system complicating pregnancy, second trimester
O99.413	Diseases of the circulatory system complicating pregnancy, third trimester
O99.43	Diseases of the circulatory system complicating the puerperium
O99.354	Diseases of the nervous system complicating childbirth
O99.355	Diseases of the nervous system complicating the puerperium
S13.111A	Dislocation of C0/C1 cervical vertebrae, initial encounter
S13.121A	Dislocation of C1/C2 cervical vertebrae, initial encounter
S13.131A	Dislocation of C2/C3 cervical vertebrae, initial encounter
S13.141A	Dislocation of C3/C4 cervical vertebrae, initial encounter
S13.151A	Dislocation of C4/C5 cervical vertebrae, initial encounter
S13.161A	Dislocation of C5/C6 cervical vertebrae, initial encounter
S13.171A	Dislocation of C6/C7 cervical vertebrae, initial encounter
S13.181A	Dislocation of C7/T1 cervical vertebrae, initial encounter
T84.021A	Dislocation of internal left hip prosthesis, initial encounter
T84.020A	Dislocation of internal right hip prosthesis, initial encounter
T84.028A	Dislocation of other internal joint prosthesis, initial encounter
S13.29XA	Dislocation of other parts of neck, initial encounter
S13.101A	Dislocation of unspecified cervical vertebrae, initial encounter
T84.029A	Dislocation of unspecified internal joint prosthesis, initial encounter
S13.20XA	Dislocation of unspecified parts of neck, initial encounter
E72.9	Disorder of amino-acid metabolism, unspecified
E70.9	Disorder of aromatic amino-acid metabolism, unspecified
E71.2	Disorder of branched-chain amino-acid metabolism, unspecified

E72.50	Disorder of glycine metabolism, unspecified
E79.9	Disorder of purine and pyrimidine metabolism, unspecified
E70.20	Disorder of tyrosine metabolism, unspecified
E72.20	Disorder of urea cycle metabolism, unspecified
E72.00	Disorders of amino-acid transport, unspecified
E74.20	Disorders of galactose metabolism, unspecified
E72.81	Disorders of gamma aminobutyric acid metabolism
E70.40	Disorders of histidine metabolism, unspecified
E71.32	Disorders of ketone metabolism
E72.3	Disorders of lysine and hydroxylysine metabolism
H47.41	Disorders of optic chiasm in (due to) inflammatory disorders
H47.42	Disorders of optic chiasm in (due to) neoplasm
H47.49	Disorders of optic chiasm in (due to) other disorders
H47.43	Disorders of optic chiasm in (due to) vascular disorders
E72.4	Disorders of ornithine metabolism
E74.4	Disorders of pyruvate metabolism and gluconeogenesis
E72.10	Disorders of sulfur-bearing amino-acid metabolism, unspecified
E70.5	Disorders of tryptophan metabolism
H47.622	Disorders of visual cortex in (due to) inflammatory disorders, left side of brain
H47.621	Disorders of visual cortex in (due to) inflammatory disorders, right side of brain
H47.629	Disorders of visual cortex in (due to) inflammatory disorders, unspecified side of brain
H47.632	Disorders of visual cortex in (due to) neoplasm, left side of brain
H47.631	Disorders of visual cortex in (due to) neoplasm, right side of brain
H47.639	Disorders of visual cortex in (due to) neoplasm, unspecified side of brain
H47.642	Disorders of visual cortex in (due to) vascular disorders, left side of brain
H47.641	Disorders of visual cortex in (due to) vascular disorders, right side of brain
H47.649	Disorders of visual cortex in (due to) vascular disorders, unspecified side of brain
H47.512	Disorders of visual pathways in (due to) inflammatory disorders, left side
H47.511	Disorders of visual pathways in (due to) inflammatory disorders, right side
H47.519	Disorders of visual pathways in (due to) inflammatory disorders, unspecified side
H47.522	Disorders of visual pathways in (due to) neoplasm, left side
H47.521	Disorders of visual pathways in (due to) neoplasm, right side
H47.529	Disorders of visual pathways in (due to) neoplasm, unspecified side
H47.532	Disorders of visual pathways in (due to) vascular disorders, left side
H47.531	Disorders of visual pathways in (due to) vascular disorders, right side
H47.539	Disorders of visual pathways in (due to) vascular disorders, unspecified side
F20.1	Disorganized schizophrenia
S72.132P	Displaced apophyseal fracture of left femur, subsequent encounter for closed fracture with malunion
S72.132K	Displaced apophyseal fracture of left femur, subsequent encounter for closed fracture with nonunion
S72.132Q	Displaced apophyseal fracture of left femur, subsequent encounter for open fracture type I or II with malunion
S72.132M	Displaced apophyseal fracture of left femur, subsequent encounter for open fracture type I or II with nonunion
S72.132R	Displaced apophyseal fracture of left femur, subsequent encounter for open fracture type IIIA, IIIB, or IIIC with malunion
S72.132N	Displaced apophyseal fracture of left femur, subsequent encounter for open fracture type IIIA, IIIB, or IIIC with nonunion
S72.131P	Displaced apophyseal fracture of right femur, subsequent encounter for closed fracture with malunion
S72.131K	Displaced apophyseal fracture of right femur, subsequent encounter for closed fracture with nonunion
S72.131Q	Displaced apophyseal fracture of right femur, subsequent encounter for open fracture type I or II with malunion
S72.131M	Displaced apophyseal fracture of right femur, subsequent encounter for open fracture type I or II with nonunion
S72.131R	Displaced apophyseal fracture of right femur, subsequent encounter for open fracture type IIIA, IIIB, or IIIC with malunion
S72.131N	Displaced apophyseal fracture of right femur, subsequent encounter for open fracture type IIIA, IIIB, or IIIC with nonunion
S72.133P	Displaced apophyseal fracture of unspecified femur, subsequent encounter for closed fracture with malunion
S72.133K	Displaced apophyseal fracture of unspecified femur, subsequent encounter for closed fracture with nonunion
S72.133Q	Displaced apophyseal fracture of unspecified femur, subsequent encounter for open fracture type I or II with malunion
S72.133M	Displaced apophyseal fracture of unspecified femur, subsequent encounter for open fracture type I or II with nonunion
S72.133R	Displaced apophyseal fracture of unspecified femur, subsequent encounter for open fracture type IIIA, IIIB, or IIIC with malunion
S72.133N	Displaced apophyseal fracture of unspecified femur, subsequent encounter for open fracture type IIIA, IIIB, or IIIC with nonunion
S72.062P	Displaced articular fracture of head of left femur, subsequent encounter for closed fracture with malunion
S72.062K	Displaced articular fracture of head of left femur, subsequent encounter for closed fracture with nonunion
S72.062Q	Displaced articular fracture of head of left femur, subsequent encounter for open fracture type I or II with malunion
S72.062M	Displaced articular fracture of head of left femur, subsequent encounter for open fracture type I or II with nonunion
S72.062R	Displaced articular fracture of head of left femur, subsequent encounter for open fracture type IIIA, IIIB, or IIIC with malunion
S72.062N	Displaced articular fracture of head of left femur, subsequent encounter for open fracture type IIIA, IIIB, or IIIC with nonunion
S72.061P	Displaced articular fracture of head of right femur, subsequent encounter for closed fracture with malunion
S72.061K	Displaced articular fracture of head of right femur, subsequent encounter for closed fracture with nonunion
S72.061Q	Displaced articular fracture of head of right femur, subsequent encounter for open fracture type I or II with malunion
S72.061M	Displaced articular fracture of head of right femur, subsequent encounter for open fracture type I or II with nonunion
S72.061R	Displaced articular fracture of head of right femur, subsequent encounter for open fracture type IIIA, IIIB, or IIIC with malunion
S72.061N	Displaced articular fracture of head of right femur, subsequent encounter for open fracture type IIIA, IIIB, or IIIC with nonunion
S72.063P	Displaced articular fracture of head of unspecified femur, subsequent encounter for closed fracture with malunion
S72.063K	Displaced articular fracture of head of unspecified femur, subsequent encounter for closed fracture with nonunion
S72.063Q	Displaced articular fracture of head of unspecified femur, subsequent encounter for open fracture type I or II with malunion
S72.063M	Displaced articular fracture of head of unspecified femur, subsequent encounter for open fracture type I or II with nonunion
S72.063R	Displaced articular fracture of head of unspecified femur, subsequent encounter for open fracture type IIIA, IIIB, or IIIC with malunion
S72.063N	Displaced articular fracture of head of unspecified femur, subsequent encounter for open fracture type IIIA, IIIB, or IIIC with nonunion
S32.462K	Displaced associated transverse-posterior fracture of left acetabulum, subsequent encounter for fracture with nonunion
S32.461K	Displaced associated transverse-posterior fracture of right acetabulum, subsequent encounter for fracture with nonunion
S32.463K	Displaced associated transverse-posterior fracture of unspecified acetabulum, subsequent encounter for fracture with nonunion
S92.152B	Displaced avulsion fracture (chip fracture) of left talus, initial encounter for open fracture
S92.152P	Displaced avulsion fracture (chip fracture) of left talus, subsequent encounter for fracture with malunion
S92.152K	Displaced avulsion fracture (chip fracture) of left talus, subsequent encounter for fracture with nonunion
S92.151B	Displaced avulsion fracture (chip fracture) of right talus, initial encounter for open fracture
S92.151P	Displaced avulsion fracture (chip fracture) of right talus, subsequent encounter for fracture with malunion
S92.151K	Displaced avulsion fracture (chip fracture) of right talus, subsequent encounter for fracture with nonunion
S92.153B	Displaced avulsion fracture (chip fracture) of unspecified talus, initial encounter for open fracture
S92.153P	Displaced avulsion fracture (chip fracture) of unspecified talus, subsequent encounter for fracture with malunion
S92.153K	Displaced avulsion fracture (chip fracture) of unspecified talus, subsequent encounter for fracture with nonunion
S32.312A	Displaced avulsion fracture of left ilium, initial encounter for closed fracture
S32.312K	Displaced avulsion fracture of left ilium, subsequent encounter for fracture with nonunion
S32.612A	Displaced avulsion fracture of left ischium, initial encounter for closed fracture
S32.612K	Displaced avulsion fracture of left ischium, subsequent encounter for fracture with nonunion
S32.311A	Displaced avulsion fracture of right ilium, initial encounter for closed fracture
S32.311K	Displaced avulsion fracture of right ilium, subsequent encounter for fracture with nonunion
S32.611A	Displaced avulsion fracture of right ischium, initial encounter for closed fracture
S32.611K	Displaced avulsion fracture of right ischium, subsequent encounter for fracture with nonunion
S92.032B	Displaced avulsion fracture of tuberosity of left calcaneus, initial encounter for open fracture
S92.032P	Displaced avulsion fracture of tuberosity of left calcaneus, subsequent encounter for fracture with malunion
S92.032K	Displaced avulsion fracture of tuberosity of left calcaneus, subsequent encounter for fracture with nonunion
S92.031B	Displaced avulsion fracture of tuberosity of right calcaneus, initial encounter for open fracture
S92.031P	Displaced avulsion fracture of tuberosity of right calcaneus, subsequent encounter for fracture with malunion
S92.031K	Displaced avulsion fracture of tuberosity of right calcaneus, subsequent encounter for fracture with nonunion
S92.033B	Displaced avulsion fracture of tuberosity of unspecified calcaneus, initial encounter for open fracture
S92.033P	Displaced avulsion fracture of tuberosity of unspecified calcaneus, subsequent encounter for fracture with malunion
S92.033K	Displaced avulsion fracture of tuberosity of unspecified calcaneus, subsequent encounter for fracture with nonunion
S32.313A	Displaced avulsion fracture of unspecified ilium, initial encounter for closed fracture
S32.313K	Displaced avulsion fracture of unspecified ilium, subsequent encounter for fracture with nonunion
S32.613A	Displaced avulsion fracture of unspecified ischium, initial encounter for closed fracture
S32.613K	Displaced avulsion fracture of unspecified ischium, subsequent encounter for fracture with nonunion
S82.142A	Displaced bicondylar fracture of left tibia, initial encounter for closed fracture
S82.142P	Displaced bicondylar fracture of left tibia, subsequent encounter for closed fracture with malunion

S82.142K Displaced bicondylar fracture of left tibia, subsequent encounter for closed fracture with nonunion

S82.142Q Displaced bicondylar fracture of left tibia, subsequent encounter for open fracture type I or II with malunion

S82.142M Displaced bicondylar fracture of left tibia, subsequent encounter for open fracture type I or II with nonunion

S82.142R Displaced bicondylar fracture of left tibia, subsequent encounter for open fracture type IIIA, IIIB, or IIIC with malunion

S82.142N Displaced bicondylar fracture of left tibia, subsequent encounter for open fracture type IIIA, IIIB, or IIIC with nonunion

S82.141A Displaced bicondylar fracture of right tibia, initial encounter for closed fracture

S82.141P Displaced bicondylar fracture of right tibia, subsequent encounter for closed fracture with malunion

S82.141K Displaced bicondylar fracture of right tibia, subsequent encounter for closed fracture with nonunion

S82.141Q Displaced bicondylar fracture of right tibia, subsequent encounter for open fracture type I or II with malunion

S82.141M Displaced bicondylar fracture of right tibia, subsequent encounter for open fracture type I or II with nonunion

S82.141R Displaced bicondylar fracture of right tibia, subsequent encounter for open fracture type IIIA, IIIB, or IIIC with malunion

S82.141N Displaced bicondylar fracture of right tibia, subsequent encounter for open fracture type IIIA, IIIB, or IIIC with nonunion

S82.143A Displaced bicondylar fracture of unspecified tibia, initial encounter for closed fracture

S82.143P Displaced bicondylar fracture of unspecified tibia, subsequent encounter for closed fracture with malunion

S82.143K Displaced bicondylar fracture of unspecified tibia, subsequent encounter for closed fracture with nonunion

S82.143Q Displaced bicondylar fracture of unspecified tibia, subsequent encounter for open fracture type I or II with malunion

S82.143M Displaced bicondylar fracture of unspecified tibia, subsequent encounter for open fracture type I or II with nonunion

S82.143R Displaced bicondylar fracture of unspecified tibia, subsequent encounter for open fracture type IIIA, IIIB, or IIIC with malunion

S82.143N Displaced bicondylar fracture of unspecified tibia, subsequent encounter for open fracture type IIIA, IIIB, or IIIC with nonunion

S82.842B Displaced bimalleolar fracture of left lower leg, initial encounter for open fracture type I or II

S82.842C Displaced bimalleolar fracture of left lower leg, initial encounter for open fracture type IIIA, IIIB, or IIIC

S82.842P Displaced bimalleolar fracture of left lower leg, subsequent encounter for closed fracture with malunion

S82.842K Displaced bimalleolar fracture of left lower leg, subsequent encounter for closed fracture with nonunion

S82.842Q Displaced bimalleolar fracture of left lower leg, subsequent encounter for open fracture type I or II with malunion

S82.842M Displaced bimalleolar fracture of left lower leg, subsequent encounter for open fracture type I or II with nonunion

S82.842R Displaced bimalleolar fracture of left lower leg, subsequent encounter for open fracture type IIIA, IIIB, or IIIC with malunion

S82.842N Displaced bimalleolar fracture of left lower leg, subsequent encounter for open fracture type IIIA, IIIB, or IIIC with nonunion

S82.841B Displaced bimalleolar fracture of right lower leg, initial encounter for open fracture type I or II

S82.841C Displaced bimalleolar fracture of right lower leg, initial encounter for open fracture type IIIA, IIIB, or IIIC

S82.841P Displaced bimalleolar fracture of right lower leg, subsequent encounter for closed fracture with malunion

S82.841K Displaced bimalleolar fracture of right lower leg, subsequent encounter for closed fracture with nonunion

S82.841Q Displaced bimalleolar fracture of right lower leg, subsequent encounter for open fracture type I or II with malunion

S82.841M Displaced bimalleolar fracture of right lower leg, subsequent encounter for open fracture type I or II with nonunion

S82.841R Displaced bimalleolar fracture of right lower leg, subsequent encounter for open fracture type IIIA, IIIB, or IIIC with malunion

S82.841N Displaced bimalleolar fracture of right lower leg, subsequent encounter for open fracture type IIIA, IIIB, or IIIC with nonunion

S82.843B Displaced bimalleolar fracture of unspecified lower leg, initial encounter for open fracture type I or II

S82.843C Displaced bimalleolar fracture of unspecified lower leg, initial encounter for open fracture type IIIA, IIIB, or IIIC

S82.843P Displaced bimalleolar fracture of unspecified lower leg, subsequent encounter for closed fracture with malunion

S82.843K Displaced bimalleolar fracture of unspecified lower leg, subsequent encounter for closed fracture with nonunion

S82.843Q Displaced bimalleolar fracture of unspecified lower leg, subsequent encounter for open fracture type I or II with malunion

S82.843M Displaced bimalleolar fracture of unspecified lower leg, subsequent encounter for open fracture type I or II with nonunion

S82.843R Displaced bimalleolar fracture of unspecified lower leg, subsequent encounter for open fracture type IIIA, IIIB, or IIIC with malunion

S82.843N Displaced bimalleolar fracture of unspecified lower leg, subsequent encounter for open fracture type IIIA, IIIB, or IIIC with nonunion

S82.042A Displaced comminuted fracture of left patella, initial encounter for closed fracture

S82.042B Displaced comminuted fracture of left patella, initial encounter for open fracture type I or II

S82.042C Displaced comminuted fracture of left patella, initial encounter for open fracture type IIIA, IIIB, or IIIC

S82.042P Displaced comminuted fracture of left patella, subsequent encounter for closed fracture with malunion

S82.042K Displaced comminuted fracture of left patella, subsequent encounter for closed fracture with nonunion

S82.042Q Displaced comminuted fracture of left patella, subsequent encounter for open fracture type I or II with malunion

S82.042M Displaced comminuted fracture of left patella, subsequent encounter for open fracture type I or II with nonunion

S82.042R Displaced comminuted fracture of left patella, subsequent encounter for open fracture type IIIA, IIIB, or IIIC with malunion

S82.042N Displaced comminuted fracture of left patella, subsequent encounter for open fracture type IIIA, IIIB, or IIIC with nonunion

S82.041A Displaced comminuted fracture of right patella, initial encounter for closed fracture

S82.041B Displaced comminuted fracture of right patella, initial encounter for open fracture type I or II

S82.041C Displaced comminuted fracture of right patella, initial encounter for open fracture type IIIA, IIIB, or IIIC

S82.041P Displaced comminuted fracture of right patella, subsequent encounter for closed fracture with malunion

S82.041K Displaced comminuted fracture of right patella, subsequent encounter for closed fracture with nonunion

S82.041Q Displaced comminuted fracture of right patella, subsequent encounter for open fracture type I or II with malunion

S82.041M Displaced comminuted fracture of right patella, subsequent encounter for open fracture type I or II with nonunion

S82.041R Displaced comminuted fracture of right patella, subsequent encounter for open fracture type IIIA, IIIB, or IIIC with malunion

S82.041N Displaced comminuted fracture of right patella, subsequent encounter for open fracture type IIIA, IIIB, or IIIC with nonunion

S42.352A Displaced comminuted fracture of shaft of humerus, left arm, initial encounter for closed fracture

S42.352P Displaced comminuted fracture of shaft of humerus, left arm, subsequent encounter for fracture with malunion

S42.352K Displaced comminuted fracture of shaft of humerus, left arm, subsequent encounter for fracture with nonunion

S42.351A Displaced comminuted fracture of shaft of humerus, right arm, initial encounter for closed fracture

S42.351P Displaced comminuted fracture of shaft of humerus, right arm, subsequent encounter for fracture with malunion

S42.351K Displaced comminuted fracture of shaft of humerus, right arm, subsequent encounter for fracture with nonunion

S42.353A Displaced comminuted fracture of shaft of humerus, unspecified arm, initial encounter for closed fracture

S42.353P Displaced comminuted fracture of shaft of humerus, unspecified arm, subsequent encounter for fracture with malunion

S42.353K Displaced comminuted fracture of shaft of humerus, unspecified arm, subsequent encounter for fracture with nonunion

S72.352P Displaced comminuted fracture of shaft of left femur, subsequent encounter for closed fracture with malunion

S72.352K Displaced comminuted fracture of shaft of left femur, subsequent encounter for closed fracture with nonunion

S72.352Q Displaced comminuted fracture of shaft of left femur, subsequent encounter for open fracture type I or II with malunion

S72.352M Displaced comminuted fracture of shaft of left femur, subsequent encounter for open fracture type I or II with nonunion

S72.352R Displaced comminuted fracture of shaft of left femur, subsequent encounter for open fracture type IIIA, IIIB, or IIIC with malunion

S72.352N Displaced comminuted fracture of shaft of left femur, subsequent encounter for open fracture type IIIA, IIIB, or IIIC with nonunion

S82.452P Displaced comminuted fracture of shaft of left fibula, subsequent encounter for closed fracture with malunion

S82.452K Displaced comminuted fracture of shaft of left fibula, subsequent encounter for closed fracture with nonunion

S82.452Q Displaced comminuted fracture of shaft of left fibula, subsequent encounter for open fracture type I or II with malunion

S82.452M Displaced comminuted fracture of shaft of left fibula, subsequent encounter for open fracture type I or II with nonunion

S82.452R Displaced comminuted fracture of shaft of left fibula, subsequent encounter for open fracture type IIIA, IIIB, or IIIC with malunion

S82.452N Displaced comminuted fracture of shaft of left fibula, subsequent encounter for open fracture type IIIA, IIIB, or IIIC with nonunion

S82.252A Displaced comminuted fracture of shaft of left tibia, initial encounter for closed fracture

S82.252P Displaced comminuted fracture of shaft of left tibia, subsequent encounter for closed fracture with malunion

S82.252K Displaced comminuted fracture of shaft of left tibia, subsequent encounter for closed fracture with nonunion

S82.252Q Displaced comminuted fracture of shaft of left tibia, subsequent encounter for open fracture type I or II with malunion

S82.252M Displaced comminuted fracture of shaft of left tibia, subsequent encounter for open fracture type I or II with nonunion

S82.252R Displaced comminuted fracture of shaft of left tibia, subsequent encounter for open fracture type IIIA, IIIB, or IIIC with malunion

S82.252N Displaced comminuted fracture of shaft of left tibia, subsequent encounter for open fracture type IIIA, IIIB, or IIIC with nonunion

S52.352A Displaced comminuted fracture of shaft of radius, left arm, initial encounter for closed fracture

S52.352P Displaced comminuted fracture of shaft of radius, left arm, subsequent encounter for closed fracture with malunion
S52.352K Displaced comminuted fracture of shaft of radius, left arm, subsequent encounter for closed fracture with nonunion
S52.352Q Displaced comminuted fracture of shaft of radius, left arm, subsequent encounter for open fracture type I or II with malunion
S52.352M Displaced comminuted fracture of shaft of radius, left arm, subsequent encounter for open fracture type I or II with nonunion
S52.352R Displaced comminuted fracture of shaft of radius, left arm, subsequent encounter for open fracture type IIIA, IIIB, or IIIC with malunion
S52.352N Displaced comminuted fracture of shaft of radius, left arm, subsequent encounter for open fracture type IIIA, IIIB, or IIIC with nonunion
S52.351A Displaced comminuted fracture of shaft of radius, right arm, initial encounter for closed fracture
S52.351P Displaced comminuted fracture of shaft of radius, right arm, subsequent encounter for closed fracture with malunion
S52.351K Displaced comminuted fracture of shaft of radius, right arm, subsequent encounter for closed fracture with nonunion
S52.351Q Displaced comminuted fracture of shaft of radius, right arm, subsequent encounter for open fracture type I or II with malunion
S52.351M Displaced comminuted fracture of shaft of radius, right arm, subsequent encounter for open fracture type I or II with nonunion
S52.351R Displaced comminuted fracture of shaft of radius, right arm, subsequent encounter for open fracture type IIIA, IIIB, or IIIC with malunion
S52.351N Displaced comminuted fracture of shaft of radius, right arm, subsequent encounter for open fracture type IIIA, IIIB, or IIIC with nonunion
S52.353A Displaced comminuted fracture of shaft of radius, unspecified arm, initial encounter for closed fracture
S52.353P Displaced comminuted fracture of shaft of radius, unspecified arm, subsequent encounter for closed fracture with malunion
S52.353K Displaced comminuted fracture of shaft of radius, unspecified arm, subsequent encounter for closed fracture with nonunion
S52.353Q Displaced comminuted fracture of shaft of radius, unspecified arm, subsequent encounter for open fracture type I or II with malunion
S52.353M Displaced comminuted fracture of shaft of radius, unspecified arm, subsequent encounter for open fracture type I or II with nonunion
S52.353R Displaced comminuted fracture of shaft of radius, unspecified arm, subsequent encounter for open fracture type IIIA, IIIB, or IIIC with malunion
S52.353N Displaced comminuted fracture of shaft of radius, unspecified arm, subsequent encounter for open fracture type IIIA, IIIB, or IIIC with nonunion
S72.351P Displaced comminuted fracture of shaft of right femur, subsequent encounter for closed fracture with malunion
S72.351K Displaced comminuted fracture of shaft of right femur, subsequent encounter for closed fracture with nonunion
S72.351Q Displaced comminuted fracture of shaft of right femur, subsequent encounter for open fracture type I or II with malunion
S72.351M Displaced comminuted fracture of shaft of right femur, subsequent encounter for open fracture type I or II with nonunion
S72.351R Displaced comminuted fracture of shaft of right femur, subsequent encounter for open fracture type IIIA, IIIB, or IIIC with malunion
S72.351N Displaced comminuted fracture of shaft of right femur, subsequent encounter for open fracture type IIIA, IIIB, or IIIC with nonunion
S82.451P Displaced comminuted fracture of shaft of right fibula, subsequent encounter for closed fracture with malunion
S82.451K Displaced comminuted fracture of shaft of right fibula, subsequent encounter for closed fracture with nonunion
S82.451Q Displaced comminuted fracture of shaft of right fibula, subsequent encounter for open fracture type I or II with malunion
S82.451M Displaced comminuted fracture of shaft of right fibula, subsequent encounter for open fracture type I or II with nonunion
S82.451R Displaced comminuted fracture of shaft of right fibula, subsequent encounter for open fracture type IIIA, IIIB, or IIIC with malunion
S82.451N Displaced comminuted fracture of shaft of right fibula, subsequent encounter for open fracture type IIIA, IIIB, or IIIC with nonunion
S82.251A Displaced comminuted fracture of shaft of right tibia, initial encounter for closed fracture
S82.251P Displaced comminuted fracture of shaft of right tibia, subsequent encounter for closed fracture with malunion
S82.251K Displaced comminuted fracture of shaft of right tibia, subsequent encounter for closed fracture with nonunion
S82.251Q Displaced comminuted fracture of shaft of right tibia, subsequent encounter for open fracture type I or II with malunion
S82.251M Displaced comminuted fracture of shaft of right tibia, subsequent encounter for open fracture type I or II with nonunion
S82.251R Displaced comminuted fracture of shaft of right tibia, subsequent encounter for open fracture type IIIA, IIIB, or IIIC with malunion
S82.251N Displaced comminuted fracture of shaft of right tibia, subsequent encounter for open fracture type IIIA, IIIB, or IIIC with nonunion
S52.252A Displaced comminuted fracture of shaft of ulna, left arm, initial encounter for closed fracture
S52.252P Displaced comminuted fracture of shaft of ulna, left arm, subsequent encounter for closed fracture with malunion
S52.252K Displaced comminuted fracture of shaft of ulna, left arm, subsequent encounter for closed fracture with nonunion
S52.252Q Displaced comminuted fracture of shaft of ulna, left arm, subsequent encounter for open fracture type I or II with malunion
S52.252M Displaced comminuted fracture of shaft of ulna, left arm, subsequent encounter for open fracture type I or II with nonunion
S52.252R Displaced comminuted fracture of shaft of ulna, left arm, subsequent encounter for open fracture type IIIA, IIIB, or IIIC with malunion
S52.252N Displaced comminuted fracture of shaft of ulna, left arm, subsequent encounter for open fracture type IIIA, IIIB, or IIIC with nonunion
S52.251A Displaced comminuted fracture of shaft of ulna, right arm, initial encounter for closed fracture
S52.251P Displaced comminuted fracture of shaft of ulna, right arm, subsequent encounter for closed fracture with malunion
S52.251K Displaced comminuted fracture of shaft of ulna, right arm, subsequent encounter for closed fracture with nonunion
S52.251Q Displaced comminuted fracture of shaft of ulna, right arm, subsequent encounter for open fracture type I or II with malunion
S52.251M Displaced comminuted fracture of shaft of ulna, right arm, subsequent encounter for open fracture type I or II with nonunion
S52.251R Displaced comminuted fracture of shaft of ulna, right arm, subsequent encounter for open fracture type IIIA, IIIB, or IIIC with malunion
S52.251N Displaced comminuted fracture of shaft of ulna, right arm, subsequent encounter for open fracture type IIIA, IIIB, or IIIC with nonunion
S52.253A Displaced comminuted fracture of shaft of ulna, unspecified arm, initial encounter for closed fracture
S52.253P Displaced comminuted fracture of shaft of ulna, unspecified arm, subsequent encounter for closed fracture with malunion
S52.253K Displaced comminuted fracture of shaft of ulna, unspecified arm, subsequent encounter for closed fracture with nonunion
S52.253Q Displaced comminuted fracture of shaft of ulna, unspecified arm, subsequent encounter for open fracture type I or II with malunion
S52.253M Displaced comminuted fracture of shaft of ulna, unspecified arm, subsequent encounter for open fracture type I or II with nonunion
S52.253R Displaced comminuted fracture of shaft of ulna, unspecified arm, subsequent encounter for open fracture type IIIA, IIIB, or IIIC with malunion
S52.253N Displaced comminuted fracture of shaft of ulna, unspecified arm, subsequent encounter for open fracture type IIIA, IIIB, or IIIC with nonunion
S72.353P Displaced comminuted fracture of shaft of unspecified femur, subsequent encounter for closed fracture with malunion
S72.353K Displaced comminuted fracture of shaft of unspecified femur, subsequent encounter for closed fracture with nonunion
S72.353Q Displaced comminuted fracture of shaft of unspecified femur, subsequent encounter for open fracture type I or II with malunion
S72.353M Displaced comminuted fracture of shaft of unspecified femur, subsequent encounter for open fracture type I or II with nonunion
S72.353R Displaced comminuted fracture of shaft of unspecified femur, subsequent encounter for open fracture type IIIA, IIIB, or IIIC with malunion
S72.353N Displaced comminuted fracture of shaft of unspecified femur, subsequent encounter for open fracture type IIIA, IIIB, or IIIC with nonunion
S82.453P Displaced comminuted fracture of shaft of unspecified fibula, subsequent encounter for closed fracture with malunion
S82.453K Displaced comminuted fracture of shaft of unspecified fibula, subsequent encounter for closed fracture with nonunion
S82.453Q Displaced comminuted fracture of shaft of unspecified fibula, subsequent encounter for open fracture type I or II with malunion
S82.453M Displaced comminuted fracture of shaft of unspecified fibula, subsequent encounter for open fracture type I or II with nonunion
S82.453R Displaced comminuted fracture of shaft of unspecified fibula, subsequent encounter for open fracture type IIIA, IIIB, or IIIC with malunion
S82.453N Displaced comminuted fracture of shaft of unspecified fibula, subsequent encounter for open fracture type IIIA, IIIB, or IIIC with nonunion
S82.253A Displaced comminuted fracture of shaft of unspecified tibia, initial encounter for closed fracture
S82.253P Displaced comminuted fracture of shaft of unspecified tibia, subsequent encounter for closed fracture with malunion
S82.253K Displaced comminuted fracture of shaft of unspecified tibia, subsequent encounter for closed fracture with nonunion
S82.253Q Displaced comminuted fracture of shaft of unspecified tibia, subsequent encounter for open fracture type I or II with malunion
S82.253M Displaced comminuted fracture of shaft of unspecified tibia, subsequent encounter for open fracture type I or II with nonunion
S82.253R Displaced comminuted fracture of shaft of unspecified tibia, subsequent encounter for open fracture type IIIA, IIIB, or IIIC with malunion
S82.253N Displaced comminuted fracture of shaft of unspecified tibia, subsequent encounter for open fracture type IIIA, IIIB, or IIIC with nonunion
S82.Ø43A Displaced comminuted fracture of unspecified patella, initial encounter for closed fracture
S82.Ø43B Displaced comminuted fracture of unspecified patella, initial encounter for open fracture type I or II
S82.Ø43C Displaced comminuted fracture of unspecified patella, initial encounter for open fracture type IIIA, IIIB, or IIIC
S82.Ø43P Displaced comminuted fracture of unspecified patella, subsequent encounter for closed fracture with malunion
S82.Ø43K Displaced comminuted fracture of unspecified patella, subsequent encounter for closed fracture with nonunion
S82.Ø43Q Displaced comminuted fracture of unspecified patella, subsequent encounter for open fracture type I or II with malunion
S82.Ø43M Displaced comminuted fracture of unspecified patella, subsequent encounter for open fracture type I or II with nonunion
S82.Ø43R Displaced comminuted fracture of unspecified patella, subsequent encounter for open fracture type IIIA, IIIB, or IIIC with malunion
S82.Ø43N Displaced comminuted fracture of unspecified patella, subsequent encounter for open fracture type IIIA, IIIB, or IIIC with nonunion
S42.422A Displaced comminuted supracondylar fracture without intercondylar fracture of left humerus, initial encounter for closed fracture
S42.422P Displaced comminuted supracondylar fracture without intercondylar fracture of left humerus, subsequent encounter for fracture with malunion

S42.422K Displaced comminuted supracondylar fracture without intercondylar fracture of left humerus, subsequent encounter for fracture with nonunion
S42.421A Displaced comminuted supracondylar fracture without intercondylar fracture of right humerus, initial encounter for closed fracture
S42.421P Displaced comminuted supracondylar fracture without intercondylar fracture of right humerus, subsequent encounter for fracture with malunion
S42.421K Displaced comminuted supracondylar fracture without intercondylar fracture of right humerus, subsequent encounter for fracture with nonunion
S42.423A Displaced comminuted supracondylar fracture without intercondylar fracture of unspecified humerus, initial encounter for closed fracture
S42.423P Displaced comminuted supracondylar fracture without intercondylar fracture of unspecified humerus, subsequent encounter for fracture with malunion
S42.423K Displaced comminuted supracondylar fracture without intercondylar fracture of unspecified humerus, subsequent encounter for fracture with nonunion
S32.482K Displaced dome fracture of left acetabulum, subsequent encounter for fracture with nonunion
S92.142B Displaced dome fracture of left talus, initial encounter for open fracture
S92.142P Displaced dome fracture of left talus, subsequent encounter for fracture with malunion
S92.142K Displaced dome fracture of left talus, subsequent encounter for fracture with nonunion
S32.481K Displaced dome fracture of right acetabulum, subsequent encounter for fracture with nonunion
S92.141B Displaced dome fracture of right talus, initial encounter for open fracture
S92.141P Displaced dome fracture of right talus, subsequent encounter for fracture with malunion
S92.141K Displaced dome fracture of right talus, subsequent encounter for fracture with nonunion
S32.483K Displaced dome fracture of unspecified acetabulum, subsequent encounter for fracture with nonunion
S92.143B Displaced dome fracture of unspecified talus, initial encounter for open fracture
S92.143P Displaced dome fracture of unspecified talus, subsequent encounter for fracture with malunion
S92.143K Displaced dome fracture of unspecified talus, subsequent encounter for fracture with nonunion
S42.432A Displaced fracture (avulsion) of lateral epicondyle of left humerus, initial encounter for closed fracture
S42.432P Displaced fracture (avulsion) of lateral epicondyle of left humerus, subsequent encounter for fracture with malunion
S42.432K Displaced fracture (avulsion) of lateral epicondyle of left humerus, subsequent encounter for fracture with nonunion
S42.431A Displaced fracture (avulsion) of lateral epicondyle of right humerus, initial encounter for closed fracture
S42.431P Displaced fracture (avulsion) of lateral epicondyle of right humerus, subsequent encounter for fracture with malunion
S42.431K Displaced fracture (avulsion) of lateral epicondyle of right humerus, subsequent encounter for fracture with nonunion
S42.433A Displaced fracture (avulsion) of lateral epicondyle of unspecified humerus, initial encounter for closed fracture
S42.433P Displaced fracture (avulsion) of lateral epicondyle of unspecified humerus, subsequent encounter for fracture with malunion
S42.433K Displaced fracture (avulsion) of lateral epicondyle of unspecified humerus, subsequent encounter for fracture with nonunion
S42.442A Displaced fracture (avulsion) of medial epicondyle of left humerus, initial encounter for closed fracture
S42.442P Displaced fracture (avulsion) of medial epicondyle of left humerus, subsequent encounter for fracture with malunion
S42.442K Displaced fracture (avulsion) of medial epicondyle of left humerus, subsequent encounter for fracture with nonunion
S42.441A Displaced fracture (avulsion) of medial epicondyle of right humerus, initial encounter for closed fracture
S42.441P Displaced fracture (avulsion) of medial epicondyle of right humerus, subsequent encounter for fracture with malunion
S42.441K Displaced fracture (avulsion) of medial epicondyle of right humerus, subsequent encounter for fracture with nonunion
S42.443A Displaced fracture (avulsion) of medial epicondyle of unspecified humerus, initial encounter for closed fracture
S42.443P Displaced fracture (avulsion) of medial epicondyle of unspecified humerus, subsequent encounter for fracture with malunion
S42.443K Displaced fracture (avulsion) of medial epicondyle of unspecified humerus, subsequent encounter for fracture with nonunion
S42.122B Displaced fracture of acromial process, left shoulder, initial encounter for open fracture
S42.122P Displaced fracture of acromial process, left shoulder, subsequent encounter for fracture with malunion
S42.122K Displaced fracture of acromial process, left shoulder, subsequent encounter for fracture with nonunion
S42.121B Displaced fracture of acromial process, right shoulder, initial encounter for open fracture
S42.121P Displaced fracture of acromial process, right shoulder, subsequent encounter for fracture with malunion
S42.121K Displaced fracture of acromial process, right shoulder, subsequent encounter for fracture with nonunion
S42.123B Displaced fracture of acromial process, unspecified shoulder, initial encounter for open fracture
S42.123P Displaced fracture of acromial process, unspecified shoulder, subsequent encounter for fracture with malunion
S42.123K Displaced fracture of acromial process, unspecified shoulder, subsequent encounter for fracture with nonunion

S32.432K Displaced fracture of anterior column [iliopubic] of left acetabulum, subsequent encounter for fracture with nonunion
S32.431K Displaced fracture of anterior column [iliopubic] of right acetabulum, subsequent encounter for fracture with nonunion
S32.433K Displaced fracture of anterior column [iliopubic] of unspecified acetabulum, subsequent encounter for fracture with nonunion
S92.022B Displaced fracture of anterior process of left calcaneus, initial encounter for open fracture
S92.022P Displaced fracture of anterior process of left calcaneus, subsequent encounter for fracture with malunion
S92.022K Displaced fracture of anterior process of left calcaneus, subsequent encounter for fracture with nonunion
S92.021B Displaced fracture of anterior process of right calcaneus, initial encounter for open fracture
S92.021P Displaced fracture of anterior process of right calcaneus, subsequent encounter for fracture with malunion
S92.021K Displaced fracture of anterior process of right calcaneus, subsequent encounter for fracture with nonunion
S92.023B Displaced fracture of anterior process of unspecified calcaneus, initial encounter for open fracture
S92.023P Displaced fracture of anterior process of unspecified calcaneus, subsequent encounter for fracture with malunion
S92.023K Displaced fracture of anterior process of unspecified calcaneus, subsequent encounter for fracture with nonunion
S32.412K Displaced fracture of anterior wall of left acetabulum, subsequent encounter for fracture with nonunion
S32.411K Displaced fracture of anterior wall of right acetabulum, subsequent encounter for fracture with nonunion
S32.413K Displaced fracture of anterior wall of unspecified acetabulum, subsequent encounter for fracture with nonunion
S62.317B Displaced fracture of base of fifth metacarpal bone, left hand, initial encounter for open fracture
S62.317P Displaced fracture of base of fifth metacarpal bone, left hand, subsequent encounter for fracture with malunion
S62.317K Displaced fracture of base of fifth metacarpal bone, left hand, subsequent encounter for fracture with nonunion
S62.316B Displaced fracture of base of fifth metacarpal bone, right hand, initial encounter for open fracture
S62.316P Displaced fracture of base of fifth metacarpal bone, right hand, subsequent encounter for fracture with malunion
S62.316K Displaced fracture of base of fifth metacarpal bone, right hand, subsequent encounter for fracture with nonunion
S62.315B Displaced fracture of base of fourth metacarpal bone, left hand, initial encounter for open fracture
S62.315P Displaced fracture of base of fourth metacarpal bone, left hand, subsequent encounter for fracture with malunion
S62.315K Displaced fracture of base of fourth metacarpal bone, left hand, subsequent encounter for fracture with nonunion
S62.314B Displaced fracture of base of fourth metacarpal bone, right hand, initial encounter for open fracture
S62.314P Displaced fracture of base of fourth metacarpal bone, right hand, subsequent encounter for fracture with malunion
S62.314K Displaced fracture of base of fourth metacarpal bone, right hand, subsequent encounter for fracture with nonunion
S72.042P Displaced fracture of base of neck of left femur, subsequent encounter for closed fracture with malunion
S72.042K Displaced fracture of base of neck of left femur, subsequent encounter for closed fracture with nonunion
S72.042Q Displaced fracture of base of neck of left femur, subsequent encounter for open fracture type I or II with malunion
S72.042M Displaced fracture of base of neck of left femur, subsequent encounter for open fracture type I or II with nonunion
S72.042R Displaced fracture of base of neck of left femur, subsequent encounter for open fracture type IIIA, IIIB, or IIIC with malunion
S72.042N Displaced fracture of base of neck of left femur, subsequent encounter for open fracture type IIIA, IIIB, or IIIC with nonunion
S72.041P Displaced fracture of base of neck of right femur, subsequent encounter for closed fracture with malunion
S72.041K Displaced fracture of base of neck of right femur, subsequent encounter for closed fracture with nonunion
S72.041Q Displaced fracture of base of neck of right femur, subsequent encounter for open fracture type I or II with malunion
S72.041M Displaced fracture of base of neck of right femur, subsequent encounter for open fracture type I or II with nonunion
S72.041R Displaced fracture of base of neck of right femur, subsequent encounter for open fracture type IIIA, IIIB, or IIIC with malunion
S72.041N Displaced fracture of base of neck of right femur, subsequent encounter for open fracture type IIIA, IIIB, or IIIC with nonunion
S72.043P Displaced fracture of base of neck of unspecified femur, subsequent encounter for closed fracture with malunion
S72.043K Displaced fracture of base of neck of unspecified femur, subsequent encounter for closed fracture with nonunion
S72.043Q Displaced fracture of base of neck of unspecified femur, subsequent encounter for open fracture type I or II with malunion
S72.043M Displaced fracture of base of neck of unspecified femur, subsequent encounter for open fracture type I or II with nonunion
S72.043R Displaced fracture of base of neck of unspecified femur, subsequent encounter for open fracture type IIIA, IIIB, or IIIC with malunion
S72.043N Displaced fracture of base of neck of unspecified femur, subsequent encounter for open fracture type IIIA, IIIB, or IIIC with nonunion

S62.318B Displaced fracture of base of other metacarpal bone, initial encounter for open fracture

S62.318P Displaced fracture of base of other metacarpal bone, subsequent encounter for fracture with malunion

S62.318K Displaced fracture of base of other metacarpal bone, subsequent encounter for fracture with nonunion

S62.311B Displaced fracture of base of second metacarpal bone, left hand, initial encounter for open fracture

S62.311P Displaced fracture of base of second metacarpal bone, left hand, subsequent encounter for fracture with malunion

S62.311K Displaced fracture of base of second metacarpal bone, left hand, subsequent encounter for fracture with nonunion

S62.310B Displaced fracture of base of second metacarpal bone, right hand, initial encounter for open fracture

S62.310P Displaced fracture of base of second metacarpal bone, right hand, subsequent encounter for fracture with malunion

S62.310K Displaced fracture of base of second metacarpal bone, right hand, subsequent encounter for fracture with nonunion

S62.313B Displaced fracture of base of third metacarpal bone, left hand, initial encounter for open fracture

S62.313P Displaced fracture of base of third metacarpal bone, left hand, subsequent encounter for fracture with malunion

S62.313K Displaced fracture of base of third metacarpal bone, left hand, subsequent encounter for fracture with nonunion

S62.312B Displaced fracture of base of third metacarpal bone, right hand, initial encounter for open fracture

S62.312P Displaced fracture of base of third metacarpal bone, right hand, subsequent encounter for fracture with malunion

S62.312K Displaced fracture of base of third metacarpal bone, right hand, subsequent encounter for fracture with nonunion

S62.319B Displaced fracture of base of unspecified metacarpal bone, initial encounter for open fracture

S62.319P Displaced fracture of base of unspecified metacarpal bone, subsequent encounter for fracture with malunion

S62.319K Displaced fracture of base of unspecified metacarpal bone, subsequent encounter for fracture with nonunion

S62.142B Displaced fracture of body of hamate [unciform] bone, left wrist, initial encounter for open fracture

S62.142P Displaced fracture of body of hamate [unciform] bone, left wrist, subsequent encounter for fracture with malunion

S62.142K Displaced fracture of body of hamate [unciform] bone, left wrist, subsequent encounter for fracture with nonunion

S62.141B Displaced fracture of body of hamate [unciform] bone, right wrist, initial encounter for open fracture

S62.141P Displaced fracture of body of hamate [unciform] bone, right wrist, subsequent encounter for fracture with malunion

S62.141K Displaced fracture of body of hamate [unciform] bone, right wrist, subsequent encounter for fracture with nonunion

S62.143B Displaced fracture of body of hamate [unciform] bone, unspecified wrist, initial encounter for open fracture

S62.143P Displaced fracture of body of hamate [unciform] bone, unspecified wrist, subsequent encounter for fracture with malunion

S62.143K Displaced fracture of body of hamate [unciform] bone, unspecified wrist, subsequent encounter for fracture with nonunion

S92.012B Displaced fracture of body of left calcaneus, initial encounter for open fracture

S92.012P Displaced fracture of body of left calcaneus, subsequent encounter for fracture with malunion

S92.012K Displaced fracture of body of left calcaneus, subsequent encounter for fracture with nonunion

S92.122B Displaced fracture of body of left talus, initial encounter for open fracture

S92.122P Displaced fracture of body of left talus, subsequent encounter for fracture with malunion

S92.122K Displaced fracture of body of left talus, subsequent encounter for fracture with nonunion

S92.011B Displaced fracture of body of right calcaneus, initial encounter for open fracture

S92.011P Displaced fracture of body of right calcaneus, subsequent encounter for fracture with malunion

S92.011K Displaced fracture of body of right calcaneus, subsequent encounter for fracture with nonunion

S92.121B Displaced fracture of body of right talus, initial encounter for open fracture

S92.121P Displaced fracture of body of right talus, subsequent encounter for fracture with malunion

S92.121K Displaced fracture of body of right talus, subsequent encounter for fracture with nonunion

S42.112B Displaced fracture of body of scapula, left shoulder, initial encounter for open fracture

S42.112P Displaced fracture of body of scapula, left shoulder, subsequent encounter for fracture with malunion

S42.112K Displaced fracture of body of scapula, left shoulder, subsequent encounter for fracture with nonunion

S42.111B Displaced fracture of body of scapula, right shoulder, initial encounter for open fracture

S42.111P Displaced fracture of body of scapula, right shoulder, subsequent encounter for fracture with malunion

S42.111K Displaced fracture of body of scapula, right shoulder, subsequent encounter for fracture with nonunion

S42.113B Displaced fracture of body of scapula, unspecified shoulder, initial encounter for open fracture

S42.113P Displaced fracture of body of scapula, unspecified shoulder, subsequent encounter for fracture with malunion

S42.113K Displaced fracture of body of scapula, unspecified shoulder, subsequent encounter for fracture with nonunion

S92.013B Displaced fracture of body of unspecified calcaneus, initial encounter for open fracture

S92.013P Displaced fracture of body of unspecified calcaneus, subsequent encounter for fracture with malunion

S92.013K Displaced fracture of body of unspecified calcaneus, subsequent encounter for fracture with nonunion

S92.123B Displaced fracture of body of unspecified talus, initial encounter for open fracture

S92.123P Displaced fracture of body of unspecified talus, subsequent encounter for fracture with malunion

S92.123K Displaced fracture of body of unspecified talus, subsequent encounter for fracture with nonunion

S62.132B Displaced fracture of capitate [os magnum] bone, left wrist, initial encounter for open fracture

S62.132P Displaced fracture of capitate [os magnum] bone, left wrist, subsequent encounter for fracture with malunion

S62.132K Displaced fracture of capitate [os magnum] bone, left wrist, subsequent encounter for fracture with nonunion

S62.131B Displaced fracture of capitate [os magnum] bone, right wrist, initial encounter for open fracture

S62.131P Displaced fracture of capitate [os magnum] bone, right wrist, subsequent encounter for fracture with malunion

S62.131K Displaced fracture of capitate [os magnum] bone, right wrist, subsequent encounter for fracture with nonunion

S62.133B Displaced fracture of capitate [os magnum] bone, unspecified wrist, initial encounter for open fracture

S62.133P Displaced fracture of capitate [os magnum] bone, unspecified wrist, subsequent encounter for fracture with malunion

S62.133K Displaced fracture of capitate [os magnum] bone, unspecified wrist, subsequent encounter for fracture with nonunion

S42.132B Displaced fracture of coracoid process, left shoulder, initial encounter for open fracture

S42.132P Displaced fracture of coracoid process, left shoulder, subsequent encounter for fracture with malunion

S42.132K Displaced fracture of coracoid process, left shoulder, subsequent encounter for fracture with nonunion

S42.131B Displaced fracture of coracoid process, right shoulder, initial encounter for open fracture

S42.131P Displaced fracture of coracoid process, right shoulder, subsequent encounter for fracture with malunion

S42.131K Displaced fracture of coracoid process, right shoulder, subsequent encounter for fracture with nonunion

S42.133B Displaced fracture of coracoid process, unspecified shoulder, initial encounter for open fracture

S42.133P Displaced fracture of coracoid process, unspecified shoulder, subsequent encounter for fracture with malunion

S42.133K Displaced fracture of coracoid process, unspecified shoulder, subsequent encounter for fracture with nonunion

S52.042P Displaced fracture of coronoid process of left ulna, subsequent encounter for closed fracture with malunion

S52.042K Displaced fracture of coronoid process of left ulna, subsequent encounter for closed fracture with nonunion

S52.042Q Displaced fracture of coronoid process of left ulna, subsequent encounter for open fracture type I or II with malunion

S52.042M Displaced fracture of coronoid process of left ulna, subsequent encounter for open fracture type I or II with nonunion

S52.042R Displaced fracture of coronoid process of left ulna, subsequent encounter for open fracture type IIIA, IIIB, or IIIC with malunion

S52.042N Displaced fracture of coronoid process of left ulna, subsequent encounter for open fracture type IIIA, IIIB, or IIIC with nonunion

S52.041P Displaced fracture of coronoid process of right ulna, subsequent encounter for closed fracture with malunion

S52.041K Displaced fracture of coronoid process of right ulna, subsequent encounter for closed fracture with nonunion

S52.041Q Displaced fracture of coronoid process of right ulna, subsequent encounter for open fracture type I or II with malunion

S52.041M Displaced fracture of coronoid process of right ulna, subsequent encounter for open fracture type I or II with nonunion

S52.041R Displaced fracture of coronoid process of right ulna, subsequent encounter for open fracture type IIIA, IIIB, or IIIC with malunion

S52.041N Displaced fracture of coronoid process of right ulna, subsequent encounter for open fracture type IIIA, IIIB, or IIIC with nonunion

S52.043P Displaced fracture of coronoid process of unspecified ulna, subsequent encounter for closed fracture with malunion

S52.043K Displaced fracture of coronoid process of unspecified ulna, subsequent encounter for closed fracture with nonunion

S52.043Q Displaced fracture of coronoid process of unspecified ulna, subsequent encounter for open fracture type I or II with malunion

S52.043M Displaced fracture of coronoid process of unspecified ulna, subsequent encounter for open fracture type I or II with nonunion

S52.043R Displaced fracture of coronoid process of unspecified ulna, subsequent encounter for open fracture type IIIA, IIIB, or IIIC with malunion

S52.043N Displaced fracture of coronoid process of unspecified ulna, subsequent encounter for open fracture type IIIA, IIIB, or IIIC with nonunion

S92.212B Displaced fracture of cuboid bone of left foot, initial encounter for open fracture

S92.212P Displaced fracture of cuboid bone of left foot, subsequent encounter for fracture with malunion

S92.212K Displaced fracture of cuboid bone of left foot, subsequent encounter for fracture with nonunion

S92.211B Displaced fracture of cuboid bone of right foot, initial encounter for open fracture

S92.211P Displaced fracture of cuboid bone of right foot, subsequent encounter for fracture with malunion

S92.211K Displaced fracture of cuboid bone of right foot, subsequent encounter for fracture with nonunion

S92.213B Displaced fracture of cuboid bone of unspecified foot, initial encounter for open fracture

S92.213P Displaced fracture of cuboid bone of unspecified foot, subsequent encounter for fracture with malunion

S92.213K Displaced fracture of cuboid bone of unspecified foot, subsequent encounter for fracture with nonunion

S92.422P Displaced fracture of distal phalanx of left great toe, subsequent encounter for fracture with malunion

S92.422K Displaced fracture of distal phalanx of left great toe, subsequent encounter for fracture with nonunion

S62.631B Displaced fracture of distal phalanx of left index finger, initial encounter for open fracture

S62.631P Displaced fracture of distal phalanx of left index finger, subsequent encounter for fracture with malunion

S62.631K Displaced fracture of distal phalanx of left index finger, subsequent encounter for fracture with nonunion

S92.532P Displaced fracture of distal phalanx of left lesser toe(s), subsequent encounter for fracture with malunion

S92.532K Displaced fracture of distal phalanx of left lesser toe(s), subsequent encounter for fracture with nonunion

S62.637B Displaced fracture of distal phalanx of left little finger, initial encounter for open fracture

S62.637P Displaced fracture of distal phalanx of left little finger, subsequent encounter for fracture with malunion

S62.637K Displaced fracture of distal phalanx of left little finger, subsequent encounter for fracture with nonunion

S62.633B Displaced fracture of distal phalanx of left middle finger, initial encounter for open fracture

S62.633P Displaced fracture of distal phalanx of left middle finger, subsequent encounter for fracture with malunion

S62.633K Displaced fracture of distal phalanx of left middle finger, subsequent encounter for fracture with nonunion

S62.635B Displaced fracture of distal phalanx of left ring finger, initial encounter for open fracture

S62.635P Displaced fracture of distal phalanx of left ring finger, subsequent encounter for fracture with malunion

S62.635K Displaced fracture of distal phalanx of left ring finger, subsequent encounter for fracture with nonunion

S62.522B Displaced fracture of distal phalanx of left thumb, initial encounter for open fracture

S62.522P Displaced fracture of distal phalanx of left thumb, subsequent encounter for fracture with malunion

S62.522K Displaced fracture of distal phalanx of left thumb, subsequent encounter for fracture with nonunion

S62.638B Displaced fracture of distal phalanx of other finger, initial encounter for open fracture

S62.638P Displaced fracture of distal phalanx of other finger, subsequent encounter for fracture with malunion

S62.638K Displaced fracture of distal phalanx of other finger, subsequent encounter for fracture with nonunion

S92.421P Displaced fracture of distal phalanx of right great toe, subsequent encounter for fracture with malunion

S92.421K Displaced fracture of distal phalanx of right great toe, subsequent encounter for fracture with nonunion

S62.630B Displaced fracture of distal phalanx of right index finger, initial encounter for open fracture

S62.630P Displaced fracture of distal phalanx of right index finger, subsequent encounter for fracture with malunion

S62.630K Displaced fracture of distal phalanx of right index finger, subsequent encounter for fracture with nonunion

S92.531P Displaced fracture of distal phalanx of right lesser toe(s), subsequent encounter for fracture with malunion

S92.531K Displaced fracture of distal phalanx of right lesser toe(s), subsequent encounter for fracture with nonunion

S62.636B Displaced fracture of distal phalanx of right little finger, initial encounter for open fracture

S62.636P Displaced fracture of distal phalanx of right little finger, subsequent encounter for fracture with malunion

S62.636K Displaced fracture of distal phalanx of right little finger, subsequent encounter for fracture with nonunion

S62.632B Displaced fracture of distal phalanx of right middle finger, initial encounter for open fracture

S62.632P Displaced fracture of distal phalanx of right middle finger, subsequent encounter for fracture with malunion

S62.632K Displaced fracture of distal phalanx of right middle finger, subsequent encounter for fracture with nonunion

S62.634B Displaced fracture of distal phalanx of right ring finger, initial encounter for open fracture

S62.634P Displaced fracture of distal phalanx of right ring finger, subsequent encounter for fracture with malunion

S62.634K Displaced fracture of distal phalanx of right ring finger, subsequent encounter for fracture with nonunion

S62.521B Displaced fracture of distal phalanx of right thumb, initial encounter for open fracture

S62.521P Displaced fracture of distal phalanx of right thumb, subsequent encounter for fracture with malunion

S62.521K Displaced fracture of distal phalanx of right thumb, subsequent encounter for fracture with nonunion

S62.639B Displaced fracture of distal phalanx of unspecified finger, initial encounter for open fracture

S62.639P Displaced fracture of distal phalanx of unspecified finger, subsequent encounter for fracture with malunion

S62.639K Displaced fracture of distal phalanx of unspecified finger, subsequent encounter for fracture with nonunion

S92.423P Displaced fracture of distal phalanx of unspecified great toe, subsequent encounter for fracture with malunion

S92.423K Displaced fracture of distal phalanx of unspecified great toe, subsequent encounter for fracture with nonunion

S92.533P Displaced fracture of distal phalanx of unspecified lesser toe(s), subsequent encounter for fracture with malunion

S92.533K Displaced fracture of distal phalanx of unspecified lesser toe(s), subsequent encounter for fracture with nonunion

S62.523B Displaced fracture of distal phalanx of unspecified thumb, initial encounter for open fracture

S62.523P Displaced fracture of distal phalanx of unspecified thumb, subsequent encounter for fracture with malunion

S62.523K Displaced fracture of distal phalanx of unspecified thumb, subsequent encounter for fracture with nonunion

S62.012B Displaced fracture of distal pole of navicular [scaphoid] bone of left wrist, initial encounter for open fracture

S62.012P Displaced fracture of distal pole of navicular [scaphoid] bone of left wrist, subsequent encounter for fracture with malunion

S62.012K Displaced fracture of distal pole of navicular [scaphoid] bone of left wrist, subsequent encounter for fracture with nonunion

S62.011B Displaced fracture of distal pole of navicular [scaphoid] bone of right wrist, initial encounter for open fracture

S62.011P Displaced fracture of distal pole of navicular [scaphoid] bone of right wrist, subsequent encounter for fracture with malunion

S62.011K Displaced fracture of distal pole of navicular [scaphoid] bone of right wrist, subsequent encounter for fracture with nonunion

S62.013B Displaced fracture of distal pole of navicular [scaphoid] bone of unspecified wrist, initial encounter for open fracture

S62.013P Displaced fracture of distal pole of navicular [scaphoid] bone of unspecified wrist, subsequent encounter for fracture with malunion

S62.013K Displaced fracture of distal pole of navicular [scaphoid] bone of unspecified wrist, subsequent encounter for fracture with nonunion

S72.022P Displaced fracture of epiphysis (separation) (upper) of left femur, subsequent encounter for closed fracture with malunion

S72.022K Displaced fracture of epiphysis (separation) (upper) of left femur, subsequent encounter for closed fracture with nonunion

S72.022Q Displaced fracture of epiphysis (separation) (upper) of left femur, subsequent encounter for open fracture type I or II with malunion

S72.022M Displaced fracture of epiphysis (separation) (upper) of left femur, subsequent encounter for open fracture type I or II with nonunion

S72.022R Displaced fracture of epiphysis (separation) (upper) of left femur, subsequent encounter for open fracture type IIIA, IIIB, or IIIC with malunion

S72.022N Displaced fracture of epiphysis (separation) (upper) of left femur, subsequent encounter for open fracture type IIIA, IIIB, or IIIC with nonunion

S72.021P Displaced fracture of epiphysis (separation) (upper) of right femur, subsequent encounter for closed fracture with malunion

S72.021K Displaced fracture of epiphysis (separation) (upper) of right femur, subsequent encounter for closed fracture with nonunion

S72.021Q Displaced fracture of epiphysis (separation) (upper) of right femur, subsequent encounter for open fracture type I or II with malunion

S72.021M Displaced fracture of epiphysis (separation) (upper) of right femur, subsequent encounter for open fracture type I or II with nonunion

S72.021R Displaced fracture of epiphysis (separation) (upper) of right femur, subsequent encounter for open fracture type IIIA, IIIB, or IIIC with malunion

S72.021N Displaced fracture of epiphysis (separation) (upper) of right femur, subsequent encounter for open fracture type IIIA, IIIB, or IIIC with nonunion

S72.023P Displaced fracture of epiphysis (separation) (upper) of unspecified femur, subsequent encounter for closed fracture with malunion

S72.023K Displaced fracture of epiphysis (separation) (upper) of unspecified femur, subsequent encounter for closed fracture with nonunion

S72.023Q Displaced fracture of epiphysis (separation) (upper) of unspecified femur, subsequent encounter for open fracture type I or II with malunion

S72.023M Displaced fracture of epiphysis (separation) (upper) of unspecified femur, subsequent encounter for open fracture type I or II with nonunion

S72.023R Displaced fracture of epiphysis (separation) (upper) of unspecified femur, subsequent encounter for open fracture type IIIA, IIIB, or IIIC with malunion

S72.023N Displaced fracture of epiphysis (separation) (upper) of unspecified femur, subsequent encounter for open fracture type IIIA, IIIB, or IIIC with nonunion

S92.352B Displaced fracture of fifth metatarsal bone, left foot, initial encounter for open fracture

S92.352P Displaced fracture of fifth metatarsal bone, left foot, subsequent encounter for fracture with malunion

S92.352K Displaced fracture of fifth metatarsal bone, left foot, subsequent encounter for fracture with nonunion

S92.351B Displaced fracture of fifth metatarsal bone, right foot, initial encounter for open fracture

S92.351P Displaced fracture of fifth metatarsal bone, right foot, subsequent encounter for fracture with malunion

S92.351K Displaced fracture of fifth metatarsal bone, right foot, subsequent encounter for fracture with nonunion

S92.353B Displaced fracture of fifth metatarsal bone, unspecified foot, initial encounter for open fracture

S92.353P Displaced fracture of fifth metatarsal bone, unspecified foot, subsequent encounter for fracture with malunion

S92.353K Displaced fracture of fifth metatarsal bone, unspecified foot, subsequent encounter for fracture with nonunion

S92.312B Displaced fracture of first metatarsal bone, left foot, initial encounter for open fracture

S92.312P Displaced fracture of first metatarsal bone, left foot, subsequent encounter for fracture with malunion

S92.312K Displaced fracture of first metatarsal bone, left foot, subsequent encounter for fracture with nonunion

S92.311B Displaced fracture of first metatarsal bone, right foot, initial encounter for open fracture

S92.311P Displaced fracture of first metatarsal bone, right foot, subsequent encounter for fracture with malunion

S92.311K Displaced fracture of first metatarsal bone, right foot, subsequent encounter for fracture with nonunion

S92.313B Displaced fracture of first metatarsal bone, unspecified foot, initial encounter for open fracture

S92.313P Displaced fracture of first metatarsal bone, unspecified foot, subsequent encounter for fracture with malunion

S92.313K Displaced fracture of first metatarsal bone, unspecified foot, subsequent encounter for fracture with nonunion

S92.342B Displaced fracture of fourth metatarsal bone, left foot, initial encounter for open fracture

S92.342P Displaced fracture of fourth metatarsal bone, left foot, subsequent encounter for fracture with malunion

S92.342K Displaced fracture of fourth metatarsal bone, left foot, subsequent encounter for fracture with nonunion

S92.341B Displaced fracture of fourth metatarsal bone, right foot, initial encounter for open fracture

S92.341P Displaced fracture of fourth metatarsal bone, right foot, subsequent encounter for fracture with malunion

S92.341K Displaced fracture of fourth metatarsal bone, right foot, subsequent encounter for fracture with nonunion

S92.343B Displaced fracture of fourth metatarsal bone, unspecified foot, initial encounter for open fracture

S92.343P Displaced fracture of fourth metatarsal bone, unspecified foot, subsequent encounter for fracture with malunion

S92.343K Displaced fracture of fourth metatarsal bone, unspecified foot, subsequent encounter for fracture with nonunion

S42.142B Displaced fracture of glenoid cavity of scapula, left shoulder, initial encounter for open fracture

S42.142P Displaced fracture of glenoid cavity of scapula, left shoulder, subsequent encounter for fracture with malunion

S42.142K Displaced fracture of glenoid cavity of scapula, left shoulder, subsequent encounter for fracture with nonunion

S42.141B Displaced fracture of glenoid cavity of scapula, right shoulder, initial encounter for open fracture

S42.141P Displaced fracture of glenoid cavity of scapula, right shoulder, subsequent encounter for fracture with malunion

S42.141K Displaced fracture of glenoid cavity of scapula, right shoulder, subsequent encounter for fracture with nonunion

S42.143B Displaced fracture of glenoid cavity of scapula, unspecified shoulder, initial encounter for open fracture

S42.143P Displaced fracture of glenoid cavity of scapula, unspecified shoulder, subsequent encounter for fracture with malunion

S42.143K Displaced fracture of glenoid cavity of scapula, unspecified shoulder, subsequent encounter for fracture with nonunion

S72.112P Displaced fracture of greater trochanter of left femur, subsequent encounter for closed fracture with malunion

S72.112K Displaced fracture of greater trochanter of left femur, subsequent encounter for closed fracture with nonunion

S72.112Q Displaced fracture of greater trochanter of left femur, subsequent encounter for open fracture type I or II with malunion

S72.112M Displaced fracture of greater trochanter of left femur, subsequent encounter for open fracture type I or II with nonunion

S72.112R Displaced fracture of greater trochanter of left femur, subsequent encounter for open fracture type IIIA, IIIB, or IIIC with malunion

S72.112N Displaced fracture of greater trochanter of left femur, subsequent encounter for open fracture type IIIA, IIIB, or IIIC with nonunion

S72.111P Displaced fracture of greater trochanter of right femur, subsequent encounter for closed fracture with malunion

S72.111K Displaced fracture of greater trochanter of right femur, subsequent encounter for closed fracture with nonunion

S72.111Q Displaced fracture of greater trochanter of right femur, subsequent encounter for open fracture type I or II with malunion

S72.111M Displaced fracture of greater trochanter of right femur, subsequent encounter for open fracture type I or II with nonunion

S72.111R Displaced fracture of greater trochanter of right femur, subsequent encounter for open fracture type IIIA, IIIB, or IIIC with malunion

S72.111N Displaced fracture of greater trochanter of right femur, subsequent encounter for open fracture type IIIA, IIIB, or IIIC with nonunion

S72.113P Displaced fracture of greater trochanter of unspecified femur, subsequent encounter for closed fracture with malunion

S72.113K Displaced fracture of greater trochanter of unspecified femur, subsequent encounter for closed fracture with nonunion

S72.113Q Displaced fracture of greater trochanter of unspecified femur, subsequent encounter for open fracture type I or II with malunion

S72.113M Displaced fracture of greater trochanter of unspecified femur, subsequent encounter for open fracture type I or II with nonunion

S72.113R Displaced fracture of greater trochanter of unspecified femur, subsequent encounter for open fracture type IIIA, IIIB, or IIIC with malunion

S72.113N Displaced fracture of greater trochanter of unspecified femur, subsequent encounter for open fracture type IIIA, IIIB, or IIIC with nonunion

S42.252A Displaced fracture of greater tuberosity of left humerus, initial encounter for closed fracture

S42.252P Displaced fracture of greater tuberosity of left humerus, subsequent encounter for fracture with malunion

S42.252K Displaced fracture of greater tuberosity of left humerus, subsequent encounter for fracture with nonunion

S42.251A Displaced fracture of greater tuberosity of right humerus, initial encounter for closed fracture

S42.251P Displaced fracture of greater tuberosity of right humerus, subsequent encounter for fracture with malunion

S42.251K Displaced fracture of greater tuberosity of right humerus, subsequent encounter for fracture with nonunion

S42.253A Displaced fracture of greater tuberosity of unspecified humerus, initial encounter for closed fracture

S42.253P Displaced fracture of greater tuberosity of unspecified humerus, subsequent encounter for fracture with malunion

S42.253K Displaced fracture of greater tuberosity of unspecified humerus, subsequent encounter for fracture with nonunion

S52.122P Displaced fracture of head of left radius, subsequent encounter for closed fracture with malunion

S52.122K Displaced fracture of head of left radius, subsequent encounter for closed fracture with nonunion

S52.122Q Displaced fracture of head of left radius, subsequent encounter for open fracture type I or II with malunion

S52.122M Displaced fracture of head of left radius, subsequent encounter for open fracture type I or II with nonunion

S52.122R Displaced fracture of head of left radius, subsequent encounter for open fracture type IIIA, IIIB, or IIIC with malunion

S52.122N Displaced fracture of head of left radius, subsequent encounter for open fracture type IIIA, IIIB, or IIIC with nonunion

S52.121P Displaced fracture of head of right radius, subsequent encounter for closed fracture with malunion

S52.121K Displaced fracture of head of right radius, subsequent encounter for closed fracture with nonunion

S52.121Q Displaced fracture of head of right radius, subsequent encounter for open fracture type I or II with malunion

S52.121M Displaced fracture of head of right radius, subsequent encounter for open fracture type I or II with nonunion

S52.121R Displaced fracture of head of right radius, subsequent encounter for open fracture type IIIA, IIIB, or IIIC with malunion

S52.121N Displaced fracture of head of right radius, subsequent encounter for open fracture type IIIA, IIIB, or IIIC with nonunion

S52.123P Displaced fracture of head of unspecified radius, subsequent encounter for closed fracture with malunion

S52.123K Displaced fracture of head of unspecified radius, subsequent encounter for closed fracture with nonunion

S52.123Q Displaced fracture of head of unspecified radius, subsequent encounter for open fracture type I or II with malunion

S52.123M Displaced fracture of head of unspecified radius, subsequent encounter for open fracture type I or II with nonunion

S52.123R Displaced fracture of head of unspecified radius, subsequent encounter for open fracture type IIIA, IIIB, or IIIC with malunion

S52.123N Displaced fracture of head of unspecified radius, subsequent encounter for open fracture type IIIA, IIIB, or IIIC with nonunion

S62.152B Displaced fracture of hook process of hamate [unciform] bone, left wrist, initial encounter for open fracture

S62.152P Displaced fracture of hook process of hamate [unciform] bone, left wrist, subsequent encounter for fracture with malunion

S62.152K Displaced fracture of hook process of hamate [unciform] bone, left wrist, subsequent encounter for fracture with nonunion

S62.151B Displaced fracture of hook process of hamate [unciform] bone, right wrist, initial encounter for open fracture

S62.151P Displaced fracture of hook process of hamate [unciform] bone, right wrist, subsequent encounter for fracture with malunion

S62.151K Displaced fracture of hook process of hamate [unciform] bone, right wrist, subsequent encounter for fracture with nonunion

S62.153B Displaced fracture of hook process of hamate [unciform] bone, unspecified wrist, initial encounter for open fracture

S62.153P Displaced fracture of hook process of hamate [unciform] bone, unspecified wrist, subsequent encounter for fracture with malunion

S62.153K Displaced fracture of hook process of hamate [unciform] bone, unspecified wrist, subsequent encounter for fracture with nonunion

S92.232B Displaced fracture of intermediate cuneiform of left foot, initial encounter for open fracture

S92.232P Displaced fracture of intermediate cuneiform of left foot, subsequent encounter for fracture with malunion

S92.232K Displaced fracture of intermediate cuneiform of left foot, subsequent encounter for fracture with nonunion

S92.231B Displaced fracture of intermediate cuneiform of right foot, initial encounter for open fracture

S92.231P Displaced fracture of intermediate cuneiform of right foot, subsequent encounter for fracture with malunion

S92.231K Displaced fracture of intermediate cuneiform of right foot, subsequent encounter for fracture with nonunion

S92.233B Displaced fracture of intermediate cuneiform of unspecified foot, initial encounter for open fracture

S92.233P Displaced fracture of intermediate cuneiform of unspecified foot, subsequent encounter for fracture with malunion

S92.233K Displaced fracture of intermediate cuneiform of unspecified foot, subsequent encounter for fracture with nonunion

S72.422A Displaced fracture of lateral condyle of left femur, initial encounter for closed fracture

S72.422P Displaced fracture of lateral condyle of left femur, subsequent encounter for closed fracture with malunion

S72.422K Displaced fracture of lateral condyle of left femur, subsequent encounter for closed fracture with nonunion

S72.422Q Displaced fracture of lateral condyle of left femur, subsequent encounter for open fracture type I or II with malunion

S72.422M Displaced fracture of lateral condyle of left femur, subsequent encounter for open fracture type I or II with nonunion

S72.422R Displaced fracture of lateral condyle of left femur, subsequent encounter for open fracture type IIIA, IIIB, or IIIC with malunion

S72.422N Displaced fracture of lateral condyle of left femur, subsequent encounter for open fracture type IIIA, IIIB, or IIIC with nonunion

S42.452A Displaced fracture of lateral condyle of left humerus, initial encounter for closed fracture

S42.452P Displaced fracture of lateral condyle of left humerus, subsequent encounter for fracture with malunion

S42.452K Displaced fracture of lateral condyle of left humerus, subsequent encounter for fracture with nonunion

S82.122A Displaced fracture of lateral condyle of left tibia, initial encounter for closed fracture

S82.122P Displaced fracture of lateral condyle of left tibia, subsequent encounter for closed fracture with malunion

S82.122K Displaced fracture of lateral condyle of left tibia, subsequent encounter for closed fracture with nonunion

S82.122Q Displaced fracture of lateral condyle of left tibia, subsequent encounter for open fracture type I or II with malunion

S82.122M Displaced fracture of lateral condyle of left tibia, subsequent encounter for open fracture type I or II with nonunion

S82.122R Displaced fracture of lateral condyle of left tibia, subsequent encounter for open fracture type IIIA, IIIB, or IIIC with malunion

S82.122N Displaced fracture of lateral condyle of left tibia, subsequent encounter for open fracture type IIIA, IIIB, or IIIC with nonunion

S72.421A Displaced fracture of lateral condyle of right femur, initial encounter for closed fracture

S72.421P Displaced fracture of lateral condyle of right femur, subsequent encounter for closed fracture with malunion

S72.421K Displaced fracture of lateral condyle of right femur, subsequent encounter for closed fracture with nonunion

S72.421Q Displaced fracture of lateral condyle of right femur, subsequent encounter for open fracture type I or II with malunion

S72.421M Displaced fracture of lateral condyle of right femur, subsequent encounter for open fracture type I or II with nonunion

S72.421R Displaced fracture of lateral condyle of right femur, subsequent encounter for open fracture type IIIA, IIIB, or IIIC with malunion

S72.421N Displaced fracture of lateral condyle of right femur, subsequent encounter for open fracture type IIIA, IIIB, or IIIC with nonunion

S42.451A Displaced fracture of lateral condyle of right humerus, initial encounter for closed fracture

S42.451P Displaced fracture of lateral condyle of right humerus, subsequent encounter for fracture with malunion

S42.451K Displaced fracture of lateral condyle of right humerus, subsequent encounter for fracture with nonunion

S82.121A Displaced fracture of lateral condyle of right tibia, initial encounter for closed fracture

S82.121P Displaced fracture of lateral condyle of right tibia, subsequent encounter for closed fracture with malunion

S82.121K Displaced fracture of lateral condyle of right tibia, subsequent encounter for closed fracture with nonunion

S82.121Q Displaced fracture of lateral condyle of right tibia, subsequent encounter for open fracture type I or II with malunion

S82.121M Displaced fracture of lateral condyle of right tibia, subsequent encounter for open fracture type I or II with nonunion

S82.121R Displaced fracture of lateral condyle of right tibia, subsequent encounter for open fracture type IIIA, IIIB, or IIIC with malunion

S82.121N Displaced fracture of lateral condyle of right tibia, subsequent encounter for open fracture type IIIA, IIIB, or IIIC with nonunion

S72.423A Displaced fracture of lateral condyle of unspecified femur, initial encounter for closed fracture

S72.423P Displaced fracture of lateral condyle of unspecified femur, subsequent encounter for closed fracture with malunion

S72.423K Displaced fracture of lateral condyle of unspecified femur, subsequent encounter for closed fracture with nonunion

S72.423Q Displaced fracture of lateral condyle of unspecified femur, subsequent encounter for open fracture type I or II with malunion

S72.423M Displaced fracture of lateral condyle of unspecified femur, subsequent encounter for open fracture type I or II with nonunion

S72.423R Displaced fracture of lateral condyle of unspecified femur, subsequent encounter for open fracture type IIIA, IIIB, or IIIC with malunion

S72.423N Displaced fracture of lateral condyle of unspecified femur, subsequent encounter for open fracture type IIIA, IIIB, or IIIC with nonunion

S42.453A Displaced fracture of lateral condyle of unspecified humerus, initial encounter for closed fracture

S42.453P Displaced fracture of lateral condyle of unspecified humerus, subsequent encounter for fracture with malunion

S42.453K Displaced fracture of lateral condyle of unspecified humerus, subsequent encounter for fracture with nonunion

S82.123A Displaced fracture of lateral condyle of unspecified tibia, initial encounter for closed fracture

S82.123P Displaced fracture of lateral condyle of unspecified tibia, subsequent encounter for closed fracture with malunion

S82.123K Displaced fracture of lateral condyle of unspecified tibia, subsequent encounter for closed fracture with nonunion

S82.123Q Displaced fracture of lateral condyle of unspecified tibia, subsequent encounter for open fracture type I or II with malunion

S82.123M Displaced fracture of lateral condyle of unspecified tibia, subsequent encounter for open fracture type I or II with nonunion

S82.123R Displaced fracture of lateral condyle of unspecified tibia, subsequent encounter for open fracture type IIIA, IIIB, or IIIC with malunion

S82.123N Displaced fracture of lateral condyle of unspecified tibia, subsequent encounter for open fracture type IIIA, IIIB, or IIIC with nonunion

S92.222B Displaced fracture of lateral cuneiform of left foot, initial encounter for open fracture

S92.222P Displaced fracture of lateral cuneiform of left foot, subsequent encounter for fracture with malunion

S92.222K Displaced fracture of lateral cuneiform of left foot, subsequent encounter for fracture with nonunion

S92.221B Displaced fracture of lateral cuneiform of right foot, initial encounter for open fracture

S92.221P Displaced fracture of lateral cuneiform of right foot, subsequent encounter for fracture with malunion

S92.221K Displaced fracture of lateral cuneiform of right foot, subsequent encounter for fracture with nonunion

S92.223B Displaced fracture of lateral cuneiform of unspecified foot, initial encounter for open fracture

S92.223P Displaced fracture of lateral cuneiform of unspecified foot, subsequent encounter for fracture with malunion

S92.223K Displaced fracture of lateral cuneiform of unspecified foot, subsequent encounter for fracture with nonunion

S42.032B Displaced fracture of lateral end of left clavicle, initial encounter for open fracture

S42.032P Displaced fracture of lateral end of left clavicle, subsequent encounter for fracture with malunion

S42.032K Displaced fracture of lateral end of left clavicle, subsequent encounter for fracture with nonunion

S42.031B Displaced fracture of lateral end of right clavicle, initial encounter for open fracture

S42.031P Displaced fracture of lateral end of right clavicle, subsequent encounter for fracture with malunion

S42.031K Displaced fracture of lateral end of right clavicle, subsequent encounter for fracture with nonunion

S42.033B Displaced fracture of lateral end of unspecified clavicle, initial encounter for open fracture

S42.033P Displaced fracture of lateral end of unspecified clavicle, subsequent encounter for fracture with malunion

S42.033K Displaced fracture of lateral end of unspecified clavicle, subsequent encounter for fracture with nonunion

S82.62XB Displaced fracture of lateral malleolus of left fibula, initial encounter for open fracture type I or II

S82.62XC Displaced fracture of lateral malleolus of left fibula, initial encounter for open fracture type IIIA, IIIB, or IIIC

S82.62XP Displaced fracture of lateral malleolus of left fibula, subsequent encounter for closed fracture with malunion

S82.62XK Displaced fracture of lateral malleolus of left fibula, subsequent encounter for closed fracture with nonunion

S82.62XQ Displaced fracture of lateral malleolus of left fibula, subsequent encounter for open fracture type I or II with malunion

S82.62XM Displaced fracture of lateral malleolus of left fibula, subsequent encounter for open fracture type I or II with nonunion

S82.62XR Displaced fracture of lateral malleolus of left fibula, subsequent encounter for open fracture type IIIA, IIIB, or IIIC with malunion

S82.62XN Displaced fracture of lateral malleolus of left fibula, subsequent encounter for open fracture type IIIA, IIIB, or IIIC with nonunion

S82.61XB Displaced fracture of lateral malleolus of right fibula, initial encounter for open fracture type I or II

S82.61XC Displaced fracture of lateral malleolus of right fibula, initial encounter for open fracture type IIIA, IIIB, or IIIC

S82.61XP Displaced fracture of lateral malleolus of right fibula, subsequent encounter for closed fracture with malunion

S82.61XK Displaced fracture of lateral malleolus of right fibula, subsequent encounter for closed fracture with nonunion

S82.61XQ Displaced fracture of lateral malleolus of right fibula, subsequent encounter for open fracture type I or II with malunion

S82.61XM Displaced fracture of lateral malleolus of right fibula, subsequent encounter for open fracture type I or II with nonunion

S82.61XR Displaced fracture of lateral malleolus of right fibula, subsequent encounter for open fracture type IIIA, IIIB, or IIIC with malunion

S82.61XN Displaced fracture of lateral malleolus of right fibula, subsequent encounter for open fracture type IIIA, IIIB, or IIIC with nonunion

S82.63XB Displaced fracture of lateral malleolus of unspecified fibula, initial encounter for open fracture type I or II

S82.63XC	Displaced fracture of lateral malleolus of unspecified fibula, initial encounter for open fracture type IIIA, IIIB, or IIIC
S82.63XP	Displaced fracture of lateral malleolus of unspecified fibula, subsequent encounter for closed fracture with malunion
S82.63XK	Displaced fracture of lateral malleolus of unspecified fibula, subsequent encounter for closed fracture with nonunion
S82.63XQ	Displaced fracture of lateral malleolus of unspecified fibula, subsequent encounter for open fracture type I or II with malunion
S82.63XM	Displaced fracture of lateral malleolus of unspecified fibula, subsequent encounter for open fracture type I or II with nonunion
S82.63XR	Displaced fracture of lateral malleolus of unspecified fibula, subsequent encounter for open fracture type IIIA, IIIB, or IIIC with malunion
S82.63XN	Displaced fracture of lateral malleolus of unspecified fibula, subsequent encounter for open fracture type IIIA, IIIB, or IIIC with nonunion
S52.512A	Displaced fracture of left radial styloid process, initial encounter for closed fracture
S52.512P	Displaced fracture of left radial styloid process, subsequent encounter for closed fracture with malunion
S52.512K	Displaced fracture of left radial styloid process, subsequent encounter for closed fracture with nonunion
S52.512Q	Displaced fracture of left radial styloid process, subsequent encounter for open fracture type I or II with malunion
S52.512M	Displaced fracture of left radial styloid process, subsequent encounter for open fracture type I or II with nonunion
S52.512R	Displaced fracture of left radial styloid process, subsequent encounter for open fracture type IIIA, IIIB, or IIIC with malunion
S52.512N	Displaced fracture of left radial styloid process, subsequent encounter for open fracture type IIIA, IIIB, or IIIC with nonunion
S82.112A	Displaced fracture of left tibial spine, initial encounter for closed fracture
S82.112P	Displaced fracture of left tibial spine, subsequent encounter for closed fracture with malunion
S82.112K	Displaced fracture of left tibial spine, subsequent encounter for closed fracture with nonunion
S82.112Q	Displaced fracture of left tibial spine, subsequent encounter for open fracture type I or II with malunion
S82.112M	Displaced fracture of left tibial spine, subsequent encounter for open fracture type I or II with nonunion
S82.112R	Displaced fracture of left tibial spine, subsequent encounter for open fracture type IIIA, IIIB, or IIIC with malunion
S82.112N	Displaced fracture of left tibial spine, subsequent encounter for open fracture type IIIA, IIIB, or IIIC with nonunion
S82.152A	Displaced fracture of left tibial tuberosity, initial encounter for closed fracture
S82.152P	Displaced fracture of left tibial tuberosity, subsequent encounter for closed fracture with malunion
S82.152K	Displaced fracture of left tibial tuberosity, subsequent encounter for closed fracture with nonunion
S82.152Q	Displaced fracture of left tibial tuberosity, subsequent encounter for open fracture type I or II with malunion
S82.152M	Displaced fracture of left tibial tuberosity, subsequent encounter for open fracture type I or II with nonunion
S82.152R	Displaced fracture of left tibial tuberosity, subsequent encounter for open fracture type IIIA, IIIB, or IIIC with malunion
S82.152N	Displaced fracture of left tibial tuberosity, subsequent encounter for open fracture type IIIA, IIIB, or IIIC with nonunion
S52.612A	Displaced fracture of left ulna styloid process, initial encounter for closed fracture
S52.612P	Displaced fracture of left ulna styloid process, subsequent encounter for closed fracture with malunion
S52.612K	Displaced fracture of left ulna styloid process, subsequent encounter for closed fracture with nonunion
S52.612Q	Displaced fracture of left ulna styloid process, subsequent encounter for open fracture type I or II with malunion
S52.612M	Displaced fracture of left ulna styloid process, subsequent encounter for open fracture type I or II with nonunion
S52.612R	Displaced fracture of left ulna styloid process, subsequent encounter for open fracture type IIIA, IIIB, or IIIC with malunion
S52.612N	Displaced fracture of left ulna styloid process, subsequent encounter for open fracture type IIIA, IIIB, or IIIC with nonunion
S72.122P	Displaced fracture of lesser trochanter of left femur, subsequent encounter for closed fracture with malunion
S72.122K	Displaced fracture of lesser trochanter of left femur, subsequent encounter for closed fracture with nonunion
S72.122Q	Displaced fracture of lesser trochanter of left femur, subsequent encounter for open fracture type I or II with malunion
S72.122M	Displaced fracture of lesser trochanter of left femur, subsequent encounter for open fracture type I or II with nonunion
S72.122R	Displaced fracture of lesser trochanter of left femur, subsequent encounter for open fracture type IIIA, IIIB, or IIIC with malunion
S72.122N	Displaced fracture of lesser trochanter of left femur, subsequent encounter for open fracture type IIIA, IIIB, or IIIC with nonunion
S72.121P	Displaced fracture of lesser trochanter of right femur, subsequent encounter for closed fracture with malunion
S72.121K	Displaced fracture of lesser trochanter of right femur, subsequent encounter for closed fracture with nonunion
S72.121Q	Displaced fracture of lesser trochanter of right femur, subsequent encounter for open fracture type I or II with malunion
S72.121M	Displaced fracture of lesser trochanter of right femur, subsequent encounter for open fracture type I or II with nonunion
S72.121R	Displaced fracture of lesser trochanter of right femur, subsequent encounter for open fracture type IIIA, IIIB, or IIIC with malunion

S72.121N	Displaced fracture of lesser trochanter of right femur, subsequent encounter for open fracture type IIIA, IIIB, or IIIC with nonunion
S72.123P	Displaced fracture of lesser trochanter of unspecified femur, subsequent encounter for closed fracture with malunion
S72.123K	Displaced fracture of lesser trochanter of unspecified femur, subsequent encounter for closed fracture with nonunion
S72.123Q	Displaced fracture of lesser trochanter of unspecified femur, subsequent encounter for open fracture type I or II with malunion
S72.123M	Displaced fracture of lesser trochanter of unspecified femur, subsequent encounter for open fracture type I or II with nonunion
S72.123R	Displaced fracture of lesser trochanter of unspecified femur, subsequent encounter for open fracture type IIIA, IIIB, or IIIC with malunion
S72.123N	Displaced fracture of lesser trochanter of unspecified femur, subsequent encounter for open fracture type IIIA, IIIB, or IIIC with nonunion
S42.262A	Displaced fracture of lesser tuberosity of left humerus, initial encounter for closed fracture
S42.262P	Displaced fracture of lesser tuberosity of left humerus, subsequent encounter for fracture with malunion
S42.262K	Displaced fracture of lesser tuberosity of left humerus, subsequent encounter for fracture with nonunion
S42.261A	Displaced fracture of lesser tuberosity of right humerus, initial encounter for closed fracture
S42.261P	Displaced fracture of lesser tuberosity of right humerus, subsequent encounter for fracture with malunion
S42.261K	Displaced fracture of lesser tuberosity of right humerus, subsequent encounter for fracture with nonunion
S42.263A	Displaced fracture of lesser tuberosity of unspecified humerus, initial encounter for closed fracture
S42.263P	Displaced fracture of lesser tuberosity of unspecified humerus, subsequent encounter for fracture with malunion
S42.263K	Displaced fracture of lesser tuberosity of unspecified humerus, subsequent encounter for fracture with nonunion
S72.442A	Displaced fracture of lower epiphysis (separation) of left femur, initial encounter for closed fracture
S72.442P	Displaced fracture of lower epiphysis (separation) of left femur, subsequent encounter for closed fracture with malunion
S72.442K	Displaced fracture of lower epiphysis (separation) of left femur, subsequent encounter for closed fracture with nonunion
S72.442Q	Displaced fracture of lower epiphysis (separation) of left femur, subsequent encounter for open fracture type I or II with malunion
S72.442M	Displaced fracture of lower epiphysis (separation) of left femur, subsequent encounter for open fracture type I or II with nonunion
S72.442R	Displaced fracture of lower epiphysis (separation) of left femur, subsequent encounter for open fracture type IIIA, IIIB, or IIIC with malunion
S72.442N	Displaced fracture of lower epiphysis (separation) of left femur, subsequent encounter for open fracture type IIIA, IIIB, or IIIC with nonunion
S72.441A	Displaced fracture of lower epiphysis (separation) of right femur, initial encounter for closed fracture
S72.441P	Displaced fracture of lower epiphysis (separation) of right femur, subsequent encounter for closed fracture with malunion
S72.441K	Displaced fracture of lower epiphysis (separation) of right femur, subsequent encounter for closed fracture with nonunion
S72.441Q	Displaced fracture of lower epiphysis (separation) of right femur, subsequent encounter for open fracture type I or II with malunion
S72.441M	Displaced fracture of lower epiphysis (separation) of right femur, subsequent encounter for open fracture type I or II with nonunion
S72.441R	Displaced fracture of lower epiphysis (separation) of right femur, subsequent encounter for open fracture type IIIA, IIIB, or IIIC with malunion
S72.441N	Displaced fracture of lower epiphysis (separation) of right femur, subsequent encounter for open fracture type IIIA, IIIB, or IIIC with nonunion
S72.443A	Displaced fracture of lower epiphysis (separation) of unspecified femur, initial encounter for closed fracture
S72.443P	Displaced fracture of lower epiphysis (separation) of unspecified femur, subsequent encounter for closed fracture with malunion
S72.443K	Displaced fracture of lower epiphysis (separation) of unspecified femur, subsequent encounter for closed fracture with nonunion
S72.443Q	Displaced fracture of lower epiphysis (separation) of unspecified femur, subsequent encounter for open fracture type I or II with malunion
S72.443M	Displaced fracture of lower epiphysis (separation) of unspecified femur, subsequent encounter for open fracture type I or II with nonunion
S72.443R	Displaced fracture of lower epiphysis (separation) of unspecified femur, subsequent encounter for open fracture type IIIA, IIIB, or IIIC with malunion
S72.443N	Displaced fracture of lower epiphysis (separation) of unspecified femur, subsequent encounter for open fracture type IIIA, IIIB, or IIIC with nonunion
S62.122B	Displaced fracture of lunate [semilunar], left wrist, initial encounter for open fracture
S62.122P	Displaced fracture of lunate [semilunar], left wrist, subsequent encounter for fracture with malunion
S62.122K	Displaced fracture of lunate [semilunar], left wrist, subsequent encounter for fracture with nonunion
S62.121B	Displaced fracture of lunate [semilunar], right wrist, initial encounter for open fracture
S62.121P	Displaced fracture of lunate [semilunar], right wrist, subsequent encounter for fracture with malunion
S62.121K	Displaced fracture of lunate [semilunar], right wrist, subsequent encounter for fracture with nonunion
S62.123B	Displaced fracture of lunate [semilunar], unspecified wrist, initial encounter for open fracture
S62.123P	Displaced fracture of lunate [semilunar], unspecified wrist, subsequent encounter for fracture with malunion

S62.123K Displaced fracture of lunate [semilunar], unspecified wrist, subsequent encounter for fracture with nonunion

S72.432A Displaced fracture of medial condyle of left femur, initial encounter for closed fracture

S72.432P Displaced fracture of medial condyle of left femur, subsequent encounter for closed fracture with malunion

S72.432K Displaced fracture of medial condyle of left femur, subsequent encounter for closed fracture with nonunion

S72.432Q Displaced fracture of medial condyle of left femur, subsequent encounter for open fracture type I or II with malunion

S72.432M Displaced fracture of medial condyle of left femur, subsequent encounter for open fracture type I or II with nonunion

S72.432R Displaced fracture of medial condyle of left femur, subsequent encounter for open fracture type IIIA, IIIB, or IIIC with malunion

S72.432N Displaced fracture of medial condyle of left femur, subsequent encounter for open fracture type IIIA, IIIB, or IIIC with nonunion

S42.462A Displaced fracture of medial condyle of left humerus, initial encounter for closed fracture

S42.462P Displaced fracture of medial condyle of left humerus, subsequent encounter for fracture with malunion

S42.462K Displaced fracture of medial condyle of left humerus, subsequent encounter for fracture with nonunion

S82.132A Displaced fracture of medial condyle of left tibia, initial encounter for closed fracture

S82.132P Displaced fracture of medial condyle of left tibia, subsequent encounter for closed fracture with malunion

S82.132K Displaced fracture of medial condyle of left tibia, subsequent encounter for closed fracture with nonunion

S82.132Q Displaced fracture of medial condyle of left tibia, subsequent encounter for open fracture type I or II with malunion

S82.132M Displaced fracture of medial condyle of left tibia, subsequent encounter for open fracture type I or II with nonunion

S82.132R Displaced fracture of medial condyle of left tibia, subsequent encounter for open fracture type IIIA, IIIB, or IIIC with malunion

S82.132N Displaced fracture of medial condyle of left tibia, subsequent encounter for open fracture type IIIA, IIIB, or IIIC with nonunion

S72.431A Displaced fracture of medial condyle of right femur, initial encounter for closed fracture

S72.431P Displaced fracture of medial condyle of right femur, subsequent encounter for closed fracture with malunion

S72.431K Displaced fracture of medial condyle of right femur, subsequent encounter for closed fracture with nonunion

S72.431Q Displaced fracture of medial condyle of right femur, subsequent encounter for open fracture type I or II with malunion

S72.431M Displaced fracture of medial condyle of right femur, subsequent encounter for open fracture type I or II with nonunion

S72.431R Displaced fracture of medial condyle of right femur, subsequent encounter for open fracture type IIIA, IIIB, or IIIC with malunion

S72.431N Displaced fracture of medial condyle of right femur, subsequent encounter for open fracture type IIIA, IIIB, or IIIC with nonunion

S42.461A Displaced fracture of medial condyle of right humerus, initial encounter for closed fracture

S42.461P Displaced fracture of medial condyle of right humerus, subsequent encounter for fracture with malunion

S42.461K Displaced fracture of medial condyle of right humerus, subsequent encounter for fracture with nonunion

S82.131A Displaced fracture of medial condyle of right tibia, initial encounter for closed fracture

S82.131P Displaced fracture of medial condyle of right tibia, subsequent encounter for closed fracture with malunion

S82.131K Displaced fracture of medial condyle of right tibia, subsequent encounter for closed fracture with nonunion

S82.131Q Displaced fracture of medial condyle of right tibia, subsequent encounter for open fracture type I or II with malunion

S82.131M Displaced fracture of medial condyle of right tibia, subsequent encounter for open fracture type I or II with nonunion

S82.131R Displaced fracture of medial condyle of right tibia, subsequent encounter for open fracture type IIIA, IIIB, or IIIC with malunion

S82.131N Displaced fracture of medial condyle of right tibia, subsequent encounter for open fracture type IIIA, IIIB, or IIIC with nonunion

S72.433A Displaced fracture of medial condyle of unspecified femur, initial encounter for closed fracture

S72.433P Displaced fracture of medial condyle of unspecified femur, subsequent encounter for closed fracture with malunion

S72.433K Displaced fracture of medial condyle of unspecified femur, subsequent encounter for closed fracture with nonunion

S72.433Q Displaced fracture of medial condyle of unspecified femur, subsequent encounter for open fracture type I or II with malunion

S72.433M Displaced fracture of medial condyle of unspecified femur, subsequent encounter for open fracture type I or II with nonunion

S72.433R Displaced fracture of medial condyle of unspecified femur, subsequent encounter for open fracture type IIIA, IIIB, or IIIC with malunion

S72.433N Displaced fracture of medial condyle of unspecified femur, subsequent encounter for open fracture type IIIA, IIIB, or IIIC with nonunion

S42.463A Displaced fracture of medial condyle of unspecified humerus, initial encounter for closed fracture

S42.463P Displaced fracture of medial condyle of unspecified humerus, subsequent encounter for fracture with malunion

S42.463K Displaced fracture of medial condyle of unspecified humerus, subsequent encounter for fracture with nonunion

S82.133A Displaced fracture of medial condyle of unspecified tibia, initial encounter for closed fracture

S82.133P Displaced fracture of medial condyle of unspecified tibia, subsequent encounter for closed fracture with malunion

S82.133K Displaced fracture of medial condyle of unspecified tibia, subsequent encounter for closed fracture with nonunion

S82.133Q Displaced fracture of medial condyle of unspecified tibia, subsequent encounter for open fracture type I or II with malunion

S82.133M Displaced fracture of medial condyle of unspecified tibia, subsequent encounter for open fracture type I or II with nonunion

S82.133R Displaced fracture of medial condyle of unspecified tibia, subsequent encounter for open fracture type IIIA, IIIB, or IIIC with malunion

S82.133N Displaced fracture of medial condyle of unspecified tibia, subsequent encounter for open fracture type IIIA, IIIB, or IIIC with nonunion

S92.242B Displaced fracture of medial cuneiform of left foot, initial encounter for open fracture

S92.242P Displaced fracture of medial cuneiform of left foot, subsequent encounter for fracture with malunion

S92.242K Displaced fracture of medial cuneiform of left foot, subsequent encounter for fracture with nonunion

S92.241B Displaced fracture of medial cuneiform of right foot, initial encounter for open fracture

S92.241P Displaced fracture of medial cuneiform of right foot, subsequent encounter for fracture with malunion

S92.241K Displaced fracture of medial cuneiform of right foot, subsequent encounter for fracture with nonunion

S92.243B Displaced fracture of medial cuneiform of unspecified foot, initial encounter for open fracture

S92.243P Displaced fracture of medial cuneiform of unspecified foot, subsequent encounter for fracture with malunion

S92.243K Displaced fracture of medial cuneiform of unspecified foot, subsequent encounter for fracture with nonunion

S82.52XB Displaced fracture of medial malleolus of left tibia, initial encounter for open fracture type I or II

S82.52XC Displaced fracture of medial malleolus of left tibia, initial encounter for open fracture type IIIA, IIIB, or IIIC

S82.52XP Displaced fracture of medial malleolus of left tibia, subsequent encounter for closed fracture with malunion

S82.52XK Displaced fracture of medial malleolus of left tibia, subsequent encounter for closed fracture with nonunion

S82.52XQ Displaced fracture of medial malleolus of left tibia, subsequent encounter for open fracture type I or II with malunion

S82.52XM Displaced fracture of medial malleolus of left tibia, subsequent encounter for open fracture type I or II with nonunion

S82.52XR Displaced fracture of medial malleolus of left tibia, subsequent encounter for open fracture type IIIA, IIIB, or IIIC with malunion

S82.52XN Displaced fracture of medial malleolus of left tibia, subsequent encounter for open fracture type IIIA, IIIB, or IIIC with nonunion

S82.51XB Displaced fracture of medial malleolus of right tibia, initial encounter for open fracture type I or II

S82.51XC Displaced fracture of medial malleolus of right tibia, initial encounter for open fracture type IIIA, IIIB, or IIIC

S82.51XP Displaced fracture of medial malleolus of right tibia, subsequent encounter for closed fracture with malunion

S82.51XK Displaced fracture of medial malleolus of right tibia, subsequent encounter for closed fracture with nonunion

S82.51XQ Displaced fracture of medial malleolus of right tibia, subsequent encounter for open fracture type I or II with malunion

S82.51XM Displaced fracture of medial malleolus of right tibia, subsequent encounter for open fracture type I or II with nonunion

S82.51XR Displaced fracture of medial malleolus of right tibia, subsequent encounter for open fracture type IIIA, IIIB, or IIIC with malunion

S82.51XN Displaced fracture of medial malleolus of right tibia, subsequent encounter for open fracture type IIIA, IIIB, or IIIC with nonunion

S82.53XB Displaced fracture of medial malleolus of unspecified tibia, initial encounter for open fracture type I or II

S82.53XC Displaced fracture of medial malleolus of unspecified tibia, initial encounter for open fracture type IIIA, IIIB, or IIIC

S82.53XP Displaced fracture of medial malleolus of unspecified tibia, subsequent encounter for closed fracture with malunion

S82.53XK Displaced fracture of medial malleolus of unspecified tibia, subsequent encounter for closed fracture with nonunion

S82.53XQ Displaced fracture of medial malleolus of unspecified tibia, subsequent encounter for open fracture type I or II with malunion

S82.53XM Displaced fracture of medial malleolus of unspecified tibia, subsequent encounter for open fracture type I or II with nonunion

S82.53XR Displaced fracture of medial malleolus of unspecified tibia, subsequent encounter for open fracture type IIIA, IIIB, or IIIC with malunion

S82.53XN Displaced fracture of medial malleolus of unspecified tibia, subsequent encounter for open fracture type IIIA, IIIB, or IIIC with nonunion

S32.472K Displaced fracture of medial wall of left acetabulum, subsequent encounter for fracture with nonunion

S32.471K Displaced fracture of medial wall of right acetabulum, subsequent encounter for fracture with nonunion

S32.473K Displaced fracture of medial wall of unspecified acetabulum, subsequent encounter for fracture with nonunion

S62.621B Displaced fracture of middle phalanx of left index finger, initial encounter for open fracture

S62.621P Displaced fracture of middle phalanx of left index finger, subsequent encounter for fracture with malunion

S62.621K Displaced fracture of middle phalanx of left index finger, subsequent encounter for fracture with nonunion

S92.522P Displaced fracture of middle phalanx of left lesser toe(s), subsequent encounter for fracture with malunion

S92.522K Displaced fracture of middle phalanx of left lesser toe(s), subsequent encounter for fracture with nonunion

S62.627B Displaced fracture of middle phalanx of left little finger, initial encounter for open fracture

S62.627P Displaced fracture of middle phalanx of left little finger, subsequent encounter for fracture with malunion

S62.627K Displaced fracture of middle phalanx of left little finger, subsequent encounter for fracture with nonunion

S62.623B Displaced fracture of middle phalanx of left middle finger, initial encounter for open fracture

S62.623P Displaced fracture of middle phalanx of left middle finger, subsequent encounter for fracture with malunion

S62.623K Displaced fracture of middle phalanx of left middle finger, subsequent encounter for fracture with nonunion

S62.625B Displaced fracture of middle phalanx of left ring finger, initial encounter for open fracture

S62.625P Displaced fracture of middle phalanx of left ring finger, subsequent encounter for fracture with malunion

S62.625K Displaced fracture of middle phalanx of left ring finger, subsequent encounter for fracture with nonunion

S62.628B Displaced fracture of middle phalanx of other finger, initial encounter for open fracture

S62.628P Displaced fracture of middle phalanx of other finger, subsequent encounter for fracture with malunion

S62.628K Displaced fracture of middle phalanx of other finger, subsequent encounter for fracture with nonunion

S62.620B Displaced fracture of middle phalanx of right index finger, initial encounter for open fracture

S62.620P Displaced fracture of middle phalanx of right index finger, subsequent encounter for fracture with malunion

S62.620K Displaced fracture of middle phalanx of right index finger, subsequent encounter for fracture with nonunion

S92.521P Displaced fracture of middle phalanx of right lesser toe(s), subsequent encounter for fracture with malunion

S92.521K Displaced fracture of middle phalanx of right lesser toe(s), subsequent encounter for fracture with nonunion

S62.626B Displaced fracture of middle phalanx of right little finger, initial encounter for open fracture

S62.626P Displaced fracture of middle phalanx of right little finger, subsequent encounter for fracture with malunion

S62.626K Displaced fracture of middle phalanx of right little finger, subsequent encounter for fracture with nonunion

S62.622B Displaced fracture of middle phalanx of right middle finger, initial encounter for open fracture

S62.622P Displaced fracture of middle phalanx of right middle finger, subsequent encounter for fracture with malunion

S62.622K Displaced fracture of middle phalanx of right middle finger, subsequent encounter for fracture with nonunion

S62.624B Displaced fracture of middle phalanx of right ring finger, initial encounter for open fracture

S62.624P Displaced fracture of middle phalanx of right ring finger, subsequent encounter for fracture with malunion

S62.624K Displaced fracture of middle phalanx of right ring finger, subsequent encounter for fracture with nonunion

S62.629B Displaced fracture of middle phalanx of unspecified finger, initial encounter for open fracture

S62.629P Displaced fracture of middle phalanx of unspecified finger, subsequent encounter for fracture with malunion

S62.629K Displaced fracture of middle phalanx of unspecified finger, subsequent encounter for fracture with nonunion

S92.523P Displaced fracture of middle phalanx of unspecified lesser toe(s), subsequent encounter for fracture with malunion

S92.523K Displaced fracture of middle phalanx of unspecified lesser toe(s), subsequent encounter for fracture with nonunion

S62.022B Displaced fracture of middle third of navicular [scaphoid] bone of left wrist, initial encounter for open fracture

S62.022P Displaced fracture of middle third of navicular [scaphoid] bone of left wrist, subsequent encounter for fracture with malunion

S62.022K Displaced fracture of middle third of navicular [scaphoid] bone of left wrist, subsequent encounter for fracture with nonunion

S62.021B Displaced fracture of middle third of navicular [scaphoid] bone of right wrist, initial encounter for open fracture

S62.021P Displaced fracture of middle third of navicular [scaphoid] bone of right wrist, subsequent encounter for fracture with malunion

S62.021K Displaced fracture of middle third of navicular [scaphoid] bone of right wrist, subsequent encounter for fracture with nonunion

S62.023B Displaced fracture of middle third of navicular [scaphoid] bone of unspecified wrist, initial encounter for open fracture

S62.023P Displaced fracture of middle third of navicular [scaphoid] bone of unspecified wrist, subsequent encounter for fracture with malunion

S62.023K Displaced fracture of middle third of navicular [scaphoid] bone of unspecified wrist, subsequent encounter for fracture with nonunion

S92.252B Displaced fracture of navicular [scaphoid] of left foot, initial encounter for open fracture

S92.252P Displaced fracture of navicular [scaphoid] of left foot, subsequent encounter for fracture with malunion

S92.252K Displaced fracture of navicular [scaphoid] of left foot, subsequent encounter for fracture with nonunion

S92.251B Displaced fracture of navicular [scaphoid] of right foot, initial encounter for open fracture

S92.251P Displaced fracture of navicular [scaphoid] of right foot, subsequent encounter for fracture with malunion

S92.251K Displaced fracture of navicular [scaphoid] of right foot, subsequent encounter for fracture with nonunion

S92.253B Displaced fracture of navicular [scaphoid] of unspecified foot, initial encounter for open fracture

S92.253P Displaced fracture of navicular [scaphoid] of unspecified foot, subsequent encounter for fracture with malunion

S92.253K Displaced fracture of navicular [scaphoid] of unspecified foot, subsequent encounter for fracture with nonunion

S62.337B Displaced fracture of neck of fifth metacarpal bone, left hand, initial encounter for open fracture

S62.337P Displaced fracture of neck of fifth metacarpal bone, left hand, subsequent encounter for fracture with malunion

S62.337K Displaced fracture of neck of fifth metacarpal bone, left hand, subsequent encounter for fracture with nonunion

S62.336B Displaced fracture of neck of fifth metacarpal bone, right hand, initial encounter for open fracture

S62.336P Displaced fracture of neck of fifth metacarpal bone, right hand, subsequent encounter for fracture with malunion

S62.336K Displaced fracture of neck of fifth metacarpal bone, right hand, subsequent encounter for fracture with nonunion

S62.252B Displaced fracture of neck of first metacarpal bone, left hand, initial encounter for open fracture

S62.252P Displaced fracture of neck of first metacarpal bone, left hand, subsequent encounter for fracture with malunion

S62.252K Displaced fracture of neck of first metacarpal bone, left hand, subsequent encounter for fracture with nonunion

S62.251B Displaced fracture of neck of first metacarpal bone, right hand, initial encounter for open fracture

S62.251P Displaced fracture of neck of first metacarpal bone, right hand, subsequent encounter for fracture with malunion

S62.251K Displaced fracture of neck of first metacarpal bone, right hand, subsequent encounter for fracture with nonunion

S62.253B Displaced fracture of neck of first metacarpal bone, unspecified hand, initial encounter for open fracture

S62.253P Displaced fracture of neck of first metacarpal bone, unspecified hand, subsequent encounter for fracture with malunion

S62.253K Displaced fracture of neck of first metacarpal bone, unspecified hand, subsequent encounter for fracture with nonunion

S62.335B Displaced fracture of neck of fourth metacarpal bone, left hand, initial encounter for open fracture

S62.335P Displaced fracture of neck of fourth metacarpal bone, left hand, subsequent encounter for fracture with malunion

S62.335K Displaced fracture of neck of fourth metacarpal bone, left hand, subsequent encounter for fracture with nonunion

S62.334B Displaced fracture of neck of fourth metacarpal bone, right hand, initial encounter for open fracture

S62.334P Displaced fracture of neck of fourth metacarpal bone, right hand, subsequent encounter for fracture with malunion

S62.334K Displaced fracture of neck of fourth metacarpal bone, right hand, subsequent encounter for fracture with nonunion

S52.132P Displaced fracture of neck of left radius, subsequent encounter for closed fracture with malunion

S52.132K Displaced fracture of neck of left radius, subsequent encounter for closed fracture with nonunion

S52.132Q Displaced fracture of neck of left radius, subsequent encounter for open fracture type I or II with malunion

S52.132M Displaced fracture of neck of left radius, subsequent encounter for open fracture type I or II with nonunion

S52.132R Displaced fracture of neck of left radius, subsequent encounter for open fracture type IIIA, IIIB, or IIIC with malunion

S52.132N Displaced fracture of neck of left radius, subsequent encounter for open fracture type IIIA, IIIB, or IIIC with nonunion

S92.112B Displaced fracture of neck of left talus, initial encounter for open fracture

S92.112P Displaced fracture of neck of left talus, subsequent encounter for fracture with malunion

S92.112K Displaced fracture of neck of left talus, subsequent encounter for fracture with nonunion

S62.338B Displaced fracture of neck of other metacarpal bone, initial encounter for open fracture

S62.338P Displaced fracture of neck of other metacarpal bone, subsequent encounter for fracture with malunion

S62.338K Displaced fracture of neck of other metacarpal bone, subsequent encounter for fracture with nonunion

S52.131P Displaced fracture of neck of right radius, subsequent encounter for closed fracture with malunion

S52.131K Displaced fracture of neck of right radius, subsequent encounter for closed fracture with nonunion

S52.131Q Displaced fracture of neck of right radius, subsequent encounter for open fracture type I or II with malunion

S52.131M Displaced fracture of neck of right radius, subsequent encounter for open fracture type I or II with nonunion

S52.131R Displaced fracture of neck of right radius, subsequent encounter for open fracture type IIIA, IIIB, or IIIC with malunion

S52.131N Displaced fracture of neck of right radius, subsequent encounter for open fracture type IIIA, IIIB, or IIIC with nonunion

S92.111B Displaced fracture of neck of right talus, initial encounter for open fracture

S92.111P Displaced fracture of neck of right talus, subsequent encounter for fracture with malunion

S92.111K Displaced fracture of neck of right talus, subsequent encounter for fracture with nonunion

S42.152B Displaced fracture of neck of scapula, left shoulder, initial encounter for open fracture

S42.152P Displaced fracture of neck of scapula, left shoulder, subsequent encounter for fracture with malunion

S42.152K Displaced fracture of neck of scapula, left shoulder, subsequent encounter for fracture with nonunion

S42.151B Displaced fracture of neck of scapula, right shoulder, initial encounter for open fracture

S42.151P Displaced fracture of neck of scapula, right shoulder, subsequent encounter for fracture with malunion

S42.151K Displaced fracture of neck of scapula, right shoulder, subsequent encounter for fracture with nonunion

S42.153B Displaced fracture of neck of scapula, unspecified shoulder, initial encounter for open fracture

S42.153P Displaced fracture of neck of scapula, unspecified shoulder, subsequent encounter for fracture with malunion

S42.153K Displaced fracture of neck of scapula, unspecified shoulder, subsequent encounter for fracture with nonunion

S62.331B Displaced fracture of neck of second metacarpal bone, left hand, initial encounter for open fracture

S62.331P Displaced fracture of neck of second metacarpal bone, left hand, subsequent encounter for fracture with malunion

S62.331K Displaced fracture of neck of second metacarpal bone, left hand, subsequent encounter for fracture with nonunion

S62.330B Displaced fracture of neck of second metacarpal bone, right hand, initial encounter for open fracture

S62.330P Displaced fracture of neck of second metacarpal bone, right hand, subsequent encounter for fracture with malunion

S62.330K Displaced fracture of neck of second metacarpal bone, right hand, subsequent encounter for fracture with nonunion

S62.333B Displaced fracture of neck of third metacarpal bone, left hand, initial encounter for open fracture

S62.333P Displaced fracture of neck of third metacarpal bone, left hand, subsequent encounter for fracture with malunion

S62.333K Displaced fracture of neck of third metacarpal bone, left hand, subsequent encounter for fracture with nonunion

S62.332B Displaced fracture of neck of third metacarpal bone, right hand, initial encounter for open fracture

S62.332P Displaced fracture of neck of third metacarpal bone, right hand, subsequent encounter for fracture with malunion

S62.332K Displaced fracture of neck of third metacarpal bone, right hand, subsequent encounter for fracture with nonunion

S62.339B Displaced fracture of neck of unspecified metacarpal bone, initial encounter for open fracture

S62.339P Displaced fracture of neck of unspecified metacarpal bone, subsequent encounter for fracture with malunion

S62.339K Displaced fracture of neck of unspecified metacarpal bone, subsequent encounter for fracture with nonunion

S52.133P Displaced fracture of neck of unspecified radius, subsequent encounter for closed fracture with malunion

S52.133K Displaced fracture of neck of unspecified radius, subsequent encounter for closed fracture with nonunion

S52.133Q Displaced fracture of neck of unspecified radius, subsequent encounter for open fracture type I or II with malunion

S52.133M Displaced fracture of neck of unspecified radius, subsequent encounter for open fracture type I or II with nonunion

S52.133R Displaced fracture of neck of unspecified radius, subsequent encounter for open fracture type IIIA, IIIB, or IIIC with malunion

S52.133N Displaced fracture of neck of unspecified radius, subsequent encounter for open fracture type IIIA, IIIB, or IIIC with nonunion

S92.113B Displaced fracture of neck of unspecified talus, initial encounter for open fracture

S92.113P Displaced fracture of neck of unspecified talus, subsequent encounter for fracture with malunion

S92.113K Displaced fracture of neck of unspecified talus, subsequent encounter for fracture with nonunion

S52.032P Displaced fracture of olecranon process with intraarticular extension of left ulna, subsequent encounter for closed fracture with malunion

S52.032K Displaced fracture of olecranon process with intraarticular extension of left ulna, subsequent encounter for closed fracture with nonunion

S52.032Q Displaced fracture of olecranon process with intraarticular extension of left ulna, subsequent encounter for open fracture type I or II with malunion

S52.032M Displaced fracture of olecranon process with intraarticular extension of left ulna, subsequent encounter for open fracture type I or II with nonunion

S52.032R Displaced fracture of olecranon process with intraarticular extension of left ulna, subsequent encounter for open fracture type IIIA, IIIB, or IIIC with malunion

S52.032N Displaced fracture of olecranon process with intraarticular extension of left ulna, subsequent encounter for open fracture type IIIA, IIIB, or IIIC with nonunion

S52.031P Displaced fracture of olecranon process with intraarticular extension of right ulna, subsequent encounter for closed fracture with malunion

S52.031K Displaced fracture of olecranon process with intraarticular extension of right ulna, subsequent encounter for closed fracture with nonunion

S52.031Q Displaced fracture of olecranon process with intraarticular extension of right ulna, subsequent encounter for open fracture type I or II with malunion

S52.031M Displaced fracture of olecranon process with intraarticular extension of right ulna, subsequent encounter for open fracture type I or II with nonunion

S52.031R Displaced fracture of olecranon process with intraarticular extension of right ulna, subsequent encounter for open fracture type IIIA, IIIB, or IIIC with malunion

S52.031N Displaced fracture of olecranon process with intraarticular extension of right ulna, subsequent encounter for open fracture type IIIA, IIIB, or IIIC with nonunion

S52.033P Displaced fracture of olecranon process with intraarticular extension of unspecified ulna, subsequent encounter for closed fracture with malunion

S52.033K Displaced fracture of olecranon process with intraarticular extension of unspecified ulna, subsequent encounter for closed fracture with nonunion

S52.033Q Displaced fracture of olecranon process with intraarticular extension of unspecified ulna, subsequent encounter for open fracture type I or II with malunion

S52.033M Displaced fracture of olecranon process with intraarticular extension of unspecified ulna, subsequent encounter for open fracture type I or II with nonunion

S52.033R Displaced fracture of olecranon process with intraarticular extension of unspecified ulna, subsequent encounter for open fracture type IIIA, IIIB, or IIIC with malunion

S52.033N Displaced fracture of olecranon process with intraarticular extension of unspecified ulna, subsequent encounter for open fracture type IIIA, IIIB, or IIIC with nonunion

S52.022P Displaced fracture of olecranon process without intraarticular extension of left ulna, subsequent encounter for closed fracture with malunion

S52.022K Displaced fracture of olecranon process without intraarticular extension of left ulna, subsequent encounter for closed fracture with nonunion

S52.022Q Displaced fracture of olecranon process without intraarticular extension of left ulna, subsequent encounter for open fracture type I or II with malunion

S52.022M Displaced fracture of olecranon process without intraarticular extension of left ulna, subsequent encounter for open fracture type I or II with nonunion

S52.022R Displaced fracture of olecranon process without intraarticular extension of left ulna, subsequent encounter for open fracture type IIIA, IIIB, or IIIC with malunion

S52.022N Displaced fracture of olecranon process without intraarticular extension of left ulna, subsequent encounter for open fracture type IIIA, IIIB, or IIIC with nonunion

S52.021P Displaced fracture of olecranon process without intraarticular extension of right ulna, subsequent encounter for closed fracture with malunion

S52.021K Displaced fracture of olecranon process without intraarticular extension of right ulna, subsequent encounter for closed fracture with nonunion

S52.021Q Displaced fracture of olecranon process without intraarticular extension of right ulna, subsequent encounter for open fracture type I or II with malunion

S52.021M Displaced fracture of olecranon process without intraarticular extension of right ulna, subsequent encounter for open fracture type I or II with nonunion

S52.021R Displaced fracture of olecranon process without intraarticular extension of right ulna, subsequent encounter for open fracture type IIIA, IIIB, or IIIC with malunion

S52.021N Displaced fracture of olecranon process without intraarticular extension of right ulna, subsequent encounter for open fracture type IIIA, IIIB, or IIIC with nonunion

S52.023P Displaced fracture of olecranon process without intraarticular extension of unspecified ulna, subsequent encounter for closed fracture with malunion

S52.023K Displaced fracture of olecranon process without intraarticular extension of unspecified ulna, subsequent encounter for closed fracture with nonunion

S52.023Q Displaced fracture of olecranon process without intraarticular extension of unspecified ulna, subsequent encounter for open fracture type I or II with malunion

S52.023M Displaced fracture of olecranon process without intraarticular extension of unspecified ulna, subsequent encounter for open fracture type I or II with nonunion

S52.023R Displaced fracture of olecranon process without intraarticular extension of unspecified ulna, subsequent encounter for open fracture type IIIA, IIIB, or IIIC with malunion

S52.023N Displaced fracture of olecranon process without intraarticular extension of unspecified ulna, subsequent encounter for open fracture type IIIA, IIIB, or IIIC with nonunion

S62.162B Displaced fracture of pisiform, left wrist, initial encounter for open fracture

S62.162P Displaced fracture of pisiform, left wrist, subsequent encounter for fracture with malunion

S62.162K Displaced fracture of pisiform, left wrist, subsequent encounter for fracture with nonunion

S62.161B Displaced fracture of pisiform, right wrist, initial encounter for open fracture

S62.161P Displaced fracture of pisiform, right wrist, subsequent encounter for fracture with malunion

S62.161K Displaced fracture of pisiform, right wrist, subsequent encounter for fracture with nonunion

S62.163B Displaced fracture of pisiform, unspecified wrist, initial encounter for open fracture

S62.163P Displaced fracture of pisiform, unspecified wrist, subsequent encounter for fracture with malunion

S62.163K Displaced fracture of pisiform, unspecified wrist, subsequent encounter for fracture with nonunion

S32.442K Displaced fracture of posterior column [ilioischial] of left acetabulum, subsequent encounter for fracture with nonunion

S32.441K Displaced fracture of posterior column [ilioischial] of right acetabulum, subsequent encounter for fracture with nonunion

S32.443K Displaced fracture of posterior column [ilioischial] of unspecified acetabulum, subsequent encounter for fracture with nonunion

S92.132B Displaced fracture of posterior process of left talus, initial encounter for open fracture

S92.132P	Displaced fracture of posterior process of left talus, subsequent encounter for fracture with malunion
S92.132K	Displaced fracture of posterior process of left talus, subsequent encounter for fracture with nonunion
S92.131B	Displaced fracture of posterior process of right talus, initial encounter for open fracture
S92.131P	Displaced fracture of posterior process of right talus, subsequent encounter for fracture with malunion
S92.131K	Displaced fracture of posterior process of right talus, subsequent encounter for fracture with nonunion
S92.133B	Displaced fracture of posterior process of unspecified talus, initial encounter for open fracture
S92.133P	Displaced fracture of posterior process of unspecified talus, subsequent encounter for fracture with malunion
S92.133K	Displaced fracture of posterior process of unspecified talus, subsequent encounter for fracture with nonunion
S32.422K	Displaced fracture of posterior wall of left acetabulum, subsequent encounter for fracture with nonunion
S32.421K	Displaced fracture of posterior wall of right acetabulum, subsequent encounter for fracture with nonunion
S32.423K	Displaced fracture of posterior wall of unspecified acetabulum, subsequent encounter for fracture with nonunion
S92.412P	Displaced fracture of proximal phalanx of left great toe, subsequent encounter for fracture with malunion
S92.412K	Displaced fracture of proximal phalanx of left great toe, subsequent encounter for fracture with nonunion
S62.611B	Displaced fracture of proximal phalanx of left index finger, initial encounter for open fracture
S62.611P	Displaced fracture of proximal phalanx of left index finger, subsequent encounter for fracture with malunion
S62.611K	Displaced fracture of proximal phalanx of left index finger, subsequent encounter for fracture with nonunion
S92.512P	Displaced fracture of proximal phalanx of left lesser toe(s), subsequent encounter for fracture with malunion
S92.512K	Displaced fracture of proximal phalanx of left lesser toe(s), subsequent encounter for fracture with nonunion
S62.617B	Displaced fracture of proximal phalanx of left little finger, initial encounter for open fracture
S62.617P	Displaced fracture of proximal phalanx of left little finger, subsequent encounter for fracture with malunion
S62.617K	Displaced fracture of proximal phalanx of left little finger, subsequent encounter for fracture with nonunion
S62.613B	Displaced fracture of proximal phalanx of left middle finger, initial encounter for open fracture
S62.613P	Displaced fracture of proximal phalanx of left middle finger, subsequent encounter for fracture with malunion
S62.613K	Displaced fracture of proximal phalanx of left middle finger, subsequent encounter for fracture with nonunion
S62.615B	Displaced fracture of proximal phalanx of left ring finger, initial encounter for open fracture
S62.615P	Displaced fracture of proximal phalanx of left ring finger, subsequent encounter for fracture with malunion
S62.615K	Displaced fracture of proximal phalanx of left ring finger, subsequent encounter for fracture with nonunion
S62.512B	Displaced fracture of proximal phalanx of left thumb, initial encounter for open fracture
S62.512P	Displaced fracture of proximal phalanx of left thumb, subsequent encounter for fracture with malunion
S62.512K	Displaced fracture of proximal phalanx of left thumb, subsequent encounter for fracture with nonunion
S62.618B	Displaced fracture of proximal phalanx of other finger, initial encounter for open fracture
S62.618P	Displaced fracture of proximal phalanx of other finger, subsequent encounter for fracture with malunion
S62.618K	Displaced fracture of proximal phalanx of other finger, subsequent encounter for fracture with nonunion
S92.411P	Displaced fracture of proximal phalanx of right great toe, subsequent encounter for fracture with malunion
S92.411K	Displaced fracture of proximal phalanx of right great toe, subsequent encounter for fracture with nonunion
S62.610B	Displaced fracture of proximal phalanx of right index finger, initial encounter for open fracture
S62.610P	Displaced fracture of proximal phalanx of right index finger, subsequent encounter for fracture with malunion
S62.610K	Displaced fracture of proximal phalanx of right index finger, subsequent encounter for fracture with nonunion
S92.511P	Displaced fracture of proximal phalanx of right lesser toe(s), subsequent encounter for fracture with malunion
S92.511K	Displaced fracture of proximal phalanx of right lesser toe(s), subsequent encounter for fracture with nonunion
S62.616B	Displaced fracture of proximal phalanx of right little finger, initial encounter for open fracture
S62.616P	Displaced fracture of proximal phalanx of right little finger, subsequent encounter for fracture with malunion
S62.616K	Displaced fracture of proximal phalanx of right little finger, subsequent encounter for fracture with nonunion
S62.612B	Displaced fracture of proximal phalanx of right middle finger, initial encounter for open fracture
S62.612P	Displaced fracture of proximal phalanx of right middle finger, subsequent encounter for fracture with malunion
S62.612K	Displaced fracture of proximal phalanx of right middle finger, subsequent encounter for fracture with nonunion
S62.614B	Displaced fracture of proximal phalanx of right ring finger, initial encounter for open fracture
S62.614P	Displaced fracture of proximal phalanx of right ring finger, subsequent encounter for fracture with malunion
S62.614K	Displaced fracture of proximal phalanx of right ring finger, subsequent encounter for fracture with nonunion
S62.511B	Displaced fracture of proximal phalanx of right thumb, initial encounter for open fracture
S62.511P	Displaced fracture of proximal phalanx of right thumb, subsequent encounter for fracture with malunion
S62.511K	Displaced fracture of proximal phalanx of right thumb, subsequent encounter for fracture with nonunion
S62.619B	Displaced fracture of proximal phalanx of unspecified finger, initial encounter for open fracture
S62.619P	Displaced fracture of proximal phalanx of unspecified finger, subsequent encounter for fracture with malunion
S62.619K	Displaced fracture of proximal phalanx of unspecified finger, subsequent encounter for fracture with nonunion
S92.413P	Displaced fracture of proximal phalanx of unspecified great toe, subsequent encounter for fracture with malunion
S92.413K	Displaced fracture of proximal phalanx of unspecified great toe, subsequent encounter for fracture with nonunion
S92.513P	Displaced fracture of proximal phalanx of unspecified lesser toe(s), subsequent encounter for fracture with malunion
S92.513K	Displaced fracture of proximal phalanx of unspecified lesser toe(s), subsequent encounter for fracture with nonunion
S62.513B	Displaced fracture of proximal phalanx of unspecified thumb, initial encounter for open fracture
S62.513P	Displaced fracture of proximal phalanx of unspecified thumb, subsequent encounter for fracture with malunion
S62.513K	Displaced fracture of proximal phalanx of unspecified thumb, subsequent encounter for fracture with nonunion
S62.032B	Displaced fracture of proximal third of navicular [scaphoid] bone of left wrist, initial encounter for open fracture
S62.032P	Displaced fracture of proximal third of navicular [scaphoid] bone of left wrist, subsequent encounter for fracture with malunion
S62.032K	Displaced fracture of proximal third of navicular [scaphoid] bone of left wrist, subsequent encounter for fracture with nonunion
S62.031B	Displaced fracture of proximal third of navicular [scaphoid] bone of right wrist, initial encounter for open fracture
S62.031P	Displaced fracture of proximal third of navicular [scaphoid] bone of right wrist, subsequent encounter for fracture with malunion
S62.031K	Displaced fracture of proximal third of navicular [scaphoid] bone of right wrist, subsequent encounter for fracture with nonunion
S62.033B	Displaced fracture of proximal third of navicular [scaphoid] bone of unspecified wrist, initial encounter for open fracture
S62.033P	Displaced fracture of proximal third of navicular [scaphoid] bone of unspecified wrist, subsequent encounter for fracture with malunion
S62.033K	Displaced fracture of proximal third of navicular [scaphoid] bone of unspecified wrist, subsequent encounter for fracture with nonunion
S52.511A	Displaced fracture of right radial styloid process, initial encounter for closed fracture
S52.511P	Displaced fracture of right radial styloid process, subsequent encounter for closed fracture with malunion
S52.511K	Displaced fracture of right radial styloid process, subsequent encounter for closed fracture with nonunion
S52.511Q	Displaced fracture of right radial styloid process, subsequent encounter for open fracture type I or II with malunion
S52.511M	Displaced fracture of right radial styloid process, subsequent encounter for open fracture type I or II with nonunion
S52.511R	Displaced fracture of right radial styloid process, subsequent encounter for open fracture type IIIA, IIIB, or IIIC with malunion
S52.511N	Displaced fracture of right radial styloid process, subsequent encounter for open fracture type IIIA, IIIB, or IIIC with nonunion
S82.111A	Displaced fracture of right tibial spine, initial encounter for closed fracture
S82.111P	Displaced fracture of right tibial spine, subsequent encounter for closed fracture with malunion
S82.111K	Displaced fracture of right tibial spine, subsequent encounter for closed fracture with nonunion
S82.111Q	Displaced fracture of right tibial spine, subsequent encounter for open fracture type I or II with malunion
S82.111M	Displaced fracture of right tibial spine, subsequent encounter for open fracture type I or II with nonunion
S82.111R	Displaced fracture of right tibial spine, subsequent encounter for open fracture type IIIA, IIIB, or IIIC with malunion
S82.111N	Displaced fracture of right tibial spine, subsequent encounter for open fracture type IIIA, IIIB, or IIIC with nonunion
S82.151A	Displaced fracture of right tibial tuberosity, initial encounter for closed fracture
S82.151P	Displaced fracture of right tibial tuberosity, subsequent encounter for closed fracture with malunion
S82.151K	Displaced fracture of right tibial tuberosity, subsequent encounter for closed fracture with nonunion
S82.151Q	Displaced fracture of right tibial tuberosity, subsequent encounter for open fracture type I or II with malunion
S82.151M	Displaced fracture of right tibial tuberosity, subsequent encounter for open fracture type I or II with nonunion
S82.151R	Displaced fracture of right tibial tuberosity, subsequent encounter for open fracture type IIIA, IIIB, or IIIC with malunion

S82.151N Displaced fracture of right tibial tuberosity, subsequent encounter for open fracture type IIIA, IIIB, or IIIC with nonunion

S52.611A Displaced fracture of right ulna styloid process, initial encounter for closed fracture

S52.611P Displaced fracture of right ulna styloid process, subsequent encounter for closed fracture with malunion

S52.611K Displaced fracture of right ulna styloid process, subsequent encounter for closed fracture with nonunion

S52.611Q Displaced fracture of right ulna styloid process, subsequent encounter for open fracture type I or II with malunion

S52.611M Displaced fracture of right ulna styloid process, subsequent encounter for open fracture type I or II with nonunion

S52.611R Displaced fracture of right ulna styloid process, subsequent encounter for open fracture type IIIA, IIIB, or IIIC with malunion

S52.611N Displaced fracture of right ulna styloid process, subsequent encounter for open fracture type IIIA, IIIB, or IIIC with nonunion

S92.322B Displaced fracture of second metatarsal bone, left foot, initial encounter for open fracture

S92.322P Displaced fracture of second metatarsal bone, left foot, subsequent encounter for fracture with malunion

S92.322K Displaced fracture of second metatarsal bone, left foot, subsequent encounter for fracture with nonunion

S92.321B Displaced fracture of second metatarsal bone, right foot, initial encounter for open fracture

S92.321P Displaced fracture of second metatarsal bone, right foot, subsequent encounter for fracture with malunion

S92.321K Displaced fracture of second metatarsal bone, right foot, subsequent encounter for fracture with nonunion

S92.323B Displaced fracture of second metatarsal bone, unspecified foot, initial encounter for open fracture

S92.323P Displaced fracture of second metatarsal bone, unspecified foot, subsequent encounter for fracture with malunion

S92.323K Displaced fracture of second metatarsal bone, unspecified foot, subsequent encounter for fracture with nonunion

S62.327B Displaced fracture of shaft of fifth metacarpal bone, left hand, initial encounter for open fracture

S62.327P Displaced fracture of shaft of fifth metacarpal bone, left hand, subsequent encounter for fracture with malunion

S62.327K Displaced fracture of shaft of fifth metacarpal bone, left hand, subsequent encounter for fracture with nonunion

S62.326B Displaced fracture of shaft of fifth metacarpal bone, right hand, initial encounter for open fracture

S62.326P Displaced fracture of shaft of fifth metacarpal bone, right hand, subsequent encounter for fracture with malunion

S62.326K Displaced fracture of shaft of fifth metacarpal bone, right hand, subsequent encounter for fracture with nonunion

S62.242B Displaced fracture of shaft of first metacarpal bone, left hand, initial encounter for open fracture

S62.242P Displaced fracture of shaft of first metacarpal bone, left hand, subsequent encounter for fracture with malunion

S62.242K Displaced fracture of shaft of first metacarpal bone, left hand, subsequent encounter for fracture with nonunion

S62.241B Displaced fracture of shaft of first metacarpal bone, right hand, initial encounter for open fracture

S62.241P Displaced fracture of shaft of first metacarpal bone, right hand, subsequent encounter for fracture with malunion

S62.241K Displaced fracture of shaft of first metacarpal bone, right hand, subsequent encounter for fracture with nonunion

S62.243B Displaced fracture of shaft of first metacarpal bone, unspecified hand, initial encounter for open fracture

S62.243P Displaced fracture of shaft of first metacarpal bone, unspecified hand, subsequent encounter for fracture with malunion

S62.243K Displaced fracture of shaft of first metacarpal bone, unspecified hand, subsequent encounter for fracture with nonunion

S62.325B Displaced fracture of shaft of fourth metacarpal bone, left hand, initial encounter for open fracture

S62.325P Displaced fracture of shaft of fourth metacarpal bone, left hand, subsequent encounter for fracture with malunion

S62.325K Displaced fracture of shaft of fourth metacarpal bone, left hand, subsequent encounter for fracture with nonunion

S62.324B Displaced fracture of shaft of fourth metacarpal bone, right hand, initial encounter for open fracture

S62.324P Displaced fracture of shaft of fourth metacarpal bone, right hand, subsequent encounter for fracture with malunion

S62.324K Displaced fracture of shaft of fourth metacarpal bone, right hand, subsequent encounter for fracture with nonunion

S42.022B Displaced fracture of shaft of left clavicle, initial encounter for open fracture

S42.022P Displaced fracture of shaft of left clavicle, subsequent encounter for fracture with malunion

S42.022K Displaced fracture of shaft of left clavicle, subsequent encounter for fracture with nonunion

S62.328B Displaced fracture of shaft of other metacarpal bone, initial encounter for open fracture

S62.328P Displaced fracture of shaft of other metacarpal bone, subsequent encounter for fracture with malunion

S62.328K Displaced fracture of shaft of other metacarpal bone, subsequent encounter for fracture with nonunion

S42.021B Displaced fracture of shaft of right clavicle, initial encounter for open fracture

S42.021P Displaced fracture of shaft of right clavicle, subsequent encounter for fracture with malunion

S42.021K Displaced fracture of shaft of right clavicle, subsequent encounter for fracture with nonunion

S62.321B Displaced fracture of shaft of second metacarpal bone, left hand, initial encounter for open fracture

S62.321P Displaced fracture of shaft of second metacarpal bone, left hand, subsequent encounter for fracture with malunion

S62.321K Displaced fracture of shaft of second metacarpal bone, left hand, subsequent encounter for fracture with nonunion

S62.320B Displaced fracture of shaft of second metacarpal bone, right hand, initial encounter for open fracture

S62.320P Displaced fracture of shaft of second metacarpal bone, right hand, subsequent encounter for fracture with malunion

S62.320K Displaced fracture of shaft of second metacarpal bone, right hand, subsequent encounter for fracture with nonunion

S62.323B Displaced fracture of shaft of third metacarpal bone, left hand, initial encounter for open fracture

S62.323P Displaced fracture of shaft of third metacarpal bone, left hand, subsequent encounter for fracture with malunion

S62.323K Displaced fracture of shaft of third metacarpal bone, left hand, subsequent encounter for fracture with nonunion

S62.322B Displaced fracture of shaft of third metacarpal bone, right hand, initial encounter for open fracture

S62.322P Displaced fracture of shaft of third metacarpal bone, right hand, subsequent encounter for fracture with malunion

S62.322K Displaced fracture of shaft of third metacarpal bone, right hand, subsequent encounter for fracture with nonunion

S42.023B Displaced fracture of shaft of unspecified clavicle, initial encounter for open fracture

S42.023P Displaced fracture of shaft of unspecified clavicle, subsequent encounter for fracture with malunion

S42.023K Displaced fracture of shaft of unspecified clavicle, subsequent encounter for fracture with nonunion

S62.329B Displaced fracture of shaft of unspecified metacarpal bone, initial encounter for open fracture

S62.329P Displaced fracture of shaft of unspecified metacarpal bone, subsequent encounter for fracture with malunion

S62.329K Displaced fracture of shaft of unspecified metacarpal bone, subsequent encounter for fracture with nonunion

S92.332B Displaced fracture of third metatarsal bone, left foot, initial encounter for open fracture

S92.332P Displaced fracture of third metatarsal bone, left foot, subsequent encounter for fracture with malunion

S92.332K Displaced fracture of third metatarsal bone, left foot, subsequent encounter for fracture with nonunion

S92.331B Displaced fracture of third metatarsal bone, right foot, initial encounter for open fracture

S92.331P Displaced fracture of third metatarsal bone, right foot, subsequent encounter for fracture with malunion

S92.331K Displaced fracture of third metatarsal bone, right foot, subsequent encounter for fracture with nonunion

S92.333B Displaced fracture of third metatarsal bone, unspecified foot, initial encounter for open fracture

S92.333P Displaced fracture of third metatarsal bone, unspecified foot, subsequent encounter for fracture with malunion

S92.333K Displaced fracture of third metatarsal bone, unspecified foot, subsequent encounter for fracture with nonunion

S62.172B Displaced fracture of trapezium [larger multangular], left wrist, initial encounter for open fracture

S62.172P Displaced fracture of trapezium [larger multangular], left wrist, subsequent encounter for fracture with malunion

S62.172K Displaced fracture of trapezium [larger multangular], left wrist, subsequent encounter for fracture with nonunion

S62.171B Displaced fracture of trapezium [larger multangular], right wrist, initial encounter for open fracture

S62.171P Displaced fracture of trapezium [larger multangular], right wrist, subsequent encounter for fracture with malunion

S62.171K Displaced fracture of trapezium [larger multangular], right wrist, subsequent encounter for fracture with nonunion

S62.173B Displaced fracture of trapezium [larger multangular], unspecified wrist, initial encounter for open fracture

S62.173P Displaced fracture of trapezium [larger multangular], unspecified wrist, subsequent encounter for fracture with malunion

S62.173K Displaced fracture of trapezium [larger multangular], unspecified wrist, subsequent encounter for fracture with nonunion

S62.182B Displaced fracture of trapezoid [smaller multangular], left wrist, initial encounter for open fracture

S62.182P Displaced fracture of trapezoid [smaller multangular], left wrist, subsequent encounter for fracture with malunion

S62.182K Displaced fracture of trapezoid [smaller multangular], left wrist, subsequent encounter for fracture with nonunion

S62.181B Displaced fracture of trapezoid [smaller multangular], right wrist, initial encounter for open fracture

S62.181P Displaced fracture of trapezoid [smaller multangular], right wrist, subsequent encounter for fracture with malunion

S62.181K Displaced fracture of trapezoid [smaller multangular], right wrist, subsequent encounter for fracture with nonunion

S62.183B Displaced fracture of trapezoid [smaller multangular], unspecified wrist, initial encounter for open fracture

S62.183P Displaced fracture of trapezoid [smaller multangular], unspecified wrist, subsequent encounter for fracture with malunion

S62.183K Displaced fracture of trapezoid [smaller multangular], unspecified wrist, subsequent encounter for fracture with nonunion

S62.112B Displaced fracture of triquetrum [cuneiform] bone, left wrist, initial encounter for open fracture

S62.112P Displaced fracture of triquetrum [cuneiform] bone, left wrist, subsequent encounter for fracture with malunion

S62.112K Displaced fracture of triquetrum [cuneiform] bone, left wrist, subsequent encounter for fracture with nonunion

S62.111B Displaced fracture of triquetrum [cuneiform] bone, right wrist, initial encounter for open fracture

S62.111P Displaced fracture of triquetrum [cuneiform] bone, right wrist, subsequent encounter for fracture with malunion

S62.111K Displaced fracture of triquetrum [cuneiform] bone, right wrist, subsequent encounter for fracture with nonunion

S62.113B Displaced fracture of triquetrum [cuneiform] bone, unspecified wrist, initial encounter for open fracture

S62.113P Displaced fracture of triquetrum [cuneiform] bone, unspecified wrist, subsequent encounter for fracture with malunion

S62.113K Displaced fracture of triquetrum [cuneiform] bone, unspecified wrist, subsequent encounter for fracture with nonunion

S52.513A Displaced fracture of unspecified radial styloid process, initial encounter for closed fracture

S52.513P Displaced fracture of unspecified radial styloid process, subsequent encounter for closed fracture with malunion

S52.513K Displaced fracture of unspecified radial styloid process, subsequent encounter for closed fracture with nonunion

S52.513Q Displaced fracture of unspecified radial styloid process, subsequent encounter for open fracture type I or II with malunion

S52.513M Displaced fracture of unspecified radial styloid process, subsequent encounter for open fracture type I or II with nonunion

S52.513R Displaced fracture of unspecified radial styloid process, subsequent encounter for open fracture type IIIA, IIIB, or IIIC with malunion

S52.513N Displaced fracture of unspecified radial styloid process, subsequent encounter for open fracture type IIIA, IIIB, or IIIC with nonunion

S82.113A Displaced fracture of unspecified tibial spine, initial encounter for closed fracture

S82.113P Displaced fracture of unspecified tibial spine, subsequent encounter for closed fracture with malunion

S82.113K Displaced fracture of unspecified tibial spine, subsequent encounter for closed fracture with nonunion

S82.113Q Displaced fracture of unspecified tibial spine, subsequent encounter for open fracture type I or II with malunion

S82.113M Displaced fracture of unspecified tibial spine, subsequent encounter for open fracture type I or II with nonunion

S82.113R Displaced fracture of unspecified tibial spine, subsequent encounter for open fracture type IIIA, IIIB, or IIIC with malunion

S82.113N Displaced fracture of unspecified tibial spine, subsequent encounter for open fracture type IIIA, IIIB, or IIIC with nonunion

S82.153A Displaced fracture of unspecified tibial tuberosity, initial encounter for closed fracture

S82.153P Displaced fracture of unspecified tibial tuberosity, subsequent encounter for closed fracture with malunion

S82.153K Displaced fracture of unspecified tibial tuberosity, subsequent encounter for closed fracture with nonunion

S82.153Q Displaced fracture of unspecified tibial tuberosity, subsequent encounter for open fracture type I or II with malunion

S82.153M Displaced fracture of unspecified tibial tuberosity, subsequent encounter for open fracture type I or II with nonunion

S82.153R Displaced fracture of unspecified tibial tuberosity, subsequent encounter for open fracture type IIIA, IIIB, or IIIC with malunion

S82.153N Displaced fracture of unspecified tibial tuberosity, subsequent encounter for open fracture type IIIA, IIIB, or IIIC with nonunion

S52.613A Displaced fracture of unspecified ulna styloid process, initial encounter for closed fracture

S52.613P Displaced fracture of unspecified ulna styloid process, subsequent encounter for closed fracture with malunion

S52.613K Displaced fracture of unspecified ulna styloid process, subsequent encounter for closed fracture with nonunion

S52.613Q Displaced fracture of unspecified ulna styloid process, subsequent encounter for open fracture type I or II with malunion

S52.613M Displaced fracture of unspecified ulna styloid process, subsequent encounter for open fracture type I or II with nonunion

S52.613R Displaced fracture of unspecified ulna styloid process, subsequent encounter for open fracture type IIIA, IIIB, or IIIC with malunion

S52.613N Displaced fracture of unspecified ulna styloid process, subsequent encounter for open fracture type IIIA, IIIB, or IIIC with nonunion

S72.142P Displaced intertrochanteric fracture of left femur, subsequent encounter for closed fracture with malunion

S72.142K Displaced intertrochanteric fracture of left femur, subsequent encounter for closed fracture with nonunion

S72.142Q Displaced intertrochanteric fracture of left femur, subsequent encounter for open fracture type I or II with malunion

S72.142M Displaced intertrochanteric fracture of left femur, subsequent encounter for open fracture type I or II with nonunion

S72.142R Displaced intertrochanteric fracture of left femur, subsequent encounter for open fracture type IIIA, IIIB, or IIIC with malunion

S72.142N Displaced intertrochanteric fracture of left femur, subsequent encounter for open fracture type IIIA, IIIB, or IIIC with nonunion

S72.141P Displaced intertrochanteric fracture of right femur, subsequent encounter for closed fracture with malunion

S72.141K Displaced intertrochanteric fracture of right femur, subsequent encounter for closed fracture with nonunion

S72.141Q Displaced intertrochanteric fracture of right femur, subsequent encounter for open fracture type I or II with malunion

S72.141M Displaced intertrochanteric fracture of right femur, subsequent encounter for open fracture type I or II with nonunion

S72.141R Displaced intertrochanteric fracture of right femur, subsequent encounter for open fracture type IIIA, IIIB, or IIIC with malunion

S72.141N Displaced intertrochanteric fracture of right femur, subsequent encounter for open fracture type IIIA, IIIB, or IIIC with nonunion

S72.143P Displaced intertrochanteric fracture of unspecified femur, subsequent encounter for closed fracture with malunion

S72.143K Displaced intertrochanteric fracture of unspecified femur, subsequent encounter for closed fracture with nonunion

S72.143Q Displaced intertrochanteric fracture of unspecified femur, subsequent encounter for open fracture type I or II with malunion

S72.143M Displaced intertrochanteric fracture of unspecified femur, subsequent encounter for open fracture type I or II with nonunion

S72.143R Displaced intertrochanteric fracture of unspecified femur, subsequent encounter for open fracture type IIIA, IIIB, or IIIC with malunion

S72.143N Displaced intertrochanteric fracture of unspecified femur, subsequent encounter for open fracture type IIIA, IIIB, or IIIC with nonunion

S92.062B Displaced intraarticular fracture of left calcaneus, initial encounter for open fracture

S92.062P Displaced intraarticular fracture of left calcaneus, subsequent encounter for fracture with malunion

S92.062K Displaced intraarticular fracture of left calcaneus, subsequent encounter for fracture with nonunion

S92.061B Displaced intraarticular fracture of right calcaneus, initial encounter for open fracture

S92.061P Displaced intraarticular fracture of right calcaneus, subsequent encounter for fracture with malunion

S92.061K Displaced intraarticular fracture of right calcaneus, subsequent encounter for fracture with nonunion

S92.063B Displaced intraarticular fracture of unspecified calcaneus, initial encounter for open fracture

S92.063P Displaced intraarticular fracture of unspecified calcaneus, subsequent encounter for fracture with malunion

S92.063K Displaced intraarticular fracture of unspecified calcaneus, subsequent encounter for fracture with nonunion

S12.040A Displaced lateral mass fracture of first cervical vertebra, initial encounter for closed fracture

S12.040K Displaced lateral mass fracture of first cervical vertebra, subsequent encounter for fracture with nonunion

S82.022A Displaced longitudinal fracture of left patella, initial encounter for closed fracture

S82.022B Displaced longitudinal fracture of left patella, initial encounter for open fracture type I or II

S82.022C Displaced longitudinal fracture of left patella, initial encounter for open fracture type IIIA, IIIB, or IIIC

S82.022P Displaced longitudinal fracture of left patella, subsequent encounter for closed fracture with malunion

S82.022K Displaced longitudinal fracture of left patella, subsequent encounter for closed fracture with nonunion

S82.022Q Displaced longitudinal fracture of left patella, subsequent encounter for open fracture type I or II with malunion

S82.022M Displaced longitudinal fracture of left patella, subsequent encounter for open fracture type I or II with nonunion

S82.022R Displaced longitudinal fracture of left patella, subsequent encounter for open fracture type IIIA, IIIB, or IIIC with malunion

S82.022N Displaced longitudinal fracture of left patella, subsequent encounter for open fracture type IIIA, IIIB, or IIIC with nonunion

S82.021A Displaced longitudinal fracture of right patella, initial encounter for closed fracture

S82.021B Displaced longitudinal fracture of right patella, initial encounter for open fracture type I or II

S82.021C Displaced longitudinal fracture of right patella, initial encounter for open fracture type IIIA, IIIB, or IIIC

S82.021P Displaced longitudinal fracture of right patella, subsequent encounter for closed fracture with malunion

S82.021K Displaced longitudinal fracture of right patella, subsequent encounter for closed fracture with nonunion

S82.021Q Displaced longitudinal fracture of right patella, subsequent encounter for open fracture type I or II with malunion

S82.021M Displaced longitudinal fracture of right patella, subsequent encounter for open fracture type I or II with nonunion

S82.021R Displaced longitudinal fracture of right patella, subsequent encounter for open fracture type IIIA, IIIB, or IIIC with malunion

S82.021N Displaced longitudinal fracture of right patella, subsequent encounter for open fracture type IIIA, IIIB, or IIIC with nonunion

S82.023A Displaced longitudinal fracture of unspecified patella, initial encounter for closed fracture

S82.023B Displaced longitudinal fracture of unspecified patella, initial encounter for open fracture type I or II

S82.023C Displaced longitudinal fracture of unspecified patella, initial encounter for open fracture type IIIA, IIIB, or IIIC

S82.023P Displaced longitudinal fracture of unspecified patella, subsequent encounter for closed fracture with malunion

S82.023K Displaced longitudinal fracture of unspecified patella, subsequent encounter for closed fracture with nonunion

S82.023Q Displaced longitudinal fracture of unspecified patella, subsequent encounter for open fracture type I or II with malunion

S82.023M Displaced longitudinal fracture of unspecified patella, subsequent encounter for open fracture type I or II with nonunion

S82.023R Displaced longitudinal fracture of unspecified patella, subsequent encounter for open fracture type IIIA, IIIB, or IIIC with malunion

S82.023N Displaced longitudinal fracture of unspecified patella, subsequent encounter for open fracture type IIIA, IIIB, or IIIC with nonunion

S82.862P Displaced Maisonneuve's fracture of left leg, subsequent encounter for closed fracture with malunion

S82.862K Displaced Maisonneuve's fracture of left leg, subsequent encounter for closed fracture with nonunion

S82.862Q Displaced Maisonneuve's fracture of left leg, subsequent encounter for open fracture type I or II with malunion

S82.862M Displaced Maisonneuve's fracture of left leg, subsequent encounter for open fracture type I or II with nonunion

S82.862R Displaced Maisonneuve's fracture of left leg, subsequent encounter for open fracture type IIIA, IIIB, or IIIC with malunion

S82.862N Displaced Maisonneuve's fracture of left leg, subsequent encounter for open fracture type IIIA, IIIB, or IIIC with nonunion

S82.861P Displaced Maisonneuve's fracture of right leg, subsequent encounter for closed fracture with malunion

S82.861K Displaced Maisonneuve's fracture of right leg, subsequent encounter for closed fracture with nonunion

S82.861Q Displaced Maisonneuve's fracture of right leg, subsequent encounter for open fracture type I or II with malunion

S82.861M Displaced Maisonneuve's fracture of right leg, subsequent encounter for open fracture type I or II with nonunion

S82.861R Displaced Maisonneuve's fracture of right leg, subsequent encounter for open fracture type IIIA, IIIB, or IIIC with malunion

S82.861N Displaced Maisonneuve's fracture of right leg, subsequent encounter for open fracture type IIIA, IIIB, or IIIC with nonunion

S82.863P Displaced Maisonneuve's fracture of unspecified leg, subsequent encounter for closed fracture with malunion

S82.863K Displaced Maisonneuve's fracture of unspecified leg, subsequent encounter for closed fracture with nonunion

S82.863Q Displaced Maisonneuve's fracture of unspecified leg, subsequent encounter for open fracture type I or II with malunion

S82.863M Displaced Maisonneuve's fracture of unspecified leg, subsequent encounter for open fracture type I or II with nonunion

S82.863R Displaced Maisonneuve's fracture of unspecified leg, subsequent encounter for open fracture type IIIA, IIIB, or IIIC with malunion

S82.863N Displaced Maisonneuve's fracture of unspecified leg, subsequent encounter for open fracture type IIIA, IIIB, or IIIC with nonunion

S72.032P Displaced midcervical fracture of left femur, subsequent encounter for closed fracture with malunion

S72.032K Displaced midcervical fracture of left femur, subsequent encounter for closed fracture with nonunion

S72.032Q Displaced midcervical fracture of left femur, subsequent encounter for open fracture type I or II with malunion

S72.032M Displaced midcervical fracture of left femur, subsequent encounter for open fracture type I or II with nonunion

S72.032R Displaced midcervical fracture of left femur, subsequent encounter for open fracture type IIIA, IIIB, or IIIC with malunion

S72.032N Displaced midcervical fracture of left femur, subsequent encounter for open fracture type IIIA, IIIB, or IIIC with nonunion

S72.031P Displaced midcervical fracture of right femur, subsequent encounter for closed fracture with malunion

S72.031K Displaced midcervical fracture of right femur, subsequent encounter for closed fracture with nonunion

S72.031Q Displaced midcervical fracture of right femur, subsequent encounter for open fracture type I or II with malunion

S72.031M Displaced midcervical fracture of right femur, subsequent encounter for open fracture type I or II with nonunion

S72.031R Displaced midcervical fracture of right femur, subsequent encounter for open fracture type IIIA, IIIB, or IIIC with malunion

S72.031N Displaced midcervical fracture of right femur, subsequent encounter for open fracture type IIIA, IIIB, or IIIC with nonunion

S72.033P Displaced midcervical fracture of unspecified femur, subsequent encounter for closed fracture with malunion

S72.033K Displaced midcervical fracture of unspecified femur, subsequent encounter for closed fracture with nonunion

S72.033Q Displaced midcervical fracture of unspecified femur, subsequent encounter for open fracture type I or II with malunion

S72.033M Displaced midcervical fracture of unspecified femur, subsequent encounter for open fracture type I or II with nonunion

S72.033R Displaced midcervical fracture of unspecified femur, subsequent encounter for open fracture type IIIA, IIIB, or IIIC with malunion

S72.033N Displaced midcervical fracture of unspecified femur, subsequent encounter for open fracture type IIIA, IIIB, or IIIC with nonunion

S42.332A Displaced oblique fracture of shaft of humerus, left arm, initial encounter for closed fracture

S42.332P Displaced oblique fracture of shaft of humerus, left arm, subsequent encounter for fracture with malunion

S42.332K Displaced oblique fracture of shaft of humerus, left arm, subsequent encounter for fracture with nonunion

S42.331A Displaced oblique fracture of shaft of humerus, right arm, initial encounter for closed fracture

S42.331P Displaced oblique fracture of shaft of humerus, right arm, subsequent encounter for fracture with malunion

S42.331K Displaced oblique fracture of shaft of humerus, right arm, subsequent encounter for fracture with nonunion

S42.333A Displaced oblique fracture of shaft of humerus, unspecified arm, initial encounter for closed fracture

S42.333P Displaced oblique fracture of shaft of humerus, unspecified arm, subsequent encounter for fracture with malunion

S42.333K Displaced oblique fracture of shaft of humerus, unspecified arm, subsequent encounter for fracture with nonunion

S72.332P Displaced oblique fracture of shaft of left femur, subsequent encounter for closed fracture with malunion

S72.332K Displaced oblique fracture of shaft of left femur, subsequent encounter for closed fracture with nonunion

S72.332Q Displaced oblique fracture of shaft of left femur, subsequent encounter for open fracture type I or II with malunion

S72.332M Displaced oblique fracture of shaft of left femur, subsequent encounter for open fracture type I or II with nonunion

S72.332R Displaced oblique fracture of shaft of left femur, subsequent encounter for open fracture type IIIA, IIIB, or IIIC with malunion

S72.332N Displaced oblique fracture of shaft of left femur, subsequent encounter for open fracture type IIIA, IIIB, or IIIC with nonunion

S82.432P Displaced oblique fracture of shaft of left fibula, subsequent encounter for closed fracture with malunion

S82.432K Displaced oblique fracture of shaft of left fibula, subsequent encounter for closed fracture with nonunion

S82.432Q Displaced oblique fracture of shaft of left fibula, subsequent encounter for open fracture type I or II with malunion

S82.432M Displaced oblique fracture of shaft of left fibula, subsequent encounter for open fracture type I or II with nonunion

S82.432R Displaced oblique fracture of shaft of left fibula, subsequent encounter for open fracture type IIIA, IIIB, or IIIC with malunion

S82.432N Displaced oblique fracture of shaft of left fibula, subsequent encounter for open fracture type IIIA, IIIB, or IIIC with nonunion

S52.332A Displaced oblique fracture of shaft of left radius, initial encounter for closed fracture

S52.332P Displaced oblique fracture of shaft of left radius, subsequent encounter for closed fracture with malunion

S52.332K Displaced oblique fracture of shaft of left radius, subsequent encounter for closed fracture with nonunion

S52.332Q Displaced oblique fracture of shaft of left radius, subsequent encounter for open fracture type I or II with malunion

S52.332M Displaced oblique fracture of shaft of left radius, subsequent encounter for open fracture type I or II with nonunion

S52.332R Displaced oblique fracture of shaft of left radius, subsequent encounter for open fracture type IIIA, IIIB, or IIIC with malunion

S52.332N Displaced oblique fracture of shaft of left radius, subsequent encounter for open fracture type IIIA, IIIB, or IIIC with nonunion

S82.232A Displaced oblique fracture of shaft of left tibia, initial encounter for closed fracture

S82.232P Displaced oblique fracture of shaft of left tibia, subsequent encounter for closed fracture with malunion

S82.232K Displaced oblique fracture of shaft of left tibia, subsequent encounter for closed fracture with nonunion

S82.232Q Displaced oblique fracture of shaft of left tibia, subsequent encounter for open fracture type I or II with malunion

S82.232M Displaced oblique fracture of shaft of left tibia, subsequent encounter for open fracture type I or II with nonunion

S82.232R Displaced oblique fracture of shaft of left tibia, subsequent encounter for open fracture type IIIA, IIIB, or IIIC with malunion

S82.232N Displaced oblique fracture of shaft of left tibia, subsequent encounter for open fracture type IIIA, IIIB, or IIIC with nonunion

S52.232A Displaced oblique fracture of shaft of left ulna, initial encounter for closed fracture

S52.232P Displaced oblique fracture of shaft of left ulna, subsequent encounter for closed fracture with malunion

S52.232K Displaced oblique fracture of shaft of left ulna, subsequent encounter for closed fracture with nonunion

S52.232Q Displaced oblique fracture of shaft of left ulna, subsequent encounter for open fracture type I or II with malunion

S52.232M Displaced oblique fracture of shaft of left ulna, subsequent encounter for open fracture type I or II with nonunion

S52.232R Displaced oblique fracture of shaft of left ulna, subsequent encounter for open fracture type IIIA, IIIB, or IIIC with malunion

S52.232N Displaced oblique fracture of shaft of left ulna, subsequent encounter for open fracture type IIIA, IIIB, or IIIC with nonunion

S72.331P Displaced oblique fracture of shaft of right femur, subsequent encounter for closed fracture with malunion

S72.331K Displaced oblique fracture of shaft of right femur, subsequent encounter for closed fracture with nonunion

S72.331Q Displaced oblique fracture of shaft of right femur, subsequent encounter for open fracture type I or II with malunion

S72.331M Displaced oblique fracture of shaft of right femur, subsequent encounter for open fracture type I or II with nonunion

S72.331R Displaced oblique fracture of shaft of right femur, subsequent encounter for open fracture type IIIA, IIIB, or IIIC with malunion

S72.331N Displaced oblique fracture of shaft of right femur, subsequent encounter for open fracture type IIIA, IIIB, or IIIC with nonunion

S82.431P Displaced oblique fracture of shaft of right fibula, subsequent encounter for closed fracture with malunion

S82.431K Displaced oblique fracture of shaft of right fibula, subsequent encounter for closed fracture with nonunion

S82.431Q Displaced oblique fracture of shaft of right fibula, subsequent encounter for open fracture type I or II with malunion

S82.431M Displaced oblique fracture of shaft of right fibula, subsequent encounter for open fracture type I or II with nonunion

S82.431R Displaced oblique fracture of shaft of right fibula, subsequent encounter for open fracture type IIIA, IIIB, or IIIC with malunion

S82.431N Displaced oblique fracture of shaft of right fibula, subsequent encounter for open fracture type IIIA, IIIB, or IIIC with nonunion

S52.331A Displaced oblique fracture of shaft of right radius, initial encounter for closed fracture

S52.331P Displaced oblique fracture of shaft of right radius, subsequent encounter for closed fracture with malunion

S52.331K Displaced oblique fracture of shaft of right radius, subsequent encounter for closed fracture with nonunion

S52.331Q Displaced oblique fracture of shaft of right radius, subsequent encounter for open fracture type I or II with malunion

S52.331M Displaced oblique fracture of shaft of right radius, subsequent encounter for open fracture type I or II with nonunion

S52.331R Displaced oblique fracture of shaft of right radius, subsequent encounter for open fracture type IIIA, IIIB, or IIIC with malunion

S52.331N Displaced oblique fracture of shaft of right radius, subsequent encounter for open fracture type IIIA, IIIB, or IIIC with nonunion

S82.231A Displaced oblique fracture of shaft of right tibia, initial encounter for closed fracture

S82.231P Displaced oblique fracture of shaft of right tibia, subsequent encounter for closed fracture with malunion

S82.231K Displaced oblique fracture of shaft of right tibia, subsequent encounter for closed fracture with nonunion

S82.231Q Displaced oblique fracture of shaft of right tibia, subsequent encounter for open fracture type I or II with malunion

S82.231M Displaced oblique fracture of shaft of right tibia, subsequent encounter for open fracture type I or II with nonunion

S82.231R Displaced oblique fracture of shaft of right tibia, subsequent encounter for open fracture type IIIA, IIIB, or IIIC with malunion

S82.231N Displaced oblique fracture of shaft of right tibia, subsequent encounter for open fracture type IIIA, IIIB, or IIIC with nonunion

S52.231A Displaced oblique fracture of shaft of right ulna, initial encounter for closed fracture

S52.231P Displaced oblique fracture of shaft of right ulna, subsequent encounter for closed fracture with malunion

S52.231K Displaced oblique fracture of shaft of right ulna, subsequent encounter for closed fracture with nonunion

S52.231Q Displaced oblique fracture of shaft of right ulna, subsequent encounter for open fracture type I or II with malunion

S52.231M Displaced oblique fracture of shaft of right ulna, subsequent encounter for open fracture type I or II with nonunion

S52.231R Displaced oblique fracture of shaft of right ulna, subsequent encounter for open fracture type IIIA, IIIB, or IIIC with malunion

S52.231N Displaced oblique fracture of shaft of right ulna, subsequent encounter for open fracture type IIIA, IIIB, or IIIC with nonunion

S72.333P Displaced oblique fracture of shaft of unspecified femur, subsequent encounter for closed fracture with malunion

S72.333K Displaced oblique fracture of shaft of unspecified femur, subsequent encounter for closed fracture with nonunion

S72.333Q Displaced oblique fracture of shaft of unspecified femur, subsequent encounter for open fracture type I or II with malunion

S72.333M Displaced oblique fracture of shaft of unspecified femur, subsequent encounter for open fracture type I or II with nonunion

S72.333R Displaced oblique fracture of shaft of unspecified femur, subsequent encounter for open fracture type IIIA, IIIB, or IIIC with malunion

S72.333N Displaced oblique fracture of shaft of unspecified femur, subsequent encounter for open fracture type IIIA, IIIB, or IIIC with nonunion

S82.433P Displaced oblique fracture of shaft of unspecified fibula, subsequent encounter for closed fracture with malunion

S82.433K Displaced oblique fracture of shaft of unspecified fibula, subsequent encounter for closed fracture with nonunion

S82.433Q Displaced oblique fracture of shaft of unspecified fibula, subsequent encounter for open fracture type I or II with malunion

S82.433M Displaced oblique fracture of shaft of unspecified fibula, subsequent encounter for open fracture type I or II with nonunion

S82.433R Displaced oblique fracture of shaft of unspecified fibula, subsequent encounter for open fracture type IIIA, IIIB, or IIIC with malunion

S82.433N Displaced oblique fracture of shaft of unspecified fibula, subsequent encounter for open fracture type IIIA, IIIB, or IIIC with nonunion

S52.333A Displaced oblique fracture of shaft of unspecified radius, initial encounter for closed fracture

S52.333P Displaced oblique fracture of shaft of unspecified radius, subsequent encounter for closed fracture with malunion

S52.333K Displaced oblique fracture of shaft of unspecified radius, subsequent encounter for closed fracture with nonunion

S52.333Q Displaced oblique fracture of shaft of unspecified radius, subsequent encounter for open fracture type I or II with malunion

S52.333M Displaced oblique fracture of shaft of unspecified radius, subsequent encounter for open fracture type I or II with nonunion

S52.333R Displaced oblique fracture of shaft of unspecified radius, subsequent encounter for open fracture type IIIA, IIIB, or IIIC with malunion

S52.333N Displaced oblique fracture of shaft of unspecified radius, subsequent encounter for open fracture type IIIA, IIIB, or IIIC with nonunion

S82.233A Displaced oblique fracture of shaft of unspecified tibia, initial encounter for closed fracture

S82.233P Displaced oblique fracture of shaft of unspecified tibia, subsequent encounter for closed fracture with malunion

S82.233K Displaced oblique fracture of shaft of unspecified tibia, subsequent encounter for closed fracture with nonunion

S82.233Q Displaced oblique fracture of shaft of unspecified tibia, subsequent encounter for open fracture type I or II with malunion

S82.233M Displaced oblique fracture of shaft of unspecified tibia, subsequent encounter for open fracture type I or II with nonunion

S82.233R Displaced oblique fracture of shaft of unspecified tibia, subsequent encounter for open fracture type IIIA, IIIB, or IIIC with malunion

S82.233N Displaced oblique fracture of shaft of unspecified tibia, subsequent encounter for open fracture type IIIA, IIIB, or IIIC with nonunion

S52.233A Displaced oblique fracture of shaft of unspecified ulna, initial encounter for closed fracture

S52.233P Displaced oblique fracture of shaft of unspecified ulna, subsequent encounter for closed fracture with malunion

S52.233K Displaced oblique fracture of shaft of unspecified ulna, subsequent encounter for closed fracture with nonunion

S52.233Q Displaced oblique fracture of shaft of unspecified ulna, subsequent encounter for open fracture type I or II with malunion

S52.233M Displaced oblique fracture of shaft of unspecified ulna, subsequent encounter for open fracture type I or II with nonunion

S52.233R Displaced oblique fracture of shaft of unspecified ulna, subsequent encounter for open fracture type IIIA, IIIB, or IIIC with malunion

S52.233N Displaced oblique fracture of shaft of unspecified ulna, subsequent encounter for open fracture type IIIA, IIIB, or IIIC with nonunion

S82.012A Displaced osteochondral fracture of left patella, initial encounter for closed fracture

S82.012B Displaced osteochondral fracture of left patella, initial encounter for open fracture type I or II

S82.012C Displaced osteochondral fracture of left patella, initial encounter for open fracture type IIIA, IIIB, or IIIC

S82.012P Displaced osteochondral fracture of left patella, subsequent encounter for closed fracture with malunion

S82.012K Displaced osteochondral fracture of left patella, subsequent encounter for closed fracture with nonunion

S82.012Q Displaced osteochondral fracture of left patella, subsequent encounter for open fracture type I or II with malunion

S82.012M Displaced osteochondral fracture of left patella, subsequent encounter for open fracture type I or II with nonunion

S82.012R Displaced osteochondral fracture of left patella, subsequent encounter for open fracture type IIIA, IIIB, or IIIC with malunion

S82.012N Displaced osteochondral fracture of left patella, subsequent encounter for open fracture type IIIA, IIIB, or IIIC with nonunion

S82.011A Displaced osteochondral fracture of right patella, initial encounter for closed fracture

S82.011B Displaced osteochondral fracture of right patella, initial encounter for open fracture type I or II

S82.011C Displaced osteochondral fracture of right patella, initial encounter for open fracture type IIIA, IIIB, or IIIC

S82.011P Displaced osteochondral fracture of right patella, subsequent encounter for closed fracture with malunion

S82.011K Displaced osteochondral fracture of right patella, subsequent encounter for closed fracture with nonunion

S82.011Q Displaced osteochondral fracture of right patella, subsequent encounter for open fracture type I or II with malunion

S82.011M Displaced osteochondral fracture of right patella, subsequent encounter for open fracture type I or II with nonunion

S82.011R Displaced osteochondral fracture of right patella, subsequent encounter for open fracture type IIIA, IIIB, or IIIC with malunion

S82.011N Displaced osteochondral fracture of right patella, subsequent encounter for open fracture type IIIA, IIIB, or IIIC with nonunion

S82.013A Displaced osteochondral fracture of unspecified patella, initial encounter for closed fracture

S82.013B Displaced osteochondral fracture of unspecified patella, initial encounter for open fracture type I or II

S82.013C Displaced osteochondral fracture of unspecified patella, initial encounter for open fracture type IIIA, IIIB, or IIIC

S82.013P Displaced osteochondral fracture of unspecified patella, subsequent encounter for closed fracture with malunion

S82.013K Displaced osteochondral fracture of unspecified patella, subsequent encounter for closed fracture with nonunion

S82.013Q Displaced osteochondral fracture of unspecified patella, subsequent encounter for open fracture type I or II with malunion

S82.013M Displaced osteochondral fracture of unspecified patella, subsequent encounter for open fracture type I or II with nonunion

S82.013R Displaced osteochondral fracture of unspecified patella, subsequent encounter for open fracture type IIIA, IIIB, or IIIC with malunion

S82.013N Displaced osteochondral fracture of unspecified patella, subsequent encounter for open fracture type IIIA, IIIB, or IIIC with nonunion

S92.052B Displaced other extraarticular fracture of left calcaneus, initial encounter for open fracture

S92.052P Displaced other extraarticular fracture of left calcaneus, subsequent encounter for fracture with malunion

S92.052K Displaced other extraarticular fracture of left calcaneus, subsequent encounter for fracture with nonunion

S92.051B Displaced other extraarticular fracture of right calcaneus, initial encounter for open fracture

S92.051P Displaced other extraarticular fracture of right calcaneus, subsequent encounter for fracture with malunion

S92.051K Displaced other extraarticular fracture of right calcaneus, subsequent encounter for fracture with nonunion

S92.053B Displaced other extraarticular fracture of unspecified calcaneus, initial encounter for open fracture

S92.053P Displaced other extraarticular fracture of unspecified calcaneus, subsequent encounter for fracture with malunion

S92.053K Displaced other extraarticular fracture of unspecified calcaneus, subsequent encounter for fracture with nonunion

S92.042B Displaced other fracture of tuberosity of left calcaneus, initial encounter for open fracture

S92.042P Displaced other fracture of tuberosity of left calcaneus, subsequent encounter for fracture with malunion

S92.042K Displaced other fracture of tuberosity of left calcaneus, subsequent encounter for fracture with nonunion

S92.041B Displaced other fracture of tuberosity of right calcaneus, initial encounter for open fracture

S92.041P Displaced other fracture of tuberosity of right calcaneus, subsequent encounter for fracture with malunion

S92.041K Displaced other fracture of tuberosity of right calcaneus, subsequent encounter for fracture with nonunion

S92.043B Displaced other fracture of tuberosity of unspecified calcaneus, initial encounter for open fracture

S92.043P Displaced other fracture of tuberosity of unspecified calcaneus, subsequent encounter for fracture with malunion

S92.043K Displaced other fracture of tuberosity of unspecified calcaneus, subsequent encounter for fracture with nonunion

S82.872B Displaced pilon fracture of left tibia, initial encounter for open fracture type I or II

S82.872C Displaced pilon fracture of left tibia, initial encounter for open fracture type IIIA, IIIB, or IIIC

S82.872P Displaced pilon fracture of left tibia, subsequent encounter for closed fracture with malunion

S82.872K Displaced pilon fracture of left tibia, subsequent encounter for closed fracture with nonunion

S82.872Q Displaced pilon fracture of left tibia, subsequent encounter for open fracture type I or II with malunion

S82.872M Displaced pilon fracture of left tibia, subsequent encounter for open fracture type I or II with nonunion

S82.872R Displaced pilon fracture of left tibia, subsequent encounter for open fracture type IIIA, IIIB, or IIIC with malunion

S82.872N Displaced pilon fracture of left tibia, subsequent encounter for open fracture type IIIA, IIIB, or IIIC with nonunion

S82.871B Displaced pilon fracture of right tibia, initial encounter for open fracture type I or II

S82.871C Displaced pilon fracture of right tibia, initial encounter for open fracture type IIIA, IIIB, or IIIC

S82.871P Displaced pilon fracture of right tibia, subsequent encounter for closed fracture with malunion

S82.871K Displaced pilon fracture of right tibia, subsequent encounter for closed fracture with nonunion

S82.871Q Displaced pilon fracture of right tibia, subsequent encounter for open fracture type I or II with malunion

S82.871M Displaced pilon fracture of right tibia, subsequent encounter for open fracture type I or II with nonunion

S82.871R Displaced pilon fracture of right tibia, subsequent encounter for open fracture type IIIA, IIIB, or IIIC with malunion

S82.871N Displaced pilon fracture of right tibia, subsequent encounter for open fracture type IIIA, IIIB, or IIIC with nonunion

S82.873B Displaced pilon fracture of unspecified tibia, initial encounter for open fracture type I or II

S82.873C Displaced pilon fracture of unspecified tibia, initial encounter for open fracture type IIIA, IIIB, or IIIC

S82.873P Displaced pilon fracture of unspecified tibia, subsequent encounter for closed fracture with malunion

S82.873K Displaced pilon fracture of unspecified tibia, subsequent encounter for closed fracture with nonunion

S82.873Q Displaced pilon fracture of unspecified tibia, subsequent encounter for open fracture type I or II with malunion

S82.873M Displaced pilon fracture of unspecified tibia, subsequent encounter for open fracture type I or II with nonunion

S82.873R Displaced pilon fracture of unspecified tibia, subsequent encounter for open fracture type IIIA, IIIB, or IIIC with malunion

S82.873N Displaced pilon fracture of unspecified tibia, subsequent encounter for open fracture type IIIA, IIIB, or IIIC with nonunion

S12.030A Displaced posterior arch fracture of first cervical vertebra, initial encounter for closed fracture

S12.030K Displaced posterior arch fracture of first cervical vertebra, subsequent encounter for fracture with nonunion

S62.222B Displaced Rolando's fracture, left hand, initial encounter for open fracture

S62.222P Displaced Rolando's fracture, left hand, subsequent encounter for fracture with malunion

S62.222K Displaced Rolando's fracture, left hand, subsequent encounter for fracture with nonunion

S62.221B Displaced Rolando's fracture, right hand, initial encounter for open fracture

S62.221P Displaced Rolando's fracture, right hand, subsequent encounter for fracture with malunion

S62.221K Displaced Rolando's fracture, right hand, subsequent encounter for fracture with nonunion

S62.223B Displaced Rolando's fracture, unspecified hand, initial encounter for open fracture

S62.223P Displaced Rolando's fracture, unspecified hand, subsequent encounter for fracture with malunion

S62.223K Displaced Rolando's fracture, unspecified hand, subsequent encounter for fracture with nonunion

S42.362A Displaced segmental fracture of shaft of humerus, left arm, initial encounter for closed fracture

S42.362P Displaced segmental fracture of shaft of humerus, left arm, subsequent encounter for fracture with malunion

S42.362K Displaced segmental fracture of shaft of humerus, left arm, subsequent encounter for fracture with nonunion

S42.361A Displaced segmental fracture of shaft of humerus, right arm, initial encounter for closed fracture

S42.361P Displaced segmental fracture of shaft of humerus, right arm, subsequent encounter for fracture with malunion

S42.361K Displaced segmental fracture of shaft of humerus, right arm, subsequent encounter for fracture with nonunion

S42.363A Displaced segmental fracture of shaft of humerus, unspecified arm, initial encounter for closed fracture

S42.363P Displaced segmental fracture of shaft of humerus, unspecified arm, subsequent encounter for fracture with malunion

S42.363K Displaced segmental fracture of shaft of humerus, unspecified arm, subsequent encounter for fracture with nonunion

S72.362P Displaced segmental fracture of shaft of left femur, subsequent encounter for closed fracture with malunion

S72.362K Displaced segmental fracture of shaft of left femur, subsequent encounter for closed fracture with nonunion

S72.362Q Displaced segmental fracture of shaft of left femur, subsequent encounter for open fracture type I or II with malunion

S72.362M Displaced segmental fracture of shaft of left femur, subsequent encounter for open fracture type I or II with nonunion

S72.362R Displaced segmental fracture of shaft of left femur, subsequent encounter for open fracture type IIIA, IIIB, or IIIC with malunion

S72.362N Displaced segmental fracture of shaft of left femur, subsequent encounter for open fracture type IIIA, IIIB, or IIIC with nonunion

S82.462P Displaced segmental fracture of shaft of left fibula, subsequent encounter for closed fracture with malunion

S82.462K Displaced segmental fracture of shaft of left fibula, subsequent encounter for closed fracture with nonunion

S82.462Q Displaced segmental fracture of shaft of left fibula, subsequent encounter for open fracture type I or II with malunion

S82.462M Displaced segmental fracture of shaft of left fibula, subsequent encounter for open fracture type I or II with nonunion

S82.462R Displaced segmental fracture of shaft of left fibula, subsequent encounter for open fracture type IIIA, IIIB, or IIIC with malunion

S82.462N Displaced segmental fracture of shaft of left fibula, subsequent encounter for open fracture type IIIA, IIIB, or IIIC with nonunion

S82.262A Displaced segmental fracture of shaft of left tibia, initial encounter for closed fracture

S82.262P Displaced segmental fracture of shaft of left tibia, subsequent encounter for closed fracture with malunion

S82.262K Displaced segmental fracture of shaft of left tibia, subsequent encounter for closed fracture with nonunion

S82.262Q Displaced segmental fracture of shaft of left tibia, subsequent encounter for open fracture type I or II with malunion

S82.262M Displaced segmental fracture of shaft of left tibia, subsequent encounter for open fracture type I or II with nonunion

S82.262R Displaced segmental fracture of shaft of left tibia, subsequent encounter for open fracture type IIIA, IIIB, or IIIC with malunion

S82.262N Displaced segmental fracture of shaft of left tibia, subsequent encounter for open fracture type IIIA, IIIB, or IIIC with nonunion

S52.362A Displaced segmental fracture of shaft of radius, left arm, initial encounter for closed fracture

S52.362P Displaced segmental fracture of shaft of radius, left arm, subsequent encounter for closed fracture with malunion

S52.362K Displaced segmental fracture of shaft of radius, left arm, subsequent encounter for closed fracture with nonunion

S52.362Q Displaced segmental fracture of shaft of radius, left arm, subsequent encounter for open fracture type I or II with malunion

S52.362M Displaced segmental fracture of shaft of radius, left arm, subsequent encounter for open fracture type I or II with nonunion

S52.362R Displaced segmental fracture of shaft of radius, left arm, subsequent encounter for open fracture type IIIA, IIIB, or IIIC with malunion

S52.362N Displaced segmental fracture of shaft of radius, left arm, subsequent encounter for open fracture type IIIB, or IIIC with nonunion

S52.361A Displaced segmental fracture of shaft of radius, right arm, initial encounter for closed fracture

S52.361P Displaced segmental fracture of shaft of radius, right arm, subsequent encounter for closed fracture with malunion

S52.361K Displaced segmental fracture of shaft of radius, right arm, subsequent encounter for closed fracture with nonunion

S52.361Q Displaced segmental fracture of shaft of radius, right arm, subsequent encounter for open fracture type I or II with malunion

S52.361M Displaced segmental fracture of shaft of radius, right arm, subsequent encounter for open fracture type I or II with nonunion

S52.361R Displaced segmental fracture of shaft of radius, right arm, subsequent encounter for open fracture type IIIA, IIIB, or IIIC with malunion

S52.361N Displaced segmental fracture of shaft of radius, right arm, subsequent encounter for open fracture type IIIA, IIIB, or IIIC with nonunion

S52.363A Displaced segmental fracture of shaft of radius, unspecified arm, initial encounter for closed fracture

S52.363P Displaced segmental fracture of shaft of radius, unspecified arm, subsequent encounter for closed fracture with malunion

S52.363K Displaced segmental fracture of shaft of radius, unspecified arm, subsequent encounter for closed fracture with nonunion

S52.363Q Displaced segmental fracture of shaft of radius, unspecified arm, subsequent encounter for open fracture type I or II with malunion

S52.363M Displaced segmental fracture of shaft of radius, unspecified arm, subsequent encounter for open fracture type I or II with nonunion

S52.363R Displaced segmental fracture of shaft of radius, unspecified arm, subsequent encounter for open fracture type IIIA, IIIB, or IIIC with malunion

S52.363N Displaced segmental fracture of shaft of radius, unspecified arm, subsequent encounter for open fracture type IIIA, IIIB, or IIIC with nonunion

S72.361P Displaced segmental fracture of shaft of right femur, subsequent encounter for closed fracture with malunion

S72.361K Displaced segmental fracture of shaft of right femur, subsequent encounter for closed fracture with nonunion

S72.361Q Displaced segmental fracture of shaft of right femur, subsequent encounter for open fracture type I or II with malunion

S72.361M Displaced segmental fracture of shaft of right femur, subsequent encounter for open fracture type I or II with nonunion

S72.361R Displaced segmental fracture of shaft of right femur, subsequent encounter for open fracture type IIIA, IIIB, or IIIC with malunion

S72.361N Displaced segmental fracture of shaft of right femur, subsequent encounter for open fracture type IIIA, IIIB, or IIIC with nonunion

S82.461P Displaced segmental fracture of shaft of right fibula, subsequent encounter for closed fracture with malunion

S82.461K Displaced segmental fracture of shaft of right fibula, subsequent encounter for closed fracture with nonunion

S82.461Q Displaced segmental fracture of shaft of right fibula, subsequent encounter for open fracture type I or II with malunion

S82.461M Displaced segmental fracture of shaft of right fibula, subsequent encounter for open fracture type I or II with nonunion

S82.461R Displaced segmental fracture of shaft of right fibula, subsequent encounter for open fracture type IIIA, IIIB, or IIIC with malunion

S82.461N Displaced segmental fracture of shaft of right fibula, subsequent encounter for open fracture type IIIA, IIIB, or IIIC with nonunion

S82.261A Displaced segmental fracture of shaft of right tibia, initial encounter for closed fracture

S82.261P Displaced segmental fracture of shaft of right tibia, subsequent encounter for closed fracture with malunion

S82.261K Displaced segmental fracture of shaft of right tibia, subsequent encounter for closed fracture with nonunion

S82.261Q Displaced segmental fracture of shaft of right tibia, subsequent encounter for open fracture type I or II with malunion

S82.261M Displaced segmental fracture of shaft of right tibia, subsequent encounter for open fracture type I or II with nonunion

S82.261R Displaced segmental fracture of shaft of right tibia, subsequent encounter for open fracture type IIIA, IIIB, or IIIC with malunion

S82.261N Displaced segmental fracture of shaft of right tibia, subsequent encounter for open fracture type IIIA, IIIB, or IIIC with nonunion

S52.262A Displaced segmental fracture of shaft of ulna, left arm, initial encounter for closed fracture

S52.262P Displaced segmental fracture of shaft of ulna, left arm, subsequent encounter for closed fracture with malunion

S52.262K Displaced segmental fracture of shaft of ulna, left arm, subsequent encounter for closed fracture with nonunion

S52.262Q Displaced segmental fracture of shaft of ulna, left arm, subsequent encounter for open fracture type I or II with malunion

S52.262M Displaced segmental fracture of shaft of ulna, left arm, subsequent encounter for open fracture type I or II with nonunion

S52.262R Displaced segmental fracture of shaft of ulna, left arm, subsequent encounter for open fracture type IIIA, IIIB, or IIIC with malunion

S52.262N Displaced segmental fracture of shaft of ulna, left arm, subsequent encounter for open fracture type IIIA, IIIB, or IIIC with nonunion

S52.261A Displaced segmental fracture of shaft of ulna, right arm, initial encounter for closed fracture

S52.261P Displaced segmental fracture of shaft of ulna, right arm, subsequent encounter for closed fracture with malunion

S52.261K Displaced segmental fracture of shaft of ulna, right arm, subsequent encounter for closed fracture with nonunion

S52.261Q Displaced segmental fracture of shaft of ulna, right arm, subsequent encounter for open fracture type I or II with malunion

S52.261M Displaced segmental fracture of shaft of ulna, right arm, subsequent encounter for open fracture type I or II with nonunion

S52.261R Displaced segmental fracture of shaft of ulna, right arm, subsequent encounter for open fracture type IIIA, IIIB, or IIIC with malunion

S52.261N Displaced segmental fracture of shaft of ulna, right arm, subsequent encounter for open fracture type IIIA, IIIB, or IIIC with nonunion

S52.263A Displaced segmental fracture of shaft of ulna, unspecified arm, initial encounter for closed fracture

S52.263P Displaced segmental fracture of shaft of ulna, unspecified arm, subsequent encounter for closed fracture with malunion

S52.263K Displaced segmental fracture of shaft of ulna, unspecified arm, subsequent encounter for closed fracture with nonunion

S52.263Q Displaced segmental fracture of shaft of ulna, unspecified arm, subsequent encounter for open fracture type I or II with malunion

S52.263M Displaced segmental fracture of shaft of ulna, unspecified arm, subsequent encounter for open fracture type I or II with nonunion

S52.263R Displaced segmental fracture of shaft of ulna, unspecified arm, subsequent encounter for open fracture type IIIA, IIIB, or IIIC with malunion

S52.263N Displaced segmental fracture of shaft of ulna, unspecified arm, subsequent encounter for open fracture type IIIA, IIIB, or IIIC with nonunion

S72.363P Displaced segmental fracture of shaft of unspecified femur, subsequent encounter for closed fracture with malunion

S72.363K Displaced segmental fracture of shaft of unspecified femur, subsequent encounter for closed fracture with nonunion

S72.363Q Displaced segmental fracture of shaft of unspecified femur, subsequent encounter for open fracture type I or II with malunion

S72.363M Displaced segmental fracture of shaft of unspecified femur, subsequent encounter for open fracture type I or II with nonunion

S72.363R Displaced segmental fracture of shaft of unspecified femur, subsequent encounter for open fracture type IIIA, IIIB, or IIIC with malunion

S72.363N Displaced segmental fracture of shaft of unspecified femur, subsequent encounter for open fracture type IIIA, IIIB, or IIIC with nonunion

S82.463P Displaced segmental fracture of shaft of unspecified fibula, subsequent encounter for closed fracture with malunion

S82.463K Displaced segmental fracture of shaft of unspecified fibula, subsequent encounter for closed fracture with nonunion

S82.463Q Displaced segmental fracture of shaft of unspecified fibula, subsequent encounter for open fracture type I or II with malunion

S82.463M Displaced segmental fracture of shaft of unspecified fibula, subsequent encounter for open fracture type I or II with nonunion

S82.463R Displaced segmental fracture of shaft of unspecified fibula, subsequent encounter for open fracture type IIIA, IIIB, or IIIC with malunion

S82.463N Displaced segmental fracture of shaft of unspecified fibula, subsequent encounter for open fracture type IIIA, IIIB, or IIIC with nonunion

S82.263A Displaced segmental fracture of shaft of unspecified tibia, initial encounter for closed fracture

S82.263P Displaced segmental fracture of shaft of unspecified tibia, subsequent encounter for closed fracture with malunion

S82.263K Displaced segmental fracture of shaft of unspecified tibia, subsequent encounter for closed fracture with nonunion

S82.263Q Displaced segmental fracture of shaft of unspecified tibia, subsequent encounter for open fracture type I or II with malunion

S82.263M Displaced segmental fracture of shaft of unspecified tibia, subsequent encounter for open fracture type I or II with nonunion

S82.263R Displaced segmental fracture of shaft of unspecified tibia, subsequent encounter for open fracture type IIIA, IIIB, or IIIC with malunion

S82.263N Displaced segmental fracture of shaft of unspecified tibia, subsequent encounter for open fracture type IIIA, IIIB, or IIIC with nonunion

S42.412A Displaced simple supracondylar fracture without intercondylar fracture of left humerus, initial encounter for closed fracture

S42.412P Displaced simple supracondylar fracture without intercondylar fracture of left humerus, subsequent encounter for fracture with malunion

S42.412K Displaced simple supracondylar fracture without intercondylar fracture of left humerus, subsequent encounter for fracture with nonunion

S42.411A Displaced simple supracondylar fracture without intercondylar fracture of right humerus, initial encounter for closed fracture

S42.411P Displaced simple supracondylar fracture without intercondylar fracture of right humerus, subsequent encounter for fracture with malunion

S42.411K Displaced simple supracondylar fracture without intercondylar fracture of right humerus, subsequent encounter for fracture with nonunion

S42.413A Displaced simple supracondylar fracture without intercondylar fracture of unspecified humerus, initial encounter for closed fracture

S42.413P Displaced simple supracondylar fracture without intercondylar fracture of unspecified humerus, subsequent encounter for fracture with malunion

S42.413K Displaced simple supracondylar fracture without intercondylar fracture of unspecified humerus, subsequent encounter for fracture with nonunion

S42.342A Displaced spiral fracture of shaft of humerus, left arm, initial encounter for closed fracture

S42.342P Displaced spiral fracture of shaft of humerus, left arm, subsequent encounter for fracture with malunion

S42.342K Displaced spiral fracture of shaft of humerus, left arm, subsequent encounter for fracture with nonunion

S42.341A Displaced spiral fracture of shaft of humerus, right arm, initial encounter for closed fracture

S42.341P Displaced spiral fracture of shaft of humerus, right arm, subsequent encounter for fracture with malunion

S42.341K Displaced spiral fracture of shaft of humerus, right arm, subsequent encounter for fracture with nonunion

S42.343A Displaced spiral fracture of shaft of humerus, unspecified arm, initial encounter for closed fracture

S42.343P Displaced spiral fracture of shaft of humerus, unspecified arm, subsequent encounter for fracture with malunion

S42.343K Displaced spiral fracture of shaft of humerus, unspecified arm, subsequent encounter for fracture with nonunion

S72.342P Displaced spiral fracture of shaft of left femur, subsequent encounter for closed fracture with malunion

S72.342K Displaced spiral fracture of shaft of left femur, subsequent encounter for closed fracture with nonunion

S72.342Q Displaced spiral fracture of shaft of left femur, subsequent encounter for open fracture type I or II with malunion

S72.342M Displaced spiral fracture of shaft of left femur, subsequent encounter for open fracture type I or II with nonunion

S72.342R Displaced spiral fracture of shaft of left femur, subsequent encounter for open fracture type IIIA, IIIB, or IIIC with malunion

S72.342N Displaced spiral fracture of shaft of left femur, subsequent encounter for open fracture type IIIA, IIIB, or IIIC with nonunion

S82.442P Displaced spiral fracture of shaft of left fibula, subsequent encounter for closed fracture with malunion

S82.442K Displaced spiral fracture of shaft of left fibula, subsequent encounter for closed fracture with nonunion

S82.442Q Displaced spiral fracture of shaft of left fibula, subsequent encounter for open fracture type I or II with malunion

S82.442M Displaced spiral fracture of shaft of left fibula, subsequent encounter for open fracture type I or II with nonunion

S82.442R Displaced spiral fracture of shaft of left fibula, subsequent encounter for open fracture type IIIA, IIIB, or IIIC with malunion

S82.442N Displaced spiral fracture of shaft of left fibula, subsequent encounter for open fracture type IIIA, IIIB, or IIIC with nonunion

S82.242A Displaced spiral fracture of shaft of left tibia, initial encounter for closed fracture

S82.242P Displaced spiral fracture of shaft of left tibia, subsequent encounter for closed fracture with malunion

S82.242K Displaced spiral fracture of shaft of left tibia, subsequent encounter for closed fracture with nonunion

S82.242Q Displaced spiral fracture of shaft of left tibia, subsequent encounter for open fracture type I or II with malunion

S82.242M Displaced spiral fracture of shaft of left tibia, subsequent encounter for open fracture type I or II with nonunion

S82.242R Displaced spiral fracture of shaft of left tibia, subsequent encounter for open fracture type IIIA, IIIB, or IIIC with malunion

S82.242N Displaced spiral fracture of shaft of left tibia, subsequent encounter for open fracture type IIIA, IIIB, or IIIC with nonunion

S52.342A Displaced spiral fracture of shaft of radius, left arm, initial encounter for closed fracture

S52.342P Displaced spiral fracture of shaft of radius, left arm, subsequent encounter for closed fracture with malunion

S52.342K Displaced spiral fracture of shaft of radius, left arm, subsequent encounter for closed fracture with nonunion

S52.342Q Displaced spiral fracture of shaft of radius, left arm, subsequent encounter for open fracture type I or II with malunion

S52.342M Displaced spiral fracture of shaft of radius, left arm, subsequent encounter for open fracture type I or II with nonunion

S52.342R Displaced spiral fracture of shaft of radius, left arm, subsequent encounter for open fracture type IIIA, IIIB, or IIIC with malunion

S52.342N Displaced spiral fracture of shaft of radius, left arm, subsequent encounter for open fracture type IIIA, IIIB, or IIIC with nonunion

S52.341A Displaced spiral fracture of shaft of radius, right arm, initial encounter for closed fracture

S52.341P Displaced spiral fracture of shaft of radius, right arm, subsequent encounter for closed fracture with malunion

S52.341K Displaced spiral fracture of shaft of radius, right arm, subsequent encounter for closed fracture with nonunion

S52.341Q Displaced spiral fracture of shaft of radius, right arm, subsequent encounter for open fracture type I or II with malunion

S52.341M Displaced spiral fracture of shaft of radius, right arm, subsequent encounter for open fracture type I or II with nonunion

S52.341R Displaced spiral fracture of shaft of radius, right arm, subsequent encounter for open fracture type IIIA, IIIB, or IIIC with malunion

S52.341N Displaced spiral fracture of shaft of radius, right arm, subsequent encounter for open fracture type IIIA, IIIB, or IIIC with nonunion

S52.343A Displaced spiral fracture of shaft of radius, unspecified arm, initial encounter for closed fracture

S52.343P Displaced spiral fracture of shaft of radius, unspecified arm, subsequent encounter for closed fracture with malunion

S52.343K Displaced spiral fracture of shaft of radius, unspecified arm, subsequent encounter for closed fracture with nonunion

S52.343Q Displaced spiral fracture of shaft of radius, unspecified arm, subsequent encounter for open fracture type I or II with malunion

S52.343M Displaced spiral fracture of shaft of radius, unspecified arm, subsequent encounter for open fracture type I or II with nonunion

S52.343R Displaced spiral fracture of shaft of radius, unspecified arm, subsequent encounter for open fracture type IIIA, IIIB, or IIIC with malunion

S52.343N Displaced spiral fracture of shaft of radius, unspecified arm, subsequent encounter for open fracture type IIIA, IIIB, or IIIC with nonunion

S72.341P Displaced spiral fracture of shaft of right femur, subsequent encounter for closed fracture with malunion

S72.341K Displaced spiral fracture of shaft of right femur, subsequent encounter for closed fracture with nonunion

S72.341Q Displaced spiral fracture of shaft of right femur, subsequent encounter for open fracture type I or II with malunion

S72.341M Displaced spiral fracture of shaft of right femur, subsequent encounter for open fracture type I or II with nonunion

S72.341R Displaced spiral fracture of shaft of right femur, subsequent encounter for open fracture type IIIA, IIIB, or IIIC with malunion

S72.341N Displaced spiral fracture of shaft of right femur, subsequent encounter for open fracture type IIIA, IIIB, or IIIC with nonunion

S82.441P Displaced spiral fracture of shaft of right fibula, subsequent encounter for closed fracture with malunion

S82.441K Displaced spiral fracture of shaft of right fibula, subsequent encounter for closed fracture with nonunion

S82.441Q Displaced spiral fracture of shaft of right fibula, subsequent encounter for open fracture type I or II with malunion

S82.441M Displaced spiral fracture of shaft of right fibula, subsequent encounter for open fracture type I or II with nonunion

S82.441R Displaced spiral fracture of shaft of right fibula, subsequent encounter for open fracture type IIIA, IIIB, or IIIC with malunion

S82.441N Displaced spiral fracture of shaft of right fibula, subsequent encounter for open fracture type IIIA, IIIB, or IIIC with nonunion

S82.241A Displaced spiral fracture of shaft of right tibia, initial encounter for closed fracture

S82.241P Displaced spiral fracture of shaft of right tibia, subsequent encounter for closed fracture with malunion

S82.241K Displaced spiral fracture of shaft of right tibia, subsequent encounter for closed fracture with nonunion

S82.241Q Displaced spiral fracture of shaft of right tibia, subsequent encounter for open fracture type I or II with malunion

S82.241M Displaced spiral fracture of shaft of right tibia, subsequent encounter for open fracture type I or II with nonunion

S82.241R Displaced spiral fracture of shaft of right tibia, subsequent encounter for open fracture type IIIA, IIIB, or IIIC with malunion

S82.241N Displaced spiral fracture of shaft of right tibia, subsequent encounter for open fracture type IIIA, IIIB, or IIIC with nonunion

S52.242A Displaced spiral fracture of shaft of ulna, left arm, initial encounter for closed fracture

S52.242P Displaced spiral fracture of shaft of ulna, left arm, subsequent encounter for closed fracture with malunion

S52.242K Displaced spiral fracture of shaft of ulna, left arm, subsequent encounter for closed fracture with nonunion

S52.242Q Displaced spiral fracture of shaft of ulna, left arm, subsequent encounter for open fracture type I or II with malunion

S52.242M Displaced spiral fracture of shaft of ulna, left arm, subsequent encounter for open fracture type I or II with nonunion

S52.242R Displaced spiral fracture of shaft of ulna, left arm, subsequent encounter for open fracture type IIIA, IIIB, or IIIC with malunion

S52.242N Displaced spiral fracture of shaft of ulna, left arm, subsequent encounter for open fracture type IIIA, IIIB, or IIIC with nonunion

S52.241A Displaced spiral fracture of shaft of ulna, right arm, initial encounter for closed fracture

S52.241P Displaced spiral fracture of shaft of ulna, right arm, subsequent encounter for closed fracture with malunion

S52.241K Displaced spiral fracture of shaft of ulna, right arm, subsequent encounter for closed fracture with nonunion

S52.241Q Displaced spiral fracture of shaft of ulna, right arm, subsequent encounter for open fracture type I or II with malunion

S52.241M Displaced spiral fracture of shaft of ulna, right arm, subsequent encounter for open fracture type I or II with nonunion

S52.241R Displaced spiral fracture of shaft of ulna, right arm, subsequent encounter for open fracture type IIIA, IIIB, or IIIC with malunion

S52.241N Displaced spiral fracture of shaft of ulna, right arm, subsequent encounter for open fracture type IIIA, IIIB, or IIIC with nonunion

S52.243A Displaced spiral fracture of shaft of ulna, unspecified arm, initial encounter for closed fracture

S52.243P Displaced spiral fracture of shaft of ulna, unspecified arm, subsequent encounter for closed fracture with malunion

S52.243K Displaced spiral fracture of shaft of ulna, unspecified arm, subsequent encounter for closed fracture with nonunion

S52.243Q Displaced spiral fracture of shaft of ulna, unspecified arm, subsequent encounter for open fracture type I or II with malunion

S52.243M Displaced spiral fracture of shaft of ulna, unspecified arm, subsequent encounter for open fracture type I or II with nonunion

S52.243R Displaced spiral fracture of shaft of ulna, unspecified arm, subsequent encounter for open fracture type IIIA, IIIB, or IIIC with malunion

S52.243N Displaced spiral fracture of shaft of ulna, unspecified arm, subsequent encounter for open fracture type IIIA, IIIB, or IIIC with nonunion

S72.343P Displaced spiral fracture of shaft of unspecified femur, subsequent encounter for closed fracture with malunion

S72.343K Displaced spiral fracture of shaft of unspecified femur, subsequent encounter for closed fracture with nonunion

S72.343Q Displaced spiral fracture of shaft of unspecified femur, subsequent encounter for open fracture type I or II with malunion

S72.343M Displaced spiral fracture of shaft of unspecified femur, subsequent encounter for open fracture type I or II with nonunion

S72.343R Displaced spiral fracture of shaft of unspecified femur, subsequent encounter for open fracture type IIIA, IIIB, or IIIC with malunion

S72.343N Displaced spiral fracture of shaft of unspecified femur, subsequent encounter for open fracture type IIIA, IIIB, or IIIC with nonunion

S82.443P Displaced spiral fracture of shaft of unspecified fibula, subsequent encounter for closed fracture with malunion

S82.443K Displaced spiral fracture of shaft of unspecified fibula, subsequent encounter for closed fracture with nonunion

S82.443Q Displaced spiral fracture of shaft of unspecified fibula, subsequent encounter for open fracture type I or II with malunion

S82.443M Displaced spiral fracture of shaft of unspecified fibula, subsequent encounter for open fracture type I or II with nonunion

S82.443R Displaced spiral fracture of shaft of unspecified fibula, subsequent encounter for open fracture type IIIA, IIIB, or IIIC with malunion

S82.443N Displaced spiral fracture of shaft of unspecified fibula, subsequent encounter for open fracture type IIIA, IIIB, or IIIC with nonunion

S82.243A Displaced spiral fracture of shaft of unspecified tibia, initial encounter for closed fracture

S82.243P Displaced spiral fracture of shaft of unspecified tibia, subsequent encounter for closed fracture with malunion

S82.243K Displaced spiral fracture of shaft of unspecified tibia, subsequent encounter for closed fracture with nonunion

S82.243Q Displaced spiral fracture of shaft of unspecified tibia, subsequent encounter for open fracture type I or II with malunion

S82.243M Displaced spiral fracture of shaft of unspecified tibia, subsequent encounter for open fracture type I or II with nonunion

S82.243R Displaced spiral fracture of shaft of unspecified tibia, subsequent encounter for open fracture type IIIA, IIIB, or IIIC with malunion

S82.243N Displaced spiral fracture of shaft of unspecified tibia, subsequent encounter for open fracture type IIIA, IIIB, or IIIC with nonunion

S72.22XP Displaced subtrochanteric fracture of left femur, subsequent encounter for closed fracture with malunion

S72.22XK Displaced subtrochanteric fracture of left femur, subsequent encounter for closed fracture with nonunion

S72.22XQ Displaced subtrochanteric fracture of left femur, subsequent encounter for open fracture type I or II with malunion

S72.22XM Displaced subtrochanteric fracture of left femur, subsequent encounter for open fracture type I or II with nonunion

S72.22XR Displaced subtrochanteric fracture of left femur, subsequent encounter for open fracture type IIIA, IIIB, or IIIC with malunion

S72.22XN Displaced subtrochanteric fracture of left femur, subsequent encounter for open fracture type IIIA, IIIB, or IIIC with nonunion

S72.21XP Displaced subtrochanteric fracture of right femur, subsequent encounter for closed fracture with malunion

S72.21XK Displaced subtrochanteric fracture of right femur, subsequent encounter for closed fracture with nonunion

S72.21XQ Displaced subtrochanteric fracture of right femur, subsequent encounter for open fracture type I or II with malunion

S72.21XM Displaced subtrochanteric fracture of right femur, subsequent encounter for open fracture type I or II with nonunion

S72.21XR Displaced subtrochanteric fracture of right femur, subsequent encounter for open fracture type IIIA, IIIB, or IIIC with malunion

S72.21XN Displaced subtrochanteric fracture of right femur, subsequent encounter for open fracture type IIIA, IIIB, or IIIC with nonunion

S72.23XP Displaced subtrochanteric fracture of unspecified femur, subsequent encounter for closed fracture with malunion

S72.23XK Displaced subtrochanteric fracture of unspecified femur, subsequent encounter for closed fracture with nonunion

S72.23XQ Displaced subtrochanteric fracture of unspecified femur, subsequent encounter for open fracture type I or II with malunion

S72.23XM Displaced subtrochanteric fracture of unspecified femur, subsequent encounter for open fracture type I or II with nonunion

S72.23XR Displaced subtrochanteric fracture of unspecified femur, subsequent encounter for open fracture type IIIA, IIIB, or IIIC with malunion

S72.23XN Displaced subtrochanteric fracture of unspecified femur, subsequent encounter for open fracture type IIIA, IIIB, or IIIC with nonunion

S72.462A Displaced supracondylar fracture with intracondylar extension of lower end of left femur, initial encounter for closed fracture

S72.462P Displaced supracondylar fracture with intracondylar extension of lower end of left femur, subsequent encounter for closed fracture with malunion

S72.462K Displaced supracondylar fracture with intracondylar extension of lower end of left femur, subsequent encounter for closed fracture with nonunion

S72.462Q Displaced supracondylar fracture with intracondylar extension of lower end of left femur, subsequent encounter for open fracture type I or II with malunion

S72.462M Displaced supracondylar fracture with intracondylar extension of lower end of left femur, subsequent encounter for open fracture type I or II with nonunion

S72.462R Displaced supracondylar fracture with intracondylar extension of lower end of left femur, subsequent encounter for open fracture type IIIA, IIIB, or IIIC with malunion

S72.462N Displaced supracondylar fracture with intracondylar extension of lower end of left femur, subsequent encounter for open fracture type IIIA, IIIB, or IIIC with nonunion

S72.461A Displaced supracondylar fracture with intracondylar extension of lower end of right femur, initial encounter for closed fracture

S72.461P Displaced supracondylar fracture with intracondylar extension of lower end of right femur, subsequent encounter for closed fracture with malunion

S72.461K Displaced supracondylar fracture with intracondylar extension of lower end of right femur, subsequent encounter for closed fracture with nonunion

S72.461Q Displaced supracondylar fracture with intracondylar extension of lower end of right femur, subsequent encounter for open fracture type I or II with malunion

S72.461M Displaced supracondylar fracture with intracondylar extension of lower end of right femur, subsequent encounter for open fracture type I or II with nonunion

S72.461R Displaced supracondylar fracture with intracondylar extension of lower end of right femur, subsequent encounter for open fracture type IIIA, IIIB, or IIIC with malunion

S72.461N Displaced supracondylar fracture with intracondylar extension of lower end of right femur, subsequent encounter for open fracture type IIIA, IIIB, or IIIC with nonunion

S72.463A Displaced supracondylar fracture with intracondylar extension of lower end of unspecified femur, initial encounter for closed fracture

S72.463P Displaced supracondylar fracture with intracondylar extension of lower end of unspecified femur, subsequent encounter for closed fracture with malunion

S72.463K Displaced supracondylar fracture with intracondylar extension of lower end of unspecified femur, subsequent encounter for closed fracture with nonunion

S72.463Q Displaced supracondylar fracture with intracondylar extension of lower end of unspecified femur, subsequent encounter for open fracture type I or II with malunion

S72.463M Displaced supracondylar fracture with intracondylar extension of lower end of unspecified femur, subsequent encounter for open fracture type I or II with nonunion

S72.463R Displaced supracondylar fracture with intracondylar extension of lower end of unspecified femur, subsequent encounter for open fracture type IIIA, IIIB, or IIIC with malunion

S72.463N Displaced supracondylar fracture with intracondylar extension of lower end of unspecified femur, subsequent encounter for open fracture type IIIA, IIIB, or IIIC with nonunion

S72.452A Displaced supracondylar fracture without intracondylar extension of lower end of left femur, initial encounter for closed fracture

S72.452P Displaced supracondylar fracture without intracondylar extension of lower end of left femur, subsequent encounter for closed fracture with malunion

S72.452K Displaced supracondylar fracture without intracondylar extension of lower end of left femur, subsequent encounter for closed fracture with nonunion

S72.452Q Displaced supracondylar fracture without intracondylar extension of lower end of left femur, subsequent encounter for open fracture type I or II with malunion

S72.452M Displaced supracondylar fracture without intracondylar extension of lower end of left femur, subsequent encounter for open fracture type I or II with nonunion

S72.452R Displaced supracondylar fracture without intracondylar extension of lower end of left femur, subsequent encounter for open fracture type IIIA, IIIB, or IIIC with malunion

S72.452N Displaced supracondylar fracture without intracondylar extension of lower end of left femur, subsequent encounter for open fracture type IIIA, IIIB, or IIIC with nonunion

S72.451A Displaced supracondylar fracture without intracondylar extension of lower end of right femur, initial encounter for closed fracture

S72.451P Displaced supracondylar fracture without intracondylar extension of lower end of right femur, subsequent encounter for closed fracture with malunion

S72.451K Displaced supracondylar fracture without intracondylar extension of lower end of right femur, subsequent encounter for closed fracture with nonunion

S72.451Q Displaced supracondylar fracture without intracondylar extension of lower end of right femur, subsequent encounter for open fracture type I or II with malunion

S72.451M Displaced supracondylar fracture without intracondylar extension of lower end of right femur, subsequent encounter for open fracture type I or II with nonunion

S72.451R Displaced supracondylar fracture without intracondylar extension of lower end of right femur, subsequent encounter for open fracture type IIIA, IIIB, or IIIC with malunion

S72.451N Displaced supracondylar fracture without intracondylar extension of lower end of right femur, subsequent encounter for open fracture type IIIA, IIIB, or IIIC with nonunion

S72.453A Displaced supracondylar fracture without intracondylar extension of lower end of unspecified femur, initial encounter for closed fracture

S72.453P Displaced supracondylar fracture without intracondylar extension of lower end of unspecified femur, subsequent encounter for closed fracture with malunion

S72.453K Displaced supracondylar fracture without intracondylar extension of lower end of unspecified femur, subsequent encounter for closed fracture with nonunion

S72.453Q Displaced supracondylar fracture without intracondylar extension of lower end of unspecified femur, subsequent encounter for open fracture type I or II with malunion

S72.453M Displaced supracondylar fracture without intracondylar extension of lower end of unspecified femur, subsequent encounter for open fracture type I or II with nonunion

S72.453R Displaced supracondylar fracture without intracondylar extension of lower end of unspecified femur, subsequent encounter for open fracture type IIIA, IIIB, or IIIC with malunion

S72.453N Displaced supracondylar fracture without intracondylar extension of lower end of unspecified femur, subsequent encounter for open fracture type IIIA, IIIB, or IIIC with nonunion

S42.472A Displaced transcondylar fracture of left humerus, initial encounter for closed fracture

S42.472P Displaced transcondylar fracture of left humerus, subsequent encounter for fracture with malunion

S42.472K Displaced transcondylar fracture of left humerus, subsequent encounter for fracture with nonunion

S42.471A Displaced transcondylar fracture of right humerus, initial encounter for closed fracture

S42.471P Displaced transcondylar fracture of right humerus, subsequent encounter for fracture with malunion

S42.471K Displaced transcondylar fracture of right humerus, subsequent encounter for fracture with nonunion

S42.473A Displaced transcondylar fracture of unspecified humerus, initial encounter for closed fracture

S42.473P Displaced transcondylar fracture of unspecified humerus, subsequent encounter for fracture with malunion

S42.473K Displaced transcondylar fracture of unspecified humerus, subsequent encounter for fracture with nonunion

S32.452K Displaced transverse fracture of left acetabulum, subsequent encounter for fracture with nonunion

S82.032A Displaced transverse fracture of left patella, initial encounter for closed fracture

S82.032B Displaced transverse fracture of left patella, initial encounter for open fracture type I or II

S82.032C Displaced transverse fracture of left patella, initial encounter for open fracture type IIIA, IIIB, or IIIC

S82.032P Displaced transverse fracture of left patella, subsequent encounter for closed fracture with malunion

S82.032K Displaced transverse fracture of left patella, subsequent encounter for closed fracture with nonunion

S82.032Q	Displaced transverse fracture of left patella, subsequent encounter for open fracture type I or II with malunion
S82.032M	Displaced transverse fracture of left patella, subsequent encounter for open fracture type I or II with nonunion
S82.032R	Displaced transverse fracture of left patella, subsequent encounter for open fracture type IIIA, IIIB, or IIIC with malunion
S82.032N	Displaced transverse fracture of left patella, subsequent encounter for open fracture type IIIA, IIIB, or IIIC with nonunion
S32.451K	Displaced transverse fracture of right acetabulum, subsequent encounter for fracture with nonunion
S82.031A	Displaced transverse fracture of right patella, initial encounter for closed fracture
S82.031B	Displaced transverse fracture of right patella, initial encounter for open fracture type I or II
S82.031C	Displaced transverse fracture of right patella, initial encounter for open fracture type IIIA, IIIB, or IIIC
S82.031P	Displaced transverse fracture of right patella, subsequent encounter for closed fracture with malunion
S82.031K	Displaced transverse fracture of right patella, subsequent encounter for closed fracture with nonunion
S82.031Q	Displaced transverse fracture of right patella, subsequent encounter for open fracture type I or II with malunion
S82.031M	Displaced transverse fracture of right patella, subsequent encounter for open fracture type I or II with nonunion
S82.031R	Displaced transverse fracture of right patella, subsequent encounter for open fracture type IIIA, IIIB, or IIIC with malunion
S82.031N	Displaced transverse fracture of right patella, subsequent encounter for open fracture type IIIA, IIIB, or IIIC with nonunion
S42.322A	Displaced transverse fracture of shaft of humerus, left arm, initial encounter for closed fracture
S42.322P	Displaced transverse fracture of shaft of humerus, left arm, subsequent encounter for fracture with malunion
S42.322K	Displaced transverse fracture of shaft of humerus, left arm, subsequent encounter for fracture with nonunion
S42.321A	Displaced transverse fracture of shaft of humerus, right arm, initial encounter for closed fracture
S42.321P	Displaced transverse fracture of shaft of humerus, right arm, subsequent encounter for fracture with malunion
S42.321K	Displaced transverse fracture of shaft of humerus, right arm, subsequent encounter for fracture with nonunion
S42.323A	Displaced transverse fracture of shaft of humerus, unspecified arm, initial encounter for closed fracture
S42.323P	Displaced transverse fracture of shaft of humerus, unspecified arm, subsequent encounter for fracture with malunion
S42.323K	Displaced transverse fracture of shaft of humerus, unspecified arm, subsequent encounter for fracture with nonunion
S72.322P	Displaced transverse fracture of shaft of left femur, subsequent encounter for closed fracture with malunion
S72.322K	Displaced transverse fracture of shaft of left femur, subsequent encounter for closed fracture with nonunion
S72.322Q	Displaced transverse fracture of shaft of left femur, subsequent encounter for open fracture type I or II with malunion
S72.322M	Displaced transverse fracture of shaft of left femur, subsequent encounter for open fracture type I or II with nonunion
S72.322R	Displaced transverse fracture of shaft of left femur, subsequent encounter for open fracture type IIIA, IIIB, or IIIC with malunion
S72.322N	Displaced transverse fracture of shaft of left femur, subsequent encounter for open fracture type IIIA, IIIB, or IIIC with nonunion
S82.422P	Displaced transverse fracture of shaft of left fibula, subsequent encounter for closed fracture with malunion
S82.422K	Displaced transverse fracture of shaft of left fibula, subsequent encounter for closed fracture with nonunion
S82.422Q	Displaced transverse fracture of shaft of left fibula, subsequent encounter for open fracture type I or II with malunion
S82.422M	Displaced transverse fracture of shaft of left fibula, subsequent encounter for open fracture type I or II with nonunion
S82.422R	Displaced transverse fracture of shaft of left fibula, subsequent encounter for open fracture type IIIA, IIIB, or IIIC with malunion
S82.422N	Displaced transverse fracture of shaft of left fibula, subsequent encounter for open fracture type IIIA, IIIB, or IIIC with nonunion
S52.322A	Displaced transverse fracture of shaft of left radius, initial encounter for closed fracture
S52.322P	Displaced transverse fracture of shaft of left radius, subsequent encounter for closed fracture with malunion
S52.322K	Displaced transverse fracture of shaft of left radius, subsequent encounter for closed fracture with nonunion
S52.322Q	Displaced transverse fracture of shaft of left radius, subsequent encounter for open fracture type I or II with malunion
S52.322M	Displaced transverse fracture of shaft of left radius, subsequent encounter for open fracture type I or II with nonunion
S52.322R	Displaced transverse fracture of shaft of left radius, subsequent encounter for open fracture type IIIA, IIIB, or IIIC with malunion
S52.322N	Displaced transverse fracture of shaft of left radius, subsequent encounter for open fracture type IIIA, IIIB, or IIIC with nonunion
S82.222A	Displaced transverse fracture of shaft of left tibia, initial encounter for closed fracture
S82.222P	Displaced transverse fracture of shaft of left tibia, subsequent encounter for closed fracture with malunion
S82.222K	Displaced transverse fracture of shaft of left tibia, subsequent encounter for closed fracture with nonunion
S82.222Q	Displaced transverse fracture of shaft of left tibia, subsequent encounter for open fracture type I or II with malunion
S82.222M	Displaced transverse fracture of shaft of left tibia, subsequent encounter for open fracture type I or II with nonunion
S82.222R	Displaced transverse fracture of shaft of left tibia, subsequent encounter for open fracture type IIIA, IIIB, or IIIC with malunion
S82.222N	Displaced transverse fracture of shaft of left tibia, subsequent encounter for open fracture type IIIA, IIIB, or IIIC with nonunion
S52.222A	Displaced transverse fracture of shaft of left ulna, initial encounter for closed fracture
S52.222P	Displaced transverse fracture of shaft of left ulna, subsequent encounter for closed fracture with malunion
S52.222K	Displaced transverse fracture of shaft of left ulna, subsequent encounter for closed fracture with nonunion
S52.222Q	Displaced transverse fracture of shaft of left ulna, subsequent encounter for open fracture type I or II with malunion
S52.222M	Displaced transverse fracture of shaft of left ulna, subsequent encounter for open fracture type I or II with nonunion
S52.222R	Displaced transverse fracture of shaft of left ulna, subsequent encounter for open fracture type IIIA, IIIB, or IIIC with malunion
S52.222N	Displaced transverse fracture of shaft of left ulna, subsequent encounter for open fracture type IIIA, IIIB, or IIIC with nonunion
S72.321P	Displaced transverse fracture of shaft of right femur, subsequent encounter for closed fracture with malunion
S72.321K	Displaced transverse fracture of shaft of right femur, subsequent encounter for closed fracture with nonunion
S72.321Q	Displaced transverse fracture of shaft of right femur, subsequent encounter for open fracture type I or II with malunion
S72.321M	Displaced transverse fracture of shaft of right femur, subsequent encounter for open fracture type I or II with nonunion
S72.321R	Displaced transverse fracture of shaft of right femur, subsequent encounter for open fracture type IIIA, IIIB, or IIIC with malunion
S72.321N	Displaced transverse fracture of shaft of right femur, subsequent encounter for open fracture type IIIA, IIIB, or IIIC with nonunion
S82.421P	Displaced transverse fracture of shaft of right fibula, subsequent encounter for closed fracture with malunion
S82.421K	Displaced transverse fracture of shaft of right fibula, subsequent encounter for closed fracture with nonunion
S82.421Q	Displaced transverse fracture of shaft of right fibula, subsequent encounter for open fracture type I or II with malunion
S82.421M	Displaced transverse fracture of shaft of right fibula, subsequent encounter for open fracture type I or II with nonunion
S82.421R	Displaced transverse fracture of shaft of right fibula, subsequent encounter for open fracture type IIIA, IIIB, or IIIC with malunion
S82.421N	Displaced transverse fracture of shaft of right fibula, subsequent encounter for open fracture type IIIA, IIIB, or IIIC with nonunion
S52.321A	Displaced transverse fracture of shaft of right radius, initial encounter for closed fracture
S52.321P	Displaced transverse fracture of shaft of right radius, subsequent encounter for closed fracture with malunion
S52.321K	Displaced transverse fracture of shaft of right radius, subsequent encounter for closed fracture with nonunion
S52.321Q	Displaced transverse fracture of shaft of right radius, subsequent encounter for open fracture type I or II with malunion
S52.321M	Displaced transverse fracture of shaft of right radius, subsequent encounter for open fracture type I or II with nonunion
S52.321R	Displaced transverse fracture of shaft of right radius, subsequent encounter for open fracture type IIIA, IIIB, or IIIC with malunion
S52.321N	Displaced transverse fracture of shaft of right radius, subsequent encounter for open fracture type IIIA, IIIB, or IIIC with nonunion
S82.221A	Displaced transverse fracture of shaft of right tibia, initial encounter for closed fracture
S82.221P	Displaced transverse fracture of shaft of right tibia, subsequent encounter for closed fracture with malunion
S82.221K	Displaced transverse fracture of shaft of right tibia, subsequent encounter for closed fracture with nonunion
S82.221Q	Displaced transverse fracture of shaft of right tibia, subsequent encounter for open fracture type I or II with malunion
S82.221M	Displaced transverse fracture of shaft of right tibia, subsequent encounter for open fracture type I or II with nonunion
S82.221R	Displaced transverse fracture of shaft of right tibia, subsequent encounter for open fracture type IIIA, IIIB, or IIIC with malunion
S82.221N	Displaced transverse fracture of shaft of right tibia, subsequent encounter for open fracture type IIIA, IIIB, or IIIC with nonunion
S52.221A	Displaced transverse fracture of shaft of right ulna, initial encounter for closed fracture
S52.221P	Displaced transverse fracture of shaft of right ulna, subsequent encounter for closed fracture with malunion
S52.221K	Displaced transverse fracture of shaft of right ulna, subsequent encounter for closed fracture with nonunion
S52.221Q	Displaced transverse fracture of shaft of right ulna, subsequent encounter for open fracture type I or II with malunion
S52.221M	Displaced transverse fracture of shaft of right ulna, subsequent encounter for open fracture type I or II with nonunion
S52.221R	Displaced transverse fracture of shaft of right ulna, subsequent encounter for open fracture type IIIA, IIIB, or IIIC with malunion
S52.221N	Displaced transverse fracture of shaft of right ulna, subsequent encounter for open fracture type IIIA, IIIB, or IIIC with nonunion
S72.323P	Displaced transverse fracture of shaft of unspecified femur, subsequent encounter for closed fracture with malunion

S72.323K Displaced transverse fracture of shaft of unspecified femur, subsequent encounter for closed fracture with nonunion
S72.323Q Displaced transverse fracture of shaft of unspecified femur, subsequent encounter for open fracture type I or II with malunion
S72.323M Displaced transverse fracture of shaft of unspecified femur, subsequent encounter for open fracture type I or II with nonunion
S72.323R Displaced transverse fracture of shaft of unspecified femur, subsequent encounter for open fracture type IIIA, IIIB, or IIIC with malunion
S72.323N Displaced transverse fracture of shaft of unspecified femur, subsequent encounter for open fracture type IIIA, IIIB, or IIIC with nonunion
S82.423P Displaced transverse fracture of shaft of unspecified fibula, subsequent encounter for closed fracture with malunion
S82.423K Displaced transverse fracture of shaft of unspecified fibula, subsequent encounter for closed fracture with nonunion
S82.423Q Displaced transverse fracture of shaft of unspecified fibula, subsequent encounter for open fracture type I or II with malunion
S82.423M Displaced transverse fracture of shaft of unspecified fibula, subsequent encounter for open fracture type I or II with nonunion
S82.423R Displaced transverse fracture of shaft of unspecified fibula, subsequent encounter for open fracture type IIIA, IIIB, or IIIC with malunion
S82.423N Displaced transverse fracture of shaft of unspecified fibula, subsequent encounter for open fracture type IIIA, IIIB, or IIIC with nonunion
S52.323A Displaced transverse fracture of shaft of unspecified radius, initial encounter for closed fracture
S52.323P Displaced transverse fracture of shaft of unspecified radius, subsequent encounter for closed fracture with malunion
S52.323K Displaced transverse fracture of shaft of unspecified radius, subsequent encounter for closed fracture with nonunion
S52.323Q Displaced transverse fracture of shaft of unspecified radius, subsequent encounter for open fracture type I or II with malunion
S52.323M Displaced transverse fracture of shaft of unspecified radius, subsequent encounter for open fracture type I or II with nonunion
S52.323R Displaced transverse fracture of shaft of unspecified radius, subsequent encounter for open fracture type IIIA, IIIB, or IIIC with malunion
S52.323N Displaced transverse fracture of shaft of unspecified radius, subsequent encounter for open fracture type IIIA, IIIB, or IIIC with nonunion
S82.223A Displaced transverse fracture of shaft of unspecified tibia, initial encounter for closed fracture
S82.223P Displaced transverse fracture of shaft of unspecified tibia, subsequent encounter for closed fracture with malunion
S82.223K Displaced transverse fracture of shaft of unspecified tibia, subsequent encounter for closed fracture with nonunion
S82.223Q Displaced transverse fracture of shaft of unspecified tibia, subsequent encounter for open fracture type I or II with malunion
S82.223M Displaced transverse fracture of shaft of unspecified tibia, subsequent encounter for open fracture type I or II with nonunion
S82.223R Displaced transverse fracture of shaft of unspecified tibia, subsequent encounter for open fracture type IIIA, IIIB, or IIIC with malunion
S82.223N Displaced transverse fracture of shaft of unspecified tibia, subsequent encounter for open fracture type IIIA, IIIB, or IIIC with nonunion
S52.223A Displaced transverse fracture of shaft of unspecified ulna, initial encounter for closed fracture
S52.223P Displaced transverse fracture of shaft of unspecified ulna, subsequent encounter for closed fracture with malunion
S52.223K Displaced transverse fracture of shaft of unspecified ulna, subsequent encounter for closed fracture with nonunion
S52.223Q Displaced transverse fracture of shaft of unspecified ulna, subsequent encounter for open fracture type I or II with malunion
S52.223M Displaced transverse fracture of shaft of unspecified ulna, subsequent encounter for open fracture type I or II with nonunion
S52.223R Displaced transverse fracture of shaft of unspecified ulna, subsequent encounter for open fracture type IIIA, IIIB, or IIIC with malunion
S52.223N Displaced transverse fracture of shaft of unspecified ulna, subsequent encounter for open fracture type IIIA, IIIB, or IIIC with nonunion
S32.453K Displaced transverse fracture of unspecified acetabulum, subsequent encounter for fracture with nonunion
S82.Ø33A Displaced transverse fracture of unspecified patella, initial encounter for closed fracture
S82.Ø33B Displaced transverse fracture of unspecified patella, initial encounter for open fracture type I or II
S82.Ø33C Displaced transverse fracture of unspecified patella, initial encounter for open fracture type IIIA, IIIB, or IIIC
S82.Ø33P Displaced transverse fracture of unspecified patella, subsequent encounter for closed fracture with malunion
S82.Ø33K Displaced transverse fracture of unspecified patella, subsequent encounter for closed fracture with nonunion
S82.Ø33Q Displaced transverse fracture of unspecified patella, subsequent encounter for open fracture type I or II with malunion
S82.Ø33M Displaced transverse fracture of unspecified patella, subsequent encounter for open fracture type I or II with nonunion
S82.Ø33R Displaced transverse fracture of unspecified patella, subsequent encounter for open fracture type IIIA, IIIB, or IIIC with malunion
S82.Ø33N Displaced transverse fracture of unspecified patella, subsequent encounter for open fracture type IIIA, IIIB, or IIIC with nonunion
S82.852B Displaced trimalleolar fracture of left lower leg, initial encounter for open fracture type I or II
S82.852C Displaced trimalleolar fracture of left lower leg, initial encounter for open fracture type IIIA, IIIB, or IIIC
S82.852P Displaced trimalleolar fracture of left lower leg, subsequent encounter for closed fracture with malunion
S82.852K Displaced trimalleolar fracture of left lower leg, subsequent encounter for closed fracture with nonunion
S82.852Q Displaced trimalleolar fracture of left lower leg, subsequent encounter for open fracture type I or II with malunion
S82.852M Displaced trimalleolar fracture of left lower leg, subsequent encounter for open fracture type I or II with nonunion
S82.852R Displaced trimalleolar fracture of left lower leg, subsequent encounter for open fracture type IIIA, IIIB, or IIIC with malunion
S82.852N Displaced trimalleolar fracture of left lower leg, subsequent encounter for open fracture type IIIA, IIIB, or IIIC with nonunion
S82.851B Displaced trimalleolar fracture of right lower leg, initial encounter for open fracture type I or II
S82.851C Displaced trimalleolar fracture of right lower leg, initial encounter for open fracture type IIIA, IIIB, or IIIC
S82.851P Displaced trimalleolar fracture of right lower leg, subsequent encounter for closed fracture with malunion
S82.851K Displaced trimalleolar fracture of right lower leg, subsequent encounter for closed fracture with nonunion
S82.851Q Displaced trimalleolar fracture of right lower leg, subsequent encounter for open fracture type I or II with malunion
S82.851M Displaced trimalleolar fracture of right lower leg, subsequent encounter for open fracture type I or II with nonunion
S82.851R Displaced trimalleolar fracture of right lower leg, subsequent encounter for open fracture type IIIA, IIIB, or IIIC with malunion
S82.851N Displaced trimalleolar fracture of right lower leg, subsequent encounter for open fracture type IIIA, IIIB, or IIIC with nonunion
S82.853B Displaced trimalleolar fracture of unspecified lower leg, initial encounter for open fracture type I or II
S82.853C Displaced trimalleolar fracture of unspecified lower leg, initial encounter for open fracture type IIIA, IIIB, or IIIC
S82.853P Displaced trimalleolar fracture of unspecified lower leg, subsequent encounter for closed fracture with malunion
S82.853K Displaced trimalleolar fracture of unspecified lower leg, subsequent encounter for closed fracture with nonunion
S82.853Q Displaced trimalleolar fracture of unspecified lower leg, subsequent encounter for open fracture type I or II with malunion
S82.853M Displaced trimalleolar fracture of unspecified lower leg, subsequent encounter for open fracture type I or II with nonunion
S82.853R Displaced trimalleolar fracture of unspecified lower leg, subsequent encounter for open fracture type IIIA, IIIB, or IIIC with malunion
S82.853N Displaced trimalleolar fracture of unspecified lower leg, subsequent encounter for open fracture type IIIA, IIIB, or IIIC with nonunion
S72.412A Displaced unspecified condyle fracture of lower end of left femur, initial encounter for closed fracture
S72.412P Displaced unspecified condyle fracture of lower end of left femur, subsequent encounter for closed fracture with malunion
S72.412K Displaced unspecified condyle fracture of lower end of left femur, subsequent encounter for closed fracture with nonunion
S72.412Q Displaced unspecified condyle fracture of lower end of left femur, subsequent encounter for open fracture type I or II with malunion
S72.412M Displaced unspecified condyle fracture of lower end of left femur, subsequent encounter for open fracture type I or II with nonunion
S72.412R Displaced unspecified condyle fracture of lower end of left femur, subsequent encounter for open fracture type IIIA, IIIB, or IIIC with malunion
S72.412N Displaced unspecified condyle fracture of lower end of left femur, subsequent encounter for open fracture type IIIA, IIIB, or IIIC with nonunion
S72.411A Displaced unspecified condyle fracture of lower end of right femur, initial encounter for closed fracture
S72.411P Displaced unspecified condyle fracture of lower end of right femur, subsequent encounter for closed fracture with malunion
S72.411K Displaced unspecified condyle fracture of lower end of right femur, subsequent encounter for closed fracture with nonunion
S72.411Q Displaced unspecified condyle fracture of lower end of right femur, subsequent encounter for open fracture type I or II with malunion
S72.411M Displaced unspecified condyle fracture of lower end of right femur, subsequent encounter for open fracture type I or II with nonunion
S72.411R Displaced unspecified condyle fracture of lower end of right femur, subsequent encounter for open fracture type IIIA, IIIB, or IIIC with malunion
S72.411N Displaced unspecified condyle fracture of lower end of right femur, subsequent encounter for open fracture type IIIA, IIIB, or IIIC with nonunion
S72.413A Displaced unspecified condyle fracture of lower end of unspecified femur, initial encounter for closed fracture
S72.413P Displaced unspecified condyle fracture of lower end of unspecified femur, subsequent encounter for closed fracture with malunion
S72.413K Displaced unspecified condyle fracture of lower end of unspecified femur, subsequent encounter for closed fracture with nonunion
S72.413Q Displaced unspecified condyle fracture of lower end of unspecified femur, subsequent encounter for open fracture type I or II with malunion
S72.413M Displaced unspecified condyle fracture of lower end of unspecified femur, subsequent encounter for open fracture type I or II with nonunion
S72.413R Displaced unspecified condyle fracture of lower end of unspecified femur, subsequent encounter for open fracture type IIIA, IIIB, or IIIC with malunion
S72.413N Displaced unspecified condyle fracture of lower end of unspecified femur, subsequent encounter for open fracture type IIIA, IIIB, or IIIC with nonunion
S92.4Ø2P Displaced unspecified fracture of left great toe, subsequent encounter for fracture with malunion
S92.4Ø2K Displaced unspecified fracture of left great toe, subsequent encounter for fracture with nonunion
S92.5Ø2P Displaced unspecified fracture of left lesser toe(s), subsequent encounter for fracture with malunion

S92.502K	Displaced unspecified fracture of left lesser toe(s), subsequent encounter for fracture with nonunion
S92.401P	Displaced unspecified fracture of right great toe, subsequent encounter for fracture with malunion
S92.401K	Displaced unspecified fracture of right great toe, subsequent encounter for fracture with nonunion
S92.501P	Displaced unspecified fracture of right lesser toe(s), subsequent encounter for fracture with malunion
S92.501K	Displaced unspecified fracture of right lesser toe(s), subsequent encounter for fracture with nonunion
S92.403P	Displaced unspecified fracture of unspecified great toe, subsequent encounter for fracture with malunion
S92.403K	Displaced unspecified fracture of unspecified great toe, subsequent encounter for fracture with nonunion
S92.503P	Displaced unspecified fracture of unspecified lesser toe(s), subsequent encounter for fracture with malunion
S92.503K	Displaced unspecified fracture of unspecified lesser toe(s), subsequent encounter for fracture with nonunion
T82.320A	Displacement of aortic (bifurcation) graft (replacement), initial encounter
T82.522A	Displacement of artificial heart, initial encounter
T85.623A	Displacement of artificial skin graft and decellularized allodermis, initial encounter
T82.523A	Displacement of balloon (counterpulsation) device, initial encounter
T85.520A	Displacement of bile duct prosthesis, initial encounter
T82.222A	Displacement of biological heart valve graft, initial encounter
T85.42XA	Displacement of breast prosthesis and implant, initial encounter
T82.120A	Displacement of cardiac electrode, initial encounter
T82.121A	Displacement of cardiac pulse generator (battery), initial encounter
T82.321A	Displacement of carotid arterial graft (bypass), initial encounter
T82.212A	Displacement of coronary artery bypass graft, initial encounter
T85.620A	Displacement of cranial or spinal infusion catheter, initial encounter
T83.020A	Displacement of cystostomy catheter, initial encounter
T84.320A	Displacement of electronic bone stimulator, initial encounter
T85.521A	Displacement of esophageal anti-reflux device, initial encounter
T82.322A	Displacement of femoral arterial graft (bypass), initial encounter
T83.22XA	Displacement of graft of urinary organ, initial encounter
T82.02XA	Displacement of heart valve prosthesis, initial encounter
T85.120A	Displacement of implanted electronic neurostimulator of brain electrode (lead), initial encounter
T85.121A	Displacement of implanted electronic neurostimulator of peripheral nerve electrode (lead), initial encounter
T85.122A	Displacement of implanted electronic neurostimulator of spinal cord electrode (lead), initial encounter
T85.123A	Displacement of implanted electronic neurostimulator, generator, initial encounter
T83.420A	Displacement of implanted penile prosthesis, initial encounter
T83.421A	Displacement of implanted testicular prosthesis, initial encounter
T83.121A	Displacement of implanted urinary sphincter, initial encounter
T83.122A	Displacement of indwelling ureteral stent, initial encounter
T82.524A	Displacement of infusion catheter, initial encounter
T85.624A	Displacement of insulin pump, initial encounter
T84.123A	Displacement of internal fixation device of bone of left forearm, initial encounter
T84.127A	Displacement of internal fixation device of bone of left lower leg, initial encounter
T84.122A	Displacement of internal fixation device of bone of right forearm, initial encounter
T84.126A	Displacement of internal fixation device of bone of right lower leg, initial encounter
T84.223A	Displacement of internal fixation device of bones of foot and toes, initial encounter
T84.220A	Displacement of internal fixation device of bones of hand and fingers, initial encounter
T84.125A	Displacement of internal fixation device of left femur, initial encounter
T84.121A	Displacement of internal fixation device of left humerus, initial encounter
T84.228A	Displacement of internal fixation device of other bones, initial encounter
T84.124A	Displacement of internal fixation device of right femur, initial encounter
T84.120A	Displacement of internal fixation device of right humerus, initial encounter
T84.129A	Displacement of internal fixation device of unspecified bone of limb, initial encounter
T84.226A	Displacement of internal fixation device of vertebrae, initial encounter
T85.22XA	Displacement of intraocular lens, initial encounter
T85.621A	Displacement of intraperitoneal dialysis catheter, initial encounter
T84.420A	Displacement of muscle and tendon graft, initial encounter
T84.328A	Displacement of other bone devices, implants and grafts, initial encounter
T82.528A	Displacement of other cardiac and vascular devices and implants, initial encounter
T82.128A	Displacement of other cardiac electronic device, initial encounter
T85.528A	Displacement of other gastrointestinal prosthetic devices, implants and grafts, initial encounter
T85.128A	Displacement of other implanted electronic stimulator of nervous system, initial encounter
T84.428A	Displacement of other internal orthopedic devices, implants and grafts, initial encounter
T85.625A	Displacement of other nervous system device, implant or graft, initial encounter
T83.428A	Displacement of other prosthetic devices, implants and grafts of genital tract, initial encounter
T85.628A	Displacement of other specified internal prosthetic devices, implants and grafts, initial enocunter

T83.128A	Displacement of other urinary devices and implants, initial encounter
T83.123A	Displacement of other urinary stents, initial encounter
T82.328A	Displacement of other vascular grafts, initial encounter
T85.622A	Displacement of permanent sutures, initial encounter
T85.321A	Displacement of prosthetic orbit of left eye, initial encounter
T85.320A	Displacement of prosthetic orbit of right eye, initial encounter
T82.520A	Displacement of surgically created arteriovenous fistula, initial encounter
T82.521A	Displacement of surgically created arteriovenous shunt, initial encounter
T82.525A	Displacement of umbrella device, initial encounter
T82.529A	Displacement of unspecified cardiac and vascular devices and implants, initial encounter
T82.129A	Displacement of unspecified cardiac electronic device, initial encounter
T82.329A	Displacement of unspecified vascular grafts, initial encounter
T83.120A	Displacement of urinary electronic stimulator device, initial encounter
T82.42XA	Displacement of vascular dialysis catheter, initial encounter
T85.02XA	Displacement of ventricular intracranial (communicating) shunt, initial encounter
T81.31XA	Disruption of external operation (surgical) wound, not elsewhere classified, initial encounter
T81.32XA	Disruption of internal operation (surgical) wound, not elsewhere classified, initial encounter
T81.33XA	Disruption of traumatic injury wound repair, initial encounter
T81.30XA	Disruption of wound, unspecified, initial encounter
F34.81	Disruptive mood dysregulation disorder
B44.7	Disseminated aspergillosis
B40.7	Disseminated blastomycosis
H30.113	Disseminated chorioretinal inflammation of posterior pole, bilateral
H30.112	Disseminated chorioretinal inflammation of posterior pole, left eye
H30.111	Disseminated chorioretinal inflammation of posterior pole, right eye
H30.119	Disseminated chorioretinal inflammation of posterior pole, unspecified eye
H30.133	Disseminated chorioretinal inflammation, generalized, bilateral
H30.132	Disseminated chorioretinal inflammation, generalized, left eye
H30.131	Disseminated chorioretinal inflammation, generalized, right eye
H30.139	Disseminated chorioretinal inflammation, generalized, unspecified eye
H30.121	Disseminated chorioretinal inflammation, peripheral right eye
H30.123	Disseminated chorioretinal inflammation, peripheral, bilateral
H30.122	Disseminated chorioretinal inflammation, peripheral, left eye
H30.129	Disseminated chorioretinal inflammation, peripheral, unspecified eye
B38.7	Disseminated coccidioidomycosis
B45.7	Disseminated cryptococcosis
B39.3	Disseminated histoplasmosis capsulati
C80.0	Disseminated malignant neoplasm, unspecified
A31.2	Disseminated mycobacterium avium-intracellulare complex (DMAC)
B41.7	Disseminated paracoccidioidomycosis
B78.7	Disseminated strongyloidiasis
B02.7	Disseminated zoster
K57.40	Diverticulitis of both small and large intestine with perforation and abscess without bleeding
K57.52	Diverticulitis of both small and large intestine without perforation or abscess without bleeding
K57.80	Diverticulitis of intestine, part unspecified, with perforation and abscess without bleeding
K57.92	Diverticulitis of intestine, part unspecified, without perforation or abscess without bleeding
K57.20	Diverticulitis of large intestine with perforation and abscess without bleeding
K57.32	Diverticulitis of large intestine without perforation or abscess without bleeding
K57.00	Diverticulitis of small intestine with perforation and abscess without bleeding
K57.12	Diverticulitis of small intestine without perforation or abscess without bleeding
Q25.45	Double aortic arch
B72	Dracunculiasis
I24.1	Dressler's syndrome
G24.02	Drug induced acute dystonia
E09.52	Drug or chemical induced diabetes mellitus with diabetic peripheral angiopathy with gangrene
O99.324	Drug use complicating childbirth
O99.321	Drug use complicating pregnancy, first trimester
O99.322	Drug use complicating pregnancy, second trimester
O99.323	Drug use complicating pregnancy, third trimester
O99.325	Drug use complicating the puerperium
E27.3	Drug-induced adrenocortical insufficiency
D59.0	Drug-induced autoimmune hemolytic anemia
E24.2	Drug-induced Cushing's syndrome
G72.0	Drug-induced myopathy
D59.2	Drug-induced nonautoimmune hemolytic anemia
L10.5	Drug-induced pemphigus
E51.11	Dry beriberi
Q43.4	Duplication of intestine
G96.11	Dural tear
A50.2	Early congenital syphilis, unspecified
A50.01	Early congenital syphilitic oculopathy
A50.02	Early congenital syphilitic osteochondropathy
A50.03	Early congenital syphilitic pharyngitis
A50.04	Early congenital syphilitic pneumonia
A50.05	Early congenital syphilitic rhinitis
A50.06	Early cutaneous congenital syphilis
A50.07	Early mucocutaneous congenital syphilis
A50.08	Early visceral congenital syphilis

G11.1	Early-onset cerebellar ataxia
B67.90	Echinococcosis, unspecified
B67.8	Echinococcosis, unspecified, of liver
B67.2	Echinococcus granulosus infection of bone
B67.0	Echinococcus granulosus infection of liver
B67.1	Echinococcus granulosus infection of lung
B67.32	Echinococcus granulosus infection, multiple sites
B67.39	Echinococcus granulosus infection, other sites
B67.31	Echinococcus granulosus infection, thyroid gland
B67.4	Echinococcus granulosus infection, unspecified
B67.5	Echinococcus multilocularis infection of liver
B67.61	Echinococcus multilocularis infection, multiple sites
B67.69	Echinococcus multilocularis infection, other sites
B67.7	Echinococcus multilocularis infection, unspecified
E24.3	Ectopic ACTH syndrome
Q43.5	Ectopic anus
Q79.60	Ehlers-Danlos syndrome, unspecified
A77.41	Ehrlichiosis chafeensis [E. chafeensis]
A77.40	Ehrlichiosis, unspecified
I74.4	Embolism and thrombosis of arteries of extremities, unspecified
I74.3	Embolism and thrombosis of arteries of the lower extremities
I74.2	Embolism and thrombosis of arteries of the upper extremities
I74.5	Embolism and thrombosis of iliac artery
I74.8	Embolism and thrombosis of other arteries
I74.19	Embolism and thrombosis of other parts of aorta
I82.3	Embolism and thrombosis of renal vein
I82.812	Embolism and thrombosis of superficial veins of left lower extremity
I82.813	Embolism and thrombosis of superficial veins of lower extremities, bilateral
I82.811	Embolism and thrombosis of superficial veins of right lower extremity
I82.819	Embolism and thrombosis of superficial veins of unspecified lower extremity
I74.11	Embolism and thrombosis of thoracic aorta
I74.9	Embolism and thrombosis of unspecified artery
I74.10	Embolism and thrombosis of unspecified parts of aorta
T82.817A	Embolism due to cardiac prosthetic devices, implants and grafts, initial encounter
T83.81XA	Embolism due to genitourinary prosthetic devices, implants and grafts, initial encounter
T84.81XA	Embolism due to internal orthopedic prosthetic devices, implants and grafts, initial encounter
T85.810A	Embolism due to nervous system prosthetic devices, implants and grafts, initial encounter
T85.810D	Embolism due to nervous system prosthetic devices, implants and grafts, subsequent encounter
T82.818A	Embolism due to vascular prosthetic devices, implants and grafts, initial encounter
O03.7	Embolism following complete or unspecified spontaneous abortion
Q01.8	Encephalocele of other sites
Q01.9	Encephalocele, unspecified
G93.40	Encephalopathy, unspecified
Z48.290	Encounter for aftercare following bone marrow transplant
Z48.21	Encounter for aftercare following heart transplant
Z48.280	Encounter for aftercare following heart-lung transplant
Z48.22	Encounter for aftercare following kidney transplant
Z48.23	Encounter for aftercare following liver transplant
Z48.24	Encounter for aftercare following lung transplant
Z43.1	Encounter for attention to gastrostomy
Z99.12	Encounter for respirator [ventilator] dependence during power failure
I42.4	Endocardial fibroelastosis
I39	Endocarditis and heart valve disorders in diseases classified elsewhere
M32.11	Endocarditis in systemic lupus erythematosus
I38	Endocarditis, valve unspecified
O86.12	Endometritis following delivery
I42.3	Endomyocardial (eosinophilic) disease
A04.6	Enteritis due to Yersinia enterocolitica
B80	Enterobiasis
A04.72	Enterocolitis due to Clostridium difficile, not specified as recurrent
A04.71	Enterocolitis due to Clostridium difficile, recurrent
A04.3	Enterohemorrhagic Escherichia coli infection
A04.2	Enteroinvasive Escherichia coli infection
A04.0	Enteropathogenic Escherichia coli infection
C86.2	Enteropathy-type (intestinal) T-cell lymphoma
K94.11	Enterostomy hemorrhage
K94.12	Enterostomy infection
K94.13	Enterostomy malfunction
A04.1	Enterotoxigenic Escherichia coli infection
A85.0	Enteroviral encephalitis
A88.0	Enteroviral exanthematous fever [Boston exanthem]
A87.0	Enteroviral meningitis
L98.3	Eosinophilic cellulitis [Wells]
P12.2	Epicranial subaponeurotic hemorrhage due to birth injury
A75.0	Epidemic louse-borne typhus fever due to Rickettsia prowazekii
L12.31	Epidermolysis bullosa due to drug
G40.911	Epilepsy, unspecified, intractable, with status epilepticus
G40.919	Epilepsy, unspecified, intractable, without status epilepticus
G40.501	Epileptic seizures related to external causes, not intractable, with status epilepticus
G40.509	Epileptic seizures related to external causes, not intractable, without status epilepticus
G40.823	Epileptic spasms, intractable, with status epilepticus
G40.824	Epileptic spasms, intractable, without status epilepticus
G40.821	Epileptic spasms, not intractable, with status epilepticus
G40.822	Epileptic spasms, not intractable, without status epilepticus
T83.24XA	Erosion of graft of urinary organ, initial encounter
T83.714A	Erosion of implanted ureteral bulking agent to surrounding organ or tissue, initial encounter
T83.713A	Erosion of implanted urethral bulking agent to surrounding organ or tissue, initial encounter
T83.712A	Erosion of implanted urethral mesh to surrounding organ or tissue, initial encounter
T83.718A	Erosion of other implanted mesh to organ or tissue, initial encounter
T83.719A	Erosion of other prosthetic materials to surrounding organ or tissue, initial encounter
L53.1	Erythema annulare centrifugum
B08.3	Erythema infectiosum [fifth disease]
L53.2	Erythema marginatum
L08.1	Erythrasma
I85.00	Esophageal varices without bleeding
K94.30	Esophagostomy complications, unspecified
K94.31	Esophagostomy hemorrhage
K94.32	Esophagostomy infection
K94.33	Esophagostomy malfunction
B47.0	Eumycetoma
D69.41	Evans syndrome
T67.02XA	Exertional heatstroke, initial encounter
L49.3	Exfoliation due to erythematous condition involving 30-39 percent of body surface
L49.4	Exfoliation due to erythematous condition involving 40-49 percent of body surface
L49.5	Exfoliation due to erythematous condition involving 50-59 percent of body surface
L49.6	Exfoliation due to erythematous condition involving 60-69 percent of body surface
L49.7	Exfoliation due to erythematous condition involving 70-79 percent of body surface
L49.8	Exfoliation due to erythematous condition involving 80-89 percent of body surface
L49.9	Exfoliation due to erythematous condition involving 90 or more percent of body surface
T83.25XA	Exposure of graft of urinary organ, initial encounter
T83.724A	Exposure of implanted ureteral bulking agent into ureter, initial encounter
T83.723A	Exposure of implanted urethral bulking agent into urethra, initial encounter
T83.722A	Exposure of implanted urethral mesh into urethra, initial encounter
T83.728A	Exposure of other implanted mesh into organ or tissue, initial encounter
T83.729A	Exposure of other prosthetic materials into organ or tissue, initial encounter
Q64.10	Exstrophy of urinary bladder, unspecified
Z16.12	Extended spectrum beta lactamase (ESBL) resistance
A28.2	Extraintestinal yersiniosis
C90.22	Extramedullary plasmacytoma in relapse
C90.21	Extramedullary plasmacytoma in remission
C90.20	Extramedullary plasmacytoma not having achieved remission
C88.4	Extranodal marginal zone B-cell lymphoma of mucosa-associated lymphoid tissue [MALT-lymphoma]
C86.0	Extranodal NK/T-cell lymphoma, nasal type
G25.9	Extrapyramidal and movement disorder, unspecified
N44.01	Extravaginal torsion of spermatic cord
T80.818A	Extravasation of other vesicant agent, initial encounter
R39.0	Extravasation of urine
T80.810A	Extravasation of vesicant antineoplastic chemotherapy, initial encounter
F68.A	Factitious disorder imposed on another
F68.10	Factitious disorder imposed on self, unspecified
F68.12	Factitious disorder imposed on self, with predominantly physical signs and symptoms
O07.39	Failed attempted termination of pregnancy with other complications
O07.30	Failed attempted termination of pregnancy with unspecified complications
O47.1	False labor at or after 37 completed weeks of gestation
O47.02	False labor before 37 completed weeks of gestation, second trimester
O47.03	False labor before 37 completed weeks of gestation, third trimester
G12.24	Familial motor neuron disease
B66.3	Fascioliasis
B66.5	Fasciolopsiasis
A81.83	Fatal familial insomnia
N73.4	Female chronic pelvic peritonitis
N82.9	Female genital tract fistula, unspecified
N82.5	Female genital tract-skin fistulae
T82.827A	Fibrosis due to cardiac prosthetic devices, implants and grafts, initial encounter
T83.82XA	Fibrosis due to genitourinary prosthetic devices, implants and grafts, initial encounter
T84.82XA	Fibrosis due to internal orthopedic prosthetic devices, implants and grafts, initial encounter
T85.820A	Fibrosis due to nervous system prosthetic devices, implants and grafts, initial encounter
T85.820D	Fibrosis due to nervous system prosthetic devices, implants and grafts, subsequent encounter
T82.828A	Fibrosis due to vascular prosthetic devices, implants and grafts, initial encounter
B74.1	Filariasis due to Brugia malayi
B74.2	Filariasis due to Brugia timori
B74.0	Filariasis due to Wuchereria bancrofti

B74.9	Filariasis, unspecified
K83.3	Fistula of bile duct
K82.3	Fistula of gallbladder
K63.2	Fistula of intestine
K11.4	Fistula of salivary gland
K31.6	Fistula of stomach and duodenum
N82.3	Fistula of vagina to large intestine
N82.2	Fistula of vagina to small intestine
G81.02	Flaccid hemiplegia affecting left dominant side
G81.04	Flaccid hemiplegia affecting left nondominant side
G81.01	Flaccid hemiplegia affecting right dominant side
G81.03	Flaccid hemiplegia affecting right nondominant side
G81.00	Flaccid hemiplegia affecting unspecified side
S22.5XXK	Flail chest, subsequent encounter for fracture with nonunion
C82.09	Follicular lymphoma grade I, extranodal and solid organ sites
C82.03	Follicular lymphoma grade I, intra-abdominal lymph nodes
C82.06	Follicular lymphoma grade I, intrapelvic lymph nodes
C82.02	Follicular lymphoma grade I, intrathoracic lymph nodes
C82.04	Follicular lymphoma grade I, lymph nodes of axilla and upper limb
C82.01	Follicular lymphoma grade I, lymph nodes of head, face, and neck
C82.05	Follicular lymphoma grade I, lymph nodes of inguinal region and lower limb
C82.08	Follicular lymphoma grade I, lymph nodes of multiple sites
C82.07	Follicular lymphoma grade I, spleen
C82.00	Follicular lymphoma grade I, unspecified site
C82.19	Follicular lymphoma grade II, extranodal and solid organ sites
C82.13	Follicular lymphoma grade II, intra-abdominal lymph nodes
C82.16	Follicular lymphoma grade II, intrapelvic lymph nodes
C82.12	Follicular lymphoma grade II, intrathoracic lymph nodes
C82.14	Follicular lymphoma grade II, lymph nodes of axilla and upper limb
C82.11	Follicular lymphoma grade II, lymph nodes of head, face, and neck
C82.15	Follicular lymphoma grade II, lymph nodes of inguinal region and lower limb
C82.18	Follicular lymphoma grade II, lymph nodes of multiple sites
C82.17	Follicular lymphoma grade II, spleen
C82.10	Follicular lymphoma grade II, unspecified site
C82.29	Follicular lymphoma grade III, unspecified, extranodal and solid organ sites
C82.23	Follicular lymphoma grade III, unspecified, intra-abdominal lymph nodes
C82.26	Follicular lymphoma grade III, unspecified, intrapelvic lymph nodes
C82.22	Follicular lymphoma grade III, unspecified, intrathoracic lymph nodes
C82.24	Follicular lymphoma grade III, unspecified, lymph nodes of axilla and upper limb
C82.21	Follicular lymphoma grade III, unspecified, lymph nodes of head, face, and neck
C82.25	Follicular lymphoma grade III, unspecified, lymph nodes of inguinal region and lower limb
C82.28	Follicular lymphoma grade III, unspecified, lymph nodes of multiple sites
C82.27	Follicular lymphoma grade III, unspecified, spleen
C82.20	Follicular lymphoma grade III, unspecified, unspecified site
C82.39	Follicular lymphoma grade IIIa, extranodal and solid organ sites
C82.33	Follicular lymphoma grade IIIa, intra-abdominal lymph nodes
C82.36	Follicular lymphoma grade IIIa, intrapelvic lymph nodes
C82.32	Follicular lymphoma grade IIIa, intrathoracic lymph nodes
C82.34	Follicular lymphoma grade IIIa, lymph nodes of axilla and upper limb
C82.31	Follicular lymphoma grade IIIa, lymph nodes of head, face, and neck
C82.35	Follicular lymphoma grade IIIa, lymph nodes of inguinal region and lower limb
C82.38	Follicular lymphoma grade IIIa, lymph nodes of multiple sites
C82.37	Follicular lymphoma grade IIIa, spleen
C82.30	Follicular lymphoma grade IIIa, unspecified site
C82.49	Follicular lymphoma grade IIIb, extranodal and solid organ sites
C82.43	Follicular lymphoma grade IIIb, intra-abdominal lymph nodes
C82.46	Follicular lymphoma grade IIIb, intrapelvic lymph nodes
C82.42	Follicular lymphoma grade IIIb, intrathoracic lymph nodes
C82.44	Follicular lymphoma grade IIIb, lymph nodes of axilla and upper limb
C82.41	Follicular lymphoma grade IIIb, lymph nodes of head, face, and neck
C82.45	Follicular lymphoma grade IIIb, lymph nodes of inguinal region and lower limb
C82.48	Follicular lymphoma grade IIIb, lymph nodes of multiple sites
C82.47	Follicular lymphoma grade IIIb, spleen
C82.40	Follicular lymphoma grade IIIb, unspecified site
C82.99	Follicular lymphoma, unspecified, extranodal and solid organ sites
C82.93	Follicular lymphoma, unspecified, intra-abdominal lymph nodes
C82.96	Follicular lymphoma, unspecified, intrapelvic lymph nodes
C82.92	Follicular lymphoma, unspecified, intrathoracic lymph nodes
C82.94	Follicular lymphoma, unspecified, lymph nodes of axilla and upper limb
C82.91	Follicular lymphoma, unspecified, lymph nodes of head, face, and neck
C82.95	Follicular lymphoma, unspecified, lymph nodes of inguinal region and lower limb
C82.98	Follicular lymphoma, unspecified, lymph nodes of multiple sites
C82.97	Follicular lymphoma, unspecified, spleen
C82.90	Follicular lymphoma, unspecified, unspecified site
T17.520A	Food in bronchus causing asphyxiation, initial encounter
T17.528A	Food in bronchus causing other injury, initial encounter
T17.820A	Food in other parts of respiratory tract causing asphyxiation, initial encounter
T17.828A	Food in other parts of respiratory tract causing other injury, initial encounter
T17.420A	Food in trachea causing asphyxiation, initial encounter
T17.428A	Food in trachea causing other injury, initial encounter
A05.4	Foodborne Bacillus cereus intoxication
A05.2	Foodborne Clostridium perfringens [Clostridium welchii] intoxication
A05.0	Foodborne staphylococcal intoxication

A05.3	Foodborne Vibrio parahaemolyticus intoxication
A05.5	Foodborne Vibrio vulnificus intoxication
O70.3	Fourth degree perineal laceration during delivery
S02.672A	Fracture of alveolus of left mandible, initial encounter for closed fracture
S02.672B	Fracture of alveolus of left mandible, initial encounter for open fracture
S02.672K	Fracture of alveolus of left mandible, subsequent encounter for fracture with nonunion
S02.670A	Fracture of alveolus of mandible, unspecified side, initial encounter for closed fracture
S02.670B	Fracture of alveolus of mandible, unspecified side, initial encounter for open fracture
S02.670K	Fracture of alveolus of mandible, unspecified side, subsequent encounter for fracture with nonunion
S02.42XA	Fracture of alveolus of maxilla, initial encounter for closed fracture
S02.42XB	Fracture of alveolus of maxilla, initial encounter for open fracture
S02.42XK	Fracture of alveolus of maxilla, subsequent encounter for fracture with nonunion
S02.671A	Fracture of alveolus of right mandible, initial encounter for closed fracture
S02.671B	Fracture of alveolus of right mandible, initial encounter for open fracture
S02.671K	Fracture of alveolus of right mandible, subsequent encounter for fracture with nonunion
S02.652A	Fracture of angle of left mandible, initial encounter for closed fracture
S02.652B	Fracture of angle of left mandible, initial encounter for open fracture
S02.652K	Fracture of angle of left mandible, subsequent encounter for fracture with nonunion
S02.650A	Fracture of angle of mandible, unspecified side, initial encounter for closed fracture
S02.650B	Fracture of angle of mandible, unspecified side, initial encounter for open fracture
S02.650K	Fracture of angle of mandible, unspecified side, subsequent encounter for fracture with nonunion
S02.651A	Fracture of angle of right mandible, initial encounter for closed fracture
S02.651B	Fracture of angle of right mandible, initial encounter for open fracture
S02.651K	Fracture of angle of right mandible, subsequent encounter for fracture with nonunion
S02.102A	Fracture of base of skull, left side, initial encounter for closed fracture
S02.102K	Fracture of base of skull, left side, subsequent encounter for fracture with nonunion
S02.101A	Fracture of base of skull, right side, initial encounter for closed fracture
S02.101K	Fracture of base of skull, right side, subsequent encounter for fracture with nonunion
S02.109A	Fracture of base of skull, unspecified side, initial encounter for closed fracture
S02.109K	Fracture of base of skull, unspecified side, subsequent encounter for fracture with nonunion
S22.22XA	Fracture of body of sternum, initial encounter for closed fracture
S22.22XK	Fracture of body of sternum, subsequent encounter for fracture with nonunion
S22.9XXA	Fracture of bony thorax, part unspecified, initial encounter for closed fracture
S22.9XXK	Fracture of bony thorax, part unspecified, subsequent encounter for fracture with nonunion
S32.2XXA	Fracture of coccyx, initial encounter for closed fracture
S32.2XXK	Fracture of coccyx, subsequent encounter for fracture with nonunion
S02.612A	Fracture of condylar process of left mandible, initial encounter for closed fracture
S02.612B	Fracture of condylar process of left mandible, initial encounter for open fracture
S02.612K	Fracture of condylar process of left mandible, subsequent encounter for fracture with nonunion
S02.610A	Fracture of condylar process of mandible, unspecified side, initial encounter for closed fracture
S02.610B	Fracture of condylar process of mandible, unspecified side, initial encounter for open fracture
S02.610K	Fracture of condylar process of mandible, unspecified side, subsequent encounter for fracture with nonunion
S02.611A	Fracture of condylar process of right mandible, initial encounter for closed fracture
S02.611B	Fracture of condylar process of right mandible, initial encounter for open fracture
S02.611K	Fracture of condylar process of right mandible, subsequent encounter for fracture with nonunion
S02.632A	Fracture of coronoid process of left mandible, initial encounter for closed fracture
S02.632B	Fracture of coronoid process of left mandible, initial encounter for open fracture
S02.632K	Fracture of coronoid process of left mandible, subsequent encounter for fracture with nonunion
S02.630A	Fracture of coronoid process of mandible, unspecified side, initial encounter for closed fracture
S02.630B	Fracture of coronoid process of mandible, unspecified side, initial encounter for open fracture
S02.630K	Fracture of coronoid process of mandible, unspecified side, subsequent encounter for fracture with nonunion
S02.631A	Fracture of coronoid process of right mandible, initial encounter for closed fracture
S02.631B	Fracture of coronoid process of right mandible, initial encounter for open fracture
S02.631K	Fracture of coronoid process of right mandible, subsequent encounter for fracture with nonunion
M96.662	Fracture of femur following insertion of orthopedic implant, joint prosthesis, or bone plate, left leg

M96.661 Fracture of femur following insertion of orthopedic implant, joint prosthesis, or bone plate, right leg

M96.669 Fracture of femur following insertion of orthopedic implant, joint prosthesis, or bone plate, unspecified leg

M96.622 Fracture of humerus following insertion of orthopedic implant, joint prosthesis, or bone plate, left arm

M96.621 Fracture of humerus following insertion of orthopedic implant, joint prosthesis, or bone plate, right arm

M96.629 Fracture of humerus following insertion of orthopedic implant, joint prosthesis, or bone plate, unspecified arm

S02.842A Fracture of lateral orbital wall, left side, initial encounter for closed fracture

S02.842B Fracture of lateral orbital wall, left side, initial encounter for open fracture

S02.842K Fracture of lateral orbital wall, left side, subsequent encounter for fracture with nonunion

S02.841A Fracture of lateral orbital wall, right side, initial encounter for closed fracture

S02.841B Fracture of lateral orbital wall, right side, initial encounter for open fracture

S02.841K Fracture of lateral orbital wall, right side, subsequent encounter for fracture with nonunion

S02.849A Fracture of lateral orbital wall, unspecified side, initial encounter for closed fracture

S02.849B Fracture of lateral orbital wall, unspecified side, initial encounter for open fracture

S02.849K Fracture of lateral orbital wall, unspecified side, subsequent encounter for fracture with nonunion

S42.92XA Fracture of left shoulder girdle, part unspecified, initial encounter for closed fracture

S42.92XP Fracture of left shoulder girdle, part unspecified, subsequent encounter for fracture with malunion

S42.92XK Fracture of left shoulder girdle, part unspecified, subsequent encounter for fracture with nonunion

S02.69XA Fracture of mandible of other specified site, initial encounter for closed fracture

S02.69XB Fracture of mandible of other specified site, initial encounter for open fracture

S02.69XK Fracture of mandible of other specified site, subsequent encounter for fracture with nonunion

S02.609A Fracture of mandible, unspecified, initial encounter for closed fracture

S02.609B Fracture of mandible, unspecified, initial encounter for open fracture

S02.609K Fracture of mandible, unspecified, subsequent encounter for fracture with nonunion

S22.21XA Fracture of manubrium, initial encounter for closed fracture

S22.21XK Fracture of manubrium, subsequent encounter for fracture with nonunion

S02.832A Fracture of medial orbital wall, left side, initial encounter for closed fracture

S02.832B Fracture of medial orbital wall, left side, initial encounter for open fracture

S02.832K Fracture of medial orbital wall, left side, subsequent encounter for fracture with nonunion

S02.831A Fracture of medial orbital wall, right side, initial encounter for closed fracture

S02.831B Fracture of medial orbital wall, right side, initial encounter for open fracture

S02.831K Fracture of medial orbital wall, right side, subsequent encounter for fracture with nonunion

S02.839A Fracture of medial orbital wall, unspecified side, initial encounter for closed fracture

S02.839B Fracture of medial orbital wall, unspecified side, initial encounter for open fracture

S02.839K Fracture of medial orbital wall, unspecified side, subsequent encounter for fracture with nonunion

S02.2XXB Fracture of nasal bones, initial encounter for open fracture

S02.2XXK Fracture of nasal bones, subsequent encounter for fracture with nonunion

S12.9XXA Fracture of neck, unspecified, initial encounter

S22.32XA Fracture of one rib, left side, initial encounter for closed fracture

S22.32XK Fracture of one rib, left side, subsequent encounter for fracture with nonunion

S22.31XA Fracture of one rib, right side, initial encounter for closed fracture

S22.31XK Fracture of one rib, right side, subsequent encounter for fracture with nonunion

S22.39XA Fracture of one rib, unspecified side, initial encounter for closed fracture

S22.39XK Fracture of one rib, unspecified side, subsequent encounter for fracture with nonunion

S02.85XA Fracture of orbit, unspecified, initial encounter for closed fracture

S02.85XB Fracture of orbit, unspecified, initial encounter for open fracture

S02.85XK Fracture of orbit, unspecified, subsequent encounter for fracture with nonunion

S02.32XA Fracture of orbital floor, left side, initial encounter for closed fracture

S02.32XB Fracture of orbital floor, left side, initial encounter for open fracture

S02.32XK Fracture of orbital floor, left side, subsequent encounter for fracture with nonunion

S02.31XA Fracture of orbital floor, right side, initial encounter for closed fracture

S02.31XB Fracture of orbital floor, right side, initial encounter for open fracture

S02.31XK Fracture of orbital floor, right side, subsequent encounter for fracture with nonunion

S02.30XA Fracture of orbital floor, unspecified side, initial encounter for closed fracture

S02.30XB Fracture of orbital floor, unspecified side, initial encounter for open fracture

S02.30XK Fracture of orbital floor, unspecified side, subsequent encounter for fracture with nonunion

S02.122A Fracture of orbital roof, left side, initial encounter for closed fracture

S02.122K Fracture of orbital roof, left side, subsequent encounter for fracture with nonunion

S02.121A Fracture of orbital roof, right side, initial encounter for closed fracture

S02.121K Fracture of orbital roof, right side, subsequent encounter for fracture with nonunion

S02.129A Fracture of orbital roof, unspecified side, initial encounter for closed fracture

S02.129K Fracture of orbital roof, unspecified side, subsequent encounter for fracture with nonunion

M96.69 Fracture of other bone following insertion of orthopedic implant, joint prosthesis, or bone plate

S42.192B Fracture of other part of scapula, left shoulder, initial encounter for open fracture

S42.192P Fracture of other part of scapula, left shoulder, subsequent encounter for fracture with malunion

S42.192K Fracture of other part of scapula, left shoulder, subsequent encounter for fracture with nonunion

S42.191B Fracture of other part of scapula, right shoulder, initial encounter for open fracture

S42.191P Fracture of other part of scapula, right shoulder, subsequent encounter for fracture with malunion

S42.191K Fracture of other part of scapula, right shoulder, subsequent encounter for fracture with nonunion

S42.199B Fracture of other part of scapula, unspecified shoulder, initial encounter for open fracture

S42.199P Fracture of other part of scapula, unspecified shoulder, subsequent encounter for fracture with malunion

S42.199K Fracture of other part of scapula, unspecified shoulder, subsequent encounter for fracture with nonunion

S32.89XA Fracture of other parts of pelvis, initial encounter for closed fracture

S32.89XK Fracture of other parts of pelvis, subsequent encounter for fracture with nonunion

S02.82XA Fracture of other specified skull and facial bones, left side, initial encounter for closed fracture

S02.82XB Fracture of other specified skull and facial bones, left side, initial encounter for open fracture

S02.82XK Fracture of other specified skull and facial bones, left side, subsequent encounter for fracture with nonunion

S02.81XA Fracture of other specified skull and facial bones, right side, initial encounter for closed fracture

S02.81XB Fracture of other specified skull and facial bones, right side, initial encounter for open fracture

S02.81XK Fracture of other specified skull and facial bones, right side, subsequent encounter for fracture with nonunion

S02.80XA Fracture of other specified skull and facial bones, unspecified side, initial encounter for closed fracture

S02.80XB Fracture of other specified skull and facial bones, unspecified side, initial encounter for open fracture

S02.80XK Fracture of other specified skull and facial bones, unspecified side, subsequent encounter for fracture with nonunion

M96.65 Fracture of pelvis following insertion of orthopedic implant, joint prosthesis, or bone plate

M96.632 Fracture of radius or ulna following insertion of orthopedic implant, joint prosthesis, or bone plate, left arm

M96.631 Fracture of radius or ulna following insertion of orthopedic implant, joint prosthesis, or bone plate, right arm

M96.639 Fracture of radius or ulna following insertion of orthopedic implant, joint prosthesis, or bone plate, unspecified arm

S02.642A Fracture of ramus of left mandible, initial encounter for closed fracture

S02.642B Fracture of ramus of left mandible, initial encounter for open fracture

S02.642K Fracture of ramus of left mandible, subsequent encounter for fracture with nonunion

S02.640A Fracture of ramus of mandible, unspecified side, initial encounter for closed fracture

S02.640B Fracture of ramus of mandible, unspecified side, initial encounter for open fracture

S02.640K Fracture of ramus of mandible, unspecified side, subsequent encounter for fracture with nonunion

S02.641A Fracture of ramus of right mandible, initial encounter for closed fracture

S02.641B Fracture of ramus of right mandible, initial encounter for open fracture

S02.641K Fracture of ramus of right mandible, subsequent encounter for fracture with nonunion

S42.91XA Fracture of right shoulder girdle, part unspecified, initial encounter for closed fracture

S42.91XP Fracture of right shoulder girdle, part unspecified, subsequent encounter for fracture with malunion

S42.91XK Fracture of right shoulder girdle, part unspecified, subsequent encounter for fracture with nonunion

S02.622A Fracture of subcondylar process of left mandible, initial encounter for closed fracture

S02.622B Fracture of subcondylar process of left mandible, initial encounter for open fracture

S02.622K Fracture of subcondylar process of left mandible, subsequent encounter for fracture with nonunion

S02.620A Fracture of subcondylar process of mandible, unspecified side, initial encounter for closed fracture

S02.620B Fracture of subcondylar process of mandible, unspecified side, initial encounter for open fracture

S02.620K Fracture of subcondylar process of mandible, unspecified side, subsequent encounter for fracture with nonunion

S02.621A Fracture of subcondylar process of right mandible, initial encounter for closed fracture

S02.621B Fracture of subcondylar process of right mandible, initial encounter for open fracture

S02.621K Fracture of subcondylar process of right mandible, subsequent encounter for fracture with nonunion

S32.512A Fracture of superior rim of left pubis, initial encounter for closed fracture

S32.512K	Fracture of superior rim of left pubis, subsequent encounter for fracture with nonunion
S32.511A	Fracture of superior rim of right pubis, initial encounter for closed fracture
S32.511K	Fracture of superior rim of right pubis, subsequent encounter for fracture with nonunion
S32.519A	Fracture of superior rim of unspecified pubis, initial encounter for closed fracture
S32.519K	Fracture of superior rim of unspecified pubis, subsequent encounter for fracture with nonunion
S02.66XA	Fracture of symphysis of mandible, initial encounter for closed fracture
S02.66XB	Fracture of symphysis of mandible, initial encounter for open fracture
S02.66XK	Fracture of symphysis of mandible, subsequent encounter for fracture with nonunion
M96.672	Fracture of tibia or fibula following insertion of orthopedic implant, joint prosthesis, or bone plate, left leg
M96.671	Fracture of tibia or fibula following insertion of orthopedic implant, joint prosthesis, or bone plate, right leg
M96.679	Fracture of tibia or fibula following insertion of orthopedic implant, joint prosthesis, or bone plate, unspecified leg
S02.5XXK	Fracture of tooth (traumatic), subsequent encounter for fracture with nonunion
S62.102B	Fracture of unspecified carpal bone, left wrist, initial encounter for open fracture
S62.102P	Fracture of unspecified carpal bone, left wrist, subsequent encounter for fracture with malunion
S62.102K	Fracture of unspecified carpal bone, left wrist, subsequent encounter for fracture with nonunion
S62.101B	Fracture of unspecified carpal bone, right wrist, initial encounter for open fracture
S62.101P	Fracture of unspecified carpal bone, right wrist, subsequent encounter for fracture with malunion
S62.101K	Fracture of unspecified carpal bone, right wrist, subsequent encounter for fracture with nonunion
S62.109B	Fracture of unspecified carpal bone, unspecified wrist, initial encounter for open fracture
S62.109P	Fracture of unspecified carpal bone, unspecified wrist, subsequent encounter for fracture with malunion
S62.109K	Fracture of unspecified carpal bone, unspecified wrist, subsequent encounter for fracture with nonunion
S92.302B	Fracture of unspecified metatarsal bone(s), left foot, initial encounter for open fracture
S92.302P	Fracture of unspecified metatarsal bone(s), left foot, subsequent encounter for fracture with malunion
S92.302K	Fracture of unspecified metatarsal bone(s), left foot, subsequent encounter for fracture with nonunion
S92.301B	Fracture of unspecified metatarsal bone(s), right foot, initial encounter for open fracture
S92.301P	Fracture of unspecified metatarsal bone(s), right foot, subsequent encounter for fracture with malunion
S92.301K	Fracture of unspecified metatarsal bone(s), right foot, subsequent encounter for fracture with nonunion
S92.309B	Fracture of unspecified metatarsal bone(s), unspecified foot, initial encounter for open fracture
S92.309P	Fracture of unspecified metatarsal bone(s), unspecified foot, subsequent encounter for fracture with malunion
S92.309K	Fracture of unspecified metatarsal bone(s), unspecified foot, subsequent encounter for fracture with nonunion
S02.602A	Fracture of unspecified part of body of left mandible, initial encounter for closed fracture
S02.602B	Fracture of unspecified part of body of left mandible, initial encounter for open fracture
S02.602K	Fracture of unspecified part of body of left mandible, subsequent encounter for fracture with nonunion
S02.600A	Fracture of unspecified part of body of mandible, unspecified side, initial encounter for closed fracture
S02.600B	Fracture of unspecified part of body of mandible, unspecified side, initial encounter for open fracture
S02.600K	Fracture of unspecified part of body of mandible, unspecified side, subsequent encounter for fracture with nonunion
S02.601A	Fracture of unspecified part of body of right mandible, initial encounter for closed fracture
S02.601B	Fracture of unspecified part of body of right mandible, initial encounter for open fracture
S02.601K	Fracture of unspecified part of body of right mandible, subsequent encounter for fracture with nonunion
S42.002B	Fracture of unspecified part of left clavicle, initial encounter for open fracture
S42.002P	Fracture of unspecified part of left clavicle, subsequent encounter for fracture with malunion
S42.002K	Fracture of unspecified part of left clavicle, subsequent encounter for fracture with nonunion
S72.002P	Fracture of unspecified part of neck of left femur, subsequent encounter for closed fracture with malunion
S72.002K	Fracture of unspecified part of neck of left femur, subsequent encounter for closed fracture with nonunion
S72.002Q	Fracture of unspecified part of neck of left femur, subsequent encounter for open fracture type I or II with malunion
S72.002M	Fracture of unspecified part of neck of left femur, subsequent encounter for open fracture type I or II with nonunion
S72.002R	Fracture of unspecified part of neck of left femur, subsequent encounter for open fracture type IIIA, IIIB, or IIIC with malunion
S72.002N	Fracture of unspecified part of neck of left femur, subsequent encounter for open fracture type IIIA, IIIB, or IIIC with nonunion
S72.001P	Fracture of unspecified part of neck of right femur, subsequent encounter for closed fracture with malunion
S72.001K	Fracture of unspecified part of neck of right femur, subsequent encounter for closed fracture with nonunion
S72.001Q	Fracture of unspecified part of neck of right femur, subsequent encounter for open fracture type I or II with malunion
S72.001M	Fracture of unspecified part of neck of right femur, subsequent encounter for open fracture type I or II with nonunion
S72.001R	Fracture of unspecified part of neck of right femur, subsequent encounter for open fracture type IIIA, IIIB, or IIIC with malunion
S72.001N	Fracture of unspecified part of neck of right femur, subsequent encounter for open fracture type IIIA, IIIB, or IIIC with nonunion
S72.009P	Fracture of unspecified part of neck of unspecified femur, subsequent encounter for closed fracture with malunion
S72.009K	Fracture of unspecified part of neck of unspecified femur, subsequent encounter for closed fracture with nonunion
S72.009Q	Fracture of unspecified part of neck of unspecified femur, subsequent encounter for open fracture type I or II with malunion
S72.009M	Fracture of unspecified part of neck of unspecified femur, subsequent encounter for open fracture type I or II with nonunion
S72.009R	Fracture of unspecified part of neck of unspecified femur, subsequent encounter for open fracture type IIIA, IIIB, or IIIC with malunion
S72.009N	Fracture of unspecified part of neck of unspecified femur, subsequent encounter for open fracture type IIIA, IIIB, or IIIC with nonunion
S42.001B	Fracture of unspecified part of right clavicle, initial encounter for open fracture
S42.001P	Fracture of unspecified part of right clavicle, subsequent encounter for fracture with malunion
S42.001K	Fracture of unspecified part of right clavicle, subsequent encounter for fracture with nonunion
S42.102B	Fracture of unspecified part of scapula, left shoulder, initial encounter for open fracture
S42.102P	Fracture of unspecified part of scapula, left shoulder, subsequent encounter for fracture with malunion
S42.102K	Fracture of unspecified part of scapula, left shoulder, subsequent encounter for fracture with nonunion
S42.101B	Fracture of unspecified part of scapula, right shoulder, initial encounter for open fracture
S42.101P	Fracture of unspecified part of scapula, right shoulder, subsequent encounter for fracture with malunion
S42.101K	Fracture of unspecified part of scapula, right shoulder, subsequent encounter for fracture with nonunion
S42.109B	Fracture of unspecified part of scapula, unspecified shoulder, initial encounter for open fracture
S42.109P	Fracture of unspecified part of scapula, unspecified shoulder, subsequent encounter for fracture with malunion
S42.109K	Fracture of unspecified part of scapula, unspecified shoulder, subsequent encounter for fracture with nonunion
S42.009B	Fracture of unspecified part of unspecified clavicle, initial encounter for open fracture
S42.009P	Fracture of unspecified part of unspecified clavicle, subsequent encounter for fracture with malunion
S42.009K	Fracture of unspecified part of unspecified clavicle, subsequent encounter for fracture with nonunion
S32.9XXA	Fracture of unspecified parts of lumbosacral spine and pelvis, initial encounter for closed fracture
S32.9XXK	Fracture of unspecified parts of lumbosacral spine and pelvis, subsequent encounter for fracture with nonunion
S62.601B	Fracture of unspecified phalanx of left index finger, initial encounter for open fracture
S62.601P	Fracture of unspecified phalanx of left index finger, subsequent encounter for fracture with malunion
S62.601K	Fracture of unspecified phalanx of left index finger, subsequent encounter for fracture with nonunion
S62.607B	Fracture of unspecified phalanx of left little finger, initial encounter for open fracture
S62.607P	Fracture of unspecified phalanx of left little finger, subsequent encounter for fracture with malunion
S62.607K	Fracture of unspecified phalanx of left little finger, subsequent encounter for fracture with nonunion
S62.603B	Fracture of unspecified phalanx of left middle finger, initial encounter for open fracture
S62.603P	Fracture of unspecified phalanx of left middle finger, subsequent encounter for fracture with malunion
S62.603K	Fracture of unspecified phalanx of left middle finger, subsequent encounter for fracture with nonunion
S62.605B	Fracture of unspecified phalanx of left ring finger, initial encounter for open fracture
S62.605P	Fracture of unspecified phalanx of left ring finger, subsequent encounter for fracture with malunion
S62.605K	Fracture of unspecified phalanx of left ring finger, subsequent encounter for fracture with nonunion
S62.502B	Fracture of unspecified phalanx of left thumb, initial encounter for open fracture
S62.502P	Fracture of unspecified phalanx of left thumb, subsequent encounter for fracture with malunion
S62.502K	Fracture of unspecified phalanx of left thumb, subsequent encounter for fracture with nonunion

S62.608B	Fracture of unspecified phalanx of other finger, initial encounter for open fracture
S62.608P	Fracture of unspecified phalanx of other finger, subsequent encounter for fracture with malunion
S62.608K	Fracture of unspecified phalanx of other finger, subsequent encounter for fracture with nonunion
S62.600B	Fracture of unspecified phalanx of right index finger, initial encounter for open fracture
S62.600P	Fracture of unspecified phalanx of right index finger, subsequent encounter for fracture with malunion
S62.600K	Fracture of unspecified phalanx of right index finger, subsequent encounter for fracture with nonunion
S62.606B	Fracture of unspecified phalanx of right little finger, initial encounter for open fracture
S62.606P	Fracture of unspecified phalanx of right little finger, subsequent encounter for fracture with malunion
S62.606K	Fracture of unspecified phalanx of right little finger, subsequent encounter for fracture with nonunion
S62.602B	Fracture of unspecified phalanx of right middle finger, initial encounter for open fracture
S62.602P	Fracture of unspecified phalanx of right middle finger, subsequent encounter for fracture with malunion
S62.602K	Fracture of unspecified phalanx of right middle finger, subsequent encounter for fracture with nonunion
S62.604B	Fracture of unspecified phalanx of right ring finger, initial encounter for open fracture
S62.604P	Fracture of unspecified phalanx of right ring finger, subsequent encounter for fracture with malunion
S62.604K	Fracture of unspecified phalanx of right ring finger, subsequent encounter for fracture with nonunion
S62.501B	Fracture of unspecified phalanx of right thumb, initial encounter for open fracture
S62.501P	Fracture of unspecified phalanx of right thumb, subsequent encounter for fracture with malunion
S62.501K	Fracture of unspecified phalanx of right thumb, subsequent encounter for fracture with nonunion
S62.609B	Fracture of unspecified phalanx of unspecified finger, initial encounter for open fracture
S62.609P	Fracture of unspecified phalanx of unspecified finger, subsequent encounter for fracture with malunion
S62.609K	Fracture of unspecified phalanx of unspecified finger, subsequent encounter for fracture with nonunion
S62.509B	Fracture of unspecified phalanx of unspecified thumb, initial encounter for open fracture
S62.509P	Fracture of unspecified phalanx of unspecified thumb, subsequent encounter for fracture with malunion
S62.509K	Fracture of unspecified phalanx of unspecified thumb, subsequent encounter for fracture with nonunion
S42.90XA	Fracture of unspecified shoulder girdle, part unspecified, initial encounter for closed fracture
S42.90XP	Fracture of unspecified shoulder girdle, part unspecified, subsequent encounter for fracture with malunion
S42.90XK	Fracture of unspecified shoulder girdle, part unspecified, subsequent encounter for fracture with nonunion
S92.202B	Fracture of unspecified tarsal bone(s) of left foot, initial encounter for open fracture
S92.202P	Fracture of unspecified tarsal bone(s) of left foot, subsequent encounter for fracture with malunion
S92.202K	Fracture of unspecified tarsal bone(s) of left foot, subsequent encounter for fracture with nonunion
S92.201B	Fracture of unspecified tarsal bone(s) of right foot, initial encounter for open fracture
S92.201P	Fracture of unspecified tarsal bone(s) of right foot, subsequent encounter for fracture with malunion
S92.201K	Fracture of unspecified tarsal bone(s) of right foot, subsequent encounter for fracture with nonunion
S92.209B	Fracture of unspecified tarsal bone(s) of unspecified foot, initial encounter for open fracture
S92.209P	Fracture of unspecified tarsal bone(s) of unspecified foot, subsequent encounter for fracture with malunion
S92.209K	Fracture of unspecified tarsal bone(s) of unspecified foot, subsequent encounter for fracture with nonunion
S02.0XXA	Fracture of vault of skull, initial encounter for closed fracture
S02.0XXK	Fracture of vault of skull, subsequent encounter for fracture with nonunion
S22.24XA	Fracture of xiphoid process, initial encounter for closed fracture
S22.24XK	Fracture of xiphoid process, subsequent encounter for fracture with nonunion
Q01.0	Frontal encephalocele
T34.3XXA	Frostbite with tissue necrosis of abdominal wall, lower back and pelvis, initial encounter
T34.812A	Frostbite with tissue necrosis of left ankle, initial encounter
T34.42XA	Frostbite with tissue necrosis of left arm, initial encounter
T34.012A	Frostbite with tissue necrosis of left ear, initial encounter
T34.532A	Frostbite with tissue necrosis of left finger(s), initial encounter
T34.822A	Frostbite with tissue necrosis of left foot, initial encounter
T34.522A	Frostbite with tissue necrosis of left hand, initial encounter
T34.62XA	Frostbite with tissue necrosis of left hip and thigh, initial encounter
T34.72XA	Frostbite with tissue necrosis of left knee and lower leg, initial encounter
T34.832A	Frostbite with tissue necrosis of left toe(s), initial encounter
T34.512A	Frostbite with tissue necrosis of left wrist, initial encounter
T34.1XXA	Frostbite with tissue necrosis of neck, initial encounter

T34.02XA	Frostbite with tissue necrosis of nose, initial encounter
T34.09XA	Frostbite with tissue necrosis of other part of head, initial encounter
T34.99XA	Frostbite with tissue necrosis of other sites, initial encounter
T34.811A	Frostbite with tissue necrosis of right ankle, initial encounter
T34.41XA	Frostbite with tissue necrosis of right arm, initial encounter
T34.011A	Frostbite with tissue necrosis of right ear, initial encounter
T34.531A	Frostbite with tissue necrosis of right finger(s), initial encounter
T34.821A	Frostbite with tissue necrosis of right foot, initial encounter
T34.521A	Frostbite with tissue necrosis of right hand, initial encounter
T34.61XA	Frostbite with tissue necrosis of right hip and thigh, initial encounter
T34.71XA	Frostbite with tissue necrosis of right knee and lower leg, initial encounter
T34.831A	Frostbite with tissue necrosis of right toe(s), initial encounter
T34.511A	Frostbite with tissue necrosis of right wrist, initial encounter
T34.2XXA	Frostbite with tissue necrosis of thorax, initial encounter
T34.819A	Frostbite with tissue necrosis of unspecified ankle, initial encounter
T34.40XA	Frostbite with tissue necrosis of unspecified arm, initial encounter
T34.019A	Frostbite with tissue necrosis of unspecified ear, initial encounter
T34.539A	Frostbite with tissue necrosis of unspecified finger(s), initial encounter
T34.829A	Frostbite with tissue necrosis of unspecified foot, initial encounter
T34.529A	Frostbite with tissue necrosis of unspecified hand, initial encounter
T34.60XA	Frostbite with tissue necrosis of unspecified hip and thigh, initial encounter
T34.70XA	Frostbite with tissue necrosis of unspecified knee and lower leg, initial encounter
T34.90XA	Frostbite with tissue necrosis of unspecified sites, initial encounter
T34.839A	Frostbite with tissue necrosis of unspecified toe(s), initial encounter
T34.519A	Frostbite with tissue necrosis of unspecified wrist, initial encounter
E74.21	Galactosemia
S52.372A	Galeazzi's fracture of left radius, initial encounter for closed fracture
S52.372P	Galeazzi's fracture of left radius, subsequent encounter for closed fracture with malunion
S52.372K	Galeazzi's fracture of left radius, subsequent encounter for closed fracture with nonunion
S52.372Q	Galeazzi's fracture of left radius, subsequent encounter for open fracture type I or II with malunion
S52.372M	Galeazzi's fracture of left radius, subsequent encounter for open fracture type I or II with nonunion
S52.372R	Galeazzi's fracture of left radius, subsequent encounter for open fracture type IIIA, IIIB, or IIIC with malunion
S52.372N	Galeazzi's fracture of left radius, subsequent encounter for open fracture type IIIA, IIIB, or IIIC with nonunion
S52.371A	Galeazzi's fracture of right radius, initial encounter for closed fracture
S52.371P	Galeazzi's fracture of right radius, subsequent encounter for closed fracture with malunion
S52.371K	Galeazzi's fracture of right radius, subsequent encounter for closed fracture with nonunion
S52.371Q	Galeazzi's fracture of right radius, subsequent encounter for open fracture type I or II with malunion
S52.371M	Galeazzi's fracture of right radius, subsequent encounter for open fracture type I or II with nonunion
S52.371R	Galeazzi's fracture of right radius, subsequent encounter for open fracture type IIIA, IIIB, or IIIC with malunion
S52.371N	Galeazzi's fracture of right radius, subsequent encounter for open fracture type IIIA, IIIB, or IIIC with nonunion
S52.379A	Galeazzi's fracture of unspecified radius, initial encounter for closed fracture
S52.379P	Galeazzi's fracture of unspecified radius, subsequent encounter for closed fracture with malunion
S52.379K	Galeazzi's fracture of unspecified radius, subsequent encounter for closed fracture with nonunion
S52.379Q	Galeazzi's fracture of unspecified radius, subsequent encounter for open fracture type I or II with malunion
S52.379M	Galeazzi's fracture of unspecified radius, subsequent encounter for open fracture type I or II with nonunion
S52.379R	Galeazzi's fracture of unspecified radius, subsequent encounter for open fracture type IIIA, IIIB, or IIIC with malunion
S52.379N	Galeazzi's fracture of unspecified radius, subsequent encounter for open fracture type IIIA, IIIB, or IIIC with nonunion
K56.3	Gallstone ileus
B56.0	Gambiense trypanosomiasis
I96	Gangrene, not elsewhere classified
T17.510A	Gastric contents in bronchus causing asphyxiation, initial encounter
T17.518A	Gastric contents in bronchus causing other injury, initial encounter
T17.810A	Gastric contents in other parts of respiratory tract causing asphyxiation, initial encounter
T17.818A	Gastric contents in other parts of respiratory tract causing other injury, initial encounter
T17.410A	Gastric contents in trachea causing asphyxiation, initial encounter
T17.418A	Gastric contents in trachea causing other injury, initial encounter
K52.0	Gastroenteritis and colitis due to radiation
A22.2	Gastrointestinal anthrax
K92.2	Gastrointestinal hemorrhage, unspecified
K92.81	Gastrointestinal mucositis (ulcerative)
C49.A1	Gastrointestinal stromal tumor of esophagus
C49.A4	Gastrointestinal stromal tumor of large intestine
C49.A9	Gastrointestinal stromal tumor of other sites
C49.A5	Gastrointestinal stromal tumor of rectum
C49.A3	Gastrointestinal stromal tumor of small intestine
C49.A2	Gastrointestinal stromal tumor of stomach
C49.A0	Gastrointestinal stromal tumor, unspecified site
A21.3	Gastrointestinal tularemia
K94.22	Gastrostomy infection

K94.23	Gastrostomy malfunction
A52.17	General paresis
A21.7	Generalized tularemia
O04.5	Genital tract and pelvic infection following (induced) termination of pregnancy
O03.5	Genital tract and pelvic infection following complete or unspecified spontaneous abortion
O08.0	Genital tract and pelvic infection following ectopic and molar pregnancy
O07.0	Genital tract and pelvic infection following failed attempted termination of pregnancy
O03.0	Genital tract and pelvic infection following incomplete spontaneous abortion
B48.3	Geotrichosis
A81.82	Gerstmann-Straussler-Scheinker syndrome
O12.21	Gestational edema with proteinuria, first trimester
O12.22	Gestational edema with proteinuria, second trimester
O12.23	Gestational edema with proteinuria, third trimester
O12.11	Gestational proteinuria, first trimester
O12.12	Gestational proteinuria, second trimester
O12.13	Gestational proteinuria, third trimester
A07.1	Giardiasis [lambliasis]
A24.0	Glanders
E76.9	Glucosaminoglycan metabolism disorder, unspecified
E71.313	Glutaric aciduria type II
E74.00	Glycogen storage disease, unspecified
E75.00	GM2 gangliosidosis, unspecified
A54.42	Gonococcal arthritis
A54.82	Gonococcal brain abscess
A54.03	Gonococcal cervicitis, unspecified
A54.31	Gonococcal conjunctivitis
A54.01	Gonococcal cystitis and urethritis, unspecified
A54.24	Gonococcal female pelvic inflammatory disease
A54.83	Gonococcal heart infection
A54.30	Gonococcal infection of eye, unspecified
A54.21	Gonococcal infection of kidney and ureter
A54.1	Gonococcal infection of lower genitourinary tract with periurethral and accessory gland abscess
A54.00	Gonococcal infection of lower genitourinary tract, unspecified
A54.40	Gonococcal infection of musculoskeletal system, unspecified
A54.23	Gonococcal infection of other male genital organs
A54.49	Gonococcal infection of other musculoskeletal tissue
A54.9	Gonococcal infection, unspecified
A54.32	Gonococcal iridocyclitis
A54.33	Gonococcal keratitis
A54.43	Gonococcal osteomyelitis
A54.85	Gonococcal peritonitis
A54.84	Gonococcal pneumonia
A54.22	Gonococcal prostatitis
A54.41	Gonococcal spondylopathy
A54.02	Gonococcal vulvovaginitis, unspecified
O98.22	Gonorrhea complicating childbirth
O98.211	Gonorrhea complicating pregnancy, first trimester
O98.212	Gonorrhea complicating pregnancy, second trimester
O98.213	Gonorrhea complicating pregnancy, third trimester
O98.23	Gonorrhea complicating the puerperium
D89.813	Graft-versus-host disease, unspecified
S42.312A	Greenstick fracture of shaft of humerus, left arm, initial encounter for closed fracture
S42.312P	Greenstick fracture of shaft of humerus, left arm, subsequent encounter for fracture with malunion
S42.312K	Greenstick fracture of shaft of humerus, left arm, subsequent encounter for fracture with nonunion
S42.311A	Greenstick fracture of shaft of humerus, right arm, initial encounter for closed fracture
S42.311P	Greenstick fracture of shaft of humerus, right arm, subsequent encounter for fracture with malunion
S42.311K	Greenstick fracture of shaft of humerus, right arm, subsequent encounter for fracture with nonunion
S42.319A	Greenstick fracture of shaft of humerus, unspecified arm, initial encounter for closed fracture
S42.319P	Greenstick fracture of shaft of humerus, unspecified arm, subsequent encounter for fracture with malunion
S42.319K	Greenstick fracture of shaft of humerus, unspecified arm, subsequent encounter for fracture with nonunion
S52.212A	Greenstick fracture of shaft of left ulna, initial encounter for closed fracture
S52.212P	Greenstick fracture of shaft of left ulna, subsequent encounter for fracture with malunion
S52.212K	Greenstick fracture of shaft of left ulna, subsequent encounter for fracture with nonunion
S52.312A	Greenstick fracture of shaft of radius, left arm, initial encounter for closed fracture
S52.312P	Greenstick fracture of shaft of radius, left arm, subsequent encounter for fracture with malunion
S52.312K	Greenstick fracture of shaft of radius, left arm, subsequent encounter for fracture with nonunion
S52.311A	Greenstick fracture of shaft of radius, right arm, initial encounter for closed fracture
S52.311P	Greenstick fracture of shaft of radius, right arm, subsequent encounter for fracture with malunion
S52.311K	Greenstick fracture of shaft of radius, right arm, subsequent encounter for fracture with nonunion
S52.319A	Greenstick fracture of shaft of radius, unspecified arm, initial encounter for closed fracture
S52.319P	Greenstick fracture of shaft of radius, unspecified arm, subsequent encounter for fracture with malunion
S52.319K	Greenstick fracture of shaft of radius, unspecified arm, subsequent encounter for fracture with nonunion
S52.211A	Greenstick fracture of shaft of right ulna, initial encounter for closed fracture
S52.211P	Greenstick fracture of shaft of right ulna, subsequent encounter for fracture with malunion
S52.211K	Greenstick fracture of shaft of right ulna, subsequent encounter for fracture with nonunion
S52.219A	Greenstick fracture of shaft of unspecified ulna, initial encounter for closed fracture
S52.219P	Greenstick fracture of shaft of unspecified ulna, subsequent encounter for fracture with malunion
S52.219K	Greenstick fracture of shaft of unspecified ulna, subsequent encounter for fracture with nonunion
P93.0	Grey baby syndrome
G61.0	Guillain-Barre syndrome
C91.40	Hairy cell leukemia not having achieved remission
C91.42	Hairy cell leukemia, in relapse
C91.41	Hairy cell leukemia, in remission
G23.0	Hallervorden-Spatz disease
R44.3	Hallucinations, unspecified
F16.150	Hallucinogen abuse with hallucinogen-induced psychotic disorder with delusions
F16.151	Hallucinogen abuse with hallucinogen-induced psychotic disorder with hallucinations
F16.121	Hallucinogen abuse with intoxication with delirium
F16.283	Hallucinogen dependence with hallucinogen persisting perception disorder (flashbacks)
F16.280	Hallucinogen dependence with hallucinogen-induced anxiety disorder
F16.250	Hallucinogen dependence with hallucinogen-induced psychotic disorder with delusions
F16.251	Hallucinogen dependence with hallucinogen-induced psychotic disorder with hallucinations
F16.259	Hallucinogen dependence with hallucinogen-induced psychotic disorder, unspecified
F16.221	Hallucinogen dependence with intoxication with delirium
F16.288	Hallucinogen dependence with other hallucinogen-induced disorder
F16.20	Hallucinogen dependence, uncomplicated
F16.950	Hallucinogen use, unspecified with hallucinogen-induced psychotic disorder with delusions
F16.951	Hallucinogen use, unspecified with hallucinogen-induced psychotic disorder with hallucinations
F16.921	Hallucinogen use, unspecified with intoxication with delirium
B33.4	Hantavirus (cardio)-pulmonary syndrome [HPS] [HCPS]
E72.02	Hartnup's disease
Z94.3	Heart and lungs transplant status
T86.22	Heart transplant failure
T86.23	Heart transplant infection
T86.21	Heart transplant rejection
Z94.1	Heart transplant status
T86.32	Heart-lung transplant failure
T86.33	Heart-lung transplant infection
T86.31	Heart-lung transplant rejection
T67.01XA	Heatstroke and sunstroke, initial encounter
C88.2	Heavy chain disease
M25.072	Hemarthrosis, left ankle
M25.022	Hemarthrosis, left elbow
M25.075	Hemarthrosis, left foot
M25.042	Hemarthrosis, left hand
M25.052	Hemarthrosis, left hip
M25.062	Hemarthrosis, left knee
M25.012	Hemarthrosis, left shoulder
M25.032	Hemarthrosis, left wrist
M25.08	Hemarthrosis, other specified site
M25.071	Hemarthrosis, right ankle
M25.021	Hemarthrosis, right elbow
M25.074	Hemarthrosis, right foot
M25.041	Hemarthrosis, right hand
M25.051	Hemarthrosis, right hip
M25.061	Hemarthrosis, right knee
M25.011	Hemarthrosis, right shoulder
M25.031	Hemarthrosis, right wrist
M25.073	Hemarthrosis, unspecified ankle
M25.029	Hemarthrosis, unspecified elbow
M25.076	Hemarthrosis, unspecified foot
M25.049	Hemarthrosis, unspecified hand
M25.059	Hemarthrosis, unspecified hip
M25.00	Hemarthrosis, unspecified joint
M25.069	Hemarthrosis, unspecified knee
M25.019	Hemarthrosis, unspecified shoulder
M25.039	Hemarthrosis, unspecified wrist
K92.0	Hematemesis
I69.352	Hemiplegia and hemiparesis following cerebral infarction affecting left dominant side
I69.354	Hemiplegia and hemiparesis following cerebral infarction affecting left non-dominant side

I69.351	Hemiplegia and hemiparesis following cerebral infarction affecting right dominant side
I69.353	Hemiplegia and hemiparesis following cerebral infarction affecting right non-dominant side
I69.359	Hemiplegia and hemiparesis following cerebral infarction affecting unspecified side
I69.152	Hemiplegia and hemiparesis following nontraumatic intracerebral hemorrhage affecting left dominant side
I69.154	Hemiplegia and hemiparesis following nontraumatic intracerebral hemorrhage affecting left non-dominant side
I69.151	Hemiplegia and hemiparesis following nontraumatic intracerebral hemorrhage affecting right dominant side
I69.153	Hemiplegia and hemiparesis following nontraumatic intracerebral hemorrhage affecting right non-dominant side
I69.159	Hemiplegia and hemiparesis following nontraumatic intracerebral hemorrhage affecting unspecified side
I69.052	Hemiplegia and hemiparesis following nontraumatic subarachnoid hemorrhage affecting left dominant side
I69.054	Hemiplegia and hemiparesis following nontraumatic subarachnoid hemorrhage affecting left non-dominant side
I69.051	Hemiplegia and hemiparesis following nontraumatic subarachnoid hemorrhage affecting right dominant side
I69.053	Hemiplegia and hemiparesis following nontraumatic subarachnoid hemorrhage affecting right non-dominant side
I69.059	Hemiplegia and hemiparesis following nontraumatic subarachnoid hemorrhage affecting unspecified side
I69.852	Hemiplegia and hemiparesis following other cerebrovascular disease affecting left dominant side
I69.854	Hemiplegia and hemiparesis following other cerebrovascular disease affecting left non-dominant side
I69.851	Hemiplegia and hemiparesis following other cerebrovascular disease affecting right dominant side
I69.853	Hemiplegia and hemiparesis following other cerebrovascular disease affecting right non-dominant side
I69.859	Hemiplegia and hemiparesis following other cerebrovascular disease affecting unspecified side
I69.252	Hemiplegia and hemiparesis following other nontraumatic intracranial hemorrhage affecting left dominant side
I69.254	Hemiplegia and hemiparesis following other nontraumatic intracranial hemorrhage affecting left non-dominant side
I69.251	Hemiplegia and hemiparesis following other nontraumatic intracranial hemorrhage affecting right dominant side
I69.253	Hemiplegia and hemiparesis following other nontraumatic intracranial hemorrhage affecting right non-dominant side
I69.259	Hemiplegia and hemiparesis following other nontraumatic intracranial hemorrhage affecting unspecified side
I69.952	Hemiplegia and hemiparesis following unspecified cerebrovascular disease affecting left dominant side
I69.954	Hemiplegia and hemiparesis following unspecified cerebrovascular disease affecting left non-dominant side
I69.951	Hemiplegia and hemiparesis following unspecified cerebrovascular disease affecting right dominant side
I69.953	Hemiplegia and hemiparesis following unspecified cerebrovascular disease affecting right non-dominant side
I69.959	Hemiplegia and hemiparesis following unspecified cerebrovascular disease affecting unspecified side
G81.92	Hemiplegia, unspecified affecting left dominant side
G81.94	Hemiplegia, unspecified affecting left nondominant side
G81.91	Hemiplegia, unspecified affecting right dominant side
G81.93	Hemiplegia, unspecified affecting right nondominant side
G81.90	Hemiplegia, unspecified affecting unspecified side
T80.919A	Hemolytic transfusion reaction, unspecified incompatibility, unspecified as acute or delayed, initial encounter
I23.0	Hemopericardium as current complication following acute myocardial infarction
I31.2	Hemopericardium, not elsewhere classified
D76.1	Hemophagocytic lymphohistiocytosis
D76.2	Hemophagocytic syndrome, infection-associated
R04.2	Hemoptysis
T82.837A	Hemorrhage due to cardiac prosthetic devices, implants and grafts, initial encounter
T83.83XA	Hemorrhage due to genitourinary prosthetic devices, implants and grafts, initial encounter
T84.83XA	Hemorrhage due to internal orthopedic prosthetic devices, implants and grafts, initial encounter
T85.830A	Hemorrhage due to nervous system prosthetic devices, implants and grafts, initial encounter
T85.830D	Hemorrhage due to nervous system prosthetic devices, implants and grafts, subsequent encounter
T82.838A	Hemorrhage due to vascular prosthetic devices, implants and grafts, initial encounter
R04.89	Hemorrhage from other sites in respiratory passages
R04.9	Hemorrhage from respiratory passages, unspecified
J95.01	Hemorrhage from tracheostomy stoma
O20.9	Hemorrhage in early pregnancy, unspecified
K62.5	Hemorrhage of anus and rectum
H31.413	Hemorrhagic choroidal detachment, bilateral
H31.412	Hemorrhagic choroidal detachment, left eye
H31.411	Hemorrhagic choroidal detachment, right eye
H31.419	Hemorrhagic choroidal detachment, unspecified eye
H35.733	Hemorrhagic detachment of retinal pigment epithelium, bilateral

H35.732	Hemorrhagic detachment of retinal pigment epithelium, left eye
H35.731	Hemorrhagic detachment of retinal pigment epithelium, right eye
H35.739	Hemorrhagic detachment of retinal pigment epithelium, unspecified eye
P53	Hemorrhagic disease of newborn
D68.32	Hemorrhagic disorder due to extrinsic circulating anticoagulants
A98.5	Hemorrhagic fever with renal syndrome
O22.41	Hemorrhoids in pregnancy, first trimester
O22.42	Hemorrhoids in pregnancy, second trimester
O22.43	Hemorrhoids in pregnancy, third trimester
O22.40	Hemorrhoids in pregnancy, unspecified trimester
O87.2	Hemorrhoids in the puerperium
J94.2	Hemothorax
B15.9	Hepatitis A without hepatic coma
C22.2	Hepatoblastoma
C86.1	Hepatosplenic T-cell lymphoma
G11.9	Hereditary ataxia, unspecified
D68.2	Hereditary deficiency of other clotting factors
E80.0	Hereditary erythropoietic porphyria
D68.1	Hereditary factor XI deficiency
D58.9	Hereditary hemolytic anemia, unspecified
D80.0	Hereditary hypogammaglobulinemia
N07.4	Hereditary nephropathy, not elsewhere classified with diffuse endocapillary proliferative glomerulonephritis
N07.2	Hereditary nephropathy, not elsewhere classified with diffuse membranous glomerulonephritis
N07.3	Hereditary nephropathy, not elsewhere classified with diffuse mesangial proliferative glomerulonephritis
N07.5	Hereditary nephropathy, not elsewhere classified with diffuse mesangiocapillary glomerulonephritis
G11.4	Hereditary spastic paraplegia
E85.2	Heredofamilial amyloidosis, unspecified
E70.331	Hermansky-Pudlak syndrome
B00.53	Herpesviral conjunctivitis
B00.2	Herpesviral gingivostomatitis and pharyngotonsillitis
B00.81	Herpesviral hepatitis
B00.51	Herpesviral iridocyclitis
B00.52	Herpesviral keratitis
B00.50	Herpesviral ocular disease, unspecified
Q43.1	Hirschsprung's disease
E70.41	Histidinemia
C96.A	Histiocytic sarcoma
C81.99	Hodgkin lymphoma, unspecified, extranodal and solid organ sites
C81.93	Hodgkin lymphoma, unspecified, intra-abdominal lymph nodes
C81.96	Hodgkin lymphoma, unspecified, intrapelvic lymph nodes
C81.92	Hodgkin lymphoma, unspecified, intrathoracic lymph nodes
C81.94	Hodgkin lymphoma, unspecified, lymph nodes of axilla and upper limb
C81.91	Hodgkin lymphoma, unspecified, lymph nodes of head, face, and neck
C81.95	Hodgkin lymphoma, unspecified, lymph nodes of inguinal region and lower limb
C81.98	Hodgkin lymphoma, unspecified, lymph nodes of multiple sites
C81.97	Hodgkin lymphoma, unspecified, spleen
C81.90	Hodgkin lymphoma, unspecified, unspecified site
E72.11	Homocystinuria
B76.9	Hookworm disease, unspecified
B20	Human immunodeficiency virus [HIV] disease
O98.72	Human immunodeficiency virus [HIV] disease complicating childbirth
O98.711	Human immunodeficiency virus [HIV] disease complicating pregnancy, first trimester
O98.712	Human immunodeficiency virus [HIV] disease complicating pregnancy, second trimester
O98.713	Human immunodeficiency virus [HIV] disease complicating pregnancy, third trimester
O98.73	Human immunodeficiency virus [HIV] disease complicating the puerperium
B97.35	Human immunodeficiency virus, type 2 [HIV 2] as the cause of diseases classified elsewhere
B97.33	Human T-cell lymphotrophic virus, type I [HTLV-I] as the cause of diseases classified elsewhere
B97.34	Human T-cell lymphotrophic virus, type II [HTLV-II] as the cause of diseases classified elsewhere
G10	Huntington's disease
E76.02	Hurler-Scheie syndrome
E76.01	Hurler's syndrome
A50.52	Hutchinson's teeth
A50.53	Hutchinson's triad
G91.9	Hydrocephalus, unspecified
N13.2	Hydronephrosis with renal and ureteral calculous obstruction
N13.1	Hydronephrosis with ureteral stricture, not elsewhere classified
N13.0	Hydronephrosis with ureteropelvic junction obstruction
K82.1	Hydrops of gallbladder
N13.4	Hydroureter
B71.0	Hymenolepiasis
E22.9	Hyperfunction of pituitary gland, unspecified
Q79.62	Hypermobile Ehlers-Danlos syndrome
E87.0	Hyperosmolality and hypernatremia
E22.1	Hyperprolactinemia
M31.0	Hypersensitivity angiitis
J67.8	Hypersensitivity pneumonitis due to other organic dusts
J67.9	Hypersensitivity pneumonitis due to unspecified organic dust
N98.1	Hyperstimulation of ovaries

I12.0	Hypertensive chronic kidney disease with stage 5 chronic kidney disease or end stage renal disease
I16.9	Hypertensive crisis, unspecified
I16.1	Hypertensive emergency
I67.4	Hypertensive encephalopathy
I13.0	Hypertensive heart and chronic kidney disease with heart failure and stage 1 through stage 4 chronic kidney disease, or unspecified chronic kidney disease
I13.2	Hypertensive heart and chronic kidney disease with heart failure and with stage 5 chronic kidney disease, or end stage renal disease
I13.11	Hypertensive heart and chronic kidney disease without heart failure, with stage 5 chronic kidney disease, or end stage renal disease
E87.1	Hypo-osmolality and hyponatremia
E23.0	Hypopituitarism
Q25.42	Hypoplasia of aorta
J18.2	Hypostatic pneumonia, unspecified organism
P91.60	Hypoxic ischemic encephalopathy [HIE], unspecified
M87.09	Idiopathic aseptic necrosis of bone, multiple sites
M87.08	Idiopathic aseptic necrosis of bone, other site
M87.072	Idiopathic aseptic necrosis of left ankle
M87.038	Idiopathic aseptic necrosis of left carpus
M87.052	Idiopathic aseptic necrosis of left femur
M87.065	Idiopathic aseptic necrosis of left fibula
M87.045	Idiopathic aseptic necrosis of left finger(s)
M87.075	Idiopathic aseptic necrosis of left foot
M87.042	Idiopathic aseptic necrosis of left hand
M87.022	Idiopathic aseptic necrosis of left humerus
M87.032	Idiopathic aseptic necrosis of left radius
M87.012	Idiopathic aseptic necrosis of left shoulder
M87.062	Idiopathic aseptic necrosis of left tibia
M87.078	Idiopathic aseptic necrosis of left toe(s)
M87.035	Idiopathic aseptic necrosis of left ulna
M87.050	Idiopathic aseptic necrosis of pelvis
M87.071	Idiopathic aseptic necrosis of right ankle
M87.037	Idiopathic aseptic necrosis of right carpus
M87.051	Idiopathic aseptic necrosis of right femur
M87.064	Idiopathic aseptic necrosis of right fibula
M87.044	Idiopathic aseptic necrosis of right finger(s)
M87.074	Idiopathic aseptic necrosis of right foot
M87.041	Idiopathic aseptic necrosis of right hand
M87.021	Idiopathic aseptic necrosis of right humerus
M87.031	Idiopathic aseptic necrosis of right radius
M87.011	Idiopathic aseptic necrosis of right shoulder
M87.061	Idiopathic aseptic necrosis of right tibia
M87.077	Idiopathic aseptic necrosis of right toe(s)
M87.034	Idiopathic aseptic necrosis of right ulna
M87.073	Idiopathic aseptic necrosis of unspecified ankle
M87.00	Idiopathic aseptic necrosis of unspecified bone
M87.039	Idiopathic aseptic necrosis of unspecified carpus
M87.059	Idiopathic aseptic necrosis of unspecified femur
M87.066	Idiopathic aseptic necrosis of unspecified fibula
M87.046	Idiopathic aseptic necrosis of unspecified finger(s)
M87.076	Idiopathic aseptic necrosis of unspecified foot
M87.043	Idiopathic aseptic necrosis of unspecified hand
M87.029	Idiopathic aseptic necrosis of unspecified humerus
M87.033	Idiopathic aseptic necrosis of unspecified radius
M87.019	Idiopathic aseptic necrosis of unspecified shoulder
M87.063	Idiopathic aseptic necrosis of unspecified tibia
M87.079	Idiopathic aseptic necrosis of unspecified toe(s)
M87.036	Idiopathic aseptic necrosis of unspecified ulna
G24.2	Idiopathic nonfamilial dystonia
J84.03	Idiopathic pulmonary hemosiderosis
K56.7	Ileus, unspecified
T69.022A	Immersion foot, left foot, initial encounter
T69.021A	Immersion foot, right foot, initial encounter
T69.029A	Immersion foot, unspecified foot, initial encounter
D69.3	Immune thrombocytopenic purpura
D80.5	Immunodeficiency with increased immunoglobulin M [IgM]
D80.9	Immunodeficiency with predominantly antibody defects, unspecified
D84.9	Immunodeficiency, unspecified
C88.3	Immunoproliferative small intestinal disease
S42.448A	Incarcerated fracture (avulsion) of medial epicondyle of left humerus, initial encounter for closed fracture
S42.448P	Incarcerated fracture (avulsion) of medial epicondyle of left humerus, subsequent encounter for fracture with malunion
S42.448K	Incarcerated fracture (avulsion) of medial epicondyle of left humerus, subsequent encounter for fracture with nonunion
S42.447A	Incarcerated fracture (avulsion) of medial epicondyle of right humerus, initial encounter for closed fracture
S42.447P	Incarcerated fracture (avulsion) of medial epicondyle of right humerus, subsequent encounter for fracture with malunion
S42.447K	Incarcerated fracture (avulsion) of medial epicondyle of right humerus, subsequent encounter for fracture with nonunion
S42.449A	Incarcerated fracture (avulsion) of medial epicondyle of unspecified humerus, initial encounter for closed fracture
S42.449P	Incarcerated fracture (avulsion) of medial epicondyle of unspecified humerus, subsequent encounter for fracture with malunion
S42.449K	Incarcerated fracture (avulsion) of medial epicondyle of unspecified humerus, subsequent encounter for fracture with nonunion
K43.0	Incisional hernia with obstruction, without gangrene
M84.752A	Incomplete atypical femoral fracture, left leg, initial encounter for fracture
M84.752P	Incomplete atypical femoral fracture, left leg, subsequent encounter for fracture with malunion
M84.752K	Incomplete atypical femoral fracture, left leg, subsequent encounter for fracture with nonunion
M84.751A	Incomplete atypical femoral fracture, right leg, initial encounter for fracture
M84.751P	Incomplete atypical femoral fracture, right leg, subsequent encounter for fracture with malunion
M84.751K	Incomplete atypical femoral fracture, right leg, subsequent encounter for fracture with nonunion
M84.753A	Incomplete atypical femoral fracture, unspecified leg, initial encounter for fracture
M84.753P	Incomplete atypical femoral fracture, unspecified leg, subsequent encounter for fracture with malunion
M84.753K	Incomplete atypical femoral fracture, unspecified leg, subsequent encounter for fracture with nonunion
O03.39	Incomplete spontaneous abortion with other complications
A30.0	Indeterminate leprosy
A48.51	Infant botulism
G12.0	Infantile spinal muscular atrophy, type I [Werdnig-Hoffman]
N43.1	Infected hydrocele
T82.6XXA	Infection and inflammatory reaction due to cardiac valve prosthesis, initial encounter
T85.735A	Infection and inflammatory reaction due to cranial or spinal infusion catheter, initial encounter
T83.510A	Infection and inflammatory reaction due to cystostomy catheter, initial encounter
T85.731A	Infection and inflammatory reaction due to implanted electronic neurostimulator of brain, electrode (lead), initial encounter
T85.732A	Infection and inflammatory reaction due to implanted electronic neurostimulator of peripheral nerve, electrode (lead), initial encounter
T85.733A	Infection and inflammatory reaction due to implanted electronic neurostimulator of spinal cord, electrode (lead), initial encounter
T85.734A	Infection and inflammatory reaction due to implanted electronic neurostimulator, generator, initial encounter
T83.61XA	Infection and inflammatory reaction due to implanted penile prosthesis, initial encounter
T83.62XA	Infection and inflammatory reaction due to implanted testicular prosthesis, initial encounter
T83.590A	Infection and inflammatory reaction due to implanted urinary neurostimulation device, initial encounter
T83.591A	Infection and inflammatory reaction due to implanted urinary sphincter, initial encounter
T83.592A	Infection and inflammatory reaction due to indwelling ureteral stent, initial encounter
T83.511A	Infection and inflammatory reaction due to indwelling urethral catheter, initial encounter
T85.72XA	Infection and inflammatory reaction due to insulin pump, initial encounter
T84.621A	Infection and inflammatory reaction due to internal fixation device of left femur, initial encounter
T84.625A	Infection and inflammatory reaction due to internal fixation device of left fibula, initial encounter
T84.611A	Infection and inflammatory reaction due to internal fixation device of left humerus, initial encounter
T84.613A	Infection and inflammatory reaction due to internal fixation device of left radius, initial encounter
T84.623A	Infection and inflammatory reaction due to internal fixation device of left tibia, initial encounter
T84.615A	Infection and inflammatory reaction due to internal fixation device of left ulna, initial encounter
T84.69XA	Infection and inflammatory reaction due to internal fixation device of other site, initial encounter
T84.620A	Infection and inflammatory reaction due to internal fixation device of right femur, initial encounter
T84.624A	Infection and inflammatory reaction due to internal fixation device of right fibula, initial encounter
T84.610A	Infection and inflammatory reaction due to internal fixation device of right humerus, initial encounter
T84.612A	Infection and inflammatory reaction due to internal fixation device of right radius, initial encounter
T84.622A	Infection and inflammatory reaction due to internal fixation device of right tibia, initial encounter
T84.614A	Infection and inflammatory reaction due to internal fixation device of right ulna, initial encounter
T84.63XA	Infection and inflammatory reaction due to internal fixation device of spine, initial encounter
T84.619A	Infection and inflammatory reaction due to internal fixation device of unspecified bone of arm, initial encounter
T84.629A	Infection and inflammatory reaction due to internal fixation device of unspecified bone of leg, initial encounter
T84.60XA	Infection and inflammatory reaction due to internal fixation device of unspecified site, initial encounter
T84.52XA	Infection and inflammatory reaction due to internal left hip prosthesis, initial encounter
T84.54XA	Infection and inflammatory reaction due to internal left knee prosthesis, initial encounter
T84.51XA	Infection and inflammatory reaction due to internal right hip prosthesis, initial encounter
T84.53XA	Infection and inflammatory reaction due to internal right knee prosthesis, initial encounter

T83.512A	Infection and inflammatory reaction due to nephrostomy catheter, initial encounter
T82.7XXA	Infection and inflammatory reaction due to other cardiac and vascular devices, implants and grafts, initial encounter
T84.59XA	Infection and inflammatory reaction due to other internal joint prosthesis, initial encounter
T84.7XXA	Infection and inflammatory reaction due to other internal orthopedic prosthetic devices, implants and grafts, initial encounter
T85.79XA	Infection and inflammatory reaction due to other internal prosthetic devices, implants and grafts, initial encounter
T85.738A	Infection and inflammatory reaction due to other nervous system device, implant or graft, initial encounter
T83.69XA	Infection and inflammatory reaction due to other prosthetic device, implant and graft in genital tract, initial encounter
T83.598A	Infection and inflammatory reaction due to other prosthetic device, implant and graft in urinary system, initial encounter
T83.518A	Infection and inflammatory reaction due to other urinary catheter, initial encounter
T83.593A	Infection and inflammatory reaction due to other urinary stents, initial encounter
T85.71XA	Infection and inflammatory reaction due to peritoneal dialysis catheter, initial encounter
T84.50XA	Infection and inflammatory reaction due to unspecified internal joint prosthesis, initial encounter
T85.730A	Infection and inflammatory reaction due to ventricular intracranial (communicating) shunt, initial encounter
N98.0	Infection associated with artificial insemination
K95.01	Infection due to gastric band procedure
K95.81	Infection due to other bariatric procedure
T81.42XA	Infection following a procedure, deep incisional surgical site, initial encounter
T81.43XA	Infection following a procedure, organ and space surgical site, initial encounter
T81.49XA	Infection following a procedure, other surgical site, initial encounter
T81.41XA	Infection following a procedure, superficial incisional surgical site, initial encounter
T81.40XA	Infection following a procedure, unspecified, initial encounter
T88.0XXA	Infection following immunization, initial encounter
T80.29XA	Infection following other infusion, transfusion and therapeutic injection, initial encounter
T87.44	Infection of amputation stump, left lower extremity
T87.42	Infection of amputation stump, left upper extremity
T87.43	Infection of amputation stump, right lower extremity
T87.41	Infection of amputation stump, right upper extremity
T87.40	Infection of amputation stump, unspecified extremity
O86.22	Infection of bladder following delivery
M46.32	Infection of intervertebral disc (pyogenic), cervical region
M46.33	Infection of intervertebral disc (pyogenic), cervicothoracic region
M46.36	Infection of intervertebral disc (pyogenic), lumbar region
M46.37	Infection of intervertebral disc (pyogenic), lumbosacral region
M46.39	Infection of intervertebral disc (pyogenic), multiple sites in spine
M46.31	Infection of intervertebral disc (pyogenic), occipito-atlanto-axial region
M46.38	Infection of intervertebral disc (pyogenic), sacral and sacrococcygeal region
M46.30	Infection of intervertebral disc (pyogenic), site unspecified
M46.34	Infection of intervertebral disc (pyogenic), thoracic region
M46.35	Infection of intervertebral disc (pyogenic), thoracolumbar region
O86.21	Infection of kidney following delivery
O23.591	Infection of other part of genital tract in pregnancy, first trimester
O23.592	Infection of other part of genital tract in pregnancy, second trimester
O23.593	Infection of other part of genital tract in pregnancy, third trimester
J95.02	Infection of tracheostomy stoma
P39.9	Infection specific to the perinatal period, unspecified
O23.11	Infections of bladder in pregnancy, first trimester
O23.12	Infections of bladder in pregnancy, second trimester
O23.13	Infections of bladder in pregnancy, third trimester
O23.511	Infections of cervix in pregnancy, first trimester
O23.512	Infections of cervix in pregnancy, second trimester
O23.513	Infections of cervix in pregnancy, third trimester
O23.01	Infections of kidney in pregnancy, first trimester
O23.02	Infections of kidney in pregnancy, second trimester
O23.03	Infections of kidney in pregnancy, third trimester
O23.31	Infections of other parts of urinary tract in pregnancy, first trimester
O23.32	Infections of other parts of urinary tract in pregnancy, second trimester
O23.33	Infections of other parts of urinary tract in pregnancy, third trimester
O23.21	Infections of urethra in pregnancy, first trimester
O23.22	Infections of urethra in pregnancy, second trimester
O23.23	Infections of urethra in pregnancy, third trimester
A09	Infectious gastroenteritis and colitis, unspecified
M60.071	Infective myositis, left ankle
M60.045	Infective myositis, left finger(s)
M60.074	Infective myositis, left foot
M60.032	Infective myositis, left forearm
M60.042	Infective myositis, left hand
M60.062	Infective myositis, left lower leg
M60.012	Infective myositis, left shoulder
M60.052	Infective myositis, left thigh
M60.077	Infective myositis, left toe(s)
M60.022	Infective myositis, left upper arm
M60.09	Infective myositis, multiple sites
M60.08	Infective myositis, other site

M60.070	Infective myositis, right ankle
M60.044	Infective myositis, right finger(s)
M60.073	Infective myositis, right foot
M60.031	Infective myositis, right forearm
M60.041	Infective myositis, right hand
M60.061	Infective myositis, right lower leg
M60.011	Infective myositis, right shoulder
M60.051	Infective myositis, right thigh
M60.076	Infective myositis, right toe(s)
M60.021	Infective myositis, right upper arm
M60.072	Infective myositis, unspecified ankle
M60.002	Infective myositis, unspecified arm
M60.046	Infective myositis, unspecified finger(s)
M60.075	Infective myositis, unspecified foot
M60.039	Infective myositis, unspecified forearm
M60.043	Infective myositis, unspecified hand
M60.001	Infective myositis, unspecified left arm
M60.004	Infective myositis, unspecified left leg
M60.005	Infective myositis, unspecified leg
M60.069	Infective myositis, unspecified lower leg
M60.000	Infective myositis, unspecified right arm
M60.003	Infective myositis, unspecified right leg
M60.019	Infective myositis, unspecified shoulder
M60.009	Infective myositis, unspecified site
M60.059	Infective myositis, unspecified thigh
M60.078	Infective myositis, unspecified toe(s)
M60.029	Infective myositis, unspecified upper arm
I30.1	Infective pericarditis
K51.414	Inflammatory polyps of colon with abscess
K51.413	Inflammatory polyps of colon with fistula
K51.412	Inflammatory polyps of colon with intestinal obstruction
K51.418	Inflammatory polyps of colon with other complication
K51.411	Inflammatory polyps of colon with rectal bleeding
K51.419	Inflammatory polyps of colon with unspecified complications
K51.40	Inflammatory polyps of colon without complications
F18.17	Inhalant abuse with inhalant-induced dementia
F18.150	Inhalant abuse with inhalant-induced psychotic disorder with delusions
F18.151	Inhalant abuse with inhalant-induced psychotic disorder with hallucinations
F18.121	Inhalant abuse with intoxication delirium
F18.280	Inhalant dependence with inhalant-induced anxiety disorder
F18.27	Inhalant dependence with inhalant-induced dementia
F18.250	Inhalant dependence with inhalant-induced psychotic disorder with delusions
F18.251	Inhalant dependence with inhalant-induced psychotic disorder with hallucinations
F18.259	Inhalant dependence with inhalant-induced psychotic disorder, unspecified
F18.221	Inhalant dependence with intoxication delirium
F18.288	Inhalant dependence with other inhalant-induced disorder
F18.20	Inhalant dependence, uncomplicated
F18.97	Inhalant use, unspecified with inhalant-induced persisting dementia
F18.950	Inhalant use, unspecified with inhalant-induced psychotic disorder with delusions
F18.951	Inhalant use, unspecified with inhalant-induced psychotic disorder with hallucinations
F18.921	Inhalant use, unspecified with intoxication with delirium
S04.42XA	Injury of abducent nerve, left side, initial encounter
S04.41XA	Injury of abducent nerve, right side, initial encounter
S04.40XA	Injury of abducent nerve, unspecified side, initial encounter
S04.72XA	Injury of accessory nerve, left side, initial encounter
S04.71XA	Injury of accessory nerve, right side, initial encounter
S04.70XA	Injury of accessory nerve, unspecified side, initial encounter
S04.62XA	Injury of acoustic nerve, left side, initial encounter
S04.61XA	Injury of acoustic nerve, right side, initial encounter
S04.60XA	Injury of acoustic nerve, unspecified side, initial encounter
S36.13XA	Injury of bile duct, initial encounter
S09.0XXA	Injury of blood vessels of head, not elsewhere classified, initial encounter
S04.52XA	Injury of facial nerve, left side, initial encounter
S04.51XA	Injury of facial nerve, right side, initial encounter
S04.50XA	Injury of facial nerve, unspecified side, initial encounter
S06.825A	Injury of left internal carotid artery, intracranial portion, not elsewhere classified with loss of consciousness greater than 24 hours with return to pre-existing conscious level, initial encounter
S06.823A	Injury of left internal carotid artery, intracranial portion, not elsewhere classified with loss of consciousness of 1 hour to 5 hours 59 minutes, initial encounter
S06.821A	Injury of left internal carotid artery, intracranial portion, not elsewhere classified with loss of consciousness of 30 minutes or less, initial encounter
S06.822A	Injury of left internal carotid artery, intracranial portion, not elsewhere classified with loss of consciousness of 31 minutes to 59 minutes, initial encounter
S06.824A	Injury of left internal carotid artery, intracranial portion, not elsewhere classified with loss of consciousness of 6 hours to 24 hours, initial encounter
S06.829A	Injury of left internal carotid artery, intracranial portion, not elsewhere classified with loss of consciousness of unspecified duration, initial encounter
S35.532A	Injury of left uterine artery, initial encounter
S35.535A	Injury of left uterine vein, initial encounter
S04.12XA	Injury of oculomotor nerve, left side, initial encounter
S04.11XA	Injury of oculomotor nerve, right side, initial encounter
S04.10XA	Injury of oculomotor nerve, unspecified side, initial encounter

S04.812A	Injury of olfactory [1st] nerve, left side, initial encounter
S04.811A	Injury of olfactory [1st] nerve, right side, initial encounter
S04.819A	Injury of olfactory [1st] nerve, unspecified side, initial encounter
S04.02XA	Injury of optic chiasm, initial encounter
S04.012A	Injury of optic nerve, left eye, initial encounter
S04.011A	Injury of optic nerve, right eye, initial encounter
S04.019A	Injury of optic nerve, unspecified eye, initial encounter
S04.032A	Injury of optic tract and pathways, left side, initial encounter
S04.031A	Injury of optic tract and pathways, right side, initial encounter
S04.039A	Injury of optic tract and pathways, unspecified side, initial encounter
S04.892A	Injury of other cranial nerves, left side, initial encounter
S04.891A	Injury of other cranial nerves, right side, initial encounter
S04.899A	Injury of other cranial nerves, unspecified side, initial encounter
S15.8XXA	Injury of other specified blood vessels at neck level, initial encounter
S36.81XA	Injury of peritoneum, initial encounter
S06.815A	Injury of right internal carotid artery, intracranial portion, not elsewhere classified with loss of consciousness greater than 24 hours with return to pre-existing conscious level, initial encounter
S06.813A	Injury of right internal carotid artery, intracranial portion, not elsewhere classified with loss of consciousness of 1 hour to 5 hours 59 minutes, initial encounter
S06.811A	Injury of right internal carotid artery, intracranial portion, not elsewhere classified with loss of consciousness of 30 minutes or less, initial encounter
S06.812A	Injury of right internal carotid artery, intracranial portion, not elsewhere classified with loss of consciousness of 31 minutes to 59 minutes, initial encounter
S06.814A	Injury of right internal carotid artery, intracranial portion, not elsewhere classified with loss of consciousness of 6 hours to 24 hours, initial encounter
S06.819A	Injury of right internal carotid artery, intracranial portion, not elsewhere classified with loss of consciousness of unspecified duration, initial encounter
S35.531A	Injury of right uterine artery, initial encounter
S35.534A	Injury of right uterine vein, initial encounter
S04.32XA	Injury of trigeminal nerve, left side, initial encounter
S04.31XA	Injury of trigeminal nerve, right side, initial encounter
S04.30XA	Injury of trigeminal nerve, unspecified side, initial encounter
S04.22XA	Injury of trochlear nerve, left side, initial encounter
S04.21XA	Injury of trochlear nerve, right side, initial encounter
S04.20XA	Injury of trochlear nerve, unspecified side, initial encounter
S15.9XXA	Injury of unspecified blood vessel at neck level, initial encounter
S04.9XXA	Injury of unspecified cranial nerve, initial encounter
S27.9XXA	Injury of unspecified intrathoracic organ, initial encounter
S35.533A	Injury of unspecified uterine artery, initial encounter
S35.536A	Injury of unspecified uterine vein, initial encounter
S04.042A	Injury of visual cortex, left side, initial encounter
S04.041A	Injury of visual cortex, right side, initial encounter
S04.049A	Injury of visual cortex, unspecified side, initial encounter
T84.023A	Instability of internal left knee prosthesis, initial encounter
T84.022A	Instability of internal right knee prosthesis, initial encounter
Q25.21	Interruption of aortic arch
J84.9	Interstitial pulmonary disease, unspecified
M51.06	Intervertebral disc disorders with myelopathy, lumbar region
M51.04	Intervertebral disc disorders with myelopathy, thoracic region
M51.05	Intervertebral disc disorders with myelopathy, thoracolumbar region
K56.52	Intestinal adhesions [bands] with complete obstruction
K56.50	Intestinal adhesions [bands], unspecified as to partial versus complete obstruction
K56.51	Intestinal adhesions [bands], with partial obstruction
B81.3	Intestinal angiostrongyliasis
B81.1	Intestinal capillariasis
B82.0	Intestinal helminthiasis, unspecified
K90.9	Intestinal malabsorption, unspecified
B78.0	Intestinal strongyloidiasis
T86.851	Intestine transplant failure
T86.852	Intestine transplant infection
T86.850	Intestine transplant rejection
Z94.82	Intestine transplant status
P39.2	Intra-amniotic infection affecting newborn, not elsewhere classified
G97.2	Intracranial hypotension following ventricular shunting
C22.1	Intrahepatic bile duct carcinoma
I97.710	Intraoperative cardiac arrest during cardiac surgery
I97.711	Intraoperative cardiac arrest during other surgery
I97.810	Intraoperative cerebrovascular infarction during cardiac surgery
I97.811	Intraoperative cerebrovascular infarction during other surgery
I97.411	Intraoperative hemorrhage and hematoma of a circulatory system organ or structure complicating a cardiac bypass
I97.410	Intraoperative hemorrhage and hematoma of a circulatory system organ or structure complicating a cardiac catheterization
I97.418	Intraoperative hemorrhage and hematoma of a circulatory system organ or structure complicating other circulatory system procedure
I97.42	Intraoperative hemorrhage and hematoma of a circulatory system organ or structure complicating other procedure
K91.61	Intraoperative hemorrhage and hematoma of a digestive system organ or structure complicating a digestive system procedure
K91.62	Intraoperative hemorrhage and hematoma of a digestive system organ or structure complicating other procedure
N99.61	Intraoperative hemorrhage and hematoma of a genitourinary system organ or structure complicating a genitourinary system procedure
N99.62	Intraoperative hemorrhage and hematoma of a genitourinary system organ or structure complicating other procedure
M96.810	Intraoperative hemorrhage and hematoma of a musculoskeletal structure complicating a musculoskeletal system procedure
M96.811	Intraoperative hemorrhage and hematoma of a musculoskeletal structure complicating other procedure
G97.31	Intraoperative hemorrhage and hematoma of a nervous system organ or structure complicating a nervous system procedure
G97.32	Intraoperative hemorrhage and hematoma of a nervous system organ or structure complicating other procedure
J95.61	Intraoperative hemorrhage and hematoma of a respiratory system organ or structure complicating a respiratory system procedure
J95.62	Intraoperative hemorrhage and hematoma of a respiratory system organ or structure complicating other procedure
E36.01	Intraoperative hemorrhage and hematoma of an endocrine system organ or structure complicating an endocrine system procedure
E36.02	Intraoperative hemorrhage and hematoma of an endocrine system organ or structure complicating other procedure
H95.21	Intraoperative hemorrhage and hematoma of ear and mastoid process complicating a procedure on the ear and mastoid process
H95.22	Intraoperative hemorrhage and hematoma of ear and mastoid process complicating other procedure
H59.113	Intraoperative hemorrhage and hematoma of eye and adnexa complicating an ophthalmic procedure, bilateral
H59.123	Intraoperative hemorrhage and hematoma of eye and adnexa complicating other procedure, bilateral
H59.112	Intraoperative hemorrhage and hematoma of left eye and adnexa complicating an ophthalmic procedure
H59.122	Intraoperative hemorrhage and hematoma of left eye and adnexa complicating other procedure
H59.111	Intraoperative hemorrhage and hematoma of right eye and adnexa complicating an ophthalmic procedure
H59.121	Intraoperative hemorrhage and hematoma of right eye and adnexa complicating other procedure
L76.01	Intraoperative hemorrhage and hematoma of skin and subcutaneous tissue complicating a dermatologic procedure
L76.02	Intraoperative hemorrhage and hematoma of skin and subcutaneous tissue complicating other procedure
D78.01	Intraoperative hemorrhage and hematoma of the spleen complicating a procedure on the spleen
D78.02	Intraoperative hemorrhage and hematoma of the spleen complicating other procedure
H59.119	Intraoperative hemorrhage and hematoma of unspecified eye and adnexa complicating an ophthalmic procedure
H59.129	Intraoperative hemorrhage and hematoma of unspecified eye and adnexa complicating other procedure
K61.4	Intrasphincteric abscess
N44.02	Intravaginal torsion of spermatic cord
P52.0	Intraventricular (nontraumatic) hemorrhage, grade 1, of newborn
P52.1	Intraventricular (nontraumatic) hemorrhage, grade 2, of newborn
P10.2	Intraventricular hemorrhage due to birth injury
K56.1	Intussusception
N30.41	Irradiation cystitis with hematuria
N30.40	Irradiation cystitis without hematuria
K04.02	Irreversible pulpitis
N28.0	Ischemia and infarction of kidney
N06.4	Isolated proteinuria with diffuse endocapillary proliferative glomerulonephritis
N06.2	Isolated proteinuria with diffuse membranous glomerulonephritis
N06.3	Isolated proteinuria with diffuse mesangial proliferative glomerulonephritis
N06.5	Isolated proteinuria with diffuse mesangiocapillary glomerulonephritis
A07.3	Isosporiasis
E71.110	Isovaleric acidemia
I49.2	Junctional premature depolarization
A96.0	Junin hemorrhagic fever
M33.02	Juvenile dermatomyositis with myopathy
M33.09	Juvenile dermatomyositis with other organ involvement
M33.01	Juvenile dermatomyositis with respiratory involvement
M33.03	Juvenile dermatomyositis without myopathy
M33.00	Juvenile dermatomyositis, organ involvement unspecified
A50.45	Juvenile general paresis
C93.32	Juvenile myelomonocytic leukemia, in relapse
C93.31	Juvenile myelomonocytic leukemia, in remission
C93.30	Juvenile myelomonocytic leukemia, not having achieved remission
G40.B11	Juvenile myoclonic epilepsy, intractable, with status epilepticus
G40.B19	Juvenile myoclonic epilepsy, intractable, without status epilepticus
G40.B01	Juvenile myoclonic epilepsy, not intractable, with status epilepticus
G40.B09	Juvenile myoclonic epilepsy, not intractable, without status epilepticus
M30.2	Juvenile polyarteritis
C46.4	Kaposi's sarcoma of gastrointestinal sites
C46.52	Kaposi's sarcoma of left lung
C46.3	Kaposi's sarcoma of lymph nodes
C46.7	Kaposi's sarcoma of other sites
C46.2	Kaposi's sarcoma of palate
C46.51	Kaposi's sarcoma of right lung
C46.0	Kaposi's sarcoma of skin
C46.1	Kaposi's sarcoma of soft tissue
C46.50	Kaposi's sarcoma of unspecified lung
C46.9	Kaposi's sarcoma, unspecified
H49.813	Kearns-Sayre syndrome, bilateral
H49.812	Kearns-Sayre syndrome, left eye
H49.811	Kearns-Sayre syndrome, right eye

H49.819	Kearns-Sayre syndrome, unspecified eye
H59.Ø13	Keratopathy (bullous aphakic) following cataract surgery, bilateral
H59.Ø12	Keratopathy (bullous aphakic) following cataract surgery, left eye
H59.Ø11	Keratopathy (bullous aphakic) following cataract surgery, right eye
H59.Ø19	Keratopathy (bullous aphakic) following cataract surgery, unspecified eye
T86.12	Kidney transplant failure
T86.13	Kidney transplant infection
T86.11	Kidney transplant rejection
Z94.Ø	Kidney transplant status
E75.23	Krabbe disease
A81.81	Kuru
A98.2	Kyasanur Forest disease
I27.1	Kyphoscoliotic heart disease
O68	Labor and delivery complicated by abnormality of fetal acid-base balance
S76.222A	Laceration of adductor muscle, fascia and tendon of left thigh, initial encounter
S76.221A	Laceration of adductor muscle, fascia and tendon of right thigh, initial encounter
S76.229A	Laceration of adductor muscle, fascia and tendon of unspecified thigh, initial encounter
S37.813A	Laceration of adrenal gland, initial encounter
S85.142A	Laceration of anterior tibial artery, left leg, initial encounter
S85.141A	Laceration of anterior tibial artery, right leg, initial encounter
S85.149A	Laceration of anterior tibial artery, unspecified leg, initial encounter
S36.53ØA	Laceration of ascending [right] colon, initial encounter
S45.212A	Laceration of axillary or brachial vein, left side, initial encounter
S45.211A	Laceration of axillary or brachial vein, right side, initial encounter
S45.219A	Laceration of axillary or brachial vein, unspecified side, initial encounter
S37.23XA	Laceration of bladder, initial encounter
S65.511A	Laceration of blood vessel of left index finger, initial encounter
S65.517A	Laceration of blood vessel of left little finger, initial encounter
S65.513A	Laceration of blood vessel of left middle finger, initial encounter
S65.515A	Laceration of blood vessel of left ring finger, initial encounter
S65.412A	Laceration of blood vessel of left thumb, initial encounter
S65.518A	Laceration of blood vessel of other finger, initial encounter
S65.51ØA	Laceration of blood vessel of right index finger, initial encounter
S65.516A	Laceration of blood vessel of right little finger, initial encounter
S65.512A	Laceration of blood vessel of right middle finger, initial encounter
S65.514A	Laceration of blood vessel of right ring finger, initial encounter
S65.411A	Laceration of blood vessel of right thumb, initial encounter
S65.519A	Laceration of blood vessel of unspecified finger, initial encounter
S65.419A	Laceration of blood vessel of unspecified thumb, initial encounter
S36.231A	Laceration of body of pancreas, unspecified degree, initial encounter
S45.112A	Laceration of brachial artery, left side, initial encounter
S45.111A	Laceration of brachial artery, right side, initial encounter
S45.119A	Laceration of brachial artery, unspecified side, initial encounter
S65.312A	Laceration of deep palmar arch of left hand, initial encounter
S65.311A	Laceration of deep palmar arch of right hand, initial encounter
S65.319A	Laceration of deep palmar arch of unspecified hand, initial encounter
S36.532A	Laceration of descending [left] colon, initial encounter
S27.8Ø3A	Laceration of diaphragm, initial encounter
S95.Ø12A	Laceration of dorsal artery of left foot, initial encounter
S95.Ø11A	Laceration of dorsal artery of right foot, initial encounter
S95.Ø19A	Laceration of dorsal artery of unspecified foot, initial encounter
S95.212A	Laceration of dorsal vein of left foot, initial encounter
S95.211A	Laceration of dorsal vein of right foot, initial encounter
S95.219A	Laceration of dorsal vein of unspecified foot, initial encounter
S36.43ØA	Laceration of duodenum, initial encounter
S56.422A	Laceration of extensor muscle, fascia and tendon of left index finger at forearm level, initial encounter
S66.321A	Laceration of extensor muscle, fascia and tendon of left index finger at wrist and hand level, initial encounter
S56.428A	Laceration of extensor muscle, fascia and tendon of left little finger at forearm level, initial encounter
S66.327A	Laceration of extensor muscle, fascia and tendon of left little finger at wrist and hand level, initial encounter
S56.424A	Laceration of extensor muscle, fascia and tendon of left middle finger at forearm level, initial encounter
S66.323A	Laceration of extensor muscle, fascia and tendon of left middle finger at wrist and hand level, initial encounter
S56.426A	Laceration of extensor muscle, fascia and tendon of left ring finger at forearm level, initial encounter
S66.325A	Laceration of extensor muscle, fascia and tendon of left ring finger at wrist and hand level, initial encounter
S66.222A	Laceration of extensor muscle, fascia and tendon of left thumb at wrist and hand level, initial encounter
S66.328A	Laceration of extensor muscle, fascia and tendon of other finger at wrist and hand level, initial encounter
S56.421A	Laceration of extensor muscle, fascia and tendon of right index finger at forearm level, initial encounter
S66.32ØA	Laceration of extensor muscle, fascia and tendon of right index finger at wrist and hand level, initial encounter
S56.427A	Laceration of extensor muscle, fascia and tendon of right little finger at forearm level, initial encounter
S66.326A	Laceration of extensor muscle, fascia and tendon of right little finger at wrist and hand level, initial encounter
S56.423A	Laceration of extensor muscle, fascia and tendon of right middle finger at forearm level, initial encounter
S66.322A	Laceration of extensor muscle, fascia and tendon of right middle finger at wrist and hand level, initial encounter
S56.425A	Laceration of extensor muscle, fascia and tendon of right ring finger at forearm level, initial encounter
S66.324A	Laceration of extensor muscle, fascia and tendon of right ring finger at wrist and hand level, initial encounter
S66.221A	Laceration of extensor muscle, fascia and tendon of right thumb at wrist and hand level, initial encounter
S56.429A	Laceration of extensor muscle, fascia and tendon of unspecified finger at forearm level, initial encounter
S66.329A	Laceration of extensor muscle, fascia and tendon of unspecified finger at wrist and hand level, initial encounter
S66.229A	Laceration of extensor muscle, fascia and tendon of unspecified thumb at wrist and hand level, initial encounter
S56.322A	Laceration of extensor or abductor muscles, fascia and tendons of left thumb at forearm level, initial encounter
S56.321A	Laceration of extensor or abductor muscles, fascia and tendons of right thumb at forearm level, initial encounter
S56.329A	Laceration of extensor or abductor muscles, fascia and tendons of unspecified thumb at forearm level, initial encounter
S56.122A	Laceration of flexor muscle, fascia and tendon of left index finger at forearm level, initial encounter
S66.121A	Laceration of flexor muscle, fascia and tendon of left index finger at wrist and hand level, initial encounter
S56.128A	Laceration of flexor muscle, fascia and tendon of left little finger at forearm level, initial encounter
S66.127A	Laceration of flexor muscle, fascia and tendon of left little finger at wrist and hand level, initial encounter
S56.124A	Laceration of flexor muscle, fascia and tendon of left middle finger at forearm level, initial encounter
S66.123A	Laceration of flexor muscle, fascia and tendon of left middle finger at wrist and hand level, initial encounter
S56.126A	Laceration of flexor muscle, fascia and tendon of left ring finger at forearm level, initial encounter
S66.125A	Laceration of flexor muscle, fascia and tendon of left ring finger at wrist and hand level, initial encounter
S56.Ø22A	Laceration of flexor muscle, fascia and tendon of left thumb at forearm level, initial encounter
S66.128A	Laceration of flexor muscle, fascia and tendon of other finger at wrist and hand level, initial encounter
S56.121A	Laceration of flexor muscle, fascia and tendon of right index finger at forearm level, initial encounter
S66.12ØA	Laceration of flexor muscle, fascia and tendon of right index finger at wrist and hand level, initial encounter
S56.127A	Laceration of flexor muscle, fascia and tendon of right little finger at forearm level, initial encounter
S66.126A	Laceration of flexor muscle, fascia and tendon of right little finger at wrist and hand level, initial encounter
S56.123A	Laceration of flexor muscle, fascia and tendon of right middle finger at forearm level, initial encounter
S66.122A	Laceration of flexor muscle, fascia and tendon of right middle finger at wrist and hand level, initial encounter
S56.125A	Laceration of flexor muscle, fascia and tendon of right ring finger at forearm level, initial encounter
S66.124A	Laceration of flexor muscle, fascia and tendon of right ring finger at wrist and hand level, initial encounter
S56.Ø21A	Laceration of flexor muscle, fascia and tendon of right thumb at forearm level, initial encounter
S56.129A	Laceration of flexor muscle, fascia and tendon of unspecified finger at forearm level, initial encounter
S66.129A	Laceration of flexor muscle, fascia and tendon of unspecified finger at wrist and hand level, initial encounter
S56.Ø29A	Laceration of flexor muscle, fascia and tendon of unspecified thumb at forearm level, initial encounter
S36.123A	Laceration of gallbladder, initial encounter
S85.312A	Laceration of greater saphenous vein at lower leg level, left leg, initial encounter
S85.311A	Laceration of greater saphenous vein at lower leg level, right leg, initial encounter
S85.319A	Laceration of greater saphenous vein at lower leg level, unspecified leg, initial encounter
S36.23ØA	Laceration of head of pancreas, unspecified degree, initial encounter
S25.512A	Laceration of intercostal blood vessels, left side, initial encounter
S25.511A	Laceration of intercostal blood vessels, right side, initial encounter
S25.519A	Laceration of intercostal blood vessels, unspecified side, initial encounter
S96.222A	Laceration of intrinsic muscle and tendon at ankle and foot level, left foot, initial encounter
S96.221A	Laceration of intrinsic muscle and tendon at ankle and foot level, right foot, initial encounter
S96.229A	Laceration of intrinsic muscle and tendon at ankle and foot level, unspecified foot, initial encounter
S66.521A	Laceration of intrinsic muscle, fascia and tendon of left index finger at wrist and hand level, initial encounter
S66.527A	Laceration of intrinsic muscle, fascia and tendon of left little finger at wrist and hand level, initial encounter
S66.523A	Laceration of intrinsic muscle, fascia and tendon of left middle finger at wrist and hand level, initial encounter
S66.525A	Laceration of intrinsic muscle, fascia and tendon of left ring finger at wrist and hand level, initial encounter
S66.422A	Laceration of intrinsic muscle, fascia and tendon of left thumb at wrist and hand level, initial encounter
S66.528A	Laceration of intrinsic muscle, fascia and tendon of other finger at wrist and hand level, initial encounter

S66.520A	Laceration of intrinsic muscle, fascia and tendon of right index finger at wrist and hand level, initial encounter
S66.526A	Laceration of intrinsic muscle, fascia and tendon of right little finger at wrist and hand level, initial encounter
S66.522A	Laceration of intrinsic muscle, fascia and tendon of right middle finger at wrist and hand level, initial encounter
S66.524A	Laceration of intrinsic muscle, fascia and tendon of right ring finger at wrist and hand level, initial encounter
S66.421A	Laceration of intrinsic muscle, fascia and tendon of right thumb at wrist and hand level, initial encounter
S66.529A	Laceration of intrinsic muscle, fascia and tendon of unspecified finger at wrist and hand level, initial encounter
S66.429A	Laceration of intrinsic muscle, fascia and tendon of unspecified thumb at wrist and hand level, initial encounter
S86.022A	Laceration of left Achilles tendon, initial encounter
S37.032A	Laceration of left kidney, unspecified degree, initial encounter
S76.122A	Laceration of left quadriceps muscle, fascia and tendon, initial encounter
S85.412A	Laceration of lesser saphenous vein at lower leg level, left leg, initial encounter
S85.411A	Laceration of lesser saphenous vein at lower leg level, right leg, initial encounter
S85.419A	Laceration of lesser saphenous vein at lower leg level, unspecified leg, initial encounter
S36.113A	Laceration of liver, unspecified degree, initial encounter
S66.022A	Laceration of long flexor muscle, fascia and tendon of left thumb at wrist and hand level, initial encounter
S66.021A	Laceration of long flexor muscle, fascia and tendon of right thumb at wrist and hand level, initial encounter
S66.029A	Laceration of long flexor muscle, fascia and tendon of unspecified thumb at wrist and hand level, initial encounter
S29.021A	Laceration of muscle and tendon of front wall of thorax, initial encounter
S96.122A	Laceration of muscle and tendon of long extensor muscle of toe at ankle and foot level, left foot, initial encounter
S96.121A	Laceration of muscle and tendon of long extensor muscle of toe at ankle and foot level, right foot, initial encounter
S96.129A	Laceration of muscle and tendon of long extensor muscle of toe at ankle and foot level, unspecified foot, initial encounter
S96.022A	Laceration of muscle and tendon of long flexor muscle of toe at ankle and foot level, left foot, initial encounter
S96.021A	Laceration of muscle and tendon of long flexor muscle of toe at ankle and foot level, right foot, initial encounter
S96.029A	Laceration of muscle and tendon of long flexor muscle of toe at ankle and foot level, unspecified foot, initial encounter
S29.029A	Laceration of muscle and tendon of unspecified wall of thorax, initial encounter
S76.022A	Laceration of muscle, fascia and tendon of left hip, initial encounter
S46.122A	Laceration of muscle, fascia and tendon of long head of biceps, left arm, initial encounter
S46.121A	Laceration of muscle, fascia and tendon of long head of biceps, right arm, initial encounter
S46.129A	Laceration of muscle, fascia and tendon of long head of biceps, unspecified arm, initial encounter
S46.222A	Laceration of muscle, fascia and tendon of other parts of biceps, left arm, initial encounter
S46.221A	Laceration of muscle, fascia and tendon of other parts of biceps, right arm, initial encounter
S46.229A	Laceration of muscle, fascia and tendon of other parts of biceps, unspecified arm, initial encounter
S76.021A	Laceration of muscle, fascia and tendon of right hip, initial encounter
S76.322A	Laceration of muscle, fascia and tendon of the posterior muscle group at thigh level, left thigh, initial encounter
S76.321A	Laceration of muscle, fascia and tendon of the posterior muscle group at thigh level, right thigh, initial encounter
S76.329A	Laceration of muscle, fascia and tendon of the posterior muscle group at thigh level, unspecified thigh, initial encounter
S46.322A	Laceration of muscle, fascia and tendon of triceps, left arm, initial encounter
S46.321A	Laceration of muscle, fascia and tendon of triceps, right arm, initial encounter
S46.329A	Laceration of muscle, fascia and tendon of triceps, unspecified arm, initial encounter
S76.029A	Laceration of muscle, fascia and tendon of unspecified hip, initial encounter
S86.222A	Laceration of muscle(s) and tendon(s) of anterior muscle group at lower leg level, left leg, initial encounter
S86.221A	Laceration of muscle(s) and tendon(s) of anterior muscle group at lower leg level, right leg, initial encounter
S86.229A	Laceration of muscle(s) and tendon(s) of anterior muscle group at lower leg level, unspecified leg, initial encounter
S86.322A	Laceration of muscle(s) and tendon(s) of peroneal muscle group at lower leg level, left leg, initial encounter
S86.321A	Laceration of muscle(s) and tendon(s) of peroneal muscle group at lower leg level, right leg, initial encounter
S86.329A	Laceration of muscle(s) and tendon(s) of peroneal muscle group at lower leg level, unspecified leg, initial encounter
S46.022A	Laceration of muscle(s) and tendon(s) of the rotator cuff of left shoulder, initial encounter
S46.021A	Laceration of muscle(s) and tendon(s) of the rotator cuff of right shoulder, initial encounter
S46.029A	Laceration of muscle(s) and tendon(s) of the rotator cuff of unspecified shoulder, initial encounter
S35.8X1A	Laceration of other blood vessels at abdomen, lower back and pelvis level, initial encounter
S95.812A	Laceration of other blood vessels at ankle and foot level, left leg, initial encounter
S95.811A	Laceration of other blood vessels at ankle and foot level, right leg, initial encounter
S95.819A	Laceration of other blood vessels at ankle and foot level, unspecified leg, initial encounter
S55.812A	Laceration of other blood vessels at forearm level, left arm, initial encounter
S55.811A	Laceration of other blood vessels at forearm level, right arm, initial encounter
S55.819A	Laceration of other blood vessels at forearm level, unspecified arm, initial encounter
S75.812A	Laceration of other blood vessels at hip and thigh level, left leg, initial encounter
S75.811A	Laceration of other blood vessels at hip and thigh level, right leg, initial encounter
S75.819A	Laceration of other blood vessels at hip and thigh level, unspecified leg, initial encounter
S85.812A	Laceration of other blood vessels at lower leg level, left leg, initial encounter
S85.811A	Laceration of other blood vessels at lower leg level, right leg, initial encounter
S85.819A	Laceration of other blood vessels at lower leg level, unspecified leg, initial encounter
S65.812A	Laceration of other blood vessels at wrist and hand level of left arm, initial encounter
S65.811A	Laceration of other blood vessels at wrist and hand level of right arm, initial encounter
S65.819A	Laceration of other blood vessels at wrist and hand level of unspecified arm, initial encounter
S25.812A	Laceration of other blood vessels of thorax, left side, initial encounter
S25.811A	Laceration of other blood vessels of thorax, right side, initial encounter
S25.819A	Laceration of other blood vessels of thorax, unspecified side, initial encounter
S56.522A	Laceration of other extensor muscle, fascia and tendon at forearm level, left arm, initial encounter
S56.521A	Laceration of other extensor muscle, fascia and tendon at forearm level, right arm, initial encounter
S56.529A	Laceration of other extensor muscle, fascia and tendon at forearm level, unspecified arm, initial encounter
S56.222A	Laceration of other flexor muscle, fascia and tendon at forearm level, left arm, initial encounter
S56.221A	Laceration of other flexor muscle, fascia and tendon at forearm level, right arm, initial encounter
S56.229A	Laceration of other flexor muscle, fascia and tendon at forearm level, unspecified arm, initial encounter
S36.893A	Laceration of other intra-abdominal organs, initial encounter
S86.822A	Laceration of other muscle(s) and tendon(s) at lower leg level, left leg, initial encounter
S86.821A	Laceration of other muscle(s) and tendon(s) at lower leg level, right leg, initial encounter
S86.829A	Laceration of other muscle(s) and tendon(s) at lower leg level, unspecified leg, initial encounter
S86.122A	Laceration of other muscle(s) and tendon(s) of posterior muscle group at lower leg level, left leg, initial encounter
S86.121A	Laceration of other muscle(s) and tendon(s) of posterior muscle group at lower leg level, right leg, initial encounter
S86.129A	Laceration of other muscle(s) and tendon(s) of posterior muscle group at lower leg level, unspecified leg, initial encounter
S56.822A	Laceration of other muscles, fascia and tendons at forearm level, left arm, initial encounter
S56.821A	Laceration of other muscles, fascia and tendons at forearm level, right arm, initial encounter
S56.829A	Laceration of other muscles, fascia and tendons at forearm level, unspecified arm, initial encounter
S46.822A	Laceration of other muscles, fascia and tendons at shoulder and upper arm level, left arm, initial encounter
S46.821A	Laceration of other muscles, fascia and tendons at shoulder and upper arm level, right arm, initial encounter
S46.829A	Laceration of other muscles, fascia and tendons at shoulder and upper arm level, unspecified arm, initial encounter
S36.538A	Laceration of other part of colon, initial encounter
S36.438A	Laceration of other part of small intestine, initial encounter
S45.812A	Laceration of other specified blood vessels at shoulder and upper arm level, left arm, initial encounter
S45.811A	Laceration of other specified blood vessels at shoulder and upper arm level, right arm, initial encounter
S45.819A	Laceration of other specified blood vessels at shoulder and upper arm level, unspecified arm, initial encounter
S27.893A	Laceration of other specified intrathoracic organs, initial encounter
S96.822A	Laceration of other specified muscles and tendons at ankle and foot level, left foot, initial encounter
S96.821A	Laceration of other specified muscles and tendons at ankle and foot level, right foot, initial encounter
S96.829A	Laceration of other specified muscles and tendons at ankle and foot level, unspecified foot, initial encounter
S76.822A	Laceration of other specified muscles, fascia and tendons at thigh level, left thigh, initial encounter
S76.821A	Laceration of other specified muscles, fascia and tendons at thigh level, right thigh, initial encounter
S76.829A	Laceration of other specified muscles, fascia and tendons at thigh level, unspecified thigh, initial encounter
S66.822A	Laceration of other specified muscles, fascia and tendons at wrist and hand level, left hand, initial encounter
S66.821A	Laceration of other specified muscles, fascia and tendons at wrist and hand level, right hand, initial encounter

S66.829A	Laceration of other specified muscles, fascia and tendons at wrist and hand level, unspecified hand, initial encounter
S37.893A	Laceration of other urinary and pelvic organ, initial encounter
S85.212A	Laceration of peroneal artery, left leg, initial encounter
S85.211A	Laceration of peroneal artery, right leg, initial encounter
S85.219A	Laceration of peroneal artery, unspecified leg, initial encounter
S95.112A	Laceration of plantar artery of left foot, initial encounter
S95.111A	Laceration of plantar artery of right foot, initial encounter
S95.119A	Laceration of plantar artery of unspecified foot, initial encounter
S27.63XA	Laceration of pleura, initial encounter
S85.172A	Laceration of posterior tibial artery, left leg, initial encounter
S85.171A	Laceration of posterior tibial artery, right leg, initial encounter
S85.179A	Laceration of posterior tibial artery, unspecified leg, initial encounter
S55.112A	Laceration of radial artery at forearm level, left arm, initial encounter
S55.111A	Laceration of radial artery at forearm level, right arm, initial encounter
S55.119A	Laceration of radial artery at forearm level, unspecified arm, initial encounter
S65.112A	Laceration of radial artery at wrist and hand level of left arm, initial encounter
S65.111A	Laceration of radial artery at wrist and hand level of right arm, initial encounter
S65.119A	Laceration of radial artery at wrist and hand level of unspecified arm, initial encounter
S36.63XA	Laceration of rectum, initial encounter
S86.021A	Laceration of right Achilles tendon, initial encounter
S37.031A	Laceration of right kidney, unspecified degree, initial encounter
S76.121A	Laceration of right quadriceps muscle, fascia and tendon, initial encounter
S36.533A	Laceration of sigmoid colon, initial encounter
S36.33XA	Laceration of stomach, initial encounter
S65.212A	Laceration of superficial palmar arch of left hand, initial encounter
S65.211A	Laceration of superficial palmar arch of right hand, initial encounter
S65.219A	Laceration of superficial palmar arch of unspecified hand, initial encounter
S45.312A	Laceration of superficial vein at shoulder and upper arm level, left arm, initial encounter
S45.311A	Laceration of superficial vein at shoulder and upper arm level, right arm, initial encounter
S45.319A	Laceration of superficial vein at shoulder and upper arm level, unspecified arm, initial encounter
S36.232A	Laceration of tail of pancreas, unspecified degree, initial encounter
S27.53XA	Laceration of thoracic trachea, initial encounter
S36.531A	Laceration of transverse colon, initial encounter
S55.012A	Laceration of ulnar artery at forearm level, left arm, initial encounter
S55.011A	Laceration of ulnar artery at forearm level, right arm, initial encounter
S55.019A	Laceration of ulnar artery at forearm level, unspecified arm, initial encounter
S65.012A	Laceration of ulnar artery at wrist and hand level of left arm, initial encounter
S65.011A	Laceration of ulnar artery at wrist and hand level of right arm, initial encounter
S65.019A	Laceration of ulnar artery at wrist and hand level of unspecified arm, initial encounter
S86.029A	Laceration of unspecified Achilles tendon, initial encounter
S35.91XA	Laceration of unspecified blood vessel at abdomen, lower back and pelvis level, initial encounter
S95.912A	Laceration of unspecified blood vessel at ankle and foot level, left leg, initial encounter
S95.911A	Laceration of unspecified blood vessel at ankle and foot level, right leg, initial encounter
S95.919A	Laceration of unspecified blood vessel at ankle and foot level, unspecified leg, initial encounter
S55.912A	Laceration of unspecified blood vessel at forearm level, left arm, initial encounter
S55.911A	Laceration of unspecified blood vessel at forearm level, right arm, initial encounter
S55.919A	Laceration of unspecified blood vessel at forearm level, unspecified arm, initial encounter
S75.912A	Laceration of unspecified blood vessel at hip and thigh level, left leg, initial encounter
S75.911A	Laceration of unspecified blood vessel at hip and thigh level, right leg, initial encounter
S75.919A	Laceration of unspecified blood vessel at hip and thigh level, unspecified leg, initial encounter
S85.912A	Laceration of unspecified blood vessel at lower leg level, left leg, initial encounter
S85.911A	Laceration of unspecified blood vessel at lower leg level, right leg, initial encounter
S85.919A	Laceration of unspecified blood vessel at lower leg level, unspecified leg, initial encounter
S45.912A	Laceration of unspecified blood vessel at shoulder and upper arm level, left arm, initial encounter
S45.911A	Laceration of unspecified blood vessel at shoulder and upper arm level, right arm, initial encounter
S45.919A	Laceration of unspecified blood vessel at shoulder and upper arm level, unspecified arm, initial encounter
S65.912A	Laceration of unspecified blood vessel at wrist and hand level of left arm, initial encounter
S65.911A	Laceration of unspecified blood vessel at wrist and hand level of right arm, initial encounter
S65.919A	Laceration of unspecified blood vessel at wrist and hand level of unspecified arm, initial encounter
S25.91XA	Laceration of unspecified blood vessel of thorax, initial encounter
S36.93XA	Laceration of unspecified intra-abdominal organ, initial encounter
S37.039A	Laceration of unspecified kidney, unspecified degree, initial encounter
S96.922A	Laceration of unspecified muscle and tendon at ankle and foot level, left foot, initial encounter
S96.921A	Laceration of unspecified muscle and tendon at ankle and foot level, right foot, initial encounter
S96.929A	Laceration of unspecified muscle and tendon at ankle and foot level, unspecified foot, initial encounter
S46.922A	Laceration of unspecified muscle, fascia and tendon at shoulder and upper arm level, left arm, initial encounter
S46.921A	Laceration of unspecified muscle, fascia and tendon at shoulder and upper arm level, right arm, initial encounter
S46.929A	Laceration of unspecified muscle, fascia and tendon at shoulder and upper arm level, unspecified arm, initial encounter
S66.922A	Laceration of unspecified muscle, fascia and tendon at wrist and hand level, left hand, initial encounter
S66.921A	Laceration of unspecified muscle, fascia and tendon at wrist and hand level, right hand, initial encounter
S66.929A	Laceration of unspecified muscle, fascia and tendon at wrist and hand level, unspecified hand, initial encounter
S86.922A	Laceration of unspecified muscle(s) and tendon(s) at lower leg level, left leg, initial encounter
S86.921A	Laceration of unspecified muscle(s) and tendon(s) at lower leg level, right leg, initial encounter
S86.929A	Laceration of unspecified muscle(s) and tendon(s) at lower leg level, unspecified leg, initial encounter
S56.922A	Laceration of unspecified muscles, fascia and tendons at forearm level, left arm, initial encounter
S56.921A	Laceration of unspecified muscles, fascia and tendons at forearm level, right arm, initial encounter
S56.929A	Laceration of unspecified muscles, fascia and tendons at forearm level, unspecified arm, initial encounter
S76.922A	Laceration of unspecified muscles, fascia and tendons at thigh level, left thigh, initial encounter
S76.921A	Laceration of unspecified muscles, fascia and tendons at thigh level, right thigh, initial encounter
S76.929A	Laceration of unspecified muscles, fascia and tendons at thigh level, unspecified thigh, initial encounter
S36.539A	Laceration of unspecified part of colon, initial encounter
S36.239A	Laceration of unspecified part of pancreas, unspecified degree, initial encounter
S36.439A	Laceration of unspecified part of small intestine, initial encounter
S76.129A	Laceration of unspecified quadriceps muscle, fascia and tendon, initial encounter
S85.112A	Laceration of unspecified tibial artery, left leg, initial encounter
S85.111A	Laceration of unspecified tibial artery, right leg, initial encounter
S85.119A	Laceration of unspecified tibial artery, unspecified leg, initial encounter
S37.93XA	Laceration of unspecified urinary and pelvic organ, initial encounter
S37.13XA	Laceration of ureter, initial encounter
S37.33XA	Laceration of urethra, initial encounter
S37.63XA	Laceration of uterus, initial encounter
S55.212A	Laceration of vein at forearm level, left arm, initial encounter
S55.211A	Laceration of vein at forearm level, right arm, initial encounter
S55.219A	Laceration of vein at forearm level, unspecified arm, initial encounter
S21.122A	Laceration with foreign body of left front wall of thorax without penetration into thoracic cavity, initial encounter
S11.22XA	Laceration with foreign body of pharynx and cervical esophagus, initial encounter
S21.121A	Laceration with foreign body of right front wall of thorax without penetration into thoracic cavity, initial encounter
S11.12XA	Laceration with foreign body of thyroid gland, initial encounter
S21.129A	Laceration with foreign body of unspecified front wall of thorax without penetration into thoracic cavity, initial encounter
S21.92XA	Laceration with foreign body of unspecified part of thorax, initial encounter
S21.112A	Laceration without foreign body of left front wall of thorax without penetration into thoracic cavity, initial encounter
S11.21XA	Laceration without foreign body of pharynx and cervical esophagus, initial encounter
S21.111A	Laceration without foreign body of right front wall of thorax without penetration into thoracic cavity, initial encounter
S11.11XA	Laceration without foreign body of thyroid gland, initial encounter
S21.119A	Laceration without foreign body of unspecified front wall of thorax without penetration into thoracic cavity, initial encounter
S21.91XA	Laceration without foreign body of unspecified part of thorax, initial encounter
G70.81	Lambert-Eaton syndrome in disease classified elsewhere
G73.1	Lambert-Eaton syndrome in neoplastic disease
G70.80	Lambert-Eaton syndrome, unspecified
A36.2	Laryngeal diphtheria
Q31.2	Laryngeal hypoplasia
Q31.3	Laryngocele
A50.54	Late congenital cardiovascular syphilis
A50.40	Late congenital neurosyphilis, unspecified
A50.55	Late congenital syphilitic arthropathy
A50.32	Late congenital syphilitic chorioretinitis
A50.31	Late congenital syphilitic interstitial keratitis
A50.30	Late congenital syphilitic oculopathy, unspecified
A50.44	Late congenital syphilitic optic nerve atrophy
A50.56	Late congenital syphilitic osteochondropathy
A50.43	Late congenital syphilitic polyneuropathy
A52.15	Late syphilitic neuropathy
A52.71	Late syphilitic oculopathy

G11.2	Late-onset cerebellar ataxia
T82.330A	Leakage of aortic (bifurcation) graft (replacement), initial encounter
T82.532A	Leakage of artificial heart, initial encounter
T82.533A	Leakage of balloon (counterpulsation) device, initial encounter
T82.223A	Leakage of biological heart valve graft, initial encounter
T85.43XA	Leakage of breast prosthesis and implant, initial encounter
T82.331A	Leakage of carotid arterial graft (bypass), initial encounter
T82.213A	Leakage of coronary artery bypass graft, initial encounter
T85.630A	Leakage of cranial or spinal infusion catheter, initial encounter
T83.030A	Leakage of cystostomy catheter, initial encounter
T82.332A	Leakage of femoral arterial graft (bypass), initial encounter
T83.23XA	Leakage of graft of urinary organ, initial encounter
T82.03XA	Leakage of heart valve prosthesis, initial encounter
T82.534A	Leakage of infusion catheter, initial encounter
T85.633A	Leakage of insulin pump, initial encounter
T85.631A	Leakage of intraperitoneal dialysis catheter, initial encounter
T82.538A	Leakage of other cardiac and vascular devices and implants, initial encounter
T85.635A	Leakage of other nervous system device, implant or graft, initial encounter
T85.638A	Leakage of other specified internal prosthetic devices, implants and grafts, initial encounter
T82.338A	Leakage of other vascular grafts, initial encounter
T82.530A	Leakage of surgically created arteriovenous fistula, initial encounter
T82.531A	Leakage of surgically created arteriovenous shunt, initial encounter
T82.535A	Leakage of umbrella device, initial encounter
T82.539A	Leakage of unspecified cardiac and vascular devices and implants, initial encounter
T82.339A	Leakage of unspecified vascular graft, initial encounter
T82.43XA	Leakage of vascular dialysis catheter, initial encounter
T85.03XA	Leakage of ventricular intracranial (communicating) shunt, initial encounter
S02.411A	LeFort I fracture, initial encounter for closed fracture
S02.411B	LeFort I fracture, initial encounter for open fracture
S02.411K	LeFort I fracture, subsequent encounter for fracture with nonunion
S02.412A	LeFort II fracture, initial encounter for closed fracture
S02.412B	LeFort II fracture, initial encounter for open fracture
S02.412K	LeFort II fracture, subsequent encounter for fracture with nonunion
S02.413A	LeFort III fracture, initial encounter for closed fracture
S02.413B	LeFort III fracture, initial encounter for open fracture
S02.413K	LeFort III fracture, subsequent encounter for fracture with nonunion
O00.212	Left ovarian pregnancy with intrauterine pregnancy
O00.202	Left ovarian pregnancy without intrauterine pregnancy
K51.514	Left sided colitis with abscess
K51.513	Left sided colitis with fistula
K51.512	Left sided colitis with intestinal obstruction
K51.518	Left sided colitis with other complication
K51.511	Left sided colitis with rectal bleeding
K51.519	Left sided colitis with unspecified complications
K51.50	Left sided colitis without complications
O00.112	Left tubal pregnancy with intrauterine pregnancy
O00.102	Left tubal pregnancy without intrauterine pregnancy
I50.1	Left ventricular failure, unspecified
G31.82	Leigh's disease
B55.9	Leishmaniasis, unspecified
G40.813	Lennox-Gastaut syndrome, intractable, with status epilepticus
G40.814	Lennox-Gastaut syndrome, intractable, without status epilepticus
G40.811	Lennox-Gastaut syndrome, not intractable, with status epilepticus
G40.812	Lennox-Gastaut syndrome, not intractable, without status epilepticus
A30.5	Lepromatous leprosy
A30.9	Leprosy, unspecified
A27.0	Leptospirosis icterohemorrhagica
A27.9	Leptospirosis, unspecified
E79.1	Lesch-Nyhan syndrome
M31.2	Lethal midline granuloma
C95.90	Leukemia, unspecified not having achieved remission
C95.92	Leukemia, unspecified, in relapse
C95.91	Leukemia, unspecified, in remission
Q24.1	Levocardia
E85.81	Light chain (AL) amyloidosis
A32.82	Listerial endocarditis
A32.11	Listerial meningitis
A32.12	Listerial meningoencephalitis
A32.9	Listeriosis, unspecified
O26.62	Liver and biliary tract disorders in childbirth
O26.611	Liver and biliary tract disorders in pregnancy, first trimester
O26.612	Liver and biliary tract disorders in pregnancy, second trimester
O26.613	Liver and biliary tract disorders in pregnancy, third trimester
C22.0	Liver cell carcinoma
K77	Liver disorders in diseases classified elsewhere
T86.42	Liver transplant failure
T86.43	Liver transplant infection
T86.41	Liver transplant rejection
Z94.4	Liver transplant status
T80.212A	Local infection due to central venous catheter, initial encounter
G40.011	Localization-related (focal) (partial) idiopathic epilepsy and epileptic syndromes with seizures of localized onset, intractable, with status epilepticus
G40.019	Localization-related (focal) (partial) idiopathic epilepsy and epileptic syndromes with seizures of localized onset, intractable, without status epilepticus
G40.001	Localization-related (focal) (partial) idiopathic epilepsy and epileptic syndromes with seizures of localized onset, not intractable, with status epilepticus
G40.009	Localization-related (focal) (partial) idiopathic epilepsy and epileptic syndromes with seizures of localized onset, not intractable, without status epilepticus
G40.211	Localization-related (focal) (partial) symptomatic epilepsy and epileptic syndromes with complex partial seizures, intractable, with status epilepticus
G40.219	Localization-related (focal) (partial) symptomatic epilepsy and epileptic syndromes with complex partial seizures, intractable, without status epilepticus
G40.201	Localization-related (focal) (partial) symptomatic epilepsy and epileptic syndromes with complex partial seizures, not intractable, with status epilepticus
G40.209	Localization-related (focal) (partial) symptomatic epilepsy and epileptic syndromes with complex partial seizures, not intractable, without status epilepticus
G40.111	Localization-related (focal) (partial) symptomatic epilepsy and epileptic syndromes with simple partial seizures, intractable, with status epilepticus
G40.119	Localization-related (focal) (partial) symptomatic epilepsy and epileptic syndromes with simple partial seizures, intractable, without status epilepticus
G40.101	Localization-related (focal) (partial) symptomatic epilepsy and epileptic syndromes with simple partial seizures, not intractable, with status epilepticus
G40.109	Localization-related (focal) (partial) symptomatic epilepsy and epileptic syndromes with simple partial seizures, not intractable, without status epilepticus
B74.3	Loiasis
E71.310	Long chain/very long chain acyl CoA dehydrogenase deficiency
O63.9	Long labor, unspecified
I48.11	Longstanding persistent atrial fibrillation
A68.0	Louse-borne relapsing fever
O44.41	Low lying placenta NOS or without hemorrhage, first trimester
O44.42	Low lying placenta NOS or without hemorrhage, second trimester
O44.43	Low lying placenta NOS or without hemorrhage, third trimester
E72.03	Lowe's syndrome
Q05.2	Lumbar spina bifida with hydrocephalus
T86.811	Lung transplant failure
T86.812	Lung transplant infection
T86.810	Lung transplant rejection
Z94.2	Lung transplant status
D68.62	Lupus anticoagulant syndrome
A69.20	Lyme disease, unspecified
C83.59	Lymphoblastic (diffuse) lymphoma, extranodal and solid organ sites
C83.53	Lymphoblastic (diffuse) lymphoma, intra-abdominal lymph nodes
C83.56	Lymphoblastic (diffuse) lymphoma, intrapelvic lymph nodes
C83.52	Lymphoblastic (diffuse) lymphoma, intrathoracic lymph nodes
C83.54	Lymphoblastic (diffuse) lymphoma, lymph nodes of axilla and upper limb
C83.51	Lymphoblastic (diffuse) lymphoma, lymph nodes of head, face, and neck
C83.55	Lymphoblastic (diffuse) lymphoma, lymph nodes of inguinal region and lower limb
C83.58	Lymphoblastic (diffuse) lymphoma, lymph nodes of multiple sites
C83.57	Lymphoblastic (diffuse) lymphoma, spleen
C83.50	Lymphoblastic (diffuse) lymphoma, unspecified site
C81.39	Lymphocyte depleted Hodgkin lymphoma, extranodal and solid organ sites
C81.33	Lymphocyte depleted Hodgkin lymphoma, intra-abdominal lymph nodes
C81.36	Lymphocyte depleted Hodgkin lymphoma, intrapelvic lymph nodes
C81.32	Lymphocyte depleted Hodgkin lymphoma, intrathoracic lymph nodes
C81.34	Lymphocyte depleted Hodgkin lymphoma, lymph nodes of axilla and upper limb
C81.31	Lymphocyte depleted Hodgkin lymphoma, lymph nodes of head, face, and neck
C81.35	Lymphocyte depleted Hodgkin lymphoma, lymph nodes of inguinal region and lower limb
C81.38	Lymphocyte depleted Hodgkin lymphoma, lymph nodes of multiple sites
C81.37	Lymphocyte depleted Hodgkin lymphoma, spleen
C81.30	Lymphocyte depleted Hodgkin lymphoma, unspecified site
C81.49	Lymphocyte-rich Hodgkin lymphoma, extranodal and solid organ sites
C81.43	Lymphocyte-rich Hodgkin lymphoma, intra-abdominal lymph nodes
C81.46	Lymphocyte-rich Hodgkin lymphoma, intrapelvic lymph nodes
C81.42	Lymphocyte-rich Hodgkin lymphoma, intrathoracic lymph nodes
C81.44	Lymphocyte-rich Hodgkin lymphoma, lymph nodes of axilla and upper limb
C81.41	Lymphocyte-rich Hodgkin lymphoma, lymph nodes of head, face, and neck
C81.45	Lymphocyte-rich Hodgkin lymphoma, lymph nodes of inguinal region and lower limb
C81.48	Lymphocyte-rich Hodgkin lymphoma, lymph nodes of multiple sites
C81.47	Lymphocyte-rich Hodgkin lymphoma, spleen
C81.40	Lymphocyte-rich Hodgkin lymphoma, unspecified site
A87.2	Lymphocytic choriomeningitis
J84.2	Lymphoid interstitial pneumonia
C91.90	Lymphoid leukemia, unspecified not having achieved remission
C91.92	Lymphoid leukemia, unspecified, in relapse
C91.91	Lymphoid leukemia, unspecified, in remission
A96.1	Machupo hemorrhagic fever
S37.022A	Major contusion of left kidney, initial encounter
S37.021A	Major contusion of right kidney, initial encounter
S36.021A	Major contusion of spleen, initial encounter
S37.029A	Major contusion of unspecified kidney, initial encounter
F33.2	Major depressive disorder, recurrent severe without psychotic features
F33.40	Major depressive disorder, recurrent, in remission, unspecified

F33.0	Major depressive disorder, recurrent, mild
F33.1	Major depressive disorder, recurrent, moderate
F33.3	Major depressive disorder, recurrent, severe with psychotic symptoms
F33.9	Major depressive disorder, recurrent, unspecified
F32.0	Major depressive disorder, single episode, mild
F32.1	Major depressive disorder, single episode, moderate
F32.3	Major depressive disorder, single episode, severe with psychotic features
F32.2	Major depressive disorder, single episode, severe without psychotic features
D81.6	Major histocompatibility complex class I deficiency
D81.7	Major histocompatibility complex class II deficiency
S36.261A	Major laceration of body of pancreas, initial encounter
S75.222A	Major laceration of greater saphenous vein at hip and thigh level, left leg, initial encounter
S75.221A	Major laceration of greater saphenous vein at hip and thigh level, right leg, initial encounter
S75.229A	Major laceration of greater saphenous vein at hip and thigh level, unspecified leg, initial encounter
S36.260A	Major laceration of head of pancreas, initial encounter
S15.022A	Major laceration of left carotid artery, initial encounter
S15.222A	Major laceration of left external jugular vein, initial encounter
S15.322A	Major laceration of left internal jugular vein, initial encounter
S15.122A	Major laceration of left vertebral artery, initial encounter
S15.021A	Major laceration of right carotid artery, initial encounter
S15.221A	Major laceration of right external jugular vein, initial encounter
S15.321A	Major laceration of right internal jugular vein, initial encounter
S15.121A	Major laceration of right vertebral artery, initial encounter
S36.262A	Major laceration of tail of pancreas, initial encounter
S15.029A	Major laceration of unspecified carotid artery, initial encounter
S15.229A	Major laceration of unspecified external jugular vein, initial encounter
S15.329A	Major laceration of unspecified internal jugular vein, initial encounter
S36.269A	Major laceration of unspecified part of pancreas, initial encounter
S15.129A	Major laceration of unspecified vertebral artery, initial encounter
K90.49	Malabsorption due to intolerance, not elsewhere classified
S02.40BA	Malar fracture, left side, initial encounter for closed fracture
S02.40BB	Malar fracture, left side, initial encounter for open fracture
S02.40BK	Malar fracture, left side, subsequent encounter for fracture with nonunion
S02.40AA	Malar fracture, right side, initial encounter for closed fracture
S02.40AB	Malar fracture, right side, initial encounter for open fracture
S02.40AK	Malar fracture, right side, subsequent encounter for fracture with nonunion
S02.400A	Malar fracture, unspecified side, initial encounter for closed fracture
S02.400B	Malar fracture, unspecified side, initial encounter for open fracture
S02.400K	Malar fracture, unspecified side, subsequent encounter for fracture with nonunion
B53.1	Malaria due to simian plasmodia
Q24.5	Malformation of coronary vessels
J95.03	Malfunction of tracheostomy stoma
R18.0	Malignant ascites
C7A.020	Malignant carcinoid tumor of the appendix
C7A.022	Malignant carcinoid tumor of the ascending colon
C7A.090	Malignant carcinoid tumor of the bronchus and lung
C7A.021	Malignant carcinoid tumor of the cecum
C7A.024	Malignant carcinoid tumor of the descending colon
C7A.010	Malignant carcinoid tumor of the duodenum
C7A.094	Malignant carcinoid tumor of the foregut, unspecified
C7A.096	Malignant carcinoid tumor of the hindgut, unspecified
C7A.012	Malignant carcinoid tumor of the ileum
C7A.011	Malignant carcinoid tumor of the jejunum
C7A.093	Malignant carcinoid tumor of the kidney
C7A.029	Malignant carcinoid tumor of the large intestine, unspecified portion
C7A.095	Malignant carcinoid tumor of the midgut, unspecified
C7A.026	Malignant carcinoid tumor of the rectum
C7A.025	Malignant carcinoid tumor of the sigmoid colon
C7A.019	Malignant carcinoid tumor of the small intestine, unspecified portion
C7A.092	Malignant carcinoid tumor of the stomach
C7A.091	Malignant carcinoid tumor of the thymus
C7A.023	Malignant carcinoid tumor of the transverse colon
C7A.00	Malignant carcinoid tumor of unspecified site
C7A.098	Malignant carcinoid tumors of other sites
T88.3XXA	Malignant hyperthermia due to anesthesia, initial encounter
C88.9	Malignant immunoproliferative disease, unspecified
C96.20	Malignant mast cell neoplasm, unspecified
C80.2	Malignant neoplasm associated with transplanted organ
C24.1	Malignant neoplasm of ampulla of Vater
C21.1	Malignant neoplasm of anal canal
C38.1	Malignant neoplasm of anterior mediastinum
C21.0	Malignant neoplasm of anus, unspecified
C75.5	Malignant neoplasm of aortic body and other paraganglia
C18.1	Malignant neoplasm of appendix
C18.2	Malignant neoplasm of ascending colon
C24.9	Malignant neoplasm of biliary tract, unspecified
C25.1	Malignant neoplasm of body of pancreas
C16.2	Malignant neoplasm of body of stomach
C41.9	Malignant neoplasm of bone and articular cartilage, unspecified
C41.0	Malignant neoplasm of bones of skull and face
C71.7	Malignant neoplasm of brain stem
C71.9	Malignant neoplasm of brain, unspecified
C16.0	Malignant neoplasm of cardia
C75.4	Malignant neoplasm of carotid body
C72.1	Malignant neoplasm of cauda equina

C18.0	Malignant neoplasm of cecum
C72.9	Malignant neoplasm of central nervous system, unspecified
C71.6	Malignant neoplasm of cerebellum
C70.0	Malignant neoplasm of cerebral meninges
C71.5	Malignant neoplasm of cerebral ventricle
C71.0	Malignant neoplasm of cerebrum, except lobes and ventricles
C21.2	Malignant neoplasm of cloacogenic zone
C18.9	Malignant neoplasm of colon, unspecified
C49.4	Malignant neoplasm of connective and soft tissue of abdomen
C49.0	Malignant neoplasm of connective and soft tissue of head, face and neck
C49.22	Malignant neoplasm of connective and soft tissue of left lower limb, including hip
C49.12	Malignant neoplasm of connective and soft tissue of left upper limb, including shoulder
C49.5	Malignant neoplasm of connective and soft tissue of pelvis
C49.21	Malignant neoplasm of connective and soft tissue of right lower limb, including hip
C49.11	Malignant neoplasm of connective and soft tissue of right upper limb, including shoulder
C49.3	Malignant neoplasm of connective and soft tissue of thorax
C49.6	Malignant neoplasm of connective and soft tissue of trunk, unspecified
C49.20	Malignant neoplasm of connective and soft tissue of unspecified lower limb, including hip
C49.10	Malignant neoplasm of connective and soft tissue of unspecified upper limb, including shoulder
C49.9	Malignant neoplasm of connective and soft tissue, unspecified
C74.02	Malignant neoplasm of cortex of left adrenal gland
C74.01	Malignant neoplasm of cortex of right adrenal gland
C74.00	Malignant neoplasm of cortex of unspecified adrenal gland
C75.2	Malignant neoplasm of craniopharyngeal duct
C18.6	Malignant neoplasm of descending colon
C17.0	Malignant neoplasm of duodenum
C75.9	Malignant neoplasm of endocrine gland, unspecified
C25.4	Malignant neoplasm of endocrine pancreas
C15.9	Malignant neoplasm of esophagus, unspecified
C24.0	Malignant neoplasm of extrahepatic bile duct
C71.1	Malignant neoplasm of frontal lobe
C16.1	Malignant neoplasm of fundus of stomach
C23	Malignant neoplasm of gallbladder
C16.6	Malignant neoplasm of greater curvature of stomach, unspecified
C25.0	Malignant neoplasm of head of pancreas
C38.0	Malignant neoplasm of heart
C18.3	Malignant neoplasm of hepatic flexure
C17.2	Malignant neoplasm of ileum
C17.1	Malignant neoplasm of jejunum
C72.42	Malignant neoplasm of left acoustic nerve
C64.2	Malignant neoplasm of left kidney, except renal pelvis
C34.02	Malignant neoplasm of left main bronchus
C72.22	Malignant neoplasm of left olfactory nerve
C72.32	Malignant neoplasm of left optic nerve
C56.2	Malignant neoplasm of left ovary
C65.2	Malignant neoplasm of left renal pelvis
C66.2	Malignant neoplasm of left ureter
C16.5	Malignant neoplasm of lesser curvature of stomach, unspecified
C22.9	Malignant neoplasm of liver, not specified as primary or secondary
C22.8	Malignant neoplasm of liver, primary, unspecified as to type
C40.22	Malignant neoplasm of long bones of left lower limb
C40.21	Malignant neoplasm of long bones of right lower limb
C40.20	Malignant neoplasm of long bones of unspecified lower limb
C34.32	Malignant neoplasm of lower lobe, left bronchus or lung
C34.31	Malignant neoplasm of lower lobe, right bronchus or lung
C34.30	Malignant neoplasm of lower lobe, unspecified bronchus or lung
C15.5	Malignant neoplasm of lower third of esophagus
C96.9	Malignant neoplasm of lymphoid, hematopoietic and related tissue, unspecified
C41.1	Malignant neoplasm of mandible
C38.3	Malignant neoplasm of mediastinum, part unspecified
C74.12	Malignant neoplasm of medulla of left adrenal gland
C74.11	Malignant neoplasm of medulla of right adrenal gland
C74.10	Malignant neoplasm of medulla of unspecified adrenal gland
C70.9	Malignant neoplasm of meninges, unspecified
C34.2	Malignant neoplasm of middle lobe, bronchus or lung
C15.4	Malignant neoplasm of middle third of esophagus
C71.4	Malignant neoplasm of occipital lobe
C72.59	Malignant neoplasm of other cranial nerves
C25.7	Malignant neoplasm of other parts of pancreas
C24.8	Malignant neoplasm of overlapping sites of biliary tract
C40.82	Malignant neoplasm of overlapping sites of bone and articular cartilage of left limb
C40.81	Malignant neoplasm of overlapping sites of bone and articular cartilage of right limb
C40.80	Malignant neoplasm of overlapping sites of bone and articular cartilage of unspecified limb
C71.8	Malignant neoplasm of overlapping sites of brain
C18.8	Malignant neoplasm of overlapping sites of colon
C49.8	Malignant neoplasm of overlapping sites of connective and soft tissue
C15.8	Malignant neoplasm of overlapping sites of esophagus
C38.8	Malignant neoplasm of overlapping sites of heart, mediastinum and pleura
C34.82	Malignant neoplasm of overlapping sites of left bronchus and lung

C25.8	Malignant neoplasm of overlapping sites of pancreas
C47.8	Malignant neoplasm of overlapping sites of peripheral nerves and autonomic nervous system
C21.8	Malignant neoplasm of overlapping sites of rectum, anus and anal canal
C48.8	Malignant neoplasm of overlapping sites of retroperitoneum and peritoneum
C34.81	Malignant neoplasm of overlapping sites of right bronchus and lung
C17.8	Malignant neoplasm of overlapping sites of small intestine
C16.8	Malignant neoplasm of overlapping sites of stomach
C34.80	Malignant neoplasm of overlapping sites of unspecified bronchus and lung
C68.8	Malignant neoplasm of overlapping sites of urinary organs
C25.9	Malignant neoplasm of pancreas, unspecified
C25.3	Malignant neoplasm of pancreatic duct
C75.0	Malignant neoplasm of parathyroid gland
C68.1	Malignant neoplasm of paraurethral glands
C71.3	Malignant neoplasm of parietal lobe
C41.4	Malignant neoplasm of pelvic bones, sacrum and coccyx
C47.9	Malignant neoplasm of peripheral nerves and autonomic nervous system, unspecified
C47.4	Malignant neoplasm of peripheral nerves of abdomen
C47.0	Malignant neoplasm of peripheral nerves of head, face and neck
C47.22	Malignant neoplasm of peripheral nerves of left lower limb, including hip
C47.12	Malignant neoplasm of peripheral nerves of left upper limb, including shoulder
C47.5	Malignant neoplasm of peripheral nerves of pelvis
C47.21	Malignant neoplasm of peripheral nerves of right lower limb, including hip
C47.11	Malignant neoplasm of peripheral nerves of right upper limb, including shoulder
C47.3	Malignant neoplasm of peripheral nerves of thorax
C47.6	Malignant neoplasm of peripheral nerves of trunk, unspecified
C47.20	Malignant neoplasm of peripheral nerves of unspecified lower limb, including hip
C47.10	Malignant neoplasm of peripheral nerves of unspecified upper limb, including shoulder
C48.2	Malignant neoplasm of peritoneum, unspecified
C75.3	Malignant neoplasm of pineal gland
C75.1	Malignant neoplasm of pituitary gland
C38.4	Malignant neoplasm of pleura
C38.2	Malignant neoplasm of posterior mediastinum
C16.3	Malignant neoplasm of pyloric antrum
C16.4	Malignant neoplasm of pylorus
C19	Malignant neoplasm of rectosigmoid junction
C20	Malignant neoplasm of rectum
C48.0	Malignant neoplasm of retroperitoneum
C41.3	Malignant neoplasm of ribs, sternum and clavicle
C72.41	Malignant neoplasm of right acoustic nerve
C64.1	Malignant neoplasm of right kidney, except renal pelvis
C34.01	Malignant neoplasm of right main bronchus
C72.21	Malignant neoplasm of right olfactory nerve
C72.31	Malignant neoplasm of right optic nerve
C56.1	Malignant neoplasm of right ovary
C65.1	Malignant neoplasm of right renal pelvis
C66.1	Malignant neoplasm of right ureter
C40.02	Malignant neoplasm of scapula and long bones of left upper limb
C40.01	Malignant neoplasm of scapula and long bones of right upper limb
C40.00	Malignant neoplasm of scapula and long bones of unspecified upper limb
C40.32	Malignant neoplasm of short bones of left lower limb
C40.12	Malignant neoplasm of short bones of left upper limb
C40.31	Malignant neoplasm of short bones of right lower limb
C40.11	Malignant neoplasm of short bones of right upper limb
C40.30	Malignant neoplasm of short bones of unspecified lower limb
C40.10	Malignant neoplasm of short bones of unspecified upper limb
C18.7	Malignant neoplasm of sigmoid colon
C17.9	Malignant neoplasm of small intestine, unspecified
C48.1	Malignant neoplasm of specified parts of peritoneum
C72.0	Malignant neoplasm of spinal cord
C70.1	Malignant neoplasm of spinal meninges
C18.5	Malignant neoplasm of splenic flexure
C16.9	Malignant neoplasm of stomach, unspecified
C25.2	Malignant neoplasm of tail of pancreas
C71.2	Malignant neoplasm of temporal lobe
C37	Malignant neoplasm of thymus
C33	Malignant neoplasm of trachea
C18.4	Malignant neoplasm of transverse colon
C72.40	Malignant neoplasm of unspecified acoustic nerve
C40.92	Malignant neoplasm of unspecified bones and articular cartilage of left limb
C40.91	Malignant neoplasm of unspecified bones and articular cartilage of right limb
C40.90	Malignant neoplasm of unspecified bones and articular cartilage of unspecified limb
C72.50	Malignant neoplasm of unspecified cranial nerve
C64.9	Malignant neoplasm of unspecified kidney, except renal pelvis
C34.00	Malignant neoplasm of unspecified main bronchus
C72.20	Malignant neoplasm of unspecified olfactory nerve
C72.30	Malignant neoplasm of unspecified optic nerve
C56.9	Malignant neoplasm of unspecified ovary
C74.92	Malignant neoplasm of unspecified part of left adrenal gland
C34.92	Malignant neoplasm of unspecified part of left bronchus or lung
C74.91	Malignant neoplasm of unspecified part of right adrenal gland
C34.91	Malignant neoplasm of unspecified part of right bronchus or lung
C74.90	Malignant neoplasm of unspecified part of unspecified adrenal gland
C34.90	Malignant neoplasm of unspecified part of unspecified bronchus or lung
C65.9	Malignant neoplasm of unspecified renal pelvis
C66.9	Malignant neoplasm of unspecified ureter
C34.12	Malignant neoplasm of upper lobe, left bronchus or lung
C34.11	Malignant neoplasm of upper lobe, right bronchus or lung
C34.10	Malignant neoplasm of upper lobe, unspecified bronchus or lung
C15.3	Malignant neoplasm of upper third of esophagus
C68.0	Malignant neoplasm of urethra
C68.9	Malignant neoplasm of urinary organ, unspecified
C41.2	Malignant neoplasm of vertebral column
C75.8	Malignant neoplasm with pluriglandular involvement, unspecified
H60.23	Malignant otitis externa, bilateral
H60.22	Malignant otitis externa, left ear
H60.21	Malignant otitis externa, right ear
H60.20	Malignant otitis externa, unspecified ear
J91.0	Malignant pleural effusion
C7A.1	Malignant poorly differentiated neuroendocrine tumors
F30.11	Manic episode without psychotic symptoms, mild
F30.12	Manic episode without psychotic symptoms, moderate
F30.10	Manic episode without psychotic symptoms, unspecified
F30.2	Manic episode, severe with psychotic symptoms
F30.13	Manic episode, severe, without psychotic symptoms
F30.9	Manic episode, unspecified
B74.4	Mansonelliasis
C83.19	Mantle cell lymphoma, extranodal and solid organ sites
C83.13	Mantle cell lymphoma, intra-abdominal lymph nodes
C83.16	Mantle cell lymphoma, intrapelvic lymph nodes
C83.12	Mantle cell lymphoma, intrathoracic lymph nodes
C83.14	Mantle cell lymphoma, lymph nodes of axilla and upper limb
C83.11	Mantle cell lymphoma, lymph nodes of head, face, and neck
C83.15	Mantle cell lymphoma, lymph nodes of inguinal region and lower limb
C83.18	Mantle cell lymphoma, lymph nodes of multiple sites
C83.17	Mantle cell lymphoma, spleen
C83.10	Mantle cell lymphoma, unspecified site
E71.0	Maple-syrup-urine disease
Q87.410	Marfan's syndrome with aortic dilation
Q87.42	Marfan's syndrome with ocular manifestations
Q87.418	Marfan's syndrome with other cardiovascular manifestations
Q87.43	Marfan's syndrome with skeletal manifestation
Q87.40	Marfan's syndrome, unspecified
C94.30	Mast cell leukemia not having achieved remission
C94.32	Mast cell leukemia, in relapse
C94.31	Mast cell leukemia, in remission
C96.22	Mast cell sarcoma
O36.0111	Maternal care for anti-D [Rh] antibodies, first trimester, fetus 1
O36.0112	Maternal care for anti-D [Rh] antibodies, first trimester, fetus 2
O36.0113	Maternal care for anti-D [Rh] antibodies, first trimester, fetus 3
O36.0114	Maternal care for anti-D [Rh] antibodies, first trimester, fetus 4
O36.0115	Maternal care for anti-D [Rh] antibodies, first trimester, fetus 5
O36.0110	Maternal care for anti-D [Rh] antibodies, first trimester, not applicable or unspecified
O36.0119	Maternal care for anti-D [Rh] antibodies, first trimester, other fetus
O36.0121	Maternal care for anti-D [Rh] antibodies, second trimester, fetus 1
O36.0122	Maternal care for anti-D [Rh] antibodies, second trimester, fetus 2
O36.0123	Maternal care for anti-D [Rh] antibodies, second trimester, fetus 3
O36.0124	Maternal care for anti-D [Rh] antibodies, second trimester, fetus 4
O36.0125	Maternal care for anti-D [Rh] antibodies, second trimester, fetus 5
O36.0120	Maternal care for anti-D [Rh] antibodies, second trimester, not applicable or unspecified
O36.0129	Maternal care for anti-D [Rh] antibodies, second trimester, other fetus
O36.0131	Maternal care for anti-D [Rh] antibodies, third trimester, fetus 1
O36.0132	Maternal care for anti-D [Rh] antibodies, third trimester, fetus 2
O36.0133	Maternal care for anti-D [Rh] antibodies, third trimester, fetus 3
O36.0134	Maternal care for anti-D [Rh] antibodies, third trimester, fetus 4
O36.0135	Maternal care for anti-D [Rh] antibodies, third trimester, fetus 5
O36.0130	Maternal care for anti-D [Rh] antibodies, third trimester, not applicable or unspecified
O36.0139	Maternal care for anti-D [Rh] antibodies, third trimester, other fetus
O33.0	Maternal care for disproportion due to deformity of maternal pelvic bones
O36.4XX1	Maternal care for intrauterine death, fetus 1
O36.4XX2	Maternal care for intrauterine death, fetus 2
O36.4XX3	Maternal care for intrauterine death, fetus 3
O36.4XX4	Maternal care for intrauterine death, fetus 4
O36.4XX5	Maternal care for intrauterine death, fetus 5
O36.4XX0	Maternal care for intrauterine death, not applicable or unspecified
O36.4XX9	Maternal care for intrauterine death, other fetus
O36.0911	Maternal care for other rhesus isoimmunization, first trimester, fetus 1
O36.0912	Maternal care for other rhesus isoimmunization, first trimester, fetus 2
O36.0913	Maternal care for other rhesus isoimmunization, first trimester, fetus 3
O36.0914	Maternal care for other rhesus isoimmunization, first trimester, fetus 4
O36.0915	Maternal care for other rhesus isoimmunization, first trimester, fetus 5
O36.0910	Maternal care for other rhesus isoimmunization, first trimester, not applicable or unspecified
O36.0919	Maternal care for other rhesus isoimmunization, first trimester, other fetus
O36.0921	Maternal care for other rhesus isoimmunization, second trimester, fetus 1
O36.0922	Maternal care for other rhesus isoimmunization, second trimester, fetus 2
O36.0923	Maternal care for other rhesus isoimmunization, second trimester, fetus 3
O36.0924	Maternal care for other rhesus isoimmunization, second trimester, fetus 4
O36.0925	Maternal care for other rhesus isoimmunization, second trimester, fetus 5

O36.0920	Maternal care for other rhesus isoimmunization, second trimester, not applicable or unspecified
O36.0929	Maternal care for other rhesus isoimmunization, second trimester, other fetus
O36.0931	Maternal care for other rhesus isoimmunization, third trimester, fetus 1
O36.0932	Maternal care for other rhesus isoimmunization, third trimester, fetus 2
O36.0933	Maternal care for other rhesus isoimmunization, third trimester, fetus 3
O36.0934	Maternal care for other rhesus isoimmunization, third trimester, fetus 4
O36.0935	Maternal care for other rhesus isoimmunization, third trimester, fetus 5
O36.0930	Maternal care for other rhesus isoimmunization, third trimester, not applicable or unspecified
O36.0939	Maternal care for other rhesus isoimmunization, third trimester, other fetus
C91.A0	Mature B-cell leukemia Burkitt-type not having achieved remission
C91.A2	Mature B-cell leukemia Burkitt-type, in relapse
C91.A1	Mature B-cell leukemia Burkitt-type, in remission
C84.99	Mature T/NK-cell lymphomas, unspecified, extranodal and solid organ sites
C84.93	Mature T/NK-cell lymphomas, unspecified, intra-abdominal lymph nodes
C84.96	Mature T/NK-cell lymphomas, unspecified, intrapelvic lymph nodes
C84.92	Mature T/NK-cell lymphomas, unspecified, intrathoracic lymph nodes
C84.94	Mature T/NK-cell lymphomas, unspecified, lymph nodes of axilla and upper limb
C84.91	Mature T/NK-cell lymphomas, unspecified, lymph nodes of head, face, and neck
C84.95	Mature T/NK-cell lymphomas, unspecified, lymph nodes of inguinal region and lower limb
C84.98	Mature T/NK-cell lymphomas, unspecified, lymph nodes of multiple sites
C84.97	Mature T/NK-cell lymphomas, unspecified, spleen
C84.90	Mature T/NK-cell lymphomas, unspecified, unspecified site
S02.40DA	Maxillary fracture, left side, initial encounter for closed fracture
S02.40DB	Maxillary fracture, left side, initial encounter for open fracture
S02.40DK	Maxillary fracture, left side, subsequent encounter for fracture with nonunion
S02.40CA	Maxillary fracture, right side, initial encounter for closed fracture
S02.40CB	Maxillary fracture, right side, initial encounter for open fracture
S02.40CK	Maxillary fracture, right side, subsequent encounter for fracture with nonunion
S02.401A	Maxillary fracture, unspecified side, initial encounter for closed fracture
S02.401B	Maxillary fracture, unspecified side, initial encounter for open fracture
S02.401K	Maxillary fracture, unspecified side, subsequent encounter for fracture with nonunion
E74.04	McArdle disease
B05.1	Measles complicated by meningitis
B05.81	Measles keratitis and keratoconjunctivitis
B05.4	Measles with intestinal complications
J95.850	Mechanical complication of respirator
T84.031A	Mechanical loosening of internal left hip prosthetic joint, initial encounter
T84.033A	Mechanical loosening of internal left knee prosthetic joint, initial encounter
T84.030A	Mechanical loosening of internal right hip prosthetic joint, initial encounter
T84.032A	Mechanical loosening of internal right knee prosthetic joint, initial encounter
T84.038A	Mechanical loosening of other internal prosthetic joint, initial encounter
T84.039A	Mechanical loosening of unspecified internal prosthetic joint, initial encounter
C17.3	Meckel's diverticulum, malignant
C85.29	Mediastinal (thymic) large B-cell lymphoma, extranodal and solid organ sites
C85.23	Mediastinal (thymic) large B-cell lymphoma, intra-abdominal lymph nodes
C85.26	Mediastinal (thymic) large B-cell lymphoma, intrapelvic lymph nodes
C85.22	Mediastinal (thymic) large B-cell lymphoma, intrathoracic lymph nodes
C85.24	Mediastinal (thymic) large B-cell lymphoma, lymph nodes of axilla and upper limb
C85.21	Mediastinal (thymic) large B-cell lymphoma, lymph nodes of head, face, and neck
C85.25	Mediastinal (thymic) large B-cell lymphoma, lymph nodes of inguinal region and lower limb
C85.28	Mediastinal (thymic) large B-cell lymphoma, lymph nodes of multiple sites
C85.27	Mediastinal (thymic) large B-cell lymphoma, spleen
C85.20	Mediastinal (thymic) large B-cell lymphoma, unspecified site
E71.311	Medium chain acyl CoA dehydrogenase deficiency
Q61.5	Medullary cystic kidney
B57.32	Megacolon in Chagas' disease
B57.31	Megaesophagus in Chagas' disease
Q04.5	Megalencephaly
E88.41	MELAS syndrome
K92.1	Melena
A24.9	Melioidosis, unspecified
R29.1	Meningismus
A69.21	Meningitis due to Lyme disease
B57.41	Meningitis in Chagas' disease
A39.83	Meningococcal arthritis
A39.9	Meningococcal infection, unspecified
A39.82	Meningococcal retrobulbar neuritis
B57.42	Meningoencephalitis in Chagas' disease
E88.42	MERRF syndrome
C45.2	Mesothelioma of pericardium
C45.1	Mesothelioma of peritoneum
C45.0	Mesothelioma of pleura
O04.83	Metabolic disorder following (induced) termination of pregnancy
O03.83	Metabolic disorder following complete or unspecified spontaneous abortion
O07.33	Metabolic disorder following failed attempted termination of pregnancy
O03.33	Metabolic disorder following incomplete spontaneous abortion
O08.5	Metabolic disorders following an ectopic and molar pregnancy
E75.25	Metachromatic leukodystrophy

D74.9	Methemoglobinemia, unspecified
E72.12	Methylenetetrahydrofolate reductase deficiency
E71.120	Methylmalonic acidemia
M31.7	Microscopic polyangiitis
G46.0	Middle cerebral artery syndrome
P91.61	Mild hypoxic ischemic encephalopathy [HIE]
J45.21	Mild intermittent asthma with (acute) exacerbation
J45.22	Mild intermittent asthma with status asthmaticus
J45.31	Mild persistent asthma with (acute) exacerbation
J45.32	Mild persistent asthma with status asthmaticus
E44.1	Mild protein-calorie malnutrition
O14.02	Mild to moderate pre-eclampsia, second trimester
O14.03	Mild to moderate pre-eclampsia, third trimester
S32.111A	Minimally displaced Zone I fracture of sacrum, initial encounter for closed fracture
S32.111K	Minimally displaced Zone I fracture of sacrum, subsequent encounter for fracture with nonunion
S32.121A	Minimally displaced Zone II fracture of sacrum, initial encounter for closed fracture
S32.121K	Minimally displaced Zone II fracture of sacrum, subsequent encounter for fracture with nonunion
S32.131A	Minimally displaced Zone III fracture of sacrum, initial encounter for closed fracture
S32.131K	Minimally displaced Zone III fracture of sacrum, subsequent encounter for fracture with nonunion
S37.012A	Minor contusion of left kidney, initial encounter
S37.011A	Minor contusion of right kidney, initial encounter
S36.020A	Minor contusion of spleen, initial encounter
S37.019A	Minor contusion of unspecified kidney, initial encounter
S36.241A	Minor laceration of body of pancreas, initial encounter
S75.212A	Minor laceration of greater saphenous vein at hip and thigh level, left leg, initial encounter
S75.211A	Minor laceration of greater saphenous vein at hip and thigh level, right leg, initial encounter
S75.219A	Minor laceration of greater saphenous vein at hip and thigh level, unspecified leg, initial encounter
S36.240A	Minor laceration of head of pancreas, initial encounter
S15.012A	Minor laceration of left carotid artery, initial encounter
S15.212A	Minor laceration of left external jugular vein, initial encounter
S15.312A	Minor laceration of left internal jugular vein, initial encounter
S37.042A	Minor laceration of left kidney, initial encounter
S15.112A	Minor laceration of left vertebral artery, initial encounter
S36.114A	Minor laceration of liver, initial encounter
S15.011A	Minor laceration of right carotid artery, initial encounter
S15.211A	Minor laceration of right external jugular vein, initial encounter
S15.311A	Minor laceration of right internal jugular vein, initial encounter
S37.041A	Minor laceration of right kidney, initial encounter
S15.111A	Minor laceration of right vertebral artery, initial encounter
S36.242A	Minor laceration of tail of pancreas, initial encounter
S15.019A	Minor laceration of unspecified carotid artery, initial encounter
S15.219A	Minor laceration of unspecified external jugular vein, initial encounter
S15.319A	Minor laceration of unspecified internal jugular vein, initial encounter
S37.049A	Minor laceration of unspecified kidney, initial encounter
S36.249A	Minor laceration of unspecified part of pancreas, initial encounter
S15.119A	Minor laceration of unspecified vertebral artery, initial encounter
E88.40	Mitochondrial metabolism disorder, unspecified
C81.29	Mixed cellularity Hodgkin lymphoma, extranodal and solid organ sites
C81.23	Mixed cellularity Hodgkin lymphoma, intra-abdominal lymph nodes
C81.26	Mixed cellularity Hodgkin lymphoma, intrapelvic lymph nodes
C81.22	Mixed cellularity Hodgkin lymphoma, intrathoracic lymph nodes
C81.24	Mixed cellularity Hodgkin lymphoma, lymph nodes of axilla and upper limb
C81.21	Mixed cellularity Hodgkin lymphoma, lymph nodes of head, face, and neck
C81.25	Mixed cellularity Hodgkin lymphoma, lymph nodes of inguinal region and lower limb
C81.28	Mixed cellularity Hodgkin lymphoma, lymph nodes of multiple sites
C81.27	Mixed cellularity Hodgkin lymphoma, spleen
C81.20	Mixed cellularity Hodgkin lymphoma, unspecified site
E87.4	Mixed disorder of acid-base balance
B81.4	Mixed intestinal helminthiases
P91.62	Moderate hypoxic ischemic encephalopathy [HIE]
S36.251A	Moderate laceration of body of pancreas, initial encounter
S36.250A	Moderate laceration of head of pancreas, initial encounter
S37.052A	Moderate laceration of left kidney, initial encounter
S37.051A	Moderate laceration of right kidney, initial encounter
S36.252A	Moderate laceration of tail of pancreas, initial encounter
S37.059A	Moderate laceration of unspecified kidney, initial encounter
S36.259A	Moderate laceration of unspecified part of pancreas, initial encounter
J45.41	Moderate persistent asthma with (acute) exacerbation
J45.42	Moderate persistent asthma with status asthmaticus
E44.0	Moderate protein-calorie malnutrition
B04	Monkeypox
C93.92	Monocytic leukemia, unspecified in relapse
C93.91	Monocytic leukemia, unspecified in remission
C93.90	Monocytic leukemia, unspecified, not having achieved remission
S52.272P	Monteggia's fracture of left ulna, subsequent encounter for closed fracture with malunion
S52.272K	Monteggia's fracture of left ulna, subsequent encounter for closed fracture with nonunion

S52.272Q	Monteggia's fracture of left ulna, subsequent encounter for open fracture type I or II with malunion
S52.272M	Monteggia's fracture of left ulna, subsequent encounter for open fracture type I or II with nonunion
S52.272R	Monteggia's fracture of left ulna, subsequent encounter for open fracture type IIIA, IIIB, or IIIC with malunion
S52.272N	Monteggia's fracture of left ulna, subsequent encounter for open fracture type IIIA, IIIB, or IIIC with nonunion
S52.271P	Monteggia's fracture of right ulna, subsequent encounter for closed fracture with malunion
S52.271K	Monteggia's fracture of right ulna, subsequent encounter for closed fracture with nonunion
S52.271Q	Monteggia's fracture of right ulna, subsequent encounter for open fracture type I or II with malunion
S52.271M	Monteggia's fracture of right ulna, subsequent encounter for open fracture type I or II with nonunion
S52.271R	Monteggia's fracture of right ulna, subsequent encounter for open fracture type IIIA, IIIB, or IIIC with malunion
S52.271N	Monteggia's fracture of right ulna, subsequent encounter for open fracture type IIIA, IIIB, or IIIC with nonunion
S52.279P	Monteggia's fracture of unspecified ulna, subsequent encounter for closed fracture with malunion
S52.279K	Monteggia's fracture of unspecified ulna, subsequent encounter for closed fracture with nonunion
S52.279Q	Monteggia's fracture of unspecified ulna, subsequent encounter for open fracture type I or II with malunion
S52.279M	Monteggia's fracture of unspecified ulna, subsequent encounter for open fracture type I or II with nonunion
S52.279R	Monteggia's fracture of unspecified ulna, subsequent encounter for open fracture type IIIA, IIIB, or IIIC with malunion
S52.279N	Monteggia's fracture of unspecified ulna, subsequent encounter for open fracture type IIIA, IIIB, or IIIC with nonunion
E66.2	Morbid (severe) obesity with alveolar hypoventilation
E76.210	Morquio A mucopolysaccharidoses
E76.211	Morquio B mucopolysaccharidoses
E76.219	Morquio mucopolysaccharidoses, unspecified
A92.9	Mosquito-borne viral fever, unspecified
G12.20	Motor neuron disease, unspecified
I67.5	Moyamoya disease
B55.2	Mucocutaneous leishmaniasis
M30.3	Mucocutaneous lymph node syndrome [Kawasaki]
E75.11	Mucolipidosis IV
E76.1	Mucopolysaccharidosis, type II
E76.3	Mucopolysaccharidosis, unspecified
N76.81	Mucositis (ulcerative) of vagina and vulva
G90.3	Multi-system degeneration of the autonomic nervous system
C96.0	Multifocal and multisystemic (disseminated) Langerhans-cell histiocytosis
C96.5	Multifocal and unisystemic Langerhans-cell histiocytosis
M35.5	Multifocal fibrosclerosis
G45.2	Multiple and bilateral precerebral artery syndromes
Q89.7	Multiple congenital malformations, not elsewhere classified
S32.810A	Multiple fractures of pelvis with stable disruption of pelvic ring, initial encounter for closed fracture
S32.810K	Multiple fractures of pelvis with stable disruption of pelvic ring, subsequent encounter for fracture with nonunion
S32.811A	Multiple fractures of pelvis with unstable disruption of pelvic ring, initial encounter for closed fracture
S32.811K	Multiple fractures of pelvis with unstable disruption of pelvic ring, subsequent encounter for fracture with nonunion
S32.82XA	Multiple fractures of pelvis without disruption of pelvic ring, initial encounter for closed fracture
S32.82XK	Multiple fractures of pelvis without disruption of pelvic ring, subsequent encounter for fracture with nonunion
S22.43XA	Multiple fractures of ribs, bilateral, initial encounter for closed fracture
S22.43XK	Multiple fractures of ribs, bilateral, subsequent encounter for fracture with nonunion
S22.42XA	Multiple fractures of ribs, left side, initial encounter for closed fracture
S22.42XK	Multiple fractures of ribs, left side, subsequent encounter for fracture with nonunion
S22.41XA	Multiple fractures of ribs, right side, initial encounter for closed fracture
S22.41XK	Multiple fractures of ribs, right side, subsequent encounter for fracture with nonunion
S22.49XA	Multiple fractures of ribs, unspecified side, initial encounter for closed fracture
S22.49XK	Multiple fractures of ribs, unspecified side, subsequent encounter for fracture with nonunion
C90.02	Multiple myeloma in relapse
C90.01	Multiple myeloma in remission
C90.00	Multiple myeloma not having achieved remission
B26.85	Mumps arthritis
B26.81	Mumps hepatitis
B26.82	Mumps myocarditis
B26.83	Mumps nephritis
B26.0	Mumps orchitis
B26.3	Mumps pancreatitis
B26.84	Mumps polyneuropathy
E71.314	Muscle carnitine palmitoyltransferase deficiency
G73.3	Myasthenic syndromes in other diseases classified elsewhere
B47.9	Mycetoma, unspecified
A31.9	Mycobacterial infection, unspecified
C84.09	Mycosis fungoides, extranodal and solid organ sites
C84.03	Mycosis fungoides, intra-abdominal lymph nodes
C84.06	Mycosis fungoides, intrapelvic lymph nodes
C84.02	Mycosis fungoides, intrathoracic lymph nodes
C84.04	Mycosis fungoides, lymph nodes of axilla and upper limb
C84.01	Mycosis fungoides, lymph nodes of head, face, and neck
C84.05	Mycosis fungoides, lymph nodes of inguinal region and lower limb
C84.08	Mycosis fungoides, lymph nodes of multiple sites
C84.07	Mycosis fungoides, spleen
C84.00	Mycosis fungoides, unspecified site
C94.6	Myelodysplastic disease, not classified
D46.C	Myelodysplastic syndrome with isolated del(5q) chromosomal abnormality
D75.81	Myelofibrosis
C92.92	Myeloid leukemia, unspecified in relapse
C92.91	Myeloid leukemia, unspecified in remission
C92.90	Myeloid leukemia, unspecified, not having achieved remission
C92.32	Myeloid sarcoma, in relapse
C92.31	Myeloid sarcoma, in remission
C92.30	Myeloid sarcoma, not having achieved remission
G99.2	Myelopathy in diseases classified elsewhere
D61.82	Myelophthisis
E79.2	Myoadenylate deaminase deficiency
R82.1	Myoglobinuria
G72.2	Myopathy due to other toxic agents
B69.81	Myositis in cysticercosis
B60.2	Naegleriasis
Q01.1	Nasofrontal encephalocele
A36.1	Nasopharyngeal diphtheria
B76.1	Necatoriasis
I77.5	Necrosis of artery
M31.9	Necrotizing vasculopathy, unspecified
P54.4	Neonatal adrenal hemorrhage
E71.511	Neonatal adrenoleukodystrophy
P70.2	Neonatal diabetes mellitus
P72.0	Neonatal goiter, not elsewhere classified
P71.2	Neonatal hypomagnesemia
P39.0	Neonatal infective mastitis
P39.4	Neonatal skin infection
P71.3	Neonatal tetany without calcium or magnesium deficiency
P39.3	Neonatal urinary tract infection
P96.1	Neonatal withdrawal symptoms from maternal use of drugs of addiction
D47.9	Neoplasm of uncertain behavior of lymphoid, hematopoietic and related tissue, unspecified
N25.1	Nephrogenic diabetes insipidus
N04.6	Nephrotic syndrome with dense deposit disease
N04.7	Nephrotic syndrome with diffuse crescentic glomerulonephritis
N04.4	Nephrotic syndrome with diffuse endocapillary proliferative glomerulonephritis
N04.2	Nephrotic syndrome with diffuse membranous glomerulonephritis
N04.3	Nephrotic syndrome with diffuse mesangial proliferative glomerulonephritis
N04.5	Nephrotic syndrome with diffuse mesangiocapillary glomerulonephritis
N04.1	Nephrotic syndrome with focal and segmental glomerular lesions
N04.0	Nephrotic syndrome with minor glomerular abnormality
N04.8	Nephrotic syndrome with other morphologic changes
N04.9	Nephrotic syndrome with unspecified morphologic changes
K59.2	Neurogenic bowel, not elsewhere classified
G21.11	Neuroleptic induced parkinsonism
R41.4	Neurologic neglect syndrome
G36.0	Neuromyelitis optica [Devic]
E75.4	Neuronal ceroid lipofuscinosis
E85.1	Neuropathic heredofamilial amyloidosis
A52.3	Neurosyphilis, unspecified
D81.4	Nezelof's syndrome
F17.203	Nicotine dependence unspecified, with withdrawal
F17.223	Nicotine dependence, chewing tobacco, with withdrawal
F17.213	Nicotine dependence, cigarettes, with withdrawal
F17.293	Nicotine dependence, other tobacco product, with withdrawal
A43.9	Nocardiosis, unspecified
C81.09	Nodular lymphocyte predominant Hodgkin lymphoma, extranodal and solid organ sites
C81.03	Nodular lymphocyte predominant Hodgkin lymphoma, intra-abdominal lymph nodes
C81.06	Nodular lymphocyte predominant Hodgkin lymphoma, intrapelvic lymph nodes
C81.02	Nodular lymphocyte predominant Hodgkin lymphoma, intrathoracic lymph nodes
C81.04	Nodular lymphocyte predominant Hodgkin lymphoma, lymph nodes of axilla and upper limb
C81.01	Nodular lymphocyte predominant Hodgkin lymphoma, lymph nodes of head, face, and neck
C81.05	Nodular lymphocyte predominant Hodgkin lymphoma, lymph nodes of inguinal region and lower limb
C81.08	Nodular lymphocyte predominant Hodgkin lymphoma, lymph nodes of multiple sites
C81.07	Nodular lymphocyte predominant Hodgkin lymphoma, spleen
C81.00	Nodular lymphocyte predominant Hodgkin lymphoma, unspecified site
C81.19	Nodular sclerosis Hodgkin lymphoma, extranodal and solid organ sites
C81.13	Nodular sclerosis Hodgkin lymphoma, intra-abdominal lymph nodes
C81.16	Nodular sclerosis Hodgkin lymphoma, intrapelvic lymph nodes
C81.12	Nodular sclerosis Hodgkin lymphoma, intrathoracic lymph nodes

C81.14	Nodular sclerosis Hodgkin lymphoma, lymph nodes of axilla and upper limb
C81.11	Nodular sclerosis Hodgkin lymphoma, lymph nodes of head, face, and neck
C81.15	Nodular sclerosis Hodgkin lymphoma, lymph nodes of inguinal region and lower limb
C81.18	Nodular sclerosis Hodgkin lymphoma, lymph nodes of multiple sites
C81.17	Nodular sclerosis Hodgkin lymphoma, spleen
C81.10	Nodular sclerosis Hodgkin lymphoma, unspecified site
T80.A0XA	Non-ABO incompatibility reaction due to transfusion of blood or blood products, unspecified, initial encounter
T80.A10A	Non-ABO incompatibility with acute hemolytic transfusion reaction, initial encounter
T80.A11A	Non-ABO incompatibility with delayed hemolytic transfusion reaction, initial encounter
T80.A19A	Non-ABO incompatibility with hemolytic transfusion reaction, unspecified, initial encounter
K90.41	Non-celiac gluten sensitivity
C83.99	Non-follicular (diffuse) lymphoma, unspecified, extranodal and solid organ sites
C83.93	Non-follicular (diffuse) lymphoma, unspecified, intra-abdominal lymph nodes
C83.96	Non-follicular (diffuse) lymphoma, unspecified, intrapelvic lymph nodes
C83.92	Non-follicular (diffuse) lymphoma, unspecified, intrathoracic lymph nodes
C83.94	Non-follicular (diffuse) lymphoma, unspecified, lymph nodes of axilla and upper limb
C83.91	Non-follicular (diffuse) lymphoma, unspecified, lymph nodes of head, face, and neck
C83.95	Non-follicular (diffuse) lymphoma, unspecified, lymph nodes of inguinal region and lower limb
C83.98	Non-follicular (diffuse) lymphoma, unspecified, lymph nodes of multiple sites
C83.97	Non-follicular (diffuse) lymphoma, unspecified, spleen
C83.90	Non-follicular (diffuse) lymphoma, unspecified, unspecified site
C85.99	Non-Hodgkin lymphoma, unspecified, extranodal and solid organ sites
C85.93	Non-Hodgkin lymphoma, unspecified, intra-abdominal lymph nodes
C85.96	Non-Hodgkin lymphoma, unspecified, intrapelvic lymph nodes
C85.92	Non-Hodgkin lymphoma, unspecified, intrathoracic lymph nodes
C85.94	Non-Hodgkin lymphoma, unspecified, lymph nodes of axilla and upper limb
C85.91	Non-Hodgkin lymphoma, unspecified, lymph nodes of head, face, and neck
C85.95	Non-Hodgkin lymphoma, unspecified, lymph nodes of inguinal region and lower limb
C85.98	Non-Hodgkin lymphoma, unspecified, lymph nodes of multiple sites
C85.97	Non-Hodgkin lymphoma, unspecified, spleen
C85.90	Non-Hodgkin lymphoma, unspecified, unspecified site
E72.51	Non-ketotic hyperglycinemia
E85.0	Non-neuropathic heredofamilial amyloidosis
L98.426	Non-pressure chronic ulcer of back with bone involvement without evidence of necrosis
L98.425	Non-pressure chronic ulcer of back with muscle involvement without evidence of necrosis
L98.428	Non-pressure chronic ulcer of back with other specified severity
L98.416	Non-pressure chronic ulcer of buttock with bone involvement without evidence of necrosis
L98.415	Non-pressure chronic ulcer of buttock with muscle involvement without evidence of necrosis
L98.418	Non-pressure chronic ulcer of buttock with other specified severity
L97.321	Non-pressure chronic ulcer of left ankle limited to breakdown of skin
L97.326	Non-pressure chronic ulcer of left ankle with bone involvement without evidence of necrosis
L97.322	Non-pressure chronic ulcer of left ankle with fat layer exposed
L97.325	Non-pressure chronic ulcer of left ankle with muscle involvement without evidence of necrosis
L97.324	Non-pressure chronic ulcer of left ankle with necrosis of bone
L97.323	Non-pressure chronic ulcer of left ankle with necrosis of muscle
L97.328	Non-pressure chronic ulcer of left ankle with other specified severity
L97.329	Non-pressure chronic ulcer of left ankle with unspecified severity
L97.221	Non-pressure chronic ulcer of left calf limited to breakdown of skin
L97.226	Non-pressure chronic ulcer of left calf with bone involvement without evidence of necrosis
L97.222	Non-pressure chronic ulcer of left calf with fat layer exposed
L97.225	Non-pressure chronic ulcer of left calf with muscle involvement without evidence of necrosis
L97.224	Non-pressure chronic ulcer of left calf with necrosis of bone
L97.223	Non-pressure chronic ulcer of left calf with necrosis of muscle
L97.228	Non-pressure chronic ulcer of left calf with other specified severity
L97.229	Non-pressure chronic ulcer of left calf with unspecified severity
L97.421	Non-pressure chronic ulcer of left heel and midfoot limited to breakdown of skin
L97.426	Non-pressure chronic ulcer of left heel and midfoot with bone involvement without evidence of necrosis
L97.422	Non-pressure chronic ulcer of left heel and midfoot with fat layer exposed
L97.425	Non-pressure chronic ulcer of left heel and midfoot with muscle involvement without evidence of necrosis
L97.424	Non-pressure chronic ulcer of left heel and midfoot with necrosis of bone
L97.423	Non-pressure chronic ulcer of left heel and midfoot with necrosis of muscle
L97.428	Non-pressure chronic ulcer of left heel and midfoot with other specified severity
L97.429	Non-pressure chronic ulcer of left heel and midfoot with unspecified severity
L97.121	Non-pressure chronic ulcer of left thigh limited to breakdown of skin
L97.126	Non-pressure chronic ulcer of left thigh with bone involvement without evidence of necrosis
L97.122	Non-pressure chronic ulcer of left thigh with fat layer exposed
L97.125	Non-pressure chronic ulcer of left thigh with muscle involvement without evidence of necrosis
L97.124	Non-pressure chronic ulcer of left thigh with necrosis of bone
L97.123	Non-pressure chronic ulcer of left thigh with necrosis of muscle
L97.128	Non-pressure chronic ulcer of left thigh with other specified severity
L97.129	Non-pressure chronic ulcer of left thigh with unspecified severity
L97.526	Non-pressure chronic ulcer of other part of left foot with bone involvement without evidence of necrosis
L97.525	Non-pressure chronic ulcer of other part of left foot with muscle involvement without evidence of necrosis
L97.528	Non-pressure chronic ulcer of other part of left foot with other specified severity
L97.821	Non-pressure chronic ulcer of other part of left lower leg limited to breakdown of skin
L97.826	Non-pressure chronic ulcer of other part of left lower leg with bone involvement without evidence of necrosis
L97.822	Non-pressure chronic ulcer of other part of left lower leg with fat layer exposed
L97.825	Non-pressure chronic ulcer of other part of left lower leg with muscle involvement without evidence of necrosis
L97.824	Non-pressure chronic ulcer of other part of left lower leg with necrosis of bone
L97.823	Non-pressure chronic ulcer of other part of left lower leg with necrosis of muscle
L97.828	Non-pressure chronic ulcer of other part of left lower leg with other specified severity
L97.829	Non-pressure chronic ulcer of other part of left lower leg with unspecified severity
L97.516	Non-pressure chronic ulcer of other part of right foot with bone involvement without evidence of necrosis
L97.515	Non-pressure chronic ulcer of other part of right foot with muscle involvement without evidence of necrosis
L97.518	Non-pressure chronic ulcer of other part of right foot with other specified severity
L97.811	Non-pressure chronic ulcer of other part of right lower leg limited to breakdown of skin
L97.816	Non-pressure chronic ulcer of other part of right lower leg with bone involvement without evidence of necrosis
L97.812	Non-pressure chronic ulcer of other part of right lower leg with fat layer exposed
L97.815	Non-pressure chronic ulcer of other part of right lower leg with muscle involvement without evidence of necrosis
L97.814	Non-pressure chronic ulcer of other part of right lower leg with necrosis of bone
L97.813	Non-pressure chronic ulcer of other part of right lower leg with necrosis of muscle
L97.818	Non-pressure chronic ulcer of other part of right lower leg with other specified severity
L97.819	Non-pressure chronic ulcer of other part of right lower leg with unspecified severity
L97.506	Non-pressure chronic ulcer of other part of unspecified foot with bone involvement without evidence of necrosis
L97.505	Non-pressure chronic ulcer of other part of unspecified foot with muscle involvement without evidence of necrosis
L97.508	Non-pressure chronic ulcer of other part of unspecified foot with other specified severity
L97.801	Non-pressure chronic ulcer of other part of unspecified lower leg limited to breakdown of skin
L97.806	Non-pressure chronic ulcer of other part of unspecified lower leg with bone involvement without evidence of necrosis
L97.802	Non-pressure chronic ulcer of other part of unspecified lower leg with fat layer exposed
L97.805	Non-pressure chronic ulcer of other part of unspecified lower leg with muscle involvement without evidence of necrosis
L97.804	Non-pressure chronic ulcer of other part of unspecified lower leg with necrosis of bone
L97.803	Non-pressure chronic ulcer of other part of unspecified lower leg with necrosis of muscle
L97.808	Non-pressure chronic ulcer of other part of unspecified lower leg with other specified severity
L97.809	Non-pressure chronic ulcer of other part of unspecified lower leg with unspecified severity
L97.311	Non-pressure chronic ulcer of right ankle limited to breakdown of skin
L97.316	Non-pressure chronic ulcer of right ankle with bone involvement without evidence of necrosis
L97.312	Non-pressure chronic ulcer of right ankle with fat layer exposed
L97.315	Non-pressure chronic ulcer of right ankle with muscle involvement without evidence of necrosis
L97.314	Non-pressure chronic ulcer of right ankle with necrosis of bone
L97.313	Non-pressure chronic ulcer of right ankle with necrosis of muscle
L97.318	Non-pressure chronic ulcer of right ankle with other specified severity
L97.319	Non-pressure chronic ulcer of right ankle with unspecified severity
L97.211	Non-pressure chronic ulcer of right calf limited to breakdown of skin
L97.216	Non-pressure chronic ulcer of right calf with bone involvement without evidence of necrosis
L97.212	Non-pressure chronic ulcer of right calf with fat layer exposed
L97.215	Non-pressure chronic ulcer of right calf with muscle involvement without evidence of necrosis
L97.214	Non-pressure chronic ulcer of right calf with necrosis of bone
L97.213	Non-pressure chronic ulcer of right calf with necrosis of muscle
L97.218	Non-pressure chronic ulcer of right calf with other specified severity
L97.219	Non-pressure chronic ulcer of right calf with unspecified severity

L97.411	Non-pressure chronic ulcer of right heel and midfoot limited to breakdown of skin	L97.913	Non-pressure chronic ulcer of unspecified part of right lower leg with necrosis of muscle
L97.416	Non-pressure chronic ulcer of right heel and midfoot with bone involvement without evidence of necrosis	L97.918	Non-pressure chronic ulcer of unspecified part of right lower leg with other specified severity
L97.412	Non-pressure chronic ulcer of right heel and midfoot with fat layer exposed	L97.919	Non-pressure chronic ulcer of unspecified part of right lower leg with unspecified severity
L97.415	Non-pressure chronic ulcer of right heel and midfoot with muscle involvement without evidence of necrosis	L97.901	Non-pressure chronic ulcer of unspecified part of unspecified lower leg limited to breakdown of skin
L97.414	Non-pressure chronic ulcer of right heel and midfoot with necrosis of bone	L97.906	Non-pressure chronic ulcer of unspecified part of unspecified lower leg with bone involvement without evidence of necrosis
L97.413	Non-pressure chronic ulcer of right heel and midfoot with necrosis of muscle	L97.902	Non-pressure chronic ulcer of unspecified part of unspecified lower leg with fat layer exposed
L97.418	Non-pressure chronic ulcer of right heel and midfoot with other specified severity	L97.905	Non-pressure chronic ulcer of unspecified part of unspecified lower leg with muscle involvement without evidence of necrosis
L97.419	Non-pressure chronic ulcer of right heel and midfoot with unspecified severity	L97.904	Non-pressure chronic ulcer of unspecified part of unspecified lower leg with necrosis of bone
L97.111	Non-pressure chronic ulcer of right thigh limited to breakdown of skin	L97.903	Non-pressure chronic ulcer of unspecified part of unspecified lower leg with necrosis of muscle
L97.116	Non-pressure chronic ulcer of right thigh with bone involvement without evidence of necrosis	L97.908	Non-pressure chronic ulcer of unspecified part of unspecified lower leg with other specified severity
L97.112	Non-pressure chronic ulcer of right thigh with fat layer exposed	L97.909	Non-pressure chronic ulcer of unspecified part of unspecified lower leg with unspecified severity
L97.115	Non-pressure chronic ulcer of right thigh with muscle involvement without evidence of necrosis	L97.101	Non-pressure chronic ulcer of unspecified thigh limited to breakdown of skin
L97.114	Non-pressure chronic ulcer of right thigh with necrosis of bone	L97.106	Non-pressure chronic ulcer of unspecified thigh with bone involvement without evidence of necrosis
L97.113	Non-pressure chronic ulcer of right thigh with necrosis of muscle	L97.102	Non-pressure chronic ulcer of unspecified thigh with fat layer exposed
L97.118	Non-pressure chronic ulcer of right thigh with other specified severity	L97.105	Non-pressure chronic ulcer of unspecified thigh with muscle involvement without evidence of necrosis
L97.119	Non-pressure chronic ulcer of right thigh with unspecified severity	L97.104	Non-pressure chronic ulcer of unspecified thigh with necrosis of bone
L98.496	Non-pressure chronic ulcer of skin of other sites with bone involvement without evidence of necrosis	L97.103	Non-pressure chronic ulcer of unspecified thigh with necrosis of muscle
L98.495	Non-pressure chronic ulcer of skin of other sites with muscle involvement without evidence of necrosis	L97.108	Non-pressure chronic ulcer of unspecified thigh with other specified severity
L98.498	Non-pressure chronic ulcer of skin of other sites with other specified severity	L97.109	Non-pressure chronic ulcer of unspecified thigh with unspecified severity
L97.301	Non-pressure chronic ulcer of unspecified ankle limited to breakdown of skin	E15	Nondiabetic hypoglycemic coma
L97.306	Non-pressure chronic ulcer of unspecified ankle with bone involvement without evidence of necrosis	S72.135P	Nondisplaced apophyseal fracture of left femur, subsequent encounter for closed fracture with malunion
L97.302	Non-pressure chronic ulcer of unspecified ankle with fat layer exposed	S72.135K	Nondisplaced apophyseal fracture of left femur, subsequent encounter for closed fracture with nonunion
L97.305	Non-pressure chronic ulcer of unspecified ankle with muscle involvement without evidence of necrosis	S72.135Q	Nondisplaced apophyseal fracture of left femur, subsequent encounter for open fracture type I or II with malunion
L97.304	Non-pressure chronic ulcer of unspecified ankle with necrosis of bone	S72.135M	Nondisplaced apophyseal fracture of left femur, subsequent encounter for open fracture type I or II with nonunion
L97.303	Non-pressure chronic ulcer of unspecified ankle with necrosis of muscle	S72.135R	Nondisplaced apophyseal fracture of left femur, subsequent encounter for open fracture type IIIA, IIIB, or IIIC with malunion
L97.308	Non-pressure chronic ulcer of unspecified ankle with other specified severity	S72.135N	Nondisplaced apophyseal fracture of left femur, subsequent encounter for open fracture type IIIA, IIIB, or IIIC with nonunion
L97.309	Non-pressure chronic ulcer of unspecified ankle with unspecified severity	S72.134P	Nondisplaced apophyseal fracture of right femur, subsequent encounter for closed fracture with malunion
L97.201	Non-pressure chronic ulcer of unspecified calf limited to breakdown of skin	S72.134K	Nondisplaced apophyseal fracture of right femur, subsequent encounter for closed fracture with nonunion
L97.206	Non-pressure chronic ulcer of unspecified calf with bone involvement without evidence of necrosis	S72.134Q	Nondisplaced apophyseal fracture of right femur, subsequent encounter for open fracture type I or II with malunion
L97.202	Non-pressure chronic ulcer of unspecified calf with fat layer exposed	S72.134M	Nondisplaced apophyseal fracture of right femur, subsequent encounter for open fracture type I or II with nonunion
L97.205	Non-pressure chronic ulcer of unspecified calf with muscle involvement without evidence of necrosis	S72.134R	Nondisplaced apophyseal fracture of right femur, subsequent encounter for open fracture type IIIA, IIIB, or IIIC with malunion
L97.204	Non-pressure chronic ulcer of unspecified calf with necrosis of bone	S72.134N	Nondisplaced apophyseal fracture of right femur, subsequent encounter for open fracture type IIIA, IIIB, or IIIC with nonunion
L97.203	Non-pressure chronic ulcer of unspecified calf with necrosis of muscle	S72.136P	Nondisplaced apophyseal fracture of unspecified femur, subsequent encounter for closed fracture with malunion
L97.208	Non-pressure chronic ulcer of unspecified calf with other specified severity	S72.136K	Nondisplaced apophyseal fracture of unspecified femur, subsequent encounter for closed fracture with nonunion
L97.209	Non-pressure chronic ulcer of unspecified calf with unspecified severity	S72.136Q	Nondisplaced apophyseal fracture of unspecified femur, subsequent encounter for open fracture type I or II with malunion
L97.401	Non-pressure chronic ulcer of unspecified heel and midfoot limited to breakdown of skin	S72.136M	Nondisplaced apophyseal fracture of unspecified femur, subsequent encounter for open fracture type I or II with nonunion
L97.406	Non-pressure chronic ulcer of unspecified heel and midfoot with bone involvement without evidence of necrosis	S72.136R	Nondisplaced apophyseal fracture of unspecified femur, subsequent encounter for open fracture type IIIA, IIIB, or IIIC with malunion
L97.402	Non-pressure chronic ulcer of unspecified heel and midfoot with fat layer exposed	S72.136N	Nondisplaced apophyseal fracture of unspecified femur, subsequent encounter for open fracture type IIIA, IIIB, or IIIC with nonunion
L97.405	Non-pressure chronic ulcer of unspecified heel and midfoot with muscle involvement without evidence of necrosis	S72.065P	Nondisplaced articular fracture of head of left femur, subsequent encounter for closed fracture with malunion
L97.404	Non-pressure chronic ulcer of unspecified heel and midfoot with necrosis of bone	S72.065K	Nondisplaced articular fracture of head of left femur, subsequent encounter for closed fracture with nonunion
L97.403	Non-pressure chronic ulcer of unspecified heel and midfoot with necrosis of muscle	S72.065Q	Nondisplaced articular fracture of head of left femur, subsequent encounter for open fracture type I or II with malunion
L97.408	Non-pressure chronic ulcer of unspecified heel and midfoot with other specified severity	S72.065M	Nondisplaced articular fracture of head of left femur, subsequent encounter for open fracture type I or II with nonunion
L97.409	Non-pressure chronic ulcer of unspecified heel and midfoot with unspecified severity	S72.065R	Nondisplaced articular fracture of head of left femur, subsequent encounter for open fracture type IIIA, IIIB, or IIIC with malunion
L97.921	Non-pressure chronic ulcer of unspecified part of left lower leg limited to breakdown of skin	S72.065N	Nondisplaced articular fracture of head of left femur, subsequent encounter for open fracture type IIIA, IIIB, or IIIC with nonunion
L97.926	Non-pressure chronic ulcer of unspecified part of left lower leg with bone involvement without evidence of necrosis	S72.064P	Nondisplaced articular fracture of head of right femur, subsequent encounter for closed fracture with malunion
L97.922	Non-pressure chronic ulcer of unspecified part of left lower leg with fat layer exposed	S72.064K	Nondisplaced articular fracture of head of right femur, subsequent encounter for closed fracture with nonunion
L97.925	Non-pressure chronic ulcer of unspecified part of left lower leg with muscle involvement without evidence of necrosis	S72.064Q	Nondisplaced articular fracture of head of right femur, subsequent encounter for open fracture type I or II with malunion
L97.924	Non-pressure chronic ulcer of unspecified part of left lower leg with necrosis of bone	S72.064M	Nondisplaced articular fracture of head of right femur, subsequent encounter for open fracture type I or II with nonunion
L97.923	Non-pressure chronic ulcer of unspecified part of left lower leg with necrosis of muscle	S72.064R	Nondisplaced articular fracture of head of right femur, subsequent encounter for open fracture type IIIA, IIIB, or IIIC with malunion
L97.928	Non-pressure chronic ulcer of unspecified part of left lower leg with other specified severity		
L97.929	Non-pressure chronic ulcer of unspecified part of left lower leg with unspecified severity		
L97.911	Non-pressure chronic ulcer of unspecified part of right lower leg limited to breakdown of skin		
L97.916	Non-pressure chronic ulcer of unspecified part of right lower leg with bone involvement without evidence of necrosis		
L97.912	Non-pressure chronic ulcer of unspecified part of right lower leg with fat layer exposed		
L97.915	Non-pressure chronic ulcer of unspecified part of right lower leg with muscle involvement without evidence of necrosis		
L97.914	Non-pressure chronic ulcer of unspecified part of right lower leg with necrosis of bone		

S72.064N	Nondisplaced articular fracture of head of right femur, subsequent encounter for open fracture type IIIA, IIIB, or IIIC with nonunion
S72.066P	Nondisplaced articular fracture of head of unspecified femur, subsequent encounter for closed fracture with malunion
S72.066K	Nondisplaced articular fracture of head of unspecified femur, subsequent encounter for closed fracture with nonunion
S72.066Q	Nondisplaced articular fracture of head of unspecified femur, subsequent encounter for open fracture type I or II with malunion
S72.066M	Nondisplaced articular fracture of head of unspecified femur, subsequent encounter for open fracture type I or II with nonunion
S72.066R	Nondisplaced articular fracture of head of unspecified femur, subsequent encounter for open fracture type IIIA, IIIB, or IIIC with malunion
S72.066N	Nondisplaced articular fracture of head of unspecified femur, subsequent encounter for open fracture type IIIA, IIIB, or IIIC with nonunion
S32.465K	Nondisplaced associated transverse-posterior fracture of left acetabulum, subsequent encounter for fracture with nonunion
S32.464K	Nondisplaced associated transverse-posterior fracture of right acetabulum, subsequent encounter for fracture with nonunion
S32.466K	Nondisplaced associated transverse-posterior fracture of unspecified acetabulum, subsequent encounter for fracture with nonunion
S92.155B	Nondisplaced avulsion fracture (chip fracture) of left talus, initial encounter for open fracture
S92.155P	Nondisplaced avulsion fracture (chip fracture) of left talus, subsequent encounter for fracture with malunion
S92.155K	Nondisplaced avulsion fracture (chip fracture) of left talus, subsequent encounter for fracture with nonunion
S92.154B	Nondisplaced avulsion fracture (chip fracture) of right talus, initial encounter for open fracture
S92.154P	Nondisplaced avulsion fracture (chip fracture) of right talus, subsequent encounter for fracture with malunion
S92.154K	Nondisplaced avulsion fracture (chip fracture) of right talus, subsequent encounter for fracture with nonunion
S92.156B	Nondisplaced avulsion fracture (chip fracture) of unspecified talus, initial encounter for open fracture
S92.156P	Nondisplaced avulsion fracture (chip fracture) of unspecified talus, subsequent encounter for fracture with malunion
S92.156K	Nondisplaced avulsion fracture (chip fracture) of unspecified talus, subsequent encounter for fracture with nonunion
S32.315A	Nondisplaced avulsion fracture of left ilium, initial encounter for closed fracture
S32.315K	Nondisplaced avulsion fracture of left ilium, subsequent encounter for fracture with nonunion
S32.615A	Nondisplaced avulsion fracture of left ischium, initial encounter for closed fracture
S32.615K	Nondisplaced avulsion fracture of left ischium, subsequent encounter for fracture with nonunion
S32.314A	Nondisplaced avulsion fracture of right ilium, initial encounter for closed fracture
S32.314K	Nondisplaced avulsion fracture of right ilium, subsequent encounter for fracture with nonunion
S32.614A	Nondisplaced avulsion fracture of right ischium, initial encounter for closed fracture
S32.614K	Nondisplaced avulsion fracture of right ischium, subsequent encounter for fracture with nonunion
S92.035B	Nondisplaced avulsion fracture of tuberosity of left calcaneus, initial encounter for open fracture
S92.035P	Nondisplaced avulsion fracture of tuberosity of left calcaneus, subsequent encounter for fracture with malunion
S92.035K	Nondisplaced avulsion fracture of tuberosity of left calcaneus, subsequent encounter for fracture with nonunion
S92.034B	Nondisplaced avulsion fracture of tuberosity of right calcaneus, initial encounter for open fracture
S92.034P	Nondisplaced avulsion fracture of tuberosity of right calcaneus, subsequent encounter for fracture with malunion
S92.034K	Nondisplaced avulsion fracture of tuberosity of right calcaneus, subsequent encounter for fracture with nonunion
S92.036B	Nondisplaced avulsion fracture of tuberosity of unspecified calcaneus, initial encounter for open fracture
S92.036P	Nondisplaced avulsion fracture of tuberosity of unspecified calcaneus, subsequent encounter for fracture with malunion
S92.036K	Nondisplaced avulsion fracture of tuberosity of unspecified calcaneus, subsequent encounter for fracture with nonunion
S32.316A	Nondisplaced avulsion fracture of unspecified ilium, initial encounter for closed fracture
S32.316K	Nondisplaced avulsion fracture of unspecified ilium, subsequent encounter for fracture with nonunion
S32.616A	Nondisplaced avulsion fracture of unspecified ischium, initial encounter for closed fracture
S32.616K	Nondisplaced avulsion fracture of unspecified ischium, subsequent encounter for fracture with nonunion
S82.145A	Nondisplaced bicondylar fracture of left tibia, initial encounter for closed fracture
S82.145P	Nondisplaced bicondylar fracture of left tibia, subsequent encounter for closed fracture with malunion
S82.145K	Nondisplaced bicondylar fracture of left tibia, subsequent encounter for closed fracture with nonunion
S82.145Q	Nondisplaced bicondylar fracture of left tibia, subsequent encounter for open fracture type I or II with malunion
S82.145M	Nondisplaced bicondylar fracture of left tibia, subsequent encounter for open fracture type I or II with nonunion
S82.145R	Nondisplaced bicondylar fracture of left tibia, subsequent encounter for open fracture type IIIA, IIIB, or IIIC with malunion
S82.145N	Nondisplaced bicondylar fracture of left tibia, subsequent encounter for open fracture type IIIA, IIIB, or IIIC with nonunion
S82.144A	Nondisplaced bicondylar fracture of right tibia, initial encounter for closed fracture
S82.144P	Nondisplaced bicondylar fracture of right tibia, subsequent encounter for closed fracture with malunion
S82.144K	Nondisplaced bicondylar fracture of right tibia, subsequent encounter for closed fracture with nonunion
S82.144Q	Nondisplaced bicondylar fracture of right tibia, subsequent encounter for open fracture type I or II with malunion
S82.144M	Nondisplaced bicondylar fracture of right tibia, subsequent encounter for open fracture type I or II with nonunion
S82.144R	Nondisplaced bicondylar fracture of right tibia, subsequent encounter for open fracture type IIIA, IIIB, or IIIC with malunion
S82.144N	Nondisplaced bicondylar fracture of right tibia, subsequent encounter for open fracture type IIIA, IIIB, or IIIC with nonunion
S82.146A	Nondisplaced bicondylar fracture of unspecified tibia, initial encounter for closed fracture
S82.146P	Nondisplaced bicondylar fracture of unspecified tibia, subsequent encounter for closed fracture with malunion
S82.146K	Nondisplaced bicondylar fracture of unspecified tibia, subsequent encounter for closed fracture with nonunion
S82.146Q	Nondisplaced bicondylar fracture of unspecified tibia, subsequent encounter for open fracture type I or II with malunion
S82.146M	Nondisplaced bicondylar fracture of unspecified tibia, subsequent encounter for open fracture type I or II with nonunion
S82.146R	Nondisplaced bicondylar fracture of unspecified tibia, subsequent encounter for open fracture type IIIA, IIIB, or IIIC with malunion
S82.146N	Nondisplaced bicondylar fracture of unspecified tibia, subsequent encounter for open fracture type IIIA, IIIB, or IIIC with nonunion
S82.845B	Nondisplaced bimalleolar fracture of left lower leg, initial encounter for open fracture type I or II
S82.845C	Nondisplaced bimalleolar fracture of left lower leg, initial encounter for open fracture type IIIA, IIIB, or IIIC
S82.845P	Nondisplaced bimalleolar fracture of left lower leg, subsequent encounter for closed fracture with malunion
S82.845K	Nondisplaced bimalleolar fracture of left lower leg, subsequent encounter for closed fracture with nonunion
S82.845Q	Nondisplaced bimalleolar fracture of left lower leg, subsequent encounter for open fracture type I or II with malunion
S82.845M	Nondisplaced bimalleolar fracture of left lower leg, subsequent encounter for open fracture type I or II with nonunion
S82.845R	Nondisplaced bimalleolar fracture of left lower leg, subsequent encounter for open fracture type IIIA, IIIB, or IIIC with malunion
S82.845N	Nondisplaced bimalleolar fracture of left lower leg, subsequent encounter for open fracture type IIIA, IIIB, or IIIC with nonunion
S82.844B	Nondisplaced bimalleolar fracture of right lower leg, initial encounter for open fracture type I or II
S82.844C	Nondisplaced bimalleolar fracture of right lower leg, initial encounter for open fracture type IIIA, IIIB, or IIIC
S82.844P	Nondisplaced bimalleolar fracture of right lower leg, subsequent encounter for closed fracture with malunion
S82.844K	Nondisplaced bimalleolar fracture of right lower leg, subsequent encounter for closed fracture with nonunion
S82.844Q	Nondisplaced bimalleolar fracture of right lower leg, subsequent encounter for open fracture type I or II with malunion
S82.844M	Nondisplaced bimalleolar fracture of right lower leg, subsequent encounter for open fracture type I or II with nonunion
S82.844R	Nondisplaced bimalleolar fracture of right lower leg, subsequent encounter for open fracture type IIIA, IIIB, or IIIC with malunion
S82.844N	Nondisplaced bimalleolar fracture of right lower leg, subsequent encounter for open fracture type IIIA, IIIB, or IIIC with nonunion
S82.846B	Nondisplaced bimalleolar fracture of unspecified lower leg, initial encounter for open fracture type I or II
S82.846C	Nondisplaced bimalleolar fracture of unspecified lower leg, initial encounter for open fracture type IIIA, IIIB, or IIIC
S82.846P	Nondisplaced bimalleolar fracture of unspecified lower leg, subsequent encounter for closed fracture with malunion
S82.846K	Nondisplaced bimalleolar fracture of unspecified lower leg, subsequent encounter for closed fracture with nonunion
S82.846Q	Nondisplaced bimalleolar fracture of unspecified lower leg, subsequent encounter for open fracture type I or II with malunion
S82.846M	Nondisplaced bimalleolar fracture of unspecified lower leg, subsequent encounter for open fracture type I or II with nonunion
S82.846R	Nondisplaced bimalleolar fracture of unspecified lower leg, subsequent encounter for open fracture type IIIA, IIIB, or IIIC with malunion
S82.846N	Nondisplaced bimalleolar fracture of unspecified lower leg, subsequent encounter for open fracture type IIIA, IIIB, or IIIC with nonunion
S82.045A	Nondisplaced comminuted fracture of left patella, initial encounter for closed fracture
S82.045B	Nondisplaced comminuted fracture of left patella, initial encounter for open fracture type I or II
S82.045C	Nondisplaced comminuted fracture of left patella, initial encounter for open fracture type IIIA, IIIB, or IIIC
S82.045P	Nondisplaced comminuted fracture of left patella, subsequent encounter for closed fracture with malunion
S82.045K	Nondisplaced comminuted fracture of left patella, subsequent encounter for closed fracture with nonunion

S82.045Q Nondisplaced comminuted fracture of left patella, subsequent encounter for open fracture type I or II with malunion

S82.045M Nondisplaced comminuted fracture of left patella, subsequent encounter for open fracture type I or II with nonunion

S82.045R Nondisplaced comminuted fracture of left patella, subsequent encounter for open fracture type IIIA, IIIB, or IIIC with malunion

S82.045N Nondisplaced comminuted fracture of left patella, subsequent encounter for open fracture type IIIA, IIIB, or IIIC with nonunion

S82.044A Nondisplaced comminuted fracture of right patella, initial encounter for closed fracture

S82.044B Nondisplaced comminuted fracture of right patella, initial encounter for open fracture type I or II

S82.044C Nondisplaced comminuted fracture of right patella, initial encounter for open fracture type IIIA, IIIB, or IIIC

S82.044P Nondisplaced comminuted fracture of right patella, subsequent encounter for closed fracture with malunion

S82.044K Nondisplaced comminuted fracture of right patella, subsequent encounter for closed fracture with nonunion

S82.044Q Nondisplaced comminuted fracture of right patella, subsequent encounter for open fracture type I or II with malunion

S82.044M Nondisplaced comminuted fracture of right patella, subsequent encounter for open fracture type I or II with nonunion

S82.044R Nondisplaced comminuted fracture of right patella, subsequent encounter for open fracture type IIIA, IIIB, or IIIC with malunion

S82.044N Nondisplaced comminuted fracture of right patella, subsequent encounter for open fracture type IIIA, IIIB, or IIIC with nonunion

S42.355A Nondisplaced comminuted fracture of shaft of humerus, left arm, initial encounter for closed fracture

S42.355P Nondisplaced comminuted fracture of shaft of humerus, left arm, subsequent encounter for fracture with malunion

S42.355K Nondisplaced comminuted fracture of shaft of humerus, left arm, subsequent encounter for fracture with nonunion

S42.354A Nondisplaced comminuted fracture of shaft of humerus, right arm, initial encounter for closed fracture

S42.354P Nondisplaced comminuted fracture of shaft of humerus, right arm, subsequent encounter for fracture with malunion

S42.354K Nondisplaced comminuted fracture of shaft of humerus, right arm, subsequent encounter for fracture with nonunion

S42.356A Nondisplaced comminuted fracture of shaft of humerus, unspecified arm, initial encounter for closed fracture

S42.356P Nondisplaced comminuted fracture of shaft of humerus, unspecified arm, subsequent encounter for fracture with malunion

S42.356K Nondisplaced comminuted fracture of shaft of humerus, unspecified arm, subsequent encounter for fracture with nonunion

S72.355P Nondisplaced comminuted fracture of shaft of left femur, subsequent encounter for closed fracture with malunion

S72.355K Nondisplaced comminuted fracture of shaft of left femur, subsequent encounter for closed fracture with nonunion

S72.355Q Nondisplaced comminuted fracture of shaft of left femur, subsequent encounter for open fracture type I or II with malunion

S72.355M Nondisplaced comminuted fracture of shaft of left femur, subsequent encounter for open fracture type I or II with nonunion

S72.355R Nondisplaced comminuted fracture of shaft of left femur, subsequent encounter for open fracture type IIIA, IIIB, or IIIC with malunion

S72.355N Nondisplaced comminuted fracture of shaft of left femur, subsequent encounter for open fracture type IIIA, IIIB, or IIIC with nonunion

S82.455P Nondisplaced comminuted fracture of shaft of left fibula, subsequent encounter for closed fracture with malunion

S82.455K Nondisplaced comminuted fracture of shaft of left fibula, subsequent encounter for closed fracture with nonunion

S82.455Q Nondisplaced comminuted fracture of shaft of left fibula, subsequent encounter for open fracture type I or II with malunion

S82.455M Nondisplaced comminuted fracture of shaft of left fibula, subsequent encounter for open fracture type I or II with nonunion

S82.455R Nondisplaced comminuted fracture of shaft of left fibula, subsequent encounter for open fracture type IIIA, IIIB, or IIIC with malunion

S82.455N Nondisplaced comminuted fracture of shaft of left fibula, subsequent encounter for open fracture type IIIA, IIIB, or IIIC with nonunion

S82.255A Nondisplaced comminuted fracture of shaft of left tibia, initial encounter for closed fracture

S82.255P Nondisplaced comminuted fracture of shaft of left tibia, subsequent encounter for closed fracture with malunion

S82.255K Nondisplaced comminuted fracture of shaft of left tibia, subsequent encounter for closed fracture with nonunion

S82.255Q Nondisplaced comminuted fracture of shaft of left tibia, subsequent encounter for open fracture type I or II with malunion

S82.255M Nondisplaced comminuted fracture of shaft of left tibia, subsequent encounter for open fracture type I or II with nonunion

S82.255R Nondisplaced comminuted fracture of shaft of left tibia, subsequent encounter for open fracture type IIIA, IIIB, or IIIC with malunion

S82.255N Nondisplaced comminuted fracture of shaft of left tibia, subsequent encounter for open fracture type IIIA, IIIB, or IIIC with nonunion

S52.355A Nondisplaced comminuted fracture of shaft of radius, left arm, initial encounter for closed fracture

S52.355P Nondisplaced comminuted fracture of shaft of radius, left arm, subsequent encounter for closed fracture with malunion

S52.355K Nondisplaced comminuted fracture of shaft of radius, left arm, subsequent encounter for closed fracture with nonunion

S52.355Q Nondisplaced comminuted fracture of shaft of radius, left arm, subsequent encounter for open fracture type I or II with malunion

S52.355M Nondisplaced comminuted fracture of shaft of radius, left arm, subsequent encounter for open fracture type I or II with nonunion

S52.355R Nondisplaced comminuted fracture of shaft of radius, left arm, subsequent encounter for open fracture type IIIA, IIIB, or IIIC with malunion

S52.355N Nondisplaced comminuted fracture of shaft of radius, left arm, subsequent encounter for open fracture type IIIA, IIIB, or IIIC with nonunion

S52.354A Nondisplaced comminuted fracture of shaft of radius, right arm, initial encounter for closed fracture

S52.354P Nondisplaced comminuted fracture of shaft of radius, right arm, subsequent encounter for closed fracture with malunion

S52.354K Nondisplaced comminuted fracture of shaft of radius, right arm, subsequent encounter for closed fracture with nonunion

S52.354Q Nondisplaced comminuted fracture of shaft of radius, right arm, subsequent encounter for open fracture type I or II with malunion

S52.354M Nondisplaced comminuted fracture of shaft of radius, right arm, subsequent encounter for open fracture type I or II with nonunion

S52.354R Nondisplaced comminuted fracture of shaft of radius, right arm, subsequent encounter for open fracture type IIIA, IIIB, or IIIC with malunion

S52.354N Nondisplaced comminuted fracture of shaft of radius, right arm, subsequent encounter for open fracture type IIIA, IIIB, or IIIC with nonunion

S52.356A Nondisplaced comminuted fracture of shaft of radius, unspecified arm, initial encounter for closed fracture

S52.356P Nondisplaced comminuted fracture of shaft of radius, unspecified arm, subsequent encounter for closed fracture with malunion

S52.356K Nondisplaced comminuted fracture of shaft of radius, unspecified arm, subsequent encounter for closed fracture with nonunion

S52.356Q Nondisplaced comminuted fracture of shaft of radius, unspecified arm, subsequent encounter for open fracture type I or II with malunion

S52.356M Nondisplaced comminuted fracture of shaft of radius, unspecified arm, subsequent encounter for open fracture type I or II with nonunion

S52.356R Nondisplaced comminuted fracture of shaft of radius, unspecified arm, subsequent encounter for open fracture type IIIA, IIIB, or IIIC with malunion

S52.356N Nondisplaced comminuted fracture of shaft of radius, unspecified arm, subsequent encounter for open fracture type IIIA, IIIB, or IIIC with nonunion

S72.354P Nondisplaced comminuted fracture of shaft of right femur, subsequent encounter for closed fracture with malunion

S72.354K Nondisplaced comminuted fracture of shaft of right femur, subsequent encounter for closed fracture with nonunion

S72.354Q Nondisplaced comminuted fracture of shaft of right femur, subsequent encounter for open fracture type I or II with malunion

S72.354M Nondisplaced comminuted fracture of shaft of right femur, subsequent encounter for open fracture type I or II with nonunion

S72.354R Nondisplaced comminuted fracture of shaft of right femur, subsequent encounter for open fracture type IIIA, IIIB, or IIIC with malunion

S72.354N Nondisplaced comminuted fracture of shaft of right femur, subsequent encounter for open fracture type IIIA, IIIB, or IIIC with nonunion

S82.454P Nondisplaced comminuted fracture of shaft of right fibula, subsequent encounter for closed fracture with malunion

S82.454K Nondisplaced comminuted fracture of shaft of right fibula, subsequent encounter for closed fracture with nonunion

S82.454Q Nondisplaced comminuted fracture of shaft of right fibula, subsequent encounter for open fracture type I or II with malunion

S82.454M Nondisplaced comminuted fracture of shaft of right fibula, subsequent encounter for open fracture type I or II with nonunion

S82.454R Nondisplaced comminuted fracture of shaft of right fibula, subsequent encounter for open fracture type IIIA, IIIB, or IIIC with malunion

S82.454N Nondisplaced comminuted fracture of shaft of right fibula, subsequent encounter for open fracture type IIIA, IIIB, or IIIC with nonunion

S82.254A Nondisplaced comminuted fracture of shaft of right tibia, initial encounter for closed fracture

S82.254P Nondisplaced comminuted fracture of shaft of right tibia, subsequent encounter for closed fracture with malunion

S82.254K Nondisplaced comminuted fracture of shaft of right tibia, subsequent encounter for closed fracture with nonunion

S82.254Q Nondisplaced comminuted fracture of shaft of right tibia, subsequent encounter for open fracture type I or II with malunion

S82.254M Nondisplaced comminuted fracture of shaft of right tibia, subsequent encounter for open fracture type I or II with nonunion

S82.254R Nondisplaced comminuted fracture of shaft of right tibia, subsequent encounter for open fracture type IIIA, IIIB, or IIIC with malunion

S82.254N Nondisplaced comminuted fracture of shaft of right tibia, subsequent encounter for open fracture type IIIA, IIIB, or IIIC with nonunion

S52.255A Nondisplaced comminuted fracture of shaft of ulna, left arm, initial encounter for closed fracture

S52.255P Nondisplaced comminuted fracture of shaft of ulna, left arm, subsequent encounter for closed fracture with malunion

S52.255K Nondisplaced comminuted fracture of shaft of ulna, left arm, subsequent encounter for closed fracture with nonunion

S52.255Q Nondisplaced comminuted fracture of shaft of ulna, left arm, subsequent encounter for open fracture type I or II with malunion

S52.255M Nondisplaced comminuted fracture of shaft of ulna, left arm, subsequent encounter for open fracture type I or II with nonunion

S52.255R Nondisplaced comminuted fracture of shaft of ulna, left arm, subsequent encounter for open fracture type IIIA, IIIB, or IIIC with malunion

S52.255N Nondisplaced comminuted fracture of shaft of ulna, left arm, subsequent encounter for open fracture type IIIA, IIIB, or IIIC with nonunion

S52.254A Nondisplaced comminuted fracture of shaft of ulna, right arm, initial encounter for closed fracture

S52.254P Nondisplaced comminuted fracture of shaft of ulna, right arm, subsequent encounter for closed fracture with malunion

S52.254K Nondisplaced comminuted fracture of shaft of ulna, right arm, subsequent encounter for closed fracture with nonunion
S52.254Q Nondisplaced comminuted fracture of shaft of ulna, right arm, subsequent encounter for open fracture type I or II with malunion
S52.254M Nondisplaced comminuted fracture of shaft of ulna, right arm, subsequent encounter for open fracture type I or II with nonunion
S52.254R Nondisplaced comminuted fracture of shaft of ulna, right arm, subsequent encounter for open fracture type IIIA, IIIB, or IIIC with malunion
S52.254N Nondisplaced comminuted fracture of shaft of ulna, right arm, subsequent encounter for open fracture type IIIA, IIIB, or IIIC with nonunion
S52.256A Nondisplaced comminuted fracture of shaft of ulna, unspecified arm, initial encounter for closed fracture
S52.256P Nondisplaced comminuted fracture of shaft of ulna, unspecified arm, subsequent encounter for closed fracture with malunion
S52.256K Nondisplaced comminuted fracture of shaft of ulna, unspecified arm, subsequent encounter for closed fracture with nonunion
S52.256Q Nondisplaced comminuted fracture of shaft of ulna, unspecified arm, subsequent encounter for open fracture type I or II with malunion
S52.256M Nondisplaced comminuted fracture of shaft of ulna, unspecified arm, subsequent encounter for open fracture type I or II with nonunion
S52.256R Nondisplaced comminuted fracture of shaft of ulna, unspecified arm, subsequent encounter for open fracture type IIIA, IIIB, or IIIC with malunion
S52.256N Nondisplaced comminuted fracture of shaft of ulna, unspecified arm, subsequent encounter for open fracture type IIIA, IIIB, or IIIC with nonunion
S72.356P Nondisplaced comminuted fracture of shaft of unspecified femur, subsequent encounter for closed fracture with malunion
S72.356K Nondisplaced comminuted fracture of shaft of unspecified femur, subsequent encounter for closed fracture with nonunion
S72.356Q Nondisplaced comminuted fracture of shaft of unspecified femur, subsequent encounter for open fracture type I or II with malunion
S72.356M Nondisplaced comminuted fracture of shaft of unspecified femur, subsequent encounter for open fracture type I or II with nonunion
S72.356R Nondisplaced comminuted fracture of shaft of unspecified femur, subsequent encounter for open fracture type IIIA, IIIB, or IIIC with malunion
S72.356N Nondisplaced comminuted fracture of shaft of unspecified femur, subsequent encounter for open fracture type IIIA, IIIB, or IIIC with nonunion
S82.456P Nondisplaced comminuted fracture of shaft of unspecified fibula, subsequent encounter for closed fracture with malunion
S82.456K Nondisplaced comminuted fracture of shaft of unspecified fibula, subsequent encounter for closed fracture with nonunion
S82.456Q Nondisplaced comminuted fracture of shaft of unspecified fibula, subsequent encounter for open fracture type I or II with malunion
S82.456M Nondisplaced comminuted fracture of shaft of unspecified fibula, subsequent encounter for open fracture type I or II with nonunion
S82.456R Nondisplaced comminuted fracture of shaft of unspecified fibula, subsequent encounter for open fracture type IIIA, IIIB, or IIIC with malunion
S82.456N Nondisplaced comminuted fracture of shaft of unspecified fibula, subsequent encounter for open fracture type IIIA, IIIB, or IIIC with nonunion
S82.256A Nondisplaced comminuted fracture of shaft of unspecified tibia, initial encounter for closed fracture
S82.256P Nondisplaced comminuted fracture of shaft of unspecified tibia, subsequent encounter for closed fracture with malunion
S82.256K Nondisplaced comminuted fracture of shaft of unspecified tibia, subsequent encounter for closed fracture with nonunion
S82.256Q Nondisplaced comminuted fracture of shaft of unspecified tibia, subsequent encounter for open fracture type I or II with malunion
S82.256M Nondisplaced comminuted fracture of shaft of unspecified tibia, subsequent encounter for open fracture type I or II with nonunion
S82.256R Nondisplaced comminuted fracture of shaft of unspecified tibia, subsequent encounter for open fracture type IIIA, IIIB, or IIIC with malunion
S82.256N Nondisplaced comminuted fracture of shaft of unspecified tibia, subsequent encounter for open fracture type IIIA, IIIB, or IIIC with nonunion
S82.Ø46A Nondisplaced comminuted fracture of unspecified patella, initial encounter for closed fracture
S82.Ø46B Nondisplaced comminuted fracture of unspecified patella, initial encounter for open fracture type I or II
S82.Ø46C Nondisplaced comminuted fracture of unspecified patella, initial encounter for open fracture type IIIA, IIIB, or IIIC
S82.Ø46P Nondisplaced comminuted fracture of unspecified patella, subsequent encounter for closed fracture with malunion
S82.Ø46K Nondisplaced comminuted fracture of unspecified patella, subsequent encounter for closed fracture with nonunion
S82.Ø46Q Nondisplaced comminuted fracture of unspecified patella, subsequent encounter for open fracture type I or II with malunion
S82.Ø46M Nondisplaced comminuted fracture of unspecified patella, subsequent encounter for open fracture type I or II with nonunion
S82.Ø46R Nondisplaced comminuted fracture of unspecified patella, subsequent encounter for open fracture type IIIA, IIIB, or IIIC with malunion
S82.Ø46N Nondisplaced comminuted fracture of unspecified patella, subsequent encounter for open fracture type IIIA, IIIB, or IIIC with nonunion
S42.425A Nondisplaced comminuted supracondylar fracture without intercondylar fracture of left humerus, initial encounter for closed fracture
S42.425P Nondisplaced comminuted supracondylar fracture without intercondylar fracture of left humerus, subsequent encounter for fracture with malunion
S42.425K Nondisplaced comminuted supracondylar fracture without intercondylar fracture of left humerus, subsequent encounter for fracture with nonunion
S42.424A Nondisplaced comminuted supracondylar fracture without intercondylar fracture of right humerus, initial encounter for closed fracture
S42.424P Nondisplaced comminuted supracondylar fracture without intercondylar fracture of right humerus, subsequent encounter for fracture with malunion
S42.424K Nondisplaced comminuted supracondylar fracture without intercondylar fracture of right humerus, subsequent encounter for fracture with nonunion
S42.426A Nondisplaced comminuted supracondylar fracture without intercondylar fracture of unspecified humerus, initial encounter for closed fracture
S42.426P Nondisplaced comminuted supracondylar fracture without intercondylar fracture of unspecified humerus, subsequent encounter for fracture with malunion
S42.426K Nondisplaced comminuted supracondylar fracture without intercondylar fracture of unspecified humerus, subsequent encounter for fracture with nonunion
S32.485K Nondisplaced dome fracture of left acetabulum, subsequent encounter for fracture with nonunion
S92.145B Nondisplaced dome fracture of left talus, initial encounter for open fracture
S92.145P Nondisplaced dome fracture of left talus, subsequent encounter for fracture with malunion
S92.145K Nondisplaced dome fracture of left talus, subsequent encounter for fracture with nonunion
S32.484K Nondisplaced dome fracture of right acetabulum, subsequent encounter for fracture with nonunion
S92.144B Nondisplaced dome fracture of right talus, initial encounter for open fracture
S92.144P Nondisplaced dome fracture of right talus, subsequent encounter for fracture with malunion
S92.144K Nondisplaced dome fracture of right talus, subsequent encounter for fracture with nonunion
S32.486K Nondisplaced dome fracture of unspecified acetabulum, subsequent encounter for fracture with nonunion
S92.146B Nondisplaced dome fracture of unspecified talus, initial encounter for open fracture
S92.146P Nondisplaced dome fracture of unspecified talus, subsequent encounter for fracture with malunion
S92.146K Nondisplaced dome fracture of unspecified talus, subsequent encounter for fracture with nonunion
S42.435A Nondisplaced fracture (avulsion) of lateral epicondyle of left humerus, initial encounter for closed fracture
S42.435P Nondisplaced fracture (avulsion) of lateral epicondyle of left humerus, subsequent encounter for fracture with malunion
S42.435K Nondisplaced fracture (avulsion) of lateral epicondyle of left humerus, subsequent encounter for fracture with nonunion
S42.434A Nondisplaced fracture (avulsion) of lateral epicondyle of right humerus, initial encounter for closed fracture
S42.434P Nondisplaced fracture (avulsion) of lateral epicondyle of right humerus, subsequent encounter for fracture with malunion
S42.434K Nondisplaced fracture (avulsion) of lateral epicondyle of right humerus, subsequent encounter for fracture with nonunion
S42.436A Nondisplaced fracture (avulsion) of lateral epicondyle of unspecified humerus, initial encounter for closed fracture
S42.436P Nondisplaced fracture (avulsion) of lateral epicondyle of unspecified humerus, subsequent encounter for fracture with malunion
S42.436K Nondisplaced fracture (avulsion) of lateral epicondyle of unspecified humerus, subsequent encounter for fracture with nonunion
S42.445A Nondisplaced fracture (avulsion) of medial epicondyle of left humerus, initial encounter for closed fracture
S42.445P Nondisplaced fracture (avulsion) of medial epicondyle of left humerus, subsequent encounter for fracture with malunion
S42.445K Nondisplaced fracture (avulsion) of medial epicondyle of left humerus, subsequent encounter for fracture with nonunion
S42.444A Nondisplaced fracture (avulsion) of medial epicondyle of right humerus, initial encounter for closed fracture
S42.444P Nondisplaced fracture (avulsion) of medial epicondyle of right humerus, subsequent encounter for fracture with malunion
S42.444K Nondisplaced fracture (avulsion) of medial epicondyle of right humerus, subsequent encounter for fracture with nonunion
S42.446A Nondisplaced fracture (avulsion) of medial epicondyle of unspecified humerus, initial encounter for closed fracture
S42.446P Nondisplaced fracture (avulsion) of medial epicondyle of unspecified humerus, subsequent encounter for fracture with malunion
S42.446K Nondisplaced fracture (avulsion) of medial epicondyle of unspecified humerus, subsequent encounter for fracture with nonunion
S42.125B Nondisplaced fracture of acromial process, left shoulder, initial encounter for open fracture
S42.125P Nondisplaced fracture of acromial process, left shoulder, subsequent encounter for fracture with malunion
S42.125K Nondisplaced fracture of acromial process, left shoulder, subsequent encounter for fracture with nonunion
S42.124B Nondisplaced fracture of acromial process, right shoulder, initial encounter for open fracture
S42.124P Nondisplaced fracture of acromial process, right shoulder, subsequent encounter for fracture with malunion
S42.124K Nondisplaced fracture of acromial process, right shoulder, subsequent encounter for fracture with nonunion
S42.126B Nondisplaced fracture of acromial process, unspecified shoulder, initial encounter for open fracture
S42.126P Nondisplaced fracture of acromial process, unspecified shoulder, subsequent encounter for fracture with malunion
S42.126K Nondisplaced fracture of acromial process, unspecified shoulder, subsequent encounter for fracture with nonunion
S32.435K Nondisplaced fracture of anterior column [iliopubic] of left acetabulum, subsequent encounter for fracture with nonunion
S32.434K Nondisplaced fracture of anterior column [iliopubic] of right acetabulum, subsequent encounter for fracture with nonunion

S32.436K Nondisplaced fracture of anterior column [iliopubic] of unspecified acetabulum, subsequent encounter for fracture with nonunion

S92.025B Nondisplaced fracture of anterior process of left calcaneus, initial encounter for open fracture

S92.025P Nondisplaced fracture of anterior process of left calcaneus, subsequent encounter for fracture with malunion

S92.025K Nondisplaced fracture of anterior process of left calcaneus, subsequent encounter for fracture with nonunion

S92.024B Nondisplaced fracture of anterior process of right calcaneus, initial encounter for open fracture

S92.024P Nondisplaced fracture of anterior process of right calcaneus, subsequent encounter for fracture with malunion

S92.024K Nondisplaced fracture of anterior process of right calcaneus, subsequent encounter for fracture with nonunion

S92.026B Nondisplaced fracture of anterior process of unspecified calcaneus, initial encounter for open fracture

S92.026P Nondisplaced fracture of anterior process of unspecified calcaneus, subsequent encounter for fracture with malunion

S92.026K Nondisplaced fracture of anterior process of unspecified calcaneus, subsequent encounter for fracture with nonunion

S32.415K Nondisplaced fracture of anterior wall of left acetabulum, subsequent encounter for fracture with nonunion

S32.414K Nondisplaced fracture of anterior wall of right acetabulum, subsequent encounter for fracture with nonunion

S32.416K Nondisplaced fracture of anterior wall of unspecified acetabulum, subsequent encounter for fracture with nonunion

S62.347B Nondisplaced fracture of base of fifth metacarpal bone, left hand, initial encounter for open fracture

S62.347P Nondisplaced fracture of base of fifth metacarpal bone, left hand, subsequent encounter for fracture with malunion

S62.347K Nondisplaced fracture of base of fifth metacarpal bone, left hand, subsequent encounter for fracture with nonunion

S62.346B Nondisplaced fracture of base of fifth metacarpal bone, right hand, initial encounter for open fracture

S62.346P Nondisplaced fracture of base of fifth metacarpal bone, right hand, subsequent encounter for fracture with malunion

S62.346K Nondisplaced fracture of base of fifth metacarpal bone, right hand, subsequent encounter for fracture with nonunion

S62.345B Nondisplaced fracture of base of fourth metacarpal bone, left hand, initial encounter for open fracture

S62.345P Nondisplaced fracture of base of fourth metacarpal bone, left hand, subsequent encounter for fracture with malunion

S62.345K Nondisplaced fracture of base of fourth metacarpal bone, left hand, subsequent encounter for fracture with nonunion

S62.344B Nondisplaced fracture of base of fourth metacarpal bone, right hand, initial encounter for open fracture

S62.344P Nondisplaced fracture of base of fourth metacarpal bone, right hand, subsequent encounter for fracture with malunion

S62.344K Nondisplaced fracture of base of fourth metacarpal bone, right hand, subsequent encounter for fracture with nonunion

S72.045P Nondisplaced fracture of base of neck of left femur, subsequent encounter for closed fracture with malunion

S72.045K Nondisplaced fracture of base of neck of left femur, subsequent encounter for closed fracture with nonunion

S72.045Q Nondisplaced fracture of base of neck of left femur, subsequent encounter for open fracture type I or II with malunion

S72.045M Nondisplaced fracture of base of neck of left femur, subsequent encounter for open fracture type I or II with nonunion

S72.045R Nondisplaced fracture of base of neck of left femur, subsequent encounter for open fracture type IIIA, IIIB, or IIIC with malunion

S72.045N Nondisplaced fracture of base of neck of left femur, subsequent encounter for open fracture type IIIA, IIIB, or IIIC with nonunion

S72.044P Nondisplaced fracture of base of neck of right femur, subsequent encounter for closed fracture with malunion

S72.044K Nondisplaced fracture of base of neck of right femur, subsequent encounter for closed fracture with nonunion

S72.044Q Nondisplaced fracture of base of neck of right femur, subsequent encounter for open fracture type I or II with malunion

S72.044M Nondisplaced fracture of base of neck of right femur, subsequent encounter for open fracture type I or II with nonunion

S72.044R Nondisplaced fracture of base of neck of right femur, subsequent encounter for open fracture type IIIA, IIIB, or IIIC with malunion

S72.044N Nondisplaced fracture of base of neck of right femur, subsequent encounter for open fracture type IIIA, IIIB, or IIIC with nonunion

S72.046P Nondisplaced fracture of base of neck of unspecified femur, subsequent encounter for closed fracture with malunion

S72.046K Nondisplaced fracture of base of neck of unspecified femur, subsequent encounter for closed fracture with nonunion

S72.046Q Nondisplaced fracture of base of neck of unspecified femur, subsequent encounter for open fracture type I or II with malunion

S72.046M Nondisplaced fracture of base of neck of unspecified femur, subsequent encounter for open fracture type I or II with nonunion

S72.046R Nondisplaced fracture of base of neck of unspecified femur, subsequent encounter for open fracture type IIIA, IIIB, or IIIC with malunion

S72.046N Nondisplaced fracture of base of neck of unspecified femur, subsequent encounter for open fracture type IIIA, IIIB, or IIIC with nonunion

S62.348B Nondisplaced fracture of base of other metacarpal bone, initial encounter for open fracture

S62.348P Nondisplaced fracture of base of other metacarpal bone, subsequent encounter for fracture with malunion

S62.348K Nondisplaced fracture of base of other metacarpal bone, subsequent encounter for fracture with nonunion

S62.341B Nondisplaced fracture of base of second metacarpal bone, left hand, initial encounter for open fracture

S62.341P Nondisplaced fracture of base of second metacarpal bone, left hand, subsequent encounter for fracture with malunion

S62.341K Nondisplaced fracture of base of second metacarpal bone, left hand, subsequent encounter for fracture with nonunion

S62.340B Nondisplaced fracture of base of second metacarpal bone, right hand, initial encounter for open fracture

S62.340P Nondisplaced fracture of base of second metacarpal bone, right hand, subsequent encounter for fracture with malunion

S62.340K Nondisplaced fracture of base of second metacarpal bone, right hand, subsequent encounter for fracture with nonunion

S62.343B Nondisplaced fracture of base of third metacarpal bone, left hand, initial encounter for open fracture

S62.343P Nondisplaced fracture of base of third metacarpal bone, left hand, subsequent encounter for fracture with malunion

S62.343K Nondisplaced fracture of base of third metacarpal bone, left hand, subsequent encounter for fracture with nonunion

S62.342B Nondisplaced fracture of base of third metacarpal bone, right hand, initial encounter for open fracture

S62.342P Nondisplaced fracture of base of third metacarpal bone, right hand, subsequent encounter for fracture with malunion

S62.342K Nondisplaced fracture of base of third metacarpal bone, right hand, subsequent encounter for fracture with nonunion

S62.349B Nondisplaced fracture of base of unspecified metacarpal bone, initial encounter for open fracture

S62.349P Nondisplaced fracture of base of unspecified metacarpal bone, subsequent encounter for fracture with malunion

S62.349K Nondisplaced fracture of base of unspecified metacarpal bone, subsequent encounter for fracture with nonunion

S62.145B Nondisplaced fracture of body of hamate [unciform] bone, left wrist, initial encounter for open fracture

S62.145P Nondisplaced fracture of body of hamate [unciform] bone, left wrist, subsequent encounter for fracture with malunion

S62.145K Nondisplaced fracture of body of hamate [unciform] bone, left wrist, subsequent encounter for fracture with nonunion

S62.144B Nondisplaced fracture of body of hamate [unciform] bone, right wrist, initial encounter for open fracture

S62.144P Nondisplaced fracture of body of hamate [unciform] bone, right wrist, subsequent encounter for fracture with malunion

S62.144K Nondisplaced fracture of body of hamate [unciform] bone, right wrist, subsequent encounter for fracture with nonunion

S62.146B Nondisplaced fracture of body of hamate [unciform] bone, unspecified wrist, initial encounter for open fracture

S62.146P Nondisplaced fracture of body of hamate [unciform] bone, unspecified wrist, subsequent encounter for fracture with malunion

S62.146K Nondisplaced fracture of body of hamate [unciform] bone, unspecified wrist, subsequent encounter for fracture with nonunion

S92.015B Nondisplaced fracture of body of left calcaneus, initial encounter for open fracture

S92.015P Nondisplaced fracture of body of left calcaneus, subsequent encounter for fracture with malunion

S92.015K Nondisplaced fracture of body of left calcaneus, subsequent encounter for fracture with nonunion

S92.125B Nondisplaced fracture of body of left talus, initial encounter for open fracture

S92.125P Nondisplaced fracture of body of left talus, subsequent encounter for fracture with malunion

S92.125K Nondisplaced fracture of body of left talus, subsequent encounter for fracture with nonunion

S92.014B Nondisplaced fracture of body of right calcaneus, initial encounter for open fracture

S92.014P Nondisplaced fracture of body of right calcaneus, subsequent encounter for fracture with malunion

S92.014K Nondisplaced fracture of body of right calcaneus, subsequent encounter for fracture with nonunion

S92.124B Nondisplaced fracture of body of right talus, initial encounter for open fracture

S92.124P Nondisplaced fracture of body of right talus, subsequent encounter for fracture with malunion

S92.124K Nondisplaced fracture of body of right talus, subsequent encounter for fracture with nonunion

S42.115B Nondisplaced fracture of body of scapula, left shoulder, initial encounter for open fracture

S42.115P Nondisplaced fracture of body of scapula, left shoulder, subsequent encounter for fracture with malunion

S42.115K Nondisplaced fracture of body of scapula, left shoulder, subsequent encounter for fracture with nonunion

S42.114B Nondisplaced fracture of body of scapula, right shoulder, initial encounter for open fracture

S42.114P Nondisplaced fracture of body of scapula, right shoulder, subsequent encounter for fracture with malunion

S42.114K Nondisplaced fracture of body of scapula, right shoulder, subsequent encounter for fracture with nonunion

S42.116B Nondisplaced fracture of body of scapula, unspecified shoulder, initial encounter for open fracture

S42.116P Nondisplaced fracture of body of scapula, unspecified shoulder, subsequent encounter for fracture with malunion

S42.116K Nondisplaced fracture of body of scapula, unspecified shoulder, subsequent encounter for fracture with nonunion

S92.016B	Nondisplaced fracture of body of unspecified calcaneus, initial encounter for open fracture
S92.016P	Nondisplaced fracture of body of unspecified calcaneus, subsequent encounter for fracture with malunion
S92.016K	Nondisplaced fracture of body of unspecified calcaneus, subsequent encounter for fracture with nonunion
S92.126B	Nondisplaced fracture of body of unspecified talus, initial encounter for open fracture
S92.126P	Nondisplaced fracture of body of unspecified talus, subsequent encounter for fracture with malunion
S92.126K	Nondisplaced fracture of body of unspecified talus, subsequent encounter for fracture with nonunion
S62.135B	Nondisplaced fracture of capitate [os magnum] bone, left wrist, initial encounter for open fracture
S62.135P	Nondisplaced fracture of capitate [os magnum] bone, left wrist, subsequent encounter for fracture with malunion
S62.135K	Nondisplaced fracture of capitate [os magnum] bone, left wrist, subsequent encounter for fracture with nonunion
S62.134B	Nondisplaced fracture of capitate [os magnum] bone, right wrist, initial encounter for open fracture
S62.134P	Nondisplaced fracture of capitate [os magnum] bone, right wrist, subsequent encounter for fracture with malunion
S62.134K	Nondisplaced fracture of capitate [os magnum] bone, right wrist, subsequent encounter for fracture with nonunion
S62.136B	Nondisplaced fracture of capitate [os magnum] bone, unspecified wrist, initial encounter for open fracture
S62.136P	Nondisplaced fracture of capitate [os magnum] bone, unspecified wrist, subsequent encounter for fracture with malunion
S62.136K	Nondisplaced fracture of capitate [os magnum] bone, unspecified wrist, subsequent encounter for fracture with nonunion
S42.135B	Nondisplaced fracture of coracoid process, left shoulder, initial encounter for open fracture
S42.135P	Nondisplaced fracture of coracoid process, left shoulder, subsequent encounter for fracture with malunion
S42.135K	Nondisplaced fracture of coracoid process, left shoulder, subsequent encounter for fracture with nonunion
S42.134B	Nondisplaced fracture of coracoid process, right shoulder, initial encounter for open fracture
S42.134P	Nondisplaced fracture of coracoid process, right shoulder, subsequent encounter for fracture with malunion
S42.134K	Nondisplaced fracture of coracoid process, right shoulder, subsequent encounter for fracture with nonunion
S42.136B	Nondisplaced fracture of coracoid process, unspecified shoulder, initial encounter for open fracture
S42.136P	Nondisplaced fracture of coracoid process, unspecified shoulder, subsequent encounter for fracture with malunion
S42.136K	Nondisplaced fracture of coracoid process, unspecified shoulder, subsequent encounter for fracture with nonunion
S52.045P	Nondisplaced fracture of coronoid process of left ulna, subsequent encounter for closed fracture with malunion
S52.045K	Nondisplaced fracture of coronoid process of left ulna, subsequent encounter for closed fracture with nonunion
S52.045Q	Nondisplaced fracture of coronoid process of left ulna, subsequent encounter for open fracture type I or II with malunion
S52.045M	Nondisplaced fracture of coronoid process of left ulna, subsequent encounter for open fracture type I or II with nonunion
S52.045R	Nondisplaced fracture of coronoid process of left ulna, subsequent encounter for open fracture type IIIA, IIIB, or IIIC with malunion
S52.045N	Nondisplaced fracture of coronoid process of left ulna, subsequent encounter for open fracture type IIIA, IIIB, or IIIC with nonunion
S52.044P	Nondisplaced fracture of coronoid process of right ulna, subsequent encounter for closed fracture with malunion
S52.044K	Nondisplaced fracture of coronoid process of right ulna, subsequent encounter for closed fracture with nonunion
S52.044Q	Nondisplaced fracture of coronoid process of right ulna, subsequent encounter for open fracture type I or II with malunion
S52.044M	Nondisplaced fracture of coronoid process of right ulna, subsequent encounter for open fracture type I or II with nonunion
S52.044R	Nondisplaced fracture of coronoid process of right ulna, subsequent encounter for open fracture type IIIA, IIIB, or IIIC with malunion
S52.044N	Nondisplaced fracture of coronoid process of right ulna, subsequent encounter for open fracture type IIIA, IIIB, or IIIC with nonunion
S52.046P	Nondisplaced fracture of coronoid process of unspecified ulna, subsequent encounter for closed fracture with malunion
S52.046K	Nondisplaced fracture of coronoid process of unspecified ulna, subsequent encounter for closed fracture with nonunion
S52.046Q	Nondisplaced fracture of coronoid process of unspecified ulna, subsequent encounter for open fracture type I or II with malunion
S52.046M	Nondisplaced fracture of coronoid process of unspecified ulna, subsequent encounter for open fracture type I or II with nonunion
S52.046R	Nondisplaced fracture of coronoid process of unspecified ulna, subsequent encounter for open fracture type IIIA, IIIB, or IIIC with malunion
S52.046N	Nondisplaced fracture of coronoid process of unspecified ulna, subsequent encounter for open fracture type IIIA, IIIB, or IIIC with nonunion
S92.215B	Nondisplaced fracture of cuboid bone of left foot, initial encounter for open fracture
S92.215P	Nondisplaced fracture of cuboid bone of left foot, subsequent encounter for fracture with malunion
S92.215K	Nondisplaced fracture of cuboid bone of left foot, subsequent encounter for fracture with nonunion
S92.214B	Nondisplaced fracture of cuboid bone of right foot, initial encounter for open fracture
S92.214P	Nondisplaced fracture of cuboid bone of right foot, subsequent encounter for fracture with malunion
S92.214K	Nondisplaced fracture of cuboid bone of right foot, subsequent encounter for fracture with nonunion
S92.216B	Nondisplaced fracture of cuboid bone of unspecified foot, initial encounter for open fracture
S92.216P	Nondisplaced fracture of cuboid bone of unspecified foot, subsequent encounter for fracture with malunion
S92.216K	Nondisplaced fracture of cuboid bone of unspecified foot, subsequent encounter for fracture with nonunion
S92.425P	Nondisplaced fracture of distal phalanx of left great toe, subsequent encounter for fracture with malunion
S92.425K	Nondisplaced fracture of distal phalanx of left great toe, subsequent encounter for fracture with nonunion
S62.661B	Nondisplaced fracture of distal phalanx of left index finger, initial encounter for open fracture
S62.661P	Nondisplaced fracture of distal phalanx of left index finger, subsequent encounter for fracture with malunion
S62.661K	Nondisplaced fracture of distal phalanx of left index finger, subsequent encounter for fracture with nonunion
S92.535P	Nondisplaced fracture of distal phalanx of left lesser toe(s), subsequent encounter for fracture with malunion
S92.535K	Nondisplaced fracture of distal phalanx of left lesser toe(s), subsequent encounter for fracture with nonunion
S62.667B	Nondisplaced fracture of distal phalanx of left little finger, initial encounter for open fracture
S62.667P	Nondisplaced fracture of distal phalanx of left little finger, subsequent encounter for fracture with malunion
S62.667K	Nondisplaced fracture of distal phalanx of left little finger, subsequent encounter for fracture with nonunion
S62.663B	Nondisplaced fracture of distal phalanx of left middle finger, initial encounter for open fracture
S62.663P	Nondisplaced fracture of distal phalanx of left middle finger, subsequent encounter for fracture with malunion
S62.663K	Nondisplaced fracture of distal phalanx of left middle finger, subsequent encounter for fracture with nonunion
S62.665B	Nondisplaced fracture of distal phalanx of left ring finger, initial encounter for open fracture
S62.665P	Nondisplaced fracture of distal phalanx of left ring finger, subsequent encounter for fracture with malunion
S62.665K	Nondisplaced fracture of distal phalanx of left ring finger, subsequent encounter for fracture with nonunion
S62.525B	Nondisplaced fracture of distal phalanx of left thumb, initial encounter for open fracture
S62.525P	Nondisplaced fracture of distal phalanx of left thumb, subsequent encounter for fracture with malunion
S62.525K	Nondisplaced fracture of distal phalanx of left thumb, subsequent encounter for fracture with nonunion
S62.668B	Nondisplaced fracture of distal phalanx of other finger, initial encounter for open fracture
S62.668P	Nondisplaced fracture of distal phalanx of other finger, subsequent encounter for fracture with malunion
S62.668K	Nondisplaced fracture of distal phalanx of other finger, subsequent encounter for fracture with nonunion
S92.424P	Nondisplaced fracture of distal phalanx of right great toe, subsequent encounter for fracture with malunion
S92.424K	Nondisplaced fracture of distal phalanx of right great toe, subsequent encounter for fracture with nonunion
S62.660B	Nondisplaced fracture of distal phalanx of right index finger, initial encounter for open fracture
S62.660P	Nondisplaced fracture of distal phalanx of right index finger, subsequent encounter for fracture with malunion
S62.660K	Nondisplaced fracture of distal phalanx of right index finger, subsequent encounter for fracture with nonunion
S92.534P	Nondisplaced fracture of distal phalanx of right lesser toe(s), subsequent encounter for fracture with malunion
S92.534K	Nondisplaced fracture of distal phalanx of right lesser toe(s), subsequent encounter for fracture with nonunion
S62.666B	Nondisplaced fracture of distal phalanx of right little finger, initial encounter for open fracture
S62.666P	Nondisplaced fracture of distal phalanx of right little finger, subsequent encounter for fracture with malunion
S62.666K	Nondisplaced fracture of distal phalanx of right little finger, subsequent encounter for fracture with nonunion
S62.662B	Nondisplaced fracture of distal phalanx of right middle finger, initial encounter for open fracture
S62.662P	Nondisplaced fracture of distal phalanx of right middle finger, subsequent encounter for fracture with malunion
S62.662K	Nondisplaced fracture of distal phalanx of right middle finger, subsequent encounter for fracture with nonunion
S62.664B	Nondisplaced fracture of distal phalanx of right ring finger, initial encounter for open fracture
S62.664P	Nondisplaced fracture of distal phalanx of right ring finger, subsequent encounter for fracture with malunion
S62.664K	Nondisplaced fracture of distal phalanx of right ring finger, subsequent encounter for fracture with nonunion
S62.524B	Nondisplaced fracture of distal phalanx of right thumb, initial encounter for open fracture

S62.524P Nondisplaced fracture of distal phalanx of right thumb, subsequent encounter for fracture with malunion
S62.524K Nondisplaced fracture of distal phalanx of right thumb, subsequent encounter for fracture with nonunion
S62.669B Nondisplaced fracture of distal phalanx of unspecified finger, initial encounter for open fracture
S62.669P Nondisplaced fracture of distal phalanx of unspecified finger, subsequent encounter for fracture with malunion
S62.669K Nondisplaced fracture of distal phalanx of unspecified finger, subsequent encounter for fracture with nonunion
S92.426P Nondisplaced fracture of distal phalanx of unspecified great toe, subsequent encounter for fracture with malunion
S92.426K Nondisplaced fracture of distal phalanx of unspecified great toe, subsequent encounter for fracture with nonunion
S92.536P Nondisplaced fracture of distal phalanx of unspecified lesser toe(s), subsequent encounter for fracture with malunion
S92.536K Nondisplaced fracture of distal phalanx of unspecified lesser toe(s), subsequent encounter for fracture with nonunion
S62.526B Nondisplaced fracture of distal phalanx of unspecified thumb, initial encounter for open fracture
S62.526P Nondisplaced fracture of distal phalanx of unspecified thumb, subsequent encounter for fracture with malunion
S62.526K Nondisplaced fracture of distal phalanx of unspecified thumb, subsequent encounter for fracture with nonunion
S62.015B Nondisplaced fracture of distal pole of navicular [scaphoid] bone of left wrist, initial encounter for open fracture
S62.015P Nondisplaced fracture of distal pole of navicular [scaphoid] bone of left wrist, subsequent encounter for fracture with malunion
S62.015K Nondisplaced fracture of distal pole of navicular [scaphoid] bone of left wrist, subsequent encounter for fracture with nonunion
S62.014B Nondisplaced fracture of distal pole of navicular [scaphoid] bone of right wrist, initial encounter for open fracture
S62.014P Nondisplaced fracture of distal pole of navicular [scaphoid] bone of right wrist, subsequent encounter for fracture with malunion
S62.014K Nondisplaced fracture of distal pole of navicular [scaphoid] bone of right wrist, subsequent encounter for fracture with nonunion
S62.016B Nondisplaced fracture of distal pole of navicular [scaphoid] bone of unspecified wrist, initial encounter for open fracture
S62.016P Nondisplaced fracture of distal pole of navicular [scaphoid] bone of unspecified wrist, subsequent encounter for fracture with malunion
S62.016K Nondisplaced fracture of distal pole of navicular [scaphoid] bone of unspecified wrist, subsequent encounter for fracture with nonunion
S72.025P Nondisplaced fracture of epiphysis (separation) (upper) of left femur, subsequent encounter for closed fracture with malunion
S72.025K Nondisplaced fracture of epiphysis (separation) (upper) of left femur, subsequent encounter for closed fracture with nonunion
S72.025Q Nondisplaced fracture of epiphysis (separation) (upper) of left femur, subsequent encounter for open fracture type I or II with malunion
S72.025M Nondisplaced fracture of epiphysis (separation) (upper) of left femur, subsequent encounter for open fracture type I or II with nonunion
S72.025R Nondisplaced fracture of epiphysis (separation) (upper) of left femur, subsequent encounter for open fracture type IIIA, IIIB, or IIIC with malunion
S72.025N Nondisplaced fracture of epiphysis (separation) (upper) of left femur, subsequent encounter for open fracture type IIIA, IIIB, or IIIC with nonunion
S72.024P Nondisplaced fracture of epiphysis (separation) (upper) of right femur, subsequent encounter for closed fracture with malunion
S72.024K Nondisplaced fracture of epiphysis (separation) (upper) of right femur, subsequent encounter for closed fracture with nonunion
S72.024Q Nondisplaced fracture of epiphysis (separation) (upper) of right femur, subsequent encounter for open fracture type I or II with malunion
S72.024M Nondisplaced fracture of epiphysis (separation) (upper) of right femur, subsequent encounter for open fracture type I or II with nonunion
S72.024R Nondisplaced fracture of epiphysis (separation) (upper) of right femur, subsequent encounter for open fracture type IIIA, IIIB, or IIIC with malunion
S72.024N Nondisplaced fracture of epiphysis (separation) (upper) of right femur, subsequent encounter for open fracture type IIIA, IIIB, or IIIC with nonunion
S72.026P Nondisplaced fracture of epiphysis (separation) (upper) of unspecified femur, subsequent encounter for closed fracture with malunion
S72.026K Nondisplaced fracture of epiphysis (separation) (upper) of unspecified femur, subsequent encounter for closed fracture with nonunion
S72.026Q Nondisplaced fracture of epiphysis (separation) (upper) of unspecified femur, subsequent encounter for open fracture type I or II with malunion
S72.026M Nondisplaced fracture of epiphysis (separation) (upper) of unspecified femur, subsequent encounter for open fracture type I or II with nonunion
S72.026R Nondisplaced fracture of epiphysis (separation) (upper) of unspecified femur, subsequent encounter for open fracture type IIIA, IIIB, or IIIC with malunion
S72.026N Nondisplaced fracture of epiphysis (separation) (upper) of unspecified femur, subsequent encounter for open fracture type IIIA, IIIB, or IIIC with nonunion
S92.355B Nondisplaced fracture of fifth metatarsal bone, left foot, initial encounter for open fracture
S92.355P Nondisplaced fracture of fifth metatarsal bone, left foot, subsequent encounter for fracture with malunion
S92.355K Nondisplaced fracture of fifth metatarsal bone, left foot, subsequent encounter for fracture with nonunion
S92.354B Nondisplaced fracture of fifth metatarsal bone, right foot, initial encounter for open fracture
S92.354P Nondisplaced fracture of fifth metatarsal bone, right foot, subsequent encounter for fracture with malunion
S92.354K Nondisplaced fracture of fifth metatarsal bone, right foot, subsequent encounter for fracture with nonunion
S92.356B Nondisplaced fracture of fifth metatarsal bone, unspecified foot, initial encounter for open fracture
S92.356P Nondisplaced fracture of fifth metatarsal bone, unspecified foot, subsequent encounter for fracture with malunion
S92.356K Nondisplaced fracture of fifth metatarsal bone, unspecified foot, subsequent encounter for fracture with nonunion
S92.315B Nondisplaced fracture of first metatarsal bone, left foot, initial encounter for open fracture
S92.315P Nondisplaced fracture of first metatarsal bone, left foot, subsequent encounter for fracture with malunion
S92.315K Nondisplaced fracture of first metatarsal bone, left foot, subsequent encounter for fracture with nonunion
S92.314B Nondisplaced fracture of first metatarsal bone, right foot, initial encounter for open fracture
S92.314P Nondisplaced fracture of first metatarsal bone, right foot, subsequent encounter for fracture with malunion
S92.314K Nondisplaced fracture of first metatarsal bone, right foot, subsequent encounter for fracture with nonunion
S92.316B Nondisplaced fracture of first metatarsal bone, unspecified foot, initial encounter for open fracture
S92.316P Nondisplaced fracture of first metatarsal bone, unspecified foot, subsequent encounter for fracture with malunion
S92.316K Nondisplaced fracture of first metatarsal bone, unspecified foot, subsequent encounter for fracture with nonunion
S92.345B Nondisplaced fracture of fourth metatarsal bone, left foot, initial encounter for open fracture
S92.345P Nondisplaced fracture of fourth metatarsal bone, left foot, subsequent encounter for fracture with malunion
S92.345K Nondisplaced fracture of fourth metatarsal bone, left foot, subsequent encounter for fracture with nonunion
S92.344B Nondisplaced fracture of fourth metatarsal bone, right foot, initial encounter for open fracture
S92.344P Nondisplaced fracture of fourth metatarsal bone, right foot, subsequent encounter for fracture with malunion
S92.344K Nondisplaced fracture of fourth metatarsal bone, right foot, subsequent encounter for fracture with nonunion
S92.346B Nondisplaced fracture of fourth metatarsal bone, unspecified foot, initial encounter for open fracture
S92.346P Nondisplaced fracture of fourth metatarsal bone, unspecified foot, subsequent encounter for fracture with malunion
S92.346K Nondisplaced fracture of fourth metatarsal bone, unspecified foot, subsequent encounter for fracture with nonunion
S42.145B Nondisplaced fracture of glenoid cavity of scapula, left shoulder, initial encounter for open fracture
S42.145P Nondisplaced fracture of glenoid cavity of scapula, left shoulder, subsequent encounter for fracture with malunion
S42.145K Nondisplaced fracture of glenoid cavity of scapula, left shoulder, subsequent encounter for fracture with nonunion
S42.144B Nondisplaced fracture of glenoid cavity of scapula, right shoulder, initial encounter for open fracture
S42.144P Nondisplaced fracture of glenoid cavity of scapula, right shoulder, subsequent encounter for fracture with malunion
S42.144K Nondisplaced fracture of glenoid cavity of scapula, right shoulder, subsequent encounter for fracture with nonunion
S42.146B Nondisplaced fracture of glenoid cavity of scapula, unspecified shoulder, initial encounter for open fracture
S42.146P Nondisplaced fracture of glenoid cavity of scapula, unspecified shoulder, subsequent encounter for fracture with malunion
S42.146K Nondisplaced fracture of glenoid cavity of scapula, unspecified shoulder, subsequent encounter for fracture with nonunion
S72.115P Nondisplaced fracture of greater trochanter of left femur, subsequent encounter for closed fracture with malunion
S72.115K Nondisplaced fracture of greater trochanter of left femur, subsequent encounter for closed fracture with nonunion
S72.115Q Nondisplaced fracture of greater trochanter of left femur, subsequent encounter for open fracture type I or II with malunion
S72.115M Nondisplaced fracture of greater trochanter of left femur, subsequent encounter for open fracture type I or II with nonunion
S72.115R Nondisplaced fracture of greater trochanter of left femur, subsequent encounter for open fracture type IIIA, IIIB, or IIIC with malunion
S72.115N Nondisplaced fracture of greater trochanter of left femur, subsequent encounter for open fracture type IIIA, IIIB, or IIIC with nonunion
S72.114P Nondisplaced fracture of greater trochanter of right femur, subsequent encounter for closed fracture with malunion
S72.114K Nondisplaced fracture of greater trochanter of right femur, subsequent encounter for closed fracture with nonunion
S72.114Q Nondisplaced fracture of greater trochanter of right femur, subsequent encounter for open fracture type I or II with malunion
S72.114M Nondisplaced fracture of greater trochanter of right femur, subsequent encounter for open fracture type I or II with nonunion
S72.114R Nondisplaced fracture of greater trochanter of right femur, subsequent encounter for open fracture type IIIA, IIIB, or IIIC with malunion
S72.114N Nondisplaced fracture of greater trochanter of right femur, subsequent encounter for open fracture type IIIA, IIIB, or IIIC with nonunion
S72.116P Nondisplaced fracture of greater trochanter of unspecified femur, subsequent encounter for closed fracture with malunion
S72.116K Nondisplaced fracture of greater trochanter of unspecified femur, subsequent encounter for closed fracture with nonunion
S72.116Q Nondisplaced fracture of greater trochanter of unspecified femur, subsequent encounter for open fracture type I or II with malunion

S72.116M Nondisplaced fracture of greater trochanter of unspecified femur, subsequent encounter for open fracture type I or II with nonunion

S72.116R Nondisplaced fracture of greater trochanter of unspecified femur, subsequent encounter for open fracture type IIIA, IIIB, or IIIC with malunion

S72.116N Nondisplaced fracture of greater trochanter of unspecified femur, subsequent encounter for open fracture type IIIA, IIIB, or IIIC with nonunion

S42.255A Nondisplaced fracture of greater tuberosity of left humerus, initial encounter for closed fracture

S42.255P Nondisplaced fracture of greater tuberosity of left humerus, subsequent encounter for fracture with malunion

S42.255K Nondisplaced fracture of greater tuberosity of left humerus, subsequent encounter for fracture with nonunion

S42.254A Nondisplaced fracture of greater tuberosity of right humerus, initial encounter for closed fracture

S42.254P Nondisplaced fracture of greater tuberosity of right humerus, subsequent encounter for fracture with malunion

S42.254K Nondisplaced fracture of greater tuberosity of right humerus, subsequent encounter for fracture with nonunion

S42.256A Nondisplaced fracture of greater tuberosity of unspecified humerus, initial encounter for closed fracture

S42.256P Nondisplaced fracture of greater tuberosity of unspecified humerus, subsequent encounter for fracture with malunion

S42.256K Nondisplaced fracture of greater tuberosity of unspecified humerus, subsequent encounter for fracture with nonunion

S52.125P Nondisplaced fracture of head of left radius, subsequent encounter for closed fracture with malunion

S52.125K Nondisplaced fracture of head of left radius, subsequent encounter for closed fracture with nonunion

S52.125Q Nondisplaced fracture of head of left radius, subsequent encounter for open fracture type I or II with malunion

S52.125M Nondisplaced fracture of head of left radius, subsequent encounter for open fracture type I or II with nonunion

S52.125R Nondisplaced fracture of head of left radius, subsequent encounter for open fracture type IIIA, IIIB, or IIIC with malunion

S52.125N Nondisplaced fracture of head of left radius, subsequent encounter for open fracture type IIIA, IIIB, or IIIC with nonunion

S52.124P Nondisplaced fracture of head of right radius, subsequent encounter for closed fracture with malunion

S52.124K Nondisplaced fracture of head of right radius, subsequent encounter for closed fracture with nonunion

S52.124Q Nondisplaced fracture of head of right radius, subsequent encounter for open fracture type I or II with malunion

S52.124M Nondisplaced fracture of head of right radius, subsequent encounter for open fracture type I or II with nonunion

S52.124R Nondisplaced fracture of head of right radius, subsequent encounter for open fracture type IIIA, IIIB, or IIIC with malunion

S52.124N Nondisplaced fracture of head of right radius, subsequent encounter for open fracture type IIIA, IIIB, or IIIC with nonunion

S52.126P Nondisplaced fracture of head of unspecified radius, subsequent encounter for closed fracture with malunion

S52.126K Nondisplaced fracture of head of unspecified radius, subsequent encounter for closed fracture with nonunion

S52.126Q Nondisplaced fracture of head of unspecified radius, subsequent encounter for open fracture type I or II with malunion

S52.126M Nondisplaced fracture of head of unspecified radius, subsequent encounter for open fracture type I or II with nonunion

S52.126R Nondisplaced fracture of head of unspecified radius, subsequent encounter for open fracture type IIIA, IIIB, or IIIC with malunion

S52.126N Nondisplaced fracture of head of unspecified radius, subsequent encounter for open fracture type IIIA, IIIB, or IIIC with nonunion

S62.155B Nondisplaced fracture of hook process of hamate [unciform] bone, left wrist, initial encounter for open fracture

S62.155P Nondisplaced fracture of hook process of hamate [unciform] bone, left wrist, subsequent encounter for fracture with malunion

S62.155K Nondisplaced fracture of hook process of hamate [unciform] bone, left wrist, subsequent encounter for fracture with nonunion

S62.154B Nondisplaced fracture of hook process of hamate [unciform] bone, right wrist, initial encounter for open fracture

S62.154P Nondisplaced fracture of hook process of hamate [unciform] bone, right wrist, subsequent encounter for fracture with malunion

S62.154K Nondisplaced fracture of hook process of hamate [unciform] bone, right wrist, subsequent encounter for fracture with nonunion

S62.156B Nondisplaced fracture of hook process of hamate [unciform] bone, unspecified wrist, initial encounter for open fracture

S62.156P Nondisplaced fracture of hook process of hamate [unciform] bone, unspecified wrist, subsequent encounter for fracture with malunion

S62.156K Nondisplaced fracture of hook process of hamate [unciform] bone, unspecified wrist, subsequent encounter for fracture with nonunion

S92.235B Nondisplaced fracture of intermediate cuneiform of left foot, initial encounter for open fracture

S92.235P Nondisplaced fracture of intermediate cuneiform of left foot, subsequent encounter for fracture with malunion

S92.235K Nondisplaced fracture of intermediate cuneiform of left foot, subsequent encounter for fracture with nonunion

S92.234B Nondisplaced fracture of intermediate cuneiform of right foot, initial encounter for open fracture

S92.234P Nondisplaced fracture of intermediate cuneiform of right foot, subsequent encounter for fracture with malunion

S92.234K Nondisplaced fracture of intermediate cuneiform of right foot, subsequent encounter for fracture with nonunion

S92.236B Nondisplaced fracture of intermediate cuneiform of unspecified foot, initial encounter for open fracture

S92.236P Nondisplaced fracture of intermediate cuneiform of unspecified foot, subsequent encounter for fracture with malunion

S92.236K Nondisplaced fracture of intermediate cuneiform of unspecified foot, subsequent encounter for fracture with nonunion

S72.425A Nondisplaced fracture of lateral condyle of left femur, initial encounter for closed fracture

S72.425P Nondisplaced fracture of lateral condyle of left femur, subsequent encounter for closed fracture with malunion

S72.425K Nondisplaced fracture of lateral condyle of left femur, subsequent encounter for closed fracture with nonunion

S72.425Q Nondisplaced fracture of lateral condyle of left femur, subsequent encounter for open fracture type I or II with malunion

S72.425M Nondisplaced fracture of lateral condyle of left femur, subsequent encounter for open fracture type I or II with nonunion

S72.425R Nondisplaced fracture of lateral condyle of left femur, subsequent encounter for open fracture type IIIA, IIIB, or IIIC with malunion

S72.425N Nondisplaced fracture of lateral condyle of left femur, subsequent encounter for open fracture type IIIA, IIIB, or IIIC with nonunion

S42.455A Nondisplaced fracture of lateral condyle of left humerus, initial encounter for closed fracture

S42.455P Nondisplaced fracture of lateral condyle of left humerus, subsequent encounter for fracture with malunion

S42.455K Nondisplaced fracture of lateral condyle of left humerus, subsequent encounter for fracture with nonunion

S82.125A Nondisplaced fracture of lateral condyle of left tibia, initial encounter for closed fracture

S82.125P Nondisplaced fracture of lateral condyle of left tibia, subsequent encounter for closed fracture with malunion

S82.125K Nondisplaced fracture of lateral condyle of left tibia, subsequent encounter for closed fracture with nonunion

S82.125Q Nondisplaced fracture of lateral condyle of left tibia, subsequent encounter for open fracture type I or II with malunion

S82.125M Nondisplaced fracture of lateral condyle of left tibia, subsequent encounter for open fracture type I or II with nonunion

S82.125R Nondisplaced fracture of lateral condyle of left tibia, subsequent encounter for open fracture type IIIA, IIIB, or IIIC with malunion

S82.125N Nondisplaced fracture of lateral condyle of left tibia, subsequent encounter for open fracture type IIIA, IIIB, or IIIC with nonunion

S72.424A Nondisplaced fracture of lateral condyle of right femur, initial encounter for closed fracture

S72.424P Nondisplaced fracture of lateral condyle of right femur, subsequent encounter for closed fracture with malunion

S72.424K Nondisplaced fracture of lateral condyle of right femur, subsequent encounter for closed fracture with nonunion

S72.424Q Nondisplaced fracture of lateral condyle of right femur, subsequent encounter for open fracture type I or II with malunion

S72.424M Nondisplaced fracture of lateral condyle of right femur, subsequent encounter for open fracture type I or II with nonunion

S72.424R Nondisplaced fracture of lateral condyle of right femur, subsequent encounter for open fracture type IIIA, IIIB, or IIIC with malunion

S72.424N Nondisplaced fracture of lateral condyle of right femur, subsequent encounter for open fracture type IIIA, IIIB, or IIIC with nonunion

S42.454A Nondisplaced fracture of lateral condyle of right humerus, initial encounter for closed fracture

S42.454P Nondisplaced fracture of lateral condyle of right humerus, subsequent encounter for fracture with malunion

S42.454K Nondisplaced fracture of lateral condyle of right humerus, subsequent encounter for fracture with nonunion

S82.124A Nondisplaced fracture of lateral condyle of right tibia, initial encounter for closed fracture

S82.124P Nondisplaced fracture of lateral condyle of right tibia, subsequent encounter for closed fracture with malunion

S82.124K Nondisplaced fracture of lateral condyle of right tibia, subsequent encounter for closed fracture with nonunion

S82.124Q Nondisplaced fracture of lateral condyle of right tibia, subsequent encounter for open fracture type I or II with malunion

S82.124M Nondisplaced fracture of lateral condyle of right tibia, subsequent encounter for open fracture type I or II with nonunion

S82.124R Nondisplaced fracture of lateral condyle of right tibia, subsequent encounter for open fracture type IIIA, IIIB, or IIIC with malunion

S82.124N Nondisplaced fracture of lateral condyle of right tibia, subsequent encounter for open fracture type IIIA, IIIB, or IIIC with nonunion

S72.426A Nondisplaced fracture of lateral condyle of unspecified femur, initial encounter for closed fracture

S72.426P Nondisplaced fracture of lateral condyle of unspecified femur, subsequent encounter for closed fracture with malunion

S72.426K Nondisplaced fracture of lateral condyle of unspecified femur, subsequent encounter for closed fracture with nonunion

S72.426Q Nondisplaced fracture of lateral condyle of unspecified femur, subsequent encounter for open fracture type I or II with malunion

S72.426M Nondisplaced fracture of lateral condyle of unspecified femur, subsequent encounter for open fracture type I or II with nonunion

S72.426R Nondisplaced fracture of lateral condyle of unspecified femur, subsequent encounter for open fracture type IIIA, IIIB, or IIIC with malunion

S72.426N Nondisplaced fracture of lateral condyle of unspecified femur, subsequent encounter for open fracture type IIIA, IIIB, or IIIC with nonunion

S42.456A Nondisplaced fracture of lateral condyle of unspecified humerus, initial encounter for closed fracture

Alphabetic & Numeric Lists of CCs

S42.456P Nondisplaced fracture of lateral condyle of unspecified humerus, subsequent encounter for fracture with malunion

S42.456K Nondisplaced fracture of lateral condyle of unspecified humerus, subsequent encounter for fracture with nonunion

S82.126A Nondisplaced fracture of lateral condyle of unspecified tibia, initial encounter for closed fracture

S82.126P Nondisplaced fracture of lateral condyle of unspecified tibia, subsequent encounter for closed fracture with malunion

S82.126K Nondisplaced fracture of lateral condyle of unspecified tibia, subsequent encounter for closed fracture with nonunion

S82.126Q Nondisplaced fracture of lateral condyle of unspecified tibia, subsequent encounter for open fracture type I or II with malunion

S82.126M Nondisplaced fracture of lateral condyle of unspecified tibia, subsequent encounter for open fracture type I or II with nonunion

S82.126R Nondisplaced fracture of lateral condyle of unspecified tibia, subsequent encounter for open fracture type IIIA, IIIB, or IIIC with malunion

S82.126N Nondisplaced fracture of lateral condyle of unspecified tibia, subsequent encounter for open fracture type IIIA, IIIB, or IIIC with nonunion

S92.225B Nondisplaced fracture of lateral cuneiform of left foot, initial encounter for open fracture

S92.225P Nondisplaced fracture of lateral cuneiform of left foot, subsequent encounter for fracture with malunion

S92.225K Nondisplaced fracture of lateral cuneiform of left foot, subsequent encounter for fracture with nonunion

S92.224B Nondisplaced fracture of lateral cuneiform of right foot, initial encounter for open fracture

S92.224P Nondisplaced fracture of lateral cuneiform of right foot, subsequent encounter for fracture with malunion

S92.224K Nondisplaced fracture of lateral cuneiform of right foot, subsequent encounter for fracture with nonunion

S92.226B Nondisplaced fracture of lateral cuneiform of unspecified foot, initial encounter for open fracture

S92.226P Nondisplaced fracture of lateral cuneiform of unspecified foot, subsequent encounter for fracture with malunion

S92.226K Nondisplaced fracture of lateral cuneiform of unspecified foot, subsequent encounter for fracture with nonunion

S42.035B Nondisplaced fracture of lateral end of left clavicle, initial encounter for open fracture

S42.035P Nondisplaced fracture of lateral end of left clavicle, subsequent encounter for fracture with malunion

S42.035K Nondisplaced fracture of lateral end of left clavicle, subsequent encounter for fracture with nonunion

S42.034B Nondisplaced fracture of lateral end of right clavicle, initial encounter for open fracture

S42.034P Nondisplaced fracture of lateral end of right clavicle, subsequent encounter for fracture with malunion

S42.034K Nondisplaced fracture of lateral end of right clavicle, subsequent encounter for fracture with nonunion

S42.036B Nondisplaced fracture of lateral end of unspecified clavicle, initial encounter for open fracture

S42.036P Nondisplaced fracture of lateral end of unspecified clavicle, subsequent encounter for fracture with malunion

S42.036K Nondisplaced fracture of lateral end of unspecified clavicle, subsequent encounter for fracture with nonunion

S82.65XB Nondisplaced fracture of lateral malleolus of left fibula, initial encounter for open fracture type I or II

S82.65XC Nondisplaced fracture of lateral malleolus of left fibula, initial encounter for open fracture type IIIA, IIIB, or IIIC

S82.65XP Nondisplaced fracture of lateral malleolus of left fibula, subsequent encounter for closed fracture with malunion

S82.65XK Nondisplaced fracture of lateral malleolus of left fibula, subsequent encounter for closed fracture with nonunion

S82.65XQ Nondisplaced fracture of lateral malleolus of left fibula, subsequent encounter for open fracture type I or II with malunion

S82.65XM Nondisplaced fracture of lateral malleolus of left fibula, subsequent encounter for open fracture type I or II with nonunion

S82.65XR Nondisplaced fracture of lateral malleolus of left fibula, subsequent encounter for open fracture type IIIA, IIIB, or IIIC with malunion

S82.65XN Nondisplaced fracture of lateral malleolus of left fibula, subsequent encounter for open fracture type IIIA, IIIB, or IIIC with nonunion

S82.64XB Nondisplaced fracture of lateral malleolus of right fibula, initial encounter for open fracture type I or II

S82.64XC Nondisplaced fracture of lateral malleolus of right fibula, initial encounter for open fracture type IIIA, IIIB, or IIIC

S82.64XP Nondisplaced fracture of lateral malleolus of right fibula, subsequent encounter for closed fracture with malunion

S82.64XK Nondisplaced fracture of lateral malleolus of right fibula, subsequent encounter for closed fracture with nonunion

S82.64XQ Nondisplaced fracture of lateral malleolus of right fibula, subsequent encounter for open fracture type I or II with malunion

S82.64XM Nondisplaced fracture of lateral malleolus of right fibula, subsequent encounter for open fracture type I or II with nonunion

S82.64XR Nondisplaced fracture of lateral malleolus of right fibula, subsequent encounter for open fracture type IIIA, IIIB, or IIIC with malunion

S82.64XN Nondisplaced fracture of lateral malleolus of right fibula, subsequent encounter for open fracture type IIIA, IIIB, or IIIC with nonunion

S82.66XB Nondisplaced fracture of lateral malleolus of unspecified fibula, initial encounter for open fracture type I or II

S82.66XC Nondisplaced fracture of lateral malleolus of unspecified fibula, initial encounter for open fracture type IIIA, IIIB, or IIIC

S82.66XP Nondisplaced fracture of lateral malleolus of unspecified fibula, subsequent encounter for closed fracture with malunion

S82.66XK Nondisplaced fracture of lateral malleolus of unspecified fibula, subsequent encounter for closed fracture with nonunion

S82.66XQ Nondisplaced fracture of lateral malleolus of unspecified fibula, subsequent encounter for open fracture type I or II with malunion

S82.66XM Nondisplaced fracture of lateral malleolus of unspecified fibula, subsequent encounter for open fracture type I or II with nonunion

S82.66XR Nondisplaced fracture of lateral malleolus of unspecified fibula, subsequent encounter for open fracture type IIIA, IIIB, or IIIC with malunion

S82.66XN Nondisplaced fracture of lateral malleolus of unspecified fibula, subsequent encounter for open fracture type IIIA, IIIB, or IIIC with nonunion

S52.515A Nondisplaced fracture of left radial styloid process, initial encounter for closed fracture

S52.515P Nondisplaced fracture of left radial styloid process, subsequent encounter for closed fracture with malunion

S52.515K Nondisplaced fracture of left radial styloid process, subsequent encounter for closed fracture with nonunion

S52.515Q Nondisplaced fracture of left radial styloid process, subsequent encounter for open fracture type I or II with malunion

S52.515M Nondisplaced fracture of left radial styloid process, subsequent encounter for open fracture type I or II with nonunion

S52.515R Nondisplaced fracture of left radial styloid process, subsequent encounter for open fracture type IIIA, IIIB, or IIIC with malunion

S52.515N Nondisplaced fracture of left radial styloid process, subsequent encounter for open fracture type IIIA, IIIB, or IIIC with nonunion

S82.115A Nondisplaced fracture of left tibial spine, initial encounter for closed fracture

S82.115P Nondisplaced fracture of left tibial spine, subsequent encounter for closed fracture with malunion

S82.115K Nondisplaced fracture of left tibial spine, subsequent encounter for closed fracture with nonunion

S82.115Q Nondisplaced fracture of left tibial spine, subsequent encounter for open fracture type I or II with malunion

S82.115M Nondisplaced fracture of left tibial spine, subsequent encounter for open fracture type I or II with nonunion

S82.115R Nondisplaced fracture of left tibial spine, subsequent encounter for open fracture type IIIA, IIIB, or IIIC with malunion

S82.115N Nondisplaced fracture of left tibial spine, subsequent encounter for open fracture type IIIA, IIIB, or IIIC with nonunion

S82.155A Nondisplaced fracture of left tibial tuberosity, initial encounter for closed fracture

S82.155P Nondisplaced fracture of left tibial tuberosity, subsequent encounter for closed fracture with malunion

S82.155K Nondisplaced fracture of left tibial tuberosity, subsequent encounter for closed fracture with nonunion

S82.155Q Nondisplaced fracture of left tibial tuberosity, subsequent encounter for open fracture type I or II with malunion

S82.155M Nondisplaced fracture of left tibial tuberosity, subsequent encounter for open fracture type I or II with nonunion

S82.155R Nondisplaced fracture of left tibial tuberosity, subsequent encounter for open fracture type IIIA, IIIB, or IIIC with malunion

S82.155N Nondisplaced fracture of left tibial tuberosity, subsequent encounter for open fracture type IIIA, IIIB, or IIIC with nonunion

S52.615A Nondisplaced fracture of left ulna styloid process, initial encounter for closed fracture

S52.615P Nondisplaced fracture of left ulna styloid process, subsequent encounter for closed fracture with malunion

S52.615K Nondisplaced fracture of left ulna styloid process, subsequent encounter for closed fracture with nonunion

S52.615Q Nondisplaced fracture of left ulna styloid process, subsequent encounter for open fracture type I or II with malunion

S52.615M Nondisplaced fracture of left ulna styloid process, subsequent encounter for open fracture type I or II with nonunion

S52.615R Nondisplaced fracture of left ulna styloid process, subsequent encounter for open fracture type IIIA, IIIB, or IIIC with malunion

S52.615N Nondisplaced fracture of left ulna styloid process, subsequent encounter for open fracture type IIIA, IIIB, or IIIC with nonunion

S72.125P Nondisplaced fracture of lesser trochanter of left femur, subsequent encounter for closed fracture with malunion

S72.125K Nondisplaced fracture of lesser trochanter of left femur, subsequent encounter for closed fracture with nonunion

S72.125Q Nondisplaced fracture of lesser trochanter of left femur, subsequent encounter for open fracture type I or II with malunion

S72.125M Nondisplaced fracture of lesser trochanter of left femur, subsequent encounter for open fracture type I or II with nonunion

S72.125R Nondisplaced fracture of lesser trochanter of left femur, subsequent encounter for open fracture type IIIA, IIIB, or IIIC with malunion

S72.125N Nondisplaced fracture of lesser trochanter of left femur, subsequent encounter for open fracture type IIIA, IIIB, or IIIC with nonunion

S72.124P Nondisplaced fracture of lesser trochanter of right femur, subsequent encounter for closed fracture with malunion

S72.124K Nondisplaced fracture of lesser trochanter of right femur, subsequent encounter for closed fracture with nonunion

S72.124Q Nondisplaced fracture of lesser trochanter of right femur, subsequent encounter for open fracture type I or II with malunion

S72.124M Nondisplaced fracture of lesser trochanter of right femur, subsequent encounter for open fracture type I or II with nonunion

S72.124R Nondisplaced fracture of lesser trochanter of right femur, subsequent encounter for open fracture type IIIA, IIIB, or IIIC with malunion

S72.124N Nondisplaced fracture of lesser trochanter of right femur, subsequent encounter for open fracture type IIIA, IIIB, or IIIC with nonunion

S72.126P Nondisplaced fracture of lesser trochanter of unspecified femur, subsequent encounter for closed fracture with malunion

S72.126K Nondisplaced fracture of lesser trochanter of unspecified femur, subsequent encounter for closed fracture with nonunion

S72.126Q Nondisplaced fracture of lesser trochanter of unspecified femur, subsequent encounter for open fracture type I or II with malunion

S72.126M Nondisplaced fracture of lesser trochanter of unspecified femur, subsequent encounter for open fracture type I or II with nonunion

S72.126R Nondisplaced fracture of lesser trochanter of unspecified femur, subsequent encounter for open fracture type IIIA, IIIB, or IIIC with malunion

S72.126N Nondisplaced fracture of lesser trochanter of unspecified femur, subsequent encounter for open fracture type IIIA, IIIB, or IIIC with nonunion

S42.265A Nondisplaced fracture of lesser tuberosity of left humerus, initial encounter for closed fracture

S42.265P Nondisplaced fracture of lesser tuberosity of left humerus, subsequent encounter for fracture with malunion

S42.265K Nondisplaced fracture of lesser tuberosity of left humerus, subsequent encounter for fracture with nonunion

S42.264A Nondisplaced fracture of lesser tuberosity of right humerus, initial encounter for closed fracture

S42.264P Nondisplaced fracture of lesser tuberosity of right humerus, subsequent encounter for fracture with malunion

S42.264K Nondisplaced fracture of lesser tuberosity of right humerus, subsequent encounter for fracture with nonunion

S42.266A Nondisplaced fracture of lesser tuberosity of unspecified humerus, initial encounter for closed fracture

S42.266P Nondisplaced fracture of lesser tuberosity of unspecified humerus, subsequent encounter for fracture with malunion

S42.266K Nondisplaced fracture of lesser tuberosity of unspecified humerus, subsequent encounter for fracture with nonunion

S72.445A Nondisplaced fracture of lower epiphysis (separation) of left femur, initial encounter for closed fracture

S72.445P Nondisplaced fracture of lower epiphysis (separation) of left femur, subsequent encounter for closed fracture with malunion

S72.445K Nondisplaced fracture of lower epiphysis (separation) of left femur, subsequent encounter for closed fracture with nonunion

S72.445Q Nondisplaced fracture of lower epiphysis (separation) of left femur, subsequent encounter for open fracture type I or II with malunion

S72.445M Nondisplaced fracture of lower epiphysis (separation) of left femur, subsequent encounter for open fracture type I or II with nonunion

S72.445R Nondisplaced fracture of lower epiphysis (separation) of left femur, subsequent encounter for open fracture type IIIA, IIIB, or IIIC with malunion

S72.445N Nondisplaced fracture of lower epiphysis (separation) of left femur, subsequent encounter for open fracture type IIIA, IIIB, or IIIC with nonunion

S72.444A Nondisplaced fracture of lower epiphysis (separation) of right femur, initial encounter for closed fracture

S72.444P Nondisplaced fracture of lower epiphysis (separation) of right femur, subsequent encounter for closed fracture with malunion

S72.444K Nondisplaced fracture of lower epiphysis (separation) of right femur, subsequent encounter for closed fracture with nonunion

S72.444Q Nondisplaced fracture of lower epiphysis (separation) of right femur, subsequent encounter for open fracture type I or II with malunion

S72.444M Nondisplaced fracture of lower epiphysis (separation) of right femur, subsequent encounter for open fracture type I or II with nonunion

S72.444R Nondisplaced fracture of lower epiphysis (separation) of right femur, subsequent encounter for open fracture type IIIA, IIIB, or IIIC with malunion

S72.444N Nondisplaced fracture of lower epiphysis (separation) of right femur, subsequent encounter for open fracture type IIIA, IIIB, or IIIC with nonunion

S72.446A Nondisplaced fracture of lower epiphysis (separation) of unspecified femur, initial encounter for closed fracture

S72.446P Nondisplaced fracture of lower epiphysis (separation) of unspecified femur, subsequent encounter for closed fracture with malunion

S72.446K Nondisplaced fracture of lower epiphysis (separation) of unspecified femur, subsequent encounter for closed fracture with nonunion

S72.446Q Nondisplaced fracture of lower epiphysis (separation) of unspecified femur, subsequent encounter for open fracture type I or II with malunion

S72.446M Nondisplaced fracture of lower epiphysis (separation) of unspecified femur, subsequent encounter for open fracture type I or II with nonunion

S72.446R Nondisplaced fracture of lower epiphysis (separation) of unspecified femur, subsequent encounter for open fracture type IIIA, IIIB, or IIIC with malunion

S72.446N Nondisplaced fracture of lower epiphysis (separation) of unspecified femur, subsequent encounter for open fracture type IIIA, IIIB, or IIIC with nonunion

S62.125B Nondisplaced fracture of lunate [semilunar], left wrist, initial encounter for open fracture

S62.125P Nondisplaced fracture of lunate [semilunar], left wrist, subsequent encounter for fracture with malunion

S62.125K Nondisplaced fracture of lunate [semilunar], left wrist, subsequent encounter for fracture with nonunion

S62.124B Nondisplaced fracture of lunate [semilunar], right wrist, initial encounter for open fracture

S62.124P Nondisplaced fracture of lunate [semilunar], right wrist, subsequent encounter for fracture with malunion

S62.124K Nondisplaced fracture of lunate [semilunar], right wrist, subsequent encounter for fracture with nonunion

S62.126B Nondisplaced fracture of lunate [semilunar], unspecified wrist, initial encounter for open fracture

S62.126P Nondisplaced fracture of lunate [semilunar], unspecified wrist, subsequent encounter for fracture with malunion

S62.126K Nondisplaced fracture of lunate [semilunar], unspecified wrist, subsequent encounter for fracture with nonunion

S72.435A Nondisplaced fracture of medial condyle of left femur, initial encounter for closed fracture

S72.435P Nondisplaced fracture of medial condyle of left femur, subsequent encounter for closed fracture with malunion

S72.435K Nondisplaced fracture of medial condyle of left femur, subsequent encounter for closed fracture with nonunion

S72.435Q Nondisplaced fracture of medial condyle of left femur, subsequent encounter for open fracture type I or II with malunion

S72.435M Nondisplaced fracture of medial condyle of left femur, subsequent encounter for open fracture type I or II with nonunion

S72.435R Nondisplaced fracture of medial condyle of left femur, subsequent encounter for open fracture type IIIA, IIIB, or IIIC with malunion

S72.435N Nondisplaced fracture of medial condyle of left femur, subsequent encounter for open fracture type IIIA, IIIB, or IIIC with nonunion

S42.465A Nondisplaced fracture of medial condyle of left humerus, initial encounter for closed fracture

S42.465P Nondisplaced fracture of medial condyle of left humerus, subsequent encounter for fracture with malunion

S42.465K Nondisplaced fracture of medial condyle of left humerus, subsequent encounter for fracture with nonunion

S82.135A Nondisplaced fracture of medial condyle of left tibia, initial encounter for closed fracture

S82.135P Nondisplaced fracture of medial condyle of left tibia, subsequent encounter for closed fracture with malunion

S82.135K Nondisplaced fracture of medial condyle of left tibia, subsequent encounter for closed fracture with nonunion

S82.135Q Nondisplaced fracture of medial condyle of left tibia, subsequent encounter for open fracture type I or II with malunion

S82.135M Nondisplaced fracture of medial condyle of left tibia, subsequent encounter for open fracture type I or II with nonunion

S82.135R Nondisplaced fracture of medial condyle of left tibia, subsequent encounter for open fracture type IIIA, IIIB, or IIIC with malunion

S82.135N Nondisplaced fracture of medial condyle of left tibia, subsequent encounter for open fracture type IIIA, IIIB, or IIIC with nonunion

S72.434A Nondisplaced fracture of medial condyle of right femur, initial encounter for closed fracture

S72.434P Nondisplaced fracture of medial condyle of right femur, subsequent encounter for closed fracture with malunion

S72.434K Nondisplaced fracture of medial condyle of right femur, subsequent encounter for closed fracture with nonunion

S72.434Q Nondisplaced fracture of medial condyle of right femur, subsequent encounter for open fracture type I or II with malunion

S72.434M Nondisplaced fracture of medial condyle of right femur, subsequent encounter for open fracture type I or II with nonunion

S72.434R Nondisplaced fracture of medial condyle of right femur, subsequent encounter for open fracture type IIIA, IIIB, or IIIC with malunion

S72.434N Nondisplaced fracture of medial condyle of right femur, subsequent encounter for open fracture type IIIA, IIIB, or IIIC with nonunion

S42.464A Nondisplaced fracture of medial condyle of right humerus, initial encounter for closed fracture

S42.464P Nondisplaced fracture of medial condyle of right humerus, subsequent encounter for fracture with malunion

S42.464K Nondisplaced fracture of medial condyle of right humerus, subsequent encounter for fracture with nonunion

S82.134A Nondisplaced fracture of medial condyle of right tibia, initial encounter for closed fracture

S82.134P Nondisplaced fracture of medial condyle of right tibia, subsequent encounter for closed fracture with malunion

S82.134K Nondisplaced fracture of medial condyle of right tibia, subsequent encounter for closed fracture with nonunion

S82.134Q Nondisplaced fracture of medial condyle of right tibia, subsequent encounter for open fracture type I or II with malunion

S82.134M Nondisplaced fracture of medial condyle of right tibia, subsequent encounter for open fracture type I or II with nonunion

S82.134R Nondisplaced fracture of medial condyle of right tibia, subsequent encounter for open fracture type IIIA, IIIB, or IIIC with malunion

S82.134N Nondisplaced fracture of medial condyle of right tibia, subsequent encounter for open fracture type IIIA, IIIB, or IIIC with nonunion

S72.436A Nondisplaced fracture of medial condyle of unspecified femur, initial encounter for closed fracture

S72.436P Nondisplaced fracture of medial condyle of unspecified femur, subsequent encounter for closed fracture with malunion

S72.436K Nondisplaced fracture of medial condyle of unspecified femur, subsequent encounter for closed fracture with nonunion

S72.436Q Nondisplaced fracture of medial condyle of unspecified femur, subsequent encounter for open fracture type I or II with malunion

S72.436M Nondisplaced fracture of medial condyle of unspecified femur, subsequent encounter for open fracture type I or II with nonunion

S72.436R Nondisplaced fracture of medial condyle of unspecified femur, subsequent encounter for open fracture type IIIA, IIIB, or IIIC with malunion

S72.436N Nondisplaced fracture of medial condyle of unspecified femur, subsequent encounter for open fracture type IIIA, IIIB, or IIIC with nonunion

S42.466A Nondisplaced fracture of medial condyle of unspecified humerus, initial encounter for closed fracture

S42.466P Nondisplaced fracture of medial condyle of unspecified humerus, subsequent encounter for fracture with malunion

S42.466K Nondisplaced fracture of medial condyle of unspecified humerus, subsequent encounter for fracture with nonunion

S82.136A Nondisplaced fracture of medial condyle of unspecified tibia, initial encounter for closed fracture

S82.136P Nondisplaced fracture of medial condyle of unspecified tibia, subsequent encounter for closed fracture with malunion

S82.136K Nondisplaced fracture of medial condyle of unspecified tibia, subsequent encounter for closed fracture with nonunion

S82.136Q Nondisplaced fracture of medial condyle of unspecified tibia, subsequent encounter for open fracture type I or II with malunion

S82.136M Nondisplaced fracture of medial condyle of unspecified tibia, subsequent encounter for open fracture type I or II with nonunion

S82.136R Nondisplaced fracture of medial condyle of unspecified tibia, subsequent encounter for open fracture type IIIA, IIIB, or IIIC with malunion

S82.136N Nondisplaced fracture of medial condyle of unspecified tibia, subsequent encounter for open fracture type IIIA, IIIB, or IIIC with nonunion

S92.245B Nondisplaced fracture of medial cuneiform of left foot, initial encounter for open fracture

S92.245P Nondisplaced fracture of medial cuneiform of left foot, subsequent encounter for fracture with malunion

S92.245K Nondisplaced fracture of medial cuneiform of left foot, subsequent encounter for fracture with nonunion

S92.244B Nondisplaced fracture of medial cuneiform of right foot, initial encounter for open fracture

S92.244P Nondisplaced fracture of medial cuneiform of right foot, subsequent encounter for fracture with malunion

S92.244K Nondisplaced fracture of medial cuneiform of right foot, subsequent encounter for fracture with nonunion

S92.246B Nondisplaced fracture of medial cuneiform of unspecified foot, initial encounter for open fracture

S92.246P Nondisplaced fracture of medial cuneiform of unspecified foot, subsequent encounter for fracture with malunion

S92.246K Nondisplaced fracture of medial cuneiform of unspecified foot, subsequent encounter for fracture with nonunion

S82.55XB Nondisplaced fracture of medial malleolus of left tibia, initial encounter for open fracture type I or II

S82.55XC Nondisplaced fracture of medial malleolus of left tibia, initial encounter for open fracture type IIIA, IIIB, or IIIC

S82.55XP Nondisplaced fracture of medial malleolus of left tibia, subsequent encounter for closed fracture with malunion

S82.55XK Nondisplaced fracture of medial malleolus of left tibia, subsequent encounter for closed fracture with nonunion

S82.55XQ Nondisplaced fracture of medial malleolus of left tibia, subsequent encounter for open fracture type I or II with malunion

S82.55XM Nondisplaced fracture of medial malleolus of left tibia, subsequent encounter for open fracture type I or II with nonunion

S82.55XR Nondisplaced fracture of medial malleolus of left tibia, subsequent encounter for open fracture type IIIA, IIIB, or IIIC with malunion

S82.55XN Nondisplaced fracture of medial malleolus of left tibia, subsequent encounter for open fracture type IIIA, IIIB, or IIIC with nonunion

S82.54XB Nondisplaced fracture of medial malleolus of right tibia, initial encounter for open fracture type I or II

S82.54XC Nondisplaced fracture of medial malleolus of right tibia, initial encounter for open fracture type IIIA, IIIB, or IIIC

S82.54XP Nondisplaced fracture of medial malleolus of right tibia, subsequent encounter for closed fracture with malunion

S82.54XK Nondisplaced fracture of medial malleolus of right tibia, subsequent encounter for closed fracture with nonunion

S82.54XQ Nondisplaced fracture of medial malleolus of right tibia, subsequent encounter for open fracture type I or II with malunion

S82.54XM Nondisplaced fracture of medial malleolus of right tibia, subsequent encounter for open fracture type I or II with nonunion

S82.54XR Nondisplaced fracture of medial malleolus of right tibia, subsequent encounter for open fracture type IIIA, IIIB, or IIIC with malunion

S82.54XN Nondisplaced fracture of medial malleolus of right tibia, subsequent encounter for open fracture type IIIA, IIIB, or IIIC with nonunion

S82.56XB Nondisplaced fracture of medial malleolus of unspecified tibia, initial encounter for open fracture type I or II

S82.56XC Nondisplaced fracture of medial malleolus of unspecified tibia, initial encounter for open fracture type IIIA, IIIB, or IIIC

S82.56XP Nondisplaced fracture of medial malleolus of unspecified tibia, subsequent encounter for closed fracture with malunion

S82.56XK Nondisplaced fracture of medial malleolus of unspecified tibia, subsequent encounter for closed fracture with nonunion

S82.56XQ Nondisplaced fracture of medial malleolus of unspecified tibia, subsequent encounter for open fracture type I or II with malunion

S82.56XM Nondisplaced fracture of medial malleolus of unspecified tibia, subsequent encounter for open fracture type I or II with nonunion

S82.56XR Nondisplaced fracture of medial malleolus of unspecified tibia, subsequent encounter for open fracture type IIIA, IIIB, or IIIC with malunion

S82.56XN Nondisplaced fracture of medial malleolus of unspecified tibia, subsequent encounter for open fracture type IIIA, IIIB, or IIIC with nonunion

S32.475K Nondisplaced fracture of medial wall of left acetabulum, subsequent encounter for fracture with nonunion

S32.474K Nondisplaced fracture of medial wall of right acetabulum, subsequent encounter for fracture with nonunion

S32.476K Nondisplaced fracture of medial wall of unspecified acetabulum, subsequent encounter for fracture with nonunion

S62.651B Nondisplaced fracture of middle phalanx of left index finger, initial encounter for open fracture

S62.651P Nondisplaced fracture of middle phalanx of left index finger, subsequent encounter for fracture with malunion

S62.651K Nondisplaced fracture of middle phalanx of left index finger, subsequent encounter for fracture with nonunion

S92.525P Nondisplaced fracture of middle phalanx of left lesser toe(s), subsequent encounter for fracture with malunion

S92.525K Nondisplaced fracture of middle phalanx of left lesser toe(s), subsequent encounter for fracture with nonunion

S62.657B Nondisplaced fracture of middle phalanx of left little finger, initial encounter for open fracture

S62.657P Nondisplaced fracture of middle phalanx of left little finger, subsequent encounter for fracture with malunion

S62.657K Nondisplaced fracture of middle phalanx of left little finger, subsequent encounter for fracture with nonunion

S62.653B Nondisplaced fracture of middle phalanx of left middle finger, initial encounter for open fracture

S62.653P Nondisplaced fracture of middle phalanx of left middle finger, subsequent encounter for fracture with malunion

S62.653K Nondisplaced fracture of middle phalanx of left middle finger, subsequent encounter for fracture with nonunion

S62.655B Nondisplaced fracture of middle phalanx of left ring finger, initial encounter for open fracture

S62.655P Nondisplaced fracture of middle phalanx of left ring finger, subsequent encounter for fracture with malunion

S62.655K Nondisplaced fracture of middle phalanx of left ring finger, subsequent encounter for fracture with nonunion

S62.658B Nondisplaced fracture of middle phalanx of other finger, initial encounter for open fracture

S62.658P Nondisplaced fracture of middle phalanx of other finger, subsequent encounter for fracture with malunion

S62.658K Nondisplaced fracture of middle phalanx of other finger, subsequent encounter for fracture with nonunion

S62.650B Nondisplaced fracture of middle phalanx of right index finger, initial encounter for open fracture

S62.650P Nondisplaced fracture of middle phalanx of right index finger, subsequent encounter for fracture with malunion

S62.650K Nondisplaced fracture of middle phalanx of right index finger, subsequent encounter for fracture with nonunion

S92.524P Nondisplaced fracture of middle phalanx of right lesser toe(s), subsequent encounter for fracture with malunion

S92.524K Nondisplaced fracture of middle phalanx of right lesser toe(s), subsequent encounter for fracture with nonunion

S62.656B Nondisplaced fracture of middle phalanx of right little finger, initial encounter for open fracture

S62.656P Nondisplaced fracture of middle phalanx of right little finger, subsequent encounter for fracture with malunion

S62.656K Nondisplaced fracture of middle phalanx of right little finger, subsequent encounter for fracture with nonunion

S62.652B Nondisplaced fracture of middle phalanx of right middle finger, initial encounter for open fracture

S62.652P Nondisplaced fracture of middle phalanx of right middle finger, subsequent encounter for fracture with malunion

S62.652K Nondisplaced fracture of middle phalanx of right middle finger, subsequent encounter for fracture with nonunion

S62.654B Nondisplaced fracture of middle phalanx of right ring finger, initial encounter for open fracture

S62.654P Nondisplaced fracture of middle phalanx of right ring finger, subsequent encounter for fracture with malunion

S62.654K Nondisplaced fracture of middle phalanx of right ring finger, subsequent encounter for fracture with nonunion

S62.659B Nondisplaced fracture of middle phalanx of unspecified finger, initial encounter for open fracture

S62.659P Nondisplaced fracture of middle phalanx of unspecified finger, subsequent encounter for fracture with malunion

S62.659K Nondisplaced fracture of middle phalanx of unspecified finger, subsequent encounter for fracture with nonunion

S92.526P Nondisplaced fracture of middle phalanx of unspecified lesser toe(s), subsequent encounter for fracture with malunion

S92.526K Nondisplaced fracture of middle phalanx of unspecified lesser toe(s), subsequent encounter for fracture with nonunion

S62.025B Nondisplaced fracture of middle third of navicular [scaphoid] bone of left wrist, initial encounter for open fracture

S62.025P Nondisplaced fracture of middle third of navicular [scaphoid] bone of left wrist, subsequent encounter for fracture with malunion

S62.025K Nondisplaced fracture of middle third of navicular [scaphoid] bone of left wrist, subsequent encounter for fracture with nonunion

S62.024B Nondisplaced fracture of middle third of navicular [scaphoid] bone of right wrist, initial encounter for open fracture

S62.024P Nondisplaced fracture of middle third of navicular [scaphoid] bone of right wrist, subsequent encounter for fracture with malunion

S62.024K Nondisplaced fracture of middle third of navicular [scaphoid] bone of right wrist, subsequent encounter for fracture with nonunion

S62.026B Nondisplaced fracture of middle third of navicular [scaphoid] bone of unspecified wrist, initial encounter for open fracture

S62.026P Nondisplaced fracture of middle third of navicular [scaphoid] bone of unspecified wrist, subsequent encounter for fracture with malunion

S62.026K Nondisplaced fracture of middle third of navicular [scaphoid] bone of unspecified wrist, subsequent encounter for fracture with nonunion

S92.255B Nondisplaced fracture of navicular [scaphoid] of left foot, initial encounter for open fracture

S92.255P Nondisplaced fracture of navicular [scaphoid] of left foot, subsequent encounter for fracture with malunion

S92.255K Nondisplaced fracture of navicular [scaphoid] of left foot, subsequent encounter for fracture with nonunion

S92.254B Nondisplaced fracture of navicular [scaphoid] of right foot, initial encounter for open fracture

S92.254P Nondisplaced fracture of navicular [scaphoid] of right foot, subsequent encounter for fracture with malunion

S92.254K Nondisplaced fracture of navicular [scaphoid] of right foot, subsequent encounter for fracture with nonunion

S92.256B Nondisplaced fracture of navicular [scaphoid] of unspecified foot, initial encounter for open fracture

S92.256P Nondisplaced fracture of navicular [scaphoid] of unspecified foot, subsequent encounter for fracture with malunion

S92.256K Nondisplaced fracture of navicular [scaphoid] of unspecified foot, subsequent encounter for fracture with nonunion

S62.367B Nondisplaced fracture of neck of fifth metacarpal bone, left hand, initial encounter for open fracture

S62.367P Nondisplaced fracture of neck of fifth metacarpal bone, left hand, subsequent encounter for fracture with malunion

S62.367K Nondisplaced fracture of neck of fifth metacarpal bone, left hand, subsequent encounter for fracture with nonunion

S62.366B Nondisplaced fracture of neck of fifth metacarpal bone, right hand, initial encounter for open fracture

S62.366P Nondisplaced fracture of neck of fifth metacarpal bone, right hand, subsequent encounter for fracture with malunion

S62.366K Nondisplaced fracture of neck of fifth metacarpal bone, right hand, subsequent encounter for fracture with nonunion

S62.255B Nondisplaced fracture of neck of first metacarpal bone, left hand, initial encounter for open fracture

S62.255P Nondisplaced fracture of neck of first metacarpal bone, left hand, subsequent encounter for fracture with malunion

S62.255K Nondisplaced fracture of neck of first metacarpal bone, left hand, subsequent encounter for fracture with nonunion

S62.254B Nondisplaced fracture of neck of first metacarpal bone, right hand, initial encounter for open fracture

S62.254P Nondisplaced fracture of neck of first metacarpal bone, right hand, subsequent encounter for fracture with malunion

S62.254K Nondisplaced fracture of neck of first metacarpal bone, right hand, subsequent encounter for fracture with nonunion

S62.256B Nondisplaced fracture of neck of first metacarpal bone, unspecified hand, initial encounter for open fracture

S62.256P Nondisplaced fracture of neck of first metacarpal bone, unspecified hand, subsequent encounter for fracture with malunion

S62.256K Nondisplaced fracture of neck of first metacarpal bone, unspecified hand, subsequent encounter for fracture with nonunion

S62.365B Nondisplaced fracture of neck of fourth metacarpal bone, left hand, initial encounter for open fracture

S62.365P Nondisplaced fracture of neck of fourth metacarpal bone, left hand, subsequent encounter for fracture with malunion

S62.365K Nondisplaced fracture of neck of fourth metacarpal bone, left hand, subsequent encounter for fracture with nonunion

S62.364B Nondisplaced fracture of neck of fourth metacarpal bone, right hand, initial encounter for open fracture

S62.364P Nondisplaced fracture of neck of fourth metacarpal bone, right hand, subsequent encounter for fracture with malunion

S62.364K Nondisplaced fracture of neck of fourth metacarpal bone, right hand, subsequent encounter for fracture with nonunion

S52.135P Nondisplaced fracture of neck of left radius, subsequent encounter for closed fracture with malunion

S52.135K Nondisplaced fracture of neck of left radius, subsequent encounter for closed fracture with nonunion

S52.135Q Nondisplaced fracture of neck of left radius, subsequent encounter for open fracture type I or II with malunion

S52.135M Nondisplaced fracture of neck of left radius, subsequent encounter for open fracture type I or II with nonunion

S52.135R Nondisplaced fracture of neck of left radius, subsequent encounter for open fracture type IIIA, IIIB, or IIIC with malunion

S52.135N Nondisplaced fracture of neck of left radius, subsequent encounter for open fracture type IIIA, IIIB, or IIIC with nonunion

S92.115B Nondisplaced fracture of neck of left talus, initial encounter for open fracture

S92.115P Nondisplaced fracture of neck of left talus, subsequent encounter for fracture with malunion

S92.115K Nondisplaced fracture of neck of left talus, subsequent encounter for fracture with nonunion

S62.368B Nondisplaced fracture of neck of other metacarpal bone, initial encounter for open fracture

S62.368P Nondisplaced fracture of neck of other metacarpal bone, subsequent encounter for fracture with malunion

S62.368K Nondisplaced fracture of neck of other metacarpal bone, subsequent encounter for fracture with nonunion

S52.134P Nondisplaced fracture of neck of right radius, subsequent encounter for closed fracture with malunion

S52.134K Nondisplaced fracture of neck of right radius, subsequent encounter for closed fracture with nonunion

S52.134Q Nondisplaced fracture of neck of right radius, subsequent encounter for open fracture type I or II with malunion

S52.134M Nondisplaced fracture of neck of right radius, subsequent encounter for open fracture type I or II with nonunion

S52.134R Nondisplaced fracture of neck of right radius, subsequent encounter for open fracture type IIIA, IIIB, or IIIC with malunion

S52.134N Nondisplaced fracture of neck of right radius, subsequent encounter for open fracture type IIIA, IIIB, or IIIC with nonunion

S92.114B Nondisplaced fracture of neck of right talus, initial encounter for open fracture

S92.114P Nondisplaced fracture of neck of right talus, subsequent encounter for fracture with malunion

S92.114K Nondisplaced fracture of neck of right talus, subsequent encounter for fracture with nonunion

S42.155B Nondisplaced fracture of neck of scapula, left shoulder, initial encounter for open fracture

S42.155P Nondisplaced fracture of neck of scapula, left shoulder, subsequent encounter for fracture with malunion

S42.155K Nondisplaced fracture of neck of scapula, left shoulder, subsequent encounter for fracture with nonunion

S42.154B Nondisplaced fracture of neck of scapula, right shoulder, initial encounter for open fracture

S42.154P Nondisplaced fracture of neck of scapula, right shoulder, subsequent encounter for fracture with malunion

S42.154K Nondisplaced fracture of neck of scapula, right shoulder, subsequent encounter for fracture with nonunion

S42.156B Nondisplaced fracture of neck of scapula, unspecified shoulder, initial encounter for open fracture

S42.156P Nondisplaced fracture of neck of scapula, unspecified shoulder, subsequent encounter for fracture with malunion

S42.156K Nondisplaced fracture of neck of scapula, unspecified shoulder, subsequent encounter for fracture with nonunion

S62.361B Nondisplaced fracture of neck of second metacarpal bone, left hand, initial encounter for open fracture

S62.361P Nondisplaced fracture of neck of second metacarpal bone, left hand, subsequent encounter for fracture with malunion

S62.361K Nondisplaced fracture of neck of second metacarpal bone, left hand, subsequent encounter for fracture with nonunion

S62.360B Nondisplaced fracture of neck of second metacarpal bone, right hand, initial encounter for open fracture

S62.360P Nondisplaced fracture of neck of second metacarpal bone, right hand, subsequent encounter for fracture with malunion

S62.360K Nondisplaced fracture of neck of second metacarpal bone, right hand, subsequent encounter for fracture with nonunion

S62.363B Nondisplaced fracture of neck of third metacarpal bone, left hand, initial encounter for open fracture

S62.363P Nondisplaced fracture of neck of third metacarpal bone, left hand, subsequent encounter for fracture with malunion

S62.363K Nondisplaced fracture of neck of third metacarpal bone, left hand, subsequent encounter for fracture with nonunion

S62.362B Nondisplaced fracture of neck of third metacarpal bone, right hand, initial encounter for open fracture

S62.362P Nondisplaced fracture of neck of third metacarpal bone, right hand, subsequent encounter for fracture with malunion

S62.362K Nondisplaced fracture of neck of third metacarpal bone, right hand, subsequent encounter for fracture with nonunion

S62.369B Nondisplaced fracture of neck of unspecified metacarpal bone, initial encounter for open fracture

S62.369P Nondisplaced fracture of neck of unspecified metacarpal bone, subsequent encounter for fracture with malunion

S62.369K Nondisplaced fracture of neck of unspecified metacarpal bone, subsequent encounter for fracture with nonunion

S52.136P Nondisplaced fracture of neck of unspecified radius, subsequent encounter for closed fracture with malunion

S52.136K Nondisplaced fracture of neck of unspecified radius, subsequent encounter for closed fracture with nonunion

S52.136Q Nondisplaced fracture of neck of unspecified radius, subsequent encounter for open fracture type I or II with malunion

S52.136M Nondisplaced fracture of neck of unspecified radius, subsequent encounter for open fracture type I or II with nonunion

S52.136R Nondisplaced fracture of neck of unspecified radius, subsequent encounter for open fracture type IIIA, IIIB, or IIIC with malunion

S52.136N Nondisplaced fracture of neck of unspecified radius, subsequent encounter for open fracture type IIIA, IIIB, or IIIC with nonunion

S92.116B Nondisplaced fracture of neck of unspecified talus, initial encounter for open fracture

S92.116P Nondisplaced fracture of neck of unspecified talus, subsequent encounter for fracture with malunion

S92.116K Nondisplaced fracture of neck of unspecified talus, subsequent encounter for fracture with nonunion

S52.035P Nondisplaced fracture of olecranon process with intraarticular extension of left ulna, subsequent encounter for closed fracture with malunion

S52.035K Nondisplaced fracture of olecranon process with intraarticular extension of left ulna, subsequent encounter for closed fracture with nonunion

S52.035Q Nondisplaced fracture of olecranon process with intraarticular extension of left ulna, subsequent encounter for open fracture type I or II with malunion

S52.035M Nondisplaced fracture of olecranon process with intraarticular extension of left ulna, subsequent encounter for open fracture type I or II with nonunion

S52.035R Nondisplaced fracture of olecranon process with intraarticular extension of left ulna, subsequent encounter for open fracture type IIIA, IIIB, or IIIC with malunion

S52.035N Nondisplaced fracture of olecranon process with intraarticular extension of left ulna, subsequent encounter for open fracture type IIIA, IIIB, or IIIC with nonunion

S52.034P Nondisplaced fracture of olecranon process with intraarticular extension of right ulna, subsequent encounter for closed fracture with malunion

S52.034K Nondisplaced fracture of olecranon process with intraarticular extension of right ulna, subsequent encounter for closed fracture with nonunion

S52.034Q Nondisplaced fracture of olecranon process with intraarticular extension of right ulna, subsequent encounter for open fracture type I or II with malunion

S52.034M Nondisplaced fracture of olecranon process with intraarticular extension of right ulna, subsequent encounter for open fracture type I or II with nonunion

S52.034R Nondisplaced fracture of olecranon process with intraarticular extension of right ulna, subsequent encounter for open fracture type IIIA, IIIB, or IIIC with malunion

S52.034N Nondisplaced fracture of olecranon process with intraarticular extension of right ulna, subsequent encounter for open fracture type IIIA, IIIB, or IIIC with nonunion

S52.036P Nondisplaced fracture of olecranon process with intraarticular extension of unspecified ulna, subsequent encounter for closed fracture with malunion

S52.036K Nondisplaced fracture of olecranon process with intraarticular extension of unspecified ulna, subsequent encounter for closed fracture with nonunion

S52.036Q Nondisplaced fracture of olecranon process with intraarticular extension of unspecified ulna, subsequent encounter for open fracture type I or II with malunion

S52.036M Nondisplaced fracture of olecranon process with intraarticular extension of unspecified ulna, subsequent encounter for open fracture type I or II with nonunion

S52.036R Nondisplaced fracture of olecranon process with intraarticular extension of unspecified ulna, subsequent encounter for open fracture type IIIA, IIIB, or IIIC with malunion

S52.036N Nondisplaced fracture of olecranon process with intraarticular extension of unspecified ulna, subsequent encounter for open fracture type IIIA, IIIB, or IIIC with nonunion

S52.025P Nondisplaced fracture of olecranon process without intraarticular extension of left ulna, subsequent encounter for closed fracture with malunion

S52.025K Nondisplaced fracture of olecranon process without intraarticular extension of left ulna, subsequent encounter for closed fracture with nonunion

S52.025Q Nondisplaced fracture of olecranon process without intraarticular extension of left ulna, subsequent encounter for open fracture type I or II with malunion

S52.025M Nondisplaced fracture of olecranon process without intraarticular extension of left ulna, subsequent encounter for open fracture type I or II with nonunion

S52.025R Nondisplaced fracture of olecranon process without intraarticular extension of left ulna, subsequent encounter for open fracture type IIIA, IIIB, or IIIC with malunion

S52.025N Nondisplaced fracture of olecranon process without intraarticular extension of left ulna, subsequent encounter for open fracture type IIIA, IIIB, or IIIC with nonunion

S52.024P Nondisplaced fracture of olecranon process without intraarticular extension of right ulna, subsequent encounter for closed fracture with malunion

S52.024K Nondisplaced fracture of olecranon process without intraarticular extension of right ulna, subsequent encounter for closed fracture with nonunion

S52.024Q Nondisplaced fracture of olecranon process without intraarticular extension of right ulna, subsequent encounter for open fracture type I or II with malunion

S52.024M Nondisplaced fracture of olecranon process without intraarticular extension of right ulna, subsequent encounter for open fracture type I or II with nonunion

S52.024R Nondisplaced fracture of olecranon process without intraarticular extension of right ulna, subsequent encounter for open fracture type IIIA, IIIB, or IIIC with malunion

S52.024N Nondisplaced fracture of olecranon process without intraarticular extension of right ulna, subsequent encounter for open fracture type IIIA, IIIB, or IIIC with nonunion

S52.026P Nondisplaced fracture of olecranon process without intraarticular extension of unspecified ulna, subsequent encounter for closed fracture with malunion

S52.026K Nondisplaced fracture of olecranon process without intraarticular extension of unspecified ulna, subsequent encounter for closed fracture with nonunion

S52.026Q Nondisplaced fracture of olecranon process without intraarticular extension of unspecified ulna, subsequent encounter for open fracture type I or II with malunion

S52.026M Nondisplaced fracture of olecranon process without intraarticular extension of unspecified ulna, subsequent encounter for open fracture type I or II with nonunion

S52.026R Nondisplaced fracture of olecranon process without intraarticular extension of unspecified ulna, subsequent encounter for open fracture type IIIA, IIIB, or IIIC with malunion

S52.026N Nondisplaced fracture of olecranon process without intraarticular extension of unspecified ulna, subsequent encounter for open fracture type IIIA, IIIB, or IIIC with nonunion

S62.165B Nondisplaced fracture of pisiform, left wrist, initial encounter for open fracture

S62.165P Nondisplaced fracture of pisiform, left wrist, subsequent encounter for fracture with malunion

S62.165K Nondisplaced fracture of pisiform, left wrist, subsequent encounter for fracture with nonunion

S62.164B Nondisplaced fracture of pisiform, right wrist, initial encounter for open fracture

S62.164P Nondisplaced fracture of pisiform, right wrist, subsequent encounter for fracture with malunion

S62.164K Nondisplaced fracture of pisiform, right wrist, subsequent encounter for fracture with nonunion

S62.166B Nondisplaced fracture of pisiform, unspecified wrist, initial encounter for open fracture

S62.166P Nondisplaced fracture of pisiform, unspecified wrist, subsequent encounter for fracture with malunion

S62.166K Nondisplaced fracture of pisiform, unspecified wrist, subsequent encounter for fracture with nonunion

S32.445K Nondisplaced fracture of posterior column [ilioischial] of left acetabulum, subsequent encounter for fracture with nonunion

S32.444K Nondisplaced fracture of posterior column [ilioischial] of right acetabulum, subsequent encounter for fracture with nonunion

S32.446K Nondisplaced fracture of posterior column [ilioischial] of unspecified acetabulum, subsequent encounter for fracture with nonunion

S92.135B Nondisplaced fracture of posterior process of left talus, initial encounter for open fracture

S92.135P Nondisplaced fracture of posterior process of left talus, subsequent encounter for fracture with malunion

S92.135K Nondisplaced fracture of posterior process of left talus, subsequent encounter for fracture with nonunion

S92.134B Nondisplaced fracture of posterior process of right talus, initial encounter for open fracture

S92.134P Nondisplaced fracture of posterior process of right talus, subsequent encounter for fracture with malunion

S92.134K Nondisplaced fracture of posterior process of right talus, subsequent encounter for fracture with nonunion

S92.136B Nondisplaced fracture of posterior process of unspecified talus, initial encounter for open fracture

S92.136P Nondisplaced fracture of posterior process of unspecified talus, subsequent encounter for fracture with malunion

S92.136K Nondisplaced fracture of posterior process of unspecified talus, subsequent encounter for fracture with nonunion

S32.425K Nondisplaced fracture of posterior wall of left acetabulum, subsequent encounter for fracture with nonunion

S32.424K Nondisplaced fracture of posterior wall of right acetabulum, subsequent encounter for fracture with nonunion

S32.426K Nondisplaced fracture of posterior wall of unspecified acetabulum, subsequent encounter for fracture with nonunion

S92.415P Nondisplaced fracture of proximal phalanx of left great toe, subsequent encounter for fracture with malunion

S92.415K Nondisplaced fracture of proximal phalanx of left great toe, subsequent encounter for fracture with nonunion

S62.641B Nondisplaced fracture of proximal phalanx of left index finger, initial encounter for open fracture

S62.641P Nondisplaced fracture of proximal phalanx of left index finger, subsequent encounter for fracture with malunion

S62.641K Nondisplaced fracture of proximal phalanx of left index finger, subsequent encounter for fracture with nonunion

S92.515P Nondisplaced fracture of proximal phalanx of left lesser toe(s), subsequent encounter for fracture with malunion

S92.515K Nondisplaced fracture of proximal phalanx of left lesser toe(s), subsequent encounter for fracture with nonunion

S62.647B Nondisplaced fracture of proximal phalanx of left little finger, initial encounter for open fracture

S62.647P Nondisplaced fracture of proximal phalanx of left little finger, subsequent encounter for fracture with malunion

S62.647K Nondisplaced fracture of proximal phalanx of left little finger, subsequent encounter for fracture with nonunion

S62.643B Nondisplaced fracture of proximal phalanx of left middle finger, initial encounter for open fracture

S62.643P Nondisplaced fracture of proximal phalanx of left middle finger, subsequent encounter for fracture with malunion

S62.643K Nondisplaced fracture of proximal phalanx of left middle finger, subsequent encounter for fracture with nonunion

S62.645B Nondisplaced fracture of proximal phalanx of left ring finger, initial encounter for open fracture

S62.645P Nondisplaced fracture of proximal phalanx of left ring finger, subsequent encounter for fracture with malunion

S62.645K Nondisplaced fracture of proximal phalanx of left ring finger, subsequent encounter for fracture with nonunion

S62.515B Nondisplaced fracture of proximal phalanx of left thumb, initial encounter for open fracture

S62.515P Nondisplaced fracture of proximal phalanx of left thumb, subsequent encounter for fracture with malunion

S62.515K Nondisplaced fracture of proximal phalanx of left thumb, subsequent encounter for fracture with nonunion

S62.648B Nondisplaced fracture of proximal phalanx of other finger, initial encounter for open fracture

S62.648P Nondisplaced fracture of proximal phalanx of other finger, subsequent encounter for fracture with malunion

S62.648K Nondisplaced fracture of proximal phalanx of other finger, subsequent encounter for fracture with nonunion

S92.414P Nondisplaced fracture of proximal phalanx of right great toe, subsequent encounter for fracture with malunion

S92.414K Nondisplaced fracture of proximal phalanx of right great toe, subsequent encounter for fracture with nonunion

S62.640B Nondisplaced fracture of proximal phalanx of right index finger, initial encounter for open fracture

S62.640P Nondisplaced fracture of proximal phalanx of right index finger, subsequent encounter for fracture with malunion

S62.640K Nondisplaced fracture of proximal phalanx of right index finger, subsequent encounter for fracture with nonunion

S92.514P Nondisplaced fracture of proximal phalanx of right lesser toe(s), subsequent encounter for fracture with malunion

S92.514K Nondisplaced fracture of proximal phalanx of right lesser toe(s), subsequent encounter for fracture with nonunion

S62.646B Nondisplaced fracture of proximal phalanx of right little finger, initial encounter for open fracture

S62.646P Nondisplaced fracture of proximal phalanx of right little finger, subsequent encounter for fracture with malunion

S62.646K Nondisplaced fracture of proximal phalanx of right little finger, subsequent encounter for fracture with nonunion

S62.642B Nondisplaced fracture of proximal phalanx of right middle finger, initial encounter for open fracture

S62.642P Nondisplaced fracture of proximal phalanx of right middle finger, subsequent encounter for fracture with malunion

S62.642K Nondisplaced fracture of proximal phalanx of right middle finger, subsequent encounter for fracture with nonunion

S62.644B Nondisplaced fracture of proximal phalanx of right ring finger, initial encounter for open fracture

S62.644P Nondisplaced fracture of proximal phalanx of right ring finger, subsequent encounter for fracture with malunion

S62.644K Nondisplaced fracture of proximal phalanx of right ring finger, subsequent encounter for fracture with nonunion

S62.514B Nondisplaced fracture of proximal phalanx of right thumb, initial encounter for open fracture

S62.514P Nondisplaced fracture of proximal phalanx of right thumb, subsequent encounter for fracture with malunion

S62.514K Nondisplaced fracture of proximal phalanx of right thumb, subsequent encounter for fracture with nonunion

S62.649B Nondisplaced fracture of proximal phalanx of unspecified finger, initial encounter for open fracture

S62.649P Nondisplaced fracture of proximal phalanx of unspecified finger, subsequent encounter for fracture with malunion

S62.649K Nondisplaced fracture of proximal phalanx of unspecified finger, subsequent encounter for fracture with nonunion

S92.416P Nondisplaced fracture of proximal phalanx of unspecified great toe, subsequent encounter for fracture with malunion

S92.416K Nondisplaced fracture of proximal phalanx of unspecified great toe, subsequent encounter for fracture with nonunion

S92.516P Nondisplaced fracture of proximal phalanx of unspecified lesser toe(s), subsequent encounter for fracture with malunion

S92.516K Nondisplaced fracture of proximal phalanx of unspecified lesser toe(s), subsequent encounter for fracture with nonunion

S62.516B Nondisplaced fracture of proximal phalanx of unspecified thumb, initial encounter for open fracture

S62.516P Nondisplaced fracture of proximal phalanx of unspecified thumb, subsequent encounter for fracture with malunion

S62.516K Nondisplaced fracture of proximal phalanx of unspecified thumb, subsequent encounter for fracture with nonunion

S62.035B Nondisplaced fracture of proximal third of navicular [scaphoid] bone of left wrist, initial encounter for open fracture

S62.035P Nondisplaced fracture of proximal third of navicular [scaphoid] bone of left wrist, subsequent encounter for fracture with malunion

S62.035K Nondisplaced fracture of proximal third of navicular [scaphoid] bone of left wrist, subsequent encounter for fracture with nonunion

S62.034B Nondisplaced fracture of proximal third of navicular [scaphoid] bone of right wrist, initial encounter for open fracture

S62.034P Nondisplaced fracture of proximal third of navicular [scaphoid] bone of right wrist, subsequent encounter for fracture with malunion

S62.034K Nondisplaced fracture of proximal third of navicular [scaphoid] bone of right wrist, subsequent encounter for fracture with nonunion

S62.036B Nondisplaced fracture of proximal third of navicular [scaphoid] bone of unspecified wrist, initial encounter for open fracture

S62.036P Nondisplaced fracture of proximal third of navicular [scaphoid] bone of unspecified wrist, subsequent encounter for fracture with malunion

S62.036K Nondisplaced fracture of proximal third of navicular [scaphoid] bone of unspecified wrist, subsequent encounter for fracture with nonunion

S52.514A Nondisplaced fracture of right radial styloid process, initial encounter for closed fracture

S52.514P Nondisplaced fracture of right radial styloid process, subsequent encounter for closed fracture with malunion

S52.514K Nondisplaced fracture of right radial styloid process, subsequent encounter for closed fracture with nonunion

S52.514Q Nondisplaced fracture of right radial styloid process, subsequent encounter for open fracture type I or II with malunion

S52.514M Nondisplaced fracture of right radial styloid process, subsequent encounter for open fracture type I or II with nonunion

S52.514R Nondisplaced fracture of right radial styloid process, subsequent encounter for open fracture type IIIA, IIIB, or IIIC with malunion

S52.514N Nondisplaced fracture of right radial styloid process, subsequent encounter for open fracture type IIIA, IIIB, or IIIC with nonunion

S82.114A Nondisplaced fracture of right tibial spine, initial encounter for closed fracture

S82.114P Nondisplaced fracture of right tibial spine, subsequent encounter for closed fracture with malunion

S82.114K Nondisplaced fracture of right tibial spine, subsequent encounter for closed fracture with nonunion

S82.114Q Nondisplaced fracture of right tibial spine, subsequent encounter for open fracture type I or II with malunion

S82.114M Nondisplaced fracture of right tibial spine, subsequent encounter for open fracture type I or II with nonunion

S82.114R Nondisplaced fracture of right tibial spine, subsequent encounter for open fracture type IIIA, IIIB, or IIIC with malunion

S82.114N Nondisplaced fracture of right tibial spine, subsequent encounter for open fracture type IIIA, IIIB, or IIIC with nonunion

S82.154A Nondisplaced fracture of right tibial tuberosity, initial encounter for closed fracture

S82.154P Nondisplaced fracture of right tibial tuberosity, subsequent encounter for closed fracture with malunion

S82.154K Nondisplaced fracture of right tibial tuberosity, subsequent encounter for closed fracture with nonunion

S82.154Q Nondisplaced fracture of right tibial tuberosity, subsequent encounter for open fracture type I or II with malunion

S82.154M Nondisplaced fracture of right tibial tuberosity, subsequent encounter for open fracture type I or II with nonunion

S82.154R Nondisplaced fracture of right tibial tuberosity, subsequent encounter for open fracture type IIIA, IIIB, or IIIC with malunion

S82.154N Nondisplaced fracture of right tibial tuberosity, subsequent encounter for open fracture type IIIA, IIIB, or IIIC with nonunion

S52.614A Nondisplaced fracture of right ulna styloid process, initial encounter for closed fracture

S52.614P Nondisplaced fracture of right ulna styloid process, subsequent encounter for closed fracture with malunion

S52.614K Nondisplaced fracture of right ulna styloid process, subsequent encounter for closed fracture with nonunion

S52.614Q Nondisplaced fracture of right ulna styloid process, subsequent encounter for open fracture type I or II with malunion

S52.614M Nondisplaced fracture of right ulna styloid process, subsequent encounter for open fracture type I or II with nonunion

S52.614R Nondisplaced fracture of right ulna styloid process, subsequent encounter for open fracture type IIIA, IIIB, or IIIC with malunion

S52.614N Nondisplaced fracture of right ulna styloid process, subsequent encounter for open fracture type IIIA, IIIB, or IIIC with nonunion

S92.325B Nondisplaced fracture of second metatarsal bone, left foot, initial encounter for open fracture

S92.325P Nondisplaced fracture of second metatarsal bone, left foot, subsequent encounter for fracture with malunion

S92.325K Nondisplaced fracture of second metatarsal bone, left foot, subsequent encounter for fracture with nonunion

S92.324B Nondisplaced fracture of second metatarsal bone, right foot, initial encounter for open fracture

S92.324P Nondisplaced fracture of second metatarsal bone, right foot, subsequent encounter for fracture with malunion

S92.324K Nondisplaced fracture of second metatarsal bone, right foot, subsequent encounter for fracture with nonunion

S92.326B Nondisplaced fracture of second metatarsal bone, unspecified foot, initial encounter for open fracture

S92.326P Nondisplaced fracture of second metatarsal bone, unspecified foot, subsequent encounter for fracture with malunion

S92.326K Nondisplaced fracture of second metatarsal bone, unspecified foot, subsequent encounter for fracture with nonunion

S62.357B Nondisplaced fracture of shaft of fifth metacarpal bone, left hand, initial encounter for open fracture

S62.357P Nondisplaced fracture of shaft of fifth metacarpal bone, left hand, subsequent encounter for fracture with malunion

S62.357K Nondisplaced fracture of shaft of fifth metacarpal bone, left hand, subsequent encounter for fracture with nonunion

S62.356B Nondisplaced fracture of shaft of fifth metacarpal bone, right hand, initial encounter for open fracture

S62.356P Nondisplaced fracture of shaft of fifth metacarpal bone, right hand, subsequent encounter for fracture with malunion

S62.356K Nondisplaced fracture of shaft of fifth metacarpal bone, right hand, subsequent encounter for fracture with nonunion

S62.245B Nondisplaced fracture of shaft of first metacarpal bone, left hand, initial encounter for open fracture

S62.245P Nondisplaced fracture of shaft of first metacarpal bone, left hand, subsequent encounter for fracture with malunion

S62.245K Nondisplaced fracture of shaft of first metacarpal bone, left hand, subsequent encounter for fracture with nonunion

S62.244B Nondisplaced fracture of shaft of first metacarpal bone, right hand, initial encounter for open fracture

S62.244P Nondisplaced fracture of shaft of first metacarpal bone, right hand, subsequent encounter for fracture with malunion

S62.244K Nondisplaced fracture of shaft of first metacarpal bone, right hand, subsequent encounter for fracture with nonunion

S62.246B Nondisplaced fracture of shaft of first metacarpal bone, unspecified hand, initial encounter for open fracture

S62.246P Nondisplaced fracture of shaft of first metacarpal bone, unspecified hand, subsequent encounter for fracture with malunion

S62.246K Nondisplaced fracture of shaft of first metacarpal bone, unspecified hand, subsequent encounter for fracture with nonunion

S62.355B Nondisplaced fracture of shaft of fourth metacarpal bone, left hand, initial encounter for open fracture

S62.355P Nondisplaced fracture of shaft of fourth metacarpal bone, left hand, subsequent encounter for fracture with malunion

S62.355K Nondisplaced fracture of shaft of fourth metacarpal bone, left hand, subsequent encounter for fracture with nonunion

S62.354B Nondisplaced fracture of shaft of fourth metacarpal bone, right hand, initial encounter for open fracture

S62.354P Nondisplaced fracture of shaft of fourth metacarpal bone, right hand, subsequent encounter for fracture with malunion

S62.354K Nondisplaced fracture of shaft of fourth metacarpal bone, right hand, subsequent encounter for fracture with nonunion

S42.025B Nondisplaced fracture of shaft of left clavicle, initial encounter for open fracture

S42.025P Nondisplaced fracture of shaft of left clavicle, subsequent encounter for fracture with malunion

S42.025K Nondisplaced fracture of shaft of left clavicle, subsequent encounter for fracture with nonunion

S62.358B Nondisplaced fracture of shaft of other metacarpal bone, initial encounter for open fracture

S62.358P Nondisplaced fracture of shaft of other metacarpal bone, subsequent encounter for fracture with malunion

S62.358K Nondisplaced fracture of shaft of other metacarpal bone, subsequent encounter for fracture with nonunion

S42.024B Nondisplaced fracture of shaft of right clavicle, initial encounter for open fracture

S42.024P Nondisplaced fracture of shaft of right clavicle, subsequent encounter for fracture with malunion

S42.024K Nondisplaced fracture of shaft of right clavicle, subsequent encounter for fracture with nonunion

S62.351B Nondisplaced fracture of shaft of second metacarpal bone, left hand, initial encounter for open fracture

S62.351P Nondisplaced fracture of shaft of second metacarpal bone, left hand, subsequent encounter for fracture with malunion

S62.351K Nondisplaced fracture of shaft of second metacarpal bone, left hand, subsequent encounter for fracture with nonunion

S62.350B Nondisplaced fracture of shaft of second metacarpal bone, right hand, initial encounter for open fracture

S62.350P Nondisplaced fracture of shaft of second metacarpal bone, right hand, subsequent encounter for fracture with malunion

S62.350K Nondisplaced fracture of shaft of second metacarpal bone, right hand, subsequent encounter for fracture with nonunion

S62.353B Nondisplaced fracture of shaft of third metacarpal bone, left hand, initial encounter for open fracture

S62.353P Nondisplaced fracture of shaft of third metacarpal bone, left hand, subsequent encounter for fracture with malunion

S62.353K Nondisplaced fracture of shaft of third metacarpal bone, left hand, subsequent encounter for fracture with nonunion

S62.352B Nondisplaced fracture of shaft of third metacarpal bone, right hand, initial encounter for open fracture

S62.352P Nondisplaced fracture of shaft of third metacarpal bone, right hand, subsequent encounter for fracture with malunion

S62.352K Nondisplaced fracture of shaft of third metacarpal bone, right hand, subsequent encounter for fracture with nonunion

S42.026B Nondisplaced fracture of shaft of unspecified clavicle, initial encounter for open fracture

S42.026P Nondisplaced fracture of shaft of unspecified clavicle, subsequent encounter for fracture with malunion

S42.026K Nondisplaced fracture of shaft of unspecified clavicle, subsequent encounter for fracture with nonunion

S62.359B Nondisplaced fracture of shaft of unspecified metacarpal bone, initial encounter for open fracture

S62.359P Nondisplaced fracture of shaft of unspecified metacarpal bone, subsequent encounter for fracture with malunion

S62.359K Nondisplaced fracture of shaft of unspecified metacarpal bone, subsequent encounter for fracture with nonunion

S42.018B Nondisplaced fracture of sternal end of left clavicle, initial encounter for open fracture

S42.018P Nondisplaced fracture of sternal end of left clavicle, subsequent encounter for fracture with malunion

S42.018K Nondisplaced fracture of sternal end of left clavicle, subsequent encounter for fracture with nonunion

S42.017B Nondisplaced fracture of sternal end of right clavicle, initial encounter for open fracture

S42.017P Nondisplaced fracture of sternal end of right clavicle, subsequent encounter for fracture with malunion

S42.017K Nondisplaced fracture of sternal end of right clavicle, subsequent encounter for fracture with nonunion

S42.019B Nondisplaced fracture of sternal end of unspecified clavicle, initial encounter for open fracture

S42.019P Nondisplaced fracture of sternal end of unspecified clavicle, subsequent encounter for fracture with malunion

S42.019K Nondisplaced fracture of sternal end of unspecified clavicle, subsequent encounter for fracture with nonunion

S92.335B Nondisplaced fracture of third metatarsal bone, left foot, initial encounter for open fracture

S92.335P Nondisplaced fracture of third metatarsal bone, left foot, subsequent encounter for fracture with malunion

S92.335K Nondisplaced fracture of third metatarsal bone, left foot, subsequent encounter for fracture with nonunion

S92.334B Nondisplaced fracture of third metatarsal bone, right foot, initial encounter for open fracture

S92.334P Nondisplaced fracture of third metatarsal bone, right foot, subsequent encounter for fracture with malunion

S92.334K Nondisplaced fracture of third metatarsal bone, right foot, subsequent encounter for fracture with nonunion

S92.336B Nondisplaced fracture of third metatarsal bone, unspecified foot, initial encounter for open fracture

S92.336P Nondisplaced fracture of third metatarsal bone, unspecified foot, subsequent encounter for fracture with malunion

S92.336K Nondisplaced fracture of third metatarsal bone, unspecified foot, subsequent encounter for fracture with nonunion

S62.175B Nondisplaced fracture of trapezium [larger multangular], left wrist, initial encounter for open fracture

S62.175P Nondisplaced fracture of trapezium [larger multangular], left wrist, subsequent encounter for fracture with malunion

S62.175K Nondisplaced fracture of trapezium [larger multangular], left wrist, subsequent encounter for fracture with nonunion

S62.174B Nondisplaced fracture of trapezium [larger multangular], right wrist, initial encounter for open fracture

S62.174P Nondisplaced fracture of trapezium [larger multangular], right wrist, subsequent encounter for fracture with malunion

S62.174K Nondisplaced fracture of trapezium [larger multangular], right wrist, subsequent encounter for fracture with nonunion

S62.176B Nondisplaced fracture of trapezium [larger multangular], unspecified wrist, initial encounter for open fracture

S62.176P Nondisplaced fracture of trapezium [larger multangular], unspecified wrist, subsequent encounter for fracture with malunion

S62.176K Nondisplaced fracture of trapezium [larger multangular], unspecified wrist, subsequent encounter for fracture with nonunion

S62.185B Nondisplaced fracture of trapezoid [smaller multangular], left wrist, initial encounter for open fracture

S62.185P Nondisplaced fracture of trapezoid [smaller multangular], left wrist, subsequent encounter for fracture with malunion

S62.185K Nondisplaced fracture of trapezoid [smaller multangular], left wrist, subsequent encounter for fracture with nonunion

S62.184B Nondisplaced fracture of trapezoid [smaller multangular], right wrist, initial encounter for open fracture

S62.184P Nondisplaced fracture of trapezoid [smaller multangular], right wrist, subsequent encounter for fracture with malunion

S62.184K Nondisplaced fracture of trapezoid [smaller multangular], right wrist, subsequent encounter for fracture with nonunion

S62.186B Nondisplaced fracture of trapezoid [smaller multangular], unspecified wrist, initial encounter for open fracture

S62.186P Nondisplaced fracture of trapezoid [smaller multangular], unspecified wrist, subsequent encounter for fracture with malunion

S62.186K Nondisplaced fracture of trapezoid [smaller multangular], unspecified wrist, subsequent encounter for fracture with nonunion

S62.115B Nondisplaced fracture of triquetrum [cuneiform] bone, left wrist, initial encounter for open fracture

S62.115P Nondisplaced fracture of triquetrum [cuneiform] bone, left wrist, subsequent encounter for fracture with malunion

S62.115K Nondisplaced fracture of triquetrum [cuneiform] bone, left wrist, subsequent encounter for fracture with nonunion

S62.114B Nondisplaced fracture of triquetrum [cuneiform] bone, right wrist, initial encounter for open fracture

S62.114P Nondisplaced fracture of triquetrum [cuneiform] bone, right wrist, subsequent encounter for fracture with malunion

S62.114K Nondisplaced fracture of triquetrum [cuneiform] bone, right wrist, subsequent encounter for fracture with nonunion

S62.116B Nondisplaced fracture of triquetrum [cuneiform] bone, unspecified wrist, initial encounter for open fracture

S62.116P Nondisplaced fracture of triquetrum [cuneiform] bone, unspecified wrist, subsequent encounter for fracture with malunion

S62.116K Nondisplaced fracture of triquetrum [cuneiform] bone, unspecified wrist, subsequent encounter for fracture with nonunion

S52.516A Nondisplaced fracture of unspecified radial styloid process, initial encounter for closed fracture

S52.516P Nondisplaced fracture of unspecified radial styloid process, subsequent encounter for closed fracture with malunion

S52.516K Nondisplaced fracture of unspecified radial styloid process, subsequent encounter for closed fracture with nonunion

S52.516Q Nondisplaced fracture of unspecified radial styloid process, subsequent encounter for open fracture type I or II with malunion

S52.516M Nondisplaced fracture of unspecified radial styloid process, subsequent encounter for open fracture type I or II with nonunion

S52.516R Nondisplaced fracture of unspecified radial styloid process, subsequent encounter for open fracture type IIIA, IIIB, or IIIC with malunion

S52.516N Nondisplaced fracture of unspecified radial styloid process, subsequent encounter for open fracture type IIIA, IIIB, or IIIC with nonunion

S82.116A Nondisplaced fracture of unspecified tibial spine, initial encounter for closed fracture

S82.116P Nondisplaced fracture of unspecified tibial spine, subsequent encounter for closed fracture with malunion

S82.116K Nondisplaced fracture of unspecified tibial spine, subsequent encounter for closed fracture with nonunion

S82.116Q Nondisplaced fracture of unspecified tibial spine, subsequent encounter for open fracture type I or II with malunion

S82.116M Nondisplaced fracture of unspecified tibial spine, subsequent encounter for open fracture type I or II with nonunion

S82.116R Nondisplaced fracture of unspecified tibial spine, subsequent encounter for open fracture type IIIA, IIIB, or IIIC with malunion

S82.116N Nondisplaced fracture of unspecified tibial spine, subsequent encounter for open fracture type IIIA, IIIB, or IIIC with nonunion

S82.156A Nondisplaced fracture of unspecified tibial tuberosity, initial encounter for closed fracture

S82.156P Nondisplaced fracture of unspecified tibial tuberosity, subsequent encounter for closed fracture with malunion

S82.156K Nondisplaced fracture of unspecified tibial tuberosity, subsequent encounter for closed fracture with nonunion

S82.156Q Nondisplaced fracture of unspecified tibial tuberosity, subsequent encounter for open fracture type I or II with malunion

S82.156M Nondisplaced fracture of unspecified tibial tuberosity, subsequent encounter for open fracture type I or II with nonunion

S82.156R Nondisplaced fracture of unspecified tibial tuberosity, subsequent encounter for open fracture type IIIA, IIIB, or IIIC with malunion

S82.156N Nondisplaced fracture of unspecified tibial tuberosity, subsequent encounter for open fracture type IIIA, IIIB, or IIIC with nonunion

S52.616A Nondisplaced fracture of unspecified ulna styloid process, initial encounter for closed fracture

S52.616P Nondisplaced fracture of unspecified ulna styloid process, subsequent encounter for closed fracture with malunion

S52.616K Nondisplaced fracture of unspecified ulna styloid process, subsequent encounter for closed fracture with nonunion

S52.616Q Nondisplaced fracture of unspecified ulna styloid process, subsequent encounter for open fracture type I or II with malunion

S52.616M Nondisplaced fracture of unspecified ulna styloid process, subsequent encounter for open fracture type I or II with nonunion

S52.616R Nondisplaced fracture of unspecified ulna styloid process, subsequent encounter for open fracture type IIIA, IIIB, or IIIC with malunion

S52.616N Nondisplaced fracture of unspecified ulna styloid process, subsequent encounter for open fracture type IIIA, IIIB, or IIIC with nonunion

S72.145P Nondisplaced intertrochanteric fracture of left femur, subsequent encounter for closed fracture with malunion

S72.145K Nondisplaced intertrochanteric fracture of left femur, subsequent encounter for closed fracture with nonunion

S72.145Q Nondisplaced intertrochanteric fracture of left femur, subsequent encounter for open fracture type I or II with malunion

S72.145M Nondisplaced intertrochanteric fracture of left femur, subsequent encounter for open fracture type I or II with nonunion

S72.145R Nondisplaced intertrochanteric fracture of left femur, subsequent encounter for open fracture type IIIA, IIIB, or IIIC with malunion

S72.145N Nondisplaced intertrochanteric fracture of left femur, subsequent encounter for open fracture type IIIA, IIIB, or IIIC with nonunion

S72.144P Nondisplaced intertrochanteric fracture of right femur, subsequent encounter for closed fracture with malunion

S72.144K Nondisplaced intertrochanteric fracture of right femur, subsequent encounter for closed fracture with nonunion

S72.144Q Nondisplaced intertrochanteric fracture of right femur, subsequent encounter for open fracture type I or II with malunion

S72.144M Nondisplaced intertrochanteric fracture of right femur, subsequent encounter for open fracture type I or II with nonunion

S72.144R Nondisplaced intertrochanteric fracture of right femur, subsequent encounter for open fracture type IIIA, IIIB, or IIIC with malunion

S72.144N Nondisplaced intertrochanteric fracture of right femur, subsequent encounter for open fracture type IIIA, IIIB, or IIIC with nonunion

S72.146P Nondisplaced intertrochanteric fracture of unspecified femur, subsequent encounter for closed fracture with malunion

S72.146K Nondisplaced intertrochanteric fracture of unspecified femur, subsequent encounter for closed fracture with nonunion

S72.146Q Nondisplaced intertrochanteric fracture of unspecified femur, subsequent encounter for open fracture type I or II with malunion

S72.146M Nondisplaced intertrochanteric fracture of unspecified femur, subsequent encounter for open fracture type I or II with nonunion

S72.146R Nondisplaced intertrochanteric fracture of unspecified femur, subsequent encounter for open fracture type IIIA, IIIB, or IIIC with malunion

S72.146N Nondisplaced intertrochanteric fracture of unspecified femur, subsequent encounter for open fracture type IIIA, IIIB, or IIIC with nonunion

S92.065B Nondisplaced intraarticular fracture of left calcaneus, initial encounter for open fracture

S92.065P Nondisplaced intraarticular fracture of left calcaneus, subsequent encounter for fracture with malunion

S92.065K Nondisplaced intraarticular fracture of left calcaneus, subsequent encounter for fracture with nonunion

S92.064B Nondisplaced intraarticular fracture of right calcaneus, initial encounter for open fracture

S92.064P Nondisplaced intraarticular fracture of right calcaneus, subsequent encounter for fracture with malunion

S92.064K Nondisplaced intraarticular fracture of right calcaneus, subsequent encounter for fracture with nonunion

S92.066B Nondisplaced intraarticular fracture of unspecified calcaneus, initial encounter for open fracture

S92.066P Nondisplaced intraarticular fracture of unspecified calcaneus, subsequent encounter for fracture with malunion

S92.066K Nondisplaced intraarticular fracture of unspecified calcaneus, subsequent encounter for fracture with nonunion

S12.041A Nondisplaced lateral mass fracture of first cervical vertebra, initial encounter for closed fracture

S12.041K Nondisplaced lateral mass fracture of first cervical vertebra, subsequent encounter for fracture with nonunion

S82.025A Nondisplaced longitudinal fracture of left patella, initial encounter for closed fracture

S82.025B Nondisplaced longitudinal fracture of left patella, initial encounter for open fracture type I or II

S82.025C Nondisplaced longitudinal fracture of left patella, initial encounter for open fracture type IIIA, IIIB, or IIIC

S82.025P Nondisplaced longitudinal fracture of left patella, subsequent encounter for closed fracture with malunion

S82.025K Nondisplaced longitudinal fracture of left patella, subsequent encounter for closed fracture with nonunion

S82.025Q Nondisplaced longitudinal fracture of left patella, subsequent encounter for open fracture type I or II with malunion

S82.025M Nondisplaced longitudinal fracture of left patella, subsequent encounter for open fracture type I or II with nonunion

S82.025R Nondisplaced longitudinal fracture of left patella, subsequent encounter for open fracture type IIIA, IIIB, or IIIC with malunion

S82.025N Nondisplaced longitudinal fracture of left patella, subsequent encounter for open fracture type IIIA, IIIB, or IIIC with nonunion

S82.024A Nondisplaced longitudinal fracture of right patella, initial encounter for closed fracture

S82.024B Nondisplaced longitudinal fracture of right patella, initial encounter for open fracture type I or II

S82.024C Nondisplaced longitudinal fracture of right patella, initial encounter for open fracture type IIIA, IIIB, or IIIC

S82.024P Nondisplaced longitudinal fracture of right patella, subsequent encounter for closed fracture with malunion

S82.024K Nondisplaced longitudinal fracture of right patella, subsequent encounter for closed fracture with nonunion

S82.024Q Nondisplaced longitudinal fracture of right patella, subsequent encounter for open fracture type I or II with malunion

S82.024M Nondisplaced longitudinal fracture of right patella, subsequent encounter for open fracture type I or II with nonunion

S82.024R Nondisplaced longitudinal fracture of right patella, subsequent encounter for open fracture type IIIA, IIIB, or IIIC with malunion

S82.024N Nondisplaced longitudinal fracture of right patella, subsequent encounter for open fracture type IIIA, IIIB, or IIIC with nonunion

S82.026A Nondisplaced longitudinal fracture of unspecified patella, initial encounter for closed fracture

S82.026B Nondisplaced longitudinal fracture of unspecified patella, initial encounter for open fracture type I or II

S82.026C Nondisplaced longitudinal fracture of unspecified patella, initial encounter for open fracture type IIIA, IIIB, or IIIC

S82.026P Nondisplaced longitudinal fracture of unspecified patella, subsequent encounter for closed fracture with malunion

S82.026K Nondisplaced longitudinal fracture of unspecified patella, subsequent encounter for closed fracture with nonunion

S82.026Q Nondisplaced longitudinal fracture of unspecified patella, subsequent encounter for open fracture type I or II with malunion

S82.026M Nondisplaced longitudinal fracture of unspecified patella, subsequent encounter for open fracture type I or II with nonunion

S82.026R Nondisplaced longitudinal fracture of unspecified patella, subsequent encounter for open fracture type IIIA, IIIB, or IIIC with malunion

S82.026N Nondisplaced longitudinal fracture of unspecified patella, subsequent encounter for open fracture type IIIA, IIIB, or IIIC with nonunion

S82.865P Nondisplaced Maisonneuve's fracture of left leg, subsequent encounter for closed fracture with malunion

S82.865K Nondisplaced Maisonneuve's fracture of left leg, subsequent encounter for closed fracture with nonunion

S82.865Q Nondisplaced Maisonneuve's fracture of left leg, subsequent encounter for open fracture type I or II with malunion

S82.865M Nondisplaced Maisonneuve's fracture of left leg, subsequent encounter for open fracture type I or II with nonunion

S82.865R Nondisplaced Maisonneuve's fracture of left leg, subsequent encounter for open fracture type IIIA, IIIB, or IIIC with malunion

S82.865N Nondisplaced Maisonneuve's fracture of left leg, subsequent encounter for open fracture type IIIA, IIIB, or IIIC with nonunion

S82.864P Nondisplaced Maisonneuve's fracture of right leg, subsequent encounter for closed fracture with malunion

S82.864K Nondisplaced Maisonneuve's fracture of right leg, subsequent encounter for closed fracture with nonunion

S82.864Q Nondisplaced Maisonneuve's fracture of right leg, subsequent encounter for open fracture type I or II with malunion

S82.864M Nondisplaced Maisonneuve's fracture of right leg, subsequent encounter for open fracture type I or II with nonunion

S82.864R Nondisplaced Maisonneuve's fracture of right leg, subsequent encounter for open fracture type IIIA, IIIB, or IIIC with malunion

S82.864N Nondisplaced Maisonneuve's fracture of right leg, subsequent encounter for open fracture type IIIA, IIIB, or IIIC with nonunion

S82.866P Nondisplaced Maisonneuve's fracture of unspecified leg, subsequent encounter for closed fracture with malunion

S82.866K Nondisplaced Maisonneuve's fracture of unspecified leg, subsequent encounter for closed fracture with nonunion

S82.866Q Nondisplaced Maisonneuve's fracture of unspecified leg, subsequent encounter for open fracture type I or II with malunion

S82.866M Nondisplaced Maisonneuve's fracture of unspecified leg, subsequent encounter for open fracture type I or II with nonunion

S82.866R Nondisplaced Maisonneuve's fracture of unspecified leg, subsequent encounter for open fracture type IIIA, IIIB, or IIIC with malunion

S82.866N Nondisplaced Maisonneuve's fracture of unspecified leg, subsequent encounter for open fracture type IIIA, IIIB, or IIIC with nonunion

S72.035P Nondisplaced midcervical fracture of left femur, subsequent encounter for closed fracture with malunion

S72.035K Nondisplaced midcervical fracture of left femur, subsequent encounter for closed fracture with nonunion

S72.035Q Nondisplaced midcervical fracture of left femur, subsequent encounter for open fracture type I or II with malunion

S72.035M Nondisplaced midcervical fracture of left femur, subsequent encounter for open fracture type I or II with nonunion

S72.035R Nondisplaced midcervical fracture of left femur, subsequent encounter for open fracture type IIIA, IIIB, or IIIC with malunion

S72.035N Nondisplaced midcervical fracture of left femur, subsequent encounter for open fracture type IIIA, IIIB, or IIIC with nonunion

S72.034P Nondisplaced midcervical fracture of right femur, subsequent encounter for closed fracture with malunion

S72.034K Nondisplaced midcervical fracture of right femur, subsequent encounter for closed fracture with nonunion

S72.034Q Nondisplaced midcervical fracture of right femur, subsequent encounter for open fracture type I or II with malunion

S72.034M Nondisplaced midcervical fracture of right femur, subsequent encounter for open fracture type I or II with nonunion

S72.034R Nondisplaced midcervical fracture of right femur, subsequent encounter for open fracture type IIIA, IIIB, or IIIC with malunion

S72.034N	Nondisplaced midcervical fracture of right femur, subsequent encounter for open fracture type IIIA, IIIB, or IIIC with nonunion
S72.036P	Nondisplaced midcervical fracture of unspecified femur, subsequent encounter for closed fracture with malunion
S72.036K	Nondisplaced midcervical fracture of unspecified femur, subsequent encounter for closed fracture with nonunion
S72.036Q	Nondisplaced midcervical fracture of unspecified femur, subsequent encounter for open fracture type I or II with malunion
S72.036M	Nondisplaced midcervical fracture of unspecified femur, subsequent encounter for open fracture type I or II with nonunion
S72.036R	Nondisplaced midcervical fracture of unspecified femur, subsequent encounter for open fracture type IIIA, IIIB, or IIIC with malunion
S72.036N	Nondisplaced midcervical fracture of unspecified femur, subsequent encounter for open fracture type IIIA, IIIB, or IIIC with nonunion
S42.335A	Nondisplaced oblique fracture of shaft of humerus, left arm, initial encounter for closed fracture
S42.335P	Nondisplaced oblique fracture of shaft of humerus, left arm, subsequent encounter for fracture with malunion
S42.335K	Nondisplaced oblique fracture of shaft of humerus, left arm, subsequent encounter for fracture with nonunion
S42.334A	Nondisplaced oblique fracture of shaft of humerus, right arm, initial encounter for closed fracture
S42.334P	Nondisplaced oblique fracture of shaft of humerus, right arm, subsequent encounter for fracture with malunion
S42.334K	Nondisplaced oblique fracture of shaft of humerus, right arm, subsequent encounter for fracture with nonunion
S42.336A	Nondisplaced oblique fracture of shaft of humerus, unspecified arm, initial encounter for closed fracture
S42.336P	Nondisplaced oblique fracture of shaft of humerus, unspecified arm, subsequent encounter for fracture with malunion
S42.336K	Nondisplaced oblique fracture of shaft of humerus, unspecified arm, subsequent encounter for fracture with nonunion
S72.335P	Nondisplaced oblique fracture of shaft of left femur, subsequent encounter for closed fracture with malunion
S72.335K	Nondisplaced oblique fracture of shaft of left femur, subsequent encounter for closed fracture with nonunion
S72.335Q	Nondisplaced oblique fracture of shaft of left femur, subsequent encounter for open fracture type I or II with malunion
S72.335M	Nondisplaced oblique fracture of shaft of left femur, subsequent encounter for open fracture type I or II with nonunion
S72.335R	Nondisplaced oblique fracture of shaft of left femur, subsequent encounter for open fracture type IIIA, IIIB, or IIIC with malunion
S72.335N	Nondisplaced oblique fracture of shaft of left femur, subsequent encounter for open fracture type IIIA, IIIB, or IIIC with nonunion
S82.435P	Nondisplaced oblique fracture of shaft of left fibula, subsequent encounter for closed fracture with malunion
S82.435K	Nondisplaced oblique fracture of shaft of left fibula, subsequent encounter for closed fracture with nonunion
S82.435Q	Nondisplaced oblique fracture of shaft of left fibula, subsequent encounter for open fracture type I or II with malunion
S82.435M	Nondisplaced oblique fracture of shaft of left fibula, subsequent encounter for open fracture type I or II with nonunion
S82.435R	Nondisplaced oblique fracture of shaft of left fibula, subsequent encounter for open fracture type IIIA, IIIB, or IIIC with malunion
S82.435N	Nondisplaced oblique fracture of shaft of left fibula, subsequent encounter for open fracture type IIIA, IIIB, or IIIC with nonunion
S52.335A	Nondisplaced oblique fracture of shaft of left radius, initial encounter for closed fracture
S52.335P	Nondisplaced oblique fracture of shaft of left radius, subsequent encounter for closed fracture with malunion
S52.335K	Nondisplaced oblique fracture of shaft of left radius, subsequent encounter for closed fracture with nonunion
S52.335Q	Nondisplaced oblique fracture of shaft of left radius, subsequent encounter for open fracture type I or II with malunion
S52.335M	Nondisplaced oblique fracture of shaft of left radius, subsequent encounter for open fracture type I or II with nonunion
S52.335R	Nondisplaced oblique fracture of shaft of left radius, subsequent encounter for open fracture type IIIA, IIIB, or IIIC with malunion
S52.335N	Nondisplaced oblique fracture of shaft of left radius, subsequent encounter for open fracture type IIIA, IIIB, or IIIC with nonunion
S82.235A	Nondisplaced oblique fracture of shaft of left tibia, initial encounter for closed fracture
S82.235P	Nondisplaced oblique fracture of shaft of left tibia, subsequent encounter for closed fracture with malunion
S82.235K	Nondisplaced oblique fracture of shaft of left tibia, subsequent encounter for closed fracture with nonunion
S82.235Q	Nondisplaced oblique fracture of shaft of left tibia, subsequent encounter for open fracture type I or II with malunion
S82.235M	Nondisplaced oblique fracture of shaft of left tibia, subsequent encounter for open fracture type I or II with nonunion
S82.235R	Nondisplaced oblique fracture of shaft of left tibia, subsequent encounter for open fracture type IIIA, IIIB, or IIIC with malunion
S82.235N	Nondisplaced oblique fracture of shaft of left tibia, subsequent encounter for open fracture type IIIA, IIIB, or IIIC with nonunion
S52.235A	Nondisplaced oblique fracture of shaft of left ulna, initial encounter for closed fracture
S52.235P	Nondisplaced oblique fracture of shaft of left ulna, subsequent encounter for closed fracture with malunion
S52.235K	Nondisplaced oblique fracture of shaft of left ulna, subsequent encounter for closed fracture with nonunion
S52.235Q	Nondisplaced oblique fracture of shaft of left ulna, subsequent encounter for open fracture type I or II with malunion
S52.235M	Nondisplaced oblique fracture of shaft of left ulna, subsequent encounter for open fracture type I or II with nonunion
S52.235R	Nondisplaced oblique fracture of shaft of left ulna, subsequent encounter for open fracture type IIIA, IIIB, or IIIC with malunion
S52.235N	Nondisplaced oblique fracture of shaft of left ulna, subsequent encounter for open fracture type IIIA, IIIB, or IIIC with nonunion
S72.334P	Nondisplaced oblique fracture of shaft of right femur, subsequent encounter for closed fracture with malunion
S72.334K	Nondisplaced oblique fracture of shaft of right femur, subsequent encounter for closed fracture with nonunion
S72.334Q	Nondisplaced oblique fracture of shaft of right femur, subsequent encounter for open fracture type I or II with malunion
S72.334M	Nondisplaced oblique fracture of shaft of right femur, subsequent encounter for open fracture type I or II with nonunion
S72.334R	Nondisplaced oblique fracture of shaft of right femur, subsequent encounter for open fracture type IIIA, IIIB, or IIIC with malunion
S72.334N	Nondisplaced oblique fracture of shaft of right femur, subsequent encounter for open fracture type IIIA, IIIB, or IIIC with nonunion
S82.434P	Nondisplaced oblique fracture of shaft of right fibula, subsequent encounter for closed fracture with malunion
S82.434K	Nondisplaced oblique fracture of shaft of right fibula, subsequent encounter for closed fracture with nonunion
S82.434Q	Nondisplaced oblique fracture of shaft of right fibula, subsequent encounter for open fracture type I or II with malunion
S82.434M	Nondisplaced oblique fracture of shaft of right fibula, subsequent encounter for open fracture type I or II with nonunion
S82.434R	Nondisplaced oblique fracture of shaft of right fibula, subsequent encounter for open fracture type IIIA, IIIB, or IIIC with malunion
S82.434N	Nondisplaced oblique fracture of shaft of right fibula, subsequent encounter for open fracture type IIIA, IIIB, or IIIC with nonunion
S52.334A	Nondisplaced oblique fracture of shaft of right radius, initial encounter for closed fracture
S52.334P	Nondisplaced oblique fracture of shaft of right radius, subsequent encounter for closed fracture with malunion
S52.334K	Nondisplaced oblique fracture of shaft of right radius, subsequent encounter for closed fracture with nonunion
S52.334Q	Nondisplaced oblique fracture of shaft of right radius, subsequent encounter for open fracture type I or II with malunion
S52.334M	Nondisplaced oblique fracture of shaft of right radius, subsequent encounter for open fracture type I or II with nonunion
S52.334R	Nondisplaced oblique fracture of shaft of right radius, subsequent encounter for open fracture type IIIA, IIIB, or IIIC with malunion
S52.334N	Nondisplaced oblique fracture of shaft of right radius, subsequent encounter for open fracture type IIIA, IIIB, or IIIC with nonunion
S82.234A	Nondisplaced oblique fracture of shaft of right tibia, initial encounter for closed fracture
S82.234P	Nondisplaced oblique fracture of shaft of right tibia, subsequent encounter for closed fracture with malunion
S82.234K	Nondisplaced oblique fracture of shaft of right tibia, subsequent encounter for closed fracture with nonunion
S82.234Q	Nondisplaced oblique fracture of shaft of right tibia, subsequent encounter for open fracture type I or II with malunion
S82.234M	Nondisplaced oblique fracture of shaft of right tibia, subsequent encounter for open fracture type I or II with nonunion
S82.234R	Nondisplaced oblique fracture of shaft of right tibia, subsequent encounter for open fracture type IIIA, IIIB, or IIIC with malunion
S82.234N	Nondisplaced oblique fracture of shaft of right tibia, subsequent encounter for open fracture type IIIA, IIIB, or IIIC with nonunion
S52.234A	Nondisplaced oblique fracture of shaft of right ulna, initial encounter for closed fracture
S52.234P	Nondisplaced oblique fracture of shaft of right ulna, subsequent encounter for closed fracture with malunion
S52.234K	Nondisplaced oblique fracture of shaft of right ulna, subsequent encounter for closed fracture with nonunion
S52.234Q	Nondisplaced oblique fracture of shaft of right ulna, subsequent encounter for open fracture type I or II with malunion
S52.234M	Nondisplaced oblique fracture of shaft of right ulna, subsequent encounter for open fracture type I or II with nonunion
S52.234R	Nondisplaced oblique fracture of shaft of right ulna, subsequent encounter for open fracture type IIIA, IIIB, or IIIC with malunion
S52.234N	Nondisplaced oblique fracture of shaft of right ulna, subsequent encounter for open fracture type IIIA, IIIB, or IIIC with nonunion
S72.336P	Nondisplaced oblique fracture of shaft of unspecified femur, subsequent encounter for closed fracture with malunion
S72.336K	Nondisplaced oblique fracture of shaft of unspecified femur, subsequent encounter for closed fracture with nonunion
S72.336Q	Nondisplaced oblique fracture of shaft of unspecified femur, subsequent encounter for open fracture type I or II with malunion
S72.336M	Nondisplaced oblique fracture of shaft of unspecified femur, subsequent encounter for open fracture type I or II with nonunion
S72.336R	Nondisplaced oblique fracture of shaft of unspecified femur, subsequent encounter for open fracture type IIIA, IIIB, or IIIC with malunion
S72.336N	Nondisplaced oblique fracture of shaft of unspecified femur, subsequent encounter for open fracture type IIIA, IIIB, or IIIC with nonunion
S82.436P	Nondisplaced oblique fracture of shaft of unspecified fibula, subsequent encounter for closed fracture with malunion
S82.436K	Nondisplaced oblique fracture of shaft of unspecified fibula, subsequent encounter for closed fracture with nonunion

S82.436Q Nondisplaced oblique fracture of shaft of unspecified fibula, subsequent encounter for open fracture type I or II with malunion

S82.436M Nondisplaced oblique fracture of shaft of unspecified fibula, subsequent encounter for open fracture type I or II with nonunion

S82.436R Nondisplaced oblique fracture of shaft of unspecified fibula, subsequent encounter for open fracture type IIIA, IIIB, or IIIC with malunion

S82.436N Nondisplaced oblique fracture of shaft of unspecified fibula, subsequent encounter for open fracture type IIIA, IIIB, or IIIC with nonunion

S52.336A Nondisplaced oblique fracture of shaft of unspecified radius, initial encounter for closed fracture

S52.336P Nondisplaced oblique fracture of shaft of unspecified radius, subsequent encounter for closed fracture with malunion

S52.336K Nondisplaced oblique fracture of shaft of unspecified radius, subsequent encounter for closed fracture with nonunion

S52.336Q Nondisplaced oblique fracture of shaft of unspecified radius, subsequent encounter for open fracture type I or II with malunion

S52.336M Nondisplaced oblique fracture of shaft of unspecified radius, subsequent encounter for open fracture type I or II with nonunion

S52.336R Nondisplaced oblique fracture of shaft of unspecified radius, subsequent encounter for open fracture type IIIA, IIIB, or IIIC with malunion

S52.336N Nondisplaced oblique fracture of shaft of unspecified radius, subsequent encounter for open fracture type IIIA, IIIB, or IIIC with nonunion

S82.236A Nondisplaced oblique fracture of shaft of unspecified tibia, initial encounter for closed fracture

S82.236P Nondisplaced oblique fracture of shaft of unspecified tibia, subsequent encounter for closed fracture with malunion

S82.236K Nondisplaced oblique fracture of shaft of unspecified tibia, subsequent encounter for closed fracture with nonunion

S82.236Q Nondisplaced oblique fracture of shaft of unspecified tibia, subsequent encounter for open fracture type I or II with malunion

S82.236M Nondisplaced oblique fracture of shaft of unspecified tibia, subsequent encounter for open fracture type I or II with nonunion

S82.236R Nondisplaced oblique fracture of shaft of unspecified tibia, subsequent encounter for open fracture type IIIA, IIIB, or IIIC with malunion

S82.236N Nondisplaced oblique fracture of shaft of unspecified tibia, subsequent encounter for open fracture type IIIA, IIIB, or IIIC with nonunion

S52.236A Nondisplaced oblique fracture of shaft of unspecified ulna, initial encounter for closed fracture

S52.236P Nondisplaced oblique fracture of shaft of unspecified ulna, subsequent encounter for closed fracture with malunion

S52.236K Nondisplaced oblique fracture of shaft of unspecified ulna, subsequent encounter for closed fracture with nonunion

S52.236Q Nondisplaced oblique fracture of shaft of unspecified ulna, subsequent encounter for open fracture type I or II with malunion

S52.236M Nondisplaced oblique fracture of shaft of unspecified ulna, subsequent encounter for open fracture type I or II with nonunion

S52.236R Nondisplaced oblique fracture of shaft of unspecified ulna, subsequent encounter for open fracture type IIIA, IIIB, or IIIC with malunion

S52.236N Nondisplaced oblique fracture of shaft of unspecified ulna, subsequent encounter for open fracture type IIIA, IIIB, or IIIC with nonunion

S82.015A Nondisplaced osteochondral fracture of left patella, initial encounter for closed fracture

S82.015B Nondisplaced osteochondral fracture of left patella, initial encounter for open fracture type I or II

S82.015C Nondisplaced osteochondral fracture of left patella, initial encounter for open fracture type IIIA, IIIB, or IIIC

S82.015P Nondisplaced osteochondral fracture of left patella, subsequent encounter for closed fracture with malunion

S82.015K Nondisplaced osteochondral fracture of left patella, subsequent encounter for closed fracture with nonunion

S82.015Q Nondisplaced osteochondral fracture of left patella, subsequent encounter for open fracture type I or II with malunion

S82.015M Nondisplaced osteochondral fracture of left patella, subsequent encounter for open fracture type I or II with nonunion

S82.015R Nondisplaced osteochondral fracture of left patella, subsequent encounter for open fracture type IIIA, IIIB, or IIIC with malunion

S82.015N Nondisplaced osteochondral fracture of left patella, subsequent encounter for open fracture type IIIA, IIIB, or IIIC with nonunion

S82.014A Nondisplaced osteochondral fracture of right patella, initial encounter for closed fracture

S82.014B Nondisplaced osteochondral fracture of right patella, initial encounter for open fracture type I or II

S82.014C Nondisplaced osteochondral fracture of right patella, initial encounter for open fracture type IIIA, IIIB, or IIIC

S82.014P Nondisplaced osteochondral fracture of right patella, subsequent encounter for closed fracture with malunion

S82.014K Nondisplaced osteochondral fracture of right patella, subsequent encounter for closed fracture with nonunion

S82.014Q Nondisplaced osteochondral fracture of right patella, subsequent encounter for open fracture type I or II with malunion

S82.014M Nondisplaced osteochondral fracture of right patella, subsequent encounter for open fracture type I or II with nonunion

S82.014R Nondisplaced osteochondral fracture of right patella, subsequent encounter for open fracture type IIIA, IIIB, or IIIC with malunion

S82.014N Nondisplaced osteochondral fracture of right patella, subsequent encounter for open fracture type IIIA, IIIB, or IIIC with nonunion

S82.016A Nondisplaced osteochondral fracture of unspecified patella, initial encounter for closed fracture

S82.016B Nondisplaced osteochondral fracture of unspecified patella, initial encounter for open fracture type I or II

S82.016C Nondisplaced osteochondral fracture of unspecified patella, initial encounter for open fracture type IIIA, IIIB, or IIIC

S82.016P Nondisplaced osteochondral fracture of unspecified patella, subsequent encounter for closed fracture with malunion

S82.016K Nondisplaced osteochondral fracture of unspecified patella, subsequent encounter for closed fracture with nonunion

S82.016Q Nondisplaced osteochondral fracture of unspecified patella, subsequent encounter for open fracture type I or II with malunion

S82.016M Nondisplaced osteochondral fracture of unspecified patella, subsequent encounter for open fracture type I or II with nonunion

S82.016R Nondisplaced osteochondral fracture of unspecified patella, subsequent encounter for open fracture type IIIA, IIIB, or IIIC with malunion

S82.016N Nondisplaced osteochondral fracture of unspecified patella, subsequent encounter for open fracture type IIIA, IIIB, or IIIC with nonunion

S92.055B Nondisplaced other extraarticular fracture of left calcaneus, initial encounter for open fracture

S92.055P Nondisplaced other extraarticular fracture of left calcaneus, subsequent encounter for fracture with malunion

S92.055K Nondisplaced other extraarticular fracture of left calcaneus, subsequent encounter for fracture with nonunion

S92.054B Nondisplaced other extraarticular fracture of right calcaneus, initial encounter for open fracture

S92.054P Nondisplaced other extraarticular fracture of right calcaneus, subsequent encounter for fracture with malunion

S92.054K Nondisplaced other extraarticular fracture of right calcaneus, subsequent encounter for fracture with nonunion

S92.056B Nondisplaced other extraarticular fracture of unspecified calcaneus, initial encounter for open fracture

S92.056P Nondisplaced other extraarticular fracture of unspecified calcaneus, subsequent encounter for fracture with malunion

S92.056K Nondisplaced other extraarticular fracture of unspecified calcaneus, subsequent encounter for fracture with nonunion

S92.045B Nondisplaced other fracture of tuberosity of left calcaneus, initial encounter for open fracture

S92.045P Nondisplaced other fracture of tuberosity of left calcaneus, subsequent encounter for fracture with malunion

S92.045K Nondisplaced other fracture of tuberosity of left calcaneus, subsequent encounter for fracture with nonunion

S92.044B Nondisplaced other fracture of tuberosity of right calcaneus, initial encounter for open fracture

S92.044P Nondisplaced other fracture of tuberosity of right calcaneus, subsequent encounter for fracture with malunion

S92.044K Nondisplaced other fracture of tuberosity of right calcaneus, subsequent encounter for fracture with nonunion

S92.046B Nondisplaced other fracture of tuberosity of unspecified calcaneus, initial encounter for open fracture

S92.046P Nondisplaced other fracture of tuberosity of unspecified calcaneus, subsequent encounter for fracture with malunion

S92.046K Nondisplaced other fracture of tuberosity of unspecified calcaneus, subsequent encounter for fracture with nonunion

S82.875B Nondisplaced pilon fracture of left tibia, initial encounter for open fracture type I or II

S82.875C Nondisplaced pilon fracture of left tibia, initial encounter for open fracture type IIIA, IIIB, or IIIC

S82.875P Nondisplaced pilon fracture of left tibia, subsequent encounter for closed fracture with malunion

S82.875K Nondisplaced pilon fracture of left tibia, subsequent encounter for closed fracture with nonunion

S82.875Q Nondisplaced pilon fracture of left tibia, subsequent encounter for open fracture type I or II with malunion

S82.875M Nondisplaced pilon fracture of left tibia, subsequent encounter for open fracture type I or II with nonunion

S82.875R Nondisplaced pilon fracture of left tibia, subsequent encounter for open fracture type IIIA, IIIB, or IIIC with malunion

S82.875N Nondisplaced pilon fracture of left tibia, subsequent encounter for open fracture type IIIA, IIIB, or IIIC with nonunion

S82.874B Nondisplaced pilon fracture of right tibia, initial encounter for open fracture type I or II

S82.874C Nondisplaced pilon fracture of right tibia, initial encounter for open fracture type IIIA, IIIB, or IIIC

S82.874P Nondisplaced pilon fracture of right tibia, subsequent encounter for closed fracture with malunion

S82.874K Nondisplaced pilon fracture of right tibia, subsequent encounter for closed fracture with nonunion

S82.874Q Nondisplaced pilon fracture of right tibia, subsequent encounter for open fracture type I or II with malunion

S82.874M Nondisplaced pilon fracture of right tibia, subsequent encounter for open fracture type I or II with nonunion

S82.874R Nondisplaced pilon fracture of right tibia, subsequent encounter for open fracture type IIIA, IIIB, or IIIC with malunion

S82.874N Nondisplaced pilon fracture of right tibia, subsequent encounter for open fracture type IIIA, IIIB, or IIIC with nonunion

S82.876B Nondisplaced pilon fracture of unspecified tibia, initial encounter for open fracture type I or II

S82.876C Nondisplaced pilon fracture of unspecified tibia, initial encounter for open fracture type IIIA, IIIB, or IIIC

S82.876P Nondisplaced pilon fracture of unspecified tibia, subsequent encounter for closed fracture with malunion

S82.876K Nondisplaced pilon fracture of unspecified tibia, subsequent encounter for closed fracture with nonunion

S82.876Q Nondisplaced pilon fracture of unspecified tibia, subsequent encounter for open fracture type I or II with malunion
S82.876M Nondisplaced pilon fracture of unspecified tibia, subsequent encounter for open fracture type I or II with nonunion
S82.876R Nondisplaced pilon fracture of unspecified tibia, subsequent encounter for open fracture type IIIA, IIIB, or IIIC with malunion
S82.876N Nondisplaced pilon fracture of unspecified tibia, subsequent encounter for open fracture type IIIA, IIIB, or IIIC with nonunion
S12.Ø31A Nondisplaced posterior arch fracture of first cervical vertebra, initial encounter for closed fracture
S12.Ø31K Nondisplaced posterior arch fracture of first cervical vertebra, subsequent encounter for fracture with nonunion
S62.225B Nondisplaced Rolando's fracture, left hand, initial encounter for open fracture
S62.225P Nondisplaced Rolando's fracture, left hand, subsequent encounter for fracture with malunion
S62.225K Nondisplaced Rolando's fracture, left hand, subsequent encounter for fracture with nonunion
S62.224B Nondisplaced Rolando's fracture, right hand, initial encounter for open fracture
S62.224P Nondisplaced Rolando's fracture, right hand, subsequent encounter for fracture with malunion
S62.224K Nondisplaced Rolando's fracture, right hand, subsequent encounter for fracture with nonunion
S62.226B Nondisplaced Rolando's fracture, unspecified hand, initial encounter for open fracture
S62.226P Nondisplaced Rolando's fracture, unspecified hand, subsequent encounter for fracture with malunion
S62.226K Nondisplaced Rolando's fracture, unspecified hand, subsequent encounter for fracture with nonunion
S42.365A Nondisplaced segmental fracture of shaft of humerus, left arm, initial encounter for closed fracture
S42.365P Nondisplaced segmental fracture of shaft of humerus, left arm, subsequent encounter for fracture with malunion
S42.365K Nondisplaced segmental fracture of shaft of humerus, left arm, subsequent encounter for fracture with nonunion
S42.364A Nondisplaced segmental fracture of shaft of humerus, right arm, initial encounter for closed fracture
S42.364P Nondisplaced segmental fracture of shaft of humerus, right arm, subsequent encounter for fracture with malunion
S42.364K Nondisplaced segmental fracture of shaft of humerus, right arm, subsequent encounter for fracture with nonunion
S42.366A Nondisplaced segmental fracture of shaft of humerus, unspecified arm, initial encounter for closed fracture
S42.366P Nondisplaced segmental fracture of shaft of humerus, unspecified arm, subsequent encounter for fracture with malunion
S42.366K Nondisplaced segmental fracture of shaft of humerus, unspecified arm, subsequent encounter for fracture with nonunion
S72.365P Nondisplaced segmental fracture of shaft of left femur, subsequent encounter for closed fracture with malunion
S72.365K Nondisplaced segmental fracture of shaft of left femur, subsequent encounter for closed fracture with nonunion
S72.365Q Nondisplaced segmental fracture of shaft of left femur, subsequent encounter for open fracture type I or II with malunion
S72.365M Nondisplaced segmental fracture of shaft of left femur, subsequent encounter for open fracture type I or II with nonunion
S72.365R Nondisplaced segmental fracture of shaft of left femur, subsequent encounter for open fracture type IIIA, IIIB, or IIIC with malunion
S72.365N Nondisplaced segmental fracture of shaft of left femur, subsequent encounter for open fracture type IIIA, IIIB, or IIIC with nonunion
S82.465P Nondisplaced segmental fracture of shaft of left fibula, subsequent encounter for closed fracture with malunion
S82.465K Nondisplaced segmental fracture of shaft of left fibula, subsequent encounter for closed fracture with nonunion
S82.465Q Nondisplaced segmental fracture of shaft of left fibula, subsequent encounter for open fracture type I or II with malunion
S82.465M Nondisplaced segmental fracture of shaft of left fibula, subsequent encounter for open fracture type I or II with nonunion
S82.465R Nondisplaced segmental fracture of shaft of left fibula, subsequent encounter for open fracture type IIIA, IIIB, or IIIC with malunion
S82.465N Nondisplaced segmental fracture of shaft of left fibula, subsequent encounter for open fracture type IIIA, IIIB, or IIIC with nonunion
S82.265A Nondisplaced segmental fracture of shaft of left tibia, initial encounter for closed fracture
S82.265P Nondisplaced segmental fracture of shaft of left tibia, subsequent encounter for closed fracture with malunion
S82.265K Nondisplaced segmental fracture of shaft of left tibia, subsequent encounter for closed fracture with nonunion
S82.265Q Nondisplaced segmental fracture of shaft of left tibia, subsequent encounter for open fracture type I or II with malunion
S82.265M Nondisplaced segmental fracture of shaft of left tibia, subsequent encounter for open fracture type I or II with nonunion
S82.265R Nondisplaced segmental fracture of shaft of left tibia, subsequent encounter for open fracture type IIIA, IIIB, or IIIC with malunion
S82.265N Nondisplaced segmental fracture of shaft of left tibia, subsequent encounter for open fracture type IIIA, IIIB, or IIIC with nonunion
S52.365A Nondisplaced segmental fracture of shaft of radius, left arm, initial encounter for closed fracture
S52.365P Nondisplaced segmental fracture of shaft of radius, left arm, subsequent encounter for closed fracture with malunion
S52.365K Nondisplaced segmental fracture of shaft of radius, left arm, subsequent encounter for closed fracture with nonunion
S52.365Q Nondisplaced segmental fracture of shaft of radius, left arm, subsequent encounter for open fracture type I or II with malunion
S52.365M Nondisplaced segmental fracture of shaft of radius, left arm, subsequent encounter for open fracture type I or II with nonunion
S52.365R Nondisplaced segmental fracture of shaft of radius, left arm, subsequent encounter for open fracture type IIIA, IIIB, or IIIC with malunion
S52.365N Nondisplaced segmental fracture of shaft of radius, left arm, subsequent encounter for open fracture type IIIA, IIIB, or IIIC with nonunion
S52.364A Nondisplaced segmental fracture of shaft of radius, right arm, initial encounter for closed fracture
S52.364P Nondisplaced segmental fracture of shaft of radius, right arm, subsequent encounter for closed fracture with malunion
S52.364K Nondisplaced segmental fracture of shaft of radius, right arm, subsequent encounter for closed fracture with nonunion
S52.364Q Nondisplaced segmental fracture of shaft of radius, right arm, subsequent encounter for open fracture type I or II with malunion
S52.364M Nondisplaced segmental fracture of shaft of radius, right arm, subsequent encounter for open fracture type I or II with nonunion
S52.364R Nondisplaced segmental fracture of shaft of radius, right arm, subsequent encounter for open fracture type IIIA, IIIB, or IIIC with malunion
S52.364N Nondisplaced segmental fracture of shaft of radius, right arm, subsequent encounter for open fracture type IIIA, IIIB, or IIIC with nonunion
S52.366A Nondisplaced segmental fracture of shaft of radius, unspecified arm, initial encounter for closed fracture
S52.366P Nondisplaced segmental fracture of shaft of radius, unspecified arm, subsequent encounter for closed fracture with malunion
S52.366K Nondisplaced segmental fracture of shaft of radius, unspecified arm, subsequent encounter for closed fracture with nonunion
S52.366Q Nondisplaced segmental fracture of shaft of radius, unspecified arm, subsequent encounter for open fracture type I or II with malunion
S52.366M Nondisplaced segmental fracture of shaft of radius, unspecified arm, subsequent encounter for open fracture type I or II with nonunion
S52.366R Nondisplaced segmental fracture of shaft of radius, unspecified arm, subsequent encounter for open fracture type IIIA, IIIB, or IIIC with malunion
S52.366N Nondisplaced segmental fracture of shaft of radius, unspecified arm, subsequent encounter for open fracture type IIIA, IIIB, or IIIC with nonunion
S72.364P Nondisplaced segmental fracture of shaft of right femur, subsequent encounter for closed fracture with malunion
S72.364K Nondisplaced segmental fracture of shaft of right femur, subsequent encounter for closed fracture with nonunion
S72.364Q Nondisplaced segmental fracture of shaft of right femur, subsequent encounter for open fracture type I or II with malunion
S72.364M Nondisplaced segmental fracture of shaft of right femur, subsequent encounter for open fracture type I or II with nonunion
S72.364R Nondisplaced segmental fracture of shaft of right femur, subsequent encounter for open fracture type IIIA, IIIB, or IIIC with malunion
S72.364N Nondisplaced segmental fracture of shaft of right femur, subsequent encounter for open fracture type IIIA, IIIB, or IIIC with nonunion
S82.464P Nondisplaced segmental fracture of shaft of right fibula, subsequent encounter for closed fracture with malunion
S82.464K Nondisplaced segmental fracture of shaft of right fibula, subsequent encounter for closed fracture with nonunion
S82.464Q Nondisplaced segmental fracture of shaft of right fibula, subsequent encounter for open fracture type I or II with malunion
S82.464M Nondisplaced segmental fracture of shaft of right fibula, subsequent encounter for open fracture type I or II with nonunion
S82.464R Nondisplaced segmental fracture of shaft of right fibula, subsequent encounter for open fracture type IIIA, IIIB, or IIIC with malunion
S82.464N Nondisplaced segmental fracture of shaft of right fibula, subsequent encounter for open fracture type IIIA, IIIB, or IIIC with nonunion
S82.264A Nondisplaced segmental fracture of shaft of right tibia, initial encounter for closed fracture
S82.264P Nondisplaced segmental fracture of shaft of right tibia, subsequent encounter for closed fracture with malunion
S82.264K Nondisplaced segmental fracture of shaft of right tibia, subsequent encounter for closed fracture with nonunion
S82.264Q Nondisplaced segmental fracture of shaft of right tibia, subsequent encounter for open fracture type I or II with malunion
S82.264M Nondisplaced segmental fracture of shaft of right tibia, subsequent encounter for open fracture type I or II with nonunion
S82.264R Nondisplaced segmental fracture of shaft of right tibia, subsequent encounter for open fracture type IIIA, IIIB, or IIIC with malunion
S82.264N Nondisplaced segmental fracture of shaft of right tibia, subsequent encounter for open fracture type IIIA, IIIB, or IIIC with nonunion
S52.265A Nondisplaced segmental fracture of shaft of ulna, left arm, initial encounter for closed fracture
S52.265P Nondisplaced segmental fracture of shaft of ulna, left arm, subsequent encounter for closed fracture with malunion
S52.265K Nondisplaced segmental fracture of shaft of ulna, left arm, subsequent encounter for closed fracture with nonunion
S52.265Q Nondisplaced segmental fracture of shaft of ulna, left arm, subsequent encounter for open fracture type I or II with malunion
S52.265M Nondisplaced segmental fracture of shaft of ulna, left arm, subsequent encounter for open fracture type I or II with nonunion
S52.265R Nondisplaced segmental fracture of shaft of ulna, left arm, subsequent encounter for open fracture type IIIA, IIIB, or IIIC with malunion
S52.265N Nondisplaced segmental fracture of shaft of ulna, left arm, subsequent encounter for open fracture type IIIA, IIIB, or IIIC with nonunion
S52.264A Nondisplaced segmental fracture of shaft of ulna, right arm, initial encounter for closed fracture

S52.264P Nondisplaced segmental fracture of shaft of ulna, right arm, subsequent encounter for closed fracture with malunion

S52.264K Nondisplaced segmental fracture of shaft of ulna, right arm, subsequent encounter for closed fracture with nonunion

S52.264Q Nondisplaced segmental fracture of shaft of ulna, right arm, subsequent encounter for open fracture type I or II with malunion

S52.264M Nondisplaced segmental fracture of shaft of ulna, right arm, subsequent encounter for open fracture type I or II with nonunion

S52.264R Nondisplaced segmental fracture of shaft of ulna, right arm, subsequent encounter for open fracture type IIIA, IIIB, or IIIC with malunion

S52.264N Nondisplaced segmental fracture of shaft of ulna, right arm, subsequent encounter for open fracture type IIIA, IIIB, or IIIC with nonunion

S52.266A Nondisplaced segmental fracture of shaft of ulna, unspecified arm, initial encounter for closed fracture

S52.266P Nondisplaced segmental fracture of shaft of ulna, unspecified arm, subsequent encounter for closed fracture with malunion

S52.266K Nondisplaced segmental fracture of shaft of ulna, unspecified arm, subsequent encounter for closed fracture with nonunion

S52.266Q Nondisplaced segmental fracture of shaft of ulna, unspecified arm, subsequent encounter for open fracture type I or II with malunion

S52.266M Nondisplaced segmental fracture of shaft of ulna, unspecified arm, subsequent encounter for open fracture type I or II with nonunion

S52.266R Nondisplaced segmental fracture of shaft of ulna, unspecified arm, subsequent encounter for open fracture type IIIA, IIIB, or IIIC with malunion

S52.266N Nondisplaced segmental fracture of shaft of ulna, unspecified arm, subsequent encounter for open fracture type IIIA, IIIB, or IIIC with nonunion

S72.366P Nondisplaced segmental fracture of shaft of unspecified femur, subsequent encounter for closed fracture with malunion

S72.366K Nondisplaced segmental fracture of shaft of unspecified femur, subsequent encounter for closed fracture with nonunion

S72.366Q Nondisplaced segmental fracture of shaft of unspecified femur, subsequent encounter for open fracture type I or II with malunion

S72.366M Nondisplaced segmental fracture of shaft of unspecified femur, subsequent encounter for open fracture type I or II with nonunion

S72.366R Nondisplaced segmental fracture of shaft of unspecified femur, subsequent encounter for open fracture type IIIA, IIIB, or IIIC with malunion

S72.366N Nondisplaced segmental fracture of shaft of unspecified femur, subsequent encounter for open fracture type IIIA, IIIB, or IIIC with nonunion

S82.466P Nondisplaced segmental fracture of shaft of unspecified fibula, subsequent encounter for closed fracture with malunion

S82.466K Nondisplaced segmental fracture of shaft of unspecified fibula, subsequent encounter for closed fracture with nonunion

S82.466Q Nondisplaced segmental fracture of shaft of unspecified fibula, subsequent encounter for open fracture type I or II with malunion

S82.466M Nondisplaced segmental fracture of shaft of unspecified fibula, subsequent encounter for open fracture type I or II with nonunion

S82.466R Nondisplaced segmental fracture of shaft of unspecified fibula, subsequent encounter for open fracture type IIIA, IIIB, or IIIC with malunion

S82.466N Nondisplaced segmental fracture of shaft of unspecified fibula, subsequent encounter for open fracture type IIIA, IIIB, or IIIC with nonunion

S82.266A Nondisplaced segmental fracture of shaft of unspecified tibia, initial encounter for closed fracture

S82.266P Nondisplaced segmental fracture of shaft of unspecified tibia, subsequent encounter for closed fracture with malunion

S82.266K Nondisplaced segmental fracture of shaft of unspecified tibia, subsequent encounter for closed fracture with nonunion

S82.266Q Nondisplaced segmental fracture of shaft of unspecified tibia, subsequent encounter for open fracture type I or II with malunion

S82.266M Nondisplaced segmental fracture of shaft of unspecified tibia, subsequent encounter for open fracture type I or II with nonunion

S82.266R Nondisplaced segmental fracture of shaft of unspecified tibia, subsequent encounter for open fracture type IIIA, IIIB, or IIIC with malunion

S82.266N Nondisplaced segmental fracture of shaft of unspecified tibia, subsequent encounter for open fracture type IIIA, IIIB, or IIIC with nonunion

S42.415A Nondisplaced simple supracondylar fracture without intercondylar fracture of left humerus, initial encounter for closed fracture

S42.415P Nondisplaced simple supracondylar fracture without intercondylar fracture of left humerus, subsequent encounter for fracture with malunion

S42.415K Nondisplaced simple supracondylar fracture without intercondylar fracture of left humerus, subsequent encounter for fracture with nonunion

S42.414A Nondisplaced simple supracondylar fracture without intercondylar fracture of right humerus, initial encounter for closed fracture

S42.414P Nondisplaced simple supracondylar fracture without intercondylar fracture of right humerus, subsequent encounter for fracture with malunion

S42.414K Nondisplaced simple supracondylar fracture without intercondylar fracture of right humerus, subsequent encounter for fracture with nonunion

S42.416A Nondisplaced simple supracondylar fracture without intercondylar fracture of unspecified humerus, initial encounter for closed fracture

S42.416P Nondisplaced simple supracondylar fracture without intercondylar fracture of unspecified humerus, subsequent encounter for fracture with malunion

S42.416K Nondisplaced simple supracondylar fracture without intercondylar fracture of unspecified humerus, subsequent encounter for fracture with nonunion

S42.345A Nondisplaced spiral fracture of shaft of humerus, left arm, initial encounter for closed fracture

S42.345P Nondisplaced spiral fracture of shaft of humerus, left arm, subsequent encounter for fracture with malunion

S42.345K Nondisplaced spiral fracture of shaft of humerus, left arm, subsequent encounter for fracture with nonunion

S42.344A Nondisplaced spiral fracture of shaft of humerus, right arm, initial encounter for closed fracture

S42.344P Nondisplaced spiral fracture of shaft of humerus, right arm, subsequent encounter for fracture with malunion

S42.344K Nondisplaced spiral fracture of shaft of humerus, right arm, subsequent encounter for fracture with nonunion

S42.346A Nondisplaced spiral fracture of shaft of humerus, unspecified arm, initial encounter for closed fracture

S42.346P Nondisplaced spiral fracture of shaft of humerus, unspecified arm, subsequent encounter for fracture with malunion

S42.346K Nondisplaced spiral fracture of shaft of humerus, unspecified arm, subsequent encounter for fracture with nonunion

S72.345P Nondisplaced spiral fracture of shaft of left femur, subsequent encounter for closed fracture with malunion

S72.345K Nondisplaced spiral fracture of shaft of left femur, subsequent encounter for closed fracture with nonunion

S72.345Q Nondisplaced spiral fracture of shaft of left femur, subsequent encounter for open fracture type I or II with malunion

S72.345M Nondisplaced spiral fracture of shaft of left femur, subsequent encounter for open fracture type I or II with nonunion

S72.345R Nondisplaced spiral fracture of shaft of left femur, subsequent encounter for open fracture type IIIA, IIIB, or IIIC with malunion

S72.345N Nondisplaced spiral fracture of shaft of left femur, subsequent encounter for open fracture type IIIA, IIIB, or IIIC with nonunion

S82.445P Nondisplaced spiral fracture of shaft of left fibula, subsequent encounter for closed fracture with malunion

S82.445K Nondisplaced spiral fracture of shaft of left fibula, subsequent encounter for closed fracture with nonunion

S82.445Q Nondisplaced spiral fracture of shaft of left fibula, subsequent encounter for open fracture type I or II with malunion

S82.445M Nondisplaced spiral fracture of shaft of left fibula, subsequent encounter for open fracture type I or II with nonunion

S82.445R Nondisplaced spiral fracture of shaft of left fibula, subsequent encounter for open fracture type IIIA, IIIB, or IIIC with malunion

S82.445N Nondisplaced spiral fracture of shaft of left fibula, subsequent encounter for open fracture type IIIA, IIIB, or IIIC with nonunion

S82.245A Nondisplaced spiral fracture of shaft of left tibia, initial encounter for closed fracture

S82.245P Nondisplaced spiral fracture of shaft of left tibia, subsequent encounter for closed fracture with malunion

S82.245K Nondisplaced spiral fracture of shaft of left tibia, subsequent encounter for closed fracture with nonunion

S82.245Q Nondisplaced spiral fracture of shaft of left tibia, subsequent encounter for open fracture type I or II with malunion

S82.245M Nondisplaced spiral fracture of shaft of left tibia, subsequent encounter for open fracture type I or II with nonunion

S82.245R Nondisplaced spiral fracture of shaft of left tibia, subsequent encounter for open fracture type IIIA, IIIB, or IIIC with malunion

S82.245N Nondisplaced spiral fracture of shaft of left tibia, subsequent encounter for open fracture type IIIA, IIIB, or IIIC with nonunion

S52.345A Nondisplaced spiral fracture of shaft of radius, left arm, initial encounter for closed fracture

S52.345P Nondisplaced spiral fracture of shaft of radius, left arm, subsequent encounter for closed fracture with malunion

S52.345K Nondisplaced spiral fracture of shaft of radius, left arm, subsequent encounter for closed fracture with nonunion

S52.345Q Nondisplaced spiral fracture of shaft of radius, left arm, subsequent encounter for open fracture type I or II with malunion

S52.345M Nondisplaced spiral fracture of shaft of radius, left arm, subsequent encounter for open fracture type I or II with nonunion

S52.345R Nondisplaced spiral fracture of shaft of radius, left arm, subsequent encounter for open fracture type IIIA, IIIB, or IIIC with malunion

S52.345N Nondisplaced spiral fracture of shaft of radius, left arm, subsequent encounter for open fracture type IIIA, IIIB, or IIIC with nonunion

S52.344A Nondisplaced spiral fracture of shaft of radius, right arm, initial encounter for closed fracture

S52.344P Nondisplaced spiral fracture of shaft of radius, right arm, subsequent encounter for closed fracture with malunion

S52.344K Nondisplaced spiral fracture of shaft of radius, right arm, subsequent encounter for closed fracture with nonunion

S52.344Q Nondisplaced spiral fracture of shaft of radius, right arm, subsequent encounter for open fracture type I or II with malunion

S52.344M Nondisplaced spiral fracture of shaft of radius, right arm, subsequent encounter for open fracture type I or II with nonunion

S52.344R Nondisplaced spiral fracture of shaft of radius, right arm, subsequent encounter for open fracture type IIIA, IIIB, or IIIC with malunion

S52.344N Nondisplaced spiral fracture of shaft of radius, right arm, subsequent encounter for open fracture type IIIA, IIIB, or IIIC with nonunion

S52.346A Nondisplaced spiral fracture of shaft of radius, unspecified arm, initial encounter for closed fracture

S52.346P Nondisplaced spiral fracture of shaft of radius, unspecified arm, subsequent encounter for closed fracture with malunion

S52.346K Nondisplaced spiral fracture of shaft of radius, unspecified arm, subsequent encounter for closed fracture with nonunion

S52.346Q Nondisplaced spiral fracture of shaft of radius, unspecified arm, subsequent encounter for open fracture type I or II with malunion

S52.346M Nondisplaced spiral fracture of shaft of radius, unspecified arm, subsequent encounter for open fracture type I or II with nonunion

S52.346R Nondisplaced spiral fracture of shaft of radius, unspecified arm, subsequent encounter for open fracture type IIIA, IIIB, or IIIC with malunion

S52.346N Nondisplaced spiral fracture of shaft of radius, unspecified arm, subsequent encounter for open fracture type IIIA, IIIB, or IIIC with nonunion

S72.344P Nondisplaced spiral fracture of shaft of right femur, subsequent encounter for closed fracture with malunion

S72.344K Nondisplaced spiral fracture of shaft of right femur, subsequent encounter for closed fracture with nonunion

S72.344Q Nondisplaced spiral fracture of shaft of right femur, subsequent encounter for open fracture type I or II with malunion

S72.344M Nondisplaced spiral fracture of shaft of right femur, subsequent encounter for open fracture type I or II with nonunion

S72.344R Nondisplaced spiral fracture of shaft of right femur, subsequent encounter for open fracture type IIIA, IIIB, or IIIC with malunion

S72.344N Nondisplaced spiral fracture of shaft of right femur, subsequent encounter for open fracture type IIIA, IIIB, or IIIC with nonunion

S82.444P Nondisplaced spiral fracture of shaft of right fibula, subsequent encounter for closed fracture with malunion

S82.444K Nondisplaced spiral fracture of shaft of right fibula, subsequent encounter for closed fracture with nonunion

S82.444Q Nondisplaced spiral fracture of shaft of right fibula, subsequent encounter for open fracture type I or II with malunion

S82.444M Nondisplaced spiral fracture of shaft of right fibula, subsequent encounter for open fracture type I or II with nonunion

S82.444R Nondisplaced spiral fracture of shaft of right fibula, subsequent encounter for open fracture type IIIA, IIIB, or IIIC with malunion

S82.444N Nondisplaced spiral fracture of shaft of right fibula, subsequent encounter for open fracture type IIIA, IIIB, or IIIC with nonunion

S82.244A Nondisplaced spiral fracture of shaft of right tibia, initial encounter for closed fracture

S82.244P Nondisplaced spiral fracture of shaft of right tibia, subsequent encounter for closed fracture with malunion

S82.244K Nondisplaced spiral fracture of shaft of right tibia, subsequent encounter for closed fracture with nonunion

S82.244Q Nondisplaced spiral fracture of shaft of right tibia, subsequent encounter for open fracture type I or II with malunion

S82.244M Nondisplaced spiral fracture of shaft of right tibia, subsequent encounter for open fracture type I or II with nonunion

S82.244R Nondisplaced spiral fracture of shaft of right tibia, subsequent encounter for open fracture type IIIA, IIIB, or IIIC with malunion

S82.244N Nondisplaced spiral fracture of shaft of right tibia, subsequent encounter for open fracture type IIIA, IIIB, or IIIC with nonunion

S52.245A Nondisplaced spiral fracture of shaft of ulna, left arm, initial encounter for closed fracture

S52.245P Nondisplaced spiral fracture of shaft of ulna, left arm, subsequent encounter for closed fracture with malunion

S52.245K Nondisplaced spiral fracture of shaft of ulna, left arm, subsequent encounter for closed fracture with nonunion

S52.245Q Nondisplaced spiral fracture of shaft of ulna, left arm, subsequent encounter for open fracture type I or II with malunion

S52.245M Nondisplaced spiral fracture of shaft of ulna, left arm, subsequent encounter for open fracture type I or II with nonunion

S52.245R Nondisplaced spiral fracture of shaft of ulna, left arm, subsequent encounter for open fracture type IIIA, IIIB, or IIIC with malunion

S52.245N Nondisplaced spiral fracture of shaft of ulna, left arm, subsequent encounter for open fracture type IIIA, IIIB, or IIIC with nonunion

S52.244A Nondisplaced spiral fracture of shaft of ulna, right arm, initial encounter for closed fracture

S52.244P Nondisplaced spiral fracture of shaft of ulna, right arm, subsequent encounter for closed fracture with malunion

S52.244K Nondisplaced spiral fracture of shaft of ulna, right arm, subsequent encounter for closed fracture with nonunion

S52.244Q Nondisplaced spiral fracture of shaft of ulna, right arm, subsequent encounter for open fracture type I or II with malunion

S52.244M Nondisplaced spiral fracture of shaft of ulna, right arm, subsequent encounter for open fracture type I or II with nonunion

S52.244R Nondisplaced spiral fracture of shaft of ulna, right arm, subsequent encounter for open fracture type IIIA, IIIB, or IIIC with malunion

S52.244N Nondisplaced spiral fracture of shaft of ulna, right arm, subsequent encounter for open fracture type IIIA, IIIB, or IIIC with nonunion

S52.246A Nondisplaced spiral fracture of shaft of ulna, unspecified arm, initial encounter for closed fracture

S52.246P Nondisplaced spiral fracture of shaft of ulna, unspecified arm, subsequent encounter for closed fracture with malunion

S52.246K Nondisplaced spiral fracture of shaft of ulna, unspecified arm, subsequent encounter for closed fracture with nonunion

S52.246Q Nondisplaced spiral fracture of shaft of ulna, unspecified arm, subsequent encounter for open fracture type I or II with malunion

S52.246M Nondisplaced spiral fracture of shaft of ulna, unspecified arm, subsequent encounter for open fracture type I or II with nonunion

S52.246R Nondisplaced spiral fracture of shaft of ulna, unspecified arm, subsequent encounter for open fracture type IIIA, IIIB, or IIIC with malunion

S52.246N Nondisplaced spiral fracture of shaft of ulna, unspecified arm, subsequent encounter for open fracture type IIIA, IIIB, or IIIC with nonunion

S72.346P Nondisplaced spiral fracture of shaft of unspecified femur, subsequent encounter for closed fracture with malunion

S72.346K Nondisplaced spiral fracture of shaft of unspecified femur, subsequent encounter for closed fracture with nonunion

S72.346Q Nondisplaced spiral fracture of shaft of unspecified femur, subsequent encounter for open fracture type I or II with malunion

S72.346M Nondisplaced spiral fracture of shaft of unspecified femur, subsequent encounter for open fracture type I or II with nonunion

S72.346R Nondisplaced spiral fracture of shaft of unspecified femur, subsequent encounter for open fracture type IIIA, IIIB, or IIIC with malunion

S72.346N Nondisplaced spiral fracture of shaft of unspecified femur, subsequent encounter for open fracture type IIIA, IIIB, or IIIC with nonunion

S82.446P Nondisplaced spiral fracture of shaft of unspecified fibula, subsequent encounter for closed fracture with malunion

S82.446K Nondisplaced spiral fracture of shaft of unspecified fibula, subsequent encounter for closed fracture with nonunion

S82.446Q Nondisplaced spiral fracture of shaft of unspecified fibula, subsequent encounter for open fracture type I or II with malunion

S82.446M Nondisplaced spiral fracture of shaft of unspecified fibula, subsequent encounter for open fracture type I or II with nonunion

S82.446R Nondisplaced spiral fracture of shaft of unspecified fibula, subsequent encounter for open fracture type IIIA, IIIB, or IIIC with malunion

S82.446N Nondisplaced spiral fracture of shaft of unspecified fibula, subsequent encounter for open fracture type IIIA, IIIB, or IIIC with nonunion

S82.246A Nondisplaced spiral fracture of shaft of unspecified tibia, initial encounter for closed fracture

S82.246P Nondisplaced spiral fracture of shaft of unspecified tibia, subsequent encounter for closed fracture with malunion

S82.246K Nondisplaced spiral fracture of shaft of unspecified tibia, subsequent encounter for closed fracture with nonunion

S82.246Q Nondisplaced spiral fracture of shaft of unspecified tibia, subsequent encounter for open fracture type I or II with malunion

S82.246M Nondisplaced spiral fracture of shaft of unspecified tibia, subsequent encounter for open fracture type I or II with nonunion

S82.246R Nondisplaced spiral fracture of shaft of unspecified tibia, subsequent encounter for open fracture type IIIA, IIIB, or IIIC with malunion

S82.246N Nondisplaced spiral fracture of shaft of unspecified tibia, subsequent encounter for open fracture type IIIA, IIIB, or IIIC with nonunion

S72.25XP Nondisplaced subtrochanteric fracture of left femur, subsequent encounter for closed fracture with malunion

S72.25XK Nondisplaced subtrochanteric fracture of left femur, subsequent encounter for closed fracture with nonunion

S72.25XQ Nondisplaced subtrochanteric fracture of left femur, subsequent encounter for open fracture type I or II with malunion

S72.25XM Nondisplaced subtrochanteric fracture of left femur, subsequent encounter for open fracture type I or II with nonunion

S72.25XR Nondisplaced subtrochanteric fracture of left femur, subsequent encounter for open fracture type IIIA, IIIB, or IIIC with malunion

S72.25XN Nondisplaced subtrochanteric fracture of left femur, subsequent encounter for open fracture type IIIA, IIIB, or IIIC with nonunion

S72.24XP Nondisplaced subtrochanteric fracture of right femur, subsequent encounter for closed fracture with malunion

S72.24XK Nondisplaced subtrochanteric fracture of right femur, subsequent encounter for closed fracture with nonunion

S72.24XQ Nondisplaced subtrochanteric fracture of right femur, subsequent encounter for open fracture type I or II with malunion

S72.24XM Nondisplaced subtrochanteric fracture of right femur, subsequent encounter for open fracture type I or II with nonunion

S72.24XR Nondisplaced subtrochanteric fracture of right femur, subsequent encounter for open fracture type IIIA, IIIB, or IIIC with malunion

S72.24XN Nondisplaced subtrochanteric fracture of right femur, subsequent encounter for open fracture type IIIA, IIIB, or IIIC with nonunion

S72.26XP Nondisplaced subtrochanteric fracture of unspecified femur, subsequent encounter for closed fracture with malunion

S72.26XK Nondisplaced subtrochanteric fracture of unspecified femur, subsequent encounter for closed fracture with nonunion

S72.26XQ Nondisplaced subtrochanteric fracture of unspecified femur, subsequent encounter for open fracture type I or II with malunion

S72.26XM Nondisplaced subtrochanteric fracture of unspecified femur, subsequent encounter for open fracture type I or II with nonunion

S72.26XR Nondisplaced subtrochanteric fracture of unspecified femur, subsequent encounter for open fracture type IIIA, IIIB, or IIIC with malunion

S72.26XN Nondisplaced subtrochanteric fracture of unspecified femur, subsequent encounter for open fracture type IIIA, IIIB, or IIIC with nonunion

S72.465A Nondisplaced supracondylar fracture with intracondylar extension of lower end of left femur, initial encounter for closed fracture

S72.465P Nondisplaced supracondylar fracture with intracondylar extension of lower end of left femur, subsequent encounter for closed fracture with malunion

S72.465K Nondisplaced supracondylar fracture with intracondylar extension of lower end of left femur, subsequent encounter for closed fracture with nonunion

S72.465Q Nondisplaced supracondylar fracture with intracondylar extension of lower end of left femur, subsequent encounter for open fracture type I or II with malunion

S72.465M Nondisplaced supracondylar fracture with intracondylar extension of lower end of left femur, subsequent encounter for open fracture type I or II with nonunion

S72.465R Nondisplaced supracondylar fracture with intracondylar extension of lower end of left femur, subsequent encounter for open fracture type IIIA, IIIB, or IIIC with malunion

S72.465N Nondisplaced supracondylar fracture with intracondylar extension of lower end of left femur, subsequent encounter for open fracture type IIIA, IIIB, or IIIC with nonunion

S72.464A Nondisplaced supracondylar fracture with intracondylar extension of lower end of right femur, initial encounter for closed fracture

S72.464P Nondisplaced supracondylar fracture with intracondylar extension of lower end of right femur, subsequent encounter for closed fracture with malunion

S72.464K Nondisplaced supracondylar fracture with intracondylar extension of lower end of right femur, subsequent encounter for closed fracture with nonunion

S72.464Q Nondisplaced supracondylar fracture with intracondylar extension of lower end of right femur, subsequent encounter for open fracture type I or II with malunion

S72.464M Nondisplaced supracondylar fracture with intracondylar extension of lower end of right femur, subsequent encounter for open fracture type I or II with nonunion

S72.464R Nondisplaced supracondylar fracture with intracondylar extension of lower end of right femur, subsequent encounter for open fracture type IIIA, IIIB, or IIIC with malunion

S72.464N Nondisplaced supracondylar fracture with intracondylar extension of lower end of right femur, subsequent encounter for open fracture type IIIA, IIIB, or IIIC with nonunion

S72.466A Nondisplaced supracondylar fracture with intracondylar extension of lower end of unspecified femur, initial encounter for closed fracture

S72.466P Nondisplaced supracondylar fracture with intracondylar extension of lower end of unspecified femur, subsequent encounter for closed fracture with malunion

S72.466K Nondisplaced supracondylar fracture with intracondylar extension of lower end of unspecified femur, subsequent encounter for closed fracture with nonunion

S72.466Q Nondisplaced supracondylar fracture with intracondylar extension of lower end of unspecified femur, subsequent encounter for open fracture type I or II with malunion

S72.466M Nondisplaced supracondylar fracture with intracondylar extension of lower end of unspecified femur, subsequent encounter for open fracture type I or II with nonunion

S72.466R Nondisplaced supracondylar fracture with intracondylar extension of lower end of unspecified femur, subsequent encounter for open fracture type IIIA, IIIB, or IIIC with malunion

S72.466N Nondisplaced supracondylar fracture with intracondylar extension of lower end of unspecified femur, subsequent encounter for open fracture type IIIA, IIIB, or IIIC with nonunion

S72.455A Nondisplaced supracondylar fracture without intracondylar extension of lower end of left femur, initial encounter for closed fracture

S72.455P Nondisplaced supracondylar fracture without intracondylar extension of lower end of left femur, subsequent encounter for closed fracture with malunion

S72.455K Nondisplaced supracondylar fracture without intracondylar extension of lower end of left femur, subsequent encounter for closed fracture with nonunion

S72.455Q Nondisplaced supracondylar fracture without intracondylar extension of lower end of left femur, subsequent encounter for open fracture type I or II with malunion

S72.455M Nondisplaced supracondylar fracture without intracondylar extension of lower end of left femur, subsequent encounter for open fracture type I or II with malunion

S72.455R Nondisplaced supracondylar fracture without intracondylar extension of lower end of left femur, subsequent encounter for open fracture type IIIA, IIIB, or IIIC with malunion

S72.455N Nondisplaced supracondylar fracture without intracondylar extension of lower end of left femur, subsequent encounter for open fracture type IIIA, IIIB, or IIIC with nonunion

S72.454A Nondisplaced supracondylar fracture without intracondylar extension of lower end of right femur, initial encounter for closed fracture

S72.454P Nondisplaced supracondylar fracture without intracondylar extension of lower end of right femur, subsequent encounter for closed fracture with malunion

S72.454K Nondisplaced supracondylar fracture without intracondylar extension of lower end of right femur, subsequent encounter for closed fracture with nonunion

S72.454Q Nondisplaced supracondylar fracture without intracondylar extension of lower end of right femur, subsequent encounter for open fracture type I or II with malunion

S72.454M Nondisplaced supracondylar fracture without intracondylar extension of lower end of right femur, subsequent encounter for open fracture type I or II with nonunion

S72.454R Nondisplaced supracondylar fracture without intracondylar extension of lower end of right femur, subsequent encounter for open fracture type IIIA, IIIB, or IIIC with malunion

S72.454N Nondisplaced supracondylar fracture without intracondylar extension of lower end of right femur, subsequent encounter for open fracture type IIIA, IIIB, or IIIC with nonunion

S72.456A Nondisplaced supracondylar fracture without intracondylar extension of lower end of unspecified femur, initial encounter for closed fracture

S72.456P Nondisplaced supracondylar fracture without intracondylar extension of lower end of unspecified femur, subsequent encounter for closed fracture with malunion

S72.456K Nondisplaced supracondylar fracture without intracondylar extension of lower end of unspecified femur, subsequent encounter for closed fracture with nonunion

S72.456Q Nondisplaced supracondylar fracture without intracondylar extension of lower end of unspecified femur, subsequent encounter for open fracture type I or II with malunion

S72.456M Nondisplaced supracondylar fracture without intracondylar extension of lower end of unspecified femur, subsequent encounter for open fracture type I or II with nonunion

S72.456R Nondisplaced supracondylar fracture without intracondylar extension of lower end of unspecified femur, subsequent encounter for open fracture type IIIA, IIIB, or IIIC with malunion

S72.456N Nondisplaced supracondylar fracture without intracondylar extension of lower end of unspecified femur, subsequent encounter for open fracture type IIIA, IIIB, or IIIC with nonunion

S42.475A Nondisplaced transcondylar fracture of left humerus, initial encounter for closed fracture

S42.475P Nondisplaced transcondylar fracture of left humerus, subsequent encounter for fracture with malunion

S42.475K Nondisplaced transcondylar fracture of left humerus, subsequent encounter for fracture with nonunion

S42.474A Nondisplaced transcondylar fracture of right humerus, initial encounter for closed fracture

S42.474P Nondisplaced transcondylar fracture of right humerus, subsequent encounter for fracture with malunion

S42.474K Nondisplaced transcondylar fracture of right humerus, subsequent encounter for fracture with nonunion

S42.476A Nondisplaced transcondylar fracture of unspecified humerus, initial encounter for closed fracture

S42.476P Nondisplaced transcondylar fracture of unspecified humerus, subsequent encounter for fracture with malunion

S42.476K Nondisplaced transcondylar fracture of unspecified humerus, subsequent encounter for fracture with nonunion

S32.455K Nondisplaced transverse fracture of left acetabulum, subsequent encounter for fracture with nonunion

S82.035A Nondisplaced transverse fracture of left patella, initial encounter for closed fracture

S82.035B Nondisplaced transverse fracture of left patella, initial encounter for open fracture type I or II

S82.035C Nondisplaced transverse fracture of left patella, initial encounter for open fracture type IIIA, IIIB, or IIIC

S82.035P Nondisplaced transverse fracture of left patella, subsequent encounter for closed fracture with malunion

S82.035K Nondisplaced transverse fracture of left patella, subsequent encounter for closed fracture with nonunion

S82.035Q Nondisplaced transverse fracture of left patella, subsequent encounter for open fracture type I or II with malunion

S82.035M Nondisplaced transverse fracture of left patella, subsequent encounter for open fracture type I or II with nonunion

S82.035R Nondisplaced transverse fracture of left patella, subsequent encounter for open fracture type IIIA, IIIB, or IIIC with malunion

S82.035N Nondisplaced transverse fracture of left patella, subsequent encounter for open fracture type IIIA, IIIB, or IIIC with nonunion

S32.454K Nondisplaced transverse fracture of right acetabulum, subsequent encounter for fracture with nonunion

S82.034A Nondisplaced transverse fracture of right patella, initial encounter for closed fracture

S82.034B Nondisplaced transverse fracture of right patella, initial encounter for open fracture type I or II

S82.034C Nondisplaced transverse fracture of right patella, initial encounter for open fracture type IIIA, IIIB, or IIIC

S82.034P Nondisplaced transverse fracture of right patella, subsequent encounter for closed fracture with malunion

S82.034K Nondisplaced transverse fracture of right patella, subsequent encounter for closed fracture with nonunion

S82.034Q Nondisplaced transverse fracture of right patella, subsequent encounter for open fracture type I or II with malunion

S82.034M Nondisplaced transverse fracture of right patella, subsequent encounter for open fracture type I or II with nonunion

S82.034R Nondisplaced transverse fracture of right patella, subsequent encounter for open fracture type IIIA, IIIB, or IIIC with malunion

S82.034N Nondisplaced transverse fracture of right patella, subsequent encounter for open fracture type IIIA, IIIB, or IIIC with nonunion

S42.325A Nondisplaced transverse fracture of shaft of humerus, left arm, initial encounter for closed fracture

S42.325P Nondisplaced transverse fracture of shaft of humerus, left arm, subsequent encounter for fracture with malunion

S42.325K Nondisplaced transverse fracture of shaft of humerus, left arm, subsequent encounter for fracture with nonunion

S42.324A Nondisplaced transverse fracture of shaft of humerus, right arm, initial encounter for closed fracture

S42.324P Nondisplaced transverse fracture of shaft of humerus, right arm, subsequent encounter for fracture with malunion

S42.324K Nondisplaced transverse fracture of shaft of humerus, right arm, subsequent encounter for fracture with nonunion

S42.326A Nondisplaced transverse fracture of shaft of humerus, unspecified arm, initial encounter for closed fracture

S42.326P Nondisplaced transverse fracture of shaft of humerus, unspecified arm, subsequent encounter for fracture with malunion

S42.326K Nondisplaced transverse fracture of shaft of humerus, unspecified arm, subsequent encounter for fracture with nonunion

S72.325P Nondisplaced transverse fracture of shaft of left femur, subsequent encounter for closed fracture with malunion

S72.325K Nondisplaced transverse fracture of shaft of left femur, subsequent encounter for closed fracture with nonunion

S72.325Q Nondisplaced transverse fracture of shaft of left femur, subsequent encounter for open fracture type I or II with malunion

S72.325M Nondisplaced transverse fracture of shaft of left femur, subsequent encounter for open fracture type I or II with nonunion

S72.325R Nondisplaced transverse fracture of shaft of left femur, subsequent encounter for open fracture type IIIA, IIIB, or IIIC with malunion

S72.325N Nondisplaced transverse fracture of shaft of left femur, subsequent encounter for open fracture type IIIA, IIIB, or IIIC with nonunion

S82.425P Nondisplaced transverse fracture of shaft of left fibula, subsequent encounter for closed fracture with malunion

S82.425K Nondisplaced transverse fracture of shaft of left fibula, subsequent encounter for closed fracture with nonunion

S82.425Q Nondisplaced transverse fracture of shaft of left fibula, subsequent encounter for open fracture type I or II with malunion

S82.425M Nondisplaced transverse fracture of shaft of left fibula, subsequent encounter for open fracture type I or II with nonunion

S82.425R Nondisplaced transverse fracture of shaft of left fibula, subsequent encounter for open fracture type IIIA, IIIB, or IIIC with malunion

S82.425N Nondisplaced transverse fracture of shaft of left fibula, subsequent encounter for open fracture type IIIA, IIIB, or IIIC with nonunion

S52.325A Nondisplaced transverse fracture of shaft of left radius, initial encounter for closed fracture

S52.325P Nondisplaced transverse fracture of shaft of left radius, subsequent encounter for closed fracture with malunion

S52.325K Nondisplaced transverse fracture of shaft of left radius, subsequent encounter for closed fracture with nonunion

S52.325Q Nondisplaced transverse fracture of shaft of left radius, subsequent encounter for open fracture type I or II with malunion

S52.325M Nondisplaced transverse fracture of shaft of left radius, subsequent encounter for open fracture type I or II with nonunion

S52.325R Nondisplaced transverse fracture of shaft of left radius, subsequent encounter for open fracture type IIIA, IIIB, or IIIC with malunion

S52.325N Nondisplaced transverse fracture of shaft of left radius, subsequent encounter for open fracture type IIIA, IIIB, or IIIC with nonunion

S82.225A Nondisplaced transverse fracture of shaft of left tibia, initial encounter for closed fracture

S82.225P Nondisplaced transverse fracture of shaft of left tibia, subsequent encounter for closed fracture with malunion

S82.225K Nondisplaced transverse fracture of shaft of left tibia, subsequent encounter for closed fracture with nonunion

S82.225Q Nondisplaced transverse fracture of shaft of left tibia, subsequent encounter for open fracture type I or II with malunion

S82.225M Nondisplaced transverse fracture of shaft of left tibia, subsequent encounter for open fracture type I or II with nonunion

S82.225R Nondisplaced transverse fracture of shaft of left tibia, subsequent encounter for open fracture type IIIA, IIIB, or IIIC with malunion

S82.225N Nondisplaced transverse fracture of shaft of left tibia, subsequent encounter for open fracture type IIIA, IIIB, or IIIC with nonunion

S52.225A Nondisplaced transverse fracture of shaft of left ulna, initial encounter for closed fracture

S52.225P Nondisplaced transverse fracture of shaft of left ulna, subsequent encounter for closed fracture with malunion

S52.225K Nondisplaced transverse fracture of shaft of left ulna, subsequent encounter for closed fracture with nonunion

S52.225Q Nondisplaced transverse fracture of shaft of left ulna, subsequent encounter for open fracture type I or II with malunion

S52.225M Nondisplaced transverse fracture of shaft of left ulna, subsequent encounter for open fracture type I or II with nonunion

S52.225R Nondisplaced transverse fracture of shaft of left ulna, subsequent encounter for open fracture type IIIA, IIIB, or IIIC with malunion

S52.225N Nondisplaced transverse fracture of shaft of left ulna, subsequent encounter for open fracture type IIIA, IIIB, or IIIC with nonunion

S72.324P Nondisplaced transverse fracture of shaft of right femur, subsequent encounter for closed fracture with malunion

S72.324K Nondisplaced transverse fracture of shaft of right femur, subsequent encounter for closed fracture with nonunion

S72.324Q Nondisplaced transverse fracture of shaft of right femur, subsequent encounter for open fracture type I or II with malunion

S72.324M Nondisplaced transverse fracture of shaft of right femur, subsequent encounter for open fracture type I or II with nonunion

S72.324R Nondisplaced transverse fracture of shaft of right femur, subsequent encounter for open fracture type IIIA, IIIB, or IIIC with malunion

S72.324N Nondisplaced transverse fracture of shaft of right femur, subsequent encounter for open fracture type IIIA, IIIB, or IIIC with nonunion

S82.424P Nondisplaced transverse fracture of shaft of right fibula, subsequent encounter for closed fracture with malunion

S82.424K Nondisplaced transverse fracture of shaft of right fibula, subsequent encounter for closed fracture with nonunion

S82.424Q Nondisplaced transverse fracture of shaft of right fibula, subsequent encounter for open fracture type I or II with malunion

S82.424M Nondisplaced transverse fracture of shaft of right fibula, subsequent encounter for open fracture type I or II with nonunion

S82.424R Nondisplaced transverse fracture of shaft of right fibula, subsequent encounter for open fracture type IIIA, IIIB, or IIIC with malunion

S82.424N Nondisplaced transverse fracture of shaft of right fibula, subsequent encounter for open fracture type IIIA, IIIB, or IIIC with nonunion

S52.324A Nondisplaced transverse fracture of shaft of right radius, initial encounter for closed fracture

S52.324P Nondisplaced transverse fracture of shaft of right radius, subsequent encounter for closed fracture with malunion

S52.324K Nondisplaced transverse fracture of shaft of right radius, subsequent encounter for closed fracture with nonunion

S52.324Q Nondisplaced transverse fracture of shaft of right radius, subsequent encounter for open fracture type I or II with malunion

S52.324M Nondisplaced transverse fracture of shaft of right radius, subsequent encounter for open fracture type I or II with nonunion

S52.324R Nondisplaced transverse fracture of shaft of right radius, subsequent encounter for open fracture type IIIA, IIIB, or IIIC with malunion

S52.324N Nondisplaced transverse fracture of shaft of right radius, subsequent encounter for open fracture type IIIA, IIIB, or IIIC with nonunion

S82.224A Nondisplaced transverse fracture of shaft of right tibia, initial encounter for closed fracture

S82.224P Nondisplaced transverse fracture of shaft of right tibia, subsequent encounter for closed fracture with malunion

S82.224K Nondisplaced transverse fracture of shaft of right tibia, subsequent encounter for closed fracture with nonunion

S82.224Q Nondisplaced transverse fracture of shaft of right tibia, subsequent encounter for open fracture type I or II with malunion

S82.224M Nondisplaced transverse fracture of shaft of right tibia, subsequent encounter for open fracture type I or II with nonunion

S82.224R Nondisplaced transverse fracture of shaft of right tibia, subsequent encounter for open fracture type IIIA, IIIB, or IIIC with malunion

S82.224N Nondisplaced transverse fracture of shaft of right tibia, subsequent encounter for open fracture type IIIA, IIIB, or IIIC with nonunion

S52.224A Nondisplaced transverse fracture of shaft of right ulna, initial encounter for closed fracture

S52.224P Nondisplaced transverse fracture of shaft of right ulna, subsequent encounter for closed fracture with malunion

S52.224K Nondisplaced transverse fracture of shaft of right ulna, subsequent encounter for closed fracture with nonunion

S52.224Q Nondisplaced transverse fracture of shaft of right ulna, subsequent encounter for open fracture type I or II with malunion

S52.224M Nondisplaced transverse fracture of shaft of right ulna, subsequent encounter for open fracture type I or II with nonunion

S52.224R Nondisplaced transverse fracture of shaft of right ulna, subsequent encounter for open fracture type IIIA, IIIB, or IIIC with malunion

S52.224N Nondisplaced transverse fracture of shaft of right ulna, subsequent encounter for open fracture type IIIA, IIIB, or IIIC with nonunion

S72.326P Nondisplaced transverse fracture of shaft of unspecified femur, subsequent encounter for closed fracture with malunion

S72.326K Nondisplaced transverse fracture of shaft of unspecified femur, subsequent encounter for closed fracture with nonunion

S72.326Q Nondisplaced transverse fracture of shaft of unspecified femur, subsequent encounter for open fracture type I or II with malunion

S72.326M Nondisplaced transverse fracture of shaft of unspecified femur, subsequent encounter for open fracture type I or II with nonunion

S72.326R Nondisplaced transverse fracture of shaft of unspecified femur, subsequent encounter for open fracture type IIIA, IIIB, or IIIC with malunion

S72.326N Nondisplaced transverse fracture of shaft of unspecified femur, subsequent encounter for open fracture type IIIA, IIIB, or IIIC with nonunion

S82.426P Nondisplaced transverse fracture of shaft of unspecified fibula, subsequent encounter for closed fracture with malunion

S82.426K Nondisplaced transverse fracture of shaft of unspecified fibula, subsequent encounter for closed fracture with nonunion

S82.426Q Nondisplaced transverse fracture of shaft of unspecified fibula, subsequent encounter for open fracture type I or II with malunion

S82.426M Nondisplaced transverse fracture of shaft of unspecified fibula, subsequent encounter for open fracture type I or II with nonunion

S82.426R Nondisplaced transverse fracture of shaft of unspecified fibula, subsequent encounter for open fracture type IIIA, IIIB, or IIIC with malunion

S82.426N Nondisplaced transverse fracture of shaft of unspecified fibula, subsequent encounter for open fracture type IIIA, IIIB, or IIIC with nonunion

S52.326A Nondisplaced transverse fracture of shaft of unspecified radius, initial encounter for closed fracture

S52.326P Nondisplaced transverse fracture of shaft of unspecified radius, subsequent encounter for closed fracture with malunion

S52.326K Nondisplaced transverse fracture of shaft of unspecified radius, subsequent encounter for closed fracture with nonunion

S52.326Q Nondisplaced transverse fracture of shaft of unspecified radius, subsequent encounter for open fracture type I or II with malunion

S52.326M Nondisplaced transverse fracture of shaft of unspecified radius, subsequent encounter for open fracture type I or II with nonunion

S52.326R Nondisplaced transverse fracture of shaft of unspecified radius, subsequent encounter for open fracture type IIIA, IIIB, or IIIC with malunion

S52.326N Nondisplaced transverse fracture of shaft of unspecified radius, subsequent encounter for open fracture type IIIA, IIIB, or IIIC with nonunion

S82.226A Nondisplaced transverse fracture of shaft of unspecified tibia, initial encounter for closed fracture

S82.226P Nondisplaced transverse fracture of shaft of unspecified tibia, subsequent encounter for closed fracture with malunion

S82.226K Nondisplaced transverse fracture of shaft of unspecified tibia, subsequent encounter for closed fracture with nonunion

S82.226Q Nondisplaced transverse fracture of shaft of unspecified tibia, subsequent encounter for open fracture type I or II with malunion

S82.226M Nondisplaced transverse fracture of shaft of unspecified tibia, subsequent encounter for open fracture type I or II with nonunion

S82.226R Nondisplaced transverse fracture of shaft of unspecified tibia, subsequent encounter for open fracture type IIIA, IIIB, or IIIC with malunion

S82.226N Nondisplaced transverse fracture of shaft of unspecified tibia, subsequent encounter for open fracture type IIIA, IIIB, or IIIC with nonunion

S52.226A Nondisplaced transverse fracture of shaft of unspecified ulna, initial encounter for closed fracture

S52.226P Nondisplaced transverse fracture of shaft of unspecified ulna, subsequent encounter for closed fracture with malunion

S52.226K Nondisplaced transverse fracture of shaft of unspecified ulna, subsequent encounter for closed fracture with nonunion

S52.226Q Nondisplaced transverse fracture of shaft of unspecified ulna, subsequent encounter for open fracture type I or II with malunion

S52.226M Nondisplaced transverse fracture of shaft of unspecified ulna, subsequent encounter for open fracture type I or II with nonunion

S52.226R Nondisplaced transverse fracture of shaft of unspecified ulna, subsequent encounter for open fracture type IIIA, IIIB, or IIIC with malunion

S52.226N Nondisplaced transverse fracture of shaft of unspecified ulna, subsequent encounter for open fracture type IIIA, IIIB, or IIIC with nonunion

S32.456K Nondisplaced transverse fracture of unspecified acetabulum, subsequent encounter for fracture with nonunion

S82.036A Nondisplaced transverse fracture of unspecified patella, initial encounter for closed fracture

S82.036B Nondisplaced transverse fracture of unspecified patella, initial encounter for open fracture type I or II

S82.036C Nondisplaced transverse fracture of unspecified patella, initial encounter for open fracture type IIIA, IIIB, or IIIC

S82.036P Nondisplaced transverse fracture of unspecified patella, subsequent encounter for closed fracture with malunion

S82.036K Nondisplaced transverse fracture of unspecified patella, subsequent encounter for closed fracture with nonunion

S82.036Q Nondisplaced transverse fracture of unspecified patella, subsequent encounter for open fracture type I or II with malunion

S82.036M Nondisplaced transverse fracture of unspecified patella, subsequent encounter for open fracture type I or II with nonunion

S82.036R Nondisplaced transverse fracture of unspecified patella, subsequent encounter for open fracture type IIIA, IIIB, or IIIC with malunion

S82.036N Nondisplaced transverse fracture of unspecified patella, subsequent encounter for open fracture type IIIA, IIIB, or IIIC with nonunion

S82.855B Nondisplaced trimalleolar fracture of left lower leg, initial encounter for open fracture type I or II

S82.855C Nondisplaced trimalleolar fracture of left lower leg, initial encounter for open fracture type IIIA, IIIB, or IIIC

S82.855P Nondisplaced trimalleolar fracture of left lower leg, subsequent encounter for closed fracture with malunion

S82.855K Nondisplaced trimalleolar fracture of left lower leg, subsequent encounter for closed fracture with nonunion

S82.855Q Nondisplaced trimalleolar fracture of left lower leg, subsequent encounter for open fracture type I or II with malunion

S82.855M Nondisplaced trimalleolar fracture of left lower leg, subsequent encounter for open fracture type I or II with nonunion

S82.855R Nondisplaced trimalleolar fracture of left lower leg, subsequent encounter for open fracture type IIIA, IIIB, or IIIC with malunion

S82.855N Nondisplaced trimalleolar fracture of left lower leg, subsequent encounter for open fracture type IIIA, IIIB, or IIIC with nonunion

S82.854B Nondisplaced trimalleolar fracture of right lower leg, initial encounter for open fracture type I or II

S82.854C Nondisplaced trimalleolar fracture of right lower leg, initial encounter for open fracture type IIIA, IIIB, or IIIC

S82.854P Nondisplaced trimalleolar fracture of right lower leg, subsequent encounter for closed fracture with malunion

S82.854K Nondisplaced trimalleolar fracture of right lower leg, subsequent encounter for closed fracture with nonunion

S82.854Q Nondisplaced trimalleolar fracture of right lower leg, subsequent encounter for open fracture type I or II with malunion

S82.854M Nondisplaced trimalleolar fracture of right lower leg, subsequent encounter for open fracture type I or II with nonunion

S82.854R Nondisplaced trimalleolar fracture of right lower leg, subsequent encounter for open fracture type IIIA, IIIB, or IIIC with malunion

S82.854N Nondisplaced trimalleolar fracture of right lower leg, subsequent encounter for open fracture type IIIA, IIIB, or IIIC with nonunion

S82.856B Nondisplaced trimalleolar fracture of unspecified lower leg, initial encounter for open fracture type I or II

S82.856C Nondisplaced trimalleolar fracture of unspecified lower leg, initial encounter for open fracture type IIIA, IIIB, or IIIC

S82.856P Nondisplaced trimalleolar fracture of unspecified lower leg, subsequent encounter for closed fracture with malunion

S82.856K Nondisplaced trimalleolar fracture of unspecified lower leg, subsequent encounter for closed fracture with nonunion

S82.856Q Nondisplaced trimalleolar fracture of unspecified lower leg, subsequent encounter for open fracture type I or II with malunion

S82.856M Nondisplaced trimalleolar fracture of unspecified lower leg, subsequent encounter for open fracture type I or II with nonunion

S82.856R Nondisplaced trimalleolar fracture of unspecified lower leg, subsequent encounter for open fracture type IIIA, IIIB, or IIIC with malunion

S82.856N Nondisplaced trimalleolar fracture of unspecified lower leg, subsequent encounter for open fracture type IIIA, IIIB, or IIIC with nonunion

S12.112A Nondisplaced Type II dens fracture, initial encounter for closed fracture

S12.112K Nondisplaced Type II dens fracture, subsequent encounter for fracture with nonunion

S72.415A Nondisplaced unspecified condyle fracture of lower end of left femur, initial encounter for closed fracture

S72.415P Nondisplaced unspecified condyle fracture of lower end of left femur, subsequent encounter for closed fracture with malunion

S72.415K Nondisplaced unspecified condyle fracture of lower end of left femur, subsequent encounter for closed fracture with nonunion

S72.415Q Nondisplaced unspecified condyle fracture of lower end of left femur, subsequent encounter for open fracture type I or II with malunion

S72.415M Nondisplaced unspecified condyle fracture of lower end of left femur, subsequent encounter for open fracture type I or II with nonunion

S72.415R Nondisplaced unspecified condyle fracture of lower end of left femur, subsequent encounter for open fracture type IIIA, IIIB, or IIIC with malunion

S72.415N Nondisplaced unspecified condyle fracture of lower end of left femur, subsequent encounter for open fracture type IIIA, IIIB, or IIIC with nonunion

S72.414A Nondisplaced unspecified condyle fracture of lower end of right femur, initial encounter for closed fracture

S72.414P Nondisplaced unspecified condyle fracture of lower end of right femur, subsequent encounter for closed fracture with malunion

S72.414K Nondisplaced unspecified condyle fracture of lower end of right femur, subsequent encounter for closed fracture with nonunion

S72.414Q Nondisplaced unspecified condyle fracture of lower end of right femur, subsequent encounter for open fracture type I or II with malunion

S72.414M Nondisplaced unspecified condyle fracture of lower end of right femur, subsequent encounter for open fracture type I or II with nonunion

S72.414R Nondisplaced unspecified condyle fracture of lower end of right femur, subsequent encounter for open fracture type IIIA, IIIB, or IIIC with malunion

S72.414N Nondisplaced unspecified condyle fracture of lower end of right femur, subsequent encounter for open fracture type IIIA, IIIB, or IIIC with nonunion

S72.416A Nondisplaced unspecified condyle fracture of lower end of unspecified femur, initial encounter for closed fracture

S72.416P Nondisplaced unspecified condyle fracture of lower end of unspecified femur, subsequent encounter for closed fracture with malunion

S72.416K Nondisplaced unspecified condyle fracture of lower end of unspecified femur, subsequent encounter for closed fracture with nonunion

S72.416Q Nondisplaced unspecified condyle fracture of lower end of unspecified femur, subsequent encounter for open fracture type I or II with malunion

S72.416M Nondisplaced unspecified condyle fracture of lower end of unspecified femur, subsequent encounter for open fracture type I or II with nonunion

S72.416R Nondisplaced unspecified condyle fracture of lower end of unspecified femur, subsequent encounter for open fracture type IIIA, IIIB, or IIIC with malunion

S72.416N Nondisplaced unspecified condyle fracture of lower end of unspecified femur, subsequent encounter for open fracture type IIIA, IIIB, or IIIC with nonunion

S92.405P Nondisplaced unspecified fracture of left great toe, subsequent encounter for fracture with malunion

S92.405K Nondisplaced unspecified fracture of left great toe, subsequent encounter for fracture with nonunion

S92.505P Nondisplaced unspecified fracture of left lesser toe(s), subsequent encounter for fracture with malunion

S92.505K Nondisplaced unspecified fracture of left lesser toe(s), subsequent encounter for fracture with nonunion

S92.404P Nondisplaced unspecified fracture of right great toe, subsequent encounter for fracture with malunion

S92.404K Nondisplaced unspecified fracture of right great toe, subsequent encounter for fracture with nonunion

S92.504P Nondisplaced unspecified fracture of right lesser toe(s), subsequent encounter for fracture with malunion

S92.504K Nondisplaced unspecified fracture of right lesser toe(s), subsequent encounter for fracture with nonunion

S92.406P Nondisplaced unspecified fracture of unspecified great toe, subsequent encounter for fracture with malunion

S92.406K Nondisplaced unspecified fracture of unspecified great toe, subsequent encounter for fracture with nonunion

S92.506P Nondisplaced unspecified fracture of unspecified lesser toe(s), subsequent encounter for fracture with malunion

S92.506K Nondisplaced unspecified fracture of unspecified lesser toe(s), subsequent encounter for fracture with nonunion

S32.110A Nondisplaced Zone I fracture of sacrum, initial encounter for closed fracture

S32.110K Nondisplaced Zone I fracture of sacrum, subsequent encounter for fracture with nonunion

S32.120A Nondisplaced Zone II fracture of sacrum, initial encounter for closed fracture

S32.120K Nondisplaced Zone II fracture of sacrum, subsequent encounter for fracture with nonunion

S32.130A Nondisplaced Zone III fracture of sacrum, initial encounter for closed fracture

S32.130K Nondisplaced Zone III fracture of sacrum, subsequent encounter for fracture with nonunion

D80.1 Nonfamilial hypogammaglobulinemia

I67.6 Nonpyogenic thrombosis of intracranial venous system

M79.A3 Nontraumatic compartment syndrome of abdomen

M79.A22 Nontraumatic compartment syndrome of left lower extremity

M79.A12 Nontraumatic compartment syndrome of left upper extremity

M79.A9 Nontraumatic compartment syndrome of other sites

M79.A21 Nontraumatic compartment syndrome of right lower extremity

M79.A11 Nontraumatic compartment syndrome of right upper extremity

M79.A29 Nontraumatic compartment syndrome of unspecified lower extremity

M79.A19 Nontraumatic compartment syndrome of unspecified upper extremity

I62.9 Nontraumatic intracranial hemorrhage, unspecified

A92.1 O'nyong-nyong fever

O71.6 Obstetric damage to pelvic joints and ligaments

O71.7 Obstetric hematoma of pelvis

O71.4 Obstetric high vaginal laceration alone

O71.3 Obstetric laceration of cervix

A34 Obstetrical tetanus

T81.526A Obstruction due to foreign body accidentally left in body following aspiration, puncture or other catheterization, initial encounter

T81.524A Obstruction due to foreign body accidentally left in body following endoscopic examination, initial encounter

T81.525A Obstruction due to foreign body accidentally left in body following heart catheterization, initial encounter

T81.521A Obstruction due to foreign body accidentally left in body following infusion or transfusion, initial encounter

T81.523A Obstruction due to foreign body accidentally left in body following injection or immunization, initial encounter

T81.522A Obstruction due to foreign body accidentally left in body following kidney dialysis, initial encounter

T81.528A Obstruction due to foreign body accidentally left in body following other procedure, initial encounter

T81.527A Obstruction due to foreign body accidentally left in body following removal of catheter or packing, initial encounter

T81.520A	Obstruction due to foreign body accidentally left in body following surgical operation, initial encounter
T81.529A	Obstruction due to foreign body accidentally left in body following unspecified procedure, initial encounter
K31.5	Obstruction of duodenum
K82.0	Obstruction of gallbladder
G91.1	Obstructive hydrocephalus
I42.1	Obstructive hypertrophic cardiomyopathy
S73.025A	Obturator dislocation of left hip, initial encounter
S73.024A	Obturator dislocation of right hip, initial encounter
S73.026A	Obturator dislocation of unspecified hip, initial encounter
S73.022A	Obturator subluxation of left hip, initial encounter
S73.021A	Obturator subluxation of right hip, initial encounter
S73.023A	Obturator subluxation of unspecified hip, initial encounter
Q01.2	Occipital encephalocele
E70.319	Ocular albinism, unspecified
S05.22XA	Ocular laceration and rupture with prolapse or loss of intraocular tissue, left eye, initial encounter
S05.21XA	Ocular laceration and rupture with prolapse or loss of intraocular tissue, right eye, initial encounter
S05.20XA	Ocular laceration and rupture with prolapse or loss of intraocular tissue, unspecified eye, initial encounter
S05.32XA	Ocular laceration without prolapse or loss of intraocular tissue, left eye, initial encounter
S05.31XA	Ocular laceration without prolapse or loss of intraocular tissue, right eye, initial encounter
S05.30XA	Ocular laceration without prolapse or loss of intraocular tissue, unspecified eye, initial encounter
E70.329	Oculocutaneous albinism, unspecified
A32.81	Oculoglandular listeriosis
A21.1	Oculoglandular tularemia
O41.01X1	Oligohydramnios, first trimester, fetus 1
O41.01X2	Oligohydramnios, first trimester, fetus 2
O41.01X3	Oligohydramnios, first trimester, fetus 3
O41.01X4	Oligohydramnios, first trimester, fetus 4
O41.01X5	Oligohydramnios, first trimester, fetus 5
O41.01X0	Oligohydramnios, first trimester, not applicable or unspecified
O41.01X9	Oligohydramnios, first trimester, other fetus
O41.02X1	Oligohydramnios, second trimester, fetus 1
O41.02X2	Oligohydramnios, second trimester, fetus 2
O41.02X3	Oligohydramnios, second trimester, fetus 3
O41.02X4	Oligohydramnios, second trimester, fetus 4
O41.02X5	Oligohydramnios, second trimester, fetus 5
O41.02X0	Oligohydramnios, second trimester, not applicable or unspecified
O41.02X9	Oligohydramnios, second trimester, other fetus
O41.03X1	Oligohydramnios, third trimester, fetus 1
O41.03X2	Oligohydramnios, third trimester, fetus 2
O41.03X3	Oligohydramnios, third trimester, fetus 3
O41.03X4	Oligohydramnios, third trimester, fetus 4
O41.03X5	Oligohydramnios, third trimester, fetus 5
O41.03X0	Oligohydramnios, third trimester, not applicable or unspecified
O41.03X9	Oligohydramnios, third trimester, other fetus
P38.1	Omphalitis with mild hemorrhage
P38.9	Omphalitis without hemorrhage
A98.1	Omsk hemorrhagic fever
B73.01	Onchocerciasis with endophthalmitis
B73.00	Onchocerciasis with eye involvement, unspecified
B73.02	Onchocerciasis with glaucoma
B73.09	Onchocerciasis with other eye involvement
B73.1	Onchocerciasis without eye disease
S21.152A	Open bite of left front wall of thorax without penetration into thoracic cavity, initial encounter
S11.25XA	Open bite of pharynx and cervical esophagus, initial encounter
S21.151A	Open bite of right front wall of thorax without penetration into thoracic cavity, initial encounter
S11.15XA	Open bite of thyroid gland, initial encounter
S21.159A	Open bite of unspecified front wall of thorax without penetration into thoracic cavity, initial encounter
S21.95XA	Open bite of unspecified part of thorax, initial encounter
F11.121	Opioid abuse with intoxication delirium
F11.150	Opioid abuse with opioid-induced psychotic disorder with delusions
F11.151	Opioid abuse with opioid-induced psychotic disorder with hallucinations
F11.221	Opioid dependence with intoxication delirium
F11.222	Opioid dependence with intoxication with perceptual disturbance
F11.250	Opioid dependence with opioid-induced psychotic disorder with delusions
F11.251	Opioid dependence with opioid-induced psychotic disorder with hallucinations
F11.259	Opioid dependence with opioid-induced psychotic disorder, unspecified
F11.281	Opioid dependence with opioid-induced sexual dysfunction
F11.282	Opioid dependence with opioid-induced sleep disorder
F11.288	Opioid dependence with other opioid-induced disorder
F11.23	Opioid dependence with withdrawal
F11.20	Opioid dependence, uncomplicated
F11.921	Opioid use, unspecified with intoxication delirium
F11.950	Opioid use, unspecified with opioid-induced psychotic disorder with delusions
F11.951	Opioid use, unspecified with opioid-induced psychotic disorder with hallucinations
F11.93	Opioid use, unspecified with withdrawal
B66.0	Opisthorchiasis
H46.03	Optic papillitis, bilateral
H46.02	Optic papillitis, left eye
H46.01	Optic papillitis, right eye
H46.00	Optic papillitis, unspecified eye
E85.4	Organ-limited amyloidosis
A93.0	Oropouche virus disease
B45.3	Osseous cryptococcosis
Q78.0	Osteogenesis imperfecta
H05.023	Osteomyelitis of bilateral orbits
H05.022	Osteomyelitis of left orbit
H05.021	Osteomyelitis of right orbit
H05.029	Osteomyelitis of unspecified orbit
M46.22	Osteomyelitis of vertebra, cervical region
M46.23	Osteomyelitis of vertebra, cervicothoracic region
M46.26	Osteomyelitis of vertebra, lumbar region
M46.27	Osteomyelitis of vertebra, lumbosacral region
M46.21	Osteomyelitis of vertebra, occipito-atlanto-axial region
M46.28	Osteomyelitis of vertebra, sacral and sacrococcygeal region
M46.20	Osteomyelitis of vertebra, site unspecified
M46.24	Osteomyelitis of vertebra, thoracic region
M46.25	Osteomyelitis of vertebra, thoracolumbar region
M86.9	Osteomyelitis, unspecified
M87.138	Osteonecrosis due to drugs of left carpus
M87.132	Osteonecrosis due to drugs of left radius
M87.135	Osteonecrosis due to drugs of left ulna
M87.137	Osteonecrosis due to drugs of right carpus
M87.131	Osteonecrosis due to drugs of right radius
M87.134	Osteonecrosis due to drugs of right ulna
M87.139	Osteonecrosis due to drugs of unspecified carpus
M87.133	Osteonecrosis due to drugs of unspecified radius
M87.136	Osteonecrosis due to drugs of unspecified ulna
M87.180	Osteonecrosis due to drugs, jaw
M87.172	Osteonecrosis due to drugs, left ankle
M87.152	Osteonecrosis due to drugs, left femur
M87.165	Osteonecrosis due to drugs, left fibula
M87.145	Osteonecrosis due to drugs, left finger(s)
M87.175	Osteonecrosis due to drugs, left foot
M87.142	Osteonecrosis due to drugs, left hand
M87.122	Osteonecrosis due to drugs, left humerus
M87.112	Osteonecrosis due to drugs, left shoulder
M87.162	Osteonecrosis due to drugs, left tibia
M87.178	Osteonecrosis due to drugs, left toe(s)
M87.19	Osteonecrosis due to drugs, multiple sites
M87.188	Osteonecrosis due to drugs, other site
M87.150	Osteonecrosis due to drugs, pelvis
M87.171	Osteonecrosis due to drugs, right ankle
M87.151	Osteonecrosis due to drugs, right femur
M87.164	Osteonecrosis due to drugs, right fibula
M87.144	Osteonecrosis due to drugs, right finger(s)
M87.174	Osteonecrosis due to drugs, right foot
M87.141	Osteonecrosis due to drugs, right hand
M87.121	Osteonecrosis due to drugs, right humerus
M87.111	Osteonecrosis due to drugs, right shoulder
M87.161	Osteonecrosis due to drugs, right tibia
M87.177	Osteonecrosis due to drugs, right toe(s)
M87.173	Osteonecrosis due to drugs, unspecified ankle
M87.10	Osteonecrosis due to drugs, unspecified bone
M87.159	Osteonecrosis due to drugs, unspecified femur
M87.166	Osteonecrosis due to drugs, unspecified fibula
M87.146	Osteonecrosis due to drugs, unspecified finger(s)
M87.176	Osteonecrosis due to drugs, unspecified foot
M87.143	Osteonecrosis due to drugs, unspecified hand
M87.129	Osteonecrosis due to drugs, unspecified humerus
M87.119	Osteonecrosis due to drugs, unspecified shoulder
M87.163	Osteonecrosis due to drugs, unspecified tibia
M87.179	Osteonecrosis due to drugs, unspecified toe(s)
M87.238	Osteonecrosis due to previous trauma of left carpus
M87.232	Osteonecrosis due to previous trauma of left radius
M87.235	Osteonecrosis due to previous trauma of left ulna
M87.237	Osteonecrosis due to previous trauma of right carpus
M87.231	Osteonecrosis due to previous trauma of right radius
M87.234	Osteonecrosis due to previous trauma of right ulna
M87.239	Osteonecrosis due to previous trauma of unspecified carpus
M87.233	Osteonecrosis due to previous trauma of unspecified radius
M87.236	Osteonecrosis due to previous trauma of unspecified ulna
M87.272	Osteonecrosis due to previous trauma, left ankle
M87.252	Osteonecrosis due to previous trauma, left femur
M87.265	Osteonecrosis due to previous trauma, left fibula
M87.245	Osteonecrosis due to previous trauma, left finger(s)
M87.275	Osteonecrosis due to previous trauma, left foot
M87.242	Osteonecrosis due to previous trauma, left hand
M87.222	Osteonecrosis due to previous trauma, left humerus
M87.212	Osteonecrosis due to previous trauma, left shoulder
M87.262	Osteonecrosis due to previous trauma, left tibia
M87.278	Osteonecrosis due to previous trauma, left toe(s)
M87.29	Osteonecrosis due to previous trauma, multiple sites
M87.28	Osteonecrosis due to previous trauma, other site

M87.250	Osteonecrosis due to previous trauma, pelvis
M87.271	Osteonecrosis due to previous trauma, right ankle
M87.251	Osteonecrosis due to previous trauma, right femur
M87.264	Osteonecrosis due to previous trauma, right fibula
M87.244	Osteonecrosis due to previous trauma, right finger(s)
M87.274	Osteonecrosis due to previous trauma, right foot
M87.241	Osteonecrosis due to previous trauma, right hand
M87.221	Osteonecrosis due to previous trauma, right humerus
M87.211	Osteonecrosis due to previous trauma, right shoulder
M87.261	Osteonecrosis due to previous trauma, right tibia
M87.277	Osteonecrosis due to previous trauma, right toe(s)
M87.273	Osteonecrosis due to previous trauma, unspecified ankle
M87.20	Osteonecrosis due to previous trauma, unspecified bone
M87.256	Osteonecrosis due to previous trauma, unspecified femur
M87.266	Osteonecrosis due to previous trauma, unspecified fibula
M87.246	Osteonecrosis due to previous trauma, unspecified finger(s)
M87.276	Osteonecrosis due to previous trauma, unspecified foot
M87.243	Osteonecrosis due to previous trauma, unspecified hand
M87.229	Osteonecrosis due to previous trauma, unspecified humerus
M87.219	Osteonecrosis due to previous trauma, unspecified shoulder
M87.263	Osteonecrosis due to previous trauma, unspecified tibia
M87.279	Osteonecrosis due to previous trauma, unspecified toe(s)
M90.572	Osteonecrosis in diseases classified elsewhere, left ankle and foot
M90.532	Osteonecrosis in diseases classified elsewhere, left forearm
M90.542	Osteonecrosis in diseases classified elsewhere, left hand
M90.562	Osteonecrosis in diseases classified elsewhere, left lower leg
M90.512	Osteonecrosis in diseases classified elsewhere, left shoulder
M90.552	Osteonecrosis in diseases classified elsewhere, left thigh
M90.522	Osteonecrosis in diseases classified elsewhere, left upper arm
M90.59	Osteonecrosis in diseases classified elsewhere, multiple sites
M90.58	Osteonecrosis in diseases classified elsewhere, other site
M90.571	Osteonecrosis in diseases classified elsewhere, right ankle and foot
M90.531	Osteonecrosis in diseases classified elsewhere, right forearm
M90.541	Osteonecrosis in diseases classified elsewhere, right hand
M90.561	Osteonecrosis in diseases classified elsewhere, right lower leg
M90.511	Osteonecrosis in diseases classified elsewhere, right shoulder
M90.551	Osteonecrosis in diseases classified elsewhere, right thigh
M90.521	Osteonecrosis in diseases classified elsewhere, right upper arm
M90.579	Osteonecrosis in diseases classified elsewhere, unspecified ankle and foot
M90.539	Osteonecrosis in diseases classified elsewhere, unspecified forearm
M90.549	Osteonecrosis in diseases classified elsewhere, unspecified hand
M90.569	Osteonecrosis in diseases classified elsewhere, unspecified lower leg
M90.519	Osteonecrosis in diseases classified elsewhere, unspecified shoulder
M90.50	Osteonecrosis in diseases classified elsewhere, unspecified site
M90.559	Osteonecrosis in diseases classified elsewhere, unspecified thigh
M90.529	Osteonecrosis in diseases classified elsewhere, unspecified upper arm
M87.9	Osteonecrosis, unspecified
Q78.2	Osteopetrosis
T80.39XA	Other ABO incompatibility reaction due to transfusion of blood or blood products, initial encounter
J39.1	Other abscess of pharynx
B60.19	Other acanthamebic disease
L12.35	Other acquired epidermolysis bullosa
K35.890	Other acute appendicitis without perforation or gangrene
K35.891	Other acute appendicitis without perforation, with gangrene
N17.8	Other acute kidney failure
M86.172	Other acute osteomyelitis, left ankle and foot
M86.152	Other acute osteomyelitis, left femur
M86.142	Other acute osteomyelitis, left hand
M86.122	Other acute osteomyelitis, left humerus
M86.132	Other acute osteomyelitis, left radius and ulna
M86.112	Other acute osteomyelitis, left shoulder
M86.162	Other acute osteomyelitis, left tibia and fibula
M86.19	Other acute osteomyelitis, multiple sites
M86.18	Other acute osteomyelitis, other site
M86.171	Other acute osteomyelitis, right ankle and foot
M86.151	Other acute osteomyelitis, right femur
M86.141	Other acute osteomyelitis, right hand
M86.121	Other acute osteomyelitis, right humerus
M86.131	Other acute osteomyelitis, right radius and ulna
M86.111	Other acute osteomyelitis, right shoulder
M86.161	Other acute osteomyelitis, right tibia and fibula
M86.179	Other acute osteomyelitis, unspecified ankle and foot
M86.159	Other acute osteomyelitis, unspecified femur
M86.149	Other acute osteomyelitis, unspecified hand
M86.129	Other acute osteomyelitis, unspecified humerus
M86.139	Other acute osteomyelitis, unspecified radius and ulna
M86.119	Other acute osteomyelitis, unspecified shoulder
M86.10	Other acute osteomyelitis, unspecified site
M86.169	Other acute osteomyelitis, unspecified tibia and fibula
T81.69XA	Other acute reaction to foreign substance accidentally left during a procedure, initial encounter
I01.8	Other acute rheumatic heart disease
D81.39	Other adenosine deaminase deficiency
E27.49	Other adrenocortical insufficiency
E27.0	Other adrenocortical overactivity
J93.82	Other air leak
E70.338	Other albinism with hematologic abnormality
J84.09	Other alveolar and parieto-alveolar conditions

A06.82	Other amebic genitourinary infections
A06.89	Other amebic infections
E85.89	Other amyloidosis
K43.6	Other and unspecified ventral hernia with obstruction, without gangrene
S73.035A	Other anterior dislocation of left hip, initial encounter
S73.034A	Other anterior dislocation of right hip, initial encounter
S73.036A	Other anterior dislocation of unspecified hip, initial encounter
S73.032A	Other anterior subluxation of left hip, initial encounter
S73.031A	Other anterior subluxation of right hip, initial encounter
S73.033A	Other anterior subluxation of unspecified hip, initial encounter
P28.4	Other apnea of newborn
A96.8	Other arenaviral hemorrhagic fevers
I74.09	Other arterial embolism and thrombosis of abdominal aorta
R18.8	Other ascites
P28.19	Other atelectasis of newborn
Q64.39	Other atresia and stenosis of urethra and bladder neck
Q25.29	Other atresia of aorta
A81.89	Other atypical virus infections of central nervous system
D59.1	Other autoimmune hemolytic anemias
F31.89	Other bipolar disorder
E71.118	Other branched-chain organic acidurias
A23.8	Other brucellosis
I42.8	Other cardiomyopathies
A52.09	Other cardiovascular syphilis
A52.12	Other cerebrospinal syphilis
I67.89	Other cerebrovascular disease
A52.05	Other cerebrovascular syphilis
I67.848	Other cerebrovascular vasospasm and vasoconstriction
F84.3	Other childhood disintegrative disorder
K83.09	Other cholangitis
K80.81	Other cholelithiasis with obstruction
H30.893	Other chorioretinal inflammations, bilateral
H30.892	Other chorioretinal inflammations, left eye
H30.891	Other chorioretinal inflammations, right eye
H30.899	Other chorioretinal inflammations, unspecified eye
L53.3	Other chronic figurate erythema
M86.572	Other chronic hematogenous osteomyelitis, left ankle and foot
M86.552	Other chronic hematogenous osteomyelitis, left femur
M86.542	Other chronic hematogenous osteomyelitis, left hand
M86.522	Other chronic hematogenous osteomyelitis, left humerus
M86.532	Other chronic hematogenous osteomyelitis, left radius and ulna
M86.512	Other chronic hematogenous osteomyelitis, left shoulder
M86.562	Other chronic hematogenous osteomyelitis, left tibia and fibula
M86.59	Other chronic hematogenous osteomyelitis, multiple sites
M86.58	Other chronic hematogenous osteomyelitis, other site
M86.571	Other chronic hematogenous osteomyelitis, right ankle and foot
M86.551	Other chronic hematogenous osteomyelitis, right femur
M86.541	Other chronic hematogenous osteomyelitis, right hand
M86.521	Other chronic hematogenous osteomyelitis, right humerus
M86.531	Other chronic hematogenous osteomyelitis, right radius and ulna
M86.511	Other chronic hematogenous osteomyelitis, right shoulder
M86.561	Other chronic hematogenous osteomyelitis, right tibia and fibula
M86.579	Other chronic hematogenous osteomyelitis, unspecified ankle and foot
M86.559	Other chronic hematogenous osteomyelitis, unspecified femur
M86.549	Other chronic hematogenous osteomyelitis, unspecified hand
M86.529	Other chronic hematogenous osteomyelitis, unspecified humerus
M86.539	Other chronic hematogenous osteomyelitis, unspecified radius and ulna
M86.519	Other chronic hematogenous osteomyelitis, unspecified shoulder
M86.50	Other chronic hematogenous osteomyelitis, unspecified site
M86.569	Other chronic hematogenous osteomyelitis, unspecified tibia and fibula
M86.672	Other chronic osteomyelitis, left ankle and foot
M86.642	Other chronic osteomyelitis, left hand
M86.622	Other chronic osteomyelitis, left humerus
M86.632	Other chronic osteomyelitis, left radius and ulna
M86.612	Other chronic osteomyelitis, left shoulder
M86.652	Other chronic osteomyelitis, left thigh
M86.662	Other chronic osteomyelitis, left tibia and fibula
M86.69	Other chronic osteomyelitis, multiple sites
M86.68	Other chronic osteomyelitis, other site
M86.671	Other chronic osteomyelitis, right ankle and foot
M86.641	Other chronic osteomyelitis, right hand
M86.621	Other chronic osteomyelitis, right humerus
M86.631	Other chronic osteomyelitis, right radius and ulna
M86.611	Other chronic osteomyelitis, right shoulder
M86.651	Other chronic osteomyelitis, right thigh
M86.661	Other chronic osteomyelitis, right tibia and fibula
M86.679	Other chronic osteomyelitis, unspecified ankle and foot
M86.649	Other chronic osteomyelitis, unspecified hand
M86.629	Other chronic osteomyelitis, unspecified humerus
M86.639	Other chronic osteomyelitis, unspecified radius and ulna
M86.619	Other chronic osteomyelitis, unspecified shoulder
M86.60	Other chronic osteomyelitis, unspecified site
M86.659	Other chronic osteomyelitis, unspecified thigh
M86.669	Other chronic osteomyelitis, unspecified tibia and fibula
K86.1	Other chronic pancreatitis
N11.8	Other chronic tubulo-interstitial nephritis
B18.8	Other chronic viral hepatitis
D81.89	Other combined immunodeficiencies

D83.8	Other common variable immunodeficiencies
K56.691	Other complete intestinal obstruction
T86.19	Other complication of kidney transplant
J95.859	Other complication of respirator [ventilator]
T82.49XA	Other complication of vascular dialysis catheter, initial encounter
N98.8	Other complications associated with artificial fertilization
O08.89	Other complications following an ectopic and molar pregnancy
T88.1XXA	Other complications following immunization, not elsewhere classified, initial encounter
T86.838	Other complications of bone graft
T86.09	Other complications of bone marrow transplant
K94.09	Other complications of colostomy
T86.848	Other complications of corneal transplant
K94.19	Other complications of enterostomy
K94.39	Other complications of esophagostomy
T81.596A	Other complications of foreign body accidentally left in body following aspiration, puncture or other catheterization, initial encounter
T81.594A	Other complications of foreign body accidentally left in body following endoscopic examination, initial encounter
T81.595A	Other complications of foreign body accidentally left in body following heart catheterization, initial encounter
T81.591A	Other complications of foreign body accidentally left in body following infusion or transfusion, initial encounter
T81.593A	Other complications of foreign body accidentally left in body following injection or immunization, initial encounter
T81.592A	Other complications of foreign body accidentally left in body following kidney dialysis, initial encounter
T81.598A	Other complications of foreign body accidentally left in body following other procedure, initial encounter
T81.597A	Other complications of foreign body accidentally left in body following removal of catheter or packing, initial encounter
T81.590A	Other complications of foreign body accidentally left in body following surgical operation, initial encounter
T81.599A	Other complications of foreign body accidentally left in body following unspecified procedure, initial encounter
K95.09	Other complications of gastric band procedure
T86.298	Other complications of heart transplant
T86.39	Other complications of heart-lung transplant
K91.858	Other complications of intestinal pouch
T86.858	Other complications of intestine transplant
T86.49	Other complications of liver transplant
T86.818	Other complications of lung transplant
K95.89	Other complications of other bariatric procedure
T86.898	Other complications of other transplanted tissue
T86.828	Other complications of skin graft (allograft) (autograft)
T86.99	Other complications of unspecified transplanted organ and tissue
O31.8X11	Other complications specific to multiple gestation, first trimester, fetus 1
O31.8X12	Other complications specific to multiple gestation, first trimester, fetus 2
O31.8X13	Other complications specific to multiple gestation, first trimester, fetus 3
O31.8X14	Other complications specific to multiple gestation, first trimester, fetus 4
O31.8X15	Other complications specific to multiple gestation, first trimester, fetus 5
O31.8X10	Other complications specific to multiple gestation, first trimester, not applicable or unspecified
O31.8X19	Other complications specific to multiple gestation, first trimester, other fetus
O31.8X21	Other complications specific to multiple gestation, second trimester, fetus 1
O31.8X22	Other complications specific to multiple gestation, second trimester, fetus 2
O31.8X23	Other complications specific to multiple gestation, second trimester, fetus 3
O31.8X24	Other complications specific to multiple gestation, second trimester, fetus 4
O31.8X25	Other complications specific to multiple gestation, second trimester, fetus 5
O31.8X20	Other complications specific to multiple gestation, second trimester, not applicable or unspecified
O31.8X29	Other complications specific to multiple gestation, second trimester, other fetus
O31.8X31	Other complications specific to multiple gestation, third trimester, fetus 1
O31.8X32	Other complications specific to multiple gestation, third trimester, fetus 2
O31.8X33	Other complications specific to multiple gestation, third trimester, fetus 3
O31.8X34	Other complications specific to multiple gestation, third trimester, fetus 4
O31.8X35	Other complications specific to multiple gestation, third trimester, fetus 5
O31.8X30	Other complications specific to multiple gestation, third trimester, not applicable or unspecified
O31.8X39	Other complications specific to multiple gestation, third trimester, other fetus
A69.29	Other conditions associated with Lyme disease
M30.8	Other conditions related to polyarteritis nodosa
P61.4	Other congenital anemias, not elsewhere classified
Q67.8	Other congenital deformities of chest
Q43.2	Other congenital functional disorders of colon
Q87.19	Other congenital malformation syndromes predominantly associated with short stature
Q87.5	Other congenital malformation syndromes with other skeletal changes
Q25.49	Other congenital malformations of aorta
Q44.5	Other congenital malformations of bile ducts
Q76.8	Other congenital malformations of bony thorax
Q32.4	Other congenital malformations of bronchus
Q39.8	Other congenital malformations of esophagus
Q44.1	Other congenital malformations of gallbladder
Q26.8	Other congenital malformations of great veins
Q31.8	Other congenital malformations of larynx
Q44.7	Other congenital malformations of liver
Q25.8	Other congenital malformations of other great arteries

Q45.3	Other congenital malformations of pancreas and pancreatic duct
Q22.3	Other congenital malformations of pulmonary valve
Q76.6	Other congenital malformations of ribs
Q32.1	Other congenital malformations of trachea
D61.09	Other constitutional aplastic anemia
G95.29	Other cord compression
A81.09	Other Creutzfeldt-Jakob disease
I23.8	Other current complications following acute myocardial infarction
E24.8	Other Cushing's syndrome
Q61.8	Other cystic kidney diseases
N99.518	Other cystostomy complication
B25.8	Other cytomegaloviral diseases
Q93.89	Other deletions from the autosomes
Q93.59	Other deletions of part of a chromosome
M33.12	Other dermatomyositis with myopathy
M33.19	Other dermatomyositis with other organ involvement
M33.11	Other dermatomyositis with respiratory involvement
M33.13	Other dermatomyositis without myopathy
M33.10	Other dermatomyositis, organ involvement unspecified
B57.39	Other digestive system involvement in Chagas' disease
A36.89	Other diphtheritic complications
O99.12	Other diseases of the blood and blood-forming organs and certain disorders involving the immune mechanism complicating childbirth
O99.111	Other diseases of the blood and blood-forming organs and certain disorders involving the immune mechanism complicating pregnancy, first trimester
O99.112	Other diseases of the blood and blood-forming organs and certain disorders involving the immune mechanism complicating pregnancy, second trimester
O99.113	Other diseases of the blood and blood-forming organs and certain disorders involving the immune mechanism complicating pregnancy, third trimester
O99.119	Other diseases of the blood and blood-forming organs and certain disorders involving the immune mechanism complicating pregnancy, unspecified trimester
O99.13	Other diseases of the blood and blood-forming organs and certain disorders involving the immune mechanism complicating the puerperium
E72.09	Other disorders of amino-acid transport
E70.8	Other disorders of aromatic amino-acid metabolism
E71.19	Other disorders of branched-chain amino-acid metabolism
E71.39	Other disorders of fatty-acid metabolism
E71.318	Other disorders of fatty-acid oxidation
E74.29	Other disorders of galactose metabolism
E76.8	Other disorders of glucosaminoglycan metabolism
E72.59	Other disorders of glycine metabolism
E70.49	Other disorders of histidine metabolism
E71.518	Other disorders of peroxisome biogenesis
E71.128	Other disorders of propionate metabolism
E79.8	Other disorders of purine and pyrimidine metabolism
E72.19	Other disorders of sulfur-bearing amino-acid metabolism
H59.093	Other disorders of the eye following cataract surgery, bilateral
H59.092	Other disorders of the left eye following cataract surgery
H59.091	Other disorders of the right eye following cataract surgery
E70.29	Other disorders of tyrosine metabolism
H59.099	Other disorders of unspecified eye following cataract surgery
E72.29	Other disorders of urea cycle metabolism
S12.120A	Other displaced dens fracture, initial encounter for closed fracture
S12.120K	Other displaced dens fracture, subsequent encounter for fracture with nonunion
S62.232B	Other displaced fracture of base of first metacarpal bone, left hand, initial encounter for open fracture
S62.232P	Other displaced fracture of base of first metacarpal bone, left hand, subsequent encounter for fracture with malunion
S62.232K	Other displaced fracture of base of first metacarpal bone, left hand, subsequent encounter for fracture with nonunion
S62.231B	Other displaced fracture of base of first metacarpal bone, right hand, initial encounter for open fracture
S62.231P	Other displaced fracture of base of first metacarpal bone, right hand, subsequent encounter for fracture with malunion
S62.231K	Other displaced fracture of base of first metacarpal bone, right hand, subsequent encounter for fracture with nonunion
S62.233B	Other displaced fracture of base of first metacarpal bone, unspecified hand, initial encounter for open fracture
S62.233P	Other displaced fracture of base of first metacarpal bone, unspecified hand, subsequent encounter for fracture with malunion
S62.233K	Other displaced fracture of base of first metacarpal bone, unspecified hand, subsequent encounter for fracture with nonunion
S12.490A	Other displaced fracture of fifth cervical vertebra, initial encounter for closed fracture
S12.490K	Other displaced fracture of fifth cervical vertebra, subsequent encounter for fracture with nonunion
S12.090A	Other displaced fracture of first cervical vertebra, initial encounter for closed fracture
S12.090K	Other displaced fracture of first cervical vertebra, subsequent encounter for fracture with nonunion
S12.390A	Other displaced fracture of fourth cervical vertebra, initial encounter for closed fracture
S12.390K	Other displaced fracture of fourth cervical vertebra, subsequent encounter for fracture with nonunion
S42.492A	Other displaced fracture of lower end of left humerus, initial encounter for closed fracture
S42.492P	Other displaced fracture of lower end of left humerus, subsequent encounter for fracture with malunion

S42.492K	Other displaced fracture of lower end of left humerus, subsequent encounter for fracture with nonunion
S42.491A	Other displaced fracture of lower end of right humerus, initial encounter for closed fracture
S42.491P	Other displaced fracture of lower end of right humerus, subsequent encounter for fracture with malunion
S42.491K	Other displaced fracture of lower end of right humerus, subsequent encounter for fracture with nonunion
S42.493A	Other displaced fracture of lower end of unspecified humerus, initial encounter for closed fracture
S42.493P	Other displaced fracture of lower end of unspecified humerus, subsequent encounter for fracture with malunion
S42.493K	Other displaced fracture of lower end of unspecified humerus, subsequent encounter for fracture with nonunion
S12.190A	Other displaced fracture of second cervical vertebra, initial encounter for closed fracture
S12.190K	Other displaced fracture of second cervical vertebra, subsequent encounter for fracture with nonunion
S12.690A	Other displaced fracture of seventh cervical vertebra, initial encounter for closed fracture
S12.690K	Other displaced fracture of seventh cervical vertebra, subsequent encounter for fracture with nonunion
S12.590A	Other displaced fracture of sixth cervical vertebra, initial encounter for closed fracture
S12.590K	Other displaced fracture of sixth cervical vertebra, subsequent encounter for fracture with nonunion
S12.290A	Other displaced fracture of third cervical vertebra, initial encounter for closed fracture
S12.290K	Other displaced fracture of third cervical vertebra, subsequent encounter for fracture with nonunion
S42.292A	Other displaced fracture of upper end of left humerus, initial encounter for closed fracture
S42.292P	Other displaced fracture of upper end of left humerus, subsequent encounter for fracture with malunion
S42.292K	Other displaced fracture of upper end of left humerus, subsequent encounter for fracture with nonunion
S42.291A	Other displaced fracture of upper end of right humerus, initial encounter for closed fracture
S42.291P	Other displaced fracture of upper end of right humerus, subsequent encounter for fracture with malunion
S42.291K	Other displaced fracture of upper end of right humerus, subsequent encounter for fracture with nonunion
S42.293A	Other displaced fracture of upper end of unspecified humerus, initial encounter for closed fracture
S42.293P	Other displaced fracture of upper end of unspecified humerus, subsequent encounter for fracture with malunion
S42.293K	Other displaced fracture of upper end of unspecified humerus, subsequent encounter for fracture with nonunion
G24.09	Other drug induced dystonia
G21.19	Other drug induced secondary parkinsonism
G24.8	Other dystonia
A50.09	Other early congenital syphilis, symptomatic
B67.99	Other echinococcosis
O00.81	Other ectopic pregnancy with intrauterine pregnancy
O00.80	Other ectopic pregnancy without intrauterine pregnancy
P83.39	Other edema specific to newborn
Q79.69	Other Ehlers-Danlos syndromes
A77.49	Other ehrlichiosis
G93.49	Other encephalopathy
H44.19	Other endophthalmitis
G40.803	Other epilepsy, intractable, with status epilepticus
G40.804	Other epilepsy, intractable, without status epilepticus
G40.801	Other epilepsy, not intractable, with status epilepticus
G40.802	Other epilepsy, not intractable, without status epilepticus
Q64.19	Other exstrophy of urinary bladder
S52.552A	Other extraarticular fracture of lower end of left radius, initial encounter for closed fracture
S52.552P	Other extraarticular fracture of lower end of left radius, subsequent encounter for closed fracture with malunion
S52.552K	Other extraarticular fracture of lower end of left radius, subsequent encounter for closed fracture with nonunion
S52.552Q	Other extraarticular fracture of lower end of left radius, subsequent encounter for open fracture type I or II with malunion
S52.552M	Other extraarticular fracture of lower end of left radius, subsequent encounter for open fracture type I or II with nonunion
S52.552R	Other extraarticular fracture of lower end of left radius, subsequent encounter for open fracture type IIIA, IIIB, or IIIC with malunion
S52.552N	Other extraarticular fracture of lower end of left radius, subsequent encounter for open fracture type IIIA, IIIB, or IIIC with nonunion
S52.551A	Other extraarticular fracture of lower end of right radius, initial encounter for closed fracture
S52.551P	Other extraarticular fracture of lower end of right radius, subsequent encounter for closed fracture with malunion
S52.551K	Other extraarticular fracture of lower end of right radius, subsequent encounter for closed fracture with nonunion
S52.551Q	Other extraarticular fracture of lower end of right radius, subsequent encounter for open fracture type I or II with malunion
S52.551M	Other extraarticular fracture of lower end of right radius, subsequent encounter for open fracture type I or II with nonunion
S52.551R	Other extraarticular fracture of lower end of right radius, subsequent encounter for open fracture type IIIA, IIIB, or IIIC with malunion

S52.551N	Other extraarticular fracture of lower end of right radius, subsequent encounter for open fracture type IIIA, IIIB, or IIIC with nonunion
S52.559A	Other extraarticular fracture of lower end of unspecified radius, initial encounter for closed fracture
S52.559P	Other extraarticular fracture of lower end of unspecified radius, subsequent encounter for closed fracture with malunion
S52.559K	Other extraarticular fracture of lower end of unspecified radius, subsequent encounter for closed fracture with nonunion
S52.559Q	Other extraarticular fracture of lower end of unspecified radius, subsequent encounter for open fracture type I or II with malunion
S52.559M	Other extraarticular fracture of lower end of unspecified radius, subsequent encounter for open fracture type I or II with nonunion
S52.559R	Other extraarticular fracture of lower end of unspecified radius, subsequent encounter for open fracture type IIIA, IIIB, or IIIC with malunion
S52.559N	Other extraarticular fracture of lower end of unspecified radius, subsequent encounter for open fracture type IIIA, IIIB, or IIIC with nonunion
N82.8	Other female genital tract fistulae
N82.4	Other female intestinal-genital tract fistulae
N82.1	Other female urinary-genital tract fistulae
B74.8	Other filariases
T17.590A	Other foreign object in bronchus causing asphyxiation, initial encounter
T17.598A	Other foreign object in bronchus causing other injury, initial encounter
T17.890A	Other foreign object in other parts of respiratory tract causing asphyxiation, initial encounter
T17.898A	Other foreign object in other parts of respiratory tract causing other injury, initial encounter
T17.490A	Other foreign object in trachea causing asphyxiation, initial encounter
T17.498A	Other foreign object in trachea causing other injury, initial encounter
A42.89	Other forms of actinomycosis
I24.8	Other forms of acute ischemic heart disease
I30.8	Other forms of acute pericarditis
A22.8	Other forms of anthrax
B44.89	Other forms of aspergillosis
A44.8	Other forms of bartonellosis
B40.89	Other forms of blastomycosis
B38.89	Other forms of coccidioidomycosis
B45.8	Other forms of cryptococcosis
A30.8	Other forms of leprosy
A27.89	Other forms of leptospirosis
A32.89	Other forms of listeriosis
A43.8	Other forms of nocardiosis
B41.8	Other forms of paracoccidioidomycosis
A21.8	Other forms of tularemia
S02.19XA	Other fracture of base of skull, initial encounter for closed fracture
S02.19XK	Other fracture of base of skull, subsequent encounter for fracture with nonunion
S32.058A	Other fracture of fifth lumbar vertebra, initial encounter for closed fracture
S32.058K	Other fracture of fifth lumbar vertebra, subsequent encounter for fracture with nonunion
S62.397B	Other fracture of fifth metacarpal bone, left hand, initial encounter for open fracture
S62.397P	Other fracture of fifth metacarpal bone, left hand, subsequent encounter for fracture with malunion
S62.397K	Other fracture of fifth metacarpal bone, left hand, subsequent encounter for fracture with nonunion
S62.396B	Other fracture of fifth metacarpal bone, right hand, initial encounter for open fracture
S62.396P	Other fracture of fifth metacarpal bone, right hand, subsequent encounter for fracture with malunion
S62.396K	Other fracture of fifth metacarpal bone, right hand, subsequent encounter for fracture with nonunion
S32.018A	Other fracture of first lumbar vertebra, initial encounter for closed fracture
S32.018K	Other fracture of first lumbar vertebra, subsequent encounter for fracture with nonunion
S62.292B	Other fracture of first metacarpal bone, left hand, initial encounter for open fracture
S62.292P	Other fracture of first metacarpal bone, left hand, subsequent encounter for fracture with malunion
S62.292K	Other fracture of first metacarpal bone, left hand, subsequent encounter for fracture with nonunion
S62.291B	Other fracture of first metacarpal bone, right hand, initial encounter for open fracture
S62.291P	Other fracture of first metacarpal bone, right hand, subsequent encounter for fracture with malunion
S62.291K	Other fracture of first metacarpal bone, right hand, subsequent encounter for fracture with nonunion
S62.299B	Other fracture of first metacarpal bone, unspecified hand, initial encounter for open fracture
S62.299P	Other fracture of first metacarpal bone, unspecified hand, subsequent encounter for fracture with malunion
S62.299K	Other fracture of first metacarpal bone, unspecified hand, subsequent encounter for fracture with nonunion
S22.018A	Other fracture of first thoracic vertebra, initial encounter for closed fracture
S22.018K	Other fracture of first thoracic vertebra, subsequent encounter for fracture with nonunion
S32.048A	Other fracture of fourth lumbar vertebra, initial encounter for closed fracture
S32.048K	Other fracture of fourth lumbar vertebra, subsequent encounter for fracture with nonunion
S62.395B	Other fracture of fourth metacarpal bone, left hand, initial encounter for open fracture

Alphabetic & Numeric Lists of CCs

S62.395P	Other fracture of fourth metacarpal bone, left hand, subsequent encounter for fracture with malunion
S62.395K	Other fracture of fourth metacarpal bone, left hand, subsequent encounter for fracture with nonunion
S62.394B	Other fracture of fourth metacarpal bone, right hand, initial encounter for open fracture
S62.394P	Other fracture of fourth metacarpal bone, right hand, subsequent encounter for fracture with malunion
S62.394K	Other fracture of fourth metacarpal bone, right hand, subsequent encounter for fracture with nonunion
S22.048A	Other fracture of fourth thoracic vertebra, initial encounter for closed fracture
S22.048K	Other fracture of fourth thoracic vertebra, subsequent encounter for fracture with nonunion
S72.092P	Other fracture of head and neck of left femur, subsequent encounter for closed fracture with malunion
S72.092K	Other fracture of head and neck of left femur, subsequent encounter for closed fracture with nonunion
S72.092Q	Other fracture of head and neck of left femur, subsequent encounter for open fracture type I or II with malunion
S72.092M	Other fracture of head and neck of left femur, subsequent encounter for open fracture type I or II with nonunion
S72.092R	Other fracture of head and neck of left femur, subsequent encounter for open fracture type IIIA, IIIB, or IIIC with malunion
S72.092N	Other fracture of head and neck of left femur, subsequent encounter for open fracture type IIIA, IIIB, or IIIC with nonunion
S72.091P	Other fracture of head and neck of right femur, subsequent encounter for closed fracture with malunion
S72.091K	Other fracture of head and neck of right femur, subsequent encounter for closed fracture with nonunion
S72.091Q	Other fracture of head and neck of right femur, subsequent encounter for open fracture type I or II with malunion
S72.091M	Other fracture of head and neck of right femur, subsequent encounter for open fracture type I or II with nonunion
S72.091R	Other fracture of head and neck of right femur, subsequent encounter for open fracture type IIIA, IIIB, or IIIC with malunion
S72.091N	Other fracture of head and neck of right femur, subsequent encounter for open fracture type IIIA, IIIB, or IIIC with nonunion
S72.099P	Other fracture of head and neck of unspecified femur, subsequent encounter for closed fracture with malunion
S72.099K	Other fracture of head and neck of unspecified femur, subsequent encounter for closed fracture with nonunion
S72.099Q	Other fracture of head and neck of unspecified femur, subsequent encounter for open fracture type I or II with malunion
S72.099M	Other fracture of head and neck of unspecified femur, subsequent encounter for open fracture type I or II with nonunion
S72.099R	Other fracture of head and neck of unspecified femur, subsequent encounter for open fracture type IIIA, IIIB, or IIIC with malunion
S72.099N	Other fracture of head and neck of unspecified femur, subsequent encounter for open fracture type IIIA, IIIB, or IIIC with nonunion
S72.8X2P	Other fracture of left femur, subsequent encounter for closed fracture with malunion
S72.8X2K	Other fracture of left femur, subsequent encounter for closed fracture with nonunion
S72.8X2Q	Other fracture of left femur, subsequent encounter for open fracture type I or II with malunion
S72.8X2M	Other fracture of left femur, subsequent encounter for open fracture type I or II with nonunion
S72.8X2R	Other fracture of left femur, subsequent encounter for open fracture type IIIA, IIIB, or IIIC with malunion
S72.8X2N	Other fracture of left femur, subsequent encounter for open fracture type IIIA, IIIB, or IIIC with nonunion
S92.812B	Other fracture of left foot, initial encounter for open fracture
S92.812P	Other fracture of left foot, subsequent encounter for fracture with malunion
S92.812K	Other fracture of left foot, subsequent encounter for fracture with nonunion
S92.492P	Other fracture of left great toe, subsequent encounter for fracture with malunion
S92.492K	Other fracture of left great toe, subsequent encounter for fracture with nonunion
S32.392A	Other fracture of left ilium, initial encounter for closed fracture
S32.392K	Other fracture of left ilium, subsequent encounter for fracture with nonunion
S92.592P	Other fracture of left lesser toe(s), subsequent encounter for fracture with malunion
S92.592K	Other fracture of left lesser toe(s), subsequent encounter for fracture with nonunion
S82.892B	Other fracture of left lower leg, initial encounter for open fracture type I or II
S82.892C	Other fracture of left lower leg, initial encounter for open fracture type IIIA, IIIB, or IIIC
S82.892P	Other fracture of left lower leg, subsequent encounter for closed fracture with malunion
S82.892K	Other fracture of left lower leg, subsequent encounter for closed fracture with nonunion
S82.892Q	Other fracture of left lower leg, subsequent encounter for open fracture type I or II with malunion
S82.892M	Other fracture of left lower leg, subsequent encounter for open fracture type I or II with nonunion
S82.892R	Other fracture of left lower leg, subsequent encounter for open fracture type IIIA, IIIB, or IIIC with malunion
S82.892N	Other fracture of left lower leg, subsequent encounter for open fracture type IIIA, IIIB, or IIIC with nonunion
S82.092A	Other fracture of left patella, initial encounter for closed fracture
S82.092B	Other fracture of left patella, initial encounter for open fracture type I or II
S82.092C	Other fracture of left patella, initial encounter for open fracture type IIIA, IIIB, or IIIC
S82.092P	Other fracture of left patella, subsequent encounter for closed fracture with malunion
S82.092K	Other fracture of left patella, subsequent encounter for closed fracture with nonunion
S82.092Q	Other fracture of left patella, subsequent encounter for open fracture type I or II with malunion
S82.092M	Other fracture of left patella, subsequent encounter for open fracture type I or II with nonunion
S82.092R	Other fracture of left patella, subsequent encounter for open fracture type IIIA, IIIB, or IIIC with malunion
S82.092N	Other fracture of left patella, subsequent encounter for open fracture type IIIA, IIIB, or IIIC with nonunion
S92.192B	Other fracture of left talus, initial encounter for open fracture
S92.192P	Other fracture of left talus, subsequent encounter for fracture with malunion
S92.192K	Other fracture of left talus, subsequent encounter for fracture with nonunion
S72.492A	Other fracture of lower end of left femur, initial encounter for closed fracture
S72.492P	Other fracture of lower end of left femur, subsequent encounter for closed fracture with malunion
S72.492K	Other fracture of lower end of left femur, subsequent encounter for closed fracture with nonunion
S72.492Q	Other fracture of lower end of left femur, subsequent encounter for open fracture type I or II with malunion
S72.492M	Other fracture of lower end of left femur, subsequent encounter for open fracture type I or II with nonunion
S72.492R	Other fracture of lower end of left femur, subsequent encounter for open fracture type IIIA, IIIB, or IIIC with malunion
S72.492N	Other fracture of lower end of left femur, subsequent encounter for open fracture type IIIA, IIIB, or IIIC with nonunion
S82.392B	Other fracture of lower end of left tibia, initial encounter for open fracture type I or II
S82.392C	Other fracture of lower end of left tibia, initial encounter for open fracture type IIIA, IIIB, or IIIC
S82.392P	Other fracture of lower end of left tibia, subsequent encounter for closed fracture with malunion
S82.392K	Other fracture of lower end of left tibia, subsequent encounter for closed fracture with nonunion
S82.392Q	Other fracture of lower end of left tibia, subsequent encounter for open fracture type I or II with malunion
S82.392M	Other fracture of lower end of left tibia, subsequent encounter for open fracture type I or II with nonunion
S82.392R	Other fracture of lower end of left tibia, subsequent encounter for open fracture type IIIA, IIIB, or IIIC with malunion
S82.392N	Other fracture of lower end of left tibia, subsequent encounter for open fracture type IIIA, IIIB, or IIIC with nonunion
S52.692A	Other fracture of lower end of left ulna, initial encounter for closed fracture
S52.692P	Other fracture of lower end of left ulna, subsequent encounter for closed fracture with malunion
S52.692K	Other fracture of lower end of left ulna, subsequent encounter for closed fracture with nonunion
S52.692Q	Other fracture of lower end of left ulna, subsequent encounter for open fracture type I or II with malunion
S52.692M	Other fracture of lower end of left ulna, subsequent encounter for open fracture type I or II with nonunion
S52.692R	Other fracture of lower end of left ulna, subsequent encounter for open fracture type IIIA, IIIB, or IIIC with malunion
S52.692N	Other fracture of lower end of left ulna, subsequent encounter for open fracture type IIIA, IIIB, or IIIC with nonunion
S72.491A	Other fracture of lower end of right femur, initial encounter for closed fracture
S72.491P	Other fracture of lower end of right femur, subsequent encounter for closed fracture with malunion
S72.491K	Other fracture of lower end of right femur, subsequent encounter for closed fracture with nonunion
S72.491Q	Other fracture of lower end of right femur, subsequent encounter for open fracture type I or II with malunion
S72.491M	Other fracture of lower end of right femur, subsequent encounter for open fracture type I or II with nonunion
S72.491R	Other fracture of lower end of right femur, subsequent encounter for open fracture type IIIA, IIIB, or IIIC with malunion
S72.491N	Other fracture of lower end of right femur, subsequent encounter for open fracture type IIIA, IIIB, or IIIC with nonunion
S82.391B	Other fracture of lower end of right tibia, initial encounter for open fracture type I or II
S82.391C	Other fracture of lower end of right tibia, initial encounter for open fracture type IIIA, IIIB, or IIIC
S82.391P	Other fracture of lower end of right tibia, subsequent encounter for closed fracture with malunion
S82.391K	Other fracture of lower end of right tibia, subsequent encounter for closed fracture with nonunion
S82.391Q	Other fracture of lower end of right tibia, subsequent encounter for open fracture type I or II with malunion
S82.391M	Other fracture of lower end of right tibia, subsequent encounter for open fracture type I or II with nonunion
S82.391R	Other fracture of lower end of right tibia, subsequent encounter for open fracture type IIIA, IIIB, or IIIC with malunion
S82.391N	Other fracture of lower end of right tibia, subsequent encounter for open fracture type IIIA, IIIB, or IIIC with nonunion
S52.691A	Other fracture of lower end of right ulna, initial encounter for closed fracture
S52.691P	Other fracture of lower end of right ulna, subsequent encounter for closed fracture with malunion

S52.691K Other fracture of lower end of right ulna, subsequent encounter for closed fracture with nonunion

S52.691Q Other fracture of lower end of right ulna, subsequent encounter for open fracture type I or II with malunion

S52.691M Other fracture of lower end of right ulna, subsequent encounter for open fracture type I or II with nonunion

S52.691R Other fracture of lower end of right ulna, subsequent encounter for open fracture type IIIA, IIIB, or IIIC with malunion

S52.691N Other fracture of lower end of right ulna, subsequent encounter for open fracture type IIIA, IIIB, or IIIC with nonunion

S72.499A Other fracture of lower end of unspecified femur, initial encounter for closed fracture

S72.499P Other fracture of lower end of unspecified femur, subsequent encounter for closed fracture with malunion

S72.499K Other fracture of lower end of unspecified femur, subsequent encounter for closed fracture with nonunion

S72.499Q Other fracture of lower end of unspecified femur, subsequent encounter for open fracture type I or II with malunion

S72.499M Other fracture of lower end of unspecified femur, subsequent encounter for open fracture type I or II with nonunion

S72.499R Other fracture of lower end of unspecified femur, subsequent encounter for open fracture type IIIA, IIIB, or IIIC with malunion

S72.499N Other fracture of lower end of unspecified femur, subsequent encounter for open fracture type IIIA, IIIB, or IIIC with nonunion

S82.399B Other fracture of lower end of unspecified tibia, initial encounter for open fracture type I or II

S82.399C Other fracture of lower end of unspecified tibia, initial encounter for open fracture type IIIA, IIIB, or IIIC

S82.399P Other fracture of lower end of unspecified tibia, subsequent encounter for closed fracture with malunion

S82.399K Other fracture of lower end of unspecified tibia, subsequent encounter for closed fracture with nonunion

S82.399Q Other fracture of lower end of unspecified tibia, subsequent encounter for open fracture type I or II with malunion

S82.399M Other fracture of lower end of unspecified tibia, subsequent encounter for open fracture type I or II with nonunion

S82.399R Other fracture of lower end of unspecified tibia, subsequent encounter for open fracture type IIIA, IIIB, or IIIC with malunion

S82.399N Other fracture of lower end of unspecified tibia, subsequent encounter for open fracture type IIIA, IIIB, or IIIC with nonunion

S52.699A Other fracture of lower end of unspecified ulna, initial encounter for closed fracture

S52.699P Other fracture of lower end of unspecified ulna, subsequent encounter for closed fracture with malunion

S52.699K Other fracture of lower end of unspecified ulna, subsequent encounter for closed fracture with nonunion

S52.699Q Other fracture of lower end of unspecified ulna, subsequent encounter for open fracture type I or II with malunion

S52.699M Other fracture of lower end of unspecified ulna, subsequent encounter for open fracture type I or II with nonunion

S52.699R Other fracture of lower end of unspecified ulna, subsequent encounter for open fracture type IIIA, IIIB, or IIIC with malunion

S52.699N Other fracture of lower end of unspecified ulna, subsequent encounter for open fracture type IIIA, IIIB, or IIIC with nonunion

S02.11HA Other fracture of occiput, left side, initial encounter for closed fracture

S02.11HK Other fracture of occiput, left side, subsequent encounter for fracture with nonunion

S02.11GA Other fracture of occiput, right side, initial encounter for closed fracture

S02.11GK Other fracture of occiput, right side, subsequent encounter for fracture with nonunion

S02.118A Other fracture of occiput, unspecified side, initial encounter for closed fracture

S02.118K Other fracture of occiput, unspecified side, subsequent encounter for fracture with nonunion

S62.398B Other fracture of other metacarpal bone, initial encounter for open fracture

S62.398P Other fracture of other metacarpal bone, subsequent encounter for fracture with malunion

S62.398K Other fracture of other metacarpal bone, subsequent encounter for fracture with nonunion

S72.8X1P Other fracture of right femur, subsequent encounter for closed fracture with malunion

S72.8X1K Other fracture of right femur, subsequent encounter for closed fracture with nonunion

S72.8X1Q Other fracture of right femur, subsequent encounter for open fracture type I or II with malunion

S72.8X1M Other fracture of right femur, subsequent encounter for open fracture type I or II with nonunion

S72.8X1R Other fracture of right femur, subsequent encounter for open fracture type IIIA, IIIB, or IIIC with malunion

S72.8X1N Other fracture of right femur, subsequent encounter for open fracture type IIIA, IIIB, or IIIC with nonunion

S92.811B Other fracture of right foot, initial encounter for open fracture

S92.811P Other fracture of right foot, subsequent encounter for fracture with malunion

S92.811K Other fracture of right foot, subsequent encounter for fracture with nonunion

S92.491P Other fracture of right great toe, subsequent encounter for fracture with malunion

S92.491K Other fracture of right great toe, subsequent encounter for fracture with nonunion

S32.391A Other fracture of right ilium, initial encounter for closed fracture

S32.391K Other fracture of right ilium, subsequent encounter for fracture with nonunion

S92.591P Other fracture of right lesser toe(s), subsequent encounter for fracture with malunion

S92.591K Other fracture of right lesser toe(s), subsequent encounter for fracture with nonunion

S82.891B Other fracture of right lower leg, initial encounter for open fracture type I or II

S82.891C Other fracture of right lower leg, initial encounter for open fracture type IIIA, IIIB, or IIIC

S82.891P Other fracture of right lower leg, subsequent encounter for closed fracture with malunion

S82.891K Other fracture of right lower leg, subsequent encounter for closed fracture with nonunion

S82.891Q Other fracture of right lower leg, subsequent encounter for open fracture type I or II with malunion

S82.891M Other fracture of right lower leg, subsequent encounter for open fracture type I or II with nonunion

S82.891R Other fracture of right lower leg, subsequent encounter for open fracture type IIIA, IIIB, or IIIC with malunion

S82.891N Other fracture of right lower leg, subsequent encounter for open fracture type IIIA, IIIB, or IIIC with nonunion

S82.091A Other fracture of right patella, initial encounter for closed fracture

S82.091B Other fracture of right patella, initial encounter for open fracture type I or II

S82.091C Other fracture of right patella, initial encounter for open fracture type IIIA, IIIB, or IIIC

S82.091P Other fracture of right patella, subsequent encounter for closed fracture with malunion

S82.091K Other fracture of right patella, subsequent encounter for closed fracture with nonunion

S82.091Q Other fracture of right patella, subsequent encounter for open fracture type I or II with malunion

S82.091M Other fracture of right patella, subsequent encounter for open fracture type I or II with nonunion

S82.091R Other fracture of right patella, subsequent encounter for open fracture type IIIA, IIIB, or IIIC with malunion

S82.091N Other fracture of right patella, subsequent encounter for open fracture type IIIA, IIIB, or IIIC with nonunion

S92.191B Other fracture of right talus, initial encounter for open fracture

S92.191P Other fracture of right talus, subsequent encounter for fracture with malunion

S92.191K Other fracture of right talus, subsequent encounter for fracture with nonunion

S32.19XA Other fracture of sacrum, initial encounter for closed fracture

S32.19XK Other fracture of sacrum, subsequent encounter for fracture with nonunion

S32.028A Other fracture of second lumbar vertebra, initial encounter for closed fracture

S32.028K Other fracture of second lumbar vertebra, subsequent encounter for fracture with nonunion

S62.391B Other fracture of second metacarpal bone, left hand, initial encounter for open fracture

S62.391P Other fracture of second metacarpal bone, left hand, subsequent encounter for fracture with malunion

S62.391K Other fracture of second metacarpal bone, left hand, subsequent encounter for fracture with nonunion

S62.390B Other fracture of second metacarpal bone, right hand, initial encounter for open fracture

S62.390P Other fracture of second metacarpal bone, right hand, subsequent encounter for fracture with malunion

S62.390K Other fracture of second metacarpal bone, right hand, subsequent encounter for fracture with nonunion

S22.028A Other fracture of second thoracic vertebra, initial encounter for closed fracture

S22.028K Other fracture of second thoracic vertebra, subsequent encounter for fracture with nonunion

S72.392P Other fracture of shaft of left femur, subsequent encounter for closed fracture with malunion

S72.392K Other fracture of shaft of left femur, subsequent encounter for closed fracture with nonunion

S72.392Q Other fracture of shaft of left femur, subsequent encounter for open fracture type I or II with malunion

S72.392M Other fracture of shaft of left femur, subsequent encounter for open fracture type I or II with nonunion

S72.392R Other fracture of shaft of left femur, subsequent encounter for open fracture type IIIA, IIIB, or IIIC with malunion

S72.392N Other fracture of shaft of left femur, subsequent encounter for open fracture type IIIA, IIIB, or IIIC with nonunion

S82.492P Other fracture of shaft of left fibula, subsequent encounter for closed fracture with malunion

S82.492K Other fracture of shaft of left fibula, subsequent encounter for closed fracture with nonunion

S82.492Q Other fracture of shaft of left fibula, subsequent encounter for open fracture type I or II with malunion

S82.492M Other fracture of shaft of left fibula, subsequent encounter for open fracture type I or II with nonunion

S82.492R Other fracture of shaft of left fibula, subsequent encounter for open fracture type IIIA, IIIB, or IIIC with malunion

S82.492N Other fracture of shaft of left fibula, subsequent encounter for open fracture type IIIA, IIIB, or IIIC with nonunion

S42.392A Other fracture of shaft of left humerus, initial encounter for closed fracture

S42.392P Other fracture of shaft of left humerus, subsequent encounter for fracture with malunion

S42.392K Other fracture of shaft of left humerus, subsequent encounter for fracture with nonunion

S82.292A Other fracture of shaft of left tibia, initial encounter for closed fracture

S82.292P Other fracture of shaft of left tibia, subsequent encounter for closed fracture with malunion

S82.292K Other fracture of shaft of left tibia, subsequent encounter for closed fracture with nonunion

S82.292Q Other fracture of shaft of left tibia, subsequent encounter for open fracture type I or II with malunion

S82.292M Other fracture of shaft of left tibia, subsequent encounter for open fracture type I or II with nonunion

S82.292R Other fracture of shaft of left tibia, subsequent encounter for open fracture type IIIA, IIIB, or IIIC with malunion

S82.292N Other fracture of shaft of left tibia, subsequent encounter for open fracture type IIIA, IIIB, or IIIC with nonunion

S52.292A Other fracture of shaft of left ulna, initial encounter for closed fracture

S52.292P Other fracture of shaft of left ulna, subsequent encounter for closed fracture with malunion

S52.292K Other fracture of shaft of left ulna, subsequent encounter for closed fracture with nonunion

S52.292Q Other fracture of shaft of left ulna, subsequent encounter for open fracture type I or II with malunion

S52.292M Other fracture of shaft of left ulna, subsequent encounter for open fracture type I or II with nonunion

S52.292R Other fracture of shaft of left ulna, subsequent encounter for open fracture type IIIA, IIIB, or IIIC with malunion

S52.292N Other fracture of shaft of left ulna, subsequent encounter for open fracture type IIIA, IIIB, or IIIC with nonunion

S52.392A Other fracture of shaft of radius, left arm, initial encounter for closed fracture

S52.392P Other fracture of shaft of radius, left arm, subsequent encounter for closed fracture with malunion

S52.392K Other fracture of shaft of radius, left arm, subsequent encounter for closed fracture with nonunion

S52.392Q Other fracture of shaft of radius, left arm, subsequent encounter for open fracture type I or II with malunion

S52.392M Other fracture of shaft of radius, left arm, subsequent encounter for open fracture type I or II with nonunion

S52.392R Other fracture of shaft of radius, left arm, subsequent encounter for open fracture type IIIA, IIIB, or IIIC with malunion

S52.392N Other fracture of shaft of radius, left arm, subsequent encounter for open fracture type IIIA, IIIB, or IIIC with nonunion

S52.391A Other fracture of shaft of radius, right arm, initial encounter for closed fracture

S52.391P Other fracture of shaft of radius, right arm, subsequent encounter for closed fracture with malunion

S52.391K Other fracture of shaft of radius, right arm, subsequent encounter for closed fracture with nonunion

S52.391Q Other fracture of shaft of radius, right arm, subsequent encounter for open fracture type I or II with malunion

S52.391M Other fracture of shaft of radius, right arm, subsequent encounter for open fracture type I or II with nonunion

S52.391R Other fracture of shaft of radius, right arm, subsequent encounter for open fracture type IIIA, IIIB, or IIIC with malunion

S52.391N Other fracture of shaft of radius, right arm, subsequent encounter for open fracture type IIIA, IIIB, or IIIC with nonunion

S52.399A Other fracture of shaft of radius, unspecified arm, initial encounter for closed fracture

S52.399P Other fracture of shaft of radius, unspecified arm, subsequent encounter for closed fracture with malunion

S52.399K Other fracture of shaft of radius, unspecified arm, subsequent encounter for closed fracture with nonunion

S52.399Q Other fracture of shaft of radius, unspecified arm, subsequent encounter for open fracture type I or II with malunion

S52.399M Other fracture of shaft of radius, unspecified arm, subsequent encounter for open fracture type I or II with nonunion

S52.399R Other fracture of shaft of radius, unspecified arm, subsequent encounter for open fracture type IIIA, IIIB, or IIIC with malunion

S52.399N Other fracture of shaft of radius, unspecified arm, subsequent encounter for open fracture type IIIA, IIIB, or IIIC with nonunion

S72.391P Other fracture of shaft of right femur, subsequent encounter for closed fracture with malunion

S72.391K Other fracture of shaft of right femur, subsequent encounter for closed fracture with nonunion

S72.391Q Other fracture of shaft of right femur, subsequent encounter for open fracture type I or II with malunion

S72.391M Other fracture of shaft of right femur, subsequent encounter for open fracture type I or II with nonunion

S72.391R Other fracture of shaft of right femur, subsequent encounter for open fracture type IIIA, IIIB, or IIIC with malunion

S72.391N Other fracture of shaft of right femur, subsequent encounter for open fracture type IIIA, IIIB, or IIIC with nonunion

S82.491P Other fracture of shaft of right fibula, subsequent encounter for closed fracture with malunion

S82.491K Other fracture of shaft of right fibula, subsequent encounter for closed fracture with nonunion

S82.491Q Other fracture of shaft of right fibula, subsequent encounter for open fracture type I or II with malunion

S82.491M Other fracture of shaft of right fibula, subsequent encounter for open fracture type I or II with nonunion

S82.491R Other fracture of shaft of right fibula, subsequent encounter for open fracture type IIIA, IIIB, or IIIC with malunion

S82.491N Other fracture of shaft of right fibula, subsequent encounter for open fracture type IIIA, IIIB, or IIIC with nonunion

S42.391A Other fracture of shaft of right humerus, initial encounter for closed fracture

S42.391P Other fracture of shaft of right humerus, subsequent encounter for fracture with malunion

S42.391K Other fracture of shaft of right humerus, subsequent encounter for fracture with nonunion

S82.291A Other fracture of shaft of right tibia, initial encounter for closed fracture

S82.291P Other fracture of shaft of right tibia, subsequent encounter for closed fracture with malunion

S82.291K Other fracture of shaft of right tibia, subsequent encounter for closed fracture with nonunion

S82.291Q Other fracture of shaft of right tibia, subsequent encounter for open fracture type I or II with malunion

S82.291M Other fracture of shaft of right tibia, subsequent encounter for open fracture type I or II with nonunion

S82.291R Other fracture of shaft of right tibia, subsequent encounter for open fracture type IIIA, IIIB, or IIIC with malunion

S82.291N Other fracture of shaft of right tibia, subsequent encounter for open fracture type IIIA, IIIB, or IIIC with nonunion

S52.291A Other fracture of shaft of right ulna, initial encounter for closed fracture

S52.291P Other fracture of shaft of right ulna, subsequent encounter for closed fracture with malunion

S52.291K Other fracture of shaft of right ulna, subsequent encounter for closed fracture with nonunion

S52.291Q Other fracture of shaft of right ulna, subsequent encounter for open fracture type I or II with malunion

S52.291M Other fracture of shaft of right ulna, subsequent encounter for open fracture type I or II with nonunion

S52.291R Other fracture of shaft of right ulna, subsequent encounter for open fracture type IIIA, IIIB, or IIIC with malunion

S52.291N Other fracture of shaft of right ulna, subsequent encounter for open fracture type IIIA, IIIB, or IIIC with nonunion

S72.399P Other fracture of shaft of unspecified femur, subsequent encounter for closed fracture with malunion

S72.399K Other fracture of shaft of unspecified femur, subsequent encounter for closed fracture with nonunion

S72.399Q Other fracture of shaft of unspecified femur, subsequent encounter for open fracture type I or II with malunion

S72.399M Other fracture of shaft of unspecified femur, subsequent encounter for open fracture type I or II with nonunion

S72.399R Other fracture of shaft of unspecified femur, subsequent encounter for open fracture type IIIA, IIIB, or IIIC with malunion

S72.399N Other fracture of shaft of unspecified femur, subsequent encounter for open fracture type IIIA, IIIB, or IIIC with nonunion

S82.499P Other fracture of shaft of unspecified fibula, subsequent encounter for closed fracture with malunion

S82.499K Other fracture of shaft of unspecified fibula, subsequent encounter for closed fracture with nonunion

S82.499Q Other fracture of shaft of unspecified fibula, subsequent encounter for open fracture type I or II with malunion

S82.499M Other fracture of shaft of unspecified fibula, subsequent encounter for open fracture type I or II with nonunion

S82.499R Other fracture of shaft of unspecified fibula, subsequent encounter for open fracture type IIIA, IIIB, or IIIC with malunion

S82.499N Other fracture of shaft of unspecified fibula, subsequent encounter for open fracture type IIIA, IIIB, or IIIC with nonunion

S42.399A Other fracture of shaft of unspecified humerus, initial encounter for closed fracture

S42.399P Other fracture of shaft of unspecified humerus, subsequent encounter for fracture with malunion

S42.399K Other fracture of shaft of unspecified humerus, subsequent encounter for fracture with nonunion

S82.299A Other fracture of shaft of unspecified tibia, initial encounter for closed fracture

S82.299P Other fracture of shaft of unspecified tibia, subsequent encounter for closed fracture with malunion

S82.299K Other fracture of shaft of unspecified tibia, subsequent encounter for closed fracture with nonunion

S82.299Q Other fracture of shaft of unspecified tibia, subsequent encounter for open fracture type I or II with malunion

S82.299M Other fracture of shaft of unspecified tibia, subsequent encounter for open fracture type I or II with nonunion

S82.299R Other fracture of shaft of unspecified tibia, subsequent encounter for open fracture type IIIA, IIIB, or IIIC with malunion

S82.299N Other fracture of shaft of unspecified tibia, subsequent encounter for open fracture type IIIA, IIIB, or IIIC with nonunion

S52.299A Other fracture of shaft of unspecified ulna, initial encounter for closed fracture

S52.299P Other fracture of shaft of unspecified ulna, subsequent encounter for closed fracture with malunion

S52.299K Other fracture of shaft of unspecified ulna, subsequent encounter for closed fracture with nonunion

S52.299Q Other fracture of shaft of unspecified ulna, subsequent encounter for open fracture type I or II with malunion

S52.299M Other fracture of shaft of unspecified ulna, subsequent encounter for open fracture type I or II with nonunion

S52.299R Other fracture of shaft of unspecified ulna, subsequent encounter for open fracture type IIIA, IIIB, or IIIC with malunion

S52.299N Other fracture of shaft of unspecified ulna, subsequent encounter for open fracture type IIIA, IIIB, or IIIC with nonunion

S22.088A Other fracture of T11-T12 vertebra, initial encounter for closed fracture

S22.088K Other fracture of T11-T12 vertebra, subsequent encounter for fracture with nonunion

S22.058A Other fracture of T5-T6 vertebra, initial encounter for closed fracture

S22.058K Other fracture of T5-T6 vertebra, subsequent encounter for fracture with nonunion

S22.068A Other fracture of T7-T8 thoracic vertebra, initial encounter for closed fracture

S22.068K Other fracture of T7-T8 thoracic vertebra, subsequent encounter for fracture with nonunion

S22.078A Other fracture of T9-T10 vertebra, initial encounter for closed fracture

S22.078K Other fracture of T9-T10 vertebra, subsequent encounter for fracture with nonunion

S32.038A Other fracture of third lumbar vertebra, initial encounter for closed fracture

S32.038K Other fracture of third lumbar vertebra, subsequent encounter for fracture with nonunion

S62.393B Other fracture of third metacarpal bone, left hand, initial encounter for open fracture

S62.393P Other fracture of third metacarpal bone, left hand, subsequent encounter for fracture with malunion

S62.393K Other fracture of third metacarpal bone, left hand, subsequent encounter for fracture with nonunion

S62.392B Other fracture of third metacarpal bone, right hand, initial encounter for open fracture

S62.392P Other fracture of third metacarpal bone, right hand, subsequent encounter for fracture with malunion

S62.392K Other fracture of third metacarpal bone, right hand, subsequent encounter for fracture with nonunion

S22.038A Other fracture of third thoracic vertebra, initial encounter for closed fracture

S22.038K Other fracture of third thoracic vertebra, subsequent encounter for fracture with nonunion

S72.8X9P Other fracture of unspecified femur, subsequent encounter for closed fracture with malunion

S72.8X9K Other fracture of unspecified femur, subsequent encounter for closed fracture with nonunion

S72.8X9Q Other fracture of unspecified femur, subsequent encounter for open fracture type I or II with malunion

S72.8X9M Other fracture of unspecified femur, subsequent encounter for open fracture type I or II with nonunion

S72.8X9R Other fracture of unspecified femur, subsequent encounter for open fracture type IIIA, IIIB, or IIIC with malunion

S72.8X9N Other fracture of unspecified femur, subsequent encounter for open fracture type IIIA, IIIB, or IIIC with nonunion

S92.819B Other fracture of unspecified foot, initial encounter for open fracture

S92.819P Other fracture of unspecified foot, subsequent encounter for fracture with malunion

S92.819K Other fracture of unspecified foot, subsequent encounter for fracture with nonunion

S92.499P Other fracture of unspecified great toe, subsequent encounter for fracture with malunion

S92.499K Other fracture of unspecified great toe, subsequent encounter for fracture with nonunion

S32.399A Other fracture of unspecified ilium, initial encounter for closed fracture

S32.399K Other fracture of unspecified ilium, subsequent encounter for fracture with nonunion

S92.599P Other fracture of unspecified lesser toe(s), subsequent encounter for fracture with malunion

S92.599K Other fracture of unspecified lesser toe(s), subsequent encounter for fracture with nonunion

S82.899B Other fracture of unspecified lower leg, initial encounter for open fracture type I or II

S82.899C Other fracture of unspecified lower leg, initial encounter for open fracture type IIIA, IIIB, or IIIC

S82.899P Other fracture of unspecified lower leg, subsequent encounter for closed fracture with malunion

S82.899K Other fracture of unspecified lower leg, subsequent encounter for closed fracture with nonunion

S82.899Q Other fracture of unspecified lower leg, subsequent encounter for open fracture type I or II with malunion

S82.899M Other fracture of unspecified lower leg, subsequent encounter for open fracture type I or II with nonunion

S82.899R Other fracture of unspecified lower leg, subsequent encounter for open fracture type IIIA, IIIB, or IIIC with malunion

S82.899N Other fracture of unspecified lower leg, subsequent encounter for open fracture type IIIA, IIIB, or IIIC with nonunion

S32.008A Other fracture of unspecified lumbar vertebra, initial encounter for closed fracture

S32.008K Other fracture of unspecified lumbar vertebra, subsequent encounter for fracture with nonunion

S62.399B Other fracture of unspecified metacarpal bone, initial encounter for open fracture

S62.399P Other fracture of unspecified metacarpal bone, subsequent encounter for fracture with malunion

S62.399K Other fracture of unspecified metacarpal bone, subsequent encounter for fracture with nonunion

S82.099A Other fracture of unspecified patella, initial encounter for closed fracture

S82.099B Other fracture of unspecified patella, initial encounter for open fracture type I or II

S82.099C Other fracture of unspecified patella, initial encounter for open fracture type IIIA, IIIB, or IIIC

S82.099P Other fracture of unspecified patella, subsequent encounter for closed fracture with malunion

S82.099K Other fracture of unspecified patella, subsequent encounter for closed fracture with nonunion

S82.099Q Other fracture of unspecified patella, subsequent encounter for open fracture type I or II with malunion

S82.099M Other fracture of unspecified patella, subsequent encounter for open fracture type I or II with nonunion

S82.099R Other fracture of unspecified patella, subsequent encounter for open fracture type IIIA, IIIB, or IIIC with malunion

S82.099N Other fracture of unspecified patella, subsequent encounter for open fracture type IIIA, IIIB, or IIIC with nonunion

S92.199B Other fracture of unspecified talus, initial encounter for open fracture

S92.199P Other fracture of unspecified talus, subsequent encounter for fracture with malunion

S92.199K Other fracture of unspecified talus, subsequent encounter for fracture with nonunion

S22.008A Other fracture of unspecified thoracic vertebra, initial encounter for closed fracture

S22.008K Other fracture of unspecified thoracic vertebra, subsequent encounter for fracture with nonunion

S82.832P Other fracture of upper and lower end of left fibula, subsequent encounter for closed fracture with malunion

S82.832K Other fracture of upper and lower end of left fibula, subsequent encounter for closed fracture with nonunion

S82.832Q Other fracture of upper and lower end of left fibula, subsequent encounter for open fracture type I or II with malunion

S82.832M Other fracture of upper and lower end of left fibula, subsequent encounter for open fracture type I or II with nonunion

S82.832R Other fracture of upper and lower end of left fibula, subsequent encounter for open fracture type IIIA, IIIB, or IIIC with malunion

S82.832N Other fracture of upper and lower end of left fibula, subsequent encounter for open fracture type IIIA, IIIB, or IIIC with nonunion

S82.831P Other fracture of upper and lower end of right fibula, subsequent encounter for closed fracture with malunion

S82.831K Other fracture of upper and lower end of right fibula, subsequent encounter for closed fracture with nonunion

S82.831Q Other fracture of upper and lower end of right fibula, subsequent encounter for open fracture type I or II with malunion

S82.831M Other fracture of upper and lower end of right fibula, subsequent encounter for open fracture type I or II with nonunion

S82.831R Other fracture of upper and lower end of right fibula, subsequent encounter for open fracture type IIIA, IIIB, or IIIC with malunion

S82.831N Other fracture of upper and lower end of right fibula, subsequent encounter for open fracture type IIIA, IIIB, or IIIC with nonunion

S82.839P Other fracture of upper and lower end of unspecified fibula, subsequent encounter for closed fracture with malunion

S82.839K Other fracture of upper and lower end of unspecified fibula, subsequent encounter for closed fracture with nonunion

S82.839Q Other fracture of upper and lower end of unspecified fibula, subsequent encounter for open fracture type I or II with malunion

S82.839M Other fracture of upper and lower end of unspecified fibula, subsequent encounter for open fracture type I or II with nonunion

S82.839R Other fracture of upper and lower end of unspecified fibula, subsequent encounter for open fracture type IIIA, IIIB, or IIIC with malunion

S82.839N Other fracture of upper and lower end of unspecified fibula, subsequent encounter for open fracture type IIIA, IIIB, or IIIC with nonunion

S52.182P Other fracture of upper end of left radius, subsequent encounter for closed fracture with malunion

S52.182K Other fracture of upper end of left radius, subsequent encounter for closed fracture with nonunion

S52.182Q Other fracture of upper end of left radius, subsequent encounter for open fracture type I or II with malunion

S52.182M Other fracture of upper end of left radius, subsequent encounter for open fracture type I or II with nonunion

S52.182R Other fracture of upper end of left radius, subsequent encounter for open fracture type IIIA, IIIB, or IIIC with malunion

S52.182N Other fracture of upper end of left radius, subsequent encounter for open fracture type IIIA, IIIB, or IIIC with nonunion

S82.192A Other fracture of upper end of left tibia, initial encounter for closed fracture

S82.192P Other fracture of upper end of left tibia, subsequent encounter for closed fracture with malunion

S82.192K Other fracture of upper end of left tibia, subsequent encounter for closed fracture with nonunion

S82.192Q Other fracture of upper end of left tibia, subsequent encounter for open fracture type I or II with malunion

S82.192M Other fracture of upper end of left tibia, subsequent encounter for open fracture type I or II with nonunion

S82.192R Other fracture of upper end of left tibia, subsequent encounter for open fracture type IIIA, IIIB, or IIIC with malunion

S82.192N Other fracture of upper end of left tibia, subsequent encounter for open fracture type IIIA, IIIB, or IIIC with nonunion

S52.092P Other fracture of upper end of left ulna, subsequent encounter for closed fracture with malunion

S52.092K Other fracture of upper end of left ulna, subsequent encounter for closed fracture with nonunion

S52.092Q Other fracture of upper end of left ulna, subsequent encounter for open fracture type I or II with malunion

S52.092M Other fracture of upper end of left ulna, subsequent encounter for open fracture type I or II with nonunion

S52.092R Other fracture of upper end of left ulna, subsequent encounter for open fracture type IIIA, IIIB, or IIIC with malunion

S52.092N Other fracture of upper end of left ulna, subsequent encounter for open fracture type IIIA, IIIB, or IIIC with nonunion

S52.181P Other fracture of upper end of right radius, subsequent encounter for closed fracture with malunion

S52.181K	Other fracture of upper end of right radius, subsequent encounter for closed fracture with nonunion
S52.181Q	Other fracture of upper end of right radius, subsequent encounter for open fracture type I or II with malunion
S52.181M	Other fracture of upper end of right radius, subsequent encounter for open fracture type I or II with nonunion
S52.181R	Other fracture of upper end of right radius, subsequent encounter for open fracture type IIIA, IIIB, or IIIC with malunion
S52.181N	Other fracture of upper end of right radius, subsequent encounter for open fracture type IIIA, IIIB, or IIIC with nonunion
S82.191A	Other fracture of upper end of right tibia, initial encounter for closed fracture
S82.191P	Other fracture of upper end of right tibia, subsequent encounter for closed fracture with malunion
S82.191K	Other fracture of upper end of right tibia, subsequent encounter for closed fracture with nonunion
S82.191Q	Other fracture of upper end of right tibia, subsequent encounter for open fracture type I or II with malunion
S82.191M	Other fracture of upper end of right tibia, subsequent encounter for open fracture type I or II with nonunion
S82.191R	Other fracture of upper end of right tibia, subsequent encounter for open fracture type IIIA, IIIB, or IIIC with malunion
S82.191N	Other fracture of upper end of right tibia, subsequent encounter for open fracture type IIIA, IIIB, or IIIC with nonunion
S52.091P	Other fracture of upper end of right ulna, subsequent encounter for closed fracture with malunion
S52.091K	Other fracture of upper end of right ulna, subsequent encounter for closed fracture with nonunion
S52.091Q	Other fracture of upper end of right ulna, subsequent encounter for open fracture type I or II with malunion
S52.091M	Other fracture of upper end of right ulna, subsequent encounter for open fracture type I or II with nonunion
S52.091R	Other fracture of upper end of right ulna, subsequent encounter for open fracture type IIIA, IIIB, or IIIC with malunion
S52.091N	Other fracture of upper end of right ulna, subsequent encounter for open fracture type IIIA, IIIB, or IIIC with nonunion
S52.189P	Other fracture of upper end of unspecified radius, subsequent encounter for closed fracture with malunion
S52.189K	Other fracture of upper end of unspecified radius, subsequent encounter for closed fracture with nonunion
S52.189Q	Other fracture of upper end of unspecified radius, subsequent encounter for open fracture type I or II with malunion
S52.189M	Other fracture of upper end of unspecified radius, subsequent encounter for open fracture type I or II with nonunion
S52.189R	Other fracture of upper end of unspecified radius, subsequent encounter for open fracture type IIIA, IIIB, or IIIC with malunion
S52.189N	Other fracture of upper end of unspecified radius, subsequent encounter for open fracture type IIIA, IIIB, or IIIC with nonunion
S82.199A	Other fracture of upper end of unspecified tibia, initial encounter for closed fracture
S82.199P	Other fracture of upper end of unspecified tibia, subsequent encounter for closed fracture with malunion
S82.199K	Other fracture of upper end of unspecified tibia, subsequent encounter for closed fracture with nonunion
S82.199Q	Other fracture of upper end of unspecified tibia, subsequent encounter for open fracture type I or II with malunion
S82.199M	Other fracture of upper end of unspecified tibia, subsequent encounter for open fracture type I or II with nonunion
S82.199R	Other fracture of upper end of unspecified tibia, subsequent encounter for open fracture type IIIA, IIIB, or IIIC with malunion
S82.199N	Other fracture of upper end of unspecified tibia, subsequent encounter for open fracture type IIIA, IIIB, or IIIC with nonunion
S52.099P	Other fracture of upper end of unspecified ulna, subsequent encounter for closed fracture with malunion
S52.099K	Other fracture of upper end of unspecified ulna, subsequent encounter for closed fracture with nonunion
S52.099Q	Other fracture of upper end of unspecified ulna, subsequent encounter for open fracture type I or II with malunion
S52.099M	Other fracture of upper end of unspecified ulna, subsequent encounter for open fracture type I or II with nonunion
S52.099R	Other fracture of upper end of unspecified ulna, subsequent encounter for open fracture type IIIA, IIIB, or IIIC with malunion
S52.099N	Other fracture of upper end of unspecified ulna, subsequent encounter for open fracture type IIIA, IIIB, or IIIC with nonunion
S52.592A	Other fractures of lower end of left radius, initial encounter for closed fracture
S52.592P	Other fractures of lower end of left radius, subsequent encounter for closed fracture with malunion
S52.592K	Other fractures of lower end of left radius, subsequent encounter for closed fracture with nonunion
S52.592Q	Other fractures of lower end of left radius, subsequent encounter for open fracture type I or II with malunion
S52.592M	Other fractures of lower end of left radius, subsequent encounter for open fracture type I or II with nonunion
S52.592R	Other fractures of lower end of left radius, subsequent encounter for open fracture type IIIA, IIIB, or IIIC with malunion
S52.592N	Other fractures of lower end of left radius, subsequent encounter for open fracture type IIIA, IIIB, or IIIC with nonunion
S52.591A	Other fractures of lower end of right radius, initial encounter for closed fracture
S52.591P	Other fractures of lower end of right radius, subsequent encounter for closed fracture with malunion
S52.591K	Other fractures of lower end of right radius, subsequent encounter for closed fracture with nonunion
S52.591Q	Other fractures of lower end of right radius, subsequent encounter for open fracture type I or II with malunion
S52.591M	Other fractures of lower end of right radius, subsequent encounter for open fracture type I or II with nonunion
S52.591R	Other fractures of lower end of right radius, subsequent encounter for open fracture type IIIA, IIIB, or IIIC with malunion
S52.591N	Other fractures of lower end of right radius, subsequent encounter for open fracture type IIIA, IIIB, or IIIC with nonunion
S52.599A	Other fractures of lower end of unspecified radius, initial encounter for closed fracture
S52.599P	Other fractures of lower end of unspecified radius, subsequent encounter for closed fracture with malunion
S52.599K	Other fractures of lower end of unspecified radius, subsequent encounter for closed fracture with nonunion
S52.599Q	Other fractures of lower end of unspecified radius, subsequent encounter for open fracture type I or II with malunion
S52.599M	Other fractures of lower end of unspecified radius, subsequent encounter for open fracture type I or II with nonunion
S52.599R	Other fractures of lower end of unspecified radius, subsequent encounter for open fracture type IIIA, IIIB, or IIIC with malunion
S52.599N	Other fractures of lower end of unspecified radius, subsequent encounter for open fracture type IIIA, IIIB, or IIIC with nonunion
E75.19	Other gangliosidosis
G40.411	Other generalized epilepsy and epileptic syndromes, intractable, with status epilepticus
G40.419	Other generalized epilepsy and epileptic syndromes, intractable, without status epilepticus
A52.76	Other genitourinary symptomatic late syphilis
E74.09	Other glycogen storage disease
E75.09	Other GM2 gangliosidosis
A54.39	Other gonococcal eye infection
A54.29	Other gonococcal genitourinary infections
A54.09	Other gonococcal infection of lower genitourinary tract
A54.89	Other gonococcal infections
E71.53	Other group 2 peroxisomal disorders
E71.542	Other group 3 peroxisomal disorders
R44.2	Other hallucinations
T67.09XA	Other heatstroke and sunstroke, initial encounter
D68.318	Other hemorrhagic disorder due to intrinsic circulating anticoagulants, antibodies, or inhibitors
G11.8	Other hereditary ataxias
I67.858	Other hereditary cerebrovascular disease
B02.39	Other herpes zoster eye disease
B00.59	Other herpesviral disease of eye
B00.89	Other herpesviral infection
D76.3	Other histiocytosis syndromes
C81.79	Other Hodgkin lymphoma, extranodal and solid organ sites
C81.73	Other Hodgkin lymphoma, intra-abdominal lymph nodes
C81.76	Other Hodgkin lymphoma, intrapelvic lymph nodes
C81.72	Other Hodgkin lymphoma, intrathoracic lymph nodes
C81.74	Other Hodgkin lymphoma, lymph nodes of axilla and upper limb
C81.71	Other Hodgkin lymphoma, lymph nodes of head, face, and neck
C81.75	Other Hodgkin lymphoma, lymph nodes of inguinal region and lower limb
C81.78	Other Hodgkin lymphoma, lymph nodes of multiple sites
C81.77	Other Hodgkin lymphoma, spleen
C81.70	Other Hodgkin lymphoma, unspecified site
B76.8	Other hookworm diseases
G91.8	Other hydrocephalus
N13.39	Other hydronephrosis
E22.8	Other hyperfunction of pituitary gland
E70.1	Other hyperphenylalaninemias
I42.2	Other hypertrophic cardiomyopathy
O72.1	Other immediate postpartum hemorrhage
D80.8	Other immunodeficiencies with predominantly antibody defects
K56.49	Other impaction of intestine
O99.834	Other infection carrier state complicating childbirth
O99.830	Other infection carrier state complicating pregnancy
O99.835	Other infection carrier state complicating the puerperium
T80.218A	Other infection due to central venous catheter, initial encounter
O86.19	Other infection of genital tract following delivery
O98.32	Other infections with a predominantly sexual mode of transmission complicating childbirth
O98.311	Other infections with a predominantly sexual mode of transmission complicating pregnancy, first trimester
O98.312	Other infections with a predominantly sexual mode of transmission complicating pregnancy, second trimester
O98.313	Other infections with a predominantly sexual mode of transmission complicating pregnancy, third trimester
O98.33	Other infections with a predominantly sexual mode of transmission complicating the puerperium
G12.1	Other inherited spinal muscular atrophy
S05.8X2A	Other injuries of left eye and orbit, initial encounter
S27.392A	Other injuries of lung, bilateral, initial encounter
S27.391A	Other injuries of lung, unilateral, initial encounter
S27.399A	Other injuries of lung, unspecified, initial encounter
S05.8X1A	Other injuries of right eye and orbit, initial encounter
S05.8X9A	Other injuries of unspecified eye and orbit, initial encounter
S37.818A	Other injury of adrenal gland, initial encounter

S36.590A	Other injury of ascending [right] colon, initial encounter
S37.29XA	Other injury of bladder, initial encounter
S36.291A	Other injury of body of pancreas, initial encounter
S36.592A	Other injury of descending [left] colon, initial encounter
S27.808A	Other injury of diaphragm, initial encounter
S36.490A	Other injury of duodenum, initial encounter
S36.128A	Other injury of gallbladder, initial encounter
S36.290A	Other injury of head of pancreas, initial encounter
S26.09XA	Other injury of heart with hemopericardium, initial encounter
S26.19XA	Other injury of heart without hemopericardium, initial encounter
S26.99XA	Other injury of heart, unspecified with or without hemopericardium, initial encounter
S36.118A	Other injury of liver, initial encounter
S36.898A	Other injury of other intra-abdominal organs, initial encounter
S36.598A	Other injury of other part of colon, initial encounter
S36.498A	Other injury of other part of small intestine, initial encounter
S27.898A	Other injury of other specified intrathoracic organs, initial encounter
S37.898A	Other injury of other urinary and pelvic organ, initial encounter
S27.69XA	Other injury of pleura, initial encounter
S36.69XA	Other injury of rectum, initial encounter
S36.593A	Other injury of sigmoid colon, initial encounter
S36.09XA	Other injury of spleen, initial encounter
S36.39XA	Other injury of stomach, initial encounter
S36.292A	Other injury of tail of pancreas, initial encounter
S27.59XA	Other injury of thoracic trachea, initial encounter
S36.591A	Other injury of transverse colon, initial encounter
S36.99XA	Other injury of unspecified intra-abdominal organ, initial encounter
S36.599A	Other injury of unspecified part of colon, initial encounter
S36.299A	Other injury of unspecified part of pancreas, initial encounter
S36.499A	Other injury of unspecified part of small intestine, initial encounter
S37.99XA	Other injury of unspecified urinary and pelvic organ, initial encounter
S37.19XA	Other injury of ureter, initial encounter
S37.39XA	Other injury of urethra, initial encounter
S37.69XA	Other injury of uterus, initial encounter
A04.4	Other intestinal Escherichia coli infections
K90.89	Other intestinal malabsorption
K56.699	Other intestinal obstruction unspecified as to partial versus complete obstruction
S52.572A	Other intraarticular fracture of lower end of left radius, initial encounter for closed fracture
S52.572P	Other intraarticular fracture of lower end of left radius, subsequent encounter for closed fracture with malunion
S52.572K	Other intraarticular fracture of lower end of left radius, subsequent encounter for closed fracture with nonunion
S52.572Q	Other intraarticular fracture of lower end of left radius, subsequent encounter for open fracture type I or II with malunion
S52.572M	Other intraarticular fracture of lower end of left radius, subsequent encounter for open fracture type I or II with nonunion
S52.572R	Other intraarticular fracture of lower end of left radius, subsequent encounter for open fracture type IIIA, IIIB, or IIIC with malunion
S52.572N	Other intraarticular fracture of lower end of left radius, subsequent encounter for open fracture type IIIA, IIIB, or IIIC with nonunion
S52.571A	Other intraarticular fracture of lower end of right radius, initial encounter for closed fracture
S52.571P	Other intraarticular fracture of lower end of right radius, subsequent encounter for closed fracture with malunion
S52.571K	Other intraarticular fracture of lower end of right radius, subsequent encounter for closed fracture with nonunion
S52.571Q	Other intraarticular fracture of lower end of right radius, subsequent encounter for open fracture type I or II with malunion
S52.571M	Other intraarticular fracture of lower end of right radius, subsequent encounter for open fracture type I or II with nonunion
S52.571R	Other intraarticular fracture of lower end of right radius, subsequent encounter for open fracture type IIIA, IIIB, or IIIC with malunion
S52.571N	Other intraarticular fracture of lower end of right radius, subsequent encounter for open fracture type IIIA, IIIB, or IIIC with nonunion
S52.579A	Other intraarticular fracture of lower end of unspecified radius, initial encounter for closed fracture
S52.579P	Other intraarticular fracture of lower end of unspecified radius, subsequent encounter for closed fracture with malunion
S52.579K	Other intraarticular fracture of lower end of unspecified radius, subsequent encounter for closed fracture with nonunion
S52.579Q	Other intraarticular fracture of lower end of unspecified radius, subsequent encounter for open fracture type I or II with malunion
S52.579M	Other intraarticular fracture of lower end of unspecified radius, subsequent encounter for open fracture type I or II with nonunion
S52.579R	Other intraarticular fracture of lower end of unspecified radius, subsequent encounter for open fracture type IIIA, IIIB, or IIIC with malunion
S52.579N	Other intraarticular fracture of lower end of unspecified radius, subsequent encounter for open fracture type IIIA, IIIB, or IIIC with nonunion
M96.89	Other intraoperative and postprocedural complications and disorders of the musculoskeletal system
I97.790	Other intraoperative cardiac functional disturbances during cardiac surgery
I97.791	Other intraoperative cardiac functional disturbances during other surgery
H95.88	Other intraoperative complications and disorders of the ear and mastoid process, not elsewhere classified
K91.81	Other intraoperative complications of digestive system
H59.88	Other intraoperative complications of eye and adnexa, not elsewhere classified
G97.81	Other intraoperative complications of nervous system
J95.88	Other intraoperative complications of respiratory system, not elsewhere classified
I97.88	Other intraoperative complications of the circulatory system, not elsewhere classified
D78.81	Other intraoperative complications of the spleen
A50.49	Other late congenital neurosyphilis
A50.59	Other late congenital syphilis, symptomatic
A50.39	Other late congenital syphilitic oculopathy
C91.Z0	Other lymphoid leukemia not having achieved remission
C91.Z2	Other lymphoid leukemia, in relapse
C91.Z1	Other lymphoid leukemia, in remission
B53.8	Other malaria, not elsewhere classified
Q28.1	Other malformations of precerebral vessels
C88.8	Other malignant immunoproliferative diseases
C96.29	Other malignant mast cell neoplasm
C7A.8	Other malignant neuroendocrine tumors
E51.8	Other manifestations of thiamine deficiency
D47.09	Other mast cell neoplasms of uncertain behavior
O98.82	Other maternal infectious and parasitic diseases complicating childbirth
O98.811	Other maternal infectious and parasitic diseases complicating pregnancy, first trimester
O98.812	Other maternal infectious and parasitic diseases complicating pregnancy, second trimester
O98.813	Other maternal infectious and parasitic diseases complicating pregnancy, third trimester
O98.83	Other maternal infectious and parasitic diseases complicating the puerperium
C84.Z9	Other mature T/NK-cell lymphomas, extranodal and solid organ sites
C84.Z3	Other mature T/NK-cell lymphomas, intra-abdominal lymph nodes
C84.Z6	Other mature T/NK-cell lymphomas, intrapelvic lymph nodes
C84.Z2	Other mature T/NK-cell lymphomas, intrathoracic lymph nodes
C84.Z4	Other mature T/NK-cell lymphomas, lymph nodes of axilla and upper limb
C84.Z1	Other mature T/NK-cell lymphomas, lymph nodes of head, face, and neck
C84.Z5	Other mature T/NK-cell lymphomas, lymph nodes of inguinal region and lower limb
C84.Z8	Other mature T/NK-cell lymphomas, lymph nodes of multiple sites
C84.Z7	Other mature T/NK-cell lymphomas, spleen
C84.Z0	Other mature T/NK-cell lymphomas, unspecified site
B05.89	Other measles complications
T82.390A	Other mechanical complication of aortic (bifurcation) graft (replacement), initial encounter
T82.592A	Other mechanical complication of artificial heart, initial encounter
T85.693A	Other mechanical complication of artificial skin graft and decellularized allodermis, initial encounter
T82.593A	Other mechanical complication of balloon (counterpulsation) device, initial encounter
T85.590A	Other mechanical complication of bile duct prosthesis, initial encounter
T82.228A	Other mechanical complication of biological heart valve graft, initial encounter
T85.49XA	Other mechanical complication of breast prosthesis and implant, initial encounter
T82.190A	Other mechanical complication of cardiac electrode, initial encounter
T82.191A	Other mechanical complication of cardiac pulse generator (battery), initial encounter
T82.391A	Other mechanical complication of carotid arterial graft (bypass), initial encounter
T82.218A	Other mechanical complication of coronary artery bypass graft, initial encounter
T85.690A	Other mechanical complication of cranial or spinal infusion catheter, initial encounter
T83.090A	Other mechanical complication of cystostomy catheter, initial encounter
T84.390A	Other mechanical complication of electronic bone stimulator, initial encounter
T85.591A	Other mechanical complication of esophageal anti-reflux device, initial encounter
T82.392A	Other mechanical complication of femoral arterial graft (bypass), initial encounter
T83.29XA	Other mechanical complication of graft of urinary organ, initial encounter
T82.09XA	Other mechanical complication of heart valve prosthesis, initial encounter
T85.190A	Other mechanical complication of implanted electronic neurostimulator of brain electrode (lead), initial encounter
T85.191A	Other mechanical complication of implanted electronic neurostimulator of peripheral nerve electrode (lead), initial encounter
T85.192A	Other mechanical complication of implanted electronic neurostimulator of spinal cord electrode (lead), initial encounter
T85.193A	Other mechanical complication of implanted electronic neurostimulator, generator, initial encounter
T83.490A	Other mechanical complication of implanted penile prosthesis, initial encounter
T83.491A	Other mechanical complication of implanted testicular prosthesis, initial encounter
T83.191A	Other mechanical complication of implanted urinary sphincter, initial encounter
T83.192A	Other mechanical complication of indwelling ureteral stent, initial encounter
T82.594A	Other mechanical complication of infusion catheter, initial encounter
T85.694A	Other mechanical complication of insulin pump, initial encounter
T84.193A	Other mechanical complication of internal fixation device of bone of left forearm, initial encounter
T84.197A	Other mechanical complication of internal fixation device of bone of left lower leg, initial encounter

T84.192A	Other mechanical complication of internal fixation device of bone of right forearm, initial encounter
T84.196A	Other mechanical complication of internal fixation device of bone of right lower leg, initial encounter
T84.293A	Other mechanical complication of internal fixation device of bones of foot and toes, initial encounter
T84.290A	Other mechanical complication of internal fixation device of bones of hand and fingers, initial encounter
T84.195A	Other mechanical complication of internal fixation device of left femur, initial encounter
T84.191A	Other mechanical complication of internal fixation device of left humerus, initial encounter
T84.298A	Other mechanical complication of internal fixation device of other bones, initial encounter
T84.194A	Other mechanical complication of internal fixation device of right femur, initial encounter
T84.190A	Other mechanical complication of internal fixation device of right humerus, initial encounter
T84.199A	Other mechanical complication of internal fixation device of unspecified bone of limb, initial encounter
T84.296A	Other mechanical complication of internal fixation device of vertebrae, initial encounter
T84.091A	Other mechanical complication of internal left hip prosthesis, initial encounter
T84.093A	Other mechanical complication of internal left knee prosthesis, initial encounter
T84.090A	Other mechanical complication of internal right hip prosthesis, initial encounter
T84.092A	Other mechanical complication of internal right knee prosthesis, initial encounter
T85.29XA	Other mechanical complication of intraocular lens, initial encounter
T85.691A	Other mechanical complication of intraperitoneal dialysis catheter, initial encounter
T84.490A	Other mechanical complication of muscle and tendon graft, initial encounter
T84.398A	Other mechanical complication of other bone devices, implants and grafts, initial encounter
T82.598A	Other mechanical complication of other cardiac and vascular devices and implants, initial encounter
T82.198A	Other mechanical complication of other cardiac electronic device, initial encounter
T85.598A	Other mechanical complication of other gastrointestinal prosthetic devices, implants and grafts, initial encounter
T85.199A	Other mechanical complication of other implanted electronic stimulator of nervous system, initial encounter
T84.098A	Other mechanical complication of other internal joint prosthesis, initial encounter
T84.498A	Other mechanical complication of other internal orthopedic devices, implants and grafts, initial encounter
T85.695A	Other mechanical complication of other nervous system device, implant or graft, initial encounter
T83.498A	Other mechanical complication of other prosthetic devices, implants and grafts of genital tract, initial encounter
T85.698A	Other mechanical complication of other specified internal prosthetic devices, implants and grafts, initial encounter
T83.198A	Other mechanical complication of other urinary devices and implants, initial encounter
T83.193A	Other mechanical complication of other urinary stent, initial encounter
T82.398A	Other mechanical complication of other vascular grafts, initial encounter
T85.692A	Other mechanical complication of permanent sutures, initial encounter
T85.391A	Other mechanical complication of prosthetic orbit of left eye, initial encounter
T85.390A	Other mechanical complication of prosthetic orbit of right eye, initial encounter
T82.590A	Other mechanical complication of surgically created arteriovenous fistula, initial encounter
T82.591A	Other mechanical complication of surgically created arteriovenous shunt, initial encounter
T82.595A	Other mechanical complication of umbrella device, initial encounter
T82.599A	Other mechanical complication of unspecified cardiac and vascular devices and implants, initial encounter
T82.199A	Other mechanical complication of unspecified cardiac device, initial encounter
T84.099A	Other mechanical complication of unspecified internal joint prosthesis, initial encounter
T82.399A	Other mechanical complication of unspecified vascular grafts, initial encounter
T83.190A	Other mechanical complication of urinary electronic stimulator device, initial encounter
T85.09XA	Other mechanical complication of ventricular intracranial (communicating) shunt, initial encounter
K59.39	Other megacolon
A24.3	Other melioidosis
A39.89	Other meningococcal infections
D74.8	Other methemoglobinemias
Q93.88	Other microdeletions
E88.49	Other mitochondrial metabolism disorders
C93.Z2	Other monocytic leukemia, in relapse
C93.Z1	Other monocytic leukemia, in remission
C93.Z0	Other monocytic leukemia, not having achieved remission
G12.29	Other motor neuron disease
E76.29	Other mucopolysaccharidoses
B26.89	Other mumps complications

A18.09	Other musculoskeletal tuberculosis
A31.8	Other mycobacterial infections
C92.Z0	Other myeloid leukemia not having achieved remission
C92.Z2	Other myeloid leukemia, in relapse
C92.Z1	Other myeloid leukemia, in remission
P71.1	Other neonatal hypocalcemia
B57.49	Other nervous system involvement in Chagas' disease
A69.22	Other neurologic disorders in Lyme disease
B06.09	Other neurological complications of rubella
T80.A9XA	Other non-ABO incompatibility reaction due to transfusion of blood or blood products, initial encounter
C83.89	Other non-follicular lymphoma, extranodal and solid organ sites
C83.83	Other non-follicular lymphoma, intra-abdominal lymph nodes
C83.86	Other non-follicular lymphoma, intrapelvic lymph nodes
C83.82	Other non-follicular lymphoma, intrathoracic lymph nodes
C83.84	Other non-follicular lymphoma, lymph nodes of axilla and upper limb
C83.81	Other non-follicular lymphoma, lymph nodes of head, face, and neck
C83.85	Other non-follicular lymphoma, lymph nodes of inguinal region and lower limb
C83.88	Other non-follicular lymphoma, lymph nodes of multiple sites
C83.87	Other non-follicular lymphoma, spleen
C83.80	Other non-follicular lymphoma, unspecified site
D59.4	Other nonautoimmune hemolytic anemias
S12.121A	Other nondisplaced dens fracture, initial encounter for closed fracture
S12.121K	Other nondisplaced dens fracture, subsequent encounter for fracture with nonunion
S62.235B	Other nondisplaced fracture of base of first metacarpal bone, left hand, initial encounter for open fracture
S62.235P	Other nondisplaced fracture of base of first metacarpal bone, left hand, subsequent encounter for fracture with malunion
S62.235K	Other nondisplaced fracture of base of first metacarpal bone, left hand, subsequent encounter for fracture with nonunion
S62.234B	Other nondisplaced fracture of base of first metacarpal bone, right hand, initial encounter for open fracture
S62.234P	Other nondisplaced fracture of base of first metacarpal bone, right hand, subsequent encounter for fracture with malunion
S62.234K	Other nondisplaced fracture of base of first metacarpal bone, right hand, subsequent encounter for fracture with nonunion
S62.236B	Other nondisplaced fracture of base of first metacarpal bone, unspecified hand, initial encounter for open fracture
S62.236P	Other nondisplaced fracture of base of first metacarpal bone, unspecified hand, subsequent encounter for fracture with malunion
S62.236K	Other nondisplaced fracture of base of first metacarpal bone, unspecified hand, subsequent encounter for fracture with nonunion
S12.491A	Other nondisplaced fracture of fifth cervical vertebra, initial encounter for closed fracture
S12.491K	Other nondisplaced fracture of fifth cervical vertebra, subsequent encounter for fracture with nonunion
S12.091A	Other nondisplaced fracture of first cervical vertebra, initial encounter for closed fracture
S12.091K	Other nondisplaced fracture of first cervical vertebra, subsequent encounter for fracture with nonunion
S12.391A	Other nondisplaced fracture of fourth cervical vertebra, initial encounter for closed fracture
S12.391K	Other nondisplaced fracture of fourth cervical vertebra, subsequent encounter for fracture with nonunion
S42.495A	Other nondisplaced fracture of lower end of left humerus, initial encounter for closed fracture
S42.495P	Other nondisplaced fracture of lower end of left humerus, subsequent encounter for fracture with malunion
S42.495K	Other nondisplaced fracture of lower end of left humerus, subsequent encounter for fracture with nonunion
S42.494A	Other nondisplaced fracture of lower end of right humerus, initial encounter for closed fracture
S42.494P	Other nondisplaced fracture of lower end of right humerus, subsequent encounter for fracture with malunion
S42.494K	Other nondisplaced fracture of lower end of right humerus, subsequent encounter for fracture with nonunion
S42.496A	Other nondisplaced fracture of lower end of unspecified humerus, initial encounter for closed fracture
S42.496P	Other nondisplaced fracture of lower end of unspecified humerus, subsequent encounter for fracture with malunion
S42.496K	Other nondisplaced fracture of lower end of unspecified humerus, subsequent encounter for fracture with nonunion
S12.191A	Other nondisplaced fracture of second cervical vertebra, initial encounter for closed fracture
S12.191K	Other nondisplaced fracture of second cervical vertebra, subsequent encounter for fracture with nonunion
S12.691A	Other nondisplaced fracture of seventh cervical vertebra, initial encounter for closed fracture
S12.691K	Other nondisplaced fracture of seventh cervical vertebra, subsequent encounter for fracture with nonunion
S12.591A	Other nondisplaced fracture of sixth cervical vertebra, initial encounter for closed fracture
S12.591K	Other nondisplaced fracture of sixth cervical vertebra, subsequent encounter for fracture with nonunion
S12.291A	Other nondisplaced fracture of third cervical vertebra, initial encounter for closed fracture
S12.291K	Other nondisplaced fracture of third cervical vertebra, subsequent encounter for fracture with nonunion

S42.295A	Other nondisplaced fracture of upper end of left humerus, initial encounter for closed fracture
S42.295P	Other nondisplaced fracture of upper end of left humerus, subsequent encounter for fracture with malunion
S42.295K	Other nondisplaced fracture of upper end of left humerus, subsequent encounter for fracture with nonunion
S42.294A	Other nondisplaced fracture of upper end of right humerus, initial encounter for closed fracture
S42.294P	Other nondisplaced fracture of upper end of right humerus, subsequent encounter for fracture with malunion
S42.294K	Other nondisplaced fracture of upper end of right humerus, subsequent encounter for fracture with nonunion
S42.296A	Other nondisplaced fracture of upper end of unspecified humerus, initial encounter for closed fracture
S42.296P	Other nondisplaced fracture of upper end of unspecified humerus, subsequent encounter for fracture with malunion
S42.296K	Other nondisplaced fracture of upper end of unspecified humerus, subsequent encounter for fracture with nonunion
O71.5	Other obstetric injury to pelvic organs
N13.8	Other obstructive and reflux uropathy
Q62.39	Other obstructive defects of renal pelvis and ureter
E70.318	Other ocular albinism
E70.328	Other oculocutaneous albinism
H46.8	Other optic neuritis
M86.8X7	Other osteomyelitis, ankle and foot
M86.8X3	Other osteomyelitis, forearm
M86.8X4	Other osteomyelitis, hand
M86.8X6	Other osteomyelitis, lower leg
M86.8X0	Other osteomyelitis, multiple sites
M86.8X8	Other osteomyelitis, other site
M86.8X1	Other osteomyelitis, shoulder
M86.8X5	Other osteomyelitis, thigh
M86.8X9	Other osteomyelitis, unspecified sites
M86.8X2	Other osteomyelitis, upper arm
M87.838	Other osteonecrosis of left carpus
M87.832	Other osteonecrosis of left radius
M87.835	Other osteonecrosis of left ulna
M87.837	Other osteonecrosis of right carpus
M87.831	Other osteonecrosis of right radius
M87.834	Other osteonecrosis of right ulna
M87.839	Other osteonecrosis of unspecified carpus
M87.833	Other osteonecrosis of unspecified radius
M87.836	Other osteonecrosis of unspecified ulna
M87.872	Other osteonecrosis, left ankle
M87.852	Other osteonecrosis, left femur
M87.865	Other osteonecrosis, left fibula
M87.845	Other osteonecrosis, left finger(s)
M87.875	Other osteonecrosis, left foot
M87.842	Other osteonecrosis, left hand
M87.822	Other osteonecrosis, left humerus
M87.812	Other osteonecrosis, left shoulder
M87.862	Other osteonecrosis, left tibia
M87.878	Other osteonecrosis, left toe(s)
M87.89	Other osteonecrosis, multiple sites
M87.88	Other osteonecrosis, other site
M87.850	Other osteonecrosis, pelvis
M87.871	Other osteonecrosis, right ankle
M87.851	Other osteonecrosis, right femur
M87.864	Other osteonecrosis, right fibula
M87.844	Other osteonecrosis, right finger(s)
M87.874	Other osteonecrosis, right foot
M87.841	Other osteonecrosis, right hand
M87.821	Other osteonecrosis, right humerus
M87.811	Other osteonecrosis, right shoulder
M87.861	Other osteonecrosis, right tibia
M87.877	Other osteonecrosis, right toe(s)
M87.873	Other osteonecrosis, unspecified ankle
M87.80	Other osteonecrosis, unspecified bone
M87.859	Other osteonecrosis, unspecified femur
M87.869	Other osteonecrosis, unspecified fibula
M87.849	Other osteonecrosis, unspecified finger(s)
M87.876	Other osteonecrosis, unspecified foot
M87.843	Other osteonecrosis, unspecified hand
M87.829	Other osteonecrosis, unspecified humerus
M87.819	Other osteonecrosis, unspecified shoulder
M87.863	Other osteonecrosis, unspecified tibia
M87.879	Other osteonecrosis, unspecified toe(s)
M80.872A	Other osteoporosis with current pathological fracture, left ankle and foot, initial encounter for fracture
M80.872P	Other osteoporosis with current pathological fracture, left ankle and foot, subsequent encounter for fracture with malunion
M80.872K	Other osteoporosis with current pathological fracture, left ankle and foot, subsequent encounter for fracture with nonunion
M80.852A	Other osteoporosis with current pathological fracture, left femur, initial encounter for fracture
M80.852P	Other osteoporosis with current pathological fracture, left femur, subsequent encounter for fracture with malunion
M80.852K	Other osteoporosis with current pathological fracture, left femur, subsequent encounter for fracture with nonunion

M80.832A	Other osteoporosis with current pathological fracture, left forearm, initial encounter for fracture
M80.832P	Other osteoporosis with current pathological fracture, left forearm, subsequent encounter for fracture with malunion
M80.832K	Other osteoporosis with current pathological fracture, left forearm, subsequent encounter for fracture with nonunion
M80.842A	Other osteoporosis with current pathological fracture, left hand, initial encounter for fracture
M80.842P	Other osteoporosis with current pathological fracture, left hand, subsequent encounter for fracture with malunion
M80.842K	Other osteoporosis with current pathological fracture, left hand, subsequent encounter for fracture with nonunion
M80.822A	Other osteoporosis with current pathological fracture, left humerus, initial encounter for fracture
M80.822P	Other osteoporosis with current pathological fracture, left humerus, subsequent encounter for fracture with malunion
M80.822K	Other osteoporosis with current pathological fracture, left humerus, subsequent encounter for fracture with nonunion
M80.862A	Other osteoporosis with current pathological fracture, left lower leg, initial encounter for fracture
M80.862P	Other osteoporosis with current pathological fracture, left lower leg, subsequent encounter for fracture with malunion
M80.862K	Other osteoporosis with current pathological fracture, left lower leg, subsequent encounter for fracture with nonunion
M80.812A	Other osteoporosis with current pathological fracture, left shoulder, initial encounter for fracture
M80.812P	Other osteoporosis with current pathological fracture, left shoulder, subsequent encounter for fracture with malunion
M80.812K	Other osteoporosis with current pathological fracture, left shoulder, subsequent encounter for fracture with nonunion
M80.871A	Other osteoporosis with current pathological fracture, right ankle and foot, initial encounter for fracture
M80.871P	Other osteoporosis with current pathological fracture, right ankle and foot, subsequent encounter for fracture with malunion
M80.871K	Other osteoporosis with current pathological fracture, right ankle and foot, subsequent encounter for fracture with nonunion
M80.851A	Other osteoporosis with current pathological fracture, right femur, initial encounter for fracture
M80.851P	Other osteoporosis with current pathological fracture, right femur, subsequent encounter for fracture with malunion
M80.851K	Other osteoporosis with current pathological fracture, right femur, subsequent encounter for fracture with nonunion
M80.831A	Other osteoporosis with current pathological fracture, right forearm, initial encounter for fracture
M80.831P	Other osteoporosis with current pathological fracture, right forearm, subsequent encounter for fracture with malunion
M80.831K	Other osteoporosis with current pathological fracture, right forearm, subsequent encounter for fracture with nonunion
M80.841A	Other osteoporosis with current pathological fracture, right hand, initial encounter for fracture
M80.841P	Other osteoporosis with current pathological fracture, right hand, subsequent encounter for fracture with malunion
M80.841K	Other osteoporosis with current pathological fracture, right hand, subsequent encounter for fracture with nonunion
M80.821A	Other osteoporosis with current pathological fracture, right humerus, initial encounter for fracture
M80.821P	Other osteoporosis with current pathological fracture, right humerus, subsequent encounter for fracture with malunion
M80.821K	Other osteoporosis with current pathological fracture, right humerus, subsequent encounter for fracture with nonunion
M80.861A	Other osteoporosis with current pathological fracture, right lower leg, initial encounter for fracture
M80.861P	Other osteoporosis with current pathological fracture, right lower leg, subsequent encounter for fracture with malunion
M80.861K	Other osteoporosis with current pathological fracture, right lower leg, subsequent encounter for fracture with nonunion
M80.811A	Other osteoporosis with current pathological fracture, right shoulder, initial encounter for fracture
M80.811P	Other osteoporosis with current pathological fracture, right shoulder, subsequent encounter for fracture with malunion
M80.811K	Other osteoporosis with current pathological fracture, right shoulder, subsequent encounter for fracture with nonunion
M80.879A	Other osteoporosis with current pathological fracture, unspecified ankle and foot, initial encounter for fracture
M80.879P	Other osteoporosis with current pathological fracture, unspecified ankle and foot, subsequent encounter for fracture with malunion
M80.879K	Other osteoporosis with current pathological fracture, unspecified ankle and foot, subsequent encounter for fracture with nonunion
M80.859A	Other osteoporosis with current pathological fracture, unspecified femur, initial encounter for fracture
M80.859P	Other osteoporosis with current pathological fracture, unspecified femur, subsequent encounter for fracture with malunion
M80.859K	Other osteoporosis with current pathological fracture, unspecified femur, subsequent encounter for fracture with nonunion
M80.839A	Other osteoporosis with current pathological fracture, unspecified forearm, initial encounter for fracture
M80.839P	Other osteoporosis with current pathological fracture, unspecified forearm, subsequent encounter for fracture with malunion
M80.839K	Other osteoporosis with current pathological fracture, unspecified forearm, subsequent encounter for fracture with nonunion

M80.849A Other osteoporosis with current pathological fracture, unspecified hand, initial encounter for fracture

M80.849P Other osteoporosis with current pathological fracture, unspecified hand, subsequent encounter for fracture with malunion

M80.849K Other osteoporosis with current pathological fracture, unspecified hand, subsequent encounter for fracture with nonunion

M80.829A Other osteoporosis with current pathological fracture, unspecified humerus, initial encounter for fracture

M80.829P Other osteoporosis with current pathological fracture, unspecified humerus, subsequent encounter for fracture with malunion

M80.829K Other osteoporosis with current pathological fracture, unspecified humerus, subsequent encounter for fracture with nonunion

M80.869A Other osteoporosis with current pathological fracture, unspecified lower leg, initial encounter for fracture

M80.869P Other osteoporosis with current pathological fracture, unspecified lower leg, subsequent encounter for fracture with malunion

M80.869K Other osteoporosis with current pathological fracture, unspecified lower leg, subsequent encounter for fracture with nonunion

M80.819A Other osteoporosis with current pathological fracture, unspecified shoulder, initial encounter for fracture

M80.819P Other osteoporosis with current pathological fracture, unspecified shoulder, subsequent encounter for fracture with malunion

M80.819K Other osteoporosis with current pathological fracture, unspecified shoulder, subsequent encounter for fracture with nonunion

M80.80XA Other osteoporosis with current pathological fracture, unspecified site, initial encounter for fracture

M80.80XP Other osteoporosis with current pathological fracture, unspecified site, subsequent encounter for fracture with malunion

M80.80XK Other osteoporosis with current pathological fracture, unspecified site, subsequent encounter for fracture with nonunion

M80.88XA Other osteoporosis with current pathological fracture, vertebra(e), initial encounter for fracture

M80.88XP Other osteoporosis with current pathological fracture, vertebra(e), subsequent encounter for fracture with malunion

M80.88XK Other osteoporosis with current pathological fracture, vertebra(e), subsequent encounter for fracture with nonunion

M35.1 Other overlap syndromes

D61.818 Other pancytopenia

K56.690 Other partial intestinal obstruction

L12.8 Other pemphigoid

L10.89 Other pemphigus

E71.548 Other peroxisomal disorders

I48.19 Other persistent atrial fibrillation

F84.8 Other pervasive developmental disorders

Q85.8 Other phakomatoses, not elsewhere classified

S49.192A Other physeal fracture of lower end of humerus, left arm, initial encounter for closed fracture

S49.192P Other physeal fracture of lower end of humerus, left arm, subsequent encounter for fracture with malunion

S49.192K Other physeal fracture of lower end of humerus, left arm, subsequent encounter for fracture with nonunion

S49.191A Other physeal fracture of lower end of humerus, right arm, initial encounter for closed fracture

S49.191P Other physeal fracture of lower end of humerus, right arm, subsequent encounter for fracture with malunion

S49.191K Other physeal fracture of lower end of humerus, right arm, subsequent encounter for fracture with nonunion

S49.199A Other physeal fracture of lower end of humerus, unspecified arm, initial encounter for closed fracture

S49.199P Other physeal fracture of lower end of humerus, unspecified arm, subsequent encounter for fracture with malunion

S49.199K Other physeal fracture of lower end of humerus, unspecified arm, subsequent encounter for fracture with nonunion

S79.192A Other physeal fracture of lower end of left femur, initial encounter for closed fracture

S79.192P Other physeal fracture of lower end of left femur, subsequent encounter for fracture with malunion

S79.192K Other physeal fracture of lower end of left femur, subsequent encounter for fracture with nonunion

S89.392P Other physeal fracture of lower end of left fibula, subsequent encounter for fracture with malunion

S89.392K Other physeal fracture of lower end of left fibula, subsequent encounter for fracture with nonunion

S89.192P Other physeal fracture of lower end of left tibia, subsequent encounter for fracture with malunion

S89.192K Other physeal fracture of lower end of left tibia, subsequent encounter for fracture with nonunion

S59.292A Other physeal fracture of lower end of radius, left arm, initial encounter for closed fracture

S59.292P Other physeal fracture of lower end of radius, left arm, subsequent encounter for fracture with malunion

S59.292K Other physeal fracture of lower end of radius, left arm, subsequent encounter for fracture with nonunion

S59.291A Other physeal fracture of lower end of radius, right arm, initial encounter for closed fracture

S59.291P Other physeal fracture of lower end of radius, right arm, subsequent encounter for fracture with malunion

S59.291K Other physeal fracture of lower end of radius, right arm, subsequent encounter for fracture with nonunion

S59.299A Other physeal fracture of lower end of radius, unspecified arm, initial encounter for closed fracture

S59.299P Other physeal fracture of lower end of radius, unspecified arm, subsequent encounter for fracture with malunion

S59.299K Other physeal fracture of lower end of radius, unspecified arm, subsequent encounter for fracture with nonunion

S79.191A Other physeal fracture of lower end of right femur, initial encounter for closed fracture

S79.191P Other physeal fracture of lower end of right femur, subsequent encounter for fracture with malunion

S79.191K Other physeal fracture of lower end of right femur, subsequent encounter for fracture with nonunion

S89.391P Other physeal fracture of lower end of right fibula, subsequent encounter for fracture with malunion

S89.391K Other physeal fracture of lower end of right fibula, subsequent encounter for fracture with nonunion

S89.191P Other physeal fracture of lower end of right tibia, subsequent encounter for fracture with malunion

S89.191K Other physeal fracture of lower end of right tibia, subsequent encounter for fracture with nonunion

S59.092A Other physeal fracture of lower end of ulna, left arm, initial encounter for closed fracture

S59.092P Other physeal fracture of lower end of ulna, left arm, subsequent encounter for fracture with malunion

S59.092K Other physeal fracture of lower end of ulna, left arm, subsequent encounter for fracture with nonunion

S59.091A Other physeal fracture of lower end of ulna, right arm, initial encounter for closed fracture

S59.091P Other physeal fracture of lower end of ulna, right arm, subsequent encounter for fracture with malunion

S59.091K Other physeal fracture of lower end of ulna, right arm, subsequent encounter for fracture with nonunion

S59.099A Other physeal fracture of lower end of ulna, unspecified arm, initial encounter for closed fracture

S59.099P Other physeal fracture of lower end of ulna, unspecified arm, subsequent encounter for fracture with malunion

S59.099K Other physeal fracture of lower end of ulna, unspecified arm, subsequent encounter for fracture with nonunion

S79.199A Other physeal fracture of lower end of unspecified femur, initial encounter for closed fracture

S79.199P Other physeal fracture of lower end of unspecified femur, subsequent encounter for fracture with malunion

S79.199K Other physeal fracture of lower end of unspecified femur, subsequent encounter for fracture with nonunion

S89.399P Other physeal fracture of lower end of unspecified fibula, subsequent encounter for fracture with malunion

S89.399K Other physeal fracture of lower end of unspecified fibula, subsequent encounter for fracture with nonunion

S89.199P Other physeal fracture of lower end of unspecified tibia, subsequent encounter for fracture with malunion

S89.199K Other physeal fracture of lower end of unspecified tibia, subsequent encounter for fracture with nonunion

S49.092A Other physeal fracture of upper end of humerus, left arm, initial encounter for closed fracture

S49.092P Other physeal fracture of upper end of humerus, left arm, subsequent encounter for fracture with malunion

S49.092K Other physeal fracture of upper end of humerus, left arm, subsequent encounter for fracture with nonunion

S49.091A Other physeal fracture of upper end of humerus, right arm, initial encounter for closed fracture

S49.091P Other physeal fracture of upper end of humerus, right arm, subsequent encounter for fracture with malunion

S49.091K Other physeal fracture of upper end of humerus, right arm, subsequent encounter for fracture with nonunion

S49.099A Other physeal fracture of upper end of humerus, unspecified arm, initial encounter for closed fracture

S49.099P Other physeal fracture of upper end of humerus, unspecified arm, subsequent encounter for fracture with malunion

S49.099K Other physeal fracture of upper end of humerus, unspecified arm, subsequent encounter for fracture with nonunion

S79.092P Other physeal fracture of upper end of left femur, subsequent encounter for fracture with malunion

S79.092K Other physeal fracture of upper end of left femur, subsequent encounter for fracture with nonunion

S89.292P Other physeal fracture of upper end of left fibula, subsequent encounter for fracture with malunion

S89.292K Other physeal fracture of upper end of left fibula, subsequent encounter for fracture with nonunion

S89.092A Other physeal fracture of upper end of left tibia, initial encounter for closed fracture

S89.092P Other physeal fracture of upper end of left tibia, subsequent encounter for fracture with malunion

S89.092K Other physeal fracture of upper end of left tibia, subsequent encounter for fracture with nonunion

S59.192P Other physeal fracture of upper end of radius, left arm, subsequent encounter for fracture with malunion

S59.192K Other physeal fracture of upper end of radius, left arm, subsequent encounter for fracture with nonunion

S59.191P Other physeal fracture of upper end of radius, right arm, subsequent encounter for fracture with malunion

S59.191K Other physeal fracture of upper end of radius, right arm, subsequent encounter for fracture with nonunion

S59.199P	Other physeal fracture of upper end of radius, unspecified arm, subsequent encounter for fracture with malunion
S59.199K	Other physeal fracture of upper end of radius, unspecified arm, subsequent encounter for fracture with nonunion
S79.091P	Other physeal fracture of upper end of right femur, subsequent encounter for fracture with malunion
S79.091K	Other physeal fracture of upper end of right femur, subsequent encounter for fracture with nonunion
S89.291P	Other physeal fracture of upper end of right fibula, subsequent encounter for fracture with malunion
S89.291K	Other physeal fracture of upper end of right fibula, subsequent encounter for fracture with nonunion
S89.091A	Other physeal fracture of upper end of right tibia, initial encounter for closed fracture
S89.091P	Other physeal fracture of upper end of right tibia, subsequent encounter for fracture with malunion
S89.091K	Other physeal fracture of upper end of right tibia, subsequent encounter for fracture with nonunion
S79.099P	Other physeal fracture of upper end of unspecified femur, subsequent encounter for fracture with malunion
S79.099K	Other physeal fracture of upper end of unspecified femur, subsequent encounter for fracture with nonunion
S89.299P	Other physeal fracture of upper end of unspecified fibula, subsequent encounter for fracture with malunion
S89.299K	Other physeal fracture of upper end of unspecified fibula, subsequent encounter for fracture with nonunion
S89.099A	Other physeal fracture of upper end of unspecified tibia, initial encounter for closed fracture
S89.099P	Other physeal fracture of upper end of unspecified tibia, subsequent encounter for fracture with malunion
S89.099K	Other physeal fracture of upper end of unspecified tibia, subsequent encounter for fracture with nonunion
J93.83	Other pneumothorax
Q61.19	Other polycystic kidney, infantile type
E80.29	Other porphyria
B02.29	Other postherpetic nervous system involvement
I97.190	Other postprocedural cardiac functional disturbances following cardiac surgery
I97.191	Other postprocedural cardiac functional disturbances following other surgery
K91.89	Other postprocedural complications and disorders of digestive system
H59.89	Other postprocedural complications and disorders of eye and adnexa, not elsewhere classified
G97.82	Other postprocedural complications and disorders of nervous system
J95.89	Other postprocedural complications and disorders of respiratory system, not elsewhere classified
I97.89	Other postprocedural complications and disorders of the circulatory system, not elsewhere classified
H95.89	Other postprocedural complications and disorders of the ear and mastoid process, not elsewhere classified
D78.89	Other postprocedural complications of the spleen
E89.89	Other postprocedural endocrine and metabolic complications and disorders
O24.811	Other pre-existing diabetes mellitus in pregnancy, first trimester
O24.812	Other pre-existing diabetes mellitus in pregnancy, second trimester
O24.813	Other pre-existing diabetes mellitus in pregnancy, third trimester
O24.819	Other pre-existing diabetes mellitus in pregnancy, unspecified trimester
O24.83	Other pre-existing diabetes mellitus in the puerperium
N48.39	Other priapism
D68.59	Other primary thrombophilia
F19.121	Other psychoactive substance abuse with intoxication delirium
F19.17	Other psychoactive substance abuse with psychoactive substance-induced persisting dementia
F19.150	Other psychoactive substance abuse with psychoactive substance-induced psychotic disorder with delusions
F19.151	Other psychoactive substance abuse with psychoactive substance-induced psychotic disorder with hallucinations
F19.221	Other psychoactive substance dependence with intoxication delirium
F19.222	Other psychoactive substance dependence with intoxication with perceptual disturbance
F19.288	Other psychoactive substance dependence with other psychoactive substance-induced disorder
F19.280	Other psychoactive substance dependence with psychoactive substance-induced anxiety disorder
F19.26	Other psychoactive substance dependence with psychoactive substance-induced persisting amnestic disorder
F19.27	Other psychoactive substance dependence with psychoactive substance-induced persisting dementia
F19.250	Other psychoactive substance dependence with psychoactive substance-induced psychotic disorder with delusions
F19.251	Other psychoactive substance dependence with psychoactive substance-induced psychotic disorder with hallucinations
F19.259	Other psychoactive substance dependence with psychoactive substance-induced psychotic disorder, unspecified
F19.281	Other psychoactive substance dependence with psychoactive substance-induced sexual dysfunction
F19.282	Other psychoactive substance dependence with psychoactive substance-induced sleep disorder
F19.231	Other psychoactive substance dependence with withdrawal delirium
F19.232	Other psychoactive substance dependence with withdrawal with perceptual disturbance
F19.230	Other psychoactive substance dependence with withdrawal, uncomplicated
F19.239	Other psychoactive substance dependence with withdrawal, unspecified
F19.20	Other psychoactive substance dependence, uncomplicated
F19.921	Other psychoactive substance use, unspecified with intoxication with delirium
F19.97	Other psychoactive substance use, unspecified with psychoactive substance-induced persisting dementia
F19.950	Other psychoactive substance use, unspecified with psychoactive substance-induced psychotic disorder with delusions
F19.951	Other psychoactive substance use, unspecified with psychoactive substance-induced psychotic disorder with hallucinations
F19.931	Other psychoactive substance use, unspecified with withdrawal delirium
F19.932	Other psychoactive substance use, unspecified with withdrawal with perceptual disturbance
F19.930	Other psychoactive substance use, unspecified with withdrawal, uncomplicated
F19.939	Other psychoactive substance use, unspecified with withdrawal, unspecified
B44.1	Other pulmonary aspergillosis
J98.19	Other pulmonary collapse
P93.8	Other reactions and intoxications due to drugs administered to newborn
M02.872	Other reactive arthropathies, left ankle and foot
M02.822	Other reactive arthropathies, left elbow
M02.842	Other reactive arthropathies, left hand
M02.852	Other reactive arthropathies, left hip
M02.862	Other reactive arthropathies, left knee
M02.812	Other reactive arthropathies, left shoulder
M02.832	Other reactive arthropathies, left wrist
M02.89	Other reactive arthropathies, multiple sites
M02.871	Other reactive arthropathies, right ankle and foot
M02.821	Other reactive arthropathies, right elbow
M02.841	Other reactive arthropathies, right hand
M02.851	Other reactive arthropathies, right hip
M02.861	Other reactive arthropathies, right knee
M02.811	Other reactive arthropathies, right shoulder
M02.831	Other reactive arthropathies, right wrist
M02.879	Other reactive arthropathies, unspecified ankle and foot
M02.829	Other reactive arthropathies, unspecified elbow
M02.849	Other reactive arthropathies, unspecified hand
M02.859	Other reactive arthropathies, unspecified hip
M02.869	Other reactive arthropathies, unspecified knee
M02.819	Other reactive arthropathies, unspecified shoulder
M02.80	Other reactive arthropathies, unspecified site
M02.839	Other reactive arthropathies, unspecified wrist
M02.88	Other reactive arthropathies, vertebrae
F33.8	Other recurrent depressive disorders
A15.8	Other respiratory tuberculosis
I42.5	Other restrictive cardiomyopathy
H33.8	Other retinal detachments
T80.49XA	Other Rh incompatibility reaction due to transfusion of blood or blood products, initial encounter
B06.89	Other rubella complications
C22.4	Other sarcomas of liver
B65.8	Other schistosomiasis
F20.89	Other schizophrenia
C7B.8	Other secondary neuroendocrine tumors
M87.338	Other secondary osteonecrosis of left carpus
M87.332	Other secondary osteonecrosis of left radius
M87.335	Other secondary osteonecrosis of left ulna
M87.337	Other secondary osteonecrosis of right carpus
M87.331	Other secondary osteonecrosis of right radius
M87.334	Other secondary osteonecrosis of right ulna
M87.339	Other secondary osteonecrosis of unspecified carpus
M87.333	Other secondary osteonecrosis of unspecified radius
M87.336	Other secondary osteonecrosis of unspecified ulna
M87.372	Other secondary osteonecrosis, left ankle
M87.352	Other secondary osteonecrosis, left femur
M87.365	Other secondary osteonecrosis, left fibula
M87.345	Other secondary osteonecrosis, left finger(s)
M87.375	Other secondary osteonecrosis, left foot
M87.342	Other secondary osteonecrosis, left hand
M87.322	Other secondary osteonecrosis, left humerus
M87.312	Other secondary osteonecrosis, left shoulder
M87.362	Other secondary osteonecrosis, left tibia
M87.378	Other secondary osteonecrosis, left toe(s)
M87.39	Other secondary osteonecrosis, multiple sites
M87.38	Other secondary osteonecrosis, other site
M87.350	Other secondary osteonecrosis, pelvis
M87.371	Other secondary osteonecrosis, right ankle
M87.351	Other secondary osteonecrosis, right femur
M87.364	Other secondary osteonecrosis, right fibula
M87.344	Other secondary osteonecrosis, right finger(s)
M87.374	Other secondary osteonecrosis, right foot
M87.341	Other secondary osteonecrosis, right hand
M87.321	Other secondary osteonecrosis, right humerus
M87.311	Other secondary osteonecrosis, right shoulder
M87.361	Other secondary osteonecrosis, right tibia
M87.377	Other secondary osteonecrosis, right toe(s)
M87.373	Other secondary osteonecrosis, unspecified ankle
M87.30	Other secondary osteonecrosis, unspecified bone
M87.353	Other secondary osteonecrosis, unspecified femur
M87.366	Other secondary osteonecrosis, unspecified fibula

M87.346	Other secondary osteonecrosis, unspecified finger(s)
M87.376	Other secondary osteonecrosis, unspecified foot
M87.343	Other secondary osteonecrosis, unspecified hand
M87.329	Other secondary osteonecrosis, unspecified humerus
M87.319	Other secondary osteonecrosis, unspecified shoulder
M87.363	Other secondary osteonecrosis, unspecified tibia
M87.379	Other secondary osteonecrosis, unspecified toe(s)
G21.8	Other secondary parkinsonism
A51.39	Other secondary syphilis of skin
A51.49	Other secondary syphilitic conditions
G40.89	Other seizures
T80.61XA	Other serum reaction due to administration of blood and blood products, initial encounter
T80.69XA	Other serum reaction due to other serum, initial encounter
T80.62XA	Other serum reaction due to vaccination, initial encounter
B50.8	Other severe and complicated Plasmodium falciparum malaria
B37.89	Other sites of candidiasis
K45.0	Other specified abdominal hernia with obstruction, without gangrene
G36.8	Other specified acute disseminated demyelination
B17.8	Other specified acute viral hepatitis
E70.39	Other specified albinism
A93.8	Other specified arthropod-borne viral fevers
A05.8	Other specified bacterial foodborne intoxications
A04.8	Other specified bacterial intestinal infections
C22.7	Other specified carcinomas of liver
B71.8	Other specified cestode infections
D68.8	Other specified coagulation defects
T82.897A	Other specified complication of cardiac prosthetic devices, implants and grafts, initial encounter
T83.89XA	Other specified complication of genitourinary prosthetic devices, implants and grafts, initial encounter
T84.89XA	Other specified complication of internal orthopedic prosthetic devices, implants and grafts, initial encounter
T85.890A	Other specified complication of nervous system prosthetic devices, implants and grafts, initial encounter
T85.890D	Other specified complication of nervous system prosthetic devices, implants and grafts, subsequent encounter
T82.898A	Other specified complication of vascular prosthetic devices, implants and grafts, initial encounter
T83.79XA	Other specified complications due to other genitourinary prosthetic materials, initial encounter
I45.89	Other specified conduction disorders
Q87.89	Other specified congenital malformation syndromes, not elsewhere classified
Q89.8	Other specified congenital malformations
Q04.8	Other specified congenital malformations of brain
Q28.8	Other specified congenital malformations of circulatory system
Q43.8	Other specified congenital malformations of intestine
G23.8	Other specified degenerative diseases of basal ganglia
G37.8	Other specified demyelinating diseases of central nervous system
E13.52	Other specified diabetes mellitus with diabetic peripheral angiopathy with gangrene
I31.8	Other specified diseases of pericardium
G95.89	Other specified diseases of spinal cord
E72.89	Other specified disorders of amino-acid metabolism
E74.8	Other specified disorders of carbohydrate metabolism
B66.8	Other specified fluke infections
S32.492K	Other specified fracture of left acetabulum, subsequent encounter for fracture with nonunion
S32.692A	Other specified fracture of left ischium, initial encounter for closed fracture
S32.692K	Other specified fracture of left ischium, subsequent encounter for fracture with nonunion
S32.592A	Other specified fracture of left pubis, initial encounter for closed fracture
S32.592K	Other specified fracture of left pubis, subsequent encounter for fracture with nonunion
S32.491K	Other specified fracture of right acetabulum, subsequent encounter for fracture with nonunion
S32.691A	Other specified fracture of right ischium, initial encounter for closed fracture
S32.691K	Other specified fracture of right ischium, subsequent encounter for fracture with nonunion
S32.591A	Other specified fracture of right pubis, initial encounter for closed fracture
S32.591K	Other specified fracture of right pubis, subsequent encounter for fracture with nonunion
S32.499K	Other specified fracture of unspecified acetabulum, subsequent encounter for fracture with nonunion
S32.699A	Other specified fracture of unspecified ischium, initial encounter for closed fracture
S32.699K	Other specified fracture of unspecified ischium, subsequent encounter for fracture with nonunion
S32.599A	Other specified fracture of unspecified pubis, initial encounter for closed fracture
S32.599K	Other specified fracture of unspecified pubis, subsequent encounter for fracture with nonunion
D58.8	Other specified hereditary hemolytic anemias
D84.8	Other specified immunodeficiencies
P39.8	Other specified infections specific to the perinatal period
S85.152A	Other specified injury of anterior tibial artery, left leg, initial encounter
S85.151A	Other specified injury of anterior tibial artery, right leg, initial encounter
S85.159A	Other specified injury of anterior tibial artery, unspecified leg, initial encounter
S45.292A	Other specified injury of axillary or brachial vein, left side, initial encounter

S45.291A	Other specified injury of axillary or brachial vein, right side, initial encounter
S45.299A	Other specified injury of axillary or brachial vein, unspecified side, initial encounter
S65.591A	Other specified injury of blood vessel of left index finger, initial encounter
S65.597A	Other specified injury of blood vessel of left little finger, initial encounter
S65.593A	Other specified injury of blood vessel of left middle finger, initial encounter
S65.595A	Other specified injury of blood vessel of left ring finger, initial encounter
S65.492A	Other specified injury of blood vessel of left thumb, initial encounter
S65.598A	Other specified injury of blood vessel of other finger, initial encounter
S65.590A	Other specified injury of blood vessel of right index finger, initial encounter
S65.596A	Other specified injury of blood vessel of right little finger, initial encounter
S65.592A	Other specified injury of blood vessel of right middle finger, initial encounter
S65.594A	Other specified injury of blood vessel of right ring finger, initial encounter
S65.491A	Other specified injury of blood vessel of right thumb, initial encounter
S65.599A	Other specified injury of blood vessel of unspecified finger, initial encounter
S65.499A	Other specified injury of blood vessel of unspecified thumb, initial encounter
S45.192A	Other specified injury of brachial artery, left side, initial encounter
S45.191A	Other specified injury of brachial artery, right side, initial encounter
S45.199A	Other specified injury of brachial artery, unspecified side, initial encounter
S65.392A	Other specified injury of deep palmar arch of left hand, initial encounter
S65.391A	Other specified injury of deep palmar arch of right hand, initial encounter
S65.399A	Other specified injury of deep palmar arch of unspecified hand, initial encounter
S95.092A	Other specified injury of dorsal artery of left foot, initial encounter
S95.091A	Other specified injury of dorsal artery of right foot, initial encounter
S95.099A	Other specified injury of dorsal artery of unspecified foot, initial encounter
S95.292A	Other specified injury of dorsal vein of left foot, initial encounter
S95.291A	Other specified injury of dorsal vein of right foot, initial encounter
S95.299A	Other specified injury of dorsal vein of unspecified foot, initial encounter
S75.292A	Other specified injury of greater saphenous vein at hip and thigh level, left leg, initial encounter
S75.291A	Other specified injury of greater saphenous vein at hip and thigh level, right leg, initial encounter
S75.299A	Other specified injury of greater saphenous vein at hip and thigh level, unspecified leg, initial encounter
S85.392A	Other specified injury of greater saphenous vein at lower leg level, left leg, initial encounter
S85.391A	Other specified injury of greater saphenous vein at lower leg level, right leg, initial encounter
S85.399A	Other specified injury of greater saphenous vein at lower leg level, unspecified leg, initial encounter
S25.592A	Other specified injury of intercostal blood vessels, left side, initial encounter
S25.591A	Other specified injury of intercostal blood vessels, right side, initial encounter
S25.599A	Other specified injury of intercostal blood vessels, unspecified side, initial encounter
S15.092A	Other specified injury of left carotid artery, initial encounter
S15.292A	Other specified injury of left external jugular vein, initial encounter
S15.392A	Other specified injury of left internal jugular vein, initial encounter
S09.392A	Other specified injury of left middle and inner ear, initial encounter
S15.192A	Other specified injury of left vertebral artery, initial encounter
S85.492A	Other specified injury of lesser saphenous vein at lower leg level, left leg, initial encounter
S85.491A	Other specified injury of lesser saphenous vein at lower leg level, right leg, initial encounter
S85.499A	Other specified injury of lesser saphenous vein at lower leg level, unspecified leg, initial encounter
S35.8X8A	Other specified injury of other blood vessels at abdomen, lower back and pelvis level, initial encounter
S95.892A	Other specified injury of other blood vessels at ankle and foot level, left leg, initial encounter
S95.891A	Other specified injury of other blood vessels at ankle and foot level, right leg, initial encounter
S95.899A	Other specified injury of other blood vessels at ankle and foot level, unspecified leg, initial encounter
S55.892A	Other specified injury of other blood vessels at forearm level, left arm, initial encounter
S55.891A	Other specified injury of other blood vessels at forearm level, right arm, initial encounter
S55.899A	Other specified injury of other blood vessels at forearm level, unspecified arm, initial encounter
S75.892A	Other specified injury of other blood vessels at hip and thigh level, left leg, initial encounter
S75.891A	Other specified injury of other blood vessels at hip and thigh level, right leg, initial encounter
S75.899A	Other specified injury of other blood vessels at hip and thigh level, unspecified leg, initial encounter
S85.892A	Other specified injury of other blood vessels at lower leg level, left leg, initial encounter
S85.891A	Other specified injury of other blood vessels at lower leg level, right leg, initial encounter
S85.899A	Other specified injury of other blood vessels at lower leg level, unspecified leg, initial encounter
S65.892A	Other specified injury of other blood vessels at wrist and hand level of left arm, initial encounter
S65.891A	Other specified injury of other blood vessels at wrist and hand level of right arm, initial encounter
S65.899A	Other specified injury of other blood vessels at wrist and hand level of unspecified arm, initial encounter
S25.892A	Other specified injury of other blood vessels of thorax, left side, initial encounter

S25.891A	Other specified injury of other blood vessels of thorax, right side, initial encounter
S25.899A	Other specified injury of other blood vessels of thorax, unspecified side, initial encounter
S45.892A	Other specified injury of other specified blood vessels at shoulder and upper arm level, left arm, initial encounter
S45.891A	Other specified injury of other specified blood vessels at shoulder and upper arm level, right arm, initial encounter
S45.899A	Other specified injury of other specified blood vessels at shoulder and upper arm level, unspecified arm, initial encounter
S85.292A	Other specified injury of peroneal artery, left leg, initial encounter
S85.291A	Other specified injury of peroneal artery, right leg, initial encounter
S85.299A	Other specified injury of peroneal artery, unspecified leg, initial encounter
S95.192A	Other specified injury of plantar artery of left foot, initial encounter
S95.191A	Other specified injury of plantar artery of right foot, initial encounter
S95.199A	Other specified injury of plantar artery of unspecified foot, initial encounter
S85.182A	Other specified injury of posterior tibial artery, left leg, initial encounter
S85.181A	Other specified injury of posterior tibial artery, right leg, initial encounter
S85.189A	Other specified injury of posterior tibial artery, unspecified leg, initial encounter
S55.192A	Other specified injury of radial artery at forearm level, left arm, initial encounter
S55.191A	Other specified injury of radial artery at forearm level, right arm, initial encounter
S55.199A	Other specified injury of radial artery at forearm level, unspecified arm, initial encounter
S65.192A	Other specified injury of radial artery at wrist and hand level of left arm, initial encounter
S65.191A	Other specified injury of radial artery at wrist and hand level of right arm, initial encounter
S65.199A	Other specified injury of radial artery at wrist and hand level of unspecified arm, initial encounter
S15.091A	Other specified injury of right carotid artery, initial encounter
S15.291A	Other specified injury of right external jugular vein, initial encounter
S15.391A	Other specified injury of right internal jugular vein, initial encounter
S09.391A	Other specified injury of right middle and inner ear, initial encounter
S15.191A	Other specified injury of right vertebral artery, initial encounter
S65.292A	Other specified injury of superficial palmar arch of left hand, initial encounter
S65.291A	Other specified injury of superficial palmar arch of right hand, initial encounter
S65.299A	Other specified injury of superficial palmar arch of unspecified hand, initial encounter
S45.392A	Other specified injury of superficial vein at shoulder and upper arm level, left arm, initial encounter
S45.391A	Other specified injury of superficial vein at shoulder and upper arm level, right arm, initial encounter
S45.399A	Other specified injury of superficial vein at shoulder and upper arm level, unspecified arm, initial encounter
S55.092A	Other specified injury of ulnar artery at forearm level, left arm, initial encounter
S55.091A	Other specified injury of ulnar artery at forearm level, right arm, initial encounter
S55.099A	Other specified injury of ulnar artery at forearm level, unspecified arm, initial encounter
S65.092A	Other specified injury of ulnar artery at wrist and hand level of left arm, initial encounter
S65.091A	Other specified injury of ulnar artery at wrist and hand level of right arm, initial encounter
S65.099A	Other specified injury of ulnar artery at wrist and hand level of unspecified arm, initial encounter
S35.99XA	Other specified injury of unspecified blood vessel at abdomen, lower back and pelvis level, initial encounter
S95.992A	Other specified injury of unspecified blood vessel at ankle and foot level, left leg, initial encounter
S95.991A	Other specified injury of unspecified blood vessel at ankle and foot level, right leg, initial encounter
S95.999A	Other specified injury of unspecified blood vessel at ankle and foot level, unspecified leg, initial encounter
S55.992A	Other specified injury of unspecified blood vessel at forearm level, left arm, initial encounter
S55.991A	Other specified injury of unspecified blood vessel at forearm level, right arm, initial encounter
S55.999A	Other specified injury of unspecified blood vessel at forearm level, unspecified arm, initial encounter
S75.992A	Other specified injury of unspecified blood vessel at hip and thigh level, left leg, initial encounter
S75.991A	Other specified injury of unspecified blood vessel at hip and thigh level, right leg, initial encounter
S75.999A	Other specified injury of unspecified blood vessel at hip and thigh level, unspecified leg, initial encounter
S85.992A	Other specified injury of unspecified blood vessel at lower leg level, left leg, initial encounter
S85.991A	Other specified injury of unspecified blood vessel at lower leg level, right leg, initial encounter
S85.999A	Other specified injury of unspecified blood vessel at lower leg level, unspecified leg, initial encounter
S45.992A	Other specified injury of unspecified blood vessel at shoulder and upper arm level, left arm, initial encounter
S45.991A	Other specified injury of unspecified blood vessel at shoulder and upper arm level, right arm, initial encounter
S45.999A	Other specified injury of unspecified blood vessel at shoulder and upper arm level, unspecified arm, initial encounter
S65.992A	Other specified injury of unspecified blood vessel at wrist and hand of left arm, initial encounter
S65.991A	Other specified injury of unspecified blood vessel at wrist and hand of right arm, initial encounter
S65.999A	Other specified injury of unspecified blood vessel at wrist and hand of unspecified arm, initial encounter
S25.99XA	Other specified injury of unspecified blood vessel of thorax, initial encounter
S15.099A	Other specified injury of unspecified carotid artery, initial encounter
S15.299A	Other specified injury of unspecified external jugular vein, initial encounter
S15.399A	Other specified injury of unspecified internal jugular vein, initial encounter
S09.399A	Other specified injury of unspecified middle and inner ear, initial encounter
S85.122A	Other specified injury of unspecified tibial artery, left leg, initial encounter
S85.121A	Other specified injury of unspecified tibial artery, right leg, initial encounter
S85.129A	Other specified injury of unspecified tibial artery, unspecified leg, initial encounter
S15.199A	Other specified injury of unspecified vertebral artery, initial encounter
S55.292A	Other specified injury of vein at forearm level, left arm, initial encounter
S55.291A	Other specified injury of vein at forearm level, right arm, initial encounter
S55.299A	Other specified injury of vein at forearm level, unspecified arm, initial encounter
B81.8	Other specified intestinal helminthiases
S06.895A	Other specified intracranial injury with loss of consciousness greater than 24 hours with return to pre-existing conscious level, initial encounter
S06.893A	Other specified intracranial injury with loss of consciousness of 1 hour to 5 hours 59 minutes, initial encounter
S06.891A	Other specified intracranial injury with loss of consciousness of 30 minutes or less, initial encounter
S06.892A	Other specified intracranial injury with loss of consciousness of 31 minutes to 59 minutes, initial encounter
S06.894A	Other specified intracranial injury with loss of consciousness of 6 hours to 24 hours, initial encounter
S06.899A	Other specified intracranial injury with loss of consciousness of unspecified duration, initial encounter
C94.80	Other specified leukemias not having achieved remission
C94.82	Other specified leukemias, in relapse
C94.81	Other specified leukemias, in remission
C96.Z	Other specified malignant neoplasms of lymphoid, hematopoietic and related tissue
A92.8	Other specified mosquito-borne viral fevers
O30.821	Other specified multiple gestation with two or more monoamniotic fetuses, first trimester
O30.822	Other specified multiple gestation with two or more monoamniotic fetuses, second trimester
O30.823	Other specified multiple gestation with two or more monoamniotic fetuses, third trimester
O30.811	Other specified multiple gestation with two or more monochorionic fetuses, first trimester
O30.812	Other specified multiple gestation with two or more monochorionic fetuses, second trimester
O30.813	Other specified multiple gestation with two or more monochorionic fetuses, third trimester
O30.831	Other specified multiple gestation, number of chorions and amnions are both equal to the number of fetuses, first trimester
O30.832	Other specified multiple gestation, number of chorions and amnions are both equal to the number of fetuses, second trimester
O30.833	Other specified multiple gestation, number of chorions and amnions are both equal to the number of fetuses, third trimester
O30.891	Other specified multiple gestation, unable to determine number of placenta and number of amniotic sacs, first trimester
O30.892	Other specified multiple gestation, unable to determine number of placenta and number of amniotic sacs, second trimester
O30.893	Other specified multiple gestation, unable to determine number of placenta and number of amniotic sacs, third trimester
O30.801	Other specified multiple gestation, unspecified number of placenta and unspecified number of amniotic sacs, first trimester
O30.802	Other specified multiple gestation, unspecified number of placenta and unspecified number of amniotic sacs, second trimester
O30.803	Other specified multiple gestation, unspecified number of placenta and unspecified number of amniotic sacs, third trimester
B48.8	Other specified mycoses
M31.8	Other specified necrotizing vasculopathies
D47.Z9	Other specified neoplasms of uncertain behavior of lymphoid, hematopoietic and related tissue
F34.89	Other specified persistent mood disorders
J94.8	Other specified pleural conditions
A07.8	Other specified protozoal intestinal diseases
A79.89	Other specified rickettsioses
A02.8	Other specified salmonella infections
M35.8	Other specified systemic involvement of connective tissue
P72.8	Other specified transitory neonatal endocrine disorders
C85.89	Other specified types of non-Hodgkin lymphoma, extranodal and solid organ sites
C85.83	Other specified types of non-Hodgkin lymphoma, intra-abdominal lymph nodes
C85.86	Other specified types of non-Hodgkin lymphoma, intrapelvic lymph nodes
C85.82	Other specified types of non-Hodgkin lymphoma, intrathoracic lymph nodes
C85.84	Other specified types of non-Hodgkin lymphoma, lymph nodes of axilla and upper limb

C85.81	Other specified types of non-Hodgkin lymphoma, lymph nodes of head, face, and neck
C85.85	Other specified types of non-Hodgkin lymphoma, lymph nodes of inguinal region and lower limb
C85.88	Other specified types of non-Hodgkin lymphoma, lymph nodes of multiple sites
C85.87	Other specified types of non-Hodgkin lymphoma, spleen
C85.80	Other specified types of non-Hodgkin lymphoma, unspecified site
A85.8	Other specified viral encephalitis
A98.8	Other specified viral hemorrhagic fevers
A88.8	Other specified viral infections of central nervous system
A28.8	Other specified zoonotic bacterial diseases, not elsewhere classified
E75.29	Other sphingolipidosis
G12.8	Other spinal muscular atrophies and related syndromes
M47.12	Other spondylosis with myelopathy, cervical region
M47.13	Other spondylosis with myelopathy, cervicothoracic region
M47.16	Other spondylosis with myelopathy, lumbar region
M47.11	Other spondylosis with myelopathy, occipito-atlanto-axial region
M47.10	Other spondylosis with myelopathy, site unspecified
M47.14	Other spondylosis with myelopathy, thoracic region
M47.15	Other spondylosis with myelopathy, thoracolumbar region
A77.8	Other spotted fevers
F15.121	Other stimulant abuse with intoxication delirium
F15.150	Other stimulant abuse with stimulant-induced psychotic disorder with delusions
F15.151	Other stimulant abuse with stimulant-induced psychotic disorder with hallucinations
F15.221	Other stimulant dependence with intoxication delirium
F15.222	Other stimulant dependence with intoxication with perceptual disturbance
F15.288	Other stimulant dependence with other stimulant-induced disorder
F15.280	Other stimulant dependence with stimulant-induced anxiety disorder
F15.250	Other stimulant dependence with stimulant-induced psychotic disorder with delusions
F15.251	Other stimulant dependence with stimulant-induced psychotic disorder with hallucinations
F15.259	Other stimulant dependence with stimulant-induced psychotic disorder, unspecified
F15.281	Other stimulant dependence with stimulant-induced sexual dysfunction
F15.282	Other stimulant dependence with stimulant-induced sleep disorder
F15.23	Other stimulant dependence with withdrawal
F15.20	Other stimulant dependence, uncomplicated
F15.921	Other stimulant use, unspecified with intoxication delirium
F15.950	Other stimulant use, unspecified with stimulant-induced psychotic disorder with delusions
F15.951	Other stimulant use, unspecified with stimulant-induced psychotic disorder with hallucinations
F15.93	Other stimulant use, unspecified with withdrawal
M00.272	Other streptococcal arthritis, left ankle and foot
M00.222	Other streptococcal arthritis, left elbow
M00.242	Other streptococcal arthritis, left hand
M00.252	Other streptococcal arthritis, left hip
M00.262	Other streptococcal arthritis, left knee
M00.212	Other streptococcal arthritis, left shoulder
M00.232	Other streptococcal arthritis, left wrist
M00.271	Other streptococcal arthritis, right ankle and foot
M00.221	Other streptococcal arthritis, right elbow
M00.241	Other streptococcal arthritis, right hand
M00.251	Other streptococcal arthritis, right hip
M00.261	Other streptococcal arthritis, right knee
M00.211	Other streptococcal arthritis, right shoulder
M00.231	Other streptococcal arthritis, right wrist
M00.279	Other streptococcal arthritis, unspecified ankle and foot
M00.229	Other streptococcal arthritis, unspecified elbow
M00.249	Other streptococcal arthritis, unspecified hand
M00.259	Other streptococcal arthritis, unspecified hip
M00.20	Other streptococcal arthritis, unspecified joint
M00.269	Other streptococcal arthritis, unspecified knee
M00.219	Other streptococcal arthritis, unspecified shoulder
M00.239	Other streptococcal arthritis, unspecified wrist
M00.28	Other streptococcal arthritis, vertebrae
M00.29	Other streptococcal polyarthritis
A52.79	Other symptomatic late syphilis
A52.19	Other symptomatic neurosyphilis
A52.06	Other syphilitic heart involvement
D68.69	Other thrombophilia
B58.09	Other toxoplasma oculopathy
J95.09	Other tracheostomy complication
G45.8	Other transient cerebral ischemic attacks and related syndromes
P61.6	Other transient neonatal disorders of coagulation
P70.8	Other transitory disorders of carbohydrate metabolism of newborn
P74.8	Other transitory metabolic disturbances of newborn
P71.8	Other transitory neonatal disorders of calcium and magnesium metabolism
P72.2	Other transitory neonatal disorders of thyroid function, not elsewhere classified
T86.891	Other transplanted tissue failure
T86.892	Other transplanted tissue infection
T86.890	Other transplanted tissue rejection
S12.450A	Other traumatic displaced spondylolisthesis of fifth cervical vertebra, initial encounter for closed fracture
S12.450K	Other traumatic displaced spondylolisthesis of fifth cervical vertebra, subsequent encounter for fracture with nonunion
S12.350A	Other traumatic displaced spondylolisthesis of fourth cervical vertebra, initial encounter for closed fracture
S12.350K	Other traumatic displaced spondylolisthesis of fourth cervical vertebra, subsequent encounter for fracture with nonunion
S12.150A	Other traumatic displaced spondylolisthesis of second cervical vertebra, initial encounter for closed fracture
S12.150K	Other traumatic displaced spondylolisthesis of second cervical vertebra, subsequent encounter for fracture with nonunion
S12.650A	Other traumatic displaced spondylolisthesis of seventh cervical vertebra, initial encounter for closed fracture
S12.650K	Other traumatic displaced spondylolisthesis of seventh cervical vertebra, subsequent encounter for fracture with nonunion
S12.550A	Other traumatic displaced spondylolisthesis of sixth cervical vertebra, initial encounter for closed fracture
S12.550K	Other traumatic displaced spondylolisthesis of sixth cervical vertebra, subsequent encounter for fracture with nonunion
S12.250A	Other traumatic displaced spondylolisthesis of third cervical vertebra, initial encounter for closed fracture
S12.250K	Other traumatic displaced spondylolisthesis of third cervical vertebra, subsequent encounter for fracture with nonunion
S12.451A	Other traumatic nondisplaced spondylolisthesis of fifth cervical vertebra, initial encounter for closed fracture
S12.451K	Other traumatic nondisplaced spondylolisthesis of fifth cervical vertebra, subsequent encounter for fracture with nonunion
S12.351A	Other traumatic nondisplaced spondylolisthesis of fourth cervical vertebra, initial encounter for closed fracture
S12.351K	Other traumatic nondisplaced spondylolisthesis of fourth cervical vertebra, subsequent encounter for fracture with nonunion
S12.151A	Other traumatic nondisplaced spondylolisthesis of second cervical vertebra, initial encounter for closed fracture
S12.151K	Other traumatic nondisplaced spondylolisthesis of second cervical vertebra, subsequent encounter for fracture with nonunion
S12.651A	Other traumatic nondisplaced spondylolisthesis of seventh cervical vertebra, initial encounter for closed fracture
S12.651K	Other traumatic nondisplaced spondylolisthesis of seventh cervical vertebra, subsequent encounter for fracture with nonunion
S12.551A	Other traumatic nondisplaced spondylolisthesis of sixth cervical vertebra, initial encounter for closed fracture
S12.551K	Other traumatic nondisplaced spondylolisthesis of sixth cervical vertebra, subsequent encounter for fracture with nonunion
S12.251A	Other traumatic nondisplaced spondylolisthesis of third cervical vertebra, initial encounter for closed fracture
S12.251K	Other traumatic nondisplaced spondylolisthesis of third cervical vertebra, subsequent encounter for fracture with nonunion
A18.59	Other tuberculosis of eye
C82.89	Other types of follicular lymphoma, extranodal and solid organ sites
C82.83	Other types of follicular lymphoma, intra-abdominal lymph nodes
C82.86	Other types of follicular lymphoma, intrapelvic lymph nodes
C82.82	Other types of follicular lymphoma, intrathoracic lymph nodes
C82.84	Other types of follicular lymphoma, lymph nodes of axilla and upper limb
C82.81	Other types of follicular lymphoma, lymph nodes of head, face, and neck
C82.85	Other types of follicular lymphoma, lymph nodes of inguinal region and lower limb
C82.88	Other types of follicular lymphoma, lymph nodes of multiple sites
C82.87	Other types of follicular lymphoma, spleen
C82.80	Other types of follicular lymphoma, unspecified site
K51.814	Other ulcerative colitis with abscess
K51.813	Other ulcerative colitis with fistula
K51.812	Other ulcerative colitis with intestinal obstruction
K51.818	Other ulcerative colitis with other complication
K51.811	Other ulcerative colitis with rectal bleeding
K51.819	Other ulcerative colitis with unspecified complications
K51.80	Other ulcerative colitis without complications
O86.29	Other urinary tract infection following delivery
B37.49	Other urogenital candidiasis
B01.89	Other varicella complications
K55.8	Other vascular disorders of intestine
O04.85	Other venous complications following (induced) termination of pregnancy
O08.7	Other venous complications following an ectopic and molar pregnancy
O03.85	Other venous complications following complete or unspecified spontaneous abortion
O07.35	Other venous complications following failed attempted termination of pregnancy
O03.35	Other venous complications following incomplete spontaneous abortion
O22.8X1	Other venous complications in pregnancy, first trimester
O22.8X2	Other venous complications in pregnancy, second trimester
O22.8X3	Other venous complications in pregnancy, third trimester
O22.8X9	Other venous complications in pregnancy, unspecified trimester
O87.8	Other venous complications in the puerperium
A69.1	Other Vincent's infections
O98.52	Other viral diseases complicating childbirth
O98.511	Other viral diseases complicating pregnancy, first trimester
O98.512	Other viral diseases complicating pregnancy, second trimester
O98.513	Other viral diseases complicating pregnancy, third trimester
O98.53	Other viral diseases complicating the puerperium
A08.39	Other viral enteritis
A87.8	Other viral meningitis
E71.528	Other X-linked adrenoleukodystrophy

T82.847A	Pain due to cardiac prosthetic devices, implants and grafts, initial encounter
T83.84XA	Pain due to genitourinary prosthetic devices, implants and grafts, initial encounter
T84.84XA	Pain due to internal orthopedic prosthetic devices, implants and grafts, initial encounter
T85.840A	Pain due to nervous system prosthetic devices, implants and grafts, initial encounter
T85.840D	Pain due to nervous system prosthetic devices, implants and grafts, subsequent encounter
T82.848A	Pain due to vascular prosthetic devices, implants and grafts, initial encounter
Z94.83	Pancreas transplant status
K90.3	Pancreatic steatorrhea
H44.013	Panophthalmitis (acute), bilateral
H44.012	Panophthalmitis (acute), left eye
H44.011	Panophthalmitis (acute), right eye
H44.019	Panophthalmitis (acute), unspecified eye
H44.113	Panuveitis, bilateral
H44.112	Panuveitis, left eye
H44.111	Panuveitis, right eye
H44.119	Panuveitis, unspecified eye
H47.11	Papilledema associated with increased intracranial pressure
B41.9	Paracoccidioidomycosis, unspecified
B66.4	Paragonimiasis
K56.0	Paralytic ileus
L10.81	Paraneoplastic pemphigus
F20.0	Paranoid schizophrenia
G82.21	Paraplegia, complete
G82.22	Paraplegia, incomplete
G82.20	Paraplegia, unspecified
H21.333	Parasitic cyst of iris, ciliary body or anterior chamber, bilateral
H21.332	Parasitic cyst of iris, ciliary body or anterior chamber, left eye
H21.331	Parasitic cyst of iris, ciliary body or anterior chamber, right eye
H21.339	Parasitic cyst of iris, ciliary body or anterior chamber, unspecified eye
H33.123	Parasitic cyst of retina, bilateral
H33.122	Parasitic cyst of retina, left eye
H33.121	Parasitic cyst of retina, right eye
H33.129	Parasitic cyst of retina, unspecified eye
H44.123	Parasitic endophthalmitis, unspecified, bilateral
H44.122	Parasitic endophthalmitis, unspecified, left eye
H44.121	Parasitic endophthalmitis, unspecified, right eye
H44.129	Parasitic endophthalmitis, unspecified, unspecified eye
K43.3	Parastomal hernia with obstruction, without gangrene
A01.1	Paratyphoid fever A
A01.2	Paratyphoid fever B
A01.3	Paratyphoid fever C
A01.4	Paratyphoid fever, unspecified
Q26.3	Partial anomalous pulmonary venous connection
K56.600	Partial intestinal obstruction, unspecified as to cause
O44.21	Partial placenta previa NOS or without hemorrhage, first trimester
O44.22	Partial placenta previa NOS or without hemorrhage, second trimester
O44.23	Partial placenta previa NOS or without hemorrhage, third trimester
H34.213	Partial retinal artery occlusion, bilateral
H34.212	Partial retinal artery occlusion, left eye
H34.211	Partial retinal artery occlusion, right eye
H34.219	Partial retinal artery occlusion, unspecified eye
S58.022A	Partial traumatic amputation at elbow level, left arm, initial encounter
S58.021A	Partial traumatic amputation at elbow level, right arm, initial encounter
S58.029A	Partial traumatic amputation at elbow level, unspecified arm, initial encounter
S88.022A	Partial traumatic amputation at knee level, left lower leg, initial encounter
S88.021A	Partial traumatic amputation at knee level, right lower leg, initial encounter
S88.029A	Partial traumatic amputation at knee level, unspecified lower leg, initial encounter
S78.022A	Partial traumatic amputation at left hip joint, initial encounter
S48.022A	Partial traumatic amputation at left shoulder joint, initial encounter
S58.122A	Partial traumatic amputation at level between elbow and wrist, left arm, initial encounter
S58.121A	Partial traumatic amputation at level between elbow and wrist, right arm, initial encounter
S58.129A	Partial traumatic amputation at level between elbow and wrist, unspecified arm, initial encounter
S88.122A	Partial traumatic amputation at level between knee and ankle, left lower leg, initial encounter
S88.121A	Partial traumatic amputation at level between knee and ankle, right lower leg, initial encounter
S88.129A	Partial traumatic amputation at level between knee and ankle, unspecified lower leg, initial encounter
S78.122A	Partial traumatic amputation at level between left hip and knee, initial encounter
S48.122A	Partial traumatic amputation at level between left shoulder and elbow, initial encounter
S78.121A	Partial traumatic amputation at level between right hip and knee, initial encounter
S48.121A	Partial traumatic amputation at level between right shoulder and elbow, initial encounter
S78.129A	Partial traumatic amputation at level between unspecified hip and knee, initial encounter
S48.129A	Partial traumatic amputation at level between unspecified shoulder and elbow, initial encounter
S78.021A	Partial traumatic amputation at right hip joint, initial encounter

S48.021A	Partial traumatic amputation at right shoulder joint, initial encounter
S78.029A	Partial traumatic amputation at unspecified hip joint, initial encounter
S48.029A	Partial traumatic amputation at unspecified shoulder joint, initial encounter
S98.022A	Partial traumatic amputation of left foot at ankle level, initial encounter
S98.922A	Partial traumatic amputation of left foot, level unspecified, initial encounter
S58.922A	Partial traumatic amputation of left forearm, level unspecified, initial encounter
S68.422A	Partial traumatic amputation of left hand at wrist level, initial encounter
S78.922A	Partial traumatic amputation of left hip and thigh, level unspecified, initial encounter
S88.922A	Partial traumatic amputation of left lower leg, level unspecified, initial encounter
S98.322A	Partial traumatic amputation of left midfoot, initial encounter
S48.922A	Partial traumatic amputation of left shoulder and upper arm, level unspecified, initial encounter
S98.021A	Partial traumatic amputation of right foot at ankle level, initial encounter
S98.921A	Partial traumatic amputation of right foot, level unspecified, initial encounter
S58.921A	Partial traumatic amputation of right forearm, level unspecified, initial encounter
S68.421A	Partial traumatic amputation of right hand at wrist level, initial encounter
S78.921A	Partial traumatic amputation of right hip and thigh, level unspecified, initial encounter
S88.921A	Partial traumatic amputation of right lower leg, level unspecified, initial encounter
S98.321A	Partial traumatic amputation of right midfoot, initial encounter
S48.921A	Partial traumatic amputation of right shoulder and upper arm, level unspecified, initial encounter
S98.029A	Partial traumatic amputation of unspecified foot at ankle level, initial encounter
S98.929A	Partial traumatic amputation of unspecified foot, level unspecified, initial encounter
S58.929A	Partial traumatic amputation of unspecified forearm, level unspecified, initial encounter
S68.429A	Partial traumatic amputation of unspecified hand at wrist level, initial encounter
S78.929A	Partial traumatic amputation of unspecified hip and thigh, level unspecified, initial encounter
S88.929A	Partial traumatic amputation of unspecified lower leg, level unspecified, initial encounter
S98.329A	Partial traumatic amputation of unspecified midfoot, initial encounter
S48.929A	Partial traumatic amputation of unspecified shoulder and upper arm, level unspecified, initial encounter
S68.722A	Partial traumatic transmetacarpal amputation of left hand, initial encounter
S68.721A	Partial traumatic transmetacarpal amputation of right hand, initial encounter
S68.729A	Partial traumatic transmetacarpal amputation of unspecified hand, initial encounter
B34.3	Parvovirus infection, unspecified
A28.0	Pasteurellosis
Q25.0	Patent ductus arteriosus
M84.559A	Pathological fracture in neoplastic disease, hip, unspecified, initial encounter for fracture
M84.559P	Pathological fracture in neoplastic disease, hip, unspecified, subsequent encounter for fracture with malunion
M84.559K	Pathological fracture in neoplastic disease, hip, unspecified, subsequent encounter for fracture with nonunion
M84.572A	Pathological fracture in neoplastic disease, left ankle, initial encounter for fracture
M84.572P	Pathological fracture in neoplastic disease, left ankle, subsequent encounter for fracture with malunion
M84.572K	Pathological fracture in neoplastic disease, left ankle, subsequent encounter for fracture with nonunion
M84.552A	Pathological fracture in neoplastic disease, left femur, initial encounter for fracture
M84.552P	Pathological fracture in neoplastic disease, left femur, subsequent encounter for fracture with malunion
M84.552K	Pathological fracture in neoplastic disease, left femur, subsequent encounter for fracture with nonunion
M84.564A	Pathological fracture in neoplastic disease, left fibula, initial encounter for fracture
M84.564P	Pathological fracture in neoplastic disease, left fibula, subsequent encounter for fracture with malunion
M84.564K	Pathological fracture in neoplastic disease, left fibula, subsequent encounter for fracture with nonunion
M84.575A	Pathological fracture in neoplastic disease, left foot, initial encounter for fracture
M84.575P	Pathological fracture in neoplastic disease, left foot, subsequent encounter for fracture with malunion
M84.575K	Pathological fracture in neoplastic disease, left foot, subsequent encounter for fracture with nonunion
M84.542A	Pathological fracture in neoplastic disease, left hand, initial encounter for fracture
M84.542P	Pathological fracture in neoplastic disease, left hand, subsequent encounter for fracture with malunion
M84.542K	Pathological fracture in neoplastic disease, left hand, subsequent encounter for fracture with nonunion
M84.522A	Pathological fracture in neoplastic disease, left humerus, initial encounter for fracture
M84.522P	Pathological fracture in neoplastic disease, left humerus, subsequent encounter for fracture with malunion
M84.522K	Pathological fracture in neoplastic disease, left humerus, subsequent encounter for fracture with nonunion

M84.534A Pathological fracture in neoplastic disease, left radius, initial encounter for fracture

M84.534P Pathological fracture in neoplastic disease, left radius, subsequent encounter for fracture with malunion

M84.534K Pathological fracture in neoplastic disease, left radius, subsequent encounter for fracture with nonunion

M84.512A Pathological fracture in neoplastic disease, left shoulder, initial encounter for fracture

M84.512P Pathological fracture in neoplastic disease, left shoulder, subsequent encounter for fracture with malunion

M84.512K Pathological fracture in neoplastic disease, left shoulder, subsequent encounter for fracture with nonunion

M84.562A Pathological fracture in neoplastic disease, left tibia, initial encounter for fracture

M84.562P Pathological fracture in neoplastic disease, left tibia, subsequent encounter for fracture with malunion

M84.562K Pathological fracture in neoplastic disease, left tibia, subsequent encounter for fracture with nonunion

M84.532A Pathological fracture in neoplastic disease, left ulna, initial encounter for fracture

M84.532P Pathological fracture in neoplastic disease, left ulna, subsequent encounter for fracture with malunion

M84.532K Pathological fracture in neoplastic disease, left ulna, subsequent encounter for fracture with nonunion

M84.58XA Pathological fracture in neoplastic disease, other specified site, initial encounter for fracture

M84.58XP Pathological fracture in neoplastic disease, other specified site, subsequent encounter for fracture with malunion

M84.58XK Pathological fracture in neoplastic disease, other specified site, subsequent encounter for fracture with nonunion

M84.550A Pathological fracture in neoplastic disease, pelvis, initial encounter for fracture

M84.550P Pathological fracture in neoplastic disease, pelvis, subsequent encounter for fracture with malunion

M84.550K Pathological fracture in neoplastic disease, pelvis, subsequent encounter for fracture with nonunion

M84.571A Pathological fracture in neoplastic disease, right ankle, initial encounter for fracture

M84.571P Pathological fracture in neoplastic disease, right ankle, subsequent encounter for fracture with malunion

M84.571K Pathological fracture in neoplastic disease, right ankle, subsequent encounter for fracture with nonunion

M84.551A Pathological fracture in neoplastic disease, right femur, initial encounter for fracture

M84.551P Pathological fracture in neoplastic disease, right femur, subsequent encounter for fracture with malunion

M84.551K Pathological fracture in neoplastic disease, right femur, subsequent encounter for fracture with nonunion

M84.563A Pathological fracture in neoplastic disease, right fibula, initial encounter for fracture

M84.563P Pathological fracture in neoplastic disease, right fibula, subsequent encounter for fracture with malunion

M84.563K Pathological fracture in neoplastic disease, right fibula, subsequent encounter for fracture with nonunion

M84.574A Pathological fracture in neoplastic disease, right foot, initial encounter for fracture

M84.574P Pathological fracture in neoplastic disease, right foot, subsequent encounter for fracture with malunion

M84.574K Pathological fracture in neoplastic disease, right foot, subsequent encounter for fracture with nonunion

M84.541A Pathological fracture in neoplastic disease, right hand, initial encounter for fracture

M84.541P Pathological fracture in neoplastic disease, right hand, subsequent encounter for fracture with malunion

M84.541K Pathological fracture in neoplastic disease, right hand, subsequent encounter for fracture with nonunion

M84.521A Pathological fracture in neoplastic disease, right humerus, initial encounter for fracture

M84.521P Pathological fracture in neoplastic disease, right humerus, subsequent encounter for fracture with malunion

M84.521K Pathological fracture in neoplastic disease, right humerus, subsequent encounter for fracture with nonunion

M84.533A Pathological fracture in neoplastic disease, right radius, initial encounter for fracture

M84.533P Pathological fracture in neoplastic disease, right radius, subsequent encounter for fracture with malunion

M84.533K Pathological fracture in neoplastic disease, right radius, subsequent encounter for fracture with nonunion

M84.511A Pathological fracture in neoplastic disease, right shoulder, initial encounter for fracture

M84.511P Pathological fracture in neoplastic disease, right shoulder, subsequent encounter for fracture with malunion

M84.511K Pathological fracture in neoplastic disease, right shoulder, subsequent encounter for fracture with nonunion

M84.561A Pathological fracture in neoplastic disease, right tibia, initial encounter for fracture

M84.561P Pathological fracture in neoplastic disease, right tibia, subsequent encounter for fracture with malunion

M84.561K Pathological fracture in neoplastic disease, right tibia, subsequent encounter for fracture with nonunion

M84.531A Pathological fracture in neoplastic disease, right ulna, initial encounter for fracture

M84.531P Pathological fracture in neoplastic disease, right ulna, subsequent encounter for fracture with malunion

M84.531K Pathological fracture in neoplastic disease, right ulna, subsequent encounter for fracture with nonunion

M84.573A Pathological fracture in neoplastic disease, unspecified ankle, initial encounter for fracture

M84.573P Pathological fracture in neoplastic disease, unspecified ankle, subsequent encounter for fracture with malunion

M84.573K Pathological fracture in neoplastic disease, unspecified ankle, subsequent encounter for fracture with nonunion

M84.553A Pathological fracture in neoplastic disease, unspecified femur, initial encounter for fracture

M84.553P Pathological fracture in neoplastic disease, unspecified femur, subsequent encounter for fracture with malunion

M84.553K Pathological fracture in neoplastic disease, unspecified femur, subsequent encounter for fracture with nonunion

M84.576A Pathological fracture in neoplastic disease, unspecified foot, initial encounter for fracture

M84.576P Pathological fracture in neoplastic disease, unspecified foot, subsequent encounter for fracture with malunion

M84.576K Pathological fracture in neoplastic disease, unspecified foot, subsequent encounter for fracture with nonunion

M84.549A Pathological fracture in neoplastic disease, unspecified hand, initial encounter for fracture

M84.549P Pathological fracture in neoplastic disease, unspecified hand, subsequent encounter for fracture with malunion

M84.549K Pathological fracture in neoplastic disease, unspecified hand, subsequent encounter for fracture with nonunion

M84.529A Pathological fracture in neoplastic disease, unspecified humerus, initial encounter for fracture

M84.529P Pathological fracture in neoplastic disease, unspecified humerus, subsequent encounter for fracture with malunion

M84.529K Pathological fracture in neoplastic disease, unspecified humerus, subsequent encounter for fracture with nonunion

M84.519A Pathological fracture in neoplastic disease, unspecified shoulder, initial encounter for fracture

M84.519P Pathological fracture in neoplastic disease, unspecified shoulder, subsequent encounter for fracture with malunion

M84.519K Pathological fracture in neoplastic disease, unspecified shoulder, subsequent encounter for fracture with nonunion

M84.50XA Pathological fracture in neoplastic disease, unspecified site, initial encounter for fracture

M84.50XP Pathological fracture in neoplastic disease, unspecified site, subsequent encounter for fracture with malunion

M84.50XK Pathological fracture in neoplastic disease, unspecified site, subsequent encounter for fracture with nonunion

M84.569A Pathological fracture in neoplastic disease, unspecified tibia and fibula, initial encounter for fracture

M84.569P Pathological fracture in neoplastic disease, unspecified tibia and fibula, subsequent encounter for fracture with malunion

M84.569K Pathological fracture in neoplastic disease, unspecified tibia and fibula, subsequent encounter for fracture with nonunion

M84.539A Pathological fracture in neoplastic disease, unspecified ulna and radius, initial encounter for fracture

M84.539P Pathological fracture in neoplastic disease, unspecified ulna and radius, subsequent encounter for fracture with malunion

M84.539K Pathological fracture in neoplastic disease, unspecified ulna and radius, subsequent encounter for fracture with nonunion

M84.659A Pathological fracture in other disease, hip, unspecified, initial encounter for fracture

M84.659P Pathological fracture in other disease, hip, unspecified, subsequent encounter for fracture with malunion

M84.659K Pathological fracture in other disease, hip, unspecified, subsequent encounter for fracture with nonunion

M84.672A Pathological fracture in other disease, left ankle, initial encounter for fracture

M84.672P Pathological fracture in other disease, left ankle, subsequent encounter for fracture with malunion

M84.672K Pathological fracture in other disease, left ankle, subsequent encounter for fracture with nonunion

M84.652A Pathological fracture in other disease, left femur, initial encounter for fracture

M84.652P Pathological fracture in other disease, left femur, subsequent encounter for fracture with malunion

M84.652K Pathological fracture in other disease, left femur, subsequent encounter for fracture with nonunion

M84.664A Pathological fracture in other disease, left fibula, initial encounter for fracture

M84.664P Pathological fracture in other disease, left fibula, subsequent encounter for fracture with malunion

M84.664K Pathological fracture in other disease, left fibula, subsequent encounter for fracture with nonunion

M84.675A Pathological fracture in other disease, left foot, initial encounter for fracture

M84.675P Pathological fracture in other disease, left foot, subsequent encounter for fracture with malunion

M84.675K Pathological fracture in other disease, left foot, subsequent encounter for fracture with nonunion

M84.642A Pathological fracture in other disease, left hand, initial encounter for fracture

M84.642P Pathological fracture in other disease, left hand, subsequent encounter for fracture with malunion

M84.642K Pathological fracture in other disease, left hand, subsequent encounter for fracture with nonunion

M84.622A Pathological fracture in other disease, left humerus, initial encounter for fracture

M84.622P Pathological fracture in other disease, left humerus, subsequent encounter for fracture with malunion

M84.622K Pathological fracture in other disease, left humerus, subsequent encounter for fracture with nonunion

M84.634A Pathological fracture in other disease, left radius, initial encounter for fracture

M84.634P Pathological fracture in other disease, left radius, subsequent encounter for fracture with malunion

M84.634K Pathological fracture in other disease, left radius, subsequent encounter for fracture with nonunion

M84.612A Pathological fracture in other disease, left shoulder, initial encounter for fracture

M84.612P Pathological fracture in other disease, left shoulder, subsequent encounter for fracture with malunion

M84.612K Pathological fracture in other disease, left shoulder, subsequent encounter for fracture with nonunion

M84.662A Pathological fracture in other disease, left tibia, initial encounter for fracture

M84.662P Pathological fracture in other disease, left tibia, subsequent encounter for fracture with malunion

M84.662K Pathological fracture in other disease, left tibia, subsequent encounter for fracture with nonunion

M84.632A Pathological fracture in other disease, left ulna, initial encounter for fracture

M84.632P Pathological fracture in other disease, left ulna, subsequent encounter for fracture with malunion

M84.632K Pathological fracture in other disease, left ulna, subsequent encounter for fracture with nonunion

M84.68XA Pathological fracture in other disease, other site, initial encounter for fracture

M84.68XP Pathological fracture in other disease, other site, subsequent encounter for fracture with malunion

M84.68XK Pathological fracture in other disease, other site, subsequent encounter for fracture with nonunion

M84.650A Pathological fracture in other disease, pelvis, initial encounter for fracture

M84.650P Pathological fracture in other disease, pelvis, subsequent encounter for fracture with malunion

M84.650K Pathological fracture in other disease, pelvis, subsequent encounter for fracture with nonunion

M84.671A Pathological fracture in other disease, right ankle, initial encounter for fracture

M84.671P Pathological fracture in other disease, right ankle, subsequent encounter for fracture with malunion

M84.671K Pathological fracture in other disease, right ankle, subsequent encounter for fracture with nonunion

M84.651A Pathological fracture in other disease, right femur, initial encounter for fracture

M84.651P Pathological fracture in other disease, right femur, subsequent encounter for fracture with malunion

M84.651K Pathological fracture in other disease, right femur, subsequent encounter for fracture with nonunion

M84.663A Pathological fracture in other disease, right fibula, initial encounter for fracture

M84.663P Pathological fracture in other disease, right fibula, subsequent encounter for fracture with malunion

M84.663K Pathological fracture in other disease, right fibula, subsequent encounter for fracture with nonunion

M84.674A Pathological fracture in other disease, right foot, initial encounter for fracture

M84.674P Pathological fracture in other disease, right foot, subsequent encounter for fracture with malunion

M84.674K Pathological fracture in other disease, right foot, subsequent encounter for fracture with nonunion

M84.641A Pathological fracture in other disease, right hand, initial encounter for fracture

M84.641P Pathological fracture in other disease, right hand, subsequent encounter for fracture with malunion

M84.641K Pathological fracture in other disease, right hand, subsequent encounter for fracture with nonunion

M84.621A Pathological fracture in other disease, right humerus, initial encounter for fracture

M84.621P Pathological fracture in other disease, right humerus, subsequent encounter for fracture with malunion

M84.621K Pathological fracture in other disease, right humerus, subsequent encounter for fracture with nonunion

M84.633A Pathological fracture in other disease, right radius, initial encounter for fracture

M84.633P Pathological fracture in other disease, right radius, subsequent encounter for fracture with malunion

M84.633K Pathological fracture in other disease, right radius, subsequent encounter for fracture with nonunion

M84.611A Pathological fracture in other disease, right shoulder, initial encounter for fracture

M84.611P Pathological fracture in other disease, right shoulder, subsequent encounter for fracture with malunion

M84.611K Pathological fracture in other disease, right shoulder, subsequent encounter for fracture with nonunion

M84.661A Pathological fracture in other disease, right tibia, initial encounter for fracture

M84.661P Pathological fracture in other disease, right tibia, subsequent encounter for fracture with malunion

M84.661K Pathological fracture in other disease, right tibia, subsequent encounter for fracture with nonunion

M84.631A Pathological fracture in other disease, right ulna, initial encounter for fracture

M84.631P Pathological fracture in other disease, right ulna, subsequent encounter for fracture with malunion

M84.631K Pathological fracture in other disease, right ulna, subsequent encounter for fracture with nonunion

M84.673A Pathological fracture in other disease, unspecified ankle, initial encounter for fracture

M84.673P Pathological fracture in other disease, unspecified ankle, subsequent encounter for fracture with malunion

M84.673K Pathological fracture in other disease, unspecified ankle, subsequent encounter for fracture with nonunion

M84.653A Pathological fracture in other disease, unspecified femur, initial encounter for fracture

M84.653P Pathological fracture in other disease, unspecified femur, subsequent encounter for fracture with malunion

M84.653K Pathological fracture in other disease, unspecified femur, subsequent encounter for fracture with nonunion

M84.676A Pathological fracture in other disease, unspecified foot, initial encounter for fracture

M84.676P Pathological fracture in other disease, unspecified foot, subsequent encounter for fracture with malunion

M84.676K Pathological fracture in other disease, unspecified foot, subsequent encounter for fracture with nonunion

M84.649A Pathological fracture in other disease, unspecified hand, initial encounter for fracture

M84.649P Pathological fracture in other disease, unspecified hand, subsequent encounter for fracture with malunion

M84.649K Pathological fracture in other disease, unspecified hand, subsequent encounter for fracture with nonunion

M84.629A Pathological fracture in other disease, unspecified humerus, initial encounter for fracture

M84.629P Pathological fracture in other disease, unspecified humerus, subsequent encounter for fracture with malunion

M84.629K Pathological fracture in other disease, unspecified humerus, subsequent encounter for fracture with nonunion

M84.619A Pathological fracture in other disease, unspecified shoulder, initial encounter for fracture

M84.619P Pathological fracture in other disease, unspecified shoulder, subsequent encounter for fracture with malunion

M84.619K Pathological fracture in other disease, unspecified shoulder, subsequent encounter for fracture with nonunion

M84.60XA Pathological fracture in other disease, unspecified site, initial encounter for fracture

M84.60XP Pathological fracture in other disease, unspecified site, subsequent encounter for fracture with malunion

M84.60XK Pathological fracture in other disease, unspecified site, subsequent encounter for fracture with nonunion

M84.669A Pathological fracture in other disease, unspecified tibia and fibula, initial encounter for fracture

M84.669P Pathological fracture in other disease, unspecified tibia and fibula, subsequent encounter for fracture with malunion

M84.669K Pathological fracture in other disease, unspecified tibia and fibula, subsequent encounter for fracture with nonunion

M84.639A Pathological fracture in other disease, unspecified ulna and radius, initial encounter for fracture

M84.639P Pathological fracture in other disease, unspecified ulna and radius, subsequent encounter for fracture with malunion

M84.639K Pathological fracture in other disease, unspecified ulna and radius, subsequent encounter for fracture with nonunion

M84.459A Pathological fracture, hip, unspecified, initial encounter for fracture

M84.459P Pathological fracture, hip, unspecified, subsequent encounter for fracture with malunion

M84.459K Pathological fracture, hip, unspecified, subsequent encounter for fracture with nonunion

M84.472A Pathological fracture, left ankle, initial encounter for fracture

M84.472P Pathological fracture, left ankle, subsequent encounter for fracture with malunion

M84.472K Pathological fracture, left ankle, subsequent encounter for fracture with nonunion

M84.452A Pathological fracture, left femur, initial encounter for fracture

M84.452P Pathological fracture, left femur, subsequent encounter for fracture with malunion

M84.452K Pathological fracture, left femur, subsequent encounter for fracture with nonunion

M84.464A Pathological fracture, left fibula, initial encounter for fracture

M84.464P Pathological fracture, left fibula, subsequent encounter for fracture with malunion

M84.464K Pathological fracture, left fibula, subsequent encounter for fracture with nonunion

M84.445A Pathological fracture, left finger(s), initial encounter for fracture

M84.445P Pathological fracture, left finger(s), subsequent encounter for fracture with malunion

M84.445K Pathological fracture, left finger(s), subsequent encounter for fracture with nonunion

M84.475A Pathological fracture, left foot, initial encounter for fracture

M84.475P Pathological fracture, left foot, subsequent encounter for fracture with malunion

M84.475K Pathological fracture, left foot, subsequent encounter for fracture with nonunion

M84.442A Pathological fracture, left hand, initial encounter for fracture

M84.442P Pathological fracture, left hand, subsequent encounter for fracture with malunion

M84.442K Pathological fracture, left hand, subsequent encounter for fracture with nonunion

M84.422A Pathological fracture, left humerus, initial encounter for fracture

M84.422P Pathological fracture, left humerus, subsequent encounter for fracture with malunion

M84.422K Pathological fracture, left humerus, subsequent encounter for fracture with nonunion

M84.434A Pathological fracture, left radius, initial encounter for fracture

M84.434P Pathological fracture, left radius, subsequent encounter for fracture with malunion

M84.434K Pathological fracture, left radius, subsequent encounter for fracture with nonunion

M84.412A Pathological fracture, left shoulder, initial encounter for fracture

M84.412P Pathological fracture, left shoulder, subsequent encounter for fracture with malunion

M84.412K Pathological fracture, left shoulder, subsequent encounter for fracture with nonunion

M84.462A Pathological fracture, left tibia, initial encounter for fracture

M84.462P Pathological fracture, left tibia, subsequent encounter for fracture with malunion

M84.462K Pathological fracture, left tibia, subsequent encounter for fracture with nonunion

M84.478A Pathological fracture, left toe(s), initial encounter for fracture

M84.478P Pathological fracture, left toe(s), subsequent encounter for fracture with malunion

M84.478K Pathological fracture, left toe(s), subsequent encounter for fracture with nonunion

M84.432A Pathological fracture, left ulna, initial encounter for fracture

M84.432P Pathological fracture, left ulna, subsequent encounter for fracture with malunion

M84.432K Pathological fracture, left ulna, subsequent encounter for fracture with nonunion

M84.48XA Pathological fracture, other site, initial encounter for fracture

M84.48XP Pathological fracture, other site, subsequent encounter for fracture with malunion

M84.48XK Pathological fracture, other site, subsequent encounter for fracture with nonunion

M84.454A Pathological fracture, pelvis, initial encounter for fracture

M84.454P Pathological fracture, pelvis, subsequent encounter for fracture with malunion

M84.454K Pathological fracture, pelvis, subsequent encounter for fracture with nonunion

M84.471A Pathological fracture, right ankle, initial encounter for fracture

M84.471P Pathological fracture, right ankle, subsequent encounter for fracture with malunion

M84.471K Pathological fracture, right ankle, subsequent encounter for fracture with nonunion

M84.451A Pathological fracture, right femur, initial encounter for fracture

M84.451P Pathological fracture, right femur, subsequent encounter for fracture with malunion

M84.451K Pathological fracture, right femur, subsequent encounter for fracture with nonunion

M84.463A Pathological fracture, right fibula, initial encounter for fracture

M84.463P Pathological fracture, right fibula, subsequent encounter for fracture with malunion

M84.463K Pathological fracture, right fibula, subsequent encounter for fracture with nonunion

M84.444A Pathological fracture, right finger(s), initial encounter for fracture

M84.444P Pathological fracture, right finger(s), subsequent encounter for fracture with malunion

M84.444K Pathological fracture, right finger(s), subsequent encounter for fracture with nonunion

M84.474A Pathological fracture, right foot, initial encounter for fracture

M84.474P Pathological fracture, right foot, subsequent encounter for fracture with malunion

M84.474K Pathological fracture, right foot, subsequent encounter for fracture with nonunion

M84.441A Pathological fracture, right hand, initial encounter for fracture

M84.441P Pathological fracture, right hand, subsequent encounter for fracture with malunion

M84.441K Pathological fracture, right hand, subsequent encounter for fracture with nonunion

M84.421A Pathological fracture, right humerus, initial encounter for fracture

M84.421P Pathological fracture, right humerus, subsequent encounter for fracture with malunion

M84.421K Pathological fracture, right humerus, subsequent encounter for fracture with nonunion

M84.433A Pathological fracture, right radius, initial encounter for fracture

M84.433P Pathological fracture, right radius, subsequent encounter for fracture with malunion

M84.433K Pathological fracture, right radius, subsequent encounter for fracture with nonunion

M84.411A Pathological fracture, right shoulder, initial encounter for fracture

M84.411P Pathological fracture, right shoulder, subsequent encounter for fracture with malunion

M84.411K Pathological fracture, right shoulder, subsequent encounter for fracture with nonunion

M84.461A Pathological fracture, right tibia, initial encounter for fracture

M84.461P Pathological fracture, right tibia, subsequent encounter for fracture with malunion

M84.461K Pathological fracture, right tibia, subsequent encounter for fracture with nonunion

M84.477A Pathological fracture, right toe(s), initial encounter for fracture

M84.477P Pathological fracture, right toe(s), subsequent encounter for fracture with malunion

M84.477K Pathological fracture, right toe(s), subsequent encounter for fracture with nonunion

M84.431A Pathological fracture, right ulna, initial encounter for fracture

M84.431P Pathological fracture, right ulna, subsequent encounter for fracture with malunion

M84.431K Pathological fracture, right ulna, subsequent encounter for fracture with nonunion

M84.473A Pathological fracture, unspecified ankle, initial encounter for fracture

M84.473P Pathological fracture, unspecified ankle, subsequent encounter for fracture with malunion

M84.473K Pathological fracture, unspecified ankle, subsequent encounter for fracture with nonunion

M84.453A Pathological fracture, unspecified femur, initial encounter for fracture

M84.453P Pathological fracture, unspecified femur, subsequent encounter for fracture with malunion

M84.453K Pathological fracture, unspecified femur, subsequent encounter for fracture with nonunion

M84.446A Pathological fracture, unspecified finger(s), initial encounter for fracture

M84.446P Pathological fracture, unspecified finger(s), subsequent encounter for fracture with malunion

M84.446K Pathological fracture, unspecified finger(s), subsequent encounter for fracture with nonunion

M84.476A Pathological fracture, unspecified foot, initial encounter for fracture

M84.476P Pathological fracture, unspecified foot, subsequent encounter for fracture with malunion

M84.476K Pathological fracture, unspecified foot, subsequent encounter for fracture with nonunion

M84.443A Pathological fracture, unspecified hand, initial encounter for fracture

M84.443P Pathological fracture, unspecified hand, subsequent encounter for fracture with malunion

M84.443K Pathological fracture, unspecified hand, subsequent encounter for fracture with nonunion

M84.429A Pathological fracture, unspecified humerus, initial encounter for fracture

M84.429P Pathological fracture, unspecified humerus, subsequent encounter for fracture with malunion

M84.429K Pathological fracture, unspecified humerus, subsequent encounter for fracture with nonunion

M84.419A Pathological fracture, unspecified shoulder, initial encounter for fracture

M84.419P Pathological fracture, unspecified shoulder, subsequent encounter for fracture with malunion

M84.419K Pathological fracture, unspecified shoulder, subsequent encounter for fracture with nonunion

M84.40XA Pathological fracture, unspecified site, initial encounter for fracture

M84.40XP Pathological fracture, unspecified site, subsequent encounter for fracture with malunion

M84.40XK Pathological fracture, unspecified site, subsequent encounter for fracture with nonunion

M84.469A Pathological fracture, unspecified tibia and fibula, initial encounter for fracture

M84.469P Pathological fracture, unspecified tibia and fibula, subsequent encounter for fracture with malunion

M84.469K Pathological fracture, unspecified tibia and fibula, subsequent encounter for fracture with nonunion

M84.479A Pathological fracture, unspecified toe(s), initial encounter for fracture

M84.479P Pathological fracture, unspecified toe(s), subsequent encounter for fracture with malunion

M84.479K Pathological fracture, unspecified toe(s), subsequent encounter for fracture with nonunion

M84.439A Pathological fracture, unspecified ulna and radius, initial encounter for fracture

M84.439P Pathological fracture, unspecified ulna and radius, subsequent encounter for fracture with malunion

M84.439K Pathological fracture, unspecified ulna and radius, subsequent encounter for fracture with nonunion

L12.9 Pemphigoid, unspecified

L10.4 Pemphigus erythematosus

L10.2 Pemphigus foliaceous

L10.1 Pemphigus vegetans

L10.0 Pemphigus vulgaris

L10.9 Pemphigus, unspecified

S05.42XA Penetrating wound of orbit with or without foreign body, left eye, initial encounter

S05.41XA Penetrating wound of orbit with or without foreign body, right eye, initial encounter

S05.40XA Penetrating wound of orbit with or without foreign body, unspecified eye, initial encounter

S05.52XA Penetrating wound with foreign body of left eyeball, initial encounter

S05.51XA Penetrating wound with foreign body of right eyeball, initial encounter

S05.50XA Penetrating wound with foreign body of unspecified eyeball, initial encounter

B48.4 Penicillosis

T81.536A Perforation due to foreign body accidentally left in body following aspiration, puncture or other catheterization, initial encounter

T81.534A Perforation due to foreign body accidentally left in body following endoscopic examination, initial encounter

T81.535A	Perforation due to foreign body accidentally left in body following heart catheterization, initial encounter
T81.531A	Perforation due to foreign body accidentally left in body following infusion or transfusion, initial encounter
T81.533A	Perforation due to foreign body accidentally left in body following injection or immunization, initial encounter
T81.532A	Perforation due to foreign body accidentally left in body following kidney dialysis, initial encounter
T81.538A	Perforation due to foreign body accidentally left in body following other procedure, initial encounter
T81.537A	Perforation due to foreign body accidentally left in body following removal of catheter or packing, initial encounter
T81.530A	Perforation due to foreign body accidentally left in body following surgical operation, initial encounter
T81.539A	Perforation due to foreign body accidentally left in body following unspecified procedure, initial encounter
K82.A2	Perforation of gallbladder in cholecystitis
I31.3	Pericardial effusion (noninflammatory)
I32	Pericarditis in diseases classified elsewhere
M32.12	Pericarditis in systemic lupus erythematosus
R06.3	Periodic breathing
L03.213	Periorbital cellulitis
H05.033	Periostitis of bilateral orbits
H05.032	Periostitis of left orbit
H05.031	Periostitis of right orbit
H05.039	Periostitis of unspecified orbit
C84.49	Peripheral T-cell lymphoma, not classified, extranodal and solid organ sites
C84.43	Peripheral T-cell lymphoma, not classified, intra-abdominal lymph nodes
C84.46	Peripheral T-cell lymphoma, not classified, intrapelvic lymph nodes
C84.42	Peripheral T-cell lymphoma, not classified, intrathoracic lymph nodes
C84.44	Peripheral T-cell lymphoma, not classified, lymph nodes of axilla and upper limb
C84.41	Peripheral T-cell lymphoma, not classified, lymph nodes of head, face, and neck
C84.45	Peripheral T-cell lymphoma, not classified, lymph nodes of inguinal region and lower limb
C84.48	Peripheral T-cell lymphoma, not classified, lymph nodes of multiple sites
C84.47	Peripheral T-cell lymphoma, not classified, spleen
C84.40	Peripheral T-cell lymphoma, not classified, unspecified site
M97.22XA	Periprosthetic fracture around internal prosthetic left ankle joint, initial encounter
M97.42XA	Periprosthetic fracture around internal prosthetic left elbow joint, initial encounter
M97.02XA	Periprosthetic fracture around internal prosthetic left hip joint, initial encounter
M97.12XA	Periprosthetic fracture around internal prosthetic left knee joint, initial encounter
M97.32XA	Periprosthetic fracture around internal prosthetic left shoulder joint, initial encounter
M97.21XA	Periprosthetic fracture around internal prosthetic right ankle joint, initial encounter
M97.41XA	Periprosthetic fracture around internal prosthetic right elbow joint, initial encounter
M97.01XA	Periprosthetic fracture around internal prosthetic right hip joint, initial encounter
M97.11XA	Periprosthetic fracture around internal prosthetic right knee joint, initial encounter
M97.31XA	Periprosthetic fracture around internal prosthetic right shoulder joint, initial encounter
M97.8XXA	Periprosthetic fracture around other internal prosthetic joint, initial encounter
M97.9XXA	Periprosthetic fracture around unspecified internal prosthetic joint, initial encounter
T84.051A	Periprosthetic osteolysis of internal prosthetic left hip joint, initial encounter
T84.053A	Periprosthetic osteolysis of internal prosthetic left knee joint, initial encounter
T84.050A	Periprosthetic osteolysis of internal prosthetic right hip joint, initial encounter
T84.052A	Periprosthetic osteolysis of internal prosthetic right knee joint, initial encounter
T84.058A	Periprosthetic osteolysis of other internal prosthetic joint, initial encounter
T84.059A	Periprosthetic osteolysis of unspecified internal prosthetic joint, initial encounter
J36	Peritonsillar abscess
I48.21	Permanent atrial fibrillation
E71.50	Peroxisomal disorder, unspecified
Q43.7	Persistent cloaca
Q26.1	Persistent left superior vena cava
G43.611	Persistent migraine aura with cerebral infarction, intractable, with status migrainosus
G43.619	Persistent migraine aura with cerebral infarction, intractable, without status migrainosus
G43.601	Persistent migraine aura with cerebral infarction, not intractable, with status migrainosus
G43.609	Persistent migraine aura with cerebral infarction, not intractable, without status migrainosus
F34.9	Persistent mood [affective] disorder, unspecified
T81.83XA	Persistent postprocedural fistula, initial encounter
R40.3	Persistent vegetative state
F84.9	Pervasive developmental disorder, unspecified
Q85.9	Phakomatosis, unspecified
A36.0	Pharyngeal diphtheria

I80.13	Phlebitis and thrombophlebitis of femoral vein, bilateral
I80.213	Phlebitis and thrombophlebitis of iliac vein, bilateral
I80.12	Phlebitis and thrombophlebitis of left femoral vein
I80.212	Phlebitis and thrombophlebitis of left iliac vein
I80.242	Phlebitis and thrombophlebitis of left peroneal vein
I80.222	Phlebitis and thrombophlebitis of left popliteal vein
I80.232	Phlebitis and thrombophlebitis of left tibial vein
I80.292	Phlebitis and thrombophlebitis of other deep vessels of left lower extremity
I80.293	Phlebitis and thrombophlebitis of other deep vessels of lower extremity, bilateral
I80.291	Phlebitis and thrombophlebitis of other deep vessels of right lower extremity
I80.299	Phlebitis and thrombophlebitis of other deep vessels of unspecified lower extremity
I80.243	Phlebitis and thrombophlebitis of peroneal vein, bilateral
I80.223	Phlebitis and thrombophlebitis of popliteal vein, bilateral
I80.11	Phlebitis and thrombophlebitis of right femoral vein
I80.211	Phlebitis and thrombophlebitis of right iliac vein
I80.241	Phlebitis and thrombophlebitis of right peroneal vein
I80.221	Phlebitis and thrombophlebitis of right popliteal vein
I80.231	Phlebitis and thrombophlebitis of right tibial vein
I80.233	Phlebitis and thrombophlebitis of tibial vein, bilateral
I80.202	Phlebitis and thrombophlebitis of unspecified deep vessels of left lower extremity
I80.203	Phlebitis and thrombophlebitis of unspecified deep vessels of lower extremities, bilateral
I80.201	Phlebitis and thrombophlebitis of unspecified deep vessels of right lower extremity
I80.209	Phlebitis and thrombophlebitis of unspecified deep vessels of unspecified lower extremity
I80.10	Phlebitis and thrombophlebitis of unspecified femoral vein
I80.219	Phlebitis and thrombophlebitis of unspecified iliac vein
I80.249	Phlebitis and thrombophlebitis of unspecified peroneal vein
I80.229	Phlebitis and thrombophlebitis of unspecified popliteal vein
I80.239	Phlebitis and thrombophlebitis of unspecified tibial vein
L05.01	Pilonidal cyst with abscess
L05.02	Pilonidal sinus with abscess
E24.0	Pituitary-dependent Cushing's disease
C90.12	Plasma cell leukemia in relapse
C90.11	Plasma cell leukemia in remission
C90.10	Plasma cell leukemia not having achieved remission
E88.02	Plasminogen deficiency
B50.0	Plasmodium falciparum malaria with cerebral complications
B52.0	Plasmodium malariae malaria with nephropathy
B52.8	Plasmodium malariae malaria with other complications
B52.9	Plasmodium malariae malaria without complication
B53.0	Plasmodium ovale malaria
B51.8	Plasmodium vivax malaria with other complications
B51.0	Plasmodium vivax malaria with rupture of spleen
B51.9	Plasmodium vivax malaria without complication
J91.8	Pleural effusion in other conditions classified elsewhere
J90	Pleural effusion, not elsewhere classified
M00.172	Pneumococcal arthritis, left ankle and foot
M00.122	Pneumococcal arthritis, left elbow
M00.142	Pneumococcal arthritis, left hand
M00.152	Pneumococcal arthritis, left hip
M00.162	Pneumococcal arthritis, left knee
M00.112	Pneumococcal arthritis, left shoulder
M00.132	Pneumococcal arthritis, left wrist
M00.171	Pneumococcal arthritis, right ankle and foot
M00.121	Pneumococcal arthritis, right elbow
M00.141	Pneumococcal arthritis, right hand
M00.151	Pneumococcal arthritis, right hip
M00.161	Pneumococcal arthritis, right knee
M00.111	Pneumococcal arthritis, right shoulder
M00.131	Pneumococcal arthritis, right wrist
M00.179	Pneumococcal arthritis, unspecified ankle and foot
M00.129	Pneumococcal arthritis, unspecified elbow
M00.149	Pneumococcal arthritis, unspecified hand
M00.159	Pneumococcal arthritis, unspecified hip
M00.10	Pneumococcal arthritis, unspecified joint
M00.169	Pneumococcal arthritis, unspecified knee
M00.119	Pneumococcal arthritis, unspecified shoulder
M00.139	Pneumococcal arthritis, unspecified wrist
M00.18	Pneumococcal arthritis, vertebrae
M00.19	Pneumococcal polyarthritis
J93.9	Pneumothorax, unspecified
M30.0	Polyarteritis nodosa
M30.1	Polyarteritis with lung involvement [Churg-Strauss]
M00.89	Polyarthritis due to other bacteria
Q61.2	Polycystic kidney, adult type
Q61.3	Polycystic kidney, unspecified
M33.22	Polymyositis with myopathy
M33.29	Polymyositis with other organ involvement
M33.21	Polymyositis with respiratory involvement
M33.20	Polymyositis, organ involvement unspecified
E74.02	Pompe disease
E80.1	Porphyria cutanea tarda
K76.6	Portal hypertension
R56.1	Post traumatic seizures

D47.Z1	Post-transplant lymphoproliferative disorder (PTLD)
G91.3	Post-traumatic hydrocephalus, unspecified
M02.172	Postdysenteric arthropathy, left ankle and foot
M02.122	Postdysenteric arthropathy, left elbow
M02.142	Postdysenteric arthropathy, left hand
M02.152	Postdysenteric arthropathy, left hip
M02.162	Postdysenteric arthropathy, left knee
M02.112	Postdysenteric arthropathy, left shoulder
M02.132	Postdysenteric arthropathy, left wrist
M02.19	Postdysenteric arthropathy, multiple sites
M02.171	Postdysenteric arthropathy, right ankle and foot
M02.121	Postdysenteric arthropathy, right elbow
M02.141	Postdysenteric arthropathy, right hand
M02.151	Postdysenteric arthropathy, right hip
M02.161	Postdysenteric arthropathy, right knee
M02.111	Postdysenteric arthropathy, right shoulder
M02.131	Postdysenteric arthropathy, right wrist
M02.179	Postdysenteric arthropathy, unspecified ankle and foot
M02.129	Postdysenteric arthropathy, unspecified elbow
M02.149	Postdysenteric arthropathy, unspecified hand
M02.159	Postdysenteric arthropathy, unspecified hip
M02.169	Postdysenteric arthropathy, unspecified knee
M02.119	Postdysenteric arthropathy, unspecified shoulder
M02.10	Postdysenteric arthropathy, unspecified site
M02.139	Postdysenteric arthropathy, unspecified wrist
M02.18	Postdysenteric arthropathy, vertebrae
G21.3	Postencephalitic parkinsonism
G46.2	Posterior cerebral artery syndrome
S73.015A	Posterior dislocation of left hip, initial encounter
S43.225A	Posterior dislocation of left sternoclavicular joint, initial encounter
S73.014A	Posterior dislocation of right hip, initial encounter
S43.224A	Posterior dislocation of right sternoclavicular joint, initial encounter
S73.016A	Posterior dislocation of unspecified hip, initial encounter
S43.226A	Posterior dislocation of unspecified sternoclavicular joint, initial encounter
S42.015B	Posterior displaced fracture of sternal end of left clavicle, initial encounter for open fracture
S42.015P	Posterior displaced fracture of sternal end of left clavicle, subsequent encounter for fracture with malunion
S42.015K	Posterior displaced fracture of sternal end of left clavicle, subsequent encounter for fracture with nonunion
S42.014B	Posterior displaced fracture of sternal end of right clavicle, initial encounter for open fracture
S42.014P	Posterior displaced fracture of sternal end of right clavicle, subsequent encounter for fracture with malunion
S42.014K	Posterior displaced fracture of sternal end of right clavicle, subsequent encounter for fracture with nonunion
S42.016B	Posterior displaced fracture of sternal end of unspecified clavicle, initial encounter for open fracture
S42.016P	Posterior displaced fracture of sternal end of unspecified clavicle, subsequent encounter for fracture with malunion
S42.016K	Posterior displaced fracture of sternal end of unspecified clavicle, subsequent encounter for fracture with nonunion
S12.111A	Posterior displaced Type II dens fracture, initial encounter for closed fracture
S12.111K	Posterior displaced Type II dens fracture, subsequent encounter for fracture with nonunion
S73.012A	Posterior subluxation of left hip, initial encounter
S43.222A	Posterior subluxation of left sternoclavicular joint, initial encounter
S73.011A	Posterior subluxation of right hip, initial encounter
S43.221A	Posterior subluxation of right sternoclavicular joint, initial encounter
S73.013A	Posterior subluxation of unspecified hip, initial encounter
S43.223A	Posterior subluxation of unspecified sternoclavicular joint, initial encounter
B02.21	Postherpetic geniculate ganglionitis
B02.23	Postherpetic polyneuropathy
B02.22	Postherpetic trigeminal neuralgia
I23.7	Postinfarction angina
A39.84	Postmeningococcal arthritis
O71.2	Postpartum inversion of uterus
E89.6	Postprocedural adrenocortical (-medullary) hypofunction
J95.812	Postprocedural air leak
I97.120	Postprocedural cardiac arrest following cardiac surgery
I97.121	Postprocedural cardiac arrest following other surgery
I97.110	Postprocedural cardiac insufficiency following cardiac surgery
I97.111	Postprocedural cardiac insufficiency following other surgery
I97.820	Postprocedural cerebrovascular infarction following cardiac surgery
I97.821	Postprocedural cerebrovascular infarction following other surgery
K91.32	Postprocedural complete intestinal obstruction
I97.130	Postprocedural heart failure following cardiac surgery
I97.131	Postprocedural heart failure following other surgery
I97.630	Postprocedural hematoma of a circulatory system organ or structure following a cardiac catheterization
I97.631	Postprocedural hematoma of a circulatory system organ or structure following cardiac bypass
I97.638	Postprocedural hematoma of a circulatory system organ or structure following other circulatory system procedure
I97.621	Postprocedural hematoma of a circulatory system organ or structure following other procedure
K91.870	Postprocedural hematoma of a digestive system organ or structure following a digestive system procedure
K91.871	Postprocedural hematoma of a digestive system organ or structure following other procedure
N99.840	Postprocedural hematoma of a genitourinary system organ or structure following a genitourinary system procedure
N99.841	Postprocedural hematoma of a genitourinary system organ or structure following other procedure
M96.840	Postprocedural hematoma of a musculoskeletal structure following a musculoskeletal system procedure
M96.841	Postprocedural hematoma of a musculoskeletal structure following other procedure
G97.61	Postprocedural hematoma of a nervous system organ or structure following a nervous system procedure
G97.62	Postprocedural hematoma of a nervous system organ or structure following other procedure
J95.860	Postprocedural hematoma of a respiratory system organ or structure following a respiratory system procedure
J95.861	Postprocedural hematoma of a respiratory system organ or structure following other procedure
E89.820	Postprocedural hematoma of an endocrine system organ or structure following an endocrine system procedure
E89.821	Postprocedural hematoma of an endocrine system organ or structure following other procedure
H95.51	Postprocedural hematoma of ear and mastoid process following a procedure on the ear and mastoid process
H95.52	Postprocedural hematoma of ear and mastoid process following other procedure
H59.333	Postprocedural hematoma of eye and adnexa following an ophthalmic procedure, bilateral
H59.343	Postprocedural hematoma of eye and adnexa following other procedure, bilateral
H59.332	Postprocedural hematoma of left eye and adnexa following an ophthalmic procedure
H59.342	Postprocedural hematoma of left eye and adnexa following other procedure
H59.331	Postprocedural hematoma of right eye and adnexa following an ophthalmic procedure
H59.341	Postprocedural hematoma of right eye and adnexa following other procedure
L76.31	Postprocedural hematoma of skin and subcutaneous tissue following a dermatologic procedure
L76.32	Postprocedural hematoma of skin and subcutaneous tissue following other procedure
D78.31	Postprocedural hematoma of the spleen following a procedure on the spleen
D78.32	Postprocedural hematoma of the spleen following other procedure
H59.339	Postprocedural hematoma of unspecified eye and adnexa following an ophthalmic procedure
H59.349	Postprocedural hematoma of unspecified eye and adnexa following other procedure
I97.610	Postprocedural hemorrhage of a circulatory system organ or structure following a cardiac catheterization
I97.611	Postprocedural hemorrhage of a circulatory system organ or structure following cardiac bypass
I97.618	Postprocedural hemorrhage of a circulatory system organ or structure following other circulatory system procedure
I97.620	Postprocedural hemorrhage of a circulatory system organ or structure following other procedure
K91.840	Postprocedural hemorrhage of a digestive system organ or structure following a digestive system procedure
K91.841	Postprocedural hemorrhage of a digestive system organ or structure following other procedure
N99.820	Postprocedural hemorrhage of a genitourinary system organ or structure following a genitourinary system procedure
N99.821	Postprocedural hemorrhage of a genitourinary system organ or structure following other procedure
M96.830	Postprocedural hemorrhage of a musculoskeletal structure following a musculoskeletal system procedure
M96.831	Postprocedural hemorrhage of a musculoskeletal structure following other procedure
G97.51	Postprocedural hemorrhage of a nervous system organ or structure following a nervous system procedure
G97.52	Postprocedural hemorrhage of a nervous system organ or structure following other procedure
J95.830	Postprocedural hemorrhage of a respiratory system organ or structure following a respiratory system procedure
J95.831	Postprocedural hemorrhage of a respiratory system organ or structure following other procedure
E89.810	Postprocedural hemorrhage of an endocrine system organ or structure following an endocrine system procedure
E89.811	Postprocedural hemorrhage of an endocrine system organ or structure following other procedure
H95.41	Postprocedural hemorrhage of ear and mastoid process following a procedure on the ear and mastoid process
H95.42	Postprocedural hemorrhage of ear and mastoid process following other procedure
H59.313	Postprocedural hemorrhage of eye and adnexa following an ophthalmic procedure, bilateral
H59.323	Postprocedural hemorrhage of eye and adnexa following other procedure, bilateral
H59.312	Postprocedural hemorrhage of left eye and adnexa following an ophthalmic procedure
H59.322	Postprocedural hemorrhage of left eye and adnexa following other procedure

H59.311	Postprocedural hemorrhage of right eye and adnexa following an ophthalmic procedure
H59.321	Postprocedural hemorrhage of right eye and adnexa following other procedure
L76.21	Postprocedural hemorrhage of skin and subcutaneous tissue following a dermatologic procedure
L76.22	Postprocedural hemorrhage of skin and subcutaneous tissue following other procedure
D78.21	Postprocedural hemorrhage of the spleen following a procedure on the spleen
D78.22	Postprocedural hemorrhage of the spleen following other procedure
H59.319	Postprocedural hemorrhage of unspecified eye and adnexa following an ophthalmic procedure
H59.329	Postprocedural hemorrhage of unspecified eye and adnexa following other procedure
K91.82	Postprocedural hepatic failure
K91.83	Postprocedural hepatorenal syndrome
E89.1	Postprocedural hypoinsulinemia
K91.30	Postprocedural intestinal obstruction, unspecified as to partial versus complete
K91.31	Postprocedural partial intestinal obstruction
J95.811	Postprocedural pneumothorax
K68.11	Postprocedural retroperitoneal abscess
I97.640	Postprocedural seroma of a circulatory system organ or structure following a cardiac catheterization
I97.641	Postprocedural seroma of a circulatory system organ or structure following cardiac bypass
I97.648	Postprocedural seroma of a circulatory system organ or structure following other circulatory system procedure
I97.622	Postprocedural seroma of a circulatory system organ or structure following other procedure
K91.872	Postprocedural seroma of a digestive system organ or structure following a digestive system procedure
K91.873	Postprocedural seroma of a digestive system organ or structure following other procedure
N99.842	Postprocedural seroma of a genitourinary system organ or structure following a genitourinary system procedure
N99.843	Postprocedural seroma of a genitourinary system organ or structure following other procedure
M96.842	Postprocedural seroma of a musculoskeletal structure following a musculoskeletal system procedure
M96.843	Postprocedural seroma of a musculoskeletal structure following other procedure
G97.63	Postprocedural seroma of a nervous system organ or structure following a nervous system procedure
G97.64	Postprocedural seroma of a nervous system organ or structure following other procedure
J95.862	Postprocedural seroma of a respiratory system organ or structure following a respiratory system procedure
J95.863	Postprocedural seroma of a respiratory system organ or structure following other procedure
E89.822	Postprocedural seroma of an endocrine system organ or structure following an endocrine system procedure
E89.823	Postprocedural seroma of an endocrine system organ or structure following other procedure
H95.53	Postprocedural seroma of ear and mastoid process following a procedure on the ear and mastoid process
H95.54	Postprocedural seroma of ear and mastoid process following other procedure
H59.353	Postprocedural seroma of eye and adnexa following an ophthalmic procedure, bilateral
H59.363	Postprocedural seroma of eye and adnexa following other procedure, bilateral
H59.352	Postprocedural seroma of left eye and adnexa following an ophthalmic procedure
H59.362	Postprocedural seroma of left eye and adnexa following other procedure
H59.351	Postprocedural seroma of right eye and adnexa following an ophthalmic procedure
H59.361	Postprocedural seroma of right eye and adnexa following other procedure
L76.33	Postprocedural seroma of skin and subcutaneous tissue following a dermatologic procedure
L76.34	Postprocedural seroma of skin and subcutaneous tissue following other procedure
D78.33	Postprocedural seroma of the spleen following a procedure on the spleen
D78.34	Postprocedural seroma of the spleen following other procedure
H59.359	Postprocedural seroma of unspecified eye and adnexa following an ophthalmic procedure
H59.369	Postprocedural seroma of unspecified eye and adnexa following other procedure
T81.10XA	Postprocedural shock unspecified, initial encounter
H95.813	Postprocedural stenosis of external ear canal, bilateral
H95.812	Postprocedural stenosis of left external ear canal
H95.811	Postprocedural stenosis of right external ear canal
H95.819	Postprocedural stenosis of unspecified external ear canal
J95.5	Postprocedural subglottic stenosis
K91.2	Postsurgical malabsorption, not elsewhere classified
I87.033	Postthrombotic syndrome with ulcer and inflammation of bilateral lower extremity
I87.032	Postthrombotic syndrome with ulcer and inflammation of left lower extremity
I87.031	Postthrombotic syndrome with ulcer and inflammation of right lower extremity
I87.039	Postthrombotic syndrome with ulcer and inflammation of unspecified lower extremity
I87.013	Postthrombotic syndrome with ulcer of bilateral lower extremity
I87.012	Postthrombotic syndrome with ulcer of left lower extremity
I87.011	Postthrombotic syndrome with ulcer of right lower extremity
I87.019	Postthrombotic syndrome with ulcer of unspecified lower extremity
Q60.6	Potter's syndrome
K91.850	Pouchitis
Q87.11	Prader-Willi syndrome
O10.02	Pre-existing essential hypertension complicating childbirth
O10.011	Pre-existing essential hypertension complicating pregnancy, first trimester
O10.012	Pre-existing essential hypertension complicating pregnancy, second trimester
O10.013	Pre-existing essential hypertension complicating pregnancy, third trimester
O10.411	Pre-existing secondary hypertension complicating pregnancy, first trimester
O10.412	Pre-existing secondary hypertension complicating pregnancy, second trimester
O10.413	Pre-existing secondary hypertension complicating pregnancy, third trimester
O10.43	Pre-existing secondary hypertension complicating the puerperium
O24.011	Pre-existing type 1 diabetes mellitus, in pregnancy, first trimester
O24.012	Pre-existing type 1 diabetes mellitus, in pregnancy, second trimester
O24.013	Pre-existing type 1 diabetes mellitus, in pregnancy, third trimester
O24.019	Pre-existing type 1 diabetes mellitus, in pregnancy, unspecified trimester
O24.03	Pre-existing type 1 diabetes mellitus, in the puerperium
O24.111	Pre-existing type 2 diabetes mellitus, in pregnancy, first trimester
O24.112	Pre-existing type 2 diabetes mellitus, in pregnancy, second trimester
O24.113	Pre-existing type 2 diabetes mellitus, in pregnancy, third trimester
O24.119	Pre-existing type 2 diabetes mellitus, in pregnancy, unspecified trimester
O24.13	Pre-existing type 2 diabetes mellitus, in the puerperium
R71.0	Precipitous drop in hematocrit
O26.831	Pregnancy related renal disease, first trimester
O26.832	Pregnancy related renal disease, second trimester
O26.833	Pregnancy related renal disease, third trimester
Z95.812	Presence of fully implantable artificial heart
Z95.811	Presence of heart assist device
O60.10X1	Preterm labor with preterm delivery, unspecified trimester, fetus 1
O60.10X2	Preterm labor with preterm delivery, unspecified trimester, fetus 2
O60.10X3	Preterm labor with preterm delivery, unspecified trimester, fetus 3
O60.10X4	Preterm labor with preterm delivery, unspecified trimester, fetus 4
O60.10X5	Preterm labor with preterm delivery, unspecified trimester, fetus 5
O60.10X0	Preterm labor with preterm delivery, unspecified trimester, not applicable or unspecified
O60.10X9	Preterm labor with preterm delivery, unspecified trimester, other fetus
N48.32	Priapism due to disease classified elsewhere
N48.31	Priapism due to trauma
N48.33	Priapism, drug-induced
N48.30	Priapism, unspecified
E27.1	Primary adrenocortical insufficiency
P28.0	Primary atelectasis of newborn
S36.510A	Primary blast injury of ascending [right] colon, initial encounter
S36.512A	Primary blast injury of descending [left] colon, initial encounter
S36.410A	Primary blast injury of duodenum, initial encounter
S09.313A	Primary blast injury of ear, bilateral, initial encounter
S09.312A	Primary blast injury of left ear, initial encounter
S27.312A	Primary blast injury of lung, bilateral, initial encounter
S27.311A	Primary blast injury of lung, unilateral, initial encounter
S27.319A	Primary blast injury of lung, unspecified, initial encounter
S36.518A	Primary blast injury of other part of colon, initial encounter
S36.418A	Primary blast injury of other part of small intestine, initial encounter
S36.61XA	Primary blast injury of rectum, initial encounter
S09.311A	Primary blast injury of right ear, initial encounter
S36.513A	Primary blast injury of sigmoid colon, initial encounter
S27.51XA	Primary blast injury of thoracic trachea, initial encounter
S36.511A	Primary blast injury of transverse colon, initial encounter
S09.319A	Primary blast injury of unspecified ear, initial encounter
S36.519A	Primary blast injury of unspecified part of colon, initial encounter
S36.419A	Primary blast injury of unspecified part of small intestine, initial encounter
C86.6	Primary cutaneous CD30-positive T-cell proliferations
E72.53	Primary hyperoxaluria
H20.013	Primary iridocyclitis, bilateral
H20.012	Primary iridocyclitis, left eye
H20.011	Primary iridocyclitis, right eye
H20.019	Primary iridocyclitis, unspecified eye
G12.23	Primary lateral sclerosis
I27.0	Primary pulmonary hypertension
A15.7	Primary respiratory tuberculosis
K83.01	Primary sclerosing cholangitis
P28.3	Primary sleep apnea of newborn
J93.11	Primary spontaneous pneumothorax
F73	Profound intellectual disabilities
G12.22	Progressive bulbar palsy
A81.2	Progressive multifocal leukoencephalopathy
G12.25	Progressive spinal muscle atrophy
G23.1	Progressive supranuclear ophthalmoplegia [Steele-Richardson-Olszewski]
I67.3	Progressive vascular leukoencephalopathy
C91.30	Prolymphocytic leukemia of B-cell type not having achieved remission
C91.32	Prolymphocytic leukemia of B-cell type, in relapse
C91.31	Prolymphocytic leukemia of B-cell type, in remission
C91.60	Prolymphocytic leukemia of T-cell type not having achieved remission

C91.62	Prolymphocytic leukemia of T-cell type, in relapse
C91.61	Prolymphocytic leukemia of T-cell type, in remission
E71.121	Propionic acidemia
B38.81	Prostatic coccidioidomycosis
D68.52	Prothrombin gene mutation
O98.62	Protozoal diseases complicating childbirth
O98.611	Protozoal diseases complicating pregnancy, first trimester
O98.612	Protozoal diseases complicating pregnancy, second trimester
O98.613	Protozoal diseases complicating pregnancy, third trimester
O98.63	Protozoal diseases complicating the puerperium
A07.9	Protozoal intestinal disease, unspecified
M96.0	Pseudarthrosis after fusion or arthrodesis
K86.3	Pseudocyst of pancreas
F06.2	Psychotic disorder with delusions due to known physiological condition
F06.0	Psychotic disorder with hallucinations due to known physiological condition
A42.0	Pulmonary actinomycosis
J84.02	Pulmonary alveolar microlithiasis
B40.2	Pulmonary blastomycosis, unspecified
B38.2	Pulmonary coccidioidomycosis, unspecified
B45.0	Pulmonary cryptococcosis
J82	Pulmonary eosinophilia, not elsewhere classified
Q24.3	Pulmonary infundibular stenosis
A31.0	Pulmonary mycobacterial infection
A43.0	Pulmonary nocardiosis
B41.0	Pulmonary paracoccidioidomycosis
A21.2	Pulmonary tularemia
S21.142A	Puncture wound with foreign body of left front wall of thorax without penetration into thoracic cavity, initial encounter
S11.24XA	Puncture wound with foreign body of pharynx and cervical esophagus, initial encounter
S21.141A	Puncture wound with foreign body of right front wall of thorax without penetration into thoracic cavity, initial encounter
S11.14XA	Puncture wound with foreign body of thyroid gland, initial encounter
S21.149A	Puncture wound with foreign body of unspecified front wall of thorax without penetration into thoracic cavity, initial encounter
S21.94XA	Puncture wound with foreign body of unspecified part of thorax, initial encounter
S21.132A	Puncture wound without foreign body of left front wall of thorax without penetration into thoracic cavity, initial encounter
S11.23XA	Puncture wound without foreign body of pharynx and cervical esophagus, initial encounter
S21.131A	Puncture wound without foreign body of right front wall of thorax without penetration into thoracic cavity, initial encounter
S11.13XA	Puncture wound without foreign body of thyroid gland, initial encounter
S21.139A	Puncture wound without foreign body of unspecified front wall of thorax without penetration into thoracic cavity, initial encounter
S21.93XA	Puncture wound without foreign body of unspecified part of thorax, initial encounter
D81.5	Purine nucleoside phosphorylase [PNP] deficiency
N28.84	Pyelitis cystica
N28.85	Pyeloureteritis cystica
O88.319	Pyemic and septic embolism in pregnancy, unspecified trimester
L88	Pyoderma gangrenosum
M00.9	Pyogenic arthritis, unspecified
N13.6	Pyonephrosis
O75.2	Pyrexia during labor, not elsewhere classified
O86.4	Pyrexia of unknown origin following delivery
A78	Q fever
O30.221	Quadruplet pregnancy with two or more monoamniotic fetuses, first trimester
O30.222	Quadruplet pregnancy with two or more monoamniotic fetuses, second trimester
O30.223	Quadruplet pregnancy with two or more monoamniotic fetuses, third trimester
O30.211	Quadruplet pregnancy with two or more monochorionic fetuses, first trimester
O30.212	Quadruplet pregnancy with two or more monochorionic fetuses, second trimester
O30.213	Quadruplet pregnancy with two or more monochorionic fetuses, third trimester
O30.231	Quadruplet pregnancy, quadrachorionic/quadra-amniotic, first trimester
O30.232	Quadruplet pregnancy, quadrachorionic/quadra-amniotic, second trimester
O30.233	Quadruplet pregnancy, quadrachorionic/quadra-amniotic, third trimester
O30.291	Quadruplet pregnancy, unable to determine number of placenta and number of amniotic sacs, first trimester
O30.292	Quadruplet pregnancy, unable to determine number of placenta and number of amniotic sacs, second trimester
O30.293	Quadruplet pregnancy, unable to determine number of placenta and number of amniotic sacs, third trimester
O30.201	Quadruplet pregnancy, unspecified number of placenta and unspecified number of amniotic sacs, first trimester
O30.202	Quadruplet pregnancy, unspecified number of placenta and unspecified number of amniotic sacs, second trimester
O30.203	Quadruplet pregnancy, unspecified number of placenta and unspecified number of amniotic sacs, third trimester
A82.9	Rabies, unspecified
A25.9	Rat-bite fever, unspecified
I73.01	Raynaud's syndrome with gangrene
I47.0	Re-entry ventricular arrhythmia
A75.1	Recrudescent typhus [Brill's disease]
K61.1	Rectal abscess
H20.023	Recurrent acute iridocyclitis, bilateral
H20.022	Recurrent acute iridocyclitis, left eye
H20.021	Recurrent acute iridocyclitis, right eye
H20.029	Recurrent acute iridocyclitis, unspecified eye
N02.6	Recurrent and persistent hematuria with dense deposit disease
N02.7	Recurrent and persistent hematuria with diffuse crescentic glomerulonephritis
N02.4	Recurrent and persistent hematuria with diffuse endocapillary proliferative glomerulonephritis
N02.2	Recurrent and persistent hematuria with diffuse membranous glomerulonephritis
N02.3	Recurrent and persistent hematuria with diffuse mesangial proliferative glomerulonephritis
N02.5	Recurrent and persistent hematuria with diffuse mesangiocapillary glomerulonephritis
N02.1	Recurrent and persistent hematuria with focal and segmental glomerular lesions
N02.0	Recurrent and persistent hematuria with minor glomerular abnormality
N02.8	Recurrent and persistent hematuria with other morphologic changes
N02.9	Recurrent and persistent hematuria with unspecified morphologic changes
D46.22	Refractory anemia with excess of blasts 2
G60.1	Refsum's disease
M02.372	Reiter's disease, left ankle and foot
M02.322	Reiter's disease, left elbow
M02.342	Reiter's disease, left hand
M02.352	Reiter's disease, left hip
M02.362	Reiter's disease, left knee
M02.312	Reiter's disease, left shoulder
M02.332	Reiter's disease, left wrist
M02.39	Reiter's disease, multiple sites
M02.371	Reiter's disease, right ankle and foot
M02.321	Reiter's disease, right elbow
M02.341	Reiter's disease, right hand
M02.351	Reiter's disease, right hip
M02.361	Reiter's disease, right knee
M02.311	Reiter's disease, right shoulder
M02.331	Reiter's disease, right wrist
M02.379	Reiter's disease, unspecified ankle and foot
M02.329	Reiter's disease, unspecified elbow
M02.349	Reiter's disease, unspecified hand
M02.359	Reiter's disease, unspecified hip
M02.369	Reiter's disease, unspecified knee
M02.319	Reiter's disease, unspecified shoulder
M02.30	Reiter's disease, unspecified site
M02.339	Reiter's disease, unspecified wrist
M02.38	Reiter's disease, vertebrae
A68.9	Relapsing fever, unspecified
Q60.1	Renal agenesis, bilateral
Q60.0	Renal agenesis, unilateral
Q60.2	Renal agenesis, unspecified
Q61.4	Renal dysplasia
Q60.4	Renal hypoplasia, bilateral
Q60.3	Renal hypoplasia, unilateral
Q60.5	Renal hypoplasia, unspecified
F20.5	Residual schizophrenia
Z16.32	Resistance to antifungal drug(s)
Z16.31	Resistance to antiparasitic drug(s)
Z16.33	Resistance to antiviral drug(s)
Z16.24	Resistance to multiple antibiotics
Z16.35	Resistance to multiple antimicrobial drugs
Z16.342	Resistance to multiple antimycobacterial drugs
Z16.29	Resistance to other single specified antibiotic
Z16.39	Resistance to other specified antimicrobial drug
Z16.19	Resistance to other specified beta lactam antibiotics
Z16.11	Resistance to penicillins
Z16.23	Resistance to quinolones and fluoroquinolones
Z16.341	Resistance to single antimycobacterial drug
Z16.20	Resistance to unspecified antibiotic
Z16.30	Resistance to unspecified antimicrobial drugs
Z16.10	Resistance to unspecified beta lactam antibiotics
Z16.21	Resistance to vancomycin
Z16.22	Resistance to vancomycin related antibiotics
P28.11	Resorption atelectasis without respiratory distress syndrome
A15.9	Respiratory tuberculosis unspecified
K91.86	Retained cholelithiasis following cholecystectomy
E45	Retarded development following protein-calorie malnutrition
H34.233	Retinal artery branch occlusion, bilateral
H34.232	Retinal artery branch occlusion, left eye
H34.231	Retinal artery branch occlusion, right eye
H34.239	Retinal artery branch occlusion, unspecified eye
H35.82	Retinal ischemia
H46.13	Retrobulbar neuritis, bilateral
H46.12	Retrobulbar neuritis, left eye
H46.11	Retrobulbar neuritis, right eye
H46.10	Retrobulbar neuritis, unspecified eye
A18.39	Retroperitoneal tuberculosis
J39.0	Retropharyngeal and parapharyngeal abscess
F84.2	Rett's syndrome

I67.841	Reversible cerebrovascular vasoconstriction syndrome
K04.01	Reversible pulpitis
T80.40XA	Rh incompatibility reaction due to transfusion of blood or blood products, unspecified, initial encounter
T80.410A	Rh incompatibility with acute hemolytic transfusion reaction, initial encounter
T80.411A	Rh incompatibility with delayed hemolytic transfusion reaction, initial encounter
T80.419A	Rh incompatibility with hemolytic transfusion reaction, unspecified, initial encounter
M62.82	Rhabdomyolysis
I02.0	Rheumatic chorea with heart involvement
I02.9	Rheumatic chorea without heart involvement
I09.81	Rheumatic heart failure
I09.0	Rheumatic myocarditis
M05.472	Rheumatoid myopathy with rheumatoid arthritis of left ankle and foot
M05.422	Rheumatoid myopathy with rheumatoid arthritis of left elbow
M05.442	Rheumatoid myopathy with rheumatoid arthritis of left hand
M05.452	Rheumatoid myopathy with rheumatoid arthritis of left hip
M05.462	Rheumatoid myopathy with rheumatoid arthritis of left knee
M05.412	Rheumatoid myopathy with rheumatoid arthritis of left shoulder
M05.432	Rheumatoid myopathy with rheumatoid arthritis of left wrist
M05.49	Rheumatoid myopathy with rheumatoid arthritis of multiple sites
M05.471	Rheumatoid myopathy with rheumatoid arthritis of right ankle and foot
M05.421	Rheumatoid myopathy with rheumatoid arthritis of right elbow
M05.441	Rheumatoid myopathy with rheumatoid arthritis of right hand
M05.451	Rheumatoid myopathy with rheumatoid arthritis of right hip
M05.461	Rheumatoid myopathy with rheumatoid arthritis of right knee
M05.411	Rheumatoid myopathy with rheumatoid arthritis of right shoulder
M05.431	Rheumatoid myopathy with rheumatoid arthritis of right wrist
M05.479	Rheumatoid myopathy with rheumatoid arthritis of unspecified ankle and foot
M05.429	Rheumatoid myopathy with rheumatoid arthritis of unspecified elbow
M05.449	Rheumatoid myopathy with rheumatoid arthritis of unspecified hand
M05.459	Rheumatoid myopathy with rheumatoid arthritis of unspecified hip
M05.469	Rheumatoid myopathy with rheumatoid arthritis of unspecified knee
M05.419	Rheumatoid myopathy with rheumatoid arthritis of unspecified shoulder
M05.40	Rheumatoid myopathy with rheumatoid arthritis of unspecified site
M05.439	Rheumatoid myopathy with rheumatoid arthritis of unspecified wrist
E71.540	Rhizomelic chondrodysplasia punctata
B56.1	Rhodesiense trypanosomiasis
E53.0	Riboflavin deficiency
E55.0	Rickets, active
A79.1	Rickettsialpox due to Rickettsia akari
A79.81	Rickettsiosis due to Ehrlichia sennetsu
A79.9	Rickettsiosis, unspecified
A92.4	Rift Valley fever
Q25.47	Right aortic arch
O00.211	Right ovarian pregnancy with intrauterine pregnancy
O00.201	Right ovarian pregnancy without intrauterine pregnancy
O00.111	Right tubal pregnancy with intrauterine pregnancy
O00.101	Right tubal pregnancy without intrauterine pregnancy
B33.1	Ross River disease
A08.0	Rotaviral enteritis
B06.82	Rubella arthritis
B06.02	Rubella meningitis
B06.81	Rubella pneumonia
B06.00	Rubella with neurological complication, unspecified
I77.2	Rupture of artery
I23.3	Rupture of cardiac wall without hemopericardium as current complication following acute myocardial infarction
Q05.3	Sacral spina bifida with hydrocephalus
A02.23	Salmonella arthritis
A02.0	Salmonella enteritis
A02.9	Salmonella infection, unspecified
A02.24	Salmonella osteomyelitis
A02.25	Salmonella pyelonephritis
A02.29	Salmonella with other localized infection
O23.521	Salpingo-oophoritis in pregnancy, first trimester
O23.522	Salpingo-oophoritis in pregnancy, second trimester
O23.523	Salpingo-oophoritis in pregnancy, third trimester
S49.112A	Salter-Harris Type I physeal fracture of lower end of humerus, left arm, initial encounter for closed fracture
S49.112P	Salter-Harris Type I physeal fracture of lower end of humerus, left arm, subsequent encounter for fracture with malunion
S49.112K	Salter-Harris Type I physeal fracture of lower end of humerus, left arm, subsequent encounter for fracture with nonunion
S49.111A	Salter-Harris Type I physeal fracture of lower end of humerus, right arm, initial encounter for closed fracture
S49.111P	Salter-Harris Type I physeal fracture of lower end of humerus, right arm, subsequent encounter for fracture with malunion
S49.111K	Salter-Harris Type I physeal fracture of lower end of humerus, right arm, subsequent encounter for fracture with nonunion
S49.119A	Salter-Harris Type I physeal fracture of lower end of humerus, unspecified arm, initial encounter for closed fracture
S49.119P	Salter-Harris Type I physeal fracture of lower end of humerus, unspecified arm, subsequent encounter for fracture with malunion
S49.119K	Salter-Harris Type I physeal fracture of lower end of humerus, unspecified arm, subsequent encounter for fracture with nonunion
S79.112A	Salter-Harris Type I physeal fracture of lower end of left femur, initial encounter for closed fracture
S79.112P	Salter-Harris Type I physeal fracture of lower end of left femur, subsequent encounter for fracture with malunion
S79.112K	Salter-Harris Type I physeal fracture of lower end of left femur, subsequent encounter for fracture with nonunion
S89.312P	Salter-Harris Type I physeal fracture of lower end of left fibula, subsequent encounter for fracture with malunion
S89.312K	Salter-Harris Type I physeal fracture of lower end of left fibula, subsequent encounter for fracture with nonunion
S89.112P	Salter-Harris Type I physeal fracture of lower end of left tibia, subsequent encounter for fracture with malunion
S89.112K	Salter-Harris Type I physeal fracture of lower end of left tibia, subsequent encounter for fracture with nonunion
S59.212A	Salter-Harris Type I physeal fracture of lower end of radius, left arm, initial encounter for closed fracture
S59.212P	Salter-Harris Type I physeal fracture of lower end of radius, left arm, subsequent encounter for fracture with malunion
S59.212K	Salter-Harris Type I physeal fracture of lower end of radius, left arm, subsequent encounter for fracture with nonunion
S59.211A	Salter-Harris Type I physeal fracture of lower end of radius, right arm, initial encounter for closed fracture
S59.211P	Salter-Harris Type I physeal fracture of lower end of radius, right arm, subsequent encounter for fracture with malunion
S59.211K	Salter-Harris Type I physeal fracture of lower end of radius, right arm, subsequent encounter for fracture with nonunion
S59.219A	Salter-Harris Type I physeal fracture of lower end of radius, unspecified arm, initial encounter for closed fracture
S59.219P	Salter-Harris Type I physeal fracture of lower end of radius, unspecified arm, subsequent encounter for fracture with malunion
S59.219K	Salter-Harris Type I physeal fracture of lower end of radius, unspecified arm, subsequent encounter for fracture with nonunion
S79.111A	Salter-Harris Type I physeal fracture of lower end of right femur, initial encounter for closed fracture
S79.111P	Salter-Harris Type I physeal fracture of lower end of right femur, subsequent encounter for fracture with malunion
S79.111K	Salter-Harris Type I physeal fracture of lower end of right femur, subsequent encounter for fracture with nonunion
S89.311P	Salter-Harris Type I physeal fracture of lower end of right fibula, subsequent encounter for fracture with malunion
S89.311K	Salter-Harris Type I physeal fracture of lower end of right fibula, subsequent encounter for fracture with nonunion
S89.111P	Salter-Harris Type I physeal fracture of lower end of right tibia, subsequent encounter for fracture with malunion
S89.111K	Salter-Harris Type I physeal fracture of lower end of right tibia, subsequent encounter for fracture with nonunion
S59.012A	Salter-Harris Type I physeal fracture of lower end of ulna, left arm, initial encounter for closed fracture
S59.012P	Salter-Harris Type I physeal fracture of lower end of ulna, left arm, subsequent encounter for fracture with malunion
S59.012K	Salter-Harris Type I physeal fracture of lower end of ulna, left arm, subsequent encounter for fracture with nonunion
S59.011A	Salter-Harris Type I physeal fracture of lower end of ulna, right arm, initial encounter for closed fracture
S59.011P	Salter-Harris Type I physeal fracture of lower end of ulna, right arm, subsequent encounter for fracture with malunion
S59.011K	Salter-Harris Type I physeal fracture of lower end of ulna, right arm, subsequent encounter for fracture with nonunion
S59.019A	Salter-Harris Type I physeal fracture of lower end of ulna, unspecified arm, initial encounter for closed fracture
S59.019P	Salter-Harris Type I physeal fracture of lower end of ulna, unspecified arm, subsequent encounter for fracture with malunion
S59.019K	Salter-Harris Type I physeal fracture of lower end of ulna, unspecified arm, subsequent encounter for fracture with nonunion
S79.119A	Salter-Harris Type I physeal fracture of lower end of unspecified femur, initial encounter for closed fracture
S79.119P	Salter-Harris Type I physeal fracture of lower end of unspecified femur, subsequent encounter for fracture with malunion
S79.119K	Salter-Harris Type I physeal fracture of lower end of unspecified femur, subsequent encounter for fracture with nonunion
S89.319P	Salter-Harris Type I physeal fracture of lower end of unspecified fibula, subsequent encounter for fracture with malunion
S89.319K	Salter-Harris Type I physeal fracture of lower end of unspecified fibula, subsequent encounter for fracture with nonunion
S89.119P	Salter-Harris Type I physeal fracture of lower end of unspecified tibia, subsequent encounter for fracture with malunion
S89.119K	Salter-Harris Type I physeal fracture of lower end of unspecified tibia, subsequent encounter for fracture with nonunion
S49.012A	Salter-Harris Type I physeal fracture of upper end of humerus, left arm, initial encounter for closed fracture
S49.012P	Salter-Harris Type I physeal fracture of upper end of humerus, left arm, subsequent encounter for fracture with malunion
S49.012K	Salter-Harris Type I physeal fracture of upper end of humerus, left arm, subsequent encounter for fracture with nonunion
S49.011A	Salter-Harris Type I physeal fracture of upper end of humerus, right arm, initial encounter for closed fracture
S49.011P	Salter-Harris Type I physeal fracture of upper end of humerus, right arm, subsequent encounter for fracture with malunion
S49.011K	Salter-Harris Type I physeal fracture of upper end of humerus, right arm, subsequent encounter for fracture with nonunion

Alphabetic & Numeric Lists of CCs

S49.019A Salter-Harris Type I physeal fracture of upper end of humerus, unspecified arm, initial encounter for closed fracture

S49.019P Salter-Harris Type I physeal fracture of upper end of humerus, unspecified arm, subsequent encounter for fracture with malunion

S49.019K Salter-Harris Type I physeal fracture of upper end of humerus, unspecified arm, subsequent encounter for fracture with nonunion

S79.012P Salter-Harris Type I physeal fracture of upper end of left femur, subsequent encounter for fracture with malunion

S79.012K Salter-Harris Type I physeal fracture of upper end of left femur, subsequent encounter for fracture with nonunion

S89.212P Salter-Harris Type I physeal fracture of upper end of left fibula, subsequent encounter for fracture with malunion

S89.212K Salter-Harris Type I physeal fracture of upper end of left fibula, subsequent encounter for fracture with nonunion

S89.012A Salter-Harris Type I physeal fracture of upper end of left tibia, initial encounter for closed fracture

S89.012P Salter-Harris Type I physeal fracture of upper end of left tibia, subsequent encounter for fracture with malunion

S89.012K Salter-Harris Type I physeal fracture of upper end of left tibia, subsequent encounter for fracture with nonunion

S59.112P Salter-Harris Type I physeal fracture of upper end of radius, left arm, subsequent encounter for fracture with malunion

S59.112K Salter-Harris Type I physeal fracture of upper end of radius, left arm, subsequent encounter for fracture with nonunion

S59.111P Salter-Harris Type I physeal fracture of upper end of radius, right arm, subsequent encounter for fracture with malunion

S59.111K Salter-Harris Type I physeal fracture of upper end of radius, right arm, subsequent encounter for fracture with nonunion

S59.119P Salter-Harris Type I physeal fracture of upper end of radius, unspecified arm, subsequent encounter for fracture with malunion

S59.119K Salter-Harris Type I physeal fracture of upper end of radius, unspecified arm, subsequent encounter for fracture with nonunion

S79.011P Salter-Harris Type I physeal fracture of upper end of right femur, subsequent encounter for fracture with malunion

S79.011K Salter-Harris Type I physeal fracture of upper end of right femur, subsequent encounter for fracture with nonunion

S89.211P Salter-Harris Type I physeal fracture of upper end of right fibula, subsequent encounter for fracture with malunion

S89.211K Salter-Harris Type I physeal fracture of upper end of right fibula, subsequent encounter for fracture with nonunion

S89.011A Salter-Harris Type I physeal fracture of upper end of right tibia, initial encounter for closed fracture

S89.011P Salter-Harris Type I physeal fracture of upper end of right tibia, subsequent encounter for fracture with malunion

S89.011K Salter-Harris Type I physeal fracture of upper end of right tibia, subsequent encounter for fracture with nonunion

S79.019P Salter-Harris Type I physeal fracture of upper end of unspecified femur, subsequent encounter for fracture with malunion

S79.019K Salter-Harris Type I physeal fracture of upper end of unspecified femur, subsequent encounter for fracture with nonunion

S89.219P Salter-Harris Type I physeal fracture of upper end of unspecified fibula, subsequent encounter for fracture with malunion

S89.219K Salter-Harris Type I physeal fracture of upper end of unspecified fibula, subsequent encounter for fracture with nonunion

S89.019A Salter-Harris Type I physeal fracture of upper end of unspecified tibia, initial encounter for closed fracture

S89.019P Salter-Harris Type I physeal fracture of upper end of unspecified tibia, subsequent encounter for fracture with malunion

S89.019K Salter-Harris Type I physeal fracture of upper end of unspecified tibia, subsequent encounter for fracture with nonunion

S49.122A Salter-Harris Type II physeal fracture of lower end of humerus, left arm, initial encounter for closed fracture

S49.122P Salter-Harris Type II physeal fracture of lower end of humerus, left arm, subsequent encounter for fracture with malunion

S49.122K Salter-Harris Type II physeal fracture of lower end of humerus, left arm, subsequent encounter for fracture with nonunion

S49.121A Salter-Harris Type II physeal fracture of lower end of humerus, right arm, initial encounter for closed fracture

S49.121P Salter-Harris Type II physeal fracture of lower end of humerus, right arm, subsequent encounter for fracture with malunion

S49.121K Salter-Harris Type II physeal fracture of lower end of humerus, right arm, subsequent encounter for fracture with nonunion

S49.129A Salter-Harris Type II physeal fracture of lower end of humerus, unspecified arm, initial encounter for closed fracture

S49.129P Salter-Harris Type II physeal fracture of lower end of humerus, unspecified arm, subsequent encounter for fracture with malunion

S49.129K Salter-Harris Type II physeal fracture of lower end of humerus, unspecified arm, subsequent encounter for fracture with nonunion

S79.122A Salter-Harris Type II physeal fracture of lower end of left femur, initial encounter for closed fracture

S79.122P Salter-Harris Type II physeal fracture of lower end of left femur, subsequent encounter for fracture with malunion

S79.122K Salter-Harris Type II physeal fracture of lower end of left femur, subsequent encounter for fracture with nonunion

S89.322P Salter-Harris Type II physeal fracture of lower end of left fibula, subsequent encounter for fracture with malunion

S89.322K Salter-Harris Type II physeal fracture of lower end of left fibula, subsequent encounter for fracture with nonunion

S89.122P Salter-Harris Type II physeal fracture of lower end of left tibia, subsequent encounter for fracture with malunion

S89.122K Salter-Harris Type II physeal fracture of lower end of left tibia, subsequent encounter for fracture with nonunion

S59.222A Salter-Harris Type II physeal fracture of lower end of radius, left arm, initial encounter for closed fracture

S59.222P Salter-Harris Type II physeal fracture of lower end of radius, left arm, subsequent encounter for fracture with malunion

S59.222K Salter-Harris Type II physeal fracture of lower end of radius, left arm, subsequent encounter for fracture with nonunion

S59.221A Salter-Harris Type II physeal fracture of lower end of radius, right arm, initial encounter for closed fracture

S59.221P Salter-Harris Type II physeal fracture of lower end of radius, right arm, subsequent encounter for fracture with malunion

S59.221K Salter-Harris Type II physeal fracture of lower end of radius, right arm, subsequent encounter for fracture with nonunion

S59.229A Salter-Harris Type II physeal fracture of lower end of radius, unspecified arm, initial encounter for closed fracture

S59.229P Salter-Harris Type II physeal fracture of lower end of radius, unspecified arm, subsequent encounter for fracture with malunion

S59.229K Salter-Harris Type II physeal fracture of lower end of radius, unspecified arm, subsequent encounter for fracture with nonunion

S79.121A Salter-Harris Type II physeal fracture of lower end of right femur, initial encounter for closed fracture

S79.121P Salter-Harris Type II physeal fracture of lower end of right femur, subsequent encounter for fracture with malunion

S79.121K Salter-Harris Type II physeal fracture of lower end of right femur, subsequent encounter for fracture with nonunion

S89.321P Salter-Harris Type II physeal fracture of lower end of right fibula, subsequent encounter for fracture with malunion

S89.321K Salter-Harris Type II physeal fracture of lower end of right fibula, subsequent encounter for fracture with nonunion

S89.121P Salter-Harris Type II physeal fracture of lower end of right tibia, subsequent encounter for fracture with malunion

S89.121K Salter-Harris Type II physeal fracture of lower end of right tibia, subsequent encounter for fracture with nonunion

S59.022A Salter-Harris Type II physeal fracture of lower end of ulna, left arm, initial encounter for closed fracture

S59.022P Salter-Harris Type II physeal fracture of lower end of ulna, left arm, subsequent encounter for fracture with malunion

S59.022K Salter-Harris Type II physeal fracture of lower end of ulna, left arm, subsequent encounter for fracture with nonunion

S59.021A Salter-Harris Type II physeal fracture of lower end of ulna, right arm, initial encounter for closed fracture

S59.021P Salter-Harris Type II physeal fracture of lower end of ulna, right arm, subsequent encounter for fracture with malunion

S59.021K Salter-Harris Type II physeal fracture of lower end of ulna, right arm, subsequent encounter for fracture with nonunion

S59.029A Salter-Harris Type II physeal fracture of lower end of ulna, unspecified arm, initial encounter for closed fracture

S59.029P Salter-Harris Type II physeal fracture of lower end of ulna, unspecified arm, subsequent encounter for fracture with malunion

S59.029K Salter-Harris Type II physeal fracture of lower end of ulna, unspecified arm, subsequent encounter for fracture with nonunion

S79.129A Salter-Harris Type II physeal fracture of lower end of unspecified femur, initial encounter for closed fracture

S79.129P Salter-Harris Type II physeal fracture of lower end of unspecified femur, subsequent encounter for fracture with malunion

S79.129K Salter-Harris Type II physeal fracture of lower end of unspecified femur, subsequent encounter for fracture with nonunion

S89.329P Salter-Harris Type II physeal fracture of lower end of unspecified fibula, subsequent encounter for fracture with malunion

S89.329K Salter-Harris Type II physeal fracture of lower end of unspecified fibula, subsequent encounter for fracture with nonunion

S89.129P Salter-Harris Type II physeal fracture of lower end of unspecified tibia, subsequent encounter for fracture with malunion

S89.129K Salter-Harris Type II physeal fracture of lower end of unspecified tibia, subsequent encounter for fracture with nonunion

S49.022A Salter-Harris Type II physeal fracture of upper end of humerus, left arm, initial encounter for closed fracture

S49.022P Salter-Harris Type II physeal fracture of upper end of humerus, left arm, subsequent encounter for fracture with malunion

S49.022K Salter-Harris Type II physeal fracture of upper end of humerus, left arm, subsequent encounter for fracture with nonunion

S49.021A Salter-Harris Type II physeal fracture of upper end of humerus, right arm, initial encounter for closed fracture

S49.021P Salter-Harris Type II physeal fracture of upper end of humerus, right arm, subsequent encounter for fracture with malunion

S49.021K Salter-Harris Type II physeal fracture of upper end of humerus, right arm, subsequent encounter for fracture with nonunion

S49.029A Salter-Harris Type II physeal fracture of upper end of humerus, unspecified arm, initial encounter for closed fracture

S49.029P Salter-Harris Type II physeal fracture of upper end of humerus, unspecified arm, subsequent encounter for fracture with malunion

S49.029K Salter-Harris Type II physeal fracture of upper end of humerus, unspecified arm, subsequent encounter for fracture with nonunion

S89.222P Salter-Harris Type II physeal fracture of upper end of left fibula, subsequent encounter for fracture with malunion

S89.222K Salter-Harris Type II physeal fracture of upper end of left fibula, subsequent encounter for fracture with nonunion

S89.022A Salter-Harris Type II physeal fracture of upper end of left tibia, initial encounter for closed fracture

S89.022P Salter-Harris Type II physeal fracture of upper end of left tibia, subsequent encounter for fracture with malunion

S89.022K Salter-Harris Type II physeal fracture of upper end of left tibia, subsequent encounter for fracture with nonunion

S59.122P Salter-Harris Type II physeal fracture of upper end of radius, left arm, subsequent encounter for fracture with malunion

S59.122K Salter-Harris Type II physeal fracture of upper end of radius, left arm, subsequent encounter for fracture with nonunion

S59.121P Salter-Harris Type II physeal fracture of upper end of radius, right arm, subsequent encounter for fracture with malunion

S59.121K Salter-Harris Type II physeal fracture of upper end of radius, right arm, subsequent encounter for fracture with nonunion

S59.129P Salter-Harris Type II physeal fracture of upper end of radius, unspecified arm, subsequent encounter for fracture with malunion

S59.129K Salter-Harris Type II physeal fracture of upper end of radius, unspecified arm, subsequent encounter for fracture with nonunion

S89.221P Salter-Harris Type II physeal fracture of upper end of right fibula, subsequent encounter for fracture with malunion

S89.221K Salter-Harris Type II physeal fracture of upper end of right fibula, subsequent encounter for fracture with nonunion

S89.021A Salter-Harris Type II physeal fracture of upper end of right tibia, initial encounter for closed fracture

S89.021P Salter-Harris Type II physeal fracture of upper end of right tibia, subsequent encounter for fracture with malunion

S89.021K Salter-Harris Type II physeal fracture of upper end of right tibia, subsequent encounter for fracture with nonunion

S89.229P Salter-Harris Type II physeal fracture of upper end of unspecified fibula, subsequent encounter for fracture with malunion

S89.229K Salter-Harris Type II physeal fracture of upper end of unspecified fibula, subsequent encounter for fracture with nonunion

S89.029A Salter-Harris Type II physeal fracture of upper end of unspecified tibia, initial encounter for closed fracture

S89.029P Salter-Harris Type II physeal fracture of upper end of unspecified tibia, subsequent encounter for fracture with malunion

S89.029K Salter-Harris Type II physeal fracture of upper end of unspecified tibia, subsequent encounter for fracture with nonunion

S49.132A Salter-Harris Type III physeal fracture of lower end of humerus, left arm, initial encounter for closed fracture

S49.132P Salter-Harris Type III physeal fracture of lower end of humerus, left arm, subsequent encounter for fracture with malunion

S49.132K Salter-Harris Type III physeal fracture of lower end of humerus, left arm, subsequent encounter for fracture with nonunion

S49.131A Salter-Harris Type III physeal fracture of lower end of humerus, right arm, initial encounter for closed fracture

S49.131P Salter-Harris Type III physeal fracture of lower end of humerus, right arm, subsequent encounter for fracture with malunion

S49.131K Salter-Harris Type III physeal fracture of lower end of humerus, right arm, subsequent encounter for fracture with nonunion

S49.139A Salter-Harris Type III physeal fracture of lower end of humerus, unspecified arm, initial encounter for closed fracture

S49.139P Salter-Harris Type III physeal fracture of lower end of humerus, unspecified arm, subsequent encounter for fracture with malunion

S49.139K Salter-Harris Type III physeal fracture of lower end of humerus, unspecified arm, subsequent encounter for fracture with nonunion

S79.132A Salter-Harris Type III physeal fracture of lower end of left femur, initial encounter for closed fracture

S79.132P Salter-Harris Type III physeal fracture of lower end of left femur, subsequent encounter for fracture with malunion

S79.132K Salter-Harris Type III physeal fracture of lower end of left femur, subsequent encounter for fracture with nonunion

S89.132P Salter-Harris Type III physeal fracture of lower end of left tibia, subsequent encounter for fracture with malunion

S89.132K Salter-Harris Type III physeal fracture of lower end of left tibia, subsequent encounter for fracture with nonunion

S59.232A Salter-Harris Type III physeal fracture of lower end of radius, left arm, initial encounter for closed fracture

S59.232P Salter-Harris Type III physeal fracture of lower end of radius, left arm, subsequent encounter for fracture with malunion

S59.232K Salter-Harris Type III physeal fracture of lower end of radius, left arm, subsequent encounter for fracture with nonunion

S59.231A Salter-Harris Type III physeal fracture of lower end of radius, right arm, initial encounter for closed fracture

S59.231P Salter-Harris Type III physeal fracture of lower end of radius, right arm, subsequent encounter for fracture with malunion

S59.231K Salter-Harris Type III physeal fracture of lower end of radius, right arm, subsequent encounter for fracture with nonunion

S59.239A Salter-Harris Type III physeal fracture of lower end of radius, unspecified arm, initial encounter for closed fracture

S59.239P Salter-Harris Type III physeal fracture of lower end of radius, unspecified arm, subsequent encounter for fracture with malunion

S59.239K Salter-Harris Type III physeal fracture of lower end of radius, unspecified arm, subsequent encounter for fracture with nonunion

S79.131A Salter-Harris Type III physeal fracture of lower end of right femur, initial encounter for closed fracture

S79.131P Salter-Harris Type III physeal fracture of lower end of right femur, subsequent encounter for fracture with malunion

S79.131K Salter-Harris Type III physeal fracture of lower end of right femur, subsequent encounter for fracture with nonunion

S89.131P Salter-Harris Type III physeal fracture of lower end of right tibia, subsequent encounter for fracture with malunion

S89.131K Salter-Harris Type III physeal fracture of lower end of right tibia, subsequent encounter for fracture with nonunion

S59.032A Salter-Harris Type III physeal fracture of lower end of ulna, left arm, initial encounter for closed fracture

S59.032P Salter-Harris Type III physeal fracture of lower end of ulna, left arm, subsequent encounter for fracture with malunion

S59.032K Salter-Harris Type III physeal fracture of lower end of ulna, left arm, subsequent encounter for fracture with nonunion

S59.031A Salter-Harris Type III physeal fracture of lower end of ulna, right arm, initial encounter for closed fracture

S59.031P Salter-Harris Type III physeal fracture of lower end of ulna, right arm, subsequent encounter for fracture with malunion

S59.031K Salter-Harris Type III physeal fracture of lower end of ulna, right arm, subsequent encounter for fracture with nonunion

S59.039A Salter-Harris Type III physeal fracture of lower end of ulna, unspecified arm, initial encounter for closed fracture

S59.039P Salter-Harris Type III physeal fracture of lower end of ulna, unspecified arm, subsequent encounter for fracture with malunion

S59.039K Salter-Harris Type III physeal fracture of lower end of ulna, unspecified arm, subsequent encounter for fracture with nonunion

S79.139A Salter-Harris Type III physeal fracture of lower end of unspecified femur, initial encounter for closed fracture

S79.139P Salter-Harris Type III physeal fracture of lower end of unspecified femur, subsequent encounter for fracture with malunion

S79.139K Salter-Harris Type III physeal fracture of lower end of unspecified femur, subsequent encounter for fracture with nonunion

S89.139P Salter-Harris Type III physeal fracture of lower end of unspecified tibia, subsequent encounter for fracture with malunion

S89.139K Salter-Harris Type III physeal fracture of lower end of unspecified tibia, subsequent encounter for fracture with nonunion

S49.032A Salter-Harris Type III physeal fracture of upper end of humerus, left arm, initial encounter for closed fracture

S49.032P Salter-Harris Type III physeal fracture of upper end of humerus, left arm, subsequent encounter for fracture with malunion

S49.032K Salter-Harris Type III physeal fracture of upper end of humerus, left arm, subsequent encounter for fracture with nonunion

S49.031A Salter-Harris Type III physeal fracture of upper end of humerus, right arm, initial encounter for closed fracture

S49.031P Salter-Harris Type III physeal fracture of upper end of humerus, right arm, subsequent encounter for fracture with malunion

S49.031K Salter-Harris Type III physeal fracture of upper end of humerus, right arm, subsequent encounter for fracture with nonunion

S49.039A Salter-Harris Type III physeal fracture of upper end of humerus, unspecified arm, initial encounter for closed fracture

S49.039P Salter-Harris Type III physeal fracture of upper end of humerus, unspecified arm, subsequent encounter for fracture with malunion

S49.039K Salter-Harris Type III physeal fracture of upper end of humerus, unspecified arm, subsequent encounter for fracture with nonunion

S89.032A Salter-Harris Type III physeal fracture of upper end of left tibia, initial encounter for closed fracture

S89.032P Salter-Harris Type III physeal fracture of upper end of left tibia, subsequent encounter for fracture with malunion

S89.032K Salter-Harris Type III physeal fracture of upper end of left tibia, subsequent encounter for fracture with nonunion

S59.132P Salter-Harris Type III physeal fracture of upper end of radius, left arm, subsequent encounter for fracture with malunion

S59.132K Salter-Harris Type III physeal fracture of upper end of radius, left arm, subsequent encounter for fracture with nonunion

S59.131P Salter-Harris Type III physeal fracture of upper end of radius, right arm, subsequent encounter for fracture with malunion

S59.131K Salter-Harris Type III physeal fracture of upper end of radius, right arm, subsequent encounter for fracture with nonunion

S59.139P Salter-Harris Type III physeal fracture of upper end of radius, unspecified arm, subsequent encounter for fracture with malunion

S59.139K Salter-Harris Type III physeal fracture of upper end of radius, unspecified arm, subsequent encounter for fracture with nonunion

S89.031A Salter-Harris Type III physeal fracture of upper end of right tibia, initial encounter for closed fracture

S89.031P Salter-Harris Type III physeal fracture of upper end of right tibia, subsequent encounter for fracture with malunion

S89.031K Salter-Harris Type III physeal fracture of upper end of right tibia, subsequent encounter for fracture with nonunion

S89.039A Salter-Harris Type III physeal fracture of upper end of unspecified tibia, initial encounter for closed fracture

S89.039P Salter-Harris Type III physeal fracture of upper end of unspecified tibia, subsequent encounter for fracture with malunion

S89.039K Salter-Harris Type III physeal fracture of upper end of unspecified tibia, subsequent encounter for fracture with nonunion

S49.142A Salter-Harris Type IV physeal fracture of lower end of humerus, left arm, initial encounter for closed fracture

S49.142P Salter-Harris Type IV physeal fracture of lower end of humerus, left arm, subsequent encounter for fracture with malunion

S49.142K Salter-Harris Type IV physeal fracture of lower end of humerus, left arm, subsequent encounter for fracture with nonunion

S49.141A Salter-Harris Type IV physeal fracture of lower end of humerus, right arm, initial encounter for closed fracture

S49.141P Salter-Harris Type IV physeal fracture of lower end of humerus, right arm, subsequent encounter for fracture with malunion

S49.141K Salter-Harris Type IV physeal fracture of lower end of humerus, right arm, subsequent encounter for fracture with nonunion

S49.149A Salter-Harris Type IV physeal fracture of lower end of humerus, unspecified arm, initial encounter for closed fracture

S49.149P Salter-Harris Type IV physeal fracture of lower end of humerus, unspecified arm, subsequent encounter for fracture with malunion

S49.149K Salter-Harris Type IV physeal fracture of lower end of humerus, unspecified arm, subsequent encounter for fracture with nonunion

S79.142A Salter-Harris Type IV physeal fracture of lower end of left femur, initial encounter for closed fracture

S79.142P Salter-Harris Type IV physeal fracture of lower end of left femur, subsequent encounter for fracture with malunion

S79.142K Salter-Harris Type IV physeal fracture of lower end of left femur, subsequent encounter for fracture with nonunion

S89.142P Salter-Harris Type IV physeal fracture of lower end of left tibia, subsequent encounter for fracture with malunion

S89.142K Salter-Harris Type IV physeal fracture of lower end of left tibia, subsequent encounter for fracture with nonunion

S59.242A Salter-Harris Type IV physeal fracture of lower end of radius, left arm, initial encounter for closed fracture

S59.242P Salter-Harris Type IV physeal fracture of lower end of radius, left arm, subsequent encounter for fracture with malunion

S59.242K Salter-Harris Type IV physeal fracture of lower end of radius, left arm, subsequent encounter for fracture with nonunion

S59.241A Salter-Harris Type IV physeal fracture of lower end of radius, right arm, initial encounter for closed fracture

S59.241P Salter-Harris Type IV physeal fracture of lower end of radius, right arm, subsequent encounter for fracture with malunion

S59.241K Salter-Harris Type IV physeal fracture of lower end of radius, right arm, subsequent encounter for fracture with nonunion

S59.249A Salter-Harris Type IV physeal fracture of lower end of radius, unspecified arm, initial encounter for closed fracture

S59.249P Salter-Harris Type IV physeal fracture of lower end of radius, unspecified arm, subsequent encounter for fracture with malunion

S59.249K Salter-Harris Type IV physeal fracture of lower end of radius, unspecified arm, subsequent encounter for fracture with nonunion

S79.141A Salter-Harris Type IV physeal fracture of lower end of right femur, initial encounter for closed fracture

S79.141P Salter-Harris Type IV physeal fracture of lower end of right femur, subsequent encounter for fracture with malunion

S79.141K Salter-Harris Type IV physeal fracture of lower end of right femur, subsequent encounter for fracture with nonunion

S89.141P Salter-Harris Type IV physeal fracture of lower end of right tibia, subsequent encounter for fracture with malunion

S89.141K Salter-Harris Type IV physeal fracture of lower end of right tibia, subsequent encounter for fracture with nonunion

S59.042A Salter-Harris Type IV physeal fracture of lower end of ulna, left arm, initial encounter for closed fracture

S59.042P Salter-Harris Type IV physeal fracture of lower end of ulna, left arm, subsequent encounter for fracture with malunion

S59.042K Salter-Harris Type IV physeal fracture of lower end of ulna, left arm, subsequent encounter for fracture with nonunion

S59.041A Salter-Harris Type IV physeal fracture of lower end of ulna, right arm, initial encounter for closed fracture

S59.041P Salter-Harris Type IV physeal fracture of lower end of ulna, right arm, subsequent encounter for fracture with malunion

S59.041K Salter-Harris Type IV physeal fracture of lower end of ulna, right arm, subsequent encounter for fracture with nonunion

S59.049A Salter-Harris Type IV physeal fracture of lower end of ulna, unspecified arm, initial encounter for closed fracture

S59.049P Salter-Harris Type IV physeal fracture of lower end of ulna, unspecified arm, subsequent encounter for fracture with malunion

S59.049K Salter-Harris Type IV physeal fracture of lower end of ulna, unspecified arm, subsequent encounter for fracture with nonunion

S79.149A Salter-Harris Type IV physeal fracture of lower end of unspecified femur, initial encounter for closed fracture

S79.149P Salter-Harris Type IV physeal fracture of lower end of unspecified femur, subsequent encounter for fracture with malunion

S79.149K Salter-Harris Type IV physeal fracture of lower end of unspecified femur, subsequent encounter for fracture with nonunion

S89.149P Salter-Harris Type IV physeal fracture of lower end of unspecified tibia, subsequent encounter for fracture with malunion

S89.149K Salter-Harris Type IV physeal fracture of lower end of unspecified tibia, subsequent encounter for fracture with nonunion

S49.042A Salter-Harris Type IV physeal fracture of upper end of humerus, left arm, initial encounter for closed fracture

S49.042P Salter-Harris Type IV physeal fracture of upper end of humerus, left arm, subsequent encounter for fracture with malunion

S49.042K Salter-Harris Type IV physeal fracture of upper end of humerus, left arm, subsequent encounter for fracture with nonunion

S49.041A Salter-Harris Type IV physeal fracture of upper end of humerus, right arm, initial encounter for closed fracture

S49.041P Salter-Harris Type IV physeal fracture of upper end of humerus, right arm, subsequent encounter for fracture with malunion

S49.041K Salter-Harris Type IV physeal fracture of upper end of humerus, right arm, subsequent encounter for fracture with nonunion

S49.049A Salter-Harris Type IV physeal fracture of upper end of humerus, unspecified arm, initial encounter for closed fracture

S49.049P Salter-Harris Type IV physeal fracture of upper end of humerus, unspecified arm, subsequent encounter for fracture with malunion

S49.049K Salter-Harris Type IV physeal fracture of upper end of humerus, unspecified arm, subsequent encounter for fracture with nonunion

S89.042A Salter-Harris Type IV physeal fracture of upper end of left tibia, initial encounter for closed fracture

S89.042P Salter-Harris Type IV physeal fracture of upper end of left tibia, subsequent encounter for fracture with malunion

S89.042K Salter-Harris Type IV physeal fracture of upper end of left tibia, subsequent encounter for fracture with nonunion

S59.142P Salter-Harris Type IV physeal fracture of upper end of radius, left arm, subsequent encounter for fracture with malunion

S59.142K Salter-Harris Type IV physeal fracture of upper end of radius, left arm, subsequent encounter for fracture with nonunion

S59.141P Salter-Harris Type IV physeal fracture of upper end of radius, right arm, subsequent encounter for fracture with malunion

S59.141K Salter-Harris Type IV physeal fracture of upper end of radius, right arm, subsequent encounter for fracture with nonunion

S59.149P Salter-Harris Type IV physeal fracture of upper end of radius, unspecified arm, subsequent encounter for fracture with malunion

S59.149K Salter-Harris Type IV physeal fracture of upper end of radius, unspecified arm, subsequent encounter for fracture with nonunion

S89.041A Salter-Harris Type IV physeal fracture of upper end of right tibia, initial encounter for closed fracture

S89.041P Salter-Harris Type IV physeal fracture of upper end of right tibia, subsequent encounter for fracture with malunion

S89.041K Salter-Harris Type IV physeal fracture of upper end of right tibia, subsequent encounter for fracture with nonunion

S89.049A Salter-Harris Type IV physeal fracture of upper end of unspecified tibia, initial encounter for closed fracture

S89.049P Salter-Harris Type IV physeal fracture of upper end of unspecified tibia, subsequent encounter for fracture with malunion

S89.049K Salter-Harris Type IV physeal fracture of upper end of unspecified tibia, subsequent encounter for fracture with nonunion

A93.1 Sandfly fever

E75.01 Sandhoff disease

E76.22 Sanfilippo mucopolysaccharidoses

C96.4 Sarcoma of dendritic cells (accessory cells)

B97.21 SARS-associated coronavirus as the cause of diseases classified elsewhere

A38.1 Scarlet fever with myocarditis

A38.8 Scarlet fever with other complications

A38.0 Scarlet fever with otitis media

A38.9 Scarlet fever, uncomplicated

E76.03 Scheie's syndrome

B65.0 Schistosomiasis due to Schistosoma haematobium [urinary schistosomiasis]

B65.2 Schistosomiasis due to Schistosoma japonicum

B65.1 Schistosomiasis due to Schistosoma mansoni [intestinal schistosomiasis]

B65.9 Schistosomiasis, unspecified

F20.81 Schizophreniform disorder

P83.0 Sclerema neonatorum

K65.4 Sclerosing mesenteritis

C77.3 Secondary and unspecified malignant neoplasm of axilla and upper limb lymph nodes

C77.4 Secondary and unspecified malignant neoplasm of inguinal and lower limb lymph nodes

C77.2 Secondary and unspecified malignant neoplasm of intra-abdominal lymph nodes

C77.5 Secondary and unspecified malignant neoplasm of intrapelvic lymph nodes

C77.1 Secondary and unspecified malignant neoplasm of intrathoracic lymph nodes

C77.9 Secondary and unspecified malignant neoplasm of lymph node, unspecified

C77.0 Secondary and unspecified malignant neoplasm of lymph nodes of head, face and neck

C77.8 Secondary and unspecified malignant neoplasm of lymph nodes of multiple regions

C7B.03 Secondary carcinoid tumors of bone

C7B.01 Secondary carcinoid tumors of distant lymph nodes

C7B.02 Secondary carcinoid tumors of liver

C7B.09 Secondary carcinoid tumors of other sites

C7B.04 Secondary carcinoid tumors of peritoneum

I85.10 Secondary esophageal varices without bleeding

N25.81 Secondary hyperparathyroidism of renal origin

H20.033 Secondary infectious iridocyclitis, bilateral

H20.032 Secondary infectious iridocyclitis, left eye

H20.031 Secondary infectious iridocyclitis, right eye

H20.039 Secondary infectious iridocyclitis, unspecified eye

C79.11 Secondary malignant neoplasm of bladder

C79.51 Secondary malignant neoplasm of bone

C79.52 Secondary malignant neoplasm of bone marrow

C79.31 Secondary malignant neoplasm of brain

C79.81 Secondary malignant neoplasm of breast

C79.32 Secondary malignant neoplasm of cerebral meninges

C79.82 Secondary malignant neoplasm of genital organs

C78.5 Secondary malignant neoplasm of large intestine and rectum

C79.72 Secondary malignant neoplasm of left adrenal gland

C79.02 Secondary malignant neoplasm of left kidney and renal pelvis

C78.02 Secondary malignant neoplasm of left lung

C79.62 Secondary malignant neoplasm of left ovary

C78.7 Secondary malignant neoplasm of liver and intrahepatic bile duct

C78.1 Secondary malignant neoplasm of mediastinum

C78.89 Secondary malignant neoplasm of other digestive organs

C79.49 Secondary malignant neoplasm of other parts of nervous system

C78.39 Secondary malignant neoplasm of other respiratory organs

C79.89 Secondary malignant neoplasm of other specified sites

C79.19	Secondary malignant neoplasm of other urinary organs
C78.2	Secondary malignant neoplasm of pleura
C78.6	Secondary malignant neoplasm of retroperitoneum and peritoneum
C79.71	Secondary malignant neoplasm of right adrenal gland
C79.01	Secondary malignant neoplasm of right kidney and renal pelvis
C78.01	Secondary malignant neoplasm of right lung
C79.61	Secondary malignant neoplasm of right ovary
C79.2	Secondary malignant neoplasm of skin
C78.4	Secondary malignant neoplasm of small intestine
C79.70	Secondary malignant neoplasm of unspecified adrenal gland
C78.80	Secondary malignant neoplasm of unspecified digestive organ
C79.00	Secondary malignant neoplasm of unspecified kidney and renal pelvis
C78.00	Secondary malignant neoplasm of unspecified lung
C79.60	Secondary malignant neoplasm of unspecified ovary
C79.40	Secondary malignant neoplasm of unspecified part of nervous system
C78.30	Secondary malignant neoplasm of unspecified respiratory organ
C79.9	Secondary malignant neoplasm of unspecified site
C79.10	Secondary malignant neoplasm of unspecified urinary organs
G21.2	Secondary parkinsonism due to other external agents
G21.9	Secondary parkinsonism, unspecified
J93.12	Secondary spontaneous pneumothorax
A51.42	Secondary syphilitic female pelvic disease
A51.45	Secondary syphilitic hepatitis
A51.44	Secondary syphilitic nephritis
A51.43	Secondary syphilitic oculopathy
A51.46	Secondary syphilitic osteopathy
E85.3	Secondary systemic amyloidosis
F13.121	Sedative, hypnotic or anxiolytic abuse with intoxication delirium
F13.150	Sedative, hypnotic or anxiolytic abuse with sedative, hypnotic or anxiolytic-induced psychotic disorder with delusions
F13.151	Sedative, hypnotic or anxiolytic abuse with sedative, hypnotic or anxiolytic-induced psychotic disorder with hallucinations
F13.221	Sedative, hypnotic or anxiolytic dependence with intoxication delirium
F13.288	Sedative, hypnotic or anxiolytic dependence with other sedative, hypnotic or anxiolytic-induced disorder
F13.280	Sedative, hypnotic or anxiolytic dependence with sedative, hypnotic or anxiolytic-induced anxiety disorder
F13.26	Sedative, hypnotic or anxiolytic dependence with sedative, hypnotic or anxiolytic-induced persisting amnestic disorder
F13.27	Sedative, hypnotic or anxiolytic dependence with sedative, hypnotic or anxiolytic-induced persisting dementia
F13.250	Sedative, hypnotic or anxiolytic dependence with sedative, hypnotic or anxiolytic-induced psychotic disorder with delusions
F13.251	Sedative, hypnotic or anxiolytic dependence with sedative, hypnotic or anxiolytic-induced psychotic disorder with hallucinations
F13.259	Sedative, hypnotic or anxiolytic dependence with sedative, hypnotic or anxiolytic-induced psychotic disorder, unspecified
F13.281	Sedative, hypnotic or anxiolytic dependence with sedative, hypnotic or anxiolytic-induced sexual dysfunction
F13.282	Sedative, hypnotic or anxiolytic dependence with sedative, hypnotic or anxiolytic-induced sleep disorder
F13.231	Sedative, hypnotic or anxiolytic dependence with withdrawal delirium
F13.232	Sedative, hypnotic or anxiolytic dependence with withdrawal with perceptual disturbance
F13.230	Sedative, hypnotic or anxiolytic dependence with withdrawal, uncomplicated
F13.239	Sedative, hypnotic or anxiolytic dependence with withdrawal, unspecified
F13.20	Sedative, hypnotic or anxiolytic dependence, uncomplicated
F13.921	Sedative, hypnotic or anxiolytic use, unspecified with intoxication delirium
F13.97	Sedative, hypnotic or anxiolytic use, unspecified with sedative, hypnotic or anxiolytic-induced persisting dementia
F13.950	Sedative, hypnotic or anxiolytic use, unspecified with sedative, hypnotic or anxiolytic-induced psychotic disorder with delusions
F13.951	Sedative, hypnotic or anxiolytic use, unspecified with sedative, hypnotic or anxiolytic-induced psychotic disorder with hallucinations
F13.931	Sedative, hypnotic or anxiolytic use, unspecified with withdrawal delirium
F13.932	Sedative, hypnotic or anxiolytic use, unspecified with withdrawal with perceptual disturbances
F13.930	Sedative, hypnotic or anxiolytic use, unspecified with withdrawal, uncomplicated
F13.939	Sedative, hypnotic or anxiolytic use, unspecified with withdrawal, unspecified
D80.2	Selective deficiency of immunoglobulin A [IgA]
D80.3	Selective deficiency of immunoglobulin G [IgG] subclasses
D80.4	Selective deficiency of immunoglobulin M [IgM]
O04.87	Sepsis following (induced) termination of pregnancy
T81.44XA	Sepsis following a procedure, initial encounter
O03.87	Sepsis following complete or unspecified spontaneous abortion
O08.82	Sepsis following ectopic and molar pregnancy
O07.37	Sepsis following failed attempted termination of pregnancy
O03.37	Sepsis following incomplete spontaneous abortion
I76	Septic arterial embolism
Q04.4	Septo-optic dysplasia of brain
E64.0	Sequelae of protein-calorie malnutrition
H31.423	Serous choroidal detachment, bilateral
H31.422	Serous choroidal detachment, left eye
H31.421	Serous choroidal detachment, right eye
H31.429	Serous choroidal detachment, unspecified eye
H35.723	Serous detachment of retinal pigment epithelium, bilateral
H35.722	Serous detachment of retinal pigment epithelium, left eye
H35.721	Serous detachment of retinal pigment epithelium, right eye
H35.729	Serous detachment of retinal pigment epithelium, unspecified eye
H33.23	Serous retinal detachment, bilateral
H33.22	Serous retinal detachment, left eye
H33.21	Serous retinal detachment, right eye
H33.20	Serous retinal detachment, unspecified eye
D81.2	Severe combined immunodeficiency [SCID] with low or normal B-cell numbers
D81.1	Severe combined immunodeficiency [SCID] with low T- and B-cell numbers
D81.0	Severe combined immunodeficiency [SCID] with reticular dysgenesis
D81.31	Severe combined immunodeficiency due to adenosine deaminase deficiency
F72	Severe intellectual disabilities
J45.51	Severe persistent asthma with (acute) exacerbation
J45.52	Severe persistent asthma with status asthmaticus
S32.112A	Severely displaced Zone I fracture of sacrum, initial encounter for closed fracture
S32.112K	Severely displaced Zone I fracture of sacrum, subsequent encounter for fracture with nonunion
S32.122A	Severely displaced Zone II fracture of sacrum, initial encounter for closed fracture
S32.122K	Severely displaced Zone II fracture of sacrum, subsequent encounter for fracture with nonunion
S32.132A	Severely displaced Zone III fracture of sacrum, initial encounter for closed fracture
S32.132K	Severely displaced Zone III fracture of sacrum, subsequent encounter for fracture with nonunion
C84.19	Sezary disease, extranodal and solid organ sites
C84.13	Sezary disease, intra-abdominal lymph nodes
C84.16	Sezary disease, intrapelvic lymph nodes
C84.12	Sezary disease, intrathoracic lymph nodes
C84.14	Sezary disease, lymph nodes of axilla and upper limb
C84.11	Sezary disease, lymph nodes of head, face, and neck
C84.15	Sezary disease, lymph nodes of inguinal region and lower limb
C84.18	Sezary disease, lymph nodes of multiple sites
C84.17	Sezary disease, spleen
C84.10	Sezary disease, unspecified site
T74.4XXA	Shaken infant syndrome, initial encounter
A03.0	Shigellosis due to Shigella dysenteriae
T88.2XXA	Shock due to anesthesia, initial encounter
R57.9	Shock, unspecified
E71.312	Short chain acyl CoA dehydrogenase deficiency
Q77.2	Short rib syndrome
M35.03	Sicca syndrome with myopathy
R56.00	Simple febrile convulsions
Q89.3	Situs inversus
T86.821	Skin graft (allograft) (autograft) failure
T86.822	Skin graft (allograft) (autograft) infection
T86.820	Skin graft (allograft) rejection
C83.09	Small cell B-cell lymphoma, extranodal and solid organ sites
C83.03	Small cell B-cell lymphoma, intra-abdominal lymph nodes
C83.06	Small cell B-cell lymphoma, intrapelvic lymph nodes
C83.02	Small cell B-cell lymphoma, intrathoracic lymph nodes
C83.04	Small cell B-cell lymphoma, lymph nodes of axilla and upper limb
C83.01	Small cell B-cell lymphoma, lymph nodes of head, face, and neck
C83.05	Small cell B-cell lymphoma, lymph nodes of inguinal region and lower limb
C83.08	Small cell B-cell lymphoma, lymph nodes of multiple sites
C83.07	Small cell B-cell lymphoma, spleen
C83.00	Small cell B-cell lymphoma, unspecified site
B03	Smallpox
E78.72	Smith-Lemli-Opitz syndrome
S52.542A	Smith's fracture of left radius, initial encounter for closed fracture
S52.542P	Smith's fracture of left radius, subsequent encounter for closed fracture with malunion
S52.542K	Smith's fracture of left radius, subsequent encounter for closed fracture with nonunion
S52.542Q	Smith's fracture of left radius, subsequent encounter for open fracture type I or II with malunion
S52.542M	Smith's fracture of left radius, subsequent encounter for open fracture type I or II with nonunion
S52.542R	Smith's fracture of left radius, subsequent encounter for open fracture type IIIA, IIIB, or IIIC with malunion
S52.542N	Smith's fracture of left radius, subsequent encounter for open fracture type IIIA, IIIB, or IIIC with nonunion
S52.541A	Smith's fracture of right radius, initial encounter for closed fracture
S52.541P	Smith's fracture of right radius, subsequent encounter for closed fracture with malunion
S52.541K	Smith's fracture of right radius, subsequent encounter for closed fracture with nonunion
S52.541Q	Smith's fracture of right radius, subsequent encounter for open fracture type I or II with malunion
S52.541M	Smith's fracture of right radius, subsequent encounter for open fracture type I or II with nonunion
S52.541R	Smith's fracture of right radius, subsequent encounter for open fracture type IIIA, IIIB, or IIIC with malunion
S52.541N	Smith's fracture of right radius, subsequent encounter for open fracture type IIIA, IIIB, or IIIC with nonunion
S52.549A	Smith's fracture of unspecified radius, initial encounter for closed fracture
S52.549P	Smith's fracture of unspecified radius, subsequent encounter for closed fracture with malunion
S52.549K	Smith's fracture of unspecified radius, subsequent encounter for closed fracture with nonunion

S52.549Q	Smith's fracture of unspecified radius, subsequent encounter for open fracture type I or II with malunion
S52.549M	Smith's fracture of unspecified radius, subsequent encounter for open fracture type I or II with nonunion
S52.549R	Smith's fracture of unspecified radius, subsequent encounter for open fracture type IIIA, IIIB, or IIIC with malunion
S52.549N	Smith's fracture of unspecified radius, subsequent encounter for open fracture type IIIA, IIIB, or IIIC with nonunion
C90.32	Solitary plasmacytoma in relapse
C90.31	Solitary plasmacytoma in remission
C90.30	Solitary plasmacytoma not having achieved remission
B70.1	Sparganosis
G80.1	Spastic diplegic cerebral palsy
G81.12	Spastic hemiplegia affecting left dominant side
G81.14	Spastic hemiplegia affecting left nondominant side
G81.11	Spastic hemiplegia affecting right dominant side
G81.13	Spastic hemiplegia affecting right nondominant side
G81.10	Spastic hemiplegia affecting unspecified side
G80.2	Spastic hemiplegic cerebral palsy
G12.9	Spinal muscular atrophy, unspecified
A25.0	Spirillosis
A77.3	Spotted fever due to Rickettsia australis
A77.1	Spotted fever due to Rickettsia conorii
A77.0	Spotted fever due to Rickettsia rickettsii
A77.2	Spotted fever due to Rickettsia siberica
A77.9	Spotted fever, unspecified
S32.051A	Stable burst fracture of fifth lumbar vertebra, initial encounter for closed fracture
S32.051K	Stable burst fracture of fifth lumbar vertebra, subsequent encounter for fracture with nonunion
S12.01XA	Stable burst fracture of first cervical vertebra, initial encounter for closed fracture
S12.01XK	Stable burst fracture of first cervical vertebra, subsequent encounter for fracture with nonunion
S32.011A	Stable burst fracture of first lumbar vertebra, initial encounter for closed fracture
S32.011K	Stable burst fracture of first lumbar vertebra, subsequent encounter for fracture with nonunion
S22.011A	Stable burst fracture of first thoracic vertebra, initial encounter for closed fracture
S22.011K	Stable burst fracture of first thoracic vertebra, subsequent encounter for fracture with nonunion
S32.041A	Stable burst fracture of fourth lumbar vertebra, initial encounter for closed fracture
S32.041K	Stable burst fracture of fourth lumbar vertebra, subsequent encounter for fracture with nonunion
S22.041A	Stable burst fracture of fourth thoracic vertebra, initial encounter for closed fracture
S22.041K	Stable burst fracture of fourth thoracic vertebra, subsequent encounter for fracture with nonunion
S32.021A	Stable burst fracture of second lumbar vertebra, initial encounter for closed fracture
S32.021K	Stable burst fracture of second lumbar vertebra, subsequent encounter for fracture with nonunion
S22.021A	Stable burst fracture of second thoracic vertebra, initial encounter for closed fracture
S22.021K	Stable burst fracture of second thoracic vertebra, subsequent encounter for fracture with nonunion
S22.081A	Stable burst fracture of T11-T12 vertebra, initial encounter for closed fracture
S22.081K	Stable burst fracture of T11-T12 vertebra, subsequent encounter for fracture with nonunion
S22.051A	Stable burst fracture of T5-T6 vertebra, initial encounter for closed fracture
S22.051K	Stable burst fracture of T5-T6 vertebra, subsequent encounter for fracture with nonunion
S22.061A	Stable burst fracture of T7-T8 vertebra, initial encounter for closed fracture
S22.061K	Stable burst fracture of T7-T8 vertebra, subsequent encounter for fracture with nonunion
S22.071A	Stable burst fracture of T9-T10 vertebra, initial encounter for closed fracture
S22.071K	Stable burst fracture of T9-T10 vertebra, subsequent encounter for fracture with nonunion
S32.031A	Stable burst fracture of third lumbar vertebra, initial encounter for closed fracture
S32.031K	Stable burst fracture of third lumbar vertebra, subsequent encounter for fracture with nonunion
S22.031A	Stable burst fracture of third thoracic vertebra, initial encounter for closed fracture
S22.031K	Stable burst fracture of third thoracic vertebra, subsequent encounter for fracture with nonunion
S32.001A	Stable burst fracture of unspecified lumbar vertebra, initial encounter for closed fracture
S32.001K	Stable burst fracture of unspecified lumbar vertebra, subsequent encounter for fracture with nonunion
S22.001A	Stable burst fracture of unspecified thoracic vertebra, initial encounter for closed fracture
S22.001K	Stable burst fracture of unspecified thoracic vertebra, subsequent encounter for fracture with nonunion
M00.072	Staphylococcal arthritis, left ankle and foot
M00.022	Staphylococcal arthritis, left elbow
M00.042	Staphylococcal arthritis, left hand
M00.052	Staphylococcal arthritis, left hip

M00.062	Staphylococcal arthritis, left knee
M00.012	Staphylococcal arthritis, left shoulder
M00.032	Staphylococcal arthritis, left wrist
M00.071	Staphylococcal arthritis, right ankle and foot
M00.021	Staphylococcal arthritis, right elbow
M00.041	Staphylococcal arthritis, right hand
M00.051	Staphylococcal arthritis, right hip
M00.061	Staphylococcal arthritis, right knee
M00.011	Staphylococcal arthritis, right shoulder
M00.031	Staphylococcal arthritis, right wrist
M00.079	Staphylococcal arthritis, unspecified ankle and foot
M00.029	Staphylococcal arthritis, unspecified elbow
M00.049	Staphylococcal arthritis, unspecified hand
M00.059	Staphylococcal arthritis, unspecified hip
M00.00	Staphylococcal arthritis, unspecified joint
M00.069	Staphylococcal arthritis, unspecified knee
M00.019	Staphylococcal arthritis, unspecified shoulder
M00.039	Staphylococcal arthritis, unspecified wrist
M00.08	Staphylococcal arthritis, vertebrae
M00.09	Staphylococcal polyarthritis
Z94.84	Stem cells transplant status
T83.85XA	Stenosis due to genitourinary prosthetic devices, implants and grafts, initial encounter
T84.85XA	Stenosis due to internal orthopedic prosthetic devices, implants and grafts, initial encounter
T85.850A	Stenosis due to nervous system prosthetic devices, implants and grafts, initial encounter
T85.850D	Stenosis due to nervous system prosthetic devices, implants and grafts, subsequent encounter
T82.855A	Stenosis of coronary artery stent, initial encounter
T82.857A	Stenosis of other cardiac prosthetic devices, implants and grafts, initial encounter
T82.858A	Stenosis of other vascular prosthetic devices, implants and grafts, initial encounter
T82.856A	Stenosis of peripheral vascular stent, initial encounter
S22.23XA	Sternal manubrial dissociation, initial encounter for closed fracture
S22.23XK	Sternal manubrial dissociation, subsequent encounter for fracture with nonunion
L51.1	Stevens-Johnson syndrome
L51.3	Stevens-Johnson syndrome-toxic epidermal necrolysis overlap syndrome
G25.82	Stiff-man syndrome
A25.1	Streptobacillosis
M84.359P	Stress fracture, hip, unspecified, subsequent encounter for fracture with malunion
M84.359K	Stress fracture, hip, unspecified, subsequent encounter for fracture with nonunion
M84.372P	Stress fracture, left ankle, subsequent encounter for fracture with malunion
M84.372K	Stress fracture, left ankle, subsequent encounter for fracture with nonunion
M84.352P	Stress fracture, left femur, subsequent encounter for fracture with malunion
M84.352K	Stress fracture, left femur, subsequent encounter for fracture with nonunion
M84.364P	Stress fracture, left fibula, subsequent encounter for fracture with malunion
M84.364K	Stress fracture, left fibula, subsequent encounter for fracture with nonunion
M84.345P	Stress fracture, left finger(s), subsequent encounter for fracture with malunion
M84.345K	Stress fracture, left finger(s), subsequent encounter for fracture with nonunion
M84.375P	Stress fracture, left foot, subsequent encounter for fracture with malunion
M84.375K	Stress fracture, left foot, subsequent encounter for fracture with nonunion
M84.342P	Stress fracture, left hand, subsequent encounter for fracture with malunion
M84.342K	Stress fracture, left hand, subsequent encounter for fracture with nonunion
M84.322P	Stress fracture, left humerus, subsequent encounter for fracture with malunion
M84.322K	Stress fracture, left humerus, subsequent encounter for fracture with nonunion
M84.334P	Stress fracture, left radius, subsequent encounter for fracture with malunion
M84.334K	Stress fracture, left radius, subsequent encounter for fracture with nonunion
M84.312P	Stress fracture, left shoulder, subsequent encounter for fracture with malunion
M84.312K	Stress fracture, left shoulder, subsequent encounter for fracture with nonunion
M84.362P	Stress fracture, left tibia, subsequent encounter for fracture with malunion
M84.362K	Stress fracture, left tibia, subsequent encounter for fracture with nonunion
M84.378P	Stress fracture, left toe(s), subsequent encounter for fracture with malunion
M84.378K	Stress fracture, left toe(s), subsequent encounter for fracture with nonunion
M84.332P	Stress fracture, left ulna, subsequent encounter for fracture with malunion
M84.332K	Stress fracture, left ulna, subsequent encounter for fracture with nonunion
M84.38XP	Stress fracture, other site, subsequent encounter for fracture with malunion
M84.38XK	Stress fracture, other site, subsequent encounter for fracture with nonunion
M84.350P	Stress fracture, pelvis, subsequent encounter for fracture with malunion
M84.350K	Stress fracture, pelvis, subsequent encounter for fracture with nonunion
M84.371P	Stress fracture, right ankle, subsequent encounter for fracture with malunion
M84.371K	Stress fracture, right ankle, subsequent encounter for fracture with nonunion
M84.351P	Stress fracture, right femur, subsequent encounter for fracture with malunion
M84.351K	Stress fracture, right femur, subsequent encounter for fracture with nonunion
M84.363P	Stress fracture, right fibula, subsequent encounter for fracture with malunion
M84.363K	Stress fracture, right fibula, subsequent encounter for fracture with nonunion
M84.344P	Stress fracture, right finger(s), subsequent encounter for fracture with malunion

M84.344K	Stress fracture, right finger(s), subsequent encounter for fracture with nonunion
M84.374P	Stress fracture, right foot, subsequent encounter for fracture with malunion
M84.374K	Stress fracture, right foot, subsequent encounter for fracture with nonunion
M84.341P	Stress fracture, right hand, subsequent encounter for fracture with malunion
M84.341K	Stress fracture, right hand, subsequent encounter for fracture with nonunion
M84.321P	Stress fracture, right humerus, subsequent encounter for fracture with malunion
M84.321K	Stress fracture, right humerus, subsequent encounter for fracture with nonunion
M84.333P	Stress fracture, right radius, subsequent encounter for fracture with malunion
M84.333K	Stress fracture, right radius, subsequent encounter for fracture with nonunion
M84.311P	Stress fracture, right shoulder, subsequent encounter for fracture with malunion
M84.311K	Stress fracture, right shoulder, subsequent encounter for fracture with nonunion
M84.361P	Stress fracture, right tibia, subsequent encounter for fracture with malunion
M84.361K	Stress fracture, right tibia, subsequent encounter for fracture with nonunion
M84.377P	Stress fracture, right toe(s), subsequent encounter for fracture with malunion
M84.377K	Stress fracture, right toe(s), subsequent encounter for fracture with nonunion
M84.331P	Stress fracture, right ulna, subsequent encounter for fracture with malunion
M84.331K	Stress fracture, right ulna, subsequent encounter for fracture with nonunion
M84.373P	Stress fracture, unspecified ankle, subsequent encounter for fracture with malunion
M84.373K	Stress fracture, unspecified ankle, subsequent encounter for fracture with nonunion
M84.353P	Stress fracture, unspecified femur, subsequent encounter for fracture with malunion
M84.353K	Stress fracture, unspecified femur, subsequent encounter for fracture with nonunion
M84.346P	Stress fracture, unspecified finger(s), subsequent encounter for fracture with malunion
M84.346K	Stress fracture, unspecified finger(s), subsequent encounter for fracture with nonunion
M84.376P	Stress fracture, unspecified foot, subsequent encounter for fracture with malunion
M84.376K	Stress fracture, unspecified foot, subsequent encounter for fracture with nonunion
M84.343P	Stress fracture, unspecified hand, subsequent encounter for fracture with malunion
M84.343K	Stress fracture, unspecified hand, subsequent encounter for fracture with nonunion
M84.329P	Stress fracture, unspecified humerus, subsequent encounter for fracture with malunion
M84.329K	Stress fracture, unspecified humerus, subsequent encounter for fracture with nonunion
M84.319P	Stress fracture, unspecified shoulder, subsequent encounter for fracture with malunion
M84.319K	Stress fracture, unspecified shoulder, subsequent encounter for fracture with nonunion
M84.30XP	Stress fracture, unspecified site, subsequent encounter for fracture with malunion
M84.30XK	Stress fracture, unspecified site, subsequent encounter for fracture with nonunion
M84.369P	Stress fracture, unspecified tibia and fibula, subsequent encounter for fracture with malunion
M84.369K	Stress fracture, unspecified tibia and fibula, subsequent encounter for fracture with nonunion
M84.379P	Stress fracture, unspecified toe(s), subsequent encounter for fracture with malunion
M84.379K	Stress fracture, unspecified toe(s), subsequent encounter for fracture with nonunion
M84.339P	Stress fracture, unspecified ulna and radius, subsequent encounter for fracture with malunion
M84.339K	Stress fracture, unspecified ulna and radius, subsequent encounter for fracture with nonunion
G23.2	Striatonigral degeneration
B78.9	Strongyloidiasis, unspecified
A24.2	Subacute and chronic melioidosis
G32.0	Subacute combined degeneration of spinal cord in diseases classified elsewhere
M86.272	Subacute osteomyelitis, left ankle and foot
M86.252	Subacute osteomyelitis, left femur
M86.242	Subacute osteomyelitis, left hand
M86.222	Subacute osteomyelitis, left humerus
M86.232	Subacute osteomyelitis, left radius and ulna
M86.212	Subacute osteomyelitis, left shoulder
M86.262	Subacute osteomyelitis, left tibia and fibula
M86.29	Subacute osteomyelitis, multiple sites
M86.28	Subacute osteomyelitis, other site
M86.271	Subacute osteomyelitis, right ankle and foot
M86.251	Subacute osteomyelitis, right femur
M86.241	Subacute osteomyelitis, right hand
M86.221	Subacute osteomyelitis, right humerus
M86.231	Subacute osteomyelitis, right radius and ulna
M86.211	Subacute osteomyelitis, right shoulder
M86.261	Subacute osteomyelitis, right tibia and fibula
M86.279	Subacute osteomyelitis, unspecified ankle and foot
M86.259	Subacute osteomyelitis, unspecified femur
M86.249	Subacute osteomyelitis, unspecified hand

M86.229	Subacute osteomyelitis, unspecified humerus
M86.239	Subacute osteomyelitis, unspecified radius and ulna
M86.219	Subacute osteomyelitis, unspecified shoulder
M86.20	Subacute osteomyelitis, unspecified site
M86.269	Subacute osteomyelitis, unspecified tibia and fibula
A81.1	Subacute sclerosing panencephalitis
C86.3	Subcutaneous panniculitis-like T-cell lymphoma
M99.11	Subluxation complex (vertebral) of cervical region
M99.10	Subluxation complex (vertebral) of head region
M99.18	Subluxation complex (vertebral) of rib cage
S13.110A	Subluxation of C0/C1 cervical vertebrae, initial encounter
S13.120A	Subluxation of C1/C2 cervical vertebrae, initial encounter
S13.130A	Subluxation of C2/C3 cervical vertebrae, initial encounter
S13.140A	Subluxation of C3/C4 cervical vertebrae, initial encounter
S13.150A	Subluxation of C4/C5 cervical vertebrae, initial encounter
S13.160A	Subluxation of C5/C6 cervical vertebrae, initial encounter
S13.170A	Subluxation of C6/C7 cervical vertebrae, initial encounter
S13.180A	Subluxation of C7/T1 cervical vertebrae, initial encounter
S13.100A	Subluxation of unspecified cervical vertebrae, initial encounter
H70.013	Subperiosteal abscess of mastoid, bilateral
H70.012	Subperiosteal abscess of mastoid, left ear
H70.011	Subperiosteal abscess of mastoid, right ear
H70.019	Subperiosteal abscess of mastoid, unspecified ear
H53.133	Sudden visual loss, bilateral
H53.132	Sudden visual loss, left eye
H53.131	Sudden visual loss, right eye
H53.139	Sudden visual loss, unspecified eye
R45.851	Suicidal ideations
E75.26	Sulfatase deficiency
S36.030A	Superficial (capsular) laceration of spleen, initial encounter
T33.3XXA	Superficial frostbite of abdominal wall, lower back and pelvis, initial encounter
T33.812A	Superficial frostbite of left ankle, initial encounter
T33.42XA	Superficial frostbite of left arm, initial encounter
T33.012A	Superficial frostbite of left ear, initial encounter
T33.532A	Superficial frostbite of left finger(s), initial encounter
T33.822A	Superficial frostbite of left foot, initial encounter
T33.522A	Superficial frostbite of left hand, initial encounter
T33.62XA	Superficial frostbite of left hip and thigh, initial encounter
T33.72XA	Superficial frostbite of left knee and lower leg, initial encounter
T33.832A	Superficial frostbite of left toe(s), initial encounter
T33.512A	Superficial frostbite of left wrist, initial encounter
T33.1XXA	Superficial frostbite of neck, initial encounter
T33.02XA	Superficial frostbite of nose, initial encounter
T33.09XA	Superficial frostbite of other part of head, initial encounter
T33.99XA	Superficial frostbite of other sites, initial encounter
T33.811A	Superficial frostbite of right ankle, initial encounter
T33.41XA	Superficial frostbite of right arm, initial encounter
T33.011A	Superficial frostbite of right ear, initial encounter
T33.531A	Superficial frostbite of right finger(s), initial encounter
T33.821A	Superficial frostbite of right foot, initial encounter
T33.521A	Superficial frostbite of right hand, initial encounter
T33.61XA	Superficial frostbite of right hip and thigh, initial encounter
T33.71XA	Superficial frostbite of right knee and lower leg, initial encounter
T33.831A	Superficial frostbite of right toe(s), initial encounter
T33.511A	Superficial frostbite of right wrist, initial encounter
T33.2XXA	Superficial frostbite of thorax, initial encounter
T33.819A	Superficial frostbite of unspecified ankle, initial encounter
T33.40XA	Superficial frostbite of unspecified arm, initial encounter
T33.019A	Superficial frostbite of unspecified ear, initial encounter
T33.539A	Superficial frostbite of unspecified finger(s), initial encounter
T33.829A	Superficial frostbite of unspecified foot, initial encounter
T33.529A	Superficial frostbite of unspecified hand, initial encounter
T33.60XA	Superficial frostbite of unspecified hip and thigh, initial encounter
T33.70XA	Superficial frostbite of unspecified knee and lower leg, initial encounter
T33.90XA	Superficial frostbite of unspecified sites, initial encounter
T33.839A	Superficial frostbite of unspecified toe(s), initial encounter
T33.519A	Superficial frostbite of unspecified wrist, initial encounter
O22.21	Superficial thrombophlebitis in pregnancy, first trimester
O22.22	Superficial thrombophlebitis in pregnancy, second trimester
O22.23	Superficial thrombophlebitis in pregnancy, third trimester
O22.20	Superficial thrombophlebitis in pregnancy, unspecified trimester
O87.0	Superficial thrombophlebitis in the puerperium
Q25.3	Supravalvular aortic stenosis
I47.1	Supraventricular tachycardia
Q64.11	Supravesical fissure of urinary bladder
A82.0	Sylvatic rabies
A95.0	Sylvatic yellow fever
H44.133	Sympathetic uveitis, bilateral
H44.132	Sympathetic uveitis, left eye
H44.131	Sympathetic uveitis, right eye
H44.139	Sympathetic uveitis, unspecified eye
A52.73	Symptomatic late syphilis of other respiratory organs
A52.10	Symptomatic neurosyphilis, unspecified
E22.2	Syndrome of inappropriate secretion of antidiuretic hormone
O98.12	Syphilis complicating childbirth
O98.111	Syphilis complicating pregnancy, first trimester
O98.112	Syphilis complicating pregnancy, second trimester

O98.113	Syphilis complicating pregnancy, third trimester
O98.13	Syphilis complicating the puerperium
A52.77	Syphilis of bone and joint
A52.75	Syphilis of kidney and ureter
A52.74	Syphilis of liver and other viscera
A52.72	Syphilis of lung and bronchus
A52.78	Syphilis of other musculoskeletal tissue
A51.32	Syphilitic alopecia
A52.01	Syphilitic aneurysm of aorta
A52.02	Syphilitic aortitis
A52.04	Syphilitic cerebral arteritis
A52.03	Syphilitic endocarditis
A50.57	Syphilitic saddle nose
G95.0	Syringomyelia and syringobulbia
A44.0	Systemic bartonellosis
R65.10	Systemic inflammatory response syndrome (SIRS) of non-infectious origin without acute organ dysfunction
D47.02	Systemic mastocytosis
M34.81	Systemic sclerosis with lung involvement
M34.82	Systemic sclerosis with myopathy
A52.11	Tabes dorsalis
B68.1	Taenia saginata taeniasis
B68.0	Taenia solium taeniasis
B68.9	Taeniasis, unspecified
I51.81	Takotsubo syndrome
B08.71	Tanapox virus disease
E75.02	Tay-Sachs disease
O60.20X1	Term delivery with preterm labor, unspecified trimester, fetus 1
O60.20X2	Term delivery with preterm labor, unspecified trimester, fetus 2
O60.20X3	Term delivery with preterm labor, unspecified trimester, fetus 3
O60.20X4	Term delivery with preterm labor, unspecified trimester, fetus 4
O60.20X5	Term delivery with preterm labor, unspecified trimester, fetus 5
O60.20X0	Term delivery with preterm labor, unspecified trimester, not applicable or unspecified
O60.20X9	Term delivery with preterm labor, unspecified trimester, other fetus
R29.0	Tetany
E51.9	Thiamine deficiency, unspecified
O70.21	Third degree perineal laceration during delivery, IIIa
O70.22	Third degree perineal laceration during delivery, IIIb
O70.23	Third degree perineal laceration during delivery, IIIc
O70.20	Third degree perineal laceration during delivery, unspecified
O72.0	Third-stage hemorrhage
Q05.1	Thoracic spina bifida with hydrocephalus
O20.0	Threatened abortion
I82.1	Thrombophlebitis migrans
T82.867A	Thrombosis due to cardiac prosthetic devices, implants and grafts, initial encounter
T83.86XA	Thrombosis due to genitourinary prosthetic devices, implants and grafts, initial encounter
T84.86XA	Thrombosis due to internal orthopedic prosthetic devices, implants and grafts, initial encounter
T85.860A	Thrombosis due to nervous system prosthetic devices, implants and grafts, initial encounter
T85.860D	Thrombosis due to nervous system prosthetic devices, implants and grafts, subsequent encounter
T82.868A	Thrombosis due to vascular prosthetic devices, implants and grafts, initial encounter
I23.6	Thrombosis of atrium, auricular appendage, and ventricle as current complications following acute myocardial infarction
A68.1	Tick-borne relapsing fever
B44.2	Tonsillar aspergillosis
N44.04	Torsion of appendix epididymis
N44.03	Torsion of appendix testis
N83.529	Torsion of fallopian tube, unspecified side
N83.522	Torsion of left fallopian tube
N83.512	Torsion of left ovary and ovarian pedicle
N83.519	Torsion of ovary and ovarian pedicle, unspecified side
N83.53	Torsion of ovary, ovarian pedicle and fallopian tube
N83.521	Torsion of right fallopian tube
N83.511	Torsion of right ovary and ovarian pedicle
N44.00	Torsion of testis, unspecified
Q25.46	Tortuous aortic arch
S72.472A	Torus fracture of lower end of left femur, initial encounter for closed fracture
S72.472P	Torus fracture of lower end of left femur, subsequent encounter for fracture with malunion
S72.472K	Torus fracture of lower end of left femur, subsequent encounter for fracture with nonunion
S82.822P	Torus fracture of lower end of left fibula, subsequent encounter for fracture with malunion
S82.822K	Torus fracture of lower end of left fibula, subsequent encounter for fracture with nonunion
S42.482A	Torus fracture of lower end of left humerus, initial encounter for closed fracture
S42.482P	Torus fracture of lower end of left humerus, subsequent encounter for fracture with malunion
S42.482K	Torus fracture of lower end of left humerus, subsequent encounter for fracture with nonunion
S52.522A	Torus fracture of lower end of left radius, initial encounter for closed fracture

S52.522P	Torus fracture of lower end of left radius, subsequent encounter for fracture with malunion
S52.522K	Torus fracture of lower end of left radius, subsequent encounter for fracture with nonunion
S82.312A	Torus fracture of lower end of left tibia, initial encounter for closed fracture
S82.312P	Torus fracture of lower end of left tibia, subsequent encounter for fracture with malunion
S82.312K	Torus fracture of lower end of left tibia, subsequent encounter for fracture with nonunion
S52.622A	Torus fracture of lower end of left ulna, initial encounter for closed fracture
S52.622P	Torus fracture of lower end of left ulna, subsequent encounter for fracture with malunion
S52.622K	Torus fracture of lower end of left ulna, subsequent encounter for fracture with nonunion
S72.471A	Torus fracture of lower end of right femur, initial encounter for closed fracture
S72.471P	Torus fracture of lower end of right femur, subsequent encounter for fracture with malunion
S72.471K	Torus fracture of lower end of right femur, subsequent encounter for fracture with nonunion
S82.821P	Torus fracture of lower end of right fibula, subsequent encounter for fracture with malunion
S82.821K	Torus fracture of lower end of right fibula, subsequent encounter for fracture with nonunion
S42.481A	Torus fracture of lower end of right humerus, initial encounter for closed fracture
S42.481P	Torus fracture of lower end of right humerus, subsequent encounter for fracture with malunion
S42.481K	Torus fracture of lower end of right humerus, subsequent encounter for fracture with nonunion
S52.521A	Torus fracture of lower end of right radius, initial encounter for closed fracture
S52.521P	Torus fracture of lower end of right radius, subsequent encounter for fracture with malunion
S52.521K	Torus fracture of lower end of right radius, subsequent encounter for fracture with nonunion
S82.311A	Torus fracture of lower end of right tibia, initial encounter for closed fracture
S82.311P	Torus fracture of lower end of right tibia, subsequent encounter for fracture with malunion
S82.311K	Torus fracture of lower end of right tibia, subsequent encounter for fracture with nonunion
S52.621A	Torus fracture of lower end of right ulna, initial encounter for closed fracture
S52.621P	Torus fracture of lower end of right ulna, subsequent encounter for fracture with malunion
S52.621K	Torus fracture of lower end of right ulna, subsequent encounter for fracture with nonunion
S72.479A	Torus fracture of lower end of unspecified femur, initial encounter for closed fracture
S72.479P	Torus fracture of lower end of unspecified femur, subsequent encounter for fracture with malunion
S72.479K	Torus fracture of lower end of unspecified femur, subsequent encounter for fracture with nonunion
S82.829P	Torus fracture of lower end of unspecified fibula, subsequent encounter for fracture with malunion
S82.829K	Torus fracture of lower end of unspecified fibula, subsequent encounter for fracture with nonunion
S42.489A	Torus fracture of lower end of unspecified humerus, initial encounter for closed fracture
S42.489P	Torus fracture of lower end of unspecified humerus, subsequent encounter for fracture with malunion
S42.489K	Torus fracture of lower end of unspecified humerus, subsequent encounter for fracture with nonunion
S52.529A	Torus fracture of lower end of unspecified radius, initial encounter for closed fracture
S52.529P	Torus fracture of lower end of unspecified radius, subsequent encounter for fracture with malunion
S52.529K	Torus fracture of lower end of unspecified radius, subsequent encounter for fracture with nonunion
S82.319A	Torus fracture of lower end of unspecified tibia, initial encounter for closed fracture
S82.319P	Torus fracture of lower end of unspecified tibia, subsequent encounter for fracture with malunion
S82.319K	Torus fracture of lower end of unspecified tibia, subsequent encounter for fracture with nonunion
S52.629A	Torus fracture of lower end of unspecified ulna, initial encounter for closed fracture
S52.629P	Torus fracture of lower end of unspecified ulna, subsequent encounter for fracture with malunion
S52.629K	Torus fracture of lower end of unspecified ulna, subsequent encounter for fracture with nonunion
S82.812P	Torus fracture of upper end of left fibula, subsequent encounter for fracture with malunion
S82.812K	Torus fracture of upper end of left fibula, subsequent encounter for fracture with nonunion
S42.272A	Torus fracture of upper end of left humerus, initial encounter for closed fracture
S42.272P	Torus fracture of upper end of left humerus, subsequent encounter for fracture with malunion
S42.272K	Torus fracture of upper end of left humerus, subsequent encounter for fracture with nonunion
S52.112A	Torus fracture of upper end of left radius, initial encounter for closed fracture
S52.112P	Torus fracture of upper end of left radius, subsequent encounter for fracture with malunion

S52.112K	Torus fracture of upper end of left radius, subsequent encounter for fracture with nonunion
S82.162A	Torus fracture of upper end of left tibia, initial encounter for closed fracture
S82.162P	Torus fracture of upper end of left tibia, subsequent encounter for fracture with malunion
S82.162K	Torus fracture of upper end of left tibia, subsequent encounter for fracture with nonunion
S52.012A	Torus fracture of upper end of left ulna, initial encounter for closed fracture
S52.012P	Torus fracture of upper end of left ulna, subsequent encounter for fracture with malunion
S52.012K	Torus fracture of upper end of left ulna, subsequent encounter for fracture with nonunion
S82.811P	Torus fracture of upper end of right fibula, subsequent encounter for fracture with malunion
S82.811K	Torus fracture of upper end of right fibula, subsequent encounter for fracture with nonunion
S42.271A	Torus fracture of upper end of right humerus, initial encounter for closed fracture
S42.271P	Torus fracture of upper end of right humerus, subsequent encounter for fracture with malunion
S42.271K	Torus fracture of upper end of right humerus, subsequent encounter for fracture with nonunion
S52.111A	Torus fracture of upper end of right radius, initial encounter for closed fracture
S52.111P	Torus fracture of upper end of right radius, subsequent encounter for fracture with malunion
S52.111K	Torus fracture of upper end of right radius, subsequent encounter for fracture with nonunion
S82.161A	Torus fracture of upper end of right tibia, initial encounter for closed fracture
S82.161P	Torus fracture of upper end of right tibia, subsequent encounter for fracture with malunion
S82.161K	Torus fracture of upper end of right tibia, subsequent encounter for fracture with nonunion
S52.011A	Torus fracture of upper end of right ulna, initial encounter for closed fracture
S52.011P	Torus fracture of upper end of right ulna, subsequent encounter for fracture with malunion
S52.011K	Torus fracture of upper end of right ulna, subsequent encounter for fracture with nonunion
S82.819P	Torus fracture of upper end of unspecified fibula, subsequent encounter for fracture with malunion
S82.819K	Torus fracture of upper end of unspecified fibula, subsequent encounter for fracture with nonunion
S42.279A	Torus fracture of upper end of unspecified humerus, initial encounter for closed fracture
S42.279P	Torus fracture of upper end of unspecified humerus, subsequent encounter for fracture with malunion
S42.279K	Torus fracture of upper end of unspecified humerus, subsequent encounter for fracture with nonunion
S52.119A	Torus fracture of upper end of unspecified radius, initial encounter for closed fracture
S52.119P	Torus fracture of upper end of unspecified radius, subsequent encounter for fracture with malunion
S52.119K	Torus fracture of upper end of unspecified radius, subsequent encounter for fracture with nonunion
S82.169A	Torus fracture of upper end of unspecified tibia, initial encounter for closed fracture
S82.169P	Torus fracture of upper end of unspecified tibia, subsequent encounter for fracture with malunion
S82.169K	Torus fracture of upper end of unspecified tibia, subsequent encounter for fracture with nonunion
S52.019A	Torus fracture of upper end of unspecified ulna, initial encounter for closed fracture
S52.019P	Torus fracture of upper end of unspecified ulna, subsequent encounter for fracture with malunion
S52.019K	Torus fracture of upper end of unspecified ulna, subsequent encounter for fracture with nonunion
Q26.2	Total anomalous pulmonary venous connection
L51.2	Toxic epidermal necrolysis [Lyell]
L53.0	Toxic erythema
K52.1	Toxic gastroenteritis and colitis
K59.31	Toxic megacolon
B58.01	Toxoplasma chorioretinitis
B58.1	Toxoplasma hepatitis
B58.82	Toxoplasma myositis
B58.00	Toxoplasma oculopathy, unspecified
B58.83	Toxoplasma tubulo-interstitial nephropathy
B58.89	Toxoplasmosis with other organ involvement
B58.9	Toxoplasmosis, unspecified
J95.04	Tracheo-esophageal fistula following tracheostomy
H33.43	Traction detachment of retina, bilateral
H33.42	Traction detachment of retina, left eye
H33.41	Traction detachment of retina, right eye
H33.40	Traction detachment of retina, unspecified eye
J95.84	Transfusion-related acute lung injury (TRALI)
G45.9	Transient cerebral ischemic attack, unspecified
D80.7	Transient hypogammaglobulinemia of infancy
P94.0	Transient neonatal myasthenia gravis
R29.5	Transient paralysis
H34.03	Transient retinal artery occlusion, bilateral
H34.02	Transient retinal artery occlusion, left eye
H34.01	Transient retinal artery occlusion, right eye

H34.00	Transient retinal artery occlusion, unspecified eye
H53.123	Transient visual loss, bilateral
H53.122	Transient visual loss, left eye
H53.121	Transient visual loss, right eye
H53.129	Transient visual loss, unspecified eye
P74.6	Transitory hyperammonemia of newborn
P76.1	Transitory ileus of newborn
P71.9	Transitory neonatal disorder of calcium and magnesium metabolism, unspecified
P72.1	Transitory neonatal hyperthyroidism
P71.4	Transitory neonatal hypoparathyroidism
P74.5	Transitory tyrosinemia of newborn
S28.1XXA	Traumatic amputation (partial) of part of thorax, except breast, initial encounter
T79.A3XA	Traumatic compartment syndrome of abdomen, initial encounter
T79.A22A	Traumatic compartment syndrome of left lower extremity, initial encounter
T79.A12A	Traumatic compartment syndrome of left upper extremity, initial encounter
T79.A9XA	Traumatic compartment syndrome of other sites, initial encounter
T79.A21A	Traumatic compartment syndrome of right lower extremity, initial encounter
T79.A11A	Traumatic compartment syndrome of right upper extremity, initial encounter
T79.A29A	Traumatic compartment syndrome of unspecified lower extremity, initial encounter
T79.A19A	Traumatic compartment syndrome of unspecified upper extremity, initial encounter
S27.0XXA	Traumatic pneumothorax, initial encounter
S13.0XXA	Traumatic rupture of cervical intervertebral disc, initial encounter
S09.22XA	Traumatic rupture of left ear drum, initial encounter
S09.21XA	Traumatic rupture of right ear drum, initial encounter
S09.20XA	Traumatic rupture of unspecified ear drum, initial encounter
T79.2XXA	Traumatic secondary and recurrent hemorrhage and seroma, initial encounter
M48.32	Traumatic spondylopathy, cervical region
M48.33	Traumatic spondylopathy, cervicothoracic region
M48.36	Traumatic spondylopathy, lumbar region
M48.37	Traumatic spondylopathy, lumbosacral region
M48.31	Traumatic spondylopathy, occipito-atlanto-axial region
M48.38	Traumatic spondylopathy, sacral and sacrococcygeal region
M48.30	Traumatic spondylopathy, site unspecified
M48.34	Traumatic spondylopathy, thoracic region
M48.35	Traumatic spondylopathy, thoracolumbar region
T79.7XXA	Traumatic subcutaneous emphysema, initial encounter
A79.0	Trench fever
B75	Trichinellosis
B81.2	Trichostrongyliasis
B79	Trichuriasis
I45.3	Trifascicular block
E72.52	Trimethylaminuria
O30.121	Triplet pregnancy with two or more monoamniotic fetuses, first trimester
O30.122	Triplet pregnancy with two or more monoamniotic fetuses, second trimester
O30.123	Triplet pregnancy with two or more monoamniotic fetuses, third trimester
O30.111	Triplet pregnancy with two or more monochorionic fetuses, first trimester
O30.112	Triplet pregnancy with two or more monochorionic fetuses, second trimester
O30.113	Triplet pregnancy with two or more monochorionic fetuses, third trimester
O30.131	Triplet pregnancy, trichorionic/triamniotic, first trimester
O30.132	Triplet pregnancy, trichorionic/triamniotic, second trimester
O30.133	Triplet pregnancy, trichorionic/triamniotic, third trimester
O30.191	Triplet pregnancy, unable to determine number of placenta and number of amniotic sacs, first trimester
O30.192	Triplet pregnancy, unable to determine number of placenta and number of amniotic sacs, second trimester
O30.193	Triplet pregnancy, unable to determine number of placenta and number of amniotic sacs, third trimester
O30.101	Triplet pregnancy, unspecified number of placenta and unspecified number of amniotic sacs, first trimester
O30.102	Triplet pregnancy, unspecified number of placenta and unspecified number of amniotic sacs, second trimester
O30.103	Triplet pregnancy, unspecified number of placenta and unspecified number of amniotic sacs, third trimester
Q91.5	Trisomy 13, mosaicism (mitotic nondisjunction)
Q91.4	Trisomy 13, nonmosaicism (meiotic nondisjunction)
Q91.6	Trisomy 13, translocation
Q91.7	Trisomy 13, unspecified
Q91.1	Trisomy 18, mosaicism (mitotic nondisjunction)
Q91.0	Trisomy 18, nonmosaicism (meiotic nondisjunction)
Q91.2	Trisomy 18, translocation
Q91.3	Trisomy 18, unspecified
G04.1	Tropical spastic paraplegia
K90.1	Tropical sprue
A30.1	Tuberculoid leprosy
O98.02	Tuberculosis complicating childbirth
O98.011	Tuberculosis complicating pregnancy, first trimester
O98.012	Tuberculosis complicating pregnancy, second trimester
O98.013	Tuberculosis complicating pregnancy, third trimester
O98.03	Tuberculosis complicating the puerperium
A18.6	Tuberculosis of (inner) (middle) ear
A18.7	Tuberculosis of adrenal glands
A18.12	Tuberculosis of bladder
A18.16	Tuberculosis of cervix
A18.83	Tuberculosis of digestive tract organs, not elsewhere classified

A18.5Ø	Tuberculosis of eye, unspecified
A18.1Ø	Tuberculosis of genitourinary system, unspecified
A18.84	Tuberculosis of heart
A15.4	Tuberculosis of intrathoracic lymph nodes
A18.11	Tuberculosis of kidney and ureter
A15.5	Tuberculosis of larynx, trachea and bronchus
A15.Ø	Tuberculosis of lung
A17.9	Tuberculosis of nervous system, unspecified
A18.Ø3	Tuberculosis of other bones
A18.82	Tuberculosis of other endocrine glands
A18.18	Tuberculosis of other female genital organs
A18.15	Tuberculosis of other male genital organs
A18.89	Tuberculosis of other sites
A18.13	Tuberculosis of other urinary organs
A18.14	Tuberculosis of prostate
A18.4	Tuberculosis of skin and subcutaneous tissue
A18.Ø1	Tuberculosis of spine
A18.85	Tuberculosis of spleen
A18.81	Tuberculosis of thyroid gland
A18.Ø2	Tuberculous arthritis of other joints
A18.53	Tuberculous chorioretinitis
A18.32	Tuberculous enteritis
A18.51	Tuberculous episcleritis
A18.17	Tuberculous female pelvic inflammatory disease
A18.54	Tuberculous iridocyclitis
A18.52	Tuberculous keratitis
A18.2	Tuberculous peripheral lymphadenopathy
A15.6	Tuberculous pleurisy
Q85.1	Tuberous sclerosis
N12	Tubulo-interstitial nephritis, not specified as acute or chronic
A21.9	Tularemia, unspecified
E1Ø.52	Type 1 diabetes mellitus with diabetic peripheral angiopathy with gangrene
S32.14XA	Type 1 fracture of sacrum, initial encounter for closed fracture
S32.14XK	Type 1 fracture of sacrum, subsequent encounter for fracture with nonunion
E11.52	Type 2 diabetes mellitus with diabetic peripheral angiopathy with gangrene
S32.15XA	Type 2 fracture of sacrum, initial encounter for closed fracture
S32.15XK	Type 2 fracture of sacrum, subsequent encounter for fracture with nonunion
S32.16XA	Type 3 fracture of sacrum, initial encounter for closed fracture
S32.16XK	Type 3 fracture of sacrum, subsequent encounter for fracture with nonunion
S32.17XA	Type 4 fracture of sacrum, initial encounter for closed fracture
S32.17XK	Type 4 fracture of sacrum, subsequent encounter for fracture with nonunion
SØ2.11BA	Type I occipital condyle fracture, left side, initial encounter for closed fracture
SØ2.11BK	Type I occipital condyle fracture, left side, subsequent encounter for fracture with nonunion
SØ2.11AA	Type I occipital condyle fracture, right side, initial encounter for closed fracture
SØ2.11AK	Type I occipital condyle fracture, right side, subsequent encounter for fracture with nonunion
SØ2.11ØA	Type I occipital condyle fracture, unspecified side, initial encounter for closed fracture
SØ2.11ØK	Type I occipital condyle fracture, unspecified side, subsequent encounter for fracture with nonunion
SØ2.11DA	Type II occipital condyle fracture, left side, initial encounter for closed fracture
SØ2.11DK	Type II occipital condyle fracture, left side, subsequent encounter for fracture with nonunion
SØ2.11CA	Type II occipital condyle fracture, right side, initial encounter for closed fracture
SØ2.11CK	Type II occipital condyle fracture, right side, subsequent encounter for fracture with nonunion
SØ2.111A	Type II occipital condyle fracture, unspecified side, initial encounter for closed fracture
SØ2.111K	Type II occipital condyle fracture, unspecified side, subsequent encounter for fracture with nonunion
SØ2.11FA	Type III occipital condyle fracture, left side, initial encounter for closed fracture
SØ2.11FK	Type III occipital condyle fracture, left side, subsequent encounter for fracture with nonunion
SØ2.11EA	Type III occipital condyle fracture, right side, initial encounter for closed fracture
SØ2.11EK	Type III occipital condyle fracture, right side, subsequent encounter for fracture with nonunion
SØ2.112A	Type III occipital condyle fracture, unspecified side, initial encounter for closed fracture
SØ2.112K	Type III occipital condyle fracture, unspecified side, subsequent encounter for fracture with nonunion
S12.44XA	Type III traumatic spondylolisthesis of fifth cervical vertebra, initial encounter for closed fracture
S12.44XK	Type III traumatic spondylolisthesis of fifth cervical vertebra, subsequent encounter for fracture with nonunion
S12.34XA	Type III traumatic spondylolisthesis of fourth cervical vertebra, initial encounter for closed fracture
S12.34XK	Type III traumatic spondylolisthesis of fourth cervical vertebra, subsequent encounter for fracture with nonunion
S12.14XA	Type III traumatic spondylolisthesis of second cervical vertebra, initial encounter for closed fracture
S12.14XK	Type III traumatic spondylolisthesis of second cervical vertebra, subsequent encounter for fracture with nonunion
S12.64XA	Type III traumatic spondylolisthesis of seventh cervical vertebra, initial encounter for closed fracture
S12.64XK	Type III traumatic spondylolisthesis of seventh cervical vertebra, subsequent encounter for fracture with nonunion
S12.54XA	Type III traumatic spondylolisthesis of sixth cervical vertebra, initial encounter for closed fracture
S12.54XK	Type III traumatic spondylolisthesis of sixth cervical vertebra, subsequent encounter for fracture with nonunion
S12.24XA	Type III traumatic spondylolisthesis of third cervical vertebra, initial encounter for closed fracture
S12.24XK	Type III traumatic spondylolisthesis of third cervical vertebra, subsequent encounter for fracture with nonunion
AØ1.Ø4	Typhoid arthritis
AØ1.Ø2	Typhoid fever with heart involvement
AØ1.Ø9	Typhoid fever with other complications
AØ1.ØØ	Typhoid fever, unspecified
AØ1.Ø1	Typhoid meningitis
AØ1.Ø5	Typhoid osteomyelitis
AØ1.Ø3	Typhoid pneumonia
A75.3	Typhus fever due to Rickettsia tsutsugamushi
A75.2	Typhus fever due to Rickettsia typhi
A75.9	Typhus fever, unspecified
I48.3	Typical atrial flutter
E7Ø.32Ø	Tyrosinase negative oculocutaneous albinism
E7Ø.321	Tyrosinase positive oculocutaneous albinism
E7Ø.21	Tyrosinemia
K62.6	Ulcer of anus and rectum
K22.1Ø	Ulcer of esophagus without bleeding
K63.3	Ulcer of intestine
K51.Ø14	Ulcerative (chronic) pancolitis with abscess
K51.Ø13	Ulcerative (chronic) pancolitis with fistula
K51.Ø12	Ulcerative (chronic) pancolitis with intestinal obstruction
K51.Ø18	Ulcerative (chronic) pancolitis with other complication
K51.Ø11	Ulcerative (chronic) pancolitis with rectal bleeding
K51.Ø19	Ulcerative (chronic) pancolitis with unspecified complications
K51.ØØ	Ulcerative (chronic) pancolitis without complications
K51.214	Ulcerative (chronic) proctitis with abscess
K51.213	Ulcerative (chronic) proctitis with fistula
K51.212	Ulcerative (chronic) proctitis with intestinal obstruction
K51.218	Ulcerative (chronic) proctitis with other complication
K51.211	Ulcerative (chronic) proctitis with rectal bleeding
K51.219	Ulcerative (chronic) proctitis with unspecified complications
K51.2Ø	Ulcerative (chronic) proctitis without complications
K51.314	Ulcerative (chronic) rectosigmoiditis with abscess
K51.313	Ulcerative (chronic) rectosigmoiditis with fistula
K51.312	Ulcerative (chronic) rectosigmoiditis with intestinal obstruction
K51.318	Ulcerative (chronic) rectosigmoiditis with other complication
K51.311	Ulcerative (chronic) rectosigmoiditis with rectal bleeding
K51.319	Ulcerative (chronic) rectosigmoiditis with unspecified complications
K51.3Ø	Ulcerative (chronic) rectosigmoiditis without complications
K51.914	Ulcerative colitis, unspecified with abscess
K51.913	Ulcerative colitis, unspecified with fistula
K51.912	Ulcerative colitis, unspecified with intestinal obstruction
K51.918	Ulcerative colitis, unspecified with other complication
K51.911	Ulcerative colitis, unspecified with rectal bleeding
K51.919	Ulcerative colitis, unspecified with unspecified complications
K51.9Ø	Ulcerative colitis, unspecified, without complications
A21.Ø	Ulceroglandular tularemia
K42.Ø	Umbilical hernia with obstruction, without gangrene
C96.6	Unifocal Langerhans-cell histiocytosis
K41.3Ø	Unilateral femoral hernia, with obstruction, without gangrene, not specified as recurrent
K41.31	Unilateral femoral hernia, with obstruction, without gangrene, recurrent
K4Ø.3Ø	Unilateral inguinal hernia, with obstruction, without gangrene, not specified as recurrent
K4Ø.31	Unilateral inguinal hernia, with obstruction, without gangrene, recurrent
K46.Ø	Unspecified abdominal hernia with obstruction, without gangrene
H2Ø.ØØ	Unspecified acute and subacute iridocyclitis
K35.8Ø	Unspecified acute appendicitis
T81.6ØXA	Unspecified acute reaction to foreign substance accidentally left during a procedure, initial encounter
E27.4Ø	Unspecified adrenocortical insufficiency
T74.91XA	Unspecified adult maltreatment, confirmed, initial encounter
T76.91XA	Unspecified adult maltreatment, suspected, initial encounter
A94	Unspecified arthropod-borne viral fever
J45.9Ø1	Unspecified asthma with (acute) exacerbation
J45.9Ø2	Unspecified asthma with status asthmaticus
P28.1Ø	Unspecified atelectasis of newborn
I48.92	Unspecified atrial flutter
C85.19	Unspecified B-cell lymphoma, extranodal and solid organ sites
C85.13	Unspecified B-cell lymphoma, intra-abdominal lymph nodes
C85.16	Unspecified B-cell lymphoma, intrapelvic lymph nodes
C85.12	Unspecified B-cell lymphoma, intrathoracic lymph nodes
C85.14	Unspecified B-cell lymphoma, lymph nodes of axilla and upper limb
C85.11	Unspecified B-cell lymphoma, lymph nodes of head, face, and neck
C85.15	Unspecified B-cell lymphoma, lymph nodes of inguinal region and lower limb
C85.18	Unspecified B-cell lymphoma, lymph nodes of multiple sites
C85.17	Unspecified B-cell lymphoma, spleen
C85.1Ø	Unspecified B-cell lymphoma, unspecified site
T74.92XA	Unspecified child maltreatment, confirmed, initial encounter
T76.92XA	Unspecified child maltreatment, suspected, initial encounter

H30.93	Unspecified chorioretinal inflammation, bilateral
H30.92	Unspecified chorioretinal inflammation, left eye
H30.91	Unspecified chorioretinal inflammation, right eye
H30.90	Unspecified chorioretinal inflammation, unspecified eye
H31.403	Unspecified choroidal detachment, bilateral
H31.402	Unspecified choroidal detachment, left eye
H31.401	Unspecified choroidal detachment, right eye
H31.409	Unspecified choroidal detachment, unspecified eye
I50.40	Unspecified combined systolic (congestive) and diastolic (congestive) heart failure
O08.9	Unspecified complication following an ectopic and molar pregnancy
O03.80	Unspecified complication following complete or unspecified spontaneous abortion
O03.30	Unspecified complication following incomplete spontaneous abortion
T86.839	Unspecified complication of bone graft
T86.00	Unspecified complication of bone marrow transplant
T82.9XXA	Unspecified complication of cardiac and vascular prosthetic device, implant and graft, initial encounter
T86.849	Unspecified complication of corneal transplant
T81.506A	Unspecified complication of foreign body accidentally left in body following aspiration, puncture or other catheterization, initial encounter
T81.504A	Unspecified complication of foreign body accidentally left in body following endoscopic examination, initial encounter
T81.505A	Unspecified complication of foreign body accidentally left in body following heart catheterization, initial encounter
T81.501A	Unspecified complication of foreign body accidentally left in body following infusion or transfusion, initial encounter
T81.503A	Unspecified complication of foreign body accidentally left in body following injection or immunization, initial encounter
T81.502A	Unspecified complication of foreign body accidentally left in body following kidney dialysis, initial encounter
T81.508A	Unspecified complication of foreign body accidentally left in body following other procedure, initial encounter
T81.507A	Unspecified complication of foreign body accidentally left in body following removal of catheter or packing, initial encounter
T81.500A	Unspecified complication of foreign body accidentally left in body following surgical operation, initial encounter
T81.509A	Unspecified complication of foreign body accidentally left in body following unspecified procedure, initial encounter
T83.9XXA	Unspecified complication of genitourinary prosthetic device, implant and graft, initial encounter
T86.20	Unspecified complication of heart transplant
T86.30	Unspecified complication of heart-lung transplant
T84.9XXA	Unspecified complication of internal orthopedic prosthetic device, implant and graft, initial encounter
T86.859	Unspecified complication of intestine transplant
T86.10	Unspecified complication of kidney transplant
T86.40	Unspecified complication of liver transplant
T86.819	Unspecified complication of lung transplant
T86.899	Unspecified complication of other transplanted tissue
T86.829	Unspecified complication of skin graft (allograft) (autograft)
T86.90	Unspecified complication of unspecified transplanted organ and tissue
S36.029A	Unspecified contusion of spleen, initial encounter
G95.20	Unspecified cord compression
F03.91	Unspecified dementia with behavioral disturbance
O24.911	Unspecified diabetes mellitus in pregnancy, first trimester
O24.912	Unspecified diabetes mellitus in pregnancy, second trimester
O24.913	Unspecified diabetes mellitus in pregnancy, third trimester
O24.919	Unspecified diabetes mellitus in pregnancy, unspecified trimester
O24.93	Unspecified diabetes mellitus in the puerperium
I50.30	Unspecified diastolic (congestive) heart failure
S73.005A	Unspecified dislocation of left hip, initial encounter
S43.205A	Unspecified dislocation of left sternoclavicular joint, initial encounter
S73.004A	Unspecified dislocation of right hip, initial encounter
S43.204A	Unspecified dislocation of right sternoclavicular joint, initial encounter
S73.006A	Unspecified dislocation of unspecified hip, initial encounter
S43.206A	Unspecified dislocation of unspecified sternoclavicular joint, initial encounter
S12.400A	Unspecified displaced fracture of fifth cervical vertebra, initial encounter for closed fracture
S12.400K	Unspecified displaced fracture of fifth cervical vertebra, subsequent encounter for fracture with nonunion
S12.000A	Unspecified displaced fracture of first cervical vertebra, initial encounter for closed fracture
S12.000K	Unspecified displaced fracture of first cervical vertebra, subsequent encounter for fracture with nonunion
S12.300A	Unspecified displaced fracture of fourth cervical vertebra, initial encounter for closed fracture
S12.300K	Unspecified displaced fracture of fourth cervical vertebra, subsequent encounter for fracture with nonunion
S12.100A	Unspecified displaced fracture of second cervical vertebra, initial encounter for closed fracture
S12.100K	Unspecified displaced fracture of second cervical vertebra, subsequent encounter for fracture with nonunion
S12.600A	Unspecified displaced fracture of seventh cervical vertebra, initial encounter for closed fracture
S12.600K	Unspecified displaced fracture of seventh cervical vertebra, subsequent encounter for fracture with nonunion
S12.500A	Unspecified displaced fracture of sixth cervical vertebra, initial encounter for closed fracture
S12.500K	Unspecified displaced fracture of sixth cervical vertebra, subsequent encounter for fracture with nonunion
S42.212A	Unspecified displaced fracture of surgical neck of left humerus, initial encounter for closed fracture
S42.212P	Unspecified displaced fracture of surgical neck of left humerus, subsequent encounter for fracture with malunion
S42.212K	Unspecified displaced fracture of surgical neck of left humerus, subsequent encounter for fracture with nonunion
S42.211A	Unspecified displaced fracture of surgical neck of right humerus, initial encounter for closed fracture
S42.211P	Unspecified displaced fracture of surgical neck of right humerus, subsequent encounter for fracture with malunion
S42.211K	Unspecified displaced fracture of surgical neck of right humerus, subsequent encounter for fracture with nonunion
S42.213A	Unspecified displaced fracture of surgical neck of unspecified humerus, initial encounter for closed fracture
S42.213P	Unspecified displaced fracture of surgical neck of unspecified humerus, subsequent encounter for fracture with malunion
S42.213K	Unspecified displaced fracture of surgical neck of unspecified humerus, subsequent encounter for fracture with nonunion
S12.200A	Unspecified displaced fracture of third cervical vertebra, initial encounter for closed fracture
S12.200K	Unspecified displaced fracture of third cervical vertebra, subsequent encounter for fracture with nonunion
H30.103	Unspecified disseminated chorioretinal inflammation, bilateral
H30.102	Unspecified disseminated chorioretinal inflammation, left eye
H30.101	Unspecified disseminated chorioretinal inflammation, right eye
H30.109	Unspecified disseminated chorioretinal inflammation, unspecified eye
O00.91	Unspecified ectopic pregnancy with intrauterine pregnancy
O00.90	Unspecified ectopic pregnancy without intrauterine pregnancy
P83.30	Unspecified edema specific to newborn
T75.1XXA	Unspecified effects of drowning and nonfatal submersion, initial encounter
S06.305A	Unspecified focal traumatic brain injury with loss of consciousness greater than 24 hours with return to pre-existing conscious level, initial encounter
S06.303A	Unspecified focal traumatic brain injury with loss of consciousness of 1 hour to 5 hours 59 minutes, initial encounter
S06.301A	Unspecified focal traumatic brain injury with loss of consciousness of 30 minutes or less, initial encounter
S06.302A	Unspecified focal traumatic brain injury with loss of consciousness of 31 minutes to 59 minutes, initial encounter
S06.304A	Unspecified focal traumatic brain injury with loss of consciousness of 6 hours to 24 hours, initial encounter
S06.309A	Unspecified focal traumatic brain injury with loss of consciousness of unspecified duration, initial encounter
T17.500A	Unspecified foreign body in bronchus causing asphyxiation, initial encounter
T17.508A	Unspecified foreign body in bronchus causing other injury, initial encounter
T17.800A	Unspecified foreign body in other parts of respiratory tract causing asphyxiation, initial encounter
T17.808A	Unspecified foreign body in other parts of respiratory tract causing other injury, initial encounter
T17.400A	Unspecified foreign body in trachea causing asphyxiation, initial encounter
T17.408A	Unspecified foreign body in trachea causing other injury, initial encounter
S02.92XA	Unspecified fracture of facial bones, initial encounter for closed fracture
S02.92XB	Unspecified fracture of facial bones, initial encounter for open fracture
S02.92XK	Unspecified fracture of facial bones, subsequent encounter for fracture with nonunion
S32.059A	Unspecified fracture of fifth lumbar vertebra, initial encounter for closed fracture
S32.059K	Unspecified fracture of fifth lumbar vertebra, subsequent encounter for fracture with nonunion
S62.307B	Unspecified fracture of fifth metacarpal bone, left hand, initial encounter for open fracture
S62.307P	Unspecified fracture of fifth metacarpal bone, left hand, subsequent encounter for fracture with malunion
S62.307K	Unspecified fracture of fifth metacarpal bone, left hand, subsequent encounter for fracture with nonunion
S62.306B	Unspecified fracture of fifth metacarpal bone, right hand, initial encounter for open fracture
S62.306P	Unspecified fracture of fifth metacarpal bone, right hand, subsequent encounter for fracture with malunion
S62.306K	Unspecified fracture of fifth metacarpal bone, right hand, subsequent encounter for fracture with nonunion
S32.019A	Unspecified fracture of first lumbar vertebra, initial encounter for closed fracture
S32.019K	Unspecified fracture of first lumbar vertebra, subsequent encounter for fracture with nonunion
S62.202B	Unspecified fracture of first metacarpal bone, left hand, initial encounter for open fracture
S62.202P	Unspecified fracture of first metacarpal bone, left hand, subsequent encounter for fracture with malunion
S62.202K	Unspecified fracture of first metacarpal bone, left hand, subsequent encounter for fracture with nonunion
S62.201B	Unspecified fracture of first metacarpal bone, right hand, initial encounter for open fracture
S62.201P	Unspecified fracture of first metacarpal bone, right hand, subsequent encounter for fracture with malunion
S62.201K	Unspecified fracture of first metacarpal bone, right hand, subsequent encounter for fracture with nonunion
S62.209B	Unspecified fracture of first metacarpal bone, unspecified hand, initial encounter for open fracture

S62.209P Unspecified fracture of first metacarpal bone, unspecified hand, subsequent encounter for fracture with malunion

S62.209K Unspecified fracture of first metacarpal bone, unspecified hand, subsequent encounter for fracture with nonunion

S22.019A Unspecified fracture of first thoracic vertebra, initial encounter for closed fracture

S22.019K Unspecified fracture of first thoracic vertebra, subsequent encounter for fracture with nonunion

S32.049A Unspecified fracture of fourth lumbar vertebra, initial encounter for closed fracture

S32.049K Unspecified fracture of fourth lumbar vertebra, subsequent encounter for fracture with nonunion

S62.305B Unspecified fracture of fourth metacarpal bone, left hand, initial encounter for open fracture

S62.305P Unspecified fracture of fourth metacarpal bone, left hand, subsequent encounter for fracture with malunion

S62.305K Unspecified fracture of fourth metacarpal bone, left hand, subsequent encounter for fracture with nonunion

S62.304B Unspecified fracture of fourth metacarpal bone, right hand, initial encounter for open fracture

S62.304P Unspecified fracture of fourth metacarpal bone, right hand, subsequent encounter for fracture with malunion

S62.304K Unspecified fracture of fourth metacarpal bone, right hand, subsequent encounter for fracture with nonunion

S22.049A Unspecified fracture of fourth thoracic vertebra, initial encounter for closed fracture

S22.049K Unspecified fracture of fourth thoracic vertebra, subsequent encounter for fracture with nonunion

S72.052P Unspecified fracture of head of left femur, subsequent encounter for closed fracture with malunion

S72.052K Unspecified fracture of head of left femur, subsequent encounter for closed fracture with nonunion

S72.052Q Unspecified fracture of head of left femur, subsequent encounter for open fracture type I or II with malunion

S72.052M Unspecified fracture of head of left femur, subsequent encounter for open fracture type I or II with nonunion

S72.052R Unspecified fracture of head of left femur, subsequent encounter for open fracture type IIIA, IIIB, or IIIC with malunion

S72.052N Unspecified fracture of head of left femur, subsequent encounter for open fracture type IIIA, IIIB, or IIIC with nonunion

S72.051P Unspecified fracture of head of right femur, subsequent encounter for closed fracture with malunion

S72.051K Unspecified fracture of head of right femur, subsequent encounter for closed fracture with nonunion

S72.051Q Unspecified fracture of head of right femur, subsequent encounter for open fracture type I or II with malunion

S72.051M Unspecified fracture of head of right femur, subsequent encounter for open fracture type I or II with nonunion

S72.051R Unspecified fracture of head of right femur, subsequent encounter for open fracture type IIIA, IIIB, or IIIC with malunion

S72.051N Unspecified fracture of head of right femur, subsequent encounter for open fracture type IIIA, IIIB, or IIIC with nonunion

S72.059P Unspecified fracture of head of unspecified femur, subsequent encounter for closed fracture with malunion

S72.059K Unspecified fracture of head of unspecified femur, subsequent encounter for closed fracture with nonunion

S72.059Q Unspecified fracture of head of unspecified femur, subsequent encounter for open fracture type I or II with malunion

S72.059M Unspecified fracture of head of unspecified femur, subsequent encounter for open fracture type I or II with nonunion

S72.059R Unspecified fracture of head of unspecified femur, subsequent encounter for open fracture type IIIA, IIIB, or IIIC with malunion

S72.059N Unspecified fracture of head of unspecified femur, subsequent encounter for open fracture type IIIA, IIIB, or IIIC with nonunion

S32.402K Unspecified fracture of left acetabulum, subsequent encounter for fracture with nonunion

S92.002B Unspecified fracture of left calcaneus, initial encounter for open fracture

S92.002P Unspecified fracture of left calcaneus, subsequent encounter for fracture with malunion

S92.002K Unspecified fracture of left calcaneus, subsequent encounter for fracture with nonunion

S72.92XP Unspecified fracture of left femur, subsequent encounter for closed fracture with malunion

S72.92XK Unspecified fracture of left femur, subsequent encounter for closed fracture with nonunion

S72.92XQ Unspecified fracture of left femur, subsequent encounter for open fracture type I or II with malunion

S72.92XM Unspecified fracture of left femur, subsequent encounter for open fracture type I or II with nonunion

S72.92XR Unspecified fracture of left femur, subsequent encounter for open fracture type IIIA, IIIB, or IIIC with malunion

S72.92XN Unspecified fracture of left femur, subsequent encounter for open fracture type IIIA, IIIB, or IIIC with nonunion

S92.902B Unspecified fracture of left foot, initial encounter for open fracture

S92.902P Unspecified fracture of left foot, subsequent encounter for fracture with malunion

S92.902K Unspecified fracture of left foot, subsequent encounter for fracture with nonunion

S52.92XA Unspecified fracture of left forearm, initial encounter for closed fracture

S52.92XP Unspecified fracture of left forearm, subsequent encounter for closed fracture with malunion

S52.92XK Unspecified fracture of left forearm, subsequent encounter for closed fracture with nonunion

S52.92XQ Unspecified fracture of left forearm, subsequent encounter for open fracture type I or II with malunion

S52.92XM Unspecified fracture of left forearm, subsequent encounter for open fracture type I or II with nonunion

S52.92XR Unspecified fracture of left forearm, subsequent encounter for open fracture type IIIA, IIIB, or IIIC with malunion

S52.92XN Unspecified fracture of left forearm, subsequent encounter for open fracture type IIIA, IIIB, or IIIC with nonunion

S32.302A Unspecified fracture of left ilium, initial encounter for closed fracture

S32.302K Unspecified fracture of left ilium, subsequent encounter for fracture with nonunion

S32.602A Unspecified fracture of left ischium, initial encounter for closed fracture

S32.602K Unspecified fracture of left ischium, subsequent encounter for fracture with nonunion

S82.92XB Unspecified fracture of left lower leg, initial encounter for open fracture type I or II

S82.92XC Unspecified fracture of left lower leg, initial encounter for open fracture type IIIA, IIIB, or IIIC

S82.92XP Unspecified fracture of left lower leg, subsequent encounter for closed fracture with malunion

S82.92XK Unspecified fracture of left lower leg, subsequent encounter for closed fracture with nonunion

S82.92XQ Unspecified fracture of left lower leg, subsequent encounter for open fracture type I or II with malunion

S82.92XM Unspecified fracture of left lower leg, subsequent encounter for open fracture type I or II with nonunion

S82.92XR Unspecified fracture of left lower leg, subsequent encounter for open fracture type IIIA, IIIB, or IIIC with malunion

S82.92XN Unspecified fracture of left lower leg, subsequent encounter for open fracture type IIIA, IIIB, or IIIC with nonunion

S82.002A Unspecified fracture of left patella, initial encounter for closed fracture

S82.002B Unspecified fracture of left patella, initial encounter for open fracture type I or II

S82.002C Unspecified fracture of left patella, initial encounter for open fracture type IIIA, IIIB, or IIIC

S82.002P Unspecified fracture of left patella, subsequent encounter for closed fracture with malunion

S82.002K Unspecified fracture of left patella, subsequent encounter for closed fracture with nonunion

S82.002Q Unspecified fracture of left patella, subsequent encounter for open fracture type I or II with malunion

S82.002M Unspecified fracture of left patella, subsequent encounter for open fracture type I or II with nonunion

S82.002R Unspecified fracture of left patella, subsequent encounter for open fracture type IIIA, IIIB, or IIIC with malunion

S82.002N Unspecified fracture of left patella, subsequent encounter for open fracture type IIIA, IIIB, or IIIC with nonunion

S32.502A Unspecified fracture of left pubis, initial encounter for closed fracture

S32.502K Unspecified fracture of left pubis, subsequent encounter for fracture with nonunion

S92.102B Unspecified fracture of left talus, initial encounter for open fracture

S92.102P Unspecified fracture of left talus, subsequent encounter for fracture with malunion

S92.102K Unspecified fracture of left talus, subsequent encounter for fracture with nonunion

S92.912P Unspecified fracture of left toe(s), subsequent encounter for fracture with malunion

S92.912K Unspecified fracture of left toe(s), subsequent encounter for fracture with nonunion

S62.92XB Unspecified fracture of left wrist and hand, initial encounter for open fracture

S62.92XP Unspecified fracture of left wrist and hand, subsequent encounter for fracture with malunion

S62.92XK Unspecified fracture of left wrist and hand, subsequent encounter for fracture with nonunion

S72.402A Unspecified fracture of lower end of left femur, initial encounter for closed fracture

S72.402P Unspecified fracture of lower end of left femur, subsequent encounter for closed fracture with malunion

S72.402K Unspecified fracture of lower end of left femur, subsequent encounter for closed fracture with nonunion

S72.402Q Unspecified fracture of lower end of left femur, subsequent encounter for open fracture type I or II with malunion

S72.402M Unspecified fracture of lower end of left femur, subsequent encounter for open fracture type I or II with nonunion

S72.402R Unspecified fracture of lower end of left femur, subsequent encounter for open fracture type IIIA, IIIB, or IIIC with malunion

S72.402N Unspecified fracture of lower end of left femur, subsequent encounter for open fracture type IIIA, IIIB, or IIIC with nonunion

S42.402A Unspecified fracture of lower end of left humerus, initial encounter for closed fracture

S42.402P Unspecified fracture of lower end of left humerus, subsequent encounter for fracture with malunion

S42.402K Unspecified fracture of lower end of left humerus, subsequent encounter for fracture with nonunion

S82.302B Unspecified fracture of lower end of left tibia, initial encounter for open fracture type I or II

S82.302C Unspecified fracture of lower end of left tibia, initial encounter for open fracture type IIIA, IIIB, or IIIC

S82.302P Unspecified fracture of lower end of left tibia, subsequent encounter for closed fracture with malunion

S82.302K Unspecified fracture of lower end of left tibia, subsequent encounter for closed fracture with nonunion

S82.302Q Unspecified fracture of lower end of left tibia, subsequent encounter for open fracture type I or II with malunion

S82.302M Unspecified fracture of lower end of left tibia, subsequent encounter for open fracture type I or II with nonunion

S82.302R Unspecified fracture of lower end of left tibia, subsequent encounter for open fracture type IIIA, IIIB, or IIIC with malunion

S82.302N Unspecified fracture of lower end of left tibia, subsequent encounter for open fracture type IIIA, IIIB, or IIIC with nonunion

S52.602A Unspecified fracture of lower end of left ulna, initial encounter for closed fracture

S52.602P Unspecified fracture of lower end of left ulna, subsequent encounter for closed fracture with malunion

S52.602K Unspecified fracture of lower end of left ulna, subsequent encounter for closed fracture with nonunion

S52.602Q Unspecified fracture of lower end of left ulna, subsequent encounter for open fracture type I or II with malunion

S52.602M Unspecified fracture of lower end of left ulna, subsequent encounter for open fracture type I or II with nonunion

S52.602R Unspecified fracture of lower end of left ulna, subsequent encounter for open fracture type IIIA, IIIB, or IIIC with malunion

S52.602N Unspecified fracture of lower end of left ulna, subsequent encounter for open fracture type IIIA, IIIB, or IIIC with nonunion

S72.401A Unspecified fracture of lower end of right femur, initial encounter for closed fracture

S72.401P Unspecified fracture of lower end of right femur, subsequent encounter for closed fracture with malunion

S72.401K Unspecified fracture of lower end of right femur, subsequent encounter for closed fracture with nonunion

S72.401Q Unspecified fracture of lower end of right femur, subsequent encounter for open fracture type I or II with malunion

S72.401M Unspecified fracture of lower end of right femur, subsequent encounter for open fracture type I or II with nonunion

S72.401R Unspecified fracture of lower end of right femur, subsequent encounter for open fracture type IIIA, IIIB, or IIIC with malunion

S72.401N Unspecified fracture of lower end of right femur, subsequent encounter for open fracture type IIIA, IIIB, or IIIC with nonunion

S42.401A Unspecified fracture of lower end of right humerus, initial encounter for closed fracture

S42.401P Unspecified fracture of lower end of right humerus, subsequent encounter for fracture with malunion

S42.401K Unspecified fracture of lower end of right humerus, subsequent encounter for fracture with nonunion

S82.301B Unspecified fracture of lower end of right tibia, initial encounter for open fracture type I or II

S82.301C Unspecified fracture of lower end of right tibia, initial encounter for open fracture type IIIA, IIIB, or IIIC

S82.301P Unspecified fracture of lower end of right tibia, subsequent encounter for closed fracture with malunion

S82.301K Unspecified fracture of lower end of right tibia, subsequent encounter for closed fracture with nonunion

S82.301Q Unspecified fracture of lower end of right tibia, subsequent encounter for open fracture type I or II with malunion

S82.301M Unspecified fracture of lower end of right tibia, subsequent encounter for open fracture type I or II with nonunion

S82.301R Unspecified fracture of lower end of right tibia, subsequent encounter for open fracture type IIIA, IIIB, or IIIC with malunion

S82.301N Unspecified fracture of lower end of right tibia, subsequent encounter for open fracture type IIIA, IIIB, or IIIC with nonunion

S52.601A Unspecified fracture of lower end of right ulna, initial encounter for closed fracture

S52.601P Unspecified fracture of lower end of right ulna, subsequent encounter for closed fracture with malunion

S52.601K Unspecified fracture of lower end of right ulna, subsequent encounter for closed fracture with nonunion

S52.601Q Unspecified fracture of lower end of right ulna, subsequent encounter for open fracture type I or II with malunion

S52.601M Unspecified fracture of lower end of right ulna, subsequent encounter for open fracture type I or II with nonunion

S52.601R Unspecified fracture of lower end of right ulna, subsequent encounter for open fracture type IIIA, IIIB, or IIIC with malunion

S52.601N Unspecified fracture of lower end of right ulna, subsequent encounter for open fracture type IIIA, IIIB, or IIIC with nonunion

S72.409A Unspecified fracture of lower end of unspecified femur, initial encounter for closed fracture

S72.409P Unspecified fracture of lower end of unspecified femur, subsequent encounter for closed fracture with malunion

S72.409K Unspecified fracture of lower end of unspecified femur, subsequent encounter for closed fracture with nonunion

S72.409Q Unspecified fracture of lower end of unspecified femur, subsequent encounter for open fracture type I or II with malunion

S72.409M Unspecified fracture of lower end of unspecified femur, subsequent encounter for open fracture type I or II with nonunion

S72.409R Unspecified fracture of lower end of unspecified femur, subsequent encounter for open fracture type IIIA, IIIB, or IIIC with malunion

S72.409N Unspecified fracture of lower end of unspecified femur, subsequent encounter for open fracture type IIIA, IIIB, or IIIC with nonunion

S42.409A Unspecified fracture of lower end of unspecified humerus, initial encounter for closed fracture

S42.409P Unspecified fracture of lower end of unspecified humerus, subsequent encounter for fracture with malunion

S42.409K Unspecified fracture of lower end of unspecified humerus, subsequent encounter for fracture with nonunion

S82.309B Unspecified fracture of lower end of unspecified tibia, initial encounter for open fracture type I or II

S82.309C Unspecified fracture of lower end of unspecified tibia, initial encounter for open fracture type IIIA, IIIB, or IIIC

S82.309P Unspecified fracture of lower end of unspecified tibia, subsequent encounter for closed fracture with malunion

S82.309K Unspecified fracture of lower end of unspecified tibia, subsequent encounter for closed fracture with nonunion

S82.309Q Unspecified fracture of lower end of unspecified tibia, subsequent encounter for open fracture type I or II with malunion

S82.309M Unspecified fracture of lower end of unspecified tibia, subsequent encounter for open fracture type I or II with nonunion

S82.309R Unspecified fracture of lower end of unspecified tibia, subsequent encounter for open fracture type IIIA, IIIB, or IIIC with malunion

S82.309N Unspecified fracture of lower end of unspecified tibia, subsequent encounter for open fracture type IIIA, IIIB, or IIIC with nonunion

S52.609A Unspecified fracture of lower end of unspecified ulna, initial encounter for closed fracture

S52.609P Unspecified fracture of lower end of unspecified ulna, subsequent encounter for closed fracture with malunion

S52.609K Unspecified fracture of lower end of unspecified ulna, subsequent encounter for closed fracture with nonunion

S52.609Q Unspecified fracture of lower end of unspecified ulna, subsequent encounter for open fracture type I or II with malunion

S52.609M Unspecified fracture of lower end of unspecified ulna, subsequent encounter for open fracture type I or II with nonunion

S52.609R Unspecified fracture of lower end of unspecified ulna, subsequent encounter for open fracture type IIIA, IIIB, or IIIC with malunion

S52.609N Unspecified fracture of lower end of unspecified ulna, subsequent encounter for open fracture type IIIA, IIIB, or IIIC with nonunion

S62.002B Unspecified fracture of navicular [scaphoid] bone of left wrist, initial encounter for open fracture

S62.002P Unspecified fracture of navicular [scaphoid] bone of left wrist, subsequent encounter for fracture with malunion

S62.002K Unspecified fracture of navicular [scaphoid] bone of left wrist, subsequent encounter for fracture with nonunion

S62.001B Unspecified fracture of navicular [scaphoid] bone of right wrist, initial encounter for open fracture

S62.001P Unspecified fracture of navicular [scaphoid] bone of right wrist, subsequent encounter for fracture with malunion

S62.001K Unspecified fracture of navicular [scaphoid] bone of right wrist, subsequent encounter for fracture with nonunion

S62.009B Unspecified fracture of navicular [scaphoid] bone of unspecified wrist, initial encounter for open fracture

S62.009P Unspecified fracture of navicular [scaphoid] bone of unspecified wrist, subsequent encounter for fracture with malunion

S62.009K Unspecified fracture of navicular [scaphoid] bone of unspecified wrist, subsequent encounter for fracture with malunion

S02.119A Unspecified fracture of occiput, initial encounter for closed fracture

S02.119K Unspecified fracture of occiput, subsequent encounter for fracture with nonunion

S62.308B Unspecified fracture of other metacarpal bone, initial encounter for open fracture

S62.308P Unspecified fracture of other metacarpal bone, subsequent encounter for fracture with malunion

S62.308K Unspecified fracture of other metacarpal bone, subsequent encounter for fracture with nonunion

S32.401K Unspecified fracture of right acetabulum, subsequent encounter for fracture with nonunion

S92.001B Unspecified fracture of right calcaneus, initial encounter for open fracture

S92.001P Unspecified fracture of right calcaneus, subsequent encounter for fracture with malunion

S92.001K Unspecified fracture of right calcaneus, subsequent encounter for fracture with nonunion

S72.91XP Unspecified fracture of right femur, subsequent encounter for closed fracture with malunion

S72.91XK Unspecified fracture of right femur, subsequent encounter for closed fracture with nonunion

S72.91XQ Unspecified fracture of right femur, subsequent encounter for open fracture type I or II with malunion

S72.91XM Unspecified fracture of right femur, subsequent encounter for open fracture type I or II with nonunion

S72.91XR Unspecified fracture of right femur, subsequent encounter for open fracture type IIIA, IIIB, or IIIC with malunion

S72.91XN Unspecified fracture of right femur, subsequent encounter for open fracture type IIIA, IIIB, or IIIC with nonunion

S92.901B Unspecified fracture of right foot, initial encounter for open fracture

S92.901P Unspecified fracture of right foot, subsequent encounter for fracture with malunion

S92.901K Unspecified fracture of right foot, subsequent encounter for fracture with nonunion

S52.91XA Unspecified fracture of right forearm, initial encounter for closed fracture

S52.91XP Unspecified fracture of right forearm, subsequent encounter for closed fracture with malunion

S52.91XK Unspecified fracture of right forearm, subsequent encounter for closed fracture with nonunion

S52.91XQ Unspecified fracture of right forearm, subsequent encounter for open fracture type I or II with malunion

S52.91XM Unspecified fracture of right forearm, subsequent encounter for open fracture type I or II with nonunion

S52.91XR Unspecified fracture of right forearm, subsequent encounter for open fracture type IIIA, IIIB, or IIIC with malunion

S52.91XN Unspecified fracture of right forearm, subsequent encounter for open fracture type IIIA, IIIB, or IIIC with nonunion

S32.301A Unspecified fracture of right ilium, initial encounter for closed fracture

S32.301K Unspecified fracture of right ilium, subsequent encounter for fracture with nonunion

S32.601A Unspecified fracture of right ischium, initial encounter for closed fracture

S32.601K Unspecified fracture of right ischium, subsequent encounter for fracture with nonunion

S82.91XB Unspecified fracture of right lower leg, initial encounter for open fracture type I or II

S82.91XC Unspecified fracture of right lower leg, initial encounter for open fracture type IIIA, IIIB, or IIIC

S82.91XP Unspecified fracture of right lower leg, subsequent encounter for closed fracture with malunion

S82.91XK Unspecified fracture of right lower leg, subsequent encounter for closed fracture with nonunion

S82.91XQ Unspecified fracture of right lower leg, subsequent encounter for open fracture type I or II with malunion

S82.91XM Unspecified fracture of right lower leg, subsequent encounter for open fracture type I or II with nonunion

S82.91XR Unspecified fracture of right lower leg, subsequent encounter for open fracture type IIIA, IIIB, or IIIC with malunion

S82.91XN Unspecified fracture of right lower leg, subsequent encounter for open fracture type IIIA, IIIB, or IIIC with nonunion

S82.001A Unspecified fracture of right patella, initial encounter for closed fracture

S82.001B Unspecified fracture of right patella, initial encounter for open fracture type I or II

S82.001C Unspecified fracture of right patella, initial encounter for open fracture type IIIA, IIIB, or IIIC

S82.001P Unspecified fracture of right patella, subsequent encounter for closed fracture with malunion

S82.001K Unspecified fracture of right patella, subsequent encounter for closed fracture with nonunion

S82.001Q Unspecified fracture of right patella, subsequent encounter for open fracture type I or II with malunion

S82.001M Unspecified fracture of right patella, subsequent encounter for open fracture type I or II with nonunion

S82.001R Unspecified fracture of right patella, subsequent encounter for open fracture type IIIA, IIIB, or IIIC with malunion

S82.001N Unspecified fracture of right patella, subsequent encounter for open fracture type IIIA, IIIB, or IIIC with nonunion

S32.501A Unspecified fracture of right pubis, initial encounter for closed fracture

S32.501K Unspecified fracture of right pubis, subsequent encounter for fracture with nonunion

S92.101B Unspecified fracture of right talus, initial encounter for open fracture

S92.101P Unspecified fracture of right talus, subsequent encounter for fracture with malunion

S92.101K Unspecified fracture of right talus, subsequent encounter for fracture with nonunion

S92.911P Unspecified fracture of right toe(s), subsequent encounter for fracture with malunion

S92.911K Unspecified fracture of right toe(s), subsequent encounter for fracture with nonunion

S62.91XB Unspecified fracture of right wrist and hand, initial encounter for open fracture

S62.91XP Unspecified fracture of right wrist and hand, subsequent encounter for fracture with malunion

S62.91XK Unspecified fracture of right wrist and hand, subsequent encounter for fracture with nonunion

S32.10XA Unspecified fracture of sacrum, initial encounter for closed fracture

S32.10XK Unspecified fracture of sacrum, subsequent encounter for fracture with nonunion

S32.029A Unspecified fracture of second lumbar vertebra, initial encounter for closed fracture

S32.029K Unspecified fracture of second lumbar vertebra, subsequent encounter for fracture with nonunion

S62.301B Unspecified fracture of second metacarpal bone, left hand, initial encounter for open fracture

S62.301P Unspecified fracture of second metacarpal bone, left hand, subsequent encounter for fracture with malunion

S62.301K Unspecified fracture of second metacarpal bone, left hand, subsequent encounter for fracture with nonunion

S62.300B Unspecified fracture of second metacarpal bone, right hand, initial encounter for open fracture

S62.300P Unspecified fracture of second metacarpal bone, right hand, subsequent encounter for fracture with malunion

S62.300K Unspecified fracture of second metacarpal bone, right hand, subsequent encounter for fracture with nonunion

S22.029A Unspecified fracture of second thoracic vertebra, initial encounter for closed fracture

S22.029K Unspecified fracture of second thoracic vertebra, subsequent encounter for fracture with nonunion

S42.302A Unspecified fracture of shaft of humerus, left arm, initial encounter for closed fracture

S42.302P Unspecified fracture of shaft of humerus, left arm, subsequent encounter for fracture with malunion

S42.302K Unspecified fracture of shaft of humerus, left arm, subsequent encounter for fracture with nonunion

S42.301A Unspecified fracture of shaft of humerus, right arm, initial encounter for closed fracture

S42.301P Unspecified fracture of shaft of humerus, right arm, subsequent encounter for fracture with malunion

S42.301K Unspecified fracture of shaft of humerus, right arm, subsequent encounter for fracture with nonunion

S42.309A Unspecified fracture of shaft of humerus, unspecified arm, initial encounter for closed fracture

S42.309P Unspecified fracture of shaft of humerus, unspecified arm, subsequent encounter for fracture with malunion

S42.309K Unspecified fracture of shaft of humerus, unspecified arm, subsequent encounter for fracture with nonunion

S72.302P Unspecified fracture of shaft of left femur, subsequent encounter for closed fracture with malunion

S72.302K Unspecified fracture of shaft of left femur, subsequent encounter for closed fracture with nonunion

S72.302Q Unspecified fracture of shaft of left femur, subsequent encounter for open fracture type I or II with malunion

S72.302M Unspecified fracture of shaft of left femur, subsequent encounter for open fracture type I or II with nonunion

S72.302R Unspecified fracture of shaft of left femur, subsequent encounter for open fracture type IIIA, IIIB, or IIIC with malunion

S72.302N Unspecified fracture of shaft of left femur, subsequent encounter for open fracture type IIIA, IIIB, or IIIC with nonunion

S82.402P Unspecified fracture of shaft of left fibula, subsequent encounter for closed fracture with malunion

S82.402K Unspecified fracture of shaft of left fibula, subsequent encounter for closed fracture with nonunion

S82.402Q Unspecified fracture of shaft of left fibula, subsequent encounter for open fracture type I or II with malunion

S82.402M Unspecified fracture of shaft of left fibula, subsequent encounter for open fracture type I or II with nonunion

S82.402R Unspecified fracture of shaft of left fibula, subsequent encounter for open fracture type IIIA, IIIB, or IIIC with malunion

S82.402N Unspecified fracture of shaft of left fibula, subsequent encounter for open fracture type IIIA, IIIB, or IIIC with nonunion

S52.302A Unspecified fracture of shaft of left radius, initial encounter for closed fracture

S52.302P Unspecified fracture of shaft of left radius, subsequent encounter for closed fracture with malunion

S52.302K Unspecified fracture of shaft of left radius, subsequent encounter for closed fracture with nonunion

S52.302Q Unspecified fracture of shaft of left radius, subsequent encounter for open fracture type I or II with malunion

S52.302M Unspecified fracture of shaft of left radius, subsequent encounter for open fracture type I or II with nonunion

S52.302R Unspecified fracture of shaft of left radius, subsequent encounter for open fracture type IIIA, IIIB, or IIIC with malunion

S52.302N Unspecified fracture of shaft of left radius, subsequent encounter for open fracture type IIIA, IIIB, or IIIC with nonunion

S82.202A Unspecified fracture of shaft of left tibia, initial encounter for closed fracture

S82.202P Unspecified fracture of shaft of left tibia, subsequent encounter for closed fracture with malunion

S82.202K Unspecified fracture of shaft of left tibia, subsequent encounter for closed fracture with nonunion

S82.202Q Unspecified fracture of shaft of left tibia, subsequent encounter for open fracture type I or II with malunion

S82.202M Unspecified fracture of shaft of left tibia, subsequent encounter for open fracture type I or II with nonunion

S82.202R Unspecified fracture of shaft of left tibia, subsequent encounter for open fracture type IIIA, IIIB, or IIIC with malunion

S82.202N Unspecified fracture of shaft of left tibia, subsequent encounter for open fracture type IIIA, IIIB, or IIIC with nonunion

S52.202A Unspecified fracture of shaft of left ulna, initial encounter for closed fracture

S52.202P Unspecified fracture of shaft of left ulna, subsequent encounter for closed fracture with malunion

S52.202K Unspecified fracture of shaft of left ulna, subsequent encounter for closed fracture with nonunion

S52.202Q Unspecified fracture of shaft of left ulna, subsequent encounter for open fracture type I or II with malunion

S52.202M Unspecified fracture of shaft of left ulna, subsequent encounter for open fracture type I or II with nonunion

S52.202R Unspecified fracture of shaft of left ulna, subsequent encounter for open fracture type IIIA, IIIB, or IIIC with malunion

S52.202N Unspecified fracture of shaft of left ulna, subsequent encounter for open fracture type IIIA, IIIB, or IIIC with nonunion

S72.301P Unspecified fracture of shaft of right femur, subsequent encounter for closed fracture with malunion

S72.301K Unspecified fracture of shaft of right femur, subsequent encounter for closed fracture with nonunion

S72.301Q Unspecified fracture of shaft of right femur, subsequent encounter for open fracture type I or II with malunion

S72.301M Unspecified fracture of shaft of right femur, subsequent encounter for open fracture type I or II with nonunion

S72.301R Unspecified fracture of shaft of right femur, subsequent encounter for open fracture type IIIA, IIIB, or IIIC with malunion

S72.301N Unspecified fracture of shaft of right femur, subsequent encounter for open fracture type IIIA, IIIB, or IIIC with nonunion

S82.401P Unspecified fracture of shaft of right fibula, subsequent encounter for closed fracture with malunion

S82.401K Unspecified fracture of shaft of right fibula, subsequent encounter for closed fracture with nonunion

S82.401Q Unspecified fracture of shaft of right fibula, subsequent encounter for open fracture type I or II with malunion

S82.401M Unspecified fracture of shaft of right fibula, subsequent encounter for open fracture type I or II with nonunion

S82.401R Unspecified fracture of shaft of right fibula, subsequent encounter for open fracture type IIIA, IIIB, or IIIC with malunion

S82.401N Unspecified fracture of shaft of right fibula, subsequent encounter for open fracture type IIIA, IIIB, or IIIC with nonunion

S52.301A Unspecified fracture of shaft of right radius, initial encounter for closed fracture

S52.301P Unspecified fracture of shaft of right radius, subsequent encounter for closed fracture with malunion

S52.301K Unspecified fracture of shaft of right radius, subsequent encounter for closed fracture with nonunion

S52.301Q Unspecified fracture of shaft of right radius, subsequent encounter for open fracture type I or II with malunion

S52.301M Unspecified fracture of shaft of right radius, subsequent encounter for open fracture type I or II with nonunion

S52.301R Unspecified fracture of shaft of right radius, subsequent encounter for open fracture type IIIA, IIIB, or IIIC with malunion

S52.301N Unspecified fracture of shaft of right radius, subsequent encounter for open fracture type IIIA, IIIB, or IIIC with nonunion

S82.201A Unspecified fracture of shaft of right tibia, initial encounter for closed fracture

S82.201P Unspecified fracture of shaft of right tibia, subsequent encounter for closed fracture with malunion

S82.201K Unspecified fracture of shaft of right tibia, subsequent encounter for closed fracture with nonunion

S82.201Q Unspecified fracture of shaft of right tibia, subsequent encounter for open fracture type I or II with malunion

S82.201M Unspecified fracture of shaft of right tibia, subsequent encounter for open fracture type I or II with nonunion

S82.201R Unspecified fracture of shaft of right tibia, subsequent encounter for open fracture type IIIA, IIIB, or IIIC with malunion

S82.201N Unspecified fracture of shaft of right tibia, subsequent encounter for open fracture type IIIA, IIIB, or IIIC with nonunion

S52.201A Unspecified fracture of shaft of right ulna, initial encounter for closed fracture

S52.201P Unspecified fracture of shaft of right ulna, subsequent encounter for closed fracture with malunion

S52.201K Unspecified fracture of shaft of right ulna, subsequent encounter for closed fracture with nonunion

S52.201Q Unspecified fracture of shaft of right ulna, subsequent encounter for open fracture type I or II with malunion

S52.201M Unspecified fracture of shaft of right ulna, subsequent encounter for open fracture type I or II with nonunion

S52.201R Unspecified fracture of shaft of right ulna, subsequent encounter for open fracture type IIIA, IIIB, or IIIC with malunion

S52.201N Unspecified fracture of shaft of right ulna, subsequent encounter for open fracture type IIIA, IIIB, or IIIC with nonunion

S72.309P Unspecified fracture of shaft of unspecified femur, subsequent encounter for closed fracture with malunion

S72.309K Unspecified fracture of shaft of unspecified femur, subsequent encounter for closed fracture with nonunion

S72.309Q Unspecified fracture of shaft of unspecified femur, subsequent encounter for open fracture type I or II with malunion

S72.309M Unspecified fracture of shaft of unspecified femur, subsequent encounter for open fracture type I or II with nonunion

S72.309R Unspecified fracture of shaft of unspecified femur, subsequent encounter for open fracture type IIIA, IIIB, or IIIC with malunion

S72.309N Unspecified fracture of shaft of unspecified femur, subsequent encounter for open fracture type IIIA, IIIB, or IIIC with nonunion

S82.409P Unspecified fracture of shaft of unspecified fibula, subsequent encounter for closed fracture with malunion

S82.409K Unspecified fracture of shaft of unspecified fibula, subsequent encounter for closed fracture with nonunion

S82.409Q Unspecified fracture of shaft of unspecified fibula, subsequent encounter for open fracture type I or II with malunion

S82.409M Unspecified fracture of shaft of unspecified fibula, subsequent encounter for open fracture type I or II with nonunion

S82.409R Unspecified fracture of shaft of unspecified fibula, subsequent encounter for open fracture type IIIA, IIIB, or IIIC with malunion

S82.409N Unspecified fracture of shaft of unspecified fibula, subsequent encounter for open fracture type IIIA, IIIB, or IIIC with nonunion

S52.309A Unspecified fracture of shaft of unspecified radius, initial encounter for closed fracture

S52.309P Unspecified fracture of shaft of unspecified radius, subsequent encounter for closed fracture with malunion

S52.309K Unspecified fracture of shaft of unspecified radius, subsequent encounter for closed fracture with nonunion

S52.309Q Unspecified fracture of shaft of unspecified radius, subsequent encounter for open fracture type I or II with malunion

S52.309M Unspecified fracture of shaft of unspecified radius, subsequent encounter for open fracture type I or II with nonunion

S52.309R Unspecified fracture of shaft of unspecified radius, subsequent encounter for open fracture type IIIA, IIIB, or IIIC with malunion

S52.309N Unspecified fracture of shaft of unspecified radius, subsequent encounter for open fracture type IIIA, IIIB, or IIIC with nonunion

S82.209A Unspecified fracture of shaft of unspecified tibia, initial encounter for closed fracture

S82.209P Unspecified fracture of shaft of unspecified tibia, subsequent encounter for closed fracture with malunion

S82.209K Unspecified fracture of shaft of unspecified tibia, subsequent encounter for closed fracture with nonunion

S82.209Q Unspecified fracture of shaft of unspecified tibia, subsequent encounter for open fracture type I or II with malunion

S82.209M Unspecified fracture of shaft of unspecified tibia, subsequent encounter for open fracture type I or II with nonunion

S82.209R Unspecified fracture of shaft of unspecified tibia, subsequent encounter for open fracture type IIIA, IIIB, or IIIC with malunion

S82.209N Unspecified fracture of shaft of unspecified tibia, subsequent encounter for open fracture type IIIA, IIIB, or IIIC with nonunion

S52.209A Unspecified fracture of shaft of unspecified ulna, initial encounter for closed fracture

S52.209P Unspecified fracture of shaft of unspecified ulna, subsequent encounter for closed fracture with malunion

S52.209K Unspecified fracture of shaft of unspecified ulna, subsequent encounter for closed fracture with nonunion

S52.209Q Unspecified fracture of shaft of unspecified ulna, subsequent encounter for open fracture type I or II with malunion

S52.209M Unspecified fracture of shaft of unspecified ulna, subsequent encounter for open fracture type I or II with nonunion

S52.209R Unspecified fracture of shaft of unspecified ulna, subsequent encounter for open fracture type IIIA, IIIB, or IIIC with malunion

S52.209N Unspecified fracture of shaft of unspecified ulna, subsequent encounter for open fracture type IIIA, IIIB, or IIIC with nonunion

S02.91XA Unspecified fracture of skull, initial encounter for closed fracture

S02.91XK Unspecified fracture of skull, subsequent encounter for fracture with nonunion

S22.20XA Unspecified fracture of sternum, initial encounter for closed fracture

S22.20XK Unspecified fracture of sternum, subsequent encounter for fracture with nonunion

S22.089A Unspecified fracture of T11-T12 vertebra, initial encounter for closed fracture

S22.089K Unspecified fracture of T11-T12 vertebra, subsequent encounter for fracture with nonunion

S22.059A Unspecified fracture of T5-T6 vertebra, initial encounter for closed fracture

S22.059K Unspecified fracture of T5-T6 vertebra, subsequent encounter for fracture with nonunion

S22.069A Unspecified fracture of T7-T8 vertebra, initial encounter for closed fracture

S22.069K Unspecified fracture of T7-T8 vertebra, subsequent encounter for fracture with nonunion

S22.079A Unspecified fracture of T9-T10 vertebra, initial encounter for closed fracture

S22.079K Unspecified fracture of T9-T10 vertebra, subsequent encounter for fracture with nonunion

S52.502A Unspecified fracture of the lower end of left radius, initial encounter for closed fracture

S52.502P Unspecified fracture of the lower end of left radius, subsequent encounter for closed fracture with malunion

S52.502K Unspecified fracture of the lower end of left radius, subsequent encounter for closed fracture with nonunion

S52.502Q Unspecified fracture of the lower end of left radius, subsequent encounter for open fracture type I or II with malunion

S52.502M Unspecified fracture of the lower end of left radius, subsequent encounter for open fracture type I or II with nonunion

S52.502R Unspecified fracture of the lower end of left radius, subsequent encounter for open fracture type IIIA, IIIB, or IIIC with malunion

S52.502N Unspecified fracture of the lower end of left radius, subsequent encounter for open fracture type IIIA, IIIB, or IIIC with nonunion

S52.501A Unspecified fracture of the lower end of right radius, initial encounter for closed fracture

S52.501P Unspecified fracture of the lower end of right radius, subsequent encounter for closed fracture with malunion

S52.501K Unspecified fracture of the lower end of right radius, subsequent encounter for closed fracture with nonunion

S52.501Q Unspecified fracture of the lower end of right radius, subsequent encounter for open fracture type I or II with malunion

S52.501M Unspecified fracture of the lower end of right radius, subsequent encounter for open fracture type I or II with nonunion

S52.501R Unspecified fracture of the lower end of right radius, subsequent encounter for open fracture type IIIA, IIIB, or IIIC with malunion

S52.501N Unspecified fracture of the lower end of right radius, subsequent encounter for open fracture type IIIA, IIIB, or IIIC with nonunion

S52.509A Unspecified fracture of the lower end of unspecified radius, initial encounter for closed fracture

S52.509P Unspecified fracture of the lower end of unspecified radius, subsequent encounter for closed fracture with malunion

S52.509K Unspecified fracture of the lower end of unspecified radius, subsequent encounter for closed fracture with nonunion

S52.509Q Unspecified fracture of the lower end of unspecified radius, subsequent encounter for open fracture type I or II with malunion

S52.509M Unspecified fracture of the lower end of unspecified radius, subsequent encounter for open fracture type I or II with nonunion

S52.509R Unspecified fracture of the lower end of unspecified radius, subsequent encounter for open fracture type IIIA, IIIB, or IIIC with malunion

S52.509N Unspecified fracture of the lower end of unspecified radius, subsequent encounter for open fracture type IIIA, IIIB, or IIIC with nonunion

S32.039A	Unspecified fracture of third lumbar vertebra, initial encounter for closed fracture
S32.039K	Unspecified fracture of third lumbar vertebra, subsequent encounter for fracture with nonunion
S62.303B	Unspecified fracture of third metacarpal bone, left hand, initial encounter for open fracture
S62.303P	Unspecified fracture of third metacarpal bone, left hand, subsequent encounter for fracture with malunion
S62.303K	Unspecified fracture of third metacarpal bone, left hand, subsequent encounter for fracture with nonunion
S62.302B	Unspecified fracture of third metacarpal bone, right hand, initial encounter for open fracture
S62.302P	Unspecified fracture of third metacarpal bone, right hand, subsequent encounter for fracture with malunion
S62.302K	Unspecified fracture of third metacarpal bone, right hand, subsequent encounter for fracture with nonunion
S22.039A	Unspecified fracture of third thoracic vertebra, initial encounter for closed fracture
S22.039K	Unspecified fracture of third thoracic vertebra, subsequent encounter for fracture with nonunion
S32.409K	Unspecified fracture of unspecified acetabulum, subsequent encounter for fracture with nonunion
S92.009B	Unspecified fracture of unspecified calcaneus, initial encounter for open fracture
S92.009P	Unspecified fracture of unspecified calcaneus, subsequent encounter for fracture with malunion
S92.009K	Unspecified fracture of unspecified calcaneus, subsequent encounter for fracture with nonunion
S72.90XP	Unspecified fracture of unspecified femur, subsequent encounter for closed fracture with malunion
S72.90XK	Unspecified fracture of unspecified femur, subsequent encounter for closed fracture with nonunion
S72.90XQ	Unspecified fracture of unspecified femur, subsequent encounter for open fracture type I or II with malunion
S72.90XM	Unspecified fracture of unspecified femur, subsequent encounter for open fracture type I or II with nonunion
S72.90XR	Unspecified fracture of unspecified femur, subsequent encounter for open fracture type IIIA, IIIB, or IIIC with malunion
S72.90XN	Unspecified fracture of unspecified femur, subsequent encounter for open fracture type IIIA, IIIB, or IIIC with nonunion
S92.909B	Unspecified fracture of unspecified foot, initial encounter for open fracture
S92.909P	Unspecified fracture of unspecified foot, subsequent encounter for fracture with malunion
S92.909K	Unspecified fracture of unspecified foot, subsequent encounter for fracture with nonunion
S52.90XA	Unspecified fracture of unspecified forearm, initial encounter for closed fracture
S52.90XP	Unspecified fracture of unspecified forearm, subsequent encounter for closed fracture with malunion
S52.90XK	Unspecified fracture of unspecified forearm, subsequent encounter for closed fracture with nonunion
S52.90XQ	Unspecified fracture of unspecified forearm, subsequent encounter for open fracture type I or II with malunion
S52.90XM	Unspecified fracture of unspecified forearm, subsequent encounter for open fracture type I or II with nonunion
S52.90XR	Unspecified fracture of unspecified forearm, subsequent encounter for open fracture type IIIA, IIIB, or IIIC with malunion
S52.90XN	Unspecified fracture of unspecified forearm, subsequent encounter for open fracture type IIIA, IIIB, or IIIC with nonunion
S32.309A	Unspecified fracture of unspecified ilium, initial encounter for closed fracture
S32.309K	Unspecified fracture of unspecified ilium, subsequent encounter for fracture with nonunion
S32.609A	Unspecified fracture of unspecified ischium, initial encounter for closed fracture
S32.609K	Unspecified fracture of unspecified ischium, subsequent encounter for fracture with nonunion
S82.90XB	Unspecified fracture of unspecified lower leg, initial encounter for open fracture type I or II
S82.90XC	Unspecified fracture of unspecified lower leg, initial encounter for open fracture type IIIA, IIIB, or IIIC
S82.90XP	Unspecified fracture of unspecified lower leg, subsequent encounter for closed fracture with malunion
S82.90XK	Unspecified fracture of unspecified lower leg, subsequent encounter for closed fracture with nonunion
S82.90XQ	Unspecified fracture of unspecified lower leg, subsequent encounter for open fracture type I or II with malunion
S82.90XM	Unspecified fracture of unspecified lower leg, subsequent encounter for open fracture type I or II with nonunion
S82.90XR	Unspecified fracture of unspecified lower leg, subsequent encounter for open fracture type IIIA, IIIB, or IIIC with malunion
S82.90XN	Unspecified fracture of unspecified lower leg, subsequent encounter for open fracture type IIIA, IIIB, or IIIC with nonunion
S32.009A	Unspecified fracture of unspecified lumbar vertebra, initial encounter for closed fracture
S32.009K	Unspecified fracture of unspecified lumbar vertebra, subsequent encounter for fracture with nonunion
S62.309B	Unspecified fracture of unspecified metacarpal bone, initial encounter for open fracture
S62.309P	Unspecified fracture of unspecified metacarpal bone, subsequent encounter for fracture with malunion
S62.309K	Unspecified fracture of unspecified metacarpal bone, subsequent encounter for fracture with nonunion
S82.009A	Unspecified fracture of unspecified patella, initial encounter for closed fracture
S82.009B	Unspecified fracture of unspecified patella, initial encounter for open fracture type I or II
S82.009C	Unspecified fracture of unspecified patella, initial encounter for open fracture type IIIA, IIIB, or IIIC
S82.009P	Unspecified fracture of unspecified patella, subsequent encounter for closed fracture with malunion
S82.009K	Unspecified fracture of unspecified patella, subsequent encounter for closed fracture with nonunion
S82.009Q	Unspecified fracture of unspecified patella, subsequent encounter for open fracture type I or II with malunion
S82.009M	Unspecified fracture of unspecified patella, subsequent encounter for open fracture type I or II with nonunion
S82.009R	Unspecified fracture of unspecified patella, subsequent encounter for open fracture type IIIA, IIIB, or IIIC with malunion
S82.009N	Unspecified fracture of unspecified patella, subsequent encounter for open fracture type IIIA, IIIB, or IIIC with nonunion
S32.509A	Unspecified fracture of unspecified pubis, initial encounter for closed fracture
S32.509K	Unspecified fracture of unspecified pubis, subsequent encounter for fracture with nonunion
S92.109B	Unspecified fracture of unspecified talus, initial encounter for open fracture
S92.109P	Unspecified fracture of unspecified talus, subsequent encounter for fracture with malunion
S92.109K	Unspecified fracture of unspecified talus, subsequent encounter for fracture with nonunion
S22.009A	Unspecified fracture of unspecified thoracic vertebra, initial encounter for closed fracture
S22.009K	Unspecified fracture of unspecified thoracic vertebra, subsequent encounter for fracture with nonunion
S92.919P	Unspecified fracture of unspecified toe(s), subsequent encounter for fracture with malunion
S92.919K	Unspecified fracture of unspecified toe(s), subsequent encounter for fracture with nonunion
S62.90XB	Unspecified fracture of unspecified wrist and hand, initial encounter for open fracture
S62.90XP	Unspecified fracture of unspecified wrist and hand, subsequent encounter for fracture with malunion
S62.90XK	Unspecified fracture of unspecified wrist and hand, subsequent encounter for fracture with nonunion
S42.202A	Unspecified fracture of upper end of left humerus, initial encounter for closed fracture
S42.202P	Unspecified fracture of upper end of left humerus, subsequent encounter for fracture with malunion
S42.202K	Unspecified fracture of upper end of left humerus, subsequent encounter for fracture with nonunion
S52.102P	Unspecified fracture of upper end of left radius, subsequent encounter for closed fracture with malunion
S52.102K	Unspecified fracture of upper end of left radius, subsequent encounter for closed fracture with nonunion
S52.102Q	Unspecified fracture of upper end of left radius, subsequent encounter for open fracture type I or II with malunion
S52.102M	Unspecified fracture of upper end of left radius, subsequent encounter for open fracture type I or II with nonunion
S52.102R	Unspecified fracture of upper end of left radius, subsequent encounter for open fracture type IIIA, IIIB, or IIIC with malunion
S52.102N	Unspecified fracture of upper end of left radius, subsequent encounter for open fracture type IIIA, IIIB, or IIIC with nonunion
S82.102A	Unspecified fracture of upper end of left tibia, initial encounter for closed fracture
S82.102P	Unspecified fracture of upper end of left tibia, subsequent encounter for closed fracture with malunion
S82.102K	Unspecified fracture of upper end of left tibia, subsequent encounter for closed fracture with nonunion
S82.102Q	Unspecified fracture of upper end of left tibia, subsequent encounter for open fracture type I or II with malunion
S82.102M	Unspecified fracture of upper end of left tibia, subsequent encounter for open fracture type I or II with nonunion
S82.102R	Unspecified fracture of upper end of left tibia, subsequent encounter for open fracture type IIIA, IIIB, or IIIC with malunion
S82.102N	Unspecified fracture of upper end of left tibia, subsequent encounter for open fracture type IIIA, IIIB, or IIIC with nonunion
S52.002P	Unspecified fracture of upper end of left ulna, subsequent encounter for closed fracture with malunion
S52.002K	Unspecified fracture of upper end of left ulna, subsequent encounter for closed fracture with nonunion
S52.002Q	Unspecified fracture of upper end of left ulna, subsequent encounter for open fracture type I or II with malunion
S52.002M	Unspecified fracture of upper end of left ulna, subsequent encounter for open fracture type I or II with nonunion
S52.002R	Unspecified fracture of upper end of left ulna, subsequent encounter for open fracture type IIIA, IIIB, or IIIC with malunion
S52.002N	Unspecified fracture of upper end of left ulna, subsequent encounter for open fracture type IIIA, IIIB, or IIIC with nonunion
S42.201A	Unspecified fracture of upper end of right humerus, initial encounter for closed fracture
S42.201P	Unspecified fracture of upper end of right humerus, subsequent encounter for fracture with malunion

S42.201K	Unspecified fracture of upper end of right humerus, subsequent encounter for fracture with nonunion
S52.101P	Unspecified fracture of upper end of right radius, subsequent encounter for closed fracture with malunion
S52.101K	Unspecified fracture of upper end of right radius, subsequent encounter for closed fracture with nonunion
S52.101Q	Unspecified fracture of upper end of right radius, subsequent encounter for open fracture type I or II with malunion
S52.101M	Unspecified fracture of upper end of right radius, subsequent encounter for open fracture type I or II with nonunion
S52.101R	Unspecified fracture of upper end of right radius, subsequent encounter for open fracture type IIIA, IIIB, or IIIC with malunion
S52.101N	Unspecified fracture of upper end of right radius, subsequent encounter for open fracture type IIIA, IIIB, or IIIC with nonunion
S82.101A	Unspecified fracture of upper end of right tibia, initial encounter for closed fracture
S82.101P	Unspecified fracture of upper end of right tibia, subsequent encounter for closed fracture with malunion
S82.101K	Unspecified fracture of upper end of right tibia, subsequent encounter for closed fracture with nonunion
S82.101Q	Unspecified fracture of upper end of right tibia, subsequent encounter for open fracture type I or II with malunion
S82.101M	Unspecified fracture of upper end of right tibia, subsequent encounter for open fracture type I or II with nonunion
S82.101R	Unspecified fracture of upper end of right tibia, subsequent encounter for open fracture type IIIA, IIIB, or IIIC with malunion
S82.101N	Unspecified fracture of upper end of right tibia, subsequent encounter for open fracture type IIIA, IIIB, or IIIC with nonunion
S52.001P	Unspecified fracture of upper end of right ulna, subsequent encounter for closed fracture with malunion
S52.001K	Unspecified fracture of upper end of right ulna, subsequent encounter for closed fracture with nonunion
S52.001Q	Unspecified fracture of upper end of right ulna, subsequent encounter for open fracture type I or II with malunion
S52.001M	Unspecified fracture of upper end of right ulna, subsequent encounter for open fracture type I or II with nonunion
S52.001R	Unspecified fracture of upper end of right ulna, subsequent encounter for open fracture type IIIA, IIIB, or IIIC with malunion
S52.001N	Unspecified fracture of upper end of right ulna, subsequent encounter for open fracture type IIIA, IIIB, or IIIC with nonunion
S42.209A	Unspecified fracture of upper end of unspecified humerus, initial encounter for closed fracture
S42.209P	Unspecified fracture of upper end of unspecified humerus, subsequent encounter for fracture with malunion
S42.209K	Unspecified fracture of upper end of unspecified humerus, subsequent encounter for fracture with nonunion
S52.109P	Unspecified fracture of upper end of unspecified radius, subsequent encounter for closed fracture with malunion
S52.109K	Unspecified fracture of upper end of unspecified radius, subsequent encounter for closed fracture with nonunion
S52.109Q	Unspecified fracture of upper end of unspecified radius, subsequent encounter for open fracture type I or II with malunion
S52.109M	Unspecified fracture of upper end of unspecified radius, subsequent encounter for open fracture type I or II with nonunion
S52.109R	Unspecified fracture of upper end of unspecified radius, subsequent encounter for open fracture type IIIA, IIIB, or IIIC with malunion
S52.109N	Unspecified fracture of upper end of unspecified radius, subsequent encounter for open fracture type IIIA, IIIB, or IIIC with nonunion
S82.109A	Unspecified fracture of upper end of unspecified tibia, initial encounter for closed fracture
S82.109P	Unspecified fracture of upper end of unspecified tibia, subsequent encounter for closed fracture with malunion
S82.109K	Unspecified fracture of upper end of unspecified tibia, subsequent encounter for closed fracture with nonunion
S82.109Q	Unspecified fracture of upper end of unspecified tibia, subsequent encounter for open fracture type I or II with malunion
S82.109M	Unspecified fracture of upper end of unspecified tibia, subsequent encounter for open fracture type I or II with nonunion
S82.109R	Unspecified fracture of upper end of unspecified tibia, subsequent encounter for open fracture type IIIA, IIIB, or IIIC with malunion
S82.109N	Unspecified fracture of upper end of unspecified tibia, subsequent encounter for open fracture type IIIA, IIIB, or IIIC with nonunion
S52.009P	Unspecified fracture of upper end of unspecified ulna, subsequent encounter for closed fracture with malunion
S52.009K	Unspecified fracture of upper end of unspecified ulna, subsequent encounter for closed fracture with nonunion
S52.009Q	Unspecified fracture of upper end of unspecified ulna, subsequent encounter for open fracture type I or II with malunion
S52.009M	Unspecified fracture of upper end of unspecified ulna, subsequent encounter for open fracture type I or II with nonunion
S52.009R	Unspecified fracture of upper end of unspecified ulna, subsequent encounter for open fracture type IIIA, IIIB, or IIIC with malunion
S52.009N	Unspecified fracture of upper end of unspecified ulna, subsequent encounter for open fracture type IIIA, IIIB, or IIIC with nonunion
E75.10	Unspecified gangliosidosis
O23.91	Unspecified genitourinary tract infection in pregnancy, first trimester
O23.92	Unspecified genitourinary tract infection in pregnancy, second trimester
O23.93	Unspecified genitourinary tract infection in pregnancy, third trimester
N13.30	Unspecified hydronephrosis
T80.219A	Unspecified infection due to central venous catheter, initial encounter
O23.41	Unspecified infection of urinary tract in pregnancy, first trimester
O23.42	Unspecified infection of urinary tract in pregnancy, second trimester
O23.43	Unspecified infection of urinary tract in pregnancy, third trimester
S37.819A	Unspecified injury of adrenal gland, initial encounter
S85.132A	Unspecified injury of anterior tibial artery, left leg, initial encounter
S85.131A	Unspecified injury of anterior tibial artery, right leg, initial encounter
S85.139A	Unspecified injury of anterior tibial artery, unspecified leg, initial encounter
S36.500A	Unspecified injury of ascending [right] colon, initial encounter
S45.202A	Unspecified injury of axillary or brachial vein, left side, initial encounter
S45.201A	Unspecified injury of axillary or brachial vein, right side, initial encounter
S45.209A	Unspecified injury of axillary or brachial vein, unspecified side, initial encounter
S37.20XA	Unspecified injury of bladder, initial encounter
S65.501A	Unspecified injury of blood vessel of left index finger, initial encounter
S65.507A	Unspecified injury of blood vessel of left little finger, initial encounter
S65.503A	Unspecified injury of blood vessel of left middle finger, initial encounter
S65.505A	Unspecified injury of blood vessel of left ring finger, initial encounter
S65.402A	Unspecified injury of blood vessel of left thumb, initial encounter
S65.508A	Unspecified injury of blood vessel of other finger, initial encounter
S65.500A	Unspecified injury of blood vessel of right index finger, initial encounter
S65.506A	Unspecified injury of blood vessel of right little finger, initial encounter
S65.502A	Unspecified injury of blood vessel of right middle finger, initial encounter
S65.504A	Unspecified injury of blood vessel of right ring finger, initial encounter
S65.401A	Unspecified injury of blood vessel of right thumb, initial encounter
S65.509A	Unspecified injury of blood vessel of unspecified finger, initial encounter
S65.409A	Unspecified injury of blood vessel of unspecified thumb, initial encounter
S36.201A	Unspecified injury of body of pancreas, initial encounter
S45.102A	Unspecified injury of brachial artery, left side, initial encounter
S45.101A	Unspecified injury of brachial artery, right side, initial encounter
S45.109A	Unspecified injury of brachial artery, unspecified side, initial encounter
S65.302A	Unspecified injury of deep palmar arch of left hand, initial encounter
S65.301A	Unspecified injury of deep palmar arch of right hand, initial encounter
S65.309A	Unspecified injury of deep palmar arch of unspecified hand, initial encounter
S36.502A	Unspecified injury of descending [left] colon, initial encounter
S27.809A	Unspecified injury of diaphragm, initial encounter
S95.002A	Unspecified injury of dorsal artery of left foot, initial encounter
S95.001A	Unspecified injury of dorsal artery of right foot, initial encounter
S95.009A	Unspecified injury of dorsal artery of unspecified foot, initial encounter
S95.202A	Unspecified injury of dorsal vein of left foot, initial encounter
S95.201A	Unspecified injury of dorsal vein of right foot, initial encounter
S95.209A	Unspecified injury of dorsal vein of unspecified foot, initial encounter
S36.400A	Unspecified injury of duodenum, initial encounter
S36.129A	Unspecified injury of gallbladder, initial encounter
S75.202A	Unspecified injury of greater saphenous vein at hip and thigh level, left leg, initial encounter
S75.201A	Unspecified injury of greater saphenous vein at hip and thigh level, right leg, initial encounter
S75.209A	Unspecified injury of greater saphenous vein at hip and thigh level, unspecified leg, initial encounter
S85.302A	Unspecified injury of greater saphenous vein at lower leg level, left leg, initial encounter
S85.301A	Unspecified injury of greater saphenous vein at lower leg level, right leg, initial encounter
S85.309A	Unspecified injury of greater saphenous vein at lower leg level, unspecified leg, initial encounter
S36.200A	Unspecified injury of head of pancreas, initial encounter
S26.00XA	Unspecified injury of heart with hemopericardium, initial encounter
S26.10XA	Unspecified injury of heart without hemopericardium, initial encounter
S26.90XA	Unspecified injury of heart, unspecified with or without hemopericardium, initial encounter
S25.502A	Unspecified injury of intercostal blood vessels, left side, initial encounter
S25.501A	Unspecified injury of intercostal blood vessels, right side, initial encounter
S25.509A	Unspecified injury of intercostal blood vessels, unspecified side, initial encounter
S15.002A	Unspecified injury of left carotid artery, initial encounter
S15.202A	Unspecified injury of left external jugular vein, initial encounter
S05.92XA	Unspecified injury of left eye and orbit, initial encounter
S15.302A	Unspecified injury of left internal jugular vein, initial encounter
S37.002A	Unspecified injury of left kidney, initial encounter
S09.302A	Unspecified injury of left middle and inner ear, initial encounter
S15.102A	Unspecified injury of left vertebral artery, initial encounter
S85.402A	Unspecified injury of lesser saphenous vein at lower leg level, left leg, initial encounter
S85.401A	Unspecified injury of lesser saphenous vein at lower leg level, right leg, initial encounter
S85.409A	Unspecified injury of lesser saphenous vein at lower leg level, unspecified leg, initial encounter
S36.119A	Unspecified injury of liver, initial encounter
S27.302A	Unspecified injury of lung, bilateral, initial encounter
S27.301A	Unspecified injury of lung, unilateral, initial encounter
S27.309A	Unspecified injury of lung, unspecified, initial encounter
S35.8X9A	Unspecified injury of other blood vessels at abdomen, lower back and pelvis level, initial encounter
S95.802A	Unspecified injury of other blood vessels at ankle and foot level, left leg, initial encounter
S95.801A	Unspecified injury of other blood vessels at ankle and foot level, right leg, initial encounter
S95.809A	Unspecified injury of other blood vessels at ankle and foot level, unspecified leg, initial encounter

S55.802A	Unspecified injury of other blood vessels at forearm level, left arm, initial encounter
S55.801A	Unspecified injury of other blood vessels at forearm level, right arm, initial encounter
S55.809A	Unspecified injury of other blood vessels at forearm level, unspecified arm, initial encounter
S75.802A	Unspecified injury of other blood vessels at hip and thigh level, left leg, initial encounter
S75.801A	Unspecified injury of other blood vessels at hip and thigh level, right leg, initial encounter
S75.809A	Unspecified injury of other blood vessels at hip and thigh level, unspecified leg, initial encounter
S85.802A	Unspecified injury of other blood vessels at lower leg level, left leg, initial encounter
S85.801A	Unspecified injury of other blood vessels at lower leg level, right leg, initial encounter
S85.809A	Unspecified injury of other blood vessels at lower leg level, unspecified leg, initial encounter
S65.802A	Unspecified injury of other blood vessels at wrist and hand level of left arm, initial encounter
S65.801A	Unspecified injury of other blood vessels at wrist and hand level of right arm, initial encounter
S65.809A	Unspecified injury of other blood vessels at wrist and hand level of unspecified arm, initial encounter
S25.802A	Unspecified injury of other blood vessels of thorax, left side, initial encounter
S25.801A	Unspecified injury of other blood vessels of thorax, right side, initial encounter
S25.809A	Unspecified injury of other blood vessels of thorax, unspecified side, initial encounter
S36.899A	Unspecified injury of other intra-abdominal organs, initial encounter
S36.508A	Unspecified injury of other part of colon, initial encounter
S36.408A	Unspecified injury of other part of small intestine, initial encounter
S45.802A	Unspecified injury of other specified blood vessels at shoulder and upper arm level, left arm, initial encounter
S45.801A	Unspecified injury of other specified blood vessels at shoulder and upper arm level, right arm, initial encounter
S45.809A	Unspecified injury of other specified blood vessels at shoulder and upper arm level, unspecified arm, initial encounter
S27.899A	Unspecified injury of other specified intrathoracic organs, initial encounter
S37.899A	Unspecified injury of other urinary and pelvic organ, initial encounter
S85.202A	Unspecified injury of peroneal artery, left leg, initial encounter
S85.201A	Unspecified injury of peroneal artery, right leg, initial encounter
S85.209A	Unspecified injury of peroneal artery, unspecified leg, initial encounter
S95.102A	Unspecified injury of plantar artery of left foot, initial encounter
S95.101A	Unspecified injury of plantar artery of right foot, initial encounter
S95.109A	Unspecified injury of plantar artery of unspecified foot, initial encounter
S27.60XA	Unspecified injury of pleura, initial encounter
S85.162A	Unspecified injury of posterior tibial artery, left leg, initial encounter
S85.161A	Unspecified injury of posterior tibial artery, right leg, initial encounter
S85.169A	Unspecified injury of posterior tibial artery, unspecified leg, initial encounter
S55.102A	Unspecified injury of radial artery at forearm level, left arm, initial encounter
S55.101A	Unspecified injury of radial artery at forearm level, right arm, initial encounter
S55.109A	Unspecified injury of radial artery at forearm level, unspecified arm, initial encounter
S65.102A	Unspecified injury of radial artery at wrist and hand level of left arm, initial encounter
S65.101A	Unspecified injury of radial artery at wrist and hand level of right arm, initial encounter
S65.109A	Unspecified injury of radial artery at wrist and hand level of unspecified arm, initial encounter
S36.60XA	Unspecified injury of rectum, initial encounter
S15.001A	Unspecified injury of right carotid artery, initial encounter
S15.201A	Unspecified injury of right external jugular vein, initial encounter
S05.91XA	Unspecified injury of right eye and orbit, initial encounter
S15.301A	Unspecified injury of right internal jugular vein, initial encounter
S37.001A	Unspecified injury of right kidney, initial encounter
S09.301A	Unspecified injury of right middle and inner ear, initial encounter
S15.101A	Unspecified injury of right vertebral artery, initial encounter
S36.503A	Unspecified injury of sigmoid colon, initial encounter
S36.00XA	Unspecified injury of spleen, initial encounter
S36.30XA	Unspecified injury of stomach, initial encounter
S65.202A	Unspecified injury of superficial palmar arch of left hand, initial encounter
S65.201A	Unspecified injury of superficial palmar arch of right hand, initial encounter
S65.209A	Unspecified injury of superficial palmar arch of unspecified hand, initial encounter
S45.302A	Unspecified injury of superficial vein at shoulder and upper arm level, left arm, initial encounter
S45.301A	Unspecified injury of superficial vein at shoulder and upper arm level, right arm, initial encounter
S45.309A	Unspecified injury of superficial vein at shoulder and upper arm level, unspecified arm, initial encounter
S36.202A	Unspecified injury of tail of pancreas, initial encounter
S27.50XA	Unspecified injury of thoracic trachea, initial encounter
S36.501A	Unspecified injury of transverse colon, initial encounter
S55.002A	Unspecified injury of ulnar artery at forearm level, left arm, initial encounter
S55.001A	Unspecified injury of ulnar artery at forearm level, right arm, initial encounter
S55.009A	Unspecified injury of ulnar artery at forearm level, unspecified arm, initial encounter
S65.002A	Unspecified injury of ulnar artery at wrist and hand level of left arm, initial encounter
S65.001A	Unspecified injury of ulnar artery at wrist and hand level of right arm, initial encounter
S65.009A	Unspecified injury of ulnar artery at wrist and hand level of unspecified arm, initial encounter
S35.90XA	Unspecified injury of unspecified blood vessel at abdomen, lower back and pelvis level, initial encounter
S95.902A	Unspecified injury of unspecified blood vessel at ankle and foot level, left leg, initial encounter
S95.901A	Unspecified injury of unspecified blood vessel at ankle and foot level, right leg, initial encounter
S95.909A	Unspecified injury of unspecified blood vessel at ankle and foot level, unspecified leg, initial encounter
S55.902A	Unspecified injury of unspecified blood vessel at forearm level, left arm, initial encounter
S55.901A	Unspecified injury of unspecified blood vessel at forearm level, right arm, initial encounter
S55.909A	Unspecified injury of unspecified blood vessel at forearm level, unspecified arm, initial encounter
S75.902A	Unspecified injury of unspecified blood vessel at hip and thigh level, left leg, initial encounter
S75.901A	Unspecified injury of unspecified blood vessel at hip and thigh level, right leg, initial encounter
S75.909A	Unspecified injury of unspecified blood vessel at hip and thigh level, unspecified leg, initial encounter
S85.902A	Unspecified injury of unspecified blood vessel at lower leg level, left leg, initial encounter
S85.901A	Unspecified injury of unspecified blood vessel at lower leg level, right leg, initial encounter
S85.909A	Unspecified injury of unspecified blood vessel at lower leg level, unspecified leg, initial encounter
S45.902A	Unspecified injury of unspecified blood vessel at shoulder and upper arm level, left arm, initial encounter
S45.901A	Unspecified injury of unspecified blood vessel at shoulder and upper arm level, right arm, initial encounter
S45.909A	Unspecified injury of unspecified blood vessel at shoulder and upper arm level, unspecified arm, initial encounter
S65.902A	Unspecified injury of unspecified blood vessel at wrist and hand level of left arm, initial encounter
S65.901A	Unspecified injury of unspecified blood vessel at wrist and hand level of right arm, initial encounter
S65.909A	Unspecified injury of unspecified blood vessel at wrist and hand level of unspecified arm, initial encounter
S25.90XA	Unspecified injury of unspecified blood vessel of thorax, initial encounter
S15.009A	Unspecified injury of unspecified carotid artery, initial encounter
S15.209A	Unspecified injury of unspecified external jugular vein, initial encounter
S15.309A	Unspecified injury of unspecified internal jugular vein, initial encounter
S36.90XA	Unspecified injury of unspecified intra-abdominal organ, initial encounter
S37.009A	Unspecified injury of unspecified kidney, initial encounter
S09.309A	Unspecified injury of unspecified middle and inner ear, initial encounter
S36.509A	Unspecified injury of unspecified part of colon, initial encounter
S36.209A	Unspecified injury of unspecified part of pancreas, initial encounter
S36.409A	Unspecified injury of unspecified part of small intestine, initial encounter
S85.102A	Unspecified injury of unspecified tibial artery, left leg, initial encounter
S85.101A	Unspecified injury of unspecified tibial artery, right leg, initial encounter
S85.109A	Unspecified injury of unspecified tibial artery, unspecified leg, initial encounter
S37.90XA	Unspecified injury of unspecified urinary and pelvic organ, initial encounter
S15.109A	Unspecified injury of unspecified vertebral artery, initial encounter
S37.10XA	Unspecified injury of ureter, initial encounter
S37.30XA	Unspecified injury of urethra, initial encounter
S37.60XA	Unspecified injury of uterus, initial encounter
S55.202A	Unspecified injury of vein at forearm level, left arm, initial encounter
S55.201A	Unspecified injury of vein at forearm level, right arm, initial encounter
S55.209A	Unspecified injury of vein at forearm level, unspecified arm, initial encounter
K56.609	Unspecified intestinal obstruction, unspecified as to partial versus complete obstruction
S72.012P	Unspecified intracapsular fracture of left femur, subsequent encounter for closed fracture with malunion
S72.012K	Unspecified intracapsular fracture of left femur, subsequent encounter for closed fracture with nonunion
S72.012Q	Unspecified intracapsular fracture of left femur, subsequent encounter for open fracture type I or II with malunion
S72.012M	Unspecified intracapsular fracture of left femur, subsequent encounter for open fracture type I or II with nonunion
S72.012R	Unspecified intracapsular fracture of left femur, subsequent encounter for open fracture type IIIA, IIIB, or IIIC with malunion
S72.012N	Unspecified intracapsular fracture of left femur, subsequent encounter for open fracture type IIIA, IIIB, or IIIC with nonunion
S72.011P	Unspecified intracapsular fracture of right femur, subsequent encounter for closed fracture with malunion
S72.011K	Unspecified intracapsular fracture of right femur, subsequent encounter for closed fracture with nonunion
S72.011Q	Unspecified intracapsular fracture of right femur, subsequent encounter for open fracture type I or II with malunion
S72.011M	Unspecified intracapsular fracture of right femur, subsequent encounter for open fracture type I or II with nonunion
S72.011R	Unspecified intracapsular fracture of right femur, subsequent encounter for open fracture type IIIA, IIIB, or IIIC with malunion
S72.011N	Unspecified intracapsular fracture of right femur, subsequent encounter for open fracture type IIIA, IIIB, or IIIC with nonunion

S72.019P	Unspecified intracapsular fracture of unspecified femur, subsequent encounter for closed fracture with malunion
S72.019K	Unspecified intracapsular fracture of unspecified femur, subsequent encounter for closed fracture with nonunion
S72.019Q	Unspecified intracapsular fracture of unspecified femur, subsequent encounter for open fracture type I or II with malunion
S72.019M	Unspecified intracapsular fracture of unspecified femur, subsequent encounter for open fracture type I or II with nonunion
S72.019R	Unspecified intracapsular fracture of unspecified femur, subsequent encounter for open fracture type IIIA, IIIB, or IIIC with malunion
S72.019N	Unspecified intracapsular fracture of unspecified femur, subsequent encounter for open fracture type IIIA, IIIB, or IIIC with nonunion
S06.9X5A	Unspecified intracranial injury with loss of consciousness greater than 24 hours with return to pre-existing conscious level, initial encounter
S06.9X3A	Unspecified intracranial injury with loss of consciousness of 1 hour to 5 hours 59 minutes, initial encounter
S06.9X1A	Unspecified intracranial injury with loss of consciousness of 30 minutes or less, initial encounter
S06.9X2A	Unspecified intracranial injury with loss of consciousness of 31 minutes to 59 minutes, initial encounter
S06.9X4A	Unspecified intracranial injury with loss of consciousness of 6 hours to 24 hours, initial encounter
S06.9X9A	Unspecified intracranial injury with loss of consciousness of unspecified duration, initial encounter
P52.3	Unspecified intraventricular (nontraumatic) hemorrhage of newborn
H20.9	Unspecified iridocyclitis
R17	Unspecified jaundice
S36.039A	Unspecified laceration of spleen, initial encounter
B54	Unspecified malaria
O16.1	Unspecified maternal hypertension, first trimester
O16.2	Unspecified maternal hypertension, second trimester
O16.3	Unspecified maternal hypertension, third trimester
O98.92	Unspecified maternal infectious and parasitic disease complicating childbirth
O98.911	Unspecified maternal infectious and parasitic disease complicating pregnancy, first trimester
O98.912	Unspecified maternal infectious and parasitic disease complicating pregnancy, second trimester
O98.913	Unspecified maternal infectious and parasitic disease complicating pregnancy, third trimester
O98.93	Unspecified maternal infectious and parasitic disease complicating the puerperium
B49	Unspecified mycosis
N05.4	Unspecified nephritic syndrome with diffuse endocapillary proliferative glomerulonephritis
N05.2	Unspecified nephritic syndrome with diffuse membranous glomerulonephritis
N05.3	Unspecified nephritic syndrome with diffuse mesangial proliferative glomerulonephritis
N05.5	Unspecified nephritic syndrome with diffuse mesangiocapillary glomerulonephritis
S12.401A	Unspecified nondisplaced fracture of fifth cervical vertebra, initial encounter for closed fracture
S12.401K	Unspecified nondisplaced fracture of fifth cervical vertebra, subsequent encounter for fracture with nonunion
S12.001A	Unspecified nondisplaced fracture of first cervical vertebra, initial encounter for closed fracture
S12.001K	Unspecified nondisplaced fracture of first cervical vertebra, subsequent encounter for fracture with nonunion
S12.301A	Unspecified nondisplaced fracture of fourth cervical vertebra, initial encounter for closed fracture
S12.301K	Unspecified nondisplaced fracture of fourth cervical vertebra, subsequent encounter for fracture with nonunion
S12.101A	Unspecified nondisplaced fracture of second cervical vertebra, initial encounter for closed fracture
S12.101K	Unspecified nondisplaced fracture of second cervical vertebra, subsequent encounter for fracture with nonunion
S12.601A	Unspecified nondisplaced fracture of seventh cervical vertebra, initial encounter for closed fracture
S12.601K	Unspecified nondisplaced fracture of seventh cervical vertebra, subsequent encounter for fracture with nonunion
S12.501A	Unspecified nondisplaced fracture of sixth cervical vertebra, initial encounter for closed fracture
S12.501K	Unspecified nondisplaced fracture of sixth cervical vertebra, subsequent encounter for fracture with nonunion
S42.215A	Unspecified nondisplaced fracture of surgical neck of left humerus, initial encounter for closed fracture
S42.215P	Unspecified nondisplaced fracture of surgical neck of left humerus, subsequent encounter for fracture with malunion
S42.215K	Unspecified nondisplaced fracture of surgical neck of left humerus, subsequent encounter for fracture with nonunion
S42.214A	Unspecified nondisplaced fracture of surgical neck of right humerus, initial encounter for closed fracture
S42.214P	Unspecified nondisplaced fracture of surgical neck of right humerus, subsequent encounter for fracture with malunion
S42.214K	Unspecified nondisplaced fracture of surgical neck of right humerus, subsequent encounter for fracture with nonunion
S42.216A	Unspecified nondisplaced fracture of surgical neck of unspecified humerus, initial encounter for closed fracture
S42.216P	Unspecified nondisplaced fracture of surgical neck of unspecified humerus, subsequent encounter for fracture with malunion

S42.216K	Unspecified nondisplaced fracture of surgical neck of unspecified humerus, subsequent encounter for fracture with nonunion
S12.201A	Unspecified nondisplaced fracture of third cervical vertebra, initial encounter for closed fracture
S12.201K	Unspecified nondisplaced fracture of third cervical vertebra, subsequent encounter for fracture with nonunion
S02.113A	Unspecified occipital condyle fracture, initial encounter for closed fracture
S02.113K	Unspecified occipital condyle fracture, subsequent encounter for fracture with nonunion
S01.102A	Unspecified open wound of left eyelid and periocular area, initial encounter
S21.102A	Unspecified open wound of left front wall of thorax without penetration into thoracic cavity, initial encounter
S11.20XA	Unspecified open wound of pharynx and cervical esophagus, initial encounter
S01.101A	Unspecified open wound of right eyelid and periocular area, initial encounter
S21.101A	Unspecified open wound of right front wall of thorax without penetration into thoracic cavity, initial encounter
S11.10XA	Unspecified open wound of thyroid gland, initial encounter
S01.109A	Unspecified open wound of unspecified eyelid and periocular area, initial encounter
S21.109A	Unspecified open wound of unspecified front wall of thorax without penetration into thoracic cavity, initial encounter
S21.90XA	Unspecified open wound of unspecified part of thorax, initial encounter
H46.9	Unspecified optic neuritis
O00.219	Unspecified ovarian pregnancy with intrauterine pregnancy
O00.209	Unspecified ovarian pregnancy without intrauterine pregnancy
H47.10	Unspecified papilledema
S49.102A	Unspecified physeal fracture of lower end of humerus, left arm, initial encounter for closed fracture
S49.102P	Unspecified physeal fracture of lower end of humerus, left arm, subsequent encounter for fracture with malunion
S49.102K	Unspecified physeal fracture of lower end of humerus, left arm, subsequent encounter for fracture with nonunion
S49.101A	Unspecified physeal fracture of lower end of humerus, right arm, initial encounter for closed fracture
S49.101P	Unspecified physeal fracture of lower end of humerus, right arm, subsequent encounter for fracture with malunion
S49.101K	Unspecified physeal fracture of lower end of humerus, right arm, subsequent encounter for fracture with nonunion
S49.109A	Unspecified physeal fracture of lower end of humerus, unspecified arm, initial encounter for closed fracture
S49.109P	Unspecified physeal fracture of lower end of humerus, unspecified arm, subsequent encounter for fracture with malunion
S49.109K	Unspecified physeal fracture of lower end of humerus, unspecified arm, subsequent encounter for fracture with nonunion
S79.102A	Unspecified physeal fracture of lower end of left femur, initial encounter for closed fracture
S79.102P	Unspecified physeal fracture of lower end of left femur, subsequent encounter for fracture with malunion
S79.102K	Unspecified physeal fracture of lower end of left femur, subsequent encounter for fracture with nonunion
S89.302P	Unspecified physeal fracture of lower end of left fibula, subsequent encounter for fracture with malunion
S89.302K	Unspecified physeal fracture of lower end of left fibula, subsequent encounter for fracture with nonunion
S89.102P	Unspecified physeal fracture of lower end of left tibia, subsequent encounter for fracture with malunion
S89.102K	Unspecified physeal fracture of lower end of left tibia, subsequent encounter for fracture with nonunion
S59.202A	Unspecified physeal fracture of lower end of radius, left arm, initial encounter for closed fracture
S59.202P	Unspecified physeal fracture of lower end of radius, left arm, subsequent encounter for fracture with malunion
S59.202K	Unspecified physeal fracture of lower end of radius, left arm, subsequent encounter for fracture with nonunion
S59.201A	Unspecified physeal fracture of lower end of radius, right arm, initial encounter for closed fracture
S59.201P	Unspecified physeal fracture of lower end of radius, right arm, subsequent encounter for fracture with malunion
S59.201K	Unspecified physeal fracture of lower end of radius, right arm, subsequent encounter for fracture with nonunion
S59.209A	Unspecified physeal fracture of lower end of radius, unspecified arm, initial encounter for closed fracture
S59.209P	Unspecified physeal fracture of lower end of radius, unspecified arm, subsequent encounter for fracture with malunion
S59.209K	Unspecified physeal fracture of lower end of radius, unspecified arm, subsequent encounter for fracture with nonunion
S79.101A	Unspecified physeal fracture of lower end of right femur, initial encounter for closed fracture
S79.101P	Unspecified physeal fracture of lower end of right femur, subsequent encounter for fracture with malunion
S79.101K	Unspecified physeal fracture of lower end of right femur, subsequent encounter for fracture with nonunion
S89.301P	Unspecified physeal fracture of lower end of right fibula, subsequent encounter for fracture with malunion
S89.301K	Unspecified physeal fracture of lower end of right fibula, subsequent encounter for fracture with nonunion
S89.101P	Unspecified physeal fracture of lower end of right tibia, subsequent encounter for fracture with malunion
S89.101K	Unspecified physeal fracture of lower end of right tibia, subsequent encounter for fracture with nonunion

Alphabetic & Numeric Lists of CCs

S59.002A	Unspecified physeal fracture of lower end of ulna, left arm, initial encounter for closed fracture
S59.002P	Unspecified physeal fracture of lower end of ulna, left arm, subsequent encounter for fracture with malunion
S59.002K	Unspecified physeal fracture of lower end of ulna, left arm, subsequent encounter for fracture with nonunion
S59.001A	Unspecified physeal fracture of lower end of ulna, right arm, initial encounter for closed fracture
S59.001P	Unspecified physeal fracture of lower end of ulna, right arm, subsequent encounter for fracture with malunion
S59.001K	Unspecified physeal fracture of lower end of ulna, right arm, subsequent encounter for fracture with nonunion
S59.009A	Unspecified physeal fracture of lower end of ulna, unspecified arm, initial encounter for closed fracture
S59.009P	Unspecified physeal fracture of lower end of ulna, unspecified arm, subsequent encounter for fracture with malunion
S59.009K	Unspecified physeal fracture of lower end of ulna, unspecified arm, subsequent encounter for fracture with nonunion
S79.109A	Unspecified physeal fracture of lower end of unspecified femur, initial encounter for closed fracture
S79.109P	Unspecified physeal fracture of lower end of unspecified femur, subsequent encounter for fracture with malunion
S79.109K	Unspecified physeal fracture of lower end of unspecified femur, subsequent encounter for fracture with nonunion
S89.309P	Unspecified physeal fracture of lower end of unspecified fibula, subsequent encounter for fracture with malunion
S89.309K	Unspecified physeal fracture of lower end of unspecified fibula, subsequent encounter for fracture with nonunion
S89.109P	Unspecified physeal fracture of lower end of unspecified tibia, subsequent encounter for fracture with malunion
S89.109K	Unspecified physeal fracture of lower end of unspecified tibia, subsequent encounter for fracture with nonunion
S49.002A	Unspecified physeal fracture of upper end of humerus, left arm, initial encounter for closed fracture
S49.002P	Unspecified physeal fracture of upper end of humerus, left arm, subsequent encounter for fracture with malunion
S49.002K	Unspecified physeal fracture of upper end of humerus, left arm, subsequent encounter for fracture with nonunion
S49.001A	Unspecified physeal fracture of upper end of humerus, right arm, initial encounter for closed fracture
S49.001P	Unspecified physeal fracture of upper end of humerus, right arm, subsequent encounter for fracture with malunion
S49.001K	Unspecified physeal fracture of upper end of humerus, right arm, subsequent encounter for fracture with nonunion
S49.009A	Unspecified physeal fracture of upper end of humerus, unspecified arm, initial encounter for closed fracture
S49.009P	Unspecified physeal fracture of upper end of humerus, unspecified arm, subsequent encounter for fracture with malunion
S49.009K	Unspecified physeal fracture of upper end of humerus, unspecified arm, subsequent encounter for fracture with nonunion
S79.002P	Unspecified physeal fracture of upper end of left femur, subsequent encounter for fracture with malunion
S79.002K	Unspecified physeal fracture of upper end of left femur, subsequent encounter for fracture with nonunion
S89.202P	Unspecified physeal fracture of upper end of left fibula, subsequent encounter for fracture with malunion
S89.202K	Unspecified physeal fracture of upper end of left fibula, subsequent encounter for fracture with nonunion
S89.002A	Unspecified physeal fracture of upper end of left tibia, initial encounter for closed fracture
S89.002P	Unspecified physeal fracture of upper end of left tibia, subsequent encounter for fracture with malunion
S89.002K	Unspecified physeal fracture of upper end of left tibia, subsequent encounter for fracture with nonunion
S59.102P	Unspecified physeal fracture of upper end of radius, left arm, subsequent encounter for fracture with malunion
S59.102K	Unspecified physeal fracture of upper end of radius, left arm, subsequent encounter for fracture with nonunion
S59.101P	Unspecified physeal fracture of upper end of radius, right arm, subsequent encounter for fracture with malunion
S59.101K	Unspecified physeal fracture of upper end of radius, right arm, subsequent encounter for fracture with nonunion
S59.109P	Unspecified physeal fracture of upper end of radius, unspecified arm, subsequent encounter for fracture with malunion
S59.109K	Unspecified physeal fracture of upper end of radius, unspecified arm, subsequent encounter for fracture with nonunion
S79.001P	Unspecified physeal fracture of upper end of right femur, subsequent encounter for fracture with malunion
S79.001K	Unspecified physeal fracture of upper end of right femur, subsequent encounter for fracture with nonunion
S89.201P	Unspecified physeal fracture of upper end of right fibula, subsequent encounter for fracture with malunion
S89.201K	Unspecified physeal fracture of upper end of right fibula, subsequent encounter for fracture with nonunion
S89.001A	Unspecified physeal fracture of upper end of right tibia, initial encounter for closed fracture
S89.001P	Unspecified physeal fracture of upper end of right tibia, subsequent encounter for fracture with malunion
S89.001K	Unspecified physeal fracture of upper end of right tibia, subsequent encounter for fracture with nonunion
S79.009P	Unspecified physeal fracture of upper end of unspecified femur, subsequent encounter for fracture with malunion
S79.009K	Unspecified physeal fracture of upper end of unspecified femur, subsequent encounter for fracture with nonunion
S89.209P	Unspecified physeal fracture of upper end of unspecified fibula, subsequent encounter for fracture with malunion
S89.209K	Unspecified physeal fracture of upper end of unspecified fibula, subsequent encounter for fracture with nonunion
S89.009A	Unspecified physeal fracture of upper end of unspecified tibia, initial encounter for closed fracture
S89.009P	Unspecified physeal fracture of upper end of unspecified tibia, subsequent encounter for fracture with malunion
S89.009K	Unspecified physeal fracture of upper end of unspecified tibia, subsequent encounter for fracture with nonunion
E80.20	Unspecified porphyria
O14.92	Unspecified pre-eclampsia, second trimester
O14.93	Unspecified pre-eclampsia, third trimester
O24.311	Unspecified pre-existing diabetes mellitus in pregnancy, first trimester
O24.312	Unspecified pre-existing diabetes mellitus in pregnancy, second trimester
O24.313	Unspecified pre-existing diabetes mellitus in pregnancy, third trimester
O24.319	Unspecified pre-existing diabetes mellitus in pregnancy, unspecified trimester
O24.33	Unspecified pre-existing diabetes mellitus in the puerperium
O10.92	Unspecified pre-existing hypertension complicating childbirth
O10.911	Unspecified pre-existing hypertension complicating pregnancy, first trimester
O10.912	Unspecified pre-existing hypertension complicating pregnancy, second trimester
O10.913	Unspecified pre-existing hypertension complicating pregnancy, third trimester
E46	Unspecified protein-calorie malnutrition
H44.003	Unspecified purulent endophthalmitis, bilateral
H44.002	Unspecified purulent endophthalmitis, left eye
H44.001	Unspecified purulent endophthalmitis, right eye
H44.009	Unspecified purulent endophthalmitis, unspecified eye
H34.9	Unspecified retinal vascular occlusion
H35.70	Unspecified separation of retinal layers
Q05.4	Unspecified spina bifida with hydrocephalus
S73.002A	Unspecified subluxation of left hip, initial encounter
S43.202A	Unspecified subluxation of left sternoclavicular joint, initial encounter
S73.001A	Unspecified subluxation of right hip, initial encounter
S43.201A	Unspecified subluxation of right sternoclavicular joint, initial encounter
S73.003A	Unspecified subluxation of unspecified hip, initial encounter
S43.203A	Unspecified subluxation of unspecified sternoclavicular joint, initial encounter
I50.20	Unspecified systolic (congestive) heart failure
J95.00	Unspecified tracheostomy complication
T86.92	Unspecified transplanted organ and tissue failure
T86.93	Unspecified transplanted organ and tissue infection
T86.91	Unspecified transplanted organ and tissue rejection
S12.430A	Unspecified traumatic displaced spondylolisthesis of fifth cervical vertebra, initial encounter for closed fracture
S12.430K	Unspecified traumatic displaced spondylolisthesis of fifth cervical vertebra, subsequent encounter for fracture with nonunion
S12.330A	Unspecified traumatic displaced spondylolisthesis of fourth cervical vertebra, initial encounter for closed fracture
S12.330K	Unspecified traumatic displaced spondylolisthesis of fourth cervical vertebra, subsequent encounter for fracture with nonunion
S12.130A	Unspecified traumatic displaced spondylolisthesis of second cervical vertebra, initial encounter for closed fracture
S12.130K	Unspecified traumatic displaced spondylolisthesis of second cervical vertebra, subsequent encounter for fracture with nonunion
S12.630A	Unspecified traumatic displaced spondylolisthesis of seventh cervical vertebra, initial encounter for closed fracture
S12.630K	Unspecified traumatic displaced spondylolisthesis of seventh cervical vertebra, subsequent encounter for fracture with nonunion
S12.530A	Unspecified traumatic displaced spondylolisthesis of sixth cervical vertebra, initial encounter for closed fracture
S12.530K	Unspecified traumatic displaced spondylolisthesis of sixth cervical vertebra, subsequent encounter for fracture with nonunion
S12.230A	Unspecified traumatic displaced spondylolisthesis of third cervical vertebra, initial encounter for closed fracture
S12.230K	Unspecified traumatic displaced spondylolisthesis of third cervical vertebra, subsequent encounter for fracture with nonunion
S12.431A	Unspecified traumatic nondisplaced spondylolisthesis of fifth cervical vertebra, initial encounter for closed fracture
S12.431K	Unspecified traumatic nondisplaced spondylolisthesis of fifth cervical vertebra, subsequent encounter for fracture with nonunion
S12.331A	Unspecified traumatic nondisplaced spondylolisthesis of fourth cervical vertebra, initial encounter for closed fracture
S12.331K	Unspecified traumatic nondisplaced spondylolisthesis of fourth cervical vertebra, subsequent encounter for fracture with nonunion
S12.131A	Unspecified traumatic nondisplaced spondylolisthesis of second cervical vertebra, initial encounter for closed fracture
S12.131K	Unspecified traumatic nondisplaced spondylolisthesis of second cervical vertebra, subsequent encounter for fracture with nonunion
S12.631A	Unspecified traumatic nondisplaced spondylolisthesis of seventh cervical vertebra, initial encounter for closed fracture
S12.631K	Unspecified traumatic nondisplaced spondylolisthesis of seventh cervical vertebra, subsequent encounter for fracture with nonunion

S12.531A	Unspecified traumatic nondisplaced spondylolisthesis of sixth cervical vertebra, initial encounter for closed fracture
S12.531K	Unspecified traumatic nondisplaced spondylolisthesis of sixth cervical vertebra, subsequent encounter for fracture with nonunion
S12.231A	Unspecified traumatic nondisplaced spondylolisthesis of third cervical vertebra, initial encounter for closed fracture
S12.231K	Unspecified traumatic nondisplaced spondylolisthesis of third cervical vertebra, subsequent encounter for fracture with nonunion
S72.102P	Unspecified trochanteric fracture of left femur, subsequent encounter for closed fracture with malunion
S72.102K	Unspecified trochanteric fracture of left femur, subsequent encounter for closed fracture with nonunion
S72.102Q	Unspecified trochanteric fracture of left femur, subsequent encounter for open fracture type I or II with malunion
S72.102M	Unspecified trochanteric fracture of left femur, subsequent encounter for open fracture type I or II with nonunion
S72.102R	Unspecified trochanteric fracture of left femur, subsequent encounter for open fracture type IIIA, IIIB, or IIIC with malunion
S72.102N	Unspecified trochanteric fracture of left femur, subsequent encounter for open fracture type IIIA, IIIB, or IIIC with nonunion
S72.101P	Unspecified trochanteric fracture of right femur, subsequent encounter for closed fracture with malunion
S72.101K	Unspecified trochanteric fracture of right femur, subsequent encounter for closed fracture with nonunion
S72.101Q	Unspecified trochanteric fracture of right femur, subsequent encounter for open fracture type I or II with malunion
S72.101M	Unspecified trochanteric fracture of right femur, subsequent encounter for open fracture type I or II with nonunion
S72.101R	Unspecified trochanteric fracture of right femur, subsequent encounter for open fracture type IIIA, IIIB, or IIIC with malunion
S72.101N	Unspecified trochanteric fracture of right femur, subsequent encounter for open fracture type IIIA, IIIB, or IIIC with nonunion
S72.109P	Unspecified trochanteric fracture of unspecified femur, subsequent encounter for closed fracture with malunion
S72.109K	Unspecified trochanteric fracture of unspecified femur, subsequent encounter for closed fracture with nonunion
S72.109Q	Unspecified trochanteric fracture of unspecified femur, subsequent encounter for open fracture type I or II with malunion
S72.109M	Unspecified trochanteric fracture of unspecified femur, subsequent encounter for open fracture type I or II with nonunion
S72.109R	Unspecified trochanteric fracture of unspecified femur, subsequent encounter for open fracture type IIIA, IIIB, or IIIC with malunion
S72.109N	Unspecified trochanteric fracture of unspecified femur, subsequent encounter for open fracture type IIIA, IIIB, or IIIC with nonunion
O00.119	Unspecified tubal pregnancy with intrauterine pregnancy
O00.109	Unspecified tubal pregnancy without intrauterine pregnancy
A86	Unspecified viral encephalitis
A99	Unspecified viral hemorrhagic fever
B19.10	Unspecified viral hepatitis B without hepatic coma
B19.9	Unspecified viral hepatitis without hepatic coma
A89	Unspecified viral infection of central nervous system
S32.119A	Unspecified Zone I fracture of sacrum, initial encounter for closed fracture
S32.119K	Unspecified Zone I fracture of sacrum, subsequent encounter for fracture with nonunion
S32.129A	Unspecified Zone II fracture of sacrum, initial encounter for closed fracture
S32.129K	Unspecified Zone II fracture of sacrum, subsequent encounter for fracture with nonunion
S32.139A	Unspecified Zone III fracture of sacrum, initial encounter for closed fracture
S32.139K	Unspecified Zone III fracture of sacrum, subsequent encounter for fracture with nonunion
I20.0	Unstable angina
S32.052A	Unstable burst fracture of fifth lumbar vertebra, initial encounter for closed fracture
S32.052K	Unstable burst fracture of fifth lumbar vertebra, subsequent encounter for fracture with nonunion
S12.02XA	Unstable burst fracture of first cervical vertebra, initial encounter for closed fracture
S12.02XK	Unstable burst fracture of first cervical vertebra, subsequent encounter for fracture with nonunion
S32.012A	Unstable burst fracture of first lumbar vertebra, initial encounter for closed fracture
S32.012K	Unstable burst fracture of first lumbar vertebra, subsequent encounter for fracture with nonunion
S22.012A	Unstable burst fracture of first thoracic vertebra, initial encounter for closed fracture
S22.012K	Unstable burst fracture of first thoracic vertebra, subsequent encounter for fracture with nonunion
S32.042A	Unstable burst fracture of fourth lumbar vertebra, initial encounter for closed fracture
S32.042K	Unstable burst fracture of fourth lumbar vertebra, subsequent encounter for fracture with nonunion
S22.042A	Unstable burst fracture of fourth thoracic vertebra, initial encounter for closed fracture
S22.042K	Unstable burst fracture of fourth thoracic vertebra, subsequent encounter for fracture with nonunion
S32.022A	Unstable burst fracture of second lumbar vertebra, initial encounter for closed fracture
S32.022K	Unstable burst fracture of second lumbar vertebra, subsequent encounter for fracture with nonunion
S22.022A	Unstable burst fracture of second thoracic vertebra, initial encounter for closed fracture

S22.022K	Unstable burst fracture of second thoracic vertebra, subsequent encounter for fracture with nonunion
S22.082A	Unstable burst fracture of T11-T12 vertebra, initial encounter for closed fracture
S22.082K	Unstable burst fracture of T11-T12 vertebra, subsequent encounter for fracture with nonunion
S22.052A	Unstable burst fracture of T5-T6 vertebra, initial encounter for closed fracture
S22.052K	Unstable burst fracture of T5-T6 vertebra, subsequent encounter for fracture with nonunion
S22.062A	Unstable burst fracture of T7-T8 vertebra, initial encounter for closed fracture
S22.062K	Unstable burst fracture of T7-T8 vertebra, subsequent encounter for fracture with nonunion
S22.072A	Unstable burst fracture of T9-T10 vertebra, initial encounter for closed fracture
S22.072K	Unstable burst fracture of T9-T10 vertebra, subsequent encounter for fracture with nonunion
S32.032A	Unstable burst fracture of third lumbar vertebra, initial encounter for closed fracture
S32.032K	Unstable burst fracture of third lumbar vertebra, subsequent encounter for fracture with nonunion
S22.032A	Unstable burst fracture of third thoracic vertebra, initial encounter for closed fracture
S22.032K	Unstable burst fracture of third thoracic vertebra, subsequent encounter for fracture with nonunion
S32.002A	Unstable burst fracture of unspecified lumbar vertebra, initial encounter for closed fracture
S32.002K	Unstable burst fracture of unspecified lumbar vertebra, subsequent encounter for fracture with nonunion
S22.002A	Unstable burst fracture of unspecified thoracic vertebra, initial encounter for closed fracture
S22.002K	Unstable burst fracture of unspecified thoracic vertebra, subsequent encounter for fracture with nonunion
A82.1	Urban rabies
A95.1	Urban yellow fever
N28.86	Ureteritis cystica
N34.0	Urethral abscess
N36.0	Urethral fistula
O04.88	Urinary tract infection following (induced) termination of pregnancy
O08.83	Urinary tract infection following an ectopic and molar pregnancy
O03.88	Urinary tract infection following complete or unspecified spontaneous abortion
O86.20	Urinary tract infection following delivery, unspecified
O07.38	Urinary tract infection following failed attempted termination of pregnancy
O03.38	Urinary tract infection following incomplete spontaneous abortion
N39.0	Urinary tract infection, site not specified
O86.13	Vaginitis following delivery
A81.01	Variant Creutzfeldt-Jakob disease
B01.81	Varicella keratitis
B01.0	Varicella meningitis
B01.9	Varicella without complication
I83.223	Varicose veins of left lower extremity with both ulcer of ankle and inflammation
I83.222	Varicose veins of left lower extremity with both ulcer of calf and inflammation
I83.224	Varicose veins of left lower extremity with both ulcer of heel and midfoot and inflammation
I83.228	Varicose veins of left lower extremity with both ulcer of other part of lower extremity and inflammation
I83.221	Varicose veins of left lower extremity with both ulcer of thigh and inflammation
I83.229	Varicose veins of left lower extremity with both ulcer of unspecified site and inflammation
I83.225	Varicose veins of left lower extremity with both ulcer other part of foot and inflammation
I83.213	Varicose veins of right lower extremity with both ulcer of ankle and inflammation
I83.212	Varicose veins of right lower extremity with both ulcer of calf and inflammation
I83.214	Varicose veins of right lower extremity with both ulcer of heel and midfoot and inflammation
I83.218	Varicose veins of right lower extremity with both ulcer of other part of lower extremity and inflammation
I83.211	Varicose veins of right lower extremity with both ulcer of thigh and inflammation
I83.219	Varicose veins of right lower extremity with both ulcer of unspecified site and inflammation
I83.215	Varicose veins of right lower extremity with both ulcer other part of foot and inflammation
I83.203	Varicose veins of unspecified lower extremity with both ulcer of ankle and inflammation
I83.202	Varicose veins of unspecified lower extremity with both ulcer of calf and inflammation
I83.204	Varicose veins of unspecified lower extremity with both ulcer of heel and midfoot and inflammation
I83.208	Varicose veins of unspecified lower extremity with both ulcer of other part of lower extremity and inflammation
I83.201	Varicose veins of unspecified lower extremity with both ulcer of thigh and inflammation
I83.209	Varicose veins of unspecified lower extremity with both ulcer of unspecified site and inflammation
I83.205	Varicose veins of unspecified lower extremity with both ulcer other part of foot and inflammation

T80.1XXA	Vascular complications following infusion, transfusion and therapeutic injection, initial encounter
F01.51	Vascular dementia with behavioral disturbance
K55.9	Vascular disorder of intestine, unspecified
Q79.63	Vascular Ehlers-Danlos syndrome
A92.2	Venezuelan equine fever
O22.90	Venous complication in pregnancy, unspecified, unspecified trimester
J95.851	Ventilator associated pneumonia
Q21.0	Ventricular septal defect
I23.2	Ventricular septal defect as current complication following acute myocardial infarction
I47.2	Ventricular tachycardia
M47.022	Vertebral artery compression syndromes, cervical region
M47.021	Vertebral artery compression syndromes, occipito-atlanto-axial region
M47.029	Vertebral artery compression syndromes, site unspecified
G45.0	Vertebro-basilar artery syndrome
N32.2	Vesical fistula, not elsewhere classified
N32.1	Vesicointestinal fistula
N82.0	Vesicovaginal fistula
B33.20	Viral carditis, unspecified
B33.21	Viral endocarditis
O98.42	Viral hepatitis complicating childbirth
O98.411	Viral hepatitis complicating pregnancy, first trimester
O98.412	Viral hepatitis complicating pregnancy, second trimester
O98.413	Viral hepatitis complicating pregnancy, third trimester
O98.43	Viral hepatitis complicating the puerperium
A87.9	Viral meningitis, unspecified
B33.22	Viral myocarditis
B33.23	Viral pericarditis
B55.0	Visceral leishmaniasis
H44.023	Vitreous abscess (chronic), bilateral
H44.022	Vitreous abscess (chronic), left eye
H44.021	Vitreous abscess (chronic), right eye
H44.029	Vitreous abscess (chronic), unspecified eye
E74.01	von Gierke disease
D68.0	Von Willebrand's disease
T84.061A	Wear of articular bearing surface of internal prosthetic left hip joint, initial encounter
T84.063A	Wear of articular bearing surface of internal prosthetic left knee joint, initial encounter
T84.060A	Wear of articular bearing surface of internal prosthetic right hip joint, initial encounter
T84.062A	Wear of articular bearing surface of internal prosthetic right knee joint, initial encounter
T84.068A	Wear of articular bearing surface of other internal prosthetic joint, initial encounter
T84.069A	Wear of articular bearing surface of unspecified internal prosthetic joint, initial encounter
S32.050A	Wedge compression fracture of fifth lumbar vertebra, initial encounter for closed fracture
S32.050K	Wedge compression fracture of fifth lumbar vertebra, subsequent encounter for fracture with nonunion
S32.010A	Wedge compression fracture of first lumbar vertebra, initial encounter for closed fracture
S32.010K	Wedge compression fracture of first lumbar vertebra, subsequent encounter for fracture with nonunion
S22.010A	Wedge compression fracture of first thoracic vertebra, initial encounter for closed fracture
S22.010K	Wedge compression fracture of first thoracic vertebra, subsequent encounter for fracture with nonunion
S32.040A	Wedge compression fracture of fourth lumbar vertebra, initial encounter for closed fracture
S32.040K	Wedge compression fracture of fourth lumbar vertebra, subsequent encounter for fracture with nonunion
S22.040A	Wedge compression fracture of fourth thoracic vertebra, initial encounter for closed fracture
S22.040K	Wedge compression fracture of fourth thoracic vertebra, subsequent encounter for fracture with nonunion
S32.020A	Wedge compression fracture of second lumbar vertebra, initial encounter for closed fracture
S32.020K	Wedge compression fracture of second lumbar vertebra, subsequent encounter for fracture with nonunion
S22.020A	Wedge compression fracture of second thoracic vertebra, initial encounter for closed fracture
S22.020K	Wedge compression fracture of second thoracic vertebra, subsequent encounter for fracture with nonunion
S22.080A	Wedge compression fracture of T11-T12 vertebra, initial encounter for closed fracture
S22.080K	Wedge compression fracture of T11-T12 vertebra, subsequent encounter for fracture with nonunion
S22.050A	Wedge compression fracture of T5-T6 vertebra, initial encounter for closed fracture
S22.050K	Wedge compression fracture of T5-T6 vertebra, subsequent encounter for fracture with nonunion
S22.060A	Wedge compression fracture of T7-T8 vertebra, initial encounter for closed fracture
S22.060K	Wedge compression fracture of T7-T8 vertebra, subsequent encounter for fracture with nonunion
S22.070A	Wedge compression fracture of T9-T10 vertebra, initial encounter for closed fracture
S22.070K	Wedge compression fracture of T9-T10 vertebra, subsequent encounter for fracture with nonunion
S32.030A	Wedge compression fracture of third lumbar vertebra, initial encounter for closed fracture
S32.030K	Wedge compression fracture of third lumbar vertebra, subsequent encounter for fracture with nonunion
S22.030A	Wedge compression fracture of third thoracic vertebra, initial encounter for closed fracture
S22.030K	Wedge compression fracture of third thoracic vertebra, subsequent encounter for fracture with nonunion
S32.000A	Wedge compression fracture of unspecified lumbar vertebra, initial encounter for closed fracture
S32.000K	Wedge compression fracture of unspecified lumbar vertebra, subsequent encounter for fracture with nonunion
S22.000A	Wedge compression fracture of unspecified thoracic vertebra, initial encounter for closed fracture
S22.000K	Wedge compression fracture of unspecified thoracic vertebra, subsequent encounter for fracture with nonunion
M31.31	Wegener's granulomatosis with renal involvement
M31.30	Wegener's granulomatosis without renal involvement
E51.2	Wernicke's encephalopathy
E51.12	Wet beriberi
K90.81	Whipple's disease
A37.10	Whooping cough due to Bordetella parapertussis without pneumonia
A37.00	Whooping cough due to Bordetella pertussis without pneumonia
A37.80	Whooping cough due to other Bordetella species without pneumonia
A37.90	Whooping cough, unspecified species without pneumonia
E85.82	Wild-type transthyretin-related (ATTR) amyloidosis
Q93.82	Williams syndrome
D82.0	Wiskott-Aldrich syndrome
P96.2	Withdrawal symptoms from therapeutic use of drugs in newborn
A48.52	Wound botulism
E71.529	X-linked adrenoleukodystrophy, unspecified type
E70.310	X-linked ocular albinism
A95.9	Yellow fever, unspecified
E71.510	Zellweger syndrome
E71.541	Zellweger-like syndrome
A92.5	Zika virus disease
A28.9	Zoonotic bacterial disease, unspecified
B02.31	Zoster conjunctivitis
B02.0	Zoster encephalitis
B02.32	Zoster iridocyclitis
B02.33	Zoster keratitis
B02.30	Zoster ocular disease, unspecified
B02.34	Zoster scleritis
B02.8	Zoster with other complications
S02.40FA	Zygomatic fracture, left side, initial encounter for closed fracture
S02.40FB	Zygomatic fracture, left side, initial encounter for open fracture
S02.40FK	Zygomatic fracture, left side, subsequent encounter for fracture with nonunion
S02.40EA	Zygomatic fracture, right side, initial encounter for closed fracture
S02.40EB	Zygomatic fracture, right side, initial encounter for open fracture
S02.40EK	Zygomatic fracture, right side, subsequent encounter for fracture with nonunion
S02.402A	Zygomatic fracture, unspecified side, initial encounter for closed fracture
S02.402B	Zygomatic fracture, unspecified side, initial encounter for open fracture
S02.402K	Zygomatic fracture, unspecified side, subsequent encounter for fracture with nonunion

Numeric CC List

A00.0	A18.32	A38.0	A52.75	A87.9	B19.9	B55.2	B76.0	C34.02	C49.4
A00.1	A18.39	A38.1	A52.76	A88.0	B20	B55.9	B76.1	C34.10	C49.5
A00.9	A18.4	A38.8	A52.77	A88.8	B25.1	B56.0	B76.8	C34.11	C49.6
A01.00	A18.50	A38.9	A52.78	A89	B25.8	B56.1	B76.9	C34.12	C49.8
A01.01	A18.51	A39.82	A52.79	A90	B25.9	B56.9	B77.0	C34.2	C49.9
A01.02	A18.52	A39.83	A54.00	A91	B26.0	B57.0	B77.89	C34.30	C49.A0
A01.03	A18.53	A39.84	A54.01	A92.0	B26.3	B57.1	B77.9	C34.31	C49.A1
A01.04	A18.54	A39.89	A54.02	A92.1	B26.81	B57.2	B78.0	C34.32	C49.A2
A01.05	A18.59	A39.9	A54.03	A92.2	B26.82	B57.30	B78.7	C34.80	C49.A3
A01.09	A18.6	A42.0	A54.09	A92.4	B26.83	B57.31	B78.9	C34.81	C49.A4
A01.1	A18.7	A42.1	A54.1	A92.5	B26.84	B57.32	B79	C34.82	C49.A5
A01.2	A18.81	A42.2	A54.21	A92.8	B26.85	B57.39	B80	C34.90	C49.A9
A01.3	A18.82	A42.81	A54.22	A92.9	B26.89	B57.40	B81.0	C34.91	C56.1
A01.4	A18.83	A42.82	A54.23	A93.0	B33.1	B57.41	B81.1	C34.92	C56.2
A02.0	A18.84	A42.89	A54.24	A93.1	B33.20	B57.42	B81.2	C37	C56.9
A02.23	A18.85	A42.9	A54.29	A93.2	B33.21	B57.49	B81.3	C38.0	C64.1
A02.24	A18.89	A43.0	A54.30	A93.8	B33.22	B57.5	B81.4	C38.1	C64.2
A02.25	A21.0	A43.1	A54.31	A94	B33.23	B58.00	B81.8	C38.2	C64.9
A02.29	A21.1	A43.8	A54.32	A95.0	B33.4	B58.01	B82.0	C38.3	C65.1
A02.8	A21.2	A43.9	A54.33	A95.1	B34.3	B58.09	B97.21	C38.4	C65.2
A02.9	A21.3	A44.0	A54.39	A95.9	B37.0	B58.1	B97.33	C38.8	C65.9
A03.0	A21.7	A44.1	A54.40	A96.0	B37.41	B58.82	B97.34	C40.00	C66.1
A04.0	A21.8	A44.8	A54.41	A96.1	B37.49	B58.83	B97.35	C40.01	C66.2
A04.1	A21.9	A44.9	A54.42	A96.8	B37.81	B58.89	C15.3	C40.02	C66.9
A04.2	A22.0	A48.51	A54.43	A96.9	B37.82	B58.9	C15.4	C40.10	C68.0
A04.3	A22.2	A48.52	A54.49	A98.0	B37.83	B60.0	C15.5	C40.11	C68.1
A04.4	A22.8	A50.01	A54.82	A98.1	B37.84	B60.10	C15.8	C40.12	C68.8
A04.5	A22.9	A50.02	A54.83	A98.2	B37.89	B60.19	C15.9	C40.20	C68.9
A04.6	A23.8	A50.03	A54.84	A98.5	B38.0	B60.2	C16.0	C40.21	C70.0
A04.71	A23.9	A50.04	A54.85	A98.8	B38.1	B65.0	C16.1	C40.22	C70.1
A04.72	A24.0	A50.05	A54.89	A99	B38.2	B65.1	C16.2	C40.30	C70.9
A04.8	A24.1	A50.06	A54.9	B00.2	B38.3	B65.2	C16.3	C40.31	C71.0
A04.9	A24.2	A50.07	A68.0	B00.50	B38.7	B65.3	C16.4	C40.32	C71.1
A05.0	A24.3	A50.08	A68.1	B00.51	B38.81	B65.8	C16.5	C40.80	C71.2
A05.1	A24.9	A50.09	A68.9	B00.52	B38.89	B65.9	C16.6	C40.81	C71.3
A05.2	A25.0	A50.2	A69.1	B00.53	B38.9	B66.0	C16.8	C40.82	C71.4
A05.3	A25.1	A50.30	A69.20	B00.59	B39.3	B66.1	C16.9	C40.90	C71.5
A05.4	A25.9	A50.31	A69.21	B00.81	B40.0	B66.2	C17.0	C40.91	C71.6
A05.5	A27.0	A50.32	A69.22	B00.89	B40.1	B66.3	C17.1	C40.92	C71.7
A05.8	A27.89	A50.39	A69.23	B01.0	B40.2	B66.4	C17.2	C41.0	C71.8
A06.0	A27.9	A50.40	A69.29	B01.81	B40.3	B66.5	C17.3	C41.1	C71.9
A06.1	A28.0	A50.43	A70	B01.89	B40.7	B66.8	C17.8	C41.2	C72.0
A06.2	A28.1	A50.44	A75.0	B01.9	B40.81	B67.0	C17.9	C41.3	C72.1
A06.3	A28.2	A50.45	A75.1	B02.0	B40.89	B67.1	C18.0	C41.4	C72.20
A06.81	A28.8	A50.49	A75.2	B02.21	B40.9	B67.2	C18.1	C41.9	C72.21
A06.82	A28.9	A50.51	A75.3	B02.22	B41.0	B67.31	C18.2	C45.0	C72.22
A06.89	A30.0	A50.52	A75.9	B02.23	B41.7	B67.32	C18.3	C45.1	C72.30
A07.1	A30.1	A50.53	A77.0	B02.29	B41.8	B67.39	C18.4	C45.2	C72.31
A07.2	A30.2	A50.54	A77.1	B02.30	B41.9	B67.4	C18.5	C46.0	C72.32
A07.3	A30.3	A50.55	A77.2	B02.31	B44.1	B67.5	C18.6	C46.1	C72.40
A07.4	A30.4	A50.56	A77.3	B02.32	B44.2	B67.61	C18.7	C46.2	C72.41
A07.8	A30.5	A50.57	A77.40	B02.33	B44.7	B67.69	C18.8	C46.3	C72.42
A07.9	A30.8	A50.59	A77.41	B02.34	B44.81	B67.7	C18.9	C46.4	C72.50
A08.0	A30.9	A51.31	A77.49	B02.39	B44.89	B67.8	C19	C46.50	C72.59
A08.11	A31.0	A51.32	A77.8	B02.7	B44.9	B67.90	C20	C46.51	C72.9
A08.19	A31.1	A51.39	A77.9	B02.8	B45.0	B67.99	C21.0	C46.52	C74.00
A08.2	A31.2	A51.42	A78	B03	B45.2	B68.0	C21.1	C46.7	C74.01
A08.31	A31.8	A51.43	A79.0	B04	B45.3	B68.1	C21.2	C46.9	C74.02
A08.32	A31.9	A51.44	A79.1	B05.1	B45.7	B68.9	C21.8	C47.0	C74.10
A08.39	A32.0	A51.45	A79.81	B05.4	B45.8	B69.0	C22.0	C47.10	C74.11
A09	A32.11	A51.46	A79.89	B05.81	B45.9	B69.1	C22.1	C47.11	C74.12
A15.0	A32.12	A51.49	A79.9	B05.89	B47.0	B69.81	C22.2	C47.12	C74.90
A15.4	A32.81	A52.00	A81.00	B06.00	B47.1	B69.89	C22.3	C47.20	C74.91
A15.5	A32.82	A52.01	A81.01	B06.02	B47.9	B69.9	C22.4	C47.21	C74.92
A15.6	A32.89	A52.02	A81.09	B06.09	B48.2	B70.0	C22.7	C47.22	C75.0
A15.7	A32.9	A52.03	A81.1	B06.81	B48.3	B70.1	C22.8	C47.3	C75.1
A15.8	A34	A52.04	A81.2	B06.82	B48.4	B71.0	C22.9	C47.4	C75.2
A15.9	A36.0	A52.05	A81.81	B06.89	B48.8	B71.1	C23	C47.5	C75.3
A17.9	A36.1	A52.06	A81.82	B08.3	B49	B71.8	C24.0	C47.6	C75.4
A18.01	A36.2	A52.09	A81.83	B08.71	B50.0	B72	C24.1	C47.8	C75.5
A18.02	A36.3	A52.10	A81.89	B15.9	B50.8	B73.00	C24.8	C47.9	C75.8
A18.03	A36.81	A52.11	A81.9	B16.1	B51.0	B73.01	C24.9	C48.0	C75.9
A18.09	A36.82	A52.12	A82.0	B16.9	B51.8	B73.02	C25.0	C48.1	C77.0
A18.10	A36.83	A52.15	A82.1	B17.0	B51.9	B73.09	C25.1	C48.2	C77.1
A18.11	A36.84	A52.16	A82.9	B17.10	B52.0	B73.1	C25.2	C48.8	C77.2
A18.12	A36.85	A52.17	A85.0	B17.2	B52.8	B74.0	C25.3	C49.0	C77.3
A18.13	A36.86	A52.19	A85.1	B17.8	B52.9	B74.1	C25.4	C49.10	C77.4
A18.14	A36.89	A52.2	A85.8	B17.9	B53.0	B74.2	C25.7	C49.11	C77.5
A18.15	A36.9	A52.3	A86	B18.0	B53.1	B74.3	C25.8	C49.12	C77.8
A18.16	A37.00	A52.71	A87.0	B18.1	B53.8	B74.4	C25.9	C49.20	C77.9
A18.17	A37.10	A52.72	A87.1	B18.8	B54	B74.8	C33	C49.21	C78.00
A18.18	A37.80	A52.73	A87.2	B18.9	B55.0	B74.9	C34.00	C49.22	C78.01
A18.2	A37.90	A52.74	A87.8	B19.10	B55.1	B75	C34.01	C49.3	C78.02

C78.1	C81.21	C82.36	C83.51	C84.76	C88.9	C94.00	D76.3	E51.11	E72.53
C78.2	C81.22	C82.37	C83.52	C84.77	C90.00	C94.01	D78.01	E51.12	E72.59
C78.30	C81.23	C82.38	C83.53	C84.78	C90.01	C94.02	D78.02	E51.2	E72.81
C78.39	C81.24	C82.39	C83.54	C84.79	C90.02	C94.20	D78.11	E51.8	E72.89
C78.4	C81.25	C82.40	C83.55	C84.90	C90.10	C94.21	D78.12	E51.9	E72.9
C78.5	C81.26	C82.41	C83.56	C84.91	C90.11	C94.22	D78.21	E53.0	E74.00
C78.6	C81.27	C82.42	C83.57	C84.92	C90.12	C94.30	D78.22	E55.0	E74.01
C78.7	C81.28	C82.43	C83.58	C84.93	C90.20	C94.31	D78.31	E64.0	E74.02
C78.80	C81.29	C82.44	C83.59	C84.94	C90.21	C94.32	D78.32	E66.2	E74.03
C78.89	C81.30	C82.45	C83.70	C84.95	C90.22	C94.40	D78.33	E70.0	E74.04
C79.00	C81.31	C82.46	C83.71	C84.96	C90.30	C94.41	D78.34	E70.1	E74.09
C79.01	C81.32	C82.47	C83.72	C84.97	C90.31	C94.42	D78.81	E70.20	E74.20
C79.02	C81.33	C82.48	C83.73	C84.98	C90.32	C94.6	D78.89	E70.21	E74.21
C79.10	C81.34	C82.49	C83.74	C84.99	C91.00	C94.80	D80.0	E70.29	E74.29
C79.11	C81.35	C82.50	C83.75	C84.A0	C91.01	C94.81	D80.1	E70.30	E74.4
C79.19	C81.36	C82.51	C83.76	C84.A1	C91.02	C94.82	D80.2	E70.310	E74.8
C79.2	C81.37	C82.52	C83.77	C84.A2	C91.10	C95.00	D80.3	E70.311	E75.00
C79.31	C81.38	C82.53	C83.78	C84.A3	C91.11	C95.01	D80.4	E70.318	E75.01
C79.32	C81.39	C82.54	C83.79	C84.A4	C91.12	C95.02	D80.5	E70.319	E75.02
C79.40	C81.40	C82.55	C83.80	C84.A5	C91.30	C95.10	D80.6	E70.320	E75.09
C79.49	C81.41	C82.56	C83.81	C84.A6	C91.31	C95.11	D80.7	E70.321	E75.10
C79.51	C81.42	C82.57	C83.82	C84.A7	C91.32	C95.12	D80.8	E70.328	E75.11
C79.52	C81.43	C82.58	C83.83	C84.A8	C91.40	C95.90	D80.9	E70.329	E75.19
C79.60	C81.44	C82.59	C83.84	C84.A9	C91.41	C95.91	D81.0	E70.330	E75.23
C79.61	C81.45	C82.60	C83.85	C84.Z0	C91.42	C95.92	D81.1	E70.331	E75.25
C79.62	C81.46	C82.61	C83.86	C84.Z1	C91.50	C96.0	D81.2	E70.338	E75.26
C79.70	C81.47	C82.62	C83.87	C84.Z2	C91.51	C96.20	D81.30	E70.339	E75.29
C79.71	C81.48	C82.63	C83.88	C84.Z3	C91.52	C96.21	D81.31	E70.39	E75.4
C79.72	C81.49	C82.64	C83.89	C84.Z4	C91.60	C96.22	D81.32	E70.40	E76.01
C79.81	C81.70	C82.65	C83.90	C84.Z5	C91.61	C96.29	D81.39	E70.41	E76.02
C79.82	C81.71	C82.66	C83.91	C84.Z6	C91.62	C96.4	D81.4	E70.49	E76.03
C79.89	C81.72	C82.67	C83.92	C84.Z7	C91.90	C96.5	D81.5	E70.5	E76.1
C79.9	C81.73	C82.68	C83.93	C84.Z8	C91.91	C96.6	D81.6	E70.8	E76.210
C7A.00	C81.74	C82.69	C83.94	C84.Z9	C91.92	C96.9	D81.7	E70.9	E76.211
C7A.010	C81.75	C82.80	C83.95	C85.10	C91.A0	C96.A	D81.89	E71.0	E76.219
C7A.011	C81.76	C82.81	C83.96	C85.11	C91.A1	C96.Z	D81.9	E71.110	E76.22
C7A.012	C81.77	C82.82	C83.97	C85.12	C91.A2	D46.22	D82.0	E71.111	E76.29
C7A.019	C81.78	C82.83	C83.98	C85.13	C91.Z0	D46.C	D82.1	E71.118	E76.3
C7A.020	C81.79	C82.84	C83.99	C85.14	C91.Z1	D47.01	D83.0	E71.120	E76.8
C7A.021	C81.90	C82.85	C84.00	C85.15	C91.Z2	D47.02	D83.1	E71.121	E76.9
C7A.022	C81.91	C82.86	C84.01	C85.16	C92.00	D47.09	D83.2	E71.128	E78.71
C7A.023	C81.92	C82.87	C84.02	C85.17	C92.01	D47.1	D83.8	E71.19	E78.72
C7A.024	C81.93	C82.88	C84.03	C85.18	C92.02	D47.9	D83.9	E71.2	E79.1
C7A.025	C81.94	C82.89	C84.04	C85.19	C92.10	D47.Z1	D84.8	E71.310	E79.2
C7A.026	C81.95	C82.90	C84.05	C85.20	C92.11	D47.Z2	D84.9	E71.311	E79.8
C7A.029	C81.96	C82.91	C84.06	C85.21	C92.12	D47.Z9	D89.810	E71.312	E79.9
C7A.090	C81.97	C82.92	C84.07	C85.22	C92.20	D58.8	D89.811	E71.313	E80.0
C7A.091	C81.98	C82.93	C84.08	C85.23	C92.21	D58.9	D89.812	E71.314	E80.1
C7A.092	C81.99	C82.94	C84.09	C85.24	C92.22	D59.0	D89.813	E71.318	E80.20
C7A.093	C82.00	C82.95	C84.10	C85.25	C92.30	D59.1	E06.0	E71.32	E80.21
C7A.094	C82.01	C82.96	C84.11	C85.26	C92.31	D59.2	E08.52	E71.39	E80.29
C7A.095	C82.02	C82.97	C84.12	C85.27	C92.32	D59.4	E09.52	E71.50	E80.3
C7A.096	C82.03	C82.98	C84.13	C85.28	C92.40	D59.9	E10.52	E71.510	E84.19
C7A.098	C82.04	C82.99	C84.14	C85.29	C92.41	D61.01	E11.52	E71.511	E84.8
C7A.1	C82.05	C83.00	C84.15	C85.80	C92.42	D61.09	E13.52	E71.518	E84.9
C7A.8	C82.06	C83.01	C84.16	C85.81	C92.50	D61.818	E15	E71.520	E85.0
C7B.01	C82.07	C83.02	C84.17	C85.82	C92.51	D61.82	E22.1	E71.521	E85.1
C7B.02	C82.08	C83.03	C84.18	C85.83	C92.52	D61.9	E22.2	E71.522	E85.2
C7B.03	C82.09	C83.04	C84.19	C85.84	C92.60	D62	E22.8	E71.528	E85.3
C7B.04	C82.10	C83.05	C84.40	C85.85	C92.61	D68.0	E22.9	E71.529	E85.4
C7B.09	C82.11	C83.06	C84.41	C85.86	C92.62	D68.1	E23.0	E71.53	E85.81
C7B.8	C82.12	C83.07	C84.42	C85.87	C92.90	D68.2	E23.2	E71.540	E85.82
C80.0	C82.13	C83.08	C84.43	C85.88	C92.91	D68.311	E24.0	E71.541	E85.89
C80.2	C82.14	C83.09	C84.44	C85.89	C92.92	D68.312	E24.2	E71.542	E85.9
C81.00	C82.15	C83.10	C84.45	C85.90	C92.A0	D68.318	E24.3	E71.548	E87.0
C81.01	C82.16	C83.11	C84.46	C85.91	C92.A1	D68.32	E24.4	E72.00	E87.1
C81.02	C82.17	C83.12	C84.47	C85.92	C92.A2	D68.4	E24.8	E72.01	E87.2
C81.03	C82.18	C83.13	C84.48	C85.93	C92.Z0	D68.51	E24.9	E72.02	E87.3
C81.04	C82.19	C83.14	C84.49	C85.94	C92.Z1	D68.52	E27.0	E72.03	E87.4
C81.05	C82.20	C83.15	C84.60	C85.95	C92.Z2	D68.59	E27.1	E72.04	E88.02
C81.06	C82.21	C83.16	C84.61	C85.96	C93.00	D68.61	E27.2	E72.09	E88.40
C81.07	C82.22	C83.17	C84.62	C85.97	C93.01	D68.62	E27.3	E72.10	E88.41
C81.08	C82.23	C83.18	C84.63	C85.98	C93.02	D68.69	E27.40	E72.11	E88.42
C81.09	C82.24	C83.19	C84.64	C85.99	C93.10	D68.8	E27.49	E72.12	E88.49
C81.10	C82.25	C83.30	C84.65	C86.0	C93.11	D68.9	E27.5	E72.19	E89.1
C81.11	C82.26	C83.31	C84.66	C86.1	C93.12	D69.0	E32.1	E72.20	E89.6
C81.12	C82.27	C83.32	C84.67	C86.2	C93.30	D69.3	E34.0	E72.21	E89.810
C81.13	C82.28	C83.33	C84.68	C86.3	C93.31	D69.41	E36.01	E72.22	E89.811
C81.14	C82.29	C83.34	C84.69	C86.4	C93.32	D69.42	E36.02	E72.23	E89.820
C81.15	C82.30	C83.35	C84.70	C86.5	C93.90	D74.0	E36.11	E72.29	E89.821
C81.16	C82.31	C83.36	C84.71	C86.6	C93.91	D74.8	E36.12	E72.3	E89.822
C81.17	C82.32	C83.37	C84.72	C88.2	C93.92	D74.9	E44.0	E72.4	E89.823
C81.18	C82.33	C83.38	C84.73	C88.3	C93.Z0	D75.81	E44.1	E72.50	E89.89
C81.19	C82.34	C83.39	C84.74	C88.4	C93.Z1	D76.1	E45	E72.51	F01.51
C81.20	C82.35	C83.50	C84.75	C88.8	C93.Z2	D76.2	E46	E72.52	F02.81

F03.91	F14.121	F19.27	G12.1	G45.2	G97.82	H33.40	H47.41	H59.369	I25.758
F05	F14.150	F19.280	G12.20	G45.3	G99.0	H33.41	H47.42	H59.811	I25.759
F06.0	F14.151	F19.281	G12.21	G45.8	G99.2	H33.42	H47.43	H59.812	I25.760
F06.2	F14.20	F19.282	G12.22	G45.9	H05.011	H33.43	H47.49	H59.813	I25.761
F10.121	F14.221	F19.288	G12.23	G46.0	H05.012	H33.8	H47.511	H59.819	I25.768
F10.14	F14.222	F19.921	G12.24	G46.1	H05.013	H34.00	H47.512	H59.88	I25.769
F10.151	F14.229	F19.930	G12.25	G46.2	H05.019	H34.01	H47.519	H59.89	I25.790
F10.159	F14.23	F19.931	G12.29	G60.1	H05.021	H34.02	H47.521	H60.20	I25.791
F10.180	F14.250	F19.932	G12.8	G61.0	H05.022	H34.03	H47.522	H60.21	I25.798
F10.181	F14.251	F19.939	G12.9	G61.81	H05.023	H34.10	H47.529	H60.22	I25.799
F10.188	F14.259	F19.950	G21.11	G62.81	H05.029	H34.11	H47.531	H60.23	I25.810
F10.19	F14.280	F19.951	G21.19	G70.80	H05.031	H34.12	H47.532	H70.001	I25.811
F10.221	F14.281	F19.97	G21.2	G70.81	H05.032	H34.13	H47.539	H70.002	I25.812
F10.230	F14.282	F20.0	G21.3	G71.2	H05.033	H34.211	H47.621	H70.003	I27.0
F10.231	F14.288	F20.1	G21.8	G72.0	H05.039	H34.212	H47.622	H70.009	I27.1
F10.232	F14.921	F20.2	G21.9	G72.1	H20.00	H34.213	H47.629	H70.011	I27.82
F10.239	F14.950	F20.5	G23.0	G72.2	H20.011	H34.219	H47.631	H70.012	I28.0
F10.24	F14.951	F20.81	G23.1	G72.81	H20.012	H34.231	H47.632	H70.013	I28.1
F10.251	F15.121	F20.89	G23.2	G73.1	H20.013	H34.232	H47.639	H70.019	I30.0
F10.259	F15.150	F23	G23.8	G73.3	H20.019	H34.233	H47.641	H70.091	I30.1
F10.27	F15.151	F30.10	G23.9	G80.1	H20.021	H34.239	H47.642	H70.092	I30.8
F10.280	F15.20	F30.11	G24.02	G80.2	H20.022	H34.8110	H47.649	H70.093	I30.9
F10.281	F15.221	F30.12	G24.09	G80.3	H20.023	H34.8111	H49.811	H70.099	I31.0
F10.288	F15.222	F30.13	G24.2	G81.00	H20.029	H34.8112	H49.812	H95.21	I31.1
F10.29	F15.23	F30.2	G24.8	G81.01	H20.031	H34.8120	H49.813	H95.22	I31.2
F10.921	F15.250	F30.9	G25.82	G81.02	H20.032	H34.8121	H49.819	H95.31	I31.3
F10.94	F15.251	F31.0	G25.9	G81.03	H20.033	H34.8122	H53.121	H95.32	I31.4
F10.951	F15.259	F31.10	G31.81	G81.04	H20.039	H34.8130	H53.122	H95.41	I31.8
F10.959	F15.280	F31.11	G31.82	G81.10	H20.9	H34.8131	H53.123	H95.42	I31.9
F10.980	F15.281	F31.12	G32.0	G81.11	H21.331	H34.8132	H53.129	H95.51	I32
F10.981	F15.282	F31.13	G32.81	G81.12	H21.332	H34.8190	H53.131	H95.52	I38
F10.988	F15.288	F31.2	G36.0	G81.13	H21.333	H34.8191	H53.132	H95.53	I39
F10.99	F15.921	F31.30	G36.1	G81.14	H21.339	H34.8192	H53.133	H95.54	I42.0
F11.121	F15.93	F31.31	G36.8	G81.90	H30.101	H34.9	H53.139	H95.811	I42.1
F11.150	F15.950	F31.32	G36.9	G81.91	H30.102	H35.70	H59.011	H95.812	I42.2
F11.151	F15.951	F31.4	G37.0	G81.92	H30.103	H35.721	H59.012	H95.813	I42.3
F11.20	F16.121	F31.5	G37.1	G81.93	H30.109	H35.722	H59.013	H95.819	I42.4
F11.221	F16.150	F31.60	G37.2	G81.94	H30.111	H35.723	H59.019	H95.88	I42.5
F11.222	F16.151	F31.61	G37.3	G82.20	H30.112	H35.729	H59.031	H95.89	I42.6
F11.23	F16.20	F31.62	G37.5	G82.21	H30.113	H35.731	H59.032	I01.0	I42.7
F11.250	F16.221	F31.63	G37.8	G82.22	H30.119	H35.732	H59.033	I01.1	I42.8
F11.251	F16.250	F31.64	G37.9	G83.0	H30.121	H35.733	H59.039	I01.2	I42.9
F11.259	F16.251	F31.81	G40.001	G83.4	H30.122	H35.739	H59.091	I01.8	I43
F11.281	F16.259	F31.89	G40.009	G90.3	H30.123	H35.82	H59.092	I01.9	I44.2
F11.282	F16.280	F32.0	G40.011	G90.50	H30.129	H40.211	H59.093	I02.0	I45.2
F11.288	F16.283	F32.1	G40.019	G90.511	H30.131	H40.212	H59.099	I02.9	I45.3
F11.921	F16.288	F32.2	G40.101	G90.512	H30.132	H40.213	H59.111	I09.0	I45.89
F11.93	F16.921	F32.3	G40.109	G90.513	H30.133	H44.001	H59.112	I09.2	I47.0
F11.950	F16.950	F33.0	G40.111	G90.519	H30.139	H44.002	H59.113	I09.81	I47.1
F11.951	F16.951	F33.1	G40.119	G90.521	H30.141	H44.003	H59.119	I12.0	I47.2
F12.121	F17.203	F33.2	G40.201	G90.522	H30.142	H44.009	H59.121	I13.0	I48.11
F12.150	F17.213	F33.3	G40.209	G90.523	H30.143	H44.011	H59.122	I13.11	I48.19
F12.151	F17.223	F33.40	G40.211	G90.529	H30.149	H44.012	H59.123	I13.2	I48.20
F12.221	F17.293	F33.8	G40.219	G90.59	H30.891	H44.013	H59.129	I16.1	I48.21
F12.250	F18.121	F33.9	G40.411	G91.0	H30.892	H44.019	H59.211	I16.9	I48.3
F12.251	F18.150	F34.81	G40.419	G91.1	H30.893	H44.021	H59.212	I20.0	I48.4
F12.921	F18.151	F34.89	G40.501	G91.2	H30.899	H44.022	H59.213	I20.1	I48.92
F12.950	F18.17	F34.9	G40.509	G91.3	H30.90	H44.023	H59.219	I23.0	I49.2
F12.951	F18.20	F50.00	G40.801	G91.8	H30.91	H44.029	H59.221	I23.1	I50.1
F13.121	F18.221	F50.01	G40.802	G91.9	H30.92	H44.112	H59.222	I23.2	I50.20
F13.150	F18.250	F50.02	G40.803	G93.1	H30.93	H44.113	H59.223	I23.3	I50.22
F13.151	F18.251	F50.2	G40.804	G93.40	H31.321	H44.119	H59.229	I23.6	I50.30
F13.20	F18.259	F68.10	G40.811	G93.49	H31.322	H44.121	H59.311	I23.7	I50.32
F13.221	F18.27	F68.12	G40.812	G95.0	H31.323	H44.122	H59.312	I23.8	I50.40
F13.230	F18.280	F68.A	G40.813	G95.20	H31.329	H44.123	H59.313	I24.0	I50.42
F13.231	F18.288	F72	G40.814	G95.29	H31.401	H44.129	H59.319	I24.1	I51.0
F13.232	F18.921	F73	G40.821	G95.81	H31.402	H44.131	H59.321	I24.8	I51.81
F13.239	F18.950	F84.0	G40.822	G95.89	H31.403	H44.132	H59.322	I24.9	I62.9
F13.250	F18.951	F84.2	G40.823	G95.9	H31.409	H44.133	H59.323	I25.110	I67.3
F13.251	F18.97	F84.3	G40.824	G96.0	H31.411	H44.139	H59.329	I25.700	I67.4
F13.259	F19.121	F84.5	G40.89	G96.11	H31.412	H44.19	H59.331	I25.710	I67.5
F13.26	F19.150	F84.8	G40.911	G97.0	H31.413	H46.00	H59.332	I25.711	I67.6
F13.27	F19.151	F84.9	G40.919	G97.2	H31.419	H46.01	H59.333	I25.718	I67.7
F13.280	F19.17	G03.1	G40.A11	G97.31	H31.421	H46.02	H59.339	I25.719	I67.81
F13.281	F19.20	G03.2	G40.A19	G97.32	H31.422	H46.03	H59.341	I25.720	I67.82
F13.282	F19.221	G04.1	G40.B01	G97.41	H31.423	H46.10	H59.342	I25.721	I67.841
F13.288	F19.222	G10	G40.B09	G97.48	H31.429	H46.11	H59.343	I25.728	I67.848
F13.921	F19.230	G11.0	G40.B11	G97.49	H33.121	H46.12	H59.349	I25.729	I67.850
F13.930	F19.231	G11.1	G40.B19	G97.51	H33.122	H46.13	H59.351	I25.730	I67.858
F13.931	F19.232	G11.2	G43.601	G97.52	H33.123	H46.8	H59.352	I25.731	I67.89
F13.932	F19.239	G11.3	G43.609	G97.61	H33.129	H46.9	H59.353	I25.738	I68.2
F13.939	F19.250	G11.4	G43.611	G97.62	H33.20	H47.10	H59.359	I25.739	I69.051
F13.950	F19.251	G11.8	G43.619	G97.63	H33.21	H47.11	H59.361	I25.750	I69.052
F13.951	F19.259	G11.9	G45.0	G97.64	H33.22		H59.362	I25.751	I69.053
F13.97	F19.26	G12.0	G45.1	G97.81	H33.23		H59.363		I69.054

Alphabetic & Numeric Lists of CCs

Alphabetic & Numeric Lists of CCs

I69.059	I70.634	I82.1	I82.619	I87.331	J93.11	K50.112	K56.699	K91.32	L03.222
I69.151	I70.638	I82.210	I82.621	I87.332	J93.12	K50.113	K56.7	K91.61	L03.311
I69.152	I70.639	I82.211	I82.622	I87.333	J93.81	K50.114	K57.00	K91.62	L03.312
I69.153	I70.641	I82.290	I82.623	I87.339	J93.82	K50.118	K57.12	K91.71	L03.313
I69.154	I70.642	I82.291	I82.629	I96	J93.83	K50.119	K57.20	K91.72	L03.314
I69.159	I70.643	I82.3	I82.701	I97.110	J93.9	K50.80	K57.32	K91.81	L03.315
I69.251	I70.644	I82.401	I82.702	I97.111	J94.0	K50.811	K57.40	K91.82	L03.316
I69.252	I70.648	I82.402	I82.703	I97.120	J94.2	K50.812	K57.52	K91.83	L03.317
I69.253	I70.649	I82.403	I82.709	I97.121	J94.8	K50.813	K57.80	K91.840	L03.319
I69.254	I70.661	I82.409	I82.711	I97.130	J95.00	K50.814	K57.92	K91.841	L03.321
I69.259	I70.662	I82.411	I82.712	I97.131	J95.01	K50.818	K59.2	K91.850	L03.322
I69.351	I70.663	I82.412	I82.713	I97.190	J95.02	K50.819	K59.31	K91.858	L03.323
I69.352	I70.668	I82.413	I82.719	I97.191	J95.03	K50.90	K59.39	K91.86	L03.324
I69.353	I70.669	I82.419	I82.721	I97.410	J95.04	K50.911	K61.0	K91.870	L03.325
I69.354	I70.731	I82.421	I82.722	I97.411	J95.09	K50.912	K61.1	K91.871	L03.326
I69.359	I70.732	I82.422	I82.723	I97.418	J95.4	K50.913	K61.2	K91.872	L03.327
I69.851	I70.733	I82.423	I82.729	I97.42	J95.5	K50.914	K61.4	K91.873	L03.329
I69.852	I70.734	I82.429	I82.811	I97.51	J95.61	K50.918	K62.5	K91.89	L03.811
I69.853	I70.738	I82.431	I82.812	I97.52	J95.62	K50.919	K62.6	K92.0	L03.818
I69.854	I70.739	I82.432	I82.813	I97.610	J95.71	K51.00	K63.0	K92.1	L03.891
I69.859	I70.741	I82.433	I82.819	I97.611	J95.72	K51.011	K63.2	K92.2	L03.898
I69.951	I70.742	I82.439	I82.890	I97.618	J95.811	K51.012	K63.3	K92.81	L03.90
I69.952	I70.743	I82.441	I82.891	I97.620	J95.812	K51.013	K65.4	K94.01	L03.91
I69.953	I70.744	I82.442	I82.90	I97.621	J95.830	K51.014	K68.11	K94.02	L05.01
I69.954	I70.748	I82.443	I82.91	I97.622	J95.831	K51.018	K76.6	K94.03	L05.02
I69.959	I70.749	I82.449	I82.A11	I97.630	J95.84	K51.019	K77	K94.09	L08.1
I70.261	I70.761	I82.451	I82.A12	I97.631	J95.850	K51.20	K80.00	K94.11	L10.0
I70.262	I70.762	I82.452	I82.A13	I97.638	J95.851	K51.211	K80.01	K94.12	L10.1
I70.263	I70.763	I82.453	I82.A19	I97.640	J95.859	K51.212	K80.10	K94.13	L10.2
I70.268	I70.768	I82.459	I82.A21	I97.641	J95.860	K51.213	K80.11	K94.19	L10.3
I70.269	I70.769	I82.491	I82.A22	I97.648	J95.861	K51.214	K80.12	K94.22	L10.4
I70.331	I70.92	I82.492	I82.A23	I97.710	J95.862	K51.218	K80.18	K94.23	L10.5
I70.332	I73.01	I82.493	I82.A29	I97.711	J95.863	K51.219	K80.19	K94.30	L10.81
I70.333	I74.09	I82.499	I82.B11	I97.790	J95.88	K51.30	K80.21	K94.31	L10.89
I70.334	I74.10	I82.4Y1	I82.B12	I97.791	J95.89	K51.311	K80.30	K94.32	L10.9
I70.338	I74.11	I82.4Y2	I82.B13	I97.810	J96.10	K51.312	K80.31	K94.33	L12.0
I70.339	I74.19	I82.4Y3	I82.B19	I97.811	J96.11	K51.313	K80.32	K94.39	L12.30
I70.341	I74.2	I82.4Y9	I82.B21	I97.820	J96.12	K51.314	K80.33	K95.01	L12.31
I70.342	I74.3	I82.4Z1	I82.B22	I97.821	J98.11	K51.318	K80.34	K95.09	L12.35
I70.343	I74.4	I82.4Z2	I82.B23	I97.88	J98.19	K51.319	K80.35	K95.81	L12.8
I70.344	I74.5	I82.4Z3	I82.B29	I97.89	K04.01	K51.40	K80.36	K95.89	L12.9
I70.348	I74.8	I82.4Z9	I82.C11	J05.10	K04.02	K51.411	K80.37	L02.01	L49.3
I70.349	I74.9	I82.501	I82.C12	J18.2	K04.4	K51.412	K80.40	L02.11	L49.4
I70.361	I75.011	I82.502	I82.C13	J21.0	K11.3	K51.413	K80.41	L02.211	L49.5
I70.362	I75.012	I82.503	I82.C19	J21.1	K11.4	K51.414	K80.42	L02.212	L49.6
I70.363	I75.013	I82.509	I82.C21	J21.8	K12.2	K51.418	K80.43	L02.213	L49.7
I70.368	I75.019	I82.511	I82.C22	J21.9	K22.10	K51.419	K80.44	L02.214	L49.8
I70.369	I75.021	I82.512	I82.C23	J36	K25.3	K51.50	K80.45	L02.215	L49.9
I70.431	I75.022	I82.513	I82.C29	J39.0	K26.3	K51.511	K80.46	L02.216	L51.1
I70.432	I75.023	I82.519	I83.201	J39.1	K27.3	K51.512	K80.47	L02.219	L51.2
I70.433	I75.029	I82.521	I83.202	J44.0	K28.3	K51.513	K80.51	L02.31	L51.3
I70.434	I75.81	I82.522	I83.203	J44.1	K31.0	K51.514	K80.60	L02.411	L53.0
I70.438	I75.89	I82.523	I83.204	J45.21	K31.1	K51.518	K80.61	L02.412	L53.1
I70.439	I76	I82.529	I83.205	J45.22	K31.5	K51.519	K80.62	L02.413	L53.2
I70.441	I77.2	I82.531	I83.208	J45.31	K31.6	K51.80	K80.63	L02.414	L53.3
I70.442	I77.4	I82.532	I83.209	J45.32	K35.20	K51.811	K80.64	L02.415	L76.01
I70.443	I77.5	I82.533	I83.211	J45.41	K35.30	K51.812	K80.65	L02.416	L76.02
I70.444	I80.10	I82.539	I83.212	J45.42	K35.31	K51.813	K80.66	L02.419	L76.11
I70.448	I80.11	I82.541	I83.213	J45.51	K35.80	K51.814	K80.71	L02.511	L76.12
I70.449	I80.12	I82.542	I83.214	J45.52	K35.890	K51.818	K80.81	L02.512	L76.21
I70.461	I80.13	I82.543	I83.215	J45.901	K35.891	K51.819	K81.0	L02.519	L76.22
I70.462	I80.201	I82.549	I83.218	J45.902	K40.00	K51.90	K81.2	L02.611	L76.31
I70.463	I80.202	I82.551	I83.219	J47.0	K40.01	K51.911	K82.0	L02.612	L76.32
I70.468	I80.203	I82.552	I83.221	J47.1	K40.30	K51.912	K82.1	L02.619	L76.33
I70.469	I80.209	I82.553	I83.222	J67.7	K40.31	K51.913	K82.3	L02.811	L76.34
I70.531	I80.211	I82.559	I83.223	J67.8	K41.00	K51.914	K82.A2	L02.818	L88
I70.532	I80.212	I82.591	I83.224	J67.9	K41.01	K51.918	K83.01	L02.91	L97.101
I70.533	I80.213	I82.592	I83.225	J68.0	K41.30	K51.919	K83.09	L03.111	L97.102
I70.534	I80.219	I82.593	I83.228	J70.0	K41.31	K52.0	K83.3	L03.112	L97.103
I70.538	I80.221	I82.599	I83.229	J70.1	K42.0	K52.1	K86.0	L03.113	L97.104
I70.539	I80.222	I82.5Y1	I85.00	J81.1	K43.0	K55.1	K86.1	L03.114	L97.106
I70.541	I80.223	I82.5Y2	I85.10	J82	K43.3	K55.8	K86.2	L03.115	L97.108
I70.542	I80.229	I82.5Y3	I87.011	J84.01	K43.6	K55.9	K86.3	L03.116	L97.109
I70.543	I80.231	I82.5Y9	I87.012	J84.02	K44.0	K56.0	K90.1	L03.119	L97.111
I70.544	I80.232	I82.5Z1	I87.013	J84.03	K45.0	K56.1	K90.2	L03.121	L97.112
I70.548	I80.233	I82.5Z2	I87.019	J84.09	K46.0	K56.3	K90.3	L03.122	L97.113
I70.549	I80.239	I82.5Z3	I87.031	J84.114	K50.00	K56.49	K90.41	L03.123	L97.114
I70.561	I80.241	I82.5Z9	I87.032	J84.116	K50.011	K56.50	K90.49	L03.124	L97.115
I70.562	I80.242	I82.601	I87.033	J84.117	K50.012	K56.51	K90.81	L03.125	L97.116
I70.563	I80.243	I82.602	I87.039	J84.2	K50.013	K56.52	K90.89	L03.126	L97.118
I70.568	I80.249	I82.603	I87.1	J84.82	K50.014	K56.600	K90.9	L03.129	L97.119
I70.569	I80.291	I82.609	I87.311	J84.9	K50.018	K56.601	K91.2	L03.211	L97.121
I70.631	I80.292	I82.611	I87.312	J90	K50.019	K56.609	K91.30	L03.212	L97.122
I70.632	I80.293	I82.612	I87.313	J91.0	K50.10	K56.690	K91.31	L03.213	L97.123
I70.633	I80.299	I82.613	I87.319	J91.8	K50.111	K56.691		L03.221	

L97.124	L97.528	M00.112	M01.X52	M05.419	M35.5	M60.043	M80.069K	M84.311K	M84.419P
L97.125	L97.801	M00.119	M01.X59	M05.421	M35.8	M60.044	M80.069P	M84.311P	M84.421A
L97.126	L97.802	M00.121	M01.X61	M05.422	M36.0	M60.045	M80.071K	M84.312K	M84.421K
L97.128	L97.803	M00.122	M01.X62	M05.429	M46.20	M60.046	M80.071P	M84.312P	M84.421P
L97.129	L97.804	M00.129	M01.X69	M05.431	M46.21	M60.051	M80.072A	M84.319K	M84.422A
L97.201	L97.805	M00.131	M01.X71	M05.432	M46.22	M60.052	M80.072K	M84.319P	M84.422K
L97.202	L97.806	M00.132	M01.X72	M05.439	M46.23	M60.059	M80.072P	M84.321K	M84.422P
L97.203	L97.808	M00.139	M01.X79	M05.441	M46.24	M60.061	M80.079A	M84.321P	M84.429A
L97.204	L97.809	M00.141	M01.X8	M05.442	M46.25	M60.062	M80.079K	M84.322K	M84.429K
L97.205	L97.811	M00.142	M01.X9	M05.449	M46.26	M60.069	M80.079P	M84.322P	M84.429P
L97.206	L97.812	M00.149	M02.10	M05.451	M46.27	M60.070	M80.08XA	M84.329K	M84.431A
L97.208	L97.813	M00.151	M02.111	M05.452	M46.28	M60.071	M80.08XK	M84.329P	M84.431K
L97.209	L97.814	M00.152	M02.112	M05.459	M46.30	M60.072	M80.08XP	M84.331K	M84.431P
L97.211	L97.815	M00.159	M02.119	M05.461	M46.31	M60.073	M80.80XA	M84.331P	M84.432A
L97.212	L97.816	M00.161	M02.121	M05.462	M46.32	M60.074	M80.80XK	M84.332K	M84.432K
L97.213	L97.818	M00.162	M02.122	M05.469	M46.33	M60.075	M80.80XP	M84.332P	M84.432P
L97.214	L97.819	M00.169	M02.129	M05.471	M46.34	M60.076	M80.811A	M84.333K	M84.433A
L97.215	L97.821	M00.171	M02.131	M05.472	M46.35	M60.077	M80.811K	M84.333P	M84.433K
L97.216	L97.822	M00.172	M02.132	M05.479	M46.36	M60.08	M80.811P	M84.334K	M84.433P
L97.218	L97.823	M00.179	M02.139	M05.49	M46.37	M60.09	M80.812A	M84.334P	M84.434A
L97.219	L97.824	M00.18	M02.141	M25.00	M46.38	M62.82	M80.812K	M84.339K	M84.434K
L97.221	L97.825	M00.19	M02.142	M25.011	M46.39	M79.A11	M80.812P	M84.339P	M84.434P
L97.222	L97.826	M00.20	M02.149	M25.019	M47.011	M79.A12	M80.819A	M84.341K	M84.439A
L97.223	L97.828	M00.211	M02.151	M25.021	M47.012	M79.A19	M80.819K	M84.341P	M84.439K
L97.224	L97.829	M00.212	M02.152	M25.022	M47.013	M79.A21	M80.819P	M84.342K	M84.439P
L97.225	L97.901	M00.219	M02.159	M25.029	M47.014	M79.A22	M80.821A	M84.342P	M84.441A
L97.226	L97.902	M00.221	M02.161	M25.031	M47.015	M79.A29	M80.821K	M84.343K	M84.441K
L97.228	L97.903	M00.222	M02.162	M25.032	M47.016	M79.A3	M80.821P	M84.343P	M84.441P
L97.229	L97.904	M00.229	M02.169	M25.039	M47.019	M79.A9	M80.822A	M84.344K	M84.442A
L97.301	L97.905	M00.231	M02.171	M25.041	M47.021	M80.00XA	M80.822K	M84.344P	M84.442K
L97.302	L97.906	M00.232	M02.172	M25.041	M47.022	M80.00XK	M80.822P	M84.345K	M84.442P
L97.303	L97.908	M00.239	M02.179	M25.042	M47.029	M80.00XP	M80.829A	M84.345P	M84.443A
L97.304	L97.909	M00.241	M02.18	M25.049	M47.10	M80.011A	M80.829K	M84.346K	M84.443K
L97.305	L97.911	M00.242	M02.19	M25.051	M47.11	M80.011K	M80.829P	M84.346P	M84.443P
L97.306	L97.912	M00.249	M02.30	M25.052	M47.12	M80.011P	M80.831A	M84.350K	M84.444A
L97.308	L97.913	M00.251	M02.311	M25.059	M47.13	M80.012A	M80.831K	M84.350P	M84.444K
L97.309	L97.914	M00.252	M02.312	M25.061	M47.14	M80.012K	M80.831P	M84.351K	M84.444P
L97.311	L97.915	M00.259	M02.319	M25.062	M47.15	M80.012P	M80.832A	M84.351P	M84.445A
L97.312	L97.916	M00.261	M02.321	M25.069	M47.16	M80.019A	M80.832K	M84.352K	M84.445K
L97.313	L97.918	M00.262	M02.322	M25.071	M48.30	M80.019K	M80.832P	M84.352P	M84.445P
L97.314	L97.919	M00.269	M02.329	M25.072	M48.31	M80.019P	M80.839A	M84.353K	M84.446A
L97.315	L97.921	M00.271	M02.331	M25.073	M48.32	M80.021A	M80.839K	M84.353P	M84.446K
L97.316	L97.922	M00.272	M02.332	M25.074	M48.33	M80.021K	M80.839P	M84.359K	M84.446P
L97.318	L97.923	M00.279	M02.339	M25.075	M48.34	M80.021P	M80.841A	M84.359P	M84.451A
L97.319	L97.924	M00.28	M02.341	M25.076	M48.35	M80.022A	M80.841K	M84.361K	M84.451K
L97.321	L97.925	M00.29	M02.342	M25.08	M48.36	M80.022K	M80.841P	M84.361P	M84.451P
L97.322	L97.926	M00.80	M02.349	M30.0	M48.37	M80.022P	M80.842A	M84.362K	M84.452A
L97.323	L97.928	M00.811	M02.351	M30.1	M48.38	M80.029A	M80.842K	M84.362P	M84.452K
L97.324	L97.929	M00.812	M02.352	M30.2	M48.50XA	M80.029K	M80.842P	M84.363K	M84.452P
L97.325	L98.3	M00.819	M02.359	M30.3	M48.51XA	M80.029P	M80.849A	M84.363P	M84.453A
L97.326	L98.415	M00.821	M02.361	M30.8	M48.52XA	M80.031A	M80.849K	M84.364K	M84.453K
L97.328	L98.416	M00.822	M02.362	M31.0	M48.53XA	M80.031K	M80.849P	M84.364P	M84.453P
L97.329	L98.418	M00.829	M02.369	M31.2	M48.54XA	M80.031P	M80.851A	M84.369K	M84.454A
L97.401	L98.425	M00.831	M02.371	M31.30	M48.55XA	M80.032A	M80.851K	M84.369P	M84.454K
L97.402	L98.426	M00.832	M02.372	M31.31	M48.56XA	M80.032K	M80.851P	M84.371K	M84.454P
L97.403	L98.428	M00.839	M02.379	M31.4	M48.57XA	M80.032P	M80.852A	M84.371P	M84.459A
L97.404	L98.495	M00.841	M02.38	M31.7	M48.58XA	M80.039A	M80.852K	M84.372K	M84.459K
L97.405	L98.496	M00.842	M02.39	M31.8	M50.00	M80.039K	M80.852P	M84.372P	M84.459P
L97.406	L98.498	M00.849	M02.80	M31.9	M50.01	M80.039P	M80.859A	M84.373K	M84.461A
L97.408	M00.00	M00.851	M02.811	M32.11	M50.020	M80.041A	M80.859K	M84.373P	M84.461K
L97.409	M00.011	M00.852	M02.812	M32.12	M50.021	M80.041K	M80.859P	M84.374K	M84.461P
L97.411	M00.012	M00.859	M02.819	M33.00	M50.022	M80.041P	M80.861A	M84.374P	M84.462A
L97.412	M00.019	M00.861	M02.821	M33.01	M50.023	M80.042A	M80.861K	M84.375K	M84.462K
L97.413	M00.021	M00.862	M02.822	M33.02	M50.03	M80.042K	M80.861P	M84.375P	M84.462P
L97.414	M00.022	M00.869	M02.829	M33.03	M51.04	M80.042P	M80.862A	M84.376K	M84.463A
L97.415	M00.029	M00.871	M02.831	M33.09	M51.05	M80.049A	M80.862K	M84.376P	M84.463K
L97.416	M00.031	M00.872	M02.832	M33.10	M51.06	M80.049K	M80.862P	M84.377K	M84.463P
L97.418	M00.032	M00.879	M02.839	M33.11	M60.000	M80.049P	M80.869A	M84.377P	M84.464A
L97.419	M00.039	M00.88	M02.841	M33.12	M60.001	M80.051A	M80.869K	M84.378K	M84.464K
L97.421	M00.041	M00.89	M02.842	M33.13	M60.002	M80.051K	M80.869P	M84.378P	M84.464P
L97.422	M00.042	M00.9	M02.849	M33.19	M60.003	M80.051P	M80.871A	M84.379K	M84.469A
L97.423	M00.049	M01.X0	M02.851	M33.20	M60.004	M80.052A	M80.871K	M84.379P	M84.469K
L97.424	M00.051	M01.X11	M02.852	M33.21	M60.005	M80.052K	M80.871P	M84.38XK	M84.469P
L97.425	M00.052	M01.X12	M02.859	M33.22	M60.009	M80.052P	M80.871P	M84.38XP	M84.471A
L97.426	M00.059	M01.X19	M02.861	M33.29	M60.011	M80.059A	M80.872A	M84.40XA	M84.471K
L97.428	M00.061	M01.X21	M02.862	M33.90	M60.012	M80.059K	M80.872K	M84.40XK	M84.471P
L97.429	M00.062	M01.X22	M02.869	M33.91	M60.019	M80.059P	M80.872P	M84.40XP	M84.472A
L97.505	M00.069	M01.X29	M02.871	M33.92	M60.021	M80.061A	M80.879A	M84.411A	M84.472K
L97.506	M00.071	M01.X31	M02.872	M33.93	M60.022	M80.061K	M80.879K	M84.411K	M84.472P
L97.508	M00.072	M01.X32	M02.879	M33.99	M60.029	M80.061P	M80.879P	M84.411P	M84.473A
L97.515	M00.079	M01.X39	M02.88	M34.81	M60.031	M80.062A	M80.88XA	M84.412A	M84.473K
L97.516	M00.08	M01.X41	M02.89	M34.82	M60.032	M80.062K	M80.88XK	M84.412K	M84.473P
L97.518	M00.09	M01.X42	M05.40	M35.03	M60.039	M80.062P	M80.88XP	M84.412P	M84.474A
L97.525	M00.10	M01.X49	M05.411	M35.1	M60.041	M80.069A	M84.30XK	M84.419A	M84.474K
L97.526	M00.111	M01.X51	M05.412	M35.2	M60.042	M80.069K	M84.30XP	M84.419K	M84.474P

M84.475A	M84.563K	M84.653P	M86.059	M86.421	M87.029	M87.221	M87.819	M96.831	N28.84
M84.475K	M84.563P	M84.659A	M86.061	M86.422	M87.031	M87.222	M87.821	M96.840	N28.85
M84.475P	M84.564A	M84.659K	M86.062	M86.429	M87.032	M87.229	M87.822	M96.841	N28.86
M84.476A	M84.564K	M84.659P	M86.069	M86.431	M87.033	M87.231	M87.829	M96.842	N30.00
M84.476K	M84.564P	M84.661A	M86.071	M86.432	M87.034	M87.232	M87.831	M96.843	N30.01
M84.476P	M84.569A	M84.661K	M86.072	M86.439	M87.035	M87.233	M87.832	M96.89	N30.40
M84.477A	M84.569K	M84.661P	M86.079	M86.441	M87.036	M87.234	M87.833	M97.01XA	N30.41
M84.477K	M84.569P	M84.662A	M86.08	M86.442	M87.037	M87.235	M87.834	M97.02XA	N32.1
M84.477P	M84.571A	M84.662K	M86.09	M86.449	M87.038	M87.236	M87.835	M97.11XA	N32.2
M84.478A	M84.571K	M84.662P	M86.10	M86.451	M87.039	M87.237	M87.836	M97.12XA	N34.0
M84.478K	M84.571P	M84.663A	M86.111	M86.452	M87.041	M87.238	M87.837	M97.21XA	N36.0
M84.478P	M84.572A	M84.663K	M86.112	M86.459	M87.042	M87.239	M87.838	M97.22XA	N39.0
M84.479A	M84.572K	M84.663P	M86.119	M86.461	M87.043	M87.241	M87.839	M97.31XA	N41.0
M84.479K	M84.572P	M84.664A	M86.121	M86.462	M87.044	M87.242	M87.841	M97.32XA	N41.2
M84.479P	M84.573A	M84.664K	M86.122	M86.469	M87.045	M87.243	M87.842	M97.41XA	N43.1
M84.48XA	M84.573K	M84.664P	M86.129	M86.471	M87.046	M87.244	M87.843	M97.42XA	N44.00
M84.48XK	M84.573P	M84.669A	M86.131	M86.472	M87.050	M87.245	M87.844	M97.8XXA	N44.01
M84.48XP	M84.574A	M84.669K	M86.132	M86.479	M87.051	M87.246	M87.845	M97.9XXA	N44.02
M84.50XA	M84.574K	M84.669P	M86.139	M86.48	M87.052	M87.250	M87.849	M99.10	N44.03
M84.50XK	M84.574P	M84.671A	M86.141	M86.49	M87.059	M87.251	M87.850	M99.11	N44.04
M84.50XP	M84.575A	M84.671K	M86.142	M86.50	M87.061	M87.252	M87.851	M99.18	N45.4
M84.511A	M84.575K	M84.671P	M86.149	M86.511	M87.062	M87.256	M87.852	N02.0	N48.30
M84.511K	M84.575P	M84.672A	M86.151	M86.519	M87.063	M87.261	M87.859	N02.1	N48.31
M84.511P	M84.576A	M84.672K	M86.152	M86.521	M87.064	M87.262	M87.861	N02.2	N48.32
M84.512A	M84.576K	M84.672P	M86.159	M86.522	M87.065	M87.263	M87.862	N02.3	N48.33
M84.512K	M84.576P	M84.673A	M86.161	M86.529	M87.066	M87.264	M87.863	N02.4	N48.39
M84.512P	M84.58XA	M84.673K	M86.162	M86.531	M87.071	M87.265	M87.864	N02.5	N70.01
M84.519A	M84.58XK	M84.673P	M86.169	M86.532	M87.072	M87.266	M87.865	N02.6	N70.02
M84.519K	M84.58XP	M84.674A	M86.171	M86.539	M87.073	M87.271	M87.869	N02.7	N70.03
M84.519P	M84.60XA	M84.674K	M86.172	M86.541	M87.074	M87.272	M87.871	N02.8	N71.0
M84.521A	M84.60XK	M84.674P	M86.179	M86.542	M87.075	M87.273	M87.872	N02.9	N73.0
M84.521K	M84.60XP	M84.675A	M86.18	M86.549	M87.076	M87.274	M87.873	N03.0	N73.4
M84.521P	M84.611A	M84.675K	M86.19	M86.551	M87.077	M87.275	M87.874	N03.1	N75.1
M84.522A	M84.611K	M84.675P	M86.20	M86.552	M87.078	M87.276	M87.875	N03.2	N76.4
M84.522K	M84.611P	M84.676A	M86.211	M86.559	M87.079	M87.277	M87.876	N03.3	N76.81
M84.522P	M84.612A	M84.676K	M86.212	M86.561	M87.08	M87.278	M87.877	N03.4	N82.0
M84.529A	M84.612K	M84.676P	M86.219	M86.562	M87.09	M87.279	M87.878	N03.5	N82.1
M84.529K	M84.612P	M84.68XA	M86.221	M86.569	M87.10	M87.28	M87.879	N03.6	N82.2
M84.529P	M84.619A	M84.68XK	M86.222	M86.571	M87.111	M87.29	M87.88	N03.7	N82.3
M84.531A	M84.619K	M84.68XP	M86.229	M86.572	M87.112	M87.30	M87.89	N03.8	N82.4
M84.531K	M84.619P	M84.750A	M86.231	M86.579	M87.119	M87.311	M87.9	N03.9	N82.5
M84.531P	M84.621A	M84.750K	M86.232	M86.58	M87.121	M87.312	M90.50	N04.0	N82.8
M84.532A	M84.621K	M84.750P	M86.239	M86.59	M87.122	M87.319	M90.511	N04.1	N82.9
M84.532K	M84.621P	M84.751A	M86.241	M86.60	M87.129	M87.321	M90.512	N04.2	N83.511
M84.532P	M84.622A	M84.751K	M86.242	M86.611	M87.131	M87.322	M90.519	N04.3	N83.512
M84.533A	M84.622K	M84.751P	M86.249	M86.612	M87.132	M87.329	M90.521	N04.4	N83.519
M84.533K	M84.622P	M84.752A	M86.251	M86.619	M87.133	M87.331	M90.522	N04.5	N83.521
M84.533P	M84.629A	M84.752K	M86.252	M86.621	M87.134	M87.332	M90.529	N04.6	N83.522
M84.534A	M84.629K	M84.752P	M86.259	M86.622	M87.135	M87.333	M90.531	N04.7	N83.529
M84.534K	M84.629P	M84.753A	M86.261	M86.629	M87.136	M87.334	M90.532	N04.8	N83.53
M84.534P	M84.631A	M84.753K	M86.262	M86.631	M87.137	M87.335	M90.539	N04.9	N98.0
M84.539A	M84.631K	M84.753P	M86.269	M86.632	M87.138	M87.336	M90.541	N05.2	N98.1
M84.539K	M84.631P	M84.754A	M86.271	M86.639	M87.139	M87.337	M90.542	N05.3	N98.2
M84.539P	M84.632A	M84.754K	M86.272	M86.641	M87.141	M87.338	M90.549	N05.4	N98.3
M84.541A	M84.632K	M84.754P	M86.279	M86.642	M87.142	M87.339	M90.551	N05.5	N98.8
M84.541K	M84.632P	M84.755A	M86.28	M86.649	M87.143	M87.341	M90.552	N06.2	N98.9
M84.541P	M84.633A	M84.755K	M86.29	M86.651	M87.144	M87.342	M90.559	N06.3	N99.510
M84.542A	M84.633K	M84.756A	M86.30	M86.652	M87.145	M87.343	M90.561	N06.4	N99.511
M84.542K	M84.633P	M84.756K	M86.311	M86.659	M87.146	M87.344	M90.562	N06.5	N99.512
M84.542P	M84.634A	M84.756P	M86.312	M86.661	M87.150	M87.345	M90.569	N07.2	N99.518
M84.549A	M84.634K	M84.757A	M86.319	M86.662	M87.151	M87.346	M90.571	N07.3	N99.61
M84.549K	M84.634P	M84.757K	M86.321	M86.669	M87.152	M87.350	M90.572	N07.4	N99.62
M84.549P	M84.639A	M84.757P	M86.322	M86.671	M87.159	M87.351	M90.579	N07.5	N99.71
M84.550A	M84.639K	M84.758A	M86.329	M86.672	M87.161	M87.352	M90.58	N10	N99.72
M84.550K	M84.639P	M84.758K	M86.331	M86.679	M87.162	M87.353	M90.59	N11.1	N99.820
M84.550P	M84.641A	M84.758P	M86.332	M86.68	M87.163	M87.361	M96.0	N11.8	N99.821
M84.551A	M84.641K	M84.759A	M86.339	M86.69	M87.164	M87.362	M96.621	N11.9	N99.840
M84.551K	M84.641P	M84.759K	M86.341	M86.8X0	M87.165	M87.363	M96.622	N12	N99.841
M84.551P	M84.642A	M84.759P	M86.342	M86.8X1	M87.166	M87.364	M96.629	N13.0	N99.842
M84.552A	M84.642K	M86.00	M86.349	M86.8X2	M87.171	M87.365	M96.631	N13.1	N99.843
M84.552K	M84.642P	M86.011	M86.351	M86.8X3	M87.172	M87.366	M96.632	N13.2	O00.00
M84.552P	M84.649A	M86.012	M86.352	M86.8X4	M87.173	M87.371	M96.639	N13.30	O00.01
M84.553A	M84.649K	M86.019	M86.359	M86.8X5	M87.174	M87.372	M96.65	N13.39	O00.101
M84.553K	M84.649P	M86.021	M86.361	M86.8X6	M87.175	M87.373	M96.661	N13.4	O00.102
M84.553P	M84.650A	M86.022	M86.362	M86.8X7	M87.176	M87.374	M96.662	N13.6	O00.109
M84.559A	M84.650K	M86.029	M86.369	M86.8X8	M87.177	M87.375	M96.669	N13.8	O00.111
M84.559K	M84.650P	M86.031	M86.371	M86.8X9	M87.178	M87.376	M96.671	N17.8	O00.112
M84.559P	M84.651A	M86.032	M86.372	M86.9	M87.179	M87.377	M96.672	N17.9	O00.119
M84.561A	M84.651K	M86.039	M86.379	M87.00	M87.180	M87.378	M96.679	N18.4	O00.201
M84.561K	M84.651P	M86.041	M86.38	M87.011	M87.188	M87.379	M96.69	N18.5	O00.202
M84.561P	M84.652A	M86.042	M86.39	M87.012	M87.19	M87.38	M96.810	N20.1	O00.209
M84.562A	M84.652K	M86.049	M86.40	M87.019	M87.20	M87.39	M96.811	N20.2	O00.211
M84.562K	M84.652P	M86.051	M86.411	M87.021	M87.211	M87.80	M96.820	N25.1	O00.212
M84.562P	M84.653A	M86.052	M86.412	M87.022	M87.212	M87.811	M96.821	N25.81	O00.219
M84.563A	M84.653K		M86.419		M87.219	M87.812	M96.830	N28.0	O00.80

O00.81	O22.42	O30.191	O36.0922	O86.12	P28.0	Q25.0	Q61.01	Q93.89	S02.31XB
O00.90	O22.43	O30.192	O36.0923	O86.13	P28.10	Q25.1	Q61.02	Q93.9	S02.31XK
O00.91	O22.50	O30.193	O36.0924	O86.19	P28.11	Q25.21	Q61.11	R04.2	S02.32XA
O03.0	O22.51	O30.201	O36.0925	O86.20	P28.19	Q25.29	Q61.19	R04.81	S02.32XB
O03.30	O22.52	O30.202	O36.0929	O86.21	P28.2	Q25.3	Q61.2	R04.89	S02.32XK
O03.33	O22.53	O30.203	O36.0930	O86.22	P28.3	Q25.40	Q61.3	R04.9	S02.400A
O03.34	O22.8X1	O30.211	O36.0931	O86.29	P28.4	Q25.41	Q61.4	R06.3	S02.400B
O03.35	O22.8X2	O30.212	O36.0932	O86.4	P35.0	Q25.42	Q61.5	R09.01	S02.400K
O03.36	O22.8X3	O30.213	O36.0933	O87.0	P38.1	Q25.43	Q61.8	R17	S02.401A
O03.37	O22.8X9	O30.221	O36.0934	O87.2	P38.9	Q25.44	Q61.9	R18.0	S02.401B
O03.38	O22.90	O30.222	O36.0935	O87.3	P39.0	Q25.45	Q62.0	R18.8	S02.401K
O03.39	O23.01	O30.223	O36.0939	O87.8	P39.2	Q25.46	Q62.10	R29.0	S02.402A
O03.5	O23.02	O30.231	O36.4XX0	O88.319	P39.3	Q25.47	Q62.11	R29.1	S02.402B
O03.7	O23.03	O30.232	O36.4XX1	O98.011	P39.4	Q25.48	Q62.12	R29.5	S02.402K
O03.80	O23.11	O30.233	O36.4XX2	O98.012	P39.8	Q25.49	Q62.2	R39.0	S02.40AA
O03.83	O23.12	O30.291	O36.4XX3	O98.013	P39.9	Q25.8	Q62.31	R40.3	S02.40AB
O03.84	O23.13	O30.292	O36.4XX4	O98.02	P52.0	Q25.9	Q62.32	R41.4	S02.40AK
O03.85	O23.21	O30.293	O36.4XX5	O98.03	P52.1	Q26.0	Q62.39	R44.0	S02.40BA
O03.86	O23.22	O30.801	O36.4XX9	O98.111	P52.3	Q26.1	Q64.10	R44.2	S02.40BB
O03.87	O23.23	O30.802	O41.01X0	O98.112	P53	Q26.2	Q64.11	R44.3	S02.40BK
O03.88	O23.31	O30.803	O41.01X1	O98.113	P54.4	Q26.3	Q64.12	R45.851	S02.40CA
O03.89	O23.32	O30.811	O41.01X2	O98.12	P61.2	Q26.4	Q64.19	R47.01	S02.40CB
O04.5	O23.33	O30.812	O41.01X4	O98.13	P61.3	Q26.8	Q64.31	R56.00	S02.40CK
O04.80	O23.41	O30.813	O41.01X5	O98.211	P61.4	Q26.9	Q64.32	R56.01	S02.40DA
O04.83	O23.42	O30.821	O41.01X9	O98.212	P61.6	Q27.30	Q64.33	R56.1	S02.40DB
O04.84	O23.43	O30.822	O41.02X0	O98.213	P70.2	Q27.4	Q64.39	R57.9	S02.40DK
O04.85	O23.511	O30.823	O41.02X1	O98.22	P70.8	Q28.0	Q67.5	R64	S02.40EA
O04.86	O23.512	O30.831	O41.02X2	O98.23	P71.0	Q28.1	Q67.8	R65.10	S02.40EB
O04.87	O23.513	O30.832	O41.02X3	O98.311	P71.1	Q28.8	Q68.1	R71.0	S02.40EK
O04.88	O23.521	O30.833	O41.02X5	O98.312	P71.2	Q28.9	Q74.3	R78.81	S02.40FA
O04.89	O23.522	O30.891	O41.02X9	O98.313	P71.3	Q31.1	Q76.3	R82.0	S02.40FB
O07.0	O23.523	O30.892	O41.03X0	O98.32	P71.8	Q31.2	Q76.425	R82.1	S02.40FK
O07.1	O23.591	O30.893	O41.03X1	O98.33	P71.9	Q31.3	Q76.426	S01.101A	S02.411A
O07.30	O23.592	O31.8X10	O41.03X2	O98.411	P72.0	Q31.5	Q76.427	S01.102A	S02.411B
O07.33	O23.593	O31.8X11	O41.03X3	O98.412	P72.1	Q31.8	Q76.428	S01.109A	S02.411K
O07.34	O23.91	O31.8X12	O41.03X4	O98.413	P72.2	Q31.9	Q76.429	S02.0XXA	S02.412A
O07.35	O23.92	O31.8X13	O41.03X5	O98.42	P72.8	Q32.0	Q76.6	S02.0XXK	S02.412B
O07.36	O23.93	O31.8X14	O41.03X9	O98.43	P74.41	Q32.1	Q76.7	S02.101A	S02.412K
O07.37	O24.011	O31.8X15	O44.01	O98.511	P74.5	Q32.2	Q76.8	S02.101K	S02.413A
O07.38	O24.012	O31.8X19	O44.02	O98.512	P74.6	Q32.3	Q76.9	S02.102A	S02.413K
O07.39	O24.013	O31.8X20	O44.03	O98.513	P74.8	Q32.4	Q77.2	S02.102K	S02.42XA
O08.0	O24.019	O31.8X21	O44.21	O98.52	P76.1	Q33.0	Q78.0	S02.109A	S02.42XB
O08.1	O24.03	O31.8X22	O44.22	O98.53	P83.0	Q33.4	Q78.2	S02.109K	S02.42XK
O08.5	O24.111	O31.8X23	O44.23	O98.611	P83.30	Q39.5	Q79.60	S02.110A	S02.5XXK
O08.6	O24.112	O31.8X24	O44.41	O98.612	P83.39	Q39.6	Q79.61	S02.110K	S02.600A
O08.7	O24.113	O31.8X25	O44.42	O98.613	P91.60	Q39.8	Q79.62	S02.111A	S02.600B
O08.81	O24.119	O31.8X29	O44.43	O98.62	P91.61	Q39.9	Q79.63	S02.111K	S02.600K
O08.82	O24.13	O31.8X30	O47.02	O98.63	P91.62	Q41.0	Q79.69	S02.112A	S02.601A
O08.83	O24.311	O31.8X31	O47.03	O98.711	P93.0	Q41.1	Q85.1	S02.112K	S02.601B
O08.89	O24.312	O31.8X32	O47.1	O98.712	P93.8	Q41.2	Q85.8	S02.113A	S02.601K
O08.9	O24.313	O31.8X33	O60.10X0	O98.713	P94.0	Q41.8	Q85.9	S02.113K	S02.602A
O10.011	O24.319	O31.8X34	O60.10X1	O98.72	P96.1	Q41.9	Q87.11	S02.118A	S02.602B
O10.012	O24.33	O31.8X35	O60.10X2	O98.73	P96.2	Q42.0	Q87.19	S02.118K	S02.602K
O10.013	O24.811	O31.8X39	O60.10X3	O98.811	Q01.0	Q42.1	Q87.2	S02.119A	S02.609A
O10.02	O24.812	O33.0	O60.10X4	O98.812	Q01.1	Q42.2	Q87.3	S02.119K	S02.609B
O10.411	O24.813	O36.0110	O60.10X5	O98.813	Q01.2	Q42.3	Q87.40	S02.11AA	S02.609K
O10.412	O24.819	O36.0111	O60.10X9	O98.82	Q01.8	Q42.8	Q87.410	S02.11AK	S02.610A
O10.413	O24.83	O36.0112	O60.20X0	O98.83	Q01.9	Q42.9	Q87.418	S02.11BA	S02.610B
O10.43	O24.911	O36.0113	O60.20X1	O98.911	Q04.4	Q43.1	Q87.42	S02.11BK	S02.610K
O10.911	O24.912	O36.0114	O60.20X2	O98.912	Q04.5	Q43.2	Q87.43	S02.11CA	S02.611A
O10.912	O24.913	O36.0115	O60.20X3	O98.913	Q04.6	Q43.3	Q87.5	S02.11CK	S02.611B
O10.913	O24.919	O36.0119	O60.20X4	O98.92	Q04.8	Q43.4	Q87.81	S02.11DA	S02.611K
O10.92	O24.93	O36.0120	O60.20X5	O98.93	Q05.0	Q43.5	Q87.82	S02.11DK	S02.612A
O12.11	O26.611	O36.0121	O60.20X9	O99.111	Q05.1	Q43.6	Q87.89	S02.11EA	S02.612B
O12.12	O26.612	O36.0122	O63.9	O99.112	Q05.2	Q43.7	Q89.01	S02.11EK	S02.612K
O12.13	O26.613	O36.0123	O68	O99.113	Q05.3	Q43.8	Q89.09	S02.11FA	S02.620A
O12.21	O26.62	O36.0124	O70.20	O99.12	Q05.4	Q43.9	Q89.3	S02.11FK	S02.620B
O12.22	O26.831	O36.0125	O70.21	O99.13	Q07.02	Q44.0	Q89.7	S02.11GA	S02.620K
O12.23	O26.832	O36.0129	O70.22	O99.321	Q07.03	Q44.1	Q89.8	S02.11GK	S02.621A
O14.02	O26.833	O36.0130	O70.23	O99.322	Q20.5	Q44.4	Q91.0	S02.11HA	S02.621B
O14.03	O26.872	O36.0131	O70.3	O99.323	Q21.0	Q44.5	Q91.1	S02.11HK	S02.621K
O14.92	O26.873	O36.0132	O70.4	O99.324	Q21.1	Q44.6	Q91.2	S02.121A	S02.622A
O14.93	O26.879	O36.0133	O71.2	O99.325	Q21.2	Q44.7	Q91.3	S02.121K	S02.622B
O16.1	O30.101	O36.0134	O71.3	O99.354	Q22.1	Q45.0	Q91.4	S02.122A	S02.622K
O16.2	O30.102	O36.0135	O71.4	O99.355	Q22.2	Q45.1	Q91.5	S02.122K	S02.630A
O16.3	O30.103	O36.0139	O71.5	O99.411	Q22.3	Q45.2	Q91.6	S02.129A	S02.630B
O20.0	O30.111	O36.0910	O71.6	O99.412	Q23.0	Q45.3	Q91.7	S02.129K	S02.630K
O20.9	O30.112	O36.0911	O71.7	O99.413	Q23.1	Q60.0	Q93.3	S02.19XA	S02.631A
O22.20	O30.113	O36.0912	O72.0	O99.43	Q23.2	Q60.1	Q93.4	S02.19XK	S02.631B
O22.21	O30.121	O36.0913	O72.1	O99.830	Q23.3	Q60.2	Q93.51	S02.2XXB	S02.631K
O22.22	O30.122	O36.0914	O72.2	O99.834	Q24.0	Q60.3	Q93.59	S02.2XXK	S02.632A
O22.23	O30.123	O36.0915	O75.2	O99.835	Q24.1	Q60.4	Q93.7	S02.30XA	S02.632B
O22.30	O30.131	O36.0919	O86.11	P10.2	Q24.3	Q60.5	Q93.82	S02.30XB	S02.632K
O22.40	O30.132	O36.0920	O86.11	P12.2	Q24.5	Q60.6	Q93.88	S02.30XK	S02.640A
O22.41	O30.133	O36.0921					Q61.00	S02.31XA	

Alphabetic & Numeric Lists of CCs

S02.640B	S04.32XA	S06.9X2A	S12.201A	S12.690K	S21.122A	S22.069A	S27.319A	S32.059A	S32.441K
S02.640K	S04.40XA	S06.9X3A	S12.201K	S12.691A	S21.129A	S22.069K	S27.321A	S32.059K	S32.442K
S02.641A	S04.41XA	S06.9X4A	S12.230A	S12.691K	S21.131A	S22.070A	S27.322A	S32.10XA	S32.443K
S02.641B	S04.42XA	S06.9X5A	S12.230K	S12.9XXA	S21.132A	S22.070K	S27.329A	S32.10XK	S32.444K
S02.641K	S04.50XA	S06.9X9A	S12.231A	S13.0XXA	S21.139A	S22.071A	S27.391A	S32.110A	S32.445K
S02.642A	S04.51XA	S07.0XXA	S12.231K	S13.100A	S21.141A	S22.071K	S27.392A	S32.110K	S32.446K
S02.642B	S04.52XA	S07.1XXA	S12.24XA	S13.101A	S21.142A	S22.072A	S27.399A	S32.111A	S32.451K
S02.642K	S04.60XA	S07.8XXA	S12.24XK	S13.110A	S21.149A	S22.072K	S27.50XA	S32.111K	S32.452K
S02.650A	S04.61XA	S07.9XXA	S12.250A	S13.111A	S21.151A	S22.078A	S27.51XA	S32.112A	S32.453K
S02.650B	S04.62XA	S09.20XA	S12.250K	S13.120A	S21.152A	S22.078K	S27.52XA	S32.112K	S32.454K
S02.650K	S04.70XA	S09.21XA	S12.251A	S13.121A	S21.159A	S22.079A	S27.53XA	S32.119A	S32.455K
S02.651A	S04.71XA	S09.22XA	S12.251K	S13.130A	S21.90XA	S22.079K	S27.59XA	S32.119K	S32.456K
S02.651B	S04.72XA	S09.301A	S12.290A	S13.131A	S21.91XA	S22.20XA	S27.60XA	S32.120A	S32.461K
S02.651K	S04.811A	S09.302A	S12.290K	S13.140A	S21.92XA	S22.20XK	S27.63XA	S32.120K	S32.462K
S02.652A	S04.812A	S09.309A	S12.291A	S13.141A	S21.93XA	S22.21XA	S27.69XA	S32.121A	S32.463K
S02.652B	S04.819A	S09.311A	S12.291K	S13.150A	S21.94XA	S22.21XK	S27.802A	S32.121K	S32.464K
S02.652K	S04.891A	S09.312A	S12.300A	S13.151A	S21.95XA	S22.22XA	S27.803A	S32.122A	S32.465K
S02.66XA	S04.892A	S09.313A	S12.300K	S13.160A	S22.000A	S22.22XK	S27.808A	S32.122K	S32.466K
S02.66XB	S04.899A	S09.319A	S12.301A	S13.161A	S22.000K	S22.23XA	S27.809A	S32.129A	S32.471K
S02.66XK	S04.9XXA	S09.391A	S12.301K	S13.170A	S22.001A	S22.23XK	S27.892A	S32.129K	S32.472K
S02.670A	S05.20XA	S09.392A	S12.330A	S13.171A	S22.001K	S22.24XA	S27.893A	S32.130A	S32.473K
S02.670B	S05.21XA	S09.399A	S12.330K	S13.180A	S22.002A	S22.24XK	S27.898A	S32.130K	S32.474K
S02.670K	S05.22XA	S11.10XA	S12.331A	S13.181A	S22.002K	S22.31XA	S27.899A	S32.131A	S32.475K
S02.671A	S05.30XA	S11.11XA	S12.331K	S13.20XA	S22.008A	S22.31XK	S27.9XXA	S32.131K	S32.476K
S02.671B	S05.31XA	S11.12XA	S12.34XA	S13.29XA	S22.008K	S22.32XA	S28.1XXA	S32.132A	S32.481K
S02.671K	S05.32XA	S11.13XA	S12.34XK	S15.001A	S22.009A	S22.32XK	S29.021A	S32.132K	S32.482K
S02.672A	S05.40XA	S11.14XA	S12.350A	S15.002A	S22.009K	S22.39XA	S29.029A	S32.139A	S32.483K
S02.672B	S05.41XA	S11.15XA	S12.350K	S15.009A	S22.010A	S22.39XK	S32.000A	S32.139K	S32.484K
S02.672K	S05.42XA	S11.20XA	S12.351A	S15.011A	S22.010K	S22.41XA	S32.000K	S32.14XA	S32.485K
S02.69XA	S05.50XA	S11.21XA	S12.351K	S15.012A	S22.011A	S22.41XK	S32.001A	S32.14XK	S32.486K
S02.69XB	S05.51XA	S11.22XA	S12.390A	S15.019A	S22.011K	S22.42XA	S32.001K	S32.15XA	S32.491K
S02.69XK	S05.52XA	S11.23XA	S12.390K	S15.021A	S22.012A	S22.42XK	S32.002A	S32.15XK	S32.492K
S02.80XA	S05.70XA	S11.24XA	S12.391A	S15.022A	S22.012K	S22.43XA	S32.002K	S32.16XA	S32.499K
S02.80XB	S05.71XA	S11.25XA	S12.391K	S15.029A	S22.018A	S22.43XK	S32.008A	S32.16XK	S32.501A
S02.80XK	S05.72XA	S12.000A	S12.400A	S15.091A	S22.018K	S22.49XA	S32.008K	S32.17XA	S32.501K
S02.81XA	S05.8X1A	S12.000K	S12.400K	S15.092A	S22.019A	S22.49XK	S32.009A	S32.17XK	S32.502A
S02.81XB	S05.8X2A	S12.001A	S12.401A	S15.099A	S22.019K	S22.5XXK	S32.009K	S32.19XA	S32.502K
S02.81XK	S05.8X9A	S12.001K	S12.401K	S15.101A	S22.020A	S22.9XXA	S32.010A	S32.19XK	S32.509A
S02.82XA	S05.91XA	S12.01XA	S12.430A	S15.102A	S22.020K	S22.9XXK	S32.010K	S32.2XXA	S32.509K
S02.82XB	S05.92XA	S12.01XK	S12.430K	S15.109A	S22.021A	S25.501A	S32.011A	S32.2XXK	S32.511A
S02.82XK	S06.0X1A	S12.02XA	S12.431A	S15.111A	S22.021K	S25.502A	S32.011K	S32.301A	S32.511K
S02.831A	S06.0X9A	S12.02XK	S12.431K	S15.112A	S22.022A	S25.509A	S32.012A	S32.301K	S32.512A
S02.831B	S06.2X1A	S12.030A	S12.44XA	S15.119A	S22.022K	S25.511A	S32.012K	S32.302A	S32.512K
S02.831K	S06.2X2A	S12.030K	S12.44XK	S15.121A	S22.028A	S25.512A	S32.018A	S32.302K	S32.519A
S02.832A	S06.2X3A	S12.031A	S12.450A	S15.122A	S22.028K	S25.519A	S32.018K	S32.309A	S32.519K
S02.832B	S06.2X4A	S12.031K	S12.450K	S15.129A	S22.029A	S25.591A	S32.019A	S32.309K	S32.591A
S02.832K	S06.2X5A	S12.040A	S12.451A	S15.191A	S22.029K	S25.592A	S32.019K	S32.311A	S32.591K
S02.839A	S06.2X9A	S12.040K	S12.451K	S15.192A	S22.030A	S25.599A	S32.020A	S32.311K	S32.592A
S02.839B	S06.301A	S12.041A	S12.490A	S15.199A	S22.030K	S25.801A	S32.020K	S32.312A	S32.592K
S02.839K	S06.302A	S12.041K	S12.490K	S15.201A	S22.031A	S25.802A	S32.021A	S32.312K	S32.599A
S02.841A	S06.303A	S12.090A	S12.491A	S15.202A	S22.031K	S25.809A	S32.021K	S32.313A	S32.599K
S02.841B	S06.304A	S12.090K	S12.491K	S15.209A	S22.032A	S25.811A	S32.022A	S32.313K	S32.601A
S02.841K	S06.305A	S12.091A	S12.500A	S15.211A	S22.032K	S25.812A	S32.022K	S32.314A	S32.601K
S02.842A	S06.309A	S12.091K	S12.500K	S15.212A	S22.038A	S25.819A	S32.028A	S32.314K	S32.602A
S02.842B	S06.371A	S12.100A	S12.501A	S15.219A	S22.038K	S25.891A	S32.028K	S32.315A	S32.602K
S02.842K	S06.372A	S12.100K	S12.501K	S15.221A	S22.039A	S25.892A	S32.029A	S32.315K	S32.609A
S02.849A	S06.373A	S12.101A	S12.530A	S15.222A	S22.039K	S25.899A	S32.029K	S32.316A	S32.609K
S02.849B	S06.374A	S12.101K	S12.530K	S15.229A	S22.040A	S25.90XA	S32.030A	S32.316K	S32.611A
S02.849K	S06.375A	S12.110A	S12.531A	S15.291A	S22.040K	S25.91XA	S32.030K	S32.391A	S32.611K
S02.85XA	S06.379A	S12.110K	S12.531K	S15.292A	S22.041A	S25.99XA	S32.031A	S32.391K	S32.612A
S02.85XB	S06.381A	S12.111A	S12.54XA	S15.299A	S22.041K	S26.00XA	S32.031K	S32.392A	S32.612K
S02.85XK	S06.382A	S12.111K	S12.54XK	S15.301A	S22.042A	S26.01XA	S32.032A	S32.392K	S32.613A
S02.91XA	S06.383A	S12.112A	S12.550A	S15.302A	S22.042K	S26.09XA	S32.032K	S32.399A	S32.613K
S02.91XK	S06.384A	S12.112K	S12.550K	S15.309A	S22.048A	S26.10XA	S32.038A	S32.399K	S32.614A
S02.92XA	S06.385A	S12.120A	S12.551A	S15.311A	S22.048K	S26.11XA	S32.038K	S32.401A	S32.614K
S02.92XB	S06.389A	S12.120K	S12.551K	S15.312A	S22.049A	S26.19XA	S32.039A	S32.402A	S32.615A
S02.92XK	S06.811A	S12.121A	S12.590A	S15.319A	S22.049K	S26.90XA	S32.039K	S32.409K	S32.615K
S04.011A	S06.812A	S12.121K	S12.590K	S15.321A	S22.050A	S26.91XA	S32.040A	S32.411A	S32.616A
S04.012A	S06.813A	S12.130A	S12.591A	S15.322A	S22.050K	S26.99XA	S32.040K	S32.412A	S32.616K
S04.019A	S06.814A	S12.130K	S12.591K	S15.329A	S22.051A	S27.0XXA	S32.041A	S32.413A	S32.691A
S04.02XA	S06.815A	S12.131A	S12.600A	S15.391A	S22.051K	S27.301A	S32.041K	S32.414A	S32.691K
S04.031A	S06.819A	S12.131K	S12.600K	S15.392A	S22.052A	S27.302A	S32.042A	S32.415K	S32.692A
S04.032A	S06.821A	S12.14XA	S12.601A	S15.399A	S22.052K	S27.309A	S32.042K	S32.416A	S32.692K
S04.039A	S06.822A	S12.14XK	S12.601K	S15.8XXA	S22.058A	S27.311A	S32.048A	S32.421K	S32.699A
S04.041A	S06.823A	S12.150A	S12.630A	S15.9XXA	S22.058K	S27.312A	S32.048K	S32.422K	S32.699K
S04.042A	S06.824A	S12.150K	S12.630K	S17.0XXA	S22.059A	S27.319A	S32.049A	S32.423K	S32.810A
S04.049A	S06.825A	S12.151A	S12.631A	S17.8XXA	S22.059K	—	S32.049K	S32.424K	S32.810K
S04.10XA	S06.829A	S12.151K	S12.631K	S17.9XXA	S22.060A	—	S32.050A	S32.425K	S32.811A
S04.11XA	S06.891A	S12.190A	S12.64XA	S21.101A	S22.060K	—	S32.050K	S32.426K	S32.811K
S04.12XA	S06.892A	S12.190K	S12.64XK	S21.102A	S22.061A	—	S32.051A	S32.431K	S32.82XA
S04.20XA	S06.893A	S12.191A	S12.650A	S21.109A	S22.061K	—	S32.051K	S32.432K	S32.82XK
S04.21XA	S06.894A	S12.191K	S12.650K	S21.111A	S22.062A	—	S32.052A	S32.433K	S32.89XA
S04.22XA	S06.895A	S12.200A	S12.651A	S21.112A	S22.062K	—	S32.052K	S32.434K	S32.89XK
S04.30XA	S06.899A	S12.200K	S12.651K	S21.119A	S22.068A	—	S32.058A	S32.435K	S32.9XXA
S04.31XA	S06.9X1A	—	S12.690A	S21.121A	S22.068K	—	S32.058K	S32.436K	S32.9XXK

S35.531A	S36.513A	S42.002K	S42.113P	S42.192B	S42.256K	S42.331P	S42.409A	S42.451K	S42.91XP
S35.532A	S36.518A	S42.002P	S42.114B	S42.192K	S42.256P	S42.332A	S42.409K	S42.451P	S42.92XA
S35.533A	S36.519A	S42.009B	S42.114K	S42.192P	S42.261A	S42.332K	S42.409P	S42.452A	S42.92XK
S35.534A	S36.520A	S42.009K	S42.114P	S42.199B	S42.261K	S42.332P	S42.411A	S42.452K	S42.92XP
S35.535A	S36.521A	S42.009P	S42.115B	S42.199K	S42.261P	S42.333A	S42.411K	S42.452P	S43.201A
S35.536A	S36.522A	S42.011B	S42.115K	S42.199P	S42.262A	S42.333K	S42.411P	S42.453A	S43.202A
S35.8X1A	S36.523A	S42.011K	S42.115P	S42.201A	S42.262K	S42.333P	S42.412A	S42.453K	S43.203A
S35.8X8A	S36.528A	S42.011P	S42.116B	S42.201K	S42.262P	S42.334A	S42.412K	S42.453P	S43.204A
S35.8X9A	S36.529A	S42.012B	S42.116K	S42.201P	S42.263A	S42.334K	S42.412P	S42.454A	S43.205A
S35.90XA	S36.530A	S42.012K	S42.116P	S42.202A	S42.263K	S42.334P	S42.413A	S42.454K	S43.206A
S35.91XA	S36.531A	S42.012P	S42.121B	S42.202K	S42.263P	S42.335A	S42.413K	S42.454P	S43.211A
S35.99XA	S36.532A	S42.013B	S42.121K	S42.202P	S42.264A	S42.335K	S42.413P	S42.455A	S43.212A
S36.00XA	S36.533A	S42.013K	S42.121P	S42.209A	S42.264K	S42.335P	S42.414A	S42.455K	S43.213A
S36.020A	S36.538A	S42.013P	S42.122B	S42.209K	S42.264P	S42.336A	S42.414K	S42.455P	S43.214A
S36.021A	S36.539A	S42.014B	S42.122K	S42.209P	S42.265A	S42.336K	S42.414P	S42.456A	S43.215A
S36.029A	S36.590A	S42.014K	S42.122P	S42.211A	S42.265K	S42.336P	S42.415A	S42.456K	S43.216A
S36.030A	S36.591A	S42.014P	S42.123B	S42.211K	S42.265P	S42.341A	S42.415K	S42.456P	S43.221A
S36.039A	S36.592A	S42.015B	S42.123K	S42.211P	S42.266A	S42.341K	S42.415P	S42.461A	S43.222A
S36.09XA	S36.593A	S42.015K	S42.123P	S42.212A	S42.266K	S42.341P	S42.416A	S42.461K	S43.223A
S36.112A	S36.598A	S42.015P	S42.124B	S42.212K	S42.266P	S42.342A	S42.416K	S42.461P	S43.224A
S36.113A	S36.599A	S42.016B	S42.124K	S42.212P	S42.271A	S42.342K	S42.416P	S42.462A	S43.225A
S36.114A	S36.60XA	S42.016K	S42.124P	S42.213A	S42.271K	S42.342P	S42.421A	S42.462K	S43.226A
S36.118A	S36.61XA	S42.016P	S42.125B	S42.213K	S42.271P	S42.343A	S42.421K	S42.462P	S45.101A
S36.119A	S36.62XA	S42.017B	S42.125K	S42.213P	S42.272A	S42.343K	S42.421P	S42.463A	S45.102A
S36.122A	S36.63XA	S42.017K	S42.125P	S42.214A	S42.272K	S42.343P	S42.422A	S42.463K	S45.109A
S36.123A	S36.69XA	S42.017P	S42.126B	S42.214K	S42.272P	S42.344A	S42.422K	S42.463P	S45.111A
S36.128A	S36.81XA	S42.018B	S42.126K	S42.214P	S42.279A	S42.344K	S42.422P	S42.464A	S45.112A
S36.129A	S36.892A	S42.018K	S42.126P	S42.215A	S42.279K	S42.344P	S42.423A	S42.464K	S45.119A
S36.13XA	S36.893A	S42.018P	S42.131B	S42.215K	S42.279P	S42.345A	S42.423K	S42.464P	S45.191A
S36.200A	S36.898A	S42.019B	S42.131K	S42.215P	S42.291A	S42.345K	S42.423P	S42.465A	S45.192A
S36.201A	S36.899A	S42.019K	S42.131P	S42.216A	S42.291K	S42.345P	S42.424A	S42.465K	S45.199A
S36.202A	S36.90XA	S42.019P	S42.132B	S42.216K	S42.291P	S42.346A	S42.424K	S42.465P	S45.201A
S36.209A	S36.92XA	S42.021B	S42.132K	S42.216P	S42.292A	S42.346K	S42.424P	S42.466A	S45.202A
S36.220A	S36.93XA	S42.021K	S42.132P	S42.221A	S42.292K	S42.346P	S42.425A	S42.466K	S45.209A
S36.221A	S36.99XA	S42.021P	S42.133B	S42.221K	S42.292P	S42.351A	S42.425K	S42.466P	S45.211A
S36.222A	S37.001A	S42.022B	S42.133K	S42.221P	S42.293A	S42.351K	S42.425P	S42.471A	S45.212A
S36.229A	S37.002A	S42.022K	S42.133P	S42.222A	S42.293K	S42.351P	S42.426A	S42.471K	S45.219A
S36.230A	S37.009A	S42.022P	S42.134B	S42.222K	S42.293P	S42.352A	S42.426K	S42.471P	S45.291A
S36.231A	S37.011A	S42.023B	S42.134K	S42.222P	S42.294A	S42.352K	S42.426P	S42.472A	S45.292A
S36.232A	S37.012A	S42.023K	S42.134P	S42.223A	S42.294K	S42.352P	S42.431A	S42.472K	S45.299A
S36.239A	S37.019A	S42.023P	S42.135B	S42.223K	S42.294P	S42.353A	S42.431K	S42.472P	S45.301A
S36.240A	S37.021A	S42.024B	S42.135K	S42.223P	S42.295A	S42.353K	S42.431P	S42.473A	S45.302A
S36.241A	S37.022A	S42.024K	S42.135P	S42.224A	S42.295K	S42.353P	S42.432A	S42.473K	S45.309A
S36.242A	S37.029A	S42.024P	S42.136B	S42.224K	S42.295P	S42.354A	S42.432K	S42.473P	S45.311A
S36.249A	S37.031A	S42.025B	S42.136K	S42.224P	S42.296A	S42.354K	S42.432P	S42.474A	S45.312A
S36.250A	S37.032A	S42.025K	S42.136P	S42.225A	S42.296K	S42.354P	S42.433A	S42.474K	S45.319A
S36.251A	S37.039A	S42.025P	S42.141B	S42.225K	S42.296P	S42.355A	S42.433K	S42.474P	S45.391A
S36.252A	S37.041A	S42.026B	S42.141K	S42.225P	S42.301A	S42.355K	S42.433P	S42.475A	S45.392A
S36.259A	S37.042A	S42.026K	S42.141P	S42.226A	S42.301K	S42.355P	S42.434A	S42.475K	S45.399A
S36.260A	S37.049A	S42.026P	S42.142B	S42.226K	S42.301P	S42.356A	S42.434K	S42.475P	S45.801A
S36.261A	S37.051A	S42.031B	S42.142K	S42.226P	S42.302A	S42.356K	S42.434P	S42.476A	S45.802A
S36.262A	S37.052A	S42.031K	S42.142P	S42.231A	S42.302K	S42.356P	S42.435A	S42.476K	S45.809A
S36.269A	S37.059A	S42.031P	S42.143B	S42.231K	S42.302P	S42.361A	S42.435K	S42.476P	S45.811A
S36.290A	S37.10XA	S42.032B	S42.143K	S42.231P	S42.309A	S42.361K	S42.435P	S42.481A	S45.812A
S36.291A	S37.12XA	S42.032K	S42.143P	S42.232A	S42.309K	S42.361P	S42.436A	S42.481K	S45.819A
S36.292A	S37.13XA	S42.032P	S42.144B	S42.232K	S42.309P	S42.362A	S42.436K	S42.481P	S45.891A
S36.299A	S37.19XA	S42.033B	S42.144K	S42.232P	S42.311A	S42.362K	S42.436P	S42.482A	S45.892A
S36.30XA	S37.20XA	S42.033K	S42.144P	S42.239A	S42.311K	S42.362P	S42.441A	S42.482K	S45.899A
S36.32XA	S37.22XA	S42.033P	S42.145B	S42.239K	S42.311P	S42.363A	S42.441K	S42.482P	S45.901A
S36.33XA	S37.23XA	S42.034B	S42.145K	S42.239P	S42.312A	S42.363K	S42.441P	S42.489A	S45.902A
S36.39XA	S37.29XA	S42.034K	S42.145P	S42.241A	S42.312K	S42.363P	S42.442A	S42.489K	S45.909A
S36.400A	S37.30XA	S42.034P	S42.146B	S42.241K	S42.312P	S42.364A	S42.442K	S42.489P	S45.911A
S36.408A	S37.32XA	S42.035B	S42.146K	S42.241P	S42.319A	S42.364K	S42.442P	S42.491A	S45.912A
S36.409A	S37.33XA	S42.035K	S42.146P	S42.242A	S42.319K	S42.364P	S42.443A	S42.491K	S45.919A
S36.410A	S37.39XA	S42.035P	S42.151B	S42.242K	S42.319P	S42.365A	S42.443K	S42.491P	S45.991A
S36.418A	S37.60XA	S42.036B	S42.151K	S42.242P	S42.321A	S42.365K	S42.443P	S42.492A	S45.992A
S36.419A	S37.62XA	S42.036K	S42.151P	S42.249A	S42.321K	S42.365P	S42.444A	S42.492K	S45.999A
S36.420A	S37.63XA	S42.036P	S42.152B	S42.249K	S42.321P	S42.366A	S42.444K	S42.492P	S46.021A
S36.428A	S37.69XA	S42.101B	S42.152K	S42.249P	S42.322A	S42.366K	S42.444P	S42.493A	S46.022A
S36.429A	S37.812A	S42.101K	S42.152P	S42.251A	S42.322K	S42.366P	S42.445A	S42.493K	S46.029A
S36.430A	S37.813A	S42.101P	S42.153B	S42.251K	S42.322P	S42.391A	S42.445K	S42.493P	S46.121A
S36.438A	S37.818A	S42.102B	S42.153K	S42.251P	S42.323A	S42.391K	S42.445P	S42.494A	S46.122A
S36.439A	S37.819A	S42.102K	S42.153P	S42.252A	S42.323K	S42.391P	S42.446A	S42.494K	S46.129A
S36.490A	S37.892A	S42.102P	S42.154B	S42.252K	S42.323P	S42.392A	S42.446K	S42.494P	S46.221A
S36.498A	S37.893A	S42.109B	S42.154K	S42.252P	S42.324A	S42.392K	S42.446P	S42.495A	S46.222A
S36.499A	S37.898A	S42.109K	S42.154P	S42.253A	S42.324K	S42.392P	S42.447A	S42.495K	S46.229A
S36.500A	S37.899A	S42.109P	S42.155B	S42.253K	S42.324P	S42.399A	S42.447K	S42.495P	S46.321A
S36.501A	S37.90XA	S42.111B	S42.155K	S42.253P	S42.325A	S42.399K	S42.447P	S42.496A	S46.322A
S36.502A	S37.92XA	S42.111K	S42.155P	S42.254A	S42.325K	S42.399P	S42.448A	S42.496K	S46.329A
S36.503A	S37.93XA	S42.111P	S42.156B	S42.254K	S42.325P	S42.401A	S42.448K	S42.496P	S46.821A
S36.508A	S37.99XA	S42.112B	S42.156K	S42.254P	S42.326A	S42.401K	S42.448P	S42.90XA	S46.822A
S36.509A	S42.001B	S42.112K	S42.156P	S42.255A	S42.326K	S42.401P	S42.449A	S42.90XK	S46.829A
S36.510A	S42.001K	S42.112P	S42.191B	S42.255K	S42.326P	S42.402A	S42.449K	S42.90XP	S46.921A
S36.511A	S42.001P	S42.113B	S42.191K	S42.255P	S42.331A	S42.402K	S42.449P	S42.91XA	S46.922A
S36.512A	S42.002B	S42.113K	S42.191P	S42.256A	S42.331K	S42.402P	S42.451A	S42.91XK	S46.929A

S48.011A	S49.112K	S52.023R	S52.046K	S52.126Q	S52.219P	S52.241A	S52.261K	S52.291Q	S52.326P
S48.012A	S49.112P	S52.024K	S52.046M	S52.126R	S52.221A	S52.241K	S52.261M	S52.291R	S52.326Q
S48.019A	S49.119A	S52.024M	S52.046N	S52.131K	S52.221K	S52.241M	S52.261N	S52.292A	S52.326R
S48.021A	S49.119K	S52.024N	S52.046P	S52.131M	S52.221M	S52.241N	S52.261P	S52.292K	S52.331A
S48.022A	S49.119P	S52.024P	S52.046Q	S52.131N	S52.221N	S52.241P	S52.261Q	S52.292M	S52.331K
S48.029A	S49.121A	S52.024Q	S52.046R	S52.131P	S52.221P	S52.241Q	S52.261R	S52.292N	S52.331M
S48.111A	S49.121K	S52.024R	S52.091K	S52.131Q	S52.221Q	S52.241R	S52.262A	S52.292P	S52.331N
S48.112A	S49.121P	S52.025K	S52.091M	S52.131R	S52.221R	S52.242A	S52.262K	S52.292Q	S52.331P
S48.119A	S49.122A	S52.025M	S52.091N	S52.132K	S52.222A	S52.242K	S52.262M	S52.292R	S52.331R
S48.121A	S49.122K	S52.025N	S52.091P	S52.132M	S52.222K	S52.242M	S52.262N	S52.299A	S52.332A
S48.122A	S49.122P	S52.025P	S52.091Q	S52.132N	S52.222M	S52.242N	S52.262P	S52.299K	S52.332K
S48.129A	S49.129A	S52.025Q	S52.092K	S52.132P	S52.222P	S52.242P	S52.262Q	S52.299M	S52.332N
S48.911A	S49.129K	S52.025R	S52.092M	S52.132Q	S52.222Q	S52.242Q	S52.262R	S52.299N	S52.332P
S48.912A	S49.129P	S52.026K	S52.092N	S52.132R	S52.222R	S52.242R	S52.263A	S52.299P	S52.332Q
S48.919A	S49.131A	S52.026M	S52.092P	S52.133K	S52.223A	S52.243A	S52.263K	S52.299Q	S52.332R
S48.921A	S49.131K	S52.026N	S52.092Q	S52.133M	S52.223K	S52.243K	S52.263N	S52.299R	S52.333A
S48.922A	S49.131P	S52.026P	S52.092R	S52.133N	S52.223M	S52.243M	S52.263P	S52.301A	S52.333K
S48.929A	S49.132A	S52.026Q	S52.099K	S52.133P	S52.223N	S52.243N	S52.263Q	S52.301K	S52.333M
S49.001A	S49.132K	S52.026R	S52.099M	S52.133Q	S52.223P	S52.243P	S52.263R	S52.301M	S52.333P
S49.001K	S49.132P	S52.031K	S52.099N	S52.133R	S52.223Q	S52.243Q	S52.264A	S52.301N	S52.333Q
S49.001P	S49.139A	S52.031M	S52.099P	S52.134K	S52.223R	S52.243R	S52.264K	S52.301P	S52.333R
S49.002A	S49.139K	S52.031N	S52.099Q	S52.134M	S52.224A	S52.244A	S52.264M	S52.301Q	S52.334A
S49.002K	S49.139P	S52.031P	S52.099R	S52.134N	S52.224K	S52.244K	S52.264N	S52.301R	S52.334K
S49.002P	S49.141A	S52.031Q	S52.101K	S52.134P	S52.224M	S52.244M	S52.264Q	S52.302A	S52.334M
S49.009A	S49.141K	S52.031R	S52.101M	S52.134R	S52.224N	S52.244N	S52.264R	S52.302K	S52.334N
S49.009K	S49.141P	S52.032K	S52.101N	S52.135K	S52.224P	S52.244P	S52.265A	S52.302M	S52.334P
S49.009P	S49.142A	S52.032M	S52.101P	S52.135M	S52.224Q	S52.244Q	S52.265K	S52.302N	S52.334R
S49.011A	S49.142K	S52.032N	S52.101Q	S52.135N	S52.224R	S52.244R	S52.265M	S52.302P	S52.335A
S49.011K	S49.142P	S52.032P	S52.101R	S52.135P	S52.225A	S52.245A	S52.265N	S52.302Q	S52.335K
S49.011P	S49.149A	S52.032Q	S52.102K	S52.135Q	S52.225K	S52.245K	S52.265P	S52.302R	S52.335M
S49.012A	S49.149K	S52.032R	S52.102M	S52.135R	S52.225M	S52.245M	S52.265Q	S52.309A	S52.335N
S49.012K	S49.149P	S52.033K	S52.102N	S52.136K	S52.225N	S52.245N	S52.265R	S52.309K	S52.335Q
S49.012P	S49.191A	S52.033M	S52.102P	S52.136M	S52.225Q	S52.245P	S52.266A	S52.309M	S52.335R
S49.019A	S49.191K	S52.033N	S52.102Q	S52.136N	S52.225R	S52.245Q	S52.266K	S52.309N	S52.336A
S49.019K	S49.191P	S52.033P	S52.102R	S52.136P	S52.226A	S52.245R	S52.266N	S52.309P	S52.336K
S49.019P	S49.192A	S52.033Q	S52.109K	S52.136Q	S52.226K	S52.246A	S52.266P	S52.309Q	S52.336N
S49.021A	S49.192K	S52.033R	S52.109M	S52.136R	S52.226M	S52.246K	S52.266Q	S52.309R	S52.336P
S49.021K	S49.192P	S52.034K	S52.109N	S52.181K	S52.226N	S52.246M	S52.266R	S52.311A	S52.336Q
S49.021P	S49.199A	S52.034M	S52.109P	S52.181M	S52.226P	S52.246N	S52.271K	S52.311K	S52.336R
S49.022A	S49.199K	S52.034N	S52.109Q	S52.181N	S52.226Q	S52.246P	S52.271M	S52.311P	S52.341A
S49.022K	S49.199P	S52.034P	S52.109R	S52.181P	S52.226R	S52.246Q	S52.271N	S52.312A	S52.341K
S49.022P	S52.001K	S52.034R	S52.111A	S52.181Q	S52.231A	S52.246R	S52.271P	S52.312K	S52.341M
S49.029A	S52.001M	S52.035K	S52.111K	S52.181R	S52.231K	S52.251A	S52.271Q	S52.312P	S52.341N
S49.029K	S52.001N	S52.035M	S52.111P	S52.182K	S52.231M	S52.251K	S52.271R	S52.319A	S52.341P
S49.029P	S52.001P	S52.035P	S52.112A	S52.182M	S52.231N	S52.251M	S52.272K	S52.319K	S52.341R
S49.031A	S52.001Q	S52.035Q	S52.112K	S52.182N	S52.231P	S52.251N	S52.272M	S52.319P	S52.342A
S49.031K	S52.001R	S52.035R	S52.112P	S52.182P	S52.231Q	S52.251P	S52.272N	S52.321A	S52.342K
S49.031P	S52.002K	S52.036K	S52.119A	S52.182Q	S52.231R	S52.251Q	S52.272P	S52.321K	S52.342N
S49.032A	S52.002M	S52.036M	S52.119K	S52.182R	S52.232A	S52.251R	S52.272Q	S52.321M	S52.342P
S49.032K	S52.002N	S52.036N	S52.119P	S52.189K	S52.232K	S52.252A	S52.272R	S52.321N	S52.342Q
S49.032P	S52.002P	S52.036P	S52.121K	S52.189M	S52.232M	S52.252K	S52.279M	S52.321P	S52.342R
S49.039A	S52.002Q	S52.036Q	S52.121M	S52.189N	S52.232N	S52.252M	S52.279N	S52.321Q	S52.343A
S49.039K	S52.002R	S52.041K	S52.121N	S52.189P	S52.232P	S52.252N	S52.279P	S52.321R	S52.343K
S49.039P	S52.009K	S52.041M	S52.121P	S52.189R	S52.232Q	S52.252P	S52.279Q	S52.322A	S52.343M
S49.041A	S52.009M	S52.041N	S52.121Q	S52.201A	S52.232R	S52.252Q	S52.279R	S52.322K	S52.343N
S49.041K	S52.009N	S52.041Q	S52.121R	S52.201K	S52.233A	S52.252R	S52.281A	S52.322M	S52.343P
S49.041P	S52.009P	S52.041R	S52.122K	S52.201M	S52.233K	S52.253A	S52.281K	S52.322N	S52.343Q
S49.042A	S52.009Q	S52.042K	S52.122M	S52.201N	S52.233M	S52.253K	S52.281M	S52.322P	S52.343R
S49.042K	S52.009R	S52.042M	S52.122N	S52.201P	S52.233N	S52.253M	S52.281N	S52.322Q	S52.344A
S49.042P	S52.011A	S52.042N	S52.122P	S52.201Q	S52.233P	S52.253N	S52.281P	S52.322R	S52.344K
S49.049A	S52.011K	S52.042P	S52.122Q	S52.201R	S52.233Q	S52.253P	S52.281Q	S52.323A	S52.344M
S49.049K	S52.011P	S52.042Q	S52.123K	S52.202A	S52.233R	S52.253Q	S52.281R	S52.323K	S52.344N
S49.049P	S52.012A	S52.043K	S52.123M	S52.202K	S52.234A	S52.253R	S52.282A	S52.323M	S52.344P
S49.091A	S52.012K	S52.043M	S52.123N	S52.202M	S52.234K	S52.254A	S52.282K	S52.323N	S52.344Q
S49.091K	S52.012P	S52.043N	S52.123P	S52.202N	S52.234M	S52.254K	S52.282M	S52.323P	S52.344R
S49.091P	S52.019A	S52.043P	S52.123Q	S52.202P	S52.234N	S52.254M	S52.282N	S52.323Q	S52.345A
S49.092A	S52.019K	S52.043Q	S52.123R	S52.202Q	S52.234P	S52.254N	S52.282P	S52.323R	S52.345K
S49.092K	S52.019P	S52.043R	S52.124K	S52.202R	S52.234Q	S52.254P	S52.282Q	S52.324A	S52.345N
S49.092P	S52.021K	S52.044K	S52.124M	S52.209A	S52.234R	S52.254Q	S52.282R	S52.324K	S52.345P
S49.099A	S52.021M	S52.044M	S52.124N	S52.209K	S52.235A	S52.254R	S52.283A	S52.324M	S52.345Q
S49.099K	S52.021N	S52.044P	S52.124P	S52.209M	S52.235K	S52.255A	S52.283K	S52.324N	S52.345R
S49.099P	S52.021P	S52.044Q	S52.124Q	S52.209N	S52.235M	S52.255K	S52.283M	S52.324P	S52.346A
S49.101A	S52.021Q	S52.044R	S52.124R	S52.209P	S52.235N	S52.255M	S52.283N	S52.324Q	S52.346K
S49.101K	S52.021R	S52.045M	S52.125K	S52.209Q	S52.235P	S52.255N	S52.283P	S52.324R	S52.346M
S49.101P	S52.022K	S52.045N	S52.125M	S52.209R	S52.235Q	S52.255P	S52.283Q	S52.325A	S52.346N
S49.102A	S52.022M	S52.045P	S52.125N	S52.211A	S52.235R	S52.255Q	S52.291A	S52.325K	S52.346P
S49.102K	S52.022N	S52.045Q	S52.125P	S52.211K	S52.236A	S52.255R	S52.291K	S52.325M	
S49.102P	S52.022P	S52.045R	S52.125Q	S52.211P	S52.236K	S52.256A	S52.291M	S52.325N	
S49.109A	S52.022Q		S52.125R	S52.212A	S52.236M	S52.256K	S52.291P	S52.325P	
S49.109K	S52.023K		S52.126K	S52.212K	S52.236N	S52.256M		S52.325Q	
S49.109P	S52.023M		S52.126M	S52.212P	S52.236P	S52.256N		S52.325R	
S49.111A	S52.023N		S52.126N	S52.219A	S52.236Q	S52.256P		S52.326A	
S49.111K	S52.023P		S52.126P	S52.219K	S52.236R	S52.256Q		S52.326K	
S49.111P	S52.023Q					S52.261A		S52.326N	
S49.112A									

S52.346Q	S52.366R	S52.511A	S52.542R	S52.599A	S52.691R	S56.122A	S59.039P	S59.232A	S62.036K
S52.346R	S52.371A	S52.511K	S52.549A	S52.599K	S52.692A	S56.123A	S59.041A	S59.232K	S62.036P
S52.351A	S52.371K	S52.511M	S52.549K	S52.599M	S52.692K	S56.124A	S59.041K	S59.232P	S62.101B
S52.351K	S52.371M	S52.511N	S52.549M	S52.599N	S52.692M	S56.125A	S59.041P	S59.239A	S62.101K
S52.351M	S52.371N	S52.511P	S52.549N	S52.599P	S52.692N	S56.126A	S59.042A	S59.239K	S62.101P
S52.351N	S52.371P	S52.511Q	S52.549P	S52.599Q	S52.692P	S56.127A	S59.042K	S59.239P	S62.102B
S52.351P	S52.371Q	S52.511R	S52.549Q	S52.599R	S52.692Q	S56.128A	S59.042P	S59.241A	S62.102K
S52.351Q	S52.371R	S52.512A	S52.549R	S52.601A	S52.692R	S56.129A	S59.049A	S59.241K	S62.102P
S52.351R	S52.372A	S52.512K	S52.551A	S52.601K	S52.699A	S56.221A	S59.049K	S59.241P	S62.109B
S52.352A	S52.372K	S52.512M	S52.551K	S52.601M	S52.699K	S56.222A	S59.049P	S59.242A	S62.109K
S52.352K	S52.372M	S52.512N	S52.551M	S52.601N	S52.699M	S56.229A	S59.091A	S59.242K	S62.109P
S52.352M	S52.372N	S52.512P	S52.551N	S52.601P	S52.699N	S56.321A	S59.091K	S59.242P	S62.111B
S52.352N	S52.372P	S52.512Q	S52.551P	S52.601Q	S52.699P	S56.322A	S59.091P	S59.249A	S62.111K
S52.352P	S52.372Q	S52.512R	S52.551Q	S52.601R	S52.699Q	S56.329A	S59.092A	S59.249K	S62.111P
S52.352Q	S52.372R	S52.513A	S52.551R	S52.602A	S52.699R	S56.421A	S59.092K	S59.249P	S62.112B
S52.352R	S52.379A	S52.513K	S52.552A	S52.602K	S52.90XA	S56.422A	S59.092P	S59.291A	S62.112K
S52.353A	S52.379K	S52.513M	S52.552K	S52.602M	S52.90XK	S56.423A	S59.099A	S59.291K	S62.112P
S52.353K	S52.379M	S52.513N	S52.552M	S52.602N	S52.90XM	S56.424A	S59.099K	S59.291P	S62.113B
S52.353M	S52.379N	S52.513P	S52.552N	S52.602P	S52.90XN	S56.425A	S59.099P	S59.292A	S62.113K
S52.353N	S52.379P	S52.513Q	S52.552P	S52.602Q	S52.90XP	S56.426A	S59.101K	S59.292K	S62.113P
S52.353P	S52.379Q	S52.513R	S52.552Q	S52.602R	S52.90XQ	S56.427A	S59.101P	S59.292P	S62.114B
S52.353Q	S52.379R	S52.514A	S52.552R	S52.609A	S52.90XR	S56.428A	S59.102K	S59.299A	S62.114K
S52.353R	S52.381A	S52.514K	S52.559A	S52.609K	S52.91XA	S56.429A	S59.102P	S59.299K	S62.114P
S52.354A	S52.381K	S52.514M	S52.559K	S52.609M	S52.91XK	S56.521A	S59.109K	S59.299P	S62.115B
S52.354K	S52.381M	S52.514N	S52.559M	S52.609N	S52.91XM	S56.522A	S59.109P	S62.001B	S62.115K
S52.354M	S52.381N	S52.514P	S52.559N	S52.609P	S52.91XN	S56.529A	S59.111K	S62.001K	S62.115P
S52.354N	S52.381P	S52.514Q	S52.559P	S52.609Q	S52.91XP	S56.821A	S59.112K	S62.001P	S62.116B
S52.354P	S52.381Q	S52.514R	S52.559Q	S52.609R	S52.91XQ	S56.822A	S59.112P	S62.002B	S62.116K
S52.354Q	S52.381R	S52.515A	S52.559R	S52.611A	S52.91XR	S56.829A	S59.119K	S62.002K	S62.116P
S52.354R	S52.382A	S52.515K	S52.561A	S52.611K	S52.92XA	S56.921A	S59.121K	S62.002P	S62.121B
S52.355A	S52.382K	S52.515M	S52.561K	S52.611M	S52.92XK	S56.922A	S59.121P	S62.009B	S62.121K
S52.355K	S52.382M	S52.515N	S52.561M	S52.611N	S52.92XM	S56.929A	S59.122K	S62.009K	S62.121P
S52.355M	S52.382N	S52.515P	S52.561N	S52.611P	S52.92XN	S58.011A	S59.122P	S62.009P	S62.122B
S52.355N	S52.382P	S52.515Q	S52.561P	S52.611Q	S52.92XP	S58.012A	S59.129K	S62.011B	S62.122K
S52.355P	S52.382Q	S52.515R	S52.561Q	S52.611R	S52.92XQ	S58.019A	S59.129P	S62.011K	S62.122P
S52.355Q	S52.382R	S52.516A	S52.561R	S52.612A	S52.92XR	S58.021A	S59.131K	S62.011P	S62.123B
S52.355R	S52.389A	S52.516K	S52.562A	S52.612K	S55.001A	S58.022A	S59.131P	S62.012B	S62.123K
S52.356A	S52.389K	S52.516M	S52.562K	S52.612M	S55.002A	S58.029A	S59.132K	S62.012K	S62.123P
S52.356K	S52.389M	S52.516N	S52.562M	S52.612N	S55.009A	S58.111A	S59.132P	S62.012P	S62.124B
S52.356M	S52.389N	S52.516P	S52.562N	S52.612P	S55.011A	S58.112A	S59.139K	S62.013B	S62.124K
S52.356N	S52.389P	S52.516Q	S52.562P	S52.612Q	S55.012A	S58.119A	S59.139P	S62.013K	S62.124P
S52.356P	S52.389Q	S52.516R	S52.562Q	S52.612R	S55.019A	S58.121A	S59.141K	S62.013P	S62.125B
S52.356Q	S52.389R	S52.521A	S52.562R	S52.613A	S55.091A	S58.122A	S59.141P	S62.014B	S62.125K
S52.356R	S52.391A	S52.521K	S52.569A	S52.613K	S55.092A	S58.129A	S59.142K	S62.014K	S62.125P
S52.361A	S52.391K	S52.521P	S52.569K	S52.613M	S55.099A	S58.911A	S59.142P	S62.014P	S62.126B
S52.361K	S52.391M	S52.522A	S52.569M	S52.613N	S55.101A	S58.912A	S59.149K	S62.015B	S62.126K
S52.361M	S52.391N	S52.522K	S52.569N	S52.613P	S55.102A	S58.919A	S59.149P	S62.015K	S62.126P
S52.361N	S52.391P	S52.522P	S52.569P	S52.613Q	S55.109A	S58.921A	S59.191K	S62.015P	S62.131B
S52.361P	S52.391Q	S52.529A	S52.569Q	S52.613R	S55.111A	S58.922A	S59.191P	S62.016B	S62.131K
S52.361Q	S52.391R	S52.529K	S52.569R	S52.614A	S55.112A	S58.929A	S59.192K	S62.016K	S62.131P
S52.361R	S52.392A	S52.529P	S52.571A	S52.614K	S55.119A	S59.001A	S59.192P	S62.016P	S62.132B
S52.362A	S52.392K	S52.531A	S52.571K	S52.614M	S55.191A	S59.001K	S59.199K	S62.021B	S62.132K
S52.362K	S52.392M	S52.531K	S52.571M	S52.614N	S55.192A	S59.001P	S59.199P	S62.021K	S62.132P
S52.362M	S52.392N	S52.531M	S52.571N	S52.614P	S55.199A	S59.002A	S59.201K	S62.021P	S62.133B
S52.362N	S52.392P	S52.531N	S52.571P	S52.614Q	S55.201A	S59.002K	S59.201P	S62.022B	S62.133K
S52.362P	S52.392Q	S52.531P	S52.571Q	S52.614R	S55.202A	S59.002P	S59.202K	S62.022K	S62.133P
S52.362Q	S52.392R	S52.531Q	S52.571R	S52.615A	S55.209A	S59.009A	S59.202P	S62.022P	S62.134B
S52.362R	S52.399A	S52.531R	S52.572A	S52.615K	S55.211A	S59.009K	S59.209A	S62.023B	S62.134K
S52.363A	S52.399K	S52.532A	S52.572K	S52.615M	S55.212A	S59.009P	S59.209K	S62.023K	S62.134P
S52.363K	S52.399M	S52.532K	S52.572M	S52.615N	S55.219A	S59.011A	S59.209P	S62.023P	S62.135B
S52.363M	S52.399N	S52.532M	S52.572N	S52.615P	S55.291A	S59.011K	S59.211A	S62.024B	S62.135K
S52.363N	S52.399P	S52.532N	S52.572P	S52.615Q	S55.292A	S59.011P	S59.211K	S62.024K	S62.135P
S52.363P	S52.399Q	S52.532P	S52.572Q	S52.615R	S55.299A	S59.012A	S59.211P	S62.024P	S62.136B
S52.363Q	S52.399R	S52.532Q	S52.572R	S52.616A	S55.801A	S59.012K	S59.212A	S62.025B	S62.136K
S52.363R	S52.501A	S52.532R	S52.579A	S52.616K	S55.802A	S59.012P	S59.212K	S62.025K	S62.136P
S52.364A	S52.501K	S52.539A	S52.579K	S52.616M	S55.809A	S59.019A	S59.212P	S62.025P	S62.141B
S52.364K	S52.501M	S52.539K	S52.579M	S52.616N	S55.811A	S59.019K	S59.219A	S62.026B	S62.141K
S52.364M	S52.501N	S52.539M	S52.579N	S52.616P	S55.812A	S59.019P	S59.219K	S62.026K	S62.141P
S52.364N	S52.501P	S52.539N	S52.579P	S52.616Q	S55.819A	S59.021A	S59.219P	S62.026P	S62.142B
S52.364P	S52.501Q	S52.539P	S52.579Q	S52.616R	S55.891A	S59.021K	S59.221A	S62.031B	S62.142K
S52.364Q	S52.501R	S52.539Q	S52.579R	S52.621A	S55.892A	S59.021P	S59.221K	S62.031K	S62.142P
S52.364R	S52.502A	S52.539R	S52.591A	S52.621K	S55.899A	S59.022A	S59.221P	S62.031P	S62.143B
S52.365A	S52.502K	S52.541A	S52.591K	S52.621P	S55.901A	S59.022K	S59.222A	S62.032B	S62.143K
S52.365K	S52.502M	S52.541K	S52.591M	S52.622A	S55.902A	S59.022P	S59.222K	S62.032K	S62.143P
S52.365M	S52.502N	S52.541M	S52.591N	S52.622K	S55.909A	S59.029A	S59.222P	S62.032P	S62.144B
S52.365N	S52.502P	S52.541N	S52.591P	S52.622P	S55.911A	S59.029K	S59.229A	S62.033B	S62.144K
S52.365P	S52.502Q	S52.541P	S52.591Q	S52.629A	S55.912A	S59.029P	S59.229K	S62.033K	S62.144P
S52.365Q	S52.502R	S52.541Q	S52.591R	S52.629K	S55.919A	S59.031A	S59.229P	S62.033P	S62.145B
S52.365R	S52.509A	S52.541R	S52.592A	S52.629P	S55.991A	S59.031K	S59.231A	S62.034B	S62.145K
S52.366A	S52.509K	S52.542A	S52.592K	S52.691A	S55.992A	S59.031P	S59.231K	S62.034K	S62.145P
S52.366K	S52.509M	S52.542K	S52.592M	S52.691K	S55.999A	S59.032A	S59.231P	S62.034P	S62.146B
S52.366M	S52.509N	S52.542M	S52.592N	S52.691M	S56.021A	S59.032K		S62.035B	S62.146K
S52.366N	S52.509P	S52.542N	S52.592P	S52.691N	S56.022A	S59.032P		S62.035K	S62.146P
S52.366P	S52.509Q	S52.542P	S52.592Q	S52.691P	S56.029A	S59.039A		S62.035P	S62.151B
S52.366Q	S52.509R	S52.542Q	S52.592R	S52.691Q	S56.121A	S59.039K		S62.036B	S62.151K

Alphabetic & Numeric Lists of CCs

S62.151P	S62.213B	S62.300K	S62.328P	S62.357B	S62.513K	S62.618P	S62.647B	S65.092A	S65.999A
S62.152B	S62.213K	S62.300P	S62.329B	S62.357K	S62.513P	S62.619B	S62.647K	S65.099A	S66.021A
S62.152K	S62.213P	S62.301B	S62.329K	S62.357P	S62.514B	S62.619K	S62.647P	S65.101A	S66.022A
S62.152P	S62.221B	S62.301K	S62.329P	S62.358B	S62.514K	S62.619P	S62.648B	S65.102A	S66.029A
S62.153B	S62.221K	S62.301P	S62.330B	S62.358K	S62.514P	S62.620B	S62.648K	S65.109A	S66.120A
S62.153K	S62.221P	S62.302B	S62.330K	S62.358P	S62.515B	S62.620K	S62.648P	S65.111A	S66.121A
S62.153P	S62.222B	S62.302K	S62.330P	S62.359B	S62.515K	S62.620P	S62.649B	S65.112A	S66.122A
S62.154B	S62.222K	S62.302P	S62.331B	S62.359K	S62.515P	S62.621B	S62.649K	S65.119A	S66.123A
S62.154K	S62.222P	S62.303B	S62.331K	S62.359P	S62.516B	S62.621K	S62.649P	S65.191A	S66.124A
S62.154P	S62.223B	S62.303K	S62.331P	S62.360B	S62.516K	S62.621P	S62.650B	S65.192A	S66.125A
S62.155B	S62.223K	S62.303P	S62.332B	S62.360K	S62.516P	S62.622B	S62.650K	S65.199A	S66.126A
S62.155K	S62.223P	S62.304B	S62.332K	S62.360P	S62.521B	S62.622K	S62.650P	S65.201A	S66.127A
S62.155P	S62.224B	S62.304K	S62.332P	S62.361B	S62.521K	S62.622P	S62.651B	S65.202A	S66.128A
S62.156B	S62.224K	S62.304P	S62.333B	S62.361K	S62.521P	S62.623B	S62.651K	S65.209A	S66.129A
S62.156K	S62.224P	S62.305B	S62.333K	S62.361P	S62.522B	S62.623K	S62.651P	S65.211A	S66.221A
S62.156P	S62.225B	S62.305K	S62.333P	S62.362B	S62.522K	S62.623P	S62.652B	S65.212A	S66.222A
S62.161B	S62.225K	S62.305P	S62.334B	S62.362K	S62.522P	S62.624B	S62.652K	S65.219A	S66.229A
S62.161K	S62.225P	S62.306B	S62.334K	S62.362P	S62.523B	S62.624K	S62.652P	S65.291A	S66.320A
S62.161P	S62.226B	S62.306K	S62.334P	S62.363B	S62.523K	S62.624P	S62.653B	S65.292A	S66.321A
S62.162B	S62.226K	S62.306P	S62.335B	S62.363K	S62.523P	S62.625B	S62.653K	S65.299A	S66.322A
S62.162K	S62.226P	S62.307B	S62.335K	S62.363P	S62.524B	S62.625K	S62.653P	S65.301A	S66.323A
S62.162P	S62.231B	S62.307K	S62.335P	S62.364B	S62.524K	S62.625P	S62.654B	S65.302A	S66.324A
S62.163B	S62.231K	S62.307P	S62.336B	S62.364K	S62.524P	S62.626B	S62.654K	S65.309A	S66.325A
S62.163K	S62.231P	S62.308B	S62.336K	S62.364P	S62.525B	S62.626K	S62.654P	S65.311A	S66.326A
S62.163P	S62.232B	S62.308K	S62.336P	S62.365B	S62.525K	S62.626P	S62.655B	S65.312A	S66.327A
S62.164B	S62.232K	S62.308P	S62.337B	S62.365K	S62.525P	S62.627B	S62.655K	S65.319A	S66.328A
S62.164K	S62.232P	S62.309B	S62.337K	S62.365P	S62.526B	S62.627K	S62.655P	S65.391A	S66.329A
S62.164P	S62.233B	S62.309K	S62.337P	S62.366B	S62.526K	S62.627P	S62.656B	S65.392A	S66.421A
S62.165B	S62.233K	S62.309P	S62.338B	S62.366K	S62.526P	S62.628B	S62.656K	S65.399A	S66.422A
S62.165K	S62.233P	S62.310B	S62.338K	S62.366P	S62.600B	S62.628K	S62.656P	S65.401A	S66.429A
S62.165P	S62.234B	S62.310K	S62.338P	S62.367B	S62.600K	S62.628P	S62.657B	S65.402A	S66.520A
S62.166B	S62.234K	S62.310P	S62.339B	S62.367K	S62.600P	S62.629B	S62.657K	S65.409A	S66.521A
S62.166K	S62.234P	S62.311B	S62.339K	S62.367P	S62.601B	S62.629K	S62.657P	S65.411A	S66.522A
S62.166P	S62.235B	S62.311K	S62.339P	S62.368B	S62.601K	S62.629P	S62.658B	S65.412A	S66.523A
S62.171B	S62.235K	S62.311P	S62.340B	S62.368K	S62.601P	S62.630B	S62.658K	S65.419A	S66.524A
S62.171K	S62.235P	S62.312B	S62.340K	S62.368P	S62.602B	S62.630K	S62.658P	S65.491A	S66.525A
S62.171P	S62.236B	S62.312K	S62.340P	S62.369B	S62.602K	S62.630P	S62.659B	S65.492A	S66.526A
S62.172B	S62.236K	S62.312P	S62.341B	S62.369K	S62.602P	S62.631B	S62.659K	S65.499A	S66.527A
S62.172K	S62.236P	S62.313B	S62.341K	S62.369P	S62.603B	S62.631K	S62.659P	S65.500A	S66.528A
S62.172P	S62.241B	S62.313K	S62.341P	S62.390B	S62.603K	S62.631P	S62.660B	S65.501A	S66.529A
S62.173B	S62.241K	S62.313P	S62.342B	S62.390K	S62.603P	S62.632B	S62.660K	S65.502A	S66.821A
S62.173K	S62.241P	S62.314B	S62.342K	S62.390P	S62.604B	S62.632K	S62.660P	S65.503A	S66.822A
S62.173P	S62.242B	S62.314K	S62.342P	S62.391B	S62.604K	S62.632P	S62.661B	S65.504A	S66.829A
S62.174B	S62.242K	S62.314P	S62.343B	S62.391K	S62.604P	S62.633B	S62.661K	S65.505A	S66.921A
S62.174K	S62.242P	S62.315B	S62.343K	S62.391P	S62.605B	S62.633K	S62.661P	S65.506A	S66.922A
S62.174P	S62.243B	S62.315K	S62.343P	S62.392B	S62.605K	S62.633P	S62.662B	S65.507A	S66.929A
S62.175B	S62.243K	S62.315P	S62.344B	S62.392K	S62.605P	S62.634B	S62.662K	S65.508A	S68.411A
S62.175K	S62.243P	S62.316B	S62.344K	S62.392P	S62.606B	S62.634K	S62.662P	S65.509A	S68.412A
S62.175P	S62.244B	S62.316K	S62.344P	S62.393B	S62.606K	S62.634P	S62.663B	S65.510A	S68.419A
S62.176B	S62.244K	S62.316P	S62.345B	S62.393K	S62.606P	S62.635B	S62.663K	S65.511A	S68.421A
S62.176K	S62.244P	S62.317B	S62.345K	S62.393P	S62.607B	S62.635K	S62.663P	S65.512A	S68.422A
S62.176P	S62.245B	S62.317K	S62.345P	S62.394B	S62.607K	S62.635P	S62.664B	S65.513A	S68.429A
S62.181B	S62.245K	S62.317P	S62.346B	S62.394K	S62.607P	S62.636B	S62.664K	S65.514A	S68.711A
S62.181K	S62.245P	S62.318B	S62.346K	S62.394P	S62.608B	S62.636K	S62.664P	S65.515A	S68.712A
S62.181P	S62.246B	S62.318K	S62.346P	S62.395B	S62.608K	S62.636P	S62.665B	S65.516A	S68.719A
S62.182B	S62.246K	S62.318P	S62.347B	S62.395K	S62.608P	S62.637B	S62.665K	S65.517A	S68.721A
S62.182K	S62.246P	S62.319B	S62.347K	S62.395P	S62.609B	S62.637K	S62.665P	S65.518A	S68.722A
S62.182P	S62.251B	S62.319K	S62.347P	S62.396B	S62.609K	S62.637P	S62.666B	S65.519A	S68.729A
S62.183B	S62.251K	S62.319P	S62.348B	S62.396K	S62.609P	S62.638B	S62.666K	S65.590A	S72.001K
S62.183K	S62.251P	S62.320B	S62.348K	S62.396P	S62.610B	S62.638K	S62.666P	S65.591A	S72.001M
S62.183P	S62.252B	S62.320K	S62.348P	S62.397B	S62.610K	S62.638P	S62.667B	S65.592A	S72.001N
S62.184B	S62.252K	S62.320P	S62.349B	S62.397K	S62.610P	S62.639B	S62.667K	S65.593A	S72.001P
S62.184K	S62.252P	S62.321B	S62.349K	S62.397P	S62.611B	S62.639K	S62.667P	S65.594A	S72.001Q
S62.184P	S62.253B	S62.321K	S62.349P	S62.398B	S62.611K	S62.639P	S62.668B	S65.595A	S72.001R
S62.185B	S62.253K	S62.321P	S62.350B	S62.398K	S62.611P	S62.640B	S62.668K	S65.596A	S72.002K
S62.185K	S62.253P	S62.322B	S62.350K	S62.398P	S62.612B	S62.640K	S62.668P	S65.597A	S72.002M
S62.185P	S62.254B	S62.322K	S62.350P	S62.399B	S62.612K	S62.640P	S62.669B	S65.598A	S72.002N
S62.186B	S62.254K	S62.322P	S62.351B	S62.399K	S62.612P	S62.641B	S62.669K	S65.599A	S72.002P
S62.186K	S62.254P	S62.323B	S62.351K	S62.399P	S62.613B	S62.641K	S62.669P	S65.801A	S72.002Q
S62.186P	S62.255B	S62.323K	S62.351P	S62.501B	S62.613K	S62.641P	S62.90XB	S65.802A	S72.002R
S62.201B	S62.255K	S62.323P	S62.352B	S62.501K	S62.613P	S62.642B	S62.90XK	S65.809A	S72.009K
S62.201K	S62.255P	S62.324B	S62.352K	S62.501P	S62.614B	S62.642K	S62.90XP	S65.811A	S72.009M
S62.201P	S62.256B	S62.324K	S62.352P	S62.502B	S62.614K	S62.642P	S62.91XB	S65.812A	S72.009N
S62.202B	S62.256K	S62.324P	S62.353B	S62.502K	S62.614P	S62.643B	S62.91XK	S65.819A	S72.009P
S62.202K	S62.256P	S62.325B	S62.353K	S62.502P	S62.615B	S62.643K	S62.91XP	S65.891A	S72.009Q
S62.202P	S62.291B	S62.325K	S62.353P	S62.509B	S62.615K	S62.643P	S62.92XB	S65.892A	S72.009R
S62.209B	S62.291K	S62.325P	S62.354B	S62.509K	S62.615P	S62.644B	S62.92XK	S65.899A	S72.011K
S62.209K	S62.291P	S62.326B	S62.354K	S62.509P	S62.616B	S62.644K	S62.92XP	S65.901A	S72.011M
S62.209P	S62.292B	S62.326K	S62.354P	S62.511B	S62.616K	S62.644P	S65.001A	S65.902A	S72.011N
S62.211B	S62.292K	S62.326P	S62.355B	S62.511K	S62.616P	S62.645B	S65.002A	S65.909A	S72.011P
S62.211K	S62.292P	S62.327B	S62.355K	S62.511P	S62.617B	S62.645K	S65.009A	S65.911A	S72.011Q
S62.211P	S62.299B	S62.327K	S62.355P	S62.512B	S62.617K	S62.645P	S65.011A	S65.912A	S72.011R
S62.212B	S62.299K	S62.327P	S62.356B	S62.512K	S62.617P	S62.646B	S65.012A	S65.919A	S72.012K
S62.212K	S62.299P	S62.328B	S62.356K	S62.512P	S62.618B	S62.646K	S65.019A	S65.991A	S72.012M
S62.212P	S62.300B	S62.328K	S62.356P	S62.513B	S62.618K	S62.646P	S65.091A	S65.992A	S72.012N

S72.012P	S72.041Q	S72.066R	S72.123K	S72.145M	S72.324N	S72.346P	S72.392Q	S72.423A	S72.443K
S72.012Q	S72.041R	S72.091K	S72.123M	S72.145N	S72.324P	S72.346Q	S72.392R	S72.423K	S72.443M
S72.012R	S72.042K	S72.091M	S72.123N	S72.145P	S72.324Q	S72.346R	S72.399K	S72.423M	S72.443N
S72.019K	S72.042M	S72.091N	S72.123P	S72.145Q	S72.324R	S72.351K	S72.399M	S72.423N	S72.443P
S72.019M	S72.042N	S72.091P	S72.123Q	S72.145R	S72.325K	S72.351N	S72.399N	S72.423P	S72.443Q
S72.019N	S72.042P	S72.091Q	S72.123R	S72.146K	S72.325M	S72.351P	S72.399P	S72.423Q	S72.443R
S72.019P	S72.042Q	S72.091R	S72.124K	S72.146M	S72.325N	S72.351Q	S72.399Q	S72.423R	S72.444A
S72.019Q	S72.042R	S72.092K	S72.124M	S72.146N	S72.325P	S72.351R	S72.399R	S72.424A	S72.444K
S72.019R	S72.043K	S72.092M	S72.124N	S72.146P	S72.325Q	S72.352K	S72.401A	S72.424K	S72.444N
S72.021K	S72.043M	S72.092N	S72.124P	S72.146Q	S72.325R	S72.352M	S72.401K	S72.424M	S72.444P
S72.021M	S72.043N	S72.092P	S72.124Q	S72.146R	S72.326K	S72.352N	S72.401M	S72.424N	S72.444Q
S72.021N	S72.043P	S72.092Q	S72.124R	S72.21XK	S72.326M	S72.352P	S72.401N	S72.424P	S72.444R
S72.021P	S72.043Q	S72.092R	S72.125K	S72.21XM	S72.326N	S72.352Q	S72.401P	S72.424Q	S72.445A
S72.021Q	S72.043R	S72.099K	S72.125M	S72.21XN	S72.326P	S72.352R	S72.401Q	S72.424R	S72.445K
S72.021R	S72.044K	S72.099M	S72.125N	S72.21XP	S72.326Q	S72.353K	S72.401R	S72.425A	S72.445M
S72.022K	S72.044M	S72.099N	S72.125P	S72.21XQ	S72.326R	S72.353N	S72.402A	S72.425K	S72.445N
S72.022M	S72.044N	S72.099P	S72.125Q	S72.21XR	S72.331K	S72.353P	S72.402K	S72.425M	S72.445P
S72.022N	S72.044P	S72.099Q	S72.125R	S72.22XK	S72.331M	S72.353Q	S72.402M	S72.425N	S72.445Q
S72.022P	S72.044Q	S72.099R	S72.126K	S72.22XM	S72.331N	S72.353R	S72.402N	S72.425P	S72.445R
S72.022Q	S72.044R	S72.101K	S72.126M	S72.22XN	S72.331P	S72.354K	S72.402P	S72.425Q	S72.446A
S72.022R	S72.045K	S72.101M	S72.126N	S72.22XP	S72.331Q	S72.354M	S72.402Q	S72.425R	S72.446K
S72.023K	S72.045M	S72.101N	S72.126P	S72.22XQ	S72.331R	S72.354N	S72.402R	S72.426A	S72.446M
S72.023M	S72.045N	S72.101P	S72.126Q	S72.22XR	S72.332K	S72.354P	S72.409A	S72.426K	S72.446N
S72.023N	S72.045P	S72.101Q	S72.126R	S72.23XK	S72.332M	S72.354Q	S72.409K	S72.426M	S72.446P
S72.023Q	S72.045Q	S72.101R	S72.131K	S72.23XM	S72.332N	S72.354R	S72.409M	S72.426N	S72.446Q
S72.023R	S72.045R	S72.102K	S72.131M	S72.23XN	S72.332P	S72.355K	S72.409N	S72.426P	S72.446R
S72.024K	S72.046K	S72.102M	S72.131N	S72.23XP	S72.332Q	S72.355M	S72.409P	S72.426Q	S72.451A
S72.024M	S72.046M	S72.102N	S72.131P	S72.23XQ	S72.332R	S72.355N	S72.409Q	S72.426R	S72.451K
S72.024N	S72.046N	S72.102P	S72.131Q	S72.23XR	S72.333K	S72.355P	S72.409R	S72.431A	S72.451M
S72.024P	S72.046P	S72.102Q	S72.131R	S72.24XK	S72.333M	S72.355Q	S72.411A	S72.431K	S72.451N
S72.024Q	S72.046Q	S72.102R	S72.132K	S72.24XM	S72.333N	S72.355R	S72.411K	S72.431M	S72.451P
S72.024R	S72.046R	S72.109K	S72.132M	S72.24XN	S72.333P	S72.356K	S72.411M	S72.431N	S72.451Q
S72.025K	S72.051K	S72.109M	S72.132N	S72.24XP	S72.333Q	S72.356M	S72.411N	S72.431P	S72.451R
S72.025M	S72.051M	S72.109N	S72.132P	S72.24XQ	S72.333R	S72.356N	S72.411P	S72.431Q	S72.452A
S72.025N	S72.051N	S72.109P	S72.132Q	S72.24XR	S72.334K	S72.356P	S72.411Q	S72.431R	S72.452K
S72.025P	S72.051P	S72.109Q	S72.132R	S72.25XK	S72.334M	S72.356Q	S72.411R	S72.432A	S72.452M
S72.025Q	S72.051Q	S72.109R	S72.133K	S72.25XM	S72.334N	S72.356R	S72.412A	S72.432K	S72.452N
S72.025R	S72.051R	S72.111K	S72.133M	S72.25XN	S72.334P	S72.361K	S72.412K	S72.432M	S72.452P
S72.026K	S72.052K	S72.111M	S72.133N	S72.25XP	S72.334Q	S72.361M	S72.412M	S72.432N	S72.452Q
S72.026M	S72.052M	S72.111N	S72.133P	S72.25XQ	S72.334R	S72.361N	S72.412N	S72.432P	S72.452R
S72.026N	S72.052N	S72.111P	S72.133Q	S72.25XR	S72.335K	S72.361P	S72.412P	S72.432Q	S72.453A
S72.026P	S72.052P	S72.111Q	S72.133R	S72.26XK	S72.335M	S72.361Q	S72.412Q	S72.432R	S72.453K
S72.026Q	S72.052Q	S72.111R	S72.134K	S72.26XM	S72.335N	S72.361R	S72.412R	S72.433A	S72.453M
S72.026R	S72.052R	S72.112K	S72.134M	S72.26XN	S72.335P	S72.362K	S72.413A	S72.433K	S72.453N
S72.031K	S72.059K	S72.112M	S72.134N	S72.26XP	S72.335Q	S72.362M	S72.413K	S72.433M	S72.453P
S72.031M	S72.059M	S72.112N	S72.134P	S72.26XQ	S72.335R	S72.362N	S72.413M	S72.433N	S72.453Q
S72.031N	S72.059N	S72.112P	S72.134Q	S72.26XR	S72.336K	S72.362P	S72.413N	S72.433P	S72.453R
S72.031P	S72.059P	S72.112Q	S72.134R	S72.301K	S72.336M	S72.362Q	S72.413P	S72.433Q	S72.454A
S72.031Q	S72.059Q	S72.112R	S72.135K	S72.301M	S72.336N	S72.362R	S72.413Q	S72.433R	S72.454K
S72.031R	S72.059R	S72.113K	S72.135M	S72.301N	S72.336P	S72.363K	S72.413R	S72.434A	S72.454N
S72.032K	S72.061K	S72.113M	S72.135N	S72.301P	S72.336Q	S72.363M	S72.414A	S72.434K	S72.454N
S72.032M	S72.061M	S72.113N	S72.135P	S72.301Q	S72.336R	S72.363N	S72.414K	S72.434M	S72.454P
S72.032N	S72.061N	S72.113P	S72.135Q	S72.301R	S72.341K	S72.363Q	S72.414M	S72.434N	S72.454Q
S72.032P	S72.061P	S72.113Q	S72.135R	S72.302K	S72.341M	S72.363R	S72.414N	S72.434P	S72.454R
S72.032Q	S72.061Q	S72.113R	S72.136K	S72.302M	S72.341N	S72.364K	S72.414P	S72.434Q	S72.455A
S72.032R	S72.061R	S72.114K	S72.136M	S72.302N	S72.341P	S72.364M	S72.414Q	S72.434R	S72.455K
S72.033K	S72.062K	S72.114M	S72.136N	S72.302P	S72.341Q	S72.364N	S72.414R	S72.435A	S72.455M
S72.033M	S72.062M	S72.114N	S72.136P	S72.302Q	S72.341R	S72.364P	S72.415A	S72.435K	S72.455N
S72.033N	S72.062N	S72.114P	S72.136Q	S72.302R	S72.342K	S72.364Q	S72.415K	S72.435M	S72.455P
S72.033P	S72.062P	S72.114Q	S72.136R	S72.309K	S72.342M	S72.364R	S72.415M	S72.435N	S72.455Q
S72.033Q	S72.062Q	S72.114R	S72.141K	S72.309M	S72.342N	S72.365K	S72.415N	S72.435P	S72.455R
S72.033R	S72.062R	S72.115K	S72.141M	S72.309N	S72.342P	S72.365M	S72.415P	S72.435Q	S72.456A
S72.034K	S72.063K	S72.115M	S72.141N	S72.309P	S72.342Q	S72.365N	S72.415Q	S72.435R	S72.456K
S72.034M	S72.063M	S72.115N	S72.141P	S72.309Q	S72.342R	S72.365P	S72.415R	S72.436A	S72.456M
S72.034N	S72.063N	S72.115P	S72.141Q	S72.309R	S72.343K	S72.365Q	S72.416A	S72.436K	S72.456N
S72.034P	S72.063P	S72.115Q	S72.141R	S72.321K	S72.343M	S72.365R	S72.416K	S72.436M	S72.456P
S72.034Q	S72.063Q	S72.115R	S72.142K	S72.321M	S72.343N	S72.366K	S72.416M	S72.436N	S72.456Q
S72.034R	S72.063R	S72.116K	S72.142M	S72.321N	S72.343P	S72.366M	S72.416N	S72.436P	S72.456R
S72.035K	S72.064K	S72.116M	S72.142N	S72.321P	S72.343Q	S72.366N	S72.416P	S72.436Q	S72.461A
S72.035M	S72.064M	S72.116N	S72.142P	S72.321Q	S72.343R	S72.366P	S72.416Q	S72.436R	S72.461K
S72.035N	S72.064N	S72.116P	S72.142Q	S72.321R	S72.344K	S72.366Q	S72.416R	S72.441A	S72.461M
S72.035P	S72.064P	S72.116Q	S72.142R	S72.322K	S72.344M	S72.366R	S72.421A	S72.441K	S72.461N
S72.035Q	S72.064Q	S72.116R	S72.143K	S72.322M	S72.344N	S72.391K	S72.421K	S72.441M	S72.461P
S72.035R	S72.064R	S72.121K	S72.143M	S72.322N	S72.344P	S72.391M	S72.421M	S72.441N	S72.461Q
S72.036K	S72.065K	S72.121M	S72.143N	S72.322P	S72.344Q	S72.391N	S72.421N	S72.441P	S72.461R
S72.036M	S72.065M	S72.121N	S72.143P	S72.322Q	S72.344R	S72.391P	S72.421P	S72.441Q	S72.462A
S72.036N	S72.065N	S72.121P	S72.143Q	S72.322R	S72.345K	S72.391Q	S72.421Q	S72.441R	S72.462K
S72.036P	S72.065P	S72.121Q	S72.143R	S72.323K	S72.345M	S72.391R	S72.421R	S72.442A	S72.462M
S72.036Q	S72.065Q	S72.121R	S72.144K	S72.323M	S72.345N	S72.392K	S72.422A	S72.442K	S72.462N
S72.036R	S72.065R	S72.122K	S72.144M	S72.323N	S72.345P	S72.392M	S72.422K	S72.442M	S72.462P
S72.041K	S72.066K	S72.122M	S72.144N	S72.323P	S72.345Q	S72.392N	S72.422M	S72.442N	S72.462Q
S72.041M	S72.066M	S72.122N	S72.144P	S72.323Q	S72.345R	S72.392P	S72.422N	S72.442P	S72.462R
S72.041N	S72.066N	S72.122P	S72.144Q	S72.323R	S72.346K		S72.422P	S72.442Q	S72.463A
S72.041P	S72.066P	S72.122Q	S72.144R	S72.324K	S72.346M		S72.422Q	S72.442R	S72.463K
	S72.066Q	S72.122R	S72.145K	S72.324M	S72.346N		S72.422R	S72.443A	

Alphabetic & Numeric Lists of CCs

S72.463M	S72.91XR	S77.00XA	S79.149K	S82.016C	S82.033P	S82.091B	S82.116N	S82.136P	S82.156Q
S72.463N	S72.92XK	S77.01XA	S79.149P	S82.016K	S82.033Q	S82.091C	S82.116P	S82.136Q	S82.156R
S72.463P	S72.92XM	S77.02XA	S79.191A	S82.016M	S82.033R	S82.091K	S82.116Q	S82.136R	S82.161A
S72.463Q	S72.92XN	S77.10XA	S79.191K	S82.016N	S82.034A	S82.091M	S82.116R	S82.141A	S82.161K
S72.463R	S72.92XP	S77.11XA	S79.191P	S82.016P	S82.034B	S82.091N	S82.121A	S82.141K	S82.161P
S72.464A	S72.92XQ	S77.12XA	S79.192A	S82.016R	S82.034C	S82.091P	S82.121K	S82.141N	S82.162A
S72.464K	S72.92XR	S78.011A	S79.192K	S82.021A	S82.034K	S82.091Q	S82.121M	S82.141P	S82.162K
S72.464M	S73.001A	S78.012A	S79.192P	S82.021B	S82.034M	S82.091R	S82.121N	S82.141Q	S82.162P
S72.464N	S73.002A	S78.019A	S79.199A	S82.021C	S82.034N	S82.092A	S82.121P	S82.141R	S82.169A
S72.464P	S73.003A	S78.021A	S79.199K	S82.021K	S82.034P	S82.092B	S82.121Q	S82.142A	S82.169K
S72.464Q	S73.004A	S78.022A	S79.199P	S82.021M	S82.034Q	S82.092C	S82.121R	S82.142K	S82.169P
S72.464R	S73.005A	S78.029A	S82.001A	S82.021N	S82.034R	S82.092K	S82.122A	S82.142M	S82.191A
S72.465A	S73.006A	S78.111A	S82.001B	S82.021P	S82.035A	S82.092M	S82.122K	S82.142N	S82.191K
S72.465K	S73.011A	S78.112A	S82.001K	S82.021Q	S82.035B	S82.092N	S82.122M	S82.142P	S82.191M
S72.465M	S73.012A	S78.119A	S82.001M	S82.021R	S82.035C	S82.092Q	S82.122N	S82.142Q	S82.191N
S72.465N	S73.013A	S78.121A	S82.001N	S82.022A	S82.035K	S82.092R	S82.122P	S82.142R	S82.191P
S72.465P	S73.014A	S78.122A	S82.001P	S82.022B	S82.035M	S82.099A	S82.122Q	S82.143A	S82.191Q
S72.465Q	S73.015A	S78.129A	S82.001Q	S82.022C	S82.035P	S82.099B	S82.122R	S82.143K	S82.191R
S72.465R	S73.016A	S78.911A	S82.001R	S82.022K	S82.035Q	S82.099C	S82.123A	S82.143M	S82.192A
S72.466A	S73.021A	S78.912A	S82.002A	S82.022M	S82.035R	S82.099K	S82.123K	S82.143N	S82.192K
S72.466K	S73.022A	S78.919A	S82.002B	S82.022P	S82.036A	S82.099M	S82.123M	S82.143P	S82.192M
S72.466M	S73.023A	S78.921A	S82.002C	S82.022Q	S82.036B	S82.099P	S82.123N	S82.143Q	S82.192N
S72.466N	S73.024A	S78.922A	S82.002K	S82.022R	S82.036C	S82.099Q	S82.123P	S82.143R	S82.192P
S72.466P	S73.025A	S78.929A	S82.002M	S82.023A	S82.036K	S82.099R	S82.123Q	S82.144A	S82.192Q
S72.466Q	S73.026A	S79.001K	S82.002N	S82.023B	S82.036M	S82.101A	S82.123R	S82.144K	S82.192R
S72.466R	S73.031A	S79.001P	S82.002P	S82.023C	S82.036N	S82.101K	S82.124A	S82.144M	S82.199A
S72.471A	S73.032A	S79.002K	S82.002Q	S82.023K	S82.036P	S82.101M	S82.124K	S82.144N	S82.199K
S72.471K	S73.033A	S79.002P	S82.002R	S82.023M	S82.036Q	S82.101N	S82.124M	S82.144P	S82.199M
S72.471P	S73.034A	S79.009K	S82.009A	S82.023N	S82.036R	S82.101P	S82.124N	S82.144Q	S82.199N
S72.472A	S73.035A	S79.009P	S82.009B	S82.023P	S82.041A	S82.101Q	S82.124P	S82.144R	S82.199P
S72.472K	S73.036A	S79.011K	S82.009C	S82.023Q	S82.041B	S82.101R	S82.124Q	S82.145A	S82.199Q
S72.472P	S73.041A	S79.011P	S82.009K	S82.023R	S82.041C	S82.102A	S82.124R	S82.145K	S82.199R
S72.479A	S73.042A	S79.012K	S82.009M	S82.024A	S82.041K	S82.102K	S82.125A	S82.145M	S82.201A
S72.479K	S73.043A	S79.012P	S82.009N	S82.024B	S82.041M	S82.102M	S82.125K	S82.145N	S82.201K
S72.479P	S73.044A	S79.019K	S82.009P	S82.024C	S82.041N	S82.102N	S82.125M	S82.145P	S82.201M
S72.491A	S73.045A	S79.019P	S82.009Q	S82.024K	S82.041P	S82.102P	S82.125N	S82.145Q	S82.201N
S72.491K	S73.046A	S79.091K	S82.009R	S82.024M	S82.041Q	S82.102Q	S82.125P	S82.145R	S82.201P
S72.491M	S75.201A	S79.091P	S82.011A	S82.024N	S82.041R	S82.109A	S82.125Q	S82.146A	S82.201Q
S72.491N	S75.202A	S79.092K	S82.011B	S82.024P	S82.042A	S82.109K	S82.125R	S82.146K	S82.201R
S72.491P	S75.209A	S79.092P	S82.011C	S82.024Q	S82.042B	S82.109M	S82.126A	S82.146M	S82.202A
S72.491Q	S75.211A	S79.099K	S82.011K	S82.024R	S82.042C	S82.109N	S82.126K	S82.146N	S82.202K
S72.491R	S75.212A	S79.099P	S82.011M	S82.025A	S82.042K	S82.109P	S82.126M	S82.146P	S82.202M
S72.492A	S75.219A	S79.101A	S82.011N	S82.025B	S82.042N	S82.109Q	S82.126N	S82.146Q	S82.202N
S72.492K	S75.221A	S79.101K	S82.011P	S82.025C	S82.042P	S82.109R	S82.126P	S82.146R	S82.202P
S72.492M	S75.222A	S79.101P	S82.011Q	S82.025K	S82.042Q	S82.111A	S82.126Q	S82.151A	S82.202Q
S72.492N	S75.229A	S79.102A	S82.011R	S82.025M	S82.042R	S82.111K	S82.126R	S82.151K	S82.202R
S72.492P	S75.291A	S79.102K	S82.012A	S82.025N	S82.043A	S82.111M	S82.131A	S82.151M	S82.209A
S72.492Q	S75.292A	S79.102P	S82.012B	S82.025P	S82.043B	S82.111N	S82.131K	S82.151N	S82.209K
S72.492R	S75.299A	S79.109A	S82.012C	S82.025Q	S82.043C	S82.111P	S82.131M	S82.151P	S82.209N
S72.499A	S75.801A	S79.109K	S82.012K	S82.025R	S82.043K	S82.111Q	S82.131N	S82.151Q	S82.209P
S72.499K	S75.802A	S79.109P	S82.012M	S82.026A	S82.043M	S82.111R	S82.131P	S82.151R	S82.209Q
S72.499M	S75.809A	S79.111A	S82.012N	S82.026B	S82.043N	S82.112A	S82.131Q	S82.152A	S82.209R
S72.499N	S75.811A	S79.111K	S82.012P	S82.026C	S82.043P	S82.112K	S82.131R	S82.152K	S82.221A
S72.499P	S75.812A	S79.111P	S82.012Q	S82.026K	S82.043Q	S82.112M	S82.132A	S82.152M	S82.221K
S72.499Q	S75.819A	S79.112A	S82.012R	S82.026M	S82.044A	S82.112N	S82.132K	S82.152N	S82.221M
S72.499R	S75.891A	S79.112K	S82.013A	S82.026N	S82.044B	S82.112P	S82.132M	S82.152P	S82.221N
S72.8X1K	S75.892A	S79.112P	S82.013B	S82.026P	S82.044C	S82.112Q	S82.132N	S82.152Q	S82.221P
S72.8X1M	S75.899A	S79.119A	S82.013C	S82.026Q	S82.044M	S82.112R	S82.132P	S82.152R	S82.221Q
S72.8X1N	S75.901A	S79.119K	S82.013M	S82.026R	S82.044N	S82.113A	S82.132Q	S82.153A	S82.221R
S72.8X1P	S75.902A	S79.119P	S82.013N	S82.031A	S82.044P	S82.113K	S82.132R	S82.153K	S82.222A
S72.8X1Q	S75.909A	S79.121A	S82.013P	S82.031B	S82.044Q	S82.113M	S82.133A	S82.153M	S82.222K
S72.8X1R	S75.911A	S79.121K	S82.013Q	S82.031C	S82.044R	S82.113N	S82.133K	S82.153N	S82.222M
S72.8X2K	S75.912A	S79.121P	S82.013R	S82.031K	S82.045A	S82.113P	S82.133M	S82.153P	S82.222N
S72.8X2M	S75.919A	S79.122A	S82.014A	S82.031M	S82.045B	S82.113Q	S82.133N	S82.153Q	S82.222P
S72.8X2N	S75.991A	S79.122K	S82.014B	S82.031N	S82.045K	S82.113R	S82.133P	S82.153R	S82.222Q
S72.8X2P	S75.992A	S79.122P	S82.014C	S82.031P	S82.045M	S82.114A	S82.133Q	S82.154A	S82.222R
S72.8X2Q	S75.999A	S79.129A	S82.014K	S82.031Q	S82.045N	S82.114K	S82.133R	S82.154K	S82.223A
S72.8X2R	S76.021A	S79.129K	S82.014M	S82.031R	S82.045P	S82.114M	S82.134A	S82.154M	S82.223K
S72.8X9K	S76.022A	S79.129P	S82.014N	S82.032A	S82.045Q	S82.114N	S82.134K	S82.154N	S82.223M
S72.8X9M	S76.029A	S79.131A	S82.014P	S82.032B	S82.045R	S82.114P	S82.134M	S82.154P	S82.223N
S72.8X9N	S76.121A	S79.131K	S82.014Q	S82.032C	S82.046A	S82.114Q	S82.134N	S82.154Q	S82.223P
S72.8X9Q	S76.122A	S79.131P	S82.014R	S82.032K	S82.046B	S82.114R	S82.134P	S82.154R	S82.223Q
S72.8X9R	S76.129A	S79.132A	S82.015A	S82.032M	S82.046C	S82.115A	S82.134Q	S82.155A	S82.223R
S72.90XK	S76.221A	S79.132K	S82.015B	S82.032N	S82.046K	S82.115K	S82.134R	S82.155K	S82.224A
S72.90XM	S76.222A	S79.132P	S82.015C	S82.032P	S82.046M	S82.115M	S82.135A	S82.155M	S82.224K
S72.90XN	S76.229A	S79.139A	S82.015K	S82.032Q	S82.046N	S82.115N	S82.135K	S82.155N	S82.224M
S72.90XP	S76.321A	S79.139K	S82.015M	S82.032R	S82.046P	S82.115P	S82.135M	S82.155Q	S82.224N
S72.90XQ	S76.322A	S79.139P	S82.015N	S82.033A	S82.046Q	S82.115Q	S82.135N	S82.155R	S82.224P
S72.90XR	S76.329A	S79.141A	S82.015P	S82.033B	S82.046R	S82.115R	S82.135P	S82.156A	S82.224Q
S72.91XK	S76.821A	S79.141K	S82.015Q	S82.033C	S82.091A	S82.116A	S82.135Q	S82.156K	S82.224R
S72.91XM	S76.822A	S79.141P	S82.015R	S82.033K		S82.116K	S82.135R	S82.156M	S82.225A
S72.91XN	S76.829A	S79.142A	S82.016A	S82.033M		S82.116M	S82.136A	S82.156N	S82.225K
S72.91XP	S76.921A	S79.142K	S82.016B	S82.033N			S82.136K	S82.156P	S82.225M
S72.91XQ	S76.922A	S79.142P					S82.136M		S82.225N
	S76.929A	S79.149A					S82.136N		

S82.225P	S82.245Q	S82.265R	S82.399R	S82.436K	S82.462M	S82.55XQ	S82.839P	S82.855K	S82.875M
S82.225Q	S82.245R	S82.266A	S82.401K	S82.436M	S82.462N	S82.55XR	S82.839Q	S82.855M	S82.875N
S82.225R	S82.246A	S82.266K	S82.401M	S82.436N	S82.462P	S82.56XB	S82.839R	S82.855N	S82.875P
S82.226A	S82.246K	S82.266M	S82.401N	S82.436P	S82.462Q	S82.56XC	S82.841B	S82.855P	S82.875Q
S82.226K	S82.246M	S82.266N	S82.401P	S82.436Q	S82.462R	S82.56XK	S82.841C	S82.855Q	S82.875R
S82.226M	S82.246N	S82.266P	S82.401Q	S82.436R	S82.463K	S82.56XM	S82.841K	S82.855R	S82.876B
S82.226N	S82.246P	S82.266Q	S82.401R	S82.441K	S82.463M	S82.56XN	S82.841M	S82.856B	S82.876C
S82.226P	S82.246Q	S82.266R	S82.402K	S82.441M	S82.463N	S82.56XP	S82.841N	S82.856C	S82.876K
S82.226Q	S82.246R	S82.291A	S82.402M	S82.441N	S82.463P	S82.56XQ	S82.841P	S82.856K	S82.876M
S82.226R	S82.251A	S82.291K	S82.402N	S82.441P	S82.463Q	S82.56XR	S82.841Q	S82.856M	S82.876N
S82.231A	S82.251K	S82.291M	S82.402P	S82.441Q	S82.463R	S82.61XB	S82.841R	S82.856N	S82.876P
S82.231K	S82.251M	S82.291N	S82.402Q	S82.441R	S82.464K	S82.61XC	S82.842B	S82.856P	S82.876Q
S82.231M	S82.251N	S82.291P	S82.402R	S82.442K	S82.464M	S82.61XK	S82.842C	S82.856Q	S82.876R
S82.231N	S82.251P	S82.291Q	S82.409K	S82.442M	S82.464N	S82.61XM	S82.842K	S82.856R	S82.891B
S82.231P	S82.251Q	S82.291R	S82.409M	S82.442N	S82.464P	S82.61XN	S82.842M	S82.861K	S82.891C
S82.231Q	S82.251R	S82.292A	S82.409N	S82.442P	S82.464Q	S82.61XP	S82.842N	S82.861M	S82.891K
S82.231R	S82.252A	S82.292K	S82.409P	S82.442Q	S82.464R	S82.61XQ	S82.842P	S82.861N	S82.891M
S82.232A	S82.252K	S82.292M	S82.409Q	S82.442R	S82.465K	S82.61XR	S82.842Q	S82.861P	S82.891N
S82.232K	S82.252M	S82.292N	S82.409R	S82.443K	S82.465M	S82.62XB	S82.842R	S82.861Q	S82.891P
S82.232M	S82.252N	S82.292P	S82.421K	S82.443M	S82.465N	S82.62XC	S82.843B	S82.861R	S82.891Q
S82.232N	S82.252P	S82.292Q	S82.421M	S82.443N	S82.465P	S82.62XK	S82.843C	S82.862K	S82.891R
S82.232P	S82.252Q	S82.292R	S82.421N	S82.443P	S82.465Q	S82.62XM	S82.843K	S82.862M	S82.892B
S82.232Q	S82.252R	S82.299A	S82.421P	S82.443Q	S82.465R	S82.62XN	S82.843M	S82.862N	S82.892C
S82.232R	S82.253A	S82.299K	S82.421Q	S82.443R	S82.466K	S82.62XP	S82.843N	S82.862P	S82.892K
S82.233A	S82.253K	S82.299M	S82.421R	S82.444K	S82.466M	S82.62XQ	S82.843P	S82.862Q	S82.892M
S82.233K	S82.253M	S82.299N	S82.422K	S82.444M	S82.466N	S82.62XR	S82.843Q	S82.862R	S82.892N
S82.233M	S82.253N	S82.299P	S82.422M	S82.444N	S82.466P	S82.63XB	S82.843R	S82.863K	S82.892P
S82.233N	S82.253P	S82.299Q	S82.422N	S82.444P	S82.466Q	S82.63XC	S82.844B	S82.863M	S82.892Q
S82.233P	S82.253Q	S82.299R	S82.422P	S82.444Q	S82.466R	S82.63XK	S82.844C	S82.863N	S82.892R
S82.233Q	S82.253R	S82.301B	S82.422Q	S82.444R	S82.491K	S82.63XM	S82.844K	S82.863P	S82.899B
S82.233R	S82.254A	S82.301C	S82.422R	S82.445K	S82.491M	S82.63XN	S82.844M	S82.863Q	S82.899C
S82.234A	S82.254K	S82.301K	S82.423K	S82.445M	S82.491N	S82.63XP	S82.844N	S82.863R	S82.899K
S82.234K	S82.254M	S82.301M	S82.423M	S82.445N	S82.491P	S82.63XQ	S82.844P	S82.864K	S82.899M
S82.234M	S82.254N	S82.301N	S82.423N	S82.445P	S82.491Q	S82.63XR	S82.844Q	S82.864M	S82.899N
S82.234N	S82.254P	S82.301P	S82.423P	S82.445Q	S82.491R	S82.64XB	S82.844R	S82.864N	S82.899P
S82.234P	S82.254Q	S82.301Q	S82.423Q	S82.445R	S82.492K	S82.64XC	S82.845B	S82.864P	S82.899Q
S82.234Q	S82.254R	S82.301R	S82.423R	S82.446K	S82.492M	S82.64XK	S82.845C	S82.864Q	S82.899R
S82.234R	S82.255A	S82.302B	S82.424K	S82.446M	S82.492N	S82.64XM	S82.845K	S82.864R	S82.90XB
S82.235A	S82.255K	S82.302C	S82.424M	S82.446N	S82.492P	S82.64XN	S82.845M	S82.865K	S82.90XC
S82.235K	S82.255M	S82.302K	S82.424N	S82.446P	S82.492Q	S82.64XP	S82.845N	S82.865M	S82.90XK
S82.235M	S82.255N	S82.302M	S82.424P	S82.446Q	S82.492R	S82.64XQ	S82.845P	S82.865N	S82.90XM
S82.235N	S82.255P	S82.302N	S82.424Q	S82.446R	S82.499K	S82.64XR	S82.845Q	S82.865P	S82.90XN
S82.235P	S82.255Q	S82.302P	S82.424R	S82.451K	S82.499M	S82.65XB	S82.845R	S82.865Q	S82.90XP
S82.235Q	S82.255R	S82.302Q	S82.425K	S82.451M	S82.499N	S82.65XC	S82.846B	S82.865R	S82.90XQ
S82.235R	S82.256A	S82.302R	S82.425M	S82.451N	S82.499P	S82.65XK	S82.846C	S82.866K	S82.90XR
S82.236A	S82.256K	S82.309B	S82.425N	S82.451P	S82.499Q	S82.65XM	S82.846K	S82.866M	S82.91XB
S82.236K	S82.256M	S82.309C	S82.425P	S82.451Q	S82.499R	S82.65XN	S82.846M	S82.866N	S82.91XC
S82.236M	S82.256N	S82.309K	S82.425Q	S82.451R	S82.51XB	S82.65XP	S82.846N	S82.866P	S82.91XK
S82.236N	S82.256P	S82.309M	S82.425R	S82.452K	S82.51XC	S82.65XQ	S82.846P	S82.866Q	S82.91XM
S82.236P	S82.256Q	S82.309N	S82.426K	S82.452M	S82.51XK	S82.65XR	S82.846Q	S82.866R	S82.91XN
S82.236Q	S82.256R	S82.309P	S82.426M	S82.452N	S82.51XM	S82.66XB	S82.846R	S82.871B	S82.91XP
S82.236R	S82.261A	S82.309Q	S82.426N	S82.452P	S82.51XN	S82.66XC	S82.851B	S82.871C	S82.91XQ
S82.241A	S82.261K	S82.309R	S82.426P	S82.452Q	S82.51XP	S82.66XK	S82.851C	S82.871K	S82.91XR
S82.241K	S82.261M	S82.311A	S82.426Q	S82.452R	S82.51XQ	S82.66XM	S82.851K	S82.871M	S82.92XB
S82.241M	S82.261N	S82.311K	S82.426R	S82.453K	S82.51XR	S82.66XN	S82.851M	S82.871N	S82.92XC
S82.241N	S82.261P	S82.311P	S82.431K	S82.453M	S82.52XB	S82.66XP	S82.851N	S82.871P	S82.92XK
S82.241P	S82.261Q	S82.312A	S82.431M	S82.453N	S82.52XC	S82.66XQ	S82.851P	S82.871Q	S82.92XM
S82.241Q	S82.261R	S82.312K	S82.431N	S82.453P	S82.52XK	S82.66XR	S82.851Q	S82.871R	S82.92XN
S82.241R	S82.262A	S82.312P	S82.431P	S82.453Q	S82.52XM	S82.811K	S82.851R	S82.872B	S82.92XP
S82.242A	S82.262K	S82.319A	S82.431Q	S82.453R	S82.52XN	S82.811P	S82.852B	S82.872C	S82.92XQ
S82.242K	S82.262M	S82.319K	S82.431R	S82.454K	S82.52XP	S82.812K	S82.852C	S82.872K	S82.92XR
S82.242M	S82.262N	S82.319P	S82.432K	S82.454M	S82.52XQ	S82.812P	S82.852K	S82.872M	S85.101A
S82.242N	S82.262P	S82.391B	S82.432M	S82.454N	S82.52XR	S82.819K	S82.852M	S82.872N	S85.102A
S82.242P	S82.262Q	S82.391C	S82.432N	S82.454P	S82.53XB	S82.819P	S82.852N	S82.872P	S85.109A
S82.242Q	S82.262R	S82.391K	S82.432P	S82.454Q	S82.53XC	S82.821K	S82.852P	S82.872Q	S85.111A
S82.242R	S82.263A	S82.391M	S82.432Q	S82.454R	S82.53XK	S82.821P	S82.852Q	S82.872R	S85.112A
S82.243A	S82.263K	S82.391N	S82.432R	S82.455K	S82.53XM	S82.822K	S82.852R	S82.873B	S85.119A
S82.243K	S82.263M	S82.391P	S82.433K	S82.455M	S82.53XN	S82.822P	S82.853B	S82.873C	S85.121A
S82.243M	S82.263N	S82.391Q	S82.433M	S82.455N	S82.53XP	S82.829K	S82.853C	S82.873K	S85.122A
S82.243N	S82.263P	S82.391R	S82.433N	S82.455P	S82.53XQ	S82.829P	S82.853K	S82.873M	S85.129A
S82.243P	S82.263Q	S82.392B	S82.433P	S82.455Q	S82.53XR	S82.831K	S82.853M	S82.873N	S85.131A
S82.243Q	S82.263R	S82.392C	S82.433Q	S82.455R	S82.54XB	S82.831M	S82.853N	S82.873P	S85.132A
S82.243R	S82.264A	S82.392K	S82.433R	S82.456K	S82.54XC	S82.831N	S82.853P	S82.873Q	S85.139A
S82.244A	S82.264K	S82.392M	S82.434K	S82.456M	S82.54XK	S82.831P	S82.853Q	S82.873R	S85.141A
S82.244K	S82.264M	S82.392N	S82.434M	S82.456N	S82.54XM	S82.831Q	S82.853R	S82.874B	S85.142A
S82.244M	S82.264N	S82.392P	S82.434N	S82.456P	S82.54XN	S82.831R	S82.854B	S82.874C	S85.149A
S82.244N	S82.264P	S82.392Q	S82.434P	S82.456Q	S82.54XP	S82.832K	S82.854C	S82.874K	S85.151A
S82.244P	S82.264Q	S82.392R	S82.434Q	S82.456R	S82.54XQ	S82.832M	S82.854K	S82.874M	S85.152A
S82.244Q	S82.264R	S82.399B	S82.434R	S82.461K	S82.54XR	S82.832N	S82.854M	S82.874N	S85.159A
S82.244R	S82.265A	S82.399C	S82.435K	S82.461M	S82.55XB	S82.832P	S82.854N	S82.874P	S85.161A
S82.245A	S82.265K	S82.399K	S82.435M	S82.461N	S82.55XC	S82.832Q	S82.854P	S82.874Q	S85.162A
S82.245K	S82.265M	S82.399M	S82.435N	S82.461P	S82.55XK	S82.832R	S82.854Q	S82.874R	S85.169A
S82.245M	S82.265N	S82.399N	S82.435P	S82.461Q	S82.55XM	S82.839K	S82.854R	S82.875B	S85.171A
S82.245N	S82.265P	S82.399P	S82.435Q	S82.461R	S82.55XN	S82.839M	S82.855B	S82.875C	S85.172A
S82.245P	S82.265Q	S82.399Q	S82.435R	S82.462K	S82.55XP	S82.839N	S82.855C	S82.875K	S85.179A

S85.181A	S89.001K	S89.192K	S92.023B	S92.101K	S92.152P	S92.241B	S92.332K	S92.426P	S95.001A
S85.182A	S89.001P	S89.192P	S92.023K	S92.101P	S92.153B	S92.241K	S92.332P	S92.491K	S95.002A
S85.189A	S89.002A	S89.199K	S92.023P	S92.102B	S92.153K	S92.241P	S92.333B	S92.491P	S95.009A
S85.201A	S89.002K	S89.199P	S92.024B	S92.102K	S92.153K	S92.242K	S92.333K	S92.492K	S95.011A
S85.202A	S89.002P	S89.201K	S92.024K	S92.102P	S92.154B	S92.242P	S92.333P	S92.492P	S95.012A
S85.209A	S89.009A	S89.201P	S92.024P	S92.109B	S92.154K	S92.243B	S92.334B	S92.499K	S95.019A
S85.211A	S89.009K	S89.202K	S92.025B	S92.109K	S92.154P	S92.243K	S92.334K	S92.499P	S95.091A
S85.212A	S89.009P	S89.202P	S92.025K	S92.109P	S92.155B	S92.243P	S92.334P	S92.501K	S95.092A
S85.219A	S89.011A	S89.209K	S92.025P	S92.111B	S92.155K	S92.244B	S92.335B	S92.501P	S95.099A
S85.291A	S89.011K	S89.209P	S92.026B	S92.111K	S92.155P	S92.244K	S92.335K	S92.502K	S95.101A
S85.292A	S89.011P	S89.211K	S92.026K	S92.111P	S92.156B	S92.244P	S92.335P	S92.502P	S95.102A
S85.299A	S89.012A	S89.211P	S92.026P	S92.112B	S92.156K	S92.245B	S92.336B	S92.503K	S95.109A
S85.301A	S89.012K	S89.212K	S92.031B	S92.112K	S92.156P	S92.245K	S92.336K	S92.503P	S95.111A
S85.302A	S89.012P	S89.212P	S92.031K	S92.112P	S92.191B	S92.245P	S92.336P	S92.504K	S95.112A
S85.309A	S89.019A	S89.219K	S92.031P	S92.113B	S92.191K	S92.246B	S92.341B	S92.504P	S95.119A
S85.311A	S89.019K	S89.219P	S92.032B	S92.113K	S92.191P	S92.246K	S92.341K	S92.505K	S95.191A
S85.312A	S89.019P	S89.221K	S92.032K	S92.113P	S92.192B	S92.246P	S92.341P	S92.505P	S95.192A
S85.319A	S89.021A	S89.221P	S92.032P	S92.114B	S92.192K	S92.251B	S92.342B	S92.506K	S95.199A
S85.391A	S89.021K	S89.222K	S92.033B	S92.114K	S92.192P	S92.251K	S92.342K	S92.506P	S95.201A
S85.392A	S89.021P	S89.222P	S92.033K	S92.114P	S92.199B	S92.251P	S92.342P	S92.511K	S95.202A
S85.399A	S89.022A	S89.229K	S92.033P	S92.115B	S92.199K	S92.252B	S92.343B	S92.511P	S95.209A
S85.401A	S89.022K	S89.229P	S92.034B	S92.115K	S92.199P	S92.252K	S92.343K	S92.512K	S95.211A
S85.402A	S89.022P	S89.291K	S92.034K	S92.115P	S92.201B	S92.252P	S92.343P	S92.512P	S95.212A
S85.409A	S89.029A	S89.291P	S92.034P	S92.116B	S92.201K	S92.253B	S92.344B	S92.513K	S95.219A
S85.411A	S89.029K	S89.292K	S92.035B	S92.116K	S92.201P	S92.253K	S92.344K	S92.513P	S95.291A
S85.412A	S89.029P	S89.292P	S92.035K	S92.116P	S92.202B	S92.253P	S92.344P	S92.514K	S95.292A
S85.419A	S89.031A	S89.299K	S92.035P	S92.121B	S92.202K	S92.254B	S92.345B	S92.514P	S95.299A
S85.491A	S89.031K	S89.299P	S92.036B	S92.121K	S92.202P	S92.254K	S92.345K	S92.515K	S95.801A
S85.492A	S89.031P	S89.301K	S92.036K	S92.121P	S92.209B	S92.254P	S92.345P	S92.515P	S95.802A
S85.499A	S89.032A	S89.301P	S92.036P	S92.122B	S92.209K	S92.255B	S92.346B	S92.516K	S95.809A
S85.801A	S89.032K	S89.302K	S92.041B	S92.122K	S92.209P	S92.255K	S92.346K	S92.516P	S95.811A
S85.802A	S89.032P	S89.302P	S92.041K	S92.122P	S92.211B	S92.255P	S92.346P	S92.521K	S95.812A
S85.809A	S89.039A	S89.309K	S92.041P	S92.123B	S92.211K	S92.256B	S92.351B	S92.521P	S95.819A
S85.811A	S89.039K	S89.309P	S92.042B	S92.123K	S92.211P	S92.256K	S92.351K	S92.522K	S95.891A
S85.812A	S89.039P	S89.311K	S92.042K	S92.123P	S92.212B	S92.256P	S92.351P	S92.522P	S95.892A
S85.819A	S89.041A	S89.311P	S92.042P	S92.124B	S92.212K	S92.301B	S92.352B	S92.523K	S95.899A
S85.891A	S89.041K	S89.312K	S92.043B	S92.124K	S92.212P	S92.301K	S92.352K	S92.523P	S95.901A
S85.892A	S89.041P	S89.312P	S92.043K	S92.124P	S92.213B	S92.301P	S92.352P	S92.524K	S95.902A
S85.899A	S89.042A	S89.319K	S92.043P	S92.125B	S92.213K	S92.302B	S92.353B	S92.524P	S95.909A
S85.901A	S89.042K	S89.319P	S92.044B	S92.125K	S92.213P	S92.302K	S92.353K	S92.525K	S95.911A
S85.902A	S89.042P	S89.321K	S92.044K	S92.125P	S92.214B	S92.302P	S92.353P	S92.525P	S95.912A
S85.909A	S89.049A	S89.321P	S92.044P	S92.126B	S92.214K	S92.309B	S92.354B	S92.526K	S95.919A
S85.911A	S89.049K	S89.322K	S92.045B	S92.126K	S92.214P	S92.309K	S92.354K	S92.526P	S95.991A
S85.912A	S89.049P	S89.322P	S92.045K	S92.126P	S92.215B	S92.309P	S92.354P	S92.531K	S95.992A
S85.919A	S89.091A	S89.329K	S92.045P	S92.131B	S92.215K	S92.311B	S92.355B	S92.531P	S95.999A
S85.991A	S89.091K	S89.329P	S92.046B	S92.131K	S92.215P	S92.311K	S92.355K	S92.532K	S96.021A
S85.992A	S89.091P	S89.391K	S92.046K	S92.131P	S92.216B	S92.311P	S92.355P	S92.532P	S96.022A
S85.999A	S89.092A	S89.391P	S92.046P	S92.132B	S92.216K	S92.312B	S92.356B	S92.533K	S96.029A
S86.021A	S89.092K	S89.392K	S92.051B	S92.132K	S92.216P	S92.312K	S92.356K	S92.533P	S96.121A
S86.022A	S89.092P	S89.392P	S92.051K	S92.132P	S92.221B	S92.312P	S92.356P	S92.534K	S96.122A
S86.029A	S89.099A	S89.399K	S92.051P	S92.133B	S92.221K	S92.313B	S92.401K	S92.534P	S96.129A
S86.121A	S89.099K	S89.399P	S92.052B	S92.133K	S92.221P	S92.313K	S92.401P	S92.535K	S96.221A
S86.122A	S89.099P	S92.001B	S92.052K	S92.133P	S92.222B	S92.313P	S92.402K	S92.535P	S96.222A
S86.129A	S89.101K	S92.001K	S92.052P	S92.134B	S92.222K	S92.314B	S92.402P	S92.536K	S96.229A
S86.221A	S89.101P	S92.001P	S92.053B	S92.134K	S92.222P	S92.314K	S92.403K	S92.536P	S96.821A
S86.222A	S89.102K	S92.002B	S92.053K	S92.134P	S92.223B	S92.314P	S92.403P	S92.591B	S96.822A
S86.229A	S89.102P	S92.002K	S92.053P	S92.135B	S92.223K	S92.315B	S92.404K	S92.591P	S96.829A
S86.321A	S89.109K	S92.002P	S92.054B	S92.135K	S92.223P	S92.315K	S92.404P	S92.592K	S96.921A
S86.322A	S89.109P	S92.009B	S92.054K	S92.135P	S92.224B	S92.315P	S92.405K	S92.592P	S96.922A
S86.329A	S89.111K	S92.009K	S92.054P	S92.136B	S92.224K	S92.316B	S92.405P	S92.599B	S96.929A
S86.821A	S89.111P	S92.009P	S92.055B	S92.136K	S92.224P	S92.316K	S92.406K	S92.599P	S98.011A
S86.822A	S89.112K	S92.011B	S92.055K	S92.136P	S92.225B	S92.316P	S92.406P	S92.811B	S98.012A
S86.829A	S89.112P	S92.011K	S92.055P	S92.141B	S92.225K	S92.321B	S92.411K	S92.811K	S98.019A
S86.921A	S89.119K	S92.011P	S92.056B	S92.141K	S92.225P	S92.321K	S92.411P	S92.811P	S98.021A
S86.922A	S89.119P	S92.012B	S92.056K	S92.141P	S92.226B	S92.321P	S92.412K	S92.812B	S98.022A
S86.929A	S89.121K	S92.012K	S92.056P	S92.142B	S92.226K	S92.322B	S92.412P	S92.812K	S98.029A
S88.011A	S89.121P	S92.012P	S92.061B	S92.142K	S92.226P	S92.322K	S92.413K	S92.812P	S98.311A
S88.012A	S89.122K	S92.013B	S92.061K	S92.142P	S92.231B	S92.322P	S92.413P	S92.819B	S98.312A
S88.019A	S89.122P	S92.013K	S92.061P	S92.143B	S92.231K	S92.323B	S92.414K	S92.819K	S98.319A
S88.021A	S89.129K	S92.013P	S92.062B	S92.143K	S92.231P	S92.323K	S92.414P	S92.819P	S98.321A
S88.022A	S89.129P	S92.014B	S92.062K	S92.143P	S92.232B	S92.323P	S92.415K	S92.901B	S98.322A
S88.029A	S89.131K	S92.014K	S92.062P	S92.144B	S92.232K	S92.324B	S92.415P	S92.901K	S98.329A
S88.111A	S89.131P	S92.014P	S92.063B	S92.144K	S92.232P	S92.324K	S92.416K	S92.901P	S98.911A
S88.112A	S89.132K	S92.015B	S92.063K	S92.144P	S92.233B	S92.324P	S92.416P	S92.902B	S98.912A
S88.119A	S89.132P	S92.015K	S92.063P	S92.145B	S92.233K	S92.325B	S92.421K	S92.902K	S98.919A
S88.121A	S89.139K	S92.015P	S92.064B	S92.145K	S92.233P	S92.325K	S92.421P	S92.902P	S98.921A
S88.122A	S89.139P	S92.016B	S92.064K	S92.145P	S92.234B	S92.325P	S92.422K	S92.909B	S98.922A
S88.129A	S89.141K	S92.016K	S92.064P	S92.146B	S92.234K	S92.326B	S92.422P	S92.909K	S98.929A
S88.911A	S89.141P	S92.016P	S92.065B	S92.146K	S92.235B	S92.326K	S92.423K	S92.909P	T17.400A
S88.912A	S89.142K	S92.021B	S92.065K	S92.146P	S92.235K	S92.326P	S92.423P	S92.911K	T17.408A
S88.919A	S89.142P	S92.021K	S92.065P	S92.151B	S92.235P	S92.331B	S92.424K	S92.911P	T17.410A
S88.921A	S89.149K	S92.021P	S92.066B	S92.151K	S92.236B	S92.331K	S92.424P	S92.912K	T17.418A
S88.922A	S89.149P	S92.022B	S92.066K	S92.151P	S92.236K	S92.331P	S92.425K	S92.912P	T17.420A
S88.929A	S89.191K	S92.022K	S92.066P	S92.152B	S92.236P	S92.332B	S92.425P	S92.919K	T17.428A
S89.001A	S89.191P	S92.022P	S92.101B	S92.152K			S92.426K	S92.919P	T17.490A

T17.498A	T22.729A	T24.701A	T33.40XA	T71.141A	T80.310A	T81.599A	T82.593A	T83.85XA	T84.410A
T17.500A	T22.731A	T24.702A	T33.41XA	T71.143A	T80.311A	T81.60XA	T82.594A	T83.86XA	T84.418A
T17.508A	T22.732A	T24.709A	T33.42XA	T71.144A	T80.319A	T81.61XA	T82.595A	T83.89XA	T84.420A
T17.510A	T22.739A	T24.711A	T33.511A	T71.151A	T80.39XA	T81.69XA	T82.598A	T83.9XXA	T84.428A
T17.518A	T22.741A	T24.712A	T33.512A	T71.152A	T80.40XA	T81.710A	T82.599A	T84.010A	T84.490A
T17.520A	T22.742A	T24.719A	T33.519A	T71.153A	T80.410A	T81.711A	T82.6XXA	T84.011A	T84.498A
T17.528A	T22.749A	T24.721A	T33.521A	T71.154A	T80.411A	T81.718A	T82.7XXA	T84.012A	T84.50XA
T17.590A	T22.751A	T24.722A	T33.522A	T71.161A	T80.419A	T81.719A	T82.817A	T84.013A	T84.51XA
T17.598A	T22.752A	T24.729A	T33.529A	T71.162A	T80.49XA	T81.72XA	T82.818A	T84.018A	T84.52XA
T17.800A	T22.759A	T24.731A	T33.531A	T71.163A	T80.51XA	T81.83XA	T82.827A	T84.019A	T84.53XA
T17.808A	T22.761A	T24.732A	T33.532A	T71.164A	T80.52XA	T82.01XA	T82.828A	T84.020A	T84.54XA
T17.810A	T22.762A	T24.739A	T33.539A	T71.191A	T80.59XA	T82.02XA	T82.837A	T84.021A	T84.59XA
T17.818A	T22.769A	T24.791A	T33.60XA	T71.192A	T80.61XA	T82.03XA	T82.838A	T84.023A	T84.60XA
T17.820A	T22.791A	T24.792A	T33.61XA	T71.193A	T80.62XA	T82.09XA	T82.847A	T84.028A	T84.610A
T17.828A	T22.792A	T24.799A	T33.62XA	T71.194A	T80.69XA	T82.110A	T82.848A	T84.029A	T84.611A
T17.890A	T22.799A	T25.311A	T33.70XA	T71.20XA	T80.810A	T82.111A	T82.855A	T84.030A	T84.612A
T17.898A	T23.301A	T25.312A	T33.71XA	T71.21XA	T80.818A	T82.118A	T82.856A	T84.031A	T84.613A
T20.30XA	T23.302A	T25.319A	T33.72XA	T71.221A	T80.910A	T82.119A	T82.857A	T84.032A	T84.614A
T20.311A	T23.309A	T25.321A	T33.811A	T71.222A	T80.911A	T82.120A	T82.858A	T84.033A	T84.615A
T20.312A	T23.311A	T25.322A	T33.812A	T71.223A	T80.919A	T82.121A	T82.867A	T84.038A	T84.619A
T20.319A	T23.312A	T25.329A	T33.819A	T71.224A	T80.A0XA	T82.128A	T82.868A	T84.039A	T84.620A
T20.32XA	T23.319A	T25.331A	T33.821A	T71.231A	T80.A10A	T82.129A	T82.897A	T84.050A	T84.621A
T20.33XA	T23.321A	T25.332A	T33.822A	T71.232A	T80.A11A	T82.190A	T82.898A	T84.051A	T84.622A
T20.34XA	T23.322A	T25.339A	T33.829A	T71.233A	T80.A19A	T82.191A	T82.9XXA	T84.052A	T84.623A
T20.35XA	T23.329A	T25.391A	T33.831A	T71.234A	T80.A9XA	T82.198A	T83.010A	T84.053A	T84.624A
T20.36XA	T23.331A	T25.392A	T33.832A	T71.29XA	T81.10XA	T82.199A	T83.020A	T84.058A	T84.625A
T20.37XA	T23.332A	T25.399A	T33.839A	T71.9XXA	T81.30XA	T82.211A	T83.030A	T84.059A	T84.629A
T20.39XA	T23.339A	T25.711A	T33.90XA	T74.01XA	T81.31XA	T82.212A	T83.090A	T84.060A	T84.63XA
T20.70XA	T23.341A	T25.712A	T33.99XA	T74.02XA	T81.32XA	T82.213A	T83.110A	T84.061A	T84.69XA
T20.711A	T23.342A	T25.719A	T34.011A	T74.11XA	T81.33XA	T82.218A	T83.111A	T84.062A	T84.7XXA
T20.712A	T23.349A	T25.721A	T34.012A	T74.12XA	T81.40XA	T82.221A	T83.112A	T84.063A	T84.81XA
T20.719A	T23.351A	T25.722A	T34.019A	T74.21XA	T81.41XA	T82.222A	T83.113A	T84.068A	T84.82XA
T20.72XA	T23.352A	T25.729A	T34.02XA	T74.22XA	T81.42XA	T82.223A	T83.118A	T84.069A	T84.83XA
T20.73XA	T23.359A	T25.731A	T34.09XA	T74.32XA	T81.43XA	T82.228A	T83.120A	T84.090A	T84.84XA
T20.74XA	T23.361A	T25.732A	T34.1XXA	T74.4XXA	T81.44XA	T82.310A	T83.121A	T84.091A	T84.85XA
T20.75XA	T23.362A	T25.739A	T34.2XXA	T74.51XA	T81.49XA	T82.311A	T83.122A	T84.092A	T84.86XA
T20.76XA	T23.369A	T25.791A	T34.3XXA	T74.52XA	T81.500A	T82.312A	T83.123A	T84.093A	T84.89XA
T20.77XA	T23.371A	T25.792A	T34.40XA	T74.61XA	T81.501A	T82.318A	T83.128A	T84.098A	T84.9XXA
T20.79XA	T23.372A	T25.799A	T34.41XA	T74.62XA	T81.502A	T82.319A	T83.190A	T84.099A	T85.01XA
T21.30XA	T23.379A	T26.20XA	T34.42XA	T74.91XA	T81.503A	T82.320A	T83.191A	T84.110A	T85.02XA
T21.31XA	T23.391A	T26.21XA	T34.511A	T74.92XA	T81.504A	T82.321A	T83.192A	T84.111A	T85.03XA
T21.32XA	T23.392A	T26.22XA	T34.512A	T75.1XXA	T81.505A	T82.322A	T83.193A	T84.112A	T85.09XA
T21.33XA	T23.399A	T26.70XA	T34.519A	T76.01XA	T81.506A	T82.328A	T83.198A	T84.113A	T85.110A
T21.34XA	T23.701A	T26.71XA	T34.521A	T76.02XA	T81.507A	T82.329A	T83.21XA	T84.114A	T85.111A
T21.35XA	T23.702A	T26.72XA	T34.522A	T76.11XA	T81.508A	T82.330A	T83.22XA	T84.115A	T85.112A
T21.36XA	T23.709A	T27.0XXA	T34.529A	T76.12XA	T81.509A	T82.331A	T83.23XA	T84.116A	T85.113A
T21.37XA	T23.711A	T27.1XXA	T34.531A	T76.21XA	T81.510A	T82.332A	T83.24XA	T84.117A	T85.118A
T21.39XA	T23.712A	T27.2XXA	T34.532A	T76.22XA	T81.511A	T82.338A	T83.25XA	T84.119A	T85.120A
T21.70XA	T23.719A	T27.3XXA	T34.539A	T76.32XA	T81.512A	T82.339A	T83.29XA	T84.120A	T85.121A
T21.71XA	T23.721A	T27.4XXA	T34.60XA	T76.51XA	T81.513A	T82.390A	T83.410A	T84.121A	T85.122A
T21.72XA	T23.722A	T27.5XXA	T34.61XA	T76.52XA	T81.514A	T82.391A	T83.411A	T84.122A	T85.123A
T21.73XA	T23.729A	T27.6XXA	T34.62XA	T76.61XA	T81.515A	T82.392A	T83.418A	T84.123A	T85.128A
T21.74XA	T23.731A	T27.7XXA	T34.70XA	T76.62XA	T81.516A	T82.398A	T83.420A	T84.124A	T85.190A
T21.75XA	T23.732A	T28.1XXA	T34.71XA	T76.91XA	T81.517A	T82.399A	T83.421A	T84.125A	T85.191A
T21.76XA	T23.739A	T28.2XXA	T34.72XA	T76.92XA	T81.518A	T82.41XA	T83.428A	T84.126A	T85.192A
T21.77XA	T23.741A	T28.6XXA	T34.811A	T78.00XA	T81.519A	T82.42XA	T83.490A	T84.127A	T85.193A
T21.79XA	T23.742A	T28.7XXA	T34.812A	T78.01XA	T81.520A	T82.43XA	T83.491A	T84.129A	T85.199A
T22.30XA	T23.749A	T31.10	T34.819A	T78.02XA	T81.521A	T82.49XA	T83.498A	T84.190A	T85.21XA
T22.311A	T23.751A	T31.11	T34.821A	T78.03XA	T81.522A	T82.510A	T83.510A	T84.191A	T85.22XA
T22.312A	T23.752A	T31.20	T34.822A	T78.04XA	T81.523A	T82.511A	T83.511A	T84.192A	T85.29XA
T22.319A	T23.759A	T31.30	T34.829A	T78.05XA	T81.524A	T82.512A	T83.512A	T84.193A	T85.310A
T22.321A	T23.761A	T31.40	T34.831A	T78.06XA	T81.525A	T82.513A	T83.518A	T84.194A	T85.311A
T22.322A	T23.762A	T31.50	T34.832A	T78.07XA	T81.526A	T82.514A	T83.590A	T84.195A	T85.320A
T22.329A	T23.769A	T31.60	T34.839A	T78.08XA	T81.527A	T82.515A	T83.591A	T84.196A	T85.321A
T22.331A	T23.771A	T31.70	T34.90XA	T78.09XA	T81.528A	T82.518A	T83.592A	T84.197A	T85.390A
T22.332A	T23.772A	T31.80	T34.99XA	T78.2XXA	T81.529A	T82.519A	T83.593A	T84.199A	T85.391A
T22.339A	T23.779A	T31.90	T67.01XA	T79.2XXA	T81.530A	T82.520A	T83.598A	T84.210A	T85.41XA
T22.341A	T23.791A	T32.10	T67.02XA	T79.7XXA	T81.531A	T82.521A	T83.61XA	T84.213A	T85.42XA
T22.342A	T23.792A	T32.11	T67.09XA	T79.A0XA	T81.532A	T82.522A	T83.62XA	T84.216A	T85.43XA
T22.349A	T23.799A	T32.20	T69.021A	T79.A11A	T81.533A	T82.523A	T83.69XA	T84.218A	T85.44XA
T22.351A	T24.301A	T32.30	T69.022A	T79.A12A	T81.534A	T82.524A	T83.712A	T84.220A	T85.49XA
T22.352A	T24.302A	T32.40	T69.029A	T79.A19A	T81.535A	T82.525A	T83.713A	T84.223A	T85.510A
T22.359A	T24.309A	T32.50	T70.3XXA	T79.A21A	T81.536A	T82.528A	T83.714A	T84.226A	T85.511A
T22.361A	T24.311A	T32.60	T71.111A	T79.A22A	T81.537A	T82.529A	T83.718A	T84.228A	T85.518A
T22.362A	T24.312A	T32.70	T71.112A	T79.A29A	T81.538A	T82.530A	T83.719A	T84.290A	T85.520A
T22.369A	T24.319A	T32.80	T71.113A	T79.A3XA	T81.539A	T82.531A	T83.722A	T84.293A	T85.521A
T22.391A	T24.321A	T32.90	T71.114A	T79.A9XA	T81.590A	T82.532A	T83.723A	T84.296A	T85.528A
T22.392A	T24.322A	T33.011A	T71.121A	T80.1XXA	T81.591A	T82.533A	T83.724A	T84.298A	T85.590A
T22.399A	T24.329A	T33.012A	T71.122A	T80.211A	T81.592A	T82.534A	T83.728A	T84.310A	T85.591A
T22.70XA	T24.331A	T33.019A	T71.123A	T80.212A	T81.593A	T82.535A	T83.729A	T84.318A	T85.598A
T22.711A	T24.332A	T33.02XA	T71.124A	T80.218A	T81.594A	T82.538A	T83.79XA	T84.320A	T85.610A
T22.712A	T24.339A	T33.09XA	T71.131A	T80.219A	T81.595A	T82.539A	T83.81XA	T84.328A	T85.611A
T22.719A	T24.391A	T33.1XXA	T71.132A	T80.22XA	T81.596A	T82.590A	T83.82XA	T84.390A	T85.612A
T22.721A	T24.392A	T33.2XXA	T71.133A	T80.29XA	T81.597A	T82.591A	T83.83XA	T84.398A	T85.613A
T22.722A	T24.399A	T33.3XXA	T71.134A	T80.30XA	T81.598A	T82.592A	T83.84XA		T85.614A

T85.615A	T85.693A	T85.820D	T86.11	T86.42	T86.838	T86.90	T88.0XXA	Z16.32	Z68.44
T85.618A	T85.694A	T85.830A	T86.12	T86.43	T86.839	T86.91	T88.1XXA	Z16.33	Z68.45
T85.620A	T85.695A	T85.830D	T86.13	T86.49	T86.840	T86.92	T88.2XXA	Z16.341	Z94.0
T85.621A	T85.698A	T85.840A	T86.19	T86.5	T86.841	T86.93	T88.3XXA	Z16.342	Z94.1
T85.622A	T85.71XA	T85.840D	T86.20	T86.810	T86.842	T86.99	T88.6XXA	Z16.35	Z94.2
T85.623A	T85.72XA	T85.850A	T86.21	T86.811	T86.848	T87.0X1	Z16.10	Z16.39	Z94.3
T85.624A	T85.730A	T85.850D	T86.22	T86.812	T86.849	T87.0X2	Z16.11	Z43.1	Z94.4
T85.625A	T85.731A	T85.860A	T86.23	T86.818	T86.850	T87.0X9	Z16.12	Z48.21	Z94.81
T85.628A	T85.732A	T85.860D	T86.290	T86.819	T86.851	T87.1X1	Z16.19	Z48.22	Z94.82
T85.630A	T85.733A	T85.890A	T86.298	T86.820	T86.852	T87.1X2	Z16.20	Z48.23	Z94.83
T85.631A	T85.734A	T85.890D	T86.30	T86.821	T86.858	T87.1X9	Z16.21	Z48.24	Z94.84
T85.633A	T85.735A	T86.00	T86.31	T86.822	T86.859	T87.2	Z16.22	Z48.280	Z95.811
T85.635A	T85.738A	T86.01	T86.32	T86.828	T86.890	T87.40	Z16.23	Z48.290	Z95.812
T85.638A	T85.79XA	T86.02	T86.33	T86.829	T86.891	T87.41	Z16.24	Z68.1	Z99.11
T85.690A	T85.810A	T86.03	T86.39	T86.830	T86.892	T87.42	Z16.29	Z68.41	Z99.12
T85.691A	T85.810D	T86.09	T86.40	T86.831	T86.898	T87.43	Z16.30	Z68.42	
T85.692A	T85.820A	T86.10	T86.41	T86.832	T86.899	T87.44	Z16.31	Z68.43	

Alphabetic MCC List

S42.222B	2-part displaced fracture of surgical neck of left humerus, initial encounter for open fracture
S42.221B	2-part displaced fracture of surgical neck of right humerus, initial encounter for open fracture
S42.223B	2-part displaced fracture of surgical neck of unspecified humerus, initial encounter for open fracture
S42.225B	2-part nondisplaced fracture of surgical neck of left humerus, initial encounter for open fracture
S42.224B	2-part nondisplaced fracture of surgical neck of right humerus, initial encounter for open fracture
S42.226B	2-part nondisplaced fracture of surgical neck of unspecified humerus, initial encounter for open fracture
S42.232B	3-part fracture of surgical neck of left humerus, initial encounter for open fracture
S42.231B	3-part fracture of surgical neck of right humerus, initial encounter for open fracture
S42.239B	3-part fracture of surgical neck of unspecified humerus, initial encounter for open fracture
S42.242B	4-part fracture of surgical neck of left humerus, initial encounter for open fracture
S42.241B	4-part fracture of surgical neck of right humerus, initial encounter for open fracture
S42.249B	4-part fracture of surgical neck of unspecified humerus, initial encounter for open fracture
I71.3	Abdominal aortic aneurysm, ruptured
K75.0	Abscess of liver
J85.1	Abscess of lung with pneumonia
J85.2	Abscess of lung without pneumonia
J85.3	Abscess of mediastinum
P91.1	Acquired periventricular cysts of newborn
D60.9	Acquired pure red cell aplasia, unspecified
A42.7	Actinomycotic sepsis
K55.059	Acute (reversible) ischemia of intestine, part and extent unspecified
K55.039	Acute (reversible) ischemia of large intestine, extent unspecified
K55.019	Acute (reversible) ischemia of small intestine, extent unspecified
J95.822	Acute and chronic postprocedural respiratory failure
J96.22	Acute and chronic respiratory failure with hypercapnia
J96.21	Acute and chronic respiratory failure with hypoxia
J96.20	Acute and chronic respiratory failure, unspecified whether with hypoxia or hypercapnia
I33.9	Acute and subacute endocarditis, unspecified
K72.01	Acute and subacute hepatic failure with coma
K72.00	Acute and subacute hepatic failure without coma
I33.0	Acute and subacute infective endocarditis
K35.21	Acute appendicitis with generalized peritonitis, with abscess
K35.33	Acute appendicitis with perforation and localized peritonitis, with abscess
K35.32	Acute appendicitis with perforation and localized peritonitis, without abscess
I50.41	Acute combined systolic (congestive) and diastolic (congestive) heart failure
I50.31	Acute diastolic (congestive) heart failure
G04.00	Acute disseminated encephalitis and encephalomyelitis, unspecified
K26.2	Acute duodenal ulcer with both hemorrhage and perforation
K26.0	Acute duodenal ulcer with hemorrhage
K26.1	Acute duodenal ulcer with perforation
I82.220	Acute embolism and thrombosis of inferior vena cava
J05.11	Acute epiglottitis with obstruction
K25.2	Acute gastric ulcer with both hemorrhage and perforation
K25.0	Acute gastric ulcer with hemorrhage
K25.1	Acute gastric ulcer with perforation
K29.01	Acute gastritis with bleeding
K28.2	Acute gastrojejunal ulcer with both hemorrhage and perforation
K28.0	Acute gastrojejunal ulcer with hemorrhage
K28.1	Acute gastrojejunal ulcer with perforation
B16.0	Acute hepatitis B with delta-agent with hepatic coma
B16.2	Acute hepatitis B without delta-agent with hepatic coma
B17.11	Acute hepatitis C with hepatic coma
K55.069	Acute infarction of intestine, part and extent unspecified
K55.049	Acute infarction of large intestine, extent unspecified
K55.029	Acute infarction of small intestine, extent unspecified
G95.11	Acute infarction of spinal cord (embolic) (nonembolic)
N17.1	Acute kidney failure with acute cortical necrosis
N17.2	Acute kidney failure with medullary necrosis
N17.0	Acute kidney failure with tubular necrosis
A39.2	Acute meningococcemia
A19.0	Acute miliary tuberculosis of a single specified site
A19.1	Acute miliary tuberculosis of multiple sites
A19.2	Acute miliary tuberculosis, unspecified
I21.9	Acute myocardial infarction, unspecified
I40.9	Acute myocarditis, unspecified
G04.30	Acute necrotizing hemorrhagic encephalopathy, unspecified
N00.6	Acute nephritic syndrome with dense deposit disease
N00.7	Acute nephritic syndrome with diffuse crescentic glomerulonephritis
N00.4	Acute nephritic syndrome with diffuse endocapillary proliferative glomerulonephritis
N00.2	Acute nephritic syndrome with diffuse membranous glomerulonephritis
N00.3	Acute nephritic syndrome with diffuse mesangial proliferative glomerulonephritis
N00.5	Acute nephritic syndrome with diffuse mesangiocapillary glomerulonephritis
N00.1	Acute nephritic syndrome with focal and segmental glomerular lesions
N00.0	Acute nephritic syndrome with minor glomerular abnormality
N00.8	Acute nephritic syndrome with other morphologic changes
N00.9	Acute nephritic syndrome with unspecified morphologic changes
I50.43	Acute on chronic combined systolic (congestive) and diastolic (congestive) heart failure
I50.33	Acute on chronic diastolic (congestive) heart failure
I50.23	Acute on chronic systolic (congestive) heart failure
K85.92	Acute pancreatitis with infected necrosis, unspecified
K85.91	Acute pancreatitis with uninfected necrosis, unspecified
K85.90	Acute pancreatitis without necrosis or infection, unspecified
A80.30	Acute paralytic poliomyelitis, unspecified
A80.0	Acute paralytic poliomyelitis, vaccine-associated
A80.1	Acute paralytic poliomyelitis, wild virus, imported
A80.2	Acute paralytic poliomyelitis, wild virus, indigenous
K27.2	Acute peptic ulcer, site unspecified, with both hemorrhage and perforation
K27.0	Acute peptic ulcer, site unspecified, with hemorrhage
K27.1	Acute peptic ulcer, site unspecified, with perforation
J95.821	Acute postprocedural respiratory failure
J81.0	Acute pulmonary edema
B39.0	Acute pulmonary histoplasmosis capsulati
J95.2	Acute pulmonary insufficiency following nonthoracic surgery
J95.1	Acute pulmonary insufficiency following thoracic surgery
J80	Acute respiratory distress syndrome
J96.02	Acute respiratory failure with hypercapnia
J96.01	Acute respiratory failure with hypoxia
J96.00	Acute respiratory failure, unspecified whether with hypoxia or hypercapnia
I50.21	Acute systolic (congestive) heart failure
J04.11	Acute tracheitis with obstruction
J12.0	Adenoviral pneumonia
Q33.3	Agenesis of lung
T79.0XXA	Air embolism (traumatic), initial encounter
T80.0XXA	Air embolism following infusion, transfusion and therapeutic injection, initial encounter
O88.02	Air embolism in childbirth
O88.011	Air embolism in pregnancy, first trimester
O88.012	Air embolism in pregnancy, second trimester
O88.013	Air embolism in pregnancy, third trimester
O88.03	Air embolism in the puerperium
K85.22	Alcohol induced acute pancreatitis with infected necrosis
K85.21	Alcohol induced acute pancreatitis with uninfected necrosis
K85.20	Alcohol induced acute pancreatitis without necrosis or infection
K29.21	Alcoholic gastritis with bleeding
K70.41	Alcoholic hepatic failure with coma
J84.843	Alveolar capillary dysplasia with vein misalignment
A06.6	Amebic brain abscess
A06.4	Amebic liver abscess
A06.5	Amebic lung abscess
O88.12	Amniotic fluid embolism in childbirth
O88.111	Amniotic fluid embolism in pregnancy, first trimester
O88.112	Amniotic fluid embolism in pregnancy, second trimester
O88.113	Amniotic fluid embolism in pregnancy, third trimester
O88.13	Amniotic fluid embolism in the puerperium
Q00.0	Anencephaly
K55.21	Angiodysplasia of colon with hemorrhage
K31.811	Angiodysplasia of stomach and duodenum with bleeding
O46.011	Antepartum hemorrhage with afibrinogenemia, first trimester
O46.012	Antepartum hemorrhage with afibrinogenemia, second trimester
O46.013	Antepartum hemorrhage with afibrinogenemia, third trimester
O46.001	Antepartum hemorrhage with coagulation defect, unspecified, first trimester
O46.002	Antepartum hemorrhage with coagulation defect, unspecified, second trimester
O46.003	Antepartum hemorrhage with coagulation defect, unspecified, third trimester
O46.021	Antepartum hemorrhage with disseminated intravascular coagulation, first trimester
O46.022	Antepartum hemorrhage with disseminated intravascular coagulation, second trimester
O46.023	Antepartum hemorrhage with disseminated intravascular coagulation, third trimester
O46.091	Antepartum hemorrhage with other coagulation defect, first trimester
O46.092	Antepartum hemorrhage with other coagulation defect, second trimester
O46.093	Antepartum hemorrhage with other coagulation defect, third trimester
S14.131A	Anterior cord syndrome at C1 level of cervical spinal cord, initial encounter
S14.132A	Anterior cord syndrome at C2 level of cervical spinal cord, initial encounter
S14.133A	Anterior cord syndrome at C3 level of cervical spinal cord, initial encounter
S14.134A	Anterior cord syndrome at C4 level of cervical spinal cord, initial encounter
S14.135A	Anterior cord syndrome at C5 level of cervical spinal cord, initial encounter
S14.136A	Anterior cord syndrome at C6 level of cervical spinal cord, initial encounter
S14.137A	Anterior cord syndrome at C7 level of cervical spinal cord, initial encounter
S14.138A	Anterior cord syndrome at C8 level of cervical spinal cord, initial encounter
S24.131A	Anterior cord syndrome at T1 level of thoracic spinal cord, initial encounter

S24.134A	Anterior cord syndrome at T11-T12 level of thoracic spinal cord, initial encounter
S24.132A	Anterior cord syndrome at T2-T6 level of thoracic spinal cord, initial encounter
S24.133A	Anterior cord syndrome at T7-T1Ø level of thoracic spinal cord, initial encounter
S12.11ØB	Anterior displaced Type II dens fracture, initial encounter for open fracture
A22.7	Anthrax sepsis
D61.81Ø	Antineoplastic chemotherapy induced pancytopenia
I71.8	Aortic aneurysm of unspecified site, ruptured
D61.2	Aplastic anemia due to other external agents
QØ4.1	Arhinencephaly
Q28.2	Arteriovenous malformation of cerebral vessels
A85.2	Arthropod-borne viral encephalitis, unspecified
B77.81	Ascariasis pneumonia
A27.81	Aseptic meningitis in leptospirosis
Q44.2	Atresia of bile ducts
Q39.1	Atresia of esophagus with tracheo-esophageal fistula
Q39.Ø	Atresia of esophagus without fistula
Q25.5	Atresia of pulmonary artery
A83.4	Australian encephalitis
GØØ.9	Bacterial meningitis, unspecified
GØ4.2	Bacterial meningoencephalitis and meningomyelitis, not elsewhere classified
P36.9	Bacterial sepsis of newborn, unspecified
S52.562B	Barton's fracture of left radius, initial encounter for open fracture type I or II
S52.562C	Barton's fracture of left radius, initial encounter for open fracture type IIIA, IIIB, or IIIC
S52.561B	Barton's fracture of right radius, initial encounter for open fracture type I or II
S52.561C	Barton's fracture of right radius, initial encounter for open fracture type IIIA, IIIB, or IIIC
S52.569B	Barton's fracture of unspecified radius, initial encounter for open fracture type I or II
S52.569C	Barton's fracture of unspecified radius, initial encounter for open fracture type IIIA, IIIB, or IIIC
S52.382B	Bent bone of left radius, initial encounter for open fracture type I or II
S52.382C	Bent bone of left radius, initial encounter for open fracture type IIIA, IIIB, or IIIC
S52.282B	Bent bone of left ulna, initial encounter for open fracture type I or II
S52.282C	Bent bone of left ulna, initial encounter for open fracture type IIIA, IIIB, or IIIC
S52.381B	Bent bone of right radius, initial encounter for open fracture type I or II
S52.381C	Bent bone of right radius, initial encounter for open fracture type IIIA, IIIB, or IIIC
S52.281B	Bent bone of right ulna, initial encounter for open fracture type I or II
S52.281C	Bent bone of right ulna, initial encounter for open fracture type IIIA, IIIB, or IIIC
S52.389B	Bent bone of unspecified radius, initial encounter for open fracture type I or II
S52.389C	Bent bone of unspecified radius, initial encounter for open fracture type IIIA, IIIB, or IIIC
S52.283B	Bent bone of unspecified ulna, initial encounter for open fracture type I or II
S52.283C	Bent bone of unspecified ulna, initial encounter for open fracture type IIIA, IIIB, or IIIC
K41.1Ø	Bilateral femoral hernia, with gangrene, not specified as recurrent
K41.11	Bilateral femoral hernia, with gangrene, recurrent
K4Ø.1Ø	Bilateral inguinal hernia, with gangrene, not specified as recurrent
K4Ø.11	Bilateral inguinal hernia, with gangrene, recurrent
K85.12	Biliary acute pancreatitis with infected necrosis
K85.11	Biliary acute pancreatitis with uninfected necrosis
K85.1Ø	Biliary acute pancreatitis without necrosis or infection
P92.Ø1	Bilious vomiting of newborn
P11.9	Birth injury to central nervous system, unspecified
G93.82	Brain death
J18.Ø	Bronchopneumonia, unspecified organism
P27.1	Bronchopulmonary dysplasia originating in the perinatal period
S14.141A	Brown-Sequard syndrome at C1 level of cervical spinal cord, initial encounter
S14.142A	Brown-Sequard syndrome at C2 level of cervical spinal cord, initial encounter
S14.143A	Brown-Sequard syndrome at C3 level of cervical spinal cord, initial encounter
S14.144A	Brown-Sequard syndrome at C4 level of cervical spinal cord, initial encounter
S14.145A	Brown-Sequard syndrome at C5 level of cervical spinal cord, initial encounter
S14.146A	Brown-Sequard syndrome at C6 level of cervical spinal cord, initial encounter
S14.147A	Brown-Sequard syndrome at C7 level of cervical spinal cord, initial encounter
S14.148A	Brown-Sequard syndrome at C8 level of cervical spinal cord, initial encounter
S24.141A	Brown-Sequard syndrome at T1 level of thoracic spinal cord, initial encounter
S24.144A	Brown-Sequard syndrome at T11-T12 level of thoracic spinal cord, initial encounter
S24.142A	Brown-Sequard syndrome at T2-T6 level of thoracic spinal cord, initial encounter
S24.143A	Brown-Sequard syndrome at T7-T1Ø level of thoracic spinal cord, initial encounter
A2Ø.Ø	Bubonic plague
I82.Ø	Budd-Chiari syndrome
T31.21	Burns involving 2Ø-29% of body surface with 1Ø-19% third degree burns
T31.22	Burns involving 2Ø-29% of body surface with 2Ø-29% third degree burns
T31.31	Burns involving 3Ø-39% of body surface with 1Ø-19% third degree burns
T31.32	Burns involving 3Ø-39% of body surface with 2Ø-29% third degree burns
T31.33	Burns involving 3Ø-39% of body surface with 3Ø-39% third degree burns
T31.41	Burns involving 4Ø-49% of body surface with 1Ø-19% third degree burns
T31.42	Burns involving 4Ø-49% of body surface with 2Ø-29% third degree burns
T31.43	Burns involving 4Ø-49% of body surface with 3Ø-39% third degree burns
T31.44	Burns involving 4Ø-49% of body surface with 4Ø-49% third degree burns
T31.51	Burns involving 5Ø-59% of body surface with 1Ø-19% third degree burns
T31.52	Burns involving 5Ø-59% of body surface with 2Ø-29% third degree burns
T31.53	Burns involving 5Ø-59% of body surface with 3Ø-39% third degree burns
T31.54	Burns involving 5Ø-59% of body surface with 4Ø-49% third degree burns
T31.55	Burns involving 5Ø-59% of body surface with 5Ø-59% third degree burns
T31.61	Burns involving 6Ø-69% of body surface with 1Ø-19% third degree burns
T31.62	Burns involving 6Ø-69% of body surface with 2Ø-29% third degree burns
T31.63	Burns involving 6Ø-69% of body surface with 3Ø-39% third degree burns
T31.64	Burns involving 6Ø-69% of body surface with 4Ø-49% third degree burns
T31.65	Burns involving 6Ø-69% of body surface with 5Ø-59% third degree burns
T31.66	Burns involving 6Ø-69% of body surface with 6Ø-69% third degree burns
T31.71	Burns involving 7Ø-79% of body surface with 1Ø-19% third degree burns
T31.72	Burns involving 7Ø-79% of body surface with 2Ø-29% third degree burns
T31.73	Burns involving 7Ø-79% of body surface with 3Ø-39% third degree burns
T31.74	Burns involving 7Ø-79% of body surface with 4Ø-49% third degree burns
T31.75	Burns involving 7Ø-79% of body surface with 5Ø-59% third degree burns
T31.76	Burns involving 7Ø-79% of body surface with 6Ø-69% third degree burns
T31.77	Burns involving 7Ø-79% of body surface with 7Ø-79% third degree burns
T31.81	Burns involving 8Ø-89% of body surface with 1Ø-19% third degree burns
T31.82	Burns involving 8Ø-89% of body surface with 2Ø-29% third degree burns
T31.83	Burns involving 8Ø-89% of body surface with 3Ø-39% third degree burns
T31.84	Burns involving 8Ø-89% of body surface with 4Ø-49% third degree burns
T31.85	Burns involving 8Ø-89% of body surface with 5Ø-59% third degree burns
T31.86	Burns involving 8Ø-89% of body surface with 6Ø-69% third degree burns
T31.87	Burns involving 8Ø-89% of body surface with 7Ø-79% third degree burns
T31.88	Burns involving 8Ø-89% of body surface with 8Ø-89% third degree burns
T31.91	Burns involving 9Ø% or more of body surface with 1Ø-19% third degree burns
T31.92	Burns involving 9Ø% or more of body surface with 2Ø-29% third degree burns
T31.93	Burns involving 9Ø% or more of body surface with 3Ø-39% third degree burns
T31.94	Burns involving 9Ø% or more of body surface with 4Ø-49% third degree burns
T31.95	Burns involving 9Ø% or more of body surface with 5Ø-59% third degree burns
T31.96	Burns involving 9Ø% or more of body surface with 6Ø-69% third degree burns
T31.97	Burns involving 9Ø% or more of body surface with 7Ø-79% third degree burns
T31.98	Burns involving 9Ø% or more of body surface with 8Ø-89% third degree burns
T31.99	Burns involving 9Ø% or more of body surface with 9Ø% or more third degree burns
K8Ø.67	Calculus of gallbladder and bile duct with acute and chronic cholecystitis with obstruction
A83.5	California encephalitis
B37.6	Candidal endocarditis
B37.5	Candidal meningitis
B37.7	Candidal sepsis
I46.8	Cardiac arrest due to other underlying condition
I46.2	Cardiac arrest due to underlying cardiac condition
P29.81	Cardiac arrest of newborn
I46.9	Cardiac arrest, cause unspecified
R57.Ø	Cardiogenic shock
A2Ø.1	Cellulocutaneous plague
S14.121A	Central cord syndrome at C1 level of cervical spinal cord, initial encounter
S14.122A	Central cord syndrome at C2 level of cervical spinal cord, initial encounter
S14.123A	Central cord syndrome at C3 level of cervical spinal cord, initial encounter
S14.124A	Central cord syndrome at C4 level of cervical spinal cord, initial encounter
S14.125A	Central cord syndrome at C5 level of cervical spinal cord, initial encounter
S14.126A	Central cord syndrome at C6 level of cervical spinal cord, initial encounter
S14.127A	Central cord syndrome at C7 level of cervical spinal cord, initial encounter
S14.128A	Central cord syndrome at C8 level of cervical spinal cord, initial encounter
A84.1	Central European tick-borne encephalitis
K76.2	Central hemorrhagic necrosis of liver
P52.6	Cerebellar (nontraumatic) and posterior fossa hemorrhage of newborn
B45.1	Cerebral cryptococcosis
G93.6	Cerebral edema
P11.Ø	Cerebral edema due to birth injury
P1Ø.1	Cerebral hemorrhage due to birth injury
I63.6	Cerebral infarction due to cerebral venous thrombosis, nonpyogenic
I63.12	Cerebral infarction due to embolism of basilar artery
I63.423	Cerebral infarction due to embolism of bilateral anterior cerebral arteries
I63.133	Cerebral infarction due to embolism of bilateral carotid arteries
I63.443	Cerebral infarction due to embolism of bilateral cerebellar arteries
I63.413	Cerebral infarction due to embolism of bilateral middle cerebral arteries
I63.433	Cerebral infarction due to embolism of bilateral posterior cerebral arteries
I63.113	Cerebral infarction due to embolism of bilateral vertebral arteries
I63.422	Cerebral infarction due to embolism of left anterior cerebral artery
I63.132	Cerebral infarction due to embolism of left carotid artery
I63.442	Cerebral infarction due to embolism of left cerebellar artery
I63.412	Cerebral infarction due to embolism of left middle cerebral artery
I63.432	Cerebral infarction due to embolism of left posterior cerebral artery
I63.112	Cerebral infarction due to embolism of left vertebral artery
I63.49	Cerebral infarction due to embolism of other cerebral artery
I63.19	Cerebral infarction due to embolism of other precerebral artery
I63.421	Cerebral infarction due to embolism of right anterior cerebral artery
I63.131	Cerebral infarction due to embolism of right carotid artery
I63.441	Cerebral infarction due to embolism of right cerebellar artery
I63.411	Cerebral infarction due to embolism of right middle cerebral artery
I63.431	Cerebral infarction due to embolism of right posterior cerebral artery
I63.111	Cerebral infarction due to embolism of right vertebral artery
I63.429	Cerebral infarction due to embolism of unspecified anterior cerebral artery
I63.139	Cerebral infarction due to embolism of unspecified carotid artery
I63.449	Cerebral infarction due to embolism of unspecified cerebellar artery
I63.4Ø	Cerebral infarction due to embolism of unspecified cerebral artery
I63.419	Cerebral infarction due to embolism of unspecified middle cerebral artery
I63.439	Cerebral infarction due to embolism of unspecified posterior cerebral artery
I63.1Ø	Cerebral infarction due to embolism of unspecified precerebral artery

I63.119	Cerebral infarction due to embolism of unspecified vertebral artery
I63.02	Cerebral infarction due to thrombosis of basilar artery
I63.323	Cerebral infarction due to thrombosis of bilateral anterior cerebral arteries
I63.033	Cerebral infarction due to thrombosis of bilateral carotid arteries
I63.343	Cerebral infarction due to thrombosis of bilateral cerebellar arteries
I63.313	Cerebral infarction due to thrombosis of bilateral middle cerebral arteries
I63.333	Cerebral infarction due to thrombosis of bilateral posterior cerebral arteries
I63.013	Cerebral infarction due to thrombosis of bilateral vertebral arteries
I63.322	Cerebral infarction due to thrombosis of left anterior cerebral artery
I63.032	Cerebral infarction due to thrombosis of left carotid artery
I63.342	Cerebral infarction due to thrombosis of left cerebellar artery
I63.312	Cerebral infarction due to thrombosis of left middle cerebral artery
I63.332	Cerebral infarction due to thrombosis of left posterior cerebral artery
I63.012	Cerebral infarction due to thrombosis of left vertebral artery
I63.39	Cerebral infarction due to thrombosis of other cerebral artery
I63.09	Cerebral infarction due to thrombosis of other precerebral artery
I63.321	Cerebral infarction due to thrombosis of right anterior cerebral artery
I63.031	Cerebral infarction due to thrombosis of right carotid artery
I63.341	Cerebral infarction due to thrombosis of right cerebellar artery
I63.311	Cerebral infarction due to thrombosis of right middle cerebral artery
I63.331	Cerebral infarction due to thrombosis of right posterior cerebral artery
I63.011	Cerebral infarction due to thrombosis of right vertebral artery
I63.329	Cerebral infarction due to thrombosis of unspecified anterior cerebral artery
I63.039	Cerebral infarction due to thrombosis of unspecified carotid artery
I63.349	Cerebral infarction due to thrombosis of unspecified cerebellar artery
I63.30	Cerebral infarction due to thrombosis of unspecified cerebral artery
I63.319	Cerebral infarction due to thrombosis of unspecified middle cerebral artery
I63.339	Cerebral infarction due to thrombosis of unspecified posterior cerebral artery
I63.00	Cerebral infarction due to thrombosis of unspecified precerebral artery
I63.019	Cerebral infarction due to thrombosis of unspecified vertebral artery
I63.22	Cerebral infarction due to unspecified occlusion or stenosis of basilar artery
I63.523	Cerebral infarction due to unspecified occlusion or stenosis of bilateral anterior cerebral arteries
I63.233	Cerebral infarction due to unspecified occlusion or stenosis of bilateral carotid arteries
I63.543	Cerebral infarction due to unspecified occlusion or stenosis of bilateral cerebellar arteries
I63.513	Cerebral infarction due to unspecified occlusion or stenosis of bilateral middle cerebral arteries
I63.533	Cerebral infarction due to unspecified occlusion or stenosis of bilateral posterior cerebral arteries
I63.213	Cerebral infarction due to unspecified occlusion or stenosis of bilateral vertebral arteries
I63.522	Cerebral infarction due to unspecified occlusion or stenosis of left anterior cerebral artery
I63.232	Cerebral infarction due to unspecified occlusion or stenosis of left carotid arteries
I63.542	Cerebral infarction due to unspecified occlusion or stenosis of left cerebellar artery
I63.512	Cerebral infarction due to unspecified occlusion or stenosis of left middle cerebral artery
I63.532	Cerebral infarction due to unspecified occlusion or stenosis of left posterior cerebral artery
I63.212	Cerebral infarction due to unspecified occlusion or stenosis of left vertebral artery
I63.59	Cerebral infarction due to unspecified occlusion or stenosis of other cerebral artery
I63.29	Cerebral infarction due to unspecified occlusion or stenosis of other precerebral arteries
I63.521	Cerebral infarction due to unspecified occlusion or stenosis of right anterior cerebral artery
I63.231	Cerebral infarction due to unspecified occlusion or stenosis of right carotid arteries
I63.541	Cerebral infarction due to unspecified occlusion or stenosis of right cerebellar artery
I63.511	Cerebral infarction due to unspecified occlusion or stenosis of right middle cerebral artery
I63.531	Cerebral infarction due to unspecified occlusion or stenosis of right posterior cerebral artery
I63.211	Cerebral infarction due to unspecified occlusion or stenosis of right vertebral artery
I63.529	Cerebral infarction due to unspecified occlusion or stenosis of unspecified anterior cerebral artery
I63.239	Cerebral infarction due to unspecified occlusion or stenosis of unspecified carotid artery
I63.549	Cerebral infarction due to unspecified occlusion or stenosis of unspecified cerebellar artery
I63.50	Cerebral infarction due to unspecified occlusion or stenosis of unspecified cerebral artery
I63.519	Cerebral infarction due to unspecified occlusion or stenosis of unspecified middle cerebral artery
I63.539	Cerebral infarction due to unspecified occlusion or stenosis of unspecified posterior cerebral artery
I63.20	Cerebral infarction due to unspecified occlusion or stenosis of unspecified precerebral arteries
I63.219	Cerebral infarction due to unspecified occlusion or stenosis of unspecified vertebral artery
I63.9	Cerebral infarction, unspecified
J16.0	Chlamydial pneumonia
K65.3	Choleperitonitis

O41.1211	Chorioamnionitis, first trimester, fetus 1
O41.1212	Chorioamnionitis, first trimester, fetus 2
O41.1213	Chorioamnionitis, first trimester, fetus 3
O41.1214	Chorioamnionitis, first trimester, fetus 4
O41.1215	Chorioamnionitis, first trimester, fetus 5
O41.1210	Chorioamnionitis, first trimester, not applicable or unspecified
O41.1219	Chorioamnionitis, first trimester, other fetus
O41.1221	Chorioamnionitis, second trimester, fetus 1
O41.1222	Chorioamnionitis, second trimester, fetus 2
O41.1223	Chorioamnionitis, second trimester, fetus 3
O41.1224	Chorioamnionitis, second trimester, fetus 4
O41.1225	Chorioamnionitis, second trimester, fetus 5
O41.1220	Chorioamnionitis, second trimester, not applicable or unspecified
O41.1229	Chorioamnionitis, second trimester, other fetus
O41.1231	Chorioamnionitis, third trimester, fetus 1
O41.1232	Chorioamnionitis, third trimester, fetus 2
O41.1233	Chorioamnionitis, third trimester, fetus 3
O41.1234	Chorioamnionitis, third trimester, fetus 4
O41.1235	Chorioamnionitis, third trimester, fetus 5
O41.1230	Chorioamnionitis, third trimester, not applicable or unspecified
O41.1239	Chorioamnionitis, third trimester, other fetus
D60.0	Chronic acquired pure red cell aplasia
K29.41	Chronic atrophic gastritis with bleeding
I82.221	Chronic embolism and thrombosis of inferior vena cava
K72.11	Chronic hepatic failure with coma
A39.3	Chronic meningococcemia
K26.6	Chronic or unspecified duodenal ulcer with both hemorrhage and perforation
K26.4	Chronic or unspecified duodenal ulcer with hemorrhage
K26.5	Chronic or unspecified duodenal ulcer with perforation
K25.6	Chronic or unspecified gastric ulcer with both hemorrhage and perforation
K25.4	Chronic or unspecified gastric ulcer with hemorrhage
K25.5	Chronic or unspecified gastric ulcer with perforation
K28.6	Chronic or unspecified gastrojejunal ulcer with both hemorrhage and perforation
K28.4	Chronic or unspecified gastrojejunal ulcer with hemorrhage
K28.5	Chronic or unspecified gastrojejunal ulcer with perforation
K27.6	Chronic or unspecified peptic ulcer, site unspecified, with both hemorrhage and perforation
K27.4	Chronic or unspecified peptic ulcer, site unspecified, with hemorrhage
K27.5	Chronic or unspecified peptic ulcer, site unspecified, with perforation
B39.1	Chronic pulmonary histoplasmosis capsulati
J95.3	Chronic pulmonary insufficiency following surgery
K29.31	Chronic superficial gastritis with bleeding
Q25.71	Coarctation of pulmonary artery
B38.4	Coccidioidomycosis meningitis
S52.532B	Colles' fracture of left radius, initial encounter for open fracture type I or II
S52.532C	Colles' fracture of left radius, initial encounter for open fracture type IIIA, IIIB, or IIIC
S52.531B	Colles' fracture of right radius, initial encounter for open fracture type I or II
S52.531C	Colles' fracture of right radius, initial encounter for open fracture type IIIA, IIIB, or IIIC
S52.539B	Colles' fracture of unspecified radius, initial encounter for open fracture type I or II
S52.539C	Colles' fracture of unspecified radius, initial encounter for open fracture type IIIA, IIIB, or IIIC
R40.2324	Coma scale, best motor response, extension, 24 hours or more after hospital admission
R40.2322	Coma scale, best motor response, extension, at arrival to emergency department
R40.2323	Coma scale, best motor response, extension, at hospital admission
R40.2321	Coma scale, best motor response, extension, in the field [EMT or ambulance]
R40.2320	Coma scale, best motor response, extension, unspecified time
R40.2344	Coma scale, best motor response, flexion withdrawal, 24 hours or more after hospital admission
R40.2342	Coma scale, best motor response, flexion withdrawal, at arrival to emergency department
R40.2343	Coma scale, best motor response, flexion withdrawal, at hospital admission
R40.2341	Coma scale, best motor response, flexion withdrawal, in the field [EMT or ambulance]
R40.2340	Coma scale, best motor response, flexion withdrawal, unspecified time
R40.2314	Coma scale, best motor response, none, 24 hours or more after hospital admission
R40.2312	Coma scale, best motor response, none, at arrival to emergency department
R40.2313	Coma scale, best motor response, none, at hospital admission
R40.2311	Coma scale, best motor response, none, in the field [EMT or ambulance]
R40.2310	Coma scale, best motor response, none, unspecified time
R40.2224	Coma scale, best verbal response, incomprehensible words, 24 hours or more after hospital admission
R40.2222	Coma scale, best verbal response, incomprehensible words, at arrival to emergency department
R40.2223	Coma scale, best verbal response, incomprehensible words, at hospital admission
R40.2221	Coma scale, best verbal response, incomprehensible words, in the field [EMT or ambulance]
R40.2220	Coma scale, best verbal response, incomprehensible words, unspecified time
R40.2214	Coma scale, best verbal response, none, 24 hours or more after hospital admission
R40.2212	Coma scale, best verbal response, none, at arrival to emergency department
R40.2213	Coma scale, best verbal response, none, at hospital admission

R40.2211 Coma scale, best verbal response, none, in the field [EMT or ambulance]
R40.2210 Coma scale, best verbal response, none, unspecified time
R40.2114 Coma scale, eyes open, never, 24 hours or more after hospital admission
R40.2112 Coma scale, eyes open, never, at arrival to emergency department
R40.2113 Coma scale, eyes open, never, at hospital admission
R40.2111 Coma scale, eyes open, never, in the field [EMT or ambulance]
R40.2110 Coma scale, eyes open, never, unspecified time
R40.2124 Coma scale, eyes open, to pain, 24 hours or more after hospital admission
R40.2122 Coma scale, eyes open, to pain, at arrival to emergency department
R40.2123 Coma scale, eyes open, to pain, at hospital admission
R40.2121 Coma scale, eyes open, to pain, in the field [EMT or ambulance]
R40.2120 Coma scale, eyes open, to pain, unspecified time
Q20.0 Common arterial trunk
S14.111A Complete lesion at C1 level of cervical spinal cord, initial encounter
S14.112A Complete lesion at C2 level of cervical spinal cord, initial encounter
S14.113A Complete lesion at C3 level of cervical spinal cord, initial encounter
S14.114A Complete lesion at C4 level of cervical spinal cord, initial encounter
S14.115A Complete lesion at C5 level of cervical spinal cord, initial encounter
S14.116A Complete lesion at C6 level of cervical spinal cord, initial encounter
S14.117A Complete lesion at C7 level of cervical spinal cord, initial encounter
S14.118A Complete lesion at C8 level of cervical spinal cord, initial encounter
S24.111A Complete lesion at T1 level of thoracic spinal cord, initial encounter
S24.114A Complete lesion at T11-T12 level of thoracic spinal cord, initial encounter
S24.112A Complete lesion at T2-T6 level of thoracic spinal cord, initial encounter
S24.113A Complete lesion at T7-T10 level of thoracic spinal cord, initial encounter
S34.111A Complete lesion of L1 level of lumbar spinal cord, initial encounter
S34.112A Complete lesion of L2 level of lumbar spinal cord, initial encounter
S34.113A Complete lesion of L3 level of lumbar spinal cord, initial encounter
S34.114A Complete lesion of L4 level of lumbar spinal cord, initial encounter
S34.115A Complete lesion of L5 level of lumbar spinal cord, initial encounter
S34.131A Complete lesion of sacral spinal cord, initial encounter
S34.119A Complete lesion of unspecified level of lumbar spinal cord, initial encounter
O44.11 Complete placenta previa with hemorrhage, first trimester
O44.12 Complete placenta previa with hemorrhage, second trimester
O44.13 Complete placenta previa with hemorrhage, third trimester
G93.5 Compression of brain
S14.0XXA Concussion and edema of cervical spinal cord, initial encounter
S34.01XA Concussion and edema of lumbar spinal cord, initial encounter
S34.02XA Concussion and edema of sacral spinal cord, initial encounter
S24.0XXA Concussion and edema of thoracic spinal cord, initial encounter
P35.1 Congenital cytomegalovirus infection
Q79.0 Congenital diaphragmatic hernia
P37.3 Congenital falciparum malaria
Q24.6 Congenital heart block
Q79.51 Congenital hernia of bladder
P35.2 Congenital herpesviral [herpes simplex] infection
Q33.6 Congenital hypoplasia and dysplasia of lung
P37.9 Congenital infectious or parasitic disease, unspecified
Q22.9 Congenital malformation of tricuspid valve, unspecified
Q04.0 Congenital malformations of corpus callosum
P23.1 Congenital pneumonia due to Chlamydia
P23.4 Congenital pneumonia due to Escherichia coli
P23.6 Congenital pneumonia due to other bacterial agents
P23.8 Congenital pneumonia due to other organisms
P23.5 Congenital pneumonia due to Pseudomonas
P23.2 Congenital pneumonia due to staphylococcus
P23.3 Congenital pneumonia due to streptococcus, group B
P23.0 Congenital pneumonia due to viral agent
P23.9 Congenital pneumonia, unspecified
Q25.72 Congenital pulmonary arteriovenous malformation
Q44.3 Congenital stenosis and stricture of bile ducts
Q39.3 Congenital stenosis and stricture of esophagus
Q24.4 Congenital subaortic stenosis
P37.1 Congenital toxoplasmosis
Q39.2 Congenital tracheo-esophageal fistula without atresia
Q22.4 Congenital tricuspid stenosis
P37.0 Congenital tuberculosis
P35.9 Congenital viral disease, unspecified
P35.3 Congenital viral hepatitis
P35.4 Congenital Zika virus disease
Q89.4 Conjoined twins
S06.335A Contusion and laceration of cerebrum, unspecified, with loss of consciousness greater than 24 hours with return to pre-existing conscious level, initial encounter
S06.336A Contusion and laceration of cerebrum, unspecified, with loss of consciousness greater than 24 hours without return to pre-existing conscious level with patient surviving, initial encounter
S06.333A Contusion and laceration of cerebrum, unspecified, with loss of consciousness of 1 hour to 5 hours 59 minutes, initial encounter
S06.331A Contusion and laceration of cerebrum, unspecified, with loss of consciousness of 30 minutes or less, initial encounter
S06.332A Contusion and laceration of cerebrum, unspecified, with loss of consciousness of 31 minutes to 59 minutes, initial encounter
S06.334A Contusion and laceration of cerebrum, unspecified, with loss of consciousness of 6 hours to 24 hours, initial encounter
S06.337A Contusion and laceration of cerebrum, unspecified, with loss of consciousness of any duration with death due to brain injury prior to regaining consciousness, initial encounter

S06.338A Contusion and laceration of cerebrum, unspecified, with loss of consciousness of any duration with death due to other cause prior to regaining consciousness, initial encounter
S06.339A Contusion and laceration of cerebrum, unspecified, with loss of consciousness of unspecified duration, initial encounter
S06.330A Contusion and laceration of cerebrum, unspecified, without loss of consciousness, initial encounter
S06.325A Contusion and laceration of left cerebrum with loss of consciousness greater than 24 hours with return to pre-existing conscious level, initial encounter
S06.326A Contusion and laceration of left cerebrum with loss of consciousness greater than 24 hours without return to pre-existing conscious level with patient surviving, initial encounter
S06.323A Contusion and laceration of left cerebrum with loss of consciousness of 1 hour to 5 hours 59 minutes, initial encounter
S06.321A Contusion and laceration of left cerebrum with loss of consciousness of 30 minutes or less, initial encounter
S06.322A Contusion and laceration of left cerebrum with loss of consciousness of 31 minutes to 59 minutes, initial encounter
S06.324A Contusion and laceration of left cerebrum with loss of consciousness of 6 hours to 24 hours, initial encounter
S06.327A Contusion and laceration of left cerebrum with loss of consciousness of any duration with death due to brain injury prior to regaining consciousness, initial encounter
S06.328A Contusion and laceration of left cerebrum with loss of consciousness of any duration with death due to other cause prior to regaining consciousness, initial encounter
S06.329A Contusion and laceration of left cerebrum with loss of consciousness of unspecified duration, initial encounter
S06.320A Contusion and laceration of left cerebrum without loss of consciousness, initial encounter
S06.315A Contusion and laceration of right cerebrum with loss of consciousness greater than 24 hours with return to pre-existing conscious level, initial encounter
S06.316A Contusion and laceration of right cerebrum with loss of consciousness greater than 24 hours without return to pre-existing conscious level with patient surviving, initial encounter
S06.313A Contusion and laceration of right cerebrum with loss of consciousness of 1 hour to 5 hours 59 minutes, initial encounter
S06.311A Contusion and laceration of right cerebrum with loss of consciousness of 30 minutes or less, initial encounter
S06.312A Contusion and laceration of right cerebrum with loss of consciousness of 31 minutes to 59 minutes, initial encounter
S06.314A Contusion and laceration of right cerebrum with loss of consciousness of 6 hours to 24 hours, initial encounter
S06.317A Contusion and laceration of right cerebrum with loss of consciousness of any duration with death due to brain injury prior to regaining consciousness, initial encounter
S06.318A Contusion and laceration of right cerebrum with loss of consciousness of any duration with death due to other cause prior to regaining consciousness, initial encounter
S06.319A Contusion and laceration of right cerebrum with loss of consciousness of unspecified duration, initial encounter
S06.310A Contusion and laceration of right cerebrum without loss of consciousness, initial encounter
S27.422A Contusion of bronchus, bilateral, initial encounter
S27.421A Contusion of bronchus, unilateral, initial encounter
S27.429A Contusion of bronchus, unspecified, initial encounter
S27.812A Contusion of esophagus (thoracic part), initial encounter
S06.386A Contusion, laceration, and hemorrhage of brainstem with loss of consciousness greater than 24 hours without return to pre-existing conscious level with patient surviving, initial encounter
S06.387A Contusion, laceration, and hemorrhage of brainstem with loss of consciousness of any duration with death due to brain injury prior to regaining consciousness, initial encounter
S06.388A Contusion, laceration, and hemorrhage of brainstem with loss of consciousness of any duration with death due to other cause prior to regaining consciousness, initial encounter
S06.380A Contusion, laceration, and hemorrhage of brainstem without loss of consciousness, initial encounter
S06.376A Contusion, laceration, and hemorrhage of cerebellum with loss of consciousness greater than 24 hours without return to pre-existing conscious level with patient surviving, initial encounter
S06.377A Contusion, laceration, and hemorrhage of cerebellum with loss of consciousness of any duration with death due to brain injury prior to regaining consciousness, initial encounter
S06.378A Contusion, laceration, and hemorrhage of cerebellum with loss of consciousness of any duration with death due to other cause prior to regaining consciousness, initial encounter
S06.370A Contusion, laceration, and hemorrhage of cerebellum without loss of consciousness, initial encounter
P90 Convulsions of newborn
Q24.2 Cor triatriatum
I25.42 Coronary artery dissection
T32.21 Corrosions involving 20-29% of body surface with 10-19% third degree corrosion
T32.22 Corrosions involving 20-29% of body surface with 20-29% third degree corrosion
T32.31 Corrosions involving 30-39% of body surface with 10-19% third degree corrosion
T32.32 Corrosions involving 30-39% of body surface with 20-29% third degree corrosion

T32.33	Corrosions involving 30-39% of body surface with 30-39% third degree corrosion
T32.41	Corrosions involving 40-49% of body surface with 10-19% third degree corrosion
T32.42	Corrosions involving 40-49% of body surface with 20-29% third degree corrosion
T32.43	Corrosions involving 40-49% of body surface with 30-39% third degree corrosion
T32.44	Corrosions involving 40-49% of body surface with 40-49% third degree corrosion
T32.51	Corrosions involving 50-59% of body surface with 10-19% third degree corrosion
T32.52	Corrosions involving 50-59% of body surface with 20-29% third degree corrosion
T32.53	Corrosions involving 50-59% of body surface with 30-39% third degree corrosion
T32.54	Corrosions involving 50-59% of body surface with 40-49% third degree corrosion
T32.55	Corrosions involving 50-59% of body surface with 50-59% third degree corrosion
T32.61	Corrosions involving 60-69% of body surface with 10-19% third degree corrosion
T32.62	Corrosions involving 60-69% of body surface with 20-29% third degree corrosion
T32.63	Corrosions involving 60-69% of body surface with 30-39% third degree corrosion
T32.64	Corrosions involving 60-69% of body surface with 40-49% third degree corrosion
T32.65	Corrosions involving 60-69% of body surface with 50-59% third degree corrosion
T32.66	Corrosions involving 60-69% of body surface with 60-69% third degree corrosion
T32.71	Corrosions involving 70-79% of body surface with 10-19% third degree corrosion
T32.72	Corrosions involving 70-79% of body surface with 20-29% third degree corrosion
T32.73	Corrosions involving 70-79% of body surface with 30-39% third degree corrosion
T32.74	Corrosions involving 70-79% of body surface with 40-49% third degree corrosion
T32.75	Corrosions involving 70-79% of body surface with 50-59% third degree corrosion
T32.76	Corrosions involving 70-79% of body surface with 60-69% third degree corrosion
T32.77	Corrosions involving 70-79% of body surface with 70-79% third degree corrosion
T32.81	Corrosions involving 80-89% of body surface with 10-19% third degree corrosion
T32.82	Corrosions involving 80-89% of body surface with 20-29% third degree corrosion
T32.83	Corrosions involving 80-89% of body surface with 30-39% third degree corrosion
T32.84	Corrosions involving 80-89% of body surface with 40-49% third degree corrosion
T32.85	Corrosions involving 80-89% of body surface with 50-59% third degree corrosion
T32.86	Corrosions involving 80-89% of body surface with 60-69% third degree corrosion
T32.87	Corrosions involving 80-89% of body surface with 70-79% third degree corrosion
T32.88	Corrosions involving 80-89% of body surface with 80-89% third degree corrosion
T32.91	Corrosions involving 90% or more of body surface with 10-19% third degree corrosion
T32.92	Corrosions involving 90% or more of body surface with 20-29% third degree corrosion
T32.93	Corrosions involving 90% or more of body surface with 30-39% third degree corrosion
T32.94	Corrosions involving 90% or more of body surface with 40-49% third degree corrosion
T32.95	Corrosions involving 90% or more of body surface with 50-59% third degree corrosion
T32.96	Corrosions involving 90% or more of body surface with 60-69% third degree corrosion
T32.97	Corrosions involving 90% or more of body surface with 70-79% third degree corrosion
T32.98	Corrosions involving 90% or more of body surface with 80-89% third degree corrosion
T32.99	Corrosions involving 90% or more of body surface with 90% or more third degree corrosion
Q00.1	Craniorachischisis
B46.3	Cutaneous mucormycosis
E84.0	Cystic fibrosis with pulmonary manifestations
B25.2	Cytomegaloviral pancreatitis
B25.0	Cytomegaloviral pneumonitis
O22.31	Deep phlebothrombosis in pregnancy, first trimester
O22.32	Deep phlebothrombosis in pregnancy, second trimester
O22.33	Deep phlebothrombosis in pregnancy, third trimester
O87.1	Deep phlebothrombosis in the puerperium
E08.01	Diabetes mellitus due to underlying condition with hyperosmolarity with coma

E08.00	Diabetes mellitus due to underlying condition with hyperosmolarity without nonketotic hyperglycemic-hyperosmolar coma (NKHHC)
E08.641	Diabetes mellitus due to underlying condition with hypoglycemia with coma
E08.11	Diabetes mellitus due to underlying condition with ketoacidosis with coma
E08.10	Diabetes mellitus due to underlying condition with ketoacidosis without coma
K44.1	Diaphragmatic hernia with gangrene
K31.82	Dieulafoy lesion (hemorrhagic) of stomach and duodenum
K63.81	Dieulafoy lesion of intestine
K55.052	Diffuse acute (reversible) ischemia of intestine, part unspecified
K55.032	Diffuse acute (reversible) ischemia of large intestine
K55.012	Diffuse acute (reversible) ischemia of small intestine
K55.062	Diffuse acute infarction of intestine, part unspecified
K55.042	Diffuse acute infarction of large intestine
K55.022	Diffuse acute infarction of small intestine
S06.2X6A	Diffuse traumatic brain injury with loss of consciousness greater than 24 hours without return to pre-existing conscious level with patient surviving, initial encounter
S06.2X7A	Diffuse traumatic brain injury with loss of consciousness of any duration with death due to brain injury prior to regaining consciousness, initial encounter
S06.2X8A	Diffuse traumatic brain injury with loss of consciousness of any duration with death due to other cause prior to regaining consciousness, initial encounter
Q20.3	Discordant ventriculoarterial connection
O99.42	Diseases of the circulatory system complicating childbirth
K67	Disorders of peritoneum in infectious diseases classified elsewhere
S72.132A	Displaced apophyseal fracture of left femur, initial encounter for closed fracture
S72.132B	Displaced apophyseal fracture of left femur, initial encounter for open fracture type I or II
S72.132C	Displaced apophyseal fracture of left femur, initial encounter for open fracture type IIIA, IIIB, or IIIC
S72.131A	Displaced apophyseal fracture of right femur, initial encounter for closed fracture
S72.131B	Displaced apophyseal fracture of right femur, initial encounter for open fracture type I or II
S72.131C	Displaced apophyseal fracture of right femur, initial encounter for open fracture type IIIA, IIIB, or IIIC
S72.133A	Displaced apophyseal fracture of unspecified femur, initial encounter for closed fracture
S72.133B	Displaced apophyseal fracture of unspecified femur, initial encounter for open fracture type I or II
S72.133C	Displaced apophyseal fracture of unspecified femur, initial encounter for open fracture type IIIA, IIIB, or IIIC
S72.062A	Displaced articular fracture of head of left femur, initial encounter for closed fracture
S72.062B	Displaced articular fracture of head of left femur, initial encounter for open fracture type I or II
S72.062C	Displaced articular fracture of head of left femur, initial encounter for open fracture type IIIA, IIIB, or IIIC
S72.061A	Displaced articular fracture of head of right femur, initial encounter for closed fracture
S72.061B	Displaced articular fracture of head of right femur, initial encounter for open fracture type I or II
S72.061C	Displaced articular fracture of head of right femur, initial encounter for open fracture type IIIA, IIIB, or IIIC
S72.063A	Displaced articular fracture of head of unspecified femur, initial encounter for closed fracture
S72.063B	Displaced articular fracture of head of unspecified femur, initial encounter for open fracture type I or II
S72.063C	Displaced articular fracture of head of unspecified femur, initial encounter for open fracture type IIIA, IIIB, or IIIC
S32.462A	Displaced associated transverse-posterior fracture of left acetabulum, initial encounter for closed fracture
S32.462B	Displaced associated transverse-posterior fracture of left acetabulum, initial encounter for open fracture
S32.461A	Displaced associated transverse-posterior fracture of right acetabulum, initial encounter for closed fracture
S32.461B	Displaced associated transverse-posterior fracture of right acetabulum, initial encounter for open fracture
S32.463A	Displaced associated transverse-posterior fracture of unspecified acetabulum, initial encounter for closed fracture
S32.463B	Displaced associated transverse-posterior fracture of unspecified acetabulum, initial encounter for open fracture
S32.312B	Displaced avulsion fracture of left ilium, initial encounter for open fracture
S32.612B	Displaced avulsion fracture of left ischium, initial encounter for open fracture
S32.311B	Displaced avulsion fracture of right ilium, initial encounter for open fracture
S32.611B	Displaced avulsion fracture of right ischium, initial encounter for open fracture
S32.313B	Displaced avulsion fracture of unspecified ilium, initial encounter for open fracture
S32.613B	Displaced avulsion fracture of unspecified ischium, initial encounter for open fracture
S82.142B	Displaced bicondylar fracture of left tibia, initial encounter for open fracture type I or II
S82.142C	Displaced bicondylar fracture of left tibia, initial encounter for open fracture type IIIA, IIIB, or IIIC
S82.141B	Displaced bicondylar fracture of right tibia, initial encounter for open fracture type I or II
S82.141C	Displaced bicondylar fracture of right tibia, initial encounter for open fracture type IIIA, IIIB, or IIIC
S82.143B	Displaced bicondylar fracture of unspecified tibia, initial encounter for open fracture type I or II

S82.143C Displaced bicondylar fracture of unspecified tibia, initial encounter for open fracture type IIIA, IIIB, or IIIC

S42.352B Displaced comminuted fracture of shaft of humerus, left arm, initial encounter for open fracture

S42.351B Displaced comminuted fracture of shaft of humerus, right arm, initial encounter for open fracture

S42.353B Displaced comminuted fracture of shaft of humerus, unspecified arm, initial encounter for open fracture

S72.352A Displaced comminuted fracture of shaft of left femur, initial encounter for closed fracture

S72.352B Displaced comminuted fracture of shaft of left femur, initial encounter for open fracture type I or II

S72.352C Displaced comminuted fracture of shaft of left femur, initial encounter for open fracture type IIIA, IIIB, or IIIC

S82.452B Displaced comminuted fracture of shaft of left fibula, initial encounter for open fracture type I or II

S82.452C Displaced comminuted fracture of shaft of left fibula, initial encounter for open fracture type IIIA, IIIB, or IIIC

S82.252B Displaced comminuted fracture of shaft of left tibia, initial encounter for open fracture type I or II

S82.252C Displaced comminuted fracture of shaft of left tibia, initial encounter for open fracture type IIIA, IIIB, or IIIC

S52.352B Displaced comminuted fracture of shaft of radius, left arm, initial encounter for open fracture type I or II

S52.352C Displaced comminuted fracture of shaft of radius, left arm, initial encounter for open fracture type IIIA, IIIB, or IIIC

S52.351B Displaced comminuted fracture of shaft of radius, right arm, initial encounter for open fracture type I or II

S52.351C Displaced comminuted fracture of shaft of radius, right arm, initial encounter for open fracture type IIIA, IIIB, or IIIC

S52.353B Displaced comminuted fracture of shaft of radius, unspecified arm, initial encounter for open fracture type I or II

S52.353C Displaced comminuted fracture of shaft of radius, unspecified arm, initial encounter for open fracture type IIIA, IIIB, or IIIC

S72.351A Displaced comminuted fracture of shaft of right femur, initial encounter for closed fracture

S72.351B Displaced comminuted fracture of shaft of right femur, initial encounter for open fracture type I or II

S72.351C Displaced comminuted fracture of shaft of right femur, initial encounter for open fracture type IIIA, IIIB, or IIIC

S82.451B Displaced comminuted fracture of shaft of right fibula, initial encounter for open fracture type I or II

S82.451C Displaced comminuted fracture of shaft of right fibula, initial encounter for open fracture type IIIA, IIIB, or IIIC

S82.251B Displaced comminuted fracture of shaft of right tibia, initial encounter for open fracture type I or II

S82.251C Displaced comminuted fracture of shaft of right tibia, initial encounter for open fracture type IIIA, IIIB, or IIIC

S52.252B Displaced comminuted fracture of shaft of ulna, left arm, initial encounter for open fracture type I or II

S52.252C Displaced comminuted fracture of shaft of ulna, left arm, initial encounter for open fracture type IIIA, IIIB, or IIIC

S52.251B Displaced comminuted fracture of shaft of ulna, right arm, initial encounter for open fracture type I or II

S52.251C Displaced comminuted fracture of shaft of ulna, right arm, initial encounter for open fracture type IIIA, IIIB, or IIIC

S52.253B Displaced comminuted fracture of shaft of ulna, unspecified arm, initial encounter for open fracture type I or II

S52.253C Displaced comminuted fracture of shaft of ulna, unspecified arm, initial encounter for open fracture type IIIA, IIIB, or IIIC

S72.353A Displaced comminuted fracture of shaft of unspecified femur, initial encounter for closed fracture

S72.353B Displaced comminuted fracture of shaft of unspecified femur, initial encounter for open fracture type I or II

S72.353C Displaced comminuted fracture of shaft of unspecified femur, initial encounter for open fracture type IIIA, IIIB, or IIIC

S82.453B Displaced comminuted fracture of shaft of unspecified fibula, initial encounter for open fracture type I or II

S82.453C Displaced comminuted fracture of shaft of unspecified fibula, initial encounter for open fracture type IIIA, IIIB, or IIIC

S82.253B Displaced comminuted fracture of shaft of unspecified tibia, initial encounter for open fracture type I or II

S82.253C Displaced comminuted fracture of shaft of unspecified tibia, initial encounter for open fracture type IIIA, IIIB, or IIIC

S42.422B Displaced comminuted supracondylar fracture without intercondylar fracture of left humerus, initial encounter for open fracture

S42.421B Displaced comminuted supracondylar fracture without intercondylar fracture of right humerus, initial encounter for open fracture

S42.423B Displaced comminuted supracondylar fracture without intercondylar fracture of unspecified humerus, initial encounter for open fracture

S32.482A Displaced dome fracture of left acetabulum, initial encounter for closed fracture

S32.482B Displaced dome fracture of left acetabulum, initial encounter for open fracture

S32.481A Displaced dome fracture of right acetabulum, initial encounter for closed fracture

S32.481B Displaced dome fracture of right acetabulum, initial encounter for open fracture

S32.483A Displaced dome fracture of unspecified acetabulum, initial encounter for closed fracture

S32.483B Displaced dome fracture of unspecified acetabulum, initial encounter for open fracture

S42.432B Displaced fracture (avulsion) of lateral epicondyle of left humerus, initial encounter for open fracture

S42.431B Displaced fracture (avulsion) of lateral epicondyle of right humerus, initial encounter for open fracture

S42.433B Displaced fracture (avulsion) of lateral epicondyle of unspecified humerus, initial encounter for open fracture

S42.442B Displaced fracture (avulsion) of medial epicondyle of left humerus, initial encounter for open fracture

S42.441B Displaced fracture (avulsion) of medial epicondyle of right humerus, initial encounter for open fracture

S42.443B Displaced fracture (avulsion) of medial epicondyle of unspecified humerus, initial encounter for open fracture

S32.432A Displaced fracture of anterior column [iliopubic] of left acetabulum, initial encounter for closed fracture

S32.432B Displaced fracture of anterior column [iliopubic] of left acetabulum, initial encounter for open fracture

S32.431A Displaced fracture of anterior column [iliopubic] of right acetabulum, initial encounter for closed fracture

S32.431B Displaced fracture of anterior column [iliopubic] of right acetabulum, initial encounter for open fracture

S32.433A Displaced fracture of anterior column [iliopubic] of unspecified acetabulum, initial encounter for closed fracture

S32.433B Displaced fracture of anterior column [iliopubic] of unspecified acetabulum, initial encounter for open fracture

S32.412A Displaced fracture of anterior wall of left acetabulum, initial encounter for closed fracture

S32.412B Displaced fracture of anterior wall of left acetabulum, initial encounter for open fracture

S32.411A Displaced fracture of anterior wall of right acetabulum, initial encounter for closed fracture

S32.411B Displaced fracture of anterior wall of right acetabulum, initial encounter for open fracture

S32.413A Displaced fracture of anterior wall of unspecified acetabulum, initial encounter for closed fracture

S32.413B Displaced fracture of anterior wall of unspecified acetabulum, initial encounter for open fracture

S72.042A Displaced fracture of base of neck of left femur, initial encounter for closed fracture

S72.042B Displaced fracture of base of neck of left femur, initial encounter for open fracture type I or II

S72.042C Displaced fracture of base of neck of left femur, initial encounter for open fracture type IIIA, IIIB, or IIIC

S72.041A Displaced fracture of base of neck of right femur, initial encounter for closed fracture

S72.041B Displaced fracture of base of neck of right femur, initial encounter for open fracture type I or II

S72.041C Displaced fracture of base of neck of right femur, initial encounter for open fracture type IIIA, IIIB, or IIIC

S72.043A Displaced fracture of base of neck of unspecified femur, initial encounter for closed fracture

S72.043B Displaced fracture of base of neck of unspecified femur, initial encounter for open fracture type I or II

S72.043C Displaced fracture of base of neck of unspecified femur, initial encounter for open fracture type IIIA, IIIB, or IIIC

S52.042B Displaced fracture of coronoid process of left ulna, initial encounter for open fracture type I or II

S52.042C Displaced fracture of coronoid process of left ulna, initial encounter for open fracture type IIIA, IIIB, or IIIC

S52.041B Displaced fracture of coronoid process of right ulna, initial encounter for open fracture type I or II

S52.041C Displaced fracture of coronoid process of right ulna, initial encounter for open fracture type IIIA, IIIB, or IIIC

S52.043B Displaced fracture of coronoid process of unspecified ulna, initial encounter for open fracture type I or II

S52.043C Displaced fracture of coronoid process of unspecified ulna, initial encounter for open fracture type IIIA, IIIB, or IIIC

S72.022A Displaced fracture of epiphysis (separation) (upper) of left femur, initial encounter for closed fracture

S72.022B Displaced fracture of epiphysis (separation) (upper) of left femur, initial encounter for open fracture type I or II

S72.022C Displaced fracture of epiphysis (separation) (upper) of left femur, initial encounter for open fracture type IIIA, IIIB, or IIIC

S72.021A Displaced fracture of epiphysis (separation) (upper) of right femur, initial encounter for closed fracture

S72.021B Displaced fracture of epiphysis (separation) (upper) of right femur, initial encounter for open fracture type I or II

S72.021C Displaced fracture of epiphysis (separation) (upper) of right femur, initial encounter for open fracture type IIIA, IIIB, or IIIC

S72.023A Displaced fracture of epiphysis (separation) (upper) of unspecified femur, initial encounter for closed fracture

S72.023B Displaced fracture of epiphysis (separation) (upper) of unspecified femur, initial encounter for open fracture type I or II

S72.023C Displaced fracture of epiphysis (separation) (upper) of unspecified femur, initial encounter for open fracture type IIIA, IIIB, or IIIC

S72.112A Displaced fracture of greater trochanter of left femur, initial encounter for closed fracture

S72.112B Displaced fracture of greater trochanter of left femur, initial encounter for open fracture type I or II

S72.112C Displaced fracture of greater trochanter of left femur, initial encounter for open fracture type IIIA, IIIB, or IIIC

S72.111A Displaced fracture of greater trochanter of right femur, initial encounter for closed fracture

S72.111B Displaced fracture of greater trochanter of right femur, initial encounter for open fracture type I or II

S72.111C Displaced fracture of greater trochanter of right femur, initial encounter for open fracture type IIIA, IIIB, or IIIC

S72.113A Displaced fracture of greater trochanter of unspecified femur, initial encounter for closed fracture

S72.113B Displaced fracture of greater trochanter of unspecified femur, initial encounter for open fracture type I or II

S72.113C Displaced fracture of greater trochanter of unspecified femur, initial encounter for open fracture type IIIA, IIIB, or IIIC

S42.252B Displaced fracture of greater tuberosity of left humerus, initial encounter for open fracture

S42.251B Displaced fracture of greater tuberosity of right humerus, initial encounter for open fracture

S42.253B Displaced fracture of greater tuberosity of unspecified humerus, initial encounter for open fracture

S52.122B Displaced fracture of head of left radius, initial encounter for open fracture type I or II

S52.122C Displaced fracture of head of left radius, initial encounter for open fracture type IIIA, IIIB, or IIIC

S52.121B Displaced fracture of head of right radius, initial encounter for open fracture type I or II

S52.121C Displaced fracture of head of right radius, initial encounter for open fracture type IIIA, IIIB, or IIIC

S52.123B Displaced fracture of head of unspecified radius, initial encounter for open fracture type I or II

S52.123C Displaced fracture of head of unspecified radius, initial encounter for open fracture type IIIA, IIIB, or IIIC

S72.422B Displaced fracture of lateral condyle of left femur, initial encounter for open fracture type I or II

S72.422C Displaced fracture of lateral condyle of left femur, initial encounter for open fracture type IIIA, IIIB, or IIIC

S42.452B Displaced fracture of lateral condyle of left humerus, initial encounter for open fracture

S82.122B Displaced fracture of lateral condyle of left tibia, initial encounter for open fracture type I or II

S82.122C Displaced fracture of lateral condyle of left tibia, initial encounter for open fracture type IIIA, IIIB, or IIIC

S72.421B Displaced fracture of lateral condyle of right femur, initial encounter for open fracture type I or II

S72.421C Displaced fracture of lateral condyle of right femur, initial encounter for open fracture type IIIA, IIIB, or IIIC

S42.451B Displaced fracture of lateral condyle of right humerus, initial encounter for open fracture

S82.121B Displaced fracture of lateral condyle of right tibia, initial encounter for open fracture type I or II

S82.121C Displaced fracture of lateral condyle of right tibia, initial encounter for open fracture type IIIA, IIIB, or IIIC

S72.423B Displaced fracture of lateral condyle of unspecified femur, initial encounter for open fracture type I or II

S72.423C Displaced fracture of lateral condyle of unspecified femur, initial encounter for open fracture type IIIA, IIIB, or IIIC

S42.453B Displaced fracture of lateral condyle of unspecified humerus, initial encounter for open fracture

S82.123B Displaced fracture of lateral condyle of unspecified tibia, initial encounter for open fracture type I or II

S82.123C Displaced fracture of lateral condyle of unspecified tibia, initial encounter for open fracture type IIIA, IIIB, or IIIC

S52.512B Displaced fracture of left radial styloid process, initial encounter for open fracture type I or II

S52.512C Displaced fracture of left radial styloid process, initial encounter for open fracture type IIIA, IIIB, or IIIC

S82.112B Displaced fracture of left tibial spine, initial encounter for open fracture type I or II

S82.112C Displaced fracture of left tibial spine, initial encounter for open fracture type IIIA, IIIB, or IIIC

S82.152B Displaced fracture of left tibial tuberosity, initial encounter for open fracture type I or II

S82.152C Displaced fracture of left tibial tuberosity, initial encounter for open fracture type IIIA, IIIB, or IIIC

S52.612B Displaced fracture of left ulna styloid process, initial encounter for open fracture type I or II

S52.612C Displaced fracture of left ulna styloid process, initial encounter for open fracture type IIIA, IIIB, or IIIC

S72.122A Displaced fracture of lesser trochanter of left femur, initial encounter for closed fracture

S72.122B Displaced fracture of lesser trochanter of left femur, initial encounter for open fracture type I or II

S72.122C Displaced fracture of lesser trochanter of left femur, initial encounter for open fracture type IIIA, IIIB, or IIIC

S72.121A Displaced fracture of lesser trochanter of right femur, initial encounter for closed fracture

S72.121B Displaced fracture of lesser trochanter of right femur, initial encounter for open fracture type I or II

S72.121C Displaced fracture of lesser trochanter of right femur, initial encounter for open fracture type IIIA, IIIB, or IIIC

S72.123A Displaced fracture of lesser trochanter of unspecified femur, initial encounter for closed fracture

S72.123B Displaced fracture of lesser trochanter of unspecified femur, initial encounter for open fracture type I or II

S72.123C Displaced fracture of lesser trochanter of unspecified femur, initial encounter for open fracture type IIIA, IIIB, or IIIC

S42.262B Displaced fracture of lesser tuberosity of left humerus, initial encounter for open fracture

S42.261B Displaced fracture of lesser tuberosity of right humerus, initial encounter for open fracture

S42.263B Displaced fracture of lesser tuberosity of unspecified humerus, initial encounter for open fracture

S72.442B Displaced fracture of lower epiphysis (separation) of left femur, initial encounter for open fracture type I or II

S72.442C Displaced fracture of lower epiphysis (separation) of left femur, initial encounter for open fracture type IIIA, IIIB, or IIIC

S72.441B Displaced fracture of lower epiphysis (separation) of right femur, initial encounter for open fracture type I or II

S72.441C Displaced fracture of lower epiphysis (separation) of right femur, initial encounter for open fracture type IIIA, IIIB, or IIIC

S72.443B Displaced fracture of lower epiphysis (separation) of unspecified femur, initial encounter for open fracture type I or II

S72.443C Displaced fracture of lower epiphysis (separation) of unspecified femur, initial encounter for open fracture type IIIA, IIIB, or IIIC

S72.432B Displaced fracture of medial condyle of left femur, initial encounter for open fracture type I or II

S72.432C Displaced fracture of medial condyle of left femur, initial encounter for open fracture type IIIA, IIIB, or IIIC

S42.462B Displaced fracture of medial condyle of left humerus, initial encounter for open fracture

S82.132B Displaced fracture of medial condyle of left tibia, initial encounter for open fracture type I or II

S82.132C Displaced fracture of medial condyle of left tibia, initial encounter for open fracture type IIIA, IIIB, or IIIC

S72.431B Displaced fracture of medial condyle of right femur, initial encounter for open fracture type I or II

S72.431C Displaced fracture of medial condyle of right femur, initial encounter for open fracture type IIIA, IIIB, or IIIC

S42.461B Displaced fracture of medial condyle of right humerus, initial encounter for open fracture

S82.131B Displaced fracture of medial condyle of right tibia, initial encounter for open fracture type I or II

S82.131C Displaced fracture of medial condyle of right tibia, initial encounter for open fracture type IIIA, IIIB, or IIIC

S72.433B Displaced fracture of medial condyle of unspecified femur, initial encounter for open fracture type I or II

S72.433C Displaced fracture of medial condyle of unspecified femur, initial encounter for open fracture type IIIA, IIIB, or IIIC

S42.463B Displaced fracture of medial condyle of unspecified humerus, initial encounter for open fracture

S82.133B Displaced fracture of medial condyle of unspecified tibia, initial encounter for open fracture type I or II

S82.133C Displaced fracture of medial condyle of unspecified tibia, initial encounter for open fracture type IIIA, IIIB, or IIIC

S32.472A Displaced fracture of medial wall of left acetabulum, initial encounter for closed fracture

S32.472B Displaced fracture of medial wall of left acetabulum, initial encounter for open fracture

S32.471A Displaced fracture of medial wall of right acetabulum, initial encounter for closed fracture

S32.471B Displaced fracture of medial wall of right acetabulum, initial encounter for open fracture

S32.473A Displaced fracture of medial wall of unspecified acetabulum, initial encounter for closed fracture

S32.473B Displaced fracture of medial wall of unspecified acetabulum, initial encounter for open fracture

S52.132B Displaced fracture of neck of left radius, initial encounter for open fracture type I or II

S52.132C Displaced fracture of neck of left radius, initial encounter for open fracture type IIIA, IIIB, or IIIC

S52.131B Displaced fracture of neck of right radius, initial encounter for open fracture type I or II

S52.131C Displaced fracture of neck of right radius, initial encounter for open fracture type IIIA, IIIB, or IIIC

S52.133B Displaced fracture of neck of unspecified radius, initial encounter for open fracture type I or II

S52.133C Displaced fracture of neck of unspecified radius, initial encounter for open fracture type IIIA, IIIB, or IIIC

S52.032B Displaced fracture of olecranon process with intraarticular extension of left ulna, initial encounter for open fracture type I or II

S52.032C Displaced fracture of olecranon process with intraarticular extension of left ulna, initial encounter for open fracture type IIIA, IIIB, or IIIC

S52.031B Displaced fracture of olecranon process with intraarticular extension of right ulna, initial encounter for open fracture type I or II

S52.031C Displaced fracture of olecranon process with intraarticular extension of right ulna, initial encounter for open fracture type IIIA, IIIB, or IIIC

S52.033B Displaced fracture of olecranon process with intraarticular extension of unspecified ulna, initial encounter for open fracture type I or II

S52.033C Displaced fracture of olecranon process with intraarticular extension of unspecified ulna, initial encounter for open fracture type IIIA, IIIB, or IIIC

S52.022B Displaced fracture of olecranon process without intraarticular extension of left ulna, initial encounter for open fracture type I or II

S52.022C Displaced fracture of olecranon process without intraarticular extension of left ulna, initial encounter for open fracture type IIIA, IIIB, or IIIC

S52.021B Displaced fracture of olecranon process without intraarticular extension of right ulna, initial encounter for open fracture type I or II

S52.021C Displaced fracture of olecranon process without intraarticular extension of right ulna, initial encounter for open fracture type IIIA, IIIB, or IIIC

S52.023B Displaced fracture of olecranon process without intraarticular extension of unspecified ulna, initial encounter for open fracture type I or II

S52.023C Displaced fracture of olecranon process without intraarticular extension of unspecified ulna, initial encounter for open fracture type IIIA, IIIB, or IIIC

S32.442A Displaced fracture of posterior column [ilioischial] of left acetabulum, initial encounter for closed fracture

S32.442B Displaced fracture of posterior column [ilioischial] of left acetabulum, initial encounter for open fracture

S32.441A Displaced fracture of posterior column [ilioischial] of right acetabulum, initial encounter for closed fracture

S32.441B Displaced fracture of posterior column [ilioischial] of right acetabulum, initial encounter for open fracture

S32.443A Displaced fracture of posterior column [ilioischial] of unspecified acetabulum, initial encounter for closed fracture

S32.443B Displaced fracture of posterior column [ilioischial] of unspecified acetabulum, initial encounter for open fracture

S32.422A Displaced fracture of posterior wall of left acetabulum, initial encounter for closed fracture

S32.422B Displaced fracture of posterior wall of left acetabulum, initial encounter for open fracture

S32.421A Displaced fracture of posterior wall of right acetabulum, initial encounter for closed fracture

S32.421B Displaced fracture of posterior wall of right acetabulum, initial encounter for open fracture

S32.423A Displaced fracture of posterior wall of unspecified acetabulum, initial encounter for closed fracture

S32.423B Displaced fracture of posterior wall of unspecified acetabulum, initial encounter for open fracture

S52.511B Displaced fracture of right radial styloid process, initial encounter for open fracture type I or II

S52.511C Displaced fracture of right radial styloid process, initial encounter for open fracture type IIIA, IIIB, or IIIC

S82.111B Displaced fracture of right tibial spine, initial encounter for open fracture type I or II

S82.111C Displaced fracture of right tibial spine, initial encounter for open fracture type IIIA, IIIB, or IIIC

S82.151B Displaced fracture of right tibial tuberosity, initial encounter for open fracture type I or II

S82.151C Displaced fracture of right tibial tuberosity, initial encounter for open fracture type IIIA, IIIB, or IIIC

S52.611B Displaced fracture of right ulna styloid process, initial encounter for open fracture type I or II

S52.611C Displaced fracture of right ulna styloid process, initial encounter for open fracture type IIIA, IIIB, or IIIC

S52.513B Displaced fracture of unspecified radial styloid process, initial encounter for open fracture type I or II

S52.513C Displaced fracture of unspecified radial styloid process, initial encounter for open fracture type IIIA, IIIB, or IIIC

S82.113B Displaced fracture of unspecified tibial spine, initial encounter for open fracture type I or II

S82.113C Displaced fracture of unspecified tibial spine, initial encounter for open fracture type IIIA, IIIB, or IIIC

S82.153B Displaced fracture of unspecified tibial tuberosity, initial encounter for open fracture type I or II

S82.153C Displaced fracture of unspecified tibial tuberosity, initial encounter for open fracture type IIIA, IIIB, or IIIC

S52.613B Displaced fracture of unspecified ulna styloid process, initial encounter for open fracture type I or II

S52.613C Displaced fracture of unspecified ulna styloid process, initial encounter for open fracture type IIIA, IIIB, or IIIC

S72.142A Displaced intertrochanteric fracture of left femur, initial encounter for closed fracture

S72.142B Displaced intertrochanteric fracture of left femur, initial encounter for open fracture type I or II

S72.142C Displaced intertrochanteric fracture of left femur, initial encounter for open fracture type IIIA, IIIB, or IIIC

S72.141A Displaced intertrochanteric fracture of right femur, initial encounter for closed fracture

S72.141B Displaced intertrochanteric fracture of right femur, initial encounter for open fracture type I or II

S72.141C Displaced intertrochanteric fracture of right femur, initial encounter for open fracture type IIIA, IIIB, or IIIC

S72.143A Displaced intertrochanteric fracture of unspecified femur, initial encounter for closed fracture

S72.143B Displaced intertrochanteric fracture of unspecified femur, initial encounter for open fracture type I or II

S72.143C Displaced intertrochanteric fracture of unspecified femur, initial encounter for open fracture type IIIA, IIIB, or IIIC

S12.040B Displaced lateral mass fracture of first cervical vertebra, initial encounter for open fracture

S82.862B Displaced Maisonneuve's fracture of left leg, initial encounter for open fracture type I or II

S82.862C Displaced Maisonneuve's fracture of left leg, initial encounter for open fracture type IIIA, IIIB, or IIIC

S82.861B Displaced Maisonneuve's fracture of right leg, initial encounter for open fracture type I or II

S82.861C Displaced Maisonneuve's fracture of right leg, initial encounter for open fracture type IIIA, IIIB, or IIIC

S82.863B Displaced Maisonneuve's fracture of unspecified leg, initial encounter for open fracture type I or II

S82.863C Displaced Maisonneuve's fracture of unspecified leg, initial encounter for open fracture type IIIA, IIIB, or IIIC

S72.032A Displaced midcervical fracture of left femur, initial encounter for closed fracture

S72.032B Displaced midcervical fracture of left femur, initial encounter for open fracture type I or II

S72.032C Displaced midcervical fracture of left femur, initial encounter for open fracture type IIIA, IIIB, or IIIC

S72.031A Displaced midcervical fracture of right femur, initial encounter for closed fracture

S72.031B Displaced midcervical fracture of right femur, initial encounter for open fracture type I or II

S72.031C Displaced midcervical fracture of right femur, initial encounter for open fracture type IIIA, IIIB, or IIIC

S72.033A Displaced midcervical fracture of unspecified femur, initial encounter for closed fracture

S72.033B Displaced midcervical fracture of unspecified femur, initial encounter for open fracture type I or II

S72.033C Displaced midcervical fracture of unspecified femur, initial encounter for open fracture type IIIA, IIIB, or IIIC

S42.332B Displaced oblique fracture of shaft of humerus, left arm, initial encounter for open fracture

S42.331B Displaced oblique fracture of shaft of humerus, right arm, initial encounter for open fracture

S42.333B Displaced oblique fracture of shaft of humerus, unspecified arm, initial encounter for open fracture

S72.332A Displaced oblique fracture of shaft of left femur, initial encounter for closed fracture

S72.332B Displaced oblique fracture of shaft of left femur, initial encounter for open fracture type I or II

S72.332C Displaced oblique fracture of shaft of left femur, initial encounter for open fracture type IIIA, IIIB, or IIIC

S82.432B Displaced oblique fracture of shaft of left fibula, initial encounter for open fracture type I or II

S82.432C Displaced oblique fracture of shaft of left fibula, initial encounter for open fracture type IIIA, IIIB, or IIIC

S52.332B Displaced oblique fracture of shaft of left radius, initial encounter for open fracture type I or II

S52.332C Displaced oblique fracture of shaft of left radius, initial encounter for open fracture type IIIA, IIIB, or IIIC

S82.232B Displaced oblique fracture of shaft of left tibia, initial encounter for open fracture type I or II

S82.232C Displaced oblique fracture of shaft of left tibia, initial encounter for open fracture type IIIA, IIIB, or IIIC

S52.232B Displaced oblique fracture of shaft of left ulna, initial encounter for open fracture type I or II

S52.232C Displaced oblique fracture of shaft of left ulna, initial encounter for open fracture type IIIA, IIIB, or IIIC

S72.331A Displaced oblique fracture of shaft of right femur, initial encounter for closed fracture

S72.331B Displaced oblique fracture of shaft of right femur, initial encounter for open fracture type I or II

S72.331C Displaced oblique fracture of shaft of right femur, initial encounter for open fracture type IIIA, IIIB, or IIIC

S82.431B Displaced oblique fracture of shaft of right fibula, initial encounter for open fracture type I or II

S82.431C Displaced oblique fracture of shaft of right fibula, initial encounter for open fracture type IIIA, IIIB, or IIIC

S52.331B Displaced oblique fracture of shaft of right radius, initial encounter for open fracture type I or II

S52.331C Displaced oblique fracture of shaft of right radius, initial encounter for open fracture type IIIA, IIIB, or IIIC

S82.231B Displaced oblique fracture of shaft of right tibia, initial encounter for open fracture type I or II

S82.231C Displaced oblique fracture of shaft of right tibia, initial encounter for open fracture type IIIA, IIIB, or IIIC

S52.231B Displaced oblique fracture of shaft of right ulna, initial encounter for open fracture type I or II

S52.231C Displaced oblique fracture of shaft of right ulna, initial encounter for open fracture type IIIA, IIIB, or IIIC

S72.333A Displaced oblique fracture of shaft of unspecified femur, initial encounter for closed fracture

S72.333B Displaced oblique fracture of shaft of unspecified femur, initial encounter for open fracture type I or II

S72.333C Displaced oblique fracture of shaft of unspecified femur, initial encounter for open fracture type IIIA, IIIB, or IIIC

S82.433B Displaced oblique fracture of shaft of unspecified fibula, initial encounter for open fracture type I or II

S82.433C Displaced oblique fracture of shaft of unspecified fibula, initial encounter for open fracture type IIIA, IIIB, or IIIC

S52.333B Displaced oblique fracture of shaft of unspecified radius, initial encounter for open fracture type I or II

S52.333C Displaced oblique fracture of shaft of unspecified radius, initial encounter for open fracture type IIIA, IIIB, or IIIC

S82.233B Displaced oblique fracture of shaft of unspecified tibia, initial encounter for open fracture type I or II

S82.233C Displaced oblique fracture of shaft of unspecified tibia, initial encounter for open fracture type IIIA, IIIB, or IIIC

S52.233B Displaced oblique fracture of shaft of unspecified ulna, initial encounter for open fracture type I or II

S52.233C Displaced oblique fracture of shaft of unspecified ulna, initial encounter for open fracture type IIIA, IIIB, or IIIC

S12.030B Displaced posterior arch fracture of first cervical vertebra, initial encounter for open fracture

S42.362B Displaced segmental fracture of shaft of humerus, left arm, initial encounter for open fracture

S42.361B Displaced segmental fracture of shaft of humerus, right arm, initial encounter for open fracture

S42.363B Displaced segmental fracture of shaft of humerus, unspecified arm, initial encounter for open fracture

S72.362A Displaced segmental fracture of shaft of left femur, initial encounter for closed fracture

S72.362B Displaced segmental fracture of shaft of left femur, initial encounter for open fracture type I or II

S72.362C Displaced segmental fracture of shaft of left femur, initial encounter for open fracture type IIIA, IIIB, or IIIC

S82.462B Displaced segmental fracture of shaft of left fibula, initial encounter for open fracture type I or II

S82.462C Displaced segmental fracture of shaft of left fibula, initial encounter for open fracture type IIIA, IIIB, or IIIC

S82.262B Displaced segmental fracture of shaft of left tibia, initial encounter for open fracture type I or II

S82.262C Displaced segmental fracture of shaft of left tibia, initial encounter for open fracture type IIIA, IIIB, or IIIC

S52.362B Displaced segmental fracture of shaft of radius, left arm, initial encounter for open fracture type I or II

S52.362C Displaced segmental fracture of shaft of radius, left arm, initial encounter for open fracture type IIIA, IIIB, or IIIC

S52.361B Displaced segmental fracture of shaft of radius, right arm, initial encounter for open fracture type I or II

S52.361C Displaced segmental fracture of shaft of radius, right arm, initial encounter for open fracture type IIIA, IIIB, or IIIC

S52.363B Displaced segmental fracture of shaft of radius, unspecified arm, initial encounter for open fracture type I or II

S52.363C Displaced segmental fracture of shaft of radius, unspecified arm, initial encounter for open fracture type IIIA, IIIB, or IIIC

S72.361A Displaced segmental fracture of shaft of right femur, initial encounter for closed fracture

S72.361B Displaced segmental fracture of shaft of right femur, initial encounter for open fracture type I or II

S72.361C Displaced segmental fracture of shaft of right femur, initial encounter for open fracture type IIIA, IIIB, or IIIC

S82.461B Displaced segmental fracture of shaft of right fibula, initial encounter for open fracture type I or II

S82.461C Displaced segmental fracture of shaft of right fibula, initial encounter for open fracture type IIIA, IIIB, or IIIC

S82.261B Displaced segmental fracture of shaft of right tibia, initial encounter for open fracture type I or II

S82.261C Displaced segmental fracture of shaft of right tibia, initial encounter for open fracture type IIIA, IIIB, or IIIC

S52.262B Displaced segmental fracture of shaft of ulna, left arm, initial encounter for open fracture type I or II

S52.262C Displaced segmental fracture of shaft of ulna, left arm, initial encounter for open fracture type IIIA, IIIB, or IIIC

S52.261B Displaced segmental fracture of shaft of ulna, right arm, initial encounter for open fracture type I or II

S52.261C Displaced segmental fracture of shaft of ulna, right arm, initial encounter for open fracture type IIIA, IIIB, or IIIC

S52.263B Displaced segmental fracture of shaft of ulna, unspecified arm, initial encounter for open fracture type I or II

S52.263C Displaced segmental fracture of shaft of ulna, unspecified arm, initial encounter for open fracture type IIIA, IIIB, or IIIC

S72.363A Displaced segmental fracture of shaft of unspecified femur, initial encounter for closed fracture

S72.363B Displaced segmental fracture of shaft of unspecified femur, initial encounter for open fracture type I or II

S72.363C Displaced segmental fracture of shaft of unspecified femur, initial encounter for open fracture type IIIA, IIIB, or IIIC

S82.463B Displaced segmental fracture of shaft of unspecified fibula, initial encounter for open fracture type I or II

S82.463C Displaced segmental fracture of shaft of unspecified fibula, initial encounter for open fracture type IIIA, IIIB, or IIIC

S82.263B Displaced segmental fracture of shaft of unspecified tibia, initial encounter for open fracture type I or II

S82.263C Displaced segmental fracture of shaft of unspecified tibia, initial encounter for open fracture type IIIA, IIIB, or IIIC

S42.412B Displaced simple supracondylar fracture without intercondylar fracture of left humerus, initial encounter for open fracture

S42.411B Displaced simple supracondylar fracture without intercondylar fracture of right humerus, initial encounter for open fracture

S42.413B Displaced simple supracondylar fracture without intercondylar fracture of unspecified humerus, initial encounter for open fracture

S42.342B Displaced spiral fracture of shaft of humerus, left arm, initial encounter for open fracture

S42.341B Displaced spiral fracture of shaft of humerus, right arm, initial encounter for open fracture

S42.343B Displaced spiral fracture of shaft of humerus, unspecified arm, initial encounter for open fracture

S72.342A Displaced spiral fracture of shaft of left femur, initial encounter for closed fracture

S72.342B Displaced spiral fracture of shaft of left femur, initial encounter for open fracture type I or II

S72.342C Displaced spiral fracture of shaft of left femur, initial encounter for open fracture type IIIA, IIIB, or IIIC

S82.442B Displaced spiral fracture of shaft of left fibula, initial encounter for open fracture type I or II

S82.442C Displaced spiral fracture of shaft of left fibula, initial encounter for open fracture type IIIA, IIIB, or IIIC

S82.242B Displaced spiral fracture of shaft of left tibia, initial encounter for open fracture type I or II

S82.242C Displaced spiral fracture of shaft of left tibia, initial encounter for open fracture type IIIA, IIIB, or IIIC

S52.342B Displaced spiral fracture of shaft of radius, left arm, initial encounter for open fracture type I or II

S52.342C Displaced spiral fracture of shaft of radius, left arm, initial encounter for open fracture type IIIA, IIIB, or IIIC

S52.341B Displaced spiral fracture of shaft of radius, right arm, initial encounter for open fracture type I or II

S52.341C Displaced spiral fracture of shaft of radius, right arm, initial encounter for open fracture type IIIA, IIIB, or IIIC

S52.343B Displaced spiral fracture of shaft of radius, unspecified arm, initial encounter for open fracture type I or II

S52.343C Displaced spiral fracture of shaft of radius, unspecified arm, initial encounter for open fracture type IIIA, IIIB, or IIIC

S72.341A Displaced spiral fracture of shaft of right femur, initial encounter for closed fracture

S72.341B Displaced spiral fracture of shaft of right femur, initial encounter for open fracture type I or II

S72.341C Displaced spiral fracture of shaft of right femur, initial encounter for open fracture type IIIA, IIIB, or IIIC

S82.441B Displaced spiral fracture of shaft of right fibula, initial encounter for open fracture type I or II

S82.441C Displaced spiral fracture of shaft of right fibula, initial encounter for open fracture type IIIA, IIIB, or IIIC

S82.241B Displaced spiral fracture of shaft of right tibia, initial encounter for open fracture type I or II

S82.241C Displaced spiral fracture of shaft of right tibia, initial encounter for open fracture type IIIA, IIIB, or IIIC

S52.242B Displaced spiral fracture of shaft of ulna, left arm, initial encounter for open fracture type I or II

S52.242C Displaced spiral fracture of shaft of ulna, left arm, initial encounter for open fracture type IIIA, IIIB, or IIIC

S52.241B Displaced spiral fracture of shaft of ulna, right arm, initial encounter for open fracture type I or II

S52.241C Displaced spiral fracture of shaft of ulna, right arm, initial encounter for open fracture type IIIA, IIIB, or IIIC

S52.243B Displaced spiral fracture of shaft of ulna, unspecified arm, initial encounter for open fracture type I or II

S52.243C Displaced spiral fracture of shaft of ulna, unspecified arm, initial encounter for open fracture type IIIA, IIIB, or IIIC

S72.343A Displaced spiral fracture of shaft of unspecified femur, initial encounter for closed fracture

S72.343B Displaced spiral fracture of shaft of unspecified femur, initial encounter for open fracture type I or II

S72.343C Displaced spiral fracture of shaft of unspecified femur, initial encounter for open fracture type IIIA, IIIB, or IIIC

S82.443B Displaced spiral fracture of shaft of unspecified fibula, initial encounter for open fracture type I or II

S82.443C Displaced spiral fracture of shaft of unspecified fibula, initial encounter for open fracture type IIIA, IIIB, or IIIC

S82.243B Displaced spiral fracture of shaft of unspecified tibia, initial encounter for open fracture type I or II

S82.243C Displaced spiral fracture of shaft of unspecified tibia, initial encounter for open fracture type IIIA, IIIB, or IIIC

S72.22XA Displaced subtrochanteric fracture of left femur, initial encounter for closed fracture

S72.22XB Displaced subtrochanteric fracture of left femur, initial encounter for open fracture type I or II

S72.22XC Displaced subtrochanteric fracture of left femur, initial encounter for open fracture type IIIA, IIIB, or IIIC

S72.21XA Displaced subtrochanteric fracture of right femur, initial encounter for closed fracture

S72.21XB Displaced subtrochanteric fracture of right femur, initial encounter for open fracture type I or II

S72.21XC Displaced subtrochanteric fracture of right femur, initial encounter for open fracture type IIIA, IIIB, or IIIC

S72.23XA Displaced subtrochanteric fracture of unspecified femur, initial encounter for closed fracture

S72.23XB Displaced subtrochanteric fracture of unspecified femur, initial encounter for open fracture type I or II

S72.23XC Displaced subtrochanteric fracture of unspecified femur, initial encounter for open fracture type IIIA, IIIB, or IIIC

S72.462B Displaced supracondylar fracture with intracondylar extension of lower end of left femur, initial encounter for open fracture type I or II

S72.462C	Displaced supracondylar fracture with intracondylar extension of lower end of left femur, initial encounter for open fracture type IIIA, IIIB, or IIIC
S72.461B	Displaced supracondylar fracture with intracondylar extension of lower end of right femur, initial encounter for open fracture type I or II
S72.461C	Displaced supracondylar fracture with intracondylar extension of lower end of right femur, initial encounter for open fracture type IIIA, IIIB, or IIIC
S72.463B	Displaced supracondylar fracture with intracondylar extension of lower end of unspecified femur, initial encounter for open fracture type I or II
S72.463C	Displaced supracondylar fracture with intracondylar extension of lower end of unspecified femur, initial encounter for open fracture type IIIA, IIIB, or IIIC
S72.452B	Displaced supracondylar fracture without intracondylar extension of lower end of left femur, initial encounter for open fracture type I or II
S72.452C	Displaced supracondylar fracture without intracondylar extension of lower end of left femur, initial encounter for open fracture type IIIA, IIIB, or IIIC
S72.451B	Displaced supracondylar fracture without intracondylar extension of lower end of right femur, initial encounter for open fracture type I or II
S72.451C	Displaced supracondylar fracture without intracondylar extension of lower end of right femur, initial encounter for open fracture type IIIA, IIIB, or IIIC
S72.453B	Displaced supracondylar fracture without intracondylar extension of lower end of unspecified femur, initial encounter for open fracture type I or II
S72.453C	Displaced supracondylar fracture without intracondylar extension of lower end of unspecified femur, initial encounter for open fracture type IIIA, IIIB, or IIIC
S42.472B	Displaced transcondylar fracture of left humerus, initial encounter for open fracture
S42.471B	Displaced transcondylar fracture of right humerus, initial encounter for open fracture
S42.473B	Displaced transcondylar fracture of unspecified humerus, initial encounter for open fracture
S32.452A	Displaced transverse fracture of left acetabulum, initial encounter for closed fracture
S32.452B	Displaced transverse fracture of left acetabulum, initial encounter for open fracture
S32.451A	Displaced transverse fracture of right acetabulum, initial encounter for closed fracture
S32.451B	Displaced transverse fracture of right acetabulum, initial encounter for open fracture
S42.322B	Displaced transverse fracture of shaft of humerus, left arm, initial encounter for open fracture
S42.321B	Displaced transverse fracture of shaft of humerus, right arm, initial encounter for open fracture
S42.323B	Displaced transverse fracture of shaft of humerus, unspecified arm, initial encounter for open fracture
S72.322A	Displaced transverse fracture of shaft of left femur, initial encounter for closed fracture
S72.322B	Displaced transverse fracture of shaft of left femur, initial encounter for open fracture type I or II
S72.322C	Displaced transverse fracture of shaft of left femur, initial encounter for open fracture type IIIA, IIIB, or IIIC
S82.422B	Displaced transverse fracture of shaft of left fibula, initial encounter for open fracture type I or II
S82.422C	Displaced transverse fracture of shaft of left fibula, initial encounter for open fracture type IIIA, IIIB, or IIIC
S52.322B	Displaced transverse fracture of shaft of left radius, initial encounter for open fracture type I or II
S52.322C	Displaced transverse fracture of shaft of left radius, initial encounter for open fracture type IIIA, IIIB, or IIIC
S82.222B	Displaced transverse fracture of shaft of left tibia, initial encounter for open fracture type I or II
S82.222C	Displaced transverse fracture of shaft of left tibia, initial encounter for open fracture type IIIA, IIIB, or IIIC
S52.222B	Displaced transverse fracture of shaft of left ulna, initial encounter for open fracture type I or II
S52.222C	Displaced transverse fracture of shaft of left ulna, initial encounter for open fracture type IIIA, IIIB, or IIIC
S72.321A	Displaced transverse fracture of shaft of right femur, initial encounter for closed fracture
S72.321B	Displaced transverse fracture of shaft of right femur, initial encounter for open fracture type I or II
S72.321C	Displaced transverse fracture of shaft of right femur, initial encounter for open fracture type IIIA, IIIB, or IIIC
S82.421B	Displaced transverse fracture of shaft of right fibula, initial encounter for open fracture type I or II
S82.421C	Displaced transverse fracture of shaft of right fibula, initial encounter for open fracture type IIIA, IIIB, or IIIC
S52.321B	Displaced transverse fracture of shaft of right radius, initial encounter for open fracture type I or II
S52.321C	Displaced transverse fracture of shaft of right radius, initial encounter for open fracture type IIIA, IIIB, or IIIC
S82.221B	Displaced transverse fracture of shaft of right tibia, initial encounter for open fracture type I or II
S82.221C	Displaced transverse fracture of shaft of right tibia, initial encounter for open fracture type IIIA, IIIB, or IIIC
S52.221B	Displaced transverse fracture of shaft of right ulna, initial encounter for open fracture type I or II
S52.221C	Displaced transverse fracture of shaft of right ulna, initial encounter for open fracture type IIIA, IIIB, or IIIC
S72.323A	Displaced transverse fracture of shaft of unspecified femur, initial encounter for closed fracture
S72.323B	Displaced transverse fracture of shaft of unspecified femur, initial encounter for open fracture type I or II

S72.323C	Displaced transverse fracture of shaft of unspecified femur, initial encounter for open fracture type IIIA, IIIB, or IIIC
S82.423B	Displaced transverse fracture of shaft of unspecified fibula, initial encounter for open fracture type I or II
S82.423C	Displaced transverse fracture of shaft of unspecified fibula, initial encounter for open fracture type IIIA, IIIB, or IIIC
S52.323B	Displaced transverse fracture of shaft of unspecified radius, initial encounter for open fracture type I or II
S52.323C	Displaced transverse fracture of shaft of unspecified radius, initial encounter for open fracture type IIIA, IIIB, or IIIC
S82.223B	Displaced transverse fracture of shaft of unspecified tibia, initial encounter for open fracture type I or II
S82.223C	Displaced transverse fracture of shaft of unspecified tibia, initial encounter for open fracture type IIIA, IIIB, or IIIC
S52.223B	Displaced transverse fracture of shaft of unspecified ulna, initial encounter for open fracture type I or II
S52.223C	Displaced transverse fracture of shaft of unspecified ulna, initial encounter for open fracture type IIIA, IIIB, or IIIC
S32.453A	Displaced transverse fracture of unspecified acetabulum, initial encounter for closed fracture
S32.453B	Displaced transverse fracture of unspecified acetabulum, initial encounter for open fracture
S72.412B	Displaced unspecified condyle fracture of lower end of left femur, initial encounter for open fracture type I or II
S72.412C	Displaced unspecified condyle fracture of lower end of left femur, initial encounter for open fracture type IIIA, IIIB, or IIIC
S72.411B	Displaced unspecified condyle fracture of lower end of right femur, initial encounter for open fracture type I or II
S72.411C	Displaced unspecified condyle fracture of lower end of right femur, initial encounter for open fracture type IIIA, IIIB, or IIIC
S72.413B	Displaced unspecified condyle fracture of lower end of unspecified femur, initial encounter for open fracture type I or II
S72.413C	Displaced unspecified condyle fracture of lower end of unspecified femur, initial encounter for open fracture type IIIA, IIIB, or IIIC
I71.02	Dissection of abdominal aorta
I77.77	Dissection of artery of lower extremity
I77.76	Dissection of artery of upper extremity
I77.71	Dissection of carotid artery
I67.0	Dissection of cerebral arteries, nonruptured
I77.72	Dissection of iliac artery
I77.75	Dissection of other precerebral arteries
I77.79	Dissection of other specified artery
I77.73	Dissection of renal artery
I71.01	Dissection of thoracic aorta
I71.03	Dissection of thoracoabdominal aorta
I77.70	Dissection of unspecified artery
I71.00	Dissection of unspecified site of aorta
I77.74	Dissection of vertebral artery
B00.7	Disseminated herpesviral disease
D65	Disseminated intravascular coagulation [defibrination syndrome]
P60	Disseminated intravascular coagulation of newborn
B46.4	Disseminated mucormycosis
K57.41	Diverticulitis of both small and large intestine with perforation and abscess with bleeding
K57.53	Diverticulitis of both small and large intestine without perforation or abscess with bleeding
K57.81	Diverticulitis of intestine, part unspecified, with perforation and abscess with bleeding
K57.93	Diverticulitis of intestine, part unspecified, without perforation or abscess with bleeding
K57.21	Diverticulitis of large intestine with perforation and abscess with bleeding
K57.33	Diverticulitis of large intestine without perforation or abscess with bleeding
K57.01	Diverticulitis of small intestine with perforation and abscess with bleeding
K57.13	Diverticulitis of small intestine without perforation or abscess with bleeding
K57.51	Diverticulosis of both small and large intestine without perforation or abscess with bleeding
K57.91	Diverticulosis of intestine, part unspecified, without perforation or abscess with bleeding
K57.31	Diverticulosis of large intestine without perforation or abscess with bleeding
K57.11	Diverticulosis of small intestine without perforation or abscess with bleeding
Q20.4	Double inlet ventricle
Q20.2	Double outlet left ventricle
Q20.1	Double outlet right ventricle
K85.32	Drug induced acute pancreatitis with infected necrosis
K85.31	Drug induced acute pancreatitis with uninfected necrosis
K85.30	Drug induced acute pancreatitis without necrosis or infection
E09.01	Drug or chemical induced diabetes mellitus with hyperosmolarity with coma
E09.00	Drug or chemical induced diabetes mellitus with hyperosmolarity without nonketotic hyperglycemic-hyperosmolar coma (NKHHC)
E09.641	Drug or chemical induced diabetes mellitus with hypoglycemia with coma
E09.11	Drug or chemical induced diabetes mellitus with ketoacidosis with coma
E09.10	Drug or chemical induced diabetes mellitus with ketoacidosis without coma
D61.1	Drug-induced aplastic anemia
K29.81	Duodenitis with bleeding
A83.2	Eastern equine encephalitis
Q22.5	Ebstein's anomaly
O15.1	Eclampsia complicating labor
O15.02	Eclampsia complicating pregnancy, second trimester
O15.03	Eclampsia complicating pregnancy, third trimester
O15.2	Eclampsia complicating the puerperium

O04.7	Embolism following (induced) termination of pregnancy
O08.2	Embolism following ectopic and molar pregnancy
O07.2	Embolism following failed attempted termination of pregnancy
O03.2	Embolism following incomplete spontaneous abortion
G05.3	Encephalitis and encephalomyelitis in diseases classified elsewhere
G04.90	Encephalitis and encephalomyelitis, unspecified
N18.6	End stage renal disease
S06.4X5A	Epidural hemorrhage with loss of consciousness greater than 24 hours with return to pre-existing conscious level, initial encounter
S06.4X6A	Epidural hemorrhage with loss of consciousness greater than 24 hours without return to pre-existing conscious level with patient surviving, initial encounter
S06.4X3A	Epidural hemorrhage with loss of consciousness of 1 hour to 5 hours 59 minutes, initial encounter
S06.4X1A	Epidural hemorrhage with loss of consciousness of 30 minutes or less, initial encounter
S06.4X2A	Epidural hemorrhage with loss of consciousness of 31 minutes to 59 minutes, initial encounter
S06.4X4A	Epidural hemorrhage with loss of consciousness of 6 hours to 24 hours, initial encounter
S06.4X7A	Epidural hemorrhage with loss of consciousness of any duration with death due to brain injury prior to regaining consciousness, initial encounter
S06.4X8A	Epidural hemorrhage with loss of consciousness of any duration with death due to other causes prior to regaining consciousness, initial encounter
S06.4X9A	Epidural hemorrhage with loss of consciousness of unspecified duration, initial encounter
S06.4X0A	Epidural hemorrhage without loss of consciousness, initial encounter
A26.7	Erysipelothrix sepsis
I85.01	Esophageal varices with bleeding
Q39.4	Esophageal web
Q79.2	Exomphalos
G06.2	Extradural and subdural abscess, unspecified
A84.0	Far Eastern tick-borne encephalitis [Russian spring-summer encephalitis]
T79.1XXA	Fat embolism (traumatic), initial encounter
N73.3	Female acute pelvic peritonitis
S22.5XXA	Flail chest, initial encounter for closed fracture
S22.5XXB	Flail chest, initial encounter for open fracture
K55.051	Focal (segmental) acute (reversible) ischemia of intestine, part unspecified
K55.031	Focal (segmental) acute (reversible) ischemia of large intestine
K55.011	Focal (segmental) acute (reversible) ischemia of small intestine
K55.061	Focal (segmental) acute infarction of intestine, part unspecified
K55.041	Focal (segmental) acute infarction of large intestine
K55.021	Focal (segmental) acute infarction of small intestine
S02.102B	Fracture of base of skull, left side, initial encounter for open fracture
S02.101B	Fracture of base of skull, right side, initial encounter for open fracture
S02.109B	Fracture of base of skull, unspecified side, initial encounter for open fracture
S22.22XB	Fracture of body of sternum, initial encounter for open fracture
S22.9XXB	Fracture of bony thorax, part unspecified, initial encounter for open fracture
S32.2XXB	Fracture of coccyx, initial encounter for open fracture
S42.92XB	Fracture of left shoulder girdle, part unspecified, initial encounter for open fracture
S22.21XB	Fracture of manubrium, initial encounter for open fracture
S22.32XB	Fracture of one rib, left side, initial encounter for open fracture
S22.31XB	Fracture of one rib, right side, initial encounter for open fracture
S22.39XB	Fracture of one rib, unspecified side, initial encounter for open fracture
S02.122B	Fracture of orbital roof, left side, initial encounter for open fracture
S02.121B	Fracture of orbital roof, right side, initial encounter for open fracture
S02.129B	Fracture of orbital roof, unspecified side, initial encounter for open fracture
S12.8XXA	Fracture of other parts of neck, initial encounter
S32.89XB	Fracture of other parts of pelvis, initial encounter for open fracture
S42.91XB	Fracture of right shoulder girdle, part unspecified, initial encounter for open fracture
S32.512B	Fracture of superior rim of left pubis, initial encounter for open fracture
S32.511B	Fracture of superior rim of right pubis, initial encounter for open fracture
S32.519B	Fracture of superior rim of unspecified pubis, initial encounter for open fracture
S72.002A	Fracture of unspecified part of neck of left femur, initial encounter for closed fracture
S72.002B	Fracture of unspecified part of neck of left femur, initial encounter for open fracture type I or II
S72.002C	Fracture of unspecified part of neck of left femur, initial encounter for open fracture type IIIA, IIIB, or IIIC
S72.001A	Fracture of unspecified part of neck of right femur, initial encounter for closed fracture
S72.001B	Fracture of unspecified part of neck of right femur, initial encounter for open fracture type I or II
S72.001C	Fracture of unspecified part of neck of right femur, initial encounter for open fracture type IIIA, IIIB, or IIIC
S72.009A	Fracture of unspecified part of neck of unspecified femur, initial encounter for closed fracture
S72.009B	Fracture of unspecified part of neck of unspecified femur, initial encounter for open fracture type I or II
S72.009C	Fracture of unspecified part of neck of unspecified femur, initial encounter for open fracture type IIIA, IIIB, or IIIC
S32.9XXB	Fracture of unspecified parts of lumbosacral spine and pelvis, initial encounter for open fracture
S42.90XB	Fracture of unspecified shoulder girdle, part unspecified, initial encounter for open fracture
S02.0XXB	Fracture of vault of skull, initial encounter for open fracture
S22.24XB	Fracture of xiphoid process, initial encounter for open fracture
R53.2	Functional quadriplegia
S52.372B	Galeazzi's fracture of left radius, initial encounter for open fracture type I or II
S52.372C	Galeazzi's fracture of left radius, initial encounter for open fracture type IIIA, IIIB, or IIIC
S52.371B	Galeazzi's fracture of right radius, initial encounter for open fracture type I or II
S52.371C	Galeazzi's fracture of right radius, initial encounter for open fracture type IIIA, IIIB, or IIIC
S52.379B	Galeazzi's fracture of unspecified radius, initial encounter for open fracture type I or II
S52.379C	Galeazzi's fracture of unspecified radius, initial encounter for open fracture type IIIA, IIIB, or IIIC
J85.0	Gangrene and necrosis of lung
A48.0	Gas gangrene
K29.71	Gastritis, unspecified, with bleeding
K22.6	Gastro-esophageal laceration-hemorrhage syndrome
K29.91	Gastroduodenitis, unspecified, with bleeding
B46.2	Gastrointestinal mucormycosis
Q79.3	Gastroschisis
K65.0	Generalized (acute) peritonitis
G40.311	Generalized idiopathic epilepsy and epileptic syndromes, intractable, with status epilepticus
G40.319	Generalized idiopathic epilepsy and epileptic syndromes, intractable, without status epilepticus
G40.301	Generalized idiopathic epilepsy and epileptic syndromes, not intractable, with status epilepticus
A54.81	Gonococcal meningitis
A54.86	Gonococcal sepsis
A41.50	Gram-negative sepsis, unspecified
D57.01	Hb-SS disease with acute chest syndrome
D57.00	Hb-SS disease with crisis, unspecified
D57.02	Hb-SS disease with splenic sequestration
O14.22	HELLP syndrome (HELLP), second trimester
O14.23	HELLP syndrome (HELLP), third trimester
D59.3	Hemolytic-uremic syndrome
K66.1	Hemoperitoneum
G00.0	Hemophilus meningitis
K72.91	Hepatic failure, unspecified with coma
B15.0	Hepatitis A with hepatic coma
K76.7	Hepatorenal syndrome
D67	Hereditary factor IX deficiency
D66	Hereditary factor VIII deficiency
B00.82	Herpes simplex myelitis
B00.4	Herpesviral encephalitis
B00.3	Herpesviral meningitis
Q04.2	Holoprosencephaly
B10.01	Human herpesvirus 6 encephalitis
J12.3	Human metapneumovirus pneumonia
P56.0	Hydrops fetalis due to isoimmunization
P56.99	Hydrops fetalis due to other hemolytic disease
P56.90	Hydrops fetalis due to unspecified hemolytic disease
P83.2	Hydrops fetalis not due to hemolytic disease
Q23.4	Hypoplastic left heart syndrome
Q22.6	Hypoplastic right heart syndrome
R57.1	Hypovolemic shock
K85.02	Idiopathic acute pancreatitis with infected necrosis
K85.01	Idiopathic acute pancreatitis with uninfected necrosis
K85.00	Idiopathic acute pancreatitis without necrosis or infection
D61.3	Idiopathic aplastic anemia
S42.448B	Incarcerated fracture (avulsion) of medial epicondyle of left humerus, initial encounter for open fracture
S42.447B	Incarcerated fracture (avulsion) of medial epicondyle of right humerus, initial encounter for open fracture
S42.449B	Incarcerated fracture (avulsion) of medial epicondyle of unspecified humerus, initial encounter for open fracture
K43.1	Incisional hernia with gangrene
S34.121A	Incomplete lesion of L1 level of lumbar spinal cord, initial encounter
S34.122A	Incomplete lesion of L2 level of lumbar spinal cord, initial encounter
S34.123A	Incomplete lesion of L3 level of lumbar spinal cord, initial encounter
S34.124A	Incomplete lesion of L4 level of lumbar spinal cord, initial encounter
S34.125A	Incomplete lesion of L5 level of lumbar spinal cord, initial encounter
S34.132A	Incomplete lesion of sacral spinal cord, initial encounter
S34.129A	Incomplete lesion of unspecified level of lumbar spinal cord, initial encounter
K76.3	Infarction of liver
O41.1011	Infection of amniotic sac and membranes, unspecified, first trimester, fetus 1
O41.1012	Infection of amniotic sac and membranes, unspecified, first trimester, fetus 2
O41.1013	Infection of amniotic sac and membranes, unspecified, first trimester, fetus 3
O41.1014	Infection of amniotic sac and membranes, unspecified, first trimester, fetus 4
O41.1015	Infection of amniotic sac and membranes, unspecified, first trimester, fetus 5
O41.1010	Infection of amniotic sac and membranes, unspecified, first trimester, not applicable or unspecified
O41.1019	Infection of amniotic sac and membranes, unspecified, first trimester, other fetus
O41.1021	Infection of amniotic sac and membranes, unspecified, second trimester, fetus 1
O41.1022	Infection of amniotic sac and membranes, unspecified, second trimester, fetus 2
O41.1023	Infection of amniotic sac and membranes, unspecified, second trimester, fetus 3

O41.1024	Infection of amniotic sac and membranes, unspecified, second trimester, fetus 4
O41.1025	Infection of amniotic sac and membranes, unspecified, second trimester, fetus 5
O41.1020	Infection of amniotic sac and membranes, unspecified, second trimester, not applicable or unspecified
O41.1029	Infection of amniotic sac and membranes, unspecified, second trimester, other fetus
O41.1031	Infection of amniotic sac and membranes, unspecified, third trimester, fetus 1
O41.1032	Infection of amniotic sac and membranes, unspecified, third trimester, fetus 2
O41.1033	Infection of amniotic sac and membranes, unspecified, third trimester, fetus 3
O41.1034	Infection of amniotic sac and membranes, unspecified, third trimester, fetus 4
O41.1035	Infection of amniotic sac and membranes, unspecified, third trimester, fetus 5
O41.1030	Infection of amniotic sac and membranes, unspecified, third trimester, not applicable or unspecified
O41.1039	Infection of amniotic sac and membranes, unspecified, third trimester, other fetus
I40.0	Infective myocarditis
J09.X1	Influenza due to identified novel influenza A virus with pneumonia
J10.08	Influenza due to other identified influenza virus with other specified pneumonia
J10.01	Influenza due to other identified influenza virus with the same other identified influenza virus pneumonia
J10.00	Influenza due to other identified influenza virus with unspecified type of pneumonia
J11.08	Influenza due to unidentified influenza virus with specified pneumonia
J11.00	Influenza due to unidentified influenza virus with unspecified type of pneumonia
Q00.2	Iniencephaly
S34.3XXA	Injury of cauda equina, initial encounter
S35.512A	Injury of left iliac artery, initial encounter
S35.515A	Injury of left iliac vein, initial encounter
S06.826A	Injury of left internal carotid artery, intracranial portion, not elsewhere classified with loss of consciousness greater than 24 hours without return to pre-existing conscious level with patient surviving, initial encounter
S06.827A	Injury of left internal carotid artery, intracranial portion, not elsewhere classified with loss of consciousness of any duration with death due to brain injury prior to regaining consciousness, initial encounter
S06.828A	Injury of left internal carotid artery, intracranial portion, not elsewhere classified with loss of consciousness of any duration with death due to other cause prior to regaining consciousness, initial encounter
S35.59XA	Injury of other iliac blood vessels, initial encounter
S35.511A	Injury of right iliac artery, initial encounter
S35.514A	Injury of right iliac vein, initial encounter
S06.816A	Injury of right internal carotid artery, intracranial portion, not elsewhere classified with loss of consciousness greater than 24 hours without return to pre-existing conscious level with patient surviving, initial encounter
S06.817A	Injury of right internal carotid artery, intracranial portion, not elsewhere classified with loss of consciousness of any duration with death due to brain injury prior to regaining consciousness, initial encounter
S06.818A	Injury of right internal carotid artery, intracranial portion, not elsewhere classified with loss of consciousness of any duration with death due to other cause prior to regaining consciousness, initial encounter
S35.513A	Injury of unspecified iliac artery, initial encounter
S35.50XA	Injury of unspecified iliac blood vessel(s), initial encounter
S35.516A	Injury of unspecified iliac vein, initial encounter
P59.1	Inspissated bile syndrome
P25.0	Interstitial emphysema originating in the perinatal period
P52.4	Intracerebral (nontraumatic) hemorrhage of newborn
P52.9	Intracranial (nontraumatic) hemorrhage of newborn, unspecified
G06.0	Intracranial abscess and granuloma
G07	Intracranial and intraspinal abscess and granuloma in diseases classified elsewhere
G08	Intracranial and intraspinal phlebitis and thrombophlebitis
O67.0	Intrapartum hemorrhage with coagulation defect
G06.1	Intraspinal abscess and granuloma
P52.21	Intraventricular (nontraumatic) hemorrhage, grade 3, of newborn
P52.22	Intraventricular (nontraumatic) hemorrhage, grade 4, of newborn
B44.0	Invasive pulmonary aspergillosis
I40.1	Isolated myocarditis
A83.0	Japanese encephalitis
P57.0	Kernicterus due to isoimmunization
P57.9	Kernicterus, unspecified
E40	Kwashiorkor
S45.012A	Laceration of axillary artery, left side, initial encounter
S45.011A	Laceration of axillary artery, right side, initial encounter
S45.019A	Laceration of axillary artery, unspecified side, initial encounter
S27.432A	Laceration of bronchus, bilateral, initial encounter
S27.431A	Laceration of bronchus, unilateral, initial encounter
S27.439A	Laceration of bronchus, unspecified, initial encounter
S27.813A	Laceration of esophagus (thoracic part), initial encounter
S26.12XA	Laceration of heart without hemopericardium, initial encounter
S26.92XA	Laceration of heart, unspecified with or without hemopericardium, initial encounter
S35.341A	Laceration of inferior mesenteric vein, initial encounter
S35.412A	Laceration of left renal artery, initial encounter
S35.415A	Laceration of left renal vein, initial encounter
S27.332A	Laceration of lung, bilateral, initial encounter
S27.331A	Laceration of lung, unilateral, initial encounter
S27.339A	Laceration of lung, unspecified, initial encounter
S85.012A	Laceration of popliteal artery, left leg, initial encounter
S85.011A	Laceration of popliteal artery, right leg, initial encounter
S85.019A	Laceration of popliteal artery, unspecified leg, initial encounter
S85.512A	Laceration of popliteal vein, left leg, initial encounter
S85.511A	Laceration of popliteal vein, right leg, initial encounter
S85.519A	Laceration of popliteal vein, unspecified leg, initial encounter
S35.311A	Laceration of portal vein, initial encounter
S35.411A	Laceration of right renal artery, initial encounter
S35.414A	Laceration of right renal vein, initial encounter
S35.321A	Laceration of splenic vein, initial encounter
S35.331A	Laceration of superior mesenteric vein, initial encounter
S35.413A	Laceration of unspecified renal artery, initial encounter
S35.416A	Laceration of unspecified renal vein, initial encounter
S31.622A	Laceration with foreign body of abdominal wall, epigastric region with penetration into peritoneal cavity, initial encounter
S31.624A	Laceration with foreign body of abdominal wall, left lower quadrant with penetration into peritoneal cavity, initial encounter
S31.621A	Laceration with foreign body of abdominal wall, left upper quadrant with penetration into peritoneal cavity, initial encounter
S31.625A	Laceration with foreign body of abdominal wall, periumbilic region with penetration into peritoneal cavity, initial encounter
S31.623A	Laceration with foreign body of abdominal wall, right lower quadrant with penetration into peritoneal cavity, initial encounter
S31.620A	Laceration with foreign body of abdominal wall, right upper quadrant with penetration into peritoneal cavity, initial encounter
S31.629A	Laceration with foreign body of abdominal wall, unspecified quadrant with penetration into peritoneal cavity, initial encounter
S11.012A	Laceration with foreign body of larynx, initial encounter
S21.422A	Laceration with foreign body of left back wall of thorax with penetration into thoracic cavity, initial encounter
S21.322A	Laceration with foreign body of left front wall of thorax with penetration into thoracic cavity, initial encounter
S31.021A	Laceration with foreign body of lower back and pelvis with penetration into retroperitoneum, initial encounter
S21.421A	Laceration with foreign body of right back wall of thorax with penetration into thoracic cavity, initial encounter
S21.321A	Laceration with foreign body of right front wall of thorax with penetration into thoracic cavity, initial encounter
S11.022A	Laceration with foreign body of trachea, initial encounter
S21.429A	Laceration with foreign body of unspecified back wall of thorax with penetration into thoracic cavity, initial encounter
S21.329A	Laceration with foreign body of unspecified front wall of thorax with penetration into thoracic cavity, initial encounter
S11.032A	Laceration with foreign body of vocal cord, initial encounter
S31.612A	Laceration without foreign body of abdominal wall, epigastric region with penetration into peritoneal cavity, initial encounter
S31.614A	Laceration without foreign body of abdominal wall, left lower quadrant with penetration into peritoneal cavity, initial encounter
S31.611A	Laceration without foreign body of abdominal wall, left upper quadrant with penetration into peritoneal cavity, initial encounter
S31.615A	Laceration without foreign body of abdominal wall, periumbilic region with penetration into peritoneal cavity, initial encounter
S31.613A	Laceration without foreign body of abdominal wall, right lower quadrant with penetration into peritoneal cavity, initial encounter
S31.610A	Laceration without foreign body of abdominal wall, right upper quadrant with penetration into peritoneal cavity, initial encounter
S31.619A	Laceration without foreign body of abdominal wall, unspecified quadrant with penetration into peritoneal cavity, initial encounter
S11.011A	Laceration without foreign body of larynx, initial encounter
S21.412A	Laceration without foreign body of left back wall of thorax with penetration into thoracic cavity, initial encounter
S21.312A	Laceration without foreign body of left front wall of thorax with penetration into thoracic cavity, initial encounter
S31.011A	Laceration without foreign body of lower back and pelvis with penetration into retroperitoneum, initial encounter
S21.411A	Laceration without foreign body of right back wall of thorax with penetration into thoracic cavity, initial encounter
S21.311A	Laceration without foreign body of right front wall of thorax with penetration into thoracic cavity, initial encounter
S11.021A	Laceration without foreign body of trachea, initial encounter
S21.419A	Laceration without foreign body of unspecified back wall of thorax with penetration into thoracic cavity, initial encounter
S21.319A	Laceration without foreign body of unspecified front wall of thorax with penetration into thoracic cavity, initial encounter
S11.031A	Laceration without foreign body of vocal cord, initial encounter
A50.42	Late congenital syphilitic encephalitis
A50.41	Late congenital syphilitic meningitis
P74.0	Late metabolic acidosis of newborn
A52.14	Late syphilitic encephalitis
A52.13	Late syphilitic meningitis
A48.1	Legionnaires' disease
A32.7	Listerial sepsis
J18.1	Lobar pneumonia, unspecified organism
G83.5	Locked-in state
O44.51	Low lying placenta with hemorrhage, first trimester
O44.52	Low lying placenta with hemorrhage, second trimester
O44.53	Low lying placenta with hemorrhage, third trimester
J84.81	Lymphangioleiomyomatosis
S35.02XA	Major laceration of abdominal aorta, initial encounter
S35.292A	Major laceration of branches of celiac and mesenteric artery, initial encounter

S35.212A	Major laceration of celiac artery, initial encounter
S75.022A	Major laceration of femoral artery, left leg, initial encounter
S75.021A	Major laceration of femoral artery, right leg, initial encounter
S75.029A	Major laceration of femoral artery, unspecified leg, initial encounter
S75.122A	Major laceration of femoral vein at hip and thigh level, left leg, initial encounter
S75.121A	Major laceration of femoral vein at hip and thigh level, right leg, initial encounter
S75.129A	Major laceration of femoral vein at hip and thigh level, unspecified leg, initial encounter
S26.022A	Major laceration of heart with hemopericardium, initial encounter
S35.232A	Major laceration of inferior mesenteric artery, initial encounter
S35.12XA	Major laceration of inferior vena cava, initial encounter
S25.122A	Major laceration of left innominate or subclavian artery, initial encounter
S25.322A	Major laceration of left innominate or subclavian vein, initial encounter
S37.062A	Major laceration of left kidney, initial encounter
S25.422A	Major laceration of left pulmonary blood vessels, initial encounter
S36.116A	Major laceration of liver, initial encounter
S25.121A	Major laceration of right innominate or subclavian artery, initial encounter
S25.321A	Major laceration of right innominate or subclavian vein, initial encounter
S37.061A	Major laceration of right kidney, initial encounter
S25.421A	Major laceration of right pulmonary blood vessels, initial encounter
S36.032A	Major laceration of spleen, initial encounter
S35.222A	Major laceration of superior mesenteric artery, initial encounter
S25.22XA	Major laceration of superior vena cava, initial encounter
S25.02XA	Major laceration of thoracic aorta, initial encounter
S25.129A	Major laceration of unspecified innominate or subclavian artery, initial encounter
S25.329A	Major laceration of unspecified innominate or subclavian vein, initial encounter
S37.069A	Major laceration of unspecified kidney, initial encounter
S25.429A	Major laceration of unspecified pulmonary blood vessels, initial encounter
G21.0	Malignant neuroleptic syndrome
E42	Marasmic kwashiorkor
P26.1	Massive pulmonary hemorrhage originating in the perinatal period
O34.31	Maternal care for cervical incompetence, first trimester
O34.32	Maternal care for cervical incompetence, second trimester
O34.33	Maternal care for cervical incompetence, third trimester
B05.0	Measles complicated by encephalitis
B05.2	Measles complicated by pneumonia
P24.01	Meconium aspiration with respiratory symptoms
E84.11	Meconium ileus in cystic fibrosis
J98.51	Mediastinitis
A17.1	Meningeal tuberculoma
G03.8	Meningitis due to other specified causes
G01	Meningitis in bacterial diseases classified elsewhere
G02	Meningitis in other infectious and parasitic diseases classified elsewhere
G03.9	Meningitis, unspecified
A39.50	Meningococcal carditis, unspecified
A39.81	Meningococcal encephalitis
A39.51	Meningococcal endocarditis
A39.0	Meningococcal meningitis
A39.52	Meningococcal myocarditis
A39.53	Meningococcal pericarditis
A39.4	Meningococcemia, unspecified
G93.41	Metabolic encephalopathy
S26.020A	Mild laceration of heart with hemopericardium, initial encounter
A19.9	Miliary tuberculosis, unspecified
S32.111B	Minimally displaced Zone I fracture of sacrum, initial encounter for open fracture
S32.121B	Minimally displaced Zone II fracture of sacrum, initial encounter for open fracture
S32.131B	Minimally displaced Zone III fracture of sacrum, initial encounter for open fracture
S35.01XA	Minor laceration of abdominal aorta, initial encounter
S35.291A	Minor laceration of branches of celiac and mesenteric artery, initial encounter
S35.211A	Minor laceration of celiac artery, initial encounter
S75.012A	Minor laceration of femoral artery, left leg, initial encounter
S75.011A	Minor laceration of femoral artery, right leg, initial encounter
S75.019A	Minor laceration of femoral artery, unspecified leg, initial encounter
S75.112A	Minor laceration of femoral vein at hip and thigh level, left leg, initial encounter
S75.111A	Minor laceration of femoral vein at hip and thigh level, right leg, initial encounter
S75.119A	Minor laceration of femoral vein at hip and thigh level, unspecified leg, initial encounter
S35.231A	Minor laceration of inferior mesenteric artery, initial encounter
S35.11XA	Minor laceration of inferior vena cava, initial encounter
S25.112A	Minor laceration of left innominate or subclavian artery, initial encounter
S25.312A	Minor laceration of left innominate or subclavian vein, initial encounter
S25.412A	Minor laceration of left pulmonary blood vessels, initial encounter
S25.111A	Minor laceration of right innominate or subclavian artery, initial encounter
S25.311A	Minor laceration of right innominate or subclavian vein, initial encounter
S25.411A	Minor laceration of right pulmonary blood vessels, initial encounter
S35.221A	Minor laceration of superior mesenteric artery, initial encounter
S25.21XA	Minor laceration of superior vena cava, initial encounter
S25.01XA	Minor laceration of thoracic aorta, initial encounter
S25.119A	Minor laceration of unspecified innominate or subclavian artery, initial encounter

S25.319A	Minor laceration of unspecified innominate or subclavian vein, initial encounter
S25.419A	Minor laceration of unspecified pulmonary blood vessels, initial encounter
S26.021A	Moderate laceration of heart with hemopericardium, initial encounter
S36.115A	Moderate laceration of liver, initial encounter
S36.031A	Moderate laceration of spleen, initial encounter
S52.272B	Monteggia's fracture of left ulna, initial encounter for open fracture type I or II
S52.272C	Monteggia's fracture of left ulna, initial encounter for open fracture type IIIA, IIIB, or IIIC
S52.271B	Monteggia's fracture of right ulna, initial encounter for open fracture type I or II
S52.271C	Monteggia's fracture of right ulna, initial encounter for open fracture type IIIA, IIIB, or IIIC
S52.279B	Monteggia's fracture of unspecified ulna, initial encounter for open fracture type I or II
S52.279C	Monteggia's fracture of unspecified ulna, initial encounter for open fracture type IIIA, IIIB, or IIIC
A83.9	Mosquito-borne viral encephalitis, unspecified
B46.5	Mucormycosis, unspecified
S32.810B	Multiple fractures of pelvis with stable disruption of pelvic ring, initial encounter for open fracture
S32.811B	Multiple fractures of pelvis with unstable disruption of pelvic ring, initial encounter for open fracture
S32.82XB	Multiple fractures of pelvis without disruption of pelvic ring, initial encounter for open fracture
S22.43XB	Multiple fractures of ribs, bilateral, initial encounter for open fracture
S22.42XB	Multiple fractures of ribs, left side, initial encounter for open fracture
S22.41XB	Multiple fractures of ribs, right side, initial encounter for open fracture
S22.49XB	Multiple fractures of ribs, unspecified side, initial encounter for open fracture
I26.94	Multiple subsegmental pulmonary emboli without acute cor pulmonale
B26.2	Mumps encephalitis
B26.1	Mumps meningitis
G70.01	Myasthenia gravis with (acute) exacerbation
G05.4	Myelitis in diseases classified elsewhere
G04.91	Myelitis, unspecified
I21.A1	Myocardial infarction type 2
I41	Myocarditis in diseases classified elsewhere
E03.5	Myxedema coma
P77.9	Necrotizing enterocolitis in newborn, unspecified
K55.30	Necrotizing enterocolitis, unspecified
M72.6	Necrotizing fasciitis
P37.2	Neonatal (disseminated) listeriosis
P24.11	Neonatal aspiration of (clear) amniotic fluid and mucus with respiratory symptoms
P24.21	Neonatal aspiration of blood with respiratory symptoms
P24.31	Neonatal aspiration of milk and regurgitated food with respiratory symptoms
P91.4	Neonatal cerebral depression
P91.3	Neonatal cerebral irritability
P91.0	Neonatal cerebral ischemia
P91.2	Neonatal cerebral leukomalacia
P91.5	Neonatal coma
P59.29	Neonatal jaundice from other hepatocellular damage
P59.20	Neonatal jaundice from unspecified hepatocellular damage
P54.1	Neonatal melena
P54.2	Neonatal rectal hemorrhage
J84.841	Neuroendocrine cell hyperplasia of infancy
I21.4	Non-ST elevation (NSTEMI) myocardial infarction
S72.135A	Nondisplaced apophyseal fracture of left femur, initial encounter for closed fracture
S72.135B	Nondisplaced apophyseal fracture of left femur, initial encounter for open fracture type I or II
S72.135C	Nondisplaced apophyseal fracture of left femur, initial encounter for open fracture type IIIA, IIIB, or IIIC
S72.134A	Nondisplaced apophyseal fracture of right femur, initial encounter for closed fracture
S72.134B	Nondisplaced apophyseal fracture of right femur, initial encounter for open fracture type I or II
S72.134C	Nondisplaced apophyseal fracture of right femur, initial encounter for open fracture type IIIA, IIIB, or IIIC
S72.136A	Nondisplaced apophyseal fracture of unspecified femur, initial encounter for closed fracture
S72.136B	Nondisplaced apophyseal fracture of unspecified femur, initial encounter for open fracture type I or II
S72.136C	Nondisplaced apophyseal fracture of unspecified femur, initial encounter for open fracture type IIIA, IIIB, or IIIC
S72.065A	Nondisplaced articular fracture of head of left femur, initial encounter for closed fracture
S72.065B	Nondisplaced articular fracture of head of left femur, initial encounter for open fracture type I or II
S72.065C	Nondisplaced articular fracture of head of left femur, initial encounter for open fracture type IIIA, IIIB, or IIIC
S72.064A	Nondisplaced articular fracture of head of right femur, initial encounter for closed fracture
S72.064B	Nondisplaced articular fracture of head of right femur, initial encounter for open fracture type I or II
S72.064C	Nondisplaced articular fracture of head of right femur, initial encounter for open fracture type IIIA, IIIB, or IIIC
S72.066A	Nondisplaced articular fracture of head of unspecified femur, initial encounter for closed fracture

S72.066B Nondisplaced articular fracture of head of unspecified femur, initial encounter for open fracture type I or II

S72.066C Nondisplaced articular fracture of head of unspecified femur, initial encounter for open fracture type IIIA, IIIB, or IIIC

S32.465A Nondisplaced associated transverse-posterior fracture of left acetabulum, initial encounter for closed fracture

S32.465B Nondisplaced associated transverse-posterior fracture of left acetabulum, initial encounter for open fracture

S32.464A Nondisplaced associated transverse-posterior fracture of right acetabulum, initial encounter for closed fracture

S32.464B Nondisplaced associated transverse-posterior fracture of right acetabulum, initial encounter for open fracture

S32.466A Nondisplaced associated transverse-posterior fracture of unspecified acetabulum, initial encounter for closed fracture

S32.466B Nondisplaced associated transverse-posterior fracture of unspecified acetabulum, initial encounter for open fracture

S32.315B Nondisplaced avulsion fracture of left ilium, initial encounter for open fracture

S32.615B Nondisplaced avulsion fracture of left ischium, initial encounter for open fracture

S32.314B Nondisplaced avulsion fracture of right ilium, initial encounter for open fracture

S32.614B Nondisplaced avulsion fracture of right ischium, initial encounter for open fracture

S32.316B Nondisplaced avulsion fracture of unspecified ilium, initial encounter for open fracture

S32.616B Nondisplaced avulsion fracture of unspecified ischium, initial encounter for open fracture

S82.145B Nondisplaced bicondylar fracture of left tibia, initial encounter for open fracture type I or II

S82.145C Nondisplaced bicondylar fracture of left tibia, initial encounter for open fracture type IIIA, IIIB, or IIIC

S82.144B Nondisplaced bicondylar fracture of right tibia, initial encounter for open fracture type I or II

S82.144C Nondisplaced bicondylar fracture of right tibia, initial encounter for open fracture type IIIA, IIIB, or IIIC

S82.146B Nondisplaced bicondylar fracture of unspecified tibia, initial encounter for open fracture type I or II

S82.146C Nondisplaced bicondylar fracture of unspecified tibia, initial encounter for open fracture type IIIA, IIIB, or IIIC

S42.355B Nondisplaced comminuted fracture of shaft of humerus, left arm, initial encounter for open fracture

S42.354B Nondisplaced comminuted fracture of shaft of humerus, right arm, initial encounter for open fracture

S42.356B Nondisplaced comminuted fracture of shaft of humerus, unspecified arm, initial encounter for open fracture

S72.355A Nondisplaced comminuted fracture of shaft of left femur, initial encounter for closed fracture

S72.355B Nondisplaced comminuted fracture of shaft of left femur, initial encounter for open fracture type I or II

S72.355C Nondisplaced comminuted fracture of shaft of left femur, initial encounter for open fracture type IIIA, IIIB, or IIIC

S82.455B Nondisplaced comminuted fracture of shaft of left fibula, initial encounter for open fracture type I or II

S82.455C Nondisplaced comminuted fracture of shaft of left fibula, initial encounter for open fracture type IIIA, IIIB, or IIIC

S82.255B Nondisplaced comminuted fracture of shaft of left tibia, initial encounter for open fracture type I or II

S82.255C Nondisplaced comminuted fracture of shaft of left tibia, initial encounter for open fracture type IIIA, IIIB, or IIIC

S52.355B Nondisplaced comminuted fracture of shaft of radius, left arm, initial encounter for open fracture type I or II

S52.355C Nondisplaced comminuted fracture of shaft of radius, left arm, initial encounter for open fracture type IIIA, IIIB, or IIIC

S52.354B Nondisplaced comminuted fracture of shaft of radius, right arm, initial encounter for open fracture type I or II

S52.354C Nondisplaced comminuted fracture of shaft of radius, right arm, initial encounter for open fracture type IIIA, IIIB, or IIIC

S52.356B Nondisplaced comminuted fracture of shaft of radius, unspecified arm, initial encounter for open fracture type I or II

S52.356C Nondisplaced comminuted fracture of shaft of radius, unspecified arm, initial encounter for open fracture type IIIA, IIIB, or IIIC

S72.354A Nondisplaced comminuted fracture of shaft of right femur, initial encounter for closed fracture

S72.354B Nondisplaced comminuted fracture of shaft of right femur, initial encounter for open fracture type I or II

S72.354C Nondisplaced comminuted fracture of shaft of right femur, initial encounter for open fracture type IIIA, IIIB, or IIIC

S82.454B Nondisplaced comminuted fracture of shaft of right fibula, initial encounter for open fracture type I or II

S82.454C Nondisplaced comminuted fracture of shaft of right fibula, initial encounter for open fracture type IIIA, IIIB, or IIIC

S82.254B Nondisplaced comminuted fracture of shaft of right tibia, initial encounter for open fracture type I or II

S82.254C Nondisplaced comminuted fracture of shaft of right tibia, initial encounter for open fracture type IIIA, IIIB, or IIIC

S52.255B Nondisplaced comminuted fracture of shaft of ulna, left arm, initial encounter for open fracture type I or II

S52.255C Nondisplaced comminuted fracture of shaft of ulna, left arm, initial encounter for open fracture type IIIA, IIIB, or IIIC

S52.254B Nondisplaced comminuted fracture of shaft of ulna, right arm, initial encounter for open fracture type I or II

S52.254C Nondisplaced comminuted fracture of shaft of ulna, right arm, initial encounter for open fracture type IIIA, IIIB, or IIIC

S52.256B Nondisplaced comminuted fracture of shaft of ulna, unspecified arm, initial encounter for open fracture type I or II

S52.256C Nondisplaced comminuted fracture of shaft of ulna, unspecified arm, initial encounter for open fracture type IIIA, IIIB, or IIIC

S72.356A Nondisplaced comminuted fracture of shaft of unspecified femur, initial encounter for closed fracture

S72.356B Nondisplaced comminuted fracture of shaft of unspecified femur, initial encounter for open fracture type I or II

S72.356C Nondisplaced comminuted fracture of shaft of unspecified femur, initial encounter for open fracture type IIIA, IIIB, or IIIC

S82.456B Nondisplaced comminuted fracture of shaft of unspecified fibula, initial encounter for open fracture type I or II

S82.456C Nondisplaced comminuted fracture of shaft of unspecified fibula, initial encounter for open fracture type IIIA, IIIB, or IIIC

S82.256B Nondisplaced comminuted fracture of shaft of unspecified tibia, initial encounter for open fracture type I or II

S82.256C Nondisplaced comminuted fracture of shaft of unspecified tibia, initial encounter for open fracture type IIIA, IIIB, or IIIC

S42.425B Nondisplaced comminuted supracondylar fracture without intercondylar fracture of left humerus, initial encounter for open fracture

S42.424B Nondisplaced comminuted supracondylar fracture without intercondylar fracture of right humerus, initial encounter for open fracture

S42.426B Nondisplaced comminuted supracondylar fracture without intercondylar fracture of unspecified humerus, initial encounter for open fracture

S32.485A Nondisplaced dome fracture of left acetabulum, initial encounter for closed fracture

S32.485B Nondisplaced dome fracture of left acetabulum, initial encounter for open fracture

S32.484A Nondisplaced dome fracture of right acetabulum, initial encounter for closed fracture

S32.484B Nondisplaced dome fracture of right acetabulum, initial encounter for open fracture

S32.486A Nondisplaced dome fracture of unspecified acetabulum, initial encounter for closed fracture

S32.486B Nondisplaced dome fracture of unspecified acetabulum, initial encounter for open fracture

S42.435B Nondisplaced fracture (avulsion) of lateral epicondyle of left humerus, initial encounter for open fracture

S42.434B Nondisplaced fracture (avulsion) of lateral epicondyle of right humerus, initial encounter for open fracture

S42.436B Nondisplaced fracture (avulsion) of lateral epicondyle of unspecified humerus, initial encounter for open fracture

S42.445B Nondisplaced fracture (avulsion) of medial epicondyle of left humerus, initial encounter for open fracture

S42.444B Nondisplaced fracture (avulsion) of medial epicondyle of right humerus, initial encounter for open fracture

S42.446B Nondisplaced fracture (avulsion) of medial epicondyle of unspecified humerus, initial encounter for open fracture

S32.435A Nondisplaced fracture of anterior column [iliopubic] of left acetabulum, initial encounter for closed fracture

S32.435B Nondisplaced fracture of anterior column [iliopubic] of left acetabulum, initial encounter for open fracture

S32.434A Nondisplaced fracture of anterior column [iliopubic] of right acetabulum, initial encounter for closed fracture

S32.434B Nondisplaced fracture of anterior column [iliopubic] of right acetabulum, initial encounter for open fracture

S32.436A Nondisplaced fracture of anterior column [iliopubic] of unspecified acetabulum, initial encounter for closed fracture

S32.436B Nondisplaced fracture of anterior column [iliopubic] of unspecified acetabulum, initial encounter for open fracture

S32.415A Nondisplaced fracture of anterior wall of left acetabulum, initial encounter for closed fracture

S32.415B Nondisplaced fracture of anterior wall of left acetabulum, initial encounter for open fracture

S32.414A Nondisplaced fracture of anterior wall of right acetabulum, initial encounter for closed fracture

S32.414B Nondisplaced fracture of anterior wall of right acetabulum, initial encounter for open fracture

S32.416A Nondisplaced fracture of anterior wall of unspecified acetabulum, initial encounter for closed fracture

S32.416B Nondisplaced fracture of anterior wall of unspecified acetabulum, initial encounter for open fracture

S72.045A Nondisplaced fracture of base of neck of left femur, initial encounter for closed fracture

S72.045B Nondisplaced fracture of base of neck of left femur, initial encounter for open fracture type I or II

S72.045C Nondisplaced fracture of base of neck of left femur, initial encounter for open fracture type IIIA, IIIB, or IIIC

S72.044A Nondisplaced fracture of base of neck of right femur, initial encounter for closed fracture

S72.044B Nondisplaced fracture of base of neck of right femur, initial encounter for open fracture type I or II

S72.044C Nondisplaced fracture of base of neck of right femur, initial encounter for open fracture type IIIA, IIIB, or IIIC

S72.046A Nondisplaced fracture of base of neck of unspecified femur, initial encounter for closed fracture

S72.046B Nondisplaced fracture of base of neck of unspecified femur, initial encounter for open fracture type I or II

S72.046C   Nondisplaced fracture of base of neck of unspecified femur, initial encounter for open fracture type IIIA, IIIB, or IIIC

S52.045B   Nondisplaced fracture of coronoid process of left ulna, initial encounter for open fracture type I or II

S52.045C   Nondisplaced fracture of coronoid process of left ulna, initial encounter for open fracture type IIIA, IIIB, or IIIC

S52.044B   Nondisplaced fracture of coronoid process of right ulna, initial encounter for open fracture type I or II

S52.044C   Nondisplaced fracture of coronoid process of right ulna, initial encounter for open fracture type IIIA, IIIB, or IIIC

S52.046B   Nondisplaced fracture of coronoid process of unspecified ulna, initial encounter for open fracture type I or II

S52.046C   Nondisplaced fracture of coronoid process of unspecified ulna, initial encounter for open fracture type IIIA, IIIB, or IIIC

S72.025A   Nondisplaced fracture of epiphysis (separation) (upper) of left femur, initial encounter for closed fracture

S72.025B   Nondisplaced fracture of epiphysis (separation) (upper) of left femur, initial encounter for open fracture type I or II

S72.025C   Nondisplaced fracture of epiphysis (separation) (upper) of left femur, initial encounter for open fracture type IIIA, IIIB, or IIIC

S72.024A   Nondisplaced fracture of epiphysis (separation) (upper) of right femur, initial encounter for closed fracture

S72.024B   Nondisplaced fracture of epiphysis (separation) (upper) of right femur, initial encounter for open fracture type I or II

S72.024C   Nondisplaced fracture of epiphysis (separation) (upper) of right femur, initial encounter for open fracture type IIIA, IIIB, or IIIC

S72.026A   Nondisplaced fracture of epiphysis (separation) (upper) of unspecified femur, initial encounter for closed fracture

S72.026B   Nondisplaced fracture of epiphysis (separation) (upper) of unspecified femur, initial encounter for open fracture type I or II

S72.026C   Nondisplaced fracture of epiphysis (separation) (upper) of unspecified femur, initial encounter for open fracture type IIIA, IIIB, or IIIC

S72.115A   Nondisplaced fracture of greater trochanter of left femur, initial encounter for closed fracture

S72.115B   Nondisplaced fracture of greater trochanter of left femur, initial encounter for open fracture type I or II

S72.115C   Nondisplaced fracture of greater trochanter of left femur, initial encounter for open fracture type IIIA, IIIB, or IIIC

S72.114A   Nondisplaced fracture of greater trochanter of right femur, initial encounter for closed fracture

S72.114B   Nondisplaced fracture of greater trochanter of right femur, initial encounter for open fracture type I or II

S72.114C   Nondisplaced fracture of greater trochanter of right femur, initial encounter for open fracture type IIIA, IIIB, or IIIC

S72.116A   Nondisplaced fracture of greater trochanter of unspecified femur, initial encounter for closed fracture

S72.116B   Nondisplaced fracture of greater trochanter of unspecified femur, initial encounter for open fracture type I or II

S72.116C   Nondisplaced fracture of greater trochanter of unspecified femur, initial encounter for open fracture type IIIA, IIIB, or IIIC

S42.255B   Nondisplaced fracture of greater tuberosity of left humerus, initial encounter for open fracture

S42.254B   Nondisplaced fracture of greater tuberosity of right humerus, initial encounter for open fracture

S42.256B   Nondisplaced fracture of greater tuberosity of unspecified humerus, initial encounter for open fracture

S52.125B   Nondisplaced fracture of head of left radius, initial encounter for open fracture type I or II

S52.125C   Nondisplaced fracture of head of left radius, initial encounter for open fracture type IIIA, IIIB, or IIIC

S52.124B   Nondisplaced fracture of head of right radius, initial encounter for open fracture type I or II

S52.124C   Nondisplaced fracture of head of right radius, initial encounter for open fracture type IIIA, IIIB, or IIIC

S52.126B   Nondisplaced fracture of head of unspecified radius, initial encounter for open fracture type I or II

S52.126C   Nondisplaced fracture of head of unspecified radius, initial encounter for open fracture type IIIA, IIIB, or IIIC

S72.425B   Nondisplaced fracture of lateral condyle of left femur, initial encounter for open fracture type I or II

S72.425C   Nondisplaced fracture of lateral condyle of left femur, initial encounter for open fracture type IIIA, IIIB, or IIIC

S42.455B   Nondisplaced fracture of lateral condyle of left humerus, initial encounter for open fracture

S82.125B   Nondisplaced fracture of lateral condyle of left tibia, initial encounter for open fracture type I or II

S82.125C   Nondisplaced fracture of lateral condyle of left tibia, initial encounter for open fracture type IIIA, IIIB, or IIIC

S72.424B   Nondisplaced fracture of lateral condyle of right femur, initial encounter for open fracture type I or II

S72.424C   Nondisplaced fracture of lateral condyle of right femur, initial encounter for open fracture type IIIA, IIIB, or IIIC

S42.454B   Nondisplaced fracture of lateral condyle of right humerus, initial encounter for open fracture

S82.124B   Nondisplaced fracture of lateral condyle of right tibia, initial encounter for open fracture type I or II

S82.124C   Nondisplaced fracture of lateral condyle of right tibia, initial encounter for open fracture type IIIA, IIIB, or IIIC

S72.426B   Nondisplaced fracture of lateral condyle of unspecified femur, initial encounter for open fracture type I or II

S72.426C   Nondisplaced fracture of lateral condyle of unspecified femur, initial encounter for open fracture type IIIA, IIIB, or IIIC

S42.456B   Nondisplaced fracture of lateral condyle of unspecified humerus, initial encounter for open fracture

S82.126B   Nondisplaced fracture of lateral condyle of unspecified tibia, initial encounter for open fracture type I or II

S82.126C   Nondisplaced fracture of lateral condyle of unspecified tibia, initial encounter for open fracture type IIIA, IIIB, or IIIC

S52.515B   Nondisplaced fracture of left radial styloid process, initial encounter for open fracture type I or II

S52.515C   Nondisplaced fracture of left radial styloid process, initial encounter for open fracture type IIIA, IIIB, or IIIC

S82.115B   Nondisplaced fracture of left tibial spine, initial encounter for open fracture type I or II

S82.115C   Nondisplaced fracture of left tibial spine, initial encounter for open fracture type IIIA, IIIB, or IIIC

S82.155B   Nondisplaced fracture of left tibial tuberosity, initial encounter for open fracture type I or II

S82.155C   Nondisplaced fracture of left tibial tuberosity, initial encounter for open fracture type IIIA, IIIB, or IIIC

S52.615B   Nondisplaced fracture of left ulna styloid process, initial encounter for open fracture type I or II

S52.615C   Nondisplaced fracture of left ulna styloid process, initial encounter for open fracture type IIIA, IIIB, or IIIC

S72.125A   Nondisplaced fracture of lesser trochanter of left femur, initial encounter for closed fracture

S72.125B   Nondisplaced fracture of lesser trochanter of left femur, initial encounter for open fracture type I or II

S72.125C   Nondisplaced fracture of lesser trochanter of left femur, initial encounter for open fracture type IIIA, IIIB, or IIIC

S72.124A   Nondisplaced fracture of lesser trochanter of right femur, initial encounter for closed fracture

S72.124B   Nondisplaced fracture of lesser trochanter of right femur, initial encounter for open fracture type I or II

S72.124C   Nondisplaced fracture of lesser trochanter of right femur, initial encounter for open fracture type IIIA, IIIB, or IIIC

S72.126A   Nondisplaced fracture of lesser trochanter of unspecified femur, initial encounter for closed fracture

S72.126B   Nondisplaced fracture of lesser trochanter of unspecified femur, initial encounter for open fracture type I or II

S72.126C   Nondisplaced fracture of lesser trochanter of unspecified femur, initial encounter for open fracture type IIIA, IIIB, or IIIC

S42.265B   Nondisplaced fracture of lesser tuberosity of left humerus, initial encounter for open fracture

S42.264B   Nondisplaced fracture of lesser tuberosity of right humerus, initial encounter for open fracture

S42.266B   Nondisplaced fracture of lesser tuberosity of unspecified humerus, initial encounter for open fracture

S72.445B   Nondisplaced fracture of lower epiphysis (separation) of left femur, initial encounter for open fracture type I or II

S72.445C   Nondisplaced fracture of lower epiphysis (separation) of left femur, initial encounter for open fracture type IIIA, IIIB, or IIIC

S72.444B   Nondisplaced fracture of lower epiphysis (separation) of right femur, initial encounter for open fracture type I or II

S72.444C   Nondisplaced fracture of lower epiphysis (separation) of right femur, initial encounter for open fracture type IIIA, IIIB, or IIIC

S72.446B   Nondisplaced fracture of lower epiphysis (separation) of unspecified femur, initial encounter for open fracture type I or II

S72.446C   Nondisplaced fracture of lower epiphysis (separation) of unspecified femur, initial encounter for open fracture type IIIA, IIIB, or IIIC

S72.435B   Nondisplaced fracture of medial condyle of left femur, initial encounter for open fracture type I or II

S72.435C   Nondisplaced fracture of medial condyle of left femur, initial encounter for open fracture type IIIA, IIIB, or IIIC

S42.465B   Nondisplaced fracture of medial condyle of left humerus, initial encounter for open fracture

S82.135B   Nondisplaced fracture of medial condyle of left tibia, initial encounter for open fracture type I or II

S82.135C   Nondisplaced fracture of medial condyle of left tibia, initial encounter for open fracture type IIIA, IIIB, or IIIC

S72.434B   Nondisplaced fracture of medial condyle of right femur, initial encounter for open fracture type I or II

S72.434C   Nondisplaced fracture of medial condyle of right femur, initial encounter for open fracture type IIIA, IIIB, or IIIC

S42.464B   Nondisplaced fracture of medial condyle of right humerus, initial encounter for open fracture

S82.134B   Nondisplaced fracture of medial condyle of right tibia, initial encounter for open fracture type I or II

S82.134C   Nondisplaced fracture of medial condyle of right tibia, initial encounter for open fracture type IIIA, IIIB, or IIIC

S72.436B   Nondisplaced fracture of medial condyle of unspecified femur, initial encounter for open fracture type I or II

S72.436C   Nondisplaced fracture of medial condyle of unspecified femur, initial encounter for open fracture type IIIA, IIIB, or IIIC

S42.466B   Nondisplaced fracture of medial condyle of unspecified humerus, initial encounter for open fracture

S82.136B   Nondisplaced fracture of medial condyle of unspecified tibia, initial encounter for open fracture type I or II

S82.136C   Nondisplaced fracture of medial condyle of unspecified tibia, initial encounter for open fracture type IIIA, IIIB, or IIIC

S32.475A Nondisplaced fracture of medial wall of left acetabulum, initial encounter for closed fracture

S32.475B Nondisplaced fracture of medial wall of left acetabulum, initial encounter for open fracture

S32.474A Nondisplaced fracture of medial wall of right acetabulum, initial encounter for closed fracture

S32.474B Nondisplaced fracture of medial wall of right acetabulum, initial encounter for open fracture

S32.476A Nondisplaced fracture of medial wall of unspecified acetabulum, initial encounter for closed fracture

S32.476B Nondisplaced fracture of medial wall of unspecified acetabulum, initial encounter for open fracture

S52.135B Nondisplaced fracture of neck of left radius, initial encounter for open fracture type I or II

S52.135C Nondisplaced fracture of neck of left radius, initial encounter for open fracture type IIIA, IIIB, or IIIC

S52.134B Nondisplaced fracture of neck of right radius, initial encounter for open fracture type I or II

S52.134C Nondisplaced fracture of neck of right radius, initial encounter for open fracture type IIIA, IIIB, or IIIC

S52.136B Nondisplaced fracture of neck of unspecified radius, initial encounter for open fracture type I or II

S52.136C Nondisplaced fracture of neck of unspecified radius, initial encounter for open fracture type IIIA, IIIB, or IIIC

S52.035B Nondisplaced fracture of olecranon process with intraarticular extension of left ulna, initial encounter for open fracture type I or II

S52.035C Nondisplaced fracture of olecranon process with intraarticular extension of left ulna, initial encounter for open fracture type IIIA, IIIB, or IIIC

S52.034B Nondisplaced fracture of olecranon process with intraarticular extension of right ulna, initial encounter for open fracture type I or II

S52.034C Nondisplaced fracture of olecranon process with intraarticular extension of right ulna, initial encounter for open fracture type IIIA, IIIB, or IIIC

S52.036B Nondisplaced fracture of olecranon process with intraarticular extension of unspecified ulna, initial encounter for open fracture type I or II

S52.036C Nondisplaced fracture of olecranon process with intraarticular extension of unspecified ulna, initial encounter for open fracture type IIIA, IIIB, or IIIC

S52.025B Nondisplaced fracture of olecranon process without intraarticular extension of left ulna, initial encounter for open fracture type I or II

S52.025C Nondisplaced fracture of olecranon process without intraarticular extension of left ulna, initial encounter for open fracture type IIIA, IIIB, or IIIC

S52.024B Nondisplaced fracture of olecranon process without intraarticular extension of right ulna, initial encounter for open fracture type I or II

S52.024C Nondisplaced fracture of olecranon process without intraarticular extension of right ulna, initial encounter for open fracture type IIIA, IIIB, or IIIC

S52.026B Nondisplaced fracture of olecranon process without intraarticular extension of unspecified ulna, initial encounter for open fracture type I or II

S52.026C Nondisplaced fracture of olecranon process without intraarticular extension of unspecified ulna, initial encounter for open fracture type IIIA, IIIB, or IIIC

S32.445A Nondisplaced fracture of posterior column [ilioischial] of left acetabulum, initial encounter for closed fracture

S32.445B Nondisplaced fracture of posterior column [ilioischial] of left acetabulum, initial encounter for open fracture

S32.444A Nondisplaced fracture of posterior column [ilioischial] of right acetabulum, initial encounter for closed fracture

S32.444B Nondisplaced fracture of posterior column [ilioischial] of right acetabulum, initial encounter for open fracture

S32.446A Nondisplaced fracture of posterior column [ilioischial] of unspecified acetabulum, initial encounter for closed fracture

S32.446B Nondisplaced fracture of posterior column [ilioischial] of unspecified acetabulum, initial encounter for open fracture

S32.425A Nondisplaced fracture of posterior wall of left acetabulum, initial encounter for closed fracture

S32.425B Nondisplaced fracture of posterior wall of left acetabulum, initial encounter for open fracture

S32.424A Nondisplaced fracture of posterior wall of right acetabulum, initial encounter for closed fracture

S32.424B Nondisplaced fracture of posterior wall of right acetabulum, initial encounter for open fracture

S32.426A Nondisplaced fracture of posterior wall of unspecified acetabulum, initial encounter for closed fracture

S32.426B Nondisplaced fracture of posterior wall of unspecified acetabulum, initial encounter for open fracture

S52.514B Nondisplaced fracture of right radial styloid process, initial encounter for open fracture type I or II

S52.514C Nondisplaced fracture of right radial styloid process, initial encounter for open fracture type IIIA, IIIB, or IIIC

S82.114B Nondisplaced fracture of right tibial spine, initial encounter for open fracture type I or II

S82.114C Nondisplaced fracture of right tibial spine, initial encounter for open fracture type IIIA, IIIB, or IIIC

S82.154B Nondisplaced fracture of right tibial tuberosity, initial encounter for open fracture type I or II

S82.154C Nondisplaced fracture of right tibial tuberosity, initial encounter for open fracture type IIIA, IIIB, or IIIC

S52.614B Nondisplaced fracture of right ulna styloid process, initial encounter for open fracture type I or II

S52.614C Nondisplaced fracture of right ulna styloid process, initial encounter for open fracture type IIIA, IIIB, or IIIC

S52.516B Nondisplaced fracture of unspecified radial styloid process, initial encounter for open fracture type I or II

S52.516C Nondisplaced fracture of unspecified radial styloid process, initial encounter for open fracture type IIIA, IIIB, or IIIC

S82.116B Nondisplaced fracture of unspecified tibial spine, initial encounter for open fracture type I or II

S82.116C Nondisplaced fracture of unspecified tibial spine, initial encounter for open fracture type IIIA, IIIB, or IIIC

S82.156B Nondisplaced fracture of unspecified tibial tuberosity, initial encounter for open fracture type I or II

S82.156C Nondisplaced fracture of unspecified tibial tuberosity, initial encounter for open fracture type IIIA, IIIB, or IIIC

S52.616B Nondisplaced fracture of unspecified ulna styloid process, initial encounter for open fracture type I or II

S52.616C Nondisplaced fracture of unspecified ulna styloid process, initial encounter for open fracture type IIIA, IIIB, or IIIC

S72.145A Nondisplaced intertrochanteric fracture of left femur, initial encounter for closed fracture

S72.145B Nondisplaced intertrochanteric fracture of left femur, initial encounter for open fracture type I or II

S72.145C Nondisplaced intertrochanteric fracture of left femur, initial encounter for open fracture type IIIA, IIIB, or IIIC

S72.144A Nondisplaced intertrochanteric fracture of right femur, initial encounter for closed fracture

S72.144B Nondisplaced intertrochanteric fracture of right femur, initial encounter for open fracture type I or II

S72.144C Nondisplaced intertrochanteric fracture of right femur, initial encounter for open fracture type IIIA, IIIB, or IIIC

S72.146A Nondisplaced intertrochanteric fracture of unspecified femur, initial encounter for closed fracture

S72.146B Nondisplaced intertrochanteric fracture of unspecified femur, initial encounter for open fracture type I or II

S72.146C Nondisplaced intertrochanteric fracture of unspecified femur, initial encounter for open fracture type IIIA, IIIB, or IIIC

S12.041B Nondisplaced lateral mass fracture of first cervical vertebra, initial encounter for open fracture

S82.865B Nondisplaced Maisonneuve's fracture of left leg, initial encounter for open fracture type I or II

S82.865C Nondisplaced Maisonneuve's fracture of left leg, initial encounter for open fracture type IIIA, IIIB, or IIIC

S82.864B Nondisplaced Maisonneuve's fracture of right leg, initial encounter for open fracture type I or II

S82.864C Nondisplaced Maisonneuve's fracture of right leg, initial encounter for open fracture type IIIA, IIIB, or IIIC

S82.866B Nondisplaced Maisonneuve's fracture of unspecified leg, initial encounter for open fracture type I or II

S82.866C Nondisplaced Maisonneuve's fracture of unspecified leg, initial encounter for open fracture type IIIA, IIIB, or IIIC

S72.035A Nondisplaced midcervical fracture of left femur, initial encounter for closed fracture

S72.035B Nondisplaced midcervical fracture of left femur, initial encounter for open fracture type I or II

S72.035C Nondisplaced midcervical fracture of left femur, initial encounter for open fracture type IIIA, IIIB, or IIIC

S72.034A Nondisplaced midcervical fracture of right femur, initial encounter for closed fracture

S72.034B Nondisplaced midcervical fracture of right femur, initial encounter for open fracture type I or II

S72.034C Nondisplaced midcervical fracture of right femur, initial encounter for open fracture type IIIA, IIIB, or IIIC

S72.036A Nondisplaced midcervical fracture of unspecified femur, initial encounter for closed fracture

S72.036B Nondisplaced midcervical fracture of unspecified femur, initial encounter for open fracture type I or II

S72.036C Nondisplaced midcervical fracture of unspecified femur, initial encounter for open fracture type IIIA, IIIB, or IIIC

S42.335B Nondisplaced oblique fracture of shaft of humerus, left arm, initial encounter for open fracture

S42.334B Nondisplaced oblique fracture of shaft of humerus, right arm, initial encounter for open fracture

S42.336B Nondisplaced oblique fracture of shaft of humerus, unspecified arm, initial encounter for open fracture

S72.335A Nondisplaced oblique fracture of shaft of left femur, initial encounter for closed fracture

S72.335B Nondisplaced oblique fracture of shaft of left femur, initial encounter for open fracture type I or II

S72.335C Nondisplaced oblique fracture of shaft of left femur, initial encounter for open fracture type IIIA, IIIB, or IIIC

S82.435B Nondisplaced oblique fracture of shaft of left fibula, initial encounter for open fracture type I or II

S82.435C Nondisplaced oblique fracture of shaft of left fibula, initial encounter for open fracture type IIIA, IIIB, or IIIC

S52.335B Nondisplaced oblique fracture of shaft of left radius, initial encounter for open fracture type I or II

S52.335C Nondisplaced oblique fracture of shaft of left radius, initial encounter for open fracture type IIIA, IIIB, or IIIC

S82.235B Nondisplaced oblique fracture of shaft of left tibia, initial encounter for open fracture type I or II

S82.235C Nondisplaced oblique fracture of shaft of left tibia, initial encounter for open fracture type IIIA, IIIB, or IIIC

S52.235B Nondisplaced oblique fracture of shaft of left ulna, initial encounter for open fracture type I or II

S52.235C Nondisplaced oblique fracture of shaft of left ulna, initial encounter for open fracture type IIIA, IIIB, or IIIC

S72.334A Nondisplaced oblique fracture of shaft of right femur, initial encounter for closed fracture

S72.334B Nondisplaced oblique fracture of shaft of right femur, initial encounter for open fracture type I or II

S72.334C Nondisplaced oblique fracture of shaft of right femur, initial encounter for open fracture type IIIA, IIIB, or IIIC

S82.434B Nondisplaced oblique fracture of shaft of right fibula, initial encounter for open fracture type I or II

S82.434C Nondisplaced oblique fracture of shaft of right fibula, initial encounter for open fracture type IIIA, IIIB, or IIIC

S52.334B Nondisplaced oblique fracture of shaft of right radius, initial encounter for open fracture type I or II

S52.334C Nondisplaced oblique fracture of shaft of right radius, initial encounter for open fracture type IIIA, IIIB, or IIIC

S82.234B Nondisplaced oblique fracture of shaft of right tibia, initial encounter for open fracture type I or II

S82.234C Nondisplaced oblique fracture of shaft of right tibia, initial encounter for open fracture type IIIA, IIIB, or IIIC

S52.234B Nondisplaced oblique fracture of shaft of right ulna, initial encounter for open fracture type I or II

S52.234C Nondisplaced oblique fracture of shaft of right ulna, initial encounter for open fracture type IIIA, IIIB, or IIIC

S72.336A Nondisplaced oblique fracture of shaft of unspecified femur, initial encounter for closed fracture

S72.336B Nondisplaced oblique fracture of shaft of unspecified femur, initial encounter for open fracture type I or II

S72.336C Nondisplaced oblique fracture of shaft of unspecified femur, initial encounter for open fracture type IIIA, IIIB, or IIIC

S82.436B Nondisplaced oblique fracture of shaft of unspecified fibula, initial encounter for open fracture type I or II

S82.436C Nondisplaced oblique fracture of shaft of unspecified fibula, initial encounter for open fracture type IIIA, IIIB, or IIIC

S52.336B Nondisplaced oblique fracture of shaft of unspecified radius, initial encounter for open fracture type I or II

S52.336C Nondisplaced oblique fracture of shaft of unspecified radius, initial encounter for open fracture type IIIA, IIIB, or IIIC

S82.236B Nondisplaced oblique fracture of shaft of unspecified tibia, initial encounter for open fracture type I or II

S82.236C Nondisplaced oblique fracture of shaft of unspecified tibia, initial encounter for open fracture type IIIA, IIIB, or IIIC

S52.236B Nondisplaced oblique fracture of shaft of unspecified ulna, initial encounter for open fracture type I or II

S52.236C Nondisplaced oblique fracture of shaft of unspecified ulna, initial encounter for open fracture type IIIA, IIIB, or IIIC

S12.031B Nondisplaced posterior arch fracture of first cervical vertebra, initial encounter for open fracture

S42.365B Nondisplaced segmental fracture of shaft of humerus, left arm, initial encounter for open fracture

S42.364B Nondisplaced segmental fracture of shaft of humerus, right arm, initial encounter for open fracture

S42.366B Nondisplaced segmental fracture of shaft of humerus, unspecified arm, initial encounter for open fracture

S72.365A Nondisplaced segmental fracture of shaft of left femur, initial encounter for closed fracture

S72.365B Nondisplaced segmental fracture of shaft of left femur, initial encounter for open fracture type I or II

S72.365C Nondisplaced segmental fracture of shaft of left femur, initial encounter for open fracture type IIIA, IIIB, or IIIC

S82.465B Nondisplaced segmental fracture of shaft of left fibula, initial encounter for open fracture type I or II

S82.465C Nondisplaced segmental fracture of shaft of left fibula, initial encounter for open fracture type IIIA, IIIB, or IIIC

S82.265B Nondisplaced segmental fracture of shaft of left tibia, initial encounter for open fracture type I or II

S82.265C Nondisplaced segmental fracture of shaft of left tibia, initial encounter for open fracture type IIIA, IIIB, or IIIC

S52.365B Nondisplaced segmental fracture of shaft of radius, left arm, initial encounter for open fracture type I or II

S52.365C Nondisplaced segmental fracture of shaft of radius, left arm, initial encounter for open fracture type IIIA, IIIB, or IIIC

S52.364B Nondisplaced segmental fracture of shaft of radius, right arm, initial encounter for open fracture type I or II

S52.364C Nondisplaced segmental fracture of shaft of radius, right arm, initial encounter for open fracture type IIIA, IIIB, or IIIC

S52.366B Nondisplaced segmental fracture of shaft of radius, unspecified arm, initial encounter for open fracture type I or II

S52.366C Nondisplaced segmental fracture of shaft of radius, unspecified arm, initial encounter for open fracture type IIIA, IIIB, or IIIC

S72.364A Nondisplaced segmental fracture of shaft of right femur, initial encounter for closed fracture

S72.364B Nondisplaced segmental fracture of shaft of right femur, initial encounter for open fracture type I or II

S72.364C Nondisplaced segmental fracture of shaft of right femur, initial encounter for open fracture type IIIA, IIIB, or IIIC

S82.464B Nondisplaced segmental fracture of shaft of right fibula, initial encounter for open fracture type I or II

S82.464C Nondisplaced segmental fracture of shaft of right fibula, initial encounter for open fracture type IIIA, IIIB, or IIIC

S82.264B Nondisplaced segmental fracture of shaft of right tibia, initial encounter for open fracture type I or II

S82.264C Nondisplaced segmental fracture of shaft of right tibia, initial encounter for open fracture type IIIA, IIIB, or IIIC

S52.265B Nondisplaced segmental fracture of shaft of ulna, left arm, initial encounter for open fracture type I or II

S52.265C Nondisplaced segmental fracture of shaft of ulna, left arm, initial encounter for open fracture type IIIA, IIIB, or IIIC

S52.264B Nondisplaced segmental fracture of shaft of ulna, right arm, initial encounter for open fracture type I or II

S52.264C Nondisplaced segmental fracture of shaft of ulna, right arm, initial encounter for open fracture type IIIA, IIIB, or IIIC

S52.266B Nondisplaced segmental fracture of shaft of ulna, unspecified arm, initial encounter for open fracture type I or II

S52.266C Nondisplaced segmental fracture of shaft of ulna, unspecified arm, initial encounter for open fracture type IIIA, IIIB, or IIIC

S72.366A Nondisplaced segmental fracture of shaft of unspecified femur, initial encounter for closed fracture

S72.366B Nondisplaced segmental fracture of shaft of unspecified femur, initial encounter for open fracture type I or II

S72.366C Nondisplaced segmental fracture of shaft of unspecified femur, initial encounter for open fracture type IIIA, IIIB, or IIIC

S82.466B Nondisplaced segmental fracture of shaft of unspecified fibula, initial encounter for open fracture type I or II

S82.466C Nondisplaced segmental fracture of shaft of unspecified fibula, initial encounter for open fracture type IIIA, IIIB, or IIIC

S82.266B Nondisplaced segmental fracture of shaft of unspecified tibia, initial encounter for open fracture type I or II

S82.266C Nondisplaced segmental fracture of shaft of unspecified tibia, initial encounter for open fracture type IIIA, IIIB, or IIIC

S42.415B Nondisplaced simple supracondylar fracture without intercondylar fracture of left humerus, initial encounter for open fracture

S42.414B Nondisplaced simple supracondylar fracture without intercondylar fracture of right humerus, initial encounter for open fracture

S42.416B Nondisplaced simple supracondylar fracture without intercondylar fracture of unspecified humerus, initial encounter for open fracture

S42.345B Nondisplaced spiral fracture of shaft of humerus, left arm, initial encounter for open fracture

S42.344B Nondisplaced spiral fracture of shaft of humerus, right arm, initial encounter for open fracture

S42.346B Nondisplaced spiral fracture of shaft of humerus, unspecified arm, initial encounter for open fracture

S72.345A Nondisplaced spiral fracture of shaft of left femur, initial encounter for closed fracture

S72.345B Nondisplaced spiral fracture of shaft of left femur, initial encounter for open fracture type I or II

S72.345C Nondisplaced spiral fracture of shaft of left femur, initial encounter for open fracture type IIIA, IIIB, or IIIC

S82.445B Nondisplaced spiral fracture of shaft of left fibula, initial encounter for open fracture type I or II

S82.445C Nondisplaced spiral fracture of shaft of left fibula, initial encounter for open fracture type IIIA, IIIB, or IIIC

S82.245B Nondisplaced spiral fracture of shaft of left tibia, initial encounter for open fracture type I or II

S82.245C Nondisplaced spiral fracture of shaft of left tibia, initial encounter for open fracture type IIIA, IIIB, or IIIC

S52.345B Nondisplaced spiral fracture of shaft of radius, left arm, initial encounter for open fracture type I or II

S52.345C Nondisplaced spiral fracture of shaft of radius, left arm, initial encounter for open fracture type IIIA, IIIB, or IIIC

S52.344B Nondisplaced spiral fracture of shaft of radius, right arm, initial encounter for open fracture type I or II

S52.344C Nondisplaced spiral fracture of shaft of radius, right arm, initial encounter for open fracture type IIIA, IIIB, or IIIC

S52.346B Nondisplaced spiral fracture of shaft of radius, unspecified arm, initial encounter for open fracture type I or II

S52.346C Nondisplaced spiral fracture of shaft of radius, unspecified arm, initial encounter for open fracture type IIIA, IIIB, or IIIC

S72.344A Nondisplaced spiral fracture of shaft of right femur, initial encounter for closed fracture

S72.344B Nondisplaced spiral fracture of shaft of right femur, initial encounter for open fracture type I or II

S72.344C Nondisplaced spiral fracture of shaft of right femur, initial encounter for open fracture type IIIA, IIIB, or IIIC

S82.444B Nondisplaced spiral fracture of shaft of right fibula, initial encounter for open fracture type I or II

S82.444C Nondisplaced spiral fracture of shaft of right fibula, initial encounter for open fracture type IIIA, IIIB, or IIIC

S82.244B Nondisplaced spiral fracture of shaft of right tibia, initial encounter for open fracture type I or II

S82.244C Nondisplaced spiral fracture of shaft of right tibia, initial encounter for open fracture type IIIA, IIIB, or IIIC

S52.245B Nondisplaced spiral fracture of shaft of ulna, left arm, initial encounter for open fracture type I or II

S52.245C Nondisplaced spiral fracture of shaft of ulna, left arm, initial encounter for open fracture type IIIA, IIIB, or IIIC

S52.244B Nondisplaced spiral fracture of shaft of ulna, right arm, initial encounter for open fracture type I or II

S52.244C Nondisplaced spiral fracture of shaft of ulna, right arm, initial encounter for open fracture type IIIA, IIIB, or IIIC

S52.246B Nondisplaced spiral fracture of shaft of ulna, unspecified arm, initial encounter for open fracture type I or II
S52.246C Nondisplaced spiral fracture of shaft of ulna, unspecified arm, initial encounter for open fracture type IIIA, IIIB, or IIIC
S72.346A Nondisplaced spiral fracture of shaft of unspecified femur, initial encounter for closed fracture
S72.346B Nondisplaced spiral fracture of shaft of unspecified femur, initial encounter for open fracture type I or II
S72.346C Nondisplaced spiral fracture of shaft of unspecified femur, initial encounter for open fracture type IIIA, IIIB, or IIIC
S82.446B Nondisplaced spiral fracture of shaft of unspecified fibula, initial encounter for open fracture type I or II
S82.446C Nondisplaced spiral fracture of shaft of unspecified fibula, initial encounter for open fracture type IIIA, IIIB, or IIIC
S82.246B Nondisplaced spiral fracture of shaft of unspecified tibia, initial encounter for open fracture type I or II
S82.246C Nondisplaced spiral fracture of shaft of unspecified tibia, initial encounter for open fracture type IIIA, IIIB, or IIIC
S72.25XA Nondisplaced subtrochanteric fracture of left femur, initial encounter for closed fracture
S72.25XB Nondisplaced subtrochanteric fracture of left femur, initial encounter for open fracture type I or II
S72.25XC Nondisplaced subtrochanteric fracture of left femur, initial encounter for open fracture type IIIA, IIIB, or IIIC
S72.24XA Nondisplaced subtrochanteric fracture of right femur, initial encounter for closed fracture
S72.24XB Nondisplaced subtrochanteric fracture of right femur, initial encounter for open fracture type I or II
S72.24XC Nondisplaced subtrochanteric fracture of right femur, initial encounter for open fracture type IIIA, IIIB, or IIIC
S72.26XA Nondisplaced subtrochanteric fracture of unspecified femur, initial encounter for closed fracture
S72.26XB Nondisplaced subtrochanteric fracture of unspecified femur, initial encounter for open fracture type I or II
S72.26XC Nondisplaced subtrochanteric fracture of unspecified femur, initial encounter for open fracture type IIIA, IIIB, or IIIC
S72.465B Nondisplaced supracondylar fracture with intracondylar extension of lower end of left femur, initial encounter for open fracture type I or II
S72.465C Nondisplaced supracondylar fracture with intracondylar extension of lower end of left femur, initial encounter for open fracture type IIIA, IIIB, or IIIC
S72.464B Nondisplaced supracondylar fracture with intracondylar extension of lower end of right femur, initial encounter for open fracture type I or II
S72.464C Nondisplaced supracondylar fracture with intracondylar extension of lower end of right femur, initial encounter for open fracture type IIIA, IIIB, or IIIC
S72.466B Nondisplaced supracondylar fracture with intracondylar extension of lower end of unspecified femur, initial encounter for open fracture type I or II
S72.466C Nondisplaced supracondylar fracture with intracondylar extension of lower end of unspecified femur, initial encounter for open fracture type IIIA, IIIB, or IIIC
S72.455B Nondisplaced supracondylar fracture without intracondylar extension of lower end of left femur, initial encounter for open fracture type I or II
S72.455C Nondisplaced supracondylar fracture without intracondylar extension of lower end of left femur, initial encounter for open fracture type IIIA, IIIB, or IIIC
S72.454B Nondisplaced supracondylar fracture without intracondylar extension of lower end of right femur, initial encounter for open fracture type I or II
S72.454C Nondisplaced supracondylar fracture without intracondylar extension of lower end of right femur, initial encounter for open fracture type IIIA, IIIB, or IIIC
S72.456B Nondisplaced supracondylar fracture without intracondylar extension of lower end of unspecified femur, initial encounter for open fracture type I or II
S72.456C Nondisplaced supracondylar fracture without intracondylar extension of lower end of unspecified femur, initial encounter for open fracture type IIIA, IIIB, or IIIC
S42.475B Nondisplaced transcondylar fracture of left humerus, initial encounter for open fracture
S42.474B Nondisplaced transcondylar fracture of right humerus, initial encounter for open fracture
S42.476B Nondisplaced transcondylar fracture of unspecified humerus, initial encounter for open fracture
S32.455A Nondisplaced transverse fracture of left acetabulum, initial encounter for closed fracture
S32.455B Nondisplaced transverse fracture of left acetabulum, initial encounter for open fracture
S32.454A Nondisplaced transverse fracture of right acetabulum, initial encounter for closed fracture
S32.454B Nondisplaced transverse fracture of right acetabulum, initial encounter for open fracture
S42.325B Nondisplaced transverse fracture of shaft of humerus, left arm, initial encounter for open fracture
S42.324B Nondisplaced transverse fracture of shaft of humerus, right arm, initial encounter for open fracture
S42.326B Nondisplaced transverse fracture of shaft of humerus, unspecified arm, initial encounter for open fracture
S72.325A Nondisplaced transverse fracture of shaft of left femur, initial encounter for closed fracture
S72.325B Nondisplaced transverse fracture of shaft of left femur, initial encounter for open fracture type I or II
S72.325C Nondisplaced transverse fracture of shaft of left femur, initial encounter for open fracture type IIIA, IIIB, or IIIC
S82.425B Nondisplaced transverse fracture of shaft of left fibula, initial encounter for open fracture type I or II

S82.425C Nondisplaced transverse fracture of shaft of left fibula, initial encounter for open fracture type IIIA, IIIB, or IIIC
S52.325B Nondisplaced transverse fracture of shaft of left radius, initial encounter for open fracture type I or II
S52.325C Nondisplaced transverse fracture of shaft of left radius, initial encounter for open fracture type IIIA, IIIB, or IIIC
S82.225B Nondisplaced transverse fracture of shaft of left tibia, initial encounter for open fracture type I or II
S82.225C Nondisplaced transverse fracture of shaft of left tibia, initial encounter for open fracture type IIIA, IIIB, or IIIC
S52.225B Nondisplaced transverse fracture of shaft of left ulna, initial encounter for open fracture type I or II
S52.225C Nondisplaced transverse fracture of shaft of left ulna, initial encounter for open fracture type IIIA, IIIB, or IIIC
S72.324A Nondisplaced transverse fracture of shaft of right femur, initial encounter for closed fracture
S72.324B Nondisplaced transverse fracture of shaft of right femur, initial encounter for open fracture type I or II
S72.324C Nondisplaced transverse fracture of shaft of right femur, initial encounter for open fracture type IIIA, IIIB, or IIIC
S82.424B Nondisplaced transverse fracture of shaft of right fibula, initial encounter for open fracture type I or II
S82.424C Nondisplaced transverse fracture of shaft of right fibula, initial encounter for open fracture type IIIA, IIIB, or IIIC
S52.324B Nondisplaced transverse fracture of shaft of right radius, initial encounter for open fracture type I or II
S52.324C Nondisplaced transverse fracture of shaft of right radius, initial encounter for open fracture type IIIA, IIIB, or IIIC
S82.224B Nondisplaced transverse fracture of shaft of right tibia, initial encounter for open fracture type I or II
S82.224C Nondisplaced transverse fracture of shaft of right tibia, initial encounter for open fracture type IIIA, IIIB, or IIIC
S52.224B Nondisplaced transverse fracture of shaft of right ulna, initial encounter for open fracture type I or II
S52.224C Nondisplaced transverse fracture of shaft of right ulna, initial encounter for open fracture type IIIA, IIIB, or IIIC
S72.326A Nondisplaced transverse fracture of shaft of unspecified femur, initial encounter for closed fracture
S72.326B Nondisplaced transverse fracture of shaft of unspecified femur, initial encounter for open fracture type I or II
S72.326C Nondisplaced transverse fracture of shaft of unspecified femur, initial encounter for open fracture type IIIA, IIIB, or IIIC
S82.426B Nondisplaced transverse fracture of shaft of unspecified fibula, initial encounter for open fracture type I or II
S82.426C Nondisplaced transverse fracture of shaft of unspecified fibula, initial encounter for open fracture type IIIA, IIIB, or IIIC
S52.326B Nondisplaced transverse fracture of shaft of unspecified radius, initial encounter for open fracture type I or II
S52.326C Nondisplaced transverse fracture of shaft of unspecified radius, initial encounter for open fracture type IIIA, IIIB, or IIIC
S82.226B Nondisplaced transverse fracture of shaft of unspecified tibia, initial encounter for open fracture type I or II
S82.226C Nondisplaced transverse fracture of shaft of unspecified tibia, initial encounter for open fracture type IIIA, IIIB, or IIIC
S52.226B Nondisplaced transverse fracture of shaft of unspecified ulna, initial encounter for open fracture type I or II
S52.226C Nondisplaced transverse fracture of shaft of unspecified ulna, initial encounter for open fracture type IIIA, IIIB, or IIIC
S32.456A Nondisplaced transverse fracture of unspecified acetabulum, initial encounter for closed fracture
S32.456B Nondisplaced transverse fracture of unspecified acetabulum, initial encounter for open fracture
S12.112B Nondisplaced Type II dens fracture, initial encounter for open fracture
S72.415B Nondisplaced unspecified condyle fracture of lower end of left femur, initial encounter for open fracture type I or II
S72.415C Nondisplaced unspecified condyle fracture of lower end of left femur, initial encounter for open fracture type IIIA, IIIB, or IIIC
S72.414B Nondisplaced unspecified condyle fracture of lower end of right femur, initial encounter for open fracture type I or II
S72.414C Nondisplaced unspecified condyle fracture of lower end of right femur, initial encounter for open fracture type IIIA, IIIB, or IIIC
S72.416B Nondisplaced unspecified condyle fracture of lower end of unspecified femur, initial encounter for open fracture type I or II
S72.416C Nondisplaced unspecified condyle fracture of lower end of unspecified femur, initial encounter for open fracture type IIIA, IIIB, or IIIC
S32.110B Nondisplaced Zone I fracture of sacrum, initial encounter for open fracture
S32.120B Nondisplaced Zone II fracture of sacrum, initial encounter for open fracture
S32.130B Nondisplaced Zone III fracture of sacrum, initial encounter for open fracture
G03.0 Nonpyogenic meningitis
I62.01 Nontraumatic acute subdural hemorrhage
I62.03 Nontraumatic chronic subdural hemorrhage
I62.1 Nontraumatic extradural hemorrhage
I61.3 Nontraumatic intracerebral hemorrhage in brain stem
I61.4 Nontraumatic intracerebral hemorrhage in cerebellum
I61.1 Nontraumatic intracerebral hemorrhage in hemisphere, cortical
I61.0 Nontraumatic intracerebral hemorrhage in hemisphere, subcortical
I61.2 Nontraumatic intracerebral hemorrhage in hemisphere, unspecified
I61.5 Nontraumatic intracerebral hemorrhage, intraventricular
I61.6 Nontraumatic intracerebral hemorrhage, multiple localized
I61.9 Nontraumatic intracerebral hemorrhage, unspecified
I62.02 Nontraumatic subacute subdural hemorrhage

I60.2	Nontraumatic subarachnoid hemorrhage from anterior communicating artery
I60.4	Nontraumatic subarachnoid hemorrhage from basilar artery
I60.02	Nontraumatic subarachnoid hemorrhage from left carotid siphon and bifurcation
I60.12	Nontraumatic subarachnoid hemorrhage from left middle cerebral artery
I60.32	Nontraumatic subarachnoid hemorrhage from left posterior communicating artery
I60.52	Nontraumatic subarachnoid hemorrhage from left vertebral artery
I60.6	Nontraumatic subarachnoid hemorrhage from other intracranial arteries
I60.01	Nontraumatic subarachnoid hemorrhage from right carotid siphon and bifurcation
I60.11	Nontraumatic subarachnoid hemorrhage from right middle cerebral artery
I60.31	Nontraumatic subarachnoid hemorrhage from right posterior communicating artery
I60.51	Nontraumatic subarachnoid hemorrhage from right vertebral artery
I60.00	Nontraumatic subarachnoid hemorrhage from unspecified carotid siphon and bifurcation
I60.7	Nontraumatic subarachnoid hemorrhage from unspecified intracranial artery
I60.10	Nontraumatic subarachnoid hemorrhage from unspecified middle cerebral artery
I60.30	Nontraumatic subarachnoid hemorrhage from unspecified posterior communicating artery
I60.50	Nontraumatic subarachnoid hemorrhage from unspecified vertebral artery
I60.9	Nontraumatic subarachnoid hemorrhage, unspecified
I62.00	Nontraumatic subdural hemorrhage, unspecified
E41	Nutritional marasmus
K83.1	Obstruction of bile duct
S31.652A	Open bite of abdominal wall, epigastric region with penetration into peritoneal cavity, initial encounter
S31.654A	Open bite of abdominal wall, left lower quadrant with penetration into peritoneal cavity, initial encounter
S31.651A	Open bite of abdominal wall, left upper quadrant with penetration into peritoneal cavity, initial encounter
S31.655A	Open bite of abdominal wall, periumbilic region with penetration into peritoneal cavity, initial encounter
S31.653A	Open bite of abdominal wall, right lower quadrant with penetration into peritoneal cavity, initial encounter
S31.650A	Open bite of abdominal wall, right upper quadrant with penetration into peritoneal cavity, initial encounter
S31.659A	Open bite of abdominal wall, unspecified quadrant with penetration into peritoneal cavity, initial encounter
S11.015A	Open bite of larynx, initial encounter
S21.452A	Open bite of left back wall of thorax with penetration into thoracic cavity, initial encounter
S21.352A	Open bite of left front wall of thorax with penetration into thoracic cavity, initial encounter
S31.051A	Open bite of lower back and pelvis with penetration into retroperitoneum, initial encounter
S21.451A	Open bite of right back wall of thorax with penetration into thoracic cavity, initial encounter
S21.351A	Open bite of right front wall of thorax with penetration into thoracic cavity, initial encounter
S11.025A	Open bite of trachea, initial encounter
S21.459A	Open bite of unspecified back wall of thorax with penetration into thoracic cavity, initial encounter
S21.359A	Open bite of unspecified front wall of thorax with penetration into thoracic cavity, initial encounter
S11.035A	Open bite of vocal cord, initial encounter
D60.8	Other acquired pure red cell aplasias
I40.8	Other acute myocarditis
G04.39	Other acute necrotizing hemorrhagic encephalopathy
K85.82	Other acute pancreatitis with infected necrosis
K85.81	Other acute pancreatitis with uninfected necrosis
K85.80	Other acute pancreatitis without necrosis or infection
A80.39	Other acute paralytic poliomyelitis
K43.7	Other and unspecified ventral hernia with gangrene
G00.8	Other bacterial meningitis
P36.8	Other bacterial sepsis of newborn
I63.89	Other cerebral infarction
I63.81	Other cerebral infarction due to occlusion or stenosis of small artery
P27.8	Other chronic respiratory diseases originating in the perinatal period
P25.8	Other conditions related to interstitial emphysema originating in the perinatal period
P37.4	Other congenital malaria
Q79.59	Other congenital malformations of abdominal wall
Q79.1	Other congenital malformations of diaphragm
Q25.79	Other congenital malformations of pulmonary artery
Q22.8	Other congenital malformations of tricuspid valve
P35.8	Other congenital viral diseases
J98.59	Other diseases of mediastinum, not elsewhere classified
K68.9	Other disorders of retroperitoneum
S12.120B	Other displaced dens fracture, initial encounter for open fracture
S12.490B	Other displaced fracture of fifth cervical vertebra, initial encounter for open fracture
S12.090B	Other displaced fracture of first cervical vertebra, initial encounter for open fracture
S12.390B	Other displaced fracture of fourth cervical vertebra, initial encounter for open fracture
S42.492B	Other displaced fracture of lower end of left humerus, initial encounter for open fracture

S42.491B	Other displaced fracture of lower end of right humerus, initial encounter for open fracture
S42.493B	Other displaced fracture of lower end of unspecified humerus, initial encounter for open fracture
S12.190B	Other displaced fracture of second cervical vertebra, initial encounter for open fracture
S12.690B	Other displaced fracture of seventh cervical vertebra, initial encounter for open fracture
S12.590B	Other displaced fracture of sixth cervical vertebra, initial encounter for open fracture
S12.290B	Other displaced fracture of third cervical vertebra, initial encounter for open fracture
S42.292B	Other displaced fracture of upper end of left humerus, initial encounter for open fracture
S42.291B	Other displaced fracture of upper end of right humerus, initial encounter for open fracture
S42.293B	Other displaced fracture of upper end of unspecified humerus, initial encounter for open fracture
D61.811	Other drug-induced pancytopenia
O88.82	Other embolism in childbirth
O88.811	Other embolism in pregnancy, first trimester
O88.812	Other embolism in pregnancy, second trimester
O88.813	Other embolism in pregnancy, third trimester
O88.83	Other embolism in the puerperium
G04.81	Other encephalitis and encephalomyelitis
S52.552B	Other extraarticular fracture of lower end of left radius, initial encounter for open fracture type I or II
S52.552C	Other extraarticular fracture of lower end of left radius, initial encounter for open fracture type IIIA, IIIB, or IIIC
S52.551B	Other extraarticular fracture of lower end of right radius, initial encounter for open fracture type I or II
S52.551C	Other extraarticular fracture of lower end of right radius, initial encounter for open fracture type IIIA, IIIB, or IIIC
S52.559B	Other extraarticular fracture of lower end of unspecified radius, initial encounter for open fracture type I or II
S52.559C	Other extraarticular fracture of lower end of unspecified radius, initial encounter for open fracture type IIIA, IIIB, or IIIC
A20.8	Other forms of plague
S02.19XB	Other fracture of base of skull, initial encounter for open fracture
S32.058B	Other fracture of fifth lumbar vertebra, initial encounter for open fracture
S32.018B	Other fracture of first lumbar vertebra, initial encounter for open fracture
S22.018B	Other fracture of first thoracic vertebra, initial encounter for open fracture
S32.048B	Other fracture of fourth lumbar vertebra, initial encounter for open fracture
S22.048B	Other fracture of fourth thoracic vertebra, initial encounter for open fracture
S72.092A	Other fracture of head and neck of left femur, initial encounter for closed fracture
S72.092B	Other fracture of head and neck of left femur, initial encounter for open fracture type I or II
S72.092C	Other fracture of head and neck of left femur, initial encounter for open fracture type IIIA, IIIB, or IIIC
S72.091A	Other fracture of head and neck of right femur, initial encounter for closed fracture
S72.091B	Other fracture of head and neck of right femur, initial encounter for open fracture type I or II
S72.091C	Other fracture of head and neck of right femur, initial encounter for open fracture type IIIA, IIIB, or IIIC
S72.099A	Other fracture of head and neck of unspecified femur, initial encounter for closed fracture
S72.099B	Other fracture of head and neck of unspecified femur, initial encounter for open fracture type I or II
S72.099C	Other fracture of head and neck of unspecified femur, initial encounter for open fracture type IIIA, IIIB, or IIIC
S72.8X2A	Other fracture of left femur, initial encounter for closed fracture
S72.8X2B	Other fracture of left femur, initial encounter for open fracture type I or II
S72.8X2C	Other fracture of left femur, initial encounter for open fracture type IIIA, IIIB, or IIIC
S32.392B	Other fracture of left ilium, initial encounter for open fracture
S72.492B	Other fracture of lower end of left femur, initial encounter for open fracture type I or II
S72.492C	Other fracture of lower end of left femur, initial encounter for open fracture type IIIA, IIIB, or IIIC
S52.692B	Other fracture of lower end of left ulna, initial encounter for open fracture type I or II
S52.692C	Other fracture of lower end of left ulna, initial encounter for open fracture type IIIA, IIIB, or IIIC
S72.491B	Other fracture of lower end of right femur, initial encounter for open fracture type I or II
S72.491C	Other fracture of lower end of right femur, initial encounter for open fracture type IIIA, IIIB, or IIIC
S52.691B	Other fracture of lower end of right ulna, initial encounter for open fracture type I or II
S52.691C	Other fracture of lower end of right ulna, initial encounter for open fracture type IIIA, IIIB, or IIIC
S72.499B	Other fracture of lower end of unspecified femur, initial encounter for open fracture type I or II
S72.499C	Other fracture of lower end of unspecified femur, initial encounter for open fracture type IIIA, IIIB, or IIIC
S52.699B	Other fracture of lower end of unspecified ulna, initial encounter for open fracture type I or II
S52.699C	Other fracture of lower end of unspecified ulna, initial encounter for open fracture type IIIA, IIIB, or IIIC

S02.11HB	Other fracture of occiput, left side, initial encounter for open fracture
S02.11GB	Other fracture of occiput, right side, initial encounter for open fracture
S02.118B	Other fracture of occiput, unspecified side, initial encounter for open fracture
S72.8X1A	Other fracture of right femur, initial encounter for closed fracture
S72.8X1B	Other fracture of right femur, initial encounter for open fracture type I or II
S72.8X1C	Other fracture of right femur, initial encounter for open fracture type IIIA, IIIB, or IIIC
S32.391B	Other fracture of right ilium, initial encounter for open fracture
S32.19XB	Other fracture of sacrum, initial encounter for open fracture
S32.028B	Other fracture of second lumbar vertebra, initial encounter for open fracture
S22.028B	Other fracture of second thoracic vertebra, initial encounter for open fracture
S72.392A	Other fracture of shaft of left femur, initial encounter for closed fracture
S72.392B	Other fracture of shaft of left femur, initial encounter for open fracture type I or II
S72.392C	Other fracture of shaft of left femur, initial encounter for open fracture type IIIA, IIIB, or IIIC
S82.492B	Other fracture of shaft of left fibula, initial encounter for open fracture type I or II
S82.492C	Other fracture of shaft of left fibula, initial encounter for open fracture type IIIA, IIIB, or IIIC
S42.392B	Other fracture of shaft of left humerus, initial encounter for open fracture
S82.292B	Other fracture of shaft of left tibia, initial encounter for open fracture type I or II
S82.292C	Other fracture of shaft of left tibia, initial encounter for open fracture type IIIA, IIIB, or IIIC
S52.292B	Other fracture of shaft of left ulna, initial encounter for open fracture type I or II
S52.292C	Other fracture of shaft of left ulna, initial encounter for open fracture type IIIA, IIIB, or IIIC
S52.392B	Other fracture of shaft of radius, left arm, initial encounter for open fracture type I or II
S52.392C	Other fracture of shaft of radius, left arm, initial encounter for open fracture type IIIA, IIIB, or IIIC
S52.391B	Other fracture of shaft of radius, right arm, initial encounter for open fracture type I or II
S52.391C	Other fracture of shaft of radius, right arm, initial encounter for open fracture type IIIA, IIIB, or IIIC
S52.399B	Other fracture of shaft of radius, unspecified arm, initial encounter for open fracture type I or II
S52.399C	Other fracture of shaft of radius, unspecified arm, initial encounter for open fracture type IIIA, IIIB, or IIIC
S72.391A	Other fracture of shaft of right femur, initial encounter for closed fracture
S72.391B	Other fracture of shaft of right femur, initial encounter for open fracture type I or II
S72.391C	Other fracture of shaft of right femur, initial encounter for open fracture type IIIA, IIIB, or IIIC
S82.491B	Other fracture of shaft of right fibula, initial encounter for open fracture type I or II
S82.491C	Other fracture of shaft of right fibula, initial encounter for open fracture type IIIA, IIIB, or IIIC
S42.391B	Other fracture of shaft of right humerus, initial encounter for open fracture
S82.291B	Other fracture of shaft of right tibia, initial encounter for open fracture type I or II
S82.291C	Other fracture of shaft of right tibia, initial encounter for open fracture type IIIA, IIIB, or IIIC
S52.291B	Other fracture of shaft of right ulna, initial encounter for open fracture type I or II
S52.291C	Other fracture of shaft of right ulna, initial encounter for open fracture type IIIA, IIIB, or IIIC
S72.399A	Other fracture of shaft of unspecified femur, initial encounter for closed fracture
S72.399B	Other fracture of shaft of unspecified femur, initial encounter for open fracture type I or II
S72.399C	Other fracture of shaft of unspecified femur, initial encounter for open fracture type IIIA, IIIB, or IIIC
S82.499B	Other fracture of shaft of unspecified fibula, initial encounter for open fracture type I or II
S82.499C	Other fracture of shaft of unspecified fibula, initial encounter for open fracture type IIIA, IIIB, or IIIC
S42.399B	Other fracture of shaft of unspecified humerus, initial encounter for open fracture
S82.299B	Other fracture of shaft of unspecified tibia, initial encounter for open fracture type I or II
S82.299C	Other fracture of shaft of unspecified tibia, initial encounter for open fracture type IIIA, IIIB, or IIIC
S52.299B	Other fracture of shaft of unspecified ulna, initial encounter for open fracture type I or II
S52.299C	Other fracture of shaft of unspecified ulna, initial encounter for open fracture type IIIA, IIIB, or IIIC
S22.088B	Other fracture of T11-T12 vertebra, initial encounter for open fracture
S22.058B	Other fracture of T5-T6 vertebra, initial encounter for open fracture
S22.068B	Other fracture of T7-T8 thoracic vertebra, initial encounter for open fracture
S22.078B	Other fracture of T9-T10 vertebra, initial encounter for open fracture
S32.038B	Other fracture of third lumbar vertebra, initial encounter for open fracture
S22.038B	Other fracture of third thoracic vertebra, initial encounter for open fracture
S72.8X9A	Other fracture of unspecified femur, initial encounter for closed fracture
S72.8X9B	Other fracture of unspecified femur, initial encounter for open fracture type I or II
S72.8X9C	Other fracture of unspecified femur, initial encounter for open fracture type IIIA, IIIB, or IIIC
S32.399B	Other fracture of unspecified ilium, initial encounter for open fracture
S32.008B	Other fracture of unspecified lumbar vertebra, initial encounter for open fracture
S22.008B	Other fracture of unspecified thoracic vertebra, initial encounter for open fracture
S82.832B	Other fracture of upper and lower end of left fibula, initial encounter for open fracture type I or II
S82.832C	Other fracture of upper and lower end of left fibula, initial encounter for open fracture type IIIA, IIIB, or IIIC
S82.831B	Other fracture of upper and lower end of right fibula, initial encounter for open fracture type I or II
S82.831C	Other fracture of upper and lower end of right fibula, initial encounter for open fracture type IIIA, IIIB, or IIIC
S82.839B	Other fracture of upper and lower end of unspecified fibula, initial encounter for open fracture type I or II
S82.839C	Other fracture of upper and lower end of unspecified fibula, initial encounter for open fracture type IIIA, IIIB, or IIIC
S52.182B	Other fracture of upper end of left radius, initial encounter for open fracture type I or II
S52.182C	Other fracture of upper end of left radius, initial encounter for open fracture type IIIA, IIIB, or IIIC
S82.192B	Other fracture of upper end of left tibia, initial encounter for open fracture type I or II
S82.192C	Other fracture of upper end of left tibia, initial encounter for open fracture type IIIA, IIIB, or IIIC
S52.092B	Other fracture of upper end of left ulna, initial encounter for open fracture type I or II
S52.092C	Other fracture of upper end of left ulna, initial encounter for open fracture type IIIA, IIIB, or IIIC
S52.181B	Other fracture of upper end of right radius, initial encounter for open fracture type I or II
S52.181C	Other fracture of upper end of right radius, initial encounter for open fracture type IIIA, IIIB, or IIIC
S82.191B	Other fracture of upper end of right tibia, initial encounter for open fracture type I or II
S82.191C	Other fracture of upper end of right tibia, initial encounter for open fracture type IIIA, IIIB, or IIIC
S52.091B	Other fracture of upper end of right ulna, initial encounter for open fracture type I or II
S52.091C	Other fracture of upper end of right ulna, initial encounter for open fracture type IIIA, IIIB, or IIIC
S52.189B	Other fracture of upper end of unspecified radius, initial encounter for open fracture type I or II
S52.189C	Other fracture of upper end of unspecified radius, initial encounter for open fracture type IIIA, IIIB, or IIIC
S82.199B	Other fracture of upper end of unspecified tibia, initial encounter for open fracture type I or II
S82.199C	Other fracture of upper end of unspecified tibia, initial encounter for open fracture type IIIA, IIIB, or IIIC
S52.099B	Other fracture of upper end of unspecified ulna, initial encounter for open fracture type I or II
S52.099C	Other fracture of upper end of unspecified ulna, initial encounter for open fracture type IIIA, IIIB, or IIIC
S52.592B	Other fractures of lower end of left radius, initial encounter for open fracture type I or II
S52.592C	Other fractures of lower end of left radius, initial encounter for open fracture type IIIA, IIIB, or IIIC
S52.591B	Other fractures of lower end of right radius, initial encounter for open fracture type I or II
S52.591C	Other fractures of lower end of right radius, initial encounter for open fracture type IIIA, IIIB, or IIIC
S52.599B	Other fractures of lower end of unspecified radius, initial encounter for open fracture type I or II
S52.599C	Other fractures of lower end of unspecified radius, initial encounter for open fracture type IIIA, IIIB, or IIIC
K29.61	Other gastritis with bleeding
A41.59	Other Gram-negative sepsis
B10.09	Other human herpesvirus encephalitis
S14.151A	Other incomplete lesion at C1 level of cervical spinal cord, initial encounter
S14.152A	Other incomplete lesion at C2 level of cervical spinal cord, initial encounter
S14.153A	Other incomplete lesion at C3 level of cervical spinal cord, initial encounter
S14.154A	Other incomplete lesion at C4 level of cervical spinal cord, initial encounter
S14.155A	Other incomplete lesion at C5 level of cervical spinal cord, initial encounter
S14.156A	Other incomplete lesion at C6 level of cervical spinal cord, initial encounter
S14.157A	Other incomplete lesion at C7 level of cervical spinal cord, initial encounter
S14.158A	Other incomplete lesion at C8 level of cervical spinal cord, initial encounter
S24.151A	Other incomplete lesion at T1 level of thoracic spinal cord, initial encounter
S24.154A	Other incomplete lesion at T11-T12 level of thoracic spinal cord, initial encounter
S24.152A	Other incomplete lesion at T2-T6 level of thoracic spinal cord, initial encounter
S24.153A	Other incomplete lesion at T7-T10 level of thoracic spinal cord, initial encounter
O75.3	Other infection during labor
S35.09XA	Other injury of abdominal aorta, initial encounter
S35.298A	Other injury of branches of celiac and mesenteric artery, initial encounter
S27.492A	Other injury of bronchus, bilateral, initial encounter
S27.491A	Other injury of bronchus, unilateral, initial encounter
S27.499A	Other injury of bronchus, unspecified, initial encounter
S35.218A	Other injury of celiac artery, initial encounter
S27.818A	Other injury of esophagus (thoracic part), initial encounter
S35.238A	Other injury of inferior mesenteric artery, initial encounter
S35.19XA	Other injury of inferior vena cava, initial encounter
S37.092A	Other injury of left kidney, initial encounter

S37.091A	Other injury of right kidney, initial encounter
S35.228A	Other injury of superior mesenteric artery, initial encounter
S37.099A	Other injury of unspecified kidney, initial encounter
J84.848	Other interstitial lung diseases of childhood
S52.572B	Other intraarticular fracture of lower end of left radius, initial encounter for open fracture type I or II
S52.572C	Other intraarticular fracture of lower end of left radius, initial encounter for open fracture type IIIA, IIIB, or IIIC
S52.571B	Other intraarticular fracture of lower end of right radius, initial encounter for open fracture type I or II
S52.571C	Other intraarticular fracture of lower end of right radius, initial encounter for open fracture type IIIA, IIIB, or IIIC
S52.579B	Other intraarticular fracture of lower end of unspecified radius, initial encounter for open fracture type I or II
S52.579C	Other intraarticular fracture of lower end of unspecified radius, initial encounter for open fracture type IIIA, IIIB, or IIIC
P52.8	Other intracranial (nontraumatic) hemorrhages of newborn
P10.8	Other intracranial lacerations and hemorrhages due to birth injury
Q28.3	Other malformations of cerebral vessels
A19.8	Other miliary tuberculosis
A83.8	Other mosquito-borne viral encephalitis
G04.89	Other myelitis
I21.A9	Other myocardial infarction type
P24.81	Other neonatal aspiration with respiratory symptoms
P54.3	Other neonatal gastrointestinal hemorrhage
S12.121B	Other nondisplaced dens fracture, initial encounter for open fracture
S12.491B	Other nondisplaced fracture of fifth cervical vertebra, initial encounter for open fracture
S12.091B	Other nondisplaced fracture of first cervical vertebra, initial encounter for open fracture
S12.391B	Other nondisplaced fracture of fourth cervical vertebra, initial encounter for open fracture
S42.495B	Other nondisplaced fracture of lower end of left humerus, initial encounter for open fracture
S42.494B	Other nondisplaced fracture of lower end of right humerus, initial encounter for open fracture
S42.496B	Other nondisplaced fracture of lower end of unspecified humerus, initial encounter for open fracture
S12.191B	Other nondisplaced fracture of second cervical vertebra, initial encounter for open fracture
S12.691B	Other nondisplaced fracture of seventh cervical vertebra, initial encounter for open fracture
S12.591B	Other nondisplaced fracture of sixth cervical vertebra, initial encounter for open fracture
S12.291B	Other nondisplaced fracture of third cervical vertebra, initial encounter for open fracture
S42.295B	Other nondisplaced fracture of upper end of left humerus, initial encounter for open fracture
S42.294B	Other nondisplaced fracture of upper end of right humerus, initial encounter for open fracture
S42.296B	Other nondisplaced fracture of upper end of unspecified humerus, initial encounter for open fracture
I61.8	Other nontraumatic intracerebral hemorrhage
I60.8	Other nontraumatic subarachnoid hemorrhage
K65.8	Other peritonitis
P29.38	Other persistent fetal circulation
S79.092A	Other physeal fracture of upper end of left femur, initial encounter for closed fracture
S79.091A	Other physeal fracture of upper end of right femur, initial encounter for closed fracture
S79.099A	Other physeal fracture of upper end of unspecified femur, initial encounter for closed fracture
J18.8	Other pneumonia, unspecified organism
T81.19XA	Other postprocedural shock, initial encounter
O24.82	Other pre-existing diabetes mellitus in childbirth
O45.8X1	Other premature separation of placenta, first trimester
O45.8X2	Other premature separation of placenta, second trimester
O45.8X3	Other premature separation of placenta, third trimester
I26.09	Other pulmonary embolism with acute cor pulmonale
I26.99	Other pulmonary embolism without acute cor pulmonale
P26.8	Other pulmonary hemorrhages originating in the perinatal period
Q04.3	Other reduction deformities of brain
K68.19	Other retroperitoneal abscess
R57.8	Other shock
D57.811	Other sickle-cell disorders with acute chest syndrome
D57.819	Other sickle-cell disorders with crisis, unspecified
D57.812	Other sickle-cell disorders with splenic sequestration
K45.1	Other specified abdominal hernia with gangrene
D61.89	Other specified aplastic anemias and other bone marrow failure syndromes
P37.8	Other specified congenital infectious and parasitic diseases
E13.01	Other specified diabetes mellitus with hyperosmolarity with coma
E13.00	Other specified diabetes mellitus with hyperosmolarity without nonketotic hyperglycemic-hyperosmolar coma (NKHHC)
E13.641	Other specified diabetes mellitus with hypoglycemia with coma
E13.11	Other specified diabetes mellitus with ketoacidosis with coma
E13.10	Other specified diabetes mellitus with ketoacidosis without coma
S32.492A	Other specified fracture of left acetabulum, initial encounter for closed fracture
S32.492B	Other specified fracture of left acetabulum, initial encounter for open fracture
S32.692B	Other specified fracture of left ischium, initial encounter for open fracture

S32.592B	Other specified fracture of left pubis, initial encounter for open fracture
S32.491A	Other specified fracture of right acetabulum, initial encounter for closed fracture
S32.491B	Other specified fracture of right acetabulum, initial encounter for open fracture
S32.691B	Other specified fracture of right ischium, initial encounter for open fracture
S32.591B	Other specified fracture of right pubis, initial encounter for open fracture
S32.499A	Other specified fracture of unspecified acetabulum, initial encounter for closed fracture
S32.499B	Other specified fracture of unspecified acetabulum, initial encounter for open fracture
S32.699B	Other specified fracture of unspecified ischium, initial encounter for open fracture
S32.599B	Other specified fracture of unspecified pubis, initial encounter for open fracture
S45.092A	Other specified injury of axillary artery, left side, initial encounter
S45.091A	Other specified injury of axillary artery, right side, initial encounter
S45.099A	Other specified injury of axillary artery, unspecified side, initial encounter
S75.092A	Other specified injury of femoral artery, left leg, initial encounter
S75.091A	Other specified injury of femoral artery, right leg, initial encounter
S75.099A	Other specified injury of femoral artery, unspecified leg, initial encounter
S75.192A	Other specified injury of femoral vein at hip and thigh level, left leg, initial encounter
S75.191A	Other specified injury of femoral vein at hip and thigh level, right leg, initial encounter
S75.199A	Other specified injury of femoral vein at hip and thigh level, unspecified leg, initial encounter
S35.348A	Other specified injury of inferior mesenteric vein, initial encounter
S25.192A	Other specified injury of left innominate or subclavian artery, initial encounter
S25.392A	Other specified injury of left innominate or subclavian vein, initial encounter
S25.492A	Other specified injury of left pulmonary blood vessels, initial encounter
S35.492A	Other specified injury of left renal artery, initial encounter
S35.495A	Other specified injury of left renal vein, initial encounter
S85.092A	Other specified injury of popliteal artery, left leg, initial encounter
S85.091A	Other specified injury of popliteal artery, right leg, initial encounter
S85.099A	Other specified injury of popliteal artery, unspecified leg, initial encounter
S85.592A	Other specified injury of popliteal vein, left leg, initial encounter
S85.591A	Other specified injury of popliteal vein, right leg, initial encounter
S85.599A	Other specified injury of popliteal vein, unspecified leg, initial encounter
S35.318A	Other specified injury of portal vein, initial encounter
S25.191A	Other specified injury of right innominate or subclavian artery, initial encounter
S25.391A	Other specified injury of right innominate or subclavian vein, initial encounter
S25.491A	Other specified injury of right pulmonary blood vessels, initial encounter
S35.491A	Other specified injury of right renal artery, initial encounter
S35.494A	Other specified injury of right renal vein, initial encounter
S35.328A	Other specified injury of splenic vein, initial encounter
S35.338A	Other specified injury of superior mesenteric vein, initial encounter
S25.29XA	Other specified injury of superior vena cava, initial encounter
S25.09XA	Other specified injury of thoracic aorta, initial encounter
S25.199A	Other specified injury of unspecified innominate or subclavian artery, initial encounter
S25.399A	Other specified injury of unspecified innominate or subclavian vein, initial encounter
S25.499A	Other specified injury of unspecified pulmonary blood vessels, initial encounter
S35.493A	Other specified injury of unspecified renal artery, initial encounter
S35.496A	Other specified injury of unspecified renal vein, initial encounter
S06.896A	Other specified intracranial injury with loss of consciousness greater than 24 hours without return to pre-existing conscious level with patient surviving, initial encounter
S06.897A	Other specified intracranial injury with loss of consciousness of any duration with death due to brain injury prior to regaining consciousness, initial encounter
S06.898A	Other specified intracranial injury with loss of consciousness of any duration with death due to other cause prior to regaining consciousness, initial encounter
P57.8	Other specified kernicterus
O86.89	Other specified puerperal infections
A41.89	Other specified sepsis
A40.8	Other streptococcal sepsis
A35	Other tetanus
E05.81	Other thyrotoxicosis with thyrotoxic crisis or storm
A84.8	Other tick-borne viral encephalitis
S12.450B	Other traumatic displaced spondylolisthesis of fifth cervical vertebra, initial encounter for open fracture
S12.350B	Other traumatic displaced spondylolisthesis of fourth cervical vertebra, initial encounter for open fracture
S12.150B	Other traumatic displaced spondylolisthesis of second cervical vertebra, initial encounter for open fracture
S12.650B	Other traumatic displaced spondylolisthesis of seventh cervical vertebra, initial encounter for open fracture
S12.550B	Other traumatic displaced spondylolisthesis of sixth cervical vertebra, initial encounter for open fracture
S12.250B	Other traumatic displaced spondylolisthesis of third cervical vertebra, initial encounter for open fracture
S12.451B	Other traumatic nondisplaced spondylolisthesis of fifth cervical vertebra, initial encounter for open fracture
S12.351B	Other traumatic nondisplaced spondylolisthesis of fourth cervical vertebra, initial encounter for open fracture

Alphabetic & Numeric Lists of MCCs

S12.151B	Other traumatic nondisplaced spondylolisthesis of second cervical vertebra, initial encounter for open fracture
S12.651B	Other traumatic nondisplaced spondylolisthesis of seventh cervical vertebra, initial encounter for open fracture
S12.551B	Other traumatic nondisplaced spondylolisthesis of sixth cervical vertebra, initial encounter for open fracture
S12.251B	Other traumatic nondisplaced spondylolisthesis of third cervical vertebra, initial encounter for open fracture
A17.89	Other tuberculosis of nervous system
G95.19	Other vascular myelopathies
J12.89	Other viral pneumonia
B46.8	Other zygomycoses
J12.2	Parainfluenza virus pneumonia
K43.4	Parastomal hernia with gangrene
O44.31	Partial placenta previa with hemorrhage, first trimester
O44.32	Partial placenta previa with hemorrhage, second trimester
O44.33	Partial placenta previa with hemorrhage, third trimester
K83.2	Perforation of bile duct
K22.3	Perforation of esophagus
K82.2	Perforation of gallbladder
K63.1	Perforation of intestine (nontraumatic)
P78.0	Perinatal intestinal perforation
O90.3	Peripartum cardiomyopathy
K65.1	Peritoneal abscess
K65.9	Peritonitis, unspecified
K75.1	Phlebitis of portal vein
O41.1411	Placentitis, first trimester, fetus 1
O41.1412	Placentitis, first trimester, fetus 2
O41.1413	Placentitis, first trimester, fetus 3
O41.1414	Placentitis, first trimester, fetus 4
O41.1415	Placentitis, first trimester, fetus 5
O41.1410	Placentitis, first trimester, not applicable or unspecified
O41.1419	Placentitis, first trimester, other fetus
O41.1421	Placentitis, second trimester, fetus 1
O41.1422	Placentitis, second trimester, fetus 2
O41.1423	Placentitis, second trimester, fetus 3
O41.1424	Placentitis, second trimester, fetus 4
O41.1425	Placentitis, second trimester, fetus 5
O41.1420	Placentitis, second trimester, not applicable or unspecified
O41.1429	Placentitis, second trimester, other fetus
O41.1431	Placentitis, third trimester, fetus 1
O41.1432	Placentitis, third trimester, fetus 2
O41.1433	Placentitis, third trimester, fetus 3
O41.1434	Placentitis, third trimester, fetus 4
O41.1435	Placentitis, third trimester, fetus 5
O41.1430	Placentitis, third trimester, not applicable or unspecified
O41.1439	Placentitis, third trimester, other fetus
A20.3	Plague meningitis
A20.9	Plague, unspecified
B50.9	Plasmodium falciparum malaria, unspecified
G00.1	Pneumococcal meningitis
B59	Pneumocystosis
P25.2	Pneumomediastinum originating in the perinatal period
J15.5	Pneumonia due to Escherichia coli
J14	Pneumonia due to Hemophilus influenzae
J15.0	Pneumonia due to Klebsiella pneumoniae
J15.212	Pneumonia due to Methicillin resistant Staphylococcus aureus
J15.211	Pneumonia due to Methicillin susceptible Staphylococcus aureus
J15.7	Pneumonia due to Mycoplasma pneumoniae
J15.6	Pneumonia due to other Gram-negative bacteria
J15.8	Pneumonia due to other specified bacteria
J16.8	Pneumonia due to other specified infectious organisms
J15.29	Pneumonia due to other staphylococcus
J15.4	Pneumonia due to other streptococci
J15.1	Pneumonia due to Pseudomonas
J12.81	Pneumonia due to SARS-associated coronavirus
J15.20	Pneumonia due to staphylococcus, unspecified
J13	Pneumonia due to Streptococcus pneumoniae
J15.3	Pneumonia due to streptococcus, group B
J17	Pneumonia in diseases classified elsewhere
J18.9	Pneumonia, unspecified organism
A20.2	Pneumonic plague
J69.0	Pneumonitis due to inhalation of food and vomit
J69.1	Pneumonitis due to inhalation of oils and essences
J69.8	Pneumonitis due to inhalation of other solids and liquids
P25.3	Pneumopericardium originating in the perinatal period
P25.1	Pneumothorax originating in the perinatal period
I81	Portal vein thrombosis
S12.111B	Posterior displaced Type II dens fracture, initial encounter for open fracture
I67.83	Posterior reversible encephalopathy syndrome
B02.24	Postherpetic myelitis
G04.02	Postimmunization acute disseminated encephalitis, myelitis and encephalomyelitis
G04.32	Postimmunization acute necrotizing hemorrhagic encephalopathy
G04.01	Postinfectious acute disseminated encephalitis and encephalomyelitis (postinfectious ADEM)
G04.31	Postinfectious acute necrotizing hemorrhagic encephalopathy
O90.4	Postpartum acute kidney failure
T81.11XA	Postprocedural cardiogenic shock, initial encounter

T81.12XA	Postprocedural septic shock, initial encounter
O11.1	Pre-existing hypertension with pre-eclampsia, first trimester
O11.2	Pre-existing hypertension with pre-eclampsia, second trimester
O11.3	Pre-existing hypertension with pre-eclampsia, third trimester
O10.42	Pre-existing secondary hypertension complicating childbirth
O24.02	Pre-existing type 1 diabetes mellitus, in childbirth
O24.12	Pre-existing type 2 diabetes mellitus, in childbirth
O45.011	Premature separation of placenta with afibrinogenemia, first trimester
O45.012	Premature separation of placenta with afibrinogenemia, second trimester
O45.013	Premature separation of placenta with afibrinogenemia, third trimester
O45.001	Premature separation of placenta with coagulation defect, unspecified, first trimester
O45.002	Premature separation of placenta with coagulation defect, unspecified, second trimester
O45.003	Premature separation of placenta with coagulation defect, unspecified, third trimester
O45.021	Premature separation of placenta with disseminated intravascular coagulation, first trimester
O45.022	Premature separation of placenta with disseminated intravascular coagulation, second trimester
O45.023	Premature separation of placenta with disseminated intravascular coagulation, third trimester
O45.091	Premature separation of placenta with other coagulation defect, first trimester
O45.092	Premature separation of placenta with other coagulation defect, second trimester
O45.093	Premature separation of placenta with other coagulation defect, third trimester
O45.91	Premature separation of placenta, unspecified, first trimester
O45.92	Premature separation of placenta, unspecified, second trimester
O45.93	Premature separation of placenta, unspecified, third trimester
L89.43	Pressure ulcer of contiguous site of back, buttock and hip, stage 3
L89.44	Pressure ulcer of contiguous site of back, buttock and hip, stage 4
L89.813	Pressure ulcer of head, stage 3
L89.814	Pressure ulcer of head, stage 4
L89.523	Pressure ulcer of left ankle, stage 3
L89.524	Pressure ulcer of left ankle, stage 4
L89.323	Pressure ulcer of left buttock, stage 3
L89.324	Pressure ulcer of left buttock, stage 4
L89.023	Pressure ulcer of left elbow, stage 3
L89.024	Pressure ulcer of left elbow, stage 4
L89.623	Pressure ulcer of left heel, stage 3
L89.624	Pressure ulcer of left heel, stage 4
L89.223	Pressure ulcer of left hip, stage 3
L89.224	Pressure ulcer of left hip, stage 4
L89.143	Pressure ulcer of left lower back, stage 3
L89.144	Pressure ulcer of left lower back, stage 4
L89.123	Pressure ulcer of left upper back, stage 3
L89.124	Pressure ulcer of left upper back, stage 4
L89.893	Pressure ulcer of other site, stage 3
L89.894	Pressure ulcer of other site, stage 4
L89.513	Pressure ulcer of right ankle, stage 3
L89.514	Pressure ulcer of right ankle, stage 4
L89.313	Pressure ulcer of right buttock, stage 3
L89.314	Pressure ulcer of right buttock, stage 4
L89.013	Pressure ulcer of right elbow, stage 3
L89.014	Pressure ulcer of right elbow, stage 4
L89.613	Pressure ulcer of right heel, stage 3
L89.614	Pressure ulcer of right heel, stage 4
L89.213	Pressure ulcer of right hip, stage 3
L89.214	Pressure ulcer of right hip, stage 4
L89.133	Pressure ulcer of right lower back, stage 3
L89.134	Pressure ulcer of right lower back, stage 4
L89.113	Pressure ulcer of right upper back, stage 3
L89.114	Pressure ulcer of right upper back, stage 4
L89.153	Pressure ulcer of sacral region, stage 3
L89.154	Pressure ulcer of sacral region, stage 4
L89.503	Pressure ulcer of unspecified ankle, stage 3
L89.504	Pressure ulcer of unspecified ankle, stage 4
L89.303	Pressure ulcer of unspecified buttock, stage 3
L89.304	Pressure ulcer of unspecified buttock, stage 4
L89.003	Pressure ulcer of unspecified elbow, stage 3
L89.004	Pressure ulcer of unspecified elbow, stage 4
L89.603	Pressure ulcer of unspecified heel, stage 3
L89.604	Pressure ulcer of unspecified heel, stage 4
L89.203	Pressure ulcer of unspecified hip, stage 3
L89.204	Pressure ulcer of unspecified hip, stage 4
L89.103	Pressure ulcer of unspecified part of back, stage 3
L89.104	Pressure ulcer of unspecified part of back, stage 4
L89.93	Pressure ulcer of unspecified site, stage 3
L89.94	Pressure ulcer of unspecified site, stage 4
O60.12X1	Preterm labor second trimester with preterm delivery second trimester, fetus 1
O60.12X2	Preterm labor second trimester with preterm delivery second trimester, fetus 2
O60.12X3	Preterm labor second trimester with preterm delivery second trimester, fetus 3
O60.12X4	Preterm labor second trimester with preterm delivery second trimester, fetus 4

O60.12X5	Preterm labor second trimester with preterm delivery second trimester, fetus 5	**S21.332A**	Puncture wound without foreign body of left front wall of thorax with penetration into thoracic cavity, initial encounter
O60.12X0	Preterm labor second trimester with preterm delivery second trimester, not applicable or unspecified	**S31.031A**	Puncture wound without foreign body of lower back and pelvis with penetration into retroperitoneum, initial encounter
O60.12X9	Preterm labor second trimester with preterm delivery second trimester, other fetus	**S21.431A**	Puncture wound without foreign body of right back wall of thorax with penetration into thoracic cavity, initial encounter
O60.13X1	Preterm labor second trimester with preterm delivery third trimester, fetus 1	**S21.331A**	Puncture wound without foreign body of right front wall of thorax with penetration into thoracic cavity, initial encounter
O60.13X2	Preterm labor second trimester with preterm delivery third trimester, fetus 2	**S11.023A**	Puncture wound without foreign body of trachea, initial encounter
O60.13X3	Preterm labor second trimester with preterm delivery third trimester, fetus 3	**S21.439A**	Puncture wound without foreign body of unspecified back wall of thorax with penetration into thoracic cavity, initial encounter
O60.13X4	Preterm labor second trimester with preterm delivery third trimester, fetus 4	**S21.339A**	Puncture wound without foreign body of unspecified front wall of thorax with penetration into thoracic cavity, initial encounter
O60.13X5	Preterm labor second trimester with preterm delivery third trimester, fetus 5		
O60.13X0	Preterm labor second trimester with preterm delivery third trimester, not applicable or unspecified	**S11.033A**	Puncture wound without foreign body of vocal cord, initial encounter
O60.13X9	Preterm labor second trimester with preterm delivery third trimester, other fetus	**O88.32**	Pyemic and septic embolism in childbirth
		O88.311	Pyemic and septic embolism in pregnancy, first trimester
O60.14X1	Preterm labor third trimester with preterm delivery third trimester, fetus 1	**O88.312**	Pyemic and septic embolism in pregnancy, second trimester
O60.14X2	Preterm labor third trimester with preterm delivery third trimester, fetus 2	**O88.313**	Pyemic and septic embolism in pregnancy, third trimester
O60.14X3	Preterm labor third trimester with preterm delivery third trimester, fetus 3	**O88.33**	Pyemic and septic embolism in the puerperium
O60.14X4	Preterm labor third trimester with preterm delivery third trimester, fetus 4	**J86.0**	Pyothorax with fistula
O60.14X5	Preterm labor third trimester with preterm delivery third trimester, fetus 5	**J86.9**	Pyothorax without fistula
O60.14X0	Preterm labor third trimester with preterm delivery third trimester, not applicable or unspecified	**G82.51**	Quadriplegia, C1-C4 complete
		G82.52	Quadriplegia, C1-C4 incomplete
O60.14X9	Preterm labor third trimester with preterm delivery third trimester, other fetus	**G82.53**	Quadriplegia, C5-C7 complete
O60.02	Preterm labor without delivery, second trimester	**G82.54**	Quadriplegia, C5-C7 incomplete
O60.03	Preterm labor without delivery, third trimester	**G82.50**	Quadriplegia, unspecified
S27.412A	Primary blast injury of bronchus, bilateral, initial encounter	**N01.6**	Rapidly progressive nephritic syndrome with dense deposit disease
S27.411A	Primary blast injury of bronchus, unilateral, initial encounter	**N01.7**	Rapidly progressive nephritic syndrome with diffuse crescentic glomerulonephritis
S27.419A	Primary blast injury of bronchus, unspecified, initial encounter	**N01.4**	Rapidly progressive nephritic syndrome with diffuse endocapillary proliferative glomerulonephritis
Q79.4	Prune belly syndrome		
K68.12	Psoas muscle abscess	**N01.2**	Rapidly progressive nephritic syndrome with diffuse membranous glomerulonephritis
O85	Puerperal sepsis		
O86.81	Puerperal septic thrombophlebitis	**N01.3**	Rapidly progressive nephritic syndrome with diffuse mesangial proliferative glomerulonephritis
A22.1	Pulmonary anthrax		
B37.1	Pulmonary candidiasis	**N01.5**	Rapidly progressive nephritic syndrome with diffuse mesangiocapillary glomerulonephritis
J68.1	Pulmonary edema due to chemicals, gases, fumes and vapors		
B39.2	Pulmonary histoplasmosis capsulati, unspecified	**N01.1**	Rapidly progressive nephritic syndrome with focal and segmental glomerular lesions
P29.30	Pulmonary hypertension of newborn		
J84.842	Pulmonary interstitial glycogenosis	**N01.0**	Rapidly progressive nephritic syndrome with minor glomerular abnormality
B46.0	Pulmonary mucormycosis	**N01.8**	Rapidly progressive nephritic syndrome with other morphologic changes
B58.3	Pulmonary toxoplasmosis	**N01.9**	Rapidly progressive nephritic syndrome with unspecified morphologic changes
Q22.0	Pulmonary valve atresia		
S31.642A	Puncture wound with foreign body of abdominal wall, epigastric region with penetration into peritoneal cavity, initial encounter	**N15.1**	Renal and perinephric abscess
		O04.82	Renal failure following (induced) termination of pregnancy
S31.644A	Puncture wound with foreign body of abdominal wall, left lower quadrant with penetration into peritoneal cavity, initial encounter	**O03.82**	Renal failure following complete or unspecified spontaneous abortion
		O08.4	Renal failure following ectopic and molar pregnancy
S31.641A	Puncture wound with foreign body of abdominal wall, left upper quadrant with penetration into peritoneal cavity, initial encounter	**O07.32**	Renal failure following failed attempted termination of pregnancy
		O03.32	Renal failure following incomplete spontaneous abortion
S31.645A	Puncture wound with foreign body of abdominal wall, periumbilic region with penetration into peritoneal cavity, initial encounter	**R09.2**	Respiratory arrest
		P28.81	Respiratory arrest of newborn
S31.643A	Puncture wound with foreign body of abdominal wall, right lower quadrant with penetration into peritoneal cavity, initial encounter	**P22.0**	Respiratory distress syndrome of newborn
		P28.5	Respiratory failure of newborn
S31.640A	Puncture wound with foreign body of abdominal wall, right upper quadrant with penetration into peritoneal cavity, initial encounter	**J96.92**	Respiratory failure, unspecified with hypercapnia
		J96.91	Respiratory failure, unspecified with hypoxia
S31.649A	Puncture wound with foreign body of abdominal wall, unspecified quadrant with penetration into peritoneal cavity, initial encounter	**J96.90**	Respiratory failure, unspecified, unspecified whether with hypoxia or hypercapnia
S11.014A	Puncture wound with foreign body of larynx, initial encounter	**J12.1**	Respiratory syncytial virus pneumonia
S21.442A	Puncture wound with foreign body of left back wall of thorax with penetration into thoracic cavity, initial encounter	**G93.7**	Reye's syndrome
		B46.1	Rhinocerebral mucormycosis
S21.342A	Puncture wound with foreign body of left front wall of thorax with penetration into thoracic cavity, initial encounter	**A83.6**	Rocio virus disease
		B06.01	Rubella encephalitis
S31.041A	Puncture wound with foreign body of lower back and pelvis with penetration into retroperitoneum, initial encounter	**I23.4**	Rupture of chordae tendineae as current complication following acute myocardial infarction
		I51.1	Rupture of chordae tendineae, not elsewhere classified
S21.441A	Puncture wound with foreign body of right back wall of thorax with penetration into thoracic cavity, initial encounter	**I23.5**	Rupture of papillary muscle as current complication following acute myocardial infarction
S21.341A	Puncture wound with foreign body of right front wall of thorax with penetration into thoracic cavity, initial encounter	**I51.2**	Rupture of papillary muscle, not elsewhere classified
S11.024A	Puncture wound with foreign body of trachea, initial encounter	**O71.02**	Rupture of uterus before onset of labor, second trimester
S21.449A	Puncture wound with foreign body of unspecified back wall of thorax with penetration into thoracic cavity, initial encounter	**O71.03**	Rupture of uterus before onset of labor, third trimester
		O71.1	Rupture of uterus during labor
S21.349A	Puncture wound with foreign body of unspecified front wall of thorax with penetration into thoracic cavity, initial encounter	**I74.01**	Saddle embolus of abdominal aorta
		I26.02	Saddle embolus of pulmonary artery with acute cor pulmonale
S11.034A	Puncture wound with foreign body of vocal cord, initial encounter	**I26.92**	Saddle embolus of pulmonary artery without acute cor pulmonale
S31.632A	Puncture wound without foreign body of abdominal wall, epigastric region with penetration into peritoneal cavity, initial encounter	**A02.21**	Salmonella meningitis
		A02.22	Salmonella pneumonia
S31.634A	Puncture wound without foreign body of abdominal wall, left lower quadrant with penetration into peritoneal cavity, initial encounter	**A02.1**	Salmonella sepsis
		S79.012A	Salter-Harris Type I physeal fracture of upper end of left femur, initial encounter for closed fracture
S31.631A	Puncture wound without foreign body of abdominal wall, left upper quadrant with penetration into peritoneal cavity, initial encounter	**S79.011A**	Salter-Harris Type I physeal fracture of upper end of right femur, initial encounter for closed fracture
S31.635A	Puncture wound without foreign body of abdominal wall, periumbilic region with penetration into peritoneal cavity, initial encounter	**S79.019A**	Salter-Harris Type I physeal fracture of upper end of unspecified femur, initial encounter for closed fracture
S31.633A	Puncture wound without foreign body of abdominal wall, right lower quadrant with penetration into peritoneal cavity, initial encounter		
		I85.11	Secondary esophageal varices with bleeding
S31.630A	Puncture wound without foreign body of abdominal wall, right upper quadrant with penetration into peritoneal cavity, initial encounter	**A51.41**	Secondary syphilitic meningitis
		A41.4	Sepsis due to anaerobes
S31.639A	Puncture wound without foreign body of abdominal wall, unspecified quadrant with penetration into peritoneal cavity, initial encounter	**A41.81**	Sepsis due to Enterococcus
		A41.51	Sepsis due to Escherichia coli [E. coli]
S11.013A	Puncture wound without foreign body of larynx, initial encounter	**A41.3**	Sepsis due to Hemophilus influenzae
S21.432A	Puncture wound without foreign body of left back wall of thorax with penetration into thoracic cavity, initial encounter	**A41.02**	Sepsis due to Methicillin resistant Staphylococcus aureus

A41.01	Sepsis due to Methicillin susceptible Staphylococcus aureus
A41.1	Sepsis due to other specified staphylococcus
A41.52	Sepsis due to Pseudomonas
A41.53	Sepsis due to Serratia
A40.3	Sepsis due to Streptococcus pneumoniae
A40.0	Sepsis due to streptococcus, group A
A40.1	Sepsis due to streptococcus, group B
A41.2	Sepsis due to unspecified staphylococcus
O86.04	Sepsis following an obstetrical procedure
P36.5	Sepsis of newborn due to anaerobes
P36.4	Sepsis of newborn due to Escherichia coli
P36.39	Sepsis of newborn due to other staphylococci
P36.19	Sepsis of newborn due to other streptococci
P36.2	Sepsis of newborn due to Staphylococcus aureus
P36.0	Sepsis of newborn due to streptococcus, group B
P36.30	Sepsis of newborn due to unspecified staphylococci
P36.10	Sepsis of newborn due to unspecified streptococci
A41.9	Sepsis, unspecified organism
I26.01	Septic pulmonary embolism with acute cor pulmonale
I26.90	Septic pulmonary embolism without acute cor pulmonale
A20.7	Septicemic plague
Q33.2	Sequestration of lung
P91.63	Severe hypoxic ischemic encephalopathy [HIE]
O14.12	Severe pre-eclampsia, second trimester
O14.13	Severe pre-eclampsia, third trimester
R65.21	Severe sepsis with septic shock
R65.20	Severe sepsis without septic shock
S32.112B	Severely displaced Zone I fracture of sacrum, initial encounter for open fracture
S32.122B	Severely displaced Zone II fracture of sacrum, initial encounter for open fracture
S32.132B	Severely displaced Zone III fracture of sacrum, initial encounter for open fracture
O75.1	Shock during or following labor and delivery
O04.81	Shock following (induced) termination of pregnancy
O03.81	Shock following complete or unspecified spontaneous abortion
O08.3	Shock following ectopic and molar pregnancy
O07.31	Shock following failed attempted termination of pregnancy
O03.31	Shock following incomplete spontaneous abortion
D57.411	Sickle-cell thalassemia with acute chest syndrome
D57.419	Sickle-cell thalassemia with crisis, unspecified
D57.412	Sickle-cell thalassemia with splenic sequestration
D57.211	Sickle-cell/Hb-C disease with acute chest syndrome
D57.219	Sickle-cell/Hb-C disease with crisis, unspecified
D57.212	Sickle-cell/Hb-C disease with splenic sequestration
I26.93	Single subsegmental pulmonary embolism without acute cor pulmonale
S52.542B	Smith's fracture of left radius, initial encounter for open fracture type I or II
S52.542C	Smith's fracture of left radius, initial encounter for open fracture type IIIA, IIIB, or IIIC
S52.541B	Smith's fracture of right radius, initial encounter for open fracture type I or II
S52.541C	Smith's fracture of right radius, initial encounter for open fracture type IIIA, IIIB, or IIIC
S52.549B	Smith's fracture of unspecified radius, initial encounter for open fracture type I or II
S52.549C	Smith's fracture of unspecified radius, initial encounter for open fracture type IIIA, IIIB, or IIIC
G80.0	Spastic quadriplegic cerebral palsy
K65.2	Spontaneous bacterial peritonitis
J93.0	Spontaneous tension pneumothorax
I21.02	ST elevation (STEMI) myocardial infarction involving left anterior descending coronary artery
I21.21	ST elevation (STEMI) myocardial infarction involving left circumflex coronary artery
I21.01	ST elevation (STEMI) myocardial infarction involving left main coronary artery
I21.09	ST elevation (STEMI) myocardial infarction involving other coronary artery of anterior wall
I21.19	ST elevation (STEMI) myocardial infarction involving other coronary artery of inferior wall
I21.29	ST elevation (STEMI) myocardial infarction involving other sites
I21.11	ST elevation (STEMI) myocardial infarction involving right coronary artery
I21.3	ST elevation (STEMI) myocardial infarction of unspecified site
A83.3	St Louis encephalitis
S32.051B	Stable burst fracture of fifth lumbar vertebra, initial encounter for open fracture
S12.01XB	Stable burst fracture of first cervical vertebra, initial encounter for open fracture
S32.011B	Stable burst fracture of first lumbar vertebra, initial encounter for open fracture
S22.011B	Stable burst fracture of first thoracic vertebra, initial encounter for open fracture
S32.041B	Stable burst fracture of fourth lumbar vertebra, initial encounter for open fracture
S22.041B	Stable burst fracture of fourth thoracic vertebra, initial encounter for open fracture
S32.021B	Stable burst fracture of second lumbar vertebra, initial encounter for open fracture
S22.021B	Stable burst fracture of second thoracic vertebra, initial encounter for open fracture
S22.081B	Stable burst fracture of T11-T12 vertebra, initial encounter for open fracture
S22.051B	Stable burst fracture of T5-T6 vertebra, initial encounter for open fracture
S22.061B	Stable burst fracture of T7-T8 vertebra, initial encounter for open fracture
S22.071B	Stable burst fracture of T9-T10 vertebra, initial encounter for open fracture
S32.031B	Stable burst fracture of third lumbar vertebra, initial encounter for open fracture
S22.031B	Stable burst fracture of third thoracic vertebra, initial encounter for open fracture
S32.001B	Stable burst fracture of unspecified lumbar vertebra, initial encounter for open fracture
S22.001B	Stable burst fracture of unspecified thoracic vertebra, initial encounter for open fracture
K55.31	Stage 1 necrotizing enterocolitis
P77.1	Stage 1 necrotizing enterocolitis in newborn
K55.32	Stage 2 necrotizing enterocolitis
P77.2	Stage 2 necrotizing enterocolitis in newborn
K55.33	Stage 3 necrotizing enterocolitis
P77.3	Stage 3 necrotizing enterocolitis in newborn
G00.3	Staphylococcal meningitis
Q25.6	Stenosis of pulmonary artery
S22.23XB	Sternal manubrial dissociation, initial encounter for open fracture
G00.2	Streptococcal meningitis
A40.9	Streptococcal sepsis, unspecified
G37.4	Subacute necrotizing myelitis of central nervous system
P52.5	Subarachnoid (nontraumatic) hemorrhage of newborn
P10.3	Subarachnoid hemorrhage due to birth injury
P10.0	Subdural hemorrhage due to birth injury
I22.2	Subsequent non-ST elevation (NSTEMI) myocardial infarction
I22.0	Subsequent ST elevation (STEMI) myocardial infarction of anterior wall
I22.1	Subsequent ST elevation (STEMI) myocardial infarction of inferior wall
I22.8	Subsequent ST elevation (STEMI) myocardial infarction of other sites
I22.9	Subsequent ST elevation (STEMI) myocardial infarction of unspecified site
J04.31	Supraglottitis, unspecified, with obstruction
J84.83	Surfactant mutations of the lung
R65.11	Systemic inflammatory response syndrome (SIRS) of non-infectious origin with acute organ dysfunction
P10.4	Tentorial tear due to birth injury
O60.22X1	Term delivery with preterm labor, second trimester, fetus 1
O60.22X2	Term delivery with preterm labor, second trimester, fetus 2
O60.22X3	Term delivery with preterm labor, second trimester, fetus 3
O60.22X4	Term delivery with preterm labor, second trimester, fetus 4
O60.22X5	Term delivery with preterm labor, second trimester, fetus 5
O60.22X0	Term delivery with preterm labor, second trimester, not applicable or unspecified
O60.22X9	Term delivery with preterm labor, second trimester, other fetus
O60.23X1	Term delivery with preterm labor, third trimester, fetus 1
O60.23X2	Term delivery with preterm labor, third trimester, fetus 2
O60.23X3	Term delivery with preterm labor, third trimester, fetus 3
O60.23X4	Term delivery with preterm labor, third trimester, fetus 4
O60.23X5	Term delivery with preterm labor, third trimester, fetus 5
O60.23X0	Term delivery with preterm labor, third trimester, not applicable or unspecified
O60.23X9	Term delivery with preterm labor, third trimester, other fetus
A33	Tetanus neonatorum
Q21.3	Tetralogy of Fallot
I71.1	Thoracic aortic aneurysm, ruptured
I71.5	Thoracoabdominal aortic aneurysm, ruptured
O88.22	Thromboembolism in childbirth
O88.211	Thromboembolism in pregnancy, first trimester
O88.212	Thromboembolism in pregnancy, second trimester
O88.213	Thromboembolism in pregnancy, third trimester
O88.23	Thromboembolism in the puerperium
M31.1	Thrombotic microangiopathy
E05.41	Thyrotoxicosis factitia with thyrotoxic crisis or storm
E05.31	Thyrotoxicosis from ectopic thyroid tissue with thyrotoxic crisis or storm
E05.01	Thyrotoxicosis with diffuse goiter with thyrotoxic crisis or storm
E05.21	Thyrotoxicosis with toxic multinodular goiter with thyrotoxic crisis or storm
E05.11	Thyrotoxicosis with toxic single thyroid nodule with thyrotoxic crisis or storm
E05.91	Thyrotoxicosis, unspecified with thyrotoxic crisis or storm
A84.9	Tick-borne viral encephalitis, unspecified
G92	Toxic encephalopathy
K71.11	Toxic liver disease with hepatic necrosis, with coma
A48.3	Toxic shock syndrome
B58.2	Toxoplasma meningoencephalitis
B58.81	Toxoplasma myocarditis
P26.0	Tracheobronchial hemorrhage originating in the perinatal period
D60.1	Transient acquired pure red cell aplasia
P61.5	Transient neonatal neutropenia
P61.0	Transient neonatal thrombocytopenia
T79.5XXA	Traumatic anuria, initial encounter
S06.1X5A	Traumatic cerebral edema with loss of consciousness greater than 24 hours with return to pre-existing conscious level, initial encounter
S06.1X6A	Traumatic cerebral edema with loss of consciousness greater than 24 hours without return to pre-existing conscious level with patient surviving, initial encounter
S06.1X3A	Traumatic cerebral edema with loss of consciousness of 1 hour to 5 hours 59 minutes, initial encounter
S06.1X1A	Traumatic cerebral edema with loss of consciousness of 30 minutes or less, initial encounter
S06.1X2A	Traumatic cerebral edema with loss of consciousness of 31 minutes to 59 minutes, initial encounter

S06.1X4A Traumatic cerebral edema with loss of consciousness of 6 hours to 24 hours, initial encounter

S06.1X7A Traumatic cerebral edema with loss of consciousness of any duration with death due to brain injury prior to regaining consciousness, initial encounter

S06.1X8A Traumatic cerebral edema with loss of consciousness of any duration with death due to other cause prior to regaining consciousness, initial encounter

S06.1X9A Traumatic cerebral edema with loss of consciousness of unspecified duration, initial encounter

S06.1X0A Traumatic cerebral edema without loss of consciousness, initial encounter

S27.2XXA Traumatic hemopneumothorax, initial encounter

S06.365A Traumatic hemorrhage of cerebrum, unspecified, with loss of consciousness greater than 24 hours with return to pre-existing conscious level, initial encounter

S06.366A Traumatic hemorrhage of cerebrum, unspecified, with loss of consciousness greater than 24 hours without return to pre-existing conscious level with patient surviving, initial encounter

S06.363A Traumatic hemorrhage of cerebrum, unspecified, with loss of consciousness of 1 hours to 5 hours 59 minutes, initial encounter

S06.361A Traumatic hemorrhage of cerebrum, unspecified, with loss of consciousness of 30 minutes or less, initial encounter

S06.362A Traumatic hemorrhage of cerebrum, unspecified, with loss of consciousness of 31 minutes to 59 minutes, initial encounter

S06.364A Traumatic hemorrhage of cerebrum, unspecified, with loss of consciousness of 6 hours to 24 hours, initial encounter

S06.367A Traumatic hemorrhage of cerebrum, unspecified, with loss of consciousness of any duration with death due to brain injury prior to regaining consciousness, initial encounter

S06.368A Traumatic hemorrhage of cerebrum, unspecified, with loss of consciousness of any duration with death due to other cause prior to regaining consciousness, initial encounter

S06.369A Traumatic hemorrhage of cerebrum, unspecified, with loss of consciousness of unspecified duration, initial encounter

S06.360A Traumatic hemorrhage of cerebrum, unspecified, without loss of consciousness, initial encounter

S06.355A Traumatic hemorrhage of left cerebrum with loss of consciousness greater than 24 hours with return to pre-existing conscious level, initial encounter

S06.356A Traumatic hemorrhage of left cerebrum with loss of consciousness greater than 24 hours without return to pre-existing conscious level with patient surviving, initial encounter

S06.353A Traumatic hemorrhage of left cerebrum with loss of consciousness of 1 hours to 5 hours 59 minutes, initial encounter

S06.351A Traumatic hemorrhage of left cerebrum with loss of consciousness of 30 minutes or less, initial encounter

S06.352A Traumatic hemorrhage of left cerebrum with loss of consciousness of 31 minutes to 59 minutes, initial encounter

S06.354A Traumatic hemorrhage of left cerebrum with loss of consciousness of 6 hours to 24 hours, initial encounter

S06.357A Traumatic hemorrhage of left cerebrum with loss of consciousness of any duration with death due to brain injury prior to regaining consciousness, initial encounter

S06.358A Traumatic hemorrhage of left cerebrum with loss of consciousness of any duration with death due to other cause prior to regaining consciousness, initial encounter

S06.359A Traumatic hemorrhage of left cerebrum with loss of consciousness of unspecified duration, initial encounter

S06.350A Traumatic hemorrhage of left cerebrum without loss of consciousness, initial encounter

S06.345A Traumatic hemorrhage of right cerebrum with loss of consciousness greater than 24 hours with return to pre-existing conscious level, initial encounter

S06.346A Traumatic hemorrhage of right cerebrum with loss of consciousness greater than 24 hours without return to pre-existing conscious level with patient surviving, initial encounter

S06.343A Traumatic hemorrhage of right cerebrum with loss of consciousness of 1 hours to 5 hours 59 minutes, initial encounter

S06.341A Traumatic hemorrhage of right cerebrum with loss of consciousness of 30 minutes or less, initial encounter

S06.342A Traumatic hemorrhage of right cerebrum with loss of consciousness of 31 minutes to 59 minutes, initial encounter

S06.344A Traumatic hemorrhage of right cerebrum with loss of consciousness of 6 hours to 24 hours, initial encounter

S06.347A Traumatic hemorrhage of right cerebrum with loss of consciousness of any duration with death due to brain injury prior to regaining consciousness, initial encounter

S06.348A Traumatic hemorrhage of right cerebrum with loss of consciousness of any duration with death due to other cause prior to regaining consciousness, initial encounter

S06.349A Traumatic hemorrhage of right cerebrum with loss of consciousness of unspecified duration, initial encounter

S06.340A Traumatic hemorrhage of right cerebrum without loss of consciousness, initial encounter

S27.1XXA Traumatic hemothorax, initial encounter

T79.4XXA Traumatic shock, initial encounter

S06.6X5A Traumatic subarachnoid hemorrhage with loss of consciousness greater than 24 hours with return to pre-existing conscious level, initial encounter

S06.6X6A Traumatic subarachnoid hemorrhage with loss of consciousness greater than 24 hours without return to pre-existing conscious level with patient surviving, initial encounter

S06.6X3A Traumatic subarachnoid hemorrhage with loss of consciousness of 1 hour to 5 hours 59 minutes, initial encounter

S06.6X1A Traumatic subarachnoid hemorrhage with loss of consciousness of 30 minutes or less, initial encounter

S06.6X2A Traumatic subarachnoid hemorrhage with loss of consciousness of 31 minutes to 59 minutes, initial encounter

S06.6X4A Traumatic subarachnoid hemorrhage with loss of consciousness of 6 hours to 24 hours, initial encounter

S06.6X7A Traumatic subarachnoid hemorrhage with loss of consciousness of any duration with death due to brain injury prior to regaining consciousness, initial encounter

S06.6X8A Traumatic subarachnoid hemorrhage with loss of consciousness of any duration with death due to other cause prior to regaining consciousness, initial encounter

S06.6X9A Traumatic subarachnoid hemorrhage with loss of consciousness of unspecified duration, initial encounter

S06.6X0A Traumatic subarachnoid hemorrhage without loss of consciousness, initial encounter

S06.5X5A Traumatic subdural hemorrhage with loss of consciousness greater than 24 hours with return to pre-existing conscious level, initial encounter

S06.5X6A Traumatic subdural hemorrhage with loss of consciousness greater than 24 hours without return to pre-existing conscious level with patient surviving, initial encounter

S06.5X3A Traumatic subdural hemorrhage with loss of consciousness of 1 hour to 5 hours 59 minutes, initial encounter

S06.5X1A Traumatic subdural hemorrhage with loss of consciousness of 30 minutes or less, initial encounter

S06.5X2A Traumatic subdural hemorrhage with loss of consciousness of 31 minutes to 59 minutes, initial encounter

S06.5X4A Traumatic subdural hemorrhage with loss of consciousness of 6 hours to 24 hours, initial encounter

S06.5X7A Traumatic subdural hemorrhage with loss of consciousness of any duration with death due to brain injury before regaining consciousness, initial encounter

S06.5X8A Traumatic subdural hemorrhage with loss of consciousness of any duration with death due to other cause before regaining consciousness, initial encounter

S06.5X9A Traumatic subdural hemorrhage with loss of consciousness of unspecified duration, initial encounter

S06.5X0A Traumatic subdural hemorrhage without loss of consciousness, initial encounter

A17.81 Tuberculoma of brain and spinal cord

A17.0 Tuberculous meningitis

A17.82 Tuberculous meningoencephalitis

A17.83 Tuberculous neuritis

A18.31 Tuberculous peritonitis

E88.3 Tumor lysis syndrome

E10.641 Type 1 diabetes mellitus with hypoglycemia with coma

E10.11 Type 1 diabetes mellitus with ketoacidosis with coma

E10.10 Type 1 diabetes mellitus with ketoacidosis without coma

S32.14XB Type 1 fracture of sacrum, initial encounter for open fracture

E11.01 Type 2 diabetes mellitus with hyperosmolarity with coma

E11.00 Type 2 diabetes mellitus with hyperosmolarity without nonketotic hyperglycemic-hyperosmolar coma (NKHHC)

E11.641 Type 2 diabetes mellitus with hypoglycemia with coma

E11.11 Type 2 diabetes mellitus with ketoacidosis with coma

E11.10 Type 2 diabetes mellitus with ketoacidosis without coma

S32.15XB Type 2 fracture of sacrum, initial encounter for open fracture

S32.16XB Type 3 fracture of sacrum, initial encounter for open fracture

S32.17XB Type 4 fracture of sacrum, initial encounter for open fracture

S02.11BB Type I occipital condyle fracture, left side, initial encounter for open fracture

S02.11AB Type I occipital condyle fracture, right side, initial encounter for open fracture

S02.110B Type I occipital condyle fracture, unspecified side, initial encounter for open fracture

S02.11DB Type II occipital condyle fracture, left side, initial encounter for open fracture

S02.11CB Type II occipital condyle fracture, right side, initial encounter for open fracture

S02.111B Type II occipital condyle fracture, unspecified side, initial encounter for open fracture

S02.11FB Type III occipital condyle fracture, left side, initial encounter for open fracture

S02.11EB Type III occipital condyle fracture, right side, initial encounter for open fracture

S02.112B Type III occipital condyle fracture, unspecified side, initial encounter for open fracture

S12.44XB Type III traumatic spondylolisthesis of fifth cervical vertebra, initial encounter for open fracture

S12.34XB Type III traumatic spondylolisthesis of fourth cervical vertebra, initial encounter for open fracture

S12.14XB Type III traumatic spondylolisthesis of second cervical vertebra, initial encounter for open fracture

S12.64XB Type III traumatic spondylolisthesis of seventh cervical vertebra, initial encounter for open fracture

S12.54XB Type III traumatic spondylolisthesis of sixth cervical vertebra, initial encounter for open fracture

S12.24XB Type III traumatic spondylolisthesis of third cervical vertebra, initial encounter for open fracture

K22.11 Ulcer of esophagus with bleeding

K42.1 Umbilical hernia with gangrene

K41.40 Unilateral femoral hernia, with gangrene, not specified as recurrent

K41.41 Unilateral femoral hernia, with gangrene, recurrent

K40.40 Unilateral inguinal hernia, with gangrene, not specified as recurrent

K40.41 Unilateral inguinal hernia, with gangrene, recurrent

K46.1 Unspecified abdominal hernia with gangrene

J15.9 Unspecified bacterial pneumonia

P11.2 Unspecified brain damage due to birth injury

K29.51 Unspecified chronic gastritis with bleeding

P27.9 Unspecified chronic respiratory disease originating in the perinatal period

R40.20 Unspecified coma

S12.400B Unspecified displaced fracture of fifth cervical vertebra, initial encounter for open fracture

S12.000B Unspecified displaced fracture of first cervical vertebra, initial encounter for open fracture

S12.300B Unspecified displaced fracture of fourth cervical vertebra, initial encounter for open fracture

S12.100B Unspecified displaced fracture of second cervical vertebra, initial encounter for open fracture

S12.600B Unspecified displaced fracture of seventh cervical vertebra, initial encounter for open fracture

S12.500B Unspecified displaced fracture of sixth cervical vertebra, initial encounter for open fracture

S42.212B Unspecified displaced fracture of surgical neck of left humerus, initial encounter for open fracture

S42.211B Unspecified displaced fracture of surgical neck of right humerus, initial encounter for open fracture

S42.213B Unspecified displaced fracture of surgical neck of unspecified humerus, initial encounter for open fracture

S12.200B Unspecified displaced fracture of third cervical vertebra, initial encounter for open fracture

S06.306A Unspecified focal traumatic brain injury with loss of consciousness greater than 24 hours without return to pre-existing conscious level with patient surviving, initial encounter

S06.307A Unspecified focal traumatic brain injury with loss of consciousness of any duration with death due to brain injury prior to regaining consciousness, initial encounter

S06.308A Unspecified focal traumatic brain injury with loss of consciousness of any duration with death due to other cause prior to regaining consciousness, initial encounter

S32.059B Unspecified fracture of fifth lumbar vertebra, initial encounter for open fracture

S32.019B Unspecified fracture of first lumbar vertebra, initial encounter for open fracture

S22.019B Unspecified fracture of first thoracic vertebra, initial encounter for open fracture

S32.049B Unspecified fracture of fourth lumbar vertebra, initial encounter for open fracture

S22.049B Unspecified fracture of fourth thoracic vertebra, initial encounter for open fracture

S72.052A Unspecified fracture of head of left femur, initial encounter for closed fracture

S72.052B Unspecified fracture of head of left femur, initial encounter for open fracture type I or II

S72.052C Unspecified fracture of head of left femur, initial encounter for open fracture type IIIA, IIIB, or IIIC

S72.051A Unspecified fracture of head of right femur, initial encounter for closed fracture

S72.051B Unspecified fracture of head of right femur, initial encounter for open fracture type I or II

S72.051C Unspecified fracture of head of right femur, initial encounter for open fracture type IIIA, IIIB, or IIIC

S72.059A Unspecified fracture of head of unspecified femur, initial encounter for closed fracture

S72.059B Unspecified fracture of head of unspecified femur, initial encounter for open fracture type I or II

S72.059C Unspecified fracture of head of unspecified femur, initial encounter for open fracture type IIIA, IIIB, or IIIC

S32.402A Unspecified fracture of left acetabulum, initial encounter for closed fracture

S32.402B Unspecified fracture of left acetabulum, initial encounter for open fracture

S72.92XA Unspecified fracture of left femur, initial encounter for closed fracture

S72.92XB Unspecified fracture of left femur, initial encounter for open fracture type I or II

S72.92XC Unspecified fracture of left femur, initial encounter for open fracture type IIIA, IIIB, or IIIC

S52.92XB Unspecified fracture of left forearm, initial encounter for open fracture type I or II

S52.92XC Unspecified fracture of left forearm, initial encounter for open fracture type IIIA, IIIB, or IIIC

S32.302B Unspecified fracture of left ilium, initial encounter for open fracture

S32.602B Unspecified fracture of left ischium, initial encounter for open fracture

S32.502B Unspecified fracture of left pubis, initial encounter for open fracture

S72.402B Unspecified fracture of lower end of left femur, initial encounter for open fracture type I or II

S72.402C Unspecified fracture of lower end of left femur, initial encounter for open fracture type IIIA, IIIB, or IIIC

S42.402B Unspecified fracture of lower end of left humerus, initial encounter for open fracture

S52.602B Unspecified fracture of lower end of left ulna, initial encounter for open fracture type I or II

S52.602C Unspecified fracture of lower end of left ulna, initial encounter for open fracture type IIIA, IIIB, or IIIC

S72.401B Unspecified fracture of lower end of right femur, initial encounter for open fracture type I or II

S72.401C Unspecified fracture of lower end of right femur, initial encounter for open fracture type IIIA, IIIB, or IIIC

S42.401B Unspecified fracture of lower end of right humerus, initial encounter for open fracture

S52.601B Unspecified fracture of lower end of right ulna, initial encounter for open fracture type I or II

S52.601C Unspecified fracture of lower end of right ulna, initial encounter for open fracture type IIIA, IIIB, or IIIC

S72.409B Unspecified fracture of lower end of unspecified femur, initial encounter for open fracture type I or II

S72.409C Unspecified fracture of lower end of unspecified femur, initial encounter for open fracture type IIIA, IIIB, or IIIC

S42.409B Unspecified fracture of lower end of unspecified humerus, initial encounter for open fracture

S52.609B Unspecified fracture of lower end of unspecified ulna, initial encounter for open fracture type I or II

S52.609C Unspecified fracture of lower end of unspecified ulna, initial encounter for open fracture type IIIA, IIIB, or IIIC

S02.119B Unspecified fracture of occiput, initial encounter for open fracture

S32.401A Unspecified fracture of right acetabulum, initial encounter for closed fracture

S32.401B Unspecified fracture of right acetabulum, initial encounter for open fracture

S72.91XA Unspecified fracture of right femur, initial encounter for closed fracture

S72.91XB Unspecified fracture of right femur, initial encounter for open fracture type I or II

S72.91XC Unspecified fracture of right femur, initial encounter for open fracture type IIIA, IIIB, or IIIC

S52.91XB Unspecified fracture of right forearm, initial encounter for open fracture type I or II

S52.91XC Unspecified fracture of right forearm, initial encounter for open fracture type IIIA, IIIB, or IIIC

S32.301B Unspecified fracture of right ilium, initial encounter for open fracture

S32.601B Unspecified fracture of right ischium, initial encounter for open fracture

S32.501B Unspecified fracture of right pubis, initial encounter for open fracture

S32.10XB Unspecified fracture of sacrum, initial encounter for open fracture

S32.029B Unspecified fracture of second lumbar vertebra, initial encounter for open fracture

S22.029B Unspecified fracture of second thoracic vertebra, initial encounter for open fracture

S42.302B Unspecified fracture of shaft of humerus, left arm, initial encounter for open fracture

S42.301B Unspecified fracture of shaft of humerus, right arm, initial encounter for open fracture

S42.309B Unspecified fracture of shaft of humerus, unspecified arm, initial encounter for open fracture

S72.302A Unspecified fracture of shaft of left femur, initial encounter for closed fracture

S72.302B Unspecified fracture of shaft of left femur, initial encounter for open fracture type I or II

S72.302C Unspecified fracture of shaft of left femur, initial encounter for open fracture type IIIA, IIIB, or IIIC

S82.402B Unspecified fracture of shaft of left fibula, initial encounter for open fracture type I or II

S82.402C Unspecified fracture of shaft of left fibula, initial encounter for open fracture type IIIA, IIIB, or IIIC

S52.302B Unspecified fracture of shaft of left radius, initial encounter for open fracture type I or II

S52.302C Unspecified fracture of shaft of left radius, initial encounter for open fracture type IIIA, IIIB, or IIIC

S82.202B Unspecified fracture of shaft of left tibia, initial encounter for open fracture type I or II

S82.202C Unspecified fracture of shaft of left tibia, initial encounter for open fracture type IIIA, IIIB, or IIIC

S52.202B Unspecified fracture of shaft of left ulna, initial encounter for open fracture type I or II

S52.202C Unspecified fracture of shaft of left ulna, initial encounter for open fracture type IIIA, IIIB, or IIIC

S72.301A Unspecified fracture of shaft of right femur, initial encounter for closed fracture

S72.301B Unspecified fracture of shaft of right femur, initial encounter for open fracture type I or II

S72.301C Unspecified fracture of shaft of right femur, initial encounter for open fracture type IIIA, IIIB, or IIIC

S82.401B Unspecified fracture of shaft of right fibula, initial encounter for open fracture type I or II

S82.401C Unspecified fracture of shaft of right fibula, initial encounter for open fracture type IIIA, IIIB, or IIIC

S52.301B Unspecified fracture of shaft of right radius, initial encounter for open fracture type I or II

S52.301C Unspecified fracture of shaft of right radius, initial encounter for open fracture type IIIA, IIIB, or IIIC

S82.201B Unspecified fracture of shaft of right tibia, initial encounter for open fracture type I or II

S82.201C Unspecified fracture of shaft of right tibia, initial encounter for open fracture type IIIA, IIIB, or IIIC

S52.201B Unspecified fracture of shaft of right ulna, initial encounter for open fracture type I or II

S52.201C Unspecified fracture of shaft of right ulna, initial encounter for open fracture type IIIA, IIIB, or IIIC

S72.309A Unspecified fracture of shaft of unspecified femur, initial encounter for closed fracture

S72.309B Unspecified fracture of shaft of unspecified femur, initial encounter for open fracture type I or II

S72.309C Unspecified fracture of shaft of unspecified femur, initial encounter for open fracture type IIIA, IIIB, or IIIC

S82.409B Unspecified fracture of shaft of unspecified fibula, initial encounter for open fracture type I or II

S82.409C Unspecified fracture of shaft of unspecified fibula, initial encounter for open fracture type IIIA, IIIB, or IIIC

S52.309B Unspecified fracture of shaft of unspecified radius, initial encounter for open fracture type I or II

S52.309C Unspecified fracture of shaft of unspecified radius, initial encounter for open fracture type IIIA, IIIB, or IIIC
S82.209B Unspecified fracture of shaft of unspecified tibia, initial encounter for open fracture type I or II
S82.209C Unspecified fracture of shaft of unspecified tibia, initial encounter for open fracture type IIIA, IIIB, or IIIC
S52.209B Unspecified fracture of shaft of unspecified ulna, initial encounter for open fracture type I or II
S52.209C Unspecified fracture of shaft of unspecified ulna, initial encounter for open fracture type IIIA, IIIB, or IIIC
S02.91XB Unspecified fracture of skull, initial encounter for open fracture
S22.20XB Unspecified fracture of sternum, initial encounter for open fracture
S22.089B Unspecified fracture of T11-T12 vertebra, initial encounter for open fracture
S22.059B Unspecified fracture of T5-T6 vertebra, initial encounter for open fracture
S22.069B Unspecified fracture of T7-T8 vertebra, initial encounter for open fracture
S22.079B Unspecified fracture of T9-T10 vertebra, initial encounter for open fracture
S52.502B Unspecified fracture of the lower end of left radius, initial encounter for open fracture type I or II
S52.502C Unspecified fracture of the lower end of left radius, initial encounter for open fracture type IIIA, IIIB, or IIIC
S52.501B Unspecified fracture of the lower end of right radius, initial encounter for open fracture type I or II
S52.501C Unspecified fracture of the lower end of right radius, initial encounter for open fracture type IIIA, IIIB, or IIIC
S52.509B Unspecified fracture of the lower end of unspecified radius, initial encounter for open fracture type I or II
S52.509C Unspecified fracture of the lower end of unspecified radius, initial encounter for open fracture type IIIA, IIIB, or IIIC
S32.039B Unspecified fracture of third lumbar vertebra, initial encounter for open fracture
S22.039B Unspecified fracture of third thoracic vertebra, initial encounter for open fracture
S32.409A Unspecified fracture of unspecified acetabulum, initial encounter for closed fracture
S32.409B Unspecified fracture of unspecified acetabulum, initial encounter for open fracture
S72.90XA Unspecified fracture of unspecified femur, initial encounter for closed fracture
S72.90XB Unspecified fracture of unspecified femur, initial encounter for open fracture type I or II
S72.90XC Unspecified fracture of unspecified femur, initial encounter for open fracture type IIIA, IIIB, or IIIC
S52.90XB Unspecified fracture of unspecified forearm, initial encounter for open fracture type I or II
S52.90XC Unspecified fracture of unspecified forearm, initial encounter for open fracture type IIIA, IIIB, or IIIC
S32.309B Unspecified fracture of unspecified ilium, initial encounter for open fracture
S32.609B Unspecified fracture of unspecified ischium, initial encounter for open fracture
S32.009B Unspecified fracture of unspecified lumbar vertebra, initial encounter for open fracture
S32.509B Unspecified fracture of unspecified pubis, initial encounter for open fracture
S22.009B Unspecified fracture of unspecified thoracic vertebra, initial encounter for open fracture
S42.202B Unspecified fracture of upper end of left humerus, initial encounter for open fracture
S52.102B Unspecified fracture of upper end of left radius, initial encounter for open fracture type I or II
S52.102C Unspecified fracture of upper end of left radius, initial encounter for open fracture type IIIA, IIIB, or IIIC
S82.102B Unspecified fracture of upper end of left tibia, initial encounter for open fracture type I or II
S82.102C Unspecified fracture of upper end of left tibia, initial encounter for open fracture type IIIA, IIIB, or IIIC
S52.002B Unspecified fracture of upper end of left ulna, initial encounter for open fracture type I or II
S52.002C Unspecified fracture of upper end of left ulna, initial encounter for open fracture type IIIA, IIIB, or IIIC
S42.201B Unspecified fracture of upper end of right humerus, initial encounter for open fracture
S52.101B Unspecified fracture of upper end of right radius, initial encounter for open fracture type I or II
S52.101C Unspecified fracture of upper end of right radius, initial encounter for open fracture type IIIA, IIIB, or IIIC
S82.101B Unspecified fracture of upper end of right tibia, initial encounter for open fracture type I or II
S82.101C Unspecified fracture of upper end of right tibia, initial encounter for open fracture type IIIA, IIIB, or IIIC
S52.001B Unspecified fracture of upper end of right ulna, initial encounter for open fracture type I or II
S52.001C Unspecified fracture of upper end of right ulna, initial encounter for open fracture type IIIA, IIIB, or IIIC
S42.209B Unspecified fracture of upper end of unspecified humerus, initial encounter for open fracture
S52.109B Unspecified fracture of upper end of unspecified radius, initial encounter for open fracture type I or II
S52.109C Unspecified fracture of upper end of unspecified radius, initial encounter for open fracture type IIIA, IIIB, or IIIC
S82.109B Unspecified fracture of upper end of unspecified tibia, initial encounter for open fracture type I or II
S82.109C Unspecified fracture of upper end of unspecified tibia, initial encounter for open fracture type IIIA, IIIB, or IIIC
S52.009B Unspecified fracture of upper end of unspecified ulna, initial encounter for open fracture type I or II
S52.009C Unspecified fracture of upper end of unspecified ulna, initial encounter for open fracture type IIIA, IIIB, or IIIC
S14.101A Unspecified injury at C1 level of cervical spinal cord, initial encounter
S14.102A Unspecified injury at C2 level of cervical spinal cord, initial encounter
S14.103A Unspecified injury at C3 level of cervical spinal cord, initial encounter
S14.104A Unspecified injury at C4 level of cervical spinal cord, initial encounter
S14.105A Unspecified injury at C5 level of cervical spinal cord, initial encounter
S14.106A Unspecified injury at C6 level of cervical spinal cord, initial encounter
S14.107A Unspecified injury at C7 level of cervical spinal cord, initial encounter
S14.108A Unspecified injury at C8 level of cervical spinal cord, initial encounter
S24.101A Unspecified injury at T1 level of thoracic spinal cord, initial encounter
S24.104A Unspecified injury at T11-T12 level of thoracic spinal cord, initial encounter
S24.102A Unspecified injury at T2-T6 level of thoracic spinal cord, initial encounter
S24.103A Unspecified injury at T7-T10 level of thoracic spinal cord, initial encounter
S35.00XA Unspecified injury of abdominal aorta, initial encounter
S45.002A Unspecified injury of axillary artery, left side, initial encounter
S45.001A Unspecified injury of axillary artery, right side, initial encounter
S45.009A Unspecified injury of axillary artery, unspecified side, initial encounter
S35.299A Unspecified injury of branches of celiac and mesenteric artery, initial encounter
S27.402A Unspecified injury of bronchus, bilateral, initial encounter
S27.401A Unspecified injury of bronchus, unilateral, initial encounter
S27.409A Unspecified injury of bronchus, unspecified, initial encounter
S35.219A Unspecified injury of celiac artery, initial encounter
S27.819A Unspecified injury of esophagus (thoracic part), initial encounter
S75.002A Unspecified injury of femoral artery, left leg, initial encounter
S75.001A Unspecified injury of femoral artery, right leg, initial encounter
S75.009A Unspecified injury of femoral artery, unspecified leg, initial encounter
S75.102A Unspecified injury of femoral vein at hip and thigh level, left leg, initial encounter
S75.101A Unspecified injury of femoral vein at hip and thigh level, right leg, initial encounter
S75.109A Unspecified injury of femoral vein at hip and thigh level, unspecified leg, initial encounter
S35.239A Unspecified injury of inferior mesenteric artery, initial encounter
S35.349A Unspecified injury of inferior mesenteric vein, initial encounter
S35.10XA Unspecified injury of inferior vena cava, initial encounter
S25.102A Unspecified injury of left innominate or subclavian artery, initial encounter
S25.302A Unspecified injury of left innominate or subclavian vein, initial encounter
S25.402A Unspecified injury of left pulmonary blood vessels, initial encounter
S35.402A Unspecified injury of left renal artery, initial encounter
S35.405A Unspecified injury of left renal vein, initial encounter
S85.002A Unspecified injury of popliteal artery, left leg, initial encounter
S85.001A Unspecified injury of popliteal artery, right leg, initial encounter
S85.009A Unspecified injury of popliteal artery, unspecified leg, initial encounter
S85.502A Unspecified injury of popliteal vein, left leg, initial encounter
S85.501A Unspecified injury of popliteal vein, right leg, initial encounter
S85.509A Unspecified injury of popliteal vein, unspecified leg, initial encounter
S35.319A Unspecified injury of portal vein, initial encounter
S25.101A Unspecified injury of right innominate or subclavian artery, initial encounter
S25.301A Unspecified injury of right innominate or subclavian vein, initial encounter
S25.401A Unspecified injury of right pulmonary blood vessels, initial encounter
S35.401A Unspecified injury of right renal artery, initial encounter
S35.404A Unspecified injury of right renal vein, initial encounter
S35.329A Unspecified injury of splenic vein, initial encounter
S35.229A Unspecified injury of superior mesenteric artery, initial encounter
S35.339A Unspecified injury of superior mesenteric vein, initial encounter
S25.20XA Unspecified injury of superior vena cava, initial encounter
S25.00XA Unspecified injury of thoracic aorta, initial encounter
S25.109A Unspecified injury of unspecified innominate or subclavian artery, initial encounter
S25.309A Unspecified injury of unspecified innominate or subclavian vein, initial encounter
S25.409A Unspecified injury of unspecified pulmonary blood vessels, initial encounter
S35.403A Unspecified injury of unspecified renal artery, initial encounter
S35.406A Unspecified injury of unspecified renal vein, initial encounter
S34.101A Unspecified injury to L1 level of lumbar spinal cord, initial encounter
S34.102A Unspecified injury to L2 level of lumbar spinal cord, initial encounter
S34.103A Unspecified injury to L3 level of lumbar spinal cord, initial encounter
S34.104A Unspecified injury to L4 level of lumbar spinal cord, initial encounter
S34.105A Unspecified injury to L5 level of lumbar spinal cord, initial encounter
S34.139A Unspecified injury to sacral spinal cord, initial encounter
S34.109A Unspecified injury to unspecified level of lumbar spinal cord, initial encounter
S72.012A Unspecified intracapsular fracture of left femur, initial encounter for closed fracture
S72.012B Unspecified intracapsular fracture of left femur, initial encounter for open fracture type I or II
S72.012C Unspecified intracapsular fracture of left femur, initial encounter for open fracture type IIIA, IIIB, or IIIC
S72.011A Unspecified intracapsular fracture of right femur, initial encounter for closed fracture
S72.011B Unspecified intracapsular fracture of right femur, initial encounter for open fracture type I or II
S72.011C Unspecified intracapsular fracture of right femur, initial encounter for open fracture type IIIA, IIIB, or IIIC
S72.019A Unspecified intracapsular fracture of unspecified femur, initial encounter for closed fracture

Code	Description
S72.019B	Unspecified intracapsular fracture of unspecified femur, initial encounter for open fracture type I or II
S72.019C	Unspecified intracapsular fracture of unspecified femur, initial encounter for open fracture type IIIA, IIIB, or IIIC
S06.9X6A	Unspecified intracranial injury with loss of consciousness greater than 24 hours without return to pre-existing conscious level with patient surviving, initial encounter
S06.9X7A	Unspecified intracranial injury with loss of consciousness of any duration with death due to brain injury prior to regaining consciousness, initial encounter
S06.9X8A	Unspecified intracranial injury with loss of consciousness of any duration with death due to other cause prior to regaining consciousness, initial encounter
P10.9	Unspecified intracranial laceration and hemorrhage due to birth injury
S12.401B	Unspecified nondisplaced fracture of fifth cervical vertebra, initial encounter for open fracture
S12.001B	Unspecified nondisplaced fracture of first cervical vertebra, initial encounter for open fracture
S12.301B	Unspecified nondisplaced fracture of fourth cervical vertebra, initial encounter for open fracture
S12.101B	Unspecified nondisplaced fracture of second cervical vertebra, initial encounter for open fracture
S12.601B	Unspecified nondisplaced fracture of seventh cervical vertebra, initial encounter for open fracture
S12.501B	Unspecified nondisplaced fracture of sixth cervical vertebra, initial encounter for open fracture
S42.215B	Unspecified nondisplaced fracture of surgical neck of left humerus, initial encounter for open fracture
S42.214B	Unspecified nondisplaced fracture of surgical neck of right humerus, initial encounter for open fracture
S42.216B	Unspecified nondisplaced fracture of surgical neck of unspecified humerus, initial encounter for open fracture
S12.201B	Unspecified nondisplaced fracture of third cervical vertebra, initial encounter for open fracture
S02.113B	Unspecified occipital condyle fracture, initial encounter for open fracture
S31.602A	Unspecified open wound of abdominal wall, epigastric region with penetration into peritoneal cavity, initial encounter
S31.604A	Unspecified open wound of abdominal wall, left lower quadrant with penetration into peritoneal cavity, initial encounter
S31.601A	Unspecified open wound of abdominal wall, left upper quadrant with penetration into peritoneal cavity, initial encounter
S31.605A	Unspecified open wound of abdominal wall, periumbilic region with penetration into peritoneal cavity, initial encounter
S31.603A	Unspecified open wound of abdominal wall, right lower quadrant with penetration into peritoneal cavity, initial encounter
S31.600A	Unspecified open wound of abdominal wall, right upper quadrant with penetration into peritoneal cavity, initial encounter
S31.609A	Unspecified open wound of abdominal wall, unspecified quadrant with penetration into peritoneal cavity, initial encounter
S11.019A	Unspecified open wound of larynx, initial encounter
S21.402A	Unspecified open wound of left back wall of thorax with penetration into thoracic cavity, initial encounter
S21.302A	Unspecified open wound of left front wall of thorax with penetration into thoracic cavity, initial encounter
S31.001A	Unspecified open wound of lower back and pelvis with penetration into retroperitoneum, initial encounter
S21.401A	Unspecified open wound of right back wall of thorax with penetration into thoracic cavity, initial encounter
S21.301A	Unspecified open wound of right front wall of thorax with penetration into thoracic cavity, initial encounter
S11.029A	Unspecified open wound of trachea, initial encounter
S21.409A	Unspecified open wound of unspecified back wall of thorax with penetration into thoracic cavity, initial encounter
S21.309A	Unspecified open wound of unspecified front wall of thorax with penetration into thoracic cavity, initial encounter
S11.039A	Unspecified open wound of vocal cord, initial encounter
S79.002A	Unspecified physeal fracture of upper end of left femur, initial encounter for closed fracture
S79.001A	Unspecified physeal fracture of upper end of right femur, initial encounter for closed fracture
S79.009A	Unspecified physeal fracture of upper end of unspecified femur, initial encounter for closed fracture
O24.32	Unspecified pre-existing diabetes mellitus in childbirth
P26.9	Unspecified pulmonary hemorrhage originating in the perinatal period
E43	Unspecified severe protein-calorie malnutrition
S12.430B	Unspecified traumatic displaced spondylolisthesis of fifth cervical vertebra, initial encounter for open fracture
S12.330B	Unspecified traumatic displaced spondylolisthesis of fourth cervical vertebra, initial encounter for open fracture
S12.130B	Unspecified traumatic displaced spondylolisthesis of second cervical vertebra, initial encounter for open fracture
S12.630B	Unspecified traumatic displaced spondylolisthesis of seventh cervical vertebra, initial encounter for open fracture
S12.530B	Unspecified traumatic displaced spondylolisthesis of sixth cervical vertebra, initial encounter for open fracture
S12.230B	Unspecified traumatic displaced spondylolisthesis of third cervical vertebra, initial encounter for open fracture
S12.431B	Unspecified traumatic nondisplaced spondylolisthesis of fifth cervical vertebra, initial encounter for open fracture
S12.331B	Unspecified traumatic nondisplaced spondylolisthesis of fourth cervical vertebra, initial encounter for open fracture
S12.131B	Unspecified traumatic nondisplaced spondylolisthesis of second cervical vertebra, initial encounter for open fracture
S12.631B	Unspecified traumatic nondisplaced spondylolisthesis of seventh cervical vertebra, initial encounter for open fracture
S12.531B	Unspecified traumatic nondisplaced spondylolisthesis of sixth cervical vertebra, initial encounter for open fracture
S12.231B	Unspecified traumatic nondisplaced spondylolisthesis of third cervical vertebra, initial encounter for open fracture
S72.102A	Unspecified trochanteric fracture of left femur, initial encounter for closed fracture
S72.102B	Unspecified trochanteric fracture of left femur, initial encounter for open fracture type I or II
S72.102C	Unspecified trochanteric fracture of left femur, initial encounter for open fracture type IIIA, IIIB, or IIIC
S72.101A	Unspecified trochanteric fracture of right femur, initial encounter for closed fracture
S72.101B	Unspecified trochanteric fracture of right femur, initial encounter for open fracture type I or II
S72.101C	Unspecified trochanteric fracture of right femur, initial encounter for open fracture type IIIA, IIIB, or IIIC
S72.109A	Unspecified trochanteric fracture of unspecified femur, initial encounter for closed fracture
S72.109B	Unspecified trochanteric fracture of unspecified femur, initial encounter for open fracture type I or II
S72.109C	Unspecified trochanteric fracture of unspecified femur, initial encounter for open fracture type IIIA, IIIB, or IIIC
B19.11	Unspecified viral hepatitis B with hepatic coma
B19.21	Unspecified viral hepatitis C with hepatic coma
B19.0	Unspecified viral hepatitis with hepatic coma
S32.119B	Unspecified Zone I fracture of sacrum, initial encounter for open fracture
S32.129B	Unspecified Zone II fracture of sacrum, initial encounter for open fracture
S32.139B	Unspecified Zone III fracture of sacrum, initial encounter for open fracture
S32.052B	Unstable burst fracture of fifth lumbar vertebra, initial encounter for open fracture
S12.02XB	Unstable burst fracture of first cervical vertebra, initial encounter for open fracture
S32.012B	Unstable burst fracture of first lumbar vertebra, initial encounter for open fracture
S22.012B	Unstable burst fracture of first thoracic vertebra, initial encounter for open fracture
S32.042B	Unstable burst fracture of fourth lumbar vertebra, initial encounter for open fracture
S22.042B	Unstable burst fracture of fourth thoracic vertebra, initial encounter for open fracture
S32.022B	Unstable burst fracture of second lumbar vertebra, initial encounter for open fracture
S22.022B	Unstable burst fracture of second thoracic vertebra, initial encounter for open fracture
S22.082B	Unstable burst fracture of T11-T12 vertebra, initial encounter for open fracture
S22.052B	Unstable burst fracture of T5-T6 vertebra, initial encounter for open fracture
S22.062B	Unstable burst fracture of T7-T8 vertebra, initial encounter for open fracture
S22.072B	Unstable burst fracture of T9-T10 vertebra, initial encounter for open fracture
S32.032B	Unstable burst fracture of third lumbar vertebra, initial encounter for open fracture
S22.032B	Unstable burst fracture of third thoracic vertebra, initial encounter for open fracture
S32.002B	Unstable burst fracture of unspecified lumbar vertebra, initial encounter for open fracture
S22.002B	Unstable burst fracture of unspecified thoracic vertebra, initial encounter for open fracture
B01.11	Varicella encephalitis and encephalomyelitis
B01.12	Varicella myelitis
B01.2	Varicella pneumonia
Q93.81	Velo-cardio-facial syndrome
I49.01	Ventricular fibrillation
I49.02	Ventricular flutter
J12.9	Viral pneumonia, unspecified
K56.2	Volvulus
A39.1	Waterhouse-Friderichsen syndrome
S32.050B	Wedge compression fracture of fifth lumbar vertebra, initial encounter for open fracture
S32.010B	Wedge compression fracture of first lumbar vertebra, initial encounter for open fracture
S22.010B	Wedge compression fracture of first thoracic vertebra, initial encounter for open fracture
S32.040B	Wedge compression fracture of fourth lumbar vertebra, initial encounter for open fracture
S22.040B	Wedge compression fracture of fourth thoracic vertebra, initial encounter for open fracture
S32.020B	Wedge compression fracture of second lumbar vertebra, initial encounter for open fracture
S22.020B	Wedge compression fracture of second thoracic vertebra, initial encounter for open fracture
S22.080B	Wedge compression fracture of T11-T12 vertebra, initial encounter for open fracture
S22.050B	Wedge compression fracture of T5-T6 vertebra, initial encounter for open fracture
S22.060B	Wedge compression fracture of T7-T8 vertebra, initial encounter for open fracture
S22.070B	Wedge compression fracture of T9-T10 vertebra, initial encounter for open fracture
S32.030B	Wedge compression fracture of third lumbar vertebra, initial encounter for open fracture

S22.030B	Wedge compression fracture of third thoracic vertebra, initial encounter for open fracture
S32.000B	Wedge compression fracture of unspecified lumbar vertebra, initial encounter for open fracture
S22.000B	Wedge compression fracture of unspecified thoracic vertebra, initial encounter for open fracture
A92.31	West Nile virus infection with encephalitis
A92.39	West Nile virus infection with other complications
A92.32	West Nile virus infection with other neurologic manifestation
A92.30	West Nile virus infection, unspecified
A83.1	Western equine encephalitis
A37.11	Whooping cough due to Bordetella parapertussis with pneumonia
A37.01	Whooping cough due to Bordetella pertussis with pneumonia
A37.81	Whooping cough due to other Bordetella species with pneumonia
A37.91	Whooping cough, unspecified species with pneumonia
P27.0	Wilson-Mikity syndrome
B02.1	Zoster meningitis
B46.9	Zygomycosis, unspecified

Numeric MCC List

A02.1	A83.5	D67	G93.82	I63.019	I67.0	J95.822	K55.30	L89.303
A02.21	A83.6	E03.5	G95.11	I63.02	I67.83	J96.00	K55.31	L89.304
A02.22	A83.8	E05.01	G95.19	I63.031	I71.00	J96.01	K55.32	L89.313
A06.4	A83.9	E05.11	I21.01	I63.032	I71.01	J96.02	K55.33	L89.314
A06.5	A84.0	E05.21	I21.02	I63.033	I71.02	J96.20	K56.2	L89.323
A06.6	A84.1	E05.31	I21.09	I63.039	I71.03	J96.21	K57.01	L89.324
A17.0	A84.8	E05.41	I21.11	I63.09	I71.1	J96.22	K57.11	L89.43
A17.1	A84.9	E05.81	I21.19	I63.10	I71.3	J96.90	K57.13	L89.44
A17.81	A85.2	E05.91	I21.21	I63.111	I71.5	J96.91	K57.21	L89.503
A17.82	A92.30	E08.00	I21.29	I63.112	I71.8	J96.92	K57.31	L89.504
A17.83	A92.31	E08.01	I21.3	I63.113	I74.01	J98.51	K57.33	L89.513
A17.89	A92.32	E08.10	I21.4	I63.119	I77.70	J98.59	K57.41	L89.514
A18.31	A92.39	E08.11	I21.9	I63.12	I77.71	K22.11	K57.51	L89.523
A19.0	B00.3	E08.641	I21.A1	I63.131	I77.72	K22.3	K57.53	L89.524
A19.1	B00.4	E09.00	I21.A9	I63.132	I77.73	K22.6	K57.81	L89.603
A19.2	B00.7	E09.01	I22.0	I63.133	I77.74	K25.0	K57.91	L89.604
A19.8	B00.82	E09.10	I22.1	I63.139	I77.75	K25.1	K57.93	L89.613
A19.9	B01.11	E09.11	I22.2	I63.19	I77.76	K25.2	K63.1	L89.614
A20.0	B01.12	E09.641	I22.8	I63.20	I77.77	K25.4	K63.81	L89.623
A20.1	B01.2	E10.10	I22.9	I63.211	I77.79	K25.5	K65.0	L89.624
A20.2	B02.1	E10.11	I23.4	I63.212	I81	K25.6	K65.1	L89.813
A20.3	B02.24	E10.641	I23.5	I63.213	I82.0	K26.0	K65.2	L89.814
A20.7	B05.0	E11.00	I25.42	I63.219	I82.220	K26.1	K65.3	L89.893
A20.8	B05.2	E11.01	I26.01	I63.22	I82.221	K26.2	K65.8	L89.894
A20.9	B06.01	E11.10	I26.02	I63.231	I85.01	K26.4	K65.9	L89.93
A22.1	B10.01	E11.11	I26.09	I63.232	I85.11	K26.5	K66.1	L89.94
A22.7	B10.09	E11.641	I26.90	I63.233	J04.11	K26.6	K67	M31.1
A26.7	B15.0	E13.00	I26.92	I63.239	J04.31	K27.0	K68.12	M72.6
A27.81	B16.0	E13.01	I26.93	I63.29	J05.11	K27.1	K68.19	N00.0
A32.7	B16.2	E13.10	I26.94	I63.30	J09.X1	K27.2	K68.9	N00.1
A33	B17.11	E13.11	I26.99	I63.311	J10.00	K27.4	K70.41	N00.2
A35	B19.0	E13.641	I33.0	I63.312	J10.01	K27.5	K71.11	N00.3
A37.01	B19.11	E40	I33.9	I63.313	J10.08	K27.6	K72.00	N00.4
A37.11	B19.21	E41	I40.0	I63.319	J11.00	K28.0	K72.01	N00.5
A37.81	B25.0	E42	I40.1	I63.321	J11.08	K28.1	K72.11	N00.6
A37.91	B25.2	E43	I40.8	I63.322	J12.0	K28.2	K72.91	N00.7
A39.0	B26.1	E84.0	I40.9	I63.323	J12.1	K28.4	K75.0	N00.8
A39.1	B26.2	E84.11	I41	I63.329	J12.2	K28.5	K75.1	N00.9
A39.2	B37.1	E88.3	I46.2	I63.331	J12.3	K28.6	K76.2	N01.0
A39.3	B37.5	G00.0	I46.8	I63.332	J12.81	K29.01	K76.3	N01.1
A39.4	B37.6	G00.1	I46.9	I63.333	J12.89	K29.21	K76.7	N01.2
A39.50	B37.7	G00.2	I49.01	I63.339	J12.9	K29.31	K80.67	N01.3
A39.51	B38.4	G00.3	I49.02	I63.341	J13	K29.41	K82.2	N01.4
A39.52	B39.0	G00.8	I50.21	I63.342	J14	K29.51	K83.1	N01.5
A39.53	B39.1	G00.9	I50.23	I63.343	J15.0	K29.61	K83.2	N01.6
A39.81	B39.2	G01	I50.31	I63.349	J15.1	K29.71	K85.00	N01.7
A40.0	B44.0	G02	I50.33	I63.39	J15.20	K29.81	K85.01	N01.8
A40.1	B45.1	G03.0	I50.41	I63.40	J15.211	K29.91	K85.02	N01.9
A40.3	B46.0	G03.8	I50.43	I63.411	J15.212	K31.811	K85.10	N15.1
A40.8	B46.1	G03.9	I51.1	I63.412	J15.29	K31.82	K85.11	N17.0
A40.9	B46.2	G04.00	I51.2	I63.413	J15.3	K35.21	K85.12	N17.1
A41.01	B46.3	G04.01	I60.00	I63.419	J15.4	K35.32	K85.20	N17.2
A41.02	B46.4	G04.02	I60.01	I63.421	J15.5	K35.33	K85.21	N18.6
A41.1	B46.5	G04.2	I60.02	I63.422	J15.6	K40.10	K85.22	N73.3
A41.2	B46.8	G04.30	I60.10	I63.423	J15.7	K40.11	K85.30	O03.2
A41.3	B46.9	G04.31	I60.11	I63.429	J15.8	K40.40	K85.31	O03.31
A41.4	B50.9	G04.32	I60.12	I63.431	J15.9	K40.41	K85.32	O03.32
A41.50	B58.2	G04.39	I60.2	I63.432	J16.0	K41.10	K85.80	O03.81
A41.51	B58.3	G04.81	I60.30	I63.433	J16.8	K41.11	K85.81	O03.82
A41.52	B58.81	G04.89	I60.31	I63.439	J17	K41.40	K85.82	O04.7
A41.53	B59	G04.90	I60.32	I63.441	J18.0	K41.41	K85.90	O04.81
A41.59	B77.81	G04.91	I60.4	I63.442	J18.1	K42.1	K85.91	O04.82
A41.81	D57.00	G05.3	I60.50	I63.443	J18.8	K43.1	K85.92	O07.2
A41.89	D57.01	G05.4	I60.51	I63.449	J18.9	K43.4	L89.003	O07.31
A41.9	D57.02	G06.0	I60.52	I63.49	J68.1	K43.7	L89.004	O07.32
A42.7	D57.211	G06.1	I60.6	I63.50	J69.0	K44.1	L89.013	O08.2
A48.0	D57.212	G06.2	I60.7	I63.511	J69.1	K45.1	L89.014	O08.3
A48.1	D57.219	G07	I60.8	I63.512	J69.8	K46.1	L89.023	O08.4
A48.3	D57.411	G08	I60.9	I63.513	J80	K55.011	L89.024	O10.42
A50.41	D57.412	G21.0	I61.0	I63.519	J81.0	K55.012	L89.103	O11.1
A50.42	D57.419	G37.4	I61.1	I63.521	J84.81	K55.019	L89.104	O11.2
A51.41	D57.811	G40.301	I61.2	I63.522	J84.83	K55.021	L89.113	O11.3
A52.13	D57.812	G40.311	I61.3	I63.523	J84.841	K55.022	L89.114	O14.12
A52.14	D57.819	G40.319	I61.4	I63.529	J84.842	K55.029	L89.123	O14.13
A54.81	D59.3	G70.01	I61.5	I63.531	J84.843	K55.031	L89.124	O14.22
A54.86	D60.0	G80.0	I61.6	I63.532	J84.848	K55.032	L89.133	O14.23
A80.0	D60.1	G82.50	I61.8	I63.533	J85.0	K55.039	L89.134	O15.02
A80.1	D60.8	G82.51	I61.9	I63.539	J85.1	K55.041	L89.143	O15.03
A80.2	D60.9	G82.52	I62.00	I63.541	J85.2	K55.042	L89.144	O15.1
A80.30	D61.1	G82.53	I62.01	I63.542	J85.3	K55.049	L89.153	O15.2
A80.39	D61.2	G82.54	I62.02	I63.543	J86.0	K55.051	L89.154	O22.31
A83.0	D61.3	G83.5	I62.03	I63.549	J86.9	K55.052	L89.203	O22.32
A83.1	D61.810	G92	I62.1	I63.59	J93.0	K55.059	L89.204	O22.33
A83.2	D61.811	G93.41	I63.00	I63.6	J95.1	K55.061	L89.213	O24.02
A83.3	D61.89	G93.5	I63.011	I63.81	J95.2	K55.062	L89.214	O24.12
A83.4	D65	G93.6	I63.012	I63.89	J95.3	K55.069	L89.223	O24.32
	D66	G93.7	I63.013	I63.9	J95.821	K55.21	L89.224	O24.82

O34.31	O45.8X3	O90.3	P61.5	R40.2311	S06.339A	S11.023A	S14.111A	S22.028B
O34.32	O45.91	O90.4	P74.0	R40.2312	S06.340A	S11.024A	S14.112A	S22.029B
O34.33	O45.92	O99.42	P77.1	R40.2313	S06.341A	S11.025A	S14.113A	S22.030B
O41.1010	O45.93	P10.0	P77.2	R40.2314	S06.342A	S11.029A	S14.114A	S22.031B
O41.1011	O46.001	P10.1	P77.3	R40.2320	S06.343A	S11.031A	S14.115A	S22.032B
O41.1012	O46.002	P10.3	P77.9	R40.2321	S06.344A	S11.032A	S14.116A	S22.038B
O41.1013	O46.003	P10.4	P78.0	R40.2322	S06.345A	S11.033A	S14.117A	S22.039B
O41.1014	O46.011	P10.8	P83.2	R40.2323	S06.346A	S11.034A	S14.118A	S22.040B
O41.1015	O46.012	P10.9	P90	R40.2324	S06.347A	S11.035A	S14.121A	S22.041B
O41.1019	O46.013	P11.0	P91.0	R40.2340	S06.348A	S11.039A	S14.122A	S22.042B
O41.1020	O46.021	P11.2	P91.1	R40.2341	S06.349A	S12.000B	S14.123A	S22.048B
O41.1021	O46.022	P11.9	P91.2	R40.2342	S06.350A	S12.001B	S14.124A	S22.049B
O41.1022	O46.023	P22.0	P91.3	R40.2343	S06.351A	S12.01XB	S14.125A	S22.050B
O41.1023	O46.091	P23.0	P91.4	R40.2344	S06.352A	S12.02XB	S14.126A	S22.051B
O41.1024	O46.092	P23.1	P91.5	R53.2	S06.353A	S12.030B	S14.127A	S22.052B
O41.1025	O46.093	P23.2	P91.63	R57.0	S06.354A	S12.031B	S14.128A	S22.058B
O41.1029	O60.02	P23.3	P92.01	R57.1	S06.355A	S12.040B	S14.131A	S22.059B
O41.1030	O60.03	P23.4	Q00.0	R57.8	S06.356A	S12.041B	S14.132A	S22.060B
O41.1031	O60.12X0	P23.5	Q00.1	R65.11	S06.357A	S12.090B	S14.133A	S22.061B
O41.1032	O60.12X1	P23.6	Q00.2	R65.20	S06.358A	S12.091B	S14.134A	S22.062B
O41.1033	O60.12X2	P23.8	Q04.0	R65.21	S06.359A	S12.100B	S14.135A	S22.068B
O41.1034	O60.12X3	P23.9	Q04.1	S02.0XXB	S06.360A	S12.101B	S14.136A	S22.069B
O41.1035	O60.12X4	P24.01	Q04.2	S02.101B	S06.361A	S12.110B	S14.137A	S22.070B
O41.1039	O60.12X5	P24.11	Q04.3	S02.102B	S06.362A	S12.111B	S14.138A	S22.071B
O41.1210	O60.12X9	P24.21	Q20.0	S02.109B	S06.363A	S12.112B	S14.141A	S22.072B
O41.1211	O60.13X0	P24.31	Q20.1	S02.110B	S06.364A	S12.120B	S14.142A	S22.078B
O41.1212	O60.13X1	P24.81	Q20.2	S02.111B	S06.365A	S12.121B	S14.143A	S22.079B
O41.1213	O60.13X2	P25.0	Q20.3	S02.112B	S06.366A	S12.130B	S14.144A	S22.080B
O41.1214	O60.13X3	P25.1	Q20.4	S02.113B	S06.367A	S12.131B	S14.145A	S22.081B
O41.1215	O60.13X4	P25.2	Q21.3	S02.118B	S06.368A	S12.14XB	S14.146A	S22.082B
O41.1219	O60.13X5	P25.3	Q22.0	S02.119B	S06.369A	S12.150B	S14.147A	S22.088B
O41.1220	O60.13X9	P25.8	Q22.4	S02.11AB	S06.370A	S12.151B	S14.148A	S22.089B
O41.1221	O60.14X0	P26.0	Q22.5	S02.11BB	S06.376A	S12.190B	S14.151A	S22.20XB
O41.1222	O60.14X1	P26.1	Q22.6	S02.11CB	S06.377A	S12.191B	S14.152A	S22.21XB
O41.1223	O60.14X2	P26.8	Q22.8	S02.11DB	S06.378A	S12.200B	S14.153A	S22.22XB
O41.1224	O60.14X3	P26.9	Q22.9	S02.11EB	S06.380A	S12.201B	S14.154A	S22.23XB
O41.1225	O60.14X4	P27.0	Q23.4	S02.11FB	S06.386A	S12.230B	S14.155A	S22.24XB
O41.1229	O60.14X5	P27.1	Q24.2	S02.11GB	S06.387A	S12.231B	S14.156A	S22.31XB
O41.1230	O60.14X9	P27.8	Q24.4	S02.11HB	S06.388A	S12.24XB	S14.157A	S22.32XB
O41.1231	O60.22X0	P27.9	Q24.6	S02.121B	S06.4X0A	S12.250B	S14.158A	S22.39XB
O41.1232	O60.22X1	P28.5	Q25.5	S02.122B	S06.4X1A	S12.251B	S21.301A	S22.41XB
O41.1233	O60.22X2	P28.81	Q25.6	S02.129B	S06.4X2A	S12.290B	S21.302A	S22.42XB
O41.1234	O60.22X3	P29.30	Q25.71	S02.19XB	S06.4X3A	S12.291B	S21.309A	S22.43XB
O41.1235	O60.22X4	P29.38	Q25.72	S02.91XB	S06.4X4A	S12.300B	S21.311A	S22.49XB
O41.1239	O60.22X5	P29.81	Q25.79	S06.1X0A	S06.4X5A	S12.301B	S21.312A	S22.5XXA
O41.1410	O60.22X9	P35.1	Q28.2	S06.1X1A	S06.4X6A	S12.330B	S21.319A	S22.5XXB
O41.1411	O60.23X0	P35.2	Q28.3	S06.1X2A	S06.4X7A	S12.331B	S21.321A	S22.9XXB
O41.1412	O60.23X1	P35.3	Q33.2	S06.1X3A	S06.4X8A	S12.34XB	S21.322A	S24.0XXA
O41.1413	O60.23X2	P35.4	Q33.3	S06.1X4A	S06.4X9A	S12.350B	S21.329A	S24.101A
O41.1414	O60.23X3	P35.8	Q33.6	S06.1X5A	S06.5X0A	S12.351B	S21.331A	S24.102A
O41.1415	O60.23X4	P35.9	Q39.0	S06.1X6A	S06.5X1A	S12.390B	S21.332A	S24.103A
O41.1419	O60.23X5	P36.0	Q39.1	S06.1X7A	S06.5X2A	S12.391B	S21.339A	S24.104A
O41.1420	O60.23X9	P36.10	Q39.2	S06.1X8A	S06.5X3A	S12.400B	S21.341A	S24.111A
O41.1421	O67.0	P36.19	Q39.3	S06.1X9A	S06.5X4A	S12.401B	S21.342A	S24.112A
O41.1422	O71.02	P36.2	Q39.4	S06.2X6A	S06.5X5A	S12.430B	S21.349A	S24.113A
O41.1423	O71.03	P36.30	Q44.2	S06.2X7A	S06.5X6A	S12.431B	S21.351A	S24.114A
O41.1424	O71.1	P36.39	Q44.3	S06.2X8A	S06.5X7A	S12.44XB	S21.352A	S24.131A
O41.1425	O75.1	P36.4	Q79.0	S06.306A	S06.5X8A	S12.450B	S21.359A	S24.132A
O41.1429	O75.3	P36.5	Q79.1	S06.307A	S06.5X9A	S12.451B	S21.401A	S24.133A
O41.1430	O85	P36.8	Q79.2	S06.308A	S06.6X0A	S12.490B	S21.402A	S24.134A
O41.1431	O86.04	P36.9	Q79.3	S06.310A	S06.6X1A	S12.491B	S21.409A	S24.141A
O41.1432	O86.81	P37.0	Q79.4	S06.311A	S06.6X2A	S12.500B	S21.411A	S24.142A
O41.1433	O86.89	P37.1	Q79.51	S06.312A	S06.6X3A	S12.501B	S21.412A	S24.143A
O41.1434	O87.1	P37.2	Q79.59	S06.313A	S06.6X4A	S12.530B	S21.419A	S24.144A
O41.1435	O88.011	P37.3	Q89.4	S06.314A	S06.6X5A	S12.531B	S21.421A	S24.151A
O41.1439	O88.012	P37.4	Q93.81	S06.315A	S06.6X6A	S12.550B	S21.422A	S24.152A
O44.11	O88.013	P37.8	R09.2	S06.316A	S06.6X7A	S12.551B	S21.429A	S24.153A
O44.12	O88.02	P37.9	R40.20	S06.317A	S06.6X8A	S12.590B	S21.431A	S24.154A
O44.13	O88.03	P52.21	R40.2110	S06.318A	S06.6X9A	S12.591B	S21.432A	S25.00XA
O44.31	O88.111	P52.22	R40.2111	S06.319A	S06.816A	S12.600B	S21.439A	S25.01XA
O44.32	O88.112	P52.4	R40.2112	S06.320A	S06.817A	S12.601B	S21.441A	S25.02XA
O44.33	O88.113	P52.5	R40.2113	S06.321A	S06.818A	S12.630B	S21.442A	S25.09XA
O44.51	O88.12	P52.6	R40.2114	S06.322A	S06.826A	S12.631B	S21.449A	S25.101A
O44.52	O88.13	P52.8	R40.2120	S06.323A	S06.827A	S12.64XB	S21.451A	S25.102A
O44.53	O88.211	P52.9	R40.2121	S06.324A	S06.828A	S12.650B	S21.452A	S25.109A
O45.001	O88.212	P54.1	R40.2122	S06.325A	S06.896A	S12.651B	S21.459A	S25.111A
O45.002	O88.213	P54.2	R40.2123	S06.326A	S06.897A	S12.690B	S22.000B	S25.112A
O45.003	O88.22	P54.3	R40.2124	S06.327A	S06.898A	S12.691B	S22.001B	S25.119A
O45.011	O88.23	P56.0	R40.2210	S06.328A	S06.9X6A	S12.8XXA	S22.002B	S25.121A
O45.012	O88.311	P56.90	R40.2211	S06.329A	S06.9X7A	S14.0XXA	S22.008B	S25.122A
O45.013	O88.312	P56.99	R40.2212	S06.330A	S06.9X8A	S14.101A	S22.009B	S25.129A
O45.021	O88.313	P57.0	R40.2213	S06.331A	S11.011A	S14.102A	S22.010B	S25.191A
O45.022	O88.32	P57.8	R40.2214	S06.332A	S11.012A	S14.103A	S22.011B	S25.192A
O45.023	O88.33	P57.9	R40.2220	S06.333A	S11.013A	S14.104A	S22.012B	S25.199A
O45.091	O88.811	P59.1	R40.2221	S06.334A	S11.014A	S14.105A	S22.018B	S25.20XA
O45.092	O88.812	P59.20	R40.2222	S06.335A	S11.015A	S14.106A	S22.019B	S25.21XA
O45.093	O88.813	P59.29	R40.2223	S06.336A	S11.019A	S14.107A	S22.020B	S25.22XA
O45.8X1	O88.82	P60	R40.2224	S06.337A	S11.021A	S14.108A	S22.021B	S25.29XA
O45.8X2	O88.83	P61.0	R40.2310	S06.338A	S11.022A		S22.022B	S25.301A

S25.302A	S31.643A	S32.416B	S32.499A	S35.402A	S42.341B	S52.002B	S52.221C	S52.324B
S25.309A	S31.644A	S32.421A	S32.499B	S35.403A	S42.342B	S52.002C	S52.222B	S52.324C
S25.311A	S31.645A	S32.421B	S32.501B	S35.404A	S42.343B	S52.009B	S52.222C	S52.325B
S25.312A	S31.649A	S32.422A	S32.502B	S35.405A	S42.344B	S52.009C	S52.223B	S52.325C
S25.319A	S31.650A	S32.422B	S32.509B	S35.406A	S42.345B	S52.021B	S52.223C	S52.326B
S25.321A	S31.651A	S32.423A	S32.511B	S35.411A	S42.346B	S52.021C	S52.224B	S52.326C
S25.322A	S31.652A	S32.423B	S32.512B	S35.412A	S42.351B	S52.022B	S52.224C	S52.331B
S25.329A	S31.653A	S32.424A	S32.519B	S35.413A	S42.352B	S52.022C	S52.225B	S52.331C
S25.391A	S31.654A	S32.424B	S32.591B	S35.414A	S42.353B	S52.023B	S52.225C	S52.332B
S25.392A	S31.655A	S32.425A	S32.592B	S35.415A	S42.354B	S52.023C	S52.226B	S52.332C
S25.399A	S31.659A	S32.425B	S32.599B	S35.416A	S42.355B	S52.024B	S52.226C	S52.333B
S25.401A	S32.000B	S32.426A	S32.601B	S35.491A	S42.356B	S52.024C	S52.231B	S52.333C
S25.402A	S32.001B	S32.426B	S32.602B	S35.492A	S42.361B	S52.025B	S52.231C	S52.334B
S25.409A	S32.002B	S32.431A	S32.609B	S35.493A	S42.362B	S52.025C	S52.232B	S52.334C
S25.411A	S32.008B	S32.431B	S32.611B	S35.494A	S42.363B	S52.026B	S52.232C	S52.335B
S25.412A	S32.009B	S32.432A	S32.612B	S35.495A	S42.364B	S52.026C	S52.233B	S52.335C
S25.419A	S32.010B	S32.432B	S32.613B	S35.496A	S42.365B	S52.031B	S52.233C	S52.336B
S25.421A	S32.011B	S32.433A	S32.614B	S35.50XA	S42.366B	S52.031C	S52.234B	S52.336C
S25.422A	S32.012B	S32.433B	S32.615B	S35.511A	S42.391B	S52.032B	S52.234C	S52.341B
S25.429A	S32.018B	S32.434A	S32.616B	S35.512A	S42.392B	S52.032C	S52.235B	S52.341C
S25.491A	S32.019B	S32.434B	S32.691B	S35.513A	S42.399B	S52.033B	S52.235C	S52.342B
S25.492A	S32.020B	S32.435A	S32.692B	S35.514A	S42.401B	S52.033C	S52.236B	S52.342C
S25.499A	S32.021B	S32.435B	S32.699B	S35.515A	S42.402B	S52.034B	S52.236C	S52.343B
S26.020A	S32.022B	S32.436A	S32.810B	S35.516A	S42.409B	S52.034C	S52.241B	S52.343C
S26.021A	S32.028B	S32.436B	S32.811B	S35.59XA	S42.411B	S52.035B	S52.241C	S52.344B
S26.022A	S32.029B	S32.441A	S32.82XB	S36.031A	S42.412B	S52.035C	S52.242B	S52.344C
S26.12XA	S32.030B	S32.441B	S32.89XB	S36.032A	S42.413B	S52.036B	S52.242C	S52.345B
S26.92XA	S32.031B	S32.442A	S32.9XXB	S36.115A	S42.414B	S52.036C	S52.243B	S52.345C
S27.1XXA	S32.032B	S32.442B	S34.01XA	S36.116A	S42.415B	S52.041B	S52.243C	S52.346B
S27.2XXA	S32.038B	S32.443A	S34.02XA	S37.061A	S42.416B	S52.041C	S52.244B	S52.346C
S27.331A	S32.039B	S32.443B	S34.101A	S37.062A	S42.421B	S52.042B	S52.244C	S52.351B
S27.332A	S32.040B	S32.444A	S34.102A	S37.069A	S42.422B	S52.042C	S52.245B	S52.351C
S27.339A	S32.041B	S32.444B	S34.103A	S37.091A	S42.423B	S52.043B	S52.245C	S52.352B
S27.401A	S32.042B	S32.445A	S34.104A	S37.092A	S42.424B	S52.043C	S52.246B	S52.352C
S27.402A	S32.048B	S32.445B	S34.105A	S37.099A	S42.425B	S52.044B	S52.246C	S52.353B
S27.409A	S32.049B	S32.446A	S34.109A	S42.201B	S42.426B	S52.044C	S52.251B	S52.353C
S27.411A	S32.050B	S32.446B	S34.111A	S42.202B	S42.431B	S52.045B	S52.251C	S52.354B
S27.412A	S32.051B	S32.451A	S34.112A	S42.209B	S42.432B	S52.045C	S52.252B	S52.355B
S27.419A	S32.052B	S32.451B	S34.113A	S42.211B	S42.433B	S52.046B	S52.252C	S52.355C
S27.421A	S32.058B	S32.452A	S34.114A	S42.212B	S42.434B	S52.046C	S52.253B	S52.356B
S27.422A	S32.059B	S32.452B	S34.115A	S42.213B	S42.435B	S52.091B	S52.253C	S52.356C
S27.429A	S32.10XB	S32.453A	S34.119A	S42.214B	S42.436B	S52.091C	S52.254B	S52.361B
S27.431A	S32.110B	S32.453B	S34.121A	S42.215B	S42.441B	S52.092B	S52.254C	S52.361C
S27.432A	S32.111B	S32.454A	S34.122A	S42.216B	S42.442B	S52.092C	S52.255B	S52.362B
S27.439A	S32.112B	S32.454B	S34.123A	S42.221B	S42.443B	S52.099B	S52.255C	S52.362C
S27.491A	S32.119B	S32.455A	S34.124A	S42.222B	S42.444B	S52.099C	S52.256B	S52.363B
S27.492A	S32.120B	S32.455B	S34.125A	S42.223B	S42.445B	S52.101B	S52.256C	S52.363C
S27.499A	S32.121B	S32.456A	S34.129A	S42.224B	S42.446B	S52.101C	S52.261B	S52.364B
S27.812A	S32.122B	S32.456B	S34.131A	S42.225B	S42.447B	S52.102B	S52.261C	S52.364C
S27.813A	S32.129B	S32.461A	S34.132A	S42.226B	S42.448B	S52.102C	S52.262B	S52.365B
S27.818A	S32.130B	S32.461B	S34.139A	S42.231B	S42.449B	S52.109B	S52.262C	S52.365C
S27.819A	S32.131B	S32.462A	S34.3XXA	S42.232B	S42.451B	S52.109C	S52.263B	S52.366B
S31.001A	S32.132B	S32.462B	S35.00XA	S42.239B	S42.452B	S52.121B	S52.263C	S52.366C
S31.011A	S32.139B	S32.463A	S35.01XA	S42.241B	S42.453B	S52.121C	S52.264B	S52.371B
S31.021A	S32.14XB	S32.463B	S35.02XA	S42.242B	S42.454B	S52.122B	S52.264C	S52.371C
S31.031A	S32.15XB	S32.464A	S35.09XA	S42.249B	S42.455B	S52.122C	S52.265B	S52.372B
S31.041A	S32.16XB	S32.464B	S35.10XA	S42.251B	S42.456B	S52.123B	S52.265C	S52.372C
S31.051A	S32.17XB	S32.465A	S35.11XA	S42.252B	S42.461B	S52.123C	S52.266B	S52.379B
S31.600A	S32.19XB	S32.465B	S35.12XA	S42.253B	S42.462B	S52.124B	S52.266C	S52.379C
S31.601A	S32.2XXB	S32.466A	S35.19XA	S42.254B	S42.463B	S52.124C	S52.271B	S52.381B
S31.602A	S32.301B	S32.466B	S35.211A	S42.255B	S42.464B	S52.125B	S52.271C	S52.381C
S31.603A	S32.302B	S32.471A	S35.212A	S42.256B	S42.465B	S52.125C	S52.272B	S52.382B
S31.604A	S32.309B	S32.471B	S35.218A	S42.261B	S42.466B	S52.126B	S52.272C	S52.382C
S31.605A	S32.311B	S32.472A	S35.219A	S42.262B	S42.471B	S52.126C	S52.279B	S52.389B
S31.609A	S32.312B	S32.472B	S35.221A	S42.263B	S42.472B	S52.131B	S52.279C	S52.389C
S31.610A	S32.313B	S32.473A	S35.222A	S42.264B	S42.473B	S52.131C	S52.281B	S52.391B
S31.611A	S32.314B	S32.473B	S35.228A	S42.265B	S42.474B	S52.132B	S52.281C	S52.391C
S31.612A	S32.315B	S32.474A	S35.229A	S42.266B	S42.475B	S52.132C	S52.282B	S52.392B
S31.613A	S32.316B	S32.474B	S35.231A	S42.291B	S42.476B	S52.133B	S52.282C	S52.392C
S31.614A	S32.391B	S32.475A	S35.232A	S42.292B	S42.491B	S52.133C	S52.283B	S52.399B
S31.615A	S32.392B	S32.475B	S35.238A	S42.293B	S42.492B	S52.134B	S52.283C	S52.399C
S31.619A	S32.399B	S32.476A	S35.239A	S42.294B	S42.493B	S52.134C	S52.291B	S52.501B
S31.620A	S32.401A	S32.476B	S35.291A	S42.295B	S42.494B	S52.135B	S52.291C	S52.501C
S31.621A	S32.401B	S32.481A	S35.292A	S42.296B	S42.495B	S52.135C	S52.292B	S52.502B
S31.622A	S32.402A	S32.481B	S35.298A	S42.301B	S42.496B	S52.136B	S52.292C	S52.502C
S31.623A	S32.402B	S32.482A	S35.299A	S42.302B	S42.90XB	S52.136C	S52.299B	S52.509B
S31.624A	S32.409A	S32.482B	S35.311A	S42.309B	S42.91XB	S52.181B	S52.299C	S52.509C
S31.625A	S32.409B	S32.483A	S35.318A	S42.321B	S42.92XB	S52.181C	S52.301B	S52.511B
S31.629A	S32.411A	S32.483B	S35.319A	S42.322B	S45.001A	S52.182B	S52.301C	S52.511C
S31.630A	S32.411B	S32.484A	S35.321A	S42.323B	S45.002A	S52.182C	S52.302B	S52.512B
S31.631A	S32.412A	S32.484B	S35.328A	S42.324B	S45.009A	S52.189B	S52.302C	S52.512C
S31.632A	S32.412B	S32.485A	S35.329A	S42.325B	S45.011A	S52.189C	S52.309B	S52.513B
S31.633A	S32.413A	S32.485B	S35.331A	S42.326B	S45.012A	S52.201B	S52.309C	S52.513C
S31.634A	S32.413B	S32.486A	S35.338A	S42.331B	S45.019A	S52.201C	S52.321B	S52.514B
S31.635A	S32.414A	S32.486B	S35.339A	S42.332B	S45.091A	S52.202B	S52.321C	S52.514C
S31.639A	S32.414B	S32.491A	S35.341A	S42.333B	S45.092A	S52.202C	S52.322B	S52.515B
S31.640A	S32.415A	S32.491B	S35.348A	S42.334B	S45.099A	S52.209B	S52.322C	S52.515C
S31.641A	S32.416A	S32.492A	S35.349A	S42.335B	S52.001B	S52.209C	S52.323B	S52.516B
S31.642A		S32.492B	S35.401A	S42.336B	S52.001C	S52.221B	S52.323C	

S52.516C	S72.022B	S72.102A	S72.24XC	S72.361B	S72.455C	S82.116C	S82.243B	S82.455C
S52.531B	S72.022C	S72.102B	S72.25XA	S72.361C	S72.456B	S82.121B	S82.243C	S82.456B
S52.531C	S72.023A	S72.102C	S72.25XB	S72.362A	S72.456C	S82.121C	S82.244B	S82.456C
S52.532B	S72.023B	S72.109A	S72.25XC	S72.362B	S72.461C	S82.122B	S82.244C	S82.461B
S52.532C	S72.023C	S72.109B	S72.26XA	S72.362C	S72.462B	S82.123B	S82.245B	S82.461C
S52.539B	S72.024A	S72.109C	S72.26XB	S72.363A	S72.462C	S82.123C	S82.245C	S82.462B
S52.539C	S72.024B	S72.111A	S72.26XC	S72.363B	S72.463B	S82.124B	S82.246B	S82.462C
S52.541B	S72.024C	S72.111C	S72.301A	S72.363C	S72.463C	S82.124C	S82.246C	S82.463B
S52.541C	S72.025A	S72.112A	S72.301B	S72.364A	S72.464B	S82.125B	S82.251B	S82.463C
S52.542B	S72.025B	S72.112B	S72.301C	S72.364B	S72.464C	S82.125C	S82.251C	S82.464B
S52.542C	S72.025C	S72.112C	S72.302A	S72.364C	S72.465B	S82.126B	S82.252B	S82.464C
S52.549B	S72.026A	S72.113A	S72.302B	S72.365A	S72.465C	S82.126C	S82.252C	S82.465B
S52.549C	S72.026B	S72.113B	S72.302C	S72.365B	S72.466B	S82.131B	S82.253B	S82.465C
S52.551B	S72.026C	S72.113C	S72.309A	S72.365C	S72.466C	S82.131C	S82.253C	S82.466B
S52.551C	S72.031A	S72.114A	S72.309B	S72.366A	S72.491B	S82.132B	S82.254B	S82.466C
S52.552B	S72.031B	S72.114B	S72.309C	S72.366B	S72.491C	S82.132C	S82.254C	S82.491B
S52.552C	S72.031C	S72.114C	S72.321A	S72.366C	S72.492B	S82.133B	S82.255B	S82.491C
S52.559B	S72.032A	S72.115A	S72.321B	S72.391A	S72.492C	S82.133C	S82.255C	S82.492B
S52.559C	S72.032B	S72.115B	S72.321C	S72.391B	S72.499B	S82.134B	S82.256B	S82.492C
S52.561B	S72.032C	S72.115C	S72.322A	S72.391C	S72.499C	S82.134C	S82.256C	S82.499B
S52.561C	S72.033A	S72.116A	S72.322B	S72.392A	S72.8X1A	S82.135B	S82.261B	S82.499C
S52.562B	S72.033B	S72.116B	S72.323A	S72.392B	S72.8X1B	S82.135C	S82.261C	S82.831B
S52.562C	S72.033C	S72.116C	S72.323B	S72.392C	S72.8X1C	S82.136B	S82.262B	S82.831C
S52.569B	S72.034A	S72.121A	S72.323C	S72.399A	S72.8X2A	S82.136C	S82.262C	S82.832B
S52.569C	S72.034B	S72.121B	S72.324A	S72.399B	S72.8X2B	S82.141B	S82.263B	S82.832C
S52.571B	S72.034C	S72.121C	S72.324B	S72.399C	S72.8X2C	S82.141C	S82.263C	S82.839B
S52.571C	S72.035A	S72.122A	S72.324C	S72.401B	S72.8X9A	S82.142B	S82.264B	S82.839C
S52.572B	S72.035B	S72.122B	S72.325A	S72.401C	S72.8X9B	S82.142C	S82.264C	S82.861B
S52.572C	S72.035C	S72.122C	S72.325B	S72.402B	S72.8X9C	S82.143B	S82.265B	S82.861C
S52.579B	S72.036A	S72.123A	S72.325C	S72.402C	S72.90XA	S82.143C	S82.265C	S82.862B
S52.579C	S72.036B	S72.123B	S72.326A	S72.409B	S72.90XB	S82.144B	S82.266B	S82.862C
S52.591B	S72.036C	S72.123C	S72.326B	S72.409C	S72.90XC	S82.144C	S82.266C	S82.863B
S52.591C	S72.041A	S72.124A	S72.326C	S72.411B	S72.91XA	S82.145B	S82.291B	S82.863C
S52.592B	S72.041B	S72.124B	S72.331A	S72.411C	S72.91XB	S82.145C	S82.291C	S82.864B
S52.592C	S72.041C	S72.124C	S72.331B	S72.412B	S72.91XC	S82.146B	S82.292B	S82.864C
S52.599B	S72.042A	S72.125A	S72.331C	S72.412C	S72.92XA	S82.146C	S82.292C	S82.865B
S52.599C	S72.042B	S72.125B	S72.332A	S72.413B	S72.92XB	S82.151B	S82.299B	S82.865C
S52.601B	S72.042C	S72.125C	S72.332B	S72.413C	S72.92XC	S82.151C	S82.299C	S82.866B
S52.601C	S72.043A	S72.126A	S72.332C	S72.414B	S75.001A	S82.152B	S82.401B	S82.866C
S52.602B	S72.043B	S72.126B	S72.333A	S72.414C	S75.002A	S82.152C	S82.401C	S85.001A
S52.602C	S72.043C	S72.126C	S72.333B	S72.415B	S75.009A	S82.153B	S82.402B	S85.002A
S52.609B	S72.044A	S72.131A	S72.333C	S72.415C	S75.011A	S82.153C	S82.402C	S85.009A
S52.609C	S72.044B	S72.131B	S72.334A	S72.416B	S75.012A	S82.154B	S82.409B	S85.011A
S52.611B	S72.044C	S72.131C	S72.334B	S72.416C	S75.019A	S82.154C	S82.409C	S85.012A
S52.611C	S72.045A	S72.132A	S72.334C	S72.421B	S75.021A	S82.155B	S82.421B	S85.019A
S52.612B	S72.045B	S72.132B	S72.335A	S72.421C	S75.022A	S82.155C	S82.421C	S85.091A
S52.612C	S72.045C	S72.132C	S72.335B	S72.422B	S75.029A	S82.156B	S82.422B	S85.092A
S52.613B	S72.046A	S72.133A	S72.335C	S72.422C	S75.091A	S82.156C	S82.422C	S85.099A
S52.613C	S72.046B	S72.133B	S72.336A	S72.423B	S75.092A	S82.191B	S82.423B	S85.501A
S52.614B	S72.046C	S72.133C	S72.336B	S72.423C	S75.099A	S82.191C	S82.423C	S85.502A
S52.614C	S72.051A	S72.134A	S72.336C	S72.424B	S75.101A	S82.192B	S82.424B	S85.509A
S52.615B	S72.051B	S72.134B	S72.341A	S72.424C	S75.102A	S82.192C	S82.424C	S85.511A
S52.615C	S72.051C	S72.134C	S72.341B	S72.425B	S75.109A	S82.199B	S82.425B	S85.512A
S52.616B	S72.052A	S72.135A	S72.341C	S72.425C	S75.111A	S82.199C	S82.425C	S85.519A
S52.616C	S72.052B	S72.135B	S72.342A	S72.426B	S75.112A	S82.201B	S82.426B	S85.591A
S52.691B	S72.052C	S72.135C	S72.342B	S72.426C	S75.119A	S82.201C	S82.426C	S85.592A
S52.691C	S72.059A	S72.136A	S72.342C	S72.431B	S75.121A	S82.202B	S82.431B	S85.599A
S52.692B	S72.059B	S72.136B	S72.343A	S72.431C	S75.122A	S82.202C	S82.431C	T31.21
S52.692C	S72.059C	S72.136C	S72.343B	S72.432B	S75.129A	S82.209B	S82.432B	T31.22
S52.699B	S72.061A	S72.141A	S72.343C	S72.432C	S75.191A	S82.209C	S82.432C	T31.31
S52.699C	S72.061B	S72.141B	S72.344A	S72.433B	S75.192A	S82.221B	S82.433B	T31.32
S52.90XB	S72.061C	S72.141C	S72.344B	S72.433C	S75.199A	S82.221C	S82.433C	T31.33
S52.90XC	S72.062A	S72.142A	S72.344C	S72.434B	S79.001A	S82.222B	S82.434B	T31.41
S52.91XB	S72.062B	S72.142B	S72.345A	S72.434C	S79.002A	S82.222C	S82.434C	T31.42
S52.91XC	S72.062C	S72.142C	S72.345B	S72.435B	S79.009A	S82.223B	S82.435B	T31.43
S52.92XB	S72.063A	S72.143A	S72.345C	S72.435C	S79.011A	S82.223C	S82.435C	T31.44
S52.92XC	S72.063B	S72.143B	S72.346A	S72.436B	S79.012A	S82.224B	S82.436B	T31.51
S72.001A	S72.063C	S72.143C	S72.346B	S72.436C	S79.019A	S82.224C	S82.436C	T31.52
S72.001B	S72.064A	S72.144A	S72.346C	S72.441B	S79.091A	S82.225B	S82.441B	T31.53
S72.001C	S72.064B	S72.144B	S72.351A	S72.441C	S79.092A	S82.225C	S82.441C	T31.54
S72.002A	S72.064C	S72.144C	S72.351B	S72.442B	S79.099A	S82.226B	S82.442B	T31.55
S72.002B	S72.065A	S72.145A	S72.351C	S72.442C	S82.101B	S82.226C	S82.442C	T31.61
S72.002C	S72.065B	S72.145B	S72.352A	S72.443B	S82.101C	S82.231B	S82.443B	T31.62
S72.009A	S72.065C	S72.145C	S72.352B	S72.443C	S82.102B	S82.231C	S82.443C	T31.63
S72.009B	S72.066A	S72.145C	S72.352C	S72.444B	S82.109B	S82.232B	S82.444B	T31.64
S72.009C	S72.066B	S72.146A	S72.353A	S72.444C	S82.109C	S82.232C	S82.444C	T31.65
S72.011A	S72.066C	S72.146B	S72.353B	S72.445B	S82.111B	S82.233B	S82.445B	T31.66
S72.011B	S72.091A	S72.146C	S72.353C	S72.445C	S82.111C	S82.233C	S82.445C	T31.71
S72.011C	S72.091B	S72.21XA	S72.354A	S72.446B	S82.112B	S82.234B	S82.446B	T31.72
S72.012A	S72.091C	S72.21XB	S72.354B	S72.446C	S82.112C	S82.234C	S82.446C	T31.73
S72.012B	S72.092A	S72.21XC	S72.354C	S72.451B	S82.113B	S82.235B	S82.451B	T31.74
S72.012C	S72.092B	S72.22XA	S72.355A	S72.451C	S82.113C	S82.235C	S82.451C	T31.75
S72.019A	S72.092C	S72.22XB	S72.355B	S72.452B	S82.114B	S82.236B	S82.452B	T31.76
S72.019B	S72.099A	S72.22XC	S72.355C	S72.452C	S82.114C	S82.236C	S82.452C	T31.77
S72.019C	S72.099B	S72.23XA	S72.356A	S72.453B	S82.115B	S82.241B	S82.453B	T31.81
S72.021A	S72.099C	S72.23XB	S72.356B	S72.453C	S82.115C	S82.241C	S82.453C	T31.82
S72.021B	S72.101A	S72.23XC	S72.356C	S72.454B	S82.116B	S82.242B	S82.454B	T31.83
S72.021C	S72.101B	S72.24XA	S72.361A	S72.454C			S82.454B	T31.84
S72.022A	S72.101C	S72.24XB	S72.361A	S72.455B	S82.116B	S82.242C	S82.455B	T31.85

T31.86	T31.96	T32.33	T32.54	T32.71	T32.82	T32.92	T79.ØXXA
T31.87	T31.97	T32.41	T32.55	T32.72	T32.83	T32.93	T79.1XXA
T31.88	T31.98	T32.42	T32.61	T32.73	T32.84	T32.94	T79.4XXA
T31.91	T31.99	T32.43	T32.62	T32.74	T32.85	T32.95	T79.5XXA
T31.92	T32.21	T32.44	T32.63	T32.75	T32.86	T32.96	T80.ØXXA
T31.93	T32.22	T32.51	T32.64	T32.76	T32.87	T32.97	T81.11XA
T31.94	T32.31	T32.52	T32.65	T32.77	T32.88	T32.98	T81.12XA
T31.95	T32.32	T32.53	T32.66	T32.81	T32.91	T32.99	T81.19XA

MS-DRG Surgical Hierarchy Table

The surgical hierarchy reflects the relative resources requirement of the various surgical procedures of each major diagnostic category (MDC). The hierarchy is based upon variables such as principal diagnosis, surgical class, complications and comorbidities.

Arranging the surgical MS-DRGs in this manner allows for the assignment of patients with multiple procedures related to the principal diagnosis to a surgical MS-DRG that best reflects the resources used in the care of that patient. Since patients can be assigned to only one surgical class for each inpatient stay, patients with multiple procedures related to the principal diagnosis are assigned to the MS-DRG associated with the most resource-intensive surgical class.

Pre MDC

Heart transplant or implant of heart assist system w MCC; w/o MCC	001–002
ECMO or trach w MV 96+ hrs or PDX exc face, mouth & neck w maj O.R.; w/o maj O.R.	003–004
Liver transplant w MCC; w/o MCC or intestinal transplant	005–006
Allogeneic bone marrow transplant	014
Lung transplant	007
Simultaneous pancreas/kidney transplant	008
Autologous bone marrow transplant; or T-cell immunotherapy; w CC/MCC; w/o CC/MCC	016–017
Pancreas transplant	010
Tracheostomy for face, mouth & neck diagnoses or laryngectomy; w MCC; w CC; w/o CC/MCC	011–013

MDC 1   DISEASES & DISORDERS OF THE NERVOUS SYSTEM

Intracranial vascular procedures w PDX hemorrhage w MCC; w CC; w/o CC/MCC	020–022
Craniotomy w maj device implant or acute complex CNS PDX	023–024
Craniotomy & endovascular intracranial proc w/ MCC; w/ CC; w/o CC/MCC	025–027
Spinal procedures w MCC; w CC or spinal neurostimulators; w/o CC/MCC	028–030
Ventricular shunt procedures w MCC; w CC; w/o CC/MCC	031–033
Carotid artery stent procedures w MCC; w CC; w/o CC/MCC	034–036
Extracranial procedures w MCC; w CC; w/o CC/MCC	037–039
Periph/cranial nerve & other nerv syst proc w MCC; w CC or periph neurostim; w/o CC/MCC	040–042

MDC 2   DISEASES & DISORDERS OF THE EYE

Orbital procedures w CC/MCC; w/o CC/MCC	113–114
Extraocular procedures except orbit	115
Intraocular procedures w CC/MCC; w/o CC/MCC	116–117

MDC 3   DISEASES & DISORDERS OF THE EAR, NOSE, MOUTH & THROAT

Major head & neck procedures w CC/MCC or major device; w/o CC/MCC	129–130
Cranial/facial procedures w CC/MCC; w/o CC/MCC	131–132
Other ear, nose, mouth & throat O.R. procedures w CC/MCC; w/o CC/MCC	133–134
Sinus & mastoid procedures w CC/MCC; w/o CC/MCC	135–136
Mouth procedures w CC/MCC; w/o CC/MCC	137–138
Salivary gland procedures	139

MDC 4   DISEASES & DISORDERS OF THE RESPIRATORY SYSTEM

Major chest procedures w MCC; w CC; w/o CC/MCC	163–165
Other resp system O.R. procedures w MCC; w CC; w/o CC/MCC	166–168

MDC 5   DISEASES & DISORDERS OF THE CIRCULATORY SYSTEM

Other heart assist system implant	215
Cardiac valve & oth maj cardiothoracic proc w or w/o card cath w MCC; w CC; w/o CC/MCC	216–221
Endovascular cardiac valve replacement w MCC; w/o MCC	266–267
Cardiac defibrillator implant	222–227
Other cardiothoracic procedures w MCC; w CC; w/o CC/MCC	228–229
Coronary bypass	231–236
Aortic & heart assist procedures exc pulsation balloon w MCC; w/o MCC	268–269
Other endovascular cardiac valve proc w MCC; w/o MCC	319–320
Other maj cardiovascular procedures w MCC; w CC; w/o CC/MCC	270–272

MDC 5   DISEASES & DISORDERS OF THE CIRCULATORY SYSTEM (Continued)

Amputation for circ sys disorders exc upper limb & toe w MCC; w CC; w/o CC/MCC	239–241
Permanent cardiac pacemaker implant w MCC; w CC; w/o CC/MCC	242–244
AICD generator procedures	245
AICD lead procedures	265
Percutaneous intracardiac procedures w MCC; w/o MCC	273–274
Percutaneous cardiovascular procedures; with coronary artery/stent	246–249
Perc cardiovasc proc w/o coronary artery stent	250–251
Other vascular procedures w MCC; w CC; w/o CC/MCC	252–254
Upper limb & toe amputation for circ system disorders w MCC; w CC; w/o CC/MCC	255–257
Cardiac pacemaker device replacement w MCC; w/o MCC	258–259
Cardiac pacemaker revision except device replacement w MCC; w CC; w/o CC/MCC	260–262
Vein ligation & stripping	263
Other circulatory system O.R. procedures	264

MDC 6   DISEASES & DISORDERS OF THE DIGESTIVE SYSTEM

Stomach, esophageal & duodenal proc w MCC; w CC; w/o CC/MCC	326–328
Major small & large bowel procedures w MCC; w CC; w/o CC/MCC	329–331
Rectal resection w MCC; w CC; w/o CC/MCC	332–334
Peritoneal adhesiolysis w MCC; w CC; w/o CC/MCC	335–337
Appendectomy w; w/o complicated principal diag w MCC; w CC/MCC	338–343
Minor small & large bowel procedures w MCC; w CC; w/o CC/MCC	344–346
Anal & stomal procedures w MCC; w CC; w/o CC/MCC	347–349
Hernia procedures	350–355
Other digestive system O.R. procedures w MCC; w CC; w/o CC/MCC	356–358

MDC 7   DISEASES & DISORDERS OF THE HEPATOBILIARY SYSTEM & PANCREAS

Pancreas, liver & shunt procedures w MCC; w CC; w/o CC/MCC	405–407
Biliary tract procs except only cholecyst w or w/o c.d.e. w MCC; w CC; w/o CC/MCC	408–410
Cholecystectomy	411–419
Hepatobiliary diagnostic procedures w MCC; w CC; w/o CC/MCC	420–422
Other hepatobiliary or pancreas O.R. procedures w MCC; w CC; w/o CC/MCC	423–425

MDC 8   DISEASES & DISORDERS OF THE MUSCULOSKELETAL SYSTEM & CONNECTIVE TISSUE

Combined anterior/posterior spinal fusion w MCC; w CC; w/o CC/MCC	453–455
Spinal fus exc cerv w spinal curv/malig/infec or 9+ fus w MCC; w CC; w/o CC/MCC	456–458
Spinal fusion except cervical w MCC; w/o MCC	459–460
Bilateral or multiple major joint procs of lower extremity w MCC; w/o MCC	461–462
Wnd debrid & skn graft exc hand, for musculo-conn tiss dis w MCC; w CC; w/o CC/MCC	463–465
Revision of hip or knee replacement w MCC; w CC; w/o CC/MCC	466–468
Major hip/knee joint replacement or reattachment of lower extremity w/ MCC or total ankle replacement; w/o MCC	469–470
Cervical spinal fusion w MCC; w CC; w/o CC/MCC	471–473
Amputation for musculoskeletal sys & conn tissue dis w MCC; w CC; w/o CC/MCC	474–476
Biopsies of musculoskeletal system & connective tissue w MCC; w CC; w/o CC/MCC	477–479
Hip & femur procedures except major joint w MCC; w CC; w/o CC/MCC	480–482
Major joint & limb reattachment procs of upper extremity	483
Knee procedures	485–489
Back & neck proc exc spinal fusion w MCC or disc device/neurostim; w CC; w/o CC/MCC	518–520
Lower extrem & humer procs except hip, foot, femur w MCC; w CC; w/o CC/MCC	492–494

MDC 8 DISEASES & DISORDERS OF THE MUSCULOSKELETAL SYSTEM & CONNECTIVE TISSUE (Continued)

Local excision & removal int fix devices exc hip & femur w MCC; w CC; w/o CC/MCC	495–497
Local excision & removal int fix devices of hip & femur w CC/MCC; w/o CC/MCC	498–499
Soft tissue procedures w MCC; w CC; w/o CC/MCC	500–502
Foot procedures w MCC; w CC; w/o CC/MCC	503–505
Major thumb or joint procedures	506
Major shoulder or elbow joint procedures w CC/MCC; w/o CC/MCC	507–508
Arthroscopy	509
Shoulder, elbow or forearm procs, exc major joint procs w MCC; w CC; w/o CC/MCC	510–512
Hand or wrist procs, except major thumb or joint procs w CC/MCC; w/o CC/MCC	513–514
Other musculoskelet sys & conn tiss O.R. procs w MCC; w CC; w/o CC/MCC	515–517

MDC 9 DISEASES & DISORDERS OF THE SKIN, SUBCUTANEOUS TISSUE & BREAST

Skin graft	573–578
Skin debridement w MCC; w CC; w/o MCC/CC	570–572
Other skin, subcut tiss & breast procs w MCC; w CC; w/o CC/MCC	579–581
Mastectomy for malignancy w CC/MCC; w/o CC/MCC	582–583
Breast biopsy, local excision & other breast procedures w CC/MCC; w/o CC/MCC	584–585

MDC 10 ENDOCRINE, NUTRITIONAL, & METABOLIC DISEASES & DISORDERS

Amputat of lower limb for endocrine, nutrit, & metabol dis w MCC; w CC; w/o CC/MCC	616–618
O.R. procedures for obesity w MCC; w CC; w/o CC/MCC	619–621
Adrenal & pituitary procedures w CC/MCC; w/o CC/MCC	614–615
Skin grafts & wound debrid for endoc, nutrit & metab dis w MCC; w CC; w/o CC/MCC	622–624
Thyroid, parathyroid & thyroglossal procedures w MCC; w CC; w/o CC/MCC	625–627
Other endocrine, nutrit & metab O.R. procs w MCC; w CC; w/o CC/MCC	628–630

MDC 11 DISEASES AND DISORDERS OF THE KIDNEY & URINARY TRACT

Kidney transplant	652
Major bladder procedures w MCC; w CC; w/o CC/MCC	653–655
Kidney & ureter procedures for neoplasm or non-neoplasm w MCC; w CC; w/o CC/MCC	656–661
Minor bladder procedures w MCC; w CC; w/o CC/MCC	662–664
Prostatectomy w MCC; w CC; w/o CC/MCC	665–667
Transurethral procedures w MCC; w CC; w/o CC/MCC	668–670
Urethral procedures w CC/MCC; w/o CC/MCC	671–672
Other kidney & urinary tract procedures w MCC; w CC; w/o CC/MCC	673–675

MDC 12 DISEASES & DISORDERS OF THE MALE REPRODUCTIVE SYSTEM

Major male pelvic procedures w CC/MCC; w/o CC/MCC	707–708
Penis procedures w CC/MCC; w/o CC/MCC	709–710
Testes procedures w CC/MCC; w/o CC/MCC	711–712
Transurethral prostatectomy w CC/MCC; w/o CC/MCC	713–714
Other male reproductive system procs	715–718

MDC 13 DISEASES & DISORDERS OF THE FEMALE REPRODUCTIVE SYSTEM

Pelvic evisceration, rad hysterectomy & rad vulvectomy w CC/MCC; w/o CC/MCC	734–735
Uterine & adnexa procs for malignancy	736–741
Uterine & adnexa procs for non-malignancy w CC/MCC; w/o CC/MCC	742–743
D&C, conization, laparoscopy & tubal interruption w CC/MCC; w/o CC/MCC	744–745
Vagina, cervix & vulva procedures w CC/MCC; w/o CC/MCC	746–747
Female reproductive system reconstructive procedures	748
Other female reproductive system O.R. procedures w CC/MCC; w/o CC/MCC	749–750

MDC 14 PREGNANCY, CHILDBIRTH, & THE PUERPERIUM

Cesarean section with sterilization w MCC; w/ CC; w/o CC/MCC	783–785
Cesarean section w/o sterilization w MCC; w/ CC; w/o CC/MCC	786–788
Vaginal Delivery w O.R. proc exc sterilization and/or D&C	768
Vaginal Delivery w sterilization/D&C w MCC; w/ CC; w/o CC/MCC	796–798
Abortion w D&C, aspiration curettage or hysterotomy	770
Other antepartum diagnoses w O.R. proc w MCC; w/ CC; w/o CC/MCC	817–819
Postpartum & post abortion diagnoses w O.R. procedure	769

MDC 15 NEWBORNS & OTHER NEONATES WITH CONDITIONS ORIGINATING IN THE PERINATAL PERIOD

None	

MDC 16 DISEASES & DISORDERS OF THE BLOOD AND BLOOD FORMING ORGANS & IMMUNOLOGICAL DISORDERS

Splenectomy w MCC; w CC; w/o CC/MCC	799–801
Other O.R. proc of the blood & blood forming organs w MCC; w CC; w/o CC/MCC	802–804

MDC 17 MYELOPROLIFERATIVE DISEASES & DISORDERS, POORLY DIFFERENTIATED NEOPLASMS

Lymphoma & leukemia w major O.R. procedure w MCC; w CC; w/o CC/MCC	820–822
Lymphoma & non-acute leukemia w other O.R. proc w MCC; w CC; w/o CC/MCC	823–825
Myeloprolif dis or poorly diff neopl w major O.R proc w MCC; w CC; w/o CC/MCC	826–828
Myeloprolif dis or poorly diff neopl w other proc w CC/MCC; w/o CC/MCC	829–830

MDC 18 INFECTIOUS & PARASITIC DISEASES, SYSTEMIC OR UNSPECIFIED SITES

Postoperative or posttraumatic infections w O.R. proc w MCC; w CC; w/o CC/MCC	856–858
Infections & parasitic diseases w O.R. procedure w MCC; w CC; w/o CC/MCC	853–855

MDC 19 MENTAL DISEASES & DISORDERS

O.R. procedure w principal diagnoses of mental illness	876

MDC 20 ALCOHOL/DRUG USE & ALCOHOL/DRUG INDUCED ORGANIC MENTAL DISORDERS

None	

MDC 21 INJURIES, POISONINGS, & TOXIC EFFECTS OF DRUGS

Wound debridements for injuries w MCC; w CC; w/o CC/MCC	901–903
Skin grafts for injuries w CC/MCC; w/o CC/MCC	904–905
Hand procedures for injuries	906
Other O.R. procedures for injuries w MCC; w CC; w/o CC/MCC	907–909

MDC 22 BURNS

Extensive burns or full thickness burns w MV 96+ hrs w skin graft	927
Full thickness burn w skin graft or inhal inj w CC/MCC; w/o CC/MCC	928–929

MDC 23 FACTORS INFLUENCING HEALTH STATUS & OTHER CONTACTS WITH HEALTH SERVICES

O.R. proc w diagnoses of other contact w health services w MCC; w CC; w/o CC/MCC	939–941

MDC 24 MULTIPLE SIGNIFICANT TRAUMA

Craniotomy for multiple significant trauma	955
Limb reattachment, hip & femur procs for multiple significant trauma	956
Other O.R. procedures for multiple significant trauma w MCC; w CC; w/o CC/MCC	957–959

MDC 25 HUMAN IMMUNODEFICIENCY VIRUS INFECTIONS

HIV w extensive O.R. procedure w MCC; w/o MCC	969–970

MS-LTC-DRG Crosswalk

CMS modified the DRGs for the LTCH PPS by developing LTCH-specific relative weights to account for the fact that LTCHs generally treat patients with multiple medical problems. Therefore, CMS developed a crosswalk of IPPS MS-DRG to MS-LTC-DRG data, including RW, GMLOS, and short-stay outlier thresholds. The MS-LTC-DRG crosswalk is based on Grouper version 37.0.

MS-LTC-DRG	MS-LTC-DRG Title	FY 2018 LTCH Cases[1]	Relative Weight	Geometric Av Length of Stay	Short-Stay Outlier (SSO) Threshold[2]
1	Heart transplant or implant of heart assist system w MCC	0	0.0000	0.0	0.0
2	Heart transplant or implant of heart assist system w/o MCC	0	0.0000	0.0	0.0
3	ECMO or trach w MV >96 hrs or PDX exc face, mouth & neck w maj O.R.	333	3.8102	55.9	46.6
4	Trach w MV >96 hrs or PDX exc face, mouth & neck w/o maj O.R.	1,551	2.8150	44.4	37.0
5	Liver transplant w MCC or intestinal transplant	0	0.0000	0.0	0.0
6	Liver transplant w/o MCC	0	0.0000	0.0	0.0
7	Lung transplant	0	0.0000	0.0	0.0
8	Simultaneous pancreas/kidney transplant	0	0.0000	0.0	0.0
10	Pancreas transplant	0	0.0000	0.0	0.0
11	Tracheostomy for face, mouth & neck diagnoses or laryngectomy w MCC	0	0.4808	15.8	13.2
12	Tracheostomy for face, mouth & neck diagnoses or laryngectomy w CC	0	0.4808	15.8	13.2
13	Tracheostomy for face, mouth & neck diagnoses or laryngectomy w/o CC/MCC	0	0.4808	15.8	13.2
14	Allogeneic bone marrow transplant	0	0.6064	18.6	15.5
16	Autologous bone marrow transplant w CC/MCC or T-cell immunotherapy	0	0.6064	18.6	15.5
17	Autologous bone marrow transplant w/o CC/MCC	0	0.6064	18.6	15.5
20	Intracranial vascular procedures w PDX hemorrhage w MCC	0	0.8779	22.4	18.7
21	Intracranial vascular procedures w PDX hemorrhage w CC	0	0.6064	18.6	15.5
22	Intracranial vascular procedures w PDX hemorrhage w/o CC/MCC	0	0.4808	15.8	13.2
23	Craniotomy w major device implant or acute complex CNS PDX w MCC or chemotherapy implant or epilepsy w neurostimulator	2	1.5478	33.6	28.0
24	Cranio w major dev impl/acute complex CNS PDX w/o MCC	0	0.4808	15.8	13.2
25	Craniotomy & endovascular intracranial procedures w MCC	2	1.0554	26.2	21.8
26	Craniotomy & endovascular intracranial procedures w CC	0	0.4808	15.8	13.2
27	Craniotomy & endovascular intracranial procedures w/o CC/MCC	0	0.4808	15.8	13.2
28	Spinal procedures w MCC	1	1.0554	26.2	21.8
29	Spinal procedures w CC or spinal neurostimulators	0	0.6064	18.6	15.5
30	Spinal procedures w/o CC/MCC	0	0.6064	18.6	15.5
31	Ventricular shunt procedures w MCC	2	1.5478	33.6	28.0
32	Ventricular shunt procedures w CC	0	0.6064	18.6	15.5
33	Ventricular shunt procedures w/o CC/MCC	0	0.6064	18.6	15.5
34	Carotid artery stent procedure w MCC	0	1.7608	39.5	32.9
35	Carotid artery stent procedure w CC	0	1.7608	39.5	32.9
36	Carotid artery stent procedure w/o CC/MCC	0	1.7608	39.5	32.9
37	Extracranial procedures w MCC	2	1.5478	33.6	28.0
38	Extracranial procedures w CC	0	1.5478	33.6	28.0
39	Extracranial procedures w/o CC/MCC	0	1.5478	33.6	28.0
40	Periph/cranial nerve & other nerv syst proc w MCC	79	1.6303	35.7	29.8
41	Periph/cranial nerve & other nerv syst proc w CC or periph neurostim	3	0.6064	18.6	15.5
42	Periph/cranial nerve & other nerv syst proc w/o CC/MCC	1	0.6064	18.6	15.5
52	Spinal disorders & injuries w CC/MCC	45	1.1249	37.9	31.6
53	Spinal disorders & injuries w/o CC/MCC	0	1.1249	37.9	31.6
54	Nervous system neoplasms w MCC	14	1.5478	33.6	28.0
55	Nervous system neoplasms w/o MCC	6	1.5478	33.6	28.0
56	Degenerative nervous system disorders w MCC	567	0.8732	25.0	20.8
57	Degenerative nervous system disorders w/o MCC	328	0.6673	22.4	18.7
58	Multiple sclerosis & cerebellar ataxia w MCC	6	0.7922	21.8	18.2
59	Multiple sclerosis & cerebellar ataxia w CC	1	0.6064	18.6	15.5
60	Multiple sclerosis & cerebellar ataxia w/o CC/MCC	0	0.6064	18.6	15.5
61	Ischemic stroke, precerebral occlusion or transient ischemia w thrombolytic agent w MCC	0	0.8629	23.0	19.2

*   In determining the MS-LTC-DRG relative weights for FY 2020, these MS-LTC-DRGs were adjusted for nonmonotonicity as discussed in section VIII.B.3.g. (step 6) of the preamble of the FY 2020 IPPS/LTCH PPS final rule.

1   The count of LTCH 'standard payment rate' cases in the database of LTCH claims from the March 2019 update of the FY 2018 MedPAR files used in the MS-LTC-DRG calculations.

2   The SSO threshold is calculated as 5/6th of the geometric average length of stay of the MS-LTC-DRG (as specified in §412.529(a)).

MS-LTC-DRG	MS-LTC-DRG Title	FY 2018 LTCH Cases[1]	Relative Weight	Geometric Av Length of Stay	Short-Stay Outlier (SSO) Threshold[2]
62	Ischemic stroke, precerebral occlusion or transient ischemia w thrombolytic agent w CC	0	0.5981	19.4	16.2
63	Ischemic stroke, precerebral occlusion or transient ischemia w thrombolytic agent w/o CC/MCC	0	0.4808	15.8	13.2
64	Intracranial hemorrhage or cerebral infarction w MCC	84	0.8779	22.4	18.7
65	Intracranial hemorrhage or cerebral infarction w CC or tPA in 24 hrs	24	0.6064	18.6	15.5
66	Intracranial hemorrhage or cerebral infarction w/o CC/MCC	2	0.4808	15.8	13.2
67	Nonspecific cva & precerebral occlusion w/o infarct w MCC	0	0.5981	19.4	16.2
68	Nonspecific cva & precerebral occlusion w/o infarct w/o MCC	0	0.4808	15.8	13.2
69	Transient ischemia w/o thrombolytic	1	0.4808	15.8	13.2
70	Nonspecific cerebrovascular disorders w MCC	162	0.8629	23.0	19.2
71	Nonspecific cerebrovascular disorders w CC	43	0.5981	19.4	16.2
72	Nonspecific cerebrovascular disorders w/o CC/MCC	1	0.4808	15.8	13.2
73	Cranial & peripheral nerve disorders w MCC	39	0.9848	23.7	19.8
74	Cranial & peripheral nerve disorders w/o MCC	14	0.6064	18.6	15.5
75	Viral meningitis w CC/MCC	6	0.6064	18.6	15.5
76	Viral meningitis w/o CC/MCC	0	0.6064	18.6	15.5
77	Hypertensive encephalopathy w MCC	1	0.6064	18.6	15.5
78	Hypertensive encephalopathy w CC	0	0.6064	18.6	15.5
79	Hypertensive encephalopathy w/o CC/MCC	0	0.6064	18.6	15.5
80	Nontraumatic stupor & coma w MCC	3	1.0554	26.2	21.8
81	Nontraumatic stupor & coma w/o MCC	1	0.7922	21.8	18.2
82	Traumatic stupor & coma, coma >1 hr w MCC	84	0.8791	24.5	20.4
83	Traumatic stupor & coma, coma >1 hr w CC	19	0.4808	15.8	13.2
84	Traumatic stupor & coma, coma >1 hr w/o CC/MCC	3	0.4808	15.8	13.2
85	Traumatic stupor & coma, coma <1 hr w MCC	24	0.7922	21.8	18.2
86	Traumatic stupor & coma, coma <1 hr w CC	15	0.7922	21.8	18.2
87	Traumatic stupor & coma, coma <1 hr w/o CC/MCC	1	0.4808	15.8	13.2
88	Concussion w MCC	0	0.7922	21.8	18.2
89	Concussion w CC	0	0.7922	21.8	18.2
90	Concussion w/o CC/MCC	0	0.4808	15.8	13.2
91	Other disorders of nervous system w MCC	177	0.9846	25.5	21.3
92	Other disorders of nervous system w CC	39	0.5851	20.1	16.8
93	Other disorders of nervous system w/o CC/MCC	5	0.4808	15.8	13.2
94	Bacterial & tuberculous infections of nervous system w MCC	172	1.1890	27.5	22.9
95	Bacterial & tuberculous infections of nervous system w CC	38	0.8016	23.5	19.6
96	Bacterial & tuberculous infections of nervous system w/o CC/MCC	1	0.4808	15.8	13.2
97	Non-bacterial infect of nervous sys exc viral meningitis w MCC	59	1.0536	23.3	19.4
98	Non-bacterial infect of nervous sys exc viral meningitis w CC	12	0.6064	18.6	15.5
99	Non-bacterial infect of nervous sys exc viral meningitis w/o CC/MCC	0	0.6064	18.6	15.5
100	Seizures w MCC	37	0.8822	21.5	17.9
101	Seizures w/o MCC	18	0.7922	21.8	18.2
102	Headaches w MCC	1	0.4808	15.8	13.2
103	Headaches w/o MCC	1	0.4808	15.8	13.2
113	Orbital procedures w CC/MCC	0	0.4808	15.8	13.2
114	Orbital procedures w/o CC/MCC	0	0.4808	15.8	13.2
115	Extraocular procedures except orbit	0	1.5478	33.6	28.0
116	Intraocular procedures w CC/MCC	0	1.5478	33.6	28.0
117	Intraocular procedures w/o CC/MCC	0	0.4808	15.8	13.2
121	Acute major eye infections w CC/MCC	3	0.7922	21.8	18.2
122	Acute major eye infections w/o CC/MCC	0	0.4808	15.8	13.2
123	Neurological eye disorders	0	0.7922	21.8	18.2
124	Other disorders of the eye w MCC	1	0.6064	18.6	15.5
125	Other disorders of the eye w/o MCC	0	0.4808	15.8	13.2
129	Major head & neck procedures w CC/MCC or major device	0	1.5478	33.6	28.0

*　In determining the MS-LTC-DRG relative weights for FY 2020, these MS-LTC-DRGs were adjusted for nonmonotonicity as discussed in section VIII.B.3.g. (step 6) of the preamble of the FY 2020 IPPS/LTCH PPS final rule.

1　The count of LTCH 'standard payment rate' cases in the database of LTCH claims from the March 2019 update of the FY 2018 MedPAR files used in the MS-LTC-DRG calculations.

2　The SSO threshold is calculated as 5/6th of the geometric average length of stay of the MS-LTC-DRG (as specified in §412.529(a)).

MS-LTC-DRG Crosswalk

MS-LTC-DRG	MS-LTC-DRG Title	FY 2018 LTCH Cases[1]	Relative Weight	Geometric Av Length of Stay	Short-Stay Outlier (SSO) Threshold[2]
130	Major head & neck procedures w/o CC/MCC	0	0.4808	15.8	13.2
131	Cranial/facial procedures w CC/MCC	0	0.4808	15.8	13.2
132	Cranial/facial procedures w/o CC/MCC	0	0.4808	15.8	13.2
133	Other ear, nose, mouth & throat O.R. procedures w CC/MCC	5	1.5478	33.6	28.0
134	Other ear, nose, mouth & throat O.R. procedures w/o CC/MCC	0	0.4808	15.8	13.2
135	Sinus & mastoid procedures w CC/MCC	0	0.4808	15.8	13.2
136	Sinus & mastoid procedures w/o CC/MCC	0	0.4808	15.8	13.2
137	Mouth procedures w CC/MCC	1	1.0554	26.2	21.8
138	Mouth procedures w/o CC/MCC	0	0.4808	15.8	13.2
139	Salivary gland procedures	0	1.5478	33.6	28.0
146	Ear, nose, mouth & throat malignancy w MCC	20	0.7922	21.8	18.2
147	Ear, nose, mouth & throat malignancy w CC	3	0.7922	21.8	18.2
148	Ear, nose, mouth & throat malignancy w/o CC/MCC	0	0.7922	21.8	18.2
149	Dysequilibrium	1	0.4808	15.8	13.2
150	Epistaxis w MCC	1	0.6064	18.6	15.5
151	Epistaxis w/o MCC	0	0.6064	18.6	15.5
152	Otitis media & URI w MCC	23	1.0554	26.2	21.8
153	Otitis media & URI w/o MCC	7	1.0554	26.2	21.8
154	Other ear, nose, mouth & throat diagnoses w MCC	17	0.6064	18.6	15.5
155	Other ear, nose, mouth & throat diagnoses w CC	6	0.4808	15.8	13.2
156	Other ear, nose, mouth & throat diagnoses w/o CC/MCC	0	0.4808	15.8	13.2
157	Dental & Oral Diseases w MCC	14	1.0554	26.2	21.8
158	Dental & Oral Diseases w CC	6	0.6064	18.6	15.5
159	Dental & Oral Diseases w/o CC/MCC	0	0.4808	15.8	13.2
163	Major chest procedures w MCC	80	2.4924	40.7	33.9
164	Major chest procedures w CC	4	1.0554	26.2	21.8
165	Major chest procedures w/o CC/MCC	0	1.0554	26.2	21.8
166	Other resp system O.R. procedures w MCC	1,664	2.3392	40.5	33.8
167	Other resp system O.R. procedures w CC	84	1.6427	31.8	26.5
168	Other resp system O.R. procedures w/o CC/MCC	0	1.6427	31.8	26.5
175	Pulmonary embolism w MCC or acute cor pulmonale	41	0.6442	17.9	14.9
176	Pulmonary embolism w/o MCC	17	0.6064	18.6	15.5
177	Respiratory infections & inflammations w MCC	1,387	0.8035	21.5	17.9
178	Respiratory infections & inflammations w CC	242	0.6729	19.4	16.2
179*	Respiratory infections & inflammations w/o CC/MCC	13	0.6729	19.4	16.2
180	Respiratory neoplasms w MCC	17	1.0554	26.2	21.8
181	Respiratory neoplasms w CC	9	0.7922	21.8	18.2
182	Respiratory neoplasms w/o CC/MCC	0	0.7922	21.8	18.2
183	Major chest trauma w MCC	2	0.4808	15.8	13.2
184	Major chest trauma w CC	2	0.4808	15.8	13.2
185	Major chest trauma w/o CC/MCC	0	0.4808	15.8	13.2
186	Pleural effusion w MCC	50	0.7382	20.5	17.1
187	Pleural effusion w CC	9	0.6064	18.6	15.5
188	Pleural effusion w/o CC/MCC	0	0.6064	18.6	15.5
189	Pulmonary edema & respiratory failure	14,180	0.9616	21.5	17.9
190	Chronic obstructive pulmonary disease w MCC	528	0.7572	19.1	15.9
191	Chronic obstructive pulmonary disease w CC	94	0.5484	16.1	13.4
192*	Chronic obstructive pulmonary disease w/o CC/MCC	17	0.5484	16.1	13.4
193	Simple pneumonia & pleurisy w MCC	542	0.7520	19.3	16.1
194	Simple pneumonia & pleurisy w CC	130	0.5562	16.3	13.6
195	Simple pneumonia & pleurisy w/o CC/MCC	10	0.4808	15.8	13.2
196	Interstitial lung disease w MCC	46	0.8012	20.1	16.8
197	Interstitial lung disease w CC	3	0.7922	21.8	18.2

*   In determining the MS-LTC-DRG relative weights for FY 2020, these MS-LTC-DRGs were adjusted for nonmonotonicity as discussed in section VIII.B.3.g. (step 6) of the preamble of the FY 2020 IPPS/LTCH PPS final rule.

1   The count of LTCH 'standard payment rate' cases in the database of LTCH claims from the March 2019 update of the FY 2018 MedPAR files used in the MS-LTC-DRG calculations.

2   The SSO threshold is calculated as 5/6th of the geometric average length of stay of the MS-LTC-DRG (as specified in §412.529(a)).

MS-LTC-DRG Crosswalk

MS-LTC-DRG	MS-LTC-DRG Title	FY 2018 LTCH Cases[1]	Relative Weight	Geometric Av Length of Stay	Short-Stay Outlier (SSO) Threshold[2]
198	Interstitial lung disease w/o CC/MCC	0	0.7922	21.8	18.2
199	Pneumothorax w MCC	45	0.7100	20.2	16.8
200	Pneumothorax w CC	9	0.4808	15.8	13.2
201	Pneumothorax w/o CC/MCC	2	0.4808	15.8	13.2
202	Bronchitis & asthma w CC/MCC	40	0.6232	17.5	14.6
203	Bronchitis & asthma w/o CC/MCC	0	0.6232	17.5	14.6
204	Respiratory signs & symptoms	8	0.6064	18.6	15.5
205	Other respiratory system diagnoses w MCC	65	0.9692	23.8	19.8
206	Other respiratory system diagnoses w/o MCC	9	0.6064	18.6	15.5
207	Respiratory system diagnosis w ventilator support >96 hours	12,486	1.8628	32.1	26.8
208	Respiratory system diagnosis w ventilator support <=96 hours	1,625	1.1100	21.6	18.0
215	Other heart assist system implant	0	1.3511	28.6	23.8
216	Cardiac valve & oth maj cardiothoracic proc w card cath w MCC	0	1.3511	28.6	23.8
217	Cardiac valve & oth maj cardiothoracic proc w card cath w CC	0	1.3511	28.6	23.8
218	Cardiac valve & oth maj cardiothoracic proc w card cath w/o CC/MCC	0	1.3511	28.6	23.8
219	Cardiac valve & oth maj cardiothoracic proc w/o card cath w MCC	0	1.3511	28.6	23.8
220	Cardiac valve & oth maj cardiothoracic proc w/o card cath w CC	0	1.3511	28.6	23.8
221	Cardiac valve & oth maj cardiothoracic proc w/o card cath w/o CC/MCC	0	1.3511	28.6	23.8
222	Cardiac defib implant w cardiac cath w AMI/HF/shock w MCC	0	1.5478	33.6	28.0
223	Cardiac defib implant w cardiac cath w AMI/HF/shock w/o MCC	0	1.5478	33.6	28.0
224	Cardiac defib implant w cardiac cath w/o AMI/HF/shock w MCC	0	1.5478	33.6	28.0
225	Cardiac defib implant w cardiac cath w/o AMI/HF/shock w/o MCC	0	1.5478	33.6	28.0
226	Cardiac defibrillator implant w/o cardiac cath w MCC	5	1.5478	33.6	28.0
227	Cardiac defibrillator implant w/o cardiac cath w/o MCC	0	1.5478	33.6	28.0
228	Other cardiothoracic procedures w MCC	1	0.7922	21.8	18.2
229	Other cardiothoracic procedures w/o MCC	0	0.7922	21.8	18.2
231	Coronary bypass w PTCA w MCC	0	1.3511	28.6	23.8
232	Coronary bypass w PTCA w/o MCC	0	1.3511	28.6	23.8
233	Coronary bypass w cardiac cath w MCC	0	1.3511	28.6	23.8
234	Coronary bypass w cardiac cath w/o MCC	0	1.3511	28.6	23.8
235	Coronary bypass w/o cardiac cath w MCC	0	1.3511	28.6	23.8
236	Coronary bypass w/o cardiac cath w/o MCC	0	1.3511	28.6	23.8
239	Amputation for circ sys disorders exc upper limb & toe w MCC	36	1.7608	39.5	32.9
240	Amputation for circ sys disorders exc upper limb & toe w CC	5	1.5478	33.6	28.0
241	Amputation for circ sys disorders exc upper limb & toe w/o CC/MCC	0	1.5478	33.6	28.0
242	Permanent cardiac pacemaker implant w MCC	12	1.5478	33.6	28.0
243	Permanent cardiac pacemaker implant w CC	2	0.7922	21.8	18.2
244	Permanent cardiac pacemaker implant w/o CC/MCC	1	0.4808	15.8	13.2
245	AICD generator procedures	1	1.5478	33.6	28.0
246	Percutaneous cardiovascular procedures w drug-eluting stent w MCC or 4+ arteries or stents	0	1.5478	33.6	28.0
247	Perc cardiovasc proc w drug-eluting stent w/o MCC	0	0.7922	21.8	18.2
248	Percutaneous cardiovascular procedures w non-drug-eluting stent w MCC or 4+ arteries or stents	0	0.4808	15.8	13.2
249	Perc cardiovasc proc w non-drug-eluting stent w/o MCC	0	0.4808	15.8	13.2
250	Perc cardiovasc proc w/o coronary artery stent w MCC	0	1.5478	33.6	28.0
251	Perc cardiovasc proc w/o coronary artery stent w/o MCC	0	0.4808	15.8	13.2
252	Other vascular procedures w MCC	46	1.3511	28.6	23.8
253	Other vascular procedures w CC	2	0.7922	21.8	18.2
254	Other vascular procedures w/o CC/MCC	0	0.7922	21.8	18.2
255	Upper limb & toe amputation for circ system disorders w MCC	10	1.5478	33.6	28.0
256	Upper limb & toe amputation for circ system disorders w CC	1	0.7922	21.8	18.2
257	Upper limb & toe amputation for circ system disorders w/o CC/MCC	0	0.7922	21.8	18.2
258	Cardiac pacemaker device replacement w MCC	0	1.5478	33.6	28.0
259	Cardiac pacemaker device replacement w/o MCC	1	1.5478	33.6	28.0

* In determining the MS-LTC-DRG relative weights for FY 2020, these MS-LTC-DRGs were adjusted for nonmonotonicity as discussed in section VIII.B.3.g. (step 6) of the preamble of the FY 2020 IPPS/LTCH PPS final rule.

1 The count of LTCH 'standard payment rate' cases in the database of LTCH claims from the March 2019 update of the FY 2018 MedPAR files used in the MS-LTC-DRG calculations.

2 The SSO threshold is calculated as 5/6th of the geometric average length of stay of the MS-LTC-DRG (as specified in §412.529(a)).

MS-LTC-DRG	MS-LTC-DRG Title	FY 2018 LTCH Cases[1]	Relative Weight	Geometric Av Length of Stay	Short-Stay Outlier (SSO) Threshold[2]
260	Cardiac pacemaker revision except device replacement w MCC	2	1.5478	33.6	28.0
261	Cardiac pacemaker revision except device replacement w CC	0	0.7922	21.8	18.2
262	Cardiac pacemaker revision except device replacement w/o CC/MCC	0	0.7922	21.8	18.2
263	Vein ligation & stripping	1	0.6064	18.6	15.5
264	Other circulatory system O.R. procedures	235	1.3001	32.2	26.8
265	AICD lead procedures	0	0.7922	21.8	18.2
266	Endovascular cardiac valve replacement & supplement procedures w MCC	0	0.7922	21.8	18.2
267	Endovascular cardiac valve replacement & supplement procedures w/o MCC	0	0.7922	21.8	18.2
268	Aortic and heart assist procedures except pulsation balloon w MCC	0	1.3511	28.6	23.8
269	Aortic and heart assist procedures except pulsation balloon w/o MCC	0	1.3511	28.6	23.8
270	Other major cardiovascular procedures w MCC	7	1.5478	33.6	28.0
271	Other major cardiovascular procedures w CC	3	0.7922	21.8	18.2
272	Other major cardiovascular procedures w/o CC/MCC	0	0.7922	21.8	18.2
273	Percutaneous intracardiac procedures w MCC	2	1.5478	33.6	28.0
274	Percutaneous intracardiac procedures w/o MCC	0	1.5478	33.6	28.0
280	Acute myocardial infarction, discharged alive w MCC	205	0.7842	21.8	18.2
281	Acute myocardial infarction, discharged alive w CC	39	0.6149	18.8	15.7
282	Acute myocardial infarction, discharged alive w/o CC/MCC	4	0.4808	15.8	13.2
283*	Acute myocardial infarction, expired w MCC	22	0.7922	21.8	18.2
284*	Acute myocardial infarction, expired w CC	1	0.7922	21.8	18.2
285	Acute myocardial infarction, expired w/o CC/MCC	0	0.7922	21.8	18.2
286	Circulatory disorders except AMI, w card cath w MCC	10	1.5478	33.6	28.0
287	Circulatory disorders except AMI, w card cath w/o MCC	0	1.5478	33.6	28.0
288	Acute & subacute endocarditis w MCC	419	1.0843	26.0	21.7
289	Acute & subacute endocarditis w CC	74	0.8629	27.0	22.5
290*	Acute & subacute endocarditis w/o CC/MCC	5	0.8629	27.0	22.5
291	Heart failure & shock w MCC	1,033	0.7964	20.0	16.7
292	Heart failure & shock w CC	139	0.6008	18.8	15.7
293	Heart failure & shock w/o CC/MCC	17	0.4808	15.8	13.2
294	Deep vein thrombophlebitis w CC/MCC	0	0.6252	20.0	16.7
295	Deep vein thrombophlebitis w/o CC/MCC	0	0.6064	18.6	15.5
296	Cardiac arrest, unexplained w MCC	2	0.4808	15.8	13.2
297	Cardiac arrest, unexplained w CC	0	0.4808	15.8	13.2
298	Cardiac arrest, unexplained w/o CC/MCC	0	0.4808	15.8	13.2
299	Peripheral vascular disorders w MCC	173	0.8239	22.1	18.4
300	Peripheral vascular disorders w CC	41	0.6252	20.0	16.7
301	Peripheral vascular disorders w/o CC/MCC	2	0.6064	18.6	15.5
302	Atherosclerosis w MCC	39	0.7560	19.7	16.4
303	Atherosclerosis w/o MCC	10	0.6064	18.6	15.5
304	Hypertension w MCC	10	0.7922	21.8	18.2
305	Hypertension w/o MCC	4	0.6064	18.6	15.5
306	Cardiac congenital & valvular disorders w MCC	36	0.7444	19.8	16.5
307*	Cardiac congenital & valvular disorders w/o MCC	3	0.7444	19.8	16.5
308	Cardiac arrhythmia & conduction disorders w MCC	51	0.7783	20.7	17.3
309	Cardiac arrhythmia & conduction disorders w CC	22	0.6064	18.6	15.5
310	Cardiac arrhythmia & conduction disorders w/o CC/MCC	3	0.4808	15.8	13.2
311	Angina pectoris	5	0.4808	15.8	13.2
312	Syncope & collapse	19	0.7922	21.8	18.2
313	Chest pain	0	0.4808	15.8	13.2
314	Other circulatory system diagnoses w MCC	892	1.0363	24.2	20.2
315	Other circulatory system diagnoses w CC	68	0.7577	21.3	17.8
316	Other circulatory system diagnoses w/o CC/MCC	3	0.6064	18.6	15.5
319	Other endovascular cardiac valve procedures w MCC	0	0.7922	21.8	18.2

* In determining the MS-LTC-DRG relative weights for FY 2020, these MS-LTC-DRGs were adjusted for nonmonotonicity as discussed in section VIII.B.3.g. (step 6) of the preamble of the FY 2020 IPPS/LTCH PPS final rule.

1 The count of LTCH 'standard payment rate' cases in the database of LTCH claims from the March 2019 update of the FY 2018 MedPAR files used in the MS-LTC-DRG calculations.

2 The SSO threshold is calculated as 5/6th of the geometric average length of stay of the MS-LTC-DRG (as specified in §412.529(a)).

MS-LTC-DRG Crosswalk

MS-LTC-DRG Crosswalk

MS-LTC-DRG	MS-LTC-DRG Title	FY 2018 LTCH Cases [1]	Relative Weight	Geometric Av Length of Stay	Short-Stay Outlier (SSO) Threshold [2]
320	Other endovascular cardiac valve procedures w/o MCC	0	0.7922	21.8	18.2
326	Stomach, esophageal & duodenal proc w MCC	12	1.5478	33.6	28.0
327	Stomach, esophageal & duodenal proc w CC	0	0.4808	15.8	13.2
328	Stomach, esophageal & duodenal proc w/o CC/MCC	0	0.4808	15.8	13.2
329	Major small & large bowel procedures w MCC	16	1.5478	33.6	28.0
330	Major small & large bowel procedures w CC	2	1.5478	33.6	28.0
331	Major small & large bowel procedures w/o CC/MCC	0	0.4808	15.8	13.2
332	Rectal resection w MCC	0	1.5478	33.6	28.0
333	Rectal resection w CC	0	0.6291	18.7	15.6
334	Rectal resection w/o CC/MCC	0	0.4808	15.8	13.2
335	Peritoneal adhesiolysis w MCC	0	0.9331	23.1	19.3
336	Peritoneal adhesiolysis w CC	0	0.6291	18.7	15.6
337	Peritoneal adhesiolysis w/o CC/MCC	0	0.4808	15.8	13.2
338	Appendectomy w complicated principal diag w MCC	0	0.9331	23.1	19.3
339	Appendectomy w complicated principal diag w CC	0	0.6291	18.7	15.6
340	Appendectomy w complicated principal diag w/o CC/MCC	0	0.4808	15.8	13.2
341	Appendectomy w/o complicated principal diag w MCC	0	0.6064	18.6	15.5
342	Appendectomy w/o complicated principal diag w CC	0	0.6064	18.6	15.5
343	Appendectomy w/o complicated principal diag w/o CC/MCC	0	0.6064	18.6	15.5
344	Minor small & large bowel procedures w MCC	3	1.0554	26.2	21.8
345	Minor small & large bowel procedures w CC	0	0.6291	18.7	15.6
346	Minor small & large bowel procedures w/o CC/MCC	0	0.4808	15.8	13.2
347	Anal & stomal procedures w MCC	4	1.5478	33.6	28.0
348	Anal & stomal procedures w CC	0	0.6291	18.7	15.6
349	Anal & stomal procedures w/o CC/MCC	0	0.4808	15.8	13.2
350	Inguinal & femoral hernia procedures w MCC	0	0.9331	23.1	19.3
351	Inguinal & femoral hernia procedures w CC	0	0.6291	18.7	15.6
352	Inguinal & femoral hernia procedures w/o CC/MCC	0	0.4808	15.8	13.2
353	Hernia procedures except inguinal & femoral w MCC	3	1.5478	33.6	28.0
354	Hernia procedures except inguinal & femoral w CC	0	0.6291	18.7	15.6
355	Hernia procedures except inguinal & femoral w/o CC/MCC	0	0.4808	15.8	13.2
356	Other digestive system O.R. procedures w MCC	114	1.4825	34.0	28.3
357	Other digestive system O.R. procedures w CC	10	1.0554	26.2	21.8
358	Other digestive system O.R. procedures w/o CC/MCC	0	1.0554	26.2	21.8
368	Major esophageal disorders w MCC	22	1.0554	26.2	21.8
369	Major esophageal disorders w CC	2	1.0554	26.2	21.8
370	Major esophageal disorders w/o CC/MCC	0	1.0554	26.2	21.8
371	Major gastrointestinal disorders & peritoneal infections w MCC	499	0.9331	23.1	19.3
372	Major gastrointestinal disorders & peritoneal infections w CC	89	0.6291	18.7	15.6
373	Major gastrointestinal disorders & peritoneal infections w/o CC/MCC	6	0.4808	15.8	13.2
374	Digestive malignancy w MCC	30	0.8291	23.8	19.8
375*	Digestive malignancy w CC	7	0.8291	23.8	19.8
376	Digestive malignancy w/o CC/MCC	0	0.8291	23.8	19.8
377	G.I. hemorrhage w MCC	81	0.8018	20.9	17.4
378	G.I. hemorrhage w CC	15	0.7922	21.8	18.2
379	G.I. hemorrhage w/o CC/MCC	1	0.4808	15.8	13.2
380	Complicated peptic ulcer w MCC	40	1.0265	26.4	22.0
381	Complicated peptic ulcer w CC	4	0.7922	21.8	18.2
382	Complicated peptic ulcer w/o CC/MCC	0	0.7922	21.8	18.2
383	Uncomplicated peptic ulcer w MCC	3	1.0554	26.2	21.8
384	Uncomplicated peptic ulcer w/o MCC	2	0.4808	15.8	13.2
385	Inflammatory bowel disease w MCC	21	1.5478	33.6	28.0
386	Inflammatory bowel disease w CC	7	0.6064	18.6	15.5

*   In determining the MS-LTC-DRG relative weights for FY 2020, these MS-LTC-DRGs were adjusted for nonmonotonicity as discussed in section VIII.B.3.g. (step 6) of the preamble of the FY 2020 IPPS/LTCH PPS final rule.

1   The count of LTCH 'standard payment rate' cases in the database of LTCH claims from the March 2019 update of the FY 2018 MedPAR files used in the MS-LTC-DRG calculations.

2   The SSO threshold is calculated as 5/6th of the geometric average length of stay of the MS-LTC-DRG (as specified in §412.529(a)).

MS-LTC-DRG	MS-LTC-DRG Title	FY 2018 LTCH Cases[1]	Relative Weight	Geometric Av Length of Stay	Short-Stay Outlier (SSO) Threshold[2]
387	Inflammatory bowel disease w/o CC/MCC	0	0.6064	18.6	15.5
388	G.I. obstruction w MCC	135	0.9392	23.4	19.5
389	G.I. obstruction w CC	40	0.6453	18.7	15.6
390*	G.I. obstruction w/o CC/MCC	5	0.6453	18.7	15.6
391	Esophagitis, gastroent & misc digest disorders w MCC	266	0.9991	24.6	20.5
392	Esophagitis, gastroent & misc digest disorders w/o MCC	58	0.6165	17.6	14.7
393	Other digestive system diagnoses w MCC	537	1.0913	26.2	21.8
394	Other digestive system diagnoses w CC	83	0.7920	22.6	18.8
395*	Other digestive system diagnoses w/o CC/MCC	7	0.7920	22.6	18.8
405	Pancreas, liver & shunt procedures w MCC	2	1.0554	26.2	21.8
406	Pancreas, liver & shunt procedures w CC	0	0.7922	21.8	18.2
407	Pancreas, liver & shunt procedures w/o CC/MCC	0	0.4808	15.8	13.2
408	Biliary tract proc except only cholecyst w or w/o c.d.e. w MCC	0	0.8018	20.9	17.4
409	Biliary tract proc except only cholecyst w or w/o c.d.e. w CC	0	0.7922	21.8	18.2
410	Biliary tract proc except only cholecyst w or w/o c.d.e. w/o CC/MCC	0	0.4808	15.8	13.2
411	Cholecystectomy w c.d.e. w MCC	0	0.8018	20.9	17.4
412	Cholecystectomy w c.d.e. w CC	0	0.7922	21.8	18.2
413	Cholecystectomy w c.d.e. w/o CC/MCC	0	0.4808	15.8	13.2
414	Cholecystectomy except by laparoscope w/o c.d.e. w MCC	1	1.5478	33.6	28.0
415	Cholecystectomy except by laparoscope w/o c.d.e. w CC	0	0.6064	18.6	15.5
416	Cholecystectomy except by laparoscope w/o c.d.e. w/o CC/MCC	0	0.6064	18.6	15.5
417	Laparoscopic cholecystectomy w/o c.d.e. w MCC	10	1.0554	26.2	21.8
418	Laparoscopic cholecystectomy w/o c.d.e. w CC	1	0.6064	18.6	15.5
419	Laparoscopic cholecystectomy w/o c.d.e. w/o CC/MCC	0	0.6064	18.6	15.5
420	Hepatobiliary diagnostic procedures w MCC	0	0.6064	18.6	15.5
421	Hepatobiliary diagnostic procedures w CC	0	0.6064	18.6	15.5
422	Hepatobiliary diagnostic procedures w/o CC/MCC	0	0.6064	18.6	15.5
423	Other hepatobiliary or pancreas O.R. procedures w MCC	12	1.0554	26.2	21.8
424	Other hepatobiliary or pancreas O.R. procedures w CC	0	1.0554	26.2	21.8
425	Other hepatobiliary or pancreas O.R. procedures w/o CC/MCC	0	0.6064	18.6	15.5
432	Cirrhosis & alcoholic hepatitis w MCC	82	0.8497	21.6	18.0
433	Cirrhosis & alcoholic hepatitis w CC	11	0.6064	18.6	15.5
434	Cirrhosis & alcoholic hepatitis w/o CC/MCC	3	0.6064	18.6	15.5
435	Malignancy of hepatobiliary system or pancreas w MCC	17	1.0554	26.2	21.8
436	Malignancy of hepatobiliary system or pancreas w CC	1	0.4808	15.8	13.2
437	Malignancy of hepatobiliary system or pancreas w/o CC/MCC	0	0.4808	15.8	13.2
438	Disorders of pancreas except malignancy w MCC	153	0.9251	20.9	17.4
439	Disorders of pancreas except malignancy w CC	26	0.8336	22.0	18.3
440	Disorders of pancreas except malignancy w/o CC/MCC	1	0.4808	15.8	13.2
441	Disorders of liver except malig, cirr, alc hepa w MCC	91	0.8400	20.6	17.2
442	Disorders of liver except malig, cirr, alc hepa w CC	20	0.6064	18.6	15.5
443	Disorders of liver except malig, cirr, alc hepa w/o CC/MCC	0	0.6064	18.6	15.5
444	Disorders of the biliary tract w MCC	104	0.8779	23.0	19.2
445*	Disorders of the biliary tract w CC	18	0.7922	21.8	18.2
446*	Disorders of the biliary tract w/o CC/MCC	2	0.7922	21.8	18.2
453	Combined anterior/posterior spinal fusion w MCC	0	0.9364	23.8	19.8
454	Combined anterior/posterior spinal fusion w CC	0	0.7210	22.6	18.8
455	Combined anterior/posterior spinal fusion w/o CC/MCC	0	0.4808	15.8	13.2
456	Spinal fus exc cerv w spinal curv/malig/infec or ext fus w MCC	0	0.9364	23.8	19.8
457	Spinal fus exc cerv w spinal curv/malig/infec or ext fus w CC	0	0.7210	22.6	18.8
458	Spinal fus exc cerv w spinal curv/malig/infec or ext fus w/o CC/MCC	0	0.4808	15.8	13.2
459	Spinal fusion except cervical w MCC	0	0.9364	23.8	19.8
460	Spinal fusion except cervical w/o MCC	0	0.7210	22.6	18.8

*   In determining the MS-LTC-DRG relative weights for FY 2020, these MS-LTC-DRGs were adjusted for nonmonotonicity as discussed in section VIII.B.3.g. (step 6) of the preamble of the FY 2020 IPPS/LTCH PPS final rule.

1   The count of LTCH 'standard payment rate' cases in the database of LTCH claims from the March 2019 update of the FY 2018 MedPAR files used in the MS-LTC-DRG calculations.

2   The SSO threshold is calculated as 5/6th of the geometric average length of stay of the MS-LTC-DRG (as specified in §412.529(a)).

MS-LTC-DRG Crosswalk

MS-LTC-DRG Crosswalk

MS-LTC-DRG	MS-LTC-DRG Title	FY 2018 LTCH Cases[1]	Relative Weight	Geometric Av Length of Stay	Short-Stay Outlier (SSO) Threshold[2]
461	Bilateral or multiple major joint procs of lower extremity w MCC	0	0.9364	23.8	19.8
462	Bilateral or multiple major joint procs of lower extremity w/o MCC	0	0.7210	22.6	18.8
463	Wnd debrid & skn grft exc hand, for musculo-conn tiss dis w MCC	361	1.4780	36.7	30.6
464	Wnd debrid & skn grft exc hand, for musculo-conn tiss dis w CC	49	1.1074	32.5	27.1
465	Wnd debrid & skn grft exc hand, for musculo-conn tiss dis w/o CC/MCC	2	0.7922	21.8	18.2
466	Revision of hip or knee replacement w MCC	0	1.7458	40.4	33.7
467	Revision of hip or knee replacement w CC	0	0.7922	21.8	18.2
468	Revision of hip or knee replacement w/o CC/MCC	0	0.7922	21.8	18.2
469	Major hip and knee joint replacement or reattachment of lower extremity w MCC or total ankle replacement	0	1.7458	40.4	33.7
470	Major hip and knee joint replacement or reattachment of lower extremity w/o MCC	0	0.7922	21.8	18.2
471	Cervical spinal fusion w MCC	1	1.5478	33.6	28.0
472	Cervical spinal fusion w CC	0	0.7210	22.6	18.8
473	Cervical spinal fusion w/o CC/MCC	0	0.4808	15.8	13.2
474	Amputation for musculoskeletal sys & conn tissue dis w MCC	26	1.7458	40.4	33.7
475	Amputation for musculoskeletal sys & conn tissue dis w CC	3	0.7922	21.8	18.2
476	Amputation for musculoskeletal sys & conn tissue dis w/o CC/MCC	0	0.7922	21.8	18.2
477	Biopsies of musculoskeletal system & connective tissue w MCC	8	1.5478	33.6	28.0
478	Biopsies of musculoskeletal system & connective tissue w CC	1	1.5478	33.6	28.0
479	Biopsies of musculoskeletal system & connective tissue w/o CC/MCC	0	1.5478	33.6	28.0
480*	Hip & femur procedures except major joint w MCC	2	1.0554	26.2	21.8
481*	Hip & femur procedures except major joint w CC	1	1.0554	26.2	21.8
482	Hip & femur procedures except major joint w/o CC/MCC	0	1.0554	26.2	21.8
483	Major joint/limb reattachment procedure of upper extremities	1	0.4808	15.8	13.2
485	Knee procedures w pdx of infection w MCC	0	1.5478	33.6	28.0
486	Knee procedures w pdx of infection w CC	1	1.5478	33.6	28.0
487	Knee procedures w pdx of infection w/o CC/MCC	0	1.5478	33.6	28.0
488	Knee procedures w/o pdx of infection w CC/MCC	0	0.6064	18.6	15.5
489	Knee procedures w/o pdx of infection w/o CC/MCC	0	0.6064	18.6	15.5
492	Lower extrem & humer proc except hip, foot, femur w MCC	5	0.6064	18.6	15.5
493	Lower extrem & humer proc except hip, foot, femur w CC	0	0.6064	18.6	15.5
494	Lower extrem & humer proc except hip, foot, femur w/o CC/MCC	0	0.6064	18.6	15.5
495	Local excision & removal int fix devices exc hip & femur w MCC	2	1.0554	26.2	21.8
496	Local excision & removal int fix devices exc hip & femur w CC	1	0.7922	21.8	18.2
497	Local excision & removal int fix devices exc hip & femur w/o CC/MCC	0	0.7922	21.8	18.2
498	Local excision & removal int fix devices of hip & femur w CC/MCC	8	1.0554	26.2	21.8
499	Local excision & removal int fix devices of hip & femur w/o CC/MCC	0	1.0554	26.2	21.8
500	Soft tissue procedures w MCC	119	1.3572	32.7	27.3
501	Soft tissue procedures w CC	17	1.0554	26.2	21.8
502	Soft tissue procedures w/o CC/MCC	0	1.0554	26.2	21.8
503	Foot procedures w MCC	9	1.5478	33.6	28.0
504	Foot procedures w CC	3	0.7922	21.8	18.2
505	Foot procedures w/o CC/MCC	0	0.7922	21.8	18.2
506	Major thumb or joint procedures	0	0.4808	15.8	13.2
507	Major shoulder or elbow joint procedures w CC/MCC	0	0.7922	21.8	18.2
508	Major shoulder or elbow joint procedures w/o CC/MCC	0	0.4808	15.8	13.2
509	Arthroscopy	0	0.4808	15.8	13.2
510	Shoulder, elbow or forearm proc, exc major joint proc w MCC	4	1.0554	26.2	21.8
511	Shoulder, elbow or forearm proc, exc major joint proc w CC	1	0.7922	21.8	18.2
512	Shoulder, elbow or forearm proc, exc major joint proc w/o CC/MCC	1	0.4808	15.8	13.2
513	Hand or wrist proc, except major thumb or joint proc w CC/MCC	4	1.0554	26.2	21.8
514	Hand or wrist proc, except major thumb or joint proc w/o CC/MCC	0	1.0554	26.2	21.8
515	Other musculoskelet sys & conn tiss O.R. proc w MCC	55	1.5842	35.6	29.7
516	Other musculoskelet sys & conn tiss O.R. proc w CC	0	1.5842	35.6	29.7

* In determining the MS-LTC-DRG relative weights for FY 2020, these MS-LTC-DRGs were adjusted for nonmonotonicity as discussed in section VIII.B.3.g. (step 6) of the preamble of the FY 2020 IPPS/LTCH PPS final rule.

1 The count of LTCH 'standard payment rate' cases in the database of LTCH claims from the March 2019 update of the FY 2018 MedPAR files used in the MS-LTC-DRG calculations.

2 The SSO threshold is calculated as 5/6th of the geometric average length of stay of the MS-LTC-DRG (as specified in §412.529(a)).

MS-LTC-DRG Crosswalk

MS-LTC-DRG	MS-LTC-DRG Title	FY 2018 LTCH Cases[1]	Relative Weight	Geometric Av Length of Stay	Short-Stay Outlier (SSO) Threshold[2]
517	Other musculoskelet sys & conn tiss O.R. proc w/o CC/MCC	0	1.5842	35.6	29.7
518	Back & neck proc exc spinal fusion w MCC or disc device/neurostim	2	1.5478	33.6	28.0
519	Back & neck proc exc spinal fusion w CC	0	0.7210	22.6	18.8
520	Back & neck proc exc spinal fusion w/o CC/MCC	0	0.4808	15.8	13.2
533	Fractures of femur w MCC	1	1.0554	26.2	21.8
534	Fractures of femur w/o MCC	0	1.0554	26.2	21.8
535	Fractures of hip & pelvis w MCC	4	0.6064	18.6	15.5
536	Fractures of hip & pelvis w/o MCC	1	0.4808	15.8	13.2
537	Sprains, strains, & dislocations of hip, pelvis & thigh w CC/MCC	0	0.6064	18.6	15.5
538	Sprains, strains, & dislocations of hip, pelvis & thigh w/o CC/MCC	0	0.4808	15.8	13.2
539	Osteomyelitis w MCC	775	1.0627	28.5	23.8
540	Osteomyelitis w CC	113	0.8771	26.4	22.0
541*	Osteomyelitis w/o CC/MCC	10	0.8771	26.4	22.0
542*	Pathological fractures & musculoskelet & conn tiss malig w MCC	8	0.7922	21.8	18.2
543*	Pathological fractures & musculoskelet & conn tiss malig w CC	1	0.7922	21.8	18.2
544	Pathological fractures & musculoskelet & conn tiss malig w/o CC/MCC	0	0.7922	21.8	18.2
545	Connective tissue disorders w MCC	27	1.4055	28.0	23.3
546	Connective tissue disorders w CC	5	1.0554	26.2	21.8
547	Connective tissue disorders w/o CC/MCC	0	1.0554	26.2	21.8
548	Septic arthritis w MCC	110	1.1103	28.8	24.0
549	Septic arthritis w CC	28	0.6247	21.6	18.0
550	Septic arthritis w/o CC/MCC	3	0.4808	15.8	13.2
551	Medical back problems w MCC	56	1.0968	28.7	23.9
552	Medical back problems w/o MCC	24	0.7922	21.8	18.2
553*	Bone diseases & arthropathies w MCC	3	0.7922	21.8	18.2
554*	Bone diseases & arthropathies w/o MCC	2	0.7922	21.8	18.2
555	Signs & symptoms of musculoskeletal system & conn tissue w MCC	3	0.7922	21.8	18.2
556	Signs & symptoms of musculoskeletal system & conn tissue w/o MCC	4	0.6064	18.6	15.5
557	Tendonitis, myositis & bursitis w MCC	154	1.0665	26.8	22.3
558	Tendonitis, myositis & bursitis w/o MCC	54	0.7162	22.3	18.6
559	Aftercare, musculoskeletal system & connective tissue w MCC	779	0.9313	25.2	21.0
560	Aftercare, musculoskeletal system & connective tissue w CC	321	0.8125	24.4	20.3
561	Aftercare, musculoskeletal system & connective tissue w/o CC/MCC	13	0.4808	15.8	13.2
562*	Fx, sprn, strn & disl except femur, hip, pelvis & thigh w MCC	3	0.7922	21.8	18.2
563*	Fx, sprn, strn & disl except femur, hip, pelvis & thigh w/o MCC	4	0.7922	21.8	18.2
564	Other musculoskeletal sys & connective tissue diagnoses w MCC	150	0.9364	23.8	19.8
565	Other musculoskeletal sys & connective tissue diagnoses w CC	35	0.7210	22.6	18.8
566	Other musculoskeletal sys & connective tissue diagnoses w/o CC/MCC	1	0.4808	15.8	13.2
570	Skin debridement w MCC	313	1.2916	32.6	27.2
571	Skin debridement w CC	86	1.0104	28.7	23.9
572*	Skin debridement w/o CC/MCC	3	1.0104	28.7	23.9
573	Skin graft for skin ulcer or cellulitis w MCC	46	1.6346	42.5	35.4
574	Skin graft for skin ulcer or cellulitis w CC	22	1.5478	33.6	28.0
575	Skin graft for skin ulcer or cellulitis w/o CC/MCC	1	1.0554	26.2	21.8
576	Skin graft exc for skin ulcer or cellulitis w MCC	5	1.5478	33.6	28.0
577	Skin graft exc for skin ulcer or cellulitis w CC	2	0.6064	18.6	15.5
578	Skin graft exc for skin ulcer or cellulitis w/o CC/MCC	0	0.6064	18.6	15.5
579	Other skin, subcut tiss & breast proc w MCC	294	1.5422	35.1	29.3
580	Other skin, subcut tiss & breast proc w CC	53	1.1137	32.6	27.2
581	Other skin, subcut tiss & breast proc w/o CC/MCC	0	1.1137	32.6	27.2
582	Mastectomy for malignancy w CC/MCC	0	1.0104	28.7	23.9
583	Mastectomy for malignancy w/o CC/MCC	0	1.0104	28.7	23.9
584	Breast biopsy, local excision & other breast procedures w CC/MCC	0	1.0104	28.7	23.9

*   In determining the MS-LTC-DRG relative weights for FY 2020, these MS-LTC-DRGs were adjusted for nonmonotonicity as discussed in section VIII.B.3.g. (step 6) of the preamble of the FY 2020 IPPS/LTCH PPS final rule.

1   The count of LTCH 'standard payment rate' cases in the database of LTCH claims from the March 2019 update of the FY 2018 MedPAR files used in the MS-LTC-DRG calculations.

2   The SSO threshold is calculated as 5/6th of the geometric average length of stay of the MS-LTC-DRG (as specified in §412.529(a)).

MS-LTC-DRG Crosswalk

MS-LTC-DRG Crosswalk

MS-LTC-DRG	MS-LTC-DRG Title	FY 2018 LTCH Cases[1]	Relative Weight	Geometric Av Length of Stay	Short-Stay Outlier (SSO) Threshold[2]
585	Breast biopsy, local excision & other breast procedures w/o CC/MCC	0	1.0104	28.7	23.9
592	Skin ulcers w MCC	640	0.9629	25.3	21.1
593	Skin ulcers w CC	196	0.7183	23.4	19.5
594*	Skin ulcers w/o CC/MCC	8	0.7183	23.4	19.5
595	Major skin disorders w MCC	8	0.7922	21.8	18.2
596	Major skin disorders w/o MCC	2	0.4808	15.8	13.2
597	Malignant breast disorders w MCC	2	0.7922	21.8	18.2
598	Malignant breast disorders w CC	1	0.4808	15.8	13.2
599	Malignant breast disorders w/o CC/MCC	0	0.4808	15.8	13.2
600	Non-malignant breast disorders w CC/MCC	4	0.7922	21.8	18.2
601	Non-malignant breast disorders w/o CC/MCC	0	0.4808	15.8	13.2
602	Cellulitis w MCC	353	0.8238	22.7	18.9
603	Cellulitis w/o MCC	175	0.5678	18.0	15.0
604	Trauma to the skin, subcut tiss & breast w MCC	26	0.9019	25.6	21.3
605	Trauma to the skin, subcut tiss & breast w/o MCC	8	0.6064	18.6	15.5
606	Minor skin disorders w MCC	50	0.9652	23.4	19.5
607	Minor skin disorders w/o MCC	16	0.6064	18.6	15.5
614	Adrenal & pituitary procedures w CC/MCC	0	0.6064	18.6	15.5
615	Adrenal & pituitary procedures w/o CC/MCC	0	0.4808	15.8	13.2
616	Amputat of lower limb for endocrine, nutrit, & metabol dis w MCC	40	1.3567	34.7	28.9
617	Amputat of lower limb for endocrine, nutrit, & metabol dis w CC	26	1.2998	30.6	25.5
618	Amputat of lower limb for endocrine, nutrit, & metabol dis w/o CC/MCC	0	0.7922	21.8	18.2
619	O.R. procedures for obesity w MCC	1	1.5478	33.6	28.0
620	O.R. procedures for obesity w CC	0	1.0554	26.2	21.8
621	O.R. procedures for obesity w/o CC/MCC	0	1.0554	26.2	21.8
622	Skin grafts & wound debrid for endoc, nutrit & metab dis w MCC	201	1.3112	34.2	28.5
623	Skin grafts & wound debrid for endoc, nutrit & metab dis w CC	99	1.1241	29.8	24.8
624	Skin grafts & wound debrid for endoc, nutrit & metab dis w/o CC/MCC	0	0.6064	18.6	15.5
625	Thyroid, parathyroid & thyroglossal procedures w MCC	0	1.4640	33.5	27.9
626	Thyroid, parathyroid & thyroglossal procedures w CC	0	1.0554	26.2	21.8
627	Thyroid, parathyroid & thyroglossal procedures w/o CC/MCC	0	0.7920	22.6	18.8
628	Other endocrine, nutrit & metab O.R. proc w MCC	35	1.4640	33.5	27.9
629	Other endocrine, nutrit & metab O.R. proc w CC	24	1.0554	26.2	21.8
630	Other endocrine, nutrit & metab O.R. proc w/o CC/MCC	0	0.7920	22.6	18.8
637	Diabetes w MCC	430	1.0019	24.5	20.4
638	Diabetes w CC	306	0.8028	23.3	19.4
639	Diabetes w/o CC/MCC	1	0.4808	15.8	13.2
640	Misc disorders of nutrition, metabolism, fluids/electrolytes w MCC	193	0.9069	22.9	19.1
641	Misc disorders of nutrition, metabolism, fluids/electrolytes w/o MCC	66	0.6217	18.6	15.5
642	Inborn and other disorders of metabolism	2	1.5478	33.6	28.0
643	Endocrine disorders w MCC	12	0.6064	18.6	15.5
644	Endocrine disorders w CC	1	0.6064	18.6	15.5
645	Endocrine disorders w/o CC/MCC	1	0.4808	15.8	13.2
652	Kidney transplant	0	0.0000	0.0	0.0
653	Major bladder procedures w MCC	0	0.7922	21.8	18.2
654	Major bladder procedures w CC	0	0.7922	21.8	18.2
655	Major bladder procedures w/o CC/MCC	0	0.7922	21.8	18.2
656	Kidney & ureter procedures for neoplasm w MCC	0	1.0554	26.2	21.8
657	Kidney & ureter procedures for neoplasm w CC	1	1.0554	26.2	21.8
658	Kidney & ureter procedures for neoplasm w/o CC/MCC	0	1.0554	26.2	21.8
659	Kidney & ureter procedures for non-neoplasm w MCC	11	1.0554	26.2	21.8
660	Kidney & ureter procedures for non-neoplasm w CC	2	0.7922	21.8	18.2
661	Kidney & ureter procedures for non-neoplasm w/o CC/MCC	0	0.7922	21.8	18.2

* In determining the MS-LTC-DRG relative weights for FY 2020, these MS-LTC-DRGs were adjusted for nonmonotonicity as discussed in section VIII.B.3.g. (step 6) of the preamble of the FY 2020 IPPS/LTCH PPS final rule.

1 The count of LTCH 'standard payment rate' cases in the database of LTCH claims from the March 2019 update of the FY 2018 MedPAR files used in the MS-LTC-DRG calculations.

2 The SSO threshold is calculated as 5/6th of the geometric average length of stay of the MS-LTC-DRG (as specified in §412.529(a)).

MS-LTC-DRG	MS-LTC-DRG Title	FY 2018 LTCH Cases[1]	Relative Weight	Geometric Av Length of Stay	Short-Stay Outlier (SSO) Threshold[2]
662	Minor bladder procedures w MCC	0	1.0554	26.2	21.8
663	Minor bladder procedures w CC	2	0.6064	18.6	15.5
664	Minor bladder procedures w/o CC/MCC	0	0.4808	15.8	13.2
665	Prostatectomy w MCC	0	0.6064	18.6	15.5
666	Prostatectomy w CC	1	0.6064	18.6	15.5
667	Prostatectomy w/o CC/MCC	0	0.6064	18.6	15.5
668	Transurethral procedures w MCC	3	0.7922	21.8	18.2
669	Transurethral procedures w CC	0	0.7922	21.8	18.2
670	Transurethral procedures w/o CC/MCC	0	0.7922	21.8	18.2
671	Urethral procedures w CC/MCC	0	0.7327	20.9	17.4
672	Urethral procedures w/o CC/MCC	0	0.7327	20.9	17.4
673	Other kidney & urinary tract procedures w MCC	213	1.4304	31.1	25.9
674	Other kidney & urinary tract procedures w CC	23	1.0554	26.2	21.8
675	Other kidney & urinary tract procedures w/o CC/MCC	0	0.7327	20.9	17.4
682	Renal failure w MCC	1,235	0.9511	22.9	19.1
683	Renal failure w CC	241	0.7327	20.9	17.4
684*	Renal failure w/o CC/MCC	11	0.7327	20.9	17.4
686	Kidney & urinary tract neoplasms w MCC	7	1.0554	26.2	21.8
687	Kidney & urinary tract neoplasms w CC	0	1.0554	26.2	21.8
688	Kidney & urinary tract neoplasms w/o CC/MCC	0	0.6045	18.4	15.3
689	Kidney & urinary tract infections w MCC	397	0.7217	20.8	17.3
690	Kidney & urinary tract infections w/o MCC	139	0.5259	16.6	13.8
693	Urinary stones w MCC	13	0.7922	21.8	18.2
694	Urinary stones w/o MCC	5	0.4808	15.8	13.2
695	Kidney & urinary tract signs & symptoms w MCC	3	1.0554	26.2	21.8
696	Kidney & urinary tract signs & symptoms w/o MCC	0	1.0554	26.2	21.8
697	Urethral stricture	0	0.9618	23.0	19.2
698	Other kidney & urinary tract diagnoses w MCC	232	0.9618	23.0	19.2
699	Other kidney & urinary tract diagnoses w CC	40	0.6045	18.4	15.3
700	Other kidney & urinary tract diagnoses w/o CC/MCC	1	0.4808	15.8	13.2
707	Major male pelvic procedures w CC/MCC	0	1.0554	26.2	21.8
708	Major male pelvic procedures w/o CC/MCC	0	1.0554	26.2	21.8
709	Penis procedures w CC/MCC	5	1.5478	33.6	28.0
710	Penis procedures w/o CC/MCC	0	0.6045	18.4	15.3
711	Testes procedures w CC/MCC	2	1.5478	33.6	28.0
712	Testes procedures w/o CC/MCC	0	0.7327	20.9	17.4
713	Transurethral prostatectomy w CC/MCC	2	1.5478	33.6	28.0
714	Transurethral prostatectomy w/o CC/MCC	0	1.5478	33.6	28.0
715	Other male reproductive system O.R. proc for malignancy w CC/MCC	0	0.7327	20.9	17.4
716	Other male reproductive system O.R. proc for malignancy w/o CC/MCC	0	0.7327	20.9	17.4
717	Other male reproductive system O.R. proc exc malignancy w CC/MCC	19	1.0554	26.2	21.8
718	Other male reproductive system O.R. proc exc malignancy w/o CC/MCC	0	0.7327	20.9	17.4
722	Malignancy, male reproductive system w MCC	2	0.4808	15.8	13.2
723	Malignancy, male reproductive system w CC	1	0.4808	15.8	13.2
724	Malignancy, male reproductive system w/o CC/MCC	0	0.4808	15.8	13.2
725	Benign prostatic hypertrophy w MCC	0	0.4808	15.8	13.2
726	Benign prostatic hypertrophy w/o MCC	1	0.4808	15.8	13.2
727	Inflammation of the male reproductive system w MCC	71	0.8670	23.9	19.9
728	Inflammation of the male reproductive system w/o MCC	31	0.6401	20.3	16.9
729	Other male reproductive system diagnoses w CC/MCC	7	0.7922	21.8	18.2
730	Other male reproductive system diagnoses w/o CC/MCC	0	0.7922	21.8	18.2
734	Pelvic evisceration, rad hysterectomy & rad vulvectomy w CC/MCC	0	0.7922	21.8	18.2
735	Pelvic evisceration, rad hysterectomy & rad vulvectomy w/o CC/MCC	0	0.7922	21.8	18.2

*   In determining the MS-LTC-DRG relative weights for FY 2020, these MS-LTC-DRGs were adjusted for nonmonotonicity as discussed in section VIII.B.3.g. (step 6) of the preamble of the FY 2020 IPPS/LTCH PPS final rule.

1   The count of LTCH 'standard payment rate' cases in the database of LTCH claims from the March 2019 update of the FY 2018 MedPAR files used in the MS-LTC-DRG calculations.

2   The SSO threshold is calculated as 5/6th of the geometric average length of stay of the MS-LTC-DRG (as specified in §412.529(a)).

MS-LTC-DRG Crosswalk

MS-LTC-DRG	MS-LTC-DRG Title	FY 2018 LTCH Cases[1]	Relative Weight	Geometric Av Length of Stay	Short-Stay Outlier (SSO) Threshold[2]
736	Uterine & adnexa proc for ovarian or adnexal malignancy w MCC	0	0.7922	21.8	18.2
737	Uterine & adnexa proc for ovarian or adnexal malignancy w CC	0	0.7922	21.8	18.2
738	Uterine & adnexa proc for ovarian or adnexal malignancy w/o CC/MCC	0	0.7922	21.8	18.2
739	Uterine, adnexa proc for non-ovarian/adnexal malig w MCC	0	1.4640	33.5	27.9
740	Uterine, adnexa proc for non-ovarian/adnexal malig w CC	0	1.0554	26.2	21.8
741	Uterine, adnexa proc for non-ovarian/adnexal malig w/o CC/MCC	0	0.4808	15.8	13.2
742	Uterine & adnexa proc for non-malignancy w CC/MCC	0	0.7922	21.8	18.2
743	Uterine & adnexa proc for non-malignancy w/o CC/MCC	0	0.7922	21.8	18.2
744	D&C, conization, laparoscopy & tubal interruption w CC/MCC	0	0.7922	21.8	18.2
745	D&C, conization, laparoscopy & tubal interruption w/o CC/MCC	0	0.7922	21.8	18.2
746	Vagina, cervix & vulva procedures w CC/MCC	0	0.7922	21.8	18.2
747	Vagina, cervix & vulva procedures w/o CC/MCC	0	0.7922	21.8	18.2
748	Female reproductive system reconstructive procedures	0	0.7922	21.8	18.2
749	Other female reproductive system O.R. procedures w CC/MCC	4	0.7922	21.8	18.2
750	Other female reproductive system O.R. procedures w/o CC/MCC	0	0.7922	21.8	18.2
754*	Malignancy, female reproductive system w MCC	4	0.7922	21.8	18.2
755*	Malignancy, female reproductive system w CC	1	0.7922	21.8	18.2
756	Malignancy, female reproductive system w/o CC/MCC	0	0.7922	21.8	18.2
757	Infections, female reproductive system w MCC	37	0.8908	24.7	20.6
758	Infections, female reproductive system w CC	16	0.6064	18.6	15.5
759	Infections, female reproductive system w/o CC/MCC	2	0.6064	18.6	15.5
760	Menstrual & other female reproductive system disorders w CC/MCC	2	1.5478	33.6	28.0
761	Menstrual & other female reproductive system disorders w/o CC/MCC	0	0.7327	20.9	17.4
768	Vaginal delivery w O.R. proc except steril &/or D&C	0	0.6064	18.6	15.5
769	Postpartum & post abortion diagnoses w O.R. procedure	0	0.6064	18.6	15.5
770	Abortion w D&C, aspiration curettage or hysterotomy	0	0.6064	18.6	15.5
776	Postpartum & post abortion diagnoses w/o O.R. procedure	2	1.5478	33.6	28.0
779	Abortion w/o D&C	0	0.6064	18.6	15.5
783	Cesarean section w sterilization w MCC	0	1.0554	26.2	21.8
784	Cesarean section w sterilization w CC	0	1.0554	26.2	21.8
785	Cesarean section w sterilization w/o CC/MCC	0	1.0554	26.2	21.8
786	Cesarean section w/o sterilization w MCC	0	1.0554	26.2	21.8
787	Cesarean section w/o sterilization w CC	0	1.0554	26.2	21.8
788	Cesarean section w/o sterilization w/o CC/MCC	0	1.0554	26.2	21.8
789	Neonates, died or transferred to another acute care facility	0	0.6064	18.6	15.5
790	Extreme immaturity or respiratory distress syndrome, neonate	0	0.6064	18.6	15.5
791	Prematurity w major problems	0	0.6064	18.6	15.5
792	Prematurity w/o major problems	0	0.6064	18.6	15.5
793	Full term neonate w major problems	0	0.6064	18.6	15.5
794	Neonate w other significant problems	0	0.6064	18.6	15.5
795	Normal newborn	0	0.6064	18.6	15.5
796	Vaginal delivery w sterilization/D&C w MCC	0	0.6064	18.6	15.5
797	Vaginal delivery w sterilization/D&C w CC	0	0.6064	18.6	15.5
798	Vaginal delivery w sterilization/D&C w/o CC/MCC	0	0.6064	18.6	15.5
799	Splenectomy w MCC	0	1.4825	34.0	28.3
800	Splenectomy w CC	0	1.0554	26.2	21.8
801	Splenectomy w/o CC/MCC	0	1.0554	26.2	21.8
802	Other O.R. proc of the blood & blood forming organs w MCC	1	0.6064	18.6	15.5
803	Other O.R. proc of the blood & blood forming organs w CC	0	0.6064	18.6	15.5
804	Other O.R. proc of the blood & blood forming organs w/o CC/MCC	0	0.6064	18.6	15.5
805	Vaginal delivery w/o sterilization/D&C w MCC	0	0.7922	21.8	18.2
806	Vaginal delivery w/o sterilization/D&C w CC	0	0.7922	21.8	18.2
807	Vaginal delivery w/o sterilization/D&C w/o CC/MCC	0	0.7922	21.8	18.2

* In determining the MS-LTC-DRG relative weights for FY 2020, these MS-LTC-DRGs were adjusted for nonmonotonicity as discussed in section VIII.B.3.g. (step 6) of the preamble of the FY 2020 IPPS/LTCH PPS final rule.

1 The count of LTCH 'standard payment rate' cases in the database of LTCH claims from the March 2019 update of the FY 2018 MedPAR files used in the MS-LTC-DRG calculations.

2 The SSO threshold is calculated as 5/6th of the geometric average length of stay of the MS-LTC-DRG (as specified in §412.529(a)).

MS-LTC-DRG	MS-LTC-DRG Title	FY 2018 LTCH Cases[1]	Relative Weight	Geometric Av Length of Stay	Short-Stay Outlier (SSO) Threshold[2]
808*	Major hematol/immun diag exc sickle cell crisis & coagul w MCC	17	0.7922	21.8	18.2
809*	Major hematol/immun diag exc sickle cell crisis & coagul w CC	1	0.7922	21.8	18.2
810	Major hematol/immun diag exc sickle cell crisis & coagul w/o CC/MCC	0	0.7922	21.8	18.2
811	Red blood cell disorders w MCC	21	1.5478	33.6	28.0
812	Red blood cell disorders w/o MCC	11	0.6064	18.6	15.5
813	Coagulation disorders	23	1.0554	26.2	21.8
814	Reticuloendothelial & immunity disorders w MCC	12	0.7922	21.8	18.2
815	Reticuloendothelial & immunity disorders w CC	4	0.6064	18.6	15.5
816	Reticuloendothelial & immunity disorders w/o CC/MCC	0	0.6064	18.6	15.5
817	Other antepartum diagnoses w O.R. procedure w MCC	0	0.6064	18.6	15.5
818	Other antepartum diagnoses w O.R. procedure w CC	0	0.6064	18.6	15.5
819	Other antepartum diagnoses w O.R. procedure w/o CC/MCC	0	0.6064	18.6	15.5
820	Lymphoma & leukemia w major O.R. procedure w MCC	0	0.6064	18.6	15.5
821	Lymphoma & leukemia w major O.R. procedure w CC	0	0.6064	18.6	15.5
822	Lymphoma & leukemia w major O.R. procedure w/o CC/MCC	0	0.6064	18.6	15.5
823	Lymphoma & non-acute leukemia w other proc w MCC	1	0.7922	21.8	18.2
824	Lymphoma & non-acute leukemia w other proc w CC	0	0.7922	21.8	18.2
825	Lymphoma & non-acute leukemia w other proc w/o CC/MCC	0	0.7922	21.8	18.2
826	Myeloprolif disord or poorly diff neopl w maj O.R. proc w MCC	0	0.6064	18.6	15.5
827	Myeloprolif disord or poorly diff neopl w maj O.R. proc w CC	0	0.6064	18.6	15.5
828	Myeloprolif disord or poorly diff neopl w maj O.R. proc w/o CC/MCC	0	0.6064	18.6	15.5
829	Myeloproliferative disorders or poorly differentiated neoplasms w other procedure w CC/MCC	0	0.6064	18.6	15.5
830	Myeloproliferative disorders or poorly differentiated neoplasms w other procedure w/o CC/MCC	0	0.6064	18.6	15.5
831	Other antepartum diagnoses w/o O.R. procedure w MCC	0	0.6064	18.6	15.5
832	Other antepartum diagnoses w/o O.R. procedure w CC	0	0.6064	18.6	15.5
833	Other antepartum diagnoses w/o O.R. procedure w/o CC/MCC	0	0.6064	18.6	15.5
834	Acute leukemia w/o major O.R. procedure w MCC	2	0.6064	18.6	15.5
835	Acute leukemia w/o major O.R. procedure w CC	4	0.6064	18.6	15.5
836	Acute leukemia w/o major O.R. procedure w/o CC/MCC	0	0.6064	18.6	15.5
837	Chemo w acute leukemia as sdx or w high dose chemo agent w MCC	0	0.4808	15.8	13.2
838	Chemo w acute leukemia as sdx w CC or high dose chemo agent	0	0.4808	15.8	13.2
839	Chemo w acute leukemia as sdx w/o CC/MCC	0	0.4808	15.8	13.2
840	Lymphoma & non-acute leukemia w MCC	26	0.8798	21.4	17.8
841	Lymphoma & non-acute leukemia w CC	1	0.4808	15.8	13.2
842	Lymphoma & non-acute leukemia w/o CC/MCC	0	0.4808	15.8	13.2
843	Other myeloprolif dis or poorly diff neopl diag w MCC	2	1.0554	26.2	21.8
844	Other myeloprolif dis or poorly diff neopl diag w CC	1	0.4808	15.8	13.2
845	Other myeloprolif dis or poorly diff neopl diag w/o CC/MCC	0	0.4808	15.8	13.2
846	Chemotherapy w/o acute leukemia as secondary diagnosis w MCC	2	1.0554	26.2	21.8
847	Chemotherapy w/o acute leukemia as secondary diagnosis w CC	1	0.4808	15.8	13.2
848	Chemotherapy w/o acute leukemia as secondary diagnosis w/o CC/MCC	0	0.4808	15.8	13.2
849	Radiotherapy	4	1.5478	33.6	28.0
853	Infectious & parasitic diseases w O.R. procedure w MCC	844	1.8541	37.7	31.4
854	Infectious & parasitic diseases w O.R. procedure w CC	38	0.8897	24.4	20.3
855	Infectious & parasitic diseases w O.R. procedure w/o CC/MCC	0	0.8897	24.4	20.3
856	Postoperative or post-traumatic infections w O.R. proc w MCC	189	1.6181	35.1	29.3
857	Postoperative or post-traumatic infections w O.R. proc w CC	37	1.0915	31.4	26.2
858	Postoperative or post-traumatic infections w O.R. proc w/o CC/MCC	0	1.0915	31.4	26.2
862	Postoperative & post-traumatic infections w MCC	822	1.0778	25.7	21.4
863	Postoperative & post-traumatic infections w/o MCC	146	0.7705	22.2	18.5
864	Fever and inflammatory conditions	1	1.5478	33.6	28.0
865	Viral illness w MCC	24	0.7922	21.8	18.2
866	Viral illness w/o MCC	4	0.7922	21.8	18.2

* In determining the MS-LTC-DRG relative weights for FY 2020, these MS-LTC-DRGs were adjusted for nonmonotonicity as discussed in section VIII.B.3.g. (step 6) of the preamble of the FY 2020 IPPS/LTCH PPS final rule.

1 The count of LTCH 'standard payment rate' cases in the database of LTCH claims from the March 2019 update of the FY 2018 MedPAR files used in the MS-LTC-DRG calculations.

2 The SSO threshold is calculated as 5/6th of the geometric average length of stay of the MS-LTC-DRG (as specified in §412.529(a)).

MS-LTC-DRG	MS-LTC-DRG Title	FY 2018 LTCH Cases[1]	Relative Weight	Geometric Av Length of Stay	Short-Stay Outlier (SSO) Threshold[2]
867	Other infectious & parasitic diseases diagnoses w MCC	107	0.9878	22.7	18.9
868*	Other infectious & parasitic diseases diagnoses w CC	17	0.9878	22.7	18.9
869*	Other infectious & parasitic diseases diagnoses w/o CC/MCC	1	0.9878	22.7	18.9
870	Septicemia or severe sepsis w MV >96 hours	1,176	1.9648	29.9	24.9
871	Septicemia or severe sepsis w/o MV >96 hours w MCC	4,132	0.9217	22.7	18.9
872	Septicemia or severe sepsis w/o MV >96 hours w/o MCC	359	0.6144	19.0	15.8
876	O.R. procedure w principal diagnoses of mental illness	0	0.7881	22.9	19.1
880	Acute adjustment reaction & psychosocial dysfunction	0	0.4959	17.7	14.8
881	Depressive neuroses	0	0.6214	20.3	16.9
882	Neuroses except depressive	0	0.6214	20.3	16.9
883	Disorders of personality & impulse control	0	0.6214	20.3	16.9
884	Organic disturbances & intellectual disability	0	0.5152	24.5	20.4
885	Psychoses	0	0.4901	23.1	19.3
886	Behavioral & developmental disorders	0	0.4959	17.7	14.8
887	Other mental disorder diagnoses	0	0.4959	17.7	14.8
894	Alcohol/drug abuse or dependence, left AMA	0	0.4959	17.7	14.8
895	Alcohol/drug abuse or dependence w rehabilitation therapy	0	0.4670	25.4	21.2
896	Alcohol/drug abuse or dependence w/o rehabilitation therapy w MCC	0	0.7881	22.9	19.1
897	Alcohol/drug abuse or dependence w/o rehabilitation therapy w/o MCC	0	0.6214	20.3	16.9
901	Wound debridements for injuries w MCC	145	1.4295	34.0	28.3
902	Wound debridements for injuries w CC	25	1.1393	31.3	26.1
903	Wound debridements for injuries w/o CC/MCC	0	1.1393	31.3	26.1
904	Skin grafts for injuries w CC/MCC	21	1.0554	26.2	21.8
905	Skin grafts for injuries w/o CC/MCC	0	1.0554	26.2	21.8
906	Hand procedures for injuries	0	1.7350	38.4	32.0
907	Other O.R. procedures for injuries w MCC	74	1.7350	38.4	32.0
908	Other O.R. procedures for injuries w CC	14	0.7922	21.8	18.2
909	Other O.R. procedures for injuries w/o CC/MCC	0	0.7922	21.8	18.2
913	Traumatic injury w MCC	0	0.4808	15.8	13.2
914	Traumatic injury w/o MCC	1	0.4808	15.8	13.2
915	Allergic reactions w MCC	1	0.4808	15.8	13.2
916	Allergic reactions w/o MCC	1	0.4808	15.8	13.2
917	Poisoning & toxic effects of drugs w MCC	16	1.0554	26.2	21.8
918	Poisoning & toxic effects of drugs w/o MCC	1	0.4808	15.8	13.2
919	Complications of treatment w MCC	805	1.1584	27.5	22.9
920	Complications of treatment w CC	182	0.8294	22.7	18.9
921	Complications of treatment w/o CC/MCC	6	0.7922	21.8	18.2
922	Other injury, poisoning & toxic effect diag w MCC	9	1.0554	26.2	21.8
923	Other injury, poisoning & toxic effect diag w/o MCC	5	0.6064	18.6	15.5
927	Extensive burns or full thickness burns w MV >96 hrs w skin graft	0	0.7922	21.8	18.2
928	Full thickness burn w skin graft or inhal inj w CC/MCC	3	0.7922	21.8	18.2
929	Full thickness burn w skin graft or inhal inj w/o CC/MCC	0	0.7922	21.8	18.2
933	Extensive burns or full thickness burns w MV >96 hrs w/o skin graft	3	1.0554	26.2	21.8
934	Full thickness burn w/o skin graft or inhal inj	8	0.6064	18.6	15.5
935	Non-extensive burns	7	0.7922	21.8	18.2
939	O.R. proc w diagnoses of other contact w health services w MCC	94	1.2375	30.5	25.4
940	O.R. proc w diagnoses of other contact w health services w CC	36	1.1605	30.0	25.0
941	O.R. proc w diagnoses of other contact w health services w/o CC/MCC	2	0.6064	18.6	15.5
945	Rehabilitation w CC/MCC	0	0.6621	20.5	17.1
946	Rehabilitation w/o CC/MCC	0	0.4063	16.3	13.6
947	Signs & symptoms w MCC	33	0.7714	20.5	17.1
948	Signs & symptoms w/o MCC	12	0.6064	18.6	15.5
949	Aftercare w CC/MCC	1,499	0.7192	21.0	17.5

*   In determining the MS-LTC-DRG relative weights for FY 2020, these MS-LTC-DRGs were adjusted for nonmonotonicity as discussed in section VIII.B.3.g. (step 6) of the preamble of the FY 2020 IPPS/LTCH PPS final rule.

1   The count of LTCH 'standard payment rate' cases in the database of LTCH claims from the March 2019 update of the FY 2018 MedPAR files used in the MS-LTC-DRG calculations.

2   The SSO threshold is calculated as 5/6th of the geometric average length of stay of the MS-LTC-DRG (as specified in §412.529(a)).

MS-LTC-DRG Crosswalk

MS-LTC-DRG	MS-LTC-DRG Title	FY 2018 LTCH Cases[1]	Relative Weight	Geometric Av Length of Stay	Short-Stay Outlier (SSO) Threshold[2]
950	Aftercare w/o CC/MCC	32	0.3750	14.2	11.8
951	Other factors influencing health status	1	1.5478	33.6	28.0
955	Craniotomy for multiple significant trauma	0	0.7922	21.8	18.2
956	Limb reattachment, hip & femur proc for multiple significant trauma	0	0.4808	15.8	13.2
957	Other O.R. procedures for multiple significant trauma w MCC	3	1.5478	33.6	28.0
958	Other O.R. procedures for multiple significant trauma w CC	0	1.0554	26.2	21.8
959	Other O.R. procedures for multiple significant trauma w/o CC/MCC	0	0.7922	21.8	18.2
963	Other multiple significant trauma w MCC	6	1.0554	26.2	21.8
964	Other multiple significant trauma w CC	3	0.7922	21.8	18.2
965	Other multiple significant trauma w/o CC/MCC	0	0.6064	18.6	15.5
969	HIV w extensive O.R. procedure w MCC	11	1.5478	33.6	28.0
970	HIV w extensive O.R. procedure w/o MCC	0	1.5478	33.6	28.0
974	HIV w major related condition w MCC	103	0.9929	22.5	18.8
975*	HIV w major related condition w CC	16	0.9929	22.5	18.8
976*	HIV w major related condition w/o CC/MCC	1	0.6064	18.6	15.5
977	HIV w or w/o other related condition	12	1.5478	33.6	28.0
981	Extensive O.R. procedure unrelated to principal diagnosis w MCC	1,279	2.2324	40.4	33.7
982	Extensive O.R. procedure unrelated to principal diagnosis w CC	90	1.3500	30.1	25.1
983	Extensive O.R. procedure unrelated to principal diagnosis w/o CC/MCC	3	0.7900	21.8	18.2
987	Non-extensive O.R. proc unrelated to principal diagnosis w MCC	173	2.1200	36.9	30.8
988	Non-extensive O.R. proc unrelated to principal diagnosis w CC	25	1.4800	27.7	23.1
989	Non-extensive O.R. proc unrelated to principal diagnosis w/o CC/MCC	0	0.4800	15.8	13.2
998	Principal diagnosis invalid as discharge diagnosis	0	0.0000	0.0	0.0
999	Ungroupable	0	0.0000	0.0	0.0

*   In determining the MS-LTC-DRG relative weights for FY 2020, these MS-LTC-DRGs were adjusted for nonmonotonicity as discussed in section VIII.B.3.g. (step 6) of the preamble of the FY 2020 IPPS/LTCH PPS final rule.

1   The count of LTCH 'standard payment rate' cases in the database of LTCH claims from the March 2019 update of the FY 2018 MedPAR files used in the MS-LTC-DRG calculations.

2   The SSO threshold is calculated as 5/6th of the geometric average length of stay of the MS-LTC-DRG (as specified in §412.529(a)).

MS-LTC-DRG Crosswalk

Glossary

against medical advice. Discharge status of patients who leave the hospital after signing a form that releases the hospital from responsibility, or those who leave the hospital premises without notifying hospital personnel.

arithmetic mean length of stay. Average number of days within a given DRG-stay in the hospital, also referred to as the average length of stay. The AMLOS is used to determine payment for outlier cases.

base rate. Payment weight assigned to hospitals to calculate diagnosis-related group (DRG) reimbursement. The base payment rate is divided into labor-related and nonlabor shares. The labor-related share is adjusted by the wage index applicable to the area where the hospital is located, and if the hospital is located in Alaska or Hawaii, the nonlabor share is adjusted by a cost of living adjustment factor. This base payment rate is multiplied by the DRG relative weight to calculate DRG reimbursement.

case mix index. Sum of all DRG relative weights for cases over a given period of time, divided by the number of Medicare cases.

charges. Dollar amount assigned to a service or procedure by a provider and reported to a payer.

code cluster. Group of two or more ICD-10-CM or ICD-10-PCS codes that must be used together to replicate the meaning of one ICD-9-CM code.

complication/comorbidity (CC). Condition that, when present, leads to substantially increased hospital resource use, such as intensive monitoring, expensive and technically complex services, and extensive care requiring a greater number of caregivers. Significant acute disease, acute exacerbations of significant chronic diseases, advanced or end stage chronic diseases, and chronic diseases associated with extensive debility are representative of CC conditions.

discharge. Situation in which the patient leaves an acute care (prospective payment) hospital after receiving complete acute care treatment.

discharge status. Disposition of the patient at discharge (e.g., left against medical advice, discharged home, transferred to an acute care hospital, expired).

GEM. General equivalence mapping. Translation tool that maps codes from one system (e.g., ICD-9-CM) to another (e.g., ICD-10-CM). The mappings are generally described as forward (mapping from ICD-9-CM to ICD-10-CM or ICD-10-PCS) or backwards (mapping ICD-10-CM or ICD-10-PCS to ICD-9-CM). Size, structure, and scope of the two systems may be completely different, which may require some decision making on the part of the user.

geometric mean length of stay. Statistically adjusted value for all cases for a given diagnosis-related group, allowing for the outliers, transfer cases, and negative outlier cases that would normally skew the data. The GMLOS is used to determine payment only for transfer cases (i.e., the per diem rate).

grouper. Software program that assigns diagnosis-related groups (DRGs).

homogeneous. Group of patients consuming similar types and amounts of hospital resources.

hospital-acquired condition (HAC). A significant, reasonably preventable condition determined to have occurred during a hospital visit, identified via the assignment of certain present on admission (POA) indicators. The MCC or CC status for the code for the HAC condition is invalidated when the POA indicator is N or U, thus potentially affecting DRG reimbursement.

major complication/comorbidity (MCC). Diagnosis codes that reflect the highest level of severity and have the potential to increase DRG reimbursement. See also complication/comorbidity.

major diagnostic category (MDC). Broad classification of diagnoses typically grouped by body system.

Medicare severity-adjusted diagnosis-related group (MS-DRG). One of the 761 classifications of diagnoses in which patients demonstrate similar resource consumption and length-of-stay patterns. MS-DRGs are a modification of the prior system that more accurately reflect the severity of a patient's illness and resources used.

nonoperating room procedure. Procedure that does not normally require the use of the operating room and that can affect MS-DRG assignment.

operating room (OR) procedure. Defined group of procedures that normally require the use of an operating room.

other diagnosis. All conditions (secondary) that exist at the time of admission or that develop subsequently that affect the treatment received and/or the length of stay. Diagnoses that relate to an earlier episode and that have no bearing on the current hospital stay are not to be reported.

outliers. There are two types of outliers: cost and day outliers. A cost outlier is a case in which the costs for treating the patient are extraordinarily high compared with other cases classified to the same MS-DRG. A cost outlier is paid an amount in excess of the cut-off threshold for a given MS-DRG. Payment for day outliers was eliminated with discharges occurring on or after October 1, 1997.

per diem rate. Payment made to the hospital from which a patient is transferred for each day of stay. It is determined by dividing the full MS-DRG payment by the GMLOS for the MS-DRG. The payment rate for the first day of stay is twice the per diem rate, and subsequent days are paid at the per diem rate up to the full DRG amount.

PMDC (Pre-major diagnostic category). Fifteen MS-DRGs to which cases are directly assigned based upon procedure codes before classification to an MDC, including MS-DRGs for the heart, liver, bone marrow transplants, simultaneous pancreas/kidney transplant, pancreas transplant, lung transplant, and five MS-DRGs for tracheostomies.

present on admission (POA). CMS-mandated assignment of indicators Y (Yes), N (No), U (Unknown), W (Clinically undetermined), or 1 (Exempt) to identify each condition as present or not present at the time the order for inpatient admission occurs for Medicare patients. A POA indicator should be listed for the principal diagnosis as well as secondary diagnoses and external cause of injury codes.

principal diagnosis. Condition established after study to be chiefly responsible for occasioning the admission of the patient to the hospital for care.

principal procedure. Procedure performed for definitive treatment rather than for diagnostic or exploratory purposes, or that was necessary to treat a complication. Usually related to the principal diagnosis.

relative weight. Assigned weight that is intended to reflect the relative resource consumption associated with each MS-DRG. The higher the relative weight, the greater the payment to the hospital. The relative weights are calculated by CMS and published in the final prospective payment system rule.

surgical hierarchy. Ordering of surgical cases from most to least resource intensive. Application of this decision rule is necessary when patient stays involve multiple surgical procedures, each of which, occurring by itself, could result in assignment to a different MS-DRG. All patients must be assigned to only one MS-DRG per admission.

transfer. A situation in which the patient is transferred to another acute care hospital for related care.

MDC 01 Diseases And Disorders Of The Nervous System

A02.21	B01.11	D43.4	G04.1	G26	G43.011	G45.0	G56.31	G65.0	G83.5
A06.6	B01.12	D43.8	G04.2	G30.0	G43.019	G45.1	G56.32	G65.1	G83.81
A17.0	B02.0	D43.9	G04.30	G30.1	G43.101	G45.2	G56.33	G65.2	G83.82
A17.1	B02.1	D44.5	G04.31	G30.8	G43.109	G45.4	G56.40	G70.00	G83.83
A17.81	B02.21	D44.6	G04.32	G30.9	G43.111	G45.8	G56.41	G70.01	G83.84
A17.82	B02.22	D44.7	G04.39	G31.01	G43.119	G45.9	G56.42	G70.1	G83.89
A17.83	B02.23	D49.6	G04.81	G31.09	G43.401	G46.0	G56.43	G70.2	G83.9
A17.89	B02.24	E03.5	G04.89	G31.1	G43.409	G46.1	G56.80	G70.80	G89.0
A27.81	B02.29	E08.40	G04.90	G31.2	G43.411	G46.2	G56.81	G70.81	G89.21
A27.89	B05.0	E08.41	G04.91	G31.81	G43.419	G46.3	G56.82	G70.89	G89.22
A39.0	B06.00	E08.42	G05.3	G31.82	G43.501	G46.4	G56.83	G70.9	G89.28
A39.81	B06.01	E08.43	G05.4	G31.83	G43.509	G46.5	G56.90	G71.00	G89.29
A50.40	B06.02	E08.44	G06.0	G31.84	G43.511	G46.6	G56.91	G71.01	G89.4
A50.41	B06.09	E08.49	G06.1	G31.85	G43.519	G46.7	G56.92	G71.02	G90.01
A50.42	B10.01	E08.610	G06.2	G31.89	G43.601	G46.8	G56.93	G71.09	G90.09
A50.43	B10.09	E09.40	G07	G31.9	G43.609	G47.20	G57.00	G71.11	G90.1
A50.45	B26.1	E09.41	G08	G32.0	G43.611	G47.21	G57.01	G71.12	G90.2
A50.49	B26.2	E09.42	G09	G32.81	G43.619	G47.22	G57.02	G71.13	G90.3
A51.41	B26.84	E09.43	G10	G32.89	G43.701	G47.23	G57.03	G71.14	G90.4
A52.10	B37.5	E09.44	G11.0	G35	G43.709	G47.24	G57.10	G71.19	G90.50
A52.11	B38.4	E09.49	G11.1	G36.0	G43.711	G47.25	G57.11	G71.2	G90.511
A52.12	B45.1	E09.610	G11.2	G36.1	G43.719	G47.26	G57.12	G71.3	G90.512
A52.13	B58.2	E10.40	G11.3	G36.8	G43.801	G47.27	G57.13	G71.8	G90.513
A52.14	B90.0	E10.41	G11.4	G36.9	G43.809	G47.29	G57.20	G71.9	G90.519
A52.15	B91	E10.42	G11.8	G37.0	G43.811	G47.31	G57.21	G72.0	G90.521
A52.16	B94.1	E10.43	G11.9	G37.1	G43.819	G47.35	G57.22	G72.1	G90.522
A52.17	C70.0	E10.44	G12.0	G37.2	G43.821	G47.37	G57.23	G72.2	G90.523
A52.19	C70.1	E10.49	G12.1	G37.3	G43.829	G47.411	G57.30	G72.3	G90.529
A52.2	C70.9	E10.610	G12.20	G37.4	G43.831	G47.419	G57.31	G72.81	G90.59
A52.3	C71.0	E11.40	G12.21	G37.5	G43.839	G47.421	G57.32	G72.89	G90.8
A54.81	C71.1	E11.41	G12.22	G37.8	G43.901	G47.429	G57.33	G72.9	G90.9
A80.0	C71.2	E11.42	G12.23	G37.9	G43.909	G47.51	G57.40	G73.1	G91.0
A80.1	C71.3	E11.43	G12.24	G40.001	G43.911	G47.53	G57.41	G73.3	G91.1
A80.2	C71.4	E11.44	G12.25	G40.009	G43.919	G47.61	G57.42	G73.7	G91.2
A80.30	C71.5	E11.49	G12.29	G40.011	G43.A0	G47.62	G57.43	G80.0	G91.3
A80.39	C71.6	E11.610	G12.8	G40.019	G43.A1	G50.0	G57.50	G80.1	G91.4
A80.9	C71.7	E13.40	G12.9	G40.101	G43.B0	G50.1	G57.51	G80.2	G91.8
A81.00	C71.8	E13.41	G13.0	G40.109	G43.B1	G50.8	G57.52	G80.3	G91.9
A81.01	C71.9	E13.42	G13.1	G40.111	G43.C0	G50.9	G57.53	G80.4	G92
A81.09	C72.0	E13.43	G13.2	G40.119	G43.C1	G51.0	G57.60	G80.8	G93.0
A81.1	C72.1	E13.44	G13.8	G40.201	G43.D0	G51.1	G57.61	G80.9	G93.1
A81.2	C72.20	E13.49	G14	G40.209	G43.D1	G51.2	G57.62	G81.00	G93.2
A81.81	C72.21	E13.610	G20	G40.211	G44.001	G51.31	G57.63	G81.01	G93.40
A81.82	C72.22	E75.00	G21.0	G40.219	G44.009	G51.32	G57.70	G81.02	G93.41
A81.83	C72.30	E75.01	G21.11	G40.301	G44.011	G51.33	G57.71	G81.03	G93.49
A81.89	C72.31	E75.02	G21.19	G40.309	G44.019	G51.39	G57.72	G81.04	G93.5
A81.9	C72.32	E75.09	G21.2	G40.311	G44.021	G51.4	G57.73	G81.10	G93.6
A82.0	C72.40	E75.10	G21.3	G40.319	G44.029	G51.8	G57.80	G81.11	G93.7
A82.1	C72.41	E75.11	G21.4	G40.401	G44.031	G51.9	G57.81	G81.12	G93.81
A82.9	C72.42	E75.19	G21.8	G40.409	G44.039	G52.0	G57.82	G81.13	G93.82
A83.0	C72.50	E75.23	G21.9	G40.411	G44.041	G52.1	G57.83	G81.14	G93.89
A83.1	C72.59	E75.25	G23.0	G40.419	G44.049	G52.2	G57.90	G81.90	G93.9
A83.2	C72.9	E75.26	G23.1	G40.501	G44.051	G52.3	G57.91	G81.91	G94
A83.3	C75.3	E75.29	G23.2	G40.509	G44.059	G52.7	G57.92	G81.92	G95.0
A83.4	C75.4	E75.4	G23.8	G40.801	G44.091	G52.8	G57.93	G81.93	G95.11
A83.5	C75.5	F07.81	G23.9	G40.802	G44.099	G52.9	G58.0	G81.94	G95.19
A83.6	C79.31	F07.89	G24.01	G40.803	G44.1	G53	G58.7	G82.20	G95.20
A83.8	C79.32	F48.2	G24.02	G40.804	G44.201	G54.0	G58.8	G82.21	G95.29
A83.9	C79.40	F80.81	G24.09	G40.811	G44.209	G54.1	G58.9	G82.22	G95.81
A84.0	C79.49	F84.2	G24.1	G40.812	G44.211	G54.2	G59	G82.50	G95.89
A84.1	D18.02	F95.0	G24.2	G40.813	G44.219	G54.3	G60.0	G82.51	G95.9
A84.8	D32.0	F95.1	G24.3	G40.814	G44.221	G54.4	G60.1	G82.52	G96.0
A84.9	D32.1	F95.2	G24.4	G40.821	G44.229	G54.5	G60.2	G82.53	G96.12
A85.0	D32.9	F95.8	G24.8	G40.822	G44.301	G54.6	G60.3	G82.54	G96.19
A85.1	D33.0	F95.9	G24.9	G40.823	G44.309	G54.7	G60.8	G83.0	G96.8
A85.2	D33.1	G00.0	G25.0	G40.824	G44.311	G54.8	G60.9	G83.10	G96.9
A85.8	D33.2	G00.1	G25.1	G40.89	G44.319	G54.9	G61.0	G83.11	G97.0
A86	D33.3	G00.2	G25.2	G40.901	G44.321	G55	G61.1	G83.12	G97.1
A87.0	D33.4	G00.3	G25.3	G40.909	G44.329	G56.00	G61.81	G83.13	G97.2
A87.1	D33.7	G00.8	G25.4	G40.911	G44.40	G56.01	G61.82	G83.14	G97.31
A87.2	D33.9	G00.9	G25.5	G40.919	G44.41	G56.02	G61.89	G83.20	G97.32
A87.8	D35.4	G01	G25.61	G40.A01	G44.51	G56.03	G61.9	G83.21	G97.81
A87.9	D35.5	G02	G25.69	G40.A09	G44.52	G56.10	G62.0	G83.22	G97.82
A88.0	D35.6	G03.0	G25.70	G40.A11	G44.53	G56.11	G62.1	G83.23	G98.0
A88.1	D42.0	G03.1	G25.71	G40.A19	G44.59	G56.12	G62.2	G83.24	G98.8
A88.8	D42.1	G03.2	G25.79	G40.B01	G44.81	G56.13	G62.81	G83.30	G99.0
A89	D42.9	G03.8	G25.81	G40.B09	G44.82	G56.20	G62.82	G83.31	G99.2
A92.2	D43.0	G03.9	G25.82	G40.B11	G44.83	G56.21	G62.89	G83.32	G99.8
B00.3	D43.1	G04.00	G25.83	G40.B19	G44.84	G56.22	G62.9	G83.33	H47.10
B00.4	D43.2	G04.01	G25.89	G43.001	G44.85	G56.23	G63	G83.34	H47.11
B00.82	D43.3	G04.02	G25.9	G43.009	G44.89	G56.30	G64	G83.4	H47.141

Diagnosis Codes by MDC

H47.142	I63.133	I66.09	I69.132	I69.343	I69.954	Q76.0	R47.81	S02.129A	S04.10XS
H47.143	I63.139	I66.11	I69.133	I69.344	I69.959	Q85.00	R47.82	S02.129B	S04.11XA
H47.149	I63.19	I66.12	I69.134	I69.349	I69.961	Q85.01	R47.89	S02.19XA	S04.11XS
H47.41	I63.20	I66.13	I69.139	I69.351	I69.962	Q85.02	R47.9	S02.19XB	S04.12XA
H47.42	I63.211	I66.19	I69.141	I69.352	I69.963	Q85.03	R51	S02.19XS	S04.12XS
H47.43	I63.212	I66.21	I69.142	I69.353	I69.964	Q85.09	R56.00	S02.2XXS	S04.20XA
H47.49	I63.213	I66.22	I69.143	I69.354	I69.965	Q85.1	R56.01	S02.30XS	S04.20XS
H47.511	I63.219	I66.23	I69.144	I69.359	I69.969	R20.0	R56.1	S02.31XS	S04.21XA
H47.512	I63.22	I66.29	I69.149	I69.361	I69.990	R20.1	R56.9	S02.32XS	S04.21XS
H47.519	I63.231	I66.3	I69.151	I69.362	I69.991	R20.2	R83.0	S02.400S	S04.22XA
H47.521	I63.232	I66.8	I69.152	I69.363	I69.992	R20.3	R83.1	S02.401S	S04.22XS
H47.522	I63.233	I66.9	I69.153	I69.364	I69.993	R20.8	R83.2	S02.402S	S04.30XA
H47.529	I63.239	I67.1	I69.154	I69.365	I69.998	R20.9	R83.3	S02.40AS	S04.30XS
H47.531	I63.29	I67.2	I69.159	I69.369	I97.810	R25.0	R83.4	S02.40BS	S04.31XA
H47.532	I63.30	I67.3	I69.161	I69.390	I97.811	R25.1	R83.5	S02.40CS	S04.31XS
H47.539	I63.311	I67.4	I69.162	I69.391	I97.820	R25.2	R83.6	S02.40DS	S04.32XA
H47.611	I63.312	I67.5	I69.163	I69.392	I97.821	R25.3	R83.8	S02.40ES	S04.32XS
H47.612	I63.313	I67.6	I69.164	I69.393	M21.331	R25.8	R83.9	S02.40FS	S04.40XA
H47.619	I63.319	I67.7	I69.165	I69.398	M21.332	R25.9	R90.81	S02.411S	S04.40XS
H47.621	I63.321	I67.81	I69.169	I69.80	M21.339	R26.0	R90.82	S02.412S	S04.41XA
H47.622	I63.322	I67.82	I69.190	I69.810	M21.511	R26.1	R93.0	S02.413S	S04.41XS
H47.629	I63.323	I67.83	I69.191	I69.811	M21.512	R26.81	R94.01	S02.42XS	S04.42XA
H47.631	I63.329	I67.841	I69.192	I69.812	M21.519	R26.89	R94.02	S02.5XXS	S04.42XS
H47.632	I63.331	I67.848	I69.193	I69.813	M21.521	R26.9	R94.09	S02.600S	S04.50XA
H47.639	I63.332	I67.850	I69.198	I69.814	M21.522	R27.0	R94.118	S02.601S	S04.50XS
H47.641	I63.333	I67.858	I69.20	I69.815	M21.529	R27.8	R94.128	S02.602S	S04.51XA
H47.642	I63.339	I67.89	I69.210	I69.818	M21.531	R27.9	R94.130	S02.609S	S04.51XS
H47.649	I63.341	I67.9	I69.211	I69.819	M21.532	R29.1	R94.138	S02.610S	S04.52XA
H47.9	I63.342	I68.0	I69.212	I69.820	M21.539	R29.2	S02.0XXA	S02.611S	S04.52XS
H51.20	I63.343	I68.2	I69.213	I69.821	M34.83	R29.3	S02.0XXB	S02.612S	S04.60XS
H51.21	I63.349	I68.8	I69.214	I69.822	M53.0	R29.5	S02.0XXS	S02.620S	S04.61XS
H51.22	I63.39	I69.00	I69.215	I69.823	M53.1	R29.6	S02.101A	S02.621S	S04.62XS
H51.23	I63.40	I69.010	I69.218	I69.828	M54.10	R29.810	S02.101S	S02.622S	S04.70XA
H57.01	I63.411	I69.011	I69.219	I69.831	M54.11	R29.818	S02.102A	S02.630S	S04.70XS
I60.00	I63.412	I69.012	I69.220	I69.832	M54.12	R29.890	S02.102B	S02.631S	S04.71XA
I60.01	I63.413	I69.013	I69.221	I69.833	M54.13	R29.90	S02.102S	S02.632S	S04.71XS
I60.02	I63.419	I69.014	I69.222	I69.834	M54.18	R29.91	S02.109A	S02.640S	S04.72XA
I60.10	I63.421	I69.015	I69.223	I69.839	M79.2	R40.0	S02.109B	S02.641S	S04.72XS
I60.11	I63.422	I69.018	I69.228	I69.841	P91.2	R40.1	S02.109S	S02.642S	S04.811A
I60.12	I63.423	I69.019	I69.231	I69.842	Q00.0	R40.20	S02.110A	S02.650S	S04.811S
I60.2	I63.429	I69.020	I69.232	I69.843	Q00.1	R40.2110	S02.110B	S02.651S	S04.812A
I60.30	I63.431	I69.021	I69.233	I69.844	Q00.2	R40.2111	S02.110S	S02.652S	S04.812S
I60.31	I63.432	I69.022	I69.234	I69.849	Q01.0	R40.2112	S02.111A	S02.66XS	S04.819A
I60.32	I63.433	I69.023	I69.239	I69.851	Q01.1	R40.2113	S02.111B	S02.670S	S04.819S
I60.4	I63.439	I69.028	I69.241	I69.852	Q01.2	R40.2114	S02.111S	S02.671S	S04.891A
I60.50	I63.441	I69.031	I69.242	I69.853	Q01.8	R40.2120	S02.112A	S02.672S	S04.891S
I60.51	I63.442	I69.032	I69.243	I69.854	Q01.9	R40.2121	S02.112B	S02.69XS	S04.892A
I60.52	I63.443	I69.033	I69.244	I69.859	Q02	R40.2122	S02.112S	S02.80XS	S04.892S
I60.6	I63.449	I69.034	I69.249	I69.861	Q03.0	R40.2123	S02.113A	S02.81XS	S04.899A
I60.7	I63.49	I69.039	I69.251	I69.862	Q03.1	R40.2124	S02.113B	S02.82XS	S04.899S
I60.8	I63.50	I69.041	I69.252	I69.863	Q03.8	R40.2210	S02.113S	S02.831A	S04.9XXA
I60.9	I63.511	I69.042	I69.253	I69.864	Q03.9	R40.2211	S02.118A	S02.831B	S04.9XXS
I61.0	I63.512	I69.043	I69.254	I69.865	Q04.0	R40.2212	S02.118B	S02.832A	S06.0X0A
I61.1	I63.513	I69.044	I69.259	I69.869	Q04.1	R40.2213	S02.118S	S02.832B	S06.0X0S
I61.2	I63.519	I69.049	I69.261	I69.890	Q04.2	R40.2214	S02.119A	S02.839A	S06.0X1A
I61.3	I63.521	I69.051	I69.262	I69.891	Q04.3	R40.2220	S02.119B	S02.839B	S06.0X1S
I61.4	I63.522	I69.052	I69.263	I69.892	Q04.4	R40.2221	S02.119S	S02.841A	S06.0X9A
I61.5	I63.523	I69.053	I69.264	I69.893	Q04.5	R40.2222	S02.11AA	S02.841B	S06.0X9S
I61.6	I63.529	I69.054	I69.265	I69.898	Q04.6	R40.2223	S02.11AB	S02.842A	S06.1X0A
I61.8	I63.531	I69.059	I69.269	I69.90	Q04.8	R40.2224	S02.11AS	S02.842B	S06.1X0S
I61.9	I63.532	I69.061	I69.290	I69.910	Q04.9	R40.2310	S02.11BA	S02.849A	S06.1X1A
I62.00	I63.533	I69.062	I69.291	I69.911	Q05.0	R40.2311	S02.11BB	S02.849B	S06.1X1S
I62.01	I63.539	I69.063	I69.292	I69.912	Q05.1	R40.2312	S02.11BS	S02.85XA	S06.1X2A
I62.02	I63.541	I69.064	I69.293	I69.913	Q05.2	R40.2313	S02.11CA	S02.85XB	S06.1X2S
I62.03	I63.542	I69.065	I69.298	I69.914	Q05.3	R40.2314	S02.11CB	S02.91XA	S06.1X3A
I62.1	I63.543	I69.069	I69.30	I69.915	Q05.4	R40.2320	S02.11CS	S02.91XB	S06.1X3S
I62.9	I63.549	I69.090	I69.310	I69.918	Q05.5	R40.2321	S02.11DA	S02.91XS	S06.1X4A
I63.00	I63.59	I69.091	I69.311	I69.919	Q05.6	R40.2322	S02.11DB	S02.92XS	S06.1X4S
I63.011	I63.6	I69.092	I69.312	I69.920	Q05.7	R40.2323	S02.11DS	S04.011S	S06.1X5A
I63.012	I63.81	I69.093	I69.313	I69.921	Q05.8	R40.2324	S02.11EA	S04.012S	S06.1X5S
I63.013	I63.89	I69.098	I69.314	I69.922	Q05.9	R40.2340	S02.11EB	S04.019S	S06.1X6A
I63.019	I63.9	I69.10	I69.315	I69.923	Q06.0	R40.2341	S02.11ES	S04.02XA	S06.1X6S
I63.02	I65.01	I69.110	I69.318	I69.928	Q06.1	R40.2342	S02.11FA	S04.02XS	S06.1X7A
I63.031	I65.02	I69.111	I69.319	I69.931	Q06.2	R40.2343	S02.11FB	S04.031A	S06.1X8A
I63.032	I65.03	I69.112	I69.320	I69.932	Q06.3	R40.2344	S02.11FS	S04.031S	S06.1X8S
I63.033	I65.09	I69.113	I69.321	I69.933	Q06.4	R40.3	S02.11GA	S04.032A	S06.1X9A
I63.039	I65.1	I69.114	I69.322	I69.934	Q06.8	R41.4	S02.11GB	S04.032S	S06.1X9S
I63.09	I65.21	I69.115	I69.323	I69.939	Q06.9	R41.842	S02.11GS	S04.039A	S06.2X0A
I63.10	I65.22	I69.118	I69.328	I69.941	Q07.00	R43.0	S02.11HA	S04.039S	S06.2X0S
I63.111	I65.23	I69.119	I69.331	I69.942	Q07.01	R43.1	S02.11HB	S04.041A	S06.2X1A
I63.112	I65.29	I69.120	I69.332	I69.943	Q07.02	R43.2	S02.11HS	S04.041S	S06.2X1S
I63.113	I65.8	I69.121	I69.333	I69.944	Q07.03	R43.8	S02.121A	S04.042A	S06.2X2A
I63.119	I65.9	I69.122	I69.334	I69.949	Q07.8	R43.9	S02.121B	S04.042S	S06.2X2S
I63.12	I66.01	I69.123	I69.339	I69.951	Q07.9	R47.01	S02.122A	S04.049A	S06.2X3A
I63.131	I66.02	I69.128	I69.341	I69.952	Q28.2	R47.02	S02.122B	S04.049S	S06.2X3S
I63.132	I66.03	I69.131	I69.342	I69.953	Q28.3	R47.1		S04.10XA	S06.2X4A
									S06.2X4S

S06.2X5A	S06.342A	S06.389A	S06.825A	S14.122A	S24.101A	S34.115A	S44.92XA	S64.8X2A	S94.21XA
S06.2X5S	S06.342S	S06.389S	S06.825S	S14.122S	S24.101S	S34.115S	S44.92XS	S64.8X2S	S94.21XS
S06.2X6A	S06.343A	S06.4X0A	S06.826A	S14.123A	S24.102A	S34.119A	S54.00XA	S64.8X9A	S94.22XA
S06.2X6S	S06.343S	S06.4X0S	S06.826S	S14.123S	S24.102S	S34.119S	S54.00XS	S64.8X9S	S94.22XS
S06.2X7A	S06.344A	S06.4X1A	S06.827A	S14.124A	S24.103A	S34.121A	S54.01XA	S64.90XA	S94.30XA
S06.2X8A	S06.344S	S06.4X1S	S06.828A	S14.124S	S24.103S	S34.121S	S54.01XS	S64.90XS	S94.30XS
S06.2X9A	S06.345A	S06.4X2A	S06.829A	S14.125A	S24.104A	S34.122A	S54.02XA	S64.91XA	S94.31XA
S06.2X9S	S06.345S	S06.4X2S	S06.829S	S14.125S	S24.104S	S34.122S	S54.02XS	S64.91XS	S94.31XS
S06.300A	S06.346A	S06.4X3A	S06.890A	S14.126A	S24.109A	S34.123A	S54.10XA	S64.92XA	S94.32XA
S06.300S	S06.346S	S06.4X3S	S06.890S	S14.126S	S24.109S	S34.123S	S54.10XS	S64.92XS	S94.32XS
S06.301A	S06.347A	S06.4X4A	S06.891A	S14.127A	S24.111A	S34.124A	S54.11XA	S74.00XA	S94.8X1A
S06.301S	S06.348A	S06.4X4S	S06.891S	S14.127S	S24.111S	S34.124S	S54.11XS	S74.00XS	S94.8X1S
S06.302A	S06.349A	S06.4X5A	S06.892A	S14.128A	S24.112A	S34.125A	S54.12XA	S74.01XA	S94.8X2A
S06.302S	S06.349S	S06.4X5S	S06.892S	S14.128S	S24.112S	S34.125S	S54.12XS	S74.01XS	S94.8X2S
S06.303A	S06.350A	S06.4X6A	S06.893A	S14.129A	S24.113A	S34.129A	S54.20XA	S74.02XA	S94.8X9A
S06.303S	S06.350S	S06.4X6S	S06.893S	S14.129S	S24.113S	S34.129S	S54.20XS	S74.02XS	S94.8X9S
S06.304A	S06.351A	S06.4X7A	S06.894A	S14.131A	S24.114A	S34.131A	S54.21XA	S74.10XA	S94.90XA
S06.304S	S06.351S	S06.4X8A	S06.894S	S14.131S	S24.114S	S34.131S	S54.21XS	S74.10XS	S94.90XS
S06.305A	S06.352A	S06.4X9A	S06.895A	S14.132A	S24.119A	S34.132A	S54.22XA	S74.11XA	S94.91XA
S06.305S	S06.352S	S06.4X9S	S06.895S	S14.132S	S24.119S	S34.132S	S54.22XS	S74.11XS	S94.91XS
S06.306A	S06.353A	S06.5X0A	S06.896A	S14.133A	S24.131A	S34.139A	S54.30XA	S74.12XA	S94.92XA
S06.306S	S06.353S	S06.5X0S	S06.896S	S14.133S	S24.131S	S34.139S	S54.30XS	S74.12XS	S94.92XS
S06.307A	S06.354A	S06.5X1A	S06.897A	S14.134A	S24.132A	S34.21XA	S54.31XA	S74.20XA	T85.01XA
S06.308A	S06.354S	S06.5X1S	S06.898A	S14.134S	S24.132S	S34.21XS	S54.31XS	S74.20XS	T85.02XA
S06.309A	S06.355A	S06.5X2A	S06.899A	S14.135A	S24.133A	S34.22XA	S54.32XA	S74.21XA	T85.03XA
S06.309S	S06.355S	S06.5X2S	S06.899S	S14.135S	S24.133S	S34.22XS	S54.32XS	S74.21XS	T85.09XA
S06.310A	S06.356A	S06.5X3A	S06.9X0A	S14.136A	S24.134A	S34.3XXA	S54.8X1A	S74.22XA	T85.110A
S06.310S	S06.356S	S06.5X3S	S06.9X0S	S14.136S	S24.134S	S34.3XXS	S54.8X1S	S74.22XS	T85.111A
S06.311A	S06.357A	S06.5X4A	S06.9X1A	S14.137A	S24.139A	S34.4XXA	S54.8X2A	S74.8X1A	T85.112A
S06.311S	S06.358A	S06.5X4S	S06.9X1S	S14.137S	S24.139S	S34.4XXS	S54.8X2S	S74.8X1S	T85.113A
S06.312A	S06.359A	S06.5X5A	S06.9X2A	S14.138A	S24.141A	S34.5XXA	S54.8X9A	S74.8X2A	T85.118A
S06.312S	S06.359S	S06.5X5S	S06.9X2S	S14.138S	S24.141S	S34.5XXS	S54.8X9S	S74.8X2S	T85.120A
S06.313A	S06.360A	S06.5X6A	S06.9X3A	S14.139A	S24.142A	S34.6XXA	S54.90XA	S74.8X9A	T85.121A
S06.313S	S06.360S	S06.5X6S	S06.9X3S	S14.139S	S24.142S	S34.6XXS	S54.90XS	S74.8X9S	T85.122A
S06.314A	S06.361A	S06.5X7A	S06.9X4A	S14.141A	S24.143A	S34.8XXA	S54.91XA	S74.90XA	T85.123A
S06.314S	S06.361S	S06.5X8A	S06.9X4S	S14.141S	S24.143S	S34.8XXS	S54.91XS	S74.90XS	T85.128A
S06.315A	S06.362A	S06.5X9A	S06.9X5A	S14.142A	S24.144A	S34.9XXA	S54.92XA	S74.91XA	T85.190A
S06.315S	S06.362S	S06.5X9S	S06.9X5S	S14.142S	S24.144S	S34.9XXS	S54.92XS	S74.91XS	T85.191A
S06.316A	S06.363A	S06.6X0A	S06.9X6A	S14.143A	S24.149A	S44.00XA	S64.00XA	S74.92XA	T85.192A
S06.316S	S06.363S	S06.6X0S	S06.9X6S	S14.143S	S24.149S	S44.00XS	S64.00XS	S74.92XS	T85.193A
S06.317A	S06.364A	S06.6X1A	S06.9X7A	S14.144A	S24.151A	S44.01XA	S64.01XA	S84.00XA	T85.199A
S06.318A	S06.364S	S06.6X1S	S06.9X8A	S14.144S	S24.151S	S44.01XS	S64.01XS	S84.00XS	T85.610A
S06.319A	S06.365A	S06.6X2A	S06.9X9A	S14.145A	S24.152A	S44.02XA	S64.02XA	S84.01XA	T85.615A
S06.319S	S06.365S	S06.6X2S	S06.9X9S	S14.145S	S24.152S	S44.02XS	S64.02XS	S84.01XS	T85.620A
S06.320A	S06.366A	S06.6X3A	S14.0XXA	S14.146A	S24.153A	S44.10XA	S64.10XA	S84.02XA	T85.625A
S06.320S	S06.366S	S06.6X3S	S14.0XXS	S14.146S	S24.153S	S44.10XS	S64.10XS	S84.02XS	T85.630A
S06.321A	S06.367A	S06.6X4A	S14.101A	S14.147A	S24.154A	S44.11XA	S64.11XA	S84.10XA	T85.635A
S06.321S	S06.368A	S06.6X4S	S14.101S	S14.147S	S24.154S	S44.11XS	S64.11XS	S84.10XS	T85.690A
S06.322A	S06.369A	S06.6X5A	S14.102A	S14.148A	S24.159A	S44.12XA	S64.12XA	S84.11XA	T85.695A
S06.322S	S06.369S	S06.6X5S	S14.102S	S14.148S	S24.159S	S44.12XS	S64.12XS	S84.11XS	T85.730A
S06.323A	S06.370A	S06.6X6A	S14.103A	S14.149A	S24.2XXA	S44.20XA	S64.20XA	S84.12XA	T85.731A
S06.323S	S06.370S	S06.6X6S	S14.103S	S14.149S	S24.2XXS	S44.20XS	S64.20XS	S84.12XS	T85.732A
S06.324A	S06.371A	S06.6X7A	S14.104A	S14.151A	S24.3XXA	S44.21XA	S64.21XA	S84.20XA	T85.733A
S06.324S	S06.371S	S06.6X8A	S14.104S	S14.151S	S24.3XXS	S44.21XS	S64.21XS	S84.20XS	T85.734A
S06.325A	S06.372A	S06.6X9A	S14.105A	S14.152A	S24.4XXA	S44.22XA	S64.22XA	S84.21XA	T85.735A
S06.325S	S06.372S	S06.6X9S	S14.105S	S14.152S	S24.4XXS	S44.22XS	S64.22XS	S84.21XS	T85.738A
S06.326A	S06.373A	S06.810A	S14.106A	S14.153A	S24.8XXA	S44.30XA	S64.30XA	S84.22XA	T85.810A
S06.326S	S06.373S	S06.810S	S14.106S	S14.153S	S24.8XXS	S44.30XS	S64.30XS	S84.22XS	T85.820A
S06.327A	S06.374A	S06.811A	S14.107A	S14.154A	S24.9XXA	S44.31XA	S64.31XA	S84.801A	T85.830A
S06.328A	S06.374S	S06.811S	S14.107S	S14.154S	S24.9XXS	S44.31XS	S64.31XS	S84.801S	T85.840A
S06.329A	S06.375A	S06.812A	S14.108A	S14.155A	S34.01XA	S44.32XA	S64.32XA	S84.802A	T85.850A
S06.329S	S06.375S	S06.812S	S14.108S	S14.155S	S34.01XS	S44.32XS	S64.32XS	S84.802S	T85.860A
S06.330A	S06.376A	S06.813A	S14.109A	S14.156A	S34.02XA	S44.40XA	S64.40XA	S84.809A	T85.890A
S06.330S	S06.376S	S06.813S	S14.109S	S14.156S	S34.02XS	S44.40XS	S64.40XS	S84.809S	Z45.31
S06.331A	S06.377A	S06.814A	S14.157A	S14.157A	S34.101A	S44.41XA	S64.490A	S84.90XA	Z45.320
S06.331S	S06.378A	S06.814S	S14.111S	S14.157S	S34.101S	S44.41XS	S64.490S	S84.90XS	Z45.321
S06.332A	S06.379A	S06.815A	S14.112A	S14.158A	S34.102A	S44.42XA	S64.491A	S84.91XA	Z45.328
S06.332S	S06.379S	S06.815S	S14.112S	S14.158S	S34.102S	S44.42XS	S64.491S	S84.91XS	Z45.41
S06.333A	S06.380A	S06.816A	S14.113A	S14.159A	S34.103A	S44.50XA	S64.492A	S84.92XA	Z45.42
S06.333S	S06.380S	S06.816S	S14.113S	S14.159S	S34.103S	S44.50XS	S64.492S	S84.92XS	Z45.49
S06.334A	S06.381A	S06.817A	S14.114A	S14.2XXA	S34.104A	S44.51XA	S64.493A	S94.00XA	Z46.2
S06.334S	S06.381S	S06.818A	S14.114S	S14.2XXS	S34.104S	S44.51XS	S64.493S	S94.00XS	
S06.335A	S06.382A	S06.819A	S14.115A	S14.3XXA	S34.105A	S44.52XA	S64.494A	S94.01XA	
S06.335S	S06.382S	S06.819S	S14.115S	S14.3XXS	S34.105S	S44.52XS	S64.494S	S94.01XS	
S06.336A	S06.383A	S06.820A	S14.116A	S14.4XXA	S34.109A	S44.8X1A	S64.495A	S94.02XA	
S06.336S	S06.383S	S06.820S	S14.116S	S14.4XXS	S34.109S	S44.8X1S	S64.495S	S94.02XS	
S06.337A	S06.384A	S06.821A	S14.117A	S14.5XXA	S34.111A	S44.8X2A	S64.496A	S94.10XA	
S06.338A	S06.384S	S06.821S	S14.117S	S14.5XXS	S34.111S	S44.8X2S	S64.496S	S94.10XS	
S06.339A	S06.385A	S06.822A	S14.118A	S14.8XXA	S34.112A	S44.8X9A	S64.497A	S94.11XA	
S06.339S	S06.385S	S06.822S	S14.118S	S14.8XXS	S34.112S	S44.8X9S	S64.497S	S94.11XS	
S06.340A	S06.386A	S06.823A	S14.119A	S14.9XXA	S34.113A	S44.90XA	S64.498A	S94.12XA	
S06.340S	S06.386S	S06.823S	S14.119S	S14.9XXS	S34.113S	S44.90XS	S64.498S	S94.12XS	
S06.341A	S06.387A	S06.824A	S14.121A	S24.0XXA	S34.114A	S44.91XA	S64.8X1A	S94.20XA	
S06.341S	S06.388A	S06.824S	S14.121S	S24.0XXS	S34.114S	S44.91XS	S64.8X1S	S94.20XS	

MDC 02 Diseases And Disorders Of The Eye

A18.50	C69.32	E08.3419	E09.3599	E11.3419	E13.3599	H01.126	H02.134	H02.514	H02.871
A18.51	C69.40	E08.3491	E09.36	E11.3491	E13.36	H01.129	H02.135	H02.515	H02.872
A18.52	C69.41	E08.3492	E09.37X1	E11.3492	E13.37X1	H01.131	H02.136	H02.516	H02.873
A18.53	C69.42	E08.3493	E09.37X2	E11.3493	E13.37X2	H01.132	H02.139	H02.519	H02.874
A18.54	C69.50	E08.3499	E09.37X3	E11.3499	E13.37X3	H01.133	H02.141	H02.521	H02.875
A18.59	C69.51	E08.3511	E09.37X9	E11.3511	E13.37X9	H01.134	H02.142	H02.522	H02.876
A36.86	C69.52	E08.3512	E09.39	E11.3512	E13.39	H01.135	H02.143	H02.523	H02.879
A39.82	C69.60	E08.3513	E10.311	E11.3513	E50.0	H01.136	H02.144	H02.524	H02.881
A50.31	C69.61	E08.3519	E10.319	E11.3519	E50.1	H01.139	H02.145	H02.525	H02.882
A51.43	C69.62	E08.3521	E10.3211	E11.3521	E50.2	H01.141	H02.146	H02.526	H02.883
A52.71	C69.80	E08.3522	E10.3212	E11.3522	E50.3	H01.142	H02.149	H02.529	H02.884
A54.30	C69.81	E08.3523	E10.3213	E11.3523	E50.4	H01.143	H02.151	H02.531	H02.885
A54.31	C69.82	E08.3529	E10.3219	E11.3529	E50.5	H01.144	H02.152	H02.532	H02.886
A54.32	C69.90	E08.3531	E10.3291	E11.3531	E50.6	H01.145	H02.153	H02.533	H02.889
A54.33	C69.91	E08.3532	E10.3292	E11.3532	E50.7	H01.146	H02.154	H02.534	H02.88A
A54.39	C69.92	E08.3533	E10.3293	E11.3533	G24.5	H01.149	H02.155	H02.535	H02.88B
A71.0	D03.10	E08.3539	E10.3299	E11.3539	G45.3	H01.8	H02.156	H02.536	H02.89
A71.1	D03.111	E08.3541	E10.3311	E11.3541	H00.011	H01.9	H02.159	H02.539	H02.9
A71.9	D03.112	E08.3542	E10.3312	E11.3542	H00.012	H02.001	H02.201	H02.59	H04.001
A74.0	D03.121	E08.3543	E10.3313	E11.3543	H00.013	H02.002	H02.202	H02.70	H04.002
B00.50	D03.122	E08.3549	E10.3319	E11.3549	H00.014	H02.003	H02.203	H02.711	H04.003
B00.51	D04.10	E08.3551	E10.3391	E11.3551	H00.015	H02.004	H02.204	H02.712	H04.009
B00.52	D04.111	E08.3552	E10.3392	E11.3552	H00.016	H02.005	H02.205	H02.713	H04.011
B00.53	D04.112	E08.3553	E10.3393	E11.3553	H00.019	H02.006	H02.206	H02.714	H04.012
B00.59	D04.121	E08.3559	E10.3399	E11.3559	H00.021	H02.009	H02.209	H02.715	H04.013
B02.30	D04.122	E08.3591	E10.3411	E11.3591	H00.022	H02.011	H02.20A	H02.716	H04.019
B02.31	D09.20	E08.3592	E10.3412	E11.3592	H00.023	H02.012	H02.20B	H02.719	H04.021
B02.32	D09.21	E08.3593	E10.3413	E11.3593	H00.024	H02.013	H02.20C	H02.721	H04.022
B02.33	D09.22	E08.3599	E10.3419	E11.3599	H00.025	H02.014	H02.211	H02.722	H04.023
B02.34	D22.10	E08.36	E10.3491	E11.36	H00.026	H02.015	H02.212	H02.723	H04.029
B02.39	D22.111	E08.37X1	E10.3492	E11.37X1	H00.029	H02.016	H02.213	H02.724	H04.031
B05.81	D22.112	E08.37X2	E10.3493	E11.37X2	H00.031	H02.019	H02.214	H02.725	H04.032
B30.0	D22.121	E08.37X3	E10.3499	E11.37X3	H00.032	H02.021	H02.215	H02.726	H04.033
B30.1	D22.122	E08.37X9	E10.3511	E11.37X9	H00.033	H02.022	H02.216	H02.729	H04.039
B30.2	D23.10	E08.39	E10.3512	E11.39	H00.034	H02.023	H02.219	H02.731	H04.111
B30.3	D23.111	E09.311	E10.3513	E13.311	H00.035	H02.024	H02.21A	H02.732	H04.112
B30.8	D23.112	E09.319	E10.3519	E13.319	H00.036	H02.025	H02.21B	H02.733	H04.113
B30.9	D23.121	E09.3211	E10.3521	E13.3211	H00.039	H02.026	H02.21C	H02.734	H04.119
B58.01	D23.122	E09.3212	E10.3522	E13.3212	H00.11	H02.029	H02.221	H02.735	H04.121
B58.09	D31.00	E09.3213	E10.3523	E13.3213	H00.12	H02.031	H02.222	H02.736	H04.122
B60.12	D31.01	E09.3219	E10.3529	E13.3219	H00.13	H02.032	H02.223	H02.739	H04.123
B60.13	D31.02	E09.3291	E10.3531	E13.3291	H00.14	H02.033	H02.224	H02.79	H04.129
B94.0	D31.10	E09.3292	E10.3532	E13.3292	H00.15	H02.034	H02.225	H02.811	H04.131
C43.10	D31.11	E09.3293	E10.3533	E13.3293	H00.16	H02.035	H02.226	H02.812	H04.132
C43.111	D31.12	E09.3299	E10.3539	E13.3299	H00.19	H02.036	H02.229	H02.813	H04.133
C43.112	D31.20	E09.3311	E10.3541	E13.3311	H01.001	H02.039	H02.22A	H02.814	H04.139
C43.121	D31.21	E09.3312	E10.3542	E13.3312	H01.002	H02.041	H02.22B	H02.815	H04.141
C43.122	D31.22	E09.3313	E10.3543	E13.3313	H01.003	H02.042	H02.22C	H02.816	H04.142
C44.101	D31.30	E09.3319	E10.3549	E13.3319	H01.004	H02.043	H02.231	H02.819	H04.143
C44.1021	D31.31	E09.3391	E10.3551	E13.3391	H01.005	H02.044	H02.232	H02.821	H04.149
C44.1022	D31.32	E09.3392	E10.3552	E13.3392	H01.006	H02.045	H02.233	H02.822	H04.151
C44.1091	D31.40	E09.3393	E10.3553	E13.3393	H01.009	H02.046	H02.234	H02.823	H04.152
C44.1092	D31.41	E09.3399	E10.3559	E13.3399	H01.00A	H02.049	H02.235	H02.824	H04.153
C44.111	D31.42	E09.3411	E10.3591	E13.3411	H01.00B	H02.051	H02.236	H02.825	H04.159
C44.1121	D31.50	E09.3412	E10.3592	E13.3412	H01.011	H02.052	H02.239	H02.826	H04.161
C44.1122	D31.51	E09.3413	E10.3593	E13.3413	H01.012	H02.053	H02.23A	H02.829	H04.162
C44.1191	D31.52	E09.3419	E10.3599	E13.3419	H01.013	H02.054	H02.23B	H02.831	H04.163
C44.1192	D31.60	E09.3491	E10.36	E13.3491	H01.014	H02.055	H02.23C	H02.832	H04.169
C44.121	D31.61	E09.3492	E10.37X1	E13.3492	H01.015	H02.056	H02.30	H02.833	H04.19
C44.1221	D31.62	E09.3493	E10.37X2	E13.3493	H01.016	H02.059	H02.31	H02.834	H04.201
C44.1222	D31.90	E09.3499	E10.37X3	E13.3511	H01.019	H02.101	H02.32	H02.835	H04.202
C44.1291	D31.91	E09.3511	E10.37X9	E13.3512	H01.01A	H02.102	H02.33	H02.836	H04.203
C44.1292	D31.92	E09.3512	E10.39	E13.3513	H01.01B	H02.103	H02.34	H02.839	H04.209
C44.131	E08.311	E09.3513	E11.311	E13.3519	H01.021	H02.104	H02.35	H02.841	H04.211
C44.1321	E08.319	E09.3519	E11.319	E13.3521	H01.022	H02.105	H02.36	H02.842	H04.212
C44.1322	E08.3211	E09.3521	E11.3211	E13.3522	H01.023	H02.106	H02.401	H02.843	H04.213
C44.1391	E08.3212	E09.3522	E11.3212	E13.3523	H01.024	H02.109	H02.402	H02.844	H04.219
C44.1392	E08.3213	E09.3523	E11.3213	E13.3529	H01.025	H02.111	H02.403	H02.845	H04.221
C44.191	E08.3219	E09.3529	E11.3219	E13.3531	H01.026	H02.112	H02.409	H02.846	H04.222
C44.1921	E08.3291	E09.3531	E11.3291	E13.3532	H01.029	H02.113	H02.411	H02.849	H04.223
C44.1922	E08.3292	E09.3532	E11.3292	E13.3533	H01.02A	H02.114	H02.412	H02.851	H04.229
C44.1991	E08.3293	E09.3533	E11.3293	E13.3539	H01.02B	H02.115	H02.413	H02.852	H04.301
C44.1992	E08.3299	E09.3539	E11.3299	E13.3541	H01.111	H02.116	H02.419	H02.853	H04.302
C69.00	E08.3311	E09.3541	E11.3311	E13.3542	H01.112	H02.119	H02.421	H02.854	H04.303
C69.01	E08.3312	E09.3542	E11.3312	E13.3543	H01.113	H02.121	H02.422	H02.855	H04.309
C69.02	E08.3313	E09.3543	E11.3313	E13.3549	H01.114	H02.122	H02.423	H02.856	H04.311
C69.10	E08.3319	E09.3549	E11.3319	E13.3551	H01.115	H02.123	H02.429	H02.859	H04.312
C69.11	E08.3391	E09.3551	E11.3391	E13.3552	H01.116	H02.124	H02.431	H02.861	H04.313
C69.12	E08.3392	E09.3552	E11.3392	E13.3553	H01.119	H02.125	H02.432	H02.862	H04.319
C69.20	E08.3393	E09.3553	E11.3393	E13.3559	H01.121	H02.126	H02.433	H02.863	H04.321
C69.21	E08.3399	E09.3559	E11.3399	E13.3591	H01.122	H02.129	H02.439	H02.864	H04.322
C69.22	E08.3411	E09.3591	E11.3411	E13.3592	H01.123	H02.131	H02.511	H02.865	H04.323
C69.30	E08.3412	E09.3592	E11.3412	E13.3593	H01.124	H02.132	H02.512	H02.866	H04.329
C69.31	E08.3413	E09.3593	E11.3413	E13.3593	H01.125	H02.133	H02.513	H02.869	H04.331

H04.332	H05.222	H10.231	H11.122	H15.092	H16.142	H17.812	H18.462	H20.811	H21.531
H04.333	H05.223	H10.232	H11.123	H15.093	H16.143	H17.813	H18.463	H20.812	H21.532
H04.339	H05.229	H10.233	H11.129	H15.099	H16.149	H17.819	H18.469	H20.813	H21.533
H04.411	H05.231	H10.239	H11.131	H15.101	H16.201	H17.821	H18.49	H20.819	H21.539
H04.412	H05.232	H10.30	H11.132	H15.102	H16.202	H17.822	H18.50	H20.821	H21.541
H04.413	H05.233	H10.31	H11.133	H15.103	H16.203	H17.823	H18.51	H20.822	H21.542
H04.419	H05.239	H10.32	H11.139	H15.109	H16.209	H17.829	H18.52	H20.823	H21.543
H04.421	H05.241	H10.33	H11.141	H15.111	H16.211	H17.89	H18.53	H20.829	H21.549
H04.422	H05.242	H10.401	H11.142	H15.112	H16.212	H17.9	H18.54	H20.9	H21.551
H04.423	H05.243	H10.402	H11.143	H15.113	H16.213	H18.001	H18.55	H21.00	H21.552
H04.429	H05.249	H10.403	H11.149	H15.119	H16.219	H18.002	H18.59	H21.01	H21.553
H04.431	H05.251	H10.409	H11.151	H15.121	H16.221	H18.003	H18.601	H21.02	H21.559
H04.432	H05.252	H10.411	H11.152	H15.122	H16.222	H18.009	H18.602	H21.03	H21.561
H04.433	H05.253	H10.412	H11.153	H15.123	H16.223	H18.011	H18.603	H21.1X1	H21.562
H04.439	H05.259	H10.413	H11.159	H15.129	H16.229	H18.012	H18.609	H21.1X2	H21.563
H04.511	H05.261	H10.419	H11.211	H15.811	H16.231	H18.013	H18.611	H21.1X3	H21.569
H04.512	H05.262	H10.421	H11.212	H15.812	H16.232	H18.019	H18.612	H21.1X9	H21.81
H04.513	H05.263	H10.422	H11.213	H15.813	H16.233	H18.021	H18.613	H21.211	H21.82
H04.519	H05.269	H10.423	H11.219	H15.819	H16.239	H18.022	H18.619	H21.212	H21.89
H04.521	H05.30	H10.429	H11.221	H15.821	H16.241	H18.023	H18.621	H21.213	H21.9
H04.522	H05.311	H10.431	H11.222	H15.822	H16.242	H18.029	H18.622	H21.219	H22
H04.523	H05.312	H10.432	H11.223	H15.823	H16.243	H18.031	H18.623	H21.221	H25.011
H04.529	H05.313	H10.433	H11.229	H15.829	H16.249	H18.032	H18.629	H21.222	H25.012
H04.531	H05.319	H10.439	H11.231	H15.831	H16.251	H18.033	H18.70	H21.223	H25.013
H04.532	H05.321	H10.44	H11.232	H15.832	H16.252	H18.039	H18.711	H21.229	H25.019
H04.533	H05.322	H10.45	H11.233	H15.833	H16.253	H18.041	H18.712	H21.231	H25.031
H04.539	H05.323	H10.501	H11.239	H15.839	H16.259	H18.042	H18.713	H21.232	H25.032
H04.541	H05.329	H10.502	H11.241	H15.841	H16.261	H18.043	H18.719	H21.233	H25.033
H04.542	H05.331	H10.503	H11.242	H15.842	H16.262	H18.049	H18.721	H21.239	H25.039
H04.543	H05.332	H10.509	H11.243	H15.843	H16.263	H18.051	H18.722	H21.241	H25.041
H04.549	H05.333	H10.511	H11.249	H15.849	H16.269	H18.052	H18.723	H21.242	H25.042
H04.551	H05.339	H10.512	H11.30	H15.851	H16.291	H18.053	H18.729	H21.243	H25.043
H04.552	H05.341	H10.513	H11.31	H15.852	H16.292	H18.059	H18.731	H21.249	H25.049
H04.553	H05.342	H10.519	H11.32	H15.853	H16.293	H18.061	H18.732	H21.251	H25.091
H04.559	H05.343	H10.521	H11.33	H15.859	H16.299	H18.062	H18.733	H21.252	H25.092
H04.561	H05.349	H10.522	H11.411	H15.89	H16.301	H18.063	H18.739	H21.253	H25.093
H04.562	H05.351	H10.523	H11.412	H15.9	H16.302	H18.069	H18.791	H21.259	H25.099
H04.563	H05.352	H10.529	H11.413	H16.001	H16.303	H18.10	H18.792	H21.261	H25.10
H04.569	H05.353	H10.531	H11.419	H16.002	H16.309	H18.11	H18.793	H21.262	H25.11
H04.571	H05.359	H10.532	H11.421	H16.003	H16.311	H18.12	H18.799	H21.263	H25.12
H04.572	H05.401	H10.533	H11.422	H16.009	H16.312	H18.13	H18.811	H21.269	H25.13
H04.573	H05.402	H10.539	H11.423	H16.011	H16.313	H18.20	H18.812	H21.271	H25.20
H04.579	H05.403	H10.811	H11.429	H16.012	H16.319	H18.211	H18.813	H21.272	H25.21
H04.611	H05.409	H10.812	H11.431	H16.013	H16.321	H18.212	H18.819	H21.273	H25.22
H04.612	H05.411	H10.813	H11.432	H16.019	H16.322	H18.213	H18.821	H21.279	H25.23
H04.613	H05.412	H10.819	H11.433	H16.021	H16.323	H18.219	H18.822	H21.29	H25.811
H04.619	H05.413	H10.821	H11.439	H16.022	H16.329	H18.221	H18.823	H21.301	H25.812
H04.69	H05.419	H10.822	H11.441	H16.023	H16.331	H18.222	H18.829	H21.302	H25.813
H04.811	H05.421	H10.823	H11.442	H16.029	H16.332	H18.223	H18.831	H21.303	H25.819
H04.812	H05.422	H10.829	H11.443	H16.031	H16.333	H18.229	H18.832	H21.309	H25.89
H04.813	H05.423	H10.89	H11.449	H16.032	H16.339	H18.231	H18.833	H21.311	H25.9
H04.819	H05.429	H10.9	H11.811	H16.033	H16.391	H18.232	H18.839	H21.312	H26.001
H04.89	H05.50	H11.001	H11.812	H16.039	H16.392	H18.233	H18.891	H21.313	H26.002
H04.9	H05.51	H11.002	H11.813	H16.041	H16.393	H18.239	H18.892	H21.319	H26.003
H05.00	H05.52	H11.003	H11.819	H16.042	H16.399	H18.30	H18.893	H21.321	H26.009
H05.011	H05.53	H11.009	H11.821	H16.043	H16.401	H18.311	H18.899	H21.322	H26.011
H05.012	H05.811	H11.011	H11.822	H16.049	H16.402	H18.312	H18.9	H21.323	H26.012
H05.013	H05.812	H11.012	H11.823	H16.051	H16.403	H18.313	H20.00	H21.329	H26.013
H05.019	H05.813	H11.013	H11.829	H16.052	H16.409	H18.319	H20.011	H21.331	H26.019
H05.021	H05.819	H11.019	H11.89	H16.053	H16.411	H18.321	H20.012	H21.332	H26.031
H05.022	H05.821	H11.021	H11.9	H16.059	H16.412	H18.322	H20.013	H21.333	H26.032
H05.023	H05.822	H11.022	H15.001	H16.061	H16.413	H18.323	H20.019	H21.339	H26.033
H05.029	H05.823	H11.023	H15.002	H16.062	H16.419	H18.329	H20.021	H21.341	H26.039
H05.031	H05.829	H11.029	H15.003	H16.063	H16.421	H18.331	H20.022	H21.342	H26.041
H05.032	H05.89	H11.031	H15.009	H16.069	H16.422	H18.332	H20.023	H21.343	H26.042
H05.033	H05.9	H11.032	H15.011	H16.071	H16.423	H18.333	H20.029	H21.349	H26.043
H05.039	H10.011	H11.033	H15.012	H16.072	H16.429	H18.339	H20.031	H21.351	H26.049
H05.041	H10.012	H11.039	H15.013	H16.073	H16.431	H18.40	H20.032	H21.352	H26.051
H05.042	H10.013	H11.041	H15.019	H16.079	H16.432	H18.411	H20.033	H21.353	H26.052
H05.043	H10.019	H11.042	H15.021	H16.101	H16.433	H18.412	H20.039	H21.359	H26.053
H05.049	H10.021	H11.043	H15.022	H16.102	H16.439	H18.413	H20.041	H21.40	H26.059
H05.10	H10.022	H11.049	H15.023	H16.103	H16.441	H18.419	H20.042	H21.41	H26.061
H05.111	H10.023	H11.051	H15.029	H16.109	H16.442	H18.421	H20.043	H21.42	H26.062
H05.112	H10.029	H11.052	H15.031	H16.111	H16.443	H18.422	H20.049	H21.43	H26.063
H05.113	H10.10	H11.053	H15.032	H16.112	H16.449	H18.423	H20.051	H21.501	H26.069
H05.119	H10.11	H11.059	H15.033	H16.113	H16.8	H18.429	H20.052	H21.502	H26.09
H05.121	H10.12	H11.061	H15.039	H16.119	H16.9	H18.43	H20.053	H21.503	H26.101
H05.122	H10.13	H11.062	H15.041	H16.121	H17.00	H18.441	H20.059	H21.509	H26.102
H05.123	H10.211	H11.063	H15.042	H16.122	H17.01	H18.442	H20.10	H21.511	H26.103
H05.129	H10.212	H11.069	H15.043	H16.123	H17.02	H18.443	H20.11	H21.512	H26.109
H05.20	H10.213	H11.10	H15.049	H16.129	H17.03	H18.449	H20.12	H21.513	H26.111
H05.211	H10.219	H11.111	H15.051	H16.131	H17.10	H18.451	H20.13	H21.519	H26.112
H05.212	H10.221	H11.112	H15.052	H16.132	H17.11	H18.452	H20.20	H21.521	H26.113
H05.213	H10.222	H11.113	H15.053	H16.133	H17.12	H18.453	H20.21	H21.522	H26.119
H05.219	H10.223	H11.119	H15.059	H16.139	H17.13	H18.459	H20.22	H21.523	H26.121
H05.221	H10.229	H11.121	H15.091	H16.141	H17.811	H18.461	H20.23	H21.529	H26.122

Diagnosis Codes by MDC

H26.123	H30.131	H33.003	H34.8131	H35.22	H35.51	H40.1222	H40.231	H40.63X3	H44.2C3
H26.129	H30.132	H33.009	H34.8132	H35.23	H35.52	H40.1223	H40.232	H40.63X4	H44.2C9
H26.131	H30.133	H33.011	H34.8190	H35.30	H35.53	H40.1224	H40.233	H40.811	H44.2D1
H26.132	H30.139	H33.012	H34.8191	H35.3110	H35.54	H40.1230	H40.239	H40.812	H44.2D2
H26.133	H30.141	H33.013	H34.8192	H35.3111	H35.60	H40.1231	H40.241	H40.813	H44.2D3
H26.139	H30.142	H33.019	H34.821	H35.3112	H35.61	H40.1232	H40.242	H40.819	H44.2D9
H26.20	H30.143	H33.021	H34.822	H35.3113	H35.62	H40.1233	H40.243	H40.821	H44.2E1
H26.211	H30.149	H33.022	H34.823	H35.3114	H35.63	H40.1234	H40.249	H40.822	H44.2E2
H26.212	H30.20	H33.023	H34.829	H35.3120	H35.70	H40.1290	H40.30X0	H40.823	H44.2E3
H26.213	H30.21	H33.029	H34.8310	H35.3121	H35.711	H40.1291	H40.30X1	H40.829	H44.2E9
H26.219	H30.22	H33.031	H34.8311	H35.3122	H35.712	H40.1292	H40.30X2	H40.831	H44.30
H26.221	H30.23	H33.032	H34.8312	H35.3123	H35.713	H40.1293	H40.30X3	H40.832	H44.311
H26.222	H30.811	H33.033	H34.8320	H35.3124	H35.719	H40.1294	H40.30X4	H40.833	H44.312
H26.223	H30.812	H33.039	H34.8321	H35.3130	H35.721	H40.1310	H40.31X0	H40.839	H44.313
H26.229	H30.813	H33.041	H34.8322	H35.3131	H35.722	H40.1311	H40.31X1	H40.89	H44.319
H26.231	H30.819	H33.042	H34.8330	H35.3132	H35.723	H40.1312	H40.31X2	H40.9	H44.321
H26.232	H30.891	H33.043	H34.8331	H35.3133	H35.729	H40.1313	H40.31X3	H42	H44.322
H26.233	H30.892	H33.049	H34.8332	H35.3134	H35.731	H40.1314	H40.31X4	H43.00	H44.323
H26.239	H30.893	H33.051	H34.8390	H35.3190	H35.732	H40.1320	H40.32X0	H43.01	H44.329
H26.30	H30.899	H33.052	H34.8391	H35.3191	H35.733	H40.1321	H40.32X1	H43.02	H44.391
H26.31	H30.90	H33.053	H34.8392	H35.3192	H35.739	H40.1322	H40.32X2	H43.03	H44.392
H26.32	H30.91	H33.059	H34.9	H35.3193	H35.81	H40.1323	H40.32X3	H43.10	H44.393
H26.33	H30.92	H33.101	H35.00	H35.3194	H35.82	H40.1324	H40.32X4	H43.11	H44.399
H26.40	H30.93	H33.102	H35.011	H35.3210	H35.89	H40.1330	H40.33X0	H43.12	H44.40
H26.411	H31.001	H33.103	H35.012	H35.3211	H35.9	H40.1331	H40.33X1	H43.13	H44.411
H26.412	H31.002	H33.109	H35.013	H35.3212	H36	H40.1332	H40.33X2	H43.20	H44.412
H26.413	H31.003	H33.111	H35.019	H35.3213	H40.001	H40.1333	H40.33X3	H43.21	H44.413
H26.419	H31.009	H33.112	H35.021	H35.3220	H40.002	H40.1334	H40.33X4	H43.22	H44.419
H26.491	H31.011	H33.113	H35.022	H35.3221	H40.003	H40.1390	H40.40X0	H43.23	H44.421
H26.492	H31.012	H33.119	H35.023	H35.3222	H40.009	H40.1391	H40.40X1	H43.311	H44.422
H26.493	H31.013	H33.121	H35.029	H35.3223	H40.011	H40.1392	H40.40X2	H43.312	H44.423
H26.499	H31.019	H33.122	H35.031	H35.3230	H40.012	H40.1393	H40.40X3	H43.313	H44.429
H26.8	H31.021	H33.123	H35.032	H35.3231	H40.013	H40.1394	H40.40X4	H43.319	H44.431
H26.9	H31.022	H33.129	H35.033	H35.3232	H40.019	H40.1410	H40.41X0	H43.391	H44.432
H27.00	H31.023	H33.191	H35.039	H35.3233	H40.021	H40.1411	H40.41X1	H43.392	H44.433
H27.01	H31.029	H33.192	H35.041	H35.3290	H40.022	H40.1412	H40.41X2	H43.393	H44.439
H27.02	H31.091	H33.193	H35.042	H35.3291	H40.023	H40.1413	H40.41X3	H43.399	H44.441
H27.03	H31.092	H33.199	H35.043	H35.3292	H40.029	H40.1414	H40.41X4	H43.811	H44.442
H27.10	H31.093	H33.20	H35.049	H35.3293	H40.031	H40.1420	H40.42X0	H43.812	H44.443
H27.111	H31.099	H33.21	H35.051	H35.33	H40.032	H40.1421	H40.42X1	H43.813	H44.449
H27.112	H31.101	H33.22	H35.052	H35.341	H40.033	H40.1422	H40.42X2	H43.819	H44.50
H27.113	H31.102	H33.23	H35.053	H35.342	H40.039	H40.1423	H40.42X3	H43.821	H44.511
H27.119	H31.103	H33.301	H35.059	H35.343	H40.041	H40.1424	H40.42X4	H43.822	H44.512
H27.121	H31.109	H33.302	H35.061	H35.349	H40.042	H40.1430	H40.43X0	H43.823	H44.513
H27.122	H31.111	H33.303	H35.062	H35.351	H40.043	H40.1431	H40.43X1	H43.829	H44.519
H27.123	H31.112	H33.309	H35.063	H35.352	H40.049	H40.1432	H40.43X2	H43.89	H44.521
H27.129	H31.113	H33.311	H35.069	H35.353	H40.051	H40.1433	H40.43X3	H43.9	H44.522
H27.131	H31.119	H33.312	H35.071	H35.359	H40.052	H40.1434	H40.43X4	H44.001	H44.523
H27.132	H31.121	H33.313	H35.072	H35.361	H40.053	H40.1490	H40.50X0	H44.002	H44.529
H27.133	H31.122	H33.319	H35.073	H35.362	H40.059	H40.1491	H40.50X1	H44.003	H44.531
H27.139	H31.123	H33.321	H35.079	H35.363	H40.061	H40.1492	H40.50X2	H44.009	H44.532
H27.8	H31.129	H33.322	H35.09	H35.369	H40.062	H40.1493	H40.50X3	H44.011	H44.533
H27.9	H31.20	H33.323	H35.101	H35.371	H40.063	H40.1494	H40.50X4	H44.012	H44.539
H28	H31.21	H33.329	H35.102	H35.372	H40.069	H40.151	H40.51X0	H44.013	H44.601
H30.001	H31.22	H33.331	H35.103	H35.373	H40.10X0	H40.152	H40.51X1	H44.019	H44.602
H30.002	H31.23	H33.332	H35.109	H35.379	H40.10X1	H40.153	H40.51X2	H44.021	H44.603
H30.003	H31.29	H33.333	H35.111	H35.381	H40.10X2	H40.159	H40.51X3	H44.022	H44.609
H30.009	H31.301	H33.339	H35.112	H35.382	H40.10X3	H40.20X0	H40.51X4	H44.023	H44.611
H30.011	H31.302	H33.40	H35.113	H35.383	H40.10X4	H40.20X1	H40.52X0	H44.029	H44.612
H30.012	H31.303	H33.41	H35.119	H35.389	H40.1110	H40.20X2	H40.52X1	H44.111	H44.613
H30.013	H31.309	H33.42	H35.121	H35.40	H40.1111	H40.20X3	H40.52X2	H44.112	H44.619
H30.019	H31.311	H33.43	H35.122	H35.411	H40.1112	H40.20X4	H40.52X3	H44.113	H44.621
H30.021	H31.312	H33.8	H35.123	H35.412	H40.1113	H40.211	H40.52X4	H44.119	H44.622
H30.022	H31.313	H34.00	H35.129	H35.413	H40.1114	H40.212	H40.53X0	H44.121	H44.623
H30.023	H31.319	H34.01	H35.131	H35.419	H40.1120	H40.213	H40.53X1	H44.122	H44.629
H30.029	H31.321	H34.02	H35.132	H35.421	H40.1121	H40.219	H40.53X2	H44.123	H44.631
H30.031	H31.322	H34.03	H35.133	H35.422	H40.1122	H40.2210	H40.53X3	H44.129	H44.632
H30.032	H31.323	H34.10	H35.139	H35.423	H40.1123	H40.2211	H40.53X4	H44.131	H44.633
H30.033	H31.329	H34.11	H35.141	H35.429	H40.1124	H40.2212	H40.60X0	H44.132	H44.639
H30.039	H31.401	H34.12	H35.142	H35.431	H40.1130	H40.2213	H40.60X1	H44.133	H44.641
H30.041	H31.402	H34.13	H35.143	H35.432	H40.1131	H40.2214	H40.60X2	H44.139	H44.642
H30.042	H31.403	H34.211	H35.149	H35.433	H40.1132	H40.2220	H40.60X3	H44.19	H44.643
H30.043	H31.409	H34.212	H35.151	H35.439	H40.1133	H40.2221	H40.60X4	H44.20	H44.649
H30.049	H31.411	H34.213	H35.152	H35.441	H40.1134	H40.2222	H40.61X0	H44.21	H44.651
H30.101	H31.412	H34.219	H35.153	H35.442	H40.1190	H40.2223	H40.61X1	H44.22	H44.652
H30.102	H31.413	H34.231	H35.159	H35.443	H40.1191	H40.2224	H40.61X2	H44.23	H44.653
H30.103	H31.419	H34.232	H35.161	H35.449	H40.1192	H40.2230	H40.61X3	H44.2A1	H44.659
H30.109	H31.421	H34.233	H35.162	H35.451	H40.1193	H40.2231	H40.61X4	H44.2A2	H44.691
H30.111	H31.422	H34.239	H35.163	H35.452	H40.1194	H40.2232	H40.62X0	H44.2A3	H44.692
H30.112	H31.423	H34.8110	H35.169	H35.453	H40.1210	H40.2233	H40.62X1	H44.2A9	H44.693
H30.113	H31.429	H34.8111	H35.171	H35.459	H40.1211	H40.2234	H40.62X2	H44.2B1	H44.699
H30.119	H31.8	H34.8112	H35.172	H35.461	H40.1212	H40.2290	H40.62X3	H44.2B2	H44.701
H30.121	H31.9	H34.8120	H35.173	H35.462	H40.1213	H40.2291	H40.62X4	H44.2B3	H44.702
H30.122	H32	H34.8121	H35.179	H35.463	H40.1214	H40.2292	H40.63X0	H44.2B9	H44.703
H30.123	H33.001	H34.8122	H35.20	H35.469	H40.1220	H40.2293	H40.63X1	H44.2C1	H44.709
H30.129	H33.002	H34.8130	H35.21	H35.50	H40.1221	H40.2294	H40.63X2	H44.2C2	H44.711

H44.712	H47.039	H49.43	H50.811	H53.023	H53.483	H54.52A2	Q12.3	S01.112A	T15.10XA
H44.713	H47.091	H49.881	H50.812	H53.029	H53.489	H54.60	Q12.4	S01.119A	T15.11XA
H44.719	H47.092	H49.882	H50.89	H53.031	H53.50	H54.61	Q12.8	S01.121A	T15.12XA
H44.721	H47.093	H49.883	H50.9	H53.032	H53.51	H54.62	Q12.9	S01.122A	T15.80XA
H44.722	H47.099	H49.889	H51.0	H53.033	H53.52	H54.7	Q13.0	S01.129A	T15.81XA
H44.723	H47.12	H49.9	H51.11	H53.039	H53.53	H54.8	Q13.1	S01.131A	T15.90XA
H44.729	H47.13	H50.00	H51.12	H53.041	H53.54	H55.00	Q13.2	S01.132A	T15.91XA
H44.731	H47.20	H50.011	H51.8	H53.042	H53.55	H55.01	Q13.3	S01.139A	T15.92XA
H44.732	H47.211	H50.012	H51.9	H53.043	H53.59	H55.02	Q13.4	S01.141A	T26.00XA
H44.733	H47.212	H50.021	H52.00	H53.049	H53.60	H55.03	Q13.5	S01.142A	T26.01XA
H44.739	H47.213	H50.022	H52.01	H53.10	H53.61	H55.04	Q13.81	S01.149A	T26.02XA
H44.741	H47.219	H50.031	H52.02	H53.11	H53.62	H55.09	Q13.89	S01.151A	T26.10XA
H44.742	H47.22	H50.032	H52.03	H53.121	H53.63	H55.81	Q13.9	S01.152A	T26.11XA
H44.743	H47.231	H50.041	H52.10	H53.122	H53.69	H55.89	Q14.0	S01.159A	T26.12XA
H44.749	H47.232	H50.042	H52.11	H53.123	H53.71	H57.00	Q14.1	S02.30XA	T26.20XA
H44.751	H47.233	H50.05	H52.12	H53.129	H53.72	H57.02	Q14.2	S02.30XB	T26.21XA
H44.752	H47.239	H50.06	H52.13	H53.131	H53.8	H57.03	Q14.3	S02.31XA	T26.22XA
H44.753	H47.291	H50.07	H52.201	H53.132	H53.9	H57.04	Q14.8	S02.31XB	T26.30XA
H44.759	H47.292	H50.08	H52.202	H53.133	H54.0X33	H57.051	Q14.9	S02.32XA	T26.31XA
H44.791	H47.293	H50.10	H52.203	H53.139	H54.0X34	H57.052	Q15.0	S02.32XB	T26.32XA
H44.792	H47.299	H50.111	H52.209	H53.141	H54.0X35	H57.053	Q15.8	S04.011A	T26.40XA
H44.793	H47.311	H50.112	H52.211	H53.142	H54.0X43	H57.059	Q15.9	S04.012A	T26.41XA
H44.799	H47.312	H50.121	H52.212	H53.143	H54.0X44	H57.09	R44.1	S04.019A	T26.42XA
H44.811	H47.313	H50.122	H52.213	H53.149	H54.0X45	H57.10	R48.3	S05.00XA	T26.50XA
H44.812	H47.319	H50.131	H52.219	H53.15	H54.0X53	H57.11	R94.110	S05.01XA	T26.51XA
H44.813	H47.321	H50.132	H52.221	H53.16	H54.0X54	H57.12	R94.111	S05.02XA	T26.52XA
H44.819	H47.322	H50.141	H52.222	H53.19	H54.0X55	H57.13	R94.112	S05.10XA	T26.60XA
H44.821	H47.323	H50.142	H52.223	H53.2	H54.10	H57.811	R94.113	S05.11XA	T26.61XA
H44.822	H47.329	H50.15	H52.229	H53.30	H54.1131	H57.812	S00.10XA	S05.12XA	T26.62XA
H44.823	H47.331	H50.16	H52.31	H53.31	H54.1132	H57.813	S00.11XA	S05.20XA	T26.70XA
H44.829	H47.332	H50.17	H52.32	H53.32	H54.1141	H57.819	S00.12XA	S05.21XA	T26.71XA
H44.89	H47.333	H50.18	H52.4	H53.33	H54.1142	H57.89	S00.201A	S05.22XA	T26.72XA
H44.9	H47.339	H50.21	H52.511	H53.34	H54.1151	H57.9	S00.202A	S05.30XA	T26.80XA
H46.00	H47.391	H50.22	H52.512	H53.40	H54.1152	H59.021	S00.209A	S05.31XA	T26.81XA
H46.01	H47.392	H50.30	H52.513	H53.411	H54.1213	H59.022	S00.211A	S05.32XA	T26.82XA
H46.02	H47.393	H50.311	H52.519	H53.412	H54.1214	H59.023	S00.212A	S05.40XA	T26.90XA
H46.03	H47.399	H50.312	H52.521	H53.413	H54.1215	H59.029	S00.219A	S05.41XA	T26.91XA
H46.10	H49.00	H50.32	H52.522	H53.419	H54.1223	H59.40	S00.221A	S05.42XA	T26.92XA
H46.11	H49.01	H50.331	H52.523	H53.421	H54.1224	H59.41	S00.222A	S05.50XA	T85.21XA
H46.12	H49.02	H50.332	H52.529	H53.422	H54.1225	H59.42	S00.229A	S05.51XA	T85.22XA
H46.13	H49.03	H50.34	H52.531	H53.423	H54.2X11	H59.43	S00.241A	S05.52XA	T85.29XA
H46.2	H49.10	H50.40	H52.532	H53.429	H54.2X12	Q10.0	S00.242A	S05.60XA	T85.318A
H46.3	H49.11	H50.411	H52.533	H53.431	H54.2X21	Q10.1	S00.249A	S05.61XA	T85.328A
H46.8	H49.12	H50.412	H52.539	H53.432	H54.2X22	Q10.2	S00.251A	S05.62XA	T85.398A
H46.9	H49.13	H50.42	H52.6	H53.433	H54.3	Q10.3	S00.252A	S05.70XA	T86.840
H47.011	H49.20	H50.43	H52.7	H53.439	H54.40	Q10.4	S00.259A	S05.71XA	T86.841
H47.012	H49.21	H50.50	H53.001	H53.451	H54.413A	Q10.5	S00.261A	S05.72XA	Z90.01
H47.013	H49.22	H50.51	H53.002	H53.452	H54.414A	Q10.6	S00.262A	S05.8X1A	Z94.7
H47.019	H49.23	H50.52	H53.003	H53.453	H54.415A	Q10.7	S00.269A	S05.8X2A	Z96.1
H47.021	H49.30	H50.53	H53.009	H53.459	H54.42A3	Q11.0	S00.271A	S05.8X9A	Z97.0
H47.022	H49.31	H50.54	H53.011	H53.461	H54.42A4	Q11.1	S00.272A	S05.90XA	
H47.023	H49.32	H50.55	H53.012	H53.462	H54.42A5	Q11.2	S00.279A	S05.91XA	
H47.029	H49.33	H50.60	H53.013	H53.469	H54.50	Q11.3	S01.101A	S05.92XA	
H47.031	H49.40	H50.611	H53.019	H53.47	H54.511A	Q12.0	S01.102A	T15.00XA	
H47.032	H49.41	H50.612	H53.021	H53.481	H54.512A	Q12.1	S01.109A	T15.01XA	
H47.033	H49.42	H50.69	H53.022	H53.482	H54.52A1	Q12.2	S01.111A	T15.02XA	

MDC 03 Diseases And Disorders Of The Ear, Nose, Mouth And Throat

A18.6	C02.0	C08.0	C14.0	D00.06	D37.04	H60.22	H60.511	H60.62	H61.191
A36.0	C02.1	C08.1	C14.2	D00.07	D37.05	H60.23	H60.512	H60.63	H61.192
A36.1	C02.2	C08.9	C14.8	D00.08	D37.09	H60.311	H60.513	H60.8X1	H61.193
A36.2	C02.3	C09.0	C30.0	D02.0	D38.0	H60.312	H60.519	H60.8X2	H61.199
A54.5	C02.4	C09.1	C30.1	D10.0	G47.30	H60.313	H60.521	H60.8X3	H61.20
A56.4	C02.8	C09.8	C31.0	D10.1	G47.33	H60.319	H60.522	H60.8X9	H61.21
A66.5	C02.9	C09.9	C31.1	D10.2	G47.34	H60.321	H60.523	H60.90	H61.22
A69.0	C03.0	C10.0	C31.2	D10.30	G47.36	H60.322	H60.529	H60.91	H61.23
A69.1	C03.1	C10.1	C31.3	D10.39	G47.39	H60.323	H60.531	H60.92	H61.301
B00.1	C03.9	C10.2	C31.8	D10.4	G47.50	H60.329	H60.532	H60.93	H61.302
B00.2	C04.0	C10.3	C31.9	D10.5	G47.52	H60.331	H60.539	H61.001	H61.303
B05.3	C04.1	C10.4	C32.0	D10.6	G47.54	H60.332	H60.541	H61.002	H61.309
B08.5	C04.8	C10.8	C32.1	D10.7	G47.59	H60.333	H60.542	H61.003	H61.311
B37.0	C04.9	C10.9	C32.2	D10.9	G47.63	H60.339	H60.543	H61.009	H61.312
B37.83	C05.0	C11.0	C32.3	D11.0	G47.69	H60.391	H60.549	H61.101	H61.313
B37.84	C05.1	C11.1	C32.8	D11.7	G47.8	H60.392	H60.551	H61.102	H61.319
C00.0	C05.2	C11.2	C32.9	D11.9	H60.00	H60.393	H60.552	H61.103	H61.321
C00.1	C05.8	C11.3	C39.0	D14.0	H60.01	H60.399	H60.553	H61.109	H61.322
C00.2	C05.9	C11.8	C46.2	D14.1	H60.02	H60.40	H60.559	H61.111	H61.323
C00.3	C06.0	C11.9	C76.0	D16.5	H60.03	H60.41	H60.591	H61.112	H61.329
C00.4	C06.1	C12	D00.00	D37.01	H60.10	H60.42	H60.592	H61.113	H61.391
C00.5	C06.2	C13.0	D00.01	D37.02	H60.11	H60.43	H60.593	H61.119	H61.392
C00.6	C06.80	C13.1	D00.02	D37.030	H60.12	H60.501	H60.599	H61.121	H61.393
C00.8	C06.89	C13.2	D00.03	D37.031	H60.13	H60.502	H60.60	H61.122	H61.399
C00.9	C06.9	C13.8	D00.04	D37.032	H60.20	H60.503	H60.61	H61.123	H61.811
C01	C07	C13.9	D00.05	D37.039	H60.21	H60.509		H61.129	H61.812

H61.813	H66.3X1	H70.813	H73.90	H81.393	H92.20	J01.21	K00.4	K08.113	K12.31
H61.819	H66.3X2	H70.819	H73.91	H81.399	H92.21	J01.30	K00.5	K08.114	K12.32
H61.891	H66.3X3	H70.891	H73.92	H81.4	H92.22	J01.31	K00.6	K08.119	K12.33
H61.892	H66.3X9	H70.892	H73.93	H81.8X1	H92.23	J01.40	K00.7	K08.121	K12.39
H61.893	H66.40	H70.893	H74.01	H81.8X2	H93.011	J01.41	K00.8	K08.122	K13.0
H61.899	H66.41	H70.899	H74.02	H81.8X3	H93.012	J01.80	K00.9	K08.123	K13.1
H61.90	H66.42	H70.90	H74.03	H81.8X9	H93.013	J01.81	K01.0	K08.124	K13.21
H61.91	H66.43	H70.91	H74.09	H81.90	H93.019	J01.90	K01.1	K08.129	K13.22
H61.92	H66.90	H70.92	H74.11	H81.91	H93.091	J01.91	K02.3	K08.131	K13.23
H61.93	H66.91	H70.93	H74.12	H81.92	H93.092	J02.0	K02.51	K08.132	K13.24
H62.40	H66.92	H71.00	H74.13	H81.93	H93.093	J02.8	K02.52	K08.133	K13.29
H62.41	H66.93	H71.01	H74.19	H82.1	H93.099	J02.9	K02.53	K08.134	K13.3
H62.42	H67.1	H71.02	H74.20	H82.2	H93.11	J03.00	K02.61	K08.139	K13.4
H62.43	H67.2	H71.03	H74.21	H82.3	H93.12	J03.01	K02.62	K08.191	K13.5
H62.8X1	H67.3	H71.10	H74.22	H82.9	H93.13	J03.80	K02.63	K08.192	K13.6
H62.8X2	H67.9	H71.11	H74.23	H83.01	H93.19	J03.81	K02.7	K08.193	K13.70
H62.8X3	H68.001	H71.12	H74.311	H83.02	H93.211	J03.90	K02.9	K08.194	K13.79
H62.8X9	H68.002	H71.13	H74.312	H83.03	H93.212	J03.91	K03.0	K08.199	K14.0
H65.00	H68.003	H71.20	H74.313	H83.09	H93.213	J04.0	K03.1	K08.20	K14.1
H65.01	H68.009	H71.21	H74.319	H83.11	H93.219	J04.2	K03.2	K08.21	K14.2
H65.02	H68.011	H71.22	H74.321	H83.12	H93.221	J04.30	K03.3	K08.22	K14.3
H65.03	H68.012	H71.23	H74.322	H83.13	H93.222	J04.31	K03.4	K08.23	K14.4
H65.04	H68.013	H71.30	H74.323	H83.19	H93.223	J05.0	K03.5	K08.24	K14.5
H65.05	H68.019	H71.31	H74.329	H83.2X1	H93.229	J05.10	K03.6	K08.25	K14.6
H65.06	H68.021	H71.32	H74.391	H83.2X2	H93.231	J05.11	K03.7	K08.26	K14.8
H65.07	H68.022	H71.33	H74.392	H83.2X3	H93.232	J06.0	K03.81	K08.3	K14.9
H65.111	H68.023	H71.90	H74.393	H83.2X9	H93.233	J06.9	K03.89	K08.401	M26.00
H65.112	H68.029	H71.91	H74.399	H83.3X1	H93.239	J11.1	K03.9	K08.402	M26.01
H65.113	H68.101	H71.92	H74.40	H83.3X2	H93.241	J30.0	K04.01	K08.403	M26.02
H65.114	H68.102	H71.93	H74.41	H83.3X9	H93.242	J30.1	K04.02	K08.404	M26.03
H65.115	H68.103	H72.00	H74.42	H83.8X1	H93.243	J30.2	K04.1	K08.409	M26.04
H65.116	H68.109	H72.01	H74.43	H83.8X2	H93.249	J30.5	K04.2	K08.411	M26.05
H65.117	H68.111	H72.02	H74.8X1	H83.8X3	H93.291	J30.81	K04.3	K08.412	M26.06
H65.119	H68.112	H72.03	H74.8X2	H83.8X9	H93.292	J30.89	K04.4	K08.413	M26.07
H65.191	H68.113	H72.10	H74.8X3	H83.90	H93.293	J30.9	K04.5	K08.414	M26.09
H65.192	H68.119	H72.11	H74.8X9	H83.91	H93.299	J31.0	K04.6	K08.419	M26.10
H65.193	H68.121	H72.12	H74.90	H83.92	H93.3X1	J31.1	K04.7	K08.421	M26.11
H65.194	H68.122	H72.13	H74.91	H83.93	H93.3X2	J31.2	K04.8	K08.422	M26.12
H65.195	H68.123	H72.2X1	H74.92	H90.0	H93.3X9	J32.0	K04.90	K08.423	M26.19
H65.196	H68.129	H72.2X2	H74.93	H90.11	H93.8X1	J32.1	K04.99	K08.424	M26.20
H65.197	H68.131	H72.2X3	H75.00	H90.12	H93.8X2	J32.2	K05.00	K08.429	M26.211
H65.199	H68.132	H72.2X9	H75.01	H90.2	H93.8X3	J32.3	K05.01	K08.431	M26.212
H65.20	H68.133	H72.811	H75.02	H90.3	H93.8X8	J32.4	K05.10	K08.432	M26.213
H65.21	H68.139	H72.812	H75.03	H90.41	H93.90	J32.8	K05.11	K08.433	M26.219
H65.22	H69.00	H72.813	H75.80	H90.42	H93.91	J32.9	K05.20	K08.434	M26.220
H65.23	H69.01	H72.819	H75.81	H90.5	H93.92	J33.0	K05.211	K08.439	M26.221
H65.30	H69.02	H72.821	H75.82	H90.6	H93.93	J33.1	K05.212	K08.491	M26.23
H65.31	H69.03	H72.822	H75.83	H90.71	H93.A1	J33.8	K05.213	K08.492	M26.24
H65.32	H69.80	H72.823	H80.00	H90.72	H93.A2	J33.9	K05.219	K08.493	M26.25
H65.33	H69.81	H72.829	H80.01	H90.8	H93.A3	J34.0	K05.221	K08.494	M26.29
H65.411	H69.82	H72.90	H80.02	H90.A11	H93.A9	J34.1	K05.222	K08.499	M26.30
H65.412	H69.83	H72.91	H80.03	H90.A12	H94.00	J34.2	K05.223	K08.50	M26.31
H65.413	H69.90	H72.92	H80.10	H90.A21	H94.01	J34.3	K05.229	K08.51	M26.32
H65.419	H69.91	H72.93	H80.11	H90.A22	H94.02	J34.81	K05.30	K08.52	M26.33
H65.491	H69.92	H73.001	H80.12	H90.A31	H94.03	J34.89	K05.311	K08.530	M26.34
H65.492	H69.93	H73.002	H80.13	H90.A32	H94.80	J34.9	K05.312	K08.531	M26.35
H65.493	H70.001	H73.009	H80.20	H91.01	H94.81	J35.01	K05.313	K08.539	M26.36
H65.499	H70.002	H73.011	H80.21	H91.02	H94.82	J35.02	K05.319	K08.54	M26.37
H65.90	H70.003	H73.012	H80.22	H91.03	H94.83	J35.03	K05.321	K08.55	M26.39
H65.91	H70.009	H73.019	H80.23	H91.09	H95.00	J35.1	K05.322	K08.56	M26.4
H65.92	H70.011	H73.091	H80.80	H91.10	H95.01	J35.2	K05.323	K08.59	M26.50
H65.93	H70.012	H73.092	H80.81	H91.11	H95.02	J35.3	K05.329	K08.81	M26.51
H66.001	H70.013	H73.093	H80.82	H91.12	H95.03	J35.8	K05.4	K08.82	M26.52
H66.002	H70.019	H73.099	H80.83	H91.13	H95.111	J35.9	K05.5	K08.89	M26.53
H66.003	H70.091	H73.10	H80.90	H91.20	H95.112	J36	K05.6	K08.9	M26.54
H66.004	H70.092	H73.11	H80.91	H91.21	H95.113	J37.0	K06.010	K09.0	M26.55
H66.005	H70.093	H73.12	H80.92	H91.22	H95.119	J37.1	K06.011	K09.1	M26.56
H66.006	H70.099	H73.13	H80.93	H91.23	H95.121	J38.00	K06.012	K09.8	M26.57
H66.007	H70.10	H73.20	H81.01	H91.3	H95.122	J38.01	K06.013	K09.9	M26.59
H66.009	H70.11	H73.21	H81.02	H91.8X1	H95.123	J38.02	K06.020	K11.0	M26.6601
H66.011	H70.12	H73.22	H81.03	H91.8X2	H95.129	J38.1	K06.021	K11.1	M26.602
H66.012	H70.13	H73.23	H81.09	H91.8X3	H95.131	J38.2	K06.022	K11.20	M26.603
H66.013	H70.201	H73.811	H81.10	H91.8X9	H95.132	J38.3	K06.023	K11.21	M26.609
H66.014	H70.202	H73.812	H81.11	H91.90	H95.133	J38.4	K06.1	K11.22	M26.611
H66.015	H70.203	H73.813	H81.12	H91.91	H95.139	J38.5	K06.2	K11.23	M26.612
H66.016	H70.209	H73.819	H81.13	H91.92	H95.191	J38.6	K06.3	K11.3	M26.613
H66.017	H70.211	H73.821	H81.20	H91.93	H95.192	J38.7	K06.8	K11.4	M26.619
H66.019	H70.212	H73.822	H81.21	H92.01	H95.193	J39.0	K06.9	K11.5	M26.621
H66.10	H70.213	H73.823	H81.22	H92.02	H95.199	J39.1	K08.0	K11.6	M26.622
H66.11	H70.219	H73.829	H81.23	H92.03	J00	J39.2	K08.101	K11.7	M26.623
H66.12	H70.221	H73.891	H81.311	H92.09	J01.00	J39.3	K08.102	K11.8	M26.629
H66.13	H70.222	H73.892	H81.312	H92.10	J01.01	J39.8	K08.103	K11.9	M26.631
H66.20	H70.223	H73.891	H81.313	H92.11	J01.10	J39.9	K08.104	K12.0	M26.632
H66.21	H70.229	H73.892	H81.319	H92.12	J01.11	K00.0	K08.109	K12.1	M26.633
H66.22	H70.811	H73.893	H81.391	H92.13	J01.20	K00.1	K08.111	K12.2	M26.639
H66.23	H70.812	H73.899	H81.392			K00.2	K08.112	K12.30	M26.69
						K00.3			

M26.70	Q16.1	Q31.3	Q38.7	S01.312A	S02.401B	S02.610A	S02.66XB	S09.22XA	T16.1XXA
M26.71	Q16.2	Q31.5	Q38.8	S01.319A	S02.402A	S02.610B	S02.670A	S09.301A	T16.2XXA
M26.72	Q16.3	Q31.8	R04.0	S01.321A	S02.402B	S02.611A	S02.670B	S09.302A	T16.9XXA
M26.73	Q16.4	Q31.9	R04.1	S01.322A	S02.40AA	S02.611B	S02.671A	S09.309A	T17.0XXA
M26.74	Q16.5	Q32.0	R06.5	S01.329A	S02.40AB	S02.612A	S02.671B	S09.311A	T17.1XXA
M26.79	Q16.9	Q32.1	R06.7	S01.331A	S02.40BA	S02.612B	S02.672A	S09.312A	T17.200A
M26.81	Q17.0	Q32.2	R07.0	S01.332A	S02.40BB	S02.620A	S02.672B	S09.313A	T17.208A
M26.82	Q17.1	Q32.3	R09.81	S01.339A	S02.40CA	S02.620B	S02.69XA	S09.319A	T17.210A
M26.89	Q17.2	Q32.4	R09.82	S01.341A	S02.40CB	S02.621A	S02.69XB	S09.391A	T17.218A
M26.9	Q17.3	Q35.1	R19.6	S01.342A	S02.40DA	S02.621B	S03.00XA	S09.392A	T17.220A
M27.0	Q17.4	Q35.3	R42	S01.349A	S02.40DB	S02.622A	S03.01XA	S09.399A	T17.228A
M27.1	Q17.5	Q35.5	R49.0	S01.351A	S02.40EA	S02.622B	S03.02XA	S09.91XA	T17.290A
M27.2	Q17.8	Q35.7	R49.1	S01.352A	S02.40EB	S02.630A	S03.03XA	S11.011A	T17.298A
M27.3	Q17.9	Q35.9	R49.21	S01.359A	S02.40FA	S02.630B	S03.2XXA	S11.012A	T17.300A
M27.40	Q18.0	Q36.0	R49.22	S01.501A	S02.40FB	S02.631A	S03.40XA	S11.013A	T17.308A
M27.49	Q18.1	Q36.1	R49.8	S01.502A	S02.411A	S02.631B	S03.41XA	S11.014A	T17.310A
M27.51	Q18.2	Q36.9	R49.9	S01.511A	S02.411B	S02.632A	S03.42XA	S11.015A	T17.318A
M27.52	Q18.4	Q37.0	R68.2	S01.512A	S02.412A	S02.632B	S03.43XA	S11.019A	T17.320A
M27.53	Q18.5	Q37.1	R68.84	S01.521A	S02.412B	S02.640A	S04.60XA	S11.031A	T17.328A
M27.59	Q18.6	Q37.2	R94.120	S01.522A	S02.413A	S02.640B	S04.61XA	S11.032A	T17.390A
M27.61	Q18.7	Q37.3	R94.121	S01.531A	S02.413B	S02.641A	S04.62XA	S11.033A	T17.398A
M27.62	Q18.8	Q37.4	S01.20XA	S01.532A	S02.5XXA	S02.641B	S08.111A	S11.034A	T18.0XXA
M27.63	Q30.0	Q37.5	S01.21XA	S01.541A	S02.5XXB	S02.642A	S08.112A	S11.035A	T28.0XXA
M27.69	Q30.1	Q37.8	S01.22XA	S01.542A	S02.600A	S02.642B	S08.119A	S11.039A	T28.5XXA
M27.8	Q30.2	Q37.9	S01.23XA	S01.551A	S02.600B	S02.650A	S08.121A	S11.20XA	T70.0XXA
M27.9	Q30.3	Q38.0	S01.24XA	S01.552A	S02.601A	S02.650B	S08.122A	S11.21XA	T70.1XXA
M95.0	Q30.8	Q38.1	S01.25XA	S02.2XXA	S02.601B	S02.651A	S08.129A	S11.22XA	T75.3XXA
M95.10	Q30.9	Q38.2	S01.301A	S02.2XXB	S02.602A	S02.651B	S08.811A	S11.23XA	
M95.11	Q31.0	Q38.3	S01.302A	S02.400A	S02.602B	S02.652A	S08.812A	S11.24XA	
M95.12	Q31.1	Q38.4	S01.309A	S02.400B	S02.609A	S02.652B	S09.20XA	S11.25XA	
Q16.0	Q31.2	Q38.6	S01.311A	S02.401A	S02.609B	S02.66XA	S09.21XA	S12.8XXA	

MDC 04 Diseases And Disorders Of The Respiratory System

A02.22	C34.30	D3A.090	J15.29	J45.40	J69.8	J93.82	J98.9	R04.9	S22.5XXB
A06.5	C34.31	D49.1	J15.3	J45.41	J70.0	J93.83	J99	R05	S23.41XA
A15.0	C34.32	D86.0	J15.4	J45.42	J70.1	J93.9	K76.81	R06.00	S23.420A
A15.4	C34.80	D86.1	J15.5	J45.50	J70.2	J94.0	M05.10	R06.01	S23.421A
A15.5	C34.81	D86.2	J15.6	J45.51	J70.3	J94.1	M05.111	R06.02	S23.428A
A15.6	C34.82	D86.3	J15.7	J45.52	J70.4	J94.2	M05.112	R06.03	S23.429A
A15.7	C34.90	D86.81	J15.8	J45.901	J70.5	J94.8	M05.119	R06.09	S26.00XS
A15.8	C34.91	D86.82	J15.9	J45.902	J70.8	J94.9	M05.121	R06.1	S26.01XS
A15.9	C34.92	D86.83	J16.0	J45.909	J70.9	J95.00	M05.122	R06.2	S26.020S
A20.2	C38.1	D86.84	J16.8	J45.990	J80	J95.01	M05.129	R06.3	S26.021S
A21.2	C38.2	D86.85	J17	J45.991	J81.0	J95.02	M05.131	R06.4	S26.022S
A22.1	C38.3	D86.86	J18.0	J45.998	J81.1	J95.03	M05.132	R06.6	S26.09XS
A31.0	C38.4	D86.87	J18.1	J47.0	J82	J95.04	M05.139	R06.81	S26.10XS
A37.00	C38.8	D86.89	J18.2	J47.1	J84.01	J95.09	M05.141	R06.82	S26.11XS
A37.01	C39.9	D86.9	J18.8	J47.9	J84.02	J95.1	M05.142	R06.83	S26.12XS
A37.10	C45.0	E66.2	J18.9	J60	J84.03	J95.2	M05.149	R06.89	S26.19XS
A37.11	C46.50	E84.0	J20.0	J61	J84.09	J95.3	M05.151	R06.9	S26.90XS
A37.80	C46.51	G47.32	J20.1	J62.0	J84.10	J95.4	M05.152	R07.1	S26.91XS
A37.81	C46.52	I26.01	J20.2	J62.8	J84.111	J95.5	M05.159	R07.81	S26.92XS
A37.90	C76.1	I26.02	J20.3	J63.0	J84.112	J95.811	M05.161	R09.01	S26.99XS
A37.91	C78.00	I26.09	J20.4	J63.1	J84.113	J95.812	M05.162	R09.02	S27.0XXA
A42.0	C78.01	I26.90	J20.5	J63.2	J84.114	J95.821	M05.169	R09.1	S27.0XXS
A43.0	C78.02	I26.92	J20.6	J63.3	J84.115	J95.822	M05.171	R09.2	S27.1XXA
A48.1	C78.1	I26.93	J20.7	J63.4	J84.116	J95.84	M05.172	R09.3	S27.1XXS
A52.72	C78.2	I26.94	J20.8	J63.5	J84.117	J95.851	M05.179	R68.3	S27.2XXA
B01.2	C78.30	I26.99	J20.9	J63.6	J84.17	J95.859	M05.19	R76.11	S27.2XXS
B05.2	C78.39	I27.82	J21.0	J64	J84.2	J95.88	M34.81	R76.12	S27.301A
B25.0	C7A.090	J04.10	J21.1	J65	J84.81	J95.89	M94.0	R91.1	S27.301S
B33.0	D02.1	J04.11	J21.8	J66.0	J84.82	J96.00	M99.18	R91.8	S27.302A
B37.1	D02.20	J09.X1	J21.9	J66.1	J84.83	J96.01	P27.0	R94.2	S27.302S
B38.0	D02.21	J09.X2	J22	J66.2	J84.841	J96.02	P27.1	S11.021A	S27.309A
B38.1	D02.22	J10.00	J39.8	J66.8	J84.842	J96.10	P27.8	S11.022A	S27.309S
B38.2	D02.3	J10.01	J40	J67.0	J84.843	J96.11	P27.9	S11.023A	S27.311A
B39.0	D02.4	J10.08	J41.0	J67.1	J84.848	J96.12	Q33.0	S11.024A	S27.311S
B39.1	D14.2	J10.1	J41.1	J67.2	J84.89	J96.20	Q33.1	S11.025A	S27.312A
B39.2	D14.30	J11.00	J41.8	J67.3	J84.9	J96.21	Q33.2	S11.029A	S27.312S
B44.0	D14.31	J11.08	J42	J67.4	J85.0	J96.22	Q33.3	S22.31XA	S27.319A
B44.81	D14.32	J12.0	J43.0	J67.5	J85.1	J96.90	Q33.4	S22.31XB	S27.319S
B58.3	D14.4	J12.1	J43.1	J67.6	J85.2	J96.91	Q33.5	S22.32XA	S27.321A
B59	D15.2	J12.2	J43.2	J67.7	J85.3	J96.92	Q33.6	S22.32XB	S27.321S
B66.4	D15.7	J12.3	J43.8	J67.8	J86.0	J98.01	Q33.8	S22.39XA	S27.322A
B67.1	D15.9	J12.81	J43.9	J67.9	J86.9	J98.09	Q33.9	S22.39XB	S27.322S
B90.9	D16.7	J12.89	J44.0	J68.0	J90	J98.11	Q34.0	S22.41XA	S27.329A
C33	D17.4	J12.9	J44.1	J68.1	J91.0	J98.19	Q34.1	S22.41XB	S27.329S
C34.00	D19.0	J13	J44.9	J68.2	J91.8	J98.2	Q34.8	S22.42XA	S27.331A
C34.01	D38.1	J14	J45.20	J68.3	J92.0	J98.3	Q34.9	S22.42XB	S27.331S
C34.02	D38.2	J15.0	J45.21	J68.4	J92.9	J98.4	Q79.0	S22.43XA	S27.332A
C34.10	D38.3	J15.1	J45.22	J68.8	J93.0	J98.51	Q79.1	S22.43XB	S27.332S
C34.11	D38.4	J15.20	J45.30	J68.9	J93.11	J98.59	R04.2	S22.49XA	S27.339A
C34.12	D38.5	J15.211	J45.31	J69.0	J93.12	J98.6	R04.81	S22.49XB	S27.339S
C34.2	D38.6	J15.212	J45.32	J69.1	J93.81	J98.8	R04.89	S22.5XXA	S27.391A

S27.391S	S27.419A	S27.491S	S27.60XA	S27.813S	S43.204A	T17.400A	T17.598A	T17.990A	T86.811
S27.392A	S27.419S	S27.492A	S27.60XS	S27.818S	S43.205A	T17.408A	T17.800A	T17.998A	T86.812
S27.392S	S27.421A	S27.492S	S27.63XA	S27.819S	S43.206A	T17.410A	T17.808A	T27.0XXA	T86.818
S27.399A	S27.421S	S27.499A	S27.63XS	S27.892A	S43.211A	T17.418A	T17.810A	T27.1XXA	T86.819
S27.399S	S27.422A	S27.499S	S27.69XA	S27.892S	S43.212A	T17.420A	T17.818A	T27.2XXA	Z43.0
S27.401A	S27.422S	S27.50XA	S27.69XS	S27.893A	S43.213A	T17.428A	T17.820A	T27.3XXA	Z90.2
S27.401S	S27.429A	S27.50XS	S27.802A	S27.893S	S43.214A	T17.490A	T17.828A	T27.4XXA	Z94.2
S27.402A	S27.429S	S27.51XA	S27.802S	S27.898A	S43.215A	T17.498A	T17.890A	T27.5XXA	
S27.402S	S27.431A	S27.51XS	S27.803A	S27.898S	S43.216A	T17.500A	T17.898A	T27.6XXA	
S27.409A	S27.431S	S27.52XA	S27.803S	S27.899A	S43.221A	T17.508A	T17.900A	T27.7XXA	
S27.409S	S27.432A	S27.52XS	S27.808A	S27.899S	S43.222A	T17.510A	T17.908A	T79.0XXA	
S27.411A	S27.432S	S27.53XA	S27.808S	S27.9XXS	S43.223A	T17.518A	T17.910A	T79.1XXA	
S27.411S	S27.439A	S27.53XS	S27.809A	S43.201A	S43.224A	T17.520A	T17.918A	T79.7XXA	
S27.412A	S27.439S	S27.59XA	S27.809S	S43.202A	S43.225A	T17.528A	T17.920A	T80.0XXA	
S27.412S	S27.491A	S27.59XS	S27.812S	S43.203A	S43.226A	T17.590A	T17.928A	T86.810	

MDC 05 Diseases And Disorders Of The Circulatory System

A36.81	I08.3	I25.700	I34.1	I48.19	I70.229	I70.402	I70.549	I70.731	I75.019
A39.50	I08.8	I25.701	I34.2	I48.20	I70.231	I70.403	I70.55	I70.732	I75.021
A39.51	I08.9	I25.708	I34.8	I48.21	I70.232	I70.408	I70.561	I70.733	I75.022
A39.52	I09.0	I25.709	I34.9	I48.3	I70.233	I70.409	I70.562	I70.734	I75.023
A39.53	I09.1	I25.710	I35.0	I48.4	I70.234	I70.411	I70.563	I70.735	I75.029
A52.00	I09.2	I25.711	I35.1	I48.91	I70.235	I70.412	I70.568	I70.738	I75.89
A52.01	I09.81	I25.718	I35.2	I48.92	I70.238	I70.413	I70.569	I70.739	I76
A52.02	I09.89	I25.719	I35.8	I49.01	I70.239	I70.418	I70.591	I70.741	I77.0
A52.03	I09.9	I25.720	I35.9	I49.02	I70.241	I70.419	I70.592	I70.742	I77.1
A52.04	I10	I25.721	I36.0	I49.1	I70.242	I70.421	I70.593	I70.743	I77.2
A52.05	I11.0	I25.728	I36.1	I49.2	I70.243	I70.422	I70.598	I70.744	I77.3
A52.06	I11.9	I25.729	I36.2	I49.3	I70.244	I70.423	I70.599	I70.745	I77.5
A52.09	I13.0	I25.730	I36.8	I49.40	I70.245	I70.428	I70.601	I70.748	I77.70
A54.83	I13.2	I25.731	I36.9	I49.49	I70.248	I70.429	I70.602	I70.749	I77.71
B33.20	I15.0	I25.738	I37.0	I49.5	I70.249	I70.431	I70.603	I70.75	I77.72
B33.21	I15.1	I25.739	I37.1	I49.8	I70.25	I70.432	I70.608	I70.761	I77.74
B33.22	I15.2	I25.750	I37.2	I49.9	I70.261	I70.433	I70.609	I70.762	I77.75
B33.23	I15.8	I25.751	I37.8	I50.1	I70.262	I70.434	I70.611	I70.763	I77.76
B37.6	I15.9	I25.758	I37.9	I50.20	I70.263	I70.435	I70.612	I70.768	I77.77
B57.0	I16.0	I25.759	I38	I50.21	I70.268	I70.438	I70.613	I70.769	I77.79
B57.2	I16.1	I25.760	I39	I50.22	I70.269	I70.439	I70.618	I70.791	I77.810
B58.81	I16.9	I25.761	I40.0	I50.23	I70.291	I70.441	I70.619	I70.792	I77.811
C38.0	I20.0	I25.768	I40.1	I50.30	I70.292	I70.442	I70.621	I70.793	I77.812
C45.2	I20.1	I25.769	I40.8	I50.31	I70.293	I70.443	I70.622	I70.798	I77.819
D15.1	I20.8	I25.790	I40.9	I50.32	I70.298	I70.444	I70.623	I70.799	I77.89
D18.00	I20.9	I25.791	I41	I50.33	I70.299	I70.445	I70.628	I70.8	I77.9
D18.09	I21.01	I25.798	I42.0	I50.40	I70.301	I70.448	I70.629	I70.90	I78.0
E08.51	I21.02	I25.799	I42.1	I50.41	I70.302	I70.449	I70.631	I70.91	I78.8
E08.52	I21.09	I25.810	I42.2	I50.42	I70.303	I70.45	I70.632	I70.92	I78.9
E08.59	I21.11	I25.811	I42.3	I50.43	I70.308	I70.461	I70.633	I71.00	I79.0
E09.51	I21.19	I25.812	I42.4	I50.810	I70.309	I70.462	I70.634	I71.01	I79.1
E09.52	I21.21	I25.82	I42.5	I50.811	I70.311	I70.463	I70.635	I71.02	I79.8
E09.59	I21.29	I25.83	I42.6	I50.812	I70.312	I70.468	I70.638	I71.03	I80.00
E10.51	I21.3	I25.84	I42.7	I50.813	I70.313	I70.469	I70.639	I71.1	I80.01
E10.52	I21.4	I25.89	I42.8	I50.814	I70.318	I70.491	I70.641	I71.2	I80.02
E10.59	I21.9	I25.9	I42.9	I50.82	I70.319	I70.492	I70.642	I71.3	I80.03
E11.51	I21.A1	I27.0	I43	I50.83	I70.321	I70.493	I70.643	I71.4	I80.10
E11.52	I21.A9	I27.1	I44.0	I50.84	I70.322	I70.498	I70.644	I71.5	I80.11
E11.59	I22.0	I27.20	I44.1	I50.89	I70.323	I70.499	I70.645	I71.6	I80.12
E13.51	I22.1	I27.21	I44.2	I50.9	I70.328	I70.501	I70.648	I71.8	I80.13
E13.52	I22.2	I27.22	I44.30	I51.0	I70.329	I70.502	I70.649	I71.9	I80.201
E13.59	I22.8	I27.23	I44.39	I51.1	I70.331	I70.503	I70.65	I72.0	I80.202
I01.0	I22.9	I27.24	I44.4	I51.2	I70.332	I70.508	I70.661	I72.1	I80.203
I01.1	I23.0	I27.29	I44.5	I51.3	I70.333	I70.509	I70.662	I72.3	I80.209
I01.2	I23.1	I27.81	I44.60	I51.4	I70.334	I70.511	I70.663	I72.4	I80.211
I01.8	I23.2	I27.83	I44.69	I51.5	I70.335	I70.512	I70.668	I72.5	I80.212
I01.9	I23.3	I27.89	I44.7	I51.7	I70.338	I70.513	I70.669	I72.6	I80.213
I02.0	I23.4	I27.9	I45.0	I51.81	I70.339	I70.518	I70.691	I72.8	I80.219
I02.9	I23.5	I28.0	I45.10	I51.89	I70.341	I70.519	I70.692	I72.9	I80.221
I05.0	I23.6	I28.1	I45.19	I51.9	I70.342	I70.521	I70.693	I73.1	I80.222
I05.1	I23.7	I28.8	I45.2	I52	I70.343	I70.522	I70.698	I73.81	I80.223
I05.2	I23.8	I28.9	I45.3	I67.0	I70.344	I70.523	I70.699	I73.89	I80.229
I05.8	I24.0	I30.0	I45.4	I70.0	I70.345	I70.528	I70.701	I73.9	I80.231
I05.9	I24.1	I30.1	I45.5	I70.201	I70.348	I70.529	I70.702	I74.01	I80.232
I06.0	I24.8	I30.8	I45.6	I70.202	I70.349	I70.531	I70.703	I74.09	I80.233
I06.1	I24.9	I30.9	I45.81	I70.203	I70.35	I70.532	I70.708	I74.10	I80.239
I06.2	I25.10	I31.0	I45.89	I70.208	I70.361	I70.533	I70.709	I74.11	I80.241
I06.8	I25.110	I31.1	I45.9	I70.209	I70.362	I70.534	I70.711	I74.19	I80.242
I06.9	I25.111	I31.2	I46.2	I70.211	I70.363	I70.535	I70.712	I74.2	I80.243
I07.0	I25.118	I31.3	I46.8	I70.212	I70.368	I70.538	I70.713	I74.3	I80.249
I07.1	I25.119	I31.4	I46.9	I70.213	I70.369	I70.539	I70.718	I74.4	I80.251
I07.2	I25.2	I31.8	I47.0	I70.218	I70.391	I70.541	I70.719	I74.5	I80.252
I07.8	I25.3	I31.9	I47.1	I70.219	I70.392	I70.542	I70.721	I74.8	I80.253
I07.9	I25.41	I32	I47.2	I70.221	I70.393	I70.543	I70.722	I74.9	I80.259
I08.0	I25.42	I33.0	I47.9	I70.222	I70.398	I70.544	I70.723	I75.011	I80.291
I08.1	I25.5	I33.9	I48.0	I70.223	I70.399	I70.545	I70.728	I75.012	I80.292
I08.2	I25.6	I34.0	I48.11	I70.228	I70.401	I70.548	I70.729	I75.013	I80.293

I80.299	I82.5Y9	I83.202	I96	Q26.2	S15.292S	S26.09XA	S45.011S	S55.899S	S65.802S
I80.3	I82.5Z1	I83.203	I97.0	Q26.3	S15.299S	S26.10XA	S45.012S	S55.901S	S65.809S
I80.8	I82.5Z2	I83.204	I97.110	Q26.4	S15.301S	S26.11XA	S45.019S	S55.902S	S65.811S
I80.9	I82.5Z3	I83.205	I97.111	Q26.5	S15.302S	S26.12XA	S45.091S	S55.909S	S65.812S
I82.1	I82.5Z9	I83.208	I97.120	Q26.6	S15.309S	S26.19XA	S45.092S	S55.911S	S65.819S
I82.210	I82.601	I83.209	I97.121	Q26.8	S15.311S	S26.90XA	S45.099S	S55.912S	S65.891S
I82.211	I82.602	I83.211	I97.130	Q26.9	S15.312S	S26.91XA	S45.101S	S55.919S	S65.892S
I82.220	I82.603	I83.212	I97.131	Q27.0	S15.319S	S26.92XA	S45.102S	S55.991S	S65.899S
I82.221	I82.609	I83.213	I97.190	Q27.1	S15.321S	S26.99XA	S45.109S	S55.992S	S65.901S
I82.290	I82.611	I83.214	I97.191	Q27.2	S15.322S	S35.00XS	S45.111S	S55.999S	S65.902S
I82.291	I82.612	I83.215	I97.710	Q27.30	S15.329S	S35.01XS	S45.112S	S65.001S	S65.909S
I82.401	I82.613	I83.218	I97.711	Q27.31	S15.391S	S35.02XS	S45.119S	S65.002S	S65.911S
I82.402	I82.619	I83.219	I97.790	Q27.32	S15.392S	S35.09XS	S45.191S	S65.009S	S65.912S
I82.403	I82.621	I83.221	I97.791	Q27.33	S15.399S	S35.10XS	S45.192S	S65.011S	S65.919S
I82.409	I82.622	I83.222	I97.88	Q27.34	S15.8XXS	S35.11XS	S45.199S	S65.012S	S65.991S
I82.411	I82.623	I83.223	I97.89	Q27.39	S15.9XXS	S35.12XS	S45.201S	S65.019S	S65.992S
I82.412	I82.629	I83.224	I99.8	Q27.4	S25.00XS	S35.19XS	S45.202S	S65.091S	S65.999S
I82.413	I82.701	I83.225	I99.9	Q27.8	S25.01XS	S35.211S	S45.209S	S65.092S	S75.001S
I82.419	I82.702	I83.228	M31.8	Q27.9	S25.02XS	S35.212S	S45.211S	S65.099S	S75.002S
I82.421	I82.703	I83.229	M31.9	Q28.0	S25.09XS	S35.218S	S45.212S	S65.101S	S75.009S
I82.422	I82.709	I83.811	N26.2	Q28.1	S25.101S	S35.219S	S45.291S	S65.102S	S75.011S
I82.423	I82.711	I83.812	Q20.0	Q28.8	S25.102S	S35.221S	S45.292S	S65.109S	S75.012S
I82.429	I82.712	I83.813	Q20.1	Q28.9	S25.109S	S35.222S	S45.299S	S65.111S	S75.019S
I82.431	I82.713	I83.819	Q20.2	Q87.40	S25.111S	S35.228S	S45.301S	S65.112S	S75.021S
I82.432	I82.719	I83.891	Q20.3	Q87.410	S25.112S	S35.229S	S45.302S	S65.119S	S75.022S
I82.433	I82.721	I83.892	Q20.4	Q87.418	S25.119S	S35.231S	S45.309S	S65.191S	S75.029S
I82.439	I82.722	I83.893	Q20.5	Q87.42	S25.121S	S35.232S	S45.311S	S65.192S	S75.091S
I82.441	I82.723	I83.899	Q20.6	Q87.43	S25.122S	S35.238S	S45.312S	S65.199S	S75.092S
I82.442	I82.729	I83.90	Q20.8	R00.0	S25.129S	S35.239S	S45.319S	S65.201S	S75.099S
I82.443	I82.811	I83.91	Q20.9	R00.1	S25.191S	S35.291S	S45.391S	S65.202S	S75.101S
I82.449	I82.812	I83.92	Q21.0	R00.2	S25.192S	S35.292S	S45.392S	S65.209S	S75.102S
I82.451	I82.813	I83.93	Q21.1	R00.8	S25.199S	S35.298S	S45.399S	S65.211S	S75.109S
I82.452	I82.819	I86.0	Q21.2	R00.9	S25.20XS	S35.299S	S45.801S	S65.212S	S75.111S
I82.453	I82.890	I86.4	Q21.3	R01.0	S25.21XS	S35.311S	S45.802S	S65.219S	S75.112S
I82.459	I82.891	I86.8	Q21.4	R01.1	S25.22XS	S35.318S	S45.809S	S65.291S	S75.119S
I82.461	I82.90	I87.001	Q21.8	R01.2	S25.29XS	S35.319S	S45.811S	S65.292S	S75.121S
I82.462	I82.91	I87.002	Q21.9	R03.0	S25.301S	S35.321S	S45.812S	S65.299S	S75.122S
I82.463	I82.A11	I87.003	Q22.0	R03.1	S25.302S	S35.328S	S45.819S	S65.301S	S75.129S
I82.469	I82.A12	I87.009	Q22.1	R07.2	S25.309S	S35.329S	S45.891S	S65.302S	S75.191S
I82.491	I82.A13	I87.011	Q22.2	R07.82	S25.311S	S35.331S	S45.892S	S65.309S	S75.192S
I82.492	I82.A19	I87.012	Q22.3	R07.89	S25.312S	S35.338S	S45.899S	S65.311S	S75.199S
I82.493	I82.A21	I87.013	Q22.4	R07.9	S25.319S	S35.339S	S45.901S	S65.312S	S75.201S
I82.499	I82.A22	I87.019	Q22.5	R09.89	S25.321S	S35.341S	S45.902S	S65.319S	S75.202S
I82.4Y1	I82.A23	I87.021	Q22.6	R55	S25.322S	S35.348S	S45.909S	S65.391S	S75.209S
I82.4Y2	I82.A29	I87.022	Q22.8	R57.0	S25.329S	S35.349S	S45.911S	S65.392S	S75.211S
I82.4Y3	I82.B11	I87.023	Q22.9	R57.1	S25.391S	S35.391S	S45.912S	S65.399S	S75.212S
I82.4Y9	I82.B12	I87.029	Q23.0	R57.9	S25.392S	S35.392S	S45.919S	S65.401S	S75.219S
I82.4Z1	I82.B13	I87.031	Q23.1	R58	S25.399S	S35.401S	S45.991S	S65.402S	S75.221S
I82.4Z2	I82.B19	I87.032	Q23.2	R93.1	S25.401S	S35.402S	S45.992S	S65.409S	S75.222S
I82.4Z3	I82.B21	I87.033	Q23.3	R94.30	S25.402S	S35.403S	S45.999S	S65.411S	S75.229S
I82.4Z9	I82.B22	I87.039	Q23.4	R94.31	S25.409S	S35.404S	S55.001S	S65.412S	S75.291S
I82.501	I82.B23	I87.091	Q23.8	R94.39	S25.411S	S35.405S	S55.002S	S65.419S	S75.292S
I82.502	I82.B29	I87.092	Q23.9	S09.0XXS	S25.412S	S35.406S	S55.009S	S65.491S	S75.299S
I82.503	I82.C11	I87.093	Q24.0	S15.001S	S25.419S	S35.411S	S55.011S	S65.492S	S75.801S
I82.509	I82.C12	I87.099	Q24.1	S15.002S	S25.421S	S35.412S	S55.012S	S65.499S	S75.802S
I82.511	I82.C13	I87.1	Q24.2	S15.009S	S25.422S	S35.413S	S55.019S	S65.500S	S75.809S
I82.512	I82.C19	I87.2	Q24.3	S15.011S	S25.429S	S35.414S	S55.091S	S65.501S	S75.811S
I82.513	I82.C21	I87.301	Q24.4	S15.012S	S25.491S	S35.415S	S55.099S	S65.502S	S75.812S
I82.519	I82.C22	I87.302	Q24.5	S15.019S	S25.492S	S35.416S	S55.101S	S65.503S	S75.819S
I82.521	I82.C23	I87.303	Q24.6	S15.021S	S25.499S	S35.491S	S55.102S	S65.504S	S75.891S
I82.522	I82.C29	I87.309	Q24.8	S15.022S	S25.501S	S35.492S	S55.109S	S65.505S	S75.892S
I82.523	I83.001	I87.311	Q24.9	S15.029S	S25.502S	S35.493S	S55.111S	S65.506S	S75.899S
I82.529	I83.002	I87.312	Q25.0	S15.091S	S25.509S	S35.494S	S55.112S	S65.507S	S75.901S
I82.531	I83.003	I87.313	Q25.1	S15.092S	S25.511S	S35.495S	S55.119S	S65.508S	S75.902S
I82.532	I83.004	I87.319	Q25.21	S15.099S	S25.512S	S35.496S	S55.191S	S65.509S	S75.909S
I82.533	I83.005	I87.321	Q25.29	S15.101S	S25.519S	S35.50XS	S55.199S	S65.510S	S75.911S
I82.539	I83.008	I87.322	Q25.3	S15.102S	S25.591S	S35.511S	S55.201S	S65.511S	S75.912S
I82.541	I83.009	I87.323	Q25.40	S15.109S	S25.592S	S35.512S	S55.202S	S65.512S	S75.919S
I82.542	I83.011	I87.329	Q25.41	S15.111S	S25.599S	S35.513S	S55.209S	S65.513S	S75.991S
I82.543	I83.012	I87.331	Q25.42	S15.112S	S25.801S	S35.514S	S55.211S	S65.514S	S75.992S
I82.549	I83.013	I87.332	Q25.43	S15.119S	S25.802S	S35.515S	S55.212S	S65.515S	S75.999S
I82.551	I83.014	I87.333	Q25.44	S15.121S	S25.809S	S35.516S	S55.219S	S65.516S	S85.001S
I82.552	I83.015	I87.339	Q25.45	S15.122S	S25.811S	S35.531S	S55.291S	S65.517S	S85.002S
I82.553	I83.018	I87.391	Q25.46	S15.129S	S25.812S	S35.532S	S55.292S	S65.518S	S85.009S
I82.559	I83.019	I87.392	Q25.47	S15.191S	S25.819S	S35.533S	S55.299S	S65.519S	S85.011S
I82.561	I83.021	I87.393	Q25.48	S15.192S	S25.891S	S35.534S	S55.801S	S65.590S	S85.012S
I82.562	I83.022	I87.399	Q25.49	S15.199S	S25.892S	S35.535S	S55.802S	S65.591S	S85.019S
I82.563	I83.023	I87.8	Q25.5	S15.201S	S25.899S	S35.536S	S55.809S	S65.592S	S85.091S
I82.569	I83.024	I87.9	Q25.6	S15.202S	S25.90XS	S35.59XS	S55.811S	S65.593S	S85.092S
I82.591	I83.025	I95.0	Q25.71	S15.209S	S25.91XS	S35.8X1S	S55.812S	S65.594S	S85.099S
I82.592	I83.028	I95.1	Q25.72	S15.211S	S25.99XS	S35.8X8S	S55.819S	S65.595S	S85.101S
I82.593	I83.029	I95.2	Q25.79	S15.212S	S26.00XA	S35.8X9S	S55.891S	S65.596S	S85.102S
I82.599	I83.10	I95.3	Q25.8	S15.219S	S26.01XA	S35.90XS	S55.892S	S65.597S	S85.109S
I82.5Y1	I83.11	I95.81	Q25.9	S15.221S	S26.020A	S35.91XS	S55.899S	S65.598S	S85.111S
I82.5Y2	I83.12	I95.89	Q26.0	S15.222S	S26.021A	S45.001S	S55.891S	S65.599S	S85.112S
I82.5Y3	I83.201	I95.9	Q26.1	S15.229S	S26.022A	S45.002S	S55.892S	S65.801S	S85.119S
				S15.291S		S45.009S			

S85.121S	S85.219S	S85.512S	S95.011S	S95.809S	T81.72XA	T82.311A	T82.513A	T82.595A	T86.290
S85.122S	S85.291S	S85.519S	S95.012S	S95.811S	T82.01XA	T82.312A	T82.514A	T82.598A	T86.298
S85.129S	S85.299S	S85.591S	S95.019S	S95.812S	T82.02XA	T82.319A	T82.515A	T82.599A	T86.30
S85.131S	S85.301S	S85.592S	S95.091S	S95.819S	T82.03XA	T82.320A	T82.518A	T82.6XXA	T86.31
S85.132S	S85.302S	S85.599S	S95.092S	S95.891S	T82.09XA	T82.321A	T82.519A	T82.7XXA	T86.32
S85.139S	S85.309S	S85.801S	S95.099S	S95.892S	T82.110A	T82.322A	T82.520A	T82.817A	T86.33
S85.141S	S85.311S	S85.802S	S95.101S	S95.899S	T82.111A	T82.328A	T82.521A	T82.818A	T86.39
S85.142S	S85.312S	S85.809S	S95.102S	S95.901S	T82.118A	T82.329A	T82.522A	T82.827A	Z45.010
S85.149S	S85.319S	S85.811S	S95.109S	S95.902S	T82.119A	T82.330A	T82.523A	T82.828A	Z45.018
S85.151S	S85.391S	S85.812S	S95.111S	S95.909S	T82.120A	T82.331A	T82.524A	T82.837A	Z45.02
S85.152S	S85.392S	S85.819S	S95.112S	S95.911S	T82.121A	T82.332A	T82.525A	T82.838A	Z45.09
S85.159S	S85.399S	S85.891S	S95.119S	S95.912S	T82.128A	T82.338A	T82.528A	T82.847A	Z94.1
S85.161S	S85.401S	S85.892S	S95.191S	S95.919S	T82.129A	T82.339A	T82.529A	T82.848A	Z94.3
S85.162S	S85.402S	S85.899S	S95.192S	S95.991S	T82.190A	T82.339A	T82.530A	T82.855A	Z95.2
S85.169S	S85.409S	S85.901S	S95.199S	S95.992S	T82.191A	T82.390A	T82.531A	T82.856A	Z95.3
S85.171S	S85.411S	S85.902S	S95.201S	S95.999S	T82.198A	T82.391A	T82.532A	T82.857A	Z95.4
S85.172S	S85.412S	S85.909S	S95.202S	T80.1XXA	T82.199A	T82.392A	T82.533A	T82.858A	Z95.811
S85.179S	S85.419S	S85.911S	S95.209S	T80.211A	T82.211A	T82.398A	T82.534A	T82.867A	Z95.812
S85.181S	S85.491S	S85.912S	S95.211S	T80.212A	T82.212A	T82.399A	T82.535A	T82.868A	Z95.820
S85.182S	S85.492S	S85.919S	S95.212S	T80.218A	T82.213A	T82.41XA	T82.538A	T82.897A	Z95.828
S85.189S	S85.499S	S85.991S	S95.219S	T80.219A	T82.218A	T82.42XA	T82.539A	T82.898A	
S85.201S	S85.501S	S85.992S	S95.291S	T80.810A	T82.221A	T82.43XA	T82.590A	T82.9XXA	
S85.202S	S85.502S	S85.999S	S95.292S	T80.818A	T82.222A	T82.49XA	T82.591A	T86.20	
S85.209S	S85.509S	S95.001S	S95.299S	T80.90XA	T82.223A	T82.510A	T82.592A	T86.21	
S85.211S	S85.511S	S95.002S	S95.801S	T81.718A	T82.228A	T82.511A	T82.593A	T86.22	
S85.212S		S95.009S	S95.802S	T81.719A	T82.310A	T82.512A	T82.594A	T86.23	

MDC 06 Diseases And Disorders Of The Digestive System

A00.0	A54.6	C17.2	C7B.04	D48.4	K26.7	K35.30	K45.8	K51.413	K55.069
A00.1	A54.85	C17.3	D00.1	D49.0	K26.9	K35.31	K46.0	K51.414	K55.1
A00.9	A56.3	C17.8	D00.2	E16.4	K27.0	K35.32	K46.1	K51.418	K55.20
A02.0	B00.81	C17.9	D01.0	E73.0	K27.1	K35.33	K46.9	K51.419	K55.21
A03.0	B37.81	C18.0	D01.1	E73.1	K27.2	K35.80	K50.00	K51.50	K55.30
A03.1	B37.82	C18.1	D01.2	E73.8	K27.3	K35.890	K50.011	K51.511	K55.31
A03.2	B68.0	C18.2	D01.3	E73.9	K27.4	K35.891	K50.012	K51.512	K55.32
A03.3	B68.1	C18.3	D01.40	E74.0	K27.5	K36	K50.013	K51.513	K55.33
A03.8	B68.9	C18.4	D01.49	E74.11	K27.6	K37	K50.014	K51.514	K55.8
A03.9	B69.0	C18.5	D01.7	E74.12	K27.7	K38.0	K50.018	K51.518	K55.9
A04.0	B69.1	C18.6	D01.9	E74.19	K27.9	K38.1	K50.019	K51.519	K56.0
A04.1	B69.81	C18.7	D12.0	E74.31	K28.0	K38.2	K50.10	K51.80	K56.1
A04.2	B69.89	C18.8	D12.1	E74.39	K28.1	K38.3	K50.111	K51.811	K56.2
A04.3	B69.9	C18.9	D12.2	E84.19	K28.2	K38.8	K50.112	K51.812	K56.3
A04.4	B70.0	C19	D12.3	I77.4	K28.3	K38.9	K50.113	K51.813	K56.41
A04.5	B70.1	C20	D12.4	I85.00	K28.4	K40.00	K50.114	K51.814	K56.49
A04.6	B71.0	C21.0	D12.5	I85.01	K28.5	K40.01	K50.118	K51.818	K56.50
A04.71	B71.1	C21.1	D12.6	I85.10	K28.6	K40.10	K50.119	K51.819	K56.51
A04.72	B71.8	C21.2	D12.7	I85.11	K28.7	K40.11	K50.80	K51.90	K56.52
A04.8	B71.9	C21.8	D12.8	I88.0	K28.9	K40.20	K50.811	K51.911	K56.600
A04.9	B76.0	C26.0	D12.9	K20.0	K29.00	K40.21	K50.812	K51.912	K56.601
A05.0	B76.1	C26.9	D13.0	K20.8	K29.01	K40.30	K50.813	K51.913	K56.609
A05.2	B76.8	C45.1	D13.1	K20.9	K29.20	K40.31	K50.814	K51.914	K56.690
A05.3	B76.9	C46.4	D13.2	K21.0	K29.21	K40.40	K50.818	K51.918	K56.691
A05.4	B77.0	C48.1	D13.30	K21.9	K29.30	K40.41	K50.819	K51.919	K56.699
A05.5	B77.81	C48.2	D13.39	K22.0	K29.31	K40.90	K50.90	K52.0	K56.7
A05.8	B77.89	C48.8	D13.9	K22.10	K29.40	K40.91	K50.911	K52.1	K57.00
A05.9	B77.9	C49.A0	D17.5	K22.11	K29.41	K41.00	K50.912	K52.21	K57.01
A06.0	B78.0	C49.A1	D18.03	K22.2	K29.50	K41.01	K50.913	K52.22	K57.10
A06.1	B78.7	C49.A2	D19.1	K22.3	K29.51	K41.10	K50.914	K52.29	K57.11
A06.2	B78.9	C49.A3	D20.0	K22.4	K29.60	K41.11	K50.918	K52.3	K57.12
A07.0	B79	C49.A4	D20.1	K22.5	K29.61	K41.20	K50.919	K52.81	K57.13
A07.1	B80	C49.A5	D37.1	K22.6	K29.70	K41.21	K51.00	K52.82	K57.20
A07.2	B81.0	C49.A9	D37.2	K22.70	K29.71	K41.30	K51.011	K52.831	K57.21
A07.3	B81.1	C76.2	D37.3	K22.710	K29.80	K41.31	K51.012	K52.832	K57.30
A07.4	B81.2	C78.4	D37.4	K22.711	K29.81	K41.40	K51.013	K52.838	K57.31
A07.8	B81.3	C78.5	D37.5	K22.719	K29.90	K41.41	K51.014	K52.839	K57.32
A07.9	B81.8	C78.6	D37.8	K22.8	K29.91	K41.90	K51.018	K52.89	K57.33
A08.0	B82.0	C78.80	D37.9	K22.9	K30	K41.91	K51.019	K52.9	K57.40
A08.11	B82.9	C78.89	D3A.010	K23	K31.0	K42.0	K51.20	K55.011	K57.41
A08.19	C15.3	C7A.010	D3A.011	K25.0	K31.1	K42.1	K51.211	K55.012	K57.50
A08.2	C15.4	C7A.011	D3A.012	K25.1	K31.2	K42.9	K51.212	K55.019	K57.51
A08.31	C15.5	C7A.012	D3A.019	K25.2	K31.3	K43.0	K51.213	K55.021	K57.52
A08.32	C15.8	C7A.019	D3A.020	K25.3	K31.4	K43.1	K51.214	K55.022	K57.53
A08.39	C15.9	C7A.020	D3A.021	K25.4	K31.5	K43.2	K51.218	K55.029	K57.80
A08.4	C16.0	C7A.021	D3A.022	K25.5	K31.6	K43.3	K51.219	K55.031	K57.81
A08.8	C16.1	C7A.022	D3A.023	K25.6	K31.7	K43.4	K51.30	K55.032	K57.90
A09	C16.2	C7A.023	D3A.024	K25.7	K31.811	K43.5	K51.311	K55.039	K57.91
A18.31	C16.3	C7A.024	D3A.025	K25.9	K31.819	K43.6	K51.312	K55.041	K57.92
A18.32	C16.4	C7A.025	D3A.026	K26.0	K31.82	K43.7	K51.313	K55.042	K57.93
A18.39	C16.5	C7A.026	D3A.029	K26.1	K31.83	K43.9	K51.314	K55.049	K58.0
A18.83	C16.6	C7A.092	D3A.092	K26.2	K31.84	K44.0	K51.318	K55.051	K58.1
A21.3	C16.8	C7A.094	D3A.094	K26.3	K31.89	K44.1	K51.319	K55.052	K58.2
A22.2	C16.9	C7A.095	D3A.095	K26.4	K31.9	K44.9	K51.40	K55.059	K58.8
A42.1	C17.0	C7A.096	D3A.096	K26.5	K35.20	K45.0	K51.411	K55.061	K58.9
A51.1	C17.1		D48.3	K26.6	K35.21	K45.1	K51.412	K55.062	K59.00

K59.01	K64.9	K94.19	Q43.6	R13.11	S27.818A	S36.112S	S36.409S	S36.522A	S36.93XS
K59.02	K65.0	K94.20	Q43.7	R13.12	S27.819A	S36.113S	S36.410A	S36.522S	S36.99XA
K59.03	K65.1	K94.21	Q43.8	R13.13	S31.600A	S36.114S	S36.410S	S36.523A	S36.99XS
K59.04	K65.2	K94.22	Q43.9	R13.14	S31.601A	S36.115S	S36.418A	S36.523S	S37.001S
K59.09	K65.3	K94.23	Q45.8	R13.19	S31.602A	S36.116S	S36.418S	S36.528A	S37.002S
K59.1	K65.4	K94.29	Q45.9	R14.0	S31.603A	S36.118S	S36.419A	S36.528S	S37.009S
K59.2	K65.8	K94.30	Q79.2	R14.1	S31.604A	S36.119S	S36.419S	S36.529A	S37.011S
K59.31	K65.9	K94.31	Q79.3	R14.2	S31.605A	S36.122S	S36.420A	S36.529S	S37.012S
K59.39	K66.0	K94.32	Q79.4	R14.3	S31.609A	S36.123S	S36.420S	S36.530A	S37.019S
K59.4	K66.1	K94.33	Q79.51	R15.0	S31.610A	S36.128S	S36.428A	S36.530S	S37.021S
K59.8	K66.8	K94.39	Q79.59	R15.1	S31.611A	S36.129S	S36.428S	S36.531A	S37.022S
K59.9	K66.9	K95.01	Q89.3	R15.2	S31.612A	S36.13XS	S36.429A	S36.531S	S37.029S
K60.0	K67	K95.09	Q89.4	R15.9	S31.613A	S36.200S	S36.429S	S36.532A	S37.031S
K60.1	K68.12	K95.81	R10.0	R19.00	S31.614A	S36.201S	S36.430A	S36.532S	S37.032S
K60.2	K68.19	K95.89	R10.10	R19.01	S31.615A	S36.202S	S36.430S	S36.533A	S37.039S
K60.3	K68.9	N80.5	R10.11	R19.02	S31.619A	S36.209S	S36.438A	S36.533S	S37.041S
K60.4	K90.0	N82.2	R10.12	R19.03	S31.620A	S36.220S	S36.438S	S36.538A	S37.042S
K60.5	K90.1	N82.3	R10.13	R19.04	S31.621A	S36.221S	S36.439A	S36.538S	S37.049S
K61.0	K90.2	N82.4	R10.2	R19.05	S31.622A	S36.222S	S36.439S	S36.539A	S37.051S
K61.1	K90.3	N99.4	R10.30	R19.06	S31.623A	S36.229S	S36.490A	S36.539S	S37.052S
K61.2	K90.41	Q38.5	R10.31	R19.07	S31.624A	S36.230S	S36.490S	S36.590A	S37.059S
K61.31	K90.49	Q39.0	R10.32	R19.09	S31.625A	S36.231S	S36.498A	S36.590S	S37.061S
K61.39	K90.81	Q39.1	R10.33	R19.11	S31.629A	S36.232S	S36.498S	S36.591A	S37.062S
K61.4	K90.89	Q39.2	R10.811	R19.12	S31.630A	S36.239S	S36.499A	S36.591S	S37.069S
K61.5	K90.9	Q39.3	R10.812	R19.15	S31.631A	S36.240S	S36.499S	S36.592A	S37.091S
K62.0	K91.0	Q39.4	R10.813	R19.2	S31.632A	S36.241S	S36.500A	S36.592S	S37.092S
K62.1	K91.1	Q39.5	R10.814	R19.30	S31.633A	S36.242S	S36.500S	S36.593A	S37.099S
K62.2	K91.2	Q39.6	R10.815	R19.31	S31.634A	S36.249S	S36.501A	S36.593S	T18.100A
K62.3	K91.30	Q39.8	R10.816	R19.32	S31.635A	S36.250S	S36.501S	S36.598A	T18.108A
K62.4	K91.31	Q39.9	R10.817	R19.33	S31.639A	S36.251S	S36.502A	S36.598S	T18.110A
K62.5	K91.32	Q40.0	R10.819	R19.34	S31.640A	S36.252S	S36.502S	S36.599A	T18.118A
K62.6	K91.81	Q40.1	R10.821	R19.35	S31.641A	S36.259S	S36.503A	S36.599S	T18.120A
K62.7	K91.82	Q40.2	R10.822	R19.36	S31.642A	S36.260S	S36.503S	S36.60XA	T18.128A
K62.81	K91.83	Q40.3	R10.823	R19.37	S31.643A	S36.261S	S36.508A	S36.60XS	T18.190A
K62.82	K91.850	Q40.8	R10.824	R19.4	S31.644A	S36.262S	S36.508S	S36.61XA	T18.198A
K62.89	K91.858	Q40.9	R10.825	R19.5	S31.645A	S36.269S	S36.509A	S36.61XS	T18.2XXA
K62.9	K91.86	Q41.0	R10.826	R19.7	S31.649A	S36.290S	S36.509S	S36.62XA	T18.3XXA
K63.0	K91.89	Q41.1	R10.827	R19.8	S31.650A	S36.291S	S36.510A	S36.62XS	T18.4XXA
K63.1	K92.0	Q41.2	R10.829	R85.610	S31.651A	S36.292S	S36.510S	S36.63XA	T18.5XXA
K63.2	K92.1	Q41.8	R10.83	R85.611	S31.652A	S36.299S	S36.511A	S36.63XS	T18.8XXA
K63.3	K92.2	Q41.9	R10.84	R85.612	S31.653A	S36.30XA	S36.511S	S36.69XA	T18.9XXA
K63.4	K92.81	Q42.0	R10.9	R85.613	S31.654A	S36.30XS	S36.512A	S36.69XS	T28.1XXA
K63.5	K92.89	Q42.1	R11.0	R85.614	S31.655A	S36.32XA	S36.512S	S36.81XA	T28.2XXA
K63.81	K92.9	Q42.2	R11.10	R85.615	S31.659A	S36.32XS	S36.513A	S36.81XS	T28.6XXA
K63.89	K94.00	Q42.3	R11.11	R85.616	S36.00XS	S36.33XA	S36.513S	S36.892S	T28.7XXA
K63.9	K94.01	Q42.8	R11.12	R85.618	S36.020S	S36.33XS	S36.518A	S36.893S	T81.710A
K64.0	K94.02	Q42.9	R11.13	R85.619	S36.021S	S36.39XA	S36.518S	S36.898S	Z43.1
K64.1	K94.03	Q43.0	R11.14	R85.81	S36.029S	S36.39XS	S36.519A	S36.899S	Z43.2
K64.2	K94.09	Q43.1	R11.15	R85.82	S36.030S	S36.400A	S36.519S	S36.90XA	Z43.3
K64.3	K94.10	Q43.2	R11.2	R93.3	S36.031S	S36.400S	S36.520A	S36.90XS	Z43.4
K64.4	K94.11	Q43.3	R12	R93.5	S36.032S	S36.408A	S36.520S	S36.92XA	Z46.51
K64.5	K94.12	Q43.4	R13.0	S27.812A	S36.039S	S36.408S	S36.521A	S36.92XS	Z46.59
K64.8	K94.13	Q43.5	R13.10	S27.813A	S36.09XS	S36.409A	S36.521S	S36.93XA	

MDC 07 Diseases And Disorders Of The Hepatobiliary System And Pancreas

A06.4	B58.1	C78.7	K71.6	K75.9	K80.40	K82.4	K85.91	S36.113A	S36.259A
A51.45	B65.1	C7B.02	K71.7	K76.0	K80.41	K82.8	K85.92	S36.114A	S36.260A
A52.74	B66.0	D01.5	K71.8	K76.1	K80.42	K82.9	K86.0	S36.115A	S36.261A
B15.0	B66.1	D13.4	K71.9	K76.2	K80.43	K82.A1	K86.1	S36.116A	S36.262A
B15.9	B66.3	D13.5	K72.00	K76.3	K80.44	K82.A2	K86.2	S36.118A	S36.269A
B16.0	B66.5	D13.6	K72.01	K76.4	K80.45	K83.01	K86.3	S36.119A	S36.290A
B16.1	B67.0	D37.6	K72.10	K76.5	K80.46	K83.09	K86.81	S36.122A	S36.291A
B16.2	B67.5	E80.4	K72.11	K76.6	K80.47	K83.1	K86.89	S36.123A	S36.292A
B16.9	B67.8	E80.5	K72.90	K76.7	K80.50	K83.2	K86.9	S36.128A	S36.299A
B17.0	C22.0	E80.6	K72.91	K76.89	K80.51	K83.3	K87	S36.129A	T86.40
B17.10	C22.1	E80.7	K73.0	K76.9	K80.60	K83.4	K91.5	S36.13XA	T86.41
B17.11	C22.2	I81	K73.1	K77	K80.61	K83.5	Q44.0	S36.200A	T86.42
B17.2	C22.3	I82.0	K73.2	K80.00	K80.62	K83.8	Q44.1	S36.201A	T86.43
B17.8	C22.4	K70.0	K73.8	K80.01	K80.63	K83.9	Q44.2	S36.202A	T86.49
B17.9	C22.7	K70.10	K73.9	K80.10	K80.64	K85.00	Q44.3	S36.209A	T86.890
B18.0	C22.8	K70.11	K74.0	K80.11	K80.65	K85.01	Q44.4	S36.220A	T86.891
B18.1	C22.9	K70.2	K74.1	K80.12	K80.66	K85.02	Q44.5	S36.221A	T86.892
B18.2	C23	K70.30	K74.2	K80.13	K80.67	K85.10	Q44.6	S36.222A	T86.898
B18.8	C24.0	K70.31	K74.3	K80.18	K80.70	K85.11	Q44.7	S36.229A	T86.899
B18.9	C24.1	K70.40	K74.4	K80.19	K80.71	K85.12	Q45.0	S36.230A	Z52.6
B19.0	C24.8	K70.41	K74.5	K80.20	K80.80	K85.20	Q45.1	S36.231A	Z94.4
B19.10	C24.9	K70.9	K74.60	K80.21	K80.81	K85.21	Q45.2	S36.232A	Z94.83
B19.11	C25.0	K71.0	K74.69	K80.30	K81.0	K85.22	Q45.3	S36.239A	
B19.20	C25.1	K71.10	K75.0	K80.31	K81.1	K85.30	R16.0	S36.240A	
B19.21	C25.2	K71.11	K75.1	K80.32	K81.2	K85.31	R16.2	S36.241A	
B19.9	C25.3	K71.2	K75.2	K80.33	K81.9	K85.32	R17	S36.242A	
B25.1	C25.4	K71.3	K75.3	K80.34	K82.0	K85.80	R82.2	S36.249A	
B25.2	C25.7	K71.4	K75.4	K80.35	K82.1	K85.81	R93.2	S36.250A	
B26.3	C25.8	K71.50	K75.81	K80.36	K82.2	K85.82	R94.5	S36.251A	
B26.81	C25.9	K71.51	K75.89	K80.37	K82.3	K85.90	S36.112A	S36.252A	

MDC 08 Diseases And Disorders Of The Musculoskeletal System And Connective Tissue

A02.23	D16.4	M00.069	M01.X22	M02.262	M05.211	M05.561	M06.031	M06.862	M08.412
A02.24	D16.6	M00.071	M01.X29	M02.269	M05.212	M05.562	M06.032	M06.869	M08.419
A18.01	D16.8	M00.072	M01.X31	M02.271	M05.219	M05.569	M06.039	M06.871	M08.421
A18.02	D16.9	M00.079	M01.X32	M02.272	M05.221	M05.571	M06.041	M06.872	M08.422
A18.03	D21.0	M00.08	M01.X39	M02.279	M05.222	M05.572	M06.042	M06.879	M08.429
A18.09	D21.10	M00.09	M01.X41	M02.28	M05.229	M05.579	M06.049	M06.88	M08.431
A39.83	D21.11	M00.10	M01.X42	M02.29	M05.231	M05.59	M06.051	M06.89	M08.432
A39.84	D21.12	M00.111	M01.X49	M02.30	M05.232	M05.60	M06.052	M06.9	M08.439
A51.46	D21.20	M00.112	M01.X51	M02.311	M05.239	M05.611	M06.059	M07.60	M08.441
A52.77	D21.21	M00.119	M01.X52	M02.312	M05.241	M05.612	M06.061	M07.611	M08.442
A52.78	D21.22	M00.121	M01.X59	M02.319	M05.242	M05.619	M06.062	M07.612	M08.449
A54.40	D21.3	M00.122	M01.X61	M02.321	M05.249	M05.621	M06.069	M07.619	M08.451
A54.41	D21.4	M00.129	M01.X62	M02.322	M05.251	M05.622	M06.071	M07.621	M08.452
A54.42	D21.5	M00.131	M01.X69	M02.329	M05.252	M05.629	M06.072	M07.622	M08.459
A54.43	D21.6	M00.132	M01.X71	M02.331	M05.259	M05.631	M06.079	M07.629	M08.461
A54.49	D21.9	M00.139	M01.X72	M02.332	M05.261	M05.632	M06.08	M07.631	M08.462
A66.6	D36.10	M00.141	M01.X79	M02.339	M05.262	M05.639	M06.09	M07.632	M08.469
B06.82	D36.11	M00.142	M01.X8	M02.341	M05.269	M05.641	M06.1	M07.639	M08.471
B90.2	D36.12	M00.149	M01.X9	M02.342	M05.271	M05.642	M06.20	M07.641	M08.472
C40.00	D36.13	M00.151	M02.00	M02.349	M05.272	M05.649	M06.211	M07.642	M08.479
C40.01	D36.14	M00.152	M02.011	M02.351	M05.279	M05.651	M06.212	M07.649	M08.48
C40.02	D36.15	M00.159	M02.012	M02.352	M05.29	M05.652	M06.219	M07.651	M08.80
C40.10	D36.16	M00.161	M02.019	M02.359	M05.30	M05.659	M06.221	M07.652	M08.811
C40.11	D36.17	M00.162	M02.021	M02.361	M05.311	M05.661	M06.222	M07.659	M08.812
C40.12	D48.0	M00.169	M02.022	M02.362	M05.312	M05.662	M06.229	M07.661	M08.819
C40.20	D48.1	M00.171	M02.029	M02.369	M05.319	M05.669	M06.231	M07.662	M08.821
C40.21	D48.2	M00.172	M02.031	M02.371	M05.321	M05.671	M06.232	M07.669	M08.822
C40.22	D49.2	M00.179	M02.032	M02.372	M05.322	M05.672	M06.239	M07.671	M08.829
C40.30	D89.82	M00.18	M02.039	M02.379	M05.329	M05.679	M06.241	M07.672	M08.831
C40.31	E55.0	M00.19	M02.041	M02.38	M05.331	M05.69	M06.242	M07.679	M08.832
C40.32	E64.3	M00.20	M02.042	M02.39	M05.332	M05.70	M06.249	M07.68	M08.839
C40.80	E78.71	M00.211	M02.049	M02.80	M05.339	M05.711	M06.251	M07.69	M08.841
C40.81	E78.72	M00.212	M02.051	M02.811	M05.341	M05.712	M06.252	M08.00	M08.842
C40.82	E85.0	M00.219	M02.052	M02.812	M05.342	M05.719	M06.259	M08.011	M08.849
C40.90	E85.1	M00.221	M02.059	M02.819	M05.349	M05.721	M06.261	M08.012	M08.851
C40.91	E85.2	M00.222	M02.061	M02.821	M05.351	M05.722	M06.262	M08.019	M08.852
C40.92	E85.3	M00.229	M02.062	M02.822	M05.352	M05.729	M06.269	M08.021	M08.859
C41.0	E85.4	M00.231	M02.069	M02.829	M05.359	M05.731	M06.271	M08.022	M08.861
C41.1	E85.81	M00.232	M02.071	M02.831	M05.361	M05.732	M06.272	M08.029	M08.862
C41.2	E85.82	M00.239	M02.072	M02.832	M05.362	M05.739	M06.279	M08.031	M08.869
C41.3	E85.89	M00.241	M02.079	M02.839	M05.369	M05.741	M06.28	M08.032	M08.871
C41.4	E85.9	M00.242	M02.08	M02.841	M05.371	M05.742	M06.29	M08.039	M08.872
C41.9	G72.41	M00.249	M02.09	M02.842	M05.372	M05.749	M06.30	M08.041	M08.879
C47.0	G72.49	M00.251	M02.10	M02.849	M05.379	M05.751	M06.311	M08.042	M08.88
C47.10	H61.011	M00.252	M02.111	M02.851	M05.39	M05.752	M06.312	M08.049	M08.89
C47.11	H61.012	M00.259	M02.112	M02.852	M05.40	M05.759	M06.319	M08.051	M08.90
C47.12	H61.013	M00.261	M02.119	M02.859	M05.411	M05.761	M06.321	M08.052	M08.911
C47.20	H61.019	M00.262	M02.121	M02.861	M05.412	M05.762	M06.322	M08.059	M08.912
C47.21	H61.021	M00.269	M02.122	M02.862	M05.419	M05.769	M06.329	M08.061	M08.919
C47.22	H61.022	M00.271	M02.129	M02.869	M05.421	M05.771	M06.331	M08.062	M08.921
C47.3	H61.023	M00.272	M02.131	M02.871	M05.422	M05.772	M06.332	M08.069	M08.922
C47.4	H61.029	M00.279	M02.132	M02.872	M05.429	M05.779	M06.339	M08.071	M08.929
C47.5	H61.031	M00.28	M02.139	M02.879	M05.431	M05.79	M06.341	M08.072	M08.931
C47.6	H61.032	M00.29	M02.141	M02.88	M05.432	M05.80	M06.342	M08.079	M08.932
C47.8	H61.033	M00.80	M02.142	M02.89	M05.439	M05.811	M06.349	M08.08	M08.939
C47.9	H61.039	M00.811	M02.149	M02.9	M05.441	M05.812	M06.351	M08.09	M08.941
C49.0	I00	M00.812	M02.151	M04.1	M05.442	M05.819	M06.352	M08.1	M08.942
C49.10	I73.00	M00.819	M02.152	M04.2	M05.449	M05.821	M06.359	M08.20	M08.949
C49.11	I73.01	M00.821	M02.159	M04.8	M05.451	M05.822	M06.361	M08.211	M08.951
C49.12	I77.6	M00.822	M02.161	M04.9	M05.452	M05.829	M06.362	M08.212	M08.952
C49.20	L40.50	M00.829	M02.162	M05.00	M05.459	M05.831	M06.369	M08.219	M08.959
C49.21	L40.51	M00.831	M02.169	M05.011	M05.461	M05.832	M06.371	M08.221	M08.961
C49.22	L40.52	M00.832	M02.171	M05.012	M05.462	M05.839	M06.372	M08.222	M08.962
C49.3	L40.53	M00.839	M02.172	M05.019	M05.469	M05.841	M06.379	M08.229	M08.969
C49.4	L40.54	M00.841	M02.179	M05.021	M05.471	M05.842	M06.38	M08.231	M08.971
C49.5	L40.59	M00.842	M02.18	M05.022	M05.472	M05.849	M06.39	M08.232	M08.972
C49.6	M00.00	M00.849	M02.19	M05.029	M05.479	M05.851	M06.4	M08.239	M08.979
C49.8	M00.011	M00.851	M02.20	M05.031	M05.49	M05.852	M06.80	M08.241	M08.98
C49.9	M00.012	M00.852	M02.211	M05.032	M05.50	M05.859	M06.811	M08.242	M08.99
C79.51	M00.019	M00.859	M02.212	M05.039	M05.511	M05.861	M06.812	M08.249	M10.00
C79.52	M00.021	M00.861	M02.219	M05.041	M05.512	M05.862	M06.819	M08.251	M10.011
C7B.03	M00.022	M00.862	M02.221	M05.042	M05.519	M05.869	M06.821	M08.252	M10.012
D16.00	M00.029	M00.869	M02.222	M05.049	M05.521	M05.871	M06.822	M08.259	M10.019
D16.01	M00.031	M00.871	M02.229	M05.051	M05.522	M05.872	M06.829	M08.261	M10.021
D16.02	M00.032	M00.872	M02.231	M05.052	M05.529	M05.879	M06.831	M08.262	M10.022
D16.10	M00.039	M00.879	M02.232	M05.059	M05.531	M05.89	M06.832	M08.269	M10.029
D16.11	M00.041	M00.88	M02.239	M05.061	M05.532	M05.9	M06.839	M08.271	M10.031
D16.12	M00.042	M00.89	M02.241	M05.062	M05.539	M06.00	M06.841	M08.272	M10.032
D16.20	M00.049	M00.9	M02.242	M05.069	M05.541	M06.011	M06.842	M08.279	M10.039
D16.21	M00.051	M01.X0	M02.249	M05.071	M05.542	M06.012	M06.849	M08.28	M10.041
D16.22	M00.052	M01.X11	M02.251	M05.072	M05.549	M06.019	M06.851	M08.29	M10.042
D16.30	M00.059	M01.X12	M02.252	M05.079	M05.551	M06.021	M06.852	M08.3	M10.049
D16.31	M00.061	M01.X19	M02.259	M05.09	M05.552	M06.022	M06.859	M08.40	M10.051
D16.32	M00.062	M01.X21	M02.261	M05.20	M05.559	M06.029	M06.861	M08.411	M10.052

M10.059	M11.021	M11.869	M12.331	M12.879	M14.842	M19.171	M1A.2320	M1A.4190	M21.069
M10.061	M11.022	M11.871	M12.332	M12.88	M14.849	M19.172	M1A.2321	M1A.4191	M21.071
M10.062	M11.029	M11.872	M12.339	M12.89	M14.851	M19.179	M1A.2390	M1A.4210	M21.072
M10.069	M11.031	M11.879	M12.341	M12.9	M14.852	M19.211	M1A.2391	M1A.4220	M21.079
M10.071	M11.032	M11.88	M12.342	M13.0	M14.859	M19.212	M1A.2410	M1A.4221	M21.10
M10.072	M11.039	M11.89	M12.349	M13.10	M14.861	M19.219	M1A.2411	M1A.4290	M21.121
M10.079	M11.041	M11.9	M12.351	M13.111	M14.862	M19.221	M1A.2420	M1A.4291	M21.122
M10.08	M11.042	M12.00	M12.352	M13.112	M14.869	M19.222	M1A.2421	M1A.4310	M21.129
M10.09	M11.049	M12.011	M12.359	M13.119	M14.871	M19.229	M1A.2490	M1A.4311	M21.151
M10.10	M11.051	M12.012	M12.361	M13.121	M14.872	M19.231	M1A.2491	M1A.4320	M21.152
M10.111	M11.052	M12.019	M12.362	M13.122	M14.879	M19.232	M1A.2510	M1A.4321	M21.159
M10.112	M11.059	M12.021	M12.369	M13.129	M14.88	M19.239	M1A.2511	M1A.4390	M21.161
M10.119	M11.061	M12.022	M12.371	M13.131	M14.89	M19.241	M1A.2520	M1A.4391	M21.162
M10.121	M11.062	M12.029	M12.372	M13.132	M15.0	M19.242	M1A.2521	M1A.4410	M21.169
M10.122	M11.069	M12.031	M12.379	M13.139	M15.1	M19.249	M1A.2590	M1A.4411	M21.171
M10.129	M11.071	M12.032	M12.38	M13.141	M15.2	M19.271	M1A.2591	M1A.4420	M21.172
M10.131	M11.072	M12.039	M12.39	M13.142	M15.3	M19.272	M1A.2610	M1A.4421	M21.179
M10.132	M11.079	M12.041	M12.40	M13.149	M15.4	M19.279	M1A.2611	M1A.4490	M21.20
M10.139	M11.08	M12.042	M12.411	M13.151	M15.8	M19.90	M1A.2620	M1A.4491	M21.211
M10.141	M11.09	M12.049	M12.412	M13.152	M15.9	M19.91	M1A.2621	M1A.4510	M21.212
M10.142	M11.10	M12.051	M12.419	M13.159	M16.0	M19.92	M1A.2690	M1A.4511	M21.219
M10.149	M11.111	M12.052	M12.421	M13.161	M16.10	M19.93	M1A.2691	M1A.4520	M21.221
M10.151	M11.112	M12.059	M12.422	M13.162	M16.11	M1A.00X0	M1A.2710	M1A.4521	M21.222
M10.152	M11.119	M12.061	M12.429	M13.169	M16.12	M1A.00X1	M1A.2711	M1A.4590	M21.229
M10.159	M11.121	M12.062	M12.431	M13.171	M16.2	M1A.0110	M1A.2720	M1A.4591	M21.231
M10.161	M11.122	M12.069	M12.432	M13.172	M16.30	M1A.0111	M1A.2721	M1A.4610	M21.232
M10.162	M11.129	M12.071	M12.439	M13.179	M16.31	M1A.0120	M1A.2790	M1A.4611	M21.239
M10.169	M11.131	M12.072	M12.441	M13.80	M16.32	M1A.0121	M1A.2791	M1A.4620	M21.241
M10.171	M11.132	M12.079	M12.442	M13.811	M16.4	M1A.0190	M1A.28X0	M1A.4621	M21.242
M10.172	M11.139	M12.08	M12.449	M13.812	M16.50	M1A.0191	M1A.28X1	M1A.4690	M21.249
M10.179	M11.141	M12.09	M12.451	M13.819	M16.51	M1A.0210	M1A.29X0	M1A.4691	M21.251
M10.18	M11.142	M12.10	M12.452	M13.821	M16.52	M1A.0211	M1A.29X1	M1A.4710	M21.252
M10.19	M11.149	M12.111	M12.459	M13.822	M16.6	M1A.0220	M1A.30X0	M1A.4711	M21.259
M10.20	M11.151	M12.112	M12.461	M13.829	M16.7	M1A.0221	M1A.30X1	M1A.4720	M21.261
M10.211	M11.152	M12.119	M12.462	M13.831	M16.9	M1A.0290	M1A.3110	M1A.4721	M21.262
M10.212	M11.159	M12.121	M12.469	M13.832	M17.0	M1A.0291	M1A.3111	M1A.4790	M21.269
M10.219	M11.161	M12.122	M12.471	M13.839	M17.10	M1A.0310	M1A.3120	M1A.4791	M21.271
M10.221	M11.162	M12.129	M12.472	M13.841	M17.11	M1A.0311	M1A.3121	M1A.48X0	M21.272
M10.222	M11.169	M12.131	M12.479	M13.842	M17.12	M1A.0320	M1A.3190	M1A.48X1	M21.279
M10.229	M11.171	M12.132	M12.48	M13.849	M17.2	M1A.0321	M1A.3191	M1A.49X0	M21.371
M10.231	M11.172	M12.139	M12.49	M13.851	M17.30	M1A.0390	M1A.3210	M1A.49X1	M21.372
M10.232	M11.179	M12.141	M12.50	M13.852	M17.31	M1A.0391	M1A.3211	M1A.9XX0	M21.379
M10.239	M11.18	M12.142	M12.511	M13.859	M17.32	M1A.0410	M1A.3220	M1A.9XX1	M21.40
M10.241	M11.19	M12.149	M12.512	M13.861	M17.4	M1A.0411	M1A.3221	M20.001	M21.41
M10.242	M11.20	M12.151	M12.519	M13.862	M17.5	M1A.0420	M1A.3290	M20.002	M21.42
M10.249	M11.211	M12.152	M12.521	M13.869	M17.9	M1A.0421	M1A.3291	M20.009	M21.541
M10.251	M11.212	M12.159	M12.522	M13.871	M18.0	M1A.0490	M1A.3310	M20.011	M21.542
M10.252	M11.219	M12.161	M12.529	M13.872	M18.10	M1A.0491	M1A.3311	M20.012	M21.549
M10.259	M11.221	M12.162	M12.531	M13.879	M18.11	M1A.0510	M1A.3320	M20.019	M21.611
M10.261	M11.222	M12.169	M12.532	M13.88	M18.12	M1A.0511	M1A.3321	M20.021	M21.612
M10.262	M11.229	M12.171	M12.539	M13.89	M18.2	M1A.0520	M1A.3390	M20.022	M21.619
M10.269	M11.231	M12.172	M12.541	M14.60	M18.30	M1A.0521	M1A.3391	M20.029	M21.621
M10.271	M11.232	M12.179	M12.542	M14.611	M18.31	M1A.0590	M1A.3410	M20.031	M21.622
M10.272	M11.239	M12.18	M12.549	M14.612	M18.32	M1A.0591	M1A.3411	M20.032	M21.629
M10.279	M11.241	M12.19	M12.551	M14.619	M18.4	M1A.0610	M1A.3420	M20.039	M21.6X1
M10.28	M11.242	M12.20	M12.552	M14.621	M18.50	M1A.0611	M1A.3421	M20.091	M21.6X2
M10.29	M11.249	M12.211	M12.559	M14.622	M18.51	M1A.0620	M1A.3490	M20.092	M21.6X9
M10.40	M11.251	M12.212	M12.561	M14.629	M18.52	M1A.0621	M1A.3491	M20.099	M21.70
M10.411	M11.252	M12.219	M12.562	M14.631	M18.9	M1A.0690	M1A.3510	M20.10	M21.721
M10.412	M11.259	M12.221	M12.569	M14.632	M19.011	M1A.0691	M1A.3511	M20.11	M21.722
M10.419	M11.261	M12.222	M12.571	M14.639	M19.012	M1A.0710	M1A.3520	M20.12	M21.729
M10.421	M11.262	M12.229	M12.572	M14.641	M19.019	M1A.0711	M1A.3521	M20.20	M21.731
M10.422	M11.269	M12.231	M12.579	M14.642	M19.021	M1A.0720	M1A.3590	M20.21	M21.732
M10.429	M11.271	M12.232	M12.58	M14.649	M19.022	M1A.0721	M1A.3591	M20.22	M21.733
M10.431	M11.272	M12.239	M12.59	M14.651	M19.029	M1A.0790	M1A.3610	M20.30	M21.734
M10.432	M11.279	M12.241	M12.80	M14.652	M19.031	M1A.0791	M1A.3611	M20.31	M21.739
M10.439	M11.28	M12.242	M12.811	M14.659	M19.032	M1A.08X0	M1A.3620	M20.32	M21.751
M10.441	M11.29	M12.249	M12.812	M14.661	M19.039	M1A.08X1	M1A.3621	M20.40	M21.752
M10.442	M11.80	M12.251	M12.819	M14.662	M19.041	M1A.09X0	M1A.3690	M20.41	M21.759
M10.449	M11.811	M12.252	M12.821	M14.669	M19.042	M1A.09X1	M1A.3691	M20.42	M21.761
M10.451	M11.812	M12.259	M12.822	M14.671	M19.049	M1A.20X0	M1A.3710	M20.5X1	M21.762
M10.452	M11.819	M12.261	M12.829	M14.672	M19.071	M1A.20X1	M1A.3711	M20.5X2	M21.763
M10.459	M11.821	M12.262	M12.831	M14.679	M19.072	M1A.2110	M1A.3720	M20.5X9	M21.764
M10.461	M11.822	M12.269	M12.832	M14.68	M19.079	M1A.2111	M1A.3721	M20.60	M21.769
M10.462	M11.829	M12.271	M12.839	M14.69	M19.111	M1A.2120	M1A.3790	M20.61	M21.80
M10.469	M11.831	M12.272	M12.841	M14.80	M19.112	M1A.2121	M1A.3791	M20.62	M21.821
M10.471	M11.832	M12.279	M12.842	M14.811	M19.119	M1A.2190	M1A.38X0	M21.00	M21.822
M10.472	M11.839	M12.28	M12.849	M14.812	M19.121	M1A.2191	M1A.38X1	M21.021	M21.829
M10.479	M11.841	M12.29	M12.851	M14.819	M19.122	M1A.2210	M1A.39X0	M21.022	M21.831
M10.48	M11.842	M12.30	M12.852	M14.821	M19.129	M1A.2211	M1A.39X1	M21.029	M21.832
M10.49	M11.849	M12.311	M12.859	M14.822	M19.131	M1A.2220	M1A.40X0	M21.051	M21.839
M10.9	M11.851	M12.312	M12.861	M14.829	M19.132	M1A.2221	M1A.40X1	M21.052	M21.851
M11.00	M11.852	M12.319	M12.862	M14.831	M19.139	M1A.2290	M1A.4110	M21.059	M21.852
M11.011	M11.859	M12.321	M12.869	M14.832	M19.141	M1A.2291	M1A.4111	M21.061	M21.859
M11.012	M11.861	M12.322	M12.871	M14.839	M19.142	M1A.2310	M1A.4120	M21.062	M21.861
M11.019	M11.862	M12.329	M12.872	M14.841	M19.149	M1A.2311	M1A.4121		M21.862

M21.869	M23.251	M24.10	M24.451	M24.875	M25.332	M25.673	M33.19	M41.126	M43.3
M21.90	M23.252	M24.111	M24.452	M24.876	M25.339	M25.674	M33.20	M41.127	M43.4
M21.921	M23.259	M24.112	M24.459	M24.9	M25.341	M25.675	M33.21	M41.129	M43.5X2
M21.922	M23.261	M24.119	M24.461	M25.00	M25.342	M25.676	M33.22	M41.20	M43.5X3
M21.929	M23.262	M24.121	M24.462	M25.011	M25.349	M25.70	M33.29	M41.22	M43.5X4
M21.931	M23.269	M24.122	M24.469	M25.012	M25.351	M25.711	M33.90	M41.23	M43.5X5
M21.932	M23.300	M24.129	M24.471	M25.019	M25.352	M25.712	M33.91	M41.24	M43.5X6
M21.939	M23.301	M24.131	M24.472	M25.021	M25.359	M25.719	M33.92	M41.25	M43.5X7
M21.941	M23.302	M24.132	M24.473	M25.022	M25.361	M25.721	M33.93	M41.26	M43.5X8
M21.942	M23.303	M24.139	M24.474	M25.029	M25.362	M25.722	M33.99	M41.27	M43.5X9
M21.949	M23.304	M24.141	M24.475	M25.031	M25.369	M25.729	M34.0	M41.30	M43.6
M21.951	M23.305	M24.142	M24.476	M25.032	M25.371	M25.731	M34.1	M41.34	M43.8X1
M21.952	M23.306	M24.149	M24.477	M25.039	M25.372	M25.732	M34.2	M41.35	M43.8X2
M21.959	M23.307	M24.151	M24.478	M25.041	M25.373	M25.739	M34.82	M41.40	M43.8X3
M21.961	M23.309	M24.152	M24.479	M25.042	M25.374	M25.741	M34.89	M41.41	M43.8X4
M21.962	M23.311	M24.159	M24.50	M25.049	M25.375	M25.742	M34.9	M41.42	M43.8X5
M21.969	M23.312	M24.171	M24.511	M25.051	M25.376	M25.749	M35.00	M41.43	M43.8X6
M22.00	M23.319	M24.172	M24.512	M25.052	M25.40	M25.751	M35.01	M41.44	M43.8X7
M22.01	M23.321	M24.173	M24.519	M25.059	M25.411	M25.752	M35.02	M41.45	M43.8X8
M22.02	M23.322	M24.174	M24.521	M25.061	M25.412	M25.759	M35.03	M41.46	M43.8X9
M22.10	M23.329	M24.175	M24.522	M25.062	M25.419	M25.761	M35.04	M41.47	M43.9
M22.11	M23.331	M24.176	M24.529	M25.069	M25.421	M25.762	M35.09	M41.50	M45.0
M22.12	M23.332	M24.20	M24.531	M25.071	M25.422	M25.769	M35.1	M41.52	M45.1
M22.2X1	M23.339	M24.211	M24.532	M25.072	M25.429	M25.771	M35.2	M41.53	M45.2
M22.2X2	M23.341	M24.212	M24.539	M25.073	M25.431	M25.772	M35.3	M41.54	M45.3
M22.2X9	M23.342	M24.219	M24.541	M25.074	M25.432	M25.773	M35.4	M41.55	M45.4
M22.3X1	M23.349	M24.221	M24.542	M25.075	M25.439	M25.774	M35.5	M41.56	M45.5
M22.3X2	M23.351	M24.222	M24.549	M25.076	M25.441	M25.775	M35.7	M41.57	M45.6
M22.3X9	M23.352	M24.229	M24.551	M25.08	M25.442	M25.776	M35.8	M41.80	M45.7
M22.40	M23.359	M24.231	M24.552	M25.10	M25.449	M25.78	M35.9	M41.82	M45.8
M22.41	M23.361	M24.232	M24.559	M25.111	M25.451	M25.80	M36.0	M41.83	M45.9
M22.42	M23.362	M24.239	M24.561	M25.112	M25.452	M25.811	M36.1	M41.84	M46.00
M22.8X1	M23.369	M24.241	M24.562	M25.119	M25.459	M25.812	M36.2	M41.85	M46.01
M22.8X2	M23.40	M24.242	M24.569	M25.121	M25.461	M25.819	M36.3	M41.86	M46.02
M22.8X9	M23.41	M24.249	M24.571	M25.122	M25.462	M25.821	M36.4	M41.87	M46.03
M22.90	M23.42	M24.251	M24.572	M25.129	M25.469	M25.822	M36.8	M41.9	M46.04
M22.91	M23.50	M24.252	M24.573	M25.131	M25.471	M25.829	M40.00	M42.00	M46.05
M22.92	M23.51	M24.259	M24.574	M25.132	M25.472	M25.831	M40.03	M42.01	M46.06
M23.000	M23.52	M24.271	M24.575	M25.139	M25.473	M25.832	M40.04	M42.02	M46.07
M23.001	M23.601	M24.272	M24.576	M25.141	M25.474	M25.839	M40.05	M42.03	M46.08
M23.002	M23.602	M24.273	M24.60	M25.142	M25.475	M25.841	M40.10	M42.04	M46.09
M23.003	M23.609	M24.274	M24.611	M25.149	M25.476	M25.842	M40.12	M42.05	M46.1
M23.004	M23.611	M24.275	M24.612	M25.151	M25.48	M25.849	M40.13	M42.06	M46.20
M23.005	M23.612	M24.276	M24.619	M25.152	M25.50	M25.851	M40.14	M42.07	M46.21
M23.006	M23.619	M24.28	M24.621	M25.159	M25.511	M25.852	M40.15	M42.08	M46.22
M23.007	M23.621	M24.30	M24.622	M25.161	M25.512	M25.859	M40.202	M42.09	M46.23
M23.009	M23.622	M24.311	M24.629	M25.162	M25.519	M25.861	M40.203	M42.10	M46.24
M23.011	M23.629	M24.312	M24.631	M25.169	M25.521	M25.862	M40.204	M42.11	M46.25
M23.012	M23.631	M24.319	M24.632	M25.171	M25.522	M25.869	M40.205	M42.12	M46.26
M23.019	M23.632	M24.321	M24.639	M25.172	M25.529	M25.871	M40.209	M42.13	M46.27
M23.021	M23.639	M24.322	M24.641	M25.173	M25.531	M25.872	M40.292	M42.14	M46.28
M23.022	M23.641	M24.329	M24.642	M25.174	M25.532	M25.879	M40.293	M42.15	M46.30
M23.029	M23.642	M24.331	M24.649	M25.175	M25.539	M25.9	M40.294	M42.16	M46.31
M23.031	M23.649	M24.332	M24.651	M25.176	M25.541	M30.0	M40.295	M42.17	M46.32
M23.032	M23.671	M24.339	M24.652	M25.18	M25.542	M30.1	M40.299	M42.18	M46.33
M23.039	M23.672	M24.341	M24.659	M25.20	M25.549	M30.2	M40.30	M42.19	M46.34
M23.041	M23.679	M24.342	M24.661	M25.211	M25.551	M30.3	M40.35	M42.9	M46.35
M23.042	M23.8X1	M24.349	M24.662	M25.212	M25.552	M30.8	M40.36	M43.00	M46.36
M23.049	M23.8X2	M24.351	M24.669	M25.219	M25.559	M31.0	M40.37	M43.01	M46.37
M23.051	M23.8X9	M24.352	M24.671	M25.221	M25.561	M31.1	M40.40	M43.02	M46.38
M23.052	M23.90	M24.359	M24.672	M25.222	M25.562	M31.2	M40.45	M43.03	M46.39
M23.059	M23.91	M24.361	M24.673	M25.229	M25.569	M31.30	M40.46	M43.04	M46.40
M23.061	M23.92	M24.362	M24.674	M25.231	M25.571	M31.31	M40.47	M43.05	M46.41
M23.062	M24.00	M24.369	M24.675	M25.232	M25.572	M31.4	M40.50	M43.06	M46.42
M23.069	M24.011	M24.371	M24.676	M25.239	M25.579	M31.5	M40.55	M43.07	M46.43
M23.200	M24.012	M24.372	M24.7	M25.241	M25.60	M31.6	M40.56	M43.08	M46.44
M23.201	M24.019	M24.373	M24.80	M25.242	M25.611	M31.7	M40.57	M43.09	M46.45
M23.202	M24.021	M24.374	M24.811	M25.249	M25.612	M32.0	M41.00	M43.10	M46.46
M23.203	M24.022	M24.375	M24.812	M25.251	M25.619	M32.10	M41.02	M43.11	M46.47
M23.204	M24.029	M24.376	M24.819	M25.252	M25.621	M32.11	M41.03	M43.12	M46.48
M23.205	M24.031	M24.40	M24.821	M25.259	M25.622	M32.12	M41.04	M43.13	M46.49
M23.206	M24.032	M24.411	M24.822	M25.261	M25.629	M32.13	M41.05	M43.14	M46.50
M23.207	M24.039	M24.412	M24.829	M25.262	M25.631	M32.14	M41.06	M43.15	M46.51
M23.209	M24.041	M24.419	M24.831	M25.269	M25.632	M32.15	M41.07	M43.16	M46.52
M23.211	M24.042	M24.421	M24.832	M25.271	M25.639	M32.19	M41.08	M43.17	M46.53
M23.212	M24.049	M24.422	M24.839	M25.272	M25.641	M32.8	M41.112	M43.18	M46.54
M23.219	M24.051	M24.429	M24.841	M25.279	M25.642	M32.9	M41.113	M43.19	M46.55
M23.221	M24.052	M24.431	M24.842	M25.28	M25.649	M33.00	M41.114	M43.20	M46.56
M23.222	M24.059	M24.432	M24.849	M25.30	M25.651	M33.01	M41.115	M43.21	M46.57
M23.229	M24.071	M24.439	M24.851	M25.311	M25.652	M33.02	M41.116	M43.22	M46.58
M23.231	M24.072	M24.441	M24.852	M25.312	M25.659	M33.03	M41.117	M43.23	M46.59
M23.232	M24.073	M24.442	M24.859	M25.319	M25.661	M33.09	M41.119	M43.24	M46.80
M23.239	M24.075	M24.443	M24.871	M25.321	M25.662	M33.10	M41.122	M43.25	M46.81
M23.241	M24.075	M24.444	M24.872	M25.322	M25.669	M33.11	M41.123	M43.26	M46.82
M23.242	M24.076	M24.445	M24.873	M25.329	M25.671	M33.12	M41.124	M43.27	M46.83
M23.249	M24.08	M24.446	M24.874	M25.331	M25.672	M33.13	M41.125	M43.28	M46.84

M46.85	M48.26	M48.8X4	M53.2X4	M60.131	M61.079	M61.412	M62.161	M62.9	M65.262
M46.86	M48.27	M48.8X5	M53.2X5	M60.132	M61.08	M61.419	M62.162	M63.80	M65.269
M46.87	M48.30	M48.8X6	M53.2X6	M60.139	M61.09	M61.421	M62.169	M63.811	M65.271
M46.88	M48.31	M48.8X7	M53.2X7	M60.141	M61.10	M61.422	M62.171	M63.812	M65.272
M46.89	M48.32	M48.8X8	M53.2X8	M60.142	M61.111	M61.429	M62.172	M63.819	M65.279
M46.90	M48.33	M48.8X9	M53.2X9	M60.149	M61.112	M61.431	M62.179	M63.821	M65.28
M46.91	M48.34	M48.9	M53.3	M60.151	M61.119	M61.432	M62.18	M63.822	M65.29
M46.92	M48.35	M49.80	M53.80	M60.152	M61.121	M61.439	M62.20	M63.829	M65.30
M46.93	M48.36	M49.81	M53.81	M60.159	M61.122	M61.441	M62.211	M63.831	M65.311
M46.94	M48.37	M49.82	M53.82	M60.161	M61.129	M61.442	M62.212	M63.832	M65.312
M46.95	M48.38	M49.83	M53.83	M60.162	M61.131	M61.449	M62.219	M63.839	M65.319
M46.96	M48.40XA	M49.84	M53.84	M60.169	M61.132	M61.451	M62.221	M63.841	M65.321
M46.97	M48.40XD	M49.85	M53.85	M60.171	M61.139	M61.452	M62.222	M63.842	M65.322
M46.98	M48.40XG	M49.86	M53.86	M60.172	M61.141	M61.459	M62.229	M63.849	M65.329
M46.99	M48.40XS	M49.87	M53.87	M60.179	M61.142	M61.461	M62.231	M63.851	M65.331
M47.011	M48.41XA	M49.88	M53.88	M60.18	M61.143	M61.462	M62.232	M63.852	M65.332
M47.012	M48.41XD	M49.89	M53.9	M60.19	M61.144	M61.469	M62.239	M63.859	M65.339
M47.013	M48.41XG	M50.00	M54.03	M60.20	M61.145	M61.471	M62.241	M63.861	M65.341
M47.014	M48.41XS	M50.01	M54.04	M60.211	M61.146	M61.472	M62.242	M63.862	M65.342
M47.015	M48.42XA	M50.020	M54.05	M60.212	M61.151	M61.479	M62.249	M63.869	M65.349
M47.016	M48.42XD	M50.021	M54.06	M60.219	M61.152	M61.48	M62.251	M63.871	M65.351
M47.019	M48.42XG	M50.022	M54.07	M60.221	M61.159	M61.49	M62.252	M63.872	M65.352
M47.021	M48.42XS	M50.023	M54.08	M60.222	M61.161	M61.50	M62.259	M63.879	M65.359
M47.022	M48.43XA	M50.03	M54.09	M60.229	M61.162	M61.511	M62.261	M63.88	M65.4
M47.029	M48.43XD	M50.10	M54.14	M60.231	M61.169	M61.512	M62.262	M63.89	M65.80
M47.10	M48.43XG	M50.11	M54.15	M60.232	M61.171	M61.519	M62.269	M65.00	M65.811
M47.11	M48.43XS	M50.120	M54.16	M60.239	M61.172	M61.521	M62.271	M65.011	M65.812
M47.12	M48.44XA	M50.121	M54.17	M60.241	M61.173	M61.522	M62.272	M65.012	M65.819
M47.13	M48.44XD	M50.122	M54.2	M60.242	M61.174	M61.529	M62.279	M65.019	M65.821
M47.14	M48.44XG	M50.123	M54.30	M60.249	M61.175	M61.531	M62.28	M65.021	M65.822
M47.15	M48.44XS	M50.13	M54.31	M60.251	M61.176	M61.532	M62.3	M65.022	M65.829
M47.16	M48.45XA	M50.20	M54.32	M60.252	M61.177	M61.539	M62.40	M65.029	M65.831
M47.20	M48.45XD	M50.21	M54.40	M60.259	M61.178	M61.541	M62.411	M65.031	M65.832
M47.21	M48.45XG	M50.220	M54.41	M60.261	M61.179	M61.542	M62.412	M65.032	M65.839
M47.22	M48.45XS	M50.221	M54.42	M60.262	M61.18	M61.549	M62.419	M65.039	M65.841
M47.23	M48.46XA	M50.222	M54.5	M60.269	M61.19	M61.551	M62.421	M65.041	M65.842
M47.24	M48.46XD	M50.223	M54.6	M60.271	M61.20	M61.552	M62.422	M65.042	M65.849
M47.25	M48.46XG	M50.23	M54.81	M60.272	M61.211	M61.559	M62.429	M65.049	M65.851
M47.26	M48.46XS	M50.30	M54.89	M60.279	M61.212	M61.561	M62.431	M65.051	M65.852
M47.27	M48.47XA	M50.31	M54.9	M60.28	M61.219	M61.562	M62.432	M65.052	M65.859
M47.28	M48.47XD	M50.320	M60.000	M60.80	M61.221	M61.569	M62.439	M65.059	M65.861
M47.811	M48.47XG	M50.321	M60.001	M60.811	M61.222	M61.571	M62.441	M65.061	M65.862
M47.812	M48.47XS	M50.322	M60.002	M60.812	M61.229	M61.572	M62.442	M65.062	M65.869
M47.813	M48.48XA	M50.323	M60.003	M60.819	M61.231	M61.579	M62.449	M65.069	M65.871
M47.814	M48.48XD	M50.33	M60.004	M60.821	M61.232	M61.58	M62.451	M65.071	M65.872
M47.815	M48.48XG	M50.80	M60.005	M60.822	M61.239	M61.59	M62.452	M65.072	M65.879
M47.816	M48.48XS	M50.81	M60.009	M60.829	M61.241	M61.9	M62.459	M65.079	M65.88
M47.817	M48.50XA	M50.820	M60.011	M60.831	M61.242	M62.00	M62.461	M65.08	M65.89
M47.818	M48.50XD	M50.821	M60.012	M60.832	M61.249	M62.011	M62.462	M65.10	M65.9
M47.819	M48.50XG	M50.822	M60.019	M60.839	M61.251	M62.012	M62.469	M65.111	M66.0
M47.891	M48.50XS	M50.823	M60.021	M60.841	M61.252	M62.019	M62.471	M65.112	M66.10
M47.892	M48.51XA	M50.83	M60.022	M60.842	M61.259	M62.021	M62.472	M65.119	M66.111
M47.893	M48.51XD	M50.90	M60.029	M60.849	M61.261	M62.022	M62.479	M65.121	M66.112
M47.894	M48.51XG	M50.91	M60.031	M60.851	M61.262	M62.029	M62.48	M65.122	M66.119
M47.895	M48.51XS	M50.920	M60.032	M60.852	M61.269	M62.031	M62.49	M65.129	M66.121
M47.896	M48.52XA	M50.921	M60.039	M60.859	M61.271	M62.032	M62.50	M65.131	M66.122
M47.897	M48.52XD	M50.922	M60.041	M60.861	M61.272	M62.039	M62.511	M65.132	M66.129
M47.898	M48.52XG	M50.923	M60.042	M60.862	M61.279	M62.041	M62.512	M65.139	M66.131
M47.899	M48.52XS	M50.93	M60.043	M60.869	M61.28	M62.042	M62.519	M65.141	M66.132
M47.9	M48.53XA	M51.04	M60.044	M60.871	M61.29	M62.049	M62.521	M65.142	M66.139
M48.00	M48.53XD	M51.05	M60.045	M60.872	M61.30	M62.051	M62.522	M65.149	M66.141
M48.01	M48.53XG	M51.06	M60.046	M60.879	M61.311	M62.052	M62.529	M65.151	M66.142
M48.02	M48.53XS	M51.14	M60.051	M60.88	M61.312	M62.059	M62.531	M65.152	M66.143
M48.03	M48.54XA	M51.15	M60.052	M60.89	M61.319	M62.061	M62.532	M65.159	M66.144
M48.04	M48.54XD	M51.16	M60.059	M60.9	M61.321	M62.062	M62.539	M65.161	M66.145
M48.05	M48.54XG	M51.17	M60.061	M61.00	M61.322	M62.069	M62.541	M65.162	M66.146
M48.061	M48.54XS	M51.24	M60.062	M61.011	M61.329	M62.071	M62.542	M65.169	M66.151
M48.062	M48.55XA	M51.25	M60.069	M61.012	M61.331	M62.072	M62.549	M65.171	M66.152
M48.07	M48.55XD	M51.26	M60.070	M61.019	M61.332	M62.079	M62.551	M65.172	M66.159
M48.08	M48.55XG	M51.27	M60.071	M61.021	M61.339	M62.08	M62.552	M65.179	M66.171
M48.10	M48.55XS	M51.34	M60.072	M61.022	M61.341	M62.10	M62.559	M65.18	M66.172
M48.11	M48.56XA	M51.35	M60.073	M61.029	M61.342	M62.111	M62.561	M65.19	M66.173
M48.12	M48.56XD	M51.36	M60.074	M61.031	M61.349	M62.112	M62.562	M65.20	M66.174
M48.13	M48.56XG	M51.37	M60.075	M61.032	M61.351	M62.119	M62.569	M65.221	M66.175
M48.14	M48.56XS	M51.44	M60.076	M61.039	M61.352	M62.121	M62.571	M65.229	M66.176
M48.15	M48.57XA	M51.45	M60.077	M61.041	M61.359	M62.122	M62.572	M65.231	M66.177
M48.16	M48.57XD	M51.46	M60.078	M61.042	M61.361	M62.129	M62.579	M65.232	M66.178
M48.17	M48.57XG	M51.47	M60.08	M61.049	M61.362	M62.131	M62.58	M65.239	M66.179
M48.18	M48.57XS	M51.84	M60.09	M61.051	M61.369	M62.132	M62.59	M65.241	M66.18
M48.19	M48.58XA	M51.85	M60.10	M61.052	M61.371	M62.139	M62.81	M65.242	M66.20
M48.20	M48.58XD	M51.86	M60.111	M61.059	M61.372	M62.141	M62.82	M65.249	M66.211
M48.21	M48.58XG	M51.87	M60.112	M61.061	M61.379	M62.142	M62.830	M65.251	M66.212
M48.22	M48.58XS	M51.9	M60.119	M61.062	M61.38	M62.149	M62.831	M65.259	M66.219
M48.23	M48.8X1	M53.2X1	M60.121	M61.069	M61.39	M62.151	M62.838	M65.261	M66.221
M48.24	M48.8X2	M53.2X2	M60.122	M61.071	M61.40	M62.152	M62.84	M65.261	M66.222
M48.25	M48.8X3	M53.2X3	M60.129	M61.072	M61.411	M62.159	M62.89	M65.261	M66.229

M66.231	M67.262	M67.863	M70.911	M71.349	M75.101	M79.601	M80.031D	M80.079K	M80.849S
M66.232	M67.269	M67.864	M70.912	M71.351	M75.102	M79.602	M80.031G	M80.079P	M80.851A
M66.239	M67.271	M67.869	M70.919	M71.352	M75.110	M79.603	M80.031K	M80.079S	M80.851D
M66.241	M67.272	M67.871	M70.921	M71.359	M75.111	M79.604	M80.031P	M80.08XA	M80.851G
M66.242	M67.279	M67.872	M70.922	M71.371	M75.112	M79.605	M80.031S	M80.08XD	M80.851K
M66.249	M67.28	M67.873	M70.929	M71.372	M75.120	M79.606	M80.032A	M80.08XG	M80.851P
M66.251	M67.29	M67.874	M70.931	M71.379	M75.121	M79.609	M80.032D	M80.08XK	M80.851S
M66.252	M67.30	M67.879	M70.932	M71.38	M75.122	M79.621	M80.032G	M80.08XP	M80.852A
M66.259	M67.311	M67.88	M70.939	M71.39	M75.20	M79.622	M80.032K	M80.08XS	M80.852D
M66.261	M67.312	M67.89	M70.941	M71.40	M75.21	M79.629	M80.032S	M80.80XA	M80.852G
M66.262	M67.319	M67.90	M70.942	M71.421	M75.22	M79.631	M80.039A	M80.80XD	M80.852K
M66.269	M67.321	M67.911	M70.949	M71.422	M75.30	M79.632	M80.039D	M80.80XG	M80.852P
M66.271	M67.322	M67.912	M70.951	M71.429	M75.31	M79.639	M80.039G	M80.80XK	M80.852S
M66.272	M67.329	M67.919	M70.952	M71.431	M75.32	M79.641	M80.039P	M80.80XP	M80.859A
M66.279	M67.331	M67.921	M70.959	M71.432	M75.40	M79.642	M80.039S	M80.80XS	M80.859D
M66.28	M67.332	M67.922	M70.961	M71.439	M75.41	M79.643	M80.041A	M80.811A	M80.859G
M66.29	M67.339	M67.929	M70.962	M71.441	M75.42	M79.644	M80.041D	M80.811D	M80.859K
M66.30	M67.341	M67.931	M70.969	M71.442	M75.50	M79.645	M80.041G	M80.811G	M80.859P
M66.311	M67.342	M67.932	M70.971	M71.449	M75.51	M79.646	M80.041K	M80.811K	M80.859S
M66.312	M67.349	M67.939	M70.972	M71.451	M75.52	M79.651	M80.041P	M80.811P	M80.861A
M66.319	M67.351	M67.941	M70.979	M71.452	M75.80	M79.652	M80.041S	M80.811S	M80.861D
M66.321	M67.352	M67.942	M70.98	M71.459	M75.81	M79.659	M80.042A	M80.812A	M80.861G
M66.322	M67.359	M67.949	M70.99	M71.461	M75.82	M79.661	M80.042D	M80.812D	M80.861K
M66.329	M67.361	M67.951	M71.00	M71.462	M75.90	M79.662	M80.042G	M80.812K	M80.861S
M66.331	M67.362	M67.952	M71.011	M71.469	M75.91	M79.669	M80.042K	M80.812P	M80.862A
M66.332	M67.369	M67.959	M71.012	M71.471	M75.92	M79.671	M80.042P	M80.812S	M80.862D
M66.339	M67.371	M67.961	M71.019	M71.472	M76.00	M79.672	M80.042S	M80.819A	M80.862G
M66.341	M67.372	M67.962	M71.021	M71.479	M76.01	M79.673	M80.049A	M80.819G	M80.862K
M66.342	M67.379	M67.969	M71.022	M71.48	M76.02	M79.674	M80.049D	M80.819K	M80.862P
M66.349	M67.38	M67.971	M71.029	M71.49	M76.10	M79.675	M80.049G	M80.819P	M80.862S
M66.351	M67.39	M67.972	M71.031	M71.50	M76.11	M79.676	M80.049P	M80.819S	M80.869A
M66.352	M67.40	M67.979	M71.032	M71.521	M76.12	M79.7	M80.049S	M80.821A	M80.869D
M66.359	M67.411	M67.98	M71.039	M71.522	M76.20	M79.81	M80.051A	M80.821D	M80.869G
M66.361	M67.412	M67.99	M71.041	M71.529	M76.21	M79.89	M80.051D	M80.821G	M80.869K
M66.362	M67.419	M70.031	M71.042	M71.531	M76.22	M79.9	M80.051G	M80.821K	M80.869P
M66.369	M67.421	M70.032	M71.049	M71.532	M76.30	M79.A11	M80.051K	M80.821P	M80.869S
M66.371	M67.422	M70.039	M71.051	M71.539	M76.31	M79.A12	M80.051P	M80.821S	M80.871A
M66.372	M67.429	M70.041	M71.052	M71.541	M76.32	M79.A19	M80.051S	M80.822A	M80.871D
M66.379	M67.431	M70.042	M71.059	M71.542	M76.40	M79.A21	M80.052A	M80.822D	M80.871G
M66.38	M67.432	M70.049	M71.061	M71.549	M76.41	M79.A22	M80.052D	M80.822G	M80.871K
M66.39	M67.439	M70.10	M71.062	M71.551	M76.42	M79.A29	M80.052G	M80.822K	M80.871P
M66.80	M67.441	M70.11	M71.069	M71.552	M76.50	M79.A3	M80.052K	M80.822P	M80.871S
M66.811	M67.442	M70.12	M71.071	M71.559	M76.51	M79.A9	M80.052P	M80.822S	M80.872A
M66.812	M67.449	M70.20	M71.072	M71.561	M76.52	M80.00XA	M80.052S	M80.829A	M80.872D
M66.819	M67.451	M70.21	M71.079	M71.562	M76.60	M80.00XD	M80.059A	M80.829D	M80.872G
M66.821	M67.452	M70.22	M71.08	M71.569	M76.61	M80.00XG	M80.059D	M80.829K	M80.872K
M66.822	M67.459	M70.30	M71.09	M71.571	M76.62	M80.00XK	M80.059G	M80.829P	M80.872P
M66.829	M67.461	M70.31	M71.10	M71.572	M76.70	M80.00XP	M80.059K	M80.829S	M80.872S
M66.831	M67.462	M70.32	M71.111	M71.579	M76.71	M80.00XS	M80.059P	M80.831A	M80.879A
M66.832	M67.469	M70.40	M71.112	M71.58	M76.72	M80.011A	M80.059S	M80.831D	M80.879D
M66.839	M67.471	M70.41	M71.119	M71.80	M76.811	M80.011D	M80.061A	M80.831G	M80.879G
M66.841	M67.472	M70.42	M71.121	M71.811	M76.812	M80.011K	M80.061D	M80.831K	M80.879K
M66.842	M67.479	M70.50	M71.122	M71.812	M76.819	M80.011P	M80.061G	M80.831P	M80.879P
M66.849	M67.48	M70.51	M71.129	M71.819	M76.821	M80.011S	M80.061K	M80.831S	M80.879S
M66.851	M67.49	M70.52	M71.131	M71.821	M76.822	M80.012A	M80.061P	M80.832A	M80.88XA
M66.852	M67.50	M70.60	M71.132	M71.822	M76.829	M80.012D	M80.061S	M80.832D	M80.88XD
M66.859	M67.51	M70.61	M71.139	M71.829	M76.891	M80.012G	M80.062A	M80.832G	M80.88XG
M66.861	M67.52	M70.62	M71.141	M71.831	M76.892	M80.012K	M80.062D	M80.832K	M80.88XK
M66.862	M67.80	M70.70	M71.142	M71.832	M76.899	M80.012P	M80.062G	M80.832P	M80.88XP
M66.869	M67.811	M70.71	M71.149	M71.839	M76.9	M80.012S	M80.062K	M80.832S	M80.88XS
M66.871	M67.812	M70.72	M71.151	M71.841	M77.00	M80.019A	M80.062P	M80.839A	M81.0
M66.872	M67.813	M70.80	M71.152	M71.842	M77.01	M80.019D	M80.062S	M80.839D	M81.6
M66.879	M67.814	M70.811	M71.159	M71.849	M77.02	M80.019G	M80.069A	M80.839G	M81.8
M66.88	M67.819	M70.812	M71.161	M71.851	M77.10	M80.019K	M80.069D	M80.839K	M83.0
M66.89	M67.821	M70.819	M71.162	M71.852	M77.11	M80.019P	M80.069G	M80.839P	M83.1
M66.9	M67.822	M70.821	M71.169	M71.859	M77.12	M80.019S	M80.069K	M80.839S	M83.2
M67.00	M67.823	M70.822	M71.171	M71.861	M77.20	M80.021A	M80.069P	M80.839G	M83.3
M67.01	M67.824	M70.829	M71.172	M71.862	M77.21	M80.021D	M80.069S	M80.839K	M83.4
M67.02	M67.829	M70.831	M71.179	M71.869	M77.22	M80.021G	M80.071A	M80.841A	M83.5
M67.20	M67.831	M70.832	M71.18	M71.871	M77.30	M80.021K	M80.071D	M80.841D	M83.8
M67.211	M67.832	M70.839	M71.19	M71.872	M77.31	M80.021P	M80.071G	M80.841K	M83.9
M67.212	M67.833	M70.841	M71.20	M71.879	M77.32	M80.021S	M80.071K	M80.841P	M84.30XA
M67.219	M67.834	M70.842	M71.21	M71.88	M77.40	M80.022A	M80.071P	M80.841S	M84.30XD
M67.221	M67.839	M70.849	M71.22	M71.89	M77.41	M80.022D	M80.071S	M80.842A	M84.30XG
M67.222	M67.841	M70.851	M71.30	M71.9	M77.42	M80.022G	M80.072A	M80.842D	M84.30XK
M67.229	M67.842	M70.859	M71.311	M72.0	M77.50	M80.022K	M80.072D	M80.842G	M84.30XP
M67.231	M67.843	M70.861	M71.312	M72.1	M77.51	M80.022P	M80.072K	M80.842K	M84.30XS
M67.232	M67.844	M70.862	M71.319	M72.2	M77.52	M80.022S	M80.072P	M80.842P	M84.311A
M67.239	M67.849	M70.869	M71.321	M72.4	M77.8	M80.029A	M80.072S	M80.842S	M84.311D
M67.241	M67.851	M70.871	M71.322	M72.6	M77.9	M80.029D	M80.079A	M80.849A	M84.311G
M67.242	M67.852	M70.872	M71.329	M72.8	M79.0	M80.029G	M80.079D	M80.849D	M84.311K
M67.249	M67.853	M70.879	M71.331	M72.9	M79.10	M80.029K	M80.079G	M80.849K	M84.311P
M67.251	M67.854	M70.88	M71.332	M75.00	M79.11	M80.029P	M80.079A	M80.849P	M84.311S
M67.252	M67.859	M70.89	M71.339	M75.01	M79.12	M80.029S	M80.079D	M80.849K	M84.312A
M67.259	M67.861	M70.90	M71.341	M75.02	M79.18	M80.031A	M80.079G	M80.849P	M84.312D
M67.261	M67.862	M70.90	M71.342	M75.100	M79.5	M80.031A	M80.079G	M80.849P	M84.312D

M84.312G	M84.345P	M84.374A	M84.431G	M84.454P	M84.479A	M84.541G	M84.572P	M84.633A	M84.664G
M84.312K	M84.345S	M84.374D	M84.431K	M84.454S	M84.479D	M84.541K	M84.572S	M84.633D	M84.664K
M84.312P	M84.346A	M84.374G	M84.431P	M84.459A	M84.479G	M84.541P	M84.573A	M84.633G	M84.664P
M84.312S	M84.346D	M84.374K	M84.431S	M84.459D	M84.479K	M84.541S	M84.573D	M84.633K	M84.664S
M84.319A	M84.346G	M84.374P	M84.432A	M84.459G	M84.479P	M84.542A	M84.573K	M84.633S	M84.669D
M84.319D	M84.346K	M84.374S	M84.432D	M84.459K	M84.479S	M84.542D	M84.573P	M84.634A	M84.669G
M84.319G	M84.346P	M84.375A	M84.432G	M84.459P	M84.48XA	M84.542G	M84.573S	M84.634D	M84.669K
M84.319K	M84.346S	M84.375D	M84.432K	M84.459S	M84.48XD	M84.542K	M84.574A	M84.634G	M84.669P
M84.319P	M84.350A	M84.375G	M84.432P	M84.461A	M84.48XG	M84.542P	M84.574D	M84.634K	M84.669S
M84.319S	M84.350D	M84.375K	M84.432S	M84.461D	M84.48XK	M84.542S	M84.574G	M84.634P	M84.671A
M84.321A	M84.350G	M84.375P	M84.433A	M84.461G	M84.48XP	M84.549A	M84.574K	M84.634S	M84.671D
M84.321D	M84.350K	M84.375S	M84.433D	M84.461K	M84.48XS	M84.549D	M84.574P	M84.639A	M84.671G
M84.321G	M84.350P	M84.376A	M84.433G	M84.461P	M84.50XA	M84.549G	M84.574S	M84.639D	M84.671K
M84.321K	M84.350S	M84.376D	M84.433K	M84.461S	M84.50XD	M84.549K	M84.575A	M84.639K	M84.671P
M84.321P	M84.351A	M84.376G	M84.433P	M84.462A	M84.50XG	M84.549P	M84.575D	M84.639P	M84.671S
M84.321S	M84.351D	M84.376K	M84.433S	M84.462D	M84.50XK	M84.549S	M84.575G	M84.639S	M84.672A
M84.322A	M84.351G	M84.376P	M84.434A	M84.462G	M84.50XP	M84.550A	M84.575K	M84.641A	M84.672D
M84.322D	M84.351K	M84.376S	M84.434D	M84.462K	M84.50XS	M84.550D	M84.575P	M84.641D	M84.672K
M84.322G	M84.351P	M84.377A	M84.434G	M84.462P	M84.511A	M84.550G	M84.575S	M84.641G	M84.672P
M84.322K	M84.351S	M84.377D	M84.434K	M84.462S	M84.511D	M84.550K	M84.576A	M84.641K	M84.672S
M84.322P	M84.352A	M84.377G	M84.434P	M84.463A	M84.511G	M84.550P	M84.576D	M84.641P	M84.673A
M84.322S	M84.352D	M84.377K	M84.434S	M84.463D	M84.511K	M84.550S	M84.576G	M84.641S	M84.673D
M84.329A	M84.352G	M84.377P	M84.439A	M84.463G	M84.511P	M84.551A	M84.576K	M84.642A	M84.673G
M84.329D	M84.352K	M84.377S	M84.439D	M84.463K	M84.511S	M84.551D	M84.576P	M84.642D	M84.673K
M84.329G	M84.352P	M84.378A	M84.439G	M84.463P	M84.512A	M84.551G	M84.576S	M84.642G	M84.673P
M84.329K	M84.352S	M84.378D	M84.439K	M84.463S	M84.512D	M84.551K	M84.58XA	M84.642K	M84.673S
M84.329P	M84.353A	M84.378G	M84.439P	M84.464A	M84.512G	M84.551P	M84.58XD	M84.642P	M84.674A
M84.329S	M84.353D	M84.378K	M84.439S	M84.464D	M84.512K	M84.551S	M84.58XG	M84.642S	M84.674D
M84.331A	M84.353G	M84.378P	M84.441A	M84.464G	M84.512P	M84.552A	M84.58XK	M84.649A	M84.674G
M84.331D	M84.353K	M84.378S	M84.441D	M84.464K	M84.512S	M84.552D	M84.58XP	M84.649D	M84.674K
M84.331G	M84.353P	M84.379A	M84.441G	M84.464P	M84.519A	M84.552G	M84.58XS	M84.649G	M84.674P
M84.331K	M84.353S	M84.379D	M84.441K	M84.464S	M84.519D	M84.552K	M84.60XA	M84.649K	M84.674S
M84.331P	M84.359A	M84.379G	M84.441P	M84.469A	M84.519G	M84.552P	M84.60XD	M84.649P	M84.675A
M84.331S	M84.359D	M84.379K	M84.441S	M84.469D	M84.519K	M84.552S	M84.60XG	M84.649S	M84.675D
M84.332A	M84.359G	M84.379P	M84.442A	M84.469G	M84.519P	M84.553A	M84.60XK	M84.650A	M84.675G
M84.332D	M84.359K	M84.379S	M84.442D	M84.469K	M84.519S	M84.553D	M84.60XP	M84.650D	M84.675K
M84.332G	M84.359P	M84.38XA	M84.442G	M84.469S	M84.521A	M84.553K	M84.60XS	M84.650G	M84.675P
M84.332K	M84.359S	M84.38XD	M84.442K	M84.471A	M84.521D	M84.553P	M84.611A	M84.650K	M84.675S
M84.332P	M84.361A	M84.38XG	M84.442P	M84.471D	M84.521G	M84.553S	M84.611D	M84.650P	M84.676A
M84.332S	M84.361D	M84.38XK	M84.442S	M84.471G	M84.521K	M84.559A	M84.611G	M84.651A	M84.676D
M84.333A	M84.361G	M84.38XP	M84.443A	M84.471K	M84.521P	M84.559D	M84.611K	M84.651D	M84.676G
M84.333D	M84.361K	M84.38XS	M84.443D	M84.471P	M84.521S	M84.559G	M84.611S	M84.651G	M84.676K
M84.333G	M84.361P	M84.40XA	M84.443G	M84.471S	M84.522A	M84.559K	M84.612A	M84.651K	M84.676P
M84.333K	M84.361S	M84.40XD	M84.443K	M84.472A	M84.522D	M84.559P	M84.612D	M84.651P	M84.676S
M84.333P	M84.362A	M84.40XG	M84.443P	M84.472D	M84.522G	M84.559S	M84.612G	M84.651S	M84.68XA
M84.333S	M84.362D	M84.40XK	M84.443S	M84.472G	M84.522K	M84.561A	M84.612K	M84.652A	M84.68XD
M84.334A	M84.362G	M84.40XP	M84.444A	M84.472K	M84.522P	M84.561D	M84.612P	M84.652D	M84.68XG
M84.334D	M84.362K	M84.40XS	M84.444D	M84.472P	M84.522S	M84.561G	M84.612S	M84.652G	M84.68XK
M84.334G	M84.362P	M84.411A	M84.444G	M84.472S	M84.529A	M84.561K	M84.619A	M84.652K	M84.68XP
M84.334K	M84.362S	M84.411D	M84.444K	M84.473A	M84.529D	M84.561P	M84.619D	M84.652P	M84.68XS
M84.334P	M84.363A	M84.411G	M84.444P	M84.473D	M84.529G	M84.561S	M84.619G	M84.652S	M84.750A
M84.334S	M84.363D	M84.411K	M84.444S	M84.473G	M84.529K	M84.562A	M84.619K	M84.653A	M84.750D
M84.339A	M84.363G	M84.411P	M84.445A	M84.473K	M84.529P	M84.562D	M84.619P	M84.653D	M84.750G
M84.339D	M84.363K	M84.411S	M84.445D	M84.473P	M84.529S	M84.562G	M84.619S	M84.653G	M84.750K
M84.339G	M84.363P	M84.412A	M84.445G	M84.473S	M84.531A	M84.562K	M84.621A	M84.653K	M84.750P
M84.339K	M84.363S	M84.412D	M84.445K	M84.474A	M84.531D	M84.562P	M84.621D	M84.653P	M84.750S
M84.339P	M84.364A	M84.412G	M84.445P	M84.474D	M84.531G	M84.562S	M84.621G	M84.653S	M84.751A
M84.339S	M84.364D	M84.412K	M84.445S	M84.474G	M84.531K	M84.563A	M84.621K	M84.659A	M84.751D
M84.341A	M84.364G	M84.412P	M84.446A	M84.474K	M84.531P	M84.563D	M84.621P	M84.659D	M84.751K
M84.341D	M84.364K	M84.412S	M84.446D	M84.474P	M84.531S	M84.563G	M84.621S	M84.659G	M84.751P
M84.341A	M84.364P	M84.419A	M84.446G	M84.474S	M84.532A	M84.563K	M84.622A	M84.659K	M84.751S
M84.341K	M84.364S	M84.419D	M84.446K	M84.475A	M84.532D	M84.563P	M84.622D	M84.659S	M84.752A
M84.341P	M84.369A	M84.419G	M84.446P	M84.475D	M84.532G	M84.563S	M84.622K	M84.659P	M84.752D
M84.341S	M84.369D	M84.419K	M84.446S	M84.475G	M84.532K	M84.564A	M84.622P	M84.659S	M84.752G
M84.342A	M84.369G	M84.419P	M84.451A	M84.475K	M84.532P	M84.564D	M84.622S	M84.661A	M84.752K
M84.342D	M84.369K	M84.419S	M84.451D	M84.475P	M84.532S	M84.564G	M84.629A	M84.661D	M84.752P
M84.342G	M84.369P	M84.421A	M84.451G	M84.475S	M84.533A	M84.564K	M84.629D	M84.661G	M84.752S
M84.342K	M84.369S	M84.421D	M84.451K	M84.476A	M84.533D	M84.564P	M84.629G	M84.661P	M84.753A
M84.342P	M84.371A	M84.421G	M84.451P	M84.476D	M84.533G	M84.564S	M84.629K	M84.661S	M84.753D
M84.342S	M84.371D	M84.421K	M84.451S	M84.476K	M84.533P	M84.569A	M84.629P	M84.662A	M84.753G
M84.343A	M84.371G	M84.421P	M84.452A	M84.476P	M84.533S	M84.569D	M84.629S	M84.662D	M84.753K
M84.343D	M84.371K	M84.421S	M84.452D	M84.476S	M84.534A	M84.569G	M84.631A	M84.662G	M84.753P
M84.343G	M84.371P	M84.422A	M84.452G	M84.477A	M84.534D	M84.569K	M84.631D	M84.662K	M84.753S
M84.343K	M84.371S	M84.422D	M84.452K	M84.477D	M84.534G	M84.569P	M84.631G	M84.662P	M84.753S
M84.343P	M84.372A	M84.422K	M84.452P	M84.477G	M84.534K	M84.569S	M84.631K	M84.662S	M84.754A
M84.343S	M84.372D	M84.422P	M84.452S	M84.477K	M84.534P	M84.571A	M84.631P	M84.663A	M84.754D
M84.344A	M84.372G	M84.422S	M84.453A	M84.477G	M84.534S	M84.571D	M84.631S	M84.663D	M84.754G
M84.344D	M84.372K	M84.429A	M84.453D	M84.477S	M84.539A	M84.571G	M84.632A	M84.663G	M84.754K
M84.344G	M84.372P	M84.429D	M84.453K	M84.478A	M84.539D	M84.571K	M84.632D	M84.663K	M84.754P
M84.344K	M84.372S	M84.429G	M84.453P	M84.478D	M84.539G	M84.571P	M84.632G	M84.663P	M84.754S
M84.344P	M84.373A	M84.429K	M84.453S	M84.478G	M84.539K	M84.571S	M84.632K	M84.664A	M84.755A
M84.344S	M84.373D	M84.429P	M84.454A	M84.478P	M84.539P	M84.572A	M84.632P	M84.664D	M84.755D
M84.345A	M84.373G	M84.429S	M84.454D	M84.478S	M84.539S	M84.572D	M84.632S	M84.664G	M84.755G
M84.345D	M84.373K	M84.431A	M84.454G		M84.541A	M84.572G			M84.755K
M84.345G	M84.373P	M84.431D	M84.454K		M84.541D	M84.572K	M84.632S	M84.664D	M84.755K
M84.345K	M84.373S								

M84.755P	M85.132	M85.58	M86.142	M86.511	M87.063	M87.262	M87.862	M89.155	M89.452
M84.755S	M85.139	M85.59	M86.149	M86.512	M87.064	M87.263	M87.863	M89.156	M89.459
M84.756A	M85.141	M85.60	M86.151	M86.519	M87.065	M87.264	M87.864	M89.157	M89.461
M84.756D	M85.142	M85.611	M86.152	M86.521	M87.066	M87.265	M87.865	M89.158	M89.462
M84.756G	M85.149	M85.612	M86.159	M86.522	M87.071	M87.266	M87.869	M89.159	M89.469
M84.756K	M85.151	M85.619	M86.161	M86.529	M87.072	M87.271	M87.871	M89.160	M89.471
M84.756P	M85.152	M85.621	M86.162	M86.531	M87.073	M87.272	M87.872	M89.161	M89.472
M84.756S	M85.159	M85.622	M86.169	M86.532	M87.074	M87.273	M87.873	M89.162	M89.479
M84.757A	M85.161	M85.629	M86.171	M86.539	M87.075	M87.274	M87.874	M89.163	M89.48
M84.757D	M85.162	M85.631	M86.172	M86.541	M87.076	M87.275	M87.875	M89.164	M89.49
M84.757G	M85.169	M85.632	M86.179	M86.542	M87.077	M87.276	M87.876	M89.165	M89.50
M84.757K	M85.171	M85.639	M86.18	M86.549	M87.078	M87.277	M87.877	M89.166	M89.511
M84.757P	M85.172	M85.641	M86.19	M86.551	M87.079	M87.278	M87.878	M89.167	M89.512
M84.757S	M85.179	M85.642	M86.20	M86.552	M87.08	M87.279	M87.879	M89.168	M89.519
M84.758A	M85.18	M85.649	M86.211	M86.559	M87.09	M87.28	M87.88	M89.169	M89.521
M84.758D	M85.19	M85.651	M86.212	M86.561	M87.10	M87.29	M87.89	M89.18	M89.522
M84.758G	M85.2	M85.652	M86.219	M86.562	M87.111	M87.30	M87.9	M89.20	M89.529
M84.758K	M85.30	M85.659	M86.221	M86.569	M87.112	M87.311	M88.0	M89.211	M89.531
M84.758P	M85.311	M85.661	M86.222	M86.571	M87.119	M87.312	M88.1	M89.212	M89.532
M84.758S	M85.312	M85.662	M86.229	M86.572	M87.121	M87.319	M88.811	M89.219	M89.539
M84.759A	M85.319	M85.669	M86.231	M86.579	M87.122	M87.321	M88.812	M89.221	M89.541
M84.759D	M85.321	M85.671	M86.232	M86.58	M87.129	M87.322	M88.819	M89.222	M89.542
M84.759G	M85.322	M85.672	M86.239	M86.59	M87.131	M87.329	M88.821	M89.229	M89.549
M84.759K	M85.329	M85.679	M86.241	M86.60	M87.132	M87.331	M88.822	M89.231	M89.551
M84.759P	M85.331	M85.68	M86.242	M86.611	M87.133	M87.332	M88.829	M89.232	M89.552
M84.759S	M85.332	M85.69	M86.249	M86.612	M87.134	M87.333	M88.831	M89.233	M89.559
M84.80	M85.339	M85.80	M86.251	M86.619	M87.135	M87.334	M88.832	M89.234	M89.561
M84.811	M85.341	M85.811	M86.252	M86.621	M87.136	M87.335	M88.839	M89.239	M89.562
M84.812	M85.342	M85.812	M86.259	M86.622	M87.137	M87.336	M88.841	M89.241	M89.569
M84.819	M85.349	M85.819	M86.261	M86.629	M87.138	M87.337	M88.842	M89.242	M89.571
M84.821	M85.351	M85.821	M86.262	M86.631	M87.139	M87.338	M88.849	M89.249	M89.572
M84.822	M85.352	M85.822	M86.269	M86.632	M87.141	M87.339	M88.851	M89.251	M89.579
M84.829	M85.359	M85.829	M86.271	M86.639	M87.142	M87.341	M88.852	M89.252	M89.58
M84.831	M85.361	M85.831	M86.272	M86.641	M87.143	M87.342	M88.859	M89.259	M89.59
M84.832	M85.362	M85.832	M86.279	M86.642	M87.144	M87.343	M88.861	M89.261	M89.60
M84.833	M85.369	M85.839	M86.28	M86.649	M87.145	M87.344	M88.862	M89.262	M89.611
M84.834	M85.371	M85.841	M86.29	M86.651	M87.146	M87.345	M88.869	M89.263	M89.612
M84.839	M85.372	M85.842	M86.30	M86.652	M87.150	M87.346	M88.871	M89.264	M89.619
M84.841	M85.379	M85.849	M86.311	M86.659	M87.151	M87.350	M88.872	M89.269	M89.621
M84.842	M85.38	M85.851	M86.312	M86.661	M87.152	M87.351	M88.879	M89.271	M89.622
M84.849	M85.39	M85.852	M86.319	M86.662	M87.159	M87.352	M88.88	M89.272	M89.629
M84.851	M85.40	M85.859	M86.321	M86.669	M87.161	M87.353	M88.89	M89.279	M89.631
M84.852	M85.411	M85.861	M86.322	M86.671	M87.162	M87.361	M88.9	M89.28	M89.632
M84.859	M85.412	M85.862	M86.329	M86.672	M87.163	M87.362	M89.00	M89.29	M89.639
M84.861	M85.419	M85.869	M86.331	M86.679	M87.164	M87.363	M89.011	M89.30	M89.641
M84.862	M85.421	M85.871	M86.332	M86.68	M87.165	M87.364	M89.012	M89.311	M89.642
M84.863	M85.422	M85.872	M86.339	M86.69	M87.166	M87.365	M89.019	M89.312	M89.649
M84.864	M85.429	M85.879	M86.341	M86.8X0	M87.171	M87.366	M89.021	M89.319	M89.651
M84.869	M85.431	M85.88	M86.342	M86.8X1	M87.172	M87.371	M89.022	M89.321	M89.652
M84.871	M85.432	M85.89	M86.349	M86.8X2	M87.173	M87.372	M89.029	M89.322	M89.659
M84.872	M85.439	M85.9	M86.351	M86.8X3	M87.174	M87.373	M89.031	M89.329	M89.661
M84.879	M85.441	M86.00	M86.352	M86.8X4	M87.175	M87.374	M89.032	M89.331	M89.662
M84.88	M85.442	M86.011	M86.359	M86.8X5	M87.176	M87.375	M89.039	M89.332	M89.669
M84.9	M85.449	M86.012	M86.361	M86.8X6	M87.177	M87.376	M89.041	M89.333	M89.671
M85.00	M85.451	M86.019	M86.362	M86.8X7	M87.178	M87.377	M89.042	M89.334	M89.672
M85.011	M85.452	M86.021	M86.369	M86.8X8	M87.179	M87.378	M89.049	M89.339	M89.679
M85.012	M85.459	M86.022	M86.371	M86.8X9	M87.180	M87.379	M89.051	M89.341	M89.68
M85.019	M85.461	M86.029	M86.372	M86.9	M87.188	M87.38	M89.052	M89.342	M89.69
M85.021	M85.462	M86.031	M86.379	M87.00	M87.19	M87.39	M89.059	M89.349	M89.70
M85.022	M85.469	M86.032	M86.38	M87.011	M87.20	M87.80	M89.061	M89.351	M89.711
M85.029	M85.471	M86.039	M86.39	M87.012	M87.211	M87.811	M89.062	M89.352	M89.712
M85.031	M85.472	M86.041	M86.40	M87.019	M87.212	M87.812	M89.069	M89.359	M89.719
M85.032	M85.479	M86.042	M86.411	M87.021	M87.219	M87.819	M89.071	M89.361	M89.721
M85.039	M85.48	M86.049	M86.412	M87.022	M87.221	M87.821	M89.072	M89.362	M89.722
M85.041	M85.50	M86.051	M86.419	M87.029	M87.222	M87.822	M89.079	M89.363	M89.729
M85.042	M85.511	M86.052	M86.421	M87.031	M87.229	M87.829	M89.08	M89.364	M89.731
M85.049	M85.512	M86.059	M86.422	M87.032	M87.231	M87.831	M89.09	M89.369	M89.732
M85.051	M85.519	M86.061	M86.429	M87.033	M87.232	M87.832	M89.121	M89.371	M89.739
M85.052	M85.521	M86.062	M86.431	M87.034	M87.233	M87.833	M89.122	M89.372	M89.741
M85.059	M85.522	M86.069	M86.432	M87.035	M87.234	M87.834	M89.123	M89.379	M89.742
M85.061	M85.529	M86.071	M86.439	M87.036	M87.235	M87.835	M89.124	M89.38	M89.749
M85.062	M85.531	M86.072	M86.441	M87.037	M87.236	M87.836	M89.125	M89.39	M89.751
M85.069	M85.532	M86.079	M86.442	M87.038	M87.237	M87.837	M89.126	M89.40	M89.752
M85.071	M85.539	M86.08	M86.449	M87.039	M87.238	M87.838	M89.127	M89.411	M89.759
M85.072	M85.541	M86.09	M86.451	M87.041	M87.239	M87.839	M89.128	M89.412	M89.761
M85.079	M85.542	M86.10	M86.452	M87.042	M87.241	M87.841	M89.129	M89.419	M89.762
M85.08	M85.549	M86.111	M86.459	M87.043	M87.242	M87.842	M89.131	M89.421	M89.769
M85.09	M85.551	M86.112	M86.461	M87.044	M87.243	M87.843	M89.132	M89.422	M89.771
M85.10	M85.552	M86.119	M86.462	M87.045	M87.244	M87.844	M89.133	M89.429	M89.772
M85.111	M85.559	M86.121	M86.469	M87.046	M87.245	M87.845	M89.134	M89.431	M89.779
M85.112	M85.561	M86.122	M86.471	M87.050	M87.246	M87.849	M89.138	M89.432	M89.78
M85.119	M85.562	M86.129	M86.472	M87.051	M87.250	M87.850	M89.139	M89.439	M89.79
M85.121	M85.569	M86.131	M86.479	M87.052	M87.251	M87.851	M89.151	M89.441	M89.8X0
M85.122	M85.571	M86.132	M86.48	M87.059	M87.252	M87.852	M89.152	M89.442	M89.8X1
M85.129	M85.572	M86.139	M86.49	M87.061	M87.256	M87.859	M89.153	M89.449	M89.8X3
M85.131	M85.579	M86.141	M86.50	M87.062	M87.261	M87.861	M89.154	M89.451	

M89.8X4	M91.30	M93.812	M95.3	M99.38	Q66.50	Q71.892	Q76.8	S02.11DG	S02.610G
M89.8X5	M91.31	M93.819	M95.4	M99.39	Q66.51	Q71.893	Q76.9	S02.11DK	S02.610K
M89.8X6	M91.32	M93.821	M95.5	M99.40	Q66.52	Q71.899	Q77.0	S02.11ED	S02.611D
M89.8X7	M91.40	M93.822	M95.8	M99.41	Q66.6	Q71.90	Q77.1	S02.11EG	S02.611G
M89.8X8	M91.41	M93.829	M95.9	M99.42	Q66.70	Q71.91	Q77.2	S02.11EK	S02.611K
M89.8X9	M91.42	M93.831	M96.0	M99.43	Q66.71	Q71.92	Q77.3	S02.11FD	S02.612D
M89.9	M91.80	M93.832	M96.1	M99.44	Q66.72	Q71.93	Q77.4	S02.11FG	S02.612G
M90.50	M91.81	M93.839	M96.2	M99.45	Q66.80	Q72.00	Q77.5	S02.11FK	S02.612K
M90.511	M91.82	M93.841	M96.3	M99.46	Q66.81	Q72.01	Q77.6	S02.11GD	S02.620D
M90.512	M91.90	M93.842	M96.4	M99.47	Q66.82	Q72.02	Q77.7	S02.11GG	S02.620G
M90.519	M91.91	M93.849	M96.5	M99.48	Q66.89	Q72.03	Q77.8	S02.11GK	S02.620K
M90.521	M91.92	M93.851	M96.621	M99.49	Q66.90	Q72.10	Q77.9	S02.11HD	S02.621D
M90.522	M92.00	M93.852	M96.622	M99.50	Q66.91	Q72.11	Q78.0	S02.11HG	S02.621G
M90.529	M92.01	M93.859	M96.629	M99.51	Q66.92	Q72.12	Q78.1	S02.11HK	S02.621K
M90.531	M92.02	M93.861	M96.631	M99.52	Q67.0	Q72.13	Q78.2	S02.19XD	S02.622D
M90.532	M92.10	M93.862	M96.632	M99.53	Q67.1	Q72.20	Q78.3	S02.19XG	S02.622G
M90.539	M92.11	M93.869	M96.639	M99.54	Q67.2	Q72.21	Q78.4	S02.19XK	S02.622K
M90.541	M92.12	M93.871	M96.65	M99.55	Q67.3	Q72.22	Q78.5	S02.2XXD	S02.630D
M90.542	M92.201	M93.872	M96.661	M99.56	Q67.4	Q72.23	Q78.6	S02.2XXG	S02.630G
M90.549	M92.202	M93.879	M96.662	M99.57	Q67.5	Q72.30	Q78.8	S02.2XXK	S02.630K
M90.551	M92.209	M93.88	M96.669	M99.58	Q67.6	Q72.31	Q78.9	S02.30XD	S02.631D
M90.552	M92.211	M93.89	M96.671	M99.59	Q67.7	Q72.32	Q79.60	S02.30XG	S02.631G
M90.559	M92.212	M93.90	M96.672	M99.60	Q67.8	Q72.33	Q79.61	S02.30XK	S02.631K
M90.561	M92.219	M93.911	M96.679	M99.61	Q68.0	Q72.40	Q79.62	S02.31XD	S02.632D
M90.562	M92.221	M93.912	M96.69	M99.62	Q68.1	Q72.41	Q79.63	S02.31XG	S02.632G
M90.569	M92.222	M93.919	M97.01XA	M99.63	Q68.2	Q72.42	Q79.69	S02.31XK	S02.632K
M90.571	M92.229	M93.921	M97.01XD	M99.64	Q68.3	Q72.43	Q79.8	S02.32XD	S02.640D
M90.572	M92.291	M93.922	M97.02XA	M99.65	Q68.4	Q72.50	Q79.9	S02.32XG	S02.640G
M90.579	M92.292	M93.929	M97.02XD	M99.66	Q68.5	Q72.51	Q87.0	S02.32XK	S02.640K
M90.58	M92.299	M93.931	M97.11XA	M99.67	Q68.6	Q72.52	Q87.11	S02.400D	S02.641D
M90.59	M92.30	M93.932	M97.11XD	M99.68	Q68.8	Q72.53	Q87.19	S02.400G	S02.641G
M90.60	M92.31	M93.939	M97.12XA	M99.69	Q69.0	Q72.60	Q87.2	S02.400K	S02.641K
M90.611	M92.32	M93.941	M97.12XD	M99.70	Q69.1	Q72.61	Q87.3	S02.401D	S02.642D
M90.612	M92.40	M93.942	M97.21XA	M99.71	Q69.2	Q72.62	Q87.5	S02.401G	S02.642G
M90.619	M92.41	M93.949	M97.21XD	M99.72	Q69.9	Q72.63	Q87.81	S02.401K	S02.642K
M90.621	M92.42	M93.951	M97.22XA	M99.73	Q70.00	Q72.70	Q87.82	S02.402D	S02.650D
M90.622	M92.50	M93.952	M97.22XD	M99.74	Q70.01	Q72.71	Q87.89	S02.402G	S02.650G
M90.629	M92.51	M93.959	M97.31XA	M99.75	Q70.02	Q72.72	Q89.7	S02.402K	S02.650K
M90.631	M92.52	M93.961	M97.31XD	M99.76	Q70.03	Q72.73	Q89.8	S02.40AD	S02.651D
M90.632	M92.60	M93.962	M97.32XA	M99.77	Q70.10	Q72.811	R26.2	S02.40AG	S02.651G
M90.639	M92.61	M93.969	M97.32XD	M99.78	Q70.11	Q72.812	R29.4	S02.40AK	S02.651K
M90.641	M92.62	M93.971	M97.41XA	M99.79	Q70.12	Q72.813	R29.891	S02.40BD	S02.652D
M90.642	M92.70	M93.972	M97.41XD	M99.80	Q70.13	Q72.819	R29.898	S02.40BG	S02.652G
M90.649	M92.71	M93.979	M97.42XA	M99.81	Q70.20	Q72.891	R93.6	S02.40BK	S02.652K
M90.651	M92.72	M93.98	M97.42XD	M99.82	Q70.21	Q72.892	R93.7	S02.40CD	S02.66XD
M90.652	M92.8	M93.99	M97.8XXA	M99.83	Q70.22	Q72.893	R94.131	S02.40CG	S02.66XG
M90.659	M92.9	M94.1	M97.8XXD	M99.84	Q70.23	Q72.899	S02.0XXA	S02.40CK	S02.66XK
M90.661	M93.001	M94.20	M97.9XXA	M99.85	Q70.30	Q72.90	S02.0XXD	S02.40DD	S02.670D
M90.662	M93.002	M94.211	M97.9XXD	M99.86	Q70.31	Q72.91	S02.0XXG	S02.40DG	S02.670G
M90.669	M93.003	M94.212	M99.00	M99.87	Q70.32	Q72.92	S02.0XXK	S02.40DK	S02.670K
M90.671	M93.011	M94.219	M99.01	M99.88	Q70.33	Q72.93	S02.101D	S02.40ED	S02.671D
M90.672	M93.012	M94.221	M99.02	M99.89	Q70.4	Q73.0	S02.101G	S02.40EG	S02.671G
M90.679	M93.013	M94.222	M99.03	M99.9	Q70.9	Q73.1	S02.101K	S02.40EK	S02.671K
M90.68	M93.021	M94.229	M99.04	Q65.00	Q71.00	Q73.8	S02.102D	S02.40FD	S02.672D
M90.69	M93.022	M94.231	M99.05	Q65.01	Q71.01	Q74.0	S02.102G	S02.40FG	S02.672G
M90.80	M93.023	M94.232	M99.06	Q65.02	Q71.02	Q74.1	S02.102K	S02.40FK	S02.672K
M90.811	M93.031	M94.239	M99.07	Q65.1	Q71.03	Q74.2	S02.109D	S02.411D	S02.69XD
M90.812	M93.032	M94.241	M99.08	Q65.2	Q71.10	Q74.3	S02.109G	S02.411G	S02.69XG
M90.819	M93.033	M94.242	M99.09	Q65.30	Q71.11	Q74.8	S02.109K	S02.411K	S02.69XK
M90.821	M93.1	M94.249	M99.10	Q65.31	Q71.12	Q74.9	S02.110D	S02.412D	S02.80XA
M90.822	M93.20	M94.251	M99.11	Q65.32	Q71.13	Q75.0	S02.110G	S02.412G	S02.80XB
M90.829	M93.211	M94.252	M99.12	Q65.4	Q71.20	Q75.1	S02.110K	S02.412K	S02.80XD
M90.831	M93.212	M94.259	M99.13	Q65.5	Q71.21	Q75.2	S02.111D	S02.413D	S02.80XG
M90.832	M93.219	M94.261	M99.14	Q65.6	Q71.22	Q75.3	S02.111G	S02.413G	S02.80XK
M90.839	M93.221	M94.262	M99.15	Q65.81	Q71.23	Q75.4	S02.111K	S02.413K	S02.81XA
M90.841	M93.222	M94.269	M99.16	Q65.82	Q71.30	Q75.5	S02.112G	S02.42XA	S02.81XB
M90.842	M93.229	M94.271	M99.17	Q65.89	Q71.31	Q75.8	S02.112K	S02.42XB	S02.81XD
M90.849	M93.231	M94.272	M99.19	Q65.9	Q71.32	Q75.9	S02.113D	S02.42XD	S02.81XG
M90.851	M93.232	M94.279	M99.20	Q66.00	Q71.33	Q76.1	S02.113G	S02.42XG	S02.81XK
M90.852	M93.239	M94.28	M99.21	Q66.01	Q71.40	Q76.2	S02.113K	S02.42XK	S02.82XA
M90.859	M93.241	M94.29	M99.22	Q66.02	Q71.41	Q76.3	S02.118D	S02.5XXD	S02.82XB
M90.861	M93.242	M94.351	M99.23	Q66.10	Q71.42	Q76.411	S02.118G	S02.5XXG	S02.82XD
M90.862	M93.249	M94.352	M99.24	Q66.11	Q71.43	Q76.412	S02.118K	S02.5XXK	S02.82XG
M90.869	M93.251	M94.359	M99.25	Q66.12	Q71.50	Q76.413	S02.119D	S02.600D	S02.82XK
M90.871	M93.252	M94.8X0	M99.26	Q66.211	Q71.51	Q76.414	S02.119G	S02.600G	S02.91XD
M90.872	M93.259	M94.8X1	M99.27	Q66.212	Q71.52	Q76.415	S02.119K	S02.600K	S02.91XG
M90.879	M93.261	M94.8X2	M99.28	Q66.219	Q71.53	Q76.419	S02.11AD	S02.601D	S02.91XK
M90.88	M93.262	M94.8X3	M99.29	Q66.221	Q71.60	Q76.425	S02.11AG	S02.601G	S02.92XA
M90.89	M93.269	M94.8X4	M99.30	Q66.222	Q71.61	Q76.426	S02.11AK	S02.601K	S02.92XB
M91.0	M93.271	M94.8X5	M99.31	Q66.229	Q71.62	Q76.427	S02.11BD	S02.602D	S02.92XD
M91.10	M93.272	M94.8X6	M99.32	Q66.30	Q71.63	Q76.428	S02.11BG	S02.602G	S02.92XG
M91.11	M93.279	M94.8X7	M99.33	Q66.31	Q71.811	Q76.429	S02.11BK	S02.602K	S02.92XK
M91.12	M93.28	M94.8X8	M99.34	Q66.32	Q71.812	Q76.49	S02.11CD	S02.609D	S03.00XS
M91.20	M93.29	M94.8X9	M99.35	Q66.40	Q71.813	Q76.5	S02.11CG	S02.609G	S03.01XS
M91.21	M93.80	M94.9	M99.36	Q66.41	Q71.819	Q76.6	S02.11CK	S02.609K	S03.02XS
M91.22	M93.811	M95.2	M99.37	Q66.42	Q71.891	Q76.7	S02.11DD	S02.610D	S03.03XS

S03.1XXA	S12.110G	S12.230S	S12.391B	S12.54XG	S13.0XXA	S22.010K	S22.040A	S22.069D	S22.23XK
S03.1XXS	S12.110K	S12.231A	S12.391D	S12.54XK	S13.0XXS	S22.010S	S22.040B	S22.069G	S22.23XS
S03.40XS	S12.110S	S12.231B	S12.391G	S12.54XS	S13.100A	S22.011A	S22.040D	S22.069K	S22.24XA
S03.41XS	S12.111A	S12.231D	S12.391K	S12.550A	S13.100S	S22.011B	S22.040G	S22.069S	S22.24XB
S03.42XS	S12.111B	S12.231G	S12.391S	S12.550B	S13.101A	S22.011D	S22.040K	S22.070A	S22.24XD
S03.43XS	S12.111D	S12.231K	S12.400A	S12.550D	S13.101S	S22.011G	S22.040S	S22.070B	S22.24XG
S03.8XXA	S12.111G	S12.231S	S12.400B	S12.550G	S13.110A	S22.011K	S22.041A	S22.070D	S22.24XK
S03.8XXS	S12.111K	S12.24XA	S12.400D	S12.550K	S13.110S	S22.011S	S22.041B	S22.070G	S22.24XS
S03.9XXA	S12.111S	S12.24XB	S12.400G	S12.550S	S13.111A	S22.012A	S22.041D	S22.070K	S22.31XD
S03.9XXS	S12.112A	S12.24XD	S12.400K	S12.551A	S13.111S	S22.012B	S22.041G	S22.070S	S22.31XG
S09.11XS	S12.112B	S12.24XG	S12.400S	S12.551B	S13.120A	S22.012D	S22.041K	S22.071A	S22.31XK
S12.000A	S12.112D	S12.24XK	S12.401A	S12.551D	S13.120S	S22.012G	S22.041S	S22.071B	S22.31XS
S12.000B	S12.112G	S12.24XS	S12.401B	S12.551G	S13.121A	S22.012K	S22.042A	S22.071D	S22.32XD
S12.000D	S12.112K	S12.250A	S12.401D	S12.551K	S13.121S	S22.012S	S22.042B	S22.071G	S22.32XG
S12.000G	S12.112S	S12.250B	S12.401G	S12.551S	S13.130A	S22.018A	S22.042D	S22.071K	S22.32XK
S12.000K	S12.120A	S12.250D	S12.401K	S12.590A	S13.130S	S22.018B	S22.042G	S22.071S	S22.32XS
S12.000S	S12.120B	S12.250G	S12.401S	S12.590B	S13.131A	S22.018D	S22.042K	S22.072A	S22.39XD
S12.001A	S12.120D	S12.250K	S12.430A	S12.590D	S13.131S	S22.018G	S22.042S	S22.072B	S22.39XG
S12.001B	S12.120G	S12.250S	S12.430B	S12.590G	S13.140A	S22.018K	S22.048A	S22.072D	S22.39XK
S12.001D	S12.120K	S12.251A	S12.430D	S12.590K	S13.140S	S22.018S	S22.048B	S22.072G	S22.39XS
S12.001G	S12.120S	S12.251B	S12.430G	S12.590S	S13.141A	S22.019A	S22.048D	S22.072K	S22.41XD
S12.001K	S12.121A	S12.251D	S12.430K	S12.591A	S13.141S	S22.019B	S22.048G	S22.072S	S22.41XG
S12.001S	S12.121B	S12.251G	S12.430S	S12.591B	S13.150A	S22.019D	S22.048K	S22.078A	S22.41XK
S12.01XA	S12.121D	S12.251K	S12.431A	S12.591D	S13.150S	S22.019G	S22.048S	S22.078B	S22.41XS
S12.01XB	S12.121G	S12.251S	S12.431B	S12.591G	S13.151A	S22.019K	S22.049A	S22.078D	S22.42XD
S12.01XD	S12.121K	S12.290A	S12.431D	S12.591K	S13.151S	S22.019S	S22.049B	S22.078G	S22.42XG
S12.01XG	S12.121S	S12.290B	S12.431G	S12.591S	S13.160A	S22.020A	S22.049D	S22.078K	S22.42XK
S12.01XK	S12.130A	S12.290D	S12.431K	S12.600A	S13.160S	S22.020B	S22.049G	S22.078S	S22.42XS
S12.01XS	S12.130B	S12.290G	S12.431S	S12.600B	S13.161A	S22.020D	S22.049K	S22.079A	S22.43XD
S12.02XA	S12.130D	S12.290K	S12.44XA	S12.600D	S13.161S	S22.020G	S22.049S	S22.079B	S22.43XG
S12.02XB	S12.130G	S12.290S	S12.44XB	S12.600G	S13.170A	S22.020K	S22.050A	S22.079D	S22.43XK
S12.02XD	S12.130K	S12.291A	S12.44XD	S12.600K	S13.170S	S22.020S	S22.050B	S22.079G	S22.43XS
S12.02XG	S12.130S	S12.291B	S12.44XG	S12.600S	S13.171A	S22.021A	S22.050D	S22.079K	S22.49XD
S12.02XK	S12.131A	S12.291D	S12.44XK	S12.601A	S13.171S	S22.021B	S22.050G	S22.079S	S22.49XG
S12.02XS	S12.131B	S12.291G	S12.44XS	S12.601B	S13.180A	S22.021D	S22.050K	S22.080A	S22.49XK
S12.030A	S12.131D	S12.291K	S12.450A	S12.601D	S13.180S	S22.021G	S22.050S	S22.080B	S22.49XS
S12.030B	S12.131G	S12.291S	S12.450B	S12.601G	S13.181A	S22.021K	S22.051A	S22.080D	S22.5XXD
S12.030D	S12.131K	S12.300A	S12.450D	S12.601K	S13.181S	S22.021S	S22.051B	S22.080G	S22.5XXG
S12.030G	S12.131S	S12.300B	S12.450G	S12.601S	S13.20XA	S22.022A	S22.051D	S22.080K	S22.5XXK
S12.030K	S12.14XA	S12.300D	S12.450K	S12.630A	S13.20XS	S22.022B	S22.051G	S22.080S	S22.5XXS
S12.030S	S12.14XB	S12.300G	S12.450S	S12.630B	S13.29XA	S22.022D	S22.051K	S22.081A	S22.9XXA
S12.031A	S12.14XD	S12.300K	S12.451A	S12.630D	S13.29XS	S22.022G	S22.051S	S22.081B	S22.9XXB
S12.031B	S12.14XG	S12.300S	S12.451B	S12.630G	S13.4XXA	S22.022K	S22.052A	S22.081D	S22.9XXD
S12.031D	S12.14XK	S12.301A	S12.451D	S12.630K	S13.4XXS	S22.022S	S22.052B	S22.081G	S22.9XXG
S12.031G	S12.14XS	S12.301B	S12.451G	S12.630S	S13.5XXA	S22.028A	S22.052D	S22.081K	S22.9XXK
S12.031K	S12.150A	S12.301D	S12.451K	S12.631A	S13.5XXS	S22.028B	S22.052G	S22.081S	S22.9XXS
S12.031S	S12.150B	S12.301G	S12.451S	S12.631B	S13.8XXA	S22.028D	S22.052K	S22.082A	S23.0XXA
S12.040A	S12.150D	S12.301K	S12.490A	S12.631D	S13.8XXS	S22.028G	S22.052S	S22.082B	S23.0XXS
S12.040B	S12.150G	S12.301S	S12.490B	S12.631G	S13.9XXA	S22.028K	S22.058A	S22.082D	S23.100A
S12.040D	S12.150K	S12.330A	S12.490D	S12.631K	S13.9XXS	S22.028S	S22.058B	S22.082G	S23.100S
S12.040G	S12.150S	S12.330B	S12.490G	S12.631S	S16.1XXA	S22.029A	S22.058D	S22.082K	S23.101A
S12.040K	S12.151A	S12.330D	S12.490K	S12.64XA	S16.1XXS	S22.029B	S22.058G	S22.082S	S23.101S
S12.040S	S12.151B	S12.330G	S12.490S	S12.64XB	S22.000A	S22.029D	S22.058K	S22.088A	S23.110A
S12.041A	S12.151D	S12.330K	S12.491A	S12.64XD	S22.000B	S22.029G	S22.058S	S22.088B	S23.110S
S12.041B	S12.151G	S12.330S	S12.491B	S12.64XG	S22.000D	S22.029K	S22.059A	S22.088D	S23.111A
S12.041D	S12.151K	S12.331A	S12.491D	S12.64XK	S22.000G	S22.029S	S22.059B	S22.088G	S23.111S
S12.041G	S12.151S	S12.331B	S12.491G	S12.64XS	S22.000K	S22.030A	S22.059D	S22.088K	S23.120A
S12.041K	S12.190A	S12.331D	S12.491K	S12.650A	S22.000S	S22.030B	S22.059G	S22.088S	S23.120S
S12.041S	S12.190B	S12.331G	S12.491S	S12.650B	S22.001A	S22.030D	S22.059K	S22.089A	S23.121A
S12.090A	S12.190D	S12.331K	S12.500A	S12.650D	S22.001B	S22.030G	S22.059S	S22.089B	S23.121S
S12.090B	S12.190G	S12.331S	S12.500B	S12.650G	S22.001D	S22.030K	S22.060A	S22.089D	S23.122A
S12.090D	S12.190K	S12.34XA	S12.500D	S12.650K	S22.001G	S22.030S	S22.060B	S22.089G	S23.122S
S12.090G	S12.190S	S12.34XB	S12.500G	S12.650S	S22.001K	S22.031A	S22.060D	S22.089K	S23.123A
S12.090K	S12.191A	S12.34XD	S12.500K	S12.651A	S22.001S	S22.031B	S22.060G	S22.089S	S23.123S
S12.090S	S12.191B	S12.34XG	S12.500S	S12.651B	S22.002A	S22.031D	S22.060K	S22.20XA	S23.130A
S12.091A	S12.191D	S12.34XK	S12.501A	S12.651D	S22.002B	S22.031G	S22.060S	S22.20XB	S23.130S
S12.091B	S12.191G	S12.34XS	S12.501B	S12.651G	S22.002D	S22.031K	S22.061A	S22.20XD	S23.131A
S12.091D	S12.191K	S12.350A	S12.501D	S12.651K	S22.002G	S22.031S	S22.061B	S22.20XG	S23.131S
S12.091G	S12.191S	S12.350B	S12.501G	S12.651S	S22.002K	S22.032A	S22.061D	S22.20XK	S23.132A
S12.091K	S12.200A	S12.350D	S12.501K	S12.690A	S22.002S	S22.032B	S22.061G	S22.20XS	S23.132S
S12.091S	S12.200B	S12.350G	S12.501S	S12.690B	S22.008A	S22.032D	S22.061K	S22.21XA	S23.133A
S12.100A	S12.200D	S12.350K	S12.530A	S12.690D	S22.008B	S22.032G	S22.061S	S22.21XB	S23.133S
S12.100B	S12.200G	S12.350S	S12.530B	S12.690G	S22.008D	S22.032K	S22.062A	S22.21XD	S23.140A
S12.100D	S12.200K	S12.351A	S12.530D	S12.690K	S22.008G	S22.032S	S22.062B	S22.21XG	S23.140S
S12.100G	S12.200S	S12.351B	S12.530G	S12.690S	S22.008K	S22.038A	S22.062D	S22.21XK	S23.141A
S12.100K	S12.201A	S12.351D	S12.530K	S12.691A	S22.008S	S22.038B	S22.062G	S22.21XS	S23.141S
S12.100S	S12.201B	S12.351G	S12.530S	S12.691B	S22.009A	S22.038D	S22.062K	S22.22XA	S23.142A
S12.101A	S12.201D	S12.351K	S12.531A	S12.691D	S22.009B	S22.038G	S22.062S	S22.22XB	S23.142S
S12.101B	S12.201G	S12.351S	S12.531B	S12.691G	S22.009D	S22.038K	S22.068A	S22.22XD	S23.143A
S12.101D	S12.201K	S12.390A	S12.531D	S12.691K	S22.009G	S22.038S	S22.068B	S22.22XG	S23.143S
S12.101G	S12.201S	S12.390B	S12.531G	S12.691S	S22.009K	S22.039A	S22.068D	S22.22XK	S23.150A
S12.101K	S12.230A	S12.390D	S12.531K	S12.8XXD	S22.009S	S22.039B	S22.068G	S22.22XS	S23.150S
S12.101S	S12.230B	S12.390G	S12.531S	S12.8XXS	S22.010A	S22.039D	S22.068K	S22.23XA	S23.151A
S12.110A	S12.230D	S12.390K	S12.54XA	S12.9XXA	S22.010B	S22.039G	S22.068S	S22.23XB	S23.151S
S12.110B	S12.230G	S12.390S	S12.54XB	S12.9XXD	S22.010D	S22.039K	S22.069A	S22.23XD	S23.152A
S12.110D	S12.230K	S12.391A	S12.54XD	S12.9XXS	S22.010G	S22.039S	S22.069B	S22.23XG	S23.152S

S23.153A	S32.018G	S32.042S	S32.122B	S32.309G	S32.412S	S32.435B	S32.461G	S32.483S	S32.599B
S23.153S	S32.018K	S32.048A	S32.122D	S32.309K	S32.413A	S32.435D	S32.461K	S32.484A	S32.599D
S23.160A	S32.018S	S32.048B	S32.122G	S32.309S	S32.413D	S32.435G	S32.461S	S32.484D	S32.599G
S23.160S	S32.019A	S32.048D	S32.122K	S32.311A	S32.413G	S32.435K	S32.462A	S32.484G	S32.599K
S23.161A	S32.019B	S32.048G	S32.122S	S32.311B	S32.413K	S32.435S	S32.462B	S32.484K	S32.599S
S23.161S	S32.019D	S32.048K	S32.129A	S32.311D	S32.413S	S32.436A	S32.462D	S32.484S	S32.601A
S23.162A	S32.019G	S32.048S	S32.129B	S32.311K	S32.414A	S32.436B	S32.462G	S32.485A	S32.601B
S23.162S	S32.019K	S32.049A	S32.129G	S32.311S	S32.414B	S32.436D	S32.462K	S32.485B	S32.601G
S23.163A	S32.019S	S32.049B	S32.129K	S32.312A	S32.414D	S32.436G	S32.462S	S32.485D	S32.601K
S23.163S	S32.020A	S32.049D	S32.129S	S32.312B	S32.414G	S32.436K	S32.463A	S32.485G	S32.601S
S23.170A	S32.020B	S32.049G	S32.130A	S32.312G	S32.414K	S32.436S	S32.463B	S32.485K	S32.602A
S23.170S	S32.020D	S32.049K	S32.130B	S32.312K	S32.414S	S32.441A	S32.463D	S32.485S	S32.602B
S23.171A	S32.020G	S32.049S	S32.130D	S32.312S	S32.415A	S32.441B	S32.463K	S32.486A	S32.602D
S23.171S	S32.020K	S32.050A	S32.130G	S32.313A	S32.415B	S32.441D	S32.463S	S32.486B	S32.602G
S23.20XA	S32.020S	S32.050B	S32.130K	S32.313B	S32.415D	S32.441G	S32.464A	S32.486D	S32.602K
S23.20XS	S32.021A	S32.050D	S32.130S	S32.313D	S32.415K	S32.441K	S32.464B	S32.486G	S32.602S
S23.29XA	S32.021B	S32.050G	S32.131A	S32.313G	S32.415S	S32.441S	S32.464D	S32.486K	S32.609A
S23.29XS	S32.021D	S32.050K	S32.131B	S32.313K	S32.416A	S32.442A	S32.464G	S32.486S	S32.609B
S23.3XXA	S32.021G	S32.050S	S32.131D	S32.313S	S32.416B	S32.442B	S32.464K	S32.491A	S32.609D
S23.3XXS	S32.021K	S32.051A	S32.131G	S32.314A	S32.416D	S32.442D	S32.464S	S32.491B	S32.609G
S23.41XS	S32.021S	S32.051B	S32.131K	S32.314B	S32.416G	S32.442G	S32.465A	S32.491D	S32.609K
S23.420S	S32.022A	S32.051D	S32.131S	S32.314D	S32.416K	S32.442K	S32.465B	S32.491G	S32.609S
S23.421S	S32.022B	S32.051G	S32.132A	S32.314G	S32.416S	S32.442S	S32.465D	S32.491K	S32.611A
S23.428S	S32.022D	S32.051K	S32.132B	S32.314K	S32.421A	S32.443A	S32.465G	S32.491S	S32.611B
S23.429S	S32.022G	S32.051S	S32.132D	S32.314S	S32.421B	S32.443B	S32.465K	S32.492A	S32.611D
S23.8XXA	S32.022K	S32.052A	S32.132G	S32.315A	S32.421D	S32.443D	S32.465S	S32.492B	S32.611G
S23.8XXS	S32.022S	S32.052B	S32.132K	S32.315B	S32.421G	S32.443G	S32.466A	S32.492D	S32.611K
S23.9XXA	S32.028A	S32.052D	S32.132S	S32.315D	S32.421K	S32.443K	S32.466B	S32.492G	S32.611S
S23.9XXS	S32.028B	S32.052G	S32.139A	S32.315G	S32.421S	S32.443S	S32.466D	S32.492K	S32.612A
S29.011A	S32.028D	S32.052K	S32.139B	S32.315K	S32.422A	S32.444A	S32.466G	S32.492S	S32.612B
S29.011S	S32.028G	S32.052S	S32.139D	S32.315S	S32.422B	S32.444B	S32.466K	S32.499A	S32.612D
S29.012A	S32.028K	S32.058A	S32.139G	S32.316A	S32.422D	S32.444D	S32.466S	S32.499B	S32.612G
S29.012S	S32.028S	S32.058B	S32.139K	S32.316B	S32.422G	S32.444G	S32.471A	S32.499D	S32.612K
S29.019A	S32.029A	S32.058D	S32.139S	S32.316D	S32.422K	S32.444K	S32.471B	S32.499G	S32.612S
S29.019S	S32.029B	S32.058G	S32.14XA	S32.316G	S32.422S	S32.444S	S32.471G	S32.499K	S32.613A
S32.000A	S32.029D	S32.058K	S32.14XB	S32.316K	S32.423A	S32.445A	S32.471K	S32.499S	S32.613B
S32.000B	S32.029G	S32.058S	S32.14XD	S32.316S	S32.423B	S32.445B	S32.471S	S32.501A	S32.613D
S32.000D	S32.029K	S32.059A	S32.14XG	S32.391A	S32.423D	S32.445D	S32.472A	S32.501B	S32.613G
S32.000G	S32.029S	S32.059B	S32.14XK	S32.391B	S32.423G	S32.445G	S32.472B	S32.501D	S32.613K
S32.000K	S32.030A	S32.059D	S32.14XS	S32.391D	S32.423K	S32.445K	S32.472D	S32.501G	S32.613S
S32.000S	S32.030B	S32.059G	S32.15XA	S32.391G	S32.423S	S32.445S	S32.472G	S32.501K	S32.614A
S32.001A	S32.030D	S32.059K	S32.15XB	S32.391K	S32.424A	S32.446A	S32.472K	S32.501S	S32.614B
S32.001B	S32.030G	S32.059S	S32.15XD	S32.391S	S32.424B	S32.446B	S32.472S	S32.502A	S32.614D
S32.001D	S32.030K	S32.10XA	S32.15XG	S32.392A	S32.424D	S32.446D	S32.473A	S32.502B	S32.614G
S32.001G	S32.030S	S32.10XB	S32.15XK	S32.392B	S32.424G	S32.446G	S32.473B	S32.502D	S32.614K
S32.001K	S32.031A	S32.10XD	S32.15XS	S32.392D	S32.424K	S32.446K	S32.473D	S32.502G	S32.614S
S32.001S	S32.031B	S32.10XG	S32.16XA	S32.392K	S32.424S	S32.446S	S32.473G	S32.502K	S32.615A
S32.002A	S32.031D	S32.10XK	S32.16XB	S32.392S	S32.425A	S32.451A	S32.473K	S32.502S	S32.615B
S32.002B	S32.031G	S32.10XS	S32.16XD	S32.399A	S32.425B	S32.451B	S32.473S	S32.509A	S32.615D
S32.002D	S32.031K	S32.110A	S32.16XG	S32.399B	S32.425D	S32.451D	S32.474A	S32.509B	S32.615K
S32.002G	S32.031S	S32.110B	S32.16XK	S32.399D	S32.425G	S32.451G	S32.474B	S32.509D	S32.615S
S32.002K	S32.032A	S32.110D	S32.16XS	S32.399G	S32.425K	S32.451K	S32.474D	S32.509G	S32.616A
S32.002S	S32.032B	S32.110G	S32.17XA	S32.399K	S32.425S	S32.451S	S32.474G	S32.509K	S32.616B
S32.008A	S32.032D	S32.110K	S32.17XB	S32.399S	S32.426A	S32.452A	S32.474K	S32.509S	S32.616D
S32.008B	S32.032G	S32.110S	S32.17XD	S32.401A	S32.426B	S32.452B	S32.474S	S32.511A	S32.616G
S32.008D	S32.032K	S32.111A	S32.17XG	S32.401B	S32.426D	S32.452D	S32.475A	S32.511B	S32.616K
S32.008G	S32.032S	S32.111B	S32.17XK	S32.401D	S32.426G	S32.452G	S32.475B	S32.511D	S32.616S
S32.008K	S32.038A	S32.111D	S32.17XS	S32.401G	S32.426K	S32.452K	S32.475D	S32.511G	S32.691A
S32.008S	S32.038B	S32.111G	S32.19XA	S32.401K	S32.426S	S32.452S	S32.475G	S32.511K	S32.691B
S32.009A	S32.038D	S32.111K	S32.19XB	S32.401S	S32.431A	S32.453A	S32.475K	S32.511S	S32.691D
S32.009B	S32.038G	S32.111S	S32.19XD	S32.402A	S32.431B	S32.453B	S32.475S	S32.512A	S32.691G
S32.009D	S32.038K	S32.112A	S32.19XG	S32.402B	S32.431D	S32.453D	S32.476A	S32.512B	S32.691S
S32.009G	S32.038S	S32.112B	S32.19XK	S32.402D	S32.431G	S32.453G	S32.476B	S32.512D	S32.692A
S32.009K	S32.039A	S32.112D	S32.19XS	S32.402G	S32.431K	S32.453K	S32.476D	S32.512G	S32.692B
S32.009S	S32.039B	S32.112G	S32.2XXA	S32.402K	S32.431S	S32.453S	S32.476G	S32.512K	S32.692D
S32.010A	S32.039D	S32.112K	S32.2XXB	S32.402S	S32.432A	S32.454A	S32.476K	S32.512S	S32.692G
S32.010B	S32.039G	S32.112S	S32.2XXD	S32.409A	S32.432B	S32.454B	S32.476S	S32.519A	S32.692K
S32.010D	S32.039K	S32.119A	S32.2XXG	S32.409B	S32.432D	S32.454D	S32.481A	S32.519B	S32.692S
S32.010G	S32.039S	S32.119B	S32.2XXK	S32.409D	S32.432G	S32.454G	S32.481B	S32.519D	S32.699A
S32.010K	S32.040A	S32.119D	S32.2XXS	S32.409G	S32.432K	S32.454K	S32.481D	S32.519G	S32.699B
S32.010S	S32.040B	S32.119G	S32.301A	S32.409K	S32.432S	S32.454S	S32.481G	S32.519K	S32.699D
S32.011A	S32.040D	S32.119K	S32.301B	S32.409S	S32.433A	S32.455A	S32.481K	S32.519S	S32.699G
S32.011B	S32.040G	S32.119S	S32.301D	S32.411A	S32.433B	S32.455B	S32.481S	S32.591A	S32.699K
S32.011D	S32.040K	S32.120A	S32.301G	S32.411B	S32.433D	S32.455D	S32.482A	S32.591B	S32.699S
S32.011G	S32.040S	S32.120B	S32.301K	S32.411D	S32.433G	S32.455G	S32.482B	S32.591D	S32.810A
S32.011K	S32.041A	S32.120D	S32.301S	S32.411G	S32.433K	S32.455K	S32.482D	S32.591G	S32.810B
S32.011S	S32.041B	S32.120G	S32.302A	S32.411K	S32.433S	S32.455S	S32.482G	S32.591K	S32.810D
S32.012A	S32.041D	S32.120K	S32.302B	S32.411S	S32.434A	S32.456A	S32.482K	S32.591S	S32.810G
S32.012B	S32.041G	S32.120S	S32.302D	S32.412A	S32.434B	S32.456B	S32.482S	S32.592A	S32.810K
S32.012D	S32.041K	S32.121A	S32.302K	S32.412B	S32.434D	S32.456D	S32.483A	S32.592B	S32.810S
S32.012G	S32.041S	S32.121B	S32.302S	S32.412D	S32.434G	S32.456G	S32.483B	S32.592D	S32.811A
S32.012K	S32.042A	S32.121D	S32.309A	S32.412G	S32.434K	S32.456K	S32.483D	S32.592G	S32.811B
S32.012S	S32.042B	S32.121G	S32.309B	S32.412K	S32.434S	S32.456S	S32.483G	S32.592K	S32.811D
S32.018A	S32.042D	S32.121K	S32.309D	S32.412K	S32.435A	S32.461A	S32.483K	S32.592S	
S32.018B	S32.042G	S32.121S				S32.461B		S32.599A	

S32.811G	S42.011A	S42.024D	S42.111K	S42.131S	S42.152B	S42.212G	S42.232P	S42.263A	S42.296P
S32.811K	S42.011B	S42.024G	S42.111P	S42.132A	S42.152D	S42.212K	S42.232S	S42.263B	S42.296S
S32.811S	S42.011D	S42.024K	S42.111S	S42.132D	S42.152G	S42.212P	S42.239A	S42.263D	S42.301A
S32.82XA	S42.011G	S42.024P	S42.112A	S42.132G	S42.152K	S42.212S	S42.239B	S42.263G	S42.301B
S32.82XB	S42.011K	S42.024S	S42.112B	S42.132K	S42.152P	S42.213A	S42.239D	S42.263K	S42.301D
S32.82XD	S42.011P	S42.025A	S42.112D	S42.132P	S42.152S	S42.213B	S42.239G	S42.263P	S42.301G
S32.82XG	S42.011S	S42.025B	S42.112G	S42.132S	S42.153A	S42.213D	S42.239K	S42.263S	S42.301K
S32.82XK	S42.012A	S42.025D	S42.112K	S42.133A	S42.153B	S42.213G	S42.239P	S42.264A	S42.301P
S32.82XS	S42.012B	S42.025G	S42.112P	S42.133B	S42.153D	S42.213K	S42.239S	S42.264B	S42.301S
S32.89XA	S42.012D	S42.025K	S42.112S	S42.133D	S42.153G	S42.213P	S42.241A	S42.264D	S42.302A
S32.89XB	S42.012G	S42.025P	S42.113A	S42.133G	S42.153K	S42.213S	S42.241B	S42.264G	S42.302B
S32.89XD	S42.012K	S42.025S	S42.113B	S42.133K	S42.153P	S42.214A	S42.241D	S42.264P	S42.302D
S32.89XG	S42.012P	S42.026A	S42.113D	S42.133P	S42.153S	S42.214B	S42.241G	S42.264S	S42.302G
S32.89XK	S42.012S	S42.026B	S42.113G	S42.133S	S42.154A	S42.214D	S42.241K	S42.265A	S42.302K
S32.89XS	S42.013A	S42.026D	S42.113K	S42.134A	S42.154B	S42.214G	S42.241P	S42.265B	S42.302P
S32.9XXA	S42.013B	S42.026G	S42.113P	S42.134D	S42.154D	S42.214K	S42.241S	S42.265D	S42.302S
S32.9XXB	S42.013D	S42.026K	S42.113S	S42.134G	S42.154K	S42.214P	S42.242A	S42.265K	S42.309A
S32.9XXD	S42.013G	S42.026P	S42.114A	S42.134K	S42.154P	S42.214S	S42.242B	S42.265P	S42.309B
S32.9XXG	S42.013K	S42.026S	S42.114B	S42.134P	S42.154S	S42.215A	S42.242D	S42.265S	S42.309D
S32.9XXK	S42.013P	S42.031A	S42.114D	S42.134S	S42.155A	S42.215B	S42.242G	S42.266A	S42.309G
S32.9XXS	S42.013S	S42.031B	S42.114G	S42.135A	S42.155B	S42.215D	S42.242K	S42.266B	S42.309K
S33.0XXA	S42.014A	S42.031D	S42.114K	S42.135B	S42.155D	S42.215G	S42.242P	S42.266D	S42.309S
S33.0XXS	S42.014B	S42.031G	S42.114P	S42.135D	S42.155G	S42.215K	S42.242S	S42.266G	S42.311A
S33.100A	S42.014D	S42.031K	S42.114S	S42.135G	S42.155K	S42.215P	S42.249A	S42.266K	S42.311D
S33.100S	S42.014G	S42.031P	S42.115A	S42.135K	S42.155P	S42.215S	S42.249B	S42.266P	S42.311G
S33.101A	S42.014K	S42.031S	S42.115B	S42.135P	S42.155S	S42.216A	S42.249D	S42.266S	S42.311K
S33.101S	S42.014P	S42.032A	S42.115D	S42.135S	S42.156A	S42.216B	S42.249G	S42.271A	S42.311P
S33.110A	S42.014S	S42.032B	S42.115G	S42.136A	S42.156B	S42.216D	S42.249K	S42.271D	S42.311S
S33.110S	S42.015A	S42.032D	S42.115K	S42.136B	S42.156D	S42.216G	S42.249P	S42.271G	S42.312A
S33.111A	S42.015B	S42.032G	S42.115P	S42.136D	S42.156K	S42.216K	S42.249S	S42.271K	S42.312D
S33.111S	S42.015D	S42.032K	S42.115S	S42.136G	S42.156P	S42.216P	S42.251A	S42.271P	S42.312G
S33.120A	S42.015G	S42.032P	S42.116A	S42.136K	S42.156S	S42.216S	S42.251B	S42.271S	S42.312K
S33.120S	S42.015K	S42.032S	S42.116B	S42.136P	S42.191A	S42.221A	S42.251D	S42.272A	S42.312P
S33.121A	S42.015P	S42.033A	S42.116D	S42.136S	S42.191B	S42.221B	S42.251G	S42.272B	S42.312S
S33.121S	S42.015S	S42.033B	S42.116G	S42.141A	S42.191D	S42.221D	S42.251K	S42.272D	S42.319A
S33.130A	S42.016A	S42.033D	S42.116K	S42.141B	S42.191G	S42.221G	S42.251P	S42.272G	S42.319D
S33.130S	S42.016B	S42.033G	S42.116P	S42.141D	S42.191K	S42.221K	S42.251S	S42.272K	S42.319G
S33.131A	S42.016D	S42.033K	S42.116S	S42.141G	S42.191P	S42.221P	S42.252A	S42.272P	S42.319K
S33.131S	S42.016G	S42.033P	S42.121A	S42.141K	S42.191S	S42.221S	S42.252B	S42.272S	S42.319P
S33.140A	S42.016K	S42.033S	S42.121B	S42.141P	S42.192A	S42.222A	S42.252D	S42.279A	S42.319S
S33.140S	S42.016P	S42.034A	S42.121D	S42.141S	S42.192B	S42.222B	S42.252G	S42.279D	S42.321A
S33.141A	S42.016S	S42.034B	S42.121G	S42.142A	S42.192D	S42.222D	S42.252K	S42.279G	S42.321B
S33.141S	S42.017A	S42.034D	S42.121K	S42.142B	S42.192G	S42.222G	S42.252P	S42.279K	S42.321D
S33.2XXA	S42.017B	S42.034G	S42.121P	S42.142D	S42.192K	S42.222K	S42.252S	S42.279P	S42.321G
S33.2XXS	S42.017D	S42.034K	S42.121S	S42.142G	S42.192P	S42.222P	S42.253A	S42.279S	S42.321K
S33.30XA	S42.017G	S42.034P	S42.122A	S42.142K	S42.192S	S42.222S	S42.253B	S42.291A	S42.321P
S33.30XS	S42.017K	S42.034S	S42.122B	S42.142P	S42.199A	S42.223A	S42.253D	S42.291B	S42.321S
S33.39XA	S42.017P	S42.035A	S42.122D	S42.142S	S42.199B	S42.223B	S42.253G	S42.291D	S42.322A
S33.39XS	S42.017S	S42.035B	S42.122G	S42.143A	S42.199D	S42.223D	S42.253K	S42.291G	S42.322B
S33.4XXA	S42.018A	S42.035D	S42.122K	S42.143B	S42.199G	S42.223G	S42.253P	S42.291K	S42.322D
S33.4XXS	S42.018B	S42.035G	S42.122P	S42.143D	S42.199K	S42.223K	S42.253S	S42.291P	S42.322G
S33.5XXA	S42.018D	S42.035K	S42.122S	S42.143G	S42.199P	S42.223P	S42.254A	S42.291S	S42.322K
S33.5XXS	S42.018G	S42.035P	S42.123A	S42.143K	S42.199S	S42.223S	S42.254B	S42.292A	S42.322P
S33.6XXA	S42.018K	S42.035S	S42.123B	S42.143P	S42.201A	S42.224A	S42.254D	S42.292B	S42.322S
S33.6XXS	S42.018P	S42.036A	S42.123D	S42.143S	S42.201B	S42.224B	S42.254G	S42.292D	S42.323A
S33.8XXA	S42.018S	S42.036B	S42.123G	S42.144A	S42.201D	S42.224D	S42.254K	S42.292G	S42.323B
S33.8XXS	S42.019A	S42.036D	S42.123K	S42.144B	S42.201G	S42.224G	S42.254P	S42.292K	S42.323D
S33.9XXA	S42.019B	S42.036G	S42.123P	S42.144D	S42.201K	S42.224K	S42.254S	S42.292P	S42.323G
S33.9XXS	S42.019D	S42.036K	S42.123S	S42.144G	S42.201P	S42.224P	S42.255A	S42.292S	S42.323K
S39.011G	S42.019G	S42.036P	S42.124A	S42.144K	S42.201S	S42.224S	S42.255B	S42.293A	S42.323P
S39.011S	S42.019K	S42.036S	S42.124B	S42.144P	S42.202A	S42.225A	S42.255D	S42.293B	S42.323S
S39.012A	S42.019P	S42.101A	S42.124D	S42.144S	S42.202B	S42.225B	S42.255G	S42.293D	S42.324A
S39.012S	S42.019S	S42.101B	S42.124G	S42.145A	S42.202D	S42.225D	S42.255K	S42.293G	S42.324B
S39.013A	S42.021A	S42.101D	S42.124K	S42.145B	S42.202G	S42.225G	S42.255P	S42.293K	S42.324D
S39.013S	S42.021B	S42.101G	S42.124P	S42.145D	S42.202K	S42.225K	S42.255S	S42.293P	S42.324G
S42.001A	S42.021D	S42.101K	S42.124S	S42.145G	S42.202P	S42.225P	S42.256A	S42.293S	S42.324K
S42.001B	S42.021G	S42.101P	S42.125A	S42.145K	S42.202S	S42.225S	S42.256B	S42.294A	S42.324P
S42.001D	S42.021K	S42.101S	S42.125B	S42.145P	S42.209A	S42.226A	S42.256D	S42.294B	S42.324S
S42.001G	S42.021P	S42.102A	S42.125D	S42.145S	S42.209B	S42.226B	S42.256G	S42.294D	S42.325A
S42.001K	S42.021S	S42.102B	S42.125G	S42.145K	S42.209D	S42.226D	S42.256K	S42.294G	S42.325B
S42.001P	S42.022A	S42.102D	S42.125K	S42.146A	S42.209G	S42.226G	S42.256P	S42.294K	S42.325D
S42.001S	S42.022B	S42.102G	S42.125P	S42.146B	S42.209K	S42.226K	S42.256S	S42.294P	S42.325K
S42.002A	S42.022D	S42.102K	S42.125S	S42.146D	S42.209P	S42.226P	S42.261A	S42.294S	S42.325P
S42.002B	S42.022G	S42.102P	S42.126A	S42.146G	S42.209S	S42.226S	S42.261B	S42.295A	S42.325S
S42.002D	S42.022K	S42.102S	S42.126B	S42.146K	S42.211A	S42.231A	S42.261D	S42.295B	S42.326A
S42.002G	S42.022P	S42.109A	S42.126D	S42.146P	S42.211B	S42.231B	S42.261G	S42.295D	S42.326B
S42.002K	S42.022S	S42.109B	S42.126G	S42.146S	S42.211D	S42.231D	S42.261K	S42.295G	S42.326D
S42.002P	S42.023A	S42.109D	S42.126K	S42.151A	S42.211G	S42.231G	S42.261P	S42.295K	S42.326G
S42.002S	S42.023B	S42.109G	S42.126P	S42.151B	S42.211K	S42.231K	S42.261S	S42.295P	S42.326K
S42.009A	S42.023D	S42.109K	S42.126S	S42.151D	S42.211P	S42.231P	S42.262A	S42.295S	S42.326P
S42.009B	S42.023G	S42.109P	S42.131A	S42.151G	S42.211S	S42.231S	S42.262B	S42.296A	S42.326S
S42.009D	S42.023K	S42.109S	S42.131B	S42.151K	S42.212A	S42.232A	S42.262D	S42.296B	S42.331A
S42.009G	S42.023P	S42.111A	S42.131D	S42.151P	S42.212B	S42.232B	S42.262G	S42.296D	S42.331B
S42.009K	S42.023S	S42.111B	S42.131G	S42.151S	S42.212D	S42.232D	S42.262K	S42.296G	S42.331D
S42.009P	S42.024A	S42.111D	S42.131K	S42.152A	S42.212D	S42.232G	S42.262P	S42.296K	
S42.009S	S42.024B	S42.111G	S42.131P						

S42.331G	S42.351P	S42.392A	S42.422D	S42.442K	S42.455S	S42.476B	S42.92XS	S43.141S	S43.432S
S42.331K	S42.351S	S42.392B	S42.422G	S42.442P	S42.456A	S42.476D	S43.001A	S43.142A	S43.439A
S42.331P	S42.352A	S42.392D	S42.422K	S42.442S	S42.456B	S42.476G	S43.001S	S43.142S	S43.439S
S42.331S	S42.352B	S42.392G	S42.422P	S42.443A	S42.456D	S42.476K	S43.002S	S43.149A	S43.491A
S42.332A	S42.352D	S42.392K	S42.422S	S42.443B	S42.456G	S42.476P	S43.003A	S43.149S	S43.491S
S42.332B	S42.352G	S42.392P	S42.423A	S42.443D	S42.456K	S42.476S	S43.003S	S43.151A	S43.492A
S42.332D	S42.352K	S42.392S	S42.423B	S42.443G	S42.456P	S42.481A	S43.004A	S43.151S	S43.492S
S42.332G	S42.352P	S42.399A	S42.423D	S42.443K	S42.456S	S42.481D	S43.004S	S43.152A	S43.499A
S42.332K	S42.352S	S42.399B	S42.423G	S42.443P	S42.461A	S42.481G	S43.005A	S43.152S	S43.499S
S42.332P	S42.353A	S42.399D	S42.423K	S42.443S	S42.461B	S42.481K	S43.005S	S43.159A	S43.50XA
S42.332S	S42.353B	S42.399G	S42.423P	S42.444A	S42.461D	S42.481P	S43.006A	S43.159S	S43.50XS
S42.333A	S42.353D	S42.399K	S42.423S	S42.444B	S42.461G	S42.481S	S43.006S	S43.201S	S43.51XA
S42.333B	S42.353G	S42.399P	S42.424A	S42.444G	S42.461K	S42.482A	S43.011A	S43.202S	S43.51XS
S42.333D	S42.353K	S42.399S	S42.424B	S42.444K	S42.461P	S42.482D	S43.011S	S43.203S	S43.52XA
S42.333G	S42.353P	S42.401A	S42.424D	S42.444P	S42.461S	S42.482G	S43.012A	S43.204S	S43.52XS
S42.333K	S42.353S	S42.401B	S42.424G	S42.444S	S42.462A	S42.482K	S43.012S	S43.205S	S43.60XA
S42.333P	S42.354A	S42.401D	S42.424K	S42.445A	S42.462B	S42.482P	S43.013A	S43.206S	S43.60XS
S42.333S	S42.354B	S42.401G	S42.424P	S42.445B	S42.462D	S42.482S	S43.013S	S43.211S	S43.61XA
S42.334A	S42.354D	S42.401K	S42.424S	S42.445D	S42.462G	S42.489A	S43.014A	S43.212S	S43.61XS
S42.334B	S42.354G	S42.401P	S42.425A	S42.445G	S42.462K	S42.489D	S43.014S	S43.213S	S43.62XA
S42.334D	S42.354K	S42.401S	S42.425B	S42.445K	S42.462P	S42.489G	S43.015A	S43.214S	S43.62XS
S42.334G	S42.354P	S42.402A	S42.425D	S42.445P	S42.462S	S42.489K	S43.015S	S43.215S	S43.80XA
S42.334K	S42.354S	S42.402B	S42.425G	S42.445S	S42.463A	S42.489P	S43.016A	S43.216S	S43.80XS
S42.334P	S42.355A	S42.402D	S42.425K	S42.446A	S42.463B	S42.489S	S43.016S	S43.221S	S43.81XA
S42.334S	S42.355B	S42.402G	S42.425P	S42.446B	S42.463D	S42.491A	S43.021A	S43.222S	S43.81XS
S42.335A	S42.355D	S42.402K	S42.425S	S42.446D	S42.463G	S42.491B	S43.021S	S43.223S	S43.82XA
S42.335B	S42.355G	S42.402P	S42.426A	S42.446G	S42.463K	S42.491D	S43.022A	S43.224S	S43.82XS
S42.335D	S42.355K	S42.402S	S42.426B	S42.446K	S42.463P	S42.491G	S43.022S	S43.225S	S43.90XA
S42.335G	S42.355P	S42.409A	S42.426D	S42.446P	S42.463S	S42.491K	S43.023A	S43.226S	S43.90XS
S42.335K	S42.355S	S42.409B	S42.426G	S42.446S	S42.464A	S42.491P	S43.023S	S43.301S	S43.91XA
S42.335P	S42.356A	S42.409D	S42.426K	S42.447A	S42.464B	S42.491S	S43.024A	S43.301S	S43.91XS
S42.335S	S42.356B	S42.409G	S42.426P	S42.447B	S42.464D	S42.492A	S43.024S	S43.302A	S43.92XA
S42.336A	S42.356D	S42.409K	S42.426S	S42.447D	S42.464G	S42.492B	S43.025A	S43.302S	S43.92XS
S42.336B	S42.356G	S42.409P	S42.431A	S42.447G	S42.464K	S42.492D	S43.025S	S43.303A	S46.011A
S42.336D	S42.356K	S42.409S	S42.431B	S42.447K	S42.464P	S42.492G	S43.026A	S43.303S	S46.011S
S42.336G	S42.356P	S42.411A	S42.431D	S42.447P	S42.464S	S42.492K	S43.026S	S43.304A	S46.012A
S42.336K	S42.356S	S42.411B	S42.431G	S42.447S	S42.465A	S42.492P	S43.031A	S43.304S	S46.012S
S42.336P	S42.361A	S42.411D	S42.431K	S42.448A	S42.465B	S42.492S	S43.031S	S43.305A	S46.019A
S42.336S	S42.361B	S42.411G	S42.431P	S42.448B	S42.465D	S42.493A	S43.032A	S43.305S	S46.019S
S42.341A	S42.361D	S42.411K	S42.431S	S42.448D	S42.465G	S42.493B	S43.032S	S43.306A	S46.021A
S42.341B	S42.361G	S42.411P	S42.432A	S42.448G	S42.465K	S42.493D	S43.033A	S43.306S	S46.022A
S42.341D	S42.361K	S42.411S	S42.432B	S42.448K	S42.465P	S42.493G	S43.033S	S43.311S	S46.029A
S42.341G	S42.361P	S42.412A	S42.432D	S42.448P	S42.465S	S42.493K	S43.034A	S43.311S	S46.111A
S42.341K	S42.361S	S42.412B	S42.432G	S42.448S	S42.466A	S42.493P	S43.034S	S43.312A	S46.111S
S42.341P	S42.362A	S42.412D	S42.432K	S42.449A	S42.466B	S42.493S	S43.035A	S43.312S	S46.112A
S42.341S	S42.362B	S42.412G	S42.432P	S42.449B	S42.466D	S42.494A	S43.035S	S43.313A	S46.112S
S42.342A	S42.362D	S42.412K	S42.432S	S42.449D	S42.466G	S42.494B	S43.036A	S43.313S	S46.119A
S42.342B	S42.362G	S42.412P	S42.433A	S42.449G	S42.466K	S42.494D	S43.036S	S43.314A	S46.119S
S42.342D	S42.362K	S42.412S	S42.433B	S42.449K	S42.466P	S42.494G	S43.081A	S43.314S	S46.121A
S42.342G	S42.362P	S42.413A	S42.433D	S42.449P	S42.466S	S42.494K	S43.081S	S43.315A	S46.122A
S42.342K	S42.362S	S42.413B	S42.433G	S42.449S	S42.471A	S42.494P	S43.082A	S43.315S	S46.129A
S42.342P	S42.363A	S42.413D	S42.433K	S42.451A	S42.471B	S42.494S	S43.082S	S43.316A	S46.211A
S42.342S	S42.363B	S42.413G	S42.433P	S42.451B	S42.471D	S42.495A	S43.083A	S43.316S	S46.211S
S42.343A	S42.363D	S42.413K	S42.433S	S42.451D	S42.471G	S42.495B	S43.083S	S43.391A	S46.212A
S42.343B	S42.363G	S42.413P	S42.434A	S42.451G	S42.471K	S42.495D	S43.084A	S43.391S	S46.212S
S42.343D	S42.363K	S42.413S	S42.434B	S42.451K	S42.471P	S42.495G	S43.084S	S43.392A	S46.219A
S42.343G	S42.363P	S42.414A	S42.434D	S42.451P	S42.471S	S42.495K	S43.085A	S43.392S	S46.219S
S42.343K	S42.363S	S42.414B	S42.434G	S42.451S	S42.472A	S42.495P	S43.085S	S43.393A	S46.221A
S42.343P	S42.364A	S42.414D	S42.434K	S42.452A	S42.472B	S42.495S	S43.086A	S43.393S	S46.222A
S42.343S	S42.364B	S42.414G	S42.434P	S42.452B	S42.472D	S42.496A	S43.086S	S43.394A	S46.229A
S42.344A	S42.364D	S42.414K	S42.434S	S42.452D	S42.472G	S42.496B	S43.101A	S43.394S	S46.311A
S42.344B	S42.364G	S42.414P	S42.435A	S42.452G	S42.472K	S42.496D	S43.101S	S43.395A	S46.311S
S42.344D	S42.364K	S42.414S	S42.435B	S42.452K	S42.472P	S42.496G	S43.102A	S43.395S	S46.312A
S42.344G	S42.364P	S42.415A	S42.435G	S42.452P	S42.472S	S42.496K	S43.102S	S43.396A	S46.312S
S42.344K	S42.364S	S42.415B	S42.435K	S42.452S	S42.473A	S42.496S	S43.109A	S43.396S	S46.319A
S42.344P	S42.365A	S42.415D	S42.435P	S42.453A	S42.473B	S42.90XA	S43.109S	S43.401A	S46.319S
S42.344S	S42.365B	S42.415G	S42.435S	S42.453B	S42.473D	S42.90XB	S43.111A	S43.401S	S46.321A
S42.345A	S42.365D	S42.415K	S42.436A	S42.453D	S42.473G	S42.90XD	S43.111S	S43.402A	S46.322A
S42.345B	S42.365G	S42.415S	S42.436B	S42.453G	S42.473K	S42.90XG	S43.112A	S43.402S	S46.329A
S42.345D	S42.365K	S42.416A	S42.436D	S42.453K	S42.473P	S42.90XK	S43.112S	S43.409A	S46.811A
S42.345G	S42.365P	S42.416B	S42.436G	S42.453P	S42.473S	S42.90XP	S43.119A	S43.409S	S46.811S
S42.345K	S42.365S	S42.416D	S42.436K	S42.453S	S42.474A	S42.90XS	S43.119S	S43.411A	S46.812A
S42.345P	S42.366A	S42.416G	S42.436P	S42.454A	S42.474B	S42.91XA	S43.121A	S43.411S	S46.812S
S42.345S	S42.366B	S42.416K	S42.436S	S42.454B	S42.474D	S42.91XB	S43.121S	S43.412A	S46.819A
S42.346A	S42.366D	S42.416K	S42.441A	S42.454D	S42.474G	S42.91XD	S43.122A	S43.412S	S46.819S
S42.346B	S42.366G	S42.416P	S42.441B	S42.454G	S42.474K	S42.91XG	S43.122S	S43.419A	S46.821A
S42.346D	S42.366K	S42.416S	S42.441D	S42.454K	S42.474P	S42.91XK	S43.129A	S43.419S	S46.822A
S42.346G	S42.366P	S42.421A	S42.441G	S42.454P	S42.474S	S42.91XP	S43.129S	S43.421A	S46.829A
S42.346K	S42.366S	S42.421B	S42.441K	S42.454S	S42.475A	S42.91XS	S43.131A	S43.421S	S46.911A
S42.346P	S42.391A	S42.421D	S42.441P	S42.455A	S42.475B	S42.92XA	S43.131S	S43.422A	S46.911S
S42.346S	S42.391B	S42.421G	S42.441S	S42.455B	S42.475D	S42.92XB	S43.132A	S43.422S	S46.912A
S42.351A	S42.391D	S42.421K	S42.442A	S42.455D	S42.475G	S42.92XD	S43.132S	S43.429A	S46.912S
S42.351B	S42.391G	S42.421P	S42.442B	S42.455G	S42.475K	S42.92XG	S43.139A	S43.429S	S46.919A
S42.351D	S42.391K	S42.421S	S42.442D	S42.455K	S42.475P	S42.92XK	S43.139S	S43.431A	S46.919S
S42.351G	S42.391P	S42.422A	S42.442G	S42.455P	S42.475S	S42.92XP	S43.141A	S43.431S	S46.921A
S42.351K	S42.391S	S42.422B	S42.442G	S42.455P	S42.476A	S42.92XP	S43.141A	S43.432A	S46.922A

Diagnosis Codes by MDC

S46.929A	S49.039D	S49.122K	S52.002H	S52.023N	S52.033B	S52.042H	S52.091Q	S52.111K	S52.125H
S48.011S	S49.039G	S49.122P	S52.002J	S52.023P	S52.033C	S52.042J	S52.091R	S52.111P	S52.125J
S48.012S	S49.039K	S49.122S	S52.002K	S52.023Q	S52.033D	S52.042K	S52.091S	S52.111S	S52.125K
S48.019S	S49.039P	S49.129A	S52.002M	S52.023R	S52.033E	S52.042M	S52.092A	S52.112A	S52.125M
S48.021S	S49.039S	S49.129D	S52.002N	S52.023S	S52.033F	S52.042N	S52.092B	S52.112D	S52.125N
S48.022S	S49.041A	S49.129G	S52.002P	S52.024A	S52.033G	S52.042P	S52.092C	S52.112G	S52.125P
S48.029S	S49.041D	S49.129K	S52.002Q	S52.024B	S52.033H	S52.042Q	S52.092D	S52.112K	S52.125Q
S48.111S	S49.041G	S49.129P	S52.002R	S52.024C	S52.033J	S52.042R	S52.092E	S52.112P	S52.125R
S48.112S	S49.041K	S49.129S	S52.002S	S52.024D	S52.033K	S52.042S	S52.092F	S52.112S	S52.125S
S48.119S	S49.041P	S49.131A	S52.009A	S52.024E	S52.033M	S52.043A	S52.092G	S52.119A	S52.126A
S48.121S	S49.041S	S49.131D	S52.009B	S52.024F	S52.033N	S52.043B	S52.092H	S52.119D	S52.126B
S48.122S	S49.042A	S49.131G	S52.009C	S52.024G	S52.033P	S52.043C	S52.092J	S52.119G	S52.126C
S48.129S	S49.042D	S49.131K	S52.009D	S52.024H	S52.033Q	S52.043D	S52.092K	S52.119K	S52.126D
S48.911S	S49.042G	S49.131P	S52.009E	S52.024J	S52.033R	S52.043E	S52.092M	S52.119P	S52.126E
S48.912S	S49.042K	S49.131S	S52.009F	S52.024K	S52.033S	S52.043F	S52.092N	S52.119S	S52.126F
S48.919S	S49.042P	S49.132A	S52.009G	S52.024M	S52.034A	S52.043G	S52.092P	S52.121A	S52.126G
S48.921S	S49.042S	S49.132D	S52.009H	S52.024N	S52.034B	S52.043H	S52.092Q	S52.121B	S52.126H
S48.922S	S49.049A	S49.132G	S52.009J	S52.024P	S52.034C	S52.043J	S52.092R	S52.121C	S52.126J
S48.929S	S49.049D	S49.132K	S52.009K	S52.024Q	S52.034D	S52.043K	S52.092S	S52.121D	S52.126K
S49.001A	S49.049G	S49.132P	S52.009M	S52.024R	S52.034E	S52.043M	S52.099A	S52.121E	S52.126M
S49.001D	S49.049K	S49.132S	S52.009N	S52.024S	S52.034F	S52.043N	S52.099B	S52.121F	S52.126N
S49.001G	S49.049P	S49.139A	S52.009P	S52.025A	S52.034G	S52.043P	S52.099C	S52.121G	S52.126P
S49.001K	S49.049S	S49.139D	S52.009Q	S52.025B	S52.034H	S52.043Q	S52.099D	S52.121H	S52.126Q
S49.001P	S49.091A	S49.139G	S52.009R	S52.025C	S52.034J	S52.043R	S52.099E	S52.121J	S52.126R
S49.001S	S49.091D	S49.139K	S52.009S	S52.025D	S52.034K	S52.043S	S52.099F	S52.121K	S52.126S
S49.002A	S49.091G	S49.139P	S52.011A	S52.025E	S52.034M	S52.044A	S52.099G	S52.121M	S52.131A
S49.002D	S49.091K	S49.139S	S52.011D	S52.025F	S52.034N	S52.044B	S52.099H	S52.121N	S52.131B
S49.002G	S49.091P	S49.141A	S52.011G	S52.025G	S52.034P	S52.044C	S52.099J	S52.121P	S52.131C
S49.002K	S49.091S	S49.141D	S52.011K	S52.025H	S52.034Q	S52.044D	S52.099K	S52.121Q	S52.131D
S49.002P	S49.092A	S49.141G	S52.011P	S52.025J	S52.034R	S52.044E	S52.099M	S52.121R	S52.131E
S49.002S	S49.092D	S49.141K	S52.011S	S52.025K	S52.034S	S52.044F	S52.099N	S52.121S	S52.131F
S49.009A	S49.092G	S49.141P	S52.012A	S52.025M	S52.035A	S52.044G	S52.099P	S52.122A	S52.131G
S49.009D	S49.092K	S49.141S	S52.012D	S52.025N	S52.035B	S52.044H	S52.099Q	S52.122B	S52.131H
S49.009G	S49.092P	S49.142A	S52.012G	S52.025P	S52.035C	S52.044J	S52.099R	S52.122C	S52.131J
S49.009K	S49.092S	S49.142D	S52.012K	S52.025Q	S52.035D	S52.044K	S52.099S	S52.122D	S52.131K
S49.009P	S49.099A	S49.142G	S52.012P	S52.025R	S52.035E	S52.044M	S52.101A	S52.122E	S52.131M
S49.009S	S49.099D	S49.142K	S52.012S	S52.025S	S52.035F	S52.044N	S52.101B	S52.122F	S52.131N
S49.011A	S49.099G	S49.142P	S52.019A	S52.026A	S52.035G	S52.044P	S52.101C	S52.122G	S52.131P
S49.011D	S49.099K	S49.142S	S52.019D	S52.026B	S52.035H	S52.044Q	S52.101D	S52.122H	S52.131Q
S49.011G	S49.099P	S49.149A	S52.019G	S52.026C	S52.035J	S52.044R	S52.101E	S52.122J	S52.131R
S49.011K	S49.099S	S49.149D	S52.019K	S52.026D	S52.035K	S52.044S	S52.101F	S52.122K	S52.131S
S49.011P	S49.101A	S49.149G	S52.019P	S52.026E	S52.035M	S52.045A	S52.101G	S52.122M	S52.132A
S49.011S	S49.101D	S49.149K	S52.019S	S52.026F	S52.035N	S52.045B	S52.101H	S52.122N	S52.132B
S49.012A	S49.101G	S49.149P	S52.021A	S52.026G	S52.035P	S52.045C	S52.101J	S52.122P	S52.132C
S49.012D	S49.101K	S49.149S	S52.021B	S52.026H	S52.035Q	S52.045D	S52.101K	S52.122Q	S52.132D
S49.012G	S49.101P	S49.191A	S52.021C	S52.026J	S52.035R	S52.045E	S52.101M	S52.122R	S52.132E
S49.012K	S49.101S	S49.191D	S52.021D	S52.026K	S52.035S	S52.045F	S52.101N	S52.122S	S52.132F
S49.012P	S49.102A	S49.191G	S52.021E	S52.026M	S52.036A	S52.045G	S52.101P	S52.123A	S52.132G
S49.012S	S49.102D	S49.191K	S52.021F	S52.026N	S52.036B	S52.045H	S52.101Q	S52.123B	S52.132H
S49.019A	S49.102G	S49.191P	S52.021G	S52.026P	S52.036C	S52.045J	S52.101R	S52.123C	S52.132J
S49.019D	S49.102K	S49.191S	S52.021H	S52.026Q	S52.036D	S52.045K	S52.101S	S52.123D	S52.132K
S49.019G	S49.102P	S49.192A	S52.021J	S52.026R	S52.036E	S52.045M	S52.102A	S52.123E	S52.132M
S49.019K	S49.102S	S49.192D	S52.021K	S52.026S	S52.036F	S52.045N	S52.102B	S52.123F	S52.132N
S49.019P	S49.109A	S49.192G	S52.021M	S52.031A	S52.036G	S52.045P	S52.102C	S52.123G	S52.132P
S49.019S	S49.109D	S49.192K	S52.021N	S52.031B	S52.036H	S52.045Q	S52.102D	S52.123H	S52.132Q
S49.021A	S49.109G	S49.192P	S52.021P	S52.031C	S52.036J	S52.045R	S52.102E	S52.123J	S52.132R
S49.021D	S49.109K	S49.192S	S52.021Q	S52.031D	S52.036K	S52.045S	S52.102F	S52.123K	S52.132S
S49.021G	S49.109P	S49.199A	S52.021R	S52.031E	S52.036M	S52.046A	S52.102G	S52.123M	S52.133A
S49.021K	S49.109S	S49.199D	S52.021S	S52.031F	S52.036N	S52.046B	S52.102H	S52.123N	S52.133B
S49.021P	S49.111A	S49.199G	S52.022A	S52.031G	S52.036P	S52.046C	S52.102J	S52.123P	S52.133C
S49.021S	S49.111D	S49.199K	S52.022B	S52.031H	S52.036Q	S52.046D	S52.102K	S52.123Q	S52.133D
S49.022A	S49.111G	S49.199P	S52.022C	S52.031J	S52.036R	S52.046E	S52.102M	S52.123R	S52.133E
S49.022D	S49.111K	S49.199S	S52.022D	S52.031K	S52.036S	S52.046F	S52.102N	S52.123S	S52.133F
S49.022G	S49.111P	S52.001A	S52.022E	S52.031M	S52.041A	S52.046G	S52.102P	S52.124A	S52.133G
S49.022K	S49.111S	S52.001B	S52.022F	S52.031N	S52.041B	S52.046H	S52.102Q	S52.124B	S52.133H
S49.022P	S49.112A	S52.001C	S52.022G	S52.031P	S52.041C	S52.046J	S52.102R	S52.124C	S52.133J
S49.022S	S49.112D	S52.001D	S52.022H	S52.031Q	S52.041D	S52.046K	S52.102S	S52.124D	S52.133K
S49.029A	S49.112G	S52.001E	S52.022J	S52.031R	S52.041E	S52.046M	S52.109A	S52.124E	S52.133M
S49.029D	S49.112K	S52.001F	S52.022K	S52.031S	S52.041F	S52.046N	S52.109B	S52.124F	S52.133N
S49.029G	S49.112P	S52.001G	S52.022M	S52.032A	S52.041G	S52.046P	S52.109C	S52.124G	S52.133P
S49.029K	S49.112S	S52.001H	S52.022N	S52.032B	S52.041H	S52.046Q	S52.109D	S52.124H	S52.133Q
S49.029P	S49.119A	S52.001J	S52.022P	S52.032C	S52.041J	S52.046R	S52.109E	S52.124J	S52.133R
S49.029S	S49.119D	S52.001K	S52.022Q	S52.032D	S52.041K	S52.046S	S52.109F	S52.124K	S52.133S
S49.031A	S49.119G	S52.001M	S52.022R	S52.032E	S52.041M	S52.091A	S52.109G	S52.124M	S52.134A
S49.031D	S49.119K	S52.001N	S52.022S	S52.032F	S52.041N	S52.091B	S52.109H	S52.124N	S52.134B
S49.031G	S49.119P	S52.001P	S52.023A	S52.032G	S52.041P	S52.091C	S52.109J	S52.124P	S52.134C
S49.031K	S49.119S	S52.001Q	S52.023B	S52.032H	S52.041Q	S52.091D	S52.109K	S52.124Q	S52.134D
S49.031P	S49.121A	S52.001R	S52.023C	S52.032J	S52.041R	S52.091E	S52.109M	S52.124R	S52.134E
S49.031S	S49.121D	S52.001S	S52.023D	S52.032K	S52.041S	S52.091F	S52.109N	S52.124S	S52.134F
S49.032A	S49.121G	S52.002A	S52.023E	S52.032M	S52.042A	S52.091G	S52.109P	S52.125A	S52.134G
S49.032D	S49.121K	S52.002B	S52.023F	S52.032N	S52.042B	S52.091H	S52.109Q	S52.125B	S52.134H
S49.032G	S49.121P	S52.002C	S52.023G	S52.032P	S52.042C	S52.091J	S52.109R	S52.125C	S52.134J
S49.032K	S49.121S	S52.002D	S52.023H	S52.032Q	S52.042D	S52.091K	S52.109S	S52.125D	S52.134K
S49.032P	S49.122A	S52.002E	S52.023J	S52.032R	S52.042E	S52.091M	S52.111A	S52.125E	S52.134M
S49.032S	S49.122D	S52.002F	S52.023K	S52.032S	S52.042F	S52.091N	S52.111D	S52.125F	S52.134N
S49.039A	S49.122G	S52.002G	S52.023M	S52.033A	S52.042G	S52.091P	S52.111G	S52.125G	S52.134P

S52.134Q	S52.201D	S52.222H	S52.231Q	S52.241D	S52.246K	S52.255S	S52.265F	S52.281N	S52.301B
S52.134R	S52.201E	S52.222J	S52.231R	S52.241E	S52.246M	S52.256A	S52.265G	S52.281P	S52.301C
S52.134S	S52.201F	S52.222K	S52.231S	S52.241F	S52.246N	S52.256B	S52.265H	S52.281Q	S52.301D
S52.135A	S52.201G	S52.222M	S52.232A	S52.241G	S52.246P	S52.256C	S52.265J	S52.281R	S52.301E
S52.135B	S52.201H	S52.222N	S52.232B	S52.241H	S52.246Q	S52.256D	S52.265K	S52.281S	S52.301F
S52.135C	S52.201J	S52.222P	S52.232C	S52.241J	S52.246R	S52.256E	S52.265M	S52.282A	S52.301G
S52.135D	S52.201K	S52.222Q	S52.232D	S52.241K	S52.246S	S52.256F	S52.265N	S52.282B	S52.301H
S52.135E	S52.201M	S52.222R	S52.232E	S52.241M	S52.251A	S52.256G	S52.265P	S52.282C	S52.301J
S52.135F	S52.201N	S52.222S	S52.232F	S52.241N	S52.251B	S52.256H	S52.265Q	S52.282D	S52.301K
S52.135G	S52.201P	S52.223A	S52.232G	S52.241P	S52.251C	S52.256J	S52.265R	S52.282E	S52.301M
S52.135H	S52.201Q	S52.223B	S52.232H	S52.241Q	S52.251D	S52.256K	S52.265S	S52.282F	S52.301N
S52.135J	S52.201R	S52.223C	S52.232J	S52.241R	S52.251E	S52.256M	S52.266A	S52.282G	S52.301P
S52.135K	S52.201S	S52.223D	S52.232K	S52.241S	S52.251F	S52.256N	S52.266B	S52.282H	S52.301Q
S52.135M	S52.202A	S52.223E	S52.232M	S52.242A	S52.251G	S52.256P	S52.266C	S52.282J	S52.301R
S52.135N	S52.202B	S52.223F	S52.232N	S52.242B	S52.251H	S52.256Q	S52.266D	S52.282K	S52.301S
S52.135P	S52.202C	S52.223G	S52.232P	S52.242C	S52.251J	S52.256R	S52.266E	S52.282M	S52.302A
S52.135Q	S52.202D	S52.223H	S52.232Q	S52.242D	S52.251K	S52.256S	S52.266F	S52.282N	S52.302B
S52.135R	S52.202E	S52.223J	S52.232R	S52.242E	S52.251M	S52.261A	S52.266G	S52.282P	S52.302C
S52.135S	S52.202F	S52.223K	S52.232S	S52.242F	S52.251N	S52.261B	S52.266H	S52.282Q	S52.302D
S52.136A	S52.202G	S52.223M	S52.233A	S52.242G	S52.251P	S52.261C	S52.266J	S52.282R	S52.302E
S52.136B	S52.202H	S52.223N	S52.233B	S52.242H	S52.251Q	S52.261D	S52.266K	S52.282S	S52.302F
S52.136C	S52.202J	S52.223P	S52.233C	S52.242J	S52.251R	S52.261E	S52.266M	S52.283A	S52.302G
S52.136D	S52.202K	S52.223Q	S52.233D	S52.242K	S52.251S	S52.261F	S52.266N	S52.283B	S52.302H
S52.136E	S52.202M	S52.223R	S52.233E	S52.242M	S52.252A	S52.261G	S52.266P	S52.283C	S52.302J
S52.136F	S52.202N	S52.223S	S52.233F	S52.242N	S52.252B	S52.261H	S52.266Q	S52.283D	S52.302K
S52.136G	S52.202P	S52.224A	S52.233G	S52.242P	S52.252C	S52.261J	S52.266R	S52.283E	S52.302M
S52.136H	S52.202Q	S52.224B	S52.233H	S52.242Q	S52.252D	S52.261K	S52.266S	S52.283F	S52.302N
S52.136J	S52.202R	S52.224C	S52.233J	S52.242R	S52.252E	S52.261M	S52.271A	S52.283G	S52.302P
S52.136K	S52.202S	S52.224D	S52.233K	S52.242S	S52.252F	S52.261N	S52.271B	S52.283H	S52.302Q
S52.136M	S52.209A	S52.224E	S52.233M	S52.243A	S52.252G	S52.261P	S52.271C	S52.283J	S52.302R
S52.136N	S52.209B	S52.224F	S52.233N	S52.243B	S52.252H	S52.261Q	S52.271D	S52.283K	S52.302S
S52.136P	S52.209C	S52.224G	S52.233P	S52.243C	S52.252J	S52.261R	S52.271E	S52.283M	S52.309A
S52.136Q	S52.209D	S52.224H	S52.233Q	S52.243D	S52.252K	S52.261S	S52.271F	S52.283N	S52.309B
S52.136R	S52.209E	S52.224J	S52.233R	S52.243E	S52.252M	S52.262A	S52.271G	S52.283P	S52.309C
S52.136S	S52.209F	S52.224K	S52.233S	S52.243F	S52.252N	S52.262B	S52.271H	S52.283Q	S52.309D
S52.181A	S52.209G	S52.224M	S52.234A	S52.243G	S52.252P	S52.262C	S52.271J	S52.283R	S52.309E
S52.181B	S52.209H	S52.224N	S52.234B	S52.243H	S52.252Q	S52.262D	S52.271K	S52.283S	S52.309F
S52.181C	S52.209J	S52.224P	S52.234C	S52.243J	S52.252R	S52.262E	S52.271M	S52.291A	S52.309G
S52.181D	S52.209K	S52.224Q	S52.234D	S52.243K	S52.252S	S52.262F	S52.271N	S52.291B	S52.309H
S52.181E	S52.209M	S52.224R	S52.234E	S52.243M	S52.253A	S52.262G	S52.271P	S52.291C	S52.309J
S52.181F	S52.209N	S52.224S	S52.234F	S52.243N	S52.253B	S52.262H	S52.271Q	S52.291D	S52.309K
S52.181G	S52.209P	S52.225A	S52.234G	S52.243P	S52.253C	S52.262J	S52.271R	S52.291E	S52.309M
S52.181H	S52.209Q	S52.225B	S52.234H	S52.243Q	S52.253D	S52.262K	S52.271S	S52.291F	S52.309N
S52.181J	S52.209R	S52.225C	S52.234J	S52.243R	S52.253E	S52.262M	S52.272A	S52.291G	S52.309P
S52.181K	S52.209S	S52.225D	S52.234K	S52.243S	S52.253F	S52.262N	S52.272B	S52.291H	S52.309Q
S52.181M	S52.211A	S52.225E	S52.234M	S52.244A	S52.253G	S52.262P	S52.272C	S52.291J	S52.309R
S52.181N	S52.211B	S52.225F	S52.234N	S52.244B	S52.253H	S52.262Q	S52.272D	S52.291K	S52.309S
S52.181P	S52.211G	S52.225G	S52.234P	S52.244C	S52.253J	S52.262R	S52.272E	S52.291M	S52.311A
S52.181Q	S52.211K	S52.225H	S52.234Q	S52.244D	S52.253K	S52.262S	S52.272F	S52.291N	S52.311D
S52.181R	S52.211P	S52.225J	S52.234R	S52.244E	S52.253M	S52.263A	S52.272G	S52.291P	S52.311G
S52.181S	S52.211S	S52.225K	S52.234S	S52.244F	S52.253N	S52.263B	S52.272H	S52.291Q	S52.311K
S52.182A	S52.212A	S52.225M	S52.235A	S52.244G	S52.253P	S52.263C	S52.272J	S52.291R	S52.311S
S52.182B	S52.212D	S52.225N	S52.235B	S52.244H	S52.253Q	S52.263D	S52.272K	S52.291S	S52.312A
S52.182C	S52.212G	S52.225P	S52.235C	S52.244J	S52.253R	S52.263E	S52.272M	S52.292A	S52.312D
S52.182D	S52.212K	S52.225Q	S52.235D	S52.244K	S52.253S	S52.263F	S52.272N	S52.292B	S52.312G
S52.182E	S52.212P	S52.225S	S52.235E	S52.244M	S52.254A	S52.263G	S52.272P	S52.292C	S52.312K
S52.182F	S52.212S	S52.226A	S52.235F	S52.244N	S52.254B	S52.263H	S52.272Q	S52.292D	S52.312P
S52.182G	S52.219A	S52.226B	S52.235G	S52.244P	S52.254C	S52.263J	S52.272R	S52.292E	S52.312S
S52.182H	S52.219D	S52.226C	S52.235H	S52.244Q	S52.254D	S52.263K	S52.272S	S52.292F	S52.319A
S52.182J	S52.219G	S52.226C	S52.235J	S52.244R	S52.254E	S52.263M	S52.279A	S52.292G	S52.319D
S52.182K	S52.219K	S52.226D	S52.235K	S52.244S	S52.254F	S52.263N	S52.279B	S52.292H	S52.319G
S52.182M	S52.219P	S52.226E	S52.235M	S52.245A	S52.254G	S52.263P	S52.279C	S52.292J	S52.319K
S52.182N	S52.219S	S52.226F	S52.235N	S52.245B	S52.254H	S52.263Q	S52.279D	S52.292K	S52.319P
S52.182P	S52.221A	S52.226G	S52.235P	S52.245C	S52.254J	S52.263R	S52.279E	S52.292M	S52.319S
S52.182Q	S52.221B	S52.226H	S52.235Q	S52.245D	S52.254K	S52.263S	S52.279F	S52.292N	S52.321A
S52.182R	S52.221C	S52.226J	S52.235R	S52.245E	S52.254M	S52.264A	S52.279G	S52.292P	S52.321B
S52.182S	S52.221D	S52.226K	S52.235S	S52.245F	S52.254N	S52.264B	S52.279H	S52.292Q	S52.321C
S52.189A	S52.221E	S52.226M	S52.236A	S52.245G	S52.254P	S52.264C	S52.279J	S52.292R	S52.321D
S52.189B	S52.221F	S52.226N	S52.236B	S52.245H	S52.254Q	S52.264D	S52.279M	S52.292S	S52.321E
S52.189C	S52.221G	S52.226P	S52.236C	S52.245J	S52.254R	S52.264E	S52.279N	S52.299A	S52.321F
S52.189D	S52.221H	S52.226Q	S52.236D	S52.245K	S52.254S	S52.264F	S52.279P	S52.299B	S52.321G
S52.189E	S52.221J	S52.226R	S52.236E	S52.245M	S52.255A	S52.264G	S52.279Q	S52.299C	S52.321H
S52.189F	S52.221K	S52.226S	S52.236F	S52.245N	S52.255B	S52.264H	S52.279R	S52.299D	S52.321J
S52.189G	S52.221M	S52.231A	S52.236G	S52.245P	S52.255C	S52.264J	S52.279S	S52.299E	S52.321K
S52.189H	S52.221N	S52.231B	S52.236H	S52.245Q	S52.255D	S52.264K	S52.281A	S52.299F	S52.321M
S52.189J	S52.221P	S52.231C	S52.236J	S52.245R	S52.255E	S52.264M	S52.281B	S52.299G	S52.321N
S52.189K	S52.221Q	S52.231D	S52.236K	S52.245S	S52.255F	S52.264N	S52.281C	S52.299H	S52.321P
S52.189M	S52.221R	S52.231E	S52.236M	S52.246A	S52.255G	S52.264P	S52.281D	S52.299J	S52.321Q
S52.189N	S52.221S	S52.231F	S52.236N	S52.246B	S52.255H	S52.264Q	S52.281E	S52.299K	S52.321R
S52.189P	S52.222A	S52.231G	S52.236P	S52.246C	S52.255J	S52.264R	S52.281F	S52.299M	S52.321S
S52.189Q	S52.222B	S52.231H	S52.236Q	S52.246D	S52.255K	S52.264S	S52.281G	S52.299N	S52.322A
S52.189R	S52.222C	S52.231J	S52.236R	S52.246E	S52.255M	S52.265A	S52.281H	S52.299P	S52.322B
S52.189S	S52.222D	S52.231K	S52.236S	S52.246F	S52.255N	S52.265B	S52.281J	S52.299Q	S52.322C
S52.201A	S52.222E	S52.231M	S52.241A	S52.246G	S52.255P	S52.265C	S52.281K	S52.299S	S52.322D
S52.201B	S52.222F	S52.231N	S52.241B	S52.246H	S52.255Q	S52.265D	S52.281M	S52.301A	S52.322E
S52.201C	S52.222G	S52.231P	S52.241C	S52.246J	S52.255R	S52.265E	S52.281M	S52.301A	S52.322E

Diagnosis Codes by MDC

S52.322F	S52.331N	S52.341B	S52.346H	S52.355Q	S52.365D	S52.381K	S52.399S	S52.513F	S52.531K
S52.322G	S52.331P	S52.341C	S52.346J	S52.355R	S52.365E	S52.381M	S52.501A	S52.513G	S52.531M
S52.322H	S52.331Q	S52.341D	S52.346K	S52.355S	S52.365F	S52.381N	S52.501B	S52.513H	S52.531N
S52.322J	S52.331R	S52.341E	S52.346M	S52.356A	S52.365G	S52.381P	S52.501C	S52.513J	S52.531P
S52.322K	S52.331S	S52.341F	S52.346N	S52.356B	S52.365H	S52.381Q	S52.501D	S52.513K	S52.531Q
S52.322M	S52.332A	S52.341G	S52.346P	S52.356C	S52.365J	S52.381R	S52.501E	S52.513M	S52.531R
S52.322N	S52.332B	S52.341H	S52.346Q	S52.356D	S52.365K	S52.381S	S52.501F	S52.513N	S52.531S
S52.322P	S52.332C	S52.341J	S52.346R	S52.356E	S52.365M	S52.382A	S52.501G	S52.513P	S52.532A
S52.322Q	S52.332D	S52.341K	S52.346S	S52.356F	S52.365N	S52.382B	S52.501H	S52.513Q	S52.532B
S52.322R	S52.332E	S52.341M	S52.351A	S52.356G	S52.365P	S52.382C	S52.501J	S52.513R	S52.532C
S52.322S	S52.332F	S52.341N	S52.351B	S52.356H	S52.365Q	S52.382D	S52.501K	S52.513S	S52.532D
S52.323A	S52.332G	S52.341P	S52.351C	S52.356J	S52.365R	S52.382E	S52.501M	S52.514A	S52.532E
S52.323B	S52.332H	S52.341Q	S52.351D	S52.356K	S52.365S	S52.382F	S52.501N	S52.514B	S52.532F
S52.323C	S52.332J	S52.341R	S52.351E	S52.356M	S52.366A	S52.382G	S52.501P	S52.514C	S52.532G
S52.323D	S52.332K	S52.341S	S52.351F	S52.356N	S52.366B	S52.382H	S52.501Q	S52.514D	S52.532H
S52.323E	S52.332M	S52.342A	S52.351G	S52.356P	S52.366C	S52.382J	S52.501R	S52.514E	S52.532J
S52.323F	S52.332N	S52.342B	S52.351H	S52.356Q	S52.366D	S52.382K	S52.501S	S52.514F	S52.532K
S52.323G	S52.332P	S52.342C	S52.351J	S52.356R	S52.366E	S52.382M	S52.502A	S52.514G	S52.532M
S52.323H	S52.332Q	S52.342D	S52.351K	S52.356S	S52.366F	S52.382N	S52.502B	S52.514H	S52.532N
S52.323J	S52.332R	S52.342E	S52.351M	S52.361A	S52.366G	S52.382P	S52.502C	S52.514J	S52.532P
S52.323K	S52.332S	S52.342F	S52.351N	S52.361B	S52.366H	S52.382Q	S52.502D	S52.514K	S52.532Q
S52.323M	S52.333A	S52.342G	S52.351P	S52.361C	S52.366J	S52.382R	S52.502E	S52.514M	S52.532R
S52.323N	S52.333B	S52.342H	S52.351Q	S52.361D	S52.366K	S52.382S	S52.502F	S52.514N	S52.532S
S52.323P	S52.333C	S52.342J	S52.351R	S52.361E	S52.366M	S52.389A	S52.502G	S52.514P	S52.539A
S52.323Q	S52.333D	S52.342K	S52.351S	S52.361F	S52.366N	S52.389B	S52.502H	S52.514Q	S52.539B
S52.323R	S52.333E	S52.342M	S52.352A	S52.361G	S52.366P	S52.389C	S52.502J	S52.514R	S52.539C
S52.323S	S52.333F	S52.342N	S52.352B	S52.361H	S52.366Q	S52.389D	S52.502K	S52.514S	S52.539D
S52.324A	S52.333G	S52.342P	S52.352C	S52.361J	S52.366R	S52.389E	S52.502M	S52.515A	S52.539E
S52.324B	S52.333H	S52.342Q	S52.352D	S52.361K	S52.366S	S52.389F	S52.502N	S52.515B	S52.539F
S52.324C	S52.333J	S52.342R	S52.352E	S52.361M	S52.371A	S52.389G	S52.502P	S52.515C	S52.539G
S52.324D	S52.333K	S52.342S	S52.352F	S52.361N	S52.371B	S52.389H	S52.502Q	S52.515D	S52.539H
S52.324E	S52.333M	S52.343A	S52.352G	S52.361P	S52.371C	S52.389J	S52.502R	S52.515E	S52.539J
S52.324F	S52.333N	S52.343B	S52.352H	S52.361Q	S52.371D	S52.389K	S52.502S	S52.515F	S52.539K
S52.324G	S52.333P	S52.343C	S52.352J	S52.361R	S52.371E	S52.389M	S52.509A	S52.515G	S52.539M
S52.324H	S52.333Q	S52.343D	S52.352K	S52.361S	S52.371F	S52.389N	S52.509B	S52.515H	S52.539N
S52.324J	S52.333R	S52.343E	S52.352M	S52.362A	S52.371G	S52.389P	S52.509C	S52.515J	S52.539P
S52.324K	S52.333S	S52.343F	S52.352N	S52.362B	S52.371H	S52.389Q	S52.509D	S52.515K	S52.539Q
S52.324M	S52.334A	S52.343G	S52.352P	S52.362C	S52.371J	S52.389R	S52.509E	S52.515M	S52.539R
S52.324N	S52.334B	S52.343H	S52.352Q	S52.362D	S52.371K	S52.389S	S52.509F	S52.515N	S52.539S
S52.324P	S52.334C	S52.343J	S52.352R	S52.362E	S52.371M	S52.391A	S52.509G	S52.515P	S52.541A
S52.324Q	S52.334D	S52.343K	S52.352S	S52.362F	S52.371N	S52.391B	S52.509H	S52.515Q	S52.541B
S52.324R	S52.334E	S52.343M	S52.353A	S52.362G	S52.371P	S52.391C	S52.509J	S52.515R	S52.541C
S52.324S	S52.334F	S52.343N	S52.353B	S52.362H	S52.371Q	S52.391D	S52.509K	S52.515S	S52.541D
S52.325A	S52.334G	S52.343P	S52.353C	S52.362J	S52.371R	S52.391E	S52.509M	S52.516A	S52.541E
S52.325B	S52.334H	S52.343Q	S52.353D	S52.362K	S52.371S	S52.391F	S52.509N	S52.516B	S52.541F
S52.325C	S52.334J	S52.343R	S52.353E	S52.362M	S52.372A	S52.391G	S52.509P	S52.516C	S52.541G
S52.325D	S52.334K	S52.343S	S52.353F	S52.362N	S52.372B	S52.391H	S52.509Q	S52.516D	S52.541H
S52.325E	S52.334M	S52.344A	S52.353G	S52.362P	S52.372C	S52.391J	S52.509R	S52.516E	S52.541J
S52.325F	S52.334N	S52.344B	S52.353H	S52.362Q	S52.372D	S52.391K	S52.509S	S52.516F	S52.541K
S52.325G	S52.334P	S52.344C	S52.353J	S52.362R	S52.372E	S52.391M	S52.511A	S52.516G	S52.541M
S52.325H	S52.334Q	S52.344D	S52.353K	S52.362S	S52.372F	S52.391N	S52.511B	S52.516H	S52.541N
S52.325J	S52.334R	S52.344E	S52.353M	S52.363A	S52.372G	S52.391P	S52.511C	S52.516J	S52.541P
S52.325K	S52.334S	S52.344F	S52.353N	S52.363B	S52.372H	S52.391Q	S52.511D	S52.516K	S52.541Q
S52.325M	S52.335A	S52.344G	S52.353P	S52.363C	S52.372J	S52.391R	S52.511E	S52.516M	S52.541R
S52.325N	S52.335B	S52.344H	S52.353Q	S52.363D	S52.372K	S52.391S	S52.511F	S52.516N	S52.541S
S52.325P	S52.335C	S52.344J	S52.353R	S52.363E	S52.372M	S52.392A	S52.511G	S52.516P	S52.542A
S52.325Q	S52.335D	S52.344K	S52.353S	S52.363F	S52.372N	S52.392B	S52.511H	S52.516Q	S52.542B
S52.325R	S52.335E	S52.344M	S52.354A	S52.363G	S52.372P	S52.392C	S52.511J	S52.516R	S52.542C
S52.325S	S52.335F	S52.344N	S52.354B	S52.363H	S52.372Q	S52.392D	S52.511K	S52.516S	S52.542D
S52.326A	S52.335G	S52.344P	S52.354C	S52.363J	S52.372R	S52.392E	S52.511M	S52.521A	S52.542E
S52.326B	S52.335H	S52.344Q	S52.354D	S52.363K	S52.372S	S52.392F	S52.511N	S52.521D	S52.542F
S52.326C	S52.335J	S52.344R	S52.354E	S52.363M	S52.379A	S52.392G	S52.511P	S52.521G	S52.542G
S52.326D	S52.335K	S52.344S	S52.354F	S52.363N	S52.379B	S52.392H	S52.511Q	S52.521K	S52.542H
S52.326E	S52.335M	S52.345A	S52.354G	S52.363P	S52.379C	S52.392J	S52.511R	S52.521P	S52.542J
S52.326F	S52.335N	S52.345B	S52.354H	S52.363Q	S52.379D	S52.392K	S52.511S	S52.521S	S52.542K
S52.326G	S52.335P	S52.345C	S52.354J	S52.363R	S52.379E	S52.392M	S52.512A	S52.522A	S52.542M
S52.326H	S52.335Q	S52.345D	S52.354K	S52.363S	S52.379F	S52.392N	S52.512B	S52.522D	S52.542N
S52.326J	S52.335R	S52.345E	S52.354M	S52.364A	S52.379G	S52.392P	S52.512C	S52.522G	S52.542P
S52.326K	S52.335S	S52.345F	S52.354N	S52.364B	S52.379H	S52.392Q	S52.512D	S52.522K	S52.542Q
S52.326M	S52.336A	S52.345G	S52.354P	S52.364C	S52.379J	S52.392R	S52.512E	S52.522P	S52.542R
S52.326N	S52.336B	S52.345H	S52.354Q	S52.364D	S52.379K	S52.392S	S52.512F	S52.522S	S52.542S
S52.326P	S52.336C	S52.345J	S52.354R	S52.364E	S52.379M	S52.399A	S52.512G	S52.529A	S52.549A
S52.326Q	S52.336D	S52.345K	S52.354S	S52.364F	S52.379N	S52.399B	S52.512H	S52.529D	S52.549B
S52.326R	S52.336E	S52.345M	S52.355A	S52.364G	S52.379P	S52.399C	S52.512J	S52.529G	S52.549C
S52.326S	S52.336F	S52.345N	S52.355B	S52.364H	S52.379Q	S52.399D	S52.512K	S52.529K	S52.549D
S52.331A	S52.336G	S52.345P	S52.355C	S52.364J	S52.379R	S52.399E	S52.512M	S52.529P	S52.549E
S52.331B	S52.336H	S52.345Q	S52.355D	S52.364K	S52.379S	S52.399F	S52.512N	S52.529S	S52.549F
S52.331C	S52.336J	S52.345R	S52.355E	S52.364M	S52.381A	S52.399G	S52.512P	S52.531A	S52.549G
S52.331D	S52.336K	S52.345S	S52.355F	S52.364N	S52.381B	S52.399H	S52.512Q	S52.531B	S52.549H
S52.331E	S52.336M	S52.346A	S52.355G	S52.364P	S52.381C	S52.399J	S52.512R	S52.531C	S52.549J
S52.331F	S52.336N	S52.346B	S52.355H	S52.364Q	S52.381D	S52.399K	S52.512S	S52.531D	S52.549K
S52.331G	S52.336P	S52.346C	S52.355J	S52.364R	S52.381E	S52.399M	S52.513A	S52.531E	S52.549M
S52.331H	S52.336Q	S52.346D	S52.355K	S52.364S	S52.381F	S52.399N	S52.513B	S52.531F	S52.549N
S52.331J	S52.336R	S52.346E	S52.355M	S52.365A	S52.381G	S52.399P	S52.513C	S52.531G	S52.549P
S52.331K	S52.336S	S52.346F	S52.355N	S52.365B	S52.381H	S52.399Q	S52.513D	S52.531H	S52.549Q
S52.331M	S52.341A	S52.346G	S52.355P	S52.365C	S52.381J	S52.399R	S52.513E	S52.531J	S52.549R

S52.549S	S52.569F	S52.592N	S52.612B	S52.622D	S52.91XN	S53.106S	S53.421S	S56.415S	S59.011S
S52.551A	S52.569G	S52.592P	S52.612C	S52.622G	S52.91XP	S53.111A	S53.422A	S56.416A	S59.012A
S52.551C	S52.569H	S52.592Q	S52.612D	S52.622K	S52.91XQ	S53.111S	S53.422S	S56.416S	S59.012D
S52.551D	S52.569J	S52.592R	S52.612E	S52.622P	S52.91XR	S53.112A	S53.429A	S56.417A	S59.012G
S52.551E	S52.569K	S52.592S	S52.612F	S52.622S	S52.91XS	S53.112S	S53.429S	S56.417S	S59.012K
S52.551F	S52.569M	S52.599A	S52.612G	S52.629A	S52.92XA	S53.113A	S53.431A	S56.418A	S59.012P
S52.551G	S52.569N	S52.599B	S52.612H	S52.629D	S52.92XB	S53.113S	S53.431S	S56.418S	S59.012S
S52.551H	S52.569P	S52.599C	S52.612J	S52.629G	S52.92XC	S53.114A	S53.432A	S56.419A	S59.019A
S52.551J	S52.569Q	S52.599D	S52.612K	S52.629K	S52.92XD	S53.114S	S53.432S	S56.419S	S59.019D
S52.551K	S52.569R	S52.599E	S52.612M	S52.629P	S52.92XE	S53.115A	S53.439A	S56.421A	S59.019G
S52.551M	S52.569S	S52.599F	S52.612N	S52.629S	S52.92XF	S53.115S	S53.439S	S56.422A	S59.019K
S52.551N	S52.571A	S52.599G	S52.612P	S52.691A	S52.92XG	S53.116A	S53.441A	S56.423A	S59.019P
S52.551P	S52.571B	S52.599H	S52.612Q	S52.691B	S52.92XH	S53.116S	S53.441S	S56.424A	S59.019S
S52.551Q	S52.571C	S52.599J	S52.612R	S52.691C	S52.92XJ	S53.121A	S53.442A	S56.425A	S59.021A
S52.551R	S52.571D	S52.599K	S52.612S	S52.691D	S52.92XK	S53.121S	S53.442S	S56.426A	S59.021D
S52.551S	S52.571E	S52.599M	S52.613A	S52.691E	S52.92XM	S53.122A	S53.449A	S56.427A	S59.021G
S52.552A	S52.571F	S52.599N	S52.613B	S52.691F	S52.92XN	S53.122S	S53.449S	S56.428A	S59.021K
S52.552B	S52.571G	S52.599P	S52.613C	S52.691G	S52.92XP	S53.123A	S53.491A	S56.429A	S59.021P
S52.552C	S52.571H	S52.599Q	S52.613D	S52.691H	S52.92XQ	S53.123S	S53.491S	S56.511A	S59.021S
S52.552D	S52.571J	S52.599R	S52.613E	S52.691J	S52.92XR	S53.124A	S53.492A	S56.511S	S59.022A
S52.552E	S52.571K	S52.599S	S52.613F	S52.691K	S52.92XS	S53.124S	S53.492S	S56.512A	S59.022D
S52.552F	S52.571M	S52.601A	S52.613G	S52.691M	S53.001A	S53.125A	S53.499A	S56.512S	S59.022G
S52.552G	S52.571N	S52.601B	S52.613H	S52.691N	S53.001S	S53.125S	S53.499S	S56.519A	S59.022K
S52.552H	S52.571P	S52.601C	S52.613J	S52.691P	S53.002A	S53.126A	S56.011A	S56.519S	S59.022P
S52.552J	S52.571Q	S52.601D	S52.613K	S52.691Q	S53.002S	S53.126S	S56.011S	S56.521A	S59.022S
S52.552K	S52.571R	S52.601E	S52.613M	S52.691R	S53.003A	S53.131A	S56.012A	S56.522A	S59.029A
S52.552M	S52.571S	S52.601F	S52.613N	S52.691S	S53.003S	S53.131S	S56.012S	S56.529A	S59.029D
S52.552N	S52.572A	S52.601G	S52.613P	S52.692A	S53.004A	S53.132A	S56.019A	S56.811A	S59.029G
S52.552P	S52.572B	S52.601H	S52.613Q	S52.692B	S53.004S	S53.132S	S56.019S	S56.811S	S59.029K
S52.552Q	S52.572C	S52.601J	S52.613R	S52.692C	S53.005A	S53.133A	S56.021A	S56.812A	S59.029P
S52.552R	S52.572D	S52.601K	S52.613S	S52.692D	S53.005S	S53.133S	S56.022A	S56.812S	S59.029S
S52.552S	S52.572E	S52.601M	S52.614A	S52.692E	S53.006A	S53.134A	S56.029A	S56.819A	S59.031A
S52.559A	S52.572F	S52.601N	S52.614B	S52.692F	S53.006S	S53.134S	S56.111A	S56.819S	S59.031D
S52.559B	S52.572G	S52.601P	S52.614C	S52.692G	S53.011A	S53.135A	S56.111S	S56.821A	S59.031G
S52.559C	S52.572H	S52.601Q	S52.614D	S52.692H	S53.011S	S53.135S	S56.112A	S56.822A	S59.031K
S52.559D	S52.572J	S52.601R	S52.614E	S52.692J	S53.012A	S53.136A	S56.112S	S56.829A	S59.031P
S52.559E	S52.572K	S52.601S	S52.614F	S52.692K	S53.012S	S53.136S	S56.113A	S56.911A	S59.031S
S52.559F	S52.572M	S52.602A	S52.614G	S52.692M	S53.013A	S53.141A	S56.113S	S56.911S	S59.032A
S52.559G	S52.572N	S52.602B	S52.614H	S52.692N	S53.013S	S53.141S	S56.114A	S56.912A	S59.032D
S52.559H	S52.572P	S52.602C	S52.614J	S52.692P	S53.014A	S53.142A	S56.114S	S56.912S	S59.032G
S52.559J	S52.572Q	S52.602D	S52.614K	S52.692Q	S53.014S	S53.142S	S56.115A	S56.919A	S59.032K
S52.559K	S52.572R	S52.602E	S52.614M	S52.692R	S53.015A	S53.143A	S56.115S	S56.919S	S59.032P
S52.559M	S52.572S	S52.602F	S52.614N	S52.692S	S53.015S	S53.143S	S56.116A	S56.921A	S59.032S
S52.559N	S52.579A	S52.602G	S52.614P	S52.699A	S53.016A	S53.144A	S56.116S	S56.922A	S59.039A
S52.559P	S52.579B	S52.602H	S52.614Q	S52.699B	S53.016S	S53.144S	S56.117A	S56.929A	S59.039D
S52.559Q	S52.579C	S52.602J	S52.614R	S52.699C	S53.021A	S53.145A	S56.117S	S58.011S	S59.039G
S52.559R	S52.579D	S52.602K	S52.614S	S52.699D	S53.021S	S53.145S	S56.118A	S58.012S	S59.039K
S52.559S	S52.579E	S52.602M	S52.615A	S52.699E	S53.022A	S53.146A	S56.118S	S58.019S	S59.039P
S52.561A	S52.579F	S52.602N	S52.615B	S52.699F	S53.022S	S53.146S	S56.119A	S58.021S	S59.039S
S52.561B	S52.579G	S52.602P	S52.615C	S52.699G	S53.023A	S53.191A	S56.119S	S58.022S	S59.041A
S52.561C	S52.579H	S52.602Q	S52.615D	S52.699H	S53.023S	S53.191S	S56.121A	S58.029S	S59.041D
S52.561D	S52.579J	S52.602R	S52.615E	S52.699J	S53.024A	S53.192A	S56.122A	S58.111S	S59.041G
S52.561E	S52.579K	S52.602S	S52.615F	S52.699K	S53.024S	S53.192S	S56.123A	S58.112S	S59.041K
S52.561F	S52.579M	S52.609A	S52.615G	S52.699M	S53.025A	S53.193A	S56.124A	S58.119S	S59.041P
S52.561G	S52.579N	S52.609B	S52.615H	S52.699N	S53.025S	S53.193S	S56.125A	S58.121S	S59.041S
S52.561H	S52.579P	S52.609C	S52.615J	S52.699P	S53.026A	S53.194A	S56.126A	S58.122S	S59.042A
S52.561J	S52.579Q	S52.609D	S52.615K	S52.699Q	S53.026S	S53.194S	S56.127A	S58.129S	S59.042D
S52.561K	S52.579R	S52.609E	S52.615M	S52.699R	S53.031A	S53.195A	S56.128A	S58.911S	S59.042G
S52.561M	S52.579S	S52.609F	S52.615N	S52.699S	S53.031S	S53.195S	S56.129A	S58.912S	S59.042K
S52.561N	S52.591A	S52.609G	S52.615P	S52.90XA	S53.032A	S53.196A	S56.211A	S58.919S	S59.042P
S52.561P	S52.591B	S52.609H	S52.615Q	S52.90XB	S53.032S	S53.196S	S56.211S	S58.921S	S59.042S
S52.561Q	S52.591C	S52.609J	S52.615R	S52.90XC	S53.033A	S53.20XA	S56.212A	S58.922S	S59.049A
S52.561R	S52.591D	S52.609K	S52.615S	S52.90XD	S53.033S	S53.20XS	S56.212S	S58.929S	S59.049D
S52.561S	S52.591E	S52.609M	S52.616A	S52.90XE	S53.091A	S53.21XA	S56.219A	S59.001A	S59.049G
S52.562A	S52.591F	S52.609N	S52.616B	S52.90XF	S53.091S	S53.21XS	S56.219S	S59.001D	S59.049K
S52.562B	S52.591G	S52.609P	S52.616C	S52.90XG	S53.092A	S53.22XA	S56.221A	S59.001G	S59.049P
S52.562C	S52.591H	S52.609Q	S52.616D	S52.90XH	S53.092S	S53.22XS	S56.222A	S59.001K	S59.049S
S52.562D	S52.591J	S52.609R	S52.616E	S52.90XJ	S53.093A	S53.30XA	S56.229A	S59.001P	S59.091A
S52.562E	S52.591K	S52.609S	S52.616F	S52.90XK	S53.093S	S53.30XS	S56.311A	S59.001S	S59.091D
S52.562F	S52.591M	S52.611A	S52.616G	S52.90XM	S53.094A	S53.31XA	S56.311S	S59.002A	S59.091G
S52.562G	S52.591N	S52.611B	S52.616H	S52.90XN	S53.094S	S53.31XS	S56.312A	S59.002D	S59.091K
S52.562H	S52.591P	S52.611C	S52.616J	S52.90XP	S53.095A	S53.32XA	S56.312S	S59.002G	S59.091P
S52.562J	S52.591Q	S52.611D	S52.616K	S52.90XQ	S53.095S	S53.32XS	S56.319A	S59.002K	S59.091S
S52.562K	S52.591R	S52.611E	S52.616M	S52.90XR	S53.096A	S53.401A	S56.319S	S59.002P	S59.092A
S52.562M	S52.591S	S52.611F	S52.616N	S52.90XS	S53.096S	S53.401S	S56.321A	S59.002S	S59.092D
S52.562N	S52.592A	S52.611G	S52.616P	S52.91XA	S53.101A	S53.402A	S56.322A	S59.009A	S59.092G
S52.562P	S52.592B	S52.611H	S52.616Q	S52.91XB	S53.101S	S53.402S	S56.329A	S59.009D	S59.092K
S52.562Q	S52.592C	S52.611J	S52.616R	S52.91XC	S53.102A	S53.409A	S56.411A	S59.009G	S59.092P
S52.562R	S52.592D	S52.611K	S52.616S	S52.91XD	S53.102S	S53.409S	S56.411S	S59.009K	S59.092S
S52.562S	S52.592E	S52.611M	S52.621A	S52.91XE	S53.103A	S53.411A	S56.412A	S59.009P	S59.099A
S52.569A	S52.592F	S52.611N	S52.621D	S52.91XF	S53.103S	S53.411S	S56.412S	S59.009S	S59.099D
S52.569B	S52.592G	S52.611P	S52.621G	S52.91XG	S53.104A	S53.412A	S56.413A	S59.011A	S59.099G
S52.569C	S52.592H	S52.611Q	S52.621K	S52.91XH	S53.104S	S53.412S	S56.413S	S59.011D	S59.099K
S52.569D	S52.592J	S52.611R	S52.621P	S52.91XJ	S53.105A	S53.419A	S56.414A	S59.011G	S59.099P
S52.569E	S52.592K	S52.611S	S52.621S	S52.91XK	S53.105S	S53.419S	S56.414S	S59.011K	S59.099S
	S52.592M	S52.612A	S52.622A	S52.91XM	S53.106A	S53.421A	S56.415A	S59.011P	S59.101A

Diagnosis Codes by MDC

S59.101D	S59.149K	S59.232S	S62.014B	S62.034G	S62.121P	S62.142A	S62.162D	S62.182K	S62.222S
S59.101G	S59.149P	S59.239A	S62.014D	S62.034K	S62.121S	S62.142B	S62.162G	S62.182P	S62.223A
S59.101K	S59.149S	S59.239D	S62.014G	S62.034P	S62.122A	S62.142D	S62.162K	S62.182S	S62.223B
S59.101P	S59.191A	S59.239G	S62.014K	S62.034S	S62.122B	S62.142G	S62.162P	S62.183A	S62.223D
S59.101S	S59.191D	S59.239K	S62.014P	S62.035A	S62.122D	S62.142K	S62.162S	S62.183B	S62.223G
S59.102A	S59.191G	S59.239P	S62.014S	S62.035B	S62.122G	S62.142P	S62.163A	S62.183D	S62.223K
S59.102D	S59.191K	S59.239S	S62.015A	S62.035D	S62.122K	S62.142S	S62.163B	S62.183G	S62.223P
S59.102G	S59.191P	S59.241A	S62.015B	S62.035G	S62.122P	S62.143A	S62.163D	S62.183K	S62.223S
S59.102K	S59.191S	S59.241D	S62.015D	S62.035K	S62.122S	S62.143B	S62.163G	S62.183P	S62.224A
S59.102P	S59.192A	S59.241G	S62.015G	S62.035P	S62.123A	S62.143D	S62.163K	S62.183S	S62.224B
S59.102S	S59.192D	S59.241K	S62.015K	S62.035S	S62.123B	S62.143G	S62.163P	S62.184A	S62.224D
S59.109A	S59.192G	S59.241P	S62.015P	S62.036A	S62.123D	S62.143K	S62.163S	S62.184B	S62.224G
S59.109D	S59.192K	S59.241S	S62.015S	S62.036B	S62.123G	S62.143P	S62.164A	S62.184D	S62.224K
S59.109G	S59.192P	S59.242A	S62.016A	S62.036D	S62.123K	S62.143S	S62.164B	S62.184G	S62.224P
S59.109K	S59.192S	S59.242D	S62.016B	S62.036G	S62.123P	S62.144A	S62.164D	S62.184K	S62.224S
S59.109P	S59.199A	S59.242G	S62.016D	S62.036K	S62.123S	S62.144B	S62.164G	S62.184P	S62.225A
S59.109S	S59.199D	S59.242K	S62.016G	S62.036P	S62.124A	S62.144D	S62.164K	S62.184S	S62.225B
S59.111A	S59.199G	S59.242P	S62.016K	S62.036S	S62.124B	S62.144G	S62.164P	S62.185A	S62.225D
S59.111D	S59.199K	S59.242S	S62.016P	S62.101A	S62.124D	S62.144K	S62.164S	S62.185B	S62.225G
S59.111G	S59.199P	S59.249A	S62.016S	S62.101B	S62.124G	S62.144P	S62.165A	S62.185D	S62.225K
S59.111K	S59.199S	S59.249D	S62.021A	S62.101D	S62.124K	S62.144S	S62.165B	S62.185G	S62.225P
S59.111P	S59.201A	S59.249G	S62.021B	S62.101G	S62.124P	S62.145A	S62.165D	S62.185K	S62.225S
S59.111S	S59.201D	S59.249K	S62.021D	S62.101K	S62.124S	S62.145B	S62.165G	S62.185P	S62.226A
S59.112A	S59.201G	S59.249P	S62.021G	S62.101P	S62.125A	S62.145D	S62.165K	S62.185S	S62.226B
S59.112D	S59.201K	S59.249S	S62.021K	S62.101S	S62.125B	S62.145G	S62.165P	S62.186A	S62.226D
S59.112G	S59.201P	S59.291A	S62.021P	S62.102A	S62.125D	S62.145K	S62.165S	S62.186B	S62.226G
S59.112K	S59.201S	S59.291D	S62.021S	S62.102B	S62.125G	S62.145P	S62.166A	S62.186D	S62.226K
S59.112P	S59.202A	S59.291G	S62.022A	S62.102D	S62.125K	S62.145S	S62.166B	S62.186G	S62.226P
S59.112S	S59.202D	S59.291K	S62.022B	S62.102G	S62.125P	S62.146A	S62.166D	S62.186K	S62.226S
S59.119A	S59.202G	S59.291P	S62.022D	S62.102K	S62.125S	S62.146B	S62.166G	S62.186P	S62.231A
S59.119D	S59.202K	S59.291S	S62.022G	S62.102P	S62.126A	S62.146D	S62.166K	S62.186S	S62.231B
S59.119G	S59.202P	S59.292A	S62.022K	S62.102S	S62.126B	S62.146G	S62.166P	S62.201A	S62.231D
S59.119K	S59.202S	S59.292D	S62.022P	S62.109A	S62.126D	S62.146K	S62.166S	S62.201B	S62.231G
S59.119P	S59.209A	S59.292G	S62.022S	S62.109B	S62.126G	S62.146P	S62.171A	S62.201D	S62.231K
S59.119S	S59.209D	S59.292K	S62.023A	S62.109D	S62.126K	S62.146S	S62.171B	S62.201G	S62.231P
S59.121A	S59.209G	S59.292P	S62.023B	S62.109G	S62.126P	S62.151A	S62.171D	S62.201K	S62.231S
S59.121D	S59.209K	S59.292S	S62.023D	S62.109K	S62.126S	S62.151B	S62.171G	S62.201P	S62.232A
S59.121G	S59.209P	S59.299A	S62.023G	S62.109P	S62.131A	S62.151D	S62.171K	S62.201S	S62.232B
S59.121K	S59.209S	S59.299D	S62.023K	S62.109S	S62.131B	S62.151G	S62.171P	S62.202A	S62.232D
S59.121P	S59.211A	S59.299G	S62.023P	S62.111A	S62.131D	S62.151K	S62.171S	S62.202B	S62.232G
S59.121S	S59.211D	S59.299K	S62.023S	S62.111B	S62.131G	S62.151P	S62.172A	S62.202D	S62.232K
S59.122A	S59.211G	S59.299P	S62.024A	S62.111D	S62.131K	S62.151S	S62.172B	S62.202G	S62.232P
S59.122D	S59.211K	S59.299S	S62.024B	S62.111G	S62.131P	S62.152A	S62.172D	S62.202K	S62.232S
S59.122G	S59.211P	S62.001A	S62.024D	S62.111K	S62.131S	S62.152B	S62.172G	S62.202P	S62.233A
S59.122K	S59.211S	S62.001B	S62.024G	S62.111P	S62.132A	S62.152D	S62.172K	S62.202S	S62.233B
S59.122P	S59.212A	S62.001D	S62.024K	S62.111S	S62.132B	S62.152G	S62.172P	S62.209A	S62.233D
S59.122S	S59.212D	S62.001G	S62.024P	S62.112A	S62.132D	S62.152K	S62.172S	S62.209B	S62.233G
S59.129A	S59.212G	S62.001K	S62.024S	S62.112B	S62.132G	S62.152P	S62.173A	S62.209D	S62.233K
S59.129D	S59.212K	S62.001P	S62.025A	S62.112D	S62.132K	S62.152S	S62.173B	S62.209G	S62.233P
S59.129G	S59.212P	S62.001S	S62.025B	S62.112G	S62.132P	S62.153A	S62.173D	S62.209K	S62.233S
S59.129K	S59.212S	S62.002A	S62.025D	S62.112K	S62.132S	S62.153B	S62.173G	S62.209P	S62.234A
S59.129P	S59.219A	S62.002B	S62.025G	S62.112P	S62.133A	S62.153D	S62.173K	S62.209S	S62.234B
S59.129S	S59.219D	S62.002D	S62.025K	S62.112S	S62.133B	S62.153G	S62.173P	S62.211A	S62.234D
S59.131A	S59.219G	S62.002G	S62.025P	S62.113A	S62.133D	S62.153K	S62.173S	S62.211B	S62.234G
S59.131D	S59.219K	S62.002K	S62.025S	S62.113B	S62.133G	S62.153P	S62.174A	S62.211D	S62.234K
S59.131G	S59.219P	S62.002P	S62.026A	S62.113D	S62.133K	S62.153S	S62.174B	S62.211G	S62.234P
S59.131K	S59.219S	S62.002S	S62.026B	S62.113G	S62.133P	S62.154A	S62.174D	S62.211K	S62.234S
S59.131P	S59.221A	S62.009A	S62.026D	S62.113K	S62.133S	S62.154B	S62.174G	S62.211P	S62.235A
S59.131S	S59.221D	S62.009B	S62.026G	S62.113P	S62.134A	S62.154D	S62.174K	S62.211S	S62.235B
S59.132A	S59.221G	S62.009D	S62.026K	S62.113S	S62.134B	S62.154G	S62.174P	S62.212A	S62.235D
S59.132D	S59.221K	S62.009G	S62.026P	S62.114A	S62.134D	S62.154K	S62.174S	S62.212B	S62.235G
S59.132G	S59.221P	S62.009K	S62.026S	S62.114B	S62.134G	S62.154P	S62.175A	S62.212D	S62.235K
S59.132K	S59.221S	S62.009P	S62.031A	S62.114D	S62.134K	S62.154S	S62.175B	S62.212G	S62.235P
S59.132P	S59.222A	S62.009S	S62.031B	S62.114G	S62.134P	S62.155A	S62.175D	S62.212K	S62.235S
S59.132S	S59.222D	S62.011A	S62.031D	S62.114K	S62.134S	S62.155B	S62.175G	S62.212P	S62.236A
S59.139A	S59.222G	S62.011B	S62.031G	S62.114P	S62.135A	S62.155D	S62.175K	S62.212S	S62.236B
S59.139D	S59.222K	S62.011D	S62.031K	S62.114S	S62.135B	S62.155G	S62.175P	S62.213A	S62.236D
S59.139G	S59.222P	S62.011G	S62.031P	S62.115A	S62.135D	S62.155K	S62.175S	S62.213B	S62.236G
S59.139K	S59.222S	S62.011K	S62.031S	S62.115B	S62.135G	S62.155P	S62.176A	S62.213D	S62.236K
S59.139P	S59.229A	S62.011P	S62.032A	S62.115D	S62.135K	S62.155S	S62.176B	S62.213G	S62.236P
S59.139S	S59.229D	S62.011S	S62.032B	S62.115G	S62.135P	S62.156A	S62.176D	S62.213K	S62.236S
S59.141A	S59.229G	S62.012A	S62.032D	S62.115K	S62.135S	S62.156B	S62.176G	S62.213P	S62.241A
S59.141D	S59.229K	S62.012B	S62.032G	S62.115P	S62.136A	S62.156D	S62.176K	S62.213S	S62.241B
S59.141G	S59.229P	S62.012D	S62.032K	S62.115S	S62.136B	S62.156G	S62.176P	S62.221A	S62.241D
S59.141K	S59.229S	S62.012G	S62.032P	S62.116A	S62.136D	S62.156K	S62.176S	S62.221B	S62.241G
S59.141P	S59.231A	S62.012K	S62.032S	S62.116B	S62.136G	S62.156P	S62.181A	S62.221D	S62.241K
S59.141S	S59.231D	S62.012P	S62.033A	S62.116D	S62.136K	S62.156S	S62.181B	S62.221G	S62.241P
S59.142A	S59.231G	S62.012S	S62.033B	S62.116G	S62.136P	S62.161A	S62.181D	S62.221K	S62.241S
S59.142D	S59.231K	S62.013A	S62.033D	S62.116K	S62.136S	S62.161B	S62.181G	S62.221P	S62.242A
S59.142G	S59.231P	S62.013B	S62.033G	S62.116P	S62.141A	S62.161D	S62.181K	S62.221S	S62.242B
S59.142K	S59.231S	S62.013D	S62.033K	S62.116S	S62.141B	S62.161G	S62.181P	S62.222A	S62.242D
S59.142P	S59.232A	S62.013G	S62.033P	S62.121A	S62.141D	S62.161K	S62.181S	S62.222B	S62.242G
S59.142S	S59.232D	S62.013K	S62.034A	S62.121B	S62.141G	S62.161P	S62.182A	S62.222D	S62.242K
S59.149A	S59.232G	S62.013P	S62.034B	S62.121D	S62.141K	S62.161S	S62.182B	S62.222G	S62.242P
S59.149D	S59.232K	S62.013S	S62.034D	S62.121G	S62.141P	S62.162A	S62.182D	S62.222K	S62.242S
S59.149G	S59.232P	S62.014A	S62.034D	S62.121K	S62.141S	S62.162B	S62.182G	S62.222P	S62.243A

S62.243B	S62.299G	S62.311P	S62.324A	S62.336D	S62.348K	S62.360S	S62.393B	S62.513G	S62.602P
S62.243D	S62.299K	S62.311S	S62.324B	S62.336G	S62.348P	S62.361A	S62.393D	S62.513K	S62.602S
S62.243G	S62.299P	S62.312A	S62.324D	S62.336K	S62.348S	S62.361B	S62.393G	S62.513P	S62.603A
S62.243K	S62.299S	S62.312B	S62.324G	S62.336P	S62.349A	S62.361D	S62.393K	S62.513S	S62.603B
S62.243P	S62.300A	S62.312D	S62.324K	S62.336S	S62.349B	S62.361G	S62.393P	S62.514A	S62.603D
S62.243S	S62.300B	S62.312G	S62.324P	S62.337A	S62.349D	S62.361K	S62.393S	S62.514B	S62.603G
S62.244A	S62.300D	S62.312K	S62.324S	S62.337B	S62.349G	S62.361P	S62.394A	S62.514D	S62.603K
S62.244B	S62.300G	S62.312P	S62.325A	S62.337D	S62.349K	S62.361S	S62.394B	S62.514G	S62.603P
S62.244D	S62.300K	S62.312S	S62.325B	S62.337G	S62.349P	S62.362A	S62.394D	S62.514K	S62.603S
S62.244G	S62.300P	S62.313A	S62.325D	S62.337K	S62.349S	S62.362B	S62.394G	S62.514P	S62.604A
S62.244K	S62.300S	S62.313B	S62.325G	S62.337P	S62.350A	S62.362D	S62.394K	S62.514S	S62.604B
S62.244P	S62.301A	S62.313D	S62.325K	S62.337S	S62.350B	S62.362G	S62.394P	S62.515A	S62.604D
S62.244S	S62.301B	S62.313G	S62.325P	S62.338A	S62.350D	S62.362K	S62.394S	S62.515B	S62.604G
S62.245A	S62.301D	S62.313K	S62.325S	S62.338B	S62.350G	S62.362P	S62.395A	S62.515D	S62.604K
S62.245B	S62.301G	S62.313P	S62.326A	S62.338D	S62.350K	S62.362S	S62.395B	S62.515G	S62.604P
S62.245D	S62.301K	S62.313S	S62.326B	S62.338G	S62.350P	S62.363A	S62.395D	S62.515K	S62.604S
S62.245G	S62.301P	S62.314A	S62.326D	S62.338K	S62.350S	S62.363B	S62.395G	S62.515P	S62.605A
S62.245K	S62.301S	S62.314B	S62.326G	S62.338P	S62.351A	S62.363D	S62.395K	S62.515S	S62.605B
S62.245P	S62.302A	S62.314D	S62.326K	S62.338S	S62.351B	S62.363G	S62.395P	S62.516A	S62.605D
S62.245S	S62.302B	S62.314G	S62.326P	S62.339A	S62.351D	S62.363K	S62.395S	S62.516B	S62.605G
S62.246A	S62.302D	S62.314K	S62.326S	S62.339B	S62.351G	S62.363P	S62.396A	S62.516D	S62.605K
S62.246B	S62.302G	S62.314P	S62.327A	S62.339D	S62.351K	S62.363S	S62.396B	S62.516G	S62.605P
S62.246D	S62.302K	S62.314S	S62.327B	S62.339G	S62.351P	S62.364A	S62.396D	S62.516K	S62.605S
S62.246G	S62.302P	S62.315A	S62.327D	S62.339K	S62.351S	S62.364B	S62.396G	S62.516P	S62.606A
S62.246K	S62.303A	S62.315B	S62.327G	S62.339P	S62.352A	S62.364D	S62.396K	S62.516S	S62.606B
S62.246P	S62.303B	S62.315D	S62.327K	S62.339S	S62.352B	S62.364G	S62.396P	S62.521A	S62.606D
S62.246S	S62.303D	S62.315G	S62.327P	S62.340A	S62.352G	S62.364K	S62.396S	S62.521B	S62.606G
S62.251A	S62.303G	S62.315K	S62.327S	S62.340B	S62.352K	S62.364P	S62.397A	S62.521D	S62.606K
S62.251B	S62.303K	S62.315P	S62.328A	S62.340D	S62.352P	S62.365A	S62.397B	S62.521G	S62.606P
S62.251D	S62.303P	S62.315S	S62.328B	S62.340G	S62.352S	S62.365B	S62.397D	S62.521K	S62.606S
S62.251G	S62.303S	S62.316A	S62.328D	S62.340K	S62.353A	S62.365D	S62.397G	S62.521P	S62.607A
S62.251K	S62.304A	S62.316B	S62.328G	S62.340P	S62.353B	S62.365G	S62.397K	S62.521S	S62.607B
S62.251P	S62.304B	S62.316G	S62.328K	S62.340S	S62.353D	S62.365K	S62.397P	S62.522A	S62.607D
S62.251S	S62.304D	S62.316K	S62.328P	S62.341A	S62.353G	S62.365P	S62.397S	S62.522B	S62.607G
S62.252A	S62.304G	S62.316P	S62.328S	S62.341B	S62.353K	S62.365S	S62.398A	S62.522D	S62.607K
S62.252B	S62.304K	S62.316S	S62.329A	S62.341D	S62.353P	S62.366A	S62.398B	S62.522G	S62.607P
S62.252D	S62.304P	S62.317A	S62.329B	S62.341G	S62.353S	S62.366B	S62.398D	S62.522K	S62.607S
S62.252G	S62.304S	S62.317B	S62.329D	S62.341K	S62.354A	S62.366D	S62.398G	S62.522P	S62.608A
S62.252K	S62.305A	S62.317D	S62.329G	S62.341P	S62.354B	S62.366G	S62.398K	S62.522S	S62.608B
S62.252P	S62.305B	S62.317G	S62.329K	S62.341S	S62.354D	S62.366K	S62.398P	S62.523A	S62.608D
S62.252S	S62.305D	S62.317K	S62.329P	S62.342A	S62.354G	S62.366P	S62.398S	S62.523B	S62.608G
S62.253A	S62.305G	S62.317P	S62.329S	S62.342B	S62.354K	S62.366S	S62.399A	S62.523D	S62.608K
S62.253B	S62.305K	S62.317S	S62.330A	S62.342D	S62.354P	S62.367A	S62.399B	S62.523G	S62.608P
S62.253D	S62.305P	S62.318A	S62.330B	S62.342G	S62.354S	S62.367B	S62.399D	S62.523K	S62.608S
S62.253G	S62.305S	S62.318B	S62.330D	S62.342K	S62.355A	S62.367D	S62.399G	S62.523P	S62.609A
S62.253K	S62.306A	S62.318G	S62.330G	S62.342P	S62.355B	S62.367G	S62.399K	S62.523S	S62.609B
S62.253P	S62.306B	S62.318K	S62.330K	S62.342S	S62.355D	S62.367K	S62.399P	S62.524A	S62.609D
S62.253S	S62.306D	S62.318P	S62.330P	S62.343A	S62.355G	S62.367P	S62.399S	S62.524B	S62.609G
S62.254A	S62.306G	S62.318S	S62.330S	S62.343B	S62.355K	S62.367S	S62.501A	S62.524D	S62.609K
S62.254B	S62.306K	S62.319A	S62.331A	S62.343D	S62.355P	S62.368A	S62.501B	S62.524G	S62.609P
S62.254D	S62.306P	S62.319B	S62.331B	S62.343G	S62.355S	S62.368B	S62.501D	S62.524K	S62.609S
S62.254G	S62.306S	S62.319D	S62.331D	S62.343K	S62.356A	S62.368D	S62.501G	S62.524P	S62.610A
S62.254K	S62.307A	S62.319G	S62.331G	S62.343P	S62.356B	S62.368G	S62.501K	S62.524S	S62.610B
S62.254P	S62.307B	S62.319K	S62.331K	S62.343S	S62.356D	S62.368K	S62.501P	S62.525A	S62.610D
S62.254S	S62.307D	S62.319P	S62.331S	S62.344A	S62.356G	S62.368P	S62.501S	S62.525B	S62.610G
S62.255A	S62.307G	S62.319S	S62.332A	S62.344B	S62.356K	S62.368S	S62.502A	S62.525D	S62.610K
S62.255B	S62.307K	S62.320A	S62.332B	S62.344D	S62.356P	S62.369A	S62.502B	S62.525G	S62.610P
S62.255D	S62.307P	S62.320B	S62.332D	S62.344G	S62.356S	S62.369B	S62.502D	S62.525K	S62.610S
S62.255G	S62.307S	S62.320D	S62.332G	S62.344K	S62.357A	S62.369D	S62.502G	S62.525P	S62.611A
S62.255K	S62.308A	S62.320G	S62.332K	S62.344P	S62.357B	S62.369G	S62.502K	S62.525S	S62.611B
S62.255P	S62.308B	S62.320K	S62.332P	S62.344S	S62.357D	S62.369K	S62.502P	S62.526A	S62.611D
S62.255S	S62.308D	S62.320P	S62.332S	S62.345A	S62.357G	S62.369P	S62.502S	S62.526B	S62.611G
S62.256A	S62.308G	S62.320S	S62.333A	S62.345B	S62.357K	S62.369S	S62.509A	S62.526D	S62.611K
S62.256B	S62.308K	S62.321A	S62.333B	S62.345G	S62.357P	S62.390A	S62.509B	S62.526G	S62.611P
S62.256D	S62.308P	S62.321B	S62.333D	S62.345K	S62.357S	S62.390B	S62.509D	S62.526K	S62.611S
S62.256G	S62.308S	S62.321D	S62.333G	S62.345P	S62.358A	S62.390D	S62.509G	S62.526P	S62.612A
S62.256K	S62.309A	S62.321G	S62.333K	S62.345S	S62.358B	S62.390G	S62.509K	S62.526S	S62.612B
S62.256P	S62.309B	S62.321K	S62.333S	S62.346A	S62.358D	S62.390K	S62.509P	S62.600A	S62.612D
S62.256S	S62.309D	S62.321P	S62.334A	S62.346B	S62.358G	S62.390P	S62.509S	S62.600B	S62.612G
S62.291A	S62.309G	S62.321S	S62.334B	S62.346D	S62.358K	S62.390S	S62.511A	S62.600D	S62.612K
S62.291B	S62.309K	S62.322A	S62.334D	S62.346G	S62.358P	S62.391A	S62.511B	S62.600G	S62.612P
S62.291D	S62.309P	S62.322B	S62.334G	S62.346K	S62.358S	S62.391B	S62.511D	S62.600K	S62.612S
S62.291G	S62.309S	S62.322D	S62.334K	S62.346P	S62.359A	S62.391D	S62.511G	S62.600P	S62.613A
S62.291K	S62.310A	S62.322G	S62.334P	S62.346S	S62.359B	S62.391G	S62.511K	S62.600S	S62.613B
S62.291P	S62.310B	S62.322K	S62.334S	S62.347A	S62.359D	S62.391K	S62.511P	S62.601A	S62.613D
S62.291S	S62.310D	S62.322P	S62.335A	S62.347B	S62.359G	S62.391P	S62.511S	S62.601B	S62.613G
S62.292A	S62.310G	S62.322S	S62.335B	S62.347D	S62.359K	S62.391S	S62.512A	S62.601D	S62.613K
S62.292B	S62.310K	S62.323A	S62.335D	S62.347G	S62.359P	S62.392A	S62.512B	S62.601G	S62.613P
S62.292D	S62.310P	S62.323B	S62.335G	S62.347K	S62.359S	S62.392B	S62.512D	S62.601K	S62.613S
S62.292G	S62.310S	S62.323D	S62.335K	S62.347P	S62.360A	S62.392D	S62.512G	S62.601P	S62.614A
S62.292K	S62.311A	S62.323G	S62.335S	S62.347S	S62.360B	S62.392G	S62.512K	S62.601S	S62.614B
S62.292P	S62.311B	S62.323K	S62.336A	S62.348A	S62.360D	S62.392K	S62.512P	S62.602A	S62.614D
S62.292S	S62.311D	S62.323P	S62.336B	S62.348B	S62.360G	S62.392P	S62.512S	S62.602B	S62.614G
S62.299A	S62.311G	S62.323S	S62.335S	S62.348D	S62.360K	S62.392S	S62.513B	S62.602D	S62.614K
S62.299B	S62.311K		S62.336A	S62.348G	S62.360P	S62.393A	S62.513D	S62.602G	S62.614P
S62.299D								S62.602K	S62.614S

Diagnosis Codes by MDC

S62.615A	S62.627D	S62.639K	S62.651S	S62.664B	S63.021A	S63.102A	S63.226A	S63.269A	S63.391A
S62.615B	S62.627G	S62.639P	S62.652A	S62.664D	S63.021S	S63.102S	S63.226S	S63.269S	S63.391S
S62.615D	S62.627K	S62.639S	S62.652B	S62.664G	S63.022A	S63.103A	S63.227A	S63.270A	S63.392A
S62.615G	S62.627P	S62.640A	S62.652D	S62.664K	S63.022S	S63.103S	S63.227S	S63.270S	S63.392S
S62.615K	S62.627S	S62.640B	S62.652G	S62.664P	S63.023A	S63.104A	S63.228A	S63.271A	S63.399A
S62.615P	S62.628A	S62.640D	S62.652K	S62.664S	S63.023S	S63.104S	S63.228S	S63.271S	S63.399S
S62.615S	S62.628B	S62.640G	S62.652P	S62.665A	S63.024A	S63.105A	S63.229A	S63.272A	S63.400A
S62.616A	S62.628D	S62.640K	S62.652S	S62.665B	S63.024S	S63.105S	S63.229S	S63.272S	S63.400S
S62.616G	S62.628G	S62.640P	S62.653A	S62.665D	S63.025A	S63.106A	S63.230A	S63.273A	S63.401A
S62.616D	S62.628K	S62.640S	S62.653B	S62.665G	S63.025S	S63.106S	S63.230S	S63.273S	S63.401S
S62.616G	S62.628P	S62.641A	S62.653D	S62.665K	S63.026A	S63.111A	S63.231A	S63.274A	S63.402A
S62.616K	S62.628S	S62.641B	S62.653G	S62.665P	S63.026S	S63.111S	S63.231S	S63.274S	S63.402S
S62.616P	S62.629A	S62.641D	S62.653P	S62.665S	S63.031A	S63.112A	S63.232A	S63.275A	S63.403A
S62.616S	S62.629B	S62.641G	S62.653S	S62.666A	S63.031S	S63.112S	S63.232S	S63.275S	S63.403S
S62.617A	S62.629D	S62.641K	S62.654A	S62.666B	S63.032A	S63.113A	S63.233A	S63.276A	S63.404A
S62.617B	S62.629G	S62.641P	S62.654B	S62.666D	S63.032S	S63.113S	S63.233S	S63.276S	S63.404S
S62.617D	S62.629K	S62.641S	S62.654D	S62.666G	S63.033A	S63.114A	S63.234A	S63.277A	S63.405A
S62.617G	S62.629P	S62.642A	S62.654G	S62.666K	S63.033S	S63.114S	S63.234S	S63.277S	S63.405S
S62.617K	S62.629S	S62.642B	S62.654K	S62.666P	S63.034A	S63.115A	S63.235A	S63.278A	S63.406A
S62.617P	S62.630A	S62.642D	S62.654P	S62.666S	S63.034S	S63.115S	S63.235S	S63.278S	S63.406S
S62.617S	S62.630B	S62.642G	S62.654S	S62.667A	S63.035A	S63.116A	S63.236A	S63.279A	S63.407A
S62.618A	S62.630D	S62.642K	S62.655A	S62.667B	S63.035S	S63.116S	S63.236S	S63.279S	S63.407S
S62.618B	S62.630G	S62.642P	S62.655B	S62.667D	S63.036A	S63.121A	S63.237A	S63.280A	S63.408A
S62.618D	S62.630K	S62.642S	S62.655D	S62.667G	S63.036S	S63.121S	S63.237S	S63.280S	S63.408S
S62.618G	S62.630P	S62.643A	S62.655G	S62.667K	S63.041A	S63.122A	S63.238A	S63.281A	S63.409A
S62.618K	S62.630S	S62.643B	S62.655K	S62.667P	S63.041S	S63.122S	S63.238S	S63.281S	S63.409S
S62.618P	S62.631A	S62.643D	S62.655P	S62.667S	S63.042A	S63.123A	S63.239A	S63.282A	S63.410A
S62.618S	S62.631B	S62.643G	S62.655S	S62.668A	S63.042S	S63.123S	S63.239S	S63.282S	S63.410S
S62.619A	S62.631D	S62.643K	S62.656A	S62.668B	S63.043A	S63.124A	S63.240A	S63.283A	S63.411A
S62.619B	S62.631G	S62.643P	S62.656B	S62.668D	S63.043S	S63.124S	S63.240S	S63.283S	S63.411S
S62.619D	S62.631K	S62.643S	S62.656D	S62.668G	S63.044A	S63.125A	S63.241A	S63.284A	S63.412A
S62.619G	S62.631P	S62.644A	S62.656G	S62.668K	S63.044S	S63.125S	S63.241S	S63.284S	S63.412S
S62.619K	S62.631S	S62.644B	S62.656K	S62.668P	S63.045A	S63.126A	S63.242A	S63.285A	S63.413A
S62.619P	S62.632A	S62.644D	S62.656P	S62.668S	S63.045S	S63.126S	S63.242S	S63.285S	S63.413S
S62.619S	S62.632B	S62.644G	S62.656S	S62.669A	S63.046A	S63.200A	S63.243A	S63.286A	S63.414A
S62.620A	S62.632D	S62.644K	S62.657A	S62.669B	S63.046S	S63.200S	S63.243S	S63.286S	S63.414S
S62.620B	S62.632G	S62.644P	S62.657B	S62.669D	S63.051A	S63.201A	S63.244A	S63.287A	S63.415A
S62.620D	S62.632K	S62.644S	S62.657D	S62.669G	S63.051S	S63.201S	S63.244S	S63.287S	S63.415S
S62.620G	S62.632P	S62.645A	S62.657G	S62.669K	S63.052A	S63.202A	S63.245A	S63.288A	S63.416A
S62.620K	S62.632S	S62.645B	S62.657K	S62.669P	S63.052S	S63.202S	S63.245S	S63.288S	S63.416S
S62.620P	S62.633A	S62.645D	S62.657P	S62.669S	S63.053A	S63.203A	S63.246A	S63.289A	S63.417A
S62.620S	S62.633B	S62.645G	S62.657S	S62.90XA	S63.053S	S63.203S	S63.246S	S63.289S	S63.417S
S62.621A	S62.633D	S62.645K	S62.658A	S62.90XB	S63.054A	S63.204A	S63.247A	S63.290A	S63.418A
S62.621B	S62.633G	S62.645P	S62.658B	S62.90XD	S63.054S	S63.204S	S63.247S	S63.290S	S63.418S
S62.621D	S62.633K	S62.645S	S62.658G	S62.90XG	S63.055A	S63.205A	S63.248A	S63.291A	S63.419A
S62.621G	S62.633P	S62.646A	S62.658K	S62.90XK	S63.055S	S63.205S	S63.248S	S63.291S	S63.419S
S62.621K	S62.633S	S62.646B	S62.658P	S62.90XP	S63.056A	S63.206A	S63.249A	S63.292A	S63.420A
S62.621P	S62.634A	S62.646D	S62.658S	S62.90XS	S63.056S	S63.206S	S63.249S	S63.292S	S63.420S
S62.621S	S62.634B	S62.646G	S62.659A	S62.91XA	S63.061A	S63.207A	S63.250A	S63.293A	S63.421A
S62.622A	S62.634D	S62.646K	S62.659B	S62.91XB	S63.061S	S63.207S	S63.250S	S63.293S	S63.421S
S62.622B	S62.634G	S62.646P	S62.659D	S62.91XD	S63.062A	S63.208A	S63.251A	S63.294A	S63.422A
S62.622D	S62.634K	S62.646S	S62.659B	S62.91XG	S63.062S	S63.208S	S63.251S	S63.294S	S63.422S
S62.622G	S62.634P	S62.647A	S62.659D	S62.91XK	S63.063A	S63.209A	S63.252A	S63.295A	S63.423A
S62.622K	S62.634S	S62.647B	S62.659G	S62.91XP	S63.063S	S63.209S	S63.252S	S63.295S	S63.423S
S62.622P	S62.635A	S62.647D	S62.659P	S62.91XS	S63.064A	S63.210A	S63.253A	S63.296A	S63.424A
S62.622S	S62.635B	S62.647G	S62.659S	S62.92XA	S63.064S	S63.210S	S63.253S	S63.296S	S63.424S
S62.623A	S62.635D	S62.647K	S62.660A	S62.92XB	S63.065A	S63.211A	S63.254A	S63.297A	S63.425A
S62.623B	S62.635G	S62.647P	S62.660B	S62.92XD	S63.065S	S63.211S	S63.254S	S63.297S	S63.425S
S62.623D	S62.635K	S62.647S	S62.660D	S62.92XG	S63.066A	S63.212A	S63.255A	S63.298A	S63.426A
S62.623G	S62.635P	S62.648A	S62.660G	S62.92XK	S63.066S	S63.212S	S63.255S	S63.298S	S63.426S
S62.623K	S62.635S	S62.648B	S62.660K	S62.92XP	S63.071A	S63.213A	S63.256A	S63.299A	S63.427A
S62.623P	S62.636A	S62.648D	S62.660P	S62.92XS	S63.071S	S63.213S	S63.256S	S63.299S	S63.427S
S62.623S	S62.636B	S62.648G	S62.660S	S63.001A	S63.072A	S63.214A	S63.257A	S63.301A	S63.428A
S62.624A	S62.636D	S62.648K	S62.661A	S63.001S	S63.072S	S63.214S	S63.257S	S63.301S	S63.428S
S62.624B	S62.636G	S62.648P	S62.661B	S63.002A	S63.073A	S63.215A	S63.258A	S63.302A	S63.429A
S62.624D	S62.636K	S62.648S	S62.661D	S63.002S	S63.073S	S63.215S	S63.258S	S63.302S	S63.429S
S62.624G	S62.636P	S62.649A	S62.661G	S63.003A	S63.074A	S63.216A	S63.259A	S63.309A	S63.430A
S62.624K	S62.636S	S62.649B	S62.661K	S63.003S	S63.074S	S63.216S	S63.259S	S63.309S	S63.430S
S62.624P	S62.637A	S62.649D	S62.661P	S63.004A	S63.075A	S63.217A	S63.260A	S63.311A	S63.431A
S62.624S	S62.637B	S62.649G	S62.661S	S63.004S	S63.075S	S63.217S	S63.260S	S63.311S	S63.431S
S62.625A	S62.637D	S62.649K	S62.662A	S63.005A	S63.076A	S63.218A	S63.261A	S63.312A	S63.432A
S62.625B	S62.637G	S62.649P	S62.662B	S63.005S	S63.076S	S63.218S	S63.261S	S63.312S	S63.432S
S62.625D	S62.637K	S62.649S	S62.662D	S63.006A	S63.091A	S63.219A	S63.262A	S63.319A	S63.433A
S62.625G	S62.637P	S62.650A	S62.662G	S63.006S	S63.091S	S63.219S	S63.262S	S63.319S	S63.433S
S62.625K	S62.637S	S62.650B	S62.662K	S63.011A	S63.092A	S63.220A	S63.263A	S63.321A	S63.434A
S62.625P	S62.638A	S62.650D	S62.662P	S63.011S	S63.092S	S63.220S	S63.263S	S63.321S	S63.434S
S62.625S	S62.638B	S62.650G	S62.662S	S63.012A	S63.093A	S63.221A	S63.264A	S63.322A	S63.435A
S62.626A	S62.638D	S62.650K	S62.663A	S63.012S	S63.093S	S63.221S	S63.264S	S63.322S	S63.435S
S62.626B	S62.638G	S62.650P	S62.663B	S63.013A	S63.094A	S63.222A	S63.265A	S63.329A	S63.436A
S62.626D	S62.638K	S62.650S	S62.663D	S63.013S	S63.094S	S63.222S	S63.265S	S63.329S	S63.436S
S62.626G	S62.638P	S62.651A	S62.663G	S63.014A	S63.095A	S63.223A	S63.266A	S63.331A	S63.437A
S62.626K	S62.638S	S62.651B	S62.663K	S63.014S	S63.095S	S63.223S	S63.266S	S63.331S	S63.437S
S62.626P	S62.639A	S62.651D	S62.663P	S63.015A	S63.096A	S63.224A	S63.267A	S63.332A	S63.438A
S62.626S	S62.639B	S62.651G	S62.663S	S63.015S	S63.096S	S63.224S	S63.267S	S63.332S	S63.438S
S62.627A	S62.639D	S62.651K	S62.664A	S63.016A	S63.101A	S63.225A	S63.268A	S63.339A	S63.439A
S62.627B	S62.639G	S62.651P	S62.664A	S63.016S	S63.101S	S63.225S	S63.268S	S63.339S	S63.439S

S63.490A	S63.635A	S66.111S	S66.515S	S68.621S	S72.012H	S72.024Q	S72.034D	S72.043K	S72.052S
S63.490S	S63.635S	S66.112A	S66.516A	S68.622S	S72.012J	S72.024R	S72.034E	S72.043M	S72.059A
S63.491A	S63.636A	S66.112S	S66.516S	S68.623S	S72.012K	S72.024S	S72.034F	S72.043N	S72.059B
S63.491S	S63.636S	S66.113A	S66.517A	S68.624S	S72.012M	S72.025A	S72.034G	S72.043P	S72.059C
S63.492A	S63.637A	S66.113S	S66.517S	S68.625S	S72.012N	S72.025B	S72.034H	S72.043Q	S72.059D
S63.492S	S63.637S	S66.114A	S66.518A	S68.626S	S72.012P	S72.025C	S72.034J	S72.043R	S72.059E
S63.493A	S63.638A	S66.114S	S66.518S	S68.627S	S72.012Q	S72.025D	S72.034K	S72.043S	S72.059F
S63.493S	S63.638S	S66.115A	S66.519A	S68.628S	S72.012R	S72.025E	S72.034M	S72.044A	S72.059G
S63.494A	S63.639A	S66.115S	S66.519S	S68.629S	S72.012S	S72.025F	S72.034N	S72.044B	S72.059H
S63.494S	S63.639S	S66.116A	S66.520A	S68.711S	S72.019A	S72.025G	S72.034P	S72.044C	S72.059J
S63.495A	S63.641A	S66.116S	S66.521A	S68.712S	S72.019B	S72.025H	S72.034Q	S72.044D	S72.059K
S63.495S	S63.641S	S66.117A	S66.522A	S68.719S	S72.019C	S72.025J	S72.034R	S72.044E	S72.059M
S63.496A	S63.642A	S66.117S	S66.523A	S68.721S	S72.019D	S72.025K	S72.034S	S72.044F	S72.059N
S63.496S	S63.642S	S66.118A	S66.524A	S68.722S	S72.019E	S72.025M	S72.035A	S72.044G	S72.059P
S63.497A	S63.649A	S66.118S	S66.525A	S68.729S	S72.019F	S72.025N	S72.035B	S72.044H	S72.059Q
S63.497S	S63.649S	S66.119A	S66.526A	S72.001A	S72.019G	S72.025P	S72.035C	S72.044J	S72.059R
S63.498A	S63.650A	S66.119S	S66.527A	S72.001B	S72.019H	S72.025Q	S72.035D	S72.044K	S72.059S
S63.498S	S63.650S	S66.120A	S66.528A	S72.001C	S72.019J	S72.025R	S72.035E	S72.044M	S72.061A
S63.499A	S63.651A	S66.121A	S66.529A	S72.001D	S72.019K	S72.025S	S72.035F	S72.044N	S72.061B
S63.499S	S63.651S	S66.122A	S66.811A	S72.001E	S72.019M	S72.026A	S72.035G	S72.044P	S72.061C
S63.501A	S63.652A	S66.123A	S66.811S	S72.001F	S72.019N	S72.026B	S72.035H	S72.044Q	S72.061D
S63.501S	S63.652S	S66.124A	S66.812A	S72.001G	S72.019P	S72.026C	S72.035J	S72.044R	S72.061E
S63.502A	S63.653A	S66.125A	S66.812S	S72.001H	S72.019Q	S72.026D	S72.035K	S72.044S	S72.061F
S63.502S	S63.653S	S66.126A	S66.819A	S72.001J	S72.019R	S72.026E	S72.035M	S72.045A	S72.061G
S63.509A	S63.654A	S66.127A	S66.819S	S72.001K	S72.019S	S72.026F	S72.035N	S72.045B	S72.061H
S63.509S	S63.654S	S66.128A	S66.821A	S72.001M	S72.019A	S72.026G	S72.035P	S72.045C	S72.061J
S63.511A	S63.655A	S66.129A	S66.822A	S72.001N	S72.021A	S72.026H	S72.035Q	S72.045D	S72.061K
S63.511S	S63.655S	S66.211A	S66.829A	S72.001P	S72.021B	S72.026J	S72.035R	S72.045E	S72.061M
S63.512A	S63.656A	S66.211S	S66.911A	S72.001Q	S72.021C	S72.026K	S72.035S	S72.045F	S72.061N
S63.512S	S63.656S	S66.212A	S66.911S	S72.001R	S72.021D	S72.026M	S72.036A	S72.045G	S72.061P
S63.519A	S63.657A	S66.212S	S66.912A	S72.001S	S72.021E	S72.026N	S72.036B	S72.045H	S72.061Q
S63.519S	S63.657S	S66.219A	S66.912S	S72.002A	S72.021F	S72.026P	S72.036C	S72.045J	S72.061R
S63.521A	S63.658A	S66.219S	S66.919A	S72.002B	S72.021G	S72.026Q	S72.036D	S72.045K	S72.061S
S63.521S	S63.658S	S66.221A	S66.919S	S72.002C	S72.021H	S72.026S	S72.036E	S72.045M	S72.062A
S63.522A	S63.659A	S66.222A	S66.921A	S72.002D	S72.021J	S72.031A	S72.036F	S72.045N	S72.062B
S63.522S	S63.659S	S66.229A	S66.922A	S72.002E	S72.021K	S72.031B	S72.036G	S72.045P	S72.062C
S63.529A	S63.681A	S66.310A	S66.929A	S72.002F	S72.021M	S72.031C	S72.036H	S72.045Q	S72.062D
S63.529S	S63.681S	S66.310S	S68.011S	S72.002G	S72.021N	S72.031D	S72.036J	S72.045R	S72.062E
S63.591A	S63.682A	S66.311A	S68.012S	S72.002H	S72.021P	S72.031E	S72.036K	S72.045S	S72.062F
S63.591S	S63.682S	S66.311S	S68.019S	S72.002J	S72.021Q	S72.031F	S72.036M	S72.046A	S72.062G
S63.592A	S63.689A	S66.312A	S68.021S	S72.002K	S72.021R	S72.031G	S72.036N	S72.046B	S72.062H
S63.592S	S63.689S	S66.312S	S68.022S	S72.002M	S72.021S	S72.031H	S72.036P	S72.046C	S72.062J
S63.599A	S63.690A	S66.313A	S68.029S	S72.002N	S72.022A	S72.031J	S72.036Q	S72.046D	S72.062K
S63.599S	S63.690S	S66.313S	S68.110S	S72.002P	S72.022B	S72.031K	S72.036S	S72.046E	S72.062M
S63.601A	S63.691A	S66.314A	S68.111S	S72.002Q	S72.022C	S72.031M	S72.041A	S72.046F	S72.062N
S63.601S	S63.691S	S66.314S	S68.112S	S72.002R	S72.022D	S72.031N	S72.041B	S72.046G	S72.062P
S63.602A	S63.692A	S66.315A	S68.113S	S72.002S	S72.022E	S72.031P	S72.041C	S72.046H	S72.062Q
S63.602S	S63.692S	S66.315S	S68.114S	S72.009A	S72.022F	S72.031Q	S72.041D	S72.046J	S72.062R
S63.609A	S63.693A	S66.316A	S68.115S	S72.009B	S72.022G	S72.031R	S72.041E	S72.046K	S72.062S
S63.609S	S63.693S	S66.316S	S68.116S	S72.009C	S72.022H	S72.031S	S72.041F	S72.046M	S72.063A
S63.610A	S63.694A	S66.317A	S68.117S	S72.009D	S72.022J	S72.032A	S72.041G	S72.046N	S72.063B
S63.610S	S63.694S	S66.317S	S68.118S	S72.009E	S72.022K	S72.032B	S72.041H	S72.046P	S72.063C
S63.611A	S63.695A	S66.318A	S68.119S	S72.009F	S72.022M	S72.032C	S72.041J	S72.046Q	S72.063D
S63.611S	S63.695S	S66.318S	S68.120S	S72.009G	S72.022N	S72.032D	S72.041K	S72.046R	S72.063F
S63.612A	S63.696A	S66.319A	S68.121S	S72.009H	S72.022P	S72.032E	S72.041M	S72.046S	S72.063G
S63.612S	S63.696S	S66.319S	S68.122S	S72.009J	S72.022Q	S72.032F	S72.041N	S72.051A	S72.063H
S63.613A	S63.697A	S66.320A	S68.123S	S72.009K	S72.022R	S72.032G	S72.041P	S72.051B	S72.063J
S63.613S	S63.697S	S66.321A	S68.124S	S72.009M	S72.022S	S72.032H	S72.041Q	S72.051C	S72.063K
S63.614A	S63.698A	S66.322A	S68.125S	S72.009N	S72.023A	S72.032J	S72.041R	S72.051D	S72.063M
S63.614S	S63.698S	S66.323A	S68.126S	S72.009P	S72.023B	S72.032K	S72.041S	S72.051E	S72.063N
S63.615A	S63.699A	S66.324A	S68.127S	S72.009Q	S72.023C	S72.032M	S72.042A	S72.051F	S72.063P
S63.615S	S63.699S	S66.325A	S68.128S	S72.009R	S72.023D	S72.032N	S72.042B	S72.051G	S72.063Q
S63.616A	S63.8X1A	S66.326A	S68.129S	S72.009S	S72.023E	S72.032P	S72.042C	S72.051H	S72.063R
S63.616S	S63.8X1S	S66.327A	S68.411S	S72.011A	S72.023F	S72.032Q	S72.042D	S72.051J	S72.063S
S63.617A	S63.8X2A	S66.328A	S68.412S	S72.011B	S72.023G	S72.032R	S72.042E	S72.051K	S72.064A
S63.617S	S63.8X2S	S66.329A	S68.419S	S72.011C	S72.023H	S72.032S	S72.042F	S72.051M	S72.064B
S63.618A	S63.8X9A	S66.411A	S68.421S	S72.011D	S72.023J	S72.033A	S72.042G	S72.051N	S72.064C
S63.618S	S63.8X9S	S66.411S	S68.422S	S72.011E	S72.023K	S72.033B	S72.042H	S72.051P	S72.064D
S63.619A	S63.90XA	S66.412A	S68.429S	S72.011F	S72.023M	S72.033C	S72.042J	S72.051Q	S72.064E
S63.619S	S63.90XS	S66.412S	S68.511S	S72.011G	S72.023N	S72.033D	S72.042K	S72.051R	S72.064F
S63.621A	S63.91XA	S66.419A	S68.512S	S72.011H	S72.023P	S72.033E	S72.042M	S72.051S	S72.064G
S63.621S	S63.91XS	S66.419S	S68.519S	S72.011J	S72.023Q	S72.033F	S72.042N	S72.052A	S72.064H
S63.622A	S63.92XA	S66.421A	S68.521S	S72.011K	S72.023R	S72.033G	S72.042P	S72.052B	S72.064J
S63.622S	S63.92XS	S66.422A	S68.522S	S72.011M	S72.023S	S72.033H	S72.042Q	S72.052C	S72.064K
S63.629A	S66.011A	S66.429A	S68.529S	S72.011N	S72.024A	S72.033J	S72.042R	S72.052D	S72.064M
S63.629S	S66.011S	S66.510A	S68.610S	S72.011P	S72.024B	S72.033K	S72.042S	S72.052E	S72.064N
S63.630A	S66.012A	S66.510S	S68.611S	S72.011Q	S72.024C	S72.033M	S72.043A	S72.052F	S72.064P
S63.630S	S66.012S	S66.511A	S68.612S	S72.011R	S72.024D	S72.033N	S72.043B	S72.052G	S72.064Q
S63.631A	S66.019A	S66.511S	S68.613S	S72.011S	S72.024E	S72.033P	S72.043C	S72.052H	S72.064R
S63.631S	S66.019S	S66.512A	S68.614S	S72.012A	S72.024F	S72.033Q	S72.043D	S72.052J	S72.064S
S63.632A	S66.021A	S66.512S	S68.615S	S72.012B	S72.024G	S72.033R	S72.043E	S72.052K	S72.065A
S63.632S	S66.022A	S66.513A	S68.616S	S72.012C	S72.024H	S72.033S	S72.043F	S72.052M	S72.065B
S63.633A	S66.029A	S66.513S	S68.617S	S72.012D	S72.024J	S72.034A	S72.043G	S72.052N	S72.065C
S63.633S	S66.110A	S66.514A	S68.618S	S72.012E	S72.024K	S72.034B	S72.043H	S72.052P	S72.065D
S63.634A	S66.110S	S66.514S	S68.619S	S72.012F	S72.024M	S72.034C	S72.043J	S72.052Q	S72.065E
S63.634S	S66.111A	S66.515A	S68.620S	S72.012G	S72.024N	S72.034P		S72.052R	

Diagnosis Codes by MDC

S72.065F	S72.101N	S72.114B	S72.123H	S72.132Q	S72.142D	S72.21XK	S72.26XS	S72.323F	S72.332N
S72.065G	S72.101P	S72.114C	S72.123J	S72.132R	S72.142E	S72.21XM	S72.301A	S72.323G	S72.332P
S72.065H	S72.101Q	S72.114D	S72.123K	S72.132S	S72.142F	S72.21XN	S72.301B	S72.323H	S72.332Q
S72.065J	S72.101R	S72.114E	S72.123M	S72.133A	S72.142G	S72.21XP	S72.301C	S72.323J	S72.332R
S72.065K	S72.101S	S72.114F	S72.123N	S72.133B	S72.142H	S72.21XQ	S72.301D	S72.323K	S72.332S
S72.065M	S72.102A	S72.114G	S72.123P	S72.133C	S72.142J	S72.21XR	S72.301E	S72.323M	S72.333A
S72.065N	S72.102B	S72.114H	S72.123Q	S72.133D	S72.142K	S72.21XS	S72.301F	S72.323N	S72.333B
S72.065P	S72.102C	S72.114J	S72.123R	S72.133E	S72.142M	S72.22XA	S72.301G	S72.323P	S72.333C
S72.065Q	S72.102D	S72.114K	S72.123S	S72.133F	S72.142N	S72.22XB	S72.301H	S72.323Q	S72.333D
S72.065R	S72.102E	S72.114M	S72.124A	S72.133G	S72.142P	S72.22XC	S72.301J	S72.323R	S72.333E
S72.065S	S72.102F	S72.114N	S72.124B	S72.133H	S72.142Q	S72.22XD	S72.301K	S72.323S	S72.333F
S72.066A	S72.102G	S72.114P	S72.124C	S72.133J	S72.142R	S72.22XE	S72.301M	S72.324A	S72.333G
S72.066B	S72.102H	S72.114Q	S72.124D	S72.133K	S72.142S	S72.22XF	S72.301N	S72.324B	S72.333H
S72.066C	S72.102J	S72.114R	S72.124E	S72.133M	S72.143A	S72.22XG	S72.301P	S72.324C	S72.333J
S72.066D	S72.102K	S72.114S	S72.124F	S72.133N	S72.143B	S72.22XH	S72.301Q	S72.324D	S72.333K
S72.066E	S72.102M	S72.115A	S72.124G	S72.133P	S72.143C	S72.22XJ	S72.301R	S72.324E	S72.333M
S72.066F	S72.102N	S72.115B	S72.124H	S72.133Q	S72.143D	S72.22XK	S72.301S	S72.324F	S72.333N
S72.066G	S72.102P	S72.115C	S72.124J	S72.133R	S72.143E	S72.22XM	S72.302A	S72.324G	S72.333P
S72.066H	S72.102Q	S72.115D	S72.124K	S72.133S	S72.143F	S72.22XN	S72.302B	S72.324H	S72.333Q
S72.066J	S72.102R	S72.115E	S72.124M	S72.134A	S72.143G	S72.22XP	S72.302C	S72.324J	S72.333R
S72.066K	S72.102S	S72.115F	S72.124N	S72.134B	S72.143H	S72.22XQ	S72.302D	S72.324K	S72.333S
S72.066M	S72.109A	S72.115G	S72.124P	S72.134C	S72.143J	S72.22XR	S72.302E	S72.324M	S72.334A
S72.066N	S72.109B	S72.115H	S72.124Q	S72.134D	S72.143K	S72.22XS	S72.302F	S72.324N	S72.334B
S72.066P	S72.109C	S72.115J	S72.124R	S72.134E	S72.143M	S72.23XA	S72.302G	S72.324P	S72.334C
S72.066Q	S72.109D	S72.115K	S72.124S	S72.134F	S72.143N	S72.23XB	S72.302H	S72.324Q	S72.334D
S72.066R	S72.109E	S72.115M	S72.125A	S72.134G	S72.143P	S72.23XC	S72.302J	S72.324R	S72.334E
S72.066S	S72.109F	S72.115N	S72.125B	S72.134H	S72.143Q	S72.23XD	S72.302K	S72.324S	S72.334F
S72.091A	S72.109G	S72.115P	S72.125C	S72.134J	S72.143R	S72.23XE	S72.302M	S72.325A	S72.334G
S72.091B	S72.109H	S72.115Q	S72.125D	S72.134K	S72.143S	S72.23XF	S72.302N	S72.325B	S72.334H
S72.091C	S72.109J	S72.115R	S72.125E	S72.134M	S72.144A	S72.23XG	S72.302P	S72.325C	S72.334J
S72.091D	S72.109K	S72.115S	S72.125F	S72.134N	S72.144B	S72.23XH	S72.302Q	S72.325D	S72.334K
S72.091E	S72.109M	S72.116A	S72.125G	S72.134P	S72.144C	S72.23XJ	S72.302R	S72.325E	S72.334M
S72.091F	S72.109N	S72.116B	S72.125H	S72.134Q	S72.144D	S72.23XK	S72.302S	S72.325F	S72.334N
S72.091G	S72.109P	S72.116C	S72.125J	S72.134R	S72.144E	S72.23XM	S72.309A	S72.325G	S72.334P
S72.091H	S72.109Q	S72.116D	S72.125K	S72.134S	S72.144F	S72.23XN	S72.309B	S72.325H	S72.334Q
S72.091J	S72.109R	S72.116E	S72.125M	S72.135A	S72.144G	S72.23XP	S72.309C	S72.325J	S72.334R
S72.091K	S72.109S	S72.116F	S72.125N	S72.135B	S72.144H	S72.23XQ	S72.309D	S72.325K	S72.334S
S72.091M	S72.111A	S72.116G	S72.125P	S72.135C	S72.144J	S72.23XR	S72.309E	S72.325M	S72.335A
S72.091N	S72.111B	S72.116H	S72.125Q	S72.135D	S72.144K	S72.23XS	S72.309F	S72.325N	S72.335B
S72.091P	S72.111C	S72.116J	S72.125R	S72.135E	S72.144M	S72.24XA	S72.309G	S72.325P	S72.335C
S72.091Q	S72.111D	S72.116K	S72.125S	S72.135F	S72.144N	S72.24XB	S72.309H	S72.325Q	S72.335D
S72.091R	S72.111E	S72.116M	S72.126A	S72.135G	S72.144P	S72.24XC	S72.309J	S72.325R	S72.335E
S72.091S	S72.111F	S72.116N	S72.126B	S72.135H	S72.144Q	S72.24XD	S72.309K	S72.325S	S72.335F
S72.092A	S72.111G	S72.116P	S72.126C	S72.135J	S72.144R	S72.24XE	S72.309M	S72.326A	S72.335G
S72.092B	S72.111H	S72.116Q	S72.126D	S72.135K	S72.144S	S72.24XF	S72.309N	S72.326B	S72.335H
S72.092C	S72.111J	S72.116R	S72.126E	S72.135M	S72.145A	S72.24XG	S72.309P	S72.326C	S72.335J
S72.092D	S72.111K	S72.116S	S72.126F	S72.135N	S72.145B	S72.24XH	S72.309Q	S72.326D	S72.335K
S72.092E	S72.111M	S72.121A	S72.126G	S72.135P	S72.145C	S72.24XJ	S72.309R	S72.326E	S72.335M
S72.092F	S72.111N	S72.121B	S72.126H	S72.135Q	S72.145D	S72.24XK	S72.309S	S72.326F	S72.335N
S72.092G	S72.111P	S72.121C	S72.126J	S72.135R	S72.145E	S72.24XM	S72.321A	S72.326G	S72.335P
S72.092H	S72.111Q	S72.121D	S72.126K	S72.135S	S72.145F	S72.24XN	S72.321B	S72.326H	S72.335Q
S72.092J	S72.111R	S72.121E	S72.126M	S72.136A	S72.145G	S72.24XP	S72.321C	S72.326J	S72.335R
S72.092K	S72.111S	S72.121F	S72.126N	S72.136B	S72.145H	S72.24XQ	S72.321D	S72.326K	S72.335S
S72.092M	S72.112A	S72.121G	S72.126P	S72.136C	S72.145J	S72.24XR	S72.321E	S72.326M	S72.336A
S72.092N	S72.112B	S72.121H	S72.126Q	S72.136D	S72.145K	S72.24XS	S72.321F	S72.326N	S72.336B
S72.092P	S72.112C	S72.121J	S72.126R	S72.136E	S72.145M	S72.25XA	S72.321G	S72.326P	S72.336C
S72.092Q	S72.112D	S72.121K	S72.126S	S72.136F	S72.145N	S72.25XB	S72.321H	S72.326Q	S72.336D
S72.092R	S72.112E	S72.121M	S72.131A	S72.136G	S72.145P	S72.25XC	S72.321J	S72.326R	S72.336E
S72.092S	S72.112F	S72.121N	S72.131B	S72.136H	S72.145Q	S72.25XD	S72.321K	S72.326S	S72.336F
S72.099A	S72.112G	S72.121P	S72.131C	S72.136J	S72.145R	S72.25XE	S72.321M	S72.331A	S72.336G
S72.099B	S72.112H	S72.121Q	S72.131D	S72.136K	S72.145S	S72.25XF	S72.321N	S72.331B	S72.336H
S72.099C	S72.112J	S72.121R	S72.131E	S72.136M	S72.146A	S72.25XG	S72.321P	S72.331C	S72.336J
S72.099D	S72.112K	S72.121S	S72.131F	S72.136N	S72.146B	S72.25XH	S72.321Q	S72.331D	S72.336K
S72.099E	S72.112M	S72.122A	S72.131G	S72.136P	S72.146C	S72.25XJ	S72.321S	S72.331E	S72.336M
S72.099F	S72.112N	S72.122B	S72.131H	S72.136Q	S72.146D	S72.25XK	S72.322A	S72.331F	S72.336N
S72.099G	S72.112P	S72.122C	S72.131J	S72.136R	S72.146E	S72.25XM	S72.322B	S72.331G	S72.336P
S72.099H	S72.112Q	S72.122D	S72.131K	S72.136S	S72.146F	S72.25XN	S72.322C	S72.331H	S72.336Q
S72.099J	S72.112R	S72.122E	S72.131M	S72.141A	S72.146G	S72.25XP	S72.322D	S72.331J	S72.336R
S72.099K	S72.112S	S72.122F	S72.131N	S72.141B	S72.146H	S72.25XQ	S72.322E	S72.331K	S72.336S
S72.099M	S72.113A	S72.122G	S72.131P	S72.141C	S72.146J	S72.25XR	S72.322F	S72.331M	S72.341A
S72.099N	S72.113B	S72.122H	S72.131Q	S72.141D	S72.146K	S72.25XS	S72.322G	S72.331N	S72.341B
S72.099P	S72.113C	S72.122J	S72.131R	S72.141E	S72.146M	S72.26XA	S72.322H	S72.331P	S72.341C
S72.099Q	S72.113D	S72.122K	S72.131S	S72.141F	S72.146N	S72.26XB	S72.322J	S72.331Q	S72.341D
S72.099R	S72.113E	S72.122M	S72.132A	S72.141G	S72.146P	S72.26XC	S72.322K	S72.331R	S72.341E
S72.099S	S72.113F	S72.122N	S72.132B	S72.141H	S72.146Q	S72.26XD	S72.322M	S72.331S	S72.341F
S72.101A	S72.113G	S72.122P	S72.132C	S72.141J	S72.146R	S72.26XE	S72.322N	S72.332A	S72.341G
S72.101B	S72.113H	S72.122Q	S72.132D	S72.141K	S72.146S	S72.26XF	S72.322P	S72.332B	S72.341H
S72.101C	S72.113J	S72.122R	S72.132E	S72.141M	S72.21XA	S72.26XG	S72.322Q	S72.332C	S72.341J
S72.101D	S72.113K	S72.122S	S72.132F	S72.141N	S72.21XB	S72.26XH	S72.322R	S72.332D	S72.341K
S72.101E	S72.113M	S72.123A	S72.132G	S72.141P	S72.21XC	S72.26XJ	S72.322S	S72.332E	S72.341M
S72.101F	S72.113N	S72.123B	S72.132H	S72.141Q	S72.21XD	S72.26XK	S72.323A	S72.332F	S72.341N
S72.101G	S72.113P	S72.123C	S72.132J	S72.141R	S72.21XE	S72.26XM	S72.323B	S72.332G	S72.341P
S72.101H	S72.113Q	S72.123D	S72.132K	S72.141S	S72.21XF	S72.26XN	S72.323C	S72.332H	S72.341Q
S72.101J	S72.113R	S72.123E	S72.132M	S72.142A	S72.21XG	S72.26XP	S72.323D	S72.332J	S72.341R
S72.101K	S72.113S	S72.123F	S72.132N	S72.142B	S72.21XH	S72.26XQ	S72.323E	S72.332K	S72.341S
S72.101M	S72.114A	S72.123G	S72.132P	S72.142C	S72.21XJ	S72.26XR		S72.332M	S72.342A

S72.342B	S72.351H	S72.356Q	S72.366D	S72.402K	S72.414S	S72.424F	S72.433N	S72.443B	S72.452H
S72.342C	S72.351J	S72.356R	S72.366E	S72.402M	S72.415A	S72.424G	S72.433P	S72.443C	S72.452J
S72.342D	S72.351K	S72.356S	S72.366F	S72.402N	S72.415B	S72.424H	S72.433Q	S72.443D	S72.452K
S72.342E	S72.351M	S72.361A	S72.366G	S72.402P	S72.415C	S72.424J	S72.433R	S72.443E	S72.452M
S72.342F	S72.351N	S72.361B	S72.366H	S72.402Q	S72.415D	S72.424K	S72.433S	S72.443F	S72.452N
S72.342G	S72.351P	S72.361C	S72.366J	S72.402R	S72.415E	S72.424M	S72.434A	S72.443G	S72.452P
S72.342H	S72.351Q	S72.361D	S72.366K	S72.402S	S72.415F	S72.424N	S72.434B	S72.443H	S72.452Q
S72.342J	S72.351R	S72.361E	S72.366M	S72.409A	S72.415G	S72.424P	S72.434C	S72.443J	S72.452R
S72.342K	S72.351S	S72.361F	S72.366N	S72.409B	S72.415H	S72.424Q	S72.434D	S72.443K	S72.452S
S72.342M	S72.352A	S72.361G	S72.366P	S72.409C	S72.415J	S72.424R	S72.434E	S72.443M	S72.453A
S72.342N	S72.352B	S72.361H	S72.366Q	S72.409D	S72.415K	S72.424S	S72.434F	S72.443N	S72.453B
S72.342P	S72.352C	S72.361J	S72.366R	S72.409E	S72.415M	S72.425A	S72.434G	S72.443P	S72.453C
S72.342Q	S72.352D	S72.361K	S72.366S	S72.409F	S72.415N	S72.425B	S72.434H	S72.443Q	S72.453D
S72.342R	S72.352E	S72.361M	S72.391A	S72.409G	S72.415P	S72.425C	S72.434J	S72.443R	S72.453E
S72.342S	S72.352F	S72.361N	S72.391B	S72.409H	S72.415Q	S72.425D	S72.434K	S72.443S	S72.453F
S72.343A	S72.352G	S72.361P	S72.391C	S72.409J	S72.415R	S72.425E	S72.434M	S72.444A	S72.453G
S72.343B	S72.352H	S72.361Q	S72.391D	S72.409K	S72.415S	S72.425F	S72.434N	S72.444B	S72.453H
S72.343C	S72.352J	S72.361R	S72.391E	S72.409M	S72.416A	S72.425G	S72.434P	S72.444C	S72.453J
S72.343D	S72.352K	S72.361S	S72.391F	S72.409N	S72.416B	S72.425H	S72.434Q	S72.444D	S72.453K
S72.343E	S72.352M	S72.362A	S72.391G	S72.409P	S72.416C	S72.425J	S72.434R	S72.444E	S72.453M
S72.343F	S72.352N	S72.362B	S72.391H	S72.409Q	S72.416D	S72.425K	S72.434S	S72.444F	S72.453N
S72.343G	S72.352P	S72.362C	S72.391J	S72.409R	S72.416E	S72.425M	S72.435A	S72.444G	S72.453P
S72.343H	S72.352Q	S72.362D	S72.391K	S72.409S	S72.416F	S72.425N	S72.435B	S72.444H	S72.453Q
S72.343J	S72.352R	S72.362E	S72.391M	S72.411A	S72.416G	S72.425P	S72.435C	S72.444J	S72.453R
S72.343K	S72.352S	S72.362F	S72.391N	S72.411B	S72.416H	S72.425Q	S72.435D	S72.444K	S72.453S
S72.343M	S72.353A	S72.362G	S72.391P	S72.411C	S72.416J	S72.425R	S72.435E	S72.444M	S72.454A
S72.343N	S72.353B	S72.362H	S72.391Q	S72.411D	S72.416K	S72.425S	S72.435F	S72.444N	S72.454B
S72.343P	S72.353C	S72.362J	S72.391R	S72.411E	S72.416M	S72.426A	S72.435G	S72.444P	S72.454C
S72.343Q	S72.353D	S72.362K	S72.391S	S72.411F	S72.416N	S72.426B	S72.435H	S72.444Q	S72.454D
S72.343R	S72.353E	S72.362M	S72.392A	S72.411G	S72.416P	S72.426C	S72.435J	S72.444R	S72.454E
S72.343S	S72.353F	S72.362N	S72.392B	S72.411H	S72.416Q	S72.426D	S72.435K	S72.444S	S72.454F
S72.344A	S72.353G	S72.362P	S72.392C	S72.411J	S72.416R	S72.426E	S72.435M	S72.445A	S72.454G
S72.344B	S72.353H	S72.362Q	S72.392D	S72.411K	S72.416S	S72.426F	S72.435N	S72.445B	S72.454H
S72.344C	S72.353J	S72.362R	S72.392E	S72.411M	S72.421A	S72.426G	S72.435P	S72.445C	S72.454J
S72.344D	S72.353K	S72.362S	S72.392F	S72.411N	S72.421B	S72.426H	S72.435Q	S72.445D	S72.454K
S72.344E	S72.353M	S72.363A	S72.392G	S72.411P	S72.421C	S72.426J	S72.435R	S72.445E	S72.454M
S72.344F	S72.353N	S72.363B	S72.392H	S72.411Q	S72.421D	S72.426K	S72.435S	S72.445F	S72.454N
S72.344G	S72.353P	S72.363C	S72.392J	S72.411R	S72.421E	S72.426M	S72.436A	S72.445G	S72.454P
S72.344H	S72.353Q	S72.363D	S72.392K	S72.411S	S72.421F	S72.426N	S72.436B	S72.445H	S72.454Q
S72.344J	S72.353R	S72.363E	S72.392M	S72.412A	S72.421G	S72.426P	S72.436C	S72.445J	S72.454R
S72.344K	S72.353S	S72.363F	S72.392N	S72.412B	S72.421H	S72.426Q	S72.436D	S72.445K	S72.454S
S72.344M	S72.354A	S72.363G	S72.392P	S72.412C	S72.421J	S72.426R	S72.436E	S72.445M	S72.455A
S72.344N	S72.354B	S72.363H	S72.392Q	S72.412D	S72.421K	S72.426S	S72.436F	S72.445N	S72.455B
S72.344P	S72.354C	S72.363J	S72.392R	S72.412E	S72.421M	S72.431A	S72.436G	S72.445P	S72.455C
S72.344Q	S72.354D	S72.363K	S72.392S	S72.412F	S72.421N	S72.431B	S72.436H	S72.445Q	S72.455D
S72.344R	S72.354E	S72.363M	S72.399A	S72.412G	S72.421P	S72.431C	S72.436J	S72.445R	S72.455E
S72.344S	S72.354F	S72.363N	S72.399B	S72.412H	S72.421Q	S72.431D	S72.436K	S72.445S	S72.455F
S72.345A	S72.354G	S72.363P	S72.399C	S72.412J	S72.421R	S72.431E	S72.436M	S72.446A	S72.455G
S72.345B	S72.354H	S72.363Q	S72.399D	S72.412K	S72.421S	S72.431F	S72.436N	S72.446B	S72.455H
S72.345C	S72.354J	S72.363R	S72.399E	S72.412M	S72.422A	S72.431G	S72.436P	S72.446C	S72.455J
S72.345D	S72.354K	S72.363S	S72.399F	S72.412N	S72.422B	S72.431H	S72.436Q	S72.446D	S72.455K
S72.345E	S72.354M	S72.364A	S72.399G	S72.412P	S72.422C	S72.431J	S72.436R	S72.446E	S72.455M
S72.345F	S72.354N	S72.364B	S72.399H	S72.412Q	S72.422D	S72.431K	S72.436S	S72.446F	S72.455N
S72.345G	S72.354P	S72.364C	S72.399J	S72.412R	S72.422E	S72.431M	S72.441A	S72.446G	S72.455P
S72.345H	S72.354Q	S72.364D	S72.399K	S72.412S	S72.422F	S72.431N	S72.441B	S72.446H	S72.455Q
S72.345J	S72.354R	S72.364E	S72.399M	S72.413A	S72.422G	S72.431P	S72.441C	S72.446J	S72.455R
S72.345K	S72.354S	S72.364F	S72.399N	S72.413B	S72.422H	S72.431Q	S72.441D	S72.446K	S72.455S
S72.345M	S72.355A	S72.364G	S72.399P	S72.413C	S72.422J	S72.431R	S72.441E	S72.446M	S72.456A
S72.345N	S72.355B	S72.364H	S72.399Q	S72.413D	S72.422K	S72.431S	S72.441F	S72.446N	S72.456B
S72.345P	S72.355C	S72.364J	S72.399R	S72.413E	S72.422M	S72.432A	S72.441G	S72.446P	S72.456C
S72.345Q	S72.355D	S72.364K	S72.399S	S72.413F	S72.422N	S72.432B	S72.441H	S72.446Q	S72.456D
S72.345R	S72.355E	S72.364M	S72.401A	S72.413G	S72.422P	S72.432C	S72.441J	S72.446R	S72.456E
S72.345S	S72.355F	S72.364N	S72.401B	S72.413H	S72.422Q	S72.432D	S72.441K	S72.446S	S72.456F
S72.346A	S72.355G	S72.364P	S72.401C	S72.413J	S72.422R	S72.432E	S72.441M	S72.451A	S72.456G
S72.346B	S72.355H	S72.364Q	S72.401D	S72.413K	S72.422S	S72.432F	S72.441N	S72.451B	S72.456H
S72.346C	S72.355J	S72.364R	S72.401E	S72.413M	S72.423A	S72.432G	S72.441P	S72.451C	S72.456J
S72.346D	S72.355K	S72.364S	S72.401F	S72.413N	S72.423B	S72.432H	S72.441Q	S72.451D	S72.456K
S72.346E	S72.355M	S72.365A	S72.401G	S72.413P	S72.423C	S72.432J	S72.441R	S72.451E	S72.456M
S72.346F	S72.355N	S72.365B	S72.401H	S72.413Q	S72.423D	S72.432K	S72.441S	S72.451F	S72.456N
S72.346G	S72.355P	S72.365C	S72.401J	S72.413R	S72.423E	S72.432M	S72.442A	S72.451G	S72.456P
S72.346H	S72.355Q	S72.365D	S72.401K	S72.413S	S72.423F	S72.432N	S72.442B	S72.451H	S72.456Q
S72.346J	S72.355R	S72.365E	S72.401M	S72.414A	S72.423G	S72.432P	S72.442C	S72.451J	S72.456R
S72.346K	S72.355S	S72.365F	S72.401N	S72.414B	S72.423H	S72.432Q	S72.442D	S72.451K	S72.456S
S72.346M	S72.356A	S72.365G	S72.401P	S72.414C	S72.423J	S72.432R	S72.442E	S72.451M	S72.461A
S72.346N	S72.356B	S72.365H	S72.401Q	S72.414D	S72.423K	S72.432S	S72.442F	S72.451N	S72.461B
S72.346P	S72.356C	S72.365J	S72.401R	S72.414E	S72.423M	S72.433A	S72.442G	S72.451P	S72.461C
S72.346Q	S72.356D	S72.365K	S72.401S	S72.414F	S72.423N	S72.433B	S72.442H	S72.451Q	S72.461D
S72.346R	S72.356E	S72.365M	S72.402A	S72.414G	S72.423P	S72.433C	S72.442J	S72.451R	S72.461E
S72.346S	S72.356F	S72.365N	S72.402B	S72.414H	S72.423Q	S72.433D	S72.442K	S72.451S	S72.461F
S72.351A	S72.356G	S72.365P	S72.402C	S72.414J	S72.423R	S72.433E	S72.442M	S72.452A	S72.461G
S72.351B	S72.356H	S72.365Q	S72.402D	S72.414K	S72.423S	S72.433F	S72.442N	S72.452B	S72.461H
S72.351C	S72.356J	S72.365R	S72.402E	S72.414M	S72.424A	S72.433G	S72.442P	S72.452C	S72.461J
S72.351D	S72.356K	S72.365S	S72.402F	S72.414N	S72.424B	S72.433H	S72.442Q	S72.452D	S72.461K
S72.351E	S72.356M	S72.366A	S72.402G	S72.414P	S72.424C	S72.433J	S72.442R	S72.452E	S72.461M
S72.351F	S72.356N	S72.366B	S72.402H	S72.414Q	S72.424D	S72.433K	S72.442S	S72.452F	S72.461N
S72.351G	S72.356P	S72.366C	S72.402J	S72.414R	S72.424E	S72.433M	S72.443A	S72.452G	S72.461P

Diagnosis Codes by MDC

S72.461Q	S72.471K	S72.8X2H	S73.011S	S76.121A	S79.012S	S79.132D	S82.009H	S82.015Q	S82.025D
S72.461R	S72.471P	S72.8X2J	S73.012A	S76.122A	S79.019A	S79.132G	S82.009J	S82.015R	S82.025E
S72.461S	S72.471S	S72.8X2K	S73.012S	S76.129A	S79.019D	S79.132K	S82.009K	S82.015S	S82.025F
S72.462A	S72.472A	S72.8X2M	S73.013A	S76.211A	S79.019G	S79.132P	S82.009M	S82.016A	S82.025G
S72.462B	S72.472D	S72.8X2N	S73.013S	S76.211S	S79.019K	S79.132S	S82.009N	S82.016B	S82.025H
S72.462C	S72.472G	S72.8X2P	S73.014A	S76.212A	S79.019P	S79.139A	S82.009P	S82.016C	S82.025J
S72.462D	S72.472K	S72.8X2Q	S73.014S	S76.212S	S79.019S	S79.139D	S82.009Q	S82.016D	S82.025K
S72.462E	S72.472P	S72.8X2R	S73.015A	S76.219A	S79.091A	S79.139G	S82.009R	S82.016E	S82.025M
S72.462F	S72.472S	S72.8X2S	S73.015S	S76.219S	S79.091D	S79.139K	S82.009S	S82.016F	S82.025N
S72.462G	S72.479A	S72.8X9A	S73.016A	S76.221A	S79.091G	S79.139P	S82.011A	S82.016G	S82.025P
S72.462H	S72.479D	S72.8X9B	S73.016S	S76.222A	S79.091K	S79.139S	S82.011B	S82.016H	S82.025Q
S72.462J	S72.479G	S72.8X9C	S73.021A	S76.229A	S79.091P	S79.141A	S82.011C	S82.016J	S82.025R
S72.462K	S72.479K	S72.8X9D	S73.021S	S76.311A	S79.091S	S79.141D	S82.011D	S82.016K	S82.025S
S72.462M	S72.479P	S72.8X9E	S73.022A	S76.311S	S79.092A	S79.141G	S82.011E	S82.016M	S82.026A
S72.462N	S72.479S	S72.8X9F	S73.022S	S76.312A	S79.092D	S79.141K	S82.011F	S82.016N	S82.026B
S72.462P	S72.491A	S72.8X9G	S73.023A	S76.312S	S79.092G	S79.141P	S82.011G	S82.016P	S82.026C
S72.462Q	S72.491B	S72.8X9H	S73.023S	S76.319A	S79.092K	S79.141S	S82.011H	S82.016Q	S82.026D
S72.462R	S72.491C	S72.8X9J	S73.024A	S76.319S	S79.092P	S79.142A	S82.011J	S82.016R	S82.026E
S72.462S	S72.491D	S72.8X9K	S73.024S	S76.321A	S79.092S	S79.142D	S82.011K	S82.016S	S82.026F
S72.463A	S72.491E	S72.8X9M	S73.025A	S76.322A	S79.099A	S79.142G	S82.011M	S82.021A	S82.026G
S72.463B	S72.491F	S72.8X9N	S73.025S	S76.329A	S79.099D	S79.142K	S82.011N	S82.021B	S82.026H
S72.463C	S72.491G	S72.8X9P	S73.026A	S76.811A	S79.099G	S79.142P	S82.011P	S82.021C	S82.026J
S72.463D	S72.491H	S72.8X9Q	S73.026S	S76.811S	S79.099K	S79.142S	S82.011Q	S82.021D	S82.026K
S72.463E	S72.491J	S72.8X9R	S73.031A	S76.812A	S79.099P	S79.149A	S82.011R	S82.021E	S82.026M
S72.463F	S72.491K	S72.8X9S	S73.031S	S76.812S	S79.099S	S79.149D	S82.011S	S82.021F	S82.026N
S72.463G	S72.491M	S72.90XA	S73.032A	S76.819A	S79.101A	S79.149G	S82.012A	S82.021G	S82.026P
S72.463H	S72.491N	S72.90XB	S73.032S	S76.819S	S79.101D	S79.149K	S82.012B	S82.021H	S82.026Q
S72.463J	S72.491P	S72.90XC	S73.033A	S76.821A	S79.101G	S79.149P	S82.012C	S82.021J	S82.026R
S72.463K	S72.491Q	S72.90XD	S73.033S	S76.822A	S79.101K	S79.149S	S82.012D	S82.021K	S82.026S
S72.463M	S72.491R	S72.90XE	S73.034A	S76.829A	S79.101P	S79.191A	S82.012E	S82.021M	S82.031A
S72.463N	S72.491S	S72.90XF	S73.034S	S76.911A	S79.101S	S79.191D	S82.012F	S82.021N	S82.031B
S72.463P	S72.492A	S72.90XG	S73.035A	S76.911S	S79.102A	S79.191G	S82.012G	S82.021P	S82.031C
S72.463Q	S72.492B	S72.90XH	S73.035S	S76.912A	S79.102D	S79.191K	S82.012H	S82.021Q	S82.031D
S72.463R	S72.492C	S72.90XJ	S73.036A	S76.912S	S79.102G	S79.191P	S82.012J	S82.021R	S82.031E
S72.463S	S72.492D	S72.90XK	S73.036S	S76.919A	S79.102K	S79.191S	S82.012K	S82.021S	S82.031F
S72.464A	S72.492E	S72.90XM	S73.041A	S76.919S	S79.102P	S79.192A	S82.012M	S82.022A	S82.031G
S72.464B	S72.492F	S72.90XN	S73.041S	S76.921A	S79.102S	S79.192D	S82.012N	S82.022B	S82.031H
S72.464C	S72.492G	S72.90XP	S73.042A	S76.922A	S79.109A	S79.192G	S82.012P	S82.022C	S82.031J
S72.464D	S72.492H	S72.90XQ	S73.042S	S76.929A	S79.109D	S79.192K	S82.012Q	S82.022D	S82.031K
S72.464E	S72.492J	S72.90XR	S73.043A	S78.011S	S79.109G	S79.192P	S82.012R	S82.022E	S82.031M
S72.464F	S72.492K	S72.90XS	S73.043S	S78.012S	S79.109K	S79.192S	S82.012S	S82.022F	S82.031N
S72.464G	S72.492M	S72.91XA	S73.044A	S78.019S	S79.109P	S79.199A	S82.013A	S82.022G	S82.031P
S72.464H	S72.492N	S72.91XB	S73.044S	S78.021S	S79.109S	S79.199D	S82.013B	S82.022H	S82.031Q
S72.464J	S72.492P	S72.91XC	S73.045A	S78.022S	S79.111A	S79.199G	S82.013C	S82.022J	S82.031R
S72.464K	S72.492Q	S72.91XD	S73.045S	S78.029S	S79.111D	S79.199K	S82.013D	S82.022K	S82.031S
S72.464M	S72.492R	S72.91XE	S73.046A	S78.111S	S79.111G	S79.199P	S82.013E	S82.022M	S82.032A
S72.464N	S72.492S	S72.91XF	S73.046S	S78.112S	S79.111K	S79.199S	S82.013F	S82.022N	S82.032B
S72.464P	S72.499A	S72.91XG	S73.101A	S78.119S	S79.111P	S82.001A	S82.013G	S82.022P	S82.032C
S72.464Q	S72.499B	S72.91XH	S73.101S	S78.121S	S79.111S	S82.001B	S82.013H	S82.022Q	S82.032D
S72.464R	S72.499C	S72.91XJ	S73.102A	S78.122S	S79.112A	S82.001C	S82.013J	S82.022R	S82.032E
S72.464S	S72.499D	S72.91XK	S73.102S	S78.129S	S79.112D	S82.001D	S82.013K	S82.022S	S82.032F
S72.465A	S72.499E	S72.91XM	S73.109A	S78.911S	S79.112G	S82.001E	S82.013M	S82.023A	S82.032G
S72.465B	S72.499F	S72.91XN	S73.109S	S78.912S	S79.112K	S82.001F	S82.013N	S82.023B	S82.032H
S72.465C	S72.499G	S72.91XP	S73.111A	S78.919S	S79.112P	S82.001G	S82.013P	S82.023C	S82.032J
S72.465D	S72.499H	S72.91XQ	S73.111S	S78.921S	S79.112S	S82.001H	S82.013Q	S82.023D	S82.032K
S72.465E	S72.499J	S72.91XR	S73.112A	S78.922S	S79.119A	S82.001J	S82.013R	S82.023E	S82.032M
S72.465F	S72.499K	S72.91XS	S73.112S	S78.929S	S79.119D	S82.001K	S82.013S	S82.023F	S82.032N
S72.465G	S72.499M	S72.92XA	S73.119A	S79.001A	S79.119G	S82.001M	S82.014A	S82.023G	S82.032P
S72.465H	S72.499N	S72.92XB	S73.119S	S79.001D	S79.119K	S82.001N	S82.014B	S82.023H	S82.032Q
S72.465J	S72.499P	S72.92XC	S73.121A	S79.001G	S79.119P	S82.001P	S82.014C	S82.023J	S82.032R
S72.465K	S72.499Q	S72.92XD	S73.121S	S79.001K	S79.119S	S82.001Q	S82.014D	S82.023K	S82.032S
S72.465M	S72.499R	S72.92XE	S73.122A	S79.001P	S79.121A	S82.001R	S82.014E	S82.023M	S82.033A
S72.465N	S72.499S	S72.92XF	S73.122S	S79.001S	S79.121D	S82.001S	S82.014F	S82.023N	S82.033B
S72.465P	S72.8X1A	S72.92XG	S73.129A	S79.002A	S79.121G	S82.002A	S82.014G	S82.023P	S82.033C
S72.465Q	S72.8X1B	S72.92XH	S73.129S	S79.002D	S79.121K	S82.002B	S82.014H	S82.023Q	S82.033D
S72.465R	S72.8X1C	S72.92XJ	S73.191A	S79.002G	S79.121P	S82.002C	S82.014J	S82.023R	S82.033E
S72.465S	S72.8X1D	S72.92XK	S73.191S	S79.002K	S79.121S	S82.002D	S82.014K	S82.023S	S82.033F
S72.466A	S72.8X1E	S72.92XM	S73.192A	S79.002P	S79.122A	S82.002E	S82.014M	S82.024A	S82.033G
S72.466B	S72.8X1F	S72.92XN	S73.192S	S79.002S	S79.122D	S82.002F	S82.014N	S82.024B	S82.033H
S72.466C	S72.8X1G	S72.92XP	S73.199A	S79.009A	S79.122G	S82.002G	S82.014P	S82.024C	S82.033J
S72.466D	S72.8X1H	S72.92XQ	S73.199S	S79.009D	S79.122K	S82.002H	S82.014Q	S82.024D	S82.033K
S72.466E	S72.8X1J	S72.92XR	S76.011A	S79.009G	S79.122P	S82.002J	S82.014R	S82.024E	S82.033M
S72.466F	S72.8X1K	S72.92XS	S76.011S	S79.009K	S79.122S	S82.002K	S82.014S	S82.024F	S82.033N
S72.466G	S72.8X1M	S73.001A	S76.012A	S79.009P	S79.129A	S82.002M	S82.015A	S82.024G	S82.033P
S72.466H	S72.8X1N	S73.001S	S76.012S	S79.009S	S79.129D	S82.002N	S82.015B	S82.024H	S82.033Q
S72.466J	S72.8X1P	S73.002A	S76.019A	S79.011A	S79.129G	S82.002P	S82.015C	S82.024J	S82.033R
S72.466K	S72.8X1Q	S73.002S	S76.019S	S79.011D	S79.129K	S82.002Q	S82.015D	S82.024K	S82.033S
S72.466M	S72.8X1R	S73.003A	S76.021A	S79.011G	S79.129P	S82.002R	S82.015E	S82.024M	S82.034A
S72.466N	S72.8X1S	S73.003S	S76.022A	S79.011K	S79.129S	S82.002S	S82.015F	S82.024N	S82.034B
S72.466P	S72.8X2A	S73.004A	S76.029A	S79.011P	S79.131A	S82.009A	S82.015G	S82.024P	S82.034C
S72.466Q	S72.8X2B	S73.004S	S76.111A	S79.011S	S79.131D	S82.009B	S82.015H	S82.024Q	S82.034D
S72.466R	S72.8X2C	S73.005A	S76.111S	S79.012A	S79.131G	S82.009C	S82.015J	S82.024R	S82.034E
S72.466S	S72.8X2D	S73.005S	S76.112A	S79.012D	S79.131K	S82.009D	S82.015K	S82.024S	S82.034F
S72.471A	S72.8X2E	S73.006A	S76.112S	S79.012G	S79.131P	S82.009E	S82.015M	S82.025A	S82.034G
S72.471D	S72.8X2F	S73.006S	S76.119A	S79.012K	S79.131S	S82.009F	S82.015N	S82.025B	S82.034H
S72.471G	S72.8X2G	S73.011A	S76.119S	S79.012P	S79.132A	S82.009G	S82.015P	S82.025C	S82.034J

S82.034K	S82.043S	S82.099F	S82.112N	S82.122B	S82.131H	S82.136Q	S82.146D	S82.155K	S82.199Q
S82.034M	S82.044A	S82.099G	S82.112P	S82.122C	S82.131J	S82.136R	S82.146E	S82.155M	S82.199R
S82.034N	S82.044B	S82.099H	S82.112Q	S82.122D	S82.131K	S82.136S	S82.146F	S82.155N	S82.199S
S82.034P	S82.044C	S82.099J	S82.112R	S82.122E	S82.131M	S82.141A	S82.146G	S82.155P	S82.201A
S82.034Q	S82.044D	S82.099K	S82.112S	S82.122F	S82.131N	S82.141B	S82.146H	S82.155Q	S82.201B
S82.034R	S82.044E	S82.099M	S82.113A	S82.122G	S82.131P	S82.141C	S82.146J	S82.155S	S82.201C
S82.034S	S82.044F	S82.099N	S82.113B	S82.122H	S82.131Q	S82.141D	S82.146K	S82.156A	S82.201D
S82.035A	S82.044G	S82.099P	S82.113C	S82.122J	S82.131R	S82.141E	S82.146M	S82.156B	S82.201E
S82.035B	S82.044H	S82.099Q	S82.113D	S82.122K	S82.131S	S82.141F	S82.146N	S82.156C	S82.201F
S82.035C	S82.044J	S82.099R	S82.113E	S82.122M	S82.132A	S82.141G	S82.146P	S82.156D	S82.201G
S82.035D	S82.044K	S82.099S	S82.113F	S82.122N	S82.132B	S82.141H	S82.146Q	S82.156E	S82.201H
S82.035E	S82.044M	S82.101A	S82.113G	S82.122P	S82.132C	S82.141J	S82.146R	S82.156F	S82.201J
S82.035F	S82.044N	S82.101B	S82.113H	S82.122Q	S82.132D	S82.141K	S82.146S	S82.156G	S82.201K
S82.035G	S82.044P	S82.101C	S82.113J	S82.122R	S82.132E	S82.141M	S82.151A	S82.156H	S82.201M
S82.035H	S82.044Q	S82.101D	S82.113K	S82.122S	S82.132F	S82.141N	S82.151B	S82.156J	S82.201N
S82.035J	S82.044R	S82.101E	S82.113M	S82.123A	S82.132G	S82.141P	S82.151C	S82.156K	S82.201P
S82.035K	S82.044S	S82.101F	S82.113N	S82.123B	S82.132H	S82.141Q	S82.151D	S82.156M	S82.201Q
S82.035M	S82.045A	S82.101G	S82.113P	S82.123C	S82.132J	S82.141R	S82.151E	S82.156N	S82.201R
S82.035N	S82.045B	S82.101H	S82.113Q	S82.123D	S82.132K	S82.141S	S82.151F	S82.156P	S82.201S
S82.035P	S82.045C	S82.101J	S82.113R	S82.123E	S82.132M	S82.142A	S82.151G	S82.156Q	S82.202A
S82.035Q	S82.045D	S82.101K	S82.113S	S82.123F	S82.132N	S82.142B	S82.151H	S82.156R	S82.202B
S82.035R	S82.045E	S82.101M	S82.114A	S82.123G	S82.132P	S82.142C	S82.151J	S82.156S	S82.202C
S82.035S	S82.045F	S82.101N	S82.114B	S82.123H	S82.132Q	S82.142D	S82.151K	S82.161A	S82.202D
S82.036A	S82.045G	S82.101P	S82.114C	S82.123J	S82.132R	S82.142E	S82.151M	S82.161D	S82.202E
S82.036B	S82.045H	S82.101Q	S82.114D	S82.123K	S82.132S	S82.142F	S82.151N	S82.161G	S82.202F
S82.036C	S82.045J	S82.101R	S82.114E	S82.123M	S82.133A	S82.142G	S82.151P	S82.161K	S82.202G
S82.036D	S82.045K	S82.101S	S82.114F	S82.123N	S82.133B	S82.142H	S82.151Q	S82.161P	S82.202H
S82.036E	S82.045M	S82.102A	S82.114G	S82.123P	S82.133C	S82.142J	S82.151R	S82.161S	S82.202J
S82.036F	S82.045N	S82.102B	S82.114H	S82.123Q	S82.133D	S82.142K	S82.151S	S82.162A	S82.202K
S82.036G	S82.045P	S82.102C	S82.114J	S82.123R	S82.133F	S82.142M	S82.152A	S82.162D	S82.202M
S82.036H	S82.045Q	S82.102D	S82.114K	S82.123S	S82.133G	S82.142N	S82.152B	S82.162G	S82.202N
S82.036J	S82.045R	S82.102E	S82.114M	S82.124A	S82.133H	S82.142P	S82.152C	S82.162K	S82.202P
S82.036K	S82.045S	S82.102F	S82.114N	S82.124B	S82.133J	S82.142Q	S82.152D	S82.162P	S82.202Q
S82.036M	S82.046A	S82.102G	S82.114P	S82.124C	S82.133K	S82.142R	S82.152E	S82.162S	S82.202R
S82.036N	S82.046B	S82.102H	S82.114Q	S82.124D	S82.133M	S82.142S	S82.152F	S82.169A	S82.202S
S82.036P	S82.046C	S82.102J	S82.114R	S82.124E	S82.133N	S82.143A	S82.152G	S82.169D	S82.209A
S82.036Q	S82.046D	S82.102K	S82.114S	S82.124F	S82.133P	S82.143B	S82.152H	S82.169G	S82.209B
S82.036R	S82.046E	S82.102M	S82.115A	S82.124G	S82.133Q	S82.143C	S82.152J	S82.169K	S82.209C
S82.036S	S82.046F	S82.102N	S82.115B	S82.124H	S82.133R	S82.143D	S82.152K	S82.169P	S82.209D
S82.041A	S82.046G	S82.102P	S82.115C	S82.124J	S82.133S	S82.143E	S82.152M	S82.169S	S82.209E
S82.041B	S82.046H	S82.102Q	S82.115D	S82.124K	S82.134A	S82.143F	S82.152N	S82.191A	S82.209F
S82.041C	S82.046J	S82.102R	S82.115E	S82.124M	S82.134B	S82.143G	S82.152P	S82.191B	S82.209G
S82.041D	S82.046K	S82.102S	S82.115F	S82.124N	S82.134C	S82.143H	S82.152Q	S82.191C	S82.209H
S82.041E	S82.046M	S82.109A	S82.115G	S82.124P	S82.134D	S82.143J	S82.152R	S82.191D	S82.209J
S82.041F	S82.046N	S82.109B	S82.115H	S82.124Q	S82.134E	S82.143K	S82.152S	S82.191E	S82.209K
S82.041G	S82.046P	S82.109C	S82.115J	S82.124R	S82.134F	S82.143M	S82.153A	S82.191F	S82.209M
S82.041H	S82.046Q	S82.109D	S82.115K	S82.124S	S82.134G	S82.143N	S82.153B	S82.191G	S82.209N
S82.041J	S82.046R	S82.109E	S82.115M	S82.125A	S82.134H	S82.143P	S82.153C	S82.191H	S82.209P
S82.041K	S82.046S	S82.109F	S82.115N	S82.125B	S82.134J	S82.143Q	S82.153D	S82.191J	S82.209Q
S82.041M	S82.091A	S82.109G	S82.115P	S82.125C	S82.134K	S82.143R	S82.153E	S82.191K	S82.209R
S82.041N	S82.091B	S82.109H	S82.115Q	S82.125D	S82.134M	S82.143S	S82.153F	S82.191M	S82.209S
S82.041P	S82.091C	S82.109J	S82.115R	S82.125E	S82.134N	S82.144A	S82.153G	S82.191N	S82.221A
S82.041Q	S82.091D	S82.109K	S82.115S	S82.125F	S82.134P	S82.144B	S82.153H	S82.191P	S82.221B
S82.041R	S82.091E	S82.109M	S82.116A	S82.125G	S82.134Q	S82.144C	S82.153J	S82.191Q	S82.221C
S82.041S	S82.091F	S82.109N	S82.116B	S82.125H	S82.134R	S82.144D	S82.153K	S82.191R	S82.221D
S82.042A	S82.091G	S82.109P	S82.116C	S82.125J	S82.134S	S82.144E	S82.153M	S82.191S	S82.221E
S82.042B	S82.091H	S82.109Q	S82.116D	S82.125K	S82.135A	S82.144F	S82.153N	S82.192A	S82.221F
S82.042C	S82.091J	S82.109R	S82.116E	S82.125M	S82.135B	S82.144G	S82.153P	S82.192B	S82.221G
S82.042D	S82.091K	S82.109S	S82.116F	S82.125N	S82.135C	S82.144H	S82.153Q	S82.192C	S82.221H
S82.042E	S82.091M	S82.111A	S82.116G	S82.125P	S82.135D	S82.144J	S82.153R	S82.192D	S82.221J
S82.042F	S82.091N	S82.111B	S82.116H	S82.125Q	S82.135E	S82.144K	S82.153S	S82.192E	S82.221K
S82.042G	S82.091P	S82.111C	S82.116J	S82.125R	S82.135F	S82.144M	S82.154A	S82.192F	S82.221M
S82.042H	S82.091Q	S82.111D	S82.116K	S82.125S	S82.135G	S82.144N	S82.154B	S82.192G	S82.221N
S82.042J	S82.091R	S82.111E	S82.116M	S82.126A	S82.135H	S82.144P	S82.154C	S82.192H	S82.221P
S82.042K	S82.091S	S82.111F	S82.116N	S82.126B	S82.135J	S82.144Q	S82.154D	S82.192J	S82.221Q
S82.042M	S82.092A	S82.111G	S82.116P	S82.126C	S82.135K	S82.144R	S82.154E	S82.192K	S82.221R
S82.042N	S82.092B	S82.111H	S82.116Q	S82.126D	S82.135M	S82.144S	S82.154F	S82.192M	S82.221S
S82.042P	S82.092C	S82.111J	S82.116S	S82.126E	S82.135N	S82.145A	S82.154G	S82.192N	S82.222A
S82.042Q	S82.092D	S82.111K	S82.121A	S82.126F	S82.135P	S82.145B	S82.154H	S82.192P	S82.222B
S82.042R	S82.092E	S82.111M	S82.121B	S82.126G	S82.135Q	S82.145C	S82.154J	S82.192Q	S82.222C
S82.042S	S82.092F	S82.111N	S82.121C	S82.126H	S82.135R	S82.145D	S82.154K	S82.192R	S82.222D
S82.043A	S82.092G	S82.111P	S82.121D	S82.126J	S82.135S	S82.145E	S82.154M	S82.192S	S82.222E
S82.043B	S82.092H	S82.111Q	S82.121E	S82.126K	S82.136A	S82.145F	S82.154N	S82.199A	S82.222F
S82.043C	S82.092J	S82.111R	S82.121F	S82.126M	S82.136B	S82.145G	S82.154P	S82.199B	S82.222G
S82.043D	S82.092K	S82.111S	S82.121G	S82.126N	S82.136C	S82.145H	S82.154Q	S82.199C	S82.222H
S82.043E	S82.092M	S82.112A	S82.121H	S82.126P	S82.136D	S82.145J	S82.154R	S82.199D	S82.222J
S82.043F	S82.092N	S82.112B	S82.121J	S82.126Q	S82.136E	S82.145K	S82.154S	S82.199E	S82.222K
S82.043G	S82.092P	S82.112C	S82.121K	S82.126S	S82.136F	S82.145M	S82.155A	S82.199F	S82.222M
S82.043H	S82.092Q	S82.112D	S82.121M	S82.131A	S82.136G	S82.145N	S82.155B	S82.199G	S82.222N
S82.043J	S82.092R	S82.112E	S82.121N	S82.131B	S82.136H	S82.145P	S82.155C	S82.199H	S82.222P
S82.043K	S82.092S	S82.112F	S82.121P	S82.131C	S82.136J	S82.145Q	S82.155D	S82.199J	S82.222Q
S82.043M	S82.099A	S82.112G	S82.121Q	S82.131D	S82.136K	S82.145R	S82.155E	S82.199K	S82.222R
S82.043N	S82.099B	S82.112H	S82.121R	S82.131E	S82.136M	S82.145S	S82.155F	S82.199M	S82.222S
S82.043P	S82.099C	S82.112J	S82.121S	S82.131F	S82.136N	S82.146A	S82.155G	S82.199N	S82.223A
S82.043Q	S82.099D	S82.112K	S82.122A	S82.131G	S82.136P	S82.146B	S82.155H	S82.199P	S82.223B
S82.043R	S82.099E	S82.112M				S82.146C	S82.155J		S82.223C

S82.223D	S82.232K	S82.241S	S82.251F	S82.256N	S82.266B	S82.302H	S82.399N	S82.423B	S82.432H
S82.223E	S82.232M	S82.242A	S82.251G	S82.256P	S82.266C	S82.302J	S82.399P	S82.423C	S82.432J
S82.223F	S82.232N	S82.242B	S82.251H	S82.256Q	S82.266D	S82.302K	S82.399Q	S82.423D	S82.432K
S82.223G	S82.232P	S82.242C	S82.251J	S82.256R	S82.266E	S82.302M	S82.399R	S82.423E	S82.432M
S82.223H	S82.232Q	S82.242D	S82.251K	S82.256S	S82.266F	S82.302N	S82.399S	S82.423F	S82.432N
S82.223J	S82.232R	S82.242E	S82.251M	S82.261A	S82.266G	S82.302P	S82.401A	S82.423G	S82.432P
S82.223K	S82.232S	S82.242F	S82.251N	S82.261B	S82.266H	S82.302Q	S82.401B	S82.423H	S82.432Q
S82.223M	S82.233A	S82.242G	S82.251P	S82.261C	S82.266J	S82.302R	S82.401C	S82.423J	S82.432R
S82.223N	S82.233B	S82.242H	S82.251Q	S82.261D	S82.266K	S82.302S	S82.401D	S82.423K	S82.432S
S82.223P	S82.233C	S82.242J	S82.251R	S82.261E	S82.266M	S82.309A	S82.401E	S82.423M	S82.433A
S82.223Q	S82.233D	S82.242K	S82.251S	S82.261F	S82.266N	S82.309B	S82.401F	S82.423N	S82.433B
S82.223R	S82.233E	S82.242M	S82.252A	S82.261G	S82.266P	S82.309C	S82.401G	S82.423P	S82.433C
S82.223S	S82.233F	S82.242N	S82.252B	S82.261H	S82.266Q	S82.309D	S82.401H	S82.423Q	S82.433D
S82.224A	S82.233G	S82.242P	S82.252C	S82.261J	S82.266R	S82.309E	S82.401J	S82.423R	S82.433E
S82.224B	S82.233H	S82.242Q	S82.252D	S82.261K	S82.266S	S82.309F	S82.401K	S82.423S	S82.433F
S82.224C	S82.233J	S82.242R	S82.252E	S82.261M	S82.291A	S82.309G	S82.401M	S82.424A	S82.433G
S82.224D	S82.233K	S82.242S	S82.252F	S82.261N	S82.291B	S82.309H	S82.401N	S82.424B	S82.433H
S82.224E	S82.233M	S82.243A	S82.252G	S82.261P	S82.291C	S82.309J	S82.401P	S82.424C	S82.433J
S82.224F	S82.233N	S82.243B	S82.252H	S82.261Q	S82.291D	S82.309K	S82.401Q	S82.424D	S82.433K
S82.224G	S82.233P	S82.243C	S82.252J	S82.261R	S82.291E	S82.309M	S82.401R	S82.424E	S82.433M
S82.224H	S82.233Q	S82.243D	S82.252K	S82.261S	S82.291F	S82.309N	S82.401S	S82.424F	S82.433N
S82.224J	S82.233R	S82.243E	S82.252M	S82.262A	S82.291G	S82.309P	S82.402A	S82.424G	S82.433P
S82.224K	S82.233S	S82.243F	S82.252N	S82.262B	S82.291H	S82.309Q	S82.402B	S82.424H	S82.433Q
S82.224M	S82.234A	S82.243G	S82.252P	S82.262C	S82.291J	S82.309R	S82.402C	S82.424J	S82.433R
S82.224N	S82.234B	S82.243H	S82.252Q	S82.262D	S82.291K	S82.309S	S82.402D	S82.424K	S82.433S
S82.224P	S82.234C	S82.243J	S82.252R	S82.262E	S82.291M	S82.311A	S82.402E	S82.424M	S82.434A
S82.224Q	S82.234D	S82.243K	S82.252S	S82.262F	S82.291N	S82.311D	S82.402F	S82.424N	S82.434B
S82.224R	S82.234E	S82.243M	S82.253A	S82.262G	S82.291P	S82.311G	S82.402G	S82.424P	S82.434C
S82.224S	S82.234F	S82.243N	S82.253B	S82.262H	S82.291Q	S82.311K	S82.402H	S82.424Q	S82.434D
S82.225A	S82.234G	S82.243P	S82.253C	S82.262J	S82.291R	S82.311P	S82.402J	S82.424R	S82.434E
S82.225B	S82.234H	S82.243Q	S82.253D	S82.262K	S82.291S	S82.311S	S82.402K	S82.424S	S82.434F
S82.225C	S82.234J	S82.243R	S82.253E	S82.262M	S82.292A	S82.312A	S82.402M	S82.425A	S82.434G
S82.225D	S82.234K	S82.243S	S82.253F	S82.262N	S82.292B	S82.312D	S82.402N	S82.425B	S82.434H
S82.225E	S82.234M	S82.244A	S82.253G	S82.262P	S82.292C	S82.312G	S82.402P	S82.425C	S82.434J
S82.225F	S82.234N	S82.244B	S82.253H	S82.262Q	S82.292D	S82.312K	S82.402Q	S82.425D	S82.434K
S82.225G	S82.234P	S82.244C	S82.253J	S82.262R	S82.292E	S82.312P	S82.402R	S82.425E	S82.434M
S82.225H	S82.234Q	S82.244D	S82.253K	S82.262S	S82.292F	S82.312S	S82.402S	S82.425F	S82.434N
S82.225J	S82.234R	S82.244E	S82.253M	S82.263A	S82.292G	S82.319A	S82.409A	S82.425G	S82.434P
S82.225K	S82.234S	S82.244F	S82.253N	S82.263B	S82.292H	S82.319D	S82.409B	S82.425H	S82.434Q
S82.225M	S82.235A	S82.244G	S82.253P	S82.263C	S82.292J	S82.319G	S82.409C	S82.425J	S82.434R
S82.225N	S82.235B	S82.244H	S82.253Q	S82.263D	S82.292K	S82.319K	S82.409D	S82.425K	S82.434S
S82.225P	S82.235C	S82.244J	S82.253R	S82.263E	S82.292M	S82.319P	S82.409E	S82.425M	S82.435A
S82.225Q	S82.235D	S82.244K	S82.253S	S82.263F	S82.292N	S82.319S	S82.409F	S82.425N	S82.435B
S82.225R	S82.235E	S82.244M	S82.254A	S82.263G	S82.292P	S82.391A	S82.409G	S82.425P	S82.435C
S82.225S	S82.235F	S82.244N	S82.254B	S82.263H	S82.292Q	S82.391B	S82.409H	S82.425Q	S82.435D
S82.226A	S82.235G	S82.244P	S82.254C	S82.263J	S82.292R	S82.391C	S82.409J	S82.425R	S82.435E
S82.226B	S82.235H	S82.244Q	S82.254D	S82.263K	S82.292S	S82.391D	S82.409K	S82.425S	S82.435F
S82.226C	S82.235J	S82.244R	S82.254E	S82.263M	S82.299A	S82.391E	S82.409M	S82.426A	S82.435G
S82.226D	S82.235K	S82.244S	S82.254F	S82.263N	S82.299B	S82.391F	S82.409N	S82.426B	S82.435H
S82.226E	S82.235M	S82.245A	S82.254G	S82.263P	S82.299C	S82.391G	S82.409P	S82.426C	S82.435J
S82.226F	S82.235N	S82.245B	S82.254H	S82.263Q	S82.299D	S82.391H	S82.409Q	S82.426D	S82.435K
S82.226G	S82.235P	S82.245C	S82.254J	S82.263R	S82.299E	S82.391J	S82.409R	S82.426E	S82.435M
S82.226H	S82.235Q	S82.245D	S82.254K	S82.263S	S82.299F	S82.391K	S82.409S	S82.426F	S82.435N
S82.226J	S82.235R	S82.245E	S82.254M	S82.264A	S82.299G	S82.391M	S82.421A	S82.426G	S82.435P
S82.226K	S82.235S	S82.245F	S82.254N	S82.264B	S82.299H	S82.391N	S82.421B	S82.426H	S82.435Q
S82.226M	S82.236A	S82.245G	S82.254P	S82.264C	S82.299J	S82.391P	S82.421C	S82.426J	S82.435R
S82.226N	S82.236B	S82.245H	S82.254Q	S82.264D	S82.299K	S82.391Q	S82.421D	S82.426K	S82.435S
S82.226P	S82.236C	S82.245J	S82.254R	S82.264E	S82.299M	S82.391R	S82.421E	S82.426M	S82.436A
S82.226Q	S82.236D	S82.245K	S82.254S	S82.264F	S82.299N	S82.391S	S82.421F	S82.426N	S82.436B
S82.226R	S82.236E	S82.245M	S82.255A	S82.264G	S82.299P	S82.392A	S82.421G	S82.426P	S82.436C
S82.226S	S82.236F	S82.245N	S82.255B	S82.264H	S82.299Q	S82.392B	S82.421H	S82.426Q	S82.436D
S82.231A	S82.236G	S82.245P	S82.255C	S82.264J	S82.299R	S82.392C	S82.421J	S82.426R	S82.436E
S82.231B	S82.236H	S82.245Q	S82.255D	S82.264K	S82.299S	S82.392D	S82.421K	S82.426S	S82.436F
S82.231C	S82.236J	S82.245R	S82.255E	S82.264M	S82.301A	S82.392E	S82.421M	S82.431A	S82.436G
S82.231D	S82.236K	S82.245S	S82.255F	S82.264N	S82.301B	S82.392F	S82.421N	S82.431B	S82.436H
S82.231E	S82.236M	S82.246A	S82.255G	S82.264P	S82.301C	S82.392G	S82.421P	S82.431C	S82.436J
S82.231F	S82.236N	S82.246B	S82.255H	S82.264Q	S82.301D	S82.392H	S82.421Q	S82.431D	S82.436K
S82.231G	S82.236P	S82.246C	S82.255J	S82.264R	S82.301E	S82.392J	S82.421R	S82.431E	S82.436M
S82.231H	S82.236Q	S82.246D	S82.255K	S82.264S	S82.301F	S82.392K	S82.421S	S82.431F	S82.436N
S82.231J	S82.236R	S82.246E	S82.255M	S82.265A	S82.301G	S82.392M	S82.422A	S82.431G	S82.436P
S82.231K	S82.236S	S82.246F	S82.255N	S82.265B	S82.301H	S82.392N	S82.422B	S82.431H	S82.436Q
S82.231M	S82.241A	S82.246G	S82.255P	S82.265C	S82.301J	S82.392P	S82.422C	S82.431J	S82.436R
S82.231N	S82.241B	S82.246H	S82.255Q	S82.265D	S82.301K	S82.392Q	S82.422D	S82.431K	S82.436S
S82.231P	S82.241C	S82.246J	S82.255R	S82.265E	S82.301M	S82.392R	S82.422E	S82.431M	S82.441A
S82.231Q	S82.241D	S82.246K	S82.255S	S82.265F	S82.301N	S82.392S	S82.422F	S82.431N	S82.441B
S82.231R	S82.241E	S82.246M	S82.256A	S82.265G	S82.301P	S82.399A	S82.422G	S82.431P	S82.441C
S82.231S	S82.241F	S82.246N	S82.256B	S82.265H	S82.301Q	S82.399B	S82.422H	S82.431Q	S82.441D
S82.232A	S82.241G	S82.246P	S82.256C	S82.265J	S82.301R	S82.399C	S82.422J	S82.431R	S82.441E
S82.232B	S82.241H	S82.246Q	S82.256D	S82.265K	S82.301S	S82.399D	S82.422K	S82.431S	S82.441F
S82.232C	S82.241J	S82.246R	S82.256E	S82.265M	S82.302A	S82.399E	S82.422M	S82.432A	S82.441G
S82.232D	S82.241K	S82.246S	S82.256F	S82.265N	S82.302B	S82.399F	S82.422N	S82.432B	S82.441H
S82.232E	S82.241M	S82.251A	S82.256G	S82.265P	S82.302C	S82.399G	S82.422P	S82.432C	S82.441J
S82.232F	S82.241N	S82.251B	S82.256H	S82.265Q	S82.302D	S82.399H	S82.422Q	S82.432D	S82.441K
S82.232G	S82.241P	S82.251C	S82.256J	S82.265R	S82.302E	S82.399J	S82.422R	S82.432E	S82.441M
S82.232H	S82.241Q	S82.251D	S82.256K	S82.265S	S82.302F	S82.399K	S82.422S	S82.432F	S82.441N
S82.232J	S82.241R	S82.251E	S82.256M	S82.266A	S82.302G	S82.399M	S82.423A	S82.432G	S82.441P

S82.441Q	S82.451D	S82.456K	S82.465S	S82.52XF	S82.61XN	S82.811D	S82.841D	S82.846K	S82.855S
S82.441R	S82.451E	S82.456M	S82.466A	S82.52XG	S82.61XP	S82.811G	S82.841E	S82.846M	S82.856A
S82.441S	S82.451F	S82.456N	S82.466B	S82.52XH	S82.61XQ	S82.811K	S82.841F	S82.846N	S82.856B
S82.442A	S82.451G	S82.456P	S82.466C	S82.52XJ	S82.61XR	S82.811P	S82.841G	S82.846P	S82.856C
S82.442B	S82.451H	S82.456Q	S82.466D	S82.52XK	S82.61XS	S82.811S	S82.841H	S82.846Q	S82.856D
S82.442C	S82.451J	S82.456R	S82.466E	S82.52XM	S82.62XA	S82.812A	S82.841J	S82.846R	S82.856E
S82.442D	S82.451K	S82.456S	S82.466F	S82.52XN	S82.62XB	S82.812D	S82.841K	S82.846S	S82.856F
S82.442E	S82.451M	S82.461A	S82.466G	S82.52XP	S82.62XC	S82.812G	S82.841M	S82.851A	S82.856G
S82.442F	S82.451N	S82.461B	S82.466H	S82.52XQ	S82.62XD	S82.812K	S82.841N	S82.851B	S82.856H
S82.442G	S82.451P	S82.461C	S82.466J	S82.52XR	S82.62XE	S82.812P	S82.841P	S82.851C	S82.856J
S82.442H	S82.451Q	S82.461D	S82.466K	S82.52XS	S82.62XF	S82.812S	S82.841Q	S82.851D	S82.856K
S82.442J	S82.451R	S82.461E	S82.466M	S82.53XA	S82.62XG	S82.819A	S82.841R	S82.851E	S82.856M
S82.442K	S82.451S	S82.461F	S82.466N	S82.53XB	S82.62XH	S82.819D	S82.841S	S82.851F	S82.856N
S82.442M	S82.452A	S82.461G	S82.466P	S82.53XC	S82.62XJ	S82.819G	S82.842A	S82.851G	S82.856P
S82.442N	S82.452B	S82.461H	S82.466Q	S82.53XD	S82.62XK	S82.819K	S82.842B	S82.851H	S82.856Q
S82.442P	S82.452C	S82.461J	S82.466R	S82.53XE	S82.62XM	S82.819P	S82.842C	S82.851J	S82.856R
S82.442Q	S82.452D	S82.461K	S82.466S	S82.53XF	S82.62XN	S82.819S	S82.842D	S82.851K	S82.856S
S82.442R	S82.452E	S82.461M	S82.491A	S82.53XG	S82.62XP	S82.821A	S82.842E	S82.851M	S82.861A
S82.442S	S82.452F	S82.461N	S82.491B	S82.53XH	S82.62XQ	S82.821D	S82.842F	S82.851N	S82.861B
S82.443A	S82.452G	S82.461P	S82.491C	S82.53XJ	S82.62XR	S82.821G	S82.842G	S82.851P	S82.861C
S82.443B	S82.452H	S82.461Q	S82.491D	S82.53XK	S82.62XS	S82.821K	S82.842H	S82.851Q	S82.861D
S82.443C	S82.452J	S82.461R	S82.491E	S82.53XM	S82.63XA	S82.821P	S82.842J	S82.851R	S82.861E
S82.443D	S82.452K	S82.461S	S82.491F	S82.53XN	S82.63XB	S82.821S	S82.842K	S82.851S	S82.861F
S82.443E	S82.452M	S82.462A	S82.491G	S82.53XP	S82.63XC	S82.822A	S82.842M	S82.852A	S82.861G
S82.443F	S82.452N	S82.462B	S82.491H	S82.53XQ	S82.63XD	S82.822D	S82.842N	S82.852B	S82.861H
S82.443G	S82.452P	S82.462C	S82.491J	S82.53XR	S82.63XE	S82.822G	S82.842P	S82.852C	S82.861J
S82.443H	S82.452Q	S82.462D	S82.491K	S82.53XS	S82.63XF	S82.822K	S82.842Q	S82.852D	S82.861K
S82.443J	S82.452R	S82.462E	S82.491M	S82.54XA	S82.63XG	S82.822P	S82.842R	S82.852E	S82.861M
S82.443K	S82.452S	S82.462F	S82.491N	S82.54XB	S82.63XH	S82.822S	S82.842S	S82.852F	S82.861N
S82.443M	S82.453A	S82.462G	S82.491P	S82.54XC	S82.63XJ	S82.829A	S82.843A	S82.852G	S82.861P
S82.443N	S82.453B	S82.462H	S82.491Q	S82.54XD	S82.63XK	S82.829D	S82.843B	S82.852H	S82.861Q
S82.443P	S82.453C	S82.462J	S82.491R	S82.54XE	S82.63XM	S82.829G	S82.843C	S82.852J	S82.861R
S82.443Q	S82.453D	S82.462K	S82.491S	S82.54XF	S82.63XN	S82.829K	S82.843D	S82.852K	S82.861S
S82.443R	S82.453E	S82.462M	S82.492A	S82.54XG	S82.63XP	S82.829P	S82.843E	S82.852M	S82.862A
S82.443S	S82.453F	S82.462N	S82.492B	S82.54XH	S82.63XQ	S82.829S	S82.843F	S82.852N	S82.862B
S82.444A	S82.453G	S82.462P	S82.492C	S82.54XJ	S82.63XR	S82.831A	S82.843G	S82.852P	S82.862C
S82.444B	S82.453H	S82.462Q	S82.492D	S82.54XK	S82.63XS	S82.831B	S82.843H	S82.852Q	S82.862D
S82.444C	S82.453J	S82.462R	S82.492E	S82.54XM	S82.64XA	S82.831C	S82.843J	S82.852R	S82.862E
S82.444D	S82.453K	S82.462S	S82.492F	S82.54XN	S82.64XB	S82.831D	S82.843K	S82.852S	S82.862F
S82.444E	S82.453M	S82.463A	S82.492G	S82.54XP	S82.64XC	S82.831E	S82.843M	S82.853A	S82.862G
S82.444F	S82.453N	S82.463B	S82.492H	S82.54XQ	S82.64XD	S82.831F	S82.843N	S82.853B	S82.862H
S82.444G	S82.453P	S82.463C	S82.492J	S82.54XR	S82.64XE	S82.831G	S82.843P	S82.853C	S82.862J
S82.444H	S82.453Q	S82.463D	S82.492K	S82.54XS	S82.64XF	S82.831H	S82.843Q	S82.853D	S82.862K
S82.444J	S82.453R	S82.463E	S82.492M	S82.55XA	S82.64XG	S82.831J	S82.843R	S82.853E	S82.862M
S82.444K	S82.453S	S82.463F	S82.492N	S82.55XB	S82.64XH	S82.831K	S82.843S	S82.853F	S82.862N
S82.444M	S82.454A	S82.463G	S82.492P	S82.55XC	S82.64XJ	S82.831M	S82.844A	S82.853G	S82.862P
S82.444N	S82.454B	S82.463H	S82.492Q	S82.55XD	S82.64XK	S82.831N	S82.844B	S82.853H	S82.862Q
S82.444P	S82.454C	S82.463J	S82.492R	S82.55XE	S82.64XM	S82.831P	S82.844C	S82.853J	S82.862R
S82.444Q	S82.454D	S82.463K	S82.492S	S82.55XF	S82.64XN	S82.831Q	S82.844D	S82.853K	S82.862S
S82.444R	S82.454E	S82.463M	S82.499A	S82.55XG	S82.64XP	S82.831R	S82.844E	S82.853M	S82.863A
S82.444S	S82.454F	S82.463N	S82.499B	S82.55XH	S82.64XQ	S82.831S	S82.844F	S82.853N	S82.863B
S82.445A	S82.454G	S82.463P	S82.499C	S82.55XJ	S82.64XR	S82.832A	S82.844G	S82.853P	S82.863C
S82.445B	S82.454H	S82.463Q	S82.499D	S82.55XK	S82.64XS	S82.832B	S82.844H	S82.853Q	S82.863D
S82.445C	S82.454J	S82.463R	S82.499E	S82.55XM	S82.65XA	S82.832C	S82.844J	S82.853R	S82.863E
S82.445D	S82.454K	S82.463S	S82.499F	S82.55XN	S82.65XB	S82.832D	S82.844K	S82.853S	S82.863F
S82.445E	S82.454M	S82.464A	S82.499G	S82.55XP	S82.65XC	S82.832E	S82.844M	S82.854A	S82.863G
S82.445F	S82.454N	S82.464B	S82.499H	S82.55XQ	S82.65XD	S82.832F	S82.844N	S82.854B	S82.863H
S82.445G	S82.454P	S82.464C	S82.499J	S82.55XR	S82.65XE	S82.832G	S82.844P	S82.854C	S82.863J
S82.445H	S82.454Q	S82.464D	S82.499K	S82.55XS	S82.65XF	S82.832H	S82.844Q	S82.854D	S82.863K
S82.445J	S82.454R	S82.464E	S82.499M	S82.56XA	S82.65XG	S82.832J	S82.844R	S82.854E	S82.863M
S82.445K	S82.454S	S82.464F	S82.499N	S82.56XB	S82.65XH	S82.832K	S82.844S	S82.854F	S82.863N
S82.445M	S82.455A	S82.464G	S82.499P	S82.56XC	S82.65XJ	S82.832M	S82.845A	S82.854G	S82.863P
S82.445N	S82.455B	S82.464H	S82.499Q	S82.56XD	S82.65XK	S82.832N	S82.845B	S82.854H	S82.863Q
S82.445P	S82.455C	S82.464J	S82.499R	S82.56XE	S82.65XM	S82.832P	S82.845C	S82.854J	S82.863R
S82.445Q	S82.455D	S82.464K	S82.499S	S82.56XF	S82.65XN	S82.832Q	S82.845D	S82.854K	S82.863S
S82.445R	S82.455E	S82.464M	S82.51XA	S82.56XG	S82.65XP	S82.832R	S82.845E	S82.854M	S82.864A
S82.445S	S82.455F	S82.464N	S82.51XB	S82.56XH	S82.65XQ	S82.832S	S82.845F	S82.854N	S82.864B
S82.446A	S82.455G	S82.464P	S82.51XC	S82.56XJ	S82.65XR	S82.839A	S82.845G	S82.854P	S82.864C
S82.446B	S82.455H	S82.464Q	S82.51XD	S82.56XK	S82.65XS	S82.839B	S82.845H	S82.854Q	S82.864D
S82.446C	S82.455J	S82.464R	S82.51XE	S82.56XM	S82.66XA	S82.839C	S82.845J	S82.854R	S82.864E
S82.446D	S82.455K	S82.464S	S82.51XF	S82.56XN	S82.66XB	S82.839D	S82.845K	S82.854S	S82.864F
S82.446E	S82.455M	S82.465A	S82.51XG	S82.56XP	S82.66XC	S82.839E	S82.845M	S82.855A	S82.864G
S82.446F	S82.455N	S82.465B	S82.51XH	S82.56XQ	S82.66XD	S82.839F	S82.845N	S82.855B	S82.864H
S82.446G	S82.455P	S82.465C	S82.51XJ	S82.56XR	S82.66XE	S82.839G	S82.845P	S82.855C	S82.864J
S82.446H	S82.455Q	S82.465D	S82.51XK	S82.56XS	S82.66XF	S82.839H	S82.845Q	S82.855D	S82.864K
S82.446J	S82.455R	S82.465E	S82.51XM	S82.61XA	S82.66XG	S82.839J	S82.845R	S82.855E	S82.864M
S82.446K	S82.455S	S82.465F	S82.51XN	S82.61XB	S82.66XH	S82.839K	S82.845S	S82.855F	S82.864N
S82.446M	S82.456A	S82.465G	S82.51XP	S82.61XC	S82.66XJ	S82.839M	S82.846A	S82.855G	S82.864P
S82.446N	S82.456B	S82.465H	S82.51XQ	S82.61XD	S82.66XK	S82.839N	S82.846B	S82.855H	S82.864Q
S82.446P	S82.456C	S82.465J	S82.51XR	S82.61XE	S82.66XM	S82.839P	S82.846C	S82.855J	S82.864R
S82.446Q	S82.456D	S82.465K	S82.51XS	S82.61XF	S82.66XN	S82.839Q	S82.846D	S82.855K	S82.864S
S82.446R	S82.456E	S82.465M	S82.52XA	S82.61XG	S82.66XP	S82.839R	S82.846E	S82.855M	S82.865A
S82.446S	S82.456F	S82.465N	S82.52XB	S82.61XH	S82.66XQ	S82.839S	S82.846F	S82.855N	S82.865B
S82.451A	S82.456G	S82.465P	S82.52XC	S82.61XJ	S82.66XR	S82.841A	S82.846G	S82.855P	S82.865C
S82.451B	S82.456H	S82.465Q	S82.52XD	S82.61XK	S82.66XS	S82.841B	S82.846H	S82.855Q	S82.865D
S82.451C	S82.456J	S82.465R	S82.52XE	S82.61XM	S82.811A	S82.841C	S82.846J	S82.855R	S82.865E

Diagnosis Codes by MDC

S82.865F	S82.874N	S82.90XB	S83.102S	S83.209S	S83.521S	S88.121S	S89.041S	S89.131D	S89.219K
S82.865G	S82.874P	S82.90XC	S83.103A	S83.211A	S83.522A	S88.122S	S89.042A	S89.131G	S89.219P
S82.865H	S82.874Q	S82.90XD	S83.103S	S83.211S	S83.522S	S88.129S	S89.042D	S89.131K	S89.219S
S82.865J	S82.874R	S82.90XE	S83.104A	S83.212A	S83.529A	S88.911S	S89.042G	S89.131P	S89.221A
S82.865K	S82.874S	S82.90XF	S83.104S	S83.212S	S83.529S	S88.912S	S89.042K	S89.131S	S89.221D
S82.865M	S82.875A	S82.90XG	S83.105A	S83.219A	S83.60XA	S88.919S	S89.042P	S89.132A	S89.221G
S82.865N	S82.875B	S82.90XH	S83.105S	S83.219S	S83.60XS	S88.921S	S89.042S	S89.132D	S89.221K
S82.865P	S82.875C	S82.90XJ	S83.106A	S83.221A	S83.61XA	S88.922S	S89.049A	S89.132K	S89.221P
S82.865Q	S82.875D	S82.90XK	S83.106S	S83.221S	S83.61XS	S88.929S	S89.049D	S89.132P	S89.221S
S82.865R	S82.875E	S82.90XM	S83.111A	S83.222A	S83.62XA	S89.001A	S89.049G	S89.132S	S89.222A
S82.865S	S82.875F	S82.90XN	S83.111S	S83.222S	S83.62XS	S89.001D	S89.049K	S89.139A	S89.222D
S82.866A	S82.875G	S82.90XP	S83.112A	S83.229A	S83.8X1A	S89.001G	S89.049P	S89.139D	S89.222G
S82.866B	S82.875H	S82.90XQ	S83.112S	S83.229S	S83.8X1S	S89.001K	S89.049S	S89.139G	S89.222K
S82.866C	S82.875J	S82.90XR	S83.113A	S83.231A	S83.8X2A	S89.001P	S89.091A	S89.139K	S89.222P
S82.866D	S82.875K	S82.90XS	S83.113S	S83.231S	S83.8X2S	S89.001S	S89.091D	S89.139P	S89.222S
S82.866E	S82.875M	S82.91XA	S83.114A	S83.232A	S83.8X9A	S89.002A	S89.091G	S89.139S	S89.229A
S82.866F	S82.875N	S82.91XB	S83.114S	S83.232S	S83.8X9S	S89.002D	S89.091K	S89.141A	S89.229D
S82.866G	S82.875P	S82.91XC	S83.115A	S83.239A	S83.90XA	S89.002G	S89.091P	S89.141D	S89.229G
S82.866H	S82.875Q	S82.91XD	S83.115S	S83.239S	S83.90XS	S89.002K	S89.091S	S89.141G	S89.229K
S82.866J	S82.875R	S82.91XE	S83.116A	S83.241A	S83.91XA	S89.002P	S89.092A	S89.141K	S89.229P
S82.866K	S82.875S	S82.91XF	S83.116S	S83.241S	S83.91XS	S89.002S	S89.092D	S89.141P	S89.229S
S82.866M	S82.876A	S82.91XG	S83.121A	S83.242A	S83.92XA	S89.009A	S89.092G	S89.141S	S89.291A
S82.866N	S82.876B	S82.91XH	S83.121S	S83.242S	S83.92XS	S89.009D	S89.092K	S89.142A	S89.291D
S82.866P	S82.876C	S82.91XJ	S83.122A	S83.249A	S86.011A	S89.009G	S89.092P	S89.142D	S89.291G
S82.866Q	S82.876D	S82.91XK	S83.122S	S83.249S	S86.011S	S89.009K	S89.092S	S89.142G	S89.291K
S82.866R	S82.876E	S82.91XM	S83.123A	S83.251A	S86.012A	S89.009P	S89.099A	S89.142K	S89.291P
S82.866S	S82.876F	S82.91XN	S83.123S	S83.251S	S86.012S	S89.009S	S89.099D	S89.142P	S89.291S
S82.871A	S82.876G	S82.91XP	S83.124A	S83.252A	S86.019A	S89.011A	S89.099G	S89.142S	S89.292A
S82.871B	S82.876H	S82.91XQ	S83.124S	S83.252S	S86.019S	S89.011D	S89.099K	S89.149A	S89.292D
S82.871C	S82.876J	S82.91XR	S83.125A	S83.259A	S86.021A	S89.011G	S89.099P	S89.149D	S89.292G
S82.871D	S82.876K	S82.91XS	S83.125S	S83.259S	S86.022A	S89.011K	S89.099S	S89.149G	S89.292K
S82.871E	S82.876M	S82.92XA	S83.126A	S83.261A	S86.029A	S89.011P	S89.101A	S89.149K	S89.292P
S82.871F	S82.876N	S82.92XB	S83.126S	S83.261S	S86.111A	S89.011S	S89.101D	S89.149P	S89.292S
S82.871G	S82.876P	S82.92XC	S83.131A	S83.262A	S86.111S	S89.012A	S89.101G	S89.149S	S89.299A
S82.871H	S82.876Q	S82.92XD	S83.131S	S83.262S	S86.112A	S89.012D	S89.101K	S89.191A	S89.299D
S82.871J	S82.876R	S82.92XE	S83.132A	S83.269A	S86.112S	S89.012G	S89.101P	S89.191D	S89.299G
S82.871K	S82.876S	S82.92XF	S83.132S	S83.269S	S86.119A	S89.012K	S89.101S	S89.191G	S89.299K
S82.871M	S82.891A	S82.92XG	S83.133A	S83.271A	S86.119S	S89.012P	S89.102A	S89.191K	S89.299P
S82.871N	S82.891B	S82.92XH	S83.133S	S83.271S	S86.121A	S89.012S	S89.102D	S89.191P	S89.299S
S82.871P	S82.891C	S82.92XJ	S83.134A	S83.272A	S86.122A	S89.019A	S89.102G	S89.191S	S89.301A
S82.871Q	S82.891D	S82.92XK	S83.134S	S83.272S	S86.129A	S89.019D	S89.102K	S89.192A	S89.301D
S82.871R	S82.891E	S82.92XM	S83.135A	S83.279A	S86.211A	S89.019G	S89.102P	S89.192D	S89.301G
S82.871S	S82.891F	S82.92XN	S83.135S	S83.279S	S86.211S	S89.019K	S89.102S	S89.192G	S89.301K
S82.872A	S82.891G	S82.92XP	S83.136A	S83.281A	S86.212A	S89.019P	S89.109A	S89.192K	S89.301P
S82.872B	S82.891H	S82.92XQ	S83.136S	S83.281S	S86.212S	S89.019S	S89.109D	S89.192P	S89.301S
S82.872C	S82.891J	S82.92XR	S83.141A	S83.282A	S86.219A	S89.021A	S89.109G	S89.192S	S89.302A
S82.872D	S82.891K	S82.92XS	S83.141S	S83.282S	S86.219S	S89.021D	S89.109K	S89.199A	S89.302D
S82.872E	S82.891M	S83.001A	S83.142A	S83.289A	S86.221A	S89.021G	S89.109P	S89.199D	S89.302G
S82.872F	S82.891N	S83.001S	S83.142S	S83.289S	S86.222A	S89.021K	S89.109S	S89.199G	S89.302K
S82.872G	S82.891P	S83.002A	S83.143A	S83.30XA	S86.229A	S89.021P	S89.111A	S89.199K	S89.302P
S82.872H	S82.891Q	S83.002S	S83.143S	S83.30XS	S86.311A	S89.021S	S89.111D	S89.199P	S89.302S
S82.872J	S82.891R	S83.003A	S83.144A	S83.31XA	S86.311S	S89.022A	S89.111G	S89.199S	S89.309A
S82.872K	S82.891S	S83.003S	S83.144S	S83.31XS	S86.312A	S89.022D	S89.111K	S89.201A	S89.309D
S82.872M	S82.892A	S83.004A	S83.145A	S83.32XA	S86.312S	S89.022G	S89.111P	S89.201D	S89.309G
S82.872N	S82.892B	S83.004S	S83.145S	S83.32XS	S86.319A	S89.022K	S89.111S	S89.201G	S89.309K
S82.872P	S82.892C	S83.005A	S83.146A	S83.401A	S86.319S	S89.022P	S89.112A	S89.201K	S89.309P
S82.872Q	S82.892D	S83.005S	S83.146S	S83.401S	S86.321A	S89.022S	S89.112D	S89.201P	S89.309S
S82.872R	S82.892E	S83.006A	S83.191A	S83.402A	S86.322A	S89.029A	S89.112G	S89.201S	S89.311A
S82.872S	S82.892F	S83.006S	S83.191S	S83.402S	S86.329A	S89.029D	S89.112K	S89.202A	S89.311D
S82.873A	S82.892G	S83.011A	S83.192A	S83.409A	S86.811A	S89.029G	S89.112P	S89.202D	S89.311G
S82.873B	S82.892H	S83.011S	S83.192S	S83.409S	S86.811S	S89.029K	S89.112S	S89.202G	S89.311K
S82.873C	S82.892J	S83.012A	S83.193A	S83.411A	S86.812A	S89.029P	S89.119A	S89.202K	S89.311P
S82.873D	S82.892K	S83.012S	S83.193S	S83.411S	S86.812S	S89.029S	S89.119D	S89.202P	S89.311S
S82.873E	S82.892M	S83.013A	S83.194A	S83.412A	S86.819A	S89.031A	S89.119G	S89.202S	S89.312A
S82.873F	S82.892N	S83.013S	S83.194S	S83.412S	S86.819S	S89.031D	S89.119K	S89.209A	S89.312D
S82.873G	S82.892P	S83.014A	S83.195A	S83.419A	S86.821A	S89.031G	S89.119P	S89.209D	S89.312G
S82.873H	S82.892Q	S83.014S	S83.195S	S83.419S	S86.822A	S89.031K	S89.119S	S89.209G	S89.312K
S82.873J	S82.892R	S83.015A	S83.196A	S83.421A	S86.829A	S89.031P	S89.121A	S89.209K	S89.312P
S82.873K	S82.892S	S83.015S	S83.196S	S83.421S	S86.911A	S89.031S	S89.121D	S89.209P	S89.312S
S82.873M	S82.899A	S83.016A	S83.200A	S83.422A	S86.911S	S89.032A	S89.121G	S89.209S	S89.319A
S82.873N	S82.899B	S83.016S	S83.200S	S83.422S	S86.912A	S89.032D	S89.121K	S89.211A	S89.319D
S82.873P	S82.899C	S83.091A	S83.201A	S83.429A	S86.912S	S89.032G	S89.121P	S89.211D	S89.319G
S82.873Q	S82.899D	S83.091S	S83.201S	S83.429S	S86.919A	S89.032K	S89.121S	S89.211G	S89.319K
S82.873R	S82.899E	S83.092A	S83.202A	S83.501A	S86.919S	S89.032P	S89.122A	S89.211K	S89.319P
S82.873S	S82.899F	S83.092S	S83.202S	S83.501S	S86.921A	S89.032S	S89.122D	S89.211P	S89.319S
S82.874A	S82.899G	S83.093A	S83.203A	S83.502A	S86.922A	S89.039A	S89.122G	S89.211S	S89.321A
S82.874B	S82.899H	S83.093S	S83.203S	S83.502S	S86.929A	S89.039D	S89.122K	S89.212A	S89.321D
S82.874C	S82.899J	S83.094A	S83.204A	S83.509A	S88.011S	S89.039G	S89.122P	S89.212D	S89.321G
S82.874D	S82.899K	S83.094S	S83.204S	S83.509S	S88.012S	S89.039K	S89.122S	S89.212G	S89.321K
S82.874E	S82.899M	S83.095A	S83.205A	S83.511A	S88.019S	S89.039P	S89.129A	S89.212K	S89.321P
S82.874F	S82.899N	S83.095S	S83.205S	S83.511S	S88.021S	S89.039S	S89.129D	S89.212P	S89.321S
S82.874G	S82.899P	S83.096A	S83.206A	S83.512A	S88.022S	S89.041A	S89.129G	S89.212S	S89.322A
S82.874H	S82.899Q	S83.096S	S83.206S	S83.512S	S88.029S	S89.041D	S89.129K	S89.219A	S89.322D
S82.874J	S82.899R	S83.101A	S83.207A	S83.519A	S88.111S	S89.041G	S89.129P	S89.219D	S89.322G
S82.874K	S82.899S	S83.101S	S83.207S	S83.519S	S88.112S	S89.041K	S89.129S	S89.219G	S89.322K
S82.874M	S82.90XA	S83.102A	S83.209A	S83.521A	S88.119S	S89.041P	S89.131A		S89.322P

S89.322S	S92.016P	S92.041A	S92.061D	S92.114K	S92.134S	S92.155B	S92.215G	S92.235P	S92.256A
S89.329A	S92.016S	S92.041B	S92.061G	S92.114P	S92.135A	S92.155D	S92.215K	S92.235S	S92.256B
S89.329D	S92.021A	S92.041D	S92.061K	S92.114S	S92.135B	S92.155G	S92.215P	S92.236A	S92.256D
S89.329G	S92.021B	S92.041G	S92.061P	S92.115A	S92.135D	S92.155K	S92.215S	S92.236B	S92.256G
S89.329K	S92.021D	S92.041K	S92.061S	S92.115B	S92.135G	S92.155P	S92.216A	S92.236G	S92.256K
S89.329P	S92.021G	S92.041P	S92.062A	S92.115D	S92.135K	S92.155S	S92.216B	S92.236K	S92.256P
S89.329S	S92.021K	S92.041S	S92.062B	S92.115G	S92.135P	S92.156A	S92.216D	S92.236P	S92.256S
S89.391A	S92.021P	S92.042A	S92.062D	S92.115K	S92.135S	S92.156B	S92.216G	S92.236S	S92.301A
S89.391D	S92.021S	S92.042B	S92.062G	S92.115P	S92.136A	S92.156D	S92.216K	S92.241A	S92.301B
S89.391G	S92.022A	S92.042D	S92.062K	S92.115S	S92.136D	S92.156G	S92.216P	S92.241B	S92.301D
S89.391K	S92.022B	S92.042G	S92.062P	S92.116A	S92.136G	S92.156K	S92.216S	S92.241D	S92.301G
S89.391P	S92.022D	S92.042K	S92.062S	S92.116B	S92.136K	S92.156P	S92.221A	S92.241G	S92.301K
S89.391S	S92.022G	S92.042P	S92.063A	S92.116D	S92.136P	S92.156S	S92.221B	S92.241K	S92.301P
S89.392A	S92.022K	S92.042S	S92.063B	S92.116G	S92.136S	S92.191A	S92.221D	S92.241P	S92.301S
S89.392D	S92.022P	S92.043A	S92.063D	S92.116K	S92.141A	S92.191B	S92.221G	S92.241S	S92.302A
S89.392G	S92.022S	S92.043B	S92.063G	S92.116P	S92.141B	S92.191D	S92.221K	S92.242A	S92.302B
S89.392K	S92.023A	S92.043D	S92.063K	S92.116S	S92.141D	S92.191G	S92.221P	S92.242B	S92.302D
S89.392P	S92.023B	S92.043G	S92.063P	S92.121A	S92.141G	S92.191K	S92.221S	S92.242D	S92.302G
S89.392S	S92.023D	S92.043K	S92.063S	S92.121B	S92.141K	S92.191P	S92.222A	S92.242G	S92.302K
S89.399A	S92.023K	S92.043P	S92.064A	S92.121D	S92.141P	S92.191S	S92.222B	S92.242K	S92.302P
S89.399D	S92.023P	S92.043S	S92.064B	S92.121G	S92.141S	S92.192A	S92.222D	S92.242P	S92.302S
S89.399G	S92.023S	S92.044A	S92.064D	S92.121K	S92.142A	S92.192B	S92.222G	S92.242S	S92.309A
S89.399K	S92.024A	S92.044B	S92.064G	S92.121P	S92.142B	S92.192D	S92.222K	S92.243A	S92.309B
S89.399P	S92.024B	S92.044D	S92.064K	S92.121S	S92.142D	S92.192G	S92.222P	S92.243B	S92.309D
S89.399S	S92.024D	S92.044G	S92.064P	S92.122A	S92.142G	S92.192K	S92.222S	S92.243D	S92.309G
S92.001A	S92.024G	S92.044K	S92.064S	S92.122B	S92.142K	S92.192P	S92.223A	S92.243G	S92.309K
S92.001B	S92.024K	S92.044P	S92.065A	S92.122D	S92.142P	S92.192S	S92.223B	S92.243K	S92.309P
S92.001D	S92.024P	S92.044S	S92.065B	S92.122G	S92.142S	S92.199A	S92.223D	S92.243P	S92.309S
S92.001G	S92.024S	S92.045A	S92.065D	S92.122K	S92.143A	S92.199B	S92.223G	S92.243S	S92.311A
S92.001K	S92.025A	S92.045B	S92.065G	S92.122P	S92.143B	S92.199D	S92.223K	S92.244A	S92.311B
S92.001P	S92.025B	S92.045D	S92.065K	S92.122S	S92.143D	S92.199G	S92.223P	S92.244B	S92.311D
S92.001S	S92.025D	S92.045G	S92.065P	S92.123A	S92.143G	S92.199K	S92.223S	S92.244D	S92.311G
S92.002A	S92.025G	S92.045K	S92.065S	S92.123B	S92.143K	S92.199P	S92.224A	S92.244G	S92.311K
S92.002B	S92.025K	S92.045P	S92.066A	S92.123G	S92.143P	S92.199S	S92.224B	S92.244K	S92.311P
S92.002D	S92.025P	S92.045S	S92.066B	S92.123K	S92.143S	S92.201A	S92.224D	S92.244P	S92.311S
S92.002G	S92.025S	S92.046A	S92.066D	S92.123P	S92.144A	S92.201B	S92.224G	S92.244S	S92.312A
S92.002K	S92.026A	S92.046B	S92.066G	S92.123S	S92.144B	S92.201D	S92.224K	S92.245A	S92.312B
S92.002P	S92.026B	S92.046D	S92.066P	S92.124A	S92.144D	S92.201G	S92.224P	S92.245D	S92.312D
S92.002S	S92.026D	S92.046G	S92.066S	S92.124B	S92.144G	S92.201K	S92.224S	S92.245G	S92.312G
S92.009A	S92.026G	S92.046K	S92.101A	S92.124D	S92.144K	S92.201P	S92.225A	S92.245K	S92.312K
S92.009B	S92.026K	S92.046P	S92.101B	S92.124G	S92.144P	S92.201S	S92.225B	S92.245P	S92.312P
S92.009D	S92.026P	S92.046S	S92.101D	S92.124K	S92.144S	S92.202A	S92.225D	S92.245S	S92.312S
S92.009G	S92.026S	S92.051A	S92.101G	S92.124P	S92.145A	S92.202B	S92.225G	S92.246A	S92.313A
S92.009K	S92.031A	S92.051B	S92.101K	S92.124S	S92.145B	S92.202D	S92.225K	S92.246B	S92.313B
S92.009P	S92.031B	S92.051D	S92.101P	S92.125A	S92.145D	S92.202G	S92.225P	S92.246D	S92.313D
S92.009S	S92.031D	S92.051G	S92.101S	S92.125B	S92.145G	S92.202K	S92.225S	S92.246K	S92.313G
S92.011A	S92.031G	S92.051K	S92.102A	S92.125D	S92.145K	S92.202P	S92.226A	S92.246P	S92.313K
S92.011B	S92.031K	S92.051P	S92.102B	S92.125G	S92.145P	S92.202S	S92.226B	S92.246S	S92.313P
S92.011D	S92.031P	S92.051S	S92.102D	S92.125K	S92.145S	S92.209A	S92.226D	S92.251A	S92.313S
S92.011G	S92.031S	S92.052A	S92.102G	S92.125P	S92.146A	S92.209B	S92.226G	S92.251B	S92.314A
S92.011K	S92.032A	S92.052B	S92.102K	S92.125S	S92.146B	S92.209D	S92.226K	S92.251D	S92.314B
S92.011P	S92.032B	S92.052D	S92.102P	S92.126A	S92.146D	S92.209G	S92.226P	S92.251G	S92.314D
S92.011S	S92.032D	S92.052G	S92.102S	S92.126B	S92.146G	S92.209K	S92.226S	S92.251K	S92.314G
S92.012A	S92.032G	S92.052K	S92.109A	S92.126D	S92.146K	S92.209P	S92.231A	S92.251P	S92.314K
S92.012B	S92.032K	S92.052P	S92.109B	S92.126G	S92.146P	S92.209S	S92.231B	S92.251S	S92.314P
S92.012D	S92.032P	S92.052S	S92.109G	S92.126K	S92.146S	S92.211A	S92.231D	S92.252A	S92.314S
S92.012G	S92.032S	S92.053A	S92.109K	S92.126P	S92.151A	S92.211B	S92.231G	S92.252B	S92.315A
S92.012K	S92.033A	S92.053B	S92.109P	S92.126S	S92.151B	S92.211D	S92.231K	S92.252D	S92.315B
S92.012P	S92.033B	S92.053D	S92.109S	S92.131A	S92.151D	S92.211G	S92.231P	S92.252K	S92.315D
S92.012S	S92.033D	S92.053G	S92.111A	S92.131B	S92.151G	S92.211K	S92.231S	S92.252P	S92.315G
S92.013A	S92.033G	S92.053K	S92.111B	S92.131D	S92.151K	S92.211P	S92.232A	S92.252S	S92.315K
S92.013B	S92.033K	S92.053P	S92.111D	S92.131G	S92.151P	S92.211S	S92.232B	S92.253A	S92.315P
S92.013D	S92.033P	S92.053S	S92.111G	S92.131K	S92.151S	S92.212A	S92.232D	S92.253B	S92.315S
S92.013G	S92.033S	S92.054A	S92.111P	S92.131P	S92.152A	S92.212B	S92.232G	S92.253D	S92.316A
S92.013K	S92.034A	S92.054B	S92.111S	S92.131S	S92.152B	S92.212D	S92.232K	S92.253G	S92.316B
S92.013P	S92.034B	S92.054D	S92.112A	S92.132A	S92.152D	S92.212G	S92.232P	S92.253K	S92.316D
S92.013S	S92.034D	S92.054G	S92.112B	S92.132B	S92.152G	S92.212K	S92.232S	S92.253S	S92.316G
S92.014A	S92.034G	S92.054K	S92.112D	S92.132D	S92.152K	S92.212P	S92.233A	S92.254A	S92.316K
S92.014B	S92.034K	S92.054P	S92.112G	S92.132G	S92.152P	S92.212S	S92.233B	S92.254B	S92.316P
S92.014D	S92.034P	S92.054S	S92.112K	S92.132K	S92.152S	S92.213A	S92.233D	S92.254D	S92.316S
S92.014G	S92.034S	S92.055A	S92.112P	S92.132P	S92.153A	S92.213B	S92.233G	S92.254G	S92.321A
S92.014K	S92.035A	S92.055B	S92.112S	S92.132S	S92.153B	S92.213D	S92.233K	S92.254K	S92.321B
S92.014P	S92.035B	S92.055D	S92.113A	S92.133A	S92.153D	S92.213G	S92.233P	S92.254P	S92.321D
S92.014S	S92.035D	S92.055G	S92.113B	S92.133B	S92.153G	S92.213K	S92.233S	S92.254S	S92.321G
S92.015A	S92.035G	S92.055K	S92.113D	S92.133D	S92.153K	S92.213P	S92.234A	S92.255A	S92.321K
S92.015B	S92.035K	S92.055P	S92.113G	S92.133G	S92.153P	S92.213S	S92.234B	S92.255B	S92.321P
S92.015D	S92.035P	S92.055S	S92.113K	S92.133K	S92.153S	S92.214A	S92.234D	S92.255D	S92.321S
S92.015G	S92.035S	S92.056A	S92.113P	S92.133P	S92.154A	S92.214B	S92.234G	S92.255K	S92.322A
S92.015K	S92.036A	S92.056B	S92.113S	S92.133S	S92.154B	S92.214D	S92.234K	S92.255P	S92.322B
S92.015P	S92.036B	S92.056D	S92.114A	S92.134A	S92.154D	S92.214G	S92.234P	S92.255S	S92.322G
S92.015S	S92.036D	S92.056G	S92.114B	S92.134B	S92.154G	S92.214K	S92.234S		S92.322K
S92.016A	S92.036G	S92.056K	S92.114D	S92.134D	S92.154K	S92.214P	S92.235A		S92.322P
S92.016B	S92.036K	S92.056P	S92.114G	S92.134G	S92.154P	S92.214S	S92.235B		S92.322S
S92.016D	S92.036P	S92.056S	S92.061A	S92.134K	S92.154S	S92.215A	S92.235D		S92.323A
S92.016G	S92.036S	S92.061A	S92.061B	S92.134P	S92.155A	S92.215B	S92.235G		S92.323B
S92.016K		S92.061B				S92.215D	S92.235K		

Diagnosis Codes by MDC

Diagnosis Codes by MDC

S92.323D	S92.343K	S92.403S	S92.424B	S92.511G	S92.531P	S92.902A	S93.129S	S93.412S	S93.699S
S92.323G	S92.343P	S92.404A	S92.424D	S92.511K	S92.531S	S92.902B	S93.131A	S93.419A	S96.011S
S92.323K	S92.343S	S92.404B	S92.424G	S92.511P	S92.532A	S92.902D	S93.131S	S93.419S	S96.011A
S92.323P	S92.344A	S92.404D	S92.424K	S92.511S	S92.532B	S92.902G	S93.132A	S93.421A	S96.012A
S92.323S	S92.344B	S92.404G	S92.424P	S92.512A	S92.532D	S92.902K	S93.132S	S93.421S	S96.012S
S92.324A	S92.344D	S92.404K	S92.424S	S92.512B	S92.532G	S92.902P	S93.133A	S93.422A	S96.019A
S92.324B	S92.344G	S92.404P	S92.425A	S92.512D	S92.532K	S92.902S	S93.133S	S93.422S	S96.019S
S92.324D	S92.344K	S92.404S	S92.425B	S92.512G	S92.532P	S92.909A	S93.134A	S93.429A	S96.021A
S92.324G	S92.344P	S92.405A	S92.425D	S92.512K	S92.532S	S92.909B	S93.134S	S93.429S	S96.022A
S92.324K	S92.344S	S92.405B	S92.425G	S92.512P	S92.533A	S92.909D	S93.135A	S93.431A	S96.029A
S92.324P	S92.345A	S92.405D	S92.425K	S92.512S	S92.533D	S92.909G	S93.135S	S93.431S	S96.111A
S92.324S	S92.345B	S92.405G	S92.425P	S92.513A	S92.533G	S92.909K	S93.136A	S93.432A	S96.111S
S92.325A	S92.345D	S92.405K	S92.425S	S92.513B	S92.533K	S92.909P	S93.136S	S93.432S	S96.112A
S92.325B	S92.345G	S92.405P	S92.426A	S92.513D	S92.533P	S92.909S	S93.139A	S93.439A	S96.112S
S92.325D	S92.345K	S92.405S	S92.426B	S92.513G	S92.533S	S92.911A	S93.139S	S93.439S	S96.119A
S92.325G	S92.345P	S92.406A	S92.426G	S92.513K	S92.534A	S92.911B	S93.141A	S93.491A	S96.119S
S92.325K	S92.345S	S92.406B	S92.426K	S92.513P	S92.534B	S92.911D	S93.141S	S93.491S	S96.121A
S92.325P	S92.346A	S92.406D	S92.426P	S92.513S	S92.534D	S92.911G	S93.142A	S93.492A	S96.122A
S92.325S	S92.346B	S92.406G	S92.426S	S92.514A	S92.534G	S92.911K	S93.142S	S93.492S	S96.129A
S92.326A	S92.346D	S92.406K	S92.491A	S92.514B	S92.534K	S92.911P	S93.143A	S93.499A	S96.211A
S92.326B	S92.346G	S92.406P	S92.491B	S92.514D	S92.534P	S92.911S	S93.143S	S93.499S	S96.211S
S92.326D	S92.346K	S92.406S	S92.491D	S92.514G	S92.534S	S92.912A	S93.144A	S93.501A	S96.212A
S92.326G	S92.346P	S92.411A	S92.491G	S92.514K	S92.535A	S92.912B	S93.144S	S93.501S	S96.212S
S92.326K	S92.346S	S92.411B	S92.491K	S92.514P	S92.535D	S92.912D	S93.145A	S93.502A	S96.219A
S92.326P	S92.351A	S92.411D	S92.491P	S92.514S	S92.535G	S92.912G	S93.145S	S93.502S	S96.219S
S92.326S	S92.351B	S92.411G	S92.491S	S92.515A	S92.535K	S92.912K	S93.146A	S93.503A	S96.221A
S92.331A	S92.351D	S92.411K	S92.492A	S92.515B	S92.535P	S92.912P	S93.146S	S93.503S	S96.222A
S92.331B	S92.351G	S92.411P	S92.492B	S92.515D	S92.535S	S92.912S	S93.149A	S93.504A	S96.229A
S92.331D	S92.351K	S92.411S	S92.492D	S92.515G	S92.536A	S92.919A	S93.149S	S93.504S	S96.811A
S92.331G	S92.351P	S92.412A	S92.492G	S92.515K	S92.536B	S92.919B	S93.301A	S93.505A	S96.811S
S92.331K	S92.351S	S92.412B	S92.492K	S92.515P	S92.536D	S92.919D	S93.301S	S93.505S	S96.812A
S92.331P	S92.352A	S92.412D	S92.492P	S92.515S	S92.536G	S92.919G	S93.302A	S93.506A	S96.812S
S92.331S	S92.352B	S92.412G	S92.492S	S92.516A	S92.536K	S92.919K	S93.302S	S93.506S	S96.819A
S92.332A	S92.352G	S92.412K	S92.499A	S92.516B	S92.536P	S92.919P	S93.303A	S93.509A	S96.819S
S92.332B	S92.352K	S92.412P	S92.499B	S92.516D	S92.536S	S92.919S	S93.303S	S93.509S	S96.821A
S92.332D	S92.352P	S92.412S	S92.499D	S92.516G	S92.591A	S93.01XA	S93.304A	S93.511A	S96.822A
S92.332G	S92.352S	S92.413A	S92.499G	S92.516K	S92.591B	S93.01XS	S93.304S	S93.511S	S96.829A
S92.332K	S92.353A	S92.413B	S92.499K	S92.516P	S92.591D	S93.02XA	S93.305A	S93.512A	S96.911A
S92.332P	S92.353B	S92.413D	S92.499P	S92.516S	S92.591G	S93.02XS	S93.305S	S93.512S	S96.911S
S92.332S	S92.353D	S92.413G	S92.499S	S92.521A	S92.591K	S93.03XA	S93.306A	S93.513A	S96.912A
S92.333A	S92.353G	S92.413K	S92.501A	S92.521B	S92.591S	S93.03XS	S93.306S	S93.513S	S96.912S
S92.333B	S92.353K	S92.413P	S92.501D	S92.521D	S92.591S	S93.04XA	S93.311A	S93.514A	S96.919A
S92.333D	S92.353P	S92.413S	S92.501G	S92.521G	S92.591P	S93.04XS	S93.311S	S93.514S	S96.919S
S92.333G	S92.353S	S92.414A	S92.501K	S92.521K	S92.591S	S93.05XA	S93.312A	S93.515A	S96.921A
S92.333K	S92.354A	S92.414B	S92.501P	S92.521P	S92.592A	S93.05XS	S93.312S	S93.515S	S96.922A
S92.333P	S92.354B	S92.414D	S92.501S	S92.521S	S92.592B	S93.06XA	S93.313A	S93.516A	S96.929A
S92.333S	S92.354D	S92.414G	S92.514A	S92.522A	S92.592D	S93.06XS	S93.313S	S93.516S	S98.011S
S92.334A	S92.354G	S92.414K	S92.514P	S92.522D	S92.592G	S93.101A	S93.314A	S93.519A	S98.012S
S92.334B	S92.354K	S92.414P	S92.502A	S92.522G	S92.592K	S93.101S	S93.314S	S93.519S	S98.019S
S92.334D	S92.354P	S92.414S	S92.502B	S92.522K	S92.592P	S93.102A	S93.315A	S93.521A	S98.021S
S92.334G	S92.354S	S92.415A	S92.502D	S92.522P	S92.592S	S93.102S	S93.315S	S93.521S	S98.022S
S92.334K	S92.355A	S92.415B	S92.502G	S92.522S	S92.599A	S93.103A	S93.316A	S93.522A	S98.029S
S92.334P	S92.355B	S92.415D	S92.502K	S92.523A	S92.599D	S93.103S	S93.316S	S93.522S	S98.111S
S92.334S	S92.355D	S92.415G	S92.502P	S92.523B	S92.599G	S93.104A	S93.321A	S93.523A	S98.112S
S92.335A	S92.355G	S92.415K	S92.502S	S92.523D	S92.599K	S93.104S	S93.321S	S93.523S	S98.119S
S92.335B	S92.355K	S92.415P	S92.503A	S92.523G	S92.599P	S93.105A	S93.322A	S93.524A	S98.121S
S92.335D	S92.355P	S92.415S	S92.503B	S92.523K	S92.599S	S93.105S	S93.322S	S93.524S	S98.122S
S92.335G	S92.355S	S92.416A	S92.503D	S92.523P	S92.599S	S93.106A	S93.323A	S93.525A	S98.129S
S92.335K	S92.356A	S92.416B	S92.503G	S92.523S	S92.811A	S93.106S	S93.323S	S93.525S	S98.131S
S92.335P	S92.356B	S92.416D	S92.503K	S92.524A	S92.811B	S93.111A	S93.324A	S93.526A	S98.132S
S92.335S	S92.356D	S92.416G	S92.503P	S92.524B	S92.811D	S93.111S	S93.324S	S93.526S	S98.139S
S92.336A	S92.356G	S92.416K	S92.503S	S92.524D	S92.811G	S93.112A	S93.325A	S93.529A	S98.141S
S92.336B	S92.356K	S92.416S	S92.504A	S92.524G	S92.811K	S93.113A	S93.325S	S93.529S	S98.142S
S92.336D	S92.356P	S92.421A	S92.504B	S92.524K	S92.811P	S93.113S	S93.326A	S93.601A	S98.149S
S92.336G	S92.356S	S92.421B	S92.504D	S92.524P	S92.811S	S93.114A	S93.326S	S93.601S	S98.211S
S92.336K	S92.401A	S92.421D	S92.504K	S92.524S	S92.812A	S93.114S	S93.331A	S93.602A	S98.212S
S92.336P	S92.401B	S92.421G	S92.504P	S92.525A	S92.812B	S93.115A	S93.331S	S93.602S	S98.219S
S92.336S	S92.401D	S92.421K	S92.504S	S92.525B	S92.812D	S93.115S	S93.332A	S93.609A	S98.221S
S92.341A	S92.401G	S92.421P	S92.505A	S92.525D	S92.812G	S93.116A	S93.332S	S93.609S	S98.222S
S92.341B	S92.401K	S92.421S	S92.505B	S92.525G	S92.812K	S93.116S	S93.333A	S93.611A	S98.229S
S92.341D	S92.401P	S92.422A	S92.505D	S92.525K	S92.812P	S93.119A	S93.333S	S93.611S	S98.311S
S92.341G	S92.401S	S92.422B	S92.505G	S92.525P	S92.812S	S93.119S	S93.334A	S93.612A	S98.312S
S92.341K	S92.402A	S92.422D	S92.505K	S92.525S	S92.819A	S93.121A	S93.334S	S93.612S	S98.319S
S92.341P	S92.402B	S92.422G	S92.505P	S92.526A	S92.819B	S93.121S	S93.335A	S93.619A	S98.321S
S92.341S	S92.402D	S92.422K	S92.505S	S92.526B	S92.819D	S93.122A	S93.335S	S93.619S	S98.322S
S92.342A	S92.402G	S92.422P	S92.506A	S92.526D	S92.819G	S93.122S	S93.336A	S93.621A	S98.329S
S92.342B	S92.402K	S92.422S	S92.506B	S92.526G	S92.819K	S93.123A	S93.336S	S93.621S	S98.911S
S92.342D	S92.402P	S92.423A	S92.506D	S92.526K	S92.819P	S93.123S	S93.401A	S93.622A	S98.912S
S92.342G	S92.402S	S92.423B	S92.506G	S92.526P	S92.819S	S93.124A	S93.401S	S93.622S	S98.919S
S92.342K	S92.403A	S92.423D	S92.506K	S92.526S	S92.901A	S93.124S	S93.402A	S93.629A	S98.921S
S92.342P	S92.403B	S92.423G	S92.506P	S92.531A	S92.901B	S93.125A	S93.402S	S93.629S	S98.922S
S92.342S	S92.403D	S92.423K	S92.506S	S92.531B	S92.901D	S93.125S	S93.409A	S93.691A	S98.929S
S92.343A	S92.403DC	S92.423P	S92.511A	S92.531D	S92.901G	S93.126A	S93.409S	S93.691S	T79.6XXA
S92.343B	S92.403G	S92.423S	S92.511B	S92.531G	S92.901K	S93.126S	S93.411A	S93.692A	T84.010A
S92.343D	S92.403K	S92.424A	S92.511D	S92.531K	S92.901P	S93.129A	S93.411S	S93.692S	T84.011A
S92.343G	S92.403P	S92.424A	S92.511D	S92.531K	S92.901S	S93.129A	S93.412A	S93.699A	T84.012A

T84.013A	T84.060A	T84.120A	T84.218A	T84.50XA	T84.63XA	T87.33	Z44.021	Z52.21	Z96.661
T84.018A	T84.061A	T84.121A	T84.220A	T84.51XA	T84.69XA	T87.34	Z44.022	Z52.29	Z96.662
T84.019A	T84.062A	T84.122A	T84.223A	T84.52XA	T84.7XXA	T87.40	Z44.029	Z94.6	Z96.669
T84.020A	T84.063A	T84.123A	T84.226A	T84.53XA	T84.81XA	T87.41	Z44.101	Z96.60	Z96.691
T84.021A	T84.068A	T84.124A	T84.228A	T84.54XA	T84.82XA	T87.42	Z44.102	Z96.611	Z96.692
T84.022A	T84.069A	T84.125A	T84.290A	T84.59XA	T84.83XA	T87.43	Z44.109	Z96.612	Z96.693
T84.023A	T84.090A	T84.126A	T84.293A	T84.60XA	T84.84XA	T87.44	Z44.111	Z96.619	Z96.698
T84.028A	T84.091A	T84.127A	T84.296A	T84.610A	T84.85XA	T87.50	Z44.112	Z96.621	Z96.7
T84.029A	T84.092A	T84.129A	T84.298A	T84.611A	T84.86XA	T87.51	Z44.119	Z96.622	Z97.10
T84.030A	T84.093A	T84.190A	T84.310A	T84.612A	T84.89XA	T87.52	Z44.121	Z96.629	Z97.11
T84.031A	T84.098A	T84.191A	T84.318A	T84.613A	T84.9XXA	T87.53	Z44.122	Z96.631	Z97.12
T84.032A	T84.099A	T84.192A	T84.320A	T84.614A	T87.0X1	T87.54	Z44.129	Z96.632	Z97.13
T84.033A	T84.110A	T84.193A	T84.328A	T84.615A	T87.0X2	T87.81	Z47.1	Z96.639	Z97.14
T84.038A	T84.111A	T84.194A	T84.390A	T84.619A	T87.0X9	T87.89	Z47.2	Z96.641	Z97.15
T84.039A	T84.112A	T84.195A	T84.398A	T84.620A	T87.1X1	T87.9	Z47.31	Z96.642	Z97.16
T84.050A	T84.113A	T84.196A	T84.410A	T84.621A	T87.1X2	Z44.001	Z47.32	Z96.643	
T84.051A	T84.114A	T84.197A	T84.418A	T84.622A	T87.1X9	Z44.002	Z47.33	Z96.649	
T84.052A	T84.115A	T84.199A	T84.420A	T84.623A	T87.2	Z44.009	Z47.81	Z96.651	
T84.053A	T84.116A	T84.210A	T84.428A	T84.624A	T87.30	Z44.011	Z47.82	Z96.652	
T84.058A	T84.117A	T84.213A	T84.490A	T84.625A	T87.31	Z44.012	Z47.89	Z96.653	
T84.059A	T84.119A	T84.216A	T84.498A	T84.629A	T87.32	Z44.019	Z52.20	Z96.659	

MDC 09 Diseases And Disorders Of The Skin, Subcutaneous Tissue And Breast

A06.7	B86	C44.391	C4A.21	C50.819	D17.21	L01.01	L02.529	L03.321	L22
A18.4	B87.0	C44.399	C4A.22	C50.821	D17.22	L01.02	L02.531	L03.322	L23.0
A22.0	B87.1	C44.40	C4A.30	C50.822	D17.23	L01.03	L02.532	L03.323	L23.1
A31.1	B87.2	C44.41	C4A.31	C50.829	D17.24	L01.09	L02.539	L03.324	L23.2
A36.3	B87.3	C44.42	C4A.39	C50.911	D17.30	L01.1	L02.611	L03.325	L23.3
A42.2	B87.4	C44.49	C4A.4	C50.912	D17.39	L02.01	L02.612	L03.326	L23.4
A43.1	B87.81	C44.500	C4A.51	C50.919	D17.79	L02.02	L02.619	L03.327	L23.5
A46	B87.82	C44.501	C4A.52	C50.921	D17.9	L02.03	L02.621	L03.329	L23.6
A51.31	B87.89	C44.509	C4A.59	C50.922	D18.01	L02.11	L02.622	L03.811	L23.7
A51.32	B87.9	C44.510	C4A.60	C50.929	D22.0	L02.12	L02.629	L03.818	L23.81
A51.39	B88.0	C44.511	C4A.61	C79.2	D22.20	L02.13	L02.631	L03.891	L23.89
A63.0	B88.1	C44.519	C4A.62	C79.81	D22.21	L02.211	L02.632	L03.898	L23.9
A66.0	B88.2	C44.520	C4A.70	D03.0	D22.22	L02.212	L02.639	L03.90	L24.0
A66.1	B88.3	C44.521	C4A.71	D03.20	D22.30	L02.213	L02.811	L03.91	L24.1
A66.2	B88.8	C44.529	C4A.72	D03.21	D22.39	L02.214	L02.818	L05.01	L24.2
A66.3	B88.9	C44.590	C4A.8	D03.22	D22.4	L02.215	L02.821	L05.02	L24.3
A66.4	C43.0	C44.591	C4A.9	D03.30	D22.5	L02.216	L02.828	L05.91	L24.4
A67.0	C43.20	C44.599	C50.011	D03.39	D22.60	L02.219	L02.831	L05.92	L24.5
A67.1	C43.21	C44.601	C50.012	D03.4	D22.61	L02.221	L02.838	L08.0	L24.6
A67.3	C43.22	C44.602	C50.019	D03.51	D22.62	L02.222	L02.91	L08.1	L24.7
B00.0	C43.30	C44.609	C50.021	D03.52	D22.70	L02.223	L02.92	L08.81	L24.81
B00.9	C43.31	C44.611	C50.022	D03.59	D22.71	L02.224	L02.93	L08.82	L24.89
B02.9	C43.39	C44.612	C50.029	D03.60	D22.72	L02.225	L03.011	L08.89	L24.9
B07.0	C43.4	C44.619	C50.111	D03.61	D22.9	L02.226	L03.012	L08.9	L25.0
B07.8	C43.51	C44.621	C50.112	D03.62	D23.0	L02.229	L03.019	L10.0	L25.1
B07.9	C43.52	C44.622	C50.119	D03.70	D23.20	L02.231	L03.021	L10.1	L25.2
B08.02	C43.59	C44.629	C50.121	D03.71	D23.21	L02.232	L03.022	L10.2	L25.3
B08.03	C43.60	C44.691	C50.122	D03.72	D23.22	L02.233	L03.029	L10.3	L25.4
B08.1	C43.61	C44.692	C50.129	D03.8	D23.30	L02.234	L03.031	L10.4	L25.5
B10.81	C43.62	C44.699	C50.211	D03.9	D23.39	L02.235	L03.032	L10.5	L25.8
B10.82	C43.70	C44.701	C50.212	D04.0	D23.4	L02.236	L03.039	L10.81	L25.9
B10.89	C43.71	C44.702	C50.219	D04.20	D23.5	L02.239	L03.041	L10.89	L26
B35.0	C43.72	C44.709	C50.221	D04.21	D23.60	L02.31	L03.042	L10.9	L27.0
B35.1	C43.8	C44.711	C50.222	D04.22	D23.61	L02.32	L03.049	L11.0	L27.1
B35.2	C43.9	C44.712	C50.229	D04.30	D23.62	L02.33	L03.111	L11.1	L27.2
B35.3	C44.00	C44.719	C50.311	D04.39	D23.70	L02.411	L03.112	L11.8	L27.8
B35.4	C44.01	C44.721	C50.312	D04.4	D23.71	L02.412	L03.113	L11.9	L27.9
B35.5	C44.02	C44.722	C50.319	D04.5	D23.72	L02.413	L03.114	L12.0	L28.0
B35.6	C44.09	C44.729	C50.321	D04.60	D23.9	L02.414	L03.115	L12.1	L28.1
B35.8	C44.201	C44.791	C50.322	D04.61	D24.1	L02.415	L03.116	L12.2	L28.2
B35.9	C44.202	C44.792	C50.329	D04.62	D24.2	L02.416	L03.119	L12.30	L29.0
B36.0	C44.209	C44.799	C50.411	D04.70	D24.9	L02.419	L03.121	L12.31	L29.8
B36.1	C44.211	C44.80	C50.412	D04.71	D48.5	L02.421	L03.122	L12.35	L29.9
B36.2	C44.212	C44.81	C50.419	D04.72	D48.60	L02.422	L03.123	L12.8	L30.0
B36.3	C44.219	C44.82	C50.421	D04.8	D48.61	L02.423	L03.124	L12.9	L30.1
B36.8	C44.221	C44.89	C50.422	D04.9	D48.62	L02.424	L03.125	L13.0	L30.2
B36.9	C44.222	C44.90	C50.429	D05.00	D49.3	L02.425	L03.126	L13.1	L30.3
B37.2	C44.229	C44.91	C50.511	D05.01	E83.2	L02.426	L03.129	L13.8	L30.4
B38.3	C44.291	C44.92	C50.512	D05.02	H02.60	L02.429	L03.211	L13.9	L30.5
B38.81	C44.292	C44.99	C50.519	D05.10	H02.61	L02.431	L03.212	L14	L30.8
B47.9	C44.299	C46.0	C50.521	D05.11	H02.62	L02.432	L03.213	L20.0	L30.9
B55.1	C44.300	C46.1	C50.522	D05.12	H02.63	L02.433	L03.221	L20.81	L40.0
B55.2	C44.301	C46.7	C50.529	D05.80	H02.64	L02.434	L03.222	L20.82	L40.1
B65.3	C44.309	C46.9	C50.611	D05.81	H02.65	L02.435	L03.311	L20.83	L40.2
B78.1	C44.310	C4A.0	C50.612	D05.82	H02.66	L02.436	L03.312	L20.84	L40.4
B83.4	C44.311	C4A.10	C50.619	D05.90	I78.1	L02.439	L03.313	L20.89	L40.8
B85.0	C44.319	C4A.111	C50.621	D05.91	I89.0	L02.511	L03.314	L20.9	L40.9
B85.1	C44.320	C4A.112	C50.622	D05.92	I89.1	L02.512	L03.315	L21.0	L41.0
B85.2	C44.321	C4A.121	C50.629	D17.0	I97.2	L02.519	L03.316	L21.1	L41.1
B85.3	C44.329	C4A.122	C50.811	D17.1	L00	L02.521	L03.317	L21.8	L41.2
B85.4	C44.390	C4A.20	C50.812	D17.20	L01.00	L02.522	L03.319	L21.9	L41.3

Diagnosis Codes by MDC

L41.4	L63.0	L84	L89.212	L89.814	L97.215	L97.803	N60.01	Q84.0	S00.37XS
L41.5	L63.1	L85.0	L89.213	L89.816	L97.216	L97.804	N60.02	Q84.1	S00.401A
L41.8	L63.2	L85.1	L89.214	L89.819	L97.218	L97.805	N60.09	Q84.2	S00.401S
L41.9	L63.8	L85.2	L89.216	L89.890	L97.219	L97.806	N60.11	Q84.3	S00.402A
L42	L63.9	L85.3	L89.219	L89.891	L97.221	L97.808	N60.12	Q84.4	S00.402S
L43.0	L64.0	L85.8	L89.220	L89.892	L97.222	L97.809	N60.19	Q84.5	S00.409A
L43.1	L64.8	L85.9	L89.221	L89.893	L97.223	L97.811	N60.21	Q84.6	S00.409S
L43.2	L64.9	L86	L89.222	L89.894	L97.224	L97.812	N60.22	Q84.8	S00.411A
L43.3	L65.0	L87.0	L89.223	L89.896	L97.225	L97.813	N60.29	Q84.9	S00.411S
L43.8	L65.1	L87.1	L89.224	L89.899	L97.226	L97.814	N60.31	R21	S00.412A
L43.9	L65.2	L87.2	L89.226	L89.90	L97.228	L97.815	N60.32	R22.0	S00.412S
L44.0	L65.8	L87.8	L89.229	L89.91	L97.229	L97.816	N60.39	R22.1	S00.419A
L44.1	L65.9	L87.9	L89.300	L89.92	L97.301	L97.818	N60.41	R22.2	S00.419S
L44.2	L66.0	L88	L89.301	L89.93	L97.302	L97.819	N60.42	R22.30	S00.421A
L44.3	L66.1	L89.000	L89.302	L89.94	L97.303	L97.821	N60.49	R22.31	S00.421S
L44.8	L66.2	L89.001	L89.303	L89.95	L97.304	L97.822	N60.81	R22.32	S00.422A
L44.9	L66.3	L89.002	L89.304	L89.96	L97.305	L97.823	N60.82	R22.33	S00.422S
L45	L66.4	L89.003	L89.306	L90.0	L97.306	L97.824	N60.89	R22.40	S00.429A
L49.0	L66.8	L89.004	L89.309	L90.1	L97.308	L97.825	N60.91	R22.41	S00.429S
L49.1	L66.9	L89.006	L89.310	L90.2	L97.309	L97.826	N60.92	R22.42	S00.431A
L49.2	L67.0	L89.009	L89.311	L90.3	L97.311	L97.828	N60.99	R22.43	S00.431S
L49.3	L67.1	L89.010	L89.312	L90.4	L97.312	L97.829	N61.0	R22.9	S00.432A
L49.4	L67.8	L89.011	L89.313	L90.5	L97.313	L97.901	N61.1	R23.4	S00.432S
L49.5	L67.9	L89.012	L89.314	L90.6	L97.314	L97.902	N62	R23.8	S00.439A
L49.6	L68.0	L89.013	L89.316	L90.8	L97.315	L97.903	N63.0	R23.9	S00.439S
L49.7	L68.1	L89.014	L89.319	L90.9	L97.316	L97.904	N63.10	R61	S00.441A
L49.8	L68.2	L89.016	L89.320	L91.0	L97.318	L97.905	N63.11	R90.0	S00.441S
L49.9	L68.3	L89.019	L89.321	L91.8	L97.319	L97.906	N63.12	R92.0	S00.442A
L50.0	L68.8	L89.020	L89.322	L91.9	L97.321	L97.908	N63.13	R92.1	S00.442S
L50.1	L68.9	L89.021	L89.323	L92.0	L97.322	L97.909	N63.14	R92.2	S00.449A
L50.2	L70.0	L89.022	L89.324	L92.1	L97.323	L97.911	N63.15	R92.8	S00.449S
L50.3	L70.1	L89.023	L89.326	L92.2	L97.324	L97.912	N63.20	S00.00XA	S00.451A
L50.4	L70.2	L89.024	L89.329	L92.3	L97.325	L97.913	N63.21	S00.00XS	S00.451S
L50.5	L70.3	L89.026	L89.40	L92.8	L97.326	L97.914	N63.22	S00.01XA	S00.452A
L50.6	L70.4	L89.029	L89.41	L92.9	L97.328	L97.915	N63.23	S00.01XS	S00.452S
L50.8	L70.5	L89.100	L89.42	L93.0	L97.329	L97.916	N63.24	S00.02XA	S00.459A
L50.9	L70.8	L89.101	L89.43	L93.1	L97.401	L97.918	N63.25	S00.02XS	S00.459S
L51.0	L70.9	L89.102	L89.44	L93.2	L97.402	L97.919	N63.31	S00.03XA	S00.461A
L51.1	L71.0	L89.103	L89.45	L94.0	L97.403	L97.921	N63.32	S00.03XS	S00.461S
L51.2	L71.1	L89.104	L89.46	L94.1	L97.404	L97.922	N63.41	S00.04XA	S00.462A
L51.3	L71.8	L89.106	L89.500	L94.2	L97.405	L97.923	N63.42	S00.04XS	S00.462S
L51.8	L71.9	L89.109	L89.501	L94.3	L97.406	L97.924	N64.0	S00.05XA	S00.469A
L51.9	L72.0	L89.110	L89.502	L94.4	L97.408	L97.925	N64.1	S00.05XS	S00.469S
L52	L72.11	L89.111	L89.504	L94.5	L97.409	L97.926	N64.2	S00.06XA	S00.471A
L53.0	L72.12	L89.112	L89.506	L94.8	L97.411	L97.928	N64.3	S00.06XS	S00.471S
L53.1	L72.2	L89.113	L89.509	L94.9	L97.412	L97.929	N64.4	S00.07XA	S00.472A
L53.2	L72.3	L89.114	L89.510	L95.0	L97.413	L98.0	N64.51	S00.07XS	S00.472S
L53.3	L72.8	L89.116	L89.511	L95.1	L97.414	L98.1	N64.52	S00.10XS	S00.479A
L53.8	L72.9	L89.119	L89.512	L95.8	L97.415	L98.2	N64.53	S00.11XS	S00.479S
L53.9	L73.0	L89.120	L89.513	L95.9	L97.416	L98.3	N64.59	S00.12XS	S00.501A
L54	L73.1	L89.121	L89.514	L97.101	L97.418	L98.411	N64.81	S00.201S	S00.501S
L55.0	L73.2	L89.122	L89.516	L97.102	L97.419	L98.412	N64.82	S00.202S	S00.502A
L55.1	L73.8	L89.123	L89.519	L97.103	L97.421	L98.413	N64.89	S00.209S	S00.502S
L55.2	L73.9	L89.124	L89.520	L97.104	L97.422	L98.414	N64.9	S00.211S	S00.511A
L55.9	L74.0	L89.126	L89.521	L97.105	L97.423	L98.415	N65.0	S00.212S	S00.511S
L56.0	L74.1	L89.129	L89.522	L97.106	L97.424	L98.416	N65.1	S00.219S	S00.512A
L56.1	L74.2	L89.130	L89.523	L97.108	L97.425	L98.418	N80.6	S00.221S	S00.512S
L56.2	L74.3	L89.131	L89.524	L97.109	L97.426	L98.419	Q18.3	S00.222S	S00.521A
L56.3	L74.4	L89.132	L89.526	L97.111	L97.428	L98.421	Q18.9	S00.229S	S00.521S
L56.4	L74.510	L89.133	L89.529	L97.112	L97.429	L98.422	Q80.0	S00.241S	S00.522A
L56.5	L74.511	L89.134	L89.600	L97.113	L97.501	L98.423	Q80.1	S00.242S	S00.522S
L56.8	L74.512	L89.136	L89.601	L97.114	L97.502	L98.424	Q80.2	S00.249S	S00.531A
L56.9	L74.513	L89.139	L89.602	L97.115	L97.503	L98.426	Q80.3	S00.251S	S00.531S
L57.0	L74.519	L89.140	L89.603	L97.116	L97.504	L98.428	Q80.4	S00.252S	S00.532A
L57.1	L74.52	L89.141	L89.604	L97.118	L97.505	L98.429	Q80.8	S00.259S	S00.532S
L57.2	L74.8	L89.142	L89.606	L97.119	L97.506	L98.491	Q80.9	S00.261S	S00.541A
L57.3	L74.9	L89.143	L89.609	L97.121	L97.508	L98.492	Q81.0	S00.262S	S00.541S
L57.4	L75.0	L89.144	L89.610	L97.122	L97.509	L98.493	Q81.1	S00.269S	S00.542A
L57.5	L75.1	L89.146	L89.611	L97.123	L97.511	L98.494	Q81.2	S00.271S	S00.542S
L57.8	L75.2	L89.149	L89.612	L97.124	L97.512	L98.495	Q81.8	S00.272S	S00.551A
L57.9	L75.8	L89.150	L89.613	L97.125	L97.513	L98.496	Q81.9	S00.279S	S00.551S
L58.0	L75.9	L89.151	L89.614	L97.126	L97.514	L98.498	Q82.0	S00.30XA	S00.552A
L58.1	L80	L89.152	L89.616	L97.128	L97.515	L98.499	Q82.1	S00.30XS	S00.552S
L58.9	L81.0	L89.153	L89.619	L97.129	L97.516	L98.5	Q82.2	S00.31XA	S00.561A
L59.0	L81.1	L89.154	L89.620	L97.201	L97.518	L98.6	Q82.3	S00.31XS	S00.561S
L59.8	L81.2	L89.156	L89.621	L97.202	L97.519	L98.7	Q82.4	S00.32XA	S00.562A
L59.9	L81.3	L89.159	L89.622	L97.203	L97.521	L98.8	Q82.5	S00.32XS	S00.562S
L60.0	L81.4	L89.200	L89.623	L97.204	L97.522	L98.9	Q82.6	S00.33XA	S00.571A
L60.1	L81.5	L89.201	L89.624	L97.205	L97.523	L99	Q82.8	S00.33XS	S00.571S
L60.2	L81.6	L89.202	L89.626	L97.206	L97.524	M35.6	Q82.9	S00.34XA	S00.572A
L60.3	L81.7	L89.203	L89.629	L97.208	L97.525	M54.00	Q83.0	S00.34XS	S00.572S
L60.4	L81.8	L89.204	L89.810	L97.209	L97.526	M54.01	Q83.1	S00.35XA	S00.80XA
L60.5	L81.9	L89.206	L89.811	L97.211	L97.528	M54.02	Q83.2	S00.35XS	S00.80XS
L60.8	L82.0	L89.209	L89.812	L97.212	L97.529	M79.3	Q83.3	S00.36XA	S00.81XA
L60.9	L82.1	L89.210	L89.813	L97.213	L97.801	M79.4	Q83.8	S00.36XS	S00.81XS
L62	L83	L89.211		L97.214	L97.802		Q83.9	S00.37XA	S00.82XA

S00.82XS	S01.409S	S05.60XS	S11.029S	S20.161A	S20.441A	S21.121S	S21.449S	S30.844A	S31.050S
S00.83XA	S01.411A	S05.61XS	S11.031S	S20.161S	S20.441S	S21.122S	S21.451S	S30.844S	S31.051S
S00.83XS	S01.411S	S05.62XS	S11.032S	S20.162A	S20.442A	S21.129S	S21.452S	S30.845A	S31.100A
S00.84XA	S01.412A	S07.0XXS	S11.033S	S20.162S	S20.442S	S21.131A	S21.459S	S30.845S	S31.100S
S00.84XS	S01.412S	S07.1XXS	S11.034S	S20.169A	S20.449A	S21.132A	S21.90XA	S30.846A	S31.101A
S00.85XA	S01.419A	S07.8XXS	S11.035S	S20.169S	S20.449S	S21.132S	S21.90XS	S30.846S	S31.101S
S00.85XS	S01.419S	S07.9XXS	S11.039S	S20.171A	S20.451A	S21.139A	S21.91XA	S30.850A	S31.102A
S00.86XA	S01.421A	S08.0XXA	S11.10XS	S20.171S	S20.451S	S21.139S	S21.91XS	S30.850S	S31.102S
S00.86XS	S01.421S	S08.0XXS	S11.11XS	S20.172A	S20.452A	S21.141A	S21.92XA	S30.851A	S31.103A
S00.87XA	S01.422A	S08.111S	S11.12XS	S20.172S	S20.452S	S21.142S	S21.93XA	S30.851S	S31.103S
S00.87XS	S01.422S	S08.112S	S11.13XS	S20.179A	S20.459A	S21.149S	S21.93XS	S30.852A	S31.104A
S00.90XA	S01.429A	S08.119S	S11.14XS	S20.179S	S20.459S	S21.151A	S21.94XS	S30.852S	S31.104S
S00.90XS	S01.429S	S08.121S	S11.15XS	S20.20XA	S20.461A	S21.151S	S21.95XA	S30.853A	S31.105A
S00.91XA	S01.431A	S08.122S	S11.20XS	S20.20XS	S20.461S	S21.152A	S21.95XS	S30.853S	S31.105S
S00.91XS	S01.431S	S08.129S	S11.21XS	S20.211A	S20.462A	S21.152S	S28.0XXS	S30.854A	S31.109A
S00.92XA	S01.432A	S08.811S	S11.22XS	S20.211S	S20.462S	S21.159A	S28.1XXA	S30.854S	S31.109S
S00.92XS	S01.432S	S08.812S	S11.23XS	S20.212A	S20.469A	S21.159S	S28.1XXS	S30.855A	S31.110A
S00.93XA	S01.439A	S08.89XA	S11.24XS	S20.212S	S20.469S	S21.201A	S28.211A	S30.855S	S31.110S
S00.93XS	S01.439S	S08.89XS	S11.25XS	S20.219A	S20.471A	S21.201S	S28.211S	S30.856A	S31.111A
S00.94XA	S01.441A	S09.12XA	S11.80XA	S20.219S	S20.471S	S21.202A	S28.212A	S30.856S	S31.111S
S00.94XS	S01.441S	S09.12XS	S11.80XS	S20.221A	S20.472A	S21.202S	S28.212S	S30.857A	S31.112A
S00.95XA	S01.442A	S09.21XS	S11.81XA	S20.221S	S20.472S	S21.209A	S28.219A	S30.857S	S31.112S
S00.95XS	S01.442S	S09.22XS	S11.81XS	S20.222A	S20.479A	S21.209S	S28.219S	S30.860A	S31.113A
S00.96XA	S01.449A	S09.311S	S11.82XA	S20.222S	S20.479S	S21.211A	S28.221A	S30.860S	S31.113S
S00.96XS	S01.449S	S09.312S	S11.82XS	S20.229A	S20.90XA	S21.211S	S28.221S	S30.861A	S31.114A
S00.97XA	S01.451A	S09.313S	S11.83XA	S20.229S	S20.90XS	S21.212A	S28.222A	S30.861S	S31.114S
S00.97XS	S01.451S	S09.319S	S11.83XS	S20.301A	S20.91XA	S21.212S	S28.222S	S30.862A	S31.115A
S01.00XA	S01.452A	S10.0XXA	S11.84XA	S20.301S	S20.91XS	S21.219A	S28.229A	S30.862S	S31.115S
S01.00XS	S01.452S	S10.0XXS	S11.84XS	S20.302A	S20.92XA	S21.219S	S28.229S	S30.863A	S31.119A
S01.01XA	S01.459A	S10.10XA	S11.85XA	S20.302S	S20.92XS	S21.221A	S29.021A	S30.863S	S31.119S
S01.01XS	S01.459S	S10.10XS	S11.85XS	S20.309A	S20.94XA	S21.221S	S29.021S	S30.864A	S31.120S
S01.02XA	S01.501S	S10.11XA	S11.89XA	S20.309S	S20.94XS	S21.222A	S29.022S	S30.864S	S31.121S
S01.02XS	S01.502S	S10.11XS	S11.89XS	S20.311A	S20.95XA	S21.222S	S29.029A	S30.865A	S31.122S
S01.03XA	S01.511S	S10.12XA	S11.90XA	S20.311S	S20.95XS	S21.229A	S29.029S	S30.865S	S31.123S
S01.03XS	S01.512S	S10.12XS	S11.90XS	S20.312A	S20.96XA	S21.229S	S30.0XXA	S30.866A	S31.124S
S01.04XA	S01.521S	S10.14XA	S11.91XA	S20.312S	S20.96XS	S21.231A	S30.0XXS	S30.866S	S31.125S
S01.04XS	S01.522S	S10.14XS	S11.91XS	S20.319A	S20.97XA	S21.231S	S30.1XXA	S30.867A	S31.129S
S01.05XA	S01.531S	S10.15XA	S11.92XA	S20.319S	S20.97XS	S21.232A	S30.1XXS	S30.867S	S31.130A
S01.05XS	S01.532S	S10.15XS	S11.92XS	S20.321A	S21.001A	S21.232S	S30.201S	S30.870A	S31.130S
S01.101S	S01.541S	S10.16XA	S11.93XA	S20.321S	S21.001S	S21.239A	S30.202S	S30.870S	S31.131A
S01.102S	S01.542S	S10.16XS	S11.93XS	S20.322A	S21.002A	S21.239S	S30.21XS	S30.871A	S31.131S
S01.109S	S01.551S	S10.17XA	S11.94XA	S20.322S	S21.002S	S21.241A	S30.22XS	S30.871S	S31.132A
S01.111S	S01.552S	S10.17XS	S11.94XS	S20.329A	S21.009A	S21.241S	S30.23XS	S30.872A	S31.132S
S01.112S	S01.80XA	S10.80XA	S11.95XA	S20.329S	S21.009S	S21.242A	S30.3XXA	S30.872S	S31.133A
S01.119S	S01.80XS	S10.80XS	S11.95XS	S20.341A	S21.011A	S21.242S	S30.3XXS	S30.873A	S31.133S
S01.121S	S01.81XA	S10.81XA	S16.2XXA	S20.341S	S21.011S	S21.249A	S30.810A	S30.873S	S31.134A
S01.122S	S01.81XS	S10.81XS	S16.2XXS	S20.342A	S21.012A	S21.249S	S30.810S	S30.874A	S31.134S
S01.129S	S01.82XA	S10.82XA	S17.0XXS	S20.342S	S21.012S	S21.251A	S30.811A	S30.874S	S31.135A
S01.131S	S01.82XS	S10.82XS	S17.8XXS	S20.349A	S21.019A	S21.251S	S30.811S	S30.875A	S31.135S
S01.132S	S01.83XA	S10.83XA	S17.9XXS	S20.349S	S21.019S	S21.252A	S30.812A	S30.875S	S31.139A
S01.139S	S01.83XS	S10.83XS	S20.00XA	S20.351A	S21.021A	S21.252S	S30.812S	S30.876A	S31.139S
S01.141S	S01.84XA	S10.84XA	S20.00XS	S20.351S	S21.021S	S21.259A	S30.813A	S30.876S	S31.140S
S01.142S	S01.84XS	S10.84XS	S20.01XA	S20.352A	S21.022A	S21.259S	S30.813S	S30.877A	S31.141S
S01.149S	S01.85XA	S10.85XA	S20.01XS	S20.352S	S21.022S	S21.301S	S30.814A	S30.877S	S31.142S
S01.151S	S01.85XS	S10.85XS	S20.02XA	S20.359A	S21.029A	S21.302S	S30.814S	S30.91XA	S31.143S
S01.152S	S01.90XA	S10.86XA	S20.02XS	S20.359S	S21.029S	S21.309S	S30.815A	S30.91XS	S31.144S
S01.159S	S01.90XS	S10.86XS	S20.101A	S20.361A	S21.031A	S21.311S	S30.815S	S30.92XA	S31.145S
S01.20XS	S01.91XA	S10.87XA	S20.101S	S20.361S	S21.031S	S21.312S	S30.816A	S30.92XS	S31.149S
S01.21XS	S01.91XS	S10.87XS	S20.102A	S20.362A	S21.032A	S21.319S	S30.816S	S30.93XA	S31.150A
S01.22XS	S01.92XA	S10.90XA	S20.102S	S20.362S	S21.032S	S21.321S	S30.817A	S30.93XS	S31.150S
S01.23XS	S01.92XS	S10.90XS	S20.109A	S20.369A	S21.039A	S21.322S	S30.817S	S30.94XA	S31.151A
S01.24XS	S01.93XA	S10.91XA	S20.109S	S20.369S	S21.039S	S21.329S	S30.820A	S30.94XS	S31.151S
S01.25XS	S01.93XS	S10.91XS	S20.111A	S20.371A	S21.041A	S21.331S	S30.820S	S30.95XA	S31.152A
S01.301S	S01.94XA	S10.92XA	S20.111S	S20.371S	S21.041S	S21.332S	S30.821A	S30.95XS	S31.152S
S01.302S	S01.94XS	S10.92XS	S20.112A	S20.372A	S21.042A	S21.339S	S30.821S	S30.96XA	S31.153A
S01.309S	S01.95XA	S10.93XA	S20.112S	S20.372S	S21.042S	S21.341S	S30.822A	S30.96XS	S31.153S
S01.311S	S01.95XS	S10.94XA	S20.119A	S20.379A	S21.049A	S21.342S	S30.822S	S30.97XA	S31.154A
S01.312S	S03.2XXS	S10.94XS	S20.119S	S20.379S	S21.049S	S21.349S	S30.823A	S30.97XS	S31.154S
S01.319S	S05.00XS	S10.95XA	S20.121A	S20.401A	S21.051A	S21.351S	S30.823S	S30.98XA	S31.155A
S01.321S	S05.01XS	S10.95XS	S20.121S	S20.401S	S21.051S	S21.352S	S30.824A	S30.98XS	S31.155S
S01.322S	S05.02XS	S10.96XA	S20.122A	S20.402A	S21.052A	S21.359S	S30.824S	S31.000A	S31.159A
S01.329S	S05.10XS	S10.96XS	S20.122S	S20.402S	S21.052S	S21.401S	S30.825A	S31.000S	S31.159S
S01.331S	S05.11XS	S10.97XA	S20.129A	S20.409A	S21.059A	S21.402S	S30.825S	S31.001A	S31.20XS
S01.332S	S05.12XS	S10.97XS	S20.129S	S20.409S	S21.059S	S21.409S	S30.826A	S31.010A	S31.21XS
S01.339S	S05.20XS	S11.011S	S20.141A	S20.411A	S21.101A	S21.411S	S30.826S	S31.010S	S31.22XS
S01.341S	S05.21XS	S11.012S	S20.141S	S20.411S	S21.101S	S21.412S	S30.827A	S31.011S	S31.23XS
S01.342S	S05.22XS	S11.013S	S20.142A	S20.412A	S21.102A	S21.419S	S30.827S	S31.020A	S31.24XS
S01.349S	S05.30XS	S11.014S	S20.142S	S20.412S	S21.102S	S21.421S	S30.840A	S31.020S	S31.25XS
S01.351S	S05.31XS	S11.015S	S20.149A	S20.419A	S21.109A	S21.422S	S30.840S	S31.021S	S31.30XS
S01.352S	S05.32XS	S11.019S	S20.149S	S20.419S	S21.109S	S21.429S	S30.841A	S31.030A	S31.31XS
S01.359S	S05.40XS	S11.021S	S20.151A	S20.421A	S21.111A	S21.431S	S30.841S	S31.030S	S31.32XS
S01.401A	S05.41XS	S11.022S	S20.151S	S20.421S	S21.111S	S21.432S	S30.842A	S31.031S	S31.33XS
S01.401S	S05.42XS	S11.023S	S20.152A	S20.422A	S21.112A	S21.439S	S30.842S	S31.040A	S31.34XS
S01.402A	S05.50XS	S11.024S	S20.152S	S20.422S	S21.112S	S21.441S	S30.843A	S31.040S	S31.35XS
S01.402S	S05.51XS	S11.025S	S20.159A	S20.429A	S21.119A	S21.442S	S30.843S	S31.041S	S31.40XS
S01.409A	S05.52XS		S20.159S	S20.429S	S21.119S			S31.050A	S31.41XS

S31.42XS	S31.833S	S40.841A	S41.139S	S50.821S	S51.831A	S60.052S	S60.392S	S60.461S	S60.841A
S31.43XS	S31.834S	S40.841S	S41.141S	S50.822A	S51.831S	S60.059A	S60.399A	S60.462A	S60.842A
S31.44XS	S31.835A	S40.842A	S41.142S	S50.822S	S51.832A	S60.059S	S60.399S	S60.462S	S60.842S
S31.45XS	S31.835S	S40.842S	S41.149S	S50.829A	S51.832S	S60.10XA	S60.410A	S60.463A	S60.849A
S31.600S	S31.839A	S40.849A	S41.151A	S50.829S	S51.839A	S60.10XS	S60.410S	S60.463S	S60.849S
S31.601S	S31.839S	S40.849S	S41.151S	S50.841A	S51.839S	S60.111A	S60.411A	S60.464A	S60.851A
S31.602S	S38.001S	S40.851A	S41.152A	S50.841S	S51.841S	S60.112A	S60.411S	S60.464S	S60.851S
S31.603S	S38.002S	S40.851S	S41.152S	S50.842A	S51.842S	S60.112S	S60.412A	S60.465A	S60.852A
S31.604S	S38.01XS	S40.852A	S41.159A	S50.842S	S51.849S	S60.119A	S60.412S	S60.465S	S60.852S
S31.605S	S38.02XS	S40.852S	S41.159S	S50.849A	S51.851A	S60.119S	S60.413A	S60.466A	S60.859A
S31.609S	S38.03XS	S40.859A	S46.021S	S50.849S	S51.851S	S60.121A	S60.413S	S60.466S	S60.859S
S31.610S	S38.1XXS	S40.859S	S46.022S	S50.851A	S51.852A	S60.121S	S60.414A	S60.467A	S60.861A
S31.611S	S38.211S	S40.861A	S46.029S	S50.851S	S51.852S	S60.122A	S60.414S	S60.467S	S60.861S
S31.612S	S38.212S	S40.861S	S46.121S	S50.852A	S51.859A	S60.122S	S60.415A	S60.468A	S60.862A
S31.613S	S38.221S	S40.862A	S46.122S	S50.852S	S51.859S	S60.129A	S60.415S	S60.468S	S60.862S
S31.614S	S38.222S	S40.862S	S46.129S	S50.859A	S56.021S	S60.129S	S60.416A	S60.469A	S60.869A
S31.615S	S38.231S	S40.869A	S46.221S	S50.859S	S56.022S	S60.131A	S60.416S	S60.469S	S60.869S
S31.619S	S38.232S	S40.869S	S46.222S	S50.861S	S56.029S	S60.131S	S60.417A	S60.470A	S60.871A
S31.620S	S38.3XXA	S40.871A	S46.229S	S50.861S	S56.121S	S60.132A	S60.417S	S60.470S	S60.871S
S31.621S	S38.3XXS	S40.871S	S46.321S	S50.862A	S56.122S	S60.132S	S60.418A	S60.471A	S60.872A
S31.622S	S39.021A	S40.872A	S46.322S	S50.862S	S56.123S	S60.139A	S60.418S	S60.471S	S60.872S
S31.623S	S39.021S	S40.872S	S46.329S	S50.869A	S56.124S	S60.139S	S60.419A	S60.472A	S60.879A
S31.624S	S39.022A	S40.879A	S46.821S	S50.869S	S56.125S	S60.141A	S60.419S	S60.472S	S60.879S
S31.625S	S39.022S	S40.879S	S46.822S	S50.871A	S56.126S	S60.141S	S60.420A	S60.473A	S60.911A
S31.629S	S39.023A	S40.911A	S46.829S	S50.871S	S56.127S	S60.142A	S60.420S	S60.473S	S60.911S
S31.630S	S39.023S	S40.911S	S46.921S	S50.872A	S56.128S	S60.142S	S60.421A	S60.474A	S60.912A
S31.631S	S40.011A	S40.912A	S46.922S	S50.872S	S56.129S	S60.149A	S60.421S	S60.474S	S60.912S
S31.632S	S40.011S	S40.912S	S46.929S	S50.879A	S56.221S	S60.149S	S60.422A	S60.475A	S60.919A
S31.633S	S40.012A	S40.919A	S47.1XXS	S50.879S	S56.222S	S60.151A	S60.422S	S60.475S	S60.919S
S31.634S	S40.012S	S40.919S	S47.2XXS	S50.901A	S56.229S	S60.151S	S60.423A	S60.476A	S60.921A
S31.635S	S40.019A	S40.921A	S47.9XXS	S50.901S	S56.321S	S60.152A	S60.423S	S60.476S	S60.921S
S31.639S	S40.019S	S40.921S	S50.00XA	S50.902A	S56.322S	S60.152S	S60.424A	S60.477A	S60.922A
S31.640S	S40.021A	S40.922A	S50.00XS	S50.902S	S56.329S	S60.159A	S60.424S	S60.477S	S60.922S
S31.641S	S40.021S	S40.922S	S50.01XA	S50.909A	S56.421S	S60.159S	S60.425A	S60.478A	S60.929A
S31.642S	S40.022A	S40.929A	S50.01XS	S50.909S	S56.422S	S60.211A	S60.425S	S60.478S	S60.929S
S31.643S	S40.022S	S40.929S	S50.02XA	S50.911A	S56.423S	S60.211S	S60.426A	S60.479A	S60.931A
S31.644S	S40.029A	S41.001A	S50.02XS	S50.911S	S56.424S	S60.212A	S60.426S	S60.479S	S60.931S
S31.645S	S40.029S	S41.001S	S50.10XA	S50.912A	S56.425S	S60.212S	S60.427A	S60.511A	S60.932A
S31.649S	S40.211A	S41.002A	S50.10XS	S50.912S	S56.426S	S60.219A	S60.427S	S60.511S	S60.932S
S31.650S	S40.211S	S41.002S	S50.11XA	S50.919A	S56.427S	S60.219S	S60.428A	S60.512A	S60.939A
S31.651S	S40.212A	S41.009A	S50.11XS	S50.919S	S56.428S	S60.221A	S60.428S	S60.512S	S60.939S
S31.652S	S40.212S	S41.009S	S50.12XA	S51.001A	S56.429S	S60.221S	S60.429A	S60.519A	S60.940A
S31.653S	S40.219A	S41.011A	S50.12XS	S51.001S	S56.521S	S60.222A	S60.429S	S60.519S	S60.940S
S31.654S	S40.219S	S41.011S	S50.311A	S51.002A	S56.522S	S60.222S	S60.440A	S60.521A	S60.941A
S31.655S	S40.221A	S41.012A	S50.311S	S51.002S	S56.529S	S60.229A	S60.440S	S60.521S	S60.941S
S31.659S	S40.221S	S41.012S	S50.312A	S51.009A	S56.821S	S60.229S	S60.441A	S60.522A	S60.942A
S31.801A	S40.222A	S41.019A	S50.312S	S51.009S	S56.822S	S60.311A	S60.441S	S60.522S	S60.942S
S31.801S	S40.222S	S41.019S	S50.319A	S51.011A	S56.829S	S60.311S	S60.442A	S60.529A	S60.943A
S31.802A	S40.229A	S41.021S	S50.319S	S51.011S	S56.921S	S60.312A	S60.442S	S60.529S	S60.943S
S31.802S	S40.229S	S41.022S	S50.321A	S51.012A	S56.922S	S60.312S	S60.443A	S60.541A	S60.944A
S31.803A	S40.241A	S41.029S	S50.321S	S51.012S	S56.929S	S60.319A	S60.443S	S60.541S	S60.944S
S31.803S	S40.241S	S41.031A	S50.322A	S51.019A	S57.00XS	S60.319S	S60.444A	S60.542A	S60.945A
S31.804A	S40.242A	S41.031S	S50.322S	S51.019S	S57.01XS	S60.321A	S60.444S	S60.542S	S60.945S
S31.804S	S40.242S	S41.032A	S50.329A	S51.021S	S57.02XS	S60.321S	S60.445A	S60.549A	S60.946A
S31.805A	S40.249A	S41.032S	S50.329S	S51.022S	S57.80XS	S60.322A	S60.445S	S60.549S	S60.946S
S31.805S	S40.249S	S41.039A	S50.341A	S51.029S	S57.81XS	S60.322S	S60.446A	S60.551A	S60.947A
S31.809A	S40.251A	S41.039S	S50.341S	S51.031A	S57.82XS	S60.329A	S60.446S	S60.551S	S60.947S
S31.809S	S40.251S	S41.041S	S50.342A	S51.031S	S60.00XA	S60.329S	S60.447A	S60.552A	S60.948A
S31.811A	S40.252A	S41.042S	S50.342S	S51.032A	S60.00XS	S60.341A	S60.447S	S60.552S	S60.948S
S31.811S	S40.252S	S41.049S	S50.349A	S51.032S	S60.011A	S60.341S	S60.448A	S60.559A	S60.949A
S31.812A	S40.259A	S41.051A	S50.349S	S51.039A	S60.011S	S60.342A	S60.448S	S60.559S	S60.949S
S31.812S	S40.259S	S41.051S	S50.351A	S51.039S	S60.012A	S60.342S	S60.449A	S60.561A	S61.001A
S31.813A	S40.261A	S41.052A	S50.351S	S51.041S	S60.012S	S60.349A	S60.449S	S60.561S	S61.001S
S31.813S	S40.261S	S41.052S	S50.352A	S51.042S	S60.019A	S60.349S	S60.450A	S60.562A	S61.002A
S31.814A	S40.262A	S41.059A	S50.352S	S51.049S	S60.019S	S60.351A	S60.450S	S60.562S	S61.002S
S31.814S	S40.262S	S41.059S	S50.359A	S51.051A	S60.021A	S60.351S	S60.451A	S60.569A	S61.009A
S31.815A	S40.269A	S41.101A	S50.359S	S51.051S	S60.021S	S60.352A	S60.451S	S60.569S	S61.009S
S31.815S	S40.269S	S41.101S	S50.361A	S51.052A	S60.022A	S60.352S	S60.452A	S60.571A	S61.011A
S31.819A	S40.271A	S41.102A	S50.361S	S51.052S	S60.022S	S60.359A	S60.452S	S60.571S	S61.011S
S31.819S	S40.271S	S41.102S	S50.362A	S51.059A	S60.029A	S60.359S	S60.453A	S60.572A	S61.012A
S31.821A	S40.272A	S41.109A	S50.362S	S51.059S	S60.029S	S60.361A	S60.453S	S60.572S	S61.012S
S31.821S	S40.272S	S41.109S	S50.369A	S51.801A	S60.031A	S60.361S	S60.454A	S60.579A	S61.019A
S31.822A	S40.279A	S41.111A	S50.369S	S51.801S	S60.031S	S60.362A	S60.454S	S60.579S	S61.019S
S31.822S	S40.279S	S41.111S	S50.371A	S51.802A	S60.032A	S60.362S	S60.455A	S60.811A	S61.021S
S31.823A	S40.811A	S41.112A	S50.371S	S51.802S	S60.032S	S60.369A	S60.455S	S60.811S	S61.022S
S31.823S	S40.811S	S41.112S	S50.372A	S51.809A	S60.039A	S60.369S	S60.456A	S60.812A	S61.029S
S31.824A	S40.812A	S41.119A	S50.372S	S51.809S	S60.039S	S60.371A	S60.456S	S60.812S	S61.031A
S31.824S	S40.812S	S41.119S	S50.379A	S51.811A	S60.041A	S60.371S	S60.457A	S60.819A	S61.031S
S31.825A	S40.819A	S41.121S	S50.379S	S51.811S	S60.041S	S60.372A	S60.457S	S60.819S	S61.032A
S31.825S	S40.819S	S41.122S	S50.811A	S51.812A	S60.042A	S60.372S	S60.458A	S60.821A	S61.032S
S31.829A	S40.821A	S41.129S	S50.811S	S51.812S	S60.042S	S60.379A	S60.458S	S60.821S	S61.039A
S31.829S	S40.821S	S41.131A	S50.812A	S51.819A	S60.049A	S60.379S	S60.459A	S60.822A	S61.039S
S31.831A	S40.822A	S41.131S	S50.812S	S51.819S	S60.049S	S60.391A	S60.459S	S60.822S	S61.041S
S31.831S	S40.822S	S41.132A	S50.819A	S51.821S	S60.051A	S60.391S	S60.460A	S60.829A	S61.042S
S31.832S	S40.829A	S41.132S	S50.819S	S51.822S	S60.051S	S60.392A	S60.460S	S60.829S	S61.049S
S31.833A	S40.829S	S41.139A	S50.821A	S51.829S	S60.052A	S60.392A	S60.461A	S60.841A	S61.051A

S61.051S	S61.230S	S61.318S	S61.449S	S67.190S	S70.349S	S71.151S	S80.821A	S81.829S	S90.416A
S61.052A	S61.231A	S61.319A	S61.451A	S67.191S	S70.351A	S71.152A	S80.821S	S81.831A	S90.416S
S61.052S	S61.231S	S61.319S	S61.451S	S67.192S	S70.351S	S71.152S	S80.822A	S81.831S	S90.421A
S61.059A	S61.232A	S61.320S	S61.452A	S67.193S	S70.352A	S71.159A	S80.822S	S81.832A	S90.421S
S61.059S	S61.232S	S61.321S	S61.452S	S67.194S	S70.352S	S71.159S	S80.829A	S81.832S	S90.422A
S61.101A	S61.233A	S61.322S	S61.459A	S67.195S	S70.359A	S76.021S	S80.829S	S81.839A	S90.422S
S61.101S	S61.233S	S61.323S	S61.459S	S67.196S	S70.359S	S76.022S	S80.841A	S81.839S	S90.423A
S61.102A	S61.234A	S61.324S	S61.501A	S67.197S	S70.361A	S76.029S	S80.841S	S81.841S	S90.423S
S61.102S	S61.234S	S61.325S	S61.501S	S67.198S	S70.361S	S76.121S	S80.842A	S81.842S	S90.424A
S61.109A	S61.235A	S61.326S	S61.502A	S67.20XS	S70.362A	S76.122S	S80.842S	S81.849S	S90.424S
S61.109S	S61.235S	S61.327S	S61.502S	S67.21XS	S70.362S	S76.129S	S80.849A	S81.851A	S90.425A
S61.111A	S61.236A	S61.328S	S61.509A	S67.22XS	S70.369A	S76.221S	S80.849S	S81.851S	S90.425S
S61.111S	S61.236S	S61.329S	S61.509S	S67.30XS	S70.369S	S76.222S	S80.851A	S81.852A	S90.426A
S61.112A	S61.237A	S61.330A	S61.511A	S67.31XS	S70.371A	S76.229S	S80.851S	S81.852S	S90.426S
S61.112S	S61.237S	S61.330S	S61.511S	S67.32XS	S70.371S	S76.321S	S80.852A	S81.859A	S90.441A
S61.119A	S61.238A	S61.331A	S61.512A	S67.40XS	S70.372A	S76.322S	S80.852S	S81.859S	S90.441S
S61.119S	S61.238S	S61.331S	S61.512S	S67.41XS	S70.372S	S76.329S	S80.859A	S86.021S	S90.442A
S61.121S	S61.239A	S61.332A	S61.519A	S67.42XS	S70.379A	S76.821S	S80.859S	S86.022S	S90.442S
S61.122S	S61.239S	S61.332S	S61.519S	S67.90XS	S70.379S	S76.822S	S80.861A	S86.029S	S90.443A
S61.129S	S61.240S	S61.333A	S61.521S	S67.91XS	S70.911A	S76.829S	S80.861S	S86.121S	S90.443S
S61.131A	S61.241S	S61.333S	S61.522S	S67.92XS	S70.911S	S76.921S	S80.862A	S86.122S	S90.444A
S61.131S	S61.242S	S61.334A	S61.529S	S70.00XA	S70.912A	S76.922S	S80.862S	S86.129S	S90.444S
S61.132A	S61.243S	S61.334S	S61.531A	S70.00XS	S70.912S	S76.929S	S80.869A	S86.221S	S90.445A
S61.132S	S61.244S	S61.335A	S61.531S	S70.01XA	S70.919A	S77.00XS	S80.869S	S86.222S	S90.445S
S61.139A	S61.245S	S61.335S	S61.532A	S70.01XS	S70.919S	S77.01XS	S80.871A	S86.229S	S90.446A
S61.139S	S61.246S	S61.336A	S61.532S	S70.02XA	S70.921A	S77.02XS	S80.871S	S86.321S	S90.446S
S61.141S	S61.247S	S61.336S	S61.539A	S70.02XS	S70.921S	S77.10XS	S80.872A	S86.322S	S90.451A
S61.142S	S61.248S	S61.337A	S61.539S	S70.10XA	S70.922A	S77.11XS	S80.872S	S86.329S	S90.451S
S61.149S	S61.249S	S61.337S	S61.541S	S70.10XS	S70.922S	S77.12XS	S80.879A	S86.821S	S90.452A
S61.151A	S61.250A	S61.338A	S61.542S	S70.11XA	S70.929A	S80.00XA	S80.879S	S86.822S	S90.452S
S61.151S	S61.250S	S61.338S	S61.549S	S70.11XS	S70.929S	S80.00XS	S80.911A	S86.829S	S90.453A
S61.152A	S61.251A	S61.339A	S61.551A	S70.12XA	S71.001A	S80.01XA	S80.911S	S86.921S	S90.453S
S61.152S	S61.251S	S61.339S	S61.551S	S70.12XS	S71.001S	S80.01XS	S80.912A	S86.922S	S90.454A
S61.159A	S61.252A	S61.340S	S61.552A	S70.211A	S71.002A	S80.02XA	S80.912S	S86.929S	S90.454S
S61.159S	S61.252S	S61.341S	S61.552S	S70.211S	S71.009A	S80.02XS	S80.919A	S87.00XS	S90.455A
S61.200A	S61.253A	S61.342S	S61.559A	S70.212A	S71.009S	S80.10XA	S80.919S	S87.01XS	S90.455S
S61.200S	S61.253S	S61.343S	S61.559S	S70.212S	S71.011A	S80.10XS	S80.921A	S87.02XS	S90.456A
S61.201A	S61.254A	S61.344S	S66.021S	S70.219A	S71.011S	S80.11XA	S80.921S	S87.80XS	S90.456S
S61.201S	S61.254S	S61.345S	S66.022S	S70.219S	S71.012A	S80.11XS	S80.922A	S87.81XS	S90.461A
S61.202A	S61.255A	S61.346S	S66.029S	S70.221A	S71.012S	S80.12XA	S80.922S	S87.82XS	S90.461S
S61.202S	S61.255S	S61.347S	S66.120S	S70.221S	S71.019A	S80.12XS	S80.929A	S90.00XA	S90.462A
S61.203A	S61.256A	S61.348S	S66.121S	S70.222A	S71.019S	S80.211A	S80.929S	S90.00XS	S90.462S
S61.203S	S61.256S	S61.349S	S66.122S	S70.222S	S71.021S	S80.211S	S81.001A	S90.01XA	S90.463A
S61.204A	S61.257A	S61.350A	S66.123S	S70.229A	S71.022S	S80.212A	S81.001S	S90.01XS	S90.463S
S61.204S	S61.257S	S61.350S	S66.124S	S70.229S	S71.029S	S80.212S	S81.002A	S90.02XA	S90.464A
S61.205A	S61.258A	S61.351A	S66.125S	S70.241A	S71.031A	S80.219A	S81.002S	S90.02XS	S90.464S
S61.205S	S61.258S	S61.351S	S66.126S	S70.241S	S71.031S	S80.219S	S81.009A	S90.111A	S90.465A
S61.206A	S61.259A	S61.352A	S66.127S	S70.242A	S71.032A	S80.221A	S81.009S	S90.111S	S90.465S
S61.206S	S61.259S	S61.352S	S66.128S	S70.242S	S71.032S	S80.221S	S81.011A	S90.112A	S90.466A
S61.207A	S61.300A	S61.353A	S66.129S	S70.249A	S71.039A	S80.222A	S81.011S	S90.112S	S90.466S
S61.207S	S61.300S	S61.353S	S66.221S	S70.249S	S71.039S	S80.222S	S81.012A	S90.119A	S90.471A
S61.208A	S61.301A	S61.354A	S66.222S	S70.251A	S71.041S	S80.229A	S81.012S	S90.119S	S90.471S
S61.208S	S61.301S	S61.354S	S66.229S	S70.251S	S71.042S	S80.229S	S81.019A	S90.121A	S90.472A
S61.209A	S61.302A	S61.355A	S66.320S	S70.252A	S71.049S	S80.241A	S81.019S	S90.121S	S90.472S
S61.209S	S61.302S	S61.355S	S66.321S	S70.252S	S71.051A	S80.241S	S81.021S	S90.122A	S90.473A
S61.210A	S61.303A	S61.356A	S66.322S	S70.259A	S71.051S	S80.242A	S81.022S	S90.122S	S90.473S
S61.210S	S61.303S	S61.356S	S66.323S	S70.259S	S71.052A	S80.242S	S81.029S	S90.129A	S90.474A
S61.211A	S61.304A	S61.357A	S66.324S	S70.261A	S71.052S	S80.249A	S81.031A	S90.129S	S90.474S
S61.211S	S61.304S	S61.357S	S66.325S	S70.261S	S71.059A	S80.249S	S81.031S	S90.211A	S90.475A
S61.212A	S61.305A	S61.358A	S66.326S	S70.262A	S71.059S	S80.251A	S81.032A	S90.211S	S90.475S
S61.212S	S61.305S	S61.358S	S66.327S	S70.262S	S71.101A	S80.251S	S81.032S	S90.212A	S90.476A
S61.213A	S61.306A	S61.359A	S66.328S	S70.269A	S71.101S	S80.252A	S81.039A	S90.212S	S90.476S
S61.213S	S61.306S	S61.359S	S66.329S	S70.269S	S71.102A	S80.252S	S81.039S	S90.219A	S90.511A
S61.214A	S61.307A	S61.401A	S66.421S	S70.271A	S71.102S	S80.259A	S81.041S	S90.219S	S90.511S
S61.214S	S61.307S	S61.401S	S66.422S	S70.271S	S71.109A	S80.259S	S81.042S	S90.221A	S90.512A
S61.215A	S61.308A	S61.402A	S66.429S	S70.272A	S71.109S	S80.261A	S81.049S	S90.221S	S90.512S
S61.215S	S61.308S	S61.402S	S66.520S	S70.272S	S71.111A	S80.261S	S81.051A	S90.222A	S90.519A
S61.216A	S61.309A	S61.409A	S66.521S	S70.279A	S71.111S	S80.262A	S81.051S	S90.222S	S90.519S
S61.216S	S61.309S	S61.409S	S66.522S	S70.279S	S71.112A	S80.262S	S81.052A	S90.229A	S90.521A
S61.217A	S61.310A	S61.411A	S66.523S	S70.311A	S71.112S	S80.269A	S81.052S	S90.229S	S90.521S
S61.217S	S61.310S	S61.411S	S66.524S	S70.311S	S71.119A	S80.269S	S81.059A	S90.30XA	S90.522A
S61.218A	S61.311A	S61.412A	S66.525S	S70.312A	S71.119S	S80.271A	S81.059S	S90.30XS	S90.522S
S61.218S	S61.311S	S61.412S	S66.526S	S70.312S	S71.121S	S80.271S	S81.801A	S90.31XA	S90.529A
S61.219A	S61.312A	S61.419A	S66.527S	S70.319A	S71.122S	S80.272A	S81.801S	S90.31XS	S90.529S
S61.219S	S61.312S	S61.419S	S66.528S	S70.319S	S71.129S	S80.272S	S81.802A	S90.32XA	S90.541A
S61.220S	S61.313A	S61.421S	S66.529S	S70.321A	S71.131A	S80.279A	S81.802S	S90.32XS	S90.541S
S61.221S	S61.313S	S61.422S	S66.821S	S70.321S	S71.131S	S80.279S	S81.809A	S90.411A	S90.542A
S61.222S	S61.314A	S61.429S	S66.822S	S70.322A	S71.132A	S80.811A	S81.809S	S90.411S	S90.542S
S61.223S	S61.314S	S61.431A	S66.829S	S70.322S	S71.132S	S80.811S	S81.811A	S90.412A	S90.549A
S61.224S	S61.315A	S61.431S	S66.921S	S70.329A	S71.139A	S80.812A	S81.811S	S90.412S	S90.549S
S61.225S	S61.315S	S61.432A	S66.922S	S70.329S	S71.139S	S80.812S	S81.812A	S90.413A	S90.551A
S61.226S	S61.316A	S61.432S	S66.929S	S70.341A	S71.141S	S80.819A	S81.812S	S90.413S	S90.551S
S61.227S	S61.316S	S61.439A	S67.00XS	S70.341S	S71.142S	S80.819S	S81.819A	S90.414A	S90.552A
S61.228S	S61.317A	S61.439S	S67.01XS	S70.342A	S71.149S	S80.821A	S81.819S	S90.414S	S90.552S
S61.229S	S61.317S	S61.441S	S67.02XS	S70.342S	S71.151A	S80.819A	S81.821S	S90.415A	S90.559A
S61.230A	S61.318A	S61.442S	S67.10XS	S70.349S	S71.151S	S80.819S	S81.822S	S90.415S	S90.559S

S90.561A	S91.029S	S91.201A	S91.331S	T20.37XS	T21.44XS	T22.241S	T22.632S	T23.179S	T23.502S
S90.561S	S91.031A	S91.201S	S91.332A	T20.39XS	T21.45XS	T22.242S	T22.639S	T23.191S	T23.509S
S90.562A	S91.031S	S91.202A	S91.332S	T20.40XS	T21.46XS	T22.249S	T22.641S	T23.192S	T23.511S
S90.562S	S91.032A	S91.202S	S91.339A	T20.411S	T21.47XS	T22.251S	T22.642S	T23.199S	T23.512S
S90.569A	S91.032S	S91.203A	S91.339S	T20.412S	T21.49XS	T22.252S	T22.649S	T23.201S	T23.519S
S90.569S	S91.039A	S91.203S	S91.341S	T20.419S	T21.50XS	T22.259S	T22.651S	T23.202S	T23.521S
S90.571A	S91.039S	S91.204A	S91.342A	T20.42XS	T21.51XS	T22.261S	T22.652S	T23.209S	T23.522S
S90.571S	S91.041S	S91.204S	S91.342S	T20.43XS	T21.52XS	T22.262S	T22.659S	T23.211S	T23.529S
S90.572A	S91.042S	S91.205A	S91.349S	T20.44XS	T21.53XS	T22.269S	T22.661S	T23.212S	T23.531S
S90.572S	S91.049S	S91.205S	S91.351A	T20.45XS	T21.54XS	T22.291S	T22.662S	T23.219S	T23.532S
S90.579A	S91.051A	S91.206A	S91.351S	T20.46XS	T21.55XS	T22.292S	T22.669S	T23.221S	T23.539S
S90.579S	S91.051S	S91.206S	S91.352A	T20.47XS	T21.56XS	T22.299S	T22.691S	T23.222S	T23.541S
S90.811A	S91.052A	S91.209A	S91.352S	T20.49XS	T21.57XS	T22.30XS	T22.692S	T23.229S	T23.542S
S90.811S	S91.052S	S91.209S	S91.359A	T20.50XS	T21.59XS	T22.311S	T22.699S	T23.231S	T23.549S
S90.812A	S91.059A	S91.211A	S91.359S	T20.511S	T21.60XS	T22.312S	T22.70XS	T23.232S	T23.551S
S90.812S	S91.059S	S91.211S	S96.021S	T20.512S	T21.61XS	T22.319S	T22.711S	T23.239S	T23.552S
S90.819A	S91.101A	S91.212A	S96.022S	T20.519S	T21.62XS	T22.321S	T22.712S	T23.241S	T23.559S
S90.819S	S91.101S	S91.212S	S96.029S	T20.52XS	T21.63XS	T22.322S	T22.719S	T23.242S	T23.561S
S90.821A	S91.102A	S91.213A	S96.121S	T20.53XS	T21.64XS	T22.329S	T22.721S	T23.249S	T23.562S
S90.821S	S91.102S	S91.213S	S96.122S	T20.54XS	T21.65XS	T22.331S	T22.722S	T23.251S	T23.569S
S90.822A	S91.103A	S91.214A	S96.221S	T20.55XS	T21.66XS	T22.332S	T22.729S	T23.252S	T23.571S
S90.822S	S91.103S	S91.214S	S96.222S	T20.56XS	T21.67XS	T22.339S	T22.731S	T23.259S	T23.572S
S90.829A	S91.104A	S91.215A	S96.229S	T20.57XS	T21.69XS	T22.341S	T22.732S	T23.261S	T23.579S
S90.829S	S91.104S	S91.215S	S96.821S	T20.59XS	T21.70XS	T22.342S	T22.739S	T23.262S	T23.591S
S90.841A	S91.105A	S91.216A	S96.822S	T20.60XS	T21.71XS	T22.349S	T22.741S	T23.269S	T23.592S
S90.841S	S91.105S	S91.216S	S96.829S	T20.611S	T21.72XS	T22.351S	T22.742S	T23.271S	T23.599S
S90.842A	S91.106A	S91.219A	S96.921S	T20.612S	T21.73XS	T22.352S	T22.749S	T23.272S	T23.601S
S90.842S	S91.106S	S91.219S	S96.922S	T20.619S	T21.74XS	T22.359S	T22.751S	T23.279S	T23.602S
S90.849A	S91.109A	S91.221S	S96.929S	T20.62XS	T21.75XS	T22.361S	T22.752S	T23.291S	T23.609S
S90.849S	S91.109S	S91.222S	S97.00XS	T20.63XS	T21.76XS	T22.362S	T22.759S	T23.292S	T23.611S
S90.851A	S91.111A	S91.223S	S97.01XS	T20.64XS	T21.77XS	T22.369S	T22.761S	T23.299S	T23.612S
S90.851S	S91.111S	S91.224S	S97.02XS	T20.65XS	T21.79XS	T22.391S	T22.762S	T23.301S	T23.619S
S90.852A	S91.112A	S91.225S	S97.101S	T20.66XS	T22.00XS	T22.392S	T22.769S	T23.302S	T23.621S
S90.852S	S91.112S	S91.226S	S97.102S	T20.67XS	T22.011S	T22.399S	T22.791S	T23.309S	T23.622S
S90.859A	S91.113A	S91.229S	S97.109S	T20.69XS	T22.012S	T22.40XS	T22.792S	T23.311S	T23.629S
S90.859S	S91.113S	S91.231A	S97.111S	T20.70XS	T22.019S	T22.411S	T22.799S	T23.312S	T23.631S
S90.861A	S91.114A	S91.231S	S97.112S	T20.711S	T22.021S	T22.412S	T23.001S	T23.319S	T23.632S
S90.861S	S91.114S	S91.232A	S97.119S	T20.712S	T22.022S	T22.419S	T23.002S	T23.321S	T23.639S
S90.862A	S91.115A	S91.232S	S97.121S	T20.719S	T22.029S	T22.421S	T23.009S	T23.322S	T23.641S
S90.862S	S91.115S	S91.233A	S97.122S	T20.72XS	T22.031S	T22.422S	T23.011S	T23.329S	T23.642S
S90.869A	S91.116A	S91.233S	S97.129S	T20.73XS	T22.032S	T22.429S	T23.012S	T23.331S	T23.649S
S90.869S	S91.116S	S91.234A	S97.80XS	T20.74XS	T22.039S	T22.431S	T23.019S	T23.332S	T23.651S
S90.871A	S91.119A	S91.234S	S97.81XS	T20.75XS	T22.041S	T22.432S	T23.021S	T23.339S	T23.652S
S90.871S	S91.119S	S91.235A	S97.82XS	T20.76XS	T22.042S	T22.439S	T23.022S	T23.341S	T23.659S
S90.872A	S91.121S	S91.235S	T20.00XS	T20.77XS	T22.049S	T22.441S	T23.029S	T23.342S	T23.661S
S90.872S	S91.122S	S91.236A	T20.011S	T20.79XS	T22.051S	T22.442S	T23.031S	T23.349S	T23.662S
S90.879A	S91.123S	S91.236S	T20.012S	T21.00XS	T22.052S	T22.449S	T23.032S	T23.351S	T23.669S
S90.879S	S91.124S	S91.239A	T20.019S	T21.01XS	T22.059S	T22.451S	T23.039S	T23.352S	T23.671S
S90.911A	S91.125S	S91.239S	T20.02XS	T21.02XS	T22.061S	T22.452S	T23.041S	T23.359S	T23.672S
S90.911S	S91.126S	S91.241S	T20.03XS	T21.03XS	T22.062S	T22.459S	T23.042S	T23.361S	T23.679S
S90.912A	S91.129S	S91.242S	T20.04XS	T21.04XS	T22.069S	T22.461S	T23.049S	T23.362S	T23.691S
S90.912S	S91.131A	S91.243S	T20.05XS	T21.05XS	T22.091S	T22.462S	T23.051S	T23.369S	T23.692S
S90.919A	S91.131S	S91.244S	T20.06XS	T21.06XS	T22.092S	T22.469S	T23.052S	T23.371S	T23.699S
S90.919S	S91.132A	S91.245S	T20.07XS	T21.07XS	T22.099S	T22.491S	T23.059S	T23.372S	T23.701S
S90.921A	S91.132S	S91.246S	T20.09XS	T21.09XS	T22.10XS	T22.492S	T23.061S	T23.379S	T23.702S
S90.921S	S91.133A	S91.249S	T20.10XS	T21.10XS	T22.111S	T22.499S	T23.062S	T23.391S	T23.709S
S90.922A	S91.133S	S91.251A	T20.111S	T21.11XS	T22.112S	T22.50XS	T23.069S	T23.392S	T23.711S
S90.922S	S91.134A	S91.251S	T20.112S	T21.12XS	T22.119S	T22.511S	T23.071S	T23.399S	T23.712S
S90.929A	S91.134S	S91.252A	T20.119S	T21.13XS	T22.121S	T22.512S	T23.072S	T23.401S	T23.719S
S90.929S	S91.135A	S91.252S	T20.12XS	T21.14XS	T22.122S	T22.519S	T23.079S	T23.402S	T23.721S
S90.931A	S91.135S	S91.253A	T20.13XS	T21.15XS	T22.129S	T22.521S	T23.091S	T23.409S	T23.722S
S90.931S	S91.136A	S91.253S	T20.14XS	T21.16XS	T22.131S	T22.522S	T23.092S	T23.411S	T23.729S
S90.932A	S91.136S	S91.254A	T20.15XS	T21.17XS	T22.132S	T22.529S	T23.099S	T23.412S	T23.731S
S90.932S	S91.139A	S91.254S	T20.16XS	T21.19XS	T22.139S	T22.531S	T23.101S	T23.419S	T23.732S
S90.933A	S91.139S	S91.255A	T20.17XS	T21.20XS	T22.141S	T22.532S	T23.102S	T23.421S	T23.739S
S90.933S	S91.141S	S91.255S	T20.19XS	T21.21XS	T22.142S	T22.539S	T23.109S	T23.422S	T23.741S
S90.934A	S91.142S	S91.256A	T20.20XS	T21.22XS	T22.149S	T22.541S	T23.111S	T23.429S	T23.742S
S90.934S	S91.143S	S91.256S	T20.211S	T21.23XS	T22.151S	T22.542S	T23.112S	T23.431S	T23.749S
S90.935A	S91.144S	S91.259A	T20.212S	T21.24XS	T22.152S	T22.549S	T23.119S	T23.432S	T23.751S
S90.935S	S91.145S	S91.259S	T20.219S	T21.25XS	T22.159S	T22.551S	T23.121S	T23.439S	T23.752S
S90.936A	S91.146S	S91.301A	T20.22XS	T21.26XS	T22.161S	T22.552S	T23.122S	T23.441S	T23.759S
S90.936S	S91.149S	S91.301S	T20.23XS	T21.27XS	T22.162S	T22.559S	T23.129S	T23.442S	T23.761S
S91.001A	S91.151A	S91.302A	T20.24XS	T21.29XS	T22.169S	T22.561S	T23.131S	T23.449S	T23.762S
S91.001S	S91.151S	S91.302S	T20.25XS	T21.30XS	T22.191S	T22.562S	T23.132S	T23.451S	T23.769S
S91.002A	S91.152A	S91.309A	T20.26XS	T21.31XS	T22.192S	T22.569S	T23.139S	T23.452S	T23.771S
S91.002S	S91.152S	S91.309S	T20.27XS	T21.32XS	T22.199S	T22.591S	T23.141S	T23.459S	T23.772S
S91.009A	S91.153A	S91.311A	T20.29XS	T21.33XS	T22.20XS	T22.592S	T23.142S	T23.461S	T23.779S
S91.009S	S91.153S	S91.311S	T20.30XS	T21.34XS	T22.211S	T22.599S	T23.149S	T23.462S	T23.791S
S91.011A	S91.154A	S91.312A	T20.311S	T21.35XS	T22.212S	T22.60XS	T23.151S	T23.469S	T23.792S
S91.011S	S91.154S	S91.312S	T20.312S	T21.36XS	T22.219S	T22.611S	T23.152S	T23.471S	T23.799S
S91.012A	S91.155A	S91.319A	T20.319S	T21.37XS	T22.221S	T22.612S	T23.159S	T23.472S	T24.001S
S91.012S	S91.155S	S91.319S	T20.32XS	T21.39XS	T22.222S	T22.619S	T23.161S	T23.479S	T24.002S
S91.019A	S91.156A	S91.321S	T20.33XS	T21.40XS	T22.229S	T22.621S	T23.162S	T23.491S	T24.009S
S91.019S	S91.156S	S91.322S	T20.34XS	T21.41XS	T22.231S	T22.622S	T23.169S	T23.492S	T24.011S
S91.021S	S91.159A	S91.329S	T20.35XS	T21.42XS	T22.232S	T22.629S	T23.171S	T23.499S	T24.012S
S91.022S	S91.159S	S91.331A	T20.36XS	T21.43XS	T22.239S	T22.631S	T23.172S	T23.501S	T24.019S

T24.021S	T24.212S	T24.409S	T24.601S	T24.792S	T25.219S	T25.431S	T25.692S	T26.42XS	T28.40XS
T24.022S	T24.219S	T24.411S	T24.602S	T24.799S	T25.221S	T25.432S	T25.699S	T26.50XS	T28.411S
T24.029S	T24.221S	T24.412S	T24.609S	T25.011S	T25.222S	T25.439S	T25.711S	T26.51XS	T28.412S
T24.031S	T24.222S	T24.419S	T24.611S	T25.012S	T25.229S	T25.491S	T25.712S	T26.52XS	T28.419S
T24.032S	T24.229S	T24.421S	T24.612S	T25.019S	T25.231S	T25.492S	T25.719S	T26.60XS	T28.49XS
T24.039S	T24.231S	T24.422S	T24.619S	T25.021S	T25.232S	T25.499S	T25.721S	T26.61XS	T28.5XXS
T24.091S	T24.232S	T24.429S	T24.621S	T25.022S	T25.239S	T25.511S	T25.722S	T26.62XS	T28.6XXS
T24.092S	T24.239S	T24.431S	T24.622S	T25.029S	T25.291S	T25.512S	T25.729S	T26.70XS	T28.7XXS
T24.099S	T24.291S	T24.432S	T24.629S	T25.031S	T25.292S	T25.519S	T25.731S	T26.71XS	T28.8XXS
T24.101S	T24.292S	T24.439S	T24.631S	T25.032S	T25.299S	T25.521S	T25.732S	T26.72XS	T28.90XS
T24.102S	T24.299S	T24.491S	T24.632S	T25.039S	T25.311S	T25.522S	T25.739S	T26.80XS	T28.911S
T24.109S	T24.301S	T24.492S	T24.639S	T25.091S	T25.312S	T25.529S	T25.791S	T26.81XS	T28.912S
T24.111S	T24.302S	T24.499S	T24.691S	T25.092S	T25.319S	T25.531S	T25.792S	T26.82XS	T28.919S
T24.112S	T24.309S	T24.501S	T24.692S	T25.099S	T25.321S	T25.532S	T25.799S	T26.90XS	T28.99XS
T24.119S	T24.311S	T24.502S	T24.699S	T25.111S	T25.322S	T25.539S	T26.00XS	T26.91XS	T85.41XA
T24.121S	T24.312S	T24.509S	T24.701S	T25.112S	T25.329S	T25.591S	T26.01XS	T26.92XS	T85.42XA
T24.122S	T24.319S	T24.511S	T24.702S	T25.119S	T25.331S	T25.592S	T26.02XS	T27.0XXS	T85.43XA
T24.129S	T24.321S	T24.512S	T24.709S	T25.121S	T25.332S	T25.599S	T26.10XS	T27.1XXS	T85.44XA
T24.131S	T24.322S	T24.519S	T24.711S	T25.122S	T25.339S	T25.611S	T26.11XS	T27.2XXS	T85.49XA
T24.132S	T24.329S	T24.521S	T24.712S	T25.129S	T25.391S	T25.612S	T26.12XS	T27.3XXS	Z40.01
T24.139S	T24.331S	T24.522S	T24.719S	T25.131S	T25.392S	T25.619S	T26.20XS	T27.4XXS	Z41.1
T24.191S	T24.332S	T24.529S	T24.721S	T25.132S	T25.399S	T25.621S	T26.21XS	T27.5XXS	Z42.1
T24.192S	T24.339S	T24.531S	T24.722S	T25.139S	T25.411S	T25.622S	T26.22XS	T27.6XXS	Z42.8
T24.199S	T24.391S	T24.532S	T24.729S	T25.191S	T25.412S	T25.629S	T26.30XS	T27.7XXS	Z52.10
T24.201S	T24.392S	T24.539S	T24.731S	T25.192S	T25.419S	T25.631S	T26.31XS	T28.0XXS	Z52.11
T24.202S	T24.399S	T24.591S	T24.732S	T25.199S	T25.421S	T25.632S	T26.32XS	T28.1XXS	Z52.19
T24.209S	T24.401S	T24.592S	T24.739S	T25.211S	T25.422S	T25.639S	T26.40XS	T28.2XXS	Z94.5
T24.211S	T24.402S	T24.599S	T24.791S	T25.212S	T25.429S	T25.691S	T26.41XS	T28.3XXS	

MDC 10 Endocrine, Nutritional And Metabolic Diseases And Disorders

A18.7	E00.9	E08.641	E11.9	E25.8	E50.9	E70.20	E71.528	E75.6	E83.40
A18.81	E01.0	E08.649	E13.00	E25.9	E51.11	E70.21	E71.529	E76.01	E83.41
B67.31	E01.1	E08.65	E13.01	E26.01	E51.12	E70.29	E71.53	E76.02	E83.42
C73	E01.2	E08.69	E13.10	E26.02	E51.2	E70.30	E71.540	E76.03	E83.49
C74.00	E01.8	E08.8	E13.11	E26.09	E51.8	E70.310	E71.541	E76.1	E83.50
C74.01	E02	E08.9	E13.618	E26.1	E51.9	E70.311	E71.542	E76.210	E83.51
C74.02	E03.0	E09.00	E13.620	E26.81	E52	E70.318	E71.548	E76.211	E83.52
C74.10	E03.1	E09.01	E13.621	E26.89	E53.0	E70.319	E72.00	E76.219	E83.59
C74.11	E03.2	E09.10	E13.622	E26.9	E53.1	E70.320	E72.01	E76.22	E83.81
C74.12	E03.3	E09.11	E13.628	E27.0	E53.8	E70.321	E72.02	E76.29	E83.89
C74.90	E03.4	E09.618	E13.630	E27.1	E53.9	E70.328	E72.03	E76.3	E83.9
C74.91	E03.8	E09.620	E13.638	E27.2	E54	E70.329	E72.04	E76.8	E84.8
C74.92	E03.9	E09.621	E13.641	E27.3	E55.9	E70.330	E72.09	E76.9	E84.9
C75.0	E04.0	E09.622	E13.649	E27.40	E56.0	E70.331	E72.10	E77.0	E86.0
C75.1	E04.1	E09.628	E13.65	E27.49	E56.1	E70.338	E72.11	E77.1	E86.1
C75.2	E04.2	E09.630	E13.69	E27.5	E56.8	E70.339	E72.12	E77.8	E86.9
C75.8	E04.8	E09.638	E13.8	E27.8	E56.9	E70.39	E72.19	E77.9	E87.0
C75.9	E04.9	E09.641	E13.9	E27.9	E58	E70.40	E72.20	E78.00	E87.1
C79.70	E05.00	E09.649	E15	E29.0	E59	E70.41	E72.21	E78.01	E87.2
C79.71	E05.01	E09.65	E16.0	E29.1	E60	E70.49	E72.22	E78.1	E87.3
C79.72	E05.10	E09.69	E16.1	E29.8	E61.0	E70.5	E72.23	E78.2	E87.4
C96.5	E05.11	E09.8	E16.2	E29.9	E61.1	E70.8	E72.29	E78.3	E87.5
C96.6	E05.20	E09.9	E16.3	E30.0	E61.2	E70.9	E72.3	E78.41	E87.6
D13.7	E05.21	E10.10	E16.8	E30.1	E61.3	E71.0	E72.4	E78.49	E87.70
D34	E05.30	E10.11	E16.9	E30.8	E61.4	E71.110	E72.50	E78.5	E87.71
D35.00	E05.31	E10.618	E20.0	E30.9	E61.5	E71.111	E72.51	E78.6	E87.79
D35.01	E05.40	E10.620	E20.1	E31.0	E61.6	E71.118	E72.52	E78.70	E87.8
D35.02	E05.41	E10.621	E20.8	E31.1	E61.7	E71.120	E72.53	E78.79	E88.01
D35.1	E05.80	E10.622	E20.9	E31.20	E61.8	E71.121	E72.59	E78.81	E88.1
D35.2	E05.81	E10.628	E21.0	E31.21	E61.9	E71.128	E72.81	E78.89	E88.2
D35.3	E05.90	E10.630	E21.1	E31.22	E63.0	E71.19	E72.89	E78.9	E88.40
D35.7	E05.91	E10.638	E21.2	E31.23	E63.1	E71.2	E72.9	E79.1	E88.41
D35.9	E06.0	E10.641	E21.3	E31.8	E63.8	E71.30	E74.00	E79.2	E88.42
D44.0	E06.1	E10.649	E21.4	E31.9	E63.9	E71.310	E74.01	E79.8	E88.49
D44.10	E06.2	E10.65	E21.5	E34.0	E64.0	E71.311	E74.02	E79.9	E88.81
D44.11	E06.3	E10.69	E22.0	E34.1	E64.1	E71.312	E74.03	E80.0	E88.89
D44.12	E06.4	E10.8	E22.1	E34.2	E64.2	E71.313	E74.04	E80.1	E88.9
D44.2	E06.5	E10.9	E22.2	E34.3	E64.8	E71.314	E74.09	E80.20	E89.0
D44.3	E06.9	E11.00	E22.8	E34.4	E64.9	E71.318	E74.20	E80.21	E89.1
D44.4	E07.0	E11.01	E22.9	E34.50	E65	E71.32	E74.21	E80.29	E89.2
D44.9	E07.1	E11.10	E23.0	E34.51	E66.01	E71.39	E74.29	E80.3	E89.3
D49.7	E07.89	E11.11	E23.1	E34.52	E66.09	E71.40	E74.4	E83.00	E89.5
D81.30	E07.9	E11.618	E23.2	E34.8	E66.1	E71.41	E74.8	E83.01	E89.6
D81.31	E08.00	E11.620	E23.3	E34.9	E66.3	E71.42	E74.9	E83.09	H49.811
D81.32	E08.01	E11.621	E23.6	E35	E66.8	E71.43	E75.21	E83.10	H49.812
D81.39	E08.10	E11.622	E23.7	E40	E66.9	E71.440	E75.22	E83.110	H49.813
D81.5	E08.11	E11.628	E24.0	E41	E67.0	E71.448	E75.240	E83.111	H49.819
D81.810	E08.618	E11.630	E24.1	E42	E67.1	E71.50	E75.241	E83.118	P92.6
D81.818	E08.620	E11.638	E24.2	E43	E67.2	E71.510	E75.242	E83.119	Q89.1
D81.819	E08.621	E11.641	E24.3	E44.0	E67.3	E71.511	E75.243	E83.19	Q89.2
D84.1	E08.622	E11.649	E24.4	E44.1	E67.8	E71.518	E75.248	E83.30	R29.0
E00.0	E08.628	E11.65	E24.8	E45	E68	E71.520	E75.249	E83.31	R62.0
E00.1	E08.630	E11.69	E24.9	E46	E70.0	E71.521	E75.3	E83.32	R62.50
E00.2	E08.638	E11.8	E25.0	E50.8	E70.1	E71.522	E75.5	E83.39	R62.51

R62.52	R63.1	R63.5	R73.02	R81	S11.10XA	S11.14XA	S37.818A	Z68.43
R62.59	R63.2	R63.6	R73.03	R82.4	S11.11XA	S11.15XA	S37.819A	Z68.44
R62.7	R63.3	R63.8	R73.09	R94.6	S11.12XA	S37.812A	Z68.41	Z68.45
R63.0	R63.4	R73.01	R73.9	R94.7	S11.13XA	S37.813A	Z68.42	

MDC 11 Diseases And Disorders Of The Kidney And Urinary Tract

A18.10	D41.20	N00.6	N07.3	N25.81	N35.814	Q60.4	R33.0	S37.022A	T83.22XA
A18.11	D41.21	N00.7	N07.4	N25.89	N35.816	Q60.5	R33.8	S37.029A	T83.23XA
A18.12	D41.22	N00.8	N07.5	N25.9	N35.819	Q60.6	R33.9	S37.031A	T83.24XA
A18.13	D41.3	N00.9	N07.6	N26.1	N35.82	Q61.00	R34	S37.032A	T83.25XA
A36.85	D41.4	N01.0	N07.7	N26.9	N35.911	Q61.01	R35.0	S37.039A	T83.29XA
A52.75	D41.8	N01.1	N07.8	N27.0	N35.912	Q61.02	R35.1	S37.041A	T83.410A
A54.01	D41.9	N01.2	N07.9	N27.1	N35.913	Q61.11	R35.8	S37.042A	T83.411A
A56.11	D49.4	N01.3	N08	N27.9	N35.914	Q61.19	R36.0	S37.049A	T83.418A
A56.19	D49.511	N01.4	N10	N28.0	N35.916	Q61.2	R36.9	S37.051A	T83.420A
A98.5	D49.512	N01.5	N11.0	N28.1	N35.919	Q61.3	R39.0	S37.052A	T83.421A
B65.0	D49.519	N01.6	N11.1	N28.81	N35.92	Q61.4	R39.11	S37.059A	T83.428A
B90.1	D49.59	N01.7	N11.8	N28.82	N36.0	Q61.5	R39.12	S37.061A	T83.490A
C64.1	E08.21	N01.8	N11.9	N28.83	N36.1	Q61.8	R39.13	S37.062A	T83.491A
C64.2	E08.22	N01.9	N12	N28.84	N36.2	Q61.9	R39.14	S37.069A	T83.498A
C64.9	E08.29	N02.0	N13.0	N28.85	N36.41	Q62.0	R39.15	S37.091A	T83.510A
C65.1	E09.21	N02.1	N13.1	N28.86	N36.42	Q62.10	R39.16	S37.092A	T83.511A
C65.2	E09.22	N02.2	N13.2	N28.89	N36.43	Q62.11	R39.191	S37.099A	T83.512A
C65.9	E09.29	N02.3	N13.30	N28.9	N36.44	Q62.12	R39.192	S37.10XA	T83.518A
C66.1	E10.21	N02.4	N13.39	N29	N36.5	Q62.2	R39.198	S37.12XA	T83.590A
C66.2	E10.22	N02.5	N13.4	N30.00	N36.8	Q62.31	R39.2	S37.13XA	T83.591A
C66.9	E10.29	N02.6	N13.5	N30.01	N36.9	Q62.32	R39.81	S37.19XA	T83.592A
C67.0	E11.21	N02.7	N13.6	N30.10	N37	Q62.39	R39.82	S37.20XA	T83.593A
C67.1	E11.22	N02.8	N13.70	N30.11	N39.0	Q62.4	R39.83	S37.22XA	T83.598A
C67.2	E11.29	N02.9	N13.71	N30.20	N39.3	Q62.5	R39.84	S37.23XA	T83.61XA
C67.3	E13.21	N03.0	N13.721	N30.21	N39.41	Q62.60	R39.89	S37.29XA	T83.62XA
C67.4	E13.22	N03.1	N13.722	N30.30	N39.42	Q62.61	R39.9	S37.30XA	T83.69XA
C67.5	E13.29	N03.2	N13.729	N30.31	N39.43	Q62.62	R80.0	S37.32XA	T83.712A
C67.6	E88.3	N03.3	N13.731	N30.40	N39.44	Q62.63	R80.1	S37.33XA	T83.713A
C67.7	I12.0	N03.4	N13.732	N30.41	N39.45	Q62.69	R80.2	S37.39XA	T83.714A
C67.8	I12.9	N03.5	N13.739	N30.80	N39.46	Q62.7	R80.3	T19.0XXA	T83.718A
C67.9	I13.10	N03.6	N13.8	N30.81	N39.490	Q62.8	R80.8	T19.1XXA	T83.719A
C68.0	I13.11	N03.7	N13.9	N30.90	N39.491	Q63.0	R80.9	T19.8XXA	T83.722A
C68.1	I70.1	N03.8	N14.0	N30.91	N39.492	Q63.1	R82.0	T19.9XXA	T83.723A
C68.8	I72.2	N03.9	N14.1	N31.0	N39.498	Q63.2	R82.3	T79.5XXA	T83.724A
C68.9	I75.81	N04.0	N14.2	N31.1	N39.8	Q63.3	R82.5	T81.711A	T83.728A
C79.00	I77.73	N04.1	N14.3	N31.2	N39.9	Q63.8	R82.6	T83.010A	T83.729A
C79.01	I82.3	N04.2	N14.4	N31.8	N99.0	Q63.9	R82.71	T83.011A	T83.79XA
C79.02	M10.30	N04.3	N15.0	N31.9	N99.110	Q64.10	R82.79	T83.018A	T83.81XA
C79.10	M10.311	N04.4	N15.1	N32.0	N99.111	Q64.11	R82.81	T83.020A	T83.82XA
C79.11	M10.312	N04.5	N15.8	N32.1	N99.112	Q64.12	R82.89	T83.021A	T83.83XA
C79.19	M10.319	N04.6	N15.9	N32.2	N99.113	Q64.19	R82.90	T83.022A	T83.84XA
C7A.093	M10.321	N04.7	N16	N32.3	N99.114	Q64.2	R82.91	T83.028A	T83.85XA
D09.0	M10.322	N04.8	N17.0	N32.81	N99.115	Q64.31	R82.991	T83.030A	T83.86XA
D09.10	M10.329	N04.9	N17.1	N32.89	N99.116	Q64.32	R82.992	T83.031A	T83.89XA
D09.19	M10.331	N05.0	N17.2	N32.9	N99.12	Q64.33	R82.993	T83.032A	T83.9XXA
D17.71	M10.332	N05.1	N17.8	N33	N99.510	Q64.39	R82.994	T83.038A	T86.10
D17.72	M10.339	N05.2	N17.9	N34.0	N99.511	Q64.4	R82.998	T83.090A	T86.11
D30.00	M10.341	N05.3	N18.1	N34.1	N99.512	Q64.5	R93.41	T83.091A	T86.12
D30.01	M10.342	N05.4	N18.2	N34.2	N99.518	Q64.6	R93.421	T83.092A	T86.13
D30.02	M10.349	N05.5	N18.3	N34.3	N99.520	Q64.70	R93.422	T83.098A	T86.19
D30.10	M10.351	N05.6	N18.4	N35.010	N99.521	Q64.71	R93.429	T83.110A	Z43.5
D30.11	M10.352	N05.7	N18.5	N35.011	N99.522	Q64.72	R93.49	T83.111A	Z43.6
D30.12	M10.359	N05.8	N18.6	N35.012	N99.523	Q64.73	R94.4	T83.112A	Z46.6
D30.20	M10.361	N05.9	N18.9	N35.013	N99.524	Q64.74	R94.8	T83.113A	Z49.01
D30.21	M10.362	N06.0	N19	N35.014	N99.528	Q64.75	S31.001A	T83.118A	Z49.02
D30.22	M10.369	N06.1	N20.0	N35.016	N99.530	Q64.79	S31.011A	T83.120A	Z49.31
D30.3	M10.371	N06.2	N20.1	N35.021	N99.531	Q64.8	S31.021A	T83.121A	Z49.32
D30.4	M10.372	N06.3	N20.2	N35.028	N99.532	Q64.9	S31.031A	T83.122A	Z52.4
D30.8	M10.379	N06.4	N20.9	N35.111	N99.533	R30.0	S31.041A	T83.123A	Z90.6
D30.9	M10.38	N06.5	N21.0	N35.112	N99.534	R30.1	S31.051A	T83.128A	Z94.0
D3A.093	M10.39	N06.6	N21.1	N35.113	N99.538	R30.9	S37.002A	T83.190A	Z96.0
D41.00	N00.0	N06.7	N21.8	N35.114	N99.81	R31.0	S37.009A	T83.191A	
D41.01	N00.1	N06.8	N21.9	N35.116	N99.89	R31.1	S37.011A	T83.192A	
D41.02	N00.2	N06.9	N22	N35.119	Q60.0	R31.21	S37.012A	T83.193A	
D41.10	N00.3	N07.0	N23	N35.12	Q60.1	R31.29	S37.019A	T83.198A	
D41.11	N00.4	N07.1	N25.0	N35.811	Q60.2	R31.9	S37.021A	T83.21XA	
D41.12	N00.5	N07.2	N25.1	N35.812	Q60.3	R32			
				N35.813					

MDC 12 Diseases And Disorders Of The Male Reproductive System

A18.14	A54.23	A57	A60.02	B37.42	C62.00	C62.92	C63.7	D07.61	D29.30
A18.15	A54.29	A58	A60.09	B37.49	C62.01	C63.00	C63.8	D07.69	D29.31
A51.0	A55	A59.00	A60.1	C60.0	C62.02	C63.01	C63.9	D17.6	D29.32
A54.00	A56.00	A59.02	A60.9	C60.1	C62.10	C63.02	C76.3	D29.0	D29.4
A54.09	A56.01	A59.03	A63.8	C60.2	C62.11	C63.10	C79.82	D29.1	D29.8
A54.1	A56.09	A59.09	A64	C60.8	C62.12	C63.11	D07.4	D29.20	D29.9
A54.21	A56.2	A60.00	B26.0	C60.9	C62.90	C63.12	D07.5	D29.21	D40.0
A54.22	A56.8	A60.01	B37.41	C61	C62.91	C63.2	D07.60	D29.22	D40.10

D40.11	N42.83	N46.029	N48.39	N52.2	Q53.212	Q55.9	R86.9	S31.541A	S37.892A
D40.12	N42.89	N46.11	N48.5	N52.31	Q53.22	Q56.0	R93.811	S31.541S	S37.892S
D40.8	N42.9	N46.121	N48.6	N52.32	Q53.23	Q56.1	R93.812	S31.551A	S37.893S
D40.9	N43.0	N46.122	N48.81	N52.33	Q53.9	Q56.3	R93.813	S31.551S	S37.898A
I86.1	N43.1	N46.123	N48.82	N52.34	Q54.0	Q56.4	R93.819	S37.10XS	S37.898S
I86.2	N43.2	N46.124	N48.83	N52.35	Q54.1	Q64.0	S30.201A	S37.12XS	S37.899A
L29.1	N43.3	N46.125	N48.89	N52.36	Q54.2	Q98.0	S30.21XA	S37.13XS	S37.899S
L29.3	N43.40	N46.129	N48.9	N52.37	Q54.3	Q98.1	S31.20XA	S37.19XS	S37.90XA
N34	N43.41	N46.8	N49.0	N52.39	Q54.4	Q98.3	S31.21XA	S37.20XS	S37.90XS
N40.0	N43.42	N46.9	N49.1	N52.8	Q54.8	Q98.4	S31.22XA	S37.22XS	S37.92XA
N40.1	N44.00	N47.0	N49.2	N52.9	Q54.9	Q98.5	S31.23XA	S37.23XS	S37.92XS
N40.2	N44.01	N47.1	N49.3	N53.11	Q55.0	Q98.6	S31.24XA	S37.29XS	S37.93XA
N40.3	N44.02	N47.2	N49.8	N53.12	Q55.1	Q98.7	S31.25XA	S37.30XS	S37.93XS
N41.0	N44.03	N47.3	N49.9	N53.13	Q55.20	Q98.8	S31.30XA	S37.32XS	S37.99XA
N41.1	N44.04	N47.4	N50.0	N53.14	Q55.21	Q98.9	S31.31XA	S37.33XS	S37.99XS
N41.2	N44.1	N47.5	N50.1	N53.19	Q55.22	Q99.0	S31.32XA	S37.39XS	S38.001A
N41.3	N44.2	N47.6	N50.3	N53.8	Q55.23	Q99.1	S31.33XA	S37.812S	S38.01XA
N41.4	N44.8	N47.7	N50.811	N53.9	Q55.29	Q99.8	S31.34XA	S37.813S	S38.02XA
N41.8	N45.1	N47.8	N50.812	Q53.00	Q55.3	R36.1	S31.35XA	S37.818S	S38.221A
N41.9	N45.2	N48.0	N50.819	Q53.01	Q55.4	R86.0	S31.501A	S37.819S	S38.222A
N42.0	N45.3	N48.1	N50.82	Q53.02	Q55.5	R86.1	S31.501S	S37.822S	S38.231A
N42.1	N45.4	N48.21	N50.89	Q53.10	Q55.61	R86.2	S31.511A	S37.822S	S38.232A
N42.30	N46.01	N48.22	N50.9	Q53.111	Q55.62	R86.3	S31.511S	S37.823A	T19.4XXA
N42.31	N46.021	N48.29	N51	Q53.112	Q55.63	R86.4	S31.521A	S37.823S	Z30.2
N42.32	N46.022	N48.30	N52.01	Q53.12	Q55.64	R86.5	S31.521S	S37.828A	Z31.0
N42.39	N46.023	N48.31	N52.02	Q53.13	Q55.69	R86.6	S31.531A	S37.828S	Z41.2
N42.81	N46.024	N48.32	N52.03	Q53.20	Q55.7	R86.7	S31.531S	S37.829A	Z90.79
N42.82	N46.025	N48.33	N52.1	Q53.211	Q55.8	R86.8		S37.829S	

MDC 13 Diseases And Disorders Of The Female Reproductive System

A18.16	C56.2	E28.0	N77.1	N83.512	N90.69	N99.83	Q96.0	S31.552S	S37.529S	
A18.17	C56.9	E28.1	N80.0	N83.519	N90.7	N99.85	Q96.1	S37.10XS	S37.531A	
A18.18	C57.00	E28.2	N80.1	N83.521	N90.810	Q50.01	Q96.2	S37.12XS	S37.531S	
A51.0	C57.01	E28.310	N80.2	N83.522	N90.811	Q50.02	Q96.3	S37.13XS	S37.532A	
A54.00	C57.02	E28.319	N80.3	N83.529	N90.812	Q50.1	Q96.4	S37.19XS	S37.532S	
A54.02	C57.10	E28.39	N80.4	N83.53	N90.813	Q50.2	Q96.8	S37.20XS	S37.539A	
A54.03	C57.11	E28.8	N80.8	N83.6	N90.818	Q50.31	Q96.9	S37.22XS	S37.539S	
A54.09	C57.12	E28.9	N80.9	N83.7	N90.89	Q50.32	Q97.0	S37.23XS	S37.591A	
A54.1	C57.20	E89.40	N81.0	N83.8	N90.9	Q50.39	Q97.1	S37.29XS	S37.591S	
A54.21	C57.21	E89.41	N81.10	N83.9	N91.0	Q50.4	Q97.2	S37.30XS	S37.592A	
A54.24	C57.22	F52.5	N81.11	N84.0	N91.1	Q50.5	Q97.3	S37.32XS	S37.592S	
A54.29	C57.3	I86.2	N81.12	N84.1	N91.2	Q50.6	Q97.8	S37.33XS	S37.599A	
A55	C57.4	I86.3	N81.2	N84.2	N91.3	Q51.0	Q97.9	S37.39XS	S37.599S	
A56.00	C57.7	L29.2	N81.3	N84.3	N91.4	Q51.10	Q98.5	S37.401A	S37.60XA	
A56.01	C57.8	L29.3	N81.4	N84.8	N91.5	Q51.11	Q99.0	S37.401S	S37.60XS	
A56.02	C57.9	N34.1	N81.5	N84.9	N92.0	Q51.20	Q99.1	S37.402A	S37.62XA	
A56.09	C58	N39.3	N81.6	N85.00	N92.1	Q51.21	Q99.8	S37.402S	S37.62XS	
A56.2	C76.3	N70.01	N81.81	N85.01	N92.2	Q51.22	R87.610	S37.409A	S37.63XA	
A56.8	C79.60	N70.02	N81.82	N85.02	N92.3	Q51.28	R87.611	S37.409S	S37.63XS	
A57	C79.61	N70.03	N81.83	N85.2	N92.4	Q51.3	R87.612	S37.421A	S37.69XA	
A58	C79.62	N70.11	N81.84	N85.3	N92.5	Q51.4	R87.613	S37.421S	S37.69XS	
A59.00	C79.82	N70.12	N81.85	N85.4	N92.6	Q51.5	R87.614	S37.422A	S37.812S	
A59.01	D06.0	N70.13	N81.89	N85.5	N93.0	Q51.6	R87.615	S37.422S	S37.813S	
A59.03	D06.1	N70.91	N81.9	N85.6	N93.1	Q51.7	R87.616	S37.429A	S37.818S	
A59.09	D06.7	N70.92	N82.0	N85.7	N93.8	Q51.810	R87.620	S37.429S	S37.819S	
A60.00	D06.9	N70.93	N82.1	N85.8	N93.9	Q51.811	R87.621	S37.431A	S37.892A	
A60.03	D07.0	N71.0	N82.5	N85.9	N94.0	Q51.818	R87.622	S37.431S	S37.892S	
A60.04	D07.1	N71.1	N82.8	N86	N94.10	Q51.820	R87.623	S37.432A	S37.893A	
A60.09	D07.2	N71.9	N82.9	N87.0	N94.11	Q51.821	R87.624	S37.432S	S37.893S	
A60.1	D07.30	N72	N83.00	N87.1	N94.12	Q51.828	R87.625	S37.439A	S37.898A	
A60.9	D07.39	N73.0	N83.01	N87.9	N94.19	Q51.9	R87.628	S37.439S	S37.898S	
A63.8	D25.0	N73.1	N83.02	N88.0	N94.2	Q52.0	R87.810	S37.491A	S37.899A	
A64	D25.1	N73.2	N83.10	N88.1	N94.3	Q52.10	R87.811	S37.491S	S37.899S	
B37.3	D25.2	N73.3	N83.11	N88.2	N94.4	Q52.11	R87.820	S37.492A	S37.90XA	
B37.41	D25.9	N73.4	N83.12	N88.3	N94.5	Q52.120	R87.821	S37.492S	S37.90XS	
B37.49	D26.0	N73.5	N83.201	N88.4	N94.6	Q52.121	S30.202A	S37.499A	S37.92XA	
C51.0	D26.1	N73.6	N83.202	N88.8	N94.810	Q52.122	S30.23XA	S37.499S	S37.92XS	
C51.1	D26.7	N73.8	N83.209	N88.9	N94.818	Q52.123	S31.40XA	S37.501A	S37.93XA	
C51.2	D26.9	N73.9	N83.291	N89.0	N94.819	Q52.124	S31.41XA	S37.501S	S37.93XS	
C51.8	D27.0	N74	N83.292	N89.1	N94.89	Q52.129	S31.42XA	S37.502A	S37.99XA	
C51.9	D27.1	N75.0	N83.299	N89.3	N94.9	Q52.2	S31.43XA	S37.502S	S37.99XS	
C52	D27.9	N75.1	N83.311	N89.4	N95.0	Q52.3	S31.44XA	S37.509A	S38.002A	
C53.0	D28.0	N75.8	N83.312	N89.5	N95.1	Q52.4	S31.45XA	S37.509S	S38.03XA	
C53.1	D28.1	N75.9	N83.319	N89.6	N95.2	Q52.5	S31.50XA	S37.511A	S38.211A	
C53.8	D28.2	N76.0	N83.321	N89.7	N95.8	Q52.6	S31.502S	S37.511S	S38.212A	
C53.9	D28.7	N76.1	N83.322	N89.8	N95.9	Q52.70	S31.512A	S37.512A	T19.2XXA	
C54.0	D28.9	N76.2	N83.329	N89.9	N96	Q52.71	S31.512S	S37.512S	T19.3XXA	
C54.1	D39.0	N76.3	N83.331	N90.0	N97.0	Q52.79	S31.522A	S37.519A	T83.31XA	
C54.2	D39.10	N76.4	N83.332	N90.1	N97.1	Q52.8	S31.522S	S37.519S	T83.32XA	
C54.3	D39.11	N76.5	N83.339	N90.3	N97.2	Q52.9	S31.532A	S37.521A	T83.39XA	
C54.8	D39.12	N76.6	N83.40	N90.4	N97.8	Q56.0	S31.532S	S37.521S	T83.711A	
C54.9	D39.2	N76.81	N83.41	N90.5	N97.9	Q56.2	S31.542A	S37.522A	T83.721A	
C55	D39.8	N76.89	N83.42	N90.60	N99.2	Q56.3	S31.542S	S37.522S	Z30.2	
C56.1	D39.9	N77.0	N83.511	N90.61	N99.3	Q56.4	S31.552A	S37.529A	Z31.0	

Z40.02	Z40.03	Z43.7	Z64.1	Z90.710	Z90.711	Z90.712	Z90.721	Z90.722	Z90.79

MDC 14 Pregnancy, Childbirth And The Puerperium

A34	O07.4	O10.019	O14.94	O23.529	O26.611	O29.292	O30.223	O31.12X5	O31.8X32
O00.00	O08.0	O10.02	O14.95	O23.591	O26.612	O29.293	O30.229	O31.12X9	O31.8X33
O00.01	O08.1	O10.03	O15.00	O23.592	O26.613	O29.299	O30.231	O31.13X0	O31.8X34
O00.101	O08.2	O10.111	O15.02	O23.593	O26.619	O29.3X1	O30.232	O31.13X1	O31.8X35
O00.102	O08.3	O10.112	O15.03	O23.599	O26.62	O29.3X2	O30.233	O31.13X2	O31.8X39
O00.109	O08.4	O10.113	O15.1	O23.90	O26.63	O29.3X9	O30.239	O31.13X3	O31.8X90
O00.111	O08.5	O10.119	O15.2	O23.91	O26.711	O29.40	O30.291	O31.13X4	O31.8X91
O00.112	O08.6	O10.12	O15.9	O23.92	O26.712	O29.41	O30.292	O31.13X5	O31.8X92
O00.119	O08.7	O10.13	O16.1	O23.93	O26.713	O29.42	O30.293	O31.13X9	O31.8X93
O00.201	O08.81	O10.211	O16.2	O24.011	O26.719	O29.43	O30.299	O31.20X0	O31.8X94
O00.202	O08.82	O10.212	O16.3	O24.012	O26.72	O29.5X1	O30.801	O31.20X1	O31.8X95
O00.209	O08.83	O10.213	O16.4	O24.013	O26.73	O29.5X2	O30.802	O31.20X2	O31.8X99
O00.211	O08.89	O10.219	O16.5	O24.019	O26.811	O29.5X3	O30.803	O31.20X3	O32.0XX0
O00.212	O08.9	O10.22	O16.9	O24.02	O26.812	O29.5X9	O30.809	O31.20X4	O32.0XX1
O00.219	O09.00	O10.23	O20.0	O24.03	O26.813	O29.60	O30.811	O31.20X5	O32.0XX2
O00.80	O09.01	O10.311	O20.8	O24.111	O26.819	O29.61	O30.812	O31.20X9	O32.0XX3
O00.81	O09.02	O10.312	O20.9	O24.112	O26.821	O29.62	O30.813	O31.21X0	O32.0XX4
O00.90	O09.03	O10.313	O21.0	O24.113	O26.822	O29.63	O30.819	O31.21X1	O32.0XX5
O00.91	O09.10	O10.319	O21.1	O24.119	O26.823	O29.8X1	O30.821	O31.21X2	O32.0XX9
O01.0	O09.11	O10.32	O21.2	O24.12	O26.829	O29.8X2	O30.822	O31.21X3	O32.1XX0
O01.1	O09.12	O10.33	O21.8	O24.13	O26.831	O29.8X3	O30.823	O31.21X4	O32.1XX1
O01.9	O09.13	O10.411	O21.9	O24.311	O26.832	O29.8X9	O30.829	O31.21X5	O32.1XX2
O02.0	O09.211	O10.412	O22.00	O24.312	O26.833	O29.90	O30.831	O31.21X9	O32.1XX3
O02.1	O09.212	O10.413	O22.01	O24.313	O26.839	O29.91	O30.832	O31.22X0	O32.1XX4
O02.81	O09.213	O10.419	O22.02	O24.319	O26.841	O29.92	O30.833	O31.22X1	O32.1XX5
O02.89	O09.219	O10.42	O22.03	O24.32	O26.842	O29.93	O30.839	O31.22X2	O32.1XX9
O02.9	O09.291	O10.43	O22.10	O24.33	O26.843	O30.001	O30.891	O31.22X3	O32.2XX0
O03.0	O09.292	O10.911	O22.11	O24.410	O26.849	O30.002	O30.892	O31.22X4	O32.2XX1
O03.1	O09.293	O10.912	O22.12	O24.414	O26.851	O30.003	O30.893	O31.22X5	O32.2XX2
O03.2	O09.299	O10.913	O22.13	O24.415	O26.852	O30.009	O30.899	O31.22X9	O32.2XX3
O03.30	O09.30	O10.919	O22.20	O24.419	O26.853	O30.011	O30.90	O31.23X0	O32.2XX4
O03.31	O09.31	O10.92	O22.21	O24.420	O26.859	O30.012	O30.91	O31.23X1	O32.2XX5
O03.32	O09.32	O10.93	O22.22	O24.424	O26.86	O30.013	O30.92	O31.23X2	O32.2XX9
O03.33	O09.33	O11.1	O22.23	O24.425	O26.872	O30.019	O30.93	O31.23X3	O32.3XX0
O03.34	O09.40	O11.2	O22.30	O24.429	O26.873	O30.021	O31.00X0	O31.23X4	O32.3XX1
O03.35	O09.41	O11.3	O22.31	O24.430	O26.879	O30.022	O31.00X1	O31.23X5	O32.3XX2
O03.36	O09.42	O11.4	O22.32	O24.434	O26.891	O30.023	O31.00X2	O31.23X9	O32.3XX3
O03.37	O09.43	O11.5	O22.33	O24.435	O26.892	O30.029	O31.00X3	O31.30X0	O32.3XX4
O03.38	O09.511	O11.9	O22.40	O24.439	O26.893	O30.031	O31.00X4	O31.30X1	O32.3XX9
O03.39	O09.512	O12.00	O22.41	O24.811	O26.899	O30.032	O31.00X5	O31.30X2	O32.4XX0
O03.4	O09.513	O12.01	O22.42	O24.812	O26.90	O30.033	O31.00X9	O31.30X3	O32.4XX1
O03.5	O09.519	O12.02	O22.43	O24.813	O26.91	O30.039	O31.01X0	O31.30X4	O32.4XX2
O03.6	O09.521	O12.03	O22.50	O24.819	O26.92	O30.041	O31.01X1	O31.30X5	O32.4XX3
O03.7	O09.522	O12.04	O22.51	O24.82	O26.93	O30.042	O31.01X2	O31.30X9	O32.4XX4
O03.80	O09.523	O12.05	O22.52	O24.83	O28.0	O30.043	O31.01X3	O31.31X0	O32.4XX5
O03.81	O09.529	O12.10	O22.53	O24.911	O28.1	O30.049	O31.01X4	O31.31X1	O32.4XX9
O03.82	O09.611	O12.11	O22.8X1	O24.912	O28.2	O30.091	O31.01X5	O31.31X2	O32.6XX0
O03.83	O09.612	O12.12	O22.8X2	O24.913	O28.3	O30.092	O31.01X9	O31.31X3	O32.6XX1
O03.84	O09.613	O12.13	O22.8X3	O24.919	O28.4	O30.093	O31.02X0	O31.31X4	O32.6XX2
O03.85	O09.619	O12.14	O22.8X9	O24.92	O28.5	O30.099	O31.02X1	O31.31X5	O32.6XX3
O03.86	O09.621	O12.15	O22.90	O24.93	O28.8	O30.101	O31.02X2	O31.31X9	O32.6XX4
O03.87	O09.622	O12.20	O22.91	O25.10	O28.9	O30.102	O31.02X3	O31.32X0	O32.6XX5
O03.88	O09.623	O12.21	O22.92	O25.11	O29.011	O30.103	O31.02X4	O31.32X1	O32.6XX9
O03.89	O09.629	O12.22	O22.93	O25.12	O29.012	O30.109	O31.02X5	O31.32X2	O32.8XX0
O03.9	O09.70	O12.23	O23.00	O25.13	O29.013	O30.111	O31.02X9	O31.32X3	O32.8XX1
O04.5	O09.71	O12.24	O23.01	O25.2	O29.019	O30.112	O31.03X0	O31.32X4	O32.8XX2
O04.6	O09.72	O12.25	O23.02	O25.3	O29.021	O30.113	O31.03X1	O31.32X5	O32.8XX3
O04.7	O09.73	O13.1	O23.03	O26.00	O29.022	O30.119	O31.03X2	O31.32X9	O32.8XX4
O04.80	O09.811	O13.2	O23.10	O26.01	O29.023	O30.121	O31.03X3	O31.33X0	O32.8XX5
O04.81	O09.812	O13.3	O23.11	O26.02	O29.029	O30.122	O31.03X4	O31.33X1	O32.8XX9
O04.82	O09.813	O13.4	O23.12	O26.03	O29.091	O30.123	O31.03X5	O31.33X2	O32.9XX0
O04.83	O09.819	O13.5	O23.13	O26.10	O29.092	O30.129	O31.03X9	O31.33X3	O32.9XX1
O04.84	O09.821	O13.9	O23.20	O26.11	O29.093	O30.129	O31.10X0	O31.33X4	O32.9XX2
O04.85	O09.822	O14.00	O23.21	O26.12	O29.099	O30.131	O31.10X1	O31.33X5	O32.9XX3
O04.86	O09.823	O14.02	O23.22	O26.13	O29.111	O30.132	O31.10X2	O31.33X9	O32.9XX4
O04.87	O09.829	O14.03	O23.23	O26.20	O29.112	O30.133	O31.10X3	O31.8X10	O32.9XX5
O04.88	O09.891	O14.04	O23.30	O26.21	O29.113	O30.139	O31.10X4	O31.8X11	O32.9XX9
O04.89	O09.892	O14.05	O23.31	O26.22	O29.119	O30.191	O31.10X5	O31.8X12	O33.0
O07.0	O09.893	O14.10	O23.32	O26.23	O29.121	O30.192	O31.10X9	O31.8X13	O33.1
O07.1	O09.899	O14.12	O23.33	O26.30	O29.122	O30.193	O31.11X0	O31.8X14	O33.2
O07.2	O09.90	O14.13	O23.40	O26.31	O29.123	O30.199	O31.11X1	O31.8X15	O33.3XX0
O07.30	O09.91	O14.14	O23.41	O26.32	O29.129	O30.201	O31.11X2	O31.8X19	O33.3XX1
O07.31	O09.92	O14.15	O23.42	O26.33	O29.191	O30.202	O31.11X3	O31.8X20	O33.3XX2
O07.32	O09.93	O14.20	O23.43	O26.40	O29.192	O30.203	O31.11X4	O31.8X21	O33.3XX3
O07.33	O09.A0	O14.22	O23.511	O26.41	O29.193	O30.209	O31.11X5	O31.8X22	O33.3XX4
O07.34	O09.A1	O14.23	O23.512	O26.42	O29.199	O30.211	O31.11X9	O31.8X23	O33.3XX5
O07.35	O09.A2	O14.24	O23.513	O26.43	O29.211	O30.212	O31.12X0	O31.8X24	O33.3XX9
O07.36	O09.A3	O14.25	O23.519	O26.50	O29.212	O30.213	O31.12X1	O31.8X25	O33.4XX0
O07.37	O10.011	O14.90	O23.521	O26.51	O29.213	O30.219	O31.12X2	O31.8X29	O33.4XX1
O07.38	O10.012	O14.92	O23.522	O26.52	O29.219	O30.221	O31.12X3	O31.8X30	O33.4XX2
O07.39	O10.013	O14.93	O23.523	O26.53	O29.291	O30.222	O31.12X4	O31.8X31	

O33.4XX3	O35.1XX0	O36.0192	O36.1994	O36.5939	O36.8191	O36.8993	O41.03X5	O41.8X10	O43.111
O33.4XX4	O35.1XX1	O36.0193	O36.1995	O36.5990	O36.8192	O36.8994	O41.03X9	O41.8X11	O43.112
O33.4XX5	O35.1XX2	O36.0194	O36.1999	O36.5991	O36.8193	O36.8995	O41.1010	O41.8X12	O43.113
O33.4XX9	O35.1XX3	O36.0195	O36.20X0	O36.5992	O36.8194	O36.8999	O41.1011	O41.8X13	O43.119
O33.5XX0	O35.1XX4	O36.0199	O36.20X1	O36.5993	O36.8195	O36.90X0	O41.1012	O41.8X14	O43.121
O33.5XX1	O35.1XX5	O36.0910	O36.20X2	O36.5994	O36.8199	O36.90X1	O41.1013	O41.8X15	O43.122
O33.5XX2	O35.1XX9	O36.0911	O36.20X3	O36.5995	O36.8210	O36.90X2	O41.1014	O41.8X19	O43.123
O33.5XX3	O35.2XX0	O36.0912	O36.20X4	O36.5999	O36.8211	O36.90X4	O41.1015	O41.8X20	O43.129
O33.5XX4	O35.2XX1	O36.0913	O36.20X5	O36.60X0	O36.8212	O36.90X5	O41.1019	O41.8X21	O43.191
O33.5XX5	O35.2XX2	O36.0914	O36.20X9	O36.60X1	O36.8213	O36.90X9	O41.1020	O41.8X22	O43.192
O33.5XX9	O35.2XX3	O36.0915	O36.21X0	O36.60X2	O36.8214	O36.91X0	O41.1021	O41.8X23	O43.193
O33.6XX0	O35.2XX4	O36.0919	O36.21X1	O36.60X3	O36.8215	O36.91X1	O41.1022	O41.8X24	O43.199
O33.6XX1	O35.2XX5	O36.0920	O36.21X2	O36.60X4	O36.8219	O36.91X2	O41.1023	O41.8X25	O43.211
O33.6XX2	O35.2XX9	O36.0921	O36.21X3	O36.60X5	O36.8220	O36.91X3	O41.1024	O41.8X29	O43.212
O33.6XX3	O35.3XX0	O36.0922	O36.21X4	O36.60X9	O36.8221	O36.91X4	O41.1025	O41.8X30	O43.213
O33.6XX4	O35.3XX1	O36.0923	O36.21X5	O36.61X0	O36.8222	O36.91X5	O41.1029	O41.8X31	O43.219
O33.6XX5	O35.3XX2	O36.0924	O36.21X9	O36.61X1	O36.8223	O36.91X9	O41.1030	O41.8X32	O43.221
O33.6XX9	O35.3XX3	O36.0925	O36.22X0	O36.61X2	O36.8224	O36.92X0	O41.1031	O41.8X33	O43.222
O33.7XX0	O35.3XX4	O36.0929	O36.22X1	O36.61X3	O36.8225	O36.92X1	O41.1032	O41.8X34	O43.223
O33.7XX1	O35.3XX5	O36.0930	O36.22X2	O36.61X4	O36.8229	O36.92X2	O41.1033	O41.8X35	O43.229
O33.7XX2	O35.3XX9	O36.0931	O36.22X3	O36.61X5	O36.8230	O36.92X3	O41.1034	O41.8X39	O43.231
O33.7XX3	O35.4XX0	O36.0932	O36.22X4	O36.61X9	O36.8231	O36.92X4	O41.1035	O41.8X90	O43.232
O33.7XX4	O35.4XX1	O36.0933	O36.22X5	O36.62X0	O36.8232	O36.92X5	O41.1039	O41.8X91	O43.233
O33.7XX5	O35.4XX2	O36.0934	O36.22X9	O36.62X1	O36.8233	O36.92X9	O41.1090	O41.8X92	O43.239
O33.7XX9	O35.4XX3	O36.0935	O36.23X0	O36.62X2	O36.8234	O36.93X0	O41.1091	O41.8X93	O43.811
O33.8	O35.4XX4	O36.0939	O36.23X1	O36.62X3	O36.8235	O36.93X1	O41.1092	O41.8X94	O43.812
O33.9	O35.4XX5	O36.0990	O36.23X2	O36.62X4	O36.8239	O36.93X2	O41.1093	O41.8X95	O43.813
O34.00	O35.4XX9	O36.0991	O36.23X3	O36.62X5	O36.8290	O36.93X3	O41.1094	O41.8X99	O43.819
O34.01	O35.5XX0	O36.0992	O36.23X4	O36.62X9	O36.8291	O36.93X4	O41.1095	O41.90X0	O43.891
O34.02	O35.5XX1	O36.0993	O36.23X5	O36.63X0	O36.8292	O36.93X5	O41.1099	O41.90X1	O43.892
O34.03	O35.5XX2	O36.0994	O36.23X9	O36.63X1	O36.8293	O36.93X9	O41.1210	O41.90X2	O43.893
O34.10	O35.5XX3	O36.0995	O36.4XX0	O36.63X2	O36.8294	O40.1XX0	O41.1211	O41.90X3	O43.899
O34.11	O35.5XX4	O36.0999	O36.4XX1	O36.63X3	O36.8295	O40.1XX1	O41.1212	O41.90X4	O43.90
O34.12	O35.5XX5	O36.1110	O36.4XX2	O36.63X4	O36.8299	O40.1XX2	O41.1213	O41.90X5	O43.91
O34.13	O35.5XX9	O36.1111	O36.4XX3	O36.63X5	O36.8310	O40.1XX3	O41.1214	O41.90X9	O43.92
O34.211	O35.6XX0	O36.1112	O36.4XX4	O36.63X9	O36.8311	O40.1XX4	O41.1215	O41.91X0	O43.93
O34.212	O35.6XX1	O36.1113	O36.4XX5	O36.70X0	O36.8312	O40.1XX5	O41.1219	O41.91X1	O44.00
O34.219	O35.6XX2	O36.1114	O36.4XX9	O36.70X1	O36.8313	O40.1XX9	O41.1220	O41.91X2	O44.01
O34.29	O35.6XX3	O36.1115	O36.5110	O36.70X2	O36.8314	O40.2XX0	O41.1221	O41.91X3	O44.02
O34.30	O35.6XX4	O36.1119	O36.5111	O36.70X3	O36.8315	O40.2XX1	O41.1222	O41.91X4	O44.03
O34.31	O35.6XX5	O36.1120	O36.5112	O36.70X4	O36.8319	O40.2XX2	O41.1223	O41.91X5	O44.10
O34.32	O35.6XX9	O36.1121	O36.5113	O36.70X5	O36.8320	O40.2XX3	O41.1224	O41.91X9	O44.11
O34.33	O35.7XX0	O36.1122	O36.5114	O36.70X9	O36.8321	O40.2XX4	O41.1225	O41.92X0	O44.12
O34.40	O35.7XX1	O36.1123	O36.5115	O36.71X0	O36.8322	O40.2XX9	O41.1229	O41.92X1	O44.13
O34.41	O35.7XX2	O36.1124	O36.5119	O36.71X1	O36.8323	O40.3XX0	O41.1230	O41.92X2	O44.20
O34.42	O35.7XX3	O36.1125	O36.5120	O36.71X2	O36.8324	O40.3XX1	O41.1231	O41.92X3	O44.21
O34.43	O35.7XX4	O36.1129	O36.5121	O36.71X3	O36.8325	O40.3XX2	O41.1232	O41.92X4	O44.22
O34.511	O35.7XX5	O36.1130	O36.5122	O36.71X4	O36.8329	O40.3XX3	O41.1233	O41.92X5	O44.23
O34.512	O35.7XX9	O36.1131	O36.5123	O36.71X5	O36.8330	O40.3XX4	O41.1234	O41.92X9	O44.30
O34.513	O35.8XX0	O36.1132	O36.5124	O36.71X9	O36.8331	O40.3XX5	O41.1235	O41.93X0	O44.31
O34.519	O35.8XX1	O36.1133	O36.5125	O36.72X0	O36.8332	O40.3XX9	O41.1239	O41.93X1	O44.32
O34.521	O35.8XX2	O36.1134	O36.5129	O36.72X1	O36.8333	O40.9XX0	O41.1290	O41.93X2	O44.33
O34.522	O35.8XX3	O36.1135	O36.5130	O36.72X2	O36.8334	O40.9XX1	O41.1291	O41.93X3	O44.40
O34.523	O35.8XX4	O36.1139	O36.5131	O36.72X3	O36.8335	O40.9XX2	O41.1292	O41.93X4	O44.41
O34.529	O35.8XX5	O36.1190	O36.5132	O36.72X4	O36.8339	O40.9XX3	O41.1293	O41.93X5	O44.42
O34.531	O35.8XX9	O36.1191	O36.5133	O36.72X5	O36.8390	O40.9XX4	O41.1294	O41.93X9	O44.43
O34.532	O35.9XX0	O36.1192	O36.5134	O36.72X9	O36.8391	O40.9XX5	O41.1295	O42.00	O44.50
O34.533	O35.9XX1	O36.1193	O36.5135	O36.73X0	O36.8392	O40.9XX9	O41.1299	O42.011	O44.51
O34.539	O35.9XX2	O36.1194	O36.5139	O36.73X1	O36.8393	O41.00X0	O41.1410	O42.012	O44.52
O34.591	O35.9XX3	O36.1195	O36.5190	O36.73X2	O36.8394	O41.00X1	O41.1411	O42.013	O44.53
O34.592	O35.9XX4	O36.1199	O36.5191	O36.73X3	O36.8395	O41.00X2	O41.1412	O42.019	O45.001
O34.593	O35.9XX5	O36.1910	O36.5192	O36.73X4	O36.8399	O41.00X4	O41.1413	O42.02	O45.002
O34.599	O35.9XX9	O36.1911	O36.5193	O36.73X5	O36.8910	O41.00X5	O41.1414	O42.10	O45.003
O34.60	O36.0110	O36.1912	O36.5194	O36.73X9	O36.8911	O41.00X9	O41.1415	O42.111	O45.009
O34.61	O36.0111	O36.1913	O36.5195	O36.80X0	O36.8912	O41.01X0	O41.1419	O42.112	O45.011
O34.62	O36.0112	O36.1914	O36.5199	O36.80X1	O36.8913	O41.01X1	O41.1420	O42.113	O45.012
O34.63	O36.0113	O36.1915	O36.5910	O36.80X2	O36.8914	O41.01X2	O41.1421	O42.119	O45.013
O34.70	O36.0114	O36.1919	O36.5911	O36.80X3	O36.8915	O41.01X3	O41.1422	O42.12	O45.019
O34.71	O36.0115	O36.1920	O36.5912	O36.80X4	O36.8919	O41.01X4	O41.1423	O42.90	O45.021
O34.72	O36.0119	O36.1921	O36.5913	O36.80X5	O36.8920	O41.01X5	O41.1424	O42.911	O45.022
O34.73	O36.0120	O36.1922	O36.5914	O36.80X9	O36.8921	O41.01X9	O41.1425	O42.912	O45.023
O34.80	O36.0121	O36.1923	O36.5915	O36.8120	O36.8922	O41.02X0	O41.1429	O42.913	O45.029
O34.81	O36.0122	O36.1924	O36.5919	O36.8121	O36.8923	O41.02X1	O41.1430	O42.919	O45.091
O34.82	O36.0123	O36.1925	O36.5920	O36.8122	O36.8924	O41.02X2	O41.1431	O42.92	O45.092
O34.83	O36.0124	O36.1929	O36.5921	O36.8123	O36.8925	O41.02X4	O41.1432	O43.011	O45.093
O34.90	O36.0125	O36.1930	O36.5922	O36.8124	O36.8929	O41.02X5	O41.1433	O43.012	O45.099
O34.91	O36.0129	O36.1931	O36.5923	O36.8125	O36.8930	O41.02X9	O41.1434	O43.013	O45.8X1
O34.92	O36.0130	O36.1932	O36.5924	O36.8129	O36.8931	O41.03X0	O41.1435	O43.019	O45.8X2
O34.93	O36.0131	O36.1933	O36.5925	O36.8130	O36.8932	O41.03X1	O41.1439	O43.021	O45.8X3
O35.0XX0	O36.0132	O36.1934	O36.5929	O36.8131	O36.8933	O41.03X2	O41.1490	O43.022	O45.8X9
O35.0XX1	O36.0133	O36.1935	O36.5930	O36.8132	O36.8935	O41.03X3	O41.1491	O43.023	O45.90
O35.0XX2	O36.0134	O36.1939	O36.5931	O36.8133	O36.8939	O41.03X4	O41.1492	O43.029	O45.91
O35.0XX3	O36.0139	O36.1990	O36.5932	O36.8134	O36.8990	O41.03X1	O41.1493	O43.101	O45.92
O35.0XX4	O36.0190	O36.1991	O36.5933	O36.8135	O36.8991	O41.03X2	O41.1494	O43.102	O45.93
O35.0XX5	O36.0191	O36.1992	O36.5934	O36.8139	O36.8992	O41.03X3	O41.1495	O43.103	O46.001
O35.0XX9		O36.1993	O36.5935	O36.8190		O41.03X4	O41.1499	O43.109	O46.002

O46.003	O60.20X1	O64.3XX5	O69.1XX2	O70.0	O86.04	O90.1	O98.212	O99.212	O99.719
O46.009	O60.20X2	O64.3XX9	O69.1XX3	O70.1	O86.09	O90.2	O98.213	O99.213	O99.72
O46.011	O60.20X3	O64.4XX0	O69.1XX4	O70.20	O86.11	O90.3	O98.219	O99.214	O99.73
O46.012	O60.20X4	O64.4XX1	O69.1XX5	O70.21	O86.12	O90.4	O98.22	O99.215	O99.810
O46.013	O60.20X5	O64.4XX2	O69.1XX9	O70.22	O86.13	O90.5	O98.23	O99.280	O99.814
O46.019	O60.20X9	O64.4XX3	O69.2XX0	O70.23	O86.19	O90.6	O98.311	O99.281	O99.815
O46.021	O60.22X0	O64.4XX4	O69.2XX1	O70.3	O86.20	O90.81	O98.312	O99.282	O99.820
O46.022	O60.22X1	O64.4XX5	O69.2XX2	O70.4	O86.21	O90.89	O98.313	O99.283	O99.824
O46.023	O60.22X2	O64.4XX9	O69.2XX3	O70.9	O86.22	O90.9	O98.319	O99.284	O99.825
O46.029	O60.22X3	O64.5XX0	O69.2XX4	O71.00	O86.29	O91.011	O98.32	O99.285	O99.830
O46.091	O60.22X4	O64.5XX1	O69.2XX5	O71.02	O86.4	O91.012	O98.33	O99.310	O99.834
O46.092	O60.22X5	O64.5XX2	O69.2XX9	O71.03	O86.81	O91.013	O98.411	O99.311	O99.835
O46.093	O60.22X9	O64.5XX3	O69.3XX0	O71.1	O86.89	O91.019	O98.412	O99.312	O99.840
O46.099	O60.23X0	O64.5XX4	O69.3XX1	O71.2	O87.0	O91.02	O98.413	O99.313	O99.841
O46.8X1	O60.23X1	O64.5XX5	O69.3XX2	O71.3	O87.1	O91.03	O98.419	O99.314	O99.842
O46.8X2	O60.23X2	O64.5XX9	O69.3XX3	O71.4	O87.2	O91.111	O98.42	O99.315	O99.843
O46.8X3	O60.23X3	O64.8XX0	O69.3XX4	O71.5	O87.3	O91.112	O98.43	O99.320	O99.844
O46.8X9	O60.23X4	O64.8XX1	O69.3XX5	O71.6	O87.4	O91.113	O98.511	O99.321	O99.845
O46.90	O60.23X5	O64.8XX2	O69.3XX9	O71.7	O87.8	O91.119	O98.512	O99.322	O99.89
O46.91	O60.23X9	O64.8XX3	O69.4XX0	O71.81	O87.9	O91.12	O98.513	O99.323	Z33.2
O46.92	O61.0	O64.8XX4	O69.4XX1	O71.82	O88.011	O91.13	O98.519	O99.324	O9A.111
O46.93	O61.1	O64.8XX5	O69.4XX2	O71.89	O88.012	O91.211	O98.52	O99.325	O9A.112
O47.00	O61.8	O64.8XX9	O69.4XX3	O71.9	O88.013	O91.212	O98.53	O99.330	O9A.113
O47.02	O61.9	O64.9XX0	O69.4XX4	O72.0	O88.019	O91.213	O98.611	O99.331	O9A.119
O47.03	O62.0	O64.9XX1	O69.4XX5	O72.1	O88.02	O91.219	O98.612	O99.332	O9A.12
O47.1	O62.1	O64.9XX2	O69.4XX9	O72.2	O88.03	O91.22	O98.613	O99.333	O9A.13
O47.9	O62.2	O64.9XX3	O69.5XX0	O72.3	O88.111	O91.23	O98.619	O99.334	O9A.211
O48.0	O62.3	O64.9XX4	O69.5XX1	O73.0	O88.112	O92.011	O98.62	O99.335	O9A.212
O48.1	O62.4	O64.9XX5	O69.5XX2	O73.1	O88.113	O92.012	O98.63	O99.340	O9A.213
O60.00	O62.8	O64.9XX9	O69.5XX3	O74.0	O88.119	O92.013	O98.711	O99.341	O9A.219
O60.02	O62.9	O65.0	O69.5XX4	O74.1	O88.12	O92.019	O98.712	O99.342	O9A.22
O60.03	O63.0	O65.1	O69.5XX5	O74.2	O88.13	O92.02	O98.713	O99.343	O9A.23
O60.10X0	O63.1	O65.2	O69.5XX9	O74.3	O88.211	O92.03	O98.719	O99.344	O9A.311
O60.10X1	O63.2	O65.3	O69.81X0	O74.4	O88.212	O92.111	O98.72	O99.345	O9A.312
O60.10X2	O63.9	O65.4	O69.81X1	O74.5	O88.213	O92.112	O98.73	O99.350	O9A.313
O60.10X3	O64.0XX0	O65.5	O69.81X2	O74.6	O88.219	O92.113	O98.811	O99.351	O9A.319
O60.10X4	O64.0XX1	O65.8	O69.81X3	O74.7	O88.22	O92.119	O98.812	O99.352	O9A.32
O60.10X5	O64.0XX2	O65.9	O69.81X4	O74.8	O88.23	O92.13	O98.813	O99.353	O9A.33
O60.10X9	O64.0XX3	O66.0	O69.81X5	O74.9	O88.311	O92.20	O98.819	O99.354	O9A.411
O60.12X0	O64.0XX4	O66.1	O69.81X9	O75.0	O88.312	O92.29	O98.82	O99.355	O9A.412
O60.12X1	O64.0XX5	O66.2	O69.82X0	O75.1	O88.313	O92.3	O98.83	O99.411	O9A.413
O60.12X2	O64.0XX9	O66.3	O69.82X1	O75.2	O88.319	O92.4	O98.911	O99.412	O9A.419
O60.12X3	O64.1XX0	O66.40	O69.82X2	O75.3	O88.32	O92.5	O98.912	O99.413	O9A.42
O60.12X4	O64.1XX1	O66.41	O69.82X3	O75.4	O88.33	O92.6	O98.913	O99.419	O9A.43
O60.12X5	O64.1XX2	O66.5	O69.82X4	O75.5	O88.811	O92.70	O98.919	O99.42	O9A.511
O60.12X9	O64.1XX3	O66.6	O69.82X9	O75.81	O88.812	O92.79	O98.92	O99.43	O9A.512
O60.13X0	O64.1XX4	O66.8	O69.89X0	O75.82	O88.813	O94	O98.93	O99.511	O9A.513
O60.13X1	O64.1XX5	O66.9	O69.89X1	O75.89	O88.819	O98.011	O99.011	O99.512	O9A.519
O60.13X2	O64.1XX9	O67.0	O69.89X2	O75.9	O88.82	O98.012	O99.012	O99.513	O9A.52
O60.13X3	O64.2XX0	O67.8	O69.89X3	O76	O88.83	O98.013	O99.013	O99.519	O9A.53
O60.13X4	O64.2XX1	O67.9	O69.89X4	O77.0	O89.01	O98.019	O99.019	O99.52	Z33.2
O60.13X5	O64.2XX2	O68	O69.89X5	O77.1	O89.09	O98.02	O99.02	O99.53	Z39.0
O60.13X9	O64.2XX3	O69.0XX0	O69.89X9	O77.8	O89.1	O98.03	O99.03	O99.611	Z64.0
O60.14X0	O64.2XX4	O69.0XX1	O69.9XX0	O77.9	O89.2	O98.111	O99.111	O99.612	
O60.14X1	O64.2XX5	O69.0XX2	O69.9XX1	O80	O89.3	O98.112	O99.112	O99.613	
O60.14X2	O64.2XX9	O69.0XX3	O69.9XX2	O82	O89.4	O98.113	O99.113	O99.619	
O60.14X3	O64.3XX0	O69.0XX4	O69.9XX3	O85	O89.5	O98.119	O99.119	O99.62	
O60.14X4	O64.3XX1	O69.0XX5	O69.9XX4	O86.00	O89.6	O98.12	O99.12	O99.63	
O60.14X5	O64.3XX2	O69.0XX9	O69.9XX5	O86.01	O89.8	O98.13	O99.13	O99.711	
O60.14X9	O64.3XX3	O69.1XX0	O69.9XX9	O86.02	O89.9	O98.211	O99.210	O99.712	
O60.20X0	O64.3XX4	O69.1XX1		O86.03	O90.0		O99.211	O99.713	

MDC 15 Newborns And Other Neonates With Conditions Originating In The Perinatal Period

A33	P02.0	P03.811	P04.49	P05.15	P07.24	P10.4	P13.3	P19.2	P24.30
E84.11	P02.1	P03.819	P04.5	P05.16	P07.25	P10.8	P13.4	P19.9	P24.31
P00.0	P02.20	P03.82	P04.6	P05.17	P07.26	P10.9	P13.8	P22.0	P24.80
P00.1	P02.29	P03.89	P04.81	P05.18	P07.30	P11.0	P13.9	P22.1	P24.81
P00.3	P02.3	P03.9	P04.89	P05.19	P07.31	P11.1	P14.0	P22.8	P24.9
P00.4	P02.4	P04.0	P04.9	P05.2	P07.32	P11.2	P14.1	P22.9	P25.0
P00.5	P02.5	P04.11	P05.00	P05.9	P07.33	P11.3	P14.2	P23.0	P25.1
P00.6	P02.60	P04.12	P05.01	P07.00	P07.34	P11.4	P14.3	P23.1	P25.2
P00.7	P02.69	P04.13	P05.02	P07.01	P07.35	P11.5	P14.8	P23.2	P25.3
P00.81	P02.70	P04.14	P05.03	P07.02	P07.36	P11.9	P14.9	P23.3	P25.8
P00.9	P02.78	P04.15	P05.04	P07.03	P07.37	P12.0	P15.0	P23.4	P26.0
P01.0	P02.8	P04.16	P05.05	P07.10	P07.38	P12.1	P15.1	P23.5	P26.1
P01.1	P02.9	P04.17	P05.06	P07.14	P07.39	P12.2	P15.2	P23.6	P26.8
P01.2	P03.0	P04.18	P05.07	P07.15	P08.0	P12.3	P15.3	P23.8	P26.9
P01.3	P03.1	P04.19	P05.08	P07.16	P08.1	P12.4	P15.4	P23.9	P28.0
P01.4	P03.2	P04.1A	P05.09	P07.17	P08.21	P12.81	P15.5	P24.00	P28.10
P01.5	P03.3	P04.2	P05.10	P07.18	P08.22	P12.89	P15.6	P24.01	P28.11
P01.6	P03.4	P04.3	P05.11	P07.20	P10.0	P12.9	P15.8	P24.10	P28.19
P01.7	P03.5	P04.40	P05.12	P07.21	P10.1	P13.0	P15.9	P24.11	P28.2
P01.8	P03.6	P04.41	P05.13	P07.22	P10.2	P13.1	P19.0	P24.20	P28.3
P01.9	P03.810	P04.42	P05.14	P07.23	P10.3	P13.2	P19.1	P24.21	P28.4

P28.5	P36.30	P50.2	P54.5	P59.20	P71.3	P76.2	P83.2	P92.09	P96.9
P28.81	P36.39	P50.3	P54.6	P59.29	P71.4	P76.8	P83.30	P92.1	Q86.0
P28.89	P36.4	P50.4	P54.8	P59.3	P71.8	P76.9	P83.39	P92.2	Q86.1
P28.9	P36.5	P50.5	P54.9	P59.8	P71.9	P77.1	P83.4	P92.3	Q86.2
P29.0	P36.8	P50.8	P55.0	P59.9	P72.0	P77.2	P83.5	P92.4	Q86.8
P29.11	P36.9	P50.9	P55.1	P60	P72.1	P77.3	P83.6	P92.5	Z38.00
P29.12	P37.0	P51.0	P55.8	P61.0	P72.2	P77.9	P83.81	P92.8	Z38.01
P29.2	P37.1	P51.8	P55.9	P61.1	P72.8	P78.0	P83.88	P92.9	Z38.1
P29.30	P37.2	P51.9	P56.0	P61.2	P72.9	P78.1	P83.9	P93.0	Z38.2
P29.38	P37.3	P52.0	P56.90	P61.3	P74.0	P78.2	P84	P93.8	Z38.30
P29.4	P37.4	P52.1	P56.99	P61.4	P74.1	P78.3	P90	P94.0	Z38.31
P29.81	P37.5	P52.21	P57.0	P61.5	P74.21	P78.81	P91.0	P94.1	Z38.4
P29.89	P37.8	P52.22	P57.8	P61.6	P74.22	P78.82	P91.1	P94.2	Z38.5
P29.9	P37.9	P52.3	P57.9	P61.8	P74.31	P78.83	P91.3	P94.8	Z38.61
P35.0	P38.1	P52.4	P58.0	P61.9	P74.32	P78.84	P91.4	P94.9	Z38.62
P35.1	P38.9	P52.5	P58.1	P70.0	P74.41	P78.89	P91.5	P95	Z38.63
P35.2	P39.0	P52.6	P58.2	P70.1	P74.421	P78.9	P91.60	P96.0	Z38.64
P35.3	P39.1	P52.8	P58.3	P70.2	P74.422	P80.0	P91.61	P96.1	Z38.65
P35.4	P39.2	P52.9	P58.41	P70.3	P74.49	P80.8	P91.62	P96.2	Z38.66
P35.8	P39.3	P53	P58.42	P70.4	P74.5	P80.9	P91.63	P96.3	Z38.68
P35.9	P39.4	P54.0	P58.5	P70.8	P74.6	P81.0	P91.811	P96.5	Z38.69
P36.0	P39.8	P54.1	P58.8	P70.9	P74.8	P81.8	P91.819	P96.81	Z38.7
P36.10	P39.9	P54.2	P58.9	P71.0	P74.9	P81.9	P91.88	P96.82	Z38.8
P36.19	P50.0	P54.3	P59.0	P71.1	P76.0	P83.0	P91.9	P96.83	
P36.2	P50.1	P54.4	P59.1	P71.2	P76.1	P83.1	P92.01	P96.89	

MDC 16 Diseases And Disorders Of The Blood And Blood- Forming Organs And Immunological Disorders

A18.2	D51.9	D57.212	D61.09	D68.32	D72.0	D75.89	D82.8	I88.9	S36.09XA
A18.85	D52.0	D57.219	D61.1	D68.4	D72.1	D75.9	D82.9	I89.8	T80.30XA
A28.1	D52.1	D57.3	D61.2	D68.51	D72.810	D75.A	D83.0	I89.9	T80.310A
D15.0	D52.8	D57.40	D61.3	D68.52	D72.818	D76.1	D83.1	L04.0	T80.311A
D18.1	D52.9	D57.411	D61.810	D68.59	D72.819	D76.2	D83.2	L04.1	T80.319A
D36.0	D53.0	D57.412	D61.811	D68.61	D72.820	D76.3	D83.8	L04.2	T80.39XA
D3A.091	D53.1	D57.419	D61.818	D68.62	D72.821	D77	D83.9	L04.3	T80.40XA
D46.0	D53.2	D57.80	D61.89	D68.69	D72.822	D80.0	D84.0	L04.8	T80.410A
D46.1	D53.8	D57.811	D61.9	D68.8	D72.823	D80.1	D84.8	L04.9	T80.411A
D46.20	D53.9	D57.812	D62	D68.9	D72.824	D80.2	D84.9	Q89.01	T80.419A
D46.21	D55.0	D57.819	D63.0	D69.0	D72.825	D80.3	D89.0	Q89.09	T80.49XA
D46.22	D55.1	D58.0	D63.1	D69.1	D72.828	D80.4	D89.2	R16.1	T80.89XA
D46.4	D55.2	D58.1	D63.8	D69.2	D72.829	D80.5	D89.3	R23.3	T80.910A
D46.9	D55.3	D58.2	D64.0	D69.3	D72.89	D80.6	D89.40	R59.0	T80.911A
D46.A	D55.8	D58.8	D64.1	D69.41	D72.9	D80.7	D89.41	R59.1	T80.919A
D46.B	D55.9	D58.9	D64.2	D69.42	D73.0	D80.8	D89.42	R59.9	T80.92XA
D46.C	D56.0	D59.0	D64.3	D69.49	D73.1	D80.9	D89.43	R71.0	T80.A0XA
D46.Z	D56.1	D59.1	D64.4	D69.51	D73.2	D81.0	D89.49	R71.8	T80.A10A
D47.2	D56.2	D59.2	D64.81	D69.59	D73.3	D81.1	D89.810	R75	T80.A11A
D47.3	D56.3	D59.3	D64.89	D69.6	D73.4	D81.2	D89.811	R76.0	T80.A19A
D47.4	D56.4	D59.4	D64.9	D69.8	D73.5	D81.4	D89.812	R76.8	T80.A9XA
D50.0	D56.5	D59.5	D65	D69.9	D73.81	D81.6	D89.813	R76.9	T86.00
D50.1	D56.8	D59.6	D66	D70.0	D73.89	D81.7	D89.89	S36.00XA	T86.01
D50.8	D56.9	D59.8	D67	D70.1	D73.9	D81.89	D89.9	S36.020XA	T86.02
D50.9	D57.00	D59.9	D68.0	D70.2	D74.0	D81.9	E32.0	S36.021A	T86.03
D51.0	D57.01	D60.0	D68.1	D70.3	D74.8	D82.0	E32.1	S36.029A	T86.09
D51.1	D57.02	D60.1	D68.2	D70.4	D74.9	D82.1	E32.8	S36.030A	Z94.81
D51.2	D57.1	D60.8	D68.311	D70.8	D75.0	D82.2	E32.9	S36.031A	Z94.84
D51.3	D57.20	D60.9	D68.312	D70.9	D75.1	D82.3	I88.1	S36.032A	
D51.8	D57.211	D61.01	D68.318	D71	D75.82	D82.4	I88.8	S36.039A	

MDC 17 Myeloproliferative Diseases And Disorders And Poorly Differentiated Neoplasms

C26.1	C7A.091	C81.12	C81.36	C81.90	C82.14	C82.38	C82.62	C82.96	C83.30
C37	C7A.098	C81.13	C81.37	C81.91	C82.15	C82.39	C82.63	C82.97	C83.31
C45.7	C7A.1	C81.14	C81.38	C81.92	C82.16	C82.40	C82.64	C82.98	C83.32
C45.9	C7A.8	C81.15	C81.39	C81.93	C82.17	C82.41	C82.65	C82.99	C83.33
C46.3	C7B.00	C81.16	C81.40	C81.94	C82.18	C82.42	C82.66	C83.00	C83.34
C48.0	C7B.01	C81.17	C81.41	C81.95	C82.19	C82.43	C82.67	C83.01	C83.35
C76.40	C7B.09	C81.18	C81.42	C81.96	C82.20	C82.44	C82.68	C83.02	C83.36
C76.41	C7B.1	C81.19	C81.43	C81.97	C82.21	C82.45	C82.69	C83.03	C83.37
C76.42	C7B.8	C81.20	C81.44	C81.98	C82.22	C82.46	C82.80	C83.04	C83.38
C76.50	C80.0	C81.21	C81.45	C81.99	C82.23	C82.47	C82.81	C83.05	C83.39
C76.51	C80.1	C81.22	C81.46	C82.00	C82.24	C82.48	C82.82	C83.06	C83.50
C76.52	C80.2	C81.23	C81.47	C82.01	C82.25	C82.49	C82.83	C83.07	C83.51
C76.8	C81.00	C81.24	C81.48	C82.02	C82.26	C82.50	C82.84	C83.08	C83.52
C77.0	C81.01	C81.25	C81.49	C82.03	C82.27	C82.51	C82.85	C83.09	C83.53
C77.1	C81.02	C81.26	C81.70	C82.04	C82.28	C82.52	C82.86	C83.10	C83.54
C77.2	C81.03	C81.27	C81.71	C82.05	C82.29	C82.53	C82.87	C83.11	C83.55
C77.3	C81.04	C81.28	C81.72	C82.06	C82.30	C82.54	C82.88	C83.12	C83.56
C77.4	C81.05	C81.29	C81.73	C82.07	C82.31	C82.55	C82.89	C83.13	C83.57
C77.5	C81.06	C81.30	C81.74	C82.08	C82.32	C82.56	C82.90	C83.14	C83.58
C77.8	C81.07	C81.31	C81.75	C82.09	C82.33	C82.57	C82.91	C83.15	C83.59
C77.9	C81.08	C81.32	C81.76	C82.10	C82.34	C82.58	C82.92	C83.16	C83.70
C79.89	C81.09	C81.33	C81.77	C82.11	C82.35	C82.59	C82.93	C83.17	C83.71
C79.9	C81.10	C81.34	C81.78	C82.12	C82.36	C82.60	C82.94	C83.18	C83.72
C7A.00	C81.11	C81.35	C81.79	C82.13	C82.37	C82.61	C82.95	C83.19	C83.73

C83.74	C84.12	C84.90	C85.18	C86.6	C91.91	C93.00	C95.91	E88.09	Z85.48
C83.75	C84.13	C84.91	C85.19	C88.0	C91.92	C93.01	C95.92	Q85.8	Z85.49
C83.76	C84.14	C84.92	C85.20	C88.2	C91.A0	C93.02	C96.0	Q85.9	Z85.50
C83.77	C84.15	C84.93	C85.21	C88.3	C91.A1	C93.10	C96.20	Z08	Z85.51
C83.78	C84.16	C84.94	C85.22	C88.4	C91.A2	C93.11	C96.21	Z51.0	Z85.520
C83.79	C84.17	C84.95	C85.23	C88.8	C91.Z0	C93.12	C96.22	Z51.11	Z85.528
C83.80	C84.18	C84.96	C85.24	C88.9	C91.Z1	C93.30	C96.29	Z51.12	Z85.53
C83.81	C84.19	C84.97	C85.25	C90.00	C91.Z2	C93.31	C96.4	Z85.00	Z85.54
C83.82	C84.40	C84.98	C85.26	C90.01	C92.00	C93.32	C96.9	Z85.01	Z85.59
C83.83	C84.41	C84.99	C85.27	C90.02	C92.01	C93.90	C96.A	Z85.020	Z85.6
C83.84	C84.42	C84.A0	C85.28	C90.10	C92.02	C93.91	C96.Z	Z85.028	Z85.71
C83.85	C84.43	C84.A1	C85.29	C90.11	C92.10	C93.92	D09.3	Z85.030	Z85.72
C83.86	C84.44	C84.A2	C85.80	C90.12	C92.11	C93.Z0	D09.8	Z85.038	Z85.79
C83.87	C84.45	C84.A3	C85.81	C90.20	C92.12	C93.Z1	D09.9	Z85.040	Z85.810
C83.88	C84.46	C84.A4	C85.82	C90.21	C92.20	C93.Z2	D19.7	Z85.048	Z85.818
C83.89	C84.47	C84.A5	C85.83	C90.22	C92.21	C94.00	D19.9	Z85.05	Z85.819
C83.90	C84.48	C84.A6	C85.84	C90.30	C92.22	C94.01	D36.7	Z85.060	Z85.820
C83.91	C84.49	C84.A7	C85.85	C90.31	C92.30	C94.02	D36.9	Z85.068	Z85.821
C83.92	C84.60	C84.A8	C85.86	C90.32	C92.31	C94.20	D3A.00	Z85.07	Z85.828
C83.93	C84.61	C84.A9	C85.87	C91.00	C92.32	C94.21	D3A.098	Z85.09	Z85.830
C83.94	C84.62	C84.Z0	C85.88	C91.01	C92.40	C94.22	D3A.8	Z85.110	Z85.831
C83.95	C84.63	C84.Z1	C85.89	C91.02	C92.41	C94.30	D45	Z85.118	Z85.840
C83.96	C84.64	C84.Z2	C85.90	C91.10	C92.42	C94.31	D47.01	Z85.12	Z85.841
C83.97	C84.65	C84.Z3	C85.91	C91.11	C92.50	C94.32	D47.02	Z85.20	Z85.848
C83.98	C84.66	C84.Z4	C85.92	C91.12	C92.51	C94.40	D47.09	Z85.21	Z85.850
C83.99	C84.67	C84.Z5	C85.93	C91.30	C92.52	C94.41	D47.1	Z85.22	Z85.858
C84.00	C84.68	C84.Z6	C85.94	C91.31	C92.60	C94.42	D47.9	Z85.230	Z85.89
C84.01	C84.69	C84.Z7	C85.95	C91.32	C92.61	C94.6	D47.Z2	Z85.238	Z85.9
C84.02	C84.70	C84.Z8	C85.96	C91.40	C92.62	C94.80	D47.Z9	Z85.29	Z87.410
C84.03	C84.71	C84.Z9	C85.97	C91.41	C92.90	C94.81	D48.7	Z85.3	
C84.04	C84.72	C85.10	C85.98	C91.42	C92.91	C94.82	D48.9	Z85.40	
C84.05	C84.73	C85.11	C85.99	C91.50	C92.92	C95.00	D49.81	Z85.41	
C84.06	C84.74	C85.12	C86.0	C91.51	C92.A0	C95.01	D49.89	Z85.42	
C84.07	C84.75	C85.13	C86.1	C91.52	C92.A1	C95.02	D49.9	Z85.43	
C84.08	C84.76	C85.14	C86.2	C91.60	C92.A2	C95.10	D61.82	Z85.44	
C84.09	C84.77	C85.15	C86.3	C91.61	C92.Z0	C95.11	D75.81	Z85.45	
C84.10	C84.78	C85.16	C86.4	C91.62	C92.Z1	C95.12	D89.1	Z85.46	
C84.11	C84.79	C85.17	C86.5	C91.90	C92.Z2	C95.90	E88.02	Z85.47	

MDC 18 Infectious And Parasitic Diseases, Systemic or Unspecified Sites

A01.00	A22.8	A32.9	A44.1	A51.42	A77.0	A98.3	B26.85	B40.3	B48.2
A01.01	A22.9	A35	A44.8	A51.44	A77.1	A98.4	B26.89	B40.7	B48.3
A01.02	A23.0	A36.82	A44.9	A51.49	A77.2	A98.8	B26.9	B40.81	B48.4
A01.03	A23.1	A36.83	A48.0	A51.5	A77.3	A99	B27.00	B40.89	B48.8
A01.04	A23.2	A36.84	A48.2	A51.9	A77.40	B00.7	B27.01	B40.9	B49
A01.05	A23.3	A36.89	A48.3	A52.73	A77.41	B00.89	B27.02	B41.0	B50.0
A01.09	A23.8	A36.9	A48.4	A52.76	A77.49	B01.0	B27.09	B41.7	B50.8
A01.1	A23.9	A38.0	A48.51	A52.79	A77.8	B01.81	B27.10	B41.8	B50.9
A01.2	A24.0	A38.1	A48.52	A52.8	A77.9	B01.89	B27.11	B41.9	B51.0
A01.3	A24.1	A38.8	A48.8	A52.9	A78	B01.9	B27.12	B42.0	B51.8
A01.4	A24.2	A38.9	A49.01	A53.0	A79.0	B02.7	B27.19	B42.1	B51.9
A02.1	A24.3	A39.1	A49.02	A53.9	A79.1	B02.8	B27.80	B42.7	B52.0
A02.20	A24.9	A39.2	A49.1	A54.82	A79.81	B03	B27.81	B42.81	B52.8
A02.25	A25.0	A39.3	A49.2	A54.84	A79.89	B04	B27.82	B42.82	B52.9
A02.29	A25.1	A39.4	A49.3	A54.86	A79.9	B05.1	B27.89	B42.89	B53.0
A02.8	A25.9	A39.89	A49.8	A54.89	A80.4	B05.4	B27.90	B42.9	B53.1
A02.9	A26.0	A39.9	A49.9	A54.9	A90	B05.89	B27.91	B43.0	B53.8
A05.1	A26.7	A40.0	A50.01	A59.8	A91	B05.9	B27.92	B43.1	B54
A06.3	A26.8	A40.1	A50.02	A59.9	A92.0	B06.81	B27.99	B43.2	B55.0
A06.81	A26.9	A40.3	A50.03	A65	A92.1	B06.89	B33.1	B43.8	B55.9
A06.82	A27.0	A40.8	A50.04	A66.7	A92.30	B06.9	B33.24	B43.9	B56.0
A06.89	A27.9	A40.9	A50.05	A66.8	A92.31	B08.010	B33.3	B44.1	B56.1
A06.9	A28.0	A41.01	A50.06	A66.9	A92.32	B08.011	B33.4	B44.2	B56.9
A17.9	A28.2	A41.02	A50.07	A67.2	A92.39	B08.04	B33.8	B44.7	B57.1
A18.82	A28.8	A41.1	A50.08	A67.9	A92.4	B08.09	B34.0	B44.89	B57.30
A18.84	A28.9	A41.2	A50.09	A68.0	A92.5	B08.20	B34.1	B44.9	B57.31
A18.89	A30.0	A41.3	A50.1	A68.1	A92.8	B08.21	B34.2	B45.0	B57.32
A19.0	A30.1	A41.4	A50.2	A68.9	A92.9	B08.22	B34.3	B45.2	B57.39
A19.1	A30.2	A41.50	A50.30	A69.20	A93.0	B08.3	B34.4	B45.3	B57.40
A19.2	A30.3	A41.51	A50.32	A69.21	A93.1	B08.4	B34.8	B45.7	B57.41
A19.8	A30.4	A41.52	A50.39	A69.22	A93.2	B08.60	B34.9	B45.8	B57.42
A19.9	A30.5	A41.53	A50.44	A69.23	A93.8	B08.61	B37.7	B45.9	B57.49
A20.0	A30.8	A41.59	A50.51	A69.29	A94	B08.62	B37.89	B46.0	B57.5
A20.1	A30.9	A41.81	A50.52	A69.8	A95.0	B08.69	B37.9	B46.1	B58.00
A20.3	A31.2	A41.89	A50.53	A69.9	A95.1	B08.70	B38.7	B46.2	B58.82
A20.7	A31.8	A41.9	A50.54	A70	A95.9	B08.71	B38.89	B46.3	B58.83
A20.8	A31.9	A42.7	A50.55	A74.81	A96.0	B08.72	B38.9	B46.4	B58.89
A20.9	A32.0	A42.81	A50.56	A74.89	A96.1	B08.79	B39.3	B46.5	B58.9
A21.0	A32.11	A42.82	A50.57	A74.9	A96.2	B08.8	B39.4	B46.8	B60.0
A21.1	A32.12	A42.89	A50.59	A75.0	A96.8	B09	B39.5	B46.9	B60.10
A21.7	A32.7	A42.9	A50.6	A75.1	A96.9	B25.8	B39.9	B47.0	B60.11
A21.8	A32.81	A43.8	A50.7	A75.2	A98.0	B25.9	B40.0	B47.1	B60.19
A21.9	A32.82	A43.9	A50.9	A75.3	A98.1	B26.82	B40.1	B48.0	B60.2
A22.7	A32.89	A44.0	A51.2	A75.9	A98.2	B26.83	B40.2	B48.1	B60.8

Diagnosis Codes by MDC

B64	B67.99	B81.4	B95.2	B96.3	B97.30	J09.X3	N98.0	T80.22XA	Z16.21
B65.2	B72	B83.0	B95.3	B96.4	B97.31	J09.X9	R50.2	T80.29XA	Z16.22
B65.8	B73.00	B83.1	B95.4	B96.5	B97.32	J10.2	R50.81	T81.40XA	Z16.23
B65.9	B73.01	B83.2	B95.5	B96.6	B97.33	J10.81	R50.82	T81.41XA	Z16.24
B66.2	B73.02	B83.3	B95.61	B96.7	B97.34	J10.82	R50.83	T81.42XA	Z16.29
B66.8	B73.09	B83.8	B95.62	B96.81	B97.35	J10.83	R50.84	T81.43XA	Z16.30
B66.9	B73.1	B83.9	B95.7	B96.82	B97.39	J10.89	R50.9	T81.44XA	Z16.31
B67.2	B74.0	B89	B95.8	B96.89	B97.4	J11.2	R57.1	T81.49XA	Z16.32
B67.32	B74.1	B90.8	B96.0	B97.0	B97.5	J11.81	R57.8	T88.0XXA	Z16.33
B67.39	B74.2	B92	B96.1	B97.10	B97.6	J11.82	R65.10	T88.1XXA	Z16.341
B67.4	B74.3	B94.2	B96.20	B97.11	B97.7	J11.83	R65.11	Z16.10	Z16.342
B67.61	B74.4	B94.8	B96.21	B97.12	B97.81	J11.89	R65.20	Z16.11	Z16.35
B67.69	B74.8	B94.9	B96.22	B97.19	B97.89	K68.11	R65.21	Z16.12	Z16.39
B67.7	B74.9	B95.0	B96.23	B97.21	B99.8	L44.4	R78.81	Z16.19	Z21
B67.90	B75	B95.1	B96.29	B97.29	B99.9	L94.6	R89.9	Z16.20	

MDC 19 Mental Diseases And Disorders

F01.50	F29	F32.0	F40.241	F44.7	F51.8	F64.9	F82	G47.01	R41.843
F01.51	F30.10	F32.1	F40.242	F44.81	F51.9	F65.0	F84.0	G47.09	R41.844
F02.80	F30.11	F32.2	F40.243	F44.89	F52.0	F65.1	F84.3	G47.10	R41.89
F02.81	F30.12	F32.3	F40.248	F44.9	F52.1	F65.2	F84.5	G47.11	R44.0
F03.90	F30.13	F32.4	F40.290	F45.0	F52.21	F65.3	F84.8	G47.12	R44.2
F03.91	F30.2	F32.5	F40.291	F45.1	F52.22	F65.4	F84.9	G47.13	R44.3
F04	F30.3	F32.81	F40.298	F45.20	F52.31	F65.50	F88	G47.14	R45.0
F05	F30.4	F32.89	F40.8	F45.21	F52.32	F65.51	F89	G47.19	R45.1
F06.0	F30.8	F32.9	F40.9	F45.22	F52.4	F65.52	F90.0	G47.9	R45.2
F06.1	F30.9	F33.0	F41.0	F45.29	F52.6	F65.81	F90.1	H93.25	R45.3
F06.2	F31.0	F33.1	F41.1	F45.41	F52.8	F65.89	F90.2	Q90.0	R45.4
F06.30	F31.10	F33.2	F41.3	F45.42	F52.9	F65.9	F90.8	Q90.1	R45.5
F06.31	F31.11	F33.3	F41.8	F45.8	F53.0	F66	F90.9	Q90.2	R45.6
F06.32	F31.12	F33.40	F41.9	F45.9	F53.1	F68.10	F91.0	Q90.9	R45.7
F06.33	F31.13	F33.41	F42.2	F48.1	F54	F68.11	F91.1	Q91.0	R45.81
F06.34	F31.2	F33.42	F42.3	F48.8	F59	F68.12	F91.2	Q91.1	R45.82
F06.4	F31.30	F33.8	F42.4	F48.9	F60.0	F68.13	F91.3	Q91.2	R45.851
F06.8	F31.31	F33.9	F42.8	F50.00	F60.1	F68.8	F91.8	Q91.3	R45.86
F07.0	F31.32	F34.0	F42.9	F50.01	F60.2	F68.A	F91.9	Q91.4	R45.87
F07.9	F31.4	F34.1	F43.0	F50.02	F60.3	F69	F93.0	Q91.5	R45.89
F09	F31.5	F34.81	F43.10	F50.2	F60.4	F70	F93.8	Q91.6	R48.0
F20.0	F31.60	F34.89	F43.11	F50.81	F60.5	F71	F93.9	Q91.7	R48.1
F20.1	F31.61	F34.9	F43.12	F50.82	F60.6	F72	F94.0	Q93.3	R48.2
F20.2	F31.62	F39	F43.20	F50.89	F60.7	F73	F94.1	Q93.4	R48.8
F20.3	F31.63	F40.00	F43.21	F50.9	F60.81	F78	F94.2	Q93.51	R48.9
F20.5	F31.64	F40.01	F43.22	F51.01	F60.89	F79	F94.8	Q93.59	R54
F20.81	F31.70	F40.02	F43.23	F51.02	F60.9	F80.0	F94.9	Q93.7	Z72.810
F20.89	F31.71	F40.10	F43.24	F51.03	F63.0	F80.1	F98.0	Q93.81	Z72.811
F20.9	F31.72	F40.11	F43.25	F51.04	F63.1	F80.2	F98.1	Q93.82	Z87.890
F21	F31.73	F40.210	F43.29	F51.05	F63.2	F80.4	F98.21	Q93.88	
F22	F31.74	F40.218	F43.8	F51.09	F63.3	F80.82	F98.29	Q93.89	
F23	F31.75	F40.220	F43.9	F51.11	F63.81	F80.89	F98.3	Q93.9	
F24	F31.76	F40.228	F44.0	F51.12	F63.89	F80.9	F98.4	Q99.2	
F25.0	F31.77	F40.230	F44.1	F51.13	F63.9	F81.0	F98.5	R37	
F25.1	F31.78	F40.231	F44.2	F51.19	F64.0	F81.2	F98.8	R40.4	
F25.8	F31.81	F40.232	F44.4	F51.3	F64.1	F81.81	F98.9	R41.81	
F25.9	F31.89	F40.233	F44.5	F51.4	F64.2	F81.89	F99	R41.840	
F28	F31.9	F40.240	F44.6	F51.5	F64.8	F81.9	G47.00	R41.841	

MDC 20 Alcohol/Drug Use And Alcohol/Drug-Induced Organic Mental Disorders

F10.10	F10.259	F11.122	F11.920	F12.21	F13.120	F13.27	F14.11	F14.281	F15.151
F10.11	F10.26	F11.129	F11.921	F12.220	F13.121	F13.280	F14.120	F14.282	F15.159
F10.120	F10.27	F11.14	F11.922	F12.221	F13.129	F13.281	F14.121	F14.288	F15.180
F10.121	F10.280	F11.150	F11.929	F12.222	F13.14	F13.282	F14.122	F14.29	F15.181
F10.129	F10.281	F11.151	F11.93	F12.229	F13.150	F13.288	F14.129	F14.90	F15.182
F10.14	F10.282	F11.159	F11.94	F12.23	F13.151	F13.29	F14.14	F14.920	F15.188
F10.150	F10.288	F11.181	F11.950	F12.250	F13.159	F13.90	F14.150	F14.921	F15.19
F10.151	F10.29	F11.182	F11.951	F12.251	F13.180	F13.920	F14.151	F14.922	F15.20
F10.159	F10.920	F11.188	F11.959	F12.259	F13.181	F13.921	F14.159	F14.929	F15.21
F10.180	F10.921	F11.19	F11.981	F12.280	F13.182	F13.929	F14.180	F14.94	F15.220
F10.181	F10.929	F11.20	F11.982	F12.288	F13.188	F13.930	F14.181	F14.950	F15.221
F10.182	F10.94	F11.21	F11.988	F12.29	F13.19	F13.931	F14.182	F14.951	F15.222
F10.188	F10.950	F11.220	F11.99	F12.90	F13.20	F13.932	F14.188	F14.959	F15.229
F10.19	F10.951	F11.221	F12.10	F12.920	F13.21	F13.939	F14.19	F14.980	F15.23
F10.20	F10.959	F11.222	F12.11	F12.921	F13.220	F13.94	F14.20	F14.981	F15.24
F10.21	F10.96	F11.229	F12.120	F12.922	F13.221	F13.950	F14.21	F14.982	F15.250
F10.220	F10.97	F11.23	F12.121	F12.929	F13.229	F13.951	F14.220	F14.988	F15.251
F10.221	F10.980	F11.24	F12.122	F12.93	F13.230	F13.959	F14.221	F14.99	F15.259
F10.229	F10.981	F11.250	F12.129	F12.950	F13.231	F13.96	F14.222	F15.10	F15.280
F10.230	F10.982	F11.251	F12.150	F12.951	F13.232	F13.97	F14.229	F15.11	F15.281
F10.231	F10.988	F11.259	F12.151	F12.959	F13.239	F13.980	F14.23	F15.120	F15.282
F10.232	F10.99	F11.281	F12.159	F12.980	F13.24	F13.981	F14.24	F15.121	F15.288
F10.239	F11.10	F11.282	F12.180	F12.988	F13.250	F13.982	F14.250	F15.122	F15.29
F10.24	F11.11	F11.288	F12.188	F12.99	F13.251	F13.988	F14.251	F15.129	F15.90
F10.250	F11.120	F11.29	F12.19	F13.10	F13.259	F13.99	F14.259	F15.14	F15.920
F10.251	F11.121	F11.90	F12.20	F13.11	F13.26	F14.10	F14.280	F15.150	F15.921

F15.922	F16.129	F16.259	F17.203	F18.14	F18.27	F19.11	F19.21	F19.282	F19.97
F15.929	F16.14	F16.280	F17.208	F18.150	F18.280	F19.120	F19.220	F19.288	F19.980
F15.93	F16.150	F16.283	F17.209	F18.151	F18.288	F19.121	F19.221	F19.29	F19.981
F15.94	F16.151	F16.288	F17.213	F18.159	F18.29	F19.122	F19.222	F19.90	F19.982
F15.950	F16.159	F16.29	F17.218	F18.17	F18.90	F19.129	F19.229	F19.920	F19.988
F15.951	F16.180	F16.90	F17.219	F18.180	F18.920	F19.14	F19.230	F19.921	F19.99
F15.959	F16.183	F16.920	F17.223	F18.188	F18.921	F19.150	F19.231	F19.922	F55.0
F15.980	F16.188	F16.921	F17.228	F18.19	F18.929	F19.151	F19.232	F19.929	F55.1
F15.981	F16.19	F16.929	F17.229	F18.20	F18.94	F19.159	F19.239	F19.930	F55.2
F15.982	F16.20	F16.94	F17.293	F18.21	F18.950	F19.16	F19.24	F19.931	F55.3
F15.988	F16.21	F16.950	F17.298	F18.220	F18.951	F19.17	F19.250	F19.932	F55.4
F15.99	F16.220	F16.951	F17.299	F18.221	F18.959	F19.180	F19.251	F19.939	F55.8
F16.10	F16.221	F16.959	F18.10	F18.229	F18.97	F19.181	F19.259	F19.94	R78.0
F16.11	F16.229	F16.980	F18.11	F18.24	F18.980	F19.182	F19.26	F19.950	
F16.120	F16.24	F16.983	F18.120	F18.250	F18.988	F19.188	F19.27	F19.951	
F16.121	F16.250	F16.988	F18.121	F18.251	F18.99	F19.19	F19.280	F19.959	
F16.122	F16.251	F16.99	F18.129	F18.259	F19.10	F19.20	F19.281	F19.96	

MDC 21 Injuries, Poisonings And Toxic Effects Of Drugs

D47.Z1	H59.313	J95.71	M1A.1621	S05.8X2S	S15.292A	S21.409A	S25.511A	S35.222A	S38.1XXA
D78.01	H59.319	J95.72	M1A.1690	S05.8X9S	S15.299A	S21.411A	S25.512A	S35.228A	S39.001A
D78.02	H59.321	J95.830	M1A.1691	S05.90XS	S15.301A	S21.412A	S25.519A	S35.229A	S39.001S
D78.11	H59.322	J95.831	M1A.1710	S05.91XS	S15.302A	S21.419A	S25.591A	S35.231A	S39.002A
D78.12	H59.323	J95.860	M1A.1711	S05.92XS	S15.309A	S21.421A	S25.592A	S35.232A	S39.002S
D78.21	H59.329	J95.861	M1A.1720	S07.0XXA	S15.311A	S21.422A	S25.599A	S35.238A	S39.003A
D78.22	H59.331	J95.862	M1A.1721	S07.1XXA	S15.312A	S21.429A	S25.801A	S35.239A	S39.003S
D78.31	H59.332	J95.863	M1A.1790	S07.8XXA	S15.319A	S21.431A	S25.802A	S35.291A	S39.091A
D78.32	H59.333	K91.61	M1A.1791	S07.9XXA	S15.321A	S21.432A	S25.809A	S35.292A	S39.091S
D78.33	H59.339	K91.62	M1A.18X0	S09.0XXA	S15.322A	S21.439A	S25.811A	S35.298A	S39.092A
D78.34	H59.341	K91.71	M1A.18X1	S09.10XA	S15.329A	S21.441A	S25.812A	S35.299A	S39.092S
D78.81	H59.342	K91.72	M1A.19X0	S09.10XS	S15.391A	S21.442A	S25.819A	S35.311A	S39.093A
D78.89	H59.343	K91.840	M1A.19X1	S09.11XA	S15.392A	S21.449A	S25.891A	S35.318A	S39.093S
E36.01	H59.349	K91.841	M96.810	S09.19XA	S15.399A	S21.451A	S25.892A	S35.319A	S39.81XA
E36.02	H59.351	K91.870	M96.811	S09.19XS	S15.8XXA	S21.452A	S25.899A	S35.321A	S39.81XS
E36.11	H59.352	K91.871	M96.820	S09.20XS	S16.8XXA	S21.459A	S25.90XA	S35.328A	S39.82XA
E36.12	H59.353	K91.872	M96.821	S09.301S	S16.8XXS	S21.92XA	S25.91XA	S35.329A	S39.82XS
E36.8	H59.359	K91.873	M96.830	S09.302S	S16.9XXA	S21.94XA	S25.99XA	S35.331A	S39.83XA
E89.810	H59.361	L76.01	M96.831	S09.309S	S16.9XXS	S25.00XA	S27.9XXA	S35.338A	S39.83XS
E89.811	H59.362	L76.02	M96.840	S09.391S	S17.0XXA	S25.01XA	S28.0XXA	S35.339A	S39.840A
E89.820	H59.363	L76.11	M96.841	S09.392S	S17.8XXA	S25.02XA	S29.001A	S35.341A	S39.840S
E89.821	H59.369	L76.12	M96.842	S09.399S	S17.9XXA	S25.09XA	S29.001S	S35.348A	S39.848A
E89.822	H59.811	L76.21	M96.843	S09.8XXA	S19.80XA	S25.101A	S29.002A	S35.349A	S39.848S
E89.823	H59.812	L76.22	M96.89	S09.8XXS	S19.80XS	S25.102A	S29.002S	S35.401A	S39.91XA
E89.89	H59.813	L76.31	M97.01XS	S09.90XA	S19.81XA	S25.109A	S29.009A	S35.402A	S39.91XS
G96.11	H59.819	L76.32	M97.02XS	S09.90XS	S19.81XS	S25.111A	S29.009S	S35.403A	S39.92XA
G97.41	H59.88	L76.33	M97.11XS	S09.91XS	S19.82XA	S25.112A	S29.091A	S35.404A	S39.92XS
G97.48	H59.89	L76.34	M97.12XS	S09.92XA	S19.82XS	S25.119A	S29.091S	S35.405A	S39.93XA
G97.49	H95.21	L76.81	M97.21XS	S09.92XS	S19.83XA	S25.121A	S29.092A	S35.406A	S39.93XS
G97.51	H95.22	L76.82	M97.22XS	S09.93XA	S19.83XS	S25.122A	S29.092S	S35.411A	S39.94XA
G97.52	H95.31	M1A.10X0	M97.31XS	S09.93XS	S19.84XA	S25.129A	S29.099A	S35.412A	S39.94XS
G97.61	H95.32	M1A.10X1	M97.32XS	S15.001A	S19.84XS	S25.191A	S29.099S	S35.413A	S41.021A
G97.62	H95.41	M1A.1110	M97.41XS	S15.002A	S19.85XA	S25.192A	S29.8XXA	S35.414A	S41.022A
G97.63	H95.42	M1A.1111	M97.42XS	S15.009A	S19.85XS	S25.199A	S29.8XXS	S35.415A	S41.029A
G97.64	H95.51	M1A.1120	M97.8XXS	S15.011A	S19.89XA	S25.20XA	S29.9XXA	S35.416A	S41.041A
H59.011	H95.52	M1A.1121	M97.9XXS	S15.012A	S19.89XS	S25.21XA	S29.9XXS	S35.491A	S41.042A
H59.012	H95.53	M1A.1190	N98.1	S15.019A	S19.9XXA	S25.22XA	S31.120A	S35.492A	S41.049A
H59.013	H95.54	M1A.1191	N98.2	S15.021A	S19.9XXS	S25.29XA	S31.121A	S35.493A	S41.121A
H59.019	H95.811	M1A.1210	N98.3	S15.022A		S25.301A	S31.122A	S35.494A	S41.122A
H59.031	H95.812	M1A.1211	N98.8	S15.029A		S25.302A	S31.123A	S35.495A	S41.129A
H59.032	H95.813	M1A.1220	N98.9	S15.091A		S25.309A	S31.124A	S35.496A	S41.141A
H59.033	H95.819	M1A.1221	N99.61	S15.092A		S25.311A	S31.125A	S35.50XA	S41.142A
H59.039	H95.88	M1A.1290	N99.62	S15.099A		S25.312A	S31.129A	S35.511A	S41.149A
H59.091	H95.89	M1A.1291	N99.71	S15.101A		S25.319A	S31.140A	S35.512A	S45.001A
H59.092	I97.3	M1A.1310	N99.72	S15.102A		S25.321A	S31.141A	S35.513A	S45.002A
H59.093	I97.410	M1A.1311	N99.820	S15.109A		S25.322A	S31.142A	S35.514A	S45.009A
H59.099	I97.411	M1A.1320	N99.821	S15.111A		S25.329A	S31.143A	S35.515A	S45.011A
H59.111	I97.418	M1A.1321	N99.840	S15.112A		S25.391A	S31.144A	S35.516A	S45.012A
H59.112	I97.42	M1A.1390	N99.841	S15.119A		S25.392A	S31.145A	S35.531A	S45.019A
H59.113	I97.51	M1A.1391	N99.842	S15.121A		S25.399A	S31.149A	S35.532A	S45.091A
H59.119	I97.52	M1A.1410	N99.843	S15.122A		S25.401A	S31.832A	S35.533A	S45.092A
H59.121	I97.610	M1A.1411	S02.121S	S15.129A		S25.402A	S31.834A	S35.534A	S45.099A
H59.122	I97.611	M1A.1420	S02.122S	S15.191A		S25.409A	S35.00XA	S35.535A	S45.101A
H59.123	I97.618	M1A.1421	S02.129S	S15.192A		S25.411A	S35.01XA	S35.536A	S45.102A
H59.129	I97.620	M1A.1490	S02.831S	S15.199A		S25.412A	S35.02XA	S35.59XA	S45.109A
H59.211	I97.621	M1A.1491	S02.832S	S15.201A		S25.419A	S35.09XA	S35.8X1A	S45.111A
H59.212	I97.622	M1A.1510	S02.839S	S15.202A		S25.421A	S35.10XA	S35.8X8A	S45.112A
H59.213	I97.630	M1A.1511	S02.841S	S15.209A		S25.422A	S35.11XA	S35.8X9A	S45.119A
H59.219	I97.631	M1A.1520	S02.842S	S15.211A		S25.429A	S35.12XA	S35.90XA	S45.191A
H59.221	I97.638	M1A.1521	S02.849S	S15.212A		S25.491A	S35.19XA	S35.91XA	S45.192A
H59.222	I97.640	M1A.1590	S02.85XS	S15.219A		S25.492A	S35.211A	S35.99XA	S45.199A
H59.223	I97.641	M1A.1591	S05.70XS	S15.221A		S25.499A	S35.212A	S36.892A	S45.201A
H59.229	I97.648	M1A.1610	S05.71XS	S15.222A		S25.501A	S35.218A	S36.893A	S45.202A
H59.311	J95.61	M1A.1611	S05.72XS	S15.229A		S25.502A	S35.219A	S36.898A	S45.209A
H59.312	J95.62	M1A.1620	S05.8X1S	S15.291A		S25.509A	S35.221A	S36.899A	S45.211A

S45.212A	S46.891A	S55.219A	S56.309A	S58.011A	S61.342A	S65.591A	S66.291S	S66.594S	S68.411A
S45.219A	S46.891S	S55.291A	S56.309S	S58.012A	S61.343A	S65.592A	S66.292A	S66.595A	S68.412A
S45.291A	S46.892A	S55.292A	S56.391A	S58.019A	S61.344A	S65.593A	S66.292S	S66.595S	S68.419A
S45.292A	S46.892S	S55.299A	S56.391S	S58.021A	S61.345A	S65.594A	S66.299A	S66.596A	S68.421A
S45.299A	S46.899A	S55.801A	S56.392A	S58.022A	S61.346A	S65.595A	S66.299S	S66.596S	S68.422A
S45.301A	S46.899S	S55.802A	S56.392S	S58.029A	S61.347A	S65.596A	S66.300A	S66.597A	S68.429A
S45.302A	S46.901A	S55.809A	S56.399A	S58.111A	S61.348A	S65.597A	S66.300S	S66.597S	S68.511A
S45.309A	S46.901S	S55.811A	S56.399S	S58.112A	S61.349A	S65.598A	S66.301A	S66.598A	S68.512A
S45.311A	S46.902A	S55.812A	S56.401A	S58.119A	S61.421A	S65.599A	S66.301S	S66.598S	S68.519A
S45.312A	S46.902S	S55.819A	S56.401S	S58.121A	S61.422A	S65.801A	S66.302A	S66.599A	S68.521A
S45.319A	S46.909A	S55.891A	S56.402A	S58.122A	S61.429A	S65.802A	S66.302S	S66.599S	S68.522A
S45.391A	S46.909S	S55.892A	S56.402S	S58.129A	S61.441A	S65.809A	S66.303A	S66.801A	S68.529A
S45.392A	S46.991A	S55.899A	S56.403A	S58.911A	S61.442A	S65.811A	S66.303S	S66.801S	S68.610A
S45.399A	S46.991S	S55.901A	S56.403S	S58.912A	S61.449A	S65.812A	S66.304A	S66.802A	S68.611A
S45.801A	S46.992A	S55.902A	S56.404A	S58.919A	S61.521A	S65.819A	S66.304S	S66.802S	S68.612A
S45.802A	S46.992S	S55.909A	S56.404S	S58.921A	S61.522A	S65.891A	S66.305A	S66.809A	S68.613A
S45.809A	S46.999A	S55.911A	S56.405A	S58.922A	S61.529A	S65.892A	S66.305S	S66.809S	S68.614A
S45.811A	S46.999S	S55.912A	S56.405S	S58.929A	S61.541A	S65.899A	S66.306A	S66.891A	S68.615A
S45.812A	S47.1XXA	S55.919A	S56.406A	S59.801A	S61.542A	S65.901A	S66.306S	S66.892A	S68.616A
S45.819A	S47.2XXA	S55.991A	S56.406S	S59.801S	S61.549A	S65.902A	S66.307A	S66.892S	S68.617A
S45.891A	S47.9XXA	S55.992A	S56.407A	S59.802A	S65.001A	S65.909A	S66.307S	S66.899A	S68.618A
S45.892A	S48.011A	S55.999A	S56.407S	S59.802S	S65.002A	S65.911A	S66.308A	S66.899S	S68.619A
S45.899A	S48.012A	S56.001A	S56.408A	S59.809A	S65.009A	S65.912A	S66.308S	S66.901A	S68.620A
S45.901A	S48.019A	S56.001S	S56.408S	S59.809S	S65.011A	S65.919A	S66.309A	S66.901S	S68.621A
S45.902A	S48.021A	S56.002A	S56.409A	S59.811A	S65.012A	S65.991A	S66.309S	S66.902A	S68.622A
S45.909A	S48.022A	S56.002S	S56.409S	S59.811S	S65.019A	S65.992A	S66.390A	S66.902S	S68.623A
S45.911A	S48.029A	S56.009A	S56.491A	S59.812A	S65.091A	S65.999A	S66.390S	S66.909A	S68.624A
S45.912A	S48.111A	S56.009S	S56.491S	S59.812S	S65.092A	S66.001A	S66.391A	S66.909S	S68.625A
S45.919A	S48.112A	S56.091A	S56.492A	S59.819A	S65.099A	S66.001S	S66.391S	S66.991A	S68.626A
S45.991A	S48.119A	S56.091S	S56.492S	S59.819S	S65.101A	S66.002A	S66.392A	S66.991S	S68.627A
S45.992A	S48.121A	S56.092A	S56.493A	S59.901A	S65.102A	S66.002S	S66.392S	S66.992A	S68.628A
S45.999A	S48.122A	S56.092S	S56.493S	S59.901S	S65.109A	S66.009A	S66.393A	S66.992S	S68.629A
S46.001A	S48.129A	S56.099A	S56.494A	S59.902A	S65.111A	S66.009S	S66.393S	S66.999A	S68.711A
S46.001S	S48.911A	S56.099S	S56.494S	S59.902S	S65.112A	S66.091A	S66.394A	S66.999S	S68.712A
S46.002A	S48.912A	S56.101A	S56.495A	S59.909A	S65.119A	S66.091S	S66.394S	S67.00XA	S68.719A
S46.002S	S48.919A	S56.101S	S56.495S	S59.909S	S65.191A	S66.092A	S66.395A	S67.01XA	S68.721A
S46.009A	S48.921A	S56.102A	S56.496A	S59.911A	S65.192A	S66.092S	S66.395S	S67.02XA	S68.722A
S46.009S	S48.922A	S56.102S	S56.496S	S59.911S	S65.199A	S66.099A	S66.396A	S67.10XA	S68.729A
S46.091A	S48.929A	S56.103A	S56.497A	S59.912A	S65.201A	S66.099S	S66.396S	S67.190A	S69.80XA
S46.091S	S49.80XA	S56.103S	S56.497S	S59.912S	S65.202A	S66.100A	S66.397A	S67.191A	S69.80XS
S46.092A	S49.80XS	S56.104A	S56.498A	S59.919A	S65.209A	S66.100S	S66.397S	S67.192A	S69.81XA
S46.092S	S49.81XA	S56.104S	S56.498S	S59.919S	S65.211A	S66.101A	S66.398A	S67.193A	S69.81XS
S46.099A	S49.81XS	S56.105A	S56.499A	S61.021A	S65.212A	S66.101S	S66.398S	S67.194A	S69.82XA
S46.099S	S49.82XA	S56.105S	S56.499S	S61.022A	S65.219A	S66.102A	S66.399A	S67.195A	S69.82XS
S46.101A	S49.82XS	S56.106A	S56.501A	S61.029A	S65.291A	S66.102S	S66.399S	S67.196A	S69.90XA
S46.101S	S49.90XA	S56.106S	S56.501S	S61.041A	S65.292A	S66.103A	S66.401A	S67.197A	S69.90XS
S46.102A	S49.90XS	S56.107A	S56.502A	S61.042A	S65.299A	S66.103S	S66.401S	S67.198A	S69.91XA
S46.102S	S49.91XA	S56.107S	S56.502S	S61.049A	S65.301A	S66.104A	S66.402A	S67.20XA	S69.91XS
S46.109A	S49.91XS	S56.108A	S56.509A	S61.121A	S65.302A	S66.104S	S66.402S	S67.21XA	S69.92XA
S46.109S	S49.92XA	S56.108S	S56.509S	S61.122A	S65.309A	S66.105A	S66.409A	S67.22XA	S69.92XS
S46.191A	S49.92XS	S56.109A	S56.591A	S61.129A	S65.311A	S66.105S	S66.409S	S67.30XA	S71.021A
S46.191S	S51.021A	S56.109S	S56.591S	S61.141A	S65.312A	S66.106A	S66.491A	S67.31XA	S71.022A
S46.192A	S51.022A	S56.191A	S56.592A	S61.142A	S65.319A	S66.106S	S66.491S	S67.32XA	S71.029A
S46.192S	S51.029A	S56.191S	S56.592S	S61.149A	S65.391A	S66.107A	S66.492A	S67.40XA	S71.041A
S46.199A	S51.041A	S56.192A	S56.599A	S61.220A	S65.392A	S66.107S	S66.492S	S67.41XA	S71.042A
S46.199S	S51.042A	S56.192S	S56.599S	S61.221A	S65.399A	S66.108A	S66.499A	S67.42XA	S71.049A
S46.201A	S51.049A	S56.193A	S56.801A	S61.222A	S65.401A	S66.108S	S66.499S	S67.90XA	S71.121A
S46.201S	S51.821A	S56.193S	S56.801S	S61.223A	S65.402A	S66.109A	S66.500A	S67.91XA	S71.122A
S46.202A	S51.822A	S56.194A	S56.802A	S61.224A	S65.409A	S66.109S	S66.500S	S67.92XA	S71.129A
S46.202S	S51.829A	S56.194S	S56.802S	S61.225A	S65.411A	S66.190A	S66.501A	S68.011A	S71.141A
S46.209A	S51.841A	S56.195A	S56.809A	S61.226A	S65.412A	S66.190S	S66.501S	S68.012A	S71.142A
S46.209S	S51.842A	S56.195S	S56.809S	S61.227A	S65.419A	S66.191A	S66.502A	S68.019A	S71.149A
S46.291A	S51.849A	S56.196A	S56.891A	S61.228A	S65.491A	S66.191S	S66.502S	S68.021A	S75.001A
S46.291S	S55.001A	S56.196S	S56.891S	S61.229A	S65.492A	S66.192A	S66.503A	S68.022A	S75.002A
S46.292A	S55.002A	S56.197A	S56.892A	S61.240A	S65.499A	S66.192S	S66.503S	S68.029A	S75.009A
S46.292S	S55.009A	S56.197S	S56.892S	S61.241A	S65.500A	S66.193A	S66.504A	S68.110A	S75.011A
S46.299A	S55.011A	S56.198A	S56.899A	S61.242A	S65.501A	S66.193S	S66.504S	S68.111A	S75.012A
S46.299S	S55.012A	S56.198S	S56.899S	S61.243A	S65.502A	S66.194A	S66.505A	S68.112A	S75.019A
S46.301A	S55.019A	S56.199A	S56.901A	S61.244A	S65.503A	S66.194S	S66.505S	S68.113A	S75.021A
S46.301S	S55.091A	S56.199S	S56.901S	S61.245A	S65.504A	S66.195A	S66.506A	S68.114A	S75.022A
S46.302A	S55.092A	S56.201A	S56.902A	S61.246A	S65.505A	S66.195S	S66.506S	S68.115A	S75.029A
S46.302S	S55.099A	S56.201S	S56.902S	S61.247A	S65.506A	S66.196A	S66.507A	S68.116A	S75.091A
S46.309A	S55.101A	S56.202A	S56.909A	S61.248A	S65.507A	S66.196S	S66.507S	S68.117A	S75.092A
S46.309S	S55.102A	S56.202S	S56.909S	S61.249A	S65.508A	S66.197A	S66.508A	S68.118A	S75.099A
S46.391A	S55.109A	S56.209A	S56.991A	S61.320A	S65.509A	S66.197S	S66.508S	S68.119A	S75.101A
S46.391S	S55.111A	S56.209S	S56.991S	S61.321A	S65.510A	S66.198A	S66.509A	S68.120A	S75.102A
S46.392A	S55.112A	S56.291A	S56.992A	S61.322A	S65.511A	S66.198S	S66.509S	S68.121A	S75.109A
S46.392S	S55.119A	S56.291S	S56.992S	S61.323A	S65.512A	S66.199A	S66.590A	S68.122A	S75.111A
S46.399A	S55.191A	S56.292A	S56.999A	S61.324A	S65.513A	S66.199S	S66.590S	S68.123A	S75.112A
S46.399S	S55.192A	S56.292S	S56.999S	S61.325A	S65.514A	S66.201A	S66.591A	S68.124A	S75.119A
S46.801A	S55.199A	S56.299A	S57.00XA	S61.326A	S65.515A	S66.201S	S66.591S	S68.125A	S75.121A
S46.801S	S55.201A	S56.299S	S57.01XA	S61.327A	S65.516A	S66.202A	S66.592A	S68.126A	S75.122A
S46.802A	S55.202A	S56.301A	S57.02XA	S61.328A	S65.517A	S66.202S	S66.592S	S68.127A	S75.129A
S46.802S	S55.209A	S56.301S	S57.80XA	S61.329A	S65.518A	S66.209A	S66.593A	S68.128A	S75.191A
S46.809A	S55.211A	S56.302A	S57.81XA	S61.340A	S65.519A	S66.209S	S66.593S	S68.129A	S75.192A
S46.809S	S55.212A	S56.302S	S57.82XA	S61.341A	S65.590A	S66.291A	S66.594A		S75.199A

Diagnosis Codes by MDC

S75.201A	S76.892A	S85.092A	S86.002S	S88.129A	S95.801A	S97.119A	S99.049B	S99.222A	T17.220S
S75.202A	S76.892S	S85.099A	S86.009A	S88.911A	S95.802A	S97.121A	S99.049S	S99.222B	T17.228S
S75.209A	S76.899A	S85.101A	S86.009S	S88.912A	S95.809A	S97.122A	S99.091A	S99.222S	T17.290S
S75.211A	S76.899S	S85.102A	S86.091A	S88.919A	S95.811A	S97.129A	S99.091B	S99.229A	T17.298S
S75.212A	S76.901A	S85.109A	S86.091S	S88.921A	S95.812A	S97.80XA	S99.091S	S99.229B	T17.300S
S75.219A	S76.901S	S85.111A	S86.092A	S88.922A	S95.819A	S97.81XA	S99.092A	S99.229S	T17.308S
S75.221A	S76.902A	S85.112A	S86.092S	S88.929A	S95.891A	S97.82XA	S99.092B	S99.231A	T17.310S
S75.222A	S76.902S	S85.119A	S86.099A	S89.80XA	S95.892A	S98.011A	S99.092S	S99.231B	T17.318S
S75.229A	S76.909A	S85.121A	S86.099S	S89.80XS	S95.899A	S98.012A	S99.099A	S99.231S	T17.320S
S75.291A	S76.909S	S85.122A	S86.101A	S89.81XA	S95.901A	S98.019A	S99.099B	S99.232A	T17.328S
S75.292A	S76.991A	S85.129A	S86.101S	S89.81XS	S95.902A	S98.021A	S99.099S	S99.232B	T17.390S
S75.299A	S76.991S	S85.131A	S86.102A	S89.82XA	S95.909A	S98.022A	S99.101A	S99.232S	T17.398S
S75.801A	S76.992A	S85.132A	S86.102S	S89.82XS	S95.911A	S98.029A	S99.101B	S99.239A	T17.400S
S75.802A	S76.992S	S85.139A	S86.109A	S89.90XA	S95.912A	S98.111A	S99.101S	S99.239B	T17.408S
S75.809A	S76.999A	S85.141A	S86.109S	S89.90XS	S95.919A	S98.112A	S99.102A	S99.239S	T17.410S
S75.811A	S76.999S	S85.142A	S86.191A	S89.91XA	S95.991A	S98.119A	S99.102B	S99.241A	T17.418S
S75.812A	S77.00XA	S85.149A	S86.191S	S89.91XS	S95.992A	S98.121A	S99.102S	S99.241B	T17.420S
S75.819A	S77.01XA	S85.151A	S86.192A	S89.92XA	S95.999A	S98.122A	S99.109A	S99.241S	T17.428S
S75.891A	S77.02XA	S85.152A	S86.192S	S89.92XS	S96.001A	S98.129A	S99.109B	S99.242A	T17.490S
S75.892A	S77.10XA	S85.159A	S86.199A	S91.021A	S96.001S	S98.131A	S99.109S	S99.242B	T17.498S
S75.899A	S77.11XA	S85.161A	S86.199S	S91.022A	S96.002A	S98.132A	S99.111A	S99.242S	T17.500S
S75.901A	S77.12XA	S85.162A	S86.201A	S91.029A	S96.002S	S98.139A	S99.111B	S99.249A	T17.508S
S75.902A	S77.20XA	S85.169A	S86.201S	S91.041A	S96.009A	S98.141A	S99.111S	S99.249B	T17.510S
S75.909A	S77.21XA	S85.171A	S86.202A	S91.042A	S96.009S	S98.142A	S99.112A	S99.249S	T17.518S
S75.911A	S77.22XA	S85.172A	S86.202S	S91.049A	S96.091A	S98.149A	S99.112B	S99.291A	T17.520S
S75.912A	S78.011A	S85.179A	S86.209A	S91.121A	S96.091S	S98.211A	S99.112S	S99.291B	T17.528S
S75.919A	S78.012A	S85.181A	S86.209S	S91.122A	S96.092A	S98.212A	S99.119A	S99.291S	T17.590S
S75.991A	S78.019A	S85.182A	S86.291A	S91.123A	S96.092S	S98.219A	S99.119B	S99.292A	T17.598S
S75.992A	S78.021A	S85.189A	S86.291S	S91.124A	S96.099A	S98.221A	S99.119S	S99.292B	T17.800S
S75.999A	S78.022A	S85.201A	S86.292A	S91.125A	S96.099S	S98.222A	S99.121A	S99.292S	T17.808S
S76.001A	S78.029A	S85.202A	S86.292S	S91.126A	S96.101A	S98.229A	S99.121B	S99.299A	T17.810S
S76.001S	S78.111A	S85.209A	S86.299A	S91.129A	S96.101S	S98.311A	S99.121S	S99.299B	T17.818S
S76.002A	S78.112A	S85.211A	S86.299S	S91.141A	S96.102A	S98.312A	S99.122A	S99.299S	T17.820S
S76.002S	S78.119A	S85.212A	S86.301A	S91.142A	S96.102S	S98.319A	S99.122B	S99.811A	T17.828S
S76.009A	S78.121A	S85.219A	S86.301S	S91.143A	S96.109A	S98.321A	S99.122S	S99.811S	T17.890S
S76.009S	S78.122A	S85.291A	S86.302A	S91.144A	S96.109S	S98.322A	S99.129A	S99.812A	T17.898S
S76.091A	S78.129A	S85.292A	S86.302S	S91.145A	S96.191A	S98.329A	S99.129B	S99.812S	T17.900S
S76.091S	S78.911A	S85.299A	S86.309A	S91.146A	S96.191S	S98.911A	S99.129S	S99.819A	T17.908S
S76.092A	S78.912A	S85.301A	S86.309S	S91.149A	S96.192A	S98.912A	S99.131A	S99.819S	T17.910S
S76.092S	S78.919A	S85.302A	S86.391A	S91.221A	S96.192S	S98.919A	S99.131B	S99.821A	T17.918S
S76.099A	S78.921A	S85.309A	S86.391S	S91.222A	S96.199A	S98.921A	S99.131S	S99.821S	T17.920S
S76.099S	S78.922A	S85.311A	S86.392A	S91.223A	S96.199S	S98.922A	S99.132A	S99.822A	T17.928S
S76.101A	S78.929A	S85.312A	S86.392S	S91.224A	S96.201A	S98.929A	S99.132B	S99.822S	T17.990S
S76.101S	S79.811A	S85.319A	S86.399A	S91.225A	S96.201S	S99.001A	S99.132S	S99.829A	T17.998S
S76.102A	S79.811S	S85.391A	S86.399S	S91.226A	S96.202A	S99.001B	S99.139A	S99.829S	T18.0XXS
S76.102S	S79.812A	S85.392A	S86.801A	S91.229A	S96.202S	S99.001S	S99.139B	S99.911A	T18.100S
S76.109A	S79.812S	S85.399A	S86.801S	S91.241A	S96.209A	S99.002A	S99.139S	S99.911S	T18.108S
S76.109S	S79.819A	S85.399S	S86.802A	S91.242A	S96.209S	S99.002B	S99.141A	S99.912A	T18.110S
S76.191A	S79.819S	S85.401A	S86.802S	S91.243A	S96.291A	S99.002S	S99.141B	S99.912S	T18.118S
S76.191S	S79.821A	S85.402A	S86.809A	S91.244A	S96.291S	S99.009A	S99.141S	S99.919A	T18.120S
S76.192A	S79.821S	S85.409A	S86.809S	S91.245A	S96.292A	S99.009B	S99.142A	S99.919S	T18.128S
S76.192S	S79.822A	S85.411A	S86.891A	S91.246A	S96.292S	S99.009S	S99.142B	S99.921A	T18.190S
S76.199A	S79.822S	S85.412A	S86.891S	S91.249A	S96.299A	S99.011A	S99.142S	S99.921S	T18.198S
S76.199S	S79.829A	S85.419A	S86.892A	S91.321A	S96.299S	S99.011B	S99.149A	S99.922A	T18.2XXS
S76.201A	S79.829S	S85.491A	S86.892S	S91.322A	S96.801A	S99.011S	S99.149B	S99.922S	T18.3XXS
S76.201S	S79.911A	S85.492A	S86.899A	S91.329A	S96.801S	S99.012A	S99.149S	S99.929A	T18.4XXS
S76.202A	S79.911S	S85.499A	S86.899S	S91.341A	S96.802A	S99.012B	S99.191A	S99.929S	T18.5XXS
S76.202S	S79.912A	S85.501A	S86.901A	S91.342A	S96.802S	S99.012S	S99.191B	T07.XXXA	T18.8XXS
S76.209A	S79.912S	S85.502A	S86.901S	S91.349A	S96.809A	S99.019A	S99.191S	T07.XXXS	T18.9XXS
S76.209S	S79.919A	S85.509A	S86.902A	S95.001A	S96.809S	S99.019B	S99.192A	T14.8XXA	T19.0XXS
S76.291A	S79.921A	S85.511A	S86.902S	S95.002A	S96.891A	S99.019S	S99.192B	T14.8XXS	T19.1XXS
S76.291S	S79.921S	S85.512A	S86.909A	S95.009A	S96.891S	S99.021A	S99.192S	T14.90XA	T19.2XXS
S76.292A	S79.922A	S85.519A	S86.909S	S95.011A	S96.892A	S99.021B	S99.199A	T14.90XS	T19.3XXS
S76.292S	S79.922S	S85.591A	S86.991A	S95.012A	S96.892S	S99.021S	S99.199B	T14.91XA	T19.4XXS
S76.299A	S79.929A	S85.592A	S86.991S	S95.019A	S96.899A	S99.022A	S99.199S	T14.91XS	T19.8XXS
S76.299S	S79.929S	S85.599A	S86.992A	S95.091A	S96.899S	S99.022B	S99.201A	T15.00XS	T19.9XXS
S76.301A	S81.021A	S85.801A	S86.992S	S95.092A	S96.901A	S99.022S	S99.201B	T15.01XS	T33.011A
S76.301S	S81.022A	S85.802A	S86.999A	S95.099A	S96.901S	S99.029A	S99.201S	T15.02XS	T33.011S
S76.302A	S81.029A	S85.809A	S86.999S	S95.101A	S96.902A	S99.029B	S99.202A	T15.10XS	T33.012A
S76.302S	S81.041A	S85.811A	S87.01XA	S95.102A	S96.902S	S99.029S	S99.202B	T15.11XS	T33.012S
S76.309A	S81.042A	S85.812A	S87.02XA	S95.109A	S96.909A	S99.031A	S99.202S	T15.12XS	T33.019A
S76.309S	S81.049A	S85.819A	S87.80XA	S95.111A	S96.909S	S99.031B	S99.209A	T15.80XS	T33.019S
S76.391A	S81.821A	S85.891A	S87.81XA	S95.112A	S96.991A	S99.031S	S99.209B	T15.81XS	T33.02XA
S76.391S	S81.822A	S85.892A	S87.82XA	S95.119A	S96.991S	S99.032A	S99.209S	T15.82XS	T33.02XS
S76.392A	S81.829A	S85.901A	S88.011A	S95.191A	S96.992A	S99.032B	S99.211A	T15.90XS	T33.09XA
S76.392S	S81.841A	S85.902A	S88.012A	S95.192A	S96.992S	S99.032S	S99.211B	T15.91XS	T33.09XS
S76.399A	S81.842A	S85.909A	S88.019A	S95.199A	S96.999A	S99.039A	S99.211S	T15.92XS	T33.1XXA
S76.399S	S81.849A	S85.911A	S88.021A	S95.201A	S96.999S	S99.039B	S99.212A	T16.1XXS	T33.1XXS
S76.801A	S85.001A	S85.912A	S88.022A	S95.202A	S97.00XA	S99.039S	S99.212B	T16.2XXS	T33.2XXA
S76.801S	S85.002A	S85.919A	S88.029A	S95.209A	S97.01XA	S99.041A	S99.212S	T16.9XXS	T33.2XXS
S76.802A	S85.009A	S85.991A	S88.111A	S95.211A	S97.02XA	S99.041B	S99.219A	T17.0XXS	T33.3XXA
S76.802S	S85.011A	S85.992A	S88.112A	S95.212A	S97.101A	S99.041S	S99.219B	T17.1XXS	T33.3XXS
S76.809A	S85.012A	S85.999A	S88.119A	S95.219A	S97.102A	S99.042A	S99.219S	T17.200S	T33.40XA
S76.809S	S85.019A	S86.001A	S88.121A	S95.291A	S97.109A	S99.042B	S99.221A	T17.208S	T33.40XS
S76.891A	S85.091A	S86.001S	S88.122A	S95.292A	S97.111A	S99.042S	S99.221B	T17.210S	T33.41XA
S76.891S	S85.091S	S86.002A		S95.299A	S97.112A	S99.049A	S99.221S	T17.218S	T33.41XS

T33.42XA	T34.529A	T36.4X3A	T37.3X1A	T38.3X4A	T38.992A	T39.8X5A	T40.694A	T41.3X3A	T42.6X1A
T33.42XS	T34.529S	T36.4X3S	T37.3X1S	T38.3X4S	T38.992S	T39.8X5S	T40.694S	T41.3X3S	T42.6X1S
T33.511A	T34.531A	T36.4X4A	T37.3X2A	T38.3X5A	T38.993A	T39.91XA	T40.695A	T41.3X4A	T42.6X2A
T33.511S	T34.531S	T36.4X4S	T37.3X2S	T38.3X5S	T38.993S	T39.91XS	T40.695S	T41.3X5A	T42.6X2S
T33.512A	T34.532A	T36.4X5A	T37.3X3A	T38.4X1A	T38.994A	T39.92XA	T40.7X1A	T41.3X5S	T42.6X3A
T33.512S	T34.532S	T36.4X5S	T37.3X3S	T38.4X1S	T38.994S	T39.92XS	T40.7X1S	T41.41XA	T42.6X3S
T33.519A	T34.539A	T36.5X1A	T37.3X4A	T38.4X2A	T38.995A	T39.93XA	T40.7X2A	T41.41XS	T42.6X4A
T33.519S	T34.539S	T36.5X1S	T37.3X4S	T38.4X2S	T38.995S	T39.93XS	T40.7X2S	T41.42XA	T42.6X4S
T33.521A	T34.60XA	T36.5X2A	T37.3X5A	T38.4X3A	T39.011A	T39.94XA	T40.7X3A	T41.42XS	T42.6X5A
T33.521S	T34.60XS	T36.5X2S	T37.3X5S	T38.4X3S	T39.011S	T39.94XS	T40.7X3S	T41.43XA	T42.6X5S
T33.522A	T34.61XA	T36.5X3A	T37.4X1A	T38.4X4A	T39.012A	T39.95XA	T40.7X4A	T41.43XS	T42.71XA
T33.522S	T34.61XS	T36.5X3S	T37.4X1S	T38.4X4S	T39.012S	T39.95XS	T40.7X4S	T41.44XA	T42.71XS
T33.529A	T34.62XA	T36.5X4A	T37.4X2A	T38.4X5A	T39.013A	T40.0X1A	T40.7X5A	T41.44XS	T42.72XA
T33.529S	T34.62XS	T36.5X4S	T37.4X2S	T38.4X5S	T39.013S	T40.0X1S	T40.7X5S	T41.45XA	T42.72XS
T33.531A	T34.70XA	T36.5X5A	T37.4X3A	T38.5X1A	T39.014A	T40.0X2A	T40.8X1A	T41.45XS	T42.73XA
T33.531S	T34.70XS	T36.5X5S	T37.4X3S	T38.5X1S	T39.014S	T40.0X2S	T40.8X1S	T41.5X1A	T42.73XS
T33.532A	T34.71XA	T36.6X1A	T37.4X4A	T38.5X2A	T39.015A	T40.0X3A	T40.8X2A	T41.5X1S	T42.74XA
T33.532S	T34.71XS	T36.6X1S	T37.4X4S	T38.5X2S	T39.015S	T40.0X3S	T40.8X2S	T41.5X2A	T42.74XS
T33.539A	T34.72XA	T36.6X2A	T37.4X5A	T38.5X3A	T39.091A	T40.0X4A	T40.8X3A	T41.5X2S	T42.75XA
T33.539S	T34.72XS	T36.6X2S	T37.4X5S	T38.5X3S	T39.091S	T40.0X4S	T40.8X3S	T41.5X3A	T42.75XS
T33.60XA	T34.811A	T36.6X3A	T37.5X1A	T38.5X4A	T39.092A	T40.0X5A	T40.8X4A	T41.5X3S	T42.8X1A
T33.60XS	T34.811S	T36.6X3S	T37.5X1S	T38.5X4S	T39.092S	T40.0X5S	T40.8X4S	T41.5X4A	T42.8X1S
T33.61XA	T34.812A	T36.6X4A	T37.5X2A	T38.5X5A	T39.093A	T40.1X1A	T40.901A	T41.5X4S	T42.8X2A
T33.61XS	T34.812S	T36.6X4S	T37.5X2S	T38.5X5S	T39.093S	T40.1X1S	T40.901S	T41.5X5A	T42.8X2S
T33.62XA	T34.819A	T36.6X5A	T37.5X3A	T38.6X1A	T39.094A	T40.1X2A	T40.902A	T41.5X5S	T42.8X3A
T33.62XS	T34.819S	T36.6X5S	T37.5X3S	T38.6X1S	T39.094S	T40.1X2S	T40.902S	T42.0X1A	T42.8X3S
T33.70XA	T34.821A	T36.7X1A	T37.5X4A	T38.6X2A	T39.095A	T40.1X3A	T40.903A	T42.0X1S	T42.8X4A
T33.70XS	T34.821S	T36.7X1S	T37.5X4S	T38.6X2S	T39.095S	T40.1X3S	T40.903S	T42.0X2A	T42.8X4S
T33.71XA	T34.822A	T36.7X2A	T37.5X5A	T38.6X3A	T39.1X1A	T40.1X4A	T40.904A	T42.0X2S	T42.8X5A
T33.71XS	T34.822S	T36.7X2S	T37.5X5S	T38.6X3S	T39.1X1S	T40.1X4S	T40.904S	T42.0X3A	T42.8X5S
T33.72XA	T34.829A	T36.7X3A	T37.8X1A	T38.6X4A	T39.1X2A	T40.2X1A	T40.905A	T42.0X3S	T43.011A
T33.72XS	T34.829S	T36.7X3S	T37.8X1S	T38.6X4S	T39.1X2S	T40.2X1S	T40.905S	T42.0X4A	T43.011S
T33.811A	T34.831A	T36.7X4A	T37.8X2A	T38.6X5A	T39.1X3A	T40.2X2A	T40.991A	T42.0X4S	T43.012A
T33.811S	T34.831S	T36.7X4S	T37.8X2S	T38.6X5S	T39.1X3S	T40.2X2S	T40.991S	T42.0X5A	T43.012S
T33.812A	T34.832A	T36.7X5A	T37.8X3A	T38.7X1A	T39.1X4A	T40.2X3A	T40.992A	T42.0X5S	T43.013A
T33.812S	T34.832S	T36.7X5S	T37.8X3S	T38.7X1S	T39.1X4S	T40.2X3S	T40.992S	T42.1X1A	T43.013S
T33.819A	T34.839A	T36.8X1A	T37.8X4A	T38.7X2A	T39.1X5A	T40.2X4A	T40.993A	T42.1X1S	T43.014A
T33.819S	T34.839S	T36.8X1S	T37.8X4S	T38.7X2S	T39.1X5S	T40.2X4S	T40.993S	T42.1X2A	T43.014S
T33.821A	T34.90XA	T36.8X2A	T37.8X5A	T38.7X3A	T39.2X1A	T40.2X5A	T40.994A	T42.1X2S	T43.015A
T33.821S	T34.90XS	T36.8X2S	T37.8X5S	T38.7X3S	T39.2X1S	T40.2X5S	T40.994S	T42.1X3A	T43.015S
T33.822A	T34.99XA	T36.8X3A	T37.91XA	T38.7X4A	T39.2X2A	T40.3X1A	T40.995A	T42.1X3S	T43.021A
T33.822S	T34.99XS	T36.8X3S	T37.91XS	T38.7X4S	T39.2X2S	T40.3X1S	T40.995S	T42.1X4A	T43.021S
T33.829A	T36.0X1A	T36.8X4A	T37.92XA	T38.7X5A	T39.2X3A	T40.3X2A	T41.0X1A	T42.1X4S	T43.022A
T33.829S	T36.0X1S	T36.8X4S	T37.92XS	T38.7X5S	T39.2X3S	T40.3X2S	T41.0X1S	T42.1X5A	T43.022S
T33.831A	T36.0X2A	T36.8X5A	T37.93XA	T38.801A	T39.2X4A	T40.3X3A	T41.0X2A	T42.1X5S	T43.023A
T33.831S	T36.0X2S	T36.8X5S	T37.93XS	T38.801S	T39.2X4S	T40.3X3S	T41.0X2S	T42.2X1A	T43.023S
T33.832A	T36.0X3A	T36.91XA	T37.94XA	T38.802A	T39.2X5A	T40.3X4A	T41.0X3A	T42.2X1S	T43.024A
T33.832S	T36.0X3S	T36.91XS	T37.94XS	T38.802S	T39.2X5S	T40.3X4S	T41.0X3S	T42.2X2A	T43.024S
T33.839A	T36.0X4A	T36.92XA	T37.95XA	T38.803A	T39.311A	T40.3X5A	T41.0X4A	T42.2X2S	T43.025A
T33.839S	T36.0X4S	T36.92XS	T37.95XS	T38.803S	T39.311S	T40.3X5S	T41.0X4S	T42.2X3A	T43.025S
T33.90XA	T36.0X5A	T36.93XA	T38.0X1A	T38.804A	T39.312A	T40.4X1A	T41.0X5A	T42.2X3S	T43.1X1A
T33.90XS	T36.0X5S	T36.93XS	T38.0X1S	T38.804S	T39.312S	T40.4X1S	T41.0X5S	T42.2X4A	T43.1X1S
T33.99XA	T36.1X1A	T36.94XA	T38.0X2A	T38.805A	T39.313A	T40.4X2A	T41.1X1A	T42.2X4S	T43.1X2A
T33.99XS	T36.1X1S	T36.94XS	T38.0X2S	T38.805S	T39.313S	T40.4X2S	T41.1X1S	T42.2X5A	T43.1X2S
T34.011A	T36.1X2A	T36.95XA	T38.0X3A	T38.811A	T39.314A	T40.4X3A	T41.1X2A	T42.2X5S	T43.1X3A
T34.011S	T36.1X2S	T36.95XS	T38.0X3S	T38.811S	T39.314S	T40.4X3S	T41.1X2S	T42.3X1A	T43.1X3S
T34.012A	T36.1X3A	T37.0X1A	T38.0X4A	T38.812A	T39.315A	T40.4X4A	T41.1X3A	T42.3X1S	T43.1X4A
T34.012S	T36.1X3S	T37.0X1S	T38.0X4S	T38.812S	T39.315S	T40.4X4S	T41.1X3S	T42.3X2A	T43.1X4S
T34.019A	T36.1X4A	T37.0X2A	T38.0X5A	T38.813A	T39.391A	T40.4X5A	T41.1X4A	T42.3X2S	T43.1X5A
T34.019S	T36.1X4S	T37.0X2S	T38.0X5S	T38.813S	T39.391S	T40.4X5S	T41.1X4S	T42.3X3A	T43.1X5S
T34.02XA	T36.1X5A	T37.0X3A	T38.1X1A	T38.814A	T39.392A	T40.5X1A	T41.1X5A	T42.3X3S	T43.201A
T34.02XS	T36.1X5S	T37.0X3S	T38.1X1S	T38.814S	T39.392S	T40.5X1S	T41.1X5S	T42.3X4A	T43.201S
T34.09XA	T36.2X1A	T37.0X4A	T38.1X2A	T38.815A	T39.393A	T40.5X2A	T41.201A	T42.3X4S	T43.202A
T34.09XS	T36.2X1S	T37.0X4S	T38.1X2S	T38.815S	T39.393S	T40.5X2S	T41.201S	T42.3X5A	T43.202S
T34.1XXA	T36.2X2A	T37.0X5A	T38.1X3A	T38.891A	T39.394A	T40.5X3A	T41.202A	T42.3X5S	T43.203A
T34.1XXS	T36.2X2S	T37.0X5S	T38.1X3S	T38.891S	T39.394S	T40.5X3S	T41.202S	T42.4X1A	T43.203S
T34.2XXA	T36.2X3A	T37.1X1A	T38.1X4A	T38.892A	T39.395A	T40.5X4A	T41.203A	T42.4X1S	T43.204A
T34.2XXS	T36.2X3S	T37.1X1S	T38.1X4S	T38.892S	T39.395S	T40.5X4S	T41.203S	T42.4X2A	T43.204S
T34.3XXA	T36.2X4A	T37.1X2A	T38.1X5A	T38.893A	T39.4X1A	T40.5X5A	T41.204A	T42.4X2S	T43.205A
T34.3XXS	T36.2X4S	T37.1X2S	T38.1X5S	T38.893S	T39.4X1S	T40.5X5S	T41.204S	T42.4X3A	T43.205S
T34.40XA	T36.2X5A	T37.1X3A	T38.2X1A	T38.894A	T39.4X2A	T40.601A	T41.205A	T42.4X3S	T43.211A
T34.40XS	T36.2X5S	T37.1X3S	T38.2X1S	T38.894S	T39.4X2S	T40.601S	T41.205S	T42.4X4A	T43.211S
T34.41XA	T36.3X1A	T37.1X4A	T38.2X2A	T38.895A	T39.4X3A	T40.602A	T41.291A	T42.4X4S	T43.212A
T34.41XS	T36.3X1S	T37.1X4S	T38.2X2S	T38.895S	T39.4X3S	T40.602S	T41.291S	T42.4X5A	T43.212S
T34.42XA	T36.3X2A	T37.1X5A	T38.2X3A	T38.901A	T39.4X4A	T40.603A	T41.292A	T42.4X5S	T43.213A
T34.42XS	T36.3X2S	T37.1X5S	T38.2X3S	T38.901S	T39.4X4S	T40.603S	T41.292S	T42.5X1A	T43.213S
T34.511A	T36.3X3A	T37.2X1A	T38.2X4A	T38.902A	T39.4X5A	T40.604A	T41.293A	T42.5X1S	T43.214A
T34.511S	T36.3X3S	T37.2X1S	T38.2X4S	T38.902S	T39.4X5S	T40.604S	T41.293S	T42.5X2A	T43.214S
T34.512A	T36.3X4A	T37.2X2A	T38.2X5A	T38.903A	T39.8X1A	T40.605A	T41.294A	T42.5X2S	T43.215A
T34.512S	T36.3X4S	T37.2X2S	T38.2X5S	T38.903S	T39.8X1S	T40.605S	T41.294S	T42.5X3A	T43.215S
T34.519A	T36.3X5A	T37.2X3A	T38.3X1A	T38.904A	T39.8X2A	T40.691A	T41.295A	T42.5X3S	T43.221A
T34.519S	T36.3X5S	T37.2X3S	T38.3X1S	T38.904S	T39.8X2S	T40.691S	T41.295S	T42.5X4A	T43.221S
T34.521A	T36.4X1A	T37.2X4A	T38.3X2A	T38.905A	T39.8X3A	T40.692A	T41.3X1A	T42.5X4S	T43.222A
T34.521S	T36.4X1S	T37.2X4S	T38.3X2S	T38.905S	T39.8X3S	T40.692S	T41.3X1S	T42.5X5A	T43.222S
T34.522A	T36.4X2A	T37.2X5A	T38.3X3A	T38.991A	T39.8X4A	T40.693A	T41.3X2A	T42.5X5S	T43.223A
T34.522S	T36.4X2S	T37.2X5S	T38.3X3S	T38.991S	T39.8X4S	T40.693S	T41.3X2S		T43.223S

T43.224A	T43.632A	T44.4X1A	T45.1X4A	T45.692A	T46.4X5A	T47.2X3A	T48.1X1A	T48.994A	T49.8X2A
T43.224S	T43.632S	T44.4X1S	T45.1X4S	T45.692S	T46.4X5S	T47.2X3S	T48.1X1S	T48.994S	T49.8X2S
T43.225A	T43.633A	T44.4X2A	T45.1X5A	T45.693A	T46.5X1A	T47.2X4A	T48.1X2A	T48.995A	T49.8X3A
T43.225S	T43.633S	T44.4X2S	T45.1X5S	T45.693S	T46.5X1S	T47.2X4S	T48.1X2S	T48.995S	T49.8X3S
T43.291A	T43.634A	T44.4X3A	T45.2X1A	T45.694A	T46.5X2A	T47.2X5A	T48.1X3A	T49.0X1A	T49.8X4A
T43.291S	T43.634S	T44.4X3S	T45.2X1S	T45.694S	T46.5X2S	T47.2X5S	T48.1X3S	T49.0X1S	T49.8X4S
T43.292A	T43.635A	T44.4X4A	T45.2X2A	T45.695A	T46.5X3A	T47.3X1A	T48.1X4A	T49.0X2A	T49.8X5A
T43.292S	T43.635S	T44.4X4S	T45.2X2S	T45.695S	T46.5X3S	T47.3X1S	T48.1X4S	T49.0X2S	T49.8X5S
T43.293A	T43.641A	T44.4X5A	T45.2X3A	T45.7X1A	T46.5X4A	T47.3X2A	T48.1X5A	T49.0X3A	T49.91XA
T43.293S	T43.641S	T44.4X5S	T45.2X3S	T45.7X1S	T46.5X4S	T47.3X2S	T48.1X5S	T49.0X3S	T49.91XS
T43.294A	T43.642A	T44.5X1A	T45.2X4A	T45.7X2A	T46.5X5A	T47.3X3A	T48.201A	T49.0X4A	T49.92XA
T43.294S	T43.642S	T44.5X1S	T45.2X4S	T45.7X2S	T46.5X5S	T47.3X3S	T48.201S	T49.0X4S	T49.92XS
T43.295A	T43.643A	T44.5X2A	T45.2X5A	T45.7X3A	T46.6X1A	T47.3X4A	T48.202A	T49.0X5A	T49.93XA
T43.295S	T43.643S	T44.5X2S	T45.2X5S	T45.7X3S	T46.6X1S	T47.3X4S	T48.202S	T49.0X5S	T49.93XS
T43.3X1A	T43.644A	T44.5X3A	T45.3X1A	T45.7X4A	T46.6X2A	T47.3X5A	T48.203A	T49.1X1A	T49.94XA
T43.3X1S	T43.644S	T44.5X3S	T45.3X1S	T45.7X4S	T46.6X2S	T47.3X5S	T48.203S	T49.1X1S	T49.94XS
T43.3X2A	T43.691A	T44.5X4A	T45.3X2A	T45.7X5A	T46.6X3A	T47.4X1A	T48.204A	T49.1X2A	T49.95XA
T43.3X2S	T43.691S	T44.5X4S	T45.3X2S	T45.7X5S	T46.6X3S	T47.4X1S	T48.204S	T49.1X2S	T49.95XS
T43.3X3A	T43.692A	T44.5X5A	T45.3X3A	T45.8X1A	T46.6X4A	T47.4X2A	T48.205A	T49.1X3A	T50.0X1A
T43.3X3S	T43.692S	T44.5X5S	T45.3X3S	T45.8X1S	T46.6X4S	T47.4X2S	T48.205S	T49.1X3S	T50.0X1S
T43.3X4A	T43.693A	T44.6X1A	T45.3X4A	T45.8X2A	T46.6X5A	T47.4X3A	T48.291A	T49.1X4A	T50.0X2A
T43.3X4S	T43.693S	T44.6X1S	T45.3X4S	T45.8X2S	T46.6X5S	T47.4X3S	T48.291S	T49.1X4S	T50.0X2S
T43.3X5A	T43.694A	T44.6X2A	T45.3X5A	T45.8X3A	T46.7X1A	T47.4X4A	T48.292A	T49.1X5A	T50.0X3A
T43.3X5S	T43.694S	T44.6X2S	T45.3X5S	T45.8X3S	T46.7X1S	T47.4X4S	T48.292S	T49.1X5S	T50.0X3S
T43.4X1A	T43.695A	T44.6X3A	T45.4X1A	T45.8X4A	T46.7X2A	T47.4X5A	T48.293A	T49.2X1A	T50.0X4A
T43.4X1S	T43.695S	T44.6X3S	T45.4X1S	T45.8X4S	T46.7X2S	T47.4X5S	T48.293S	T49.2X1S	T50.0X4S
T43.4X2A	T43.8X1A	T44.6X4A	T45.4X2A	T45.8X5A	T46.7X3A	T47.5X1A	T48.294A	T49.2X2A	T50.0X5A
T43.4X2S	T43.8X1S	T44.6X4S	T45.4X2S	T45.8X5S	T46.7X3S	T47.5X1S	T48.294S	T49.2X2S	T50.0X5S
T43.4X3A	T43.8X2A	T44.6X5A	T45.4X3A	T45.91XA	T46.7X4A	T47.5X2A	T48.295A	T49.2X3A	T50.1X1A
T43.4X3S	T43.8X2S	T44.6X5S	T45.4X3S	T45.91XS	T46.7X4S	T47.5X2S	T48.295S	T49.2X3S	T50.1X1S
T43.4X4A	T43.8X3A	T44.7X1A	T45.4X4A	T45.92XA	T46.7X5A	T47.5X3A	T48.3X1A	T49.2X4A	T50.1X2A
T43.4X4S	T43.8X3S	T44.7X1S	T45.4X4S	T45.92XS	T46.7X5S	T47.5X3S	T48.3X1S	T49.2X4S	T50.1X2S
T43.4X5A	T43.8X4A	T44.7X2A	T45.4X5A	T45.93XA	T46.8X1A	T47.5X4A	T48.3X2A	T49.2X5A	T50.1X3A
T43.4X5S	T43.8X4S	T44.7X2S	T45.4X5S	T45.93XS	T46.8X1S	T47.5X4S	T48.3X2S	T49.2X5S	T50.1X3S
T43.501A	T43.8X5A	T44.7X3A	T45.511A	T45.94XA	T46.8X2A	T47.5X5A	T48.3X3A	T49.3X1A	T50.1X4A
T43.501S	T43.8X5S	T44.7X3S	T45.511S	T45.94XS	T46.8X2S	T47.5X5S	T48.3X3S	T49.3X1S	T50.1X4S
T43.502A	T43.91XA	T44.7X4A	T45.512A	T45.95XA	T46.8X3A	T47.6X1A	T48.3X4A	T49.3X2A	T50.1X5A
T43.502S	T43.91XS	T44.7X4S	T45.512S	T45.95XS	T46.8X3S	T47.6X1S	T48.3X4S	T49.3X2S	T50.1X5S
T43.503A	T43.92XA	T44.7X5A	T45.513A	T46.0X1A	T46.8X4A	T47.6X2A	T48.3X5A	T49.3X3A	T50.2X1A
T43.503S	T43.92XS	T44.7X5S	T45.513S	T46.0X1S	T46.8X4S	T47.6X2S	T48.3X5S	T49.3X3S	T50.2X1S
T43.504A	T43.93XA	T44.8X1A	T45.514A	T46.0X2A	T46.8X5A	T47.6X3A	T48.4X1A	T49.3X4A	T50.2X2A
T43.504S	T43.93XS	T44.8X1S	T45.514S	T46.0X2S	T46.8X5S	T47.6X3S	T48.4X1S	T49.3X4S	T50.2X2S
T43.505A	T43.94XA	T44.8X2A	T45.515A	T46.0X3A	T46.901A	T47.6X4A	T48.4X2A	T49.3X5A	T50.2X3A
T43.505S	T43.94XS	T44.8X2S	T45.515S	T46.0X3S	T46.901S	T47.6X4S	T48.4X2S	T49.3X5S	T50.2X3S
T43.591A	T43.95XA	T44.8X3A	T45.521A	T46.0X4A	T46.902A	T47.6X5A	T48.4X3A	T49.4X1A	T50.2X4A
T43.591S	T43.95XS	T44.8X3S	T45.521S	T46.0X4S	T46.902S	T47.6X5S	T48.4X3S	T49.4X1S	T50.2X4S
T43.592A	T44.0X1A	T44.8X4A	T45.522A	T46.0X5A	T46.903A	T47.7X1A	T48.4X4A	T49.4X2A	T50.2X5A
T43.592S	T44.0X1S	T44.8X4S	T45.522S	T46.0X5S	T46.903S	T47.7X1S	T48.4X4S	T49.4X2S	T50.2X5S
T43.593A	T44.0X2A	T44.8X5A	T45.523A	T46.1X1A	T46.904A	T47.7X2A	T48.4X5A	T49.4X3A	T50.3X1A
T43.593S	T44.0X2S	T44.8X5S	T45.523S	T46.1X1S	T46.904S	T47.7X2S	T48.4X5S	T49.4X3S	T50.3X1S
T43.594A	T44.0X3A	T44.901A	T45.524A	T46.1X2A	T46.905A	T47.7X3A	T48.5X1A	T49.4X4A	T50.3X2A
T43.594S	T44.0X3S	T44.901S	T45.524S	T46.1X2S	T46.905S	T47.7X3S	T48.5X1S	T49.4X4S	T50.3X2S
T43.595A	T44.0X4A	T44.902A	T45.525A	T46.1X3A	T46.991A	T47.7X4A	T48.5X2A	T49.4X5A	T50.3X3A
T43.595S	T44.0X4S	T44.902S	T45.525S	T46.1X3S	T46.991S	T47.7X4S	T48.5X2S	T49.4X5S	T50.3X3S
T43.601A	T44.0X5A	T44.903A	T45.601A	T46.1X4A	T46.992A	T47.7X5A	T48.5X3A	T49.5X1A	T50.3X4A
T43.601S	T44.0X5S	T44.903S	T45.601S	T46.1X4S	T46.992S	T47.7X5S	T48.5X3S	T49.5X1S	T50.3X4S
T43.602A	T44.1X1A	T44.904A	T45.602A	T46.1X5A	T46.993A	T47.8X1A	T48.5X4A	T49.5X2A	T50.3X5A
T43.602S	T44.1X1S	T44.904S	T45.602S	T46.1X5S	T46.993S	T47.8X1S	T48.5X4S	T49.5X2S	T50.3X5S
T43.603A	T44.1X2A	T44.905A	T45.603A	T46.2X1A	T46.994A	T47.8X2A	T48.5X5A	T49.5X3A	T50.4X1A
T43.603S	T44.1X2S	T44.905S	T45.603S	T46.2X1S	T46.994S	T47.8X2S	T48.5X5S	T49.5X3S	T50.4X1S
T43.604A	T44.1X3A	T44.991A	T45.604A	T46.2X2A	T46.995A	T47.8X3A	T48.6X1A	T49.5X4A	T50.4X2A
T43.604S	T44.1X3S	T44.991S	T45.604S	T46.2X2S	T46.995S	T47.8X3S	T48.6X1S	T49.5X4S	T50.4X2S
T43.605A	T44.1X4A	T44.992A	T45.605A	T46.2X3A	T47.0X1A	T47.8X4A	T48.6X2A	T49.5X5A	T50.4X3A
T43.605S	T44.1X4S	T44.992S	T45.605S	T46.2X3S	T47.0X1S	T47.8X4S	T48.6X2S	T49.5X5S	T50.4X3S
T43.611A	T44.1X5A	T44.993A	T45.611A	T46.2X4A	T47.0X2A	T47.8X5A	T48.6X3A	T49.6X1A	T50.4X4A
T43.611S	T44.1X5S	T44.993S	T45.611S	T46.2X4S	T47.0X2S	T47.8X5S	T48.6X3S	T49.6X1S	T50.4X4S
T43.612A	T44.2X1A	T44.994A	T45.612A	T46.2X5A	T47.0X3A	T47.91XA	T48.6X4A	T49.6X2A	T50.4X5A
T43.612S	T44.2X1S	T44.994S	T45.612S	T46.2X5S	T47.0X3S	T47.91XS	T48.6X4S	T49.6X2S	T50.4X5S
T43.613A	T44.2X2A	T44.995A	T45.613A	T46.3X1A	T47.0X4A	T47.92XA	T48.6X5A	T49.6X3A	T50.5X1A
T43.613S	T44.2X2S	T44.995S	T45.613S	T46.3X1S	T47.0X4S	T47.92XS	T48.6X5S	T49.6X3S	T50.5X1S
T43.614A	T44.2X3A	T45.0X1A	T45.614A	T46.3X2A	T47.0X5A	T47.93XA	T48.901A	T49.6X4A	T50.5X2A
T43.614S	T44.2X3S	T45.0X1S	T45.614S	T46.3X2S	T47.0X5S	T47.93XS	T48.901S	T49.6X4S	T50.5X2S
T43.615A	T44.2X4A	T45.0X2A	T45.615A	T46.3X3A	T47.1X1A	T47.94XA	T48.902A	T49.6X5A	T50.5X3A
T43.615S	T44.2X4S	T45.0X2S	T45.615S	T46.3X3S	T47.1X1S	T47.94XS	T48.902S	T49.6X5S	T50.5X3S
T43.621A	T44.2X5A	T45.0X3A	T45.621A	T46.3X4A	T47.1X2A	T47.95XA	T48.903A	T49.7X1A	T50.5X4A
T43.621S	T44.2X5S	T45.0X3S	T45.621S	T46.3X4S	T47.1X2S	T47.95XS	T48.903S	T49.7X1S	T50.5X4S
T43.622A	T44.3X1A	T45.0X4A	T45.622A	T46.3X5A	T47.1X3A	T48.0X1A	T48.904A	T49.7X2A	T50.5X5A
T43.622S	T44.3X1S	T45.0X4S	T45.622S	T46.3X5S	T47.1X3S	T48.0X1S	T48.904S	T49.7X2S	T50.5X5S
T43.623A	T44.3X2A	T45.0X5A	T45.623A	T46.4X1A	T47.1X4A	T48.0X2A	T48.905A	T49.7X3A	T50.6X1A
T43.623S	T44.3X2S	T45.0X5S	T45.623S	T46.4X1S	T47.1X4S	T48.0X2S	T48.905S	T49.7X3S	T50.6X1S
T43.624A	T44.3X3A	T45.1X1A	T45.624A	T46.4X2A	T47.1X5A	T48.0X3A	T48.991A	T49.7X4A	T50.6X2A
T43.624S	T44.3X3S	T45.1X1S	T45.624S	T46.4X2S	T47.1X5S	T48.0X3S	T48.991S	T49.7X4S	T50.6X2S
T43.625A	T44.3X4A	T45.1X2A	T45.625A	T46.4X3A	T47.2X1A	T48.0X4A	T48.992A	T49.7X5A	T50.6X3A
T43.625S	T44.3X4S	T45.1X2S	T45.625S	T46.4X3S	T47.2X1S	T48.0X4S	T48.992S	T49.7X5S	T50.6X3S
T43.631A	T44.3X5A	T45.1X3A	T45.691A	T46.4X4A	T47.2X2A	T48.0X5A	T48.993A	T49.8X1A	T50.6X4A
T43.631S	T44.3X5S	T45.1X3S	T45.691S	T46.4X4S	T47.2X2S	T48.0X5S	T48.993S	T49.8X1S	T50.6X4S

T5Ø.6X5A	T5Ø.B12S	T52.ØX1S	T53.3X4S	T55.ØX3S	T56.892S	T58.8X1S	T59.814S	T61.13XS	T63.Ø12S
T5Ø.6X5S	T5Ø.B13A	T52.ØX2A	T53.4X1A	T55.ØX4A	T56.893A	T58.8X2S	T59.891A	T61.14XA	T63.Ø13A
T5Ø.7X1A	T5Ø.B13S	T52.ØX2S	T53.4X1S	T55.ØX4S	T56.893S	T58.8X2S	T59.891S	T61.14XS	T63.Ø13S
T5Ø.7X1S	T5Ø.B14A	T52.ØX3A	T53.4X2A	T55.1X1A	T56.894A	T58.8X3A	T59.892A	T61.771A	T63.Ø14A
T5Ø.7X2A	T5Ø.B14S	T52.ØX3S	T53.4X2S	T55.1X1S	T56.894S	T58.8X3S	T59.892S	T61.771S	T63.Ø14S
T5Ø.7X2S	T5Ø.B15A	T52.ØX4A	T53.4X3A	T55.1X2A	T56.91XA	T58.8X4A	T59.893A	T61.772A	T63.Ø21A
T5Ø.7X3A	T5Ø.B15S	T52.ØX4S	T53.4X3S	T55.1X2S	T56.91XS	T58.8X4S	T59.893S	T61.772S	T63.Ø21S
T5Ø.7X3S	T5Ø.B91A	T52.1X1A	T53.4X4A	T55.1X3A	T56.92XA	T58.91XA	T59.894A	T61.773A	T63.Ø22A
T5Ø.7X4A	T5Ø.B91S	T52.1X1S	T53.4X4S	T55.1X3S	T56.92XS	T58.91XS	T59.894S	T61.773S	T63.Ø22S
T5Ø.7X4S	T5Ø.B92A	T52.1X2A	T53.5X1A	T55.1X4A	T56.93XA	T58.92XA	T59.91XA	T61.774A	T63.Ø23A
T5Ø.7X5A	T5Ø.B92S	T52.1X2S	T53.5X1S	T55.1X4S	T56.93XS	T58.92XS	T59.91XS	T61.774S	T63.Ø23S
T5Ø.7X5S	T5Ø.B93A	T52.1X3A	T53.5X2A	T56.ØX1A	T56.94XA	T58.93XA	T59.92XA	T61.781A	T63.Ø24A
T5Ø.8X1A	T5Ø.B93S	T52.1X3S	T53.5X2S	T56.ØX1S	T56.94XS	T58.93XS	T59.92XS	T61.781S	T63.Ø24S
T5Ø.8X1S	T5Ø.B94A	T52.1X4A	T53.5X3A	T56.ØX2A	T57.ØX1A	T58.94XA	T59.93XA	T61.782A	T63.Ø31A
T5Ø.8X2A	T5Ø.B94S	T52.1X4S	T53.5X3S	T56.ØX2S	T57.ØX1S	T58.94XS	T59.93XS	T61.782S	T63.Ø31S
T5Ø.8X2S	T5Ø.B95A	T52.2X1A	T53.5X4A	T56.ØX3A	T57.ØX2A	T59.ØX1A	T59.94XA	T61.783A	T63.Ø32A
T5Ø.8X3A	T5Ø.B95S	T52.2X1S	T53.5X4S	T56.ØX3S	T57.ØX2S	T59.ØX1S	T59.94XS	T61.783S	T63.Ø32S
T5Ø.8X3S	T5Ø.Z11A	T52.2X2A	T53.6X1A	T56.ØX4A	T57.ØX3A	T59.ØX2A	T6Ø.ØX1A	T61.784A	T63.Ø33A
T5Ø.8X4A	T5Ø.Z11S	T52.2X2S	T53.6X1S	T56.ØX4S	T57.ØX3S	T59.ØX2S	T6Ø.ØX1S	T61.784S	T63.Ø33S
T5Ø.8X4S	T5Ø.Z12A	T52.2X3A	T53.6X2A	T56.1X1A	T57.ØX4A	T59.ØX3A	T6Ø.ØX2A	T61.8X1A	T63.Ø34A
T5Ø.8X5A	T5Ø.Z12S	T52.2X3S	T53.6X2S	T56.1X1S	T57.ØX4S	T59.ØX3S	T6Ø.ØX2S	T61.8X1S	T63.Ø34S
T5Ø.8X5S	T5Ø.Z13A	T52.2X4A	T53.6X3A	T56.1X2A	T57.1X1A	T59.ØX4A	T6Ø.ØX3A	T61.8X2A	T63.Ø41A
T5Ø.9Ø1A	T5Ø.Z13S	T52.2X4S	T53.6X3S	T56.1X2S	T57.1X1S	T59.ØX4S	T6Ø.ØX3S	T61.8X2S	T63.Ø41S
T5Ø.9Ø1S	T5Ø.Z14A	T52.3X1A	T53.6X4A	T56.1X3A	T57.1X2A	T59.1X1A	T6Ø.ØX4A	T61.8X3A	T63.Ø42A
T5Ø.9Ø2A	T5Ø.Z14S	T52.3X1S	T53.6X4S	T56.1X3S	T57.1X2S	T59.1X1S	T6Ø.ØX4S	T61.8X3S	T63.Ø42S
T5Ø.9Ø2S	T5Ø.Z15A	T52.3X2A	T53.7X1A	T56.1X4A	T57.1X3A	T59.1X2A	T6Ø.1X1A	T61.8X4A	T63.Ø43A
T5Ø.9Ø3A	T5Ø.Z15S	T52.3X2S	T53.7X1S	T56.1X4S	T57.1X3S	T59.1X2S	T6Ø.1X1S	T61.8X4S	T63.Ø43S
T5Ø.9Ø3S	T5Ø.Z91A	T52.3X3A	T53.7X2A	T56.2X1A	T57.1X4A	T59.1X3A	T6Ø.1X2A	T61.91XA	T63.Ø44A
T5Ø.9Ø4A	T5Ø.Z91S	T52.3X3S	T53.7X2S	T56.2X1S	T57.1X4S	T59.1X3S	T6Ø.1X2S	T61.91XS	T63.Ø44S
T5Ø.9Ø4S	T5Ø.Z92A	T52.3X4A	T53.7X3A	T56.2X2A	T57.2X1A	T59.1X4A	T6Ø.1X3A	T61.92XA	T63.Ø61A
T5Ø.9Ø5A	T5Ø.Z92S	T52.3X4S	T53.7X3S	T56.2X2S	T57.2X1S	T59.1X4S	T6Ø.1X3S	T61.92XS	T63.Ø61S
T5Ø.9Ø5S	T5Ø.Z93A	T52.4X1A	T53.7X4A	T56.2X3A	T57.2X2A	T59.2X1A	T6Ø.1X4A	T61.93XA	T63.Ø62A
T5Ø.911A	T5Ø.Z93S	T52.4X1S	T53.7X4S	T56.2X3S	T57.2X2S	T59.2X1S	T6Ø.1X4S	T61.93XS	T63.Ø62S
T5Ø.911S	T5Ø.Z94A	T52.4X2A	T53.91XA	T56.2X4A	T57.2X3A	T59.2X2A	T6Ø.2X1A	T61.94XA	T63.Ø63A
T5Ø.912A	T5Ø.Z94S	T52.4X2S	T53.91XS	T56.2X4S	T57.2X3S	T59.2X2S	T6Ø.2X1S	T61.94XS	T63.Ø63S
T5Ø.912S	T5Ø.Z95A	T52.4X3A	T53.92XA	T56.3X1A	T57.2X4A	T59.2X3A	T6Ø.2X2A	T62.ØX1A	T63.Ø64A
T5Ø.913A	T5Ø.Z95S	T52.4X3S	T53.92XS	T56.3X1S	T57.2X4S	T59.2X3S	T6Ø.2X2S	T62.ØX1S	T63.Ø64S
T5Ø.913S	T51.ØX1A	T52.4X4A	T53.93XA	T56.3X2A	T57.3X1A	T59.2X4A	T6Ø.2X3S	T62.ØX2S	T63.Ø71A
T5Ø.914A	T51.ØX1S	T52.4X4S	T53.93XS	T56.3X2S	T57.3X1S	T59.2X4S	T6Ø.2X4A	T62.ØX3A	T63.Ø71S
T5Ø.914S	T51.ØX2A	T52.8X1A	T53.94XA	T56.3X3A	T57.3X2A	T59.3X1A	T6Ø.2X4S	T62.ØX3S	T63.Ø72A
T5Ø.915A	T51.ØX2S	T52.8X1S	T53.94XS	T56.3X3S	T57.3X2S	T59.3X1S	T6Ø.3X1A	T62.ØX4A	T63.Ø72S
T5Ø.915S	T51.ØX3A	T52.8X2A	T54.ØX1A	T56.3X4A	T57.3X3A	T59.3X2A	T6Ø.3X1S	T62.ØX4S	T63.Ø73A
T5Ø.916S	T51.ØX3S	T52.8X2S	T54.ØX1S	T56.3X4S	T57.3X3S	T59.3X2S	T6Ø.3X2A	T62.1X1A	T63.Ø73S
T5Ø.991A	T51.ØX4A	T52.8X3A	T54.ØX2A	T56.4X1A	T57.3X4A	T59.3X3A	T6Ø.3X2S	T62.1X1S	T63.Ø74A
T5Ø.991S	T51.ØX4S	T52.8X3S	T54.ØX2S	T56.4X1S	T57.3X4S	T59.3X3S	T6Ø.3X3A	T62.1X2A	T63.Ø74S
T5Ø.992A	T51.1X1A	T52.8X4A	T54.ØX3A	T56.4X2A	T57.8X1A	T59.3X4A	T6Ø.3X3S	T62.1X2S	T63.Ø81A
T5Ø.992S	T51.1X1S	T52.8X4S	T54.ØX3S	T56.4X2S	T57.8X1S	T59.3X4S	T6Ø.3X4A	T62.1X3A	T63.Ø81S
T5Ø.993A	T51.1X2A	T52.91XA	T54.ØX4A	T56.4X3A	T57.8X2A	T59.4X1A	T6Ø.3X4S	T62.1X3S	T63.Ø82A
T5Ø.993S	T51.1X2S	T52.91XS	T54.ØX4S	T56.4X3S	T57.8X2S	T59.4X1S	T6Ø.4X1A	T62.1X4A	T63.Ø82S
T5Ø.994A	T51.1X3A	T52.92XA	T54.1X1A	T56.4X4A	T57.8X3A	T59.4X2A	T6Ø.4X1S	T62.1X4S	T63.Ø83A
T5Ø.994S	T51.1X3S	T52.92XS	T54.1X1S	T56.4X4S	T57.8X3S	T59.4X2S	T6Ø.4X2A	T62.2X1A	T63.Ø83S
T5Ø.995A	T51.1X4A	T52.93XA	T54.1X2A	T56.5X1A	T57.8X4A	T59.4X3A	T6Ø.4X2S	T62.2X1S	T63.Ø84A
T5Ø.995S	T51.1X4S	T52.93XS	T54.1X2S	T56.5X1S	T57.8X4S	T59.4X3S	T6Ø.4X3A	T62.2X2A	T63.Ø84S
T5Ø.A11A	T51.2X1A	T52.94XA	T54.1X3A	T56.5X2A	T57.91XA	T59.4X4A	T6Ø.4X3S	T62.2X2S	T63.Ø91A
T5Ø.A11S	T51.2X1S	T52.94XS	T54.1X3S	T56.5X2S	T57.91XS	T59.4X4S	T6Ø.4X4A	T62.2X3A	T63.Ø91S
T5Ø.A12A	T51.2X2A	T53.ØX1A	T54.1X4A	T56.5X3A	T57.92XA	T59.5X1A	T6Ø.4X4S	T62.2X3S	T63.Ø92A
T5Ø.A12S	T51.2X2S	T53.ØX1S	T54.1X4S	T56.5X3S	T57.92XS	T59.5X1S	T6Ø.8X1A	T62.2X4A	T63.Ø92S
T5Ø.A13A	T51.2X3A	T53.ØX2A	T54.2X1A	T56.5X4A	T57.93XA	T59.5X2A	T6Ø.8X1S	T62.2X4S	T63.Ø93A
T5Ø.A13S	T51.2X3S	T53.ØX2S	T54.2X1S	T56.5X4S	T57.93XS	T59.5X2S	T6Ø.8X2A	T62.8X1A	T63.Ø93S
T5Ø.A14A	T51.2X4A	T53.ØX3A	T54.2X2A	T56.6X1A	T57.94XA	T59.5X3A	T6Ø.8X2S	T62.8X1S	T63.Ø94A
T5Ø.A14S	T51.2X4S	T53.ØX3S	T54.2X2S	T56.6X1S	T57.94XS	T59.5X3S	T6Ø.8X3A	T62.8X2A	T63.Ø94S
T5Ø.A15A	T51.3X1A	T53.ØX4A	T54.2X3A	T56.6X2A	T58.Ø1XA	T59.5X4A	T6Ø.8X3S	T62.8X2S	T63.111A
T5Ø.A15S	T51.3X1S	T53.ØX4S	T54.2X3S	T56.6X2S	T58.Ø1XS	T59.5X4S	T6Ø.8X4A	T62.8X3A	T63.111S
T5Ø.A21A	T51.3X2A	T53.1X1A	T54.2X4A	T56.6X3A	T58.Ø2XA	T59.6X1A	T6Ø.8X4S	T62.8X3S	T63.112A
T5Ø.A21S	T51.3X2S	T53.1X1S	T54.2X4S	T56.6X3S	T58.Ø2XS	T59.6X1S	T6Ø.91XA	T62.8X4A	T63.112S
T5Ø.A22A	T51.3X3A	T53.1X2A	T54.3X1A	T56.6X4A	T58.Ø3XA	T59.6X2A	T6Ø.91XS	T62.8X4S	T63.113A
T5Ø.A22S	T51.3X3S	T53.1X2S	T54.3X1S	T56.6X4S	T58.Ø3XS	T59.6X2S	T6Ø.92XA	T62.91XA	T63.113S
T5Ø.A23A	T51.3X4A	T53.1X3A	T54.3X2A	T56.7X1A	T58.Ø4XA	T59.6X3A	T6Ø.92XS	T62.91XS	T63.114A
T5Ø.A23S	T51.3X4S	T53.1X3S	T54.3X2S	T56.7X1S	T58.Ø4XS	T59.6X3S	T6Ø.93XA	T62.92XA	T63.114S
T5Ø.A24A	T51.8X1A	T53.1X4A	T54.3X3A	T56.7X2A	T58.11XA	T59.6X4A	T6Ø.93XS	T62.92XS	T63.121A
T5Ø.A24S	T51.8X1S	T53.1X4S	T54.3X3S	T56.7X2S	T58.11XS	T59.6X4S	T6Ø.94XA	T62.93XA	T63.121S
T5Ø.A25A	T51.8X2A	T53.2X1A	T54.3X4A	T56.7X3A	T58.12XA	T59.7X1A	T6Ø.94XS	T62.93XS	T63.122A
T5Ø.A25S	T51.8X2S	T53.2X1S	T54.3X4S	T56.7X3S	T58.12XS	T59.7X1S	T61.Ø1XA	T62.94XA	T63.122S
T5Ø.A91A	T51.8X3A	T53.2X2A	T54.91XA	T56.7X4A	T58.13XA	T59.7X2A	T61.Ø1XS	T62.94XS	T63.123A
T5Ø.A91S	T51.8X3S	T53.2X2S	T54.91XS	T56.7X4S	T58.13XS	T59.7X2S	T61.Ø2XA	T63.ØØ1A	T63.123S
T5Ø.A92A	T51.8X4A	T53.2X3A	T54.92XA	T56.811A	T58.14XA	T59.7X3A	T61.Ø2XS	T63.ØØ1S	T63.124A
T5Ø.A92S	T51.8X4S	T53.2X3S	T54.92XS	T56.811S	T58.14XS	T59.7X3S	T61.Ø3XA	T63.ØØ2A	T63.124S
T5Ø.A93A	T51.91XA	T53.2X4A	T54.93XA	T56.812A	T58.2X1A	T59.7X4A	T61.Ø3XS	T63.ØØ2S	T63.191A
T5Ø.A93S	T51.91XS	T53.2X4S	T54.93XS	T56.812S	T58.2X1S	T59.7X4S	T61.Ø4XA	T63.ØØ3A	T63.191S
T5Ø.A94A	T51.92XA	T53.3X1A	T54.94XA	T56.813A	T58.2X2A	T59.811A	T61.Ø4XS	T63.ØØ3S	T63.192A
T5Ø.A94S	T51.92XS	T53.3X1S	T54.94XS	T56.813S	T58.2X2S	T59.811S	T61.11XA	T63.ØØ4A	T63.192S
T5Ø.A95A	T51.93XA	T53.3X2A	T55.ØX1A	T56.814A	T58.2X3A	T59.812A	T61.11XS	T63.ØØ4S	T63.193A
T5Ø.A95S	T51.93XS	T53.3X2S	T55.ØX1S	T56.814S	T58.2X3S	T59.812S	T61.12XA	T63.Ø11A	T63.193S
T5Ø.B11A	T51.94XA	T53.3X3A	T55.ØX2A	T56.891A	T58.2X4A	T59.813A	T61.12XS	T63.Ø11S	T63.194A
T5Ø.B11S	T51.94XS	T53.3X3S	T55.ØX2S	T56.891S	T58.2X4S	T59.813S	T61.13XA	T63.Ø12A	T63.194S
T5Ø.B12A	T52.ØX1A	T53.3X4A	T55.ØX3A	T56.892A	T58.8X1A	T59.814A	T61.13XA	T63.Ø12A	T63.2X1A

Diagnosis Codes by MDC

T63.2X1S	T63.454S	T63.813S	T65.292S	T67.1XXS	T71.153S	T75.00XS	T78.8XXA	T81.31XA	T81.537A
T63.2X2A	T63.461A	T63.814A	T65.293A	T67.2XXA	T71.154A	T75.01XA	T78.8XXS	T81.31XS	T81.537S
T63.2X2S	T63.461S	T63.814S	T65.293S	T67.2XXS	T71.154S	T75.01XS	T79.0XXS	T81.32XA	T81.538A
T63.2X3A	T63.462A	T63.821A	T65.294A	T67.3XXA	T71.161A	T75.09XA	T79.1XXS	T81.32XS	T81.538S
T63.2X3S	T63.462S	T63.821S	T65.294S	T67.3XXS	T71.161S	T75.09XS	T79.2XXA	T81.33XA	T81.539A
T63.2X4A	T63.463A	T63.822A	T65.3X1A	T67.4XXA	T71.162A	T75.1XXA	T79.2XXS	T81.33XS	T81.539S
T63.2X4S	T63.463S	T63.822S	T65.3X1S	T67.4XXS	T71.162S	T75.1XXS	T79.4XXA	T81.40XS	T81.590A
T63.301A	T63.464A	T63.823A	T65.3X2A	T67.5XXA	T71.163A	T75.20XA	T79.4XXS	T81.41XS	T81.590S
T63.301S	T63.464S	T63.823S	T65.3X2S	T67.5XXS	T71.163S	T75.20XS	T79.5XXS	T81.42XS	T81.591A
T63.302A	T63.481A	T63.824A	T65.3X3A	T67.6XXA	T71.164A	T75.21XA	T79.6XXS	T81.43XS	T81.591S
T63.302S	T63.481S	T63.824S	T65.3X3S	T67.6XXS	T71.164S	T75.21XS	T79.7XXS	T81.44XS	T81.592A
T63.303A	T63.482A	T63.831A	T65.3X4A	T67.7XXA	T71.191A	T75.22XA	T79.8XXA	T81.49XS	T81.592S
T63.303S	T63.482S	T63.831S	T65.3X4S	T67.7XXS	T71.191S	T75.22XS	T79.8XXS	T81.500A	T81.593A
T63.304A	T63.483A	T63.832A	T65.4X1A	T67.8XXA	T71.192A	T75.23XA	T79.9XXA	T81.500S	T81.593S
T63.304S	T63.483S	T63.832S	T65.4X1S	T67.8XXS	T71.192S	T75.23XS	T79.9XXS	T81.501A	T81.594A
T63.311A	T63.484A	T63.833A	T65.4X2A	T67.9XXA	T71.193A	T75.29XA	T79.A0XA	T81.501S	T81.594S
T63.311S	T63.484S	T63.833S	T65.4X2S	T67.9XXS	T71.193S	T75.29XS	T79.A0XS	T81.502A	T81.595A
T63.312A	T63.511A	T63.834A	T65.4X3A	T68.XXXA	T71.194A	T75.3XXS	T79.A11A	T81.502S	T81.595S
T63.312S	T63.511S	T63.834S	T65.4X3S	T68.XXXS	T71.194S	T75.4XXA	T79.A11S	T81.503A	T81.596A
T63.313A	T63.512A	T63.891A	T65.4X4A	T69.011A	T71.20XA	T75.4XXS	T79.A12A	T81.503S	T81.596S
T63.313S	T63.512S	T63.891S	T65.4X4S	T69.011S	T71.20XS	T75.81XA	T79.A12S	T81.504A	T81.597A
T63.314A	T63.513A	T63.892A	T65.5X1A	T69.012A	T71.21XA	T75.81XS	T79.A19A	T81.504S	T81.597S
T63.314S	T63.513S	T63.892S	T65.5X1S	T69.012S	T71.21XS	T75.82XA	T79.A19S	T81.505A	T81.598A
T63.321A	T63.514A	T63.893A	T65.5X2A	T69.019A	T71.221A	T75.82XS	T79.A21A	T81.505S	T81.598S
T63.321S	T63.514S	T63.893S	T65.5X2S	T69.019S	T71.221S	T75.89XA	T79.A21S	T81.506A	T81.599A
T63.322A	T63.591A	T63.894A	T65.5X3A	T69.021A	T71.222A	T75.89XS	T79.A22A	T81.506S	T81.599S
T63.322S	T63.591S	T63.894S	T65.5X3S	T69.021S	T71.222S	T76.01XA	T79.A22S	T81.507A	T81.60XA
T63.323A	T63.592A	T63.91XA	T65.5X4A	T69.022A	T71.223A	T76.01XS	T79.A29A	T81.507S	T81.60XS
T63.323S	T63.592S	T63.91XS	T65.5X4S	T69.022S	T71.223S	T76.02XA	T79.A29S	T81.508A	T81.61XA
T63.324A	T63.593A	T63.92XA	T65.6X1A	T69.029A	T71.224A	T76.02XS	T79.A3XA	T81.508S	T81.61XS
T63.324S	T63.593S	T63.92XS	T65.6X1S	T69.029S	T71.224S	T76.11XA	T79.A3XS	T81.509A	T81.69XA
T63.331A	T63.594A	T63.93XA	T65.6X2A	T69.1XXA	T71.231A	T76.11XS	T79.A9XA	T81.509S	T81.69XS
T63.331S	T63.594S	T63.93XS	T65.6X2S	T69.1XXS	T71.231S	T76.12XA	T79.A9XS	T81.510A	T81.710S
T63.332A	T63.611A	T63.94XA	T65.6X3A	T69.8XXA	T71.232A	T76.12XS	T80.0XXS	T81.510S	T81.711S
T63.332S	T63.611S	T63.94XS	T65.6X3S	T69.8XXS	T71.232S	T76.21XA	T80.1XXS	T81.511A	T81.718S
T63.333A	T63.612A	T64.01XA	T65.6X4A	T69.9XXA	T71.233A	T76.21XS	T80.211S	T81.511S	T81.719S
T63.333S	T63.612S	T64.01XS	T65.6X4S	T69.9XXS	T71.233S	T76.22XA	T80.212S	T81.512A	T81.72XS
T63.334A	T63.613A	T64.02XA	T65.811A	T70.0XXS	T71.234A	T76.22XS	T80.218S	T81.512S	T81.81XA
T63.334S	T63.613S	T64.02XS	T65.811S	T70.1XXS	T71.234S	T76.31XA	T80.219S	T81.513A	T81.81XS
T63.391A	T63.614A	T64.03XA	T65.812A	T70.20XA	T71.29XA	T76.31XS	T80.22XS	T81.513S	T81.82XA
T63.391S	T63.614S	T64.03XS	T65.812S	T70.20XS	T71.29XS	T76.32XA	T80.29XS	T81.514A	T81.82XS
T63.392A	T63.621A	T64.04XA	T65.813A	T70.29XA	T71.9XXA	T76.32XS	T80.30XS	T81.514S	T81.83XA
T63.392S	T63.621S	T64.04XS	T65.813S	T70.29XS	T71.9XXS	T76.51XA	T80.310S	T81.515A	T81.83XS
T63.393A	T63.622A	T64.81XA	T65.814A	T70.3XXA	T73.0XXA	T76.51XS	T80.311S	T81.515S	T81.89XA
T63.393S	T63.622S	T64.81XS	T65.814S	T70.3XXS	T73.0XXS	T76.52XA	T80.319S	T81.516A	T81.89XS
T63.394A	T63.623A	T64.82XA	T65.821A	T70.4XXA	T73.1XXA	T76.52XS	T80.39XS	T81.516S	T81.9XXA
T63.394S	T63.623S	T64.82XS	T65.821S	T70.4XXS	T73.1XXS	T76.61XA	T80.40XS	T81.517A	T81.9XXS
T63.411A	T63.624A	T64.83XA	T65.822A	T70.8XXA	T73.2XXA	T76.61XS	T80.410S	T81.517S	T82.01XS
T63.411S	T63.624S	T64.83XS	T65.822S	T70.8XXS	T73.2XXS	T76.62XA	T80.411S	T81.518A	T82.02XS
T63.412A	T63.631A	T64.84XA	T65.823A	T70.9XXA	T73.3XXA	T76.62XS	T80.419S	T81.518S	T82.03XS
T63.412S	T63.631S	T64.84XS	T65.823S	T70.9XXS	T73.3XXS	T76.91XA	T80.49XS	T81.519A	T82.09XS
T63.413A	T63.632A	T65.0X1A	T65.824A	T71.111A	T73.8XXA	T76.91XS	T80.51XA	T81.519S	T82.110S
T63.413S	T63.632S	T65.0X1S	T65.824S	T71.111S	T73.8XXS	T76.92XA	T80.51XS	T81.520A	T82.111S
T63.414A	T63.633A	T65.0X2A	T65.831A	T71.112A	T73.9XXA	T76.92XS	T80.52XA	T81.520S	T82.118S
T63.414S	T63.633S	T65.0X2S	T65.831S	T71.112S	T73.9XXS	T78.00XA	T80.52XS	T81.521A	T82.119S
T63.421A	T63.634A	T65.0X3A	T65.832A	T71.113A	T74.01XA	T78.00XS	T80.59XA	T81.521S	T82.120S
T63.421S	T63.634S	T65.0X3S	T65.832S	T71.113S	T74.01XS	T78.01XA	T80.59XS	T81.522A	T82.121S
T63.422A	T63.691A	T65.0X4A	T65.833A	T71.114A	T74.02XA	T78.01XS	T80.61XA	T81.522S	T82.128S
T63.422S	T63.691S	T65.0X4S	T65.833S	T71.114S	T74.02XS	T78.02XA	T80.61XS	T81.523A	T82.129S
T63.423A	T63.692A	T65.1X1A	T65.834A	T71.121A	T74.11XA	T78.02XS	T80.62XA	T81.523S	T82.190S
T63.423S	T63.692S	T65.1X1S	T65.834S	T71.121S	T74.11XS	T78.03XA	T80.62XS	T81.524A	T82.191S
T63.424A	T63.693A	T65.1X2A	T65.891A	T71.122A	T74.12XA	T78.03XS	T80.69XA	T81.524S	T82.198S
T63.424S	T63.693S	T65.1X2S	T65.891S	T71.122S	T74.12XS	T78.04XA	T80.69XS	T81.525A	T82.199S
T63.431A	T63.694A	T65.1X3A	T65.892A	T71.123A	T74.21XA	T78.04XS	T80.810S	T81.525S	T82.211S
T63.431S	T63.694S	T65.1X3S	T65.892S	T71.123S	T74.21XS	T78.05XA	T80.818S	T81.526A	T82.212S
T63.432A	T63.711A	T65.1X4A	T65.893A	T71.124A	T74.22XA	T78.05XS	T80.89XS	T81.526S	T82.213S
T63.432S	T63.711S	T65.1X4S	T65.893S	T71.124S	T74.22XS	T78.06XA	T80.90XS	T81.527A	T82.218S
T63.433A	T63.712A	T65.211A	T65.894A	T71.131A	T74.31XA	T78.06XS	T80.910S	T81.527S	T82.221S
T63.433S	T63.712S	T65.211S	T65.894S	T71.131S	T74.31XS	T78.07XA	T80.911S	T81.528A	T82.222S
T63.434A	T63.713A	T65.212A	T65.91XA	T71.132A	T74.32XA	T78.07XS	T80.919S	T81.528S	T82.223S
T63.434S	T63.713S	T65.212S	T65.91XS	T71.132S	T74.32XS	T78.08XA	T80.92XS	T81.529A	T82.228S
T63.441A	T63.714A	T65.213A	T65.92XA	T71.133A	T74.4XXA	T78.08XS	T80.A0XS	T81.529S	T82.310S
T63.441S	T63.714S	T65.213S	T65.92XS	T71.133S	T74.4XXS	T78.09XA	T80.A10S	T81.530A	T82.311S
T63.442A	T63.791A	T65.214A	T65.93XA	T71.134A	T74.51XA	T78.09XS	T80.A11S	T81.530S	T82.312S
T63.442S	T63.791S	T65.214S	T65.93XS	T71.134S	T74.51XS	T78.1XXA	T80.A19S	T81.531A	T82.318S
T63.443A	T63.792A	T65.221A	T65.94XA	T71.141A	T74.52XA	T78.1XXS	T80.A9XS	T81.531S	T82.319S
T63.443S	T63.792S	T65.221S	T65.94XS	T71.141S	T74.52XS	T78.2XXA	T81.10XA	T81.532A	T82.320S
T63.444A	T63.793A	T65.222A	T66.XXXA	T71.143A	T74.61XA	T78.2XXS	T81.10XS	T81.532S	T82.321S
T63.444S	T63.793S	T65.222S	T66.XXXS	T71.143S	T74.61XS	T78.3XXA	T81.11XA	T81.533A	T82.322S
T63.451A	T63.794A	T65.223A	T67.01XA	T71.144A	T74.62XA	T78.3XXS	T81.11XS	T81.533S	T82.328S
T63.451S	T63.794S	T65.223S	T67.01XS	T71.144S	T74.62XS	T78.40XA	T81.12XA	T81.534A	T82.329S
T63.452A	T63.811A	T65.224A	T67.02XA	T71.151A	T74.91XA	T78.40XS	T81.12XS	T81.534S	T82.330S
T63.452S	T63.811S	T65.224S	T67.02XS	T71.151S	T74.91XS	T78.41XA	T81.19XA	T81.535A	T82.331S
T63.453A	T63.812A	T65.291A	T67.09XA	T71.152A	T74.92XA	T78.41XS	T81.19XS	T81.535S	T82.332S
T63.453S	T63.812S	T65.291S	T67.09XS	T71.152S	T74.92XS	T78.49XA	T81.30XA	T81.536A	T82.338S
T63.454A	T63.813A	T65.292A	T67.1XXA	T71.153A	T75.00XA	T78.49XS	T81.30XS	T81.536S	T82.339S

T82.390S	T82.828S	T83.22XS	T83.85XS	T84.116S	T84.51XS	T85.191S	T85.611A	T85.72XS	T86.849
T82.391S	T82.837S	T83.23XS	T83.86XS	T84.117S	T84.52XS	T85.192S	T85.611S	T85.730S	T86.850
T82.392S	T82.838S	T83.24XS	T83.89XS	T84.119S	T84.53XS	T85.193S	T85.612A	T85.731S	T86.851
T82.398S	T82.847S	T83.25XS	T83.9XXS	T84.120S	T84.54XS	T85.199S	T85.612S	T85.732S	T86.852
T82.399S	T82.848S	T83.29XS	T84.010S	T84.121S	T84.59XS	T85.21XS	T85.613A	T85.733S	T86.858
T82.41XS	T82.855S	T83.31XS	T84.011S	T84.122S	T84.60XS	T85.22XS	T85.613S	T85.734S	T86.859
T82.42XS	T82.856S	T83.32XS	T84.012S	T84.123S	T84.610S	T85.29XS	T85.614A	T85.735S	T86.90
T82.43XS	T82.857S	T83.39XS	T84.013S	T84.124S	T84.611S	T85.310A	T85.614S	T85.738S	T86.91
T82.49XS	T82.858S	T83.410S	T84.018S	T84.125S	T84.612S	T85.310S	T85.615S	T85.79XA	T86.92
T82.510S	T82.867S	T83.411S	T84.019S	T84.126S	T84.613S	T85.311A	T85.618A	T85.79XS	T86.93
T82.511S	T82.868S	T83.418S	T84.020S	T84.127S	T84.614S	T85.311S	T85.618S	T85.810S	T86.99
T82.512S	T82.897S	T83.420S	T84.021S	T84.129S	T84.615S	T85.318S	T85.620S	T85.818A	T88.0XXS
T82.513S	T82.898S	T83.421S	T84.022S	T84.190S	T84.619S	T85.320A	T85.621A	T85.818S	T88.1XXS
T82.514S	T82.9XXS	T83.428S	T84.023S	T84.191S	T84.620S	T85.320S	T85.621S	T85.820S	T88.2XXA
T82.515S	T83.010S	T83.490S	T84.028S	T84.192S	T84.621S	T85.321A	T85.622A	T85.828S	T88.2XXS
T82.518S	T83.011S	T83.491S	T84.029S	T84.193S	T84.622S	T85.321S	T85.622S	T85.830S	T88.3XXA
T82.519S	T83.012S	T83.498S	T84.030S	T84.194S	T84.623S	T85.328S	T85.623A	T85.838A	T88.3XXS
T82.520S	T83.018S	T83.510S	T84.031S	T84.195S	T84.624S	T85.390A	T85.623S	T85.838S	T88.4XXA
T82.521S	T83.020S	T83.511S	T84.032S	T84.196S	T84.625S	T85.390S	T85.624A	T85.840S	T88.4XXS
T82.522S	T83.021S	T83.512S	T84.038S	T84.197S	T84.629S	T85.391A	T85.624S	T85.848A	T88.51XA
T82.523S	T83.022S	T83.518S	T84.039S	T84.199S	T84.63XS	T85.391S	T85.625S	T85.848S	T88.51XS
T82.524S	T83.028S	T83.590S	T84.050S	T84.210S	T84.69XS	T85.398S	T85.628A	T85.850S	T88.52XA
T82.525S	T83.030S	T83.591S	T84.051S	T84.213S	T84.7XXS	T85.41XS	T85.628S	T85.858A	T88.52XS
T82.528S	T83.031S	T83.592S	T84.052S	T84.216S	T84.81XS	T85.42XS	T85.630S	T85.858S	T88.53XA
T82.529S	T83.032S	T83.593S	T84.053S	T84.218S	T84.82XS	T85.43XS	T85.631S	T85.860S	T88.53XS
T82.530S	T83.038S	T83.598S	T84.058S	T84.220S	T84.83XS	T85.44XS	T85.633A	T85.868A	T88.59XA
T82.531S	T83.090S	T83.61XS	T84.059S	T84.223S	T84.84XS	T85.49XS	T85.633S	T85.868S	T88.59XS
T82.532S	T83.091S	T83.62XS	T84.060S	T84.226S	T84.85XS	T85.510A	T85.635S	T85.890S	T88.6XXA
T82.533S	T83.092S	T83.69XS	T84.061S	T84.228S	T84.86XS	T85.510S	T85.638A	T85.898A	T88.6XXS
T82.534S	T83.098S	T83.711S	T84.062S	T84.290S	T84.89XS	T85.511A	T85.638S	T85.898S	T88.7XXA
T82.535S	T83.110S	T83.712S	T84.063S	T84.293S	T84.9XXS	T85.511S	T85.690S	T85.9XXA	T88.7XXS
T82.538S	T83.111S	T83.713S	T84.068S	T84.296S	T85.01XS	T85.518A	T85.691A	T85.9XXS	T88.8XXA
T82.539S	T83.112S	T83.714S	T84.069S	T84.298S	T85.02XS	T85.518S	T85.691S	T86.5	T88.8XXS
T82.590S	T83.113S	T83.718S	T84.090S	T84.310S	T85.03XS	T85.520A	T85.692S	T86.820	T88.9XXA
T82.591S	T83.118S	T83.719S	T84.091S	T84.318S	T85.09XS	T85.520S	T85.692S	T86.821	T88.9XXS
T82.592S	T83.120S	T83.721S	T84.092S	T84.320S	T85.110S	T85.521A	T85.693A	T86.822	Z04.1
T82.593S	T83.121S	T83.722S	T84.093S	T84.328S	T85.111S	T85.521S	T85.693S	T86.828	Z04.2
T82.594S	T83.122S	T83.723S	T84.098S	T84.390S	T85.112S	T85.528A	T85.694A	T86.829	Z04.3
T82.595S	T83.123S	T83.724S	T84.099S	T84.398S	T85.113S	T85.528S	T85.694S	T86.830	
T82.598S	T83.128S	T83.728S	T84.110S	T84.410S	T85.118S	T85.590A	T85.695S	T86.831	
T82.599S	T83.190S	T83.729S	T84.111S	T84.418S	T85.120S	T85.590S	T85.698A	T86.832	
T82.6XXS	T83.191S	T83.79XS	T84.112S	T84.420S	T85.121S	T85.591A	T85.698S	T86.838	
T82.7XXS	T83.192S	T83.81XS	T84.113S	T84.428S	T85.122S	T85.591S	T85.71XA	T86.839	
T82.817S	T83.193S	T83.82XS	T84.114S	T84.490S	T85.123S	T85.598A	T85.71XS	T86.842	
T82.818S	T83.198S	T83.83XS	T84.115S	T84.498S	T85.128S	T85.598S	T85.72XA	T86.848	
T82.827S	T83.21XS	T83.84XS		T84.50XS	T85.190S	T85.610S			

MDC 22 Burns

T20.00XA	T20.319A	T20.64XA	T21.22XA	T21.62XA	T22.092A	T22.249A	T22.421A	T22.569A	T22.741A
T20.011A	T20.32XA	T20.65XA	T21.23XA	T21.63XA	T22.099A	T22.251A	T22.422A	T22.591A	T22.742A
T20.012A	T20.33XA	T20.66XA	T21.24XA	T21.64XA	T22.10XA	T22.252A	T22.429A	T22.592A	T22.749A
T20.019A	T20.34XA	T20.67XA	T21.25XA	T21.65XA	T22.111A	T22.259A	T22.431A	T22.599A	T22.751A
T20.02XA	T20.35XA	T20.69XA	T21.26XA	T21.66XA	T22.112A	T22.261A	T22.432A	T22.60XA	T22.752A
T20.03XA	T20.36XA	T20.70XA	T21.27XA	T21.67XA	T22.119A	T22.262A	T22.439A	T22.611A	T22.759A
T20.04XA	T20.37XA	T20.711A	T21.29XA	T21.69XA	T22.121A	T22.269A	T22.441A	T22.612A	T22.761A
T20.05XA	T20.39XA	T20.712A	T21.30XA	T21.70XA	T22.122A	T22.291A	T22.442A	T22.619A	T22.762A
T20.06XA	T20.40XA	T20.719A	T21.31XA	T21.71XA	T22.129A	T22.292A	T22.449A	T22.621A	T22.769A
T20.07XA	T20.411A	T20.72XA	T21.32XA	T21.72XA	T22.131A	T22.299A	T22.451A	T22.622A	T22.791A
T20.09XA	T20.412A	T20.73XA	T21.33XA	T21.73XA	T22.132A	T22.30XA	T22.452A	T22.629A	T22.792A
T20.10XA	T20.419A	T20.74XA	T21.34XA	T21.74XA	T22.139A	T22.311A	T22.459A	T22.631A	T22.799A
T20.111A	T20.42XA	T20.75XA	T21.35XA	T21.75XA	T22.141A	T22.312A	T22.461A	T22.632A	T23.001A
T20.112A	T20.43XA	T20.76XA	T21.36XA	T21.76XA	T22.142A	T22.319A	T22.462A	T22.639A	T23.002A
T20.119A	T20.44XA	T20.77XA	T21.37XA	T21.77XA	T22.149A	T22.321A	T22.469A	T22.641A	T23.009A
T20.12XA	T20.45XA	T20.79XA	T21.39XA	T21.79XA	T22.151A	T22.322A	T22.491A	T22.642A	T23.011A
T20.13XA	T20.46XA	T21.00XA	T21.40XA	T22.00XA	T22.152A	T22.329A	T22.492A	T22.649A	T23.012A
T20.14XA	T20.47XA	T21.01XA	T21.41XA	T22.011A	T22.159A	T22.331A	T22.499A	T22.651A	T23.019A
T20.15XA	T20.49XA	T21.02XA	T21.42XA	T22.012A	T22.161A	T22.332A	T22.50XA	T22.652A	T23.021A
T20.16XA	T20.50XA	T21.03XA	T21.43XA	T22.019A	T22.162A	T22.339A	T22.511A	T22.659A	T23.022A
T20.17XA	T20.511A	T21.04XA	T21.44XA	T22.021A	T22.169A	T22.341A	T22.512A	T22.661A	T23.029A
T20.19XA	T20.512A	T21.05XA	T21.45XA	T22.022A	T22.191A	T22.342A	T22.519A	T22.662A	T23.031A
T20.20XA	T20.519A	T21.06XA	T21.46XA	T22.029A	T22.192A	T22.349A	T22.521A	T22.669A	T23.032A
T20.211A	T20.52XA	T21.07XA	T21.47XA	T22.031A	T22.199A	T22.351A	T22.522A	T22.691A	T23.039A
T20.212A	T20.53XA	T21.09XA	T21.49XA	T22.032A	T22.20XA	T22.352A	T22.529A	T22.692A	T23.041A
T20.219A	T20.54XA	T21.10XA	T21.50XA	T22.039A	T22.211A	T22.359A	T22.531A	T22.699A	T23.042A
T20.22XA	T20.55XA	T21.11XA	T21.51XA	T22.041A	T22.212A	T22.361A	T22.532A	T22.70XA	T23.049A
T20.23XA	T20.56XA	T21.12XA	T21.52XA	T22.042A	T22.219A	T22.362A	T22.539A	T22.711A	T23.051A
T20.24XA	T20.57XA	T21.13XA	T21.53XA	T22.049A	T22.221A	T22.369A	T22.541A	T22.712A	T23.059A
T20.25XA	T20.59XA	T21.14XA	T21.54XA	T22.051A	T22.222A	T22.391A	T22.542A	T22.719A	T23.061A
T20.26XA	T20.60XA	T21.15XA	T21.55XA	T22.052A	T22.229A	T22.392A	T22.549A	T22.721A	T23.062A
T20.27XA	T20.611A	T21.16XA	T21.56XA	T22.059A	T22.231A	T22.399A	T22.551A	T22.722A	T23.069A
T20.29XA	T20.612A	T21.17XA	T21.57XA	T22.061A	T22.232A	T22.40XA	T22.552A	T22.729A	T23.071A
T20.30XA	T20.619A	T21.19XA	T21.59XA	T22.062A	T22.239A	T22.411A	T22.559A	T22.731A	T23.072A
T20.311A	T20.62XA	T21.20XA	T21.60XA	T22.069A	T22.241A	T22.412A	T22.561A	T22.732S	T23.079A
T20.312A	T20.63XA	T21.21XA	T21.61XA	T22.091A	T22.242A	T22.419A	T22.562A	T22.739A	

Diagnosis Codes by MDC

T23.091A	T23.291A	T23.491A	T23.691A	T24.131A	T24.511A	T25.111A	T25.531A	T31.40	T32.33
T23.092A	T23.292A	T23.492A	T23.692A	T24.132A	T24.512A	T25.112A	T25.532A	T31.41	T32.40
T23.099A	T23.299A	T23.499A	T23.699A	T24.139A	T24.519A	T25.119A	T25.539A	T31.42	T32.41
T23.101A	T23.301A	T23.501A	T23.701A	T24.191A	T24.521A	T25.121A	T25.591A	T31.43	T32.42
T23.102A	T23.302A	T23.502A	T23.702A	T24.192A	T24.522A	T25.122A	T25.592A	T31.44	T32.43
T23.109A	T23.309A	T23.509A	T23.709A	T24.199A	T24.529A	T25.129A	T25.599A	T31.50	T32.44
T23.111A	T23.311A	T23.511A	T23.711A	T24.201A	T24.531A	T25.131A	T25.611A	T31.51	T32.50
T23.112A	T23.312A	T23.512A	T23.712A	T24.202A	T24.532A	T25.132A	T25.612A	T31.52	T32.51
T23.119A	T23.319A	T23.519A	T23.719A	T24.209A	T24.539A	T25.139A	T25.619A	T31.53	T32.52
T23.121A	T23.321A	T23.521A	T23.721A	T24.211A	T24.591A	T25.191A	T25.621A	T31.54	T32.53
T23.122A	T23.322A	T23.522A	T23.722A	T24.212A	T24.592A	T25.192A	T25.622A	T31.55	T32.54
T23.129A	T23.329A	T23.529A	T23.729A	T24.219A	T24.599A	T25.199A	T25.629A	T31.60	T32.55
T23.131A	T23.331A	T23.531A	T23.731A	T24.221A	T24.601A	T25.211A	T25.631A	T31.61	T32.60
T23.132A	T23.332A	T23.532A	T23.732A	T24.222A	T24.602A	T25.212A	T25.632A	T31.62	T32.61
T23.139A	T23.339A	T23.539A	T23.739A	T24.229A	T24.609A	T25.219A	T25.639A	T31.63	T32.62
T23.141A	T23.341A	T23.541A	T23.741A	T24.231A	T24.611A	T25.221A	T25.691A	T31.64	T32.63
T23.142A	T23.342A	T23.542A	T23.742A	T24.232A	T24.612A	T25.222A	T25.692A	T31.65	T32.64
T23.149A	T23.349A	T23.549A	T23.749A	T24.239A	T24.619A	T25.229A	T25.699A	T31.66	T32.65
T23.151A	T23.351A	T23.551A	T23.751A	T24.291A	T24.621A	T25.231A	T25.711A	T31.70	T32.66
T23.152A	T23.352A	T23.552A	T23.752A	T24.292A	T24.622A	T25.232A	T25.712A	T31.71	T32.70
T23.159A	T23.359A	T23.559A	T23.759A	T24.299A	T24.629A	T25.239A	T25.719A	T31.72	T32.71
T23.161A	T23.361A	T23.561A	T23.761A	T24.301A	T24.631A	T25.291A	T25.721A	T31.73	T32.72
T23.162A	T23.362A	T23.562A	T23.762A	T24.302A	T24.632A	T25.292A	T25.722A	T31.74	T32.73
T23.169A	T23.369A	T23.569A	T23.769A	T24.309A	T24.639A	T25.299A	T25.729A	T31.75	T32.74
T23.171A	T23.371A	T23.571A	T23.771A	T24.311A	T24.691A	T25.311A	T25.731A	T31.76	T32.75
T23.172A	T23.372A	T23.572A	T23.772A	T24.312A	T24.692A	T25.312A	T25.732A	T31.77	T32.76
T23.179A	T23.379A	T23.579A	T23.779A	T24.319A	T24.699A	T25.319A	T25.739A	T31.80	T32.77
T23.191A	T23.391A	T23.591A	T23.791A	T24.321A	T24.701A	T25.321A	T25.791A	T31.81	T32.80
T23.192A	T23.392A	T23.592A	T23.792A	T24.322A	T24.702A	T25.322A	T25.792A	T31.82	T32.81
T23.199A	T23.399A	T23.599A	T23.799A	T24.329A	T24.709A	T25.329A	T25.799A	T31.83	T32.82
T23.201A	T23.401A	T23.601A	T24.001A	T24.331A	T24.711A	T25.331A	T28.3XXA	T31.84	T32.83
T23.202A	T23.402A	T23.602A	T24.002A	T24.332A	T24.712A	T25.332A	T28.40XA	T31.85	T32.84
T23.209A	T23.409A	T23.609A	T24.009A	T24.339A	T24.719A	T25.339A	T28.411A	T31.86	T32.85
T23.211A	T23.411A	T23.611A	T24.011A	T24.391A	T24.721A	T25.391A	T28.412A	T31.87	T32.86
T23.212A	T23.412A	T23.612A	T24.012A	T24.392A	T24.722A	T25.392A	T28.419A	T31.88	T32.87
T23.219A	T23.419A	T23.619A	T24.019A	T24.399A	T24.729A	T25.399A	T28.49XA	T31.90	T32.88
T23.221A	T23.421A	T23.621A	T24.021A	T24.401A	T24.731A	T25.411A	T28.8XXA	T31.91	T32.90
T23.222A	T23.422A	T23.622A	T24.022A	T24.402A	T24.732A	T25.412A	T28.90XA	T31.92	T32.91
T23.229A	T23.429A	T23.629A	T24.029A	T24.409A	T24.739A	T25.419A	T28.911A	T31.93	T32.92
T23.231A	T23.431A	T23.631A	T24.031A	T24.411A	T24.791A	T25.421A	T28.912A	T31.94	T32.93
T23.232A	T23.432A	T23.632A	T24.032A	T24.412A	T24.792A	T25.422A	T28.919A	T31.95	T32.94
T23.239A	T23.439A	T23.639A	T24.039A	T24.419A	T24.799A	T25.429A	T28.99XA	T31.96	T32.95
T23.241A	T23.441A	T23.641A	T24.091A	T24.421A	T25.011A	T25.431A	T30.0	T31.97	T32.96
T23.242A	T23.442A	T23.642A	T24.092A	T24.422A	T25.012A	T25.432A	T30.4	T31.98	T32.97
T23.249A	T23.449A	T23.649A	T24.099A	T24.429A	T25.019A	T25.439A	T31.0	T31.99	T32.98
T23.251A	T23.451A	T23.651A	T24.101A	T24.431A	T25.021A	T25.491A	T31.10	T32.0	T32.99
T23.252A	T23.452A	T23.652A	T24.102A	T24.432A	T25.022A	T25.492A	T31.11	T32.10	
T23.259A	T23.459A	T23.659A	T24.109A	T24.439A	T25.029A	T25.499A	T31.20	T32.11	
T23.261A	T23.461A	T23.661A	T24.111A	T24.491A	T25.031A	T25.511A	T31.21	T32.20	
T23.262A	T23.462A	T23.662A	T24.112A	T24.492A	T25.032A	T25.512A	T31.22	T32.21	
T23.269A	T23.469A	T23.669A	T24.119A	T24.499A	T25.039A	T25.519A	T31.30	T32.22	
T23.271A	T23.471A	T23.671A	T24.121A	T24.501A	T25.091A	T25.521A	T31.31	T32.30	
T23.272A	T23.472A	T23.672A	T24.122A	T24.502A	T25.092A	T25.522A	T31.32	T32.31	
T23.279A	T23.479A	T23.679A	T24.129A	T24.509A	T25.099A	T25.529A	T31.33	T32.32	

MDC 23 Factors Influencing Health Status And Other Contacts With Health Services

E07.81	Q92.9	R29.711	R29.739	R40.2254	R40.2432	R46.81	R77.0	R84.6	R88.8
E79.0	Q93.0	R29.712	R29.740	R40.2330	R40.2433	R46.89	R77.1	R84.7	R89.0
F17.200	Q93.1	R29.713	R29.741	R40.2331	R40.2434	R52	R77.2	R84.8	R89.1
F17.201	Q93.2	R29.714	R29.742	R40.2332	R40.2440	R53.0	R77.8	R84.9	R89.2
F17.210	Q95.0	R29.715	R40.2130	R40.2333	R40.2441	R53.1	R77.9	R85.0	R89.3
F17.211	Q95.1	R29.716	R40.2131	R40.2334	R40.2442	R53.2	R78.1	R85.1	R89.4
F17.220	Q95.2	R29.717	R40.2132	R40.2350	R40.2443	R53.81	R78.2	R85.2	R89.5
F17.221	Q95.3	R29.718	R40.2133	R40.2351	R40.2444	R53.82	R78.3	R85.3	R89.6
F17.290	Q95.5	R29.719	R40.2134	R40.2352	R41.0	R53.83	R78.4	R85.4	R89.7
F17.291	Q95.8	R29.720	R40.2140	R40.2353	R41.1	R60.0	R78.5	R85.5	R89.8
G89.11	Q95.9	R29.721	R40.2141	R40.2354	R41.2	R60.1	R78.6	R85.69	R90.89
G89.12	Q99.9	R29.722	R40.2142	R40.2360	R41.3	R60.9	R78.71	R85.7	R93.89
G89.18	R18.0	R29.723	R40.2143	R40.2361	R41.82	R64	R78.79	R85.89	R93.9
G89.3	R18.8	R29.724	R40.2144	R40.2362	R41.83	R68.0	R78.89	R85.9	R97.0
G93.3	R23.0	R29.725	R40.2230	R40.2363	R41.9	R68.11	R78.9	R87.0	R97.1
J95.850	R23.1	R29.726	R40.2231	R40.2364	R44.8	R68.12	R79.0	R87.1	R97.20
P00.2	R23.2	R29.727	R40.2232	R40.2410	R44.9	R68.13	R79.1	R87.2	R97.21
P00.89	R29.700	R29.728	R40.2233	R40.2411	R45.83	R68.19	R79.81	R87.3	R97.8
P09	R29.701	R29.729	R40.2234	R40.2412	R45.84	R68.81	R79.82	R87.4	R99
Q89.9	R29.702	R29.730	R40.2240	R40.2413	R45.850	R68.82	R79.89	R87.5	S00.00XD
Q92.0	R29.703	R29.731	R40.2241	R40.2414	R46.0	R68.83	R79.9	R87.618	S00.01XD
Q92.1	R29.704	R29.732	R40.2242	R40.2420	R46.1	R68.89	R82.1	R87.619	S00.02XD
Q92.2	R29.705	R29.733	R40.2243	R40.2421	R46.2	R69	R84.0	R87.629	S00.03XD
Q92.5	R29.706	R29.734	R40.2244	R40.2422	R46.3	R70.0	R84.1	R87.69	S00.04XD
Q92.61	R29.707	R29.735	R40.2250	R40.2423	R46.4	R70.1	R84.2	R87.7	S00.05XD
Q92.62	R29.708	R29.736	R40.2251	R40.2424	R46.5	R74.0	R84.3	R87.89	S00.06XD
Q92.7	R29.709	R29.737	R40.2252	R40.2430	R46.6	R74.8	R84.4	R87.9	S00.07XD
Q92.8	R29.710	R29.738	R40.2253	R40.2431	R46.7	R74.9	R84.5	R88.0	S00.10XD

S00.11XD	S00.97XD	S01.91XD	S05.01XD	S06.346D	S06.9X4D	S11.13XD	S14.143D	S19.9XXD	S21.019D
S00.12XD	S01.00XD	S01.92XD	S05.02XD	S06.349D	S06.9X5D	S11.14XD	S14.144D	S20.01XD	S21.021D
S00.201D	S01.01XD	S01.93XD	S05.10XD	S06.350D	S06.9X6D	S11.15XD	S14.145D	S20.02XD	S21.022D
S00.202D	S01.02XD	S01.94XD	S05.11XD	S06.351D	S06.9X9D	S11.20XD	S14.146D	S20.101D	S21.029D
S00.209D	S01.03XD	S01.95XD	S05.12XD	S06.352D	S07.0XXD	S11.21XD	S14.147D	S20.102D	S21.031D
S00.211D	S01.04XD	S02.121D	S05.20XD	S06.353D	S07.1XXD	S11.22XD	S14.148D	S20.109D	S21.032D
S00.212D	S01.05XD	S02.121G	S05.21XD	S06.354D	S07.8XXD	S11.23XD	S14.149D	S20.111D	S21.039D
S00.219D	S01.101D	S02.121K	S05.22XD	S06.355D	S07.9XXD	S11.24XD	S14.151D	S20.112D	S21.041D
S00.221D	S01.102D	S02.122D	S05.30XD	S06.356D	S08.0XXD	S11.25XD	S14.152D	S20.119D	S21.042D
S00.222D	S01.109D	S02.122G	S05.31XD	S06.359D	S08.111D	S11.80XD	S14.153D	S20.121D	S21.049D
S00.229D	S01.111D	S02.122K	S05.32XD	S06.360D	S08.112D	S11.81XD	S14.154D	S20.122D	S21.051D
S00.241D	S01.112D	S02.129D	S05.40XD	S06.361D	S08.119D	S11.82XD	S14.155D	S20.129D	S21.052D
S00.242D	S01.119D	S02.129G	S05.41XD	S06.362D	S08.121D	S11.83XD	S14.156D	S20.141D	S21.059D
S00.249D	S01.121D	S02.129K	S05.42XD	S06.363D	S08.122D	S11.84XD	S14.157D	S20.142D	S21.101D
S00.251D	S01.122D	S02.831D	S05.50XD	S06.364D	S08.129D	S11.85XD	S14.158D	S20.149D	S21.102D
S00.252D	S01.129D	S02.831G	S05.51XD	S06.365D	S08.811D	S11.89XD	S14.159D	S20.151D	S21.109D
S00.259D	S01.131D	S02.831K	S05.52XD	S06.366D	S08.812D	S11.90XD	S14.2XXD	S20.152D	S21.111D
S00.261D	S01.132D	S02.832D	S05.60XD	S06.369D	S08.89XD	S11.91XD	S14.3XXD	S20.159D	S21.112D
S00.262D	S01.139D	S02.832G	S05.61XD	S06.370D	S09.0XXD	S11.92XD	S14.4XXD	S20.161D	S21.119D
S00.269D	S01.141D	S02.832K	S05.62XD	S06.371D	S09.10XD	S11.93XD	S14.5XXD	S20.162D	S21.121D
S00.271D	S01.142D	S02.839D	S05.70XD	S06.372D	S09.11XD	S11.94XD	S14.8XXD	S20.169D	S21.122D
S00.272D	S01.149D	S02.839G	S05.71XD	S06.373D	S09.12XD	S11.95XD	S14.9XXD	S20.171D	S21.129D
S00.279D	S01.151D	S02.839K	S05.72XD	S06.374D	S09.19XD	S13.0XXD	S15.001D	S20.172D	S21.131D
S00.30XD	S01.152D	S02.841D	S05.8X1D	S06.375D	S09.20XD	S13.100D	S15.002D	S20.179D	S21.132D
S00.31XD	S01.159D	S02.841G	S05.8X2D	S06.376D	S09.21XD	S13.101D	S15.009D	S20.20XD	S21.139D
S00.32XD	S01.20XD	S02.841K	S05.8X9D	S06.379D	S09.22XD	S13.110D	S15.011D	S20.211D	S21.141D
S00.33XD	S01.21XD	S02.842D	S05.90XD	S06.380D	S09.301D	S13.111D	S15.012D	S20.212D	S21.142D
S00.34XD	S01.22XD	S02.842G	S05.91XD	S06.381D	S09.302D	S13.120D	S15.019D	S20.219D	S21.149D
S00.35XD	S01.23XD	S02.842K	S05.92XD	S06.382D	S09.309D	S13.121D	S15.021D	S20.221D	S21.151D
S00.36XD	S01.24XD	S02.849D	S06.0X0D	S06.383D	S09.311D	S13.130D	S15.022D	S20.222D	S21.152D
S00.37XD	S01.25XD	S02.849G	S06.0X1D	S06.384D	S09.312D	S13.131D	S15.029D	S20.229D	S21.159D
S00.401D	S01.301D	S02.849K	S06.0X9D	S06.385D	S09.313D	S13.140D	S15.091D	S20.301D	S21.201D
S00.402D	S01.302D	S02.85XD	S06.1X0D	S06.386D	S09.319D	S13.141D	S15.092D	S20.302D	S21.202D
S00.409D	S01.309D	S02.85XG	S06.1X1D	S06.389D	S09.391D	S13.150D	S15.099D	S20.309D	S21.209D
S00.411D	S01.311D	S02.85XK	S06.1X2D	S06.4X0D	S09.392D	S13.151D	S15.101D	S20.311D	S21.211D
S00.412D	S01.312D	S03.00XD	S06.1X3D	S06.4X1D	S09.399D	S13.160D	S15.102D	S20.312D	S21.212D
S00.419D	S01.319D	S03.01XD	S06.1X4D	S06.4X2D	S09.8XXD	S13.161D	S15.109D	S20.319D	S21.219D
S00.421D	S01.321D	S03.02XD	S06.1X5D	S06.4X3D	S09.90XD	S13.170D	S15.111D	S20.321D	S21.221D
S00.422D	S01.322D	S03.03XD	S06.1X6D	S06.4X4D	S09.91XD	S13.171D	S15.112D	S20.322D	S21.222D
S00.429D	S01.329D	S03.1XXD	S06.1X9D	S06.4X5D	S09.92XD	S13.180D	S15.119D	S20.329D	S21.229D
S00.431D	S01.331D	S03.2XXD	S06.2X0D	S06.4X6D	S09.93XD	S13.181D	S15.121D	S20.341D	S21.231D
S00.432D	S01.332D	S03.40XD	S06.2X1D	S06.4X9D	S10.0XXD	S13.20XD	S15.122D	S20.342D	S21.232D
S00.439D	S01.339D	S03.41XD	S06.2X2D	S06.5X0D	S10.10XD	S13.29XD	S15.129D	S20.349D	S21.239D
S00.441D	S01.341D	S03.42XD	S06.2X3D	S06.5X1D	S10.11XD	S13.4XXD	S15.191D	S20.351D	S21.241D
S00.442D	S01.342D	S03.43XD	S06.2X4D	S06.5X2D	S10.12XD	S13.5XXD	S15.192D	S20.352D	S21.242D
S00.449D	S01.349D	S03.8XXD	S06.2X5D	S06.5X3D	S10.14XD	S13.8XXD	S15.199D	S20.359D	S21.249D
S00.451D	S01.351D	S03.9XXD	S06.2X6D	S06.5X4D	S10.15XD	S13.9XXD	S15.201D	S20.361D	S21.251D
S00.452D	S01.352D	S04.011D	S06.2X9D	S06.5X5D	S10.16XD	S14.0XXD	S15.202D	S20.362D	S21.252D
S00.459D	S01.359D	S04.012D	S06.300D	S06.5X6D	S10.17XD	S14.101D	S15.209D	S20.369D	S21.259D
S00.461D	S01.401D	S04.019D	S06.301D	S06.5X9D	S10.80XD	S14.102D	S15.211D	S20.371D	S21.301D
S00.462D	S01.402D	S04.02XD	S06.302D	S06.6X0D	S10.81XD	S14.103D	S15.212D	S20.372D	S21.302D
S00.469D	S01.409D	S04.031D	S06.303D	S06.6X1D	S10.82XD	S14.104D	S15.219D	S20.379D	S21.309D
S00.471D	S01.411D	S04.032D	S06.304D	S06.6X2D	S10.83XD	S14.105D	S15.221D	S20.401D	S21.311D
S00.472D	S01.412D	S04.039D	S06.305D	S06.6X3D	S10.84XD	S14.106D	S15.222D	S20.402D	S21.312D
S00.479D	S01.419D	S04.041D	S06.306D	S06.6X4D	S10.85XD	S14.107D	S15.229D	S20.409D	S21.319D
S00.501D	S01.421D	S04.042D	S06.309D	S06.6X5D	S10.86XD	S14.108D	S15.291D	S20.411D	S21.321D
S00.502D	S01.422D	S04.049D	S06.310D	S06.6X6D	S10.87XD	S14.109D	S15.292D	S20.412D	S21.322D
S00.511D	S01.429D	S04.10XD	S06.311D	S06.6X9D	S10.90XD	S14.111D	S15.299D	S20.419D	S21.329D
S00.512D	S01.431D	S04.11XD	S06.312D	S06.810D	S10.91XD	S14.112D	S15.301D	S20.421D	S21.331D
S00.521D	S01.432D	S04.12XD	S06.313D	S06.811D	S10.92XD	S14.113D	S15.302D	S20.422D	S21.332D
S00.522D	S01.439D	S04.20XD	S06.314D	S06.812D	S10.93XD	S14.114D	S15.309D	S20.429D	S21.339D
S00.531D	S01.441D	S04.21XD	S06.315D	S06.813D	S10.94XD	S14.115D	S15.311D	S20.441D	S21.341D
S00.532D	S01.442D	S04.22XD	S06.316D	S06.814D	S10.95XD	S14.116D	S15.312D	S20.442D	S21.342D
S00.541D	S01.449D	S04.30XD	S06.319D	S06.815D	S10.96XD	S14.117D	S15.319D	S20.449D	S21.349D
S00.542D	S01.451D	S04.31XD	S06.320D	S06.816D	S10.97XD	S14.118D	S15.321D	S20.451D	S21.351D
S00.551D	S01.452D	S04.32XD	S06.321D	S06.819D	S11.011D	S14.119D	S15.322D	S20.452D	S21.352D
S00.552D	S01.459D	S04.40XD	S06.322D	S06.820D	S11.012D	S14.121D	S15.329D	S20.459D	S21.359D
S00.561D	S01.501D	S04.41XD	S06.323D	S06.821D	S11.013D	S14.122D	S15.391D	S20.461D	S21.401D
S00.562D	S01.502D	S04.42XD	S06.324D	S06.822D	S11.014D	S14.123D	S15.392D	S20.462D	S21.402D
S00.571D	S01.511D	S04.50XD	S06.325D	S06.823D	S11.015D	S14.124D	S15.399D	S20.469D	S21.409D
S00.572D	S01.512D	S04.51XD	S06.326D	S06.824D	S11.019D	S14.125D	S15.8XXD	S20.471D	S21.411D
S00.80XD	S01.521D	S04.52XD	S06.329D	S06.825D	S11.021D	S14.126D	S15.9XXD	S20.472D	S21.412D
S00.81XD	S01.522D	S04.60XD	S06.330D	S06.826D	S11.022D	S14.127D	S16.1XXD	S20.479D	S21.419D
S00.82XD	S01.531D	S04.61XD	S06.331D	S06.829D	S11.023D	S14.128D	S16.2XXD	S20.90XD	S21.421D
S00.83XD	S01.532D	S04.62XD	S06.332D	S06.890D	S11.024D	S14.129D	S16.8XXD	S20.91XD	S21.422D
S00.84XD	S01.541D	S04.70XD	S06.333D	S06.891D	S11.025D	S14.131D	S16.9XXD	S20.92XD	S21.429D
S00.85XD	S01.542D	S04.71XD	S06.334D	S06.892D	S11.029D	S14.132D	S17.0XXD	S20.94XD	S21.431D
S00.86XD	S01.551D	S04.72XD	S06.335D	S06.893D	S11.031D	S14.133D	S17.8XXD	S20.95XD	S21.432D
S00.87XD	S01.552D	S04.811D	S06.336D	S06.894D	S11.032D	S14.134D	S17.9XXD	S20.96XD	S21.439D
S00.90XD	S01.80XD	S04.812D	S06.339D	S06.895D	S11.033D	S14.135D	S19.80XD	S20.97XD	S21.441D
S00.91XD	S01.81XD	S04.819D	S06.340D	S06.896D	S11.034D	S14.136D	S19.81XD	S21.001D	S21.442D
S00.92XD	S01.82XD	S04.891D	S06.341D	S06.899D	S11.035D	S14.137D	S19.82XD	S21.002D	S21.449D
S00.93XD	S01.83XD	S04.892D	S06.342D	S06.9X0D	S11.039D	S14.138D	S19.83XD	S21.009D	S21.451D
S00.94XD	S01.84XD	S04.899D	S06.343D	S06.9X1D	S11.10XD	S14.139D	S19.84XD	S21.011D	S21.452D
S00.95XD	S01.85XD	S04.9XXD	S06.344D	S06.9X2D	S11.11XD	S14.141D	S19.85XD	S21.012D	S21.459D
S00.96XD	S01.90XD	S05.00XD	S06.345D	S06.9X3D	S11.12XD	S14.142D	S19.89XD		S21.90XD

Diagnosis Codes by MDC

S21.91XD	S25.191D	S27.409D	S30.846D	S31.159D	S31.822D	S35.318D	S36.250D	S37.039D	S39.002D
S21.92XD	S25.192D	S27.411D	S30.850D	S31.20XD	S31.823D	S35.319D	S36.251D	S37.041D	S39.003D
S21.93XD	S25.199D	S27.412D	S30.851D	S31.21XD	S31.824D	S35.321D	S36.252D	S37.042D	S39.011D
S21.94XD	S25.20XD	S27.419D	S30.852D	S31.22XD	S31.825D	S35.328D	S36.259D	S37.049D	S39.012D
S21.95XD	S25.21XD	S27.421D	S30.853D	S31.23XD	S31.829D	S35.329D	S36.260D	S37.051D	S39.013D
S23.0XXD	S25.22XD	S27.422D	S30.854D	S31.24XD	S31.831D	S35.331D	S36.261D	S37.052D	S39.021D
S23.100D	S25.29XD	S27.429D	S30.855D	S31.25XD	S31.832D	S35.338D	S36.262D	S37.059D	S39.022D
S23.101D	S25.301D	S27.431D	S30.856D	S31.30XD	S31.833D	S35.339D	S36.269D	S37.061D	S39.023D
S23.110D	S25.302D	S27.432D	S30.857D	S31.31XD	S31.834D	S35.341D	S36.290D	S37.062D	S39.091D
S23.111D	S25.309D	S27.439D	S30.860D	S31.32XD	S31.835D	S35.348D	S36.291D	S37.069D	S39.092D
S23.120D	S25.311D	S27.491D	S30.861D	S31.33XD	S31.839D	S35.349D	S36.292D	S37.091D	S39.093D
S23.121D	S25.312D	S27.492D	S30.862D	S31.34XD	S33.0XXD	S35.401D	S36.299D	S37.092D	S39.81XD
S23.122D	S25.319D	S27.499D	S30.863D	S31.35XD	S33.100D	S35.402D	S36.30XD	S37.099D	S39.82XD
S23.123D	S25.321D	S27.50XD	S30.864D	S31.40XD	S33.101D	S35.403D	S36.32XD	S37.10XD	S39.83XD
S23.130D	S25.322D	S27.51XD	S30.865D	S31.41XD	S33.110D	S35.404D	S36.33XD	S37.12XD	S39.840D
S23.131D	S25.329D	S27.52XD	S30.866D	S31.42XD	S33.111D	S35.405D	S36.39XD	S37.13XD	S39.848D
S23.132D	S25.391D	S27.53XD	S30.867D	S31.43XD	S33.120D	S35.406D	S36.400D	S37.19XD	S39.91XD
S23.133D	S25.392D	S27.59XD	S30.870D	S31.44XD	S33.121D	S35.411D	S36.408D	S37.20XD	S39.92XD
S23.140D	S25.399D	S27.60XD	S30.871D	S31.45XD	S33.130D	S35.412D	S36.409D	S37.22XD	S39.93XD
S23.141D	S25.401D	S27.63XD	S30.872D	S31.501D	S33.131D	S35.413D	S36.410D	S37.23XD	S39.94XD
S23.142D	S25.402D	S27.69XD	S30.873D	S31.502D	S33.140D	S35.414D	S36.418D	S37.29XD	S40.011D
S23.143D	S25.409D	S27.802D	S30.874D	S31.511D	S33.141D	S35.415D	S36.419D	S37.30XD	S40.012D
S23.150D	S25.411D	S27.803D	S30.875D	S31.512D	S33.2XXD	S35.416D	S36.420D	S37.32XD	S40.019D
S23.151D	S25.412D	S27.808D	S30.876D	S31.521D	S33.30XD	S35.491D	S36.428D	S37.33XD	S40.021D
S23.152D	S25.419D	S27.809D	S30.877D	S31.522D	S33.39XD	S35.492D	S36.429D	S37.39XD	S40.022D
S23.153D	S25.421D	S27.812D	S30.91XD	S31.531D	S33.4XXD	S35.493D	S36.430D	S37.401D	S40.029D
S23.160D	S25.422D	S27.813D	S30.92XD	S31.532D	S33.5XXD	S35.494D	S36.438D	S37.402D	S40.211D
S23.161D	S25.429D	S27.818D	S30.93XD	S31.541D	S33.6XXD	S35.495D	S36.439D	S37.409D	S40.212D
S23.162D	S25.491D	S27.819D	S30.94XD	S31.542D	S33.8XXD	S35.496D	S36.490D	S37.421D	S40.219D
S23.163D	S25.492D	S27.892D	S30.95XD	S31.551D	S33.9XXD	S35.50XD	S36.498D	S37.422D	S40.221D
S23.170D	S25.499D	S27.893D	S30.96XD	S31.552D	S34.01XD	S35.511D	S36.499D	S37.429D	S40.222D
S23.171D	S25.501D	S27.898D	S30.97XD	S31.600D	S34.02XD	S35.512D	S36.500D	S37.431D	S40.229D
S23.20XD	S25.502D	S27.899D	S30.98XD	S31.601D	S34.101D	S35.513D	S36.501D	S37.432D	S40.241D
S23.29XD	S25.509D	S27.9XXD	S31.000D	S31.602D	S34.102D	S35.514D	S36.502D	S37.439D	S40.242D
S23.3XXD	S25.511D	S28.0XXD	S31.001D	S31.603D	S34.103D	S35.515D	S36.503D	S37.491D	S40.249D
S23.41XD	S25.512D	S28.1XXD	S31.010D	S31.604D	S34.104D	S35.516D	S36.508D	S37.492D	S40.251D
S23.420D	S25.519D	S28.211D	S31.011D	S31.605D	S34.105D	S35.531D	S36.509D	S37.499D	S40.252D
S23.421D	S25.591D	S28.212D	S31.020D	S31.609D	S34.109D	S35.532D	S36.510D	S37.501D	S40.259D
S23.428D	S25.592D	S28.219D	S31.021D	S31.610D	S34.111D	S35.533D	S36.511D	S37.502D	S40.261D
S23.429D	S25.599D	S28.221D	S31.030D	S31.611D	S34.112D	S35.534D	S36.512D	S37.509D	S40.262D
S23.8XXD	S25.801D	S28.222D	S31.031D	S31.612D	S34.113D	S35.535D	S36.513D	S37.511D	S40.269D
S23.9XXD	S25.802D	S28.229D	S31.040D	S31.613D	S34.114D	S35.536D	S36.518D	S37.512D	S40.271D
S24.0XXD	S25.809D	S29.001D	S31.041D	S31.614D	S34.115D	S35.59XD	S36.519D	S37.519D	S40.272D
S24.101D	S25.811D	S29.002D	S31.050D	S31.615D	S34.119D	S35.8X1D	S36.520D	S37.521D	S40.279D
S24.102D	S25.812D	S29.009D	S31.051D	S31.619D	S34.121D	S35.8X8D	S36.521D	S37.522D	S40.811D
S24.103D	S25.819D	S29.011D	S31.100D	S31.620D	S34.122D	S35.8X9D	S36.522D	S37.529D	S40.812D
S24.104D	S25.891D	S29.012D	S31.101D	S31.621D	S34.123D	S35.90XD	S36.523D	S37.531D	S40.819D
S24.109D	S25.892D	S29.019D	S31.102D	S31.622D	S34.124D	S35.91XD	S36.528D	S37.532D	S40.821D
S24.111D	S25.899D	S29.021D	S31.103D	S31.623D	S34.125D	S35.99XD	S36.529D	S37.539D	S40.822D
S24.112D	S25.90XD	S29.022D	S31.104D	S31.624D	S34.129D	S36.00XD	S36.530D	S37.591D	S40.829D
S24.113D	S25.91XD	S29.029D	S31.105D	S31.625D	S34.131D	S36.020D	S36.531D	S37.592D	S40.841D
S24.114D	S25.99XD	S29.091D	S31.109D	S31.629D	S34.132D	S36.021D	S36.532D	S37.599D	S40.842D
S24.119D	S26.00XD	S29.092D	S31.110D	S31.630D	S34.139D	S36.029D	S36.533D	S37.60XD	S40.849D
S24.131D	S26.01XD	S29.099D	S31.111D	S31.631D	S34.21XD	S36.030D	S36.538D	S37.62XD	S40.851D
S24.132D	S26.020D	S29.8XXD	S31.112D	S31.632D	S34.22XD	S36.031D	S36.539D	S37.63XD	S40.852D
S24.133D	S26.021D	S29.9XXD	S31.113D	S31.633D	S34.3XXD	S36.032D	S36.590D	S37.69XD	S40.859D
S24.134D	S26.022D	S30.0XXD	S31.114D	S31.634D	S34.4XXD	S36.039D	S36.591D	S37.812D	S40.861D
S24.139D	S26.09XD	S30.1XXD	S31.115D	S31.635D	S34.5XXD	S36.09XD	S36.592D	S37.813D	S40.862D
S24.141D	S26.10XD	S30.201D	S31.119D	S31.639D	S34.6XXD	S36.112D	S36.593D	S37.818D	S40.869D
S24.142D	S26.11XD	S30.202D	S31.120D	S31.640D	S34.8XXD	S36.113D	S36.598D	S37.819D	S40.871D
S24.143D	S26.12XD	S30.21XD	S31.121D	S31.641D	S34.9XXD	S36.114D	S36.599D	S37.822D	S40.872D
S24.144D	S26.19XD	S30.22XD	S31.122D	S31.642D	S35.00XD	S36.115D	S36.60XD	S37.823D	S40.879D
S24.149D	S26.90XD	S30.23XD	S31.123D	S31.643D	S35.01XD	S36.116D	S36.61XD	S37.828D	S40.911D
S24.151D	S26.91XD	S30.3XXD	S31.124D	S31.644D	S35.02XD	S36.118D	S36.62XD	S37.829D	S40.912D
S24.152D	S26.92XD	S30.810D	S31.125D	S31.645D	S35.09XD	S36.119D	S36.63XD	S37.892D	S40.919D
S24.153D	S26.99XD	S30.811D	S31.129D	S31.649D	S35.10XD	S36.122D	S36.69XD	S37.893D	S40.921D
S24.154D	S27.0XXD	S30.812D	S31.130D	S31.650D	S35.11XD	S36.123D	S36.81XD	S37.898D	S40.922D
S24.159D	S27.1XXD	S30.813D	S31.131D	S31.651D	S35.12XD	S36.128D	S36.892D	S37.899D	S40.929D
S24.2XXD	S27.2XXD	S30.814D	S31.132D	S31.652D	S35.19XD	S36.129D	S36.893D	S37.90XD	S41.001D
S24.3XXD	S27.301D	S30.815D	S31.133D	S31.653D	S35.211D	S36.13XD	S36.898D	S37.92XD	S41.002D
S24.4XXD	S27.302D	S30.816D	S31.134D	S31.654D	S35.212D	S36.200D	S36.899D	S37.93XD	S41.009D
S24.8XXD	S27.309D	S30.817D	S31.135D	S31.655D	S35.218D	S36.201D	S36.90XD	S37.99XD	S41.011D
S24.9XXD	S27.311D	S30.820D	S31.139D	S31.659D	S35.219D	S36.202D	S36.92XD	S38.001D	S41.012D
S25.00XD	S27.312D	S30.821D	S31.140D	S31.801D	S35.221D	S36.209D	S36.93XD	S38.002D	S41.019D
S25.01XD	S27.319D	S30.822D	S31.141D	S31.802D	S35.222D	S36.220D	S36.99XD	S38.01XD	S41.021D
S25.02XD	S27.321D	S30.823D	S31.142D	S31.803D	S35.228D	S36.221D	S37.001D	S38.02XD	S41.022D
S25.09XD	S27.322D	S30.824D	S31.143D	S31.804D	S35.229D	S36.222D	S37.002D	S38.03XD	S41.029D
S25.101D	S27.329D	S30.825D	S31.144D	S31.805D	S35.231D	S36.229D	S37.009D	S38.1XXD	S41.031D
S25.102D	S27.331D	S30.826D	S31.145D	S31.809D	S35.232D	S36.230D	S37.011D	S38.211D	S41.032D
S25.109D	S27.332D	S30.827D	S31.149D	S31.811D	S35.238D	S36.231D	S37.012D	S38.212D	S41.039D
S25.111D	S27.339D	S30.840D	S31.150D	S31.812D	S35.239D	S36.232D	S37.019D	S38.221D	S41.041D
S25.112D	S27.391D	S30.841D	S31.151D	S31.813D	S35.291D	S36.239D	S37.021D	S38.222D	S41.042D
S25.119D	S27.392D	S30.842D	S31.152D	S31.814D	S35.292D	S36.240D	S37.022D	S38.231D	S41.049D
S25.121D	S27.399D	S30.843D	S31.153D	S31.815D	S35.298D	S36.241D	S37.029D	S38.232D	S41.051D
S25.122D	S27.401D	S30.844D	S31.154D	S31.819D	S35.299D	S36.242D	S37.031D	S38.3XXD	S41.052D
S25.129D	S27.402D	S30.845D	S31.155D	S31.821D	S35.311D	S36.249D	S37.032D	S39.001D	S41.059D

S41.101D	S43.303D	S45.202D	S46.811D	S50.869D	S53.122D	S55.211D	S56.309D	S57.81XD	S60.372D
S41.102D	S43.304D	S45.209D	S46.812D	S50.871D	S53.123D	S55.212D	S56.311D	S57.82XD	S60.379D
S41.109D	S43.305D	S45.211D	S46.819D	S50.872D	S53.124D	S55.219D	S56.312D	S58.011D	S60.391D
S41.111D	S43.306D	S45.212D	S46.821D	S50.879D	S53.125D	S55.291D	S56.319D	S58.012D	S60.392D
S41.112D	S43.311D	S45.219D	S46.822D	S50.901D	S53.126D	S55.292D	S56.321D	S58.019D	S60.399D
S41.119D	S43.312D	S45.291D	S46.829D	S50.902D	S53.131D	S55.299D	S56.322D	S58.021D	S60.410D
S41.121D	S43.313D	S45.292D	S46.891D	S50.909D	S53.132D	S55.801D	S56.329D	S58.022D	S60.411D
S41.122D	S43.314D	S45.299D	S46.892D	S50.911D	S53.133D	S55.802D	S56.391D	S58.029D	S60.412D
S41.129D	S43.315D	S45.301D	S46.899D	S50.912D	S53.134D	S55.809D	S56.392D	S58.111D	S60.413D
S41.131D	S43.316D	S45.302D	S46.901D	S50.919D	S53.135D	S55.811D	S56.399D	S58.112D	S60.414D
S41.132D	S43.391D	S45.309D	S46.902D	S51.001D	S53.136D	S55.812D	S56.401D	S58.119D	S60.415D
S41.139D	S43.392D	S45.311D	S46.909D	S51.002D	S53.141D	S55.819D	S56.402D	S58.121D	S60.416D
S41.141D	S43.393D	S45.312D	S46.911D	S51.009D	S53.142D	S55.891D	S56.403D	S58.122D	S60.417D
S41.142D	S43.394D	S45.319D	S46.912D	S51.011D	S53.143D	S55.892D	S56.404D	S58.129D	S60.418D
S41.149D	S43.395D	S45.391D	S46.919D	S51.012D	S53.144D	S55.899D	S56.405D	S58.911D	S60.419D
S41.151D	S43.396D	S45.392D	S46.921D	S51.019D	S53.145D	S55.901D	S56.406D	S58.912D	S60.420D
S41.152D	S43.401D	S45.399D	S46.922D	S51.021D	S53.146D	S55.902D	S56.407D	S58.919D	S60.421D
S41.159D	S43.402D	S45.801D	S46.929D	S51.022D	S53.191D	S55.909D	S56.408D	S58.921D	S60.422D
S43.001D	S43.409D	S45.802D	S46.991D	S51.029D	S53.192D	S55.911D	S56.409D	S58.922D	S60.423D
S43.002D	S43.411D	S45.809D	S46.992D	S51.031D	S53.193D	S55.912D	S56.411D	S58.929D	S60.424D
S43.003D	S43.412D	S45.811D	S46.999D	S51.032D	S53.194D	S55.919D	S56.412D	S59.801D	S60.425D
S43.004D	S43.419D	S45.812D	S47.1XXD	S51.039D	S53.195D	S55.991D	S56.413D	S59.802D	S60.426D
S43.005D	S43.421D	S45.819D	S47.2XXD	S51.041D	S53.196D	S55.992D	S56.414D	S59.809D	S60.427D
S43.006D	S43.422D	S45.891D	S47.9XXD	S51.042D	S53.20XD	S55.999D	S56.415D	S59.811D	S60.428D
S43.011D	S43.429D	S45.892D	S48.011D	S51.049D	S53.21XD	S56.001D	S56.416D	S59.812D	S60.429D
S43.012D	S43.431D	S45.899D	S48.012D	S51.051D	S53.22XD	S56.002D	S56.417D	S59.819D	S60.440D
S43.013D	S43.432D	S45.901D	S48.019D	S51.052D	S53.30XD	S56.009D	S56.418D	S59.901D	S60.441D
S43.014D	S43.439D	S45.902D	S48.021D	S51.059D	S53.31XD	S56.011D	S56.419D	S59.902D	S60.442D
S43.015D	S43.491D	S45.909D	S48.022D	S51.801D	S53.32XD	S56.012D	S56.421D	S59.909D	S60.443D
S43.016D	S43.492D	S45.911D	S48.029D	S51.802D	S53.401D	S56.019D	S56.422D	S59.911D	S60.444D
S43.021D	S43.499D	S45.912D	S48.111D	S51.809D	S53.402D	S56.021D	S56.423D	S59.912D	S60.445D
S43.022D	S43.50XD	S45.919D	S48.112D	S51.811D	S53.409D	S56.022D	S56.424D	S59.919D	S60.446D
S43.023D	S43.51XD	S45.991D	S48.119D	S51.812D	S53.411D	S56.029D	S56.425D	S60.00XD	S60.447D
S43.024D	S43.52XD	S45.992D	S48.121D	S51.819D	S53.412D	S56.091D	S56.426D	S60.011D	S60.448D
S43.025D	S43.60XD	S45.999D	S48.122D	S51.821D	S53.419D	S56.092D	S56.427D	S60.012D	S60.449D
S43.026D	S43.61XD	S46.001D	S48.129D	S51.822D	S53.421D	S56.099D	S56.428D	S60.019D	S60.450D
S43.031D	S43.62XD	S46.002D	S48.911D	S51.829D	S53.422D	S56.101D	S56.429D	S60.021D	S60.451D
S43.032D	S43.80XD	S46.009D	S48.912D	S51.831D	S53.429D	S56.102D	S56.491D	S60.022D	S60.452D
S43.033D	S43.81XD	S46.011D	S48.919D	S51.832D	S53.431D	S56.103D	S56.492D	S60.029D	S60.453D
S43.034D	S43.82XD	S46.012D	S48.921D	S51.839D	S53.432D	S56.104D	S56.493D	S60.031D	S60.454D
S43.035D	S43.90XD	S46.019D	S48.922D	S51.841D	S53.439D	S56.105D	S56.494D	S60.032D	S60.455D
S43.036D	S43.91XD	S46.021D	S48.929D	S51.842D	S53.441D	S56.106D	S56.495D	S60.039D	S60.456D
S43.081D	S43.92XD	S46.022D	S49.80XD	S51.849D	S53.442D	S56.107D	S56.496D	S60.041D	S60.457D
S43.082D	S44.00XD	S46.029D	S49.81XD	S51.851D	S53.449D	S56.108D	S56.497D	S60.042D	S60.458D
S43.083D	S44.01XD	S46.091D	S49.82XD	S51.852D	S53.491D	S56.109D	S56.498D	S60.049D	S60.459D
S43.084D	S44.02XD	S46.092D	S49.90XD	S51.859D	S53.492D	S56.111D	S56.499D	S60.051D	S60.460D
S43.085D	S44.10XD	S46.099D	S49.91XD	S53.001D	S53.499D	S56.112D	S56.501D	S60.052D	S60.461D
S43.086D	S44.11XD	S46.101D	S49.92XD	S53.002D	S54.00XD	S56.113D	S56.502D	S60.059D	S60.462D
S43.101D	S44.12XD	S46.102D	S50.00XD	S53.003D	S54.01XD	S56.114D	S56.509D	S60.10XD	S60.463D
S43.102D	S44.20XD	S46.109D	S50.01XD	S53.004D	S54.02XD	S56.115D	S56.511D	S60.111D	S60.464D
S43.109D	S44.21XD	S46.111D	S50.02XD	S53.005D	S54.10XD	S56.116D	S56.512D	S60.112D	S60.465D
S43.111D	S44.22XD	S46.112D	S50.10XD	S53.006D	S54.11XD	S56.117D	S56.519D	S60.119D	S60.466D
S43.112D	S44.30XD	S46.119D	S50.11XD	S53.011D	S54.12XD	S56.118D	S56.521D	S60.121D	S60.467D
S43.119D	S44.31XD	S46.121D	S50.12XD	S53.012D	S54.20XD	S56.119D	S56.522D	S60.122D	S60.468D
S43.121D	S44.32XD	S46.122D	S50.311D	S53.013D	S54.21XD	S56.121D	S56.529D	S60.129D	S60.469D
S43.122D	S44.40XD	S46.129D	S50.312D	S53.014D	S54.22XD	S56.122D	S56.591D	S60.131D	S60.470D
S43.129D	S44.41XD	S46.191D	S50.319D	S53.015D	S54.30XD	S56.123D	S56.592D	S60.132D	S60.471D
S43.131D	S44.42XD	S46.192D	S50.321D	S53.016D	S54.31XD	S56.124D	S56.599D	S60.139D	S60.472D
S43.132D	S44.50XD	S46.199D	S50.322D	S53.021D	S54.32XD	S56.125D	S56.801D	S60.141D	S60.473D
S43.139D	S44.51XD	S46.201D	S50.329D	S53.022D	S54.8X1D	S56.126D	S56.802D	S60.142D	S60.474D
S43.141D	S44.52XD	S46.202D	S50.341D	S53.023D	S54.8X2D	S56.127D	S56.809D	S60.149D	S60.475D
S43.142D	S44.8X1D	S46.209D	S50.342D	S53.024D	S54.8X9D	S56.128D	S56.811D	S60.151D	S60.476D
S43.149D	S44.8X2D	S46.211D	S50.349D	S53.025D	S54.90XD	S56.129D	S56.812D	S60.152D	S60.477D
S43.151D	S44.8X9D	S46.212D	S50.351D	S53.026D	S54.91XD	S56.191D	S56.819D	S60.159D	S60.478D
S43.152D	S44.90XD	S46.219D	S50.352D	S53.031D	S54.92XD	S56.192D	S56.821D	S60.211D	S60.479D
S43.159D	S44.91XD	S46.221D	S50.359D	S53.032D	S55.001D	S56.193D	S56.822D	S60.212D	S60.511D
S43.201D	S44.92XD	S46.222D	S50.361D	S53.033D	S55.002D	S56.194D	S56.829D	S60.219D	S60.512D
S43.202D	S45.001D	S46.229D	S50.362D	S53.091D	S55.009D	S56.195D	S56.891D	S60.221D	S60.519D
S43.203D	S45.002D	S46.291D	S50.369D	S53.092D	S55.011D	S56.196D	S56.892D	S60.222D	S60.521D
S43.204D	S45.009D	S46.292D	S50.371D	S53.093D	S55.012D	S56.197D	S56.899D	S60.229D	S60.522D
S43.205D	S45.011D	S46.299D	S50.372D	S53.094D	S55.019D	S56.198D	S56.901D	S60.311D	S60.529D
S43.206D	S45.012D	S46.301D	S50.379D	S53.095D	S55.091D	S56.199D	S56.902D	S60.312D	S60.541D
S43.211D	S45.019D	S46.302D	S50.811D	S53.096D	S55.092D	S56.201D	S56.909D	S60.319D	S60.542D
S43.212D	S45.091D	S46.309D	S50.812D	S53.101D	S55.099D	S56.202D	S56.911D	S60.321D	S60.549D
S43.213D	S45.092D	S46.311D	S50.819D	S53.102D	S55.101D	S56.209D	S56.912D	S60.322D	S60.551D
S43.214D	S45.099D	S46.312D	S50.821D	S53.103D	S55.102D	S56.211D	S56.919D	S60.329D	S60.552D
S43.215D	S45.101D	S46.319D	S50.822D	S53.104D	S55.109D	S56.212D	S56.921D	S60.341D	S60.559D
S43.216D	S45.102D	S46.321D	S50.829D	S53.105D	S55.111D	S56.219D	S56.922D	S60.342D	S60.561D
S43.221D	S45.109D	S46.322D	S50.841D	S53.106D	S55.112D	S56.221D	S56.929D	S60.349D	S60.562D
S43.222D	S45.111D	S46.329D	S50.842D	S53.111D	S55.119D	S56.222D	S56.991D	S60.351D	S60.569D
S43.223D	S45.112D	S46.391D	S50.849D	S53.112D	S55.191D	S56.229D	S56.992D	S60.352D	S60.571D
S43.224D	S45.119D	S46.392D	S50.851D	S53.113D	S55.192D	S56.291D	S56.999D	S60.359D	S60.572D
S43.225D	S45.191D	S46.399D	S50.852D	S53.114D	S55.199D	S56.292D	S57.00XD	S60.361D	S60.579D
S43.226D	S45.192D	S46.801D	S50.859D	S53.115D	S55.201D	S56.299D	S57.01XD	S60.362D	S60.811D
S43.301D	S45.199D	S46.802D	S50.861D	S53.116D	S55.202D	S56.301D	S57.02XD	S60.369D	S60.812D
S43.302D	S45.201D	S46.809D	S50.862D	S53.121D	S55.209D	S56.302D	S57.80XD	S60.371D	S60.819D

S60.821D	S61.216D	S61.342D	S63.053D	S63.246D	S63.417D	S63.689D	S65.419D	S66.122D	S66.504D
S60.822D	S61.217D	S61.343D	S63.054D	S63.247D	S63.418D	S63.690D	S65.491D	S66.123D	S66.505D
S60.829D	S61.218D	S61.344D	S63.055D	S63.248D	S63.419D	S63.691D	S65.492D	S66.124D	S66.506D
S60.841D	S61.219D	S61.345D	S63.056D	S63.249D	S63.420D	S63.692D	S65.499D	S66.125D	S66.507D
S60.842D	S61.220D	S61.346D	S63.061D	S63.250D	S63.421D	S63.693D	S65.500D	S66.126D	S66.508D
S60.849D	S61.221D	S61.347D	S63.062D	S63.251D	S63.422D	S63.694D	S65.501D	S66.127D	S66.509D
S60.852D	S61.222D	S61.348D	S63.063D	S63.252D	S63.423D	S63.695D	S65.502D	S66.128D	S66.510D
S60.852D	S61.223D	S61.349D	S63.064D	S63.253D	S63.424D	S63.696D	S65.503D	S66.129D	S66.511D
S60.859D	S61.224D	S61.350D	S63.065D	S63.254D	S63.425D	S63.697D	S65.504D	S66.190D	S66.512D
S60.861D	S61.225D	S61.351D	S63.066D	S63.255D	S63.426D	S63.698D	S65.505D	S66.191D	S66.513D
S60.862D	S61.226D	S61.352D	S63.071D	S63.256D	S63.427D	S63.699D	S65.506D	S66.192D	S66.514D
S60.869D	S61.227D	S61.353D	S63.072D	S63.257D	S63.428D	S63.8X1D	S65.507D	S66.193D	S66.515D
S60.871D	S61.228D	S61.354D	S63.073D	S63.258D	S63.429D	S63.8X2D	S65.508D	S66.194D	S66.516D
S60.872D	S61.229D	S61.355D	S63.074D	S63.259D	S63.430D	S63.8X9D	S65.509D	S66.195D	S66.517D
S60.879D	S61.230D	S61.356D	S63.075D	S63.260D	S63.431D	S63.90XD	S65.510D	S66.196D	S66.518D
S60.911D	S61.231D	S61.357D	S63.076D	S63.261D	S63.432D	S63.91XD	S65.511D	S66.197D	S66.519D
S60.912D	S61.232D	S61.358D	S63.091D	S63.262D	S63.433D	S63.92XD	S65.512D	S66.198D	S66.520D
S60.919D	S61.233D	S61.359D	S63.092D	S63.263D	S63.434D	S64.00XD	S65.513D	S66.199D	S66.521D
S60.921D	S61.234D	S61.401D	S63.093D	S63.264D	S63.435D	S64.01XD	S65.514D	S66.201D	S66.522D
S60.922D	S61.235D	S61.402D	S63.094D	S63.265D	S63.436D	S64.02XD	S65.515D	S66.202D	S66.523D
S60.929D	S61.236D	S61.409D	S63.095D	S63.266D	S63.437D	S64.10XD	S65.516D	S66.209D	S66.524D
S60.931D	S61.237D	S61.411D	S63.096D	S63.267D	S63.438D	S64.11XD	S65.517D	S66.211D	S66.525D
S60.932D	S61.238D	S61.412D	S63.101D	S63.268D	S63.439D	S64.12XD	S65.518D	S66.212D	S66.526D
S60.939D	S61.239D	S61.419D	S63.102D	S63.269D	S63.490D	S64.20XD	S65.519D	S66.219D	S66.527D
S60.940D	S61.240D	S61.421D	S63.103D	S63.270D	S63.491D	S64.21XD	S65.590D	S66.221D	S66.528D
S60.941D	S61.241D	S61.422D	S63.104D	S63.271D	S63.492D	S64.22XD	S65.591D	S66.222D	S66.529D
S60.942D	S61.242D	S61.429D	S63.105D	S63.272D	S63.493D	S64.30XD	S65.592D	S66.229D	S66.590D
S60.943D	S61.243D	S61.431D	S63.106D	S63.273D	S63.494D	S64.31XD	S65.593D	S66.291D	S66.591D
S60.944D	S61.244D	S61.432D	S63.111D	S63.274D	S63.495D	S64.32XD	S65.594D	S66.292D	S66.592D
S60.945D	S61.245D	S61.439D	S63.112D	S63.275D	S63.496D	S64.40XD	S65.595D	S66.299D	S66.593D
S60.946D	S61.246D	S61.441D	S63.113D	S63.276D	S63.497D	S64.490D	S65.596D	S66.300D	S66.594D
S60.947D	S61.247D	S61.442D	S63.114D	S63.277D	S63.498D	S64.491D	S65.597D	S66.301D	S66.595D
S60.948D	S61.248D	S61.449D	S63.115D	S63.278D	S63.499D	S64.492D	S65.598D	S66.302D	S66.596D
S60.949D	S61.249D	S61.451D	S63.116D	S63.279D	S63.501D	S64.493D	S65.599D	S66.303D	S66.597D
S61.001D	S61.250D	S61.452D	S63.121D	S63.280D	S63.502D	S64.494D	S65.801D	S66.304D	S66.598D
S61.002D	S61.251D	S61.459D	S63.122D	S63.281D	S63.509D	S64.495D	S65.802D	S66.305D	S66.599D
S61.009D	S61.252D	S61.501D	S63.123D	S63.282D	S63.511D	S64.496D	S65.809D	S66.306D	S66.801D
S61.011D	S61.253D	S61.502D	S63.124D	S63.283D	S63.512D	S64.497D	S65.811D	S66.307D	S66.802D
S61.012D	S61.254D	S61.509D	S63.125D	S63.284D	S63.519D	S64.498D	S65.812D	S66.308D	S66.809D
S61.019D	S61.255D	S61.511D	S63.126D	S63.285D	S63.521D	S64.8X1D	S65.819D	S66.309D	S66.811D
S61.021D	S61.256D	S61.512D	S63.200D	S63.286D	S63.522D	S64.8X2D	S65.891D	S66.310D	S66.812D
S61.022D	S61.257D	S61.519D	S63.201D	S63.287D	S63.529D	S64.8X9D	S65.892D	S66.311D	S66.819D
S61.029D	S61.258D	S61.521D	S63.202D	S63.288D	S63.591D	S64.90XD	S65.899D	S66.312D	S66.821D
S61.031D	S61.259D	S61.522D	S63.203D	S63.289D	S63.592D	S64.91XD	S65.901D	S66.313D	S66.822D
S61.032D	S61.300D	S61.529D	S63.204D	S63.290D	S63.599D	S64.92XD	S65.902D	S66.314D	S66.829D
S61.039D	S61.301D	S61.531D	S63.205D	S63.291D	S63.601D	S65.001D	S65.909D	S66.315D	S66.891D
S61.041D	S61.302D	S61.532D	S63.206D	S63.292D	S63.602D	S65.002D	S65.911D	S66.316D	S66.892D
S61.042D	S61.303D	S61.539D	S63.207D	S63.293D	S63.609D	S65.009D	S65.912D	S66.317D	S66.899D
S61.049D	S61.304D	S61.541D	S63.208D	S63.294D	S63.610D	S65.011D	S65.919D	S66.318D	S66.901D
S61.051D	S61.305D	S61.542D	S63.209D	S63.295D	S63.611D	S65.012D	S65.991D	S66.319D	S66.902D
S61.052D	S61.306D	S61.549D	S63.210D	S63.296D	S63.612D	S65.019D	S65.992D	S66.320D	S66.909D
S61.059D	S61.307D	S61.551D	S63.211D	S63.297D	S63.613D	S65.091D	S65.999D	S66.321D	S66.911D
S61.101D	S61.308D	S61.552D	S63.212D	S63.298D	S63.614D	S65.092D	S66.001D	S66.322D	S66.912D
S61.102D	S61.309D	S61.559D	S63.213D	S63.299D	S63.615D	S65.099D	S66.002D	S66.323D	S66.919D
S61.109D	S61.310D	S63.001D	S63.214D	S63.301D	S63.616D	S65.101D	S66.009D	S66.324D	S66.921D
S61.111D	S61.311D	S63.002D	S63.215D	S63.302D	S63.617D	S65.102D	S66.011D	S66.325D	S66.922D
S61.112D	S61.312D	S63.003D	S63.216D	S63.309D	S63.618D	S65.109D	S66.012D	S66.326D	S66.929D
S61.119D	S61.313D	S63.004D	S63.217D	S63.311D	S63.619D	S65.111D	S66.019D	S66.327D	S66.991D
S61.121D	S61.314D	S63.005D	S63.218D	S63.312D	S63.621D	S65.112D	S66.021D	S66.328D	S66.992D
S61.122D	S61.315D	S63.006D	S63.219D	S63.319D	S63.622D	S65.119D	S66.022D	S66.329D	S66.999D
S61.129D	S61.316D	S63.011D	S63.220D	S63.321D	S63.629D	S65.191D	S66.029D	S66.390D	S67.00XD
S61.131D	S61.317D	S63.012D	S63.221D	S63.322D	S63.630D	S65.192D	S66.091D	S66.391D	S67.01XD
S61.132D	S61.318D	S63.013D	S63.222D	S63.329D	S63.631D	S65.199D	S66.092D	S66.392D	S67.02XD
S61.139D	S61.319D	S63.014D	S63.223D	S63.331D	S63.632D	S65.201D	S66.099D	S66.393D	S67.10XD
S61.141D	S61.320D	S63.015D	S63.224D	S63.332D	S63.633D	S65.202D	S66.100D	S66.394D	S67.190D
S61.142D	S61.321D	S63.016D	S63.225D	S63.339D	S63.634D	S65.209D	S66.101D	S66.395D	S67.191D
S61.149D	S61.322D	S63.021D	S63.226D	S63.391D	S63.635D	S65.211D	S66.102D	S66.396D	S67.192D
S61.151D	S61.323D	S63.022D	S63.227D	S63.392D	S63.636D	S65.212D	S66.103D	S66.397D	S67.193D
S61.152D	S61.324D	S63.023D	S63.228D	S63.399D	S63.637D	S65.219D	S66.104D	S66.398D	S67.194D
S61.159D	S61.325D	S63.024D	S63.229D	S63.400D	S63.638D	S65.291D	S66.105D	S66.399D	S67.195D
S61.200D	S61.326D	S63.025D	S63.230D	S63.401D	S63.639D	S65.292D	S66.106D	S66.401D	S67.196D
S61.201D	S61.327D	S63.026D	S63.231D	S63.402D	S63.641D	S65.299D	S66.107D	S66.402D	S67.197D
S61.202D	S61.328D	S63.031D	S63.232D	S63.403D	S63.642D	S65.301D	S66.108D	S66.409D	S67.198D
S61.203D	S61.329D	S63.032D	S63.233D	S63.404D	S63.649D	S65.302D	S66.109D	S66.411D	S67.20XD
S61.204D	S61.330D	S63.033D	S63.234D	S63.405D	S63.650D	S65.309D	S66.110D	S66.412D	S67.21XD
S61.205D	S61.331D	S63.034D	S63.235D	S63.406D	S63.651D	S65.311D	S66.111D	S66.419D	S67.22XD
S61.206D	S61.332D	S63.035D	S63.236D	S63.407D	S63.652D	S65.312D	S66.112D	S66.421D	S67.30XD
S61.207D	S61.333D	S63.036D	S63.237D	S63.408D	S63.653D	S65.319D	S66.113D	S66.422D	S67.31XD
S61.208D	S61.334D	S63.041D	S63.238D	S63.409D	S63.654D	S65.391D	S66.114D	S66.429D	S67.32XD
S61.209D	S61.335D	S63.042D	S63.239D	S63.410D	S63.655D	S65.392D	S66.115D	S66.491D	S67.40XD
S61.210D	S61.336D	S63.043D	S63.240D	S63.411D	S63.656D	S65.399D	S66.116D	S66.492D	S67.41XD
S61.211D	S61.337D	S63.044D	S63.241D	S63.412D	S63.657D	S65.401D	S66.117D	S66.499D	S67.42XD
S61.212D	S61.338D	S63.045D	S63.242D	S63.413D	S63.658D	S65.402D	S66.118D	S66.500D	S67.90XD
S61.213D	S61.339D	S63.046D	S63.243D	S63.414D	S63.659D	S65.409D	S66.119D	S66.501D	S67.91XD
S61.214D	S61.340D	S63.051D	S63.244D	S63.415D	S63.681D	S65.411D	S66.120D	S66.502D	S67.92XD
S61.215D	S61.341D	S63.052D	S63.245D	S63.416D	S63.682D	S65.412D	S66.121D	S66.503D	S68.011D

S68.012D	S70.259D	S73.032D	S75.911D	S77.22XD	S81.022D	S83.203D	S85.109D	S86.022D	S88.921D
S68.019D	S70.261D	S73.033D	S75.912D	S78.011D	S81.029D	S83.204D	S85.111D	S86.029D	S88.922D
S68.021D	S70.262D	S73.034D	S75.919D	S78.012D	S81.031D	S83.205D	S85.112D	S86.091D	S88.929D
S68.022D	S70.269D	S73.035D	S75.991D	S78.019D	S81.032D	S83.206D	S85.119D	S86.092D	S89.80XD
S68.029D	S70.271D	S73.036D	S75.992D	S78.021D	S81.039D	S83.207D	S85.121D	S86.099D	S89.81XD
S68.110D	S70.272D	S73.041D	S75.999D	S78.022D	S81.041D	S83.209D	S85.122D	S86.101D	S89.82XD
S68.111D	S70.279D	S73.042D	S76.001D	S78.029D	S81.042D	S83.211D	S85.129D	S86.102D	S89.90XD
S68.112D	S70.311D	S73.043D	S76.002D	S78.111D	S81.049D	S83.212D	S85.131D	S86.109D	S89.91XD
S68.113D	S70.312D	S73.044D	S76.009D	S78.112D	S81.051D	S83.219D	S85.132D	S86.111D	S89.92XD
S68.114D	S70.319D	S73.045D	S76.011D	S78.119D	S81.052D	S83.221D	S85.139D	S86.112D	S90.00XD
S68.115D	S70.321D	S73.046D	S76.012D	S78.121D	S81.059D	S83.222D	S85.141D	S86.119D	S90.01XD
S68.116D	S70.322D	S73.101D	S76.019D	S78.122D	S81.801D	S83.229D	S85.142D	S86.121D	S90.02XD
S68.117D	S70.329D	S73.102D	S76.021D	S78.129D	S81.802D	S83.231D	S85.149D	S86.122D	S90.111D
S68.118D	S70.341D	S73.109D	S76.022D	S78.911D	S81.809D	S83.232D	S85.151D	S86.129D	S90.112D
S68.119D	S70.342D	S73.111D	S76.029D	S78.912D	S81.811D	S83.239D	S85.152D	S86.191D	S90.119D
S68.120D	S70.349D	S73.112D	S76.091D	S78.919D	S81.812D	S83.241D	S85.159D	S86.192D	S90.121D
S68.121D	S70.351D	S73.119D	S76.092D	S78.921D	S81.819D	S83.242D	S85.161D	S86.199D	S90.122D
S68.122D	S70.352D	S73.121D	S76.099D	S78.922D	S81.821D	S83.249D	S85.162D	S86.201D	S90.129D
S68.123D	S70.359D	S73.122D	S76.101D	S78.929D	S81.822D	S83.251D	S85.169D	S86.202D	S90.211D
S68.124D	S70.361D	S73.129D	S76.102D	S79.811D	S81.829D	S83.252D	S85.171D	S86.209D	S90.212D
S68.125D	S70.362D	S73.191D	S76.109D	S79.812D	S81.831D	S83.259D	S85.172D	S86.211D	S90.219D
S68.126D	S70.369D	S73.192D	S76.111D	S79.819D	S81.832D	S83.261D	S85.179D	S86.212D	S90.221D
S68.127D	S70.371D	S73.199D	S76.112D	S79.821D	S81.839D	S83.262D	S85.181D	S86.219D	S90.222D
S68.128D	S70.372D	S74.00XD	S76.119D	S79.822D	S81.841D	S83.269D	S85.182D	S86.221D	S90.229D
S68.129D	S70.379D	S74.01XD	S76.121D	S79.829D	S81.842D	S83.271D	S85.189D	S86.222D	S90.30XD
S68.411D	S70.911D	S74.02XD	S76.122D	S79.911D	S81.849D	S83.272D	S85.201D	S86.229D	S90.31XD
S68.412D	S70.912D	S74.10XD	S76.129D	S79.912D	S81.851D	S83.279D	S85.202D	S86.291D	S90.32XD
S68.419D	S70.919D	S74.11XD	S76.191D	S79.919D	S81.852D	S83.281D	S85.209D	S86.292D	S90.411D
S68.421D	S70.921D	S74.12XD	S76.192D	S79.921D	S81.859D	S83.282D	S85.211D	S86.299D	S90.412D
S68.422D	S70.922D	S74.20XD	S76.199D	S79.922D	S83.001D	S83.289D	S85.212D	S86.301D	S90.413D
S68.429D	S70.929D	S74.21XD	S76.201D	S79.929D	S83.002D	S83.30XD	S85.219D	S86.302D	S90.414D
S68.511D	S71.001D	S74.22XD	S76.202D	S80.00XD	S83.003D	S83.31XD	S85.291D	S86.309D	S90.415D
S68.512D	S71.002D	S74.8X1D	S76.209D	S80.01XD	S83.004D	S83.32XD	S85.292D	S86.311D	S90.416D
S68.519D	S71.009D	S74.8X2D	S76.211D	S80.02XD	S83.005D	S83.401D	S85.299D	S86.312D	S90.421D
S68.521D	S71.011D	S74.8X9D	S76.212D	S80.10XD	S83.006D	S83.402D	S85.301D	S86.319D	S90.422D
S68.522D	S71.012D	S74.90XD	S76.219D	S80.11XD	S83.011D	S83.409D	S85.302D	S86.321D	S90.423D
S68.529D	S71.019D	S74.91XD	S76.221D	S80.12XD	S83.012D	S83.411D	S85.309D	S86.322D	S90.424D
S68.610D	S71.021D	S74.92XD	S76.222D	S80.211D	S83.013D	S83.412D	S85.311D	S86.329D	S90.425D
S68.611D	S71.022D	S75.001D	S76.229D	S80.212D	S83.014D	S83.419D	S85.312D	S86.391D	S90.426D
S68.612D	S71.029D	S75.002D	S76.291D	S80.219D	S83.015D	S83.421D	S85.319D	S86.392D	S90.441D
S68.613D	S71.031D	S75.009D	S76.292D	S80.221D	S83.016D	S83.422D	S85.391D	S86.399D	S90.442D
S68.614D	S71.032D	S75.011D	S76.299D	S80.222D	S83.091D	S83.429D	S85.392D	S86.801D	S90.443D
S68.615D	S71.039D	S75.012D	S76.301D	S80.229D	S83.092D	S83.501D	S85.399D	S86.802D	S90.444D
S68.616D	S71.041D	S75.019D	S76.302D	S80.241D	S83.093D	S83.502D	S85.401D	S86.809D	S90.445D
S68.617D	S71.042D	S75.021D	S76.309D	S80.242D	S83.094D	S83.509D	S85.402D	S86.811D	S90.446D
S68.618D	S71.049D	S75.022D	S76.311D	S80.249D	S83.095D	S83.511D	S85.409D	S86.812D	S90.451D
S68.619D	S71.051D	S75.029D	S76.312D	S80.251D	S83.096D	S83.512D	S85.411D	S86.819D	S90.452D
S68.620D	S71.052D	S75.091D	S76.319D	S80.252D	S83.101D	S83.519D	S85.412D	S86.821D	S90.453D
S68.621D	S71.059D	S75.092D	S76.321D	S80.259D	S83.102D	S83.521D	S85.419D	S86.822D	S90.454D
S68.622D	S71.101D	S75.099D	S76.322D	S80.261D	S83.103D	S83.522D	S85.491D	S86.829D	S90.455D
S68.623D	S71.102D	S75.101D	S76.329D	S80.262D	S83.104D	S83.529D	S85.492D	S86.891D	S90.456D
S68.624D	S71.109D	S75.102D	S76.391D	S80.269D	S83.105D	S83.60XD	S85.499D	S86.892D	S90.461D
S68.625D	S71.111D	S75.109D	S76.392D	S80.271D	S83.106D	S83.61XD	S85.501D	S86.899D	S90.462D
S68.626D	S71.112D	S75.111D	S76.399D	S80.272D	S83.111D	S83.62XD	S85.502D	S86.901D	S90.463D
S68.627D	S71.119D	S75.112D	S76.801D	S80.279D	S83.112D	S83.8X1D	S85.509D	S86.902D	S90.464D
S68.628D	S71.121D	S75.119D	S76.802D	S80.811D	S83.113D	S83.8X2D	S85.511D	S86.909D	S90.465D
S68.629D	S71.122D	S75.121D	S76.809D	S80.812D	S83.114D	S83.8X9D	S85.512D	S86.911D	S90.466D
S68.711D	S71.129D	S75.122D	S76.811D	S80.819D	S83.115D	S83.90XD	S85.519D	S86.912D	S90.471D
S68.712D	S71.131D	S75.129D	S76.812D	S80.821D	S83.116D	S83.91XD	S85.591D	S86.919D	S90.472D
S68.719D	S71.132D	S75.191D	S76.819D	S80.822D	S83.121D	S83.92XD	S85.592D	S86.921D	S90.473D
S68.721D	S71.139D	S75.192D	S76.821D	S80.829D	S83.122D	S84.00XD	S85.599D	S86.922D	S90.474D
S68.722D	S71.141D	S75.199D	S76.822D	S80.841D	S83.123D	S84.01XD	S85.801D	S86.929D	S90.475D
S68.729D	S71.142D	S75.201D	S76.829D	S80.842D	S83.124D	S84.02XD	S85.802D	S86.991D	S90.476D
S69.80XD	S71.149D	S75.202D	S76.891D	S80.849D	S83.125D	S84.10XD	S85.809D	S86.992D	S90.511D
S69.81XD	S71.151D	S75.209D	S76.892D	S80.851D	S83.126D	S84.11XD	S85.811D	S86.999D	S90.512D
S69.82XD	S71.152D	S75.211D	S76.899D	S80.852D	S83.131D	S84.12XD	S85.812D	S87.00XD	S90.519D
S69.90XD	S71.159D	S75.212D	S76.901D	S80.859D	S83.132D	S84.20XD	S85.819D	S87.01XD	S90.521D
S69.91XD	S73.001D	S75.219D	S76.902D	S80.861D	S83.133D	S84.21XD	S85.891D	S87.02XD	S90.522D
S69.92XD	S73.002D	S75.221D	S76.909D	S80.862D	S83.134D	S84.22XD	S85.892D	S87.80XD	S90.529D
S70.00XD	S73.003D	S75.222D	S76.911D	S80.869D	S83.135D	S84.801D	S85.899D	S87.81XD	S90.541D
S70.01XD	S73.004D	S75.229D	S76.912D	S80.871D	S83.136D	S84.802D	S85.901D	S87.82XD	S90.542D
S70.02XD	S73.005D	S75.291D	S76.919D	S80.872D	S83.141D	S84.809D	S85.902D	S88.011D	S90.549D
S70.10XD	S73.006D	S75.292D	S76.921D	S80.879D	S83.142D	S84.90XD	S85.909D	S88.019D	S90.551D
S70.11XD	S73.011D	S75.299D	S76.922D	S80.911D	S83.143D	S84.91XD	S85.911D	S88.021D	S90.552D
S70.12XD	S73.012D	S75.801D	S76.929D	S80.912D	S83.144D	S84.92XD	S85.912D	S88.022D	S90.559D
S70.211D	S73.013D	S75.802D	S76.991D	S80.919D	S83.145D	S85.001D	S85.919D	S88.029D	S90.561D
S70.212D	S73.014D	S75.809D	S76.992D	S80.921D	S83.146D	S85.002D	S85.991D	S88.111D	S90.562D
S70.219D	S73.015D	S75.811D	S76.999D	S80.922D	S83.191D	S85.009D	S85.992D	S88.112D	S90.569D
S70.221D	S73.016D	S75.812D	S77.00XD	S80.929D	S83.192D	S85.011D	S85.999D	S88.119D	S90.571D
S70.222D	S73.021D	S75.819D	S77.01XD	S81.001D	S83.193D	S85.012D	S86.001D	S88.121D	S90.572D
S70.229D	S73.022D	S75.891D	S77.02XD	S81.002D	S83.194D	S85.019D	S86.002D	S88.122D	S90.579D
S70.241D	S73.023D	S75.892D	S77.10XD	S81.009D	S83.195D	S85.091D	S86.009D	S88.129D	S90.811D
S70.242D	S73.024D	S75.899D	S77.11XD	S81.011D	S83.196D	S85.092D	S86.011D	S88.911D	S90.812D
S70.249D	S73.025D	S75.901D	S77.12XD	S81.012D	S83.200D	S85.099D	S86.012D	S88.912D	S90.819D
S70.251D	S73.026D	S75.902D	S77.20XD	S81.019D	S83.201D	S85.101D	S86.019D	S88.919D	S90.821D
S70.252D	S73.031D	S75.909D	S77.21XD	S81.021D	S83.202D	S85.102D	S86.021D	S88.919D	S90.822D

S90.829D	S91.202D	S93.132D	S94.01XD	S96.201D	S98.929D	S99.111G	S99.221P	T17.300D	T20.212D
S90.841D	S91.203D	S93.133D	S94.02XD	S96.202D	S99.001D	S99.111K	S99.222D	T17.308D	T20.219D
S90.842D	S91.204D	S93.134D	S94.10XD	S96.209D	S99.001K	S99.111P	S99.222K	T17.310D	T20.22XD
S90.849D	S91.205D	S93.135D	S94.11XD	S96.211D	S99.001P	S99.112D	S99.222P	T17.318D	T20.23XD
S90.851D	S91.206D	S93.136D	S94.12XD	S96.212D	S99.002D	S99.112G	S99.229D	T17.320D	T20.24XD
S90.852D	S91.209D	S93.139D	S94.20XD	S96.219D	S99.002G	S99.112K	S99.229G	T17.328D	T20.25XD
S90.859D	S91.211D	S93.141D	S94.21XD	S96.221D	S99.002K	S99.112P	S99.229K	T17.390D	T20.26XD
S90.861D	S91.212D	S93.142D	S94.22XD	S96.222D	S99.002P	S99.119D	S99.229P	T17.398D	T20.27XD
S90.862D	S91.213D	S93.143D	S94.30XD	S96.229D	S99.009D	S99.119G	S99.231D	T17.400D	T20.29XD
S90.869D	S91.214D	S93.144D	S94.31XD	S96.291D	S99.009G	S99.119K	S99.231G	T17.408D	T20.30XD
S90.871D	S91.215D	S93.145D	S94.32XD	S96.292D	S99.009K	S99.119P	S99.231K	T17.410D	T20.311D
S90.872D	S91.216D	S93.146D	S94.8X1D	S96.299D	S99.009P	S99.121D	S99.231P	T17.418D	T20.312D
S90.879D	S91.219D	S93.149D	S94.8X2D	S96.801D	S99.011D	S99.121G	S99.232D	T17.420D	T20.319D
S90.911D	S91.221D	S93.301D	S94.8X9D	S96.802D	S99.011G	S99.121K	S99.232G	T17.428D	T20.32XD
S90.912D	S91.222D	S93.302D	S94.90XD	S96.809D	S99.011K	S99.121P	S99.232K	T17.490D	T20.33XD
S90.919D	S91.223D	S93.303D	S94.91XD	S96.811D	S99.011P	S99.122D	S99.232P	T17.498D	T20.34XD
S90.921D	S91.224D	S93.304D	S94.92XD	S96.812D	S99.012D	S99.122G	S99.239D	T17.500D	T20.35XD
S90.922D	S91.225D	S93.305D	S95.001D	S96.819D	S99.012G	S99.122K	S99.239G	T17.508D	T20.36XD
S90.929D	S91.226D	S93.306D	S95.002D	S96.821D	S99.012K	S99.122P	S99.239K	T17.510D	T20.37XD
S90.931D	S91.229D	S93.311D	S95.009D	S96.822D	S99.012P	S99.129D	S99.239P	T17.518D	T20.39XD
S90.932D	S91.231D	S93.312D	S95.011D	S96.829D	S99.019D	S99.129G	S99.241D	T17.520D	T20.40XD
S90.933D	S91.232D	S93.313D	S95.012D	S96.891D	S99.019G	S99.129K	S99.241G	T17.528D	T20.411D
S90.934D	S91.233D	S93.314D	S95.019D	S96.892D	S99.019K	S99.129P	S99.241K	T17.590D	T20.412D
S90.935D	S91.234D	S93.315D	S95.091D	S96.899D	S99.019P	S99.131D	S99.241P	T17.598D	T20.419D
S90.936D	S91.235D	S93.316D	S95.092D	S96.901D	S99.021D	S99.131G	S99.242D	T17.800D	T20.42XD
S91.001D	S91.236D	S93.321D	S95.099D	S96.902D	S99.021G	S99.131K	S99.242G	T17.808D	T20.43XD
S91.002D	S91.239D	S93.322D	S95.101D	S96.909D	S99.021K	S99.131P	S99.242K	T17.810D	T20.44XD
S91.009D	S91.241D	S93.323D	S95.102D	S96.911D	S99.021P	S99.132D	S99.242P	T17.818D	T20.45XD
S91.011D	S91.242D	S93.324D	S95.109D	S96.912D	S99.022D	S99.132G	S99.249D	T17.820D	T20.46XD
S91.012D	S91.243D	S93.325D	S95.111D	S96.919D	S99.022G	S99.132K	S99.249K	T17.828D	T20.47XD
S91.019D	S91.244D	S93.326D	S95.112D	S96.921D	S99.022K	S99.132P	S99.249P	T17.890D	T20.49XD
S91.021D	S91.245D	S93.331D	S95.119D	S96.922D	S99.022P	S99.139D	S99.291D	T17.898D	T20.50XD
S91.022D	S91.246D	S93.332D	S95.191D	S96.929D	S99.029D	S99.139G	S99.291G	T17.900D	T20.511D
S91.029D	S91.249D	S93.333D	S95.192D	S96.991D	S99.029G	S99.139K	S99.291K	T17.908D	T20.512D
S91.031D	S91.251D	S93.334D	S95.199D	S96.992D	S99.029K	S99.139P	S99.291P	T17.910D	T20.519D
S91.032D	S91.252D	S93.335D	S95.201D	S96.999D	S99.029P	S99.141D	S99.292D	T17.918D	T20.52XD
S91.039D	S91.253D	S93.336D	S95.202D	S97.00XD	S99.031D	S99.141G	S99.292G	T17.920D	T20.53XD
S91.041D	S91.254D	S93.401D	S95.209D	S97.01XD	S99.031G	S99.141K	S99.292K	T17.928D	T20.54XD
S91.042D	S91.255D	S93.402D	S95.211D	S97.02XD	S99.031K	S99.141P	S99.292P	T17.990D	T20.55XD
S91.049D	S91.256D	S93.409D	S95.212D	S97.101D	S99.031P	S99.142D	S99.299D	T17.998D	T20.56XD
S91.051D	S91.259D	S93.411D	S95.219D	S97.102D	S99.032D	S99.142G	S99.299G	T18.0XXD	T20.57XD
S91.052D	S91.301D	S93.412D	S95.291D	S97.109D	S99.032G	S99.142K	S99.299K	T18.100D	T20.59XD
S91.059D	S91.302D	S93.419D	S95.292D	S97.111D	S99.032K	S99.142P	S99.299P	T18.108D	T20.60XD
S91.101D	S91.309D	S93.421D	S95.299D	S97.112D	S99.032P	S99.149D	S99.811D	T18.110D	T20.611D
S91.102D	S91.311D	S93.422D	S95.801D	S97.119D	S99.039D	S99.149G	S99.812D	T18.118D	T20.612D
S91.103D	S91.312D	S93.429D	S95.802D	S97.121D	S99.039G	S99.149K	S99.819D	T18.120D	T20.619D
S91.104D	S91.319D	S93.431D	S95.809D	S97.122D	S99.039K	S99.149P	S99.821D	T18.128D	T20.62XD
S91.105D	S91.321D	S93.432D	S95.811D	S97.129D	S99.039P	S99.191D	S99.822D	T18.190D	T20.63XD
S91.106D	S91.322D	S93.439D	S95.812D	S97.80XD	S99.041D	S99.191G	S99.829D	T18.198D	T20.64XD
S91.109D	S91.329D	S93.491D	S95.819D	S97.81XD	S99.041G	S99.191K	S99.911D	T18.2XXD	T20.65XD
S91.111D	S91.331D	S93.492D	S95.891D	S97.82XD	S99.041K	S99.191P	S99.912D	T18.3XXD	T20.66XD
S91.112D	S91.332D	S93.499D	S95.892D	S98.011D	S99.041P	S99.192D	S99.919D	T18.4XXD	T20.67XD
S91.113D	S91.339D	S93.501D	S95.899D	S98.012D	S99.042D	S99.192G	S99.921D	T18.5XXD	T20.69XD
S91.114D	S91.341D	S93.502D	S95.901D	S98.019D	S99.042G	S99.192K	S99.922D	T18.8XXD	T20.70XD
S91.115D	S91.342D	S93.503D	S95.902D	S98.021D	S99.042K	S99.192P	S99.929D	T18.9XXD	T20.711D
S91.116D	S91.349D	S93.504D	S95.909D	S98.022D	S99.042P	S99.199D		T19.0XXD	T20.712D
S91.119D	S91.351D	S93.505D	S95.911D	S98.029D	S99.049D	S99.199G		T19.1XXD	T20.719D
S91.121D	S91.352D	S93.506D	S95.912D	S98.111D	S99.049G	S99.199K	T07.XXXD	T19.2XXD	T20.72XD
S91.122D	S91.359D	S93.509D	S95.919D	S98.112D	S99.049K	S99.199P	T14.8XXD	T19.3XXD	T20.73XD
S91.123D	S93.01XD	S93.511D	S95.991D	S98.119D	S99.049P	S99.201D	T14.90XD	T19.4XXD	T20.74XD
S91.124D	S93.02XD	S93.512D	S95.992D	S98.121D	S99.091D	S99.201G	T14.91XD	T19.8XXD	T20.75XD
S91.125D	S93.03XD	S93.513D	S95.999D	S98.122D	S99.091G	S99.201K	T15.00XD	T19.9XXD	T20.76XD
S91.126D	S93.04XD	S93.514D	S96.001D	S98.129D	S99.091K	S99.201P	T15.01XD	T20.00XD	T20.77XD
S91.129D	S93.05XD	S93.515D	S96.002D	S98.131D	S99.091P	S99.202D	T15.02XD	T20.011D	T20.79XD
S91.131D	S93.06XD	S93.516D	S96.009D	S98.132D	S99.092D	S99.202G	T15.10XD	T20.012D	T21.00XD
S91.132D	S93.101D	S93.519D	S96.011D	S98.139D	S99.092G	S99.202K	T15.11XD	T20.019D	T21.01XD
S91.133D	S93.102D	S93.521D	S96.012D	S98.141D	S99.092K	S99.202P	T15.12XD	T20.02XD	T21.02XD
S91.134D	S93.103D	S93.522D	S96.019D	S98.142D	S99.092P	S99.209D	T15.80XD	T20.03XD	T21.03XD
S91.135D	S93.104D	S93.523D	S96.021D	S98.149D	S99.099D	S99.209G	T15.81XD	T20.04XD	T21.04XD
S91.136D	S93.105D	S93.524D	S96.022D	S98.211D	S99.099G	S99.209K	T15.82XD	T20.05XD	T21.05XD
S91.139D	S93.106D	S93.525D	S96.029D	S98.212D	S99.099K	S99.209P	T15.90XD	T20.06XD	T21.06XD
S91.141D	S93.111D	S93.526D	S96.091D	S98.219D	S99.099P	S99.211D	T15.91XD	T20.07XD	T21.07XD
S91.142D	S93.112D	S93.529D	S96.092D	S98.221D	S99.101D	S99.211G	T15.92XD	T20.09XD	T21.09XD
S91.143D	S93.113D	S93.601D	S96.099D	S98.222D	S99.101G	S99.211K	T16.1XXD	T20.10XD	T21.10XD
S91.144D	S93.114D	S93.602D	S96.101D	S98.229D	S99.101K	S99.211P	T16.2XXD	T20.111D	T21.11XD
S91.145D	S93.115D	S93.609D	S96.102D	S98.311D	S99.101P	S99.212D	T16.9XXD	T20.112D	T21.12XD
S91.146D	S93.116D	S93.611D	S96.109D	S98.312D	S99.102D	S99.212G	T17.0XXD	T20.119D	T21.13XD
S91.149D	S93.119D	S93.612D	S96.111D	S98.319D	S99.102G	S99.212K	T17.1XXD	T20.12XD	T21.14XD
S91.151D	S93.121D	S93.619D	S96.112D	S98.321D	S99.102K	S99.212P	T17.200D	T20.13XD	T21.15XD
S91.152D	S93.122D	S93.621D	S96.119D	S98.322D	S99.102P	S99.219D	T17.208D	T20.14XD	T21.16XD
S91.153D	S93.123D	S93.622D	S96.121D	S98.329D	S99.109D	S99.219G	T17.210D	T20.15XD	T21.17XD
S91.154D	S93.124D	S93.629D	S96.122D	S98.911D	S99.109G	S99.219P	T17.218D	T20.16XD	T21.20XD
S91.155D	S93.125D	S93.691D	S96.129D	S98.912D	S99.109K	S99.221D	T17.220D	T20.17XD	T21.21XD
S91.156D	S93.126D	S93.692D	S96.191D	S98.919D	S99.109P	S99.221G	T17.228D	T20.19XD	T21.22XD
S91.159D	S93.129D	S93.699D	S96.192D	S98.921D	S99.111D	S99.221K	T17.290D	T20.20XD	T21.23XD
S91.201D	S93.131D	S94.00XD	S96.199D	S98.922D	S99.111D		T17.298D	T20.211D	

T21.24XD	T22.152D	T22.549D	T23.119D	T23.432D	T23.751D	T24.499D	T25.322D	T27.0XXD	T34.70XD
T21.25XD	T22.159D	T22.551D	T23.121D	T23.439D	T23.752D	T24.501D	T25.329D	T27.1XXD	T34.71XD
T21.26XD	T22.161D	T22.552D	T23.122D	T23.441D	T23.759D	T24.502D	T25.331D	T27.2XXD	T34.72XD
T21.27XD	T22.162D	T22.559D	T23.129D	T23.442D	T23.761D	T24.509D	T25.332D	T27.3XXD	T34.811D
T21.29XD	T22.169D	T22.561D	T23.131D	T23.449D	T23.762D	T24.511D	T25.339D	T27.4XXD	T34.812D
T21.30XD	T22.191D	T22.562D	T23.132D	T23.451D	T23.769D	T24.512D	T25.391D	T27.5XXD	T34.819D
T21.31XD	T22.192D	T22.569D	T23.139D	T23.452D	T23.771D	T24.519D	T25.392D	T27.6XXD	T34.821D
T21.32XD	T22.199D	T22.591D	T23.141D	T23.459D	T23.772D	T24.521D	T25.399D	T27.7XXD	T34.822D
T21.33XD	T22.20XD	T22.592D	T23.142D	T23.461D	T23.779D	T24.522D	T25.411D	T28.0XXD	T34.829D
T21.34XD	T22.211D	T22.599D	T23.149D	T23.462D	T23.791D	T24.529D	T25.412D	T28.1XXD	T34.831D
T21.35XD	T22.212D	T22.60XD	T23.151D	T23.469D	T23.792D	T24.531D	T25.419D	T28.2XXD	T34.832D
T21.36XD	T22.219D	T22.611D	T23.152D	T23.471D	T23.799D	T24.532D	T25.421D	T28.3XXD	T34.839D
T21.37XD	T22.221D	T22.612D	T23.159D	T23.472D	T24.001D	T24.539D	T25.422D	T28.40XD	T34.90XD
T21.39XD	T22.222D	T22.619D	T23.161D	T23.479D	T24.002D	T24.591D	T25.429D	T28.411D	T34.99XD
T21.40XD	T22.229D	T22.621D	T23.162D	T23.491D	T24.009D	T24.592D	T25.431D	T28.412D	T36.0X1D
T21.41XD	T22.231D	T22.622D	T23.169D	T23.492D	T24.011D	T24.599D	T25.432D	T28.419D	T36.0X2D
T21.42XD	T22.232D	T22.629D	T23.171D	T23.499D	T24.012D	T24.601D	T25.439D	T28.49XD	T36.0X3D
T21.43XD	T22.239D	T22.631D	T23.172D	T23.501D	T24.019D	T24.602D	T25.491D	T28.5XXD	T36.0X4D
T21.44XD	T22.241D	T22.632D	T23.179D	T23.502D	T24.021D	T24.609D	T25.492D	T28.6XXD	T36.0X5D
T21.45XD	T22.242D	T22.639D	T23.191D	T23.509D	T24.022D	T24.611D	T25.499D	T28.7XXD	T36.0X6A
T21.46XD	T22.249D	T22.641D	T23.192D	T23.511D	T24.029D	T24.612D	T25.511D	T28.8XXD	T36.0X6D
T21.47XD	T22.251D	T22.642D	T23.199D	T23.512D	T24.031D	T24.619D	T25.512D	T28.90XD	T36.0X6S
T21.49XD	T22.252D	T22.649D	T23.201D	T23.519D	T24.032D	T24.621D	T25.519D	T28.911D	T36.1X1D
T21.50XD	T22.259D	T22.651D	T23.202D	T23.521D	T24.039D	T24.622D	T25.521D	T28.912D	T36.1X2D
T21.51XD	T22.261D	T22.652D	T23.209D	T23.522D	T24.091D	T24.629D	T25.522D	T28.919D	T36.1X3D
T21.52XD	T22.262D	T22.659D	T23.211D	T23.529D	T24.092D	T24.631D	T25.529D	T28.99XD	T36.1X4D
T21.53XD	T22.269D	T22.661D	T23.212D	T23.531D	T24.099D	T24.632D	T25.531D	T33.011D	T36.1X5D
T21.54XD	T22.291D	T22.662D	T23.219D	T23.532D	T24.101D	T24.639D	T25.532D	T33.012D	T36.1X6A
T21.55XD	T22.292D	T22.669D	T23.221D	T23.539D	T24.102D	T24.691D	T25.539D	T33.019D	T36.1X6D
T21.56XD	T22.299D	T22.691D	T23.222D	T23.541D	T24.109D	T24.692D	T25.591D	T33.02XD	T36.1X6S
T21.57XD	T22.30XD	T22.692D	T23.229D	T23.542D	T24.111D	T24.699D	T25.592D	T33.09XD	T36.2X1D
T21.59XD	T22.311D	T22.699D	T23.231D	T23.549D	T24.112D	T24.701D	T25.599D	T33.1XXD	T36.2X2D
T21.60XD	T22.312D	T22.70XD	T23.232D	T23.551D	T24.119D	T24.702D	T25.611D	T33.2XXD	T36.2X3D
T21.61XD	T22.319D	T22.711D	T23.239D	T23.552D	T24.121D	T24.709D	T25.612D	T33.3XXD	T36.2X4D
T21.62XD	T22.321D	T22.712D	T23.241D	T23.559D	T24.122D	T24.711D	T25.619D	T33.40XD	T36.2X5D
T21.63XD	T22.322D	T22.719D	T23.242D	T23.561D	T24.129D	T24.712D	T25.621D	T33.41XD	T36.2X6A
T21.64XD	T22.329D	T22.721D	T23.249D	T23.562D	T24.131D	T24.719D	T25.622D	T33.42XD	T36.2X6D
T21.65XD	T22.331D	T22.722D	T23.251D	T23.569D	T24.132D	T24.721D	T25.629D	T33.511D	T36.2X6S
T21.66XD	T22.332D	T22.729D	T23.252D	T23.571D	T24.139D	T24.722D	T25.631D	T33.512D	T36.3X1D
T21.67XD	T22.339D	T22.731D	T23.259D	T23.572D	T24.191D	T24.729D	T25.632D	T33.519D	T36.3X2D
T21.69XD	T22.341D	T22.732D	T23.261D	T23.579D	T24.192D	T24.731D	T25.639D	T33.521D	T36.3X3D
T21.70XD	T22.342D	T22.739D	T23.262D	T23.591D	T24.199D	T24.732D	T25.691D	T33.522D	T36.3X4D
T21.71XD	T22.349D	T22.741D	T23.269D	T23.592D	T24.201D	T24.739D	T25.692D	T33.529D	T36.3X5D
T21.72XD	T22.351D	T22.742D	T23.271D	T23.599D	T24.202D	T24.791D	T25.699D	T33.531D	T36.3X6A
T21.73XD	T22.352D	T22.749D	T23.272D	T23.601D	T24.209D	T24.792D	T25.711D	T33.532D	T36.3X6D
T21.74XD	T22.359D	T22.751D	T23.279D	T23.602D	T24.211D	T24.799D	T25.712D	T33.539D	T36.3X6S
T21.75XD	T22.361D	T22.752D	T23.291D	T23.609D	T24.212D	T25.011D	T25.719D	T33.60XD	T36.4X1D
T21.76XD	T22.362D	T22.759D	T23.292D	T23.611D	T24.219D	T25.012D	T25.721D	T33.61XD	T36.4X2D
T21.77XD	T22.369D	T22.761D	T23.299D	T23.612D	T24.221D	T25.019D	T25.722D	T33.62XD	T36.4X3D
T21.79XD	T22.391D	T22.762D	T23.301D	T23.619D	T24.222D	T25.021D	T25.729D	T33.70XD	T36.4X4D
T22.00XD	T22.392D	T22.769D	T23.302D	T23.621D	T24.229D	T25.022D	T25.731D	T33.71XD	T36.4X5D
T22.011D	T22.399D	T22.791D	T23.309D	T23.622D	T24.231D	T25.029D	T25.732D	T33.72XD	T36.4X6A
T22.012D	T22.40XD	T22.792D	T23.311D	T23.629D	T24.232D	T25.031D	T25.739D	T33.811D	T36.4X6D
T22.019D	T22.411D	T22.799D	T23.312D	T23.631D	T24.239D	T25.032D	T25.791D	T33.812D	T36.4X6S
T22.021D	T22.412D	T23.001D	T23.319D	T23.632D	T24.291D	T25.039D	T25.792D	T33.819D	T36.5X1D
T22.022D	T22.419D	T23.002D	T23.321D	T23.639D	T24.292D	T25.091D	T25.799D	T33.821D	T36.5X2D
T22.029D	T22.421D	T23.009D	T23.322D	T23.641D	T24.299D	T25.092D	T26.00XD	T33.822D	T36.5X3D
T22.031D	T22.422D	T23.011D	T23.329D	T23.642D	T24.301D	T25.099D	T26.01XD	T33.829D	T36.5X4D
T22.032D	T22.429D	T23.012D	T23.331D	T23.649D	T24.309D	T25.111D	T26.02XD	T33.831D	T36.5X5D
T22.039D	T22.431D	T23.019D	T23.332D	T23.651D	T24.311D	T25.112D	T26.10XD	T33.832D	T36.5X6A
T22.041D	T22.432D	T23.021D	T23.339D	T23.652D	T24.312D	T25.119D	T26.11XD	T33.839D	T36.5X6D
T22.042D	T22.439D	T23.022D	T23.341D	T23.659D	T24.319D	T25.121D	T26.12XD	T33.90XD	T36.5X6S
T22.049D	T22.441D	T23.029D	T23.342D	T23.661D	T24.321D	T25.122D	T26.20XD	T33.99XD	T36.6X1D
T22.051D	T22.442D	T23.031D	T23.349D	T23.662D	T24.322D	T25.129D	T26.21XD	T34.011D	T36.6X2D
T22.052D	T22.449D	T23.032D	T23.351D	T23.669D	T24.329D	T25.131D	T26.22XD	T34.012D	T36.6X3D
T22.059D	T22.451D	T23.039D	T23.352D	T23.671D	T24.331D	T25.132D	T26.30XD	T34.019D	T36.6X4D
T22.061D	T22.452D	T23.041D	T23.359D	T23.672D	T24.339D	T25.139D	T26.31XD	T34.02XD	T36.6X5D
T22.062D	T22.459D	T23.042D	T23.361D	T23.679D	T24.332D	T25.191D	T26.32XD	T34.09XD	T36.6X6A
T22.069D	T22.461D	T23.049D	T23.362D	T23.691D	T24.339D	T25.192D	T26.40XD	T34.1XXD	T36.6X6D
T22.091D	T22.462D	T23.051D	T23.369D	T23.692D	T24.391D	T25.199D	T26.41XD	T34.2XXD	T36.6X6S
T22.092D	T22.469D	T23.052D	T23.371D	T23.699D	T24.392D	T25.211D	T26.42XD	T34.3XXD	T36.7X1D
T22.099D	T22.491D	T23.059D	T23.372D	T23.701D	T24.399D	T25.212D	T26.50XD	T34.40XD	T36.7X2D
T22.10XD	T22.492D	T23.061D	T23.379D	T23.702D	T24.401D	T25.219D	T26.51XD	T34.41XD	T36.7X3D
T22.111D	T22.499D	T23.062D	T23.391D	T23.709D	T24.402D	T25.221D	T26.52XD	T34.42XD	T36.7X4D
T22.112D	T22.50XD	T23.069D	T23.392D	T23.711D	T24.409D	T25.222D	T26.60XD	T34.511D	T36.7X5D
T22.119D	T22.511D	T23.071D	T23.399D	T23.712D	T24.411D	T25.229D	T26.61XD	T34.512D	T36.7X6A
T22.121D	T22.512D	T23.072D	T23.401D	T23.719D	T24.412D	T25.231D	T26.62XD	T34.519D	T36.7X6D
T22.122D	T22.519D	T23.079D	T23.402D	T23.721D	T24.419D	T25.232D	T26.70XD	T34.521D	T36.7X6S
T22.129D	T22.521D	T23.091D	T23.409D	T23.722D	T24.421D	T25.239D	T26.71XD	T34.522D	T36.8X1D
T22.131D	T22.522D	T23.092D	T23.411D	T23.729D	T24.422D	T25.291D	T26.72XD	T34.529D	T36.8X2D
T22.132D	T22.529D	T23.099D	T23.412D	T23.731D	T24.429D	T25.292D	T26.80XD	T34.531D	T36.8X3D
T22.139D	T22.531D	T23.101D	T23.419D	T23.732D	T24.431D	T25.299D	T26.81XD	T34.532D	T36.8X4D
T22.141D	T22.532D	T23.102D	T23.421D	T23.739D	T24.432D	T25.311D	T26.82XD	T34.539D	T36.8X5D
T22.142D	T22.539D	T23.109D	T23.422D	T23.741D	T24.439D	T25.312D	T26.90XD	T34.60XD	T36.8X6A
T22.149D	T22.541D	T23.111D	T23.429D	T23.742D	T24.491D	T25.319D	T26.91XD	T34.61XD	T36.8X6D
T22.151D	T22.542D	T23.112D	T23.431D	T23.749D	T24.492D	T25.321D	T26.92XD	T34.62XD	T36.8X6S

T36.91XD	T38.1X6D	T38.995D	T40.1X3D	T41.1X1D	T42.4X6D	T43.295D	T43.8X6D	T44.905D	T45.623D
T36.92XD	T38.1X6S	T38.996A	T40.1X4D	T41.1X2D	T42.4X6S	T43.296A	T43.8X6S	T44.906A	T45.624D
T36.93XD	T38.2X1D	T38.996D	T40.2X1D	T41.1X3D	T42.5X1D	T43.296D	T43.91XD	T44.906D	T45.625D
T36.94XD	T38.2X2D	T38.996S	T40.2X2D	T41.1X4D	T42.5X2D	T43.296S	T43.92XD	T44.906S	T45.626A
T36.95XD	T38.2X3D	T39.011D	T40.2X3D	T41.1X5D	T42.5X3D	T43.3X1D	T43.93XD	T44.991D	T45.626D
T36.96XA	T38.2X4D	T39.012D	T40.2X4D	T41.1X6A	T42.5X4D	T43.3X2D	T43.94XD	T44.992D	T45.626S
T36.96XD	T38.2X5D	T39.013D	T40.2X5D	T41.1X6D	T42.5X5D	T43.3X3D	T43.95XD	T44.993D	T45.691D
T36.96XS	T38.2X6A	T39.014D	T40.2X6A	T41.1X6S	T42.5X6A	T43.3X4D	T43.96XA	T44.994D	T45.692D
T37.0X1D	T38.2X6D	T39.015D	T40.2X6D	T41.201D	T42.5X6D	T43.3X5D	T43.96XD	T44.995D	T45.693D
T37.0X2D	T38.2X6S	T39.016A	T40.2X6S	T41.202D	T42.5X6S	T43.3X6A	T43.96XS	T44.996A	T45.694D
T37.0X3D	T38.3X1D	T39.016D	T40.3X1D	T41.203D	T42.6X1D	T43.3X6D	T44.0X1D	T44.996D	T45.695D
T37.0X4D	T38.3X2D	T39.016D	T40.3X2D	T41.204D	T42.6X2D	T43.3X6S	T44.0X2D	T44.996S	T45.696A
T37.0X5D	T38.3X3D	T39.091D	T40.3X3D	T41.205D	T42.6X3D	T43.4X1D	T44.0X3D	T45.0X1D	T45.696D
T37.0X6A	T38.3X4D	T39.092D	T40.3X4D	T41.206A	T42.6X4D	T43.4X2D	T44.0X4D	T45.0X2D	T45.696S
T37.0X6D	T38.3X5D	T39.093D	T40.3X5D	T41.206D	T42.6X5D	T43.4X3D	T44.0X5D	T45.0X3D	T45.7X1D
T37.0X6S	T38.3X6A	T39.094D	T40.3X6A	T41.206S	T42.6X6A	T43.4X4D	T44.0X6A	T45.0X4D	T45.7X2D
T37.1X1D	T38.3X6D	T39.095D	T40.3X6D	T41.291D	T42.6X6D	T43.4X5D	T44.0X6D	T45.0X5D	T45.7X3D
T37.1X2D	T38.3X6S	T39.096A	T40.3X6S	T41.292D	T42.6X6S	T43.4X6A	T44.0X6S	T45.0X6A	T45.7X4D
T37.1X3D	T38.4X1D	T39.096D	T40.4X1D	T41.293D	T42.71XD	T43.4X6D	T44.1X1D	T45.0X6D	T45.7X5D
T37.1X4D	T38.4X2D	T39.096S	T40.4X2D	T41.294D	T42.72XD	T43.4X6S	T44.1X2D	T45.0X6S	T45.7X6A
T37.1X5D	T38.4X3D	T39.1X1D	T40.4X3D	T41.295D	T42.73XD	T43.501D	T44.1X3D	T45.1X1D	T45.7X6D
T37.1X6A	T38.4X4D	T39.1X2D	T40.4X4D	T41.296A	T42.74XD	T43.502D	T44.1X4D	T45.1X2D	T45.7X6S
T37.1X6D	T38.4X5D	T39.1X3D	T40.4X5D	T41.296D	T42.75XD	T43.503D	T44.1X5D	T45.1X3D	T45.8X1D
T37.1X6S	T38.4X6A	T39.1X4D	T40.4X6A	T41.296S	T42.76XA	T43.504D	T44.1X6A	T45.1X4D	T45.8X2D
T37.2X1D	T38.4X6D	T39.1X5D	T40.4X6D	T41.3X1D	T42.76XD	T43.505D	T44.1X6D	T45.1X5D	T45.8X3D
T37.2X2D	T38.4X6S	T39.1X6A	T40.4X6S	T41.3X2D	T42.76XS	T43.506A	T44.1X6S	T45.1X6A	T45.8X4D
T37.2X3D	T38.5X1D	T39.1X6D	T40.5X1D	T41.3X3D	T42.8X1D	T43.506D	T44.2X1D	T45.1X6D	T45.8X6A
T37.2X4D	T38.5X2D	T39.1X6S	T40.5X2D	T41.3X4D	T42.8X2D	T43.506S	T44.2X2D	T45.1X6S	T45.8X6D
T37.2X5D	T38.5X3D	T39.2X1D	T40.5X3D	T41.3X5D	T42.8X3D	T43.591D	T44.2X3D	T45.2X1D	T45.91XD
T37.2X6A	T38.5X4D	T39.2X2D	T40.5X4D	T41.3X6A	T42.8X4D	T43.592D	T44.2X4D	T45.2X2D	T45.92XD
T37.2X6D	T38.5X5D	T39.2X3D	T40.5X5D	T41.3X6D	T42.8X5D	T43.593D	T44.2X5D	T45.2X3D	T45.93XD
T37.2X6S	T38.5X6D	T39.2X4D	T40.5X6A	T41.3X6S	T42.8X6A	T43.594D	T44.2X6A	T45.2X4D	T45.94XD
T37.3X1D	T38.5X6S	T39.2X5D	T40.5X6D	T41.41XD	T42.8X6D	T43.595D	T44.2X6D	T45.2X5D	T45.95XD
T37.3X2D	T38.6X1D	T39.2X6A	T40.5X6S	T41.42XD	T42.8X6S	T43.596A	T44.2X6S	T45.2X6A	T45.96XA
T37.3X3D	T38.6X2D	T39.2X6S	T40.601D	T41.43XD	T43.011D	T43.596D	T44.3X1D	T45.2X6D	T45.96XD
T37.3X4D	T38.6X3D	T39.311D	T40.602D	T41.44XD	T43.012D	T43.596S	T44.3X2D	T45.2X6S	T45.96XS
T37.3X5D	T38.6X4D	T39.312D	T40.603D	T41.45XD	T43.013D	T43.601D	T44.3X3D	T45.3X1D	T46.0X1D
T37.3X6A	T38.6X5D	T39.313D	T40.604D	T41.46XA	T43.014D	T43.602D	T44.3X4D	T45.3X2D	T46.0X2D
T37.3X6D	T38.6X6A	T39.314D	T40.605D	T41.46XD	T43.015D	T43.603D	T44.3X5D	T45.3X3D	T46.0X3D
T37.3X6S	T38.6X6D	T39.315D	T40.606A	T41.46XS	T43.016A	T43.604D	T44.3X6A	T45.3X4D	T46.0X4D
T37.4X1D	T38.6X6S	T39.316A	T40.606D	T41.5X1D	T43.016D	T43.605D	T44.3X6D	T45.3X5D	T46.0X5D
T37.4X2D	T38.7X1D	T39.316D	T40.606S	T41.5X2D	T43.016S	T43.606A	T44.3X6S	T45.3X6A	T46.0X6A
T37.4X3D	T38.7X2D	T39.316S	T40.691D	T41.5X3D	T43.021D	T43.606D	T44.4X1D	T45.3X6D	T46.0X6D
T37.4X4D	T38.7X3D	T39.391D	T40.692D	T41.5X4D	T43.022D	T43.606S	T44.4X2D	T45.3X6S	T46.0X6S
T37.4X6A	T38.7X4D	T39.392D	T40.693D	T41.5X5D	T43.023D	T43.611D	T44.4X3D	T45.4X1D	T46.1X1D
T37.4X6D	T38.7X5D	T39.393D	T40.694D	T41.5X6A	T43.024D	T43.612D	T44.4X4D	T45.4X2D	T46.1X2D
T37.4X6S	T38.7X6A	T39.394D	T40.695D	T41.5X6D	T43.025D	T43.613D	T44.4X5D	T45.4X3D	T46.1X3D
T37.5X1D	T38.7X6D	T39.395D	T40.696A	T41.5X6S	T43.026A	T43.614D	T44.4X6A	T45.4X4D	T46.1X4D
T37.5X2D	T38.7X6S	T39.396A	T40.696S	T42.0X1D	T43.026D	T43.615D	T44.4X6D	T45.4X5D	T46.1X5D
T37.5X3D	T38.801D	T39.396D	T40.7X1D	T42.0X2D	T43.026S	T43.616A	T44.4X6S	T45.4X6A	T46.1X6A
T37.5X4D	T38.802D	T39.396S	T40.7X2D	T42.0X3D	T43.1X1D	T43.616D	T44.5X1D	T45.4X6D	T46.1X6D
T37.5X5D	T38.803D	T39.4X1D	T40.7X3D	T42.0X4D	T43.1X2D	T43.616S	T44.5X2D	T45.4X6S	T46.1X6S
T37.5X6A	T38.804D	T39.4X2D	T40.7X4D	T42.0X5D	T43.1X3D	T43.621D	T44.5X3D	T45.511D	T46.2X1D
T37.5X6D	T38.805D	T39.4X3D	T40.7X5D	T42.0X6A	T43.1X4D	T43.622D	T44.5X4D	T45.512D	T46.2X2D
T37.5X6S	T38.806A	T39.4X4D	T40.7X6A	T42.0X6D	T43.1X5D	T43.623D	T44.5X5D	T45.513D	T46.2X3D
T37.8X1D	T38.806D	T39.4X5D	T40.7X6D	T42.0X6S	T43.1X6A	T43.624D	T44.5X6A	T45.514D	T46.2X4D
T37.8X2D	T38.806S	T39.4X6A	T40.7X6S	T42.1X1D	T43.1X6D	T43.625D	T44.5X6D	T45.515D	T46.2X5D
T37.8X3D	T38.811D	T39.4X6D	T40.8X1D	T42.1X2D	T43.1X6S	T43.626A	T44.5X6S	T45.516A	T46.2X6A
T37.8X4D	T38.812D	T39.4X6S	T40.8X2D	T42.1X3D	T43.201D	T43.626D	T44.6X1D	T45.516D	T46.2X6D
T37.8X5D	T38.813D	T39.8X1D	T40.8X3D	T42.1X4D	T43.202D	T43.626S	T44.6X2D	T45.516S	T46.2X6S
T37.8X6A	T38.814D	T39.8X2D	T40.8X4D	T42.1X5D	T43.203D	T43.631D	T44.6X3D	T45.521D	T46.3X1D
T37.8X6D	T38.815D	T39.8X3D	T40.901D	T42.1X6A	T43.204D	T43.632D	T44.6X4D	T45.522D	T46.3X2D
T37.8X6S	T38.816A	T39.8X4D	T40.902D	T42.1X6D	T43.205D	T43.633D	T44.6X5D	T45.523D	T46.3X3D
T37.91XD	T38.816D	T39.8X5D	T40.903D	T42.1X6S	T43.206A	T43.634D	T44.6X6A	T45.524D	T46.3X4D
T37.92XD	T38.816S	T39.8X6A	T40.904D	T42.2X1D	T43.206D	T43.635D	T44.6X6D	T45.525D	T46.3X5D
T37.93XD	T38.891D	T39.8X6D	T40.905D	T42.2X2D	T43.206S	T43.636A	T44.6X6S	T45.526A	T46.3X6D
T37.94XD	T38.892D	T39.8X6S	T40.906A	T42.2X3D	T43.211D	T43.636D	T44.7X1D	T45.526D	T46.3X6S
T37.95XD	T38.893D	T39.91XD	T40.906D	T42.2X4D	T43.212D	T43.636S	T44.7X2D	T45.526S	T46.4X1D
T37.96XA	T38.894D	T39.92XD	T40.906S	T42.2X5D	T43.213D	T43.641D	T44.7X3D	T45.601D	T46.4X2D
T37.96XD	T38.895D	T39.93XD	T40.991D	T42.2X6A	T43.214D	T43.642D	T44.7X4D	T45.602D	T46.4X3D
T37.96XS	T38.896A	T39.94XD	T40.992D	T42.2X6D	T43.215D	T43.643D	T44.7X5D	T45.603D	T46.4X4D
T38.0X1D	T38.896D	T39.95XD	T40.993D	T42.2X6S	T43.216A	T43.644D	T44.7X6A	T45.604D	T46.4X5D
T38.0X2D	T38.896S	T39.96XA	T40.994D	T42.3X1D	T43.216D	T43.691D	T44.7X6D	T45.605D	T46.4X6A
T38.0X3D	T38.901D	T39.96XD	T40.995D	T42.3X2D	T43.216S	T43.692D	T44.7X6S	T45.606A	T46.4X6D
T38.0X4D	T38.902D	T39.96XS	T40.996A	T42.3X3D	T43.221D	T43.693D	T44.8X1D	T45.606D	T46.4X6S
T38.0X5D	T38.903D	T40.0X1D	T40.996D	T42.3X4D	T43.222D	T43.694D	T44.8X2D	T45.606S	T46.5X1D
T38.0X6A	T38.904D	T40.0X2D	T40.996S	T42.3X5D	T43.223D	T43.695D	T44.8X3D	T45.611D	T46.5X2D
T38.0X6D	T38.905D	T40.0X3D	T41.0X1D	T42.3X6A	T43.224D	T43.696A	T44.8X4D	T45.612D	T46.5X3D
T38.0X6S	T38.906A	T40.0X4D	T41.0X2D	T42.3X6D	T43.225D	T43.696D	T44.8X5D	T45.613D	T46.5X4D
T38.1X1D	T38.906D	T40.0X5D	T41.0X3D	T42.3X6S	T43.226A	T43.696S	T44.8X6A	T45.614D	T46.5X5D
T38.1X2D	T38.906S	T40.0X6A	T41.0X4D	T42.4X1D	T43.226D	T43.8X1D	T44.8X6S	T45.615D	T46.5X6A
T38.1X3D	T38.991D	T40.0X6D	T41.0X5D	T42.4X2D	T43.226S	T43.8X2D	T44.901D	T45.616A	T46.5X6D
T38.1X4D	T38.992D	T40.0X6S	T41.0X6A	T42.4X3D	T43.291D	T43.8X3D	T44.902D	T45.616D	T46.5X6S
T38.1X5D	T38.993D	T40.1X1D	T41.0X6D	T42.4X4D	T43.292D	T43.8X4D	T44.903D	T45.616S	
T38.1X6A	T38.994D	T40.1X2D	T41.0X6S	T42.4X5D	T43.293D	T43.8X5D	T44.904D	T45.621D	
				T42.4X6A	T43.294D	T43.8X6A		T45.622D	

T46.6X1D	T47.5X6D	T48.5X5D	T49.7X3D	T50.8X1D	T50.Z96S	T53.92XD	T57.2X4D	T60.2X2D	T63.064D
T46.6X2D	T47.5X6S	T48.5X6A	T49.7X4D	T50.8X2D	T51.0X1D	T53.93XD	T57.3X1D	T60.2X3D	T63.071D
T46.6X3D	T47.6X1D	T48.5X6D	T49.7X5D	T50.8X3D	T51.0X3D	T53.94XD	T57.3X3D	T60.2X4D	T63.072D
T46.6X4D	T47.6X2D	T48.5X6S	T49.7X6A	T50.8X4D	T51.0X4D	T54.0X1D	T57.3X4D	T60.3X1D	T63.073D
T46.6X5D	T47.6X3D	T48.6X1D	T49.7X6D	T50.8X5D	T51.1X1D	T54.0X2D	T57.8X1D	T60.3X2D	T63.074D
T46.6X6A	T47.6X4D	T48.6X2D	T49.7X6S	T50.8X6A	T51.1X2D	T54.0X3D	T57.8X2D	T60.3X3D	T63.081D
T46.6X6D	T47.6X5D	T48.6X3D	T49.8X1D	T50.8X6D	T51.1X3D	T54.0X4D	T57.8X4D	T60.3X4D	T63.082D
T46.6X6S	T47.6X6A	T48.6X4D	T49.8X2D	T50.8X6S	T51.1X4D	T54.1X1D	T57.91XD	T60.4X1D	T63.083D
T46.7X1D	T47.6X6D	T48.6X5D	T49.8X3D	T50.901D	T51.2X1D	T54.1X2D	T57.92XD	T60.4X2D	T63.084D
T46.7X2D	T47.6X6S	T48.6X6A	T49.8X4D	T50.902D	T51.2X2D	T54.1X3D	T57.93XD	T60.4X3D	T63.091D
T46.7X3D	T47.7X1D	T48.6X6D	T49.8X5D	T50.903D	T51.2X3D	T54.1X4D	T57.94XD	T60.4X4D	T63.092D
T46.7X4D	T47.7X2D	T48.6X6S	T49.8X6A	T50.904D	T51.2X4D	T54.2X1D	T58.01XD	T60.8X1D	T63.093D
T46.7X5D	T47.7X3D	T48.901D	T49.8X6D	T50.905D	T51.3X1D	T54.2X2D	T58.02XD	T60.8X2D	T63.094D
T46.7X6A	T47.7X4D	T48.902D	T49.8X6S	T50.906A	T51.3X2D	T54.2X3D	T58.03XD	T60.8X3D	T63.111D
T46.7X6D	T47.7X5D	T48.903D	T49.91XD	T50.906D	T51.3X3D	T54.2X4D	T58.04XD	T60.8X4D	T63.112D
T46.7X6S	T47.7X6A	T48.904D	T49.92XD	T50.906S	T51.3X4D	T54.3X1D	T58.11XD	T60.91XD	T63.113D
T46.8X1D	T47.7X6D	T48.905D	T49.93XD	T50.911D	T51.8X1D	T54.3X2D	T58.12XD	T60.92XD	T63.114D
T46.8X2D	T47.7X6S	T48.906A	T49.94XD	T50.912D	T51.8X2D	T54.3X3D	T58.13XD	T60.93XD	T63.121D
T46.8X3D	T47.8X1D	T48.906D	T49.95XD	T50.913D	T51.8X3D	T54.3X4D	T58.14XD	T60.94XD	T63.122D
T46.8X4D	T47.8X2D	T48.906S	T49.96XA	T50.914D	T51.8X4D	T54.91XD	T58.2X1D	T61.01XD	T63.123D
T46.8X5D	T47.8X3D	T48.991D	T49.96XD	T50.915D	T51.91XD	T54.92XD	T58.2X2D	T61.02XD	T63.124D
T46.8X6A	T47.8X4D	T48.992D	T49.96XS	T50.916A	T51.92XD	T54.93XD	T58.2X3D	T61.03XD	T63.191D
T46.8X6D	T47.8X5D	T48.993D	T50.0X1D	T50.916D	T51.93XD	T54.94XD	T58.2X4D	T61.04XD	T63.192D
T46.8X6S	T47.8X6A	T48.994D	T50.0X2D	T50.991D	T51.94XD	T55.0X1D	T58.8X1D	T61.11XD	T63.193D
T46.901D	T47.8X6D	T48.995D	T50.0X3D	T50.992D	T52.0X1D	T55.0X2D	T58.8X2D	T61.12XD	T63.194D
T46.902D	T47.8X6S	T48.996A	T50.0X4D	T50.993D	T52.0X2D	T55.0X3D	T58.8X3D	T61.13XD	T63.2X1D
T46.903D	T47.91XD	T48.996D	T50.0X5D	T50.994D	T52.0X3D	T55.0X4D	T58.8X4D	T61.14XD	T63.2X2D
T46.904D	T47.92XD	T48.996S	T50.0X6A	T50.995D	T52.0X4D	T55.1X1D	T58.91XD	T61.771D	T63.2X3D
T46.905D	T47.93XD	T49.0X1D	T50.0X6D	T50.996A	T52.1X1D	T55.1X2D	T58.92XD	T61.772D	T63.2X4D
T46.906A	T47.94XD	T49.0X2D	T50.0X6S	T50.996D	T52.1X2D	T55.1X3D	T58.93XD	T61.773D	T63.301D
T46.906D	T47.95XD	T49.0X3D	T50.1X1D	T50.996S	T52.1X3D	T55.1X4D	T58.94XD	T61.774D	T63.302D
T46.906S	T47.96XA	T49.0X4D	T50.1X2D	T50.A11D	T52.1X4D	T56.0X1D	T59.0X1D	T61.781D	T63.303D
T46.991D	T47.96XD	T49.0X5D	T50.1X3D	T50.A12D	T52.2X1D	T56.0X2D	T59.0X2D	T61.782D	T63.304D
T46.992D	T47.96XS	T49.0X6A	T50.1X4D	T50.A13D	T52.2X2D	T56.0X3D	T59.0X4D	T61.783D	T63.311D
T46.993D	T48.0X1D	T49.0X6D	T50.1X5D	T50.A14D	T52.2X3D	T56.0X4D	T59.1X1D	T61.784D	T63.312D
T46.994D	T48.0X2D	T49.0X6S	T50.1X6D	T50.A15D	T52.2X4D	T56.1X1D	T59.1X2D	T61.8X1D	T63.313D
T46.995D	T48.0X3D	T49.1X1D	T50.1X6S	T50.A16A	T52.3X1D	T56.1X2D	T59.1X3D	T61.8X2D	T63.314D
T46.996A	T48.0X4D	T49.1X2D	T50.2X1D	T50.A16D	T52.3X2D	T56.1X3D	T59.1X4D	T61.8X3D	T63.321D
T46.996D	T48.0X5D	T49.1X3D	T50.2X2D	T50.A16S	T52.3X3D	T56.1X4D	T59.2X1D	T61.8X4D	T63.322D
T46.996S	T48.0X6A	T49.1X4D	T50.2X3D	T50.A21D	T52.3X4D	T56.2X1D	T59.2X2D	T61.91XD	T63.323D
T47.0X1D	T48.0X6D	T49.1X5D	T50.2X4D	T50.A22D	T52.4X1D	T56.2X2D	T59.2X3D	T61.92XD	T63.324D
T47.0X2D	T48.0X6S	T49.1X6A	T50.2X5D	T50.A23D	T52.4X2D	T56.2X3D	T59.2X4D	T61.93XD	T63.331D
T47.0X3D	T48.1X1D	T49.1X6D	T50.2X6A	T50.A24D	T52.4X3D	T56.2X4D	T59.3X1D	T61.94XD	T63.332D
T47.0X4D	T48.1X2D	T49.1X6S	T50.2X6D	T50.A25D	T52.4X4D	T56.3X1D	T59.3X2D	T62.0X1D	T63.333D
T47.0X5D	T48.1X3D	T49.2X1D	T50.2X6S	T50.A26A	T52.8X1D	T56.3X2D	T59.3X3D	T62.0X2D	T63.334D
T47.0X6A	T48.1X4D	T49.2X2D	T50.3X1D	T50.A26D	T52.8X2D	T56.3X3D	T59.3X4D	T62.0X3D	T63.391D
T47.0X6D	T48.1X5D	T49.2X3D	T50.3X2D	T50.A26S	T52.8X3D	T56.3X4D	T59.4X1D	T62.0X4D	T63.392D
T47.0X6S	T48.1X6A	T49.2X4D	T50.3X3D	T50.A91D	T52.8X4D	T56.4X1D	T59.4X2D	T62.1X1D	T63.393D
T47.1X1D	T48.1X6D	T49.2X5D	T50.3X4D	T50.A92D	T52.91XD	T56.4X2D	T59.4X3D	T62.1X2D	T63.394D
T47.1X2D	T48.1X6S	T49.2X6A	T50.3X5D	T50.A93D	T52.92XD	T56.4X3D	T59.4X4D	T62.1X3D	T63.411D
T47.1X3D	T48.201D	T49.2X6D	T50.3X6A	T50.A94D	T52.93XD	T56.4X4D	T59.5X1D	T62.1X4D	T63.412D
T47.1X4D	T48.202D	T49.2X6S	T50.3X6D	T50.A95D	T52.94XD	T56.5X1D	T59.5X2D	T62.2X1D	T63.413D
T47.1X5D	T48.203D	T49.3X1D	T50.3X6S	T50.A96A	T53.0X1D	T56.5X2D	T59.5X3D	T62.2X2D	T63.414D
T47.1X6A	T48.204D	T49.3X2D	T50.4X1D	T50.A96D	T53.0X2D	T56.5X3D	T59.5X4D	T62.2X3D	T63.421D
T47.1X6D	T48.205D	T49.3X3D	T50.4X2D	T50.A96S	T53.0X3D	T56.5X4D	T59.6X1D	T62.2X4D	T63.422D
T47.1X6S	T48.206A	T49.3X4D	T50.4X3D	T50.B11D	T53.0X4D	T56.6X1D	T59.6X2D	T62.8X1D	T63.423D
T47.2X1D	T48.206D	T49.3X5D	T50.4X4D	T50.B12D	T53.1X1D	T56.6X2D	T59.6X3D	T62.8X2D	T63.424D
T47.2X2D	T48.206S	T49.3X6A	T50.4X5D	T50.B13D	T53.1X2D	T56.6X3D	T59.6X4D	T62.8X3D	T63.431D
T47.2X3D	T48.291D	T49.3X6D	T50.4X6A	T50.B14D	T53.1X3D	T56.6X4D	T59.7X1D	T62.91XD	T63.432D
T47.2X4D	T48.292D	T49.3X6S	T50.4X6D	T50.B15D	T53.1X4D	T56.7X1D	T59.7X2D	T62.92XD	T63.433D
T47.2X5D	T48.293D	T49.4X1D	T50.4X6S	T50.B16A	T53.2X1D	T56.7X2D	T59.7X3D	T62.93XD	T63.434D
T47.2X6A	T48.294D	T49.4X2D	T50.5X1D	T50.B16D	T53.2X2D	T56.7X3D	T59.7X4D	T62.94XD	T63.441D
T47.2X6D	T48.295D	T49.4X3D	T50.5X2D	T50.B16S	T53.2X3D	T56.7X4D	T59.811D	T63.001D	T63.442D
T47.2X6S	T48.296A	T49.4X4D	T50.5X3D	T50.B91D	T53.2X4D	T56.811D	T59.812D	T63.002D	T63.443D
T47.3X1D	T48.296D	T49.4X5D	T50.5X4D	T50.B92D	T53.3X1D	T56.812D	T59.813D	T63.003D	T63.444D
T47.3X2D	T48.296S	T49.4X6A	T50.5X5D	T50.B93D	T53.3X2D	T56.813D	T59.814D	T63.004D	T63.451D
T47.3X3D	T48.3X1D	T49.4X6D	T50.5X6A	T50.B94D	T53.3X3D	T56.814D	T59.891D	T63.011D	T63.452D
T47.3X4D	T48.3X2D	T49.4X6S	T50.5X6D	T50.B95D	T53.3X4D	T56.891D	T59.892D	T63.012D	T63.453D
T47.3X5D	T48.3X3D	T49.5X1D	T50.5X6S	T50.B96A	T53.4X1D	T56.892D	T59.893D	T63.013D	T63.454D
T47.3X6A	T48.3X4D	T49.5X2D	T50.6X1D	T50.B96D	T53.4X2D	T56.893D	T59.894D	T63.014D	T63.461D
T47.3X6D	T48.3X5D	T49.5X3D	T50.6X2D	T50.B96S	T53.4X3D	T56.894D	T59.91XD	T63.021D	T63.462D
T47.3X6S	T48.3X6A	T49.5X4D	T50.6X3D	T50.Z11D	T53.4X4D	T56.91XD	T59.92XD	T63.022D	T63.463D
T47.4X1D	T48.3X6D	T49.5X5D	T50.6X4D	T50.Z12D	T53.5X1D	T56.92XD	T59.93XD	T63.023D	T63.464D
T47.4X2D	T48.3X6S	T49.5X6A	T50.6X5D	T50.Z13D	T53.5X2D	T56.93XD	T59.94XD	T63.024D	T63.481D
T47.4X3D	T48.4X1D	T49.5X6D	T50.6X6A	T50.Z14D	T53.5X3D	T56.94XD	T59.91XD	T63.031D	T63.482D
T47.4X4D	T48.4X2D	T49.5X6S	T50.6X6D	T50.Z15D	T53.5X4D	T57.0X1D	T59.92XD	T63.032D	T63.483D
T47.4X5D	T48.4X3D	T49.6X1D	T50.6X6S	T50.Z16A	T53.6X1D	T57.0X2D	T59.93XD	T63.033D	T63.484D
T47.4X6A	T48.4X4D	T49.6X2D	T50.6X6S	T50.Z16D	T53.6X2D	T57.0X3D	T59.94XD	T63.034D	T63.511D
T47.4X6D	T48.4X5D	T49.6X3D	T50.7X1D	T50.Z16S	T53.6X3D	T57.0X4D	T60.0X1D	T63.041D	T63.512D
T47.4X6S	T48.4X6A	T49.6X4D	T50.7X2D	T50.Z91D	T53.6X4D	T57.1X1D	T60.0X2D	T63.042D	T63.513D
T47.5X1D	T48.4X6D	T49.6X5D	T50.7X3D	T50.Z92D	T53.7X1D	T57.1X2D	T60.0X3D	T63.043D	T63.514D
T47.5X2D	T48.4X6S	T49.6X6A	T50.7X4D	T50.Z93D	T53.7X2D	T57.1X4D	T60.0X4D	T63.044D	T63.591D
T47.5X3D	T48.5X1D	T49.6X6D	T50.7X5D	T50.Z94D	T53.7X3D	T57.2X1D	T60.1X1D	T63.061D	T63.592D
T47.5X4D	T48.5X2D	T49.6X6S	T50.7X6A	T50.Z95D	T53.7X4D	T57.2X2D	T60.1X2D	T63.062D	T63.593D
T47.5X5D	T48.5X3D	T49.7X1D	T50.7X6D	T50.Z96A	T53.91XD	T57.2X3D	T60.1X3D	T63.063D	T63.594D
T47.5X6A	T48.5X4D	T49.7X2D	T50.7X6S	T50.Z96D			T60.1X4D		T63.611D

T63.612D	T65.6X4D	T71.232D	T79.A29D	T81.532D	T82.519D	T83.418D	T84.121D	T85.128D	T88.3XXD
T63.613D	T65.811D	T71.233D	T79.A3XD	T81.533D	T82.520D	T83.420D	T84.122D	T85.190D	T88.4XXD
T63.614D	T65.812D	T71.234D	T79.A9XD	T81.534D	T82.521D	T83.421D	T84.123D	T85.191D	T88.51XD
T63.621D	T65.813D	T71.29XD	T80.0XXD	T81.535D	T82.522D	T83.428D	T84.124D	T85.192D	T88.52XD
T63.622D	T65.814D	T71.9XXD	T80.1XXD	T81.536D	T82.523D	T83.490D	T84.125D	T85.193D	T88.53XD
T63.623D	T65.821D	T73.0XXD	T80.211D	T81.537D	T82.524D	T83.491D	T84.126D	T85.199D	T88.59XD
T63.624D	T65.822D	T73.1XXD	T80.212D	T81.538D	T82.525D	T83.498D	T84.127D	T85.21XD	T88.6XXD
T63.631D	T65.823D	T73.2XXD	T80.218D	T81.539D	T82.528D	T83.510D	T84.129D	T85.22XD	T88.7XXD
T63.632D	T65.824D	T73.3XXD	T80.219D	T81.590D	T82.529D	T83.511D	T84.190D	T85.29XD	T88.8XXD
T63.633D	T65.831D	T73.8XXD	T80.22XD	T81.591D	T82.530D	T83.512D	T84.191D	T85.310D	T88.9XXD
T63.634D	T65.832D	T73.9XXD	T80.29XD	T81.592D	T82.531D	T83.518D	T84.192D	T85.311D	Z00.00
T63.691D	T65.833D	T74.01XD	T80.30XD	T81.593D	T82.532D	T83.590D	T84.193D	T85.318D	Z00.01
T63.692D	T65.834D	T74.02XD	T80.310D	T81.594D	T82.533D	T83.591D	T84.194D	T85.320D	Z00.110
T63.693D	T65.891D	T74.11XD	T80.311D	T81.595D	T82.534D	T83.592D	T84.195D	T85.321D	Z00.111
T63.694D	T65.892D	T74.12XD	T80.319D	T81.596D	T82.535D	T83.593D	T84.196D	T85.328D	Z00.121
T63.711D	T65.893D	T74.21XD	T80.39XD	T81.597D	T82.538D	T83.598D	T84.197D	T85.390D	Z00.129
T63.712D	T65.894D	T74.22XD	T80.40XD	T81.598D	T82.539D	T83.61XD	T84.199D	T85.391D	Z00.2
T63.713D	T65.91XD	T74.31XD	T80.410D	T81.599D	T82.590D	T83.62XD	T84.210D	T85.398D	Z00.3
T63.714D	T65.92XD	T74.32XD	T80.411D	T81.60XD	T82.591D	T83.69XD	T84.213D	T85.41XD	Z00.5
T63.791D	T65.93XD	T74.4XXD	T80.419D	T81.61XD	T82.592D	T83.711D	T84.216D	T85.42XD	Z00.6
T63.792D	T65.94XD	T74.51XD	T80.49XD	T81.69XD	T82.593D	T83.712D	T84.218D	T85.43XD	Z00.70
T63.793D	T66.XXXD	T74.52XD	T80.51XD	T81.710D	T82.594D	T83.713D	T84.220D	T85.44XD	Z00.71
T63.794D	T67.01XD	T74.61XD	T80.52XD	T81.711D	T82.595D	T83.714D	T84.223D	T85.49XD	Z00.8
T63.811D	T67.02XD	T74.62XD	T80.59XD	T81.718D	T82.598D	T83.718D	T84.226D	T85.510D	Z01.00
T63.812D	T67.09XD	T74.91XD	T80.61XD	T81.719D	T82.599D	T83.719D	T84.228D	T85.511D	Z01.01
T63.813D	T67.1XXD	T74.92XD	T80.62XD	T81.72XD	T82.6XXD	T83.721D	T84.290D	T85.518D	Z01.020
T63.814D	T67.2XXD	T75.00XD	T80.69XD	T81.81XD	T82.7XXD	T83.722D	T84.293D	T85.520D	Z01.021
T63.821D	T67.3XXD	T75.01XD	T80.810D	T81.82XD	T82.817D	T83.723D	T84.296D	T85.521D	Z01.10
T63.822D	T67.4XXD	T75.09XD	T80.818D	T81.83XD	T82.818D	T83.724D	T84.298D	T85.528D	Z01.110
T63.823D	T67.5XXD	T75.1XXD	T80.89XD	T81.89XD	T82.827D	T83.728D	T84.310D	T85.590D	Z01.118
T63.824D	T67.6XXD	T75.20XD	T80.90XD	T81.9XXD	T82.828D	T83.729D	T84.318D	T85.591D	Z01.12
T63.831D	T67.7XXD	T75.21XD	T80.910D	T82.01XD	T82.837D	T83.79XD	T84.320D	T85.598D	Z01.20
T63.832D	T67.8XXD	T75.22XD	T80.911D	T82.02XD	T82.838D	T83.81XD	T84.328D	T85.610D	Z01.21
T63.833D	T67.9XXD	T75.23XD	T80.919D	T82.03XD	T82.847D	T83.82XD	T84.390D	T85.611D	Z01.30
T63.834D	T68.XXXD	T75.29XD	T80.92XD	T82.09XD	T82.848D	T83.83XD	T84.398D	T85.612D	Z01.31
T63.891D	T69.011D	T75.3XXD	T80.A0XD	T82.110D	T82.855D	T83.84XD	T84.410D	T85.613D	Z01.411
T63.892D	T69.012D	T75.4XXD	T80.A10D	T82.111D	T82.856D	T83.85XD	T84.418D	T85.614D	Z01.419
T63.893D	T69.019D	T75.81XD	T80.A11D	T82.118D	T82.857D	T83.86XD	T84.420D	T85.615D	Z01.42
T63.894D	T69.021D	T75.82XD	T80.A19D	T82.119D	T82.858D	T83.89XD	T84.428D	T85.618D	Z01.810
T63.91XD	T69.022D	T75.89XD	T80.A9XD	T82.120D	T82.867D	T83.9XXD	T84.490D	T85.620D	Z01.811
T63.92XD	T69.029D	T76.01XD	T81.10XD	T82.121D	T82.868D	T84.010D	T84.498D	T85.621D	Z01.812
T63.93XD	T69.1XXD	T76.02XD	T81.11XD	T82.128D	T82.897D	T84.011D	T84.50XD	T85.622D	Z01.818
T63.94XD	T69.8XXD	T76.11XD	T81.12XD	T82.129D	T82.898D	T84.012D	T84.51XD	T85.623D	Z01.82
T64.01XD	T69.9XXD	T76.12XD	T81.19XD	T82.190D	T82.9XXD	T84.013D	T84.52XD	T85.624D	Z01.83
T64.02XD	T70.0XXD	T76.21XD	T81.30XD	T82.191D	T83.010D	T84.018D	T84.53XD	T85.625D	Z01.84
T64.03XD	T70.1XXD	T76.22XD	T81.31XD	T82.198D	T83.011D	T84.019D	T84.54XD	T85.628D	Z01.89
T64.04XD	T70.20XD	T76.31XD	T81.32XD	T82.199D	T83.012D	T84.020D	T84.59XD	T85.630D	Z02.0
T64.81XD	T70.29XD	T76.32XD	T81.33XD	T82.211D	T83.018D	T84.021D	T84.60XD	T85.631D	Z02.1
T64.82XD	T70.3XXD	T76.51XD	T81.40XD	T82.212D	T83.020D	T84.022D	T84.610D	T85.633D	Z02.2
T64.83XD	T70.4XXD	T76.52XD	T81.41XD	T82.213D	T83.021D	T84.023D	T84.611D	T85.635D	Z02.3
T64.84XD	T70.8XXD	T76.61XD	T81.42XD	T82.218D	T83.022D	T84.028D	T84.612D	T85.638D	Z02.4
T65.0X1D	T70.9XXD	T76.62XD	T81.43XD	T82.221D	T83.028D	T84.029D	T84.613D	T85.690D	Z02.5
T65.0X2D	T71.111D	T76.91XD	T81.44XD	T82.222D	T83.030D	T84.030D	T84.614D	T85.691D	Z02.6
T65.0X3D	T71.112D	T76.92XD	T81.49XD	T82.223D	T83.031D	T84.031D	T84.615D	T85.692D	Z02.71
T65.0X4D	T71.113D	T78.00XD	T81.500D	T82.228D	T83.032D	T84.032D	T84.619D	T85.693D	Z02.79
T65.1X1D	T71.114D	T78.01XD	T81.501D	T82.310D	T83.038D	T84.033D	T84.620D	T85.694D	Z02.81
T65.1X2D	T71.121D	T78.02XD	T81.502D	T82.311D	T83.090D	T84.038D	T84.621D	T85.695D	Z02.82
T65.1X3D	T71.122D	T78.03XD	T81.503D	T82.312D	T83.091D	T84.039D	T84.622D	T85.698D	Z02.83
T65.1X4D	T71.123D	T78.04XD	T81.504D	T82.318D	T83.092D	T84.050D	T84.623D	T85.71XD	Z02.89
T65.211D	T71.124D	T78.05XD	T81.505D	T82.319D	T83.098D	T84.051D	T84.624D	T85.72XD	Z02.9
T65.212D	T71.131D	T78.06XD	T81.506D	T82.320D	T83.110D	T84.052D	T84.625D	T85.730D	Z03.6
T65.213D	T71.132D	T78.07XD	T81.507D	T82.321D	T83.111D	T84.053D	T84.629D	T85.731D	Z03.71
T65.214D	T71.133D	T78.08XD	T81.508D	T82.322D	T83.112D	T84.058D	T84.63XD	T85.732D	Z03.72
T65.221D	T71.134D	T78.09XD	T81.509D	T82.328D	T83.113D	T84.059D	T84.69XD	T85.733D	Z03.73
T65.222D	T71.141D	T78.1XXD	T81.510D	T82.329D	T83.118D	T84.060D	T84.7XXD	T85.734D	Z03.74
T65.223D	T71.143D	T78.2XXD	T81.511D	T82.330D	T83.120D	T84.061D	T84.81XD	T85.735D	Z03.75
T65.224D	T71.144D	T78.3XXD	T81.512D	T82.331D	T83.121D	T84.062D	T84.82XD	T85.738D	Z03.79
T65.291D	T71.151D	T78.40XD	T81.513D	T82.332D	T83.122D	T84.063D	T84.83XD	T85.79XD	Z03.810
T65.292D	T71.152D	T78.41XD	T81.514D	T82.338D	T83.123D	T84.068D	T84.84XD	T85.810D	Z03.818
T65.293D	T71.153D	T78.49XD	T81.515D	T82.339D	T83.128D	T84.069D	T84.85XD	T85.818D	Z03.89
T65.294D	T71.154D	T78.8XXD	T81.516D	T82.390D	T83.190D	T84.090D	T84.86XD	T85.820D	Z04.41
T65.3X1D	T71.161D	T79.0XXD	T81.517D	T82.391D	T83.191D	T84.091D	T84.89XD	T85.828D	Z04.42
T65.3X2D	T71.162D	T79.1XXD	T81.518D	T82.392D	T83.192D	T84.092D	T84.9XXD	T85.830D	Z04.6
T65.3X3D	T71.163D	T79.2XXD	T81.519D	T82.398D	T83.193D	T84.093D	T85.01XD	T85.838D	Z04.71
T65.3X4D	T71.164D	T79.4XXD	T81.520D	T82.399D	T83.198D	T84.098D	T85.02XD	T85.840D	Z04.72
T65.4X1D	T71.191D	T79.5XXD	T81.521D	T82.41XD	T83.21XD	T84.099D	T85.03XD	T85.848D	Z04.81
T65.4X2D	T71.192D	T79.6XXD	T81.522D	T82.42XD	T83.22XD	T84.110D	T85.09XD	T85.850D	Z04.82
T65.4X3D	T71.193D	T79.7XXD	T81.523D	T82.43XD	T83.23XD	T84.111D	T85.110D	T85.858D	Z04.89
T65.4X4D	T71.194D	T79.8XXD	T81.524D	T82.49XD	T83.24XD	T84.112D	T85.111D	T85.860D	Z04.9
T65.5X1D	T71.20XD	T79.9XXD	T81.525D	T82.510D	T83.25XD	T84.113D	T85.112D	T85.868D	Z05.0
T65.5X2D	T71.21XD	T79.A0XD	T81.526D	T82.511D	T83.29XD	T84.114D	T85.113D	T85.890D	Z05.1
T65.5X3D	T71.221D	T79.A11D	T81.527D	T82.512D	T83.31XD	T84.115D	T85.118D	T85.898D	Z05.2
T65.5X4D	T71.222D	T79.A12D	T81.528D	T82.513D	T83.32XD	T84.116D	T85.120D	T85.9XXD	Z05.3
T65.6X1D	T71.223D	T79.A19D	T81.529D	T82.514D	T83.39XD	T84.117D	T85.121D	T88.0XXD	Z05.41
T65.6X2D	T71.224D	T79.A21D	T81.530D	T82.515D	T83.410D	T84.119D	T85.122D	T88.1XXD	Z05.42
T65.6X3D	T71.231D	T79.A22D	T81.531D	T82.518D	T83.411D	T84.120D	T85.123D	T88.2XXD	Z05.43

Z05.5	Z18.12	Z30.46	Z3A.12	Z48.817	Z62.29	Z71.0	Z77.9	Z86.010	Z89.201
Z05.6	Z18.2	Z30.49	Z3A.13	Z48.89	Z62.3	Z71.1	Z78.0	Z86.011	Z89.202
Z05.71	Z18.31	Z30.8	Z3A.14	Z51.5	Z62.6	Z71.2	Z78.1	Z86.012	Z89.209
Z05.72	Z18.32	Z30.9	Z3A.15	Z51.6	Z62.810	Z71.3	Z78.9	Z86.018	Z89.211
Z05.73	Z18.33	Z31.41	Z3A.16	Z51.81	Z62.811	Z71.41	Z79.01	Z86.03	Z89.212
Z05.8	Z18.39	Z31.42	Z3A.17	Z51.89	Z62.812	Z71.42	Z79.02	Z86.11	Z89.219
Z05.9	Z18.81	Z31.430	Z3A.18	Z52.000	Z62.813	Z71.51	Z79.1	Z86.12	Z89.221
Z09	Z18.83	Z31.438	Z3A.19	Z52.001	Z62.819	Z71.52	Z79.2	Z86.13	Z89.222
Z11.0	Z18.89	Z31.440	Z3A.20	Z52.008	Z62.820	Z71.6	Z79.3	Z86.14	Z89.229
Z11.1	Z18.9	Z31.441	Z3A.21	Z52.010	Z62.821	Z71.7	Z79.4	Z86.15	Z89.231
Z11.2	Z19.1	Z31.448	Z3A.22	Z52.011	Z62.822	Z71.81	Z79.51	Z86.19	Z89.232
Z11.3	Z19.2	Z31.49	Z3A.23	Z52.018	Z62.890	Z71.82	Z79.52	Z86.2	Z89.239
Z11.4	Z20.01	Z31.5	Z3A.24	Z52.090	Z62.891	Z71.83	Z79.810	Z86.31	Z89.411
Z11.51	Z20.09	Z31.61	Z3A.25	Z52.091	Z62.898	Z71.84	Z79.811	Z86.32	Z89.412
Z11.59	Z20.1	Z31.62	Z3A.26	Z52.098	Z62.9	Z71.89	Z79.818	Z86.39	Z89.419
Z11.6	Z20.2	Z31.69	Z3A.27	Z52.3	Z63.0	Z71.9	Z79.82	Z86.51	Z89.421
Z11.7	Z20.3	Z31.7	Z3A.28	Z52.5	Z63.1	Z72.0	Z79.83	Z86.59	Z89.422
Z11.8	Z20.4	Z31.81	Z3A.29	Z52.810	Z63.31	Z72.3	Z79.84	Z86.61	Z89.429
Z11.9	Z20.5	Z31.82	Z3A.30	Z52.811	Z63.32	Z72.4	Z79.890	Z86.69	Z89.431
Z12.0	Z20.6	Z31.83	Z3A.31	Z52.812	Z63.4	Z72.51	Z79.891	Z86.711	Z89.432
Z12.10	Z20.7	Z31.84	Z3A.32	Z52.813	Z63.5	Z72.52	Z79.899	Z86.718	Z89.439
Z12.11	Z20.810	Z31.89	Z3A.33	Z52.819	Z63.6	Z72.53	Z80.0	Z86.72	Z89.441
Z12.12	Z20.811	Z31.9	Z3A.34	Z52.89	Z63.71	Z72.6	Z80.1	Z86.73	Z89.442
Z12.13	Z20.818	Z32.00	Z3A.35	Z52.9	Z63.72	Z72.820	Z80.2	Z86.74	Z89.449
Z12.2	Z20.820	Z32.01	Z3A.36	Z53.01	Z63.79	Z72.821	Z80.3	Z86.79	Z89.511
Z12.31	Z20.821	Z32.02	Z3A.37	Z53.09	Z63.8	Z72.89	Z80.41	Z87.01	Z89.512
Z12.39	Z20.828	Z32.2	Z3A.38	Z53.1	Z63.9	Z72.9	Z80.42	Z87.09	Z89.519
Z12.4	Z20.89	Z32.3	Z3A.39	Z53.20	Z64.4	Z73.0	Z80.43	Z87.11	Z89.521
Z12.5	Z20.9	Z33.1	Z3A.40	Z53.21	Z65.0	Z73.1	Z80.49	Z87.19	Z89.522
Z12.6	Z22.0	Z33.3	Z3A.41	Z53.29	Z65.1	Z73.2	Z80.51	Z87.2	Z89.529
Z12.71	Z22.1	Z34.00	Z3A.42	Z53.31	Z65.2	Z73.3	Z80.52	Z87.310	Z89.611
Z12.72	Z22.2	Z34.01	Z3A.49	Z53.32	Z65.3	Z73.4	Z80.59	Z87.311	Z89.612
Z12.73	Z22.31	Z34.02	Z40.00	Z53.33	Z65.4	Z73.5	Z80.6	Z87.312	Z89.619
Z12.79	Z22.321	Z34.03	Z40.09	Z53.39	Z65.5	Z73.6	Z80.7	Z87.39	Z89.621
Z12.81	Z22.322	Z34.80	Z40.8	Z53.8	Z65.8	Z73.810	Z80.8	Z87.411	Z89.622
Z12.82	Z22.330	Z34.81	Z40.9	Z53.9	Z65.9	Z73.811	Z80.9	Z87.412	Z89.629
Z12.83	Z22.338	Z34.82	Z41.3	Z55.0	Z66	Z73.812	Z81.0	Z87.430	Z89.9
Z12.89	Z22.39	Z34.83	Z41.8	Z55.1	Z67.10	Z73.819	Z81.1	Z87.438	Z90.02
Z12.9	Z22.4	Z34.90	Z41.9	Z55.2	Z67.11	Z73.82	Z81.2	Z87.440	Z90.09
Z13.0	Z22.6	Z34.91	Z43.8	Z55.3	Z67.20	Z73.89	Z81.3	Z87.441	Z90.10
Z13.1	Z22.7	Z34.92	Z43.9	Z55.4	Z67.21	Z73.9	Z81.4	Z87.442	Z90.11
Z13.21	Z22.8	Z34.93	Z44.20	Z55.8	Z67.30	Z74.01	Z81.8	Z87.448	Z90.12
Z13.220	Z22.9	Z36.0	Z44.21	Z55.9	Z67.31	Z74.09	Z82.0	Z87.51	Z90.13
Z13.228	Z23	Z36.1	Z44.22	Z56.0	Z67.40	Z74.1	Z82.1	Z87.59	Z90.3
Z13.29	Z28.01	Z36.2	Z44.30	Z56.1	Z67.41	Z74.2	Z82.2	Z87.710	Z90.410
Z13.30	Z28.02	Z36.3	Z44.31	Z56.2	Z67.90	Z74.3	Z82.3	Z87.718	Z90.411
Z13.31	Z28.03	Z36.4	Z44.32	Z56.3	Z67.91	Z74.8	Z82.41	Z87.720	Z90.49
Z13.32	Z28.04	Z36.5	Z44.8	Z56.4	Z68.1	Z74.9	Z82.49	Z87.721	Z90.5
Z13.39	Z28.09	Z36.81	Z44.9	Z56.5	Z68.20	Z75.0	Z82.5	Z87.728	Z90.81
Z13.40	Z28.1	Z36.82	Z45.1	Z56.6	Z68.21	Z75.1	Z82.61	Z87.730	Z90.89
Z13.41	Z28.20	Z36.83	Z45.2	Z56.81	Z68.22	Z75.2	Z82.62	Z87.738	Z91.010
Z13.42	Z28.21	Z36.84	Z45.811	Z56.82	Z68.23	Z75.3	Z82.69	Z87.74	Z91.011
Z13.49	Z28.29	Z36.85	Z45.812	Z56.89	Z68.24	Z75.4	Z82.71	Z87.75	Z91.012
Z13.5	Z28.3	Z36.86	Z45.819	Z56.9	Z68.25	Z75.5	Z82.79	Z87.76	Z91.013
Z13.6	Z28.81	Z36.87	Z45.82	Z57.0	Z68.26	Z75.8	Z82.8	Z87.790	Z91.018
Z13.71	Z28.82	Z36.88	Z45.89	Z57.1	Z68.27	Z75.9	Z83.0	Z87.798	Z91.02
Z13.79	Z28.83	Z36.89	Z45.9	Z57.2	Z68.28	Z76.0	Z83.1	Z87.81	Z91.030
Z13.810	Z28.89	Z36.8A	Z46.0	Z57.31	Z68.29	Z76.1	Z83.2	Z87.820	Z91.038
Z13.811	Z28.9	Z36.9	Z46.1	Z57.39	Z68.30	Z76.2	Z83.3	Z87.821	Z91.040
Z13.818	Z29.11	Z37.0	Z46.3	Z57.4	Z68.31	Z76.3	Z83.41	Z87.828	Z91.041
Z13.820	Z29.12	Z37.1	Z46.4	Z57.5	Z68.32	Z76.4	Z83.42	Z87.891	Z91.048
Z13.828	Z29.13	Z37.2	Z46.81	Z57.6	Z68.33	Z76.5	Z83.430	Z87.892	Z91.09
Z13.83	Z29.14	Z37.3	Z46.82	Z57.7	Z68.34	Z76.81	Z83.438	Z87.898	Z91.11
Z13.84	Z29.3	Z37.4	Z46.89	Z57.8	Z68.35	Z76.82	Z83.49	Z88.0	Z91.120
Z13.850	Z29.8	Z37.50	Z46.9	Z57.9	Z68.36	Z76.89	Z83.511	Z88.1	Z91.128
Z13.858	Z29.9	Z37.51	Z48.00	Z59.0	Z68.37	Z77.010	Z83.518	Z88.2	Z91.130
Z13.88	Z30.011	Z37.52	Z48.01	Z59.1	Z68.38	Z77.011	Z83.52	Z88.3	Z91.138
Z13.89	Z30.012	Z37.53	Z48.02	Z59.2	Z68.39	Z77.012	Z83.6	Z88.4	Z91.14
Z13.9	Z30.013	Z37.54	Z48.03	Z59.3	Z68.51	Z77.018	Z83.71	Z88.5	Z91.15
Z14.01	Z30.014	Z37.59	Z48.1	Z59.4	Z68.52	Z77.020	Z83.79	Z88.6	Z91.19
Z14.02	Z30.015	Z37.60	Z48.21	Z59.5	Z68.53	Z77.021	Z84.0	Z88.7	Z91.410
Z14.1	Z30.016	Z37.61	Z48.22	Z59.6	Z68.54	Z77.028	Z84.1	Z88.8	Z91.411
Z14.8	Z30.017	Z37.62	Z48.23	Z59.7	Z69.010	Z77.090	Z84.2	Z88.9	Z91.412
Z15.01	Z30.018	Z37.63	Z48.24	Z59.8	Z69.011	Z77.098	Z84.3	Z89.011	Z91.419
Z15.02	Z30.019	Z37.64	Z48.280	Z59.9	Z69.020	Z77.110	Z84.81	Z89.012	Z91.42
Z15.03	Z30.02	Z37.69	Z48.288	Z60.0	Z69.021	Z77.111	Z84.82	Z89.019	Z91.49
Z15.04	Z30.09	Z37.7	Z48.290	Z60.2	Z69.11	Z77.112	Z84.89	Z89.021	Z91.5
Z15.09	Z30.40	Z37.9	Z48.298	Z60.3	Z69.12	Z77.118	Z86.000	Z89.022	Z91.81
Z15.81	Z30.41	Z39.1	Z48.3	Z60.4	Z69.81	Z77.120	Z86.001	Z89.029	Z91.82
Z15.89	Z30.42	Z39.2	Z48.810	Z60.5	Z69.82	Z77.121	Z86.002	Z89.111	Z91.83
Z17.0	Z30.430	Z3A.00	Z48.811	Z60.8	Z70.0	Z77.122	Z86.003	Z89.112	Z91.841
Z17.1	Z30.431	Z3A.01	Z48.812	Z60.9	Z70.1	Z77.123	Z86.004	Z89.119	Z91.842
Z18.01	Z30.432	Z3A.08	Z48.813	Z62.0	Z70.2	Z77.128	Z86.005	Z89.121	Z91.843
Z18.09	Z30.433	Z3A.09	Z48.814	Z62.1	Z70.3	Z77.21	Z86.006	Z89.122	Z91.849
Z18.10	Z30.44	Z3A.10	Z48.815	Z62.21	Z70.8	Z77.22	Z86.007	Z89.129	Z91.89
Z18.11	Z30.45	Z3A.11	Z48.816	Z62.22	Z70.9	Z77.29	Z86.008	Z89.129	Z92.0

Diagnosis Codes by MDC

Z92.21	Z92.82	Z93.50	Z94.9	Z96.22	Z96.9	Z98.3	Z98.811	Z98.890
Z92.22	Z92.83	Z93.51	Z95.0	Z96.29	Z97.2	Z98.41	Z98.818	Z98.891
Z92.23	Z92.84	Z93.52	Z95.1	Z96.3	Z97.3	Z98.42	Z98.82	Z99.0
Z92.240	Z92.89	Z93.59	Z95.5	Z96.41	Z97.4	Z98.49	Z98.83	Z99.11
Z92.241	Z93.0	Z93.6	Z95.810	Z96.49	Z97.5	Z98.51	Z98.84	Z99.12
Z92.25	Z93.1	Z93.8	Z95.818	Z96.5	Z97.8	Z98.52	Z98.85	Z99.2
Z92.29	Z93.2	Z93.9	Z95.9	Z96.81	Z98.0	Z98.61	Z98.86	Z99.3
Z92.3	Z93.3	Z94.82	Z96.20	Z96.82	Z98.1	Z98.62	Z98.870	Z99.81
Z92.81	Z93.4	Z94.89	Z96.21	Z96.89	Z98.2	Z98.810	Z98.871	Z99.89

MDC 24 Multiple Significant Trauma

M99.10	S00.479A	S01.332A	S02.11BB	S02.621A	S04.032A	S06.1X7A	S06.360A	S06.823A	S10.81XA
M99.11	S00.501A	S01.339A	S02.11CA	S02.621B	S04.039A	S06.1X8A	S06.361A	S06.824A	S10.82XA
M99.12	S00.502A	S01.341A	S02.11CB	S02.622A	S04.041A	S06.1X9A	S06.362A	S06.825A	S10.83XA
M99.13	S00.511A	S01.342A	S02.11DA	S02.622B	S04.042A	S06.2X0A	S06.363A	S06.826A	S10.84XA
M99.14	S00.512A	S01.349A	S02.11DB	S02.630A	S04.049A	S06.2X1A	S06.364A	S06.827A	S10.85XA
M99.15	S00.521A	S01.351A	S02.11EA	S02.630B	S04.10XA	S06.2X2A	S06.365A	S06.828A	S10.86XA
M99.16	S00.522A	S01.352A	S02.11EB	S02.631A	S04.11XA	S06.2X3A	S06.366A	S06.829A	S10.87XA
M99.17	S00.531A	S01.359A	S02.11FA	S02.631B	S04.12XA	S06.2X4A	S06.367A	S06.890A	S10.90XA
M99.18	S00.532A	S01.401A	S02.11FB	S02.632A	S04.20XA	S06.2X5A	S06.368A	S06.891A	S10.91XA
M99.19	S00.541A	S01.402A	S02.11GA	S02.632B	S04.21XA	S06.2X6A	S06.369A	S06.892A	S10.92XA
S00.00XA	S00.542A	S01.409A	S02.11GB	S02.640A	S04.22XA	S06.2X7A	S06.370A	S06.893A	S10.93XA
S00.01XA	S00.551A	S01.411A	S02.11HA	S02.640B	S04.30XA	S06.2X8A	S06.371A	S06.894A	S10.94XA
S00.02XA	S00.552A	S01.412A	S02.11HB	S02.641A	S04.31XA	S06.2X9A	S06.372A	S06.895A	S10.95XA
S00.03XA	S00.561A	S01.419A	S02.121A	S02.641B	S04.32XA	S06.300A	S06.373A	S06.896A	S10.96XA
S00.04XA	S00.562A	S01.421A	S02.121B	S02.642A	S04.40XA	S06.301A	S06.374A	S06.897A	S10.97XA
S00.05XA	S00.571A	S01.422A	S02.122A	S02.642B	S04.41XA	S06.302A	S06.375A	S06.898A	S11.011A
S00.06XA	S00.572A	S01.429A	S02.122B	S02.650A	S04.42XA	S06.303A	S06.376A	S06.899A	S11.012A
S00.07XA	S00.80XA	S01.431A	S02.129A	S02.650B	S04.50XA	S06.304A	S06.377A	S06.9X0A	S11.013A
S00.10XA	S00.81XA	S01.432A	S02.129B	S02.651A	S04.51XA	S06.305A	S06.378A	S06.9X1A	S11.014A
S00.11XA	S00.82XA	S01.439A	S02.19XA	S02.651B	S04.52XA	S06.306A	S06.379A	S06.9X2A	S11.015A
S00.12XA	S00.83XA	S01.441A	S02.19XB	S02.652A	S04.60XA	S06.307A	S06.380A	S06.9X3A	S11.019A
S00.201A	S00.84XA	S01.442A	S02.2XXA	S02.652B	S04.61XA	S06.309A	S06.381A	S06.9X4A	S11.021A
S00.202A	S00.85XA	S01.449A	S02.2XXB	S02.66XA	S04.62XA	S06.310A	S06.382A	S06.9X5A	S11.022A
S00.209A	S00.86XA	S01.451A	S02.30XA	S02.66XB	S04.70XA	S06.311A	S06.383A	S06.9X6A	S11.023A
S00.211A	S00.87XA	S01.452A	S02.30XB	S02.670A	S04.71XA	S06.312A	S06.384A	S06.9X7A	S11.024A
S00.212A	S00.90XA	S01.459A	S02.31XA	S02.670B	S04.72XA	S06.313A	S06.385A	S06.9X8A	S11.025A
S00.219A	S00.91XA	S01.501A	S02.31XB	S02.671A	S04.811A	S06.314A	S06.386A	S06.9X9A	S11.029A
S00.221A	S00.92XA	S01.502A	S02.32XA	S02.671B	S04.812A	S06.315A	S06.387A	S07.0XXA	S11.031A
S00.222A	S00.93XA	S01.511A	S02.32XB	S02.672A	S04.819A	S06.316A	S06.388A	S07.1XXA	S11.032A
S00.229A	S00.94XA	S01.512A	S02.400A	S02.672B	S04.891A	S06.317A	S06.389A	S07.8XXA	S11.033A
S00.241A	S00.95XA	S01.521A	S02.400B	S02.69XA	S04.892A	S06.318A	S06.4X0A	S07.9XXA	S11.034A
S00.242A	S00.96XA	S01.522A	S02.401A	S02.69XB	S04.899A	S06.319A	S06.4X1A	S08.0XXA	S11.035A
S00.249A	S00.97XA	S01.531A	S02.401B	S02.80XA	S04.9XXA	S06.320A	S06.4X2A	S08.111A	S11.039A
S00.251A	S01.00XA	S01.532A	S02.402A	S02.80XB	S05.00XA	S06.321A	S06.4X3A	S08.112A	S11.10XA
S00.252A	S01.01XA	S01.541A	S02.402B	S02.81XA	S05.01XA	S06.322A	S06.4X4A	S08.119A	S11.11XA
S00.259A	S01.02XA	S01.542A	S02.40AA	S02.81XB	S05.02XA	S06.323A	S06.4X5A	S08.121A	S11.12XA
S00.261A	S01.03XA	S01.551A	S02.40AB	S02.82XA	S05.10XA	S06.324A	S06.4X6A	S08.122A	S11.13XA
S00.262A	S01.04XA	S01.552A	S02.40BA	S02.82XB	S05.11XA	S06.325A	S06.4X7A	S08.129A	S11.14XA
S00.269A	S01.05XA	S01.80XA	S02.40BB	S02.831A	S05.12XA	S06.326A	S06.4X8A	S08.811A	S11.15XA
S00.271A	S01.101A	S01.81XA	S02.40CA	S02.831B	S05.20XA	S06.327A	S06.4X9A	S08.812A	S11.20XA
S00.272A	S01.102A	S01.82XA	S02.40CB	S02.832A	S05.21XA	S06.328A	S06.5X0A	S08.89XA	S11.21XA
S00.279A	S01.109A	S01.83XA	S02.40DA	S02.832B	S05.22XA	S06.329A	S06.5X1A	S09.0XXA	S11.22XA
S00.30XA	S01.111A	S01.84XA	S02.40DB	S02.839A	S05.30XA	S06.330A	S06.5X2A	S09.10XA	S11.23XA
S00.31XA	S01.112A	S01.85XA	S02.40EA	S02.839B	S05.31XA	S06.331A	S06.5X3A	S09.11XA	S11.24XA
S00.32XA	S01.119A	S01.90XA	S02.40EB	S02.841A	S05.32XA	S06.332A	S06.5X4A	S09.12XA	S11.25XA
S00.33XA	S01.121A	S01.91XA	S02.40FA	S02.841B	S05.40XA	S06.333A	S06.5X5A	S09.19XA	S11.80XA
S00.34XA	S01.122A	S01.92XA	S02.40FB	S02.842A	S05.41XA	S06.334A	S06.5X6A	S09.20XA	S11.81XA
S00.35XA	S01.129A	S01.93XA	S02.411A	S02.842B	S05.42XA	S06.335A	S06.5X7A	S09.21XA	S11.82XA
S00.36XA	S01.131A	S01.94XA	S02.411B	S02.849A	S05.50XA	S06.336A	S06.5X8A	S09.22XA	S11.83XA
S00.37XA	S01.132A	S01.95XA	S02.412A	S02.849B	S05.51XA	S06.337A	S06.5X9A	S09.301A	S11.84XA
S00.401A	S01.139A	S02.0XXA	S02.412B	S02.85XA	S05.52XA	S06.338A	S06.6X0A	S09.302A	S11.85XA
S00.402A	S01.141A	S02.0XXB	S02.413A	S02.85XB	S05.60XA	S06.339A	S06.6X1A	S09.309A	S11.89XA
S00.409A	S01.142A	S02.101A	S02.413B	S02.91XA	S05.61XA	S06.340A	S06.6X2A	S09.311A	S11.90XA
S00.411A	S01.149A	S02.101B	S02.42XA	S02.91XB	S05.62XA	S06.341A	S06.6X3A	S09.312A	S11.91XA
S00.412A	S01.151A	S02.102A	S02.42XB	S02.92XA	S05.70XA	S06.342A	S06.6X4A	S09.313A	S11.92XA
S00.419A	S01.152A	S02.102B	S02.5XXA	S02.92XB	S05.71XA	S06.343A	S06.6X5A	S09.319A	S11.93XA
S00.421A	S01.159A	S02.109A	S02.5XXB	S03.00XA	S05.72XA	S06.344A	S06.6X6A	S09.391A	S11.94XA
S00.422A	S01.20XA	S02.109B	S02.600A	S03.01XA	S05.8X1A	S06.345A	S06.6X7A	S09.392A	S11.95XA
S00.429A	S01.21XA	S02.110A	S02.600B	S03.02XA	S05.8X2A	S06.346A	S06.6X8A	S09.399A	S12.000A
S00.431A	S01.22XA	S02.110B	S02.601A	S03.03XA	S05.8X9A	S06.347A	S06.6X9A	S09.8XXA	S12.000B
S00.432A	S01.23XA	S02.111A	S02.601B	S03.1XXA	S05.90XA	S06.348A	S06.810A	S09.90XA	S12.001A
S00.439A	S01.24XA	S02.111B	S02.602A	S03.2XXA	S05.91XA	S06.349A	S06.811A	S09.91XA	S12.001B
S00.441A	S01.25XA	S02.112A	S02.602B	S03.40XA	S05.92XA	S06.350A	S06.812A	S09.92XA	S12.01XA
S00.442A	S01.301A	S02.112B	S02.609A	S03.41XA	S06.0X0A	S06.351A	S06.813A	S09.93XA	S12.01XB
S00.449A	S01.302A	S02.113A	S02.609B	S03.42XA	S06.0X1A	S06.352A	S06.814A	S10.0XXA	S12.02XA
S00.451A	S01.309A	S02.113B	S02.610A	S03.43XA	S06.0X9A	S06.353A	S06.815A	S10.10XA	S12.02XB
S00.452A	S01.311A	S02.118A	S02.610B	S03.8XXA	S06.1X0A	S06.354A	S06.816A	S10.11XA	S12.030A
S00.459A	S01.312A	S02.118B	S02.611A	S03.9XXA	S06.1X1A	S06.355A	S06.817A	S10.12XA	S12.030B
S00.461A	S01.319A	S02.119A	S02.611B	S04.011A	S06.1X2A	S06.356A	S06.818A	S10.14XA	S12.031A
S00.462A	S01.321A	S02.119B	S02.612A	S04.012A	S06.1X3A	S06.357A	S06.819A	S10.15XA	S12.031B
S00.469A	S01.322A	S02.11AA	S02.612B	S04.019A	S06.1X4A	S06.358A	S06.820A	S10.16XA	S12.040A
S00.471A	S01.329A	S02.11AB	S02.620A	S04.02XA	S06.1X5A	S06.359A	S06.821A	S10.17XA	S12.040B
S00.472A	S01.331A	S02.11BA	S02.620B	S04.031A	S06.1X6A		S06.822A	S10.80XA	S12.041A

Diagnosis Codes by MDC

S12.041B	S12.491B	S14.124A	S15.399A	S20.462A	S21.409A	S22.062A	S23.421A	S25.591A	S28.212A
S12.090A	S12.500A	S14.125A	S15.8XXA	S20.469A	S21.411A	S22.062B	S23.428A	S25.592A	S28.219A
S12.090B	S12.500B	S14.126A	S15.9XXA	S20.471A	S21.412A	S22.068A	S23.429A	S25.599A	S28.221A
S12.091A	S12.501A	S14.127A	S16.1XXA	S20.472A	S21.419A	S22.068B	S23.8XXA	S25.801A	S28.222A
S12.091B	S12.501B	S14.128A	S16.2XXA	S20.479A	S21.421A	S22.069A	S23.9XXA	S25.802A	S28.229A
S12.100A	S12.530A	S14.129A	S16.8XXA	S20.90XA	S21.422A	S22.069B	S24.0XXA	S25.809A	S29.001A
S12.100B	S12.530B	S14.131A	S16.9XXA	S20.91XA	S21.429A	S22.070A	S24.101A	S25.811A	S29.002A
S12.101A	S12.531A	S14.132A	S17.0XXA	S20.92XA	S21.431A	S22.070B	S24.102A	S25.812A	S29.009A
S12.101B	S12.531B	S14.133A	S17.8XXA	S20.94XA	S21.432A	S22.071A	S24.103A	S25.819A	S29.011A
S12.110A	S12.54XA	S14.134A	S17.9XXA	S20.95XA	S21.439A	S22.071B	S24.104A	S25.891A	S29.012A
S12.110B	S12.54XB	S14.135A	S19.80XA	S20.96XA	S21.441A	S22.072A	S24.109A	S25.892A	S29.019A
S12.111A	S12.550A	S14.136A	S19.81XA	S20.97XA	S21.442A	S22.072B	S24.111A	S25.899A	S29.021A
S12.111B	S12.550B	S14.137A	S19.82XA	S21.001A	S21.449A	S22.078A	S24.112A	S25.90XA	S29.022A
S12.112A	S12.551A	S14.138A	S19.83XA	S21.002A	S21.451A	S22.078B	S24.113A	S25.91XA	S29.029A
S12.112B	S12.551B	S14.139A	S19.84XA	S21.009A	S21.452A	S22.079A	S24.114A	S25.99XA	S29.091A
S12.120A	S12.590A	S14.141A	S19.85XA	S21.011A	S21.459A	S22.079B	S24.119A	S26.00XA	S29.092A
S12.120B	S12.590B	S14.142A	S19.89XA	S21.012A	S21.90XA	S22.080A	S24.131A	S26.01XA	S29.099A
S12.121A	S12.591A	S14.143A	S19.9XXA	S21.019A	S21.91XA	S22.080B	S24.132A	S26.020A	S29.8XXA
S12.121B	S12.591B	S14.144A	S20.00XA	S21.021A	S21.92XA	S22.081A	S24.133A	S26.021A	S29.9XXA
S12.130A	S12.600A	S14.145A	S20.01XA	S21.022A	S21.93XA	S22.081B	S24.134A	S26.022A	S30.0XXA
S12.130B	S12.600B	S14.146A	S20.02XA	S21.029A	S21.94XA	S22.082A	S24.139A	S26.09XA	S30.1XXA
S12.131A	S12.601A	S14.147A	S20.101A	S21.031A	S21.95XA	S22.082B	S24.141A	S26.10XA	S30.201A
S12.131B	S12.601B	S14.148A	S20.102A	S21.032A	S22.000A	S22.088A	S24.142A	S26.11XA	S30.202A
S12.14XA	S12.630A	S14.149A	S20.109A	S21.039A	S22.000B	S22.088B	S24.143A	S26.12XA	S30.21XA
S12.14XB	S12.630B	S14.151A	S20.111A	S21.041A	S22.001A	S22.089A	S24.144A	S26.19XA	S30.22XA
S12.150A	S12.631A	S14.152A	S20.112A	S21.042A	S22.001B	S22.089B	S24.149A	S26.90XA	S30.23XA
S12.150B	S12.631B	S14.153A	S20.119A	S21.049A	S22.002A	S22.20XA	S24.151A	S26.91XA	S30.3XXA
S12.151A	S12.64XA	S14.154A	S20.121A	S21.051A	S22.002B	S22.20XB	S24.152A	S26.92XA	S30.810A
S12.151B	S12.64XB	S14.155A	S20.122A	S21.052A	S22.008A	S22.21XA	S24.153A	S26.99XA	S30.811A
S12.190A	S12.650A	S14.156A	S20.129A	S21.059A	S22.008B	S22.21XB	S24.154A	S27.0XXA	S30.812A
S12.190B	S12.650B	S14.157A	S20.141A	S21.101A	S22.009A	S22.22XA	S24.159A	S27.1XXA	S30.813A
S12.191A	S12.651A	S14.158A	S20.142A	S21.102A	S22.009B	S22.22XB	S24.2XXA	S27.2XXA	S30.814A
S12.191B	S12.651B	S14.159A	S20.149A	S21.109A	S22.010A	S22.23XA	S24.3XXA	S27.301A	S30.815A
S12.200A	S12.690A	S14.2XXA	S20.151A	S21.111A	S22.010B	S22.23XB	S24.4XXA	S27.302A	S30.816A
S12.200B	S12.690B	S14.3XXA	S20.152A	S21.112A	S22.011A	S22.24XA	S24.8XXA	S27.309A	S30.817A
S12.201A	S12.691A	S14.4XXA	S20.159A	S21.119A	S22.011B	S22.24XB	S24.9XXA	S27.311A	S30.820A
S12.201B	S12.691B	S14.5XXA	S20.161A	S21.121A	S22.012A	S22.31XA	S25.00XA	S27.312A	S30.821A
S12.230A	S12.8XXA	S14.8XXA	S20.162A	S21.122A	S22.012B	S22.31XB	S25.01XA	S27.319A	S30.822A
S12.230B	S12.9XXA	S14.9XXA	S20.169A	S21.129A	S22.018A	S22.32XA	S25.02XA	S27.321A	S30.823A
S12.231A	S13.0XXA	S15.001A	S20.171A	S21.131A	S22.018B	S22.32XB	S25.09XA	S27.322A	S30.824A
S12.231B	S13.100A	S15.002A	S20.172A	S21.132A	S22.019A	S22.39XA	S25.101A	S27.329A	S30.825A
S12.24XA	S13.101A	S15.009A	S20.179A	S21.139A	S22.019B	S22.39XB	S25.102A	S27.331A	S30.826A
S12.24XB	S13.110A	S15.011A	S20.20XA	S21.141A	S22.020A	S22.41XA	S25.109A	S27.332A	S30.827A
S12.250A	S13.111A	S15.012A	S20.211A	S21.142A	S22.020B	S22.41XB	S25.111A	S27.339A	S30.840A
S12.250B	S13.120A	S15.019A	S20.212A	S21.149A	S22.021A	S22.42XA	S25.112A	S27.391A	S30.841A
S12.251A	S13.121A	S15.021A	S20.219A	S21.151A	S22.021B	S22.42XB	S25.119A	S27.392A	S30.842A
S12.251B	S13.130A	S15.022A	S20.221A	S21.152A	S22.022A	S22.43XA	S25.121A	S27.399A	S30.843A
S12.290A	S13.131A	S15.029A	S20.222A	S21.159A	S22.022B	S22.43XB	S25.122A	S27.401A	S30.844A
S12.290B	S13.140A	S15.091A	S20.229A	S21.201A	S22.028A	S22.49XA	S25.129A	S27.402A	S30.845A
S12.291A	S13.141A	S15.092A	S20.301A	S21.202A	S22.028B	S22.49XB	S25.191A	S27.409A	S30.846A
S12.291B	S13.150A	S15.099A	S20.302A	S21.209A	S22.029A	S22.5XXA	S25.192A	S27.411A	S30.850A
S12.300A	S13.151A	S15.101A	S20.309A	S21.211A	S22.029B	S22.5XXB	S25.199A	S27.412A	S30.851A
S12.300B	S13.160A	S15.102A	S20.311A	S21.212A	S22.030A	S22.9XXA	S25.20XA	S27.419A	S30.852A
S12.301A	S13.161A	S15.109A	S20.312A	S21.219A	S22.030B	S22.9XXB	S25.21XA	S27.421A	S30.853A
S12.301B	S13.170A	S15.111A	S20.319A	S21.221A	S22.031A	S23.0XXA	S25.22XA	S27.422A	S30.854A
S12.330A	S13.171A	S15.112A	S20.321A	S21.222A	S22.031B	S23.100A	S25.29XA	S27.429A	S30.855A
S12.330B	S13.180A	S15.119A	S20.322A	S21.229A	S22.032A	S23.101A	S25.301A	S27.431A	S30.856A
S12.331A	S13.181A	S15.121A	S20.329A	S21.231A	S22.032B	S23.110A	S25.302A	S27.432A	S30.857A
S12.331B	S13.20XA	S15.122A	S20.341A	S21.232A	S22.038A	S23.111A	S25.309A	S27.439A	S30.860A
S12.34XA	S13.29XA	S15.129A	S20.342A	S21.239A	S22.038B	S23.120A	S25.311A	S27.491A	S30.861A
S12.34XB	S13.4XXA	S15.191A	S20.349A	S21.241A	S22.039A	S23.121A	S25.312A	S27.492A	S30.862A
S12.350A	S13.5XXA	S15.192A	S20.351A	S21.242A	S22.039B	S23.122A	S25.319A	S27.499A	S30.863A
S12.350B	S13.8XXA	S15.199A	S20.352A	S21.249A	S22.040A	S23.123A	S25.321A	S27.50XA	S30.864A
S12.351A	S13.9XXA	S15.201A	S20.359A	S21.251A	S22.040B	S23.130A	S25.322A	S27.51XA	S30.865A
S12.351B	S14.0XXA	S15.202A	S20.361A	S21.252A	S22.041A	S23.131A	S25.329A	S27.52XA	S30.866A
S12.390A	S14.101A	S15.209A	S20.362A	S21.259A	S22.041B	S23.132A	S25.391A	S27.53XA	S30.867A
S12.390B	S14.102A	S15.211A	S20.369A	S21.301A	S22.042A	S23.133A	S25.392A	S27.59XA	S30.870A
S12.391A	S14.103A	S15.212A	S20.371A	S21.302A	S22.042B	S23.140A	S25.399A	S27.60XA	S30.871A
S12.391B	S14.104A	S15.219A	S20.372A	S21.309A	S22.048A	S23.141A	S25.401A	S27.63XA	S30.872A
S12.400A	S14.105A	S15.221A	S20.379A	S21.311A	S22.048B	S23.142A	S25.402A	S27.69XA	S30.873A
S12.400B	S14.106A	S15.222A	S20.401A	S21.312A	S22.049A	S23.143A	S25.409A	S27.802A	S30.874A
S12.401A	S14.107A	S15.229A	S20.402A	S21.319A	S22.049B	S23.150A	S25.411A	S27.803A	S30.875A
S12.401B	S14.108A	S15.291A	S20.409A	S21.321A	S22.050A	S23.151A	S25.412A	S27.808A	S30.876A
S12.430A	S14.109A	S15.292A	S20.411A	S21.322A	S22.050B	S23.152A	S25.419A	S27.809A	S30.877A
S12.430B	S14.111A	S15.299A	S20.412A	S21.329A	S22.051A	S23.153A	S25.421A	S27.812A	S30.91XA
S12.431A	S14.112A	S15.301A	S20.419A	S21.331A	S22.051B	S23.160A	S25.422A	S27.813A	S30.92XA
S12.431B	S14.113A	S15.302A	S20.421A	S21.332A	S22.052A	S23.161A	S25.429A	S27.818A	S30.93XA
S12.44XA	S14.114A	S15.309A	S20.422A	S21.339A	S22.052B	S23.162A	S25.491A	S27.819A	S30.94XA
S12.44XB	S14.115A	S15.311A	S20.429A	S21.341A	S22.058A	S23.163A	S25.492A	S27.892A	S30.95XA
S12.450A	S14.116A	S15.312A	S20.441A	S21.342A	S22.058B	S23.170A	S25.499A	S27.893A	S30.96XA
S12.450B	S14.117A	S15.319A	S20.442A	S21.349A	S22.059A	S23.171A	S25.501A	S27.898A	S30.97XA
S12.451A	S14.118A	S15.321A	S20.449A	S21.351A	S22.059B	S23.20XA	S25.502A	S27.899A	S30.98XA
S12.451B	S14.119A	S15.322A	S20.451A	S21.352A	S22.060A	S23.29XA	S25.509A	S27.9XXA	S31.000A
S12.490A	S14.121A	S15.329A	S20.452A	S21.359A	S22.060B	S23.3XXA	S25.511A	S28.0XXA	S31.001A
S12.490B	S14.122A	S15.391A	S20.459A	S21.401A	S22.061A	S23.41XA	S25.512A	S28.1XXA	S31.010A
S12.491A	S14.123A	S15.392A	S20.461A	S21.402A	S22.061B	S23.420A	S25.519A	S28.211A	S31.011A

S31.020A	S31.609A	S32.028A	S32.315A	S32.466A	S33.101A	S35.403A	S36.32XA	S37.10XA	S40.811A
S31.021A	S31.610A	S32.028B	S32.315B	S32.466B	S33.110A	S35.404A	S36.33XA	S37.12XA	S40.812A
S31.030A	S31.611A	S32.029A	S32.316A	S32.471A	S33.111A	S35.405A	S36.39XA	S37.13XA	S40.819A
S31.031A	S31.612A	S32.029B	S32.316B	S32.471B	S33.120A	S35.406A	S36.400A	S37.19XA	S40.821A
S31.040A	S31.613A	S32.030A	S32.391A	S32.472A	S33.121A	S35.411A	S36.408A	S37.20XA	S40.822A
S31.041A	S31.614A	S32.030B	S32.391B	S32.472B	S33.130A	S35.412A	S36.409A	S37.22XA	S40.829A
S31.050A	S31.615A	S32.031A	S32.392A	S32.473A	S33.131A	S35.413A	S36.410A	S37.23XA	S40.841A
S31.051A	S31.619A	S32.031B	S32.392B	S32.473B	S33.140A	S35.414A	S36.418A	S37.29XA	S40.842A
S31.100A	S31.620A	S32.032A	S32.399A	S32.474A	S33.141A	S35.415A	S36.419A	S37.30XA	S40.849A
S31.101A	S31.621A	S32.032B	S32.399B	S32.474B	S33.2XXA	S35.416A	S36.420A	S37.32XA	S40.851A
S31.102A	S31.622A	S32.038A	S32.401A	S32.475A	S33.30XA	S35.491A	S36.428A	S37.33XA	S40.852A
S31.103A	S31.623A	S32.038B	S32.401B	S32.475B	S33.39XA	S35.492A	S36.429A	S37.39XA	S40.859A
S31.104A	S31.624A	S32.039A	S32.402A	S32.476A	S33.4XXA	S35.493A	S36.430A	S37.60XA	S40.861A
S31.105A	S31.625A	S32.039B	S32.402B	S32.476B	S33.5XXA	S35.494A	S36.438A	S37.62XA	S40.862A
S31.109A	S31.629A	S32.040A	S32.409A	S32.481A	S33.6XXA	S35.495A	S36.439A	S37.63XA	S40.869A
S31.110A	S31.630A	S32.040B	S32.409B	S32.481B	S33.8XXA	S35.496A	S36.490A	S37.69XA	S40.871A
S31.111A	S31.631A	S32.041A	S32.411A	S32.482A	S33.9XXA	S35.50XA	S36.498A	S37.812A	S40.872A
S31.112A	S31.632A	S32.041B	S32.411B	S32.482B	S34.01XA	S35.511A	S36.499A	S37.813A	S40.879A
S31.113A	S31.633A	S32.042A	S32.412A	S32.483A	S34.02XA	S35.512A	S36.500A	S37.818A	S40.911A
S31.114A	S31.634A	S32.042B	S32.412B	S32.483B	S34.101A	S35.513A	S36.501A	S37.819A	S40.912A
S31.115A	S31.635A	S32.048A	S32.413A	S32.484A	S34.102A	S35.514A	S36.502A	S37.892A	S40.919A
S31.119A	S31.639A	S32.048B	S32.413B	S32.484B	S34.103A	S35.515A	S36.503A	S37.893A	S40.921A
S31.120A	S31.640A	S32.049A	S32.414A	S32.485A	S34.104A	S35.516A	S36.508A	S37.898A	S40.922A
S31.121A	S31.641A	S32.049B	S32.414B	S32.485B	S34.105A	S35.531A	S36.509A	S37.899A	S40.929A
S31.122A	S31.642A	S32.050A	S32.415A	S32.486A	S34.109A	S35.532A	S36.510A	S37.90XA	S41.001A
S31.123A	S31.643A	S32.050B	S32.415B	S32.486B	S34.111A	S35.533A	S36.511A	S37.92XA	S41.002A
S31.124A	S31.644A	S32.051A	S32.416A	S32.491A	S34.112A	S35.534A	S36.512A	S37.93XA	S41.009A
S31.125A	S31.645A	S32.051B	S32.416B	S32.491B	S34.113A	S35.535A	S36.513A	S37.99XA	S41.011A
S31.129A	S31.649A	S32.052A	S32.421A	S32.492A	S34.114A	S35.536A	S36.518A	S38.001A	S41.012A
S31.130A	S31.650A	S32.052B	S32.421B	S32.492B	S34.115A	S35.59XA	S36.519A	S38.002A	S41.019A
S31.131A	S31.651A	S32.058A	S32.422A	S32.499A	S34.119A	S35.8X1A	S36.520A	S38.01XA	S41.021A
S31.132A	S31.652A	S32.058B	S32.422B	S32.499B	S34.121A	S35.8X8A	S36.521A	S38.02XA	S41.022A
S31.133A	S31.653A	S32.059A	S32.423A	S32.501A	S34.122A	S35.8X9A	S36.522A	S38.03XA	S41.029A
S31.134A	S31.654A	S32.059B	S32.423B	S32.501B	S34.123A	S35.90XA	S36.523A	S38.1XXA	S41.031A
S31.135A	S31.655A	S32.10XA	S32.424A	S32.502A	S34.124A	S35.91XA	S36.528A	S38.211A	S41.032A
S31.139A	S31.659A	S32.10XB	S32.424B	S32.502B	S34.125A	S35.99XA	S36.529A	S38.212A	S41.039A
S31.140A	S31.801A	S32.110A	S32.425A	S32.509A	S34.129A	S36.00XA	S36.530A	S38.221A	S41.041A
S31.141A	S31.802A	S32.110B	S32.425B	S32.509B	S34.131A	S36.020A	S36.531A	S38.222A	S41.042A
S31.142A	S31.803A	S32.111A	S32.426A	S32.511A	S34.132A	S36.021A	S36.532A	S38.231A	S41.049A
S31.143A	S31.804A	S32.111B	S32.426B	S32.511B	S34.139A	S36.029A	S36.533A	S38.232A	S41.051A
S31.144A	S31.805A	S32.112A	S32.431A	S32.512A	S34.21XA	S36.030A	S36.538A	S38.3XXA	S41.052A
S31.145A	S31.809A	S32.112B	S32.431B	S32.512B	S34.22XA	S36.031A	S36.539A	S39.001A	S41.059A
S31.149A	S31.811A	S32.119A	S32.432A	S32.519A	S34.3XXA	S36.032A	S36.590A	S39.002A	S41.101A
S31.150A	S31.812A	S32.119B	S32.432B	S32.519B	S34.4XXA	S36.039A	S36.591A	S39.003A	S41.102A
S31.151A	S31.813A	S32.120A	S32.433A	S32.591A	S34.5XXA	S36.09XA	S36.592A	S39.011A	S41.109A
S31.152A	S31.814A	S32.120B	S32.433B	S32.591B	S34.6XXA	S36.112A	S36.593A	S39.012A	S41.111A
S31.153A	S31.815A	S32.121A	S32.434A	S32.592A	S34.8XXA	S36.113A	S36.598A	S39.013A	S41.112A
S31.154A	S31.819A	S32.121B	S32.434B	S32.592B	S34.9XXA	S36.114A	S36.599A	S39.021A	S41.119A
S31.155A	S31.821A	S32.122A	S32.435A	S32.599A	S35.00XA	S36.115A	S36.60XA	S39.022A	S41.121A
S31.159A	S31.822A	S32.122B	S32.435B	S32.599B	S35.01XA	S36.118A	S36.61XA	S39.023A	S41.122A
S31.20XA	S31.823A	S32.129A	S32.436A	S32.601A	S35.02XA	S36.119A	S36.62XA	S39.091A	S41.129A
S31.21XA	S31.824A	S32.129B	S32.436B	S32.601B	S35.09XA	S36.122A	S36.63XA	S39.092A	S41.131A
S31.22XA	S31.825A	S32.130A	S32.441A	S32.602A	S35.10XA	S36.123A	S36.69XA	S39.093A	S41.132A
S31.23XA	S31.829A	S32.130B	S32.441B	S32.602B	S35.11XA	S36.128A	S36.81XA	S39.81XA	S41.139A
S31.24XA	S31.831A	S32.131A	S32.442A	S32.609A	S35.12XA	S36.129A	S36.892A	S39.82XA	S41.141A
S31.25XA	S31.832A	S32.131B	S32.442B	S32.609B	S35.19XA	S36.13XA	S36.893A	S39.83XA	S41.142A
S31.30XA	S31.833A	S32.132A	S32.443A	S32.611A	S35.211A	S36.200A	S36.898A	S39.840A	S41.149A
S31.31XA	S31.834A	S32.132B	S32.443B	S32.611B	S35.212A	S36.201A	S36.899A	S39.848A	S41.151A
S31.32XA	S31.835A	S32.139A	S32.444A	S32.612A	S35.218A	S36.202A	S36.90XA	S39.91XA	S41.152A
S31.33XA	S31.839A	S32.139B	S32.444B	S32.612B	S35.219A	S36.209A	S36.92XA	S39.92XA	S41.159A
S31.34XA	S32.000A	S32.14XA	S32.445A	S32.613A	S35.221A	S36.220A	S36.93XA	S39.93XA	S42.001A
S31.35XA	S32.000B	S32.14XB	S32.445B	S32.613B	S35.222A	S36.221A	S36.99XA	S39.94XA	S42.001B
S31.40XA	S32.001A	S32.15XA	S32.446A	S32.614A	S35.228A	S36.222A	S37.001A	S40.011A	S42.002A
S31.41XA	S32.001B	S32.15XB	S32.446B	S32.614B	S35.229A	S36.229A	S37.002A	S40.012A	S42.002B
S31.42XA	S32.002A	S32.16XA	S32.451A	S32.615A	S35.231A	S36.230A	S37.009A	S40.019A	S42.009A
S31.43XA	S32.002B	S32.16XB	S32.451B	S32.615B	S35.232A	S36.231A	S37.011A	S40.021A	S42.009B
S31.44XA	S32.008A	S32.17XA	S32.452A	S32.616A	S35.238A	S36.232A	S37.012A	S40.022A	S42.011A
S31.45XA	S32.008B	S32.17XB	S32.452B	S32.616B	S35.239A	S36.239A	S37.019A	S40.029A	S42.011B
S31.501A	S32.009A	S32.19XA	S32.453A	S32.691A	S35.291A	S36.240A	S37.021A	S40.211A	S42.012A
S31.502A	S32.009B	S32.19XB	S32.453B	S32.691B	S35.292A	S36.241A	S37.022A	S40.212A	S42.012B
S31.511A	S32.010A	S32.2XXA	S32.454A	S32.692A	S35.298A	S36.242A	S37.029A	S40.219A	S42.013A
S31.512A	S32.010B	S32.2XXB	S32.454B	S32.692B	S35.299A	S36.249A	S37.031A	S40.221A	S42.013B
S31.521A	S32.011A	S32.301A	S32.455A	S32.699A	S35.311A	S36.250A	S37.032A	S40.222A	S42.014A
S31.522A	S32.011B	S32.301B	S32.455B	S32.699B	S35.318A	S36.251A	S37.039A	S40.229A	S42.014B
S31.531A	S32.012A	S32.302A	S32.456A	S32.810A	S35.319A	S36.252A	S37.041A	S40.241A	S42.015A
S31.532A	S32.012B	S32.302B	S32.456B	S32.810B	S35.321A	S36.259A	S37.042A	S40.242A	S42.015B
S31.541A	S32.018A	S32.309A	S32.461A	S32.811A	S35.328A	S36.260A	S37.049A	S40.249A	S42.016A
S31.542A	S32.018B	S32.309B	S32.461B	S32.811B	S35.329A	S36.261A	S37.051A	S40.251A	S42.016B
S31.551A	S32.019A	S32.311A	S32.462A	S32.82XA	S35.331A	S36.262A	S37.052A	S40.252A	S42.017A
S31.552A	S32.019B	S32.311B	S32.462B	S32.82XB	S35.338A	S36.269A	S37.059A	S40.259A	S42.017B
S31.600A	S32.020A	S32.312A	S32.463A	S32.89XA	S35.339A	S36.290A	S37.061A	S40.261A	S42.018A
S31.601A	S32.020B	S32.312B	S32.463B	S32.89XB	S35.341A	S36.291A	S37.062A	S40.262A	S42.018B
S31.602A	S32.021A	S32.313A	S32.464A	S32.9XXA	S35.348A	S36.292A	S37.069A	S40.269A	S42.019A
S31.603A	S32.021B	S32.313B	S32.464B	S32.9XXB	S35.349A	S36.299A	S37.091A	S40.271A	S42.019B
S31.604A	S32.022A	S32.314A	S32.465A	S33.0XXA	S35.401A	S36.30XA	S37.092A	S40.272A	S42.021A
S31.605A	S32.022B	S32.314B	S32.465B	S33.100A	S35.402A		S37.099A	S40.279A	S42.021B

S42.022A	S42.156A	S42.295B	S42.412A	S42.476A	S43.224A	S45.119A	S46.392A	S49.90XA	S51.859A
S42.022B	S42.156B	S42.296A	S42.412B	S42.476B	S43.225A	S45.191A	S46.399A	S49.91XA	S52.001A
S42.023A	S42.191A	S42.296B	S42.413A	S42.481A	S43.226A	S45.192A	S46.801A	S49.92XA	S52.001B
S42.023B	S42.191B	S42.301A	S42.413B	S42.482A	S43.301A	S45.199A	S46.802A	S50.00XA	S52.001C
S42.024A	S42.192A	S42.301B	S42.414A	S42.489A	S43.302A	S45.201A	S46.809A	S50.01XA	S52.002A
S42.024B	S42.192B	S42.302A	S42.414B	S42.491A	S43.303A	S45.202A	S46.811A	S50.02XA	S52.002B
S42.025A	S42.199A	S42.302B	S42.415A	S42.491B	S43.304A	S45.209A	S46.812A	S50.10XA	S52.002C
S42.025B	S42.199B	S42.309A	S42.415B	S42.492A	S43.305A	S45.211A	S46.819A	S50.11XA	S52.009A
S42.026A	S42.201A	S42.309B	S42.416A	S42.492B	S43.306A	S45.212A	S46.821A	S50.12XA	S52.009B
S42.026B	S42.201B	S42.311A	S42.416B	S42.493A	S43.311A	S45.219A	S46.822A	S50.311A	S52.009C
S42.031A	S42.202A	S42.312A	S42.421A	S42.493B	S43.312A	S45.291A	S46.829A	S50.312A	S52.011A
S42.031B	S42.202B	S42.319A	S42.421B	S42.494A	S43.313A	S45.292A	S46.891A	S50.319A	S52.012A
S42.032A	S42.209A	S42.321A	S42.422A	S42.494B	S43.314A	S45.299A	S46.892A	S50.321A	S52.019A
S42.032B	S42.209B	S42.321B	S42.422B	S42.495A	S43.315A	S45.301A	S46.899A	S50.322A	S52.021A
S42.033A	S42.211A	S42.322A	S42.423A	S42.495B	S43.316A	S45.302A	S46.901A	S50.329A	S52.021B
S42.033B	S42.211B	S42.322B	S42.423B	S42.496A	S43.391A	S45.309A	S46.902A	S50.341A	S52.021C
S42.034A	S42.212A	S42.323A	S42.424A	S42.496B	S43.392A	S45.311A	S46.909A	S50.342A	S52.022A
S42.034B	S42.212B	S42.323B	S42.424B	S42.90XA	S43.393A	S45.312A	S46.911A	S50.349A	S52.022B
S42.035A	S42.213A	S42.324A	S42.425A	S42.90XB	S43.394A	S45.319A	S46.912A	S50.351A	S52.022C
S42.035B	S42.213B	S42.324B	S42.425B	S42.91XA	S43.395A	S45.391A	S46.919A	S50.352A	S52.023A
S42.036A	S42.214A	S42.325A	S42.426A	S42.91XB	S43.396A	S45.392A	S46.921A	S50.359A	S52.023B
S42.036B	S42.214B	S42.325B	S42.426B	S42.92XA	S43.401A	S45.399A	S46.922A	S50.361A	S52.023C
S42.101A	S42.215A	S42.326A	S42.431A	S42.92XB	S43.402A	S45.801A	S46.929A	S50.362A	S52.024A
S42.101B	S42.215B	S42.326B	S42.431B	S43.001A	S43.409A	S45.802A	S46.991A	S50.369A	S52.024B
S42.102A	S42.216A	S42.331A	S42.432A	S43.002A	S43.411A	S45.809A	S46.992A	S50.371A	S52.024C
S42.102B	S42.216B	S42.331B	S42.432B	S43.003A	S43.412A	S45.811A	S46.999A	S50.372A	S52.025A
S42.109A	S42.221A	S42.332A	S42.433A	S43.004A	S43.419A	S45.812A	S47.1XXA	S50.379A	S52.025B
S42.109B	S42.221B	S42.332B	S42.433B	S43.005A	S43.421A	S45.819A	S47.2XXA	S50.811A	S52.025C
S42.111A	S42.222A	S42.333A	S42.434A	S43.006A	S43.422A	S45.891A	S47.9XXA	S50.812A	S52.026A
S42.111B	S42.222B	S42.333B	S42.434B	S43.011A	S43.429A	S45.892A	S48.011A	S50.819A	S52.026B
S42.112A	S42.223A	S42.334A	S42.435A	S43.012A	S43.431A	S45.899A	S48.012A	S50.821A	S52.026C
S42.112B	S42.223B	S42.334B	S42.435B	S43.013A	S43.432A	S45.901A	S48.019A	S50.822A	S52.031A
S42.113A	S42.224A	S42.335A	S42.436A	S43.014A	S43.439A	S45.902A	S48.021A	S50.829A	S52.031B
S42.113B	S42.224B	S42.335B	S42.436B	S43.015A	S43.491A	S45.909A	S48.022A	S50.841A	S52.031C
S42.114A	S42.225A	S42.336A	S42.441A	S43.016A	S43.492A	S45.911A	S48.029A	S50.842A	S52.032A
S42.114B	S42.225B	S42.336B	S42.441B	S43.021A	S43.499A	S45.912A	S48.111A	S50.849A	S52.032B
S42.115A	S42.226A	S42.341A	S42.442A	S43.022A	S43.50XA	S45.919A	S48.112A	S50.851A	S52.032C
S42.115B	S42.226B	S42.341B	S42.442B	S43.023A	S43.51XA	S45.991A	S48.119A	S50.852A	S52.033A
S42.116A	S42.231A	S42.342A	S42.443A	S43.024A	S43.52XA	S45.992A	S48.121A	S50.859A	S52.033B
S42.116B	S42.231B	S42.342B	S42.443B	S43.025A	S43.60XA	S45.999A	S48.122A	S50.861A	S52.033C
S42.121A	S42.232A	S42.343A	S42.444A	S43.026A	S43.61XA	S46.001A	S48.129A	S50.862A	S52.034A
S42.121B	S42.232B	S42.343B	S42.444B	S43.031A	S43.62XA	S46.002A	S48.911A	S50.869A	S52.034B
S42.122A	S42.239A	S42.344A	S42.445A	S43.032A	S43.80XA	S46.009A	S48.919A	S50.871A	S52.034C
S42.122B	S42.239B	S42.344B	S42.445B	S43.033A	S43.81XA	S46.011A	S48.921A	S50.872A	S52.035A
S42.123A	S42.241A	S42.345A	S42.446A	S43.034A	S43.82XA	S46.012A	S48.922A	S50.879A	S52.035B
S42.123B	S42.241B	S42.345B	S42.446B	S43.035A	S43.90XA	S46.019A	S48.929A	S50.901A	S52.035C
S42.124A	S42.242A	S42.346A	S42.447A	S43.036A	S43.91XA	S46.021A	S49.001A	S50.902A	S52.036A
S42.124B	S42.242B	S42.346B	S42.447B	S43.081A	S43.92XA	S46.022A	S49.002A	S50.909A	S52.036B
S42.125A	S42.249A	S42.351A	S42.448A	S43.082A	S44.00XA	S46.029A	S49.009A	S50.911A	S52.036C
S42.125B	S42.249B	S42.351B	S42.448B	S43.083A	S44.01XA	S46.091A	S49.011A	S50.912A	S52.041A
S42.126A	S42.251A	S42.352A	S42.449A	S43.084A	S44.02XA	S46.092A	S49.012A	S50.919A	S52.041B
S42.126B	S42.251B	S42.352B	S42.449B	S43.085A	S44.10XA	S46.099A	S49.019A	S51.001A	S52.041C
S42.131A	S42.252A	S42.353A	S42.451A	S43.086A	S44.11XA	S46.101A	S49.021A	S51.002A	S52.042A
S42.131B	S42.252B	S42.353B	S42.451B	S43.101A	S44.12XA	S46.102A	S49.022A	S51.009A	S52.042B
S42.132A	S42.253A	S42.354A	S42.452A	S43.102A	S44.20XA	S46.109A	S49.029A	S51.011A	S52.042C
S42.132B	S42.253B	S42.354B	S42.452B	S43.109A	S44.21XA	S46.111A	S49.031A	S51.012A	S52.043A
S42.133A	S42.254A	S42.355A	S42.453A	S43.111A	S44.22XA	S46.112A	S49.032A	S51.019A	S52.043B
S42.133B	S42.254B	S42.355B	S42.453B	S43.112A	S44.30XA	S46.119A	S49.039A	S51.021A	S52.043C
S42.134A	S42.255A	S42.356A	S42.454A	S43.119A	S44.31XA	S46.121A	S49.041A	S51.022A	S52.044A
S42.134B	S42.255B	S42.356B	S42.454B	S43.121A	S44.32XA	S46.122A	S49.042A	S51.029A	S52.044B
S42.135A	S42.256A	S42.361A	S42.455A	S43.122A	S44.40XA	S46.129A	S49.049A	S51.031A	S52.044C
S42.135B	S42.256B	S42.361B	S42.455B	S43.129A	S44.41XA	S46.191A	S49.091A	S51.032A	S52.045A
S42.136A	S42.261A	S42.362A	S42.456A	S43.131A	S44.42XA	S46.192A	S49.092A	S51.039A	S52.045B
S42.136B	S42.261B	S42.362B	S42.456B	S43.132A	S44.50XA	S46.199A	S49.099A	S51.041A	S52.045C
S42.141A	S42.262A	S42.363A	S42.461A	S43.139A	S44.51XA	S46.201A	S49.101A	S51.042A	S52.046A
S42.141B	S42.262B	S42.363B	S42.461B	S43.141A	S44.52XA	S46.202A	S49.102A	S51.049A	S52.046B
S42.142A	S42.263A	S42.364A	S42.462A	S43.142A	S44.8X1A	S46.209A	S49.109A	S51.051A	S52.046C
S42.142B	S42.263B	S42.364B	S42.462B	S43.149A	S44.8X2A	S46.211A	S49.111A	S51.052A	S52.091A
S42.143A	S42.264A	S42.365A	S42.463A	S43.151A	S44.8X9A	S46.212A	S49.112A	S51.059A	S52.091B
S42.143B	S42.264B	S42.365B	S42.463B	S43.152A	S44.90XA	S46.219A	S49.119A	S51.801A	S52.091C
S42.144A	S42.265A	S42.366A	S42.464A	S43.159A	S44.91XA	S46.221A	S49.121A	S51.802A	S52.092A
S42.144B	S42.265B	S42.366B	S42.464B	S43.201A	S44.92XA	S46.222A	S49.122A	S51.809A	S52.092B
S42.145A	S42.266A	S42.391A	S42.465A	S43.202A	S45.001A	S46.229A	S49.129A	S51.811A	S52.092C
S42.145B	S42.266B	S42.391B	S42.465B	S43.203A	S45.002A	S46.291A	S49.131A	S51.812A	S52.099A
S42.146A	S42.271A	S42.392A	S42.466A	S43.204A	S45.009A	S46.292A	S49.132A	S51.819A	S52.099B
S42.146B	S42.272A	S42.392B	S42.466B	S43.205A	S45.011A	S46.299A	S49.139A	S51.821A	S52.099C
S42.151A	S42.279A	S42.399A	S42.471A	S43.206A	S45.012A	S46.301A	S49.141A	S51.822A	S52.101A
S42.151B	S42.291A	S42.399B	S42.471B	S43.211A	S45.019A	S46.302A	S49.142A	S51.829A	S52.101B
S42.152A	S42.291B	S42.401A	S42.472A	S43.212A	S45.091A	S46.309A	S49.149A	S51.831A	S52.101C
S42.152B	S42.292A	S42.401B	S42.472B	S43.213A	S45.092A	S46.311A	S49.191A	S51.832A	S52.102A
S42.153A	S42.292B	S42.402A	S42.473A	S43.214A	S45.099A	S46.312A	S49.192A	S51.839A	S52.102B
S42.153B	S42.293A	S42.402B	S42.473B	S43.215A	S45.101A	S46.319A	S49.199A	S51.841A	S52.102C
S42.154A	S42.293B	S42.409A	S42.474A	S43.216A	S45.102A	S46.321A	S49.80XA	S51.842A	S52.109A
S42.154B	S42.294A	S42.409B	S42.474B	S43.221A	S45.109A	S46.322A	S49.81XA	S51.849A	S52.109B
S42.155A	S42.294B	S42.411A	S42.475A	S43.222A	S45.111A	S46.329A	S49.82XA	S51.851A	S52.109C
S42.155B	S42.295A	S42.411B	S42.475B	S43.223A	S45.112A	S46.391A		S51.852A	S52.111A

S52.112A	S52.234A	S52.292C	S52.356B	S52.541A	S52.90XC	S53.432A	S56.104A	S56.493A	S59.102A
S52.119A	S52.234B	S52.299A	S52.356C	S52.541B	S52.91XA	S53.439A	S56.105A	S56.494A	S59.109A
S52.121A	S52.234C	S52.299B	S52.361A	S52.541C	S52.91XB	S53.441A	S56.106A	S56.495A	S59.111A
S52.121B	S52.235A	S52.299C	S52.361B	S52.542A	S52.91XC	S53.442A	S56.107A	S56.496A	S59.112A
S52.121C	S52.235B	S52.301A	S52.361C	S52.542B	S52.92XA	S53.449A	S56.108A	S56.497A	S59.119A
S52.122A	S52.235C	S52.301B	S52.362A	S52.542C	S52.92XB	S53.491A	S56.109A	S56.498A	S59.121A
S52.122B	S52.236A	S52.301C	S52.362B	S52.549A	S52.92XC	S53.492A	S56.111A	S56.499A	S59.122A
S52.122C	S52.236B	S52.302A	S52.362C	S52.549B	S53.001A	S53.499A	S56.112A	S56.501A	S59.129A
S52.123A	S52.236C	S52.302B	S52.363A	S52.549C	S53.002A	S54.00XA	S56.113A	S56.502A	S59.131A
S52.123B	S52.241A	S52.302C	S52.363B	S52.551A	S53.003A	S54.01XA	S56.114A	S56.509A	S59.132A
S52.123C	S52.241B	S52.309A	S52.363C	S52.551B	S53.004A	S54.02XA	S56.115A	S56.511A	S59.139A
S52.124A	S52.241C	S52.309B	S52.364A	S52.551C	S53.005A	S54.10XA	S56.116A	S56.512A	S59.141A
S52.124B	S52.242A	S52.309C	S52.364B	S52.552A	S53.006A	S54.11XA	S56.117A	S56.519A	S59.142A
S52.124C	S52.242B	S52.311A	S52.364C	S52.552B	S53.011A	S54.12XA	S56.118A	S56.521A	S59.149A
S52.125A	S52.242C	S52.312A	S52.365A	S52.552C	S53.012A	S54.20XA	S56.119A	S56.522A	S59.191A
S52.125B	S52.243A	S52.319A	S52.365B	S52.559A	S53.013A	S54.21XA	S56.121A	S56.529A	S59.192A
S52.125C	S52.243B	S52.321A	S52.365C	S52.559B	S53.014A	S54.22XA	S56.122A	S56.591A	S59.199A
S52.126A	S52.243C	S52.321B	S52.366A	S52.559C	S53.015A	S54.30XA	S56.123A	S56.592A	S59.201A
S52.126B	S52.244A	S52.321C	S52.366B	S52.561A	S53.016A	S54.31XA	S56.124A	S56.599A	S59.202A
S52.126C	S52.244B	S52.322A	S52.366C	S52.561B	S53.021A	S54.32XA	S56.125A	S56.801A	S59.209A
S52.131A	S52.244C	S52.322B	S52.371A	S52.561C	S53.022A	S54.8X1A	S56.126A	S56.802A	S59.211A
S52.131B	S52.245A	S52.322C	S52.371B	S52.562A	S53.023A	S54.8X2A	S56.127A	S56.809A	S59.212A
S52.131C	S52.245B	S52.323A	S52.371C	S52.562B	S53.024A	S54.8X9A	S56.128A	S56.811A	S59.219A
S52.132A	S52.245C	S52.323B	S52.372A	S52.562C	S53.025A	S54.90XA	S56.129A	S56.812A	S59.221A
S52.132B	S52.246A	S52.323C	S52.372B	S52.569A	S53.026A	S54.91XA	S56.191A	S56.819A	S59.222A
S52.132C	S52.246B	S52.324A	S52.372C	S52.569B	S53.031A	S54.92XA	S56.192A	S56.821A	S59.229A
S52.133A	S52.246C	S52.324B	S52.379A	S52.569C	S53.032A	S55.001A	S56.193A	S56.822A	S59.231A
S52.133B	S52.251A	S52.324C	S52.379B	S52.571A	S53.033A	S55.002A	S56.194A	S56.829A	S59.232A
S52.133C	S52.251B	S52.325A	S52.379C	S52.571B	S53.091A	S55.009A	S56.195A	S56.891A	S59.239A
S52.134A	S52.251C	S52.325B	S52.381A	S52.571C	S53.092A	S55.011A	S56.196A	S56.892A	S59.241A
S52.134B	S52.252A	S52.325C	S52.381B	S52.572A	S53.093A	S55.012A	S56.197A	S56.899A	S59.242A
S52.134C	S52.252B	S52.326A	S52.381C	S52.572B	S53.094A	S55.019A	S56.198A	S56.901A	S59.249A
S52.135A	S52.252C	S52.326B	S52.382A	S52.572C	S53.095A	S55.091A	S56.199A	S56.902A	S59.291A
S52.135B	S52.253A	S52.326C	S52.382B	S52.579A	S53.096A	S55.092A	S56.201A	S56.909A	S59.292A
S52.135C	S52.253B	S52.331A	S52.382C	S52.579B	S53.101A	S55.099A	S56.202A	S56.911A	S59.299A
S52.136A	S52.253C	S52.331B	S52.389A	S52.579C	S53.102A	S55.101A	S56.209A	S56.912A	S59.801A
S52.136B	S52.254A	S52.331C	S52.389B	S52.591A	S53.103A	S55.102A	S56.211A	S56.919A	S59.802A
S52.136C	S52.254B	S52.332A	S52.389C	S52.591B	S53.104A	S55.109A	S56.212A	S56.921A	S59.809A
S52.181A	S52.254C	S52.332B	S52.391A	S52.591C	S53.105A	S55.111A	S56.219A	S56.922A	S59.811A
S52.181B	S52.255A	S52.332C	S52.391B	S52.592A	S53.106A	S55.112A	S56.221A	S56.929A	S59.812A
S52.181C	S52.255B	S52.333A	S52.391C	S52.592B	S53.111A	S55.119A	S56.222A	S56.991A	S59.819A
S52.182A	S52.255C	S52.333B	S52.392A	S52.592C	S53.112A	S55.191A	S56.229A	S56.992A	S59.901A
S52.182B	S52.256A	S52.333C	S52.392B	S52.599A	S53.113A	S55.192A	S56.291A	S56.999A	S59.902A
S52.182C	S52.256B	S52.334A	S52.392C	S52.599B	S53.114A	S55.199A	S56.292A	S57.00XA	S59.909A
S52.189A	S52.256C	S52.334B	S52.399A	S52.599C	S53.115A	S55.201A	S56.299A	S57.01XA	S59.911A
S52.189B	S52.261A	S52.334C	S52.399B	S52.601A	S53.116A	S55.202A	S56.301A	S57.02XA	S59.912A
S52.189C	S52.261B	S52.335A	S52.399C	S52.601B	S53.121A	S55.209A	S56.302A	S57.80XA	S59.919A
S52.201A	S52.261C	S52.335B	S52.501A	S52.601C	S53.122A	S55.211A	S56.309A	S57.81XA	S60.00XA
S52.201B	S52.262A	S52.335C	S52.501B	S52.602A	S53.123A	S55.212A	S56.311A	S57.82XA	S60.011A
S52.201C	S52.262B	S52.336A	S52.501C	S52.602B	S53.124A	S55.219A	S56.312A	S58.011A	S60.012A
S52.202A	S52.262C	S52.336B	S52.502A	S52.602C	S53.125A	S55.291A	S56.319A	S58.012A	S60.019A
S52.202B	S52.263A	S52.336C	S52.502B	S52.609A	S53.126A	S55.292A	S56.321A	S58.019A	S60.021A
S52.202C	S52.263B	S52.341A	S52.502C	S52.609B	S53.131A	S55.299A	S56.322A	S58.021A	S60.022A
S52.209A	S52.263C	S52.341B	S52.509A	S52.609C	S53.132A	S55.801A	S56.329A	S58.022A	S60.029A
S52.209B	S52.264A	S52.341C	S52.509B	S52.611A	S53.133A	S55.802A	S56.391A	S58.029A	S60.031A
S52.209C	S52.264B	S52.342A	S52.509C	S52.611B	S53.134A	S55.809A	S56.392A	S58.111A	S60.032A
S52.211A	S52.264C	S52.342B	S52.511A	S52.611C	S53.135A	S55.811A	S56.399A	S58.112A	S60.039A
S52.212A	S52.265A	S52.342C	S52.511B	S52.612A	S53.136A	S55.812A	S56.401A	S58.119A	S60.041A
S52.219A	S52.265B	S52.343A	S52.511C	S52.612B	S53.141A	S55.819A	S56.402A	S58.121A	S60.042A
S52.221A	S52.265C	S52.343B	S52.512A	S52.612C	S53.142A	S55.891A	S56.403A	S58.122A	S60.049A
S52.221B	S52.266A	S52.343C	S52.512B	S52.613A	S53.143A	S55.892A	S56.404A	S58.129A	S60.051A
S52.221C	S52.266B	S52.344A	S52.512C	S52.613B	S53.144A	S55.899A	S56.405A	S58.911A	S60.052A
S52.222A	S52.266C	S52.344B	S52.513A	S52.613C	S53.145A	S55.901A	S56.406A	S58.912A	S60.059A
S52.222B	S52.271A	S52.344C	S52.513B	S52.614A	S53.146A	S55.902A	S56.407A	S58.919A	S60.10XA
S52.222C	S52.271B	S52.345A	S52.513C	S52.614B	S53.191A	S55.909A	S56.408A	S58.921A	S60.111A
S52.223A	S52.271C	S52.345B	S52.514A	S52.614C	S53.192A	S55.911A	S56.409A	S58.922A	S60.112A
S52.223B	S52.272A	S52.345C	S52.514B	S52.615A	S53.193A	S55.912A	S56.411A	S58.929A	S60.119A
S52.223C	S52.272B	S52.346A	S52.514C	S52.615B	S53.194A	S55.919A	S56.412A	S59.001A	S60.121A
S52.224A	S52.272C	S52.346B	S52.515A	S52.615C	S53.195A	S55.991A	S56.413A	S59.002A	S60.122A
S52.224B	S52.279A	S52.346C	S52.515B	S52.616A	S53.196A	S55.992A	S56.414A	S59.009A	S60.129A
S52.224C	S52.279B	S52.351A	S52.515C	S52.616B	S53.20XA	S55.999A	S56.415A	S59.011A	S60.131A
S52.225A	S52.279C	S52.351B	S52.516A	S52.616C	S53.21XA	S56.001A	S56.416A	S59.012A	S60.132A
S52.225B	S52.281A	S52.351C	S52.516B	S52.621A	S53.22XA	S56.002A	S56.417A	S59.019A	S60.139A
S52.225C	S52.281B	S52.352A	S52.516C	S52.622A	S53.30XA	S56.009A	S56.418A	S59.021A	S60.141A
S52.226A	S52.281C	S52.352B	S52.521A	S52.629A	S53.31XA	S56.011A	S56.419A	S59.022A	S60.142A
S52.226B	S52.282A	S52.352C	S52.522A	S52.691A	S53.32XA	S56.019A	S56.421A	S59.029A	S60.149A
S52.226C	S52.282B	S52.353A	S52.529A	S52.691B	S53.401A	S56.021A	S56.422A	S59.031A	S60.151A
S52.231A	S52.282C	S52.353B	S52.531A	S52.691C	S53.402A	S56.022A	S56.423A	S59.032A	S60.152A
S52.231B	S52.283A	S52.353C	S52.531B	S52.692A	S53.409A	S56.029A	S56.424A	S59.039A	S60.159A
S52.231C	S52.283B	S52.354A	S52.531C	S52.692B	S53.411A	S56.091A	S56.425A	S59.041A	S60.211A
S52.232A	S52.283C	S52.354B	S52.532A	S52.692C	S53.412A	S56.092A	S56.426A	S59.042A	S60.212A
S52.232B	S52.291A	S52.354C	S52.532B	S52.699A	S53.419A	S56.099A	S56.427A	S59.049A	S60.219A
S52.232C	S52.291B	S52.355A	S52.532C	S52.699B	S53.421A	S56.101A	S56.428A	S59.091A	S60.221A
S52.233A	S52.291C	S52.355B	S52.539A	S52.699C	S53.422A	S56.102A	S56.429A	S59.092A	S60.222A
S52.233B	S52.292A	S52.355C	S52.539B	S52.90XA	S53.429A	S56.103A	S56.491A	S59.099A	S60.229A
S52.233C	S52.292B	S52.356A	S52.539C	S52.90XB	S53.431A		S56.492A	S59.101A	S60.311A

S60.312A	S60.541A	S61.201A	S61.327A	S62.016B	S62.154B	S62.245B	S62.332B	S62.395B	S62.623B
S60.319A	S60.542A	S61.202A	S61.328A	S62.021A	S62.155A	S62.246A	S62.333A	S62.396A	S62.624A
S60.321A	S60.549A	S61.203A	S61.329A	S62.021B	S62.155B	S62.246B	S62.333B	S62.396B	S62.624B
S60.322A	S60.551A	S61.204A	S61.330A	S62.022A	S62.156A	S62.251A	S62.334A	S62.397A	S62.625A
S60.329A	S60.552A	S61.205A	S61.331A	S62.022B	S62.156B	S62.251B	S62.334B	S62.397B	S62.625B
S60.341A	S60.559A	S61.206A	S61.332A	S62.023A	S62.161A	S62.252A	S62.335A	S62.398A	S62.626A
S60.342A	S60.561A	S61.207A	S61.333A	S62.023B	S62.161B	S62.252B	S62.335B	S62.398B	S62.626B
S60.349A	S60.562A	S61.208A	S61.334A	S62.024A	S62.162A	S62.253A	S62.336A	S62.399A	S62.627A
S60.351A	S60.569A	S61.209A	S61.335A	S62.024B	S62.162B	S62.253B	S62.336B	S62.399B	S62.627B
S60.352A	S60.571A	S61.210A	S61.336A	S62.025A	S62.163A	S62.254A	S62.337A	S62.501A	S62.628A
S60.359A	S60.572A	S61.211A	S61.337A	S62.025B	S62.163B	S62.254B	S62.337B	S62.501B	S62.628B
S60.361A	S60.579A	S61.212A	S61.338A	S62.026A	S62.164A	S62.255A	S62.338A	S62.502A	S62.629A
S60.362A	S60.811A	S61.213A	S61.339A	S62.026B	S62.164B	S62.255B	S62.338B	S62.502B	S62.629B
S60.369A	S60.812A	S61.214A	S61.340A	S62.031A	S62.165A	S62.256A	S62.339A	S62.509A	S62.630A
S60.371A	S60.819A	S61.215A	S61.341A	S62.031B	S62.165B	S62.256B	S62.339B	S62.509B	S62.630B
S60.372A	S60.821A	S61.216A	S61.342A	S62.032A	S62.166A	S62.291A	S62.340A	S62.511A	S62.631A
S60.379A	S60.822A	S61.217A	S61.343A	S62.032B	S62.166B	S62.291B	S62.340B	S62.511B	S62.631B
S60.391A	S60.829A	S61.218A	S61.344A	S62.033A	S62.171A	S62.292A	S62.341A	S62.512A	S62.632A
S60.392A	S60.841A	S61.219A	S61.345A	S62.033B	S62.171B	S62.292B	S62.341B	S62.512B	S62.632B
S60.399A	S60.842A	S61.220A	S61.346A	S62.034A	S62.172A	S62.299A	S62.342A	S62.513A	S62.633A
S60.410A	S60.849A	S61.221A	S61.347A	S62.034B	S62.172B	S62.299B	S62.342B	S62.513B	S62.633B
S60.411A	S60.851A	S61.222A	S61.348A	S62.035A	S62.173A	S62.300A	S62.343A	S62.514A	S62.634A
S60.412A	S60.852A	S61.223A	S61.349A	S62.035B	S62.173B	S62.300B	S62.343B	S62.514B	S62.634B
S60.413A	S60.859A	S61.224A	S61.350A	S62.036A	S62.174A	S62.301A	S62.344A	S62.515A	S62.635A
S60.414A	S60.861A	S61.225A	S61.351A	S62.036B	S62.174B	S62.301B	S62.344B	S62.515B	S62.635B
S60.415A	S60.862A	S61.226A	S61.352A	S62.101A	S62.175A	S62.302A	S62.345A	S62.516A	S62.636A
S60.416A	S60.869A	S61.227A	S61.353A	S62.101B	S62.175B	S62.302B	S62.345B	S62.516B	S62.636B
S60.417A	S60.871A	S61.228A	S61.354A	S62.102A	S62.176A	S62.303A	S62.346A	S62.521A	S62.637A
S60.418A	S60.872A	S61.229A	S61.355A	S62.102B	S62.176B	S62.303B	S62.346B	S62.521B	S62.637B
S60.419A	S60.879A	S61.230A	S61.356A	S62.109A	S62.181A	S62.304A	S62.347A	S62.522A	S62.638A
S60.420A	S60.911A	S61.231A	S61.357A	S62.109B	S62.181B	S62.304B	S62.347B	S62.522B	S62.638B
S60.421A	S60.912A	S61.232A	S61.358A	S62.111A	S62.182A	S62.305A	S62.348A	S62.523A	S62.639A
S60.422A	S60.919A	S61.233A	S61.359A	S62.111B	S62.182B	S62.305B	S62.348B	S62.523B	S62.639B
S60.423A	S60.921A	S61.234A	S61.401A	S62.112A	S62.183A	S62.306A	S62.349A	S62.524A	S62.640A
S60.424A	S60.922A	S61.235A	S61.402A	S62.112B	S62.183B	S62.306B	S62.349B	S62.524B	S62.640B
S60.425A	S60.929A	S61.236A	S61.409A	S62.113A	S62.184A	S62.307A	S62.350A	S62.525A	S62.641A
S60.426A	S60.931A	S61.237A	S61.411A	S62.113B	S62.184B	S62.307B	S62.350B	S62.525B	S62.641B
S60.427A	S60.932A	S61.238A	S61.412A	S62.114A	S62.185A	S62.308A	S62.351A	S62.526A	S62.642A
S60.428A	S60.939A	S61.239A	S61.419A	S62.114B	S62.185B	S62.308B	S62.351B	S62.526B	S62.642B
S60.429A	S60.940A	S61.240A	S61.421A	S62.115A	S62.186A	S62.309A	S62.352A	S62.600A	S62.643A
S60.440A	S60.941A	S61.241A	S61.422A	S62.115B	S62.186B	S62.309B	S62.352B	S62.600B	S62.643B
S60.441A	S60.942A	S61.242A	S61.429A	S62.116A	S62.201A	S62.310A	S62.353A	S62.601A	S62.644A
S60.442A	S60.943A	S61.243A	S61.431A	S62.116B	S62.201B	S62.310B	S62.353B	S62.601B	S62.644B
S60.443A	S60.944A	S61.244A	S61.432A	S62.121A	S62.202A	S62.311A	S62.354A	S62.602A	S62.645A
S60.444A	S60.945A	S61.245A	S61.439A	S62.121B	S62.202B	S62.311B	S62.354B	S62.602B	S62.645B
S60.445A	S60.946A	S61.246A	S61.441A	S62.122A	S62.209A	S62.312A	S62.355A	S62.603A	S62.646A
S60.446A	S60.947A	S61.247A	S61.442A	S62.122B	S62.209B	S62.312B	S62.355B	S62.603B	S62.646B
S60.447A	S60.948A	S61.248A	S61.449A	S62.123A	S62.211A	S62.313A	S62.356A	S62.604A	S62.647A
S60.448A	S60.949A	S61.249A	S61.451A	S62.123B	S62.211B	S62.313B	S62.356B	S62.604B	S62.647B
S60.449A	S61.001A	S61.250A	S61.452A	S62.124A	S62.212A	S62.314A	S62.357A	S62.605A	S62.648A
S60.450A	S61.002A	S61.251A	S61.459A	S62.124B	S62.212B	S62.314B	S62.357B	S62.605B	S62.648B
S60.451A	S61.009A	S61.252A	S61.501A	S62.125A	S62.213A	S62.315A	S62.358A	S62.606A	S62.649A
S60.452A	S61.011A	S61.253A	S61.502A	S62.125B	S62.213B	S62.315B	S62.358B	S62.606B	S62.649B
S60.453A	S61.012A	S61.254A	S61.509A	S62.126A	S62.221A	S62.316A	S62.359A	S62.607A	S62.650A
S60.454A	S61.019A	S61.255A	S61.511A	S62.126B	S62.221B	S62.316B	S62.359B	S62.607B	S62.650B
S60.455A	S61.021A	S61.256A	S61.512A	S62.131A	S62.222A	S62.317A	S62.360A	S62.608A	S62.651A
S60.456A	S61.022A	S61.257A	S61.519A	S62.131B	S62.222B	S62.317B	S62.360B	S62.608B	S62.651B
S60.457A	S61.029A	S61.258A	S61.521A	S62.132A	S62.223A	S62.318A	S62.361A	S62.609A	S62.652A
S60.458A	S61.031A	S61.259A	S61.522A	S62.132B	S62.223B	S62.318B	S62.361B	S62.609B	S62.652B
S60.459A	S61.032A	S61.300A	S61.529A	S62.133A	S62.224A	S62.319A	S62.362A	S62.610A	S62.653A
S60.460A	S61.039A	S61.301A	S61.531A	S62.133B	S62.224B	S62.319B	S62.362B	S62.610B	S62.653B
S60.461A	S61.041A	S61.302A	S61.532A	S62.134A	S62.225A	S62.320A	S62.363A	S62.611A	S62.654A
S60.462A	S61.042A	S61.303A	S61.539A	S62.134B	S62.225B	S62.320B	S62.363B	S62.611B	S62.654B
S60.463A	S61.049A	S61.304A	S61.541A	S62.135A	S62.226A	S62.321A	S62.364A	S62.612A	S62.655A
S60.464A	S61.051A	S61.305A	S61.542A	S62.135B	S62.226B	S62.321B	S62.364B	S62.612B	S62.655B
S60.465A	S61.052A	S61.306A	S61.549A	S62.136A	S62.231A	S62.322A	S62.365A	S62.613A	S62.656A
S60.466A	S61.059A	S61.307A	S61.551A	S62.136B	S62.231B	S62.322B	S62.365B	S62.613B	S62.656B
S60.467A	S61.101A	S61.308A	S61.552A	S62.141A	S62.232A	S62.323A	S62.366A	S62.614A	S62.657A
S60.468A	S61.102A	S61.309A	S61.559A	S62.141B	S62.232B	S62.323B	S62.366B	S62.614B	S62.657B
S60.469A	S61.109A	S61.310A	S62.001A	S62.142A	S62.233A	S62.324A	S62.367A	S62.615A	S62.658B
S60.470A	S61.111A	S61.311A	S62.001B	S62.142B	S62.233B	S62.324B	S62.367B	S62.615B	S62.659A
S60.471A	S61.112A	S61.312A	S62.002A	S62.143A	S62.234A	S62.325A	S62.368A	S62.616A	S62.659B
S60.472A	S61.119A	S61.313A	S62.002B	S62.143B	S62.234B	S62.325B	S62.368B	S62.616B	S62.660A
S60.473A	S61.121A	S61.314A	S62.009A	S62.144A	S62.235A	S62.326A	S62.369A	S62.617A	S62.660B
S60.474A	S61.122A	S61.315A	S62.009B	S62.144B	S62.235B	S62.326B	S62.369B	S62.617B	S62.661A
S60.475A	S61.129A	S61.316A	S62.011A	S62.145A	S62.236A	S62.327A	S62.390A	S62.618A	S62.661B
S60.476A	S61.131A	S61.317A	S62.011B	S62.145B	S62.236B	S62.327B	S62.390B	S62.618B	S62.662A
S60.477A	S61.132A	S61.318A	S62.012A	S62.146A	S62.241A	S62.328A	S62.391A	S62.619A	S62.662B
S60.478A	S61.139A	S61.319A	S62.012B	S62.146B	S62.241B	S62.328B	S62.391B	S62.619B	S62.663A
S60.479A	S61.141A	S61.320A	S62.013A	S62.151A	S62.242A	S62.329A	S62.392A	S62.620A	S62.663B
S60.511A	S61.142A	S61.321A	S62.013B	S62.151B	S62.242B	S62.329B	S62.392B	S62.620B	S62.664A
S60.512A	S61.149A	S61.322A	S62.014A	S62.152A	S62.243A	S62.330A	S62.393A	S62.621A	S62.664B
S60.519A	S61.151A	S61.323A	S62.014B	S62.152B	S62.243B	S62.330B	S62.393B	S62.621B	S62.665A
S60.521A	S61.152A	S61.324A	S62.015A	S62.153A	S62.244A	S62.331A	S62.394A	S62.622A	S62.665B
S60.522A	S61.159A	S61.325A	S62.015B	S62.153B	S62.244B	S62.331B	S62.394B	S62.622B	S62.666A
S60.529A	S61.200A.	S61.326A	S62.016A	S62.154A	S62.245A	S62.332A	S62.395A	S62.623A	S62.666B

S62.666B	S63.201A	S63.287A	S63.529A	S64.8X9A	S65.892A	S66.311A	S66.819A	S68.614A	S71.032A
S62.667A	S63.202A	S63.288A	S63.591A	S64.90XA	S65.899A	S66.312A	S66.821A	S68.615A	S71.039A
S62.667B	S63.203A	S63.289A	S63.592A	S64.91XA	S65.901A	S66.313A	S66.822A	S68.616A	S71.041A
S62.668A	S63.204A	S63.290A	S63.599A	S64.92XA	S65.902A	S66.314A	S66.829A	S68.617A	S71.042A
S62.668B	S63.205A	S63.291A	S63.601A	S65.001A	S65.909A	S66.315A	S66.891A	S68.618A	S71.049A
S62.669A	S63.206A	S63.292A	S63.602A	S65.002A	S65.911A	S66.316A	S66.892A	S68.619A	S71.051A
S62.669B	S63.207A	S63.293A	S63.609A	S65.009A	S65.912A	S66.317A	S66.899A	S68.620A	S71.052A
S62.90XA	S63.208A	S63.294A	S63.610A	S65.011A	S65.919A	S66.318A	S66.901A	S68.621A	S71.059A
S62.90XB	S63.209A	S63.295A	S63.611A	S65.012A	S65.991A	S66.319A	S66.902A	S68.622A	S71.101A
S62.91XA	S63.210A	S63.296A	S63.612A	S65.019A	S65.992A	S66.320A	S66.909A	S68.623A	S71.102A
S62.91XB	S63.211A	S63.297A	S63.613A	S65.091A	S65.999A	S66.321A	S66.912A	S68.624A	S71.109A
S62.92XA	S63.212A	S63.298A	S63.614A	S65.092A	S66.001A	S66.322A	S66.919A	S68.625A	S71.111A
S62.92XB	S63.213A	S63.299A	S63.615A	S65.099A	S66.002A	S66.323A	S66.921A	S68.626A	S71.112A
S63.001A	S63.214A	S63.301A	S63.616A	S65.101A	S66.009A	S66.324A	S66.922A	S68.627A	S71.119A
S63.002A	S63.215A	S63.302A	S63.617A	S65.102A	S66.011A	S66.325A	S66.929A	S68.628A	S71.121A
S63.003A	S63.216A	S63.309A	S63.618A	S65.109A	S66.012A	S66.326A	S66.991A	S68.629A	S71.122A
S63.004A	S63.217A	S63.311A	S63.619A	S65.111A	S66.019A	S66.327A	S66.992A	S68.711A	S71.129A
S63.005A	S63.218A	S63.312A	S63.621A	S65.112A	S66.021A	S66.328A	S66.999A	S68.712A	S71.131A
S63.006A	S63.219A	S63.319A	S63.622A	S65.119A	S66.022A	S66.329A	S67.00XA	S68.719A	S71.132A
S63.011A	S63.220A	S63.321A	S63.629A	S65.191A	S66.029A	S66.390A	S67.01XA	S68.721A	S71.139A
S63.012A	S63.221A	S63.322A	S63.630A	S65.192A	S66.091A	S66.391A	S67.02XA	S68.722A	S71.141A
S63.013A	S63.222A	S63.329A	S63.631A	S65.199A	S66.092A	S66.392A	S67.10XA	S68.729A	S71.142A
S63.014A	S63.223A	S63.331A	S63.632A	S65.201A	S66.099A	S66.393A	S67.190A	S69.80XA	S71.149A
S63.015A	S63.224A	S63.332A	S63.633A	S65.202A	S66.100A	S66.394A	S67.191A	S69.81XA	S71.151A
S63.016A	S63.225A	S63.339A	S63.634A	S65.209A	S66.101A	S66.395A	S67.192A	S69.82XA	S71.152A
S63.021A	S63.226A	S63.391A	S63.635A	S65.211A	S66.102A	S66.396A	S67.193A	S69.90XA	S71.159A
S63.022A	S63.227A	S63.392A	S63.636A	S65.212A	S66.103A	S66.397A	S67.194A	S69.91XA	S72.001A
S63.023A	S63.228A	S63.399A	S63.637A	S65.219A	S66.104A	S66.398A	S67.195A	S69.92XA	S72.001B
S63.024A	S63.229A	S63.400A	S63.638A	S65.291A	S66.105A	S66.399A	S67.196A	S70.00XA	S72.001C
S63.025A	S63.230A	S63.401A	S63.639A	S65.292A	S66.106A	S66.401A	S67.197A	S70.01XA	S72.002A
S63.026A	S63.231A	S63.402A	S63.641A	S65.299A	S66.107A	S66.402A	S67.198A	S70.02XA	S72.002B
S63.031A	S63.232A	S63.403A	S63.642A	S65.301A	S66.108A	S66.409A	S67.20XA	S70.10XA	S72.002C
S63.032A	S63.233A	S63.404A	S63.649A	S65.302A	S66.109A	S66.411A	S67.21XA	S70.11XA	S72.009A
S63.033A	S63.234A	S63.405A	S63.650A	S65.309A	S66.110A	S66.412A	S67.22XA	S70.12XA	S72.009B
S63.034A	S63.235A	S63.406A	S63.651A	S65.311A	S66.111A	S66.419A	S67.30XA	S70.211A	S72.009C
S63.035A	S63.236A	S63.407A	S63.652A	S65.312A	S66.112A	S66.421A	S67.31XA	S70.212A	S72.011A
S63.036A	S63.237A	S63.408A	S63.653A	S65.319A	S66.113A	S66.422A	S67.32XA	S70.219A	S72.011B
S63.041A	S63.238A	S63.409A	S63.654A	S65.391A	S66.114A	S66.429A	S67.40XA	S70.221A	S72.011C
S63.042A	S63.239A	S63.410A	S63.655A	S65.392A	S66.115A	S66.491A	S67.41XA	S70.222A	S72.012A
S63.043A	S63.240A	S63.411A	S63.656A	S65.399A	S66.116A	S66.492A	S67.42XA	S70.229A	S72.012B
S63.044A	S63.241A	S63.412A	S63.657A	S65.401A	S66.117A	S66.499A	S67.90XA	S70.241A	S72.012C
S63.045A	S63.242A	S63.413A	S63.658A	S65.402A	S66.118A	S66.500A	S67.91XA	S70.242A	S72.019A
S63.046A	S63.243A	S63.414A	S63.659A	S65.409A	S66.119A	S66.501A	S67.92XA	S70.249A	S72.019B
S63.051A	S63.244A	S63.415A	S63.681A	S65.411A	S66.120A	S66.502A	S68.011A	S70.251A	S72.019C
S63.052A	S63.245A	S63.416A	S63.682A	S65.412A	S66.121A	S66.503A	S68.012A	S70.252A	S72.021A
S63.053A	S63.246A	S63.417A	S63.689A	S65.419A	S66.122A	S66.504A	S68.019A	S70.259A	S72.021B
S63.054A	S63.247A	S63.418A	S63.690A	S65.491A	S66.123A	S66.505A	S68.021A	S70.261A	S72.021C
S63.055A	S63.248A	S63.419A	S63.691A	S65.492A	S66.124A	S66.506A	S68.022A	S70.262A	S72.022A
S63.056A	S63.249A	S63.420A	S63.692A	S65.499A	S66.125A	S66.507A	S68.029A	S70.269A	S72.022B
S63.061A	S63.250A	S63.421A	S63.693A	S65.500A	S66.126A	S66.508A	S68.110A	S70.271A	S72.022C
S63.062A	S63.251A	S63.422A	S63.694A	S65.501A	S66.127A	S66.509A	S68.111A	S70.272A	S72.023A
S63.063A	S63.252A	S63.423A	S63.695A	S65.502A	S66.128A	S66.510A	S68.112A	S70.279A	S72.023B
S63.064A	S63.253A	S63.424A	S63.696A	S65.503A	S66.129A	S66.511A	S68.113A	S70.311A	S72.023C
S63.065A	S63.254A	S63.425A	S63.697A	S65.504A	S66.190A	S66.512A	S68.114A	S70.312A	S72.024A
S63.066A	S63.255A	S63.426A	S63.698A	S65.505A	S66.191A	S66.513A	S68.115A	S70.319A	S72.024B
S63.071A	S63.256A	S63.427A	S63.699A	S65.506A	S66.192A	S66.514A	S68.116A	S70.321A	S72.024C
S63.072A	S63.257A	S63.428A	S63.8X1A	S65.507A	S66.193A	S66.515A	S68.117A	S70.322A	S72.025A
S63.073A	S63.258A	S63.429A	S63.8X2A	S65.508A	S66.194A	S66.516A	S68.118A	S70.329A	S72.025B
S63.074A	S63.259A	S63.430A	S63.8X9A	S65.509A	S66.195A	S66.517A	S68.119A	S70.341A	S72.025C
S63.075A	S63.260A	S63.431A	S63.90XA	S65.510A	S66.196A	S66.518A	S68.120A	S70.342A	S72.026A
S63.076A	S63.261A	S63.432A	S63.91XA	S65.511A	S66.197A	S66.519A	S68.121A	S70.349A	S72.026B
S63.091A	S63.262A	S63.433A	S63.92XA	S65.512A	S66.198A	S66.520A	S68.122A	S70.351A	S72.026C
S63.092A	S63.263A	S63.434A	S64.00XA	S65.513A	S66.199A	S66.521A	S68.123A	S70.352A	S72.031A
S63.093A	S63.264A	S63.435A	S64.01XA	S65.514A	S66.201A	S66.522A	S68.124A	S70.359A	S72.031B
S63.094A	S63.265A	S63.436A	S64.02XA	S65.515A	S66.202A	S66.523A	S68.125A	S70.361A	S72.031C
S63.095A	S63.266A	S63.437A	S64.10XA	S65.516A	S66.209A	S66.524A	S68.126A	S70.362A	S72.032A
S63.096A	S63.267A	S63.438A	S64.11XA	S65.517A	S66.211A	S66.525A	S68.127A	S70.369A	S72.032B
S63.101A	S63.268A	S63.439A	S64.12XA	S65.518A	S66.212A	S66.526A	S68.128A	S70.371A	S72.032C
S63.102A	S63.269A	S63.490A	S64.20XA	S65.519A	S66.219A	S66.527A	S68.129A	S70.372A	S72.033A
S63.103A	S63.270A	S63.491A	S64.21XA	S65.590A	S66.221A	S66.528A	S68.411A	S70.379A	S72.033B
S63.104A	S63.271A	S63.492A	S64.22XA	S65.591A	S66.222A	S66.529A	S68.412A	S70.911A	S72.033C
S63.105A	S63.272A	S63.493A	S64.30XA	S65.592A	S66.229A	S66.590A	S68.419A	S70.912A	S72.034A
S63.106A	S63.273A	S63.494A	S64.31XA	S65.593A	S66.291A	S66.591A	S68.421A	S70.919A	S72.034B
S63.111A	S63.274A	S63.495A	S64.32XA	S65.594A	S66.292A	S66.592A	S68.422A	S70.921A	S72.034C
S63.112A	S63.275A	S63.496A	S64.40XA	S65.595A	S66.299A	S66.593A	S68.429A	S70.922A	S72.035A
S63.113A	S63.276A	S63.497A	S64.490A	S65.596A	S66.300A	S66.594A	S68.511A	S70.929A	S72.035B
S63.114A	S63.277A	S63.498A	S64.491A	S65.597A	S66.301A	S66.595A	S68.512A	S71.001A	S72.035C
S63.115A	S63.278A	S63.499A	S64.492A	S65.598A	S66.302A	S66.596A	S68.519A	S71.002A	S72.036A
S63.116A	S63.279A	S63.501A	S64.493A	S65.599A	S66.303A	S66.597A	S68.521A	S71.009A	S72.036B
S63.121A	S63.280A	S63.502A	S64.494A	S65.801A	S66.304A	S66.598A	S68.522A	S71.011A	S72.036C
S63.122A	S63.281A	S63.509A	S64.495A	S65.802A	S66.305A	S66.599A	S68.529A	S71.012A	S72.041A
S63.123A	S63.282A	S63.511A	S64.496A	S65.809A	S66.306A	S66.801A	S68.610A	S71.019A	S72.041B
S63.124A	S63.283A	S63.512A	S64.497A	S65.811A	S66.307A	S66.802A	S68.611A	S71.021A	S72.041C
S63.125A	S63.284A	S63.519A	S64.498A	S65.812A	S66.308A	S66.809A	S68.612A	S71.022A	S72.042A
S63.126A	S63.285A	S63.521A	S64.8X1A	S65.819A	S66.309A	S66.811A	S68.613A	S71.029A	S72.042B
S63.200A	S63.286A	S63.522A	S64.8X2A	S65.891A	S66.310A	S66.812A	S68.613A	S71.031A	S72.042C

S72.043A	S72.124C	S72.326B	S72.402A	S72.453C	S73.045A	S76.011A	S78.119A	S80.862A	S82.025A
S72.043B	S72.125A	S72.326C	S72.402B	S72.454A	S73.046A	S76.012A	S78.121A	S80.869A	S82.025B
S72.043C	S72.125B	S72.331A	S72.402C	S72.454B	S73.101A	S76.019A	S78.122A	S80.871A	S82.025C
S72.044A	S72.125C	S72.331B	S72.409A	S72.454C	S73.102A	S76.021A	S78.129A	S80.872A	S82.026A
S72.044B	S72.126A	S72.331C	S72.409B	S72.455A	S73.109A	S76.022A	S78.911A	S80.879A	S82.026B
S72.044C	S72.126B	S72.332A	S72.409C	S72.455B	S73.111A	S76.029A	S78.912A	S80.911A	S82.026C
S72.045A	S72.126C	S72.332B	S72.411A	S72.455C	S73.112A	S76.091A	S78.919A	S80.912A	S82.031A
S72.045B	S72.131A	S72.332C	S72.411B	S72.456A	S73.119A	S76.092A	S78.921A	S80.919A	S82.031B
S72.045C	S72.131B	S72.333A	S72.411C	S72.456B	S73.121A	S76.099A	S78.922A	S80.921A	S82.031C
S72.046A	S72.131C	S72.333B	S72.412A	S72.456C	S73.122A	S76.101A	S78.929A	S80.922A	S82.032A
S72.046B	S72.132A	S72.333C	S72.412B	S72.461A	S73.129A	S76.109A	S79.001A	S80.929A	S82.032B
S72.046C	S72.132B	S72.334A	S72.412C	S72.461B	S73.191A	S76.111A	S79.002A	S81.001A	S82.032C
S72.051A	S72.132C	S72.334B	S72.413A	S72.461C	S73.192A	S76.112A	S79.009A	S81.002A	S82.033A
S72.051B	S72.133A	S72.334C	S72.413B	S72.462A	S73.199A	S76.119A	S79.011A	S81.009A	S82.033B
S72.051C	S72.133B	S72.335A	S72.413C	S72.462B	S74.00XA	S76.121A	S79.012A	S81.011A	S82.033C
S72.052A	S72.133C	S72.335B	S72.414A	S72.462C	S74.01XA	S76.122A	S79.019A	S81.012A	S82.034A
S72.052B	S72.134A	S72.335C	S72.414B	S72.463A	S74.02XA	S76.129A	S79.091A	S81.019A	S82.034B
S72.052C	S72.134B	S72.336A	S72.414C	S72.463B	S74.10XA	S76.191A	S79.092A	S81.021A	S82.034C
S72.059A	S72.134C	S72.336B	S72.415A	S72.463C	S74.11XA	S76.192A	S79.099A	S81.022A	S82.035A
S72.059B	S72.135A	S72.336C	S72.415B	S72.464A	S74.12XA	S76.199A	S79.101A	S81.029A	S82.035B
S72.059C	S72.135B	S72.341A	S72.415C	S72.464B	S74.20XA	S76.201A	S79.102A	S81.031A	S82.035C
S72.061A	S72.135C	S72.341B	S72.416A	S72.464C	S74.21XA	S76.202A	S79.109A	S81.032A	S82.036A
S72.061B	S72.136A	S72.341C	S72.416B	S72.465A	S74.22XA	S76.209A	S79.111A	S81.039A	S82.036B
S72.061C	S72.136B	S72.342A	S72.416C	S72.465B	S74.8X1A	S76.211A	S79.112A	S81.041A	S82.036C
S72.062A	S72.136C	S72.342B	S72.421A	S72.465C	S74.8X2A	S76.212A	S79.119A	S81.042A	S82.041A
S72.062B	S72.141A	S72.342C	S72.421B	S72.466A	S74.8X9A	S76.219A	S79.121A	S81.049A	S82.041B
S72.062C	S72.141B	S72.343A	S72.421C	S72.466B	S74.90XA	S76.221A	S79.122A	S81.051A	S82.041C
S72.063A	S72.141C	S72.343B	S72.422A	S72.466C	S74.91XA	S76.222A	S79.129A	S81.052A	S82.042A
S72.063B	S72.142A	S72.343C	S72.422B	S72.471A	S74.92XA	S76.229A	S79.131A	S81.059A	S82.042B
S72.063C	S72.142B	S72.344A	S72.422C	S72.472A	S75.001A	S76.291A	S79.132A	S81.801A	S82.042C
S72.064A	S72.142C	S72.344B	S72.423A	S72.479A	S75.002A	S76.292A	S79.139A	S81.802A	S82.043A
S72.064B	S72.143A	S72.344C	S72.423B	S72.491A	S75.009A	S76.299A	S79.141A	S81.809A	S82.043B
S72.064C	S72.143B	S72.345A	S72.423C	S72.491B	S75.011A	S76.301A	S79.142A	S81.811A	S82.043C
S72.065A	S72.143C	S72.345B	S72.424A	S72.491C	S75.012A	S76.309A	S79.149A	S81.812A	S82.044A
S72.065B	S72.144A	S72.345C	S72.424B	S72.492A	S75.019A	S76.311A	S79.191A	S81.819A	S82.044B
S72.065C	S72.144B	S72.346A	S72.424C	S72.492B	S75.021A	S76.312A	S79.192A	S81.821A	S82.044C
S72.066A	S72.144C	S72.346B	S72.425A	S72.492C	S75.022A	S76.319A	S79.199A	S81.822A	S82.045A
S72.066B	S72.145A	S72.346C	S72.425B	S72.499A	S75.029A	S76.321A	S79.811A	S81.829A	S82.045B
S72.066C	S72.145B	S72.351A	S72.425C	S72.499B	S75.091A	S76.322A	S79.812A	S81.831A	S82.045C
S72.091A	S72.145C	S72.351B	S72.426A	S72.499C	S75.092A	S76.329A	S79.819A	S81.832A	S82.046A
S72.091B	S72.146A	S72.351C	S72.426B	S72.8X1A	S75.099A	S76.391A	S79.821A	S81.839A	S82.046B
S72.091C	S72.146B	S72.352A	S72.426C	S72.8X1B	S75.101A	S76.392A	S79.822A	S81.841A	S82.046C
S72.092A	S72.146C	S72.352B	S72.431A	S72.8X1C	S75.102A	S76.399A	S79.829A	S81.842A	S82.091A
S72.092B	S72.21XA	S72.352C	S72.431B	S72.8X2A	S75.109A	S76.801A	S79.911A	S81.849A	S82.091B
S72.092C	S72.21XB	S72.353A	S72.431C	S72.8X2B	S75.111A	S76.802A	S79.912A	S81.851A	S82.091C
S72.099A	S72.21XC	S72.353B	S72.432A	S72.8X2C	S75.112A	S76.809A	S79.919A	S81.852A	S82.092A
S72.099B	S72.22XA	S72.353C	S72.432B	S72.8X9A	S75.119A	S76.811A	S79.921A	S81.859A	S82.092B
S72.099C	S72.22XB	S72.354A	S72.432C	S72.8X9B	S75.121A	S76.812A	S79.922A	S82.001A	S82.092C
S72.101A	S72.22XC	S72.354B	S72.433A	S72.8X9C	S75.122A	S76.819A	S79.929A	S82.001B	S82.099A
S72.101B	S72.23XA	S72.354C	S72.433B	S72.90XA	S75.129A	S76.821A	S80.00XA	S82.001C	S82.099B
S72.101C	S72.23XB	S72.355A	S72.433C	S72.90XB	S75.191A	S76.822A	S80.01XA	S82.002A	S82.099C
S72.102A	S72.23XC	S72.355B	S72.434A	S72.90XC	S75.192A	S76.829A	S80.02XA	S82.002B	S82.101A
S72.102B	S72.24XA	S72.355C	S72.434B	S72.91XA	S75.199A	S76.891A	S80.10XA	S82.002C	S82.101B
S72.102C	S72.24XB	S72.356A	S72.434C	S72.91XB	S75.201A	S76.892A	S80.11XA	S82.009A	S82.101C
S72.109A	S72.24XC	S72.356B	S72.435A	S72.91XC	S75.202A	S76.899A	S80.12XA	S82.009B	S82.102A
S72.109B	S72.25XA	S72.356C	S72.435B	S72.92XA	S75.209A	S76.901A	S80.211A	S82.009C	S82.102B
S72.109C	S72.25XB	S72.361A	S72.435C	S72.92XB	S75.211A	S76.902A	S80.212A	S82.011A	S82.102C
S72.111A	S72.25XC	S72.361B	S72.436A	S72.92XC	S75.212A	S76.909A	S80.219A	S82.011B	S82.109A
S72.111B	S72.26XA	S72.361C	S72.436B	S73.001A	S75.219A	S76.911A	S80.221A	S82.011C	S82.109B
S72.111C	S72.26XB	S72.362A	S72.436C	S73.002A	S75.221A	S76.912A	S80.222A	S82.012A	S82.109C
S72.112A	S72.26XC	S72.362B	S72.441A	S73.003A	S75.222A	S76.919A	S80.229A	S82.012B	S82.111A
S72.112B	S72.301A	S72.362C	S72.441B	S73.004A	S75.229A	S76.921A	S80.241A	S82.012C	S82.111B
S72.112C	S72.301B	S72.363A	S72.441C	S73.005A	S75.291A	S76.922A	S80.242A	S82.013A	S82.111C
S72.113A	S72.301C	S72.363B	S72.442A	S73.006A	S75.292A	S76.929A	S80.249A	S82.013B	S82.112A
S72.113B	S72.302A	S72.363C	S72.442B	S73.011A	S75.299A	S76.991A	S80.251A	S82.013C	S82.112B
S72.113C	S72.302B	S72.364A	S72.442C	S73.012A	S75.801A	S76.992A	S80.252A	S82.014A	S82.112C
S72.114A	S72.302C	S72.364B	S72.443A	S73.013A	S75.802A	S76.999A	S80.259A	S82.014B	S82.113A
S72.114B	S72.309A	S72.364C	S72.443B	S73.014A	S75.809A	S77.00XA	S80.261A	S82.014C	S82.113B
S72.114C	S72.309B	S72.365A	S72.443C	S73.015A	S75.811A	S77.01XA	S80.262A	S82.015A	S82.113C
S72.115A	S72.309C	S72.365B	S72.444A	S73.016A	S75.812A	S77.02XA	S80.269A	S82.015B	S82.114A
S72.115B	S72.321A	S72.365C	S72.444B	S73.021A	S75.819A	S77.10XA	S80.271A	S82.015C	S82.114B
S72.115C	S72.321B	S72.366A	S72.444C	S73.022A	S75.891A	S77.11XA	S80.272A	S82.016A	S82.114C
S72.116A	S72.321C	S72.366B	S72.445A	S73.023A	S75.892A	S77.12XA	S80.279A	S82.016B	S82.115A
S72.116B	S72.322A	S72.366C	S72.445B	S73.024A	S75.899A	S77.20XA	S80.811A	S82.016C	S82.115B
S72.116C	S72.322B	S72.391A	S72.445C	S73.025A	S75.901A	S77.21XA	S80.812A	S82.021A	S82.115C
S72.121A	S72.322C	S72.391B	S72.446A	S73.026A	S75.902A	S77.22XA	S80.819A	S82.021B	S82.116A
S72.121B	S72.323A	S72.391C	S72.446B	S73.031A	S75.909A	S78.011A	S80.821A	S82.021C	S82.116B
S72.121C	S72.323B	S72.392A	S72.446C	S73.032A	S75.911A	S78.012A	S80.822A	S82.022A	S82.116C
S72.122A	S72.323C	S72.392B	S72.451A	S73.033A	S75.912A	S78.019A	S80.829A	S82.022B	S82.121A
S72.122B	S72.324A	S72.392C	S72.451B	S73.034A	S75.919A	S78.021A	S80.841A	S82.022C	S82.121B
S72.122C	S72.324B	S72.399A	S72.451C	S73.035A	S75.991A	S78.022A	S80.842A	S82.023A	S82.121C
S72.123A	S72.324C	S72.399B	S72.452A	S73.036A	S75.992A	S78.029A	S80.849A	S82.023B	S82.122A
S72.123B	S72.325A	S72.399C	S72.452B	S73.041A	S75.999A	S78.111A	S80.851A	S82.023C	S82.122B
S72.123C	S72.325B	S72.401A	S72.452C	S73.042A	S76.001A	S78.112A	S80.852A	S82.024A	S82.122C
S72.124A	S72.325C	S72.401B	S72.453A	S73.043A	S76.002A		S80.859A	S82.024B	S82.123A
S72.124B	S72.326A	S72.401C	S72.453B	S73.044A	S76.009A		S80.861A	S82.024C	S82.123B

S82.123C	S82.221B	S82.266A	S82.443C	S82.65XB	S82.875A	S83.209A	S85.122A	S86.101A	S89.009A
S82.124A	S82.221C	S82.266B	S82.444A	S82.65XC	S82.875B	S83.211A	S85.129A	S86.102A	S89.011A
S82.124B	S82.222A	S82.266C	S82.444B	S82.66XA	S82.875C	S83.212A	S85.131A	S86.109A	S89.012A
S82.124C	S82.222B	S82.291A	S82.444C	S82.66XB	S82.876A	S83.219A	S85.132A	S86.111A	S89.019A
S82.125A	S82.222C	S82.291B	S82.445A	S82.66XC	S82.876B	S83.221A	S85.139A	S86.112A	S89.021A
S82.125C	S82.223A	S82.291C	S82.445B	S82.811A	S82.876C	S83.222A	S85.141A	S86.119A	S89.022A
S82.126A	S82.223B	S82.292A	S82.445C	S82.812A	S82.891A	S83.229A	S85.142A	S86.121A	S89.029A
S82.126B	S82.223C	S82.292B	S82.446A	S82.819A	S82.891B	S83.231A	S85.149A	S86.122A	S89.031A
S82.126C	S82.224A	S82.292C	S82.446B	S82.821A	S82.891C	S83.232A	S85.151A	S86.129A	S89.032A
S82.131A	S82.224B	S82.299A	S82.446C	S82.822A	S82.892A	S83.239A	S85.152A	S86.191A	S89.039A
S82.131B	S82.224C	S82.299B	S82.451A	S82.829A	S82.892B	S83.241A	S85.159A	S86.192A	S89.041A
S82.131C	S82.225A	S82.299C	S82.451B	S82.831A	S82.892C	S83.242A	S85.161A	S86.199A	S89.042A
S82.132A	S82.225B	S82.301A	S82.451C	S82.831B	S82.899A	S83.249A	S85.162A	S86.201A	S89.049A
S82.132B	S82.225C	S82.301B	S82.452A	S82.831C	S82.899B	S83.251A	S85.169A	S86.202A	S89.091A
S82.132C	S82.226A	S82.301C	S82.452B	S82.832A	S82.899C	S83.252A	S85.171A	S86.209A	S89.092A
S82.133A	S82.226B	S82.302A	S82.453A	S82.832B	S82.90XA	S83.259A	S85.172A	S86.211A	S89.099A
S82.133B	S82.226C	S82.302B	S82.453B	S82.832C	S82.90XB	S83.261A	S85.179A	S86.212A	S89.101A
S82.133C	S82.231A	S82.302C	S82.453C	S82.839A	S82.90XC	S83.262A	S85.181A	S86.219A	S89.102A
S82.134A	S82.231B	S82.309A	S82.454A	S82.839B	S82.91XA	S83.269A	S85.182A	S86.221A	S89.109A
S82.134B	S82.231C	S82.309B	S82.454B	S82.839C	S82.91XB	S83.271A	S85.189A	S86.222A	S89.111A
S82.134C	S82.232A	S82.309C	S82.454C	S82.841A	S82.91XC	S83.272A	S85.201A	S86.229A	S89.112A
S82.135A	S82.232B	S82.311A	S82.455A	S82.841B	S82.92XA	S83.279A	S85.202A	S86.291A	S89.119A
S82.135B	S82.232C	S82.312A	S82.455B	S82.841C	S82.92XB	S83.281A	S85.209A	S86.292A	S89.121A
S82.135C	S82.233A	S82.319A	S82.455C	S82.842A	S82.92XC	S83.282A	S85.211A	S86.299A	S89.122A
S82.136A	S82.233B	S82.391A	S82.456A	S82.842B	S83.001A	S83.289A	S85.212A	S86.301A	S89.129A
S82.136B	S82.233C	S82.391B	S82.456B	S82.842C	S83.002A	S83.30XA	S85.219A	S86.302A	S89.131A
S82.136C	S82.234A	S82.391C	S82.456C	S82.843A	S83.003A	S83.31XA	S85.291A	S86.309A	S89.132A
S82.141A	S82.234B	S82.392A	S82.461A	S82.843B	S83.004A	S83.32XA	S85.292A	S86.311A	S89.139A
S82.141B	S82.234C	S82.392B	S82.461B	S82.843C	S83.005A	S83.401A	S85.299A	S86.312A	S89.141A
S82.141C	S82.235A	S82.392C	S82.461C	S82.844A	S83.006A	S83.402A	S85.301A	S86.319A	S89.142A
S82.142A	S82.235B	S82.399A	S82.462A	S82.844B	S83.011A	S83.409A	S85.302A	S86.321A	S89.149A
S82.142B	S82.235C	S82.399B	S82.462B	S82.844C	S83.012A	S83.411A	S85.309A	S86.322A	S89.191A
S82.142C	S82.236A	S82.399C	S82.462C	S82.845A	S83.013A	S83.412A	S85.311A	S86.329A	S89.192A
S82.143A	S82.236B	S82.401A	S82.463A	S82.845B	S83.014A	S83.419A	S85.312A	S86.391A	S89.199A
S82.143B	S82.236C	S82.401B	S82.463B	S82.845C	S83.015A	S83.421A	S85.319A	S86.392A	S89.201A
S82.143C	S82.241A	S82.401C	S82.463C	S82.846A	S83.016A	S83.422A	S85.391A	S86.399A	S89.202A
S82.144A	S82.241B	S82.402A	S82.464A	S82.846B	S83.091A	S83.429A	S85.392A	S86.801A	S89.209A
S82.144B	S82.241C	S82.402B	S82.464B	S82.846C	S83.092A	S83.501A	S85.399A	S86.802A	S89.211A
S82.144C	S82.242A	S82.402C	S82.464C	S82.851A	S83.093A	S83.502A	S85.401A	S86.809A	S89.212A
S82.145A	S82.242B	S82.409A	S82.465A	S82.851B	S83.094A	S83.509A	S85.402A	S86.811A	S89.219A
S82.145B	S82.242C	S82.409B	S82.465B	S82.851C	S83.095A	S83.511A	S85.409A	S86.812A	S89.221A
S82.145C	S82.243A	S82.409C	S82.465C	S82.852A	S83.096A	S83.512A	S85.411A	S86.819A	S89.222A
S82.146A	S82.243B	S82.421A	S82.466A	S82.852B	S83.101A	S83.519A	S85.412A	S86.821A	S89.229A
S82.146B	S82.243C	S82.421B	S82.466B	S82.853A	S83.102A	S83.521A	S85.419A	S86.822A	S89.291A
S82.146C	S82.244A	S82.421C	S82.466C	S82.853B	S83.103A	S83.522A	S85.491A	S86.829A	S89.292A
S82.151A	S82.244B	S82.422A	S82.491A	S82.853C	S83.104A	S83.529A	S85.492A	S86.891A	S89.299A
S82.151B	S82.244C	S82.422B	S82.491B	S82.854A	S83.105A	S83.60XA	S85.499A	S86.892A	S89.301A
S82.151C	S82.245A	S82.422C	S82.491C	S82.854B	S83.106A	S83.61XA	S85.501A	S86.899A	S89.302A
S82.152A	S82.245B	S82.423A	S82.492A	S82.854C	S83.111A	S83.62XA	S85.502A	S86.901A	S89.309A
S82.152B	S82.245C	S82.423B	S82.492B	S82.855A	S83.112A	S83.8X1A	S85.509A	S86.902A	S89.311A
S82.152C	S82.246A	S82.423C	S82.492C	S82.855B	S83.113A	S83.8X2A	S85.511A	S86.909A	S89.312A
S82.153A	S82.246B	S82.424A	S82.499A	S82.855C	S83.114A	S83.8X9A	S85.512A	S86.911A	S89.319A
S82.153B	S82.246C	S82.424B	S82.499B	S82.856A	S83.115A	S83.90XA	S85.519A	S86.912A	S89.321A
S82.153C	S82.251A	S82.424C	S82.499C	S82.856B	S83.116A	S83.91XA	S85.591A	S86.919A	S89.322A
S82.154A	S82.251B	S82.425A	S82.51XA	S82.856C	S83.121A	S83.92XA	S85.592A	S86.921A	S89.329A
S82.154B	S82.251C	S82.425B	S82.51XB	S82.861A	S83.122A	S84.00XA	S85.599A	S86.922A	S89.391A
S82.154C	S82.252A	S82.425C	S82.51XC	S82.861B	S83.123A	S84.01XA	S85.801A	S86.929A	S89.392A
S82.155A	S82.252B	S82.426A	S82.52XA	S82.861C	S83.124A	S84.02XA	S85.802A	S86.991A	S89.399A
S82.155B	S82.252C	S82.426B	S82.52XB	S82.862A	S83.125A	S84.10XA	S85.809A	S86.992A	S89.80XA
S82.155C	S82.253A	S82.426C	S82.52XC	S82.862B	S83.126A	S84.11XA	S85.811A	S86.999A	S89.81XA
S82.156A	S82.253B	S82.431A	S82.53XA	S82.862C	S83.131A	S84.12XA	S85.812A	S87.00XA	S89.82XA
S82.156B	S82.253C	S82.431B	S82.53XB	S82.863A	S83.132A	S84.20XA	S85.819A	S87.01XA	S89.90XA
S82.156C	S82.254A	S82.431C	S82.53XC	S82.863B	S83.133A	S84.21XA	S85.891A	S87.02XA	S89.91XA
S82.161A	S82.254B	S82.432A	S82.54XA	S82.863C	S83.134A	S84.22XA	S85.892A	S87.80XA	S89.92XA
S82.162A	S82.254C	S82.432B	S82.54XB	S82.864A	S83.135A	S84.801A	S85.899A	S87.81XA	S90.00XA
S82.169A	S82.255A	S82.432C	S82.54XC	S82.864B	S83.136A	S84.802A	S85.901A	S87.82XA	S90.01XA
S82.191A	S82.255B	S82.433A	S82.55XA	S82.864C	S83.141A	S84.809A	S85.902A	S88.011A	S90.02XA
S82.191B	S82.255C	S82.433B	S82.55XB	S82.865A	S83.142A	S84.90XA	S85.909A	S88.012A	S90.111A
S82.191C	S82.256A	S82.433C	S82.55XC	S82.865B	S83.143A	S84.91XA	S85.911A	S88.019A	S90.112A
S82.192A	S82.256B	S82.434A	S82.56XA	S82.865C	S83.144A	S84.92XA	S85.912A	S88.021A	S90.119A
S82.192B	S82.256C	S82.434B	S82.56XB	S82.866A	S83.145A	S85.001A	S85.919A	S88.022A	S90.121A
S82.192C	S82.261A	S82.434C	S82.56XC	S82.866B	S83.146A	S85.002A	S85.991A	S88.029A	S90.122A
S82.199A	S82.261B	S82.435A	S82.61XA	S82.866C	S83.191A	S85.009A	S85.992A	S88.111A	S90.129A
S82.199B	S82.261C	S82.435B	S82.61XB	S82.871A	S83.192A	S85.011A	S85.999A	S88.112A	S90.211A
S82.199C	S82.262A	S82.435C	S82.61XC	S82.871B	S83.193A	S85.012A	S86.001A	S88.119A	S90.212A
S82.201A	S82.262B	S82.436A	S82.62XA	S82.871C	S83.194A	S85.019A	S86.002A	S88.121A	S90.219A
S82.201B	S82.262C	S82.436B	S82.62XB	S82.872A	S83.195A	S85.091A	S86.009A	S88.122A	S90.221A
S82.201C	S82.263A	S82.436C	S82.62XC	S82.872B	S83.196A	S85.092A	S86.011A	S88.129A	S90.222A
S82.202A	S82.263B	S82.441A	S82.63XA	S82.872C	S83.200A	S85.099A	S86.012A	S88.911A	S90.229A
S82.202B	S82.263C	S82.441B	S82.63XB	S82.873A	S83.201A	S85.101A	S86.019A	S88.912A	S90.30XA
S82.202C	S82.264A	S82.441C	S82.63XC	S82.873B	S83.202A	S85.102A	S86.021A	S88.919A	S90.31XA
S82.209A	S82.264B	S82.442A	S82.64XA	S82.873C	S83.203A	S85.109A	S86.022A	S88.921A	S90.32XA
S82.209B	S82.264C	S82.442B	S82.64XB	S82.874A	S83.204A	S85.111A	S86.029A	S88.922A	S90.411A
S82.209C	S82.265A	S82.442C	S82.64XC	S82.874B	S83.205A	S85.112A	S86.091A	S88.929A	S90.412A
S82.221A	S82.265B	S82.443A	S82.65XA	S82.874C	S83.206A	S85.119A	S86.092A	S89.001A	S90.413A
	S82.265C	S82.443B			S83.207A	S85.121A	S86.099A	S89.002A	S90.414A

S90.415A	S91.021A	S91.245A	S92.053A	S92.191A	S92.315A	S92.426A	S93.101A	S93.519A	S96.011A
S90.416A	S91.022A	S91.246A	S92.053B	S92.191B	S92.315B	S92.426B	S93.102A	S93.521A	S96.012A
S90.421A	S91.029A	S91.249A	S92.054A	S92.192A	S92.316A	S92.491A	S93.103A	S93.522A	S96.019A
S90.422A	S91.031A	S91.251A	S92.054B	S92.192B	S92.316B	S92.491B	S93.104A	S93.523A	S96.021A
S90.423A	S91.032A	S91.252A	S92.055A	S92.199A	S92.321A	S92.492A	S93.105A	S93.524A	S96.022A
S90.424A	S91.039A	S91.253A	S92.055B	S92.199B	S92.321B	S92.492B	S93.106A	S93.525A	S96.029A
S90.425A	S91.041A	S91.254A	S92.056A	S92.201A	S92.322A	S92.499A	S93.111A	S93.526A	S96.091A
S90.426A	S91.042A	S91.255A	S92.056B	S92.201B	S92.322B	S92.499B	S93.112A	S93.529A	S96.092A
S90.441A	S91.049A	S91.256A	S92.061A	S92.202A	S92.323A	S92.501A	S93.113A	S93.601A	S96.099A
S90.442A	S91.051A	S91.259A	S92.061B	S92.202B	S92.323B	S92.501B	S93.114A	S93.602A	S96.101A
S90.443A	S91.052A	S91.301A	S92.062A	S92.209A	S92.324A	S92.502A	S93.115A	S93.609A	S96.102A
S90.444A	S91.059A	S91.302A	S92.062B	S92.209B	S92.324B	S92.502B	S93.116A	S93.611A	S96.109A
S90.445A	S91.101A	S91.309A	S92.063A	S92.211A	S92.325A	S92.503A	S93.119A	S93.612A	S96.111A
S90.446A	S91.102A	S91.311A	S92.063B	S92.211B	S92.325B	S92.503B	S93.121A	S93.619A	S96.112A
S90.451A	S91.103A	S91.312A	S92.064A	S92.212A	S92.326A	S92.504A	S93.122A	S93.621A	S96.119A
S90.452A	S91.104A	S91.319A	S92.064B	S92.212B	S92.326B	S92.504B	S93.123A	S93.622A	S96.121A
S90.453A	S91.105A	S91.321A	S92.065A	S92.213A	S92.331A	S92.505A	S93.124A	S93.629A	S96.122A
S90.454A	S91.106A	S91.322A	S92.065B	S92.213B	S92.331B	S92.505B	S93.125A	S93.691A	S96.129A
S90.455A	S91.109A	S91.329A	S92.066A	S92.214A	S92.332A	S92.506A	S93.126A	S93.692A	S96.191A
S90.456A	S91.111A	S91.331A	S92.066B	S92.214B	S92.332B	S92.506B	S93.129A	S93.699A	S96.192A
S90.461A	S91.112A	S91.332A	S92.101A	S92.215A	S92.333A	S92.511A	S93.131A	S94.00XA	S96.199A
S90.462A	S91.113A	S91.339A	S92.101B	S92.215B	S92.333B	S92.511B	S93.132A	S94.01XA	S96.201A
S90.463A	S91.114A	S91.341A	S92.102A	S92.216A	S92.334A	S92.512A	S93.133A	S94.02XA	S96.202A
S90.464A	S91.115A	S91.342A	S92.102B	S92.216B	S92.334B	S92.512B	S93.134A	S94.10XA	S96.209A
S90.465A	S91.116A	S91.349A	S92.109A	S92.221A	S92.335A	S92.513A	S93.135A	S94.11XA	S96.211A
S90.466A	S91.119A	S91.351A	S92.109B	S92.221B	S92.335B	S92.513B	S93.136A	S94.12XA	S96.212A
S90.471A	S91.121A	S91.352A	S92.111A	S92.222A	S92.336A	S92.514A	S93.139A	S94.20XA	S96.219A
S90.472A	S91.122A	S91.359A	S92.111B	S92.222B	S92.336B	S92.514B	S93.141A	S94.21XA	S96.221A
S90.473A	S91.123A	S92.001A	S92.112A	S92.223A	S92.341A	S92.515A	S93.142A	S94.22XA	S96.222A
S90.474A	S91.124A	S92.001B	S92.112B	S92.223B	S92.341B	S92.515B	S93.143A	S94.30XA	S96.229A
S90.475A	S91.125A	S92.002A	S92.113A	S92.224A	S92.342A	S92.516A	S93.144A	S94.31XA	S96.291A
S90.476A	S91.126A	S92.002B	S92.113B	S92.224B	S92.342B	S92.516B	S93.145A	S94.32XA	S96.292A
S90.511A	S91.129A	S92.009A	S92.114A	S92.225A	S92.343A	S92.521A	S93.146A	S94.8X1A	S96.299A
S90.512A	S91.131A	S92.009B	S92.114B	S92.225B	S92.343B	S92.521B	S93.149A	S94.8X2A	S96.801A
S90.519A	S91.132A	S92.011A	S92.115A	S92.226A	S92.344A	S92.522A	S93.301A	S94.8X9A	S96.802A
S90.521A	S91.133A	S92.011B	S92.115B	S92.226B	S92.344B	S92.522B	S93.302A	S94.90XA	S96.809A
S90.522A	S91.134A	S92.012A	S92.116A	S92.231A	S92.345A	S92.523A	S93.304A	S94.91XA	S96.811A
S90.529A	S91.135A	S92.012B	S92.116B	S92.231B	S92.345B	S92.523B	S93.305A	S94.92XA	S96.812A
S90.541A	S91.136A	S92.013A	S92.121A	S92.232A	S92.346A	S92.524A	S93.306A	S95.001A	S96.819A
S90.542A	S91.139A	S92.013B	S92.121B	S92.232B	S92.346B	S92.524B	S93.311A	S95.002A	S96.821A
S90.549A	S91.141A	S92.014A	S92.122A	S92.233A	S92.351A	S92.525A	S93.312A	S95.009A	S96.822A
S90.551A	S91.142A	S92.014B	S92.122B	S92.233B	S92.351B	S92.525B	S93.313A	S95.011A	S96.829A
S90.552A	S91.143A	S92.015A	S92.123A	S92.234A	S92.352A	S92.526A	S93.314A	S95.012A	S96.891A
S90.559A	S91.144A	S92.015B	S92.123B	S92.234B	S92.352B	S92.526B	S93.315A	S95.019A	S96.892A
S90.561A	S91.145A	S92.016A	S92.124A	S92.235A	S92.353A	S92.531A	S93.316A	S95.091A	S96.899A
S90.562A	S91.146A	S92.016B	S92.124B	S92.235B	S92.353B	S92.531B	S93.321A	S95.092A	S96.901A
S90.569A	S91.149A	S92.021A	S92.125A	S92.236A	S92.354A	S92.532A	S93.322A	S95.099A	S96.902A
S90.571A	S91.151A	S92.021B	S92.125B	S92.236B	S92.354B	S92.532B	S93.323A	S95.101A	S96.909A
S90.572A	S91.152A	S92.022A	S92.126A	S92.241A	S92.355A	S92.533A	S93.324A	S95.102A	S96.911A
S90.579A	S91.153A	S92.022B	S92.126B	S92.241B	S92.355B	S92.533B	S93.325A	S95.109A	S96.912A
S90.811A	S91.154A	S92.023A	S92.131A	S92.242A	S92.356A	S92.534A	S93.326A	S95.111A	S96.919A
S90.812A	S91.155A	S92.023B	S92.131B	S92.242B	S92.356B	S92.534B	S93.331A	S95.112A	S96.921A
S90.819A	S91.156A	S92.024A	S92.132A	S92.243A	S92.401A	S92.535A	S93.332A	S95.119A	S96.922A
S90.821A	S91.159A	S92.024B	S92.132B	S92.243B	S92.401B	S92.535B	S93.333A	S95.191A	S96.929A
S90.822A	S91.201A	S92.025A	S92.133A	S92.244A	S92.402A	S92.536A	S93.334A	S95.192A	S96.991A
S90.829A	S91.202A	S92.025B	S92.133B	S92.244B	S92.402B	S92.536B	S93.335A	S95.199A	S96.992A
S90.841A	S91.203A	S92.026A	S92.134A	S92.245A	S92.403A	S92.591A	S93.336A	S95.201A	S96.999A
S90.842A	S91.204A	S92.026B	S92.134B	S92.245B	S92.403B	S92.591B	S93.401A	S95.202A	S97.00XA
S90.849A	S91.205A	S92.031A	S92.135A	S92.246A	S92.404A	S92.592A	S93.402A	S95.209A	S97.01XA
S90.851A	S91.206A	S92.031B	S92.135B	S92.246B	S92.404B	S92.592B	S93.409A	S95.211A	S97.02XA
S90.852A	S91.209A	S92.032A	S92.136A	S92.251A	S92.405A	S92.599A	S93.411A	S95.212A	S97.101A
S90.859A	S91.211A	S92.032B	S92.136B	S92.251B	S92.405B	S92.599B	S93.412A	S95.219A	S97.102A
S90.861A	S91.212A	S92.033A	S92.141A	S92.252A	S92.406A	S92.811A	S93.419A	S95.291A	S97.109A
S90.862A	S91.213A	S92.033B	S92.141B	S92.252B	S92.406B	S92.811B	S93.421A	S95.292A	S97.111A
S90.869A	S91.214A	S92.034A	S92.142A	S92.253A	S92.411A	S92.812A	S93.422A	S95.299A	S97.112A
S90.871A	S91.215A	S92.034B	S92.142B	S92.253B	S92.411B	S92.812B	S93.429A	S95.801A	S97.119A
S90.872A	S91.216A	S92.035A	S92.143A	S92.254A	S92.412A	S92.819A	S93.431A	S95.802A	S97.121A
S90.879A	S91.219A	S92.035B	S92.143B	S92.254B	S92.412B	S92.819B	S93.432A	S95.809A	S97.122A
S90.911A	S91.221A	S92.036A	S92.144A	S92.255A	S92.413A	S92.901A	S93.439A	S95.811A	S97.129A
S90.912A	S91.222A	S92.036B	S92.144B	S92.255B	S92.413B	S92.901B	S93.491A	S95.812A	S97.80XA
S90.919A	S91.223A	S92.041A	S92.145A	S92.256A	S92.414A	S92.902A	S93.492A	S95.819A	S97.81XA
S90.921A	S91.224A	S92.041B	S92.145B	S92.256B	S92.414B	S92.902B	S93.499A	S95.891A	S97.82XA
S90.922A	S91.225A	S92.042A	S92.146A	S92.301A	S92.415A	S92.909A	S93.501A	S95.892A	S98.011A
S90.929A	S91.226A	S92.042B	S92.146B	S92.301B	S92.415B	S92.909B	S93.502A	S95.899A	S98.012A
S90.931A	S91.229A	S92.043A	S92.151A	S92.302A	S92.416A	S92.911A	S93.503A	S95.901A	S98.019A
S90.932A	S91.231A	S92.043B	S92.151B	S92.302B	S92.416B	S92.911B	S93.504A	S95.902A	S98.021A
S90.933A	S91.232A	S92.044A	S92.152A	S92.309A	S92.421A	S92.912A	S93.505A	S95.909A	S98.022A
S90.934A	S91.233A	S92.044B	S92.152B	S92.309B	S92.421B	S92.912B	S93.506A	S95.911A	S98.029A
S90.935A	S91.234A	S92.045A	S92.153A	S92.311A	S92.422A	S92.919A	S93.509A	S95.912A	S98.111A
S90.936A	S91.235A	S92.045B	S92.153B	S92.311B	S92.422B	S92.919B	S93.511A	S95.919A	S98.112A
S91.001A	S91.236A	S92.046A	S92.154A	S92.312A	S92.423A	S93.01XA	S93.512A	S95.991A	S98.119A
S91.002A	S91.239A	S92.046B	S92.154B	S92.312B	S92.423B	S93.02XA	S93.513A	S95.992A	S98.121A
S91.009A	S91.241A	S92.051A	S92.155A	S92.313A	S92.424A	S93.03XA	S93.514A	S95.999A	S98.122A
S91.011A	S91.242A	S92.051B	S92.155B	S92.313B	S92.424B	S93.04XA	S93.515A	S96.001A	S98.129A
S91.012A	S91.243A	S92.052A	S92.156A	S92.314A	S92.425A	S93.05XA	S93.516A	S96.002A	S98.131A
S91.019A	S91.244A	S92.052B	S92.156B	S92.314B	S92.425B	S93.06XA		S96.009A	S98.132A

S98.139A	S98.912A	S99.021A	S99.049B	S99.119A	S99.142B	S99.212A	S99.241B	S99.911A	T79.8XXA
S98.141A	S98.919A	S99.021B	S99.091A	S99.119B	S99.149A	S99.212B	S99.242A	S99.912A	T79.9XXA
S98.142A	S98.921A	S99.022A	S99.091B	S99.121A	S99.149B	S99.219A	S99.242B	S99.919A	T79.A0XA
S98.149A	S98.922A	S99.022B	S99.092A	S99.121B	S99.191A	S99.219B	S99.249A	S99.921A	T79.A11A
S98.211A	S98.929A	S99.029A	S99.092B	S99.122A	S99.191B	S99.221A	S99.249B	S99.922A	T79.A12A
S98.212A	S99.001A	S99.029B	S99.099A	S99.122B	S99.192A	S99.221B	S99.291A	S99.929A	T79.A19A
S98.219A	S99.001B	S99.031A	S99.099B	S99.129A	S99.192B	S99.222A	S99.291B	T07.XXXA	T79.A21A
S98.221A	S99.002A	S99.031B	S99.101A	S99.129B	S99.199A	S99.222B	S99.292A	T14.8XXA	T79.A22A
S98.222A	S99.002B	S99.032A	S99.101B	S99.131A	S99.199B	S99.229A	S99.292B	T14.90XA	T79.A29A
S98.229A	S99.009A	S99.032B	S99.102A	S99.131B	S99.201A	S99.229B	S99.299A	T14.91XA	T79.A3XA
S98.311A	S99.009B	S99.039A	S99.102B	S99.132A	S99.201B	S99.231A	S99.299B	T79.0XXA	T79.A9XA
S98.312A	S99.011A	S99.039B	S99.109A	S99.132B	S99.202A	S99.231B	S99.811A	T79.1XXA	
S98.319A	S99.011B	S99.041A	S99.109B	S99.139A	S99.202B	S99.232A	S99.812A	T79.2XXA	
S98.321A	S99.012A	S99.041B	S99.111A	S99.139B	S99.209A	S99.232B	S99.819A	T79.4XXA	
S98.322A	S99.012B	S99.042A	S99.111B	S99.141A	S99.209B	S99.239A	S99.821A	T79.5XXA	
S98.329A	S99.019A	S99.042B	S99.112A	S99.141B	S99.211A	S99.239B	S99.822A	T79.6XXA	
S98.911A	S99.019B	S99.049A	S99.112B	S99.142A	S99.211B	S99.241A	S99.829A	T79.7XXA	

MDC 25 Human Immunodeficiency Virus Infections

A02.1	A31.9	B02.22	B47.1	C83.34	C84.79	C85.94	D80.0	E51.8	G96.9
A02.20	A40.9	B02.23	B47.9	C83.35	C84.90	C85.95	D80.1	E51.9	G98.8
A02.21	A41.01	B02.29	B48.8	C83.36	C84.91	C85.96	D80.2	E52	H35.00
A02.22	A41.02	B02.30	B58.00	C83.37	C84.92	C85.97	D80.3	E53.0	H35.011
A02.23	A41.1	B02.31	B58.01	C83.38	C84.93	C85.98	D80.4	E53.1	H35.012
A02.24	A41.2	B02.32	B58.09	C83.39	C84.94	C85.99	D80.5	E53.8	H35.013
A02.25	A41.3	B02.33	B58.1	C83.70	C84.95	C86.0	D80.6	E53.9	H35.019
A02.29	A41.4	B02.34	B58.2	C83.71	C84.96	C86.1	D80.7	E54	H35.021
A02.8	A41.50	B02.39	B58.3	C83.72	C84.97	C86.2	D80.8	E55.0	H35.022
A02.9	A41.51	B02.7	B58.81	C83.73	C84.98	C86.3	D80.9	E55.9	H35.023
A07.3	A41.52	B02.8	B58.82	C83.74	C84.99	C86.4	D81.0	E56.0	H35.029
A09	A41.53	B02.9	B58.83	C83.75	C84.A0	C86.5	D81.1	E56.1	H35.031
A15.0	A41.59	B10.01	B58.89	C83.76	C84.A1	C86.6	D81.2	E56.8	H35.032
A15.4	A41.81	B10.09	B58.9	C83.77	C84.A2	C88.4	D81.4	E56.9	H35.033
A15.5	A41.89	B20	B59	C83.78	C84.A3	D50.0	D81.6	E58	H35.039
A15.6	A41.9	B25.8	B60.8	C83.79	C84.A4	D50.1	D81.7	E59	H35.041
A15.7	A42.0	B25.9	B78.0	C83.80	C84.A5	D50.8	D81.818	E60	H35.042
A15.8	A42.1	B35.0	B78.7	C83.81	C84.A6	D50.9	D81.819	E61.0	H35.043
A15.9	A42.2	B35.1	B78.9	C83.82	C84.A7	D51.0	D81.89	E61.1	H35.049
A17.0	A42.7	B35.2	B97.10	C83.83	C84.A8	D51.1	D81.9	E61.2	H35.051
A17.1	A42.81	B35.3	B99.8	C83.84	C84.A9	D51.2	D82.0	E61.3	H35.052
A17.81	A42.82	B35.4	C46.0	C83.85	C84.Z0	D51.3	D82.1	E61.4	H35.053
A17.82	A42.89	B35.5	C46.1	C83.86	C84.Z1	D51.8	D82.2	E61.5	H35.059
A17.83	A42.9	B35.6	C46.2	C83.87	C84.Z2	D51.9	D82.3	E61.6	H35.061
A17.89	A43.0	B35.8	C46.3	C83.88	C84.Z3	D52.0	D82.4	E61.7	H35.062
A17.9	A43.1	B35.9	C46.4	C83.89	C84.Z4	D52.1	D82.8	E61.8	H35.063
A18.01	A43.8	B36.0	C46.50	C83.90	C84.Z5	D52.8	D82.9	E61.9	H35.069
A18.02	A43.9	B36.1	C46.51	C83.91	C84.Z6	D52.9	D83.0	E63.0	H35.071
A18.03	A48.1	B36.2	C46.52	C83.92	C84.Z7	D53.0	D83.1	E63.1	H35.072
A18.09	A60.00	B36.3	C46.7	C83.93	C84.Z8	D53.1	D83.2	E63.8	H35.073
A18.10	A60.01	B36.8	C46.9	C83.94	C84.Z9	D53.2	D83.8	E63.9	H35.079
A18.11	A60.04	B36.9	C82.50	C83.95	C85.10	D53.8	D83.9	E64.0	H35.09
A18.12	A60.09	B37.0	C82.51	C83.96	C85.11	D53.9	D84.0	E64.1	H54.0X33
A18.13	A60.1	B37.1	C82.52	C83.97	C85.12	D59.0	D84.8	E64.2	H54.0X34
A18.14	A60.9	B37.2	C82.53	C83.98	C85.13	D59.1	D84.9	E64.3	H54.0X35
A18.15	A74.9	B37.5	C82.54	C83.99	C85.14	D59.2	D89.3	E64.8	H54.0X43
A18.16	A81.2	B37.6	C82.55	C84.40	C85.15	D59.3	D89.40	E64.9	H54.0X44
A18.17	A81.82	B37.81	C82.56	C84.41	C85.16	D59.4	D89.41	E86.0	H54.0X45
A18.18	A81.83	B37.82	C82.57	C84.42	C85.17	D59.5	D89.42	E86.1	H54.0X53
A18.2	A81.89	B37.83	C82.58	C84.43	C85.18	D59.6	D89.43	E86.9	H54.0X54
A18.31	A81.9	B37.84	C82.59	C84.44	C85.19	D59.8	D89.49	F03.90	H54.0X55
A18.32	A85.0	B37.89	C83.00	C84.45	C85.20	D59.9	D89.82	F06.8	H54.10
A18.39	A85.1	B37.9	C83.01	C84.46	C85.21	D60.0	D89.89	F07.9	H54.1131
A18.4	A85.8	B38.0	C83.02	C84.47	C85.22	D60.1	D89.9	F09	H54.1132
A18.50	A86	B38.1	C83.03	C84.48	C85.23	D60.8	E40	F28	H54.1141
A18.51	A87.9	B38.2	C83.04	C84.49	C85.24	D60.9	E41	F29	H54.1142
A18.52	A88.8	B38.3	C83.05	C84.60	C85.25	D61.1	E42	G03.2	H54.1151
A18.53	A89	B38.4	C83.06	C84.61	C85.26	D61.2	E43	G04.81	H54.1152
A18.54	B00.0	B38.7	C83.07	C84.62	C85.27	D61.3	E44.0	G04.89	H54.1213
A18.59	B00.1	B38.81	C83.08	C84.63	C85.28	D61.89	E44.1	G04.90	H54.1214
A18.6	B00.2	B38.89	C83.09	C84.64	C85.29	D61.9	E45	G04.91	H54.1215
A18.7	B00.3	B38.9	C83.10	C84.65	C85.80	D64.9	E46	G36.9	H54.1223
A18.81	B00.4	B39.0	C83.11	C84.66	C85.81	D69.51	E50.0	G37.4	H54.1224
A18.82	B00.50	B39.1	C83.12	C84.67	C85.82	D69.59	E50.1	G37.9	H54.1225
A18.83	B00.51	B39.2	C83.13	C84.68	C85.83	D69.6	E50.2	G61.0	H54.1213
A18.84	B00.52	B39.3	C83.14	C84.69	C85.84	D70.0	E50.3	G61.9	H54.2X11
A18.85	B00.53	B39.4	C83.15	C84.70	C85.85	D70.1	E50.4	G62.9	H54.2X12
A18.89	B00.59	B39.5	C83.16	C84.71	C85.86	D70.2	E50.5	G93.3	H54.2X21
A19.0	B00.7	B39.9	C83.17	C84.72	C85.87	D70.3	E50.6	G93.40	H54.2X22
A19.1	B00.81	B45.0	C83.18	C84.73	C85.88	D70.4	E50.7	G93.41	H54.3
A19.2	B00.89	B45.2	C83.19	C84.74	C85.89	D70.8	E50.8	G93.49	H54.40
A19.8	B00.9	B45.3	C83.30	C84.75	C85.90	D70.9	E50.9	G93.9	H54.413A
A19.9	B02.0	B45.7	C83.31	C84.76	C85.91	D73.1	E51.11	G95.20	H54.414A
A31.2	B02.1	B45.8	C83.32	C84.77	C85.92	D75.82	E51.12	G95.29	H54.415A
A31.8	B02.21	B45.9	C83.33	C84.78	C85.93	D75.9	E51.2	G95.9	H54.42A3
									H54.42A4

H54.42A5	J15.211	L04.0	M00.10	M00.232	M00.861	N01.1	N04.3	N07.5	R21
H54.50	J15.212	L04.1	M00.111	M00.239	M00.862	N01.2	N04.4	N07.6	R50.2
H54.511A	J15.29	L04.2	M00.112	M00.241	M00.869	N01.3	N04.5	N07.7	R50.81
H54.512A	J15.3	L04.3	M00.119	M00.242	M00.871	N01.4	N04.6	N07.8	R50.82
H54.52A1	J15.4	L04.8	M00.121	M00.249	M00.872	N01.5	N04.7	N07.9	R50.83
H54.52A2	J15.5	L04.9	M00.122	M00.251	M00.879	N01.6	N04.8	N08	R50.84
H54.60	J15.6	L08.1	M00.129	M00.252	M00.88	N01.7	N04.9	N14.0	R50.9
H54.61	J15.8	L98.9	M00.131	M00.259	M00.89	N01.8	N05.0	N14.1	R53.0
H54.62	J15.9	M00.00	M00.132	M00.261	M00.9	N01.9	N05.1	N14.2	R53.1
H54.7	J18.1	M00.011	M00.139	M00.262	M12.9	N02.0	N05.2	N14.3	R53.81
H54.8	J18.8	M00.012	M00.141	M00.269	M54.10	N02.1	N05.3	N14.4	R53.82
I33.0	J18.9	M00.019	M00.142	M00.271	M54.18	N02.2	N05.4	N15.0	R53.83
I33.9	J84.09	M00.021	M00.149	M00.272	M79.2	N02.3	N05.5	N15.8	R59.0
I40.0	J84.111	M00.022	M00.151	M00.279	M83.0	N02.4	N05.6	N15.9	R59.1
I40.1	J84.116	M00.029	M00.152	M00.28	M83.1	N02.5	N05.7	N16	R59.9
I40.8	J84.117	M00.031	M00.159	M00.29	M83.2	N02.6	N05.8	P92.6	R61
I40.9	J84.2	M00.032	M00.161	M00.80	M83.3	N02.7	N05.9	R06.00	R62.0
I42.7	K11.9	M00.039	M00.162	M00.811	M83.4	N02.8	N06.0	R06.01	R62.50
I42.9	K13.21	M00.041	M00.169	M00.812	M83.5	N02.9	N06.1	R06.02	R62.51
I67.3	K13.3	M00.042	M00.171	M00.819	M83.8	N03.0	N06.2	R06.03	R62.52
I67.83	K52.0	M00.049	M00.172	M00.821	M83.9	N03.1	N06.3	R06.09	R62.59
J09.X1	K52.1	M00.051	M00.179	M00.822	N00.0	N03.2	N06.4	R06.2	R63.4
J10.08	K52.3	M00.052	M00.18	M00.829	N00.1	N03.3	N06.5	R06.3	R63.6
J12.3	K52.81	M00.059	M00.19	M00.831	N00.2	N03.4	N06.6	R06.4	R64
J12.81	K52.82	M00.061	M00.20	M00.832	N00.3	N03.5	N06.7	R06.81	
J12.89	K52.831	M00.062	M00.211	M00.839	N00.4	N03.6	N06.8	R06.82	
J12.9	K52.832	M00.069	M00.212	M00.841	N00.5	N03.7	N06.9	R06.83	
J13	K52.838	M00.071	M00.219	M00.842	N00.6	N03.8	N07.0	R06.89	
J14	K52.839	M00.072	M00.221	M00.849	N00.7	N03.9	N07.1	R06.9	
J15.0	K52.89	M00.079	M00.222	M00.851	N00.8	N04.0	N07.2	R16.0	
J15.1	K52.9	M00.08	M00.229	M00.852	N00.9	N04.1	N07.3	R16.1	
J15.20	K90.9	M00.09	M00.231	M00.859	N01.0	N04.2	N07.4	R16.2	

DRG Decision Trees

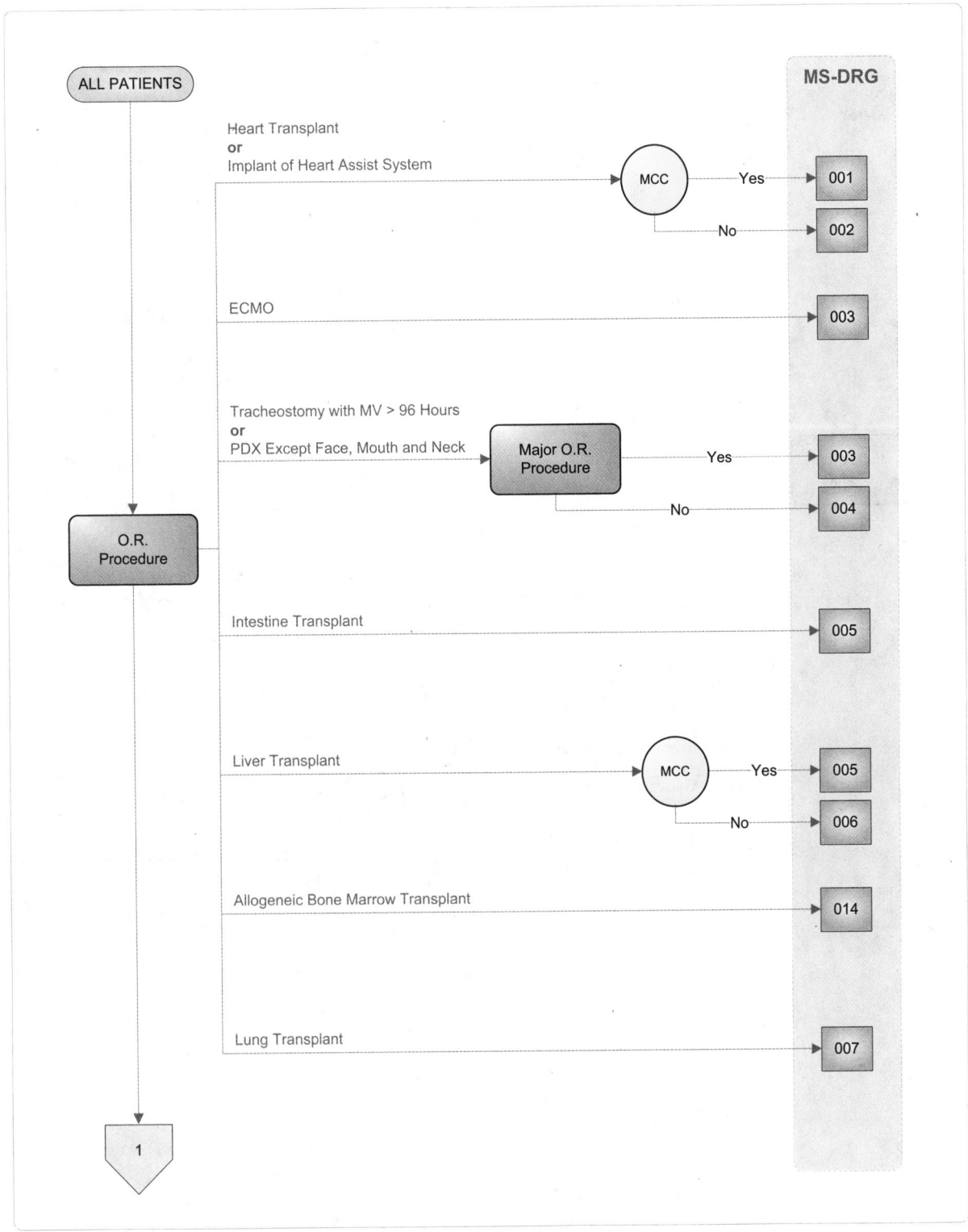

Pre-MDC

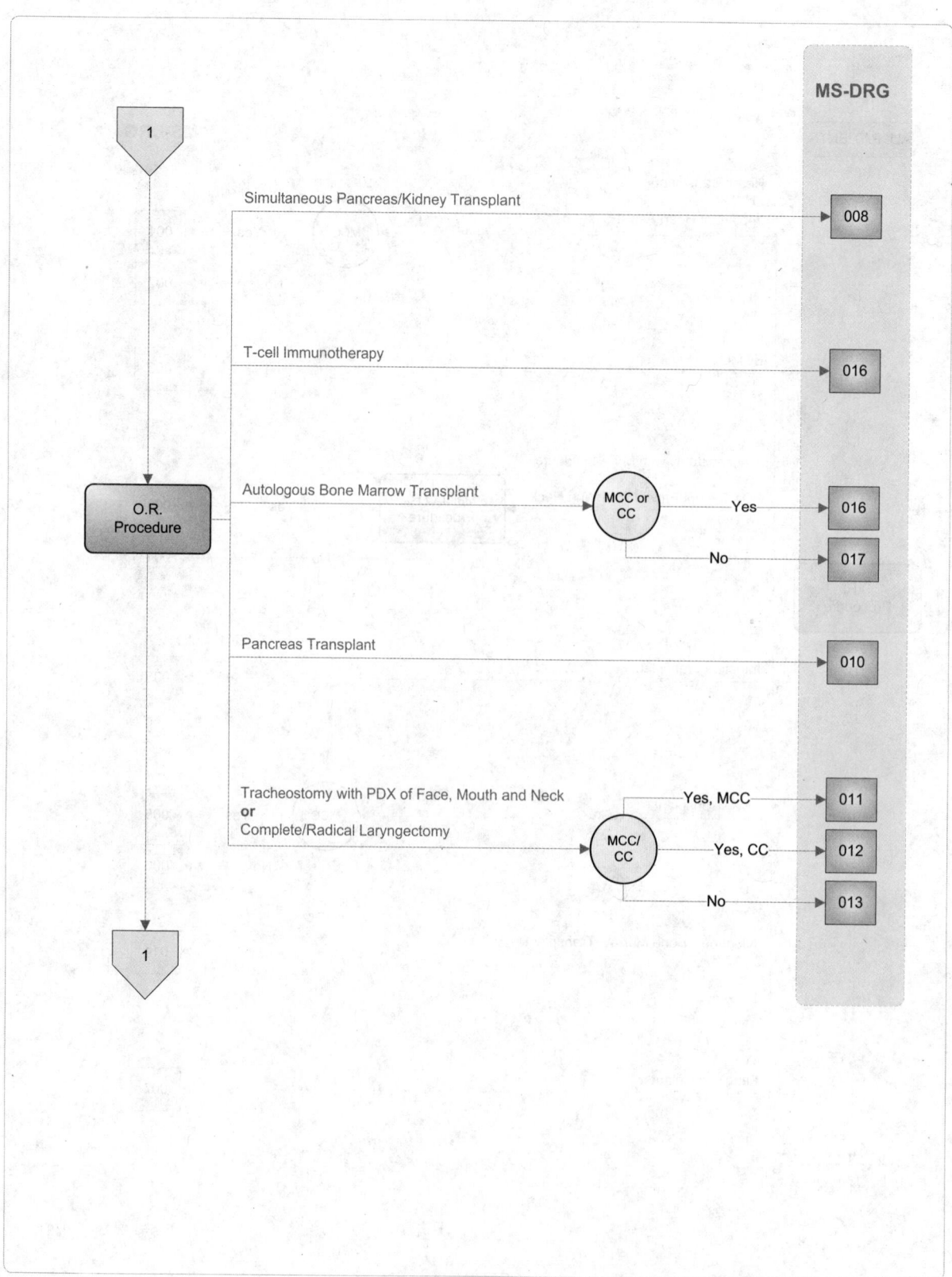

MS-DRG

1

Simultaneous Pancreas/Kidney Transplant → 008

T-cell Immunotherapy → 016

O.R. Procedure

Autologous Bone Marrow Transplant → MCC or CC — Yes → 016

No → 017

Pancreas Transplant → 010

Tracheostomy with PDX of Face, Mouth and Neck
or
Complete/Radical Laryngectomy → MCC/CC — Yes, MCC → 011

Yes, CC → 012

No → 013

1

All Patients

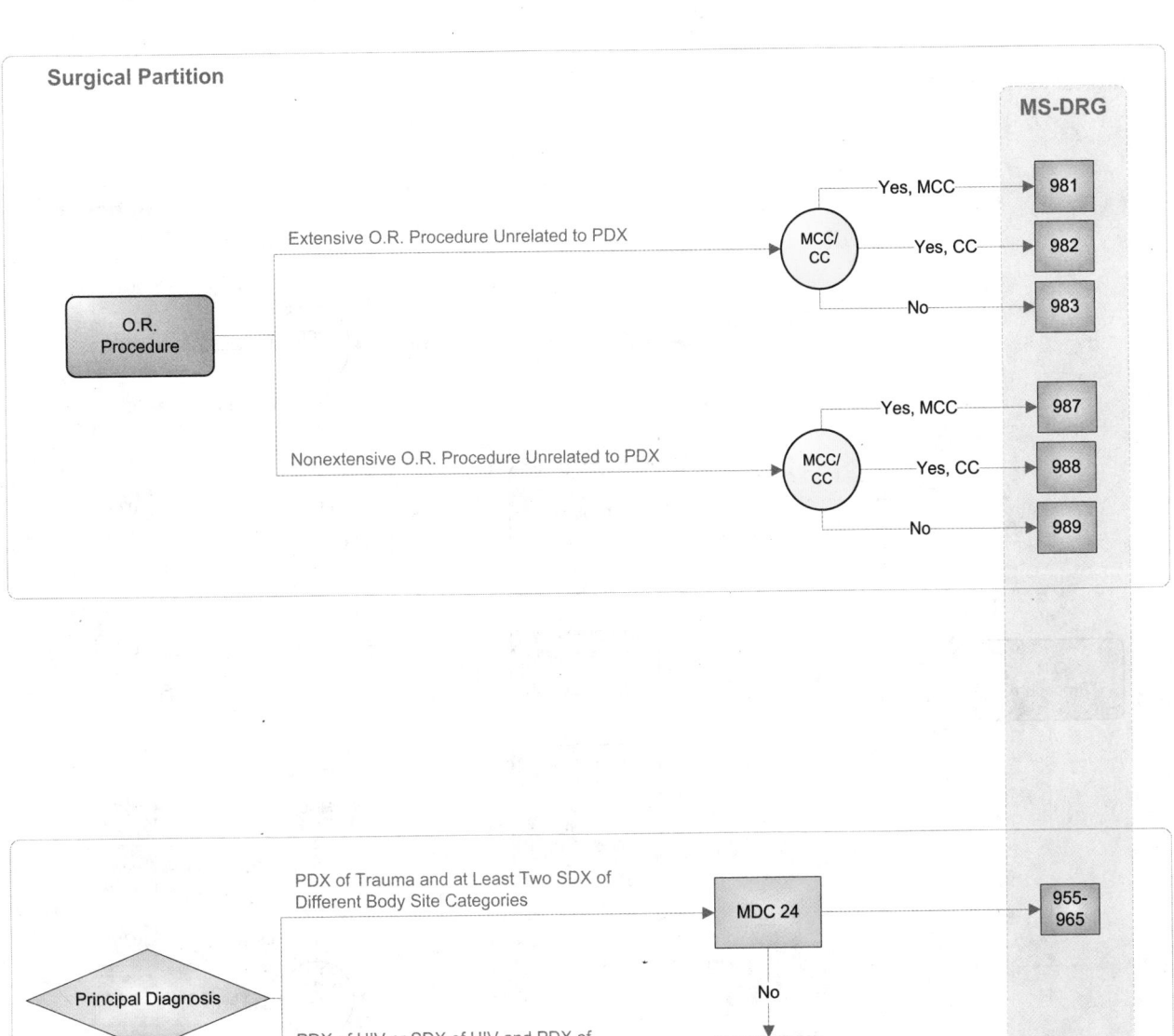

Major Diagnostic Category 1
Diseases and Disorders of the Nervous System

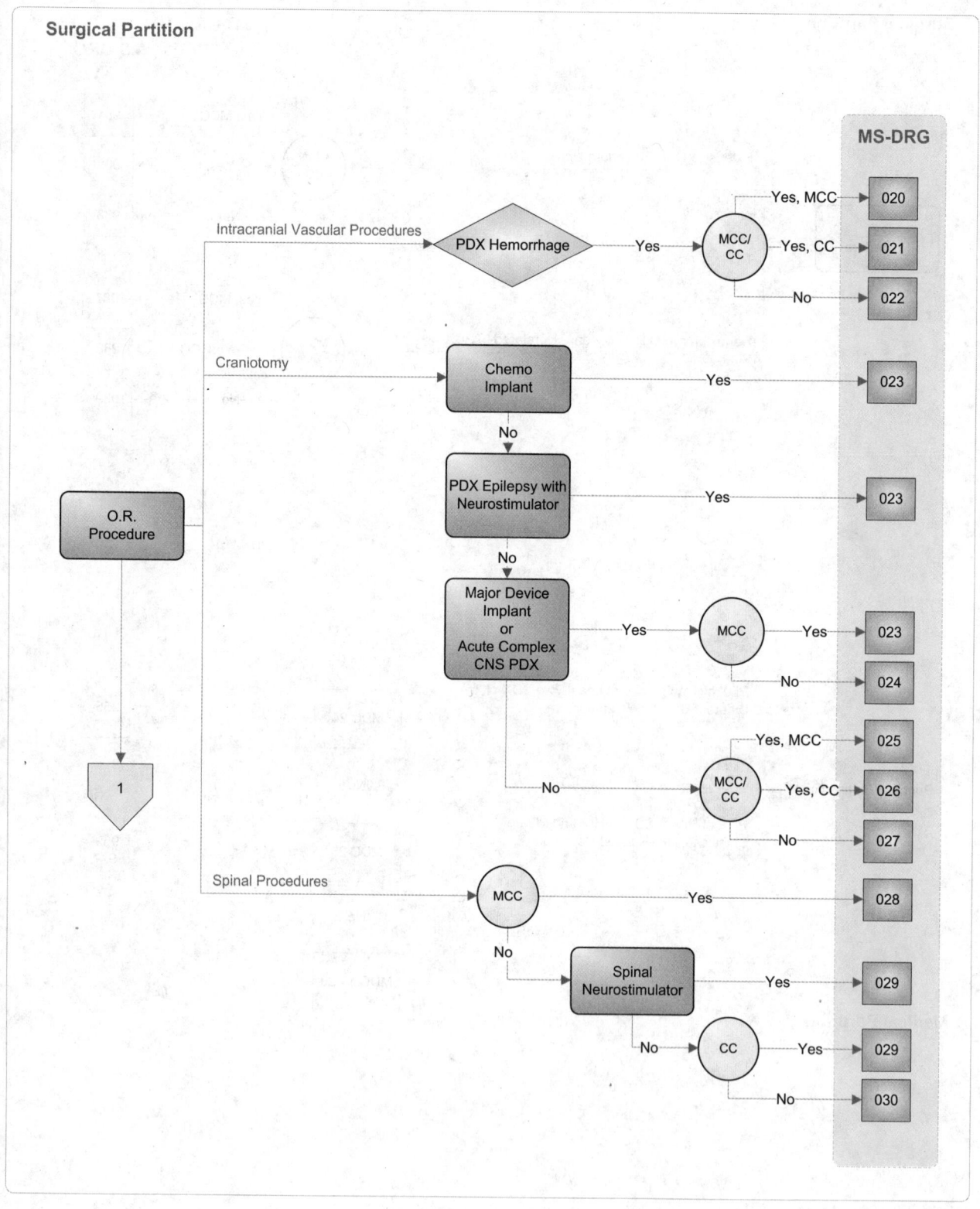

Major Diagnostic Category 1
Diseases and Disorders of the Nervous System

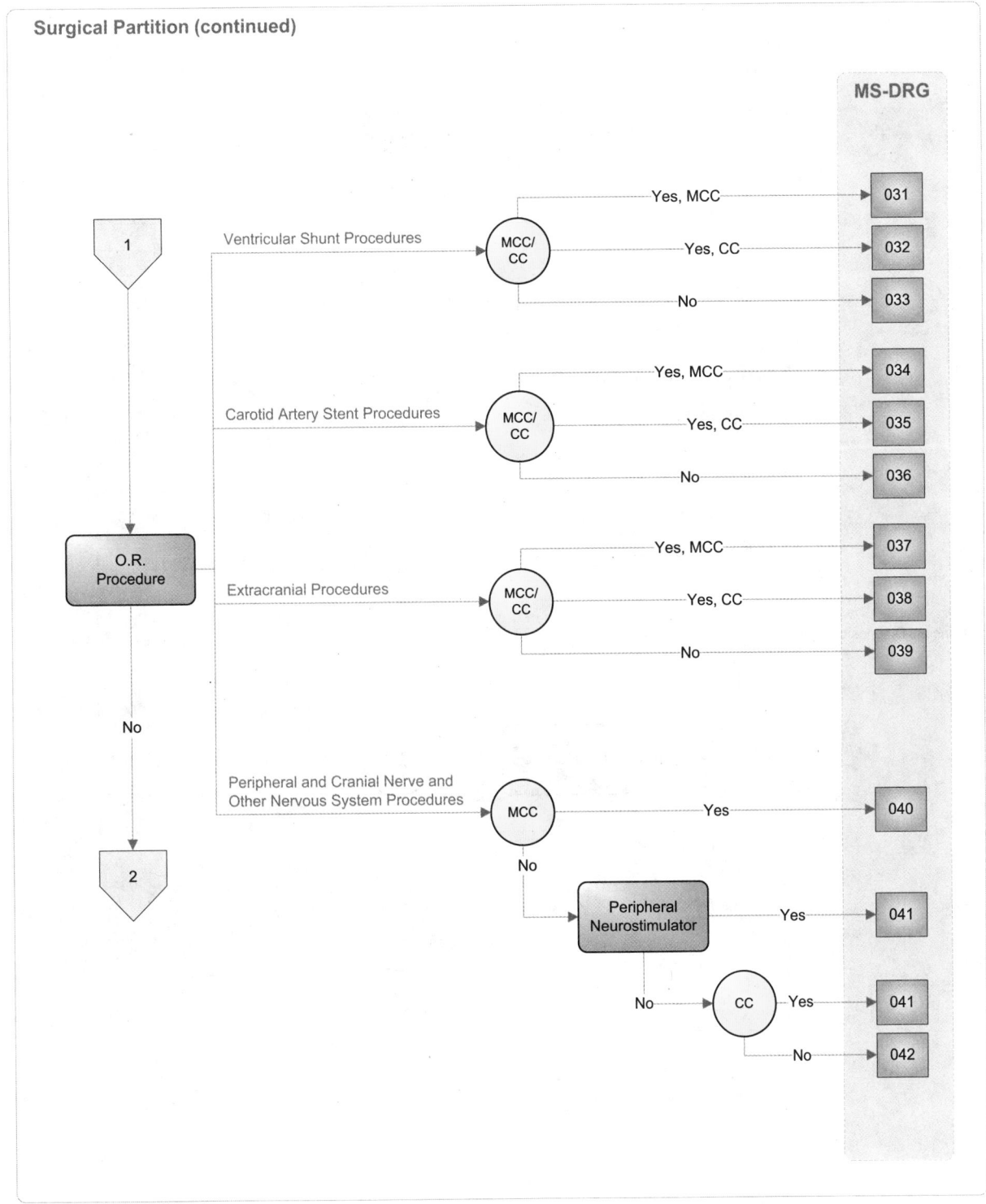

Surgical Partition (continued)

MS-DRG

1 → O.R. Procedure

Ventricular Shunt Procedures → MCC/CC
- Yes, MCC → 031
- Yes, CC → 032
- No → 033

Carotid Artery Stent Procedures → MCC/CC
- Yes, MCC → 034
- Yes, CC → 035
- No → 036

Extracranial Procedures → MCC/CC
- Yes, MCC → 037
- Yes, CC → 038
- No → 039

Peripheral and Cranial Nerve and Other Nervous System Procedures → MCC
- Yes → 040
- No → Peripheral Neurostimulator
  - Yes → 041
  - No → CC
    - Yes → 041
    - No → 042

No → 2

Major Diagnostic Category 1
Diseases and Disorders of the Nervous System

Medical Partition

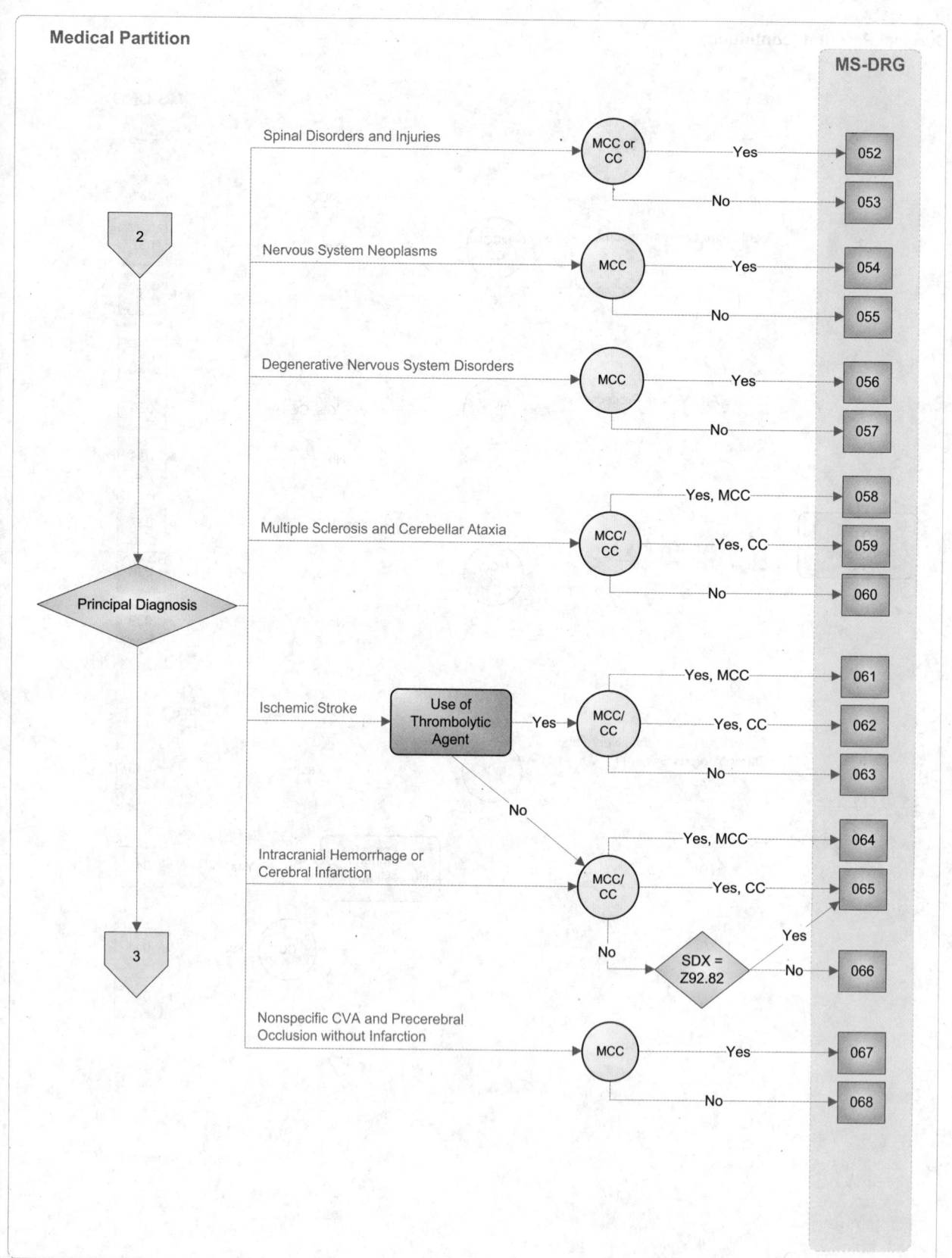

Major Diagnostic Category 1
Diseases and Disorders of the Nervous System

Medical Partition (continued)

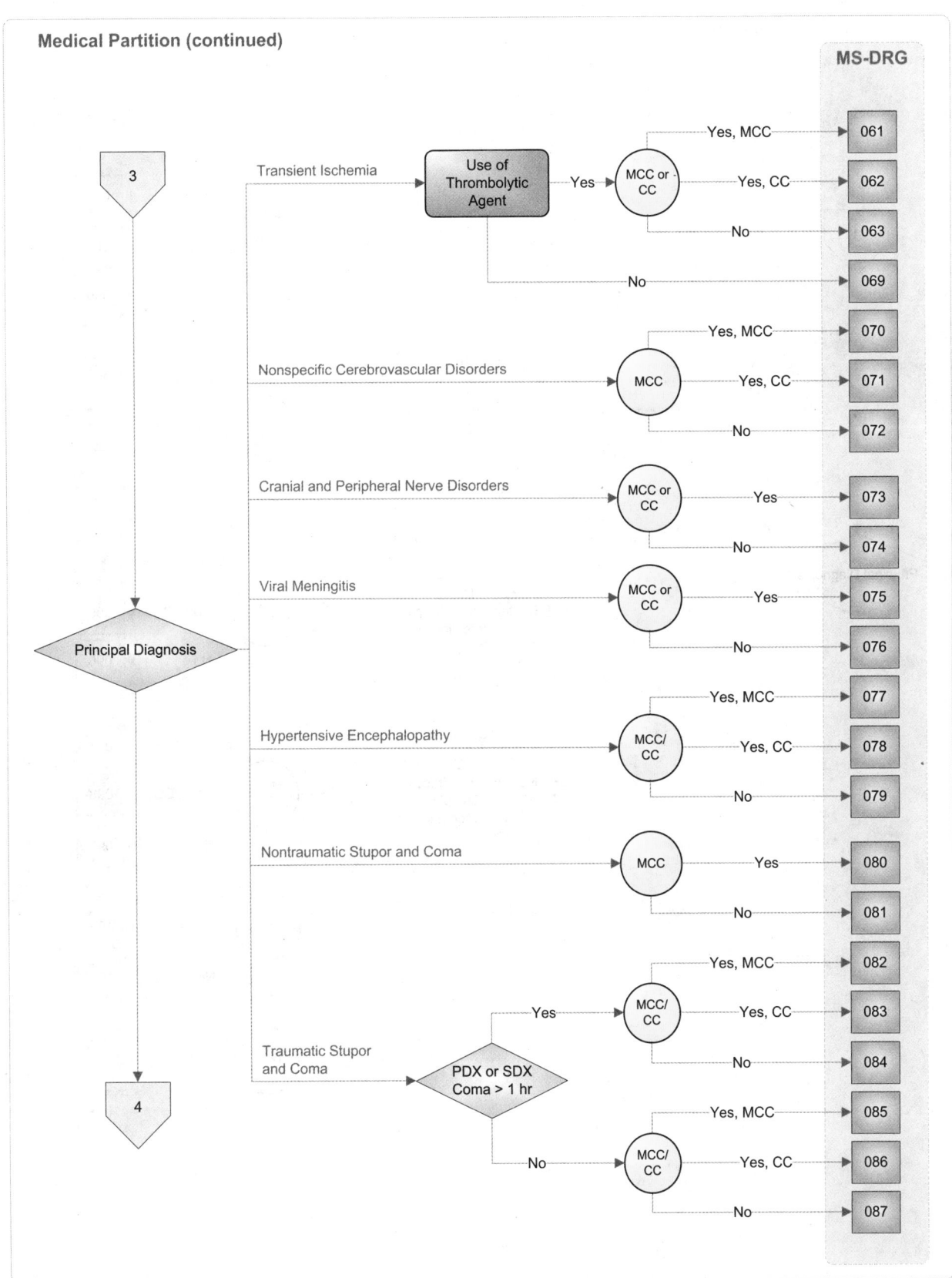

Medical Partition (continued)

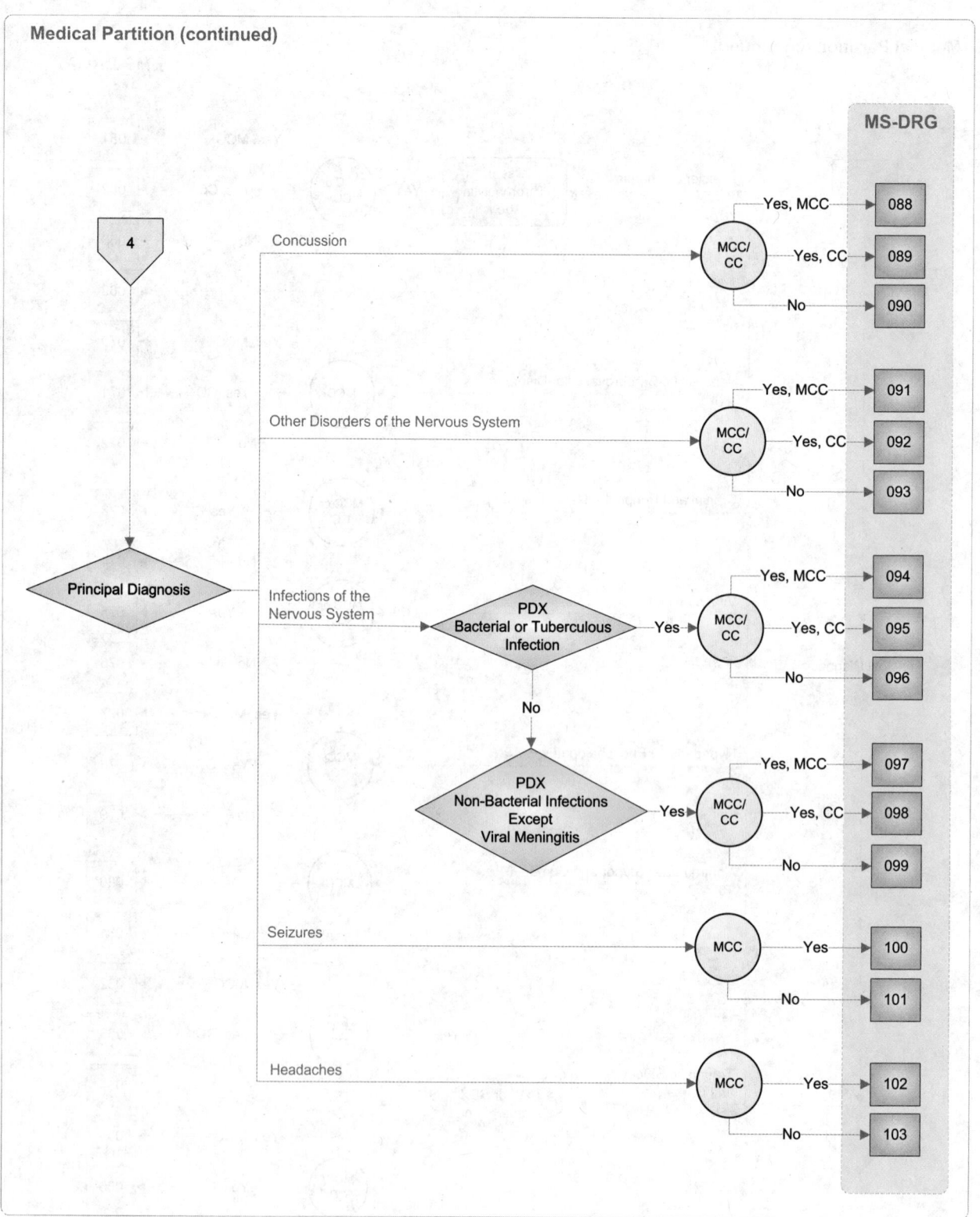

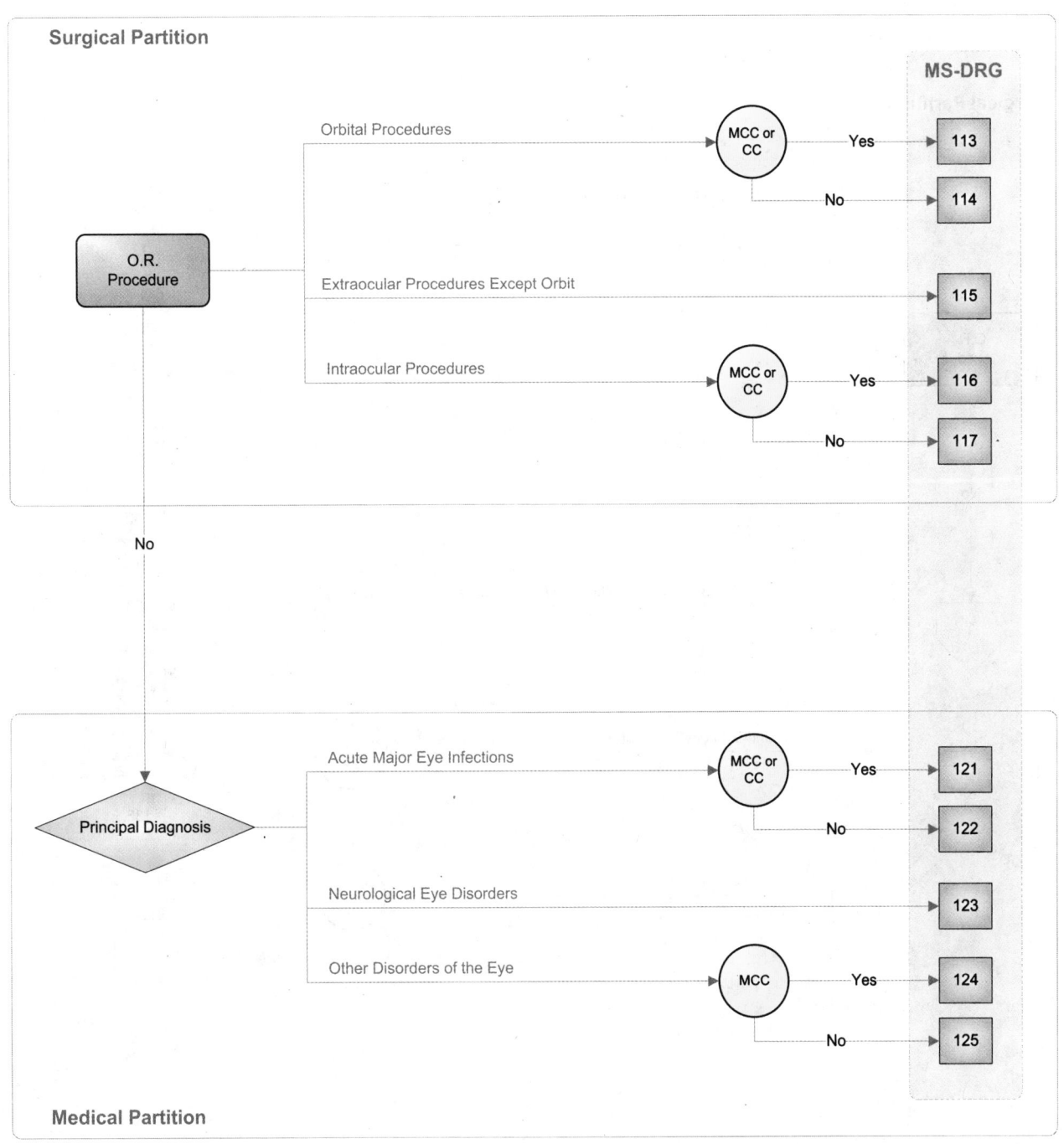

DRG Decision Trees

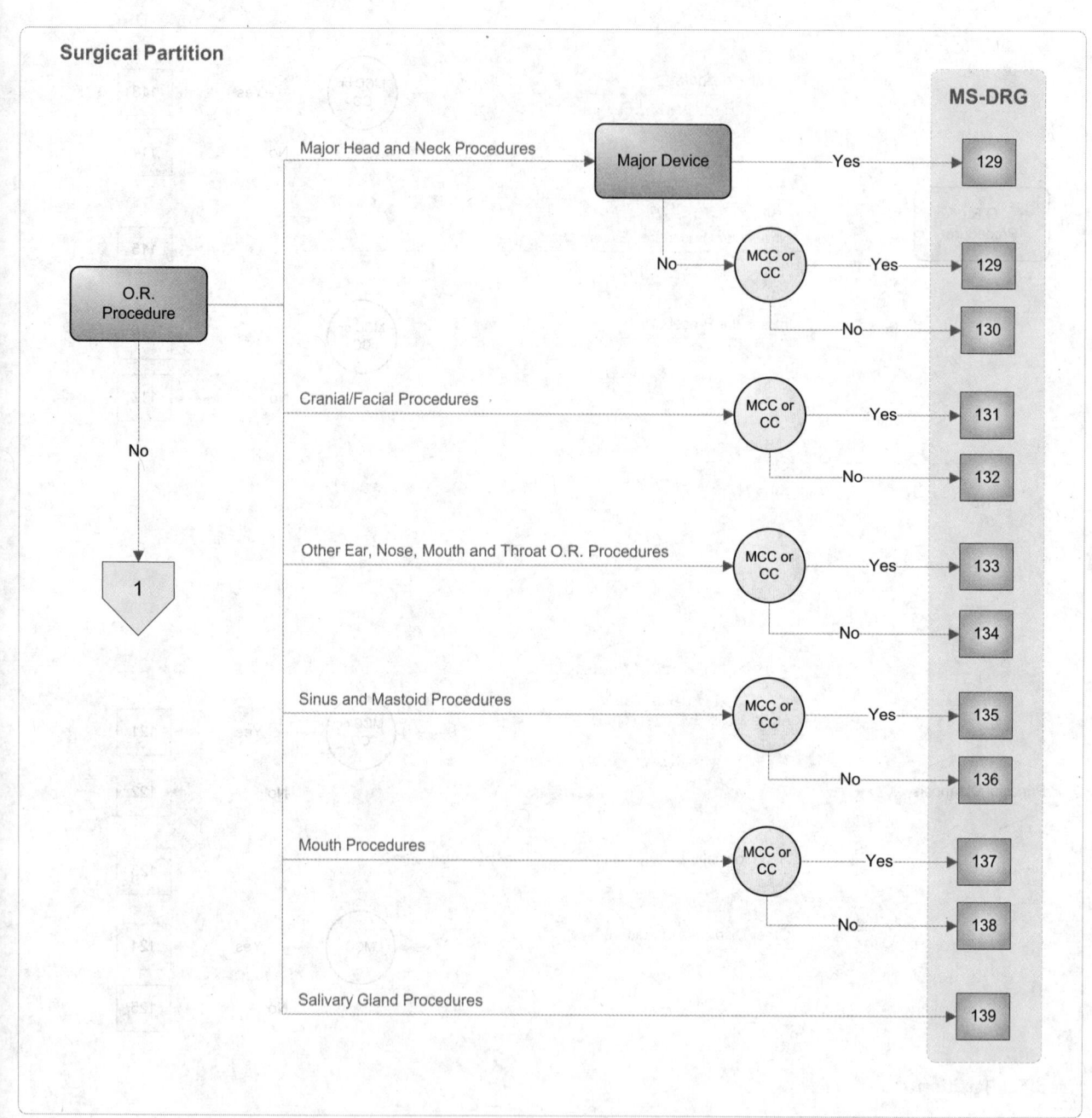

Major Diagnostic Category 3
Diseases and Disorders of the Ear, Nose, Mouth and Throat

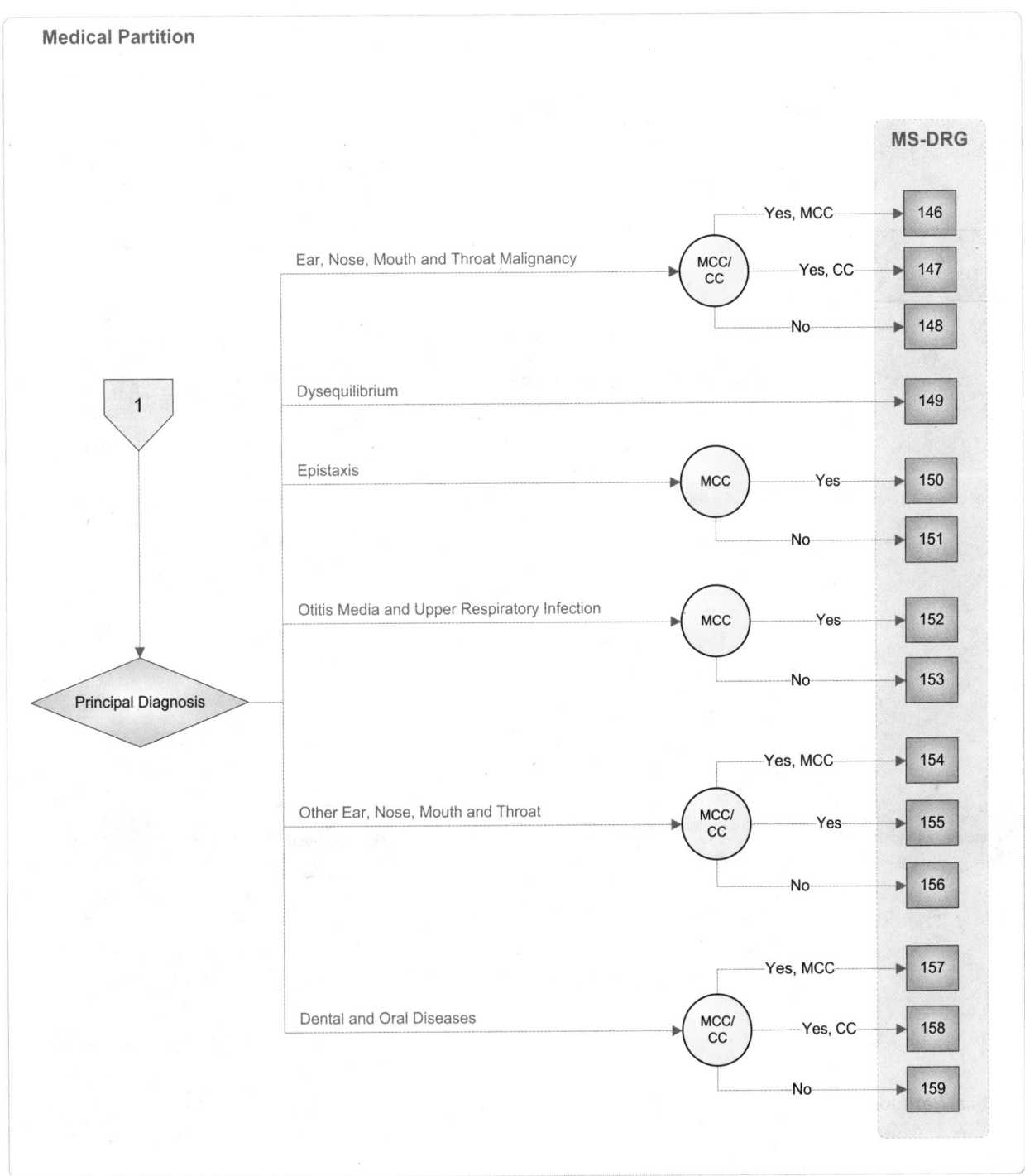

Major Diagnostic Category 4
Diseases and Disorders of the Respiratory System

Medical Partition (continued)

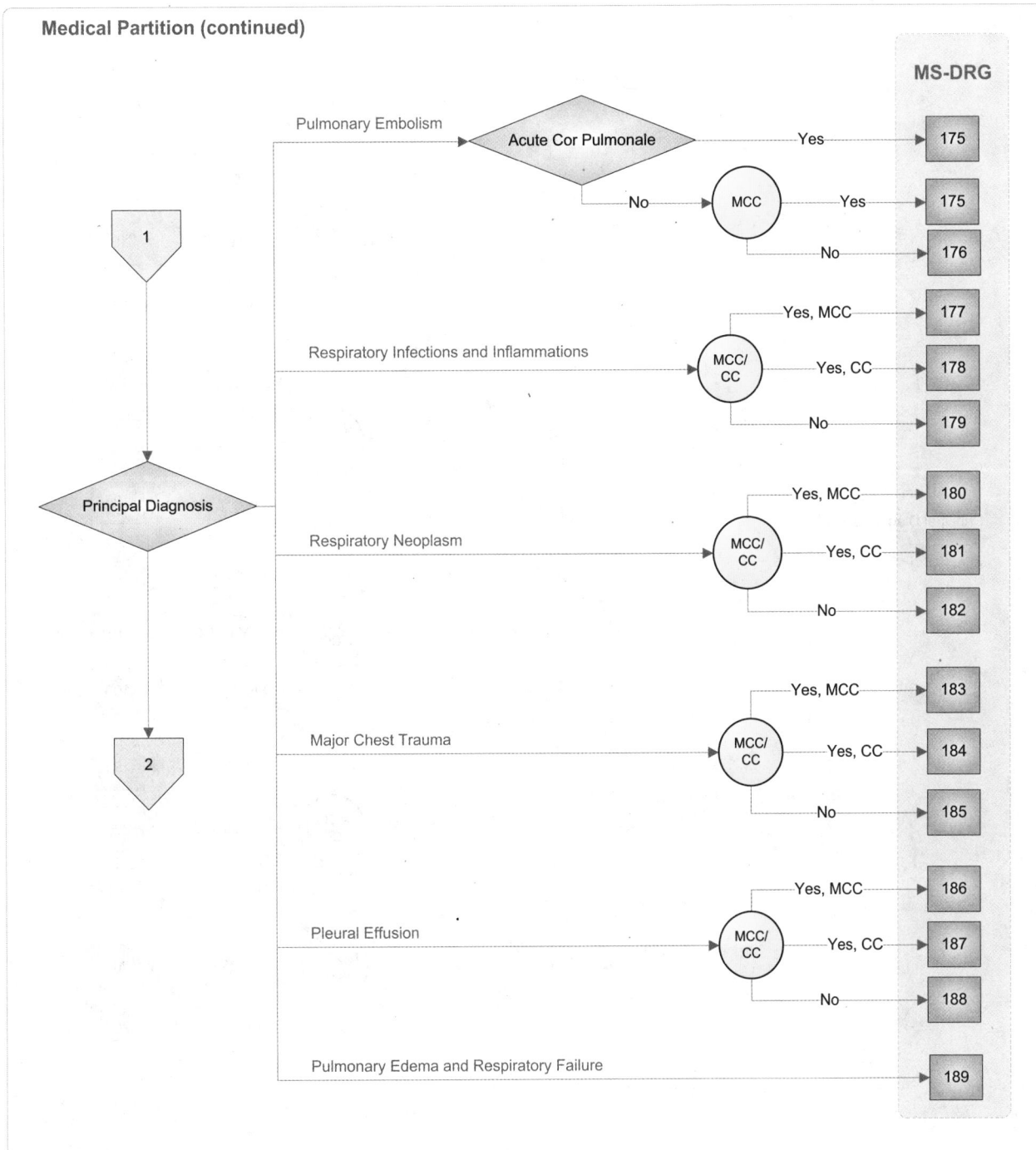

DRG Decision Trees

Medical Partition (continued)

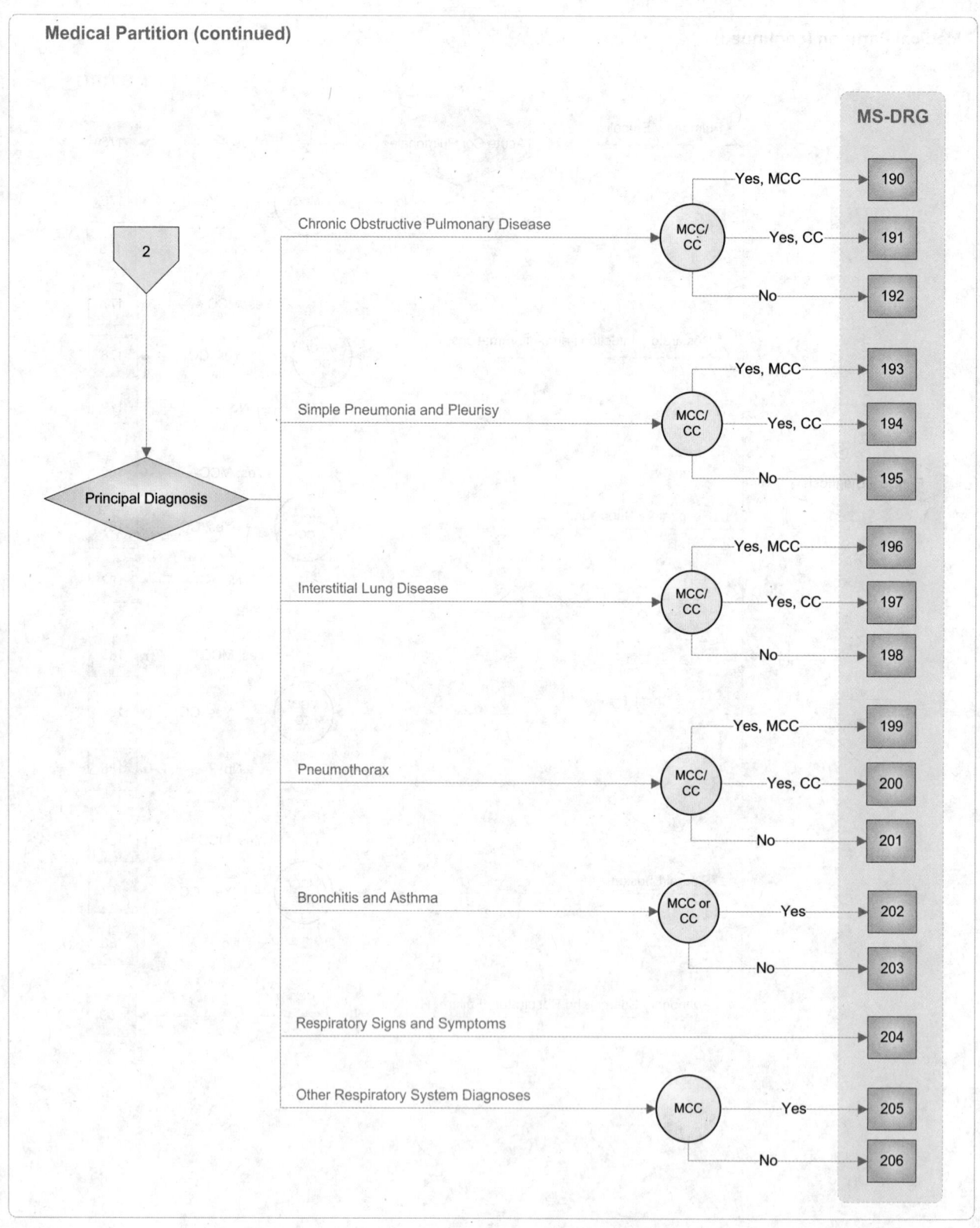

Major Diagnostic Category 5
Diseases and Disorders of the Circulatory System

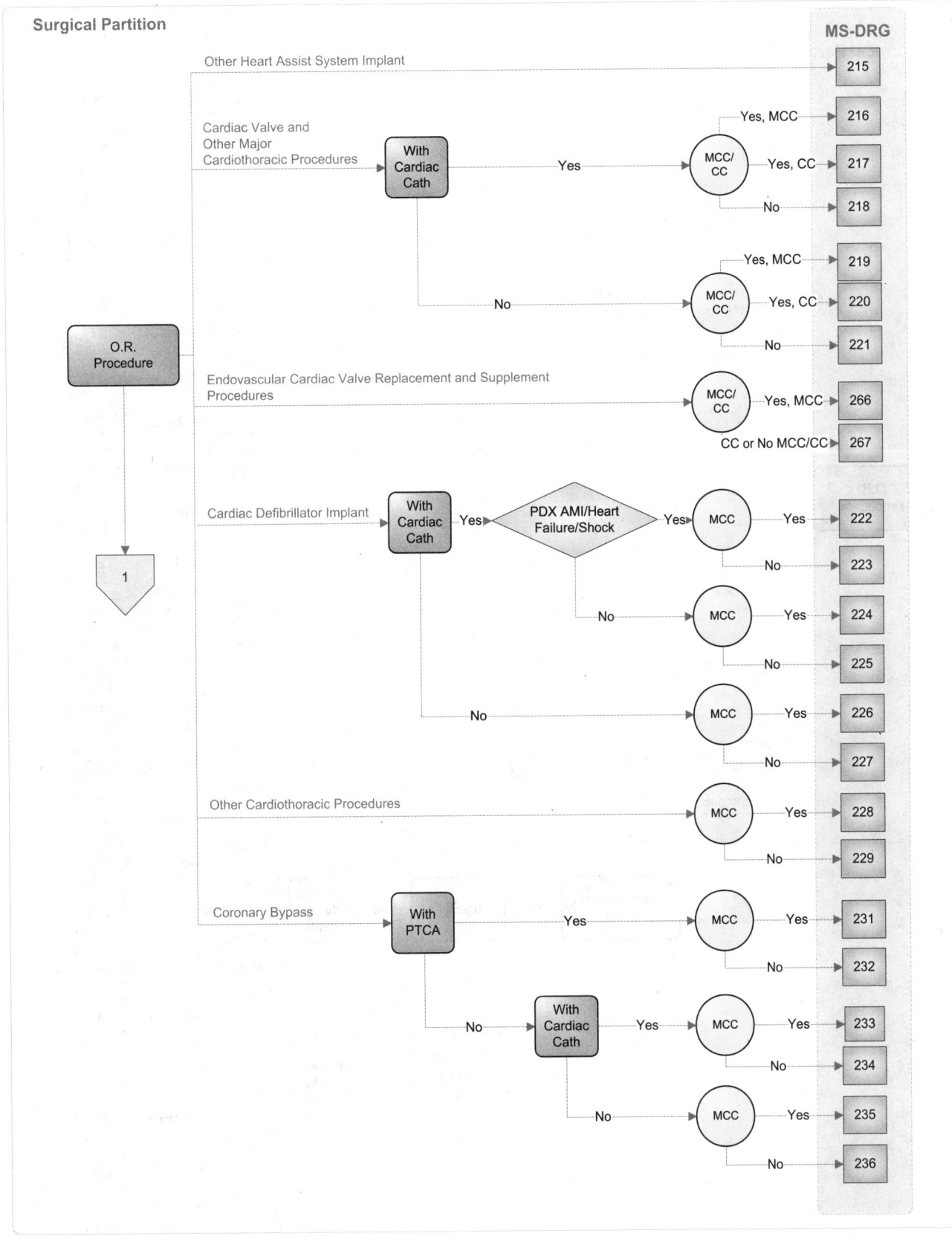

Surgical Partition

MS-DRG

Other Heart Assist System Implant → 215

Cardiac Valve and Other Major Cardiothoracic Procedures → With Cardiac Cath → Yes → MCC/CC → Yes, MCC → 216
Yes, CC → 217
No → 218

No → MCC/CC → Yes, MCC → 219
Yes, CC → 220
No → 221

Endovascular Cardiac Valve Replacement and Supplement Procedures → MCC/CC → Yes, MCC → 266
CC or No MCC/CC → 267

Cardiac Defibrillator Implant → With Cardiac Cath → Yes → PDX AMI/Heart Failure/Shock → Yes → MCC → Yes → 222
No → 223
No → MCC → Yes → 224
No → 225
No → MCC → Yes → 226
No → 227

Other Cardiothoracic Procedures → MCC → Yes → 228
No → 229

Coronary Bypass → With PTCA → Yes → MCC → Yes → 231
No → 232
No → With Cardiac Cath → Yes → MCC → Yes → 233
No → 234
No → MCC → Yes → 235
No → 236

O.R. Procedure → 1

DRG Decision Trees

Major Diagnostic Category 5
Diseases and Disorders of the Circulatory System

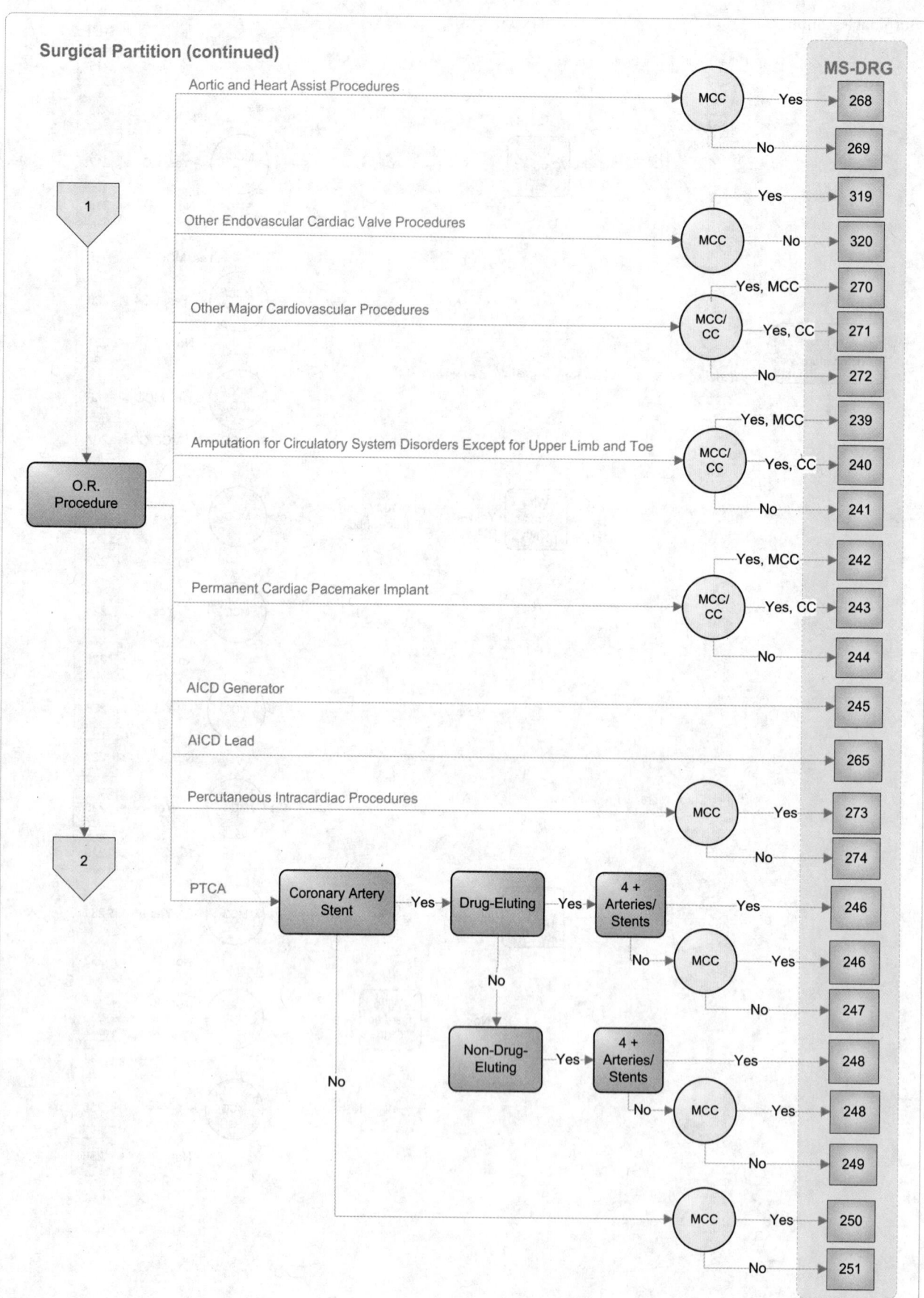

Surgical Partition (continued)

Major Diagnostic Category 5
Diseases and Disorders of the Circulatory System

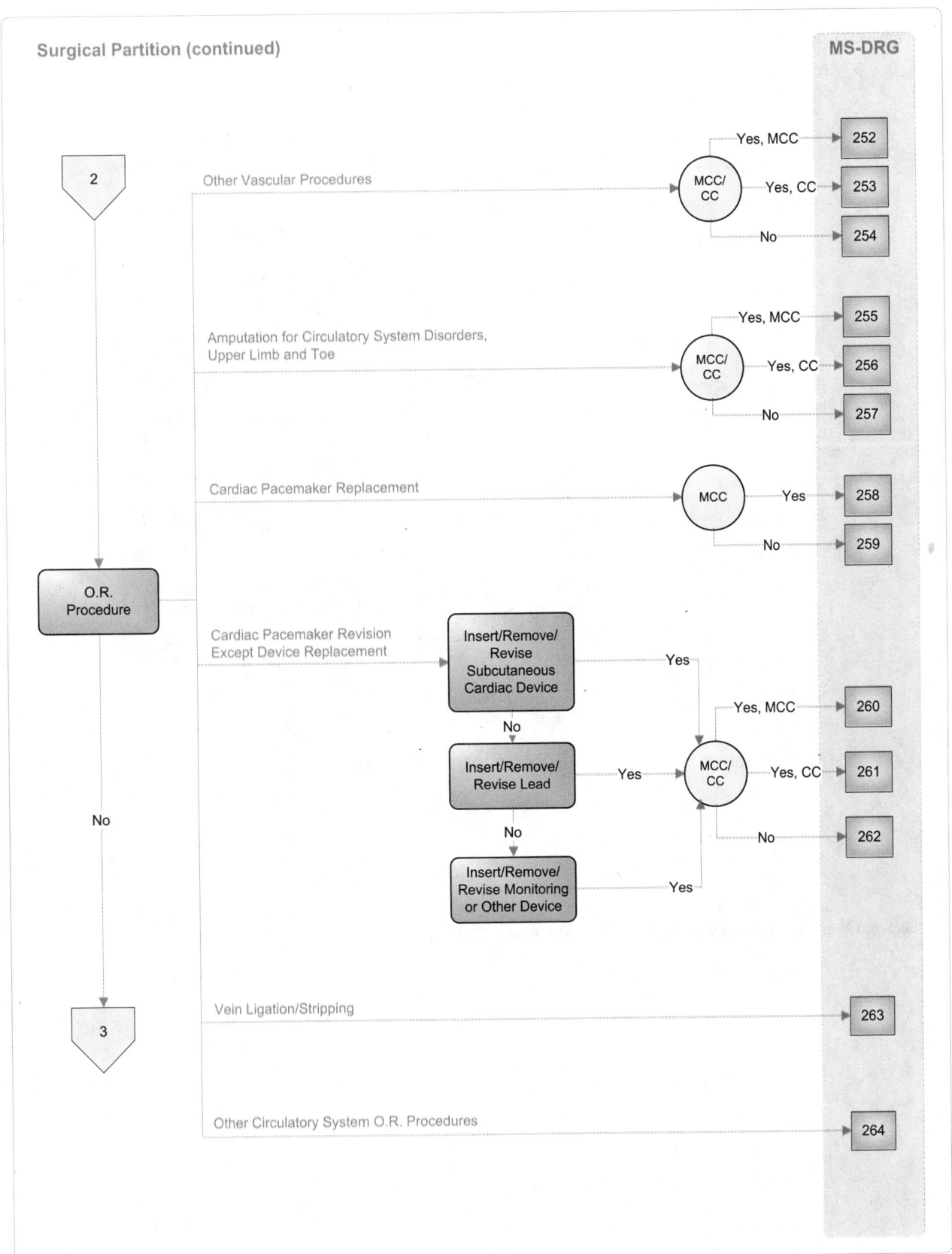

Surgical Partition (continued)

MS-DRG

Other Vascular Procedures — MCC/CC — Yes, MCC → 252 / Yes, CC → 253 / No → 254

Amputation for Circulatory System Disorders, Upper Limb and Toe — MCC/CC — Yes, MCC → 255 / Yes, CC → 256 / No → 257

Cardiac Pacemaker Replacement — MCC — Yes → 258 / No → 259

Cardiac Pacemaker Revision Except Device Replacement — Insert/Remove/Revise Subcutaneous Cardiac Device — Yes → MCC/CC — Yes, MCC → 260 / Yes, CC → 261 / No → 262

Insert/Remove/Revise Lead — Yes → MCC/CC

Insert/Remove/Revise Monitoring or Other Device — Yes → MCC/CC

Vein Ligation/Stripping → 263

Other Circulatory System O.R. Procedures → 264

O.R. Procedure

2

No

3

Major Diagnostic Category 5
Diseases and Disorders of the Circulatory System

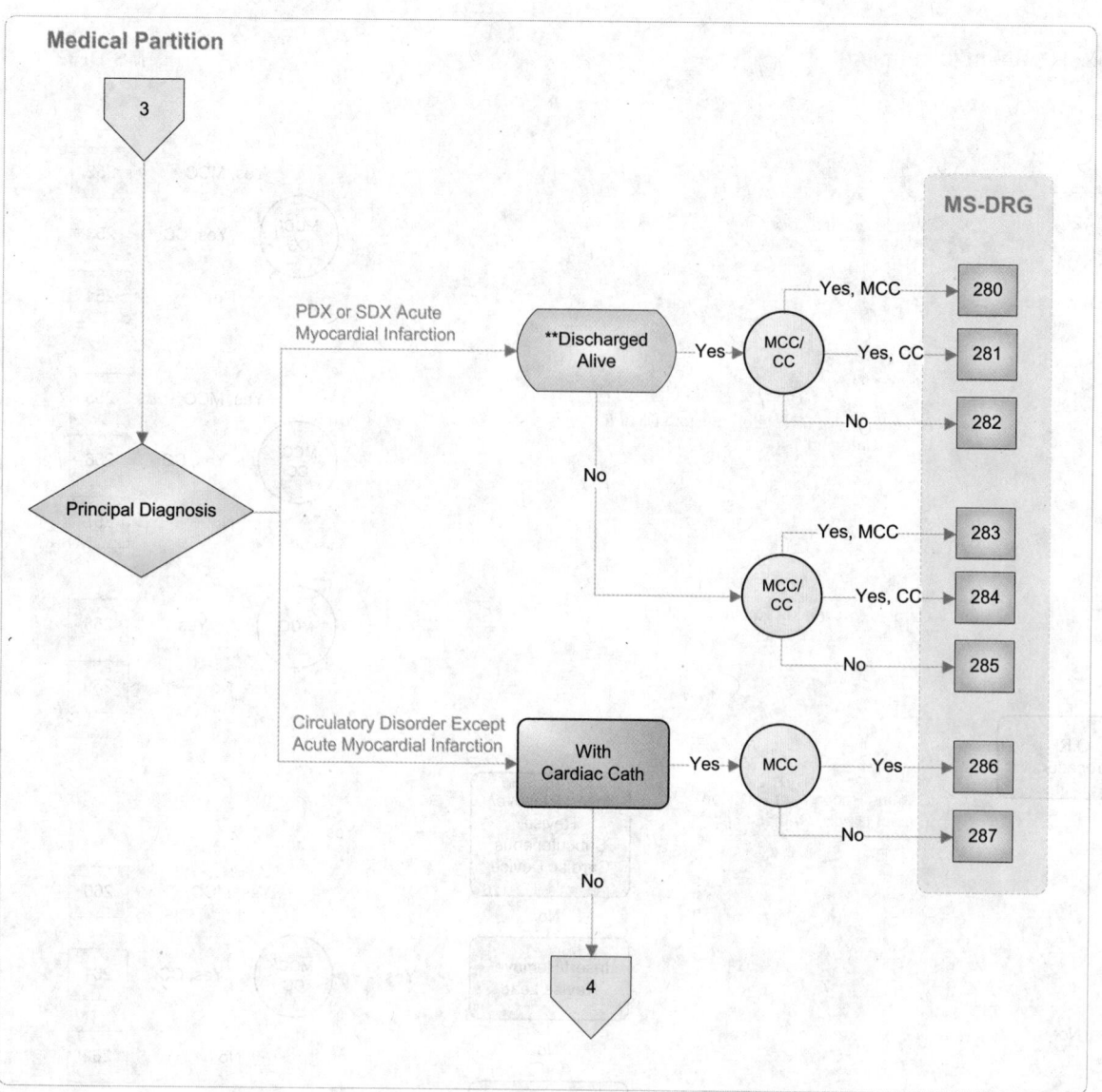

Medical Partition

**Discharged Alive = Any discharge status except for Discharge Status of 20 (Died).

Major Diagnostic Category 5
Diseases and Disorders of the Circulatory System

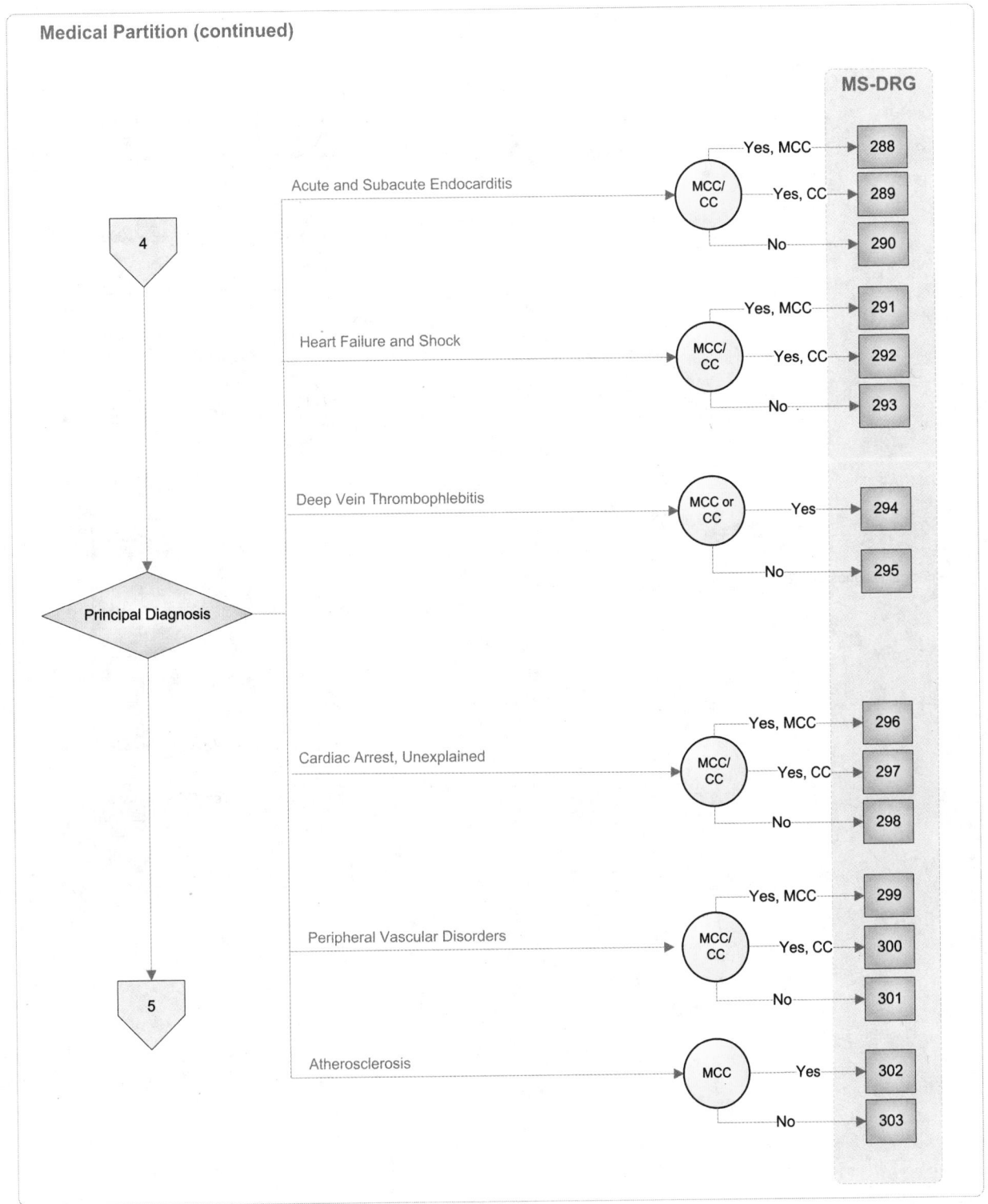

Medical Partition (continued)

Major Diagnostic Category 5
Diseases and Disorders of the Circulatory System

Medical Partition (continued)

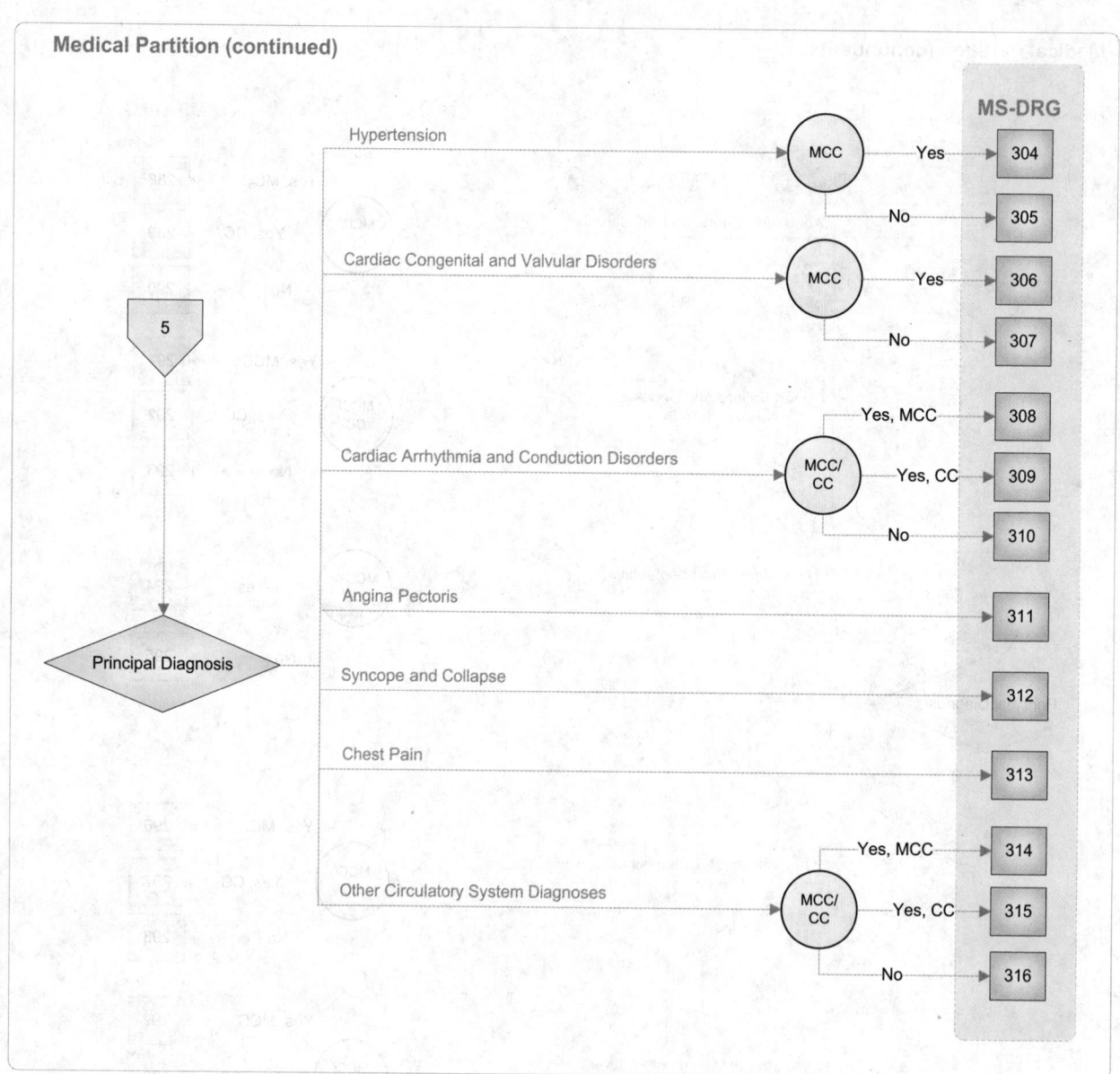

Major Diagnostic Category 6
Diseases and Disorders of the Digestive System

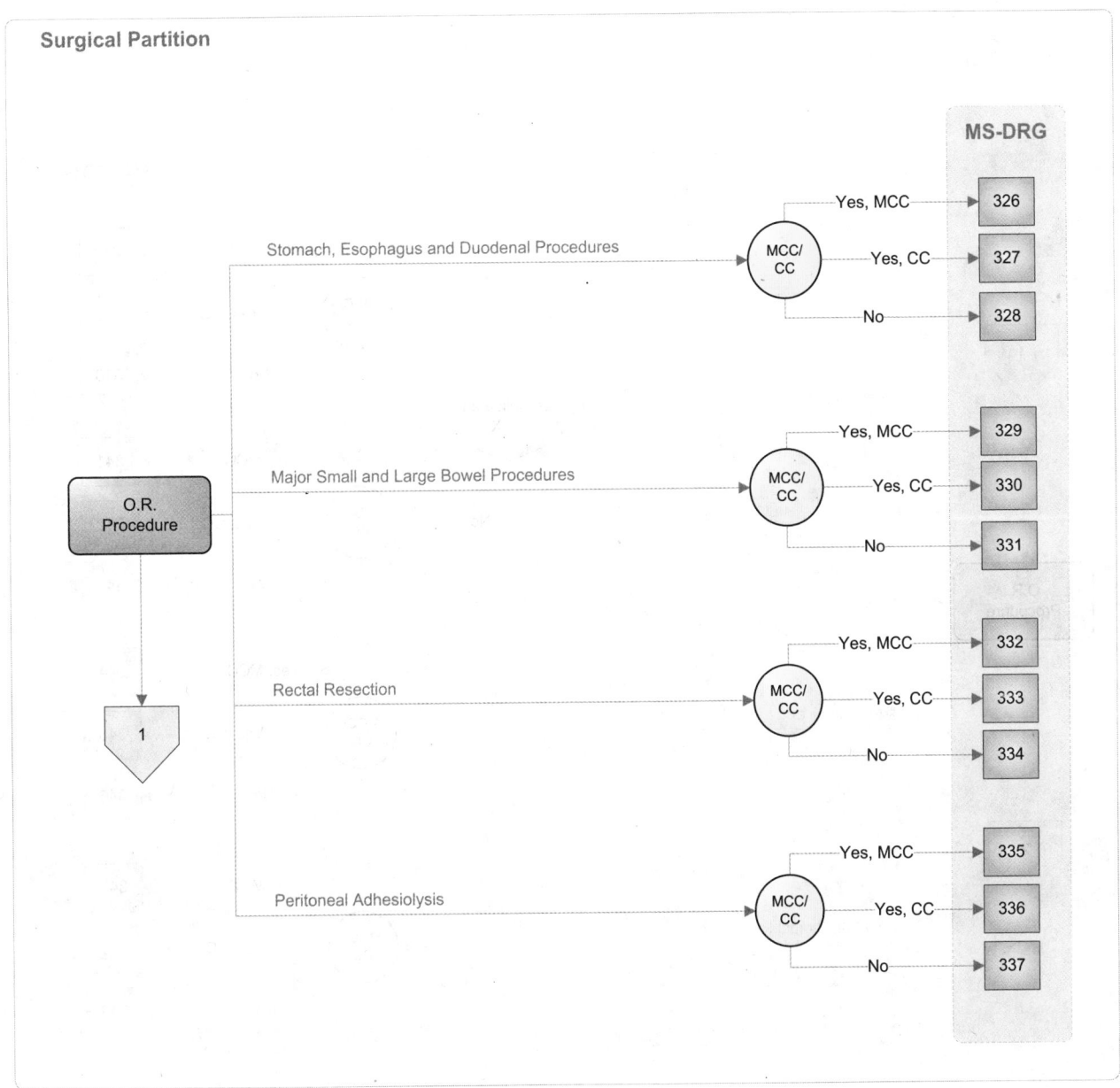

Surgical Partition

O.R. Procedure

1

MS-DRG

Stomach, Esophagus and Duodenal Procedures — MCC/CC
- Yes, MCC → 326
- Yes, CC → 327
- No → 328

Major Small and Large Bowel Procedures — MCC/CC
- Yes, MCC → 329
- Yes, CC → 330
- No → 331

Rectal Resection — MCC/CC
- Yes, MCC → 332
- Yes, CC → 333
- No → 334

Peritoneal Adhesiolysis — MCC/CC
- Yes, MCC → 335
- Yes, CC → 336
- No → 337

DRG Decision Trees

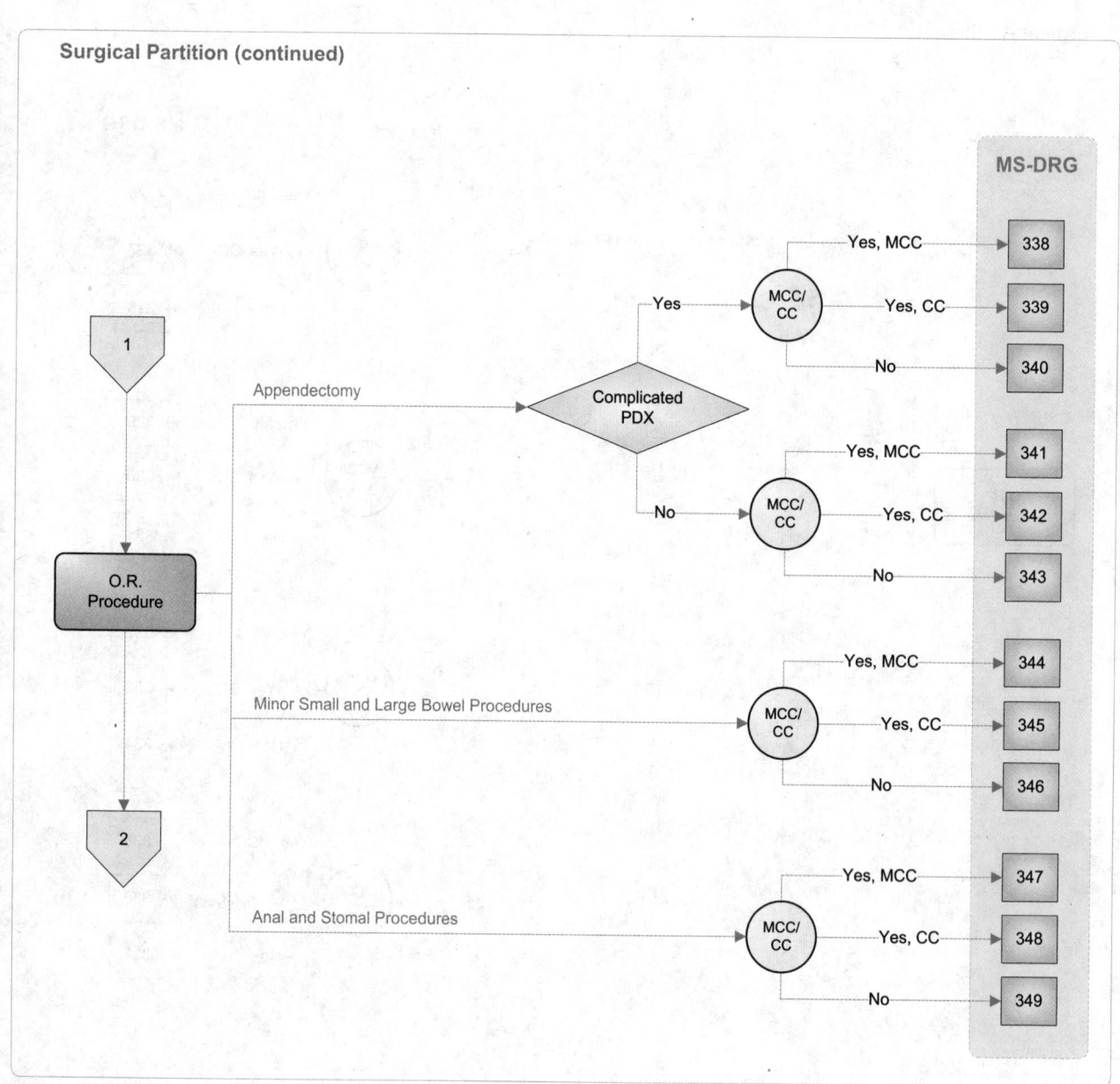

Surgical Partition (continued)

Major Diagnostic Category 6
Diseases and Disorders of the Digestive System

Surgical Partition (continued)

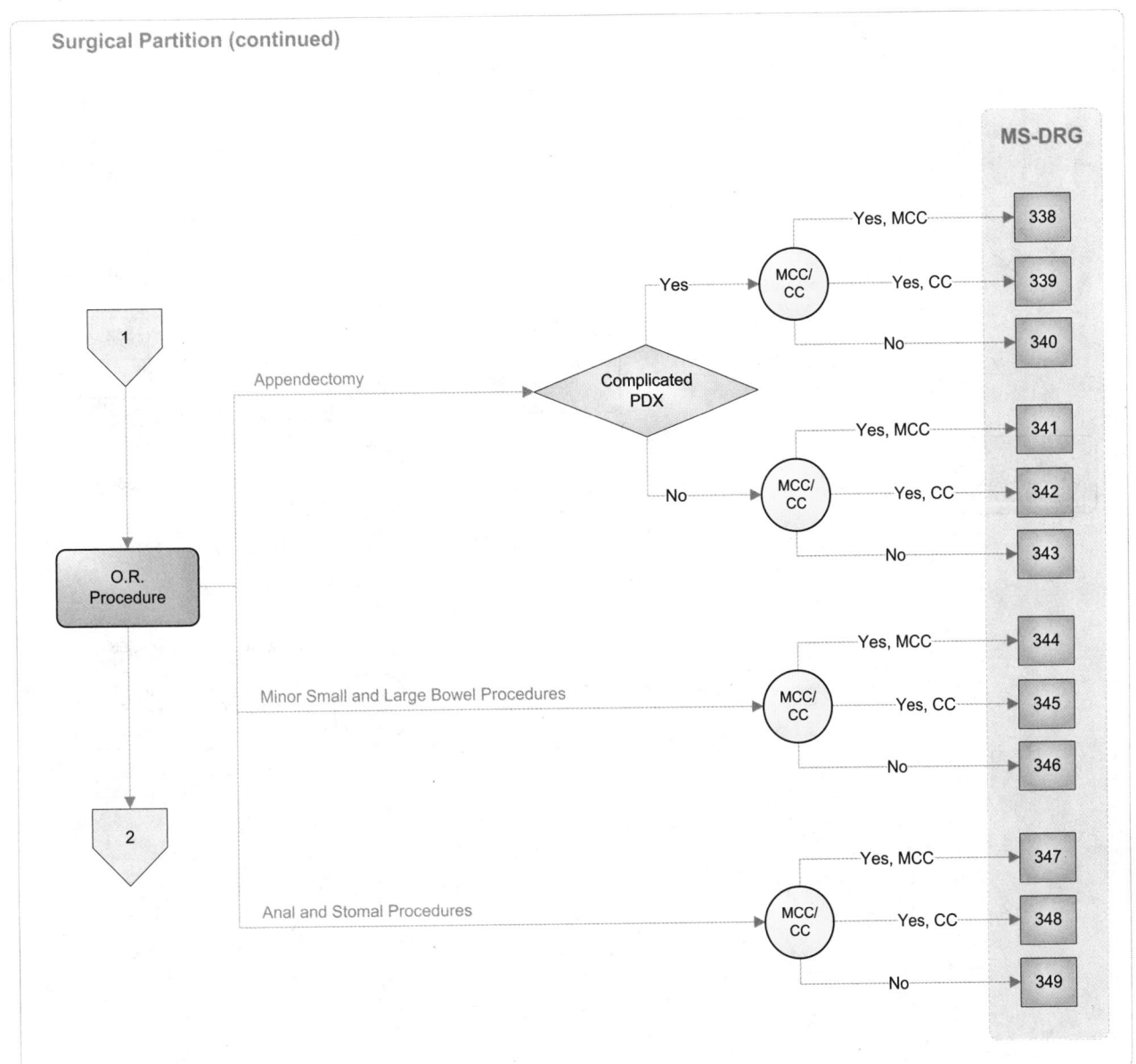

Surgical Partition (continued)

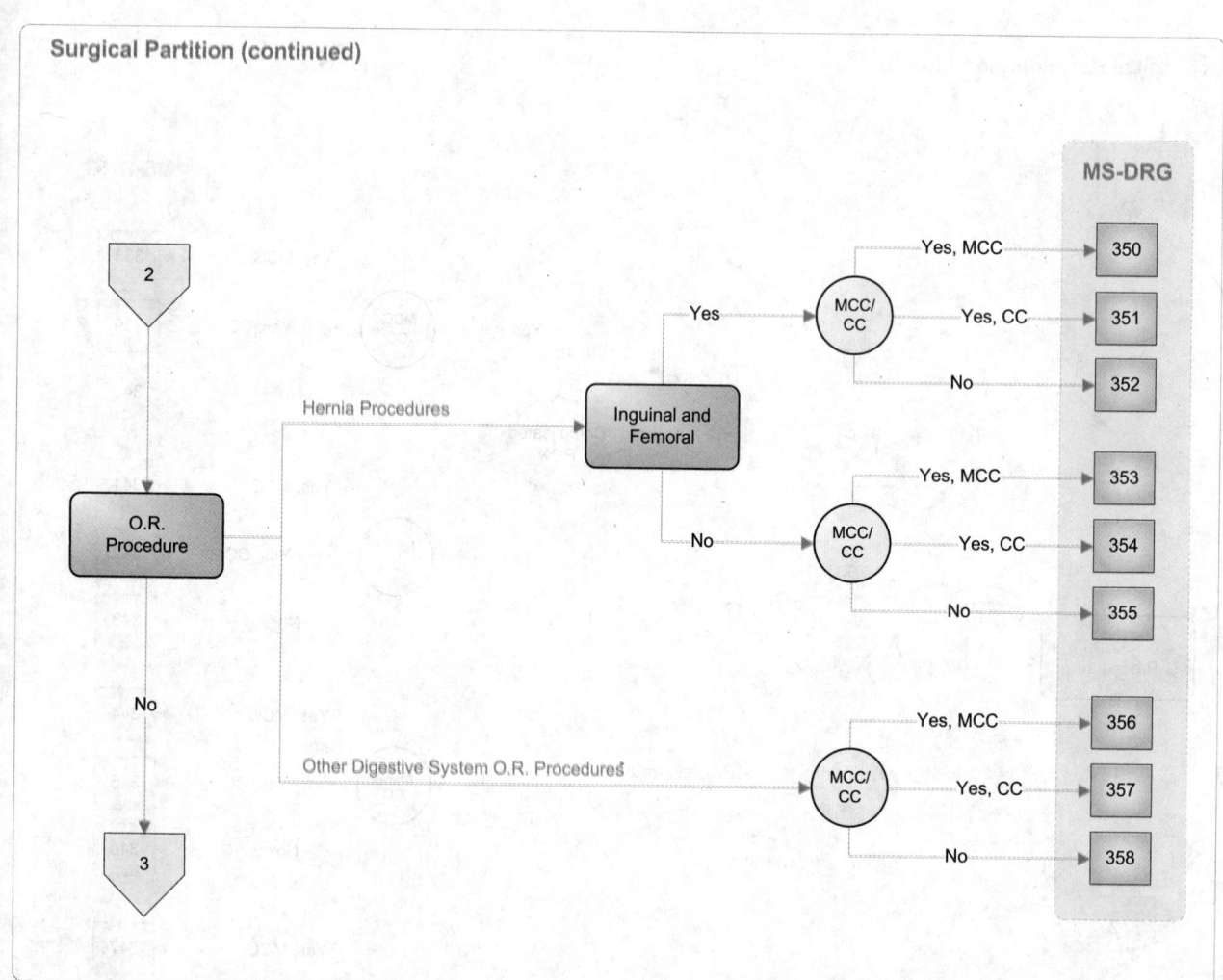

Major Diagnostic Category 6
Diseases and Disorders of the Digestive System

Medical Partition

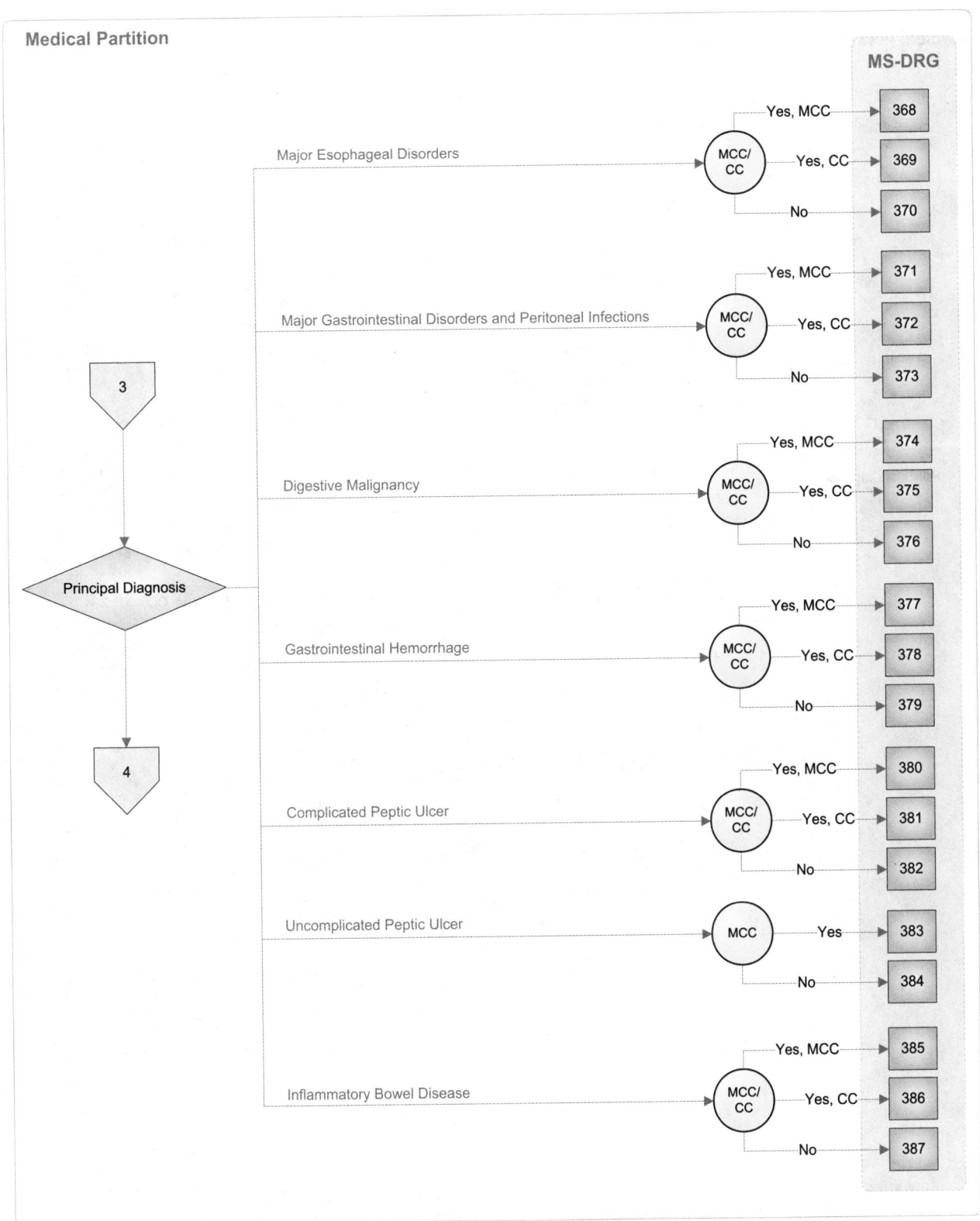

Medical Partition (continued)

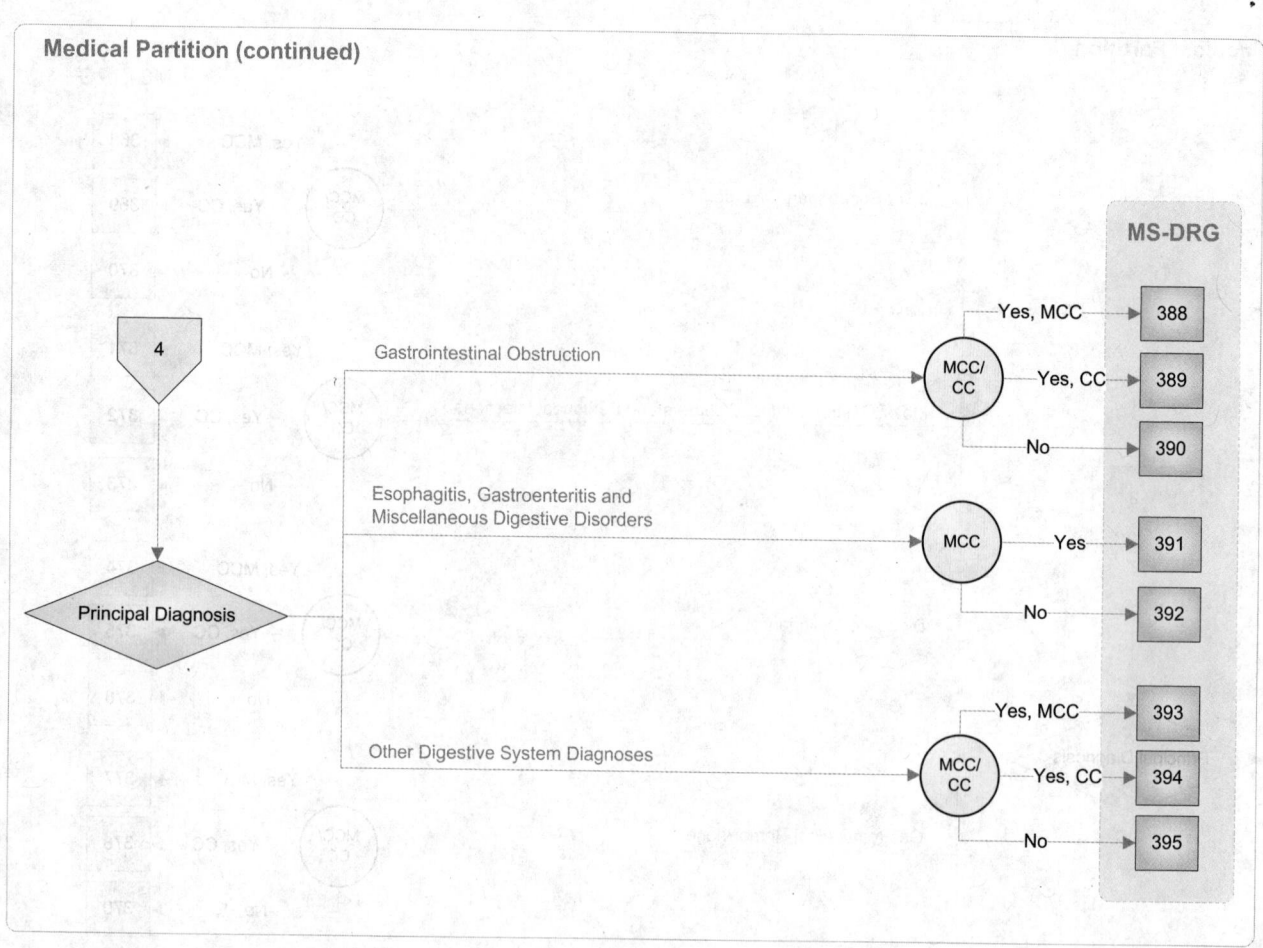

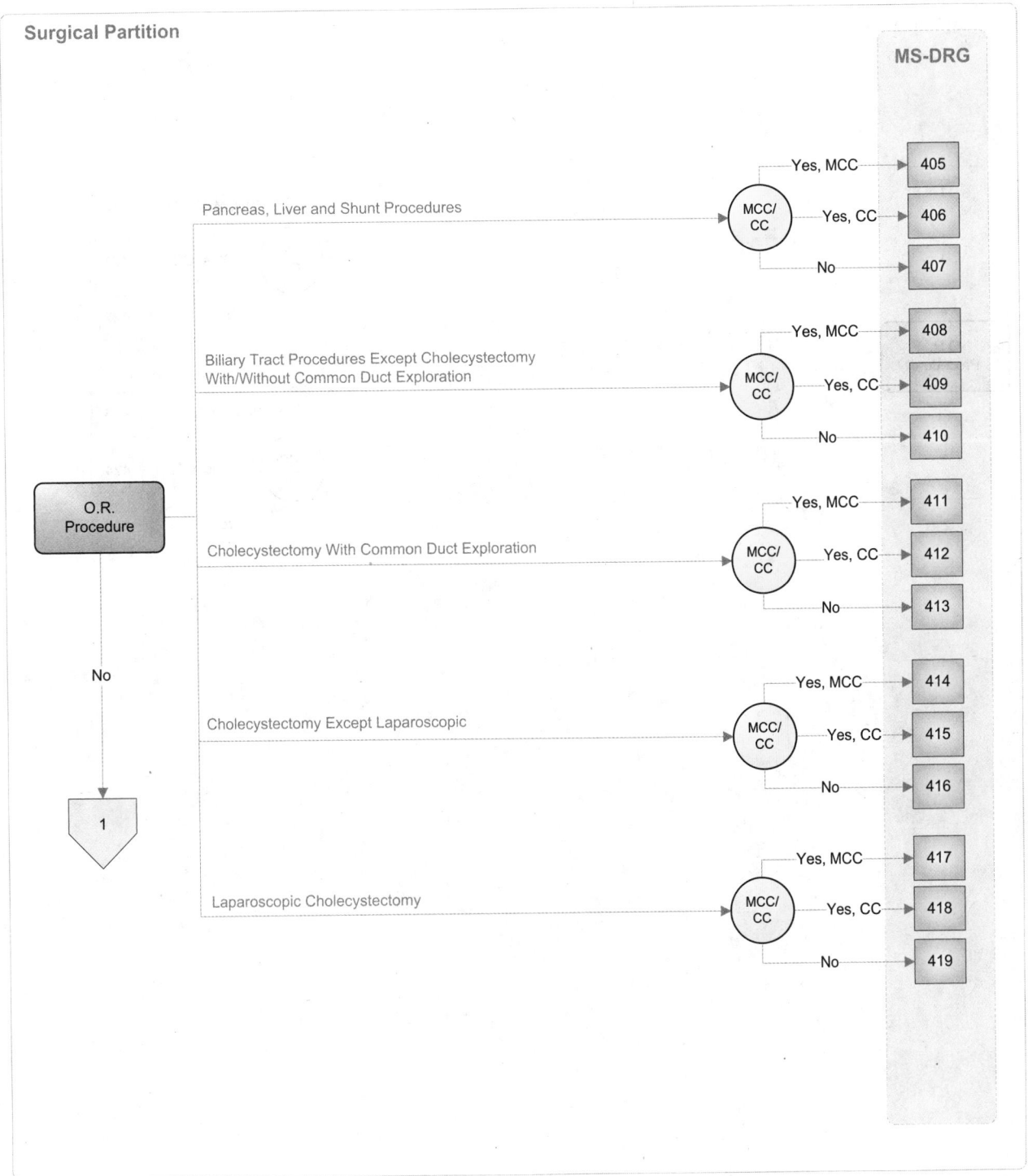

Surgical Partition

Major Diagnostic Category 7
Diseases and Disorders of the Hepatobiliary System and Pancreas

Surgical Partition (continued)

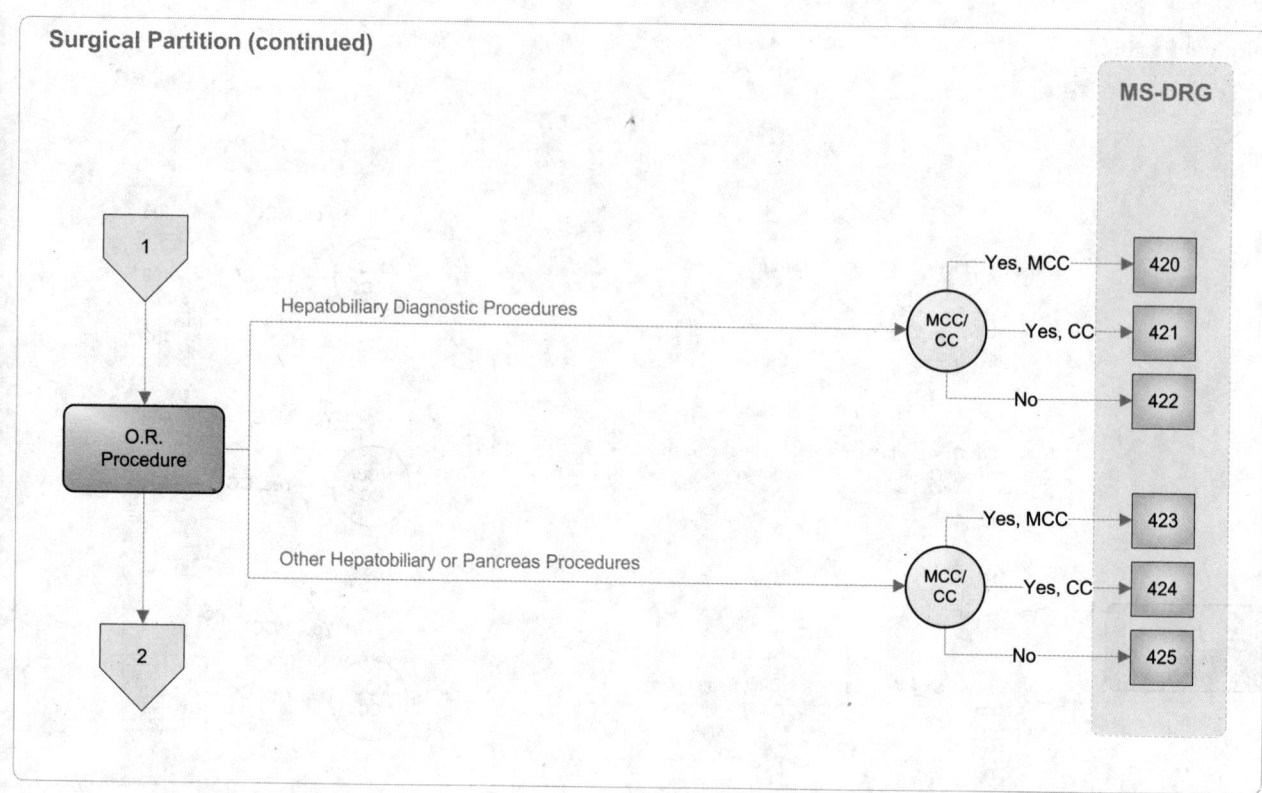

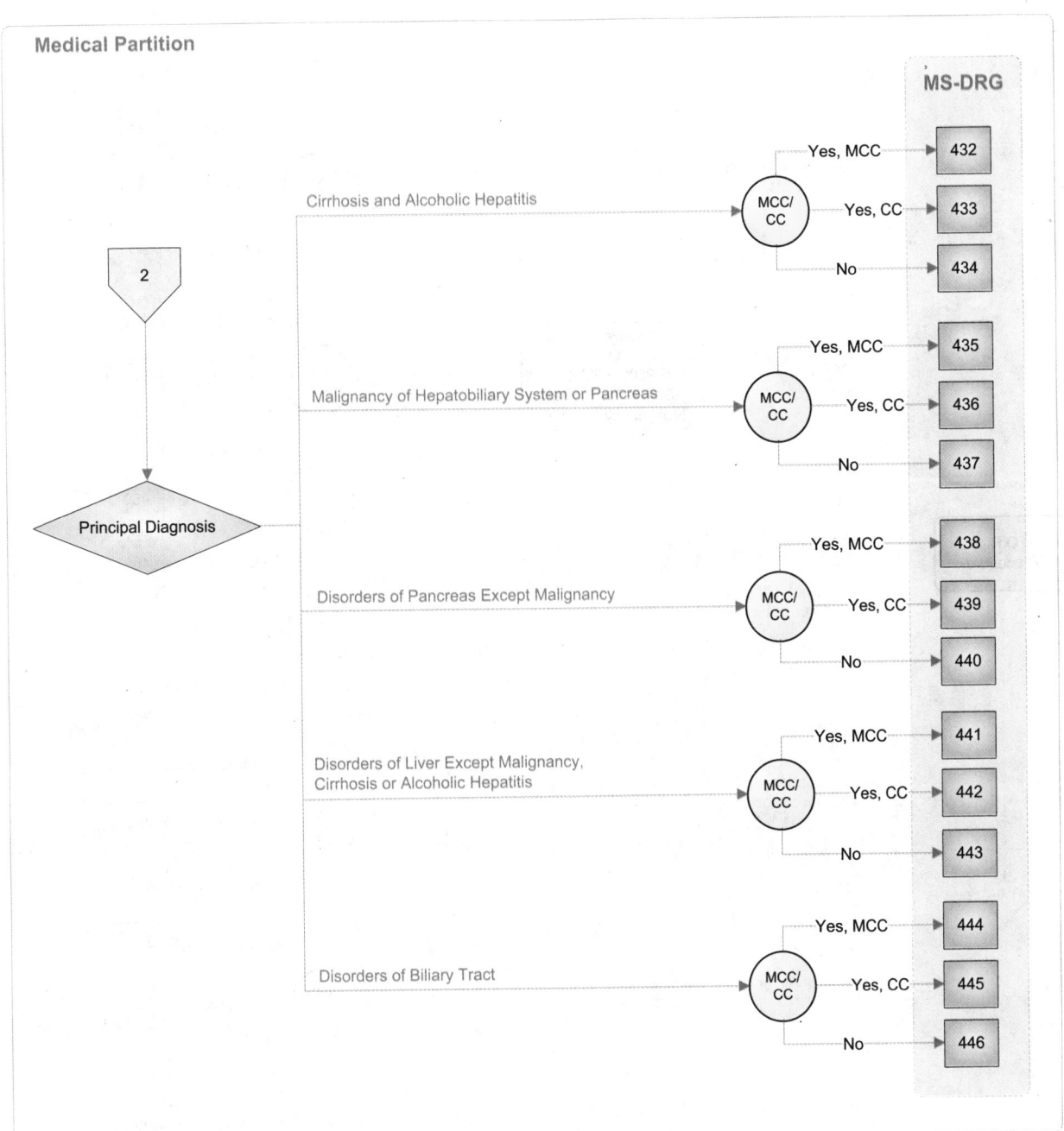

Major Diagnostic Category 8
Diseases and Disorders of the Musculoskeletal System and Connective Tissue

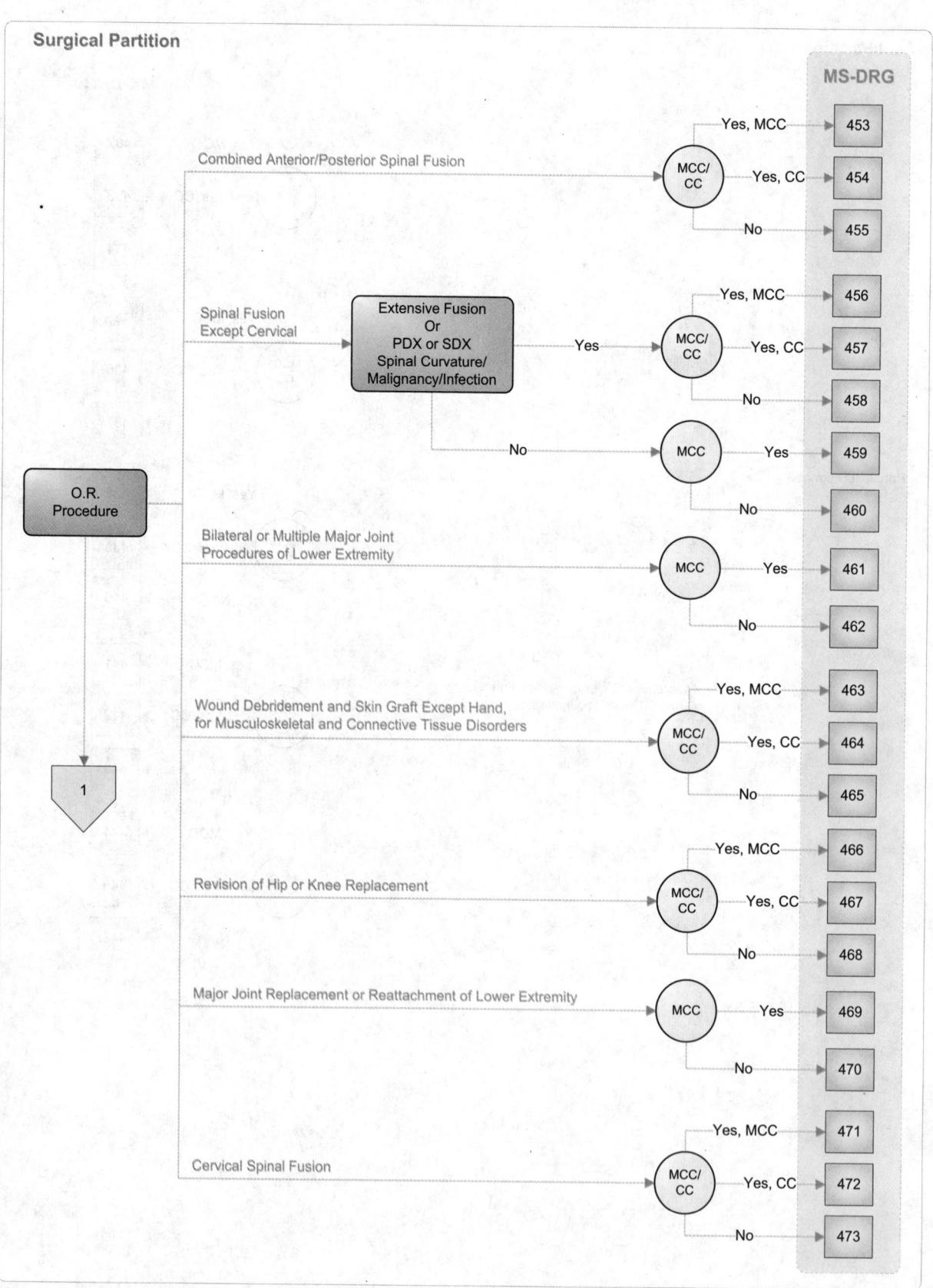

Surgical Partition

MS-DRG

Combined Anterior/Posterior Spinal Fusion — MCC/CC
- Yes, MCC → 453
- Yes, CC → 454
- No → 455

Spinal Fusion Except Cervical → Extensive Fusion Or PDX or SDX Spinal Curvature/Malignancy/Infection
- Yes → MCC/CC
  - Yes, MCC → 456
  - Yes, CC → 457
  - No → 458
- No → MCC
  - Yes → 459
  - No → 460

O.R. Procedure

1

Bilateral or Multiple Major Joint Procedures of Lower Extremity — MCC
- Yes → 461
- No → 462

Wound Debridement and Skin Graft Except Hand, for Musculoskeletal and Connective Tissue Disorders — MCC/CC
- Yes, MCC → 463
- Yes, CC → 464
- No → 465

Revision of Hip or Knee Replacement — MCC/CC
- Yes, MCC → 466
- Yes, CC → 467
- No → 468

Major Joint Replacement or Reattachment of Lower Extremity — MCC
- Yes → 469
- No → 470

Cervical Spinal Fusion — MCC/CC
- Yes, MCC → 471
- Yes, CC → 472
- No → 473

Major Diagnostic Category 8
Diseases and Disorders of the Musculoskeletal System and Connective Tissue

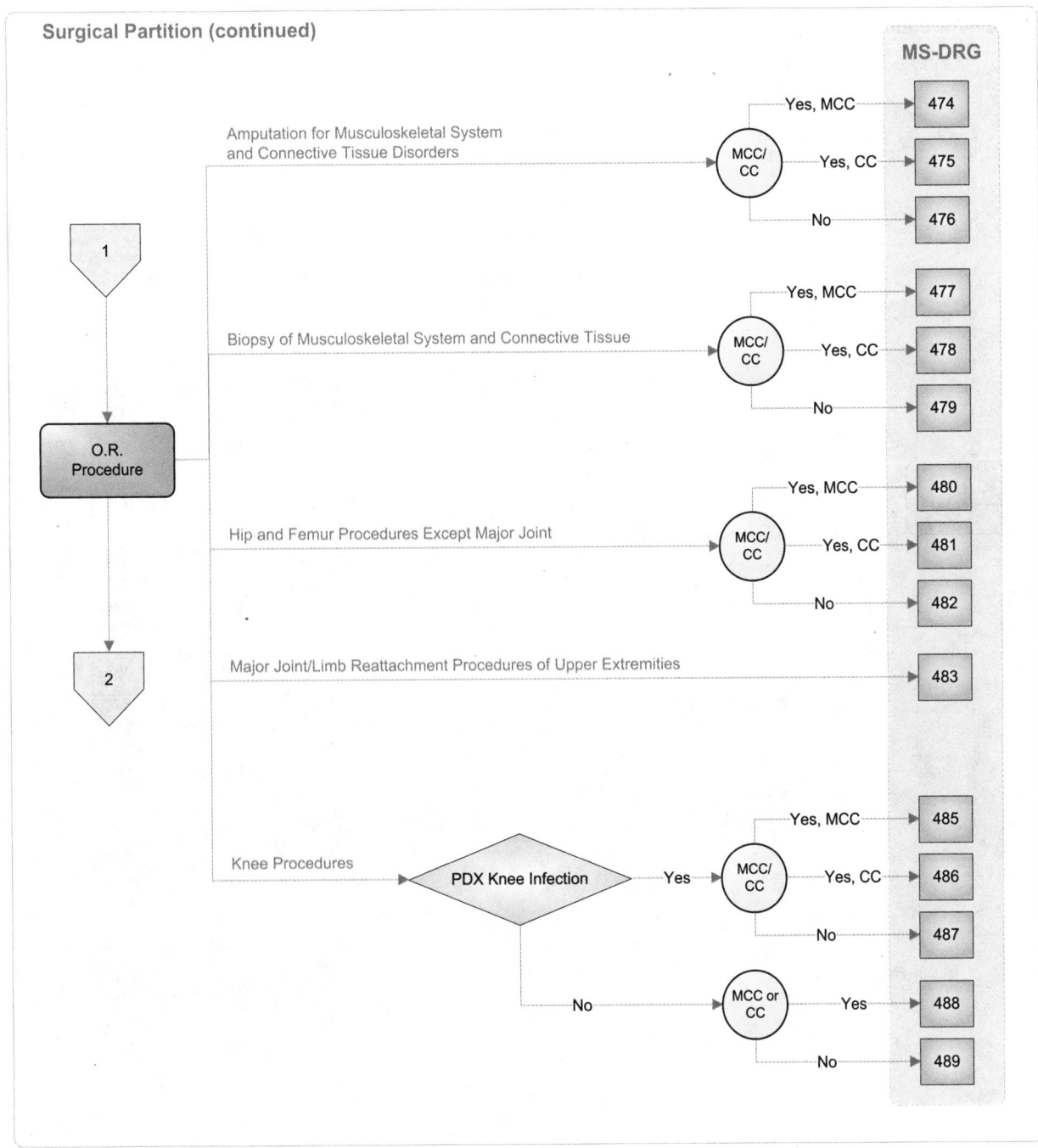

Surgical Partition (continued)

DRG Decision Trees

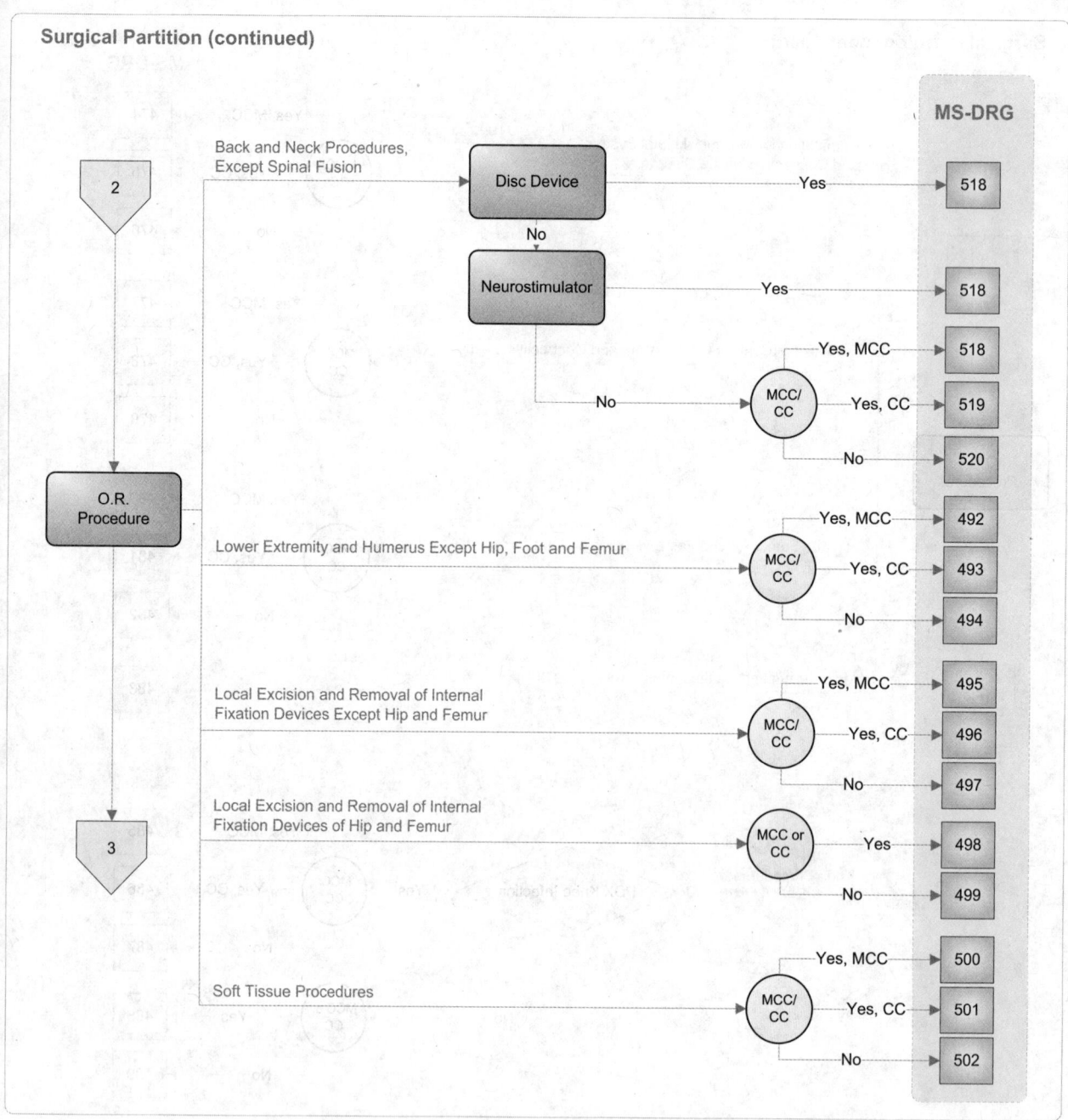

Major Diagnostic Category 8
Diseases and Disorders of the Musculoskeletal System and Connective Tissue

Surgical Partition (continued)

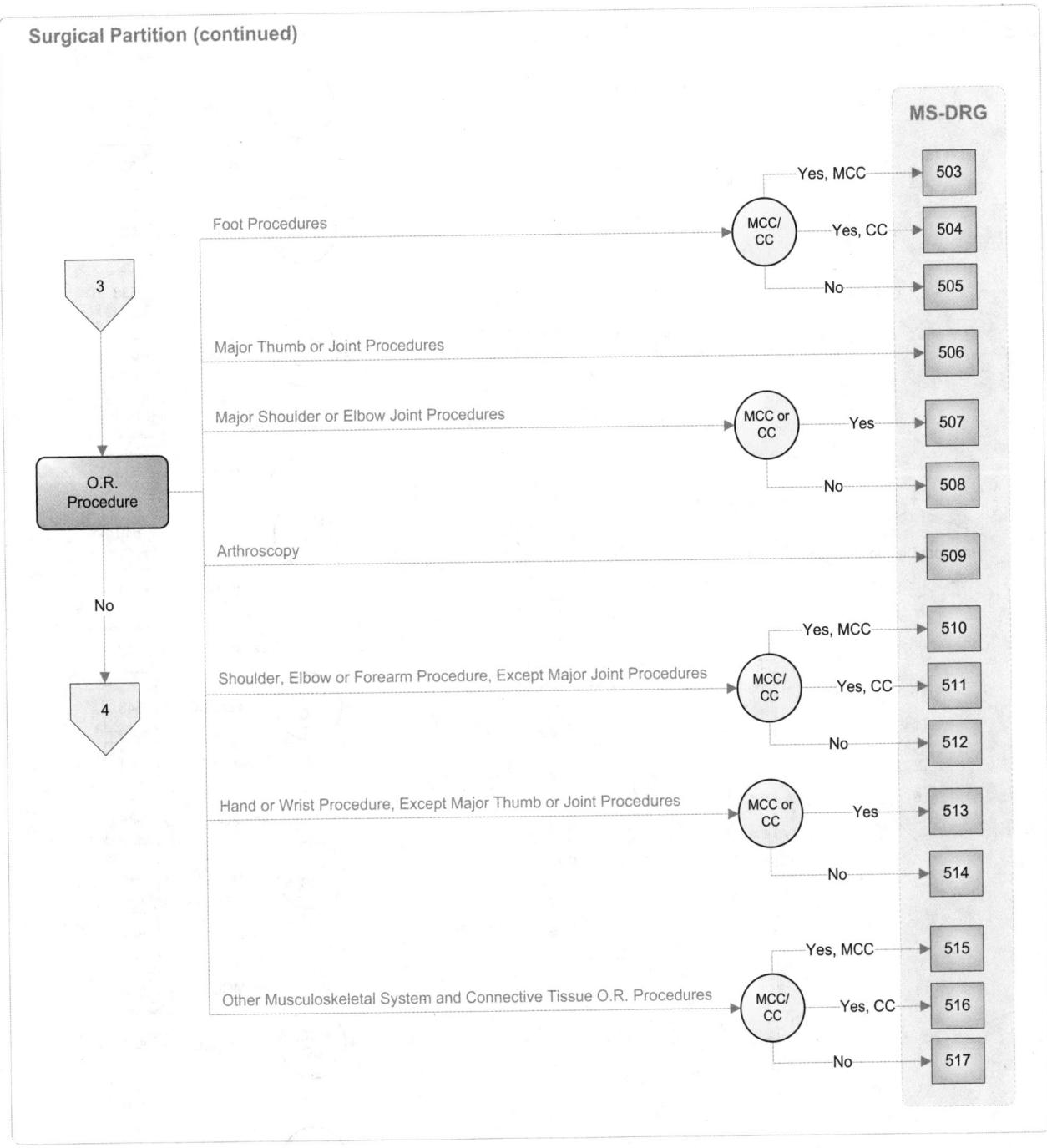

Major Diagnostic Category 8
Diseases and Disorders of the Musculoskeletal System and Connective Tissue

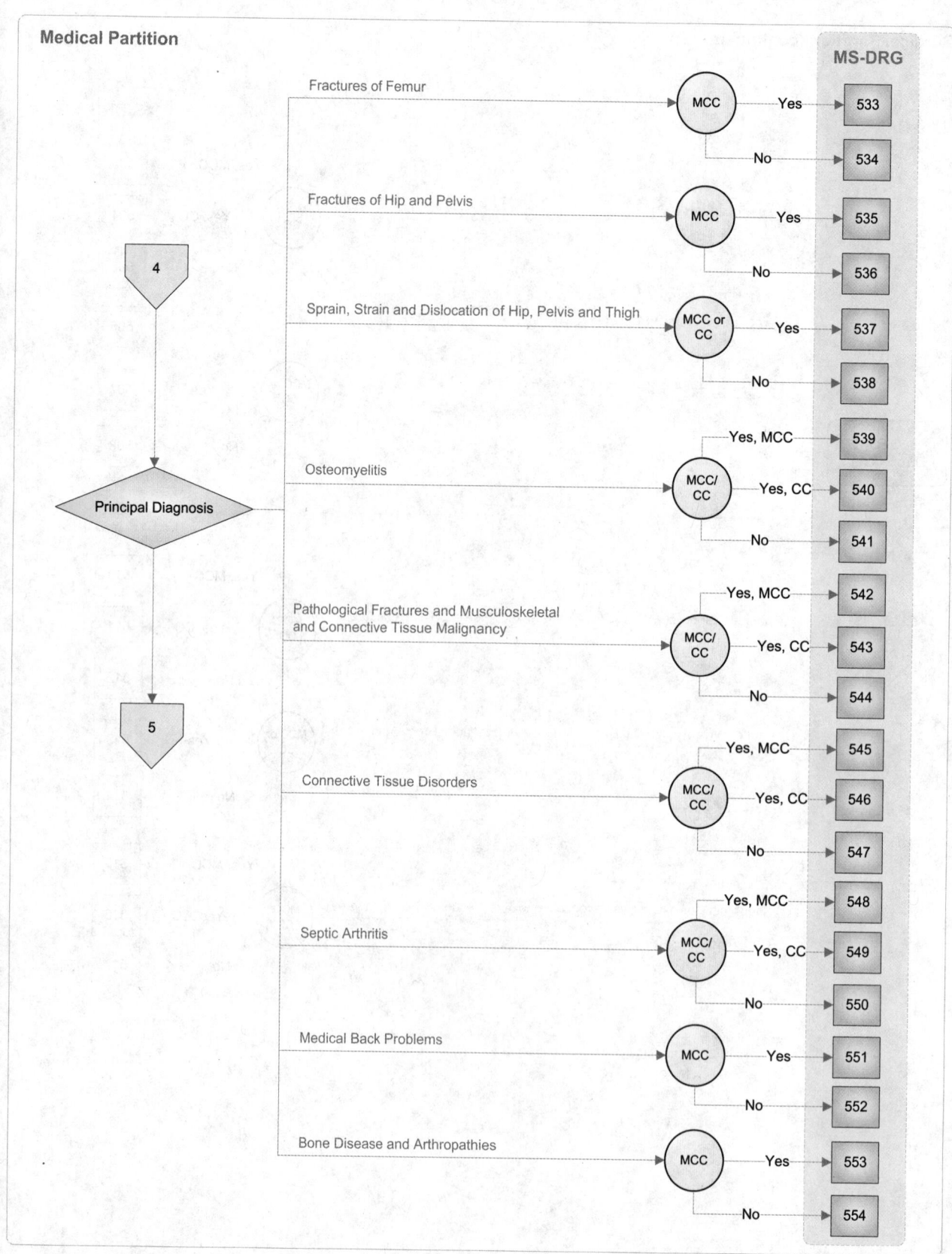

Medical Partition

MS-DRG

Category	Condition	MS-DRG
Fractures of Femur	MCC — Yes	533
	No	534
Fractures of Hip and Pelvis	MCC — Yes	535
	No	536
Sprain, Strain and Dislocation of Hip, Pelvis and Thigh	MCC or CC — Yes	537
	No	538
Osteomyelitis	MCC/CC — Yes, MCC	539
	Yes, CC	540
	No	541
Pathological Fractures and Musculoskeletal and Connective Tissue Malignancy	MCC/CC — Yes, MCC	542
	Yes, CC	543
	No	544
Connective Tissue Disorders	MCC/CC — Yes, MCC	545
	Yes, CC	546
	No	547
Septic Arthritis	MCC/CC — Yes, MCC	548
	Yes, CC	549
	No	550
Medical Back Problems	MCC — Yes	551
	No	552
Bone Disease and Arthropathies	MCC — Yes	553
	No	554

Principal Diagnosis

4

5

DRG Decision Trees

Major Diagnostic Category 8
Diseases and Disorders of the Musculoskeletal System and Connective Tissue

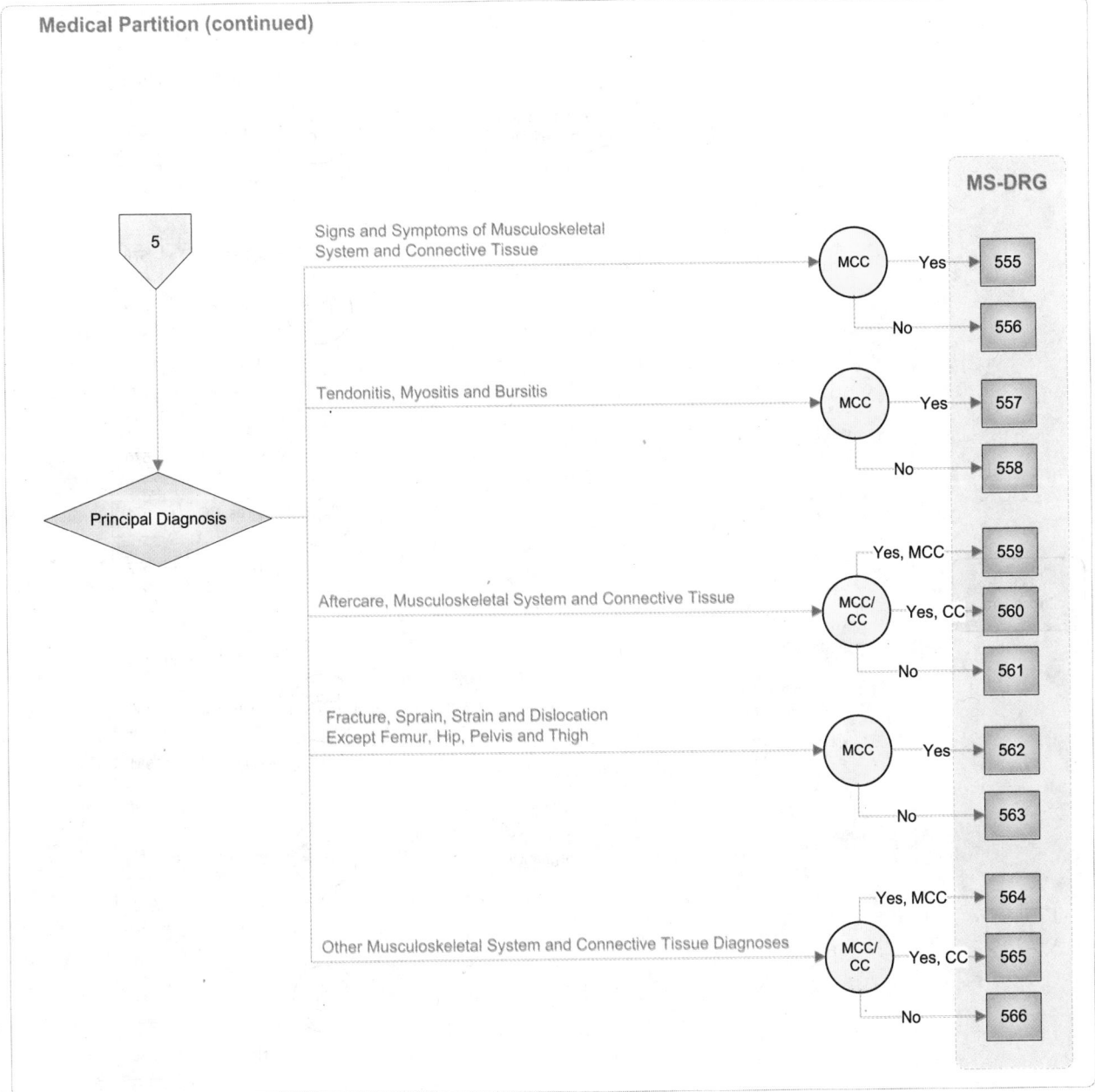

Medical Partition (continued)

DRG Decision Trees

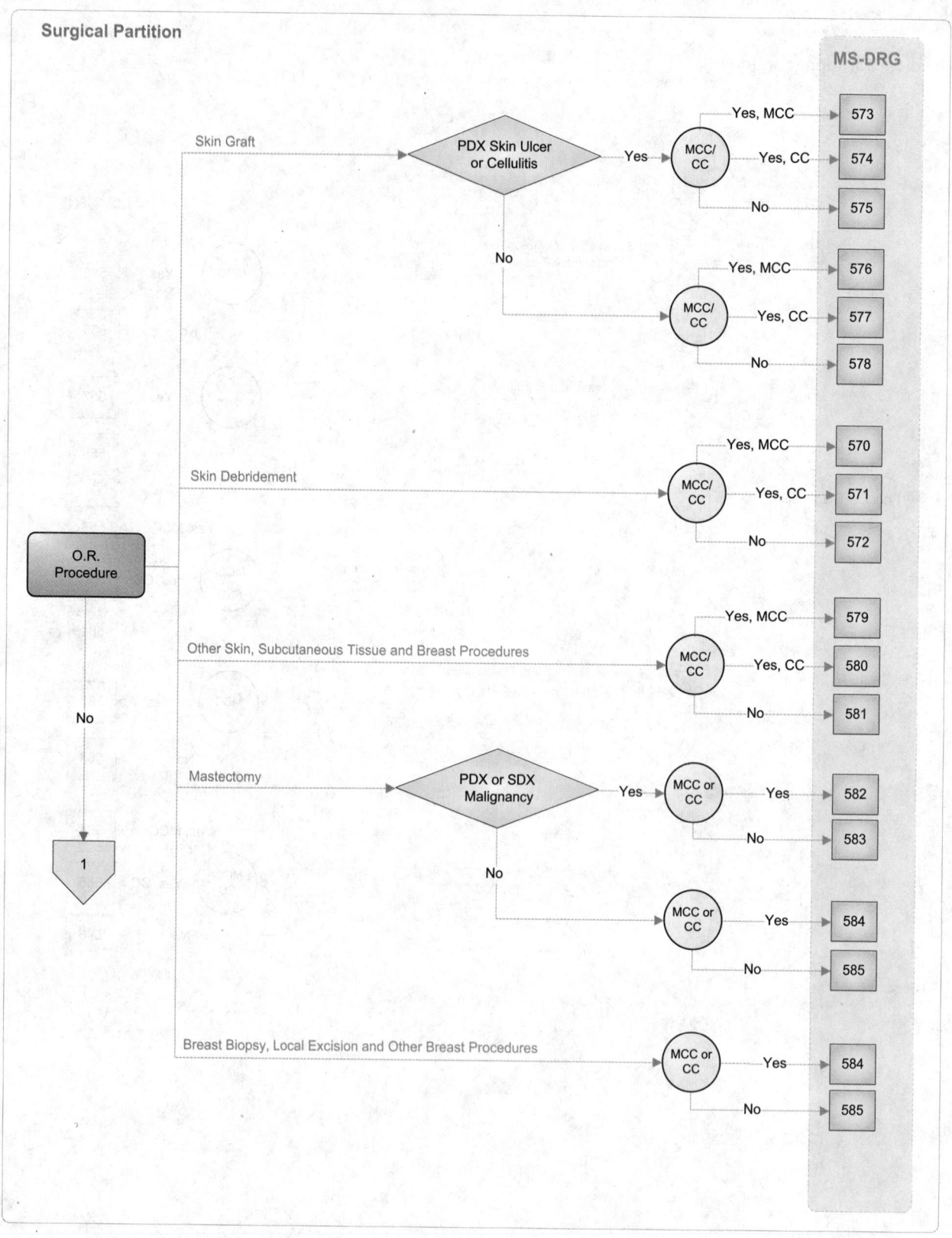

DRG Decision Trees

Major Diagnostic Category 9
Diseases and Disorders of the Skin, Subcutaneous Tissue and Breast

Medical Partition

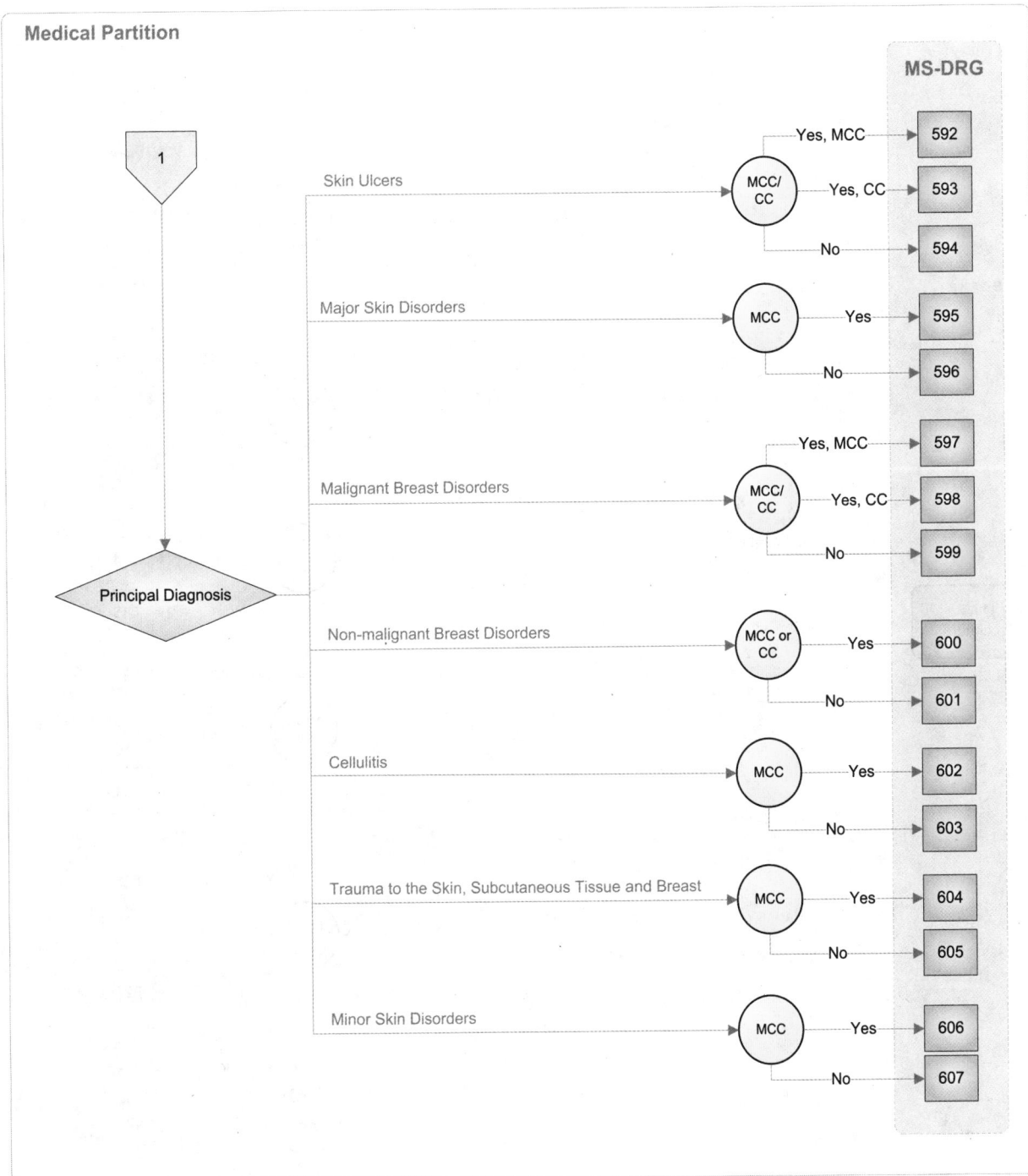

DRG Decision Trees

Surgical Partition

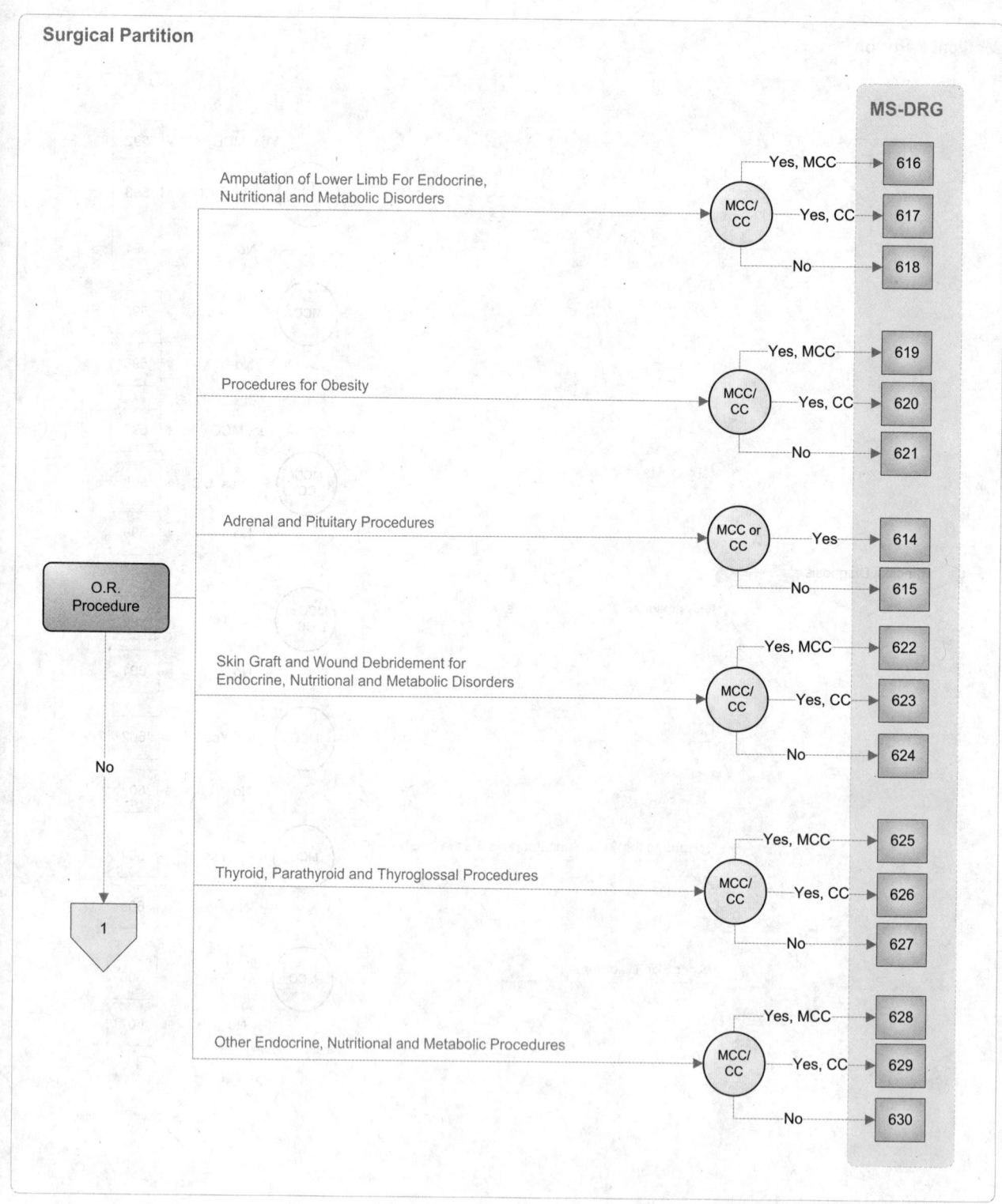

MS-DRG

Amputation of Lower Limb For Endocrine, Nutritional and Metabolic Disorders
- MCC/CC
  - Yes, MCC → 616
  - Yes, CC → 617
  - No → 618

Procedures for Obesity
- MCC/CC
  - Yes, MCC → 619
  - Yes, CC → 620
  - No → 621

Adrenal and Pituitary Procedures
- MCC or CC
  - Yes → 614
  - No → 615

O.R. Procedure

Skin Graft and Wound Debridement for Endocrine, Nutritional and Metabolic Disorders
- MCC/CC
  - Yes, MCC → 622
  - Yes, CC → 623
  - No → 624

Thyroid, Parathyroid and Thyroglossal Procedures
- MCC/CC
  - Yes, MCC → 625
  - Yes, CC → 626
  - No → 627

No → 1

Other Endocrine, Nutritional and Metabolic Procedures
- MCC/CC
  - Yes, MCC → 628
  - Yes, CC → 629
  - No → 630

DRG Decision Trees

Medical Partition

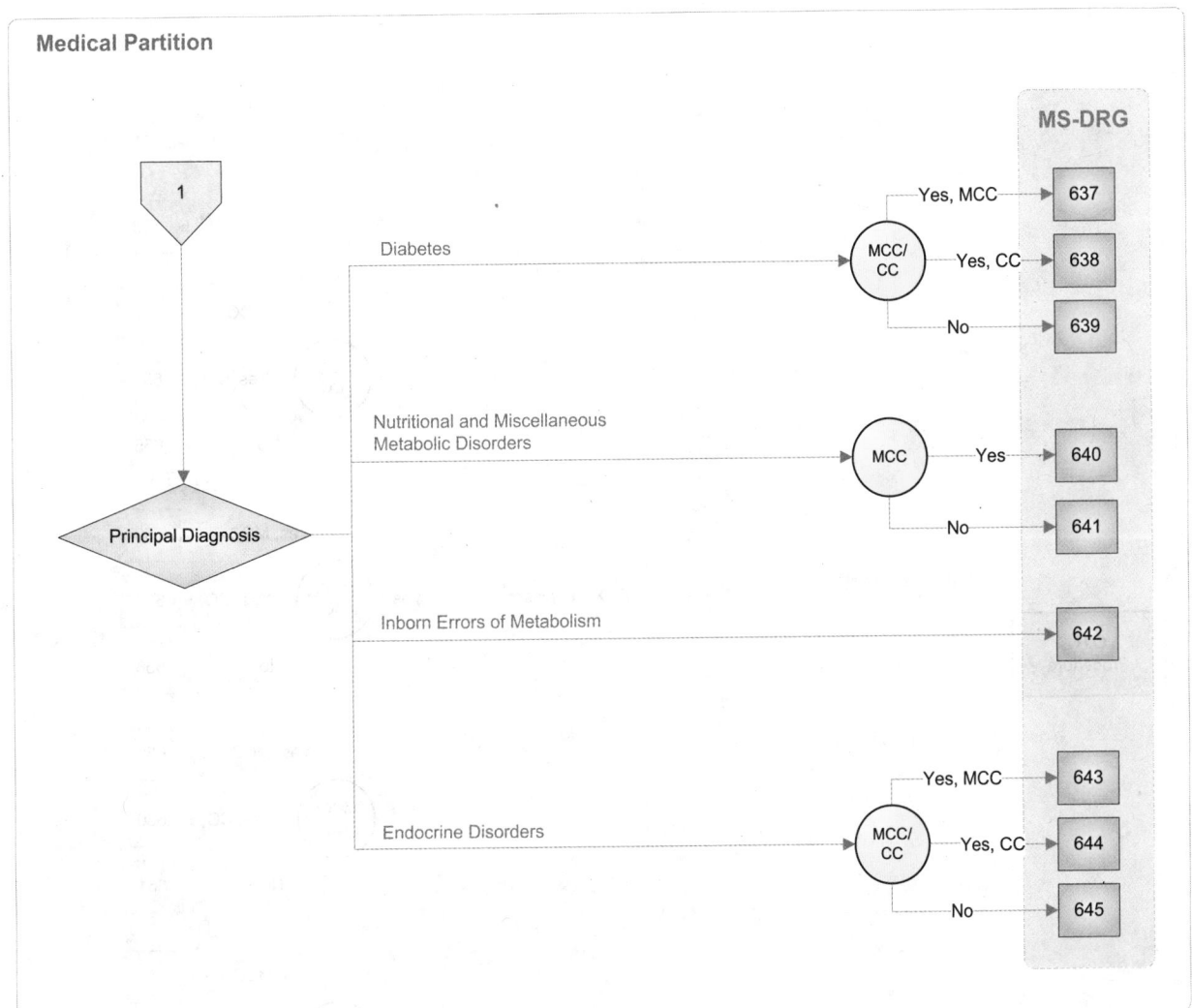

Major Diagnostic Category 11
Diseases and Disorders of the Kidney and Urinary Tract

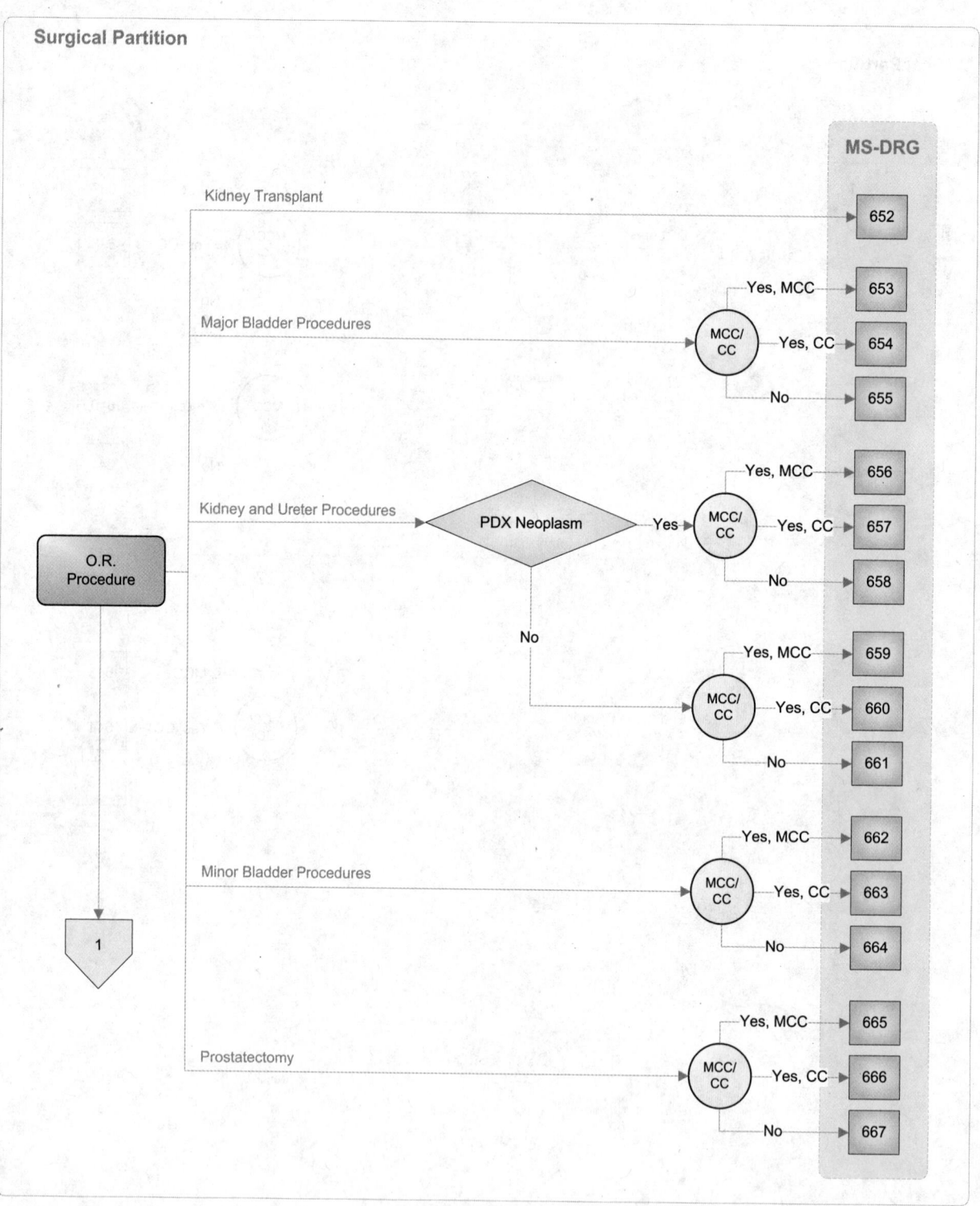

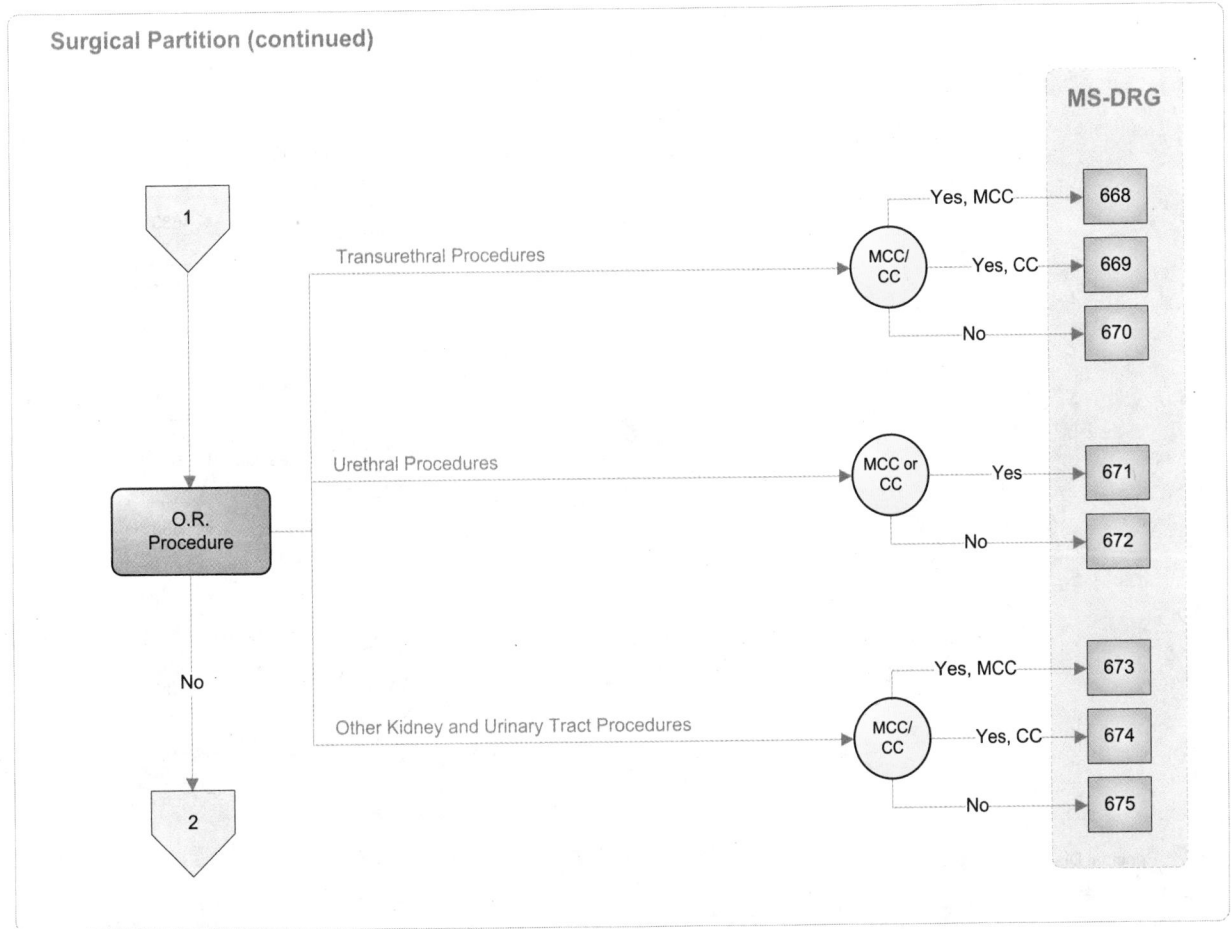

Surgical Partition (continued)

DRG Decision Trees

Major Diagnostic Category 11
Diseases and Disorders of the Kidney and Urinary Tract

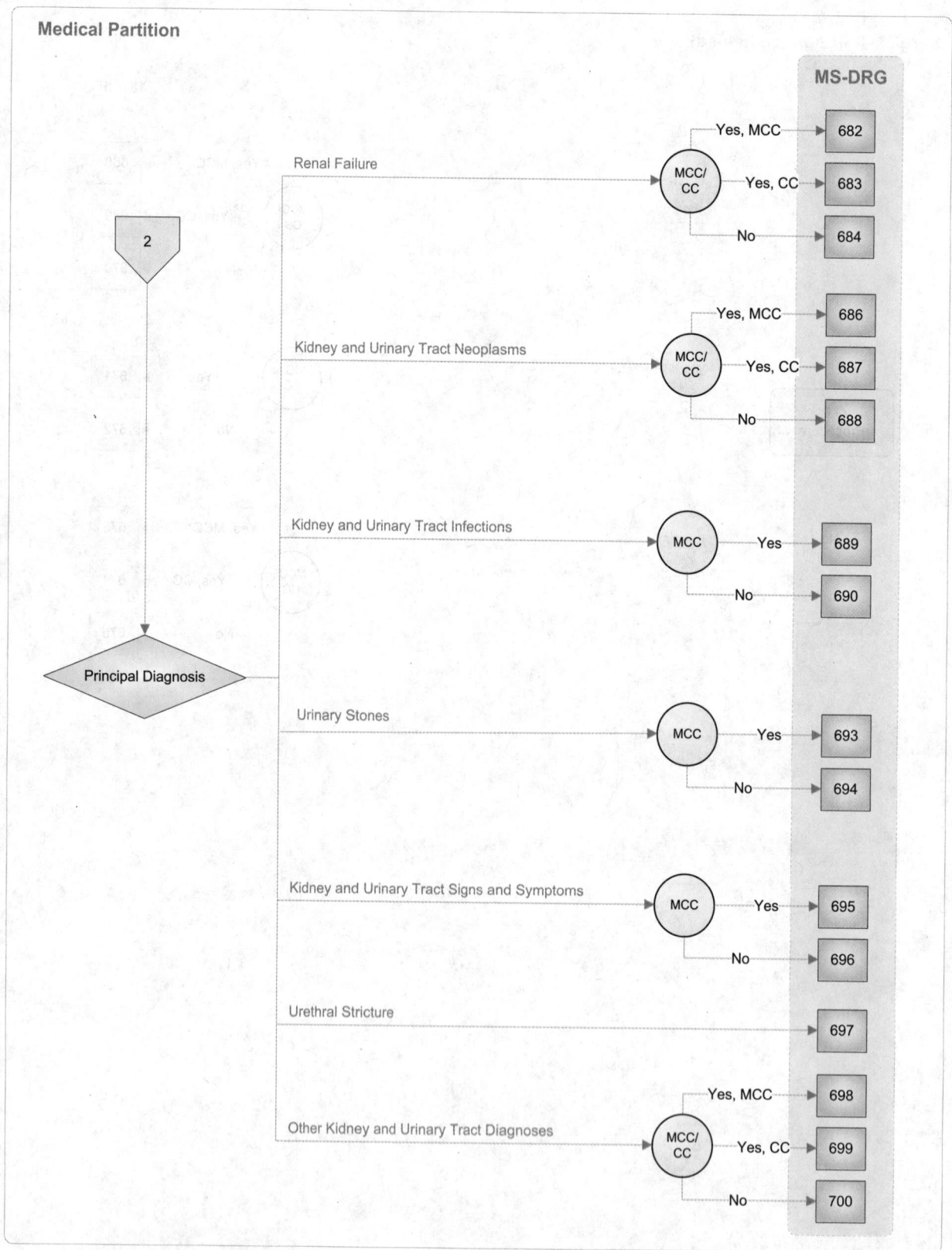

Medical Partition

MS-DRG

2

Principal Diagnosis

Renal Failure — MCC/CC
- Yes, MCC → 682
- Yes, CC → 683
- No → 684

Kidney and Urinary Tract Neoplasms — MCC/CC
- Yes, MCC → 686
- Yes, CC → 687
- No → 688

Kidney and Urinary Tract Infections — MCC
- Yes → 689
- No → 690

Urinary Stones — MCC
- Yes → 693
- No → 694

Kidney and Urinary Tract Signs and Symptoms — MCC
- Yes → 695
- No → 696

Urethral Stricture → 697

Other Kidney and Urinary Tract Diagnoses — MCC/CC
- Yes, MCC → 698
- Yes, CC → 699
- No → 700

DRG Decision Trees

Surgical Partition

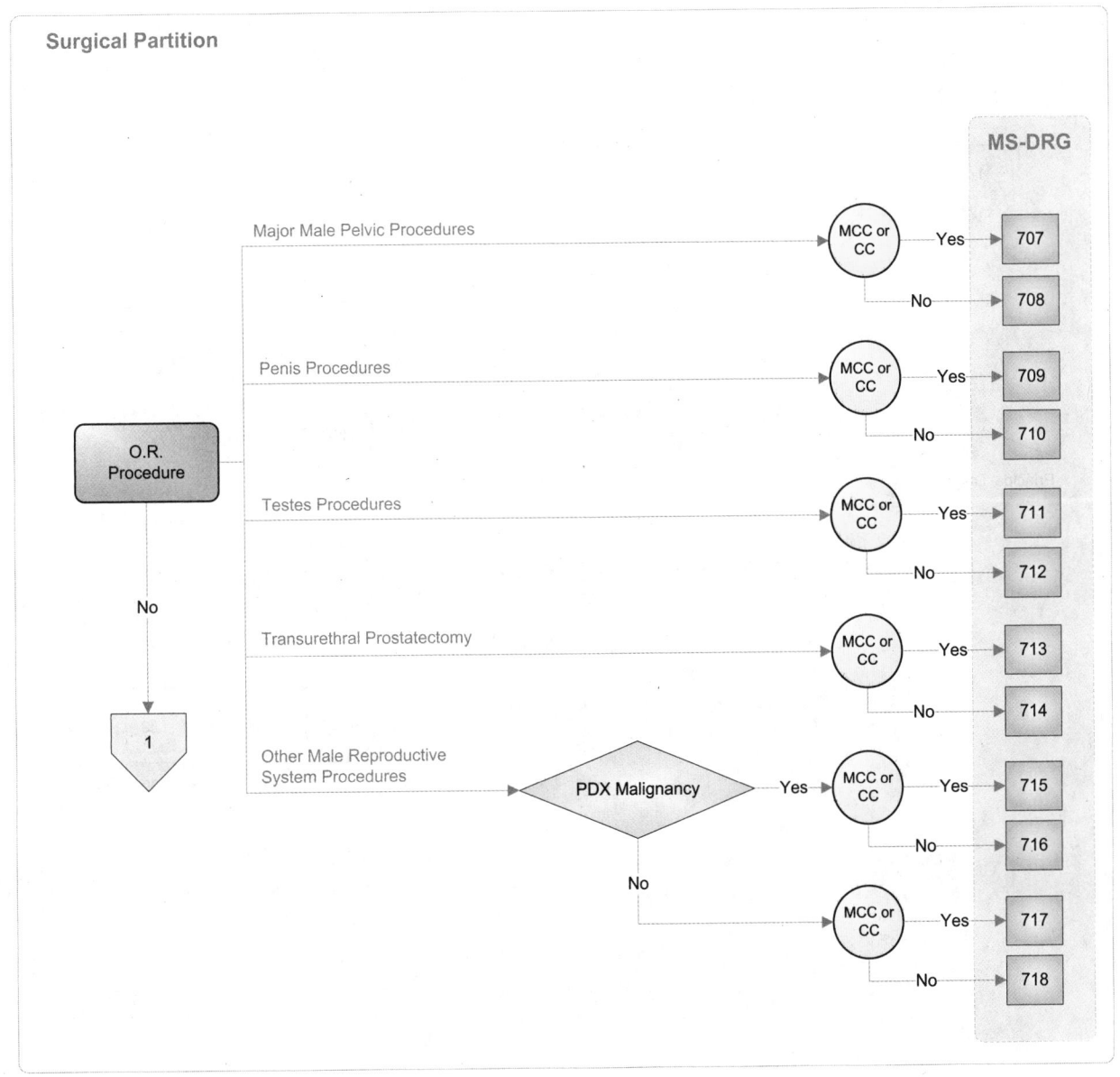

DRG Decision Trees

Medical Partition

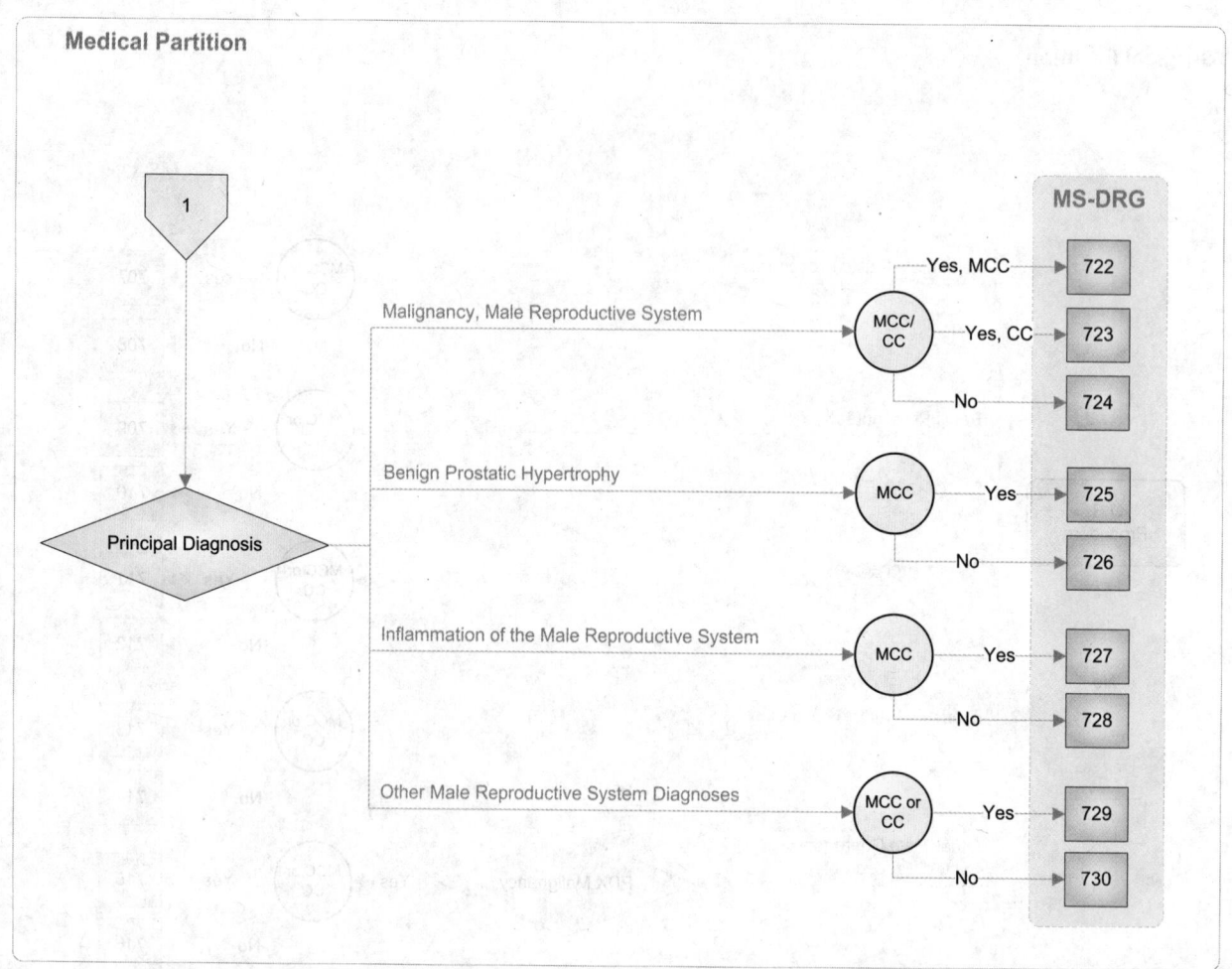

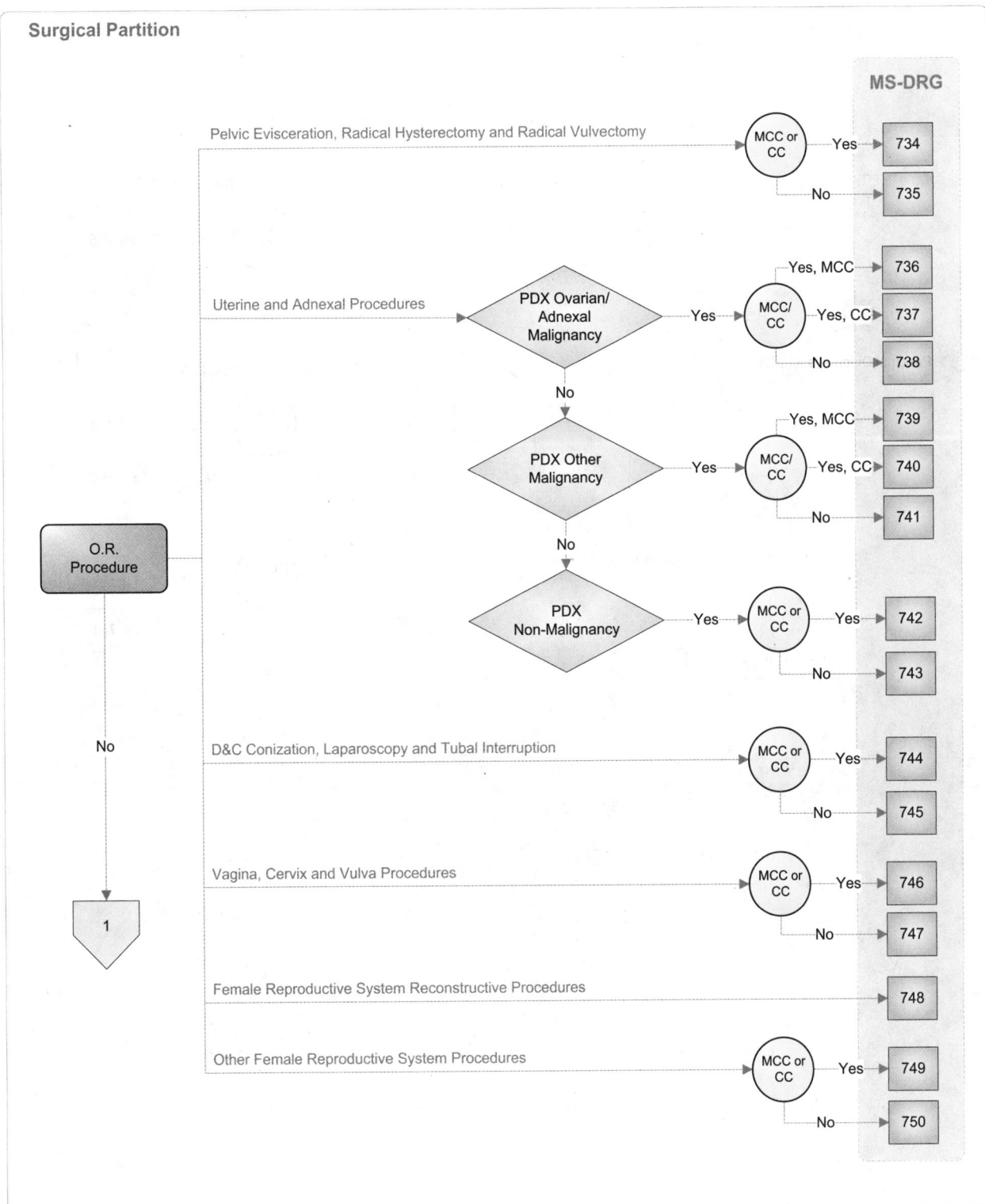

DRG Decision Trees

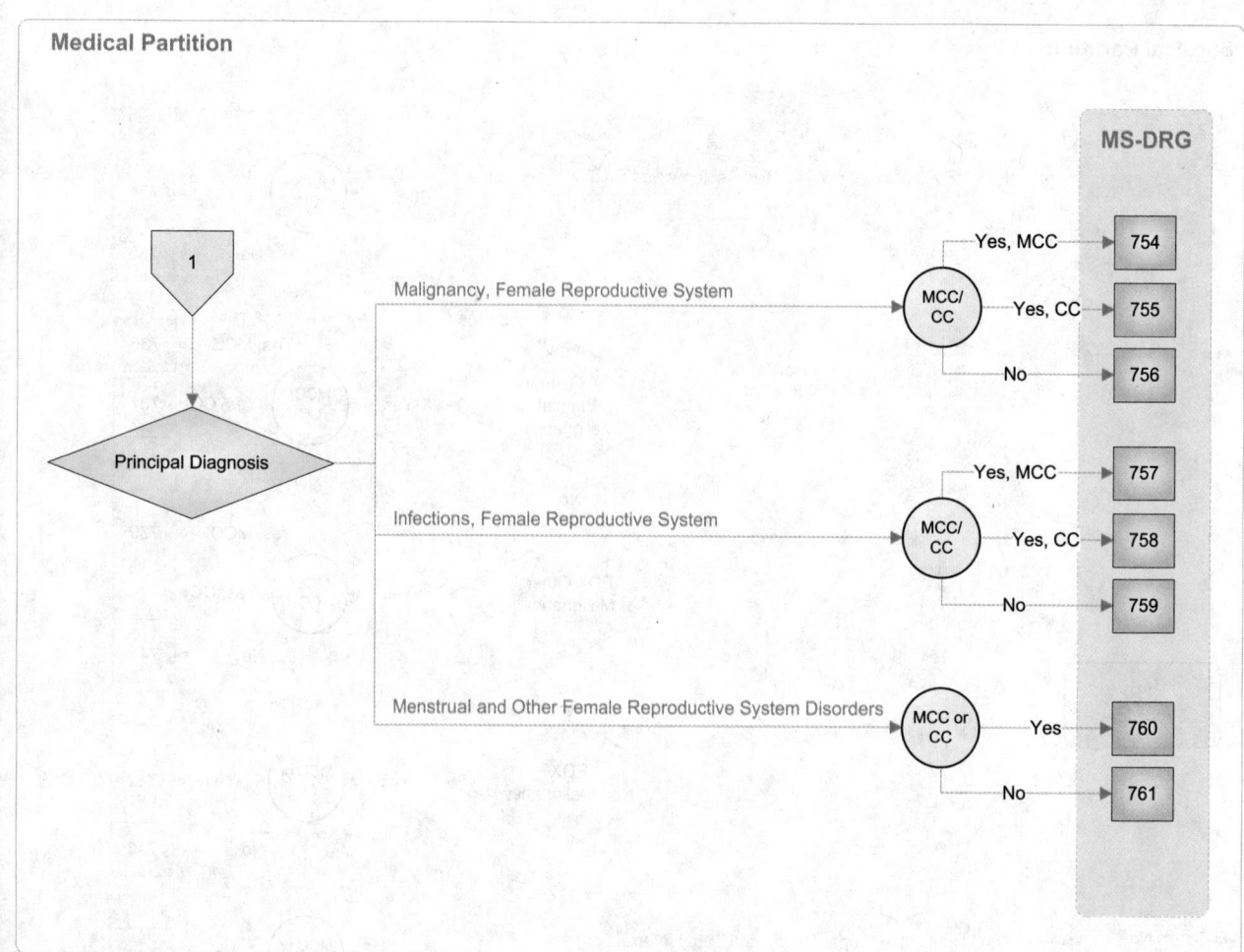

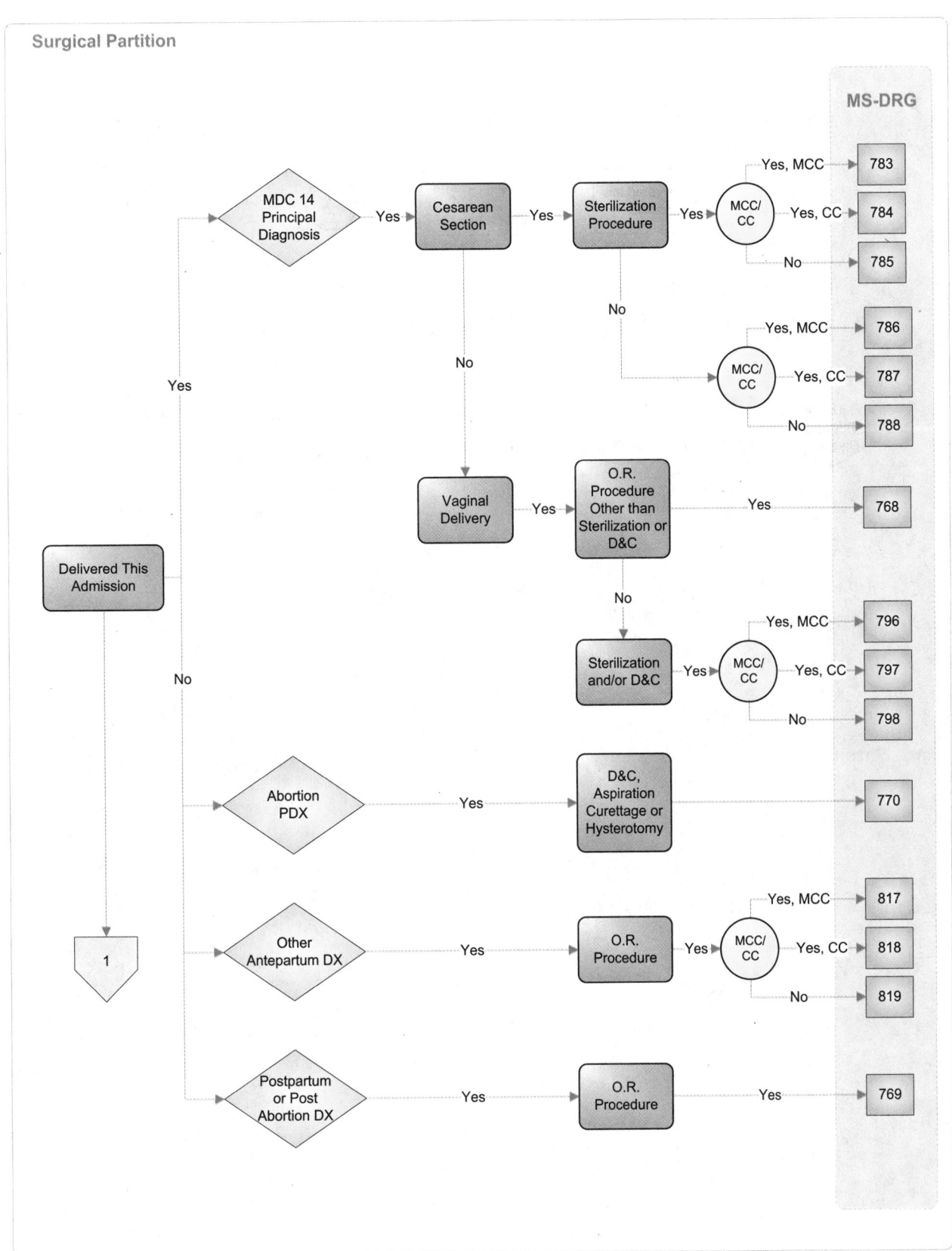

DRG Decision Trees

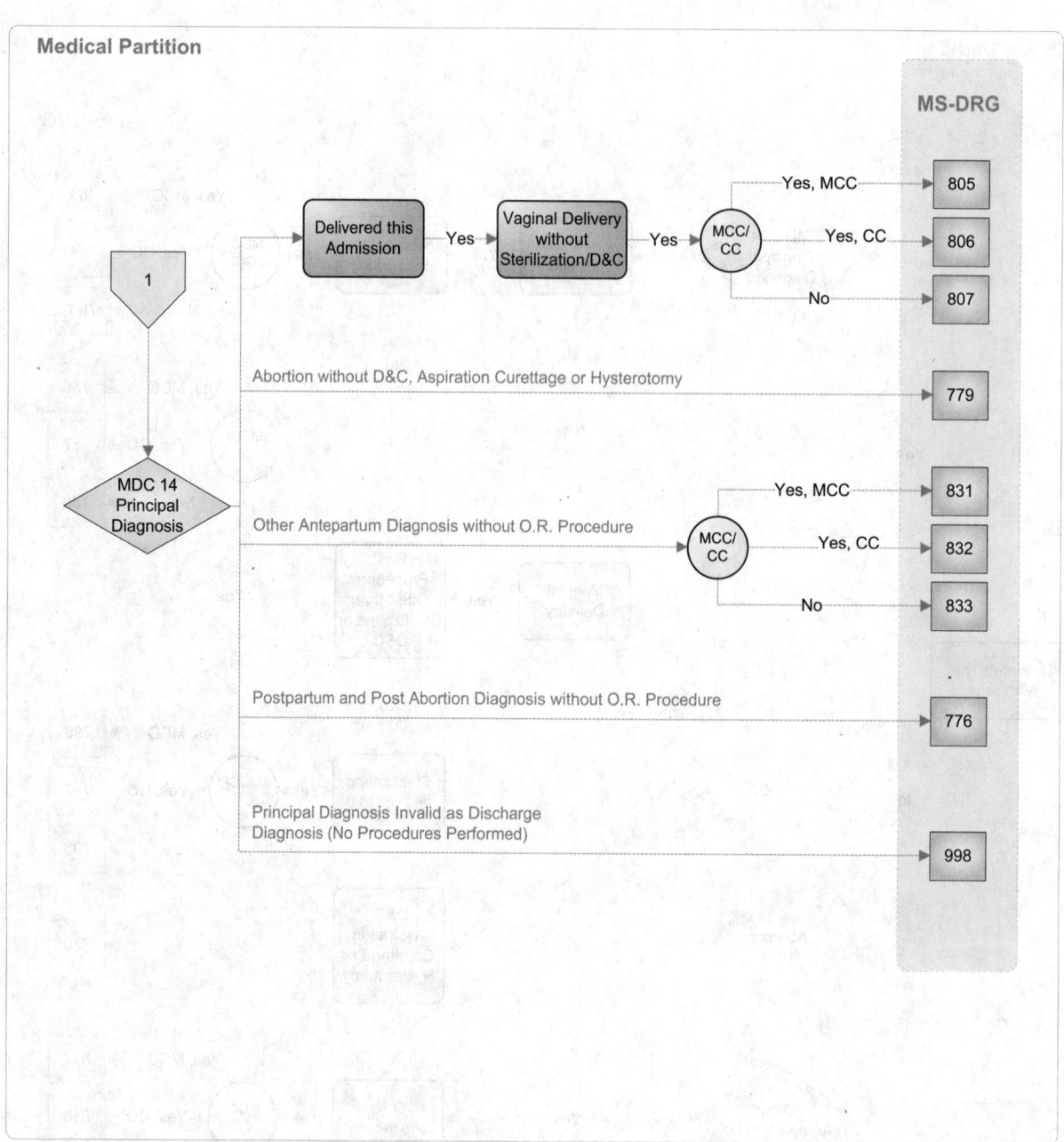

Major Diagnostic Category 15
Newborns and Other Neonates with Conditions Originating in the Perinatal Period

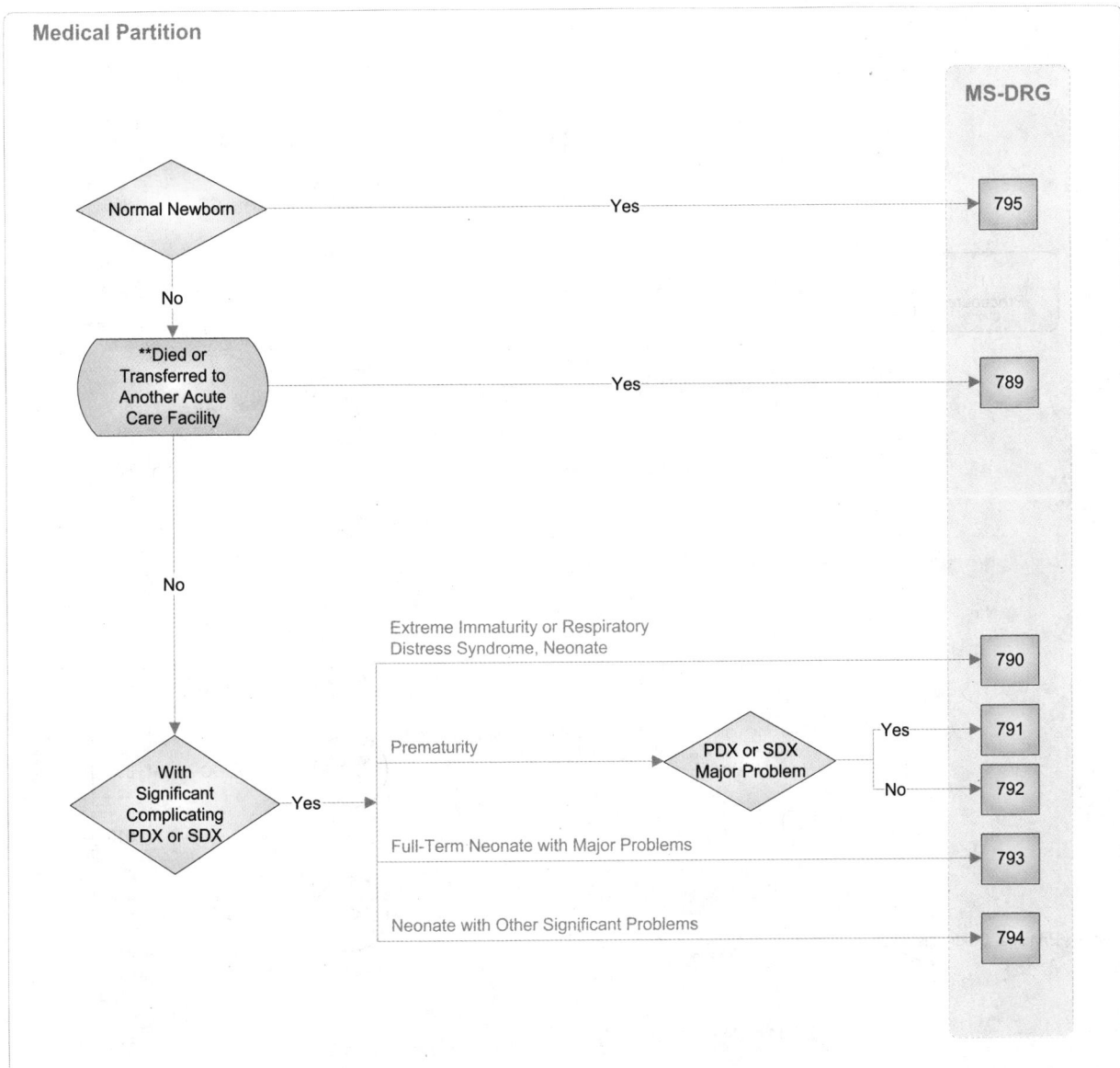

Medical Partition

**Died = Discharge Status of 20

<u>Acute Care Facilities</u>:

 Discharge Status of 02 = Short-Term General Hospital or;

 Discharge Status of 05 = Designated Cancer Center or Children's Hospital or;

 Discharge Status of 66 = Critical Access Hospital or;

 Discharge Status of 82 = Discharged/Transferred to a Short Term General Hospital for Inpatient Care with a Planned Acute Care
    Hospital Inpatient Readmission or;

 Discharge Status of 85 = Discharged/Transferred to a Designated Cancer Center or Children's Hospital with a Planned Acute Care
    Hospital Inpatient Readmission or;

 Discharge Status of 94 = Discharged/Transferred to a Critical Access Hospital (CAH) with a
    Planned Acute Care Hospital Inpatient Readmission

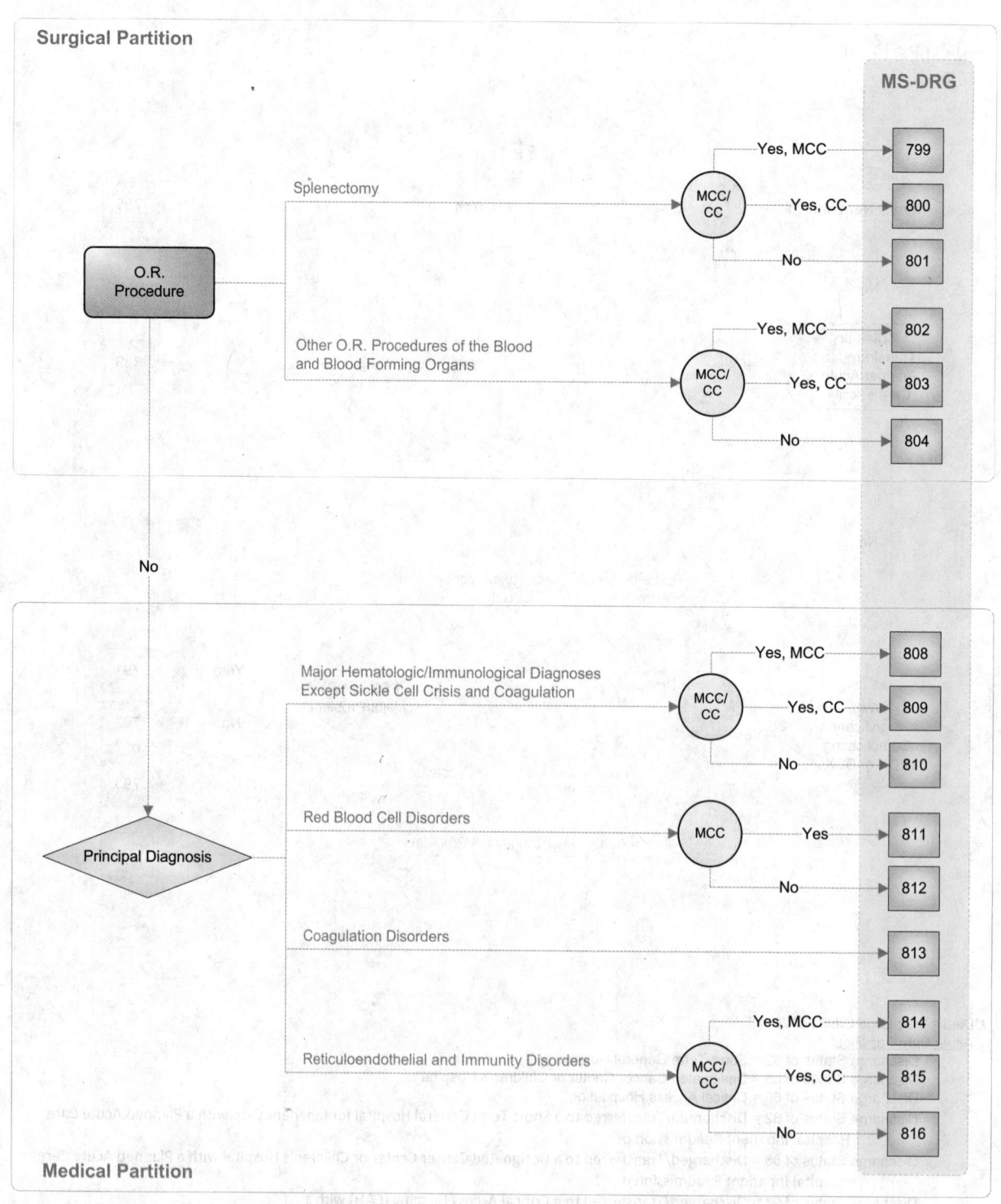

Surgical Partition

MS-DRG

O.R. Procedure

Splenectomy

MCC/CC — Yes, MCC → 799

Yes, CC → 800

No → 801

Other O.R. Procedures of the Blood and Blood Forming Organs

MCC/CC — Yes, MCC → 802

Yes, CC → 803

No → 804

No

Principal Diagnosis

Major Hematologic/Immunological Diagnoses Except Sickle Cell Crisis and Coagulation

MCC/CC — Yes, MCC → 808

Yes, CC → 809

No → 810

Red Blood Cell Disorders

MCC — Yes → 811

No → 812

Coagulation Disorders → 813

Reticuloendothelial and Immunity Disorders

MCC/CC — Yes, MCC → 814

Yes, CC → 815

No → 816

Medical Partition

Major Diagnostic Category 17
Myeloproliferative Diseases and Disorders, Poorly Differentiated Neoplasm

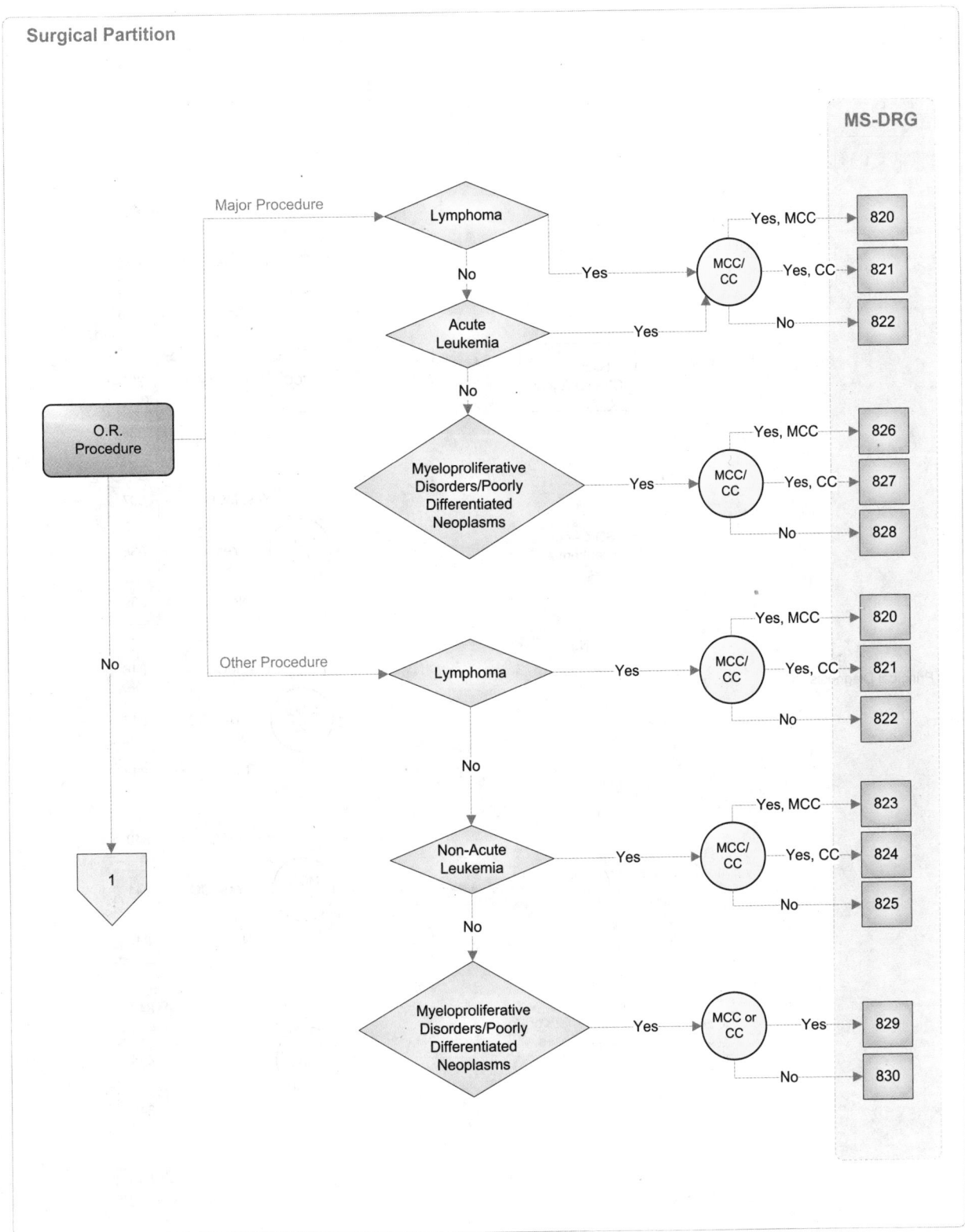

Surgical Partition

MS-DRG

Major Diagnostic Category 17
Myeloproliferative Diseases and Disorders, Poorly Differentiated Neoplasm

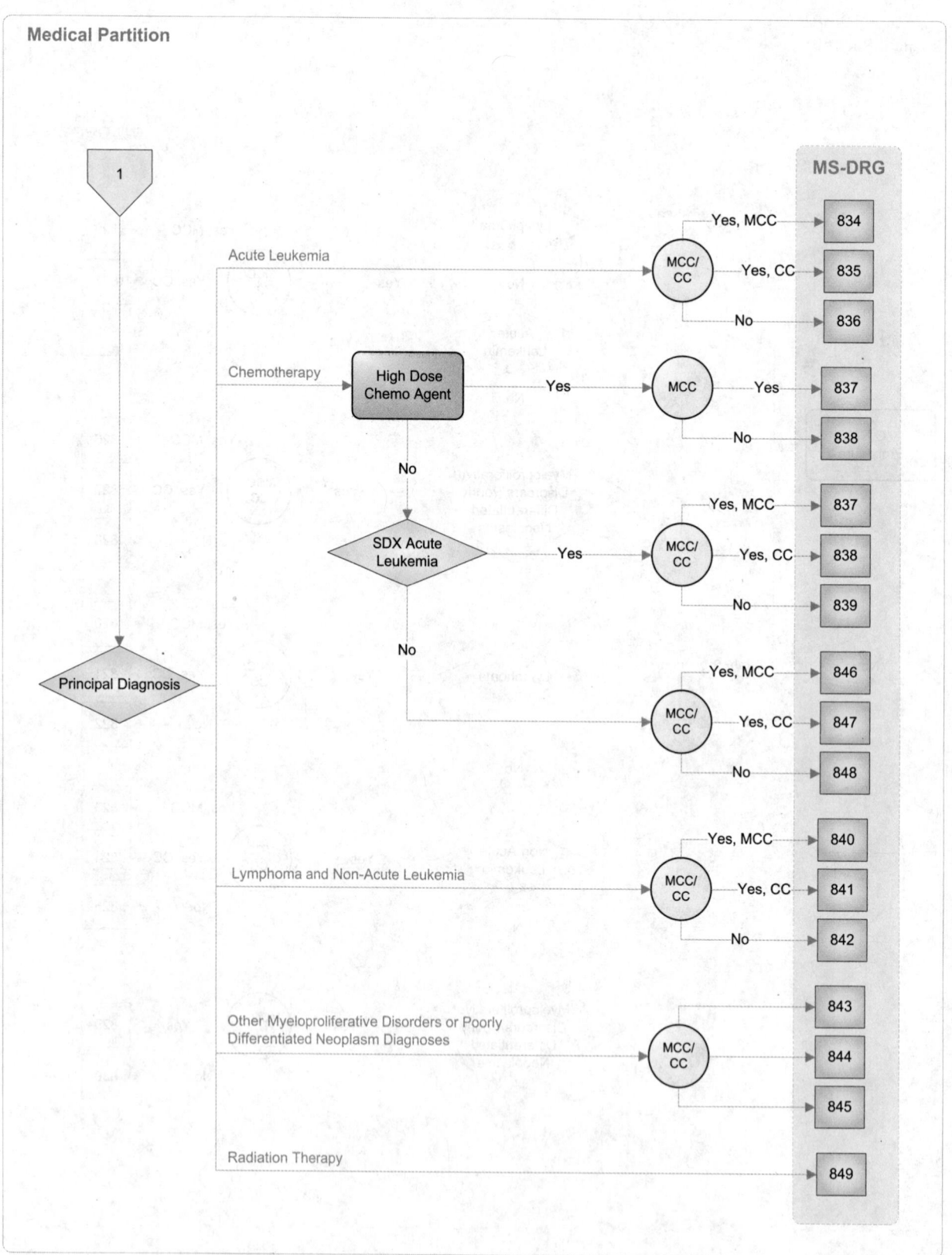

Medical Partition

Major Diagnostic Category 18
Infections and Parasitic Diseases (Systemic or Unspecified Sites)

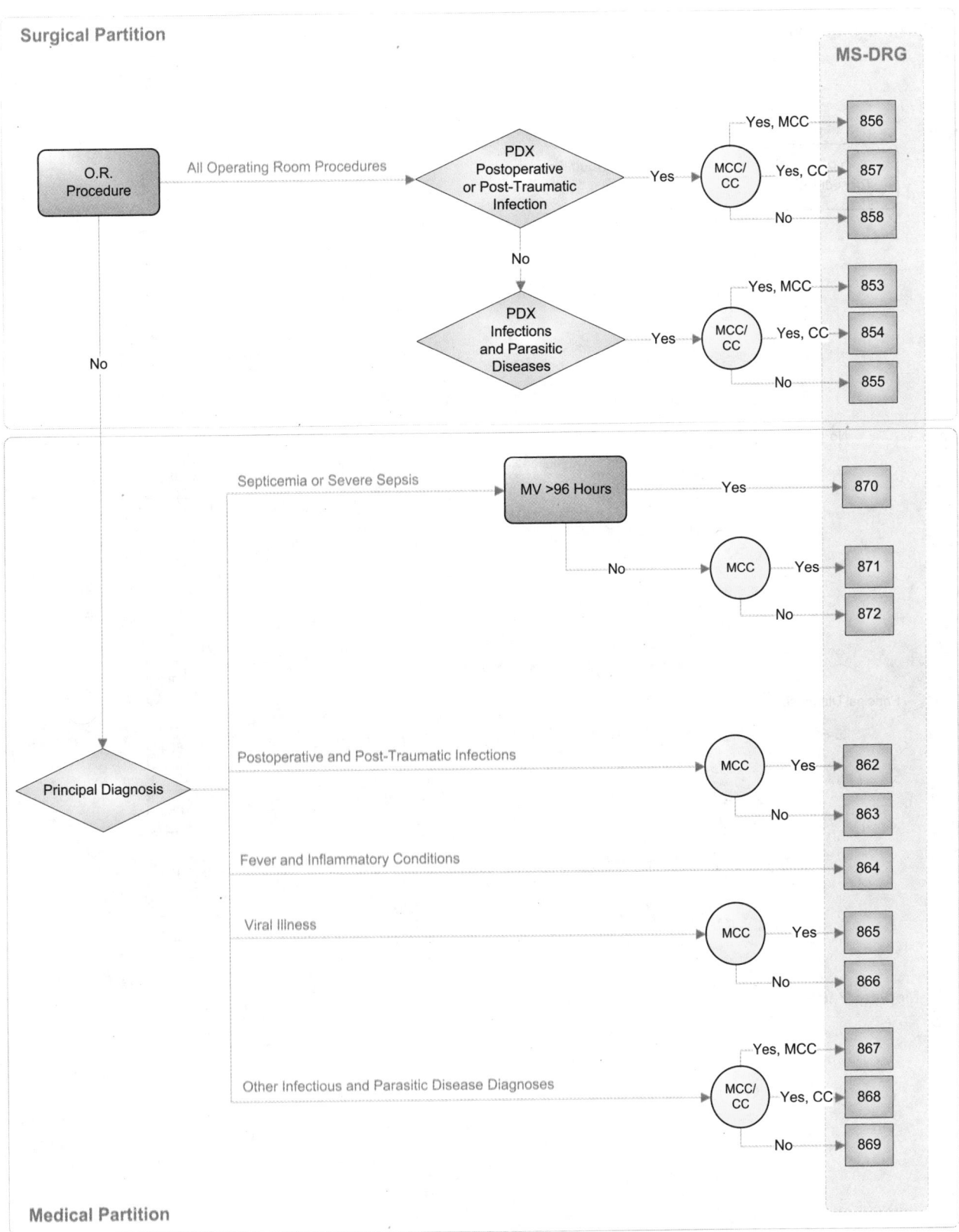

Surgical Partition

Medical Partition

DRG Decision Trees

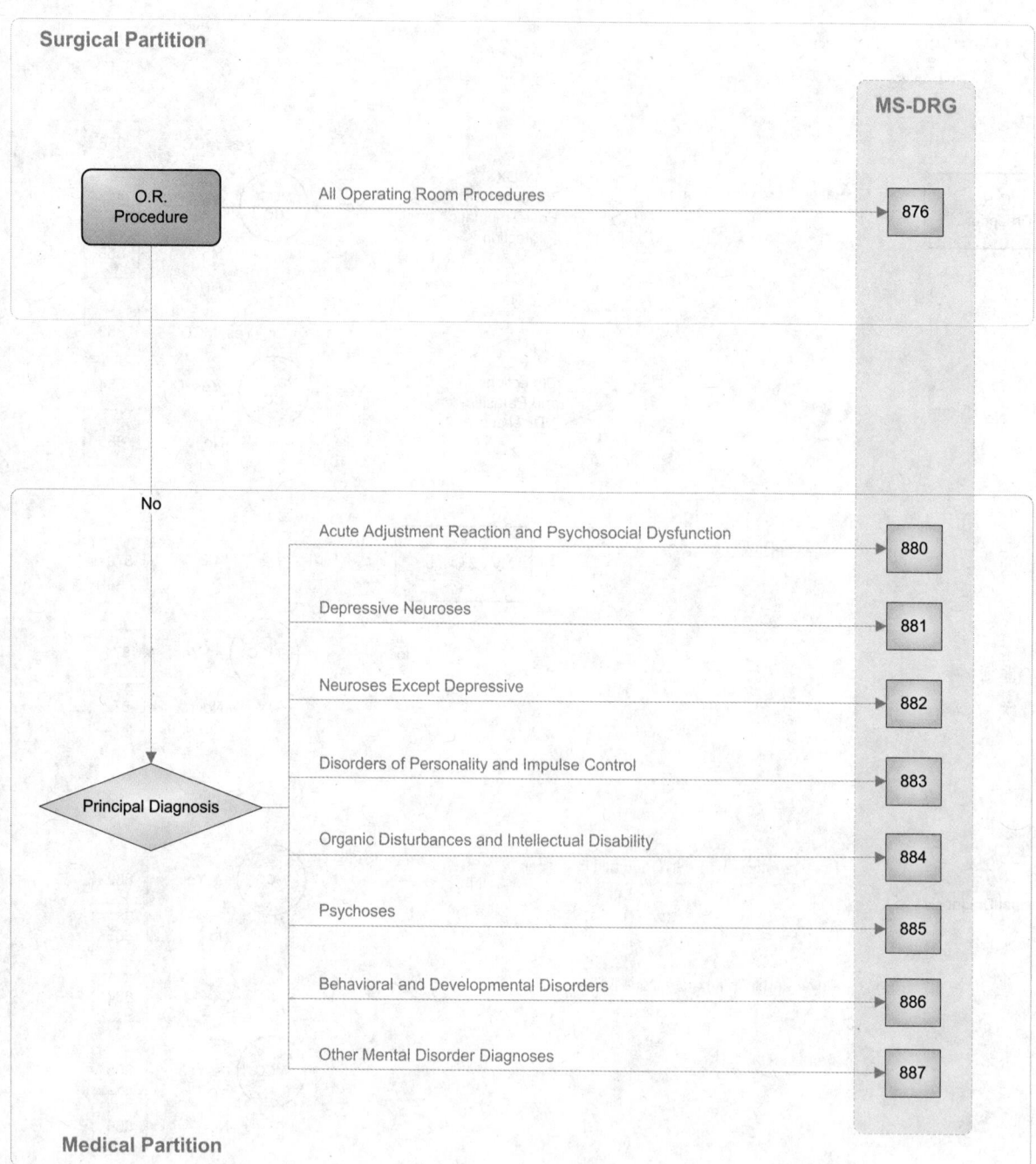

DRG Decision Trees

Medical Partition

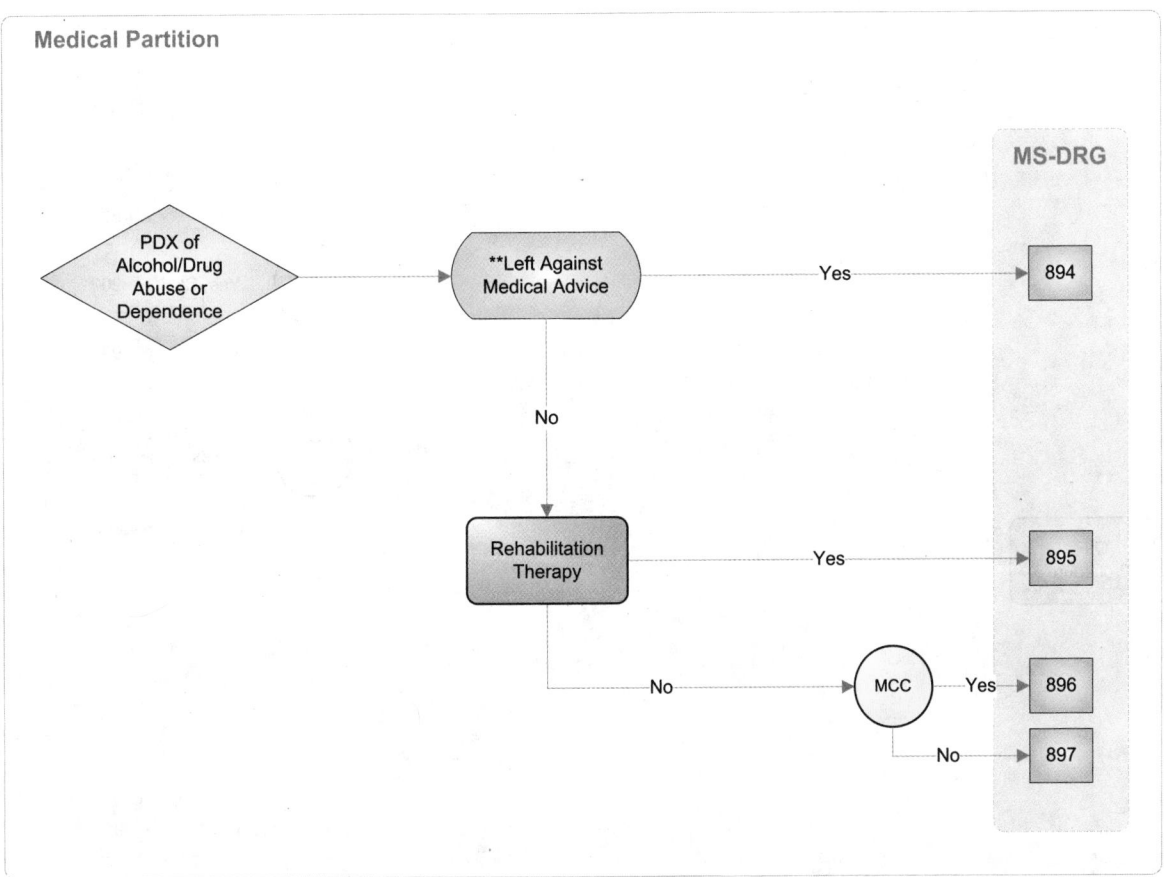

** Left Against Medical Advice = Discharge Status of 07

Major Diagnostic Category 21
Injuries, Poisonings and Toxic Effects of Drugs

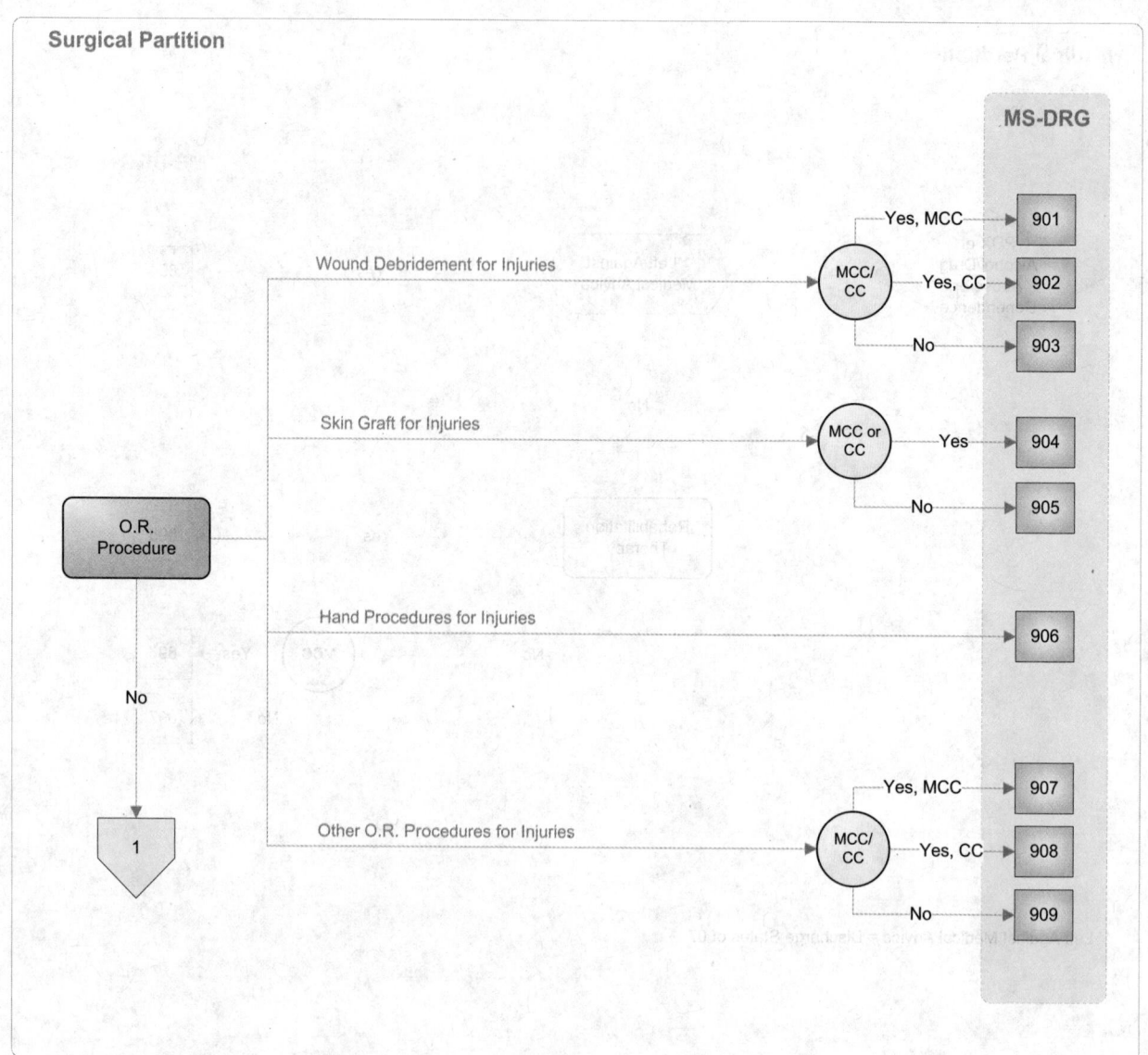

Surgical Partition

MS-DRG

Wound Debridement for Injuries → MCC/CC
- Yes, MCC → 901
- Yes, CC → 902
- No → 903

Skin Graft for Injuries → MCC or CC
- Yes → 904
- No → 905

Hand Procedures for Injuries → 906

O.R. Procedure
- No → 1

Other O.R. Procedures for Injuries → MCC/CC
- Yes, MCC → 907
- Yes, CC → 908
- No → 909

Major Diagnostic Category 21
Injuries, Poisonings and Toxic Effects of Drugs

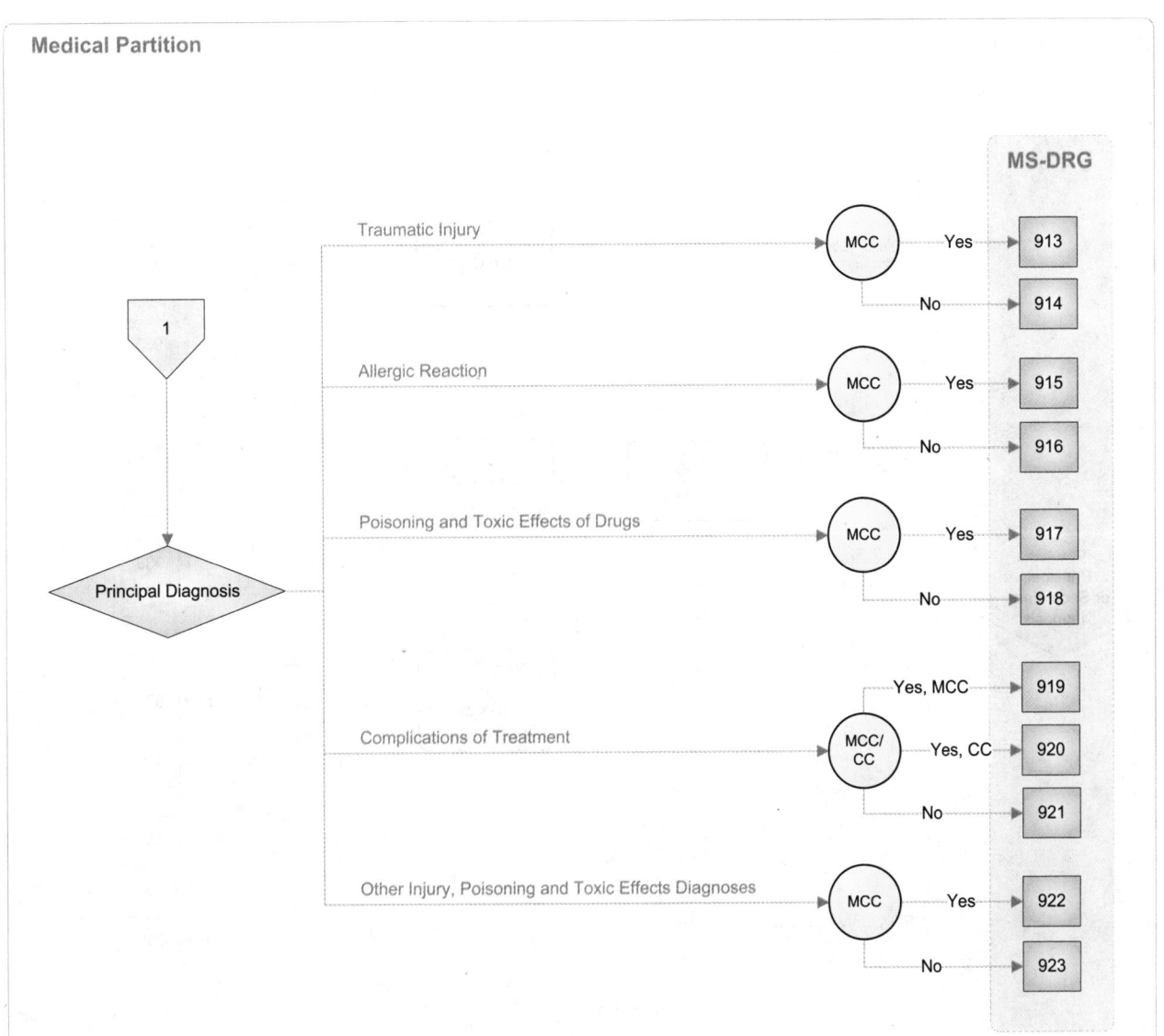

Medical Partition

Principal Diagnosis

Branch	Condition	MS-DRG
Traumatic Injury	MCC — Yes	913
	No	914
Allergic Reaction	MCC — Yes	915
	No	916
Poisoning and Toxic Effects of Drugs	MCC — Yes	917
	No	918
Complications of Treatment	MCC/CC — Yes, MCC	919
	Yes, CC	920
	No	921
Other Injury, Poisoning and Toxic Effects Diagnoses	MCC — Yes	922
	No	923

Surgical and Medical Partition

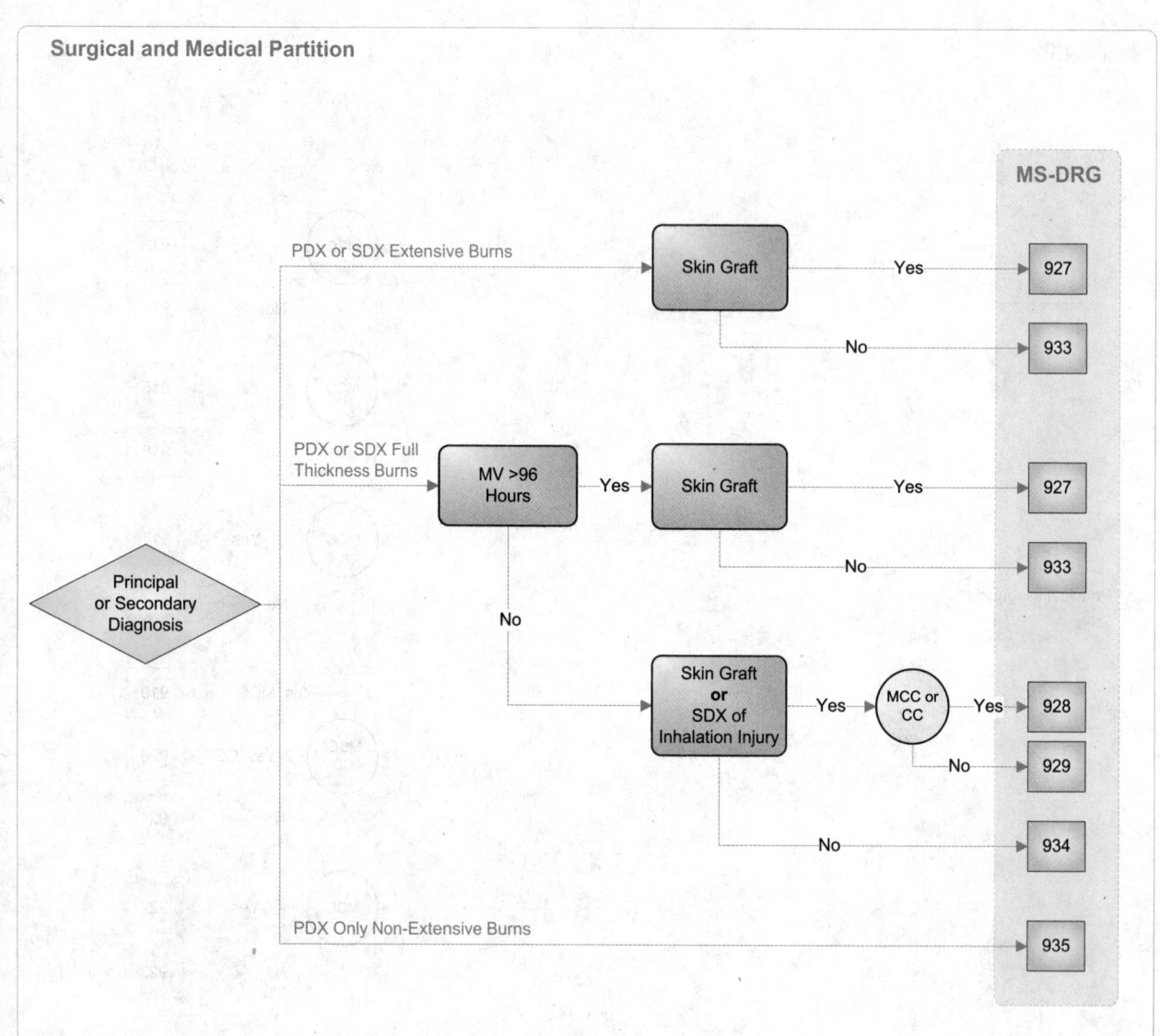

Major Diagnostic Category 23
Factors Influencing Health Status and Other Contacts with Health Services

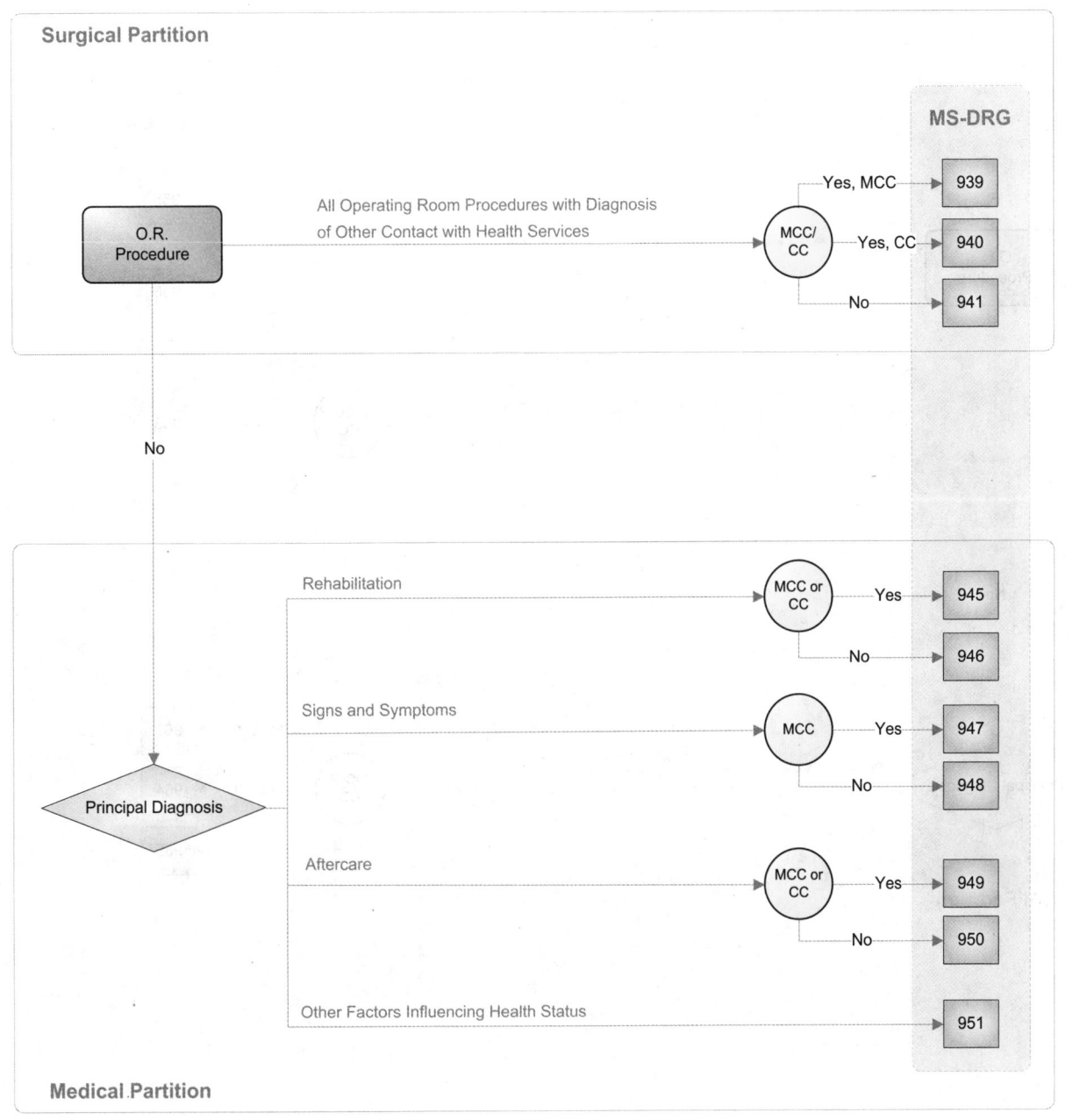

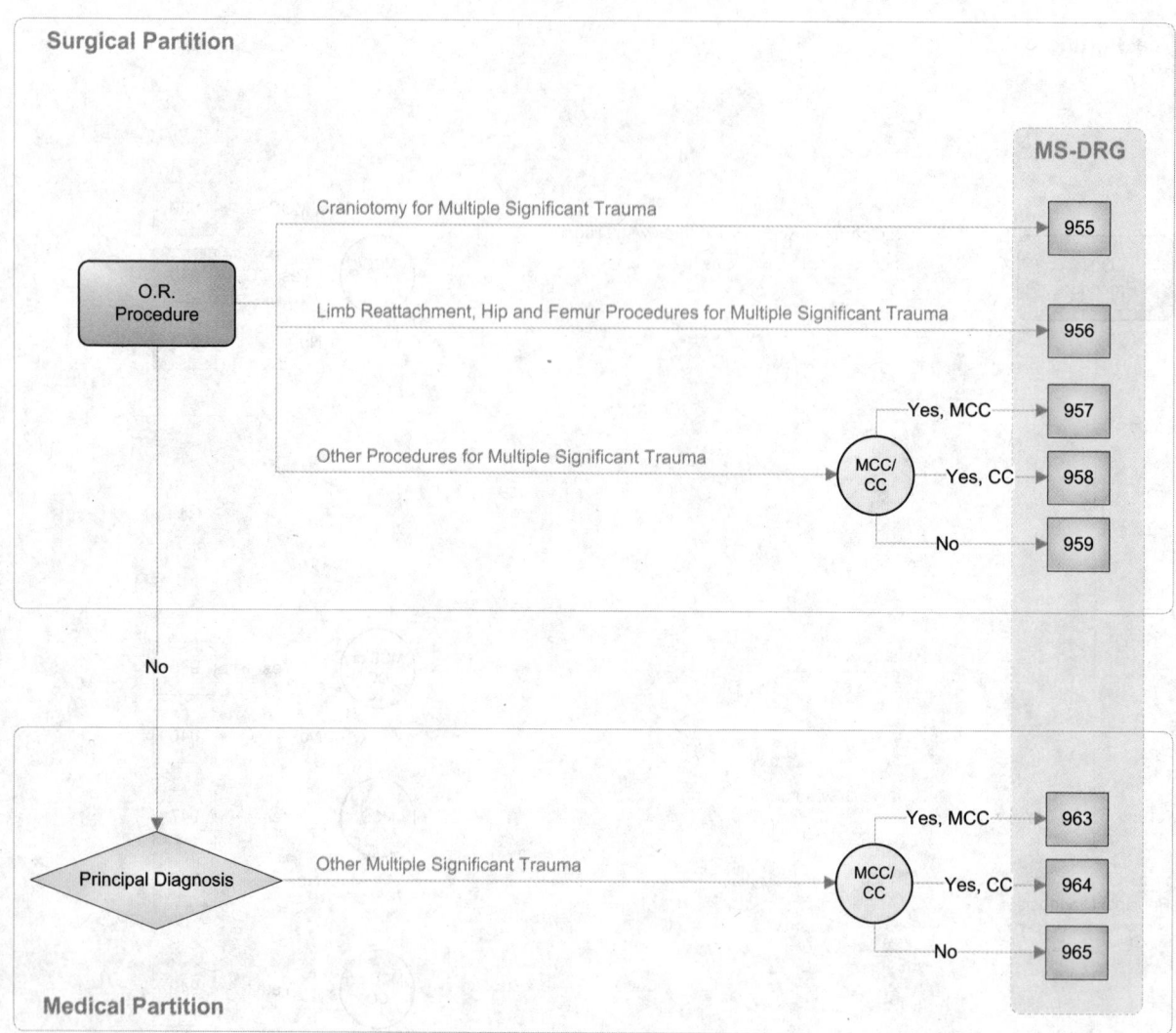

Major Diagnostic Category 25
Human Immunodeficiency Virus (HIV) Infections

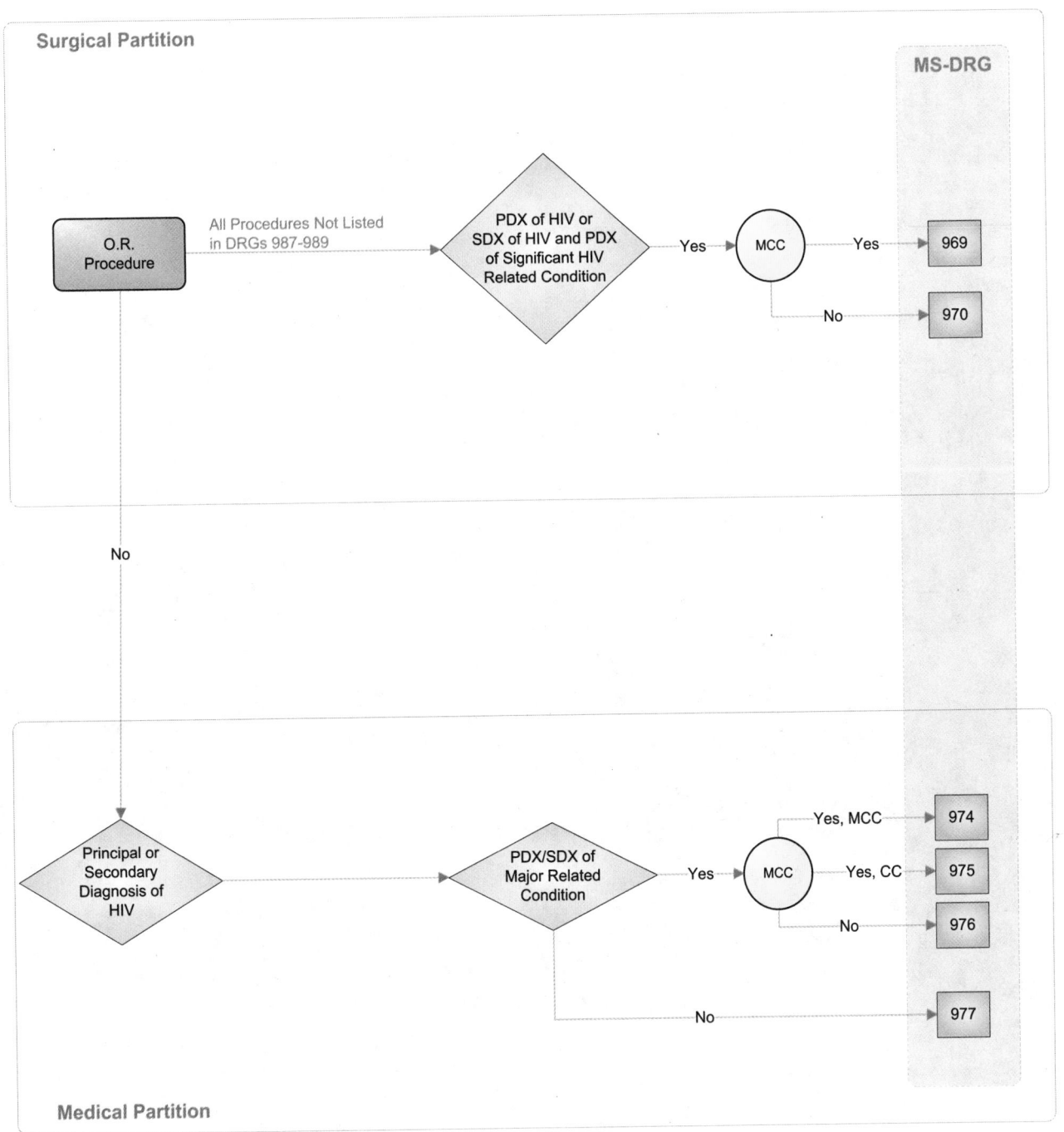